Warman's
ANTIQUES AND COLLECTIBLES
PRICE GUIDE

32ND EDITION

THE ESSENTIAL FIELD GUIDE TO THE ANTIQUES AND COLLECTIBLES MARKETPLACE

EDITED BY ELLEN T. SCHROY

Volumes in the Encyclopedia of Antiques and Collectibles

© 1998 by Krause Publications
Depression Glass Illustrations Copyright © by Jerry O'Brien

Special thanks to the auction houses and individuals who provided the photos for the cover, which are, clockwise from top right: Russian Icon, No. 488, Archangel Gabriel, holding lily, standing atop clouds, two-tone silver gilt repousse and chased riza, hallmarked Moscow, dated 1890, from workshop of Vasily Semenov, 15" h, 12" w, $4,620, photo courtesy of Jackson's Auctioneers & Appraisers; Clarice Cliff, sugar sifter, bizarre, conical, Blue Firs pattern, blue fir trees, green landscape, 5-1/2" h, $17,000, photo courtesy of Christie's, South Kensington; Cabinet, Tramp Art, blue, scratch built, embellished with pyramids, floral pattern on doors, crest, secret compartment, 22-1/2" w, 14" d, 44" h, $6,500, photo courtesy of Clifford Wallach; Marklin, racer, Model 11075, tin, wind-up kit, original key, driver missing, fenders repainted, 15" l, $1,650, photo courtesy of Jackson's Auctioneers & Appraisers; and a Toilet Bottle, Ruba Rombic, jungle green, made by Consolidated Glass Co., $375, photo courtesy of Jerry Gallagher.

Published by

krause publications

700 E. State Street • Iola, WI 54990-0001
Telephone: 715/445-2214

www.krause.com

Please call or write for our free catalog of publications. Our toll-free number to place an order or obtain a free catalog is 800-258-0929 or please use our regular business telephone 715-445-2214 for editorial comment and further information.

ISBN: 0-87341-599-X

Library of Congress Catalog Card No. 82-643543

Printed in the United States of America

Contents

iv   Contents

BOARD OF ADVISORS

INTRODUCTION

Warman's—serving the trade for 49 years

In 1994, **Warman's Antiques and Their Prices** became **Warman's Antiques and Collectibles Price Guide**. The last edition is bigger than ever–physically, that is. Longtime **Warman's** users may find it difficult to imagine that the amount of information in this larger-size book is identical to that found in the earlier smaller-size editions. Yet, it is true. While the page, text, and photograph sizes are larger, the content is the same. You can always expect more, never less from **Warman's.**

Individuals in the trade refer to this book simply as **Warman's,** a fitting tribute to E.G. Warman and the product that he created. **Warman's** has been around for 50 years, 25 years longer than its closest rival. We are proud as peacocks that Warman's continues to establish the standards for general antiques and collectibles price guides in 1997, just as it did in 1972 when its first rival appeared on the scene.

Warman's, the antiques and collectibles "bible," covers objects made between 1700 and the present. It always has. Because it reflects market trends, **Warman's** has added more and more 20th-century material to each edition. Remember, 1900 was 97 years ago–the distant past to the new generation of twentysomething and thirtysomething collectors.

The general "antiques" market consists of antiques (for the purposes of this book, objects made before 1945), collectibles (objects of the post-World War II era that enjoy an established secondary market), and desirables (contemporary objects that are collected, but speculative in price). Although **Warman's** contains information on all three market segments, its greatest emphasis is on antiques and collectibles.

Also note the book's subtitle: *The Essential Field Guide to the Antiques and Collectibles Marketplace*, first introduced in the 27th Edition. This indicates that **Warman's** is much more than a list of object descriptions and prices. It is a basic guide to the field as a whole, providing you with the key information you need every time you encounter a new object or collecting category.

'Warman's is the key'

Warman's provides the keys needed by auctioneers, collectors, dealers, and others to understand and deal with the complexities of the antiques and collectibles market. A price list is only one of many keys needed today. *Warman's 32nd Edition* contains many additional keys including: histories, marks, reference books, periodicals, collectors' clubs, museums, reproductions, videotapes, and special auctions. Useful buying and collecting hints also are provided. Used properly, there are few doors these keys will not open.

Warman's is designed to be your first key to the exciting world of antiques and collectibles. As you use the keys, this book provides to advance further in your specialized collecting areas, **Warman's** hopes you will remember with fondness where you received your start. When you encounter items outside your area of specialty, remember **Warman's** remains your key to unlocking the information you need, just as it has for over 49 years.

Organization

Listings: Objects are listed alphabetically by category, beginning with ABC Plates and ending with Zsolnay Pottery. If you have trouble identifying the category to which your object belongs, use the extensive index in the back of the book. It will guide you to the proper category.

We have made the listings descriptive enough so that specific objects can be identified. We also emphasize items that are actively being sold in the marketplace. Some harder-to-find objects are included to demonstrate market spread–useful information worth considering when you have not traded actively in a category recently.

Each year as the market changes, we carefully review our categories–adding, dropping, and combining to provide the most comprehensive coverage possible. **Warman's** quick response to developing trends in the marketplace is one of the prime reasons for its continued leadership in the field.

Krause Publications also publishes other Warman's titles. Each utilizes the **Warman's** format and concentrates on a specific collecting group, e.g., American pottery and porcelain, Americana and collectibles, coins and currency, country, English and continental pottery and porcelain, glass, and jewelry. Several are second or subsequent editions. Their expanded coverage compliments the information found in **Warman's Antiques and Collectibles Price Guide**.

History: Collectors and dealers enhance their appreciation of objects by knowing something about their history. We present a capsule history for each category. In many cases this history contains collecting hints or other useful information.

References: Books are listed in most categories to help you learn more about the objects. Included are author, title, publisher, and date of publication or most recent edition. If a book has been published by a small firm or individual, we have indicated (published by author). Beginning with this edition, the address from which to obtain these hard-to-locate sources is included when possible.

Many of the books included in the lists are hard to find. The antiques and collectibles field is blessed with a dedicated core of book dealers who stock these specialized publications. You will find them at flea markets and antiques shows and through their advertisements in trade publications. Books go out of print quickly, yet many books printed more than 25 years ago remain the standard work in a category. Used book dealers often can locate many of these valuable reference sources. Many dealers publish annual or semi-annual catalogs. Ask to be put on their mailing lists. Another new feature in this edition of **Warman's** is a list of pertinent book publishers, addresses, and phone numbers. Often the publisher can direct you to a source for their hard-to-find, currently in-print books and may even provide copies directly.

Periodicals: The newsletter or bulletin of a collectors' club usually provides the concentrated focus sought by specialty collectors and dealers. However, there are publications, not associated with collectors' clubs, about which collectors and dealers should be aware. These are listed in their appropriate category introductions.

In addition, there are several general interest newspapers and magazines which deserve to be brought to our users' attention. These are:

Antique & The Arts Weekly, Bee Publishing Company, 5 Church Hill Road, Newton, CT 06470 http://www.the-bee.com/aweb

Antique Review, P.O. Box 538, Worthington, OH 43085

Antique Trader Weekly, P.O. Box 1050, Dubuque, IA 52001; http://www.csmonline.com

AntiqueWeek, P.O. Box 90, Knightstown, IN 46148; http://www.antiqueweek.com

Antiques (The Magazine Antiques), 551 Fifth Avenue, New York, NY 10017

Antiques & Collecting 1006 South Michigan Avenue, Chicago, IL 60605

Inside Collector, 225 Main St., Suite 300, Northport, NY 11768

Maine Antique Digest, P.O. Box 358, Waldoboro, ME 04572; http://www.maineantiquedigest.com

MidAtlantic Monthly Antiques Magazine, P.O. Box 908, Henderson, NC 27536

New England Antiques Journal, 4 Church St., Ware, MA 01082

New York-Pennsylvania Collector, Drawer C, Fishers, NY 14453

Space does not permit listing all the national and regional publications in the antiques and collectibles field. The above is a sampling. See David J. Maloney, Jr.'s *Maloney's Antiques & Collectibles Resource Directory*, 4th Edition (Antique Trader Books, 1997).

Collectors' Clubs: Collectors' clubs add vitality to the antiques and collectibles field. Their publications and conventions produce knowledge which often cannot be found elsewhere. Many of these clubs are short-lived; others are so strong that they have regional and local chapters.

Museums: The best way to study a specific field is to see as many documented examples as possible. For this reason, we have listed museums where significant collections in that category are on display. Special attention must be directed to the complex of museums which make up the Smithsonian Institution in Washington, D.C.

Reproductions: Reproductions are a major concern to all collectors and dealers. Throughout this edition, boxes will alert you to known reproductions and keys to recognizing them. Most reproductions are unmarked; the newness of their appearance is often the best clue to uncovering them. Specific objects known to be reproduced are marked within the listings with an asterisk (*). The information is designed to serve as a reminder of past reproductions and prevent you from buying them believing them to be period.

We strongly recommend subscribing to *Antique & Collectors Reproduction News*, a monthly newsletter that reports on past and present reproductions, copycats, fantasies, and fakes. Send $32 for 12 issues to: ACRN, Box 71174, Des Moines, IA 50325. This newsletter has been published for several years. Consider buying all available back issues. The information they contain will be of service long into the future.

Special Auctions: In the 32nd Edition, we have chosen to again feature boxes highlighting auction houses. To qualify for placement in one of these boxes, auction houses had to meet several specific requirements. First, they must actively hold auctions solely devoted to that specialty. Second, they must provide a catalog and prices realized. Often the catalogs become an important part of a collection, serving as reference and identification guides. Many of the auction companies featured

hold more than one auction annually. Some work with a particular collectors' club or society. It is our hope that these boxes will give collectors and those searching for specific objects a better idea of who to contact. **Warman's** is designed to give collectors and dealers a lot of clues to find out what they have, what it is worth, and where to sell it!

These special auction boxes are not intended, however, to diminish the outstanding work done by the generalists, those auctioneers who handle all types of material. The fine auctions like Garth's, Skinner's, and Sloan's, provide us with excellent catalogs all through the year covering many aspects of the antiques and collectibles marketplace. Several categories had too many auction houses to list. For example, most auctioneers sell furniture, clocks, and fine arts. We just couldn't list them all. In addition to these auction house boxes, we hope you will consult the master list of auction houses included in this edition. We are sure that any one of them will be eager to assist in consigning or selling antiques and collectibles.

Index: A great deal of effort has been expended to make our index useful. Always begin by looking for the most specific reference. For example, if you have a piece of china, look first for the maker's name and second for the type. Remember, many objects can be classified in three or more categories. If at first you don't succeed, try, try again.

Black-and-White Photographs: You may encounter a piece you cannot identify well enough to use the index. Consult the photographs and marks. If you own several editions of Warman's, you have available a valuable photographic reference to the antiques and collectibles field. Learn to use it.

Price notes

In assigning prices, we assume the object is in very good condition. If otherwise, we note this in our description. It would be ideal to suggest that mint, or unused, examples of all objects exist. The reality is that objects from the past were used, whether they be glass, china, dolls, or toys. Because of this, some normal wear must be expected. In fact, if an object such as a piece of furniture does not show wear, its origins may be more suspect than if it does show wear.

Whenever possible, we have tried to provide a broad listing of prices within a category so you have a "feel" for the market. We emphasize the middle range of prices within a category, while also listing some objects of high and low value to show market spread.

We do not use ranges because they tend to confuse rather than help the collector and dealer. How do you determine if your object is at the high or low end of the range? There is a high degree of flexibility in pricing in the antiques field. If you want to set ranges, add or subtract 10 percent from our prices.

One of the hardest variants with which to deal is the regional fluctuations of prices. Victorian furniture brings widely differing prices in New York, Chicago, New Orleans, or San Francisco. We have tried to strike a balance. Know your region and subject before investing heavily. If the best buys for cameo glass are in Montreal or Toronto, then be prepared to go there if you want to save money or add choice pieces to your collection. Research and patience are key factors to building a collection of merit.

Another factor that affects prices is a sale by a leading dealer or private collector. We temper both dealer and auction house figures.

Price research

Everyone asks, "Where do you get your prices?"
They come from many sources.

First, we rely on auctions. Auction houses and auctioneers do not always command the highest prices. If they did, why do so many dealers buy from them? The key to understanding auction prices is to know when a price is high or low in the range. We think we do this and do it well. The 32nd edition represents a concentrated effort to contact more regional auction houses, both large and small. The cooperation has been outstanding and has resulted in an ever-growing pool of auction prices and trends to help us determine the most up-to-date auction prices.

Second, we work closely with dealers. We screen our contacts to make certain they have full knowledge of the market. Dealers make their living from selling antiques; they cannot afford to have a price guide which is not in touch with the market.

More than 50 antiques and collectibles magazines, newspapers, and journals come into our office regularly. They are excellent barometers of what is moving and what is not. We don't hesitate to call an advertiser and ask if his listed merchandise sold.

When the editorial staff is doing field work, we identify ourselves. Our conversations with dealers and collectors around the country have enhanced this book. Teams from Warman's are in the field at antiques shows, malls, flea markets, and auctions recording prices and taking photographs.

Collectors work closely with us. They are specialists whose devotion to research and accurate information is inspiring. Generally, they are not dealers. Whenever we have asked them for help, they have responded willingly and admirably.

Board of advisors

Our Board of Advisors is made up of specialists, both dealers and collectors, who feel a commitment to accurate information. You'll find their names listed in the front of the book. Several have authored a major reference work on their subject.

Our esteemed Board of Advisors has increased in number and scope. Participants have all provided detailed information regarding the history and reference section of their particular area of expertise, as well as preparing price listings. Many furnished excellent photographs and even shared with us their thoughts on the state of the market.

We are delighted to include those who are valuable members, officers, and founders of collectors' clubs. They are authors of books and articles, and many frequently lecture to groups about their specialties. Most of our advisors have been involved with antiques and collectibles for more than 20 years. Several are retired, and the antiques and collectibles business is a hobby which encompasses most of their free time. Others are a bit younger and either work full time or part time in the antiques and collectibles profession. We asked them about their favorite publications, and most responded with the names of specialized trade papers. Many told us they are regular readers of *AntiqueWeek* and the *Maine Antique Digest*.

One thing they all have in common is their enthusiasm for the antiques and collectibles marketplace. They are eager to share their knowledge with collectors. Many have developed wonderful friendships through their efforts and are enriched by them. If you wish to buy or sell an object in the field of expertise of any of our advisors, drop them a note along with an SASE. If time permits, they will respond.

Buyer's guide, not seller's guide

Warman's is designed to be a buyer's guide suggesting what you would have to pay to purchase an object on the open market from a dealer or collector. **It is not a seller's guide to prices**. People frequently make this mistake. In doing so, they deceive themselves. If you have an object listed in this book and wish to sell it to a dealer, you should expect to receive approximately 50 percent of the listed value. If the object will not resell quickly, expect to receive even less.

Private collectors may pay more, perhaps 70 to 80 percent of our listed price, if your object is something needed for their collection. If you have an extremely rare object or an object of exceptionally high value, these guidelines do not apply.

Examine your piece as objectively as possible. As an antiques and collectibles appraiser, I spend a great deal of time telling people their treasures are not "rare" at all, but items readily available in the marketplace.

In respect to buying and selling, a simple philosophy is that a good purchase occurs when the buyer and seller are happy with the price. Don't look back. Hindsight has little value in the antiques and collectibles field. Given time, things tend to balance out.

Always improving

Warman's is always trying to improve. Space is freely given to long price descriptions, to help you understand that the piece looks like, perhaps what's special about it. With this edition, we're arranged some old formats, using more **bold** words to help you find what you're looking for. Some categories have been arranged so that if the only thing you know is how high, you can start there. Many times identifying that you've got is the hardest part. Well, the first place to start is how big, grab that ruler and see what you can find that's a comparable size. You are still going to have make a determination about what the object is made of, be it china, glass, porcelain, wood, or other materials. Use all your senses to discover what you've got. Ask questions about your object, who made it, and why, how was it used, where and when. As you find answers to these questions, you'll be helping yourself figure out just what the treasure is all about. Now take that information and you'll be able to look it up and discover the value.

Eager to hear from readers

At **Warman's** and Krause Publications, we're always eager to hear what you think about Warman's, how we can improve it. Write to either Ellen Schroy, Warman's Editor, P.O. Box 392, Quakertown, PA 18951-0392 or e-mail at schroy@voicenet.com. The fine staff at Krause Publications can be reached at 700 E. State St., Iola, WI 54990. It's our goal to continue in the **Warman's** tradition and make it the best price guide available.

ACKNOWLEDGMENTS

As we reach the end of production for the 32nd edition of *Warman's Antiques & Collectibles Price Guide*, my thoughts turn with grateful thanks to the fine folks at Krause Publications for making this edition so special.

From the stunning cover right to the back cover, this edition is crammed full of information. The listings are new and I can now say that each and every price has gotten my personal attention and consideration, as have the introductions, the photographs, and the captions.

The Board of Advisors have done a sterling job, many providing even longer lists than before—again with an attention to detail that well deserves my praise. Many have supplied photographs and taught me more about their specialties. Also, this year, many more auction houses have provided photographs, giving this edition of Warman's a fresh look.

However, it was the Books Division, the Art Department, and the Production Department at Krause Publications that have put it all together in the form you hold in your hands. They agonize over how the words fit together, check my spelling and all those other things editors check. Kris Manty has been the editor on this project and I'm sure you'll agree that for her first Warman's, she has done a great job. Together we've made some changes to the Warman's format, some major, some so minor you may not even notice, but hopefully it will make for a more readable edition. And, because this Warman's belongs to a long series of books, it's important to me to keep the same kind of cover—something that probably naturally frustrates the Art Department, but graphic designer Tom Dupuis has done a great job.

Patsy Morrison, Production Department, deserves my thanks and all the credit for making the words fit the pages, and making sure the illustrations are right side up. Her attention to details and her patience is awe inspiring!

Add to this the more than 400 other people who make up Krause Publications and you can see that Warman's has a great new home with this team of talented folks.

I had the privilege of spending several days late in 1997 with the Krause Publications family and left with a greater appreciation for their talents; plus, I can now add their smiles to that happiness I hear in their voices.

As you may know, the Warman price guide series is now written on the East Coast and translated to the pages you see in Iola, Wis. This offers some challenges, which we've solved together with e-mail, telephone and fax.

The enthusiasm with which the Warman series is received at Krause Publications makes me very secure in the hope that Warman's now has a wonderful new home. And best of all, the staff at Krause Publications are just dedicated as I am to making each edition the best it can be!

Ellen Louise Tischbein Schroy
February 17, 1998

STATE OF THE MARKET

The state of the antiques and collectibles marketplace is holding tight in this time of widely fluctuating stocks and bond prices. Whether you're a bear or a bull, there are fascinating opportunities for you in this market. Some prices of antiques and collectibles have reached new highs, and sadly, some of loss. It can't begin to compare to those who worry daily about their stock market portfolios. Hopefully they can take some solace in their collections which are probably slowly increasing in value every year.

Throughout the past year and through travels around the country, visits to antique shops, shows, flea markets, and malls, one thing was constantly observed: people were buying–perhaps not the most expensive item in the booth, but objects and money were changing hands and keeping the economy moving. Some dealers may not have done as well as others, but is not that the way it goes with free enterprise? The next time you visit an antiques sale, watch the number of people carrying objects happily out of the door. Their smiles say a lot about the status of the antiques marketplace. It's rather infrequent to see someone leaving with a frown.

The antiques and collectibles marketplace seemed to have more energy than in past years. Auctions were still king. Major auctions of items belonging to many celebrities, and even sales of the possessions of ordinary folks, made headlines. This past year we heard about the dresses of the late Princess Diana as they were sold at Christie's. Many aspects of the market have remained highly interesting, like paintings and art work. Add to that the newly growing excitement about scientific instruments, a field being added by some of the larger auction houses. The first Scientific and Technology auction at Skinners was such an international success that more are being planned. More and more reports about auctions made the evening news, our newspapers and magazines. More and more auction house representatives and specialists in the antiques and collectibles world presented us with information through several media avenues. One must learn to listen carefully to these experts. What are they trying to tell us? Are they promoting something? Many times they will carefully avoid expressing their views about what to collect in the future, for it's too speculative a market right now.

One example of this changing market is the comic books marketplace. Several years ago, there were many individuals heavily buying comic books as investments. Today, this same comic book market has returned to those individuals who are interested in the artwork, and other aspects, not just the potential financial rewards. Several dealers of comic books feel the market has returned to its roots–those who love comic books, not just speculators. There will always be those folks trying to figure out what the next "hot" area is going to be. Would the antiques and collectibles marketplace continue to be such fun if we all had crystal balls?

Probably the biggest change in the antiques and collectibles marketplace is the expanded use of the computer and World Wide Web. One only has to explore the thousands of sites to find his heart's desire, strike a deal with e-mail or fax, and then it's back to surfing the net for more fun. In a field where a price guide or new reference book can immediately affect prices, the computer will someday also do that. To date, most dealers are sticking to the published reference books when pricing and then listing their objects for sale in cyberspace. If the piece fails to find a buyer in cyberspace, the dealer still has the option of including the same piece in his shop or show, finding a buyer the old-fashioned way.

Internet web sites, or addresses, exist for every part of the antiques and collectibles marketplace. You can go online and chat for hours about your favorite pieces, ask questions of experts, and research all kinds of information. Everyone–from auctioneers, dealers, and collectors clubs–has home pages. Some of these home pages are more exciting than others, and, like everything else, you must decide which ones suit your particular needs. The Alderfer Auction Company has an interesting site at http://www.alderfercompany.com. It lists information pertaining to its upcoming auctions and other information of interest to collectors and dealers. One sparkling site is http://www.glass.co.nz/ This site features Angela Bowery's Online Glass Museum. It's her concept of a glass museum, complete with stunning photographs, informative articles, etc. It's a treat for the eyes, as well as the mind. The first "internet" collector's club has been created by carnival glass collectors. Visit http://www.zeus.kspress.com/woodsland/carnivalglass to see this exciting new club. WWW.CGA. They've got all the features of a "live" club, but with the advantage of internet speed and convenience. Many of these web sites are growing, changing, and constantly improving. They are fun to visit and probably will become a very integral part of the antiques and collectibles marketplace as we look forward to the next century!

One area of the internet antiques world that is still coming of age is the internet auction. Some wonderful pieces are offered daily and the excitement of an auction is certainly present. What you're missing is the ability to hold and closely examine the object. If you can deal with that aspect, great; if not, perhaps it's not worth the time for you. Hopefully, all the pieces offered are as they are described, but because you can't personally handle the object, don't be afraid to ask questions, etc. It's a place where the "buyer beware" phrase is important.

Part of what makes the internet work so well is the fast exchange of ideas between participants. Antiques collectors and dealers have always been a very loosely bonded network. Ideas and information are passed on every day. **Warman's** is very fortunate to have the guidance of a Board of Advisors, whose members eagerly share their information. They not only submit information on the background of their categories and offer current price listings, but they also offer their opinions on the state of the market. Last edition in the State of the Market report, we concluded Mechanical Banks Advisor James Maxwell was realistic when he reported that some bank prices have declined in the last year. He feels that the quantity and quality of the banks coming into the marketplace over the last few months have given buyers many opportunities to add to their collections while paying less. He predicts "that this downward swing will continue for many years to come and that banks will arrive at a more realistic and much lower price level." He further predicts "lower prices will stabilize in seven years and not begin to climb again for at least 10-12 years."

This conclusion is based on James' careful study of the fluctuations in the mechanical bank market over the last 60 years. He is optimistic this downward swing will bring new collectors into the market and help keep the allure of these appealingly designed banks alive for us all.

Well, Mr. Maxwell is standing by his statement. This year he tells us, "As a general statement, many bank prices have fluctuated downward and some remained stable over the year for average condition examples of both rare and common banks. Rare banks in superb condition, for the most part, have remained stable. Common makes in like new (97% to 99% original paint) have gone up.

"Currently, I feel that common all original banks in 80% painted are underpriced and common banks with 97%+ paint are overpriced," he said. This accurate assessment can be transferred to other areas of the antiques and collectibles marketplace.

Record-setting prices

As a new feature of this year's **Warman's,** we've decided to list some record-setting prices. Everyone hopes that their special items are the most important, and some folks were delighted to have these dreams realized this past year. Some examples are:

Astronomical telescope by Alvan Clark & Son, Cambridge, MA, offered at Skinner's Auction of Science & Technology, July 19, 1997. The price realized was $14,950. Listed as a 6-inch Refractor Telescope, it measured 92" l, x 87" h when mounted with counterweight equatorial mount, it's mahogany tripod, 7 eyepiece, 1 rt angle eyepiece, tube, partial spotting scope, lens cover. It was estimated at $4,000-$6,000.

Albrecht Auctions, Vassar, MI, struck down a new carnival glass record with a Memphis pattern ice green punch bowl and base. This Northwood pattern fetched $15,000.

Gary Kisner Auctions, of Coral Springs, FL, established a new record for a Mettlach vase. This vase has an etched scene of a knight on one side, and a maiden on the reverse. It stands 48" h and is one of two examples known to exist. It is dated 1900, sgd "C. Spindler," but not numbered. The price realized was $46,000.

It is only the big auction houses that garner the high prices. The Sandwich Auction House, Sandwich, MA, discovered a fine pair of brass andirons. These 30-3/4" h andirons had fluted urns, tapered sq columns, spurred legs with fully developed ball and claw feet. The columns, skirts, and capitals were covered with engraving, including rayed ovals, starbursts, tulips with vine and leaf,

draped swag, a memorial urn and weeping willow. By the time of the auction, all the seats were taken, and excitement swelled until the hammer dropped on these andirons at $52,250, setting a new record price for American andirons.

A weather vane topped another Skinner Auction in August. This molded and gilded full bodied copper merino ram once stood atop the Abbot Worsted Mill buildings in Westford, MA. It was a striking example of form, a well weathered gilded surface with verdigris and documented provenance. The bidding ended at $68,500.

A telephone bidder won an Eskimo polychrome bentwood hunting hat with an open crown and striking decorative painting at Skinner's American Indian auction for $68,500. This bidder competed with several other telephone bidders from all across the country. It tripled it's pre-sale bid, setting a new record for this type of material.

Skinner's also sold a hand-blown tumbler by John Frederick Amelung, for $83,900. This particular tumbler had been etched "Federal" and was made to commemorate the ratification of the U.S. Constitution in 1788.

Freeman/Fine Arts, Philadelphia, sold a pair of Tucker urn/vases for $291,500 to a telephone bidder. These vases are exquisitely decorated. One has views of Sedgley Park, seat of James Fisher, and is titled below the scene, with the reverse scene featuring the Schuykill River. The other vase is decorated with a shipwreck, including a man and woman fleeing on horseback while firing a gun at Indians. These 20-3/4" and 21" h vases have gilt decorations and griffin handles.

Ron Bourgeault's Northeast Auction Sale in Manchester, NH, just sold a Boston Queen Anne wing chair for a record $387,500. This record price is even more stunning when you consider the chair was stripped down to its frame.

Butterfields in San Francisco also sold a record priced item recently. It auctioned a Massachusetts highboy which was japanned. It is a Dorr family Boston flat top high chest, which has descended through the family. The auction house noted that the family declined to have some restoration done to the piece several years ago. It is believed this helped push the price that much higher to $772,500. The new owner plans only to stabilize it in his desire to preserve it for the future.

If your collecting tastes run to sporting and fishing, you missed a record auction at Lang Sporting Collectables, Inc., 31 R. Turtle Cove, Raymond, ME 04071, on Nov. 15, 1997.

Several record prices were set at this auction, despite an early Northeastern snow storm and treacherous driving conditions. It was an auction filled with eager bidding and lots of absentee bidders.

Lang's is known as the "nation's leading fishing tackle auction," and no one was disappointed with the escalation in lure prices at the November auction. A rare Heddon #1400 Dowagiac Minnow sold for $9,900, which was twice its estimate. This wonderful lure not only set an auction record for Heddon bait, but also an auction record price for any wooden lure. This particular lure appeared in the 1913 Heddon catalog and is one of six known examples. It's got a flat bottom and an experimental triangular staple belly hook hanger.

Other Heddons also received record prices with a #1770 Minnow (frog scale) realizing $1,980; a Spindriver

An auction record price for a wooden lure of $9,900 was paid for this 1913 Heddon No. 1400 Dowagiac Minnow. Photos courtesy Lang's Collectables, Inc.

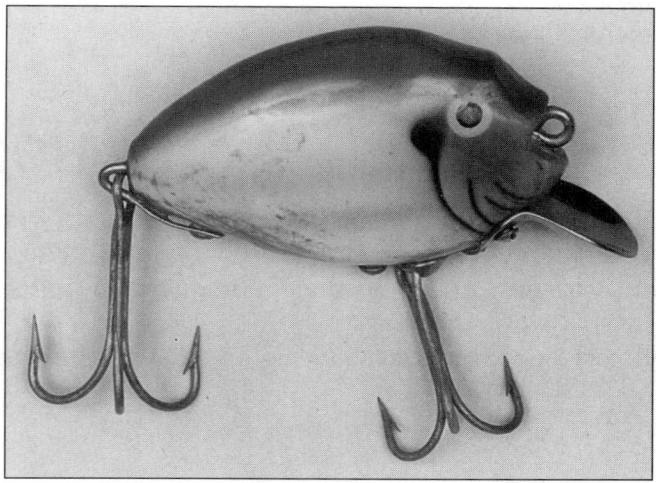

An auction price record for a Heddon Punkinseed was set when this rainbow example soared past the $400 high estimate to bring $1,320.

(green crackle back) reaching $1,650; and a Punkinseed with rainbow finish landed $1,320.

Now, if you need a record-setting bait reel to go with that lure, Lang's sold an 1896 patent Pflueger wood line winder-type reel for $1,210, setting an auction price record for any American wooden reel. An Edw. Vom Hofe, N.Y., handmade German silver and hard rubber #2 Perfection fly-reel model went for $4,400 and a Peerless model fetched a record $6,050.

In the reel accessories department, a bottle of Milam reel oil, complete with its original box, set a record at $935.

Other record-setting prices at this auction included a 4-foot Old Town Sales Sample Canoe that sold above its estimate of $6,270; a C.C.B.C. tackle catalog that sold for $605, A Heddon 1934 catalog that reeled in $440 and a 1939 one that sold for $265; a 1908 Bristol calendar print that went for $630; a 1926 Pflueger poster that sold for $550; and a "Joe's Tackle Shop" sign bought for $495. An 1870 trout fishing lithograph brought $1,045.

Who know what kinds of treasures will find their way into the antiques and collectibles market in the next few months and years. May you be the lucky finder/buyer/seller/auctioneer of such a wonderful object.

Selling for $1,100, this lure in its illustrated box set a record price for a Creek Chub Wiggler.

Auction price records were paid for this Heddon Near Surface Wiggler, top, ($1,980) and Spindiver ($1,650).

The bottle of Milam's reel oil, left, fetched a record $935, while the Horton Mfg. Meek bottle brought $550.

AUCTION HOUSES

The following auction houses cooperate with **Warman's** by providing catalogs of their auctions and price lists. This information is used to prepare *Warman's Antiques and Collectibles Price Guide*, volumes in the Warman's Encyclopedia of Antiques and Collectibles. This support is truly appreciated.

Albrecht & Cooper Auction Services
3884 Saginaw Rd.
Vassar, MI 48768
(517) 823-8835

Sanford Alderfer Auction Company
501 Fairgrounds Rd.
Hatfield, PA 19440
(215) 393-3000
web site: http://www.alderfercompany.com

Andre Ammelounx
The Stein Auction Company
P.O. Box 136
Palantine, IL 60078
(847) 991-5927

Apple Tree Auction Center
1616 W. Church St.
Newark, OH 43055
(614) 344-4282

The Armans' Collector's Sales and
Services
P.O. Box 4037
Middletown, RI 02842
(401) 849-5012

Arthur Auctioneering
RD 2, P.O. Box 155
Hughesville, PA 17737
(717) 584-3697

Aston Macek Auctioneers
& Appraisers
2825 Country Club Rd.
Endwell, NY 13760
(607) 785-6598

Auction Team Köln
Jane Herz
6731 Ashley Court
Sarasota, FL 34241
(941) 925-0385

Auction Team Köln
Postfach 501168 D 5000
Köln 50, W. Germany

Bailey's Antiques
102 E Main St.
Homer, MI 49245
(517) 568-4014

Noel Barrett Antiques & Auctions, Ltd.
P.O. Box 1001
Carversville, PA 18913
(610) 297-5109

Robert F. Batchelder
1 W. Butler Ave.
Ambler, PA 19002
(610) 643-1430

Bill Bertoia Auctions
1881 Spring Rd.
Vineland, NJ 08360
(609) 692-1881

Biders Antiques Inc.
241 S Union St.
Lawrence, MA 01843
(508) 688-4347

Brown Auction & Real Estate
900 East Kansas
Greensburg, KS 67054
(316) 723-2111

Butterfield & Butterfield
7601 Sunset Blvd.
Los Angeles, CA 90046
(213) 850-7500

Butterfield & Butterfield
220 San Bruno Ave.
San Francisco, CA 94103
(415) 861-7500

C. C. Auction Gallery
416 Court
Clay Center, KS 67432
(913) 632-6021

W. E. Channing & Co., Inc.
53 Old Santa Fe Trail
Santa Fe, NM 87501
(505) 988-1078

Chicago Art Galleries
5039 Oakton St.
Skokie, IL 60077
(847) 677-6080

Christie's
502 Park Ave.
New York, NY 10022
(212) 546-1000
web site: http://www.sirius.com/~christie/

Christie's East
219 E 67th St.
New York, NY 10021
(212) 606-0400

Cincinnati Art Galleries
635 Main St.
Cincinnati, OH 45202
(513) 381-2128

Mike Clum, Inc.
P.O. Box 2
Rushville, OH 43150
(614) 536-9220

Cohasco Inc.
Postal 821
Yonkers, NY 10702
(914) 476-8500

Samuel J. Cottonne
15 Genesee St.
Mt. Morris, NY 14510
(716) 583-3119

Craftsman Auctions
1485 W. Housatoric
Pittsfield MA 01201
(413) 442-7003

Dargate Auction Galleries
5607 Baum Blvd.
Pittsburgh, PA 15206
(412) 362-3558
web site: http://www.dargate.com

DeWolfe & Wood
P.O. Box 425
Alfred, ME 04002
(207) 490-5572

Marlin G. Denlinger
RR3, Box 3775
Morrisville, VT 05661
(802) 888-2775

Dixie Sporting Collectibles
1206 Rama Rd.
Charlotte, NC 28211
(704) 364-2900
web site: http://www.sportauction

William Doyle Galleries, Inc.
175 E. 87th St.
New York, NY 10128
(212) 427-2730
web site: http://www.doylegalleries.com

Dunbar Gallery
76 Haven St.
Milford, MA 01757
(508) 634-8697

Dunning's Auction Service
755 Church Road
Elgin, IL 60123
(847) 741-3483

Early Auction Co.
123 Main St.
Milford, OH 45150
(513) 831-4833

Fain & Co.
P.O. Box 1330
Grants Pass, OR 97526
(888) 324-6726

Ken Farmer Realty & Auction Co.
105A Harrison St.
Radford, VA 24141
(703) 639-0939
web site: http://kenfarmer.com

Fine Tool Journal
27 Fickett Rd.
Pownal, ME 04069
(207) 688-4962
web site: http://www.wowpages.com/FTJ/

Steve Finer Rare Books
P.O. Box 758
Greenfield, MA 01302
(413) 773-5811

Flomaton Antique Auction
207 Palafox St.
Flomaton, AL 36441
(334) 296-3059

William A. Fox Auctions Inc.
676 Morris Ave.
Springfield, NJ 07081
(201) 467-2366

Freeman/Fine Arts Co. of Philadelphia,
Inc.
1808 Chestnut St.
Philadelphia, PA 19103
(215) 563-9275

Garth's Auction, Inc.
2690 Stratford Rd
P.O. Box 369
Delaware, OH 43015
(614) 362-4771

Greenberg Auctions
7566 Main St.
Skysville, MD 21784
(410) 795-7447

Green Valley Auction Inc.
Route 2, Box 434
Mt Crawford, VA 22841
(540) 434-4260

Guerney's
136 E. 73rd St.
New York, NY 10021
(212) 794-2280

Hake's Americana & Collectibles
P.O. Box 1444
York, PA 17405
(717) 848-1333

Gene Harris Antique Auction Center,
Inc.
203 South 18th Ave.
P.O. Box 476
Marshalltown, IA 50158
(515) 752-0600

Norman C. Heckler & Company
Bradford Corner Rd.
Woodstock Valley, CT 06282
(203) 974-1634

High Noon
9929 Venice Blvd.
Los Angeles CA 90034
(310) 202-9010

Leslie Hindman, Inc.
215 W Ohio St.
Chicago, IL 60610
(312) 670-0010

Historical Collectible Auctions
P.O. Box 975
Burlington, N.C. 27215
(910) 570-2803

Michael Ivankovich Auction Co.
P.O. Box 2458
Doylestown, PA 18901
(215) 345-6094

Jackson's Auctioneers & Appraisers
2229 Lincoln St.
Cedar Falls, IA 50613
(319) 277-2256
e-mail: jacksons @corenet.net

James D. Julia Inc.
Rt. 201 Skowhegan Rd.
P.O. Box 830
Fairfield, ME 04937
(207) 453-7125

J.W. Auction Co.
54 Rochester Hill Road
Rochester, N.H. 03867
(603) 332-0192

Lang's Sporting Collectables
31 R. Turtle Cove
Raymond, ME 04071
(207) 655-4265

La Rue Auction Service
201 S. Miller St.,
Sweet Springs, MO 65351
(816) 335-4538

Leonard's Auction Company
1631 State Rd.
Duncannon, PA 17020
(717) 957-3324

Howard Lowery
3818 W. Magnolia Blvd.
Burbank, CA 91505
(818) 972-9080

Joy Luke
The Gallery
300 E. Grove St.
Bloomington, IL 61701
(309) 828-5533

Mapes Auctioneers & Appraisers
1729 Vestal Pkwy.
Vestal, NY 13850
(607) 754-9193

Martin Auctioneers Inc.
P.O. Box 477
Intercourse, PA 17534
(717) 768-8108

McMasters Doll Auctions
P.O. Box 1755
Cambridge, OH 43725
(614) 432-4419

Metropolitan Book Auction
123 W. 18th St., 4th Floor
New York, NY 10011
(212) 929-7099

Wm. Frost Mobley
P.O. Box 10
Schoharie, NY 12157
(518) 295-7978

Wm. Morford
RD #2
Cazenovia, NY 13035
(315) 662-7625

New England Auction Gallery
P.O. Box 2273
W Peabody, MA 01960
(508) 535-3140

New Hampshire Book Auctions
P.O. Box 460
92 Woodbury Rd.
Weare, NH 03281
(603) 529-7432

Norton Auctioneers of Michigan Inc.
50 West Pearl at Monroe
Coldwater MI 49036
(517) 279-9063

Ohio Cola Traders
Donald Stocz
4411 Bazetta Road
Cortland, OH 44410
1-800-397-6546

Old Barn Auction
10040 St. Rt. 224 West
Findlay, OH 45840
(419) 422-8531
web site: http://www.oldbarn.com

Richard Opfer Auctioneering Inc.
1919 Greenspring Dr.
Timonium, MD 21093
(410) 252-5035

Pacific Book Auction Galleries
133 Kerney St., 4th Floor
San Francisco, CA 94108
(415) 989-2665
web site: http://www.nbn.com/~pba/

Past Tyme Pleasures
101 First St. Suite 404
Los Altos, CA 94022
(510) 484-4488

Pettigrew Auction Company
1645 S.Tejon St.
Colorado Springs, CO 80906
(719) 633-7963

Phillips Fine Art Auctions
406 E. 79th St.
New York, NY 10021
(212) 570-4830

Postcards International
2321 Whitney Ave., Sutie 102
P.O. Box 5398
Hamden, CT 06518
(203) 248-6621
web site: http://www.csmon-
line.com/postcardsint/

Poster Auctions International
601 W. 26th St.
New York, NY 10001
(212) 787-4000

Provenance
P.O. Box 3487
Wallington, NJ 07057
(201) 779-8725

David Rago Auctions, Inc.
333 S. Main St.
Lambertville, NJ 08530
(609) 397-9374

Lloyd Ralston Toys
173 Post Rd.
Fairfield, CT 06432
(203) 255-1233

Mickey Reichel Auctioneer
1440 Ashley Rd.
Boonville MO 65233
(816) 882-5292

Sandy Rosnick Auctions
15 Front St.
Salem, MA 01970
(508) 741-1130

Thomas Schmidt
7099 McKean Rd.
Ypsilanti, MI 48197
(313) 485-8606

Seeck Auctions
P.O. Box 377
Mason City, IA 50402
(515) 424-1116
website: www.wil-
lowtree.com/~seeckauctions

L. H. Selman Ltd
761 Chestnut St.
Santa Cruz, CA 95060
(408) 427-1177
web site: http://www.selman.com

Sentry Auction
113 School St.
Apollo, PA 15613
(412) 478-1989

Robert W. Skinner Inc.
Bolton Gallery
357 Main St.
Bolton, MA 01740
(508) 779-6241

Skinner, Inc.
The Heritage on the Garden
63 Park Plaza
Boston MA 02116
(617) 350-5429

C. G. Sloan & Company Inc.
4920 Wyaconda Rd.
North Bethesda, MD 20852
(301) 468-4911
web site: http://www.cgsloan.com

Smith & Jones, Inc., Auctions
12 Clark Lane
Sudbury MA 01776
(508) 443-5517

Smith House Toy Sales
26 Adlington Rd.
Eliot, ME 03903
(207) 439-4614

R. M. Smythe & Co.
26 Broadway
New York, NY 10004-1710

Sotheby's
1334 York Ave.
New York, NY 10021
(212) 606-7000
web site: http://www.sothebys.com

Southern Folk Pottery Collectors
Society
1828 N. Howard Mill Rd.
Robbins, NC 27325
(910) 464-3961

Stanton's Auctioneers
P.O. Box 146
144 South Main St.
Vermontville, MI 49096
(517) 726-0181

Stout Auctions
11 W. Third St.
Williamsport, IN 47993-1119
(765) 764-6901

Michael Strawser
200 N. Main St., P.O. Box 332
Wolcottville, IN 46795
(219) 854-2859

Swann Galleries Inc.
104 E. 25th St.
New York, NY 10010
(212) 254-4710

Swartz Auction Services
2404 N. Mattis Ave.
Champaign, IL 61826-7166
(217) 357-0197
web site: http://www/SwartzAuction.com

Theriault's
P.O. Box 151
Annapolis, MD 21401
(301) 224-3655

Toy Scouts
137 Casterton Ave.
Akron, OH 44303
(216) 836-0668
e-mail: toyscout@salamander.net

Treadway Gallery, Inc.
2029 Madison Rd.
Cincinnati, OH 45208
(513) 321-6742
web site: http://www.a3c2net.com/treadwaygallery

Victorian Images
P.O. Box 284
Marlton, NJ 08053
(609) 985-7711

Victorian Lady
P.O. Box 424
Waxhaw, NC 28173
(704) 843-4467

Vintage Cover Story
P.O. Box 975
Burlington, NC 27215
(919) 584-6900

Bruce and Vicki Waasdorp
P.O. Box 434
10931 Main St.
Clarence, NY 14031
(716) 759-2361

Web Wilson Antiques
P.O. Box 506
Portsmouth, RI 02871
1-800-508-0022

Winter Associates
21 Cooke St. Box 823
Plainville, CT 06062
(203) 793-0288

Wolf's Auctioneers
1239 W. 6th St.
Cleveland, OH 44113
(614) 362-4711

Woody Auction
Douglass, KS 67039
(316) 746-2694

ABBREVIATIONS

The following are standard abbreviations which we have used throughout this edition of **Warman's**.

4to = 8" x 10"
8vo = 5" x 7"
12mo = 3" x 5"
ADS = Autograph Document Signed
adv = advertising
ah = applied handle
ALS = Autograph Letter Signed
AQS = Autograph Quotation Signed
C = century
c = circa
circ = circular
cov = cover
CS = Card Signed
d = diameter or depth
dec = decorated
dj = dust jacket
DQ = Diamond Quilted
DS = Document Signed
ed = edition
emb = embossed
ext. = exterior
Folio = 12" x 16"
ftd = footed
gal = gallon
ground = background
h = height
hp = hand painted
hs = high standard
illus = illustrated, illustration
imp = impressed
int. = interior
irid = iridescent
IVT = inverted thumbprint
j = jewels
K = karat
l = length

lb = pound
litho = lithograph
ll = lower left
lr = lower right
ls = low standard
LS = Letter Signed
mfg = manufactured
MIB = mint in box
MOP = mother-of-pearl
NE = New England
No. = number
opal = opalescent
orig = original
os = orig stopper
oz = ounce
pat = patent
pcs = pieces
pgs = pages
PUG = printed under the glaze
pr = pair
PS = Photograph Signed
pt = pint
qt = quart
rect = rectangular
sgd = signed
sngl = single
SP = silver plated
SS = Sterling silver
sq = square
TLS = Typed Letter Signed
unp = unpaged
vol = volume
w = width
yg = yellow gold
# = numbered

ABC PLATES

History: The majority of early ABC plates were manufactured in England and imported into the United States. They achieved their greatest popularity from 1780 to 1860. Since a formal education was uncommon in the early 19th century, the ABC plate was a method of educating the poor for a few pennies.

ABC plates were made of glass, pewter, porcelain, pottery, or tin. Porcelain plates range in diameter from 4-3/8 to slightly over 9-1/2 inches. The rim usually contains the alphabet and/or numbers; the center features animals, great men, maxims, or nursery rhymes.

References: Susan and Al Bagdade, *Warman's English & Continental Pottery & Porcelain*, 2nd ed., Wallace-Homestead, 1991; Mildred L. and Joseph P. Chalala, *A Collector's Guide to ABC Plates, Mugs and Things*, Pridemark Press, 1980; Irene and Ralph Lindsey, *ABC Plates & Mugs,* Collector Books, 1997; Noel Riley, *Gifts for Good Children*, Richard Dennis Publications, 1991.

Collectors' Club: ABC Plate/Mug Collectors, 67 Stevens Ave., Old Bridge, NJ 08857.

Glass

Christmas Eve, Santa on chimney, clear, 6" d......................75.00
Clock face center, Arabic and Roman numerals, alphabet center, frosted and clear, 7" d 75.00
Duck, amber, 6" d..45.00
Elephant with howdah, three waving Brownies, Ripley & Co., clear, 6" d 135.00
Frosted Stork, flake..125.00
Little Bo Peep, center scene, raised alphabet border, 6" d .50.00
Plain center, clear, white scalloped edge, 6" d 65.00
Young Girl, portrait, clear, 6" d 65.00

Pottery or Porcelain

Boy, stringed instrument, bird on fence, brown transfer, emb alphabet border, mkd "Adams," 7-1/4" d 80.00

Child reading, black transfer, polychrome enamel, Staffordshire, 5" d, short hairline, small back edge flakes 35.00
Crusoe Finding the Footprints, 7 1/2" d 80.00
Father Matthews, soft paste, enamel, minor damage 72.00
Gathering Cotton, 6" d 425.00
Keep Within Compass, soft paste, enamel, minor damage 85.00
Little Boy Blue..80.00
Make Hay, soft paste, enamel, minor damage....................55.00
Old Mother Hubbard, brown transfer, polychrome enamel trim, alphabet border, mkd "Tunstall," 7-1/2" d 200.00
Take Your Time Miss Lucy, black transfer of money and cat, polychrome enamel, titled, molded hops rim, red trim, ironstone, imp "Meakin," 6" d 125.00
Three Removes, soft paste, enamel, minor damage............85.00

Tin

Girl on swing, lithographed center, printed alphabet border, 3-1/2" d 60.00
Mary Had A Little Lamb, light rust, 9" d...............................115.00
Two kittens playing with basket of wood, 4-1/2" d...............80.00
Who Killed Cock Robin, 7-3/4" d 120.00

ADAMS ROSE

History: Adams Rose, made about 1820 to 1840 by Adams and Son in the Staffordshire district of England, is decorated with brilliant red roses and green leaves on a white ground.

G. Jones and Son, England, made a variant known as "Late Adams Rose," which has a dirty-white ground. The colors in this pattern are not as brilliant and pieces sell for less than the original Adams Rose.

Bowl, 9-1/2" d, 4-1/4" h, scalloped rim, chips....................720.00
Creamer, early..350.00
Cup and Saucer, handleless, red, green, and black dec, imp "Adams" 220.00
Cup Plate, 4-1/2" d...115.00
Milk Pitcher, 6-1/2" h, bulbous, emb...................................145.00
Plate, red, green, and black dec, imp "Adams"
    7-1/8" d, rim hairline..40.00
    8-1/2" d, late..70.00
    9-1/2" d, late..80.00
    10-1/2" d..150.00

Raised alphabet border, multicolored scene of children with kite, 6" d, $90. Photo courtesy of Susan and Al Bagdade.

Plate, green and maroon flowers, imp "Adams," 9" d, $125. Photo courtesy of Susan and Al Bagdade.

Platter, 13-1/2" l, red, green, and black dec, imp "Adams," minor scratches 385.00
Saucer, red, green, and black, blue spatter, stains 125.00
Soup Plate, 10-1/2" d, mkd "Adams" 100.00
Sugar, cov, late..185.00
Teapot, cov, late...235.00
Waste Bowl 245.00

ADVERTISING

History: Before the days of mass media, advertisers relied on colorful product labels and advertising giveaways to promote their products. Containers were made to appeal to the buyer through the use of stylish lithographs and bright colors. Many of the illustrations used the product in the advertisement so that even an illiterate buyer could identify a product.

Advertisements were put on almost every household object imaginable and were constant reminders to use the product or visit a certain establishment.

References: *Advertising & Figural Tape Measures*, L-W Book Sales, 1995; Art Anderson, *Casinos and Their Ashtrays*, 1994, printed by author (P.O. Box 4103, Flint, MI 48504); Al Bergevin, *Drugstore Tins and Their Prices*, Wallace-Homestead, 1990; A. Walker Bingham, *Snake-Oil Syndrome*, Christopher Publishing House, 1994; Michael Bruner, *Advertising Clocks*, Schiffer Publishing, 1995; ——, *Encyclopedia of Porcelain Enamel Advertising*, Schiffer Publishing, 1994;--, *More Porcelain Enamel Advertising,* Schiffer Publishing, 1997; *Collector's Digest Letter Openers: Advertising & Figural*, L-W Book Sales, 1996; Doug Collins, *America's Favorite Food: The Story of Campbell Soup Company*, Harry N Abrams, 1994; Douglas Congdon-Martin, *America for Sale*, Schiffer Publishing, 1991; ——, *Tobacco Tins*, Schiffer Publishing, 1992; Douglas Congdon-Martin and Robert Biondi, *Country Store Antiques*, Schiffer Publishing, 1991; ——, *Country Store Collectibles*, Schiffer Publishing, 1990; Fred Dodge, *Antique Tins*, 1995, 1997 value update, Collector Books; Warren Dotz, *Advertising Character Collectibles*, Collector Books, 1993, 1997 values updated; ——, *What a Character! 20th Century American Advertising Icons*, Chronicle Books, 1996; James L. Dundas, *Collecting Whistles*, Schiffer Publishing, 1995; Tony Fusco, *Posters Identification and Price Guide*, 2nd ed., Avon Books, 1994.

Ted Hake, *Hake's Guide to Advertising Collectibles*, Wallace-Homestead, 1992; Bill and Pauline Hogan, *Charlton Standard Catalogue of Canadian Country Store Collectibles*, Charlton Press, 1996; Bob and Sharon Huxford, *Huxford's Collectible Advertising*, 3rd ed., Collector Books, 1996; Thomas Patrick Jacobsen, *Pat Jacobsen's First International Price Guide to Fruit Crate Labels*, Patco Enterprise (437 Minton Ct, Pleasant Hill, CA 94523), 1994; Ray Klug, *Antique Advertising Encyclopedia*, Vol. 1 (1978, 1993 value update) and Vol. 2 (1985), L-W Promotions; Mary Jane Lamphier, *Zany Characters of the Ad World*, Collector Books, 1995; Patricia McDaniel, *Drugstore Collectibles*, Wallace-Homestead, 1994; Tom Morrison, *More Root Beer Advertising & Collectibles*, Schiffer Publishing, 1997; Gerald S. Petrone, *Tobacco Advertising*, Schiffer Publishing, 1996; Don and Carol Raycraft, *American Country Store*, Wallace-Homestead, 1994; Bob Sloan and Steve Guarnaccia, *A Stiff Drink and a Close Shave*, Chronicle Books, 1995; Louis Storino, *Chewing Tobacco Tin Tags*, Schiffer Publishing, 1995; Neil Wood, *Smoking Collectibles*, L-W Book Sales, 1994.

Periodicals: *Creamers*, P.O. Box 11, Lake Villa, IL 60046; *Paper Collectors' Marketplace*, P.O. Box 128, Scandinavia, WI 54917; *Advertising Collectors Express*, P.O. Box 221, Mayview, MO 64071.

Collectors' Clubs: Antique Advertising Assoc. of America, P.O. Box 1121, Morton Grove, IL 60053; Button Pusher, P.O. Box 4, Coopersburg, PA 18036; Inner Seal Collectors Club, 6609 Billtown Rd, Louisville, KY 40299; National Assoc of Paper and Advertising Collectibles, P.O. Box 500, Mount Joy, PA 17552; Porcelain Advertising Collectors Club, P.O. Box 381, Marshfield Hills, MA 02051; Ephemera Society of America, P.O. Box 95, Cazenovia, NY 13035; Tin Container Collectors Association, P.O. Box 440101, Aurora, CO 80014.

Museums: American Advertising Museum, Portland, OR; Museum of Transportation, Brookline, MA; National Museum of American History, Archives Center, Smithsonian Institution, Washington, DC.

Additional Listings: See *Warman's Americana & Collectibles* for more examples.

Advertisement, framed
Dr. Jane's Family Medicines, founder's portrait 425.00
Mother's Oats, baby illus...300.00
Bill Hook, "Don't Forget to Order J. G. Davis Co.'s Granite Flour," gray and dark blue, 5-1/2" x 3-5/8" 210.00
Biscuit Box, Columbia, Missouri Can Co, red, white, and blue, Miss Columbia, pre-1900 ....115.00
Biscuit Jar, 10-1/2" h, glass jar, glass lid, "Sunshine Biscuits" emb on front "Loose-Wiles Biscuit Company" on back........350.00
Bottle
Sauer's Vanilla Extract, wood box, graphic label 25.00
Stromeyer's Grape Punch, syrup bottle, reverse with glass label, orig cup lid, 12-1/2" h 200.00

Bottle Carrier
　Dad's Root Beer, wood...25.00
　7-Up, press board 10.00
Box, cardboard
　Adam's Red Rose Chewing Gum, hinged lid, graphic of well
　　dressed women, butterflies, flowers, 1886 testimonial on
　　back, 1" x 6" x 13"...575.00
　Andy Gump Sunshine Biscuits, cardboard, 5" x 3" x 2"
　　..425.00
　Fairbank's Gold Dust Washing Powder, tri-panel, 3 printed
　　panels on front and back, 19" x 9-1/4" 1,000.00
　King Brand Rolled Oats...45.00
　Williams Brothers Valvriggans, men's long underwear ...15.00
Calendar
　1885, L. L. Ferriss, boots, shoes, and rubbers, framed, 6" x 8-
　　1/2" 70.00
　1894, Nestle's Food, "Give the Babies Nestle's Food," © 1894,
　　starts with May, 1894, ends April, 1895, framed to show
　　both sides, 5-1/2" x 11-3/4" x 35-1/2" 50.00
　1909, DeLaval Cream Separator, full pad, 19-1/2" x 12-1/2"
　　..475.00
　1913, Swift's Premium, 4 pages, each with different scene, 17"
　　x 9" 20.00
　1921, McCormick-Deering, young girl sitting on fence at edge
　　of wheat field, 24" x 12" 30.00
Chair, wooden, folding, adv on both sides of backrest
　Cross-Cut Cigarettes, Victorian Lady, slogan, and illus of
　　package, 30-1/2" h 200.00
　Duke's Cigarettes, Victorian Lady and slogan, 32" h 150.00
Cigar Box, Kin-To, full...40.00
Cigar Lighter, hotel lobby type
　Midland Spark, wood base, Model L, c1920, 15" x 7-1/4" x 7"
　　..400.00
　Rising Sun Stove Polish, oak, lighter and cigar cutter, 23" x 9"
　　...1,600.00
Clip, Spencerian Pens 20.00
Counter Display
　Beech-Nut Gum, back of tin display shows little girl with pack-
　　age of gum, mounted on metal pedestal, 14-3/4" h
　　...1,450.00
　Bicycle Playing Cards, tin display, front shows royal flush,
　　sides simulated wood grain, 12-1/2" x 4-1/2" x 8" 100.00
　Dana's Sarsaparilla, metal rim and glass, fancy Art Nouveau
　　filigree on all corners, glass etched "Dana's Sarsaparilla,"
　　5-1/2" x 10" x 10" 50.00
　Ever-ready Shaving Brushes, tin, oversized shaving brush on
　　left side, right side with bald man shaves "trademark" face,
　　shaving brushes displayed behind window, 12" h, 15" w
　　..450.00
　Horseshow Tobacco, wood, hinged display box, decal on
　　glass lid, orig tax stamp, 13" x 13" x 4" 200.00

Cereal Bowl, white china, Yellow Slicker Boy, three boys, two on outside, one inside, wearing yellow slickers, 5" d, 3" h, $60.

Regal Elastic Web, slanted oak case, int. compartmentalized
　for corset supplies, 7" x 6" x 18" 400.00
Sir Walter Raleigh Tin, 6 orig pocket tins......................130.00
Cup and Saucer, Hills Bros. Tea and Coffee, china, Hills Man on
　front, 2-3/8" h, 5" d 150.00
Dispenser, Karo Tape, porcelain..25.00
Display Cabinet
　Arrow Collar, vertical, adv on front glass door, brass trim, 7"
　　x 7" x 47"...750.00
　JP Clarks, spool
　　2 drawer, "Best Six Cord Thread," and "J&P Coats" on
　　　drawers, decals on other 3 sides adv "J. & P. Coats Cot-
　　　tons," 6-1/2" x 14" x 20" 100.00
　　4 drawer, lift lid top, orig knobs, 29-1/2" x 20" 410.00
　　Slant front, oak, partial orig decal on front, roll top front, 24"
　　　x 32" x 9"...525.00
　Diamond Dyes, wooden case, emb tin panel
　　Lady drying clothes, Kellogg & Bulkeley Co., Hartford,
　　　Conn. Lithographer, orig paper label inside, 29-1/2" h, 22-
　　　1/4" w, 9-3/4" l...650.00
　　Mrs. Knight Bought a Remnant, 5 children in vintage cloth-
　　　ing playing with balloon in front of mansion, cardboard
　　　adv on back, inner compartments, plus approx. 50 packs
　　　of orig Diamond Dye, © 1908, Meek Co. Lithographer, 24-
　　　1/4" h, 15-1/4" w, 8" l..800.00
　　The Governess, children playing in park, © 1906, slight sur-
　　　face rust, 29-3/4" h, 22-1/4" w, 9-3/4" l 500.00
　Dr. Scholl's, metal, wood grain emb............................240.00
　Ferry's 5¢ Seeds, cabinet with rack, 27" x 12" x 5-1/2"
　　..200.00
　Humphrey's Remedies, wooden cabinet, tin front lists reme-
　　dies, approx. 60 unopened packages inside, 27-1/2" h, 21"
　　w, 10" d 1,250.00
　Lorillard & Co., P., countertop type, front doors stenciled, 4
　　etched panes of glass, 17-1/2" x 33" x 32-1/2" 900.00
　Putnam Dyes, wood, countertop type, trademark scene, Brit-
　　ish Red Coats chasing George Washington, 10" x 21" x 8-
　　1/4" 115.00
　Rubberite Varnish, tiger decal, 15" x 26" x 12-1/2" 40.00
　Star Braid, thread, wood...650.00
Display Case
　Ever Ready Daylo, glass, 20" x 14" x 12" 250.00
　Primley's, J. P., Gum, small countertop curved glass display
　　case, etched "J. P, Primley's California Fruit and Pepsin
　　Chewing Gum," orig silver, gold and copper paint on etch-
　　ing, 9-1/2" x 18-1/2" x 12-1/4" 900.00
Display Rack
　Samoset Chocolate, circular metal stand, metal marquee sign
　　"Samoset Chocolate Pocket Packets 10 Cents," 6" x 22"
　　..25.00
　Yello-Bole Pipe, revolving..95.00
Figure
　Dr. Scholl's Foot Comfort, meal, blue 160.00
　Nathan's Ankle Support, display foot, orig box 90.00
　Old Crow, ceramic..35.00
　William Atkinson's Bear's Grease, 15-1/4" l, earthenware bear,
　　hand modeled, ribbon extending over back with adv, En-
　　gland, c1860, firing lines, chips to ears, glaze loss to feet
　　...1,265.00
Jar, Squirrel Brand Nuts, bulbous glass jar, emb "Squirrel Brand
　Salted Nut" trademark, glass lid....................................130.00
Ledger Marker, Bagley's May-Flower Chewing Tobacco, tin, ship
　scene on left, fan with little girls picture on right, 3" x 12"
　..100.00
Lunch Box
　Fashion Cut Plug 130.00
　Pattersoin, R. A., Tobacco...25.00
　Pedro Tobacco..180.00
　Tiger Bright Sweet, red..50.00

Mirror, Ballard's Obelisk, Louisville, Parisian Nov. Co., Chicago, 1-3/4" d, $45.

Match Holder/Striker
  Dockash Stove Factory...110.00
  Juice Fruit, Wm. Wrigley..300.00
  Michigan Stove, pre-1900, cast iron...............................40.00
  Old Judson Whiskey, J. C. Stevens.............................375.00
Mirror, beveled, countertop type
  Duke's Tobacco, brass base, stenciled "Smoke and Chew Duke's Special Long Cut," w. Dukesons & Co., 17-1/2" x 10" x 6"...700.00
  Y&N Corsets, lady in her "Diagonal Seam Corset," wood frame, 25-3/4" x 16-1/2"...300.00
Mirror, Pocket, Tydol Veedol Petroleum Products, celluloid, birthstones, 2" d...80.00
Mug
  Dove Brand Ginger Ale, Penn's Bottling & Supply Co., 3 doves on branch, two hairline cracks, 5" h...........................55.00
  Good Cheer Cigar..55.00
Paint Set
  American Crayon, Pied Piper Set, 1930s......................40.00
  DeVoe Water Colors with Indian Pictures......................45.00
Paperweight, Socony Motor Oils, palm type mirror back, 3-1/2" d..160.00

Pinback Button, multicolored
  American Express, red, white, and blue corporate flag centered on "World Service" globe image, c1920..........15.00
  Forest City Paint, fleshtone arm holding black, white, and gray paint can, ivory white ground, black letters................25.00
  Hamilton Brown Shoe Co, red, white, blue, and gray, "Keep the Quality Up," 1920s...20.00
  Pontiac Strain Furs, black and white image of seated fox over gold profile of Indian head, red, blue, and gold accents...70.00
  Quaker Oats, package on white ground, red lettering....45.00
  South Bend Watch Co, image of pocket watch encased in block of ice, blue ground, white letters, c1920..........20.00
  Stephenson Underwear, red underwear shirt held by gentleman in blue and white striped dress shirt, white ground, black letters, 1920s..75.00
  Waterloo Boy Tractor, farm boy in broad brimmed straw hat, image of early 1900s steam farm tractor.................100.00
  White Rose Butter, white rose, green petals, dark blue ground, white letters...25.00
  Wilbur's Cocoa, cupid stirring cup of steaming cocoa...65.00
Pot Scraper
  Delco-Light Brand, Farm Electric Generators, never used, 3-1/4" x 2-1/2"...725.00
  Penn Furnaces/Stoves...100.00
Ruler, Toldedo Metal Co., litho tin, diecut, children playing at well, 5-1/4"...500.00
Saleman's Sample
  Calendar, titled "Advertising That Advertises," F. J. Offreman Art Works, Inc., Buffalo, IN, green Art Nouveau border, two colorful tigers in center, 1934 calendar pad, 30" x 41"...125.00
  Display Showcase, German silver steeple case curved glass, 9" x 6" x 5-1/2"...7,500.00
  Furnace, Holland Furnace, orig carrying case, cast iron and sheet metal, 12" x 13" x 10"...............................100.00
  Stove, cast iron, mkd "Little Eva N. S. Cate Boston," 19th C, 11-1/4" w, 13-1/2" d, minor rust...................................345.00
Shipping Crate
  Castile Soap, Chicago, 1900, wooden, paper label........10.00
  Warner's Safe Yeast, wooden, printed.............................20.00
Soap, Goblin Soap, wrapped bar, orig box, graphics both sides...30.00
Store Canister/Bin
  A & P Coffee, metal..200.00
  Alburn Eskimo Cigar, early 1900s, 5" x 5".....................25.00

Pencil Sharpener, Symington's Soup, light blue ground, dark blue lettering, $20.

Pinback Button, The Prudential Has the Strength of Gibraltar, rim inscriptions, $15.

Gloor, R. G. & Co. Coffee, stenciled front, pre-1900, 8-1/2" sq 120.00

Horlick's Malt Milk, raised blue enameled lettering, 4-5/8" h 475.00

Nestle's Hot Chocolate, large.......................100.00

Roundy's Mustard, stenciling, pre-1900, 7" x 5-1/2" x 9-1/2" 70.00

Sweet Cuba Fine Cut, large, yellow and orange 325.00

Sweet Mist, sq, cardboard lift top.................150.00

Thompson's Malted Milk..............................70.00

Signs

Angelus Marshmallows, diecut cardboard, Christmas scene, matted and framed, 12" x 9" 125.00

Anheuser-Busch, Budweiser, King of Bottled Beer, tin, 49" x 14-1/2"...250.00

Barrett, Lawrence, Mild Havana Cigar, 10 and 15 cents, portrait of Barrett, porcelain, 20" x 34" 125.00

Canada Dry, diecut tin, bottle shape, 40" h.................750.00

Cetacolor, "Not a Soap, Prevents Wash Good from Fading, 10 cents Package," graphic of Gibson style girl, linen, framed, 36" x 12" 125.00

Colgate's Cashmere Bouquet, two sided diecut cardboard, baby holding tin of powder, matted, framed to show both sides, 13-3/4" x 8" 150.00

Columbia Records, cardboard, Columbia Phonograph cylinder packages on either side of highly emb American eagle standing stop stars and stripes shield, 11" x 14-1/2" 200.00

Columbian Rope, linen, seaman carrying coil of rope, 49" x 29-1/2" 325.00

Cremo Cigar, litho tin, round, 17" d 225.00

Crown Prince Coffees, paper, lady in vintage clothing standing in garden, holding roses, matted and framed, 27-1/2" x 13-1/2" 400.00

Dr. Coc's Barbed Wire Liniment, Carlisle, Indiana, cardboard 150.00

Eagle Rock Wine, emb diecut cardboard, western scene, riding roping cowgirl, framed, 15-3/4" x 19" 900.00

Edgemont Tobacco, linen, shows two colorful packages, framed, 36" x 12"..70.00

Elgin National Watch Works, paper, black and white, factory scene, various horse drawn carriages and early automobiles along streets, orig wood frame mkd "Elgin," 15-1/4" x 33-1/4" 125.00

Fiske, J., Boston, figural pocket watch, wood, gold, white, and black paint, 24" h..440.00

Greenback Smoking Tobacco

Diecut cardboard, logo frog shape, matted and framed, 7-1/2" x 11" 250.00

Diecut paper, frog barber scene, "This tobacco is as fine as a frog's hair," package of tobacco added to front, wood frame, 10-1/2" x 13-1/2" 250.00

Helmar Turkish Cigarettes, porcelain, 24" x 12" 80.00

Hickman-Ebbert Co, self framed tin, couple picking apples, loading them into Ebbert wagon, "In the Shade of the Old Apple Tree," © 1906, Chas. W. Shonk Co., Litho, 25-1/2" x 37-1/2"..700.00

Hires Root Beer, diecut cardboard, 33-1/2" x 14-1/2" 200.00

Hood Dairy

Guernsey Cow and milk maid 125.00

Jersey cow...225.00

Independence Indemnity Insurance, tin litho, 15" x 18" 55.00

Illinois Springfield Watches, tin, view of Observatory of Illinois Watch Co., Springfield, orig wood frame, some surface rust to upper portion, overall fading, 17-1/2" x 23-1/2" 200.00

Kawannee, elevators, wagons, tin, 20" x 11" 55.00

Keene, Tom, Cigars 5 Cents, yellow, blue, and white, porcelain, 40" x 18" 300.00

Lipschultz 44 Cigar, two sided diecut tin litho oval, flange, 18" x 13" 250.00

London Life Cigarettes, two sided, porcelain, diecut flange, 16" 500.00

Masury's House Paints, reverse glass, corner sign, "Masury's Pure Linseed Oil House Paints," wood frame, 21" x 16-1/2" 275.00

Mellin's Food, diecut, stand-up, baby sitting in highchair, adv on back "Why Your Baby Should ......Have Mellin's Food," framed to show both sides, 12" x 10-1/4" 150.00

Moxie

Diecut, tin, two sided, Moxie Car, blue, man in Moxie coat riding white horse in blue car, patented Feb. 27, 1917, lithographer H. D. Beach Co., 6-1/2" h, 8-1/2" l 1,700.00

Self framed tin, oval, "Yes, We Sell Moxie, Very Healthy, Feeds the Nerves," Kaufmann & Strass Co., NY litho, 27" x 19-1/2" 500.00

Navy Cut Plug, emb tin, self framed, emb battleships and horse shoe designs on sides, horse shoe flags hanging in air, 35" x 23" 3,750.00

Nesbitt's Soda Pop, tin, showing bottle, 24" sq.............275.00

Nu-Wood Insulating Wall Board and Lath, porcelain, house among trees, mfg. by Veribrite Signs, 22-1/2" x 35" 100.00

Old Boone Distillery, Tixton, Millett & Co. Distillers, old time distillery in backwoods of KY, © 1904, Haeusermann M. M. Co. Litho, crease in lift side, 18" x 26" 500.00

Old English Curved Cut Pipe Tobacco, two sided diecut cardboard, man driving truck made out of product packaging, matted, framed to show both sides, 11" x 9" 175.00

Owl Cigar, two-sided diecut cardboard, owl in cage sitting atop Owl Cigar, © 1902, framed to show both sides 300.00

Pickwick Ale, self framed tin, jovial old men toasting beer at table in front of fireplace, Charles W. Shank, Chicago, Lithographer, 22" x 28-1/2" 300.00

Piedmont, the Virginia Cigarettes, porcelain, shows package

14" x 16", curved..450.00

30" x 46" 200.00

San Antonia Brewery, cardboard, western scene of "The Jersey Lilly," home of Judge Roy Bean, wood frame, 26" x 36" 550.00

Segal Key, double sided, diecut tin litho, key shape, 31" l 170.00

Shepherd, W., serpentine frame painted yellow, red scroll border, center panel painted with stars and rays above eagle and shield flanked by flag, banner, and arrows, MA, early 19th C, 59-1/4" w, 49-1/2" h 3,740.00

Sickle Cut Plug, linen, framed with plastic-pac, 36" x 12"
....65.00
Smoke Moonstruck Cigars, reverse painted under glass, early,
some restoration, 16" x 9" 450.00
St Louis Shot Tower Co., paper, factory scene, vintage horse
drawer vehicles on upper portion, lower section with successful duck hunter, A. Lambrecht & Co. Lithographer, St.
Louis Mo., wooden frame holds vials of company's different
shot sizes, 16-1/2" x 25-1/2" 3,900.00
Sullivan, R. G., Manchester, NH, two sided tin, "7-20-4 10¢ Cigars," 5-1/2" x 4-1/2" 50.00
Sunlight Soap, Cincinnati, tin...................................300.00
Tatem-Wright Dry Goods Co., diecut cardboard, 4 little ladies
dressed in Sunday best, riding in rose dec vehicle, matted
and framed, 7-1/2" x 11-1/4" 100.00
Union Leader, cardboard, Uncle Sam reading the Naval Review, images of named U. S. Fleet, c1909, framed, 17-1/2"
x 26" 700.00
U. S. Marine Cut Plug, sailor leaning out of porthole with pack-
age, double matted and framed, 19-1/2" x 25" 1,050.00
Velvet Tobacco, porcelain, 42" x 11" 225.00
Vienna Pudding, paper, comical dinner guests looking as family dog runs between butler's legs, spilling the Vienna Pudding, border trimmed, 12-1/4" x 9" 80.00
Warren, E. K. Grocery Store, pine, worn and weather black
and yellow paint, blue and yellow on crown molded frame,
20-1/2" h, 48-3/4" w 800.00
Weller, J. H., dealer in ready made clothing and sewing machines, imperfections, 21-1/4" x 74-1/4" 1,380.00
Wrigley's Spearmint Chewing Gum, countertop type, two sided, cardboard, orig metal frame, "Wrigley's" engraved on
both sides, 14" x 18" 100.00
Thermometer
American Seal Paints, Uncle Sam carrying paint bucket,
wood, 21" h, 9" w 210.00
Ex Lax, porcelain, 36" h, 8-1/4" w 140.00
Mail Pouch Chewing Tobacco Co., blue, red, and white, 39" h,
8" w, minor paint chips 400.00
Moxie, tin, Moxie Man image, 9-1/2" x 25" 425.00
Tins
Baking Powder
Clabber Girl 10.00
Rabbit's Foot Baking Powder, 5-1/2" x 3-1/4" 775.00
Royal Powder..10.00
Coffee
Anchor Coffee, 1 lb...25.00
Breakfast Call Coffee, round slip top, 3 lb, 8-1/4" x 9-1/2"
....120.00
Dining Car Brand Coffee, Johnson-Layne Coffee Co., figur-
al, railroad dining car shape, Columbia Can Co., St. Lou-
is, tin mfg., some denting to roof, overall scratching, some
paint loss, 14" x 31" x 24" h 7,500.00
Folger's Coffee, 5 lb, keywind 50.00
Gold Bond Coffee, 1 lb, screw top 30.00
Jam Boy, paper label, 1 lb, 6" x 4" 350.00
National's Best Blend, 1 lb, screw top.....................50.00
Opeko Coffee, 1 lb, keywind 35.00
Sears Coffee, 10 lb, bail handle, green vertical stripes
....20.00
Society Brand, tin litho, 2" h, 2-1/2" d 325.00
Vogel Bros. Coffee, 2 lb, paper label, no top 25.00
Waldorf-Astoria, tapered 1 lb, hotel scenes, 6-1/2" x 4-1/2"
x 3-1/2" 550.00
White Goose, 1 lb, litho tin, bright red ground, 6" x 4-1/4"
....1,300.00
White House Coffee, 1 lb, tin vacuum pack, keywind, scene
of Ye Olde Bacon, Stickney 1834 Coffee House, Bacon,
Stickney Co., Albany, NY, 3-7/8" x 5" 400.00
Wigwam Coffee, 1 lb, prytop, lid missing................40.00
Gum, Adams California Fruit Gum, illus of packs of Adams Cali-
fornia Fruit Gum on all 4 sides, 6" x 6-3/4" x 4-3/4" 550.00

Tin, Tiger Chewing Tobacco, rect, 6 x 3-3/4" x 2-1/4", $65.

Peanut Butter Pail, tin litho
Brundage Star Mail Peanut Butter, 25 lb pry top......275.00
Christmas/New Year, 1898 ....120.00
Credo, bail handle...80.00
Dixie High Grade Peanut Butter, bail handle 45.00
Frontinac, bail handle 75.00
Sultanta, bail handle 60.00
Uzar, 5 lb, bail handle 25.00
Wilson & Co., Chicago, 12 oz, bail handle, 3-1/2" x 3"
....180.00
Razor, Yankee Brand Safety Razor, hinged lid, father faced man,
eagles, 1-1/2" x 2-1/2" x 1-3/4" 825.00
Tobacco Tin
Bagdad Short Cut, pocket 115.00
Bigger Hair Tobacco, yellow 65.00
Brigg's Best, pocket size...30.00
Burley Boy, pocket 375.00
Central Union, pocket 55.00
Chicago Cub Chewing Tobacco, round, 1936.........130.00
City Club, tall, pocket 120.00
Cornell Mixture Smoking Tobacco, upright, sq corner, pre-
1900 ....25.00
Dill's Best, pocket size...30.00
Eve Cube Cut, Globe Tobacco Co, vertical, pocket, 3-1/2"
x 3-1/2" x 1-1/2" 400.00
Four Roses, pocket tin, flip top.................................60.00
Hawatha Fine Cut Dark 70.00
King Dutch Stogies, sq 25.00
Lucky Strike, R. A. Patterson Tobacco Co, short, pocket
....40.00
Lucky Strike White, pocket 300.00
Mayo's Brand, roly poly, litho tin, 7" h, 6" d
Dutchman 525.00
Satisfied Customer..425.00
Q Boid, oval, pocket 45.00
Reichard's Cadet, cigars, lift top, 4-3/4" x 3-3/4" 30.00
Sir Walter Raleigh, Christmas, multicolored, horizontal
....25.00
Stag, pocket 100.00
Sterling Fine Cut, plaid, 6-1/4" x 8-1/2" 100.00
Tiger Fine Cut, blue, horizontal, 6" x 4" 25.00
Trout Line, fisherman in stream graphics, 3-3/4" x 3-1/2" x
1-1/4" 825.00
Union Leader, pocket tin 35.00
Van Bitter, flat, pocket, full..30.00
Tip Tray
Climax Plug, colorful...115.00
DeLaval Cream Separators, lady separating cream in family
kitchen, little boy, © 1906, 4-1/4" d..........................140.00
Globe-Wernicke Sectional Bookcases, couple sorting books in
stacking bookcases, 4-1/4" d 95.00

Advertising trade card, Celluloid Waterproof Collars, Cuffs & Shirt Bosoms, green, blue, gray, tan and white, yellow lightning bolt, $15. Photo courtesy of Julie Robinson.

Junket, little girl eating bowl, "Have Some Junket," mfg. By Chr. Hansens Laboratory, Little Falls, NY, 4-1/4" d 200.00

Kenney, C. D., Co., America's Pride, patriotic stars and stripes border, sailor and solider in vintage uniforms, background shows Gatlin guns, airplanes, and battleship, 4-1/4" d 275.00

King's Pure Malt, nurse in vintage garb carrying tray of "King's Pure Malt," 6" x 4-1/4" 75.00

Krebs, E. K., adv President Suspenders, glass applied over base of tray protecting image of Grecian looking woman, wear to rim, 4-1/4" d..125.00

Lehnert's Beer, beautiful woman head, 4-1/4" d 100.00

Red Raven Splits, Red Raven logo next to vintage bottle, "For High Livers' Livers," Chas. W. Shonk Co. Litho Chicago, 4-1/4" d 50.00

Rockford Watches, lady in waiting, sitting on water's edge, scalloped edge rim, 5" x 3-1/4" 300.00

Welsbach Mantle 85.00

Tray, Hall Ice Cream, Binghamton, NY, 13" x 10-1/2" 1,650.00

Watch Fob

Green River, silvered brass, horseshoe shape, center trademark image of caretaker and horse, "Green River" jug suspended from saddle, slogan "She Was Bred In Old Kentucky," reverse inscription "Official Whiskey of the U. S. Marine Hospital Service," lists six international awards from 1900-1907...40.00

Kellogg Switchboard & Supple Co/The Service Of The Telephone Proves The Worth Of The Line, dark copper luster brass, raised image of candlestick phone, receiver off the hook, "K" circular logo, 1920s 60.00

King Musical Instruments, dark brass, yellowed black and white celluloid inset of young lady opening coronet case, reverse imp "A King' Booster/H.N. White/Cleveland, Ohio," c1920..50.00

ADVERTISING TRADE CARDS

History: Advertising trade cards are small, thin cardboard cards made to advertise the merits of a product. They usually bear the name and address of a merchant.

With the invention of lithography, colorful trade cards became a popular way to advertise in the late 19th and early 20th centuries. They were made to appeal especially to children. Young and old alike collected and treasured them in albums and scrapbooks. Very few are dated; the prime years for trade card production were 1880 to 1893; cards made between 1810 and 1850 can be found, but rarely. By 1900 trade cards were rapidly losing their popularity, and by 1910 they had all but vanished.

References: Kit Barry, *Advertising Trade Card*, Book 1, published by author, 1981; Dave Cheadle, *Victorian Trade Cards*, Collector Books, 1996; Robert Jay, *Trade Card in Nineteenth-Century America*, University of Missouri Press, 1987; Murray Cards (International) Ltd. (comp.), *Cigarette Card Values*, Murray Cards (International) Ltd., 1994.

Periodicals: *Card Times*, 70 Winified Lane, Aughton, Ormskirk, Lancashire L38 5DL England; *Trade Card Journal*, 109 Main St, Brattleboro, VT 05301.

Collectors' Club: Trade Card Collector's Assoc., P.O. Box 284, Marlton, NJ 08053

Additional Listings: See *Warman's Americana & Collectibles* for more examples.

Beverages

Ayer's Sarsaparilla

"Ayer's Sarsaparilla Makes the Weak Strong," two gentlemen 18.00

"The Old Folks at Home," 8" x 12", bottle of tonic..........325.00

Duff's Malt Whiskey, man in red jacket working on formula 30.00

Hermitage Sour Mash Whiskey, two rats and bottle.............30.00

Lion Coffee, canaries and parakeets 12.00

Gibson's Pure Rye Whiskey...35.00

Buckeye Force Pump, Krebs Litho Co., Cincinnati, 6" x 3-1/2", $10.

Mayer Brewing, Palest Brewery, New York, diecut 65.00
Union Pacific Tea, young lad sailors with American flag, includes Easter greeting 8.00

Clothing

Ball's Corsets, center corset illus, child and mother holding baby..25.00
Drown Co., Umbrellas & Parasols, black and white............18.00
Hapke Knit Goods, 1876 Centennial, light green knitting machine vignette 45.00
Solar Tip Shoes, Girard College, Philadelphia, Where Boys Wear our Solar Tip Shoes 20.00
Strauss, Levi & Co., multi-fold, multiple images of children and adults wearing jeans, when folded it's shape of pair of Levi Strauss jeans showing both front and back pockets 275.00
Thompson's Glove Fitting Corsets, lady and cupids............35.00

Farm Machinery & Supplies

Gale Mfg. Co., Daisy Sulky Hay Rake, folder type, 4 panels, field scene 75.00
Keystone Agricultural Implements, Uncle Sam talking to world representatives, metamorphic..75.00
Mast & Foos Columbia Steel Wind Mill, folder type, child with pump 45.00
New Essay Lawn Mower, scene of Statue of Liberty, New York harbor 35.00
Reid's Flower Seeds, two high wheeled bicyclers admiring flowers held by three ladies 15.00
Sheridan's, To Make Hens Lay, Use Sheridan's Condition Powder, before and after views of farmer in chicken house 25.00

Food

Czar Baking Powder, black woman and boy with giant biscuit 25.00
Enterprise Meat and Food Chopper.....................................45.00
Heinz Apple Butter, diecut, pickle shape.............................45.00
Hornby's Oats, diecut of girl peeking out of box..................35.00
Pearl Baking Powder, light blue and sepia, reverse with order blank, c1890 ....35.00
Royal Hams, Chief Joseph & His Tribe examining barrel of hams 48.00
Thurber Connoisseur Ketchup, product label illus...............70.00
E. Tunison Grocer, elf standing next to pansies...................15.00
Woolson Spice, Lion Coffee, young children portraying Cinderella 25.00

National Blue Flame Oil Stove, adv on back for Loraine, OH, National Vapor Store Co., 5-13/16" x 4-5/8", $5.

Kerr & Co., loading safe in front of factory, 3-1/4" x 4-3/4", $10.

Health and Beauty

Ayer's Hair Vigor, four mermaids, ship in background 7.00
Golf Queen Perfume, Ricksecker Co., c1895, blotter type 12.00
Hill's Hair and Whisker Dye, New York proprietor 40.00
Hoyt's German Cologne, E. M. Hoyt & Co., mother cat and kittens 25.00

Laundry and Soaps

Empire Wringer Co, Auburn, NY, child helping "I Can Help Mama" 35.00
Higgin's Soap, comical black scene showing various uses for soap, set of 7 cards, framed, 29-1/2" x 8" 150.00
Ivorine Cleanser, lettering on side of elephant, other animals 15.00
Mrs. Potts' Sad Irons, sign painters.....................................35.00
Sapolio Soap, young black face peering out of watermelon center 18.00
Soapine, Kendall Mfg. Co, Providence, RI
    Carriage 15.00
    Soapine on mantle, product box plus name spelled out over mantle 15.00
    Steam Engine 10.00
    Street Scene 10.00
    Wizard, lady talking to wizard.......................................10.00
The Fort Wayne Improved Western Washer, Horton Manufacturing Co, Fort Wayne, Ind, one lady watching as other works new machine 35.00

Medicine

Dr. Kilmer & Co, Binghamton, NY, 36" x 60", Standard Herbal Remedies, detailed graphics 395.00
King of the Blood Medicine, Automation Musical Band, Barnum's Traveling Museum 45.00
Perry Davis, Pain Killer for Wounds, armored man of war ships battle scene 25.00
Quaker Bitters, Standard Family Medicine, child in barrel 17.50
Scott's Emulsion of Cod Liver Oil, man with large fish over back, vertical format 20.00
Shaker Family Pills, little girl in white bonnet 38.00

Miscellaneous

Auburn County Fair, dressed up cats, dates 6.00
Bear Hunt Bank, J. & E. Stevens Co....................................60.00
Diamond Dyes, Class in Economy, one lady teaching other well dressed ladies 15.00
Emerson Piano Co., black and white illus 40.00

Forbes, C. P., Jewelry, Greenfield, MA, Santa in front of fireplace, toys on table 15.00
Granite Iron Ware, 3 ladies gossiping over tea 25.00
Schwarz, Henry, toy store, Christmas scene.........................30.00
The American Machine Co., Manufacturers of Hardware Specialties, three women ironing, vertical format.....................40.00
Two-Headed Lady, 8th Wonder of the World 150.00

Stoves and Ranges

Andes Stove, black children..15.00
Dixon's Stove Polish, Brownies illus 20.00
Florence Oil Stove, colorful illus of 2 women and 2 children
....40.00
Rising Sun Stove Polish, folder type, "The Modern Cinderella"
....50.00
Rutland Stove Lining, child talking to parrot.......................115.00

Thread and Sewing

Brooks' Spool Cotton, 3 kittens playing instruments made from spools 25.00
Clark's Thread, Mile End Spool Cotton
    Two children riding high wheeled bike made from spools, others falling 12.00
    Two circus clowns 15.00
Singer Manufacturing Co., choir of children singing as bird's listen 20.00
White Sewing Machine Co, elves working at sewing machine
....15.00

Tobacco

Capadura Cigar, two baseball players, "Judgment, Judgment is always decided in favor of the Capadura Cigar" 30.00
49 Cut Plug, miners scene 225.00
Horsehead Tobacco, Dansman Tobacco Co, horse head illus
....15.00

AGATA GLASS

History: Agata glass was invented in 1887 by Joseph Locke of the New England Glass Company, Cambridge, Massachusetts.

Tumbler, experimental type, 3-3/4" h, $1,350.

Agata glass was produced by coating a piece of peachblow glass with metallic stain, spattering the surface with alcohol, and firing. The resulting high-gloss, mottled finish looked like oil droplets floating on a watery surface. Shading usually ranged from opaque pink to dark rose, although pieces in a pastel opaque green also exist. A few pieces have been found in a satin finish.

Bowl
    5-1/4" d, 3" h, ruffled, peachblow opaque body, allover bright blue staining spots 750.00
    8" d, 4" h, green opaque body, staining and gold trim
....1,150.00
Celery Vase, 7" h, sq, fluted top 625.00
Creamer..1,200.00
Finger Bowl, 5-1/4" d, 2-5/8" h, crushed raspberry shading to creamy pink, all over gold mottling, blue accents.........995.00
Pitcher, 6-3/8" h, crimped rim..1,750.00
Spooner, 4-1/2" h, 2-1/2" w, sq top, wild rose peachblow ground, small areas of wear...400.00
Toothpick Holder, 2-1/4" h, flared, green opaque, orig blue oil spots, green trim..795.00
Tumbler, 3-7/8" h, peachblow ground, gold tracery, bold black splotches 785.00
Vase, 8" h, lily, shiny surface, crimson peachblow ground, large black splotches 1,085.00

AMBERINA GLASS

History: Joseph Locke developed Amberina glass in 1883 for the New England Glass Works. "Amberina," a trade name, describes a transparent glass which shades from deep ruby to amber. It was made by adding powdered gold to the ingredients for an amber-glass batch. A portion of the glass was reheated later to produce the shading effect. Usually it was the bottom which was reheated to form the deep red; however, reverse examples have been found.

Most early Amberina is flint-quality glass, blown or pattern molded. Patterns include Diamond Quilted, Daisy and Button, Venetian Diamond, Diamond and Star, and Thumbprint.

In addition to the New England Glass Works, the Mount. Washington Glass Company of New Bedford, Massachusetts, copied the glass in the 1880s and sold it at first under the Amberina trade name and later as "Rose Amber." It is difficult to distinguish pieces from these two New England factories. Boston and Sandwich Glass Works never produced the glass.

Amberina glass also was made in the 1890s by several Midwest factories, among which was Hobbs, Brockunier & Co. Trade names included "Ruby Amber Ware" and "Watermelon." The Midwest glass shaded from cranberry to amber, and the color resulted from the application of a thin flashing of cranberry to the reheated portion. This created a sharp demarcation between the two colors. This less-expensive version was the death knell for the New England variety.

In 1884, Edward D. Libbey was given the use of the trade name "Amberina" by the New England Glass Works. Production took place during 1900, but ceased shortly thereafter. In the 1920s Edward Libbey renewed production at his Toledo, Ohio, plant for a short period. The glass was of high quality.

Marks: Amberina made by Edward Libbey in the 1920s is marked "Libbey" in script on the pontil.

References: Gary Baker et al., *Wheeling Glass 1829-1939*, Oglebay Institute, 1994 (distributed by Antique Publications); Neila and Tom Bredehoft, *Hobbs, Brockunier & Co. Glass*, Collector Books, 1997; Kenneth Wilson, *American Glass 1760-1930*, 2 Vols., Hudson Hill Press and The Toledo Museum of Art, 1994.

REPRODUCTION ALERT
Reproductions abound.

Additional Listings: Mount Washington.

Beverage Set, Optic Diamond Quilted pattern, 7" h pitcher, 3 punch cups, 2 tumblers, New England, 6 pcs 825.00

Bonbon, 7" d, 1-1/2" h, wavy six-pointed 1-1/2" w rim, fuchsia shading to pale amber, sgd "Libbey" 625.00

Bowl
   4-1/4" h, 8-3/4" d, Optic Diamond Quilted pattern, stand-up color 585.00
   4-1/2" d, 2-1/4" h, tricorn, fuchsia shading to amber, Venetian Diamond design 325.00

Butter Pat, 2-3/4" d, Daisy and Button pattern, sq, notched corners, pr 250.00

Celery Boat, 14" l, 5" w, 2-1/2" h, Daisy and Button pattern, Hobbs, Brockunier, minute roughness on bow 750.00

Celery Vase
   Inverted Thumbprint pattern 145.00
   Optic Expanded Diamond pattern, New England Glass Works, 6-1/2" h........345.00

Centerpiece, 14" l, canoe, Daisy and Button pattern, Hobbs Brockunier 950.00

Cordial, 4-1/2" h, trumpet shape........225.00

Cracker Jar, cov, 8" h, 5-3/4" d, Inverted Thumbprint pattern, barrel shape, rare glass cov, applied amber knob finial, attributed to Hobbs, c1885 ....785.00

Creamer and Sugar, 4-1/2" h, Diamond Quilted pattern, crimped top, amber reeded handles........650.00

Cruet, 5-1/2" h, Inverted Thumbprint pattern, fuchsia trefoil spout, neck, and shoulder, Mt.Washington........435.00

Decanter
   Optic Diamond Quilted pattern, solid amber faceted stopper, 12" h 485.00
   Reverse Inverted Thumbprint pattern, ground and polished pontil 125.00

Ice Cream Plate, 5-1/2" sq, Daisy and Button pattern, Hobbs Brockunier 95.00

Juice Tumbler, 3-3/4" h, 2-1/2" d, applied reeded amber handle, slight ribbing, tapered body, New England Glass Co...395.00

Pickle Castor Insert, 4-1/4" h, 4" d, Inverted Thumbprint pattern, Mt. Washington........425.00

Pitcher
   4-1/2" h, sq top, Inverted Thumbprint pattern, applied amber reeded handle 325.00
   5" h, Daisy and Button pattern, Hobbs Brockunier........425.00

Celery Vase, DQ, sq top, ground pontil, 6-1/8" h, $225. Photo courtesy of Gene Harris Antique Auction Center.

8" h, 5" d, amberina-opalescent, clear reeded handle, ruffled top, wide flange petticoat shape 650.00
10" h, 4-3/4" d, Optic Diamond Quilted pattern, applied amber handle, ground pontil 235.00

Punch Cup, 2-1/2" h, applied reeded amber handle, slight ribbing, tapered body, attributed to Mt Washington 245.00

Sauce, Daisy and Button pattern........40.00

Spooner, 4-1/2" h, Inverted Thumbprint pattern, New England Glass Works........100.00

Syrup Pitcher, Hobnail pattern, orig pewter top std "Pat. Jan 29 84," hobbs, Brockunier & Co, 3 hobs chipped 300.00

Toothpick Holder
   Baby Inverted Thumbprint pattern
      Square top, 2-1/4" h, 1-1/2" w 295.00
      Tricorn........275.00
   Optic Diamond Quilted pattern, sq
      2-3/8" h........295.00
      2-1/2" h, shape #8, Mt. Washington........285.00

Vase
   6-3/4" h, roll down lip, optic diamond body........300.00
   10" h, lily, fuchsia highlights 675.00
   10-1/2" h, swagged and ruffled lip, snake form entwined around neck, heavy enameled goldfinches perched on thistle blossoms, attributed to Le Gras, c1890........595.00
   12-1/4" h, 3-1/4" d, swirled calla lily shape, cranberry shading to golden amber foot, amber applied spiral trim 165.00
   11-1/4" h, shape #3004, sgd "Libbey"........1,200.00
   15" h, lily shape, deep red shading to amber, large lily top, flint, c1880........825.00

AMBERINA GLASS, PLATED

History: The New England Glass Company, Cambridge, Massachusetts, first made Plated Amberina in 1886; Edward Libbey patented the process for the company in 1889.

Plated Amberina was made by taking a gather of chartreuse or cream opalescent glass, dipping it in Amberina, and working the two, often utilizing a mold. The finished product had a deep amber to deep ruby red shading, a fiery opalescent lining, and often vertical ribbing for enhancement. Designs ranged from simple forms to complex pieces with collars, feet, gilding, and etching.

A cased Wheeling glass of similar appearance had an opaque white lining but is not opalescent and does not have a ribbed body.

Bowl, 8" w, 3-1/2" h, border of deep dark mahogany, 12 vertical stripes alternating with 12 vertical opalescent fuchsia stripes, off-white casing 7,500.00
Celery Vase 2,750.00
Cruet, 6-3/4" h, faceted amber stopper..........................3,200.00
Lamp Shade, 14" d, hanging, swirled, ribbed.................4,750.00
Milk Pitcher, applied amber handle, orig "Aurora" label
....7,500.00
Punch Cup, vertical ribs, applied handle.......................1,500.00
Salt Shaker, vertical ribs, orig top..................................1,200.00
Tumbler, 9 optic ribs, fuchsia top shading to butter cream
....1,750.00
Vase, 7-1/4" h, lily shape, raspberry red shading to bright amber, opal white casing..2,750.00

AMPHORA

History: The Amphora Porcelain Works was one of several pottery companies located in the Teplitz-Turn region of Bohemia in the late 19th and early 20th centuries. It is best known for art pottery, especially Art Nouveau and Art Deco pieces.

Marks: Several markings were used, including the name and location of the pottery and the Imperial mark, which included a crown. Prior to World War I, Bohemia was part of the Austro-Hungarian Empire, so the word "Austria" may appear as part of the mark. After World War I, the word "Czechoslovakia" may be part of the mark.

Additional Listings: Teplitz.

Bowl, 12" x 15", reticulated, ftd, applied leaves and chestnuts, 2 double twisted gold handles, sgd 645.00
Creamer, 5-1/4" h, gold trim, raised flowers, sgd "Turin, Teplitz, Amphora"...215.00
Ewer, 14-1/2" h, pink, gold, and green floral dec, gold accents, salamander entwined handle, c1900 ....575.00

Vase, octagonal, mottled gold, tan stripes, enameled tear drop, red and white ram's head on base, aqua band behind head, mkd "Made in Czecho-slavakia," 10-3/4" h, $210.

Figure
16-1/4" h, peasant woman carries basket on back, reaching for another basket at feet, tan clothes, gold highlights, crown mark and "Austria".......................................550.00
18-1/2" h, peasant woman empties apron of greens into basket, tan, gold highlights, crown mark and "Austria" .550.00
Pitcher, 11" h, emb owl sitting on branch..........................165.00
Vase
10" h, 9-1/2" w, applied blackberry clusters, cream basketweave ground, braided shoulder handles, sgd ..650.00
11" h, 5" w, bulbous, two handles, flaring base with four handles, two raised leaves under pink, green, and blue, imp "Crown, Austria, Amphora"......................................460.00
12" h, cobalt blue majolica, George Jones, pr 2,310.00
17-3/4" h, basket-form, three cherubs mounted to one side, floral applied drapery, imp and printed marks, early 20th C, restorations 230.00

ANIMAL COLLECTIBLES

History: The representation of animals in fine arts, decorative arts, and on utilitarian products dates back to antiquity. Some religions endowed certain animals with mystical properties. Authors throughout written history used human characteristics when portraying animals.

Glass has been a popular material in making animal-related collectibles. Dishes with an animal-theme cover were fashionable in the early 19th century. In the years between World Wars I and II, glass manufacturers such as Fostoria Glass Company and A. H. Heisey & Company created a number of glass animal figures for the novelty and decorative-accessory markets. In the 1950s and early 1960s, a second glass-animal craze swept America led by companies such as Duncan & Miller and New Martinsville-Viking Glass Company. A third craze struck in the early 1980s when companies such as Boyd Crystal Art Glass, Guernsey Glass, Pisello Art Glass, and Summit Art Glass began offering the same animal figure in a wide variety of collectible glass colors, with some colors in limited production.

The formation of collectors' clubs and marketing crazes, e.g., flamingo, pig, and penguin, during the 1970s increased the popularity of this collecting field.

References: Elaine Butler, *Poodle Collectibles of the 50s & 60s*, L-W Book Sales, 1995; Diana Callow et al., *Charlton Price Guide to Beswick Animals*, The Charlton Press, 1994; Jean Dale, *Charlton Standard Catalogue of Royal Doulton Animals*, The Charlton Press, 1994; ——, *Charlton Standard Catalogue of Royal Doulton Beswick Storybook Figurines*, The Charlton Press, 1994; Marbena Jean Fyke, *Collectible Cats*, Book I (1993, 1995 value update), Book II (1996), Collector Books; Lee Garmon and Dick Spencer, *Glass Animals of the Depression Era*, Collector Books, 1993; Everett Grist, *Covered Animal Dishes*, Collector Books, 1988, 1993 value update; Frank L. Hahn and Paul Kikeli, *Collector's Guide to Heisey and Heisey By Imperial Glass Animals*, Golden Era Publications, 1991; Todd Holmes, *Boyd Glass Workbook*, published by author, 1992; Jan Lindenberger, *501 Collectible Horses*, Schiffer Publishing, 1996; Jessie Walker, *Country Living Collectibles: Rabbits*, Hearst Books, 1996.

Periodicals: *Boyd Crystal Art Glass Newsletter*, P.O. Box 127, 1203 Morton Ave., Cambridge, OH 43725; *Canine Collector's Companion*, P.O. Box 2948, Portland, OR 97208; *Collieactively Speaking*, 428 Philadelphia Rd., Joppa, MD 21085 *Collie Courier*, 428 Philadelphia Rd., Joppa, MD 21085; *Hobby Horse News*, 5492 Tallapoosa Rd., Tallahassee, FL 32303; *Jody & Darrell's Glass Collectibles Newsletter*, P.O. Box 180833, Arlington, TX 76096; *Jumbo Jargon*, 1002 West 25th St., Erie, PA 16502; *MOOsletter*, 240 Wahl Ave., Evans City, PA 16033; *TRR Pony Express*, 71 Aloha Circle, Little Rock, AR 72120.

Collectors' Clubs: Boyd Art Glass Collectors Guild, P.O. Box 52, Hatboro, PA 19040; Canine Collectibles Club of America, Suite 314, 736 N. Western Ave., Lake Forest, IL 60045; Cat Collectors, 33161 Wendy Dr., Sterling Heights, MI 48310; Folk Art Society of America, P.O. Box 17041, Richmond, VA 23226; Frog Pond, P.O. Box 193, Beech Grove, IN 46107; National Elephant Collector's Society, 380 Medford St., Somerville, MA 02145; Squirrel Lovers Club, 318 W. Fremont Ave., Elmhurst, IL 60126; Wee Scots, Inc., P.O. Box 1512, Columbus, IN 47202.

Museums: American Kennel Club, New York, NY; American Saddle Horse Museum Assoc., Lexington, KY; Dog Museum, St. Louis, MO; Frog Fantasies Museum, Eureka Springs, AR; International Museum of the Horse, Lexington, KY; Stradling Museum of the Horse, Patagonia, AZ.

Additional Listings: See specific animal collectible categories in *Warman's Americana & Collectibles*.

Advisor: Jocelyn C. Mousley.

Note: Prices for glass animal figures are for the colorless variety unless otherwise noted.

Barnyard

Bank, mechanical, cast iron
  Tricky Pig Bank, old repaint, 7-1/2" l, teller replaced 420.00
  Trick Pony, worn polychrome 1,210.00
Bank, still, 5" l, pig, white ironstone, black spatter spots, one ear replaced 110.00
Bottle, 7-1/2" h, pig, dark brown Albany slip, incised "Good Old Rye in Hogs" and "Our oil diggins, pure lard in a flowing well," Anna Pottery, IL 880.00
Cookie Jar, hen on nest, Brush 125.00
Creamer, Moo Cow, plastic, Whirley Industries, c1950 ....20.00
Figure
  4-1/2" h, cow and calf, white clay, dark brown glaze 580.00
  4-3/4" h, rooster, bronze, cold painted in naturalistic tones, stamped "Austria," c1920......................................1,035.00
  6-1/2" h, pig, porcelain, realistic brown and beige enamel 110.00
  6-1/2" l, ram, carved green stone, on stand, orig box 66.00
  9" l, sheep, sewer pipe, rough textured coat, chips......165.00
Memorial Sculpture, 5-1/2" l, marble, lamb, inscribed "Annie," chips 65.00
Painting, oil on canvas
  10-1/2" x 14", Cow Grazing, sgd "John B. Johnston," identified on label on reverse, c1870, framed.........................805.00

Painting, oil on canvas, Cows, Aldophe Jacobs, Belgium, signed lower right, 29" x 36", $3,550. Photo courtesy of Sanford Alderfer Auction Co.

  23-3/4" x 29-3/4", barn scene with sheep and rooster, sgd "C. H. Clair," gilt frame 1,045.00
Pitcher, Rooster, Watt Pottery..150.00
Planter, pig, American Bisque..25.00
Rug, hooked, 25" x 38", cow in landscape with foliage in spandrels, edge stripes, rows of scalloped gray felt, red, brown, blue, gray, olive, and white, some fading.....................615.00
Soap, lamb-shaped, Bo Peep brand, 3 bars, orig box 15.00
Spaghetti Bowl, Rooster, Watt Pottery..................................315.00
Weathervane, 20-3/4" h, pig, zinc, cast iron directional arrow 415.00

Birds

Andirons, pr, 15-1/2" h, owls, cast iron, yellow and black glass eyes 85.00
Ashtray, Rook, Rookwood, #1139 ....325.00
Bank, still, 5-1/4" h, duck in top hat, "Save For A Rainy Day," polychrome dec 215.00
Candy Container, figural, baby chick..................................195.00
Child's Riding Toy, 39-1/2" l, wood, cutout silhouettes of roosters, orig dark red, green, and yellow paint, adjustable seat, rockers and folding wheels, wear and edge damage, partial paper label on bottom 715.00
Dish, 14-1/4" l, swan, sterling silver, Mexican 140.00
Doorstop, parrot, cast iron..140.00
Figure
  6" h, rooster, carved wood, worn polychrome, edge damage 770.00
  8-1/4" h, owl, sewer pipe, solid, incised "Tim Gibson" ..140.00
  11" l, mother bird facing baby bird, black, red, yellow, and white, metal feet, wooden base 1,100.00
  12-1/2" h, owl, matte finish, polychrome enamel, mkd "Great Horned Owl by Andrea," 60.00
  22" l, pheasants, bronze, worn polychrome dec, pr......770.00
  24-1/2" h, owl, earthenware, redware body, naturalistic colored enamels, inset glass eyes, German, 19th C, repair to branch 2,415.00
Game Plate, 11-5/8" d, pair of quail, sgd "A. Broussilion," gilt rim, mkd "Coronet, Limoges, France," 140.00
Hen on Nest, Staffordshire, porcelain, polychrome dec
  7-1/2" l, egg cup insert, one cup damaged and glued .635.00
  10-1/2" l, good color, minor edge wear, chips on inner flange 715.00

Painting, 18" x 12", oil on canvas, Parrot Perched in a Sunset Landscape, sgd and dated "J. O'B Inman April 8 '90," (John Edward O'Brien Inman, 1890,) framed 1,150.00

Plate, 9-1/2" d, peacock, blue Royal Bayreuth mark 600.00

Prints, 12-1/2 x 10-1/2", handcolored engravings, sgd "George Edwards," book pages with English and French text on reverse side, old gilt frames vary, set of 6 .... 885.50

Shooting Gallery Target, 3" h, cast iron, set of 2 .... 100.00

Stuffed Toy, 6" h, Peggy Penguin, Steiff 60.00

Tape Dispenser, pelican, cast metal 130.00

Toy, tin wind-up
  4" l, pecking chickens, finger activated, good polychrome dec 360.00
  7-1/2" l, duck pulls cart with three small ducks, Lehmann 315.00

Weathervane, rooster
  21-1/4" x 25", sheet metal, traces of old paint, 20th C, modern base 360.00
  25-1/4" h, tin silhouette, double cone base 470.00
  31" x 31-1/2", sheet metal, cast iron, and zinc, red tin tail, Rochester Ironwork 1,500.00
  32" x 34", cast and sheet iron, American, c1850 .... 4,890.00

Cats

Band, 11-1/2" h, cold painted bronze, Austrian, c1920, 8 pc 1,035.00

Bank, still, blue, abstract, Carlton 55.00

Figure
  3-1/4" h, white Persian, green eyes, sitting 30.00
  7" h, sewer pipe, solid, seated 165.00
  10-7/8" h, seated, redware, black glaze, yellow glass eyes, imp "Zanesware, Made in U.S.A." 105.00
  13" h, Galle Faience, yellow enamel ground, black trimmed blue dec, glass eyes, imp mark, early 20th C, restored 230.00

Painting, 21" x 25-3/4", oil on canvas, sgd "Brunel Neuville," French, 1879-1907, framed 3,100.00

Pip-Squeak, 7-1/4" h, wood and composition, worn white flannel and painted brown and gray cat, white button eyes, worn painted pupils, neck and voice box damaged 110.00

Print, 11-7/8" x 9-1/4", lithograph on paper, numbered "49/90," sgd "T. L. Foujita," Japanese, 1886-1968, matted 1,610.00

Quilt, 84-1/2" x 63", pierced and appliquéd, repeating design of seated cats, America, c1930 .... 1,265.00

Shooting Gallery Target, 14-3/4" h, stuffed canvas, painted features, leather strap added to weighted base 110.00

Dogs

Advertising Sign
  20" w, 31" h, self-framed tin, "To school well fed on Grape-Nuts, There's a Reason," little girl walking beside St. Bernard, dog carrying bag in mouth 1,600.00
  36" x 47", tin, setter on chain through fence, sgd "Alexander Pope," orig metal decal on front "Friedman, Keiler & Company Distillers, Paducah, Kentucky," oak frame 700.00

Bank, still, cast iron
  Speaking Dog, polychrome, child with dog, 7" h, minor wear 1,430.00
  St. Bernard, black with gold, minor wear 130.00
  Trick Dog, clown, dog with barrel, gold polychrome color, 8-3/4" l 35.00

Book, Terhune, *Lad,* dj 15.00

Calendar, beautiful cowgirl twirls lariat around herself and sitting dog, Rolf Armstrong 65.00

Candy Container, top hat, filled, pr 55.00

Doorstop, double Scotties 95.00

Figure
  1-1/2" x 3", Scottie, bronze, mkd "J. B." 80.00
  5-5/8" h, seated, free standing front legs, oval base, traces of red paint cast iron 110.00
  6-3/4" h, 5-1/2" d, Poodle, white, tan base, brown collar, blue bow, gold trim padlock 155.00
  9-1/2" h, Ohio buff clay, black painted finish, glitter trim 412.50
  9-1/2" l, Harlequin Great Dane, laying down, gray and white 65.00
  10" h, seated, Ohio pottery, unglazed buff clay, reddish paint stain, black painted details, attributed to Newcomerstown 550.00
  10-1/4" h, sewer pipe, seated, free standing front legs, solid 220.00
  13-1/2" h, Staffordshire, seated, red and white, gold, black, and ochre trim, mkd "Staffordshire, Kent, Made in England," pr 385.00
  27" h, Foo Dog, cast stone, 20th C 115.00
  Cocker Spaniel, standing, Royal Doulton 75.00
  Dachshund, Beswick, begging 55.00

Game Plate, 10" d, dog with deer, gold trim, mkd "Limoges" 135.00

Glasses, RCA Nipper giveaway, pr 30.00

Lamp Base, 15" h, Bulldogs, cold painted white metal, dogs standing by tree, electrified, 20th C 1,265.00

Match Safe, Bulldog with American flag 145.00

Painting, oil on canvas
  16-7/8" x 21", black and white Spaniel, with pheasant, found condition, back with London preparer's label, modern frame 412.50
  21" h, 32-7/8" w, St. Bernard with rescued child, sgd "Speck, 1903," found condition, worn gilt 26" l x 37-1/2" w gilt frame 330.00

Paperweight, 2" d, black and white hunter with dog, heart, turtle, shamrock, rabbit, and floral canes, Kazium silhouette . 865.00

Perfume Bottle, 3-1/2" h, Russian Wolfhound, bottle tied at neck, Czarina perfume 40.00

Pip-Squeak, 7" h, wood and composition, worn white flannel dog, white button eyes, worn painted pupils, worn whiskers, one leg broken, mouth opens, voice box silent 160.00

Plate, 10" d, dog with deer, gold trim, mkd "Limoges" 135.00

Stuffed Toy, Tige, Buster Brown, Steiff, all jointed 550.00

Dog, Meissen figure, standing, blue collar, oval rocky plinth, 7-3/4" h, $2,100. Photo courtesy of Freeman\Fine Arts.

Tile, 8-1/4" d, sitting white dog, white glaze, green ground, imp Walley Pottery marks 320.00
Watercolor, 7-3/8" x 8-1/2", "Beagles...Small Hounds in Landscape," sgd "Vernon Stokes," framed, three beagles in field 865.00

Horses

Advertising Sign, Bickmore Gall Salve, diecut cardboard of horse, 12" x 18" 140.00
Bank
    Circus Horse, 5-3/8" h, tub, black, brown, silver, and red 140.00
    Trick Pony, worn polychrome 1,210.00
Candy Container, papier-mâché, prancing, orig saddle and reins 250.00
Figure
    5" x 4", papier-mâché and wood, on platform, wheels, Germany 125.00
    28-1/2" x 24-3/4" h, full figured head, carved walnut, mounted in molded frame, late 19th C, minor losses 690.00
    Dappled Grey Foal, Cybis 325.00
    Draft Horse, large, Melbaware 100.00
    Palomino, large, Goebel 125.00
Plate, Plough Horses, Royal Doulton...................................85.00
Rug, hooked yarn
    23" x 35", braided yarn border, horse head, brown, beige, black, and white, light green ground......................200.00
    30-1/2" x 51", pictorial ground, saddled horse on variegated ground, New England, 19th C, mounted...............2,185.00
Toy, painted cast iron, bell toy, wild mule 1,150.00
Weather Vane
    15" x 17-1/2", zinc and copper, trotting, applied mane and tail, C. J. Howard, Bridgewater, MA, late 19th C 2,300.00
    15-1/2" x 25", copper, running, fine verdigris surface, one bullet hole, America, late 19th C 1,380.00
    25-1/2" x 34", gilt copper, WA Snow, Boston, late 19th C 2,415.00
Windmill Weight, 17" l, 16-1/2" h, cast iron, Dempster Mill Manufacturing Co, Beatrice, NE, old black paint 385.00

Wild Life

Bank, still, cast iron
    Begging Bear, gold paint, some wear............................90.00
    Polar Bear, white, some wear, 5-1/4" h.........................385.00
Bread Plate, two handles, lion in center 65.00
Candy Container, 7" h, rabbit, papier-mâché, orig white paint, pink and red trim, glass eyes, wooden legs, mkd "Germany" 110.00

Eagle, covered dish, eggs and nest base, front emb "The American Hen," mkd "Porto Rico/Cuba/Philippines, $75.

Center Bowl, 14" d, majolica, lion mask relief, torsos terminating in paw feet supporting bowl, shaped triangular base, Italian, 19th C, rim chips, glaze flakes 980.00
Display Jar, 14-1/2" h, "Squirrel Brand Salted Nuts," name and squirrel emb on front 395.00
Figure
    3" h, elephant, carved wood, orig gray paint, black, red, white, and yellow, mkd "Joe" on blanket 27.50
    3-1/2" h, walrus, carved ivory 85.00
    5-1/2" l, bear, bronze, cold painted in browns and white, Austrian, c1920..980.00
    5-7/8" h, 5-1/2" d, frog, blue overlay diamond quilted glass, crystal legs, climbing glass tree stump, fancy scalloped base, applied crystal eyes and legs, mouth open, white lining...275.00
    6" l, frog, sewer pipe, hollow int. incised "Al Frail March 5, 1908" and "Alfred Frail March 5, 1908," chips and short hairline 175.00
    6-3/4" h, squirrel, sewer pipe, yellow slip eye, solid, imp "cm1980" 27.50
    7" l, frog, sewer pipe, solid 105.00
    7-1/4" l, lions, recumbent, pressed colorless glass, oval base, imp anchor symbol of Davidson, English registry mark for July 4, 1874, very minor chips, pr 115.00
    15-1/4" l, raccoon, sewer pipe, white slip detail, green painted eyes, incised "J. C." 165.00
Hunting Set, fox with hounds, lead, orig box, Germany.....125.00
Perfume Bottle, monkey, brown, Schuco 385.00
Stuffed Toy, Camel with the Wrinkled Knees, Germany.....250.00

ARCHITECTURAL ELEMENTS

History: Architectural elements, many of which are handcrafted, are those items which have been removed or salvaged from buildings, ships, or gardens. Part of their desirability is due to the fact that it would be extremely costly to duplicate the items today.

Beginning about 1840, decorative building styles began to feature carved wood and stone, stained glass, and ornate ironwork. At the same time, builders and manufacturers also began to use fancy doorknobs, doorplates, hinges, bells, window locks, shutter pulls, and other decorative hardware as finishing touches to elaborate new homes and commercial buildings.

Hardware was primarily produced from bronze, brass, and iron, and doorknobs also were made from clear, colored, and cut glass. Highly ornate hardware began appearing in the late 1860s and remained popular through the early 1900s. Figural pieces that featured animals, birds, and heroic and mythological images were very popular, as were ornate and very graphic designs that complimented the many architectural styles that emerged in the late 19th century.

Fraternal groups, government and educational institutions, and individual businesses all ordered special hardware for their buildings. Catalogs from the era show hundreds of patterns, often with a dozen different pieces available in each design.

The current trends of preservation and recycling of architectural elements has led to the establishment and growth of organized salvage operations that specialize in removal and resale of elements. Special auctions are now held to sell architectural elements from churches, mansions, office buildings, etc. Today's decorators often design an entire room around one architectural element, such as a Victorian marble bar or mural, or use several as key accent pieces.

References: Ronald S. Barlow (comp.), *Victorian Houseware, Hardware and Kitchenware*, Windmill Publishing, 1991; Margarete Baur-Heinhold, *Decorative Ironwork*, Schiffer Publishing, 1996; Len Blumin, *Victorian Decorative Art*, available from ADCA (P.O. Box 126, Eola, IL 60519), n.d.; Michael Breza and Craig R. Olson (eds.), *Identification and Dating of Round Oak Heating Stoves*, Southwestern Michigan College Museum (58900 Cherry Grove Rd., Dowagiac, MI 49047), 1995; Maude Eastwood wrote several books about doorknobs which are available from P.O. Box 126, Eola, IL 60519; Constance M Greiff, *Early Victorian*, Abbeville Press, 1995; Philip G. Knobloch, *A Treasure of Fine Construction Design*, Astragal Press, 1995; Henrie Martinie, *Art Deco Ornamental Ironwork*, Dover Publications, 1996; James Massey and Shirley Maxwell, *Arts & Crafts*, Abbeville Press, 1995; Ted Menten (comp.), *Art Nouveau Decorative Ironwork*, Dover Publications, n.d.; *Ornamental French Hardware Designs*, Dover Publications, 1995; Ernest Rettelbusch, *Handbook of Historic Ornament from Ancient Times to Biedermeier*, Dover Publications, 1996; Edward Shaw, *Modern Architect* (reprint), Dover Publications, 1996; *Turn of the Century Doors, Windows and Decorative Millwork*, Dover Publications, 1995 reprint; Stanley Shuler, *Architectal Details from Old New England Homes*, Schiffer Publishing, 1997; Web Wilson, *Great Glass in American Architecture*, E. P. Dutton, New York, 1986.

Periodical: *American Bungalow*, P.O. Box 756, Sierra Madre, CA 91204.

Collectors' Club: Antique Doorknob Collectors of America, Inc., P.O. Box 126, Eola, IL 60519.

Additional Listings: Doorknobs & Builders' Hardware, Stained Glass.

SPECIAL AUCTION

**Web Wilson Antique Hardware Auction
P.O. Box 506
Portsmouth, RI 02871
(800) 508-0022**

Advertising Flyer, 5" x 6-3/4", American Sea Green Slate, Granville, NY, 16 pgs, c1922, sketches 12.00
Bird Bath, 32" h, 24" d, carved stone, circular, steeply tapering sides, separate sq section pyramidal stand, 19th C.....395.00
Bracket Shelf, 10-3/4" w, 9" h, eagle detailed carved pine, gesso and old worn gilt, old edge damage 600.00
Cafe Curtain Holders, brass, Germany, set of 12 .... 45.00
Catalog
    Badger Wire & Iron Works, Milwaukee, WI, c1929, 64 pgs, 7-1/2" x 9-3/4", Ornamental & Iron Work, lamp standards, entrance gates, balconies, stairways, terraces, fire escapes, etc. 48.00
    Berger Mfg Co, Canton, OH, 1920, 175 pgs, 8-1/2" x 10-3/4", Cat. No. 23, metal ceilings, chair rails, moldings, cornices, etc. 50.00

Brown-Blodgett Co., St. Paul, MN, 1927, 100 pgs,. 9" x 12", Service Bureau Book of 100 Homes, 100 Designs and Floor Plans 35.00
Farley & Loetscher Mfg, Dubuque, IA, 1952, 132 pgs, 8-1/2" x 11", spiral bound, Quality Built Woodwork Price No. 9 .... 40.00
Indiana Limestone Quarrymen's, Bedford, IN, 1923, 40 pgs, 8-1/2" x 11", Vol. 27, Library Series, Designs for Houses Featuring Indiana Limestone 40.00
Kenneth Lynch & Sons, Wilton, CT, 1961, 136 pgs, 11" x 17", International Collection, garden ornaments, spheres, weathervanes, sundials, etc. 50.00
Mohawk Carpet Mills, Amsterdam, NY, 1937, 63 pgs, 9-1/4" x 12-1/2", spiral bound, From the Looms of Mohawk, laid in samples 35.00
Montgomery Ward Co., Chicago, IL, 1926, 100 pgs, 7-1/2" x 10", Wardway Homes 30.00
Door, 27" w, 69" h, grain painted, batten type, red and gray decorative painting, repairs, New England, early 19th C.... 175.00
Door Lintel, 51-3/4" l, 5-1/2" h, Indian, polychrome dec, glass insert, parcel-gilt, late 19th C 145.00
Eagle
    24" h, 30-1/2" w, Bellamy type, America, 20th C, repainted, cracks, minor losses 3,335.00
    27" h, 50" w, carved gilt gesso, orig weathered surface and gilding, attributed to MA, early 19th C, losses 2,875.00
Eagle's Head, 12" l, carved wood, traces of gilt, 19th C, cracks, losses to beak 345.00
Element
    8-1/2" h, 9-1/2" w, painted wood, lion's head, 19th C, minor imperfections 460.00
    33" h, 78" w, molded copper, figural lion's head, flanked by scrolls, verdigris surface, America, late 19th C, minor imperfections 2,645.00
Elevator Door, 19" w, 71" h, Aesthetic Movement, brass borders, ascending design, drilled 275.00
Fencing, 47" l, 41" h, cast iron, America, 19th C 450.00
Figure
    Rabbit, 12" h, cast iron, full bodied, old white repaint...385.00
    Stag, one 54" h, 51" l, 22" d, other 40" h, 44-1/2" l, 16" d, one standing, other lying with one front leg extended, life size, cast iron, made by Whitman Massachusetts Foundry, mold cut by H. Mansbach, 1880-85, some repairs, pr...7,475.00
Finial
    15-1/2" h, urn form, painted wood, 19th C, imperfections, pr 460.00
    73-1/2" h, copper, fine verdigris surface, tall spire over round orb, extending to layered pyramid base, American, 19th C 2,575.00
Fountain, 40" h, cast iron, attributed to J. W. Fiske, NY, late 19th C, losses, surface rust 1,200.00
Furniture, cast iron
    Chair, Vintage pattern, white repaint, 14" h seat, 27-1/4" h, 4 pc set 200.00
    Garden Bench, old white repaint, welded repairs to legs, 46-1/2" l 380.00
    Settee, Vintage pattern, one back foot replaced, white repaint, 57" l 175.00

Eagle, carved wood, in the style of Bellamy, traces of paint, varnished, 20th C, 44" w, $935. Photo courtesy of Garth's Auctions.

Suite, Coalbrookdale style, settee and 4 chairs, fern and blackberry design, indistinct registry stamp on back of chairs, slate blue paint, England, late 19th C, 59-1/2" l x 35-1/4" h settee, 5 pc set 5,750.00

Table, round pierced top, shaped baluster dec with herons, pierced tripod base, slate blue paint, 22 3-4" d, 28-1/2" h 815.00

Table, round pierced top, four legs, old white repaint, 40" d, 26" h 110.00

Gates, pr, 36" h, 32" w, painted wood, New England, 19th C, arched molded rails above baluster cut-outs flanked by chamfered posts, old gray weathered paint 635.00

Hitching Post, cast iron
37-1/2" h, jockey, polychrome repaint 360.00
38-1/2" h, horse head 90.00

Lever, 33-3/4" l, gilt bronze, cast fully molded cherub, snake, and bird, floral and foliate dec, Continental, pr 1,100.00

Mantel, 62-3/4" h, 87" w, Federal, Hudson, NY, c1790, carved wood, raised panel of 2 carved fans flanked by recessed fans and carved and molded pilasters, imperfections.......2,760.00

Panel, 82" h, 42-1/2" w, New England, 18th C, 3 vertical fielded panels, centering small horizontal panels and 3 vertical panels below, several coats of old paint....................................460.00

Snow Bird, 6-1/2" wing span, 7-1/4" h, eagles, cast iron, 4 pcs 95.00

Sundial, 41" h, Carrara marble, acanthus carved baluster, fluted and volute carved capital, chamfered gray, marble sq top, cast bronze dial, Greek Key plinth, Neoclassical, Continental, 19th C 2,400.00

Switch Plate Cover, Channel 7, 5 3/4" h brass cover, "7" logo 35.00

Urn
25" h, cast iron, sq plinth, old black repaint 165.00
34-1/4" h, cast iron, labeled "C. E. Walbridge, Pat Jan 26, 1873, Buffalo, NY," old white repaint........................250.00

Valance Fragment, Aubusson, France, 19th C, flowers, fruits, and vines, navy blue, sky blue, red, rose, maroon, gold, green, and blue-green, variegated deep gold, brown, tan, and olive field, 65" l, 8" h 230.00

Wall Sconce
15" h, bronze dore, drop crystals, cast foliate dec, French, pr 600.00
36" h, carved and gilded, three-light, foliate and bow dec, Venetian, price for 3 pc set......................................1,500.00

Window, 72-1/2" h, 50-3/4" w, painted pine, pr forms gothic arch, glazed, America, 19th C, imperfections 375.00

ART DECO

History: The Art Deco period was named after an exhibition, "l'Exposition Internationale des Arts Déecorative et Industriels Modernes," held in Paris in 1927. Its beginnings succeed those of the Art Nouveau period, but the two overlap in time as well as in style.

Art Deco designs are angular with simple lines. This was the period of skyscrapers, movie idols, and the Cubist works of Picasso and Legras. Art Deco motifs were used for every conceivable object being produced in the 1920s and 1930s (ceramics, furniture, glass, and metals) not only in Europe but in America as well.

References: Victor Arwas, *Glass: Art Nouveau to Art Deco*, Rizzoli, 1977; Lillian Baker, *Art Nouveau & Art Deco Jewelry*, Collector Books, 1981, 1994 value update; Bry-

an Catley, *Art Deco and Other Figures*, Antique Collectors' Club, n.d.; Jean L. Druesedow (ed.), *Authentic Art Deco Interiors and Furniture in Full Color,* Dover Pub., 1997; Alfred W. Edward, *Art Deco Sculpture and Metalware*, Schiffer Publishing, 1996; Tony Fusco, *Art Deco Identification and Price Guide*, Avon Books, 1993; Mary Gaston, *Collector's Guide to Art Deco*, 2nd ed., Collector Books, 1997; Steven Heller and Louise Fili, *Italian Art Deco: Graphic Design between the Wars*, Chronicle Books, 1993; ——, *Streamline: American Art Deco Graphic Design*, Chronicle Books, 1995; Francis Joseph, *Collecting Carlton Ware*, Francis Joseph Publications, 1994; Henrie Martinie, *Art Deco Ornamental Ironwork*, Dover Publications, 1996; Theodore Menten, *Art Deco Style*, Dover Publications, n.d.; Paul Ockner and Leslie Piña, *Art Deco Aluminum: Kensington,* Schiffer Publishing, 1997; Francis Salmon, *Collecting Susie Cooper*, Francis Joseph Books, 1995; Wolf Uecker, *Art Nouveau and Art Deco Lamps and Candlesticks*, Abbeville Press, 1986; Howard and Pat Watson, *Collecting Art Deco Ceramics*, Kevin Francis, 1993.

Periodical: *Echoes Report*, P.O. Box 2321, Mashpee, MA 02649.

Collectors' Clubs: Canadian Art Deco Society, #302-884 Bute St., Vancouver, British Columbia V6E 1YA Canada; Carlton Ware International, P.O. Box 161, Sevenoaks, Kent TN15 6GA England; Chase Collectors Society, 2149 W Jibsail Loop, Mesa, AZ 85202; International Coalition of Art Deco Societies, One Murdock Terrace, Brighton, MA 02135; Miami Design Preservation League, P.O. Bin L, Miami Beach, FL 33119; Twentieth Century Society, 70 Cowcross St., London EC1M 6DR England.

Museums: Art Institute of Chicago, Chicago, IL; Cooper-Hewitt Museum, National Museum of Design, Smithsonian Institution, New York, NY; Corning Museum of Glass, Corning, NY; Jones Museum of Glass and Ceramics, Sebago, ME; Virginia Museum of Fine Arts, Richmond, VA.

Additional Listings: Furniture; Jewelry. Also check glass, pottery, and metal categories.

Bottle
8-1/4" h, angular squared colorless body, overlaid black geometric designs in Josef Hoffman style, faceted edges, polished base, European, stopper possible replacement 375.00

13-5/8" h, 4-1/2" d, 3 sided, amethyst, gold, green, and red enamel designs, 3-sided amethyst spear-shaped stopper 195.00

Bowl, 10" d, 301/2" h, mottled beige ground, orange, tan, green, and copper flowers, and leaves, sgd "Charlotte Rhead," mkd "Crown Ducal" 235.00

Box, agate, gold strapwork findings, highlighted by sapphire cabochon and center diamond set initial clasp, fitted Cartier case 3,000.00

Left, garden bench, cast iron, fern detail, old black repaint, old break in seat, 59-1/2" l, $825; right: garden arm chair, cast iron, lily of the valley detail, old black repaint, old break in seat, 33-1/2" l, $825; front: cast iron horse head hitching post, old black repaint, 62" l, repairs to one of pr, $615. Photo courtesy of Garth's Auctions.

Cigarette Lighter, woman's head, heating coil in mouth 250.00

Clock

Alarm, 3-1/2" x 5" x 5-1/2", plastic, mkd "Tele-vision," lighted and dated 1959, mahogany red, cream, and gold, minor wear to case, working..................................75.00

Mantel, 19" l, 12-1/2" h, black and gold marble, stylized female nude, white metal clock face, sgd "Geo-Luc," France, 1925..350.00

Cocktail Set, sterling silver, 9-1/4" cocktail shaker with finely cut-out strainer, 25 troy oz., twelve 2-1/2" d x 4" h goblets, 4 troy oz. each, mkd "Tiffany & Co, 1885 makers, 1512," price for 13-pc. set 1,265.00

Desk Set, Bakelite, butterscotch, ink tray, two note pad holders 225.00

Dinnerware, partial, Susie Cooper

Daffodil pattern, 2 cov tureens, gravy boat, meat platter, 6 soup bowls with underplates, 6 side dishes, 6 salad plates, 6 dinner plates..300.00

Dresden Spray pattern, 2 cov tureens, 3 oval serving plates, 6 salad plates, fish plate, 6 handled soup bowls and matching saucers, 6 tea cups and saucers, sugar bowl, printed marks "Susie Cooper Production Crown Works, Burslem England," minor damage..900.00

Dish, 7-1/4" l, 2-1/4" h, free-form oval, colorless glass, internally dec with alternating white and dark aubergine purple stripes, sgd "Walter" between two stripes (Almeric Walter).......635.00

Figure, dog, cobalt blue, gold trim, Grindley 125.00

Furniture

Chest of Drawers, 44-1/2" x 35", parchment covered, rect top, 3 tapering drawers, pyramid mirrored stiles, bracket feet, back branded "Quigley," French, c1925..............2,750.00

Vanity, 33-1/2" w, 22-1/2" d, 67" h, brass and Carrara marble, swivel oval mirror flanked by pr of glass sconces, rect top over 2 drawers, sq legs joined by stretchers, early 20th C 1,100.00

Lamp

Cast metal, slave girl holding leaded multicolored cull de vere glass globe over one knee, dark bronze finish, black stone base, 14-3/4" l, 12" h..425.00

Chrome airplane, vertical glass airship, chrome base..525.00

Lorgnette, platinum, line of round diamonds within an openwork textured mount, suspended from 34" l navette link chain highlighted by collet diamond..1,400.00

Mirror, 22-1/2" w, 42" h, wrought iron, imp marks, attributed to Paul Kiss, c1925 ....1,2400.00

Pitcher, 11-1/2" h, tankard, cut daisy dec, Honsdale.........325.00

Plaque, 23-3/4" w, 42" h, carved and polychrome dec wood panel depicting bicycle racing, Federal Art Project, c1930, some damage 525.00

Cigarette Lighter, AS Solingen, Germany, 3-3/4" h, $60.

Clock, Sessions, Golden Girl, gold finished pot metal, wood base, $195.

Rug, 3' 10" x 2', two diagonal rows of dark red, gold, aubergine, royal blue, tan, and green half circles, stippled field, Chinese, good pile, slight edge wear 300.00

Tea Service, partial, Susie Cooper, Rex shape, painted underglaze dark brown, smoke-brown, brown crayon lines, aubergine glaze, cov teapot, 4 cups and saucers, 4 plates, minor damage 200.00

Tile, 8" sq, rust, tan, off-white, and purple lady, four short round feet, mkd "Longway France Primavera" with shield and crown.. 415.00

Umbrella Stand, 18-1/2" h, sewer pipe, molded Art Deco shoulder design, glazed over rim chips, drainage hole drilled in bottom.. 75.00

Vanity Case, 14kt yg, polished surface, band of calibre cut sapphires, diamonds, and emeralds, link chain, 72.1 dwt 1,750.00

Vase
6" d, ball shape, mottled blue, #601, mkd "Rumrill" 125.00
9-1/2" h, Boch Freres, designed by Charles Catteau, Belgium, c1925, ceramic, matte yellow, blue and white stylized leaves, black ground, artist sgd, stamp mark 500.00
19" h, flared trumpet of mottled white and colorless glass, layered in bright royal blue, etched repeating stylized foliate devices, side sgd "Degue," base mkd "Made in France" 1,380.00

ART NOUVEAU

History: Art Nouveau is the French term for the "new art" which had its beginning in the early 1890s and continued for the next 40 years. The flowing and sensuous female forms used in this period were popular in Europe and America. Among the most recognized artists of this period were Gallé, Lalique, and Tiffany.

The Art Nouveau style can be identified by flowing, sensuous lines, florals, insects, and the feminine form.

These designs were incorporated into almost everything produced during the period, from art glass to furniture, silver, and personal objects. Later wares demonstrate some of the characteristics of the evolving Art Deco style.

References: Victor Arwas, *Glass: Art Nouveau to Art Deco*, Rizzoli, 1977; Lillian Baker, *Art Nouveau & Art Deco Jewelry*, Collector Books, 1981, 1994 value update; Constance M Greiff, *Art Nouveau*, Abbeville Press, 1995; Ted Menten (comp.), *Art Nouveau Decorative Ironwork*, Dover Publications, n.d.; Bengt Nystrom, *Rorstrand Porcelain*, Abbeville Press, 1995; Albert Christian Revi, *American Art Nouveau Glass*, reprint, Schiffer Publishing, 1981; Wolf Uecker, *Art Nouveau and Art Deco Lamps and Candlesticks*, Abbeville Press, 1986; Roberta Waddell, *Art Nouveau Style*, Dover Publications, n.d.; Kenneth Wilson, *American Glass 1760-1930*, 2 Vols., Hudson Hill Press and The Toledo Museum of Art, 1994.

Museum: Virginia Museum of Fine Arts, Richmond, VA.

Additional Listings: Furniture; Jewelry. Also check glass, pottery, and metal categories.

Basket, 13-1/4" x 9-1/2" x 3-1/4", silverplated, grapes dec, 1904 hallmark 135.00

Belt Buckle, polychrome enamel, silver mount, minor enamel loss 245.00

Bird Cage, 33" h, beechwood, onion domed body, wirework sides, scrolled feet 800.00

Bowl, 9" d, 3-1/4" h, German silver, foliate design, two handles, cut-out design, imp marks, approx. 16 troy oz.............. 460.00

Candelabrum, pr, 12-1/4" h, silvered metal, stylized arms, flaring sq post and base, imp mark, bobeche missing, dents. 625.00

Charger, 20" d, pewter, large emb profile center bust portrait of woman, long flying hair, thin gown, wide rim emb with daisies, long stems, scrolling leaves, hallmarked, c1900 .... 675.00

Cigar Lighter, 18" h, chrome plated, woman holding long horn 850.00

Clock, 25" h, green bisque, gold and pink highlights, gilt metal, imp Charenton marks, France, c1900, hand missing, nicks 825.00

Desk Set, onyx, inlaid lapis lazuli band, two inkwells, blotter, note pad, card, and pen holders, imp hallmarks, London, c1921, 6 pc set 296.00

Candy Dish, sterling silver, water lily motif, 7-5/8" x 6-5/8" x 1-1/2", $240.

Jewelry Box, rabbit and oak leaf relief, pink satin int., bronze finish, mkd "Trademark J. B. Signifies the Best 298," 4-7/8" x 3" x 4", $65.

Dresser Set, silver, blue guillouche enamel, Birmingham hallmarks for 1919-20, mirror, four brushes, and comb, worn fitted case 550.00

Figure, 14-1/2" h, gilt bronze, girl, long skirt, low girdle and breast-plates over mesh bodice, draped beaded necklace, ivory head, arms, and feet, coved circular gray-green and black marble base, incised "A. Gori" 3,200.00

Fire Screen, 28" h, 20" w, brass, translucent floral design of seed beads and brass channeling between glass panels 800.00

Furniture

    Desk Chair, attributed to Louis Majorelle, France, mahogany, curved crest rail continues to outward flaring arms, 3 upholstered panels over D-shaped over-upholstered seat, outward curving molded legs, back uprights supporting setback arms continuing downward as rear leg braces, dark green leatherette upholstery 9,500.00

    Parlor Suite, Majorelle style, Escargot pattern, carved mahogany, 55" l settee, 2 armchairs, 2 side chairs, molded and dipped crest rails, carved and pierced stiles, rect upholstered seats, cabriole legs, 5 pc set 4,750.00

Inkwell, 5" d, 1-1/2" h, conical pewter body, raised stylized foliage design, blue-green enamel buttons, glass insert, imp "English Pewter 0521" 275.00

Lorgnette, 14k yg, collet set with 3 round diamonds, foliate mount, Krementz hallmark..1,400.00

Magnifying Glass, 2-1/8" d glass, 6-1/4" l hollow sterling silver handle, scrolled leaves dec, mkd "Blackinton, 1904" ..125.00

Match Safe, 14K yg, griffin and serpentine images, c1898, 26.7 dwt 525.00

Mirror, 19-1/2" h, cast bronze, Rococo kidney shape 250.00

Picture Frame, 4-3/4 x 6-1/2", rect, silver, English................90.00

Plaque, 17" d, pink, white, and green Limoges style dec, blue ground, gold highlights, incised sgd "E. Kiliert," back imp "Longway D/1182" 900.00

Tazza, 12-1/2" d, 9-3/4" h, gilt bronze, high relief teasel and stalks, fluted bronze stem, brown/green patina, black marble base, inscribed "A. Marionnet"..675.00

Tile, 32-1/2" l, 22" w, shoreline scene, Barbitone School, attributed to Armand Desire Gautier, incised "A. Gautier L.L." on reverse, painted cipher "DG," framed, c1800..........................1,200.00

Umbrella Stand, 28-1/2" h, cast iron, emb floral dec, old green re-paint 150.00

Vase, 11" h, floral polychrome dec, cream ground, imp mark, Carter, Stabler, and Adams, Poole, England, 1925 ......295.00

ART POTTERY (GENERAL)

History: America's interest in art pottery can be traced to the Centennial Exposition in Philadelphia, Pennsylvania, in 1877, where Europe's finest producers of decorative art displayed an impressive selection of their wares. Our burgeoning artists rose to the challenge immediately, and by 1900, native artisans were winning gold medals for decorative ceramics in European competitions.

The Art Pottery "Movement" in America lasted from about 1880 until the first World War. During this time, more than 200 companies, in most states, produced decorative ceramics ranging from borderline production ware to intricately decorated, labor intensive artware establishing America as a decorative art powerhouse.

Below is a listing of the work by various factories and studios, with pricing, from a number of these companies. The location of these outlets are included to give the reader a sense of how nationally-based the industry was.

References: Susan and Al Bagdade, *Warman's Americana Pottery and Porcelain*, Wallace-Homestead, 1994; Carol and Jim Carlton, *Colorado Pottery*, Collector Books, 1994; Paul Evans, *Art Pottery of the United States*, 2nd ed., Feingold & Lewis Publishing, 1987; Lucile Henzke, *Art Pottery of America*, revised ed., Schiffer Publishing, 1996; Ralph and Terry Kovel, *Kovels' American Art Pottery*, Crown Publishers, 1993; Richard and Hilary Myers, *William Morris Tiles*, Richard Dennis (distributed by Antique Collectors' Club), 1996; David Rago, *American Art Pottery,* Knickerbocker Press, 1997.

Periodical: *Style 1900*, 17 S. Main St., Lambertville, NJ 08530.

Collectors' Clubs: American Art Pottery Assoc., P.O. Box 525, Cedar Hill, MO 63016; Pottery Lovers Reunion, 4969 Hudson Dr., Stow, OH 44224.

Videotapes: Ralph and Terry Kovel, *Collecting with the Kovels: American Art Pottery*, two tapes, Antiques, Inc., 1995.

Museums: Cincinnati Art Museum, Cincinnati, OH; Everson Museum of Art of Syracuse and Onondaga County, Syracuse, NY; Newcomb College Art Gallery, New Orleans, LA; Zanesville Art Center, Zanesville, OH.

Additional Listings: See Clewell; Clifton; Cowan; Dedham; Fulper; Grueby; Jugtown; Marblehead; Moorcroft; Newcomb; North Dakota School of Mines; Ohr; Paul Revere; Peters and Reed; Rookwood; Roseville; Van Briggle; Weller; Zanesville.

Notes: Condition, design, and glaze quality are the key considerations when buying art pottery. This category includes only companies not found elsewhere in this book.

Advisor: David Rago.

Arequipa Pottery, Fairfax, CA
Cabinet Vase, 5" h, 3" d, squeezebag dec, stylized blue and yellow leaves, green ground, blue mark 2,500.00
Vase, 6" h, 4" d, hand modeled, stylized flowers, blue matte glaze, imp mark 850.00

Crook, Russel
Vessel
8" h, 4" d, ovoid, stoneware, gray mouse in tall trees, black ground, minor glaze flecks to rim, unmarked 1,700.00
9" h, 9" d, stoneware, herd of moose in clay color, black ground, firing lines through body, chips to rim, incised palette mark 950.00

Denaura, Denver, vase, 8-1/2" h, 5" d, ovoid, small opening, incised with tulips, cover in smooth green glaze, ink mark and "Denaura/Denver/1903/160" 2,400.00

FHR Pottery, Los Angeles, vase, 6" h, 3" d, crystalline, silvery crystals on flowing brown ground, imp mark 1,000.00

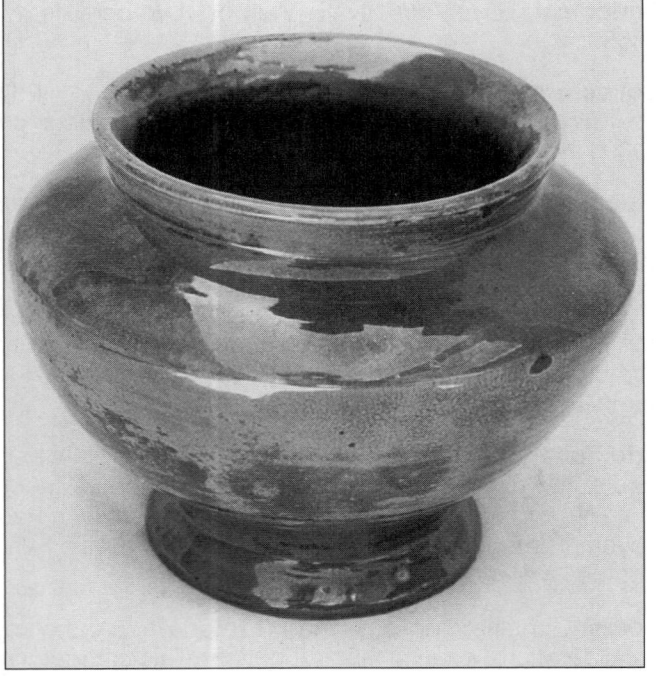

Pewabic Pottery, vase, irid purple and turquoise high glaze, orig paper label, 5" d, 4" h, $250.

Lucie Rie
Bowl
5-1/4" d, 3-1/2" h, ftd, matte white glaze, bronze colored rim 7-3/4" d, 3-3/4" h, flaring, ftd, crackled yellow glaze, bronze band 2,750.00
Vase
11" h, 5-1/4" d, bulbous rim, flaring rim, thin green vertical lines, broad bronze bands, restoration to small chip 2,750.00
7-1/2" h, 4-1/2" d, flat flaring rim with ribs, light green and raspberry matte glaze, dark brown base 4,500.00

Merrimac Pottery, Newburyport, MA
Cabinet Vase, 4" h, 3-1/2" d, feathered matte green and gunmetal glaze, mark partially obscured by glaze 450.00
Pitcher, 6-3/4" h, 6-1/2" h, rich matte green glaze, restoration to chip at rim, stamped 300.00

Overbeck Pottery, vase, 15" h, incised dec of wisteria vine and blossoms, two kiln marks, c1931 .... 11,200.00

Owens Pottery, Roseville and Zanesville, OH
Creamer, 3-1/2" h, Aqua Verdi, green matte, imp mark 75.00
Inkwell, 3-3/4" d, lime leaves, brown ground, sgd 110.00
Vase
5" h, Chinese Translation, white flowing glaze 120.00
11" h, Lotus, morning glories dec, artist sgd "Charles Fouts" 185.00

Pewabic Pottery, Detroit, MI
Bowl, 5" d, 2" h, ext. covered in shimmering burgundy glaze, int. with richly lustered gold glaze, stamped 450.00
Vase
7" h, 5" d, bulbous, flaring rim, rich metallic lustered blue and gray glaze, circular imp mark 865.00
8-1/4" h, 5-1/4" d, tapering shoulder, lustered gold, green, and burgundy glaze, mark partially obscured by glaze 1,300.00
9-1/4" h, 7-1/4" d, bulbous, lustered cobalt blue glaze, slight bruise to side, in making, circular stamp 1,000.00
9-3/4" h, 5-3/4" d, classically shaped, flaring rim, blue-green crystalline glaze, imp mark, paper label 2,000.00

Roblin Pottery, San Francisco, CA, miniature vase, 3" h, 2" d, bulbous, beaded rim, buff clay, imp mark 350.00

Teco, Terra Cotta, IL
Vase
6" h, 4-3/4" d, bulbous, flaring rim, satin matte green glaze, imp "Teco" twice 410.00
10-1/4" h, 5-1/2" d, buttress, satin matte green glaze, imp "Teco" three times 2,300.00
11" h, 5-3/4" d, ikebana, emb tulips and tall intertwining leaves, smooth matte green glaze, minor restoration to one leaf tip, imp "TECO" 5,500.00
13" h, 10" w, #119, circular form, four buttress handles, satin green finish, imp "Teco 119," repair to rim chips, repair to glaze nicks 4,000.00

University City Pottery, St. Louis, MO
Trivet, pate-sur-pate, pink maple leaves, cream ground, dec by Taxile Doat 2,500.00
Vase, 7" h, 4" d, crystalline, gold snowflake crystals on cream ground, imp mark 1,000.00

Valentien Pottery, San Diego, CA, vase, 7" h, 3" d, painted stylized Greek key design, matte painting technique, imp mark 2,500.00

Walley Pottery, West Sterling, MA
Candlestick, 10" h, 4-1/4" h, bulbous top, flared base, striated brown-yellow high glaze, smooth green ground, looped handle, imp "WJW" 290.00
Mug, 5" h, 4" d, molded head of devil with garnet eyes, imp mark 800.00
Tile, 7-1/2" d, circular form, large relief turtle design, thick crackle matte green glaze, imp "WJW" 460.00

Arequipa, Squeezebag Ware by F. H. Rhead, left, $9,350; right, $6,325. Photo courtesy of David Rago Auctions, Inc.

Walrath Pottery, candleholder, seated cherub on pedestal warming hands over candle opening, light green, imp "Walrath Pottery/1914," 7-1/4" h, $450.

Vase

4-1/2" h, 3-1/2" d, elongated neck, mottled, dripping green high glaze, imp mark 345.00

4-1/2" h, 4" d, oviform, pinkish gray, irid high gloss glaze rippling on one side, smoother on other, imp "WJW" 460.00

5-1/2" h, 5-3/4" d, high gloss glaze, brown speckles with yellowish brown striation on olive green ground, imp "WSH" mark for "Worcester State Hospital," minor glaze nick and scratches 575.00

6" h, 3-1/2" h, bulbous, tapering to slightly flared base, speckled white, striated brown high glaze, imp "WJW".....435.00

7" h, 7" d, oviform, overlapping leaves in high relief, deep matte green glaze, slivery black edges, imp "WJW," glaze imperfections, minor glaze nick.............................1,725.00

8-1/2" h, 5" d, bulbous shoulder tapering to foot, imp stylized Oriental floral under predominately brown high glaze green ground, some speckling on shoulder, imp "WJW" 815.00

13-1/2" h, 5-1/4" d, tapering cylindrical form, four rising handles mounted with rolled rim enclosing int. rim with scalloped edges, thick sliding green high glaze rippling towards base on brown ground, imp "WJW" 6,325.00

Walrath Pottery, Rochester, NY

Chamberstick, 5" h 250.00

Mug, 4-1/2" w, 3-1/4" h, reddish-brown foliate design, brown ground, imp mark, price for pr 435.00

Vase, 7-3/4" h, 3-3/4" d, stylized blue leaf forms, light matte blue ground, tight hairline...1,380.00

Wheatley Pottery Co., Cincinnati, OH

Lamp Base, 11-1/2" h, 9-1/2" d, buttressed, curdled matte green glaze, glaze scrape small nicks to feet 2,600.00

Vase

10" h, 5" d, handle, emb leaves, matte green finish, imp mark 1,500.00

12-3/4" h, ovoid, white and green flowers, mottled blue and light blue high glaze, inscribed "J. T. Wheatley, Cincinnati, 1879" 865.00

Vessel, 11" h, 10" d, matte green glaze, overlaid with silver leaves, branches, and simulated net, minor losses...............2,500.00

ARTS AND CRAFTS MOVEMENT

History: The Arts and Crafts Movement in American decorative arts took place between 1895 and 1920. Leading proponents of the movement were Elbert Hubbard and his Roycrofters, the brothers Stickley, Frank Lloyd Wright, Charles and Henry Greene, George Niedecken, and Lucia and Arthur Mathews.

The movement was marked by individualistic design (although the movement was national in scope) and re-emphasis on handcraftsmanship and appearance. A reform of industrial society was part of the long-range goal. Most pieces of furniture favored a rectilinear approach and were made of oak.

The Arts and Crafts Movement embraced all aspects of the decorative arts, including metalwork, ceramics, embroidery, woodblock printing, and the crafting of jewelry.

References: Steven Adams, *Arts & Crafts Movement*, Chartwell Books, 1987; *Arts and Crafts Furniture: The Complete Brooks Catalog of 1912*, Dover Publications, 1996; Michael E. Clark and Jill Thomas-Clark (eds.), *J. M. Young Arts and Crafts Furniture*, Dover Publications, 1994; Paul Evans, *Art Pottery of the United States*, 2nd ed., Feingold & Lewis Publishing, 1987; *Furniture of the Arts & Crafts Period With Prices*, L-W Book Sales, 1992, 1995 value update; Bruce Johnson, *Official Identification and Price Guide to Arts and Crafts*, 2nd ed., House of Collectibles, 1992; ——, *Pegged Joint*, Knock on Wood Publications, 1995; Elyse Zorn Karlin, *Jewelry and Metalwork in the Arts and Crafts Tradition*, Schiffer Publishing, 1993; *Limbert Arts and Crafts Furniture: The Complete 1903 Catalog*, Dover Publications, n.d.; Thomas K. Maher, *The Jarvie Shop: The Candlesticks and Metalwork of Robert R. Jarvie*, Turn of the Century Editions, 1997; James Massey and Shirley Maxwell, *Arts & Crafts*, Abbeville Press, 1995; Kevin McConnell, *More Roycroft Art Metal*, Schiffer Publishing, 1995; Richard and Hilary Myers, *William Morris Tiles*, Richard Dennis (distributed by Antique Collectors' Club), 1996; David Rago, *American Art Pottery*, Knickerbocker Press, 1997; Roycrofters, *Roycroft Furniture Catalog, 1906*, Dover Publications, 1994; Paul Royka, *Mission Furniture, from the American Arts & Crafts Movement*, Schiffer Publishing, 1997; Joanna Wissinger, *Arts and Crafts: Metalwork and Silver* and *Pottery and Ceramics*, Chronicle Books, 1994.

Periodicals: *American Bungalow*, P.O. Box 756, Sierra Madre, CA 91204; *Style 1900*, 333 N. Main St., Lambertville, NJ 08530. *American Bungalow* focuses on the contemporary owner of Period homes and the refurbishing of same. *Style 1900* has a more historically oriented approach to the turn of the century artisans.

Collectors' Clubs: Foundation for the Study of the Arts & Crafts Movement, Roycroft Campus, 31 S. Grove St., East Aurora, NY 14052; Roycrofters-At-Large Assoc., P.O. Box 417, East Aurora, NY 14052; William Morris Soc. of Canada, 1942 Delaney Dr., Mississaugua, Ontario, L5J 3L1, Canada. Students of the Arts and Crafts Movement are encouraged to participate in the two major confer-

ences now available. The Grove Park Inn Conference is held annually in Ashville, NC, in February, by Bruce Johnson. An Arts and Crafts College will be held in Princeton, NJ, in 1998, under the guidance of David Rago.

Museums: Elbert Hubbard Library-Museum, East Aurora, NY; Museum of Modern Art, New York, NY.

Advisor: David Rago.

Additional Listings: Roycroft; Stickleys; art pottery categories.

Andirons, pr, 56" h, 19" w, 28" d, wrought iron, wrapped with protruding animal faces, attributed to Samuel Yetlin, c1920 ....2,300.00

Bowl, 5-3/4" d, 2-3/4" h, copper and silver, chased and repousse waves highlighted with silver beads of spray and silver rim, rich patina, early imp Arthur J Stone mark, c1901-12 6,325.00

Box
    4" sq, 2-1/2" h, copper, small brass mushrooms and decorative stone, rich dark patina, price for pr 750.00
    4-1/2" w, 3-1/4" d, 1-3/4" h, hand-hammered, enameled black lined sailing ship, yellow ground 260.00

Creamer, 3-1/4" h, silver, oviform, rolled rim, mkd with Arthur Stone logo and initial "G" for Herman Glendenning, c1920, approx. 6 troy oz 290.00

Book Stand, oak, rect top, two shelves, pairs of parallel side supports, shelves mortised to supports, bracket feet, Roycroft, 26" w, 14" d, 26-1/2" d, $495.

Fish Tureen, 12" d, 12-1/2" h, hand hammered pewter, applied fish handles, orig ladle, imp Old Newbury marks 460.00

Furniture

Bookcase

33-3/4" l, 14" d, 50-1/2" h, J. M. Young, single glazed door with 12 mullions, refinished 1,725.00

20-3/4" sq, 44" h, revolving, three int. shelves, dark finish, mortise and tenons..575.00

Cabinet, 39" w, 13" d, 76-1/2" h, attributed to England, c1910, oak, two leaded glass doors, copper hinges and pulls over open shelf, orig finish, breaks to glass, minor wear .920.00

Chair

Arm, pagoda-form crest rail, padded back, lattice work splat and arm supports, drop-in seat, paneled seat rail, sq tapering leg, polychrome Chinoiserie dec on black Japanned ground, English....................................275.00

Dining, price for 8 pc set

17-1/2" w, 16-1/2" d, 37-1/2" h, one arm chair, seven side chairs, refinished....................................865.00

18-1/2" w, 18-1/2" h, 36-1/2" h, three vertical slats, orig black leather and tacks seat 1,150.00

China Cabinet, 48" w, 14" d, 60" h, two doors, mullioned windows, deeply woven brown finish, unmarked 800.00

Hall Mirror, 48-3/4" w, 28-1/4" h, Lifetime, similar to #512, two color glass, orig finish and pulls, inverted "V" crest rail 490.00

Morris Chair, 31-1/4" w, 36" d, 40" h, four vertical slats to the floor, through tenons, adjustable pins, orig finish .1,495.00

Settle

72" l, 30" d, 36" h, even arms with slats all around, orig dark brown finish, mkd "J. M. Young and Company" .2,000.00

74" l, 29" d, 34-1/2" h, Conant Furniture Co., 15 vertical back slats, sloping side rails, five vertical side slats, orig finish, new leather upholstery 2,300.00

74" l, 30" d, 36" h, Limbert, oak, eight vertical back slats, three vertical side slats, orig medium brown finish, some wear, missing cushions..2,990.00

77" l, 26-1/4" d, 43" h, 14 vertical back slats, four vertical side slats, orig dark finish, nicks to wood, missing cushion....................................290.00

Sewing Rocker, 17" w, 15-1/4" d, 32-1/4" h, three vertical slats, orig finish 460.00

Stand, 42 1/2" h, 20 1/2" w, 12 1/2" d, Limbert, horizontal support stretchers under top and bottom shelves on four sides gently arched on underside, support stretchers mortised through the vertical posts, 3 middle shelves held with round pegs, burned in mark, number 303, orig condition 1,025.00

Table

Dining

54" d, 28-1/2" h, five tapered legs, two leaves, refinished....................................345.00

54" d, 30" h, quarter-sawn oak, mortise and tenon stretcher base, orig finish, veneer chips...........920.00

Lamp, 30" h, 30" w, round top and round lower shelf, supported by 4 legs, orig medium-dark brown finish, Paine Furniture Co 60.00

Library, 48" w, 28" d, 30" h, two drawers, flat medial stretcher, worn orig dark brown finish, Stickley Brother/Quaint label 750.00

Limbert

36-1/2" d, 26-1/4" h, round, stretcher base, through tenons, cut down, orig finish 575.00

45" l, 30" d, 29" h, #146, oak, square cut outs and arched apron, branded mark, orig finish, some color added 2,990.00

Jewelry, brooch, attributed to S. G. Panis, silver, foliate pattern mounted with two sapphires, three diamonds, marked "S.G.P., STERLING," 2-1/4" l 800.00

Lamp

Chandelier, 27" d, 18" h, yellow, caramel, and green slag glass, some damage 1,380.00

Floor, 72" h, 24-1/2" sq shade, three bookshelves with oval cutouts, red, green, yellow, and white leaded glass shade over orig oil burner lamp, orig dark finish, paper label, "Shop of the Crafters, #153" 4,600.00

Hanging, 32" h, 9" w, brass patina cattail overlay, yellow and green slag glass 1,150.00

Table

18" h, 18" d, Dirk Van Erp, copper and mica, paneled shade, orig dark patina, 3 lights, mica panel, imp mark 10,000.00

21" h, 16" sq shade, painted gold metal frame, geometric panels over purple, blue, and yellow slag glass, Prairie School, Bradley and Hubbard 1,380.00

24" h, 11" w, four green and white glass panels in shade and base, oak frame 415.00

Loving Cup, 6-1/2" w, 6-1/4" h, silver, two applied angular handles, bulbous form, chased with wave and spray dec, monogrammed, minor scratched, marked with Stone logo and initial "T" for Herbert Taylor, underside engraved as Red Cross presentation, 12 troy oz....................635.00

Match Striker, 7" h, 5" w, inlaid wall hanging, glass butterflies on copper mount, imp "Burdick" 1,500.00

Plaque, 11" h, 14" w, patinated repousse copper, semi-precious stones, executed by Maria Longwoth Nichols Storer, Cincinnati, OH, 1909, rect, eight crabs and starfish in midst of irid pagination and raking, sgd "MLS/1915," wood frame 4,025.00

Porringer, 6-1/4" d, 1-3/4" h, silver, finely pierced and chased handle, engraved "Mary Louise Lawser-Christmas 1909 - from Auntie Mary," mkd with Arthur Stone logo, initial "B" for William Blair, 6 troy oz. 460.00

Print

Color linoleumcut on paper, Moonlight on Cape Cod, Tod Lindenmuth, sgd "Tod Lindenmuth" in pencil lower right, titled in pencil lower left, identified on label on mat, image size 9-1/4 x 7", matted....................1,265.00

Color woodblock on paper, William Rice, lone pine off the Carmel, CA, coat, 6" x 4" 1,000.00

Color woodcut on paper, Gearhart, Frances Hammel, sgd "Frances H. Gearhart" in pencil lower right, initialed in block lower left, identified on label on mat 7-3/4" x 4-1/2", Coastal Scene, matted....................1,495.00

8" x 4-1/2", Point Lobos, matted............................1,380.00

Salt, 3-1/4" w, 1-1/4" h, silver, oblong, flared base, set of six, four marked with Arthur Stone logo, and initial "T" for Herbert Taylor, other two with stone logo and initial "C," 18 troy oz.460.00

Serving Piece, silver, 8-1/2" l, hammered finish, pierced and engraved dec, monogram, imp "F. Porter, Sterling," c1925, 2 troy oz....................210.00

Smoking Stand, 9-1/4" sq, 25" h, copper top, new pyramid tacks, push button lock, caned sides and door, quarter-sawn oak, unmarked 1,100.00

Tray, 9" w, 12" l, silver, openwork handles, mid with Arthur Stone logo, initial "C," minor scratches, 15 troy oz..................865.00

Vase

Derby, 7" h, 11" d, silver plate, bulbous, hand hammered surface, rim dec with four riveted mounts 320.00

Heinz Art Metal Shop, bronze

8" h, 3-1/2" d, applied silver tree design, imp logo, patent Aug. 27, 12, D, orig patina, some denting 175.00

8" h, 5" d, silver foliate design, good patina, imp mark 290.00

8-1/2" h, bulbous top tapering to base, silver foliate design, cleaned 400.00

AUSTRIAN WARE

History: More than 100 potteries were located in the Austro-Hungarian Empire in the late 19th and early 20th centuries. Although Carlsbad was the center of the industry, the factories spread as far as the modern-day Czech Republic.

Many of the factories were either owned or supported by Americans; hence, their wares were produced mainly for export to the United States.

Marks: Many wares do not have a factory mark but only the word "Austrian" in response to the 1891 law specifying that the country of origin had to be marked on imported products.

Additional Listings: Amphora; Carlsbad; Royal Dux; Royal Vienna.

Bowl, 10-1/2" d, glazed pottery, gnarled branch section, grape bunch at one end, incised mark, c1900........................325.00
Celery Tray, 12" l, scalloped border, pink roses, green leaves, gold trim..75.00
Ewer
   5-5/8" h, 2-7/8" d, dark green, maroon, tan, and cream, gold trim, Alhambra pattern......................................90.00
   11-3/4" h, 6" d, rococo gold scroll, hp pink and yellow wild roses, gold outlines, 4 ftd..125.00
Figure
   3-1/2" h, bronze, robin, cold painted, c1920................230.00
   3-3/4" h, bronze, huntsman, cold painted, c1920.........320.00
   4" h, bronze, monkey holding shell, cold painted.........230.00
   4" l, bronze, recumbent puppy, cold painted in brown tones, c1920..290.00
   4-1/4" h, bronze, courting couple, cold painted............750.00
   6" h, Harem Girl with leopard, Oriental carpet form base, A. Chotka, c1920..815.00
   8" h, porcelain, five children in various poses, mounted on circular base, printed beehive mark, late 19th C, restoration 175.00
   14" h, bronze, farmer, dark brown and green patina, sgd "Andor Ruff"...460.00
Lamp, 15-1/2" h, 9" d metal shade dec with three red glass inserts, three foliate stem arms, reticulated bronzed Secessionist-inspired base 750.00

Pitcher, light green ground shaded to brown, purple grapes with white and green leaves, brown handle, gold rim, mkd "Vienna, Austria" 200.00
Portrait Vase, 34-1/2" h, cov, oval cartouche, polychrome enameled female portrait, burgundy luster ground, raised gilt scrolled foliate design, sgd "Rosley," beehive mark, early 20th C, rim repair, lines to handles....................................2,875.00
Salt, 3" h, figural, donkey, 2 dish shaped baskets on back, c1915 ....265.00
Stamp Box, cov, 4-1/4" x 3-1/8", ftd, two compartments, hp, roses, gold trim...50.00
Tankard, 14" h, hp Dutch scene, mkd "Made in Austria, 159 Haag" 400.00
Tray, 7" h, 2 bronze dancers, round green and white marble base, imp ark, c1925, abrasions 175.00
Vase
   10" h, divided rim forms 2 spouts, large dolphin handles, gold scales, raised gold florals, cream ground...............125.00
   10-1/2" h, 4-1/2" w, pedestal, reticulated handles, peacock on balcony scene, aqua, roses, green, brown, mkd "Carlsbad, Austria" 265.00
   13-3/8" h, 6-1/2" d, hp florals and holly, shaded ground, raised enameling, mkd "Carlsbad," pr 320.00

AUTOGRAPHS

History: Autographs appear on a wide variety of formats—letters, documents, photographs, books, cards, etc. Most collectors focus on a particular person, country, or category, e.g., signers of the Declaration of Independence.

References: Mark Allen Baker, *All-Sport Autographs*, Krause Publications, 1995; ——, *Collector's Guide to Celebrity Autographs*, Krause Publications, 1996; George S. Lowry, *Autographs: Identification and Price Guide*, Avon Books, 1994; J. B. Muns, *Musical Autographs*, 2nd Supplement, published by author, 1994; Susan and Steve Raab, *Movie Star Autographs of the Golden Era*, published by authors, 1994; Kenneth W. Rendell, *Forging History: The Detection of Fake Letters & Documents*, University of Oklahoma Press, 1994; ——, *History Comes to Life*, University of Oklahoma Press, 1996; George Sanders, Helen Sanders and Ralph Roberts, *Sanders Price Guide to Sports Autographs*, 1994 ed., Scott Publishing, 1993; ——*1994 Sanders Price Guide to Autographs*, Number 3, Alexander Books, 1994.

Periodicals: *Autograph Collector*, 510-A S. Corona Mall, Corona, CA 91720; *Autograph Review*, 305 Carlton Rd., Syracuse, NY 13207; *Autograph Times*, 2303 N. 44th St., No. 225, Phoenix, AZ 85008; *Autographs & Memorabilia*, P.O. Box 224, Coffeyville, KS 67337; *The Collector*, P.O. Box 255, Hunter, NY 12442.

Collectors' Clubs: Manuscript Society, 350 N. Niagara St., Burbank, CA 95105; Universal Autograph Collectors Club, P.O. Box 6181, Washington, DC 20044.

Additional Listings: See *Warman's Americana & Collectibles* for more examples.

Notes: The condition and content of letters and documents bear significantly on value. Collectors should know their source since forgeries abound and copy machines compound the problem. Further, some signatures of re-

Plate, 9-3/4" d, rose dec, scalloped and beaded edge, gold border, crown over capital mark, 9-3/4" d, $40.

cent presidents and movie stars were done by machine rather than by the persons themselves. A good dealer or advanced collector can help spot the differences.

Abbreviations: The following are used to describe autograph materials and their sizes.

Materials:

ADS	Autograph Document Signed
ALS	Autograph Letter Signed
AQS	Autograph Quotation Signed
CS	Card Signed
DS	Document Signed
FDC	First Day Cover
LS	Letter Signed
PS	Photograph Signed
TLS	Typed Letter Signed

Sizes (approximate):

Folio	12 x 16 inches
4to	8 x 10 inches
8vo	7 x 7 inches
12mo	3 x 5 inches

Colonial America

Adams, John, DS, "Recd of John Adams Four Pounds twelve shillings of lawful money..." also sgd by Jonathan Webb, Braintree, 22 Dec. 1763, 1 pg, oblong 8vo, folds, minor repairs, backed, statement of authentication by Adam's grandson, Charles French Adams" 1,100.00

Adams, Samuel, ALS, as Congressman to Henry Bromfield, telling military news, sgd "Saml. Adams," Philadelphia, Sept. 2, 1777, 1 pg, folio, addressed and docketed on verso 9,200.00

Austin, Stephen Fl, DS, Texian Loan Certificate, issued to Robert Triplett in the amount of $32, first installment of $320 loan to the Government of Texas, 8% interest, partially printed, New Orleans, Jan. 11, 1836, cross-cut cancellation, triangular piece missing at top of cancellation, also sgd by other Commissioners, B. T. Archer and W. H. Wharton... 1,100.00

Burr, Aaron, ALS, to his Aunt Mary Clarke, sending requested funds and expressing mortification that she would be hesitant to ask for anything in his power, sgd "A. Burr," 1 pg, 8vo, integral address leaf 1,150.00

Clymer, George, ALS, to William Wells, negotiating for a black indentured servant, sgd "Geo, Clymer," Philadelphia Nov. 13, 1794, 3 pgs, 4to, integral address leaf, docketed 1,380.00

Dalton, Trestram, ALS, to Elbridge Gerry, Chairman of the Committee of Supply, about supplying Indians in Maine and keeping their friendship, pleading for additional supplies, especially gunpowder, Newburyport, Oct. 21, 1775, 4 pgs, 4to, on 2 sheets, minor repairs 1,265.00

Jefferson, Thomas, ALS, to Mt. De Poirey, announcing the successful outcome of his efforts to secure compensation for de Poirey's services as Lafayette's aide-de-camp during the Revolution, explaining circumstances for delay, 1 full pg, 4to, sgd "Th. Jefferson," framed with portrait and clipping dated March 1819..14,950.00

Washington, George, LS, to Captain Brewster, discussing prisoners and his inability to release more troops, sgd "Go. Washington," headquarters, New Windsor, Feb. 23, 1781, 1 pg, folio, silked, uniformly browned, chips in right edge 10,350.00

Foreign

Bonaparte, Napoleon, DS, 1 pg, 17" x 23-1/2", sgd as Emperor of France, 29 Oct. 1809, concerning Senator Giassano being awarded title of Count of the Empire of France, sgd as Napol," 4-1/2" d wax seal showing Napoleon on his throne, Giassano's coat of arms hand painted in upper left of document, framed 2,530.00

Charles I, King of England, 1625-1649, DS, license for foreigners to fish in English waters, countersigned by Sir Balthazar Gerbier, 1 pg folio, mid 1630s...2,250.00

Louis XVI, King of France, 1774-1792, DS, tax of officers of justice for the district of Auch, district of Armagnac, offices of Senechal and President, account of sums payable, 6 pgs folio, Jan. 31, 1789, some chipping and soil to edges, text and signatures unaffected 1,250.00

Rosenberg, Alfred, Nazi, sgd and inscribed book, copy of his *Schriften und Reden,* Munich, 1943, 624 pgs, 8vo, bound in gold-stamped blue cloth, German inscription on fly-leaf regarding thanks for work in office to Party member G. Ebert, some wear on covers 875.00

General

Barton, Clara, ALS, personal letter to Miss Kensel, regarding busy schedule of travel and activities, ...Don't work too hard—There is a Hereafter...," 1 pg, small 8vo, Glen Echo, MD, May 7, 1908..450.00

Calamity Jane (Martha Jane Burke), CS, cabinet card, sgd 26,450.00

Clement VIII, Ippolito Aldobrandini, pope, ALS, to Monsignor Cerasio our Treasurer, ordering some grain to be sold and proceeds paid to the Treasurer of the Marches, in Italian, 1 pg, 4to, Monte Cavallio, Sept. 25, 1597...........................1,800.00

Dalton, Emmett, American outlaw, sgd and inscribed 8vo pg from his personal copy of his book, *When the Daltons Rode,* in blank area above heading for Chapter V 1,100.00

Edison, Thomas, PS, bust portrait, youthful, sgd 2,875.00

Longacre, James B., American engraver, DS, receipt for payment of subscription 950.00

Oakley, Annie, printed photo of Annie on card signed and shot through by her, large printed red heart with bullet hole, left with sq red printed photograph of Annie on horseback, name printed below, sgd on black area at center bottom with date "2 26 22," 2" x 4-5/8" oblong..5,500.00

Schwab, Charles, TLS, to Maurence T. Fleisher of Philadelphia regarding permission to order photograph of a painting lent by Schwab to the Metropolitan Museum of Art, 1 pg 4to, personal letterhead, NY, Feb. 25, 1937......................................450.00

Rockefeller, John D., TLS, to Charles H. Brown, Jr., of Yonkers, NY, with orig envelope, thanking him for gift of a putter, 1 pg, 8vo, letterhead of Pocantico Hills, NY, Jan. 12, 1912 ....1,400.00

Literature

Hemingway, Ernest, Modern Library copy of *The Sun Also Rises,* inscribed and sgd by Hemingway on half title page..2,200.00

Keller, Helen, TLS, dealing with horrors of blindness and deafness in appeals for funds for foundation, 1 full pg, 4to, Nov. 3, 1948 ....550.00

Shaw, George Bernard, English playwright, ALS, to Gilbert Murray, 2 pgs, oblong 8vo, Old House, Harmer Green, Welwyn, June 21, 1905 ....875.00

Stowe, Harriet Beecher, AQS, Biblical quote, 1 pg, 8vo, Andover Jan. 24, 1864...475.00

Twain, Mark, (Samuel L. Clemens,) ALS, 2 separate pgs, 4to, Hartford, April 11, 1883 ....2,750.00

Whitman, Walt, American poet, book sgd, on title page of conclusion of printed poem, and on flyleaf *Dr. Benjamin from the author, May 26, 1883,* author's edition of *Leaves of Grass,* accompanied by orig photo of Dr. Benjamin, taken in 1925, cloth folding case 4,000.00

Whittier, John Greenleaf, American poet, AQS, last stanza from poem "*Child Songs,*" 1 pg, 8vo, Amesbury, June 5, 1874 ....385.00

Military

Grant, U. S., ALS, to Captain Edward Brown turning down invitation for Declaration Day parade, New York City, 12 April, 1882, 1 pg, small 8vo, matted with engraving of Grant with his horse and sgd card from Chicago, 1879 ....1,150.00

Jackson, Andrew, DS, 1 pg, 19-1/4" x 15", military appointment of Alfred Morton as 2nd Lieutenant in 9th US Infantry, sgd as Pres of US 200.00

McClellan, George B., ALS, to William C. Biddle commenting on problems of his family, 3 pages 8vo, as Gov of New Jersey, Trenton, c1878-79 ....350.00

Santa Anna, Antonio Lopez De, Mexican General, DS, military commission for Don Julio Castaneda, sgd as dictator, in Spanish, partially printed, 1 pg folio, Palace of the National Government, June 5, 1854 ....1,400.00

Toombs, Robert A., Confederate general, Secretary of State, ALS, to Navy Secretary John P. Kennedy, asking if there is a vacancy as a surgeon's make for Dr. Whitlock of Washington, 1 pg, 4to, Washington, Oct. 3, 1852 ....285.00

Music

Gershwin, George, PS, by Miskikin, NY, sgd, sepia 3,737.00

Giuseppe Verdi, Italian composer, LS, Nov. 30, 1882 to Baron Hoffman 4,025.00

Herbert, Victor, Irish-American light opera composer, TLS, to Misses Hoyt, thanking them for tickets, 1 pg, 4to, New York, April 13, 1916 ....175.00

Kern, Jerome, DS, contract with publisher T. B. Harms Co., for song *Day Dreaming,* partially printed, 4 pgs, 4 to, New York Sept 10, 1941, sgd on 4th pg......................................375.00

Newman, Paul, PS, playing Buffalo Bill, 1976, black and white, sgd in black pen...82.00

Powell, Eleanor, PS, 8" x 10", black and white, inscribed "Harriet, a sweet girl I'm happy I know-you couldn't be anything else with the wonderful mother you have, Good Luck," sgd in ink, 1939..41.00

Ravel, Maurice, French composer, musical quotation sgd, inscribed to Mlle. Thérèse (Moss), 4 bars of music, mkd "*Simplicidato,*" 1 pg, 4to, Nov. 21, 1927..............................3,500.00

Sousa, John Philip, American composer and bandmaster, ALS, to "Dear Little Lady," Mrs. Ralph Willis, 1 pg 8vo, Feb. 19, 1925, with orig envelope 250.00

Presidents

Buchanan, James, ALS, to David Mann, Esq., asking to be paid "liberal compensation" for work in case of Commonwealth vs Aurand, Lancaster, Aug. 26, 1829, 1 pg, oblong 8vo ...690.00

Bush, George, LS, as VP, to Jim Hier, providing letter for collection, 1 pg, 8vo, vice-presidential stationery, framed with photo sgd by George and Barbara Bush 330.00

Carter, James, PS, sgd and inscribed, color, 8" x 10", standing in library, American flag to right 250.00

Cleveland, Grover, DS, sgd as President, authorizing Secretary of State to affix the Seal of the United States to a letter responding to the "Emperor of Austria-Hungary announcing the marriage of the arch Duchess Maria Dorothea to Duke Louis Philippe Robert of Orleans," Executive Mansion, Washington,

Jan. 5, 1897, partially printed, 1 pg, 8vo, horizontal folds 345.00

Ford, Gerald R., DS, granting Richard Nixon "a full, free, and absolute pardon...for all offenses against the United States which he...has committed or may have committed or taken part in...," Washington, 8 Sept. 1974, souvenir copy, sgd at later date by Ford, 1 pg, 4to 490.00

Garfield, James, A., Washington, April 29, 1881, partially printed document..8,050.00

Hoover, Herbert, LS, to Jess Hoover Chevalier, sending thanks for birthday greetings, 1 pg, small 4vo, engraved White House stationery, Aug. 10, 1931..175.00

Kennedy, John F., typed letter to Gov Edmund G Brown, CA, Jan. 26, 1963...3,162.00

Lincoln, Abraham, DS, partially printed one page 5,175.00

Truman, Harry S., PS, smiling Truman holding up Chicago Daily Tribune with famous "Dewey Defeats Truman" headline, inscribe din brown ink "My best to my good friend Nathan Lichtblau who made a great contribution towards making above statement false," 9-1/2" x 12-1/2"..................................2,760.00

Tyler, John, DS, sgd as President, Washington, May 12, 1842, directing Secretary of State to affix U.S. seal to pardon of William H. Thornberry, partially printed, 1 pg, 4to 550.00

Show Business

Bogart, Humphrey, DS, agreement with Aurelio Salazar, an employee, to purchase a truck for him and to deduct $100 a month from Salazar's salary to pay for same, 1 pg, 4to, Dec. 30, 1947 ....1,400.00

Davis, Sammy, dressing gown, signed by hundreds of visitors to Sammy Davis Jr.'s shows, autographs embroidered over in black silk thread, includes Ronald Reagan, Stevie Wonder's thumbprints 4,592.00

Clark Gable, DS, Gone with the Wind contract, MGM stationery, Culver City, Aug. 3, 1939...6,325.00

Garland, Judy, DS, receipt for travelers checks, sgd as "Judy Garland Luft," 1 pg, 4to, Aug. 14, 1957 ....550.00

Monroe, Marilyn, LS, addressed to son of Lefty O'Doul, dated San Francisco, 1954...10,350.00

Swanson, Gloria, CS, printed instructions for Security First National Bank, sgd by her, but not filled in with information....150.00

Sports

Aaron, Hank, sgd on 1966 Topps #500 card 50.00

Baer, Max, PS, 8" x 10", jacket and tie, arms folded, personalized, 1934..180.00

Cobb, Ty, check, 1945, First National Bank of Nevada, cancellation marks 110.00

Gehringer, Charles, salutation sgd on exhibit card............125.00

Greenberg, Hank, LS, handwritten, thanking author for complimentary copy of book, *Baseball's Best,* April 20, 1978, personal Beverly Hills stationery, orig envelope.......................695.00

Henie, Sonja, PS, bust pose, green ink sentiment and signature, 4to 165.00

Hodges, Gil, LS, handwritten, regarding taxes and accountant, Jan. 30, 1958, orig envelope, postmarked Brooklyn NY 795.00

Jeffries, James, photograph, oversized, sgd, prizefighter and heavyweight champion...2,875.00

Mantle, Mickey and Joe DiMaggio, 1961 Sport magazine, Sept. issue with two players on cover, sgd boldly in blue ink across jerseys 395.00

Rizzuto, Phil, orig wire photo, 7" x 9", shows Phil, wife, and family after being voted most popular Yankee and new prize sports car..60.00

Smith, Emmitt, sgd jersey 210.00

Williams, Ted, sgd on Topps #539 card..............................65.00

Statesmen

Clay, Henry, ALS, sgd as Secretary of State, to R. Smith, bank cashier, re collection of funds, 1 pg, 4to, Aug. 12, 1826 ....350.00

Davis, Jefferson, ALS, April 29, 1853, concerns Allegheny Valley RR Co. 495.00

Franklin, Benjamin, ALS, to wife Deborah in Philadelphia, waiting from word from home, news of grand sons, 6-1/2 lines of text, 1 pg, 3-3/4" x 7-3/8" oblong, London, c1774 .... 14,700.00

Henry, Patrick, DS, partially printed 2,875.00

Jay, John, ALS, to son Peter Augustus, discussing personal matters and grandchildren, 1 pg, 8vo, Bedford, June 24, 1822 ....2,200.00

Marshall, Thurgood, CS, 4-1/2" x 6" 225.00

Souter, David, Associate Justice, first day cover, eagle image 60.00

Webster, Noah, book from personal library, *The History of Great Britain,* 8vo, fully bound in calf, sgd on flyleaf, with bookplate of descendant, Robert Webster Day 975.00

AUTOMOBILES

History: Automobiles can be classified into several categories. In 1947 the Antique Automobile Club of America devised a system whereby any motor vehicle (car, bus, motorcycle, etc.) made prior to 1930 is considered an "antique." The Classic Car Club of America expanded the list focusing on luxury models from 1925 to 1948. The Milestone Car Society developed a list for cars for the years 1948 to 1964.

Some states, such as Pennsylvania, have devised a dual registration system for older cars—antique and classic. Models from the 1960s and 1970s, especially convertibles and limited-production models, fall into the "classic" designation, if they are used accordingly.

References: Robert Ackerson, *Standard Catalog of 4x4s, 1945-1993,* Krause Publications, 1993; Dennis A. Adler, *Corvettes,* Krause Publications, 1996; Quentin Craft, *Classic Old Car Value Guide,* 23rd ed., published by author, 1989; John Chevedden & Ron Kowalke, *Standard Catalog of Oldsmobile, 1897-1997,* Krause Publications, 1997; James M. Flammang, *Standard Catalog of American Cars, 1976–1986,* 2nd ed., Krause Publications, 1989; ——, *Standard Catalog of Imported Cars, 1946–1990,* Krause Publications, 1992; ——, *Volkswagen Beetles, Buses and Beyond,* Krause Publications, 1996; Patrick R. Foster, *American Motors, The Last Independent,* Krause Publications, 1993; *The Metropolitan Story,* Krause Publications, 1996; John Gunnell, *American Work Trucks,* Krause Publications, 1994; --, *Marques of America,* Krause Publications, 1994; —— (ed.), *100 Years of American Cars,* Krause Publications, 1993; --, *Standard Catalog of American Light Duty Trucks, 1896-1986,* 2nd ed., Krause Publications, 1993; --, *Standard Catalog of Chevrolet Trucks, Pickups & Other Light Duty Trucks, 1918-1995,* Krause Publications, 1995; Beverly Kimes and Henry Austin Clark, Jr., *Standard Catalog of American Cars, 1805–1942,* 3rd ed., Krause Publications, 1996; Ron Kowalke, *Old Car Wrecks,* Krause Publications, 1997; --, *Standard Guide to American Cars, 1946-1975,* 3rd ed., Krause Publications, 1997; --, *Standard Guide to Amercian Muscle Cars, 1949-1995,* 2nd ed.,

Krause Publications, 1996; Jim Lenzke and Ken Buttolph, *Standard Guide to Cars & Prices,* 10th ed., Krause Publications, 1997; Albert Mroz, *The Illustrated Encyclopedia of American Trucks & Commercial Vehicles,* Krause Publications, 1996; Robert Murfin (ed.), *Miller's Collectors Cars Price Guide,* Reed International Books (distributed by Antique Collectors' Club), 1996; Gerald Perschbacher, *Wheels in Motion,* Krause Publications, 1996; Edwin J. Sanow, *Chevrolet Police Cars,* Krause Publications, 1997; Donald F. Wood and Wayne Sorensen, *Big City Fire Trucks, 1951-1997,,* Krause Publications, Vol. I, 1996, Vol. II, 1997. Krause Publications' *Standard Catalog* series includes special marque volumes, including *Standard Catalog of Cadillac,1903-1990; Standard Catalog of Chrysler, 1925-1990; Standard Catalog of Pontiac, 1926-1995; Standard Catalog of Ford, 1903-1990; Standard Catalog of Chevrolet, 1912-1990; Standard Catalog of American Motors, 1902-1987; Standard Catalog of Oldsmobile, 1897-1997; Standard Catalog of Buick, 1903-1990.*

Periodicals: *Auto Trader Old Car Book,* 14549 62nd St. N., Clearwater, FL 34620; *Automobile Quarterly,* 15040 Kutztown Rd., P.O. Box 348, Kutztown, PA 19530; *Car Collector & Car Classics,* 1241 Canton St., Roswell, GA 30076; *Cars & Parts,* P.O. Box 482, Sidney, OH 45365; *DuPont Registry,* 2502 N. Rocky Point Dr. #1095, Tampa, FL 33607; *Hemmings Motor News,* P.O. Box 256, Bennington, VT 05201; *Old Cars Price Guide,* 700 E State St., Iola, WI 54990; *Old Cars Weekly, News & Markeplace,* 700 E. State St., Iola, WI 54990.

Collectors' Clubs: Antique Automobile Club of America, 501 West Governor Rd., P.O. Box 417, Hershey, PA 17033; Classic Car Club of America, 1645 Des Plaines River Rd., Suite 7, Des Plaines, IL 60018; Milestone Car Society, P.O. Box 24612, Indianapolis, IN 46224; Veteran Motor Car Club of America, P.O. Box 360788, Strongsville, OH 44136; Willys/Kaiser/AMC Jeep Club, 1511 19th Ave. W., Bradenton, FL 34205.

Advisors: Jim and Nancy Schaut.

Notes: The prices below are for cars in running condition, with a high proportion of original parts and somewhere between 60% and 80% restoration. *Prices can vary by as much as 30% in either direction.* Many older cars, especially if restored, are now worth more than $15,000. Their limited availability makes them difficult to price. Auctions, more than any other source, are the true determinant of value at this level.

Auburn, 1935, Model 653, sedan, 6 cyl. 8,500.00
Bentley, 1953, Park Ward, convertible, 4.6 litre engine 28,000.00
Bricklin, 1975, Model SV-1, gullwing coupe...................8,000.00
Buick
    1908, Model 10, touring, 4 cyl. 15,000.00
    1941, Roadmaster, sedan, 8 cyl.............................12,000.00
Cadillac
    1931, Model 370, cabriolet, V-12 ....60,000.00
    1956, sedan, blue body, cream top 8,400.00
Chandler, 1927, Big Six, sedan, 6 cyl. 4,800.00
Chevrolet
    1931, Model AE, two-door sedan, 6 cyl. 10,000.00
    1933, Eagle, coupe, rumble seat, 6 cyl.....................9,600.00

1965, Corvair, convertible, 6 cyl. 4,000.00
1967, Corvette, convertible 15,000.00
Chrysler
    1932, Imperial, sedan, 6 cyl. 9,000.00
    1956, New Yorker, hemi-engine 9,000.00
    1959, Saratoga, sedan, V-8 ....4,000.00
Columbia, 1925, Six, sedan, 6 cyl. 8,000.00
Cunningham, 1929, Model V9, roadster, 6 cyl. 20,000.00
Daniels, 1920, Submarine, speedster, V-8 ....24,500.00
Dayton, 1913, Tandem, Cycle, 2 cyl. 3,000.00
Delahaye, 1935, Superflux, roadster, 6 cyl. 12,000.00
DeSoto, 1931, Model 31, coupe, rumble seat, 6 cyl. 4,200.00
Dodge
    1921, Model 21, touring, 4 cyl. 5,000.00
    1949, Wayfarer, roadster, 6 cyl. 9,200.00
Dort, 1924, Model 27, touring, 6 cyl. 4,000.00
Dragon, 1906, Model 25, touring, 4 cyl. 5,500.00
Drexel, 1916, Model 7-60, 7 passenger touring, 4 cyl. ...5,000.00
Durant, 1928, Model M, sedan, 4 cyl. 4,800.00
Edsel, 1959, Ranger, V-8 engine 3,200.00
Excalibur SS, 1973, Model SSK, roadster, V-8 ....11,500.00
Falcon, 1922, touring, 4 cyl. 5,000.00
Ferrari, 1956, Tip 375, touring, V-12 ....27,000.00
Ford
    1927, Model T, coupe, green 5,000.00
    1929, Model A, coupe, rumble seat, orig title 7,000.00
    1957, Thunderbird, convertible 19,000.00
    1960, Galaxie, sedan, V-8, hardtop 6,400.00
    1963, Falcon, convertible 4,500.00
    1970, Mustang, Shelby GT, convertible 20,000.00
Fritchle, 1916, touring, 4 cyl. 5,000.00
Gardner, 1929, Model 130, roadster, 8 cyl. 12,000.00
Graham-Paige, 1941, Hollywood, convertible couple, 6 cyl.
    ....10,000.00
Grant, 1921, Model HZ, sedan, 6 cyl. 4,500.00
Hillman, 1967, Huskey, station wagon, 1.7 litre 1,250.00
Hudson, 1935, Terraplane Fordor, sedan, black, brown int.
    ....5,000.00
Jaguar
    1951, Mark VII, sedan, 6 cyl. 6,600.00
    1966, SKE, Sport Roadster, 4.2 litre 22,000.00
Julian, 1922, Model 60, coupe, 6 cyl. 10,000.00
Lambert, 1909, roadster, 6 cyl. 8,000.00
LaSalle
    1939, hearse 14,500.00
    1940, Model 52, club coupe, V-8 ....5,000.00
Lincoln, 1935, Dietrich, convertible coupe, V-12 ....28,000.00
Lotus, 1966, Mark 46 European, coupe, V-8 ....5,000.00
Mercedes-Benz
    1935, Model 170-V, limousine 15,000.00
    1956, Model 190SL, convertible, 4 cyl. 12,000.00

Mercury
    1940, Series C9A, convertible, 8 cyl. 10,000.00
    1955, Monterey, sedan 4,500.00
Nash, 1954, Ambassador, two-door hardtop, 8 cyl. 3,800.00
Oldsmobile, 1942, Model 66, station wagon, 6 cyl. 9,000.00
Opel, 1938, Admiral, drophead coupe, 3.6 litre 2,500.00
Packard
    1928, Model 426, roadster, 6 cyl. 18,000.00
    1940, Darrin, convertible Victoria, 8 cyl. 50,000.00
Pittsburgh, 1911, touring, 7 passenger, 6 cyl. 6,500.00
Plymouth
    1942, Model P145, sedan, 6 cyl. 2,500.00
    1957, Fury, convertible, V-8 engine 7,500.00
Pontiac
    1955, Star Chief, custom Safari 7,500.00
    1966, GTO, convertible, V-8 ....7,200.00
Porsche, 1969, Model 911 T, coupe, 4 cyl. 7,800.00
Renault, 1955, Fregate, convertible, 2 litre 2,000.00
Rolls Royce
    1952, Silver Dawn, touring limousine, 6 cyl. 18,000.00
    1971, Corniche Coupe 22,000.00
Studebaker
    1949, Champion, convertible, 6 cyl. 3,800.00
    1963, Avanti, coupe, V-8 ....7,500.00
Stutz
    1914, Bearcat, roadster, 6 cyl. 45,000.00
    1927, Black Hawk, speedster, 8 cyl. 8,000.00
Miscellaneous
Fire Engine
    Diamond T, 1947, pumper 2,500.00
    Dodge, 1945, pumper, American LaFrance, 6 cyl. 2,500.00
    Ford, 1940, pumper, flat V-8 ....6,500.00
    Mack, 1936, pumper, Hale pump 4,000.00
Motorcycle
    BSA, 1943, Military 3,800.00
    Harley-Davidson, 1952, Model K 1,800.00
    Indian
        1930, Scout, model 101 ....5,500.00
        1948, Chief 7,500.00
    Triumph, 1921, Baby 1,500.00
Truck
    Chevrolet
        1932, huckster 6,000.00
        1937, sedan delivery, 6 cyl. 5,500.00
        1957, pickup, 1/2 ton, short bed, V-6 ....3,500.00
    Dodge, 1937, pickup, 3/4 ton, slant 6 ....2,500.00
    Ford
        1941, F-1, stake, V-8 ....2,500.00
        1956, F-100, custom cab, V-8 ....3,200.00
    Plymouth, 1938, pickup, high side, slant 6 ....2,500.00
    Stewart, pickup, 1 ton, 4 cyl. 3,200.00
    VW, pickup, short bed, 1600 cc 1,500.00
    Willys, 1928, Model 70, 6 cyl. 2,600.00

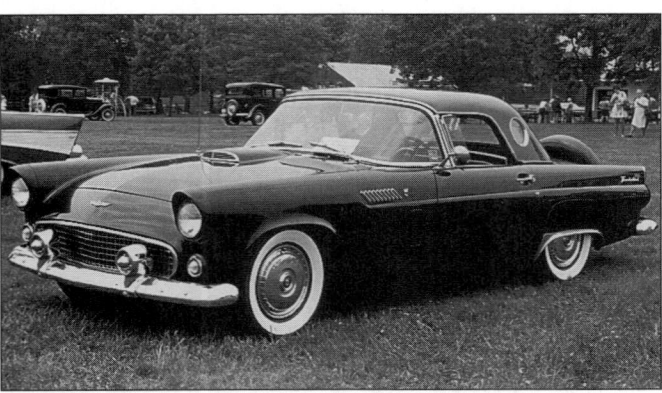

Ford, 1956 Thunderbird, removable hard top, $8,500.

AUTOMOBILIA

History: The number of items related to the automobile is endless. Collectors seem to fit into three groups—those collecting parts to restore a car, those collecting information about a company or certain model for research purposes, and those trying to use automobile items for decorative purposes. Most material changes hands at the hundreds of swap meets and auto shows around the country.

References: Mark Anderton and Sherry Mullen, *Gas Station Collectibles*, Wallace-Homestead/Krause, 1994; Mark Allen Baker, *Auto Racing Memorabilia and Price Guide*, Krause Publications, 1996; David K. Bausch, *The*

Official Price Guide to Automobilia, House of Collectibles, 1996; Scott Benjamin and Wayne Henderson, *Gas Pump Globes,* Motorbooks International, 1993; Mike Bruner, *Gasoline Treasures,* Schiffer Publishing, 1996; Bob and Chuck Crisler, *License Plates of the United States,* Interstate Directory Publishing Co. (420 Jericho Tpk., Jericho, NY 11753), 1997; Leila Dunbar, *Motorcycle Collectibles,* Schiffer Publishing, 1996; John A. Gunnell, *Car Memorabilia Price Guide,* Krause Publications, 1995; James K. Fox, *License Plates of the United States, A Pictorial History 1903 to the Present,* Interstate Directory Publishing Co., 1996; Todd Helms, *Conoco Collector's Bible,* Schiffer Publishing, 1995; Todd Helms and Chip Flohe, *A Collection of Vintage Gas Station Photographs,* Schiffer Publishing, 1997; Ron Kowalke and Ken Buttolph, *Car Memorabilia Price Guide,* 2nd ed., Krause Publications, 1997; Rick Pease, *A Tour With Texaco,* Schiffer Publishing, 1997; --, *Service Station Collectibles,* Schiffer Publishing, 1996; Jim and Nancy Schaut, *American Automobilia,* Wallace-Homestead, 1994; Don Stewart, *Antique Classic Marque Car Keys,* 2nd ed., Key Collectors International, 1993.

Periodicals: *Hemmings Motor News,* P.O. Box 256, Bennington, VT 05201; *Mobilia,* P.O. Box 575, Middlebury, VT 05753; *Petroleum Collectibles Monthly,* 411 Forest St., LaGrange, OH 44050; PL8S, P.O. Box 222, East Texas, PA 18046; *WOCCO,* 36100 Chardon Rd., Willoughby, OH 44094.

Collectors' Clubs: Automobile Objects D'Art Club, 252 N. 7th St., Allentown, PA 18102; Classic Gauge & Oiler Hounds, Rte. 1, Box 9, Farview, SD 57027; Hubcap Collectors Club, P.O. Box 54, Buckley, MI 49620; International Petroliana Collectors Assoc., P.O. Box 937, Powell, OH 43065; Spark Plug Collectors of America, 14018 NE. 85th St., Elk River, MN 55330.

Advisors: Jim and Nancy Schaut.

Badge, 3" d, Sinclair Grease, attendant's type, celluloid ... 150.00
Blotter, Kelly Tires, c1910 .... 30.00
Box, tin, Mobil Oil, designed to hold lubrication charts 20.00
Calendar, Chevrolet, 1920, 30-1/2" h, 16" w, green, white lettering 145.00
Can, 1 qt, tin litho, motor oil
    Banner, Clarkson & Ford Co., red, white, and blue 350.00
    Ronson, Wayne Oil Co., Philadelphia, racing streamlined train, airplane, and car, full, 5-1/2" h, 4" d 1,050.00
    Wm. Tell, Canfield Oil Co, red, white, and black 400.00
Carburetor, Buick, 1924-25 .... 25.00
Clock
    Atlas Tires & Batteries, wall, 1950s 175.00
    Firestone, 15-1/4" h, 15-1/4" w, sq, glass front, wood frame 150.00
    Studebaker, 15-1/4" h, gold metal rim, red and blue emblem, electric 250.00
Compression Tester, Hasting's adv on dial 30.00
Decanter, spark plug, Motorcraft 25.00
Display
    Champion Spark Plugs, 12" h, 19" w, 5-1/2" d, tin, yellow, black lettering 200.00
    Exide Battery, 40" h, tin and metal, black and orange lettering 185.00
    Gilmer Fan Belts, 22-1/4" h, 16-1/2" w, 24" d, tin, painted, orange, blue trim 135.00

Display Cabinet
    Auto Lite Spark Plug, 18-1/2" h, 13-1/8" w, metal, painted, green, glass front 45.00
    Firestone Spark Plugs, 15-1/4" h, 20-1/8" w, tin, painted, 1940-50 .... 225.00
Emblem, porcelain, Toledo Motor Club AAA 30.00
First Aid Kit, Mobil Flying Fed Horse 60.00
Gas Cap, Ford, metal 8.00
Gas Globe, Spartan Ethyl, helmet logo, metal rim, mounted on wood base, electrified, 19" x 17-1/2" x 7" 200.00
Hubcap
    Chevrolet, 1957 .... 15.00
    Edsel, spinner type 35.00
    License Plate Attachment, Automobile Club of Pittsburgh, 3-1/2" h, 3-1/2" d, porcelain, white, black lettering, maroon, and green emblem 75.00
Key Fob, Esso Tiger, dark luster metal, raised tiger head, logo, slogan "Put A Tiger In Your Tank," reverse with engraved serial number, Houston, c1960 .... 10.00
Map Rack, wall, Cities Service, green 55.00
Plate, 6" d, Mobil Flying Red Horse emblem 35.00
Radiator Cap, brass, figural, woman's head, wings 50.00
Radio, Champion Spark Plug, 14" h, spark plug shape, gray and white 55.00
Sign
    Aetna Automobile Insurance Co., 12" h, 24" w, tin, painted, black lettering 75.00
    Cooper Tires, 12" h, 32-1/2" w, tin, painted, emb, orange and blue ground, cream and blue lettering 200.00
    Delco Battery, 22" h, 30" w, tin, painted, yellow and orange, blue lettering 160.00
    Essolube Motor Oil, porcelain, 2-1/4" h, 6-1/2" l 160.00
    Hudson Rambler, 30" h, 42" w, porcelain, dark blue, white logo 475.00
    National Batteries, 12" h, 20" w, tin, orange, dark blue raised letters 150.00
    Seiberling Tires, 16" h, 30" w, porcelain, double sided, dark blue, orange letters 200.00
    Veedol Brand Motor Oil, figural, tin litho, blond woman shaker 525.00

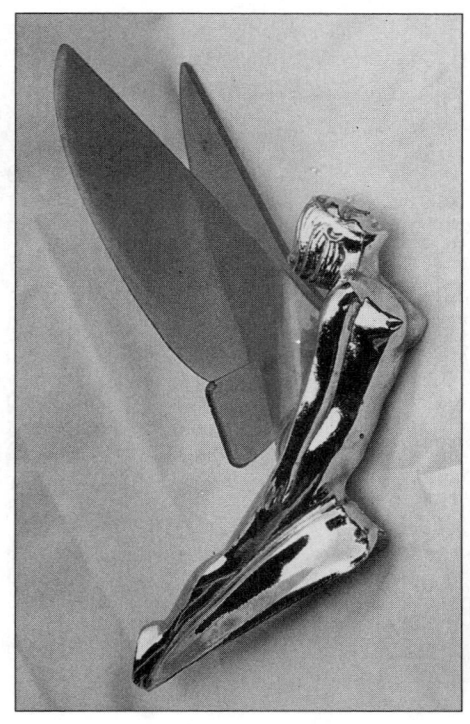

Hood Ornament, chrome, yellow plastic wings, Art Deco woman, mkd #511 on base, 7-1/2" x 4-1/4" x 9", $50.

Spark Plug, Rentz Visable 55.00
Thermometer
    Buick Motor Cars, 27" h, porcelain, blue, emblem, c1915
    ....275.00
Gold Medal Motor Oils, 9-1/8" d, metal, painted 180.00
Tire Pump, brass, Ford script on base 55.00
Visor, Ford, 1932, full length...125.00
Watch Fob, Shell Oil, Golden Brand Motor Oil, cloisonné enam-
    eled metal, 1-3/8" d..160.00
Weathervane, 27" x 32", Mobil service station, two sided, porce-
    lain, figural red flying Pegasus, early replacement base
    ....1,500.00

BACCARAT GLASS

History: The Sainte-Anne glassworks at Baccarat in Voges, France, was founded in 1764 and produced utilitarian soda glass. In 1816, Aime-Gabriel d'Artiques purchased the glassworks, and a Royal Warrant was issued in 1817 for the opening of Verrerie de Vonâoche éa Baccarat. The firm concentrated on lead-crystal glass products. In 1824, a limited company was created.

From 1823 to 1857, Baccarat and Saint-Louis glassworks had a commercial agreement and used the same outlets. No merger occurred. Baccarat began the production of paperweights in 1846. In the late 19th century, the firm achieved an international reputation for cut-glass table services, chandeliers, display vases, centerpieces, and sculptures. Products eventually included all forms of glassware. The firm still is active today.

Reference: Jean-Louis Curtis, *Baccarat*, Harry N. Abrams, 1992; Paul Jokelson and Dena Tarshis, *Baccarat Paperweights and Related Glass*, Paperweight Press, 1990 (distributed by Charles E. Tuttle Co.).

Additional Listings: Paperweights.

Bowl, 14" d, 3-1/2" h, wide flattened rim, narrow knopped foot,
    etched "Baccarat, France" 500.00
Box, cov, 2-3/4" d, 2-1/4" h, white airplane design on sides,
    etched mark...125.00
Candelabra, pr, crystal, 32" h, four light, diamond cut baluster
    standard, four scrolling candle arms terminating I urn form
    sockets, etched glass globes hung with prisms 2,000.00
Chandelier, 42" h, 29" w, 12 scrolling candle arms, foliate crown
    surmounting figures, prisms 12,365.00
Cigar Lighter, Rose Tiente, SP top 150.00
Cologne Bottle, 7" h, crystal, frosted rosette ground, gold floral
    swags and bows, cut faceted stopper, pr.....................335.00
Decanter, 9-3/4" h, Rose Tiente, orig stopper 125.00
Epergne, 10-3/4" h, 4 cranberry overlay cut to clear vases, gilt
    metal holder..550.00
Finger Bowl, 4-3/4" d, 6-3/4" d underplate, ruby ground, gold me-
    dallions and flowers dec...350.00
Jar, cov, 7" d, cameo cut, gilt metal mounts, imp "Baccarat"
    ....350.00
Pitcher, 9-1/4" h, Rose Tiente, Helical Twist pattern...........295.00
Paperweight, Zodiac, sulphide, Libra, c1955 ....165.00
Rose Bowl, 5-1/2" h, 2-1/4" d opening, Cuir, round seal mark
    ....400.00
Toothpick Holder, 2-1/2" h, Rose Tiente 110.00
Vase, 6-1/8" h, cobalt blue, white lace dec 250.00

BANKS, MECHANICAL

History: Banks which display some form of action while accepting a coin are considered mechanical banks. Mechanical banks date back to ancient Greece and Rome, but the majority of collectors are interested in those made between 1867 and 1928 in Germany, England, and the United States. Recently, there has been an upsurge of interest in later types, some of which date into the 1970s.

Initial research suggested that approximately 250 to 300 different or variant designs of banks were made in the early period. Today that number has been revised to 2,000-3,000 types and varieties. The field remains ripe for discovery and research.

More than 80% of all cast-iron mechanical banks produced between 1869 and 1928 were made by J. E. Stevens Co., Cromwell, Connecticut. Tin banks are usually of German origin.

References: Collectors Encyclopedia of Toys and Banks, L-W Book Sales, 1986, 1993 value update; Al Davidson, Penny Lane, A History of Antique Mechanical Toy Banks, Long's Americana, 1987; Don Duer, A Penny Saved: Still and Mechanical Banks, Schiffer Publishing, 1993; Bill Norman, The Bank Book: The Encyclopedia of Mechanical Bank Collecting, Collectors' Showcase, 1984.

Collectors' Club: Mechanical Bank Collectors of America, P.O. Box 128, Allegan, MI 49010.

Notes: While rarity is a factor in value, appeal of design, action, quality of manufacture, country of origin, and history of collector interest also are important. Radical price fluctuations may occur when there is an imbalance in these factors. Rare banks may sell for a few hundred dollars, while one of more common design with greater appeal will sell in the thousands.

The values in the list below accurately represent the selling prices of banks in the specialized collectors' market. Some banks are hard to find, and establishing a price outside auction is difficult.

The prices listed are for original old mechanical banks with minor repairs, in sound operating condition, and with a majority of the original paint intact.

Advisor: James S. Maxwell, Jr.

Note: Prices quoted are for 100% original examples, no repairs, no repaint, and have excellent original paint; * indicates casual reproductions; † denotes examples where casual reproductions and serious fakes exist.

REPRODUCTION ALERT

Reproductions, fakes, and forgeries exist for many banks. Forgeries of some mechanical banks were made as early as 1937, so age alone is not a guarantee of authenticity. In the following price listing, two asterisks indicate banks for which serious forgeries exist, and one asterisk indicates banks for which casual reproductions have been made.

†Acrobat 1,500.00
†Afghanistan 600.00
African Bank, black bust, back emb "African Bank" 750.00
American Bank, sewing machine 500.00
*Artillery 1,800.00
Atlas, iron, steel, wood, paper..........................750.00
Automatic Chocolate Vending, tin 650.00
Automatic Coin Savings, predicts future, tin 250.00
Automatic Fortune Bank, tin 4,500.00
Automatic Savings Bank, tin, soldier 300.00
Automatic Savings Bank, tin, sailor 200.00
Automatic Surprise Money Box, wood 6,500.00
†Baby Elephant X-O'clock, lead and wood.............2,000.00
*Bad Accident 3,700.00
Bambovila, black bust, back emb "Bambula".........3,000.00
Bank Teller, man behind 3-sided fancy grillwork......5,500.00
Bank of Education and Economy, must have orig paper reel
....2,800.00
Barking Dog, wood 500.00
Bear, tin 375.00
†Bear and Tree Stump 3,500.00
†Bears, slot in chest 400.00
†Bill E. Grin 400.00
†Billy Goat Bank 350.00
Bird In Cage, tin..250.00
†Bird on Roof 1,500.00
†Bismark Bank..15,000.00
Bonzo, tin..350.00
Book-Keepers Magic Bank, tin........................22,000.00
Bow-ery Bank, iron, paper, wood 2,500.00
Bowing Man in Empola 3,200.00
†Bowling Alley 4,500.00
†Boy Robbing Birds Nest 2,200.00
*Boy Scout Camp 2,500.00
†Boy and bull dog 8,500.00
†Boy on trapeze 6,000
†Boys stealing watermelons 1,500.00
Bread Winners 2,700.00
British Clown, tin 12,000.00
†Bucking Mule 3,500.00
*Bull Dog, place coin on nose 3,700.00
†Bull and Bear 75,000.00
Bull Dog Savings, clockwork 1,000.00
†Bull Dog, standing 1,500.00
Bureau, wood, Serrill patent 4,500.00
Bureau, Lewando's, wood 18,000.00
Bureau, wood, John R. Jennings Patent 5,500.00
Burnett Postman, tin man with tray 3,500.00
†Butting Buffalo 850.00
†Butting Goat...2,700.00
†Butting Ram...375.00
*Cabin, black man flips 1,400.00
Caller Vending, tine 2,500.00
†Calamity...4,500.00
†Called Out...2,800.00
Calumet, tin and cardboard, with Calumet kid.........100.00
Calumet, tin and cardboard, with sailor 12,000.00
Calumet, tin and Cardboard, with soldier.............15,000.00
†Camera 1,100.00
*Cat and Mouse...1,200.00
†Cat and Mouse, giant cat standing on top 30,000.00
Chandlers 2,000.00
Chandlers with clock 350.00
*Chief Big Moon..1,800.00
Child's Bank, wood 850.00
Monkey, pot metal, nods head 750.00
Monkey, chimpanzee in ornate circular blgd, iron 1,050.00
Chinaman in Boat, lead 3,500.00
Chinaman with queue, tin...............................400.00
Chocolate Menier, tin....................................1,500.00
†Chrysler Pig 400.00

Cigarette Vending, tin.....................................500.00
Cigarette Vending, lead...................................2,000.00
Circus, clown on card in circular ring...................2,000.00
†Circus, ticket collector 350.00
Clever Dick, tin 200.00
Clown Bust, iron 5,050.00
Clown, Chein, tin...65.00
†Clown on Bar, tin and iron 2,800.00
*Clown on Globe...5,500.00
Clown and Dog, tin 250.00
Clown with arched top, tin 250.00
Clown with black face, tin.................................2,000.00
Clown with white face, tin 125.00
Clown with white face, round, tin 3,700.00
Cockatoo Pelican, tin......................................200.00
Coin Registering, many variants...................25-1,000.00
Columbian Magic Savings, iron...........................200.00
Columbian magic Savings, wood and Paper 15,000.00
Confectionery 2,200.00
Coolie Bust, lead 400.00
Cowboy with tray, tin......................................350.00
†Creedmoor..1,275.00
Crescent Cash Register 3,700.00
Cross Legged Minstrel, tin 350.00
Crowing Rooster, circular base, tin 5,500.00
Cupid at Piano, pot metal, musical........................750.00
†Cupola 1,050.00
Dapper Dan, tin 2,500.00
*Darktown Battery...3,500.00
Darky Bust, tin, tiny size 200.00
†Darky Fisherman, lead....................................8,500.00
†Darky Watermelon, man kicks football at watermelon...7,500.00
†Dentist..3,700.00
Dinah, iron 400.00
Dinah, aluminum 250.00
Ding Dong Bell, tin, windup................................3,500.00
Dog on turntable 950.00
†Dog with tray...650.00
Domed vending, tin 4,000.00
Driver's Service Vending, tin 2,800.00

Clown on Bar, C. G. Bush & Co., Norman 1920, $2,800.

Droste Chocolate...1,200.00
*Eagle and Eaglettes 1,200.00
Electric Safe, steel...1,800.00
*Elephant and Three Clowns..1,850.00
*Elephant, locked howdah...450.00
Elephant, made in Canada..6,500.00
Elephant, man pops out, wood, cloth, iron.......................550.00
†Elephant, no stars..3,700.00
*Elephant, pull tail...850.00
Elephant, three stars...1,200.00
*Elephant, trunk swings, large..350.00
*Elephant, trunk swings, small...250.00
Elephant, trunk swings, raised coin slot........................1,500.00
†Elephant with tusks, on wheels.......................................500.00
Empire Cinema, tin..700.00
English Bulldog, tin..450.00
Feed the Goose, pot metal...800.00
5 cents Adding 250.00
Flip the Frog, tin...375.00
Football, English football 1,800.00
Fortune Savings, tin, horse race.....................................1,050.00
Fortune Teller, Savings, safe...2,200.00
†Fowler 2,200.00
†Freedman's Bank, wood, lead, brass, tin, paper, etc. 75,000.00
Frog on arched track, tin...1,200.00
Frog on rock 1,400.00
*Frog on round base...950.00
†Frogs, two frogs...1,200.00
Fun Producing Savings, tin...1,800.00
*Gem, dog with blgd..2,800.00
German Sportsman, lead and iron 1,500.00
German Vending, tin..1,200.00
†Germania Exchange, iron, lead, tin...............................2,000.00
†Giant in Tower...1,200.00
†Giant, standing by rock 2,700.00
Girl Feeding Geese, tin, paper, lead.............................22,000.00
†Girl Skipping Rope 16,000.00
†Girl in Victorian chair 2,000.00
Give Me A Penny, wood 8,000.00
Grenadier..1,875.00
Guessing, man's figure, lead, steel, iron 8,800.00

Dog on Turntable, Judd Mfg. Co, Norman 2170, $950.

Guessing, woman's figure, iron 2,200.00
Guessing, woman's figure, lead 1,400.00
Gwenda Money Box, tin 3,500.00
Hall's Excelsior, iron, wood..750.00
Hall's Liliput, no tray 400.00
Hall's Liliput, with tray..250.00
†Harlequin 7,500.00
Harold Lloyd, tin 450.00
Hartwig and Vogel, vending, tin 1,200.00
Hen and Chick...1,650.00
Highwayman, tin..650.00
Hillman Coin Target...1,500.00
*Hindu, bust..750.00
†Hold the Fort, 2 varieties...........................each 1,050.00
Home, tin building 750.00
*Home, iron...400.00
Hoop-La...5,500.00
*Horse Race, 2 varieties.............................2,000.00 each
†Humpty Dumpty, bust of clown with name on back, iron
     ....2,800.00
Humpty Dumpty, aluminum, English 350.00
Huntley and Palmas, tin, vending...................................1,400.00
*I Always Did 'spise a Mule, black man on bench 1,050.00
*I Always Did 'spise a Mule, black man on mule..............1,800.00
Ideal Bureau, tin 3,700.00
*Indian and Bear...1,050.00
†Indian Chief, black man bust with Indian feathered headdress,
     aluminum 750.00
Indiana Paddlewheel Boat..1,050.00
†Initiating Bank, first degree..1,000.00
Initiating Bank, second degree 1,200.00
*Jolly Nigger, American..650.00
*Jolly Nigger, English 350.00
Jolly Nigger, lettering in Greek..375.00
Jolly Nigger, lettering in Arabic.....................................1,500.00
*Jolly Nigger, raises hat, lead..1,200.00
*Jolly Nigger, raises hat, iron...2,200.00
*Jolly Nigger, stationary ears..250.00
*Jolly Nigger, stationary eyes..450.00
*Jolly Nigger, with fez, aluminum 750.00
Japanese Ball Tosser, tin, wood, paper 5,500.00
John R. Jennings Trick Drawer Money Box, wood........15,000.00
Joe Socko Novelty Bank, tin..250.00
John Bull's Money Box 2,000.00
Jolly Joe Clown, tin..3,200.00
Jolly Sambo Bank...2,800.00
*Jonah and The Whale Bank, large rectangular base.....2,000.00
†Jonah and The Whale Bank, stands on 2 ornate legs with rect-
     angular coin box at center.......................................8,500.00
†Jumbo, elephant on wheels...500.00
Kick Inn Bank, wood...1,800.00
Kiltie...650.00
Lawrence Steinberg's Bureau Bank, wood 12,000.00
†Leap Frog...2,200.00
Lehmann Berlin Tower, tin..350.00
Lehmann,. London Tower, tin...400.00
†Light of Asia..450.00
†Lighthouse Bank..400.00
Lion, tin..575.00
Lion Hunter..1,650.00
†Lion and Two Monkeys...1,850.00
*Little High Hat...1,500.00
Little Jocko, tin...650.00
*Little Joe Bank..950.00
Little Moe Bank...350.00
Lucky wheel Money Box, tin..3,500.00
*Magic Bank, iron house 650.00
Magic Bank, tin...200.00
Magic, safe, tin...450.00
†Magician...1,800.00
†Mama Katzenjammer..2,650.00

†Mammy and Child 2,000.00
*Mason...2,800.00
Memorial Money Box 400.00
*Merry-Go-Round, mechanical, coin activates...............2,800.00
†Merry-Go-Round, semi-mechanical, spin by hand 575.00
Mickey Mouse, tin...2,350.00
Mikado Bank...7,500.00
†Milking Cow 3,600.00
Minstrel, tin...2,8800.00
Model Railroad Drink Dispenser, tin.......................15,000.00
Model Savings Bank, tin, cash register 3,700.00
*Monkey and Coconut...1,600.00
Monkey and Parrot, tin.......................................1,200.00
†Monkey Bank 1,450.00
Monkey Face, tin with carched top 3,200.00
†Monkey, slot in stomach 350.00
Monkey, tin, tips hat...450.00
Monkey with Tray, tin 875.00
Mosque...450.00
Motor Bank, coin activates trolley...........................2,000.00
Mule Entering Barn 1,875.00
Music Bank, tin...375.00
Musical Church, wood 575.00
Musical Savings Bank, Regina 2,800.00
Musical Savings, tin...325.00
Musical Savings, velvet covered easel 450.00
Musical Savings, velvet covered frame 500.00
Musical Savings, wood house 950.00
National Bank 950.00
National, Your Savings, cash register 2,800.00
Nestle's Automatic Chocolate, cardboard, vending 2,300.00
*New Bank, lever at center 400.00
*New Bank, lever at left 300.00
†New Creedmoor Bank 3,200.00
Nodding Clown, pewter and Brass 675.00
Nodding Dog, painted tin 375.00
†North Pole Bank...1,875.00
*Novelty Bank 1,450.00
Octagonal Fort Bank...1,600.00
Old Mother Hubbard, tin..750.00
*Organ Bank, boy and girl 875.00
*Organ Bank, cat and dog 675.00
*Organ Bank, medium, only monkey figure..................400.00
*Organ Bank, tiny, only monkey figure 350.00
Organ Grinder and Dancing Bear 1,275.00
Owl, slot in book 275.00
Owl, slot in head 325.00
*Owl, turns head 400.00
*Paddy and the Pig...1,850.00
Panorama Bank 1,675.00
Paseall Chocolate Cigarettes, vending, tin 1,800.00
Patronize the Blind Man..1,200.00
Pay Phone Bank, iron 2,800.00
Pay Phone Bank, tin...350.00
†Peg-Leg Beggar 675.00
*Pelican, Arab head pops out 575.00
*Pelican, Mammy head pops out 525.00
*Pelican, man thumbs nose 500.00
*Pelican, rabbit pops out 375.00
†Perfection Registering, girl and dog at blackboard 1,850.00
Piano, musical 450.00
*Picture Gallery...2,650.00
Pig in High Chair..450.00
Pinball Vending, tin...1,600.00
Pistol Bank, iron..575.00
Pistol Bank, iron, Uncle Sam figure pops out 2,200.00
Pistol Bank, litho, tin..3,700.00
Pistol Bank, sheet steel......................................1,200.00
Policeman, tin...500.00
Popeye Knockout, tin...1,400.00
Post Office Savings, steel....................................1,700.00

†Preacher in the Pulpit 9,500.00
†Presto, iron building..950.00
Presto, mouse on roof, wood and paper 950.00
*Presto, penny changes optically to quarter 1,275.00
*Professor Pug Frog 4,200.00
Pump and Bucket..4,700.00
*Punch and Judy, iron 2,450.00
Punch and Judy, iron front, tin back.........................750.00
Punch and Judy, litho tin, circa 1910 ....475.00
Punch and Judy, litho tin, circa 1930 ....275.00
†Queen Victoria. bust, brass.................................2,800.00
†Queen Victoria, bust, iron...................................4,200.00
Rabbit in Cabbage 350.00
†Rabbit Standing, large...675.00
†Rabbit Standing, small...375.00
Reclining Chinaman with cards 2,100.00
Record Money Box, tin scales...............................5,500.00
†Red Riding Hood, iron..3,300.00
Red Riding Hood, tin, vending 1,500.00
†Rival Bank..2,650.00
Robot Bank, aluminum 575.00
Robot Bank, iron...1,050.00
Roller-Skating Bank..2,850.00
Rooster 1,600.00
Royal Trick Elephant, tin......................................5,500.00
Safe Deposit Bank, tin, elephant 1,650.00
Safety Locomotive, semi.......................................1,850.00
Sailor Face, tin, pointed top...................................3,200.00
Sailor Money Box, wood 450.00
Saluting Sailor, tin...850.00
Sam Segal's Aim to Save, brass and wood...................1,300.00
Sam Segal's Aim to Save, iron...............................1,800.00
*Santa Claus..1,650.00
Savo, circular, tin 650.00
Savo, rectangular, tin..575.00
†Schley Bottling Up Cevera 975.00
Schokolade Automat, tin, vending...........................1,200.00
School Teacher, tin and wood, American 1,200.00
School Teacher, tin, German...................................675.00
Scotchman, tin..1,875.00
Seek Him Frisk..3,200.00
Sentry Bank, tin...375.00
Sentry Bugler, tin 275.00
†Shoot That Hat Bank...2,700.00
†Shoot the Chute Bank..2,300.00
Signal Cabin, tin 1,875.00
†Smith X-ray Bank...1,275.00
Snake and Frog in Pond, tin 12,000.00
*Snap-It Bank...1,200.00
Snow White, tin and lead 875.00
*Speaking Dog 1,875.00
Spring Jawed Alligator, pot metal 250.00
Spring Jawed Bonzo, pot metal 250.00
Spring Jawed Bulldog, pot metal 225.00
Spring Jawed Cat, pot metal 275.00
Spring Jawed Chinaman, pot metal 1,400.00
Spring Jawed Donkey, pot metal 225.00
Spring Jawed Felix the Cat, pot metal.......................3,700.00
Spring Jawed Mickey Mouse, pot metal 12,500.00
Spring Jawed Monkey, pot metal 225.00
Spring Jawed Parrot, pot metal 250.00
Spring Jawed Penguin, pot metal 275.00
Springing Cat...4,200.00
†Squirrel and Tree Stump.......................................675.00
Starkies Aeroplane, aluminum, cardboard 12,000.00
Starkies Aeroplane, aluminum, steel 16,000.00
Stollwerk Bros., vending, tin 950.00
Stollwerk Bros., 2 penny, vending, tin 1,200.00
Stollwerk Bros., Progressive Sampler, tin....................275.00
Stollwerk Bros., Victoria, spar-automat, tin..................850.00
Stollwerk Bros., large vending, tin...........................1,400.00

*Stump Speaker Bank 2,800.00
Sweet Thrift, tin, vending 875.00
Symphonium Musical Savings, wood 2,400.00
†Tabby..375.00
*Tammany Bank 375.00
Tank and Cannon, aluminum.......................................2,000.00
Tank and Cannon, iron 2,800.00
†Target Bank 875.00
†Target In Vestibule..950.00
*Teddy and The Bear 1,650.00
Ten Cent Adding Bank 3,800.00
Thrifty Animal Bank, tin 850.00
Thrift Scotchman, wood, paper 4,500.00
Thrifty Tom's Jigger, tin 2,500.00
Tid-Bits Money Box, tin 350.00
Tiger, tin 450.00
Time Is Money 1,050.00
Time Lock Savings 575.00
Time Registering Bank 750.00
*Toad on Stump 750.00
Toilet Bank, tin 450.00
Tommy Bank 950.00
Treasure Chest Music Bank 250.00
*Trick Dog, 6 part base 2,300.00
*Trick Dog, solid base 850.00
*Trick Pony Bank 1,200.00
Trick Savings, wood, end drawer 950.00
Trick Savings, wood, side drawer 950.00
Tropical Chocolate Vending, tin 2,700.00
Try your Weight, tin, semi 950.00
Try Your Weight, tin, mechanical...............................2,600.00
†Turtle Bank..3,200.00
Twentieth Century Savings Bank.................................500.00
Two Ducks Bank, lead..9,000.00
U.S. Bank, Building..850.00
†U.S. and Spain...1,200.00
†Uncle Remus Bank 1,275.00
†Uncle Sam Bank, standing figure with satchel.............1,875.00
†Uncle Sam, bust 400.00
†Uncle Tom, no lapels, with star 425.00
†Uncle Tom, lapels, with star 400.00
†Uncle Tom, no star 350.00
United States Bank, safe...550.00
Viennese soldier 1,050.00
Volunteer bank..950.00
Watch Bank, blank face, tin 200.00
Watch Bank, dime disappears, tin 275.00
Watch Bank, stamped face, tin 100.00
Watchdog Safe 575.00
Weeden's Plantation, tin, wood 850.00
Weight Lifter, tin...650.00
Whale Bank, pot metal..850.00
*William Tell, iron 2,175.00
William Tell, crossbow, Australian, sheet steel, aluminum ...3,200.00
Wimbledon Bank 1,500.00
Winner Savings Bank, tin...1,050.00
Wireless Bank, tin, wood, iron 875.00
Woodpecker Bank, tin 875.00
World's Banker, tin...750.00
*World's Fair Bank 1,200.00
Zentral Sparkasse, steel..1,150.00
Zig Zag Bank, iron, tin, papier-mâché..........................4,200.00
*Zoo 1,500.00

BANKS, STILL

History: Banks with no mechanical action are known as still banks. The first still banks were made of wood or pottery or from gourds. Redware and stoneware banks,

made by America's early potters, are prized possessions of today's collectors.

Still banks reached a golden age with the arrival of the cast-iron bank. Leading manufacturing companies include Arcade Mfg. Co., J. Chein & Co., Hubley, J. & E. Stevens, and A. C. Williams. The banks often were ornately painted to enhance their appeal. During the cast-iron era, banks and other businesses used the still bank as a form of advertising.

The tin lithograph bank, again frequently a tool for advertising, reach its zenith during the years 1930 to 1955. The tin bank was an important premium, whether a Pabst Blue Ribbon beer can bank or a Gerber's Orange Juice bank. Most tin advertising banks resembled the packaging of the product.

Almost every substance has been used to make a still bank—die-cast white metal, aluminum, brass, plastic, glass, etc. Many of the early glass candy containers also converted to a bank after the candy was eaten. Thousands of varieties of still banks were made, and hundreds of new varieties appear on the market each year.

References: Savi Arbola and Marco Onesti, *Piggy Banks*, Chronicle Books, 1992; *Collector's Encyclopedia of Toys and Banks*, L-W Book Sales, 1986, 1993 value update; Don Duer, *Penny Banks Around the World*, Schiffer Publishing, 1997; Earnest Ida and Jane Pitman, *Dictionary of Still Banks*, Long's Americana, 1980; Andy and Susan Moore, *Penny Bank Book, Collecting Still Banks*, Schiffer Publishing, 1984, 1997 value update; Tom and Loretta Stoddard, *Ceramic Coin Banks*, Collector Books, 1997.

Periodical: *Glass Bank Collector*, P.O. Box 155, Poland, NY 13431.

Collectors' Club: Still Bank Collectors Club of America, 4175 Millersville Rd., Indianapolis, IN 46205.

Museum: Margaret Woodbury Strong Museum, Rochester, NY.

Aluminum

Lindy, 6-1/2" h, aluminum and painted gold metal, Grannis & Tolton, US, bust type, wearing hat and goggles, c1928...125.00

Brass

Beehive, 4" h, 4-1/2" d, EOS, well detailed, base mkd "A.B. Dalames Bank" 385.00

Cast Iron

Auto, 3-1/2" x 6-3/4" l, A.C. Williams, painted green, slot on door, gold painted spoked wheels, three passengers 1,430.00
Bear with Honey Pot, 6-1/2" h, Hubley, painted brown, white and yellow coin pot...605.00
Boston Bull Terrier, 5-1/4" x 5-3/4", Vindex, painted brown and white 415.00
Buffalo, 5-1/4" x 8", detailed fur, emb "Amherst Stoves" 310.00
Building
    2-1/2" h, 2" w, John Brown's Fort, slotted sides..........1,100.00
    2-3/4" to 4-3/4" h, Kyser & Rex, Town Hall and Log Cabin, chimney on left side, "Town Hall Bank" painted yellow, c1882 ....260.00

3-1/4" h, Kenton, State, japanned, gold and bronze highlights
....180.00
3-3/4" h, Grey Iron Ceiling Co, bungalow, porch, painted
....470.00
Cab, Arcade
7-3/4" l, Yellow Cab, painted orange and black, stenciling on
doors, seated driver, rubber tires, painted metal wheels,
coin slot in roof 935.00
8" l, Yellow Cab, painted orange and black, iron wheels, rubber tires, stenciled "Yellow Cab Main 4321" on door, spare
tire missing 3,575.00
8-1/4" l, Green Cab, painted green, white, and black, coin slot
in front hood, head lamps, seated figure, disc wheels, new
license plate, spare tire attached to rear..............1,870.00
Cat with Ball, 2-1/2" x 5-11/16", A.C. Williams, painted gray, gold
ball 190.00
Cat with Bow, 4-1/8" h, Hubley, painted black and white, yellow
box 415.00
Circus Elephant, 3-7/8" h, Hubley, colorfully painted, seated position 180.00
Coronation, 6-5/8" h, Syndeham & McOustra, England, ornately
detained, emb busts in center, England, c1911 ....200.00
Dresser, 6-3/4" h, very detailed casting, columned panel, simulated wood carving, key lock opens center drawer, painted
brown and black..990.00
Duck, 4-3/4" h, Hubley, colorfully painted, outstretched wings,
slot on back 165.00
Dutch Boy and Girl, 5-1/4" and 5-1/8" h, Hubley, colorfully painted, boy on barrel, girl holding flowers, c1930, price for pr
....260.00
Egyptian Tomb, 6-1/4" x 5-1/4", green finish, pharaoh's tomb entrance, hieroglyphics on front panel......................275.00
Elk, 9-1/2" h, painted gold, full antlers 154.00
Globe Safe, 5" h, Kenton, round sphere, claw feet, nickeled com-
bination lock on front hinged door.......................105.00
Hall Clock, 5-3/4" h, swinging pendulum visible through panel
....110.00
Horseshoe, 4-1/4" x 4-3/4", Arcade, Buster Brown and Tige with
horse, painted black and gold 125.00
Husky, 5" h, Grey Iron Casting Co, painted brown, black eyes,
yellow box, repaired 365.00
Jewel Chest, 6-1/8" x 4-5/8", ornate casting, ftd bank, brass combination lock on front, top lifts for coin retrieval, crack at corner..90.00
Kodak, 4-1/4" x 5" w, J & E Stevens, nickeled, highly detailed casting, intricate pattern, emb "Kodak Bank" on front opening panel, c1905 ....225.00
Merry-Go-Round, 4-5/8" x 4-3/8", nickeled, Grey Iron Casting Co,
ornate, round merry-go-round mounted on pedestal for spinning, replaced shaft.....................................105.00
North Pole, 4-1/4" h, nickeled, Grey Iron Casting Co, depicts
wooden pole with handle, emb lettering 415.00
Mailbox, 5-1/2" h, Hubley, painted green, emb "Air Mail," with eagle, standing type..220.00
Maine, 4-5/8" l, Grey Iron Casting Co, japanned, gold highlights,
c1900 ....660.00
Mammy, 5-1/4" h, Hubley, hands on hips, colorfully painted
....300.00
Pagoda, 5" x 3" x 3", England, gold trim, c1889 ....245.00
Pershing, General, 7-3/4" h, Grey Iron Casting Co, full bust, detailed casting 55.00
Pig, 2-1/2" h, 5-1/4" l, Hubley, laughing, painted brown, trap on
bottom 120.00
Professor Pug Frog, 3-1/4" h, A.C. Williams, painted gold, blue
jacket, new twist pin 195.00
Radio, Kenton
2-7/8" h, 4-1/2" w, painted red, nickeled combination on front
panel, three dial style, orig Kenton tag..................440.00
4-1/2" h, metal sides and back, painted green, nickeled front
panel in Art Deco style 435.00

Tramp Art, wood, secret access to coins, 4" w, 4" d, 6" h, $335. Photo courtesy of Clifford Wallach.

Reindeer, 9-1/2" h, 5-1/4" l, A.C. Williams, painted gold, full rack
of antlers, replaced screw................................55.00
Rumplestiltskin, 6" h, painted gold, long red hat, base and feet,
mkd "Do You Know Me," c1910 ....210.00
Safe
3-9/16" h, 2-5/8" w, painted black, nickeled scroll design, key
lock on front door, factory flaw 190.00
4-1/8" h, 2-7/8" w, Kyser & Rex, Old Homestead, japanned, nickeled combination lock on front panel, emb "Old Homestead"
....470.00
4-3/8" h, Kyser & Rex, Young America, japanned, intricate
casting, emb at top, c1882 ....275.00
4-3/16" h, IXL, Kyser & Rex, vault safe shape, painted green,
gold highlights, emb front door, c1881 ....140.00
4-1/2" h, 3-1/4" w, Junior, painted black, gold highlights, emb
floral casting, combination lock on front, c1892.......220.00
4-9/16" h, 4-1/4" h, Kyser & Rex, Arabian, japanned, ornate
emb 90.00
5-3/8" h, Kyser & Rex, Japanese-style, japanned, cast Oriental
designs, c1882 ....85.00
5-3/4" h, 4-3/16" w, cast iron and metal, National Safe Deposit, ornate emb, combo lock on front, black, gold highlights .190.00
5-11/16" h, 4-1/4" w, J & E Stevens, Burglar Proof House, scalloped edges, combination lock, promising phrase..160.00
6" h, 6-3/8" w, Kenton Hardware, Chicago & NY Bank, double
vault, two separate combination locks 385.00
6-1/2" h, 4-11/16" w, Mudd Mfg. Co, Liberatas, copper electroplated, emb eagle and combination lock on front door
....605.00
6-3/4" h, 4-7/8" w, Kenton, Bank of Commerce, nickeled, vault
safe, heavily emb with Miss Liberty, scroll work, lettering
....550.00
6-3/4" h, 6" h, Kenton, Army and Navy, double sided vault, emb
military service men.....................................935.00
8" h, 5-3/4" w, nickeled, Coin Deposit, heavily emb, handle on
top, front combo 150.00
Seal 3-1/2" x 4-1/4", Arcade, painted japanned, basking on rock
platform...75.00
Sharecropper, 5-1/2" h, A.C. Williams, painted black, gold, and
red, toes visible on one foot 240.00
Spitz, 4-1/4" x 4-1/2" h, Grey Iron Casting Co., painted gold, repaired 165.00
Steamboat, 7-1/2" l, Arcade, painted gold 190.00

Stove

3-3/4" x 3-3/4", Roper, arcade, cast iron and sheet metal, painted white, burner cover lifts open 1,045.00

4-3/4" h, Gem, Abendroth Bros, traces of bronzing, back mkd "Gem Heaters Save Money" 275.00

5-1/2" x 4", gas, Berstein Co, NY, cast iron and sheet metal, metallic scale version of early stove, railed handle on top 150.00

5-3/4" h, upright, enameled violet color, mkd "Tiger" on back, removable base plate 360.00

6-7/8" h, parlor, nickeled finial and center bands, ornately cast, free standing 360.00

Tank, 9-1/2" l, 4" w, Ferrosteel, side mounted guns, rear spoke wheels, emb on sides, c1919 .... 385.00

US Mail

4-3/4" h, Kenton, painted silver, red highlights on lettering, small combo trap on back panel 195.00

5-1/8" h, Kenton, painted silver, gold painted emb eagle, red lettering large trap on back panel 180.00

6-7/8" h, 4-3/8" w, D.B. Fish, painted silver, red emb lettering, nickeled combination lock on front panel, c1903 ..... 130.00

World Time, 4-1/8 x 2-5/8", Arcade, paper time-tables of various cities around the world 315.00

Yellow Cab, 7-3/4" l, Arcade, painted yellow and black, slot on door, stenciled on doors 2,970.00

Chalk

Winston Churchill, 5-1/4" h, bust, painted green, back etched "Save for Victory," wood base 55.00

Glass

Charles Chaplin, 3-3/4" h, Geo Borgfeldt & Co., painted figure standing next to barrel slotted on lid, name emb on base 220.00

Lead

Boxer, 2-5/8" h, Germany, head, painted brown, black facial details, lock on collar, bent in back 130.00

Burro, 3-1/2" x 3-1/2", Japan, lock on saddle mkd "Plymouth, VT" 125.00

Ocean Liner, 2-3/4" x 7-5/8" l, bronze electroplated, three smoking stacks, hinged trap on deck, small hole 180.00

Pug, 2-3/4" h, Germany, painted, stenciled "Hershey Park" on side, lock on collar 300.00

Pottery

Cat, 3" h, head, white clay, green glaze 275.00

Dog, 2-1/2" h, head, white clay, dark green glaze, flake at coin slot 110.00

Pig, Germany, two pigs on see-saw on top of money bag 120.00

Steel

Life Boat, 14" l, pressed, painted yellow and blue, boat length decal mkd "Contributions for Royal National Life Boat Institution," deck lifts for coin removal, over painted 360.00

Piano, 5-1/8" x 5-7/8", lyon & Healy's, free standing, etched wording on cabinet panel 380.00

Postal Savings, 4-5/8" h, 5-3/8" w, copper finish, glass view front panel, paper registering strips, emb "U.S.Mail" on sides, top lifts to reveal four coin slots, patent 1902 .... 95.00

Tin Lithograph

Panama-Pacific Expo, Bliss Can Manuf Co., talc can shape, 4" h, 2-1/2"w, 1-1/4" d 150.00

White Metal

Amish Boy, seated on bale of straw, 4-3/4" x 3-3/8", U.S., painted in bright colors, key lock trap on bottom 55.00

Cat with Bow, 4-1/8" h, painted white, blue bow 155.00

Gorilla, colorfully painted in brown hues, seated position, trap on bottom 165.00

Pig, 4-3/8" h, painted white, decal mkd "West Point, N.Y." on belly 30.00

Rabbit, 4-1/2" h, seated, painted brown, painted eyes, trap on bottom, crack in ear 30.00

Santa, 5-7/8" l, colorfully painted, full figure of standing Santa, holding toy bag, book and box mkd "York National Trust Co" 165.00

Spaniel, seated, 4-1/2" h, painted white, black highlights .. 470.00

Uncle Sam Hat, 3-1/2" h, painted red, white, and blue, stars on brim, slot on top, trap on bottom 135.00

BARBER BOTTLES

History: Barber bottles, colorful glass bottles found on shelves and counters in barber shops, held the liquids barbers used daily. A specific liquid was kept in a specific bottle, which the barber knew by color, design, or lettering. The bulk liquids were kept in utilitarian containers under the counter or in a storage room.

Barber bottles are found in many types of glass–art glass with various decorations, pattern glass, and commercially prepared and labeled bottles.

References: *Barbershop Collectibles*, L-W Book Sales, 1996; Keith E. Estep, *Shaving Mug & Barber Bottle Book*, Schiffer Publishing, 1995; Richard Holiner, *Collecting Barber Bottles*, Collector Books, 1986; Ralph & Terry Kovel, *Kovels' Bottles Price List*, 10th ed., Crown Publishers, 1996; John Odell, *Digger Odell's Official Antique Bottle and Glass Collector Magazine Price Guide Series*, Vol. 1, published by author (1910 Shawhan Rd., Morrow, OH 45152), 1995.

Note: Prices are for bottles without original stoppers unless otherwise noted.

Advertising

Koken's Quinine Tonic for the Hair, 7-1/2" h, clear, label under glass 195.00

Lucky tiger, red, green, yellow, black, and gilt label under glass, emb on reverse 85.00

Vegederma, cylindrical, bulbous, long neck, amethyst, white enamel dec of bust of woman with long flower hair, tooled mouth, pontil scar, 8" h 130.00

Amber, Hobb's Hobnail 250.00

Amethyst, Mary Gregory type dec, white enameled child and flowers, 8" h 250.00

Cobalt Blue, cylindrical, bulbous body, long neck, white enamel, traces of gold dec, tooled mouth, pontil scar, 7-1/4" h . 100.00

Emerald Green, cylindrical bell form, long neck, orange and white enameled floral dec, sheared mouth, pontil scar, some int. haze, 8-1/2" h 210.00

Latticino, cylindrical, bulbous, long neck, clear frosted glass, white, red, and pale green vertical stripes, tooled mouth, pontil scar, 8-1/4" h 200.00

Lime Green, Amethyst, cylindrical, bulbous bodies, long necks, profuse floral gilt dec, tooled mouth, pontil scar, 8" h, matched pr 350.00

Lime Green, satin glass, classical bird claw grasping ball, ground mouth, smooth base, 7" h, pr 100.00

Milk Glass, Witch Hazel, painted letters and flowers, 9" h . 115.00

Opalescent

Coin Spot, blue 300.00

Seaweed, cranberry, bulbous 465.00

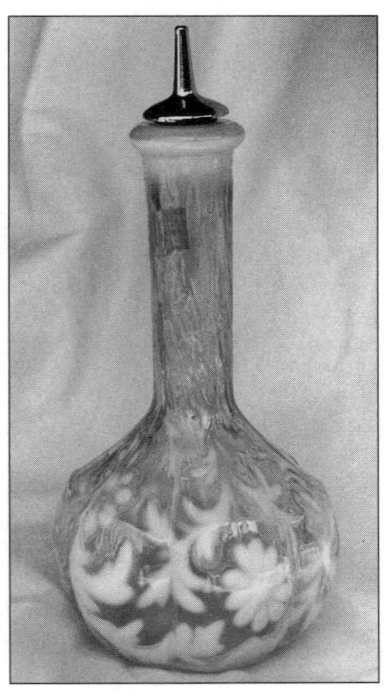

Vaseline, opalescent Daisy pattern, blown, 8-1/2" h, $85.

Spanish Lace, electric blue ground, sq, long neck, tooled mouth, smooth base, 7-7/8" h, pr 250.00

Stars and Stripes, cranberry, pale blue, tooled mouth, smooth base, 7-1/4" h, pr 600.00

Sapphire Blue

Enameled white and yellow daisies, green leaves, 8-5/8" h 125.00

Mary Gregory type dec, white enamel dec of girl playing tennis, c ylindrical bulbous form, long neck, tooled mouth, pontil scar, 8" h 150.00

BAROMETERS

History: A barometer is an instrument which measures atmospheric pressure, which, in turn, aids weather forecasting. Low pressure indicates the coming of rain, snow, or storm; high pressure signifies fair weather.

Most barometers use an evacuated and graduated glass tube which contains a column of mercury. These are classified by the shape of the case. An aneroid barometer has no liquid and works by a needle connected to the top of a metal box in which a partial vacuum is maintained. The movement of the top moves the needle.

3-1/2" d, brass, "The Hughes - Owens Co. Ltd, Montreal," leatherized case 165.00

33" d, wheel, carved oak, foliage and C-scrolls, English, late 19th C 230.00

34" l, stick, sgd E. Kendall, N. Lebanon, mahogany, etched steel face, mirrored well cov 550.00

37" h, stick, Central Scientific Co, Chicago, IL, engraved silver brass scale, ebonized backboard................................200.00

38" h, Timby's Patent, rosewood rippled frame, label reads "sold by John M. Merrick & Co., Worcester, MA," c1857, barometer and thermometer 750.00

38-1/4" h, banjo, mahogany inlaid, T. and H. Doublet, Moorgate St. Bank, early 19th C, shaped case with engraved thermometer and barometer dials, convex mirror, restoration 750.00

38-3/4" h, banjo, mahogany, dial engraved "P. Nossi & Co. Boston," broken pediment cresting above shaped case with thermometer, circular barometer dial flanked by inlaid paterae 690.00

39" h, wall, pierced crest above paper dial in rect frame, scrolling brackets continuing to shaped base with applied boss, painted black, Thomas Shaw, England, early 19th C, minor imperfections 690.00

39-1/2" h, stick, Georgian style, mahogany, swan's neck cresting, carved well cov, engraved steel face, 20th C 290.00

39-3/4" h, banjo, shell inlaid, painted black, Kirner Bros., Oxford, Victorian, mid-19th C 460.00

41" h, stick, retailer plaque Williams, Page & Co, Boston, paper labels, two thermometers, Victorian, c1850, losses 290.00

41-1/2" h, cased, Storm King, E. C. Spooner, Boston, late 19th C 445.00

42" h, wheel, L. Solomons, Bath Warantes, Regency period, early 19th C, shaped case 850.00

BASKETS

History: Baskets were invented when man first required containers to gather, store, and transport goods. Today's collectors, influenced by the country look, focus on baskets made of splint, rye straw, or willow. Emphasis is placed on handmade examples. Nails or staples, wide splints which are thin and evenly cut, or a wire bail handle denote factory construction which can date back to the mid-19th century. Decorated painted or woven baskets rarely are handmade, unless they are American Indian in origin.

Baskets are collected by (a) type–berry, egg, or field, (b) region–Nantucket or Shaker, and (c) composition–splint, rye, or willow.

Reference: Don and Carol Raycraft, *Collector's Guide to Country Baskets*, Collector Books, 1985, 1994 value update.

Museums: Heard Museum, Phoenix, AZ; Old Salem, Inc., Winston-Salem, NC.

REPRODUCTION ALERT

Modern reproductions abound, made by diverse groups ranging from craft revivalists to foreign manufacturers.

Note: Limit purchases to baskets in very good condition; damaged ones are a poor investment, even at a low price.

Baby, Windsor type, wood bottom, oval bent wood top supported by sq tapered spindles, splint basket weaving, 19-1/2" w, 12" d, 35-1/2" l 750.00

Nantucket

5" to 11-7/8" d, nested set of 7, 20th C, minute breaks and losses, 7 pc set 12,650.00

5-7/8" d, 4-1/2" h, turned wooden bottom, splint and cane, bentwood swivel handle, traces of paper label, two small holes in one side 525.00

6" h, pocketbook style, whalebone plaque on lid, imperfections 175.00

7-3/4" d, 4-7/8" h, paper label on base "Lightship Basket made by Fred S. Chadwick Nantucket Mass. 4 Pine St.," early 20th C 920.00

Potato, woven oak splint, oval form, tightly woven ends, fitted with bentwood ash carrying handle, Lehigh County, PA, 19th C, 16" l, 12" h, $1,150. Photo courtesy of Sotheby's.

10" d, 7-1/4" h, 20th C, minor imperfections 1,100.00
11" d, 7" h, early 20th C, scattered minor breaks and losses 575.00
Oak, 11-1/2" h, 14" d top, peach, initials "CMT" 235.00
Rye Straw
    23" d, dough rising, shallow, hickory splint binding, PA, late 19th C 125.00
    24" d, domed lid, wear, edge damage, one bentwood rim handle missing 300.00
Splint Oak, 24" d, 17" h, two strong handles, feather type . 420.00
Woven Splint, bentwood handle
    7" x 7-1/2" x 4" h, buttocks, 38 ribs, natural patina 140.00
    7-1/4" x 7-1/4" x 4-1/4" h, buttocks, 26 ribs, natural patina, faded red and green 220.00
    10-1/2" d, 5-1/2" h, round, good patina 275.00
    10-1/2" x 13" x 5-3/4", rect, courses of splint have unfaded dyed color, red, blue, yellow, and brown 385.00
    11" x 13" x 6-1/2" h, buttocks, old dark green paint, some dam, 28 ribs, wear and holes in bottom 275.00
    12-1/2" x 12-1/2" x 6-1/2" h, buttocks, 58 ribs, old orange-tan pigmented varnish, twisted detail at handle 550.00
    13" x 16-1/2" x 9" h, buttocks, 44 ribs, scrubbed finish, some exposure damage 110.00
    13-1/4" d, 7" h, old green paint 440.00
    13-1/2" x 14" x 7" h, buttocks, 40 ribs, old gray paint 60.00
    13-1/2" x 16-1/2" x 8-1/2" h, buttocks, 22 ribs, blue and black stripes 140.00
    14" d, buttocks, single handle 160.00
    15" d, melon shaped, single handle, minor loss 85.00
    15-1/2" x 23" x 10-3/4" h, yellow bands, blue potato print designs, bentwood swivel handle, minor damage 275.00
    16" d, market type, single handle 90.00

BATTERSEA ENAMELS

History: Battersea enamel is a generic term for English enamel-on-copper objects of the 18th century.

In 1753, Stephen Theodore Janssen established a factory to produce "Trinkets and Curiosities Enamelled on Copper" at York House, Battersea, London. Here the new invention of transfer printing developed to a high degree of excellence, and the resulting trifles delighted fashionable Georgian society.

Recent research has shown that enamels actually were being produced in London and the Midlands sever-al years before York House was established. However, most enamel trinkets still are referred to as "Battersea Enamels," even though they were probably made in other workshops in London, Birmingham, Bilston, Wednesbury, or Liverpool.

All manner of charming items were made, including snuff and patch boxes bearing mottos and memory gems. (By adding a mirror inside the lid, a snuff box became a patch box). Many figural whimsies, called "toys," were created to amuse a gay and fashionable world. Many other elaborate articles, e.g., candlesticks, salts, tea caddies, and bonbonnières, were made for the tables of the newly rich middle classes.

Reference: Susan Benjamin, *English Enamel Boxes*, Merrimack Publishers Circle, 1978.

Bonbonniere, reclining cow, natural colors, grassy mound, floral lid, Bilston, c1770 .... 3,750.00
Box, 1-3/4" l, With Greatful Heart this Trifle I Present as such accept it & I'm Content, enamel on copper, blue inscription, white lid, polychrome lovebirds, professional repair 220.00
Candlesticks, pr, 6" h, pink ground, allover nosegays, pastels, Bilston, 1770 .... 3,500.00
Etui, white tapered column, pastoral scenes within reserves, gilt scrolling and diaper work, int. fitted with perfume bottle, writing slide, pencil, and bodkin, Bilston, c1770 .... 3,400.00
Mirror Knobs, 2-7/8" d, rural genre scenes, woman on shore, two restored, 3 pc set 300.00
Patch Box, oval
    1-1/2" l, pastoral riverside scene, full color, pale green top and base, Bilston, c1780 .... 650.00
    2-1/2" x 1-3/4" x 1-1/2", black and white King Charles Spaniel, pink ground, floral dec, around sides 2,750.00
Portrait Medallion, 4" l, oval, enameled portrait of George II, third quarter 18th C, painted en grisaille 1,265.00

Scent Bottle Holder, white ground, purple dec, green leaves, rose and blue flowers, bow and arrow sheaf on reverse, 1-2" x 1-1/4" x 2-1/4", $400.

Snuff Box, 3" l, molded spaniel cover, landscape painted base, lines 1,265.00
Tiebacks, 2-1/2" d, enamel and brass, Cupid dec, pr 150.00
Topsy-Turvy Box, 2-3/4" l, oval, white, Before and After Marriage, humorous drawing of couple whose smiles turn into frowns with box is turned upside down, Bilston, c1780 .... 1,500.00

BAVARIAN CHINA

History: Bavaria, Germany, was an important porcelain production center, similar to the Staffordshire district in England. The phrase "Bavarian China" refers to the products of companies operating in Bavaria, among which were Hutschenreuther, Thomas, and Zeh, Scherzer & Co. (Z. S. & Co.). Very little of the production from this area was imported into the United States prior to 1870.

Bowl, 9-1/2" d, large orange poppies, green leaves 85.00
Celery Tray, 11" l, center with basket of fruit, luster edge, c1900 .... 45.00
Charger, scalloped rim, game bird in woodland scene, bunches of pink and yellow roses, connecting garlands 95.00
Chocolate Set, cov chocolate pot, 6 cups and saucers, shaded blue and white, large white leaves, pink, red, and white roses, crown mark 295.00
Creamer and Sugar, purple and white pansy dec, mkd "Meschendorf, Bavaria" 65.00
Cup and Saucer, roses and foliage, gold handle 25.00
Figure, 10-1/2" h, dark blue and pale orange marabou standing beside tan and navy cactus, mkd "Hutschenreuther Selb-Bavaria, K. Tutter" 285.00
Fish Set, 13 plates, matching sauce boat, artist sgd 295.00
Hair Receiver, 3-1/2" x 2-1/2" apple blossom dec, mkd "T. S. & Co." 60.00
Pitcher, 9" h, bulbous, blackberry dec, shaded ground, burnished gold lizard handle, sgd "D. Churchill" 125.00
Plate
    8-1/2" d, hp, poinsettia dec 50.00
    9-1/2" d, red berries, green leaves, white ground, scalloped border 35.00
Portrait Plate, 16" l, side view of lady, sgd "L. B. Chaffee, R. C. Bavaria" 95.00

Plate, hp, pink, blue, and purple morning glories, leaves, buds, sgd "E. H. Koeher," stamped "Louise, Bavaria," 8-3/4" d, $25.

Ramekin, underplate, ruffled, small red roses with green foliage, gold rim.. 45.00
Salt and Pepper Shakers, pr, pink apple blossom sprays, white ground, reticulated gold tops, pr.................................. 35.00
Shaving Mug, pink carnations, mkd "Royal Bavarian" 65.00
Sugar Shaker, hp, pastel pansies 60.00
Vase, 4-3/4" h, hp, florals, sgd.. 40.00

BELLEEK

History: Belleek, a thin, ivory-colored, almost-iridescent porcelain, was first made in 1857 in county Fermanagh, Ireland. Production continued until World War I, was discontinued for a period of time, and then resumed. The Shamrock pattern is most familiar, but many patterns were made, including Limpet, Tridacna, and Grasses.

There is an Irish saying: If a newly married couple receives a gift of Belleek, their marriage will be blessed with lasting happiness.

Several American firms made a Belleek-type porcelain. The first was Ott and Brewer Co. of Trenton, New Jersey, in 1884, followed by Willets. Other firms producing this ware included The Ceramic Art Co. (1889), American Art China Works (1892), Columbian Art Co. (1893), and Lenox, Inc. (1904).

Marks: The European Belleek company used specific marks during given time periods, which makes it relatively easy to date a piece of Irish Belleek. Variations in mark color are important, as well as the symbols and words.

First mark	Black	Harp, Hound, and Castle	1863-1890
Second mark	Black	Harp, Hound, and Castle and the words "Co. Fermanagh, Ireland"	1891-1826
Third mark	Black	"Deanta in Eirinn" added	1926-1946
Fourth mark	Green	same as third mark except for color	1946-1955
Fifth mark	Green	"R" inside a circle added	1955-1965
Sixth mark	Green	"Co. Fermanagh" omitted	1965-March 1980
Seventh mark	Gold	"Deanta in Eirinn" omitted	April 1980-December 1992
Eighth mark	Blue	Blue version of the second mark with "R" inside a circle added	January 1993-present

References: Susan and Al Bagdade, *Warman's English & Continental Pottery & Porcelain*, 2nd ed., Wallace-Homestead, 1991; Richard K. Degenhardt, *Belleek*, 2nd ed., Wallace-Homestead, 1993; Mary Frank Gaston, *Collector's Encyclopedia of Knowles, Taylor & Knowles China*, Collector Books, 1996; Timothy J. Kearns, *Knowles, Taylor & Knowles*, Schiffer Publishing, 1994; Marion Langham, *Belleek Irish Porcelain*, Quiller Press, 1993.

Collectors' Club: The Belleek Collectors' Society, 144 W. Britannia St., Taunton, MA 02780.

Museum: Museum of Ceramics at East Liverpool, East Liverpool, OH.

Additional Listings: Lenox.

American

Bowl, 9" d, green, heavy gold trim, white curled handle, Lenox green wreath mark.................................95.00

Cup and Saucer, 6" h, sq pedestal base, undecorated, Willets brown mark.................................45.00

Dresser Set, cov powder box, pink tray, buffer and container, nail brush, pin cushion, hp violets, artist sgd "M. R.," Willets brown mark 600.00

Figure, 4" h, Lenox green wreath mark
  Elephant, white 325.00
  Swan, green.................................75.00

Loving Cup, 3 handles, wine keeper in wine cellar dec, artist sgd, SS repousse collar, CAC mark 195.00

Mustache Cup, gold leaves, butterflies.................................100.00

Perfume Bottle, figural, rabbit, white, Lenox green wreath mark 550.00

Powder Box, 4" x 6", pink, gold wheat on lid, Lenox green wreath mark.................................60.00

Salt, 2" d, gold ftd, green ground, pink roses, Lenox green palette mark.................................40.00

Vase
  5" h, 5" d, tree trunk shape, transfer printed flowers, polychrome dec, red Ott & Brewer stamp 450.00
  18-1/2" h, enamel and gilt dec, female within landscape, floral bouquet, artist sgd "J. Wallbridge," printed "Ceramic Art Co." NJ mark, c1900, restoration 320.00

Irish

Basket, 8" d, Melvin, sq, decorative border, twig handles, turquoise-blue, 4 applied violet floral sprays, green leaves 625.00

Box, cov, 3" h, Forget-Me-Not, globular, ftd, applied flowerheads, conical knob, pearl luster glaze, 3BM 395.00

Butter Dish, cov, figural, cottage, 6th mark 160.00

Cake Plate, Limpet pattern, 2BM.................................195.00

Creamer, Lotus pattern, green handle, 2BM.................................95.00

Cup and Saucer, Shamrock pattern, 2BM 200.00

Demitasse Cup and Saucer, Shamrock pattern, 6th mark ..55.00

Dish, coral and shell, 6th mark.................................35.00

Figure
  3-1/2" h, terrier, 4GM 45.00
  5-1/2" h, fish on rocky pedestal, 7th mark 75.00

Flower Holder, 3-1/2" h, Seahorse, one with one head, other with brown, 1BM, pr.................................1,400.00

Mustache Cup, Tridacna pattern, first black mark 125.00

Plate, 9" d, Harp and Shamrock pattern, 5th mark.................................60.00

Sandwich Tray, Mask pattern, 2BM.................................285.00

Spill Jug, 7" h, Limerick pattern, 5th mark 60.00

Tea and Toast Set, Tridacna pattern, 6th mark 90.00

Tub, 3-1/4" d, Shamrock pattern, 3BM 65.00

Vase, 6-1/2" h, Harp and Shamrock pattern, 5GM 60.00

BELLS

History: Bells have been used for centuries for many different purposes. They have been traced as far back as 2697 B.C., though at that time they did not have any true tone. One of the oldest bells is the "crotal," a tiny sphere with small holes, a ball, and a stone or metal interior. This type now appears as sleigh bells.

True bell making began when bronze, a mixture of tin and copper, was invented. Bells are now made out of many types of materials–almost as many materials as there are uses for them.

Bells of the late 19th century show a high degree of workmanship and artistic style. Glass bells from this period are examples of the glassblower's talent and the glass manufacturer's product.

Collectors' Clubs: American Bell Association, Alter Rd., Box 386, Natrona Heights, PA 15065; American Bell Association International, Inc., 7210 Bellbrook Dr., San Antonio, TX 78227.

Museum: Bell Haven, Tarentum, PA.

Vase, tree trunk, three openings, green dec, third black mark, 6-1/4" h, 4-1/2" d, $175.

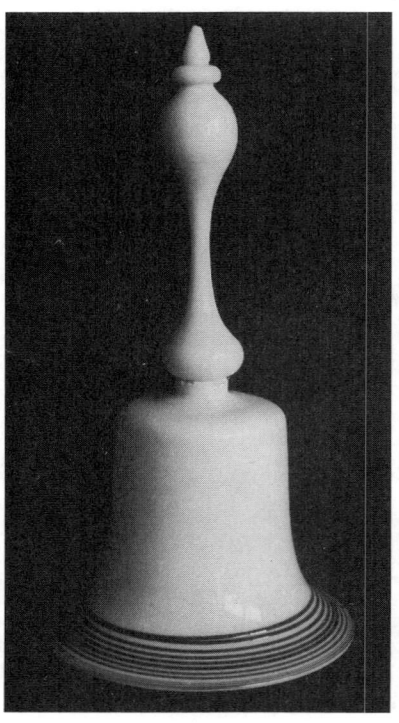

Milk glass, red bands at base, brass clapper with faceted colored glass ball, 11" h, $120.

Bicycle, cast brass, nickel plated, eagle..............................90.00
Brass, 4" h, 3-1/4" d, Jacobean head finial, emb figures around sides 120.00
Church, cast brass
   20" h, wrought-iron ringer, suspended from chain, Reading, PA, late 18th C...980.00
   24" h, mounted on wrought iron frame, c1772, from Manheim, Lancaster County, PA church...............................8,000.00
Desk, bronze, white marble base, side tap, c1875.............65.00
Glass
   Amethyst, flint, metal lace trim, painted crowing rooster on top of handle..375.00
   Custard, souvenir, "Alamo-Built 1718, San Antonio, Texas," gilt band 120.00
   Vaseline, flint, ornate metal lace trim, elephant with green eyes and red mouth on top of handle..............................350.00
Hemony, 6-3/4" h, 3-3/8" d, brass, figural knight handle, figures emb around sides, name "Hemony" 120.00
Locomotive, 17" x 17", brass, cradle and yoke.................850.00
School, 10-1/4" h, turned curly maple handle...................385.00
Sleigh, leather strap, 24 bells..110.00
Table, 4-5/8" h, sterling silver, cupid blowing horn, figural handle, foliate strap work border, frosted finish, Gorham, c1870
....750.00

BENNINGTON AND BENNINGTON-TYPE POTTERY

History: In 1845, Christopher Webber Fenton joined Julius Norton, his brother-in-law, in the manufacturing of stoneware pottery in Bennington, Vermont. Fenton sought to expand the company's products and glazes; Norton wanted to concentrate solely on stoneware. In 1847, Fenton broke away and established his own factory.

Fenton introduced to America the famous Rockingham glaze, developed in England and named after the Marquis of Rockingham. In 1849, he patented a flint enamel glaze, "Fenton's Enamel," which added flecks, spots, or streaks of color (usually blues, greens, yellows, and oranges) to the brown Rockingham glaze. Forms included candlesticks, coachman bottles, cow creamers, poodles, sugar bowls, and toby pitchers.

Fenton produced the little-known scroddled ware, commonly called lava or agate ware. Scroddled ware is composed of differently colored clays which are mixed with cream-colored clay, molded, turned on a potter's wheel, coated with feldspar and flint, and fired. It was not produced in quantity as there was little demand for it.

Fenton also introduced Parian ware to America. Parian was developed in England in 1842 and known as "Statuary ware." Parian is a translucent porcelain which has no glaze and resembles marble. Bennington made the blue and white variety in the form of vases, cologne bottles, and trinkets.

The hound-handled pitcher is probably the best-known Bennington piece. Hound-handled pitchers were made by about 30 different potteries in over 55 variations. Rockingham glaze was used by more than 150 potteries in 11 states, mainly in the Midwest, between 1830 and 1900.

Marks: Five different marks were used, with many variations. Only about 20% of the pieces carried any mark; some forms were almost always marked, others never. Marks include:

1849 mark (4 variations) for flint enamel and Rockingham
E. Fenton's Works, 1845-1847, on Parian and occasionally on scroddled ware
U. S. Pottery Co., ribbon mark, 1852-1858, on Parian and blue and white porcelain
U. S. Pottery Co., lozenge mark, 1852-1858, on Parian
U. S. Pottery, oval mark, 1853-1858, mainly on scroddled ware.

References: Richard Carter Barret, *How to Identify Bennington Pottery*, Stephen Greene Press, 1964; William C. Ketchum, Jr., *American Pottery and Porcelain*, Avon Books, 1994.

Museums: Bennington Museum, Bennington, VT; East Liverpool Museum of Ceramics, East Liverpool, OH.

Additional Listings: Stoneware.

SPECIAL AUCTION

The Armans Collector's Sales and Services
P.O. Box 4037
Middletown, RI 02842
(401) 849-5012

Bank, 6-1/2" h, flint enamel, c1850-60...............................865.00
Bowl, 7-1/8" d, shallow, brown and yellow Rockingham glaze, Fenton's 1849 mark...775.00
Candlestick, 8-1/4" h, flint enamel glaze..........................875.00
Churn, stoneware, 6 gallon, cobalt blue cornucopia of flowers, orig dasher, mkd "A. J. Norton & Co"......................8,800.00
Curtain Tiebacks, 4-1/2" l, 1849-58, Barrett plate 200, one chipped, pr...175.00
Figure
   7-1/2" h, 10" l, lion, facing left, coleslaw mane, tongue up, flint enamel, Barrett plate 377, minor repair to tail, repaired on chip on paw...4,315.00
   8-1/2" h, 9" l, poodle, standing, basket in mouth, Barrett plate 367, repairs to tail and hind quarters....................2,500.00

Flask, book shape, "Bennington Battle," dense brown and tan bottled glaze, 1840-80, age lines run along one side and across base, 5-5/8" h, $210. Photo courtesy of Norman C. Heckler & Company.

Flask, book, flint enamel, title imp on spine, 1849-58, Barrett plate 411.00
5-3/4" h, titled "Bennington Battle" 750.00
5-3/4" h, untitled 460.00
6" h, titled "Hermit's Life & Suffering" 980.00
7" h, titled "Ladies Companion" 690.00
8" h, titled "Bennington Companion G" 750.00
Jar, 4-3/8" h, 4-1/4" d, Parian, blue and white, Acanthus Leaf pattern, lid missing 85.00
Jug, 10-3/4" h, stoneware, strap handle, imp label "F. B. Norton & Co, Worcester, Mass," cobalt blue slip floral design 220.00
Nameplate, 8" l, Rockingham glaze 135.00
Paperweight, 3" h, 4-1/2" h, spaniel, 1849-58, Barrett plate 407 .... 815.00
Picture Frame, 9-1/2" h, oval, 1848-58, Barrett plate VIII, chips and repairs, pr 230.00
Pie Plate, 9" d, brown and yellow Rockingham glaze, Fenton's 1848-58 mark, minor wear 925.00
Pitcher
8" h, hunting scene, Barrett pate 26, chips 175.00
9-1/2" h, hound handle, 1852-67, Barrett plate 32, crack and repair to spout 345.00
Planter, 11" h, stump form, stoneware, base mkd "F. B. Norton & Co, Worcester," minor chips 320.00
Spittoon, 9-1/2" d, flint enamel glaze, rare 1849 mark 450.00
Sugar Bowl, cov, 3-3/4" h, Parian, blue and white, Repeated Oak Leaves pattern, raised grapevine dec on lid 150.00
Teapot, cov, flint enamel, Alternate Rib pattern, pierced pouring spout 425.00
Toby Bottle, 10-1/2" h, Barrett plate 421, marked on base, mold cracks, top of foot repaired, other foot chipped 550.00
Wash Bowl and Pitcher, flint enamel glaze 1,100.00

Bennington-Type

Bank, 3-1/4" h, 3-3/4" w, chest of drawers shape, Rockingham glaze, Barrett plate 428, small chip to front top edge . 150.00
Creamer, 5-1/2" h, 6-3/4" l, figural, cow, Rockingham glaze, Barrett plate 378, chipped cov, repairs 115.00

Pitcher, seated cupid, scalloped top, medium brown, shaped handle, 7" h, $185.

Flask, book
7" h, titled "Spiritual Manifestations By" imp on spine, Rockingham glaze, mid 19th C, crack 260.00
7-3/4" h, untitled, Rockingham glaze, roughness to top edge 175.00
Spittoon, 8-1/2" d, scallop shell form, Rockingham glaze, 19th C 175.00
Toby Bottle, 9" h, barrel, Rockingham glaze, mid-19th C, rim and base chips 175.00

BISCUIT JARS

History: The biscuit or cracker jar was the forerunner of the cookie jar. Biscuit jars were made of various materials by leading glassworks and potteries of the late 19th and early 20th centuries.

Note: All items listed have silver-plated mountings unless otherwise noted.

Bristol Glass, 6-1/2" h, allover enameled pink, blue, white and yellow floral dec, green leaves, SP top, rim, and handle ... 125.00
Cased Glass, 6-1/4" h, blue, enameled pink roses and green leaves, SP top, rim and handle 145.00
Cranberry Glass, 9" h, 6-1/4" d, two applied clear ring handles, applied clear feet and flower prunt pontil, ribbed finial knob 195.00
Jasperware, 6" h, white classical cameos, black ground, SP handle, rim, and lid, imp "Wedgwood" 450.00
Loetz Type, 6-1/2" h, translucent white mother-of-pearl irid green raindrop spatter, melon swirls, SP lid, rim, and handle . 225.00
New England Glass Co., melon ribbed, pink floral dec, lid and bail missing 60.00
Nippon China, 7-1/2" h, 4-1/2" w, sq, white, multicolored floral bands, gold outlines and trim 110.00

Wave Crest, multicolored florals in scrolled panels, unsgd, 7-1/2" h, $215.

Pairpoint, 9-1/2" h, burnt orange, floral dec, blown-out floral base, sgd 350.00
Royal Bayreuth, Poppy, blue mark 650.00
Satin Glass, 7-1/4" h, pink, molded shell base, enameled floral dec, SP lid and handle 315.00
Vaseline Glass, 7" h, threaded, SP rim, lid, and handle 160.00
Wave Crest, 9" h, yellow roses, molded multicolored swirl ground, incised floral and leaf dec on lid, mkd "Quadruple Plate"
.... 400.00

BISQUE

History: Bisque or biscuit china is the name given to wares that have been fired once and have not been glazed.

Bisque figurines and busts, which were popular during the Victorian era, were used on fireplace mantels, dining room buffets, and end tables. Manufacturing was centered in the United States and Europe. By the mid-20th century, Japan was the principal source of bisque items, especially character-related items.

References: Susan and Al Bagdade, *Warman's English & Continental Pottery & Porcelain*, 2nd ed., Wallace-Homestead, 1991; Elyse Karlin, *Children Figurines of Bisque and Chinawares*, Schiffer Publishing, 1990; Sharon Weintraub, *Naughties, Nudies and Bathing Beauties*, Hobby House Press, 1993.

Box, cov, egg shape, relief windmill scene, ftd 50.00
Center Bowl, 8-3/4" h, figural, pierced bowl supported by tripod feet modeled as cherubs, white, France, 19th C 575.00
Dish, cov, 9" x 6-1/2" x 5-1/2", dog, brown, and white, green blanket, white and gilt basketweave base 500.00
Figure
    12" h, 3-3/8" d, young boy, dressed in pastel blue, carries blue hat and flower, gold and lavender floral trim, gold dot trim on suit 155.00

Salt, girl, pink jacket, white skirt, blue dots, tan and black basket, 3-1/4" x 1-1/2" x 2-3/4", $65.

16" h, polychrome enameled boy and girl, each with basket over their shoulder, Germany, late 19th C, pr 290.00
20-3/4" h, man offering lady a rose, Victorian costumes, polychrome dec, German, 19th C, pr 325.00
Match Holder, figural, Dutch girl, copper and gold trim 45.00
Nodder, 2-1/2" x 3-1/2", jester, seated holding pipe, pastel peach and white, gold trim 85.00
Piano Baby
    Crawling, crying, mkd "Made in Japan" 20.00
    Lying on stomach, wearing bib, dog, and cat, 6-3/4" l, German 100.00
Planter, carriage, four wheels, pale blue and pink, white ground, gold dots, royal markings 165.00
Salt, 3" d, figural, walnut, cream, branch base, matching spoon
.... 75.00
Wall Plaque, 10-1/4" d, light green, scrolled and pierced scallop, white relief figures in center, man playing mandolin, lady wearing hat, c1900, pr 275.00

BITTERS BOTTLES

History: Bitters, a "remedy" made from natural herbs and other mixtures with an alcohol base, often was viewed as the universal cure-all. The names given to various bitter mixtures were imaginative, though the bitters seldom cured what their makers claimed.

The manufacturers of bitters needed a way to sell and advertise their products. They designed bottles in many shapes, sizes, and colors to attract the buyer. Many forms of advertising, including trade cards, billboards, signs, almanacs, and novelties, proclaimed the virtues of a specific bitter.

During the Civil War, a tax was levied on alcoholic beverages. Since bitters were identified as medicines, they were exempt from this tax. The alcoholic content was never mentioned. In 1907, when the Pure Foods Regulations went into effect, "an honest statement of content on every label" put most of the manufacturers out of business.

References: Ralph and Terry Kovel, *Kovels' Bottles Price List*, 10th ed., Crown Publishers, 1996; John Odell, *Digger Odell's Official Antique Bottle and Glass Collector Magazine Price Guide Series*, Vol. 2, published by author (1910 Shawhan Rd., Morrow, OH 45152), 1995; Carlyn Ring, *For Bitters Only*, published by author 203 Kensington Rd., Hampton Falls, NH 03844), 1980; J. H. Thompson, *Bitters Bottles*, Century House, 1947; Richard Watson, *Bitters Bottles*, Thomas Nelson and Sons, 1965.

Periodicals: *Antique Bottle and Glass Collector*, P.O. Box 187, East Greenville, PA 18041; *Bitters Report*, P.O. Box 1253, Bunnell, FL 32110.

A. S. Hopkins Union Stomach Bitters, greenish-yellow, applied tapered collar lip, smooth base, 9-1/4" h 265.00
Alpine Herb Bitters, amber, sq, smooth base, tooled lip, 9-5/8" h
.... 175.00
Baker's Orange Grove Bitters, yellowish-amber, smooth base, applied mouth, 9-1/2" h 185.00
Bell's Cocktail Bitters, Jas. M. Bell & Co., New York, amber, applied ring, smooth base, 10-1/2" h 450.00
Browns Celebrated Indian Herb Bitters/Patented Feb. 11, 1868, figural, emb, golden amber, ground lip, smooth base, 12-1/4" h
.... 350.00

Bourbon Whiskey Bitters, barrel shape, cherry puce, applied sq collar, smooth base, 9-3/4" h 500.00

Caldwell's Herb Bitters/The Great Tonic, triangular, beveled and lattice work panels, yellowish-amber, applied tapered lip, iron pontil 395.00

Clarke's Vegetable Sherry Wine Bitters, aqua, smooth base, applied mouth, 14" h........................575.00

Dr. Loew's Celebrated Stomach Bitters & Nerve Tonic, green, smooth base, tooled lip, 9-1/4" h 150.00

Drake's Plantation Bitters, puce, Arabaseque design, tapered lip, smooth base, 9-3/4" h........................295.00

Godfrey's Celebrated Cordial Bitters, NY, aqua, pontil, applied mouth, 10" h........................1,225.00

Greeley's Bourbon Bitters, barrel shape, smokey gray-brown, sq collared lip, smooth base, 9-1/4" h 225.00

Hibernia Bitters, amber, sq, smooth base, tooled lip, 9-1/4" h 125.00

Hops & Malt Bitters, golden amber, tapered collar lip, smooth base, 9-1/8" h........................250.00

J. C.& Co., molded pineapple form, deep golden amber, blown molded, 19th C, 8-1/2" h........................460.00

Kelly's Old Cabin Bitters, cabin shape, amber, sloping collar lip, smooth base, 9" h........................725.00

Keystone Bitters, barrel shape, golden amber, applied tapered collar, sq lip, smooth base, 9-3/4" h 175.00

McKeever's Army Bitters, amber, sloping collared lip, smooth base, 10-5/8" h........................1,700.00

Mist of the Morning Sole Agents Barnett & Lumley, golden amber, sloping collar lip, smooth base, 9-3/4" h 300.00

National Bitters, corn cob shape, puce amber, applied ring lip, smooth base, 12-5/8" h........................350.00

Red Jacket Bitters, Monheimer & Co, sq, amber, tooled lip, smooth base, 9-1/2" h........................100.00

Schroeder's Bitters, Louisville, KY, amber, tooled lip, smooth base, 11-3/4" h........................350.00

Simon's Centennial Bitters, George Washington bust shape, aqua, applied mouth, smooth base, 9-1/8" h 650.00

Suffolk Bitters, Philbrook & Tucker, Boston, pig shape, amber, applied mouth, smooth base, 10-1/8" l 600.00

Sunny Castle Stomach Bitters, Jos. Dudenhoefer, Milwaukee, sq, amber, tooled lip, smooth base, 9" h 125.00

Tippecanoe, Warner & Co, amber, applied mushroom lip, 9" h 95.00

Warner's Safe Bitters, amber, applied mouth, smooth base, 8-1/2" h 265.00

Zingan Bitters, amber, applied mouth, smooth base, 11-7/8" h 150.00

BLACK MEMORABILIA

History: The term "Black memorabilia" refers to a broad range of collectibles that often overlap other collecting fields, e.g., toys and postcards. It also encompasses African artifacts, items created by slaves or related to the slavery era, modern Black cultural contributions to literature, art, etc., and material associated with the Civil Rights Movement and the Black experience throughout history.

The earliest known examples of Black memorabilia include primitive African designs and tribal artifacts. Black Americana dates back to the arrival of African natives upon American shores.

The advent of the 1900s saw an incredible amount and variety of material depicting Blacks, most often in a derogatory and dehumanizing manner that clearly reflected the stereotypical attitude held toward the Black race during this period. The popularity of Black portrayals in this unflattering fashion flourished as the century wore on.

As the growth of the Civil Rights Movement escalated and aroused public awareness to the Black plight, attitudes changed. Public outrage and pressure during the early 1950s eventually put a halt to these offensive stereotypes.

Black representations are still being produced in many forms, but no longer in the demoralizing designs of the past. These modern objects, while not as historically significant as earlier examples, will become the Black memorabilia of tomorrow.

References: Patiki Gibbs, *Black Collectibles Sold in America*, Collector Books, 1987, 1996 value update; Kenneth Goings, *Mammy and Uncle Mose*, Indiana University Press, 1994; Dee Hockenberry, *Enchanting Friends: Collectible Poohs, Raggedies, Golliwoggs & Roosevelt Bears*, Schiffer Publishing, 1995; Kyle Husfloen (ed.), *Black Americana Price Guide*, Antique Trader Books, 1997; Jan Lindenberger, *More Black Memorabilia*, Schiffer Publishing, 1995; J. L. Mashburn, *Black Americana: A Century of History Preserved on Postcards*, Colonial House, 1996; Myla Perkins, *Black Dolls 1820-1991* (1993, 1995 value update), *Book II* (1995), Collector Books; Dawn Reno, *Encyclopedia of Black Collectibles*, Wallace-Homestead/Krause, 1996; J. P. Thompson, *Collecting Black Memorabilia*, L-W Book Sales, 1996; Jean Williams Turner, *Collectible Aunt Jemima*, Schiffer Publishing, 1994.

Periodical: *Blackin*, 559 22nd Ave., Rock Island, IL 61201.

Collectors' Club: Black Memorabilia Collector's Assoc., 2482 Devoe Ter, Bronx, NY 10468.

Abbotts Bitters, pewter top, raised letters, orig paper label, 9" h, $125.

Museums: Great Plains Black Museum, Omaha, NE 68110; Museum of African American History, Detroit, MI.

Andirons, pr, cast iron
    15-1/2" h, 8" w, 14" d, male and female, dressed as servants, hands resting on knees, legs curving outward to work inverted U-shaped base, horizontal bar tapering to upturned point at rear, resting on short rear leg, traces of paint, 19th C 1,200.00
    16-1/2" h, man with comical pose, old pitted surface ..385.00
Ashtray, 4" h figure, tray between legs, boy eating watermelon, ceramic and glass, black, yellow, red, and green 50.00
Autograph
    Document, small folio, Washington Co. D.C., Oct. 31, 1845, bill of sale for slave who is buying his own freedom, "Harry Heard a man of colour and my slave" has paid $300 to Susan Edwards 250.00
    Letter, Papa Bell, handwritten, Negro League, sgd "James 'Cool Papa' Bell" 695.00
    Letter, George Washington Carver, to Ralph Douberly of Columbus, GA, young poet friend, 2 full pgs, 4to, Tuskegee Institute letterhead, orig envelope, Dec. 11, 1931 ...550.00
Automata, papier-mâché, orig condition
    Alligator Bait, black child holding snake beside snapping alligator with light-up eyes, c1930 ....350.00

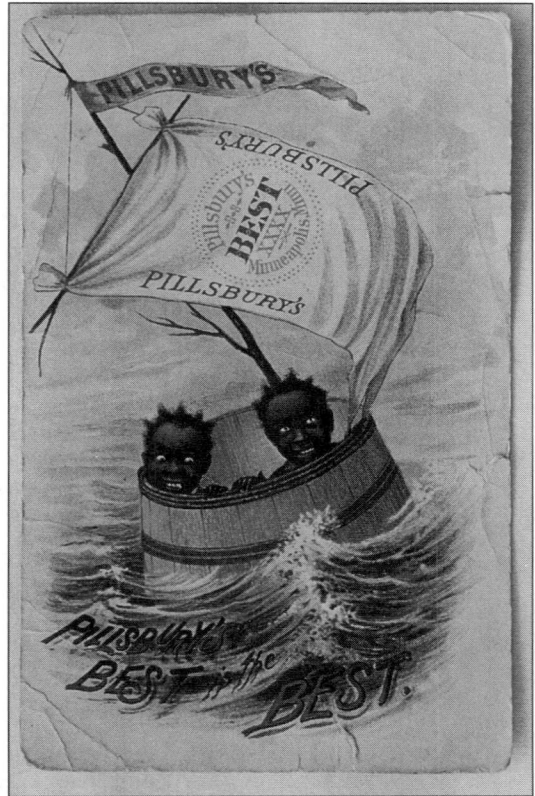

Advertising Trade Card, Pillsbury XXXX Best Flour, two black children floating in tub, flour sack for sale, multicolored, A. Hoen & Co., Baltimore, $20.

Slave woman churning, grass skirt, c1940, 63" h..........750.00
Stu and the Witch Doctor, funhouse figure created by Bill Tracy, 1950s 500.00
Badge, Aunt Jemima Breakfast Club, 4" d litho tin, sepia face, pink lips, yellow and red checkered bandanna, red background, black letters "Eat A Better Breakfast," bar pin fastener, 1960s 40.00
Bank, cast iron
    3" h, two faced boy, painted...60.00
    5-1/2" h, sharecropper, painted gold, black, and red ...125.00
    5-3/4" h, mammy with spoon, painted gold 45.00
Bottle Opener, native lady, winking eye 48.00
Bust, Ubangy Savage, side show exhibit from Gibsonton, FL, hard rubber, glass eyes, carrying case, 24" x 22".......850.00
Cane, alligator and black boy, carved staghorn, 5-1/2" l handle with alligator nipping black boy, 1/2" silver collar, natural orangewood shaft, 1-1/2" metal and iron ferrule, 1880 .... 2,640.00
Cigar Cutter, 6-1/2" h, cast iron figure, wood base, painted, Rohling & Co. 600.00
Cigar Stand, 11" x 37" x 12", carved wood, black man with nodding head, musical mechanism in back....................1,050.00
Clock, 8-1/2" h, painted composition, male face, pendulum tin tie, eyes move, Lux...395.00
Cut-Out Sheet, 8" x 10-1/2", stiff paper sheet, full color, jazz band musicians, intended to be cut out and used as table place cards, Mayfair Novelty Co., 1930s 45.00
Doll, 9" h, carved and painted wood, articulated limbs, folk art, 20th C 175.00
Doorstop, 13-1/2" h, cast iron, Mammy, painted, Littco label. 265.00
Figure
    3-3/4" h, cast lead, boy with cigar, painted, red, yellow, and green 25.00
    5-1/4" h, cast iron, African woman, removable basket on head, yellow and green 225.00
Game, target
    Chocolate Splash, Willis G. Young Mfg., Chicago, ©1916 .... 125.00
    Little Black Sambo, litho metal, stand, 23" h 85.00
Lunch Box, Dixie Kid Tobacco, tin, black child 200.00
Menu, Coon-Chicken Inn, diecut cardboard, one side with logo black face and pictures of different restaurants in various states, framed to show both sides, 12" x 18"................350.00
Notepad and Pencil Holder, 6" x 10-1/2", Mammy, painted hard plastic, 1950s 125.00
Painting, 6" h, 12" l, Cotton Pickers, sgd "WAWalker" lower left, (William Aiken Walker,) oil on board, framed 8,625.00
Pencil Holder, 5-1/2" l, celluloid, alligator with black's head in mouth, c1930 ....20.00
Plaque, 1-3/8" d, painted porcelain, low relief wax figure kneeling chained slave, "Am I not a man and a brother," period frame, 19th C, very minor pigment loss...................................750.00
Salt and Pepper Shakers, pr, boys seated on green peas ..40.00
Sign
    11" x 14", Picaninny Freeze, cardboard, black baby eating watermelon ice cream, ©1922 ....325.00
    13-1/2" x 18-3/4", Green River Whiskey, cardboard, trademark logo of black man holding horse with big jug of "Green River Whiskey," hanging from saddle, orig wood frame with adv...250.00
    15-1/2" x 7-1/2", Gold Dust, two-sided diecut cardboard, one of the Twins, framed to show both sides 150.00
    24" x 36", porcelain, black man riding away on trusty Raleigh bicycle to get away from ferocious lion 600.00
    26" x 33" x 2", plaster, 3-dimensional, three black gentlemen playing flute, guitar, and accordion, Waverly Pure Rye 500.00
    30" x 24", Lime Kiln Club Cigars, paper, comical black town meeting, Calvert Litho Co., © 1882 ....500.00
Teapot, 9" h, 11" w, silver, African man and shell handle supports, flower finial, shell thumb lift, expressive open mouthed human head spout, silver, mkd "800 Missialia"........................750.00

Painting, oil on canvas, The New Puppy, John George Brown, sgd lower right "copyright J. G. Brown N.A.," 25-1/4" h, 20" w, $19,800. Photo courtesy of Jackson's Auctioneers & Appraisers.

Tobacco Tin, pail shape, Nigger Hair Tobacco, yellow, bail handle 400.00
Toy
  8" h, Sweeping Maid, litho tin wind-up, red, yellow, green, and white, Lindstrom Corp. 225.00
  8-1/2" h, Bojangle Dances Again, mechanical, stenciled wood figure, litho tin base, arms, and hat, orig box, Clown Toy Mfg. 200.00
  9" h, Jazzbo-Jim, litho tin wind-up, Unique Art..............300.00
Vending Machine, Smilin Sam, gum, c1901, orig paint, 10" x 15" x 10" 3,200.00
Whirligig, 19" l, 15" h, painted wood, Mammy, scrubs cloths on washboard, c1930...250.00

BLOWN THREE MOLD

History: The Jamestown colony in Virginia introduced glassmaking into America. The artisans used a "free-blown" method.

Blowing molten glass into molds was not introduced into America until the early 1800s. Blown three-mold glass used a predesigned mold that consisted of two, three, or more hinged parts. The glassmaker placed a quantity of molten glass on the tip of a rod or tube, inserted it into the mold, blew air into the tube, waited until the glass cooled, and removed the finished product. The three-part mold is the most common and lends its name to this entire category.

The impressed decorations on blown-mold glass usually are reversed, i.e., what is raised or convex on the outside will be concave on the inside. This is useful in identifying the blown form.

By 1850, American-made glassware was relatively common. Increased demand led to large factories and the creation of a technology which eliminated the smaller companies.

Reference: George S. and Helen McKearin, *American Glass*, reprint, Crown Publishers, 1941, 1948.

Collectors' Club: National Early American Glass Club, P.O. Box 8489, Silver Spring, MD 20907.

Museum: Sandwich Glass Museum, Sandwich, MA.

Bottle, 7-1/4" h, olive green, McKearin GIII-16 ....330.00
Bowl, 5-3/8" d, colorless, folded rim, pontil, 12 diamond base, McKearin GII-6 ....125.00
Celery Vase, colorless, Pittsburgh, McKearin GV-21 ....650.00
Cordial, 2-7/8" h, colorless, ringed base, pontil, heavy circular foot, freehand formed, McKearinGII-18........................550.00
Creamer, 3-1/2" h, colorless, applied handle 125.00
Cruet, 7-3/4" h, cobalt blue, scroll scale pattern, ribbed base, pontil, applied handle, French.....................................265.00
Decanter
  6-3/4" h, olive-amber, pint, attributed to Marlboro Street Glass Works, Keene, NH, some abrasions.........................460.00
  8" h, colorless, 3 applied rings, McKearin GII-18, replaced wheel stopper 110.00

Decanter, three ring, rigaree neck, ground stopper, Mc-Kearin GII-22, 8-1/4" h, $125.

8-1/4" h, colorless, McKearin GII-19, replaced wheel stopper
....115.00
8-1/2" h, light sea green, Kent-Ohio pattern, McKearin GII-6
.... 2,415.00
10" h, colorless, arch and fern design, snake medallion, Mc-
Kearin GIV-7, minor chips, mold imperfections........165.00
11" h, colorless, sunburst in square, minor chips, mold imperfections 150.00
Dish, colorless
5-1/4" d, McKearin GII-16 ....65.00
5-1/2" d, McKearin GII-18 ....50.00
Flask, 5-1/4" h, colorless, arch and diamond pattern, sheared
mouth, pontil, Continental....................................300.00
Flip Glass, colorless
5-1/2" h, McKearin GII-18 ....165.00
6" h, McKearin GII-18 ....125.00
Ink Bottle, 2-1/4" d, deep olive green, McKearin GII-2.......195.00
Miniature, 2-5/8" h decanter, colorless, McKearin GIII-12..165.00
Mustard, 4-1/4" h, colorless, pontil, cork stopper, orig paper label,
McKearin GI-15 ....85.00
Pitcher, 7" h, colorless, base of handle reglued, McKearin GIII-5
....145.00
Salt, basket shape, colorless....................................120.00
Toilet Water Bottle, 5-3/4" h, cobalt blue, tam-o-shanter cap
....300.00
Tumbler, 6-1/4" h, colorless, McKearin GII-19....................155.00
Vase, 9" h, colorless, engraved flowers, leaves, and berries, McK-
earin GV-21 .... 7,500.00
Vinegar Bottle, cobalt blue, ribbed, orig stopper, McKearin GI-7
....285.00
Whiskey Glass, 2-3/8" h, colorless, applied handle, McKearin GII-
18 ....285.00

BOEHM PORCELAINS

History: Edward Marshall Boehm was born on Aug. 21, 1913. Boehm's childhood was spent at the McConogh School, a rural Baltimore County, Maryland, school. He studied animal husbandry at the University of Maryland, serving as manager of Longacre Farms on the Eastern Shore of Maryland upon graduation. After serving in the air force during World War II, Boehm moved to Great Neck, Long Island, and worked as an assistant veterinarian.

In 1949, Boehm opened a pottery studio in Trenton, New Jersey. His initial hard-paste porcelain sculptures consisted of Herefords, Percherons, and dogs. The first five to six years were a struggle, with several partnerships beginning and ending during the period. In the early 1950s, Boehm's art porcelain sculptures began appearing in major department stores. When Eisenhower presented a Boehm sculpture to Queen Elizabeth and Prince Philip during their visit to the United States in 1957, Boehm's career accelerated.

Boehm contributed the ideas for the images and the techniques used to produce the sculptures. Thousands of prototype sculptures were made, with more than 400 put into production. The actual work was done by skilled artisans. Boehm died on Jan. 29, 1969.

In the early 1970s, a second production site, called Boehm Studios, was opened in Malvern, England. The tradition begun by Boehm continues today.

Many collectors specialize in Boehm porcelain birds or flowers. Like all of Boehm's sculptures, pieces in these series are highly detailed, signed, and numbered.

Reference: Reese Palley, *Porcelain Art of Edward Marshall Boehm*, Harrison House, 1988.

Collectors' Club: Boehm Porcelain Society, P.O. Box 5051, Trenton, NJ 08638.

Birds

American Avocet, #40134 ....1,350.00
American Eagle, #498 ....1,000.00
Blue Jay, #436, 4-1/2" h 130.00
Bob White Quail, #407 ....1,400.00
California Quail, #433, pr 1,800.00
Cape May Warbler, 9-1/4" h, one leaf loose 270.00
Cardinal, female, #415, 15" h 700.00
Crested Flycatcher, baby, #458C 250.00
Fledgling Eastern Bluebird, #442 ....175.00
Hummingbird, 8-1/4" h 220.00
Kingfisher, #449..175.00
Oven Bird, 10" h 800.00
Pelican, #4016 ....1,000.00
Ruby Crowned Kinglets, #434 ....900.00
Tumbler Pigeons, #416..850.00

Flowers

Blue Nile Rose, #300-80 ....1,500.00
Crocus, 5" h 200.00
Daisies, #3002 ....800.00
Magnolia Grandiflora, #300-12 ....1,600.00
Pussy Willows, #200-28, pr 300.00
Queen Elizabeth Rose, #30091 ....1,500.00

Other

Madonna La Pieta, 4-1/2" h, c1958 ....115.00

BOHEMIAN GLASS

History: The once independent country of Bohemia, now a part of the Czech Republic, produced a variety of fine glassware: etched, cut, overlay, and colored. Its glassware, which first appeared in America in the early 1820s, continues to be exported to the U.S. today.

Bohemia is known for its "flashed" glass that was produced in the familiar ruby color, as well as in amber, green, blue, and black. Common patterns include Deer and Castle, Deer and Pine Tree, and Vintage.

Most of the Bohemian glass encountered in today's market is from 1875 to 1900. Bohemian-type glass also was made in England, Switzerland, and Germany.

References: Sylvia Petrova and Jean-Luc Olivie (eds.), *Bohemian Glass*, Abrams, 1990; Robert and Deborah Truitt, *Collectible Bohemian Glass*, R & D Glass, 1995.

Reproduction Alert.

Beaker, 5-1/2" h, amber flashed, engraved, animals and building, C scroll panels, flared foot, c1860................................125.00
Bowl, 12-1/2" d, double cut overlay, cobalt blue cut to clear
....265.00
Box, domed lid, ruby flashed, Vintage, engraved clear and frosted grape clusters and vines, gilt brass fittings 165.00
Cologne Bottle, 5" h, cobalt blue, tiered body dec, white and gold flowers and scrolls...175.00
Compote, 7" d, amber flashed, cut leaf and floral dec, green band at top, pedestal base..125.00
Cruet, amber cut to clear, floral arrangement intaglio carved on ruby flashed ground of 3 oval panels with carved frames of flo-

Vase, blue on clear, center medallion of peasant in tree, vertical panels with castle, deer, and partridge, 9" h, pr, $260.

ral swags, 5 cut-to-clear panels at neck, 3 embellished with gold scrolls, all edged in brilliant gold, 16 decorative panels edged in gold, base and stopper both sgd "4"............750.00
Decanter, 14-3/4" h, octagonal, clear with greenish tint, engraved forest and deer scene, orig stopper...........................100.00
Goblet, 6-3/4" h, white and cranberry overlay, thistle form bowl, six teardrop panels alternately enameled with floral bouquets and cut with blocks of diamonds, faceted knob and spreading scalloped foot, gilt trim....................................600.00
Jar, 6" h, quatraform, green, maroon-red threading, metal rim, swing bail handle and cover..250.00
Jug, 8-1/4" h, dark olive green spherical body, irid pulled feather silvery luster, applied offset twisted basket handle, raised pedestal foot, berry prunt at pontil............................1,265.00
Mug, 6" h, ruby flashed, engraved castle and trees, applied clear handle, sgd "Volmer, 1893"...95.00
Perfume Bottle, 7" h, ruby flashed, Deer and Castle, clear and frosted, gold dec..120.00
Powder Box, 4-1/4" d, round, straight sides, flat top, ruby flashed, etched cov with leaping stag, forest setting, landscape and birds on sides, clear base..120.00
Punch Set, 11" h, 11-1/2" d tray, curved oval bow, undertray, frosted clear glass, red glass jewels as centers of gold enameled swags and medallions, bowl elaborately engraved, dated 1875 and relating to Carl Buschbeck............................345.00
Rose Bowl, 7" d, 4" h, green irid, molded swirled organic elements, trifid pewter base rim...245.00
Spill Vase, 6-3/8" h, overlay, cut white to cranberry, 19th C, very minor chips, pr..420.00
Tumbler, 4" h, ruby flashed, cut design, gold dec, 4 pc set
....150.00
Vase
    6-3/4" h, amber etched to clear, deer and forest dec ...135.00
    7-3/8" h, ruby etched to clear, deer and architecture, foliate and abstract dec, price for pr..................................950.00
    9-1/2" h, burgundy red oval body cased with opal white, gilded scroll and swag dec, opal, green, and turquoise glass beaded highlights...435.00
Whiskey Glass, 3-1/4" h, clear, engraved, early 19th C, pr
....250.00

BOOKS, MINIATURE

History: A "miniature" book is any book under three inches high. These books are collected primarily be-

cause of size rather than content or historical significance.

Collecting miniature books was very popular in the late 17th and early 18th centuries, when they were valued for their careful and minute typography, luxurious leather or metallic bindings and generally pleasing illustrations. They were treasured curiosities of wealthy bibliophiles.

The Victorian era experienced a popularity in miniature books, especially almanacs and religious works. The best examples were printed in England and also had exquisite illustrations and bindings.

References: Allen and Patricia Ahearn, *Book Collecting: A Comprehensive Guide*, G. P. Putnam's Sons, 1995; *American Book Prices Current*, Bankcroft Parkman, published annually; Geoffrey Ashall Glaister, *Encyclopedia of the Book*, 2nd ed., available from Spoon River Press, 1996; John R. Gretton, *Baedeker's Guidebooks: A Checklist of English-Language Editions 1861-1939*, available from Spoon River Press, 1994; Sharon and Bob Huxford, *Huxford's Old Book Value Guide*, 9th ed., Collector Books, 1997; Charlie Lovett, *Everybody's Guide to Book Collecting*, available from Spoon River Press, 1993; Ian C. Ellis, *Book Finds*, available from Spoon River Press, 1996; Norma Levarie, *Art & History of Books*, available from Spoon River Press, 1995; Catherine Porter, *Collecting Books*, available from Spoon River Press, 1995; Caroline Seebohm, Estelle Ellis, and Christopher Simon Sykes, *At Home with Books: How Book Lovers Live with and Care for Their Libraries*, available from Spoon River Press, 1996; Henry Toledano, *The Modern Library Price Guide 1917-1995*, available from Spoon River Press, 1995; John Wade, *Tomart's Price Guide to 20th Century Books*, Tomart Publications, 1994; Nancy Wright, *Books: Identification and Price Guide*, Avon Books, 1993; Edward N. Zempel and Linda A. Verkler (eds.), *Book Prices: Used and Rare 1996*, Spoon River Press, 1996; —, *First Editions: A Guide to Identification*, 3rd ed., Spoon River Press, (2319C W Rohmann, Peoria, IL 61604) 1995.

Periodicals: *A B Bookman's Weekly*, P.O. Box AB, Clifton, NJ 07015; *Biblio*, 845 Willamette St., Eugene, OR 87401; *Bookseller*, P.O. Box 8183, Ann Arbor, MI 48107; *Book Source Monthly*, 2007 Syossett Dr., P.O. Box 567, Cazenovia, NY 13035; *Rare Book Bulletin*, P.O. Box 201, Peoria, IL 61650.

Additional Listings: See Miniature Books, Paperback Books, and Western Americana in *Warman's Americana & Collectibles*.

Notes: The prices listed below serve as a model for local-history publications. Compare similar items to this listing–prices are approximately the same nationwide for the identical type of material. More recent publications, i.e., within the last 25 years, rarely are valued above their initial selling price.

Remember, condition is perhaps the greatest factor in correctly pricing a book. Local and regional books will bring slightly higher prices in the areas about which they are written.

Astronomical Diary for 1842, Pocket Almanack for the Year of our Lord 1942, Boston, printed wrappers in pink and black, 88 x 48 mm 125.00

Bible
   Book of Ruth, Maverick Press, NY, 1937, English text, red and black printing, printed on 2" x 32" parchment scroll held by wooden rollers in frame, plastic case 230.00
   Codex Argenteus, Uppsala, 1959, 32 pg pamphlet of story of the Silver Bible, text in Swedish, English, French, and German, self wrappers, contained in silver metal facsimile of the orig 17th C box that houses orig codex, purple silk ribbon pull, 22 x 33 mm 115.00
   Les Pseaumes de David, Henri Dasauzet, Amsterdam, 1730, text and printed music, contemporary green roan gilt, lightly rubbed, 73 x 45 mm 375.00
   Sefer Tehillim, R. Peseach Lebenzahn, Warsaw, 1885, orig brown blindstamped cloth, worn, joints cracked, 60 x 44 mm 165.00
   Sefer Tehillim, Samuel Molcho, Pisa, 1786, Hebrew, with prayers by Chaim Joseph David Azulai, Kabbalistic amulet, 1/4 leather, moderately worn, joints repaired, 70 x 50 mm 420.00
   Tanach, Norman M. Scholtz, Warsaw, c1895, Hebrew, cloth, faded, brass book-shaped folding case, front clasp, 30 x 20 mm 750.00
   The Holy Bible, Old and New Testaments, Glasgow & London, 1911, David Bryce publisher, 28 plates by Charles Bell Birch, emb leather, magnifying glass laid in front cover, chained to wooden lectern, orig box, slightly warped, 150 mm h 345.00

Bijou Illustrations of Christ's Life, Rock & Co, London, engraved title, 31 plates, 29 x 25 mm...................................125.00
Daily Food for Daily Life, David Bryce & Son, Glasgow, From Finger Post series, red morocco with gilt-pictorial front cover, bookplate, 76 x 25 mm 60.00
De Consolation Philosphaie, Boethius, G.J. Caesius, Amsterdam, 1625, engraved title, burgundy morocco gilt, spine ends repaired, 65 x 45 mm 320.00
De Flagorum Usu in Re Veneria...Rariorus Argumenti Libellus, Johann Henrick Meibom, Paris, 1757, contemporary mottled calf, spine with gilt floral tooling, dampstained, wrinkled, bookplate..260.00
Elegy Written on a Country Church-Yard, Thomas Gray, William Lewis Washburn, Audubon, NJ, 1929, limp turquoise morocco gilt, one of 64 numbered copies, 77 x 54 mm 175.00
Enfantines, Marcilly, Paris, c1830, 6 engraved plaques, ivory-covered boards, engraved front cover, 45 x 32 mm.......60.00
Epicteti Enchiridion, et Cebetis Tabula, Epictetus, Plantin, Antwerp, 1616, contemporary morocco gilt, various ink and pencil notations and signatures on endpapers, 65 x 40 mm...420.00
History of the Bible, Lansingburgh, 1820, wood engraved illus, contemporary calf, inked ownership, signatures, foxed, 4 x 35 mm 115.00

History of England from Julius Caesar to George III, R. Snagg, London, 1902, Lilliputian Edition, half cloth, soiled, 45 x 30 mm 140.00
Les Jeux De l'Amour: Annee 1820, Paris, 64 pgs, engraved illus, red morocco with gilt borders and flower in center of each cov, traces of glue bleeding through endpapers, 26 x 19 mm 200.00
Le Petit Chansonnier 1841, Marcilly, Paris, 6 engraved plates, dark green morocco with gilt borders, rose on center of covers, few leaves creased, 25 x 18 mm..........................260.00
Of The Holy Land, J. Hamilton, Philadelphia, 1850, engraved title, 31 plates, flexible roan, cloth gilt, lightly worn, 29 x 25 mm 125.00
Petit Fabuliste, Doumenc Maulde, Paris, late 19th C, 6 plates, leather gilt, unevenly faded, 27 x 21 mm 70.00
Plaisir Et Gaite, Marcilly, Paris, 1836, 8 engraved illus, red morocco with elaborate gilt border and fruit basket on covers, bookplate, 25 x 18 mm..230.00
Schloss's English Bijou Almanac for 1839, London, entirely engraved, orig gilt-stamped stiff wrappers, slipcase, 19 x 15 mm 140.00
Seder Hamisha Ta'aniyot, Hebrew Prayer Book, Amsterdam, 1740, Sephardic rite, brown mottled boards, 80 x 50"..290.00
Taschen-Kalender Fuer Das Jahr 1815, Joseph Zaengl, Munich, 1815, engraved numismatic frontispiece, 12 hand-colored etched plates of Bavarian costume, orig boards, covers soiled, orig board slipcase, with pencil, somewhat worn, 83 x 46 mm 140.00
Taschen-Kalender Fuer Das Jahr 1855, Zittau & Leipzig, Heyn, engraved frontispiece, 4 plates, illus, orig wrappers, 50 x 32 mm 230.00
The Bijou Ministrel: Containing all the Choice, Fashionable and Popular Songs, Turner & Fisher, Philadelphia, 1840, woodcut illus, half morocco, rubbed, foxed, inked ownership name, 80 x 70 mm 460.00
The Famous History of Valentine and Orson, R. Snagg, London, 1901, Lilliputian Folio Edition, half cloth, soiled, 45 x 30 mm 140.00
The Goldfish, The Seventh Princess, Eleanor Farjeon, Rebecca Press, Hyattsville, 1993, bound in one volume, color plates by Edith Bingham, elaborate green dragon bindery, cream morocco gilt, semi-circular clear plastic overlays on front cover showing goldfish, princess on rear, silk folding case with windows, publisher's plastic case, double fore-edge paintings of goldfish on one side, group of swans on other, one of 26 numbered copies, sgd by Rebecca and Edith Bingham, 70 x 55 mm 640.00
The History of the Seven Champions of Christendom, Richard Johnson, R. Snagg, London, 1801, Lilliputian Folio edition, half cloth, soiled and worn, 45" x 30".....................................140.00
The Infant's Library, John Marshall, London, c1800, book 1, engraved plates, orig boards, lightly rubbed, 53 x 48 mm 115.00
The Lullaby Book of Poems, Eugene Field, Ward Schori, Evanston, 1963, illus, designer binding of morocco gilt, vellum, and parchment by Joseph Newman, matching quarter gray leather gilt folding case, fore-edge painting by Don Noble, sgd, 3 fisherman in shoe fishing for stars, one of 600 copies........575.00
The News-Letters of the LXIVMOS, Woodstock, VT, 196, bound volume containing 21 issues from Nov 1927 to Nov 1929, illus, cloth, dampstained, and wrinkled, 8vo 130.00
The Rose Garden...Founded on the Persian by Eben Francis Thompson, Omar Khayyam, Worcester, 1932, limp red morocco, 4 x 6 mm 460.00
Victoria Miniature Almanack and Fashionable Remembrancer for 1856, London, hand-colored litho frontispiece, later gold and multicolored woven cloth, hand-written proverbs and quotations on several blank pages, 63 x 30 mm 140.00
Wine Songs from Omar Khayyam, Omar Khayyam, William Lewis Washburn, Collingswood, NJ, c1930, printed wrappers, contents fold out to 183 x 128 mm sheet, printed envelope, bookplate, 6 x 52 mm 165.00

BOOTJACKS

History: Bootjacks are metal or wooden devices that facilitate the removal of boots. Bootjacks are used by placing the heel of the boot in the U-shaped opening, putting the other foot on the back of the bootjack, and pulling the boot off the front foot.

Brass, 10" l, beetle	95.00

Cast Iron
9-3/4" l, Naughty Nellie, old worn polychrome repair	50.00
10-1/4" l, lyre shape	50.00
11-1/2" l, intertwined scrolls form letter "M"	35.00
11-3/4" l, crick, emb lacy design	30.00
12" l, tree center	35.00

Wood
10" l, tiger stripe maple	25.00
13" l, maple, hand hewn	20.00
15" l, folk art, monkey, painted suit, c1900	35.00
22" l, walnut, heart and diamond openwork	40.00
24" l, pine, rose head nails, pierced for hanging	40.00
25" l; pine, oval ends, sq nails	30.00

Cast Iron, emb "Boot Jack" on prongs, wrench socket on one end, 13-1/2" l, $40.

BOTTLES, GENERAL

History: Cosmetic bottles held special creams, oils, and cosmetics designed to enhance the beauty of the user. Some also claimed, especially on their colorful labels, to cure or provide relief from common ailments.

A number of household items, e.g., cleaning fluids and polishes, required glass storage containers. Many are collected for their fine lithographed labels.

Mineral water bottles contained water from a natural spring. Spring water was favored by health-conscious people between the 1850s and 1900s.

Nursing bottles, used to feed the young and sickly, were a great help to the housewife because of their graduated measure markings, replaceable nipples, and the ease with which they could be cleaned, sterilized, and reused.

References: Ralph & Terry Kovel, *Kovels' Bottles Price List*, 10th ed., Crown Publishers, 1996; Peck and Audie Markota, *Western Blob Top Soda and Mineral Bottles*, 2nd ed., published by authors, 1994; John Odell, *Digger Odell's Official Antique Bottle and Glass Collector Magazine Price Guide Series*, Vols. 1 through 8, published by author (1910 Shawhan Rd., Morrow, OH 45152), 1995;

Diane Ostrander, *Guide to American Nursing Bottles*, 1984, revised ed. by American Collectors of Infant Feeders, 1992; Michael Polak, *Bottles*, Avon Books, 1994; Dick Roller (comp.), *Indiana Glass Factories Notes*, Acorn Press, 1994; Carlo and Dorothy Sellari, *The Standard Old Bottle Price Guide,* 1989, 1997 value update, Collector Books.

Periodicals: *Antique Bottle and Glass Collector*, P.O. Box 187, East Greenville, PA 18041; *Canadian Bottle and Stoneware Collector*, 179D Woodridge Crescent, Nepean, Ontario K2B 7T2 Canada.

Collectors' Clubs: American Collectors of Infant Feeders, 5161 W. 59th St., Indianapolis, IN 46254; Federation of Historical Bottle Collectors, Inc., 88 Sweetbriar Branch, Longwood, FL 32750; Midwest Antique Fruit Jar & Bottle Club, P.O. Box 38, Flat Rock, IN 47234; New England Antique Bottle Club, 120 Commonwealth Rd., Lynn, MA 01904; San Bernardino County Historical Bottle and Collectible Club, P.O. Box 6759, San Bernardino, CA 92412.

Museums: Hawaii Bottle Museum, Honolulu, Hawaii; National Bottle Museum, Ballston Spa, NY; Old Bottle Museum, Salem, NJ.

Additional Listings: Barber Bottles; Bitters Bottles; Figural Bottles; Food Bottles; Ink Bottles; Medicine Bottles; Poison Bottles; Sarsaparilla Bottles; Snuff Bottles. Also see the bottle categories in *Warman's Americana & Collectibles* for more examples.

Beverage

Arny & Shinn, Georgetown, D. C., "This Bottle Is Never Sold," soda water, squat cylindrical, yellow ground, applied heavy collared mouth, smooth base, half pink, professionally cleaned 150.00
Bay Rum, 11-1/4" h, amethyst, blown molded, paneled body, partial label, burst bubble, mold imperfections 375.00
Cole & Southey, Washington, DC, soda water, squat cylindrical, aquamarine, applied sloping collared mouth with ring, smooth base, half pint, professionally cleaned 110.00
M. Flanagan, Petersburg, Va., Philadelphia XXX Porter & Ale, squat cylindrical, green with olive tone, heavy applied collared mouth, iron pontil mark, half pint, overall ext. wear 230.00
W. H. Buck, Norfolk, VA., soda water, squat cylindrical, deep green, applied heavy collard mouth, iron pontil mark, half pint, some ext. wear and scratches 240.00

Cosmetic

De Vry's Dandero-Off Hair Tonic, clear, paper label, 6-1/2" h 15.00
Kickapoo Sage Hair Tonic, cylindrical, cobalt blue, tooled mouth, matching stopper, smooth base, 5" h 160.00
Kranks Cold Cream, milk glass, 2-3/4" h 6.50
Pompeian Massage Cream, amethyst, 2-3/4" h 9.00
Violet Dulce Vanishing Cream, eight panels, 2-1/2" h 7.50

Household

Glue, Bull Dog Brand Liquid Glue, aqua, ring collar, 3-1/2"...6.50
Ink, Waterman's, paper label with bottle of ink, wooden bullet shaped case, orig paper label, 4-1/4" h 10.00
Sewing Machine Oil, Sperm Brand, clear, 5-1/2" h 5.00
Shoe Polish, Everett & Barron Co, oval, clear, 4-3/4" 5.00

Mineral or Spring Water

Albergh A., Spring, VT, cylindrical, apricot amber, applied sloping collared mouth with ring, smooth base, quart, rare with misspelling 1,000.00
Alburgh A., Spring, VT, cylindrical, golden yellow, applied sloping collared mouth with ring, smooth base, quart 800.00
Caladonia Spring, Wheelock, VT, cylindrical, golden amber, applied sloping collared mouth with ring, smooth base, quart 130.00
Chalybeate Water Of The American Spa, Spring Co, N. J., cylindrical, light to medium blue green, olive green slag striation neck, applied heavy collared mouth, smooth base, pint 400.00
Champlain Spring, Alkaline Chalybeate, Highgate, VT, cylindrical, emerald green, applied sloping collared mouth with ring, smooth base, quart..200.00
Gettysburgh Katalysine Water, yellow olive, applied sloping collared mouth with ring, smooth base, quart....................200.00
Guilford Mineral Spring Water, Guilford, VT, cylindrical, yellow-olive, applied sloping collard mouth with ring, smooth base, quart 475.00
Hopkins Chalybeate, Baltimore, cylindrical, dense amber, applied double collared mouth, iron pontil mark, pint.......130.00
Middletown Healing Springs, Grays & Clark, Middletown, VT, cylindrical, yellow apricot amber, applied sloping collared mouth with ring, smooth base, quart 1,200.00
Missiquoi, A. Springs, cylindrical, apricot amber, applied sloping collared mouth with ring, smooth base, quart 150.00
Saratoga (star) Springs, cylindrical, dark olive green, applied sloping collared mouth with ring, smooth base, quart ..300.00
Vermont Spring, Saxe & Co., Sheldon, VT, cylindrical, citron, applied sloping collared mouth with ring, smooth base, quart 600.00

Missisquoi/A/Springs Mineral Water, cylindrical, apricot amber, applied sloping collared mouth with ring, smooth base, qt, some minor ext. wear on reverse, 1860-80, $150. Photo courtesy of Norman C. Heckler & Company.

Nursing

Acme, clear, lay-down, emb...65.00
Cala Nurser, oval, clear, emb, ring on neck, 7-1/8" h.............8.00
Empire Nursing Bottle, bent neck, 6-1/2" h 50.00
Mother's Comfort, clear, turtle type 25.00
Nonpareil Nurser, aqua, 5-1/2" h...20.00

BRASS

History: Brass is a durable, malleable, and ductile metal alloy consisting mainly of copper and zinc. The height of its popularity for utilitarian and decorative art items occurred in the 18th and 19th centuries.

References: Mary Frank Gaston, *Antique Brass & Copper*, Collector Books, 1992, 1994 value update; Rupert Gentle and Rachael Feild, *Domestic Metalwork 1640-1820*, Revised, Antique Collectors' Club, 1994; Henry J. Kaufmann, *Early American Copper, Tin & Brass*, Astragal Press, 1995.

REPRODUCTION ALERT

Many modern reproductions are being made of earlier brass forms, especially such items as buckets, fireplace equipment, and kettles.

Additional Listings: Bells; Candlesticks; Fireplace Equipment; Scientific Instruments.

Andirons, pr
   13-1/4" h, ball top..275.00
   19" h, ringed faceted finials and shaft, spurred arched legs, ball feet, matching shovel and tongs, America, c1840 ....490.00
24" h, spiral turned column and finial, shield at base, paw feet 140.00
Ashtray, 4-1/2" x 5", figural, bull's head, protruding curled horns 50.00
Basinette, 43" l, 35" h, Edwardian, crosier suspending knotted rope basket, oval brass basin, decorative stand, scrolled legs 1,200.00
Bed Warmer
   43" l, Continental, pierced and tooled lid, turned handle 140.00
   45" l, turned wood handle, 19th C 115.00
Book Stand, 9" h, folding, pierced and scrolled, rect base, English 17.00
Boot Scraper, 12" h, 15" d, brass lyre, cast iron pan..........315.00
Bucket, 22-1/2" d, tapered cylinder, rolled rim, iron bail handle, 19th C 350.00
Candlesticks, pr, 7-7/8" h, Victorian, pushups removed, stems resoldered to base...40.00
Candy Scoop, 8" l...35.00
Cigar Cutter, pocket type 40.00
Doorstop, 13" h, sheaf of wheat, green enameled center tie40.00
Fire Fender, 12" h 42-1/2" w, 11-1/2" d, wire work, 19th C, imperfections 805.00
Fire Trivet, 6-1/2" h, 47-1/2" w, 12" d, England, 19th C.......230.00
Incense Burner, 4-3/8" h, foo dog..75.00
Jardiniere, 6-1/2" x 9-1/2", engraved dragon dec, China.....65.00
Kettle
   9-1/2" d, 11-1/2" d, 12-1/2" d, spun, wire bale handle, mkd "Hayden Patent," price for set 280.00
   9-3/4" h, spun, iron bale handle, mkd "Hayden Patent", dents 45.00
Kettle Shelf, 13-3/4" l, oval, reticulated top.........................90.00
Milk Pail...300.00

Candlesticks, pr, Adams style, 7" h, $250.

Mortar and Pestle, 4-1/2" h 65.00
Pie Crimper, 4-1/2" l, wheel on each end 45.00
Plant Stand, 23" h, paw feet...85.00
Sewing Bird, 5" h, cast iron clamp....................................90.00
Skater's Lamp, 6-7/8" h, clear globe, polished, replaced tin bottom and wire bale 85.00
Sundial, 7-7/8" d, octagonal, engraved face, dated 1689..750.00
Taper Jack, 5-1/2" h, scissors form, floral dec, adjustable shaft, pierced base, mkd "H. R.," mid 18th C 420.00
Umbrella Stand, Victorian, 26" h, lozenge form, bands molded with grapevine, foliate sprays, putti..............................165.00
Wall Sconces, pr, 15" h, scrolled arm with best, mask, and foliate dec, single-light, orig gas fitted, American, 19th C.......690.00
Wash Bowl, 15" d, circular handle, Georgian, 19th C 100.00
Wick Trimmer, 9-3/4" l, matching undertray 150.00

BREAD PLATES

History: Beginning in the mid-1880s, special trays or platters were made for serving bread and rolls. Designated "bread plates" by collectors, these small trays or platters can be found in porcelain, glass (especially pattern glass), and metals.

Bread plates often were part of a china or glass set. However, many glass companies made special plates which honored national heroes, commemorated historical or special events, offered a moral maxim, or supported a religious attitude. The subject matter appears either horizontally or vertically. Most of these plates are oval and ten inches in length.

Reference: Anna Maude Stuart, *Bread Plates and Platters*, published by author, 1965.

Additional Listings: Pattern Glass.

Majolica
    Apple and Pear, brown ground, minor wear rim 385.00
    Bamboo and Fern, cobalt blue, Wardles.....................395.00
    Corn, yellow center, minor rim chip on back................440.00
    Give Us This Day Our Daily Bread, cobalt border and basket center, wheat handles 360.00

Picket Fence and Floral, cobalt blue............................385.00
    Pineapple, cobalt blue center 440.00
    Pond Lily, very minor rim repair...............................440.00
    Water Lily, 12" l, surface wear 110.00
Milk Glass, Wheat & Barley 65.00
Mottos, pressed glass, clear
    Be Industrious, handles, oval 50.00
    Give Us this Day, round, rosette center and border 65.00
    Rock of Ages, 12-7/8" l 175.00
    Waste Not Want Not 35.00
Pattern Glass, clear unless otherwise noted
    Actress, Miss Nielson 80.00
    Beaded Grape, sq...35.00
    Butterfly & Fan 40.00
    Canadian, 10" d 45.00
    Cupid and Venus, amber 85.00
    Deer and Pine Tree, amber 110.00
    Egyptian, Cleopatra center....................................60.00
    Good Luck 45.00
    Iowa, motto 80.00
    Lion, amber, lion handles, motto 135.00
    Scroll and Flowers, 12" d 40.00
    Tennessee, colored jewels 75.00
    Train..75.00
Souvenir and Commemorative
    Old State House, sapphire blue 185.00
    Three Presidents, frosted center 95.00
    Virginia Dare 135.00
    William J. Bryan, milk glass 45.00
Silver, sterling, American
    6" d, plain circular form, reeded rim, 19 oz., 2 dwt, price for 8 pc set...300.00
    11" l, oval, fluted sides, Poole, 10 oz., 4 dwt 100.00
    12" l, oval, four claw feet, Francis I pattern, acanthus dec, applied foliage and scrolls on sides, Reed & Barton, 16 oz., 8 dwt 400.00
    12-1/2" d, oval, partly fluted sides, reeded rim, Gorham, 10 oz., 6 dwt 100.00
    14-1/2" l, oval, applied scroll border rim, mkd "E. P. Roberts & Sons," 14 oz., 6 dwt...250.00
Staffordshire, 12" x 15-1/4", rect, raised sides, combed slipware, 19th C 415.00

Majolica, Pineapple, green leaves, brown center, gold, 12-1/2" x 11" w, $400.

BRIDE'S BASKETS

History: A ruffled-edge glass bowl in a metal holder was a popular wedding gift between 1880 and 1910, hence the name "bride's basket." These bowls can be found in most glass types of the period. The metal holder was generally silver plated with a bail handle, thus enhancing the basket image.

Over the years, bowls and bases became separated and married pieces resulted. If the base has been lost, the bowl should be sold separately.

Reference: John Mebane, *Collecting Bride's Baskets and Other Glass Fancies*, Wallace-Homestead, 1976.

REPRODUCTION ALERT

The glass bowls have been reproduced.

Note: Items listed below have a silver-plated holder unless otherwise noted.

8" d, 2-1/8" h, bowl only, satin overlay, shaded pink, clear edging on base, gold and silver sanded flowers and leaves dec, ruffled, off-white lining, ground pontil 155.00

8-1/4" w, sq, cased, deep rose and white ext., whit int., dragon, floral, and leaf dec, ruffled edge, Mt. Washington 675.00

9-1/4" d, Peachblow, yellow flowers dec, orig SP holder ... 225.00

9-3/8" d, cased, shaded pink int. with gold floral dec, clear ruffled rim, whit ext 110.00

9-3/4" d, 2-3/4" h, 3" d, base, bowl only, shaded pink overlay, ruffled edge, white underside, colored enameled flowers and foliage dec, clear and opaque ribbon applied edge 220.00

9-7/8" d, 3" h, 3-3/4" base, bowl only, peachblow, glossy finish, deep pink shading to pale 250.00

10" d, 11" h, Vasa Murrhina, outer amber layer, center layer with hundreds of cream colored spots, random toffee colored spots, dark veins, gold mica flakes, mulberry pink lining, crossed rod thorn handles 635.00

10" w, sq, custard, melon ribbed, enameled daisies, applied rubena crystal rim, twisted and beaded handle, ftd, emb SP frame, mkd "Wilcox" 450.00

10-1/2" d, Hobnail, pink, enameled flowers, ruffled rim, reticulated SP frame 250.00

10-3/4" d, 3-1/2" h, bowl only

Overlay, heavenly blue, enameled white flowers, green leaves, white underside, ruffled 215.00

Satin, shaded purple, white underside, dainty purple and white flowers, lacy foliage dec 225.00

11" x 15-1/2", satin, deep rose, enamel swan and floral dec, heavy bronze holder with birds perched on top 425.00

11-1/8" d, 3-3/4" h, bowl only, satin, brown shaded to cream overlay, raised dots, dainty gold and silver flowers and leaves dec, ruffled 250.00

11-3/8" d, 3-1/4" h, 2-7/8" d base, bowl only, maroon shaded to cream overlay, fancy leaf edges with circle and slot emb designs, dainty enameled pink flowers, gold leaves, white underside 215.00

11-1/2" d, 3-5/8" h, bowl only, shaded green overlay satin, ruffled emb lattice edge, white underside 210.00

14" d, satin, rose pink, scalloped, rippled, ribbed, and swirled, lacy allover enamel and gold flower pattern, figural SP base with hummingbird, sgd "Eagle & Co." 1,200.00

BRISTOL GLASS

History: Bristol glass is a designation given to a semi-opaque glass, usually decorated with enamel and cased with another color.

Initially, the term referred only to glass made in Bristol, England, in the 17th and 18th centuries. By the Victorian era, firms on the Continent and in America were copying the glass and its forms.

Cased bowl, white ext., pink int., pink ruffled edge, SP frame with foliate dec, $195.

Vases, window and curtain motif, lake scene in background, fluted, scalloped, gold highlights, pedestal foot, 11-1/8" h, pr, $80.

Biscuit Jar, 6-1/2" h, white, brown leaves and white flowers 165.00

Bowl, light blue, Cupid playing mandolin, gold trim.............40.00

Box, cov, 2-1/2" d, round, hinged, Cupid on lid, purple floral dec 150.00

Cake Stand, celadon green, enameled herons in flight, gold trim 135.00

Candlesticks, pr, 7" h, soft green, gold band......................75.00

Decanter, 11-1/2" h, ruffled stopper, enameled flowers and butterfly 75.00

Dresser Set, two cologne bottles, cov powder jar, white, gilt butterflies dec, clear stoppers..75.00

Ewer, 6-3/8" h, 2-5/8" d, pink ground, fancy gold designs, bands, and leaves, applied handle with gold trim 135.00

Finger Bowl, 4-3/8" d, blue, faceted sides, early 20th C, 8 pc set 500.00

Hatpin Holder, 6-1/8" h, ftd, blue, enameled jewels, gold dec100.00

Mug, 5" h, white, eagle and "Liberty" 375.00

Perfume Bottle, 3-1/4" h, squatty, blue, gold band, white enameled flowers and leaves, matching stopper 100.00

Puff Box, cov, round, blue, gold dec....................................35.00

Rose bowl, 3-1/2" d, shaded blue, crimped edge................65.00

Sugar Shaker, 4-3/4" h, white, hp flowers...........................60.00

Sweetmeat Jar, 3" x 5-1/2", deep pink, enameled flying duck, leaves, blue flower dec, white lining, SP rim, lid, and bail handle..110.00

Urn, 18" h, pink, boy and girl with lamp..............................550.00

Vase, 8-1/2" h, light pink shading to dark pink, hp enameled design 65.00

BRITISH ROYALTY COMMEMORATIVES

History: British commemorative china, souvenirs to commemorate coronations and other royal events, dates from the 1600s, with the early pieces being rather crude in design and form. With the development of transfer printing, c1780, the images on the wares more closely resembled the monarchs.

Few commemorative pieces predating Queen Victoria's reign are found today at popular prices. Items associated with Queen Elizabeth II and her children, e.g., the wedding of HRH Prince Andrew and Miss Sarah Ferguson and the subsequent birth of their daughter, HRH Princess Beatrice, are very common.

Some British Royalty commemoratives are easily recognized by their portraits of past or present monarchs. Some may be in silhouette profile. Royal symbols include crowns, dragons, royal coats of arms, national flowers, swords, scepters, dates, messages, and monograms.

References: Susan and Al Bagdade, *Warman's English & Continental Pottery & Porcelain*, 2nd ed., Wallace-Homestead, 1991; Douglas H. Flynn and Alan H. Bolton, *British Royalty Commemoratives*, Schiffer Publishing, 1994; Lincoln Hallinan, *British Commemoratives*, Antique Collectors' Club, 1993; Eric Knowles, *Miller's Royal Memorabilia*, Reed Consumer Books, 1994.

Collectors' Club: Commemorative Collector's Soc., The Gardens, Gainsborough Rd., Winthrope, New Newark, Nottingham NG24 2NR England.

Additional Listings: See *Warman's Americana & Collectibles* for more examples.

Autograph
   Charles II, document, sgd as king, 1 page, folio, Whitehall, May 26, 1676, ordering Lord Chancellor Heneage Finch to deliver a bill, countersigned at bottom by Thomas Osborne, Earl of Danby, as Lord High Treasurer 1,075.00

   Edward VII, letter, sgd "Albert Edward," 3 pages, 8vo, Abergeldie Castle, Sept. 1, to Choimsedale, relating to grouse hunting 250.00

   Elizabeth I, letter, sgd as Queen, 1 page, oblong folio, London, Jan. 21, 1592, "Our Trustie and wellbeloved William Colles," concerning money to be paid toward "...the defense of our Realms...," striking signature, upper right corner of letter missing, integral address intact 7,900.00

   George I, broadside, sgd as Elector of Hanover, in German, 1 page, small folio, Hanover, Dec. 31, 1701, approves request by the Duchy of Catenberg that year's tithe be paid entirely in corn, with complete translation, chip in left margin...900.00

   George II, letter, sgd as Prince of Wales, in French, 2 pages, 4to, Leicester House, Jan.11/22, 1723, to Madame Marygrove, sympathies over loss of relation 1,200.00

   Henry VII, document, sgd with woodcut stamped signature, 1 page irregularly cut, 8" x 9", Greenwich, Feb. 14 (c1509), to Sir Edward Poynings, Comptroller of the Household and Lord Warden of the Cinque Ports, regarding 7 lasts and 8 barrels of herring to be sold without delay, torn on right edge 3,500.00

   James II, document, sgd as Duke of York and Lord High Admiral, 1 page, 4to, Whitehall, June 25, 1660, concerning payment for bill 975.00

   William IV, document, sgd as king, 1 page 4to, Bushby House, Sept. 18, 1827, appoints David Davis as his personal surgeon, red wax seal next to signature 350.00

Beaker, George IV and Elizabeth, 1937 Coronation, Grindley, 4" h...45.00

Bowl
   Charles, 1969 Investiture, Aynsley, 5-1/2" d...................60.00
   Edward VII, 1937 Coronation, profile in well, pressed glass, 10" d 70.00

Pitcher, Elizabeth II Coronation, Burleigh Ware, E. T. Bailey Sculpt., 1952, 8-1/2" h, $200.

Elizabeth II, 1953 Coronation, pressed glass, 4-3/4" h ...60.00
George VI and Elizabeth, 1937 Coronation, coat of arms, Paragon, 5-1/2" d 55.00
Box, cov, Elizabeth the Queen Mother, 1980, 80th Birthday, color portrait, Crown Staffordshire, 4" d 75.00
Brochure, Canadian Visit, 1959, Queen Elizabeth II and Prince Philip, opening of St. Lawrence Seaway, 8-1/2" x 11" 15.00
Cup and Saucer
   Andrew and Sarah, 1986 Wedding, Colclough...............30.00
   Edward VII and Alexandra, 1888 Silver Wedding Anniversary, coat of arms.. 185.00
   Elizabeth II, portrait flanked by flags, coronation, pairs of flags inside cup and on saucer, mkd "Alfred Meakin England," 3" h x 3-1/4" d cup, 6" d saucer 45.00
   George V and Mary, 1911 Coronation, color portraits 60.00
Figure, 5-1/4" h, Elizabeth I, carved ivory, lower section of skirt hinged to reveal triptych of Queen and Sir Walter Raleigh, Continental, 19th C, hairlines...550.00
Handkerchief, white fabric, small red, white, and blue stitched British flag above printed full color view across Thames towards Buckingham Palace, Westminster Abbey, rural countryside scenes on border, May 1937, orig small cardboard price tag, 10-1/2" x 11" 20.00
Jug
   Elizabeth II, 1953 Coronation, emb crowning scene, Burleigh Ware, 8-1/4" h 250.00
   Victoria, 1887 Gold Jubilee, black and white portraits, 5" h 145.00
Lithophane, cup, crown, and cypher, 2-3/4" h
   Alexandra, 1902 .... 195.00
   George V, 1911 .... 165.00
Loving Cup
   Elizabeth II and Philip, 1972 Silver Wedding Anniversary, Paragon, 3" h... 175.00
   George VI and Elizabeth, 1937 Coronation, brown Marcus Adams portraits, 3-1/4" h...................................145.00
Magic Lantern Slide, Victoria and Albert.............................15.00
Medallion, Anne and Mark, 1973 Wedding, molded pale pink portraits, pink frame, Hutchenreuther 3-1/4" d.......................60.00
Mug
   Edward VIII, Coronation, 1937, sepia portrait of king flanked by multicolored flags, reverse with Union Jack and Flag of commonwealth, flanking names of some of the nations, topped by crown, gold trim, 2-1/2" h, 2-1/2" d, crest mark and "Empire England"..50.00
   Elizabeth II
      Coronation, portrait of Queen facing left, "Coronation of Her Majesty Queen Elizabeth" on reverse, gold trim, 3" h, 3" d, crown and "Radfords Bone China Made in England" mark 45.00
      Silver Jubilee, Queen in circle flanked by flags, topped by crown, 3-1/2" h, 3" d, royal crest on back, mkd "Made in England" in raised letters, red and yellow crown mark 35.00
Paperweight
   Charles and Diana, 1981 Wedding, white sulphide portraits, cobalt blue ground, CR Albret, France, 2-3/4" d 175.00
   Edward VIII, 1937 Coronation, black and white portrait, 4-1/4" d 50.00
Pinback Button
   Edward VIII, multicolored, for 1937 coronation, 7/8" d 15.00
   George V and Queen Mary Silver Jubilee, black and white oval portraits, pale turquoise ground, full color British flags, 1" d 20.00
   George VI and Elizabeth, black and white, May 2, 1937, coronation, 1-1/4"...20.00
   Prince of Wales, c1910 portrait, 7/8" d 30.00
   Prince of Wales, 1920, Australian-made, celluloid, inscribed "Souvenir Adelaide 1920", color portrait captioned "H.R.H. The Prince Of Wales Australian Tour," 1-1/4" 20.00

Plate, Edward VII & Alexandra, portraits in center, cobalt blue border, gilt trim, pierced for hanging, 9" d, $65.

   Victoria, Queen of England, multicolored, from 1900 series, 1-1/4" d...35.00
Pin Tray, Elizabeth II, 1977 Silver Jubilee, black silhouette, Coalport, 3-3/4" d..35.00
Pitcher, 8-3/4" h, marriage of Princess Charlotte and Prince Leopold, c1816, relief dec, double scroll handle, Pratt ware, minor enamel loss 1,265.00
Plate
   Edward VII and Alexandra, 1902 Coronation, blue and white, Royal Copenhagen, 7" d...200.00
   George VI and Elizabeth, Canadian visit, 1939, word "Canada" in relief under portraits in center, "King George IV, Queen Elizabeth, 1939" in relief on rim.......................65.00
   Princess Elizabeth and Duke of Edinburgh, visit to Canada, October 1951, maroon colored portraits flanked by flags of Great Britain and Canada, gold trim, mkd "Casidian Guaranteed 22K Gold," 10" d, some crazing 60.00
Program
   Prince of Wales Royal Investiture, July 1, 1969, glossy paper, 6-1/2" x 9"..12.00
   Queen Elizabeth II, Silver Jubilee, 1977, 42 pgs, glossy paper, 8-1/4" x 11-3/4"..10.00
Snuff Box, 3" d, round, bronze, round, dark patina, angel riding lion with "Regent," reverse emb inscription "In record of the reign of George III" covered by sunburst and cross, visible on int., engraved paper bust and "H.R.H. George Augustus Frederick Prince Regent...Feb 1811".............................2,100.00
Teapot
   Charlotte, 1817 In Memoriam, black and white dec, 6" h 275.00
   Victoria, 1897 Diamond Jubilee, color coat of arms, Aynsley 225.00
Tin
   Queen Elizabeth II, coronation
      Round, Queen Elizabeth II on horseback saluting, side mkd "Souvenir of the Coronation of H. M. Queen Elizabeth II, June 2nd, 1953," bottom mkd "Henry Thorne & Co, Ltd. Toffee & Chocolate Manufacturers Leeds England," 5" d, 3/4" h, top slightly pitted...35.00
      Square, Queen Elizabeth II on horseback, full view, mkd "Sharp Assorted Toffee," stamped "Made In England by

Edward Sharp & Sons Ltd. Of Maidstone Kent," 7 x 6 x 2", minor scratches and edge rubbing 40.00
Queen Elizabeth II and Prince Philip, round, coats of arms of the commonwealth nations on sides alternating with pictures of Buckingham Palace, Westminster Abbey, Windsor Castle, and Palace of Holyrood, mkd "Huntley & Palmer Biscuits Reading & London, England," 7-1/2" d.........30.00
Prince of Wales, wedding, portrait of Charles and Diana on cover and back, heraldic picture on other sides, 3-1/4" w, 3-1/4" d, 4-1/4" h, mkd "Container Made in England" 45.00

BRONZE

History: Bronze is an alloy of copper, tin, and traces of other metals. It has been used since Biblical times not only for art objects, but also for utilitarian wares. After a slump in the Middle Ages, the use of bronze was revived in the 17th century and continued to be popular until the early 20th century.

References: Harold Berman, *Bronzes: Sculptors & Founders 1800-1930*, Vols. 1-4 and Index, distributed by Schiffer Publishing, 1996; *Catalog of the Society des Beaux Arts, Paris*, Schiffer Publishing, 1995 reprint; *1886 Catalog of the French Bronze Foundry of F. Barbedienne of Paris*, Schiffer Publishing, 1995 reprint; Pierre Kjellberg, *Bronzes of the Nineteenth Century*, Schiffer Publishing, 1994; Lynne and Fritz Weber, *Jacobsen's Thirteenth Painting and Bronze Price Guide*, January 1992 to January 1994, Weber Publications, 1994.

Notes: Do not confuse a "bronzed" object with a true bronze. A bronzed item usually is made of white metal and then coated with a reddish-brown material to give it a bronze appearance. A magnet will stick to it but not to anything made of true bronze.

A signed bronze commands a higher market price than an unsigned one. There also are "signed" reproductions on the market. It is very important to know the history of the mold and the background of the foundry.

Ashtray, 7-1/2" d, circular leaf form, applied salamander, c1910 ....110.00
Bookends, pr
6-3/4" h, cupid, swathed in swirl of fabric, tip-toeing with bow in hand, other young girl with flowing hair and bouquet in hand, inscribed "Cast by Griffoul, Newark, NJ," early 20th C 420.00
9" h, daffodil silhouette, imp mark of G. Thew, 1928 .....225.00
Cake Basket, 9-1/2" d, 7-5/8" h, circular bowl, molded pedestal, flat arch handle with enameled mottled red, pink, and amber enamel, imp "Favrile, Louis C. Tiffany Furnaces, IN 511," monogram, c1918 ....1,300.00
Candelabra, pr, 21" h, 3 acanthus and scrolled arms, reeded urn form candle sockets, turned and floral banding, French Empire 1,750.00
Corkscrew, 5" l, leering bacchante, two herm figures, Victorian 420.00
Cricket Cage, 5-3/4" h 85.00
Desk Accessory, 8-1/2" h, equestrian, weight and thermometer, sgd "Zimmerman," German..............................375.00
Dresser Box, 3-1/2" l, portrait of woman on lid, sgd "Perin" 150.00
Figure
5" h, robin, cold painted, Vienna 365.00
9-1/4" h, young girl in cape, mkd "Salon des Beaux Arts, 1903, Bronze Garanti Au Titre, L.V. Deposee, #5589" 600.00

Figure, boy with ram, after Barye, 4" h, $750.

16-3/4" h, young woman, wearing bathing suit, seated, one bent leg tucked under other bent leg, extended arm resting on leg, hand clutching ankle, head turned to left.....415.00

17-1/2" h, equestrian group, falconer astride rearing horse, marble base, gold patination, after V. Tigner, inscribed "H. Miller," Austrian, 20th C 750.00

Door Push Plate, Windsor pattern, by Sargent, c1885, 16" h, 4" w, $150. Photo courtesy of Web Wilson's Antique Hardware Auctions.

32" h, nude Bacchante, sgd "I.V.I. Robert," bacchanalian beast base, 20th C 1,510.00
Match Safe, Zodiac pattern, matching ashtray, sgd "Tiffany Studios, New York" 175.00
Miniature, cannon, 10" l, barrel molded with crown, Portuguese 100.00
Pitcher, 6" h, baluster shape, tapering spout, applied scrolled handle, low relief dec, Continental, 16th C 600.00
Planter, 8" h, squatty, cut-out coin dec, cut-out handles, cylindrical feet, Japan, late 19th C 525.00
Sculpture, 13" h, 29" l, nude woman leaning back, balancing on one foot, large green marble base, figure sgd "L-32 V. Salmones 9/10" 660.00
Snuff Box, cov, 3" l, round, dark patina, angel riding lion with "Regent," reverse emb inscription "In record of the reign of George III" covered by sunburst and cross, visible on int., engraved paper bust and "H.R.H. George Augustus Frederick Prince Regent...Feb 1811" 2,100.00
Standish, 16" l, retriever flanked by pair of foliate molded inkwells, oval verte antico marble base, French, early 20th C 435.00
Statue, 20" h, Mercury, sgd "M. Amodie, Napoli," 750.00
Vase
   15" h, Neoclassical style, after Clodion, baluster form, continuous bacchanalian scene of infant satyrs, putti, and goats, light brown patina 345.00
   17-1/2" h, Neoclassical style, Barbedienne, bacchantes picking grapes, late 19th C, pr 3,110.00
Wall Plaque
   10-3/4" w, 13-1/4" h, oval, Indian head, greenish patina 165.00
   21-1/4" d, shield-form, Classical Revival, raised and pointed center section, continuous battle scene, Continental, late 19th C 500.00

BUFFALO POTTERY

History: Buffalo Pottery Co., Buffalo, New York, was chartered in 1901. The first kiln was fired in October 1903. Larkin Soap Company established Buffalo Pottery to produce premiums for its extensive mail-order business. Wares also were sold to the public by better department and jewelry stores. Elbert Hubbard and Frank Lloyd Wright, who designed the Larkin Administration Building in Buffalo in 1904, were two prominent names associated with the Larkin Company.

Early Buffalo Pottery production consisted mainly of semi-vitreous china dinner sets. Buffalo was the first pottery in the United States to produce successfully the Blue Willow pattern. Buffalo also made a line of hand-decorated, multicolored willow ware, called Gaudy Willow. Other early items include a series of game, fowl, and fish sets, pitchers, jugs, and a line of commemorative, historical, and advertising plates and mugs.

From 1908 to 1909, and again from 1921 to 1923, Buffalo Pottery produced the line for which it is most famous—Deldare Ware. The earliest of this olive green, semi-vitreous china displays hand-decorated scenes from English artist Cecil Aldin's *Fallowfield Hunt*. Hunt scenes were done only from 1908 to 1909. English village scenes also were characteristic of the ware and were used during both periods. Most pieces are artist signed.

In 1911, Buffalo Pottery produced Emerald Deldare, which used scenes from Goldsmith's *The Three Tours of Dr. Syntax* and an Art Nouveau-type border. Completely decorated Art Nouveau pieces also were made.

Abino, introduced in 1912, had a Deldare body and displayed scenes of sailboats, windmills, or the sea. Rust was the main color used, and all pieces were signed by the artist and numbered.

In 1915, the manufacturing process was modernized, giving the company the ability to produce vitrified china. Consequently, hotel and institutional ware became the main production items, with hand-decorated ware deemphasized. The Buffalo firm became a leader in producing and designing the most-famous railroad, hotel, and restaurant patterns. These wares, especially railroad items, are eagerly sought by collectors.

In the early 1920s, fine china was made for home use. Bluebird is one of the patterns from this era. In 1950 Buffalo made their first Christmas plate. These were given away to customers and employees primarily from 1950 to 1960. However, it is known that Hample Equipment Co. ordered some as late as 1962. The Christmas plates are very scarce in today's resale market.

The Buffalo China Company made "Buffalo Pottery" and "Buffalo China"—the difference being that one is semi-vitreous ware and the other vitrified. In 1956, the company was reorganized, and Buffalo China became the corporate name. Today Buffalo China is owned by Oneida Silver Company. The Larkin family no longer is involved.

Marks: Blue Willow pattern is marked "First Old Willow Ware Mfg. in America."

Reference: Seymour and Violet Altman, *Book of Buffalo Pottery*, reprinted by Schiffer Publishing, 1987.

Abino Ware

Candlestick, 9" h, sailing ships, 1913 .... 475.00
Pitcher, 7" h, Portland Head Light 700.00
Tankard, 10-1/2" h, sailing scene 900.00

Advertising Ware

Mug, 4-1/2" h, Calumet Club 110.00
Plate
   Automobile Club of Buffalo.. 25.00
   Hotel Astor, Art Nouveau 25.00
Platter, 12" l, Elkwood 25.00

Deldare

Calling Card Tray
   Street scene.. 395.00
   Three Pigeons... 450.00
Candlesticks, pr, street scene... 895.00
Cereal Bowl, Fallowfield Hunt
   6" d... 295.00
   9" d... 495.00
Chop Plate, 14" d
   Fallowfield Hunt 795.00
   Street scene.. 695.00
Cup and Saucer, street scene... 225.00
Fruit Bowl, street scene.. 575.00
Hair Receiver, street scene... 495.00
Jardiniere, street scene.. 995.00

Luncheon Service, 2-3/4" h creamer; six 6-1/4" dessert plate; six 8-1/2" d luncheon plates; 5-3/4" h pitcher; six 6" d saucers; 7" d serving bowl; 9" d serving bowl; 4" h sugar; six 4-1/4" d tea-cups; all with stamp mark, price for set......................1,955.00

Mug

   3-1/2" h

      Fallowfield Hunt 395.00

      Street scene 350.00

   4-1/2" h

      Fallowfield Hunt 475.00

      Street scene 395.00

      Three Pigeons, hairline 150.00

Pin Tray, street scene 325.00

Pitcher

   Street scene

      6" h..495.00

      7" h..550.00

      8" h..750.00

      9" h..775.00

   The Great Controversy, 7" w, 12" h, sgd "W. Fozter," stamped mark 290.00

Plate, 10" d, Fallowfield Hunt...295.00

Powder Jar, street scene...395.00

Punch Cup, Fallowfield Hunt 375.00

Soup Plate, 9" d, street scene 425.00

Tankard, Three Pigeons 1,175.00

Teapot, cov, large, street scene..395.00

Tea Tile

   Fallowfield Hunt 395.00

   Street scene...395.00

Tea Tray, street scene..650.00

Vase

   7" h, street scene..450.00

   7-3/4" h, 6-1/2" d, King Fisher, green and white dec, olive ground, stamped mark, artist signature 1,380.00

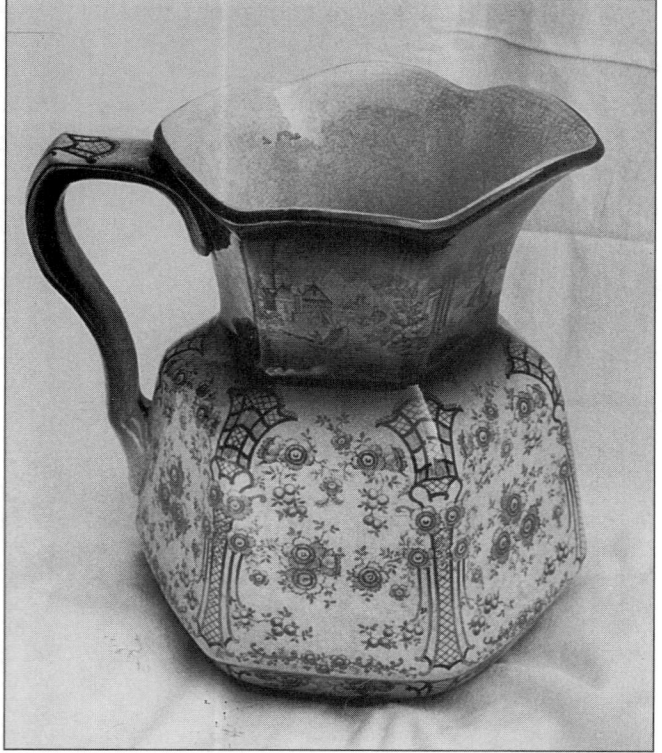

Jug, Mason, emerald green, 1907, sgd, 8-1/4" h, $325.

Emerald Deldare

Creamer...450.00

Fruit Bowl..1,450.00

Mug, 4-1/2" h 475.00

Vase, 8-1/2" h, 6-1/2" h, stylized foliate motif, shades of green and white, olive ground, stamp mark 810.00

Miscellaneous

Jug

   Chrysanthemum 495.00

   Robin Hood..550.00

   Roger Williams 595.00

Plate, Willow, 9" d 20.00

BURMESE GLASS

History: Burmese glass is a translucent art glass originated by Frederick Shirley and manufactured by the Mt. Washington Glass Co., New Bedford, Massachusetts, from 1885 to c1891.

Burmese glass colors shade from a soft lemon to a salmon pink. Uranium was used to attain the yellow color, and gold was added to the batch so that on reheating, one end turned pink. Upon reheating again, the edges would revert to the yellow coloring. The blending of the colors was so gradual that it is difficult to determine where one color ends and the other begins.

Although some of the glass has a glossy surface, most pieces were acid finished. The majority of the items were free blown, but some were blown molded in a ribbed, hobnail, or diamond-quilted design.

American-made Burmese is quite thin and, therefore, is fragile and brittle. English Burmese was made by Thos. Webb & Sons. Out of deference to Queen Victoria, they called their wares "Queen's Burmese."

Collectors Club: Mount Washington Art Glass Society, P.O. Box 24094, Fort Worth, TX 76124-1094.

REPRODUCTION ALERT

Reproductions abound in almost every form. Since uranium can no longer be used, some of the reproductions are easy to spot. In the 1950s, Gunderson produced many pieces in imitation of Burmese.

Abbreviations:

   MW   Mount Washington

   Wb   Webb

   a.f.   acid finish

   s.f.   shiny finish

Advisors: Clarence and Betty Maier.

Bon Bon Bowl, 2" h, 5-1/4" l, 4-1/2" w, Mt. Washington, smooth satin finish, rectangular bowl, bulged-out optic ribbed sides with turned-in edges 285.00

Charger, 10" d, shallow, disk shape..................................365.00

Cruet

   6-1/2" h, three striking chrysanthemum blossoms, two white and one yellow, coral colored detail stripes mushroom stopper, signed "88" in enamel 2,950.00

   7" h, shiny finish, mushroom stopper, each rib has hint of pink, refired buttery yellow tip of spout 1,250.00

Vase, Queen's Ware, Mt. Washington, 9" h, $2,750. Photo courtesy of Clarence and Betty Maier.

Fairy Lamp

    3-3/4" h, Webb, pyramid, Burmese shade, unsigned clear glass base 145.00

    4" h, pyramid, pressed glass base has molded-in "S. Clarke Fairy Pyramid" and dancing fairy logo signature 335.00

    5-1/2" h, 5-3/4" w, Webb, Cricklite, short crimped skirt flares out from the top of the bowl-shaped base, impressed signature "Thos. Webb & Sons Queens Burmeseware Patented," clear glass candle cup is signed, "S Clarke Fairy Trade Mark Patent," unused wax candle 950.00

    6" h, 7-1/2" d spreading, skirt-like, pleated base, two acid etched signatures, "Thos Webb & Sons Queen's Burmeseware Patented" and "S. Clarke's Fairy Patent Trade Mark," clear glass candle cup signed, "Clarke's Criklite Trade Mark" 950.00

Rose Bowl, 3-1/4" h, Webb, prunus blossom dec, sq top .. 285.00

Toothpick Holder, shiny, soft peach blush fading to buttery-yellow, eggshell-thin body 435.00

Tumbler, Mt. Washington

    Pastel salmon shading to a creamy-yellow 285.00

    Shiny finish, egg-shell thin satin body 375.00

Vase

    6" h, English, white, front has line-drawn, sepia-colored decoration in Chinoiserie motif depicting oriental man after releasing arrow from bow striking goose in mid air, reverse side is continuation of scene, elaborate border encircling shoulder 950.00

    7" h, Mt. Washington, lily, delicate blush to the mouth of the "lily," refired yellow rim 285.00

    8" h, gourd shape, roses and forget-me-nots, three lovely peach-colored rose blossoms cling to leafed branch which swirl down rim, around body and down to the base, entwining strands of turquoise-colored forget-me-not blossoms, double gourd shaped, 8" tall 1,250.00

    9-1/2" d, h, encrusted gold, crown Milano, thorny rose branches laden with single petaled blossoms, buds and leaves, 9-1/2" tall, original paper label 1,450.00

    11" h, 6" d base, white daisies with distinctive yellow-dot centers 1,750.00

    23-1/2" h, circa 1890 .... 1,250.00

    White, faint blush of color on collar and shoulder, golden bird flying toward golden moon decoration, swags of stylized golden bamboo, branches of baby-blue blossoms, Chinoiserie motif 750.00

    Whiskey Taster, 2-3/4" tall, molded-in elongated diamond quilted design 285.00

BUSTS

History: The portrait bust has its origins in pagan and Christian traditions. Greek and Roman heroes dominate the earliest examples. Later, images of Christian saints were used. Busts of the "ordinary man" first appeared during the Renaissance.

During the 18th and 19th centuries, nobility, poets, and other notable people were the most frequent subjects, especially on those busts designed for use in a home library. Because of the large number of these library busts, excellent examples can be found at reasonable prices, depending on artist, subject, and material.

Reference: Lynne and Fritz Weber, *Jacobsen's Thirteenth Painting and Bronze Price Guide*, January 1992 to January 1994, Weber Publications, 1994.

Additional Listings: Ivory; Parian Ware; Soapstone; Wedgwood.

Charles V, 29-1/2" h, majolica, intaglio of Order of the Golden Fleece around neck, scrolling foliage, mustard, rust, and green edge epaulets, 16th C 2,500.00

Child

    6-3/4" h, bronze, gilt, green onyx base, mkd "S. Klaber & Co. Founder, NY" 85.00

    21" h, carved sandstone, sitter Shella Estelle Russell-Taylor, Arthur Bryan 385.00

Franklin, Benjamin, 15" h, carved oak, old brown alligatored finish, black carved base, sgd "Harris" 750.00

Goddess Hera, 28" h, lead, diadem in parted hair, loose tunic tied at shoulder, 18th C 1,200.00

Joan of Arc, 61" h, carved Italian Carrara and Sienna marble, matching columnar pedestal, c1885 .... 2,875.00

Virgin Mary, 18-1/2" h, bronze, two tone finish, black granite base, sgd "F. de Luca" 115.00

Washington, George, 35" h, cast plaster, orig bronze finish
.... 125.00

George Washington, black, plaster, sgd, dated 1861, 9" h, $75.

Woman
  11" h, floral headdress, carved stone, black base, unknown
    sculptor 475.00
  16" h, alabaster, Renaissance style, marble base 425.00
  18" h, bisque, Classical, smiling, wearing silver and gold
    trimmed helmet with gilt eagle mounted on top, gold socle,
    France, 19th C 625.00
  21-3/4" h, young woman, Italian faience, polychromed Renais-
    sance attire, initialed 350.00

BUTTER PRINTS

History: There are two types of butter prints: butter molds and butter stamps. Butter molds are generally of three-piece construction–the design, the screw-in handle, and the case. Molds both shape and stamp the butter at the same time. Butter stamps are generally of one-piece construction but can be of two-piece construction if the handle is from a separate piece of wood. Stamps decorate the top of butter after it is molded.

The earliest prints are one piece and were hand carved, often heavily and deeply. Later prints were factory made with the design forced into the wood by a metal die.

Some of the most common designs are sheaves of wheat, leaves, flowers, and pineapples. Animal designs and Germanic tulips are difficult to find. Prints with designs on both sides are rare, as are those in unusual shapes, such as half-rounded or lollipop.

Reference: Paul E. Kindig, *Butter Prints and Molds*, Schiffer Publishing, 1986.

REPRODUCTION ALERT

Reproductions of butter prints were made as early as the 1940s.

Mold

2-3/4" d, anchor, carved wood 185.00
3-1/2" d, sunflower, carved wood 85.00
4-3/8" d, pineapple, carved wood 325.00
5" x 8", roses, carved maple, serrated edges 165.00

Stamp

2-1/2" d, round, turned handle, thistle 50.00
2-7/8" d, 4-1/2" l, carved fruitwood, strawberry 50.00
3-1/4" l, turned inserted handle, leaf, refinished..................50.00
3-3/8" d, round, eagle 90.00
3-5/8" d, 2-1/4" l, fruitwood, leaf and branch 65.00
3-3/4" d, pinwheel, 4 teardrop and triangular arms form design,
  old dark finish 115.00
3-7/8" d, round, one piece turned handle, stylized tulip, good col-
  or 165.00
4-1/8" d x 4-1/2", star design, similar carving on handle 145.00
4-1/4" d, round, turned handle
  Cow 150.00
  Sunflower, feather leaves, old dark finish......................435.00
  Swan 125.00
4-1/2" d, round, sturdy handle, stylized tulip 125.00
4-1/2" d, round, turned handle, sheaf 100.00
4-5/8" d, round, turned handle, pineapple 95.00
4-3/4" d, round, handle, geometric design...........................95.00

Print, scallop design, reeded lines, raised borders, 3-1/2" d, 2-5/8" h, $90.

4-3/4" d, 5-1/2" l, walnut, foliage and flowers, elaborate carving
  ....85.00
5-7/8" l, carved hardwood, lollipop style, rosette 110.00
6-3/4" l, sheaf of wheat, stylized design, notched rim band
  ....200.00
7" l, lollipop style, star, zig-zag band rim, flared end handle, old
  patina 300.00

CALENDAR PLATES

History: Calendar plates were first made in England in the late 1880s. They became popular in the United States after 1900, the peak years being 1909 to 1915. The majority of the advertising plates were made of porcelain or pottery and the design included a calendar, the name of a store or business, and either a scene, portrait, animal, or flowers. Some also were made of glass or tin.

Periodical: *The Calendar*, 710 N. Lake Shore Dr., Barrington, IL 60010.

Additional Listings: See *Warman's Americana & Collectibles* for more examples.

1907, Christmas scene, holly center 85.00
1908, hunting dog, Pittstown, PA 40.00
1908, roses center...55.00
1909, woman and man in patio garden, 9" d 35.00
1910, Betsy Ross, Dresden 35.00
1910, ships and windmills 30.00
1911, hunt scene, Markell Drug Co, Chelsea, 8" d 35.00
1911, Cash Grocery Store, W. C. Vanderberg, Hoopston, IL adv,
  cherub center...50.00
1912, Martha Washington...40.00
1913, roses and holly 30.00
1914, Point Arena, CA, 6-3/4" d...30.00
1915, black boy eating watermelon, 9" d 60.00
1916, man in canoe, IA, 7-1/2" 35.00

1911, man and woman and musical instruments, "Should auld acquaintance be forgot" in banner, scattered calendar pages, $30.

1916, eagle with shield, American flag, 8-1/4" 40.00
1917, cat center..35.00
1919, ship center...30.00
1920, The Great War, MO..30.00
1921, bluebirds and fruit, 9" d 35.00
1922, dog watching rabbit 35.00
1929, Valentine, NE, flower, 6-1/4" d 35.00

CALLING CARD CASES AND RECEIVERS

History: Calling cards, usually carried in specially designed cases, played an important social role in the United States from the Civil War until the end of World War I. When making formal visits, callers left their card in a receiver (card dish) in the front hall. Strict rules of etiquette developed. For example, the lady in a family was expected to make calls of congratulation and condolence and visits to the ill.

The cards themselves were small, embossed or engraved with the caller's name and often decorated with a floral design. Many handmade examples, especially in Spencerian script, can be found. The cards themselves are considered collectible and range in price from a few cents to several dollars.

Note: Don't confuse a calling card case with a match safe.

Case

3" x 2", 18K yg, basketweave design, sgd "Van Cleef & Arpels"
....920.00
3-3/8" l, sterling silver, chased scrolled borders, chain holder, Nathanial Mills, Birmingham, England, 1949-50 ....215.00
3-3/4" l, rect, abalone, pearl inlay, diamond pattern 85.00

Coin Silver, scenic, center cartouche of mountain lake, scale and herringbone design, American, 2-1/4" x 3-3/8", $120.

3-3/4" l, rect, tortoiseshell, ivory inlay, nacre and colored metal
....95.00
4" l, rect, ivory, wood inlay, block rows, center framed with diamond design rim band 175.00
4" x 3", white metal, bird and floral motif, green and black enamel highlights, Victorian 230.00
4-1/8" x 2-1/2", Shakudo, silver, yellow, white, and rose gold, applied dec of cranes in bamboo, reverse with vase with flowers, Victorian..635.00

Receiver

Bronze, 7" l, monkey, Victorian..135.00
Cast Metal, figural Art Deco lady, painted green.................90.00
Crystal, blown out flowers, pedestal base...........................45.00
Hand Painted China, 10" l, roses, foliage, gold handles......45.00
Majolica, 5" l, duck and bird, Continental, minor rim nicks
....90.00
Stone and Glass, polished onyx-type oval dish, fitted at each end by ribbed gold Favrile glass handles, inscribed "Schlumberger/Made in France/Tiffany" 865.00

CAMBRIDGE GLASS

History: Cambridge Glass Company, Cambridge, Ohio, was incorporated in 1901. Initially, the company made clear tableware, later expanding into colored, etched, and engraved glass. More than 40 different hues were produced in blown and pressed glass.

The plant closed in 1954. Some of the molds were later sold to the Imperial Glass Company, Bellaire, Ohio.

Marks: Five different marks were employed during the production years, but not every piece was marked.

References: Gene Florence, *Elegant Glassware of the Depression Era*, Revised 6th ed., Collector Books, 1995; National Cambridge Collectors, Inc., *Cambridge Glass*

Co., Cambridge, Ohio (reprint of 1930 catalog and supplements through 1934), Collector Books, 1976, 1996 value update; —, *Cambridge Glass Co., Cambridge, Ohio, 1949 thru 1953* (catalog reprint), Collector Books, 1976, 1996 value update; —, *Colors in Cambridge Glass*, Collector Books, 1984, 1993 value update; Naomi L. Over, *Ruby Glass of the 20th Century*, Antique Publications, 1990, 1993-94 value update; Bill and Phyllis Smith, *Cambridge Glass 1927-1929* (1986) and *Identification Guide to Cambridge Glass 1927-1929* (updated prices 1996), published by authors (4003 Old Columbus Rd., Springfield, OH 45502).

Periodical: *The Daze*, P.O. Box 57, Otisville, MI 48463.

Collectors' Club: National Cambridge Collectors, Inc., P.O. Box 416, Cambridge, OH 43725.

Museums: Cambridge Glass Museum, Cambridge, OH; Museum of the National Cambridge Collectors, Inc., Cambridge, OH.

Animal, swan, 7", crystal, sgd..................................33.00
Ashtray, Stack Away, 4 ashtrays, blue, green, pink, and yellow, wood base..55.00
Basket
   Apple Blossom, crystal, 7"..............................475.00
   Hunts Scene, pink, 11" h................................215.00
Bell, Blossom Time, crystal...................................90.00
Bonbon, Diane, crystal, 8-1/2"..............................25.00
Bookends, pr, eagle, crystal..................................55.00
Bowl
   10" d, Wildflower, crystal, gold krystol, matching 12-1/2" d plate, sgd..375.00
   15" d, Rose Point, crystal................................100.00
Butter Dish, cov
   Gadroon, crystal...45.00
   Rose Point, crystal, quarter pound................750.00
Candlestick
   Caprice, blue, 3-lite, #1338.............................75.00
   Cascade, crystal, 1-lite, pr..............................47.50
   Diane, crystal, 5"..20.00
   Doric, black, 9-1/2" h, pr................................160.00
   Rose Point, crystal, 2 lite, keyhole, pr.............95.00
Candy Dish, cov, 3 ftd
   Caprice, Alpine Blue.....................................130.00
   Wildflower, crystal, 8" d, 3 part.......................75.00
Champagne, Wildflower, crystal, 6 oz....................20.00
Cigarette Holder, Caprice, blue............................60.00
Claret, Wildflower, crystal, 4-1/2 oz......................42.00
Cocktail
   Caprice, blue..47.50
   Diane, crystal, 3 oz..14.00
   Rose Point, crystal, 3 oz.................................35.00
Comport
   Caprice, crystal, low, ftd, 7"............................19.00
   Honeycomb, rubena, 9" d, 4-3/4" h, ftd..........150.00
   Krome Kraft, 71/2" h, cutout grape motif, amethyst.........55.00
   Rose Point, crystal, 5-1/2"..............................50.00
Condiment Set, Pristine, crystal, 5 pc...................98.50
Cordial
   Caprice, blue..120.00
   Chantilly crystal..58.00
   Wildflower, crystal, 1 oz.................................60.00
Corn Dish, Portia, crystal....................................50.00
Creamer, Martha Washington, amber, clear stick handle....15.00
Creamer and Sugar
   Cascade, emerald green.................................35.00
   Decagon, blue, flat bottom..............................18.00

Creamer and Sugar, tray, Caprice, crystal..............40.00
Cream Soup, orig liner
   Decagon, green...35.00
   Willow Blue, #3400/55....................................25.00
Cup and Saucer
   Caprice, crystal...14.00
   Decagon, pink...7.00
   Martha Washington, amber..............................12.00
Decanter, Nautilus, #84482, crystal......................45.00
Decanter Set, decanter, stopper, 6 handled 2-1/2 oz. tumblers, Tally Ho, amethyst.................................185.00
Dressing Bottle, Chantilly, crystal, silver base........150.00
Finger Bowl, Adam, yellow...................................25.00
Flower Frog
   Draped Lady, 8-1/2" h
      Amber..190.00
      Crown Tuscan...................................1,850.00
      Crystal, frosted, ribbed base.................75.00
      Dark pink...150.00
      Frosted green.....................................150.00
      Green..160.00
      Light pink...160.00
   Eagle, pink..365.00
   Jay, green...365.00
   Nude, 6-1/2" h, 3-1/4" d, clear...........................95.00
   Rose Lady
      Amber..260.00
      Green..250.00
      Mocha, tall base.................................275.00
      Pink..250.00
   Seagull...65.00
   Two Kids, clear..155.00
Fruit Bowl, Decagon, pink, 5-1/2".............................5.50
Goblet
   Caprice, blue..40.00
   Cascade, crystal...13.00
   Diane, crystal...25.00
   Heirloom, crystal, 9 oz...................................17.50
   Rose Point, crystal, 10 oz..............................30.00
Ice Bucket
   Blossom Time, crystal..................................125.00
   Chrysanthemum, pink, silver handle................85.00
   Tally Ho, cobalt blue.....................................175.00
Iced Tea Tumbler, ftd
   Lexington, #7966, trumpet, 12 oz...................17.50
   Wildflower, crystal, 12 oz...............................28.00
Jam Jar, Krome Kraft base and lid, amber..............35.00
Juice Tumbler, ftd
   Candlelight etch, 5 oz., #3114........................38.50
   Diane, crystal, ftd...15.00
Lamp, Martha Washington, crystal, 9", electric, portable.....95.00
Lemon Plate, Caprice, blue, 5" d..........................15.00
Martini Pitcher, Rose Point, crystal......................700.00
Mustard, cov, Farber Brothers, cobalt blue.............50.00

Dresser Compact, #681, light cutting, Emerald with Peach-blow rose knob, $210.

Oil Cruet, Chantilly etch, 4 oz. 95.00
Oyster Cocktail, Portia, crystal 40.00
Pitcher
    Mt. Vernon, forest green 300.00
    Tally Ho, crystal, metal spout and lid 105.00
Plate
    Apple Blossom, pink, 8-1/2" d 20.00
    Caprice, crystal, 9-1/2" d 38.00
    Crown Tuscan, 7" d 45.00
    Decagon, pink, 8" 5.00
    Martha Washington, amber, lunch 12.00
    Rose Point, crystal, 8" d, ftd 70.00
Platter, Caprice, crystal, 14" l, ftd 30.00
Relish
    Mt. Vernon, crystal, 5 part 35.00
    Rose Point, crystal, 12" l, 5 part 100.00
    Tally Ho, blue, 8-1/4" l, 3 part, handle 25.00
Salad Bowl, Caprice, blue, 10" d 250.00
Salt Shaker
    Decagon, cobalt blue 40.00
    Farber Brothers, amethyst, pr......................40.00
Seafood Cocktail, Seashell, #110, Crown Tuscan, 4-1/2" oz.
    ....95.00
Server, center handle
    Apple Blossom, amber 30.00
    Decagon, blue 16.00
Sherbet
    Caprice, blue..325.00
    Carmine, crystal 17.00
    Diane, crystal, low 14.00
    Regency, low 12.00
    Rose Point, crystal, 7 oz. 24.00
Sherry, Portia, gold encrusted..............................60.00
Sugar, Martha Washington, crystal 17.50
Torte Plate, Rose Point, crystal, 13" d, 3 ftd 95.00
Tray, #3500/112, 3 part, 15" 38.50
Tumbler
    Adam, yellow, ftd 25.00
    Caprice
        Blue, 12 oz., ftd..40.00
        Crystal, 5 oz., ftd......................................14.00
    Carmine, crystal, 12 oz. 25.00
    Decagon, blue, ftd
        5 oz. 10.00
        8 oz. 12.00
        12 oz. 20.00
Vase
    Crown Tuscan
        Flying nude, hp roses and violets dec, creamy pink molded shell bowl held by nude woman, 9" h, 12" l............175.00
        Nautilus, ftd, 7" h.......................................67.50
    Rose Point, #278, gold encrusted, 11" h 475.00
    Diane, crystal, keyhole, 12" h 110.00
    Songbird and Butterfly, #402, 12" h, blue.....375.00
    Tall Flat Panel, swung, 19-1/4" h, sgd 105.00
    Wildflower, 12" h, flip 800.00
Whiskey, Caprice, blue, 2-1/2 oz............................225.00
Wine
    Caprice, crystal 24.00
    Diane, crystal, 2-1/2 oz.................................30.00
    Rose Point, crystal, 2-1/2 oz. 57.50

CAMEO GLASS

History: Cameo glass is a form of cased glass. A shell of glass was prepared; then one or more layers of glass of a different color(s) was faced to the first. A design was then cut through the outer layer(s) leaving the inner layer(s) exposed.

This type of art glass originated in Alexandria, Egypt between 100 and 200 A.D. The oldest and most famous example of cameo glass is the Barberini or Portland vase which was found near Rome in 1582. It contained the ashes of Emperor Alexander Serverus, who was assassinated in 235 A.D.

Emile Gallé is probably one of the best-known cameo glass artists. He established a factory at Nancy, France, in 1884. Although much of the glass bears his signature, he was primarily the designer. Assistants did the actual work on many pieces, even signing Gallé's name. Other makers of French cameo glass include D'Argental, Daum Nancy, LeGras, and Delatte.

English cameo pieces do not have as many layers of glass (colors) and cuttings as do French pieces. The outer layer is usually white, and cuttings are very fine and delicate. Most pieces are not signed. The best-known makers are Thomas Webb & Sons and Stevens and Williams.

Marks: A star before the name Gallé on a piece by that company indicates that it was made after Gallé's death in 1904.

References: Victor Arwas, *Glass Art Nouveau to Art Deco*, Rizzoli International Publications, 1977; Alastair Duncan and George DeBartha, *Glass by Gallé*, Harry N. Abrams, 1984; Ray and Lee Grover, *English Cameo Glass*, Crown Publishers, 1980; Albert C. Revi, *Nineteenth Century Glass*, reprint, Schiffer Publishing, 1981; John A. Shuman, III, *Collector's Encyclopedia of American Art Glass*, Collector Books, 1988, 1994 value update.

American

Gillander American Glass Co, attributed to, 4" h, overlaid in white, cameo etched morning glory blossoms, buds, and leafy vines, shaded blue cased to white oval body 825.00
Harrach, vase, 8" h, 4" d, bright white carved daffodils, leaves, and stems, frosted and green ground...........................950.00
Honesdale Glass, vase, 12" h, green etched to clear, gold dec trim..1,295.00
Mount Washington
    Bowl, 8" d, 4" h, sq, ruffled edge, two winged Griffins holding up scroll and spray of flowers design, blue over white ground 1,475.00

Table Ware, blue rim, blue cameo landscape of lake, trees, and mountains, vaseline bases, faceted stems and fan cut bases on stemware, five (repaired) water goblets, 12 white wines, eight champagnes, 12 finger bowls, 12 underplates, nine after dinner liquors, price for set, $1,2500. Photo courtesy of Freeman\Fine Arts.

Lamp
    17" h, 10" d shade, fluid font and shade composed of opal
    white opaque glass overlaid in bright rose pink, acid
    etched butterflies, ribbons, and bouquets centering cameo
    portrait medallions in classical manner, mounted on silver-
    plated metal fittings, imp "Pairpoint Mfg. Co 3013," electri-
    fied 3,105.00
    21" h, 10" d shade, bright deep yellow over white, base figural
    woman with basket of flowers, matching floral design on
    shade, fancy brass base and font, orig chimney ..8,500.00
    24" h, deep rose over white, portrait of woman dec on shade
    and base, silver-plated fittings 7,500.00

English

Florentine Art, cruet, 6-1/2" h, ruby-red body, textured white
    enamel meadowland scene, Meadowlark on tall plant stalk,
    smaller scene on reverse, white rim, trefoil spout, clear frosted
    handle, teardrop shaped stopper, pontil mark sgd "59"
    ....750.00
Stevens and Williams
    Vase
        4-1/2" h, broad bright blue oval, overlaid in opaque white
        glass, cameo etched and cut clusters of cherries on leafy
        boughs, circular mark on base "Stevens & Williams Art
        Glass Stourbridge" 1,265.00
        6-1/4" h, Rose du Barry, lush pink rose oval body, etched with
        white six-petaled blossoms and buds, intricate leaves, but-
        terfly at reverse, linear border 1,610.00
Unknown Maker
    Plaque, 5-1/2" l, 3-1/2" w, citron yellow, five white carved car-
        nation flowers, leaf..1,275.00
    Vase, 7" h, 5" w, corset shape, cranberry, white overlay,
        carved sprays of sweet peas, leaves, branches, butterfly in
        flight 1,750.00
Webb
    Cup and Saucer, handleless, 2-3/4" h, 5" d, cranberry over
        crystal, prunous blossom carving, leaves, and branches,
        10 blossoms on cup with large butterfly and 25 buds
        ....550.00
    Perfume Bottle
        3-3/4" l, flattened teardrop shape, bright blue, etched forget-
        me-nots all around, two butterflies on shoulder, one chip on
        surface flower, wear to gilt metal screw cap 435.00
        5-1/2" l, 2-3/4" w, sq, citron yellow, white overlay, allover
        carved wild roses, leaves, and buds, orig silver spring-
        hinge cov 2,750.00

**LeGras, vase, rust cut to orange to gray to green, black sunset
scene, 5" x 3-1/2" x 4-3/4", $500.**

Scent Bottle, 4" l, flattened teardrop shape, sapphire blue,
    white ferns and grasses dec, butterfly at side, gilt metal
    hinged cover...920.00
Vase
    4-1/2" h, pale raison color oval body, layered in white cam-
        eo, leafy bough and delicate blossom clusters etched
        around shoulder, linear border above 575.00
    7" h, simulated ivory bulbous body, cameo etched ivy
        above berries on leafy vines, motif enhanced by sepia
        coloration, semicircular mark on base "Thos. Webb &
        Sons" 815.00
    7-1/2" h, 6-1/2" w, pillow, brilliant blue, white cameo wild
        rose dec, two large roses, 12 leaves, large butterfly in
        flight, full signature 2,750.00

French

Arsall, vase, 5" h, flared, pink mottled yellow overlaid ground,
    green layer etched as decumbent blossoms, buds, and leafy
    stems, sgd "Arsall" in design 325.00
Crystallerie D'Art, vase, 13" h, creamy opal white oval, bright for-
    est green over pastel green layers, etched stylized Art Deco
    blossoms and leaves, sgd and mkd on base " o. 31 of 100 ex-
    emplaries"..880.00
D'Argental, atomizer, 4" h, cylindrical amber perfume bottle,
    green and brown overlay, etched landscape of leafy trees,
    wild geese in flight, sgd " d'Argental" on side, gilt metal fittings
    mkd " le Parisien Made in France," "BTE, S.G.D.G." 825.00
Daum Nancy
    Bowl, 4-3/4" d, deep blue grape pods, autumn color leaves
        and vines, mottled yellow, pink, and amethyst ground,
        quad fold trim, cameo sgd 900.00
    Box, cov, 4-3/4" x 2-3/4", green grapes and leaves, tan
        ground 500.00
    Cologne Bottle, 4" h, deeply carved red poppies and green
        leaves, pink ground, vertical lines, gold rim and stopper
        with dragonflies, sgd, cross mark 5,000.00
    Dish, 6-1/4" d, 3-1/4" h, tricorn, mottled green, amber, and col-
        orless, padded white trumpet blossoms, green leafy vines,
        rim sgd " daum Nancy (cross) 1875" 750.00
    Vase
        4-1/2" h, oval bud, fiery opalescent amber with red stria-
            tions, etched thistle pods and thorny stems, enameled
            burgundy-red, sgd " daum Nancy (cross)" at side
            ....815.00
        11-1/2" h, mold blown, woodland scene, dark green foli-
            age, peering village, mottled orange and yellow sky, sgd
            on bottom 10,200.00
De Vez
    Rose Bowl, 3-1/2" d, cobalt blue foliated trees and mountains,
        pink to yellow sky and water, scalloped rim, sgd.....500.00
    Vase, 8" h, tubular, three color scenic brown castle and trees,
        blue mountains, frosted ground, sgd 1,400.00
Galle
    Bowl, 5" l, 2-1/2" h, oval, flared mottled green gray oval, cased
        to pink, layered with mauve, acid etched stylized leafy
        plants, sgd "Galle" at side.......................................635.00
    Ceiling Shade, Plaffonier, 11-1/2" d, 6-1/2" d, conical flared
        shale, frosted shades of green and gray layered in burgun-
        dy red-maroon over green, cameo cut and etched buds
        and blossoms, leafy stems around rim, sgd "Galle" at side
        in motif, three gilt metal chains and ceiling mount
        ....3,220.00
    Lamp, boudoir, 10-1/2" h, 10" d conical flared shade, oval
        base, colorless glass cased to fiery yellow, layered in dark
        maroon under burnt umber, cameo etched and cut as ex-
        otic blossoms and leafy stems, sgd "Galle" on shade and
        base, two circular "Galle/Nancy/Paris" paper labels on
        base..8,625.00

Toothpick Holder, 2-1/2" h, chartreuse and medium green seed pods and leafy branches, frosted and orange ground, sgd..500.00

Vase
4-1/4" h, bright frosted red oval body layered in aubergine-black, etched as wild geranium blossoms and leafy stems, sgd "Galle" on motif, collar ridge for atomizer 435.00

5-3/4" h, flattened oval, elliptical rim, amethyst and green layers, cameo etched with raised center blossoms, leafy vines, sgd "Galle" at side, two small chips to stems 490.00

8" h, olive green over colorless glass cased to bright orange, acid-etched water lilies and water grasses, sgd "Galle" on side 1,380.00

8-1/4" h, flattened bulbous body, elongated neck, cased pink layered in amethyst and green, cameo etched wisteria clusters and leafy stems, sgd "Galle" on side 920.00

8-3/4" h, bud, trumpet form, fiery amber layered in blue and purple, cameo etched and cut wild rose blossoms and buds, leaf border below, sgd "Galle" in design 1,380.00

11" h, bud, tall flattened bottle-form, amethyst overlay, cameo etched blossoms, bud, and vines, sgd "Galle" on back 1,150.00

13" h, flattened oval, colorless shaded to blue body, layered in bright pink and olive green, cameo etched and cut decumbent bleeding heart blossoms and leafy stems, sgd "Galle" in design on side 5,175.00

13-1/4" h, large conical frosted colorless body, layered in pale green and dark green, cameo cut and carved as tall iris blossoms and spike leaves, Oriental-style, "Galle" vertically on one spike, four tiny leaf edge chips.....1,380.00

16" h, flared trumpet-form oval, frosted pale blue and colorless glass layered in amethyst and mauve green, cameo etched hydrangea blossom clusters, leafy stems, sgd "Galle" in design on reverse 2,645.00

Legras
Bowl, 4-3/4" l, 1-3/4" h, frosted colorless shaped oval, scenic dec of shepherd and flock of sheep among mountainous landscape, enameled natural colors, sgd " legras" at end, rim roughness 175.00

Vase, 8-3/4" h, scalloped oval shape, landscape scene, green, brown, peach, and frosty white......................50.00

Richard
Bowl, 6" l, 2-3/4" h, brilliant cased poppy red, brown overlay, acid-etched stylized foliate motif, sgd "Richard" at side 460.00

Vase, 7-1/4" h, yellow cased oval, layered in brown, cameo etched mountainous village waterfront scene, applied brown-black handles at each side, sgd "Richard" at side 825.00

Wine, 7-3/4" h, cobalt blue scenic water and sailboats, frosted ground, notched stem 400.00

Velez, vase, 8-1/2" h, ftd, tapered, deep cranberry shaded sky silhouettes autumn green trees and woodland grasses, pale green hills and trees along river bank, sgd "Velez" 1,100.00

CAMERAS

History: Although photography generally is considered to have had its beginning in 1839, it is very unusual to find a camera made before 1880. These cameras and others made before 1925 are considered to be antique cameras. Most cameras made after 1925 that are no longer in production are considered to be classic cameras. American, German, and Japanese cameras are found most often.

References: John S. Craig, *General Catalog of Photographica*, published by author, 1993; James and Joan McKeown (eds.), *Price Guide to Antique & Classic Cameras, 1992-1995*, 9th ed., Centennial Photo Service, 1994; Douglas St. Denny (ed.), *Hove International Blue Book Guide Prices for Classic and Collectable Cameras*, Hove Foto Books, 1992.

Periodicals: *Camera Shopper*, 313 N. Quaker Lane, P.O. Box 370279, West Hartford, CT 06137; *Shutterbug*, P.O. Box F, Titusville, FL 32781.

Collectors' Clubs: American Photographic Historical Society, Inc., 1150 Avenue of the Americas, New York, NY 10036; American Society of Camera Collectors, 4918 Alcove Ave., North Hollywood, CA 91607; International Kodak Historical Society, P.O. Box 21, Flourtown, PA 19301; Leica Historical Society of America, 7611 Dornoch Lane, Dallas, TX 75248; Movie Machine Society, 50 Old Country Rd., Hudson, MA 01749; National Stereoscopic Assoc., P.O. Box 14801, Columbus, OH 43214; Nikon Historical Society, P.O .Box 3213, Munster, IN 46321; Photographic Historical Society, P.O. Box 39563, Rochester, NY 14604; Zeiss Historical Society, P.O. Box 631, Clifton, NJ 07012.

Museums: Cameras & Images International, Boston, MA; Fleetwood Museum, North Plainfield, NJ; George Eastman Museum, Rochester, NY; International Cinema Museum, Chicago, IL; Smithsonian Institution, Washington, DC.

Additional Listings: See *Warman's Americana & Collectibles* for more examples.

Advisor: Tom Hoepf.

Notes: Value of cameras is affected by both exterior and mechanical conditions. Particular attention must be given to the condition of the bellows, if cameras have them.

Bell & Howell, Dial 35, half-frame 35 mm, c1963-67, spring-powered auto wind, unique styling, molded plastic case, also found with Canon nameplate...60.00

Eastman Kodak
Retina IIIc, 35 mm rangefinder, c1954, f2/50mm Xenon C lens, built-in exposure meter, excellent condition.............200.00

Leica, Model M-3, single stroke conversation, 5cm 1.5 summarit lens, $1,375. Photo courtesy of Jackson's Auctioneers & Appraisers.

Retina IIIC, c 1958, f2/50 mm Xenon lens, built-in exposure meter, similar to earlier IIIc except viewfinder windows are same size and bigger, near mint, everready case ... 750.00
Kodak Signet 35, 1951-58, f3.5/44mm lens, Kodak Synchro 300 shutter 25.00
Kodak Town & Country Outfit featuring Bantam RF Camera, case, flash, cord, hang tag, mint in original box, c 1953-1957 .... 45.00
Franke & Heidecke, Germany
Heidoscop, three-lens stereo camera, c 1925-1941, Carl Zeiss Jena Tessar f4.5 55 mm lenses, 45 x 107 mm exposure size 600.00
Rolleiflex Gray Baby, twin lens reflex, c 1958, f3.5 Xenar, with flash, filters, lens hoods 275.00
Rolleiflex Automat 2.8C, twin lens reflex, c 1954, Xenotar f2.8 lens 300.00
Gundlach, Korona 4 x 5 view camera, c 1900-1950, polished cherrywood, antique lens 175.00
Ihagee, Germany, Kine Exakta I, 35mm single lens reflex, rect focusing magnifier, c1937-49, with Tessar or Exaktar f3.5/50mm lens 175.00
Kamera Werkstatten, Germany, Patent Etui, 9x12cm folding camera, c 1937, f6.3 Tessar lens, Compur shutter, black leather covering body and bellow, with sheet film holder 100.00
Kemper, Kombi, miniature box camera, c 1890s, metal body doubles as a transparency viewer, engraved decorated front 300.00
Konica, Japan
Baby Pearl, c 1940 folding camera, f4.5/50mm Hexar lens, 127 film 125.00
Konica, 35 mm rangefinder, original model, c 1948, f2.8 Hexar lens, marked "Made in Occupied Japan" 75.00
Nikon, Japan, Nikon S2, 35mm rangefinder, f1.4/50mm lens, c 1955, chrome finish with black leather, case, near mint 700.00
Paillard (Switzerland), Bolex-H-16 movie camera, 3-lens turret 225.00
Stirn, Concealed Vest Camera No. 2, c1890, round metal" detective" camera, 7" diameter, takes 4 pictures on round glass negatives, original neck string 2,500.00
Thornton-Pickard, England
Folding Ruby, c1920 3-1/4" x 4-1/4" folding plate camera, polished wood interior, Cooke Anastigmat lens 250.00
Stereo Puck, c 1925, simple stereo box camera, 120 roll film 150.00
Voigtlander, Germany, Sterophotoskop, 45x107mm stereo camera, c 1907, with magazine back for 12 plates, f4.5 Herliers lens 400.00
Whittaker, Micro 16, 16mm subminiature, c1950, Achromatic doublet lens, single shutter speed, with slide-on metal viewfinder and film cartridge, chrome body 65.00
Ziess, Germany
Box Tengor 54/2, c1935, box camera, 6x9 cm image on 120 film 30.00
Ikoflex Ic, twin lens reflex, c1956, f3.5/75mm Tessar, working meter, near mint 300.00
Nettar 515/2, folding camera, f4.5/11cm Nettar lens, c1937, black paint chipping off edges of black body 25.00

CAMPHOR GLASS

History: Camphor glass derives its name from its color. Most pieces have a cloudy white appearance, similar to gum camphor; others have a pale tint. Camphor glass is made by treating the glass with hydrofluoric acid vapors.

Bowl, 10" d, fluted rim, polished pontil 125.00
Box, cov, 5" d, hinged, enameled holly spray 75.00
Candlesticks, pr, 7" h, hp roses 75.00
Creamer, 3-1/4" h 25.00

Powder Jar, pink salmon, emb florals on lid, 4-1/2" h, 5" d, $45.

Cruet, hp enameled roses, orig stopper 45.00
Perfume Bottle, 8-1/2" h, pinch type, mushroom cap 50.00
Place Card Holder, 3-3/4" h, ftd 35.00
Plate, 7-1/4" d, hp owl 40.00
Rose Bowl, hp violets, green leaves 50.00
Salt and Pepper Shakers, pr, Swirl pattern, blue, orig tops . 45.00
Toothpick Holder, bucket shape 30.00
Vase, 8" h, fan shape, clear leaf design and trim 85.00

CANDLESTICKS

History: The domestic use of candlesticks is traced to the 14th century. The earliest was a picket type, named for the sharp point used to hold the candle. The socket type was established by the mid-1660s.

From 1700 to the present, candlestick design mirrored furniture design. By the late 17th century, a baluster stem was introduced, replacing the earlier Doric or clustered column stem. After 1730, candlesticks reflected rococo ornateness. Neoclassic styles followed in the 1760s. Each new era produced a new style of candlesticks; however, some styles became universal and remained in production for centuries. Therefore, when attempting to date a candlestick, it is important to try to determine the techniques used to manufacture the piece.

References: Margaret and Douglas Archer, *Collector's Encyclopedia of Glass Candlesticks*, Collector Books, 1983; Veronika Baur, *Metal Candlesticks*, Schiffer Publishing, 1996; Kenneth Wilson, *American Glass 1760-1930*, 2 Vols., Hudson Hills Press and The Toledo Museum of Art, 1994.

Brass
5-7/8" h, sq base, spool stem, one base slightly battered, pr 440.00

Porcelain, Samson, pastel colors, gold anchor marks, 8-1/4" h, $250.

6-1/2" h, Queen Anne, first half 18th C, petal base, old repair, minor dents 575.00
7" h, Queen Anne, octagonal base and stem, one with old repair to base, pr 965.00
7-1/4" h, Queen Anne, one with old repair to lip, pr ... 1,100.00
7-7/8" h, Queen Anne, petal base, pushup 935.00
8-1/8" h, Queen Anne, petal base, poorly resoldered stem and base 275.00
9" h, scalloped base, segmented stem, drip pan under socket 110.00
9-5/8" h, Victorian, beehive and diamond detail, pushups, mkd "England, " pr 140.00
11-1/4" h, Victorian, pushups and diamond detail, English registry marks 140.00
Bronze, 20-1/2" h, rod shafts, wide circular base, gold Favrile swirled glass shades, Tiffany & Co., pr 1,200.00
Copper, 6" h, sq base, handle stamped "6," battered, replaced pushup 95.00
Gilt Metal, 12-3/4" h, Napoleon II, urn form socket above foliate molded standard flanked by phoenixes, caryatid and swag molded base, pr 275.00
Glass
  6" h, blue flint glass, one with glass lamp insert, pr ... 2,310.00
  7-5/8" h, pressed, blue, paneled hexagonal form, American, 19th C, minor chips, gaffering marks 815.00
  9-1/4" h, clambroth and blue pressed glass, acanthus leaf dec on blue sockets, 19th C, minor chips, pr 550.00
  9-3/4" h, clambroth and blue pressed glass, dolphin form, 19th C, cracks, chips, pr 690.00
Hogscraper
  6-3/8" h, pushup knob replaced, lip hanger 115.00
  6-3/4" h, pushup, lip hanger, brass ring, dents in ring .. 385.00
  7" h, pushup, lip hanger, brass ring 495.00
  8-1/4" h, pushup mkd "Shaw's Brim," lip repair, hanger missing 100.00
Pewter
  7-1/2" h, Jack-O-Diamonds, English, 19th C, pr............ 100.00
  8-3/4" h, push-up, English, 1800-25 .... 375.00
Silver, 13-1/2" h, English, Birmingham, Mappin, and Webb, 1807, Corinthian column wrapped with trailing vines, spread foot, acanthus and urn dec, weighted 2,000.00
Wrought Iron, 11-1/2" h, scrolled feet, lip handle, notched pushup with scrolled handle, pr 550.00
Wrought Iron and Tin, 6-1/4" h, side pushup 225.00
Wrought Steel, 7-1/4" h, wooden base, spiral pushup 275.00

CANDY CONTAINERS

History: In 1876, Croft, Wilbur and Co. filled small glass Liberty Bells with candy and sold them at the Centennial Exposition in Philadelphia. From that date until the 1960s, glass candy containers remained popular. They reflect historical changes, particularly in transportation.

Jeannette, Pennsylvania, a center for the packaging of candy in containers, was home for J. C. Crosetti, J. H. Millstein, T. H. Stough, and Victory Glass. Other early manufacturers included: George Borgfeldt, New York, New York; Cambridge Glass, Cambridge, Ohio; Eagle Glass, Wheeling, West Virginia; L. E. Smith, Mt. Pleasant, Pennsylvania; and West Brothers, Grapeville, Pennsylvania.

References: *Candy Containers*, L-W Book Sales, 1996; Douglas M. Dezso, J. Lion Poirier & Rose D. Poirier, *Collector's Guide to Candy Containers,* Collector Books, 1997; George Eikelberner and Serge Agadjanian, *Complete American Glass Candy Containers Handbook*, revised and published by Adele L. Bowden, 1986; Jennie Long, *Album of Candy Containers*, published by author, Vol. I (1978), Vol. II (1983).

Collectors' Club: Candy Container Collectors of America, P.O. Box 352, Cleveland, OH 01824.

Museums: Cambridge Glass Museum, Cambridge, OH; L. E. Smith Glass, Mt. Pleasant, PA.

Additional Listings: See *Warman's Americana & Collectibles* for more examples.

Notes: Candy containers with original paint, candy, and closures command a high premium, but beware of reproduced parts and repainting. The closure is a critical part of each container; if it is missing, the value of the container drops considerably.

Small figural perfumes and other miniatures often are sold as candy containers.

Airplane, Liberty Motor, clear, orig closure, replaced wheels 1,100.00
Amos & Andy, glass, car, 2-3/4" x 4-1/2" x 1-1/2" 525.00
Barney Google and Bank
  Orig paint, orig closure 700.00
  Repainted, orig closure 550.00
Barney Google and Bell, 70% orig paint, orig closure 350.00
Barney Google on Pedestal, orig closure 250.00
Baseball Player with Bat, 50% orig paint, orig closure 500.00
Bear on Circus Tub, orig tin, orig closure 500.00
Begging Dog, 3-1/2" h, pressed glass, clear, no closure .. 150.00
Black Cat for Luck, repainted, replaced closure 2,000.00
Bird on Mount, orig whistle, 80% orig paint, orig closure, some chips 550.00
Boat
  F-6 Submarine, replaced periscope 450.00
  USN Dreadnaught, orig closure 350.00
Boot, 3" h, clear glass, etched "Rick I Love You Penny" 35.00
Bulldog, 4-1/4" h, screw closure 60.00
Bus
  Chicago, replaced closure 270.00
  New York-San Francisco, orig closure 375.00
  Victory Glass Co., replaced closure 300.00
Cannon
  Cannon #1, orig carriage, orig closure 375.00

Rapid Fire Gun, orig closure 425.00
U. S. Defense Field Gun #17, orig closure 380.00
Two Wheel Mount #1, orig carriage, orig closure..........180.00
Two Wheel Mount #2, orig carriage, orig closure, one replaced
    wheel 260.00
Cash Register, orig paint, orig closure............................600.00
Chick, composition
    3" h, painted, orange, yellow, and white, lead legs.........65.00
    5" h, cardboard, base, Germany 20.00
Clarinet, musical, tin whistle, cardboard tube 35.00
Delivery Truck, cream colored tin canopy, red lettering
    Bakery Truck, small chip 1,100.00
    Express Truck 2,100.00
    Grocery Truck, small chip 2,100.00
    Ice Truck...690.00
    Laundry Truck, small chip, crack on wheel flank 2,100.00
Elf on Rocking Horse, 3-1/2" h, pressed glass, no closure
    ....160.00
Felix the Cat, repainted, replaced closure 550.00
Fire Truck, with ladders..25.00
Flossie Fisher's Bed, yellow tin bed, dec with black silhouettes of
    children and animals 3,600.00
Football, tin, Germany 20.00
Ghost Head, 3-1/2" h, papier-mâché, flannel shroud.........150.00
Girl, celluloid, crepe paper dress.....................................30.00
Goblin Head, 60% orig paint, orig closure 625.00
Green Taxi, orig wheels, orig closure, small chip 600.00
Gun, 5-3/4" l, West Specialty Co.....................................20.00
Horse and Wagon, pressed glass....................................35.00
Hot Doggie, traces of paint, orig closure 525.00
Indian, 5" l, pressed glass, riding motorcycle with sidecar, no clo-
    sure..350.00
Jack-o-lantern
    Open top, 95% orig paint, no closure 350.00
    Pop eyed, 75% orig paint, orig closure, orig bail..........475.00
    Screw on lid, 95% orig paint..360.00

Kettle, 2" h, 2-1/4" d, pressed glass, clear, T. H. Stough, card-
    board closure 50.00
Kewpie on radio, orig paint, orig closure 650.00
Lantern, 3-3/4" h, mkd "Pat. Dec. 20, "04" 35.00
Lawn Swing, orig red and white tin canopy, orig closure ..650.00
Limousine, orig wheels, orig closure, small chip...............600.00
Lynne Clock Bank...750.00
Nursing Bottle, pressed glass, clear, natural wood nipple closure,
    T. H. Stough, 1940-50..20.00
Pumper, 5" l, pressed glass, tin wheels and bottom 110.00
Pumpkin Head Witch, 50% orig paint, orig closure............650.00
Puppy, 2-1/2" h, papier-mâché, painted, white, black muzzle,
    glass eyes..35.00
Rabbit
    Rabbit Emerging from Tree Trunk, lamp, missing shade
    ....1,250.00
    Rabbit Family, 95% orig paint, no closure....................650.00
    Rabbit Family, repainted, replaced closure 525.00
    Rabbit Mother and Daughter, orig closure, chipped tail
    ....675.00
    Rabbit Pushing Chick in Shell Cart, orig closure..........500.00
    Rabbit Wearing Hat, 90% orig paint above waist, repainted
        below waist, orig closure 900.00
    Rabbit With Feet Together Round Nose #2, orig closure
    ....650.00
Record Player with Horn..200.00
Rooster, 6-1/2" h, papier-mâché, pewter feet, orig polychrome
    paint, mkd "Germany" 225.00
Santa Clause, 6-1/2" h, cardboard, painted face, Germany
    ....150.00
Soldier by the Tent, 95% orig paint, orig closure 2,700.00
Statue of Liberty, 5-3/4" h, pressed glass, clear, lead top
    ....1,200.00
Swan Boat with Rabbit and Chick, repainted, replaced closure
    ....650.00
Telephone, candlestick type, bell and crank 325.00
Toonerville Depot Line, orig paint, orig closure.................575.00
Turkey, papier-mâché 25.00

CANES

History: Canes and walking sticks were important accessories in a gentleman's wardrobe in the 18th and 19th
centuries. They often served both a decorative and utilitarian function. Glass canes and walking sticks were
glassmakers' whimsies, ornamental rather than practical.

References: Linda L. Beeman, *Cane Collector's Directo-
ry*, published by author, 1993; Joyce E. Blake, *Glasshouse
Whimsies*, published by author, 1984; Catherine Dike,
Cane Curiosa, Cane Curiosa Press (250 Dielman Rd., Ladue, MO 63124), 1983; ——, *Canes in the United States*,
Cane Curiosa Press (250 Dielman Rd., Ladue, MO 63124),
1994; ——, *La Cane Object díArt;* Cane Curiosa Press (250
Dielman Rd., Ladue, MO 63124), 1988; Ulrich Klever,
Walkingsticks, Schiffer Publishing, 1996; George H. Meyer, *American Folk Art Canes,* Sandringham Press, 1992,
Francis H. Monek, *Canes through the Ages*, Schiffer Publishing, 1995; Jeffrey B. Snyder, *Canes from the Seven-
teenth to the Twentieth Century*, Schiffer Publishing, 1993.

Periodical: *Cane Collector's Chronicle*, 99 Ludlum Crescent, Lower Hutt Welling, New Zealand.

Collectors' Club: International Cane Collectors, 24 Magnolia Ave., Manchester-by-the-Sea, MA 01944; The Cane Collector's Chronicle, 99 Ludlum Crescent, Lower Hutt,

Lantern, J. C. Crosetti, Co., glass, orig metal closure, $20.

Weelington, New Zealand.

Museums: Essex Institute, Salem, MA; Remington Gun Museum, Ilion, NY; Valley Forge Historical Soc., Valley Forge, PA.

Notes: Carved wood and ivory canes are frequently considered folk art and collectors pay higher prices for them.

Cane

Commemorative, Civil War
"Devil's Den, Gettysburg, May 29, 1895," 9" figure, 36" l cane, carved and painted officer with glass eyes, brass tack buttons as hands, plain shaft....................................4,100.00
Gettysburg Reunion, 1913, relief and incised carving of cannon with flag, Washington monument, clasped hands, animals, birds, slogans, initials and "Edinburgh, VA, Sept. 21, 1913" 11,000.00
Folk Art
29" l, child's, carved and painted dogwood, carved red bird with head held high, perched on green nest, upward turned yellow hand, tapering black shaft, wear to tip of beak, paint chips, attributed to Schtockschnitzler Simmons, PA, c1900..1,725.00
36-1/2" l, carved dogwood, curved handle, tapered shaft, relief carved soldiers on horseback, spread winged American eagle, US shield, floral sprigs, insects, fish, stag, butterfly, coat of arms, PA, c1900 ....1,380.00
36-3/4" l, carved dogwood, curved handle carved in the round with figure of a horse standing on plateau, relief carved cluster of blossoms over entwined snake, PA, c1900, minor shrinkage cracks 850.00
37" h, carved dogwood, curved handle carved with goat leaping through barrel, dog leaping through the other end clutching a box, bearded gentleman seated astride keg fitted with metal spigot, holding a bottle and glass, eyes and buttons with colored glass beads, tapered shaft, attributed to Bally Carver, R. Heniz, Bally, Berks County 575.00
38-5/8" l, carved and painted wood, The House That Jack Built, various carved animal, figural, and human motifs, America, 19th C, minor cracks, very minor paint loss 3,500.00
38-1/2" l, carved wood, baboon head knob encloses sundial and compass, various carved human and animal motifs, one head enclosing 3 dice, America, 19th C, minor losses, cracks 2,990.00

Folk Art type, carved rattlesnake, ivory knob, textured finish, America, late 19th C, $235. Photo courtesy of Aston Macek Auctioneers & Appraisers.

Gun, 43" l, Remington, 3-1/2" l, dog head molded gutta percha handle, nickel silver collar, gutta percha cov shaft, Remington mark and "Pat. 1872" above separation, 22-caliber concealed gun..5,940.00
Ivory, 2-5/8" h x 1-1/4" handle with phrenology head, dark rosewood shaft, Continental, c1850 ....4,400.00
Opera, Frankie Feathers
Carved handle, carved shaft with eagle's head, floral, and geometric forms, inscribed "Truth, Faith, Hope, Love, Charity, In God We Trust, June 1937," brass ferrule.....4,180.00
Knob carved as helmeted man's head, black walnut or mahogany shaft carved with plant forms and geometric designs, inscribed "N. D. Crum Walkersville, By Industry We Thrive," brass ferrule 1,500.00
Sword
Elephant ivory handle, man in early dress, round boxwood hat, knotted scarf and coat with wood buttons, 15-1/2" diamond shaped blade, Continental, c1840 ....2,100.00
Elephant ivory handle, 2-1/4" h,1-3/4" d, fluted ivory and snakewood, 24-3/4" l blade, Continental, c1860 ...1,600.00
Silver topped, 2" h, 1-3/8" d, gutta percha shaft, 12-1/2" triangular blade with bluing and gold gilding, white metal and iron ferrule, 34" l, America, c1860 ....590.00
Tiffany, 2" h handle, 1" d, owner's initials on top, 12" l platinum fleur-de-lis around dark tone malacca shaft, 2-1/2" l black horn ferrule, mkd "Tiffany and Co., Makers 18K gold and platinum," c1902-07 ....6,100.00

Walking Stick

Baleen and shark vertebrae, 33-7/8" l, tapering baleen knob, alternating vertebrae and baleen spacers continuing to tapering vertebrae, 19th C, cracks 375.00
Dogwood, carved, PA, c1900
29-3/4" h, knopped handle, tapered shaft with relief carving of bands of stars, two horses, American eagle, scrolled banner with stars, stag and rearing stallion.................1,265.00
32-1/4" l, handle carved in high relief as reclining dog, tapered shaft carved at top with squirrel hooding nut, initialed "AK," metal tip, attributed to Adam Krauss, Montgomery County 345.00
33" h, carved clenched fist handle, tapered shaft with buckled belt over snake, inset white bead eyes, scrolled grapevine, metal tip 1,380.00
35" l, curved handle carved with head of duck, inset glass eyes, tapered shaft, metal tip, shrinkage crack 690.00
37" l, slightly knobbed handle, tapered shaft finely relief carved with American eagle, lion, two horses, gilt with pony, blossom in a pot, butterfly, stag, and hen, metal tip 1,150.00
Ivory and whalebone
35-1/4" l, rounded knob, scribe line dec, paneled whalebone shaft with ivory inlay, concave paneled section continuing to spiral carving, 19th C, inlay loss, minor cracks 1,150.00
36" l, ivory inlaid polyhedron-form knob, shaped ivory neck, rounded tapering whalebone shaft with inlaid ebony ending in brass finial, 19th C, inlay loss, minor cracks ..345.00
Tortoiseshell, 34" l, handle with repousse and chased foliage, Continental, 19th C 1,200.00

CANTON CHINA

History: Canton china is a type of Oriental porcelain made in the Canton region of China from the late 18th century to the present. It was produced largely for export. Canton china has a hand-decorated light- to dark-blue underglaze on white ground. Design motifs include houses, mountains, trees, boats, and bridges. A design similar to willow pattern is the most common.

Borders on early Canton feature a rain and cloud motif (a thick band of diagonal lines with a scalloped bottom). Later pieces usually have a straight-line border.

Early, c1790-1840, plates are very heavy and often have an unfinished bottom, while serving pieces have an overall "orange peel" bottom. Early covered pieces, such as tureens, vegetable dishes, and sugars, have strawberry finials and twisted handles. Later ones have round finials and a straight, single handle.

Marks: The markings "Made in China" and "China" indicate wares which date after 1891.

REPRODUCTION ALERT

Several museum gift shops and private manufacturers are issuing reproductions of Canton china.

Bowl
    9-1/4" d, 4-3/4" h, cut corner, gilt highlights, minute glaze chips 920.00
    9-3/4" d, lobed, gilt rim, base chips, gilt wear 865.00
Box, cov, sq, domed top, cloud and rain border on lids, early 19th C, pr 6,270.00
Cider Jug
    8-1/4" h..1,610.00
    9-1/2" h, mismatched cover, spout, and finial chips ..1,610.00
Coffeepot, 7-1/4" h, mismatched cover 750.00
Creamer, 4-1/4" h, helmet-shape, chips, damage to one spout, pr 815.00
Dish, 8-7/8" d, scalloped rim, blue and white, 1/4" glued rim chip 300.00
Egg Cup, 2-1/4" h, chips, cracked, 9 pc set 345.00
Fish Platter, 13-1/2" l, glaze roughness 1,265.00
Fruit Basket
    9-1/4" d, minor chips...690.00
    10-1/2" l, reticulated, undertray 1,100.00
    11" l, reticulated, mismatched undertray, star crack, minor chips 345.00
Ginger Jar, cov..230.00
Milk Pitcher, 6-1/8" h, very minor chips 575.00

Ginger Jar, 19th C, blue and white peony motif, 8-1/2" h, later lid, $110. Photo courtesy of Sanford Alderfer Auction Co.

Pitcher, 3" to 6-1/2" h, chips, 4 pc set..............................2,760.00
Plate, early, c1820-30
    6" d, bread and butter 65.00
    7-1/2" d, salad...85.00
    8" d, dessert 95.00
    9" d, lunch 115.00
    10" d, dinner 150.00
Platter
    13-3/4" l, deep, minor glaze chips..................................375.00
    16-1/8" l, indented tree, gilt rim, very minor chips, gilt wear 575.00
    18-3/8" l, rim chips, knife marks, pr 1,265.00
Pot de Creme, 4" h, 3 pc set 325.00
Salad Bowl, 9-3/4" d, rim roughness 815.00
Salt, 3-3/4" l, trench, chips, 3 pc set................................550.00
Sauce Tureen
    6" l, minor chips 245.00
    8-1/2" l, mismatched cover 865.00
Serving Plate, 12" d, minor chips 435.00
Shrimp Dish, 10-1/4" d, minor edge roughness, pr 690.00
Soup Tureen, 9" h, 11-3/4" d, mismatched cover 635.00
Syllabub, 3" h, imperfections, 16 pc set............................850.00
Tea Canister, cov, 11-1/2" h, restoration to lids, damage to one base, pr 3,336.00
Tureen, 12" l, minor chips, star cracks 750.00
Tureen, cov, undertray, 12-1/2" l, mismatched, cracks, chips 815.00
Vegetable Dish, cov
    9-1/2" l, chips 250.00
    9-3/4" l, minute chips 400.00
    10-1/4" l, chips 265.00
Warming Dish, cov
    9" d, 3 pc set..500.00
    10-1/2" d, circular, pr 525.00

CAPO-DI-MONTE

History: In 1743, King Charles of Naples established a soft-paste porcelain factory near Naples. The firm made figurines and dinnerware. In 1760, many of the workmen and most of the molds were moved to Buen Retiro, near Madrid, Spain. A new factory, which also made hard-paste porcelains, opened in Naples in 1771. In 1834, the Doccia factory in Florence purchased the molds and continued production with them in Italy.

Capo-di-Monte was copied heavily by other factories in Hungary, Germany, France, and Italy.

REPRODUCTION ALERT

Many of the pieces in today's market are of recent vintage. Do not be fooled by the crown over the "N" mark; it also was copied.

Box, cov, gilt mounting
    6-1/8" l, hinged, rect, relief molded, 3 maidens and young, sides molded with baby Bacchantes tending to grapevine, overglaze blue crowned "N" mark.........................1,200.00
    11-1/2" l, oval, Greek gods molded on lid, ribbon tied floral garland, gilt ground, side frieze of mask flanked by 2 sphinxes between scrolling acanthus above gilt guilouche band enclosing flowerheads, underglaze blue crowned "N" mark 1,350.00

Figure, girl reading, blue coat, yellow pants, boy with garland, yellow coat, pink garments, 6" h, $525.

Candleholder, 3" h, raised flowers and nude figures 120.00

Compote, cov, 9" h, oval, relief molded cherubs on sides, cherub finial and handles 250.00

Cup and Saucer, molded cup ext. with sea nymphs swimming in the ocean, gilt int. with painted floral sprigs, molded putti on saucers, underglaze blue crowned "N" mark, set of 12 .... 2,500.00

Demitasse Set, covered coffeepot, creamer, sugar, six ftd cups and saucers, large round ftd tray, artist sgd, 17 pc set 275.00

Ferner, 11" l, oval, relief molded and enameled allegorical figures, full relief female mask at each end 110.00

Figure, 14" h, African Crowned Crane, one foot in water, other with water plants on base, sgd "G. Armani" 190.00

Plate, 9" d, raised classical figure in border surrounding central armorial crests, sgd on reverse "Palazzo Reale Napoli," 19th C, slight surface wear, 12 pc set 1,495.00

Snuff Box, 3-1/4" d, hinged lid, cartouche shape, molded basketweave and flowerhead ext., painted int. with court lady and page examining portrait of gentlemen, gold mountings, c1740, minor restoration 1,650.00

Urn, cov, 21-1/8" h, ovoid, central molded frieze of Nerieds and putti, molded floral garlands, gadroon upper section, acanthus molded lower section, socle foot with putti, sq plinth base, applied ram's head handles, domed cov, acorn finial, underglaze crowned "N" mark, minor chips and losses, pr 1,650.00

Wall Plaque, 27" h, shield shape, tooled leather frame, late 19th C, wear 865.00

CARLSBAD CHINA

History: Because of changing European boundaries during the last 100 years, German-speaking Carlsbad has found itself located first in the Austro-Hungarian Empire, then in Germany, and currently in the Czech Republic. Carlsbad was one of the leading pottery manufacturing centers in Bohemia.

Wares from the numerous Carlsbad potteries are lumped together under the term "Carlsbad China." Most pieces on the market are post-1891, although several potteries date to the early 19th century.

Ashtray, 5-1/4" d, multicolored Dutch men and women strolling waterfront 18.00

Bowl, 8-3/4" d, shallow, gold center with death of King Lear scene, green border, artist sgd 85.00

Butter Dish, cov, 7-1/4" d, pink flowers, green leaves, wavy gold lines, white ground 65.00

Chocolate Pot, cov, 10" h, blue, scenic portrait, mkd "Carlsbad Victoria" 115.00

Creamer and Sugar, Bluebird pattern, mkd "Victoria Carlsbad" 70.00

Ewer, 14" h, handles, light green, floral dec, gold trim, mkd "Carlsbad Victoria" 85.00

Hair Receiver, 4" d, cobalt blue flowers, emb basketweave at top, gold trim, white ground.................................... 45.00

Oyster Plate, 9-3/4" d, lavender flowers, gold outlining, white ground 125.00

Pin Tray, 8-1/2" l, irregular scalloped shape, roses, green leaves, white ground, mkd "Victoria Carlsbad Austria" 40.00

Pitcher, 8" h, gold floral dec, cream ground, ornate handle 65.00

Plate, 9" d, hp cherries, artist sgd 35.00

Sugar Shaker, 5-1/2" h, egg shape, floral dec 70.00

Urn, 14-1/2" h, rose bouquet, shaded ivory ground, mkd "Carlsbad Austria" 155.00

Vase, 9-1/2" h, center medallion of 4 Grecian figures, dark blue-green ground, ornate cream handles" 65.00

Vase, handle, blue to and base with gold circles, pink chrysanthemums, cream ground, small blue flowers, mkd "Victoria, Carlsbad, Austria," 10-1/4" h, 4-1/2" d, $175.

CARNIVAL GLASS

History: Carnival glass, an American invention, is colored pressed glass with a fired-on iridescent finish. It was first manufactured about 1905 and immensely popular both in America and abroad. More than 1,000 different patterns have been identified. Production of old carnival glass patterns ended in 1930.

Most of the popular patterns of carnival glass were produced by five companies–Dugan, Fenton, Imperial, Millersburg, and Northwood.

Marks: Northwood patterns frequently are found with the "N" trademark. Dugan used a diamond trademark on several patterns.

References: Gary E. Baker et al., *Wheeling Glass*, Oglebay Institute, 1994 (distributed by Antique Publications); Elaine and Fred Blair, *Carnival Hunte's Companion: A Guide to Pattern Recognition*, published by authors (P.O. Box 116335, Carrolton, TX 75011), 1995; Carol O. Burns, *Collector's Guide to Northwood Carnival Glass*, L-W Book Sales, 1994; Bill Edwards, *Standard Encyclopedia of Carnival Glass*, 5th ed., Collector Books, 1996; Marion T.

Hartung, *First Book of Carnival Glass to Tenth Book of Carnival Glass* (series of 10 books), published by author, 1968 to 1982; William Heacock, James Measell and Berry Wiggins, *Dugan/Diamond*, Antique Publications, 1993; ––, *Harry Northwood, The Wheeling Years, 1901–1925*, Antique Publications, 1991; Marie McGee, *Millersburg Glass*, Antique Publications, 1995; Tom and Sharon Mordini, *Carnival Glass Auction Price for Auctions Conducted in 1995*, published by authors (36 N. Mernitz, Freeport, IL 61032), 1996.

Collectors' Clubs: American Carnival Glass Assoc., 9621 Springwater Lane, Miamisburg, OH 45342; Canadian Carnival Glass Assoc., 107 Montcalm Dr., Kitchner, Ontario N2B 2R4 Canada; Collectible Carnival Glass Assoc., 3103 Brentwood Circle, Grand Island, NE 68801;

Heart of America Carnival Glass Assoc., 4305 W. 78th St., Prairie Village, KS 66208; International Carnival Glass Assoc., P.O. Box 306, Mentone, IN 46539; Lincoln-Land Carnival Glass Club, N951, Hwy. 27, Conrath, WI 54731; National Duncan Glass Society, P.O. Box 965, Washington, PA 15301; New England Carnival Glass Club, 27 Wells Rd., Broad Brooks, CT 06016; Tampa Bay Carnival Glass Club, 101st Ave. N., Pinellas Park, FL 34666; WWW.CGA at http://www.woodsland.com.

Museums: National Duncan Glass Society, Washington, PA; Fenton Art Glass Co, Williamstown, WV.

Notes: Color is the most important factor in pricing carnival glass. The color of a piece is determined by holding it to the light and looking through it.

Acanthus, Imperial, bowl, 7-1/2" d, smoke 50.00
Acorn, Fenton, bowl, 8" d, marigold 100.00
Amaryllis, Northwood, compote, pastel............................150.00
Apple Blossom Twigs, Dugan, bowl, low, ruffled, marigold.70.00
April Showers, Fenton, vase
    6" h, squatty, amethyst 125.00
    13" h, blue..50.00
Beaded Bulls Eye, Imperial, vase, 9" h, pastel..................170.00
Blackberry Wreath, Millersburg, sauce, 3 in 1, green..........85.00
Brocaded Acorns, Fostoria, plate, 7-1/2" d, lavender 225.00
Bushel Basket, Northwood
    Amethyst...250.00
    White...200.00
Butterfly and Berry, Fenton, vase, 7" h, tightly crimped edge,
    blue...80.00
Butterfly and Fern, Fenton, tumbler, amethyst 50.00
Cosmos, ice cream bowl, 6" d, green 65.00
Cut Flowers, Jenkins, vase, 10", h.....................................110.00
Diamond Point, Northwood, vase, 10" h, ice blue 300.00
Diamond Rib, vase, 10" h, green...90.00
Dogwood Sprays, Dugan, bowl, tricorn, dome ftd, peach opalescent..50.00
Double Stem, rose bowl, domed foot, peach opalescent..160.00
Dragon and Lotus, Fenton
    Bowl, ruffled, plain back, amber....................................120.00
    Bowl, 3 in 1, light amethyst, irid pink and blue highlights..225.00
    Ice Cream Bowl, chip, marigold..40.00
Drapery, Northwood
    Candy Dish, N mark, marigold 135.00
    Rose Bowl, white 425.00
    Vase, 8" h, marigold, small chip 35.00

Cherry Circles, Fenton, bonbon, red, $5,600. Photo courtesy of Albrecht Auction.

Christmas, Dugan, compote, purple, $5,250. Photo courtesy of Albrecht Auction.

Dutch Mill, ashtray, marigold..30.00
Embroidered Mums, Northwood, bowl, ruffled, marigold ..400.00
Fanciful, Dugan
 Bowl, ruffled, peach opalescent....................................160.00
 Ice Cream Bowl, peach opalescent 160.00
Fashion, Imperial, rose bowl, green 300.00
Fine Cut, Jenkins, vase, 10" h, marigold.............................80.00
Fine Cut and Roses, Northwood, rose bowl
 Ice Blue...195.00
 White..225.00
Flowering Dill, Fenton, hat, amethyst....................................40.00
Flute, berry bowl, aqua..20.00
Good Luck, Northwood
 Bowl, pie crust edge, basketweave ext., green 225.00
 Bowl, ruffled, amethyst 100.00
Grape, Imperial
 Cup and Saucer, marigold 40.00
 Decanter, stopper, marigold 75.00
 Tumbler, pastel..30.00
Grape and Cable, Northwood
 Bowl, 7-1/4" d, basketweave back, green.........................80.00
 Bowl, ruffled, basketweave ext., marigold........................35.00

Hattie, Imperial, chop plate, amber, 10-1/2" d, $3,850. Photo courtesy of Albrecht Auction.

Breakfast Creamer, purple 100.00
Candle Lamp, marigold..600.00
Cracker Jar, cov, marigold 350.00
Hatpin Holder, green..350.00
Ice Cream Bowl, 10-1/2" l, white, sgd................................175.00
Orange Bowl, banded, blue..800.00
Plate, 7-3/4" d, hand grip, basketweave ext., green, sgd
....135.00
Plate, 8" d, 2 sides up, basketweave ext., green 120.00
Plate, 9" d, plain back, marigold..80.00
Spooner, marigold, chip 25.00
Sugar Bowl, cov, green 175.00
Grape Delight, Dugan
 Nut Bowl, white...90.00
 Rose Bowl, white 100.00
Grapevine Lattice, Dugan, bowl, low, ruffled, white.............85.00
Hearts and Flowers, Northwood
 Bowl, ruffled, ice blue..270.00
 Compote, white...150.00
Holly, Fenton
 Bowl, crimped, ruffled edge, 9" d, marigold.................135.00
 Bowl, ruffled, aqua...85.00
 Hat, 4 sides up, aqua 60.00
 Ice Cream Bowl, scalloped, 9" d, marigold 25.00
 Plate, 9-1/4" d, white..300.00
Holly and Berry, Dugan, bowl, ruffled, peach opalescent .110.00
Lattice and Points, Dugan, vase, 9-1/2" h, marigold 40.00
Leaf Column, Northwood, vase, 10" h, white......................125.00
Lined Lattice, Dugan, vase, 11" h, light lavender/smoke ...220.00
Long Thumbprint, Dugan, vase, 7" h, aqua...........................35.00
Lotus and Grape, Fenton
 Bowl, low, ruffled, marigold 65.00
 Bowl, 7" d, ftd, marigold 25.00
Lustre Rose, Imperial
 Ice Cream Bowl, 10" d, ftd, pastel 220.00
 Plate, 9" d, amber...120.00
Memphis, Northwood, punch cup, marigold...........................7.50
Mikado, Fenton, compote, ruffled, blue..............................650.00
Northern Star, Fenton, plate, 6" d, two sides turned up, very light
 marigold...20.00
Octagon, Imperial, wine, marigold 25.00
Omnibus, U. S. Glass, tumbler, marigold...........................225.00
Orange Tree, Fenton
 Bowl, ruffled, 9" d, white 110.00
 Mug, Persian Blue 60.00
 Orange Bowl, blue...150.00

Hobnail Swirl, Millersburg, lady's spittoon, green, small chip, $7,000. Photo courtesy of Albrecht Auction.

Plate, trunk base, white 175.00
Tumbler, marigold 70.00
Pansy, Imperial, dresser tray, stippled amber 135.00
Peacock and Grape, Fenton, ice cream bowl, spatula foot, green
....60.00
Peacock and Urn, Fenton
    Compote, blue..45.00
    Ice Cream Bowl, dark marigold...............................600.00
    Plate, 9" d, deep marigold..................................260.00
Peacock at Fountain, Northwood
    Compote, ice blue...1,100.00
    Pitcher, light blue.......................................2,000.00
    Tumbler, light blue..100.00
Peacocks, Northwood, bowl, ruffled, ribbed back, marigold
....325.00
Persian Garden, Dugan
    Bowl, 10-1/2" d, deep, ruffled, peach......................450.00
    Plate, 6" d, white..65.00
Persian Medallion, Fenton
    Bowl, aqua..75.00
    Plate, 6" d, marigold 50.00
Pine Cone, Fenton, plate, 6"
    Blue, silvery iridescent....................................95.00
    Marigold..70.00
Plume Panels, Fenton
    Compote, green..40.00
    Vase, 10-1/2" h, red.......................................650.00
    Vase, 12" h, green...100.00
Poppy Show, Northwood, plate, amethyst 1,150.00
Rainbow, Northwood
    Bowl, basketweave back, green 105.00
    Compote, amethyst...95.00
Ribbon Tie, Fenton, bowl, 3 in 1, amethyst 130.00
Ripple, Imperial, vase, 10-1/2" h, green 50.00
Rococo, Imperial, bowl, ruffled, marigold 20.00
Round-Up, Dugan, bowl, low, ruffled, marigold..................85.00
Rustic, Fenton, vase
    6-1/2" h, white...70.00
    20" h, 5" dbase, green....................................1,500.00
Sailboats, Fenton, bowl, 6" d, ruffled, marigold..................75.00
Scroll Embossed, Imperial
    Compote, large, deep amethyst...............................80.00
    Plate, green 60.00

Poppy Show, Northwood, plate, green, 9" d, $3,000. Photo courtesy of Mickey Reichel Auction Service.

Tornado, Northwood, vase, marigold, pastel green tornado centers, $2,100. Photo courtesy of Mickey Reichel Auction Service.

Singing Birds, Northwood
    Berry Bowl, master, green 2,500.00
    Mug, amethyst...75.00
    Mug, light blue..550.00
Single Flower, Dugan
    Bowl, 3-1, peach opalescent.................................35.00
    Plate, 7" d, peach opalescent...............................40.00
Ski Star, Dugan
    Banana Boat, peach opalescent...............................50.00
    Bowl, ruffled, 8", peach opalescent.........................50.00
Springtime, Northwood
    Tumbler, green..65.00
    Water Pitcher, green.......................................900.00
S-Repeat, Dugan, punch cup, amethyst 12.50
Stag and Holly, Fenton, ice cream bowl, 8" d, spatula foot, marigold..90.00
Star of David and Bows, Northwood, bowl, amethyst 70.00
Stippled Rays, Northwood, bowl, amethyst.......................60.00
Stippled Strawberries, Jenkins, plate, 9" d, ribbed back, green
....1,250.00
Stork and Rushes, Dugan, tumbler, blue 35.00
Strawberry, Millersburg and Northwood
    Bowl, 8-1/2" d, pie crust edge, stippled, blue 450.00
    Bowl, 9" d, plain back, pastel marigold 200.00
    Compote, amethyst 400.00
    Ice Cream Bowl, amethyst...................................150.00
Plate, basketweave ext., marigold................................76.00
Sunflower, Millersburg, pin tray, green...........................90.00
Swan, master salt, celeste blue.................................20.00
Swirl, Northwood, compote, tricorn, 3-1/2" d, marigold......100.00
Thistle, Fenton
    Banana Boat, deep marigold 140.00
    Bowl, 9" d, 3 in 1, green...................................70.00
Three Fruits, Northwood
    Bowl, ruffled, meander ext., stippled, ftd, butterscotch aqua
      opal..450.00
    Bowl, stippled, ribbed back, collar base, white 250.00
    Plate, basketweave ext., green 200.00
    Plate, stippled, ribbed back, amethyst.....................450.00
Tree Trunk, Northwood, vase, 12" h, 4-3/4" dbase, amethyst, sgd
....245.00
Tulip and Cane, Imperial, goblet, marigold.......................40.00
Two Flowers, Fenton, rose bowl, ftd, blue.......................100.00
Vineyard, Dugan, water pitcher, marigold.........................90.00
Vintage, Fenton, Millersburg, Northwood
    Bowl, 8" d, candy ribbon edge, green.......................175.00
    Bowl, 9" d, ruffled, green..................................60.00
    Plate, 7-1/2" d, amethyst..................................450.00

Whirling Leaves, Millersburg, bowl, ruffled
    Amethyst..150.00
    Green, radium iridescent..100.00
Wide Rib, Dugan, vase, 11" h, cobalt blue.........................50.00
Wishbone, Northwood
    Bowl, ruffled, 3 ftd, white 300.00
    Epergne, single lily, green...550.00
Zig Zag, Millersburg, bowl, amethyst, 3 in 1, amethyst......450.00

CAROUSEL FIGURES

History: By the late 17th century, carousels were found in most capital cities of Europe. In 1867, Gustav Dentzel carved America's first carousel. Other leading American firms include Charles I. D. Looff, Allan Herschell, Charles Parker, and William F. Mangels.

References: Charlotte Dinger, *Art of the Carousel*, Carousel Art, 1983; Tobin Fraley, *The Carousel Animal*, Tobin Fraley Studios, 1983; Frederick Fried, *Pictorial History of the Carousel*, Vestal Press, 1964; William Manns, Peggy Shank, and Marianne Stevens, *Painted Ponies*, Zon International Publishing, 1986.

Periodicals: *Carousel Collecting & Crafting*, 3755 Avocado Blvd., Suite 164, La Mesa, CA 91941; *Carousel News & Trader*, Suite 206, 87 Park Avenue West, Mansfield, OH 44902; *Carousel Shopper*, Zon International Publishing, P.O. Box 6459, Santa Fe, NM 87502.

Collectors' Clubs: American Carousel Society, 3845 Telegraph Rd., Elkton, MD 21921; National Amusement Park Historical Assoc., P.O. Box 83, Mount Prospect, IL 60056; National Carousel Assoc., P.O. Box 4333, Evansville, IN 47724.

Museums: Carousel Museum of America, San Francisco, CA; Heritage Plantation of Sandwich, Sandwich, MA; Herschell Carrousel Factory Museum, North Tonawanda, NY; International Museum of Carousel Art, Portland, OR; Merry-Go-Round Museum, Sandusky, OH; New England Carousel Museum, Inc., Bristol, CT.

Notes: Since carousel figures were repainted annually, original paint is not a critical factor to collectors. "Park paint" indicates layers of accumulated paint; "stripped" means paint has been removed to show carving; "restored" involves stripping and repainting in the original colors.

Barber Chair, Stein & Goldstein 5,000.00
Camel
    European, 1890 ....2,000.00
    Loeff..7,000.00
    Morris, E. Joy..8,000.00
Chariot Bench
    Loeff, gilded...625.00
    Parker, C. W..12,500.00
    Spillman, with flowers 300.00
    Unknown maker, one panel having applied carved flowers, other side with applied carved eagle and horse, 52" x 29" 800.00
Cow, Bayol, France 5,000.00
Elephant, fiberglass..600.00
Deer, P.T.C., orig paint...20,000.00
Donkey, Illions, from Willow Grove Amusement Park, Willow Grove, PA 17,000.00

Horse, Philadelphia Toboggan Co., carved and painted, c1918, 70" l, 65" h, $11,000.

Giraffe, Loeff...13,000.00
Goat, Loeff...7,500.00
Horse
    Anderson, J. R., jumper...5,000.00
    Bayol, France, jumper 3,000.00
    Carmel, jumper..3,700.00
    Dare, Charles W. F., New York Carousel Manufacturing Company, Brooklyn, NY, jumper
        56" l, 39" h, orig paint, old repair, minor imperfections 9,775.00
        60" l, 39" h, orig paint, very minor losses, paint wear and loss 8,625.00
    Dentzel
        Escape Jumper, restored in fiber glass 7,750.00
        Jumper, top knot..5,000.00
        Prancer, orig paint 8,000.00
    Herschell, Allen
        Combination wood and fiber glass...........................650.00
        Jumper, all wood, 1920 ....2,000.00
        Metal, restored..800.00
        Trojan, restored 3,750.00
    Herschell-Spillman, North Tonawanda, NY, jumper, orange, green, and blue, 60" x 56" x 12" cast iron stand....2,750.00
    Heyn, Frederick 4,100.00
    Hubner, prancer, fully restored 4,250.00
    Illions
        Jumper, inside row, from Seaside Heights, NJ, amusement park 2,950.00
        Jumper, second row, from Seaside Heights, NJ, amusement park 7,000.00
        Jumper, from Willow Grove Amusement Park, Willow Grove, PA...5,000.00
        Stander, armored, from Willow Grove Amusement Park, Willow Grove, PA....................................75,000.00
        Stander, from Willow Grove Amusement Park, Willow Grove, PA...13,000.00
    Loeff, stander, closed mouth, from Wilkes-Barre, PA 14,200.00
    Morris, E. J., stander..10,500.00
    Norman & Evans 1,500.00
    Ortega, jumper 300.00
    Parker, C.W. Abilene, KA, c1905, carved mane, saddle, American flag, glass eyes, old polychrome repaint, 56" h,

added base and brass post, replaced tail and stirrups, old sheet metal repairs over seams and breaks in legs 1,760.00

P.T.C., jumper..3,250.00

Spillman
　Jumper, restored 3,300.00
　Stander, animal pelt..4,600.00
　Stander, from New York park........................10,000.00

Stein & Goldstein
　Jumper 2,750.00
　Stander 11,000.00

Indian Pony
　Parker, C.W., pelt saddle.......................................9,000.00
　Spillman 4,500.00

Panel, wood
　12" x 21" x 2", carved leaf patter panels, pr...................100.00
　37-1/2" x 45", cowboy on bucking bronco in panoramic view 200.00
　63" x 13", carved, cherub at top, carved leaves overall 450.00

Pig
　Dentzel, restored 12,000.00
　Spillman, with pear, from Las Vegas 5,000.00

Sign, C.W. Parker, paper, "Jumping Horse Carry-Us-All Carousel," 21" x 28" 525.00

CASTLEFORD

History: Castleford is a soft-paste porcelain made in Yorkshire, England, in the 1800s for the American trade. The wares have a warm, white ground, scalloped rims (resembling castle tops), and are trimmed in deep blue. Occasionally pieces are decorated further with a coat of arms, eagles, or Lady Liberty.

Creamer, 4-1/4" h, Parian, white, deep blue striping, emb classical scenes of cherubs 100.00
Milk Jug, 4-3/4" h, oval, relief of American eagle on one side, Liberty and cap on reverse, acanthus leaf border 165.00
Sugar, cov, relief of classical figure leaning on urn, acanthus leaf panel, blue enamel border, scalloped edge, 3 enameled bands on cov 250.00
Teapot, cov, 6" h, molded eagle dec, early 19th C, minor imperfections 245.00

Sugar Bowl, cov, $250.

CASTOR SETS

History: A castor set consists of matched condiment bottles held within a frame or holder. The bottles are for condiments such as salt, pepper, oil, vinegar, and mustard. The most commonly found castor sets consist of three, four, or five glass bottles in a silver-plated frame.

Although castor sets were made as early as the 1700s, most of the sets encountered today date from 1870 to 1915, the period when they enjoyed their greatest popularity.

3 Bottle, clear, Daisy and Button pattern, toothpick holder center, matching glass holder 125.00
3 Bottle, clear, Ribbed Palm pattern, pewter tops and frame 185.00
4 Bottle, clear, mold blown, pewter lids and frame, domed based, loop handle, mkd "I. Trask," early 19th C, 8" h..............320.00
4 Bottle, cranberry bottles and jars, clear pressed glass frame, silver plated look handle, two brass caps, one pewter, 9-1/2" h...275.00
4 Bottle, green cut to clear, sq bottles, SP frame..............340.00
4 Bottle, rubena, Venecia pattern, glass frame 200.00
4 Bottle, ruby stained, Ruby Thumbprint pattern, glass frame 360.00
5 Bottle, clear, Bellflower pattern, pressed stoppers, pewter frame with pedestal 295.00
5 Bottle, clear, allover cut linear and geometric design, SS mounts and frame, shell shaped foot, English hallmarks, c1750, 8-1-2/" h 625.00
5 Bottle, clear, Honeycomb pattern, ornate Wilcox frame 265.00
5 Bottle, cut glass, ornate Rogers & Bros. frame 295.00
5 Bottle, etched, wreath and polka dots pattern, rib trimmed frame..195.00
6 Bottle, china, Willow ware, matching frame....................150.00
6 Bottle, clear, pressed bottles, SP Simpson Hall & Miller frame 150.00

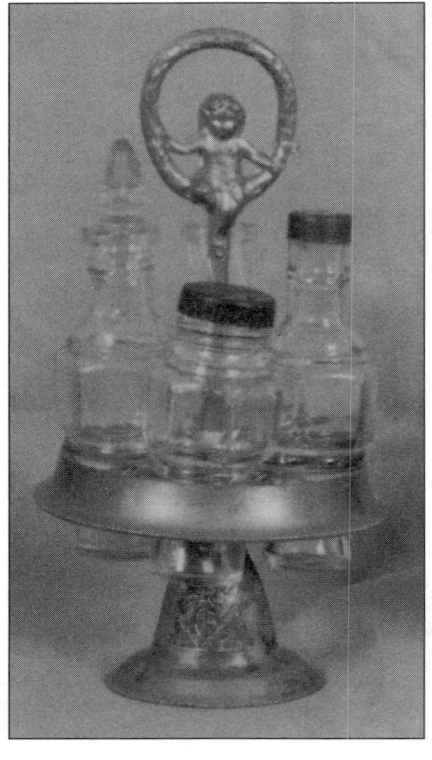

Four Bottle, Flute pattern, Girl in Ring metal holder, child's size, $200. Photo courtesy of Gene Harris Antique Auction Center.

6 Bottle, cut, diamond point panels, rotating sterling silver frame, all over flowers, paw feet, loop handle, Gorham Mfg. Co., c1880, 11-1/2" h 2,500.00
6 Bottle, cut, pewter frame with mechanical door housing, Gleason 1,500.00

CATALOGS

History: The first American mail-order catalog was issued by Benjamin Franklin in 1744. This popular advertising tool helped to spread inventions, innovations, fashions, and necessities of life to rural America. Catalogs were profusely illustrated and are studied today to date an object, identify its manufacturer, study its distribution, and determine its historical importance.

References: Ron Barlow and Ray Reynolds, *Insider's Guide to Old Books, Magazines, Newspapers, Trade Catalogs*, Windmill Publishing (2147 Windmill View Rd., Cajon, CA 92020), 1995; Lawrence B. Romaine, *Guide to American Trade Catalogs 1744-1900*, Dover Publications, n.d.

Museums: Grand Rapids Public Museum, Grand Rapids, MI; National Museum of Health and Medicine, Walter Reed Medical Center, Washington, DC.

Additional Listings: See *Warman's Americana & Collectibles* for more examples.

Advisor: Kenneth Schneringer.

Abercrombie & Fitch, New York, NY, 1956, 7-1/2" x 9-3/4", Fall Book 28.00
Alfred Peats Co., Chicago, IL, 1925, 48 pgs, 6-1/2" x 9-1/2", Peat's Catalog of Paints and Decorators Supplies 21.00
American Bed Co., St. Louis, MO, 1927, 48 pgs, 5-1/4" x 10", Cat. No. 23, enameled steel beds 28.00
Berlin Tanning & Mfg. Co., Berlin, WI, c1923, 5-1/4" x 7-1/2", gloves and mittens 24.00
Bryce Brothers, Mt. Pleasant, PA, 1963, 24 pgs, 8-1/2" x 11", 12 pgs price list and laid-in letter, glassware 28.00
Cadillac Motor Car Division, Detroit, MI, 1973, 87 pgs, 10-1/4" x 11-1/2", salesman's merchandising guide, swatches of upholstery, high gloss illus, fold-up leather book, metallic silver Cadillac insignia on front 60.00
Carl Fischer, Inc., New York, NY, 1928, 55 pgs, 8" x 10", Catalog of Violin and Stringed Instruments, 5 colored sheets, front wrap loose 66.00
Carr & Baal Co., Des Moines, IA, c1925, 403 pgs, 6-1/2" x 9-3/4", Bilt-Well Millwork 44.00
Columbia Recording Corp., New York, NY, 1943, 5-1/2" x 8-1/4", Columbia Record Catalog 15.00
Decorators Supply Co., Chicago, IL, 1917, 288 pgs, 9" x 12-1/4", Illustrated Catalog of Plastic Ornaments Cast in Plaster for Interiors and Composition of Exteriors, hard cover 50.00
Dennison Manufacturing Co., Boston, MA, 1904, 104 pgs, 6" x 8-1/2", tissue and crepe paper art and decorative ideas ... 23.00
Edison Lamp Works, Cleveland, OH, 1930, 40 pgs 4" x 6-1/2", stand and intermediate price schedules for Edison Mazda lamps, illus 42.00
Ed Spring & Summer Styles 48.00
Eureka Mower Co., Towanda, PA, 1879, 16 pgs, 5-3/4" x 8-1/2", Wilber's Eureka Mower, 2 pictures of mower in action, other pictures of parts, supplies, prices 48.00
Frost's Stamp & Stencil, Worcester, PA, c1904, 104 pgs, 6" x 9", Cat. N.10, A Feast of Appliances For Producing Graphicware & Samples 65.00

Starrett Precision Tools, Athol, MA, Catalog 26, copyright 1938, 4-7/8" x 7", $35.

Garden City Watch Co., Chicago, IL, 1900, 228 pgs, 7-3/4" x 10", watches and jewelry, illus 44.00
Grand Rapids Fibre Cord., Grand Rapids, MI, 1927, 161 pgs, 6" x 9", Art Fibre Weaving of Furniture, illus 28.00
Granite State Evaporator, Marlow, NH, 1897, 32 pgs, 5-3/4" x 8-1/4", Illustrated Catalogue of Sugar Makers' Supplies, cuts and illus 60.00
John Dunn, Inc., Boston MA, 1953, 268 pgs, 8-1/2" x 11", Fall & Winter Catalog of Toys 85.00
John Lewis Childs, Inc., Floral Park, NY, 1922, 64 pgs, 7" x 10", Bulbs That Bloom, wraps loose 11.00
J. T. King & Co., Baltimore, MD, 1852, 24 pgs, 4-3/4" x 7-1/2", description & Philosophy of King's Patent Washing Apparatus & Washing Liquid, printed wrapper, creased, rubbed, soiled, engraving of prototypical clothes washer inside and on front cover, cuts of various parts 72.00
Kenneth Lynch & Sons, Inc., Wilton, CT, 1966, 176 pgs, 11" x 16", International Garden Ornaments No. 2066, price list and catalog supply list laid in 46.00
Kentucky Metal Products Co., Louisville, KY, 76 pgs, 8" x 10", Cat. No. 50, Blue Book of Wire Work 31.00
Lafayette Radio Corp., Chicago, IL, 1942, 128 pgs, 7" x 10", Cat. No. 87, Radio Supplies & Accessories 20.00
Lyon & Healy, Chicago, IL, 1880, 186 pgs, 6" x 9-1/4", McCoch's Guide for Amateur Brass Bands, old rebinding 395.00
Magee Picture & Frame Co., Pochantas, AR, 1972, 42 pgs, 8-1/2" x 11", frames and all types of pictures 11.00
Manufacturers' Price List, US, 1907, 298 pgs, 7-3/4" x 10-1/4", No. 80, jewelry items, cut glass, hand painted china, pipes, guns, etc. 110.00
Marks Arnheim, Inc., New York, NY, 1913, 16 pgs, 4-1/2" x 6-1/2", The Sign of the Ram's Head, custom made clothes for men 32.00
Merrill Woolen Mills Co., Merrill, WI, c1929, 8 pgs, 6-1/2" x 10", orig company mailing envelope 23.00
Middletown Machine Co., NY, 1908, 16 pgs, 3-1/2" x 6-1/4", Appleton wood saws, tools 22.00
Norwalk Lock Co., New York, Y, c1945, 34 pgs, 8-1/4" x 10-3/4", Segal locks and hardware 30.00
Olson Rug Co., Chicago, IL, 1945, 40 pgs, 8-1/2" x 11-1/4", illus of rugs, room settings 14.00
Pittsburgh Plate Glass Co, Pittsburgh, PA, 1942, 24 pgs, 8-1/2" x 11", "Natures Colors in Lasting Beauty, Building Morale Through The Proper Use of Color, "cuts of rooms inside home 11.00

R. H. Macy & Co., New York, NY, c1900, 480 pgs, 6-1/2" x 9-1/4", department store products, hard cover 90.00

Rostand Manufacturing Co., Milford, CT, c1925, 78 pgs, 9-3/8" x 12", Cat. No. 7, Fireplace Fixtures 60.00

Rough Notes Co., Indianapolis, IN, 1911, 84 pgs, 5-3/4" x 8-3/4", everything for the insurance man, forms to filing cabinets 31.00

Sears, Roebuck & Co., Chicago, IL, 1918, 56 pgs, 8" x 11", The Book of Barns, Honor-Bilt, Already Cut Modern Dairy Barns, floor plans, details 76.00

Seth Thomas Clock Co., Thomaston, CT, 1881, 32 pgs, 6" x 9-1/4", illus of mantel clocks, 1 per page........................250.00

Silver Dome, Inc., Detroit, MI, 1936, 20 pgs, 6-3/4" x 9-1/2", Silver Dome for 1936 Motorized Travel Homes, illus of interiors, different models...38.00

Sperry & Hutchinson Co., New York, NY, 1927, 9" x 12-3/4", S & H Green Stamps Merchants Redemption Catalog, hard cover 65.00

Starr Bros. Bell Co., East Hampton, CT, 1922, 15 pgs, 6-1/4" x 7-3/4", bicycle bells...55.00

Standard-Gillett Light Co., Chicago, IL, 1911, 24 pgs, 5" x 9", Standard Vacuum Machines, 2 halftone views 48.00

Standard Sanitary Mfg. Co., Pittsburgh, PA, 1915, 329 pgs, 9-1/4" x 12-1/4", Cat. "PF," Standard Porcelain Enameled Vitreous China & Brass Plumbing Goods, hard cover 65.00

Stover Mfg. & Engine Co., Freeport, IL, c1940, 12 pgs, 4" x 9", Stover Power Shellers, slight damage 14.00

T. Noonan & Sons, Co., Boston, MA, c1929, 56 pgs, 8-1/2" x 11", "Chrometal" Barber Shop Equipment..............................92.00

Ward's Natural Science, Rochester, NY, 1885, 121 pgs, 5-3/4" x 9", Catalogue of Specimens of Mollusca for Sale, illus ...65.00

Westinghouse Electric Corp., Metuchen, NJ, 1956, 72 pgs, 8-3/4" x 11", spiral bound, television and radio catalog 39.00

CELADON

History: The term "celadon," meaning a pale grayish green color, is derived from the theatrical character Celadon, who wore costumes of varying shades of grayish green, in Honore d'Urfe's 17th-century pastoral romance, *L'Astree.* French Jesuits living in China used the name to refer to a specific type of Chinese porcelain.

Celadon divides into two types. Northern celadon, made during the Sung Dynasty up to the 1120s, has a gray to brownish body, relief decoration, and monochromatic olive green glaze. Southern (Lung-ch'uan) celadon, made during the Sung Dynasty and much later, is paint-decorated with floral and other scenic designs and is found in forms which would appeal to the European and American export market. Many of the southern pieces date from 1825 to 1885. A blue square with Chinese or pseudo-Chinese characters appears on pieces after 1850. Later pieces also have a larger and sparser decorative patterning.

Reproduction Alert.

Bowl
7" d, café au lait jade, ornate wooden stand, Ming Dynasty, Chinese..1,3200.00
14-3/4" d, deep rounded sides, waisted rim, everted lip, ext. with interwoven bands of flowering magnolias, 3 cylindrical applied monster head feet, pale gray-green glaze, unglazed base, Chinese...950.00
Censor, 10-3/4" d, compressed globular form, 3 monster head supports, etc. carved with Eight Trigrams, thick gray-green crackle glaze, int. central portion and base unglazed, kiln flaws, Longquan, Ming Dynasty 675.00

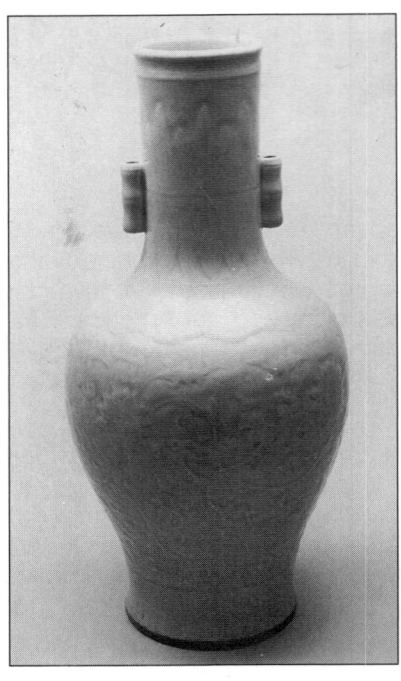

Vase, body of molded lingzhi and reticulared foliage, stick neck with acanthus band, bamboo handles, 14" h, $1,400.

Dish, 6-3/4" d, steel sides, everted rim, small ring foot, muted green glaze, wide crackle pattern, Korean, Koryo Dynasty 295.00

Ginger Jar, 6" h, bulbous, multicolored relief floral dec, dark green leaves, gold trim...175.00

Libation Cup, 3-3/4" h, steep tapering sides, foliate rim, dragon and clouds, blue-green glaze, 19th C 225.00

Snuff Bottle, carved gourd, foliate, and butterfly dec, russet jade stopper, Chinese 175.00

Vase, 7-3/4" h, Hu form, lower relief, handles.................1,750.00

CELLULOID ITEMS

History: In 1869, Albany, New York, printer John W. Hyatt developed and patented the world's first commercially successful semi-synthetic thermoplastic. Made from camphor and pyroxylin, a type of cellulose nitrate, Hyatt and his brother Isaiah named the material "Celluloid," a contraction of the words cellulose and colloid.

By the mid-1870s, the Hyatts were successfully making pyroxylin plastic in imitation of expensive luxury materials at the Celluloid Manufacturing Company of Newark, NJ. In the early days of its commercial development, celluloid was used for only a few utilitarian applications. However, by the 1880s, fabricating companies were busy molding the plastic into a variety of fancy articles, fashion accessories, and novelty items.

As the industry grew, several other factories went into business making pyroxylin plastic identical to Hyatts' Celluloid, but licensed under different trade names: Pyralin (manufactured by Arlington Co., Arlington, New Jersey), Fiberloid (Fiberloid Corp., Indian Orchard, Massachusetts), and Viscoloid (Viscoloid Co., Leominster, Massachusetts). Even though these companies branded their products with proper trade names, today the word "celluloid" is used generically and encompasses all forms of this early plastic.

The ease with which celluloid can be manipulated and the abundance of available man-made material helped the industry to grow tremendously. However, pyroxylin plastic did have one major drawback, because of the cellulose nitrate used in its production, it was dangerously flammable. Nevertheless, because celluloid products imitated expensive luxury items, the plastic copies became increasingly popular with the working and middle classes.

Used as a replacement for ivory, amber, and tortoiseshell in hundreds of different utilitarian and novelty applications, it wasn't until the development of the motion picture industry that celluloid gained it's own special purpose. In addition to camera film, it was also used by animation artists who drew cartoons on transparent sheet cels. By fulfilling these unique roles, celluloid was no longer viewed exclusively as a imitation for expensive natural materials.

By 1930 and the advent of the modern plastics age, the use of celluloid began to decline dramatically. Development of nonflammable safety film eventually ended the use of celluloid in the movies, and by 1950 production in the United States had ceased altogether. However, Japan, France, Italy and Korea continue to manufacture celluloid in small amounts today for specialty items such as musical-instrument inlay and ping-pong balls, designer fountain pens and jewelry.

Beware of celluloid items that show signs of deterioration: oily residue, cracking, discoloration, and crystallization. Take care when cleaning celluloid items. It is best to use mild soap and water, avoiding alcohol or acetone based cleaners. Never expose celluloid to excessive heat or flame and avoid extreme sunlight.

Marks: Viscoloid Co. manufactured a large variety of small hollow animals that ranged in size from 2 to 8 inches. Most of these toys are embossed with one of three trademarks: "Made in USA," an intertwined "VCO," or an eagle with a shield.

Advisor: Julie P. Robinson.

Advertising & Souvenir Keepsake Items

Bookmark, 4-1/2" l, diecut ivory grained celluloid, poinsettia motif in red, yellow & green, Psalm 22, David C. Cook Publishing Co. 25.00
Clothing Brush, 3" d, circular brush, shows black and white photograph of Gettysburg Memorial, Gettysburg, PA...........35.00

Combination ruler, ink blotter, 8-3/4" x 1-1/2" wood grained celluloid, tan and light brown tones, features 1917 calendar for "Jennison Co. Engineers & Contractors," mfg. By Brown & Bigelow, St. Paul 30.00
Compact
1-1/4" x 2" metal powder compact with celluloid top, featuring scenic view of Cypress Gardens................................15.00
1-3/4" octagonal metal compact with inset pearlized celluloid lid in light amber tone, pink & blue floral motif; reverse has shield shaped medallion of Harrisburg, PA...............12.00
Fan, 4" h, mottled turquoise and cream celluloid Brise, light blue ribbon, shows the Washington Monument and words "Washington D.C." in gold tone paint 15.00
Ink Blotter, 2-1/2" x 6" rect, booklet of blotters with decorative celluloid cover, shepherds overseeing sheep; A Merry Christmas; Keller Mfg. Co. of Allentown, PA, Christmas 1921, printed by Whitehead and Hoag Co 25.00
Letter Opener, 6-3/4" l, round bookmark medallion features Indian profile while the pointed letter knife mkd "SOUVENIR OF QUEBEC" 18.00
Match Safe
2-1/2" x 1-1/2" ivory grained, blue and black graphics "New England Made Cigars, Carry This Blue Union Label On The Box & Before Purchasing A Cigar Be Sure & See that This Blue Label is on The Box" 65.00
2-1/2" x 1-1/2", celluloid photo dec in green tones feature scenic views of Atlantic City, NJ 15.00
Note Pad, 4-1/4" x 2-1/2" leather bound celluloid cover, children with bird and advertisement "Presented By Germania Savings Bank, Pittsburgh, PA," reverse has 1906 Calendar.........25.00
Pocket Mirror
Oval shaped, pink rose motif; "Use Mennen's Flesh Tint Talcum Powder" 50.00
Round, 1-1/2" d, Bedford Peanut Butter, colorful graphics on cream ground features a jar of peanut butter 75.00
Pyro Print, 7-7/8" x 4-5/16" black ink over ivory grained celluloid sheet, featuring image of boy and girl at waters edge, "Smoke Mellow Mixture" printed by the Pyro Photo Company, NY, imp patent date Aug. 11, 1891..110.00
Shoe Horn, 5-1/2" l, two tone amber and cream pearlescent, "HR Holden & Co. Inc-Shoe Store Supplies, 184 Summer St. Boston," c1925 ....15.00
Tape Measure
1-1/4" d with pull out tape; colorful picture of pretty girl with flowers, advertisement for "The First National Bank of Boswell, The Same Old Bank in its New Home" printed by P.N. Co. (Parisian Novelty Co. of Chicago) and Patent 7-10-17 emb in the side 65.00

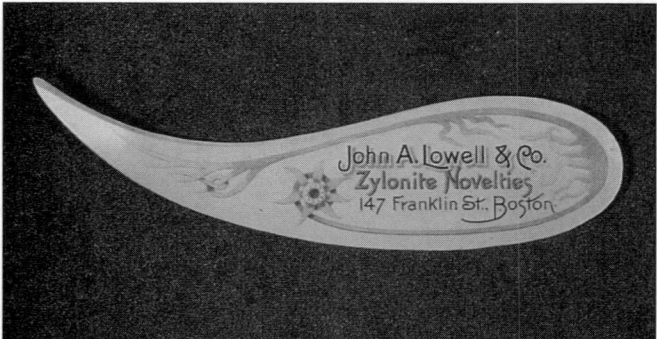

Advertising letter opener, ivory grained, sickle shaped, adv for Zylonite Novelties, $85. Photo courtesy of Julie Robinson.

Autograph album, celluloid cover, ocean scene with sea gulls, c1907, 5-1/2" x 4." Photo courtesy of Julie Robinson.

1-1/2" d, cream, black lettering, "JR Kramer Inc. Butter, NY.," mfg. by JB Carroll Co. of Chicago..............................15.00

2-5/8" h, red celluloid bear on round pink tape measure base, Souvenir of Old Orchard Beach, Maine......................65.00

Template, 3-7/16" x 1-13/16", typewriter correction template, "Remtico Typewriter Supplies" Remington Typewriter Co., printed by Whitehead & Hoag of Newark, NJ.................20.00

Decorative Items and Fancy Goods

Autograph Album, 4" x 5-1/2", printed celluloid with ocean scene, sea gulls, predominately green and blue colors.............45.00

Candle Holders, pr, 6-1/2" h, with round weighted base, trademark Tuskoid in triangular outline......................................65.00

Clock
3-1/2" w x 4-1/2" h, ivory grained rect mantle clock........30.00
6-1/2" x 5-1/2", classical design with columns, pink pearlescence celluloid, round clock face, working order, c1930 ....45.00

Collar Box, triangular shape, 10" on w end and 5" on back, 6-1/2" h, completely covered in brown imitation wood grained celluloid with bright yellow rose motif on the top.....................55.00

Dresser Box
3-1/2" deep, 8" x 6-1/4" embossed white celluloid with floral motif, fitted with imitation ivory brush, mirror, salve box, file and nail cleaner, mkd "Celluloid, 62" on the mirror, deep maroon satin lining, c1890..150.00
4-1/2" w, 4-1/2" h, grained ivory celluloid fashioned in the shape of a grand Piano, lift top with celluloid prop, blue velvet lining, no trademark...65.00

Dresser Set
Arch Amerith, Beverly Pattern, Ivory with amber edging, scalloped beveled edge, mirror, comb, rect clothing brush, imitation ivory tray with amber trimming, matching powder jar and hair receiver, perfume bottle with celluloid holder, ivory pin cushion base with scalloped amber trim, mkd Arch Amerith, Beverly...125.00
Black with green pearlescent surface, dresser tray with oval glass center, comb, brush, mirror, glass powder jar with matching celluloid lid, c1930......................................35.00
Fiberloid, Fairfax pattern, variegated brown and gold, Fairfax pattern, includes 11 pieces, powder box, hair receiver, mir-ror, brush, comb, file, 2 button hooks, scissors and clothing brush..85.00
Pyralin, DuBarry pattern, vanity set in ivory, brush and comb, button hook, clothing brush, dresser tray, hair receiver, hand mirror, manicure implements, buffer and slave box, powder box, vase and frame...................................145.00

Frame
2-3/4" x 4-1/4" filigree lace edge with oval opening, easel back..20.00
5-1/2" x 4" peach celluloid, semi-oval with footed scalloped bottom, oval metal decoration in black and gold floral design, oval 3" x 5" opening......................................15-20.00
6" x 8" oval in ivory celluloid, celluloid easel back...........18.00

Hat Pin Holder
Circular weighted base from cream celluloid with cranberry colored velvet cushion, 5" h, center post with round circular disc on top features various openings to hold hat pins 85.00
Conical shaped holder fashioned from cream colored celluloid, weighted rect base, very plain..........................15.00

Glove Box, 13" x 4", blue satin lining, reverse painted Arts & Crafts type geometric design in cream, brown and coral.........65.00

Handkerchief Box, 3-1/2" h, 6" x 6" square, pale green embossed celluloid with reverse painted center motif in cream of a classical woman petting a little dog, Wedgwood type design 75.00

Manicure Set, rolled up leather pouch with fitted manicure tools, salve jars and scissors, deep purple velvet lining, mkd "French Ivory"...35.00

Music Box, 14" x 9" x 6" h, green floral embossed celluloid with center motif of a beautiful woman in a flowing gown....175.00

Photograph Album
8" x 11", picture of a pretty child holding kitten, yellow and turquoise..125.00
18" x 6", printed picture of standing lady in red draped flowing dress..250.00

Vase
7" h, yellow, bulbous bottom, narrow opening with fluted top, painted pink and blue floral motif on bottom, no trademark 20.00
12" h, conical shape with round weighted base, imitation tortoise shell..30.00

Dresser Set, Fiberloid Fairfax, mottled brown and gold celluloid, floral trim, 9 pc, $85. Photo courtesy of Julie Robinson.

Fashion Accessories

Bar Pin
2-1/2" l ivory grained rect, hp floral pink and green motif
....10.00
3" black, flared ends, applied pink, blue and yellow celluloid
flowers, c-clasp 12.00
Belt, 22" l, 3-4" x 1-1/2" rect mottled green celluloid slabs, applied
silver tone filigree decorations, slabs linked together by chain
....35.00
Brooch
1-1/4" oval, imitation coral, molded flowers, filigree edging,
mkd "Made In Japan," blue ink on back 20.00
1-1/2" x 1-1/8" oval brooch in amber pearlessence with black
silhouette of a swan, c1926 ....25.00
Bracelet, 3" d
Link, 4 oblong two tone cream and ivory links, attached with
round creme links of smaller size, unusual 30.00
Molded imitation coral, imitation ivory or imitation jade celluloid
bangle with all over floral designs, Made in Japan, blue ink
stamp inside 15.00
Cuff Links
Kum-a-Part, separable links, square brown celluloid face with
circular center opening for metal disc, orig paper display
....25.00
Toggle back, realistic molded celluloid owls, glass eyes,
c1896 ....95.00
Dress Clips, pr, molded lily in semi-translucent cream celluloid
mkd "Japan" 25.00
Eyeglasses, Harold Lloyd type with black frames.................20.00
Hair Comb
Imitation ivory back comb with regal filigree design topped
with celluloid balls, English, c1890............................70.00
Imitation tortoise shell back comb with decorative metal work
with scarab beetles among flowers and leaves, rhinestone
trim, wide row of multiple teeth, c1900........................85.00
Pale amber celluloid with embedded red rhinestones in a
whimsical floral motif, c1926 ....40.00
Side combs, pr of 4-1/2" imitation amber side ornaments
shaped like long hair pins, painted with delicate floral mo-
tif 25.00
Hat Pin
4" l imitation ivory elephant head with tusks and black glass
eyes 95.00
12" l, imitation tortoise, hollow tusk shape 18.00
12" l, Question mark shape, pearlized gray and cream swirled,
hollow..45.00
Hat Ornament
3-1/2" h, Art Deco ornament with pearlized red and pearlized
cream half circles, rhinestone trimming 32.00
4" translucent pale amber feather with black center, studded
with rhinestones...10.00
4-1/2" calla lily, amber celluloid with applied gold paint, studded with yellow rhinestones 30.00
Necklace
1" imitation ivory elephant pendant on celluloid linked chain
....35.00
2" elegant Art Nouveau filigree pendant, cream celluloid with
oval cameo, profile of a beautiful woman, suspended from
20"cream celluloid beaded necklace, fine detailing ..95.00
Purse
4-1/2" h, x 3" w, oval cream molded basket weave design,
dyed olive green, celluloid chain...............................120.00
6" long linked chain bag with satin lining, lid is solid celluloid,
4" x 3" oval shaped with painted flowers, 4" w at top and
goes to a point at the bottom....................................135.00

Holiday Items

Christmas
Nodder, Santa, 4-1/2" h, Made in Japan 95.00

Viscoloid Santa Express, blow mold, $125. Photo courtesy of Julie Robinson.

Ornament, roly poly type house with opening in back for a
small bulb, shows Santa approaching door, red and white,
intertwined VCO/USA trademark 85.00
Santa, 4-1/2" figure, holding lantern in one hand and waving
the other, Made In Japan 40.00
Easter
Car, 3" peach with mottled green movable wheels, driven by
bunny, VCO/USA 65.00
Rabbit, 3-1/2" Roly Poly, cream with aqua trim, VCO/USA
....75.00
Woven Basket with lid, 1-3/4" tall, 1-1/2" diameter, bright red,
string handle, bright blue Easter bunny with egg in hand
painted on lid..35.00
Independence Day, 5-1/4" Uncle Sam figural in white celluloid
with painted red white and blue patriotic clothing 65-90.00
Halloween
2-3/4" witch driving a pumpkin vehicle, VCO 150.00
3" owl, roly poly, VCO trademark....................................85.00
4" h, horn, favor, orange celluloid with black stencil witch,
VCO 45.00
St. Patrick's Day, toy, Paddy riding the Pig, 4-3/4" tall figure of a
pig with movable legs, little boy with dunce cap riding on the
back, Japan 185.00
Thanksgiving, 2-1/2" realistic turkey in gray with molded detailing
highlighted with red and black, on roly poly base 55.00

Novelties

Bookmark, child's, 4-1/2" l x 1/2" w, thick cream colored celluloid,
folded over to clasp onto paper, top formed into a cute bunny
head with painted pink and blue features 22.00
Compact, 1-1/2" d, dark blue celluloid base with lid with reverse
painted dancing girl, decorated with glitter, "Made in France"
....65.00
Comb, 2-1/2" folding, comb, tear drop shaped, cream celluloid
with black embossed floral trim and rhinestones 25.00
Comb with Case, 3-1/4" x 1" pearlized red and gray rhinestone
studded case, 3" cream colored comb 15.00
Letter Opener
5" curved sword with butterfly motif on handle, hand painted
garish colors over thin ivory celluloid 10.00
7-1/4" l, cream, bull dog figural top, VCO trademark 30.00
8" l, saber shape, embossed fern motif, heavy thick ivory
grained celluloid, mfg. by Celluloid Novelty Co., c1898
....90.00
Pocket Mirror, round, 2-1/8" d, black dwg, cream ground, 1920s
style woman holding hand mirror, scene reverses to naughty
scene when turned upside down 25.00
Tape Measure, figural
Billiken, cream colored, applied brown highlights, sitting on
circular tape measure base, mkd "Japan" on tape mea-
sure..125.00

Dice, 1-1/8" sq, cream colored, black dots 120.00
Fruit, 1-1/4" pear with lady bug tape measure pull........ 175.00
Girl, basket of flowers and little dog near skirt, cream, blue, and maroon, Japan 110.00
Pig with piglet, cream colored, mkd "Made in Occupied Japan" 60.00

Animals

Alligator
3" green with white tail tip, VCO/USA 6.00-8.00
5-3/4" tan with red and black detailing, facing left, VCO/USA trademark 32.00
Bear
5" w, ream bear with pink & gray highlights, VCO/USA .. 15.00
5" w, cream bear with pink & gray highlights, VCO/USA 15.00
5-1/4" l, white polar bear, made in USA............................ 5.00
Bison, 3-1/4" long dark Brown, eagle and shield trademark 18.00
Boar, 3-1/4" brown, Paul Haneaus of Germany/PH trademark 65.00
Camel
2-1/4" l cream camel with light brown highlights, Made in USA trademark 12.00
3-1/2" tan with brown highlights, Diamond S2 trademark, mkd "Made In Japan" 15.00
Cat
3" peach with black highlights, floral trademark, mkd "JAPAN" 25.00
5-1/4" cream cat with pink & black highlights, molded collar and bell, Made In USA trademark, rare....................... 50.00
Chicken, 3" standing hen in grass, cream with gray, yellow feet, VCO/USA trademark... 15.00
Circus animals, elephant, gorilla, giraffe, tiger, lion, and hippo, garish bright colors, mkd "Made In Occupied Japan".... 45.00
Cow
5-1/2" purple and cream with red rhinestone eyes, crossed circle mark, "Made in Japan" 25.00
7-1/2" gray cow with purple highlights, eagle and shield trademark 35.00
Dog
3" sitting German Shepherd, cream, plaster filled, MC, mkd "Made In Japan" 40.00
3-1/4" collie, yellow and tan, excellent realistic detail, Noris trademark 55.00
3-1/4" St. Bernard, tan with black highlights, VCO/Circle 15.00
4-1/2" Scotty, all black with VCO/USA 20.00
4-3/4" bull dog, cream with black highlights, VCO/USA.. 25.00
5-3/4" hound dog with long tail, gray, VCO/Circle mark 25.00
5-3/4" Scotty, purple & gray with red rhinestone eyes, Royal Japan.. 20.00

Animals, blow molded, deigned by Dr. Paul Haneus, boar, $75; large duck, $20; small duck, $15; rhino $35. Photo courtesy of Julie Robinson.

Donkey
2-1/4" cream with pink and black highlights, Made in USA 12.00
3-1/2" cream & lavender with molded saddle in red and peach, VCO/USA trademark.. 30.00
Duck
3-1/2" yellow with green highlights, VCO/USA & Circle... 12.00
4"g lossy surface with red & green, VCO/USA 15.00
Elephant
3-1/2" cream elephant with painted red floral blanket, Made In USA.. 12.00
6-3/4" gray with painted tusks, Made In USA mark 20.00
Fish
4-1/2" yellow & red with molded scales, Made in USA...... 8.00
6-3/4" white and red fish, smooth shiny surface, molded fin, VCO/USA 15.00
Frog
1-1/4" yellow frog with stripe on back, VCO/USA 10.00
2-3/8" green celluloid frog with spotted back, VCO/USA 12.00
Giraffe, yellow with brown spots, excellent molding by Petticolin of France, eagle head trademark 75.00
Goat, 3-1/2" white with gray, Billy Goat with beard & horns, VCO/USA 22.00
Hippopotamus, 3-1/2" peach with open mouth, Made in Tokyo Japan, TS 15.00
Horse
4" yellow horse with orange highlights, painted reigns and saddle, rattles, Made in USA.................................. 20.00
7" cream with purple & pink highlights, Made in USA..... 25.00
Lion, 3" orange with black highlights, Made in USA............. 12.00
Pig, 4-1/2" or 1-1/8" pink pig with painted eyes, Made in USA 22.00
Ram
2-1/2" cream with gray highlights, Made in USA 8.00
4-1/2" cream ram with gray highlights, Made in USA...... 18.00
Rhinoceros, 2-1/2" gray and peach rhino, Made in USA.... 12.00
Seal, 4-1/2" gray balancing red ball, VCO/USA 55.00
Squirrel, 2-7/8" brown celluloid, holding a nut, Made in USA 30.00
Stork, 6-3/4" standing stork, white with pink legs, flower mark & Japan... 18.00
Swan, 4" cream swan with gray, pink and orange highlights, VCO/USA 18.00
Tiger, 4" tan with black stripes, 2 stickmen trademark & Japan 15.00
Turkey, 2-1/2" cream with dark blue, wire spring legs, PH...35.00
Turtle
1-3/8" two tone, brown top, yellow bottom...................... 10.00
3" cream with brown highlights, VCO/USA with Circle 12.00

Dolls, Toys and Rattles

Doll
4-3/4" realistic child doll with movable arms and legs, short blond molded hair, Shell trademark on back 55.00
6" side glancing Kewpie carnival doll with top hat, cane and feathers, crossed circle, Japan 18.00
9-1/2" girl and boy dressed in ethnic costumes, Turtle in Diamond trademark, Rheinische Gummiund Celluloid Fabrik Co, of Germany, pr 125.00
10" Carnival Kewpie with feathers, top hat and cane, Royal Japan, fleur-de-lis trademark 30.00
12" realistic baby doll, Made in USA by Viscoloid Co 95.00
Figural Toy
4" double figural showing two little girls with umbrella in pink and green bathing suit, floral trademark, mkd "Made in Japan" 55.00
4-1/2" flesh tone Aviator with purple highlights, gray and black detailing, Made in Japan 35.00

6-1/4" Beefeater with British Flag, standing on bright green base, House in Circle with Japan 35.00

Rattle

    Egg shape on solid handle with ring, cream, pink, and blue floral motif 12.00

    Stork, 6" long, Made in Japan, rabbit trademark............35.00

Roly Poly

    1-1/2" Commodore Vanderbilt Navy Blue Officers Suit, PH trademark 105.00

    2-1/2" aqua and cream ball with balancing elephant, trunk raised, no trademark 35.00

    3-1/2" clown, pink & white base with balancing clown, feather on hat, Germany 55.00

Toy Boat, 3-3/4" Gun Boat, purple with cream and pink flag, bow trademark, Made In Japan 20.00

Toy Dish, 3-3/4", cake on round platter, brightly colored, intertwined VCO..95.00

Whistle, 2"

    Green and white whistle, no trademark...........................8.00

    Red bird whistle..12.00

Utilitarian Items

Cutlery, solid imitation ivory grained handle utensils, 8 forks and 8 knives in original box, Standard Mfg. Co. 30.00

Crumb Tray Set, two dust pan shaped trays in ivory colored celluloid, one large and one small, scalloped and curved rim, no trademark 12.00

Napkin Ring, 1-1/2" wide, lacy embossed ivory celluloid 8.00-10.00

Soap Container, two piece cream box, rectangular with round corners, overall emb fleur-de-lis motif 12.00

Powder Box with Puff, 3-1/4" h, 2-3/4" h, hp forget me not motif, marked "Celluloid" with an easel trademark 35.00

Straight Razor, molded cream celluloid, handle formed to represent an ear of corn, Germany...20.00

Toothbrush, imitation ivory with hog hair bristles, no trademark 4.00

Toothbrush Case, rectangular, 1" x 7" peach mottled celluloid, hinged opening on top with ventilating holes....................8.00

Toothbrush Holder, 4" wall mount holder of mottled green with four compartments for toothbrushes, "The Guardian" 15.00

CHALKWARE

History: William Hutchinson, an Englishman, invented chalkware in 1848. It was a substance used by sculptors to imitate marble and also was used to harden plaster of paris, creating confusion between the two products.

Chalkware pieces, which often copied many of the popular Staffordshire items made between 1820 and 1870, was cheap, gaily decorated, and sold by vendors. The Pennsylvania German folk art pieces are from this period.

Carnivals, circuses, fairs, and amusement parks gave away chalkware prizes during the late 19th and the 20th centuries. These pieces often were poorly made and gaudy.

References: Thomas G. Morris, *The Carnival Chalk Prize*, Prize Publishers, 1985; ——, *The Carnival Chalk Prize II*, Prize Publishers, 1994.

Additional Listings: See Carnival Chalkware in Warman's Americana & Collectibles.

Notes: Don't confuse the chalkware carnival giveaways with the earlier pieces. Prices for the later chalkware items range from $10 to $50.

Bank, 11" h, dove, worn orig polychrome paint..................350.00

Bookends, pr, 8" h, Arabian Nights, male and female, red, gold, and brown..85.00

Bust, Sheherazade, painted to resemble bronze..............250.00

Figure

    5" h, squirrel, worn red and green, base flakes.............250.00

    5-1/4" h, cat, red and black details, PA, 19th C 200.00

    5-1/2" h, dog, molded detail, painted brown, black spots, red collar, PA, 19th C, pr 375.00

    6-3/8" h, reclining eye and lamb, grassy base, yellow border, PA, 19th C, one ear repaired 325.00

Frame, lace edge, cream colored, easel back, 3" x 5", $20. Photo courtesy of Julie Robinson.

Bust, woman on pedestal, titled "Micaela," numbered on back, painted black, 11-1/4", $140.

15" h hen, 20" h rooster, full bodied, comb, wattle, and feather detail, inset glass eyes, quatrefoil base, scrolled acanthus support, repairs, pr 1,495.00

Mantel Ornaments, 12-1/2" h, fruit and foliage design, American, 19th C, restoration, paint wear, pr 460.00

Match Holder, 6" h, figural, man with long nose and beard, Northwestern National Insurance Co. adv, c1890 .... 110.00

Nodder, 8-1/2" l, cat, white, black spots, late 19th C 1,495.00

Plaque, 9" h, horse head, orig polychrome paint 100.00

Wall Pocket, basket shape 35.00

CHARACTER AND PERSONALITY ITEMS

History: In many cases, toys and other products using the images of fictional comic, movie, and radio characters occur simultaneously with the origin of the character. The first Dick Tracy toy was manufactured within less than a year after the strip first appeared.

The golden age of character material is the TV era of the mid-1950s through the late 1960s. Some radio premium collectors might argue this point. Today, television and movie producers often have their product licensing arranged well in advance of the initial release.

Do not overlook the characters created by advertising agencies, e.g., Tony the Tiger. They represent a major collecting subcategory.

References: Pauline Bartel, *Everything Elvis*, Taylor Publishing, 1995; Bill Blackbeard (ed.*), R. F. Outcault's The Yellow Kid*, Kitchen Sink Press, 1995; Bill Bruegman, *Cartoon Friends of the Baby Boom Era*, Cap'n Penny Productions, 1993; —, *Superhero Collectibles*, Toy Scouts, 1996; *Cartoon & Character Toys of the 50s, 60s, & 70s*, L-W Book Sales, 1995; Rudy D'Angelo, *Cowboy Hero Cap Pistols*, Antique Trader Books, 1997; Warren Dotz, *Advertising Character Collectibles*, Collector Books, 1993; —, *What a Character! 20th Century American Advertising Icons*, Chronicle Books, 1996; Ted Hake, *Hake's Guide to Cowboy Character Collectibles*, Wallace-Homestead, 1994; —, *Hake's Price Guide to Character Toy Premiums*, Gemstone Publishing (1996 Greenspring Dr., Ste. 405, Timonium, MD 21093), 1996; Jim Harmon, *Radio & TV Premiums,* Krause Publications, 1997.

Jack Koch, *Howdy Doody*, Collector Books, 1996; Mary Jane Lamphier, *Zany Characters of the Ad World*, Collector Books, 1995; Cynthia Boris Liljeblad, *TV Toys and the Shows That Inspired Them*, Krause Publications, 1996; Jan Lindenberger, *More Snoopy Collectibles, An Unauthorized Guide with Values,* Schiffer Publishing, 1997; David Longest, *Character Toys and Collectibles* (1984, 1992 value update), 2nd Series (1987, 1990 value update), Collector Books; Richard O'Brien, *Collecting Toys*, 7th ed., Books Americana, 1993; Maxine A. Pinsky, *Marx Toys: Robots, Space, Comic, Disney & TV Characters*, Schiffer Publishing, 1996; Susan and Steve Raab, *Movie Star Autographs of the Golden Era*, published by authors, 1994; Jon D. Swartz and Robert C. Reinehr, *Handbook of Old-Time Radio*, Scarecrow Press, 1993; Jon R. Warren, *Collecting Hollywood: The Movie Poster*

Price Guide, 3rd ed., American Collectors Exchange, 1994; Dian Zillner, *Hollywood Collectibles* (1991), *The Sequel* (1994) Schiffer Publishing.

Periodicals: *Autograph Times*, 2303 N. 44th St., #225, Phoenix, AZ 85008; *Baby Boomer*, P.O. Box 1050, Dubuque, IA 52004; *Big Reel*, P.O. Box 1050, Dubuque, IA 52004; *Celebrity Collector*, P.O. Box 1115, Boston, MA 02117; *Classic Images*, P.O. Box 809, Muscatine, IA 52761; *Collecting Hollywood*, American Collectors Exchange, 2401 Broad St., Chattanooga, TN 37408; *Cowboy Collector Newsletter*, P.O. Box 7486, Long Beach, CA 90807; *Frostbite Falls Far-Flung Flier*, P.O. Box 39, Macedonia, OH 44056; *Hollywood & Vine*, Box 717, Madison, NC 27025; *Hollywood Collectibles*, 4099 McEwen Dr., Suite 350, Dallas, TX 75224; *Movie Advertising Collector*, P.O. Box 28587, Philadelphia, PA 19149; *Movie Collector's World*, 17230 13 Mile Rd., Roseville, MI 48066; *Television History Magazine*, 700 E. Macoupin St., Staunton, IL 62088; *TV Collector Magazine*, P.O. Box 1088, Easton, MA 02334.

Collectors' Clubs: All About Marilyn, P.O. Box 291176, Hollywood, CA 90029; Beatles Fan Club, 397 Edgewood Ave., New Haven, CT 06511; Betty Boop Fan Club, 6025 Fullerton Ave., Apt. 2, Buena Park, CA 90621; C.A.L./N-X-211 Collectors Society, 727 Youn Kin Pkwy So., Columbus, OH 43207; Camel Joe & Friends, 2205 Hess Dr., Cresthill, IL 60435; Charlie Tuna Collectors Club, 7812 NW Hampton Rd, Kansas City, MO 64152; Dagwood-Blondie Fan Club, 541 El Paso, Jacksonville, TX 75766; Dick Tracy Fan Club, P.O. Box 632, Manitou Springs, CO 80829; Dionne Quint Collectors, P.O. Box 2527, Woburn, MA 01888; Howdy Doody Memorabilia Collectors Club, 8 Hunt Ct., Flemington, NJ 08822; Official Popeye Fan Club, 1001 State St., Chester, IL 62233; R. F. Outcault Society, 103 Doubloon Dr., Slidell, LA 70461; Three Stooges Fan Club, P.O. Box 747, Gwynedd Valley, PA 19437.

Videotapes: *Dionne Quintuplet Dolls: 1934-1939*, Sirocco Productions, 1992; *Shirley Temple Dolls & Memorabilia*, Sirocco Productions, 1994.

Additional Listings: See *Warman's Americana & Collectibles* for expanded listings in Cartoon Characters, Cowboy Collectibles, Movie Personalities and Memorabilia, Shirley Temple, Space Adventurers, and TV Personalities and Memorabilia.

Character

Andy Gump, pinback button

7/8" d, Andy Gump/The Gumps by Syndey Smith, black, white, and red, issued by Western Theatre Premium Co, 1930s 22.00

1" d, "Schutter's Old Gold Candy," black and white litho, colorful image of Andy in green jacket, red bow tie, "Investigator Gum Charities Giving Away $1,000,000,000.00," 1930s 20.00

1-1/4" d, "Andy Gump For President/I Endorse The Atwater Kent Receiving Set," red, white, blue, and fleshtone 40.00

Betty Boop

Decal Sheet, c1920, set of 12 ....15.00
Perfume Bottle, 3-1/2" h, figural, glass, c1930 ....46.00
Wall Pocket, Betty and Bimbo, luster glaze, © Fleischer Studios 110.00

Brownies, Palmer Cox

Book, *The Brownie Primer,* Flanagan Co, Chicago, 1905, hard cover, 6" x 8", 96 pgs 40.00

Pinback Button, 1-1/4" d, blue on white, 8 Brownies around board fence imprinted with calendar page for January, 1897, Whitehead & Hoag 20.00

Plate, 7" d, octagonal, china, full color illus of 3 Brownies, dressed as Uncle Sam, Scotsman, and golfer, soft blue ground, gold trim, sgd "La Francaise Porcelain" 95.00

Buster Brown

Bank, iron, horse shoe shape, Buster, Tige, and horse 145.00

Drawing Book, 8 pgs, thin film tracing sheets between each page, Emerson Piano Co., unused 70.00

Mask, diecut, stiff paper, Froggy the Gremlin, 1946 ....45.00

Paddle Board, 5" x 10", cardboard, rubber ball attached by string, 1946 ....65.00

Pinback Button

Buster Brown Bread, multicolored, yellow rim, red letters 20.00

New York Herald Young Folks, Buster with dripping paint brush, c1905, 1-1/4" d 85.00

Sign, 39" x 55", diecut, tin, Buster Brown in shoe being pulled by diecut Tiger 1,900.00

Whistle, Buster Brown Shoes, litho tin, image of Buster, black inscriptions, ivory ground, bright gold underside, 1930s 65.00

Campbell Kid

Children's Dishes, "Campbell's Lunch Time," 4" x 14" x 17-1/2" unopened display carton, service for 6, child's hard plastic soup bowls and coaster plates, cups, saucers, spoons, and forks, prominent Campbell's marking, sealed in orig clear shrink wrap, six miniature placements on back, © 1984 ....45.00

Menu Book, 5-1/2" x 7-1/2", softcover, © 1910, 48 pgs, menus for 30 days of the month, full color Campbell Kid art on cov 20.00

Salt and Pepper Shakers, pr, 4-1/2" h, painted hard plastic, red and white outfits, yellow molded hair, © Campbell Soup 40.00

Sign, 11-1/2" x 17-1/2", tin, Kid holding spoon, red, white, and yellow 250.00

Charlie the Tuna

Animation Cel, 10-1/2" x 12" clear acetate sheet, centered smiling full figured 4"image of Charlie gesturing toward 4" image of goldfish holding scissors, 10-1/2" x 12-1/2" white paper sheet with matching blue/lead pencil 4"tall image of Charlie, c1960 ....150.00

Figure, 7-1/2" h, soft vinyl, blue, dark pink opened mouth, black rimmed eyeglasses, orange cap inscribed "Charlie," © 1973 ....30.00

Wristwatch, 1-1/2" dbright gold luster bezel, full color image of Charlie on silver background, © 1971 Star-Kist Foods, grained purple leather band 60.00

Dutch Boy, string holder, 14-1/2" x 30", diecut tin, Dutch Boy sitting on swing painting the sign for this product, White Lead Paint Bucket houses ball of string 300.00

Elsie The Cow, Borden

Display, mechanical milk carton, cardboard and papier-mâché, figural milk carton rocks back and forth, eyes and mouth move from side to side, made for MN state fair circuit, 1940s 500.00

Lamp, 4" x 4" x 10", Elsie and Baby, hollow ceramic figure base, Elsie reading to baby nestled on her lap, brass socket, c1950 ....125.00

Mug, 3-1/4" h, white china, full color image of Elmer, gold accent line, orig sq box with image of child's alphabet block including panels "E for Elsie" and "B for Borden," Elmer pictured on one side panel, © 1950 ....95.00

Felix the Cat

Figure, 1" h, dark copper colored plastic, loop at top, 1950s 10.00

Pinback Button, 1" d, Herald and Examiner, c1930s 45.00

Place Card Holder, 1-3/4" h celluloid Felix, arched back black cat, base, glossy black holder, Japanese, 1930s 85.00

Valentine, diecut, jointed cardboard, full color, "Purr Around If You Want To Be My Valentine" inscription, © Pat Sullivan, c1920 ....20.00

Vending Label, 3" x 3", red, white, blue, black, and fleshtone, Little King and Felix the Cat illus, for Popeye "Kid Kartoon Komics" button, King Features ©, mid 1940s 15.00

Yarn Holder, 6-1/2", diecut wood, black images, inscription "Felix Keeps On Knitting," Pathe Presents" symbol in center, c1930 ....38.00

Happy Hooligan

Figure, 8-1/4" h, bisque, worried expression, tin can hat, orange, black, blue, and yellow 75.00

Jiggs and Maggie, chalkware figures, multicolored, Jiggs 8-1/2" h, Maggie 9-3/4" h, pr, $225.

Pinback Button, 11-16" d, brown and cream, profile, inscribed "Son Of Rest," initials below "G.T.A.T.," c1910 ....30.00

Stickpin, 2-1/4" l, brass 25.00

Howdy Doody

Bank, 6-1/2" x 5", ceramic, riding pig 65.00

Belt, suede, emb face 35.00

Cake Decorating Set, unused 40.00

Handkerchief, 8" x 8-1/4", cotton 20.00

Pencil Case, vinyl, red 25.00

Jiggs and Maggie

Paperweight glass 40.00

Pinback Button

3/4" d, The Knoxville Sentinel, black white image of Jiggs, red bow tie, c1920 ....15.00

1" d, Herald And Examiner, black image, bright yellow ground, 1930s 30.00

Salt and Pepper Shakers, pr, ceramic 48.00

Krazy Kat, pinback button

7/8" d, full color, cigarette premium, c1912, Tokio back paper 20.00

1-3/8" d, "Cash Prices See Comic Pages Daily," Los Angeles Evening Herald & Express, black on green litho, 1930s 30.00

Little Annie Rooney, pinback button, 1-1/4" d, comic strip contest button, serial number type, c1930 ....25.00

Little Orphan Annie

Clicker, red, white, and black, Mysto members, 1941 ....40.00

Doll, ABC Toys, c1940 ....50.00

Mug, Ovaltine 70.00

Whistle, tin, signal type, 3 tones 40.00

Little Oscar, Oscar Mayer

Doll, 30" inflatable soft vinyl, chef hat, white chef outfit, red inscriptions, 1970s 25.00

Post Card, 3-1/2" x 5-1/2", traveling Wienermobile, sgd "Jerry Maren," portrayed Little Oscar in 1950s 10.00

Ring, red plastic top, c1970 ....18.00

Toy, 3" w, 10" l, 4-1/2" h, Wienermobile, pull toy, wheels turn and diecut Little Oscar moves up and down, c1950s 150.00

Mr. Peanut

Ashtray, Golden Jubilee, 50th Anniversary, gold plated metal, figural, orig attached booklet, orig box, 5" h, 5-3/4" h 130.00

Bank, 8-1/2" x 4", full figure, orange plastic 725.00

Booklet, *Mr. Peanuts Guide to Tennis,* 6" x 9", © 1960, 24 illus pgs 20.00

Box, Planters Chocolate Covered Nut Assortment, silver alligator texture, 2 early Mr. Peanut figures, 8-1/4" sq 350.00

Case, salesman's sample, attaché, 9 different unopened vacuum pack display cans, orig promotional divider 475.00

Paint Book, *Planter's Paint Book No. 2,* 7-1/4" x 10-1/2", © 1929, 32 pgs 35.00

Salad Set, ceramic tops, wooden fork and spoon, rhinestone monocle, 10" h 170.00

Shipping Box, corrugated cardboard, adv for Planters Salted Peanut 5¢ cellophane bags, 1950s, 17" x 14" x 11" 140.00

Toy, trailer truck, red cab, yellow and blue plastic trailer, 5-1/2" l 275.00

Mr. Zip

Bank, 2-1/4" x 4" x 5-3/4", tin litho, mail box, red, white, and blue, photos of coins, chart on back, trap missing 15.00

Decal, 6" d, red, white, and blue glossy paper, May, 1963, unused 5.00

First Day Cover, 3-1/2" x 6-1/2", with Zip Code commemorative stamp, "Saluting the U.S. Postal Service Zip Code System 1974" 10.00

Popeye

Charm, 1" h, bright copper luster plastic figure of Olive Oyl, 1930s 10.00

Children's Book, *Popeye Borrows A Baby Nurse,* Whitman, #712 ....45.00

Figure, 14" h, chalkware 140.00

Mug, 4" h, Olive Oyl, figural 20.00

Pencil Sharpener, figural, Catalin plastic, dark yellow, multicolored decal, 1930s 60.00

Sticker Book, Lowe #263 ....140.00

Tie Bar, 2-1/2" l, 3/4" h enameled figure of Popeye, 1930s 45.00

Reddy Kilowatt

Bib, 10" x 10" fabric, printed nursery rhyme and Reddy, c1950 ....65.00

Employee Cap, white canvas fabric, 2" bright red, white, blue, and yellow fabric patch for PA Power and Light Co, 1920-1996 commemorative date 10.00

Hot Pad, 6" d, laminated heat resistant cardboard, textured top surface with art and verse inscription "My name is Reddy Kilowatt-I keep things cold. I make things hot. I'm your cheap electric servant. Always ready on the spot," c1940 ....40.00

Pinback Button

Inspectors Club, multicolored, silver rim, for nuclear plant of Consumers Power Co., c1960 ....45.00

Please Don't Litter, blue and white, 1950s 15.00

Pocket Knife, metal cast, red figure image and title on one side, single knife blade, Zippo, c1950 ....60.00

Statuette, 5" h, 1-1/2" x 3" black plastic base, ivory white glow plastic head, gloves, and boots, translucent red body, c1950 ....195.00

Stickpin, red enamel and silvered metal miniature diecut figure, c1950 ....30.00

Rocky Jones, Space Ranger

Coloring Book, Whitman, cockpit cov, 1951 ....40.00

Pinback Button, membership type 45.00

Wings, pin 40.00

Sambo

Doll, 4" x 6-1/2" x 9", tiger, plush stuffed, ear tag and name tags, 1977 ©, R. Dakin Co., orange striped, black and white muzzle, inset glass eyes, Sambo's name stamped in red on chest 40.00

Pinback Button, Sambo's Pancakes, brown, orange, and white, c1960 ....15.00

Token, wooden disk, printed in red on both sides, Sambo and tiger image on one side, other side with coffee cup "What This Country Needs Is A Good Cup of Coffee-Sambo's Has It," c1960 ....8.00

Yellow Kid, pin cushion, silvered metal, "I'm Weightin For Yer "See," 4-5/8" h, $145.

Yellow Kid

Cigar Box, 3-1/2" x 4-1/4" x 9", wood, illus and name inscription in bright gold, brass hinges, label inside "Smoke Yellow Kid Cigars/Manuf'd by B. R. Fleming, Curwesville, Pa," tax label strips on back, c1896 ....225.00

Fireworks, 5" l, 5/8" d, "Yellow Kid Salute," orig cartoon illus of Kid holding lit firecracker under his arm, "Don't touch me when I'se Lit," fuse missing 850.00

Pinback Button

"There is Only One Yellow Kid/Big Bubble Chewing Gum," bright yellow and black, fleshtone details on Kid's head, c1910, 7/8" d 40.00

"Yellow Kid No. 1," Kid with huge beer mug, no back paper, blue number and copyright......................................75.00

"Yellow Kid No. 13," Kid with wooden horse, Napoleon-style hat, text reference to Napoleon 20.00

"Yellow Kid No. 15," Kid with money and can of red paint, ready to "Paint new York Red," high Admiral Cigarettes on black tin reverse 20.00

"Yellow Kid No. 16," Kid hanging stocking for "Santie Klaws," orig back paper..20.00

"Yellow Kid No. 72," Kid with Vassar pennant...........25.00

"Yellow Kid No. 146," Kid with earrings, hair in pigtails, holds rifle and Madagascar flag 60.00

Personality

Amos and Andy

Ashtray and match holder, plaster 30.00

Diecut, 3" x 5", cardboard, Amos, Andy, and Kingfish, 1931 ....22.00

Poster, 13" x 29", multicolored, Campbell's Soup ad, radio show listings, framed 145.00

Toy, Fresh Air Taxi, litho tin wind-up, Marx, 1929..........425.00

Ball, Lucille

Magazine, Life, April 6, 1953, 5 pg article, full color cover of Lucy, Desi Arnaz, Desi IV, and Lucy Desiree.............30.00

Movie Lobby Card, 11" x 14", full color, 1949 Columbia Picture "Miss Grant Takes Richmond"....................................40.00

Captain Kangaroo

Badge, 2-1/4" h, emb tin shield, came on 1960s doll......15.00

Puzzle, 10" x 14", frame tray, Captain and nursery rhyme characters, 1956, Milton Bradley...20.00

Whisk Broom, 7" h, wood handle, blue and fleshtones, black, white, red, and yellow accents, © R.K.A., 1960 ....40.00

Cassidy, Hopalong

Badge, silvered metal, star shape, raised center portrait, c1950...25.00

Coloring Book, 1950, large size 30.00

Rug, chenille..100.00

Tablet, 8" x 10", color photo cov, facsimile signature, unused 24.00

Hopalong Cassidy, spurs, $200. Photo courtesy of Jackson's Auctioneers & Appraisers.

Dionne Quintuplets

Advertisement, 5" x 7", Quintuplet Bread, Schultz Baking Co., diecut cardboard, loaf of bread, brown crust, bright red and blue letters, named silhouette portraits, text on reverse 70.00

Book, Now We Are Five, Jas Brough, 256 pgs, dj 7.50

Fan, 8-1/4" x 8-3/4", diecut cardboard, titled "Sweethearts Of The World," full color tinted portraits, light blue ground, © 1936, funeral director name on reverse 35.00

Garland, Judy

Pinback Button

1" h, "Judy Garland Doll," black and white photo, used on c1930 Ideal doll, name appears on curl, also "Metro-Goldwyn-Mayer Star" in tiny letters 125.00

1-1/4" d, "Oz/Your Dollars Will Work Magic in Hecht Month," Baltimore department store, multicolored..............275.00

Sheet Music, On The Atchison, Topeka, and the Sante Fe," 1945 MGM movie "The Harvey Girls," sepia photo, purple, light pink, and brown cov 35.00

Gleason, Jackie

Coloring Book, "Jackie Gleason's Dan Dan Dandy Color Book," Abbott, © 1956, unused.................................25.00

Magazine, TV Guide, May 21, 1955, Philadelphia edition, 3 pg article on the Honeymooners....................................18.00

Pinback Button, 1-5/8" d, "Jackie Gleason Fan Club/And Awa-a-ay We Go!," blue on cream litho, checkered suit, 1950s 65.00

Houdini, Harry, big little book, Houdini's Big Little Book of Magic, Whitman, 1927, premium or American Oil and Amoco Gas, 192 pgs..35.00

Henie, Sonja

Pinback Button, 1-3/4" d, "Sonja Henie Ice Review," orange on blue, illus of skater, c1940s 20.00

Portrait Art, 15-1/2" x 19-1/2", rigid white art board, 12-1/2" x 16-1/2" paint and ink portrait by John Cullen Murphy, figure skater wearing cap with Olympic rings symbols, bottom margin with title in red pencil, "Once In A Lifetime," for nostalgia feature in Jan 1948 Sports Magazine 300.00

Lone Ranger

Badge, 1" d, Safety Scout..20.00

Guitar, 30" l, Jefferson, orig box 95.00

Hartland Figure, orig box...250.00

Pencil Case, 1" x 4" x 8-1/4", textured stiff cardboard, gold cov design, dark blue ground, American Lead Pencil Co., 1930s 45.00

Print Set, orig box, unused, 1940s 45.00

Marx Brothers

Book, Beds, hardbound 45.00

Sheet Music, 9-1/2" x 12-1/4", Alone from MGM musical "A Night At The Opera," 1935, orange, blue, and white cov, blue tone photos of Groucho, Chico, Harpo, Allan Jones, and Kitty Carlisle..30.00

Rogers, Roy

Bank, Roy on Trigger, porcelain, sgd "Roy Rogers" and "Trigger" 200.00

Ring, litho tin, Post's Raisin Bran premium, Dale Evans, © 1942..45.00

Toy, Roy Fit It Stagecoach, figure, Bullet, 2 horses, complete accessories 95.00

Temple, Shirley

Children's Book, Shirley Temple's Birthday Book, Dell Publishing Co, c1934, soft cover, 24 pgs 100.00

Figure, 6-1/2" h, salt-glazed...85.00

Handkerchief, Little Colonel, boxed set of 3 ....200.00

Magazine Advertisement, Lane Hope Chests, 1945.........8.00

Magazine

Life, July 11, 1938, cover with young Shirley in field, article...28.00

Parade, Oct. 20, 1957, Shirley and her children on cov 22.00

Three Stooges
    Autograph, letter, 4-1/2" x 5-1/2" mailing envelope, two folded 6" x 8" sheets of Three Stooges letterhead, personally inked response to fan, sgd "Moe Howard," March 10, 1964 Los Angeles postmark..200.00
    Badge, 4" d, cello, black and white upper face image of Curly-Joe on purple background, Clark Oil employee type 20.00
    Movie Poster
        14" x 36", The Three Stooges Meet Hercules," paper insert for 1961 Columbia Pictures movie, folded...............60.00
        27" x 41", "Snow White and The Three Stooges," 1961 20th Century Fox film, folded..60.00
    Photo, 4" x 5" glossy black and white, facsimile signatures of Curly-Joe, Larry, and Moe, plus personal inscription in blue ink by Moe 95.00
    Pinback Button, 7/8" d, black and white photo of Moe, series issued by "Button-Up Co." on the curl.........................8.00
Valentino, Rudolph, book, *Sons of the Sheik*, Photo Play movie edition, orig dj..60.00

CHILDREN'S BOOKS

History: Because there is a bit of the child in all of us, collectors always have been attracted to children's books. In the 19th century, books were popular gifts for children, with many of the children's classics written and published during this time. These books were treasured and often kept throughout a lifetime.

Developments in printing made it possible to include more attractive black and white illustrations and color plates. The work of artists and illustrators has added value beyond the text itself.

References: E. Lee Baumgarten, *Price Guide for Children's & Illustrated Books for the Years 1880-1960 Sorted by Artist* and *Sorted by Author*, published by author, 1996; David & Virginia Brown, *Whitman Juvenile Books*, Collector Books, 1996; Richard E. Dickerson, *Brownie Bibliography*, 2nd ed., Golden Pippin Press, 1995; Virginia Haviland, *Children's Literature, a Guide to Reference Sources* (1966), first supplement (1972), second supplement (1977), third supplement (1982), Library of Congress; Alan Horne, *Dictionary of 20th Century British Book Illustrators*, available from Spoon River Press, 1994; Simon Houfe, *Dictionary of 19th Century British Book Illustrators*, revised ed., available from Spoon River Press, 1996; Diane McClure Jones and Rosemary Jones, *Collector's Guide to Children's Books, 1850 to 1950*, Collector Books, 1997; Jack Matthews, *Toys Go to War*, Pictorial Histories Publishing, 1994; Edward S. Postal, *Price Guide & Bibliography to Children's & Illustrated Books*, M & P Press (available from Spoon River Press, 2319C W. Rohmann, Peoria, IL 61604), 1995; *Price Guide to Big Little Books & Better Little, Jumbo Tiny Tales, A Fast Action Story, etc.*, L-W Book Sales, 1995; Steve Santi, *Collecting Little Golden Books*, 2nd ed., Books Americana, 1994.

Periodicals: *Book Source Monthly*, 2007 Syossett Dr., P.O. Box 567, Cazenovia, NY 13035; *Martha's KidLit Newsletter*, P.O. Box 1488, Ames, IA 50010; *Mystery & Adventure Series Review*, P.O. Box 3488, Tucson, AZ 85722; *Yellowback Library*, P.O .Box 36172, Des Moines, IA 50315.

Collectors' Clubs: Horatio Alger Society, 4907 Allison Dr., Lansing, MI 48910; Society of Phanton Friends, 4100 Cornelia Way, North Highlands, CA 95660.

Libraries: American Antiquarian Society, Worcester, MA; Free Library of Philadelphia, Philadelphia, PA; Library of Congress, Washington, DC; Lucile Clark Memorial Children's Library, Central Michigan University, Mount Pleasant, MI; Pierpont Morgan Library, New York, NY; Toronto Public Library, Toronto, Ontario, Canada.

Additional Listings: See *Warman's Americana & Collectibles* for more examples and an extensive listing of collectors' clubs.

Abbreviations:

dj	dust jacket
n.d.	no date
pgs	pages
teg	top edges gilt
unp	unpaged
wraps	paper covers

ABC, Easy Steps Picture Book, Samuel Lowe Co., 1945, folio, wraps 21.00

A Brighter Garden, Emily Dickinson poems, illus by Tasha Tudor, Philomel, 1990, 1st ed., 4to 32.00

A Child's Garden of Verses, Robert Louis Stevenson, 10 color plates with tissue guards by Jessie Wilcox Smith, Scribner, 1905, 1st ed...65.00

A Happy Pair, Frederic E. Weatherly, 6 Beatrix Potter illus, 1890 ....63,000.00

Alice in Wonderland, Lewis Carroll, color plates by Edwin John Prittie, black and white illus by Tenniel, John Winston Publishers, 1923, 1st printing...35.00

A Very Little Child's Book of Stories, Ada & Eleanor Skinner, 8 color plates, color cov insert by Jessie Wilcox Smith, Duffield, 1924 ....42.00

Bread An' Jam, Wymond Garthwaite, Harper, 1928, 1st ed., poetry and pen and ink dwgs each page 10.00

Captain Salt in Oz, Ruth Plumly Thompson, illus by John R. Neill, Reilly & Lee Co., 1936, minor damage to cover........45.00

Dicken's Children, Jessie Wilcox Smith, Scribner, 1912, 10 color plates by Smith..65.00

Dorothy Dainty's Castle, Amy Brooks, Lothrop, Lee, 1923, 6 black and white illus, picture green cloth cover, dj..............12.00

Eloise in Moscow, Kay Thompson, Simon & Schuster, 1959, 1st printing..50.00

Fun with Dick and Jane, Scott Foreman, 1940, blue cover 25.00

Gene Autry and the Golden Ladder Gang, W. H. Hutchinson, illus by Andrew Benson, Whitman, 1950, 250 pgs, pgs yellowed 8.50

Handy Mandy In Oz, Ruth Plumly Thompson, illus by John R. Neill, Reilly & Lee Co., 1937, binding loose 45.00

Heidi, Spyri, translated by Phillip Allen, Univ of Chicago, 8 color plates by Maginel Wright Enright, Rand McNally, 1921, 1st ed...25.00

Horton Hatches the Egg, Dr. Seuss, Random House, 1940, 11" x 8-1/2"..12.50

Little Black Sambo and the Gingerbread Man, Rand McNally & Co., 1936, color illus, 20 pgs...90.00

Little Rudy & Other Stories, Hans Christian Anderson, James Miller, 1965, 167 pgs, 16mo, blind and gilt stamped covers 18.00

Little Women, Louisa M. Alcott, Robert Bros., 1971, 2 volumes 135.00

Lucy Locket, The Doll with the Pocket, John Rae, Saalfield, 1928, 1st ed...75.00

Mother Goose and Nursery Rhymes, color wood engravings, Philip Reed, Athenum, 1968, 2nd ed., dec cov, gold lettering, 11" x 8".. 12.50

Mother Goose and Other Stories, black and white illus, The Goldsmith Pub. Co., 1930 .... 15.00

Mother Goose Nursery Rhymes, Samuel Lowe Co., 1944, 4to, wraps 18.00

My Book House, ed. O.B. Miller, published by The Book House for Children, set of 12 volumes, blue picture covers, 31st printing, 1947 .... 80.00

Old Fashioned Girl, Alcott Publishing, 1914, illus of Jessie Wilcox Smith, dec cov, gold top pgs 28.00

One Little Indian, Grace Moon, color illus by Carl Moon, Whitman, 1951, paste label, school stamp 20.00

Out to Old Aunt Mary's, James Whitcomb Riley, tinted picture of children, Howard Chandler Christy, Bobbs-Merr, 1904 .... 35.00

Peter and Wendy, J. M. Barrie, Schribner, 1911, 1st ed., 13 plates by F. D. Beford, green cov with gold dec 17.50

Peter Pan, A Bonnie Television Book, color illus by Nan Pollard, based on J. M. Barrie play, Samuel Lowe Co., 1953 ...... 15.00

Raggedy Ann and Andy with Animated Illustrations in Color, Julian Wehr, hardcover, spiral bound, working animations, Saalfield, 1944 .... 60.00

Riley Child Rhymes, Bowen-Merr, 1899, Vawter picture, moss green shading to tan cov....................................... 17.50

Rip Van Winkle, Washington Irving, illus by Frances Brundage, Saalfield, 1927, 1st ed., picture cov 22.50

Second Bubble Book, The Harper Columbia Book That Sings, nursery rhymes, three 5" records in pockets, 16 pgs, 1918 .... 22.00

Stories from Uncle Remus, Joel Chandler Harris, color illus, A. B. Frost illus, Saalfield, c1940.................................. 35.00

Take Joy! The Tasha Tudor Christmas Book, Philomel, 1966, dj 12.00

Tales From Woodsey Newton, illus by Horace Faithful, Young World Prod. Ltd, London, 1969, 61 pgs, 4to 10.00

Tasha Tudor's Favorite Stories, color and black and white illus by Tasha Tudor, J. B. Lippincott, 1965, 1st edition, 10 stories, 131 pgs, 8vo.. 88.00

Teenie Weenie Days, William Donahey, Whittlesey House, 1944, 2nd ed., 11 pgs of illus 30.00

The Adventures of O'Mistah Buzzard, Thornton Burgess, 6 glossy plates by Harrison Cady, Little-Brown, 1922................... 20.00

The Arrow of Tee-May, Grace Moon, illus by Carl Moon, Burt, 1931 .... 10.00

The Dutch Twins, Lucy Fitch Perkins, black and white illus by author, Houghton Mifflin Co., and, beige cover 30.00

The Happy Hollisters at Pony Hill Farm, Jerry West, illus by Helen Hamilton, Garden City, 1956 .... 4.00

The King of the Golden River, John Ruskin, color illus by Arthur Rackham, Lippincott, 1932, inscribed, 1st ed., orange cloth cover 95.00

The Lord Will Love Thee, Sara Klein Clark, illus by Tasha Tudor, Westminster Press, 1959 .... 46.00

The Lost Princess of Oz, L. Frank Baum, illus by John R. Neill, 12 color plates and black and white illus, Reilly & Lee Co., 1930s 55.00

The Secret Garden, Frances Burnett, color illus by Maria Kirk, Frederick, Stokes, 1911, 2nd ed., picture cov..................... 38.00

Titty Mouse and Tatty Mouse, Rand McNally & Co., 1936, color illus, 20 pgs.. 90.00

Trixie Belden & The Mystery Off Glen Road, Julie Campbell, Whitman, 1960, picture cover.. 4.00

Walt Disney IM Talder Biber, German, IM Bertelsmann Lesering, color photo illus, 1957 .... 15.00

When We Were Very Young, Milne, illus by Shepard, Dutton, 1926, 5th printing, red cov, told trim 20.00

Wings From The Wind, An Anthology of Poems Selected and Illustrated by Tasha Tudor, color and black and white illus, J. B. Lippincott, 1964, 5th printing.. 45.00

Winnie-Ille-Pu (Winnie the Pooh in Latin), Milne, illus by Shepard, Dutton, 1961, 9th printing, dj.. 25.00

CHILDREN'S FEEDING DISHES

History: Unlike toy dishes meant for play, children's feeding dishes are the items actually used in the feeding of a child. Their colorful designs of animals, nursery rhymes, and children's activities are meant to appeal to the child and make mealtimes fun. Many plates have a unit to hold hot water, thus keeping the food warm.

Although glass and porcelain examples from the late 19th and early 20th centuries are most popular, collectors are beginning to seek some of the plastic examples from the 1920s to 1940s, especially those with Disney designs on them.

References: Maureen Batkin, *Gifts for Good Children, Part II, 1890-1990*, Antique Collectors' Club, 1996; Doris Lechler, *Children's Glass Dishes, China and Furniture*, Vol. I (1983), Vol. II (1986, 1993 value update), Collector Books; Noel Riley, *Gifts for Good Children: The History of Children's China, Part I, 1790-1890*, Richard Dennis Publications (available from Antique Collectors' Club), 1991; Margaret and Kenn Whitmyer, *Collector's Encyclopedia of Children's Dishes: An Illustrated Value Guide*, Collector Books, 1993.

Bowl
   6" d, black cats chasing mouse 45.00
   6-1/4" d, Darling Doggy 45.00
Cereal Set, Nursery Rhyme, amber, divided plate, Humpty Dumpty on mug and bowl, Tiara 125.00
Cup, Raggedy Ann, Johnny Gruelle, 1941, Crooksville China
.... 65.00
Cup Plate, 4-5/8" d, "Constant dropping wears away stones and little strokes fell great oaks," green transfer, polychrome enamel dec.. 90.00
Feeding Dish
   Bunnies, puppies, Nippon.. 45.00

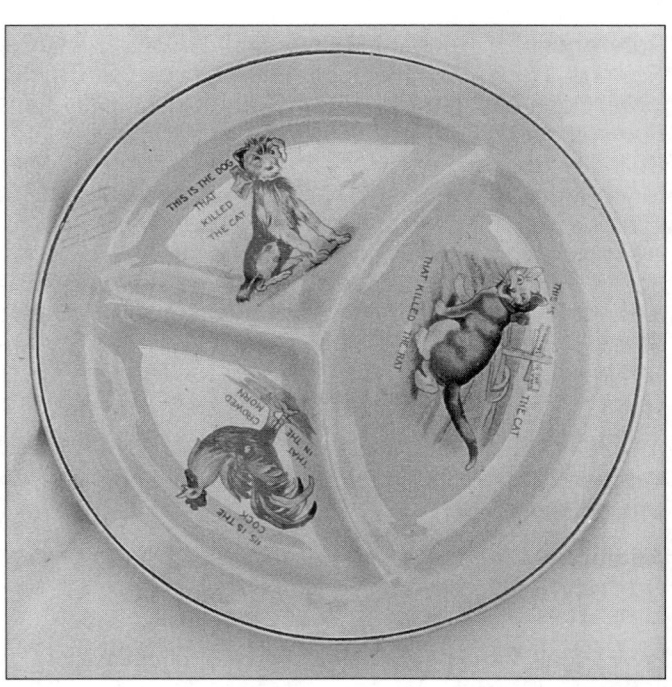

Divided, decal of cat, dog, and cock, mkd "Roma," 7-3/8" d, $50.

Kiddieware, pink, Stangl..75.00
Nursery Rhyme, green enamelware, mkd "Made in Germany"
....40.00
Raggedy Ann, Johnny Gruelle, 1941, Crooksville China, 8-3/4" d
....85.00
Mug, yellow glazed, transfer print, England, c1850, glaze and
transfer wear
    1-3/4" h, "A rabbit for William" 225.00
    2-1/8" h, "Keep thy shop and thy shop will keep thee," luster
    rim, minor chip..195.00
    2-1/8" h, two sheep reserve, luster rim 220.00
    2-1/4" h, red and green flower, leaf handle 200.00
    2-3/8" h, "A new doll for Margaret," very minor chips
    ....490.00
    2-3/8" h, reddish brown transfer "My Son, if sinners entice thee,
    consent thou not lest disgrace come upon thee," leaf han-
    dle, small lip flakes 420.00
    2-1/2" h, "A rocking horse for John," minor chips..........460.00
    2-1/2" h, reserve of townscape with bridge, luster rim
    ....200.00
Plate
    6" d, Buster Brown, 1910, mint center image 135.00
    8" d, Nursery Rhymes, glass, green 30.00
    8" d, Where Are You Going My Pretty Maid, See Saw Margery
    Daw, 3 part, transparent green Depression-era glass
    ....35.00
Sherbet, white Depression-era glass, red dec of Three Little
Pigs..12.00

CHILDREN'S NURSERY ITEMS

History: The nursery is a place where children live in a miniature world. Things come in two sizes. Child scale designates items actually used for the care, housing, and feeding of the child. Toy or doll scale denotes items used by the child in play and for creating a fantasy environment which copies that of an adult or his own.

Cheap labor and building costs during the Victorian era encouraged the popularity of the nursery. Most collectors focus on items from the years 1880 to 1930.

References: Marguerite *Fawdry, International Survey of Rocking Horse Manufacture*, New Cavendish Books, 1992; Doris Lechler, *Children's Glass Dishes, China and Furniture*, Vol. I (1983), Vol. II (1986, 1993 value update), Collector Books; Patricia Mullins, *Rocking Horse: A History of Moving Toy Horses*, New Cavendish Books, 1992; Lorraine May Punchard, *Playtime Kitchen Items and Table Accessories*, published by author, 1993; Herbert F. Schiffer and Peter B. Schiffer, *Miniature Antique Furniture: Doll House and Children's Furniture from the United States & Europe*, Schiffer Publishing, 1995; Tony Stevenson and Eva Marsden, *Rocking Horses: The Collector's Guide to Selecting, Restoring, and Enjoying New and Vintage Rocking Horses*, Courage Books, 1993.

Museum: The Victorian Perambulator Museum of Jefferson, Jefferson, OH.

Additional Listings: Children's Books; Children's Feeding Dishes; Children's Toy Dishes; Dolls; Games; Miniatures; Toys.

Baby Buggy, wicker, adjustable back, cast iron parasol holder, 1890s 375.00
Bib Clips, sterling silver, clothespin type 75.00

Painting, oil on canvas, untitled, young boy holding drum, blue costume, white lace and pantaloons, 39-1/4" h, 32" w, $2,200. Photo courtesy of Jackson's Auctioneers & Appraisers.

Blocks
    Boxed set, ABC's, animals, litho of Noah and ark on cov, Victorian...185.00
    23 wooden blocks, colored litho dec of sailors, letters, etc.
    ....250.00
Boat, play, ice, 24" l, wood with iron runners, c1900..........460.00
Chair, 28" h, 9" h seat, New England, 18th C, arm, slat back, old splint seat, needlepoint cushion, old refinish, minor height loss
....490.00
Chamber Pot, 8" d, 4-3/4" h, blue and white Oriental scene
....165.00
Cradle Quilt, pieced cotton calico
    36" x 35", delectable Mountain, blue, gray, red, and yellow patches, printed baby-blocks fabric back, diagonal line quilting, Mennonite, PA, late 19th C 3,165.00
    41" x 40", Sunburst, pink, red, green, navy blue, and orange patches, reverse with paisley fabric, field outline and diagonal line quilting, PA, early 20th C...........................865.00
    42" x 36", Star of Bethlehem, brown, green, pink, and blue and white calico patches, straight line quilting, Lehigh County, PA, early 20th C 230.00
Dog Cart, 60" l, two wooden wheels, painted dec of two birds and nest on sides, worn, incomplete....................................495.00
Highchair, New England, early 19th C
    32-1/2" h, 17-3/4" seat, old red paint, "TH" carved on underside of seat, minor surface imperfections 1,150.00
    35" h, 22" h seat, old black paint, mustard highlights, rush seat, imperfections 345.00
Jack in the Box, 6-1/2" l, pine box, paper covering, wooden figure with cloth costume, lace, and printed round cardboard head
....470.00
Pram Coverlet, quilted silk, satin rosebud dec....................60.00
Quilt
    40" x 58", nursery rhyme characters, embroidered names
    ....100.00

Teether and rattle, Santa Claus head, bag of toys on back, MOP teether, SS, English, 5-1/" l, $295.

CHILDREN'S TOY DISHES

History: Dishes made for children often served a dual purpose–playthings and a means of learning social graces. Dish sets came in two sizes. The first was for actual use by the child when entertaining friends. The second, a smaller size than the first, was for use with dolls.

Children's dish sets often were made as a sideline to a major manufacturing line, either as a complement to the family service or as a way to use up the last of the day's batch of materials. The artwork of famous illustrators, such as Palmer Cox, Kate Greenaway, and Rose O'Neill, can be found on porcelain children's sets.

References: Doris Lechler, *Children's Glass Dishes, China and Furniture*, Vol. I (1983), Vol. II (1986, 1993 value update), Collector Books; Lorraine May Punchard, *Playtime Kitchen Items and Table Accessories*, published by author, 1993; ——, *Playtime Pottery & Porcelain from Europe and Asia*, Schiffer Publishing, 1996; ——, *Playtime Pottery and Porcelain from the United Kingdom and the United States*, Schiffer Publishing, 1996; Margaret and Kenn Whitmyer, *Collector's Encyclopedia of Children's Dishes*, Collector Books, 1993.

Collectors' Club: Toy Dish Collectors, P.O. Box 159, Bethlehem, CT 06751.

Akro Agate
    Tea Set, Octagonal, large, green and white, Little American Maid, orig box, 17 pcs 225.00
    Water Set, Play Time, pink and blue, orig box, 7 pcs ... 125.00
    Bohemian glass, decanter set, ruby flashed, Vintage dec, 5 pcs 135.00
China
    Cheese Dish, cov, hunting scene, Royal Bayreuth 65.00
    Chocolate Pot, Model T car with passengers 90.00
    Creamer, Phoenix Bird 20.00
    Cup and Saucer
        Phoenix Bird 15.00
        Willow Ware 10.00
    Dinner Set, Moss Rose, 23 pcs 90.00
    Tea Set
        Children playing, cov teapot, creamer, cov sugar, 6 cups, saucers, and tea plates, German, Victorian 285.00
        Willow Ware, cov teapot, creamer, cov sugar, 4 cups, saucers and plates, Japan, orig box 250.00
Depression Glass, 14 pc set
    Cherry Blossom, pink 390.00
    Laurel, McKee, red trim 355.00
    Moderntone, tuqruoise, gold 210.00

45" x 37", cotton, appliquéd, four geometric cross motifs, chain, foliate vine, and vertical bar quilting, pale gray and black, Amish, Ohio, c1930 .... 350.00

Rattle, 3-3/4" l, bone, whistle 95.00

Rocking Horse, 45" l, 24-1/2" h, worn old dapple gray paint, traces of red on rockers, worn remains of saddle, harness, mane, and tail, rocker platform incomplete 500.00

Rocking Toy, 30" l, two duck silhouettes, platform base with turned spindle sides, orig ivory paint, black, gold and red trim, some paint missing, upholstered seat missing 165.00

Scooter, 43" l, 30-3/4" h, steel frame and wheels, wooden platform and handle, worn orig red paint, black and yellow striping, partial label "… Arrow Deluxe" 140.00

Sled, wooden
    Iron rod tipped runners, scrolled finials, worn black paint, polychrome striping, flowers, small landscape, and "Black Bird" 395.00
    Peaked runners, red painted and polychrome dec, poplar and oak, shaped deck, turned frontal stretcher on rect legs with chamfered corners, seat dec with galloping horse in red, black, and white with yellow highlights, PA, 19th C, metal braces added, some loss to paint 990.00
    Steel runners, old green paint, yellow striping on runners, polychrome foliage in a circle on top, touch-up repaint, 35-1/2" l 235.00

Wagon
    15" l, 25" tongue, wood, orig dark blue and yellow paint, orange and black striping, gold stenciled "Express," stenciled label "Pat. Jan. 12, 1869" 1,185.00
    40" l, wood, metal fittings, Roller Bearing Coaster, black stenciled label, old red and brown paint, some orig paint, old repaint touchup repair 385.00
    42" l, wood, metal fittings, Studebaker Junior, orig green paint, black and yellow striping, red wheels, old added tongue, orig dog cart harness frame and tongue included, minor damage 1,845.00

Wheelbarrow, 26-1/2" l, wood, orig red paint, black stenciled horse 250.00

Pattern Glass, creamer and sugar, Tulip & Honeycomb, $45.

Milk Glass
    Creamer, Wild Rose................................65.00
    Cup, Nursery Rhyme 24.00
    Ice Cream Platter, Wild Rose....................60.00
Pattern Glass
    Berry Set, Wheat Sheaf, 7 pcs..................85.00
    Butter, cov, Hobnail with Thumbprint base, blue 95.00
    Cake Stand
        Beautiful Lady, 4" h, 5" d, c1905................25.00
        Palm Leaf Fan.......................................35.00
    Creamer
        Buzz Saw 15.00
        Drum 70.00
        Lamb 75.00
    Cup and Saucer, Lion...............................50.00
        Pitcher, Oval Star, clear........................20.00
        Punch Set, Wheat Sheaf, 7 pcs 75.00
    Spooner
        Mardi Gras 45.00
        Tulip and Honeycomb 20.00
    Sugar, cov
        Beaded Swirl 40.00
        Mardi Gras 65.00
    Water Set, Nursery Rhyme, pitcher, 6 tumblers 225.00

CHINESE CERAMICS

History: The Chinese pottery tradition has existed for thousands of years. By the 16th century Chinese ceramic wares were being exported to India, Persia, and Egypt. During the Ming Dynasty (1368-1643), earthenwares became more highly developed. The Ch'ien Lung period (1736-1795) of the Ch'ing dynasty marked the golden age of interchange with the West.

Trade between China and the West began in the 16th century when the Portuguese established Macao. The Dutch entered the trade early in the 17th century. With the establishment of the English East India Company, all of Europe sought Chinese-made pottery and porcelain. Styles, shapes, and colors were developed to suit Western tastes, a tradition which continued until the late 19th century.

Fine Oriental ceramics continued to be made into the 20th century, and modern artists enjoy equal fame with older counterparts.

Reference: Gloria and Robert Mascarelli, *Warman's Oriental Antiques*, Wallace-Homestead, 1992; Nancy N. Schiffer, *Imari, Satsuma, and Other Japanese Export Ceramics,* Schiffer Publishing, 1997.

Periodical: *Orientalia Journal*, P.O. Box 94, Little Neck, NY 11363.

Collectors' Club: China Student's Club, 59 Standish Rd., Wellesley, MA 02181.

Museums: Art Institute of Chicago, Chicago, IL; Asian Art Museum of San Francisco, San Francisco, CA; George Walter Vincent Smith Art Museum, Springfield, MA; Morikami Museum & Japanese Gardens, Delray Beach, FL; Pacific Asia Museum, Pasadena, CA.

Additional Listings: Canton; Fitzhugh; Imari; Kutani; Nanking; Rose Medallion; Satsuma.

Chinese Ceramics

Bowl, 6-3/4" d, flared sides, cut foot, molded int. with twin fish medallion at well, pale crackled blue-green glaze, Song Dynasty 265.00
Brush Washer, 4-3/4" d, compressed circular form, splayed base, incurved rim, thick bluish-gray crackle glaze...............175.00
Censer, 3-1/2" h, compressed globular form, splayed raised foot, everted rim, countersunk band dec, 2 scroll handles, white glaze, 19th C................395.00
Cup, 2-1/4" h, Blanc-De-Chine, molded animal and foliate dec, Qing dynasty, 18th C................100.00
Dish
    9-1/4" d, blue and white porcelain, scalloped, central figural scene surrounded by shaped panels alternating with figures and flowering prunus branches, price for pr....450.00
    11" d, shaped rim, incised floral dec, celadon glaze, Ming dynasty 1,200.00
Figure, 16" h, horse, standing, draped trappings and saddle, green, chestnut, and honey glaze, Tang style 650.00
Garden Set, blue and white, 18-1/2" h................635.00
Ginger Jar, cov, 3-1/2" h, blue and white porcelain, figural procession dec, wood cover 300.00
Jar, cov, blue and white porcelain
    3-3/4" h, petal shaped panels, figures and flower-filled jardinieres, Kangxi................225.00
    8" h, shaped panels with kylins on blue ground, floral dec, carved wood lid, Kangxi................425.00
    11" h, flowering prunus branch dec, crackled ice ground, fu dog finials, Qing Dynasty, 19th C, price for pr.........275.00
Jardiniere, 14" d, iron red and white, dragon chasing flaming pearl of wisdom dec 150.00
Lamp Base, 16" h vase, celadon and blue ovoid form, warriors in landscape dec................150.00
Moon Flask, 8-1/4" h, blue and white porcelain, two central bird and flower-filled panels, all-over scrolling floral and foliate dec, c1830................425.00
Plate
    8-1/2" d, blue and white, Ming Dynasty................395.00
    9-3/8" d, Cabbage Leaf and Butterfly, 19th C, minor chips, gilt and enamel wear, cracks, 9 pc set 345.00
Soup Plate, 9-5/8" d, Cabbage Leaf and Butterfly, 19th C, minor chips, gilt and enamel wear, 4 pc set 175.00
Urn, 17" h, baluster, blue and white, scrolling foliate, floral and shou dec, pr 450.00
Vase
    2-3/4" l, globular, underglaze blue and celadon, two handles, molded fluting, Yuan dynasty 200.00
    5" h, ovoid, blue and white porcelain, all-over floral and foliate dec, Kangxi 175.00
    8-3/4" h, gu form, raised mid-section, 2 countersunk bands, thick ivory colored glaze, 18th C 800.00
    12" h, baluster body, flared neck, fluted rim, incised scroll and applied Imperial dragon dec, Sing Dynasty............600.00
    16-1/2" h, club form, celadon and blue glazed, figures in landscape dec................150.00

Chinese Export

Bottle, 16" h, painted reserves of floral and bird scenes, light blue ground, 19th C, wear................230.00
Bough Pot, 8-1/2" h, 8-1/4" w, 5-1/4" w base, 7-7/8" d, octagonal, applied dec of squirrels among grapes on canted corners which flank shaped lanes, central floral sprays, gilt dec base, famille rose palette, gilt rope twist handles, inserts with 5 circular apertures, gilt edges, European market, c1775-85, gilt wear, 3 insert handles missing, pr............13,800.00
Bowl, 10-1/4" d, rose to pink and pale salmon petals, 3 reserve gilt edged quatrefoil panels with iron-red edged gold hibiscus sprays, stylized floral springs on rim, central spray of iron-red edged gilt chrysanthemums and prunus with blossom and scroll border int., c1760................1,800.00

Chinese Export, Armorial, Rose Medallion, basin, celadon ground, first half 19th C, 16-1/4" d, $3,600. Photo courtesy of Freeman\Fine Arts.

Chamber Pot, cov, 9-3/4" d, polychrome floral motifs, gilt highlights, 19th C, minor chips..435.00

Coffeepot
   9" h, fruit final, intertwined handle with flowers and foliage, sepia colored and gilt dec landscape in almond-shaped reserve 550.00
   9-1/8" h, berry lid finial, intertwined handle with flower and leaf detail, round medallions with geese, red, blue, and gilt, minor wear and roughness at spout...........................1,100.00
   9-3/4" h, berry lid finial, intertwined handled with flower and leaf detail, red, blue, and gilt armorial, spout reglued 880.00

Dish, 8-3/4" l, leaf-shape, blue enamel and gilt armorial design and handles, orange peel glaze, old label on back implying prior ownership by Thomas Mifflen, PA Governor, 1773 ....495.00

Figure
   8-1/4" h, Fu lions, male with left paw on reticulated ball, female with pup, gilt pale pink, green, orange, light blue, and yellow paint dec, reticulated rect section plinth with floral spray dec, late 19th C, pr......................................1,200.00
   9-1/4" h, parrot, standing on blue glazed rockwork, green glaze, coral-red beak and feet, pr..........................1,250.00

Garden Set, 18-1/2" h, celadon glaze, birds among flowering branches, strapwork entwined antiques, studded ext., 20th C, pr 815.00

Jar, 4" h, blue and white porcelain, floral and foliate dec, Yongzheng..200.00

Lamp Base, 12-1/4" h, tin tea canister, green painted and stenciled, pr...1,380.00

Miniature, 4-1/2" h, tall pot, side spout, underglaze blue floral dec, red enamel and gilt dec 550.00

Plate
   9" d, armorial
      Arms of Beauple of Devon and Cornwall impaling Bettesworthy of Tyning in Sussex and the Isle of Wight, gilt and enamel wear, 3 pc set...1,840.00
      Arms of Ross of Balnagowan Castle, rim chips, gilt, and enamel wear...490.00
      Unknown coat of arms, quartered shield below a shell and crown flanked by dogs, very minor chips, gilt, and enamel wear..375.00
   9-1/8" d, armorial
      Arms of Beatson of Kelrie and Rossend and later by Beatsons of Knowle Farm in Sussex, chip, gilt and enamel wear...520.00
      Unknown coat of arms, unicorn below crown flanked by two rampant unicorns, restoration to one, gilt and enamel wear, minor chips, 4 pc set................................1,380.00
   9-1/2" d, center sepia butterfly design, floral and gilt borders, 19th C, pr...750.00

Platter, 17-3/4" l, pierced insert, painted armorial of New York State, extensive restoration 375.00

Punch Bowl, sepia landscape medallion, white gilt and blue enamel border, late 18th C, hairline firing blemishes 1,265.00

Salad Bowl, 9-1/2" d, armorial, some rim roughness..........460.00

Teabowl and Saucer, floral spray painted in underglaze blue, rose, iron-red, green, turquoise blue, gold, underglaze blue trellis diaper int. border with 4 rose stylized blossom panels, 1765-75, set of 12..2,400.00

Tea Caddy
   5" h, gilt, blue, gray, and red enameled love birds in sunburst medallion, yellowed neck repair, no lid 65.00
   5-1/4" h
      Blue and gold urn and floral borders, fruit finial, wear, repair to neck...440.00
      Round medallions, polychrome enameled woman and dog waiting for returning ships, old yellowed repairs ...440.00

Teapot, 5" h, dec en grisaille, Diana and reserves of hunt scenes, minor gilt and enamel wear, late 18th C, chips to strainer 400.00

Tea Service, gilt and blue enamel border and monogram, lighthouse-shaped coffeepot, 2 teapots, tea caddy, 2 sugar bowls, 2 helmet-shaped creamers, waste bowl, 7 tea bowls, 7 cups, 4 plates, 26 saucers, chips and hairline, 55 pc set....2,070.00

Vase
   9-1/8" h, baluster, Tobacco Leaf pattern, iron-red pheasants perched on flowering branch, enameled yellow, turquoise, green, and blue leaves, rose and yellow tobacco blossom, insects and floral springs on reverse, gilt ruyi lappet border with floral springs dec on iron-red hatchwork ground, gilt husk and dot band, ormolu pierced foliate scroll base, c1785...1,750.00
   14-1/2" h, polychrome dec, celadon ground, gilt highlights, 19th C, electrified, minor gilt wear............................550.00

CHRISTMAS ITEMS

History: The celebration of Christmas dates back to Roman times. Several customs associated with modern Christmas celebrations are traced back to early pagan rituals.

Father Christmas, believed to have evolved in Europe in the 7th century, was a combination of the pagan god Thor, who judged and punished the good and bad, and St. Nicholas, the generous Bishop of Myra. Kris Kringle originated in Germany and was brought to America by the Germans and Swiss who settled in Pennsylvania in the late 18th century.

In 1822 Clement C. Moore wrote "A Visit From St. Nicholas" and developed the character of Santa Claus into the one we know today. Thomas Nast did a series of drawings for Harper's Weekly from 1863 until 1886 and further solidified the character and appearance of Santa Claus.

References: Robert Brenner, *Christmas Past*, 3rd ed., Schiffer Publishing, 1996; ——, *Christmas through the Decades*, Schiffer Publishing, 1993; Barbara Fahs Charles and J. R. Taylor, *Dream of Santa,* Gramercy Books, 1992; Beth Dees, *Santa's Guide to Contemporary Christmas Collectibles,* Krause Publications, 1997; Jill Gallina, *Christmas Pins Past and Present*, Collector Books, 1996; George Johnson, *Christmas Ornaments, Lights & Decorations* (1987, 1998 value update), Vol. II (1996), Vol. III (1996), Collector Books; Chris Kirk, *Joy of Christmas Col-*

lecting, L-W Book Sales, 1994; James S. Morrison, *Vintage View of Christmas Past*, Shuman Heritage Press, 1995; Mary Morrison, *Snow Babies, Santas and Elves: Collecting Christmas Bisque Figures*, Schiffer Publishing, 1993; Margaret Schiffer, *Christmas Ornaments: A Festive Study*, Schiffer Publisher, 1984, 1995 value update; Clara Johnson Scroggins, *Silver Christmas Ornaments*, Krause Publications, 1997; Lissa and Dick Smith, *Christmas Collectibles*, Chartwell Books, 1993; Margaret and Kenn Whitmyer, *Christmas Collectibles*, 2nd ed., 1994, 1996 value update, Collector Books.

Collectors' Club: Golden Glow of Christmas Past, 6401 Winsdale St., Golden Valley, MN 55427.

Additional Listings: See *Warman's Americana & Collectibles* for more examples.

Advisors: Lissa Bryan-Smith and Richard M. Smith.

Advertising
  Bank, molded rubber, Santa Claus holding a coin, toys in pack, mkd "Christmas Club A. Corp, N.Y. 1972" 6.00
  Booklet, "When All The World Is Kin," 5" x 4", collection of Christmas stories, Christmas giveaway, Fowler, Dick, and Walker, The Boston Store, Wilkes-Barre, PA" 7.00
  Calendar, 3" h, 7" l, celluloid, Christmas scene with holly border and 1929 calendar, giveaway from the Penny Specialty Shop, Selinsgrove, PA 15.00
  Candy Tin, 9" l, rect, red and green holly on white ground, mkd "Satin Finish, hard candies, div. of Luden's Inc., Reading, PA" 18.00
  Catalog, Boston Store, Milwaukee, WI, 1945, 48 pgs, 8-1/2" x 11", "For An American Christmas" 20.00
  Cracker Tin, 2-1/2" h, 11" l, 8" w, Christmas scene on hinged lid, red and gold trim on sides, mkd "NBC" on base .25.00
  Matches, 4" x 2", "Season's Greetings," winter scene on cover, intact matches create Christmas scene, Boehmer's Garage, Milton, MA 15.00
  Trade Card, child holding snowballs, "The White is King of all Sewing Machines, 80,000 now in use," reverse reads "J. Saltzer, Pianos, Organs, and Sewing Machines, Bloomsburg, Pa." 10.00
Candy Box, cardboard
  4-1/2" l, 3" h, Christmas Greetings, three carolers, USA ...4.00
  6" x 5", pocketbook style, tuck-in flap, Merry Christmas, Santa in store window with children outside, mkd "USA".....15.00
  8" h, four sided cornucopia, Merry Christmas, Santa, sleigh, and reindeer over village rooftops, string bail, USA...35.00
Children's Book
  The Night Before Christmas, Clement C. Moore, Corrine Malvern illustrator, A Golden Book, Golden Press, 1975.....8.00
  Rudolph The Red-Nosed Reindeer, Robert I. May, Maxton Publishers, Inc., 1939 ....12.00
  The Littlest Snowman, Charles Tazewell, Grosset Dunlap, NY, 1958..18.00
Feather Tree, 4' h, green goose feather wrapped branches with metal candleholders, painted white with green trim round wooden base, mkd "Germany" 400.00
Figure
  Father Christmas
    7" h, composition, pink face, red cloth coat, painted blue pants, black boots, mounted on mica-covered cardboard base, mkd "Japan"...90.00
    8" h, papier-mâché, hollow molded, plaster covered, white coat, black boots, sprinkled with mica..................300.00
  Nativity, 7" h, composition, shepherd holding lamb, mkd "Germany"...12.00

Reindeer
  1" h, pot metal, mkd "Germany" 18.00
  4" h, celluloid, white 7.00
Santa Claus
  3" h, bisque, long red coat, mkd "Japan"..................25.00
  3" h, cotton batting, red, attached to cardboard house, mkd "Japan"..48.00
  3" l, celluloid, molded, one-piece Santa, sleigh, and reindeer...35.00
  5" h, hard plastic, Santa on green plastic skis, USA 120.00
  10" h, pressed cardboard, red hat and jacket, black boots 90.00
  14" h, pressed cardboard, head, store display..........95.00
Sheep, 3" h, composition body, carved wooden legs, covered with cloth or wool, glass eyes 40.00
Greeting Card
  "Christmas Greetings," booklet style, emb diecut cov, color litho pictures on int. pgs, The Art Lithographic Publishing Co. 18.00
  "Loving Greetings," flat card, two girls pictured hanging garland, c1910, mkd "Germany" 8.00
  "Merry Christmas," series of 6 envelopes, decreasing in size, small card in last envelope, American Greeting Publishers, Cleveland, USA, 1933 .... 12.00
  "Sincere Good Wishes," purple pansy with green leaves, greeting inside, Raphael Tuck & Sons, 1892 ....7.00
House, cardboard
  2" x 2", mica covered, wire loop on top, mkd "Czechoslovakia" 7.00
  4" x 5", house and fence, sponge trees, mkd "USA".......10.00
Lantern, 8" h, four sided, peaked top, wire bail, metal candleholder in base, black cardboard, colored tissue paper scenes, 1940s 25.00

Ornament
Angel
  4" h, wax over composition, human hair wig, spun glass wings, cloth dress, Germany 55.00
  8" h, chromolithograph, tinsel and lametta trim, pr.....15.00
Ball, 2" d, silvered glass, any color....................................3.00
Beads, 72" l, glass, half inch multicolored beads, paper label mkd "Japan" 8.00
Bulldog, 3" h, Dresden, three-dimensional, mkd "Germany" 250.00
Camel,. 4" h, cotton batting, Germany 160.00
Cross, 4" h, beaded, 2-sided, silvered, wire hanger, paper label mkd "Czechoslovakia"......................................18.00
Drummer Boy, 3" h, wax, hollow, metal ring hanger, USA 5.00
Father Christmas on Donkey, 10" h, chromolithograph, blue robe, tinsel trim 25.00
Mandolin, 5" h, unsilvered glass, wrapped in lametta and tinsel 45.00
Parakeet, 5" h, multicolored glass, spun glass tail, mounted on metal clip 23.00
Pear, 3" h, cotton batting, mica highlights, paper leaf, wire hanger, Japan 12.00

Putz, village scene, three buildings and church, mkd "Germany," 8" h, $35. Photo courtesy of Lissa Bryan-Smith and Richard M. Smith.

Scrap Book, brown leather cover, emb Father Christmas figures and holly leaves, mkd "Pat. March 1876," 11-1/2" h, $125. Photo courtesy of Lissa Bryan-Smith and Richard M. Smith.

Santa Claus in Chimney, 4" h, glass, Germany 75.00
Swan, 5" x 6", Dresden, flat, gold with silver, green, and red highlights 150.00
Tree Top, 11" h, 3 spheres stacked with small clear glass balls, silvered, lametta and tinsel trim, attached to blown glass hooks 90.00

Postcard, Germany
"Happy Christmas Wishes," Santa steering ship 10.00
"May Your Christmas Be Merry and Gay," photo card, sepia tones, Father Christmas peeking between 2 large wooden doors, wearing fur cap 18.00

Putz
Brush Tree, 6" h, green, mica-covered branches, wooden base 8.00
Christmas Tree Fence
Cast iron, silver, ornate gold trim, fifteen 10" l segments with posts, Germany 600.00
Wood, folding red and green sections, 48" l, USA 35.00
Choir Boy, 3" h, hard plastic, red and white 4.00
Penny Wooden, two children on seesaw, hand carved wood, multicolored, Nurenberg or Erzgebrige 32.00

Toy
Jack-in-the-Box, 9-1/2" h, "Santa Pops," hard plastic, red felt hat, orig box, Tigrette Industries, 1956 .... 30.00
Merry-Go-Round, wind-up, celluloid, green and red base, 4 white reindeer heads, Santa sitting under umbrella, Santa spins around, stars hanging from umbrella bounce of bobbing deer heads, orig box, Japan 65.00
Santa, 10" h, battery operated, metal covered with red and white plush suit and hat, soft plastic face, holding metal want with white star light, wand moves up and down and lights up while Santa turns head 90.00

CIGAR CUTTERS

History: Counter and pocket cigar cutters were used at the end of the 19th and the beginning of the 20th centuries. They were a popular form of advertising. Pocket-type cigar cutters often were a fine piece of jewelry that attached to a watch chain.

Reference: Jerry Terranova and Douglas Congdon-Martin, *Antique Cigar Cutters and Lighters*, Schiffer Publishing, 1996; —, *Great Cigar Stuff for Collectors,* Schiffer Publishing, 1997.

Advertising
Brown's Mule Tobacco Plug 50.00
Dutch Masters, full 115.00
General Daniel Morgan 15.00
Miss Detroit 75.00
Old Mortality 25.00

Pocket, figural, man, $35.

Piedmont Cigarettes, cigarette and match holder, graphics on front under glass 600.00
Red Seal Cigars, cast iron, cutter and gambling machine, ball dropped on top of figural donkey, ears or tails would wiggle, denoting heads or tails, 8-1/2" x 7 x 2-1/2" 1,950.00
Spear Head Tobacco, P. J. Sorg, spear shape 65.00
Antler handle, large, three holes 17.00
Brass, pig 475.00
Desk Top, figural cat and floral design, hole cutter and "V" cutter 375.00

Fob, gold filled
Blimp 110.00
Dragon, wings 295.00
Horseshoe and 4 diamonds, engraved 250.00
Rectangular 85.00
Snake, entwined 195.00

Pocket
Bottle shaped, horn 110.00
German Silver, engraved "El Roi-Tan Perfect Cigars" 75.00
Pearl handled 95.00
Scissors, nickel, engraved 75.00
Sterling
Hammered finish 110.00
Oval, engraved 120.00
Rectangle 65.00
Swirls 110.00
Trick Lock 45.00

CIGAR STORE FIGURES

History: Cigar store figures were familiar sights in front of cigar stores and tobacco shops starting about 1840. Figural themes included Sir Walter Raleigh, sailors, Punch figures, and ladies, with Indians being the most popular.

Most figures were carved in wood, although some also were made in metal and papier mâché for a short time. Most carvings were life size or slightly smaller and were brightly painted. A coating of tar acted as a preservative against the weather. Of the few surviving figures, only a small number have their original bases. Most replacements were necessary because of years of wear and usage by dogs.

Use of figures declined when local ordinances were passed requiring shopkeepers to move the figures inside at night. This soon became too much trouble, and other forms of advertising developed.

Indian maiden, carved polychrome, brown and gray fringed dress with beaded necklace, fringed leggings, black moccasins, holding of cigars in right hand, rect plinth base, right arm restored, 69" h, $4,675.

References: Edwin O. Christensen, *Early American Wood Carvings*, Dover Publications, out of print; A.W. Pendergast and W. Porter Ware, *Cigar Store Figures*, The Lightner Publishing Corp., out of print.

Indian
   Brave, 88" h, standing, left hand extended, looking to left, detailed carving 21,000.00
   Chief, 70-1/4" h, pine, carved and painted, wearing red, white, and blue feathered headdress, gold and red gown, holds dagger in right hand, tobacco and cigars in left, black painted pedestal base, 19th C 2,750.00
   Maiden, 28" h, pine, carved and painted, wearing 3 feathered headdress, standing on circular base, missing one arm, c1870 .... 3,750.00
   Princess, 79" h, pine, carved and painted, feathered headdress and sash, red and green costume, carved and yellow painted fringe, blue leggings and moccasins, 1 foot raised on tobacco block, holding tobacco leaves and pink rose in right hand, platform base, c1875 .... 11,000.00
Punch, 50" h, pine, carved and painted, holding bunch of cigars in one hand, other hand raised, circular base, early 20th C 3,000.00
Virginian, 80" h, pine, carved and painted, black man wearing crown of red, green, orange, and gold tobacco leaves, tobacco leaves kilt and armbands, composition base, black painted wood frame, c1970 .... 14,000.00

CINNABAR

History: Cinnabar, a ware made of numerous layers of a heavy mercuric sulfide, often is referred to as vermilion because of the red hue of most pieces. It was carved into boxes, buttons, snuff bottles, and vases. The best examples were made in China.

Box, 5-3/4" l, carved figures in landscape, floral and foliate dec, Qianlong mark, Chinese 450.00
Cigarette Case, 6-1/8" l, rect hinged top, cinnabar lacquer and ivory, carved courtly scene, key fret band border 370.00

Dish, 14-1/2", carved, 3 maidens in palace courtyard scene, lotus scrolls on sides, barbed and lobed rim 225.00
Ginger Jar, 9" h, mkd "China," pr 850.00
Snuff Bottle, 3-1/2" h, carved scene, figures in garden, carved matching stopper, c1825 .... 250.00
Table Screen, 22-1/4", figural scene with monk rowing boat, reverse with 3 dragons above rock, flower scroll border, stand 315.00
Vase, 12-1/4" h, 6 lobed shape, carved with flowering plants, scrolls at neck, 19th C 215.00

CLAMBROTH GLASS

History: Clambroth glass is a semi-opaque, grayish-white glass which resembles the color of the broth from clams. Pieces are found in both a smooth finish and a rough sandy finish. The Sandwich Glass Co. and other manufacturers made clambroth glass.

Barber Bottle... 70.00
Candlestick
   6-5/8" h, hexagonal petal socket, loop base, ground base with chips, small flakes, roughness 90.00
   7" h, hexagonal petal socket, loop base, small flakes, roughness 110.00
Ewer, 10-7/8" h, green applied handle and band, pewter fittings 65.00
Ladle, 9-1/2" l 45.00
Mug, Lacy Medallion, souvenir... 35.00
Pomade Jar, 3-3/4" h, figural bear, made for F. B. Strouse, NY 375.00
Salt, master, Sawtooth, Sandwich, c1850 .... 65.00
Talcum Shaker... 35.00

CLEWELL POTTERY

History: Charles Walter Clewell was first a metal worker and secondarily a potter. In the early 1900s he opened a small shop in Canton, Ohio, to produce metal overlay pottery.

Metal on pottery was not a new idea, but Clewell was perhaps the first to completely mask the ceramic body with copper, brass or "silvered" or "bronzed" metals. One result was a product whose patina added to the character of the piece over time.

Since Clewell operated on a small scale with little outside assistance, only a limited quantity of his artwork exists. He retired at the age of 79 in 1955, choosing not to reveal his technique to anyone else.

Marks: Most of the wares are marked with a simple incised "Clewell" along with a code number. Because Clewell used pottery blanks from other firms, the names "Owens" or "Weller" are sometimes found.

References: Paul Evans, *Art Pottery of the United States*, 2nd ed., Feingold & Lewis Publishing Corp., 1987; Ralph and Terry Kovel, *Kovels' American Art Pottery*, Crown Publishers, 1993.

Museum: John Besser Museum, Alpena, MI.

Ashtray, 3-3/4" d, copper clad, label "Compliments Canton Bridge Co." 65.00
Bowl, 8" d, blue- green patina 150.00
Jardiniere, 14" h, ovoid, matte finish................................. 95.00
Mug, 4-1/2" h, copper clad, riveted design, applied monogram, relief signature 45.00

Ashtray, copper clad, imp mark in circle, 1922, 3-3/4" d, 1-1/4" h, $160.

Pitcher, 5-3/4" h, copper clad, green patina 195.00
Vase
    4" h, ovoid, glossy green and brown patina 350.00
    8" h, ovoid, brown to green foot, sgd "Clewell 45936"
    .... 395.00
    9-1/2" h, cylinder, pinched rim, veined copper foot 200.00

CLARICE CLIFF

History: Clarice Cliff, born Jan. 20, 1899, in Tunstall, Staffordshire, England, has come to symbolize art deco pottery for collectors around the world. As early as 1931, she was hailed as 'a pioneer of advanced thought' and buyers were urged to look upon her work as a future heirloom. In March 1997, Sotheby's in London auctioned at Age of Jazz figure for $19,000–a record for a single piece of Clarice.

A member of a large working class family in the Potteries, Clarice Cliff left school at 13 and apprenticed at Lingard, Webster and Company. In 1916, the firm of A. J. Wilkinson hired Clarice for its lithography department. She attended evening classes and spent all her spare time at the factory learning about each technical progress. In time her employers recognized her ability; in 1927, Clarice went to the Royal College of Art in London for a few months and then on to Paris.

When Wilkinson bought the Newport Pottery in 1920, it inherited a warehouse with literally hundreds of pieces of undecorated ware. Clarice and an ever-growing group of young girls hid the defects in this ware with brightly colored geometric designs. The company marketed these early pieces under the name "Bizarre Ware." Success came very quickly and orders poured in. It is impossible to describe all the patterns and shapes Clarice designed or supervised from 1927-1935. Newport Pottery made such enormous profits in 1929 that a new series of designs were issued under the name Fantasque and classed as part of the Wilkinson production for tax purposes.

An extraordinary range of patterns and shapes poured out of the Newport Pottery in the first half of the 1930s. Cla-

rice took her ideas from everywhere and the company's skill at marketing kept them in the public eye. Unfortunately, changing fashions and ever-deepening world-wide Depression spelled the end of this remarkable creative flurry. By 1935, even the name 'Bizarre' had been phased out and replaced with 'Clarice Cliff, Newport Pottery or Wilkinson Ltd. England.' Although Clarice Cliff continued to design for many years, few of the patterns achieved the success of the earlier work. There have been few collectors for the post-war production, aside from "Crocus" which was in production from 1928-1963 and the "Greetings from Canada" tee-pee teapot.

Clarice Cliff sold the factory to Midwinter in 1964 and the trademark now belongs to Wedgwood Ltd., which took over Midwinter in the 1980s.

References: Richard Green and Des Jones, *The Rich Designs of Clarice Cliff,* published by authors, 1995 (available from Carole A. Berk, Ltd. 8020 Norfolk Ave., Bethesda, MD, 20814); Leonard R. Griffin and Louis and Susan Pear Meisel, *Clarice Cliff,* Harry N. Abrams, 1994; Leonard Griffin, *Taking Tea with Clarice,* Pavilion Books Ltd., 1966; Howard and Pat Watson, *The Clarice Cliff Colour Price Guide,* Francis Joseph Books, 1995.

Collectors' Club: Clarice Cliff Collector's Club, Fantasque House, Tennis Drive, The Park, Nottingham, NG7, 1AE, England.

Reproductions vs. Fakes: Interest in Clarice Cliff seems to grow every year. In 1985, Midwinter introduced a series of limited edition reproductions including six conical sugar dredgers and a conical bowl. Wedgwood launched an eight piece series in 1992, each piece was limited to 250 and is clearly marked "Wedgwood." The second series was introduced a year later and included an Age of Jazz figure. The Museum of Modern Art has, for several years, offered a group of pieces based on Clarice Cliff designed and impressed ©1992MMA. None of these pieces were intended to deceive and the Midwinter and Wedgwood series are becoming collectible in their own right.

However, as prices rise, a number of fakes have appeared. In 1995, a Lotus jug in Orange Roof Cottage and Conical Sugar Shakes in Red Roofs, Orange Erin, Sungray and House & Bridge started to show up in auction and general fairs in England. They are quite well modeled, but the painting is poor and there are gaps between the banding. Forgers have been taking plain Clarice Cliff plates with banding and adding desirable patterns. Check the impressed date stamp on the bottom of suspect plates; it is usually the late 1930s plain plates which are used. Louis Meisel has reported that fakes have been appearing in the Northeast United States in 1997.

Advisor: Susan Scott.

Celtic Harvest Jugs, gold, emb basketweave, sheaf of wheat, multicolored flowers, and fruit handle, green mark, 11" h, pr, $500.

Lotus Jug, single handle
  11-3/8" h, Fantasque Bizarre, Oranges, stylized oranges, blue and green leaves between orange bands, printed factory marks 3,000.00
  11-1/2" h, Bizarre, Crocus, stylized flowers painted in blue, purple, orange, and green with banding, printed factory marks 900.00
  11-5/8" h, Fantasque Bizarre, Rhodathe, large marigold type flowers, painted in yellow, orange, and brown, printed factory marks 800.00
Miniature Vase, 2-3/4" h, Original Bizarre, painted with band of orange and brown triangles outlined in green, printed factory marks 360.00
Plate
  6" d, Bizarre, side, Gibraltar, blue sea and the Rock of Gibraltar painted pink, blue, and green with yellow, pink, and blue bands, printed factory marks 425.00
  9-3/4" d, Bizarre, Blue Chintz, painted green, pink and blue inside blue bands, printed factory marks....................625.00
  9-3/4" d, Bizarre, Appliqué Orange Lucerne, inside yellow, red, and black bands 1,700.00
Sandwich Plate, 10-1/2" d, Bizarre, Gayday, orange and purple flowers, green leaves inside yellow band......................400.00
Sugar Sifter
  5" h, Bizarre, Lynton shape, Viscaria, tall marigold-like flowers in pink and yellow, long green stems, printed factory marks 425.00
  5-1/2" h, Bizarre, conical, Crocus, stylized flowers painted in blue, purple, orange, and green with banding, printed factory marks 625.00
  5-1/2" h, Bizarre, conical, Blue Firs, blue fir trees in mainly green landscape, printed factory marks 1,700.00
  5-1/2" h, Fantasque Bizarre, conical, Pastel Melon, band of overlapping fruit painted pink, yellow, and green, pink and blue bands...1,175.00
Tea for Two, cov teapot, milk, and sugar, two cups and saucers, side plate, price for set
  Bon Jour, 5" h cov teapot, Taormina, orange trees on cliff overlooking sea, printed factory marks 1,975.00
  Stamford, 4-3/4" h cov teapot, painted bands in shades of yellow, orange, and black, printed factory marks 1,250.00
Vase
  8-1/2" h, shape 186, Melon, stylized fruit painted in yellow, blue, red, and orange between orange bands, printed factory marks 1,250.00
  10" h, Fantasque Bizarre, Pastel Trees and House, painted in colors between blue and orange bands, printed factory marks 1,400.00

9-1/2" h, Bizarre, Isis, Inscription Caprice, painted in shades of blue, purple, and ochre, turquoise ground, printed and painted marks...1,800.00
11-1/2" h, Bizarre, single-handled Lotus Inn Crocus, stylized flowers painted in blue, purple, orange, and green with banding, printed factory marks 900.00
Wall Mask, 6-7/8" h, Bizarre, Marlene, painted shades of green, yellow, and red, printed factory marks, price for pr ... 1,075.00

CLIFTON POTTERY

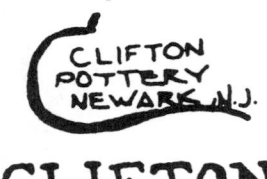

History: The Clifton Art Pottery, Newark, New Jersey, was established by William A. Long, once associated with Lonhuda Pottery, and Fred Tschirner, a chemist.

Production consisted of two major lines: Crystal Patina, which resembled true porcelain with a subdued crystal-like glaze, and Indian Ware or Western Influence, an adaptation of the American Indians' unglazed and decorated pottery with a high-glazed black interior. Other lines included Robin's-Egg Blue and Tirrube. Robin's-Egg Blue is a variation of the crystal patina line but in blue-green instead of straw-colored hues and with a less-prominent crushed-crystal effect in the glaze. Tirrube, which is often artist signed, features brightly colored, slip-decorated flowers on a terra-cotta ground.

Marks: Marks are incised or impressed. Early pieces may be dated and impressed with a shape number. Indian wares are identified by tribes.

References: Paul Evans, *Art Pottery of the United States*, 2nd ed., Feingold & Lewis Publishing Corp., 1987; Ralph and Terry Kovel, *Kovels' American Art Pottery*, Crown Publishers, 1993.

Bowl, 8" d, 5" h, Indian Ware, small neck and rim, squatty bulbous body, dark brown bands, redware ground, Four Mile Ruin, AZ, inspired design, stamped...195.00

Bowl, Indian Ware, brown, stamped "Clifton Indian Cooking Ware," 8-7/8" d, 4" h, $70.

Vase, Crystal Patina
- 3-1/2" h, 4" d, spherical, fish and waves in relief, green glaze, incised "Clifton Pottery/1906" 700.00
- 3-1/2" h, 6" d, squatty, two handles, golden glaze, incised "Clifton Pottery/1906" 100.00
- 4-1/2" h, 5" d, two handles, silver overlay, incised "Clifton Pottery/1906" 1,000.00
- 5" w, 4" d, bulbous
  - Overlaid in silver, trellis pattern, incised "Clifton Pottery/1906" 1,000.00
  - Stove pipe neck, incised "Clifton Pottery" 325.00
- 7" h, 3" w, gourd shape, celadon glaze, incised "Clifton Pottery/1906" 325.00
- 7" h, 5" w, emb with poppies under turquoise glaze, imp "Clifton Pottery/1905," short, tight hairline to rim............. 400.00

CLOCKS

History: The sundial was the first man-made device for measuring time. Its basic disadvantage is well expressed by the saying: "Do like the sundial, count only the sunny days."

Needing greater dependability, man developed the water clock, oil clock, and the sand clock, respectively. All these clocks worked on the same principle–time was measured by the amount of material passing from one container to another.

The wheel clock was the next major step. These clocks can be traced back to the 13th century. Many improvements on the basic wheel clock were made and continue to be made. In 1934, the quartz crystal movement was introduced.

The recently invented atomic clock, which measures time by radiation frequency, only varies one second in a thousand years.

References: Robert W. D. Ball, *American Shelf and Wall Clocks*, Schiffer Publishing, 1992; Philip Collins, *Pastime*, Chronicle Books, 1993; Brian Loomes, *Painted Dial Clocks*, Antique Collector's Club, 1994; Tran Duy Ly, *Seth Thomas Clocks & Movements*, Arlington Book Co., 1996; Derek Roberts, *Carriage and Other Traveling Clocks*, Schiffer Publishing, 1993; John Ware Willard, *Simon Willard and His Clocks*, Dover Publications, n.d.

Periodicals: *Clocks*, 4314 W. 238th St., Torrance, CA 90505.

Collectors' Club: National Association of Watch and Clock Collectors, Inc., 514 Poplar St., Columbia, PA 17512.

Museums: American Clock & Watch Museum, Bristol, CT; Greensboro Clock Museum, Greensboro, NC; National Assoc. of Watch and Clock Collectors Museum, Columbia, PA; National Museum of American History, Washington, DC; Old Clock Museum, Pharr, TX; The Time Museum, Rockford, IL; Willard House & Clock Museum, Grafton, MA.

Notes: Identifying the proper model name for a clock is critical in establishing price. Condition of the works also is a critical factor. Examine the works to see how many original parts remain. If repairs are needed, try to include this in your estimate of purchase price. Few clocks are purchased purely for decorative value.

Advertising

Amalie Pennsylvania Motor Oil, octagonal, glass and metal and neon, 18".. 600.00
Calumet Baking Powder, wall clock, reverse lettering on bottom glass panel "Time to Buy Calumet Baking Powder - Best by Test," 17" x 39".. 750.00
Gem Damaskeene Razor, jovial man sitting in chair shaving while baby on knee trying to escape, 21" x 28" 1,400.00
Halls Ice Cream, Waterbury Clock Co., Waterbury, CT, 1890, pressed oak case, black and gold tablet, 8 day time movement with pendulum, paper on tin dial, 38" h 450.00
Strauss Bros, cast iron, heavily emb, elaborate casting, emb lettering "Strauss Brothers American's Leading Tailors" around dial, "Chicago Orders Taken Here" around pendulum opening, 17-1/2" x 34".. 3,000.00

Alarm

Ansonia Clock Co., Ansonia, CT, patented April 23, 1878, nickel plated case, beveled glass, bell on top, 30 hour time and alarm movement with winding mechanism, sgd dial and case, 4" h.. 95.00
Gilbert Clock Co., Winsted, CT, c1890, nickel plated case, top mounted with rolling bell swings back and forth causing hammer to strike, paper dial, 30 hour time and alarm lever movement, 10-3/4" h.. 95.00
Parker Clock Co., Meriden CT, 1900, Model #60, brass case mounted on brass bell, beveled glass, painted dial, inscribed, 5" h 150.00
Seth Thomas Clock Co., Thomaston, CT, 1885, student lever model, nickel plated and gilded case, paper on zinc dial, 30 hour time and alarm lever movement, 7" h 95.00
Terry Clock Co., Terryville, CT, 1875, ebonized cast iron case, paper on zinc dial, 30 hour time and alarm movement, fixed pendulum, paper label, 6" h 45.00
Westclox, America, c1925, Art Deco white metal case, silvered dial, 30 hour time and alarm movement, 3" h 40.00

Automated

Thomas Armstrong & Bros., Manchester, England, 1880, ship's hull cross section shape, engine room, crankshaft powered by spring movement, deck mounted with timepiece, inscribed silver dial, aneroid barometer, thermometer, compass, and cannons, brass and nickel plated brass case, 8 day time lever movement, carved stone base, 17-1/4" h.................. 8,900.00

Blinking Eye, figural

Dog, Bradley & Hubbard, cast iron case, orig paint, paper on zinc dial, 20 hour movement, fixed pendulum, 8-1/2" h 1,540.00
John Bull, Chauncey Jerome, Bristol, CT, 1870, 30 hour time and movement, paper on zinc dial, 16" h 1,200.00
Lion, Bradley & Hubbard, cast iron case, orig paint, paper on zinc dial, 30 hour movement, fixed pendulum, 8" h 1,950.00
Organ Grinder, Waterbury Clock Co., Waterbury, CT, 1870, painted cast iron case, eyes move up and down, paper on zinc dial, 30 hour lever movement, 17-1/4" h.......................... 1,800.00
Owl, German, c1900, nickel plated front, green eyes, paper dial, 30 hour lever movement, 6-1/2" h 500.00
Topsy, Waterbury Clock Co., Waterbury, CT, 1870, balance wheel, 30 hour time movement, 17" h........................... 750.00

Carriage

French
- Gilt bronze and Limoges enamel, c1900, purple and green, sides with portrait profiles of women, silvered dial, alarm, minor cracking to one panel, 4-1/2" h.................... 7,475.00
- Gilt metal, beveled glass, retailed by Bigelow, Kennard, & Co., alarm, leather case, early 20th C............................. 520.00
- Glass and brass, works stamped "H. & H.," early 20th C 215.00

German, brass cased, alarm and subsidiary second dial, cast etched with foliage, musical, early 20th C.....................350.00

Chime

Regina, disc operated, tall case shape, mechanism utilizes 12-1/8" metal disc to play six tunes on 14 brass bells, can be set to play on the hour..4,750.00

Cottage

Open fretwork, mahogany, glass box frame, dated 1887, 35" h
....1,840.00

Desk

French, gilt metal and porcelain, figural cat seated among flowering vines, early 20th C, minor losses, 3-1/2" h...............260.00

Welch, E. N., Mfg. Co., octagonal amber glass paperweight case, porcelain dial, 30 hour lever movement, 4" h 195.00

Gravity

European, 19-3/4" h, engraved silvered brass dial, pierced brass hands, 30 hour movement with crown wheel escapement
....4,750.00

German, carved base, 30 hour time movement, sawtooth bar driven, porcelain dial inscribed "Anno 1750," 26-1/2" h
....425.00

Mantel

Ansonia Brass & Copper CO., Ansonia, CT, 1870, calendar, rosewood veneered case, drop finials, painted tablet, enameled zinc dial, 8 day time and strike movement with iron weights and pendulum, 32-3/4" h 750.00

Bartholomew, E. and G.W., Bristol, CT, c1825, Classical, mahogany, eagle carved crest over glazed door, giltwood dial, 30 hr wooden movement flanked by turned acanthus carved columns, claw feet, refinished, restoration, 35-1/2" h.........520.00

Burwell Mfg. Co., Bristol, CT, c1860, calendar, rosewood veneered case, laminated and turned bezels, black and gold tablets, upper paper on zinc dial, lower enameled zinc dial, 8 day time and strike movement with rolling pinions, 2 iron weights and pendulum, 36" h 750.00

Left: bracket, late 18th C, ebony case, loop brass bail handle, four metal urn finials, arched door, conforming steel face, mkd "Edwd. Stevens Boston," four gilt metal cast winged claw and ball feet, 19-1/2" h, $3,700; right: mantel, bronze, figural, mid-19th C, seated figure of Benjamin Franklin beside Independence of the United States of America, July 4, 1776, rect base, scroll and leafage feet, 22-1/4" h, $950. Photo courtesy of Freeman\Fine Arts.

Davis Clock Co., Texarkana, AK, 1890, pressed and carved oak case, 2 black and gold tablets, paper on zinc dial, 8 day time and strike movement, simple calendar mechanism, pressed brass pendulum, 27-1/2" h 750.00

English
  Edwardian, c1895, brass and silvered metal, windmill shape, retailed by Shreve, Crump U& Low, subsidiary barometer/thermometer, 17" h 2,415.00
  Winterholder & Hoffmeyer, oak, quarter-striking, foliate cast mounts, late 19th C...460.00

French
  Brass and glass, Gothic style, arched case, mercury filled pendulum, retailed by Tiffany & Co., 10" h, wear 375.00
  Ebonized wood and cast brass, fire gilt brass cast pendulum of American eagle shield and stars, c1840, minor imperfections, 17-1/2" h 1,495.00
  Gilded brass, classical figure of Diana with butterfly, works mkd "Pons. Melaille Dargen, 1823," key and pendulum, back missing from works, 18" h............................1,210.00
  Gilded brass, porcelain inserts, two children, bird, and nest, polychrome floral dec, case mkd "C. Budtz," works mkd "Jafry Freres, Edaille Dor," key and pendulum, back missing from works, 16-1/4" h..715.00
  Gilt bronze and Limoges enamel, mounted sedan chair-form, late 19th C, painted, rect and oval portrait roundels, face with engine turned enamel, case cased with figures and foliage in high relief, two side panels sgd with initials, 11" h
  ....3,750.00
  Gilded cast metal, equestrian figure of Richard I, enameled numbers on clock face, case mkd "F. H. Mourey," works mkd "Japy Fils,. Exp 1855 Medailles 1944-1849," key and pendulum, damage, horse missing one back foreleg, breaks, back cover of works missing, 29" h 330.00
  Gothic Revival, gilt bronze and glass, mid 19th C, cathedral facade form, beast-form feet, minor chips, 23-1/2" h
  ....6,900.00

Ingraham, E., Clock Co., Bristol, CT, rosewood, veneered case, laminated bezels, painted tablet, enameled zinc dial, 8 day time and strike movement with pendulum, Josiah K Seem calendar dial, 22" h...950.00

Ithaca Calendar Clock Co., Ithaca, NY, c1870, No. 3-1/2, parlor, walnut ebonized wood trim, 2 dials, black paper with silver numerals upper, lower with silver numbers and maker's name, 8 day time and strike movement, cut glass pendulum, 20-1/2" h
....3,500.00

Louis Philippe, c1840, gilt and patinated bronze, movement sgd "Guyerdet Aine, Paris, boy seated with scrolls and books, 13-1/4" h, 10" l..635.00

Louis XVI
  Cronier, Paris, c1790, gilt bronze and white marble, figural, Diana with bird and foliate mounts, giltwood oval base, glass dome, minor losses, 14-1/2" h 3,105.00
  LeRoy, Paris, late 19th C, gilt bronze mounted white marble, lyre form, dial sgd, foliate cast mounts, 6" h..........2,300.00

Terry, Eli, Classical, mahogany, carved eagle and foliate carved crest, glazed door with eglomise tablet, polychrome and gilt floral dec dial flanked by stenciled columns, carved hairy paw feet, labeled "Invented by Eli Terry made and sold by Seth Thomas Plymouth Connecticut," c1825, old finish, some imperfections, 30" h 750.00

Terryville Manufacturing Co., Terryville, CT, 1852, candlestick, brass spring driven movement, circular dial inscribed "Terryville Mft Co. Terryville, Conn." mounted on cobalt blue molded glass baluster base, dome broken, 10-1/2" h 3,450.00

Welch, E. N., Forestville, CT, c1870, ripple front mahogany, star design tablet, 30 hr sprig movement, 18-1/2" h 520.00

Whiting, Riley, Winchester, CT, c1825, Classical, mahogany, carved cresting of basket of fruit above glazed door, gilt and painted wooden dial flanked by carved columns, 30 hr wooden movement, 34-3/4" h...435.00

Night Light

American
   1890, milk glass dial, brass mounts, 30 hour lever movement, 6" h...75.00
   1895, Standard Novelty Co., New York, nickel plated case, revolving milk glass shade, 30 hour time lever movement, 6-1/2" h 300.00

French, Arlandaux, Paris, c1850, cast iron base, gilt brass mounts lacy style clear glass, frosted glass dial, 30 hour fusee verge escapement movement, pierced and engraved balance cock, 14" h...800.00

Novelty

Birdcage, metal cage, gold painted, two plastic birds, one moves with balance wheel, other with alarm mechanism, 30 hour lever movement, 7" h...90.00
Commemorative, Admiral Dewey, gilded iron case, 30 hour lever movement, 10" h...225.00
Doll, Ansonia Clock Co., Ansonia, CT, c1900, swinging boy, gilded and cast white metal case, paper dial, 30 hour time movement, 11-3/4" h..850.00
Train, Ansonia Clock Co., New York, pat 1878, white metal train front case, includes engineers and amber reflector, 30 hour balance wheel movement with paper dial, gilt highlights, 8" h 625.00

Shelf

Ansonia Clock Co., Ansonia, CT, c1890
   Beehive, rosewood case, 30 hour time and strike movements, 18-3/4" h..100.00
   Gingerbread, carved and pressed walnut case, paper on zinc dial, silver dec glass, 8 day time and strike movement with pendulum, 22" h...150.00
Bartholomew, E. and G. W., Bristol, CT, c1830, classical, mahogany, flat molded cornice above glazed door flanking black painted and stenciled columns, eglomise table of landscape enc. painted wood dial, gilt spandrels, 30 hr wooden weight driven movement, 29-3/4" h, 16-1/2" d 690.00
Beals, J. J. Boston, MA, 1860, overpasted label, mahogany veneered beehive case, enameled zinc dial, J. C. Brown 8 day time, strike, and alarm movement, 18-3/4" h 300.00
Birge and Ives, Bristol, CT, c1825, triple decker, classical, mahogany, 8-day weight driven movement, gilt carved basket of fruit cresting painted dial, mirror, and eglomise tablets flanked by columns, carved claw feet, regilded, orig tablet with losses, 36" h..575.00
Brown, J. C., and Forestville Mfg. Co., laminated rosewood veneered acorn case, painted tablet with floral dec and geometric designs, painted zinc dial, 8 day time and strike double fusee movement with pendulum, 19" h.......................5,000.00
Chauncey, Jerome, Bristol, CT, 1860, ebonized wood box case, MOP inlay, gold dec, inscribed enameled zinc dial, 30 hour time and strike fusee movement, 13" h...........................450.00
Downes, Ephraim, Bristol, CT, c1825, mahogany, pillar and scroll, 30 hr wooden weight driven movement, old finish, imperfections, 31" h 920.00
Eli Terry and Sons, Plymouth, CT, c1820-40, late Federal, pillar and scroll, mahogany, brass finials over painted wood dial, glazed door with reverse glass painted tablet, flanked by tapering cylindrical columns, bracket feet, 17-1/2" w, 31" h 1,400.00
Federal, attributed to Eli Terri, Plymouth, CT, c1818, pillar and scroll, mahogany, wooden 30 hr weight drive movement, outside escapement, refinished, restored, 28-3/4" h.......2,070.00
Forestville Mfg. Co., Bristol, CT, 1847, laminated wood acorn case, 8 day time and strike lyre movement, detailed fusees mounted on case bottom, painted dial and glass table, pendulum, 24-1/2" h..4,500.00

Gilbert Mfg. Co., Winstead, CT, 1875, rosewood veneered box case, gilded moldings, dec tablet, enameled zinc dial, paper label, 8 day time and strike movement, pendulum, 13-1/2" h 100.00
Gothic Style, German, Black Forest, castle form, carved figure of knight, 21" h...2,070.00
Ingraham, E.& A., Bristol, CT
   Beehive, 1850, mahogany veneered case, etched glass tablet, enameled zinc dial, 8 day time and strike movement with pendulum, 19" h..350.00
   Gingerbread, c1900, oak case, Capitol dome pressed on crest, gold dec tablet, paper on zinc dial, 8 day time and strike movement with calendar mechanism and pendulum, paper label on reverse of case, 22" h......................325.00
Leavenworth, Mark, and Son, Waterbury, CT, c1825, pillar and scroll, mahogany, 30 hr wooden movement, imperfections, 16-1/2" w, 4-1/2" d, 29-3/4" h.....................................920.00
Manross, Elisha, Bristol, CT, 1845, mahogany veneered steeple case, 2 geometric tablets, painted zinc dial, 8 day time and strike fusee strap brass movement with pendulum, 23-1/2" h 750.00
New England Clock Co., Bristol, CT, c1850, box case, painted tablet, painted zinc dial, 30 hour time and alarm movement with pendulum, 11" h...450.00
Seth Thomas, pillar and scroll, refinished mahogany and curly maple veneer case, wooden works, painted wooden face, painted paper label "Seth Thomas, Plymouth, Connecticut," worn orig reverse painted glass with landscape and house, old touch up repair, weights, key, pendulum, replaced brass finials and goosenecks, 31" h....................................1,265.00
Smith & Goodrich, Bristol, CT, 1845, mahogany veneered steeple case, tablet with balloon and American flags, painted zinc dial, 30 hour time and strike fusee movement with pendulum, 20" h..650.00
Terry & Andrews, Bristol, CT, 1850, mahogany veneered steeple case, painted tablet, painted zinc dial, 8 day time and strike lyre movement with pendulum, 19-1/2" h 625.00
Whiting, Riley, Winchester, CT, mahogany, pillar and scroll, 30 hr wooden weight driven movement, old finish, imperfections, 30-1/4" h...1,200.00
Willard, Aaron, Jr., Boston, c1815, Federal, mahogany and bull's eye maple, inlaid geometric stringing and crossbanding, white painted and gilt iron dial inscribed "A. Willard Jr.; Boston," 8 day weight driven movement with drop ball hour strike, refinished, restoration, 40" h....................................10,350.00
Willard, Simon and Son, 1824-32, Classical, ebonized wood and ormolu, fire gilt brass lyre-form finial above fire gilt bezel and white porcelain circular dial inscribed "Simon Willard and Son patent no. 154," 8 day brass weight driven movement, black painted slightly domed iron plate, fluted ebonized column flaring at iron plate, fluted ebonized column flaring at brass fire gilt mounting, conforming fluted columnar base, imperfections, glass dome missing, 25" h 101,500.00

Ship

Ashcroft Mfg. Co., New York, c1920, cast brass case mounted on walnut base, engraved brass dial, seconds indicator, 8 day double wind time lever movement, chipped bezel glass, 12-1/2" h 450.00
Seth Thomas, Thomaston, CT, 1900, brass case, silver dial inscribed "Kelvin White & Co. Nautical Instruments Boston-New York, Seth Thomas," 30 hour lever movement, bell strike, later mahogany base, 10-1/4" h..425.00
Waterbury Clock Co., Waterbury, CT, 1940, cast brass case, ship's wheel bezel, silvered dial, 8 day jeweled lever movement, bell strike, 8" d 350.00

Tall Case

Automation, Victorian, mahogany and inlay, chiming, late 19th C, 95" h..4,600.00
Barron, William, London, mid to late 18th C, Chinoiserie case, caddy top, 8 day count wheel works, ornate brass dial, sil-

vered chapter ring, brass spandrels with face in center, half hour mark between each Roman numeral, second hand dial and calendar, orig weights, brass weight shells, later case dec, feet reduced, some paint loss, 7' 10-1/2" h........3,100.00

Best, Samuel, Cincinnati, OH, cherry, old finish, dovetailed bonnet, freestanding columns and broken arch pediment with molded goosenecks, carved floral rosettes, molded edge door with cut-out corners, fluted quarter columns, cove molding between sections, applied base panel, ogee feet, brass works, painted face with phases of moon dial, calendar movement, second hand and "Samuel Best," orig operating instructions in pen and ink inside with "Sold by S. Best, June 2, 1806 Cincinnati, Ohio," feet replaced, minor repairs to case and works, orig weights and pendulum, 95-1/2" h 8,250.00

Chippendale

New England, late 18th C, butternut, hood with fretwork joining 3 reeded plinths above tombstone glazed door, painted iron dial with portrait of bearded man in arch, articulated eyes, dial flanked by free standing base stop fluted columns, molded tombstone waist door flanked by brass stop fluted reeded quarter columns on base, ogee bracket feet, old finish, imperfections, 93" h...............................4,025.00

Pennsylvania, Reading, 1784, Henry Hahn, grain painted, flat top, overhanging cornice, engraved columnar supports, center glazed door opening to brass dial with gilt spandrels, Roman and Arabic numerals, calendar aperture, sgd "Henry Hahn Reading, No. 61," waisted case below with arched molded door, incised on reverse "1784," flanked by quarter columns, flaring molding on rect base, stepped molding, ogee bracket feet, mustard colored ground 23,000.00

Colonial Manufacturing Co., Zeeland, MI, walnut case, broken pediment, final over corner columns, brass face dial with moon phase, arch door with beveled glass, brass weights, five tone pipes, 81-1/2" h, 19" w, damage to int. floor..........440.00

Federal

Massachusetts, c1810, cherry, hood with reeded plinths above arched molded cornice, glazed tombstone door flanked by freestanding reeded columns, white painted moon phase dial, polychrome and gilt American shield spandrels, 8 day weight drive movement, molded rect waist door on inlaid base, flaring French feet, old finish, imperfections, 85" h...6,900.00

Tall Case, Walter H. Durfee, retailed by Tiffany & Co, NY, 1890, mahogany, tombstone top with carved fan and carved acanthus molding supporting split arched bonnet with full twist columns, waist with full twist columns flanking beveled glass front access door, base with full twist columns on bronze mounts, claw foot, John Elliot of London eight-day precision quarter hour chime on gongs, hour strike movement, precision mercury compensating pendulum with gold washed filigree dial, silver chapter ring, raised gold washed Arabic numeral below hp scenic moon phase dial, 96" h, $8,800. Photo courtesy of Jackson's Auctioneers & Appraisers.

New England, c1820, maple inlaid, scrolled fret joining 3 plinths with brass ball finials above arched cornice molding, glazed door flanked by freestanding columns, white painted polychrome and gilt dec dial with red drapery at the arch, fruit spandrels with seconds indicator, calendar aperture, 8 day brass weight driven movement, rect waist door, bird's eye maple veneer, mahogany cross-banding, flanking quarter columns on base with grain paint and simulated stringing, old finish, imperfections, 84" h....4,600.00

New York or New Jersey, c1800, mahogany inlaid, hood with molded swans neck cresting centering urn finial, flat molded cornice with arched molding, tombstone glazed door flanked by free standing string inlaid columns, brass dial with engraved silver chapter ring, second hand and calendar aperture engraved "Tho. Wagstaffe, London," cast gilt metal spandrels on oval inlaid waist door flanked by string inlaid quarter columns on base with circular panel in inlaid mitered frame, French feet, refinished, movement of different origin, other imperfections, 99" h 7,150.00

George III, mahogany, oak, and inlay, painted dial inscribed "McDowall Pontefract," dial depicts continents, c1800, restorations, 94" h 1,495.00

Goddard, Nicholas, Rutland, VT, early 19th C, Federal, cherry inlaid, hood with scrolled crest flanked by turned finials and diagonal contrasting bands above glazed inlaid door, flanked by reeded columns, painted moon phase iron dial inscribed "Nicholas Goddard Rutland No. 138," waist inlaid with stringing diagonal banding and contrasting ovals flanked by reeded quarter columns on base with 2 inlaid ovals bordered by stringing, old finish, imperfections, 89-1/4" h 5,175.00

Hepplewhite, refinished mahogany figured veneer, curved cornice with fretwork crest and brass finials on reeded plinths, free standing front reeded columns on bonnet with brass sittings, reeded quarter columns with brass fittings, molding between sections, cross banded veneer with banded inlay around base, French feet, brass works, painted metal face are period, but orig to clock, second hand, calendar movement, and rocking ship, weights and pendulum, minor veneer damage, 94-1/2" h 7,150.00

Hewlett, John, Bristol, England, 8 day, Chinoiserie case, brass dial, brass floral and shell spandrels, calendar and second dials, finals missing, loss to feet, 7' 4" h 2,145.00

Krauss, John Samuel, Bethlehem, PA, c1810, Moravian, 8 day second hand and calendar dial, moon dial, dial framed in gesso beading, cherry case with inlay, chamfered corners, tiger maple inlay on case and bonnet, 5 replaced bonnet finials, 4 columns, 8' 6"...12,100.00

Massachusetts, southeastern, 1790-1810, birch, case inlaid with stringing, paterae and quarter fans, hood atop fluted columns and waist quarter columns, dial with polychrome dec, seconds and calendar apertures, refinished, 8 day brass weight driven movement, restoration, 86-3/4" h.....................6,325.00

Murphy, John, Northampton (Allentown), PA, c1775, 8 day, orig non-functioning painted moon dial in good condition, walnut case, bonnet with turned columns, tan top door with orig trunk door lock, bear skin panel on lower base, feet reduced, 8' 1" h..22,000.00

Parker, Gardner, Westborough, MA, Federal, cherry, hood with arched cornice molding above inlaid glazed tombstone door, white painted iron dial with polychrome floral gilt designs, seconds hand, and calendar aperture, mkd "warranted by G. Parker," 8 day brass movement flanked by reeded columns, rect inlaid waist with center oval flanked by reeded quarter columns, conforming inlaid base, old finish, imperfections, 78" h 9,775.00

Rogers, Samuel, Plymouth, MA, c1810, Federal, mahogany, inlaid stringing, crossbanding, brass stop fluted hood columns, waist quarter columns, polychrome floral dec on dial, seconds hand inscribed "Saml. Rogers," brass 8 day weight driven movement, old refinish, restoration, 89-1/4" h 10,350.00

Tall Case, Chester County, PA, 18th C, walnut, double scroll top, rosettes, three flame urn finials, arched brass face with moon phases, engraved leaves and flowers, sweep second hand, sgd "Eli Bentley, West Whiteland," rect lip molded waist door, recessed panel below, quarter round fluted corners, ogival bracket feet, 96" h, $15,000. Photo courtesy of Freeman\Fine Arts.

Taylor, Joseph, Perth, Scotland, c1780, Chinoiserie case, 8 day, brass dial, brass floral spandrels, calendar and second dials, 7' 11-1/2" h...2,145.00

Willard, Aaron, Jr., Boston, c1800, Federal, mahogany, inlaid stringing, crossbanded, brass stop fluted freestanding hood columns and waist quarter columns, door with label "Aaron Willard Jun. Washington - Street, Boston (near Roxbury) Massachusetts," moon phase dial with seconds hand and calendar aperture inscribed "Aaron Willard Jr., Boston," emb with gilt and polychrome American shields, old refinish, 8 day brass weight driven movement, restoration, 95-1/2" h 19,550.00

Willard, Simon, Boston, c1800, Federal, mahogany, inlaid stringing and quarter fans, brass stop fluted hood, columns, waste quarter columns, moon phase dial with floral painted spandrels, second hand and calendar aperture, inscribed "warranted for Mr. Daniel Phillips Simon Willard," old refinish, restoration, 96-1/2" h.................40,250.00

Williams, W. A., Albany, c1825, Federal, mahogany and mahogany veneer inlaid, hood with molded swan's neck cresting, center molded keystone above glazed tombstone door, flanking turned spiral carved columns, painted iron moon phase dial with shell spandrels, inlaid molded waste door flanked by canted corners, base bordered by stringing and mahogany crossbanding, ogee bracket feet, 100" h 5,175.00

Wingate, Frederick, Augusta, ME, c1817, Federal, painted birch, dark brown stained case, ring turned brass mounted quarter columns, rocking ship polychrome dial with Arabic numerals, gilt dec spandrels, seconds, and calendar aperture, maker's orig label, old refinish, restoration, 90" h 4,890.00

Wall

Banjo
21" h, Federal, mahogany, attributed to Lemuel Curtis, Concord, MA, c1820, restored dial, retouched 1,100.00
32-1/4" h, Federal, Simon Willard, Roxbury, c1815, mahogany inlaid, circular brass molded bezel enclosing white painted dial, 8 day brass weight drive movement with "T bridge" above trapezoidal throat, white eglomise tablet and pendulum box below inscribed "S. Willards Patent," framed by

mahogany cross banding and stringing, flanking pierced brass brackets, old finish, restoration 1,610.00
32-3/4" h, mahogany and mahogany veneer, brass trim, old flaking reverse painted glass tablet, scene of chariot in sky, replaced brass eagle finial, repainted face, weight, key, pendulum.. 1,265.00
33-1/2" h, Federal, John Wawin, Boston, early 19th C, mahogany, gilt gesso, painted dial inscribed "Sawin" about gilt framed eglomise tablets, lower showing sea battle "The Wasp and Reindeer," restored 1,265.00
34" h, Federal, attributed to NH, c1820, mahogany, molded brass bezel, white painted dial above flat veneered framed throat eglomise table inscribed patent, pendulum tablet inscribed "Constitutions Escape," flanking brass pierced brackets, 8 day weight driven movement, imperfections 1,610.00
34" h, Federal, Currier and Foster, Salem, MA, mahogany, gilt gesso rope moldings framing red and white eglomise tablets, lower label with eagle inscribed "Currier & Foster, Salem," brass full striking weight driven movement, glasses replaced, restored 2,875.00
35" h, MA, c1820, mahogany, carved giltwood eagle finial, flat mahogany frame with projecting corner blocks enclosing eglomise tablets of "The Constitution's Escape," restored 920.00
39" h, Aaron Willard, Boston, early 19th C, Federal, mahogany and gilt gesso, eglomise throat glass with scrolled leaf design in orange and green on white, scene of Mount Vernon below, restored, imperfections 1,380.00
40" h, New England, early 19th C, mahogany and gilt gesso, presentation, gilt rope moldings enclosing eglomise tablets showing chariot, restored 750.00
41" h, attributed to Lemuel Curtis, mahogany case, gilded facade, bracket and brass trim, replaced acorn on bracket, old regilding with repairs to facade, replaced reverse painted scene of battle of Lake Erie, replaced finial, weight, key, pendulum...3,300.00

Classical Mirror, Benjamin B. Torry, Hanover, MA, c1825, mahogany, pillar and scroll cresting above flat cornice molding, glazed door of 2 eglomise tablets, mirror with flanking turned columns, door opens to access iron white painted dished dial inscribed "Benji B. Torrey Hanover," striking 8 day weight driven movement, refinished, restoration, 37" h, 17" w.....2,415.00

Gallery
Ingraham, E. & Co., Bristol, CT, c1870, gilt gesso, molded circular glazed frame, white painted metal dial, 8 day spring driven movement, minor imperfections, 20" d 1,955.00
Little, W. Torrey, New England, early 19th C, gilt gesso, molded circular frame, convex painted wooden dial inscribed "W. Torrey Little, Inc., Boston-Marshfield," 8 day weight driven movement, repainted dial, restoration, 29" d 1,495.00

Regulator, W. Morrison, London, mahogany, 19th C, 66-1/2" h 1,955.00

Wag on the Wall, 8-1/2" x 6", northern Europe, early 19th C, painted tombstone dial, brass alarm wheel, pull-up weight driven movement 100.00

Water, English, 29" h, oak, chip carving, brass fittings, name plate engraved "John West, 1674, Warwick" 715.00

CLOISONNÉ

History: Cloisonné is the art of enameling on metal. The design is drawn on the metal body, then wires, which follow the design, are glued or soldered on. The cells thus created are packed with enamel and fired; this step is repeated several times until the level of enamel is higher than the wires. A buffing and polishing process brings the level of enamels flush to the surface of the wires.

This art form has been practiced in various countries since 1300 B.C. and in the Orient since the early 15th century. Most cloisonné found today is from the late Victorian era, 1870–1900, and was made in China or Japan.

Reference: Lawrence A. Cohen and Dorothy C. Ferster, *Japanese Cloisonné,* Charles E. Tuttle Co., 1990.

Collectors' Club: Cloisonne Collectors Club, P.O. Box 96, Rockport, MA 01966.

Museum: George Walter Vincent Smith Art Museum, Springfield, MA.

Beaker, 19-1/2" h, spheroid, long flaring neck, galleried rim, stepped foot, brocade dec, green ground, Japanese, mid 19th C, pr 800.00
Bowl, 12" d, 3-1/2" h, turned l rim, marine blue, variety of large lotus blossoms, clusters of small circles cloisonnés, cobalt border with silk-worm cloisonnés, overlapping pomegranates on bottom, Chinese 550.00
Box, cov, 12" d, steep sloping sides, high splayed foot, int. polychrome enameled medallion of Buddha flanked by two arhats, lotus pond, two kinnara flying through cloud scrolls, turquoise ground, etc., with sinuous dragons winding through flowering lotus plants and Chinese characters of longevity and happiness, two character base mark of "Daimin," Chinese, Meiji period..650.00
Brush Pot, 5" h, asters and butterfly dec, light blue ground, sgd "Takeuchi," Japanese, c1875.......................................225.00
Charger
    12" d, bird and floral dec, Chinese, 19th C, repairs 175.00
    14" d, roosters and floral dec, black ground, Chinese late 19th C, surface scratches 180.00
Cigarette Case, green, 3 dragons, multicolored, Chinese. 165.00
Clock, 10" h, oval, multicolored bands of foliage, French, c1900 ....690.00
Figure, Chinese, teakwood base
    3" h, 3" l, singing frogs, pr...195.00
    3" h, 7-1/2" l, fantailed goldfish, pr.............................350.00
    4" h, 5" l, lounging horses, pr..250.00
Incense Burner, 5" h, lotus-form, Chinese, 19th C 295.00

Lamp Base, 18" h, vase form, multicolored foliage and mask-form handles, Chinese, late 19th C 1,840.00
Libation Cup, 5-1/2" l, figural, ram's head, blue, multicolored swirl and dragon design 265.00
Plate, 9-3/4" d, marine blue, 2 white cranes, scenic terrain, peonies, foliage, Japanese...300.00
Seal Paste Box, 3-3/4" d, cov dec with two shaped panels, one green, other orange, floral sprays on blue ground, allover scrolling vine dec, Japanese, Meiji period...................125.00
Tureen, cov, 14-1/2" l handle to handle, blue ground, scrolled foliate design surrounding characters, Chinese, 19th C
....460.00
Vase
    8-1/2" h, 3-1/8" d, dark colors, wide rust band, small colored flowers, bird in flight, goldstone in band, Japanese
....235.00
    11" h, shaped panels depicting birds and flowering branches, blue ground with butterflies, Japanese, Meiji period 400.00
    16" h, green, overall floral dec, electrified, some damage
....115.00
    19-3/4" h, quadrangular, 2 sinuous dragons chasing flaming jewel, bands of taotie masks, archaistic motifs, waisted neck with stylized archastic ruyi-lappet band, gilt rims, four character Xuande mark, minor restorations, pr........800.00

CLOTHING AND CLOTHING ACCESSORIES

History: While museums and a few private individuals have collected clothing for decades, it is only recently that collecting clothing has achieved a widespread popularity. Clothing reflects the social attitudes of a historical period.

Christening and wedding gowns abound and, hence, are not in large demand. Among the hardest items to find are men's clothing from the 19th and early 20th centuries. The most sought after clothing is by designers, such as Fortuny, Poirret, and Vionnet.

References: Maryanne Dolan, *Vintage Clothing,* 3rd ed., Books Americana, 1995; Roseanne Ettinger, *'50s Popular Fashions for Men, Women, Boys & Girls,* Schiffer Publishing, 1995; Roselyn Gerson, *Vintage & Contemporary Purse Accessories,* Collector Books, 1997; ——, *Vintage Ladies Compacts,* Collector Books, 1996; ——, *Vintage Vanity Bags and Purses,* Collector Books, 1994; Michael Jay Goldberg, *The Ties That Blind,* Schiffer Publishing, 1997; Carol Belanger Grafton, *Fashions of the Thirties,* Dover Publications, 1993; Kristina Harris, *Victorian & Edwardian Fashions for Women,* Schiffer Publishing, 1995; ——, *Vintage Fashions for Women,* Schiffer Publishing, 1996; Richard Holiner, *Antique Purses,* Collector Books, 1996 value upate; Susan Langley, *Vintage Hats & Bonnets, 1770-1970,* Collector Books, 1997; Ellie Laubner, *Fashions of the Roarings '20s,* Schiffer Publishing, 1996; Jan Lindenberger, *Clothing & Accessories from the '40s, '50s, & '60s,* Schiffer Publishing, 1996; Phillip Livoni (ed.), *Russell's Standard Fashions: 1915–1919,* Dover Publications, 1996; Sally C. Luscomb, *The Collector's Encyclopedia of Buttons,* Schiffer Publishing, 1997; Desire Smith, *Hats,* Schiffer Publishing, 1996; ——, *Vintage Styles: 1920-1960,* Schiffer Publishing, 1997; Pamela Smith, *Vintage Fashion & Fabrics,* Alliance Publishers, 1995; Jeffrey B. Snyder, *Stetson Hats & The John B. Stetson*

Button, red ground, 1-1/4" d, $25.

Company 1865-1970, Schiffer Publishing, 1997; Diane Snyder-Haug, *Antique & Vintage Clothing*, Collector Books, 1996; Geoffrey Warren, *Fashion & Accessories, 1840-1980,* Schiffer Publishing, 1997; Debra Wisniewski, *Antique and Collectible Buttons,* Collector Books, 1997.

Periodicals: *Glass Slipper*, 653 S. Orange Ave., Sarasota, FL 34236; *Lady's Gallery*, P.O. Box 1761, Independence, MO 64055; *Lill's Vintage Clothing Newsletter*, 19 Jamestown Dr., Cincinnati, OH 45241; *Vintage Clothing Newsletter*, P.O. Box 88892, Seattle, WA 98138; *Vintage Connection*, 904 N. 65th St., Springfield, OR 97478; *Vintage Gazette*, 194 Amity St., Amherst, MA 01002.

Collectors' Clubs: The Costume Society of America, P.O. Box 73, Earleville, MD 21919; Vintage Fashion and Costume Jewelry Club, P.O. Box 265, Glen Oaks, NY 11004.

Museums: Bata Shoe Museum, Toronto, Canada; Fashion Institute of Technology, New York, NY; Los Angeles County Museum (Costume and Textile Dept.), Los Angeles, CA; Metropolitan Museum of Art, New York, NY; Museum of Costume, Bath, England; Philadelphia Museum of Art, Philadelphia, PA; Smithsonian Institution (Inaugural Gown Collection), Washington, DC; Wadsworth Athenaeum, Hartford, CT; Whiting and Davis Handbag Museum, Attleboro Falls, MA.

Additional Listings: See *Warman's Americana & Collectibles* for more examples.

Note: Condition, size, age, and completeness are critical factors in purchasing clothing. Collectors divide into two groups: those collecting for aesthetic and historic value and those desiring to wear the garment. Prices are higher on the West coast; major auction houses focus on designer clothes and high-fashion items.

Apron, cotton, hand sewn
　　Christmas design, printed fabric, c1940 ....20.00
　　Green and white check 40.00
　　Patchwork design, waist length.....................25.00
Bed Jacket
　　Satin, pale yellow, floral design in material 45.00
　　Sheer, lingerie type, light blue, floral embroidery, tie at waist 42.00
Blazer, man's
　　Imported Cotton, shades of brown, gold, dark red, and navy blue, size 42, "Charka Batik, 100% Imported Cotton, Dry Clean" and "Designed and Tailored by Gordon-Ford" labels 45.00
　　Perma Press Cotton, small check in gray and black, 3 button, 2 front pockets with flaps, size 42-1/2", 1960s, "Kingsridge Flex Tailored Jas. T. Mullin & Sons Inc. Wilmington" label, 2nd label with washing instructions............35.00
　　Wool, red, navy blue, and dark green plaid, 2 button front, 2 pockets with flaps, 4 buttons on sleeve, split tail, size 38/40, "Saks Fifth Avenue, 100% Wool" label 45.00
Blouse
　　Cotton
　　　Black, dragon design on sleeves, design at neck 40.00
　　　Shirt Waist, eyelet lace, button front, long mutton sleeves, puffy shoulders, late 1880s 150.00
　　Lace, black, long sleeves, 1920s 35.00
　　Nylon/chiffon, shades of pink and rose, lined, short sleeve, 4 covered buttons, finished at hem, size 8/10, 1940s.............35.00

Nylon, white, satin trim, long sleeves, 1930s........................20.00
Silk taffeta, pale green, handmade bobbin lace trim, 1900 ....400.00
Boas, Marabou feather, black, 7' long 22.00
Bodice, satin, beige, fully lined, 9 satin-lace covered buttons, pleated tail back, 22" fitted waist line, 9-1/2" ruffled cuff trim, semi-high neckline, lace overlay 35.00
Bonnet, baby
　　Crochet, ribbon insert, newborn....................15.00
　　Organdy, white, blue ribbon and trim..........................20.00
Cape
　　Gauze, black, stenciled foliate scrolls, tied at shoulders, hem threaded with striped Venetian glass beads, Fortuny, 36" l 500.00
　　Velvet, black, white fur collar and sleeves, 1930s.........125.00
　　Wool, medium brown, dark brown fur trim at neck, hemline, dark brown silk lining, finger tip length, tie closure, c1890 ....425.00
Catalog
　　Alfred H. Cammeyer Co., New York, NY, 1896, 50 pgs, 7-1/4" x 10", orig mailing envelope, shoes, boots, slippers, and rubbers for men and women 48.00
　　Bellas Hess & Co., New York, NY, 1927, 243 pgs, 11" x 14", NY's Latest Fashions for Spring and Summer, Cat. #128 ....30.00
　　Hamilton Garment Co., New York, NY, 1917, 42 pgs, 7" x 9-1/4", fall and winter ladies styles.................30.00
　　Missouri Distributing Co., Chillicothe, MO, 1954, 48 pgs, 8-1/4" x 11", Special Summer Issue #129, World's Largest Distributors of Gloves..............30.00
　　National Cloak & Suit Co., New York, NY, 1908, 96 pgs, 6-3/4" x 9-1/4", ladies fashions..............38.00
　　Straus & Schram, Chicago, IL, 1929, 88 pgs, 7" x 8-3/4", Fashion's Authentic Style Book, fall and winter, ladies and men's fashions 20.00
　　Work Bros. & Co., Chicago, IL, 1893, 4-1/4" x 7-1/2", illustrated price list, men's clothes 40.00
Chaps, women's, leather, belt buckle front closure, leather tie in back, fringe and pockets, "Jim Burke Maker Paris, Texas" label..............175.00
Christening, cotton batiste dress, lace tiers, matching cap.95.00
Coat
　　Crepe, black, dots, fox trim, fringed neck, 1920s 250.00
　　Gabardine, lavender-gray, flaring form, panels of blue and gray silk, floral embroidery, gray rabbit fur collar.....145.00
　　Leather, wrap style, lavender, long, tie belt, cuffed dolman sleeves, slash pockets, irid taffeta lining 125.00
　　Velvet Brocade, opera, gold and brown, gold satin lining, 3/4 sleeve, one button at neck closure, small rounded collar, size 14/16, 1950s.....................95.00
　　Wool, red-orange, mink collar, cuffs, and hood trip, wrap style, red taffeta lining, small size 7 ....5.00
Collar, velvet, black, rhinestones, beads and pearls, 1930s 35.00
Dress
　　Cotton, turquoise, high neck, lace inserts, ruffled sleeves, 1895..................200.00
　　Leather, Vakko, red, zipper front, 2 front patch pockets, belted in back, snap cuffs, fully lined, size 6.........75.00
　　Rayon, pink, blue piping, padded shoulders, 1935-45...50.00
Evening Dress
　　Chanel, black lace, grosgrain ribbon center bowl, flared skirt, size 4-6, 1930s..............5,750.00
　　Christian Dior, strapless, train, taffeta chiné, full blown roses, shades of pink and green, matching pumps by C. Sybille, dress label "Christian Dior Paris Printemps/Été 1957" 17,250.00
　　Jean Desses, strapless, yellow silk chiffon, draped bodice, c1960..............9,200.00

Homemade, black crepe bodice with shirred front, ivory brocade princess seamed skirt, replaced zipper, tea length 20.00

Lace, peach, a-line slip dress, white lace overdress, dropped waist, V neck, flared skirt, scalloped lace edging at hemline, criss-cross spaghetti straps, back zipper, ankle length 45.00

Lord & Taylor, yellow knit, long, empire waist, V-neck, two rows of fat piping under bust, back zipper, fully lined, full skirt, c1970 ....55.00

Victor Costa for Saks Fifth Ave., 2 pc strapless black and white dress, wide belt, matching jacket, size 4, c1980 ....75.00

Worth, ivory satin, pointed bodice, trained skirt heavily embroidered with flowers, plumes, and foliage, pearlescent beads, sequins, and rhinestones, late 1890s........3,220.00

Yves Saint Laurent for Christian Dior, beaded short dress, crystal beads, matching satin belt, pink, c1959..10,350.00

Fur
Jacket, Persian lamb, waist length, 3/4 length sleeves, hand tailored, shawl collar, one button at top, small size, c1950 ....125.00

Stole, silver fox, shoulder wrap, beige satin lining, frog closure 45.00

Gloves, 4-3/4" l, infant's, leather, white kidskin, silvered metal button snap, imp "Dent's" 30.00

Handbag
Brocade, Art Deco, evening style, engraved gold filled framed 75.00

Faille, black, marcasite set mount, green onyx monogram, c1930 ....65.00

Plastic, lunch box style, pumpkin colored striations 50.00

Hat
Derby, riding, black, wear to inside lining 45.00

Felt
Black, trimmed in black ostrich feathers, small bowl crown, brim short in back, wide in front, black ribbon with bow in back, "Yowell Drew Ivey Co., Daytona Beach" label 125.00

Dark Brown, man's, 1-3/4" brim, label "Berg Fifth Ave. NY," 1940s..25.00

Brown, wide brim, beige feathers, green netting, 1930s 125.00

Rose, net and chiffon layers, flowers and pearls, wire frame on each side for secure fit, "Mary Louis Shaker-Shaker Heights" label...28.00

Sapphire Blue, Art Deco style, small matching bow and netting 35.00

Velour, brown, rolled brim, 1960s................................42.00

Velvet, black
Moss green velvet bow, silk rose, c1930 ....80.00

Red poppies, fully lined, wire in brim, 2" w front brim narrows in back 38.00

Fur, black beaver, pill box style..................................65.00

Stetson, man's, wool felt
Grey, size 7-1/8", turned up edge on brim, c1950 .....35.00

Royal, dark gray, inside brim measurement 22-1/2" ..45.00

Straw
Black, large brim, crown fabric, 20-1/2", Schiparallei Jr. Paris label..65.00

Black, pink, rose, and white flowers, green leaves, Neiman Marcus label..30.00

Navy, feather and veil, small turned up brim, "Gage Brothers & Co., Chicago, New York Since 1856" 35.00

Skimmer, size 7-1/4" d, old store stock, unused 55.00

Suede, man's, light beige, size 7-1/4", feather on side, "Custom Made Bee Hats" label 35.00

Top, silk, black, "Reeds" label, early 1900s 95.00

Magazine, *Altman Magazine,* B. Altman & Co., New York, NY, 1931, 50 pgs, 9" x 12", fall and winter fashions 25.00

Muff, black fur, black velvet strap, 10" w, 26" d..................65.00

Nightgown, silk, lace edge neckline, embroidered, 1930s..90.00

Parasol
Child's, silk, black...85.00

Lady's, white, embroidered, c1910 ....75.00

Robe
Gauze, black, gilt foliate scrolls and medallions, Fortuny, 44" l 1,200.00

Silk, blue ground 8 couched gold dragons chasing flaming pearls, stylized clouds and bats, boashan haishui band at hem, Chinese, mid 19th C 1,800.00

Shawl
Chantilly type lace, black 35.00

Kashimir, paisley, rose...225.00

Sheer, pastel Art Deco florals.......................................45.00

Wool, black, black satin embroidery, silk fringe.............85.00

Shoes
Capezio, yellow plastic, size 6-1/2", 1970s 22.00

High Button, leather, black 55.00

Platforms, gold, size 10 ....45.00

Spats, 4 buttons, foot strap, mkd "English box cloth, Standard Spats," pr...35.00

Stockings, white, stamped "Imperial Lisle," orig box 12.00

Hat, John B. Stetson, Phila, black, leather band, silk lining, $40.

Petticoat, white batiste, drawstring top, scalloped bottom, $45.

Suit, lady's
 Knitted, mohair and wool, winter white, pink embroidered
  snowflakes, skirt with elastic waist, lined, size 10, c1960,
  "75% Mohair, 25% Wool, Soufle, A Beldoch Popper Pro-
  duc" label 45.00
Suit, man's, Zoot style, peacock blue, double button, double
 breasted jacket size 40, tux style color, 3 pockets on jacket,
 30" pants with cuffs, white lining, label reads "Retro made in
 USA" 95.00
Sweater
 Acrylic, cardigan, red and gold flowers, avocado leaves,
  beige background, size small, "Featherknits, 100% Orlon
  Acrylic" label...15.00
 Angora
  Chinese red, charcoal, and beige diamonds, size small,
   1970s, slight pilling, "Sportempos has that Suburbia
   look!"label 25.00
  Green, cardigan, small, "James Kenrob by Dalton, Kauf-
   man's, Pittsburgh" label 20.00
 Cashmere, waist length, blue, 4 frog closures, hooks and eyes
  under frogs, lined bodice, sating binding, 3/4 length sleeves,
  lining faded, size medium, "Exclusively hand tailored by
  ASHA'S custom tailors, Hong Kong" label 35.00
 Wool, dark and light green floral design, fully lined 60.00
Tux
 Black, wool, size 38 coat, wise labels, 3 buttons each side,
  split tails, black satin lining, 34 waist pants..............250.00
 White, jacket only, shawl collar, 2 front pockets, 1 button front
  closure, white lining, size 44, "Palm Crest-Tailored by Palm
  Beach Co." 65.00

COALPORT

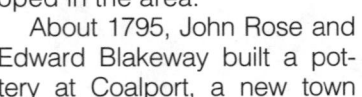

History: In the mid-1750s, Ambrose Gallimore established a pottery at Caughley in the Severn Gorge, Shropshire, England. Several other potteries, including Jackfield, developed in the area.

About 1795, John Rose and Edward Blakeway built a pottery at Coalport, a new town founded along the right-of-way of the Shropshire Canal. Other potteries located adjacent to the canal were those of Walter Bradley and Anstice, Horton, and Rose. In 1799, Rose and Blakeway bought the Royal Salopian China Manufactory at Caughley. In 1814 this operation was moved to Coalport.

A bankruptcy in 1803 led to refinancing and a new name–John Rose and Company. In 1814, Anstice, Horton, and Rose was acquired. The South Wales potteries at Swansea and Nantgarw were added. The expanded firm made fine-quality, highly decorated ware. The plant enjoyed a renaissance from 1888 to 1900.

World War I, decline in trade, and shift of the pottery industry away from the Severn Gorge brought hard times to Coalport. In 1926 the firm, now owned by Cauldon Potteries, moved from Coalport to Shelton. Later owners included Crescent Potteries, Brain & Co., Ltd., and finally, in 1967, Wedgwood.

References: Susan and Al Bagdade, *Warman's English & Continental Pottery & Porcelain*, 2nd ed., Wallace-Homestead, 1991; Michael Messenger, *Coalport 1795-*

Tureen, polychrome Imari style dec, c1805-10, 9"d, 10-1/2" l, $750.

1926, Antique Collectors' Club, 1990; Tom Power, *The Charlton Standard Catalogue of Coalport Figures,* Charlton Press, 1997.

Additional Listings: Indian Tree Pattern.

Bough Pot, 11-1/2" h, hp landscape scene with 2 British soldiers,
 gilt floral dec, yellow ground, c1809 ....365.00
Compote, 12" d, round, pedestal on sq foot, gilt scroll molded rim,
 flower sprays within gilt and foliage surrounds, red ground,
 c1830...475.00
Cup and Saucer, Harebell pattern 35.00
Dish, leaf shape, apple green, garden flower bouquet, gilt foliage,
 c1820...95.00
Figure
 6-1/4" h, Annette, pink and mauve dress, pink shawl and bonnet, c1920..525.00
 6-3/4" h, Lady Bountiful, pink overskirt, green collar and under-
  skirt, blue bows, pink bonnet with blue ribbon, c1949
  ....445.00
 7-3/4" h, The Fire Fighter, black and orange, limited edition,
  1985..275.00
 8" h, Stephanie, yellow, 1984.......................................265.00
 9-1/2" h, Harlequin, multicolored, limited edition, 1983.775.00
Ginger Jar, cov, Blue Willow pattern 75.00
Jug, 7-1/2" h, Lotus, majolica 4,675.00
Plate, 9" d, pink, roses, green garlands, heavy gold, artist sgd,
 made for Davis Collamore, NY 95.00
Spill Vase, 5" h, pink, garden flowers and gilt scroll bands, bird's
 head handles with gilt rings, flared rim, sq base, 3 pc set
 ....950.00
Vase, 7" h, waisted, pierced lip dec with leaf sprays and applied
 flowerheads, body with gilt highlighted leaf scrolls which form
 pierced handles, painted butterflies and floral sprays, magenta glazed lower section, scroll molded foot, quatrefoil base,
 underglaze blue mark...250.00

COCA-COLA ITEMS

History: The originator of Coca-Cola was John Pemberton, a pharmacist from Atlanta, Georgia. In 1886, Dr. Pemberton introduced a patent medicine to relieve headaches, stomach disorders, and other minor maladies. Unfortunately, his failing health and meager finances forced him to sell his interest.

In 1888, Asa G. Candler became the sole owner of Coca-Cola. Candler improved the formula, increased the advertising budget, and widened the distribution. A "patient" was accidentally given a dose of the syrup mixed with carbonated water instead of still water. The result was a tastier, more refreshing drink.

As sales increased in the 1890s, Candler recognized that the product was more suitable for the soft-drink market and began advertising it as such. From these beginnings, a myriad of advertising items have been issued to invite all to "Drink Coca-Cola."

References: Gael de Courtivron, *Collectible Coca-Cola Toy Trucks*, Collector Books, 1995; Steve Ebner, *Vintage Coca-Cola Machines*, Vol. II, published by author (available from FunTronics, Inc., P.O. Box 448, Middletown, MD 21769; Shelly Goldstein, *Goldstein's Coca-Cola Collectibles*, Collector Books, 1991, 1996 value update; *Coca-Cola Trays*, William McClintock, Schiffer Publishing, 1996; Allan Petretti, *Petretti's Coca-Cola Collectibles Price Guide*, 10th ed., Antique Trader Books, 1997; Randy Schaeffer and Bill Bateman, *Coca-Cola*, Running Books, 1995; B. J. Summers, *B. J. Summers' Guide to Coca-Cola*, Collector Books, 1996; Jeff Walters, *Complete Guide to Collectible Picnic Coolers & Ice Chests*, Memory Lane Publishing, 1994; Al Wilson, *Collectors Guide to Coca-Cola Items*, Vol. I (revised: 1987, 1993 value update), Vol. II (1987, 1993 value update), L-W Book Sales; Al and Helen Wilson, *Wilson's Coca-Cola Guide*, Schiffer Publishing, 1997.

Collectors' Club: Coca-Cola Collectors Club, P.O. Box 49166, Atlanta, GA 30359.

Museums: Coca-Cola Memorabilia Museum of Elizabethtown, Inc., Elizabethtown, KY; World of Coca-Cola Pavilion, Atlanta, GA.

Additional Listings: See *Warman's Americana & Collectibles* for more examples.

Notes: Dates of interest: "Coke" was first used in advertising in 1941. The distinctively shaped bottle was registered as a trademark on April 12, 1960.

Album
    Cotton Material for a Thousand Needs, copyright 1943, 16 pgs, 20 insert cards..25.00
    Steel a Modern Essential, copyright 1942, 16 pgs, 20 insert cards..25.00
    Transportation Builds a Nation, copyright 1943, 16 pgs, 20 insert cards...25.00
Badge, 2-1/2" d, white celluloid, black letters, Coca-Cola in red, cello window for name strip, 1950s................................40.00
Barrel, miniature, solid wood, metal bands, red wash paint, early paper label on end, 4-1/2" h, 2-3/4" d........................1,850.00
Baseball Scorekeeper, perpetual counter.........................415.00
Booklet, 2" x 6-1/4", tour plant souvenir, bottle shaped diecut, fold-out type, c1950..35.00
Bottle Mold, 8 3/4" h, 4" w, heavy metal, polished int., background painted black, c1960...15.00
Calendar, 1930, girl in bathing suit, pad begins with August, orig metal rim at top, 24-1/2" x 12".....................................200.00
Charm Bracelet, gold luster metal chair link bracelet, miniature locket booklet inscribed "Eddie Fisher" on front and "Coke Time" on back, black and white photo of Fisher, other charms plastic records with Fisher song titles and RCA Victor markings, c1953...60.00
Clock
    9" x 19-1/2" d, light-up, "Drink Coca-Cola," some oxidation and pitting to gold plating..500.00
    17-1/2" d, tin, silver background, 1951..........................250.00
Cuff Links, 1-1/2" d silvered brass, white on red celluloid insert, c1920, pr..60.00

Magazine, *The Red Barrel*, March 15, 1931, full color cover of camping Boy Scouts enjoying Coke, 28 pgs..................20.00
Notepad, 1-1/2" x 2-1/2" celluloid cov, full color cover portrait art, back cover lists gallons from 1886 to 1901 using Washington Monument as pictorial comparison, vintage pencil notes on two remaining stiff paper sheets....................................500.00
Penlight, 3/4" d, 5-1/2" l, metal and plastic, pocket clip, red, silver and black accents, slogan in silver lettering, c1950s.....65.00
Pinback Button
    Insignia Series, 15-1/6" d, celluloid, Parisian Novelty Co., insert back paper with "Drink Coca-Cola" trademark along with designation of insignia, and series number, 1940s
        No. 10, 99th Bombardment Squadron, red buffalo, blue accents..75.00
        No. 13, Patrol Squadron, white Pegasus, yellow wings, gray ground, red circle...75.00
Radio, 7" x 12" x 9-1/2", cooler shape, c1950, working......550.00
Salesman's Sample Cooler
    7-1/2" x 12" x 10", open front type, inside top lids are pages entitled "A Business Builder" attached to ring binder, pages show different types of coolers available, 1939, some main loss, wear to bottle holder.......................................2,00.00
    13-1/4" x 7-1/2" x 10-1/2", Glascock, orig carrying case, 4 cases of bottles, 1929...17,000.00
Selling Kit, 19" x 17" x 3", orig contents, 1955....................250.00
Sign
    8" x 19-1/2" d, light up, "Have a Coke Drink Coca-Cola," metal frame, glass front, c1950, some minor scratching to metal frame...400.00
    10" d, emb tin, octagon, designed and mfg. by Kay Displays Inc., NY, some paint loss to bottle........................200.00
    12" x 25", tin over cardboard, bottle and different scenes of people enjoying Coca-Cola, "Pause...Refresh Yourself," some scratching..250.00
    17-1/2" x 54", tin, bottle of Coca-Cola, "Drink Coca-Cola Enjoy That Refreshing New Feeling"..............................300.00

Serving Tray, 1950-52, screened background, 10-1/2" x 13-1/4", $50.

20" x 16-1/2" d, self-framed tin, Hilda Clark, gold border with white and purple chrysanthemums, Chas. W. Shonk lithographer, 1903 .... 72,500.00

54" x 16", tin, bottle of Coca-Cola with Coke button attached to top of sign, c1950 .... 600.00

61" x 41", two sided, porcelain, "Drug Store Drink Coca-Cola Delicious and Refreshing," iron ext. frame 1,050.00

Stand, 7-1/2" x 14", diecut, Santa Claus helping himself to bottle of Coke out of refrigerator, ©1948 .... 150.00

Thermometer, 2-1/4" x 7", wall, diecut tin, dimensional bottle, c1956 .... 40.00

Tip Tray

4", 1904, pretty lady, Victorian dress "Delicious" and "Refreshing" on border 200.00

6" x 4-1/4"

1912, lady in large hat, drinking from flared glass, etched with Coca-Cola adv 70.00

1916, lady in vintage clothing drinking from flared glass, etched with Coca-Cola adv 110.00

Tray

10-1/2" x 13-1/2" x 1", color litho, c1953 .... 60.00

13" x 10-1/2" d, young lady enjoying Coca-Cola from flared glass at World's Fair, H. D. Beach Co. litho, 1909, light surface scratching 3,000.00

Wallet, 50th Anniversary, 3-1/4" x 9", tan pigskin, gold markings for c1956 anniversary, unused 60.00

COFFEE MILLS

History: Coffee mills or grinders are utilitarian objects designed to grind fresh coffee beans. Before the advent of stay-fresh packaging, coffee mills were a necessity.

The first home-size coffee grinders were introduced about 1890. The large commercial grinders designed for use in stores, restaurants, and hotels often bear an earlier patent date.

Landers, Frary & Clark, New Britain, CT, No. 2, two wheels, cast iron, 12" h, $475.

Reference: Joseph Edward MacMillan, *MacMillan Index of Antique Coffee Mills*, Cherokee Publishing (657 Old Mountain Rd., Marietta, GA 30064), 1995; Michael L. White and Derek S. White, *Early American Coffee Mills*, published by authors (P.O. Box 483, Fraser, CO 80442).

Collectors' Club: Association of Coffee Mill Enthusiasts, 657 Old Mountain Rd., Marietta, GA 30064.

Cast Iron

7-1/2" h, cast iron, brass trim, lion and unicorn label, English . 140.00

12" h, S & H, drawer 450.00

27" h, Coles Mfg. No. 7, patented 1887 .... 525.00

60" h, Elgin National, red, store type 375.00

72" h, Fairbanks Morse, brass hopper 1,350.00

72" h, Starr 995.00

Ceramic, 14-1/2" h, blue and white Delft design, cast iron fittings, German, wall mounted 90.00

Wood, cast iron fittings

4" h, cherry, dovetailed, brass hopper 170.00

8-1/2" h, refinished poplar, pewter hopper, bottom renailed 115.00

11" h, Arcade Imperial 95.00

COIN-OPERATED ITEMS

History: Coin-operated items include amusement games, pinball machines, jukeboxes, slot machines, vending machines, cash registers, and other items operated by coins.

The first jukebox was developed about 1934 and played 78-RPM records. Jukeboxes were important to teen-agers before the advent of portable radios and television.

The first pinball machine was introduced in 1931 by Gottlieb. Pinball machines continued to be popular until the advent of solid-state games in 1977 and advanced electronic video games after that.

The first three-reel slot machine, the Liberty Bell, was invented in 1905 by Charles Fey in San Francisco. In 1910 Mills Novelty Company copyrighted the classic fruit symbols. Improvements and advancements have led to the sophisticated machines of today.

Vending machines for candy, gum, and peanuts were popular from 1910 until 1940 and can be found in a wide range of sizes and shapes.

References: Michael Adams, Jurgen Lukas, and Thomas Maschke, *Jukeboxes*, Schiffer Publishing, 1995; Michael F. Baute, *Always Jukin' Official Guide to Collectible Jukeboxes*, published by author (221 Yesler Way, Seattle, WA 98104), 1996; Richard M. Bueschel, *Collector's Guide to Vintage Coin Machines*, Schiffer Publishing, 1995; ——, *Guide to Vintage Trade Stimulators & Counter Games*, Schiffer Publishing, 1997; ——, *Lemons, Cherries and Bell-Fruit-Gum*, Royal Bell Books, 1995; ——, *Pinball 1*, Hoflin Publishing, 1988; ——, *Slots 1*, Hoflin Publishing, 1989; Richard Bueschel and Steve Gronowski, *Arcade 1*, Hoflin Publishing, 1993; Herbert Eiden and Jurgen Lukas, *Pinball Machines*, Schiffer Publishing, 1992, values updated 1997; Bill Enes, *Silent Salesmen Too, The Encyclopedia of Collectible Vending Machines*, published by author (8520 Lewis Dr., Lenexa, KS 66227),

1995; Eric Hatchell and Dick Bueschel, *Coin-Ops on Location*, published by authors, 1993; Bill Kurtz, *Arcade Treasures*, Schiffer Publishing, 1994.

Periodicals: *Always Jukin'*, 221 Yesler Way, Seattle, WA 98104; *Antique Amusements Slot Machines & Jukebox Gazette*, 909 26th St. NW, Washington, DC 20037; *Around the Vending Wheel*, 5417 Castana Ave., Lakewood, CA 90712; *Coin Drop International*, 5815 W. 52nd Ave., Denver, CO 80212; *Coin Machine Trader*, 569 Kansas SE, P.O. Box 602, Huron, SD 57350; *Coin-Op Classics*, 17844 Toiyabe St, Fountain Valley, CA 92708; *Coin Slot*, 4401 Zephyr St., Wheat Ridge, Co. 80033; *Gameroom Magazine*, 1014 Mt. Tabor Rd., New Albany, IN 47150; *Jukebox Collector*, 2545 SE 60th St., Des Moines, IA 50317; *Loose Change*, 1515 S. Commerce St., Las Vegas, NV 89102; *Pin Game Journal*, 31937 Olde Franklin Dr., Farmington, MI, 48334; *Scopitone Newsletter*, 810 Courtland Dr., Ballwin, MO 63021.

Collectors' Club: Bubble-Gum Charm, 24 Seafoam St., Staten Island, NY 10306

Museum: Liberty Belle Saloon and Slot Machine Collection, Reno, NV.

Additional Listings: See *Warman's Americana & Collectibles* for separate categories for Jukeboxes, Pinball Machines, Slot Machines, and Vending Machines.

Advisor: Bob Levy.

Notes: Because of the heavy usage these coin-operated items received, many are restored or, at the very least, have been repainted by either the operator or manufacturer. Using reproduced mechanisms to restore pieces is acceptable in many cases, especially when the restored piece will then perform as originally intended.

Arcade

Duck Hunter, 1¢, shoots penny at target, received gum ball, ABT Silver King, c1949................................250.00
Kicker/Catcher, 5¢, 3 balls, skill game, Baker Mfg., c1940 ....400.00
Merchandiser, 5¢, upright wooden machine, to retrieve prizes, exhibit supply, c1940 ....1,800.00
Shuffle Alley, 10¢, tavern bowling game, United, c1953....350.00
Tally-Ho, 5¢, wood rail pinball machine with flippers, exhibit, c1948..250.00

Gum Machines

Columbus Model K, 1¢, dome glass, Lehman and Son, c1920 ....400.00
Lions Club, 1¢, glass dome, chrome base, ball gum, Ford Mfg., c1950..65.00
Master, 1¢, metal, glass, flat sided confection machine, Norris, c1930..200.00
Pulver, 1¢, wall hanging, 2 column, gum stick vending machine, rotating Woody Woodpecker figure, c1940..................500.00
Zeno, 1¢, wooden case, dispenses stick of gum, c1910...600.00

Jukeboxes

AMI, Model E, 1953 ....1,500.00
Mills, Model 951, Constellation, 1947.............................1,300.00
Rockola, Model 1426, 1947...5,000.00
Seeburg, Model KD 100, 1957 ....2,500.00

Wurlitzer
    Model 1015, Bubbler, 1946 ....7,500.00
    Model 1600, 1953...2,500.00

Miscellaneous

Card Vendor, Novelty, 1930s 200.00
Cigar Vendor, Malkin Phillies, 1930s..............................125.00
Cigarette Machine, Rowe Special, 1935 ....450.00
Match Merchandiser, Northwestern, 1930 ....75.00
Perfume Vendor, Sabelle, #5, 1950..................................50.00
Prophylactic, Harmon, 1960 ....75.00
Razor Blades, Gillette, 1940...60.00
Stamp Machine, Shipman, 1960.......................................35.00

Scales

American Scale, Fortune, 1937 ....225.00
Mills, Modern, 1931 ....300.00
Watling, Fortune Telling, #400, 1948...............................400.00

Slot Machines

Caillie, Silent Sphinx, 1932, introduced to capitalized on popularity of King Tut Tomb discovery 2,000.00
Columbia, Deluxe, 25¢, 1938, wear and damage.............500.00
Jennings
    Buckeroo, four reel, 1954 ....2,000.00
    Four Star Chief, 1936...1,500.00
    Little Duke, 1932, 1¢..1,600.00
    Standard Chief, 1947..1,300.00
Mills
    Black Cherry, 1946 ....1,200.00
    Extraordinary, 1934 ....1,400.00
    Firebird "QT," 1936..1,000.00
    Liberty Bell, 1907...7,500.00
    Lions Head, 1931 ....1,500.00
    Operator Bell, 1924..1,200.00
    21 Bell Hightop, 1949...1,200.00
Pace
    Bantam, 1929 ....1,100.00
    Deluxe Comet, 1940..900.00
Watling
    Blue Seal, 1932...1,000.00
    Rolatop, 1937 ....2,800.00
    Treasury, 1934 ....3,500.00

Slot Machine, The Little Duke, 1¢, early 1930s, 24-3/4" h, $2,100.

COMIC BOOKS

History: Shortly after comics first appeared in newspapers of the 1890s, they were reprinted in book format and often used as promotional giveaways by manufacturers, movie theaters, and candy and stationery stores. The first modern-format comic was issued in 1933.

The magic date in comic collecting is June 1938, when DC issued Action Comics No. 1, marking the first appearance of Superman. Thus began the golden age of comics, which lasted until the mid-1950s and witnessed the birth of the major comic book publishers, titles, and characters.

In 1954, Fredric Wertham authored *Seduction of the Innocent*, a book which pointed a guilt-laden finger at the comic industry for corrupting youth, causing juvenile delinquency, and undermining American values. Many publishers were forced out of business while others established a "comics code" to assure parents that their comics were compliant with morality and decency standards upheld by the code authority.

The silver age of comics, mid-1950s through the end of the 1960s, witnessed the revival of many of the characters from the golden age in new comic formats. The era began with Showcase No. 4 in October 1956, which marked the origin and first appearance of the Silver-Age Flash.

While comics survived into the 1970s, it was a low point for the genre; but in the early 1980s, a revival occurred. In 1983, comic book publishers, other than Marvel and DC, issued more titles than had existed in total during the previous 40 years. The mid- and late 1980s were a boom time, a trend which appears to be continuing into the 1990s.

References: *Comic Buyer's Guide Annual*, Krause Publications, issued annually; Alex G. Malloy, *Comics Values Annual 1998*, Antique Trader Books, 1997; Duncan McAlpine (comp.), *Comic Values Annual*, 1996 ed., Antique Trader Books, 1995; Robert M. Overstreet, *Overstreet Comic Book Price Guide*, 27th ed., Avon Books, 1997; Don and Maggie Thompson (eds.), *Comic Book Superstars*, Krause Publications, 1993; —— (eds.), *Marvel Comics Checklist & Price Guide*, Krause Publications, 1993; Maggie Thompson and Brent Frankenhoff, *Comic Book Checklist & Price Guide*, 4th ed., Krause Publications, 1997; Maggie Thompson and John Jackson Miller, *Comic Buyer's Guide 1997 Annual,* 6th ed., Krause Publications, 1996; Stuart W. Wells and Alex G. Malloy, *Comics Collectibles and Their Values*, Wallace-Homestead, 1996.

Periodicals: *Archie Fan Magazine*, 185 Ashland St., Holliston, MA 01746; *Comic Book Market Place*, P.O. Box 180900, Coronado, CO 92178; *Comics Buyer's Guide*, 700 E. State St., Iola, WI 54990; *Comics Interview*, 234 Fifth Ave., New York, NY 10001; *Comics Source*, 2401 Broad St., Chattanooga, TN 37408; *Duckburg Times*, 3010 Wilshire Blvd #362, Los Angeles, CA 90010; *Hogan's Alley*, P.O. Box 47684, Atlanta, GA 30362; *Overstreet Comic Book Marketplace*, 1996 Greenspring Dr., Suite 405, Timonium, MD 21093; *Western Comics Journal*, 1703 N Aster Place, Broken Arrow, OK 74012; *Wizard: The Guide To Comics*, 151 Wells Ave., Congers, NY 10920.

Collectors' Clubs: American Comics Exchange, 351-T Baldwin Rd, Hempstead, NY 11550; Fawcett Collectors of America & Magazine Enterprise, too!, 301 E. Buena Vista Ave., North Augusta, SC 29841.

Videotape: *Overstreet World of Comic Books*, Overstreet Productions and Tom Barker Video, 1994.

Museums: International Museum of Cartoon Art, 300 SE 5th Ave., #5150, Boca Raton, FL 33432; Museum of Cartoon Art, Rye, NY.

REPRODUCTION ALERT

Publishers frequently reprint popular stories, even complete books, so the buyer must pay strict attention to the title, not just the portion printed in oversized letters on the front cover. If there is any doubt, look inside at the fine print on the bottom of the inside cover or first page. The correct title will be printed there in capital letters.

Also pay attention to the dimensions of the comic book. Reprints often differ in size from the original.

Note: The comics listed below are in near-mint condition, meaning they have a flat, clean, shiny cover that has no wear other than tiny corner creases; no subscription creases, writing, yellowing at margins, or tape repairs; staples are straight and rust free; pages are supple and like new; generally just-off-the-shelf quality.

Action, DC
 #29, Lois Lane cover 195.00
 #73...125.00
Adventure, DC
 #49...210.00
 #86, damage to cover 250.00
 #210, first Kryto...260.00
Adventures of the Fly, Archie, #1 ....1,250.00
All American, DC
 #30...295.00
 #42...135.00
All Star, DC
 #8, 1st appear Wonder Woman.................................4,500.00
 #21, rusty staples 395.00
All Winners, Timely
 #2...400.00
 #14..1,200.00
Amazing Spiderman, Marvel
 #1..16,500.00
 #3...2,550.00
 #9...950.00
America's Best, Nedor, #15, Schomburg cover..................35.00
Archie, MLJ, #11, piece out of front cover 20.00
Atom, DC
 #7, Hawkman cross over..300.00
 #18...65.00
Avengers, Marvel
 #1...2,950.00
 #3...395.00
 #4, reprint 115.00
 #11..245.00
 #63..32.00
 #100..75.00

Barbie & Ken, Dell, #2 ....275.00
Batman, DC
  #20 ....2,200.00
  #27 ....890.00
  #35 ....395.00
Battle, Atlas, #46 ....65.00
Beyond, Ace, #13 ....85.00
Black Terror, Nedor, #13, Schomburg cover 495.00
Bob Hope, DC, #1 ....850.00
Brave & The Bold, DC
  #28, 1st Justice League 4,800.00
  #34, 1st SA Hawkman 1,500.00
  #62 ....250.00
Captain America, Timely
  #6 ....6,800.00
  #19 ....2,450.00
  #54, Schomburg cover 495.00
Captain Marvel, Fawcett, #24 ....140.00
Catman, Holyoke, #23 ....60.00
Daredevil, Marvel
  #1 ....3,450.00
  #2 ....775.00
  #4 ....345.00
Detective, DC
  #35 ....1,300.00
  #38, 1st appearance Robin 3,500.00
  #140, 1st appearance Riddler 310.00
  #357 ....52.00
Famous Funnies, Eastern Color
  #98 ....10.00
  #102 ....30.00
Fantastic Four, Marvel
  #1, professionally cleaned 9,750.00
  #13 ....300.00
  #16 ....375.00
  #26 ....650.00
  #71 ....50.00
  #100 ....25.00
Feature Comics, Quality, #66 ....20.00
Fighting Yank, Nedor, #12, Schomburg cover 120.00
Flash, DC
  #24 ....160.00
  #105 ....250.00
  #153 ....60.00
  #175 ....50.00
Forbidden Love, Quality, #2 ....450.00
Four Color, Dell
  #1, Series II 95.00
  #18, Series I 35.00
Giant Size X-Men, Marvel, #1 ....475.00
Green Hornet, Harvey
  #18 ....90.00
  #19, Schomburg cover 140.00
  #42, file copy 200.00
Green Lantern, DC
  #1 ....850.00
  #16 ....160.00
  #33 ....120.00
  #41 ....80.00
Hawkman, DC
  #1 ....900.00
  #4 ....180.00
  #7 ....130.00
Hopalong Cassidy, DC, #101 ....100.00
House of Mystery, DC
  #3 ....1,200.00
  #141 ....58.00
  #145 ....110.00
Human Torch, Timely
  #10 ....245.00
  #28 ....1,150.00

Incredible Hulk, Marvel
  #1 ....11,150.00
  #180 ....95.00
Jo-Jo, Fox, #18 ....575.00
Justice League America, DC
  #1 ....3,200.00
  #9 ....850.00
  #11 ....210.00
  #24 ....140.00
  #49 ....46.00
Little Orphan Annie, Quaker 25.00
Looney Tunes, Dell
  #6 ....65.00
  #18 ....90.00
  #43 ....13.00
Mad, EC
  #1 ....475.00
  #24 ....90.00
Marvel Mystery, Timely
  #10 ....950.00
  #82, 1st appearance Namora 200.00
Millie the Model, Timely, #6 ....225.00
More Fun, DC
  #8 ....150.00
  #23 ....325.00
  #54, 3rd Spectre 1,900.00
  #98 ....235.00
Mystery in Space, DC
  #1 ....250.00
  #82 ....75.00
Quick Trigger Western, Atlas, #17 ....95.00
Rawhide Kid, Atlas
  #12 ....175.00
  #15 ....175.00
Sgt. Fury, Marvel
  #1 ....1,350.00
  #5 ....325.00
  #14 ....125.00
  #26 ....45.00
Shock Suspenstories, EC, #7 ....85.00

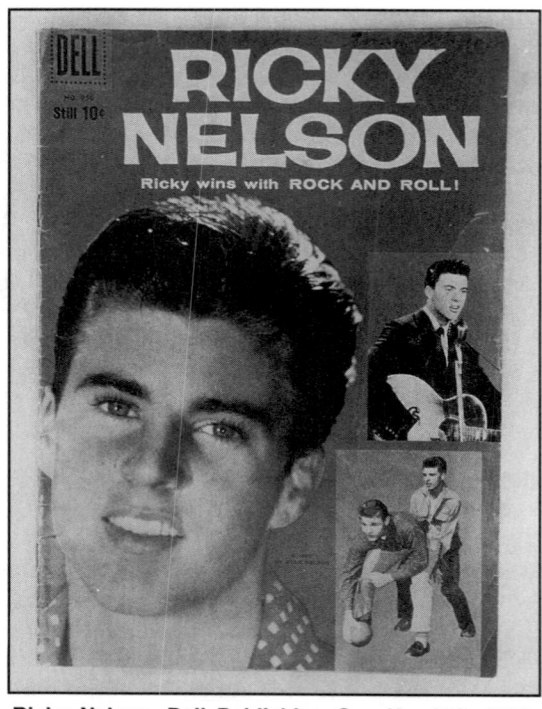

Ricky Nelson, Dell Publishing Co., No. 956, 1958, $10.

Showcase, DC
#4 .... 1,350.00
#8 .... 2,300.00
Silver Streak, New Friday Publications
#11, bind holes 135.00
#12 .... 95.00
Silver Surfer, Marvel
#1 .... 475.00
#3 .... 145.00
#5 .... 75.00
#13 .... 45.00
Sparkler, United Features Syndicate, #13 ..... 45.00
Star Spangled, DC
#11 .... 115.00
#22 .... 195.00
#33 .... 175.00
Star Trek, Gold Key
#2 .... 285.00
#9 .... 165.00
Stars and Stripes, Centaur, #2 .... 200.00
Strange Tales, Marvel
#101 .... 250.00
#110 .... 4,975.00
#113 .... 150.00
#144 .... 125.00
#150 .... 90.00
Super, Dell
#1 .... 295.00
#53 .... 30.00
Superman, DC
#9 .... 210.00
#11, Back from the Dead, 1993, sealed in package 100.00
#26 .... 260.00
#34, Funeral for a Friend Epilogue, 1993 .... 90.00
Tales of Suspense, Marvel
#39 .... 4,450.00
#41 .... 650.00
#49 .... 375.00
#68 .... 150.00
#77 .... 60.00
#91 .... 70.00
#98 .... 70.00
Tales to Astonish, Marvel
#39 .... 950.00
#45 .... 495.00
#60 .... 475.00
#86 .... 85.00
#98 .... 75.00
Tom Mix, Ralston-Purina, #1 .... 225.00
Tomahawk, DC
#4 .... 125.00
#8 .... 130.00
#36 .... 88.00
Walt Disney Comics & Stories, Dell
Vol. 2, #3 .... 90.00
Vol. 3, #8 .... 110.00
Whiz, Fawcett
#44 .... 95.00
#65 .... 50.00
X-Men, Marvel
#2 .... 2,650.00
#3 .... 395.00
GS1 .... 400.00
Young Allies, Timely, #16 .... 800.00

COMPACTS

History: In the first quarter of the 20th century, attitudes regarding cosmetics changed drastically. The use of make-up during the day was no longer looked upon with disdain. As women became "liberated," and as more and more of them entered the business world, the use of cosmetics became a routine and necessary part of a woman's grooming. Portable containers for cosmetics became a necessity.

Compacts were made in myriad shapes, styles, combinations and motifs, all reflecting the mood of the times. Every conceivable natural or man-made material was used in the manufacture of compacts. Commemorative, premium, souvenir, patriotic, figural, Art Deco, and enamel compacts are a few examples of the types of compacts that were made in the United States and abroad. Compacts combined with other forms, such as cigarette cases, music boxes, watches, hatpins, canes, and lighters, also were very popular.

Compacts were made and used until the late 1950s, when women opted for the "Au Naturel" look. The term "vintage" is used to describe the compacts from the first half of the 20th century as distinguished from contemporary examples.

References: Juliette Edwards, *Compacts*, published by author, 1994; Roselyn Gerson, *Ladies Compacts*, Collector Books, 1996; ——, *Vintage Ladies Compacts*, Collector Books, 1996; ——, *Vintage Vanity Bags and Purses: An Identification and Value Guide*, 1994, 1997 value update, Collector Books; Frances Johnson, *Compacts, Powder and Paint*, Schiffer Publishing, 1996; Laura M. Mueller, *Collector's Encyclopedia of Compacts, Carryalls & Face Powder Boxes* (1994, 1996 value update), Vol. II (1997), Collector Books.

Collectors' Club: Compact Collectors Club, P.O. Box 40, Lynbrook, NY 11563.

Additional Listings: See *Warman's Americana & Collectibles* for more examples.

Advisor: Roselyn Gerson.

American Maid, heart shape, goldtone, brocade lid, c1930 ..... 50.00
Amita, damascene with inlaid gold and silver Mt Fuji scene, black matte finish lid, Japan, c1920 .... 140.00
Black, Starr and Frost, Retro, 14 K, yellow, rose and green gold, 5 single 1.2 to 2.1 cut round diamonds, textured geometric ground, sgd, 1-1/2" sq, 35 dwt 375.00
Coro, Flying Colors, gilt metal, spread eagle shape, red, white, and blue lipstick tube center, orig presentation box, c1940 .... 225.00
Croco, sq, leather, white, zippered, multicolored cord in lid, Israel 65.00
Dorette, snakeskin, pale blue paper, floral spray on lid, 1950s 55.00
Dunhill Vanity, silvered, cigarette lighter shape, sliding lipstick, c1920 .... 145.00
Eastern Star, enameled jeweled 50.00
Fiato, Paul, Retro, 14K rose gold, 10 full cut 2.5 mm round diamonds, cut out star pattern, sgd "Paul Fiato," 2-3/4" sq, 60 dwt 2,975.00
French
18K yg, 71 rose cut .9 mm round diamonds, Chinoiserie scene with flowers and dots, French maker's mark and hallmarks, 2-5/8" x 1-5/8", 70 dwt 2,300.00
Vanity Case, Art Deco
18K yg, 1 carved and pierced 22.15 mm round jadeite, 330 rose cut .98 to 1.1 round diamonds, black enamel, French hallmarks, 3-3/4" x 1-1/4", 124 dwt 6,325.00
18K yg, 200 rose cut 1.2 mm round diamonds, black enam-

el case and ring, French hallmarks, 2-3/4" x 1-5/8", 86 dwt...2,875.00
Grey, Kamra-Pak, confetti plastic case, camera shape, compartments and slide-out lipstick, 1930-40.............................75.00
Harmony, Boston, box shape, tan, snap closure, 1920s 65.00
Illinois Watch Co., compact and watch, goldtone, engraved design on lid, 1930-50 ....145.00
Lacloche Freres, Paris, Art Deco design, 18K yg, 47 rose cut 1.1 to 2.2 mm round diamonds, enamel, sgd, 1-5/8" x 1-3/4", 48 dwt 2,530.00
Line Vautrin, enameled, 1950s..2,415.00
Marathon, goldtone, heart on lid, lid reveals locket 70.00
Rex, mesh, vanity pouch, white plastic beads, c1930.........60.00
Richard Hudnut, vanity clutch, fabric, white and gold, Tree of Life motif with green stones, 1940s......................................95.00
T & Co., silver gilt, Art Deco design, cabochon cut oval 14 x 10.5 mm jadeite, sgd, 2-7/8 x 1-1/2", 90 dwt 1,955.00
Timepact, enamel, black, elongated horseshoe shape, case and watch, powder and rouge compartments 185.00
Udall & Bailou
  14K, yellow, white, and rose gold, basketweave design, 3-1/4" d round, sgd, 1960s, 38 dwt 575.00
  Platinum, Art Deco design, 21 rose cut .75 to 1.5 mm diamonds, satin finish, 2 cabochon cut rubies, sgd, 2" x 1-5/8", 46 dwt 2,300.00
Unknown Maker
  Alligator, pull-out mirror 80.00
  Hand Mirror shape, goldtone, dec and engraved lid......95.00
  Horseshoe shape, gilt metal, tooled leather inserts on lid and back 115.00
  Jadeite, YG, carved 16.18 x 12.47 mm jadeite plaque (cracked), 27 rose cut diamonds, 2-1/8" x 1-5/8" 1,610.00
Verdura, 14K yg, 1 cabochon cut round stone, sgd, 1970s, 2-1/2" d, 77.7 dwt...2,415.00
Wadsworh, Compakit, plastic, black, camera shape, compartment on front, lipstick and cigarette lighter on top, cigarette compartment on bottom, c1940 ....195.00
Whiting & Davis, vanity bag, silvered mesh, etched and engraved lid, braided carrying chain, 1920s................................425.00

CONSOLIDATED GLASS COMPANY

History: The Consolidated Lamp and Glass Company was formed as a result of the 1893 merger of the Wallace and McAfee Company, glass and lamp jobbers of Pittsburgh, and the Fostoria Shade & Lamp Company of Fostoria, Ohio. When the Fostoria, Ohio, plant burned down in 1895, Corapolis, Pennsylvania, donated a seven-acre tract of land near the center of town for a new factory. In 1911 the company was the largest lamp, globe, and shade works in the United States, employing more than 400 workers.

In 1925, Reuben Haley, owner of an independent design firm, convinced John Lewis, president of Consolidated, to enter the giftware field utilizing a series of designs inspired by the 1925 Paris Exposition (l'Exposition Internationale des Arts Décorative et Industriels Modernes) and the work of René Lalique. Initially, the glass was marketed by Howard Selden through his showroom at 225 Fifth Avenue in New York City. The first two lines were Catalonian and Martele.

Additional patterns were added in the late 1920s: Florentine (January 1927), Chintz (January 1927), Ruba Rombic (January 1928), and Line 700 (January 1929). On April 2, 1932, Consolidated closed its doors. Kenneth Harley moved about 40 molds to Phoenix. In March 1936,

Consolidated reopened under new management, and the "Harley" molds were returned. During this period, the famous Dancing Nymph line, based on an eight-inch salad plate in the 1926 Martele series, was introduced.

In August 1962, Consolidated was sold to Dietz Brothers. A major fire damaged the plant during a 1963 labor dispute and in 1964 the company permanently closed its doors.

References: Ann Gilbert McDonald, *Evolution of the Night Lamp*, Wallace-Homestead, 1979; Jack D. Wilson, *Phoenix & Consolidated Art Glass, 1926-1980*, Antique Publications, 1989.

Collectors' Club: Phoenix and Consolidated Glass Collectors, P.O. Box 81974, Chicago, IL 60681.

Basket, Catalonian, green 48.00
Berry Bowl, master, Cone, pink, glossy, silverplated rim ...110.00
Bowl
  8" d, Ruba Rhombic, Smokey Topaz...........................900.00
  9-1/2" d, Catalonian, yellow 45.00
Butter Dish, cov
  Cosmos, pink band 200.00
  Guttate, white, gold trim 150.00
Candlestick, Five Fruits, Martele line, green 30.00
Celery Tray, Florette, pink...35.00
Cigarette Box, cov, Phlox, slate blue.................................150.00
Compote, Fish, green...90.00
Cracker jar, cov, pink satin, glass lid 195.00
Creamer, Cosmos..165.00
Cruet, orig stopper, Cone, yellow satin 295.00
Cup and Saucer, Catalonian, green 30.00
Jug, Five Fruits, half gallon, French Crystal 250.00
Lamp, Dogwood, brown and white 135.00
Old Fashioned Tumbler, 3-7/8" h, Catalonian, yellow...........20.00
Pickle Castor, Cosmos 525.00
Pitcher, Catalonian, yellow 135.00
Plate
  7" d, Catalonian, yellow 15.00
  8-1/4" d, Dancing Nude, pink 145.00
  8-1/2" d, Five Fruits, green...40.00
  10-1/4" d, Catalonian, yellow 40.00
Puff Box, cov, Lovebirds, blue..95.00
Salt and Pepper Shakers, pr, Cosmos 65.00
Scent Bottle, Cosmos, pink and blue floral, orig stopper...140.00
Sherbet, ftd
  Catalonian, green 20.00
  Dance of the Nudes, French Crystal 80.00
Spooner, Cosmos 140.00
Sugar Bowl, cov, Catalonian, yellow 40.00

Lamp, blown-out floral shade, silvered base, 10" h, $660. Photo courtesy of Jackson's Auctioneers & Appraisers.

Sugar Shaker, Cone, green, orig top.....................................95.00
Syrup
    Cone, squatty, pink...295.00
    Cosmos...275.00
Tumbler
    5-1/4" h, Catalonian, ftd, green......................................30.00
    5-1/2" h, Ruba Rhombic, jade..325.00
    6" d, Dance of the Nudes, frosted pink 175.00
Vase
    5-1/2" h, Hummingbird, #2588, turquoise on satin custard
    ....90.00
    6-5/8" h, fan, Calatonian, lavender 45.00
    8-1/2", Katydid, white frosted, fan shaped top 165.00
    9" x 9", bulbous, cream ground, aqua cockatoos, beige
        branches, lavender berries 325.00
    9-1/2" h, Ruba Rhombic, French Silver......................4,000.00
    10" h, Catalonian, #1101, triangle, rubena 90.00
Water Pitcher, Florette, pink satin......................................195.00

CONTINENTAL CHINA AND PORCELAIN (GENERAL)

History: By 1700, porcelain factories existed in large numbers throughout Europe. In the mid-18th century, the German factories at Meissen and Nymphenburg were dominant. As the century ended, French potteries assumed the leadership role. The 1740s to the 1840s were the golden age of Continental china and porcelains.

Americans living in the last half of the 19th century eagerly sought the masterpieces of the European porcelain factories. In the early 20th century, this style of china and porcelain was considered "blue chip" by antiques collectors.

References: Susan and Al Bagdade, *Warman's English & Continental Pottery & Porcelain*, 2nd ed., Wallace-Homestead, 1991; Rachael Feild, *Macdonald Guide to Buying Antique Pottery & Porcelain*, Wallace-Homestead, 1987; Geoffrey Godden, *Godden's Guide to European Porcelain*, Random House, 1993.

Additional Listings: French–Haviland, Limoges, Old Paris, Sarreguemines, and Sevres; German–Austrian Ware, Bavarian China, Carlsbad China, Dresden/Meissen, Rosenthal, Royal Bayreuth, Royal Bonn, Royal Rudolstadt, Royal Vienna, Schlegelmilch, and Villeroy and Boch; Italian–Capo-di-Monte.

French

Faience
    Jardiniere, 22-1/2" d, yellow, green, and blue, painted chrysanthemums, scalloped rim 495.00
    Plate, 9-3/4" d, blue, red, and green floral, insects in center, mkd "Rouen"...195.00
Jacob Petit
    Clock Case, 15-3/4", portrait of French courtesan, sgd, c1840, chips 1,100.00
    Vase, 7" h, cornucopia shape, multicolored floral garland, green ground, molded foliate scrollwork, shaped base with scroll molding and emb floral springs and gilt highlights, underglaze blue "J. P." mark 400.00
Mennency, figure, 9" h, seated lady, polychrome and gilt dec, 1755, minor damage 3,500.00
Niderviller, charger, scalloped, Bleuet dec, cobalt blue rim, Count Philibert De Custine mark, c1780..................................400.00

French Faience, bell, figural, peasant woman, multicolored, unglazed clapper, "Bayeux" mark, 8-1/4" h, $90. Photo courtesy of Susan and Al Bagdade.

St. Cloud
    Bonbonniere, cov, cat form, SS mountings, late 19th C 245.00
    Chamber Pot, cov, 4-1/2" h, SS mountings, c1740 ....1,200.00
    Cup and Saucer, pr, tremleuse, c1750 ....650.00
Unknown Maker, figure, 10-3/4" h, Cupid, other young female, white glaze, printed marks, early 20th C, pr..................200.00
Vieux Paris
    Clock, 13" h, vase form, yellow ground, minor chips, c1820
    ....975.00
    Tray, 13-1/2", sq, mythological dec, iron red factory, Duc d'Angouleme factory, c1800 ....475.00
    Vase, 14-3/4" h, floral medallion, lavender ground, handles, sq marble plinth base, mounted as lamp, c1815, pr .3,500.00
Yellow Glaze, 8-11/16" d, plate, grape and foliate border, central reserve of genre scene with castle ruins, imp "L. L. & T." on base, knife marks, minute chips, glaze wear 175.00

German

Berlin, plaque, 10-1/2" x 14-1/4", domestic int. scene, painted in the manner of Felix Schlesinger, c1870 ....3,850.00
Frankenthal, figure, 8" h, lyre player, 19th C 495.00

Boch Feres, vase, blue, turquoise, and yellow bands on neck, geometric center patterns, ivory cracked ground, 8-1/4" h, $365. Photo courtesy of Susan and Al Bagdade.

Furstenburg

Cup and Saucer, purple dec, underglaze blue "F" mark, c1765...550.00

Platter, 14" d, circular, laurel leaves edge band, polychrome bird in tree center, late 18th C.................................725.00

Hochst

Figure, 11" h, group of lovers, rococo arbor entwined with grapes, underglaze wheel mark, incised triangle, c1765, minor restoration...9,500.00

Sugar Bowl, 6-1/4" d, Meissen type dec, polychrome village scene, randomly scattered sprigs and sprays, underglaze blue crowned wheel mark 650.00

Hutschenreuther

Plaque, 5-1/8" x 6-7/8", oval, Madonna and Child, giltwood frame, late 19th C 575.00

Portrait Plate, 9-5/8" d, Princess de Lambelle, yellow roses and pink ribbons in hair, white ruffled dress, gray ground, imp factory mark, blue "lamb Dresden 135K" artist sgd "Vorberger"
....850.00

Service Plate, 10-7/8" d, central dec, summer flowers within heavily gilt cavetto, rim worked with scrolling acanthus, textured ground, underglaze green factory marks, minor rubbing, 12 pc set..1,450.00

Nymphenberg

Soup Plate, 9-1/2" d, raised beadwork border, central landscape cartouche in black, framed in gilt banded blue enamel ribbon, late 19th C, minor rim chips, 12 pc set
....920.00

Vase, 9-3/4" h, bottle-form, floral dec, price for pr 325.00

Potschappel

Clock, 13-1/2" h, monkey, woman, and humpback masked man gathered around rockery supporting urn, repairs
....425.00

Urn, covered, 19th C

19" h, cartouche with three women and musical instruments enclosed by applied fruit and floral dec, sq plinth base with applied floral enclosed neoclassical style and floral cartouches 400.00

47" h, on stand, central cartouche painted with four women in landscape, sgd "N. A. Schram," enclosed with applied fruit and floral dec, fully molded figure of woman with basket of flowers seated on shoulder, two gilt scrolling flowering vine handles with mask dec, floral dec verso, figural scene and applied swag on foot, lid with two fully molded females seated on rockery, applied fruit and flower enclosed cartouche with two putto, octagonal base with applied flower swag enclosing triptych neoclassical figural scene, five floral filled panels, underglazed blue T above crossed lines, incised "2207".............................8,000.00

Sitzendorf, figure

8" h, 5-1/2" d, polar bear, white body, gray claws, eyes, nose, and teeth, blue underglaze Sitzendorf mark 255.00

8-1/2" h, young girl holding bird, pink trim 200.00

Unknown Maker

Candelabra, pr, 19" h, two figures of children seated on shoulder of base, scroll molded body with applied and painted floral dec, unmarked, restorations............................345.00

Candlesticks, pr

9" h, cherubs, one with ewer and wine goblet, other carrying wheat, late 19th C, restorations........................260.00

11-1/4" h, green porcelain, male and female figures, three-light candlesticks, sconces set top branches applied with leaves and flowers, scrolled freeform bases, late 19th C
....635.00

Compote

8" h, bowl supported by 4 figures of children, bowl and base with applied leaves and flowers, restoration to one head 190.00

12" h, pierced bowl, applied leaves and flowers, supported by steam surrounded by male and female figures, printed "Thieme" mark, late 19th C 960.00

Picture Frame, 8-3/4" h, modeled as a child dressed as a jester supporting rococo style oval frame 520.00

Plaque, 12-1/2" w, 15-1/2" h, oval portrait medallion, family in opulent int., gilt border with anthemion dec corners, sgd and dated "V. Treverret 1828" 3,250.00

Plate, 9-1/2" d, molded lattice borders, enamel painted birds and insects, gilded rims, AR underglaze mark, gilt rim wear, c1900, 12 pc set 750.00

Volkestedt

Figure

7-3/4" h, female figure flanked by cherubs, raised rect base, white biscuit, printed mark, c1900...............115.00

12-3/4" h, Cupid and Psyche, mounted on rock molded circular base, white biscuit, printed mark, late 19th C, restorations..230.00

Teapot, swelled circular, faint ridging, dome cov, applied purple berry finial, purple floral springs, applied scroll handles, underglaze blue crossed pitchforks mark, handle restored, mid 18th C 300.00

Italian

Doccia

Charger, 15-3/4" d, Imari style, cobalt blue, iron-red, and gold, branches of flowering prunus and peonies, trellis, diaper, and floral panel borders, c1755 ....325.00

Tea Bowl, 3-1/4" d, Chinoiserie figures, c1700..............475.00

Naples, ewer, 20" h, relief dec, bacchic scene in orchard, female rising from leaf ornaments handle, late 19th C..............365.00

COOKIE JARS

History: Cookie jars, colorful and often whimsical, are now an established collecting category. Do not be misled by the high prices realized at the 1988 Andy Warhol auction. Many of the same cookie jars that sold for more than $1,000 each can be found in the field for less than $100.

Cookie jars often were redesigned to reflect newer tastes. Hence, the same jar may be found in several different variations.

Marks: Many cookie jar shapes were manufactured by more than one company and, as a result, can be found with different marks. This often happened because of mergers or separations, e.g., Brush-McCoy, which became Nelson McCoy. Molds also were traded and sold among companies.

References: Mary Jane Giacomini, *American Bisque*, Schiffer Publishing, 1994; *1995 Cookie Jar Express Pricing Guide to Cookie Jars*, Paradise Publications, 1995; Fred and Joyce Roerig, *Collector's Encyclopedia of Cookie Jars*, Book I (1991, 1993 value update), Book II (1994), Book III (1997), Collector Books; Mark and Ellen Supnick, *Wonderful World of Cookie Jars*, L-W Book Sales (1995, 1997 value update); Ermagene Westfall, *Illustrated Value Guide to Cookie Jars*, Book I (1983, 1995 value update), Book II (1993, 1995 value update), Collector Books.

Periodicals: *Cookie Jar Collectors Express*, P.O. Box 221, Mayview, MO 64071; *Cookie Jarrin'*, RR 2, Box 504, Walterboro, SC 29488.

Collectors' Club: The Cookie Jar Collector's Club, 595 Cross River Rd, Katonah, NY 10536.

Hull Pottery, Little Red Riding Hood, each $400. Photo courtesy of Joan Hull.

Museum: The Cookie Jar Museum, Lemont, IL.

American Bisque
    Baby Elephant 140.00
    Barney Rubble House 650.00
    Casper the Friendly Ghost, marked "Harvey Publications Inc., USA" 775.00
    Clown, flasher 350.00
    Cow Jumped Over the Moon, flasher 950.00
    Dino, with golf clubs 850.00
    Fred and Wilma Flintstone 300.00
    Liberty Bell 185.00
    Little Audrey 6,700.00
    Little Mo, Mohawk Carpet Co. advertising 1,600.00
    Sandman Dog, flasher, minor factory flaw on lid 300.00
    Spaceship with Astronaut 1,400.00
    Wilma, on the telephone 800.00
Brush
    Donkey with cart 225.00
    Humpty Dumpty 75.00
    Lantern 85.00
California Originals
    Pinocchio Head 1,500.00
    Tigger 165.00
    Winnie The Pooh, bee on head 140.00
    Wonder Woman, Cookie Bank, 1970s 900.00
Goebel, owl 125.00
Maddux of California
    Humpty Dumpty 95.00
    Queen of Tarts 525.00
McCoy
    Asparagus 60.00
    Chipmunk 75.00
    Lamb's head on cylinder 185.00
    Little Miss Muffet 95.00
    Penguin 85.00
    Winnie the Pooh 145.00
Metlox
    Cookie Girl 115.00
    Raggedy Andy 185.00
Regal China
    Alice in Wonderland, Walt Disney Productions copyright, "Alice in Wonderland" mark, 1950s, several small paint flakes 3,300.00
    Hubert the Lion, wire glasses, made for Harris Bank of Chicago, IL, December, 1982, limited to 1,500 pcs 1,250.00

Robinson Ransbottom
    Dutch Boy 75.00
    Jocko the Monkey 70.00
    Oscar 70.00
Shawnee
    Cardinal French Chef 125.00
    Dutch Boy 165.00
    Winnie Pig, shamrock 320.00
Sierra Vista
    Rocking Horse 140.00
    Stagecoach 90.00
Twin Winton
    Baby Bear 45.00
    Cow Spots 65.00
    Happy Bull 65.00
    Jack In Box 70.00
    Nestle Tollhouse 110.00

COPELAND AND SPODE

History: In 1749, Josiah Spode was apprenticed to Thomas Whieldon and in 1754 worked for William Banks in Stoke-on-Trent. In the early 1760s, Spode started his own pottery, making cream-colored earthenware and blue-printed whiteware. In 1770, he returned to Banks' factory as master, purchasing it in 1776.

Spode pioneered the use of steam-powered pottery-making machinery and mastered the art of transfer printing from copper plates. Spode opened a London shop in 1778 and sent William Copeland there about 1784. A number of larger London locations followed. At the turn of the century, Spode introduced bone china. In 1805, Josiah Spode II and William Copeland entered into a partnership for the London business. A series of partnerships between Josiah Spode II, Josiah Spode III, and William Taylor Copeland resulted.

In 1833, Copeland acquired Spode's London operations and seven years later the Stoke plants. William Taylor Copeland managed the business until his death in 1868. The firm remained in the hands of Copeland heirs. In 1923 the plant was electrified; other modernization followed.

In 1976, Spode merged with Worcester Royal Porcelain to become Royal Worcester Spode, Ltd.

References: Susan and Al Bagdade, *Warman's English & Continental Pottery & Porcelain*, 2nd ed., Wallace-Homestead, 1991; D. Drakard & P. Holdway, *Spode Printed Wares*, Longmans, 1983; L. Whiter, *Spode: A History of the Family, Factory, and Wares, 1733-1833*, Barrie & Jenkins, 1970.

Creamer, 5-1/2" l, underglaze blue floral dec, polychrome enamel and gilt, mkd "1645 Spode" 125.00
Cup and Saucer, Rosalie 10.00
Dinner Service, assorted place settings and service pieces
    Black floral transfer, underglaze blue and red enamel, chips and stains, 55 pc set 990.00

Creamer, blue band, gold trim, ivory ground, 1810, No. 89, 3 -1/4" h, 5-1/2" w, $45.

Fleur de lis and foliate dec, gray and white, silver highlights, 73 pc set 1,700.00

Dish, 11-1/2" w, 2 handles, mushroom ground, gilt foliage, gilt scroll molded handles, puce Spode Felspar mark, c1800 .... 145.00

Figure, 21-1/2" h, Parian, barefoot boy wearing breeches and jacket, scarf tied at throat, sickle lying on ground, pointed to letter concealed in tree stump, titled "The Trysting Tree," incised "C. Halse, Sc/Pubd 1874, " imp "Copeland/Copyright Reserved" 650.00

Jar, cov, 10" h, globular, handled, Oriental style, apple green, birds on flowering branches, iron-red, pink, and gilt, gilt knob finial, Spode mark, Pat. #3086, c1820 .... 725.00

Jug, 6-1/2" d, 7-1/4" h, bright blue ground, raised ivory figures on front and back, raised leaf trim around top, Copeland, made for Columbian Expo, 1893 .... 215.00

Pitcher, 7-1/2" h, deep blue glaze, raised white figures, tavern scenes and berries 215.00

Plate
    8-3/4" d, creamware, pink shell motif, gilt flowering foliage, brown net pattern ground, gilt rim, imp Spode mark, c1920 .... 85.00
    9-1/2" d, bird perched on snowy branch, holly leaves and berries 115.00

Platter, 10-1/2" l, oval, creamware, pierced rim, Spode, mkd, c1920 .... 85.00

Potpourri Jar, 10" h, pierced cov, flared rim and foot, Imari style, flowering plants, gilt knop finial, Spode mark, Pat. #967, c1810 .... 625.00

Soup Plate, black transfer print, multicolored insect and flowering plants, scrolling floral border, Spode mark, pattern #2148, c1810, 12 pc set 500.00

Spill Vase, 4-3/4" h, flared rim, pale lilac, gilt octagonal panels with portrait of bearded man, band of pearls on rims and bases, Spode, c1920 .... 415.00

Tray, 11-1/2" w, sq, rose spray center, floral bouquet in corners, bale ground with gilt scale pattern, Pat. #1163, iron-red Spode, c1800 .... 365.00

Urn, cov, 15" h, Louis XVI style, cobalt blue ground, medallions on each side with bouquet of roses, majolica, repair to one handle, nick to one lid, pr 880.00

Warming Dish, 9-3/8" d, New Stone China, polychrome dec blue transfer print of Oriental foliate landscapes, imp marks, c1810, pr 225.00

COPPER

History: Copper objects, such as kettles, teakettles, warming pans, and measures, played an important part in the 19th-century household. Outdoors, the apple-butter kettle and still were the two principal copper items. Copper culinary objects were lined with a thin protective coating of tin to prevent poisoning. They were relined as needed.

References: Mary Frank Gaston, *Antique Brass & Copper*, Collector Books, 1992, 1994 value update; Henry J. Kauffman, *Early American Copper, Tin, and Brass: Handcrafted Metalware from Colonial Times*, Astragal Press, 1995.

REPRODUCTION ALERT

Many modern reproductions exist.

Additional Listings: Arts and Crafts Movement; Roycroft.

Notes: Collectors place great emphasis on signed pieces, especially those by American craftsmen. Since copper objects were made abroad as well, it is hard to identify unsigned examples.

Ale Warmer, 12-1/2" l 300.00

Baking Pan, 11" d, turk's head, swirled design, dovetailed construction, worn tin lining 65.00

Bed Warmer, 38-1/2" l, engraved lid, wood handle, wrought iron ferule, European 75.00

Bowl, 6-1/2" d, globular form, hand hammered, scrolled rim, brown patina, stamped "Harry Dixon San Francisco," c1920 .... 350.00

Box, cov, 7" x 4" x 3", rect, red enamel floral dec, stylized green and black enamel motifs, hinged lid, scroll feet, dark patina, Buffalo, NY, c1910 .... 450.00

Chamberstick, 9" h, 7" d, hammered, riveted spade shaped handle, orig patina and bobeche, Gustave Stickley Als Ik Kan mark 550.00

Coal Shuttle, 18" x 22" x 15", Art Nouveau, brass shovel, emb with stylized flowers, English, break to two hinges 250.00

Colander, 10-3/4" d, punched star design 75.00

Desk Set, hammered, blotter, letter holder, bookends, stamp box, each with cabochon of bone carvd with branch and berry motif, Potter Studio, fine orig patina, die-stamp mar, 5 pc set 700.00

Fish Poacher, cov, 20-1/2" l, oval, rolled rim, iron swing bail handle, C form handle on lid, 19th C 350.00

Jug, 14-1/2" h, iron hoop base, Continental, late 19th C 325.00

Haystack Measure, 18-1/2" h, dovetailed construction, conical body, flared rim, tubular scroll handle, loop handle on front, mkd "Anderson Brothers Makers Glasgow, 4 gallons," Scotland, 19th C 150.00

Cauldron, circular form, hinged bail handle, riveted tabs, circular wrought iron stand on three splayed legs, PA, late 18th C, 12" d, 9" h, $345. Photo courtesy of Sotheby's.

Lantern, 15" h, hexagonal beveled glass panels, circular handle, 19th C 265.00
Milk Pail, 12" h, swing handle, stamped "1870" dutch.......500.00
Pill Box, 1-1/4" x 3-1/4", hammered, Arts & Crafts, repousse and enameled top, opal cabochon 250.00
Prick Stick, 10" h, Gothic style, gold overlay, floral terminations 470.00
Sauce Pan, 7" d, dovetailed construction, cast iron handle.65.00
Skillet, 10-1/2" d, wrought sheet handle, stamped "Colony RI" 90.00
Tea Kettle
    7" h, bulbous, hinged handle, goose neck, brass finial ..45.00
    8-1/4" h, sturdy construction, swivel handle stamped "1840" 200.00
    9" d, porcelain knob, sheet copper 50.00
Tray, hammered
    14-1/2" x 9-3/4", rect, Dirk Van Erp, imp mark, wear to orig patina 400.00
    16-1/2" x 11-3/4", rect, wrought handles, Arts & Crafts, enameled peacocks, medium brown ground, some wear to orig patina 75.00
    24" x 16", oval, Dirk Van Erp, tooled and painted leather image of rooster, covered in glass, orig light brown patina, leather sgd "G. M. Lee, 1912," imp windmill 1,800.00
Umbrella Stand, 25" h, hand hammered, flared rim, cylindrical body, two strap work loop handles, repousse medallion, riveted flared foot, c1910 ....650.00
Vase, 11-3/4" h, hand hammered, baluster form, waisted neck, flared mouth, brown patina, imp "Juchens, Old Copper Shop, 36," 1915-16 ....425.00
Warming Pan, pierced lid, wrought iron and wood handle 165.00

CORALENE

History: Coralene refers to glass or china objects which have the design painted on the surface of the piece along with tiny colorless glass beads which were applied with a fixative. The piece was placed in a muffle to fix the enamel and set the beads.

Several American and English companies made glass coralene in the 1880s. Seaweed or coral were the most common design. Other motifs were Wheat Sheaf and Fleur-de-Lis. Most of the base glass was satin finished.

China and pottery coralene, made from the late 1890s until after World War II, is referred to as Japanese coralene. The beading is opaque and inserted into the soft clay. Hence, it is only one-half to three-quarters visible.

REPRODUCTION ALERT

Reproductions are on the market, some using an old glass base. The beaded decoration on new coralene has been glued and can be scraped off.

China

Condiment Set, open salt, cov mustard, pepper shaker, white opaque ground, floral coralene dec, SP stand 250.00
Pitcher, 4-1/2" h, 1909 pattern, red and brown ground, beaded yellow daffodil dec...950.00
Vase, 8" h, 6-3/4" w, melon ribbed, sq top, yellow drape coralene, rose shaded to pink ground, white int. 850.00

Vase, dark pink shaded to white, DQ, yellow seaweed coralene, 4-1/4" h, $300. Photo courtesy of Gene Harris Antique Auction Center.

Glass

Bowl, 5-1/2" d, blue MOP satin herringbone pattern, pink seaweed coralene, deeply crimped top, applied rim 625.00
Cruet, pink satin, yellow coralene, orig stopper 410.00
Fairy Lamp, 7" h, six rows of yellow coralene, white opaque shade with yellow tinting, brass colored metal holder 375.00
Tumbler, 3-3/4" h, satin glass, medium to light pink, white int., gold seaweed coralene, gold rim...............................225.00
Vase
    5-1/2" h, 4-5/8" d, fan shaped top, opaque pink satin ground blends to frosted base, all over dec of yellow three leaf sprays with coralene beads 235.00
    7" h, pink shaded and cased to white, diamond pattern, gold beading within design, price for pr 440.00
    8-1/2" h, yellow shaded to pale pink cased to opal white, diamond and cross pattern, yellow beading, gold trim, slight bead loss 175.00
    8-1/2" h, 7" w, sapphire blue, two pastel colored coralene lilies, stems, and foliage, reverse with cream colored foliage, 4 clear scrolled feet, gold enamel trim, Moser, some loss of glass beads 950.00

COWAN POTTERY

History: R. Guy Cowan founded the Cowan Pottery in 1913 in Cleveland, Ohio. The establishment remained in almost continuous operation until 1931, when financial difficulties forced closure.

Early production was redware pottery. Later a porcelain-like finish was perfected with special emphasis placed on glazes, with lustreware being one of the most common types. Commercial wares marked "Lakeware" were produced from 1927 to 1931.

Marks: Early marks include an incised "Cowan Pottery" on the redware (1913-1917), an impressed "Cowan," and an impressed "Lakewood." The imprinted stylized semi-circle, with or without the initials "R. G.," came later.

References: Mark Bassett and Victorian Naumann, *Cowan Pottery and the Cleveland School,* Schiffer Publishing, 1997; Leslie Piña, *Pottery, Modern Wares 1920-1960,* Schiffer Publishing, 1994; Tim and Jamie Saloff, *Collector's Encyclopedia of Cowan Pottery: Identification and Values,* Collector Books, 1994.

Vase, redware body, incised name and monogram, 12" h, $95.

Museums: Cowan Pottery Museum, Rocky River Public Library, Rocky River, OH; Everson Museum of Art, Syracuse, NY.

Bookend, 7-1/4" h, 4" w, figural, little girl in sunbonnet, matte green crystalline glaze, imp mark 100.00
Bowl, 5-1/4" h, 5-1/2" d, ftd, cinnabar glaze, some glaze cracking at foot joint, imp mark 150.00
Candlestick, 9" h, 5" d, figural, beaver holding open work which reads "Light Seek High Light Doth Light of Light Beguille," matte green and gunmetal glaze, inscribed "Rowfant Club 1925, number 152 of 156 copies, R. G. Cowan" 1,100.00
Charger, 11-1/4" d, emb undersea motif, light green fish and plants, blue-green ground, imp "Cowan" 500.00
Figure
    Art Deco Russian set, dancer, 3 musicians, glossy beige glaze, stamped "Cowan" and numbered, restoration to accordion player's foot, 4 pcs 5,250.00
    Horse, 9-1/2" x 9", mahogany and gold flambé glaze, imp mark 1,700.00
Flower Frog, 8", nude, #680.. 325.00
Jar, cov, 5-3/4" h, 5" d, ribbed, blue-green crystalline glaze, imp mark 200.00
Nut Dish, figural, clown... 115.00
Trivet, 6-1/2" d, woman's head and flowers, blue, cream, yellow, and pink, minor usage scratches, die-stamped Cowan/flower 450.00
Vase
    5" h, pillow, handles, yellow... 65.00
    6-1/2" h, Orange Luster, fluted 70.00
    7-1/4" h, 5" d, classical shape, dripping brown crystalline glaze, mirrored orange glaze, ink mark.................... 300.00
    12" h, 6-1/4" d, ribbed, glossy mahogany glaze, die-stamped mark.. 300.00

CRANBERRY GLASS

History: Cranberry glass is transparent and named for its color, achieved by adding powdered gold to a molten batch of amber glass and reheating at a low temperature to develop the cranberry or ruby color. The glass color first appeared in the last half of the 17th century but was not made in American glass factories until the last half of the 19th century.

Cranberry glass was blown, mold blown, or pressed. Examples often are decorated with gold or enamel. Less-expensive cranberry glass, made by substituting copper for gold, can be identified by its bluish purple tint.

Reference: William Heacock and William Gamble, Encyclopedia of Victorian Colored Pattern Glass: Book 9, Cranberry Opalescent from A to Z, Antique Publications, 1987.

REPRODUCTION ALERT
Reproductions abound. These pieces are heavier, off-color, and lack the quality of older examples.

Additional Listings: See specific categories, such as Bride's Baskets; Cruets; Jack-in-the-Pulpit Vases; etc.

Basket
    5-1/2" h, 6" w, star shaped top, ruffled edge, crystal thorn loop handle, c1890 .... 195.00
    7" h, 5" w, ruffled edge, petticoat shape, crystal loop handle, c1890 .... 250.00
Bottle
    7-3/4" h, 4" d, flattened bulbous, frosted, gold church scene, small boats on back, gold around top 135.00
    8" h, 3" d, gold mid-band, white enameled trim, clear faceted stopper 145.00
    8-1/2" h, 3-1/4" d, Inverted Thumbprint pattern, white enameled dot flowers and bands, gold trim, clear cut faceted stopper 155.00
Bowl, 7-3/4" d, paneled, flower dec, brass standard, mirrored base... 120.00
Butter Dish, cov, round, Hobnail pattern 125.00
Candlestick, 10-1/2" h, applied yellow eel dec 120.00
Cologne Bottle, 7" h, dainty blue, white, and yellow enameled flowers, green leaves, gold outlines and trim, orig clear ball stopper 195.00
Creamer, 5" h, 2-3/4" d, Optic pattern, fluted top, applied clear handle.. 95.00
Cruet, 13" h, 4" d, heavy gold roses dec, clear cut faceted stopper 195.00

Vase, gold enameled fern like dec, cup neck, ormolu stand, 4-1/4" h, $75.

Cup and Saucer, gold bands, enameled purple and white violets, gold handle 135.00
Epergne, 19" h, 11" d, 5 pc, large ruffled bowl, tall center lily, 3 jack-in-the-pulpit vases 1,150.00
Finger Bowl, scalloped, matching underplate 145.00
Perfume Bottle, 7-1/4" d, 2-3/4" d, gold stars dec, star cut under base, clear bubble stopper 150.00
Pitcher
   6-1/4" h, 4-3/8" d, Ripple pattern, bulbous, round mouth, applied clear handle 110.00
   6-1/2" h, 4-1/8" d, Ripple and Thumbprint pattern, bulbous, round moth, applied clear handle 110.00
   7-1/2" h, 4-1/2" d, Optic pattern, bulbous, round mouth, applied clear reeded handle 145.00
   10" h, 5" d, bulbous, ice bladder int., applied clear handle 220.00
   11-3/8" h, 9" w, bulbous shape, crystal loop handle, white and blue floral leaf dec, int. vertical ribs, c1895 .... 275.00
Salt, master, ftd, enameled floral dec 200.00
Sauce, Hobbs Hobnail pattern 45.00
Sugar Bowl, cov, 6-1/8" h, 4" d, applied wafer foot, clear ribbed bubble finial 110.00
Tumble-Up, Inverted Thumbprint pattern 195.00
Tumbler, Inverted Thumbprint pattern 65.00
Urn, 11-1/2" h, 2 applied clear handles, enameled flowers and leaves 400.00
Vase
   6-3/8" h, 4-3/8" d, frosted, white daisies, blue forget-me-nots, green leaves, price for pr 210.00
   7-1/2" h, emb ribs, applied clear feet, 3 swirled applied clear leaves around base 110.00
   8-7/8" h, bulbous, white enameled lilies of the valley dec, cylinder neck 115.00
Wine Decanter
   8-1/2" h, 4-1/2" d, small gold stars dec, orig gold trim cranberry bubble stopper 165.00
   10-3/4" h, 4-3/4" d, flattened bulbous shape, clear wafer foot, applied clear spun rope handle, orig bubble stopper 185.00
   12" h, opaque white cased over cranberry, enameled flowers and gilt scrollwork dec, pr 500.00
   13" h, 4" d, gold roses and foliage dec, applied clear handle, clear cut faceted stopper 200.00
   13-1/2" h, blown swirl, clear applied ruffled top, 3 clear applied feet, gilt and enamel surface dec of leaves and flowers, some paint wear 350.00

CROWN MILANO

History: Crown Milano is an American art glass produced by the Mt. Washington Glass Works, New Bedford, Massachusetts. The original patent was issued in 1886 to Frederick Shirley and Albert Steffin.

Normally, it is an opaque-white satin glass finished with light-beige or ivory-colored ground embellished with fancy florals, decorations, and elaborate and thick raised gold.

Collectors Club: Mount Washington Art Glass Society, PO Box 24094, Fort Worth, TX 76124.-1094

Marks: Marked pieces have a purple enamel entwined "CM" with a crown on the base. Sometimes paper labels

Vase, spring floral bouquet, pastel hues, reverse with white flowering dogwood branches, 6" h, $1,950. Photo courtesy of Clarence and Betty Maier.

were used. Since both Mount Washington and Pairpoint supplied mountings, the silver-plated mounts often have "MW" impressed or a Pairpoint mark.

Advisors: Clarence and Betty Maier.

Biscuit Jar, 7-1/2" d, 9" h, colorful painting of couple in Colonial garb covers entire front, reverse side is a small white reserve, outlined in raised gold, gold line-drawn florals, cream colored body, base is signed "3912/80," lid is signed, "M.W.4419/c" 975.00
Muffineer, 3" h, 4" d, melon-ribbed shape, chalk-white body, sprays of violet-colored Johnny-Jump-Up blossoms, silvery-bright metal collar and lid, embossed with butterfly, dragonfly, and blossoms 585.00
Salt Shaker, 4" h, ribbed, dainty blue and white daisy blossoms, Burmese-colored background 185.00
Vase
   6" h, 5-3/4" d, cream-colored body, 24 swirling molded-in ribs, white peony blossoms 1,250.00
   6" h, 6" d, springtime blossoms, glorious pastel hues, opposite side of flowering white dogwood, 4 raised gold circular embellishment, large circle with cherub riding mystical sea creature, 1 with a sun face surrounded by stylized dolphins, 2 smaller circles with geometric designs, Crown Milano logo and "583" 1,950.00
   9-1/4" h, opaque white body, cup-shaped top, exquisite floral decoration, 2 applied handles, orig paper label ... 1,750.00

CRUETS

History: Cruets are small glass bottles used on the table and holding condiments such as oil, vinegar, and wine. The pinnacle of cruet use occurred during the Victorian era when a myriad of glass manufacturers made cruets in a wide assortment of patterns, colors, and sizes. All cruets had stoppers; most had handles.

References: Elaine Ezell and George Newhouse, *Cruets, Cruets, Cruets*, Vol. I, Antique Publications, 1991; William Heacock, *Encyclopedia of Victorian Colored Pattern Glass: Book 6, Oil Cruets from A to Z*, Antique Publications, 1981.

Additional Listings: Pattern Glass and specific glass categories such as Amberina, Cranberry, and Satin.

Amberina, 7" h, IVT, three petal top, amber applied handle, cut faceted stopper 185.00
Art Glass, 6" h, ruby cut to clear, intricate design cut into body, oval panels cut in to neck, notches cut into spout, 16 pointed

Cranberry, bulbous base, applied clear handle, clear faceted stopper, 6-1/2" h, $70.

star cut into base, clear glass handle, orig faceted stopper 400.00
Burmese, 6-1/4" h, ribbed, orig stopper, Mt Washington ...720.00
Cranberry, 6" h, 4" w, Diamond Quilted pattern, blown molded, clear applied handle, cut stopper 125.00
Custard Glass, 6-1/2" h, Wild Bouquet pattern, fired-on dec 525.00
Cut Glass, sgd "Sinclair" 125.00
Opalescent Glass
    Daisy Fern, blue opalescent, Parian mold, no stopper .195.00
    Parian Swirl, blue opalescent 495.00
    Stripes, pale blue, orig hollow stopper, solid amber handle, 7-1/4" h, polished pontil mark 345.00
    Swag with Brackets, green opalescent 485.00
    Wild Bouquet, blue opalescent 495.00
Pattern Glass
    Argonaut Shell, custard, gold trim.......................975.00
    Big Button, ruby stained 250.00
    Column Block, vaseline 295.00
    Chrysanthemum Sprig
        Blue, opaque 1,250.00
        Custard 495.00
    Croesus, large, green, gold trim.........................395.00
    Double Circle, apple green 225.00
    Empress, green, os 295.00
    Esther, green, gold trim 465.00
    Everglades, vaseline, gold trim 595.00
    Fluted Scrolls, blue, dec 295.00
    Inverted Thumbprint, cranberry...........................265.00
    Jackson, vaseline 225.00
    Louis XV, green, gold trim 350.00
    Medallion Sprig, green 395.00
    Millard, amber stain 345.00
    O'Hara's Diamond, ruby stained 295.00
    Riverside's Ranson, vaseline 210.00
    Royal Ivy, rubena..465.00
    Stars and Stripes, cranberry, heat check.................650.00
    Tiny Optic, green, dec...................................140.00
    Truncated Cube, ruby stained.............................285.00
Peachblow
    6-1/2" h, petticoat shape, orig cut amber stopper, Wheeling 1,750.00
    8" h, acid finish, applied reeded handle.................775.00
Rubena Verde, 6-3/4" h, 4" w, IVT, petticoat shape, orig cut vaseline stopper, Wheeling...................................395.00
Satin, 8-1/4" h, DQ, white shaded to gold, clear frosted handle, orig frosted clear knobby stopper 595.00
Slag, 6-3/4" h, Hobstars pattern, matching stopper 65.00

CUP PLATES

History: Many early cups were handleless and came with deep saucers. The hot liquid was poured into the saucer and sipped from it. This necessitated another plate for the cup, hence the "cup plate."

The first cup plates made of pottery were of the Staffordshire variety. From the mid-1830s to 1840s, glass cup plates were favored. The Boston and Sandwich Glass Company was one of the main manufacturers of the lacy glass type.

References: Ruth Webb Lee and James H. Rose, *American Glass Cup Plates*, published by author, 1948, Charles E. Tuttle Co. reprint, 1985; Kenneth Wilson, *American Glass 1760-1930*, 2 Vols., Hudson Hills Press and The Toledo Museum of Art, 1994.

Collectors' Club: Pairpoint Cup Plate Collectors of America, P.O. Box 890052, East Weymouth, MA 02189.

Notes: It is extremely difficult to find glass cup plates in outstanding (mint) condition. Collectors expect some signs of use, such as slight rim roughness, minor chipping (best if under the rim), and, in rarer patterns, portions of scallops missing.

The numbers used are from the Lee-Rose book in which all plates are illustrated.

Prices are based on plates in average condition.

Glass

LR 11, 2-13/16", clear, New England origin, small shallow rim chips and roughage 85.00
LR 22-B, 3-7/16" d, clear pontil, New England origin, slight roughage..95.00
LR 26, 3-7/17" d, clear, attributed to Sandwich..................165.00
LR 45, 3-9/16" d, pale opalescent, attributed to Sandwich, mold overfill, slag deposit near center 120.00
LR 51, 3-3/4" d, clear, pontil, eastern orig, moderate rim roughage, few shallow flakes...............................185.00
LR 75-A, 3-13/16" d, clear, New England origin, one tiny rim flake 90.00
LR 80, 3-3//4" d, opalescent, New England origin.............250.00
LR 81, 3-3/4" d, fiery red opalescent, New England origin 360.00
LR 95, 3-5/8" d, opalescent opaque, New England origin 180.00
LR 100, 3-1/4" d, clear, attributed to Philadelphia area, normal mold roughness...110.00
LR 121, 3-16" d, clear, lacy midwestern, slight rim roughage 115.00
LR 242-A, 3-1/2" d, black amethyst, lacy, eastern origin ...675.00

Glass, log cabin with flag in center, $65.

LR 247, 3-7-16" d, emerald green, attributed to Sandwich, small chip on one scallop 750.00
LR 259, 3-7/16" d, clear, eastern origin 200.00
LR 276, 3-7/16" d, blue, lacy, Boston and Sandwich Glass Co. 395.00
LR 279, 2-7/8" d, light green, lacy, eastern origin 295.00
LR 399, 3-5/16" d, clear, eastern origin, normal mold roughness 110.00
LR 433, 4-1/8" d, clear, two chips, mold roughness.............80.00
LR 459M, jade opaque, 12 hearts 475.00

Glass, Historical

LR 568, 3-7/16" d, clear, attributed to Sandwich, mold roughness 85.00
LR 586-B, clear, Ringgold, Palo alto, stippled ground, small letters, Philadelphia area, 1847-48......................650.00
LR 615-A, 3-7/8" d, clear, unknown origin, Constitution 650.00
LR 695, 3" d, clear, midwestern origin, normal mold roughness 150.00

Porcelain or Pottery

Gaudy Dutch, Butterfly pattern...............................75.00
Leeds, 3-3/4" d, soft paste, gaudy blue and white floral dec 275.00
Pearlware, 4" d, blue feather edge, later enameled eagle, pr 110.00
Staffordshire, historical, dark blue
  Franklin Tomb, 3-1/2" d, Wood 625.00
  Landing of Lafayette, 4-3/8" d, full border, Clews 450.00
  Unidentified view of Country Estate, 4-5/8" d, grapevine border series, Wood..............................90.00
Staffordshire, romantic, Garden Scenery, 12 sided, pink transfer, Mayer..45.00

CUSTARD GLASS

History: Custard glass was developed in England in the early 1880s. Harry Northwood made the first American custard glass at his Indiana, Pennsylvania, factory in 1898.

From 1898 until 1915, many manufacturers produced custard glass patterns, e.g., Dugan Glass, Fenton, A. H. Heisey Glass Co., Jefferson Glass, Northwood, Tarentum Glass, and U.S. Glass. Cambridge and McKee continued the production of custard glass into the Depression.

The ivory or creamy yellow custard color is achieved by adding uranium salts to the molten hot glass. The chemical content makes the glass glow when held under a black light. The more uranium, the more luminous the color. Northwood's custard glass has the smallest amount of uranium, creating an ivory color; Heisey used more, creating a deep yellow color.

Custard glass was made in patterned tableware pieces. It also was made as souvenir items and novelty pieces. Souvenir pieces are include a place name or hand-painted decorations, e.g., flowers. Patterns of custard glass often were highlighted in gold, enameled colors, and stains.

References: Gary E. Baker et al., *Wheeling Glass 1829-1939*, Oglebay Institute, 1994, distributed by Antique Publications; William Heacock, *Encyclopedia of Victorian Colored Pattern Glass, Book IV: Custard Glass from A to Z*, Peacock Publications, 1980; William Heacock, James Measell and Berry Wiggins, *Harry Northwood: The Early Years 1881-1900*, Antique Publications, 1990.

Additional Listings: Pattern Glass.

Banana Boat, Geneva, 11" l, oval 145.00
Berry Bowl, individual size
  Fan..45.00
  Louis XV, gold trim..45.00
  Ring Band, gold and rose dec 48.00
Berry Bowl, master
  Diamond with Peg 225.00
  Louis XV, gold trim..145.00
Berry Set
  Chrysanthemum Sprig, master and six individual bowls, sgd "Northwood" in script................................590.00
  Everglades, gold trim 395.00
  Geneva, master and four sauces 225.00
Bowl, Grape and Cable, 7-1/2" d, basketweave ext., nutmeg stain, Northwood..60.00
Butter Dish, cov
  Everglades..375.00
  Georgia Gem, enamel dec 150.00
  Tiny Thumbprint, Tarentum, dec 300.00
  Victoria..300.00
Celery
  Georgia Gem 195.00
  Ring Band 300.00
Compote
  Argonaut Shell 80.00
  Geneva 45.00
  Ring Band, roses dec, gold trim.......................170.00
Condiment Set, Creased Bale, 4 pcs 200.00
Creamer
  Chrysanthemum Sprig, blue, gold dec 395.00
  Fluted Scrolls..85.00
  Geneva 85.00
  Heart with Thumbprint 80.00
Cruet, Chrysanthemum Sprig, clear stopper, goofus dec . 125.00
Dresser Tray, Grape, nutmeg stain 225.00
Goblet, Grape and Gothic Arches, nutmeg stain................75.00
Hair Receiver, Winged Scroll...125.00
Ice Cream Bowl, Peacock and Urn, individual size 40.00
Napkin Ring, Diamond with Peg..150.00
Nappy
  Northwood Grape 60.00
  Prayer Rug..65.00

Bonbon, Scroll, green, emb maple leaf with chrysanthemum dec, sgd "Northwood," 5-7/8" l, 3-3/9" w, 2-5/8" h, $45.

Pitcher
    Argonaut Shell 325.00
    Diamond with Peg, tankard 275.00
Plate, Grape and Cable, Northwood 55.00
Punch Cup
    Diamond with Peg 70.00
    Northwood Grape 50.00
Rose Bowl, Grape and Gothic Arches 90.00
Salt and Pepper Shakers, pr
    Chrysanthemum Sprig 175.00
    Punty Band 90.00
Sauce
    Cane Insert 35.00
    Intaglio 35.00
    Klondyke 45.00
Spooner
    Argonaut Shell, 4-3/4" h, Northwood script signature, bright
      gold dec, scalloped rim.............................275.00
    Grape and Gothic Arches 95.00
    Intaglio 95.00
Sugar, cov, Chrysanthemum Sprig, blue 395.00
Syrup, Ring Band 315.00
Table Set, cov butter, creamer, cov sugar, spooner
    Argonaut Shell 425.00
    Intaglio 500.00
Toothpick Holder, Fan and Feather, 2-1/2" h......875.00
Tumbler
    Beaded Circle, Northwood, 4" h, enameled blue blossoms, six
      tiny flowers with green leaves, slight loss to gold highlights
      ....250.00
    Cherry Scale 50.00
    Geneva, red and green enamel dec 60.00
    Inverted Fan and Feather 90.00
    Louis XV, gold trim..60.00
    Vermont 110.00
    Wild Bouquet 35.00

CUT GLASS, AMERICAN

History: Glass is cut by grinding decorations into the glass by means of abrasive-carrying metal or stone wheels. A very ancient craft, it was revived in 1600 by Bohemians and spread through Europe to Great Britain and America.

American cut glass came of age at the Centennial Exposition in 1876 and the World Columbian Exposition in 1893. The American public recognized American cut glass to be exceptional in quality and workmanship. America's most significant output of this high-quality glass occurred from 1880 to 1917, a period now known as the Brilliant Period.

Marks: Around 1890, some companies began adding an acid-etched "signature" to their glass. This signature may be the actual company name, its logo, or a chosen symbol. Today, signed pieces command a premium over unsigned pieces since the signature clearly establishes the origin. However, signatures should be carefully verified for authenticity since objects with forged signatures have been in existence for some time. One way to check is to run a finger tip or fingernail lightly over the signature area. As a general rule, a genuine signature cannot be felt; a forged signature has a raised surface.

Many companies never used the acid-etched signature on their glass and may or may not have affixed paper labels to the items originally. Dorflinger Glass and the Meriden Glass Co. made cut glass of the highest quality, yet never used an acid-etched signature. Furthermore, cut glass made before the 1890s was not signed. Many of these wood-polished items, cut on blown blanks, were of excellent quality and often won awards at exhibitions.

References: Bill and Louis Boggess, *Identifying American Brilliant Cut Glass*, 3rd ed., Schiffer Publishing, 1996; ——, *Reflections on American Brilliant Cut Glass*, Schiffer Publishing, 1995; Jo Evers, *Evers' Standard Cut Glass Value Guide*, Collector Books, 1975, 1995 value update; Bob Page and Dale Fredericksen, *A Collection of American Crystal*, Page-Fredericksen Publishing, 1995; ——, *Seneca Glass Company 1891-1983*, Page-Fredericksen Publishing, 1995; J. Michael Pearson, *Encyclopedia of American Cut & Engraved Glass*, Vols. I to III, published by author, 1975; Albert C. Revi, *American Cut & Engraved Glass*, Schiffer Publishing, 1965; Martha Louise Swan, *American Cut and Engraved Glass*, Wallace-Homestead, 1986, 1994 value update; Kenneth Wilson, *American Glass 1760-1930*, 2 Vols., Hudson Hills Press and The Toledo Museum of Art, 1994.

Collectors' Club: American Cut Glass Assoc., P.O. Box 482, Ramona, CA 92065.

Museums: Corning Museum of Glass, Corning, NY; High Museum of Art, Atlanta, GA; Huntington Galleries, Huntington, WV; Lightner Museum, St. Augustine, FL; Toledo Museum of Art, Toledo, OH.

Basket, 7" d, 8" h, hobstars, fans, tiny buttons, cut scalloped rim, 3 applied feet, cut notched applied handle 295.00
Bowl
    7" d, low, Pontiac pattern, sgd "Clark" 60.00
    8" d, Checker Board pattern.........................250.00
    8" d, Heart pattern 250.00
    8" d, low, circle motifs of hobstar and cane 150.00
    8" d, low, "Y" in center, 3 large hobstars 80.00
    8" sq, 4 large hobstars in corners, double-mitre vesicas with cane and Russian motifs 115.00
    9" d, Manitou pattern, clear uncut tusk surrounded by brilliant overall cutting, Hoare 400.00
    9" d, 4" h, hobstar, fan 125.00
    9" d, 5-1/2" h, hobstar, checkerboard, American Brilliant Period..135.00
    12" d, Holland pattern, rolled rim, sgd "Hawkes" 700.00
Bread Tray
    11-1/2" x 8", Blazed Star 90.00
    12" x 7-1/2", wedgemere pattern, Libbey, tooth chip 250.00
Candlesticks, 10" h, faceted cut knobs, large teardrop stems, ray base..425.00
Candy Dish, 7-3/4" l, oval, deeply cut Elfin pattern, Hoare ..90.00

Ice Cream Set, 15" d charger, 12 7" d plates, J. Hoare, pattern #587 (Boggess, pg 156), $6,750. Photo courtesy of Woody Auction.

Celery Dish

10" l, 4-1/2" w, hobstar center, buzzstars, American Brilliant Period 85.00

11" x 6", Pattern #70450, Marshall Field catalog, Boggess, pg 156, #568 ....140.00

12" l, Bakers Gothic pattern, folded, sgd "Libbey" 85.00

Celery Vase, 7-3/4" h, blown, scalloped rim, bowl cut with panels, strawberry diamonds, and fans, knop stem, star cut foot, Pittsburgh 275.00

Centerpiece, 10-3/4" d, wheel cut and etched, molded, fruiting foliage, chips 490.00

Champagne, stone engraved rock crystal, Dorflinger, c1890 ....85.00

Champagne Pitcher

10" h, hobstars and cane, double thumbprint handle ...210.00

11" h, Prism pattern, triple notch handle, monogram sterling silver top 425.00

13-1/4" h, allover cut hobstars, cane bars, stars, and fan, 24 point hobstar base, triple notch handle, fluted spout 600.00

Cider Pitcher

Hobstar, cross-cut diamond, jewels and fan, zipper cut and tear drop handle 325.00

Pinwheel and chain of hobstar cut, triple notch handle 220.00

Split vesica motifs, hobstar, star, and tan, triple notch handle 150.00

Cologne Bottle

5-1/4" h, alternating bull's eye and cross-cut squares, faceted cup stopper, sgd "Libbey" 325.00

7-1/2" h, Holland pattern, faceted cut stopper 275.00

Compote

Pairpoint, intaglio cut fruit 445.00

Pittsburgh, 9-1/4" d, 7" h, blown, cut panels, strawberry diamonds and fans, foliage band at rim, finely scalloped lip, knob stem, star cut foot, minor wear and scratches 385.00

Creamer and Sugar

Hobstar, 3" h, American Brilliant Period 50.00

Zenda, sgd "Libbey" 90.00

Decanter, orig stopper

6-1/2" h, blown, colorless, cut panels, fans, and diamond point roundels, applied foot and 2 rings, Pittsburgh, small chips 220.00

7-1/4" h, blown, colorless, cut flutes, diamond point, strawberry diamonds and panels, 3 applied rings, Pittsburgh, small flakes, lip ground 110.00

7-3/8" h, blown, colorless, cut panels, strawberry diamonds and fans, 3 applied rings, Pittsburgh, pinpoint flakes, mismatched stopper 55.00

8" h, blown, colorless, cut panels, strawberry diamonds and fans, applied foot, 3 applied rings, Pittsburgh, slight stain in bottom, very small chips 250.00

8-1/2" h, blown, colorless, cut panels and fans, 3 applied rings, Pittsburgh, small flakes..140.00

13" h, cranberry cut to clear, bulbous body, fan and diamond cutting, notched panel neck, applied cut handle, faceted stopper, star-cut base, American Brilliant Period..3,450.00

Dish

5" d, heart shape, handle, American Brilliant Period 45.00

5" d, hobstar, pineapple, palm leaf, American Brilliant Period 45.00

Epergne, 11" h, one piece, bowl cut in intaglio thistle, lily cut in honeycomb and cross hatch, rolled rim 850.00

Goblet

Buzzstar, pineapple, 7" h, marked "B & B," American Brilliant Period 40.00

Intaglio vintage cut, 8-1/2" h, sgd "Sinclaire" 80.00

Strawberry diamond, pinwheel, and fan, notched stem, 7 pc set 350.00

Hair Receiver, 5-1/2" d, Harvard pattern, 2 pc 140.00

Ice Cream Set, Russian pattern, eight 7" d dishes, 8-1/2" d serving bowl, 11" d cake plate, some chips to edges, American Brilliant Period, price for 10 pc set 500.00

Ice Cream Tray, 14" x 7-1/2", 24 point hobstar center surrounded by cane, pinwheel border...100.00

Ice Tub, two handles, hobstars, American Brilliant Period.395.00

Lamp, 18" h, mushroom shade, Pattern #69359, orig pendants, T. B. Clark 2,450.00

Liquor, stemmed, buzzstar, pineapple, marked, "B & B," American Brilliant Period..25.00

Loving Cup, 6-1/2" h, sterling rim, prism cut, three triple notched handles, American Brilliant Period 575.00

Nappy, two handles

6" d, hobstar center, intaglio floral, strawberry diamond button border, 6" d..45.00

6" x 7", step-cut pulled handle, checker board bottom, diamond cut sides 70.00

7" d, Four part, hobstar in each section, double thumbprint handles, 7" 160.00

Pickle Tray, 7" x 3", checkerboard, hobstar..........................45.00

Pitcher, 6-3/8" h, blown, cut panels, strawberry diamonds, fans, roundels, and rays with foliage rim, fluted lip, Pittsburgh, recut rim with chip 95.00

Plate

10" d, Carolyn pattern, J. Hoare 525.00

12" d, alternating hobstar and pinwheel......................100.00

Powder Box, cov, 4-1/2" d, flashed hobstar on top, alternating pinwheel and vesica motif 120.00

Punch Bowl, 11" x 10", 2 pc, Elgin pattern, Quaker City 600.00

Relish, 8" l, two handles, divided, Jupiter pattern, Meriden 120.00

Rose Bowl, 8" d, 7-1/2" h, ftd, all over strawberry diamond, ray base, Mt Washington..575.00

Scent Bottle, 6-1/4" l, cane pattern, tapered bottle, hinged cover and rim, imp "Tiffany & Co. Sterling," American Brilliant Period, cover mis-aligned, glass stopper missing.....................175.00

Tankard, 11" h, hobstar, strawberry diamond, notched prism and fan, flared base with bull's eye, double thumbprint handle 275.00

Tray

10" l, allover hobstars, American Brilliant Period...........495.00

12", similar to Hawkes Nelson pattern, sgd "Straus" 700.00

Tobacco Jar, 9" h, 6" d, straight sided canister, panels of fine cut cane pattern alternating with faceted thumbprints, matching cut glass top with star cutting repeated on base, American Brilliant Period...1,150.00

Tumbler, 3-1/8" h, flint, cut panels, fans, sheaves, roundels, strawberry diamonds, Pittsburgh 40.00

Lamp, mushroom shade, hobstars, prism, strawberry diamond, feathered fan, $3,000. Photo courtesy of Woody Auction.

Vase, intaglio wild floral dec, sgd "Hawkes Gravic," 17-1/2" h, $2,400. Photo courtesy of Woody Auction.

Vase
  8" h, monogrammed and inscribed silver flared neck, body cut with thumb notching and elongated panels, American Brilliant Period, c1901, minor chips 230.00
  9" h, cylindrical, star, strawberry diamond, cross-cut diamond and fan, attributed to Dorflinger 130.00
  12" h, strawberry diamond, buzzstars. American Brilliant Period..150.00
  14" h, bowling pin shape, Comet pattern, sgd "J. Hoare," professionally repaired 200.00
  14" h, bowling pin shape, three 24 point hobstars on sides surrounded by notched prisms, strawberry diamond, hobstars, star, and checkered diamond fields...............700.00
  15" h, corset shape, Primrose pattern, Dorlinger 1,250.00
  16 h, corset shape, well cut hobstar, strawberry diamond, prism, flashed star and fan.......................................300.00
  17" h, 7" w at widest point, tulip shape, hobstar, strawberry diamond and fan, 24 point hobstar base 425.00
  19-1/2" h, funeral, hobstars, strawberry diamond, and fan motifs 500.00
Water Carafe
  Brunswick pattern, thin neck, sgd "Hawkes" 240.00
  Thumbprint and chain of hobstar, honeycomb neck, sgd "Hawkes" 180.00
Water Pitcher, pinwheel, strawberry diamond and notched fan 90.00
Water Set, pitcher and tumblers, two bands of hobstars, flat pillar cut, 3 panels of intaglio wild florals, sgd "Sinclaire," 6 pcs 575.00
Whiskey Jug, 6-1/4" h, bulbous, thistle and grape cutting, orig stopper, sgd "Sinclaire"..295.00
Wine
  4" h, flint, cut panels, strawberry diamonds, and fans, Pittsburgh 60.00
  4-1/8" h, flint, Gothic Arch, sheaf like ferns, Pittsburgh ...75.00
  4-1/4" h, flint, strawberry diamonds, fans, leaves, and panels, Pittsburgh 65.00

CUT VELVET

History: Several glass manufacturers made cut velvet during the late Victorian era, c1870–1900. An outer layer of pastel color was applied over a white casing. The piece then was molded or cut in a high-relief ribbed or diamond shape, exposing portions of the casing. The finish had a satin velvety feel, hence the name "cut velvet."

Biscuit Jar, cov, pink, SP mountings and lid 275.00
Celery Vase, 6-1/2" h, deep blue over white, DQ, box-pleated top..725.00

Creamer, 3-1/2" h, DQ, cranberry, applied multicolored enamel dec..385.00
Cruet, 6" h, shiny pink, DQ body, clear faceted stopper, clear handle..750.00
Finger Bowl, 4-1/2" d, DQ, blue...185.00
Vase
  7-1/2" h, 3-1/2" w, bulbous shape, ruffled top, Herringbone, deep Alice Blue, white lining, c1880 ....450.00
  9" h, slight flare to end of elongated neck, robin's egg blue, diamond quilt body, daisy blossom like design at base 385.00
  9" h, 6" tall cylinder over short bulbous base, deeply ruffled 9" w top, deep orange DQ...675.00
  13-1/2" h, 6" d base, double gourd shape, long pumpkin stem neck, pale gold, DQ 650.00

CZECHOSLOVAKIAN ITEMS

History: Objects marked "Made in Czechoslovakia" were produced after 1918 when the country claimed its independence from the Austro-Hungarian Empire. The people became more cosmopolitan and liberated and expanded the scope of their lives. Their porcelains, pottery, and glassware reflect many influences.

Marks: A specific manufacturer's mark may include a date which precedes 1918, but this only indicates the factory existed during the years of the Bohemian or Austro-Hungarian Empire.

References: Dale and Diane Barta and Helen M. Rose, *Czechoslovakian Glass & Collectibles* (1992, 1995 values), Book II (1996) Collector Books; *Bohemian Glass*, n.d., distributed by Antique Publications; Ruth A. Forsythe, *Made in Czechoslovakia*, Antique Publications, 1993; Jacquelyne Y. Jones-North, *Czechoslovakian Perfume Bottles and Boudoir Accessories*, Antique Publications, 1990.

Periodical: *New Glass Review*, Bardounova 2140 149 00 Praha 4, Prague, Czech Republic.

Collectors' Club: Czechoslovakian Collectors Guild International, P.O. Box 901395, Kansas City, MO 64190.

Museum: Friends of the Glass Museum of Novy Bor, Kensington, MD.

Atomizer, 7-1/2" h, brilliant period cut glass.......................115.00
Bowl, cased, yellow int., black ext., polished pontil.............60.00
Console Set, 10" x 6" x 2-1/2" bowl, Art Deco design, turquoise raised drapery, knotted corners, bowl and pr candlesticks 85.00
Jack In The Pulpit Vase, 12" h, white and yellow irid, deep red interior, green-red criss-cross looping, mkd "Czechoslovakia" 325.00
Lamp Shade, beaded...50.00
Luncheon Set, partial, flowing irid magenta, orange, brown and lavender, mother of pearl ground, sgd, 40 pcs.............280.00
Perfume Bottle, 6-3/4" h, amber, large intaglio floral stopper . 175.00
Plate, 9-1/2" d, gilt foliate designs, wide burgundy border, Epiag, early 20th C, light wear, 11 pc set................................290.00
Powder Box, cov, round, yellow, black knop 60.00
Vase
  4-3/4" h, blue, ftd, applied black rim, cased 70.00
  7-1/4" h, yellow and orange, ftd, applied black rim, cased 65.00

Candlestick, tortoiseshell type glass, mkd "Made in Czechoslovakia," 7-3/4" h, $100.

8-1/2" h, red and white mottled ground, black snake dec, ruffled 125.00
9" h, wrought iron reticulated frame, blown-in glass body with splotched blue, orange and green cased to white, base stamped "Czechoslovakia" 460.00
14-3/4" h, raised rim, irid colorless oval body cased to opal glass, internal layer of bright red, green, orange, and olive green splotched dec, base stamped "Czechoslovakia" 520.00

DAIRY ITEMS

History: The history of collecting dairy related items is as varied as there are items. Advertising pieces can go back to mid 1800s. Post cards, trade cards, and pinback buttons were used as advertising, as well as more household utilitarian items, such as match holders and pot holders. The cream separator, milk cans, various testing equipment and cow bells followed as more advertising items were developed. In more recent years, these items are used as promotion or give-aways by the numerous dairy companies.

There were hundreds of small dairies and creameries scattered throughout the United States during the late 19th to mid 20th centuries. Many gave away a variety of materials to promote their products.

Eventually regional cooperatives expanded the marketing regions, and many smaller dairies closed. Companies such as Borden distributed products on a national level. Borden created the advertising character of "Elsie, the Borden Cow" to help sell its products. Additional consolidation of firms occurred, encouraged in part by state milk marketing boards and federal subsidies.

One area of Dairy Collecting that is popular is the collecting of milk bottle caps. Prices for these range from $.25 to $2.00 for the hundreds of dairies commonly found throughout the United States. Milk bottle caps issued for special events or by special organizations can range from $1.00 to $2.50 or higher. Bottle caps with war time slogans are also in the $2.50 range.

Many collectors specialize, for instance, in cream separators, milk cans, farm equipment, or creamers used in the diners across America. Individually, or in combination, there will be competition with other collectors of similar items. As with almost any type of collecting, dairy collectibles can be enhanced by so-called "go withs." dairy items, such as post cards, trade cards, cream separators, and other advertising items can enrich a milk bottle collection. Dairy collecting continues to gain in popularity.

Reference: Paul Dettloff, *Cream Separator Guide,* D. V. M., published by author, 1993; C. H. Wendel, *Encyclopedia of American Farm Implements & Antiques,* Krause Publications, 1997.

Collectors' Clubs: Cream Separator and Dairy Collectors, Rt. 3, P.O. Box 488, Arcadia, WI 54612; National Association of Milk Bottle Collectors, 4 Ox Bow Rd., Westport, CT 06880; National Association of Soda Jerks, P.O. Box 115, Omaha, NE, 68101.

Periodicals: Creamers, P.O. Box 11, Lake Villa, IL 60046; Cream Separator and Dairy Collectors Newsletter, Route 3, P.O. Box 488, Arcadia, WI 54612; Fiz Biz, P.O. Box 115, Omaha, NE, 68101. The Milk Route, 4 Ox Bow Rd., Westport, CT 06880.

Museums: Museum Village, Monroe, NY; New York State Historical Association Farmers Museum, Cooperstown, NY.

Advisors: Tony Knipp and Tom Gallagher.

Also see: Milk Bottles.

Baseball Cap, name of dairy 8.00
Britains, cow, metal 15.00
Butter Churn, wooden, plunger, blue paint 250.00
Butter Paddles, wood, pr......................................45.00
Change Tray, DeLaval..85.00
Churn, Daisy, 1 gallon, glass base.......................55.00
Clock, Dairyman's League, electric.....................150.00
Condensed Milk Can Holder, holder, lid, and underplate, floral pattern, Nippon...125.00
Container, round, Horton Ice Cream, pint, cardboard 6.00
Cook Book, Borden's, 1939 World's Fair, Elsie 8.00
Creamer, ceramic, Paradise Hotel 15.00

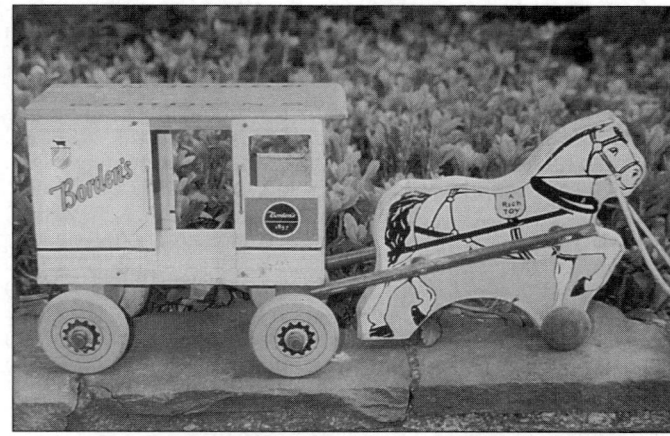

Toy, Borden horse drawn milk wagon, Rich Toys, $450. Photo courtesy of Anthony J. Knipp.

Creamer, glass, 3/4 oz.
    Amsterdam Dairy 18.00
    Bowman 16.00
    Foremost 8.00
    Lehigh Valley 12.00
    Tuscan Dairy: 8.00
Cream Separator, Sanitary Economy King #2 .... 125.00
Game, Borden Milk Co., boxed board 150.00
Letterhead
    Beaks Dairy Co. 3.00
    Brown & Bailey, woodcut cow and farm scene 9.00
    Frank Charlton, Milk dealer 2.50
    E. L. Crawford, Dealers in Pure Milk 2.60
Match Holder, DeLaval, metal, separator shape 125.00
Milk Bottle Cap Pick, Sheffield 8.00
Milk Box, wood, carrying type, 4 quart 10.00
Milk Cup, child's
    Elsie, head with daisy necklace 50.00
    Hopalong Cassidy 18.00
Patent Model, milk can, NY design 8" h 200.00
Pencil, Sweet Clover Milk Co. 3.50
Photograph, 8-1/2" x 10"
    Dutch Belted Cow 10.00
    Early Dairy Wagon, horse drawn 10.00
Post Card, Borden plant, Deposit, NY 5.00
Pot Holder, Superior dairy 6.00
Ruler, 12" l, wood, Breyers Ice Cream 8.00
Shipping Tag, various creameries 3.50
Sign, 10" x 14", porcelain, DeLaval Cream Separator 125.00
Spoon, cream top, 1929 patent 10.00
Toy
    Borden horse drawn milk wagon, Rich Toys 450.00
    Milk truck, name of typical dairy 45.00
Trade Card, diecut, Borden milk wagon pulled by horse 25.00
Train, toy, car, Carnation Milk, HO 12.00

DAVENPORT

History: John Davenport opened a pottery in Longport, Staffordshire, England, in 1793. His high-quality light-weight wares are cream colored with a beautiful velvety texture.

The firm's output included soft-paste (Old Blue) products, luster-trimmed pieces, and pink luster wares with black transfer. Pieces of Gaudy Dutch and Spatterware also have been found with the Davenport mark. Later Davenport became a leading maker of ironstone and early flow blue. His famous Cyprus pattern in mulberry became very popular. His heirs continued the business until the factory closed in 1886.

Charger, 17-1/2" l, oval, Venetian harbor scene, light blue transfer 80.00
Compote, 2-1/2" h, 8-1/2" d, turquoise and gold band, tiny raised flowers, hp scene with man fishing, cows at edge of lake, c1860, pr 225.00
Creamer, tan, jasperware, basketweave, incised anchor mark 60.00
Cup Plate, Teaberry pattern, pink luster 40.00
Dish, ftd, tricorn, Belvoir Castle dec 90.00
Ewer, 9" h, floral dec, multicolored, c1930 .... 190.00
Plate, 9-1/8" d, Legend of Montrose, transfer, c1850 .... 65.00
Platter
    18-1/4", stone china, polychrome dec blue transfer print bird and floral pattern, printed mark, c1810, glaze wear 230.00

Jug, blue and orange Oriental design, green serpent handle, gilt trim, mkd, c1805, $195. Photo courtesy of Susan and Al Bagdade.

    19-1/8" l, purple transfer, idyllic scene, boat and church, mkd "Davenport" 440.00
Sauce Tureen, cov, ladle, creamware, molded leaves, lime green veining, early 450.00
Soup Tureen, matching stand, 13-1/4" l, stone china, polychrome dec blue transfer printed bird and floral patter, gilded lion mask handles, printed marks, c1810, large hairline on stand, glaze wear 1,610.00
Tea Set, cov teapot, creamer, and ftd sugar, blue and white, mkd "Davenport," c1880 .... 140.00
Vegetable Dish, Berry pattern, imp, sgd, anchor mark 60.00

DECOYS

History: During the past several years, carved wooden decoys, used to lure ducks and geese to the hunter, have become widely recognized as an indigenous American folk art form. Many decoys are from 1880 to 1930, when commercial gunners commonly hunted using rigs of several hundred decoys. Many fine carvers also worked through the 1930s and 1940s. Fish decoys were also carved by individuals and commercial decoy makers.

Because decoys were both hand made and machine made, and many examples exist, firm pricing is difficult to establish. The skill of the carver, rarity, type of bird, and age all effect the value.

References: Joel Barber, *Wild Fowl Decoys*, Dover Publications, n.d.; Russell J. Goldberger and Alan G. Haid, *Mason Decoys–A Complete Pictorial Guide,* Decoy Magazine, 1993; Bob and Sharon Huxford, *Collector's Guide to Decoys*, Vol. II, Collector Books, 1992; Linda and Gene Kangas, *Collector's Guide to Decoys*, Wallace-Homestead, 1992; Carl F. Luckey, *Collecting Antique Bird Decoys and Duck Calls: An Identification & Value Guide*, 2nd ed., Books Americana, 1992; Donald J. Peterson, *Folk Art Fish Decoys*, Schiffer Publishing, 1996.

Periodicals: *Decoy Magazine*, P.O. Box 787, Lewes, DE, 19558; *North America Decoys*, P.O. Box 246, Spanish Fork, UT 84660; *Sporting Collector's Monthly*, RW Publishing, P.O. Box 305, Camden, DE 19934; *Wildfowl Art*, Ward Foundation, 909 South Schumaker Dr., Salisbury, MD 21801; *Wildfowl Carving & Collecting*, 500 Vaughn St., Harrisburg, PA 17110.

Collectors' Clubs: Midwest Collectors Assoc., 1100 Bayview Dr., Fox River Grove, IL 60021; Minnesota Decoy Collectors Assoc., P.O. Box 130084, St. Paul, MN 55113; Ohio Decoy Collectors & Carvers Assoc., P.O. Box 499, Richfield, OH 44286.

Museums: Havre de Grace Decoy Museum, Havre de Grace, MD; Museum at Stony Brook, Stony Brook, NY; Noyes Museum of Art, Oceanville, NJ; Peabody Museum of Salem, Salem, MA; Refuge Waterfowl Museum, Chincoteague, VA; Shelburne Museum, Inc., Shelburne, VT; Ward Museum of Wildfowl Art, Salisbury, MD.

Reproduction Alert.

Notes: A decoy's value is based on several factors: (1) fame of the carver, (2) quality of the carving, (3) species of wild fowl–the most desirable are herons, swans, mergansers, and shorebirds–and (4) condition of the original paint.

The inexperienced collector should be aware of several facts. The age of a decoy, per se, is usually of no importance in determining value. However, age does have some influence when it comes to a rare or important example. Since very few decoys were ever signed, it is quite difficult to attribute most decoys to known carvers. Anyone who has not examined a known carver's work will be hard pressed to determine if the paint on one of his decoys is indeed original. Repainting severely decreases a decoy's value. In addition, there are many fakes and reproductions on the market and even experienced collectors are occasionally fooled. Decoys represent a subject where dealing with a reputable dealer or auction house is important, especially those who offer a guarantee as to authenticity.

Decoys listed below are of average wear unless otherwise noted.

SPECIAL AUCTION

Gary Guyette & Frank Schmidt Inc.
P.O. Box 522
West Farmington, ME 04992
(207) 778-6256

Black Breasted Plover, Harry C. Shourds, orig paint 2,650.00
Black Duck
    Charles Thomas, MA, glass eyes, orig paint 365.00
    Ira Hudson, preening, raised wings, outstretched neck, scratch feather paint.. 8,500.00
    Mason Factory, challenge grade, snakey head, orig grade stamp on bottom.. 1,700.00
    Unknown Maker, carved balsa body, wood head, glass eyes, orig pant, 15-1/2" l 150.00
    Wildfowler, CT, inlet head, glass eyes, worn orig paint, green overpaint on bottom on sides, 13" l, c1900 .... 220.00
Black-Breasted Plover, A.E. Crowell, oval brand on bottom 2,750.00
Bluebill, matted pr, Mason Factory, standard grade, glass eyes 1,400.00
Bluebill Drake
    Jim Kelson, Mt. Clemens, MI, carved wing detail, feather stamping, glass eyes, orig paint, orig keep and weight, 13-1/2" l, c1930 .... 295.00

Sandusky, well shaped head, tack eyes, orig paint traces, 19th C 350.00
Bluebill Hen
    Irving Miller, Monroe, MI, carved wood, glass eyes, orig paint, 11-1/2" l 165.00
    Thomas Chambers, Canada Club, hollow body, glass eyes, old repaint, 15-3/4" l, c1900 .... 550.00
Blue-Wing Teal Drake, Mason Factory, premier grade, replaced eyes 850.00
Brant, Ward Brothers, MD, carved, hollow body, head turned left, sgd "Lem and Steve," dated 1917 .... 1,650.00
Bufflehead Drake
    Bob Kerr, carved detail, glass eyes, orig paint, scratch carved signature, 10-1/2" l, c1980 .... 250.00
    Harry M. Shrouds, carved, hollow body, painted eyes 1,800.00
Canada Goose
    Bill Eminght, Toledo, OH, cork body, wood head and keep, orig paint shot scars, sgd and dated 1968, 24-1/2" l 650.00
Castle Haven, orig paint, branded mark, minor age cracks, 22" l 310.00
Hurley Conklin, carved, hollow body, swimming position, branded "H. Conklin" on bottom 600.00
Canvasback Drake
    Thomas Chambers, Canada Club, Ontario, Canada, hollow body, glass eyes, worn orig paint, 14-1/2" l 600.00
    Miles Smith, Marine City, MI, high head, balsa body, glass eyes, orig paint, 19" l, c1933 .... 200.00
Canvasback Hen
    Charles Bean, carved wood, glass eyes, orig paint, 14-3/4" l 250.00
    Frank Schmidt, orig paint, glass eyes, relief carved wing tips, 16-1/4" l 165.00
Curlew
    A. E. Crowell, hollow carved, orig paint......................... 850.00
    Harry V. Shrouds, orig paint 2,000.00
    William Bowman, Long Island, NY, 1870-90 .... 57,500.00
    William Gibian, carved wings and feathers, head turned back carved neck muscle, sgd on bottom 600.00
Elder Drake, unknown Maine maker, carved bill, inlet neck, chip carved body, turned-up tail, orig paint 700.00
Golden Eye Drake
    A. Elmer Crowell, East Harwich, MA, minor paint wear, miniature, rect stamp, 3" h 630.00
    Stevens Factory, repainted, branded on bottom........... 460.00
Green Wing Teal, matted pair, Robert Weeks.................... 275.00
Heron, unknown maker, carved wig and tail, wrought iron legs 900.00
Herring Gull, Charles Wiber, Highland Heights, NJ, Barnegat Bay style, hollow body, carved splint wing tip, glass eyes, orig paint, 19" l.. 350.00
Mallard Drake
    Ben Schmidt, Detroit, relief carved, feather stamping, glass eyes, orig paint, orig keep, mkd "Mallard drake Benj Schmidt, Detroit 1960," 15-1/4" l 450.00
    Bert Graves, carved, hollow body, orig weighted bottom, branded "E. I. Rogers" and "Cleary" 900.00
    Mason Factory, standard grand, carved wood, glass eyes, orig paint, 15-3/4" l 225.00
Mallard Hen
    Ralph Johnston, Detroit, MI, high head, glass eyes, orig paint mkd "R. D. Johnston orig keel 1948" in pencil, 17-1/2" l 250.00
    Robert Elliston, carved, hollow body, orig paint......... 1,800.00
Merganser Drake
    A. Elmer Crowell, East Harwich, MA, miniature, rect stamp, 2-7/8" h 690.00
    Mason Factory, challenge grade, orig paint 700.00
Merganser Hen
    George Boyd, head turned slightly, feathered paint .. 7,000.00

Top: Golden Eye or Whistler, Joe Wooster, sgd "Good Hunting, Josef Wooster, '70," orig paint, glass eyes, very good detail, 14-1/2" l, $360; middle: Merganser Hen, Joe Wooster, sgd "Good Hunting Joseph 'Buckeye Joe' Wooster," orig paint, glass eyes, very good detail, minor paint separation, 21-1/2" l, $200; bottom: Merganser Drake, Joe Wooster, mate to one above, sgd the same, minor wedge wear, $385. Photo courtesy of Garth's Auctions.

Hurley Conklin, hollow body, carved wing tips, branded "H. Conklin" on bottom 375.00

Pigeon, carved and painted wood, America, late 19th/early 20th C, 12-1/4" l 575.00

Pintail Drake
    Mason Factory, premier grade, sloping breast, orig paint
    ....750.00
    Zeke McDonald, MI, high head, hollow body, glass eyes, orig paint, c1910 ....550.00

Pintail Hen, Mason Factory, premier grade, sloping breast, orig paint, mkd "Big Point Co. Pathcourt, Ont. James S. Meredith, member 1900-1920" 2,400.00

Plover, Joe Lincoln, winter plumage, feather painting, orig paint
    ....800.00

Red Breasted Merganser Drake
    Amos Wallace, ME, inlet neck, carved crest, detailed feathered paint 2,000.00
    George Boyd, NH, carved, orig paint........................8,000.00

Redhead Drake
    R Madison Mitchell, carved wood, orig paint, unused, 13" l
    ....300.00
    Frank Schmidt, Detroit, MI, orig paint, glass eyes, relief carved wing tips, 15-1/2" l 250.00

Robin Snipe, Obediah Verity, carved wings and eyes, orig paint
    ....4,400.00

Ruddy Duck Drake, Len Carmeghi, Mt. Clemens, MI, hollow body, glass eyes, orig paint, sgd and dated, 10-3/4" l .250.00

Sickle Bill Curlew, unknown maker, carved wood, glass eyes, pitchfork tine beak, orig paint, 22" l 150.00

Swan, unknown Chesapeake Bay, MD, maker, carved wood, braced neck, white paint, 30" l; 900.00

Widgeon, matted pair, Charlie Joiner, MD, sgd on bottom
    ....800.00
Yellowlegs, Joe Lincoln, carved wings, split tail, stippled paint, branded "S" on bottom 1,750.00

DEDHAM POTTERY

History: Alexander W. Robertson established a pottery in Chelsea, Massachusetts, about 1866. After his brother, Hugh Cornwall Robertson, joined him in 1868, the firm was called A. W. & H. C. Robertson. Their father, James Robertson, joined his sons in 1872, and the name Chelsea Keramic Art Works Robertson and Sons was used.

Their initial products were simple flower and bean pots, but the firm quickly expanded its output to include a wide variety of artistic pottery. It produced a very fine redware body used in classical forms, some with black backgrounds imitating ancient Greek and Apulian works. The firm experimented with underglaze slip decoration on vases. The Chelsea Keramic Art Works Pottery also produced high-glazed vases, pitchers, and plaques with a buff clay body with either sculpted or molded applied decoration.

James Robertson died in 1880 and Alexander moved to California in 1884 leaving Hugh C. Robertson alone in Chelsea, where his tireless experiments eventually yielded a stunning imitation of the prized Chinese Ming-era blood-red glaze. Hugh's vases with that glaze were marked with an impressed "CKAW." Creating these red-glazed vases was very expensive, and even though they received great critical acclaim, the company declared bankruptcy in 1889.

Recapitalized by a circle of Boston art patrons in 1891, Hugh started the Chelsea Pottery U.S., which produced gray crackle-glazed dinnerware with cobalt blue decorations, the rabbit pattern being the most popular.

The business moved to new facilities in Dedham, Massachusetts, and began production in 1896 under the name Dedham Pottery. Hugh's son and grandson operated the business until it closed in 1943, by which time between 50 and 80 patterns had been produced, some very briefly.

Marks: The following marks help determine the approximate age of items:

"Chelsea Keramic Art Works Robertson and Sons," impressed, 1874-1880
"CKAW," impressed, 1875-1889
"CPUS," impressed in a cloverleaf, 1891-1895
Foreshortened rabbit only, impressed, 1894-1896
Conventional rabbit with "Dedham Pottery" in square blue stamped mark along with one impressed foreshortened rabbit, 1896-1928
Blue rabbit stamped mark with "registered" beneath along with two impressed foreshortened rabbit marks, 1929-1943

References: Lloyd E. Hawes, *Dedham Pottery and the Earlier Robertson's Chelsea Potteries*, Dedham Historical Soc., 1968; Paul Evans, *Art Pottery of the United States*, Feingold & Lewis, 1974; Ralph and Terry Kovel, *Kovels'*

American Art Pottery, Crown Publishers, 1993.

Collectors' Club: Dedham Pottery Collectors Society, 248 Highland St., Dedham, MA 02026.

Museum: Dedham Historical Society, Dedham, MA.

REPRODUCTION ALERT

Two companies make Dedham-like reproductions primarily utilizing the rabbit pattern, but always mark their work very differently from the original.

Advisor: James D. Kaufman.

Bowl, 8-1/2" sq
    Rabbit pattern, reg. stamp 600.00
    Rabbit pattern, reg. stamp, hairline crack 275.00
    Swan pattern, reg. stamp 725.00
Candlesticks, pr
    Elephant pattern, reg. blue stamp................................525.00
    Rabbit pattern, reg. blue stamp 325.00
Creamer and Sugar, type #1, 3-1/4" h, Duck pattern, blue stamp
    ....650.00
Demitasse Cup and Saucer, Rabbit pattern, blue stamp ..320.00
Knife Rest, Rabbit form, blue reg. stamp 575.00
Paperweight, Rabbit form, blue reg. stamp 495.00
Pickle Dish, 10-1/2" l, Elephant pattern, blue reg. stamp ...750.00
Pitcher
    5" h, Rabbit pattern, blue stamp...................................325.00
    5-1/8" h, Chickens pattern, blue stamp 2,300.00
    7" h, Turkey pattern, blue stamp...................................585.00
    9" h, Rabbit pattern, blue stamp...................................700.00
    Style of 1850, blue reg. stamp.....................................975.00
Plate
  6" d
    Clover pattern, reg. stamp...625.00
    Dolphin pattern, blue reg. stamp, chip.....................225.00

Plate, Duck pattern, blue stamp, Maude Davenport's "O" rebus, 8-1/2" d, $375. Photo courtesy of James Kaufman.

  Iris pattern, blue stamp, Maude Davenport's "O" rebus
    ....280.00
    Rabbit pattern, blue stamp 145.00
8" d, Iris pattern, reg. stamp 230.00
8-1/2" d
    Chicken pattern, reg. blue stamp.......................1,450.00
    Crab central design, blue stamp...........................550.00
    Duck pattern, blue stamp, Maude Davenport's "O" rebus
    ....375.00
    Elephant pattern, blue reg. stamp........................650.00
    French Mushroom pattern, blue stamp 1,100.00
    Lobster central design, blue stamp........................575.00
    Magnolia pattern, blue stamp.................................165.00
    Rabbit pattern, blue stamp.....................................170.00
    Rabbit pattern, blue stamp, Maude Davenport's "O" rebus
    ....235.00
    Snow Tree pattern, blue stamp 210.00
    Upside down dolphin, CPUS...................................900.00
10" d
    Clover pattern, blue stamp 825.00
    Dolphin pattern, blue reg. stamp............................875.00
    Elephant pattern, blue reg. stamp..........................900.00
    Elephant pattern, blue reg. stamp, three small rim nicks
    ....450.00
    Pine Apple pattern, CPUS 775.00
    Turkey pattern, blue stamp, Maude Davenport's "O" rebus
    ....475.00
    Turtle pattern, reg. blue stamp 1,125.00
Platter, 14" x 8", oval, steak platter, Rabbit pattern, blue reg. stamp 825.00
Sherbet, two handles, Rabbit pattern, blue stamp.............350.00

Pitcher, Chickens pattern, blue stamp, 5-1/8" h, $2,300. Photo courtesy of James Kaufman.

Plate, Turkey pattern, blue stamp, Maude Davenport's "O" rebus, 10" d. $475. Photo courtesy of James Kaufman.

Tea Cup and Saucer
    Azalea pattern, reg. stamp 130.00
    Butterfly pattern, blue stamp 345.00
    Duck pattern, reg. stamp...190.00
    Iris pattern, reg. stamp 155.00
    Rabbit pattern, reg. stamp 155.00
    Turtle pattern, reg. stamp 680.00
    Water Lily pattern, reg. stamp 130.00
Teapot, 6-1/8" h, Rabbit pattern, blue stamp 875.00

DELFTWARE

History: Delftware is pottery with a soft, red-clay body and tin-enamel glaze. The white, dense, opaque color came from adding tin ash to lead glaze. The first examples had blue designs on a white ground. Polychrome examples followed.

The name originally applied to pottery made in the region around Delft, Holland, beginning in the 16th century and ending in the late 18th century. The tin used came from the Cornish mines in England. By the 17th and 18th centuries English potters in London, Bristol, and Liverpool were copying the glaze and designs. Some designs unique to English potters also developed.

In Germany and France the ware is known as Faience, and in Italy as Majolica.

REPRODUCTION ALERT

Since the late 19th century, much Delft-type souvenir material has been produced to appeal to the foreign traveler. Don't confuse these modern pieces with the older examples.

Bottle, 8-3/4" h, blue and white floral dec, attributed to Lambeth, lip chipped..385.00
Bowl
    7-1/2" d, blue and white, Chinese pavilion in landscape, England, 18th C 325.00
    8-3/4" d, shallow, blue and white, figure of young woman with bough 475.00
    12" d, shallow, blue and white, landscape with figure, edge chips 550.00
    12-1/2" d, 6-1/2" h, blue and white, broken, poorly repaired 1,155.00
Bowl, attached strainer, 8-3/4" d, 3-1/2" h, blue and white floral dec, hairlines and deteriorating old repair 470.00
Charger
    12" d, blue and white, floral rim, landscape, edge chips 200.00
    13" d, floral design, building scene, manganese and blue, edge chips..615.00
    13-1/8" d, blue and white, foliate devices, Dutch, 19th C, chips, glaze wear 410.00
    13-1/4" d, polychrome floral design, blue, red, yellow, green, and black, edge chips..............................880.00
    13-1/4" d, polychrome floral Fazackerly pattern, iron red, yellow, green, and blue, attributed to Liverpool, edge chips 825.00
    13-5/8" d, blue and white, foliate devices, 19th C, chips, glass wear, restoration 320.00
    14" d, polychrome floral dec, tree, edge chips 550.00
    16 1/2" d, center branch with fruiting blossoms, two birds, conforming florals on wide rim, sgd "G. A. Kleynoven," c1655 ....2,250.00

Dish
    8-1/4" d, molded rim, blue and white, stylized landscape and floral design, edge chips..........................315.00
    12-3/8" l, fluted oval, blue and white floral design, attributed to Lambeth, chips..................................440.00
Flower Brick, 4-5/8" l, 2-1/2" h, blue and white, Chinese figures in landscape, Dutch, 18th C, chips, cracks 375.00
Inkwell, 4-1/2" h, heart shape, blue and white floral dec, wear and edge chips..495.00
Jar, 5" h, blue and white, chips, pr.....................................715.00
Model, 17-1/2" h, tall case clock, blue dec white ground, panels of figural and architectural landscapes between scrolled foliate borders, 19th C, slight glaze wear 320.00
Mug, 6-3/8" h, blue and white, armorial surrounded by exotic landscape, palm trees, mkd on base, Dutch, 19th C, minor chips, glaze wear 490.00
Plate
    8-1/2" d, blue and white, floral, pots of flowers and insects, small edge chips, 5 pc set 825.00
    8-5/8" d, blue and white, central reserves of foliate devices, neoclassical urn, Continental, 18th C......................175.00
    8-3/4" d, manganese, iron red, yellow, and underglaze blue floral design, chips 200.00
    9" d, blue and white floral dec, Dutch inscription on front, another on back, edge chips 200.00
    9" d, blue scene, bianco-sopra-bianco border, attributed to Bristol, hairline and chips 200.00
    9" d, polychrome central reserve of basket of flowers, surrounded by foliate border, Dutch, early 19th C, minor chips and cracks, glaze wear, pr.......................................635.00
    9" d, polychrome floral design, manganese, green, iron-red, and blue, edge chips 615.00

Tiles, set of nine in brass frame, blue and white painted picturesque scene, 12-1/" sq, $200. Photo courtesy of Aston Macek Auction.

9" d, polychrome iron red, yellow, and manganese, underglaze blue, Fazackerly design, chips, some touch-up repair to red and yellow 165.00

9" d, polychrome Oriental bridge scene, blue acanthus leaf border, chips 275.00

10-1/4" d, blue and white Bible illustration, small over reserve with bible reference and date "MAT 2:IV.00, 1752," small edge chips..770.00

Posset Pot

4-3/4" h, blue and white, birds among foliage, England, 19th C, minor chips and cracks 920.00

7-1/4" h, blue and white floral dec with bird, attributed to Lambeth, mismatched lid, base hairlines, minor edge chips 1,650.00

Sauce Boat, 8-1/4" l, applied scrolled handles, fluted flaring lip, blue and white Oriental design, edge chips and hairline, later added yellow enamel rim 440.00

Saucer, 8-3/4" d, table ring, blue, iron-red, yellow, and manganese bowl of flowers dec.....................................825.00

Strainer Bowl, 9-1/8" d, blue and white floral design, three short feet, chips..520.00

Tea Caddy, 5-7/8" h, blue and white floral dec, scalloped bottom edge, mkd "MVS 1750," cork closure, wear, edge flakes, old filled in chip on lid..550.00

Tobacco Jar, 10" h, blue and white, Indians and "Siville," older brass stepped lid, chips... 1,870.00

Wall Pocket, 7-3/4" h, blue and white, cornucopia with cherub's head, attributed to Liverpool, small edge chips......... 1,100.00

DEPRESSION GLASS

History: Depression glass was made from 1920 to 1940. It was an inexpensive machine-made glass and produced by several companies in various patterns and colors. The number of forms made in different patterns also varied.

Depression glass was sold through variety stores, given away as premiums, or packaged with certain products. Movie houses gave it away from 1935 until well into the 1940s.

Like pattern glass, knowing the proper name of a pattern is the key to collecting. Collectors should be prepared to do research.

References: Gene Florence, *Collectible Glassware from the 40's, 50's, 60's*, 4th ed., Collector Books, 1997; ——, *Collector's Encyclopedia of Depression Glass*, 13th ed., Collector Books, 1997; ——, *Elegant Glassware of the Depression Era*, 7th ed., Collector Books, 1997; ——, *Pocket Guide to Depression Glass & More, 1920-1960s*, 10th ed., Collector Books, 1996; ——, *Stemware Identification Featuring Cordials with Values, 1920s-1960s*, Collector Books, 1997; ——, *Very Rare Glassware of the Depression Era*, 1st Series (1988, 1991 value update), 2nd Series (1991), 3rd Series (1993), 4th Series (1996), 5th Series (1996), Collector Books; Ralph and Terry Kovel, *Kovels' Depression Glass & American Dinnerware Price List*, 5th ed., Crown, 1995; Carl F. Luckey and Mary Burris, *Identification & Value Guide to Depression Era Glassware*, 3rd ed., Books Americana, 1994; Ellen T. Schroy, *Warman's Depression Glass*, Krause Publications, 1997; Kent G. Washburn, *Price Survey*, 4th ed., published by author, 1994; Hazel Marie Weatherman, *Colored Glassware of the Depression Era*, Book 2, published by author 1974, available in reprint; ——, 1984 *Supplement & Price Trends for Colored Glassware of the Depression Era, Book 1*, published by author, 1984.

Periodical: *The Daze*, P.O. Box 57, Otisville, MI 48463.

Collectors' Clubs: Canadian Depression Glass Club, P.O. Box 104, Mississaugua, Ontario L53 2K1 Canada; National Depression Glass Assoc., Inc., P.O. Box 8264, Wichita, KS 67209; 20-30-40 Society, Inc., P.O. Box 856, LaGrange, IL 60525.

Videotape: *Living Glass: Popular Patterns of the Depression Era*, 2 Vols., Ro Cliff Communications, 1993.

Additional Listings: See *Warman's Americana & Collectibles* for more examples.

REPRODUCTION ALERT

The following is a partial listing of Depression Glass patterns that have been reproduced. When available, the name of the reproduction manufacturer, shapes, and colors are given.

Adam (produced in the Far East and distributed through AA Importing of St. Louis) butter dish, pink.

Avocado (Indiana Glass Company) pitcher and tumbler, in amethyst, blue, green, pink, frosted pink, red, and yellow.

Cherry Blossom (large number of manufacturers and importers) numerous forms including two-handled tray, cup and saucer, and children's set, in blue, cobalt blue, Delphite, green, iridized colors, pink, and red.

Madrid (Indiana Glass Company) goblet, grill plate, shakers, vase, and more, in crystal (clear), blue, pink, and teal.

Mayfair, cookie jars, juice pitchers, shakers, shot glasses, and more, in amethyst, blue, cobalt blue, green, pink, and red.

Miss America, covered butter dish, pitcher, shakers, and tumbler, in cobalt blue, crystal (clear), green, ice blue, pink, and red amberina.

Sharon (privately produced) covered butter in blue, cobalt blue, green (light and dark), opalescent blue, red, and umber (burnt).

Send a self-addressed stamped business envelope to *The Daze* and request a copy of its glass reproduction list. It is one of the best bargains in the antiques business.

AURORA

Manufactured by Hazel Atlas Glass Company, Clarksburg, WV, and Zanesville, OH, in the late 1930s. Made in cobalt (Ritz) blue, crystal, green, and pink.

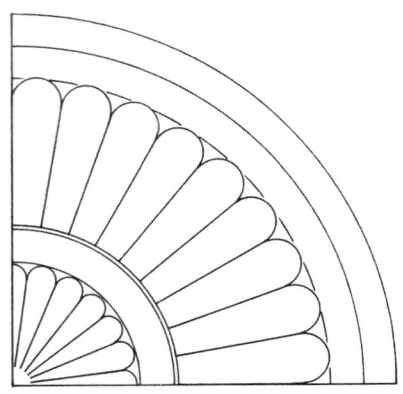

	Cobalt Blue	Crystal	Green	Pink
Bowl, 4-1/2" d	50.00	—	—	50.00
Breakfast Set, 24 pcs, service for 4	488.00	—	—	—
Cereal Bowl, 5-3/8" d.............................	17.50	10.00	7.50	14.00
Cup..	18.00	5.00	9.00	13.50
Milk Pitcher	24.00	—	—	22.00
Plate, 6-1/2" d	12.00	—	—	12.00
Saucer	6.00	2.00	3.00	6.00
Tumbler, 10 oz., 4-3/4" h	22.00	—	—	22.00

BLOCK OPTIC, Block

Manufactured by Hocking Glass Company, Lancaster, OH, from 1929 to 1933. Made in amber, crystal, green, pink, and yellow.

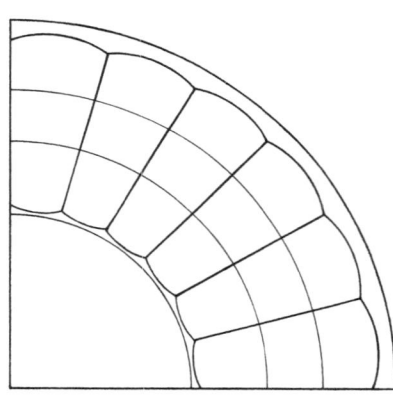

	Crystal	Green	Pink	Yellow
Berry Bowl, 8-1/2" d............................	20.00	35.00	40.00	—
Bowl, 4-1/4" d, 1-3/8" h	4.00	8.00	10.00	—
Bowl, 4-1/2" d, 1-1/2" h	—	28.00	—	—
Butter Dish, cov..................................	—	50.00	—	—
Cake Plate, 10" d, ftd.........................	18.00	—	—	—
Candlesticks, pr, 1-3/4" h	—	100.00	80.00	—
Candy Jar, cov, 2-1/4" h	30.00	60.00	55.00	65.00
Candy Jar, cov, 6-1/4" h	40.00	80.00	60.00	—
Cereal Bowl, 5-1/2" d.........................	—	16.00	27.50	—
Champagne, 4-3/4" h	10.00	27.50	16.50	15.00
Cocktail, 4" h	—	35.00	35.00	—
Comport, 4" wide...............................	—	36.00	70.00	—
Console Bowl, 11-3/4" d, rolled edge	—	70.00	95.00	—
Creamer*	10.00	12.50	18.00	15.00
Cup*	6.00	7.00	6.50	6.50
Goblet, 9 oz., 5-3/4" h........................	10.00	24.00	30.00	
Goblet, 9 oz., 7-1/2" h, thin...............	15.00	—	—	22.00
Ice Bucket	—	40.00	48.00	—
Ice Tub, open	—	48.00		—
Mug	—	35.00		—
Pitcher, 54 oz., 7-5/8" h, bulbous	—	70.00	70.00	—
Pitcher, 54 oz., 8-1/2" h	—	42.00	40.00	—
Pitcher, 80 oz., 8" h	—	88.50	80.00	—

	Crystal	Green	Pink	Yellow
Plate, 6" d, sherbet	1.50	3.50	3.25	3.50
Plate, 8" d, luncheon	3.50	5.50	7.00	8.50
Plate, 9" d, dinner	11.00	27.50	35.00	42.00
Plate, 9" d, dinner, snowflake center	—	16.50	—	—
Plate, 9" d, grill	15.00	27.50	30.00	42.00
Salad Bowl, 7-1/4" d	—	155.00	—	—
Salt and Pepper Shakers, pr, ftd	—	37.50	80.00	80.00
Salt and Pepper Shakers, pr, squatty	—	90.00	—	—
Sandwich Plate, 10-1/4" d	—	27.50	30.00	—
Sandwich Server, center handle	—	65.00	50.00	—
Saucer, 5-3/4" d	—	12.00	10.00	—
Saucer, 6-1/8" d	2.00	8.00	10.00	3.50
Sherbet, cone	—	6.00	5.50	—
Sherbet, 5-1/2 oz., 3-1/4" h	—	6.50	9.50	7.50
Sherbet, 6 oz., 4-3/4" h	7.00	15.50	15.00	16.00
Sugar, cone	—	12.00	9.50	12.00
Sugar, flat	—	10.00	10.00	—
Sugar, round, ftd	10.00	12.00	18.00	—
Tumbler, 3 oz., 2-5/8" h	—	27.50	25.00	—
Tumbler, 3 oz., 3-1/4" h, ftd	—	27.50	25.00	—
Tumbler, 5 oz., 3-1/2" h, flat	—	20.00	17.50	—
Tumbler, 5-3/8" h, ftd	—	—	19.50	18.00
Tumbler, 9" h, ftd	—	—	17.50	22.00
Tumbler, 9-1/2 oz., 3-13/16" h, flat	—	17.50	14.00	—
Tumbler, 10 oz., 6" h, ftd	10.00	—	—	—
Tumbler, 10 or 11 oz., 5" h, flat	—	24.00	22.00	—
Tumbler, 12 oz., 4-7/8" h, flat	—	27.50	24.00	—
Tumbler, 15 oz., 5-1/4" h, flat	—	27.50	24.00	—
Tumble-Up, 3" h tumbler and bottle	—	87.50	75.00	—
Vase, 5-3/4" h, blown	—	285.00	—	—
Whiskey, 1 oz., 1-5/8" h	20.00	40.00	45.00	—
Whiskey, 2 oz., 2-1/4" h	15.00	35.00	30.00	—
Wine, 3-1/2" h	—	415.00	415.00	—
Wine, 4-1/2" h	15.00	35.00	32.00	—

Production in amber was very limited. A 11-3/4" d console bowl is valued at $50, while a pair of matching 1-3/4" h candlesticks are valued at $110.00.
*There are five styles of creamers and four styles of cups, each have a relative value.

DEWDROP

Manufactured by Jeannette Glass Company, Jeannette, PA, from 1953 to 1956. Made in crystal.

	Crystal
Bowl, 4-3/4" d	7.00
Bowl, 8-1/2" d	20.00
Bowl, 10-3/8" d	20.00
Butter, cov	30.00
Candy Dish, cov, 7" d	24.00
Casserole, cov	24.00
Creamer	8.50
Iced Tea Tumbler, 15 oz.	17.50

	Crystal
Lazy Susan, 13" d tray	29.00
Pitcher, 1/2 gallon, ftd	48.00
Plate, 11-1/2" d	20.00
Punch Cup	4.00
Punch Bowl Set, bowl, 12 cups	65.00
Snack Cup	4.00
Snack Plate, indent for cup	5.00
Relish, leaf-shape, handle	9.00
Sugar, cov	14.00
Tumbler, 9 oz.	15.00

DOGWOOD, Apple Blossom, Wild Rose

Manufactured by Mac Beth Evans Company, Charleroi, PA, from 1929 to 1932. Made in Cremax, crystal, green, Monax, pink, and yellow.

	Cremax or Monax	Green	Pink
Berry Bowl, 8-1/2" d	40.00	100.00	65.00
Cake Plate, 11" d, heavy solid foot	—	—	650.00
Cake Plate, 13" d, heavy solid foot	185.00	130.00	165.00
Cereal Bowl, 5-1/2" d	6.00	32.00	32.00
Coaster, 3-1/4" d	—	—	500.00
Creamer, 2-1/2" h, thin	—	48.00	18.00
Creamer, 3-1/4" h, thick	—	—	17.50
Cup, thin	—	32.00	14.00
Cup, thick	36.00	40.00	25.00
Fruit Bowl, 10-1/4" d	100.00	250.00	435.00
Pitcher, 8" h, 80 oz., (American Sweetheart style)	—	—	420.00
Pitcher, 8" h, 80 oz., decorated	—	500.00	265.00
Plate, 6" d, bread & butter	22.00	10.00	9.50
Plate, 8" d, luncheon	—	9.00	9.00

	Cremax or Monax	Green	Pink
Plate, 9-1/4" d, dinner	—	—	38.00
Plates, 10-1/2" d, grill, AOP or border design only	—	20.00	20.00
Platter, 12" d, oval.............................	—	—	500.00
Salver, 12" d.....................................	20.00	—	35.00
Saucer	20.00	10.00	7.00
Sherbet, low, ftd...............................	—	95.00	40.00
Sugar, 2-1/2" h, thin	—	50.00	18.00
Sugar, 3-1/4" h, thick, ftd	—	—	18.50
Tidbit, 2 tier	—	—	88.00
Tumbler, 10 oz., 4" h, decorated	—	85.00	53.00
Tumbler, 11 oz., 4-3/4" h, decorated	—	95.00	75.00
Tumbler, 12 oz., 5" h, decorated	—	100.00	65.00
Tumbler, moulded band	—	—	25.00

Yellow is rare, a cereal bowl is known and valued at $85.00. Crystal items are valued at 50% less than green.

ENGLISH HOBNAIL, Line #555

Manufactured by Westmoreland Glass Company, Grapeville, PA, from the 1920s to 1983. Made in amber, cobalt blue, crystal, crystal with various color treatments, green, ice blue, pink, red, and turquoise blue.

	Amber	Crystal	Green	Ice Blue	Pink
Ashtray, 3" d	20.00	20.00	22.00	—	22.00
Ashtray, 4-1/2" d	9.00	9.00	15.00	24.00	15.00
Ashtray, 4-1/2" sq	9.50	9.50	15.00	—	15.00
Basket, 6" d, handle, tall............................	36.00	36.00	—	—	43.00
Bonbon, 6-1/2" h, handle	15.00	16.00	27.50	38.00	27.50
Bowl, 7" d, 6 part	17.50	17.50	—	—	—
Bowl, 8" d, ftd	28.00	28.00	48.00	—	48.00
Bowl, 8" d, hexagonal foot, 2 handles	38.00	38.00	75.00	115.00	75.00
Bowl, 9-1/2" d, round, crimped	30.00	30.00	—	—	—
Bowl, 10" d, flared	30.00	30.00	40.00	—	40.00
Bowl, 10" l, oval, crimped	35.00	35.00	—	—	—
Bowl, 11" d, rolled edge	35.00	35.00	40.00	85.00	40.00

	Amber	Crystal	Green	Ice Blue	Pink
Bowl, 12" d, flared	32.00	32.00	40.00	—	95.00
Bowl,12" l, oval crimped	32.00	32.00	—	—	—
Candelabra, 2 lite	18.00	18.00	—	—	—
Candlesticks, pr, 3-1/2" h, round base	18.00	32.00	36.00	—	60.00
Candlesticks, pr, 5-1/2" h, sq base	30.00	32.00	—	—	—
Candlesticks, pr, 9" h, round base	50.00	36.00	72.00	—	125.00
Candy Dish, 3 foot	35.00	38.00	50.00	—	50.00
Candy Dish, cov, 1/2 lb, cone shape	35.00	40.00	55.00	—	90.00
Celery, 12" l, oval	24.00	45.00	36.00	—	36.00
Celery, 9" d	18.00	20.00	32.00	—	32.00
Champagne, two ball, round foot	8.00	7.00	20.00	—	20.00
Chandelier, 17" shade, 200 prisms	425.00	400.00	—	—	—
Cheese, cov, 6" d	40.00	42.00	—	—	—
Cheese, cov, 8-3/4" d	50.00	48.00	—	—	—
Cigarette Box, cov, 4-1/2" x 2-1/2"	24.50	24.50	30.00	—	55.00
Cigarette Jar, cov, round	16.00	18.00	25.00	—	65.00
Claret, 5 oz., round	15.00	17.50	—	—	—
Coaster, 3"	5.00	5.00	—	—	—
Cocktail, 3 oz., round	8.50	12.00	—	—	37.50
Cocktail, 3-1/2 oz., round, ball	15.00	17.50	—	—	—
Compote, 5" d, round, round foot	22.00	20.00	25.00	—	25.00
Compote, 5" d, round, sq foot	24.00	24.00	—	—	—
Compote, 5-1/2" d, bell	12.00	15.00	—	—	—
Compote, 5-1/2" d, bell, sq foot	20.00	20.00	—	—	—
Console Bowl, 12" d, flange	30.00	30.00	40.00	—	40.00
Cordial, 1 oz., round, ball	15.00	15.00	—	—	—
Cordial, 1 oz., round, foot	15.00	15.00	—	—	—
Cream Soup Bowl	12.00	12.00	—	—	—
Cream Soup Liner, round	5.00	5.00	—	—	—
Creamer, hexagonal foot	20.00	20.00	25.00	—	48.00
Creamer, low, flat	10.00	10.00	—	—	—
Creamer, sq foot	24.00	24.00	45.00	—	45.00
Cruet, 12 oz.	—	25.00	—	—	—
Cup	6.50	6.50	18.00	—	25.00
Decanter, 20 oz.	55.00	55.00	—	—	—
Demitasse Cup	17.50	17.50	55.00	—	55.00
Dish, 6" d, crimped	15.00	15.00	—	—	—
Egg Cup	10.00	10.00	—	—	—
Finger Bowl, 4-1/2" d	7.00	7.00	15.00	35.00	15.00
Finger Bowl, 4-1/2" sq, foot	8.50	8.50	18.00	40.00	18.00
Finger Bowl Liner, 6" sq	6.00	6.00	20.00	—	20.00
Finger Bowl Liner, 6-1/2" d, round	12.00	12.00	10.00	—	10.00
Ginger Ale Tumbler, 5 oz., flat	10.00	10.00	18.00	—	20.00
Ginger Ale Tumbler, 5 oz., sq foot	8.00	8.00	32.00	—	35.00
Goblet, 8 oz., 6-1/4" h, round, water	11.00	11.00	—	50.00	35.00
Goblet, 8 oz., sq foot, water	9.00	9.00	—	—	50.00

	Amber	Crystal	Green	Ice Blue	Pink
Grapefruit Bowl, 6-1/2" d	12.00	12.00	22.00	—	24.00
Hat	15.00	15.00	—	—	—
Honey Compote, 6" d, round foot	18.00	18.00	35.00	—	35.00
Ice Tub, 4" h	18.00	18.00	50.00	—	85.00
Ice Tub, 5-1/2" h	36.00	36.00	65.00	—	100.00
Iced Tea Tumbler, 10 oz.	14.00	14.00	30.00	—	30.00
Iced Tea Tumbler, 12 oz., flat	14.00	14.00	32.00	—	32.00
Icer, sq base, patterned insert	45.00	45.00	—	—	—
Ivy Bowl, 6-1/2" d, sq foot, crimp top	35.00	35.00	—	—	—
Juice Tumbler, 7 oz., round foot	7.50	7.50	—	—	—
Juice Tumbler, 7 oz., sq foot	6.50	6.50	—	—	—
Lamp Shade, 17" d	17500	165.00	—	—	—
Lamp, 9-1/2" d, electric	45.00	45.00	115.00	—	115.00
Lamp, candlestick	32.00	32.00	—	—	—
Marmalade, cov	40.00	40.00	45.00	—	70.00
Mayonnaise, 6"	12.00	12.00	22.00	—	22.00
Mustard, cov, sq, foot	18.00	18.00	—	—	—
Nappy, 4-1/2" d, round	8.00	8.00	15.00	30.00	15.00
Nappy, 5" d, round	10.00	10.00	15.00	35.00	15.00
Nappy, 6" d, round	10.00	10.00	17.50	—	17.50
Nappy, 6" d, sq	10.00	10.00	17.50	—	17.50
Nappy, 6-1/2" d, round	12.50	12.50	20.00	—	20.00
Nappy, 7" d, round	14.00	14.00	24.00	—	24.00
Nappy, 8" d, cupped	22.00	22.00	30.00	—	30.00
Nappy, 8" d, round	22.00	22.00	35.00	—	35.00
Nut, individual, ftd	6.00	6.00	14.50	—	14.50
Old Fashioned Tumbler, 5 oz.	12.00	12.00	—	—	—
Oyster Cocktail, 5 oz., sq foot	10.00	10.00	17.50	—	17.50
Parfait, round foot	15.00	15.00	—	—	—
Pickle, 8" d	15.00	15.00	—	—	—
Pitcher, 23 oz., rounded	48.00	48.00	150.00	—	165.00
Pitcher, 32 oz., straight side	50.00	50.00	175.00	—	175.00
Pitcher, 38 oz., rounded	62.00	62.00	215.00	—	215.00
Pitcher, 60 oz., rounded	65.00	65.00	295.00	—	295.00
Pitcher, 64 oz, straight side	7500	72.00	310.00	—	310.00
Plate, 5-1/2" d, round	7.00	7.00	10.00	—	10.00
Plate, 6" w, sq	5.00	5.00	—	—	—
Plate, 6-1/2" d, round	6.25	6.25	10.00	—	10.00
Plate, 6-1/2" d, round, depressed center	6.00	6.00	—	—	—
Plate, 8" d, round	9.00	9.00	14.00	—	14.00
Plate, 8" d, round, ftd	13.00	13.00	—	—	—
Plate, 8-1/2" d, plain edge	9.00	9.00	—	—	—
Plate, 8-1/2" d, round	7.00	9.00	17.50	—	28.00
Plate, 8-3/4" w, sq	9.25	9.25	—	—	—
Plate, 10" d, round	14.00	14.00	45.00	—	65.00

	Amber	Crystal	Green	Ice Blue	Pink
Plate, 10" w, sq	14.00	14.00	—	—	—
Plate, 10-1/2" d, round, grill	15.00	15.00	—	—	—
Preserve, 8" d	15.00	15.00	—	—	—
Puff Box, cov, 6" d, round	20.00	20.00	47.50	—	80.00
Punch Bowl and Stand	215.00	215.00	—	—	—
Punch Cup	7.00	7.00	—	—	—
Relish, 8" d, 3 part	18.00	18.00	—	—	—
Rose Bowl, 4" d	17.50	17.50	48.00	—	50.00
Rose Bowl, 6" d	20.00	20.00	—	—	—
Salt and Pepper Shakers, pr, round foot	24.00	24.00	150.00	—	165.00
Salt and Pepper Shakers, pr, sq, foot	10.00	10.00	—	—	—
Saucer, Demitasse, round	10.00	10.00	15.00	—	17.50
Saucer, Demitasse, sq	10.00	10.00	—	—	—
Saucer, round	2.00	2.00	6.00	—	6.00
Saucer, sq	2.00	2.00	—	—	—
Sherbet, high, round foot	7.00	7.00	18.00	—	37.50
Sherbet, high, sq foot	8.00	8.00	18.00	—	—
Sherbet, high, two ball, round foot	10.00	10.00	—	—	—
Sherbet, low, one ball, round foot	9.00	8.25	—	—	15.00
Sherbet, low, round foot	12.50	7.00	—	—	—
Sherbet, low, sq foot	6.50	6.00	15.00	—	17.50
Straw Jar, 10" h	60.00	58.00	—	—	—
Sundae	9.00	9.00	—	—	—
Sugar, hexagonal, ftd	9.00	9.00	25.00	—	48.00
Sugar, low, flat	8.00	8.00	—	—	—
Sugar, sq foot	9.00	9.00	48.00	—	55.00
Sweetmeat, 5-1/2" d, ball stem	28.00	28.00	—	—	—
Sweetmeat, 8" d, ball stem	39.00	39.00	60.00	—	65.00
Tidbit, 2 tier	26.00	26.00	65.00	85.00	80.00
Toilet Bottle, 5 oz.	24.00	24.00	40.00	65.00	40.00
Torte Plate, 14" d, round	35.00	30.00	48.00	—	48.00
Torte Plate, 20-1/2" round	55.00	50.00	—	—	—
Tumbler, 8 oz., water	10.00	10.00	24.00	—	24.00
Tumbler, 9 oz., round, ball, water	10.00	10.00	—	—	—
Tumbler, 9 oz., round or sq, ftd water	10.00	10.00	—	—	—
Urn, cov, 11" h	35.00	35.00	350.00	—	350.00
Vase, 6-1/2" h, sq foot	24.00	24.00	—	—	—
Vase, 7-1/2" h, flip	27.50	27.50	70.00	—	70.00
Vase, 7-1/2" h, flip jar with cov	55.00	55.00	85.00	—	85.00
Vase, 8-1/2" h, flared top	40.00	40.00	120.00	—	235.00
Wine, 2 oz., round foot	13.00	13.00	—	—	—
Wine, 2 oz., sq ft	15.00	15.00	35.00	—	65.00

Values for cobalt blue, red, or turquoise blue pieces would be approximately 25% higher than ice blue values. Crystal pieces with a color accent would be slightly higher than crystal values.

FLORAGOLD, Louisa

Manufactured by Jeannette Glass Company, Jeannette, PA, 1950s. Made in iridescent. Some large comports were later made in ice blue, crystal, red-yellow, and shell pink.

	Iridescent
Ashtray, 4" d	10.00
Bowl, 4-1/2" sq	6.50
Bowl, 5-1/4" d, ruffled	16.00
Bowl, 8-1/2" d, sq	8.00
Bowl, 8-1/2" d, ruffled	12.00
Butter Dish, cov, 1/4 pound, oblong	24.00
Butter Dish, cov, round, 5-1/2" sq base	675.00
Candlesticks, pr, double branch	50.00
Candy Dish, 1 handle	15.00
Candy or Cheese Dish, cov, 6-3/4" d	110.00
Candy, 5-3/4" l, 4 feet	7.50
Celery Vase	395.00
Cereal Bowl, 5-1/2" d, round	35.00
Coaster, 4" d	10.00
Comport, 5-1/4", plain top	595.00
Comport, 5-1/4", ruffled top	695.00
Creamer	10.00
Cup	5.00
Fruit Bowl, 5-1/2" d, ruffled	8.50

	Iridescent
Fruits Bowl, 12" d, ruffled, large	8.00
Nappy, 5" d, one handle	11.00
Pitcher, 64 oz.	40.00
Plate, 5-1/4" d, sherbet	15.00
Plate, 8-1/2" d, dinner	35.00
Platter, 11-1/4" d	22.00
Salad Bowl, 9-1/2" d, deep	42.50
Salt and Pepper Shakers, pr, plastic tops	35.00
Saucer, 5-1/4" d	12.00
Sherbet, low, ftd	16.00
Sugar	15.00
Sugar Lid	15.00
Tidbit, wooden post	35.00
Tray, 13-1/2" d	22.50
Tray, 13-1/2" d, with indent	45.00
Tumbler, 11 oz. ftd	18.00
Tumbler, 10 oz. ftd	18.00
Tumbler, 15 oz. ftd	110.00
Vase	395.00

FLOWER GARDEN WITH BUTTERFLIES, Butterflies and Roses

Manufactured by U.S. Glass Company, Pittsburgh, PA, late 1920s. Made in amber, black, blue, blue-green, canary yellow, crystal, green, and pink.

	Amber or Crystal	Black	Blue-Green or Green or Pink	Blue or Canary Yellow
Ashtray	175.00	—	185.00	195.00
Bonbon, cov, 6-5/8" d	—	265.00	—	—
Bowl, 9" d, rolled edge	—	225.00	—	—
Candlesticks, pr, 4" h	50.00	—	60.00	100.00
Candlesticks, pr, 8" h	80.00	285.00	145.00	145.00
Candy, cov, 6" d, flat	135.00	—	165.00	—
Candy, cov, 7-1/2" cone shape	90.00	100.00	165.00	175.00
Candy, cov, heart shape	—	—	1,750.00	3,200.00
Cologne Bottle, 7-1/2" h	—	—	195.00	352.00
Comport, 2-7/8" h	—	250.00	40.00	45.00
Comport, 3" h	25.00	—	30.00	35.00
Comport, 4-1/4" h, 4-3/4" w	—	—	—	65.00
Comport, 4-3/4" h, 10-1/4" w	50.00	250.00	70.00	90.00
Comport, 5-7/8" h, 11" w	60.00	—	—	95.00
Comport, 7-1/4" h, 8-1/4" w	65.00	175.00	85.00	—
Creamer	—	—	75.00	—
Cup	—	—	70.00	—
Mayonnaise, ftd, 4-3/4" h, 6-1/4" w, 7" d plate, ladle	70.00	—	85.00	125.00
Orange Bowl, 11" d, ftd	—	250.00	—	—
Plate, 7" d	20.00	—	25.00	30.00
Plate, 8" d	17.50	—	20.00	27.50
Plate, 10" d	—	—	45.00	50.00
Plate, 10" d, indent	35.00	150.00	45.00	50.00
Powder Jar, 3-1/2", flat	—	—	75.00	—
Powder Jar, 6-1/4" h, ftd	80.00	—	130.00	175.00
Powder Jar, 7-1/2" h, ftd	85.00	—	135.00	195.00
Sandwich Server, center handle	55.00	135.00	75.00	100.00
Saucer	—	—	30.00	—
Tray, 5-1/2 x 10", oval	50.00	—	75.00	9.00
Tray, 11-3/4 x 7-3/4", rect	50.00	—	75.00	90.00
Tumbler, 7-1/2 oz	175.00	—	—	—
Vase, 6-1/4" h	75.00	145.00	135.00	145.00
Vase, 8" h, Dahlia, cupped	—	225.00	—	—
Vase, 10" h, 2 handles	—	245.00	—	—
Vase, 10-1/2" h	—	—	140.00	225.00
Wall Pocket, 9" l	—	350.00	—	—

GEORGIAN, Lovebirds

Manufactured by Federal Glass Company, Columbus, OH, from 1931 to 1936. Made in green.

	Green
Berry Bowl, 4-1/2" d.............................	7.00
Berry Bowl, 7-1/2" d, large.....................	62.00
Bowl, 6-1/2" d, deep.............................	65.00
Butter Dish, cov..................................	80.00
Cereal Bowl, 5-3/4" d...........................	26.00
Cold Cuts Server, 18-1/2" d, wood, seven openings for 5" d coasters......	825.00
Creamer, 3" d, ftd................................	15.00
Creamer, 4" d, ftd................................	15.00
Cup..	6.50
Cup and Saucer..................................	12.75
Hot Plate, 5" d, center design	48.00
Plate, 6" d, sherbet..............................	6.50

	Green
Plate, 8" d, luncheon	10.00
Plate, 9-1/4" d, center design only	25.00
Plate, 9-1/4" d, dinner...........................	30.00
Platter, 11-1/2" l, closed handle..............	70.00
Saucer	3.50
Sherbet, ftd..	16.00
Sugar Cover, 3" d	35.00
Sugar Cover, 4" d	35.00
Sugar, 3" d, ftd	15.00
Sugar, 4" d, ftd	15.00
Tumbler, 9 oz. 4" h, flat..........................	60.00
Tumbler 12 oz., 5-1/4" h, flat	135.00
Vegetable Bowl, 9" l, oval......................	65.00

A crystal hot plate is valued at $25.00.

HERITAGE

Manufactured by Federal Glass Company, Columbus, OH, from 1940 to 1955. Made in blue, crystal, green, and pink.

	Blue	Crystal	Green	Pink
Berry Bowl, 5" d	55.00	8.00	50.00	42.00
Berry Bowl, 8-1/2" d..................	190.00	45.00	190.00	115.00
Creamer, ftd	—	30.00	—	—
Cup..	—	7.00	—	—
Fruit Bowl, 10-1/2" d	—	15.00	—	—
Plate, 8" d, luncheon................	—	8.50	—	—
Plate, 9-1/4" d, dinner	—	12.00	—	—
Sandwich Plate, 12" d..............	—	15.00	—	—
Saucer	—	4.00	—	—
Sugar, open, ftd........................	—	22.00	—	—

HOBNAIL

Manufactured by Hocking Glass Company, Lancaster, OH, from 1934 to 1936. Made in crystal, crystal with red trim, and pink.

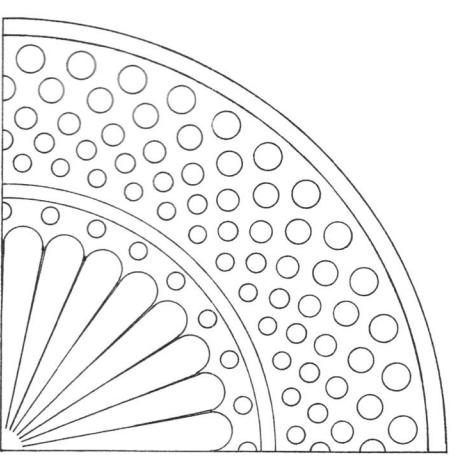

	Crystal	Crystal, red trim	Pink
Cereal Bowl, 5-1/2" d	4.25	4.25	—
Cordial, 5 oz., ftd	6.00	6.00	—
Creamer, ftd	4.00	4.00	—
Cup	4.00	4.00	5.00
Decanter and stopper, 32 oz.	27.50	27.50	—
Goblet, 10 oz.	7.50	7.50	—
Iced Tea Goblet, 13 oz.	8.50	8.50	—
Iced Tea Tumbler, 15 oz.	8.50	8.50	—
Juice Tumbler, 5 oz.	4.00	4.00	—
Milk Pitcher, 18 oz.	22.00	22.00	—
Pitcher, 67 oz.	25.00	25.00	—
Plate, 6" d, sherbet	2.00	2.00	3.00
Plate, 8-1/2" d, luncheon	5.50	5.50	4.50
Salad Bowl, 7" d	5.00	5.00	—
Saucer	2.00	2.00	3.00
Sherbet	4.00	4.00	5.00
Sugar, ftd	4.00	4.00	—
Tumbler, 9 oz., 4-3/4" h, flat	5.00	5.00	—
Whiskey, 1-1/2 oz.	5.00	5.00	—
Wine, 3 oz., ftd	6.50	6.50	—

HOMESPUN, Fine Rib

Manufactured by Jeannette Glass Company, Jeannette, PA, from 1939 to 1949. Made in crystal and pink.

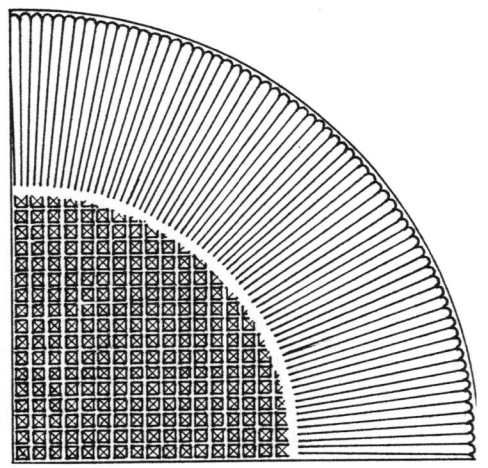

	Crystal	Pink
Ashtray	6.00	6.00
Berry Bowl, 4-1/2" d, closed handles	12.00	13.00
Berry Bowl, 8-1/4" d	20.00	20.00
Butter Dish, cov	50.00	55.00

	Crystal	Pink
Cereal Bowl, 5" d, closed handles	25.00	25.00
Coaster	6.00	6.00
Creamer, ftd	12.50	12.50
Cup	12.00	12.00
Iced Tea Tumbler, 13 oz., 5-1/4" h	32.00	32.00
Plate, 6" d, sherbet	7.50	7.50
Plate, 9-1/4" d, dinner	17.00	17.00
Platter, 13" d, closed handles	18.00	18.00
Saucer	5.50	5.50
Sherbet, low, flat	17.50	19.00
Sugar, ftd	12.50	12.50
Tumbler, 5 oz., 4" h, ftd	8.00	8.00
Tumbler, 6 oz., 3-7/8" h, straight	7.00	7.00
Tumbler, 9 oz., 4" h, flared top	17.50	17.50
Tumbler, 9 oz., 4-1/4" h, band at top	17.50	17.50
Tumbler, 15 oz., 6-1/4" h, ftd	38.00	38.00
Tumbler, 15 oz., 6-3/8" h, ftd	36.00	36.00

JUBILEE

Manufactured by Lancaster Glass Company, Lancaster, OH, early 1930s. Made in pink and yellow.

	Pink	Yellow
Bowl, 8" d, 5-1/8" h, 3 legs	265.00	215.00
Bowl, 11-1/2" d, 3 legs	250.00	250.00
Bowl, 11-1/2" d, 3 legs, curved in	—	250.00
Bowl, 13" d, 3 legs	250.00	235.00
Cake Tray, 11" d, 2 handles	75.00	85.00
Candlesticks, pr	190.00	190.00
Candy Jar, cov, 3 legs	325.00	325.00
Cheese and Cracker Set	265.00	255.00
Cordial, 1 oz., 4" h	—	245.00
Creamer	45.00	30.00
Cup	40.00	15.00
Fruit Bowl, 9" d, handle	—	125.00
Fruit Bowl, 11-1/2" h, flat	200.00	165.00
Goblet, 3 oz., 4-7/8" h	—	150.00
Goblet, 11 oz., 7-1/2" h	—	75.00
Iced Tea Tumbler, 12-1/2 oz., 6 1/8" h	—	135.00
Juice Tumbler, 6 oz., 5" h, ftd	—	100.00
Mayonnaise, plate, orig ladle	315.00	285.00
Mayonnaise Underplate	125.00	110.00
Plate, 7" d, salad	25.00	14.00
Plate, 8-3/4" d, luncheon	30.00	16.50
Plate, 14" d, 3 legs	—	210.00
Sandwich Plate, 13-1/2" d	95.00	65.00
Sandwich Tray, 11" d, center handle	200.00	250.00
Saucer	15.00	8.00
Sherbet, 8 oz., 3" h	—	75.00
Sherbet/Champagne, 7 oz., 5-1/2" h	—	75.00
Sugar	40.00	24.00
Tumbler, 10 oz., 6" h, ftd	75.00	50.00
Vase, 12" h	—	365.00

LACED EDGE, Katy Blue

Manufactured by Imperial Glass Company, Bellaire, OH, early 1930s. Made in blue and green with opalescent edges.

	Blue	Green
Bowl, 5" d	40.00	40.00
Bowl, 5-1/2" d	37.50	37.50
Bowl, 5-7/8" d	40.00	40.00
Bowl, 11" l, oval	285.00	285.00
Bowl, 11" l, oval, divided	130.00	130.00
Candlesticks, pr, double lite	165.00	180.00
Creamer	45.00	40.00
Cup	35.00	35.00
Fruit Bowl, 4-1/2" d	32.00	30.00
Mayonnaise, 3 piece	100.00	125.00

	Blue	Green
Plate, 6-1/2" d, bread and butter	20.00	20.00
Plate, 8" d, salad	32.00	32.00
Plate, 10" d, dinner	90.00	85.00
Plate, 12" d, luncheon	85.00	80.00
Platter, 13" l	165.00	150.00
Saucer	18.00	15.00
Soup Bowl, 7" d	85.00	80.00
Sugar	45.00	40.00
Tidbit, 2 tiers, 8 and 10" plates	110.00	100.00
Tumbler, 9 oz.	60.00	60.00
Vegetable Bowl, 9" d	95.00	95.00

MODERNTONE

Manufactured by Hazel Atlas Glass Company, Clarksburg, WV, and Zanesville, OH, from 1934 to 1942, later in the late 1940s to early 1950s. Made in amethyst, cobalt blue, crystal, pink, and Platonite fired-on colors. Later period production saw plain white, as well as white with blue or red stripes, a Willow-type design in blue or red on white.

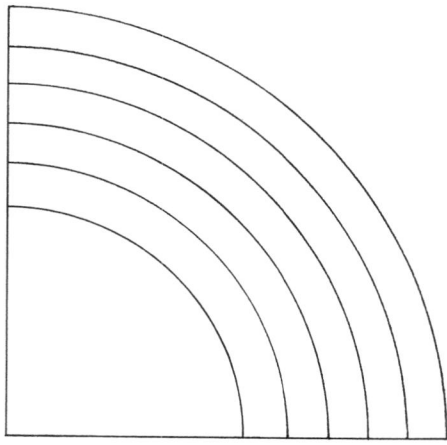

	Amethyst	Cobalt Blue	Platonite, Darker Shades	Platonite, Pastel Shades	White or White with Dec	Willow-Type Dec
Ashtray, 7-3/4" d, match holder center	—	165.00	—	—	—	—
Berry Bowl, 5" d, rim...................................	22.00	26.00	—	4.00	4.00	14.00
Berry Bowl, 5" d, without rim	—	—	12.50	25.00	—	—
Berry Bowl, 8-3/4" d...................................	42.00	45.00	—	—	7.50	28.00
Bowl, 8" d, no rim	—	—	36.00	50.00	—	—
Bowl, 8" d, rim	—	—	—	15.00	6.00	28.00
Butter Dish, metal cov	—	98.00	—	—	—	—
Cereal Bowl, 5" d, deep, no white	—	—	16.00	8.00	—	—
Cereal Bowl, 5" d, deep, with white............	—	—	—	9.00	4.50	—
Cereal Bowl, 6-1/2" d.................................	70.00	70.00	—	—	—	—
Cheese Dish, 7" d, metal cov	—	460.00	—	—	—	—
Cream Soup, 4-3/4" d..................................	19.00	22.00	—	6.50	5.00	22.00
Cream Soup, 5" d, ruffled...........................	30.00	48.00	—	—	—	—
Creamer	18.00	12.00	12.00	5.50	4.50	20.00
Cup..	9.00	16.00	9.00	4.00	2.50	22.00
Custard Cup...	15.00	18.00	—	—	—	—
Mug, 4" h, 8 oz.	—	—	—	—	8.50	—
Mustard, metal lid.......................................	—	25.00	—	—	—	—
Plate, 5-7/8" d, sherbet..............................	9.00	6.50	—	—	—	—
Plate, 6-3/4" d, salad	10.00	12.00	9.00	5.00	3.00	8.50
Plate, 7-3/4" d, luncheon	10.00	15.00	—	—	—	—
Plate, 8-7/8" d, dinner	12.00	19.00	15.00	7.00	4.00	20.00
Platter, 11" l, oval.......................................	40.00	45.00	—	—	14.00	30.00
Platter, 12" l, oval.......................................	48.00	72.00	32.00	15.00	10.00	35.00
Salt and Pepper Shakers, pr	37.50	42.50	—	10.00	12.00	—
Sandwich Plate, 10-1/2" d	18.00	60.00	—	17.50	8.50	—
Saucer..	4.50	5.00	7.50	1.00	1.50	4.50
Sherbet...	11.00	13.00	10.00	6.00	2.50	12.00
Soup Bowl, 7-1/2" d....................................	95.00	135.00	—	—	—	—
Sugar..	18.00	12.00	12.00	6.00	4.50	20.00
Tumbler, 5 oz.	30.00	50.00	—	—	—	—
Tumbler, 9 oz.	27.50	37.50	24.00	9.00	—	—
Tumbler, 12 oz.	85.00	95.00	—	—	—	—
Tumbler, cone, ftd	—	—	—	—	4.00	—
Whiskey, 1-1/2 oz.	—	42.50	—	10.00	—	—

Collector interest in crystal is limited and prices remain low, less than 50% of platonite.

NORMANDIE, Bouquet and Lattice

Manufactured by Federal Glass Company, Columbus, OH, from 1933 to 1940. Made in amber, crystal, iridescent, and pink.

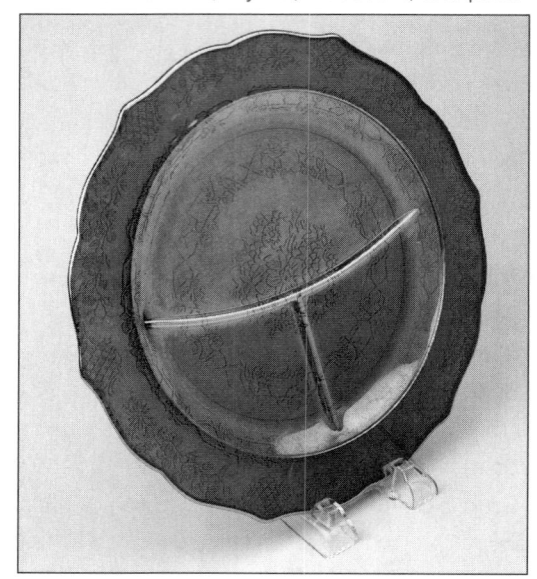

	Amber	Crystal	Iridescent	Pink
Berry Bowl, 5" d	5.00	4.00	5.00	11.00
Berry Bowl, 8-1/2" d	17.50	12.00	15.00	42.00
Cereal Bowl, 6-1/2" d	25.00	15.00	8.00	30.00
Creamer, ftd	16.00	6.00	4.00	12.00
Cup	7.50	3.50	5.50	8.50
Iced Tea Tumbler, 12 oz., 5" h	50.00	—	—	—
Juice Tumbler, 5 oz., 4" h	38.00	—	—	—
Pitcher, 80 oz., 8" h	89.00	—	—	245.00
Plate, 6" d, sherbet	4.50	2.00	3.00	5.00
Plate, 7-3/4" d, salad	10.00	5.00	55.00	14.00
Plate, 9-1/4" d, luncheon	12.50	6.00	16.50	100.00
Plate, 11" d, dinner	32.00	15.00	10.00	18.00
Plate, 11" d, grill	15.00	8.00	8.00	25.00
Platter, 11-3/4" l	24.00	10.00	12.00	80.00
Salt and Pepper Shakers, pr	50.00	20.00	—	4.00
Saucer	4.00	1.50	3.50	10.00
Sherbet	7.50	5.00	9.00	8.00
Sugar	8.00	6.00	7.00	12.00
Tumbler, 9 oz., 4-1/4" h	25.00	10.00	—	50.00
Vegetable Bowl, 10" l, oval	20.00	10.00	18.50	36.00

PATRICK

Manufactured by Lancaster Glass Company, Lancaster, OH, early 1930s.
Made in pink and yellow.

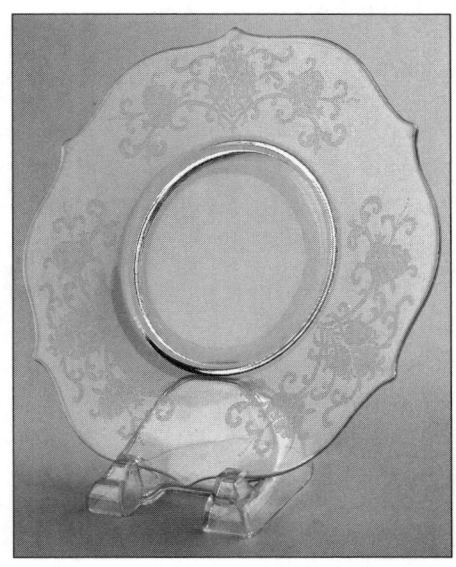

	Pink	Yellow		Pink	Yellow
Candlesticks, pr	150.00	160.00	Juice Goblet, 6 oz., 4-3/4" h	95.00	75.00
Candy Dish, 3 ftd	155.00	165.00	Mayonnaise, 3 piece	185.00	80.00
Cheese and Cracker Set	150.00	130.00	Plate, 7" d, sherbet	20.00	15.00
Cocktail, 4" h	85.00	85.00	Plate, 7-1/2" d, salad	25.00	20.00
Console Bowl, 11" d	150.00	150.00	Plate, 8" d, luncheon	45.00	30.00
Creamer	75.00	40.00	Saucer	20.00	12.00
Cup	70.00	40.00	Sherbet, 4-3/4" d	65.00	40.00
Fruit Bowl, 9" d, handle	172.00	120.00	Sugar	75.00	38.00
Goblet, 10 oz., 6" h	100.00	75.00	Tray, 11" d, center handle	85.00	95.00
			Tray, 11" d, two handles	145.00	65.00

PINEAPPLE AND FLORAL, No. 618

Manufactured by Indiana Glass Company, Dunkirk, IN, from 1932 to 1937. Made in amber, avocado (late 1960s), cobalt blue (1980s), crystal, fired-on green, fired-on red, and pink (1980s).

Reproductions: † Salad bowl and diamond shaped comport have been reproduced in several different colors.

	Amber	Crystal	Red
Ashtray, 4-1/2" d	20.00	16.50	20.00
Berry Bowl, 4-3/4" d	22.00	20.00	22.00
Cereal Bowl, 6" d	22.00	25.00	22.00
Comport, diamond-shape	10.00	3.00	10.00
Creamer, diamond-shape	10.00	7.50	10.00
Cream Soup	16.50	18.00	16.50
Cup	10.00	10.00	10.00
Plate, 6" d, sherbet	6.00	5.00	6.00
Plate, 8-3/8" d, salad	8.00	8.00	8.00
Plate, 9-3/8" d, dinner	15.00	17.50	15.00
Plate, 9-3/4" d, indentation	—	25.00	—
Plate, 11" d, closed handles	18.00	17.00	18.00
Plate, 11-1/2" d, indentation	—	25.00	—

	Amber	Crystal	Red
Platter, 11" l, closed handles........................	15.00	18.00	15.00
Relish, 11-1/2" d, divided	20.00	16.50	20.00
Salad Bowl, 7" d †	10.00	3.00	10.00
Sandwich Plate, 11-1/2" d	13.00	20.00	13.00
Saucer	5.00	6.00	5.00
Sherbet, ftd.............................	24.00	20.00	24.00
Sugar, diamond-shape............	10.00	6.00	10.00
Tumbler, 8 oz., 4-1/4" h	40.00	40.00	40.00
Tumbler, 12 oz., 5" h	48.00	47.50	48.00
Vase, cone shape	45.00	42.50	45.00
Vegetable Bowl, 10" l, oval......	30.00	30.00	30.00

PYRAMID, No. 610

Manufactured by Indiana Glass Company, Dunkirk, IN, from 1926 to 1932. Made in black (1974-75 by Tiara), blue, crystal, green, pink, white, and yellow.

	Crystal	Green	Pink	Yellow
Berry Bowl, 4-3/4" d	10.00	25.00	20.00	40.00
Berry Bowl, 8-1/2" d	17.50	65.00	32.00	60.00
Bowl, 9-1/2" l, oval	25.00	45.00	35.00	55.00
Creamer..	15.00	30.00	30.00	40.00
Creamer and Sugar, tray	50.00	175.00	175.00	105.00
Ice Tub..	55.00	90.00	80.00	185.00
Pickle Dish, 9-1/2" l, 5-3/4" w	20.00	35.00	35.00	65.00
Pitcher..	350.00	210.00	475.00	450.00
Relish, 4 part, handles...........................	25.00	48.00	50.00	65.00
Salt and Pepper Shakers, pr	16.00	—	—	—
Sugar	15.00	30.00	30.00	40.00
Tray for creamer and sugar	20.00	25.00	25.00	35.00
Tumbler, 8 oz., ftd.................................	50.00	45.00	50.00	75.00
Tumbler, 11 oz., ftd...............................	60.00	50.00	45.00	70.00

Production limited in blue and white. Prices for black not firmly established in secondary market at this time.

RIBBON

Manufactured by Hazel Atlas Glass Company, Clarksburg, WV, and Zanesville, OH, early 1930s. Made in black, crystal, green, and pink.

	Black	Crystal	Green
Berry Bowl, 4" d	—	20.00	22.00
Berry Bowl, 8" d	—	27.50	30.00
Candy Dish, cov	38.50	30.00	32.00
Cereal Bowl, 5" d	—	20.00	25.00
Creamer, ftd	—	10.00	15.00
Cup	—	3.50	5.50
Plate, 6-1/4" d, sherbet	—	2.50	3.50
Plate, 8" d, luncheon	15.00	4.00	5.50
Salt and Pepper Shakers, pr	45.00	22.00	32.00
Saucer	—	1.00	2.50
Sherbet	—	4.00	6.00
Sugar, ftd	—	10.00	12.00
Tumbler, 10 oz., 6" h	—	27.00	30.00

Production in pink was limited to salt and pepper shakers, valued at $40.00.

ROXANA

Manufactured by Hazel Atlas Glass Company, Clarksburg, WV, and Zanesville, OH, in 1932. Made in crystal, golden topaz, and white.

	Crystal	Golden Topaz
Berry Bowl, 5" d	6.00	12.00
Bowl, 4-1/2 x 2-3/8"	6.00	12.00
Cereal Bowl, 6" d	7.50	15.00
Plate, 5-1/2" d	4.50	9.00
Plate, 6" d, sherbet	4.00	8.00
Sherbet, ftd	6.00	12.00
Tumbler, 9 oz., 4-1/4" h	8.50	17.00

Production in white was limited to a 4-1/2" bowl, valued at $15.00

SANDWICH

Manufactured by Hocking Glass Company, and later Anchor Hocking Corporation, from 1939 to 1964. Made in crystal, Desert Gold, 1961-64; Forest Green, 1956-1960s; pink, 1939-1940; Royal Ruby, 1938-1939; white/ivory (opaque) 1957-1960s.
Reproductions: † The cookie jar has been reproduced in crystal.

	Crystal	Desert Gold	Forest Green	Pink	Royal Ruby	White
Bowl, 4-5/16" d, smooth	3.00	—	2.00	—	—	—
Bowl, 4-7/8" d, smooth	3.00	3.50	—	4.50	17.50	—
Bowl, 4-7/8" d, crimped	12.00	—	—	—	—	—
Bowl, 5-1/4" d, scalloped	5.00	6.00	—	—	20.00	—
Bowl, 5-1/4" d, smooth	—	—	—	7.00	20.00	—
Bowl, 6-1/2" d, scalloped	5.00	8.00	40.00	—	27.50	—
Bowl, 6-1/2" d, smooth	7.50	8.00	—	—	—	—
Bowl, 7-1/4" d, scalloped	6.00	—	—	—	—	—
Bowl, 8-1/4" d, oval	5.00	—	—	—	—	—
Bowl, 8-1/4" d, scalloped	6.00	—	70.00	18.00	55.00	—
Butter Dish, cov	40.00	—	—	—	—	—
Cereal Bowl, 6-3/4" d	32.00	12.00	—	—	—	—
Cookie Jar, cov † *	35.00	40.00	20.00	—	—	—
Creamer	5.50	—	25.00	—	—	—
Cup, coffee	2.00	11.00	24.00	—	—	—
Cup, tea	3.00	11.00	24.00	—	—	—
Custard Cup	7.00	—	1.00	—	—	—
Custard Cup Liner	5.50	—	1.50	—	—	—
Custard Cup, crimped	12.50	—	—	—	—	—
Dessert Bowl, 5" d, crimped	10.50	—	—	—	—	—
Juice Pitcher, 6" h	75.00	—	135.00	—	—	—
Juice Tumbler, 3 oz., 3-3/8" h	12.00	—	6.00	—	—	—
Juice Tumbler, 5 oz., 3-9/16" h	7.50	—	2.50	—	—	—
Pitcher, half gallon, ice lip	80.00	—	350.00	—	—	—
Plate, 6" d	3.00	—	—	—	—	—
Plate, 7" d, dessert	10.00	—	—	—	—	—
Plate, 8" d, luncheon	4.00	—	—	—	—	—
Plate, 9" d, dinner	18.00	9.00	85.00	6.00	—	—
Plate, 9" d, indent for punch cup	6.00	—	—	—	—	—
Punch Bowl, 9-3/4" d	18.00	—	—	—	—	15.00
Punch Bowl and Stand	32.00	—	—	—	—	30.00

	Crystal	Desert Gold	Forest Green	Pink	Royal Ruby	White
Punch Bowl Set, bowl, base, 12 cups ...	60.00	—	—	—	—	—
Punch Cup	3.00	—	—	—	—	2.00
Salad Bowl, 7" d...................................	8.00	25.00	—	—	—	—
Salad Bowl, 7-5/8" d.............................	—	—	60.00	—	—	—
Salad Bowl, 9" d...................................	24.00	—	—	—	—	—
Sandwich Plate, 12" d	14.00	17.50	—	—	—	—
Saucer..	2.00	4.00	15.00	—	—	—
Sherbet, ftd	8.00	8.00	—	—	—	—
Snack Set, plate and cup......................	9.00	—	—	—	—	—
Sugar, cov..	30.00	—	—	—	—	—
Sugar, no cover.....................................	5.50	—	25.00	—	—	—
Tumbler, 9 oz., ftd	27.50	125.00	—	—	—	—
Tumbler, 9 oz., water	9.00	—	5.00	—	—	—
Vase	—	—	24.00	—	—	—
Vegetable, 8-1/2" l, oval	6.00	—	—	—	—	—

* No cover is known for cookie jar in Forest Green.

SPIRAL

Manufactured by Hocking Glass Company, Lancaster, OH, from 1928 to 1930. Made in crystal, green, and pink. Collector interest is strongest in green.

	Green			Green
Berry Bowl, 4-3/4" d.....................	6.00	Plate, 8" d, luncheon		4.00
Berry Bowl, 8" d...........................	14.00	Platter, 12" l		30.00
Butter Tub....................................	25.00	Preserve, cov		30.00
Creamer, flat................................	8.00	Salt and Pepper Shakers, pr		37.50
Creamer, footed	8.00	Sandwich Server, center handle ..		30.00
Cup..	5.00	Saucer		2.00
Ice Tub	25.00	Sherbet...		5.00
Juice Tumbler, 5 oz., 3" h.............	5.00	Sugar, flat		8.00
Mixing Bowl, 7" d.........................	9.00	Sugar, footed................................		8.00
Pitcher, 58 oz., 7-5/8" h	35.00	Tumbler, 5-7/8" h, ftd...................		24.00
Plate, 6" d, sherbet	3.00	Tumbler, 9 oz., 5" h		10.00

THUMBPRINT

Manufactured by Federal Glass Company, Columbus, OH, from
1927 to 1930. Made in green.

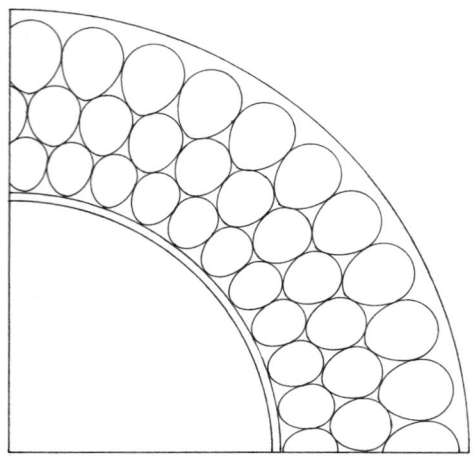

	Green
Berry Bowl, 4-3/4" d	7.00
Berry Bowl, 8" d	10.00
Cereal Bowl, 5" d	9.00
Creamer, ftd	8.00
Cup	6.00
Juice Tumbler, 4" h	6.00
Plate, 6" d, sherbet	3.00
Plate, 8" d, luncheon	5.00
Plate, 9-1/4" d, dinner	7.00
Salt and Pepper Shakers, pr.	25.00
Saucer	2.00
Sherbet	7.00
Sugar, ftd	8.00
Tumbler, 5" h	8.00
Tumbler, 5-1/2" h	10.00
Whiskey, 2-1/4" h	6.50

WATERFORD, Waffle

Manufactured by Hocking Glass Company, Lancaster, OH, from
1938 to 1944. Made in crystal, forest green (1950s), pink, white,
and yellow.

	Crystal	Pink
Ashtray, 4" d	5.00	5.00
Berry Bowl, 4-3/4" d	7.50	16.00
Berry Bowl, 8-1/4" d	10.00	27.00
Butter Dish, cov	28.00	225.00
Cake Plate, 10-1/4" d, handles	11.50	16.00
Cereal Bowl, 5-1/2" d	17.50	30.00
Coaster, 4" d	2.50	—
Creamer, Miss America style	37.50	—
Creamer, oval	5.00	12.00
Cup	6.50	15.00
Cup, Miss America style	—	42.00
Goblet, 5-1/2" h, Miss America style	35.00	85.00
Goblet, 5-1/4" h	12.00	—
Goblet, 5-5/8" h	17.50	—
Juice Pitcher, 42 oz., tilted	28.00	—
Juice Tumbler, 5 oz., 3-1/2" h, Miss America style	—	62.00
Lamp, 4" spherical base	28.00	—
Pitcher, 80 oz., tilted, ice lip	32.00	150.00
Plate, 6" d, sherbet	3.50	6.50
Plate, 7-1/8" d, salad	7.00	8.00
Plate, 9-5/8" d, dinner	12.50	24.00
Platter, 14" l	8.00	—
Relish, 13-3/4" d, 5 part	16.00	—
Salt and Pepper Shakers, pr	6.50	—
Sandwich Plate, 13-3/4" d	12.00	30.00
Saucer	3.00	5.00
Sherbet, ftd	3.50	15.00
Sherbet, ftd, scalloped base	8.00	—
Sugar	5.00	12.00
Sugar, Miss America style	35.00	—
Sugar Lid, oval	5.00	25.00
Tray	6.00	—
Tumbler, 10 oz., 4-7/8" h, ftd	16.00	23.00

Forest Green production was limited, currently an ashtray is valued at $4.00. Yellow was also limited, and a small berry bowl is valued
at $3.50. Collector interest is low in white.

DISNEYANA

History: Walt Disney and the creations of the famous Disney Studios hold a place of fondness and enchantment in the hearts of people throughout the world. The 1928 release of "Steamboat Willie," featuring Mickey Mouse, heralded an entertainment empire.

Walt and his brother, Roy, were shrewd businessmen. From the beginning they licensed the reproduction of Disney characters on products ranging from wristwatches to clothing.

In 1984, Donald Duck celebrated his 50th birthday, and collectors took a renewed interest in material related to him.

References: Ted Hake, *Hake's Guide to Character Toy Premiums*, Gemstone Publishing (1966 Greenspring, Ste. 405, Timonium, MD 21093), 1996; Robert Heide and John Gilman, Disneyana, Hyperion, 1994; Maxine A. Pinsky, *Marx Toys: Robots, Space, Comic, Disney & TV Characters*, Schiffer Publishing, 1996; Carol J. Smith, *Identification & Price Guide to Winnie the Pooh Collectibles*, Hobby House Press, 1994; Tom Tumbusch, *Tomart's Illustrated Disneyana Catalog and Price Guide*, Vols. 1, 2, 3, and 4, Tomart Publications, 1985; ——, *Tomart's Illustrated Disneyana Catalog and Price Guide, Condensed Edition*, Wallace-Homestead, 1989.

Periodicals: *Baby Boomer Collectibles*, P.O. Box 437, Waupaca, WI 54981; *Mouse Rap Monthly*, P.O. Box 1064, Ojai, CA 93024; *Tomart's Disneyana Digest*, 3300 Encrete Ln., Dayton, OH 45439; *Tomart's Disneyana Update*, 3300 Encrete Ln., Dayton, OH 45439.

Collectors' Clubs: Imagination Guild, P.O. Box 907, Boulder Creek, CA 95006; Mouse Club East, P.O. Box 3195, Wakefield, MA 01880; National Fantasy Fan Club for Disneyana Collectors and Enthusiasts, P.O .Box 19212, Irvine, CA 92713.

Archives/Museum: Walt Disney Archives, Burbank, CA 91521.

Additional Listings: See *Warman's Americana & Collectibles* for more examples.

Advisor: Ted Hake.

SPECIAL AUCTION

Hake's Americana & Collectibles
P.O. Box 1444, Dept 344
York, PA 17405
(717) 848-1333

Joe Carioca, Three Caballeros

Pencil Drawing, 10" x 12" sheet of animation paper, 4-1/4" x 5-3/4" image in lead pencil, from numbered sequence, 1950s 275.00
Pencil Sharpener, 1-1/8" dark red translucent plastic, full color decal on top, 1940s 30.00

Disney Studios

Book, hardcover, *The Art of Walt Disney, New Concise Edition,* Abrams, copyright 1975, 9" x 11-1/2," 160 pgs, 251 illus, 170 full color plates 30.00
Certificate, 8" x 10", war bond, issued by "Untied States Treasury War Finance Committee," 1944, center text surrounded by full color character portraits, unsigned 150.00
Christmas Card
    5-1/4" x 7-3/4," stiff glossy thin cardboard, color scene of Mickey, Donald, Pluto and Goofy filling stockings hanging around fireplace, inside with additional color scene of trail of Disney cartoon characters pictured in chronological order, 1981 ....30.00
    7-3/16" x 9-1/8", semi-gloss crescent board art stick, Mickey, Minnie, Pluto looking through window of Pigs' house as Pigs sing, play instruments, and dance on top of grinning (but deceased) Big Bad Wolf, who lies on floor like bearskin rug, bottom right corner mkd "Printed in USA," 1943 ....275.00
Glass, 4-1/4" h, 1939 Walt Disney All Star Parade, wrap-around design of Mickey, Minnie, Pluto, and parrot, orange, yellow title 60.00
Lunch Box, 7" x 9" x 4-1/2", Walt Disney School Bus, metal dome, orange, Aladdin, 1960s 80.00

Donald Duck

Bank, 2-1/2" d, 4-3/4" h, standard glass jar, color label on front, blue and yellow tin lid, Nash-Underwood label, coin slot not punched, 1950s 80.00
Book, *Walt Disney's Donald Duck,* Whitman, #948, copyright 1935, 9-1/2" x 13", linen type, 12 pgs, large color story art 275.00
Button, 1-1/4" d, Donald Duck Jackets, blue, white, and orange, Donald standing with blue streams simulating raindrops, inscription "Dry in Any Weather/Norwich Knitting Co, Norwich, N.Y.," c1936...500.00
Figure
    3" h, bisque, Donald holding silver sword, incised "S1336," on reverse..110.00
    4" h, castile soap, Lightfoot Schultz Co, c1938, orig 2-1/2" x 2-1/2" x 5", box 110.00
Greeting Card, 5-1/4" x 6-1/4", Easter, Hallmark, copyright 1946, 13 different images..30.00
Ink Blotter, 4" x 6-3/4," Sunoco, Donald/car in front of "Nu-Blue Sunoco" gas pump, copyright 1940...............................25.00
Lamp, plaster, 3-dimensional Donald figure atop circular base, 4" d base, 9-1/2" h, LaMode Studios, 1938, orig cord.......425.00
Light Bulb, 4" h, tube shaped glass bulb, threaded brass socket, stamped metal filament figure of Donald, 1930s...........275.00
Little Golden Book, Simon & Schuster, 6-1/2" x 8"
    Donald Duck and the Witch, copyright 1953, first printing, 28 pgs...30.00
    Donald Duck's Toy Train, copyright 1950, first printing ..20.00
Premium Comic, *Donald Duck's Atom Bomb,* Cheerios, 3-1/4" x 7", 32 pgs, copyright 1947 ....350.00
Production Cel, 12-1/2" x 16", acetate sheet, 3" x 4" cel image, 1960s..500.00
Soaky, 7" h, soft plastic, blue and yellow 30.00
Tea Set, white and irid blue, Donald illus in blue, red, and brown, Japanese, 1930s, one saucer missing, 14 pc set.........225.00

Dumbo

Book, *Dumbo The Story Of The Flying Elephant,* Whitman, #710, copyright 1942, 10-1/4" x 11", stiff color paper covers, 20 pgs, with black and white and full color art.............................80.00
Button, 1-1/4" d, "Walt Disney's Dumbo/D-X," gasoline club type, red, black, and gray, back paper with image of Mickey running, c1941..40.00

Fantasia

Book, *Walt Disney Presents Fantasia,* Western Printing Co, copyright 1940, 9-1/2" x 12-1/2", souvenir, soft cover 60.00
Figure, 3" x 3" x 5", hippo, painted and glazed, mkd Vernon Kilns, incised "34, 1940 copyright" 600.00

Ferdinand The Bull

Book, *Ferdinand the Bull,* Whitman, copyright 1938, 32 pgs, 8" x 10-3/4", color stiff paper cov, brown, tan, and white feature story art 45.00
Doll, 5" x 9" x 8", composition, jointed, movable head, dark brown, facial accents, red nostrils and tongue, stenciled name on leg, bee design, fabric flower missing, Ideal, c1938 .... 250.00
Sheet Music, *Ferdinand The Bull,* 9" x 12", 4 pgs, copyright 1938 ABC Music Co 20.00

Goofy

Figure, 7" x 15" x 16" h, inflatable vinyl, red jersey, "Sport Goofy" logo, yellow shorts, red, white, and blue sneakers, back mkd "Magic Kingdom of Ice" logo, early 1980s 30.00
Magic Slate, 8-1/2" x 13-1/2," stiff cardboard, color illus of Goofy, Mickey's and Donald's nephews, unused, plastic stylus still attached in plastic blister, Whitman, c1970 .... 14.00
Soaky, 8-1/2" h, soft plastic, white design, black and red accents, red cap, 1950s 30.00
Toy, 5" x 7" colorful blister card, 2-1/2" l hard plastic "Goofy stunt Car," "Azrak-Hamway," c1970 .... 35.00

Jungle Book

Concept sketch, 12-1/2" x 17" sheet of animation paper, 4" x 7-1/2" lead pencil sketch of Mowgli holding banana in one hand, c1967 .... 80.00

Mickey Mouse

Alarm Clock, 4-1/2" x 5-1/4" x 8-3/4" h, hard plastic, Bradley Time, 1970s, orig box 40.00
Bank, 6-1/2" h, hard vinyl, one movable arm and head, black jacket, white shirt, orange bow tie, red pants, orig cardboard tag and price sticker on one ear, 1970s 30.00
Big Little Book, Whitman
  Mickey Mouse Runs His Own Newspaper, #1409, copyright 1937 .... 40.00
  Mickey Mouse The Mail Pilot, 1933 copyright, softcover version 75.00
Bottle, 3-1/4" h, ceramic, 3-dimensional, painted and glazed, black and white Mickey, blue bow tie, tan accents on pants, green base, European, 1930s 110.00

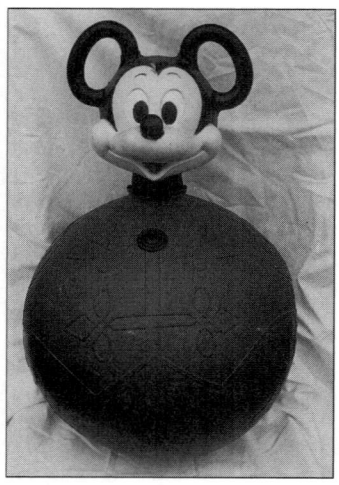

Mickey Mouse, jumping ball, Walt Disney Productions, Sun Products Corp., 23" h, $40.

Button
  1-1/4" d, Mickey in black on cream background, waving pose, text below his feet "Copy. 1928-1930 by W. E. Disney," movie club type, Philadelphia Badge Co., orig back paper 150.00
  1-1/4" d, Mickey Mouse Glove Trotters/Member, black imprint "Drink More Meyer Milk Daily," 1938 .... 65.00
  1-1/2" d, "Happy Birthday Mickey," full color photograph of Mickey Mouse telephone, white background, 1978 .... 15.00
  1-1/2" d, "I Grew Up On Mickey Mouse, black, white, and red, Mickey as conductor, c1970 .... 30.00
  1-3/4" d, "Mickey Mouse 60th Anniversary 1928-1988," full color, back view of Mickey in very modern clothes looking into mirror which reflects 1928 image, Disney company copyright, inscribed "Distributed by One Stop Posters" 5.00
Club Member's Badge, 1" d, Mickey Mouse Chums, enamel on brass, English, 1930s 110.00
Coloring Book, *Another Mickey Mouse Coloring Book,* Saalfield, copyright 1935, 10-3/4" x 15-1/4," somewhat curled, 6 pgs neatly colored 150.00
Fireplace Fork, 17-1/2" l, brass, 1-3/4" x 3" oval design at top with relief figure of Mickey, 1930s 110.00
Guitar, 6 x 17", black, white, and blue display card, 15" l, hard plastic guitar, Carnival Toy, 1970s 60.00
Magazine
  Life, Nov. 1978, Mickey's 50th Anniversary 20.00
  Mickey Mouse Magazine, 5-1/4" x 7-1/4", Vol. 1, #2, December 1933, Laher's sponsor, 16 pgs, red and green cover, green and white contents, 5 pg article titled "Seeing The Stars On The Milky Way," photos of movie stars drinking milk, including Dickie Moore and Claudette Corbet, puzzle page 110.00
Pencil Holder, 1-3/4" d base, 3" h, thick diecut celluloid figure, pink celluloid tube attached to back to hold pencil, crescent-shaped celluloid piece as pencil rest, moving head, 1930s 375.00
Pinback, 7/8" d, textured brass, fabric insert of Mickey in classic black and white pose against dark red background, early 1930s 110.00
Premium Book, *Merry Christmas From Mickey Mouse,* 7" x 10", thick newsprint, copyright 1939 K. K. Publications, color cover, black and white contents, full color illus, stories, puzzles, games, pictures to color, wear, covers loose, small tears, chips 110.00
Toothbrush Holder, 2-3/4" x 3-1/4" x 5", bisque, one arm connected to body, other arm movable, late 1930s, string tail missing, paint worn 225.00
Wristwatch, Ingersoll, 1" x 1-5/8" chrome luster metal case, dial illus of black, white, red, and yellow Mickey, hands point to numbers, 1939 version 250.00

Minnie Mouse

Book, *Minnie Mouse and the Antique chair,* Whitman, Walt Disney Productions 1948 copyright, 5" x 5" 20.00
Bowl, 6-1/2" d, glazed china, colorful transfer image, mkd "Wade-heath Ware/Made in England," Disney permission notice, minor wear and damage 45.00
Cereal Premium
  Face Mask, 8" x 10," colored stiff paper, Disney copyright, Einson-Freeman 65.00
  Ring, Sugar Jets, green plastic, high relief head of Minnie against shield design, her name below, 1956 .... 60.00
Figure, 3" h, bisque, Minnie in seated position on wood and cardboard seat suspended by 4 threads from horizontal pole across unpainted wooden frame, 1930s, Japanese 98.00

Pinocchio

Book, *Pinocchio Linen-Like*, Whitman, 7-1/4" x 8", 12 pgs, copyright 1940, color art, imprint "Compliments of Montgomery Ward, Albany, NY"...80.00

Charm, 3/4" h, Jiminy Cricket, bronze colored plastic, loop, c1950..8.00

Clicker, litho tin, Jiminy Cricket, green on bright yellow, inscribed "You Help More The United Way," Productions copyright on bottom edge, c1960..18.00

Doll, composition and wood, jointed, 7-1/2" h Pinocchio and 8-1/4" h Jiminy Cricket, Ideal, c1940, repairs and restoration to both, pr...275.00

Fan Card, 7-1/4" x 9-14," "Pinocchio/Jiminy Cricket," studio issued, color images, c1940.............................65.00

Glass, 4-3/4" h, illus and poem in orange, Cleo, 1940 dairy premium...30.00

Little Golden Book, *Pinocchio,* Simon & Schuster, 1948........8.00

Pencil Case, 5" x 8-1/2", white vinyl, colorful illus on front, Productions copyright, c1960...........................24.00

Spoon, 5" l, silverplate, showing Pinocchio and the donkey, c1940..23.00

Valentine, 3" x 5", Gideon, movable head, 1939 copyright 18.00

Pluto

Bank, 4" x 4" x 6-1/2" h, painted composition, glossy finish, trap missing, early 1950s.....................................35.00

Card, 3-1/2" x 5-1/2", RPM Motor Oil, stiff paper ad, color illus of Pluto with container of RPM oil, 1939 copyright, dealer's name lower left margin 30.00

Clock, 4" x 5" x 9-1/2" h, hard plastic, figural, Allied Mfg., Co., mid-1950s black, white, blue, orange, and red box.............275.00

Cup, 3-1/2" h, Bettleware, white plastic, yellow and black image, raised name, W.D. Inc. copyright, c1937...............42.00

Soaky, 8-1/2" h, deep orange, black and red accents, red cap, 1960s...20.00

Toy, 1-1/2" x 2" x 1", Pluto Boxed Sports Car, white and red Mercedes Benz with 3-dimensional figure of Pluto, 2" l hard plastic car, Elm Toys, c1960.................................35.00

Silly Symphony

Book, *Peculiar Penguins From A Walt Disney Silly Symphony,* David McCay Co, copyright 1934, 6-1/4" x 8-1/4", 45 pgs, small color illus 75.00

Calendar, 1938, Brown & Bigelow, 11 of 12 pgs, spiral bound, 9" x 16-1/2"..400.00

Sleeping Beauty

Book, *Sleeping Beauty,* Whitman, Story Hour Series, copyright 1959, 7-1/2" x 8-1/4"......................................35.00

Snow White

Advertisement, 3-1/4" x 5-3/4" two sided glossy paper, blue and white adv for series of 8 glasses, issued with cottage cheese, mkd "Sheffield Farms," photo of Dopey glass, reverse with recipe for cottage cheese pie, c1938 ....60.00

Bagatelle, 10-1/4" x 20-1/2" x 3" deep, wood, pinball type game, Chad Valley, late 1930s, thick cardboard underside, attached black and white instruction sheet, green and black sticker with Disney name....................................275.00

Button, 1-1/4" d, "Snow White Jingle Club/Member," red, white and blue, Snow White surrounded by dwarfs, c1938 .....30.00

Candy Wrapper, 4-1/2" x 5," Grumpy, waxed paper, color image in center, copyright 1938, Consolidated Biscuit Co........30.00

Figure, 3" x 3-1/2" x 7-1/4" h, hollow plaster, replica of Seiberling rubber Happy, orange and brown outfit, green hat and base, fleshtone face, black, white, and red accents, white beard, c1938...110.00

Snow White, alarm clock, Bayard, mkd "Made in France, Par Autorisation Walt Disney," $120.

Hand Bill, 7" x 9", white, black lettering and illus, Fords Theater, Washington, DC "Walt Disney's Snow White production done as a holiday musical by a Baltimore Actors group," late 1930s...20.00

Pin, 1-5/8" h, composition, painted wood, Dopey, brown, green enamel paint on hat, small red accent on tongue, two yellow shirt buttons, white accent on candle, 1938.....................35.00

Premium, book, *Dopey's Christmas Tree,* 8-1/2" x 11-1/4", 16 pgs, stiff newsprint, green and red illus, copyright 1938, imprint for "Joslin's Mass. Toy Store" 60.00

Salt and Pepper Shakers, pr, 2-1/2" h, glazed ceramic, one Bashful, other Sleepy, orig cork stoppers, marked "Foreign," Japanese made for European market, late 1930s...............70.00

Serigraph, 10-3/4" x 14" acetate sheet, 3" x 8-1/2" image of Snow White and 5" x 5-1/2" image of Sleepy, Bashful and Happy, limited edition, "Walt Disney Company" seal at lower right, black felt tip signature of Marc Davis, and blue felt tip pen signature of "Adriana Caselotti, Voice of Snow White".................500.00

Souvenir Program, "Snow White and the Seven Dwarfs' Radio City Music Hall," 6-3/4" x 9", 16 pgs, Jan. 27, 1938...............40.00

Wristwatch, 4-1/4" x 5-1/2" x 1-1/2" d oval shaped box, 7/8" chromed metal case, orig red fabric straps, Ingersoll/US Time, 1950..175.00

Zorro

Little Golden Book, *Zorro and the Secret Plan,* Simon & Schuster, 1958...8.00

Mug, 2" x 6" x 4-3/4", boot shape, yellow soft plastic, glossy sticker on front, Z-shaped handle, c1958..................................40.00

Pez Dispenser, 4-1/4" h, red stem, name on side, fleshtone head, black hat, mask, painted mustache worn off...................60.00

Puzzle, 11" x 14," frame tray, Jaymar, c1975, color photo of Zorro and Capt. Monastario sword fighting 20.00

Ring, silver plastic, black plastic top inscribed in gold, octagonal, 1950s...30.00

DOLLHOUSES

History: Dollhouses date from the 18th century to modern times. Early dollhouses often were handmade, sometimes with only one room. The most common type was made for a young girl to fill with replicas of furniture scaled especially to fit into a dollhouse. Specially sized dolls also were made for dollhouses. All types of accessories in all types of styles were available, and dollhouses could portray any historical period.

References: Evelyn Ackerman, *Genius of Moritz Gottschalk*, Gold House Publishing, 1994; Mary Brett, *Tomart's Price Guide to Tin Litho Doll Houses and Plastic Doll House Furnishings*, Tomart Publications, 1997; Caroline Clifton-Mogg, *Dollhouse Sourcebook*, Abbeville Press, 1993; Nora Earnshaw, *Collecting Dolls' Houses and Miniatures*, Pincushion Press, 1993; Flora Bill Jacobs, *Dolls' Houses in America: Historic Preservation in Miniature*, Charles Scribner's Sons, 1974; Margaret Towner, *Dollhouse Furniture*, Courage Books, 1993; Dian Zillner, *American Dollhouses and Furniture from the 20th Century*, Schiffer Publishing, 1995.

Periodicals: *Doll Castle News*, P.O. Box 247, Washington, NJ 07882; *International Dolls' House News*, P.O. Box 79, Southampton S09 7EZ England; *Miniature Collector*, 30595 Eight Mill, Livonia, MI 48152; *Miniatures Showcase*, P.O. Box 1612, Waukesha, WI 53187; *Nutshell News*, 21027 Crossroads Circle, P.O. Box 1612, Waukesha, WI 53187.

Collectors' Clubs: Dollhouse & Miniature Collectors, 9451 Lee Hwy #515, Fairfax, VA 22302; National Assoc. of Miniature Enthusiasts, P.O. Box 69, Carmel, IN 46032; National Organization of Miniaturists and Dollers, 1300 Schroder, Normal, IL 61761.

Museums: Art Institute of Chicago, Chicago, IL; Margaret Woodbury Strong Museum, Rochester, NY; Museums at Stony Brook, Stony Brook, NY; Toy and Miniature Museum of Kansas City, Kansas City, MO; Washington Dolls' House and Toy Museum, Washington, DC.

American, hand made
- 15" h, half inch scale, c1980, 3 story townhouse, turntable base, living room, bedroom, and nursery settings, living room and bedroom furniture by Mel Prescott, metal, glass, wood, and cloth accessories, gazebo, and lawn furniture, plants and fencing 520.00
- 19-1/4" w, 10-1/" d, 18-3/4" h, 1920s, bungalow, red gambrel roof, front porch opens, front dormer, 2 room first floor, 1 room second, opens at either end, assorted wood and lacquered board furniture 1,150.00
- 75" w, 34" w, 52" h, late 19th C, wood, 6 rooms, electrified, simulated shingle roof, 1 over 1 opening glass sash, old wallpapers, parlor, kitchen, hallways, master bedroom, nursery, grandfather room in attic, family of 4, assembled furniture and accessories in various scales, modification, some restoration 2,300.00
- Bing, Germany, garage, lithographed tin, double doors, extensive graphics, houses 2 autos, sedan and roadster 550.00
- Bliss, Victorian, 27" x 18" x 11", litho on wood, 2 rooms, 2 story, high steeple roof, dormer windows, spindled porch railing, second floor balcony 1,200.00

McLoughlin Folding Doll House, two rooms, highly dec interiors, orig box, 16" h, 17" l, 12" d, $950.

Converse, cottage, red and green litho on redwood, printed bay windows, stone base, roof dormer 500.00
French, carved oak, 2 stories, mansard roof, hinged shutters, 40" h, 33" w, 27" d, later black painted stand 1,955.00
Germany, carriage house, 35-1/2" w, 16-1/2" d, 25" h, painted wood, lithographed paper, 2 horse stalls, office, carriage stall, and hay loft, missing loft doors and 2 gates 1,725.00
Gottschalk, Saxony, 1870s, lithograph paper on wood, elaborate German villa style, 2 rooms down, 2 rooms up, separate front steps, orig int. papers, blue roof, roof tower missing, some paper and wood damage, 26-1/2" w, 18-5/16" d, 31" h 9,200.00
McLoughlin, 12" x 17" x 16", folding, house, 2 rooms, dec int., orig box..900.00
Schoenhut, 29" x 26" x 30", mansion, 2 story, 8 rooms, attic, tan brick design, red roof, large dormer, 20 glass windows, orig decal, 1923...1,750.00
Tootsietoy, dollhouse, furniture, and accessories, printed Masonite, half-timbered style, 2 rooms down, 2 up removable roof, open back, 21" w, 10-1/8" d, 16" h, orchid and pink bedroom sets, orchid bathroom, brown dining room set, flocked sofa and chairs, green and white kitchen pcs, piano, bench, lamps, telephone, cane-back sofa, rocker, some damage and wear to 3/4" scale furniture 460.00

DOLLS

History: Dolls have been children's play toys for centuries. Dolls also have served other functions. From the 14th through 18th centuries, doll making was centered in Europe, mainly in Germany and France. The French dolls produced in this era were representations of adults and were dressed in the latest couturier designs. They were not children's toys.

During the mid-19th century, child and baby dolls, made in wax, cloth, bisque, and porcelain, were introduced. Facial features were hand painted; wigs were made of mohair and human hair; and the dolls were dressed in the current fashions for babies or children.

Doll making in the United States began to flourish in the 1900s with companies such as Effanbee, Madame Alexander, and Ideal.

Marks: Marks of the various manufacturers are found on the back of the head or neck or on the doll's back. These marks are very important in identifying a doll and its date of manufacture.

References: Johana Gast Anderton, *More Twentieth Century Dolls from Bisque to Vinyl*, Vols. A-H, I-Z, revised ed.s, Wallace-Homestead, 1974; Kim Avery, *The World of Raggedy Ann Collectibles,* Collector Books, 1997; John Axe, *Encyclopedia of Celebrity Dolls*, Hobby House Press, 1983; Carol Corson, *Schoenhut Dolls*, Hobby House Press, 1993; Carla Marie Cross, *Modern Doll Rarities,* Antique Trader Books, 1997; Jan Foulke, *Doll Classics*, Hobby House Press, 1997; ––, *Insider's Guide to China Doll Collecting*, Hobby House Press, 1995; ––, *Insider's Guide to Doll Buying and Selling*, Hobby House Press, 1995; ––, *Insider's Guide to Germany "Dolly" Collecting*, Hobby House Press, 1995; ––, *32th Blue Book Dolls and Values*, Hobby House Press, 1997; Cynthia Gaskill, *Legendary Dolls of Madame Alexander*, Theriault's, 1995; Patricia Hall, *Johnny Gruelle: Creator of Raggedy Ann and Andy*, Pelican Publishing (1101 Monroe St., Gretna, LA 70053), 1993; Dawn Herlocher, *200 Years of Dolls*, Antique Trader Books, 1996; Judith Izen and Carol Sover, *Collector's Guide to Vogue Dolls*, Collector Books, 1997; Polly Judd, *African and Asian Costumed Dolls*, Hobby House Press, 1995: ––, *Cloth Dolls*, Hobby House Press, 1990; Polly and Pam Judd, *Composition Dolls*, Vol. I (1991), Vol. II (1994), Hobby House Press; ––, *European Costume Dolls*, Hobby House Press, 1994; ––, *Glamour Dolls of the 1950s & 1960s*, revised ed., Hobby House Press, 1993; ––, *Hard Plastic Dolls*, 3rd ed. (1993), Book II (1994), Hobby House Press; A. Glenn Mandeville, *Alexander Dolls*, 2nd ed., Hobby House Press, 1995; ––, *Ginny*, 2nd ed., Hobby House Press, 1994; Marcie Melilo, *The Ultimate Barbie Doll Book,* Krause Publications, 1997; Patsy Moyer, *Doll Values, Antique to Modern*, Collector Books, 1997; ––, *Modern Collectible Dolls*, Collector Books, 1997; Myra Yellin Outwater, *Advertising Dolls,* Schiffer Publishing, 1997; Edward R. Pardella, *Shirley Temple Dolls and Fashion*, Schiffer Publishing, 1992; Sabine Reinelt, *Magic of Character Dolls*, Hobby House Press, 1993.

Lydia Richter, *China, Parian, and Bisque German Dolls*, Hobby House Press, 1993; Lydia and Joachim F. Richter, *Bru Dolls*, Hobby House Press, 1989; Lydia Richter and Karin Schmelcher, *Heubach Character Dolls and Figurines*, Hobby House Press, 1992; Joyce Rinehart, *Wonderful Raggedy Anns,* Schiffer Publishing, 1997; Jane Sarasohn-Kahn, *Contemporary Barbie,* Antique Trader Books, 1997; Patricia R. Smith, *Antique Collector's Dolls*, Vol. I (1975, 1991 value update), Vol. II (1976, 1991 Value update), Collector Books; ––, *Effanbee Dolls,* Collector Books, 1998 values update; ––, *Madame Alexander Collector's Dolls Price Guide #20*, Collector Books, 1995; ––, *Madame Alexander Dolls 1965-1990*, 1991, 1997 values update, Collector Books; ––, *Modern Collector's Dolls*, Series I through VIII (1973–1996 value updates), Collector Books; ––, *Patricia Smith's Doll Values Antique to Modern*, Eleventh Series, Collector Books, 1995; ––, *Shirley Temple Dolls and Collectibles*, Vol. I (1977, 1992 value update), Vol. II (1979, 1992 value up-

date), Collector Books; Evelyn Robson Stahlendorf, *Charlton Standard Catalogue of Canadian Dolls*, 3rd ed., Charlton Press, 1995; Carl P. Stirn, *Turn-of-the-Century Dolls, Toys and Games* (1893 catalog reprint), Dover Publications, 1990; Margaret Whitton, *Jumeau Doll*, Dover Publications, 1981.

Periodicals: *Antique Doll World*, 225 Main St., Suite 300, Northport, NY 11768; *Cloth Doll Magazine*, P.O. Box 2167 Lake Oswego, OR 97035; *Costume Quarterly for Doll Collectors*, 118-01 Sutter Ave, Jamaica, NY 11420; *Doll Castle News*, P.O. Box 247, Washington, NJ 07882; *Doll Collector's Price Guide*, 306 East Parr Rd., Berne, IN 46711; Doll Life, 243 Newton-Sparta Rd, Newton, NJ 07860; *Doll Reader*, 6405 Flank Dr., Harrisburg, PA 17112; *Doll Times*, 218 W. Woodin Blvd, Dallas, TX 75224; *Doll World*, 306 East Parr Rd., Berne, IN 46711; *Dollmasters*, P.O. Box 151, Annapolis, MD 21404; *Dolls–The Collector's Magazine*, 170 Fifth Ave, 12th Floor, New York, NY 10010; *National Doll & Teddy Bear Collector*, P.O. Box 4032, Portland, OR 97208.

Collectors' Clubs: Doll Collector International, P.O. Box 2761, Oshkosh, WI 54903; Madame Alexander Fan Club, P.O. Box 330, Mundeline, IL 60060; United Federation of Doll Clubs, P.O. Box 14146, Parkville, MO 64152.

Videotapes: Doll Makers: Women Entrepreneurs 1865-1945, Sirocco Productions, 1995; Dolls of the Golden Age: 1880-1915, Sirocco Productions, 1993; Extraordinary World of Doll Collecting, Cinebar Productions, 1994.

Museums: Aunt Len's Doll House, Inc., New York, NY; Children's Museum, Detroit, MI; Doll Castle Doll Museum, Washington, NJ; Doll Museum, Newport, RI; Toy and Miniature Museum of Kansas City, Kansas City, MO; Gay Nineties Button & Doll Museum, Eureka Springs, AR; Margaret Woodbury Strong Museum, Rochester, NY; Mary Merritt Doll Museum, Douglassville, PA; Mary Miller Doll Museum, Brunswick, GA; Prairie Museum of Art & History, Colby, KS; Washington Dolls' House & Toy Museum, Washington, DC; Yesteryears Museum, Sandwich, MA.

Additional Listings: See *Warman's Americana & Collectibles* for more examples.

Alabama Doll Co.

22-1/2" h, rag face, neck, and bust fabric stuffed, neck and bust sewn to torso, ears sewn to head, body, arms, legs and hands also stuffed, flesh colored waterproof paint, painted over features, painted black shoes and white socks, orig cloths, c1900, mkd "Mrs. S. S. Smith Manufacturer and Dealer to The Alabama Indestructible Doll, Roanoke, Ala. Patented Sept. 26, 1905," 2,750.00

Alt, Beck, & Gottschalk

22" h, bisque turned shoulder head, brown glass stationary eyes, closed mouth, chestnut human hair wig, kid body, cloth lower legs, composition hands, imp "698," damage to body . 750.00

26" h, Sweet Nell, bisque socket head, gray glass sleep eyes, real lashes, painted features, open, 4 porcelain teeth, brunette human hair wig, composition wood ball jointed body, old clothes, c1910, mkd "1362 Made in Germany" 900.00

Arranbee Doll Co.

13" h, Bottletot, all composition, blue sleep eyes, open mouth, molded painted hair, baby body with bent arms and legs, celluloid hands, orig clothes, right hand holds bottle mkd "Arranbee/Pat Aug. 10, 25," 225.00

16" h, Nancy, all composition, painted eyes, closed mouth, molded hair, body jointed at neck, shoulders, and hips, mkd "Arranbee" 275.00

20" h, Debu teen, all composition, swivel head, shoulder plate, sleep eyes with lashes, closed mouth, human hair wig, composition body jointed at neck, shoulders, and hips, orig clothes, c1938, mkd "R & B" 295.00

Averill

10" h, Topsy & Eva, double-ended cloth doll, hp faces, one black with yarn hair, other white with painted hair, orig polka-dot cotton flip dress, red/white to blue/white, c1930, paper tag mkd "Georgene Novelties" 150.00

A. M., 310 Just Me, 9" h, $1,050. Photo courtesy of McMasters Doll Auctions.

16-1/2" h, Bonnie Babe, celluloid head, brown set glass eyes, smiling open/closed mouth, 2 teeth, molded painted hair, cloth body, arms, and legs all stuffed but movable, old clothing, c1926, mkd "BONNIE BABE/Reg. U. S. PAT OFF/Copyright by Georgene Averill/Germany 34" and turtle mark 700.00

Bahr & Proschild

22" h, Character Baby, bisque socket head, brown glass sleep eyes, open mouth, 2 upper teeth, brunette human hair wig, composition bent baby limb body, c1915, mkd "BP 585 Germany"..800.00

Bergmann, C. M.

15" h, bisque socket head, almond shaped small gray glass sleep eyes, open mouth, 2 porcelain upper teeth, brunette mohair wig, composition bent limb baby body, nicely dressed, mkd "Simon & Halbig, C. M. Bergmann 612 Germany"
....1,500.00

Bru

13" h, Bru Jne Black Child, dark brown bisque socket head on shoulder plate, brown paperweight eyes, closed mouth, black lamb's wool wig, dark bisque lower arms, brown kid jointed body, wooden, lower legs, nicely dressed in old fabric clothing, mkd "BRU JNE" 1,500.00

16" h, Bebe, bisque swivel head on shoulder plate with molded bosom, brown paperweight eyes, painted lashes, black eyeliner, rose-blushed eyelids, softly feathered brows, closed mouth, shaded and accented lips, pierced ears, old French lamb's skin wig, orig gusset-jointed kid body, bisque forearms, antique clothes, incised circle and dot mark ...8,500.00

16" h, French Fashion, very pale bisque, paperweight set eyes, human hair wig, early pierced ears, swivel neck, wood jointed body, articulated arms..6,750.00

16" h, Smiling Fashion, bisque, blue-green paperweight eyes, closed smiling mouth, mohair wig, swivel neck, gusset-jointed kid body, rare bisque Bru hands, orig fashion dress and hat 3,600.00

23-1/2" h, Jne R #10, big brown eyes, open mouth, orig blond human hair wig, Bru Jne body, orig clothes, old mkd Bru shoes
....7,500.00

Cameo Doll Company

10" h, Margie, composition head, painted eyes, nose, and mouth, molded painted hair, wooden segmented spool-like body, arms, and legs, undressed, c1929, red triangular decal label on chest "MARGIE Des. & Copyright by Jos. Kallus" ...350.00

12" h, Betty Boop, composition swivel head, side glancing eyes, tiny closed mouth, molded and painted black hair, composition torso with molded and painted swim suit, wooden segmented spool-like arms, and legs, old cotton print dress, c1932, heart shaped label on chest "BETTY BOOP Des. & Copyright by Fleischer Studios" 700.00

15" h, Scootles, all composition, painted side glancing eyes, smiling closed mouth, molded and painted hair, toddler body, jointed at neck, shoulders, and hips, undressed, c1925, orig wrist tags 650.00

Chase, Martha

21" h, painted blond hair, stockinette body painted and weighted, touch up to painted facial features, body, hands and legs, fabric weak at several places 345.00

Dressel, Cuno & Otto

7" h, toddler, bisque socket head, almond shaped blue glass sleep eyes, open mouth, hair wig, 5 pc composition toddler body, nicely dressed, painted shoes and socks, c1910-22, mkd "Jutta 1914 8" 600.00

Gebruder Heubach, walking doll, 11" h, $2,000. Photo courtesy of McMasters Doll Auctions.

Effanbee

14" h, Patsy, all composition, painted eyes glance to the side, open/closed smiling mouth, detailed molded hair, nicely dressed in old fabric clothes, c1926, mkd "Effanbee/Patsy" 700.00

24" h, Dy-Dee baby, hard plastic head, painted eyes, open drinker mouth, molded painted hair, soft rubber inset ears, soft rubber jointed body, orig coat and hat outfit, mkd "Effanbee/Dy-Dee Baby/U. S. Pat 1-857-485/Enbland 880-00/France 723-980/Germany 5-85-647/Other Pat. Pending" 400.00

Gaultier

2-5/8" h shoulder head, bisque, swivel, light blue paperweight eyes, closed mouth, pierced ears, cork pate imp 3/0, right shoulder imp "3/0," imp "FG" on left shoulder, c1815 ... 575.00

Greiner, Ludwig

25" h, papier-mâché shoulder head, painted blue upper glancing eyes, closed mouth, painted hair, muslin body, brown leather arms, stitched fingers, well dressed, c1860, mkd: "Greiner Improved Patent Heads, Pat. March 30th '58" 800.00

Handwerck

18-1/2" h, bisque socket head, brown sleep eyes, open mouth, pierced ears, orig blond mohair wig, fully jointed composition body, imp "119" mark..550.00

20" h, bisque socket head, brown glass sleep eyes, open mouth, 4 porcelain teeth, pierced ears, brunette human hair wig, composition and wood ball jointed body, well dressed, c1900, mkd "Handwerck 109-11 Germany"....................................795.00

Hertel, Schwab & Co.

12" h, bisque socket head, blue glass side glancing googlie eyes, closed mouth, watermelon smile, blond mohair wig, composition bent limb baby body, well dressed, c1910, mkd "165," 3,000.00

Heubach, Ernst

23" h, child, bisque socket head, brown glass sleep eyes, open mouth, 4 teeth, brown wig, fully jointed composition body, c1888, mkd "Heubach Koppelsdorf 250 Germany"......650.00

Heubach, Gebruder

10" h, baby, bisque shoulder head, blue intaglio eyes, closed mouth, 2 white beaded teeth, blond forehead curls, muslin baby body, composition lower arms and legs, nicely dressed, c1915..500.00

Ideal Novelty Co.

18" h, Shirley Temple, composition, orig blond mohair wig, fine craquelure overall, eyes crazed, needs restringing, 1936 ....150.00

Jumeau

18" h, standard face, bisque head on shoulder plate, paperweight eyes, closed mouth, pierced ears, old wig, wood body, bisque arms and legs, fashionably dressed, old fabric clothing, c1870, mkd "Jumeau Medallie d'Or Paris"................5,500.00

30" h, bisque, open mouth, pierced ears, stationary set blue glass eyes, French long curls brown hair wig, jointed composition body, orig ivory dress, matching cap and purse, mkd "1907" 2,850.00

Jumeau, 31" h, bisque head, brown glass sleep eyes, open mouth, human hair wig, $2,900. Photo courtesy of McMasters Doll Auctions.

Jumeau, bisque head, blue glass sleep eyes, closed mouth, brunette wig, pierced ears, 16-1/2" h, mkd "E. D.," $2,600. Photo courtesy of McMasters Doll Auctions.

Kammer & Reinhardt

8" h, bisque head, blue glass sleep eyes, open mouth, orig blond mohair wig, composition body, jointed at shoulder and hips, imp "Halbig K star R" mark, paint wear, foot damage, needs restringing..230.00

12" h, Character Toddler, bisque socket head, brown glass sleep eyes, open mouth, 2 porcelain teeth, spring tongue, brunette mohair wig, composition bent limb toddler body, voice box, nicely dressed, c1915, mkd "K star R Simon and Halbig 122 28" 1,500.00

Kestner

13-1/2" h, bisque head, brown glass sleep eyes, closed mouth, orig blond mohair wig, fully jointed composition body, imp "169" mark, needs restringing....................................2,185.00

16-1/2" h, bisque shoulder head, blue sleep eyes, open mouth, replaced wig, painted kid body, bisque hands, imp "154" mark..260.00

Krass, Gebruder

23" h, bisque head, brown glass sleep eyes, open mouth, orig brown mohair wig, fully jointed composition body, imp "GK165," hairline right side of head..............................225.00

Kruse, Kathy

15" h, celluloid socket head, blue inset eyes, closed mouth, blond human air wig, celluloid jointed body, orig clothes, c1958, mkd "Modell Kathy Kruse T40"..............................475.00

Lenci

20" h, child, all felt, swivel head, cloth body jointed at shoulders and hips, painted features, side glancing eyes, orig felt and or-

gandy clothes, c1920, mkd "Lenci, Made in Italy" on cloth and paper tags, also stamped "Lenci" on bottom of foot..1,800.00

Madame Alexander

7-1/2" h, Dionne Quintuplets, 5 composition babies, painted brown eyes glancing to the side, single-stroke brows, painted upper lashes, closed mouths, molded and painted hair, 5 pc composition baby bodies with bent legs, orig tagged rompers and matching bonnets, socks, and shoes, name pins, 5 extra tagged organdy dresses, extra clothing tied on lid of orig basket with pink ribbons, orig tray with pink lace trimmed insert, mkd "Alexander" on back of head and back, "Genuine Dionne Quintuplet Dolls, All Rights Reserved, Madame Alexander, N.Y." on clothing tabs, minor damage to dolls...........1,650.00

14" h, Snow White, all hard plastic, socket head, painted features, green plastic sleep eyes, real lashes, closed mouth, black saran wig, 5 pc body jointed at shoulders and hips, orig tagged ivory satin gown, gold leaf patterned brocade vest, c1952, mkd "Walt Disney Snow White Madame Alexander U.S.A."
....750.00

Marseilles, Armand

20" h, bisque socket head, brown glass sleep eyes, open mouth, blond mohair wig, composition and wood ball jointed body, nicely dressed in old fabric clothing, c1890, mkd "390 ASM, Made in Germany"..400.00

Moramuri

11" h, character, bisque head, blue glass sleep eyes, open mouth, orig mohair wig, bent limb composition body, imp mark, c1920, repairs..115.00

Putnam, Grace Storey

13" h, Bye-Lo Baby, bisque head, blue glass sleep eyes, cloth body and legs, celluloid hands, orig lawn christening dress, cloth label, 1920s 375.00

Schoenhut

Wood head, jointed wood body

12" h, blond wig, painted blue eyes, worn blue garments, patent 1911, decals on head..................................100.00

14" h, painted eyes, blond wig, blue jacket, yellow pants, patent 1911, decals on head and body 470.00

Grace Putnum Storey, Bye-Lo Toddler, 12" h, 10" circ, orig layette box and contents, $2,500. Photo courtesy of McMasters Doll Auctions.

15" l, blue painted eyes, open mouth with four painted teeth, brown wig, brown striped suit, name incised on body, restored..200.00

17" l, body jointed at hips, one piece legs, molded hair, painted blue eyes, white suit, blue collar, patent 1911, partial decal on head, over painted...220.00

20" l, brown sleep eyes, open mouth with four painted teeth, long blond wig, long cotton print dress....................750.00

Simon & Halbig

17-1/2" h, bisque head, gray glass sleep eyes, open mouth, pierced ears, orig human hair wig, fully jointed composition body, imp "S 17-1/2H 939," eyes fixed in open position, small flake off left ear, wear to body 1,035.00

23-3/4" h, bisque head, blue glass sleep eyes, open mouth, pierced ears, orig light brown mohair wig, fully jointed composition body, imp "S12H 719," glaze chips front of head, wear and scuffing to body..1,495.00

Societe Francaise de Bebes et Jouets (SFBJ)

19-1/2" h, Bluette, brown glass sleep eyes, open mouth, pierced ears, orig brown mohair wig, composition body, fully jointed arms, straight legs, walking mechanism, imp "SFBJ 301 Paris," damage to back edge of head, clock works need adjustment...920.00

27" h, Character Toddler, bisque socket head, half moon shaped brown glass sleep eyes, open mouth, beaded upper teeth, wobbler tongue, human hair wig, composition and wood hip jointed toddler body, orig clothes, orig paper label on body, c1915, mkd "21 S.F.B.J. 251 Paris 12".......................2,890.00

Left: Schoenhut, 16" h, pouty expression, $750; right: Simon &Halbig, 15" h, blue glass sleep eyes, closed mouth, brunette wig, $1,900. Photo courtesy of McMasters Doll Auctions.

Steiner, Jules

20" h, bisque head, clockwork, blue glass stationary eyes, open mouth, pierced ears, orig blond lambskin wig, cloth covered torso, kidskin lower body and upper legs, composition arms and legs, slight color loss over right eyes, fine hairline at neck, one hand damaged, some paint wear 1,035.00

Unknown Maker

15" h, bisque shoulder head, blue paperweight stationary eyes, closed mouth, round head with small top opening, unmarked, remnants of orig blond mohair wig, cloth body and limbs, firing blemish on forehead...375.00

15" h, Frozen Charlie, German, porcelain, realistically painted, blond hair, blue eyes..320.00

21" h, bisque head, brown glass sleep eyes, closed mouth, brown synthetic wing, straight wrist composition body, imp "14" on back of head, body yellowed, hands scrubbed...........690.00

Wax Over Composition Head

England or Germany, mid-19th C, pink tinted wax, stationary brown pupil-less eyes, painted mouth, brown glued on human hair wig, cloth body, tan leather arms, orig pink tarlatan and white lace costume, fine cracks in wax 230.00

DOORKNOBS AND OTHER BUILDER'S HARDWARE

History: Man's home has always been his castle, whether grand and ornate, or simple and homey. The use of decorative doorknobs, back plates, doorbells, knockers, and mail slots helped decorate and distinguish one's door. Creating a grand entrance was as important to our ancestors as it is today.

Before the advent of the mechanical bell or electrical buzzer and chime, a doorknocker was considered an essential door ornament to announce the arrival of visitors. Metal was used to cast or forge the various forms; many cast-iron examples were painted. Collectors like to find doorknockers with English registry marks.

Collectors of doorknobs and other types of builders' hardware are growing as we learn to treasure the decorative elements of our past. Often old house lovers seek out these elements to refurbish their homes, adding to the demand.

References: Ronald S. Barlow (comp.), *Victorian Houseware, Hardware and Kitchenware*, Windmill Publishing, 1991; Margarete Baur-Heinhold, *Decorative Ironwork*, Schiffer Publishing, 1996; Len Blumin, *Victorian Decorative Art*, available from ADCA (P.O. Box 126, Eola, IL 60519), n.d.; Maude Eastwood wrote several books about doorknobs which are available from P.O. Box 126, Eola, IL 60519; Constance M Greiff, *Early Victorian*, Abbeville Press, 1995; Philip G. Knobloch, *A Treasure of Fine Construction Design*, Astragal Press, 1995; Henrie Martinie, *Art Deco Ornamental Ironwork*, Dover Publications, 1996; James Massey and Shirley Maxwell, *Arts & Crafts*, Abbeville Press, 1995; Ted Menten (comp.), *Art Nouveau Decorative Ironwork*, Dover Publications, n.d.; *Ornamental French Hardware Designs*, Dover Publications, 1995; Ernest Rettelbusch, *Handbook of Historic Ornament from Ancient Times to Biedermeier*, Dover Publications, 1996; Alan Robertson, *Architectural An-*

tiques, Chronicle Books, 1987; Edward Shaw, *Modern Architect* (reprint), Dover Publications, 1996; *Turn of the Century Doors, Windows and Decorative Millwork*, Dover Publications, 1995 reprint; Web Wilson, *Great Glass in American Architecture,* E. P. Dutton, New York, 1986.

Periodical: *American Bungalow,* P.O. Box 756, Sierra Madre, CA 91204.

Collectors' Club: Antique Doorknob Collectors of America, Inc., P.O. Box 126, Eola, IL 60519.

Additional Listings: Architectural Elements, Stained Glass.

Advisor: Web Wilson.

Door Bell
    Connell's Patent of 1873, dec, 6" d 70.00
    Mechanical, brass 125.00
Door Bell Plate
    Marshall Field & Co, brass 25.00
    Neoclassic, Toulon pattern, Reading, 6" l, 2-1/4" w.........55.00
Door Knob
    Arts and Crafts, stamped metal, rose motif, one nickel plate, other copper plated, 2" d knobs, matching 9" h x 1-1/2" plates, pr.................45.00
    Cherub and sunburst, Corbin Special Hardware, c1890, 2-1/4" d.................300.00

Knob and heavy dec plate from Cook County Office Building, Chicago, $65. Photo courtesy of Web Wilson's Antique Hardware Auctions.

Cook County Office Building, Chicago, 2-1/2" d heavy dec knob, 11" h x 3-1/2" w plate 65.00
Eastlake style, brass.................35.00
Gold washed surface, Veroccio pattern, RH Co., 2-1/4" knobs, 9-1/4" h, 2-1/2" w plates, 4 pcs 110.00
Gutta Percha, figural, cherub and dog running through woods, 2-1/2" d, some wear.................140.00
La Salle Hotel, Chicago, mkd "LS" on knob, one ext., one int..................185.00

Bronze, hammered, thumb action, tapered pickets and serrated ends, 12-1/2" x 3-3/4", $250. Photo courtesy of Web Wilson's Antique Hardware Auctions.

Ludwig Kruzinger designed lion knob (with second mark) and massive backplate, Neo-Grec taste, $2,300. Photo courtesy of Web Wilson's Antique Hardware Auctions.

Lion, Ludwig Kruzinger design, with 2nd mark (MCCC/R&E), massive MCCC Neo-Grec taste backplate, 2-3/4" w knob, 9" h x 3-1/2" w backplate 2,300.00

Mineral, multicolored, brass shank, 2-1/4" d 30.00

Passage, Gothic trefoil design, heavy, 2-1/4" d 70.00

Passage, sunburst vase and foliage, Branford, c1880 ...35.00

Porcelain, hp, fixed brass rosette, mkd "H&S Pitts Patent," 19th C, 2-1/2" d 275.00

Door Knocker, 6-1/2" h, 4" w, dog, heavy cast iron, old tan paint, American, mid 19th C...................................235.00

Door Knocker and Peep Hole Combination, Masonic, brass, 20th C 60.00

Door Pull

Art Nouveau style, Flora pattern, Corbin, 1905, 21" l, 4-1/2" w, one with nick, pr 650.00

Cast Iron, bluebird and butterfly pattern, Norwalk, pr.....90.00

Entry Set, Norwalk, large and small knob, large double key-hole plate, rosette, fancy lock, nightworks, 1888 ....300.00

Mail Slot Cover, 7 3/4" w, "Letters," brass, Victorian 45.00

Push Plate, bronze, Windsor pattern, Sargent, c1885, 16" x 4" 150.00

Thumb Action Handle, 12-1/2" h, 3-3/4" w, hammered bronze, tapered "pickets" with serrated ends as back plate.........250.00

DOORSTOPS

History: Doorstops became popular in the late 19th century. They are either flat or three dimensional and were made out of a variety of different materials, such as cast iron, bronze, or wood. Hubley, a leading toy manufacturer, made many examples.

References: Jeanne Bertoia, *Doorstops*, Collector Books, 1985, 1996 value update; Douglas Congdon–Martin, *Figurative Cast Iron*, Schiffer Publishing, 1994.

Collectors' Club: Doorstop Collectors of America, 2413 Madison Ave., Vineland, NJ 08630.

Videotape: *Off the Ground & Off the Wall*, Gary Roma, Iron Frog Productions.

REPRODUCTION ALERT

Reproductions are proliferating as prices on genuine doorstops continue to rise. A reproduced piece generally is slightly smaller than the original unless an original mold is used. The overall casting of reproductions is not as smooth as on the originals. Reproductions also lack the detail apparent in originals, including the appearance of the painted areas. Any bright orange rusting is strongly indicative of a new piece. Beware. If it looks too good to be true, it usually is.

Notes: Pieces described below contain at least 80% or more of the original paint and are in very good condition. Repainting drastically reduces price and desirability. Poor original paint is preferred over repaint.

All listings are cast-iron and flat-back castings unless otherwise noted.

Doorstops marked with an asterisk are currently being reproduced.

Basket, 11" h, rose, ivory wicker basket, natural flowers, handle with bow, sgd "Hubley 121" 145.00

Bear, 15" h, holding and looking at honey pot, brown furl, black highlights 625.00

Bellhop, 7-1/2" h, carrying satchel, facing sideways, orange-red uniform and cap 400.00

Bowl, 7" x 7", green-blue, natural colored fruit, sgd "Hubley 456" 125.00

Boy, 10-5/8" h, wearing diapers, directing traffic, police hat, red scarf, brown dog at side.................................465.00

*Caddie, 8" h, carrying brown and tan bag, white, brown knickers, red jacket..350.00

*Cat, 8" h, black, red ribbon and bow around neck, on pillow 125.00

Child, 17" h, reaching naked, flesh color, short brown curly hair 625.00

Clown, 10" h, full figure, 2 sided, red suit, white collar, blue hat, black shoes 575.00

Cottage, 8-5/8" l, 5-3/4" h, Cape type, blue roof, flowers, fenced garden, path, sgd "Eastern Specialty Mfg. Co. 14" 150.00

Dancer, 8-7/8" h, Art Deco couple doing Charleston, pink dress, black tux, red and black base, "FISH" on front, sgd "Hubley 270" 495.00

Dog

7" h, three puppies in basket, natural colors, sgd "Copyright 1932 M. Rosenstein, Lancaster, PA, USA" 275.00

8-1/2" x 9", full figure facing forward, brown, tan markings 200.00

9" h, full figure, Boston Bull, facing left, black, tan markings 150.00

Doormen In Livery, 12" h, twin men, worn orig paint, mkd "Fish," hubley 1,760.00

Drum Major, 12-5/8" h, full figure, ivory pants, red hat with feather, yellow baton in right hand, left hand on waist, sq base 275.00

Duck, 7-1/2" h, white, green bush and grass 245.00

Dutch Boy, 11" h, full figure, hands in pockets, blue suit and hat, red belt and collar, brow shoes, blond hair...................425.00

Basket of Flowers, cast iron, yellow basket, blue, red, and yellow tulips, green stems, 8-1/2" h, $90.

Elephant, 14" h, with palm tree, early 20th C, very minor paint wear 210.00

Fisherman, 6-1/4" h, standing at wheel, hand over eyes, rain gear 150.00

Frog, 3" h, full figure, sitting, yellow and green 60.00

Giraffe, 20-1/4" h, tan, brown spots, squared off lines to casting 600.00

Girl
8-3/4" h, dark blue outfit and beanie, high white collar, black shoes, red hair, incised "663" 395.00
*13-3/4" h, 9-3/4" l, white hat, flowing cape, holding orange jack-o-lantern with red cutout eyes, nose, and mouth 800.00

Goldenrods, 7-1/8" h, natural color, sgd "Hubley 268" 200.00

*Golfer, 10" h, overhand swing, hat and ball on ground, Hubley 300.00

Indian Chief, 9-3/4" h, orange and tan headdress, yellow pants with blue stripes, red patches at ankles, green grass, sgd "A. A. Richardson," copyright 1928 ....295.00

Lighthouse, 14" h, green rocks, black path, white lighthouse, red window and door trim..225.00

*Mammy, 10" h, white, scarf and apron, dark blue dress, red kerchief on head..325.00

Monkey, 14-3/8" h, hand reaching up, brown, tan and white 500.00

Old Mill, 6-1/4" h, brown log mill, tan roof, white path, green shrubbery..235.00

Owl, 9-1/2" h, sits on books, sgd "Eastern Spec. Co" 245.00

Pan, 7" h, with flute, sitting on mushroom, green outfit, red hat and sleeves, green grass base 150.00

Parrot, 13-3/4" h, in ring, two sided, heavy gold base, sgd "B & H"..250.00

Peasant Woman, 8-3/4" h, blue dress, black hair, fruit basket on head..145.00

Penguin, 10" h, full figure, facing sideways, black, white chest, top hat and bow tie, yellow feet and beak, unsgd Hubley 295.00

*Pheasant, 9-1/2" h, leaning on red fire hydrant, blue uniform and tilted hat, comic character face, tan base, "Safety First" on front..650.00

Prancing Horse, 11" h, scrolled and molded base, "Greenlees Glasgow" imp on base, cast iron 175.00

*Quail, 7-1/4" h, 2 brown, tan, and yellow birds, green, white, and yellow grass, Fred Everett on front, sgd "Hubley 459" 265.00

Rabbit, 8-1/8" h, eating carrot, red sweater, brown pants 300.00

Rooster, 13" h, red comb, black and brown tail 325.00

Ship, 5-1/4" h, clipper, full sails, American flag on top mast, wave base, 2 rubber stoppers, sgd "CJO"...........................65.00

Squirrel, 9" h, sitting on stump eating nut, brown and tan 200.00

Storybook
4-1/2" h, Humpty Dumpty, full figure, sgd "661"............295.00
7-3/4" h, Little Miss Muffet, sitting on mushroom, blue dress, blond hair..175.00
9-1/2" h, Little Red Riding Hood, basket at side, red cape, tan dress with blue pattern, blond hair, sgd "Hubley" ...395.00
12-1/2" h, Huckleberry Finn, floppy hat, pail, stick, Littco Products label..395.00

Sunbonnet Girl, pink dress..245.00

Tiger, 8-1/2" h, tan, black stripes, baseball bat on shoulder black base..400.00

Whistler, 20-1/4" h, boy, hands in tan knickers, yellow striped baggy shirt, sgd "B & H"..950.00

*Windmill, 6-3/4" h, ivory, red roof, house at side, green base 100.00

*Woman, 11" h, flowers and shawl 140.00

Zinnias, 11-5/8" h, multicolored flowers, blue and black vase, sgd "B & H"..185.00

DRESDEN/MEISSEN

History: Augustus II, Elector of Saxony and King of Poland, founded the Royal Saxon Porcelain Manufactory in the Albrechtsburg, Meissen, in 1710. Johann Frederick Boettger, an alchemist, and Tschirnhaus, a nobleman, experimented with kaolin from the Dresden area to produce porcelain. By 1720, the factory produced a whiter hard-paste porcelain than that from the Far East. The factory experienced its golden age from the 1730s to the 1750s under the leadership of Samuel Stolzel, kiln master, and Johann Gregor Herold, enameler.

The Meissen factory was destroyed and looted by forces of Frederick the Great during the Seven Years' War (1756-1763). It was reopened, but never achieved its former greatness.

In the 19th century, the factory reissued some of its earlier forms. These later wares are called "Dresden" to differentiate them from the earlier examples. Further, there were several other porcelain factories in the Dresden region and their products also are grouped under the "Dresden" designation.

Marks: Many marks were used by the Meissen factory. The first was a pseudo-Oriental mark in a square. The famous crossed swords mark was adopted in 1724. A small dot between the hilts was used from 1763 to 1774, and a star between the hilts from 1774 to 1814. Two modern marks are swords with a hammer and sickle and swords with a crown.

References: Susan and Al Bagdade, *Warman's English & Continental Pottery & Porcelain*, 2nd ed., Wallace-Homestead, 1991; Robert E. Röntgen, *The Book of Meissen*, revised ed., Schiffer Publishing, 1996.

Dresden

Basket, 12-3/4" l, reticulated, center medallion of couple in landscape, puce interlocking circles, four feet, two handles, gilt, floral, and foliate dec, price for pr 1,600.00

Compote, 14-1/4" h, figural, shaped pierced oval bowl with applied florets, support stems mounted with 2 figures of children, printed marks, late 19th/early 20th C, pr 345.00

Cup, 3-1/2" d, white, relief prunus dec, two handles, attributed to Boettger, unmarked, 1715..260.00

Demitasse Cup and Saucer, floral reserves, blue ground 275.00

Dessert Plate, 9" d, central female portrait, heavy gilt, green ground, mkd, c1910, 12 pc set 1,200.00

Figure
7" h, Ballerina, young girl, white and pink lace dress, pink shoes, red hair, applied flowers on dress 250.00
8" x 10-1/2", Gypsy Lady with Goat, seated, sandals, red kerchief, young goat, crown mark 450.00

Loving Cup, 6-1/2" h, 3 handles, woodland scene with nymph, gold trim..475.00

Plate, 8-1/4" d, enamel floral dec, c1900, 12 pc set..........520.00

Tea Caddy, 5-1/4" h, 3-1/2" w, sq, lacy gold flowers on 2 panels, scene of courting boy and girl, crossed swords mark, "H" and "Dresden" 250.00

Urn, cov, 12" h, 2 panels of lowers, garden setting, red ground, floral dec, c1860-1920..400.00
Vase, 8-1/2" h, portrait scene, cobalt blue ground, raised gold dec, artist sgd..375.00

Meissen

Bowl, 7" sq, scalloped, four panels, two with floral scenes, two with scenes of court couples, 19th C 225.00
Cup and Saucer, 5-1/4" d, Imari palette, Marcolini period 300.00
Dessert Plate, 7" d, polychrome floral dec, price for 4 pc set 50.00
Figure
   3-1/2" h, child with wig stand..350.00
   4-1/2" h, girl with doll, factory marks, 20th C 920.00
   5" h, young girl with spotted dog, factory marks, 20th C 920.00
   5-3/4" h, two flute players, mandolin player, dancing lady, price for 4 pc set 1,600.00
   7" h, cupid with birdbath, factory marks, late 19th C, minor chip..1,495.00
   13" h, 13-1/2" w, two neoclassical style women in garden, one with cupid, other feeding birds on lap...................4,500.00
   13-1/2" and 14," Malabars, male adorned with bow, arrow, sword, and shield, female carrying basket of fruit and cov pot, crossed words mark, incised "823" and "764," pr 4,600.00
   13-3/4" h, muse and putti with tree stump, Roman soldier style costume, flags and weapons 3,250.00
   16-1/2" h, allegorical figure, woman, seated on scrolled free-form base, late 19th/early 20th C
     Holding script, incised "#369/4," printed mark 2,990.00
     Holding staff, incised #369/5," printed mark 3,220.00
     Holding stringed instrument, incised "#369/6,".....2,990.00
Lamp, oil, 4" h, molded applied polychrome floral dec, 18th-19th C 600.00
Plate
   9-1/2" d, enamel dec bird and insect dec, gilded border, 19th C, gilt wear, 11 pc set...1,150.00

Potpourri Bowl, gilded garland and flame top, openwork lid and bowl, four ram's head handles, oval floral medallions, sq tapering fluted feet, int. painted with flowers, Meissen, 18th/19th C, 12" d, $3,100. Photo courtesy of Freeman\Fine Arts.

9-3/4" d, reticulated, still life of fruit, gilded edge, 19th C factory marks, pr..690.00
Serving Dish, 11-1/3" h, gilt trim, enamel dec fruit cartouches, printed mark, 20th C, pr 435.00
Tea Caddy, 5" h, ovoid, gilt and grisaille floral dec, festooned floral finial, Marcolini period 325.00
Tea Cup and Saucer, 3-7/8" d, Konigstein topographical scene, cobalt blue ground, late 19th C 1,380.00
Teapot
   5" h, globular
     Polychrome rose dec, 19th C 200.00
     White porcelain, chrysanthemum form finial 100.00
   11" h, enameled scenes of hunters, c1900, chips to floral finial 230.00
Tea Set, partial, 4-1/2" h ovoid teapot, key form handle, festooned floral final, five cups and saucers, gilt and grisaille floral dec 1,400.00
Urn, 10-3/4" h, white, gilt trim, two double snake-form handles, price for pr...550.00
Vase
   7-1/4" h, new gold trim, enamel floral dec, c1900 ....460.00
   10" h, cobalt blue ground, foliage reserve, factory marks, 20th C 260.00
   13-1/4" h, two men and woman in forest scene.............225.00

DUNCAN AND MILLER

History: George Duncan, Harry B. and James B., his sons, and Augustus Heisey, his son-in-law, formed George Duncan & Sons in Pittsburgh, Pennsylvania, in 1865. The factory was located just two blocks from the Monongahela River, providing easy and inexpensive access by barge for materials needed to produce glass. The men, from Pittsburgh's south side, were descendants of generations of skilled glassmakers.

The plant burned to the ground in 1892. James E. Duncan, Sr., selected a site for a new factory in Washington, Pennsylvania, where operations began on Feb. 9, 1893. The plant prospered, producing fine glassware and table services for many years.

John E. Miller, one of the stockholders, was responsible for designing many fine patterns, the most famous being Three Face. The firm incorporated and used the name The Duncan and Miller Glass Company until the plant closed in 1955. The company's slogan was "The Loveliest Glassware in America." The U.S. Glass Co. purchased the molds, equipment, and machinery in 1956.

References: Gene Florence, *Elegant Glassware of the Depression Era*, 6th ed., Collector Books, 1995; Naomi L. Over, *Ruby Glass of the 20th Century*, Antique Publications, 1990, 1993-94 value update.

Collectors' Club: National Duncan Glass Society, P.O. Box 965, Washington, PA 15301.

Additional Listings: Pattern Glass.

Animal
   Donkey and pheasant 425.00
   Goose, fat 275.00
   Heron..95.00
   Swan
     6-1/2", opal pink..95.00
     7-1/2", crystal bowl 12.00
     7-1/2", red bowl...40.00
     10-1/2", crystal bowl...24.00

10-1/2", dark green bowl 55.00
10-1/2", red bowl 75.00
Ashtray, Terrace, red, sq 35.00
Bowl
    Caribbean, blue, 8-1/2" d 70.00
    Chrysanthemum, blue, 13-1/2" d 145.00
    First Love, crystal, 10" d, flared 50.00
Bud Vase, First Love, crystal, 9" h 75.00
Candelabra, pr
    First Love, crystal, 2-lite, #30 ....75.00
    Sandwich, crystal, 3-lite, 16" h, bobeches and prisms .225.00
Candlesticks, pr, Hobnail, amethyst 75.00
Candy Box, cov, Canterbury, crystal, 3 part, 6" d, 3-1/2" h
    ....65.00
Candy Jar, cov, Sandwich, chartreuse, 8-1/2" h 95.00
Champagne
    First Love, crystal 16.00
    Terrace, red 95.00
Cigarette Box, Sandwich, red, small 125.00
Cocktail, Caribbean, blue, 3-3/4" oz., 4-1/8" h 45.00
Console Bowl, #16, winged shape, cobalt blue 250.00
Cordial, Astaire, red 45.00
Cornucopia Vase
    First Love, crystal, #117 ....60.00
    #121, Swirl, blue opalescent, shape #2, upswept tail 75.00
    #131, 14" h, shape #3, deep ruby 125.00
Creamer and Sugar
    Passion Flower, #38, crystal 40.00
    Radiance, light blue 45.00
Cup and Saucer, Radiance, light blue 20.00
Decanter, First Love, crystal, 32 oz 295.00
Finger Bowl, Astaire, red 35.00
Flower Arranger, Canterbury, citrone 65.00
Fruit Bowl, Sandwich, crystal, 12" d, flared 45.00
Goblet
    Caribbean, blue 38.00
    Festival of Flowers, crystal 28.50
    Plaza, cobalt blue 37.50
Milk Pitcher, Caribbean, blue 295.00
Oyster Cocktail
    Canterbury, citrone 14.00

First Love, crystal, 3-3/4" 22.00
Language of Flowers, crystal 15.00
Plate
    Astaire, red, 7-1/2" d 12.50
    Caribbean, blue, 6" d, handle 18.00
    Radiance, light blue, 8-1/2" d 16.50
Sandwich, green, 8" 10.00
Spiral Flute, crystal, 10-3/8" d, dinner 22.00
Terrace, cobalt blue, 7-1/2" d 37.50
Relish
    Caribbean, blue, 2 part, round, 6" d 30.00
    First Love, crystal, 10" d, 5 part 65.00
    Terrace, crystal, 5 part, gold trim 125.00
Sherbet
    Language of Flowers, crystal 15.00
    Sandwich, green 10.00
Sugar Shaker, Duncan Block, crystal 40.00
Tumbler, Terrace, red 37.50
Violet Vase, Hobnail, green, ftd, ruffled 30.00
Whiskey, Seahorse, etch #502, red and crystal, ftd, 2 oz 45.00
Wine
    Caribbean, sapphire blue, 3 oz, 4-3/4" h 45.00
    Festival of Flowers, crystal 26.50

DURAND

History: Victor Durand (1870-1931), born in Baccarat, France, apprenticed at the Baccarat glassworks, where several generations of his family had worked. In 1884, Victor came to America to join his father at Whitall-Tatum & Co. in New Jersey. In 1897, father and son leased the Vineland Glass Manufacturing Company in Vineland, New Jersey. Products included inexpensive bottles, jars, and glass for scientific and medical purposes. By 1920, four separate companies existed.

When Quezal Art Glass and Decorating Company failed, Victor Durand recruited Martin Bach, Jr., Emil J. Larsen, William Wiedebine, and other Quezal men and opened an art-glass shop at Vineland in December 1924. Quezal-style iridescent pieces were made. New innovations included cameo and intaglio designs, geometric Art Deco shapes, Venetian Lace, and Oriental-style pieces. In 1928, crackled glass, called Moorish Crackle and Egyptian Crackle, was made.

Durand died in 1931. The Vineland Flint Glass Works was merged with Kimble Glass Company a year later, and the art glass line was discontinued.

Marks: Many Durand glass pieces are not marked. Some have a sticker with the words "Durand Art Glass," others have the name "Durand" scratched on the pontil or "Durand" inside a large V. Etched numbers may be part of the marking.

Bowl
    5" h, luster glass, opal and blue floral, sgd and numbered
    ....3,350.00
    9-3/4" d, butterscotch, partial silver sgd 325.00
Candlesticks, pr, 2-3/4" h, mushroom, red, opal pulled florals, pale yellow base 700.00
Compote, cov, 10-1/2" h, Spanish yellow cased glass, etched and wheel-cut Bridgeton Rose floral dec cut to clear, conforming matching cover, base marked with "Durand" in "V," possibly added latter 375.00
Decanter, 12" h, blue cut to clear, mushroom shaped stopper, unsgd 600.00
Jar, 8-1/2" h, gold ground, blue swirl vine dec 1,200.00

Candleholders, Carribean, two-lite, sapphire blue, pr, $295.

Lamp Base, Moorish crackle, orange, greenish highlights, 9-1/4" h, $125.

Lamp Base, 12" h vase, blue, green, orange King Tut dec, opal ground, drilled 400.00
Mint Bowl, 6" d, shallow, gold scalloped rim, sgd "V. Durand" 195.00
Rose Bowl, 4" h, clear, air traps, sgd and numbered.........350.00
Stemware, cobalt blue cut to clear......................................175.00
Vase
    6-1/4" h, King Tut, classic baluster form, irid green swirls and coils, warm orange glass cased to white, lustered orange int., Larson foot 690.00
    7" h, irid amber, intaglio florals, unsgd 195.00
    8-1/2" h, fold over white rim, light green, shiny, sgd and numbered 600.00
    9" h, flared, bulbous, irid blue, sgd and numbered....1,600.00
    9-3/4" h, Lady Gay Rose, flared orange lined oval body, cased to white, red-rose surface, King Tut irid swirling gold and silver design 1,495.00
    12" h, flared cylinder, bright transparent green shaded to clear, five pulled green and white striped pulled peacock feathers 750.00

EARLY AMERICAN GLASS

History: The term "Early American glass" covers glass made in America from the colonial period through the mid-19th century. As such, it includes the early pressed glass and lacy glass made between 1827 and 1840.

Major glass-producing centers prior to 1850 were Massachusetts (New England Glass Company and the Boston and Sandwich Glass Company), South Jersey, Pennsylvania (Stiegel's Manheim factory and many Pittsburgh-area firms), and Ohio (several different companies in Kent, Mantua, and Zanesville).

Early American glass was popular with collectors from 1920 to 1950. It has now regained some of its earlier prominence. Leading auction sources for early American glass include Garth's, Heckler & Company, James D. Julia, and Skinner, Inc.

References: William E. Covill, *Ink Bottles and Inkwells*, William S. Sullwold Publishing, out of print; George and Helen McKearin, American Glass, Crown, 1975; ——, *Two Hundred Years of American Blown Glass*, Doubleday and Company, 1950; Helen McKearin and Kenneth Wilson, *American Bottles and Flasks*, Crown, 1978; Dick Roller (comp.), *Indiana Glass Factories Notes*, Acorn Press, 1994; Jane S. Spillman, *American and European Pressed Glass*, Corning Museum of Glass, 1981; Kenneth Wilson, *American Glass 1760-1930*, 2 Vols., Hudson Hills Press and The Toledo Museum of Art, 1994; ——, *New England Glass and Glassmaking*, Crowell, 1972.

Periodicals: *Antique Bottle & Glass Collector*, P.O. Box 187, East Greenville, PA 18041; *Glass Collector's Digest*, Antique Publications, P.O. Box 553, Marietta, OH 45750.

Collectors' Clubs: Early American Glass Traders, RD 5, Box 638, Milford, DE 19963; Early American Pattern Glass Society, P.O. Box 266, Colesburg, IA 52035; Glass Research Soc. of New Jersey, Wheaton Village, Glasstown Rd, Millville, NJ 08332; National Early American Glass Club, P.O. Box 8489, Silver Spring, MD 20907.

Museums: Bennington Museum, Bennington, VT; Chrysler Museum, Norfolk, VA; Corning Museum of Glass, Corning, NY; Glass Museum, Dunkirk, IN; Glass Museum Foundation, Redlands, CA; New Bedford Glass Museum, New Bedford, MA; Sandwich Glass Museum, Sandwich, MA; Toledo Museum of Art, Toledo, OH; Wheaton Historical Village Assoc. Museum of Glass, Millville, NJ.

Additional Listings: Blown Three Mold; Cup Plates; Flasks; Sandwich Glass; Stiegel-Type Glass.

Back Bar Bottle, 10-1/4" h, fancy pattern mold, cylindrical, pale opalescent yellow green, opalescent stripes swirled to the right, rolled mouth, ground pontil scar, 1870-1900 ....200.00
Bottle
    5" h, opaque white, polychrome enameled floral dec, some opalescent, pewter fittings and cap 360.00
    6-3/8" h, colorless, blown, cased, finely engraved floral swags with bows, medallion with "B. R.," mismatched stopper 125.00
    7-5/8" h, blown, amber, globular, 24 swirled ribs, applied lip, appears to have terminal ring, minor wear and scratches, tiny broken blister, small stones, trace of stain, Zanesville, OH 330.00
    7-7/8" h, blown, deep amber, globular, 24 swirled ribs, Zanesville, OH, minor int. stain..470.00
Bowl
    4-3/4" d, 3-1/8" h, blown, cobalt blue, expanded diamond, applied foot 250.00
    5" d, 3-5/8" h, blown, cobalt blue, 15 swirled ribs, flared lip, applied foot 440.00
    5-7/8" d, 3" h, blown, amber, folded rim, early 19th C, minor burst bubble 690.00
    6-1/2" d, 1-7/8" h, blown, light green, lily pad dec, rolled rim, attributed to NJ 1,495.00

6-1/2" d, 4-5/8" h, blown, amber, folded rim, Midwestern
....715.00

Candlesticks, pr
6-7/8" h, clambroth, hexagonal......................................500.00
9-1/8" h, flint, dolphin base, hexagonal socket, small edge
flakes, one glued socket, pr 110.00

Canister, blown, colorless
9-5/8" h, 2 applied rings and finial, Pittsburgh 110.00
11" h, 2 applied rings, pressed lid with chips 140.00
11-1/8" h, 3 applied blue rings, colorless applied finial, Pittsburgh 770.00

Celery Vase
8-1/4" h, cut, waisted with band of alternating cross hatched
diamonds and ovals, foliate band at rim, Bakewell, Pitts-
burgh, c1825..375.00
8-3/8" h, flint, colorless, cut sheaf of wheat pattern, Pittsburgh,
rim chips 385.00
10" h, flint, colorless, round foot, hexagonal foot and bowl with
oval and round thumbprint and Gothic Arches, chips on
foot 145.00

Cologne, 5-1/2" h, hexagonal, canary yellow, Star and Punty, cut
stopper with ground edges 330.00

Compote
5-3/4" d, 5-7/8" h, fiery opalescent, Colonial, rim chip
....535.00
10" d, 7-3/4" h, flint, colorless, blown bowl with cut sheaf of
wheat pattern, knop stem, star foot, Pittsburgh, wear and
small flakes 385.00

Creamer
3-1/4" h, pattern molded, sapphire blue, faint darker blue striations, 14 ribs, tooled rim with pour spout, applied handle,
attributed to Pittsburgh, 1820-60, small pc of rigaree at tail
end of handle missing 150.00
3-1/2" h, cobalt blue, expanded diamond, applied handle,
check at handle 165.00

Decanter, colorless, blown
9-3/8" h, cut fluting and panels, engraved swags and tassels,
lip flakes 165.00
9-1/2" h, copper wheel engraved floral design, stopper re-
ground 110.00
9-3/4" h, blown, colorless, applied chain dec, attributed to Th-
omas Cains, Boston, first half 19th C, very minor chips,
scratches to int. 230.00
10-5/8" h, pillar molded, 8 pillar mold, colorless with amethyst
highlights on each rib, heavy collar molded mouth, ground
pontil scar, attributed to Pittsburgh, 1835-70 ....1,000.00

Dish, 5-1/8" d, fiery opalescent, Plume, minor chips..........165.00

Ewer, 11-3/4" h, flint, colorless, pillar mold, applied foot and handle, pewter top, hinged lid with finial, Pittsburgh 495.00

Gaffing Tool Holder, 4-3/4" h, blown, peacock blue, applied base,
segmented stem...580.00

Jigger, 2-1/8" h, fiery opalescent, paneled...........................75.00

Lamp, flint
8-1/8" h, canary, pressed, loop design, hexagonal base, minor
cracks..375.00
10-1/4" h, colorless, hexagonal base, comet font, soldered re-
pair on brass collar, chips on foot 165.00
12-1/4" h, colorless, sq base, hexagonal stem, four printee
font, pewter collar 180.00

Pan, 7" d, blown, colorless, applied cobalt blue rim, ground pon-
til 165.00

Pitkin
7" h, blown, aqua, half post neck, 30 ribs with broken swirl,
flake at pontil and bottom edge................................330.00
7-1/4" h, blown, olive green, half post neck, 36 ribs with broken
swirl..275.00

Pitcher
4-3/8" h, blown, deep olive green, applied foot and handle, Mt.
Vernon Glass Works 1,760.00

Scent Bottles, various shapes, colors; some with orig pewter screw-on tops, others with brass fixtures, some with internal stoppers, prices range from $50 to $65. Photo courtesy of Gene Harris Antique Auction Center.

4-5/8" h, lily-pad, blown, amber, applied handle, broken blister
in second gather near one pulled up peak, Ellenville, NY
....2,255.00
5" h, blown, colorless, applied chain dec, attributed to Thomas
Cains, Boston, first half 19th C, minor crack to handle
....690.00
5-1/2" h, blown, amber, incised rim, applied ribbed handle,
petal foot, Midwestern, minute chips....................4,315.00
5-3/4" h, pillar mold, flint, colorless, applied handle and tooled
lip, Pittsburgh..315.00
7" h, blown, colorless with slight blue-gray tint, threaded neck,
applied handle, check at base of handle, Midwestern
....220.00
9" h, mold blown, flint, Cleat pattern, applied handle, minor
edge roughness 300.00

Preserving Jar, 7-1/4" h, blown, colorless, tin lid, recessed gallery
lip for wax 220.00

Salt
2-1/2" h, blown molded, light green, diamond pattern on petal
foot, late 18th C/early 19th C, minute chips 815.00
2-7/8" h, pattern molded, cobalt blue, 16 ribs swirled slightly to
the right, double ogee bowl, short stem of same gather, applied circular foot, sheared mouth, pontil scar, Midwest,
1820-60..90.00
3-5/8" h, pattern molded, colorless with pale gray cast, 15 ribs,
outward folded rim, pontil scar, freeblown foot, flat rim
chip..170.00

Spooner
4-1/8" h, cobalt blue, Bigler variant 415.00
4-3/8" h, fiery opalescent, Excelsior, chips on base......330.00

Sugar Bowl, cov
5-1/8" h, blown, colorless, applied chain dec, attributed to Thomas Cains, Boston, first half 19th C 920.00
5-3/8" h, flint, vaseline, Gothic Arch, octagonal, acanthus leaf
lid, small flakes on base, lid with rim chips 550.00

Sugar Bowl, open
5-5/8" h, deep blue, paneled, small flakes on foot 200.00
8-3/4" h, cobalt blue, paneled, small flakes...................660.00

Syrup, 8-1/4" h, colorless, hexagonal, Star and Punty, applied hollow handle, tin top with hinged lid, pewter finial............220.00

Tumbler
3-1/8" h, blown, cobalt blue, paneled, pinpoint flakes on foot
....125.00
3-1/8" h, blown, cobalt blue, Ashburton, pinpoint flakes on
foot..150.00
4" h, blown, olive green, old paper label, broken blisters, Midwestern 715.00

Vase, 8" h, blown, emerald green, flared baluster, circular foot, attributed to Pittsburgh, 19th C 2,185.00

Whiskey Bottle, 7-1/4" h, blown molded, amber, pear-shape, applied handle, "Griffith Hyatt & Co. Baltimore" around semicircular panel enclosing paper label, circular panel on reverse enclosing paper label of *U.S.S. Constitution*, wear, losses to labels 750.00

ENGLISH CHINA AND PORCELAIN (GENERAL)

History: By the 19th century, more than 1,000 china and porcelain manufacturers were scattered throughout England, with the majority of the factories located in the Staffordshire district.

By the 19th century, English china and porcelain had achieved a worldwide reputation for excellence. American stores imported large quantities for their customers. The special-production English pieces of the 18th and early 19th centuries held a position of great importance among early American antiques collectors.

References: Susan and Al Bagdade, *Warman's English & Continental Pottery & Porcelain*, 2nd ed., Wallace-Homestead, 1991; John A. Bartlett, *British Ceramic Art: 1870-1940*, Schiffer Publishing, 1993; David Battie and Michael Turner, *19th and 20th Century British Porcelain Price Guide*, Antique Collectors' Club, 1994; Peter Bradshaw, *English Eighteenth Century Porcelain Figures, 1745-1795*, Antiques Collectors' Club, 1980; John and Margaret Cushion, *Collector's History of British Porcelain*, Antique Collectors' Club, 1992; Rachael Feild, *Macdonald Guide to Buying Antique Pottery & Porcelain*, Wallace-Homestead, 1987; Mary J. Finegan, *Johnson Brothers Dinnerware: Pattern Directory & Price Guide*, Marfine Antiques, 1993; Geoffrey A. Godden, *Godden's Guide to Mason's China and the Ironstone Wares*, Antique Collectors' Club, out of print; ——, *Godden's Guide to English Porcelain*, Wallace-Homestead, 1992; Pat Halfpenny, *English Earthenware Figures 1740-1840*, Antique Collectors' Club, 1992; R. K. Henrywood, *Relief Molded Jugs, 1820-1900*, Antique Collectors' Club; Kathy Hughes, *Collector's Guide to Nineteenth-Century Jugs* (Routledge Kegan Paul, 1985), Vol. II (Taylor Publishing, 1991); Llewellyn Jewitt, *Ceramic Art of Great Britain*, Sterling Publishing, 1985 (reprint of 1883 classic); Griselda Lewis, *Collector's History of English Pottery*, Antique Collectors' Club, 1987.

Additional Listings: Castleford; Chelsea; Coalport; Copeland and Spode; Liverpool; Royal Crown Derby; Royal Doulton; Royal Worcester; Staffordshire, Historical; Staffordshire, Romantic; Wedgwood; Whieldon.

Bargeware

Teapot, 7-1/2" h, all over brown glaze, enamel floral relief dec, imp motto "Mr. A. Aldredge, Foleshill 1886," minor nicks 250.00

Bodley, E.

Plate, 9-3/8" d, 1875-1892, scallop shell shape, painted whimsical undersea plants, wear, 12 pc set 230.00

Bow

Bowl, 4-1/2" d, blue trailing vine, white ground, c1770 ...... 175.00

Chelsea, dish, Hans Sloan, multicolored botanical design, named on reverse, red anchor mark, 12-1/2" l, $40.

Candlesticks, pr, two birds on flowering branches, dog and sheep on grassy base, wood stand, c1755 .... 1,200.00

Egg Cup, 2-1/2" h, 2 half-flower panels, powder blue ground, pseudo Oriental mark, c1760 .... 900.00

Figure, 9-1/2" h, gardener, puce jacket, underglaze blue hat, turquoise breeches, black shoes, blue, puce, and gilt base, c1765 .... 775.00

Plate, 9" d, Turk's Cap Lily, dragonfly and moths, c1755 ... 850.00

Bradley

Candlesticks, pr, 8-3/8" h, gilt dec white bodies supporting sconces, towing freeform shaped dishes, imp marks, c1885 .... 420.00

Chelsea

Bowl, 8-3/4" d, swirled ribs, scalloped, foliage and floral dec 75.00

Candlesticks, pr, 7-1/2" h, figural, draped putti, sitting on tree stump holding flower, scroll molded base, encircled in puce, gilt, wax pan 850.00

Cup and Saucer, multicolored exotic birds, white ground, gold anchor mark, c1765 .... 750.00

Plate, 8-1/2" d, multicolored floral design, scalloped rim, gold anchor mark 475.00

Scent Bottle, 3" h, cupid at altar, applied flowers, c1760 .... 2,500.00

Coalbrookdale

Cologne Bottle, 7-1/2" h, raised floral dec, 1820, pr 750.00

Inkstand, 10" l, floral encrusted, molded asters, leafy ground, scrolling handle, early 19th C 250.00

Vase, cov, 15" h, pear shape, raised floral dec, gilt rim and cov, flower spray finial, c1840, pr 850.00

Derby

Figure, 8" h, 8-1/2" h, pastoral, boy resting against tree stump playing bagpipe, black hat, bleu-do-roi jacket, gilt trim, yellow breeches, girl with green hat, bleu-du-roi bodice, pink skirt, white apron with iron-red flowerheads, gilt centers, leaves, scroll molded mound base, crown and incised iron-red D mark, pr 2,200.00

Jar, cov, 22" h, octagonal, iron-red, bottle green and leaf green, alternating cobalt blue and white grounds, gilding, grotesque sea serpent handles, now fitted as lamp with carved base, 19th C, pr 10,000.00

Plaque, cluster of fruit, carved giltwood frame, c1830, pr 2,200.00

Flight, Barr & Barr

Crocus Pot, 9" w, 4" d, 6-1/4" h, D-form, molded columns and architrave, peach ground panels, ruined abbey landscape reserve, gilding 2,400.00
Pastille Burner, 3-1/2" h, cottage, four open chimneys, mkd, c1815 ....425.00
Plate, 8" d, armorial, iron-red, gold, blue, and black arms and crest, Abbot quartering Bryan impaling Harris quartering another, iron-red and gray mantling, pink banderole, motto "Toujours Prest," gilt edged rim and salmon ground border, incised letter mark, crowned and plumed brown oval mark, c1804-09 ....995.00

Jackfield

Creamer, 4-1/4" h, bulbous, emb grapes design, leaves, and tendrils, gilt highlights, 3 pr paw feet, ear shape handle ... 175.00
Pitcher, 6-1/2" h, applied handle, black, traces of enameling, bird, initials and "1763," wear, small flakes 125.00
Sugar Bowl, cov, 4-1/2" h, 3-3/4" d, scalloped SS rims, SS mounted cov and ornate pierced finial....................................250.00

Lowestoft

Coffeepot, cov, 9" h, dark blue, underglaze river scene, Chinese man fishing, trellis diaper border, c1770-75 ....950.00
Demitasse Cup and Saucer, blue underglaze dec 150.00
Milk Jug, 3-1/4" h, dark blue underglaze, Chinese river scene, diaper border, brown rim, c1775......................................210.00

Masons

Creamer, 4" h, Oriental style shape, mkd "Mason's Patent Ironstone"...85.00
Jug, 8" h, octagonal, Hydra pattern, waisted straight neck, green enameled handle, lion head terminal, underglaze blue and iron-red flowers and vase, 2 imp marks and printed rounded crown mark, c1813-30..320.00
Platter, 13-1/2" x 10-3/4", double Landscape pattern, Oriental motif, deep green and brick red, c1883..............................265.00
Potpourri Vase, cov, 25-1/4" h, hexagonal body, cobalt blue, large gold stylized peony blossom, chrysanthemums, prunus, and butterflies, gold and blue dragon handles, and knobs, trellis diaper rim border, c1820-25 ....1,750.00

Moore Bros.

Centerpiece, 13" l, figural, oval basketweave molded bowl, applied oak leaves and acorns, cherub figures set to each side, gilt foot rim, c1875, staining, hairlines to base 750.00

Coalbrookdale, basket, blue ext. white int., multicolored flowers, roses, carnations, mkd, c1830, 9" l, 5" w, 7" h, $900.

New Hall

Creamer, Chinese figure on terrace, c1790 ....190.00
Dessert Set, 2 oval dishes, 8 plates, printed and colored named views, lavender-blue borders, light blue ground, c1815 ....450.00
Tea Set, interwoven ribbon and leaf trails, blue and gilt oval medallion border, c1790, minor repairs, 44 pcs 1,500.00

Woods

Bust, 15-3/8" h, Sir Isaac Newton, gray hair, brown drape, waisted rect marbled green and pink socle, c1800 ....475.00
Cup and Saucer, handleless, Woods Rose..........................65.00
Dish, 8" l, 6" w, dark blue transfer of castle, imp "Wood" ...165.00
Jug, 5-3/4" h, ovoid, cameos of Queen Caroline, pink luster ground, beaded edge, molded and painted floral border, c1820...425.00
Plate, 9" d, Woods Rose, scalloped edge 125.00
Stirrup Cub, 5-1/2" l, modeled hound's head, translucent shades of brown, c1760..2,200.00
Whistle, 3-7/8" h, modeled as seated sphinx, blue accents, oval green base, c1770 ....600.00

Worcester

Creamer, 3-5/8" h, blue and white, Dr. Wall crescent mark 250.00
Cup and Saucer, handleless, molded flutes, underglaze blue, worn gilt thistles, hairline in saucer................................45.00
Serving Tray, 16" x 10", light blue florals, dark blue border, dated 1883...100.00

ENGLISH SOFT PASTE

History: Between 1820 and 1860, a large number of potteries in England's Staffordshire district produced decorative wares with a soft earthenware (creamware) base and a plain white or yellow glazed ground.

Design or "stick" spatterware was created by a cut sponge (stamp), hand painting, or transfers. Blue was the predominant color. The earliest patterns were carefully arranged geometrics, which generally covered the entire piece. Later pieces had a decorative border with a central motif, usually a tulip. In the 1850s, Elsmore and Foster developed the Holly Leaf pattern.

King's Rose features a large, cabbage-type rose in red, pale red, or pink. The pink rose often is called "Queen's Rose." Secondary colors are pastels–yellow, pink, and, occasionally, green. The borders vary: a solid band, vined, lined, or sectional. The King's Rose exists in an oyster motif.

Strawberry China ware comes in three types: strawberries and strawberry leaves (often called strawberry luster), green featherlike leaves with pink flowers (often called cut-strawberry, primrose, or old strawberry), and relief decoration. Rust-red moldings characterize the first two types. Most pieces have a cream ground. Davenport was only one of the many potteries which made this ware.

Yellow-glazed earthenware (canary luster) has a canary yellow ground, a transfer design that is usually in black, and occasional luster decoration. The earliest pieces date from the 1780s and have a fine creamware base. A few hand-painted pieces are known. Not every piece has luster decoration.

Because the base material is soft paste, the ware is subject to cracking and chipping. Enamel colors and other types of decoration do not hold well. It is not unusual to see a piece with the decoration worn off.

Marks: Marked pieces are uncommon.

Additional Listings: Adams Rose; Gaudy Dutch; Salopian Ware; Staffordshire Items.

Creamware

Basket and Undertray, 11-1/2" l, pierced, early 19th C, hairline on rim of tray..865.00
Dish, 15" d, scalloped edge, late 18th C, rim chips...........320.00
Figure, 2-1/2" h, monkey, brown sponging, base chips.....250.00
Plate, 8-3/8" sq, red, blue, pink, green, and worn gilt........110.00
Sugar Bowl, 5-1/8" d, 2-3/4" h, int. with red and green enamel floral dec, purple luster and underglaze blue, ext. mkd "Be Canny with the Sugar" flanked by small flowers..................385.00
Teapot
    4" h, floral dec, early 19th C, hairline along spout and handle
    ....115.00
    4-3/4" h, molded acanthus spout, ribbed handle, small flakes
    ....385.00

Design Spatterware

Bowl, 7-1/2" d, 4" h, polychrome stripes.....................85.00
Creamer, 4-3/8" h, gaudy floral dec, red, green, blue, and black, mkd "Baker & Co., England" 75.00
Cup, oversize, gaudy floral dec, red, blue, and green, 6-1/8" d
    ....200.00
Jug, 7" h, barrel shape, blue, rosettes and fern prongs.....185.00
Miniature
    Cup and saucer, green and black, polychrome center flower
    ....75.00
    Tea set, Five pieces, 5-3/4" h teapot, creamer, sugar, two handleless cups and saucers, blue and white design spatter, teapot finial restored, chips 440.00
Mug, 4" h, octagonal, red, blue, and green stripes............135.00
Plate, 9-1/2" d, red and green design spatter border and center, 8 pc set...660.00
Sugar Bowl, cov, 5" h, white, blue, and red flowers, green leaves, closed ring and shell handles 120.00

King's Rose

Bowl, 7-3/4" d, Rose, broken solid border, flakes 55.00
Cup and Saucer, handleless
    Oyster pattern, hairline cracks 40.00
    Rose, solid border 100.00
    Rose, vine border 150.00
Plate
    5-5/8" d, pink border, wear......................................55.00
    6-1/2" d, broken solid border, flakes 55.00
    6-1/2" d, vine border, wear......................................80.00
    7-3/8" d, some flaking..90.00
    8-1/4" d, scalloped borders and edges, some flakes, 6 pcs
    ....275.00
    8-1/4" d, pink border, wear......................................70.00
    8-1/4" d, vine border, 3 pcs 255.00
    9-3/4" d, scalloped border, 4 pcs............................220.00
Soup Plate, 9-1/2" d, broken solid border, scalloped edges, some flakes, 3 pcs 360.00
Teapot, 5-3/4" h, broken solid border, some flakes............140.00

Pearlware

Coffeepot, cov, 9-1/4" h, blue Chinoiserie dec, early 19th C, chips to underside of cover......................................805.00
Cup and Saucer, red transfer of ship with American flag, eagle, and anchor on shore, Clermont, Fulton's steamship also on cup, luster rim, minor damage 65.00

Design Spatterware, mug, blue top band, green and red center, 4-1/4" h, 4" d base, $550.

Figure
    3" l, sheep, brown, blue, and yellow ochre sponging, small edge flakes 275.00
    3-1/4" h, squirrel, nut and collar with ring, polychrome, orange coat, attributed to Derby, minor wear and small flakes on base...635.00
    3-7/8" h, cat, seated, green base, yellow and brown polka dots, attributed to Wood, repairs, hairline in base, small flakes 550.00
    6-3/4" h, Autumn, molded base, green, brown, yellow, orange, black, and pink flesh tones, chips on base, old repair
    ....330.00
Jar, cov, 12-1/4" h, blue transfer, willow pattern, gilt highlights, c1830..550.00
Pitcher
    6-5/8" h, gaudy floral dec, red, blue, green, and black, minor enamel wear, deteriorating professional repair........110.00
    8-5/8" h, Leeds floral dec, green, brown, blue, and tan, later added row of peacocks, very flaked, stains, chips on spout..275.00
Plate
    5-3/4" d, rose dec, molded luster rim, wear 85.00
    7-3/4" d, blue and white Oriental dec, imp "Turner," minor wear 165.00
Platter, 20-3/4" l, blue feather edge, Leeds blue and white Oriental dec, wear, scratches, edge chips, old puttied repair ...500.00
Teapot, 5-3/4" h, octagonal, molded designs, swan finial, Oriental transfer, polychrome enamel, attributed to T. Harley, some edge flakes and professional repair............................425.00
Vase, 7" h, five finger type, underglaze blue, enameled birds and foliage, yellow ochre, brown, and green, silver luster highlights, chips and crazing, pr...500.00

Queen's Rose

Cream Pitcher and Sugar, cov, vine border, some flakes
    ....250.00
Cup and Saucer, handleless, broken solid border 495.00
Plate
    6-1/2" d, broken solid border.....................................50.00
    7-1/2" d, solid border..75.00
    8-1/4" d, vine border, scalloped edge..........................85.00
    10" d, vine border..110.00
Teapot and cov sugar, shell form, some flakes................420.00

Strawberry, saucer, 5-5/8" d, $175.

Strawberry China

Bowl, 4" d 165.00
Cup and Saucer, pink border, scalloped edge 225.00
Plate, 8-1/2" d, Cut Strawberry 200.00
Sugar Bowl, cov, raised strawberries, strawberry knob 175.00
Tea Bowl and Saucer, vine border 250.00

Yellow Glaze

Mug, 2-3/8" h, rural scene transfer print, mkd "Montread," rim chip and hairline 195.00
Pitcher, 4-3/4" h, transfer dec of foliate devices, reserve of shepherd with milkmaid, hand painted dec, c1850 .... 635.00
Plate, 8-1/4" d, brown transfer print, Wild Rose pattern, imp "Montread" 250.00
Soup Bowl, 8-1/4" d, molded border, Cabbage Rose pattern, iron-red and green dec 400.00
Sugar Bowl, cov, 5-1/2" h, printed transfer of The Tea Party, fishing scene, iron-red painted rims 1,250.00
Tea Bowl and Saucer, iron-red print of two cupids, mkd "Sewell" 250.00
Teapot, 5-1/2" h, printed transfer of The Party, iron-red painted rims, minor hairline, spout damage 850.00
Waste Bowl, 5-5/8" d, 3" h, crenulated rim, Cabbage Rose pattern, iron-red and green dec, restored hairline 425.00

FAIRY LAMPS

History: Fairy lamps, which originated in England in the 1840s, are candle-burning night lamps. They were used in nurseries, hallways, and dim corners of the home.

Two leading candle manufacturers, the Price Candle Company and the Samuel Clarke Company, promoted fairy lamps as a means to sell candles. Both contracted with glass, porcelain, and metal manufacturers to produce the needed shades and cups. For example, Clarke used Worcester Royal Porcelain Company, Stuart & Sons, and Red House Glass Works in England, plus firms in France and Germany.

Fittings were produced in a wide variety of styles. Shades ranged from pressed to cut glass, from Burmese to Nailsea. Cups are found in glass, porcelain, brass, nickel, and silver plate.

American firms selling fairy lamps included Diamond Candle Company of Brooklyn, Blue Cross Safety Candle Co., and Hobbs-Brockunier of Wheeling, West Virginia.

Two-piece (cup and shade) and three-piece (cup with matching shade and saucer) fairy lamps can be found. Married pieces are common.

Marks: Clarke's trademark was a small fairy with a wand surrounded by the words "Clarke Fairy Pyramid, Trade Mark."

References: Bob and Pat Ruf, *Fairy Lamps*, Schiffer Publishing, 1996; John F. Solverson (comp.), *Those Fascinating Little Lamps: Miniature Lamps Value Guide*, Antique Publications, 1988.

Periodical: *Light Revival*, 35 West Elm Ave., Quincy, MA 02170.

Collectors' Club: Night Light Club, 38619 Wakefield Ct., Northville, MI 48167.

REPRODUCTION ALERT
Reproductions abound.

Bisque, 4" h, figural, owl, cat, and dog, glass eyes, clear mkd Clarke candle cup 265.00
Burmese, 7" h, salmon pink shaded to yellow, acid finish, matching ruffled base mkd "Clarke's Patent Fairy Lamp," clear mkd Clarke candle cup, brass frame with 2 scrolling arms .. 825.00
Cranberry, 4-1/2" h, crown shape, overshot shade, clear base, clear mkd Clarke candle cup, c1887 .... 220.00
Overshot, 3-1/2" h, yellow swirl, cased, clear mkd Clarke candle cup 125.00
Peachblow, 3-7/8" h, cream lining, acid finished rose shaded pink, black lacy flower and leaf dec, clear mkd Clarke candle cup, gold washed metal stand, attributed to Thomas Webb .. 350.00
Sapphire Blue, 4-5/8" h, DQ, melon ribbed, clear mkd Clarke candle cup 175.00
Satin
   3-5/8" h, apple green opaque shade, emb Swirl pattern, clear mkd Clarke candle cup 150.00
   6" d, lavender ruffled dome top, 3 gold inset jeweled medallions, ruffled base 350.00
Spatter, 5-1/2" h, white spatter, chartreuse cased in crystal ground, swirled rib mold, heavy applied crystal feet and base trim, clear mkd Clarke candle cup 550.00
Verre Moiré (Nailsea)
   4" h, red frosted ground, white loopings, clear Clarke candle cup mkd "S. Clarke's Patent Pyramid Trade Mark" and "C.W.S. Night Light" 495.00
   5-1/4" h, cranberry frosted ground, white loopings, clear base, clear mkd Clarke candle cup 250.00
   6-1/2" h, 8" w, sweeping white loopings blend into delicate blue background, done shaped shade, triangular shaped base with pinch-in folds, clear glass cup holder with ruffled edge, sgd "S. Clarke Patent Trade Mark Fairy" 945.00

FAMILLE ROSE

History: Famille Rose is Chinese export enameled porcelain on which the pink color predominates. It was made

Plate, 8-1/4" d, $225.

primarily in the 18th and 19th centuries. Other porcelains in the same group are Famille Jaune (yellow), Famille Noire (black), and Famille Verte (green).

Decorations include courtyard and home scenes, birds, and insects. Secondary colors are yellow, green, blue, aubergine, and black.

Rose Canton, Rose Mandarin, and Rose Medallion are mid- to late 19th-century Chinese export wares which are similar to Famille Rose.

Famille Jeune, lamp, 33" h, triple gourd shape, yellow ground, blue dec medallions, scrolled leaf and floral designs, late 19th C 320.00

Famille Rose
Basket and Undertray, 11" l, reticulated, figure, bird, and insect-filled panels, c1850 ....1,200.00
Bowl, 15-1/4" d, painted figural cartouches alternating with floral cartouches, Qianlong 2,400.00
Cache Pot, 9" h, floral and scrolling foliate dec, price for pr 150.00
Charger, 13" d, millefiore dec, Qing dynasty 225.00
Dish
    8" d, European subject figural dec, Qianlong, c1780 ...350.00
    9" d, floriform, allover lotus flower and floral dec, Yongcheng 350.00
Plate
    6" d, armorial, floral garland border, Browne arms, Qianlong, c1775, price for pr 550.00
    8" d, center figures in punt, insect, and floral border, Qianlong, c1770..200.00
    8-1/8" d, reticulated rim, fine detail, small flake.............290.00
    8-3/4" d, lobed dec, floral dec, Qianlong, c1740, price for pr 375.00
    8-3/4" d, octagonal, cockerel and floral dec, Qianlong, c1740 ....400.00
Sauce Tureen, cov, 8" h, ftd, trellis work, Chinese figures, gilded foliage, English painted ironstone, mid 19th C, pr 435.00
Snuff Bottle, blue ground, floral and scrolling foliate design, Qing dynasty, Chinese 80.00
Tureen, 7-1/2" l, cov, undertray, central floral filled basket dec, spear head border, animal form handles, fruit form finial, Qianlong, some damage, price for pr..........................2,200.00

Vase
    8-1/2" h, Rouleau form, figures in landscape, drilled, price for pr 225.00
    10" h, cov, baluster, allover floral dec, mounted as lamps, price for pr 250.00
    13-1/4" h, baluster, 19th C, chips, enamel wear, pr 345.00
    14" h, cov, flattened baluster form, molded floral, foliate, branch, and squirrel dec on neck, twig form handles, Qianlong, c1780, price for pr 4,000.00
    15" h, floral dec, price for pr 275.00
    20-3/4" h, cov, tapering rect, figural handles, female form finial, central panels with figural procession, verso with figures in architectural landscape on white ground, allover floral spray and bird dec, c1830, price for pr 5,500.00
    24-3/4" h, Rouleau, shaped panels of birds, flowers, and scenes from Peking Opera, gold ground dec with pink flowers and green tendrils, Jiaquing Period, 1796-1820 .... 1,380.00
Wig Stand, 11-1/4" h, hexagonal, figures holding floral sprays in landscape, white ground, pierced lozenge form cut-outs, Qing dynasty, 19th C, price for pr..750.00
Famille Verte
Dish, 9" d, center flower filled vase dec, pomegranate dec border, cavetto with floral and foliage dec, blue hatched ground, Qianlong dynasty, price for pr......................................600.00

FANS

History: Today, people tend to think of fans as fragile, frivolous accessories used by women; yet the origin of the fan was no doubt highly practical. Early man may have used it to winnow his grain, shoo flies, and cool his brow. This simple tool eventually became a symbol of power: ancient lore maintains that Emperor Hsien Yuan (c2697 B.C.) used fans; the tomb of Egypt's Tutankhamen (1350 b.c.) yielded two ostrich-feather fans with gold mounts. Fans also began to assume religious significance and were used to whisk flies from altars. Early Christians recognized the practicality of this device and included a flabellum, or fixed fly-whisk, in their early services. Meanwhile, the Chinese and Japanese continued to use fans in their courts, often incorporating precious materials such as ivory, gold, and jade.

Until the 7th century a.d., fans were non-folding. Then, according to Japanese legend, Emperor Jen-ji noticed the logic of a bat's folded wings and applied his insight to a new fan design. Later, European traders returned from the East with samples of these wonders. By the 16th century sophisticated Italian women had appropriated the fan, use of which soon became de rigueur throughout Europe. Now primarily feminine fashion accessories, their styles changed to complement the ever-changing dress styles. Fans' popularity led to experimentation in their production and merchandising. They also became popular as a way for artists to test their skills–a fan leaf's curved, folding surface offered challenges in perspective.

World War I brought about the end of the slow-paced lifestyle; the 1920s raced at a frenetic speed. The modern woman set aside her ubiquitous fan, freeing both hands to drive her roadster or carry her political banner. Fans became more an advertising tool than a fashion statement.

Twentieth century advertising fans are readily available, ranging from church and funeral home fans starting under $1 each to the ubiquitous ones for Putnam Dyes, 666 Salve, Alka Seltzer, and other well known products. Because of their number, such fans are nominally priced. However, the surge of interest in earlier advertising, worlds' fair collectibles, certain illustrators, celebrities, and specialized areas such as transportation and machinery, has helped raise prices of fans in those areas.

The fan collector's concerns include not only the product, but artistic quality, physical condition, and rarity. Thus, the experienced collector knows that despite Moxie's popularity, not all fans advertising the drink are of equal value: the 8" (20.3 cm.) cdbd. one, dated 1925, of the woman looking in a compact, is fairly common and frequently priced around $35; earlier diecut Moxie fans made between 1915 and 1919 feature actresses of the day and more interesting graphics–their prices are accordingly higher. The 5 fans featuring Muriel Ostriche, the first Moxie model, may range from $40 for her 1919 one (8 1/4"/20.7cm.) to 3 or 4 times that sum for her 1916 one (10"/25.4 cm.), in which she holds a Moxie celluloid fan.

The collector also quickly learns the impact of location and supply and demand on prices. Those just given are common on the coasts; prices in the Midwest and Central states, which have fewer fan collectors, are often much lower.

Some basic guidelines are:

19th-century artisans copied 18th-century styles. True Georgian figures should have gray hair; if the wigs are white, the fan is probably more recent. The later fans will often have a heavier appearance, and anachronistic costuming.

Empire fans were also copied. The period ones have sequins made by flattening circles of wire; a tiny line shows where the wire ends meet. Later sequins were stamped whole out of sheet metal and have no joining line.

Ivory, bone, celluloid, and plastic may look somewhat alike. Ivory often has a subtle, textureless graining pattern and may feel smooth and buttery; bone frequently has channels. Look for mold marks in plastic. The Victorians were excited by new technology and made ample use of faux ivories, except for brisé fans and those made in the Orient, most seemingly ivory fans made after 1860 are really ivory substitutes. Look for mold marks in plastic, or if feasible, use a hot needle, if it pierces the surface, the material is plastic, organic materials will fluoresce under ultraviolet light, plastics will appear dull, mottled.

Many leaves became damaged with wear and were replaced. These "married" fans can still be delightful collectibles, but beware of dating a fan merely based on one component.

Loops are uncommon on most 18th C fans.

Framing a fan often causes its sticks to warp, its leaf to lose its elasticity and ability to fold. It is also difficult to tell if a fan has been sewn or glued to its backing, making its removal difficult.

The number of degrees a folding fan opens is a key to dating.

Handle fans gently, unfolding from left to right.

Fan Terminology:

Artificial Ivory–introduced at London's Great Exhibition in 1851, these imitations, which eventually included Cellu-

loid, Cellonite, Xylonite, Pyralin, French Ivory, Ivorine, hair combs, the imitations were also popular for fans. Many later Victorian, American and European fans are misidentified as ivory, when they are in fact one of the *faux* ivories or bone.

Brisé–fan with no leaf, but made of rigid, overlapping sticks held together at base by a rivet and at the other end by a ribbon.

Cartouche–ornamental frame, usually oval; also, the small scene or design element surrounded by that frame.

Celluloid–John W. Hyatt invented his artificial ivory in 1865, then improved his product and began marketing it as "Celluloid" in 1867, Made of nitrocellulose, alcohol, and camphor, celluloid was the first synthetic plastic. Considered a marvel of technology, it replaced elephant ivory in many products, including fans, piano keys, and billiard balls. Unfortunately, celluloid is flammable and can even decompose and self-combust. For that reason, celluloid fans should be stored in fireproof containers, separate from fans made of other materials.

Chickenskin–common but misleading name for very fine skin (usually kid), with a somewhat pebbled appearance and smooth, "powdered" feel.

Cockade–pleated fan opening to form complete circle.

Fixed Fan–one which, having no pleated leaf, remains in one position. Hand screens and flag fans are examples.

Folding fan–fan with a flexible, pleated leaf mounted on sticks.

Fontange–shape of folding fans c1890-1935, with center of leaf longer than guards.

Gorge–lower portion of the sticks, often marked by a tapering or change of shape.

Gouache–opaque watercolor mixed with a preparation of gum.

Guards–two outermost sticks, usually height of fan. Heavier than the other sticks, they help protect the fan.

Handscreen–rigid fan, often oval or round, mounted on a handle. Often used to protect a woman's complexion from the fire, earlier handscreens were made in pairs to display atop the mantelpiece. During the latter part of the 19th c., handscreens became popular as advertising tools.

Head–lower part of the sticks which contain the rivet and which rests in the hand when the fan is held open.

"Jenny Lind" –small, brisé fan purportedly favored by the Swedish-born coloratura soprano who toured the United States, 1850 - 52, under the aegis of famed promoter P.T. Barnum. Each stick of a "Jenny" is topped with a piece of shaped fabric, often resembling a feather.

Leaf or mount–flexible, pleated material which unites the upper parts of a folding fan's sticks.

Lithograph–printing process invented in 1797, often subsequently hand-colored.

Loop–often U-shaped finger holder attached to rivet at base of fan; rare before 1830.

Mai ogi–Japanese folding dance fan. Because this style has few sticks, the pleats in its leaf are wide; the fan is ideally suited for use as an autograph or "scrap" fan. The latter term refers to the fad in which women cut bits of paper, such as letterheads from colleges, famous hotels, or re-sorts, and glued them to their fans.

Medallion–pictorial representation, usually circular or oval, in leaf.

Mother-of-pearl–smooth, lustrous internal layer of certain mollusks (such as abalone, snail), used to make fan sticks/guards and *goldfish*.

Piqué-point–decorative small gold or silver points or pins set flush with surface or sticks or guards.

Protein–usually preceded by "processed," "reconstituted," or : "re-formed," the term refers to organic material. After being made soft and pliable by heat, the protein was shaped by pressing or molding into the desired stick or guard shape, tinted, and polished. The result may resemble blonde tortoise shell or amber.

Putto–a baby angel, usually a boy, who represents the innocence of first love. Especially popular in fan decoration during the latter part of the 19th century. Plural from: *putti.*

Recto–front or public side of a fan.

Reserve–small oval or shield background for monogram or scene.

Ribbon–the length of silk, thread, or cord connecting the sticks of a brisé fan. Period ribbon has no selvages (slightly thicker woven edges), which are too thick to allow a fan to lie securely closed.

Rivet–pin about which sticks of a folding fan pivot.

Shoulder—area of the stick/guards immediately below the leaf's lower edge; demarcation between the sticks and the slips.

Slips (also called ribs) –slender extensions of the *sticks,* used to support leaf from behind.

Sticks–rigid framework of a folding fan.

Studs–exposed end of rivet, sometimes shaped as decorative paste "gem."

Verso–rear side of a fan; often the decoration is not as detailed as that on the *recto* (front)

Washer–small disk to prevent friction between end of rivet and fan.

References: Hélène Alexander, *Fans,* Shire Publications, 1989; Nancy Armstrong, *Book of Fans,* Mayflower Books, out of print; ——, *Collector's History of Fans,* Clarkson N. Potter, 1974; ——, *Fans,* Souvenir Press, 1984; Anna Gray Bennett and Ruth Berson, *Fans in Fashion,* San Francisco Art Museum, 1981; ——, *Unfolding Beauty-The Art of the Fan,* Thames and Hudson, 1988; Durian-Ress, Saskia and Elisabeth Heller-Winter, *Fücher: Kunst und Mode aus Fünf Jahr-hunderten,* Bayerischen Nationalmusuem, Munich, 1987; Mary S. Frazier, *Hunt and Allen Fans,* Braintree Historical Society, 1988; Berthe de Vere Green, *Fans Over The Ages, a Collector's Guide,* Frederick Muller, 1975; Julia Hutt and Hèléne Alexander, *Ogi a History of the Japanese Fan,* Dauphine Publishing, 1992; Neville John Irons, *Fans of Imperial China,* Kaiserreich Kunst, 1982; ——, *Fans of Imperial Japan,* Kaiserreich Kunst, 1982; Christl Kammerl, *Der Fücher: Kunstobjekt und Billetdoux,* Himmer Verlag, 1989; Carol E. Mayer, *Fans,* Vancouver Museum, New World Press, 1983, Susan Mayor, *A Collector's Guide to Fans,* Wellfleet Books, 1990; Francoise de Perthuis and

Vincent Meylan, *Eventail,* Hermé, 1989; Dr. Aileen Ribeiro (ed.), *Fans-The Costume Accessories Series,* B. T. Batsford, 1984; Mary E. G. Rhoads, *Fan Directory: A Guide to Decorative Fans for Museums and Collectors*, 2nd ed., Fan Collectors Press, 1993; Paul van Saanen and Peter Greenhaigh, *From Court to Confectionery/Des Courtesans aux artisans,* Imprimeries Reunies Laussane, 1994; Grazia Gobbi Sica, *Il Ventaglio Pullicatario 1890-1940,* Catini & C., 1991; Maryse Volet, *Imagination and its Contribution to Fans: Patents for Fans Filed In France During the 20th Century,* printed by author, 1986.

Collectors' Clubs: FANA, Fan Association of North America, Suite 128, 1409 N. Cedar Crest Blvd., Allentown, PA 18104.

Advisor: Wendy Hamilton Blue.

Note: Condition is important above all! Any tear or split in a leaf, any break in a stick, any missing part drastically reduces a fan's value, often by half or more. Most fans available on the U.S. market were produced in plentiful numbers, and many have survived in good to excellent condition.

Abbreviations:

cdbd	cardboard
chlth	chromolithograph
dbl	double leaf
gl	guard length
h	height
hp	handpainted
litho	lithograph
mop	mother of pearl
op	width when opened
#//#	number of sticks/number of guards

American and European

c1760, silk, ivory, folding, pleated fan, Dutch, painted silk leaf depicts biblical scene: Jacob's dream of angels ascending ladder into heaven; verso has vignette, painted in muted tones, of small island, mountainous island with farmhouse, carved sticks, pierced with figures, 12//2; gl. 11"; op. 20".........350.00

c1780, skin, ivory, folding, pleated fan, Italian/Chinese, souvenir of the Grand Tour, "chickenskin" leaf, painted in Italy, 3 circular vignettes of classical ruins, Chinese sticks are carved and pierced, a central monogram; guards are carved with buildings, 14//2; gl. 11".........300.00

c1793, paper, wood, folding, pleated fan, French, paper leaf is printed with assortment of playing cards and *assignats* (currency issued by France's revolutionary governments), in tones of red, black, and brown, unadorned simple wood sticks, 14//2, gl. 9".........300.00

c1805, paper, wood, folding, pleated fan, English, titled "New Roscius Country Dance Fan for 1805, the leaf is printed with 3 stipple engravings of *putti* and child musicians, and etched with *trompe l'oeil* (fool the eye) rendition of twelve music sheets for dances, simple wood sticks, gl. 7".........375.00

c1855, silk, mop. Folding, brisé fan, American, each individual "feather" is hp with daisies and poppies, pierced mop sticks and clouté with cut steels, metal rivet, silk tassel. Shaped, layered pulp box mkd "Tiffany," 12//2; gl. 8"; op. 14".........550.00

c1865, silk, mop, folding, brisé fan, French, silk, shaped "feather" panels are printed with a litho, hand-colored, scene of the christening of the Prince Imperial, son of Empress Eugenie and Napoleon III, mop sticks, metal rivet, washer, paste stud, gl. 8".........225.00

Mourning, cockade, glazed black fabric, emb paper over wood sticks, wire clip, 8-1/2" d open size, $50.

c1870, ivory, gilt metal, folding, brisé dance card fan, European, 7 shaped ivory plain, interior leaves, allowing room for user to pencil in names of her dance partners, shaped metal gilt guards, enameled with touches of red, white, and blue, shaped, metal swivel loop, also gilt and enameled, 7//2; gl. 2-1/4"; op. 4"..175.00

Late 19th c.

Tortoise shell, folding, brisé fan, European, probably French or Austrian, unadorned interior sticks are thin sheets of tortoise shell, sticks are also tortoise, decorated with gilded copper and enamel, highlighted by glass, imitation turquoise, and garnet cabochons, metal rivet; tortoise shell, shaped loop, silk tassel, 18//2; gl. 9-1/4"; op. 16-3/4".......................650.00

Silk, protein, folding, pleated fan, French, sgd in left reserve "Van Garden," silk leaf, hp in gouache, depicts lovers' meeting near gated wall; grooms wait with nearby coach and four, leaf is backed with translucent gauze, mounted á la anglaise (directly to the slips, leaving them exposed on the verso) portion of the right guard above the shoulder in mop, topped with intertwining tendrils of protein which extend from guard's lower portion, gold metal rivet, loop; protein washer; orig box, mkd "Duvelleroy," with street address, 18//2; gl. 8-1/2"; op. 15-1/2" 360.00

c1880, tortoise shell, folding, brisé fan, European, finial (tip) of each shaped tortoise shell stick is carved with coronet, metal rivet, tortoise shell loop, 16//2; gl. 8"; op. 14"................275.00

c1890, lace, tortoise shell, folding, pleated fan, European, black silk bobbin lace, commonly called Chantilly, features graceful swirls of feathery, pendant flowers, unadorned simple tortoise shell sticks, tortoise loop, brass rivet, 16//2; gl. 14"; op. 27"...175.00

c1900, gauze, protein, folding, pleated fan, European, black gauze leaf, in a palmette shape, dec with spangles, blonde, processed protein sticks are set, clouté, with steel. guards are similar, but somewhat more ornately, dec, paste stud, 12//2; gl. 11"...185.00

Early 20th C, net, lace, tortoise shell, folding, pleated fan, European, black net leaf is dec with applied Brussels bobbin and needle lace, a spray of flowers to one side and smaller blossoms near the top border, small sequins highlight the floral motif, simple sticks are decorated piqué point, gl. 13-1/2"
....195.00

American and European Souvenir, Commemorative, and Advertising

1867, paper, wood, folding, pleated fan, French, paper leaf is engraving by Truillot (2 Rue Grange aux Belles), hand colored, labeled "Souvenir de L'Exposition Universelle de 1867," recto presents panoramic view of fair; verso has simplified map in the center, simple wood sticks, metal rivet, 14//2; gl. 11"; op. 18-1/2"..200.00

1876, raffia, wood, folding, pleated cockade fan, probably Austrian, border of circular raffia leaf is dec with patriotic emblems, including picture of George Washington and seal of United States, leaf is inscribed: "International Exhibition 1876 Philadelphia" and "M Coffani, Vienna, Austria," fan was probably made as a souvenir of the Austrian pavilion, 9-5/8" l.....175.00

c1888, cdbd, advertising handscreen, American, young Japanese girl, dressed in kimono and holding an uchiwa (Fixed fan with paper leaf over a split bamboo frame), demurely looks to right. Over her right shoulder is adv: "Dr. Fahrney's Teething Syrup for Infants," design © 1888, by Charles E. Hayes, verso contains text telling mothers "what a blessing" the syrup is, reinforced cdbd. handle, scalloped at top, attached with 3 metal rivets; rivet at base of handle, screen 7-3/8" h, 6-1/2" w......................70.00

Late 19th C, cdbd., wood, American, recto chlth. on rounded square screen of Japanese woman in blue kimono, large red fan held behind her head, verso is simple text, in black print, adv "Clark's Cove Guano Co." of New Bedford, Mass., manufacturers of "The Bay State Fertilizer," wood stick, slightly rounded, and higher in back than front, attached by 2 vertical staples, screen 6-1/2" h; 6-1/2" w 75.00

1890. cdbd, wood, Advertising handscreen, America, circular screen has chlth. of young girl in peach dress and lace bonnet, surrounded by trompe l'oeil sheets from the "Ladies Calendar 1890," calendar is presented "Compliments of E.W. Hoyt & Co., Proprietors of Hoyt's German Cologne and Rubifoam for the Teeth," equally colorful verso shows a bottle of tooth powder and one of cologne, each with appropriate advertising text, screen is mounted atop rounded, split wood stick, attached at top, screen 7-3/4" d...................150.00

1895, cdbd, wood, advertising handscreen, American, recto of somewhat shield-shaped screen, wider at top than at base, has 6 black and white photo images of Boston, in arrangement "Designed by John Sample, Jr.," beneath the photo collage is ad: "Drink Queen Sherbet, 5c at all Soda Fountains, Mantd by W.P. Sheldon, Malden, Mass," verso explains screen is a "Souvenir of the 14th International YPSCE Convention at Boston, July 10-14 1895," and provides the lyrics for a song by Pres. of the Massachusetts Christian Endeavor Union, shaped wooden handle attached with 2 small, short nails, screen 7-1/2" h, 6-3/4" w 65.00

Early 20th C, cdbd, advertising handscreen, American, young boy beckons to girl who is leaving drug store, ready to put her purchases in express wagon pulled by boy's terrier. Fan's self-handle advertises "Tums for the Tummy," verso, printed in black, shows tin of "Nature's Remedy" tablets, and roll of Tums, screen 7-5/8" h; 6" w 25.00

Early 20th C, cdbd, wood, advertising handscreen, American, smiling infant, seated on red wooden sled, and wearing only strategically placed pale blue ribbon, holds Thermos in either upraised hand, bottom left corner text: "Clear the way for Thermos," verso has 8 black and white scenes showing when and where Thermos "Serves you right," split wood stick, higher on verso, attached with 2 vertical, metal staples, screen 9-1/4" h; 8-1/2" w 75.00

c1909, cdbd, wood, advertising handscreen, diecut, American, recto of colorful fan, shaped like man's head, presents the full face of comical police officer, one eye closed, his chin bristling with short beard, gray helmet, with "23" in gold, on head, design was © in 1909 by F.A. Schneider, verso advertises Poole pianos, split wood stick, longer on verso, attached with 2 vertical staples, screen 9-3/4" h; 6-7/8" w 95.00

c1904-14, cdbd, wood, commemorative handscreen, American, central scene is black and white artist's depiction of an aerial map of the Panama Canal, text at center, top, gives statistics of the canal, each rounded corners has circular photo, showing Col. Goethals and parts of canal, listing beginning and completion dates, verso plain text, advertising Weaver pianos, split wood stick, longer on verso, attached with 2 vertical metal staples, screen 8-1/4" h; 7-5/8" w...110.00

c1916, cdbd, wood, advertising handscreen, American, recto of the ovoid screen has central, sepia tone photo of ship going through locks of Panama Canal; 8 smaller photos of other types of transport, ranging from camels to biplane, surround central photo and the legend, "Progress," verso shows "True Reproduction of Buick Model D-48. Price $985 F.O.B. Factory," and note that "1916 Prices range from $90 to $1485," split wood handle, higher on verso than recto, screen 8-3/8" h; 7-1/4" w 60.00

c1920-39, cdbd, wood, political advertising handscreen, American, Friends' Peace Committee used this rectangular handscreen, with Statue of Liberty silhouetted against an orange sun, to urge others to prevent war, 3 blocks of text on verso explain the Friends' position, which include "Co.-operation, through the World Court, the League of Nations, and other means. . ." split wooden stick, longer on verso, attached with 2 vertical staples, screen 9" h; 6-3/8" w 30.00

1934, cdbd, advertising handscreen, American, recto of rect screen has color rendition of train in front of American Snuff Co.; verso, printed in blue, shows aerial view of factory, surrounded by calendar leaves for 1934 and 1935, split wood stick, longer on verso, attached with 2 vertical staples, screen 9-1/4" h; 7-3/4" w 75.00

Mid 20th C, cdbd, wood, advertising handscreen, American, young woman clutches armful of marigolds on recto of slightly shield shaped fan, verso, printed primarily in green with some red, advertises Derr Bros., Bottlers, Manufacturers and Jobbers, flat wooden stick, wider at base, attached with 2 horizontal staples, screen 7-3/8" h.; 7-7/8" w 8.00

1952, cdbd, political handscreen and tally card, American, recto of this large, rect dark blue handscreen urges voters to "Keep up on the campaign with the Chicago Sun-Times." Verso is tally sheet, for delegates at the Republican convention to keep track of votes for candidates for nomination: Warren, Taft, Stassen, and Eisenhower, thumbhole at bottom, center, screen 10-1/4" h; 13-5/8" w...45.00

Oriental, Pacific

c1790, ivory, folding brisé fan, Cantonese, ivory sticks, connected by silk ribbon, are single side carved and pierced with pagodas, and other buildings, mountains, bats, birds, and flowers, finials carved with birds and flowers, central *gorge* area has space for monogram, guards repeat the birds and flowers motif, mop washer, brass (?) rivet, 26//2; gl.10-3/8" op. 15"...450.00

c1800, feather, ivory, folding, brisé fan, Cantonese, made for export, simple white goose feathers mounted atop ivory sticks, feathers painted with large, pink roses and butterflies; sticks are carved and pierced with figures, gl. 12" 150.00

c1800, silk, ivory, folding, pleated fan, Chinese, hp leaf, central scene of pagodas near mountain river, oval scene of birds and flowers on either side, sticks are carved and pierced in floral design, 10" 150.00

c1860, paper, lacquer, folding, pleated fan, Cantonese, recto of paper leaf hp view of Canton; verso has various figures, their faces of small applied ovals of ivory, applied silk clothes, sticks, lacquer over what is probably light wood, painted in pinks and blues with flowers and birds, gl. 11".............200.00

Late 19th C, reed, wood, fixed flag fan, east Indian, scalloped reed leaf, bound in red cotton and dec with beetle wings, attached to turned and painted wooden handle, when stick is lightly swirled, leaf rotates around the handle, creating a breeze, which both refreshes the user and carries his prayers heavenward; handle 18" l; leaf 13 1/2" h 80.00

Late 19th C, silk, bone, folding, pleated fan, Burmese, hp leaf, court scene and mounted atop pierced bone sticks, gl. 13" 70.00

Late 19th C, tortoise shell folding, brisé fan, Japanese, flat tortoise shell sticks, lacquered, in gold, with birds and bamboo, gl. 14"...290.00

Late 19th C, wood, *Tanto*, Japanese, appears as closed, wooden fan with bamboo guards actually a carved sheath for hidden dagger. Overall length 9"...150.00

c1880, paper, bamboo, wood, folding, pleated fan, Japanese, scalloped leaf painted with women in garden; verso painted with landscape, plain sticks are bamboo, heavier, wooden guards painted to look like bamboo, gl. 17"...................135.00

Indeterminate age, paper, reed, wood, fixed fan, Korean, *pu-ch'ae*, or fixed fan, traditional design popular in Korea for many years, lacquered paper, placed atop reed framework, painted in red and ochre with triple jewel design (3 broad swirls of color), simple stained black wood handle, 13-3/4" l...........................50.00

FENTON GLASS

History: The Fenton Art Glass Company began as a cutting shop in Martins Ferry, Ohio, in 1905. In 1906, Frank L. Fenton started to build a plant in Williamstown, West Virginia, and produced the first piece of glass there in 1907. Early production included carnival, chocolate, custard, and pressed glass, plus mold-blown opalescent glass. In the 1920s, stretch glass, Fenton dolphins, jade green, ruby, and art glass were added.

In the 1930s, boudoir lamps, Dancing Ladies, and slag glass in various colors were produced. The 1940s saw crests of different colors being added to each piece by hand. Hobnail, opalescent, and two-color overlay pieces were popular items. Handles were added to different shapes, making the baskets they created as popular today as then.

Through the years Fenton has beautified its glass by decorating it with hand painting, acid etching, color staining, and copper-wheel cutting.

Marks: Several different paper labels have been used. In 1970, an oval raised trademark also was adopted.

References: William Heacock, *Fenton Glass: The First Twenty-Five Years* (1978), *The Second Twenty-Five Years* (1980), *The Third Twenty-Five Years* (1989), available from Antique Publications; Alan Linn, *Fenton Story of Glass Making*, Antique Publications, 1996; James Measell (ed.), *Fenton Glass: The 1980s Decade*, Antique Publications, 1996; Naomi L. Over, *Ruby Glass of the 20th Century*, Antique Publications, 1990, 1993–94 value update; Ferill J. Rice (ed.), *Caught in the Butterfly Net*, Fenton Art Glass Collectors of America, Inc., 1991; Margaret and Kenn Whitmyer, *Fenton Art Glass 1907–1939*, Collector Books, 1996.

Periodical: *Butterfly Net*, 302 Pheasant Run, Kaukauna, WI 54130.

Collectors' Clubs: Fenton Art Glass Collectors of America, Inc., P.O. Box 384, Williamstown, WV 26187; National Fenton Glass Society, P.O. Box 4008, Marietta, OH 45750; Pacific Northwest Fenton Assoc., 8225 Kilchis River Rd., Tillamook, OR 97141.

Videotape: *Glass Artistry in the Making Fenton*, Fenton Art Glass, 1992.

Museum: Fenton Art Glass Co., Williamstown, WV.

Advisor: Ferill J. Rice.

Additional Listings: Carnival Glass.

Ashtray
    Lincoln Inn, Aqua or Ruby 25.00
    #848 2 Ruby, three feet 20.00
    #848 Mandarin Red 75.00
Basket
    #7237 7" h Rose Crest 45.00
    #6137 Beatty Waffle, Green Opal 47.50
    #7437 Burmese, Maple Leaf Decal 75.00
    #7437 DV Violets in the Snow on MI 75.00
    #1523 Aquacrest, 13" t 250.00
    #3830 10" Cranberry Opal, Hobnail 95.00
Bell
    #9064 Velva Rose,Whitton..............................25.00
    #7466 CV hp Christmas Morn 45.00
    #8466 OI Faberge, Teal Marigold 55.00
    #8466 RE Fabergé, Rosalene.........................45.00
Bon bon
    #8230 Rosalene Butterfly, two handled...........35.00
    #1621 Dolphin Handled, Green.......................32.50
Bowl
    Gold Crest, 8" d 40.00
    Peach Crest, Charleton dec 105.00
    #846 Pekin Blue, cupped 37.50
    #848 8 Petal, Chinese Yellow 45.00
    #1562 Satin Etched Silvertone, oblong bowl....55.00
    #7423 Milk Glass bowl, hp Yellow roses 65.00
    #8222 Rosalene, Basketweave 30.00
Candlestick, single
    #951 Silvercrest Cornucopia 37.50
    #7272 Silver Crest 17.50
Candy Box, cov
    Ruby Iridized, Butterfly, for FAGCA...............100.00
    #7380 Custard hp Pink Daffodils Louise Piper dt'd/March 1975...160.00

Bowl, #1790 Jade Green, Leaf Tiers, flared, c1932, $175. Photo courtesy of Ferill J. Rice.

Jardiniere, #3994, Hobnail, Patriot Red, experimental piece, rare, c1975-65, 4-1/2" h, $95. Photo courtesy of Ferill J. Rice.

    #9394 UE 3 pc. Ogee, Blue Burmese 110.00
    #9394 RE 3 pc. Ogee, Rosalene 100.00
Comport
    #3728 PO Plum Opal Hobnail 5-1/2" 75.00
    #8422 Waterlily ftd, Rosalene 30.00
    #8422 Flowered, ftd. Rosalene 30.00
Cocktail Shaker, #6120 Plymouth, Crystal.............55.00
Cracker Jar
    Lilac Big Cookies, no lid, handle 250.00
    #1681 Big Cookies, Jade 125.00
Creamer
    #1502 Diamond Optic, Black 35.00
    #1502 Diamond Optic, Ruby 30.00
    #6464 RG Aventurine Green w/Pink, Vasa Murrhina.......45.00
Creatures (Animals and Birds)
    #5174 Springtime Green Iridized Blown Rabbit 45.00
    #5178 Springtime Green Iridized Blown Owl 45.00
    #5193 RE Rosalene Fish, paperweight 25.00
    #5197 Happiness Bird, Cardinals in Winter 32.50
    #5197 Happiness Bird, Rosalene....................40.00
Cruet, #7701 QJ 7" Burmese, Petite Floral 175.00
Cup and Saucer, #7208 Aqua Crest 35.00
Epergne
    #3902 Petite Blue, Opal 4" h..........................125.00
    #3902 Petite French Opal, 4" h 40.00
    #7308 SC Silvercrest, 3 Horn 125.00
Fairy Light
    #1167 RV Rose Magnolia Hobnail 3 pc. Persian Pearl Crest, Signed Shelly Fenton 80.00
    #3380 CR Hobnail, 3 pc. Cranberry Opal 75.00
    #3804 CA Hobnail 3 pc. Colonial Amber 25.00
    #3804 CG Hobnail 3 pc. Colonial Green..........20.00
    #8406 WT Heart, Wisteria 65.00
    #8406 PE Heart, Shell Pink 25.50
    #8408 VR Persian Medallion, 3 pc. Velva Rose - 75th Anniv 75.00
    #8408 BA Persian Medallion 3 pc. Blue Satin 35.00
Ginger Jar, #893 Persian Pearl w/base and top................150.00
Goblet, #1942 Flower Windows Blue......................55.00
Hat, #1922 Swirl Optic, French Opal......................110.00
Jug, #6068 Cased Lilac, Handled, 6-1/2"...............50.00
Lamp
    #2606 Candy Stripe French Colonial, 20".......650.00
    #2700 Ruby Overlay Mariners 150.00
    #3782 CA Courting, Amber Hobnail, Kerosene 65.00

Lamp, G70, Chinese Yellow, etched leaf and peacock design, encrusted with gold, c1931, $350. Photo courtesy of Ferill J. Rice.

#7312 BD Hurricane Candle Lamp, 5 Petal Blue Dogwood
....75.00
#7398 Black Rose, Hurricane, White Base, 9" h............100.00
Liquor Set, #1934 Flower Stopper, floral silver overlay, 8 pc. Set
....250.00
Nut Bowl, Sailboats, Marigold Carnival 50.00
Pitcher
  Christmas Snowflake, Cranberry Opal, water (L.G. Wright)
  ....350.00
  Christmas Snowflake, Cobalt, water, with six tumblers Tumblers (L.G. Wright) 210.00
  Daisy & Fern, Topaz Opal, water (L.G. Wright) 170.00
  Plum Opal, Hobnail, water, 80 oz. 190.00
  #100 Honeycomb & Clover, Crystal/Gold 45.00
Powder Box
  #6080 Blue Overlay, Wave Crest.................................90.00
  #6080 Coral, Wave Crest..226.00
Plate
  Lafayette & Washington, Light Blue Iridized, Sample 80.00
  #107 Ming Rose 8"...30.00
  #1614 9-1/2" Green Opal w Label New World................65.00
  #1621 Dolphin Handled, Fenton Rose, 6" 25.00
  #5118 Leaf, 11" Rosalene (Sample) 120.00
Rose Bowl, Black Rose, 6-1/2" 40.00
Salt & Pepper Shakers, pr, #3806 Cranberry Opal, Hobnail, flat
....47.50
Sherbet
  #1942 Flower Windows, Crystal 35.00

#4441 Small, Thumbprint, Colonial Blue 35.00
#4443 Thumbprint, Colonial Blue 20.00
Sugar & Creamer, #9103 Cov'd Sugar & Creamer, Fine Cut & Block (OVG)...20.00
Temple Jar, #7488 Chocolate Roses on Cameo Satin.........25.00
Tumbler
  #1634 Diamond Optic, Aqua..6.00
  #3700, Grecian Gold, grape cut....................................15.00
Vase
  Aristocrat Bud Vase, #98 Cutting, Fenton Rose.............45.00
  Ivory Crest, 10" 65.00
  #847 Periwinkle Blue, Fan 62.50
  #3759 Plum Opal, Hobnail, Swung...............................150.00
  #7460 Amberina Overlay crimped, 6-1/2" 80.00
  #7547 Burmese, hp Pink Dogwood, 5-1/2" h.................75.00
  #8254 Mermaid Planter/Vase, Dark Carnival................100.00
  #8802 12" French Blue, Oval, Sandcarved 160.00

FIESTA

History: The Homer Laughlin China Company introduced Fiesta dinnerware in January 1936 at the Pottery and Glass Show in Pittsburgh, Pennsylvania. Frederick Rhead designed the pattern; Arthur Kraft and Bill Bensford molded it. Dr. A. V. Bleininger and H. W. Thiemecke developed the glazes.

The original five colors were red, dark blue, light green (with a trace of blue), brilliant yellow, and ivory. A vigorous marketing campaign took place between 1939 and 1943. In mid-1937, turquoise was added. Red was removed in 1943 because some of the chemicals used to produce it were essential to the war effort; it did not reappear until 1959. In 1951, light green, dark blue, and ivory were retired and forest green, rose, chartreuse, and gray were added to the line. Other color changes took place in the late 1950s, including the addition of a medium green.

Fiesta ware was redesigned in 1969 and discontinued about 1972. In 1986, Fiesta was reintroduced by Homer Laughlin China Company. The new china body shrinks more than the old semi-vitreous and ironstone pieces, thus making the new pieces slightly smaller than the earlier pieces. The modern colors are also different in tone or hue, e.g., the cobalt blue is darker than the old blue. Other modern colors are black, white, apricot, and rose.

References: Susan and Al Bagdade, *Warman's American Pottery and Porcelain*, Wallace-Homestead, 1994; Sharon and Bob Huxford, *Collector's Encyclopedia of Fiesta*, Revised 7th ed., Collector Books, 1996; Jeffrey B. Snyder, *Fiesta, Homer Laughlin China Company's Colorful Dinnerware,* Schiffer Publishing, 1997.

Collectors' Clubs: Fiesta Club of America, P.O. Box 15383, Loves Park, IL 61115; Fiesta Collectors Club, 19238 Dorchester Circle, Strongsville, OH 44136.

Reproduction Alert.

Additional Listings: See *Warman's Americana & Collectibles* for more examples.

After Dinner Coffeepot, cov, cobalt blue............................550.00
After Dinner Cup and Saucer
    Charcoal...550.00
    Chartreuse...625.00
    Cobalt blue...95.00
    Gray...550.00
    Green..85.00
Ashtray, red...50.00
Bowl, 5-1/2" d
    Green..60.00
    Red..34.00
Cake Plate, green.....................................1,950.00
Candlesticks, pr
  Bulb
    Ivory..125.00
    Turquoise..110.00
  Tripod
    Cobalt blue...950.00
    Turquoise..890.00
    Yellow...550.00
Carafe
    Turquoise..380.00
    Yellow...275.00
Casserole, cov
    Red...275.00
    Turquoise..135.00
Casserole, French
    Yellow...275.00
Chop Plate, 13" d
    Gray...95.00
    Ivory..45.00
Coffeepot, turquoise...................................235.00
Comport, 12" d, Ivory, mkd............................225.00
Creamer, stick handle
    Ivory..75.00
    Red..75.00
    Turquoise..115.00
    Yellow...45.00
Cream Soup
    Gray...60.00
    Ivory..60.00
    Rose...95.00
Cup
    Cobalt blue...35.00
    Dark green...45.00
    Light green...25.00
    Medium green..70.00
    Turquoise..25.00
    Yellow...25.00
Dessert Bowl, 6" d
    Red..45.00
    Rose...45.00
Egg Cup
    Green..50.00
    Red..70.00
Fruit Bowl, 4-3/4" d
    Cobalt blue...25.00
    Medium green..550.00
Fruit Bowl, 11-3/4" d, cobalt blue....................485.00
Gravy, turquoise...30.00

Juice Pitcher, red..750.00
Juice Tumbler
    Cobalt blue...40.00
    Rose...65.00
    Yellow...40.00
Marmalade
    Turquoise..325.00
    Yellow...360.00
Mixing Bowl
    #1, cobalt blue.......................................375.00
    #2, cobalt blue.......................................195.00
    #2, yellow..140.00
    #4, green...195.00
    #5, ivory...275.00
    #7, ivory...580.00
Mug
    Dark green...90.00
    Ivory, marked..125.00
    Rose...95.00
Mustard, cov
    Cobalt blue...325.00
    Turquoise..275.00
Nappy, 5-1/2" d, turquoise.............................25.00
Onion Soup, cov
    Green..895.00
    Ivory..950.00
Pitcher, disk
    Chartreuse...275.00
    Turquoise..110.00
Pitcher, ice lip
    Green..135.00
    Turquoise..195.00
Plate, deep
    Gray...42.00
    Rose...42.00

Coffeepot, green, 10-1/2" h, $50.

Plate, 6" d
   Dark green 13.00
   Ivory 7.00
   Light green 9.00
   Turquoise 8.00
   Yellow 5.00
Plate, 7" d
   Chartreuse 13.00
   Ivory 10.00
   Light green 8.50
   Medium green 30.00
   Rose 14.00
   Turquoise 8.50
Plate, 9" d
   Cobalt blue 15.00
   Ivory 14.00
   Red 15.00
   Yellow 8.00
Plate, 10" d, dinner
   Gray 42.00
   Light green 28.00
   Medium green 125.00
   Red 35.00
   Turquoise 30.00
Plate, 15" d, cobalt blue 62.00
Platter, oval
   Gray 35.00
   Ivory 25.00
   Red 45.00
   Yellow 22.00
Relish
   Ivory base and center, turquoise inserts 285.00
   Red, base and inserts 425.00
Salt and Pepper Shakers, pr
   Red 24.00
   Turquoise 135.00
Saucer
   Light green 5.00
   Turquoise 5.00
Soup Plate
   Ivory 36.00
   Turquoise 29.00
Sugar Bowl, cov
   Chartreuse 65.00
   Gray 75.00
   Rose 75.00
Syrup
   Green 450.00
   Ivory 600.00
   Red 495.00
Sweets Compote, yellow 65.00
Tea Cup, flat bottom, cobalt blue 100.00
Teapot, cov
   Cobalt blue, large 335.00
   Red
      Large 225.00
      Medium 250.00
   Rose, medium 350.00
Tumbler, cobalt blue 75.00
Utility Tray, red 55.00
Vase, 12" h, ivory 1,200.00

FIGURAL BOTTLES

History: Porcelain figural bottles, which have an average height of three to eight and were made either in a glazed or bisque finish, achieved popularity in the late 1800s and remained popular into the 1930s. The majority of figural bottles were made in Germany, with Austria and Japan accounting for the balance.

Your Health, flask shape, bisque front, tree bark back, 4-1/2" x 4", $35.

Empty figural bottles were shipped to the United States and filled upon arrival. They were then given away to customers by brothels, dance halls, hotels, liquor stores, and taverns. Some were lettered with the names and addresses of the establishment, others had paper labels. Many were used for holidays, e.g., Christmas and New Year.

Figural bottles also were made in glass and other materials. The glass bottles held perfumes, food, or beverages.

References: Ralph & Terry Kovel, *Kovels' Bottles Price List*, 10th ed., Crown Publishers, 1996; Kenneth Wilson, *American Glass 1760-1930*, 2 vols., Hudson Hills Press and The Toledo Museum of Art, 1994.

Periodical: *Antique Bottle and Glass Collector*, P.O. Box 187, East Greenville, PA 18041.

Collectors' Clubs: Federation of Historical Bottle Clubs, 88 Sweetbriar Branch, Longwood, FL 32750; New England Antique Bottle Club, 120 Commonwealth Rd., Lynn, MA 01904.

Museums: National Bottle Museum, Ballston Spa, NY; National Bottle Museum, Barnsley, S Yorkshire, England; Old Bottle Museum, Salem, NJ.

Bisque
Man, 4-1/2" h, toasting, "Your Health," flask style, tree bark back
.... 85.00
Sailor, 6-1/2" h, white pants, blue blouse, hat, high gloss front,
   mkd "Made in Germany" 115.00
Turkey Trot, 6-3/4" h, tree trunk back, mkd "Made in Germany"
.... 150.00

Glass
Ballet Dancer, 12" h, milk glass, pink and brown paint dec highlights, sheared mouth, removable head as closure, pontil scar, attributed to America, 1860-90 .... 525.00

Bear, 10-5/8" h, dense yellow amber, sheared mouth, applied face, Russia, 1860-80, flat chip on back 400.00

Big Stick, Teddy Roosevelt's, 7-1/2" h, golden amber, sheared mouth, smooth base, flat flake at mouth........................170.00

Bull, John, 11-3/4" h, bright orange amber, tooled mouth, smooth base, attributed to England, 1870-1900 ....160.00

Cherub Holding Medallion, 11-1/8" h, blue opaque milk glass, sq collared mouth, ground pontil scar, attributed to America, 1860-90 ....120.00

Chinaman, 5-3/4" h, seated form, milk glass, ground mouth, orig painted metal atomizer head, smooth base, America, 1860-90............................120.00

Fish, 11-1/2" h, "Doctor Fisch's Bitters," golden amber, applied small round collared mouth, smooth base, America, 1860-80, some ext. highpoint wear, burst bubble on base..........160.00

Garfield, James, President, 8" h, colorless glass bust set in turned wood base, ground mouth, smooth base, America, 1880-1900...80.00

Indian Maiden, 12-1/4" h, "Brown's Celebrated Indian Herb Bitters," yellow amber, inward rolled mouth, smooth base, America, 1860-80 ....600.00

Shoe, dark amethyst, ground mouth, smooth base 125.00

Washington, George, 10" h, "Simon's Centennial Bitters," aquamarine, applied double collared mouth, smooth base, America, 1860-80................................650.00

Pottery and Porcelain

Book, 10-1/2" h, Bennington Battle, brown, tan, cream, and green flint enamel 1,000.00

Canteen, painted bust of Lincoln, Garfield, and McKinley, half pint...375.00

Cucumber, 11-3/4" l, stoneware, green and cream mottled glaze..100.00

FINDLAY ONYX GLASS

History: Findlay onyx glass, produced by Dalzell, Gilmore & Leighton Company, Findlay, Ohio, was patented for the firm in 1889 by George W. Leighton. Due to high production costs resulting from a complex manufacturing process, the glass was made only for a short time.

Layers of glass were plated to a bulb of opalescent glass through repeated dippings into a glass pot. Each layer was cooled and reheated to develop opalescent qualities. A pattern mold then was used to produce raised decorations of flowers and leaves. A second mold gave the glass bulb its full shape and form.

A platinum luster paint, producing pieces identified as silver or platinum onyx, was applied to the raised decorations. The color was fixed in a muffle kiln. Other colors such as cinnamon, cranberry, cream, raspberry, and rose were achieved by using an outer glass plating which reacted strongly to reheating. For example, a purple or orchid color came from the addition of manganese and cobalt to the glass mixture.

References: Neila and Tom Bredenhoft, *Findlay Toothpick Holders*, Cherry Hill Publications, 1995; James Measell and Don E. Smith, *Findlay Glass: The Glass Tableware Manufacturers, 1886-1902*, Antique Publications, 1986.

Collectors' Club: Collectors of Findlay Glass, P.O. Box 256, Findlay, OH 45839.

Celery, cream 450.00
Creamer, 4-1/2" h, cream 265.00

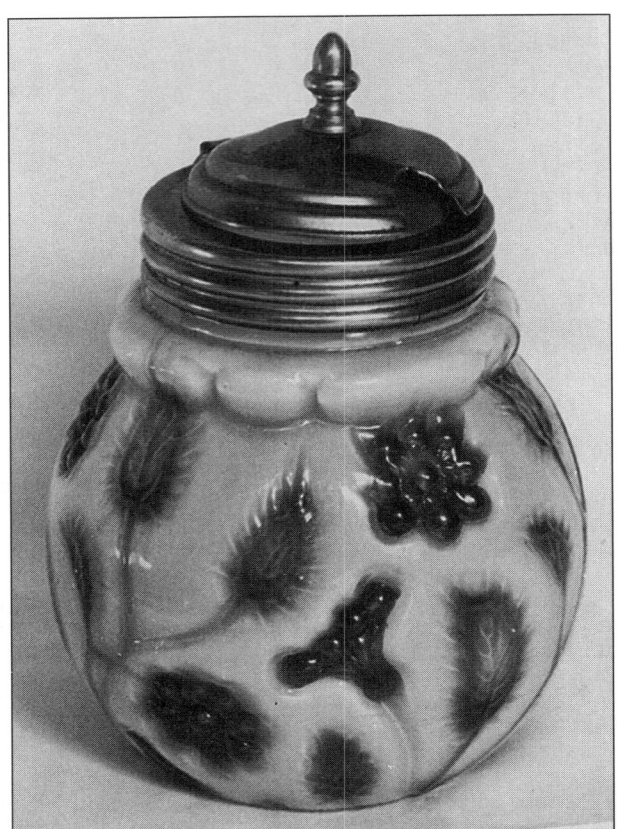
Mustard Jar, cov, raspberry, SP cover, 3-3/8" h, $1,350.

Dresser Box, cov, 5" d, cream..675.00
Pitcher, 7-1/2" h, cream, applied opalescent handle, polished rim chip..800.00
Spooner, 4-1/2" h, satin surface, bright silver dec, few small rim flakes..485.00
Sugar Bowl, cov, 5-1/2" h, cream 375.00
Sugar Shaker, raspberry 495.00
Syrup, 7" h, 4" w, silver dec, applied opalescent handle 1,150.00
Toothpick Holder, cream 375.00

FINE ARTS

Notes: There is no way a listing of less than one hundred paintings can accurately represent the breadth and depth of the examples sold during the last year. To attempt to make such a list would be ludicrous.

In any calendar year, tens, if not hundreds, of thousands of paintings are sold. Prices range from a few dollars to millions. Since each painting is essentially a unique creation, it is difficult to compare prices.

Since an essential purpose of *Warman's Antiques And Collectibles Price Guide* is to assist its users in finding information about a category, this Fine Arts introduction has been written primarily to identify the reference books that you will need to find out more about a painting in your possession.

Artist Dictionaries: Emmanuel Benezit, *Dictionnaire Critique et Documentaire des Peintres, Sculpteurs, Dessinateurs et Graveurs*, 10 volumes, 3rd ed., Grund, 1976; John Castagno, *Old Masters: Signatures and Monograms*, Scarecrow Press, 1996; Ian Chilvers, *Concise Ox-*

ford Dictionary of Arts & Artists, 2nd ed., Oxford University Press, 1996; Peter Hastings Falk, Dictionary of Signatures & Monograms of American Artists, Sound View Press, 1988; Mantle Fielding, Dictionary of American Painters, Sculptors and Engravers, Apollo Books, 1983; J. Johnson and A. Greutzner, Dictionary of British Artists, 1880-1940: An Antique Collector's Club Research Project Listing 41,000 Artists, Antique Collector's Club, 1976; Les Krantz, American Artists, Facts on File, 1985.

Introductory Information: Alan Bamberger, Buy Art Smart, Wallace-Homestead Book Company, 1990; ——, How to Buy Fine Art You Can Afford, Wallace-Homestead, 1994.

Price Guide References, Basic: Art at Auction in America, 1994 ed., Krexpress, 1994; William T. Currier (comp.), Currier's Price Guide to American Artists 1645-1945 at Auction, Currier Publications, 1997; -- (comp.), Currier's Price Guide to American and European Prints at Auction, Currier Publications, 1997; —— (comp.), Currier's Price Guide to European Artists 1545-1945 at Auction, Currier Publications, 1997.

Price Guide References, Advanced: R. J. Davenport, Davenport's Art Reference & Price Guide: 1996-97, 8th ed., Davenport Publishing, 1996; Peter Hastings Falk (ed.), Art Price Index International '96, Sound View Press (859 Boston Post Rd., Madison, CT 06443), 1995; Richard Hislop (ed.), Annual Art Sales Index, 28th ed., Art Sales Index Ltd., 1996; Enrique Mayer, International Auction Record, Paris, Editions Enrique Mayer, since 1967; Judith and Martin Miller (comps. & eds.), Miller's Picture Price Guide, Millers Publications, 1996; Susan Theran (ed.), Leonard's Price Index of Art Auctions, Auction Index, since 1980.

Museum Directories: American Art Directory, R. R. Bowker, 1995; American Association of Museums, Official Museum Directory: United States and Canada, R. R. Bowker, updated periodically.

Painting, Northern Hills, Jonas Lie, oil on canvas, sgd and dated lower right, 1922, 29-1/2" h, 39-1/2" w, $9,900. Photo courtesy of Jackson's Auctioneers & Appraisers.

Collectors' Club: American Art Collectors, 610 N. Delaware Ave., Roswell, NM 88201.

FIREARM ACCESSORIES

History: Muzzle-loading weapons of the 18th and early 19th centuries varied in caliber and required the owner to carry a variety of equipment, including a powder horn or flask, patches, flints or percussion caps, bullets, and bullet molds. In addition, military personnel were responsible for bayonets, slings, and miscellaneous cleaning equipment and spare parts.

During the French and Indian War, soldiers began to personalize their powder horns with intricate engraving, in addition to the usual name or initial used for identification. Sometimes professional hornsmiths were employed to customize these objects, which have been elevated to a form of folk art by some collectors.

In the mid-19th century, cartridge weapons replaced their black-powder ancestors. Collectors seek anything associated with early ammunition—from the cartridges themselves to advertising material. Handling old ammunition can be extremely dangerous because of decomposition of compounds. Seek advice from an experienced collector before becoming involved in this area.

References: Ralf Coykendall, Jr., Coykendall's Complete Guide to Sporting Collectibles, Wallace-Homestead, 1996; John Delph, Firearms and Tackle Memorabilia, Schiffer Publishing, 1991; Jim Dresslar, Folk Art of Early America–The Engraved Powder Horn, Dresslar Publishing (P.O. Box 635, Bargersville, IN 46106), 1996; Jim and Vivian Karsnitz, Sporting Collectibles, Schiffer Publishing, 1992.

Periodical: Military Trader, P.O. Box 1050, Dubuque, IA 52004.

Museums: Fort Ticonderoga Museum, Ticonderoga, NY; Huntington Museum of Art, Huntington, WV.

REPRODUCTION ALERT

There are a large number of reproduction and fake powder horns. Be very cautious!

Notes: Military-related firearm accessories generally are worth more than their civilian counterparts.

Additional Listings: Militaria.

Belt, 36" l, 2" w, 30 nickel metal clips for holding shot shells, canvas shoulder straps, nickel plated buckle with Savage Arms logo cast into it, nickel plated hook 350.00

Canteen, 7" d, 2-5/8" deep, painted, cheesebox style, dark red paint overall, one side painted l gold with a large primitive eagle with shield breast, the top of the shield red with cream lettering "No. 37," other side painted in gold letters, "Lt. Rufus Cook," pewter nozzle, sq nail construction, strap loops missing...1,650.00

Cartridge Box
  3-7/8" x 2" x 1", Hall and Hubbard, .22 caliber, green and black label "100 No. 1/22-100/Pistol Cartridges," cov with molded cream and black paper, empty, missing about half green side label 300.00

Powder Horn, engraved map of Fort Lebanon, three fish, and duck, inscribed "CAPT. JACOB MORGAN, FT. LEBANON, 1856" within laurel heart surround, rim with scrolling band of tulips, fitted with domed wood base plug with knob finial, wood stopper, 10-1/4" l, $3,450. Photo courtesy of Sotheby's.

3-7/8" x 2-1/8" x 1-1/4", Phoenix Metallic Cartridge Co., early green and black label, "50 Cartridges/32-100 Caliber Long," opened, but full 250.00
4" x 2-1/8" x 1-1/4", Union Metallic Cartridge Co., .32 caliber, cream and black label "Fifth .32 caliber/No. 2/Pistol Cartridges," engraving of Smith & Wesson 1st Model 3rd Issue, checked covering, orange and black side labels, unopened 210.00
Catalog, Stoeger Arms Corp, New York, NY, 1945, 512 pgs, 8" x 10", The Shooter's Bible, No. 36 .... 45.00
Dagger, Caucasian Kinjahl, Cossack, c1750 .... 750.00
Dirk, Naval, American, scabbard 600.00
Dress Knife, Sir Lanka, c1800, fine chisel engraving on blade and hilt, silver and gold inlay, silver scabbard, damage to scabbard 700.00
Epaulets, pr, military, gilt, office, large, "MASSACHUSETTS" buttons with standing Indian warrior, orig purple carton with green edging, orig label "MILITIA ESTABLISHMENTS/BENT & BUSH/Boston" 265.00
Flask, powder, 7-5/8" l, brass, threaded brass top, mkd "A. M. Flask & Cap. Co.," fitted with 4 carrying rings, orig green carrying cord, brass body emb on 1 side with crossed revolvers, stars, eagle with shield breast, cannon with eagle American flag to each side, ground with various military weapons and accessories, missing spout screw, body with 90% orig dark lacquer.................. 450.00
Hari-Kiri, Samurai, ornamental blade 1,200.00
Katar, Indian
    Piercing blade 450.00
    Split blade, silver inlay, c1750 .... 900.00
Powder Horn
    4-1/4" l, engraved spread eagle clutching American flag and arrows, ship under sail, various geometric and heart motifs, 19th C, losses, cracks 375.00
    6-1/2" h, E. K. B. 1831 Horn NH, dec foliate border, heats, star, and patriotic banner, rounded plug dec with hearts, centers inset brass button depicting eagle surrounded by stars 1,955.00
    9" l, whale's tooth, engraved ship under sail, crosshatched diamond design, losses, cracks.................. 350.00
    13" l, "Daniel Chase his horn made in August ye 1786," dec with British coat of arms, townscape, hunt scene, reverse with gentleman, minor cracks and flaking 1,035.00
    13" l, engraved fish, Indian hunting deer, fanciful figures and flowers, inscribed "John Mills his horn made at Crown Point, Ocf [sic] 4br 1758," minor insect damage, minor imperfections 2,000.00
    13" l, engraved, initialed and dated "AB 1807," floral and geometric motifs 980.00
Shot Flask, leather, 7" l, black pigskin body stamped "Sykes/Extra/lb/1," fitted with carrying ring, 2" German silver top with bright steel dispenser stamped "Skyes Extra" 85.00

Target Ball, 2-3/4" d, Bogardus, molded, amber glass, surface with overall net patter, bottom with raised sunburst pattern, middle with 1/2" band "Bogardus Glass Ball Patd April 18, 1877," chips at neck 200.00
Tinder Box, 4-3/8" d, tin, candle socket, inside damper, flint, and steel 330.00
Tinder Lighter, flintlock
    5-1/2" l, rosewood pistol grip, tooled brass fittings 750.00
    6-1/2" l, compartment for extra flint, taper holder 550.00

FIREARMS

History: The 15th-century Matchlock Harquebus was the forerunner of the modern firearm. The Germans refined the wheelock firing mechanism during the 16th and 17th centuries. English settlers arrived in America with the smoothbore musket; German settlers had rifled arms. Both used the new flintlock firing mechanism.

A major advance was achieved when Whitney introduced interchangeable parts into the manufacturing of rifles. Continued refinements in firearms continued in the 19th century. The percussion ignition system was developed by the 1840s. Minie, a French military officer, produced a viable projectile. By the end of the 19th century cartridge weapons dominated the field.

References: Robert W. D. Ball, *Mauser Military Rifles of the World*, Krause Publications, 1996; ——, *Remington Firearms*, Krause Publications; ——, *Springfield Armory Shoulder Weapons, 1795-1968*, Antique Trader Books, 1997; Ralf Coykendall, Jr., *Coykendall's Complete Guide to Sporting Collectibles*, Wallace-Homestead, 1996; Norman Flayderman, *Flayderman's Guide to Antique American Firearms And Their Values*, 6th ed., DBI Books, 1995; *Gun Trader's Guide*, 15th ed., Stoeger Publishing, 1992; Herbert G. Houze, *Colt Rifles and Muskets from 1847-1870*, Krause Publications, 1996; ——, *History of Winchester Repeating Arms Company*, Krause Publications, 1994; Russell and Steve Quertermous, *Modern Guns Identification & Values*, 11th ed., Collector Books, 1997; Ned Schwing, *Browning Superposed*, Krause Publications, 1996; Ned Schwing and Herbert Houze, *Standard Catalog of Firearms*, 7th ed., Krause Publications, 1997; Jim Supica and Richard Nahas, *Standard Catalog of Smith & Wesson*, Krause Publications, 1996; John Taffin, *Big Bore Sixguns,* Krause Publications, 1997; --, *Modern Custom Guns*, Krause Publications, 1997; Ken Warner (ed.), *Gun Digest 1998,* 52nd ed., Krause Publications, 1997; Frederick Wilkinson, Handguns, New Burlington Books, 1993; A. B. Zhuk, *Illustrated Encyclopedia of Handguns*, Greenhill Books, 1995.

Periodicals: *Gun List*, 700 E. State St., Iola, WI 54990; *Gun Report*, P.O. Box 38, Aledo, IL 61231; *Historic Weapons & Relics*, 2650 Palmyra Rd., Palmyra, TN 37142; *Man at Arms*, P.O. Box 460, Lincoln, RI 02865; *Military Trader*, P.O. Box 1050, Dubuque, IA 52004; *Sporting Gun*, P.O. Box 301369, Escondido, CA 92030; *Wildcat Collectors Journal*, 15158 NE. 6 Ave., Miami, FL 33162.

Collectors' Clubs: American Society of Military History, Los Angeles Patriotic Hall, 1816 S. Figuerora, Los Angeles, CA 90015; Winchester Arms Collectors Assoc., Inc., P.O. Box 6754, Great Falls, MT 59406.

Museums: Battlefield Military Museum, Gettysburg, PA; National Firearms Museum, Washington, DC; Remington Gun Museum, Ilion, NY; Springfield Armory National Historic Site, Springfield, MA; Winchester Mystery House, Historic Firearms Museum, San Jose, CA.

Notes: Two factors control the pricing of firearms: condition and rarity. Variations in these factors can cause a wide range in the value of antique firearms. For instance, a Colt 1849 pocket-model revolver with a 5-inch barrel can be priced from $100 to $700 depending on whether all the component parts are original, whether some are missing, how much of the original finish (bluing) remains on the barrel and frame, how much silver plating remains on the brass trigger guard and back strap, and the condition and finish of the walnut grips.

Be careful to note a weapon's negative qualities. A Colt Peterson belt revolver in fair condition will command a much higher price than the Colt pocket model in very fine condition. Know the production run of a firearm before buying it.

SPECIAL AUCTION

James D. Julia, Inc.
P.O. Box 830
Fairfield, ME 04937
(207) 453-7125

Flintlock Pistols-Single Shot

English, Tower, 60 caliber, 12" round barrel, full length military stock, brass trigger guard, butt cap and sidelined, lockplate mkd Tower behind hammer and crown over "GR" forward of hammer, proofed on left side of barrel at breech, crown on tang behind tang screw, good condition, re-browned and cleaned, replaced front sight, working order 700.00
European, blunderbuss, 70 caliber, 16" brass barrel, brass trigger guard and buttplate, full stock, lock plate mkd with crown over "R" under pan, good condition, mellow brass patina, working order, all orig 750.00
French Huguenot, dueling, sgd "Piere Laffemand, Paris," c1640-80, 23" l, ivory stocks from pistol butt to barrel tip, barrels, butts, and trigger guards gold engraved with battle scenes, price for matched pr 12,200.00
Halsbach & Sons, Baltimore, MD, holster pistol, c1785 to early 1800s, 9" brass part round, part octagon barrel, 65 caliber, lock mkd "Halsbach & Sons," large brass butt cap with massive spread wing eagle (primitive) in high relief surrounded by cluster of 13 stars, large relief shell carving around tang of barrel, full walnut stock, pin-fastened 1,750.00
Kentucky, T. B. Cherington, 12-1/2" octagonal smooth bore barrel, stamped "T. P. Cherington" on barrel and lockplate, 45 caliber, brightly polished iron parts, walnut stock...........2,500.00
U.S. Model 1805, 10" round iron barrel with iron rib underneath holding ramrod pipe, lockplate mkd with spread eagle and shield over "US" and vertically at rear "Harper's Ferry" over "1808," 54 caliber, walnut half stock with brass buttplate and trigger guard, Flayderman 6A-008 ....3,000.00
U.S. Model 1819, Simeon North, Middletown, CT, c1819-23, 10" round barrel, 54 caliber, smooth bore, barrel mkd at breech J//P//US, lock mkd ahead of hammer S. North over American eagle and shield motif with letters U and S at either side over bottom line MIDLTN CONN., date of production mkd at rear of lock below safety bolt, swivel type ramrod, iron mountings,

sliding safety bolt, brass blade front sight, oval shaped rear sight on tang.................................850.00

Percussion Pistols-Single Shot

Note: Conversation of flintlock pistols to percussion was common practice. Most English and U.S. military flintlock pistols listed above can be found in percussion. Values for these percussion converted pistols are from 40% to 60% of the flintlock values as given.

Blunt & Syms side hammer, Blunt & Syms, NY, c1840-50, 6" octagon barrel, 44 caliber, barrel mkd "B & S New York," dec broad scroll engraving on frame, iron forend, ramrod mounted beneath, bag shaped handle, walnut grips 350.00
Caucasian Miguelet, extensive gold and silver inlay on stock, c1690-1720, butt had 1-1/2" split 5,000.00
German, dueling, sgd "A. J. Freund in Suhl," c1850 ....700.00
Mule Ear, 9-1/4" overall, 5-1/8" octagonal rifled barrel, 44 caliber, large dovetailed brass front sight, open rear sight, simple mule ear lock with external mainspring, tiger striped full stock with simple brass forend cap and trigger guard, sear and corresponding notch of hammer restored, two small cracks in stock 500.00

Percussion Pistols-Multi-Shot

Belgian, side-by-side 4" round barrels, approx. .45 cal, double trigger boxlock percussion action and checkered bag grip, needs tuning.......................................90.00
Colt
  Navy, Model 1861, 7-1/2" round barrel, 36 caliber, 6 shot, creeping style loading lever, barrel stamped "Address Co. Saml Colt New-York, U.S. America-.36 cal," cylinder roll scene depicts battle between Texas, Navy, and that of Mexico, one piece walnut grip 1,200.00
  Pocket, Model 1849, 3", 4", 5" and 6" barrel length, 31 caliber, 5 or 6 shot, octagon barrel with attached loading lever, barrel stamped "Address Co. Saml Colt New-York, U.S. America," cylinder engraved with stagecoach holdup scene, round trigger guard, walnut grips...........................600.00
Remington
  Belt, New Model, 6-1/2" octagon barrel, 36 caliber, 6 shot, barrel stamped "Patented Sept. 14, 1856/E. Remington & Sons, Ilion, New York USA/New Model," round cylinder, threads visible at breech end, safety notches on cylinder shoulders between nipples 600.00
  Navy, 1861, 7-3/8" octagon barrel, 36 caliber, 6 shot, barrel stamped "Patented Dec. 17, 1861/Manufactured by Remington's Ilion, N.Y.," round cylinder, walnut grips.....675.00
Remington-Beals 3rd Model Pocket Revolver, cased, 4" octagon barrel, 31 caliber, 5 shot, barrel stamped "Beal's Patent 1856 7 57 758/Manufactured by Remington's Ilion, N.Y.," orig cardboard box with brass bullet mold, quantity of bullets, eagle and shield flask, mushroom shaped cleaning rod with screw-in type extension, extra pawl spring, can of Eley percussion caps.......................................2,500.00

Revolvers

Colt
  1917 Military, 34 caliber, non-factory nickel finish, bottom of barrel mkd "United States Property," bottom of butt with normal markings, grips sanded and refinished........150.00
  Flat Top, officer's model, target, .38 cal, 7-1/2" barrel, adjustable front and rear sights, silver medallion checkered walnut grips, 98% bright blue finish.............................400.00
  Frontier Six Shooter, 44-40 caliber, nickeled finish, 7-1/2" roll marked barrel, black powder ram with rampant Colt black composition grips, accompanied by factory letter regarding 1893 shipment to Montgomery Ward in Chicago, 95% orig bright nickel, solid grips 4,000.00

Flintlock long rifles, top: VA, curly maple stock with good figure, relief carving, old mellow varnished finish, brass hardware includes engraved and pierced patchbox, "Ketland" lock skillfully reconverted back to flint, silver thumb piece inlay, 41-1/2" l barrel and forend shortened slightly, top flat engraved "H.B.," $3,300; bottom: PA, attributed to W. Haga of the Reading School, 50-1/2" octagon to round barrel, maple stock with relief carving and incised detail, brass hardware with a flintlock, some age cracks, glued repair, patch box lid replaced, $1,760. Photo courtesy of Garth's Auctions.

M.1901 Army, 38 caliber, blue finish, 6" barrel, half moon sight with smooth walnut grips, lanyard loop through butt, left side rear frame mkd with inspector initials "RAC" and "LEB," orig type commercial black flap holster........200.00

SAA, 32 caliber, standard blue and case color finish, 5-1/2" barrel, deluxe walnut medallion fleur-de-lis checkered grips, 97% bright orig bluing, orig case colors, bright bore 2,500.00

Smith & Wesson

M.686-3 DA, 357 caliber, 4-1/8" full lug barrel, red ramp, white outline sights, checked medallion magnum grips....200.00

M.1955, target, 45 caliber, blue finish, 6-1/2" barrel, partridge front sight, adjustable rear, target trigger and hammer and magnum checkered walnut grips, orig presentation box and paperwork 350.00

Flintlock Long Arms

Kentucky, N. Beyer, 50 caliber, orig smooth bore, 58-1/2" overall, 42-1/2" part rounded barrel, orig front sight mounted on light engraved brass oval, sgd in script "N. Beyer" on top flat and secured to stock with incise carving on the forend to the faceted brass tailpipe, 2 faceted brass ramrod pipes and brass forend cap, beveled brass sideplate, raised scroll carving about tang with lightly engraved silver oval wrist escutcheon, incise carving at wrist on right side, left side with raised carved scrolls, a large raised carved scroll to rear of cheekpiece, engraved brass patch box with bird finial, typical Beyer beveled brass trigger guard, reconverted barrel and lock 3,650.00

Pennsylvania, attributed to W. Haga, Reading School, 50-1/2" l octagon to round barrel, maple stock, relief carving, incised details, brass hardware with flintlock, some age cracks, glued repair, good patina, replaced patch box lid..............1,760.00

U.S. Model 1808, Thomas French, Canton, MA, Contract Musket, Harpers Ferry pattern, tail of lock stamped "Canton/1810," below the pan with the eagle and "US" over "FRENCH" (well struck with no trace of "T"), barrel stamped "US/V," with sunken eagle head CT proof (Flayderman 9A-131)..........1,200.00

Virginia, curly maple stock with good figure, relief carving, old mellow varnished finish, brass hardware, engraved and pierced patch box, Ketland lock reconverted back to flint, silver thumb piece inlay, 41-1/2" l barrel and forend shortened slightly, small pierced repair at breech area, top flat engraved "H. B." 3,300.00

Percussion Long Arms

Note: Conversion of flintlock long arms to percussion was common practice. Most English, French, and U.S. military flintlock model long arms listed in the previous section can be found in percussion. Values of these percussion converted long arms are from 40 to 60% of the flintlock values previously noted.

English, 577 Rifled Musket, 39-1/4" barrel fitted with folding leaf long range sight, lockplate stamped with crown and "1863/Tower," walnut full stock with brass forend cap, trigger guard, and butt plate, orig nipple protector, complete with correct style English bayonet, excellent to mint condition 1,500.00

Kentucky Rifle, swivel breech, 51" overall, deeply rifled 38 caliber octagonal barrels, sgd "Jon Shuler/Liverpool PA," on both top flats, one side of the barrel group is a flat piece of steel, the other with four brass ramrod pipes, tiger stripped butt stock with engraved brass sideplate, light engraved brass trigger guard with double set triggers, engraved brass patchbox and toe plate, lightly engraved German silver escutcheon at right, 2" inlay on left side, back action lock sgd "N. Ashmore," old ramrod, probably not orig..1,200.00

U. S. Model 1863, Rifle Musket, Type II (a.k.a. Model 1864), Springfield Armory, c1864-65, 58 caliber, single shot, muzzleloader, 40" round barrel, 3 barrel bands, lock stamped with eagle motif to right of hammer, "U.S./Springfield" beneath nipple bolster, "1864" at angle at rear section of lock, single leaf rear sight, walnut stock (Flayderman 9A-341) 850.00

Winchester, M.1866 musket, standard factory engraving, scrolls on right side of frame, similar scrolls on left side, standing stag within a round panel, light scroll engraving on top and bottom of frame with further scroll small area on top of buttplate, cleaning rod missing, accompanied by letter "...shipped from the warehouse on March 24, 1877, with 345 other arms to order number 8365"..16,000.00

Rifles

Browning, safari grade, bolt action, cal. 257 Roberts, standard grade configuration, 22" pencil barrel on FN action, checkered wood with pistol grip Monte Carlo stock and engraved floor plate/trigger guard, high luster on wood, accompanied by 2 Browning letters stating this was special order..........1,000.00

Marlin

Model 94, lever action, cal. 38-40, standard grade, 24" octagon barrel, full magazine, straight drip stock with smooth steel buttplate, case colored receiver, 96% orig bluing, most orig varnish, brilliant shiny bore.......................350.00

Model 1893 SRC, cal. 38-55, standard carbine configuration, 20" barrel, full magazine, carbine ladder sight, plain wood with straight stock and carbine steel buttplate, 95% orig bluing, old refinish, shiny bore 400.00

Winchester

M.67, single shot, 22 caliber, 27" tapered round barrel, open sights, nickeled bolt, blued trigger and trigger guard, 1 pc walnut stock, black composition buttplate, no serial number 125.00

M.68, single shot, 22 caliber, 27" tapered round barrel, ramp front sight with hood and Dockendorfer barrel mounted peep sight, nickeled bolt and trigger, 1 pc walnut stock, black logo composition buttplate, no serial number 165,99

M.75, target, 22 caliber, 28" round barrel, Lyman 17A front sight, Winchester rear peep sight, barrel mounted with scope blocks, receiver drilled and tapped 215.00

Model 94, deluxe factory presentation, 30 caliber, 26" part round barrel, ivory bead Lyman front sight, 3 leaf express sight, half magazine take down and 4-X pistol grip wood C-style carving and checkered in rare pattern, forearm with 90% coverage in 28 and 32 line checkering with scallops and florals with rect and circular patterns, pistol grip stock also carved and checkered with identical patterns having

single major panel of 28 line and 3 smaller panels of 32 line checkering, adjacent to the receiver on either side are carved fleur-de-lis and half diamond patterns with scallops and modified lined carving at the pistol grip, left side of receiver embellished "Compliments of/Winchester Repeating Arms Co.," upper tang equipped with Lyman style tang sight, buttplate is case colored crescent steel.... 13,500.00
Model 1890 case colored 2nd model pump, .22 cal, 24-1/2" tapered octagon barrel, fixed front sight, sight blank in the dovetail and Lyman tang sight installed, small ribbed forearm and straight drip stock with crescent steel buttplate, 95% bluing, 70% fading case colors, 90% orig varnish, shiny bore 1,000.00

Shotguns

Ithaca, Grade 2E NID, 4-barrel set, cal. 10 ga, 32, 30, and two 28" barrels, all numbered to receiver and all fitted with ejectors and marked 3-1/2" chambers, one set of 28" barrels appears to be of later origin (mkd SB & Co.), all four sets mkd with Grade 2 designation, double beads, received fitted with single trigger and cocked indicators, typical Grade 2 engraved with standing quail on left side and woodcock on right with light coarse floral engraving to back and bottom, professional replacement wood with wide carved and checkered beavertail forearm, heavy carved and checkered cheekpiece buttstock, 14-7/8" over an Ithaca recoil pad, refinished trigger guard 2,000.00
Parker GHE, double barrel, cal. 28 ga, standard Parker configuration, 26" barrels on double "O" frame, double triggers and ejectors, splinter forearm, pistol grip stock, 14-3/8" over an ancient leather faced pad, receiver is game scene engraved with flying mallards, quail, and pheasants, surrounded by Arabesque patterns, 96% orig bright barrel blue, numerous small handing marks.................6,250.00
Savage Model 720, 12 gauge, 4-shot tubular, 30" cylinder bore, full coke, Browning patent, semi-automatic, hammerless, blued, checkered walnut pistol grip stock and forearm, plain receiver...200.00
Stevens, Model 970, 12 gauge, single shot, 32" l round barrel with octagonal breech, top lever break-open, hammerless, automatic shell ejector, automatic safety, blued, case hardened frame, checkered walnut pistol grip stock and forearm 95.00

FIREHOUSE COLLECTIBLES

History: The volunteer fire company has played a vital role in the protection and social growth of many towns and rural areas. Paid professional firemen usually are found only in large metropolitan areas. Each fire company prided itself on equipment and uniforms. Conventions and parades gave the fire companies a chance to show off their equipment. These events produced a wealth of firehouse-related memorabilia.

References: Andrew G. Gurka, *Hot Stuff! Firefighting Collectibles*, L-W Book Sales, 1994; James Piatti, *Firehouse Memorabilia: Identification and Price Guide*, Avon Books, 1994; Donald F. Wood and Wayne Sorensen, *American Volunteer Fire Trucks*, Krause Publications, 1995; --. *Big City Fire Trucks, 1900-1950*, Krause Publications, 1996 (Vol. I), 1997 (Vol. II).

Periodical: *Fire Apparatus Journal*, P.O. Box 141295, Staten Island, NY 10314.

Collectors' Clubs: Antique Fire Apparatus Club of America, 5420 S. Kedvale Ave., Chicago, IL 60632; Fire Collectors Club, P.O. Box 992, Milwaukee, WI 53201; Fire

Mark Circle of the Americas, 2859 Marlin Dr., Chamblee, GA 30341; Great Lakes International Antique Fire Apparatus Assoc., 4457 285th St., Toledo, OH 43611; International Fire Buff Associates, Inc., 7509 Chesapeake Ave., Baltimore, MD 21219; International Fire Photographers Assoc., P.O. Box 8337, Rolling Meadows, IL 60008; Society for the Preservation & Appreciation of Motor Fire Apparatus in America, P.O. Box 2005, Syracuse, NY 13320.

Museums: American Museum of Fire Fighting, Corton Falls, NY; Fire Museum of Maryland, Lutherville, MD; Hall of Flame, Scottsdale, AZ; Insurance Company of North America (INA) Museum, Philadelphia, PA; New England Fire & History Museum, Brewster, MA; New York City Fire Museum, New York, NY; Oklahoma State Fireman's Association Museum, Oklahoma City, OK; San Francisco Fire Dept. Memorial Museum, San Francisco, CA.

Additional Listings: See *Warman's Americana & Collectibles* for more examples.

Advertising
    Calendar, Quincy Mutual Fire Insurance Co., 1889, 3 rats playing with box of stick matches, burnt claws, coming to cat holding Quincy Fire policy, 9-3/4" x 6-1/2"................575.00
    Ledger Marker, Caisse General Fire Insurance, statue of Liberty illus, multicolored, tin litho, 12-1/4" l, 3" w..........275.00
Alarm Box, mkd "Gamewell" and "Telegraph Station," 1880s 95.00
Badge, brass
    Allison H. & L. Co., No. 2, pendant with 1" gray/black cello insert picture PA State Capitol Bldg, inscribed "Harrisburg, PA, State Fireman's Convention, PA, Oct. 3-4-5, 1923" 15.00
    C.B.F.D. No. 1/Cresson, PA, silvered, pale bronze luster over raised center relief image of fire fighting symbols, 1930s 20.00
Bell, 11", brass, iron back...125.00
Belt, red, black, and white, 43" l, mkd "Hampden" 85.00
Fire Bucket, leather, America, 19th C
    10" h, leather, repair, traces of red and white paint, some damage..165.00
    14" h, sgd "T. Newman," imperfections.........................320.00

Red Comet Fire Extinquisher. Red Comet Inc., Littleton, Colo.; $30.

Fire Extinguisher
  Babcock, American La France Fire Engine Co., Elmire, NY, grenade, amber glass 500.00
  Hayward's Hand Fire Grenade, yellow, ground mouth, smooth base, 6-1/4" h, c1870...85.00
  Red Comet, red metal canister, red glass bulb 50.00
Fire Mark, cast iron, oval
  8" x 11-1/2", relief molded design, pumper framed by "Fire Department Insurance," polychrome paint 495.00
  8" x 12", black, gold eagle and banner dec, mkd "Eagle Ins. Co. Cin O"...950.00
Helmet
  Leather, 4 comb type, painted red, black brim, gilt inscribed shield, "o. 3-EBD," orig padded straw liner, early 19th C 1,800.00
  Oil Cloth, blue, tin shield inscribed "Niagara 3 Brunswick," red underbrim, early 19th C..1,200.00
Lantern, Dietz, King Fire Dept., copper bottom 150.00
Magazine, *Blazes,* March-June issue, American-Lafrance-Foamite, Elmira, NY, 1950, 28 pgs, 8-1/2" x 11", articles and illus relating to fires, fire fighting 18.00
Nozzle, hose, 16" l, brass, double handle, mkd "Akron Brass Mfg. Co., Inc."...165.00
Parade Hat, 6-1/2" h, painted leather, polychrome dec, green ground, front with eagle and harp, banner above "Hibernia," back inscribed "1752" in gilt, "1" on top, red brim underside, some age cracks, small losses to brim edge.............3,335.00
Presentation Trumpet, 16-1/4" h, coin silver, derby-style bell, inscribed "Presented by the City of Lowell to Mazeppa Engine Company No. 10 for the Third Best Horizontal Playing July 4, 1856" 1,500.00
Print, 9-1/2" x 13-1/2", hand colored lithograph, "Prairie Fires of the Great West," Currier and Ives, publishers, identified in inscriptions in matrix, period frame 320.00
Toy
  Boxed Set, Hubley, orig box
    9" x 12", Scale Models Fire Department, cast iron motorcycle with policeman, plastic hook and ladder, fire pumper, fire chief's car, two cast axes, flap tears on box....435.00
    9-1/2" x 14", Hubley Fire Dept., cast iron pumper, fire chief's car, hose reel truck, Harley Davidson with police driver, painted red, silver highlights..............................2,640.00
    11" x 14-1/4", Fire Apparatus, metal ladder truck, fire chief's car, water truck, cast iron motorcycle with policeman, ladders and axes 660.00
  Fire Chief Coupe, cast iron, painted red
    5" l, Arcade, cast bell on hood, emb "Chief" on doors, orig decal on front hood, rubber tires 1,650.00
    5-5/8" l, Kenton, emb "Chief" on side, cast bell on hood, nickel disc wheels 660.00
  Fire Engine, Hubley, cast iron, Ahrens Fox, rubber tires
    7" l, 4th size...315.00
    7-1/2" l, 5th size 470.00
    11" l, hose reel, two ladders, removable nickeled driver, nickeled engine, repaired bumper, new hose reel 2,200.00
  Fire Engine House, 8-1/2" x 15-1/4" x 12" h, Ives, clockwork, cast iron facade, detailed brick work, wooden sided, cast iron windows, horse drawn pumper rolls out, brick work repaired 2,970.00
  Fire Pumper, cast iron, painted red
    Arcade, 13" l, 1941 Ford, emb sides, cast fireman, hose reel on bed, rubber tires, repaired fender 440.00
    Hubley, 13" l, detailed nickel boiler cranks, figures, steam values, ornament, and search light mounted on hood, rubber tires, spoked wheels.................................1,045.00
    Kenton, gold highlights on boiler, and ball, emb sides, disc wheels with spoke centers 615.00
    Williams, AC
      7-1/2" l, gold highlights, cast driver, bell, and boiler, rear platform with railing, rubber tires 315.00

      10-1/2" l, gold trim, cast headlights and seated figure, rear platform, disc wheels, repainted 300.00
  Hook and Ladder Truck, cast iron, painted red
    7-1/4" l, AC Williams, nickeled grill, bell, running boards, and cast ladders, rubber tires............................1,320.00
    13-1/2" l, Hubley, cast windshield and driver's compartment, white body with water guns and ladder supports, new rubber tires, seated driver, ladders with one rubber hose..350.00
  Horse Drawn Fire Pumper, 21" l, sheet metal, painted red, gold and silver boiler, wood values, cast iron spoke wheels, pulled by three cast iron horses supported on two spoke wheeled frame..650.00
  Horse Drawn Ladder Wagon, 26" l, Kingsbury, sheet metal, pained red, wire supports, holding yellow wooden ladders, two seated drivers, pulled by two black horses, yellow spoke wheels, bell on frame rings as toy is pulled 2,090.00
  Ladder Truck, cast iron, painted red, rubber tires
    9-1/4" l, Arcade, two cast fireman, bed contains ladder supports, open frame design......................................440.00
    9-3/4" l, Arcade, nickeled grill, cast driver, standing fireman, two yellow tin ladders.................................1,320.00
    10-3/4" l, nickeled grill, headlights, bumper, hose reel and ladder extender, full rear platform, two seated figures, ladders, painted silver full running boards 660.00
    22" l, ladder supports, nickeled hose reel and bumper, water tanks cast along sides, spoked wheels, seated driver, replaced utility bucket..1,210.00
  Water Tower Truck, Kenton, cast iron, painted red, gold highlights
    12" l, emb water cans, open frame body, blue water extension crane, disc wheels, factory sample.............1,760.00
    16" l, large painted blue water extension crane, open body frame, ladders cast to side, seated driver, spoke wheels, repainted 1,430.00
  Water Tower Wagon, 29" l, cast iron, painted green, white extension tower, nozzle tip, red spoke wheels, drawn by three horses 1,760.00

FIREPLACE EQUIPMENT

History: In the colonial home, the fireplace was the gathering point for heat, meals, and social interaction. It maintained its dominant position until the introduction of central heating in the mid-19th century.

Because of the continued popularity of the fireplace, accessories still are manufactured, usually in an early-American motif.

References: Rupert Gentle and Rachael Feild, *Domestic Metalwork 1640-1820*, Revised, Antique Collectors' Club, 1994; George C. Neumann, *Early American Antique Country Furnishings*, L-W Book Sales, 1984, 1993 reprint.

REPRODUCTION ALERT
Modern blacksmiths are reproducing many old iron implements.

Additional Listings: Brass; Ironware.

Andirons, pr
  15" h, brass, belted ball top, matching tongs and shovel, America, early 19th C, 4 pc set 550.00
  15-1/2" h, brass, belted ball top, matching tongs and shovel, Boston, c1800, 4 pc set..690.00

15-1/2" h, cast iron, building form, 20th C, minor losses
....1,495.00

17-1/2" h, brass, belted double lemon tops, beaded edge, attributed to NY, early 19th C 750.00

18" h, brass, steeple top, spurred arched legs, NY, early 19th C 635.00

18-1/2" h, brass, acorn finials, baluster turned shaft, spurred arched legs, ball feet, America, c1800, replaced log rests
....375.00

19" h, brass, belted urn-top, double spurred legs, America, early 19th C 375.00

19" h, brass, urn finial, matching tongs and shovel, NY, early 19th C, 4 pc set 2,070.00

19" h, brass, whale form, 20th C......................................435.00

20" h, wrought iron, knife blade, penny feet, brass urn finials, bars stamped "I.SHB," old splint in base of one finial
....330.00

20-1/4" h, brass, belted ball top, attributed to R. Wittingham, NY, early 19th C, matching tongs and shovel, 4 pcs.....1,610.00

20-1/4" h, brass, belted ball top, attributed to New York, c1800, replaced log stops.....................................375.00

20-1/2" h, brass and wrought iron, American, late 18th C, minor imperfections 375.00

20-1/2" h, cast iron, George Washington commemorative, painted...550.00

21" h, brass, steeple top, New England, c1800 ....920.00

22" h, brass, belted ball top, plinths engraved with urn and willow motif and foliate devices, attributed to R. Wittingham, New York, early 19th C 4,890.00

22-1/2" h, brass and wrought iron, knife blade, one brass shield mkd "I.C.," America, c1780 ....1,840.00

36" h, wrought iron and brass, Baroque style, Scottish, late 19th C 1,100.00

Bellows

17" l, turtle back

Orig green paint, red trim, yellow stenciled fruit and foliage, brass nozzle, old latter in tatters, wear, chip on handle
.... 165.00

Bellows, turtle back, orig green paint with red trim, yellow stenciled fruit and foliage, brass nozzle, old leather in tatters, chip on handle, 17" l, $165. Photo courtesy of Garth's Auctions.

Orig yellow paint, stenciled and free hand fruit and foliage, red, black, green, and gold, brass nozzle, professionally releathered, chips on handle 440.00

17-3/4" l, orig red paint, vintage dec, two tone gold and black, sheet brass nozzle, old worn releathering................220.00

18" l, orig smoked yellow paint, stenciled and freehand fruit and foliage dec, gold, green, black, and red, brass nozzle, professionally releathered 880.00

Coal Hod, 25" h, brass, hammered, emb tavern scenes 75.00

Dummy Board, 8-1/2" h, face, painted in naturalistic tones, mounted on wood panel, Continental, 19th C 435.00

Fireback

32" h, 23-1/2" w, cast iron, molded, arched crest, knight's head and foliate motifs, figure of gentleman with fleur-de-lis and celestial motifs, flanked by turned pilasters, Continental, 17th-18th C 250.00

45" h, 31 w, cast iron, cast allegorical group, floral border, dated "1653," Scottish 800.00

Fire Board

12-1/4" h, 18-3/4" w, figural, Papillon spaniel, painted sheet metal, 19th C, areas of repaint, minor paint loss 520.00

30" h, 43-1/4" w, oval louvered panel centering carved rosette framed by molded and reeded border joining 2 sq carved corner rosettes, painted, America, early 19th C, minor imperfections 1,840.00

30-1/2" h, 43-3/4" w, 9-1/4" d, pine, shadow box format, borders with floral printed and marbleized wallpaper, center harbor view with figures, American, early 19th C, paper loss, staining...460.00

Fire Fender, brass and wire

37-1/2" w, 9" d, 9-1/2" h, English, early 19th C 550.00

52-1/2" w, 18" d, American, early 19th C 1,265.00

Firescreen

Beadwork, heraldic device, painted and parcel-gilt, rococo, period stand, late Victorian.......................................375.00

Mahogany, turned, urn form finial above flaring shaft, orig sq molded flame-stitched adjustable panel, ring-turned flaring standard, hexagonal plinth, 3 cabriole legs, slipper feet, Queen Anne, New England, c1750, one foot replaced, minor losses to needlework panel, 24" d, 48" h.........1,150.00

Rosewood, carved frame with simulated gilt painted stringing, needlework panel flanked by turned columns, acanthus carved scrolled legs, cast foliate cap fire gilt casters, old finish, Classical, New York, c1830, 24" w, 38" h
....21,850.00

Frieze, 45" w, 41-1/2" h, 17 tiles, Providential, two hunters and dog chasing deer, brown glaze thinning at edges, some chips, center tile cracked...435.00

Hearth Rug, 39" x 84", hooked, diamond border enclosing field of stars, flowerheads, and geometric motifs, purple, blue, green, red, and olive yarns, sand field, America, 19th C, backed, fading, fraying 2,415.00

Mantel Lamp, 14" h, squat chimney-form glass shade, enameled painted stylized green trees against red-orange background, silvered metal candlestick-form electrolier, imp "P" in diamond E3072, Pairpoint, some glass rim chips, silver finish worn 230.00

Mantle, 74-1/2" w, 58-3/4" h, striped pine and composition, central dec depicting flight of Athena, George III, late 18th C
....2,990.00

Tools, brass, America, early 19th C

22-1/2" and 28-3/4" l, brass and steel, urn top, tongs, shovel, and poker 520.00

29" l, matched pr of belted ball tongs and shovel, minor dents
....490.00

30" l, matched pr of belted ball tongs and shovel.........200.00

32" l, pr of urn-top tongs 115.00

34" l, steeple-top shovel, minor dents 115.00

FISCHER CHINA

FISCHER J.
BUDAPEST.

History: In 1893, Moritz Fischer founded his factory in Herend, Hungary, a center of porcelain production since the 1790s.

Confusion exists about Fischer china because of its resemblance to Meissen, Sevres, and Oriental export wares. It often was bought and sold as the product of these firms.

Fischer's Herend is hard-paste ware with luminosity and exquisite decoration. Pieces are designated by pattern names, the best known being Chantilly Fruit, Rothschild Bird, Chinese Bouquet, Victoria Butterfly, and Parsley.

Fischer also made figural birds and animal groups, Magyar figures (individually and in groups), and Herend eagles poised for flight.

Marks: Forged marks of other potteries are found on Herend pieces. The initials "MF," often joined together, is the mark of Moritz Fischer's pottery.

Cache Pot, 5" h, Rothchild Bird pattern, handled.............175.00
Charger, 13" d, multicolored enameled floral dec, gold grim
....350.00
Ewer, 16-1/2" h, reticulated body, roe, blue, green, and gold enameled floral dec..295.00
Jar, cov, 7-1/4" h, multicolored floral motif, raised relief medallions with reticulated fleur-de-lis, white ground, matching oval reticulated finial 275.00
Nappy, 4-1/2", triangular shape, Victoria Butterfly pattern, gold trim..150.00
Pitcher, 12" h, reticulated, multicolored floral dec..............350.00
Plate, 7-1/2" d, Chantilly Fruit pattern 90.00

Vase, cornucopia, pierced rim, painted floral motif, four feet with fish scales, stamped and imp mark, 1913, orig paper label, $295.

Sauce Boat, underplate, matching ladle, Parsley pattern..250.00
Tureen, cov, 8-1/2" l, Chantilly Fruit pattern, natural molded fruit finial, handles...350.00
Urn, 12" h, reticulated, blue floral dec, shield mark 250.00
Vase, 8" h, reticulated, blue flowers and green leaves, gold handles, shield mark 250.00

FITZHUGH

History: Fitzhugh, one of the most-recognized Chinese Export porcelain patterns, was named for the Fitzhugh family for whom the first dinner service was made. The peak years of production were 1780 to 1850.

Fitzhugh features an oval center medallion or monogram surrounded by four groups of flowers or emblems. The border is similar to that on Nanking china. Occasional border variations are found. Butterfly and honeycomb are among the rarest.

REPRODUCTION ALERT

Spode Porcelain Company, England, and Vista Alegre, Portugal, currently are producing copies of the Fitzhugh pattern. Oriental copies also are available.

Notes: Color is a key factor in pricing. Blue is the most common color; rarer colors are ranked in the following ascending order: orange, green, sepia, mulberry, yellow, black, and gold. Combinations of colors are scarce.

Basket, oval, reticulated, blue
   10-7/8" l...500.00
   11" l, matching undertray, handles...........................1,500.00
Bowl
   6-1/4" d, blue..220.00
   9-3/4" d, shallow, scalloped rim, blue..........................125.00
   10" w, sq, blue 325.00
Creamer, 5-1/2" h, helmet shape, blue...............................450.00
Cup and Saucer, blue, set of 6...395.00
Dish, 5-1/8" l, 5-1/4" w, scallop shell shape, c1770............295.00
Gravy Boat, plain sides, blue 125.00
Jug, 12-1/2" h, blue...800.00
Pitcher
   6-7/8" h, blue..850.00
   7-1/2" h, blue..850.00
Platter
   13-1/4" l, blue, very minor chips 495.00
   17-1/4" l, blue, very minor chips 525.00
Rice Bowl, blue, pr..90.00
Soap Dish, 5-1/2" l, drain, blue..375.00
Sugar Bowl, cov, 5-1/4" h, blue 565.00
Teapot, cov, 5-1/2" h, drum shape, blue 1,200.00
Tureen, cov, undertray, blue, pr..2,750.00
Vase, 13-1/4" h, beaker shape, blue, teakwood stand....1,250.00
Vegetable Dish, cov
   12-1/2" l, rect, blue, liner...1,500.00
   13" l, cov, oval, liner...1,750.00

FLASKS

History: A flask, which usually has a narrow neck, is a container for liquids. Early American glass companies frequently formed them in molds which left a relief design on the front and/or back. Historical flasks with a portrait, building, scene, or name are the most desirable.

A chestnut is hand-blown, small, and has a flattened bulbous body. The pitkin has a blown globular body with a spiral rib overlay on vertical ribs. Teardrop flasks are generally fiddle-shaped and have a scroll or geometric design.

References: Gary Baker et al., *Wheeling Glass 1829-1939*, Oglebay Institute, 1994, distributed by Antique Publications; Ralph and Terry Kovel, *Kovels' Bottles Price List*, 10th ed., Crown Publishers, 1996; George L. and Helen McKearin, *American Glass*, Crown Publishers, 1941 and 1948; John Odell, *Digger Odell's Official Antique Bottle and Glass Collector Magazine Price Guide Series*, Vol. 3, published by author (1910 Shawhan Rd., Morrow, OH 45152), 1995; Michael Polak, Bottles, Avon Books, 1994, 2nd edition, 1997; Kenneth Wilson, *American Glass 1760-1930*, 2 Vols., Hudson Hills Press and The Toledo Museum of Art, 1994.

Periodical: *Antique Bottle & Glass Collector*, P.O. Box 187, East Greenville, PA 18041.

Collectors' Clubs: Federation of Historical Bottle Clubs, 88 Sweetbriar Branch, Longwood, FL 32750; The National Early American Glass Club, P.O. Box 8489, Silver Spring, MD 20907.

Notes: Dimensions can differ for the same flask because of variations in the molding process. Color is important in determining value—aqua and amber are the most common colors; scarcer colors demand more money. Bottles with "sickness," an opalescent scaling which eliminates clarity, are worth much less.

Pitkin, 36 ribs swirled to the right, yellow olive, sheared mouth, pontil scar, New England, 1783-1830, 5" h, $400. Photo courtesy of Norman C. Heckler & Company.

SPECIAL AUCTION

Norman C. Heckler & Company
Bradford Corner Rd.
Woodstock Valley, CT 06282

Chestnut, 4-3/4" h, Zanesville, OH, blown, 24 vertical ribs, amber, half pint, minor wear 250.00

Historical

Double Eagle, attributed to Kentucky Glass Works, Louisville, KY 1850-55, brilliant copper, sheared mouth, pontil scar, pint, McKearin GII-24, 2" vertical crack 325.00

Double Eagle, Louisville Glass Works, Louisville, KY, 1955-60, vertically ribbed, pale blue green, sheared mouth, pontil scar, pint, McKearin GII-32A, manufacturer's mouth roughness, some int. haze 575.00

Eagle-Cornucopia, early Pittsburgh district, 1820-40, light greenish-aquamarine, sheared mouth, pontil scar, pint, McKearin GII-6 .... 475.00

Eagle-Stag, Coffin and Hay Manufacturers, Hammonton, NJ, 1836-47, sheared mouth, pontil scar, half pint, McKearin GII-50 .... 325.00

Eagle-Willington/Glass Co., Willington glass Works, West Willington, CT, 1860-72, bright medium yellowish-olive, applied double collared mouth, smooth base, half pint, McKearin GII-63 .... 210.00

For Pike's Peak Prospector-Hunter Shooting Deer, attributed to Ravenna Glass Works, Ravenna, OH, 1860-80, aquamarine, applied mouth with ring, smooth base, quart, McKearin GXI-47, 1/4" shallow flake 325.00

Masonic-Eagle, Keene Marlboro Street Glassworks, Keene, NH, 1815-30, pale bluish-green, tooled collared mouth, pontil scar, pint, McKearin GIV-7a 950.00

Success to the Railroad, Keene Marlboro Street Glassworks, Keene, NH, 1830-50, light yellow amber with olive tone, sheared mouth, pontil scar, pint, McKearin GV-3 .... 250.00

Pattern Molded

4-5/8" l, Midwest, 1800-30, 24 ribs swirled to the right, golden amber, sheared mouth, pontil scar 190.00

7-3/8" l, Emil Larson, NJ, c1930, swirled to the right, amethyst, sheared mouth, pontil scar, some exterior highpoint wear 250.00

Pictorial

Cornucopia-Urn, Lancaster Glass Works, NY, 1849-60, blue green, applied sloping collared mouth, pontil scar, pint, McKearin GIII-17, some minor stain 350.00

Flora Temple/Horse, Whitney Glass Works, Glassboro, NJ, 1860-80, cherry puce, applied collared mouth with ring, smooth base, pint, handle, McKearin GXIII-21 .... 170.00

Monument-Sloop, Baltimore Glass Works, Baltimore, MD, 1840-60, medium variated yellow green, sheared mouth, pontil scar, half pint, McKearin GVI-2, some exterior highpoint wear, overall dullness 1,100.00

Pitkin Type

Midwest, 1800-30, 6-1/4" l, ribbed and swirled to the right, 16 ribs, olive green with yellow tone, sheared mouth, pontil scar, some int. stain 300.00

New England, 1783-30, sheared mouth, pontil scar

   5" h, 36 ribs swirled to the right, yellow olive 400.00

   5-1/4" h, 36 swirled ribs, olive green, half post neck 255.00

   5-1/4" l, ribbed and swirled to the left, 36 ribs, light olive yellow 375.00

   6" l, ribbed and swirled to the right, distinct popcorn pattern, 36 ribs, yellow-olive, 1/4" fissure 220.00

   6-1/2" h, 31 ribs, broken swirl, olive green, half post neck 315.00

Portrait

Adams-Jefferson, New England, 1830-50, yellow amber, sheared mouth, pontil scar, half pint, McKearin GI-114 .... 325.00

General Jackson, Pittsburgh district, 1820-40, bluish-aquamarine, sheared mouth, pontil scar, pint, McKearin GI-68 .... 1,500.00

Lafayette-DeWitt Clinton, Coventry Glass Works, Coventry, CT, 1824-25, yellowish-olive, sheared mouth, pontil scar, half pint, 1/2" vertical crack, weakened impression, McKearin GI-82 .... 2,100.00

Lafayette-Masonic, Coventry Glass Works, Coventry, CT, 1824-45, yellowish-olive, sheared mouth, pontil scar, half pint, McKearin Gi-84, some minor exterior highpoint wear 1,700.00

Rough and Ready Taylor-Eagle, Midwest, 1830-40, aquamarine, sheared mouth, pontil scar, pint, McKearin GI-77 ..... 1,200.00

Washington-Albany Glass Works/NY, Albany Glass Works, Albany, NY, 1847-50, greenish-aquamarine, sheared mouth, pontil scar, half pint, McKearin GI-30....................................2,200.00
Washington-Eagle, Kensington Glass Works, Philadelphia, PA, 1820-38, bright aquamarine, sheared mouth, pontil scar, pint, McKearin GI-14 ....375.00
Washington-Sheaf of Wheat, Dyottville Glass Works, Philadelphia, PA 1840-60, medium yellow-olive, inward rolled mouth, pontil scar, half pint, McKearin GI-59.........................9,000.00
Washington-Taylor, Dyottville Glass Works, Philadelphia, PA 1840-60, bright bluish-green, applied double collared mouth, pontil scar, quart, McKearin GI-42 ....400.00
Pottery, 3-1/2" h, shield shaped, eagle, brown glaze, "McKearin Collection of American Pottery" paper sticker, threaded neck repaired, screw cap missing 550.00

FLOW BLUE

History: Flow blue, or flown blue, is the name applied to cobalt and white china whose color, when fired in a kiln, produced a flowing or blurred effect. The blue varies from dark royal cobalt to a navy or steel blue. The flow may be very slight to a heavy blur where the pattern cannot be easily recognized. The blue color does not permeate through the body of the china. The amount of flow on the back of a piece is determined by the position of the piece in the sagger during firing.

Flow blue was first produced around 1830 in the Staffordshire area of England and credit is generally given to Josiah Wedgwood. He worked in the Staffordshire area of England. Many other potters followed, including Alcock, Davenport, Grindley, Johnson Brothers, Meakin, and New Wharf. Early flow blue, 1830s to 1870s, was usually of the ironstone variety. The later patterns, 1880s to 1900s, and modern patterns, after 1910, usually were made of the more delicate semi-porcelain. Approximately 90% of the flow blue was made in England, with the remainder made in Germany, Holland, France, Belgium, Wales and Scotland. A few patterns were also made in the United States by Mercer, Warwick, and the Wheeling Pottery companies.

References: Susan and Al Bagdade, *Warman's English & Continental Pottery & Porcelain*, 2nd ed., Wallace-Homestead, 1991; Mary F. Gaston, *Collector's Encyclopedia of Flow Blue China*, Collector Books, 1983, 1993 value update; ——, *Collector's Encyclopedia of Flow Blue China*, 2nd Series, Collector Books, 1994; Ellen R. Hill, *Mulberry Ironstone: Flow Blue's Best Kept Little Secret*, published by author, 1993; Norma Jean Hoener, *Flow Blue China, Additional Patterns and New Information*, Flow Blue International Collectors' Club, Inc. (11560 W. 95th #297, Overland Park, KS 66214), 1996; Petra Williams, *Flow Blue China: An Aid to Identification*, revised ed. (1981), *Flow Blue China II* (1981), *Flow Blue China and Mulberry Ware: Similarity and Value Guide*, revised ed. (1993), Fountain House East (P.O. Box 99298, Jeffersontown, KY 40269).

Collectors' Club: Flow Blue International Collectors' Club, Inc., P.O. Box 1526, Dickenson, TX 77539.

Museum: The Margaret Woodbury Strong Museum, Rochester, New York.

Advisor: Ellen G. King.

Atlas, Grindley, 7 pc wash set, consisting of pitcher, basin, cov soap dish, chamber pot, cov waste jar 3,500.00
Abbey, Jones
    Inkwell, holds two bottles and pen 475.00
    Wash Basin and Pitcher 1,200.00
Acme, Hancock
    Cheese Dish, slant lid...450.00
    Chocolate Pot, cov...475.00
    Sweetmeat Dish, cov 325.00
Albany, Johnson Bros.
    Bone Dish 50.00
    Platter, 12" l 175.00
    Vegetable Tureen, cov 325.00
Amoy, Davenport
    Cup, handleless..250.00
    Dessert Bowl, 5-1/8" d 150.00
    Pitcher, 8-1/2" h 825.00
    Plate, 10-1/2" d 185.00
    Soap Dish, lid, strainer, base 925.00
    Soup Bowl, 10-1/2" d 155.00
    Toothbrush Holder, 8" h...450.00
    Wash Basin and Pitcher 3,500.00
Argyle, Grindley
    Butter Dish, lid, strainer, base 625.00
    Butter Pat, 3" d...50.00
    Creamer, 6" h...235.00
    Sauce Ladle..450.00
    Sauce Tureen, lid, base, tray......................................500.00
Astoria, New Wharf
    Plate, 10" d 95.00
    Tea Cup and Saucer 115.00
Beauford, Grindley
    Gravy Boat, tray...175.00
    Platter, 16-1/4" l...275.00
Bluebell, Dillwyn-Swansea
    Coffee Cup and Saucer...145.00
    Fruit Compote, pedestal, 8" h.....................................1,110.00
    Syrup Pitcher, 10-1/2" h, pewter lid 850.00
    Vegetable Tureen, cov, 11-1/2"...................................750.00

Bluebell, fruit compote, pedestal, 8" h, $1,100. Photo courtesy of Ellen King.

Brazil, Grindley, soup bowl, 9" d, flanged 65.00
Brunswick, Wood & Sons
    Tea Cup and Saucer 95.00
    Plate, 9" d...85.00
    Sugar Bowl, cov...225.00
Brushstroke, various potters
    Dahlia, 15 pc child's tea set...................1,150.00
    Fern & Tulip, cup and saucer, handleless 175.00
    Grapes & Shot, plate, 9" d........................110.00
    Spinach, bowl, 8" d round..........................195.00
    Strawberry, teapot, lid............................855.00
Buccleuch, maker unknown, but English
    Tea Cup and Saucer, handleless 95.00
    Honey Dish 70.00
    Sugar Bowl, cov, panels, large........................450.00
Cambridge, Meakin
    Plate, 10-1/8" d 65.00
    Soup Bowl, 9" d, flanged..............................55.00
Canton, Maddock
    Creamer, 5" h...475.00
    Plate, 10-1/2" d 150.00
    Sugar Bowl, cov, 8".....................................550.00
    Tea Cup and Saucer, handleless.....................145.00
Carlton, Ford, vegetable tureen, cov...................375.00
Cashmere, Morley
    Coffee Cup and Saucer................................150.00
    Creamer, 5-1/2" d 795.00
    Pitcher, two quart, spout hairline 1,750.00
    Plate, 10-1/2" d 195.00
    Sauce Tureen, lid, base, tray......................1,110.00
    Soup Bowl, 9-3/8" d, flanged......................2,854.00
    Sugar Bowl, cov, 8" d, restoration to lid.......................425.00
    Teapot, lid, 9"..1,300.00
    Vegetable Tureen, cov, 11-1/2" 2,755.00
    Wash Basin and Pitcher 4,500.00
Celtic, Grindley
    Platter, 21" l...325.00
    Tea Cup and Saucer 80.00

Buccleuch, teacup and saucer, handleless, $95. Photo courtesy of Ellen King.

Chapoo, Wedgwood
    Butter Dish, lid, base 520.00
    Creamer, 5-1/2" h.......................................850.00
    Gravy Boat 275.00
    Platter, 16" l...895.00
    Teapot, cov, restoration to spout....................495.00
    Waste Bowl, restoration to rim......................180.00
Chusan, Clementson, teapot, cov 650.00
Conway, New Wharf
    Serving Bowl, 9" d, round, open....................135.00
    Soup Bowl, 8-7/8" d, flanged 75.00
    Tea Cup and Saucer 90.00
Daisy, Burgess & Leigh
    Butter Dish, cov, base 275.00
    Dessert Bowl, 4-3/4" d 35.00
    Tea Cup and Saucer 85.00
    Vegetable Tureen, cov 295.00
Delft, Minton
    Butter Dish, cov, base 325.00
    Cheese Dish, slant lid..................................675.00
Dorothy, Upper Hanley Pottery, bone dish 42.00
Dundee, Ridgways
    Bone Dish 75.00
    Plate, 10" d...125.00
    Tea Cup and Saucer 85.00
    Vegetable Tureen, cov 350.00
Eclipse, Johnson Bros.
    Cereal Bowl, 6-1/8" d...................................60.00
    Dessert Bowl, 5-1/4" d 45.00
    Plate, 7" d...65.00
    Platter, 10-1/4" l..285.00
    Vegetable Tureen, cov 295.00
Egerton, Doulton, soup ladle, 12" l 495.00
Fairy Villas, Adams
    Butter Pat, 3' 50.00
    Creamer, 5" h..275.00
    Plate, 10-1/2" d 135.00
    Serving Bowl, 10-3/8" d, round, open................175.00

Brushstroke, Grapes & Shot, plate, 9" d, $110. Photo courtesy of Ellen King.

Cashmere, pitcher, 2 qt, spout hairline, $1,750. Photo courtesy of Ellen King.

Formosa, Mayer
    Platter, 14" l...350.00
    Tea Cup and Saucer, handleless..................250.00
Geisha, Upper Hanley Pottery
    Cake Plate, 9-1/2" d, handles.....................185.00
    Vegetable Tureen, cov................................300.00
Georgia, Johnson Bros.
    Butter Pat..45.00
    Plate, 10" d..90.00
    Platter, 14-3/8" l.....................................250.00
Gironde, Grindley
    Gravy Boat, tray......................................155.00
    Plate, 10-1/2" d......................................90.00
Grace, Grindley, platter, 15-3/4" l.......................350.00
Haddon, Grindley
    Plate, 10" d..100.00
    Sauce Ladle..125.00
    Tea Cup and Saucer 90.00
    Vegetable Tureen, cov 425.00
Hong Kong, Meigh
    Plate, 9-1/2" d..95.00
    Plate, 10-1/2" d......................................120.00
    Sauce Tureen, lid, base, tray...................1,100.00
    Vegetable Tureen, cov 850.00
Idris, Grindley
    Creamer...195.00
    Gravy Boat..85.00
    Plate, 10" d..75.00
Indian Jar, Furnival
    Plate, 10-1/2" d 225.00
    Tea Cup and Saucer, handleless..................250.00
    Vegetable Tureen, cov................................950.00
Kelvin, Meakin, plate, 7" d..............................40.00
Keele, Grindley, serving bowl, 9-7/8" d, oval, open...........175.00
Kyber, Adams
    Plate, 9" d...95.00
    Plate 10" d..120.00
    Platter, 10" l..275.00
    Sauce Tureen, lid and base 825.00
    Vegetable Tureen, cov 750.00

LaBelle, Wheeling
    Biscuit Jar, cov 425.00
    Charger Plate, 11-1/4" d 350.00
    Chocolate Pot, lid 895.00
    Creamer, 4" h...325.00
    Helmet Bowl, 12" d 400.00
    Pitcher, 7-1/2" h 425.00
    Plate, 10" d, 85.00
    Samovar, undertray, restoration to lid 5,000.00
Lakewood, Wood & Sons, cereal bowl, 6-1/2" d 65.00
Lancaster, New Wharf
    Plate, 9" d...95.00
    Tea Cup and Saucer 110.00
Le Pavot, Grindley
    Bone Dish 60.00
    Plate, 9" d...65.00
    Serving Bowl, 9" l, oval, open 150.00
Lorne, Grindley
    Butter Pat..38.00
    Gravy Boat...195.00
    Platter, 13-7/8" d.....................................210.00
    Sauce Tureen, lid, base, tray.....................550.00
    Vegetable Tureen, cov, oval.......................325.00
Madras, Doulton
    Cake Plate, 9-3/4" d 95.00
    Plate, 9-1/2" d..85.00
Manilla, Podmore & Walker
    Butter Dish, lid and base 850.00
    Dessert Bowl, 4-1/2" d 125.00
    Gravy Boat...185.00
Manhattan, Alcock
    Butter Dish, lid and base 375.00
    Butter Pat..40.00
    Dessert Bowl, 5-14" d 42.00
    Soup Bowl, 9" d, flanged 55.00

LaBelle, samovar, undertray, restoration to lid, $5,000. Photo courtesy of Ellen King.

Marguerite, fruit compote, 4-3/4" h, $250. Photo courtesy of Ellen King.

Marguerite, Grindley
Butter Pat 35.00
Fruit Compote, 4-3/4" h..250.00
Gravy Boat, tray 145.00
Tea Cup and Saucer 85.00
Melbourne, Grindley
Cake Stand, low, pedestal, 9" d 295.00
Gravy Boat, tray 235.00
Platter, 18" l..425.00
Sugar Bowl, cov..350.00
Ning Po, Hall
Dessert Bowl, 5-1/4" d...150.00
Teapot, cov..1,800.00
Non Pareil, Burgess & Leigh
Butter Dish, lid and base.......................................395.00
Gravy Boat...165.00
Plate, 9-7/8" d...125.00
Serving Bowl, 8-5/8" d, round, open.....................250.00
Soup Bowl, 8-3/4" d..135.00
Normandy, Johnson Bros.
Platter, 14" l..375.00
Sugar Bowl, cov..345.00
Oriental, Alcock
Bowl, low pedestal, 7" d 495.00
Charger Plate, 12-1/2" d...375.00
Oriental; Ridgways
Butter Pat...38.00
Dessert Bowl, 5" d 45.00
Plate, 9" d..65.00
Vegetable Tureen, cov 650.00
Oxford, Johnson Bros., vegetable tureen cov 295.00
Pansy, Warwick
Creamer..285.00
Demitasse Cup and Saucer 55.00
Dresser Tray, 8" x 10" 125.00
Paris, Wood & Sons
Soup Bowl, 9" d, flanged 60.00
Tea Cup and Saucer 85.00
Pelew, Challinor
Plate, 10" d..195.00
Tea Cup and Saucer, handleless...........................275.00
Teapot, cov..650.00
Persian Moss, Utzschneider
Dessert Bowl, 5" d 35.00
Plate, 6-1/4" d...40.00
Tea Cup and Saucer 75.00
Waste Bowl, 5-1/4" d..50.00
Richmond, Meakin
Butter Pat...35.00
Cake Plate, 10" d 250.00

Richmond, Johnson Bros., gravy boat 150.00
Roseville, Maddock
Celery Dish, flat, 11" l...245.00
Gravy Boat, tray 165.00
Soup Tureen, cov, no ladle.....................................495.00
Vegetable Tureen, cov 325.00
Scinde, Alcock
Chamber Pot..450.00
Gravy Boat...275.00
Milk Pitcher, 8" h 275.00
Platter, 20" l...1,500.00
Sugar Bowl, cov..365.00
Tea Cup and Saucer 175.00
Vegetable Tureen, cov 655.00
Shanghai, Grindley
Serving Bowl, 10-1/8" d, round 135.00
Tea Cup and Saucer 85.00
Waste Bowl, 5-1/2" d...250.00
Temple, Podmore & Walker
Dessert Bowl, 5-1/2" d 150.00
Plate, 9-7/8" d...225.00
Platter, 14" l..650.00
Touraine, Alcock
Bone Dish 100.00
Dessert Bowl, 5-1/4" d..55.00
Plate, 10" d..165.00
Serving Bowl, 9-1/2" l, oval, open.........................150.00
Soup Bowl, 9" d, flanged 135.00
Sugar Bowl, cov, 6-1/2" 475.00
Tea Cup and Saucer 110.00
Touraine, Stanley
Bacon Platter, 10" l 235.00
Bone Dish, 6-1/4" l 125.00
Cereal Bowl, 6-1/4" d 75.00
Tea Cup and Saucer 90.00
Waste Bowl 200.00
Vermont, Burgess & Leigh
Butter Pat...40.00
Platter, 14" l..350.00
Serving Bowl, 9" l, oval, open 135.00
Soup Plate, 11-1/2" d, flanged...............................125.00
Watteau, Doulton
Cream Soup, 5" d, handles.....................................145.00
Plate, 10-1/2" d...125.00
Platter, 16" l..275.00
Toothbrush Holder...225.00
Vegetable Tureen, cov 310.00
Waverly, Grindley
Plate, 10" d..90.00
Platter, 14" l..185.00
Soup Bowl, 9" d, flanged 65.00
Tea Cup and Saucer 85.00

FOLK ART

History: Exactly what constitutes folk art is a question still being vigorously debated among collectors, dealers, museum curators, and scholars. Some want to confine folk art to non-academic, handmade objects. Others are willing to include manufactured material. In truth, the term is used to cover objects ranging from crude drawings by obviously untalented children to academically trained artists' paintings of "common" people and scenery.

References: Edwin O. Christensen, *Early American Wood Carvings*, Dover Publications, n.d.; Country Living Magazine, *Living with Folk Art*, Hearst Books, 1994; Catherine Dike, *Canes in the United States*, Cane Curiosa

Press, 1995; Jim Dresslar, *Folk Art of Early America–The Engraved Powder Horn*, Dresslar Publishing (P.O. Box 635, Bargersville, IN 46106), 1996; Wendy Lavitt, *Animals in American Folk Art,* Knopf, 1990; Jean Lipman, *American Folk Art in Wood, Metal, and Stone*, Dover Publications, n.d. George H. Meyer, *American Folk Art Canes*, Sandringham Press, Museum of American Folk Art, and University of Washington Press, 1992; Donald J. Petersen, *Folk Art Fish Decoys*, Schiffer Publishing, 1996; Beatrix Rumford and Carolyn Weekly, *Treasures in American Folk Art from the Abby Aldrich Rockefeller Folk Art Center,* Little Brown, 1989.

Periodical: *Folk Art Illustrated*, P.O. Box 906, Marietta, OH 45750.

Museums: Abby Aldrich Rockefeller Folk Art Center, Williamsburg, VA; Daughters of the American Revolution Museum, Washington, DC; Landis Valley Farm Museum, Lancaster, PA; Museum of American Folk Art, New York, NY; Museum of Early Southern Decorative Arts, Winston-Salem, NC; Museum of International Folk Art, Sante Fe, NM.

Dues Box, carved wood, carved and applied doves and acorns, PA, $935. Photo courtesy of Aston Macek Auctioneers & Appraisers.

SPECIAL AUCTION

Aston Macek Auctioneers & Appraisers
2825 Country Club Rd.
Endwell, NY 13760
(607) 785-6598

Garth's Auction Inc.
2690 Stratford Rd
P.O. Box 369
Delaware, OH 43015

Birdhouse, 24" h, seacoast house shape, mansard roof and cupola, old red, gray, blue, white, and green paint, found in Kittery, Maine 1,815.00

Box, cov, 5" h, 8-1/4" w, 6" d, covered with nuts, inscribed "E...B.N. Bailey 1860," minor loss 260.00

Calligraphy, 14-1/4" h, 8-1/2" w, watercolor and ink on paper, sgd and dated "George Macness, age 12, Salem, Massachusetts, October 24, 1812," framed, some toning and foxing 1,150.00

Checkerboard, 14-1/4" sq, wood, reverse painted with caricature of Zachary Taylor, mustard and dark brown paint, 19th C, minor paint wear 2,185.00

Figure, carved and painted wood
  2-3/4" h, bird, stylized, carved wig and head detail, serrated tail, painted green and brown, wire legs, domed sq base, Deco-Tex Carver, PA, 20th C 1,100.00
  5-1/4" h, rooster, pine, cross-hatched wing detail, orange, red, yellow, pink, and green, standing on grassy mound, Carl Snavely, Lititz, Lancaster County, PA, 20th C 400.00
  5-3/4" h and 6-3/4" h, hen and rooster, rooster in feeding position, head down and tail up, hen standing with head up, realistically carved, beige, black, red, and yellow, John Reber, Germansville, PA, early 20th C, pr ... 14,950.00
  6-5/8" h, gooney bird, stylized, chip-carved wings, black and orange paint, blue and yellow details, long legs, rect base, PA, early 20th C 520.00
  8-5/8" h, horse, standing, head up, carved mane flowing to one side, ears pricked, painted brown, black and white details, John Reber, Germansville, PA, early 20th C, small chip to ears 6,325.00

10" h, fan-tailed rooster, standing, full bodied, head up, chip carved wing and tail detail, red, black, yellow, green, white, orange, and brown paint, domed mound, Schohaire County, NY, minor losses 1,380.00

13-1/2" h, elk, standing, head up and turned slightly left, ears pricked, mottled brown and black paint, mounted on later rect wood base, John Reber, Germansville, PA, early 20th C 9,775.00

31-1/2" l, fox hunting group, 5 hunters astride horses, 12 hounds, figure of man holding a fox, snake, raccoon, and 2 birds in tree, mounted on rect base, George D. Wolfskill, Fivepointville, Lancaster County, PA, early 20th C 27,600.00

Glove Box, 4-5/8" h, 24" w, 7" d, bas relief carved mahogany, lid with foliate devices, stippled ground, centered initials "TW," rope twist borders, geometric designs, and "gloves" carved into sides, pale blue silk lining, 19th C, minor imperfections 300.00

Lamp Base, 13-3/4" h, sewer pipe, tree and 4 stumps, naked lady, and lion, base incised "J. W. Moore, June 10, 1926, Uhrichsville, O. Evans Pipe Co." small chips 2,640.00

Rug, hooked, "Home Is Where The Heart Is," log cabin center, pine trees and fence 1,200.00

Scherenschnitte, (paper cutting)
  6-1/4" sq, peacock in a tree, initialed and dated "MW 1805" lower right, period circular gilt gesso frame, American School, 19th C 460.00
  12-1/4" x 11", image of Christ's face, done by Samuel Krauss, sgd in pencil lower center, Philadelphia, PA, Schwenkfelder, born in 1804 .... 35.00

Table, PA, late 19th C, circular carved top with sawtooth edge centering carved star and bordered by leafy meandering vine, underside with applied ball pendants on 4 geometric leaf carved legs centering ball and sire finials, old finish and polychrome dec, 21" d, 30" h 815.00

Tavern Sign, 41-1/4" h, 31" w, New England, c1800, black painted frame with turned flanking posts, molded paneled sign, both sides painted dark green, gilt eagle and stars dec, "Independence" across top 17,250.00

Theorem
  6-3/8" h, 8-3/8" w, watercolor on velvet, fruit, framed, toning, minor staining 920.00

Figure, carved and painted pine, fan-tailed rooster, Schoharie County, NY, standing, full bodied, chip carved wing and tail detail, standing on domed mount, painted red, black, yellow, green, white, orange, and brown, minor losses, 10" h, $1,380. Photo courtesy of Sotheby's.

8-3/4" h, 11" w, watercolor on paper, memorial type, tomb, willow, and two buildings, black green, and blue, pen and ink inscription on tomb "In Memory Of Abraham Tilton...1739-1838" 165.00
14" h, 15" w, oil on cloth, basket of flowers, unframed, minor scattered foxing, small puncture to ground 3,680.00
14-1/8" h, 18" w, watercolor on paper, table top with compote of fruit, framed, minor staining, toning 2,185.00
Watch Hutch, New England, early 19th C, carved and paint dec wood, tall case clock shape
8-1/4" h, foliate finials flanking central pediment, bracket feet...1,610.00
9-1/2" h, rounded finials flanking central peak, waisted case, wear to waist...550.00
12-1/2" h, scrolled bonnet, carved central rosette, losses, paint wear 1,840.00
Watercolor on Paper
4-3/4" h, 6" w, chicken, red, yellow, green, and blue, damage and water stains, matted and unframed...................150.00
7-3/4" h, 5-3/8" w, graphite and gouache, Martha Barnes Aged 76 Years and 6 Months, partial family history inscribed on back, framed, minor staining and toning...............1,725.00
11-1/2" h, 9-1/2" w, pen and ink, girl with flowering fabric dress, stylized tulips, and flowers, "Menta Chain 1846," green, teal blue, orange, brown, and black, old curly maple frame 1,100.00
11-1/2" h, 15-1/2" w, Bonaparte in Trouble, sgd "Executed by Jane R....ine," lower right, political cartoon with Napoleon on horseback being attached by lion and bear, lower margin inscribed "Explanation I the infernal spirit enticing Bonaparte with the Crown of Russia, 2 Bonaparte arrested ...in his progress by the Russian bear, 3 the British lion attacking him in the rear, having already wrestled from his power, the Crowns of Spain and Portugal and the Confederate Eagles of Austria and Prussia plucking the feathers of the Rhinish Confederation - The genius of Europe breaking the scepter of Bonaparte and loudly proclaiming Louis the XVIII, framed, toning, minor scattered foxing, copied from etching by Amos Doolittle, published c1814 by CT firm of Shelton & Kensett" 3,220.00

FOOD BOTTLES

History: Food bottles were made in many sizes, shapes, and colors. Manufacturers tried to make an attractive bottle that would ship well and allow the purchaser to see the product, thus giving assurance that the product was as good and as well-made as home preserves.

References: Ralph & Terry Kovel, *Kovels' Bottle Price List*, 10th ed., Crown Publishers, 1996; John Odell, *Digger Odell's Official Antique Bottle and Glass Collector Magazine Price Guide Series*, Vol. 6, published by author (1910 Shawhan Rd, Morrow, OH 45152), 1995.

Periodical: *Antique Bottle and Glass Collector*, P.O. Box 187, East Greenville, PA 18041.

Collectors' Club: Federation of Historical Bottle Collectors, Inc., 88 Sweetbriar Branch, Longwood, Fl 32750.

Blueberry, 11" h, 10 lobed flutes, medium green, tooled rolled collared mouth...160.00
Catsup, 10" h, Cuyuga County Tomato Catsup, aqua, swirl design 65.00
Celery Salt, 8" h, Crown Celery Salt, Horton Cato & Co., Detroit, yellow amber, smooth base, ground lip, orig shaker type cap 175.00
Extract
Baker's Flavoring Extracts, 4-3/4" h, aqua, sq ring lip.....15.00
L. C. Extract, label, orig box 180.00
Ginger, Sanford's orig label................................12.00
Horseradish, As You Like It, pottery, clamp 25.00
Lime Juice, 10-1/4" h, arrow motif, olive amber, smooth base, applied mouth 85.00
Peanut Butter, 5" h, Bennett Hubba.......................20.00
Pepper Sauce, 8" h, S & P Pat. Appl. For, teal blue, smooth base, tooled lip 50.00

Pickle Jar, cathedral, sq, beveled corners, two fancy cathedral designs, greenish aqua, tooled rolled mouth, smooth base, 1860-80, 11-1/2" h, $140. Photo courtesy of Norman C. Heckler & Company.

Pickle, cathedral, America, 1845-80, sq, beveled corners,
  10-5/8" h, 4 fancy cathedral arch designs, medium green, tooled rolled mouth, smooth base 650.00
  11-1/2" h, 3 fancy cathedral designs, greenish-aqua, tooled rolled mouth, smooth base 150.00
  11-3/4" h, 4 different fancy cathedral arch designs, protruding irregular panels, aquamarine, tooled sq mouth, iron pontil mark 170.00
Vinegar, Weso Biko Co. Cider Vinegar, jug shape...............45.00

FOOD MOLDS

History: Food molds were used both commercially and in the home. Generally, pewter ice cream molds and candy molds were used commercially; pottery and copper molds were used in homes. Today, both types are collected largely for decorative purposes.

The majority of pewter ice cream molds are individual serving molds. One quart of ice cream would make eight to ten pieces. Scarcer, but still available, are banquet molds which used two to four pints of ice cream. European-made pewter molds are available.

Marks: Pewter ice cream molds were made primarily by two American companies: Eppelsheimer & Co. (molds marked "E & Co., N.Y.") and Schall & Co. (marked "S & Co."). Both companies used a numbering system for their molds. The Krauss Co. bought out Schall & Co., removed the "S & Co." from some, but not all, of the molds, and added more designs (pieces marked "K" or "Krauss"). "CC" is a French mold mark.

Manufacturers of chocolate molds are more difficult to determine. Unlike the pewter ice cream molds, makers' marks were not always used or were covered by frames. Eppelsheimer & Co. of New York marked many of their molds, either with their name or with a design resembling a child's toy top and the words "Trade Mark" and "NY." Many chocolate molds were imported from Germany and Holland and were marked with the country of origin and, in some cases, the mold-maker's name.

Reference: Judene Divone, *Chocolate Moulds*, Oakton Hills Publications, 1987.

Museum: Wilbur's American Candy Museum, Lititz, PA.

Additional Listings: Butter Prints.

Chocolate Mold

Basket, 3-1/2" x 6", one cavity 50.00
Boy on bicycle, 8-1/4" h, 2 parts...395.00
Catalog, Anton Reich, 13" x 17", 86 pgs..........................2,420.00
Chick and egg, 3-1/2" h, two parts, folding, mkd "Allemagne," Germany 65.00
Easter Rabbit, 18-1/2" h, standing, two part mold, separate two part molds for ears and front legs, "Anton Reiche, Dresden, Germany" 220.00
Elephant, tin, 3 cavities..95.00
Fish 95.00
Jack O' Lantern, 2 pcs, wire clamp.......................................40.00
Hen on basket, 2 pcs, clamp type, mkd "E & Co./Toy".......60.00
Pig...95.00
Skeleton, 5-1/2" h, pressed tin...60.00
Teddy Bear, 2 pcs, clamp type, mkd "Reiche" 295.00
Witch, 4-1/2" x 2", 4 cavities..75.00

Copper, fish shaped, sgd "Kreamer," $60.

Food Mold

Butter, 4-1/2" x 6-7/8", rect cased, cherry, deep carved geometric design...125.00
Cake, rabbit, Griswold..265.00
Cheese, 5" x 13", wood, relief carved design and "Bid," pinned, branded "Los," carved scratch date 1893 ....60.00
Pudding, tin and copper
  5" x 5" x 6-1/2", oval, pineapple 95.00
  8" l, oval, lion...220.00

Ice Cream Mold, pewter

Asparagus, 3-5/8" h...35.00
Basket, replaced hinge pins...25.00
Cherub riding Easter Bunny, 4" h...45.00
Circle, mkd "Kiwanis Club" and "E & Co. NY".....................25.00
Easter Lily, 3 part..75.00
Flag, 13 stars...95.00
Man in the Moon, 5-1/2" h, mkd "E & Co. copyright 1888" 95.00
Naked lady with drape, 3 part, 5-1/4" h..............................275.00
Owl, banquet size, 4 pints, mid "S & Co. 7"........................600.00
Pear, banquet size, mkd "S & Co. 17"................................325.00
Rose, two part, 3-1/2" d...125.00
Ship, banquet size, 2 quarts...265.00
Steamboat 115.00
Tulip, 4-1/8" h, mkd "E. & Co. NY".......................................45.00

FOSTORIA GLASS

History: Fostoria Glass Co. began operations at Fostoria, Ohio, in 1887, and moved to Moundsville, West Virginia, its present location, in 1891. By 1925, Fostoria had five furnaces and a variety of special shops. In 1924, a line of colored tableware was introduced. Fostoria was purchased by Lancaster Colony in 1983 and continues to operate under the Fostoria name.

Reference: Gene Florence, *Elegant Glassware of the Depression Era*, Revised 5th ed., Collector Books, 1993; Ann Kerr, *Fostoria: An Identification and Value Guide of Pressed, Blown, & Hand Molded Shapes* (1994, 1997 values), *Etched, Carved & Cut Designs* (1996, 1997 values) Collector Books; Milbra Long and Emily Seate, *Fostoria Stemware*, Collector Books, 1995; Leslie Piña, *Fostoria Designer George Sakier*, Schiffer Publishing, 1996; ——, *Fostoria*, Schiffer Publishing, 1995; JoAnn Schleismann, *Price Guide to Fostoria*, 3rd ed., Park Avenue Publications, n.d.

Periodical: The Daze, P.O. Box 57, Otisville, MI 48463.

Collectors' Clubs: Fostoria Glass Collectors, 10221 Slater Ave. #103-396, Fountain Valley, CA 92708; Fostoria Glass Society of America, P.O. Box 826, Moundsville, WV 26041.

Museums: Fostoria Glass Museum, Moundsville, WV; Huntington Galleries, Huntington, WV.

Note: Glassware is colorless (clear, crystal, or etched) unless other color noted.

After Dinner Cup, June, topaz	25.00
After Dinner Saucer, June, rose	20.00
After Dinner Cup and Saucer, Mayfair, ebony	12.00
Almond, Colony, ftd	17.00
Animal	
Colt, standing	45.00
Pelican	65.00
Appetizer, American, individual size	35.00
Ashtray	
Coin, green, 3" x 9", oblong	20.00
Manor, #2412	15.00
Bonbon	
Chintz, 7-5/8"	28.00
Versailles, topaz	35.00
Bookend	
Eagle	125.00
Owl	250.00
Seahorse	175.00
Bouillon with liner, Pioneer, #2350, blue	20.00
Bowl	
Baroque, topaz, 7" d, ruffled, 3 feet	20.00
Chintz, 10-1/2" d, handle	65.00
Colony, 11", flared	30.00
Meadow Rose, 10-1/2" d, flared	22.00
Versailles, topaz, 9-1/2" d, scroll handles	45.00
Brandy, #6012, 2 oz.	22.00
Butter Dish, cov	
American	95.00
Century	28.75
Cake Plate, Meadow Rose, handle	22.00
Candlestick	
Acanthus, #2395, amber	55.00
Baroque, 8-1/4" h, 2 lite, 16 prisms	90.00
Buttercup, 1 lite, pr	45.00
Coin, olive green, 4-1/2", pr	20.00
Navarre, flame, 2 lite	45.00
Rebecca at the Well, frosted, pr	150.00
Royal, 3", green, pr	50.00
Versailles, topaz, 5" h, scroll, pr	60.00
Candy Dish, cov, Coin, ruby, frosted	55.00
Celery/Relish, 12" l, Navarre, 5 part	100.00
Celery Vase, Alexis, tall	35.00
Cereal Bowl, Versailles, yellow, 6-1/2" d	22.50
Champagne	
Chintz	15.00
Meadow Rose	16.76
Rogene	15.00
Romance	15.00
Willowmere	14.00
Cheese and Cracker Set, Fairfax, #2375, azure	65.00
Cheese Compote, Chintz, 3-1/2" h	24.00
Claret	
June, yellow	60.00
Wilma, blue, blank #6016	38.00
Cocktail, Chintz, 5"	22.00
Comport	
Baroque, blue, 6"	30.00
Chintz, 5-1/2" d, 4-3/4" h	30.00

Colony, low, cov	55.00
June, 6-1/2", blue	110.00
Cookie Jar, American	325.00
Cordial, Holly	35.00
Creamer, Coin, amber	10.00
Creamer and Sugar	
Alexis, hotel, cutting	95.00
Fairfax, green, ftd	20.00
Lido	40.00
Vesper, green, ftd	65.00
Cream Soup, liner	
Fairfax, yellow	15.00
Versailles, blue	55.00
Cruet, Coin, olive green, 7 oz.	50.00
Cup and Saucer	
Baroque, blue	30.00
Coronet	9.75
Fairfax, blue, ftd	15.00
Lafayette, wisteria	32.00
Mayfair, ebony	12.00
Meadow Rose	22.00
Versailles, blue	30.00
Willowmere	22.00
Decanter, Alexis, Kentucky Tavern, no stopper	75.00
Demitasse Cup and Saucer	
Versailles, pink	42.00
Willowmere	36.00
Figure, Madonna	55.00
Fruit Bowl, Versailles, yellow, 5"	18.00
Goblet, water	
American, hex, 7" h	15.00
Baroque, blue	25.00
Chintz, 6-1/8" h	25.00
Contour, set of 6	100.00

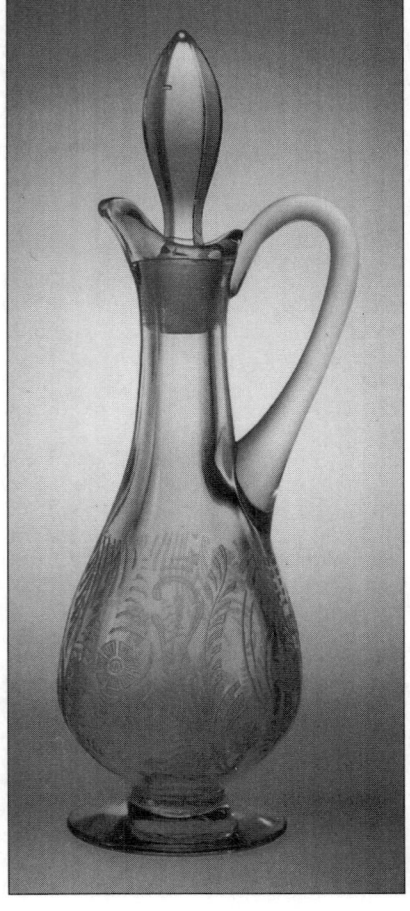

Oil, Fairfax, #2375, Azure, ftd, #283 Kasmir plate etching, $185.

Grand Majesty, etched blue bowl
    9 oz. 30.00
    13 oz. 35.00
  Holly 20.00
  Jamestown, blue 12.75
  June, azure, 8-1/4" 55.00
  Lotus, 11 oz., crystal mist base 21.00
Ice Bucket
  Fairfax, ice blue 45.00
  Vesper, amber 65.00
Iced Tea Tumbler
  American, ftd 20.00
  Holly 20.00
  Jamestown, medium blue, 6" h 20.00
  Tradition, red 22.00
Jug, Alexis, half gallon 195.00
Juice Tumbler, ftd
  Holly 20.00
  Navarre, 5 oz. 24.00
  Versailles, topaz 15.00
Lunch Tray, Oak Leaf, octagon, fleur-de-lis handle, green
  ....75.00
Mayonnaise, underplate
  Baroque, yellow 25.00
  Colony 25.00
  Versailles, topaz 40.00
Muffin Tray, Colony 35.00
Oyster Cocktail
  American, 3-1/4" 12.00
  Corsage 12.00
  Romance 22.50
  Versailles, topaz 25.00
Pickle, Kashmir, azure 28.00
Pitcher
  Beverly, amber 125.00
  Century, pint 50.00
  Jamestown, green 110.00
  Meadow Rose, bulbous, 7" h 195.00
  Priscilla, #2321, blue 67.50
  Rogene, crystal, ftd 225.00
Plate
  Baroque, 7" d, blue 10.00
  Chintz, 7-1/2" d 8.00
  Colony, 9" d, dinner 35.00
  Fairfax, 8-3/4" d, salad, green 5.00
  Fairfax, 9" d 4.50
  Holly, 7-1/2" d 20.00
  Lafayette, 8-1/2" d, wisteria 22.00
  Pioneer, #2350, blue, dinner 25.00
  Sun Ray, 16-1/2" d 70.00
  Versailles, blue, luncheon 15.00
Platter, Fairfax, 10-1/2" l, oval 25.00
Relish
  Chintz, 6" sq, 2 part 30.00
  Colony, oval 12.00
  Silver Spruce, 10" l, 3 part 35.00
  Versailles, topaz, 8-1/2" l, 2 part 28.00
  Victoria, canoe shape, satin highlights 85.00
Salad Bowl, Fairfax, green, 9-1/4" d 25.00
Salt and Pepper Shakers, pr, Romance, crystal, individual
  ....65.00
Server, center handle
  Acanthus, #2395, amber 5.00
  Chintz 25.00
Sherbet
  Baroque, blue, 5 oz., 3-3/4" 25.00
  Chintz, low, 4-3/8" 16.00
  Fairfax, yellow, 6 oz. 11.00
  Holly 20.00
  Jamestown, medium blue, 7 oz. 13.00
  June, azure, 6" 35.00

  Meadow Rose, 4-1/2" 14.75
  Navarre, 6 oz. 24.00
  Vernon, 6 oz., low 10.00
  Versailles, topaz 14.75
Sugar, Chintz, 3-1/2", ftd 15.00
Toothpick Holder
  Brazilian 55.00
  Priscillia, gold worn 65.00
Tray, Fairfax, #2375, center handle, rose 22.00
Tumbler
  Chintz, ftd, 6" h 22.50
  Vernon, etched, ftd 15.00
  Versailles, ftd 22.75
Vase
  Alexis, 8" h 65.00
  American
    9-1/2" h, flared, swung 210.00
    16" h, swung 345.00
  Royal Blue, 8" h, flared, #2292 ....175.00
  #2385, fan, azure 65.00
Vegetable Bowl, Fairfax, green, 10" l, oval 25.00
Wedding Bowl, Coin
  Amber 50.00
  Red 60.00
Whipped Cream Bowl, June, rose 35.00
Whiskey, American 15.00
Window Box, #2373, with frog
  Ebony, small 85.00
  Green, large 55.00
  Rose, small 90.00
Wine
  American 14.00
  Chintz, 4-1/2 oz. 35.00
  Holly 25.00
  Willowmere, 3-1/2 oz. 16.00

FRAKTUR

History: Fraktur, the calligraphy associated with the Pennsylvania Germans, is named for the elaborate first letter found in many of the hand-drawn examples. Throughout its history, printed, partially printed/partially hand-drawn, and fully hand-drawn works existed side by side. Frakturs often were made by schoolteachers or ministers living in rural areas of Pennsylvania, Maryland, and Virginia. Many artists are unknown.

Fraktur exists in several forms—geburts and taufschein (birth and baptismal certificates), vorschrift (writing examples, often with alphabet), haus sagen (house blessings), bookplates and bookmarks, rewards of merit, illuminated religious texts, valentines, and drawings. Although collected for decoration, the key element in fraktur is the text.

References: Donald A. Shelley, Fraktur-Writings or Illuminated Manuscripts of the Pennsylvania Germans, Pennsylvania German Society, 1961; Frederick S. Weiser and Howell J. Heaney (comps.), Pennsylvania German Fraktur of the Free Library of Philadelphia, 2 Vols., Pennsylvania German Society, 1976.

Museum: The Free Library of Philadelphia, Philadelphia, PA.

Notes: Fraktur prices rise and fall along with the American folk-art market. The key marketplaces are Pennsylvania and the Middle Atlantic states.

Account Book, 12-1/2" x 7-3/4", watercolor, pen and ink on paper, marbled covers, leather binding, several pages of full color drawings, sums, and ornamental calligraphy of David Schultz, tinsmith, Schwenkfelder, dated 1834 .... 1,955.00

Birth Certificate (Geburts and Taufschein)
5" h, 8-1/4" w, pen and ink, wove paper, brown, black, and green flourishes and German inscription, "Marie Grager, 1850, born June 4th, AD 1833 in State of Ohio," minor paper damage, 6-1/2" x 9-1/2" w frame 825.00
7-1/2" h, 8" w, Jesse Snyder, Towamencin Twp, PA, born in 1812, Schwenkfelder, 1873, orange, yellow, and green, two birds on branches 275.00
7-3/4" h, 12-1/2" w, watercolor, pen and ink on paper, red and yellow blossoms, pale green vines, for Christian Heft, Springfield Township, Bucks County, PA, dated March 10, 1816.. 2,875.00
8" x 13-1/4", watercolor, pen and ink on paper, sgd "Martin Brechall," Linn Township, Northampton County, PA, paired tulips, red and yellow blossoms, for Lea Claus, dated March 7, 1808 .... 1,035.00
12" x 15", hand-colored printed form, Frederick Krebs, watercolor elements, red and green parrots, tulips, sun faces and crown, for Henrich Ott, Bucks County, Bedminster Township, PA, dated Oct 29, 1800 .... 980.00
12" x 15-1/2", hand colored printed form, S. Baumann, for Joseph Raub, Berks County, Bern Township, PA, dated July 8, 1809 .... 460.00
12-1/4" x 15-1/2", watercolor, pen, and ink on paper, Berks County artist, winged angels, paired birds and mermaids, for Frederick Heverling, dated 1784 .... 2,100.00
12-3/4" x 15-1/2", watercolor, pen, and ink on paper, Flat Parrot artist, for Susana Gensemer, dated 1811 .... 1,265.00
13" x 15-7/8", hand colored printed form, printed by Gottlieb Jungmann, Reading, 1795, Friedrich Krebs imprint, paired parrots, blossoms, and sun faces, for Johannes Ries, Paxton Township, Dauphin County, PA, dated Aug. 28, 1799 .... 2,185.00
13" x 16", hand colored printed form, watercolor elements, Frederick Speyer, paired angels, parrots, blossoms, and mermaids, for Sarra Grill, Lehigh County, PA, dated April 18, 1789 .... 1,380.00
15-1/2" x 12-1/4", watercolor, pen and ink on paper, gilded decoupage elements, Frederick Krebs, pair of certificates for brothers Daniel Raup (1784) and Peter Raup (1791), pr 3,800.00
18-1/4" h, 16" w, printed by Blumer and Busch in 1846, records 1835 Montgomery County, PA, birth, hand colored maroon, blue, green, and yellow, glued down, minor damage, framed 220.00

Bookplate, pen, ink, and watercolor
3" h, 5" w, two birds on branches of potted tulip plant, leather bound book cover detached from book 110.00
4-3/4" h, 2-3/4" w, laid paper, red, yellow, and black tulips and heart, "Barbara Hallem 1790," attributed to Berks County, PA, some damage and repair, 6-7/8" h x 5-3/8" w frame 1,540.00
5-7/8" h, 3-3/4" w, wove paper, red, orange, blue, olive, and yellow stylized flowers and "1830," edge wear, stains, tape stain, 9" h x 6-1/2" w frame 660.00
6-3/8" h x 4" w, Rebecka Meuer the Testament 1850, very minor foxing 230.00

6-1/2" x 3-1/2", The Serpent and the Apple from Garden of Eden, attributed to Berks County, PA 495.00
6-1/2" h x 4" w, Esther Hoch, Hereford Township, Berks County, (PA), Jan. 25, 1808, hearts and tulips, drawn in red, yellow, and brown, inside first edition Germantown printed leather bound song book 1,100.00

Child's Book of Moral Instruction (Metamorphosis), watercolor, pen and ink on paper
5-3/4" x 7-1/2", dec on both sides of 4 leaves, each with upper and lower flaps showing different versus and color illus, unknown illustrator 345.00
6" x 7", printed form on paper, hand colored elements, The Great American Metamorphosis, Philadelphia, printed by Benjamin Sands, 1805-06, printed on both sides of 4 leaves, each with upper and lower flaps, engraved collar illus by Poupard 420.00
6-1/4" x 7", dec on both sides of 4 leaves, when folded reveals different versus and full-page color illus, executed by Sarah Ann Siger, Nazareth, PA, orig string hinges 575.00

Confirmation Certificate, 6" x 7-3/4", watercolor, pen and ink on paper, David Schumacher, paired tulips and hearts, for Maria Magdalena Spengler, dated 1780.............................. 4,600.00

Drawing, watercolor, pen and ink
4" x 2-3/4", red yellow and blue rooster with bushy tail, American School, 19th C 865.00
9-1/2" x 7-1/8", red, green and black interlaced calligraphic figure eight with 4 angel heads in corners, attributed to Gottschall family, PA, early 19th C 3,800.00
10-1/4" x 10-1/2", Monstrous Great Snake, called Anaconda, found in early 19th C copy book with Norristown, PA, bookstore label, American School, 19th C 4,600.00

House Blessing (Haus Segen), 15-1/2" h, 11-3/4" w, printed by Johann Ritter, Reading, hand colored, orange, green, blue, yellow, brown, and black, professionally repaired and rebacked on cloth, 18-1/4" h, 14-3/8" w old stenciled dec frame 500.00

Marriage Certificate, 8" x 12-1/2", watercolor, pen and ink on paper, Daniel Schumacher, paired red, yellow and green birds flanking an arch with crown, for Johannes Haber and Elisabeth Stimmess, Windsor Township, Berks County, PA, dated 1777 .... 1,035.00

Reward of Merit, American School, early 19th C, watercolor, pen, and ink on paper,
3-5/8" x 3-1/8", red, yellow, and blue-tailed bird perched on flowering branch 1,092.00
4-1/8" x 3-1/4", red and yellow birds, green and yellow pinwheel flower 345.00

Birth and Baptismal Certificates for brothers Daniel Raup (1784) and Peter Raup (1791), by Frederick Krebs, Adam and Eve, Apple Tree and Serpent in Garden of Eden, printed cut-out birds, watercolor, pen, and ink on paper, gilded decoupage elements, 15-1/2" h, 12-1/4" w, pr, $3,740. Photo courtesy of Sotheby's.

Song Book, 4-1/8" x 6-3/4", watercolor, pen, and ink on paper, marbled covers, leather binding, several handwritten and calligraphy pages, illuminated bookplate, David Hiestand, dated Feb 8, 1823, Macungie Township, Lehigh County, PA 1,380.00

Writing Book (Schreibbuch)

Catharine Rohr, New Britain Township, Bucks County, PA, legal size, soft cover manuscript, dating from 1784 to approx. 1824, written in German script, 45 pgs of text, 5 full page fraktur inscriptions by unidentified hand, family records, tailoring records 4,400.00

Ella M. Eisenbach, full page ink drawings, biblical quotes, Nov. 25, 1898 .... 150.00

FRANKART

History: Arthur Von Frankenberg, artist and sculptor, founded Frankart, Inc., in New York City in the mid-1920s. Frankart, Inc., mass produced practical "art objects" in the Art Deco style into the 1930s. Pieces include aquariums, ashtrays, bookends, flower vases, and lamps. Although Von Frankenberg used live female models as his subjects, his figures are characterized by their form and style rather than specific features. Nudes are the most collectible; caricatures of animals and human figures were also produced, no doubt, to increase sales.

Pieces were cast in white metal in one of the following finishes: cream–a pale iridescent white; bronzoid–oxidized copper, silver, or gold; french–medium brown with green in the crevices; gunmetal–iridescent gray; jap–very dark brown, almost black, with green in the crevices; pearl green–pale iridescent green; and verde–dull light green. Cream and bronzoid were used primarily in the 1930s.

Marks: With few exceptions, pieces were marked "Frankart, Inc.," with a patent number or "pat. appl. for."

Note: All pieces listed have totally original parts and are in very good condition unless otherwise indicated.

Ashtray

5" h, stylized duck with outstretched wings supports green glass ash receiver 120.00

6" h, nude figure kneels on cushion, holding 3" d removable pottery ashtray 225.00

9-1/2" h, seated nude figure on 3" h column, leg extends over 5" sq ceramic ashtray 395.00

Bookends, pr, seated women, white metal, 6-1/2" x 5-1/2", $250.

25" h, nude figure grows from tobacco plant to hold scalloped glass tray overhead 650.00

Bookends, pr

5" h, horse heads with flowing manes 60.00

6" h, seated cubist stylized bears 90.00

8" h, nude figures peek around edge of books 250.00

Candlesticks, pr, 12-1/2" h, nude figures standing on tiptoes, holding candle cup over head 395.00

Cigarette Box, 8" h, back to back nudes supporting removable green glass box 450.00

Lamp

11" h, 8-1/4" w, 4" d, frosted amber crackle glass shade, metal base, worn patina 345.00

13" h, two back to back dancing nude figures support 11" sq glass cylinder satin finished shade 775.00

18" h, standing nude figure holds 6" d round crackled rose glass globe 425.00

Wall Pocket, 12" h, seated nude figure supported by wrought iron metal frame work, metal pan for flowers 300.00

FRANKOMA POTTERY

History: John N. Frank founded a ceramic art department at Oklahoma University in Norman and taught there for several years. In 1933, he established his own business and began making Oklahoma's first commercial pottery. Frankoma moved from Norman to Sapulpa, Oklahoma, in 1938.

A fire completely destroyed the new plant later the same year, but rebuilding began almost immediately. The company remained in Sapulpa and continued to grow. Frankoma is the only American pottery to have pieces on permanent exhibit at the International Ceramic Museum of Italy.

In September 1983, a disastrous fire struck once again, destroying 97% of Frankoma's facilities. The rebuilt Frankoma Pottery reopened on July 2, 1984. Production has been limited to 1983 production molds. All other molds were lost in the fire.

Prior to 1954, all Frankoma pottery was made with a honey-tan-colored clay from Ada, Oklahoma. Since 1954, Frankoma has used a brick-red clay from Sapulpa. During the early 1970s, the clay became lighter and is now pink in color.

Marks: There were a number of early marks. One most eagerly sought is the leopard pacing on the "Frankoma" name. Since the 1938 fire, all pieces have carried only the name.

References: Susan and Al Bagdade, *Warman's American Pottery and Porcelain*, Wallace-Homestead, 1994; Phyllis and Tom Bess, *Frankoma and Other Oklahoma Potteries*, Schiffer Publishing, 1995; Donna Frank, *Clay in the Master's Hands*, 2nd ed., Cock-A-Hoop Publishing, 1995.

Collectors' Club: Frankoma Family Collectors Assoc., P.O. Box 32571, Oklahoma, OH 73122.

Ashtray

Fish, 7" l 15.00

Leaf-shape, price for pr 20.00

Texas, shaped like state 20.00

Bean Pot, cov, Plainsman, green and brown 15.00

Bird Feeder 25.00

Bolo Tie, Blue Gray Jade..40.00
Bottle, 11-1/2" h, morning glory blue, white int., 1979..........35.00
Bowl, 12" d, Shell..25.00
Carafe, cov, Plainsman, green and brown........................20.00
Casserole, cov, Wagon Wheel, tan glaze........................30.00
Christmas Card
    1952..75.00
    1958..70.00
    1965..65.00
    1968..65.00
    1974..60.00
Corn Tray..10.00
Dinnerware Set, service for 8 plus serving pieces, price for 45 pc
    set, orig box
    Brown Satin..75.00
    Robin's Egg Blue..150.00
Figure
    Circus Horse, Desert Gold......................................135.00
    English Setter...55.00
    Gardener Boy..115.00
    Puma, seated, Ada clay...95.00
    Swan, brown glaze..45.00
Flower Frog, mermaid..385.00
Jar, carved, #70, green...35.00
Lazy Susan, Wagon Wheel, blue....................................200.00
Mug
    Donkey, red, 1976...35.00
    GOP, blue, 1970...45.00
Planter
    Drill Bit..10.00
    Elephant...15.00
    Turtle...12.00
Plate
    7" d
        Daniel the Courageous, Teen-agers of the Bible Series,
            1979...25.00
        Peter the Fisherman, Teen-agers of the Bible Series, 1979
            25.00
        Prairie Chicken, Wildlife Series, 1974.........................35.00
    8-1/2" d, Battle for Independence, Bicentennial Series
    ....35.00
Sculpture
    Fan Dancer, Sally Rand..300.00
    Irish Setter head, c1942-60......................................105.00
Souvenir Plate, Oklahoma...35.00
Teapot, cov, Wagon Wheel, 1-1/2 cup size, green and brown
    ....15.00

Mug, donkey figural, souvenir of the 1976 Democratic convention, $35.

Tea Set, Desert Gold...55.00
Toothbrush Holder, owl...135.00
Trivet
    Horseshoes, green..15.00
    Lazybones...35.00
    Unicorn...15.00
Vase
    6-1/2" h, marked "Frank Potteries"...........................195.00
    9" h, peacock blue glaze, 1934-42.............................30.00
    9-1/2" h, octagonal, red glaze..................................40.00
Wall Mask, Comedy and Tragedy, 1963, price for pr........170.00
Wall Pocket
    Boot..25.00
    Indian Chief, Ada clay...45.00
    Phoebe, Onyx Black...80.00

FRATERNAL ORGANIZATIONS

History: Benevolent and secret societies played an important part in America from the late 18th to the mid-20th centuries. Initially, the societies were organized to aid members and their families in times of distress. They evolved from this purpose into important social clubs by the late 19th century.

In the 1950s, with the arrival of the civil rights movement, an attack occurred on the secretiveness and often discriminatory practices of these societies. Membership in fraternal organizations, with the exception of the Masonic group, dropped significantly. Many local chapters closed and sold their lodge halls. This resulted in the appearance of many fraternal items in the antiques market.

Museums: Iowa Masonic Library & Museum, Cedar Rapids, IA; Knights of Columbus Headquarters Museum, New Haven, CT; Masonic Grand Lodge Library & Museum of Texas, Waco, TX; Museum of Our National Heritage, Lexington, MA; Odd Fellows Historical Society, Caldwell, ID.

Additional Listings: See *Warman's Americana & Collectibles* for more examples.

Benevolent & Protective Order of the Elks, (BPOE)
Ashtray, brass, 3 elks..25.00
Badge, 1920 Chicago 56th Annual Reunion......................20.00
Beaker, 5" h, cream, black elk head, mkd "Mettlach, Villeroy & Boch"..110.00
Book, *National Memorial,* 1931, color illus.....................35.00
Bookends, pr, bronzed cast iron, elk in high relief..............75.00
Plate, tin, litho, Elk Lodge, Mt. Hood and elk by river scene, 1912..85.00
Shaving Mug, pink and white, gold elk head, crossed American flags and floral dec, mkd "Germany" on bottom.............90.00
Eastern Star
Demitasse Cup and Saucer, porcelain............................25.00
Pendant, SP, rhinestones and rubies..............................45.00
Ring, gold, Past Matron, star shape stone with diamond in center..150.00
Independent Order of Odd Fellows (I.O.O.F)
Badge, 1-3/4" d celluloid pinback, striped red, white, and blue fabric ribbon suspending 1-1/2" brass pendant with Odd Fellow symbols, headquarters, bale of cotton, Negro man, plus draped US flags, 1912...45.00
Goblet...48.00
Sign, 29-1/2" h, 100" l, Phillipstown Lodge 815, carved, painted, gilt lettering, 3 interlacing ropes, c1930................2,750.00
Watch Fob, 94th Anniversary, April 12, 1913....................30.00

Odd Fellows, Lodge Ax, carved and painted wood and sheet metal, Germania, PA, late 19th C, curved grain painted handle terminating in flaring head painted on one wide with heart in hand, other inscribed "GERMANIA LODGE 158," 37" l, $980. Photo courtesy of Sotheby's.

Knights Templar

Plate, 9" d, Pittsburgh Commandry, 1903, china.................50.00
Tumbler, 4" h, 36th Conclave, glass....................................75.00

Masonic

Apron
    14" x 12", leather, white, blue silk trim, white embroidery, silver fringe...35.00
    18" x 17", satin, ivory, red fringe, polychrome painted insignia 65.00
Book, *History of the Most Ancient & Honorable Fraternity of Free and Accepted Masons in New York from the Earliest Date,* Charles T. McClenachan, 1888, Grand Lodge, NY.........25.00
Catalog, Ihling Bros. Everard Co., Kalamazoo, MI, 72 pgs, 7" x 12", Cat. #82, Masonic costumes, paraphernalia, etc.....48.00
Certificate, Third Degree Freemason, Penobscot Lodge, dated Aug. 8, 1863 ....175.00
Chocolate Pot, cov, china, lodge name and officer roster dec, platinum color trim...125.00
Goblet, St. Paul, 1908...70.00
Ice Cream Mold, 3-3/4" d, pewter, symbol, mkd "E & Co., NY" 30.00
Jug, 5-5/8" h, lusterware, transfer printed and painted polychrome enamels, horseman, inscribed "James Hardman 1823," Masonic dec, royal coat of arms, minor wear....410.00
Match Holder, 11" h, wall type, walnut, pierce carved symbols 75.00
Painting, 23-1/4" h, 20" w, oil on canvas, "Our Motto," framed, retouched, craquelure 2,645.00
Watch Fob, 10K yg, raised emblem, chain and ring............90.00

Shrine

Cup and Saucer, Los Angeles, 1906 ....70.00
Dinnerware, Rajah, partial set, various marks, 52 pcs.......150.00
Goblet, St. Paul, 1908, ruby stained, pedestal foot..............70.00
Ice Cream Mold, 4-1/4" d, pewter, crescent with Egyptian head, mkd "E & Co., NY" 30.00
Mug, Syria Temple, Pittsburgh, 1895, Nantasket Beach, gold figures 125.00

FRUIT JARS

History: Fruit jars are canning jars used to preserve food. Thomas W. Dyott, one of Philadelphia's earliest and most innovative glassmakers, was promoting his glass canning jars in 1829. John Landis Mason patented his screwtype canning jar on Nov. 30, 1858. This date refers to the patent date, not the age of the jar. There are thousands of different jars and a variety of colors, types of closures, sizes, and embossings.

References: Douglas M. Leybourne, Jr., *Red Book No. 7,* published by author (P.O. Box 5417, N. Muskegon, MI 49445), 1993; Jerry McCann, *Fruit Jar Annual,* published by author (5003 W. Berwyn Ave., Chicago, IL 60630), 1995; Dick Roller (comp.), *Indiana Glass Factories Notes,* Acorn Press, 1994; Bill Schroeder, *1000 Fruit Jars: Priced and Illustrated,* 5th ed., Collector Books, 1987, 1996 value update.

Periodical: *Fruit Jar Newsletter,* 364 Gregory Ave., West Orange, NJ 07052.

Collectors' Clubs: Ball Collectors Club, 22203 Doncaster, Riverview, MI 48192; Federation of Historical Bottle Collectors, Inc., 88 Sweetbriar Branch, Longwood, FL 32750; Midwest Antique Fruit Jar & Bottle Club, P.O. Box 38, Flat Rock, IN 47234.

Additional Listings: See *Warman's Americana & Collectibles* for more examples.

Adams & Co., Manufacturers, Pittsburgh, PA, aqua, applied mouth, orig stopper, qt..540.00
Advance, Pat. Appl'd For, aqua, ground lip, qt....................95.00
A. Stone & Co./Philada, aquamarine, applied collared mouth, glass lid, smooth base, half gallon, 2 mouth chips, L #2747 ....175.00
Atlas Mason's Patent, medium yellow green, ABM lip, qt....50.00
Ball, mason, yellow green, amber striations, qt...................75.00
B. B. Wilcox, aquamarine, ground mouth, glass lid, wire bale, smooth base, half gallon, L #3000 ....100.00
Belle, pat. Dec. 14, 1869, aqua, 3 raised feet, ground lip, metal neck band, qt...75.00
Clarke Fruit Jar Co., Cleveland, OH, aqua, ground lip, lid, metal cam lever closure, 1-1/2 pt..165.00
Crystal Jar, pat. Dec. 17, 1878, clear, ground lip 70.00

Moore's Patent Dec. 3, 1861, cylindrical, aquamarine, applied collared mouth, glass lid, iron yoke clamp, smooth, base, qt, 1860-70, $120. Photo courtesy of Norman C. Heckler & Company.

Dodge Sweeney & Co.'s California, aqua, ground lip, glass insert, zinc band, 1-1/2 qt 425.00

Eagle, deep aquamarine, applied collared mouth, glass lid, iron yoke, smooth base, half gallon, # 872............................160.00

Excelsior, aqua, ground lip, insert, zinc band, qt...............575.00

Fahnestock Albree & Co., aqua, applied mouth, qt.............35.00

Franklin Fruit Jar, aqua, ground lip, zinc lid, qt..................225.00

Friedley & Cornman's, pat. Oct. 25th 1958, Ladies Choice, aquamarine, ground mouth, iron rim, gutta percha or leather insert, smooth base, half gallon, iron rim lid rusty, L #1039..1,200.00

Gilberds Improved Jar, aqua, ground lip, wire band, qt....160.00

Helmen's Railroad Mills, amber, ground lip, insert, zinc band, pt 70.00

High Grade, aqua, ground lip, zinc lid, qt...........................150.00

Johnson & Johnson, New York, cobalt blue, ground lip, orig insert, screw band, qt..325.00

Lafayette, aqua, tooled lip, orig 3 pc glass and metal stopper, qt 200.00

Mason Crystal Jar, clear, ground lip, zinc lid 65.00

Mason's, pat. Nov. 30, 1858, light green, profuse amber striations, machined mouth, zinc lid, smooth base, half gallon, some int. stain, L#1787...325.00

Moore's, pat. Dec. 3, 1861, aquamarine, applied collared mouth, glass lid, iron yoke clamp, smooth base, qt, L #2204...120.00

Peerless, aqua, applied mouth, iron yoke, half gallon 85.00

Pet, aqua, applied mouth, qt...55.00

Protector, aquamarine, ground mouth, unmarked tin lid, smooth base, qt, L #2420...70.00

Star, aqua, emb star, ground lip, zinc insert and screw band, qt 300.00

Sun, aquamarine, ground mouth, glass lid, iron clamp, smooth base, qt...130.00

The Magic (star) Fruit Jar, greenish-aqua, ground mouth, glass lid, iron clamp, smooth base, half gallon, chips to mouth, L #1606 ....180.00

The Pearl, aqua, ground lip, screw band, qt........................40.00

The Van Vilet Jar of 1881, aqua, ground lip, orig wire and iron yoke, qt 365.00

Union N1, Beaver Falls Glass Co., Beaver Falls, PA, aqua, applied wax seal ring, half gallon 45.00

Whitmore's Patent, Rochester, NY, aqua, ground lip, wire closure, qt...425.00

FRY GLASS

History: The H. C. Fry Glass Co. of Rochester, Pennsylvania, began operating in 1901 and continued in business until 1933. Its first products were brilliant-period cut glass. It later produced Depression glass tablewares. In 1922, the company patented heat-resisting ovenware in an opalescent color. This "Pearl Oven Glass," which was produced in a variety of pieces for oven and table, included casseroles, meat trays, and pie and cake pans.

Fry's beautiful art line, Foval, was produced only in 1926 and 1927. It is pearly opalescent, with jade green or delft blue trim. It is always evenly opalescent, never striped like Fenton's opalescent line.

REPRODUCTION ALERT

In the 1970s, reproductions of Foval were made in abundance in Murano, Italy. These pieces, including items such as candlesticks and toothpicks, have teal blue transparent trim.

Marks: Most pieces of the oven glass are marked "Fry" with model numbers and sizes.

Foval examples are rarely signed, except for occasional silver-overlay pieces marked "Rockwell."

Reference: Fry Glass Society, *Collector's Encyclopedia of Fry Glass*, Collector Books, 1989, 1998 value update.

Collectors' Club: H. C. Fry Glass Society, P.O. Box 41, Beaver, PA 15009.

Bowl, 8" d, cut glass, pineapple design, wheel cutting, sgd 120.00

Butter Dish, cov, Pearl Oven Ware 75.00

Canapé Plate, 6-1/4" d, 4" h, cobalt blue center handle, Foval 165.00

Candlesticks, pr, 12" h, Foval, pearl white candlesticks, jade green threading and trim..1,380.00

Creamer and Sugar, Set 200, Foval, delft blue handles 175.00

Cruet, Foval, cobalt blue handle, orig stopper...................125.00

Cup and Saucer, Foval, blue handles..................................65.00

Decanter, 9" h, ftd, Foval, applied Delft blue handle..........195.00

Fruit Bowl, 9-7/8" d, 5-1/4" h, Foval, pearl white, ridged, delft blue foot..520.00

Ice Cream Tray, 14" l, 7" w, cut glass, Nelson pattern variation, all over cutting, sgd "Fry"...290.00

Lemonade Pitcher, 10-1/2" h, 5" w, tankard, applied Delft Blue large loop handle and foot, strong pearlescence 675.00

Nappy, 6" d, cut glass, pinwheel and fan with hobstar center, sgd..60.00

Platter, 17" l, Oven Ware...65.00

Punch Cup, Crackle, clear, cobalt blue ring handle 45.00

Sherbet, 4" h, cut glass, Chicago pattern.............................75.00

Teacup and Saucer, Foval, delft blue handles.....................95.00

Trivet, 8", Oven Ware..20.00

Tumbler, cut glass, pinwheel, zipper, and fan motifs, sgd, 6 pc set..180.00

Goblet, three-Buttress, open stem, quilted optic, emerald, rare; $185.

FULPER POTTERY

History: The Fulper Pottery Company of Flemington, New Jersey, made stoneware pottery and utilitarian ware beginning in the early 1800s. It switched to the production of art pottery in 1909 and continued until about 1935.

The company's earliest artware was called the Vasekraft line (1910-1915), featuring intense glazine and rectilinear, Germanic forms. Its middle period (1915-1925) included some of the earlier shapes, but they also incorporated Oriental forms as well. Fulper's glazing at this time was less consistent but more diverse. Its last period (1925-1935) was characterized by watered-down Art-Deco forms with relatively weak glazing.

Pieces were almost always molded, though careful hand-glazing distinguished this pottery as one of the premier semi-commercial producers. Pieces from all periods are almost always marked.

Marks: A rectangular mark, FULPER, in a rectangle is known as the "ink mark" and dates from 1910-1915. The second mark, as shown, dates from 1915-1925, it was incised or in black ink. The final mark, FULPER, die-stamped, dates from about 1925 to 1935.

Left to right, vase, Cat's eye flambé, incised racetrack mark, 12" x 9-1/2", $1,100; pepper shaped vessel, matted green and purple microcrystalline glaze, rect ink mark, $605. Photo courtesy of David Rago Auctions, Inc.

References: Susan and Al Bagdade, *Warman's American Pottery and Porcelain*, Wallace-Homestead, 1994; Ralph and Terry Kovel, *Kovels' American Art Pottery*, Crown Publishers, 1993; David Rago, *American Art Pottery,* Knickerbocker Press, 1977; ---, *Fulper Pottery,* Arts & Crafts Quarterly Press, n.d.

Collectors' Club: American Art Pottery Assoc., P.O. Box 525, Cedar Hill, MO 63016; Stangl/Fulper Collectors Club, P.O. Box 64-A, Changewater, NJ 07831.

Advisor: David Rago.

Bowl
    12" d, 6" h, Effigy, 3 apes holding flat bowl, blue glossy flambé over blue matte, early mark 450.00
    13" d, 5" h, curled edge, Leopard skin Crystalline glaze, early mark...300.00
Cabinet Vase, 5" h, 4" d, cylindrical neck, squat base, ivory flambé over mustard matte glaze, early mark......................200.00
Centerpiece Bowl, flaring, flutes and ruffled edge, green flambé, late mark 200.00
Vase
    6" h, 8" d, bulbous, 3 handles, white glossy glaze, late mark
    ....125.00
    7" h, 5" d, bulbous, 3 curling handles at rim, blue semi-mate crystalline glaze, late mark 150.00
    8" h, 5" d, tapering hexagonal, Chinese blue and mahogany flambé glaze, middle mark 350.00
    10" h, 4" d, reticulated cylindrical, emb mushrooms, ivory and mahogany flambé glaze, early mark 800.00

FURNITURE

History: Two major currents dominate the American furniture marketplace–furniture made in Great Britain and furniture made in the United States. American buyers continue to show a strong prejudice for objects manufactured in the

Lamp, mushroom shaped shade, rose, yellow, and green slag glass inserts, round cabochon jewels, Mirrored Black and Flemington Green glaze, vertical box ink mark, 23" h, 17" d, $15,400.

United States. They will pay a premium for such pieces and accept them above technically superior and more aesthetically appealing English examples.

Until the last half of the 19th century, formal American styles were dictated by English examples and design books. Regional furniture, such as the Hudson River Valley (Dutch) and the Pennsylvania German styles, did develop. A less-formal furniture, often designated as "country" or vernacular style, developed throughout the 19th and early 20th centuries. These country pieces deviated from the accepted formal styles and have a charm that many collectors find irresistible.

America did contribute a number of unique decorative elements to English styles. The American Federal period is a reaction to the English Hepplewhite period. American designers created furniture, which influenced, rather than reacted to, world taste in the Gothic Revival style and Arts and Crafts, Art Deco, and Modern International movements.

Furniture styles	Approx. dates
William and Mary	1690-1730
Queen Anne	1720-1760
Chippendale	1755-1790
Federal (Hepplewhite)	1790-1815
Sheraton	1790-1810
Empire (Classical)	1805-1830
Victorian	
French Restoration	1830-1850
Gothic Revival	1840-1860
Rococo Revival	1845-1870
Elizabethan	1850-1915
Louis XIV	1850-1914
Naturalistic	1850-1914
Renaissance Revival	1850-1880
Neo-Greek	1855-1885
Eastlake	1870-1890
Art Furniture	1880-1914
Arts and Crafts	1895-1915
Art Nouveau	1896-1914
Art Deco	1920-1945
International Movement	1940-Present

REPRODUCTION ALERT

Beware of the large number of reproductions. During the 25 years following the American Centennial of 1876, there was a great revival in copying furniture styles and manufacturing techniques of earlier eras. These centennial pieces now are more than 100 years old. They confuse many dealers as well as collectors.

References: *Antique Wicker from the Heywood-Wakefield Catalog*, Schiffer Publishing, 1994; Luke Beckerdite (ed.), *American Furniture*, Chipstone Foundation, 1994; Joseph T. Butler, Field Guide to American Furniture, Facts on File Publications, 1985; Robert Judson Clark et al., *Design in America*, Harry N. Abrams, Detroit Institute of Arts and The Metropolitan Museum of Art, 1983; Wendy Cooper, *Classical Taste in America*, Abbeville Press, 1993; Madeleine Deschamps, *Empire*, Abbeville Press, 1994; Eileen and Richard Dubrow, *Styles of American Furniture, 1860-1960,* Schiffer Publishing, 1997;

Nancy Goyne Evans, *American Windsor Chairs*, Hudson Hills Press, 1996.

Fine Furniture Reproductions, Schiffer Publishing, 1996; Oscar Fitzgerald, *Four Centuries of American Furniture*, Wallace-Homestead, 1995; Tim Forrest, *Bulfinch Anatomy of Antique Furniture*, Bulfinch Press, 1996; Benno M. Forman, *American Seating Furniture*, Winterthur Museum, W. W. Norton & Company, 1988; Don Fredgant, *American Manufactured Furniture*, revised and updated ed., Schiffer Publishing, 1996; *Furniture of the Arts & Crafts Period*, L-W Book Sales, 1992, 1995 value update; Phillipe Garner, *Twentieth-Century Furniture*, Van Nostrand Reinhold, 1980; Cara Greenberg, *Mid-Century Modern*, Harmony Books, 1995; George Hepplewhite, *Cabinet-Maker and Upholsterer's Guide* (reprint), Dover Publications, 1969; Heywood Brothers and Wakefield Company, Katherine S. Howe, et al., *Herter Brothers*, Harry N. Abrams, 1994; Conover Hill, *Antique Oak Furniture,* 1997 value update, Collector Books; Bruce Johnson, *The Pegged Joint*, Knock on Wood Publications, 1995.

Myrna Kaye, F*ake, Fraud, or Genuine*, New York Graphic Society Book, 1987; William C. Ketchum, Jr., *American Cabinetmakers*, Crown, 1995; Ralph Kylloe, *History of the Old Hickory Chair Company and the Indiana Hickory Furniture Movement*, published by author, 1995; ——, Rustic Traditions, Gibbs-Smith, 1993; David P. Lindquist and Caroline C. Warren, *Colonial Revival Furniture with Prices*, Wallace-Homestead, 1993; ——, *English & Continental Furniture with Prices*, Wallace-Homestead, 1994; ——, *Victorian Furniture with Prices*, Wallace-Homestead, 1995; Robert F. McGiffin, *Furniture Care and Conservation*, revised 3rd ed., American Association for State and Local History Press, 1992; Kathryn McNerny, *Victorian Furniture, Our American Heritage,* Book I, 1997 value update, Book II, 1997 value update; Collector Books; Edgar G. Miller, Jr., *American Antique Furniture*, 2 Vols., Dover Publications, 1966; Marie Purnell Musser, *Country Chairs of Central Pennsylvania*, published by author, 1990.

Milo M. Naeve, *Identifying American Furniture*, 2nd ed., American Association for State and Local History, 1989; George C. Neumann, *Early American Antique Country Furnishings*, L-W Book Sales, 1984, 1993 reprint; Jacquelyn Peake, *How to Recognize and Refinish Antiques for Pleasure and Profit*, 3rd ed., Globe Pequot Press (P.O. Box 833, Old Saybrook, CT 06475), 1995; Peter Philip, Gillian Walkling, and John Bly, *Field Guide to Antique Furniture*, Houghton Mifflin, 1992; Leslie Piña, *Fifties Furniture*, Schiffer Publishing, 1996; Rudolf Pressler and Robin Staub, *Biedermeier Furniture*, Schiffer Publishing, 1996; Don and Carol Raycraft, *Wallace-Homestead Price Guide To American Country Antiques, 15th Edition,* Krause Publications, 1997; Ernest Rettelbusch, *Handbook of Historic Ornament from Ancient Times to Biedermeier*, Dover Publications, 1996; Michael Regan (ed.), *American & European Furniture Price Guide*, Antique Trader Books, 1995; Steve and Roger W. Rouland, *Heywood-Wakefield Modern Furniture*, 1995, 1997 value update, Collector Books; Paul Royka, *Mission Furniture from the American Arts & Crafts Movement,* Schiffer Publishing, 1997.

Albert Sack, *New Fine Points of Furniture*, Crown, 1993; *American Wooden Chairs, 1895-1907,* Schiffer Publishing, 1997; Klaus-Jurgen Sembach, *Modern Furniture Designs, 1950-1980s,* Schiffer Publishing, 1997; Nancy A. Smith, *Old Furniture,* 2nd ed., Dover Publications, 1990; Robert W. and Harriett Swedberg, *Collector's Encyclopedia of American Furniture*, Vol. 1 (1990, 1996 value update), Vol. 2 (1992, 1996 value update), Vol. 3 (1998), Collector Books; ——, *Furniture of the Depression Era*, Collector Books, 1987, 1996 value update; ——, *Swedberg's Price Guide to Antique Oak Furniture*, 1st Series, Collector Books, 1994; Thonet Co., *Thonet Bentwood and Other Furniture* (1904 catalog reprint), Dover Publications, 1980; Eli Wilner, *Antique American Frames*, Avon Books, 1995; Ghenete Zelleke, Eva B. Ottillinger, and Nina Stritzler, *Against the Grain*, The Art Institute of Chicago, 1993.

There are hundreds of specialized books on individual furniture forms and styles. Two of note are Monroe H. Fabian, *Pennsylvania-German Decorated Chest*, Universe Books, 1978, and Charles Santore, *Windsor Style In America*, Revised, vols. I and II, Dover Publications, n.d.

Videotapes: BBC Enterprises Ltd., *Story of English Furniture*, 2 Vols., Home Vision, 1981; John Bivens, *Authenticating Antique Furniture*, 2 Vols., Pilaster Publications, 1994.

Additional Listings: Arts and Craft Movement; Art Deco; Art Nouveau; Children's Nursery Items; Orientalia; Shaker Items; Stickley.

Notes: Furniture is one of the types of antiques for which regional preferences are a factor in pricing. Victorian furniture is popular in New Orleans and unpopular in New England. Oak is in demand in the Northwest, not as much so in the Middle Atlantic states.

Prices vary considerably on furniture. Shop around. Furniture is plentiful unless you are after a truly rare example. Examine all pieces thoroughly—avoid buying on impulse. Turn items upside down; take them apart. Price is heavily influenced by the amount of repairs and restoration. Make certain you know if any such work has been done to a piece before buying it.

The prices listed below are "average" prices. They are only a guide. High and low prices are given to show market range.

Beds

Adirondack-Style, double 350.00
Aesthetic Movement, suite, walnut and burl walnut, full size bed frame, Carrara marble tops, 55-1/2" w, 24" d, 87-3/4" h mirrored bureau, 38" w, 17-1/2" d, 32" h two door cupboard, 19-1/2" w, 18-1/4" d, 31-1/2" h commode, c1870, price for suite 7,500.00
Chippendale Style, Drexel mahogany, four poster, carved, 65" x 86-1/2", 67-1/2" h 750.00
Classical
Massachusetts, c1825, carved mahogany, vase and ring-turned spiral acanthus leaf and pineapple carved posts, block turned legs, joined to plain turned tapering head posts, shaped headboard, old refinish, rails extended in length, 53" w, 78" l, 62-1/2" h.. 1,725.00
New York, 1820-30, carved mahogany veneer, crest rails and supports with waterleaf carving above veneered paneled sec-

tion over foliate carved ball feet, castors, refinished, 73" l, 33" w, 37" h 2,000.00

Country
Block Turned Posts, New England, c1800, painted birch, urn finials, swelled turned legs, peaked headboard, block ring-turned swelled footposts, old red-orange mottled paint, 41-1/2" w, 75" l, 35" h... 345.00
Low Post
  New England, 18th C, birch, block turned tapering legs joined by shaped headboard, shorter conforming turned footboard, orig red paint, 49" w, 75-1/2" l, 39-1/4" h....... 865.00
  Pennsylvania, early 19th C, dark green and red painted maple and poplar, ball finials on turned posts, centering pitched headboard, shaped footboard, tall turned tapering legs, 47-1/2" w 690.00
Rope, late 18th C/early 19th C
  American, poplar and pine, red repaint, paneled headboard, turned blanket rail, turned posts with onion finials, some loss to feet, 54" w, 72" l orig rails, 50" h 275.00
  American, red paint, cylinder turned short headposts, compressed ball-turned finials, center triangular arched headboard, tapering-turned legs, conforming footposts, molded rails, 73-1/2" l, 48" w, 31" h.................................... 6,600.00
  Pennsylvania, walnut, lowpost, cylindrical turned short headposts, ball-turned finials, center arched headboard, turned tapering legs, conforming footposts and footboard, orig rails, later hardware added to support box spring, 73-3/4" l, 49-1/8" w, 31" h 850.00
Turned and Painted
  New England, c1800, block turned headpost, turned slight swelled legs, peaked headboard, low footpost, old red paint, 53-1/4" w, 76" l, 34-1/2" h 1,035.00
  Pennsylvania, c1840, posts with acorn turned finials continuing to bulbous vase and ring-turned posts joined by shaped headboard with turned spindles, blanket rail at foot, 58" w, 72-1/2" l, 51" h 950.00
Turned and Stained, poplar, Berks County, Pennsylvania, first half 19th C, ball finials, reel and vase-turned supports centering shaped head and footboard on tall tapering reel and vase-turned legs, peg feet, matching trundle bed with ball finials, similar turnings, centering plain head and footboard, ball feet, 48" w bed 2,600.00
Youth, paint dec, scroll cut outs on head and foot boards, cannon ball turnings, attributed to Jacob Leiby, Berks County, Pennsylvania, 39-1/2" w, 69-1/2" l 825.00

Day Bed, French Empire, mahogany, upholstered, bowed crest rail, ormolu mask head dec, rect flaring tapering legs, ormolu paw feet, 60" l, $1,900. Photo courtesy of Freeman\Fine Arts.

Duncan Phyfe Style, recamier, ormolu mount, rush seat, scrolled ends, horizontal splat, large scrolled back, 58" l, 18-1/2" d, 32-1/2" h..1,300.00

Empire Style, mfg. by Dauler, Close & Johns, Pittsburgh, Pennsylvania, early 20th C, deeply carved foliate and turned posts, front posts terminate in paw feet, shaped headboard and foot board, 63-1/2" l, 60" w, 54-1/2" h headboard, 74-1/2" h posts 500.00

Federal
c1810, tester, mahogany, molded shaped rect tester, four turned reeded uprights, shaped rect headboard, straight side rails, ring-turned cylindrical legs, 56-1/2" w, 77" l, 81-1/2" h..2,100.00
c1820, New England, tester, maple, foot posts with carved ring-turned swelled reeded posts joined to more simply turned head posts, refinished, 51" w, 75-1/2" l, 58-1/2" h 865.00
c1850, four post, tiger maple, ball final over ring and spiral-turned posts, straight side rails 2,100.00

Federal Style, early 20th C, 4 post, turned and reeded posts, central shell carving with foliage dec on either side of top of headboard, paneled footboard and headboard with rope edge borders, 82" l, 61" w, 84-1/2" h posts, 70" h headboard 450.00

George III Style, late 19th C, full tester, painted dec satinwood, scrolls with centered scene of couple, full size, lacking bolt covers, 83-1/4" w, 71" l, 93" h 8,625.00

Hepplewhite, country, tall post, refinished maple, old cherry finish, pine headboard, sq tapered posts, orig side rails, replaced tester frame, 50" x 70-3/4" mattress, 75-1/2" h 1,265.00

International Movement, George Nakashima, walnut
Bed, headboard: block dovetail top and doweled sides, two sliding doors, plywood back with holes for wires, orig finish, 62" w, 12" d, 36" h; platform: flush tenons and dowels, orig finish, c1957, 60" w, 74" l, 10" h..............................5,775.00
Daybed, free edge plank back, slight elevation, double through tenons at intersection of rails, wooden wedges of contrasting color, green vinyl cushion, c1957, 91" w, 34" d, 36" h 6,325.00

Louis XVI Style, double, ornate metal mount on rect fruitwood headboard, foot board with blue jasperware plaques set within ornate metal frames, banded inlay, 50" w, 57-1/2" h.....125.00

Marquetry, Dutch, 19th C, half tester, inlaid walnut, vase and ring-turned inlaid uprights, attached half-tester, scrolled supports, shaped rect inlaid headboard, straight side rails, shaped rect inlaid footboard, turned tapering feet 3,000.00

Sheraton, maple, pine headboard, tapered head posts, turned foot posts, curved canopy frame, refinished, end rails extended to full; size, orig side rails extended, minor age cracks, 54" x 77" mattress size, 59" h..............................1,650.00

Sleigh, American
Cast iron and metal, painted cream, ornate pierced design, casters, some dents, twin size 600.00
Mahogany and mahogany veneer, double size................600.00

Victorian, America, c1850, daybed, tiger maple, spool turned head and footboard, straight side rails, spool-turned legs, ball feet, 71-1/2" l, 24" d, 27-1/2" h 1,300.00

Victorian, Renaissance Revival, American, c1872, stained maple and burled maple, tester, arched headboard with center carved rosette above panel dec with opposed winged griffins and floral scrolls, panel of suspended palmettos below, gilt incised half round pilasters flanking conforming footboard, side rails, posts, and rounded quarter canopy, minor restorations, 67" w, 72" h headboard..7,000.00

Bench

Arts and Crafts, American
Limbert, Grand Rapids, MI, 1907, No. 243, window, oak, canted flat sides, 4 sq cutouts each centering seat, leather cushion,

Bench, Sheraton Windsor, country, bowed seat frame, refinished hardwood with turned spindles, posts, and rungs, old rush seat, attributed to Thomas Ash, NY, break in one arm at back post, 73" l, $770. Photo courtesy of Garth's Auctions.

branded mark, dark color, shellac finish, 24" w, 18" d, 24" h 4,750.00
Rohlf's style, 2 horizontal slats, quarter-sawn oak, refinished, screw construction, 51" w, 16" d, 40" h..............650.00

Baroque Style, late 19th C, walnut, gross point and petit point upholstered seat, 34" w, 16-1/2" d, 23-1/2" h..............635.00

Chippendale Style, mahogany, long rect padded top, cabriole lets, claw and ball feet, Verdue tapestry upholstery, late 19th C, 52" l, 13-1/2" d, 10-1/2" h..............................550.00

Country
Bucket
Birch and pine, old red stain, 5 shelves with cutout ends, molded cornice, dovetailed, turned feet painted black, 64" w, 12-1/2" d, 52-1/4" h..............................1,430.00
Pine, 3 shelves, mortised, gallery back, 36" w, 12" d, 45" h 600.00
Poplar, brown stained, 3 convex short drawers with ironstone knobs, projecting lower section with 2 doors, shelved int., sides continue to form feet, Lebanon County, Pennsylvania, c1860, 39" w, 16-1/4" d, 50-1/2" h..............460.00
Deacon's, painted blue, 141" l..............................175.00
Double mortised top
Green paint on sides and base, stencil dec, iron braces added, 19th C, 60" l, 11" w, 20-1/2" h..............825.00
Yellow over red paint, underside sgd "Wm. H. Wieand, Nov 1878 Upper Milford Lehigh County, Pennsylvania," scroll cut outs in front of legs, break to one leg, 60" l, 11" w, 19" h 495.00
Mammy, stenciled detail, black repaint, worn rockers, 46-1/2" l 750.00
Water, pine, old blue and green paint, crest, cutout ends, base shelf, 43" w, 18" d, 32-1/4" h..............................250.00

Federal, c1810, window, mahogany, upholstered seat and rolled arms, sq tapering legs, sq H stretchers, refinished, minor repair to one leg, 39-1/2" l, 16" w, 29" h..............................900.00

George III Style, late 19th C, settle, limed pine, rect paneled back, downswept arms, lift seat, paneled front, 72" w, 21" d, 60" h 650.00

Gothic Revival, late 19th C, Prie-Dieu, walnut, upholstered top rail, pierced carved backrest, over upholstered set, circular turned legs 250.00

International Movement, Oscar Bach, brass scroll work and hand beaten metal, painted, 50" l, 16-1/2" d, 44" h 3,737.00

Jacobean Style, settle, late 19th C, constructed from 17th and 18th C parts
Oak, molded cornice, carved arched panel supported by spiral-turned uprights, molded, paneled back, hinged seat, carved conforming case, molded base 1,500.00
Walnut, carved and molded arched crest rail over panel, fielded panel back with carved grotesqueries, floral molded panel, acanthus leaf carved arms, hinged seat, carved

paneled base, constructed from 17th and 18th C parts 1,200.00

Louis XVI, early 19th C, giltwood, shaped later marble top, acanthus leaf carved conforming apron, cabriole legs with cartouche and acanthus leaf carved knees, scroll feet, 24" w, 19" d, 15" h 1,850.00

Windsor, American, 19th C, kneeling, splayed, bamboo turned legs, reeded edge top, gray over olive green and red paint, 36-3/4" l, 6-3/4" w, 6" h 350.00

Bentwood

In 1856, Michael Thonet of Vienna perfected the process of bending wood using steam. Shortly after, Bentwood furniture became popular. Other manufacturers of Bentwood furniture were Jacob and Joseph Kohn; Philip Strobel and Son; Sheboygan Chair Co.; and Tidoute Chair Co. Bentwood furniture is still being produced today by the Thonet firm and others.

Bed, c1900, scrolled and carved headboard, conforming footboard, double mattress size, 60" h 850.00

Bride's Box, Continental, late 18th C, oblong, fitted lid, painted in blue, brown, orange, green, white, and place, couple dressed in formal costume, surrounded by blossoms and curlicues, border with amorous German inscription, sides with stylized blossoms and berries, 18-7/8" l, 6-3/8" h 1,610.00

Chair, c1900
    Arm, Thonet, scrolled back and arms, cane seat, splayed legs, orig label and stamp 325.00
    Side, J & J Kohn, oak, pressed wood seat insert, branded and paper label remnants, 36" h 150.00

Cradle, c1900, oval bentwood basket, shaped cradle, extended ornate scrolled support, 52" l, 36" h................................750.00

Rack, spindle back, central mirror, overhead spindle shelf, bentwood hook on outside rails, spindle containers flank horizontal rack, bentwood frame, natural color, 48-1/2" w, 17" d, 74-1/2" h 1,400.00

Rocker, Thonet, arched twined top rail, cut velvet fabric fitted back, armrests, and seat, elaborate scrolling frame, curved runners, 53" l..700.00

Table, Austria, c1900, center type, shaped oblong white marble top, narrow frieze, elaborate bentwood cruciform base with interlocking and overlapping scrolls centering on turned standard, 45-1/2" l, 28-1/2" h 325.00

Blanket Chests

Adirondack, New York, early 20th C, painted twigs, hinged top, front and side surfaces dec with applied designs, shaped skirts, old light red paint, 33-3/4" w, 16-7/8" d, 23-1/2" h 635.00

Blanket Chest, William and Mary, possibly PA, dovetailed, two drawers in base, replaced ball feet, 50-1/2" l, 24" d, 27-1/2" h, $1,200. Photo courtesy of Sanford Alderfer Auction Co.

Chinese Style, American, 19th C, pine, legs and brass fittings, red japanned style dec, 45-1/4" w..............................600.00

Decorated

Pine, Pennsylvania
    Orig blue paint, c1785, rect hinged lid, opening to well, case with mid-molding above 3 molded drawers, molded base, ogee bracket feet, moldings highlighted in red, orig brass handles and escutcheon plate, 51" l, 22-1/2" d, 27-1/2" h 5,175.00
    Orig blue grained paint, c1810, hinged rect lid, opening to well and till, base moldings, bracket feet, painted and grained allover in blue swirls, 50" l, 19-1/2" d, 23" h 12,650.00
    Orig blue paint, polychrome dec, Windsor Township, Berks County, 1787, hinged rect lid, opening to well and till with partially legible inscriptions on underside, case dec with 3 arched reserves flanked by and centering 4 pots of flowers and birds, center reserve dec with rampant unicorns and crown, flanking reserves with birds, tulips, and inverted hearts with riders on horseback wielding drawn swords, inscribed date 1787, case sides with arched reserves of tulip filled pots, molded base, straight bracket feet, central pendant, right hand top molding replaced, base molding and feet added at later date, 50" l, 22" d, 24" h 11,500.00
    Orig brown fanciful graining on faded pink-cream ground, orange-salmon undercoat, black lid trim and feet, molded lid edge with till and secret compartment, dovetailed case, three dovetailed overlapping drawers with orig oval brasses, applied molding above drawers, bracket feet with unusual glue blocks and braces, some edge damage, two drawers with rodent holes, front feet ended out, some touch up repairs to paint, very worn top, 50-3/4" w, 25-1/4" d, 29-1/4" h 2,880.00
    Orig paint, Lehigh County, 1791, rect lid fitted on int. with orig wrought iron heart strap hinges, opening to well with till, front dec with 2 arched reserves flanked by balusters centering tulips and flowers, center inscription "Lifbeth Jacobiffen 1791," molded base, bracket feet, 49-1/2" l, 22" d, 25" h..3,165.00
    Orig paint, late 18th C, 3 tombstone dec on front, one on each side, dovetailed, bat wing hinges, crab lock missing, orig feet, replaced till and patches, 52" l, 23" d, 22-1/2" h 1,100.00
    Orig red paint, stylized green and yellow tree, lid with till and applied edge molding, dovetailed case, bracket feet, replaced hinges, minor age crack in lid, attributed to Somerset County, 41-1/2" w, 20" d, 24-3/4" h 1,925.00

Pine and Poplar, New England, early 18th C, molded lift top above half rounded molded case, single drawer on bottom, bracket feet, orig paint, 36" w, 18-1/2" d, 37" h 4,600.00

Pine and Poplar, Pennsylvania, orig dark reddish brown paint, yellow striping divides front panel into 2 sections, each with 3-headed red, yellow, and green tulip, dovetailed case, till, turned feet, base and lid edge moldings, 45-1/2" w, 19" d, 24-3/4" h..935.00

Poplar, Pennsylvania, attributed to Soap Hollow area, Somerset County, orig red graining, yellow stenciled star flowers, scrolled foliage, baskets of fruit and "S.S. 1877," lid with till and edge molding, dovetailed case, bracket feet, minor wear, 50" w, 20-1/2" d, 25" h 1,540.00

Grain Painted, 6 board

Maine, early 19th C, pine, molded top lifts over case, lidded till, bracket feet, orig red and black paint simulating mahogany, 42" l, 18" d, 23" h...1,840.00

New York, Schoharie County, c1815, molded hinged top, dovetail constructed box, bracket feet, grain painted burnt umber to resemble mahogany, initialed "JAS," flanked by yellow flowering vines, 37-3/4" w, 14-1/4" d, 17-1/4" h 1,265.00

Pennsylvania, poplar, rect top with molded edge, till, mid-molding, 2 short drawers below, base molding, splayed bracket feet, allover tones of red and black paint simulating crotch mahogany, pencil inscription on lid int. "Thomas B. Reber Murall

1833 Thomas R. Reber January 16th 1837 C?D Reber Feb. 24-87 bought this chest at Uncle's sale for $3.85. Delivered to Addie May 14/03," orig drawer pulls and brass escutcheons, repairs to front left foot, 49-1/2" l, 22" d, 27-1/2" h 3,165.00

Hepplewhite, Pennsylvania, pine, orig red paint, grain painting traces, case with 3 dovetailed drawers, French feet, orig locks, wrought iron strap hinges, brass escutcheons, stenciled initials "W. H. G.," 50" l, 23' d, 29-1/4" h 2,400.00

Queen Anne, Massachusetts, c1740, pine, old red paint, 36" w, 17" d, 31-3/4" h 2,000.00

Book Cases

Art Nouveau
American, c1900, walnut, dentil molding and brackets in pediment, carved and paneled sides, some loss to finish, some elements missing, 99" l, 92" h 1,120.00
French, Majorelle, c1900, carved walnut, molded crest, carved splayed leaves, glazed door mounted with central textured purple glass panel, silvered bronze branch-form spandrels, pr of narrow cupboard doors, molded base, carved feet, 64-1/4" w, 79" h.................................3,500.00

Arts and Crafts
American, oak, glazed doors, 48" h, 48" w.........................250.00
Flint Company, #607A, double door, leaded glass, 3 adjustable shelves, orig overcoated dark finish, 36" w, 14-1/2" d, 55" h 1,600.00

Chippendale, Maryland or Pennsylvania, 1765-85, mahogany, 3 sections, upper: triangular molded and dentiled pediment, plinth with contemporary bust of William Shakespeare, plain veneered frieze, center: bookcase with double glazed cupboard doors, astragal mullions, Chinoiserie pattern, molded base; lower: chest with short thumb-molded central drawer flanked by two similar box drawers, two graduated long drawers flanked by fluted quarter columns, ogee bracket feet, 44-3/4" w, 25-1/2" d, 106-1/8" h 16,500.00

Classical, New York or New Jersey, c1825, tiger maple, flat carved molded cornice above 2 glazed doors enclosing 3 shelves, projecting case of 2 central cockbeaded short drawers flanked by deep drawer and recessed tombstone panel all above 3 cockbeaded long drawers, flanked by vase and ring-turned columns, sides with recessed panels, old refinish, replaced brasses, imperfections, feet missing, 41" w, 20-1/2" d, 88" h 5,175.00

George I, walnut, projecting molded cornice, glazed doors, shelf int. 2 short and 2 long feather banded drawers, bracket feet, 43-3/4" w, 18-1/4" d, 74-1/2" h 8,500.00

Gothic Revival, walnut, molded cornice, 3 glazed doors with quatrefoil and Gothic arched design, reeded stiles, shelved int., flattened ball feet, 54" w, 13" d, 71" h 1,250.00

Rococo Revival, European, c1870, ebonized oak, carved cornice, egg and dart molding, frieze with applied floral and leaf molding, 2 large beveled glass doors flanked by carved columns and curved glass sides, base with wreath carved edges, central double door cupboard carved with musical instruments, carved sides with applied carving in form of basket of fruit and flowers, surrounded by branches and ribbon wreath, 95" w, 21-1/2" d, 110-1/2" h..............................7,000.00

Victorian, Globe Wernicke, mahogany and mahogany veneer, barrister's, four stack, 59-1/2" h, 34" w 400.00

Boxes

Band, America, c1835, wallpaper cov, squirrel pattern on top, blue, pink, green and brown floral motif on sides, 14-1/2" l, 11" h, wear..950.00

Bible, English, 1674, oak, slant top, butterfly hinge, carved foliate dec and date, 28-1/2" w 21-1/2" d, 18-3/4" h..............1,350.00

Candle
Carved and painted maple, hanging, rect box, canted sides, hinged lid, shaped backplate, painted red, white, and green clusters of blossoms and berries, on black ground, Pennsylva-

nia, late 18th C, some wear to edges, 11-3/4" l, 4-1/4" d, 4" h 3,165.00

Carved and painted white pine, rect box fitted with sliding lid
  Painted green, black, and white stylized floral spring, wavy line on sides, Berks County, Pennsylvania, c1850, 9-7/8" l, 41/4" d, 3-1/4" h..460.00
  Vinegar painted spirals in tones of brown, Lebanon County, Pennsylvania, c1830, some wear to paint, 7-1/2" l, 4-1/8" d, 2-3/4" h 980.00
  Pine, old red paint, faint white inscription, name and date 1855, sliding lid, 14-3/4" l 495.00

Document, America, 19th C
Curly walnut, refinished, geometric walnut, cherry, maple, mahogany, and ebony inlay, int. dividers missing, lid mirror loose, some veneer damage, 13-3/4" l....................................440.00
Decoupage and grain paint, lid dec on both sides with prints of figures in landscape, sides with grain painted reserves, minor cracks, paint wear, losses to prints, 13-7/8" d, 8-7/8" d, 4-3/8" h 520.00
Dark brown over red paint, very minor losses, paint wear, 16" h, 8" d, 6-3/4" w 420.00
Inlay, covered with geometric inlay design, inlaid leaf on front with name "Mary," inside lined red velvet, fitted compartment tray, mirrored lid, 11-1/2" w, 8" d, 6-3/4" h 385.00
Smoked dec, ochre ground, turned feet, minor losses, paint wear, 18-3/4" w, 11-3/4" d, 16-1/2" h 260.00

Dome Top
Grain painted, America, 19th C, dark brown over gray-green paint, cracks, minor paint wear, 16" w, 9-1/4" d, 7-3/4" h 345.00
Vinegar paint, America, 19th C, dark green over putty paint, cracks, paint wear, 28-1/2" w, 14" d, 13" h 290.00
Painted dec, western Massachusetts, early 19th C, drapery swags and foliate devices in gold and red on black ground, reverse inscribed "Simon Chandler Sept. 17th 1822," paint wear, minute loss, 16" w, 8-1/8" d, 6-5/8" h 3,105.00

Dressing, Portsmouth, New Hampshire, c1810, Federal, tiger maple and mahogany, rect mirror framed by tiger maple, contrasting striped inlay flanked by ring-turned reeded engaged columns with urn finials, rect top with reeded edge and slightly bowed front above conforming case, 2 drawers outlined in contrasting striped inlay, flanked by ring-turned quarter engaged columns, turned feet, carved beaded lower edge, old finish, imperfections, 20" w, 15-3/4" d, 34-1/2" h 3,200.00

Hanging, walnut, dovetailed front corners, single lift lid, 1 int. partition in till, shaped hanging board, 11-3/4" w, 6" d, 5-3/4" h to lid, 12-1/2" h overall 715.00

Knife, mahogany
Country, ext. and int. inlay dec, some loss, 14-3/4" h 495.00
George III, late 18th C, serpentine outline, checkered banding, fitted int., minor losses, shrinkage, 9" w, 8-1/2" d, 14" h 375.00

Salt, carved walnut, rect slanted and hinged lid, 2 wells, pierced serpentine backplate, front fitted with 2 short drawers, brass knob, eastern Pennsylvania, early 19th C, patched and repaired backplate, 10-7/8" l, 7-1/4" d, 11-5/8" h..............865.00

Spice, refinished walnut, dovetailed, molded sliding lid, molded top edge, six compartment int., minor age cracks, 10" l 330.00

Trinket, Jacob Weber, Lancaster County, Pennsylvania, 1840-50, hinged rect lid, carved and painted, front fitted with metal hasp, bracket feet
  White pine, red, yellow, and black, tulip on black ground, painted with white and red house flanked by trees, sides with tulip, crazing to paint, 6-1/8" l, 3-7/8" d, 4-5/8" h 6,900.00
  Yellow pine, red, green, and black on ochre ground, stylized tulip, red house flanked by 2 pine trees, sides with tulip, 7" l, 4-1/4" d, 4-5/8" h 12,650.00

Wall, painted, America

Green painted, double backed, repainted, old make-do repair, 19th C, 12" w, 5-1/2" d, 7-1/2" h 890.00

Three tier, putty color, pine, late 19th C, minor surface imperfection, 11-3/4" w, 36-1/2" h 1,035.00

Work, America, mid 19th C, paint dec, "Nettie Dill," various floral devices, dark green ground, replaced hinges, paint wear, 9-1/4" w, 7-1/8" d, 5-1/2" h 920.00

Writing

Massachusetts, early 18th C, old painted olive green pine and oak, pine overhanging rect hinged slant lid, thumb-molded edge opens to int. with 2 divided oak compartments on rect box, applied molded base, 4 turned feet, 18" w, 11-1/2" d, 12-1/4" h 10,350.00

New England, southeastern, late 18th C, cherry, slant lid, int. with 6 compartments, 2 small drawers, old finish, minor imperfections, 24" w, 13" d, 10-1/2" h 1,495.00

Cabinets

Aesthetic Movement, c1880

Display, carved mahogany, arched crest, carved tendrils and leaf tip lunettes, open platform with pierced undulating foliate frame work, poppy carved stiles, rect beveled and mirrored glass door, short cabriole legs with tendril pierced spandrels, wired for int. lighting, 35-1/4" w, 98" h 2,750.00

Folio cabinet, ebonized and parcel gilt, 40-1/2" w, 6-1/4" d, 61" h 1,380.00

Baroque, Continental, 19th C, cabinet on stand, inlaid and polychrome fruitwood, two parts: upper: needlepoint covered case, fall front opens to inlaid cupboard door surrounded by ten inlaid drawers, molded base, two pull supports; lower: mask carved and pierced apron, heavily carved and painted legs, X-shaped stretcher, 20" w, 12-3/4" d, 41" h 3,700.00

Classical, middle Atlantic States, 1815-25, mahogany and mahogany veneer, vitrine, rect top with cockbeaded pedimented backboard over 2 glazed doors flanked by turned half engaged columns, turned legs, refinished, 28-3/4" w, 12-1/2" d, 33" h 1,840.00

Classical Revival, mahogany and mahogany veneer, three glazed doors flanked by three-quarter columns, four carved paw feet, some loss to finish 1,200.00

Colonial Revival, Chippendale Style, c1940, china, walnut veneer, breakfront, scrolled broken pediment, center urn finial, 2 glazed doors and panels, long drawer over 2 cupboard doors, 44" w, 15" d, 76" h 700.00

Country, New England, 19th C, spice, painted pine, traces of orig paint, imperfections, 7-3/4" w, 4" d, 10" h 1,725.00

Dutch Marquetry, 19th C, display case on chest, inlaid walnut, two parts; upper: arched cornice, centered ebonized floral carving, arched glazed door and sides; lower section with bombe-front, three long graduated drawers, shaped apron, ebonized paw feet, 41" w, 21" d, 72" h 4,500.00

Empire, c1825, pedestal, mahogany, circular gray marble top, cylindrical body, door enclosing shelves, plinth base, 16" d, 29" h 800.00

French Restoration, New York, c1820, console, mahogany and mahogany veneer, rect marble top, central swell front drawer over 2 molded cupboard doors flanked by plain columns capped with gilt capitals terminating in turned squatty bulbed feet, 42" w, 17-1/2" d, 36" h 1,900.00

George IV, English, c1825, library, mahogany, superstructure of 4 graduated bookshelves on either side, stand with 2 frieze drawers on one side, false drawers on reverse, trestle support with concentric bosses, downswept legs joined by turned cylindrical stretcher, casters, 36" w, 59" h 5,550.00

Georgian Style, side, late 19th C, inlaid mahogany, demilune, D-shaped crossbanded top, conforming inlaid apron, two tambour doors, inlaid sq tapering legs, brass casters, 31" w, 18" d, 32" w 2,800.00

Gothic Revival, American, c1830, parlor, carved rosewood, architectural pediment, 2 glass doors, 45-1/4" w, 13-3/4" d, 86" h 3,950.00

Hepplewhite, china, inlaid mahogany, leaded glass, velvet lined int., 63" w, 21" d, 75-1/2" h 700.00

Louis XV Style, side, c1880, ormolu mounted ebonized, D-shaped top, conforming boulle-work frieze, one cupboard door, oval boulle-work panel, flanked by two glazed cupboard doors, int. shelves, shaped forming base, 69-3/4" l, 16-1/2" d, 43" h 1,400.00

Napoleon III, c1875, side, rosewood and marquetry, gilt bronze mounts, 57-1/2" w, 16-1/2" d, 41-1/2" h 2,415.00

Neoclassic Style, Continental, buffet, inlaid yew, ormolu, glazed doors above mirrored backsplash, swan form supports, two aligned frieze drawers over cupboard doors in base, tapered feet, 60" w, 19-1/2" d, 82" h 1,750.00

Victorian, American, c1900

China, shaped crest with lion's head and carved foliage, curved central door flanked by curved glass to either side, 4 ball and claw feet, 48" w, 16" d, 72" h 1,400.00

Music, inlaid mahogany, bow front, single drawer over door, inlaid with instruments and flowers, some loss to finish on door 585.00

Candle Shields

Chippendale

American, 1760-65, carved mahogany, cylindrical turned pole, adjustable cartouche shape screen, molded and carved frame, clustered column pedestal with leafage carved ball, tripod scrolled legs carved with leafage and trailing pendant vines and fruit, scrolled feet on rect molded base, 61-1/4" h 39,600.00

Philadelphia, c1770, attributed to Thomas Afleck, carving attributed to Bernard and Jugiez, carved mahogany, turned cylindrical pole, adjustable screen with intricately carved frame, tapering fluted shaft, acanthus carved baluster, swirl gadroon carved ball, acanthus carved tripod cabriole legs overlaid with trailing husk and vines, carved hairy paw feet, 60" h 68,000.00

Regency Style, giltwood, rect panel with molded border, scrolling frame, shells and ornaments at corners with volutes, 33" w, 48" h 1,500.00

Victorian, English, 1840-50, walnut, octagonal needlepoint screen, ring-turned standard, shaped triangular platform, carved bun feet, 56-1/2" h 400.00

Candlestands

Chippendale

America, Dominican mahogany, dish turned tilt top, turned column, tripod base, snake feet, old finish and overvarnish, repairs to base, age cracks to column, repairs to hinge block, 21" d, 27-1/2" h 1,540.00

Connecticut, Hartford, late 18th C, cherry, shaped top, vase and ring-turned post and tripod cabriole leg base, arris pad feet on platforms, old refinish, imperfections, 25" h 920.00

Pennsylvania, Lancaster County, c1800, refinished walnut, tilt top, one board dish turned top, birdcage with turned posts, turned column, tripod base, snake feet and pads, age cracks in column, top flange cracked, short age cracks on top, 19" d, 29" h 2,310.00

Pennsylvania, Lehigh County, c1800, figured maple, sq top tilts and revolves over birdcage support, urn form standard, 3 cabriole legs, slipper feet, repairs to hinge on birdcage and standard, 15-1/2" h, 27-1/2" h 500.00

Country, screw type, New England, late 18th C, painted maple and pine, painted apple green, 11" d, 40" h 2,300.00

Federal

Connecticut, c1790, mahogany, sq top, chamfered platform with drawer, vase and ring-turned post on tripod cabriole base ending in arris pad feet on platforms, old refinish, 14-3/4" w, 14-1/2" d, 29-1/2" h 2,990.00

Massachusetts, c1780, mahogany, tilt-top circular dished top, vase and ring-turned post on tripod cabriole legs base ending in arris pad feet on platform, old refinish, top warped, 19-1/2" d, 27-1/4" h 865.00

Massachusetts, c1790, mahogany, circular top, vase and ring-turned post, cabriole tripod base ending in pad feet, old refinish, 13-3/4" d, 25-1/2" h 5,175.00

Massachusetts, c1790, mahogany, serpentine top, vase and ring-turned post on tripod cabriole leg base ending in arris pad feet on platforms, old finish, very minor imperfections, 19" w, 19-3/4" w, 27" h 5,175.00

Massachusetts or New Hampshire, c1800, birch, oval shaped tilt top, urn shaped pedestal, curving legs, spade feet, old refinish, top slightly warped, 22-3/8" w, 14-1/4" d, 28" h 650.00

Rhode Island, c1810, mahogany, tilt-top with serpentine sides and sq corners, vase and ring-turned post, tripod cabriole legs, arris pad feet, old refinish, 20-1/2" w, 28-1/4" h 600.00

Hepplewhite

New England, Wethersfield, Connecticut, refinished cherry, one board top with cutout ovolo corners, urn turned column, tripod base, snake feet, orig finish on underside of top, minor age cracks, 15-3/4" x 16-3/8" x 27-3/4" h 1,775.00

New Hampshire, refinished maple, vining inlay on oval top and post, sq tapering column, four spider legs, damage and old repairs, 12-7/8" x 17-3/8" x 28-1/4" h 1,210.00

Candlestand, Chippendale, attributed to Lancaster County, PA, tilt top, refinished walnut, one board dish turned top, birdcage with turned posts, turned column, tripod base with snake feet and pads, age cracks, birdcage may be replacement, 19" d, 29" h, $,2310. Photo courtesy of Garth's Auctions.

Refinished curly maple top, birch base, oval one board tilt top, turned column, tripod base, snake feet, traces of old red paint, latch replaced, 16-1/4" x 22-1/4" x 26-3/4" h 1,760.00

Windsor, New England, early 19th C, cherry, circular top, vase and ring-turned post, 4 splayed block, vase and ring-turned legs joined by conforming turned stretchers, old refinish, 18-1/2" d, 28-1/2" h 1,840.00

Chairs

Adam Style, arm, fruitwood, shaped crest rail, pierced splat, cane seat, dec seat rail, dec-tapered leg, 4 pc set ... 1,200.00

Aesthetic Movement, attributed to Herter Bros., New York, c1870, slipper, ebony inlaid maple, India Rubber Co. casters, restoration, 29-1/2" h 750.00

Art Modern

Arm and Side, Luigi Tagliabue, light wood, vertical ebony stripes, black seats, 39" h, pr 700.00

Lounge, c1955, black wire frame seat and frame, dec wooden arm rests, coiled spring seat support, 4 prong shaped splayed legs, 32-1/2" h, pr 995.00

Arts and Crafts

Arm

  L & J G Stickley, #822, U-form back, five vertical back slats, orig medium brown finish, 27" w, 20-3/4" d, 36" h, pr
  .... 920.00

  Limbert, 5 vertical slats, brand mark, overcoated, 25" w, 19-3/4" d, 38-1/2" h 230.00

  Unidentified Maker, 4 vertical back slats, orig finish, 26-1/4" w, 22" d, 38-1/2" w 290.00

Morris, L & J G Stickley, #471, six vertical side slats, adjustable bar on pegs, orig finish, replaced cushions, 32" w, 35" d, 41" h
.... 1,495.00

Dining, Limbert, c1910, oak, orig medium finish, branded mark, 17-1/4" w, 38" h, 6 pc set 2,200.00

Morris, Lifetime, No. 584, c1910, oak, orig medium brown finish, box spring and cushion, hinged back, remnant of paper label, retailer's metal tag, 29-3/8" w, 40-1/2" h 425.00

Baroque Style, late 19th C

Arm, stained beechwood, needlepoint upholstery, 46-1/2" h, pr
.... 1,495.00

Side, walnut, back elaborately carved with putto and fruit, spiral turned and carved legs, 37-3/4" h 490.00

Biedermeier, second quarter 19th C, side, fruitwood and marquetry, tablet back with scrolling foliate inlay, Neoclassical figure dec on splat, sq tapering legs 500.00

Chippendale

Boston-Salem area, 1755-85, mahogany, pierced splats above over upholstered seats, front cabriole legs, high pad feet, old refinish, minor repairs, 37-1/2" h, pr 6,900.00

Country, side, mahogany, pierced corner brackets, replaced seats, one with replaced stretcher, pr 1,760.00

Irish, 19th C, arm, mahogany, padded rect back, outscrolled padded arms, over upholstered seat, carved cabriole legs, carved paw feet, dark orange velvet upholstery 750.00

Massachusetts

  Lolling, c1780, mahogany, upholstered back with serpentine crest above shaped and beaded arms, concave molded supports continuing to molded Marlborough legs joined by stretchers, restored, 37-1/2" h, 16" h seat 1,495.00

  Side, c1780, carved mahogany, serpentine crest rail with carved terminals, pierced splat, raked stiles, trapezoidal slip seat, frontal cabriole legs ending in pad feet on platforms, chamfered rear legs, old refinish, 37" h 2,300.00

  Side, refinished mahogany, carved crest with shell and ears, pierced and carved splat, upholstered seat, cabriole legs, ball and claw feet, turned "H" stretchers, wear to base and feet, minor repairs to knee brackets, minor repairs, dark red velvet re-upholstery, glue blocks added to seat frame, 16" seat, 37-3/4" h 1,925.00

Pennsylvania, Philadelphia, 1760-90, mahogany, side, shaped crest rail with molded terminals, pierced scroll carved splat with beaded racked stiles, trapezoidal slip seat, carved shell on claw and ball feet, refinished, minor imperfections, 40" h, 17-1/4" w 9,200.00

Rhode Island, Newport, side, walnut, old finish, pierced splat and yoke crest, carved cross hatching and carved ears, balloon seat frame, turned "H" stretcher, cabriole legs, ball and claw feet, restored top lip of seat frame, old slip seat frame reupholstered in gold velvet, minor age crack in one top corner of splat, 17-1/4" seat, 38" h 4,950.00

Chippendale Style, side

Chinese, mahogany, back scrolled crest rail, padded back, over-upholstered seat, carved sq legs, open fretwork corners 275.00

English, mahogany, shaped eared crest rail, pierced and carved tracery splat, over-upholstered seat, cabriole legs with carved knees, claw and ball feet 120.00

Classical

Baltimore, c1820, attributed to John and Hugh Finley, side, painted light yellow, gilt and black painted fruit filled compotes flanked by scrolls bordered by contrasting black and green striping, caned seat, surface imperfections, 32" h, pr...750.00

Boston, c1820, side, mahogany, carved Grecian-style, figured mahogany crest above drapery carved splat, scrolled anthemion dec flanking molded stiles, acanthus carved molded front legs, old refinish, minor patch to crest, 32-1/2" h 980.00

Massachusetts, c1820, dining, mahogany, slightly concave rect crest bordered by carved beading, stay rail with reeded carved panel joining raked stiles to caned trapezoidal seat, sabre legs, refinished, 33-1/2" h, 4 pc set 1,610.00

New England, c1820, mahogany and mahogany veneer, concave paneled crests, horizontal plat on shaped stiles, slip sea on frontal saber legs joined by rounded seat frame, old refinish, 33" h, 6 pc set 1,725.00

New England, c1825, mahogany and mahogany veneer, side, Gondola-style, concave scrolled cresting vasiform splat, raked stiles, patterned horsehair upholstered slip seats, frontal sabre legs jointed by bowed seat rail, refinished, orig upholstery in fine condition, 32-1/2" h, 4 pc set 1,150.00

New England, c1830, tiger maple and maple, dining, concave cresting above horizontal splat, turned raked stiles, caned seat, ring-turned legs, joined by stretchers, old finish, 33-1/2" h, 8 pc set 2,645.00

New England, c1835, tiger maple, dining, concave crests, cane seats, refinished, 33" h, 8 pc set 3,333.00

Directorie, French, c1800, side, painted, straight molded crest rail, floral finials, lyre shaped splat flanked by fluted uprights, over upholstered seat, shaped and molded seat rail, fluted cylindrical tapering legs 1,300.00

Dutch Style, New England, 18th C, maple and ash, slat back, turned stiles joining three arched slats to the ring-turned arms terminating in mushroom handholds, vase and ring-turned supports, legs joined by turned double stretchers, rush seat, old refinish, 38-1/2" h 2,415.00

Eastlake, American, c1870, lady's, walnut, Minerva head carving on crest, incised lines, applied burl veneer panels and roundels dec, shaped hip brackets with conforming dec, shaped reupholstered back and seat, turned front legs, 36" h 425.00

Elizabethian Revival, George Huntzinger, New York, folding, arm, walnut, Berlin work upholstery 650.00

Empire, American, 1825-35

Arm, deep tufted barrel back, turned feet and arm trim with dark mahogany finish, reupholstered, 41-1/2" h 770.00

Bergére, walnut and cherry, tablet crest rail and foliate carved down scrolling arms, upholstered back, loose cushion seat, sabre legs, pr 3,500.00

Dining, mahogany, carved crest rail, shaped splat, needlepoint sets, shaped legs, 4 pc set 600.00

Empire Style, late 19th/early 20th C, arm, gilt bronze mounted mahogany, reupholstered, 35" h 4,025.00

Federal

Arm, c1790-1810, maple, straight crest rail over pierced shaped splat, outscrolled arms ending in paws, drop-in seat, sq molded legs 375.00

Lolling

English, late 18th C, mahogany, shaped crest rail, rect back, downswept armrests, over upholstered seat, sq molded legs joined by stretchers 1,100.00

Massachusetts, c1785-95, mahogany inlaid, upholstered serpentine back above serpentine arms, curving arm supports, H-stretcher base, sq line inlaid legs, castors, old surface, upholstered in light beige silk, imperfections, 15-1/2" h seat, 43-1/2" h 12,000.00

Side

Massachusetts, Salem, c1796, Salem, made for Elias Hasket Derby, merchant and ship owner, painted and decorated, oval back, painted white with five plume pained Prince of Wales splats gathered by blue painted and carved bows accented with gold and red, delicately dec with trailing green vines, blue flowers, and red roses on crest and front legs, over upholstered seats with serpentine front rails, bowed side rails, sq tapering vie dec front legs ending in spade feet, sq saber-like rear legs, imperfections, 21-3/4" w, 38-1/4" h, pr 178,500.00

New England, c1800, cherry, rect back enclosing 4 vertical spindles bordered by inlaid stringing over trapezoidal slip seats, inlaid sq legs joined by stretchers, old refinish, 35-5/8" h, set of 3 ....1,100.00

Pennsylvania, c1810, Lehigh County, paint and stencil dec, horizontal crest flanked by projecting stiles, 4 arrow-form spindles, serpentine sided bow front seat, turned tapering legs, ball feet, joined by stretchers, dec with flowers and foliage, green highlights, yellow ground 635.00

Pennsylvania, c1810, Philadelphia, grain painted and stencil dec, horizontal reverse scrolling crest, shaped stay rail dec with C-scrolls and palmettos, rush seat, ring-turned tapering legs, tall peg feet, joined by stretchers, stenciled fruit and foliage, black and yellow ground, gold and red highlights 2,070.00

Pennsylvania, c1855, brown painted, stenciled, arched crest and tapering stiles, vasiform splat, balloon form seat, ring-turned tapering legs joined by stretchers, fruit and flowers in green, blue, and red with cream and gold highlights dec, 6 pc set...1,725.00

Wing, New England, c1800, mahogany, upholstered in white damask, 44" h 1,265.00

French Empire, fauteuil, mahogany, shaped crest rail, over padded back, out-scrolled arms, over-upholstered seat, shaped cabriole legs, c1830 ....850.00

French Empire Style, side, ormolu mounted mahogany, turned crest rail, carved ears, centered ormolu mount, padded back, over-upholstered seat, ring-turned cylindrical legs, casters, late 19th C 400.00

George III, 19th C, library, mahogany, arched back, downswept arms, carved front legs, H-stretcher, 47" h 1,150.00

George III Style, late 19th C, side, mahogany, ribbon back, 40" h 345.00

Georgian Style, late 19th/early 20th C, dining, 2 arm chairs, 4 side chairs, mahogany, shaped back with Gothic splat, slip seat, shell carved seat rail, leaf carved legs, ball and claw feet, 40-1/2" h 2,300.00

Gothic Revival

American, late 19th C, arm, walnut, arched pediment, flanked by pierced arched spires over carved panel, padded back, hinged seat, carved downswept arms on spiral-turned arm supports, carved panel, grotesque carved feet.........1,800.00

New York City, c1850-60, side mahogany, carved curving crest and stay rail, serpentine front seat rail, old refinish, minor imperfections, 33-3/4" h, pr 990.00

Chairs, Hepplewhite, attributed to Benjamin Frothingham, Charleston, carved by Samuel McIntire, Salem, MA, c1780, shaped crest rail over pierced urn and floral swag carved back splat, carved fruit basket base, upholstered seat, molded tapering legs, joined by stretcher, pr. $20,000. Photo courtesy of Freeman\Fine Arts.

Grotto, Italian, mid 19th C, walnut, arm, swan form, losses, 26" h 1,150.00

Hepplewhite
Lolling, Martha Washington
Refinished cherry and birch frame, open arms with molded top edge, back frame with mortised vertical slats, sq tapered legs, old soiled and worn brocade upholstery, 44-1/4" h 1,870.00
Refinished mahogany frame, sq tapered legs, mortised and pinned "H" stretcher, frame has repairs, arms replaced, added casters, reupholstered, 43-1/2" h..............1,100.00
Side
Attributed to Salem, Massachusetts, mahogany, old finish, shield back, molded members, inlaid fan, worn reupholstered seat, sq molded tapered legs, "H" stretcher, 37-3/4" h, pr 2,420.00
Refinished mahogany, shield back with molded members, well detailed Prince of Wales feather and drapery swags, slip seat, sq tapered molded legs, "H" stretcher, reupholstered, two added glue blocks, 17" seat, 37-5/8" h........................550.00
Slipper, lady's, mahogany, Haines Connolly School, Philadelphia, 19th C, back with 4 carved spindles with flame tops, mid square rosettes, reeded sq tapered feet, castors, 32" h 200.00

International Movement
Arm, George Nakashima, walnut, slat back, four short flaring dowel legs, yellow and white stitch cushion, orig finish, c1957...1,495.00
Dining, George Nakashima, walnut, curved crest rail over six hand planed spindles and legs, sea grass seats, dowel construction, orig finish, c1957, 18" d, 26-1/2" h, price for 6 pc set...1,955.00
Lounge Chair and Ottoman
Bertoia, Harry, orange fabric, white metal base, 38" w, 35" d, 37-1/2" h, worn fabric, loose mounts 320.00
Eames, Charles, #670, manufactured by Herman Miller, black leather clip-on cushion, molded rosewood shell mounted to cast aluminum base, 34" w, 30" d, 31-1/2" h 1,610.00
Fiberglass Egg-Form, one piece, blue fabric upholstery, int. speakers, orig label, 38" w, 30" d, 46" h, minor wear 460.00

Side
Eames, Charles, manufactured by Herman Miller, yellow, gray, and blue fabric, black wire base, 19" w, 16" d, 32" h, price for 4 pc set...375.00
Nakashima, George, walnut, slat back, flaring dowel legs, removable back, dowel construction, orange and yellow stitch cushion, orig finish, 24" w, 31" d, 30" h 1,000.00
Ladderback, Pennsylvania
Arm, maple and hardwood, five graduated arched slats, turned finials, sturdy arms, turned posts, bulbous turned front feet and stretcher, replaced rush seat, old dark finish, one foot partially restored, minor age cracks in legs, 15" seat, 43" h 2,530.00
Side, Philadelphia, green painted, four slat back, replaced rush seat, bulbous turnings terminating in arrows, c1840 ....1,980.00

Louis XVI Style
Arm
17th-18th C, oak, padded rect back, bobbin-turned arms, over upholstered seat, bobbin-turned legs joined by bobbin-turned stretchers, tapestry upholstery.....................450.00
Late 19th C, gesso and painted, floral carved pierced crest rail, oval padded back, scrolling arms, over-upholstered seat, carved shaped seat rail, cabriole legs 125.00
Bergére, giltwood, acanthus leaf carved, curved crest rail, padded back, over-upholstered seat, out-curved molded crest rail, foliate carved, cylindrical tapering legs..................800.00
Child's, 18th C, walnut, upholstered back, bobbin-turned uprights, over upholstered seat, bobbin-turned legs, stretchers, pr 750.00

Queen Anne to Chippendale, transitional
Arm, attributed to RI, corner, birch, old worn finish, pierced slats and arm rail with crest, scrolled arms with turned posts, rush sheet, turned legs and stretchers, age cracks, repairs, 16" seat, 28-3/4" h..660.00
Side, mahogany, shell carved crest, balloon seat, drake feet, c1740, repairs..2,750.00

Chair, International Movement, Arne Jacobsen, Egg Chair, mfg. by Fritz Hansen, bright blue upholstery, 40" h, 36" d, $1,540. Photo courtesy of Jackson's Auctioneers & Appraisers.

Side, refinished mahogany, pierced splat with carved edge and crest, carved ears, reupholstered slip seat, turned rings, cabriole legs, duck feet and pads, crack in one post, one foot partially restored, 16-5/8" seat, 37-1/2" h........................715.00

Side, walnut, pierced splat with arrow motif, carved crest with ears, reupholstered slip seat, cabriole legs with duck feet and pads, repaired break in one side of seat frame, replaced glue blocks, knee brackets reattached, 16-1/2" seat, 37-1/2" h 1,155.00

Queen Anne

Arm, country, refinished birch and maple, traces of old red paint, vase splat and yoke crest, scrolled arms, replaced rush seat turned legs, Spanish feet, turned front stretcher, repaired splint on one back leg, 17-1/2" seat, 40-1/2" h 2,310.00

Arm, Massachusetts, mid 18th C, maple, shaped yoked crest rail above chamfered vasiform splat flanked by raked and blocked rounded stiles, scrolled arms, trapezoidal slip seat, frontal cabriole legs ending in pad feet, racked block turned rear legs, turned stretchers, old refinish, repairs, alternations, 42" h..2,760.00

Roundabout, attributed to RI, last half 18th C, walnut, orig Spanish brown paint, shaped crest projects above scrolled back rail ending in circular handholds on block vase, ring-turned stiles continuing to turned slightly swelled legs, frontal cabriole leg ending in pad foot on platform supporting ballooned slip set, joined by block vase and ring-turned cross stretcher, minor imperfections, 30-1/2" h, 17-1/2" h seat 4,315.00

Side

Boston, c1740-50, carved walnut, serpentine spooned crest rail, vasiform splat, rakes stiles, trapezoidal slip seat, frontal cabriole legs, pad feet, joined to rear chamfered legs by turned stretchers, shaped seat rail, old finish, 40" h 4,660.00

Newport, RI, or Boston, 1740-50, carved walnut, shaped crest rail centering carved shell, vasiform splat joining rounded raked stiles, slip balloon seat, frontal cabriole legs ending in pad feet on platform, joined to rear chamfered legs by turned stretchers, old finish, 40-1/2" h 34,500.00

Queen Anne Style

Arm, walnut, back scrolled crest rail, open vase shaped splat, out-scrolled arms, drop-in seat, concave seat rail centered with shell carving, cabriole legs, shell carved knees, pad feet, 19th C 1,600.00

Wing, mahogany, padded back, wings, and out-scrolled arms, over-upholstered seat, cabriole legs, pad feet, ring and block turned stretchers 400.00

Renaissance Revival

Arm, oak, carved and pierced backrest and front stretcher, block and cylinder H-stretcher base, some repairs and loss, 58" h 175.00

Side, plant seat and back, carved stretcher, some loss of finish, price for 10 pc set 250.00

Sheraton, American, c1800, polychrome dec

Side, slightly curved crest rail, five vertical and three horizontal bamboo-turned spindles, rush seat, bamboo-turned tapering cylindrical legs, double stretchers, orig red, gold, white, and yellow floral dec on black ground 225.00

Suite, 2 arms, 6 sides, old well executed repaint, red and black graining, yellow striping, gold stenciling, old rush seats, 18" seat, 34" h 3,300.00

Victorian, side, balloon back, walnut, molded curved crest rail, molded and curved horizontal splat, over-upholstered seat, molded cabriole legs, late 19th C, price for 5 pc set 375.00

William and Mary, side, Boston, maple, old mellow refinishing, molded crest with molded back posts and upholstered splat, old black leather upholstered seat, bulbous turned front stretcher, mortised and pinned back and side stretchers, turned front legs and feet, old nailed repairs, seat upholstery cracked, 43-1/8" h 6,710.00

Windsor

Arm

Bow back, bamboo turnings, saddle seat, paper label on underside "Frank Philips, Philips Mill, Pennsylvania, Bucks Co." 1,650.00

Comb back, New England, c1810, carved mahogany, scrolled arms, bamboo turnings, old black paint, repairs, 46" h 750.00

Continuous arm, turned maple, hickory, and pine, Rhode Island, c1760, arched line-incised crest with paddle terminals, vase and reel-turned supports, 13 flared spindles, shaped saddle seat, vase and reel-turned tapering legs joined by stretchers, one foot extended, formerly painted 1,150.00

Low back, maple, ash, and poplar, vase and ring turnings, saddle seat, old refinish, 29-1/2" h 1,265.00

Sack back, bowed crest, 11 spindles, concave stay rail, paddle-form terminals, oval seat, vase-turned tapering legs joined by bulbous stretchers, New England, late 18th C, repairs to seat, possibly later paint 950.00

High Chair, southeastern Massachusetts, c1780, painted, old worn red under black graining, freehand yellow dec, serpentine crest rail, circular terminals, five spindles, vase and ring-turned stiles joined to turned arms on vase and ring supports, shaped saddle seat, splayed vase and turned legs joined by turned stretchers, 35-3/4" h, 22" h seat 28,750.00

Side

Bow back, New England, early 19th C, ash and pine, shaped incised crest above shaped incised seat with pommel, old refinish, 38-3/4" h, pr 1,150.00

Chair, transitional, Philadelphia, c1760, walnut, serpentine crest rail, urn back splat, flaring arm, spooned supports, scroll and scroll carved grips, slip seat with straight seat rail, shell carved cabriole legs, claw and ball feet, $8,500. Photo courtesy of Freeman\Fine Arts.

Bow back, Pennsylvania, John Lackey, Reading, 1800, arched crest continuing to shaped stiles, flaring spindles, plank seat, faux bamboo legs joined by stretchers, branded mark..690.00

Brace fan back, New England, c1780, ash, cherry, and maple, serpentine crest with scroll carved terminals above 7 spindles with flanking vase and ring-turned stiles, shaped saddle seat joining 4 vase and ring-turned splayed legs joined by stretchers, 36" h..1,150.00

Decorated, imp "T. H. Brown Warranted," painted yellow, shaped splat centering painted reserve of fruit and leafy fines flanked by painted striping above 5 spindles, turned flattened stiles, incised balloon seats, bamboo turned legs joined by stretchers, late varnish, 33-1/2" h, 6 pc set plus matching child's chair 3,740.00

Decorated, orig red paint, yellow striping, yellow, green, and black shell and foliage dec on step down crest, arrowback, shaped seat, turned bamboo legs and rungs,18" seat, 35-1/2" h, pr 990.00

Fan back, DE, late 19th C, later green paint, brass supports on outside back rungs, underside stamped "Sampson Barnet," Wilmington..1,155.00

Fan back, New England, c1780, maple, pine, and ash serpentine crest terminating in scrolls above 7 spindles and vase ring-turned stiles, shaped saddle seats, splayed vase, ring-turned legs, shaped stretcher, 36-1/2" h, pr 2,990.00

Sack back, saddle seat, Philadelphia turnings, late 1700s 1,150.00

Chests of Drawers

Arts and Crafts, American, oak, Model No. 902, arched back rail, 2 top drawers, 4 horizontal drawers, oval hammered pulls, red decal in top right drawer, 39-3/4" w, 22" d, 53-1/2" h 4,200.00

Chest of Drawers, Philadelphia, c1765, cherry, rect molded top, notched front corners, graduated molded drawers, openwork brasses, quarter round fluted corners, ogival bracket feet, 30-1/2" w, 32" d, 32" h, $29,000. Photo courtesy of Freeman\Fine Arts.

Chippendale

Connecticut, c1780, cherry, rect overhanging top with molded edge, inverted corners, 4 graduated cockbeaded drawers, ogee bracket feet, old refinish, restoration, 39-1/4" w, 19" d, 33-1/2" h 2,645.00

Connecticut River Valley, c1780, carved cherry, rect top with applied molded edge, case with 4 graduated cockbeaded drawers flanked by ring-turned spiral carved quarter columns, ogee bracket feet, replaced brasses, restoration, 39" w, 19" d, 34-1/4" h..4,315.00

Massachusetts, Boston, 1760-80, mahogany, serpentine, rect molded serpentine and block fronted top overhangs conforming case, 4 graduated drawers surrounded by cockbeading, molded base, shaped ogee bracket feet, old color, old refinished surface, orig brass, 33-1/4" w, 17-3/4" d, 32" h 178,500.00

Massachusetts, c1780, cherry, serpentine, overhanging molded top with serpentine front, conforming cockbeaded case with 4 graduated drawers, ogee bracket feet, old finish, early replaced oval brass oak leaf pulls, 36-1/4" w, 19-3/4" d, 33-1/2" h 42,550.00

Massachusetts, c1780, mahogany and mahogany veneer, serpentine front, 4 graduated cockbeaded drawers, ogee bracket feet, old refinish, some old brasses, restoration, 40" w, 19-1/2" d, 35-3/4" h..2,875.00

Massachusetts, Salem, c1790, serpentine, mahogany, good figure, stripe, and color, pine secondary wood, serpentine top with thumb-molded edge, applied edge beading, inlaid stringing on invected corners, four dovetailed drawers, ogee feet, old finish, orig brass, age cracks in end, 38" w, 20-3/4 x 42" top, 33-1/4" h 13,200.00

New England, c1775, tall, carved maple, flat molded cornice, case with 6 thumb-molded graduated drawers, top drawer with central fan carving and faux three-drawer facade, bracket feet, old refinish, replaced brasses, restoration, 36" w, 18" d, 56-3/4" h 5,100.00

New England, late 18th C, birch and wavy birch, molded top overhangs 4 thumb-molded graduated drawers flanked by engaged quarter columns, scrolled bracket feet, old refinish, old brass, 41-3/4" w, 18-1/2" d, 39" h...............................2,185.00

New England, late 18th C, mahogany, desk on frame, slant hinged lid opens to int. of open cubbyholes with shaped dividers above compartments and small drawers, molded frame with sq legs and H-stretcher, orig surface, 36-3/4" w, 18-5/8" d, 37-1/2" h..2,875.00

New England, late 18th C, painted, cherry, rect overhanging top, case of 4 graduated drawers, bracket feet, replaced turned pulls, 40-1/4" w, 18-3/4" d, 42-1/2" h.........................1,265.00

New England, southeastern, late 18th C, maple, flat molded cornice over case of 2 thumb-molded short drawers, 5 long drawers, bracket feet, old refinish, replaced pulls, repairs, loss of height, 36" w, 17-1/4" d, 54" h...................................1,725.00

Pennsylvania, c1770, figured walnut, tall, overhanging cornice, 3 short drawers over 5 graduated long drawers flanked by fluted quarter columns, ogee bracket feet, 43" w, 23" d, 62-1/2" h 7,475.00

Pennsylvania, late 18th C, walnut, rect top with applied molded edge, 2 short drawers over 3 long drawers with cockbeading, flanked by reeded quarter columns, ogee bracket feet, old oval brasses, old refinish, minor repairs, 41-1/2" w, 20-1/2" d, 44" h..4,025.00

Pennsylvania, late 18th C, walnut, 3 over 2 drawers, dovetailed case, reeded corner cornice, dovetailed bracket feet, minor lip repair, replaced back boards, 38-1/2" w, 22" d, 40" h 3,575.00

Chippendale to Hepplewhite, transitional, refinished mahogany, pine secondary wood, serpentine top with thumb-molded edge, four dovetailed drawers with inlaid stringing, bandy feet with claw and ball, old replaced period brasses, age cracks in ends, 42-1/4" w, 25-1/2" x 45-1/2" top, 39-3/4" h 5,775.00

Classical

Vermont, Shaftsbury, 1816, maple, cherry, and tiger maple veneer, rect top with molded edge, 2 short drawers over 4 graduated drawers, inscribed "Made by Asa Loomis in the year 1816," 42-1/2" w, 19-3/8" d, 45" h 6,325.00

New England, c1825, tiger maple, rect top, large top drawer over 3 graduated incised beaded drawers flanked by ring-turned columns, turned legs on castors, old refinish, old emb brass pulls, 47" w, 22-1/2" d, 49-3/4" h 2,415.00

Federal

American, refinished cherry, poplar secondary wood, mahogany molding on top edge, 4 dovetailed drawers with applied edge molding, scrolled apron, reeded stiles, paneled ends, turned feet, banded inlay around base, old brass pulls, 39-1/2" w, 20" x 40" top, 41-1/4" h 1,210.00

Connecticut, c1790, cherry inlaid, rect overhanging top, molded edge above case of 4 incised beaded graduated drawers with inlaid quarter fans and stringing, ogee bracket feet, old refinish, 38-3/4" w, 18" d, 34-1/4" h 6,900.00

Massachusetts, 1800, cherry, rect top, cockbeaded case, 4 graduated drawers, inlaid base, flaring French feet, shaped skirt, old refinish, replaced brasses, very minor imperfections, 37-1/2" w, 19-1/2" d, 37-1/4" h 2,070.00

Massachusetts, c1800, mahogany inlaid, bow front, overhanging top with bow front and inlaid edge, conforming case with 4 cockbeaded drawers with bird's eye maple panels bordered by stringing and mahogany crossbanding, tall cutout feet, old finish, orig brass, minor imperfections, 38" w, 21" d, 34" h 4,890.00

Massachusetts, c1800, mahogany and mahogany veneer, bow front, shaped top, conforming case, 4 graduated cockbeaded drawers, flaring French feet, shaped skirt, old refinish, orig brass, 40-1/2" w, 20-3/4" d, 35-1/4" h 2,415.00

Massachusetts, 1815, carved mahogany and mahogany veneer, shaped top, bowed front, ovolo corners, beaded edge, conforming case, 4 graduated beaded drawers flanked by quarter engaged ring-turned reeded columns continuing to ring-turned swelled legs, old refinish, orig brass, imperfections, 41-3/4" w, 22-5/8" d, 41-3/4" h...1,380.00

Massachusetts, 1815-25, mahogany and tiger maple, bow front, top with bow front and ovolo corners, crossbanded edge over 4 cockbeaded graduated drawers, central tiger maple panel flanked by mahogany panels and borders, contrasting stringing and crossbanding, quarter engaged ring-turned reeded posts continuing to swelled feet, old refinish, turned pulls, minor imperfections, 40-1/4" w, 20-3/4" d, 38-1/4" h 2,530.00

Massachusetts or New Hampshire, c1820, wavy birch inlaid, bow front, top with ovolo corners, conforming case with 4 drawers, 2 satinwood panels bordered by mahogany crossbanding and cockbeading flanked by one-quarter engaged ring-turned and reeded columns, swelled legs, joined by valanced skirt with center satinwood panel, old refinish, imperfections, 39-1/2" w, 22" d, 41-5/8" h...3,450.00

Massachusetts, Salem, 1820, mahogany and mahogany veneer, rect top, ovolo corners and carved edge, 4 graduated cockbeaded drawers flanked by ring-turned reeded legs ending in turned swelled feet, old replaced pulls, old finish, imperfections, 40-3/4" w, 19-1/2" d, 41" h 1,150.00

New England, c1810, tiger maple, rect top, cockbeaded case, 4 graduated drawers, cutout base with applied reeded molding, refinished, old oval brasses, 40-1/2" w, 19" d, 39-3/4" h 5,750.00

New England, c1820, birch mahogany, rect overhanging top, case of 4 bird's eye maple cockbeaded graduated drawers, ring-turned swelled legs, refinished, replaced brasses, 39" w, 18-1/2" d, 38-3/4" h 1,610.00

New England, late 18th C, wavy birch, rect overhanging top above cockbeaded case, 4 graduated drawers, bracket feet, refinished, replaced brasses, 38-1/2" w, 19-1/4" d, 35" h 2,100.00

New Hampshire, 1820-30, cherry, bird's eye maple, and mahogany, 4 cockbeaded graduated drawers outlined in stringing, shaped veneered skirt, inlay accents on over turned legs, replaced brasses, 38-5/8" w, 19" d, 40-3/4" h.................4,025.00

New Hampshire, 1810-14, attributed to Joseph Clark, Portsmouth or Greenland, birch inlaid, rect overhanging top with bow front, case of 4 cockbeaded drawers with mahogany veneer flanked by contrasting inlaid stringing and wavy birch panels, all bordered by mahogany crossbanding, flaring French feet, center rect drop panel of wavy birch bordered by checkered and contrasting inlaid banding, old refinish, orig brasses, 39-1/2" w, 20-3/4" d, 38-3/4" h 8,050.00

Pennsylvania, c1800, inlaid figured maple, tall, overhanging cornice above 3 short drawers, 5 graduated long drawers, splayed feet, shaped apron, orig drawer brasses and escutcheons, 41-1/2" w, 22-1/2' d, 63" h 8,625.00

Pennsylvania, c1800, tiger maple, case with 2 cockbeaded short drawers over 4 graduated long drawers inlaid with diamond dorm escutcheons and stringing, flaring French feet, joined by shaped apron, refinished, replaced brasses, restoration, 37-1/2" w, 20-1/2" d, 53-1/2" h...4,025.00

Pennsylvania, c1810, inlaid figured cherry, bow front, oblong top with line inlaid edge, 4 graduated cockbeaded long drawers flanked by line inlaid canted corners, splayed bracket feet, patches to cockbeading, feet replaced, 41" w, 24-1/4" d, 38-1/2" h 1,035.00

Pennsylvania, Lehigh County, c1820, cherry, bow front, shaped top, reeded edge, 4 graduated cockbeaded long drawers, shaped apron, splayed bracket feet, 39-1/4" w, 22-1/4" d, 37-1/2" h 1,610.00

French Restoration Style, 1840-60, mahogany veneer, 4 long drawers, carved pilasters, flat sides, paw feet..............350.00

George III, English, c1800

Mahogany, bow front, shaped rect top, brushing slide over 4 long graduated cockbeaded drawers, outswept feet, 36-1/2" w, 20-1/2" d, 32" h...4,100.00

Mahogany, inlaid, shaped rect crossbanded top, 2 short cockbeaded drawers over 2 long cockbeaded drawers, shaped apron, bracket feet, 41-1/2" w, 20-1/2" d, 34-1/2" h 2,100.00

Mahogany, serpentine front, rect top, brushing slide over 4 long graduated drawers, flanked by molded canted corners, shaped block feet, 40" w, 22" d, 36-1/2" h...................2,750.00

Hepplewhite

American, mahogany veneer, bow front, 4 dovetailed drawers with applied edge beading, French feet, old replaced period eagle brasses, dust shelves, edge and veneer damage, old repairs, 34-1/2" w, 19-1/2" x 35-3/4" top, 37" h 1,650.00

Pennsylvania, walnut, molded edge top, 4 cockbeaded drawers, dovetailed case, French bracket feet, 39-1/2" w, 22-1/4" d, 34-1/2" h...3,025.00

International Movement, George Nakashima, walnut, block dovetail top, dowel construction, eight drawers, two walnut slab legs, orig finish, c1957, 72" w, 20" d, 32" h.........5,000.00

Queen Anne

American, 18th C, cherry, chestnut secondary wood, high chest, molded cornice, dovetailed case, 7 overlapping dovetailed drawers, bracket feet, orig brass, 4 replaced keyhole escutcheons, old mellow finish, age cracks, old pierced repair, minor restoration to feet, 36" w, 19-1/2" d, 51-3/8" h.............4,125.00

New England, 18th C, maple, flat molded top, case with 2 thumb-molded shorts drawers, 4 graduated long drawers, bracket feet, old refinish, replaced brasses, restoration, 36" w, 18-3/4" d, 44-1/2" h 3,750.00

New England, southeastern, c1760, tiger maple, flat molded cornice, case with 2 thumb-molded short drawers, 4 graduated long drawers, bracket feet, refinished, replaced brasses, 36" w, 19-1/4" d, 46" h..3,450.00

Renaissance Style, New England, 17th C, joined oak and pine, pine thumb-molded top over 4 drawers, applied raised moldings, splint spindles with paneled sides, heavy molded base on ball feet, applied split spindles, turned ebonized maple pulls, old Spanish brown color with black accents, restoration, 39" w, 21-1/2" d, 39-1/2" h..................................20,700.00

Rococo, Portuguese, late 18th C, rosewood, serpentine front, 3 drawers, stamped brass drawer pulls, claw and ball feet, 40-1/2" w, 10-1/4" d, 35" h..................................2,875.00

Sheraton, maple and cherry, bow front, curly and bird's-eye veneer, paneled ends, turned feet, scalloped apron, 4 dovetailed drawers with applied edge beading, refinished, 39-3/4" w, 44" h 2,500.00

Chests of Drawers, Other

Apothecary, poplar, old red paint, 9 drawers, wooden pulls, wire nail construction, one back board replaced, 7-1/2" x 11" x 11" 480.00

Chest On Chest

Chippendale, Massachusetts or New Hampshire, 18th C, maple, 2 part dovetailed case, molded cornice, graduated thumb-molded drawers, bracket base, old refinish, orig brass, 38-1/2" w, 18-1/2" d, 76-1/2" h..................................11,500.00

Chest on Chest, Queen Anne, New England, c1750, cherry, flat top, cove molded corners, bow straight front, four graduated thumb-molded drawers, lower section with one wide over three small molded drawers, brass bail, handles, escutcheons, and lock plates, shaped apron with acorn drops, cabriole legs, pad feet, 38" w, 21" d, 68" h, $5,500. Photo courtesy of Freeman\Fine Arts.

George III, c1790-1800

Flame mahogany, two parts, upper: dentil molded cornice, 2 short drawers over 3 long graduated drawers, flanked by fluted canted corners; lower: brushing slide, 3 long graduated drawers, shaped ogee bracket feet, 42" w, 22" d, 77-1/2" h..................................6,000.00

Mahogany, two parts, upper: molded cornice, 3 short drawers over 3 graduated long drawers, flanked by fluted canted corners, lower: 2 small drawers over 3 graduated long drawers, shaped ogee bracket feet, 43-1/2" w, 21-1/2" d, 76-1/4" h..................................4,025.00

Queen Anne, Pennsylvania or DE Valley, walnut, pine and oak secondary woods, crown molded cornice, fluted chamfered corners, dovetailed base, moldings around base and sections, bracket feet, worn orig finish, orig had pin brasses, Chippendale period batwing bale brass replacements, carved date inside bottom of top section "1738+ 3 mo.," some edge damage on back edge of top chest, 22-3/8" x 40-3/4" cornice, 22-1/2" x 41-1/2" base molding, 37-3/4" w, 69-1/4" h..................................41,800.00

Commode

Edwardian, c1900-10, paint dec satinwood, minor paint loss, shrinkage, 42-1/4" w, 18-1/2" d, 39-1/2" h..................................6,325.00

Federal, Salem, Massachusetts, 1800-15, mahogany, demilune top, conforming case, central cockbeaded molded drawer flanked by similar hinged compartment drawers, double cupboard doors with molded panels, 3 sliding trays, flanked by similar cupboard doors, shelves int., scalloped int., French feet, 55" w, 32" d, 40" h..................................46,200.00

Louis XV Style, c1900, marquetry inlaid fruitwood, shaped rect marble top, three long drawers, sq molded legs, 27" w, 16" d, 33-1/2" h 900.00

Louis XVI, 18th C, mahogany, eared Set Anne marble top, paneled sides, 3 graduated paneled drawers, fluted column front stiles, pilaster rear stiles, toupie feet, 45-1/2" l, 33-3/4" h 4,250.00

Highboy, Chest on Frame

Chippendale, Philadelphia, walnut, swan neck cresting with flower head terminals, carved shell and foliate scroll, fluted quarter columns, scroll carved apron, acanthus carved cabriole legs, claw and ball feet, 44" w, 95" h..................................6,600.00

Queen Anne

Massachusetts, c1760, tiger maple, top section with flat molded cornice above case of 4 thumb-molded graduated drawers, base with long drawer and central fan carved concave drawer flanked by drawers, cabriole legs, valanced apron with two turned drop pendants, old refinish, orig brasses, 37-3/4" w, 16-1/2" d, 69-1/2" h..................................28,750.00

Pennsylvania, c1760-80, walnut, top section with flat molded cornice above case of 3 thumb-molded short drawers, 2 half drawers, 3 graduated long drawers, 4 cabriole legs, carved pad feet, valanced apron, old finish, orig brasses, detailed Quaker provenance, 38" w, 22" d, 65" h 26,450.00

William and Mary, American, walnut and pine, burl veneer facade, 2 pcs; upper section: molded cornice, 5 dovetailed drawers; lower section: 3 dovetailed drawers, scalloped apron, herringbone cross banding, turned legs and feet, scalloped edge stretcher base, replaced legs and stretchers, beaded edge molding on apron and facade molding on base, some veneer and molding repairs to top, old replaced engraved teardrop brasses, 34-1/2" w, 20 x 36-3/8" cornice, 61-1/2" h..................................9,350.00

Linen Press, Georgian, mahogany, dovetailed case, top dentil molding, minor replacement to center molding, two over one cock beaded drawers, paneled bracket feet, 46" w, 24" d, 70" h..................................3,630.00

Lowboy

Chippendale Style, tiger and bird's eye maple, claw and ball feet 1,100.00

Highboy, Queen Anne, New England, c1750, maple, flat cove molded cornice over straight front, single top drawer with mock twin drawer facing over three wide thumb-molded drawers, lower section with mock triple drawer facing, center with shell carving, brass bail handles, escutcheons, and lockplates, shaped apron, cabriole legs, pad feet, 38-1/2" w, 29-1/2" d, 63-1/2" h, $7,500. Photo courtesy of Freeman\Fine Arts.

Queen Anne, walnut, satinwood inlay, rect molded edge top, 3 drawers, scalloped apron, round tapered legs, pad feet, 32" w, 19-1/2" d, 28-3/4" h..2,400.00

William and Mary, American, walnut, burl veneer, herringbone cross banding, turned legs and feet, undulating cross stretcher, scrolled apron, acorn drops, applied facade moldings, 3 dovetailed drawers, molded edge top with geometric veneer pattern, legs and stretcher old restorations, old replaced engraved teardrop brasses, 31" w, 23-3/8" x 36-1/2" top, 29-1/4" h 11,550.00

Sugar Chest, Sheraton, walnut, dovetailed case, int. divided into 3 sections, 1 drawer in base, fine turned legs, sgd "Read Atlantic Ga.," old refinish, 29" w, 18-3/4" d, 39" h 3,000.00

Cradle

Birch, hooded, dovetailed, cutout rockers, scalloped ends, 41" l 500.00

Cherry, mortised sides, scrolled detail, sq corner posts, turned finials, scrolled rockers, old dark finish, nailed repairs, 40" l 250.00

Grain Painted, New England, early 19th C, pine, yellow, ochre, and burnt umber painting simulating tiger maple, 37-1/2" w, 19-1/2" d, 25-1/2" h 395.00

Cradle, walnut, PA, c1800, scrolled heart-pierced head-board and footboard, flanked by canted reeded sides fitted with turned knobs on rockers, 40" l, $1,610. Photo courtesy of Sotheby's.

Mahogany, dovetailed, scrolled sides and ends, old dark finish, 49-1/2" l..500.00
Pine, America, late 18th C, pine, scalloped hood sides, plain bonnet top, orig finish 425.00
Walnut, Pennsylvania, c1800, scrolled heart-pierced headboard and footboard flanked by canted reeded sides fitted with turned knobs, rockers, 40" l........................1,610.00

Cupboards

Armoire

Dutch, 19th C, marquetry, inlaid walnut, broken arch pediment flanked by ball finials, inlaid frieze, long cupboard door inset with shaped rect beveled mirror, one long drawer, flanked by inlaid half columns, molded base, 52" w, 25" d, 80" h 2,500.00
French Provincial, fruitwood, shaped top, 2 cupboard shelves, int. shelves, shaped apron, scrolled feet, 52" w, 25" d, 84" h 2,400.00
Canning, orig blue paint 2,800.00

Corner

Baroque Style, Dutch, late 19th C/early 20th C, blue painted, arched crest over glazed cabinet doors, base with cupboard door, plain base, 40-1/2" w, 21" d, 89-1/2" h 1,850.00
Country
America, cherry, molded cornice, pr doors with 6 glazed panes each, 1 dovetailed drawer, raised panel doors, high feet with scalloped apron, old mellow refinishing, 46" w, 49" w at cornice, 78" h..4,675.00
New England, late 18th C
Cherry, upper case with glazed door, 2 int. shelves, lower case with 2 recessed paneled doors, 1 shelf int., old red paint with recent varnish, replaced pulls, 40" w, 20" d, 82" h 5,750.00
Pine, flat cove molded cornice, glazed door, 3 int. shelves, flanked by canted corners, base with 2 recessed paneled cupboard doors, one shelf int., ogee feet, old refinish, 45" w, 26" d, 91" h..2,415.00
New York State, 1830, cherry, glazed door in upper case, 3 shelved int., lower case with drawers above recessed paneled doors, one shelf int., refinished, old replaced pulls, 43" w, 21-1/4" d, 88" h...4,000.00
Country, English or Irish, architectural, stripped pine, traces of white paint, green repaint int., damage, pierced repairs, 35-1/2" w cornice, 71-3/4" h..990.00
Dutch, 19th C, inlaid walnut, bow front, inlaid cornice over scrolled vine frieze, one long cupboard door with elaborate marquetry inlay, conforming inlaid base, 14" w, 14-1/2" d, 75" h 2,200.00

Jelly Cupboard, pine, old red paint, molded cornice with overhanging top, door with four raised panels, rattail hinges, scrolled apron, applied base molding, high cut-out feet, 41-1/2" w, 68-3/4" h, $4,750. Photo courtesy of Garth's Auctions.

Federal, Lebanon County, Pennsylvania, c1830, paneled cherry, two parts, cove molding above 2 glazed and mullioned doors, shelved int., base with 2 paneled doors, bracket feet, 51-3/4" w, 82-1/4" h...1,610.00

Queen Anne, Connecticut River Valley, cherry, one pc, molded old replacement cornice, two raised panel tombstone panels over two sq panels on upper raised doors, molded mid strip, base two square over two rect panel doors, fluted stiles, base molding, pine backboards attached with rose head nails, old mellow refinishing, some repairs, 46" w at cornice, 42-3/4" w, 79-1/2" h..4,180.00

Court, Baroque, English, c1650, oak, two parts, upper: projecting frieze, carved flowers and fox heads, center initials "J.M.J.," inlaid and architectural carved recessed cupboard door, flanked by two dragon-carved cupboard doors; lower: rect top, floral carved frieze, two carved and paneled cupboard doors, block feet, reverse labeled "Stair and Andrew Ltd.," 58" w, 21-1/2" d, 62-1/2" h...2,100.00

Dresser, George III, late 18th C
Oak, married top and bottom, restorations, 55-1/2" w, 20" d, 77" h
....2,450.00

Oak and elmwood, upper section with scalloped cornice, 2 open shelves, one closed shelf base with 3 drawers over scalloped apron, sq tapered legs, 76" w, 16-1/2" d, 48" h upper section, 33-1/2" h base...4,025.00

Hutch
America, Federal, c1810, pine, two parts, upper: molded cornice over two long shelves; lower: rect surface over three short drawers, two cupboard doors, conforming base, 86" w, 24" d, 81" h...3,750.00

New England, early 19th C, grain painted, flat molded cornice above 3 open shelves over cupboard door with 2 vertical raised panels flanked by molding painted gray, dark gray swirl design, red-orange int., paint wear, 28" w, 15" d, 80" h
....5,465.00

Jelly
America, pine, old red paint, molded cornice with overhanging top board, single door with four raised panels, rattail hinges, high cutout feet with scrolled apron, applied base molding, 46-1/2 x 16" cornice, 41-1/2" w, 68-3/4" h.................4,730.00

America, walnut, dovetailed gallery, solid sides, 2 raised panel doors, 1 linen fold drawer, wooden pulls, scalloped apron, 47-1/2" w, 18" d, 48" h..350.00

New Jersey, early 19th C, pine, painted paneled and carved, molded overhanging top, cupboard with applied moldings, fluting, and raised paneled cupboard doors, bottom drawer, shaped base, 3 shelved int., old red wash, replaced hardware, minor imperfections, 40-1/2" w, 17-1/4" d, 48" h
....3,450.00

Kas
Baroque, German, 18th C, walnut, molded cornice, two long paneled cupboard doors, molded base, bun feet, 80" w, 32" d, 86" h
....4,200.00

Hudson River Valley, 18th C, cherry, heavy cornice molding over paneled doors, 2 shelved int. base with single paneled drawer, heavy turned feet, replaced pulls, refinished, restored, 62" w, 21" d, 69-3/4" h..2,415.00

Kitchen, country, pine, old worn patina, six board type construction, 1 board ends, high cutout feet, old paper can labels, 39-3/4" w, 20" d, 34-1/2" h..440.00

Pewter
Country, Lebanon County, Pennsylvania, c1770, painted blue, red, and buff, pine, two parts, upper section with overhanging cornice, 2 open shelves flanked by scrolling sides, projecting base below with molded edge, 1 long drawer with raised panel cupboard door, shelf int., molded base, bun feet, paint of later date, 48" w, 15-1/4" d, 79" h.......................................1,150.00

William and Mary, early 18th C, pine and poplar, old refinishing, some old red repaint, open shelves with cutouts for spoons, plate rails, molded cornice with scalloped rail, paneled doors with rat tail hinges, cutout and scalloped ends, bracket feet, apron drop, portions of feet restored, wear, age cracks, edge damage, found near Gettsyburg, Pennsylvania, 56" w, 12-1/2 x 61-1/2" cornice, 20 x 56" base, 80-3/4" h................6,050.00

Pie Safe
American, sliding door, attached walnut cabinet, star tin punched dec...3,600.00

Ohio, Zanesville, poplar, 2 doors with 12 punched tin panels with snowflake type designs, paint stripped, later red wash
....1,980.00

Pennsylvania, first half 19th C, walnut, rect top, 2 short drawers, 2 cupboard doors, each mounted with 3 punched tin panels depicting quarter-round spandrels centering diamond motif, sq tapering legs, 41" w, 17-3/4" w, 53-1/2" h..............2,590.00

Press, Jacobean Style, 18th C, oak, two parts: upper: overhanging carved cornice, one cupboard door; lower: two short drawers over one cupboard door, molded base, 39" w, 24-1/2" d, 68-1/2" h...1,400.00

Schrank, Pennsylvania
c1750-80, Bucks County, walnut, stepped overhanging cornice, 2 raised paneled cupboard doors, shelved int., paneled sides, mid-molding, 2 short drawers below flanked by diamond appliques, base molding below, bracket feet, orig brasses and wrought iron lock, small repair to left corner of cornice, 75" w, 26" d, 77" h...7,475.00

Pie Safe, poplar with orig red and black graining, gold stenciling and "Octagon Safe Pat'd 1870," four sides have solid raised panels, four sides have screen panels, door with two screened panels, cut-out feet, int. revolving rack holds 40 pies, molded cornice on seven sides, flat back, cast iron latch with white porcelain latch, attributed to IN, 36" w, 67-1/2" h, $1,650. Photo courtesy of Garth's Auctions.

c1770, figured walnut, overhanging cornice, 2 raised paneled cupboard doors, flanked by and centering paneled stiles, 3 short drawers below, ogee bracket feet, 86" w, 28" d, 84" h 43,700.00

Step Back, country

New England, early 19th C, painted pine, cornice molding above 3 raised panel doors, 3 shelved int. above single paneled door opening to one shelf int. base, molded base, painted red, replaced hardware, 36" w, 15-1/2" d, 80-1/2" h 2,415.00

One pc, butternut and poplar, blue repaint on case and door frames, brown finished on poplar panels, two pairs of doors, wooden latches and knobs, 35" w, 18-1/4" d, 71-1/4" h 770.00

Two pc, poplar, orig dark finish, 7' h, 42" w 3,350.00

Store, grain painted, Massachusetts, mid 19th C, glazed door, 4 shelf int., two recessed panel doors with one shelf int., old brown graining, imperfections, 70-3/4" w, 16" d, 78" h, pr 5,175.00

Cupboard, Schrank, PA, c1770, figured walnut, overhanging cornice, two cupboard doors flanked by and centering paneled stiles, sides with similar dec, three short drawers below, ogee bracket feet, orig brass hardware and finish, 7'2" w, 28" d, 7' h, $43,700. Photo courtesy of Sotheby's.

Wall

Maine, mid 19th C, grained pine, molded top, paneled door, 4 turned ball feet, orig simulated crotch mahogany graining in ochre, and red brown, turned wooden pull, minor imperfections, 41-1/2" w, 17-1/4" d, 85" h 4,600.00

New England, c1850, Gothic, shaped gallery above 3 glazed doors, arched panels flanked by conforming side panels, painted red-brown, 23-1/2" w, 9" d, 23" h 345.00

Pennsylvania, c1840, red painted poplar, two part, overhanging cornice above 2 glazed doors, shelved int., projecting lower section with 3 short drawers, 2 raised panel cupboard doors, turned tapering legs, ball feet, orig Sandwich glass drawer pulls 16,100.00

Desks

Art Nouveau, French, Majorelle, wood and gilt mounts, center drawer, pull-out wing table top with two drawers and letter holders at side, 48" l, 30" d, 48" h 17,250.00

Arts and Crafts, Gustav Stickley, c1902, partners, flat rect top, central drawer, pullout writing surface, 4 drawers on either side, wooden pulls, lower shelf with kneehole, V board sides, prominent key tenons, mirrored on opposing side, large red signature, retailer's mark, minor older surface nicks, waxed finish, 60" l, 40" d, 30" h 7,000.00

Chippendale

Boston area, 1750-70, mahogany, block front, carved slant lid, int. with fan carving, end-blocked concave and serpentine drawers, open compartments and prospect door flanked by capitals with flame finials above case of blocked graduated drawers, molded base with central drop, 4 ball and claw feet, old refinish, orig brass, 41" w, 22-1/2" d, 44-1/2" h 48,300.00

Massachusetts, block front, mahogany with good figure, slat front with fitted stepped int. with blocked detail, 3 carved fans, dovetailed drawers and pigeon holes, 4 dovetailed drawers, beaded frame, bracket feet conform to blocking on facade, old finish, several hidden drawers, old brasses, minor edge damage, old pierced repairs, two feet on one side ended out, lid lip restored on 3 edges, hinges replaced, pull out lid supports replaced, center int. door replaced as well as small hidden drawers, 41" w, 22" d, 33-1/4" writing height, 44" h 8,800.00

Massachusetts, c1780, oxbow slant front, mahogany, int. of small drawers, valanced compartments, flanking prospect door with small drawers behind, case with 4 graduated cockbeaded drawers, light finish, replaced brasses, 41-7/8" w, 22" d, 43-1/2" h..3,910.00

Massachusetts, c1785, slant front, cherry and tiger maple, fitted int. with central molded door flanked by document drawers, valanced compartments and drawers, 4 long thumb-molded drawers, bracket feet, center drop pendant, old refinish, old replaced brasses, minor imperfections, 35-5/8" w, 18-3/4" d, 41-5/8" h...4,315.00

Massachusetts, c1785, slant front, carved mahogany, fitted int. of fan carved prospect door flanked by document drawers with flame carved finials on columns and valanced compartments plus fan carved concave drawers, blocked cockbeaded case with 4 graduated drawers, shaped center pendant, carved cabriole legs ending in ball and claw feet, old refinish, replaced brasses, minor imperfections, 41-3/4" w, 22" d, 44-1/4" h 25,300.00

Massachusetts, c1785, slant front, maple, stepped int. of valanced compartments, document drawers, and small drawers, case with 3 graduated long drawers, refinished, replaced brasses, repairs, 34-5/8" w, 17-5/8" d, 43-3/8" h 4,600.00

New England, c1790, mahogany, fall front, lid opens to int. of 9 drawers, 8 valanced compartments, case with 4 incised cockbeaded graduated drawers, bracket feet, old refinish, old oval brasses, 39-1/4" w, 18-1/2" d, 42" h..............................3,740.00

Pennsylvania, Oley Valley, Berks County, c1770, carved and figured walnut, slant front, hinged molded lid, int. fitted with 8 valanced pigeonholes, 6 short drawers, centering prospect door revealing 4 graduated short drawers, case with 4 graduated thumb-molded long drawers, flanked by fluted quarter columns, ogee bracket feet, 40-1/4" w, 22-1/2" d, 43-1/4" h 9,775.00

Pennsylvania, c1780, walnut, slant front writing surface, fitted int. 8 valanced pigeon holes, 6 drawers, 2 document drawers, center compartment with 4 drawers, 4 lower drawers, reeded quarter columns, replaced feet, 39-1/2" w, 30" writing height, 40-1/2" h..2,530.00

Desk, Chippendale, American, c1790, cherry, slant front, rect dovetailed top, five drawers, six pigeon holes over three graduated drawers, later claw and ball feet, orig period brass pulls with grape cluster motif, 40" x 39" x 18", $880. Photo courtesy of Jackson's Auctioneers & Appraisers.

Rhode Island, Newport, c1750, carved mahogany, fall front opens to int. with central carved concave prospect door, 3 concave carved drawers, flanked by 2 carved valance drawers, 2 compartments, blocked drawer and shell carved drawer above 2 concave drawers, case with 4 thumb-molded graduated drawers, ogee bracket feet, refinished, orig brasses, 37" w, 19" d, 42" h...29,900.00

Colonial Revival, Governor Winthrop style, c1920, mahogany veneer, serpentine front, solid mahogany slant front, fitted int., 2 document drawers, shell carved center door, 4 long drawers, brass pulls and escutcheons 600.00

Country, New England or New York state, early 19th C, store keeper's, grain painted, pine, top lists to opening with valanced compartments and single drawer, stand with 2 drawers, shaped skirt, sq legs, stretcher base, late 19th C brown and gold graining, 33" w, 20" d, 48" h 1,840.00

Dutch Colonial, 18th C, slant lid, painted red, part ebonized, 4 long drawers, brass escutcheons and teardrop pulls, side handles, int. mkd "SSM 1743," backboards inscribed "SS MARTA GTB," areas of repaint, restorations, 38-1/4" w, 20" d, 39-1/2" h..4,600.00

Edwardian, inlaid walnut, arched backsplash, retractable mirror, green leather inset writing surface, flanked by stepped gallery, each side with spring loaded retractable pencil case, one long drawer, sq tapering legs, castors, 29-1/4" w, 21" d, 35-1/2" h 1,300.00

Edwardian Style, lady's, early 20th C, mahogany and inlay, galleried top, glazed upper section tambour enclosing drawers, writing slope and drawer, shelf stretcher, spade feet, 29-1/4" w, 19-1/2" d, 54" h..1,650.00

Empire, refinished cherry, pine and poplar secondary wood, slant front, fitted int. with curly maple trim, 6 drawers, 4 more behind center door, 4 dovetailed drawers with applied edge molding, turned and role carved pilasters with carved ionic capitals, turned legs, scalloped apron, clear lacy glass pulls on large drawers, opalescent glass pulls on int. drawers, some edge damage and age cracks to lid, 39-3/4" w, 21-1/2" d, 48-1/4" h..1,870.00

Federal

American, butler's, c1800, mahogany and bird's eye maple, shaped rect top, hinged front, leather inset writing surface, three long drawers, flanked by reeded columns, reeded cylindrical feet, castors, orig brass inscribed "W. J.," 46-1/4" w, 22" d, 43-1/4" h 1,700.00

American, slant front, c1820, walnut, rect top, hinged slant front, fitted int., four long graduated cockbeaded drawers, shaped bracket feet, 39" w, 19-1/2" d, 41-1/2" h 3,750.00

Massachusetts, c1800, mahogany and mahogany veneer inlaid, slant front, int. with central prospect door flanked by 3 drawers, 4 valanced compartments, case with 4 cockbeaded graduated drawers, flaring French feet, valanced skirt with stringing and crossbanding, old finish, old oval brasses, minor replacements, 41-1/2" w, 20" d, 42-1/2" h...................3,105.00

Massachusetts, c1820, bookcase and desk, mahogany veneer, shaped pediment above glazed doors, shelved int., small drawers over baize lined writing surface, cockbeaded drawers flanked by spiral carved columns, turned legs, old refinish, old pulls, imperfections, 36-1/4" w, 18" d, 65-1/2" h 1,610.00

Massachusetts, c1820, tiger maple and mahogany inlaid, top section with crossbanded cornice board above 2 tambour doors, int. of 9 valanced compartments, 15 drawers with mahogany cockbeaded surrounds, center prospect door, pen and ink on paper "Commandments 10" within arched glass panel set in mahogany panel and framed by tombstone stringing, lower section with fold-out writing surface, 2 cockbeaded long drawers, straight skirt joining block ring-turned tapering legs, old refinish, replaced pulls, minor restoration. 39-1/4" w, 18-1/2" d, 54" h 19,500.00

New England, early 19th C, tiger maple, fall front, int. of 7 valanced compartments, 12 drawers, case of 4 cockbeaded drawers, turned pulls, old refinish, imperfections, feet lacking, 20-3/4" w, 45-1/2" d, 50" h 3,450.00

Hepplewhite, ladies, attributed to Salem, Massachusetts

Refinished mahogany with inlay, pine secondary wood, 2 sections, upper: tambour doors and center door with fitted int., with pigeon holes and 5 dovetailed drawers, stringing on drawers, top with stringing with husks on pilasters, center door has stringing with invected corners, and oval medallion of figured veneer and banded outline, lower: fold down writing shelf, 4 dovetailed drawers, applied edge beading, bracket feet, inside backboards sgd "Made in the year of our Lord and Savior Jesus Christ 1802, by Thomas R. Williams," minor repairs to feet, top slightly warped, replaced eagle brasses, 39" w, 20-1/4" d, 47-3/4" h 3,850.00

Refinished mahogany, figured veneer, crossbanded mahogany inlays, figured satinwood, and stringing, 2 sections, upper: 3 doors, 3 drawers, fitted int. of drawers and pigeon holes, lower: fold down writing surface, 3 dovetailed drawers with applied edge beading, sq tapered legs, minor age cracks and veneer damage, hinges and brasses replaced, 42" w, 20-1/4" d, 53-1/4" h 2,420.00

Louis XVI Style, cylinder, vernis-martin painted gilt metal mounted mahogany, rect variegated white marble top with 3/4 pierced gallery, 3 paneled drawers, painted cylinder front, writing slide and drawers, circular tapering fluted legs, 36" w, 45" h 2,200.00

Queen Anne

Boston, c1750, block front, kneehole, carved mahogany, thumb-molded top with blocked front, conforming case, valanced drawer above arched raised paneled door opening to shelves flanked by tiers of short drawers, blocked molded bracket base, old refinish, old brasses, imperfections, 35" w, 19-1/4" d, 31" h..20,700.00

Country, attributed to Connecticut, refinished pine and maple, slant top lid, fitted int. with 4 drawers, pigeon holes, base frame with mortised and pinned apron with deeply scalloped edge, 1 dovetailed drawer, turned tapered legs, duck feet, replaced legs, feet with edge damage, repairs, 32-3/4" w, 18" d, 38-1/2" h, 29-3/4" writing height 7,700.00

Office Suite, Renaissance taste, Continental, 19th/20th C, hand carved oak, three pc bookcase with central glass door flanked by blind doors with carved figural busts of cavalier in plumed hat between fluted columns, base with large carved acanthus corbels and rosettes, four claw feet, cornice of scrolled acanthus and winged cherubs, egg & dart and leaf & dart moldings, 10" x 79" x 22", matching desk with eight carved claw feet, 66"x 31" x 33", executive acanthus carved claw foot armchair with leather seat, two matching chairs, $9,900. Photo courtesy of Jackson's Auctioneers & Appraisers.

Dough box, pine and turned poplar, rect removable top, tapering well, splayed-ring turned legs, ball feet, 38" w, 19-3/4" w, 29-1/2" h, PA, 19th C, $400. Photo courtesy of Sotheby's.

Massachusetts, 1730-50, walnut, slant lid, hinged lid, two inlaid stellate devices opens to int. of open valanced compartments above small drawers, stellate inlaid prospect door, flanked by turned columns, opens to int. with small drawer, case with 4 graduated line-inlaid drawers, bracket feet, replaced brasses, surface imperfections and repairs, 38" w, 19-1/2" d, 43" h 5,500.00

Renaissance Revival, Boston, c1857, oak, carving attributed to Thomas U. Walter, stamped "Doe, Hazelton & Co.,/Manufacturers/Boston, Massachusetts," brass plaque engraved "John Hill/New Jersey," provenance includes service at US Senate 14,950.00

Sheraton, school master's, country, cherry, old mellow finish, slant lid with pull out supports, fitted int., 3 dovetailed drawers, 7 pigeon holes, 1 dovetailed drawer, turned legs, 1 pigeon hole bracket missing, age cracks in lid, top board and low crest replaced, 29-1/2" w, 22" d, 38" h 770.00

Victorian

Davenport, American, c1875, mahogany and ebonized, shaped and carved backsplash, rect top over projecting, hinged slanted front, int. fitted with three drawers, one short pencil drawer, four long side drawers, paneled front, flanked by turned pilasters, bun feet, 21-1/2" w, 25" d, 32-1/2" h 350.00

English, late 19th C, burl walnut, carved pierced crest, two cupboard doors, flanked by four short drawers, projecting shaped rect surface over writing slide, one long drawer, flanked by four short drawers, carved cabriole legs, scroll feet, 44-1/2" l, 28" d, 52" h...1,200.00

Roll-Top, Boston, late 19th C, oak, rect top, retracting roll top, fitted int., two pedestal each with three short drawers and one deep drawer, 54" w, 35" d, 43-1/2" h 1,500.00

William and Mary, English, desk on stand, 33-1/2" h........495.00

Wooten, America, c1880, standard grade, orig finish..11,550.00

Dry Sinks

Chippendale, America, 19th C, cherry, 2 paneled doors on top, rect sing over 2 paneled base doors, 46" l, 23-1/2" w, 77" h 1,250.00

Country, America, mid to late 19th C

Pine, paneled doors, 1 drawer, crest, 54" l, 17-1/2" d, 30" h 500.00

Poplar, crest, off center door with swing-out attached shelf, simple cutout feet, orig cast iron thumb latch, stripped finish, 33" x 18-1/2" x 26" 395.00

Grain Painted, America, mid 19th C, simulated oak graining, cupboard top with 2 paneled doors, hood opening over dry sink, base with four graduated drawers, 2 cupboard doors, cast iron hardware, 54" w, 21-1/2" h, 78" h 1,500.00

Hat Racks and Hall Trees

Art Nouveau, French, c1900, carved walnut, thumb-molded cornice over shaped mirror plate, molded tendril border, serpentine projecting shelf, panel carved at sides with tendrils and leafy sprays, shaped feet, 50" w, 85" h 1,500.00

Arts and Crafts, Gustav Stickley, c1904, Model No. 53, 4 iron hooks on 2 tapering posts, 2 hooks on rect exposed tenon cross brace, 22" w, 65-1/2" h 1,850.00

Baroque Style, walnut, pierced scrolled crest, scrolled arms, hinged seat, 47" w, 15-1/2" d, 35-1/4" h 325.00

Classical, New England, maple, turned and acanthus carved post, 15 clothes supports, ball finial, scrolled legs, 79" h 1,400.00

Federal, New England, 1820-30, maple, acorn shaped finial, 14 shaped pegs descending full length of single post, ring-turned shaped vase base, 3 scrolled legs, 70-1/2" h 1,400.00

Victorian

Carved wood, mother bear at base of tree, bear cub near top, glass eyes, metal pan, 19" d wide base, top branches 20" w, 78" h 6,600.00

Cast Iron, Jack and the BeanStalk, figural, old green and gold repaint, English registry number, 33-1/2" h 425.00

Walnut, intricate carving, 6 small and 2 large shelves, stained, mirror back, 46" w, 14" d, 90" h 850.00

Hall tree, Victorian, mahogany, carved and molded detail, brass trim, six brass hooks, mirrors, red marble insert in base, 62-1/2" w, 85" h, $1,650. Photo courtesy of Garth's Auctions.

Magazine Racks

Arts and Crafts

Limbert, Michigan, c1910, 4 open shelves centered by flat sides, cutout circles at base, branded, refinished, 20" w, 14" d, 36-1/4" h 650.00

Michigan Chair Co., c1912, panel sided, rect top, 5 shelves each with 6 "V" grooved boards, projecting pins, dark finish, 1-3/4" w, 11-3/4" d, 45-1/2" h..725.00

Stickley, Gustav, Toby, pedestal, sq top, applied corbels on carved flat sides, 4 open shelves, orig tacked leather strips, 14" w, 12-3/4" d, 34-1/2" h...450.00

George III, 19th C, mahogany, rect case, ring-turned stiles, conforming shelf stretcher, ring-turned cylindrical legs, castors, 16-3/4" w, 14" d, 18-1/2" h...500.00

Victorian, American, c1850

Mahogany, 3 sections formed by columnar arcades, basal drawer, turned legs, 19" w, 14" d, 19" h.............................1,200.00

Walnut, 2 handles, 4 compartments, pierced scrolled ends, turned supports, castors, 23" l, 18" d, 20-1/2" h 600.00

William IV, early 19th C, rosewood, twin bow form end crest rails, scrolling supports, joined by divider rails, 2 compartments, rect dais, C-scroll legs, paw feet, 19-1/2" w, 17-1/2" d, 19" h 1,700.00

Mirrors

Art Deco, carved fruit and foliage at crest and on sides, 31" l, 41-1/2" h 75.00

Art Nouveau, wrought iron, octagonal reticulated internal edge, upper part mounted by stylized fountain and floral ground, beveled edge mirror, stamped "E Brandt" lower right corner, 43" l, 38-1/2" w 63,800.00

Arts and Crafts, Michigan Chair Co., Grand Rapids, MI, 1915, wall, shaped cutouts, center rect mirror, scalloped details, orig paper label, 35-1/2" w, 23-1/2" h 125.00

Chippendale, America or England, late 18th C, wall

Mahogany and parcel gilt, scroll, carved gilt gesso shell and foliate device in crest above molded and gilt incised liner, minor imperfections, 18-3/4" w, 36" h 1,955.00

Mahogany veneer on pine, carved moldings with old regilding, floral garlands and rosettes with phoenix finial, old mirror glass, some edge damage and old repair, 57" h, 27-1/4" w 10,450.00

Mahogany veneer on pine, scroll, gilded liner, some veneer damage, old veneer repair, 39-3/4" h, 21" w 2,100.00

Mahogany veneer on pine, scroll, regilded phoenix crest ornament and liner, orig mirror with very worn silvering, refinished, minor repairs, gilding on phoenix flaked, 30-1/2" h, 17" w 1,430.00

Walnut veneer, scroll, 15-3/4" x 9-1/4" old mirror, 26" x 15-3/4" 360.00

Walnut and gilt gesso, scrolled frame, gilt gesso phoenix in pierced cresting above molded gilt incised liner, label "Nathaniel Blake at 56 Cornhill (opposite the Statehouse) English, India & Hardware Goods," refinished, restorations, 22-3/4" w, 41" h 2,185.00

Classical, girandole, gilt gesso, eagle figure on foliate and grapevine cresting over circular molded frame, ebonized liner, flanking candle scones, repainted, imperfections, 28-1/2" w, 41-1/2" h...2,530.00

Empire, American

Pier, mahogany, rect mirror plate, surmounted by slip, conforming leaf carved, ring and block turned frame, 21" w, 35" h, c1820 .... 325.00

Two Part, frame with half turnings and corner blocks, old dark refinish, orig reverse painting with church and trees in green, yellow, white, blue, and brown, orig discolored mirror, 28-1/4" h, 13" w 275.00

Wall, flame mahogany, ogee-molded frame, rect mirror plate, c1850, 27-1/2" w, 37" h 175.00

Federal

Dressing, New England, C1820, mahogany and mahogany veneer inlaid, rect inlaid mirror frame, turned supports, projecting boxed case, 2 short drawers, turned feet, refinished, 18-1/2" w, 7-1/2" d, 21-1/2" h...300.00

Pier, giltwood, c1800

Molded cornice, spherules, floral carved tablet over eglomise painted tablet, rect mirror plate flanked by double spiral turned columns, 19-1/2" w, 33" h.............................600.00

Rect mirror plate, conforming molded frame, reverse-glass painted tablet and eagle finial, 21-1/2" w, 52" h.................4,500.00

Wall

American, c1800, giltwood, ebonized wing-spread eagle finial with suspended ball and chain in beak, plinth and beribboned crest, circular convex mirror plate, ebonized slip, spherules, acanthus leaf and acorn pendant, 25" w, 51" h 3,250.00

Boston, gilt gesso, cornice with spheres above reverse painted tablet of 2 children dancing within a stenciled foliate and star border, mirror plate with flanking molded spiral pilasters, labeled "Edward Lothrop #53 Marlborough Street, Boston," minor imperfections, 13-1/2" w, 30-1/2" h 1,150.00

Mirror, George III, c1760, mahogany and gilt carved, gesso fret scroll, gilt exotic bird cartouche with gilded leafy tendrils to edge, 48" h, 22" w, $2,800. Photo courtesy of Freeman\Fine Arts.

Boston, split baluster painted and gilded, labeled "Bittle and Copper Burnish Guilders No. 28 Court St...Boston," black painted and gilt frame, reverse painted eglomise tablet of woman standing in courtyard against red draped green ground, franked by blue above mirror plate, regilding, 20-1/4" w, 40-1/2" h 1,035.00

Massachusetts, c1810, gilt gesso, cornice with applied spiral molding and foliate banding above eglomise tablet of castle ruins, white and blue background, over mirror plate flanked by fluted half columns, minor imperfections, 24" w, 45" h..2,415.00

Massachusetts, c1815, gilt gesso, cornice with applied spheres above central panel, applied water leaf and acorns, eglomise tablet of flower filled urn framed in silver on white background above mirror plate flanked by spiral molded pilasters, 19-3/4" w, 44" h, minor imperfections 1,850.00

Massachusetts, c1820, gilt gesso, molded cornice with applied spherules above eglomise tablet of cottage, mirror plate flanked by concave molding with applied spherules, minor imperfections, 23" w, 38-1/4" h 1,035.00

New England, c1800, gilt gesso, molded cornice with applied balls, eglomise tablet with battle of Lake Erie, mirror plate flanked by pillars with applied foliage devices, 20" w, 35-3/4" h..920.00

George II, late 18th C, wall, walnut, rect mirror plate, pierced, carved, and scrolling frame, 20-1/2" w, 35" h............1,300.00

George III, c1800, walnut and parcel-gilt, rect mirror plate, parcel-gilt slip, conforming carved and scrolling frieze, 23-3/4" w, 43" h 450.00

Hepplewhite, shaving, mahogany veneer, serpentine, 3 dovetailed drawers, ogee feet, oval mirror, beaded edge standards, some edge and veneer damage, replaced wooden knobs, 17-3/4" w, 8" d, 22-1/2" h....................................495.00

Neoclassical, Scandinavian, c1825, mahogany and parcel gilt, relief swan scene above rect plate, flanked by columns, 23-1/2" w, 60" h 1,250.00

Queen Anne

American, walnut veneer on pine, scrolled crest

Applied gilded ornaments, molded frame, gilded line, old beveled glass, brief biography of previous owner, Christian Meyer, attached to backboards, minor veneer damage, refinished, gilding redone, 47" h, 19-1/4" h..............2,640.00

Fretwork side garlands, gilded liner, old refinishing, regilding work and flaking, old damage and repairs, old mirror glass, 24-1/4" w, 39-1/4" h..3,740.00

England, 1730-50, walnut and gilt gesso, scrolled crest centering pierced and carved foliate device above molded and gilt incised liner, 2 part beveled glass, old finish, 16-1/4" w, 40-1/2" h 8,625.00

Rococo, Italian, mid 18th C, wall, giltwood, rect plate, conforming frame, foliage carved corners and mirrored slips, 22" w, 27" h 1,000.00

Rococo Style, ebonized and parcel-gilt, overmantel, five shaped rect mirror plates, carved panels, conforming elaborately carved frame, surmounted by cartouche, 95" l, 44-1/2" h 1,200.00

Sheraton, attributed to Albany, New York, architectural, gilded frame, eglomise reverse glass painting, orig mirror glass discolored, replaced painting, old regilding with some flakes, 41-1/4" h, 23-3/4" w..770.00

Victorian, late 19th C, cheval, walnut, rect mirror plate, brass inlaid surround, spiraled supports with candleholders, curved legs, large brass feet, 71-1/2" h................................1,495.00

Rockers

Art Furniture, Adirondack, American, early 20th C, bent rustic twigs and branches, interwoven latticework back and downswept arms, round seat, curlicue seat 350.00

Arts and Crafts, Gustav Stickley, c1904, Model No. 303, oak, 4 horizontal back slats, canvas seat, wide seat rail, orig paper label, 14" w, 16" d, 33" h 395.00

Boston, America, mid 19th C, grain painted, gilt stenciled dec, rosewood grained seat..750.00

Eastlake, America, late 19th C, mahogany platform, incised and pierced cresting over sq panel back, center, padded reeded arms, velvet seat upholstery, reeded supports 275.00

Ladder Back, American, 19th C, walnut, bud finials, turned uprights, four out-curved horizontal splats, turned legs, joined by double stretchers, rocker base 225.00

Sheraton, country, maple, rush seat, refinished................100.00

Windsor, Middle Atlantic States, mid 19th C, painted and dec, low back, old mustard color, old black paint accents, 26-1/2" h
....635.00

Secretaries

Art Nouveau, attributed to Walter Gropius, Austria, c1900, oak and oak veneer, secretary top, adjustable shelves, slant id, butterfly spines and shaped vertical straps, fitted int., paneled sliding doors, conforming wall shelf, unsgd, remnants of Holland American Line label, veneer loss, 50-3/4" w, 16-1/2" d, 115" h..750.00

Chippendale

Boston Area, 1770-1800, carved mahogany, scrolled pediment with carved rosettes above cyma curved paneled doors flanked by pilasters, int. of open bookshelves surrounded by small valanced compartments and row of open pigeon holes above desk with blocked and fan carved int. with small drawers flanking concave prospect door flanked by columns with turned finials on stepped bases, cockbeaded case, 4 graduated block front drawers, molded ogee bracket base, replaced brasses, restoration, 40-3/8" w, 22-3/8" d, 95-1/2" h.. 14,950.00

New England, 18th C, tiger maple, broken arch top, flame finials, arched blind doors, inlaid slant top, valanced pigeon holes, 12 drawers, 2 document drawers, dovetailed case with 4 drawers, reeded quarter columns, replaced bracket feet, 36" w, 10" d, 56" h top, 38-1/4" w, 22-1/2" d, 7'5-1/2" h overall
....20,075.00

Chippendale Style, handmade, block front, claw and ball feet, fan carved lid, 35-1/2" w, 20-1/4" d, 91-3/4" h 2,400.00

Classical

New England, c1830, mahogany and mahogany veneer, flat molded cornice above 2 glazed doors, Gothic arched mullions, shelved int. above 3 short external drawers on projecting base, fold-out writing surface, ogee molded long drawer, 2 cupboard doors, ogee bracket feet, refinished, 45-1/2" w, 25" d, 83-1/2" h 4,600.00

NY, c1830, mahogany and mahogany veneer, two sections; top: flat molded cornice above 2 glazed doors, 3 short drawers incorporating flanking column on sq plinth; base: projecting with fold-out writing surface, 2 cupboard doors with raised panels and flanking turned columns on ring turned hexagonal tapering front feet, sides with recessed panels on rear stile feet, refinished, 45-1/2" w, 26" d, 93" h 5,500.00

New York, c1835, attributed to J. & W. Meeks, mahogany, straight projecting cornice above arched frieze, upper section with pr of glazed doors, flanked by columns, fitted cylinder desk with pull-out baize-lined writing surface, 2 small drawers over 2 long drawers, pull-out acanthus carved circular feet, 95" h
....6,325.00

Directoire, early 19th C, mahogany, rect gray marble top over frieze drawer, fall front writing surface, fitted int., base with three drawers, sq tapering legs, brass sabots, 37-3/4" w, 16" d, 56" h 1,800.00

Empire, Secretarie à Abattant, 2nd half 19th C, mahogany, ormolu mounts, 39" w, 17-1/4" d, 55-1/4" h 4,890.00

Secretaire a Abattant, Second Empire, French, ormolu mounted, gray variegated marble top, straight front fitted with single drawer, fall front, fitted int., mask head lock plate flanked by swan mounted ormolu column, 40" w, 16" d, 57" h, $8,250. Photo courtesy of Freeman\Fine Arts.

Federal

Baltimore, c1800, inlaid mahogany, two parts, upper: molded cornice, two glazed and mullioned cupboard doors, shelves; lower: three short drawers over roll top, lifts to reveal sliding leather inset writing surface, fitted int., three long graduated drawers, shaped apron, splay feet, 47" w, 21" d, 86" h
....7,000.00

Massachusetts, c1790, mahogany inlaid, shaped gallery with inlaid central panel above 2 molded glazed doors, shelved and valanced compartment int., projecting base with fold-out writing surface, 3 cockbeaded inlaid graduated drawers, flanked by inlaid sq tapering legs, imperfections, 40" w, 19-1/4" d, 76" h 2,990.00

New England, c1825, cherry, two parts, upper: molded cornice over two glazed and mullioned cupboard doors, shelves; lower: projecting with one long drawer, hinged drop-front, felt-lined writing surfaced, fitted int., two cupboard doors, ring-turned legs, castors, 42-1/2" w, 22" d, 85-1/2" h.........2,000.00

George II, second quarter 18th C, burl walnut, restored, molded cornice over two molded and shaped glazed doors, fall front, 4 graduated drawers, 39-1/2" w, 22-3/4" d, 78-1/2" h
....5,750.00

George III, lacquer, scarlet japanned ground, Chinoiserie dec, of people engaged in various pursuits, animals, and foliage, broken triangular cornice over pr of doors, shelved int., base with hinged slant front, fitted int., 2 short and 2 long drawers, bun feet, restorations, 37" w, 21-3/4" d, 89" h...................6,500.00

Hepplewhite, New England, late 18th C, inlaid mahogany, cupboard top with 3 int. shelves, butler style drawer, 2 long drawers in base, 40-3/4" w, 67-1/4" h 3,500.00

Napoleon III, Continental, 19th C, boulle and ebonized wood, domed cornice, urn form finials above pr of paned cabinet doors, shelves, serpentine fronted lower case with frieze drawer, cabriole legs mounted with chutes and sabots, 32" w, 19-1/2" d, 61-1/2" h 1,750.00

Renaissance Revival, America, walnut, burl veneer, turned and carved ornaments, hand carved bust of Shakespeare finial, dovetailed upper case with mirrored door, bird's-eye maple fitted int., 3 dovetailed drawers, based with turned legs and stretcher, 46-1/2" w, 22" d, 91-1/2" h 4,000.00

Sheraton, East Liverpool, OH, c1880, grain painted, two sections: upper: bookcase top with molded cornice, paneled doors, adjustable shelves; base: dovetailed case, fold-down slant front, fitted int. with 4 pigeonholes, 2 dovetailed drawers, over 3 long dovetailed drawers, turned feet, old brown graining, replaced brasses, 34" w, 19-1/4" d, 76-1/2" h 2,400.00

Settee

Biedermeier, second quarter 19th C, birch and ebonized wood, shaped scalloped back centered by triangular pediment, straight paneled sides with half round molded cappings, applied ebonized half rounded baluster uprights, block feet, beige satin upholstery, 75-1/2" w 2,550.00

Chippendale Style, Centennial, 1880-1915, carved mahogany, triple chair back, ornately carved crest rail and slats, upholstered seat, scrolled arms, claw and ball feet 1,200.00

Federal

America, c1790-1810, mahogany, shaped crest rail, over triple shield back, pierced splats, over upholstered seat, molded sq tapering legs, beige and pink floral silk upholstery, 52" l 750.00

Pennsylvania, Lehigh County, c1820, mustard painted and polychrome dec, shaped tripartite crest on turned supports centering pierced baluster-form splats, downswept scrolling arms, plank seat, ring-turned tapering legs joined by stretchers, dec in yellow, red, and green, white and black highlights, fruit and flowers on ochre ground, 76" l 1,100.00

Federal Style, mahogany, straight molded crest rail, over padded back and arms, reeded turned arm supports, over-upholstered seat, molded seat rail, turned reeded legs, castors, late 19th C, 56" l 1,000.00

George III, third quarter 18th C, mahogany, double chair back, elaborate back splats, curving arms, upholstered seat, fretwork supports and skirt molding, sq legs, worming, 48-1/4" l, 38" h 7,500.00

George III Style, late 19th C, paint dec satinwood, upholstered in striped silk, 54" l, 35" h 3,800.00

International Movement, George Nakashima, walnut, slat-back, short flaring dowel legs, white cushion with pale beige, green, and brown stitch, orig finish, c1957, 48" l, 31" d, 30" h 1,925.00

Louis XV Style, oak, shaped carved crest rail, continuing to arms, padded back, over-upholstered seat, carved and shaped seat rail, molded cabriole legs, castors, 60" l .. 950.00

Provincial, Italian, 17th-18th C, walnut, shaped rect back, outscrolled open arms, shaped uprights, over upholstered seat, shaped seat rail, cabriole legs, painted leather upholstery, 61-1/2" l 3,500.00

Sheraton, inlaid mahogany, open arms with fluted posts, seat rail with swag design inlay, ivory colored upholstered back, sides, and seat, fluted tapering front legs, turned feet, 51" w 1,750.00

Windsor, New England, 1790-1810, curving arms, shaped incised seat, early black paint, imperfections, 75" l, 35-1/2" h 6,000.00

Sideboards

Arts and Crafts

Limbert, mirrored back over 6 drawers, 2 doors, brand mark, orig worn finish, 60" w, 27-1/2" d, 57" h 4,900.00

Gustav Stickley, #816, long drawer over three center drawers flanked by two doors, arched apron, sgd Gustav red mark, partial paper label, refinished, restored veneer on sides, 48" l, 18-1/4" d, 45-1/4" h 2,300.00

Classical

New England, c1802, mahogany and mahogany veneer, veneered peaked backboard, scrolled gallery, rect top with rounded edge, case of 2 cockbeaded short drawers, 2 cupboard doors, paneled sides, turned feet, old refinish, replaced brasses, 58" w, 21" d, 44" h 3,200.00

New York State, 1830s, mahogany and mahogany veneer, leafage carving flanking central basket of fruit over 2 small convex drawers above classical columns flanking a central drawer above compartment flanked by side recessed paneled doors, one shelf int., carved paw feet, old refinish, orig glass pulls, minor imperfections, 60" w, 21" d, 50-1/2" h 2,530.00

Philadelphia, c1830, carved mahogany veneer, backboard outlined in brass inlay, center brass floral device, conforming top, 3 convex veneered drawers above brass inlaid paneled cabinet doors, flanked by Ionic columns on carved front feet, castors, old refinish, 71" w, 23-1/2" d, 45" h 9,000.00

Colonial Revival, Chippendale Style, America, c1920, mahogany, central bow front over 2 frieze drawers, 2 deep drawers flanked by 2 wine drawers, central section flanked by 2 drawers over curved cupboard doors, claw and ball feet, 46" w, 18" d, 40-1/2" h 1,200.00

Eastlake, American, rosewood, inlaid ebony door, ebonized and gilded moldings, incised carved leaf dec enhanced with gold, 60" w, 22-1/4" d, 51-3/4" h 3,750.00

Edwardian, English, c1900, Neoclassical taste inlaid and penwork dec, mahogany, inverted broken outline, maple crossbanded top with boxwood strung edges, dart and line inlaid border, concave fronted frieze drawer inlaid with ribbon tied swages of husks and flanked by simulated fluted end drawers and cupboards, each with penwork dec of classically robed maiden representing summer and music, left hand cupboard enclosing 3 fitted drawers, plinth base, 83-1/2" l, 33" h 4,750.00

Federal

America, c1810, mahogany, shaped rect top, slightly projecting center section, one long drawer over two cupboard doors flanked by two deep cellarette drawers flanked by two short drawers over two cupboard doors, flanked by fluted columns, ring-turned cylindrical tapering legs, 72" l, 23" d, 40-1/4" h 1,400.00

CT, Hartford, c1790, mahogany inlaid, serpentine edged top with line inlay and crossbanding, conforming case with drawers and central cupboard doors, sq tapering line inlaid legs with cuff inlays, old finish, old replaced brasses with American shield and anchor, 77" w, 28-1/2" d, 42" h 33,350.00

Massachusetts, c1815, mahogany, top with bowed front and ovolo corners over conforming case with 2 cockbeaded central short drawers flanked by wine drawers, 2 cupboard doors, contrasting inlaid stringing on quarter engaged ring-turned reeded posts continuing to reeded legs, old refinish, restored, 44-1/4" l, 21-1/2" d, 39-1/2" h 4,890.00

Massachusetts, early 19th C, mahogany and maple veneer, two tiered shaped tops with beaded edges, cockbeaded drawers outlined in rosewood veneer and stringing with end cabinets on turned mahogany legs, replaced brass, imperfections, 69-5/8" w, 26-1/2" d, 43-3/4" h 4,600.00

New Hampshire, Portsmouth, 1800-15, mahogany and flame birch veneer, shaped top, inlaid edge above 3 drawers outlined in crossbanded mahogany veneer and stringing over 2 central cupboard doors flanked by sectioned bottle drawer and end cabinets above 6 double tapered cuff-inlaid legs, front legs with bellflower inlay, old surface, replaced pulls, imperfections, 68-3/8" w, 26" d, 41-5/8" h....................16,675.00

Vermont, Rutland, c1825, cherry, rect top with ovolo corners and inlaid edge supporting by flanking outset columns with colonettes above reeding on turned feet, central fitted hinged desk drawer over 2 long drawers, all outlined in beading enclosing mahogany crossbanded veneer, orig surface, replaced brasses, imperfections, 46-1/8" w, 21-3/4" d, 44" h.............4,025.00

George III Style, late 19th C, mahogany and inlay, serpentine top, conforming case, center long drawer flanked by 2 shorter drawers over cupboard doors, sq tapered legs, 78-1/4" l, 24" d, 37" h...3,450.00

Hepplewhite, mahogany, oblong top with serpentine front, conforming frieze, 3 cockbeaded drawers, central recessed cupboard doors flanked by conforming doors, sq tapered legs, crossbanded cuffs, 66" w, 28" d, 41" h......................3,750.00

International Movement, George Nakasima, walnut, free edge front, six exposed walnut burls, block dovetail on one edge, 10" overhang on right, three sliding doors, three walnut slab legs, plywood int., orig finish, c1957, 8' 10" l, 29" d, 36" h 7,475.00

Regency, early 19th C, inlaid mahogany, shaped rect top, one long drawer, flanked by two deep drawers, ring-turned cylindrical tapering legs, 62-1/2" w, 25" d, 37" h................4,250.00

Renaissance Style, North or South Carolina, 1850-75, walnut inlaid, top with central rect inlay outlined by double row of light and dark inlays and stringing over 3 checkerboard inlaid drawers, 2 similarly dec, recessed paneled cupboard doors, shaped skirt, old refinish, imperfections, 44" w, 19-3/4" d, 37" h 3,740.00

William IV, second quarter 19th C, brass, inlaid mahogany, losses, 90-1/2" l, 19-1/4" d, 44" h..1,850.00

Sofas

Charles II Style, mid-18th C, walnut, carved and parcel gilt, shaped back with finial corners, turned shaped legs, stretcher, Flemish tapestry upholstery, 64" l..........................2,250.00

Chesterfield, 20th C, brown leather, minor damage, 68" l, 29" h 1,495.00

Chippendale, New York, c1770, mahogany, camel back, shaped crest, outward scrolling arm supports and seat, sq molded legs, flat stretchers, 80" l..................................10,000.00

Chippendale Style, late 19th C, mahogany, padded camel back, out-scrolled arms, padded seat, sq molded legs, 82" l 900.00

Classical

Boston, MA, 1820s, carved mahogany veneer, rolled brass trim outlines leafage carvings, punch work ground, red velvet upholstery, old refinish, minor imperfections, 84" l, 35" h 1,900.00

Sofa, Federal, mahogany frame with carving attributed to McIntire, Salem, MA, acanthus and floral carved arms and crest with swags, arrows, floral medallions, punched background, turned arm posts, sq tapered legs, 76-1/2" l, $9,350. Photo courtesy of Garth's Auctions.

New York, c1815-20, box style, carved mahogany and rosewood, carved eagle brackets, brass inlay, paw feet, cherry and pine secondary woods, slightly reduced, orig damaged brocade upholstery 2,000.00

Duncan Phyfe Style, New York, mahogany, old finish, crest with fluted panels and swag drapery with ribbon and tassels, reeded scrolled arms, turned and reeded legs and arm posts, old worn and faded upholstery, 60-1/4" l........................12,650.00

Empire

American, c1830, mahogany, carved cornucopias, acorns, oak leaves, and acanthus leaves, basket of flowers finial, refinished, gold brocade reupholstery, 83" l.....................1,800.00

English, late 19th C, mahogany, giltwood, rect top rail with ormolu mount continuing to outward turned arms, giltwood wreath and ribbon back rail above over upholstered seat, sq tapering legs, 65" w, 24-1/" d, 36-1/4" h..................................1,100.00

New York, c1835, mahogany, acanthus carved shaped crest continuing to carved scrolled arms, rounded base, acanthus carved hairy paw feet, gilt feather returns, 78" l.........1,650.00

Federal, mahogany frame

Massachusetts, carving attributed to McIntire, Salem, MA, acanthus and floral carved arms and crest with swag, arrows, floral medallions, and punched background, turned arm posts, sq tapered legs, 4 in front, 4 in back, pale blue upholstery, minor small repairs, 76-1/2" l...9,350.00

Massachusetts, c1815, shaped reeded crest rail continuing to scrolled arms on vase and ring-turned posts, fluted panels, reeded paneled seat rail joining ring-turned reeded frontal legs, raked rear legs, 78" l, 32" d, 33" h......................1,495.00

New England, c1815, reeded arm supports, gently bowed seat rail, sq tapering molded legs, no upholstery, 79" w, 25-1/2" h, 14-1/2" h seat, 36-1/2" h back....................................2,250.00

Philadelphia, c1815, carved mahogany, slightly arched crest, upholstered back flanked by leaf carved terminals, semi-exposed seat rail with flower head carved dies, reeded tapering legs, restoration to legs and crest, 74-3/4" l...............2,500.00

International Movement

Cloud-form, orig green fabric, six maple legs, 117" l, 28" d, 28" h, some staining 31,050.00

Eames, Charles, compact, manufactured by Herman Miller, green-gray wool fabric, polished chrome legs, 72" l, 30" d, 35" h 750.00

Regency, mahogany, reclining arms form chaise, black and white striped upholstery, carved, 58-1/2" l.................1,650.00

Stands

Book, Victorian, Bettemann's patent, sold by Shreve Crump and Low, walnut veneer, end pieces set with pate-sur-pate plaques of cupids playing badminton, 16" l..................600.00

Chamber, Federal, attributed to New York State, early 19th C, mahogany, replaced pulls, refinished, imperfections, 22" w, 17" d, 42" h...400.00

Coffin, folding sawhorse type, turned legs, old black paint, 21-3/4" h, pr 100.00

Dumbwaiter, Georgian, 19th C, mahogany, dishes shelves, 50-3/4" h...850.00

Easel

Aesthetic Movement, attributed to Kimbel and Cabus, New York, c1875-80, ebonized, damage to one foot, 70-1/2" l ...1,750.00

Victorian, Gothic Style, America, c1872, oak, swiveling pierced stand, tracery carved top rail, rotating on platform base, molded sq legs joined by stretchers, adjustable racks missing, stamped "1738," 31" w, 87" h, pr................................4,950.00

Etagere

Country, New England, c1830, tiger maple, rect top, 3 short drawers, 3 shelves supported by block ring-turned posts, turned legs, replaced brass pulls, old refinish, 39" w, 12" d, 53" h 3,220.00

Edwardian, mahogany, pierced carved foliate top over molded and shaped oval cartouche, conforming beveled mirror plate, single shelf with pierce-carved supports, center shaped mirror plate flanked by two "S" shaped mirror plates above 2 glazed cabinet doors, flanked by 2 glazed and foliate carved mullioned doors, sq tapering cabriole legs, shaped stretcher shelf, 54" w, 16" d, 100" h 1,600.00

Library, carousel, architectural carpentry, maple, c1900 .... 2,400.00

Music

Art Nouveau, Austrian, carved walnut, openwork foliate carved adjustable easel, carved adjustable column, carved and molded tripod cabriole legs, 67" h 850.00

Classical, England, c1800, rosewood graining, gilt striping, lyre-shaped rack with brass strings above adjustable thumbscrew collar, pedestal with gold stenciling, 3 curving legs ending in brass paw feet, orig surface, repair to dip pans, very minor surface imperfections, 45-1/2" h 4,600.00

Gilt Iron, openwork scrolled lyre work, 2 scrolling candelabra arms, adjustable column, scroll tripod feet, electrified, 54-1/2" h 250.00

Night

Biedermeier, c1820, walnut, shaped rect top, frieze drawer, ebonized wood tambour compartment flanked by canted corners, sabre legs, 12-1/2" w, 15-3/4" d, 31-1/2" h 950.00

Country, Soap Hollow, PA, dated 1875, painted red-orange on cherry, overhanging top, single drawer, 4 ring turned slightly swelled legs, drawer stenciled "1875" flanked by initials "RF," 21-3/4" w, 22 d, 29" h 1,840.00

Plant

Arts and Crafts, Paine Furniture Co, pedestal circular top with orig leatherette cov, sides tacked, 4 long corbels, 4 slender legs, orig dark finish, metal tag, 12-1/2" d, 31" h 500.00

Country, turned ash column, burl ask top, 3 cast iron branch legs, 10-1/2" d, 33-1/4" h 195.00

Edwardian, c1900, mahogany, hexagonal top with inlaid satinwood edge, paneled baluster form standard with bellflower inlay, 3 down scrolled supports, acanthus carved centerpiece, cylindrical feet, 15" w, 42" h 900.00

Plate, Louis Philippe, walnut, molded border above tapering caned body, carved claw feet, 14-3/4" d, 14" h 575.00

Shaving, Federal, mahogany, 2 drawers, bracket feet, 18-3/4" w, 9-1/4" d, 19-1/2" h 300.00

Stand, Dumbwaiter, French, 19th C, mixed woods, retractable top divides into three parts, $770. Photo courtesy of Sanford Alderfer Auction Co.

Stand, pedestal, Tramp Art, polychromed in green and black paint, 12-1/2" w, 12-1/2" d, 25" h, $950. Photo courtesy of Clifford Wallach.

Side

Federal, MA, c1800, mahogany, sq top with rounded edge, single drawer, straight skirt, 4 sq tapered legs, old refinish, old brass, minor imperfections, 16" w, 16" d, 29" h 1,035.00

Hepplewhite, Maine, poplar, orig red and black graining, yellow and green striping, gold stenciled floral design on dovetailed drawer, 1 board top, sq tapered legs, some wear, 17" x 18-3/4" x 28-1/4" h 4,290.00

Sheraton, mahogany veneer, 2 dovetailed drawers, dragon edges around top and molded edge drawers, orig glass knobs, some veneer chips, 21" w, 18" d, 29" h 440.00

Vitrine, Louis XVI Style, late 19th C, gilt metal mounted giltwood, 26-1/2" w, 37-1/4" d, 30" h 1,150.00

Wash

Empire, American, mahogany, marble backsplash with shelf, shaped rect marble top, single long projecting drawers, two cupboard doors, shaped block feet, c1850, 33" l, 20" d, 38-1/2" h 350.00

Federal Style, country, painted, green foliate dec, yellow ground, shaped backsplash over rect top, circular cut-out, ring turned cylindrical tapering legs joined by short stretcher, one drawer, second quarter 19th C, 18" w, 16" d, 40" h 250.00

Hepplewhite, Salem, MA, corner, bowfront, curly maple, dovetailed high crest with shelf, molded detail on bowed edge, top with cutouts for bowl and jars, mid shelf with one dovetailed drawer, trefoil bottom shelf, sq legs, outward curving feet, old finish, 21" w, 43-1/2" h 2,970.00

Sheraton, painted and stenciled, 2 tiers, backsplash in yellow with brown stripes, fruit stenciling, 34" w, 36" h 425.00

Wig, Queen Anne, English, washbowl holder, mahogany, pine and oak secondary woods, turned ring supporting blue transfer Copeland Spode bowl, turned and carved columns, 2 dovetailed drawers, tripod base, snake feet, 31-1/2" h 900.00

Wine Cooler, Georgian, 19th C, mahogany, oval and brass banded body, fitted with brass liner, later fitted stands, raised tapering legs, 14-3/4" w, 14" h, pr 1,200.00

Steps

Bed

Georgian Style, mahogany, green leather inset steps, turned legs, 16" w, 30" d, 17" h, pr 850.00

Regency, early 19th C, mahogany, 3 treads, inset tooled morocco leather surfaces, paneled risers, drawer, turned tapering fluted legs, 20-1/2" w, 29" d, 28" h 2,500.00

Sheraton, mid 19th C, replaced brocade 475.00

Victorian, English, c1840, mahogany, rect platforms with tooled red leather inset, 2 platforms, open to storage area, turned cylindrical legs, 28-3/4" l, 28" h 1,900.00

Library

Napoleon III, 19th C, oak, 6 steps leading to demilune barred platform, trestle base, 47" l, 81" h 1,800.00

Regency, early 19th C, mahogany, three steps, inset green leather treads, scrolling banister, sq balusters, castors, 46" w, 27" d, 56" h 23,000.00

Stools

Bar, International Movement, Alvar Aalto, designed for Artek, c1954, "X," each leg of 5 laminated ash pieces joined at seat, leather upholstery, traces of orig label, 18-1/2" w, 18" h, pr 400.00

Choir, Louis XV, Provincial, oak, molded D-shaped top, sq legs joined by stretchers, 25-1/2" h, pr 450.00

Foot

Classical

Attributed to Hancock, Holden and Adams, Boston, 1830s, over upholstered rect top, double C-scroll base centering rosettes, turned stretcher, old refinish, 16-1/2" w, 15-1/2" d, 14" h 920.00

New York City, 1810-15, mahogany, rect concave over upholstered top, conforming frame, curlicue-form base centering circular boss, joined by turned medial stretcher, old finish, 21" w, 15-1/2" d, 15" h 980.00

Empire, mahogany and mahogany flame veneer, old shiny varnish, applied pressed moldings, old floral needlepoint top, turned legs, minor wear to top, some tacks missing, 10" x 11-1/4" x 9" h 220.00

George I, c1740, walnut, oval, padded top in later figural petit point, molded frame, angled cabriole legs with bold paneled C-scroll capitals, ball and claw feet, 20" l 26,000.00

Louis XVI Style, Continental, walnut, shaped rect top, Fortuny cotton cov, floral carved apron, cabriole legs, scroll toes, pr 275.00

Mission, oak, rect, arched skirt, 4 vertical slats per side, 20-1/4" l, 14" d, 16" h 350.00

William and Mary, attributed to French Canada, 18th C, turned maple, over upholstered rect top, 4 block turned legs joined by block turned "H" stretcher, turned feet, old refinish, imperfections, 15-1/2" w, 19" d, 14-1/2" h 2,415.00

Windsor, oval, splayed base, old green repaint, 10 x 14", 10-3/4" h 225.00

Organ, Victorian, circular, upholstered top, ebonized stem, 3 fancy metal legs 195.00

Piano, Classical

New England, c1830, rosewood, circular adjustable molded top, tapering column, shaped scrolled platform, 18" h 460.00

New York, 1810-15, carved mahogany veneer and brass, curving veneered crest above lyre-shaped splat with brass strings over carved stay rail and pedestal with applied stamped brass or-

namentation, carved legs, castors, beige silk upholstery, 32" h 4,900.00

Primitive, dished out semi-circular seat, whittled legs, worn old red, 28" l, 20-1/2" h 360.00

Tables

Banquet, Classical, MA, c1825, mahogany and mahogany veneer, double hinged D-form top, conforming beaded apron centering veneered panel, flanked by panels above the ring turned, reeded spiral carved legs, old refinish, imperfections, 54" w, extends to 172-3/4" l, 28-3/4" h 6,900.00

Bow Front, Hepplewhite, refinished birch, mahogany and satinwood veneer, banded inlay, bow front top with beaded edge, two dovetailed drawers, bowfront apron, tapered legs with fluting on front surface, some veneer damage and repair, old emb brass pulls, attributed to Portsmouth, NH, 16-5/8" x 23-1/4" x 32" h 14,300.00

Breakfast

Chippendale, attributed to Newport, RI, family, walnut, old refinishing, tilt top sq top with notched corners, scroll carved legs, tripod base with elongated ball and claw feet, top and hinge block old replacements, 33-1/2" x 34-1/4" x 27" h 1,760.00

Classical, MA, c1820, mahogany carved and mahogany veneer, rect drop leaf top, straight skirt, two cockbeaded drawers at either end, turned and spiral carved cost and rect platform, 4 scrolled legs with brass rosettes, cast brass hairy paw feet, 18" w, 42" d closed, 28" h...1,150.00

Federal, New England, c1800, cherry, serpentine shaped top, shaped skirts, flanked by sq tapering molded legs, refinished, imperfections, 17-1/2" w, 35" d, 27-1/2" h...................1,035.00

Regency, early 19th C, mahogany, rect top, reeded edge, turned support, downswept molded legs, gilt bronze caps and castors, 43-3/4" w, 40" d, 28" h...1,150.00

Card

Chippendale, attributed to

Affleck, Thomas, Philadelphia, refinished mahogany, pine and poplar secondary woods, 1 overlapping dovetailed drawer, molded edge top, apron with applied gadrooned molding, Marlborough legs with inside chamfer, orig brass, minor damage to moldings on feet, gadrooning, and drawer overlap, pierced repair to leaf at hinge, 36" w, 17-3/4" d, 28-1/4" h 5,225.00

Townsend, John, RI, refinished mahogany, serpentine top with edge fluting on top leaf, conforming apron with gadrooned edge bead, fretwork brackets, sq legs with stop fluting, corner brackets replacements made by Kahil Gabran, minor edge damage, short age cracks in top, secret drawer in apron, 34-1/4" w, 17" d, 27-3/4" h 25,300.00

MA, 1750-80, cherry inlaid, rect top, fluted edge, undercut inner top with central inlaid stellate device, two paterae on frieze, sq molded legs, frontal brackets, side opening drawer, old surface, imperfections, 31-1/4" w, 13-1/2" d, 29-1/4" h..5,750.00

Classical

MA, c1820, carved and veneer mahogany, shaped top with beaded edge, conforming skirt with beaded lower edge, 4 acanthus carved ring turned spiral carved legs, old refinish, 35-1/2" w, 17-1/2" d, 29-1/4" h........................1,725.00

Massachusetts, c1825, carved and veneer mahogany, folding top with rounded corners, conforming ogee molded skirt with floral and foliate carved corners, turned and carved post, concave shaped platform, acanthus leaf scroll-carved hairy paw feet, castors, old finish, 36" w, 18-1/4" d, 30-1/4" h..990.00

New York City, 1800-15, carved mahogany and satinwood veneer, top with canted corners pivots above satinwood skirt, cyma carved deeply incised legs with flanking applied wood carved ornamentation, legs terminate in leafage carved ankles above carved animal paw feet, old refinish, 37-1/2" w, 18-3/4" d, 28-1/2" h..6,900.00

Empire, America, c1840, mahogany, round pedestal with leaf carving, quatrefoil platform, 4 claw feet, 37" l, 13" d, 28" h 425.00

Federal

c1790, Boston, inlaid mahogany, shaped top with undercut lower top, 3 paneled skirt outlined in stringing above sq tapered legs outlined in stringing with inlaid paterae and cuffs, old refinish, minor imperfections, 43-5/8" w, 18" d, 30" h...2,990.00

c1790, MA, inlaid mahogany, rect folding top with ovolo corners, checkered inlaid edge, conforming base with center inlaid oval within mitered panel flanked by panels of stringing, sq tapering legs with geometric inlay and banded cuffs, old refinish, restoration, 35-1/2" w, 16-3/4" d, 28-3/4" h...1,840.00

c1790, RI, inlaid mahogany, folding rect top with ovolo corners, inlaid edge, conforming skirt with center satin wood pane, inlaid lower edge joining four sq tapering legs inlaid with rect panels, diagonal stringing and bellflowers, cuffs, old refinish, minor imperfections, 35" w, 16-3/4" d, 28-3/8" h 3,740.00

c1800, inlaid mahogany, demilune, hinged D-shaped top, conforming apron with floral inlay, sq tapering legs, spade feet, 35" w, 17-3/4" d, 28-3/4" h................................2,100.00

c1800, New England, inlaid mahogany, demilune, hinged top with edge of inlaid stringing, conforming base, three string inlaid lozenge panels, 4 sq tapering legs with string inlay and cuffs, old refinish, restoration, 36" w, 17-3/4" d, 29-1/4" h...1,265.00

c1800, North Shore, MA, mahogany veneer, shaped top, ovolo corners above legs with leaf carving, colonettes, and reeding, orig surface, very minor surface imperfections, 36" w, 17-3/4" d, 28-1/2" h 5,500.00

c1815, MA, mahogany, bird's eye maple inlaid, folding top with half serpentine ends, bow front and sq corners inlaid with stringing and bird's eye maple, center oval panel within mitered rect, ring turned swelled reeded legs, old refinish, minor imperfections, 36-1/4" w, 17-1/2" d, 29-3/4" h 3,800.00

c1815, MA, inlaid mahogany, folding top with half serpentine ends, D-front, squared corners, edge inlaid with stringing and crossbanding, conforming skirt, center oval panel with mahogany mitered frame, flanked by satinwood panels bordered by stringing and crossbanding joining four ring turned reeded tapering legs, old refinish, 35-1/2" w, 17-1/4" d, 29-1/2" h 8,625.00

c1825, cherry and tiger maple, shaped, hinged rect top, conforming tiger maple apron, ring turned reeded cylindrical tapering legs, 36" w, 16-1/2" d, 29" h....................2,500.00

Hepplewhite

Boston, attributed to, reputed to have belonged to Joseph Bartlett, signer of Declaration of Independence, refinished mahogany, cut corner top, cut corner apron, sq tapered legs, banded inlay in top, legs with stringing, unusual stylized leather or wheat design with rectangles on all four posts and top, pierced repair to top, age cracks, 17-1/2" x 35-3/4" x 28-1/8" h...4,400.00

New York, mahogany with good figure, old finish, curved and serpentine top, conforming apron, sq tapering legs, stringing inlay on legs, banding at feet, bottom edge of apron, and edge of top, very minor veneer damage, small patch to one hinged, 35" w, 17" d, 28-3/4" h.........................3,520.00

Sheraton, attributed to Salem, MA, refinished mahogany, serpentine top and conforming apron, string and banded inlay on apron, figured satin wood veneer on rounded corners, stringing on top edge, turned and reeded legs, 36-1/2" w, 17-1/2" d, 29-1/2" h..9,350.00

Center

Empire, Boston, circular white marble top, three-sided pedestal, trefoil base, scroll feet, c1825, 34" w, 21" h................1,400.00

Empire Style, second half 19th C, ormolu mounted mahogany, round marble top, baluster pedestal with floral and acanthus carving, trefoil base with figural sphinx, paw feet, 27" d, 29-3/4" h 8,625.00

Regency Style, late 19th/early 20th C, giltwood, round marble top with composition inlay, dolphin form supports, 38" d, 29-1/2" h 2,645.00

Chair, New England, late 18th C, maple, circular top above lift top well, rect ends ending in shoe feet, old refinish, 41-3/4" d, 28" h 3,740.00

Conference, Renaissance Revival, late 19th C, U-shape, walnut, 3 section table, olive ash burl top, conforming frieze, shaped and tapering rect legs, joined by molded and shaped stretcher base, 126-1/2" w, 144" d, 30" h..............................3,100.00

Console

Federal Style, attributed to mid-Atlantic, 19th C, demilune, mahogany, D-shaped top, conforming apron, sq tapering legs, 44-1/2" w, 22-1/2" d, 28" h..500.00

French Empire, mahogany, shaped rect gray marble top, one long drawer, out-curved supports, shaped base, ring-turned feet, c1830, 38-1/4" l, 18" d, 36" h..............................1,800.00

Renaissance Revival, three drawers, carved skirt, some loss to feet...330.00

Dining

Arts and Crafts, Limbert, round top with two 12" leaves, pedestal base with center leg, orig worn finish, top overcoated, 48" d, 24" h 1,840.00

Eastlake, Victorian, American, oak, shaped rect top, shaped quatrefoil pedestal, castors, late 19th C, 37-1/2" d, 29" h ...600.00

Federal, late, c1825, mahogany, two D-shaped ends, hinged middle section, ring-turned tapering cylindrical legs, 42" w, 72-1/2" d, 29-1/2" h 1,300.00

George III Style, late 19th C, mahogany and satinwood crossbanding, two pedestals, 70" l, 51" w, 29" h.................6,900.00

Dressing

Empire, French, c1800, ebonized, marquetry and ivory inlaid mahogany, oval mirror plate, conforming inlaid frame, swiveling between inlaid turned uprights, ormolu finials, rect surface inlaid with ivory figures, oval marble inset, one long drawer, inlaid turned legs, concave, shaped stretcher, castors, 25-1/2" w, 15-1/2" d, 61" h...2,100.00

Empire, late, Charles Hale, Baltimore, flame mahogany, rect mirror plate swivels between turned uprights, rect case with two short drawers over projecting rect surface, over single long drawer, ring-turned cylindrical tapering legs, c1850, 38" l, 19-1/2" d, 59" h...1,100.00

Queen Anne, MA, c1740, walnut veneer, overhanging top with thumbnail molding, 4 matched panels of crotch veneer outlined in herringbone veneer, case with 5 similar drawers with cockbeaded surrounds, arcaded skirt with applied cockbeading, drop pendants, cockbeaded skirts, cabriole legs, pad feet, old refinish, old replaced brasses, 29" w, 18" d, 31" h 11,500.00

Drop Leaf

Biedermeier, second half 19th C, birchwood and ebonized, rect top, drop sides, circular fluted and ebonized standard, sq base, 4 scroll legs, 35" w, 27-1/2" d, 47-3/4" extended, 29-1/2" h 3,750.00

Classical, NY, c1815, mahogany, rect top, round leaves, beaded skirt with drawer, four ring turned reeded legs ending in swelled feet, cast brass hairy paw feet, refinished, restored, 36" w, 57" l open, 28-3/4" h 1,725.00

Empire, American, c1840, walnut, hinged rect top, two drop leaves, conforming apron, octagonal pedestal, quatrefoil plinth base, scroll feet, castors, 60-1/4" w, 42" d, 28-1/2" h 375.00

Table, drop leaf, Queen Anne, hardwood with old red, dovetailed apron with scalloped ends, swing legs, cabriole legs, high duck feet and pads, wrought iron butterfly hinges, 42-1/" l, 15" d, 14-3/4" leaves, 28-1/4" h, $28,600. Photo courtesy of Garth's Auctions.

Federal

Mahogany, hinged shape rect top, two drop leaves, sq tapering legs, dated 1820, 35" l, 33" d, 29" h....................500.00

Mahogany, hinged shaped rect top, two drop leaves, one short drawer, ring and spiral turned, foliate carved legs, castors, c1850, 56-1/2" l, 43" d, 28-3/4" h.................850.00

Mahogany, hinged shaped rect top, two leaves, stylized pineapple column base, 4 heavily carved hairy paw feet, brass castors, 37" w, 28-3/4" h 800.00

Hepplewhite, country

Cherry, old mellow refinishing, drop leaf top with cut corners on leaves, 1 dovetailed drawer, sq tapering legs, old brass pull, one board top has repaired crack through center, 36" w, 21" d, 10-3/4" d leaves, 28-1/4" h 440.00

Mahogany, pine secondary wood, very worn old finish, dovetailed apron with banded veneer on ends and drop leaf top, molded on 2 sides, sq tapered legs, edge damage to rule joint, stains in top, 47-1/4" l, 15-1/2" d, 16-1/4" leaves, 30" h...935.00

Queen Anne

American, hardwood, pine secondary wood, old red finish, dovetailed apron with scalloped ends, cabriole swing legs, high duck feet and pads, wrought iron butterfly hinges, pristine condition, 42-1/2" w, 15" d, 14-3/4" leaves, 28-1/4" h...28,600.00

New England, 18th C, maple, drop leaf, half round ends, turned legs, pad feet, refinished, restored, 51-1/4" w, 17-3/8" d, 27" h...1,955.00

Sheraton, cherry, single drawer, gate leg, 41" l, 19-1/2" d, two 20-1/4" leaves, 29-1/2" h 250.00

William and Mary, CT, early 18th C, cherry, overhanging oval drop leaf top, 4 splayed block vase and ring turned legs, butterfly support, turned feet, joined by beaded apron with thumb molded drawer, old refinish, restored, 40" w, 35-1/4" d, 25-1/2" h 2,4315.00

Folding Top, Renaissance, Italian, 17th C, walnut, hinged rect top, carved apron with two short drawers, ring turned cylindrical legs joined by stretchers, 60" w, 28" d, 28-1/2" h 2,600.00

Gaming, Federal, central MA, c1800, cherry inlaid, folding rect top with carved edge, 4 sq chamfered tapering legs inlaid with stringing joined by straight skirt with applied beading, refinished, top reset, 33" w, 15-1/2" d, 29" h.........................920.00

Harvest, Federal, New England, early 19th C, pine and cherry, rect overhanging top, 4 sq tapering legs, castors, vestiges of old red paint, 72" l, 37-1/2" w open, 28-3/4" h 4,025.00

Hunt

George II, c1725, mahogany, hinged oval top, two D-shaped drop leaves, sq molded legs, 44-1/2" w, 59" d, 28" h 2,900.00

George III, mahogany, top with molded edge, sq legs, restorations, 64" w, 41-1/2" d, 28" h 2,185.00

Marble, Victorian-style, turtle top, rose marble, turned and carved quadruped base, turned drop finials............................550.00

Pembroke

Chippendale

Connecticut River Valley, c1780, mahogany, exotically grained drop leaf top, 4 sq legs with inside chamfered corners, joined by straight skirt drawer, shaped flat cross stretchers, old finish, orig brass, top slightly warped, 35" w, 34-3/4" d, 27" h 2,875.00

NH, Portsmouth, late 18th C, cherry, rect drop leaf top overhangs straight skirt with drawer, 4 sq beaded legs, inside corner chamfered to shaped and pierced cross stretchers, refinished, repairs, 35" w, 21-1/2" d, 27-3/4" h.......1,610.00

Federal

Massachusetts or Connecticut, c1800, cherry, serpentine drop leaf top, frieze drawer, string inlay, lower edges of alternating inlay squares joining 4 sq double tapering legs inlaid with oval paterae, stringing and icicle motif continue to sawtooth cuffs, refinished, 20" w, 39-1/2" d, 28-3/4" h..2,645.00

Massachusetts, c1800, mahogany inlaid, rect drop leaf top with ovolo corners, single drawer, straight skirt joining 4 sq tapering legs with stringing inlay, refinished, old brass pull, 35-3/4" w, 19" d, 28-1/2" h....................................1,380.00

George III, c1800, inlaid satinwood, hinged crossbanded shaped rect top, two drop leaves, inlaid apron with one long drawer, sq tapering inlaid legs, 38" w, 30-1/4" d, 27-1/2" h.....1,500.00

Table, Pembroke, Hepplewhite, refinished cherry, serpentine drop leaf top, serpentine end aprons, conforming drawer, sq tapered lets with inside chamber, stringing inlay on legs and aprons with fans and oval paterae, fretwork brackets, 35-3/8" w, 16-3/4" d, 8-3/4" leaves, 28" h, $6,500. Photo courtesy of Garth's Auctions.

Hepplewhite
  Mahogany, inlay, old worn finish, drop leaf top, 1 dovetailed drawer, sq tapered legs, inlay stringing and banding on legs, curved end aprons, banded inlay on top, edge inlay damage, old repairs, replaced brass knob, 32" w, 17-3/4" d, 10-1/4" l leaves, 28-3/4" h 880.00
  Refinished cherry, pine and maple secondary woods, serpentine shaped drop leaf top, serpentine end aprons with conforming drawer in one end, sq tapered legs with inside chamfer, stringing inlay on lefts and aprons with fans and oval paterae, fretwork brackets, 38-5/8" w, 16-3/4" l, 8-3/4" leaves, 28" h 6,050.00

Pier
  Classical, mid-Atlantic states, 1830-40, carved mahogany and veneer, figured mahogany veneer splashboard supported by marble columns topped by carved Ionic capitals with ring turned bases, marble top, two convex veneered drawers, similar columns flank platform with concave front, backed by mirror and pilasters, old refinish, 37-1/2" w, 19" d, 41" h 3,450.00
  Federal, Faux Bois, pine, England, c1810, gray and white marbleized rect top overhangs frieze drawer dec to simulate bamboo, tapering legs, yellow painted ground accented with orange, cream, and black, 27-3/4" w, 18-3/4" d, 30-1/4" h 2,875.00

Sawbuck
  New England, late 19th C, painted pine, rect top, drawer, sawbuck base with horizontal rails, old lime green paint, paint worn on top, 30-1/4" w, 15" d, 15" h 865.00
  Pennsylvania, Montgomery County, early 19th C, green painted walnut, rect one board top, X-form supports joined by octagonal stretcher, 43" w, 27" d, 27" d 895.00

Side
  Classical, MA, c1825, mahogany and mahogany veneer, rect top with scrolled gallery above conforming case with long drawer, circular brass pulls, 4 ring-turned column supports, concave platform, turned legs, old refinish, 39" w, 18-3/4" d, 30" h 2,530.00
  International Movement, George Nakashima, walnut, free edge top
    Four flaring dowel legs, orig finish, c1957, 28" w, 28" d, 15" h 1,495.00
    Three flaring dowel legs, orig finish, c1957, 17-1/2" w, 24" d, 17" h 1,840.00
  Victorian, late 19th/early 20th C, mahogany, burlwood, and inlay, oblong base, paint frieze, trestle supports, carved cabriole legs, pad feet, turned stretcher, 38-1/2" w, 20-1/2" d, 27-1/2" h 850.00
  William and Mary, late 17th C, marquetry, walnut, inlaid rect top, molded edge, one long drawer, later barley-twist legs, shaped inlaid center stretcher, ball feet, 42-1/2" l, 24-1/2" d, 33" h 1,500.00

Tavern
  MA, 18th C, pine and maple, top with breadboard ends, overhanging single drawer above skirt with molded edge, vase and ring turned legs, turned feet, joined by stretchers, refinished, patch in top, 35" w, 25-1/2" d, 25-1/2" h 1,495.00
  New England, mid-18th C, painted pine and maple, scrubbed top with breadboard ends, side opening drawer, baluster and ring turned legs connected by 4 sq stretchers, old red paint, 37-3/4" w, 23-5/8" h, 23-1/2" h 1,840.00
  Pennsylvania, Lehigh Valley, 1780-1800, turned figured walnut, rect two-board top, 2 thumb-molded short drawers, centering reeded dye, ring-turned baluster-form legs, joined by box stretcher, turned tapering feet, orig brass drawer pulls, one with eagle dec, chips to both drawers, 60" w, 35-1/2" d, 28-1/2" h 1,610.00
  Pennsylvania, early 18th C, walnut, overhanging rect top, molded skirt with thumb molded drawer to right of smaller drawer, 4 molded block turned legs, flat box stretchers, turned feet, refinished, 32" w, 21-1/2" d, 28-1/4" h 2,530.00

Pennsylvania, late 18th/early 19th C, cherry, shaped top, incised beaded drawer, straight skirt, four block and ring turned tapering legs, button feet, imperfections, 28" w, 21-3/4" d, 26-1/2" h 1,725.00
William and Mary, New England
  Early 18th C, painted, rect overhanging top, four block, vase, and ring turned legs, turned feet, joined by molded skirt, box stretchers, old gray paint over earlier colors, repairs to 1 foot, 43" w, 27-1/2" d, 25-1/2" h 6,325.00
  Mid-18th C, maple, top overhangs molded skirt connected by splayed ring and baluster turned legs, turned feet, old refinish, restored, 34" w, 22-3/4" d, 23" h 1,150.00

Tea
Chippendale
  America, reputed to have belonged to George Clinton, first NY governor, refinished mahogany, 1 board dish turned tilt top, bird cage with turned posts, turned column with swirl fluted urn, tripod base, bulbous feet, sun bleached top, 30" d, 27-1/2" h 1,650.00
  Pennsylvania, c1740-60, turned walnut, rect two board top, beaded frieze, splayed ring-turned baluster form legs, box stretcher, ball feet, 30" l, 21" d, 28-1/4" h 7,475.00
  Pennsylvania, c1780, walnut, circular molded top, birdcage platform, vase and ring turned post, tripod cabriole legs base, paneled knees ending in pad feet on platforms, old refinish, minor imperfections, 35-1/2" d, 28-1/2" h 2,300.00
  George III, early 19th C, mahogany, circular top, tilting over baluster turned pedestal, cabriole legs, slipper feet, 35" d, 27-1/2" h 525.00
  George III Style, late 19th C, mahogany, tilt top, tripod base, 32" d, 29-3/4" h 1,265.00
Queen Anne
  New England, 18th C, cherry and maple, oval top, 4 block turned legs, pad feet on platforms, cut-out skirt, refinished, 34-3/4" w, 26" d, 25-3/4" h 4,890.00
  New England, mid-18th C, maple, overhanging oval top, valanced apron, four block turned tapering legs, button feet, old refinish, 28" w, 21-3/4" d, 26" h 2,875.00
  Pennsylvania, 1730-80, walnut, rect one board top, shaped apron, cabriole legs, sq feet, orig finish on top, 35" w, 25" d, 27-1/2" h 22,425.00
  Virginia, Williamsburg, mid-18th C, walnut, tray top overhanging slightly shaped skirt, 4 cabriole legs with shell carvings, bellflowers below, deeply carved elongated flanking scrolls above paneled trifid feet, old surface, 27-1/2" w, 18-3/4" d, 29-1/4" h 5,750.00
  Victorian, English, c1870, inlaid walnut and ebonized, circular parquetry inlaid top, pierced and scalloped apron, tilting over ring turned carved pedestal, three carved and scrolled legs, scroll feet, 29-3/8" d, 29" h 550.00
Trestle, French Provincial, 19th C, oak and walnut, rect slab top, trestle support joined by stretcher, 94-1/2" l, 34-1/2" w, 27" h 2,415.00

Work
Classical
  Boston, c1830, carved mahogany and veneer
    Attributed to Isaac Vose Jr., rect top with rounded leaves above 2 drawers top drawer fitted with adjustable work easel, lower drawer with faux two drawer facade, molded pedestal, shaped platform with carved scroll feet, old refinish, minor imperfections, 22-1/2" w, 19" d, 30" h 1,840.00
    Rect top with canted corners, half-rounded edge, conforming case with 2 drawers and bag drawer, foliate carved ring turned columns, concave shaped platform and 4 turned feet, old finish, orig brasses, 22-1/2" w, 17" d, 31-1/2" h 12,650.00
  Massachusetts, c1825, carved mahogany and veer, hinged rect top opens to int. with work surface and compartments, case with rounded drawer, recessed drawer below, flanked by

acorn pendants, turned acanthus carved post and 4 shaped acanthus-carved legs, paw feet, castors, old finish, 22-1/2" w, 17-1/2" d, 33" h 750.00

Federal

American, mahogany, c1850, hinged rect top, two drop leaves, two short drawers, ring-turned cylindrical tapering legs, 35-1/2" l, 17" d, 29" h 350.00

Massachusetts, c1790, mahogany and satinwood inlaid, octagonal top, inlaid edge, satinwood veneered conforming skirt, center bag drawer with geometric inlaid lower edge, 4 sq tapering legs, old refinish, replaced pulls, imperfections, 19-3/4" w, 16-1/4" d, 29" h 1,840.00

Massachusetts, 1815-20, carved mahogany, rect top with bird's eye maple veneer bordered by mahogany veneer crossbanding, case with 2 drawers with bird's eye maple veneer, fluted corners, ring turned reeded tapering legs, castors, refinished, old brass pulls, minor imperfections, 20-1/2" w, 17" d, 29" h..2,875.00

New England, mahogany, c1850, pine secondary wood, old finish, smooth lift top with rounded edge and turquoise felt writing surface, 2 semi-cylindrical open compartments, 2 dovetailed drawers, 1 large, 1 smaller with 9 part divided int., continuous reeding, slender turned and reeded legs, old added brasses, 23-3/4" w, 12-3/4" d, 28-5/8" h 2,860.00

Hepplewhite, mahogany and figured satinwood veneer with inlay, octagonal top and case, two dovetailed drawers, sq tapered legs with stringing and banded inlay around feet, feet ended out, bottom drawer int. rebuilt after work bag removed, dividers removed from top drawer, veneer repairs, orig brass, 20-5/8" w, 15" d, 28-1/2" h 1,980.00

Queen Anne, attributed to Chester County, PA, walnut, two drawers, pine top, beaded skirt, splay leg, replaced top and drawer runners, 51" w, 32" d, 29-1/2" h................................1,450.00

Sheraton, Boston or Salem, MA, curly maple with excellent figure, pine and walnut secondary wood, old mellow refinishing, octagonal case with single dovetailed drawer, pull-out bag frame disguised as drawer front, turned ivory pulls, slender turned legs with reeding and turned half posts at apron with biscuit corners, age crack in top, 17" w, 15-1/2" d, 27-3/4" h 20,900.00

GAME PLATES

History: Game plates, popular between 1870 and 1915, are specially decorated plates used to serve fish and game. Sets originally included a platter, serving plates, and a sauce or gravy boat. Many sets have been divided. Today, individual plates are often used as wall hangings.

Birds

Plate

9-1/2" d, bird, scalloped edge, mauve ground, gold trim, sgd "Vitet Limoges" 130.00

9-1/2" d, duck, pastel pink, blue, and cream ground, duck flying up from water, yellow flowers and grasses, sgd "Laury," mkd "Limoges," not pierced for hanging 120.00

10" d, pheasant, Limoges, sgd "Max" 95.00

10-1/2" d, game bird and two water spaniels, crimped gold rim, sgd "RK Beck" 95.00

13-1/4" d, game bird and pheasant, heavy gold, scalloped emb rococo border, mkd "Coronet Limoges, Bussilion" 250.00

Platter, 16" l, 2 handles, quail, hp gold trim, Limoges 150.00

Set

7 pcs, wild game birds, pastoral scene, molded edges, shell dec, Fazent Meheim, Bonn, Germany 250.00

12 pcs, 10-1/2" d plates, game birds in natural habitat, sgd "I. Bubedi" 3,500.00

Fish Service, platter, two serving plates, sauce boat, under plate shown, enameled fish and scrolling gilt edges, Limoges, price for set with 12 plates, and serving pcs as shown, $1,700. Photo courtesy of Freeman\Fine Arts.

Deer

Plate, 9" d, buck and doe, forest scene 60.00

Set, 13 pcs, platter, 12 plates, deer, bear, and game birds, yellow ground, scalloped border, "Haviland China," sgd "MC Haywood" 3,200.00

Fish

Plate

8" d, bass, scalloped edge, gray-green trim, fern on side of fish, Limoges 65.00

8-1/2" d, colorful fish swimming on green shaded ground, scalloped border, gold trim, sgd "Lancy," "Bairritz, W. S. or S. W. Co. Limoges, France," pierced for hanging......50.00

Platter

14" l, bass on lure, sgd "RK Beck" 125.00

23" l, hp, Charoone, Haviland......................................200.00

Set

8 pcs, 4 plates, 24" l, platter, sauce boat with attached plate, cov tureen, Rosenthal..395.00

11 pcs, 10 plates, serving platter, sgd "Limoges" 360.00

15 pcs, 12 9" plates, 24" platter, sauce boat with attached plate, cov tureen, hp, raised gold design edge, artist sgd, Limoges 800.00

GAMES

History: Board games have been commercially produced in this country since at least 1822, and card games since the 1780s. However, it was not until the 1840s that large numbers of games were produced that survive to this day. The W. & S. B. Ives Company produced many board and card games in the 1840s and 1950s. Milton Bradley and McLoughlin Brothers became major producers of games starting in the 1860s, followed by Parker Brothers in the 1880s. Other major producers of games in this period were Bliss, Chaffee and Selchow, Selchow and Righter, and Singer.

Today, most games from the 19th century are rare and highly collectible, primarily because of their spectacular lithography. McLoughlin and Bliss command a premium because of the rarity. The quality of materials, and the extraordinary art that was created to grace the covers and boards of their games.

In the 20th century, Milton Bradley, Selchow and Righter and Parker Brothers became the primary manufacturers of boxed games. They have all now been absorbed by toy giant Hasbro Corporation. Other noteworthy producers were All-Fair, Pressman, and Transogram, all of which are no longer in business. Today the hottest part of the game collecting market is in rare character games from the 1960s. Parker Brothers and All-Fair games from the 1920s to 1940s also have some excellent lithography and are highly collectible.

References: *Board Games of the 50's, 60's & 70's with Prices*, L-W Books, 1994; Mark Cooper, *Baseball Games*, Schiffer Publishing, 1995; Lee Dennis, *Warman's Antique American* Games, 1840-1940, Wallace-Homestead, 1991; *Dexterity Games and Other Hand-Held Puzzles*, L-W Book Sales, 1995; Jack Matthews, *Toys Go to War*, Pictorial Histories Publishing, 1994; Rick Polizzi, *Baby Boomer Games*, Collector Books, 1995; Rick Polizzi and Fred Schaefer, *Spin Again*, Chronicle Books, 1991; Desi Scarpone, *Board Games*, Schiffer Publishing, 1995; Carl P. Stirn, *Turn-of-the-Century Dolls, Toys and Games* (1893 catalog reprint), Dover Publications, 1990; Bruce Whitehill, *Games: American Boxed Games and Their Makers*, Wallace-Homestead, 1992.

Periodicals: *The Games Annual,* 5575 Arapahoe Rd., Suite D, Boulder, CO 80303; *Toy Shop*, 700 E. State St., Iola, WI 54990; *Toy Trader*, P.O. Box 1050, Dubuque, IA 52004.

Collectors' Clubs: American Game Collectors Assoc., P.O. Box 44, Dresher, PA, 19025; Gamers Alliance, P.O. Box 197, East Meadow, NY 11554.

Museums: Checkers Hall of Fame, Petal, MS; Essex Institute, Salem, MA; Margaret Woodbury Strong Museum, Rochester, NY; University of Waterloo Museum & Archive of Games, Waterloo, Ontario, Canada; Washington Dolls' House and Toy Museum, Washington, D.C.

Additional Listings: See *Warman's Americana & Collectibles*.

Notes: While people collect games for many reasons, it is strong graphic images that bring the highest prices. Games which are collected because they are fun to play or for nostalgic reasons are still collectible but will not bring high prices. Also, game collectors are not interested in common and "public domain" games such as checkers, tiddley winks, Authors, Anagrams, Jackstraws, Rook, Pit, Flinch, and Peter Coodles. The game market today is characterized by fairly stable prices for ordinary items, increasing discrimination for grades of condition, and continually rising prices for rare material in excellent condition. Whether you are a dealer or a collector, be careful to buy games in good condition. Avoid games with taped or split corners or other box damage. Games made after about 1950 are difficult to sell unless they are complete and in excellent condition. As games get older, there is a forgiveness factor for condition and completeness that increases with age.

These listings are for games that are complete and in excellent condition. Be sure that the game you're looking to price is the same as the one described in the listing. The 19th century makers routinely published the same title on several different versions of the game, varying in size and graphics. Dimensions listed below are rounded to the nearest half inch.

Advisor: David Oglesgy and Susan Stock..

Big Trail Game, Parker Brothers, c1930, 13-1/2" x 17", based on John Wayne's first feature film......................................250.00
Bugs Bunny Adventure Game, Milton Bradley, c1961, 9-1/2" x 19", colorful box showing Warner Bros. characters 35.00
Bullwinkle and Rocky Role Playing Party Game, TSR, c1988 ....20.00
Caper, Parker Brothers, c1970, 11" x 23", features 3 dimensional playing board 10.00
Clue, Parker Brothers, c1949, separate board and pieces box 25.00
Eldorado, Parker Brothers, c1941, 15" x 24-1/2" 125.00
Fish Pond, McLoughlin Bros., c1898, 8" x 18", children on cover 125.00
Fish Pond, Milton Bradley, c1910, 10" x 20", fisherman on cover 75.00
Flap Jacks, Alderman-Fairchild, c1931, toss game, 15-1/2" x 12-1/2"...75.00
F-Troop mini-board Card Game, Ideal, c1965, from TV show 50.00

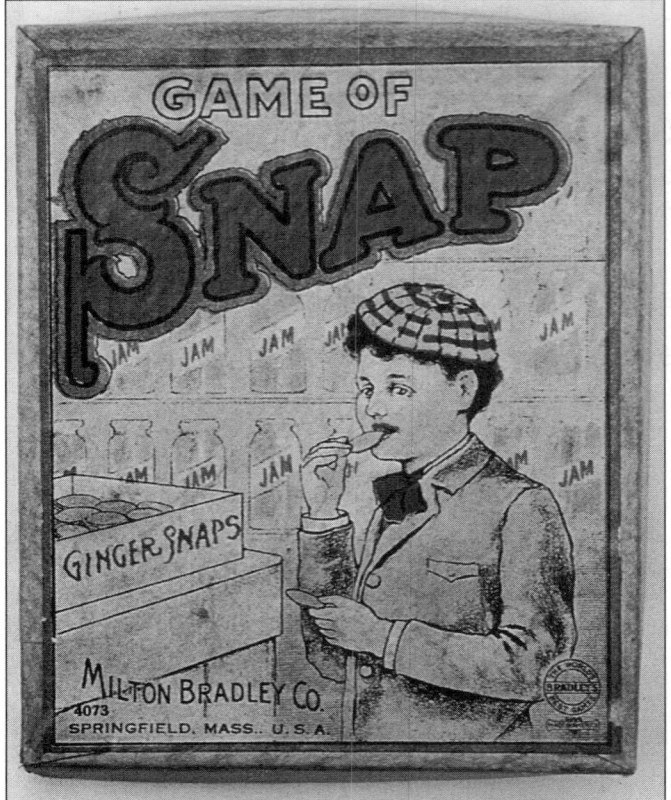

Game of Snap, Milton Bradley, #4073, $35.

Game of Battles or Fun For Boys, McLoughlin Bros., c1900, 23" x 23", cardboard soldiers and cannons 2,500.00

Game of Billy Possum, unknown mfgr, c1910, 8" x 15", cover showing Billy Possom and Teddy Bear 600.00

Game of Bo Peep, J. H. Singer, beautiful woman on cover, 8-1/2" x 14"..275.00

Game of Moon Tag, Parker Brothers, c1950, 10-1/2" x 20" 50.00

Game of Oasis, Milton Bradley, c1937, 9-1/2" x 19-1/2", rare game based on Middle East.....................................150.00

Game of Rival Policeman, McLoughlin Brothers, c1898, 12" x 21", comic style cover art, lead figural playing pieces......4,000.00

Gilligans Island Game, Game Gems, c1965, 9-1/2" x 18-1/2" 350.00

Going to Jerusalem, Parker Brothers, c1955, 10-1/2" x 20", unusual religious theme game 75.00

Jolly Darkie Target Game, Milton Bradley, c1900, 10-1/2" x 19" 750.00

Jonny Quest Card Game, Milton Bradley, c1965, 6" x 10" 75.00

Monopoly, Parker Brothers, c1935, white box edition #9, metal playing pieces and embossed hotels 150.00

Monopoly, Parker Brothers, 1946 Popular Edition, separate board and pieces box..25.00

Motorcycle Game, Milton Bradley, c1905, 9" x 9", early motorcycle on cover 250.00

Play Basketball with Bob Cousy, National Games, c1960, featuring young Bob Cousy on cover 125.00

Race To The Moon, All-Fair, c1932, early space target game, 10" x 19"..600.00

Ralph Edwards This Is Your Life, Lowell, c1955, 13" x 19" 125.00

Star Reporter, Parker Brothers, c1950, 10-1/2" x 20" 65.00

Strange Game of Forbidden Fruit, Parker Brothers, c1900, 4" x 5-1/2", card game 35.00

The Game of the Wizard of Oz, Whitman, c1939, 7" x 13-1/2" 300.00

The Limited Mail and Express Game, Parker Brothers, c1894, 14" x 21", metal train playing pieces..................................250.00

The Mansion of Happiness, Henry P. Ives (and others), c1864, sold as a board only 250.00

The Mansion of Happiness, W. & S. B. Ives, c1843, the earliest "common" American board game................................950.00

Tom Swift, Parker Brothers, c1966, 9-1/2" x 19-1/2", based on syndicated book series 250.00

Truth or Consequences, Gabriel, c1955, 14" x 19-1/2", from Ralph Edwards TV show 75.00

World's Fair Game, Milton Bradley, c1964, 9-1/2" x 13-1/2" 35.00

GAUDY DUTCH

History: Gaudy Dutch is an opaque, soft-paste ware made between 1790 and 1825 in England's Staffordshire district.

The wares first were hand decorated in an underglaze blue and fired; then additional decorations were added over the glaze. The over-glaze decoration is extensively worn on many of the antique pieces. Gaudy Dutch found a ready market in the Pennsylvania German community because it was inexpensive and extremely colorful. It had little appeal in England.

Marks: Marks of various potters, including the impressed marks of Riley and Wood, have been found on some pieces, although most are unmarked.

References: Susan and Al Bagdade, *Warman's English & Continental Pottery & Porcelain*, 2nd ed., Wallace-Homestead, 1991; Eleanor and Edward Fox, *Gaudy Dutch*, published by author, 1970, out of print; John A. Shuman, III, *Collector's Encyclopedia of Gaudy Dutch & Welsh*, Collector Books, 1990, 1998 value update.

REPRODUCTION ALERT

Cup plates, bearing the impressed mark "CYBRIS," have been reproduced and are collectible in their own right. The Henry Ford Museum has issued pieces in the Single Rose pattern, although they are porcelain rather than soft paste.

Advisor: John D. Querry.

Butterfly
    Bowl, 11" d...3,900.00
    Coffeepot 11" h..4,500.00
    Cup and Saucer, handleless, minor enamel flakes, chips on table ring...600.00
    Plate, 7 1/4" d..775.00
    Soup Plate, 8 1/2" d, wear and scratches, rim hairline
    ....495.00
    Sugar Bowl, cov...900.00
    Teapot, 5" h, squat baluster form 1,400.00
    Waste Bowl, 1,275.00
Carnation
    Bowl, 6-1/4" d..750.00
    Creamer, 4-3/4" h...700.00
    Pitcher, 6" h..675.00
    Plate, 8" d...850.00
    Teabowl and Saucer...495.00
    Teapot, cov..1,275.00
    Toddy Plate...525.00
    Waste Bowl 370.00
Dahlia
    Bowl, 6-1/4" d..675.00
    Plate, 8" d...1,100.00
    Teabowl and Saucer...700.00

Plate, Single Rose, 8-1/4" d, $325.

Double Rose
- Bowl, 6-1/4" d..400.00
- Creamer..650.00
- Gravy Boat..300.00
- Plate
  - 8-1/4" d..580.00
  - 10" d..935.00
- Sugar Bowl, cov..750.00
- Teapot, cov...800.00
- Toddy Plate, 4-1/2" d.....................................350.00
- Waste Bowl, 6-1/2" d, 3" h.............................550.00

Dove
- Creamer..675.00
- Plate
  - 7-1/2" d..770.00
  - 8 1/8" d, very worn, scratches, stains.........245.00
- Waste Bowl...650.00

Flower Basket, plate, 6-1/2" d...........................195.00

Grape
- Bowl, 6-1/2" d, lustered rim............................385.00
- Plate, 6-1/4" d..580.00
- Sugar Bowl, cov..450.00
- Teabowl and Saucer..475.00
- Toddy Plate, 5" d..395.00

Leaf, bowl, 11-1/2" d, shallow.......................4,800.00

Oyster
- Bowl, 5-1/2" d...300.00
- Coffeepot, cov, 12" h...................................3,000.00
- Plate, 9-1/2" d...575.00
- Soup Plate, 8-1/2" d..550.00
- Teabowl and Saucer..400.00
- Toddy Plate, 5-1/2" d......................................425.00

Single Rose
- Bowl, 6" d...275.00
- Coffeepot, 10-3/4" h, double-gourd form........850.00
- Cup and Saucer, handleless, pr......................850.00
- Plate, 8-1/4" d...650.00
- Quill Holder, cov...2,500.00
- Sugar Bowl, cov..700.00
- Toddy Plate, 5-1/4" d......................................250.00
- Waste Bowl, 5 1/2" d, wear, hairlines, stains, flake on table rim, glaze rim flakes.................................365.00

Sunflower
- Bowl, 6-1/2" d...900.00
- Coffeepot, cov, 9-1/2" h..............................6,500.00
- Creamer..850.00
- Cup and saucer, handleless, wear, chips.......360.00

Urn
- Creamer..350.00
- Cup and Saucer, handleless, wear and scratches.......300.00
- Plate
  - 8-1/4" d..910.00
  - 9 7/8" d, very worn, scratches, stains, rim chips......225.00
- Sugar Bowl, cov, 6-1/2" h, round, tip and base restored...295.00

War Bonnet
- Bowl, cov..225.00
- Coffeepot, cov...9,500.00
- Cup and Saucer, handleless, wear, chips, close mismatch...370.00
- Plate, 8-1/8" d, pinpoint rim flake, minor wear..............880.00
- Teapot, cov..2,400.00
- Toddy Plate, 4-1/2" d......................................525.00

GAUDY IRONSTONE

History: Gaudy Ironstone was made in England around 1850. Ironstone is an opaque, heavy-bodied earthenware which contains large proportions of flint and slag.

Gaudy Ironstone is decorated in patterns and colors similar to those of Gaudy Welsh.

Marks: Most pieces are impressed "Ironstone" and bear a registry mark.

Chop Plate, 12-3/4" d, 9 rabbits, 4 frogs and flowers, circular center, black transfer, red, blue, green, and yellow dec....990.00
Creamer, Morning Glory, 6-1/2" h, paneled, foliage handle...175.00
Cup and Saucer, handleless
- Floral..85.00
- Morning Glory...90.00
- Rose..80.00
- Strawberry..85.00
- Urn..115.00
- Urn and Flowers..135.00
Pitcher, 7-1/2" d, lion head snake handle, red, blue, and green, Mason's, mkd "Patent Ironstone China".......330.00
Plate
- 8-1/2" d...75.00
- 9-3/8" d, 6 rabbits, 3 frogs and flowers, black transfer, red, blue, green, and yellow dec.......470.00
- 9-3/8" d, 9 rabbits, 3 cabbages, 3 frogs, 3 trees, black transfer, red, blue, green, and yellow dec.......420.00
- 9-1/2" d, 8 rabbits, black transfer, red, blue, green, and yellow dec, stains and crazing.......360.00
- 9-3/4" d, twelve-sided, Urn and Flowers, blue, red, pink, and green, minor enamel flaking.......140.00
Platter, 14-7/8" l, 8 rabbits, 4 frogs and flowers, black transfer, red, blue, green, and yellow dec, stains and crazing...1,100.00
Sugar Bowl, cov
- Floral, 7-1/4" h, luster trim............................125.00
- Morning Glory, 8" h, paneled, underglaze blue, foliage handles...195.00
Teapot, cov, 10" h, Blackberry, paneled, underglaze blue and black, yellow and red enamel and luster, cock's comb handle and final glued, chips on rim and spout.......880.00
Toddy Plate, Urn, 4-3/4" d.................................200.00
Waste Bowl, Strawberry, 5-3/8" h......................185.00

Plate, shaped rim, copper luster highlights, 8-3/8" d, $75.

GAUDY WELSH

History: Gaudy Welsh is a translucent porcelain that was originally made in the Swansea area of England from 1830 to 1845. Although the designs resemble Gaudy Dutch, the body texture and weight differ. One of the characteristics is the gold luster on top of the glaze.

In 1890, Allerton made a similar ware from heavier opaque porcelain.

Marks: Allerton pieces usually bear an export mark.

References: Susan and Al Bagdade, *Warman's English & Continental Pottery & Porcelain*, 2nd ed., Wallace-Homestead, 1991; John A. Shuman, III, *Collector's Encyclopedia of Gaudy Dutch and Welsh*, Collector Books, 1990, 1991 value update, out-of-print; Howard Y. Williams, *Gaudy Welsh China*, Wallace-Homestead, out-of-print.

Columbine
  Bowl, 10" d, 5-1/2" h, ftd, underglaze blue and polychrome
    enamel floral dec 410.00
  Plate, 5-1/2" d 75.00
Daisy and Chain
  Creamer..185.00
  Cup and Saucer 95.00
  Sugar Bowl, cov...195.00
  Teapot, cov...225.00
Flower Basket
  Bowl, 10-1/2" d...195.00
  Mug, 4" h...95.00
  Plate...65.00
  Sugar Bowl, cov, luster trim...175.00

Grape
  Bowl, 5-3/4" d..50.00
  Cup and Saucer 75.00
  Mug, 2-1/2" h..70.00
  Plate, 5-1/4" d..65.00
Oyster
  Bowl, 6" d...85.00
  Creamer, 3" h..100.00
  Cup and Saucer 75.00
  Jug, 5-3/4" h..90.00
  Soup Plate, 10" d, flange rim...85.00
  Sugar Bowl, cov..100.00
Strawberry
  Creamer..90.00
  Cup and Saucer 80.00
  Plate, 8-3/4" d...150.00
Tulip
  Bowl, 6-1/4" d..60.00
  Cake Plate, 10" d, molded handles 125.00
  Creamer, 5-1/4" h...100.00
  Sugar, cov, 6-3/4" h..115.00
  Teapot, 7-1/4" h..195.00
Wagon Wheel
  Cup and Saucer 85.00
  Mug, 2-1/2" h..95.00
  Pitcher, 8-1/2" h..200.00
  Plate, 8-3/4" d..90.00

GIRANDOLES AND MANTEL LUSTRES

History: A girandole is a very elaborate branched candleholder, often featuring cut glass prisms surrounding the mountings. A mantel lustre is a glass vase with attached cut glass prisms.

Pitcher, 7-3/8" h, $85.

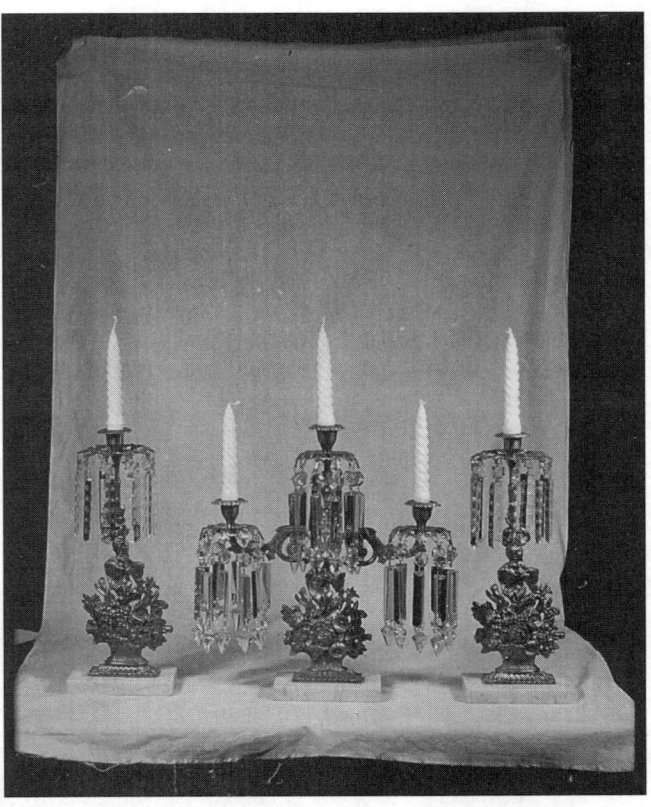

Brass, basket of flowers motif, three-candle centerpiece, two single candle side pieces, marble base, 16-1/4" h, $500.

Girandoles and mantel lustres usually are found in pairs. It is not uncommon for girandoles to be part of a large garniture set. Girandoles and mantel lustres achieved their greatest popularity in the last half of the 19th century both in the United States and Europe.

Girandoles, pr

14" h, SP and cut glass, three tiers hung with faceted drops, scrolled candle arms, c1900 .... 165.00

15" h, Victorian, pink, enameled and colored wild flowers, notched prisms 275.00

15-1/2" h, candlesticks, marble bases, figural brass stems, clear cut prisms 140.00

16-3/8" h, three arms, clear cut prisms, cast brass frame, marble base with brass boy and dog 145.00

18" h, courting couple, brass relief, triple branch with prisms, marble base 125.00

20-1/2" h, pierced and shaped rect frame, orig glass, crest, Italian Rococo, 18th C 450.00

35-1/2" h, bronze, 7 light glass drops suspended from pressed glass stars 600.00

Mantel Lusters

6-1/4" h, 8" w, cornucopia style, opaline glass horns, alternating with gilt-bronze female hand, white marble base, French, 19th C, pr 250.00

9" h, blue, enameled florals, gold trim, white beading, Waterford crystal prisms 240.00

12" h, opaline, green fold over top, white satin glass bodies, gold trim 250.00

14" h, double cut overlay, white to emerald green, prisms of alternating lengths 250.00

15-3/4" h, Bohemian, cobalt blue, gilt scrollwork dec, colored floral springs, 2 rows of crystal prisms, late 19th C 345.00

GOLDSCHEIDER

History: Friedrich Goldscheider founded a porcelain and faience factory in Vienna, Austria, in 1885. Upon his death, his widow carried on operations. In 1920, Walter and Marcell, Friedrich's sons, gained control. During the Art Deco period, the firm commissioned several artists to create figural statues, among which were Pierrettes and sleek wolfhounds. During the 1930s, the company's products were mostly traditional.

In the early 1940s, the Goldscheiders fled to the United States and re-established operations in Trenton, New Jersey. The Goldscheider Everlast Corporation was listed in Trenton City directories between 1943 and 1950. Goldscheider Ceramics, located at, 1441 Heath Avenue, Trenton, New Jersey, was listed in the *1952 Crockery and Glass Journal Directory* but was not listed in 1954.

Ashtray, 7-1/2" l, German Shepherd 48.00

Bust, 26" h, finely molded face, downcast eyes, long light brown hair looped into chignon, narrow mauve head band and straps with oval irid glass jewels, gilt draped gown, incised "Montenave," Goldschneider seal molded in relief 2,800.00

Figure
  4-1/2" h, Madonna and Child, orig label 35.00
  4-3/4" h, terrier, orange, Art Deco 45.00
  6-3/4" h, Prince of Wales 75.00
  8-1/2" h, lady with parasol, #817 .... 70.00
  10-1/2" h, Southern Belle 85.00
  13" h, flying duck, modeled by E. Straub 115.00

Figure, Lorenzl, artist, mkd "622/344/10 72/700," 16-1/4" h, $1,600.

Music Box, cov, 7" h, Colonial girl 115.00

Plaque, 13-1/2" w, 25-1/8" h, earthenware, rect, molded maiden, profile, garland of blossoms and berries in hair, large blossom and cluster on left, earth tones, designer sgd "Lamassi," c1900 .... 1,100.00

Plate, mermaid pattern, multicolored 165.00

Wall Mask, 11-1/4" h, Art Dec, curly brown haired girl, red lips, aqua scarf 200.00

GONDER POTTERY

History: Lawton Gonder established Gonder Ceramic Arts, Inc., at Zanesville, Ohio, in 1941. He had gained experience while working for other factories in the area. Gonder experimented with glazes, including Chinese crackle, gold crackle, and flambé. Lamp bases were manufactured under the name "Eglee" at a second plant location.

The company ceased operation in 1957.

Marks: Pieces are clearly marked with the word "Gonder" in various forms.

References: Susan and Al Bagdade, *Warman's American Pottery and Porcelain*, Wallace-Homestead, 1994; Ron Hoppes, *Collector's Guide and History of Gonder Pottery*, L-W Book Sales, 1992.

Collectors' Club: Gonder Collectors Club, P.O. Box 21, Crooksville, OH 43731.

Basket, pink and gray, H-39, 8-1/4" w, 7" h, $38.

Bowl, 6-1/2" d, ribbed, yellow 10.00
Candlesticks, pr, 4-3/4" h, turquoise ext., pink-coral int., mkd "E-14, Gonder" 20.00
Creamer and Sugar, dark brown drip and brown spatter 30.00
Ewer
    6" d, mottled blue, pink int. 24.00
    13" h, Shell and Star pattern, green..................................50.00
Figure
    7" h, swan, shaded blue 15.00
    10-1/2" h, elephant, raised trunk, rose and gray 45.00
Flower Frog, 7-3/4" x 7", Swirl pattern, blue and brown glossy glaze 25.00
Vase, 7-1/2" h, flower shape, pink and mottled blue glaze ..20.00

GOOFUS GLASS

History: Goofus glass, also known as Mexican ware, hooligan glass, and pickle glass, is a pressed glass with relief designs that were painted either on the back or front. The designs are usually in red and green with a metallic gold ground. It was popular from 1890 to 1920 and was used as a premium at carnivals.

It was produced by several companies: Crescent Glass Company, Wellsburg, West Virginia; Imperial Glass Corporation, Bellaire, Ohio; LaBelle Glass Works, Bridgeport, Ohio; and Northwood Glass Co., Indiana, Pennsylvania, Wheeling, West Virginia, and Bridgeport, Ohio.

Goofus glass lost its popularity when people found that the paint tarnished or scaled off after repeated washings and wear. No record of its manufacture has been found after 1920.

Marks: Goofus glass made by Northwood includes one of the following marks: "N," "N" in one circle, "N" in two circles, or one or two circles without the "N."

Periodical: *Goofus Glass Gazette*, 9 Lindenwood Ct., Sterling, VA 20165.

Bowl
    9" d, carnations..30.00
    10-1/2" d, red roses, molded, gold ground 45.00

Vase, rose, red roses, gold ground, 7-1/2" h, $50.

Cake Plate, 11" d, Dahlia and Fan, red dec, gold ground ...40.00
Candle Holder, red and gold..20.00
Compote, 9-1/2" d, strawberries and leaves, red and green dec, gold ground, ruffled..50.00
Dish, 11" d, chrysanthemum sprays, red and gold, scalloped rim 75.00
Pickle Jar, aqua, molded, gold, blue, and red painted floral design 50.00
Pitcher, red rose bud dec, gold leaves 60.00
Plate
    7-1/2" d, apples, red dec, gold ground 24.00
    11" d, roses, red and gold, scalloped rim 45.00
Salt and Pepper Shakers, pr, poppy...................................40.00
Vase
    7-1/2" h, brown, red bird..30.00
    12" h, red roses, molded, gold ground...........................60.00

GOUDA POTTERY

History: Gouda and the surrounding areas of Holland have been principal Dutch pottery centers for centuries. Originally, the potteries produced a simple utilitarian tin-glazed Delft-type earthenware and the famous clay smoker's pipes.

When pipe making declined in the early 1900s, the Gouda potteries turned to art pottery. Influenced by the Art Nouveau and Art Deco movements, artists expressed themselves with free-form and stylized designs in bold colors.

Periodical: *Dutch Potter*, 47 London Terrace, New Rochelle, NY 10804.

Bowl
  7" d, stylized floral design, black, blues, gold, red, and white, mkd "8r8/GABY/house logo/Gouda/Made in Holland/4239, other incised marks 200.00
  8-1/2" d, 3" h, handle 125.00
Box, cov, 4-1/4" l, carved, black, gold, and white, glazed, Regina mark..175.00
Candleholders, pr, 6-1/2" h, one damaged 150.00
Charger, 12" d, white magnolias, teal petals, black stems, orange and amber speckled ground, mkd "NV Kon Pazuis Unique Gouda Holland," artists monogram "JVS," (J. W. Van Schaik), c1930...450.00
Creamer, Verona pattern...50.00
Decanter, 10-1/2" h, Nadra pattern, orange, brown, and ochre floral dec, black base, handle, stopper 165.00
Jar, cov, 5-1/2" h, Aero pattern, glossy finish, Royal Zuid mark 65.00
Lantern, 6" h, Art Nouveau dec, Palzuid house mark.........165.00
Pitcher
  5" h, 3" d, brown, blue, orange, and white, mkd "ROSEVOL/Gouda/X195/house logo/AB/Made in Holland" 125.00
  5" h, 3-1/2" w, stylized flowers 90.00
Planter, 6" d, 4" at base, white, orange, blue, yellow, and black, dark blue int...125.00
Plate, 12" d, Nadra pattern 115.00
Tobacco Jar, cov, 5" h, Vernon pattern..............................115.00
Trivet, 4" w, Damascus, c1895 ....195.00
Vase, 8-1/4" h, 4-1/2" h, four buttress handles, deep green and purple stylized flowers, factory symbol "A to H" and "Zuid, Holland" 345.00
Wooden Shoe, 6" l, 2-1/2" w, 2-1/4" h, purple, yellow, orange, brown, and turquoise...90.00

Vase, black ground, blue handles, bands of red and light green, mkd, 5-1/4" h, $120.

GRANITEWARE

History: Graniteware is the name commonly given to enamel-coated iron or steel kitchenware.

The first graniteware was made in Germany in the 1830s. Graniteware was not produced in the United States until the 1860s. At the start of World War I, when European companies turned to manufacturing war weapons, American producers took over the market.

Gray and white were the most common graniteware colors, although each company made their own special color in shades of blue, green, brown, violet, cream, or red.

Older graniteware is heavier than the new. Pieces with cast-iron handles date between 1870 to 1890; wood handles between 1900 to 1910. Other dating clues are seams, wooden knobs, and tin lids.

References: Helen Greguire, *Collector's Encyclopedia of Granite Ware: Colors Shapes and Values*, Book 1 (1990, 1994 value update), Book 2 (1993, 1998 value update), Collector Books.

Collectors' Club: National Graniteware Society, P.O. Box 10013, Cedar Rapids, IA 52410.

Additional Listings: See *Warman's Americana & Collectibles* for more examples.

Berry Pail, cov, 7" d, 4-3/4" h, gray and black mottled.........50.00
Bowl, 11-3/4" d, 3-3/4" h, green and white 50.00
Bread Riser, cov, blue and white swirl, tin lid, large 175.00
Cake Pan, 7-1/2" d, robin's egg blue and white marbleized 45.00
Child's Feeding Set, cup and dish, white, chickens dec, worn 35.00
Coffee Boiler, cov, blue and white swirl 100.00
Coffeepot, cov, red swirl...235.00
Colander, 12" d, gray, pedestal base..................................30.00
Cream Can, Chrystolite, green 2,500.00
Creamer, 5" h, turquoise swirl..18.00
Cup, 2-3/4" h, blue and white medium swirl, black trim and handle 50.00
Double Boiler, red swirl 3,600.00
Frying Pan, 10-1/4" d, blue and white mottled, white int. ...135.00
Funnel, cobalt blue and white marbleized, large 50.00
Grater, medium blue...115.00
Hotplate, 2 burners, white graniteware, Hotpoint...............165.00
Kettle, cov, 9" h, 11-1/2" d, gray mottled 50.00
Measure, 1 cup, gray 45.00
Milk Pan, blue and white..35.00
Mixing Bowls, red and white, nested set of 4, 1930s.........155.00
Muffin Pan, blue and white mottled, 8 cups 250.00
Pie Pan, 6" d, cobalt blue and white marbleized.................25.00
Pitcher, 11" h, gray, ice lip...110.00
Pudding Pan, 8" d, cobalt blue and white swirl....................40.00
Refrigerator Bowls, red swirl, 4 pc set..............................585.00
Roaster, emerald green swirl, large 250.00
Skimmer, 10" l, gray mottled..25.00
Spittoon, blue and white swirl..325.00
Teapot, cov, red, cobalt blue, orange, and black swirls, early 1900s 325.00

Soap Dish, wall type, gray, $35.

Tube Pan, octagonal, gray mottled 45.00
Wash Bason, 11-3/4" d, blue and white swirl, Blue Diamond Ware 150.00
Water Pail, lime green, brown, and white swirl, early 1900s 225.00

GREENAWAY, KATE

History: Kate Greenaway, or "K.G." as she initialed her famous drawings, was born in 1846 in London. Her father was a prominent wood engraver. Kate's natural talent for drawing soon was evident, and she began art classes at the age of 12. In 1868 she had her first public exhibition.

Her talents were used primarily in illustrating. The cards she decorated for Marcus Ward are largely unsigned. China and pottery companies soon had her drawings of children appearing on many of their wares. By the 1880s she was one of the foremost children's book illustrators in England.

Reference: Ina Taylor, *Art of Kate Greenaway: A Nostalgic Portrait of Childhood*, Pelican Publishing, 1991.

Collectors' Club: Kate Greenaway Society, P.O. Box 8, Norwood, PA 19074.

REPRODUCTION ALERT

Some Greenaway buttons have been reproduced in Europe and sold in the United States.

Butter Pat, transfer print of boy and girl 35.00
Button, 3/4" d, girl with kitten on fence 12.00
Children's Play Dishes, tea set, multicolored scenes, gold trim, 15 pc set 450.00
Cup and Saucer, transfer print of girl doing laundry in wooden tub 35.00
Dish, 11" l, oval, transfer print of Jack Sprat and Sunbonnet girl 50.00
Figure, 8-1/2" h, boy with basket, satin, gold, pink, and blue trim, mkd "1893" 525.00
Hat, bisque, 3 girls sitting on brim, flowers 120.00
Inkwell, bronze, emb, 2 children 200.00
Match Safe, SP, emb children 50.00

Children's Book, Birthday Book for Children, George Routledge & Sons, 1880, first edition, $125.

Napkin Ring, SS, girl feeding yearling...............................160.00
Perfume Bottle, 2" l, SS, low relief of girls, orig stopper 200.00
Plate, 7" d, transfer print of boy chasing rabbits 65.00
Stickpin, figural, bronze, children playing ring around the rosy, c1900...25.00
Tape Measure, figural, girl holding muff...............................45.00
Teaspoon, SS, figural, girl handle, bowl engraved with Lucy Locket verse..50.00
Tile, each 6-3/8" d, transfer print, 4 seasons, one spacer, brown and white dec, blue border, stamped mark, produced by T & R Boote, 1881, framed, 5 pc set....................................325.00
Toothpick Holder, 5" h, 2-1/4" h New England shiny finish sq peachblow toothpick holder, silverplated holder metal holder, little girl holding ring over holder, cocker spaniel on opposite side, sgd "James . Tufts Boston Warranted Quadruple Plate 3404, 1148" 1,075.00

GREENTOWN GLASS

History: The Indiana Tumbler and Goblet Co., Greentown, Indiana, produced its first clear, pressed glass table and bar wares in late 1894. Initial success led to a doubling of the plant size in 1895 and other subsequent expansions, one in 1897 to allow for the manufacture of colored glass. In 1899, the firm joined the combine known as the National Glass Company.

In 1900, just before arriving in Greentown, Jacob Rosenthal developed an opaque brown glass, called "chocolate," which ranged in color from a dark, rich chocolate to a lighter coffee-with-cream hue. Production of chocolate glass saved the financially pressed Indiana Tumbler and Goblet Works. The Cactus and Leaf Bracket patterns were made almost exclusively in chocolate glass. Other popular chocolate patterns include Austrian, Dewey, Shuttle, and Teardrop and Tassel. In 1902, National Glass Company bought Rosenthal's chocolate glass formula so other plants in the combine could use the color.

In 1902, Rosenthal developed the Golden Agate and Rose Agate colors. All work ceased on June 13, 1903, when a fire of suspicious origin destroyed the Indiana Tumbler and Goblet Company Works.

After the fire, other companies, e.g., McKee and Brothers, produced chocolate glass in the same pattern designs used by Greentown. Later reproductions also have been made, with Cactus among the most-heavily copied patterns.

Reference: James Measell, *Greentown Glass*, Grand Rapids Public Museum, 1979, 1992-93 value update, distributed by Antique Publications.

Collectors' Clubs: Collectors of Findlay Glass, P.O. Box 256, Findlay, OH 45839; National Greentown Glass Assoc., 19596 Glendale Ave., South Bend, IN 46637.

Videotapes: *Centennial Exhibit of Greentown Glass* and *Reproductions of Greentown Glass*, National Greentown Glass Assoc., P.O. Box 107, Greentown, IN 46936.

Museums: Grand Rapids Public Museum, Ruth Herrick Greentown Glass Collection, Grand Rapids, MI; Greentown Glass Museum, Greentown, IN.

Additional Listings: Holly Amber; Pattern Glass.

Reproduction Alert.

Animal Covered dish
    Dolphin, chocolate, chip off tail 195.00
    Rabbit, dome top, amber 250.00
Bowl, 7-1/4" d, Herringbone Buttress, green......................135.00
Butter, cov, Cupid, chocolate..575.00
Celery Vase, Beaded Panel, clear.......................................100.00
Compote, Geneva, 4-1/2" d, 3-1/2" h, chocolate...............150.00
Cordial, Austrian, canary...125.00
Creamer
    Cactus, chocolate...85.00
    Cupid, Nile green 400.00
    Indian Head, opaque white 450.00
Cruet, orig stopper, Leaf Bracket, chocolate 275.00
Goblet
    Overall Lattice...40.00
    Shuttle, chocolate 500.00
Mug, outdoor drinking scene, Nile green.........................200.00
Mustard, cov, Daisy, opaque white......................................75.00
Nappy, Masonic, chocolate..85.00
Paperweight, Buffalo, Nile green.......................................600.00

Plate, Serenade, chocolate 85.00
Punch Cup, Cord Drapery, clear..20.00
Relish, Leaf Bracket, 8" l, oval, chocolate 75.00
Salt and Pepper Shakers, pr, Cactus, chocolate 150.00
Sugar, cov, Dewey, cobalt blue 145.00
Syrup, Indian Feather, green..175.00
Toothpick, Cactus, chocolate...75.00
Tumbler
    Cactus, chocolate..60.00
    Dewey, canary..65.00

GRUEBY POTTERY

History: William Grueby was active in the ceramic industry for several years before he developed his own method of producing matte-glazed pottery and founded the Grueby Faience Company in Boston, Massachusetts, in 1897.

The art pottery was hand thrown in natural shapes, hand molded, and hand tooled. A variety of colored glazes, singly or in combinations, were produced, but green was the most popular. In 1908, the firm was divided into the Grueby Pottery Company and the Grueby Faience and Tile Co. The Grueby Faience and Tile Company made art tile until 1917, although its pottery production was phased out about 1910.

Vase, bulbous, leaves and flowers, 12" h, $8,525. Photo courtesy of David Rago Auctions, Inc.

Salt and Pepper Shakers, pr, Cactus pattern, chocolate slag, $275. Photo courtesy of Jackson's Auctioneers & Appraisers.

Left: Vase, three-sided opening, applied full length leaves alternating with buds, frothy matte green finish, white clay body showing through leaf edges, imp "Grueby Faience," 7-3/4" h, $2,090; middle: Scarab paperweight, matte green enamel, imp mark and paper label, $715; right: Vase, six-sided lobed rim, tooled and applied yellow daffodils, rich organic matte green enamel, circular mark/ER, 11-1/4" h, $8,525. Photo courtesy of David Rago Auctions, Inc.

Minor damage is acceptable to most collectors of Grueby Pottery.

References: Paul Evans, *Art Pottery of the United States*, 2nd ed., Feingold & Lewis Publishing, 1987; Ralph and Terry Kovel, *Kovels' American Art Pottery*, Crown Publishers, 1993; Susan Montgomery, *The Ceramics of William H. Grueby,* Arts and Crafts Quarterly Press, 1993; David Rago, *American Art Pottery,* Knickerbocker Press, 1997.

Advisor: David Rago.

Bowl, 8" d, 2" h, flat, green matte ext., glossy dark green int., circle mark 300.00
Candlestick, 8" h, 3" d, tapering cylindrical, bulbous top, tooled leaves, dark blue glaze, unmarked 1,000.00
Jardiniere, 6" h, 11" d, flaring vessel, tooled leaves, yellow matte glaze, circle mark 3,000.00
Paperweight, 3" h, 4" l, Scarab beetle, matte blue glaze, circle mark, nicks to bottom edge...400.00
Vase
  7" h, 13" d, bulbous, squatty, tooled leaves, three-petal flowers, matte green glaze, circle mark........................3,000.00
  8" h, 4" d, cylindrical, green matte glaze, mkd..............500.00
  8" h, 5" d, bulbous, cylindrical neck, tooled and applied leaves and buds, green matte glaze, circle stamp mark . 1,500.00
  9" h, 5" d, five-sided, yellow daffodils and green leaves, green matte ground, circle mark, small chip to rim 4,000.00

HAIR ORNAMENTS

History: Hair ornaments, among the first accessories developed by primitive man, were used to remove tangles and keep hair out of one's face. Remnants of early combs have been found in many archaeological excavations.

As fashion styles evolved through the centuries, hair ornaments kept pace with changes in design and usage. Hair combs and other hair ornaments are made in a wide variety of materials, e.g., precious metals, ivory, tortoiseshell, plastics, and wood.

Combs were first made in America during the Revolution when imports from England were restricted. Early American combs were made of horn and treasured as toiletry articles.

Reference: Evelyn Haetig, *Antique Combs and Purses*, Gallery Graphics Press, 1983.

Collectors' Club: Antique Fancy Comb Collectors Club, 3291 N. River Rd., Libertyville, IL 60048.

Museums: Leominster Historical Society, Field School Museum, Leominster, MA; Miller's Museum of Antique Combs, Homer, AK.

Back Comb, Art Nouveau, tortoiseshell, gilt brass and turquoise glass accents 125.00
Barrette, 4" l, bar type, faux tortoiseshell with rhinestones... 10.00
Bodkin, Art Nouveau, celluloid, imitation tortoiseshell, sinuous contours, pique, rhinestones 10.00
Comb
  Art Nouveau, ivory, paste stones, French, c1910 ....45.00
  Edwardian, 3-1/2" l, 2-3/4" w, silver topped yellow and white gold, 100 round rose cut diamonds, foliated scroll motif, simulated tortoise shell comb 2,530.00
  Retro, 1-7/8" l, 1-3/4" w, 14K yg, tortoise shell combs, pr 345.00
  Victorian, 3-5/8" l, 3-5/8" w, yellow colored metal, prong and bezel set 142 old European cut round diamonds, ranging from 2.49 to 6.11 mm, hinged, textured arch, scrolling ribbons 12,650.00

Comb, celluloid, cream color, five prongs, dec filigree ornamentation with bead trimming, English, $100. Photo courtesy of Julie Robinson.

Hairpin, 15 1/2" l, carved ivory, pierced and carved handle depicting two figures, Japanese 100.00
Ornament
    4-1/2" l, plastic, simulated stones, c1935 ....65.00
    4-3/4" l, rhinestones and simulated pearls, c1925 ....40.00
Pompadour Comb, Art Nouveau, faux tortoiseshell, gilt brass and turquoise glass accents, pr 80.00

HALL CHINA COMPANY

History: Robert Hall founded the Hall China Company in 1903 in East Liverpool, Ohio. He died in 1904 and was succeeded by his son, Robert Taggart Hall. After years of experimentation, Robert T. Hall developed a leadless glaze in 1911, opening the way for production of glazed household products.

The Hall China Company made many types of kitchenware, refrigerator sets, and dinnerware in a wide variety of patterns. Some patterns were made exclusively for a particular retailer, such as Heather Rose for Sears.

One of the most popular patterns was Autumn Leaf, a premium designed by Arden Richards in 1933 for the exclusive use of the Jewel Tea Company. Still a Jewel Tea property, Autumn Leaf has not been listed in catalogs since 1978 but is produced on a replacement basis with the date stamped on the back.

References: Susan and Al Bagdade, *Warman's American Pottery and Porcelain*, Wallace-Homestead, 1994; Harvey Duke, *Hall China: Price Guide Update Two*, ELO Books, 1995; ——, *Official Price Guide to Pottery and Porcelain*, 8th ed., House of Collectibles, 1995; C. L. Miller, *Jewel Tea Grocery Products with Values*, Schiffer Publishing, 1996; ——, *Jewel Tea: Sales and Housewares Collectibles*, Schiffer Publishing, 1995; Jim and Lynn Salko, *Halls Autumn Leaf China and Jewel Tea Collectible*, published by authors (143 Topeg Dr., Severna Park, MD 21146); Margaret and Kenn Whitmyer, *Collector's Encyclopedia of Hall China*, 2nd ed., Collector Books, 1994, 1997 values update.

Periodicals: *The Daze*, P.O. Box 57, Otisville, MI 48463; *Hall China Encore*, 317 N. Pleasant St., Oberlin, OH 44074.

Collectors' Clubs: Hall Collector's Club, P.O. Box 360488, Cleveland, OH 44136; National Autumn Leaf Collectors Club, Route 16, Box 275, Tulsa, OK 74131.

Additional Listings: See *Warman's Americana & Collectibles* for more examples.

Autumn Leaf, creamer and sugar, $45.

Chinese Red, pitcher, $24.

Kitchen Ware

Bean Pot, New England, #1, Orange Poppy 100.00
Coffeepot, Great American, Orange Poppy 65.00
Fork, Feather, experimental pattern, blue 200.00
Jug, Primrose, rayed 20.00
Reamer, lettuce green 450.00
Spoon, Feather, experimental pattern, yellow 300.00
Watering Can, lilac 850.00

Patterns

Autumn Leaf
Bowl, 5-1/2" d..5.00
Butter, 1 lb 185.00
Candy Dish..525.00
Coffeepot, cov 65.00
Creamer and Sugar 45.00
Cup and Saucer 10.00
Drip Jar 15.00
Gravy Boat, underplate 15.00
Plate, 8" d..14.00
Platter, 13-1/2" l...15.00
Teacup and Saucer 9.00
Vegetable Bowl, bowl 18.00
Banded Indian Red, cookie jar.......................................100.00
Blue Bouquet
Creamer, Boston...20.00
Cup and Saucer 25.00
French Baker, round..25.00
Platter
    13" l...35.00
    15" l...40.00
Soup, flat..30.00
Spoon...100.00
Cactus, cookie jar, cov, five band 75.00
Cameo Rose
Bowl, 5-1/4" d...3.00
Butter Dish, 3/4 lb 30.00
Casserole...25.00
Creamer and Sugar 10.00
Cream Soup, 6" d 7.00
Cup and Saucer 9.00
Plate, 8" d..2.50
Teapot, cov, 6 cup..35.00
Tidbit, 3 tier...40.00

Fuji
Coffee Server 40.00
Creamer and Sugar 25.00
Gamebirds
Percolator, electric...140.00
Teapot, cov, 2 cup size
    Ducks and pheasant 195.00
    Geese and grouse 195.00
Mount Vernon
Coffeepot 125.00
Creamer...10.00
Cup...8.00
Fruit Bowl..8.00
Gravy Boat...20.00
Plate, 10" d..14.00
Saucer...3.00
Soup Bowl, 8" d, flat...6.50
Vegetable Bowl, 9-1/4" l, oval...10.00
Red Poppy
Bowl, 5-1/2" d...5.00
Cake Plate 17.50
Cake Server 65.00
Casserole, cov...25.00
Coffeepot, cov 12.00
Creamer and Sugar..15.00
Cup and Saucer...8.00
French Baker, fluted..15.00
Jug, Daniel, radiance..28.00
Plate, 9" d..6.50
Salad Bowl, 9" d...14.00
Teapot, New York..90.00
Silhouette
Bean Pot 50.00
Bowl, 7-7/8" d...50.00
Coffeepot, cov 30.00
Mug...32.00
Pretzel Jar 75.00
Tulip
Bowl, 10-1/4" l, oval...36.00
Coffee Maker, drip, Kadota, all china..............................115.00
Condiment Jar 165.00
Creamer..15.00
Cup and Saucer 15.00
Fruit Bowl, 5-1/2" d...10.00
Mixing Bowl, 6" d 27.00
Plate, 9" d, luncheon..16.00
Platter, 13-1/4" l, oval...42.00
Shakers
    Bulge-type, price for pr 110.00
    Set, salt, pepper, flour, and sugar, handles...................240.00
Sugar, cov 25.00

Teapots
Blue Blossom, airflow 950.00
Cadet, Radiance...350.00
Chinese Red, 3 cup...40.00
Cleveland, turquoise and gold 165.00
Los Angeles, cobalt blue...160.00
Philadelphia, ivory, gold label 115.00
Surfside, emerald and gold...250.00

HAMPSHIRE POTTERY

History: In 1871, James S. Taft founded the Hampshire Pottery Company in Keene, New Hampshire. Production began with redwares and stonewares, followed by majolica in 1879. A semi-porcelain, with the recognizable matte glazes plus the Royal Worcester glaze, was introduced in 1883.

Until World War I, the factory made an extensive line of utilitarian and art wares including souvenir items. After the war, the firm resumed operations but made only hotel dinnerware and tiles. The company was dissolved in 1923.

References: Susan and Al Bagdade, *Warman's American Pottery and Porcelain*, Wallace-Homestead, 1994; Ralph and Terry Kovel, *Kovels' American Art Pottery*, Crown Publishers, 1993.

Bowl, 5-1/2" d, 2-1/2" h, matte green glaze over foliate-forms, imp "Hampshire, M.O."...320.00
Candleholder, 6-1/2" h, shield back with handle, matte green glaze 200.00
Chocolate Pot, 9-1/2" h, cream, holly dec 275.00
Compote, 13-1/4" d, ftd, 2 handles, Ivory pattern, light green highlights, cream ground, red decal mark 175.00
Inkwell, 4-1/8" d, 2-3/4" h, round, large center well, 3 pen holes
....125.00
Lamp Base, 15" h, 9" d, tall cylindrical form, vertical leaves, stems, and flowers, matte green glaze 2,185.00
Mustache Mug, 4" h, applied scene of two men in canoe, titled "Successful Hunters," cream ground, gold highlights, separate mustache insert, circular mark, c1883 ....40.00
Tankard, 7" h, band of stylized dec, green matte glaze, imp "Hampshire" 100.00
Vase
    3" h, cabinet, matte green glaze, mkd....................250.00
    3-1/4" h, 4-1/4" d, squat, leathery matte green glaze, imp mark..375.00
    4-1/2" h, squat base, matte green glaze 265.00
    6-3/4" h, 4-1/4" d, alternating buds and leaves, matte yellow glaze, imp mark...500.00
    7" h, 4" d, cylindrical, flaring to base with two handles, feathered green matte glaze, imp marks "TO" 435.00
    7-1/2" h, 4" d, cylindrical, feathered matte blue glaze, imp mark "A.O." 520.00
    8-1/2" h, 6-1/2" d, bulbous, leathery matte green, blue, and brown dripping glaze, imp mark 1,000.00
    12" h, 5" d, leathery matte blue-green glaze, imp mark
....1,600.00

Compote, ftd, two handles, ivy pattern, cream ground, light green highlights, red decal mark, 13-1/4" h, $175.

HAND-PAINTED CHINA

History: Hand painting on china began in the Victorian era and remained popular through the 1920s. It was considered an accomplished art form for women in upper- and upper-middle-class households. It developed first in England, but spread rapidly to the Continent and America.

China factories in Europe, America, and the Orient made the blanks. Belleek, Haviland, Limoges, and Rosenthal were among the European manufacturers. American firms included A. H. Hews Co., Cambridge, Massachusetts; Willetts Mfg. Co., Trenton, New Jersey; and Knowles, Taylor and Knowles, East Liverpool, Ohio. Nippon blanks from Japan were used frequently during the early 20th century.

Marks: Many pieces were signed and dated by the artist.

Reference: Dorothy Kamm, *American Painted Porcelain,* Collector Books, 1997.

Collectors' Club: World Organization of China Painters, 2641 NW. 10th St., Oklahoma City, OK 73107.

Museum: World Organization of China Painters, Oklahoma City, OK.

Notes: The quality and design of the blank is a key factor in pricing. Some blanks were very elaborate. Aesthetics is critical. Value is higher for a piece which has unique decorations and pleasing and unusual designs.

Compote, 8-7/8" d, 5-1/2" h, shallow, pink roses and green leaves dec, artist sgd, dated 1907 .... 125.00

Cup and Saucer, floral dec, Silesia blank, c1870 .... 35.00

Hair Receiver, violet dec, blue and white, Limoges blank ... 50.00

Hatpin Holder, 5" h, blue forget-me-not dec, Austria blank 35.00

Ink Blotter, violets, green leaves, Haviland blank 35.00

Jug, 5-3/4" h, green and purple grapes and green leaves, gold trim 95.00

Milk Pitcher, 7" h, white, basketweave design, yellow flowers, green leaf handle 45.00

Plate

   8-1/2" d, pink roses dec, green ground, gold border, Limoges blank 40.00

   9-1/2" d, rose dec, blank mkd "Elite, France" 25.00

Platter, 23-1/2" l, yellow roses and green leaves, gold trim, artist sgd, Haviland blank 250.00

Strawberry Bowl, 8-1/2" d, 3-1/2" h, notched corners, profusely dec inside and out with strawberries and blossoms 165.00

Sugar Shaker, 3-1/2" d, 4-1/2" h, blue and white, pink roses and green leaves, gold top and feet 50.00

Tankard, 14-1/2" h, green and purple grapes, green leaves, Lenox blank 175.00

Teapot, 5" h, purple violets, green leaves, gold trim, Lenox blank 125.00

Tray, 14" d, pink, white, and red peonies, buds, and green foliage, marked "AK France" 100.00

Trinket Box, 4-1/2" x 3-1/2" x 1-1/2", couple and woodland setting, yellow ground, mkd "JBH, France" 75.00

Vase, 5" h, white orchids, black ground, artist std, Rosenthal blank 100.00

Urn, mottled green ground, multicolored floral motif, outlined in black, stamp on bottom "handpainted /MM," 9-3/4" h, $70.

HATPINS AND HATPIN HOLDERS

History: When oversized hats were in vogue, around 1850, hatpins became popular. Designers used a variety of materials to decorate the pin ends, including china, crystal, enamel, gem stones, precious metals, and shells. Decorative subjects ranged from commemorative designs to insects.

Hatpin holders, generally placed on a dresser, are porcelain containers which were designed specifically to hold these pins. The holders were produced by major manufacturers, among which were Meissen, Nippon, R. S. Germany, R. S. Prussia, and Wedgwood.

Reference: Lillian Baker, *Hatpins & Hatpin Holders: An Illustrated Value Guide*, Collector Books, 1983, 1997 value update.

Collectors' Clubs: American Hatpin Society, 20 Monticello Dr., Palos Verdes Peninsula, CA 90274; International Club for Collectors of Hatpins and Hatpin Holders, 15237 Chanera Avenue, Gardena, CA, 90249.

Museum: Los Angeles Art Museum, Costume Dept., Los Angeles, CA.

Art Deco, left, 1-1/2" d top, 9" l, $20; right, cross, 8" l, brass, $18.

Hatpins

Bakelite, black fluted disc, rhinestone dec, silver accents ..40.00
Black Glass, faceted ball, painted top, 8" l 30.00
Brass, openwork, amber setting..45.00
Carnival Glass, figural, rose, marigold 40.00
Hand Painted China, violets, gold trim.................................30.00
Ivory, ball shape, carved design...65.00
Jet, faceted top...25.00
Plique-a-jour, 2 baroque pearls, Art Deco.........................385.00
Satsuma, Geisha Girl dec..245.00
Sterling Silver, Art Nouveau, 4 sided, 12" l...........................85.00

Bavaria, china, hexagonal, floral motif, pastels, mkd "Z. S. & Co.," 4-3/4"h, $35.

Hatpin Holders

Bavarian, MOP dec, mkd "H & C Bavaria"...........................65.00
Belleek, 5-1/4" h, relief pink and maroon floral dec, green leaves,
    gold top, mkd "Willets Belleek," dated 1911 ....125.00
Hand Painted China, 4" h, violets, gold trim and beading ...75.00
Limoges, grapes, pink roses, matte finish, artist sgd...........60.00
Mt Washington, mushroom shape
    Brown ground, brown leaves, blue berries dec 325.00
    White ground, floral dec, small crack at center hole.....120.00
Nippon, hp, pink florals, gold rim 75.00
Royal Bayreuth, tapestry, portrait of lady wearing hat, blue mark
    ....575.00

HAVILAND CHINA

H&C°
L

H & C°
L
FRANCE

History: In 1842, American china importer David Haviland moved to Limoges, France, where he began manufacturing and decorating china specifically for the U.S. market. Haviland is synonymous with fine, white, translucent porcelain, although early hand-painted patterns were generally larger and darker colored on heavier whiteware blanks than were later ones.

David revolutionized French china factories by both manufacturing the whiteware blank and decorating it at the same site. In addition, Haviland and Company pioneered the use of decals in decorating china.

David's sons, Charles Edward and Theodore, split the company in 1892. In 1936, Theodore opened an American division, which still operates today. In 1941, Theodore bought out Charles Edward's heirs and recombined both companies under the original name of H. and Co. The Haviland family sold the firm in 1981.

Charles Field Haviland, cousin of Charles Edward and Theodore, worked for and then, after his marriage in 1857, ran the Casseaux Works until 1882. Items continued to carry his name as decorator until 1941.

Thousands of Haviland patterns were made, but not consistently named until after 1926. The similarities in many of the patterns makes identification difficult. Numbers assigned by Arlene Schleiger and illustrated in her books have become the identification standard.

References: Susan and Al Bagdade, *Warman's American Pottery and Porcelain*, Wallace-Homestead, 1994; Mary Frank Gaston, *Haviland Collectibles & Art Objects*, Collector Books, 1984, out of print; Arlene Schleiger, *Two Hundred Patterns of Haviland China*, Books I-V, published by author, 1950-1977; Nora Travis, *Haviland China*, Schiffer Publishing, 1997.

Collectors' Club: Haviland Collectors International Foundation, P.O. Box 802462, Santa Clarita, CA 91380.

Matching Services: Charles E. & Carol M. Ulrey, *Matching Services for Haviland China*, P.O. Box 15815, San Diego, CA 92175.

Bone Dish, 8-1/4" l, hp
    Clam dec...60.00
    Crab dec...60.00
    Turtle dec..65.00
Bouillon, underplate, Rajah pattern, mkd "Theo Haviland" ..25.00

Plate, sprays of pink morning glories, red mark "Porcelaine Theo Haviland, Limoges, France," 8" d, $15.

Bowl
   6" d, scalloped edge, gold trim 18.00
   8" d, hp, yellow roses...35.00
Butter Dish, cov, Gold Band, mkd "Theo Haviland" 45.00
Butter Pat, sq, rounded corners, gold trim 12.00
Cake Plate, 10" d, gold handles and border 35.00
Celery Dish, scalloped edge, green flowers, pale pink scroll
   ....45.00
Cream Soup, underplate, cranberry and blue scroll border
   ....30.00
Creamer and Sugar, small pink flowers, scalloped, gold trim
   ....65.00
Cup and Saucer, deep pink flowers, scalloped gold edge .30.00
Demitasse Cup and Saucer, 1885 ....30.00
Dinner Set, Gold Band, service for 12............................ 1,000.00
Fish Set, twelve 8-1/4" d plates, 19-1/2" l tray, underglaze cobalt
   blue banded borders, enamel dec transfer fish prints, c1880
   ....575.00
Gravy Boat, round, navy and rust, double handles and lips,
   matching tray, Theo Haviland...35.00
Oyster Plate, 9" d, blue and pink flowers, mkd "Haviland & Co."
   ....90.00
Plate
   6" d, Rajah pattern, mkd "Theo Haviland" 6.00
   7-1/2" d, pink flowers, gold scalloped edge....................16.00
   9" d, Fronteac 120.00
   9-1/2" d, Princess..24.00
Platter
   12" l, turquoise morning glories, gold scalloped edge....35.00
   14" l, Athena pattern 195.00
Relish Dish, blue and pink flowers 25.00
Sandwich Plate, 11-1/2" d, Drop Rose pattern 275.00
Teacup and Saucer, small blue flowers, green leaves 25.00
Vase, 5-1/2" h, 3-5/8" d, tan, brown, pink, and rose, two oval
   scenes of lady in large hat, baskets and flower garlands,
   Charles Field Haviland and GDA Limoges mark..........275.00

HEISEY GLASS

History: The A. H. Heisey Glass Co. began producing glasswares in April 1896, in Newark, Ohio. Heisey, the firm's founder, was not a newcomer to the field, having been associated with the craft since his youth.

   Many blown and molded patterns were produced in crystal, colored, milk (opalescent), and Ivorina Verde (custard) glass. Decorative techniques of cutting, etching, and silver deposit were employed. Glass figurines were introduced in 1933 and continued in production until 1957 when the factory closed. All Heisey glass is notable for its clarity.

Marks: Not all pieces have the familiar H-within-a-diamond mark.

References: Neila Bredehoft, *Collector's Encyclopedia of Heisey Glass, 1925-1938*, Collector Books, 1986, 1997 value update; Lyle Conder, *Collector's Guide to Heisey's Glassware for Your Table*, L-W Books, 1984, 1993-94 value update; Gene Florence, *Elegant Glassware of the Depression Era*, Revised 5th ed., Collector Books, 1993.

REPRODUCTION ALERT

   Some Heisey molds were sold to Imperial Glass of Bellaire, Ohio, and certain items were reissued. These pieces may be mistaken for the original Heisey. Some of the reproductions were produced in colors which were never made by Heisey and have become collectible in their own right. Examples include: the Colt family in Crystal, Caramel Slag, Ultra Blue, and Horizon Blue; the mallard with wings up in Caramel Slag; Whirlpool (Provincial) in crystal and colors; and Waverly, a 7-inch, oval, footed compote in Caramel Slag.

Collectors' Clubs: Bay State Heisey Collectors Club, 354 Washington St., East Walpole, MA 02032; Heisey Collectors of America, 169 W. Church St., Newark, OH, 43055; National Capital Heisey Collectors, P.O. Box 23, Clinton, MD 20735.

Videotape: Heisey Glass Collectors of America, Inc., *Legacy of American Craftsmanship: The National Heisey Glass Museum*, Heisey Collectors of America, Inc., 1994.

Museum: National Heisey Glass Museum, Newark, OH.

Note: Glassware is colorless (clear, crystal, or etched) unless other color indicated.

Animal
   Gazelle... 1,450.00
   Goose, wings half up...80.00
   Plug Horse, Oscar 115.00
   Pony, kicking 175.00
   Pony, standing..95.00
   Sealyham Terrier...125.00
   Sparrow 145.00
Ashtray
   Old Sandwich, #1404, moongleam, individual size 67.50
   Ridgeleigh, #1469, club shape 10.00
   Rose..35.00
Bitters Bottle, #5003, tube 165.00
Bowl
   Priscilla, 10" h, ftd, mkd 295.00
   Waverly, #1519, rose etch, seahorse foot, floral, 12" d .235.00
Buffet Plate, Lariat, #1540, 21" 70.00
Butter Dish, cov, Orchid 145.00
Cake Plate, Rose, 15" d, pedestal.....................................325.00
Camellia Bowl, Lariat, #1540, 9-1/2" d................................40.00
Candelabra, Grape Cluster, #1445, 1 lite, 4" prisms, pr 325.00
Candle Block, #1469, 3" pr..85.00

Candlesticks, pr
  Cyrstolite, 3 lite, #1503 ....75.00
  Lariat, 2 lite, #1150 ....95.00
  Little Squatter, #99 ....35.00
  Mercury, #122 ....70.00
  New Era, #3877 ....90.00
  Pinwheel, #121 ....90.00
  Pluto, #114, hawthorne, pr 155.00
  Regency, 2 light, #1504 ....98.00
  Ridgeleigh, 2" sq, #1469 ....80.00
  Thumbprint and Panel, #1433 ....140.00
  Trophy, #126, flamingo 275.00
  Windsor, #22, 7-1/2" h 140.00
Caramel, cov, Lariat, #1540, 7" 75.00
Celery, Twist, #1252, flamingo, 13" l.......................35.00
Centerpiece Bowl, Ridgeleigh, #1469, 11" d........225.00
Champagne
  Minuet 30.00
  Orchid 25.00
  Rampo pattern, moongleam green bowls, applied flamingo
    pink base, 6 pc set 360.00
  Rose Etch 26.50
  Tudor 12.00
Cheese Dish, cov, Lariat, #1540, ftd 40.00
Cheese Plate, Twist, #1252, Kraft, moongleam.......62.50
Cigarette Holder
  Crystolite 25.00
  Orchid, ftd 165.00
  Ridgeleigh 20.00
Coaster
  Colonial..10.00
  Plantation 50.00
Cocktail
  Lariat, #1540, moonglo cut 12.00
  Orchid Etch, 4 oz. 40.00
  Rooster stem..40.00
  Rose Etch 32.50
  Rosealie, 3 oz. 10.00

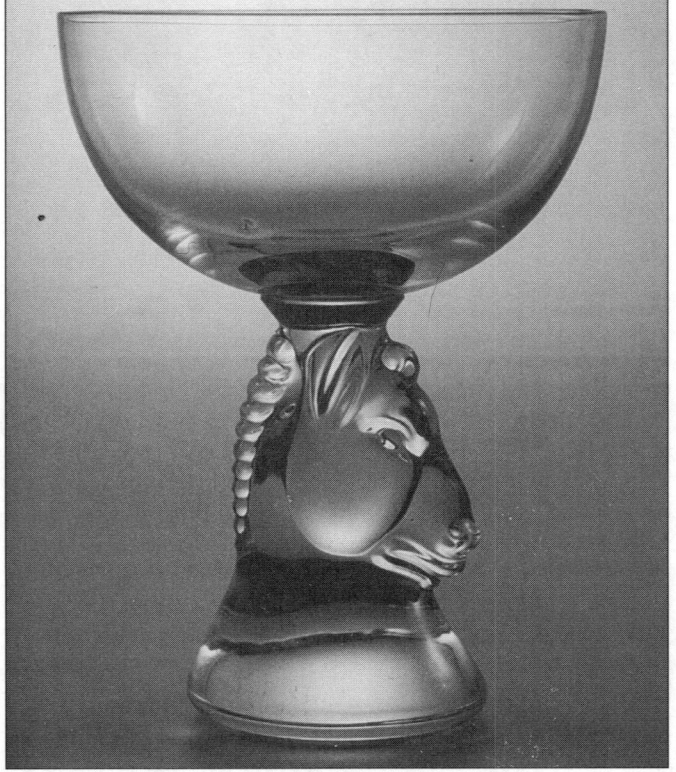

Horsehead, #5066, cocktail, rare, 4-1/4" h, $425.

Cocktail Shaker
  Cobel, #4225, quart 55.00
  Orchid Etch, sterling foot 200.00
Cologne, #1489, cut stopper, 4 oz. 155.00
Compote, Rose, #1519, low, ftd, 6-1/2".....................65.00
Cordial
  Carcassone, #390, sahara 115.00
  Old Dominion, #3380, diamond optic, sahara.......145.00
  5th Avenue-Mitchell, #829 ....45.00
Creamer, Ridgeleigh, #1469 ....20.00
Creamer and Sugar
  Twist, #1252, oval, sahara......................................165.00
  Waverly, #1519, orchid etch 75.00
Cruet, Plantation, crystal, #1567.............................155.00
Cup and Saucer
  Empress, yellow, round 40.00
  Twist, #1252, flamingo 55.00
Custard Cup, Pinwheel & Fan, moongleam 20.00
Gardenia Bowl, Crystolite, #1503, 12" d 175.00
Goblet
  Galaxy, #8005 ....25.00
  Narrow Flute, #393 ....28.50
  Old Dominion, #3380, marigold, 8-3/4" 55.00
  Provincial, #1506 ....15.00
  Rose Etch, crystal 40.00
  Spanish, #3404, cobalt blue 155.00
  Tudor 12.00
Honey, Plantation, #1567, ivy etch, 6-1/2" 80.00
Hurricane Lamp Base, Lariat, #1540, pr 85.00
Iced Tea Tumbler, ftd, Plantation, #1567 ....75.00
Jelly, Ridgeleigh, #1469, handle, 6" 20.00
Jug, Old Sandwich, #1404, sahara, half gallon.......225.00
Mayonnaise Ladle, #6, Alexandrite 245.00
Muffin Plate, Octagon #1229, 12" d, moongleam.......47.50
Mustard, cov, Flat Panel, #352 ....48.50
Nut Dish
  Empress, #1401, individual, Alexandrite 175.00
  Narrow Flute, #393, moongleam 15.00
Oyster Cocktail, Pied Piper.......................................15.00
Paperweight, rabbit 225.00
Pickle Tray, Twist, #1252, flamingo, 7" 20.00
Pitcher, Orchid, tankard 625.00
Plate
  Colonial, 4-3/4" d 4.75
  Empress, yellow
    6" d, sherbet 13.00
    8" d, salad 15.00
  Minuet, 8" d 19.75
  Orchid Etch, 7-1/4" d 18.00
  Ridgeleigh, #1469, 8" d 10.00
Punch Cup, Lariat, #1540...12.50
Punch Ladle, #11..95.00
Relish
  Empress, #1401, Minuet etch, 3 part 90.00
  Normandie etch, star, #1466 ....95.00
  Lariat, #1540, 3 part
    10-1/2"...24.00
    12" 28.00
  Provincial, #1506, 12" 35.00
  Twist, #1252, flamingo, 13" l....................................40.00
  Waverly, #1519, 6-1/2", divided, 3 ft 25.00
Rose Bowl, Plateau, #3369, flamingo 65.00
Salt Shaker, Old Sandwich, #1404 ....30.00
Sandwich Plate, Plantation, #1567, 14" d.................65.00
Serving Tray, center handle, Orchid Etch 150.00
Sherbet
  Orchid Etch, low 20.00
  Priscilla, 4 oz., high 15.00
Soda
  Coronation, #4054, 10 oz. 9.50

Creole, #3381, 12 oz., ftd, diamond optic Alexandrite bowl,
crystal foot 167.50
Duquesne, #3389, 12 oz., ftd, tangerine 210.00
Newton, #2351, 8 oz., Fronetnac etch........................... 20.00
Old Dominion, #3380, 12 oz., ftd, diamond optic Alexandrite
.... 90.00
Old Sandwich, #1404, 8 oz., moongleam 48.50
Stanhope, #4083, 8 oz., ftd, zircon bowl and foot........ 155.00
Strawberry Dip Plate, Narrow Flute, #393, with rim 195.00
Tankard, Greek Key, 3 quart 250.00
Toothpick Holder
Fancy Loop, emerald, small base flake, wear to gold trim
.... 120.00
Waldorf Astoria, #333 .... 110.00
Tumbler
Ridgeleigh, #1469, 8 oz. 45.00
Rose Etch, ftd, 12 oz. 50.00
Vase
Prison Stripe, #357, cupped, 5" 55.00
Ridgeleigh, #1469, sahara, cylinder, 8" h................... 245.00
Water Bottle
Banded Flute, #150 .... 125.00
Beaded Panel & Sunburst, #1235 .... 115.00
Wine
Minuet 65.00
Orchid etch, 3 oz. 75.00

HOLLY AMBER

History: Holly Amber, originally called Golden Agate, was produced by the Indiana Tumbler and Goblet Works of the National Glass Co., Greentown, Indiana. Jacob Rosenthal created the color in 1902. Holly Amber is a gold-colored glass with a marbleized onyx color on raised parts.

Holly (No. 450), a pattern created by Frank Jackson, was designed specifically for the Golden Agate color. Between January 1903 and June of that year, when the factory was destroyed by fire, more than 35 different forms were made in this pattern.

Reference: James Measell, *Greentown Glass, The Indiana Tumbler & Goblet Co.*, Grand Rapids Public Museum, 1979, 1992-93 value update, distributed by Antique Publications.

Collectors' Club: National Greentown Glass Assoc., 19596 Glendale Ave., South Bend, IN 46637.

Museums: Grand Rapids Public Museum, Ruth Herrick Greentown Glass Collection, Grand Rapids, MI; Greentown Glass Museum, Greentown, IN.

Additional Listings: Greentown Glass

Berry Bowl, 8-1/2" d 375.00
Butter, cov, 7-1/4" x 6-3/4" d 1,200.00
Cake Stand 2,000.00
Compote, cov, 8-1/2" d, 12" h........................... 1,800.00
Creamer and Sugar 1,550.00
Cruet, 6-1/2" h, orig stopper 2,100.00
Jelly Compote, 4-3/4" d 450.00
Match Holder 400.00
Mug, 4-1/2" h 450.00
Nappy 375.00
Parfait 575.00
Relish, oval 275.00
Salt and Pepper Shakers, pr 500.00
Sauce Dish 225.00

Spooner 425.00
Syrup, 5-3/4" h, SP hinged lid.......................... 2,000.00
Toothpick Holder, 2-1/2" h, deep amber, fiery opalescence
.... 695.00
Tumbler... 350.00

HORNS

History: For centuries, horns from animals have been used for various items, e.g., drinking cups, spoons, powder horns, and small dishes. Some pieces of horn have designs scratched in them. Around 1880, furniture made from the horns of Texas longhorn steers was popular in Texas and the southwestern United States.

Additional Listings: Firearm Accessories.

Beaker, 5" h, presentation type, silver and horn, engraved "Wilkinson 1751, To George Wildgoose," middle band engraved "Wildgoose to Mallory," base band engraved "To John Hales, 1842," bottom engraved "Henry Willing, December 25, 1893," England 375.00
Calling Card Case, horn and ivory, floral design 45.00
Chair, arm, curled horn crest, arms, and legs, black leather reupholstery, 29-1/2" w, 21" d, 41" h 475.00
Comb Case, 7-1/2" x 9", pocket type, diamond shape mirror
.... 35.00
Libation Cup, 2-1/2" h, 5" l, rhinoceros horn, ext. carved as chilong crawling among funghi and bamboo, pierced base, rim partially carved with scrolling border, Oriental, early 18th C 3,500.00
Shoe Horn, scratch carved, 1756........................... 65.00
Snuff Bottle, heart-form ivory inlay, mountainous landscape, verso with gilt inscription, Chinese 225.00
Tea Caddy, cov, 14-1/2" w, 9" d, 7-1/2" h, Ango-Indian, Vishapatnam, early 19th C, antler veneer, steer horn, ivory, int. cov compartments, etched scrolling vines, restorations... 1,850.00

Spoon, monogrammed "MBL," 1907, thistle, hallmarked, $48.

HULL POTTERY

History: In 1905, Addis E. Hull purchased the Acme Pottery Company, Crooksville, Ohio. In 1917, the A. E. Hull Pottery Company began making art pottery, novelties, stoneware, and kitchenware, later including the famous Little Red Riding Hood line. Most items had a matte finish with shades of pink and blue or brown predominating.

After a disastrous flood and fire in 1950, J. Brandon Hull reopened the factory in 1952 as the Hull Pottery Company. New, more-modern-style pieces, mostly with glossy finish, were produced. The company currently produces wares for florists, e.g. the Regal and Floraline lines.

Marks: Hull pottery molds and patterns are easily identified. Pre-1950 vases are marked "Hull USA" or "Hull Art USA" on the bottom. Many also retain their paper labels.

Post-1950 pieces are marked "Hull" in large script or "HULL" in block letters.

Each pattern has a distinctive letter or number, e.g., Wildflower has a "W" and a number; Waterlily, "L" and number; Poppy, numbers in the 600s; Orchid, in the 300s. Early stoneware pieces are marked with an "H."

References: Susan and Al Bagdade, *Warman's American Pottery and Porcelain*, Wallace-Homestead, 1994; Barbara Loveless Gick-Burke, *Collector's Guide to Hull Pottery*, Collector Books, 1993; Joan Hull, *Hull*, 5th ed., published by author (1376 Nevada, Huron, SD 57350), 1997; Brenda Roberts, *Collectors Encyclopedia of Hull Pottery*, Collector Books, 1980, 1995 value update.

Periodicals: *Hull Pottery News*, 466 Foreston Place, St. Louis, MO 63119; *Hull Pottery Newsletter*, 11023 Tunnel Hill NE., New Lexington, OH 43764.

Collectors' Club: Hull Pottery Assoc., 4 Hilltop Rd., Council Bluff, IA 51503.

Additional Listings: See *Warman's Americana & Collectibles* for more examples.

Advisor: Joan Hull.

Pre-1950 Matte

Bowknot
Basket, B-12, 10-1/2" h..............................750.00
Candleholders, pr, B-17.............................225.00
Console Bowl, B-16..................................325.00
Cornucopia, B-7......................................165.00
Vase
  B-4 6-1/2" h..200.00
  B-11, 10-1/2" h.....................................485.00
Calla Lily, vase, 520-33, 8" h....................150.00
Dogwood (Wild Rose)
Basket, 501, 8-1/2" h................................300.00
Vase, 513, 6-1/2" h..................................125.00
Little Red Riding Hood
Creamer and Sugar, side pour........................400.00
Lamp...2,500.00
Matchbox for wooden matches........................900.00
Teapot, cov..375.00
Magnolia
Floor Vase, 20, 15"..................................425.00
Pitcher, 14, 4-3/4" h.................................50.00

Open Rose, mermaid planter, 104, 10-1/2" l, $4,000. Photo courtesy of Joan Hull.

Parchment & Pine, tea set, S-11, orig box, $170. Photo courtesy of Joan Hull.

Vase
  3, 8-1/2" h...115.00
  9, 10-1/2" h..175.00
Open Rose/Camellia
Jardiniere, 114, 8-1/2" h............................375.00
Pitcher, 106, 13-1/2" h..............................575.00
Vase
  119, 8-1/2" h.......................................175.00
  127, 4-3/4" h...75.00
Orchid, vase
  301, 4-3/4" h...95.00
  302, 6" h..140.00
  303, 8" h..195.00
  304, 10-1/2" h.......................................325.00
Poppy
Basket, 601, 9" h....................................750.00
Vase
  607, 10-1/2" h......................................425.00
  6112, 6-1/2" h......................................200.00
Rosella, vase
  R-2, 5" h...35.00
  R-6, 6-1/2" h...45.00
  R-15, 8-1/2" h..75.00
Tulip, vase
101-33, 9" h...245.00
103-33, 6" h...250.00
107-33, 6" h...125.00
Water Lily
Basket, L-14, 10-1/2"................................350.00
Cornucopia, K-27, 12", double.......................225.00
Vase, L-16, 10-1/2"..................................395.00
Wildflower, vase
W-5, 6-1/2" d...80.00
W-12, 9-1/2" h.......................................155.00
W-14, 10-1/2" h......................................175.00
Wild Flower, No. Series
Basket, 66, 10-1/4" h..............................2,000.00
Vase
  53, 8-1/2" h..295.00
  61, 6-1/2" h..160.00
  71, 12" h...395.00
Woodland
Basket, W9, 8-3/4" h.................................245.00
Wall Pocket, shell, W13, 7-1/2" l....................165.00
Window Box, W14, 10-1/2".............................145.00

Wild Flower Baskets, #66 and #79, $2,000 each. Photo courtesy of Joan Hull.

Post 1950

Blossom Flite
Basket, T4, 8-1/2" h..110.00
Pitcher, T13, 12-1/2" h 150.00

Butterfly
Basket, B13, 8" h 150.00
Pitcher, B15, 13-1/2" h 185.00
Vase, B9, 9" h..55.00

Continental
Candy Dish, C62, 8-1/4".......................................45.00
Vase, C29, 12" h 95.00

Ebb Tide
Ashtray, with mermaid, E-8................................195.00
Bud Vase, E-1, 7" h..75.00
Pitcher, E-10, 13" h 250.00

Parchment and Pine
Basket, S-3, 6" h 75.00
Coffeepot, S-15, 8" h..125.00
Tea Set, S-11 and S-12.......................................150.00

Serenade
Fruit Bowl, S-15, 11-1/2" d, ftd...........................110.00
Vase
    S1, 6" h..50.00
    S11, 10-1/2" h 95.00

Sunglow
Bell...200.00
Grease Jar, 53...35.00
Wall Whisk Broom, 82...65.00
Vase, 85, 8-3/4" h, bird 45.00

Tokay/Tuscany
Cornucopia, 10, 11" l 65.00
Pitcher, 3, 8" h...95.00
Vase
    8, 10" h...125.00
    12, 12" h 110.00

Tropicana
Basket, T55, 12-3/4" h..750.00
Vase, T53, 8-1/2" h..500.00

Woodland (glossy)
Console Bowl, W19, 14" d 100.00
Vase
    W1, 5-1/2" h 45.00
    W15, 8-1/2" h, double 75.00

HUMMEL ITEMS

History: Hummel items are the original creations of Berta Hummel, who was born in 1909 in Massing, Bavaria, Germany. At age 18, she was enrolled in the Academy of Fine Arts in Munich to further her mastery of drawing and the palette. Berta entered the Convent of Siessen and became Sister Maria Innocentia in 1934. In this Franciscan cloister, she continued drawing and painting images of her childhood friends.

In 1935, W. Goebel Co. in Rodental, Germany, began producing Sister Maria Innocentia's sketches as three-dimensional bisque figurines. The Schmid Brothers of Randolph, Massachusetts, introduced the figurines to America and became Goebel's U.S. distributor.

In 1967, Goebel began distributing Hummel items in the U.S. A controversy developed between the two companies, the Hummel family, and the convent. Law suits and counter-suits ensued. The German courts finally effected a compromise: the convent held legal rights to all works produced by Sister Maria Innocentia from 1934 until her death in 1946 and licensed Goebel to reproduce these works; Schmid was to deal directly with the Hummel family for permission to reproduce any pre-convent art.

Marks: All authentic Hummel pieces bear both the signature "M. I. Hummel" and a Goebel trademark. Various trademarks were used to identify the year of production:

Crown Mark (trademark 1)	1935 through 1949
Full Bee (trademark 2)	1950–1959
Stylized Bee (trademark 3)	1957–1972
Three Line Mark (trademark 4)	1964–1972
Last Bee Mark (trademark 5)	1972–1979
Missing Bee Mark (trademark 6)	1979–1990
Current Mark or New Crown Mark (trademark 7)	1991 to the present

References: Ken Armke, *Hummel: An Illustrated History and Price Guide*, Wallace-Homestead, 1995; Carl F. Luckey, *Luckey's Hummel Figurines and Plates: A Collector's Identification and Value Guide*, 11th ed., Krause Publications, 1997; Robert L. Miller, *No. 1 Price Guide to M. I. Hummel: Figurines, Plates, More...*, 6th ed., Portfolio Press, 1995; Wolfgang Schwalto, *M. I. Hummel Collector's Handbook, Part I: Rarities and Collector Pieces*, Schwalto, GMBH, 1994; Lawrence L. Wonsch, *Hummel Copycats with Values*, Wallace-Homestead, 1987, out-of-print.

Collectors' Clubs: Hummel Collector's Club, Inc., 1261 University Dr., Yardley, PA 19067; M. I. Hummel Club, Goebel Plaza, Rte. 31, P.O. Box 11, Pennington, NJ 08534.

Museum: Hummel Museum, New Braunfels, TX.

Additional Listings: See *Warman's Americana & Collectibles* for more examples.

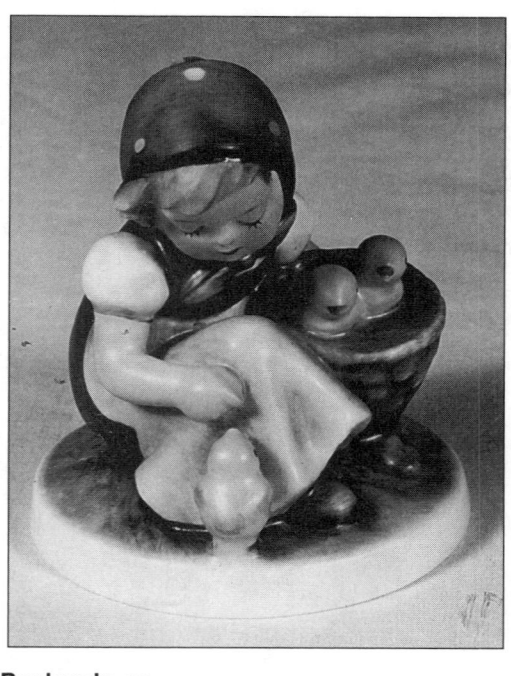

Figure, Chick Girl, 57/0, stylized bee mark, $120.

Bookends, pr
Chick Girl, #618, full bee, trademark-2 ....320.00
Playmates, #61A, full bee, trademark-2 ....320.00
Candleholder
Silent Night, #54, trademark 5 ....175.00
Watchful angel, #194, trademark 2 ....400.00
Candy Box, cov
Happy Pastime, #III/169, trademark 4 ....125.00
Joyful, #III/53, trademark 4 ....115.00
Christmas Angel
Boy, #117, trademark 3 ....45.00
Girl, #116, fir tree, 3" h, trademark 3 ....40.00
Figure
Apple Tree Girl, #141, 6" h, stamped full bee, incised crown
    mark 425.00
Band Leader, #129, trademark 5 ....120.00
Be Patient, #197/12/10, trademark 2 ....125.00
Chimney Sweep, #122/10, trademark 5 ....70.00
Congratulations, #17/0, 1971, MIB 150.00
For Father, #877, trademark 3 ....200.00
For Mother, #257, trademark 5 ....145.00
Happiness, #86, trademark 3 ....110.00
Heavenly Angel, #21/0, trademark 3 ....100.00
Just Resting, #112/13/0, trademark 4 ....90.00
Kiss Me, #311, trademark 3 ....150.00
Little Bookkeeper, #306, trademark 4 ....220.00
Little Tooter, #214/1, 3-1/4" x 5", trademark 4 ....145.00
Merry Wanderer, #11/0, trademark 2 ....215.00
Photographers, #178, trademark 4 ....215.00
Sensitive Hunter, #640, trademark 4 ....150.00
Soldier Boy, #332, trademark 4 ....300.00
Wash Day, #3211, trademark 4 ....100.00
Wayside Harmony, #111/3/0, trademark 4 ....100.00
Font
Angel Cloud, #206, trademark 5 ....45.00
Child Jesus, #26/0, MK 4 ....35.00
Guardian angel, #248, trademark 4 ....60.00
Holy Family, #246, trademark 2 ....85.00
Seated Angel, #10/1, trademark 3 ....420.00
Plaque
Madonna, #48/0, trademark 7 ....250.00
Mail Coach, #140, trademark 5 ....145.00
Merry Wanderer, #92, trademark 2 ....195.00

IMARI

History: Imari derives its name from a Japanese port city. Although Imari ware was manufactured in the 17th century, the pieces most commonly encountered are those made between 1770 and 1900.

Early Imari was decorated simply, quite unlike the later heavily decorated brocade pattern commonly associated with Imari. Most of the decorative patterns are an underglaze blue and overglaze "seal wax" red complimented by turquoise and yellow.

The Chinese copied Imari ware. The Japanese examples can be identified by grayer clay, thicker glaze, runny and darker blue, and deep red opaque hues.

The pattern and colors of Imari inspired many English and European potteries, such as Derby and Meissen, to adopt a similar style of decoration for their wares.

Reference: Nancy N. Schiffer, *Imari, Satsuma, and Other Japanese Export Ceramics,* Schiffer Publishing, 1997.

Bowl
    6-3/8" d, center flowering tree dec 375.00
    13-1/2" d, 5-1/2" h, blue and white, edge chips 715.00
    15" d, 5-3/4" h, blue and white, scalloped rim, early 20th C
    ....220.00
Charger
    14-1/2" d, scalloped, alternating floral and foliage panels, basket reserve, 19th C 200.00
    24" d, figural panel, 2 panels of phoenix birds, foliate ground, Chinese, late 19th C 750.00
Creamer and Sugar, 5-1/2" h creamer, 5-7/8" cov sugar, ovoid, dragon form handles, gilt and bright enamels, shaped reserves, dragon-like beasts, stylized animal medallions, brocade ground, high dome lid, knob, cipher mark of Mount Fuji, Fukagama Studio marks, Meiji period 500.00
Dish
    8-3/8" d, central scene with fence and flowering tree dec, shaped cartouches enclosing flowers and hares on crackle blue ground at rim, gilt highlights, Meiji period, price for pr
    ....650.00
    9-1/2" d, shaped rim, allover flowering vine dec, gilt highlights 150.00
Food Box, 6" h, 3 section, ext. and lid with phoenix and floral design, underglaze blue, iron-red, and gilt enamels, 19th C
    ....400.00
Jardiniere, 10" h, hexagonal, bulbous, short flared foot, alternating bijin figures and immortal symbols, stylized ground
    ....250.00
Plate, 14-3/4" d, scalloped, floral dec, 16-1/2" h fitted wooden table form stand 375.00
Platter, 18" d, alternating panels of figures and foliage, trelliswork ground, Japanese, late 19th C 475.00
Punch Bowl, 11" d, red and blue floral dec, scalloped rim, 19th C
    ....395.00
Teabowl and Saucer, 5" d, floriform, floral spray dec, gilt highlights on saucer 200.00
Umbrella Stand, 24" h, iron-red and blue palette, bird and floral designs, Japan, late 19th C 690.00

Charger, pictorial on dark blue ground of angled flaring rim, flowerheads and gilt foliage, center sprays of bamboo, peonies, and chrysanthemums, 18-1/2" d, $1,500. Photo courtesy of Freeman\Fine Arts.

Urn, 21" h, gilt bronze mounts, deep bowl, red, blue, and gilt floral dec, everted pierced collar, S-scroll arms of leaves and cattails, mid band of plaited reeds, flaring porcelain base banded in bronze, pierced skirt interspersing 4 foliate clasps, pr 14,000.00

IMPERIAL GLASS

History: Imperial Glass Co., Bellaire, Ohio, was organized in 1901. Its primary product was pattern (pressed) glass. Soon other lines were added, including carnival glass, Nuart, Nucut, and Near Cut. In 1916, the company introduced Free-Hand, a lustered art glass line, and Imperial Jewels, an iridescent stretch glass that carried the Imperial cross trademark. In the 1930s, the company was reorganized into the Imperial Glass Corporation, and the firm is still producing a great variety of wares.

Imperial recently acquired the molds and equipment of several other glass companies: Central, Cambridge, and Heisey. Many of the retired molds of these companies are once again in use.

Marks: The Imperial reissues are marked to distinguish them from the originals.

References: Margaret and Douglas Archer, *Imperial Glass* Collector Books, 1978, 1993 value update; Gene Florence, *Elegant Glassware of the Depression Era*, 6th ed., Collector Books, 1994; National Imperial Glass Collectors Society, *Imperial Glass Encyclopedia: Volume I, A-Cane*, Antique Publications, 1995; ——, *Imperial Glass 1966 Catalog*, reprint, 1991 price guide, Antique Publications; Mary M. Wetzel, *Candlewick: The Jewel of Imperial Price Guide II*, Revised 2nd ed., published by author, 1993, 1995 value update.

Collectors' Clubs: National Candlewick Collector's Club, 275 Milledge Terrace, Athens, GA 30606; National Imperial Glass Collectors Society, P.O. Box 534, Bellaire, OH 43906.

Videotapes: National Imperial Glass Collectors Society, *Candlewick: At Home, In Any Home, Vol. I: Imperial Beauty, Vol. II: Virginia and Mary*, RoCliff Communications, 1993; ——, *Glass of Yesteryears: The Renaissance of Slag Glass*, RoCliff Communications, 1994.

Additional Listings: See Carnival Glass; Pattern Glass; and *Warman's Americana & Collectibles* for more examples.

Engraved or Hand Cut

Bowl, 6-1/2" d, flower and leaf, molded star base	25.00
Candlesticks, pr, 7" h, Amelia	35.00
Celery Vase, 3 side stars, cut star base	25.00
Pitcher, tankard, Design No. 110, flowers, foliage, and butterfly cutting	60.00
Plate, 5-1/2" d, Design No. 12	15.00

Jewels

Bowl, 6-1/2" d, purple Pearl Green luster, mkd 75.00

Vase, orange ground, gold swirls, 10-1/2" h, $325.

Compote, 7-1/2" d, irid teal blue...65.00
Rose Bowl, amethyst, green irid...75.00
Vase, 7-3/4" h, classic baluster, white body, mirror bright tray-
  blue surface, deep orange irid int. rim 320.00

Lustered (Freehand)

Candlesticks, pr, 10-3/4" h, cobalt blue, white vine and leaf dec
  ....325.00
Hat, 9" w, ruffled rim, cobalt blue, embedded irid white vines and
  leaves 120.00
Vase
  7" h, opal white irid body, bright blue heart and vine dec, ap-
    plied cobalt blue wrap, subtle orange lustered int...800.00
  7-1/4" h, brilliant orange irid flared oval body cased to white,
    lustered green pulled dec, unsigned polished white pontil
    ....345.00
  11-1/2" h, 5" w, bright orange ground, deep blue loops over
    bright white, irid surface 875.00

Nuart

Ashtray..20.00
Lamp Shade, marigold...50.00
Vase, 7" h, bulbous, irid green 125.00

Nucut

Berry Bowl, 4-1/2" d, handles 15.00
Celery Tray, 11" l...18.00
Creamer..20.00
Fern Dish, 8" l, brass lining, ftd...30.00
Orange Bowl, 12" d, Rose Marie 48.00

Pressed

Berry Bowl, Katy, blue opalescent, flat rim............................30.00
Birthday Cake Plate, Cape Cod 325.00
Bowl, 10" d, Pillar Flutes, light blue.......................................35.00
Champagne, Cape Cod, azalea..22.00
Compote, Pillar Flutes, light blue...25.00
Creamer and Sugar, Pillar Flutes, light blue..........................48.00
Decanter, stopper, blown out grapes, orchid, IG mark........70.00
Goblet, Monticello, crystal 12.00
Ivy Ball, 4" h, Spun, red, crystal foot.....................................60.00
Juice Tumbler, Georgian, red...14.00
Marmalade, Code Cod, crystal 30.00
Nappy, 5" d, handle, Floral pattern, caramel slag, IG mark .30.00
Pitcher, 80 oz, Spun, teal...95.00
Plate, Windmill, glossy, green slag, IG mark.........................45.00
Sherbet, Cape Cod, amberina 20.00
Tumbler, Georgian, red 18.00
Wine, Wild Rose etch..16.50

INDIAN ARTIFACTS, AMERICAN

History: During the historic period, there were approximately 350 Indian tribes grouped into the following regions: Eskimo, Northeast and Woodland, Northwest Coast, Plains, and West and Southwest.

American Indian artifacts are quite popular. Currently, the market is stable following a rapid increase in prices during the 1970s.

References: Susan and Al Bagdade, *Warman's American Pottery and Porcelain*, Wallace-Homestead, 1994; C. J. Brafford and Laine Thom (comps.), *Dancing Colors: Paths of Native American Women*, Chronicle Books, 1992; Harold S. Colton, *Hopi Kachina Dolls*, revised ed., University of New Mexico Press, 1959, 1990 reprint; Gary L. Fogelman, *Identification and Price Guide for Indian Arti-*

facts of the Northeast, Fogelman Publishing, 1994; Lar Hothem, *Arrowheads & Projectile Points*, Collector Books, 1983, 1997 value update; ——, *Indian Artifacts of the Midwest*, Book I (1992, 1996 value update), Book II (1995), Book III (1997), Collector Books; ——, *Indian Axes & Related Stone Artifacts*, Collector Books, 1996; Robert M. Overstreet, *Overstreet Indian Arrowheads Identification and Price Guide*, Avon Books, 1997; Lillian Peaster, *Pueblo Pottery Families*, Schiffer Publishing, 1997; Dawn E. Reno, *Native American Collectibles*, Avon Books, 1994; Nancy N. Schiffer, *Indian Dolls*, Schiffer Publishing, 1997; Peter N. Schiffer, *Indian Jewelry on the Market*, Schiffer Publishing, 1996; Lawrence N. Tully & Steven N. Tully, *Field Guide to Flint Arrowheads & Knives of North American Indians*, Collector Books, 1997; Sarah Peabody Turnbaugh and William A. Turnbaugh, *Indian Baskets*, Schiffer Publishing, 1997.

Periodicals: *American Indian Art Magazine*, 7314 E Osborn Dr., Scottsdale, AZ 85251; *American Indian Basketry Magazine*, P.O. Box 66124, Portland, OR 97266; *Indian-Artifact Magazine*, RD #1 Box 240, Turbotville, PA 17772; *Indian Trader*, P.O. Box 1421, Gallup, NM 87305; *Whispering Wind Magazine*, 8009 Wales St., New Orleans, LA 70126.

Collectors' Club: Indian Arts & Crafts Assoc., Suite B, 122 Laveta NE, Suite B, Albuquerque, NM 87108.

Museums: Amerind Foundation, Inc., Dragoon, AZ; The Heard Museum, Phoenix, AZ; Colorado River Indian Tribes Museum, Parker, AZ; Favell Museum of Western Art & Indian Artifacts, Klamath Falls, OR; Field Museum of Natural History, Chicago, IL; Grand Rapids Public Museum, Grand Rapids, MI; Indian Center Museum, Wichita, KS; Institute of American Indian Arts Museum, Sante Fe, NM; Maryhill Museum of Art, Goldendale, WA; Museum of Classical Antiquities & Primitive Arts, Medford, NJ; Museum of the American Indian, Heye Foundation, New York, NY; US Dept. of the Interior Museum, Washington, DC; Wheelwright Museum of the American Indian, Sante Fe, NM.

Note: American Indian artifacts listed below are prehistoric or historic objects made on the North American continent.

Arrowhead
    3-1/16" fluted point, Smithton, PA, Rostraver Township, Allegheny County, PA 1,045.00
    3-3/4", Susquehanna, Bakertown, PA 860.00
    4-3/8", Archaic side notch, Adams County, OH 165.00
    4-1/2", Graham Cave, Pike County, IL 385.00
    5-1/4", F.R. Hopewell, Erie County, OH 550.00
    5-5/8", Etley, Mercer County, KY 220.00
    5-7/8", Archaic deep notch, Humphrey County, TN, slight restoration 220.00
Awl Case, 14" l, 1" w, harness leather, trimmed in beads and cones, Adams County, OH 90.00
Axe, 4-1/4", 3/4 groove, Northumberland County, PA 495.00
Bag
    Great Lakes, 10" x 17", beaded, American and British flags 110.00
    Nez Perce, 16" x 11", cornhusk, stacked triangle design, red chevrons, c1860 .... 770.00
    Parfleche, c1880s 1,650.00
Banner Stone
    2-3/4", steatite, ridged, White County, GA 300.00
    4-3/8" l, pick shape, Richland County, OH, small flake off back hole 470.00
    5-1/2" l, butterfly, found near Ney, OH, some damage 495.00
Basket
    3" h, 5" d, Paiute, beaded, coiled, cov with netted beads, orange and green geometric design, white ground, some bead loss 315.00
    4" h, 9" l, Papago, oval, saguaro cactus design, 3 women harvesting fruit, beads attached at rim, some beads and rim stitching missing 115.00
    5-1/2" h, 10-1/2" d, Yokuto, cowboys, cowgirls, and stars, polychrome, rim ticking, c1890s 4,290.00
    8-1/2" h, 8" w, 5" d, wall, splint, Northeast Woodland, 19th C, swabbed and stamped with yellow and salmon 460.00
Belt, 33-7/8" l, 2-1/8" w, beaded, Plains, c1880s 440.00
Birdstone
    3/4", popeyed, miniature head, tally marked, Berrien Co., MI 1,650.00
    4-1/2", classic glacial Kame, Allen County, OH 4,400.00
    6-1/2", popeye, Montgomery Co., OH, one eye restored 3,300.00
Blanket, 18-1/4" x 18-1/4", child's, Germantown 235.00
Bowl
    4-1/2" h, 6-1/2" d, twined basketry, Hupa, conifer root, bear grass design, some wear, stitched rim repair 30.00
    5" h, 11-1/2" d, basketry, Papago, shallow, straight sides, geometric design, devil's claw and yucca, base trim missing stitches 50.00
    5-3/4", Gila black on red ware, Anazazi, AZ, dug, petrified 1,320.00

Basket, coiled, black designs and crosses, Apache, $700.

    7-1/4", Gila River, Anazazi, excavated 1950 .... 1,650.00
    9-1/4" x 11" x 4-1/4" h, burl, worn scrubbed patina, small protruding end handles, by Solomon Jackson, American Indian, accompanied by old photo post card of Mr. Jackson 300.00
    9-1/2" h, 14" d, basketry, Makah, looped rim, alternating twined and grass bands, central band with faded images of whales, birds, and boaters, old tag reads "Makah (Tiaashaft or Klaziaht) Vancouver Island and Cape Flattery, Washington…," two rim breaks 200.00
Box, 5-7/8", birchbark, old trader slings, Objiwa, MN, c1880s 550.00
Bridle, horsehair, steel bit, Plains 415.00
Canoe, 19-1/4" l, birchbark, Chippewa, c1880 .... 330.00
Catalog, Francis E. Lester Co., Mesilla Park, MN, c1924, 20 pgs, 6" x 9", 11th Annual Gift Sale of Uncommon Native Handicraft Navajo Blankets, Indian Baskets, etc. 45.00
Celt, 9-1/8" l, Alleghany County, PA 125.00
Cradle, 6" l, child's miniature, quill and beads, Plains, 1880s 550.00
Dagger
    6" l, found near Fall River, MA, shows Viking influence in Northeast, info on old card 660.00
    11-5/8" l, Athabascan, Northwest, 1880s 910.00
Discoidal, 2-1/4" d, Scioto County, OH, Feurt Site 100.00
Doll, 6-1/2" h, buckskin, beads, c1930 .... 40.00
Dovetail, 5-1/2" l, flint, ridge, Miami County, Ohio 1,100.00
Drill, 3-3/4" l, notched, hornstone, IL 140.00
Figure
    3" h, Innuit, Eskimo, Cape Dorset Island, hunter with pouch and tool, Alaskan jade, bottom inscribed "Abraha E9 1706" 100.00
    5-3/8" l, Innuit, Eskimo, hunter carrying seal, banded graystone, bottom inscribed "A-Kan 138523" 250.00
Gorget
    5", expanded center, Adena, found in 1896, Franklin County, OH 330.00
    5-3/8" l, knobbed, found near Newark, OH 1,320.00
    6-1/8" l, 2 hole, Seneca County, OH, some flakes off end 220.00
Hammerstone, 2-5/8" d, quartz, Beaver Falls, Beaver County, PA 220.00
Hat, basketry
    3-1/4" h, 6-1/2" d, Yurok, northern CA, simple geometric design in maidenhair fern and bear grass, rim damage, three splits, misshapen 130.00
    3-1/2" h, 7" d, Whilkut, northwest CA, three banded design with diagonally staked rhomboids and zig-zag lightning in black maidenhair fern, red Woodwardia and tan bear grass, two splits at first band 300.00
    7", child's, coiled, Yokut, c1880 .... 440.00
Hat, cloth, 12-1/2" x 4-1/2", Mic Mac, Great Lakes, c1890 .... 635.00
Head Knocker, 20" l, full beaded handle, Plains, 1880s, some bead loss 440.00
Hide Scraper, 12" l, bone, Apache, hide strap, 1870s 245.00
Jacket, 23" x 30", beaded hide, men's, Cree 250.00
Jar, pottery
    4-5/8" h, 2-5/8" d, Hopi, attributed to Nampeyo, Grand Canyon Harvey House, attached partial label "From the Hopi Villages," some wear 150.00
    6-1/2" h, 7-1/2" d, Santa Clara, blackware, highly polished, Zolo paper tags, partial one reads "From the Pueblo of Santa Clara," initials on bottom, minor wear, rim chips ... 85.00
    7-1/2" h, 7-1/2" d, Acoma, umber and red ochre stylized cloud, sun, and star geometric design, white slip ground, red ochre bottom, minor wear 385.00
    7-7/8" h, 7-1/4" d, Acoma, umber hatched curvilinear design, foliage band at shoulder on white slip ground, red ochre bottom, mkd "ax $1.00," wear, green stains, rim chip 220.00

Rug, Navaho, Ganado area, double dye red, tan, carded gray and black diamond design, universal oval elements, 3' 2" x 5' 4", $440. Photo courtesy of Garth's Auctions.

11-1/2", Zuno, applied frogs and dragonfly design....3,300.00
13-1/4", laguna, 4 color......6,490.00
Knife
   6-3/4", sq base, Stewart Co., TN 300.00
   11-1/8" l, burl buffalo effigy handle, copper tack eyes, Wilson 245.00
Knife Sheaf
   12" l, brass beads, fringe, and cones, Plains......935.00
   14" l, 2-7/8" w, beaded, cones, and beaded drops, Plains, c1880......1045.00
Leggins, 15" x 13", full beaded, Cree, c1880, pr......770.00
Moccasins, pr
   5", child's, Great Lakes......165.00

Water Jug, Cochit Pueblo, NM, earthtones, c1910, 9-5/8" h, $325.

10", men's, Sioux, red and white heart beads, c1890 ......1,210.00
10-1/2", men's, quill and beaded designs, Plains, c1870s 1,375.00
Needle Case, 4-3/8" x 3-1/4", moosehair, ribbon tie, 1800s, some damage 165.00
Pendant, 4" l, anchor, Champaign Co., OH......200.00
Pen Tray, 6" l, embroidered moosehair, birchbark, Great Lakes, slight damage......55.00
Pipe
   1-3/8" pedestal, tally mark keel, Scioto County, OH......250.00
   2-1/8" l, frog effigy, Lewis County, TN 495.00
   3-7/8" l, bear effigy, Sandusky, OH 525.00
   8-1/8" l, Steatite, Flying Wing Bird, ceremonial, Smith County, TN, restored head......5,500.00
   34" l, Catlinite T, orig twisted stem, snakes incised on 4 sides of stem 800.00
Plummet, 3" l, grooved top, Humphrey County, TN......220.00
Pouch, 15" l, beaded, fringe, Great Lakes, c1890 ......300.00
Purse, 7" x 6-1/4", beaded, Iroquois 190.00
Rug, Navaho
   2'3" x 4'4", graphic design, central rect panel with serrate stripes in shades of brown, striking red and black border design, minor color run, small hole 275.00
   2'8" x 3'7", red, dark brown, and natural stepped diamond design, gray ground, slight bleeding of red 110.00
   3' x 5'8", western Reservation, black and white serrate diamond cross, tan and red terrace hook design, carded gray ground, black and white stepped diamond terrace border, warp breaks, white has pink tinge......175.00
   3'3" x 4'5", red serrate diamond center, carded gray ground, outlined black and white Greek key border, fringe ends 330.00
   3'8" x 5'9", serrate diamonds, alternating bands of red, dark brown, natural, tan, dark brown, red, carded brown, and natural, wear, some staining......880.00
   4'2" x 5'9", Eyedazzler, bright aniline reds, orange, yellow, black, and dark blue, natural and dark brown, cotton string warp, selvage worn, overall wear, repairs, hold, soiling, minor color run, c1885-1900 ......440.00
Saddle Blanket, double, Navaho
   2'9" x 4'4", interlocking serrate diamond design, gray/green, black, and white, deep double dyed red ground.....330.00
   2'10" x 4'10", serrate zig-zag design, central row of serrate diamonds, natural tan and dark brown, natural white ground, overall wear, edge damage, small hole, warp breaks, stains 165.00
Spade
   6-5/8" l, flint, KY......75.00
   10" l, Henry County, TN 80.00
Spoon
   9-3/8", wood, Wood Spirit effigy face in handle, Huron, early 1880s, slight break in spoon 275.00
   9-5/8", Menomenni, silver beaver inlay, 1880s......1,760.00
   15-5/8" l, Athabascan Horn, incised designs, bird head motif, mid 19th C......590.00
Totem Pole, 27-1/2" h, hand carved polychrome Zoomorphic figures, mkd "Southaven 1946," edge wear......90.00
Wand, 17-1/8" l, carved, head effigy, Woodland......495.00
War Club, 15-1/2", Apache, c1880......900.00
Weaving, 2'6" x 3'10", Chimayo, fine weave, red and black circular design, fringed ends 140.00

INDIAN TREE PATTERN

History: Indian Tree pattern is a popular pattern of porcelain made from the last half of the 19th century until the present. The pattern, consisting of an Oriental crooked tree branch, landscape, exotic flowers, and foliage, is found predominantly in greens, pinks, blues, and orang-

Cup and Saucer, Maddock, England, $25.

Umbrella, 12 sided, bright sapphire blue, inward rolled mouth, pontil scar, professionally cleaned, 1840-60, 2-1/8" h, $950. Photo courtesy of Norman C. Heckler & Company.

es on a white ground. Several English potteries, including Burgess and Leigh, Coalport, and Maddock, made wares in the Indian Tree pattern.

Bowl, 8-1/2" d, ftd, Minton..42.00
Butter Dish, cov Johnson Bros. 45.00
Cake Plate, 10-1/2" d, Coalport 40.00
Creamer and Sugar, scalloped, Coalport 60.00
Cup and Saucer, scalloped, Coalport......................30.00
Egg Cup, 4" h, Maddock & Sons.............................25.00
Gravy Boat, Brownfield & Sons, c1856 ....35.00
Plate, 9-1/2" d, KPM...15.00
Sauce Dish, 5" d, Johnson Bros. 7.50
Soup Plate, 7-1/2" d, Coalport 20.00
Vegetable Bowl, oval, smooth edge, Coalport 60.00

INK BOTTLES

History: Ink was sold in glass or pottery bottles in the early 1700s in England. Retailers mixed their own formula and bottled it. The commercial production of ink did not begin in England until the late 18th century and in America until the early 19th century.Initially, ink was supplied in often poorly manufactured pint or quart bottles from which smaller bottles could be filled. By the mid-19th century, when writing implements had been improved, emphasis was placed on making an "untippable" bottle. Shapes ranging from umbrellas to turtles were tried. Since ink bottles were usually displayed, shaped or molded bottles were popular.

The advent of the fountain pen relegated the ink bottle to the back drawer. Bottles lost their decorative design and became merely functional items.

References: Ralph & Terry Kovel, *Kovels' Bottles Price List*, 10th ed., Crown Publishers, 1996; John Odell, *Digger Odell's Official Antique Bottle and Glass Collector Magazine Price Guide Series*, Vol. 4, published by author (1910 Shawhan Rd, Morrow, OH 45152), 1995.

Periodical: *Antique Bottle and Glass Collector*, P.O. Box 187, East Greenville, PA 18041.

Additional Listings: See *Warman's Americana & Collectibles* for more examples.

Cylindrical, 5-5/8" h, America, 1840-60, "Harrison's Columbia Ink," cobalt blue, applied flared mouth, pontil scar, 3" crack, mouth roughness, C #764 ....140.00
Figural, America, 1860-90
  2" h, house, domed offset neck for, emb architectural features of front door and 4 windows, colorless, sheared mouth, smooth base, Carter's Ink, some remaining int. ink residue, C #614 ....650.00
  2" h, locomotive, aquamarine, ground mouth, smooth base, C #715 ....800.00
  2-3/8" h, log cabin, rect, colorless, tooled sq collared mouth, smooth base, pinhead sized hole in one base corner, some int. haze, C #680..190.00
  2-5/8" h, house, 1-1/2 story cottage form, full label on reverse "Bank of Writing Fluid, Manuf by the Senate Ink Co. Philadelphia," aquamarine, tooled sq collared mouth, smooth base, small area of label slightly faded, C# 682 ......300.00
Hexagonal, 9-7/8" h, America, 1900-20, "Carter," cathedral panels, colorless with pale yellow cast, machined mouth, smooth base, similar to C #820..700.00
Inverted Concial
  2-3/8" h, Stoddard, NH, 1846-1860, deep yellow-olive, sheared mouth, pontil scar, pinhead flake on mouth edge, C #15 ....170.00
  2-1/2" h, America, 1840-60, medium cobalt blue, tooled mouth, tubular pontil scar, C #23 ....800.00
  2-1/2" h, America, 1840-60, "Woods/Black Ink/Portland," aquamarine, inward rolled mouth, pontil scar, C #12, unearthed with some remaining stain..........................170.00
Octagonal
  G. H. Gilbert Co., West Brookfield, MA, orig label 150.00
  Harrison's Columbian Ink, light green 60.00
  Laughlin's And Bushfield Wheeling Va, 2-7/8" h, aquamarine, inward rolled mouth, pontil scar 300.00
Umbrella, America, 1840-60
  2-1/8" h, 12-sided, sapphire blue, inward rolled mouth, pontil, scar, C #182, professionally cleaned 950.00
  2-1/4" h, New England, 1840-60, octagonal, golden amber, sheared mouth, C #145 ....160.00
  2-3/8" h, octagonal, sapphire blue, inward rolled mouth, pontil, scar, C #141 ....700.00
  2-5/8" h, octagonal, lime green, labeled "Williams/Black/Empire/Ink/New York," tooled mouth, smooth base, label 95% intact, C #173 ....160.00
  2-5/8" h, octagonal, sapphire blue, inward rolled mouth, pontil, scar, C #129 ....950.00
  2-5/8" h, octagonal, yellow, inward rolled mouth, pontil, scar, C#129 1,200

INKWELLS

History: Most of the commonly found inkwells were produced in the United States or Europe between the early 1800s and the 1930s. The most popular materials were glass and pottery because these substances resisted the corrosive effects of ink.

Inkwells were a sign of the office or wealth of an individual. The common man tended to dip his ink directly from the bottle. The years between 1870 and 1920 represent the golden age of inkwells when elaborate designs were produced.

References: Veldon Badders, *Collector's Guide to Inkwells: Identification and Values*, Book I (1995), Book II, 1997, Collector Books; William E. Covill Jr., *Inkbottles and Inkwells*, William S. Sullwold Publishing, out of print.

Collectors' Clubs: St. Louis Inkwell Collectors Society, P.O. Box 29396, St. Louis, MO 63126; The Society of Inkwell Collectors, 5136 Thomas Ave. S., Minneapolis, MN 55410.

Amber Glass, 4-1/2" h, 2-1/2" sq, fine stippling on base, deep plain dimple on each side, polished brass hinged mountings 240.00

Blown Three Mold, glass

    1-5/8" h, Mount Vernon Glass Works, Vernon, NY, 1820-40, dense olive amber, tooled disc mouth, pontil scar, McKearin GII-15 .... 150.00

    1-3/4" h, Boston and Sandwich Glass Works, Sandwich, MA, 1860-90, cylindrical, vertical flues, fiery opalescent milk glass, crudely sheared mouth, smooth base, small areas of roughness and flaking, C #1173 .... 200.00

Brass, figural rose, color wash, pink/red petals, green stem 250.00

Bronze

    9-3/4" l, patinated, Zodiac pattern, sexagonal inkwell with glass liner, sq pen tray, imp "Tiffany Studios, New York/1073" 1,000.00

    12" w, 6-7/8" h, gilt bronze, 2 nude women in surf, inkwell lid in form of crab, brown composition base, Ve Leonie Ledru, France, c1900.. 525.00

Figural

    1-7/8" h, snail, America, 1830-70, colorless glass, ground mouth, smooth base, flat chip on int. 140.00

    2-3/4" h, Benjamin Franklin head shape, France, 1830-60, colorless glass with pale gray cast, sheared mouth, smooth base, C#1289 .... 230.00

Freeblown Glass, 1-3/4" h, attributed to America, 1840-60, sq, opaque electric blue, flared mouth, pontil scar............. 120.00

Gilt Metal, 11" l, 4-1/2" h, double, Moorish pattern, cast brass, two hinged-top inkwells with hooks to hold pen, base imp "Tiffany & Co.," foot restored, pen missing 345.00

Grain painted finish, stenciled dec, 5 quill holds, two orig inserts, bottom labeled "Silliman & Co., Chester, CT," 1820 ..... 260.00

Marble, 9-1/2" l, Sienna, modeled after sarcophagus of Lucius Seipio, Italian, 19th C... 2,000.00

Paperweight, 6-1/4" h, 4-1/2" d, multicolored concentric millefiore, base with 1848 date canes, Whitefriars 175.00

Pattern Molded Glass, 2" h, America, 1840-60, cylindrical, vertical ribs, cobalt blue, sheared rim, pontil scar, C #1066 ..... 140.00

Pearlware, 5-1/2" h, gilt highlights, imp "By F. Bridges, Phrenologist," and "EM" on base, England, 19th C, very minor chips, gilt wear 520.00

Pitkin Type, 1-7/8" h, New England, 1780-1830, 36 ribs swirled to left, cylindrical, deep yellow-olive, tooled mouth, pontil scar, C #1160 .... 400.00

Teakettle, ceramic

    2-1/8" h, France, 1830-60, hexagonal, mottled ruby red and white glazes.. 80.00

    2-1/2" h, attributed to America, 1830-60, hexagonal, blue glaze, transfer scene on top, gilt dec highlights, ground mouth with brass collar and cap, smooth base, C #1240 .... 450.00

Teakettle, glass, attributed to America, 1830-60, cut and polished octagonal form

    1-5/8" h, orange amber, ground mouth, applied brass collar, smooth base, brass cap missing, C #1268 .... 325.00

    2" h, opalescent electric blue, ground mouth, smooth base, C #1255 .... 400.00

    2-1/8" h, canary, ground moth, smooth base, missing closure, C #1268 .... 250.00

    2-5/8" h, brick red and burgundy slag glass, ground mouth with brass cap, smooth base, two small chips, C#1261 .... 110.00

    3-1/4" h, additional applied ink reservoir on top, opaque blue, gilt highlighted dec, ground mouth, smooth base, no collar and cap, wear to gilt... 350.00

Wood, 7" h, figural, squatting man with pipe, painted, America, 19th C, minor imperfections 865.00

IRONS

History: Ironing devices have been used for many centuries, with the earliest references dating from 1100. Irons from the medieval, Renaissance, and early industrial eras can be found in Europe but are rare. Fine engraved brass irons and hand-wrought irons predominated prior to 1850. After 1850, the iron underwent a series of rapid evolutionary changes.

Between 1850 and 1910, irons were heated in four ways: 1) a hot metal slug was inserted into the body, 2) a burning solid, e.g., coal or charcoal, was placed in the body, 3) a liquid or gas, e.g., alcohol, gasoline, or natural gas, was fed from an external tank and burned in the body, or 4) conduction heat, usually drawing heat from a stove top.

Electric irons are just beginning to find favor among iron collectors.

References: Dave Irons, *Irons by Irons*, published by author (223 Covered Bridge Rd., Northampton, PA 18067), 1994; ——, *More Irons by Irons*, published by author 1996; ——, *Pressing Iron Patents*, published by author, 1994.

Periodical: *Iron Talk*, P.O. Box 68, Waelder, TX 78959.

Collectors' Clubs: Club of the Friends of Ancient

Teakettle, barrel form, sapphire blue, gilt dec highlights at mid body, sheared mouth, applied brass collar, smooth base, missing brass cap, 1830-60, 2-1/4" h, $550. Photo courtesy of Norman C. Heckler & Company.

Smoothing Irons, P.O. Box 215, Carlsbad, CA 92008; Midwest Sad Iron Collectors Club, 24 Nob Hill Dr., St. Louis, MO 63138.

Museums: Henry Ford Museum, Dearborn, MI; Shelburne Museum, Shelburne, VT; Sturbridge Village, Sturbridge, MA.

Additional Listings: See *Warman's Americana & Collectibles* for more examples.

Advisors: David and Sue Irons.

Charcoal
Box, Colebrookdale, tall chimney, 6-1/2" 130.00
Box, German, head on latch, sawtooth upper edge, 8" 200.00
Double Chimney, Ne Plus Ultra, Oz., 7-1/4" 200.00
Pan, Oriental, ivory handle, highly decorated 210.00
Children's small size, under 5"
Charcoal, box, tall chimney, hinged top, 3-3/4" 175.00
French, Gendarme No. 1, 4" 95.00
Goffering Iron, brass barrel, "S" wire, no heater.................180.00
Slug, box, English, all iron, lift gate, 3" 250.00
Wood Grip, star with 7, 2-3/4" 175.00
Electric
K/M, flatwork ironer, round iron, 1930 ....225.00
Pacific Electric Heating Co., 1906..75.00
Flat
Cold Handle, (handle lifts off), Best on Earth, Potts 70.00
Cold Handle, (handle lifts off), Dover Sad Iron, #62, 6-1/2" ...35.00
Cold Handle, (handle lifts off), Enterprise, double ptd.........20.00
French, all cast, low profile...45.00
Ober, #6, all cast, 5-3/4" 25.00
Wrought, Mexican, bell handle...100.00
Fluters
Clamp-On, Companion, 5" roll, good paint 350.00
Combination, Magic #1, Groton, NY, 6 pcs........................375.00
Machine, English, cast frame with fine fluted rolls 225.00
Machine, Mrs. Susan R. Knox, crank, good paint..............300.00
Roller, Good Luck, 2 pcs..275.00
Roller, Sundry Mfg Co., Buffalo, NY, 3 pcs 300.00
Goffering
Clamp-On, wrought, 1700s 400.00
Double, brassQueen Anne tripod base..............................450.00
Single, "S" post, common, cast base 85.00
Wrought, single, spider base, early 1800...........................350.00
Liquid Fuel
Acme, front tank, 7" 120.00
Boudoir, British, meta fuel, 5-1/4" 130.00
Coleman, 609A, black enamel, plastic handle....................125.00
Gas/Jet, (slug style), European, decorated surface...........130.00
Modern Gasoline Iron, cylindrical tank.................................90.00
Omega, alcohol, 2 rows of side holes, 6" 180.00
Miscellaneous
Laundry Stove, Dixie, holds 8 irons around belly 300.00
Stove Top Heater, pyramid, cast, holds 3 irons 160.00

Goffering, left: Single, European, all wrought iron, small monkeytail, tripod base, early 1800, 4-3/4" w, 11" h, $600; **right:** single, European, base wrought, barrel and standard turned, spiral end feet, early 1800, 5-1/2' b, 8-7/8" h, $800. Photo courtesy of David Irons.

Flat, left: Cast, European, early 1900, 7" l, $15; **middle:** cast, Crown #2, Pat App'd For, late 1800, 6-1/2" l, $60; **right:** cast, about 1900, 6-3/4" l, $40.

Slug
Kenrick, hinged top flips, double ptd 140.00
Magic #1, top lifts off 175.00
Ox Tongue, (bullet style), brass, European, "L" handle 200.00
Wrought, French, pierced construction, early 1800 ....300.00
Smoothing/Mangle Boards
Grip Handle, geometric carved decorations........................350.00
Horse Handle, decorated with chip carving and/or painted designs, 27" 650.00
Special Purpose
Billiard Table, English, rectangular....................................110.00
Egg, on stand, French 180.00
Hat, McCoy's, all cast, concave bottom.............................130.00
Hat, Tolliker, wood with brass plate...................................120.00
Leaf/Flower, brass top and bottom......................................85.00
Long Sleeve, floral head, French, 14" 180.00
Polisher, Mahony, grid bottom, 4-1/2" 50.00
Polisher, Salter, round bottom, 5" 110.00

IRONWARE

History: Iron, a metallic element that occurs abundantly in combined forms, has been known for centuries. Items made from iron range from the utilitarian to the decorative. Early hand-forged ironwares are of considerable interest to Americana collectors.

References: *Collectors Guide to Wagner Ware and Other Companies*, L-W Book Sales, 1994; Douglas Congdon-Martin, *Figurative Cast Iron*, Schiffer Publishing, 1994; *Griswold Cast Iron*, L-W Book Sales, 1997; Jon B. Haussler, *Griswold Muffin Pans*, Schiffer Publishing, 1997; Henrie Martinie, *Art Deco Ornamental Ironwork*, Dover Publications, 1996; Kathryn McNerney, *Antique Iron Identification and Values*, Collector Books, 1984, 1998 value update; J. L. Mott Iron Works, *Mott's Illustrated Catalog of Victorian Plumbing Fixtures for Bathrooms and Kitchens* (reprint of 1888 catalog), Dover Publications, 1987; George C. Neumann, *Early American Antique Country Furnishings*, L-W Book Sales, 1984, 1993 reprint; David G. Smith and Charles Wafford, *Book of Griswold & Wagner*, Schiffer Publishing, 1995; Diane Stoneback, *Kitchen Collectibles*, Wallace-Homestead, 1994.

Periodicals: *Cast Iron Cookware News*, 28 Angela Ave., San Anselmo, CA 94960; *Kettles 'n Cookware*, Drawer B, Perrysburg, NY 14129.

Collectors' Club: Griswold & Cast Iron Cookware Assoc., 54 Macon Ave., Asheville, NC 28801.

REPRODUCTION ALERT

Use the following checklist to determine if a metal object is a period piece or modern reproduction. This checklist applies to all cast-metal items, from mechanical banks to trivets.

Period cast-iron pieces feature well-defined details, carefully fitted pieces, and carefully finished and smooth castings. Reproductions, especially those produced by making a new mold from a period piece, often lack detail in the casting (lines not well defined, surface details blurred) and parts have gaps at the seams and a rough surface. Reproductions from period pieces tend to be slightly smaller in size than the period piece from which they were copied.

Period paint mellows, i.e., softens in tone. Colors look flat. Beware of any cast-iron object whose paint is bright and fresh. Painted period pieces should show wear. Make certain the wear is in places it is supposed to be.

Period cast-iron pieces develop a surface patina that prevents rust. When rust is encountered on a period piece, it generally has a greasy feel and is dark in color. The rust on artificially aged reproductions is flaky and orange.

Additional Listings: Banks; Boot Jacks; Doorstops; Fireplace Equipment; Food Molds; Irons Kitchen Collectibles; Lamps; Tools.

Apple Roaster, 34-1/4" l, wrought, hinged apple support, pierced heat end on slightly twisted projecting handle, late 18th C 1,650.00

Baker's Lamp, 4-1/4" h, 8-1/2" l, cast iron, attached pan, hinged lid, bottom mkd "No. 2 B. L.," pitted 250.00

Boot Scraper, cast
    12" l, scroll ends, green granite base 110.00
    14" l, 9" h, pecking rooster, molded, traces of polychrome paint, 19th C 1,500.00

Candle Holder, 9-1/2" h, wrought iron, spring clamp, twisted detail, shaped saucer base, three feet, taper socket, and handle 250.00

Candlestand, 51-1/2" h, wrought iron, adjustable candle arm, two sockets, four part base, penny feet, pitted 1,265.00

Chenet, 10" to 13", cast iron, portrait bust, pitted, Continental, 3 prs 180.00

Cruisie Lamp, 7" h, wrought iron, double, ram's horn finial, twisted handle 140.00

Door Knocker, 5-1/2" l, cast, fox head, ring hangs from mouth 85.00

Hat Rack, 40-1/2" h, 33" w, cast, painted, flower basket form, late 19th C 825.00

Kettle, 8" h, cast iron, Sampson & Tiscale, NY, 19th C, mkd on side, corrosion, crack 145.00

Loom Light, 17-3/4" h, candle socket, sawtooth trammel, wrought iron 420.00

Mirror, 18" h, shaving type, old polychrome repaint 315.00

Mortar and Pestle, 10-1/2" d, 8-1/4" h, urn shape, cast iron, pitted 50.00

Peel, 46" l, ram's horn handle, wrought, pitted 110.00

Pipe Tongs, 17-1/4" l, wrought iron, 18th C 1,150.00

Shelf Brackets, pr, 5-1/2" h, swivel 20.00

Shoe Shine Chair, wire work heart shaped back, two cast foot rests, leather seat, oak arm rests 325.00

Hinges, wrought iron, left: blanket chest hinges, PA, late 18th C, articulated strap form, pierced heart finial at one end, spurred openwork heart terminal at other end, one with broken spur, pr, 25-1/2" h, $230; middle: blanket chest hinges, Jonestown, Lebanon County, PA, late 18th C, articulated form, heart terminal and spurred bulbous strap ending in spurred-ball terminals, pr, 19" h, $75; right: blanket chest hinges, PA, 19th C, penny terminals, 15-1/2" l, $50. Photo courtesy of Sotheby's.

Skillet, cast
    Griswold No. 7 .... 30.00
    Wagner, MiPet, No. 3 .... 12.00

Stove Plate, 24" h, 27-1/2" w, cast iron, Wedding Fable scene, right plate of Marlboro stove, attributed to Harrisonburg, VA, c1768, minor losses, rust 815.00

Sugar Cane Kettle, cast, wide flat rim, mkd "Kelly Kettle," 19th C 350.00

Taster, 7-1/8" l, copper bowl, tooled wrought iron handle .. 110.00

Trade Sign, 12" h, milliner's, figural top hat with trim, painted, 19th C, paint wear, corrosion 1,150.00

Trivet, 7-3/4" d, round, mkd "The Griswold Mfg. Co., Eire, PA, USA/8/Trivet/206" 35.00

Umbrella Stand, 21" h, cast iron, heron, lily pads and fish in base, old polychrome repaint 275.00

Utensil Rack, 10-3/4" l, wrought iron, scrolled crest, five hooks with acorn terminals, minor brazed repair 770.00

Wafer Iron, 5-1/4" d, 24" l, imp with seal of US, c1800, minor imperfections 550.00

Wall Frame, 8-1/2" h, 6" d, cast iron, gilt eagle crest, elaborately dec frame, C-scrolls and foliate devices, 19th C 575.00

Windmill Weight, cast iron
    10-1/2" l, crescent, "Eclipse," Fairbanks, Morris & Co., Chicago 250.00
    16" l, figural "W," Althouse Wheeler Co., Waupen, WI, paint stripped 360.00
    16-1/2" h, 17" w, bobtail horse, Dempster Mill Manufacturing, Beatrice, NE, old black repaint 110.00

IVORY

History: Ivory, a yellowish white organic material, comes from the teeth or tusks of animals and lends itself to carving. Many cultures have used it for centuries to make artistic and utilitarian items.

A cross section of elephant ivory will have a reticulated crisscross pattern. Hippopotamus teeth, walrus tusks, whale teeth, narwhal tusks, and boar tusks also are forms of ivory. Vegetable ivory, bone, stag horn, and plastic are ivory substitutes which often confuse collectors. For information on how to identify real ivory, see Bernard Rosett's "Is It Genuine Ivory" in Sandra Andacht's *Oriental Antiques & Art: An Identification and Value Guide* (Wallace-Homestead, 1987).

References: Edgard O. Espinoza and Mary-Jacque Mann, *Identification for Ivory and Ivory Substitutes*, 2nd ed., World Wildlife Fund, 1992.

Periodical: *Netsuke & Ivory Carving Newsletter*, 3203 Adams Way, Ambler, PA 19002.

Collectors' Club: International Ivory Society, 11109 Nicholas Dr., Wheaton, MD 20902.

Note: Dealers and collectors should be familiar with The Endangered Species Act of 1973, amended in 1978, which limits the importation and sale of antique ivory and tortoiseshell items.

Box, 3-5/8" l, almond-shape, silver inlay and fittings, engraved monogram, mirror on int. lid, floral petit point lining 175.00
Brush Pot, 4" h, carved, figures and pavilions, Chinese, c1885 .... 1,000.00
Chess Set, fully carved, red stained opposition, Chinese Export, later box, wear 750.00
Cup, cov, foliate finial, oval body, carved frieze of putti with hound, mask and acanthus baluster stem, round foot, Continental, early 18th C 1,200.00
Dipper, 14-1/4" l whale ivory, rosewood, and coconut, baleen spacers, 19th C, cracks to dipper, repair to handle 490.00
Door Knobs, pr, 7-1/4" l, carved whale ivory, cracks, very minor losses 980.00

Grouping, Minstrel Band, carved figures in period dress, whimsical expressions, various musical instruments, mounted on single wood base, additional ivory fence rail and sign post, Continental, 18th C, 13" l, 8" h, $3,300. Photo courtesy of Jackson's Auctioneers & Appraisers.

Figure
3" h, eagle attacking monkey, Japanese 475.00
4-1/4" l, Medicine Woman, Chinese 425.00
5-1/4" l, Medicine Woman, Chinese 400.00
5-1/2" h, Basket Seller, etched geometric designs and foliage, Japanese, late 19th C 815.00
Jagging Wheel, 19th C
5-3/4" l, pierced carved, whalebone, minute losses ... 2,875.00
6-1/4" l, open carved handle, minor cracks, minute chips 920.00
7-1/8" l, figural, unicorn, inlaid eyes and nostrils, minor losses 4,600.00
7-1/4" l, pistol handle, baleen spacer, cracks, old repair 230.00
Measure, 14-7/8" l, whalebone, ivory, and exotic wood, American shield inlay, inscribed "WH," 19th C, minor imperfections 195.00
Pickwick, 3-1/4" h, carved, 19th C, minor losses, repair 210.00
Plaque, 14" h, elephant's head, realistically molded bronze skin, ivory tusks, Japanese, discolored 1,100.00
Pointer, 24-2/4" l, whalebone and ivory, carved eagle's head handle, exotic wood spacers, 19th C, minor cracks 980.00
Rolling Pin, 19th C, minor insect damage
13-5/8" l, exotic wood, baleen spacers, 19th C, cracks 225.00
15-3/4" l, walrus ivory and exotic wood, baleen spacers, red sealing wax inlaid scribe lines 375.00
Sander, 2-1/4" h, miniature, walrus ivory, scribe line dec, 19th C, minor chips 320.00
Seal, 3-7/8" l, intaglio, handle, 19th C, cracks 400.00
Sewing Bird, 4-1/8" l, four side mounted spools, geometric and heart exotic wood inlay, 19th C, inlay loss and replacements 1,150.00
Sewing Egg, 2-1/2" l, walrus ivory, unscrews to reveal ivory spool, thimble, and needle case, 19th C 920.00
Square, 10" l, whalebone and ivory inlaid walnut, diamond motif inlay, 19th C, cracks to ivory 1,095.00
Stand, 7" h, pierced relief, pink and cream flowers, peony and lotus flowers, green stones 425.00
Toy, 2-7/8" l, top, carved, sealing wax inlaid scribe lines, 19th C, minor cracks and chips 350.00

JACK-IN-THE-PULPIT VASES

History: Trumpet-shaped jack-in-the-pulpit glass vases were in vogue during the late 19th and early 20th centuries. The vases were made in a wide variety of patterns, colors, and sizes.

Additional Listings: See specific glass categories.

5-1/2" h, 3-1/2" w, spangled blue, yellow, and brown, white ground, all over silver flecks, applied crystal edge, swirled, Mt. Washington 250.00
6" h, vaseline, clear bulging opalescent body, cranberry flared rim, ftd 165.00
6" h, 5" w, frosted pink and white stripes, large bulbous base, broad flange, Webb 375.00
6-1/2" h, 3" w top, Burmese, matte finish, ruffled top, Mt. Washington, c1880 .... 425.00
6-3/4" h, Stevens and Williams, rainbow swirl, trefoil crimped top 500.00
7-1/4" h, creamy opaque ext., white and yellow flowers, green leaves gold trim, deep rose pink int., amber edge, ormolu leaf feet 165.00
7-1/2" h, opalescent, chartreuse, ruffled 90.00
8-1/2" h, spatter, white, green, and cranberry 115.00
9" h, 5" w, cranberry, white opal edge, applied crystal base, Hobbs 325.00

Peachblow, New England, 7-3/4" h, $450. Photo courtesy of Gene Harris Antique Auction Center.

9-1/2" h, 5" w, lusterless white, Mt. Washington, randomly scattered floral dec, flared pie crimped top..........................300.00

9-3/4" h, 4-3/4" d top, Crown Milano, painted opalware, Burmese yellow base, Peachblow pink top, white mid section, small flower and leaves floral dec, 36 crimps at top, Mt. Washington..........................785.00

12" h, Loetz, green, silver-blue irid spots, c1920...............450.00

14" h, purple stretch, butterscotch pulled feather design on base..........................270.00

JADE

History: Jade is the generic name for two distinct minerals: nephrite and jadeite. Nephrite, an amphibole mineral from Central Asia that was used in pre-18th-century pieces, has a waxy surface and hues that range from white to an almost-black green. Jadeite, a pyroxene mineral found in Burma and used from 1700 to the present, has a glassy appearance and comes in various shades of white, green, yellow-brown, and violet.

Jade cannot be carved because of its hardness. Shapes are achieved by sawing and grinding with wet abrasives such as quartz, crushed garnets, and carborundum.

Prior to 1800, few items were signed or dated. Stylistic considerations are used to date pieces. The Ch'ien Lung period (1736-1795) is considered the golden age of jade.

Periodical: *Bulletin of the Friends of Jade*, 5004 Ensign St., San Diego, CA 92117.

Museum: Avery Brundage Collection, de Young Museum, San Francisco, CA.

Bowl, 8-3/4" d, spinach green, hemispherical, ftd, polished surface, sgd "H. Wolf"......................1,100.00
Box, 3-3/8" l, rect, silver mounted, early 20th C.................320.00
Brush Pot, 4-1/4" h, scrolling cloud pattern, Chinese, 19th C..........................320.00
Candlesticks, pr, 12-7/8" h, dark green, carved low relief goose with out-spread wings, stands on tortoise, head supports 3 tiered pricket, tripod bowl with int. carving, reticulated wood base with carved key scroll motifs and floral scrolls.....550.00
Dish, 5-1/2", octagonal, green spinach...............................150.00
Figure
    2-1/4" h, Buddha with monkey, white jade, Chinese.....200.00

6-3/4" h, grotto, wrinkled elephant and attendant on ledge beneath rocky outcrop and pine trees on front, reverse with gnarled pine and sage on flight of stairs with climbing monkey, late 17th C..........................16,500.00
7-1/8" h, Meiren, standing, holding peach bough and hoe, mint green, China......................2,000.00
Inkstone, 3-5/8" l, oval, depression to one side, black and white mottling, incised rim band..........................200.00
Letter Opener, 10-3/4" l, carved interlocking C scrolls between keyfret bands handle, SS knife..........................250.00
Libation Cup, 5" l, celadon jade, incised dec, dragon head handles, Chinese, Qing Dynasty, price for pr.....................425.00
Plaque, 5-1/4" l, carved figure in mountainous riverscape, Chinese, Qing Dynasty..........................600.00
Snuff Bottle
    Grayish-white, mottled russet skin on one side, rose quartz stopper..........................550.00
    Greenish-white, sloping shoulder, oval foot, 1880-80, pr..........................650.00
Urn, 8" h, ovoid, incised mask dec, narrow neck, handles, domed lid with suspending carved chains, yoke shape hanger..........................700.00
Vase, 7" h, cov, celadon to gray jade, carved, two loose ring and fu dog head handles, foliate and stylized dec, fu dog finial, Chinese..........................250.00

JAPANESE CERAMICS

History: Like the Chinese, the Japanese spent centuries developing their ceramic arts. Each region established its own forms, designs, and glazes. Individual artists added their unique touches.

Japanese ceramics began to be exported to the West in the mid-19th century. Their beauty quickly made them favorites of the patrician class.

Fine Japanese ceramics continued to be made into the 20th century, and modern artists enjoy equal fame with older counterparts.

References: Christopher Dresser, *Traditional Arts and Crafts of Japan*, Dover Publications, 1994; Gloria and Robert Mascarelli, *Warman's Oriental Antiques*, Wallace-Homestead, 1992; Nancy N. Schiffer, *Imari, Satsuma, and Other Japanese Export Ceramics,* Schiffer Publishing, 1997.

Periodical: *Orientalia Journal*, P.O. Box 94, Little Neck, NY 11363.

Collectors' Club: China Student's Club, 59 Standish Rd., Wellesley, MA 02181.

Museums: Art Institute of Chicago, Chicago, IL; Asian Art Museum of San Francisco, San Francisco, CA; George Walter Vincent Smith Art Museum, Springfield, MA; Morikami Museum & Japanese Gardens, Delray Beach, FL; Pacific Asia Museum, Pasadena, CA.

Basket, 5" h, abstract figures related to tea ceremony, greens, bail handle, Oribe..........................95.00
Bowl, 6-3/4" d, painted iron-red, green, deep turquoise, black, gray, and gold int., chrysanthemum spray tied with tasseled gilt ribbon, molded base with incised petal border on ext., gold highlights, Arita, 18th C..........................1,200.00
Charger, 13-1/4" d, two large iron oxide carp, underglaze blue ground, peonies, stylized waves, and flowering branches, Meiji period..........................295.00
Dish, 8-1/8" d, Nabeshima style, blossoming cherry branches on int., late 19th C..........................675.00

Teapot, Seven Gods of Wisdom, glazed and unglazed clay, polychrome, Banko, 5" h, 5-1/2" w, $450.

Ewer, 10-1/2" h, red and gilt motif, riverscape and figure dec, loop handle, dragon finial, Kaga, late 19th C 550.00

Figure, 3" h, seated Sumo wrestler, left hand on ground, right hand raised, Sumida 1,200.00

Nodder, 5-1/2" h, Fukujurojin, seated figure robe with knotted tie cord on chest, polychrome dec, Banko 475.00

Plate

    8-1/2" d, Nabeschima style, relief and underglaze blue hibiscus dec, c1900 .... 220.00

Sake Bottle, 7-1/4" h, rect, underglaze blue, 2 pine trees and 3 pavilions, stylized landscape scene, sq top with leaf and cloud dec, sq spout and pierced hole, Arita, late 17th C 675.00

Tea Bowl, 4-3/4" d, hand modeled, irregular straight sides, small recessed ring foot, central well of flower heads, peach glaze, double crackle pattern, Raku 185.00

Teapot, 5-1/2" x 5", gray ware, polychrome, 7 gods of wisdom, glazed and unglazed, Banko 450.00

JASPERWARE

History: Jasperware is a hard, unglazed porcelain with a colored ground varying from the most common blues and greens to lavender, yellow, red, or black. The white designs, often classical in nature, are applied in relief. Jasperware was first produced at Wedgwood's Etruria Works in 1775. Josiah Wedgwood described it as "a fine terra-cotta of great beauty and delicacy proper for cameos."

In addition to Wedgwood, many other English potters produced jasperware. Two of the leaders were Adams and Copeland and Spode. Several Continental potters, e.g., Heubach, also produced the ware.

References: Susan and Al Bagdade, *Warman's English & Continental Pottery & Porcelain*, 2nd ed., Wallace-Homestead, 1991; R. K. Henrywood, *Relief-Moulded Jugs*, 1820-1900, Antique Collectors' Club, out of print.

Note: This category includes jasperware pieces which were made by companies other than Wedgwood. Wedgwood jasperware is found in the Wedgwood listing.

Cheese Dish, 11" d, 11-1/4" h, high domed blue cov, panels of white relief classical ladies, rolled rim base with white relief flower and leaf band, acorn finial, Dudson Bros., England 550.00

Creamer, 2-1/2" h, sage green ground, pale pink frolicking Kewpies, sgd "O'Neill" 195.00

Hatpin, 4-1/2", star form, multi-faceted steel beading surrounded by blue jasper dip button, white floret in relief, England, late 18th C 450.00

Jewelry, brooch, 1-5/8" x 2-1/8", oval, pale blue jasper dip, white classical figure, Turner imp mark, late 18th C, 14k gold frame 275.00

Jug, 4-7/8" h, 4-3/8" d, blue ground, white relief hunting scene with men on horses, dogs, and stag, white relief rim band, Copeland 85.00

Pitcher, 7-7/8" h, 5" d, dark blue ground, cylindrical, band of white relief floral swags around rim, band of small white classical figures at base, angled white handle, Copeland 120.00

Pitcher, brown, Copeland & Sons, $185.

Plaque, 3-3/8" x 4-1/2", solid blue, white classical relief figures, Enoch Wood imp marks, late 18th C, brass frame, 3 pc set 395.00

Serving Dish, 11-1/8" l, oval, light blue dip, white applied classical angelic figures between male masks, unmarked, England, late 18th C, base hairlines....................................1,100.00

Tobacco Jar, cov, 6-1/4" h, cylindrical, dark blue ground, white relief band around base, SP rim, bail handle, and cov, ivory finial, imp "Adams, Tunstall, England" 120.00

JEWEL BOXES

History: The evolution of jewelry was paralleled by the development of boxes in which to store it. Jewel-box design followed the fashion trends dictated by furniture styles. Many jewel boxes are lined.

2-1/4" h, 6-1/2" d, sapphire blue glass, lift off lid, round, center scene of two cavaliers talking to pretty lady, fancy gold border with pink enameled flowers and green leaves 240.00

4-1/2" x 2-1/2", malachite, veneer, rect, raised feet, satin lining, Russian, 19th C 250.00

4-1/2" x 2-3/4", cranberry glass, enameled floral dec, silverplated rim..165.00

4-5/8" h, 4-3/8" d, golden amber, inverted thumbprint, round, hinged, ormolu feet, sapphire blue serpent applied to lid, small enameled flowers and green leaves dec.............235.00

4-3/4" h, 4-3/8" d, egg shape, clear, cream colored enamel scroll trim and edging, white enamel flower on top, fine sanded ground, gold trim, ormolu feet......................................185.00

4-3/4" x 8-3/4", Russian Silver, rect, sky blue, deep red, and white enameled diapering pattern, stylized flower heads, raised studded bands, swing handles on lid and sides, pale blue padded satin lining, 4 bun feet...................................2,500.00

6" h, 10" w, 6-3/4" d, engraved whalebone, top polychrome dec of elegant ladies and child flanked by birds among trees, sides with reserves of birds among foliage, top lists to reveal a removable tray, four cov compartments and door, dec with snakes, fish, and foliate devices, shaped bracket feet, minor imperfections 5,660.00

6-1/4" h, 10" d, 7" d, exotic woods, various geometric motifs, late 19th C, minor losses 320.00

6-1/2" l, German Silver, heavily molded and bellied sides, winged dolphin form feet, early 19th C, 13 oz. 850.00

6-1/2" h, 11-1/4" w, 8" d, decoupage, cigar box construction, stamps dec, two drawers, America, early 20th C, minor imperfections 175.00

7" x 6-1/2", wave Crest, puffy egg crate mold, hp lid, child with bow and arrow, satin finish, ftd, orig lining................1,200.00

8" x 5" x 3", silverplated, rococo floral design......................90.00

Tramp Art, covered with hearts, painted silver over gold, velvet lined, 11" w, 6" d, 6" h, $595. Photo courtesy of Clifford Wallach.

8-1/2" x 5-1/2" x 4-3/4", ivory, rect, hinged lid, delicate engraved and repousse mounts....................................200.00

9-1/2" h, 16" w, gilt bronze, elaborate Moorish design, semi precious stones, enamel dec....................................900.00

10" x 8" x 7", Art Nouveau, ormolu, raised figural and floral dec, plaque dated 1903 ....245.00

10" h, 11-1/2" w, 10-1/2" d, Victorian, painted and decoupage, lift top, pr of doors opening to small drawers, Chinese scenes on mustard yellow ground 815.00

11-3/4" l, ebony, allover scrolling flowering foliage dec, inlaid ivory, 19th C 300.00

12" h, 10" w, 10" d, painted papier-mâché, lit top, fitted int., 2 doors enclosing small drawers, Victorian, mid 19th, minor restorations 520.00

13" x 5" x 4", sterling silver, repousse sides, small petal-like beaded edges, fancy feet, red velvet lining, mkd "Meriden" 160.00

JEWELRY

History: Jewelry has been a part of every culture. It is a way of displaying wealth, power, or love of beauty. In the current antiques marketplace, it is easiest to find jewelry dating after 1830.

Jewelry items were treasured and handed down as heirlooms from generation to generation. In the United States, antique jewelry is any jewelry at least 100 years old, a definition linked to U.S. Customs law. Pieces that do not meet the antique criteria but are at least 25 years old are called "period" or "heirloom/estate" jewelry.

The names of historical periods are commonly used when describing jewelry. The following list indicates the approximate dates for each era.

Georgian	1714-1830
Victorian	1837-1901
Edwardian	1890-1920
Arts and Crafts	1890-1920
Art Nouveau	1895-1910
Art Deco	1920-1935
Retro Modern	1935-1945
Post-War Modern	1945-1965

References: Lillian Baker, *Art Nouveau & Art Deco Jewelry*, Collector Books, 1981, 1994 value update; ——, *100 Years of Collectible Jewelry, 1850-1950*, Collector Books, 1978, 1997 value update; Howard L. Bell, Jr., *Cuff Jewelry*, published by author (P.O. Box 11695, Raytown, MO 64138), 1994; Jeanne Bell, *Answers to Questions about Old Jewelry*, 4th ed., Books Americana, 1996; David Bennett and Daniela Mascetti, *Understanding Jewellery*, revised ed., Antique Collectors' Club, 1994; France Borel, *Splendor of Ethnic Jewelry*, Harry N. Abrams, 1994; Shirley Bury, *Jewellery 1789-1910*, Vols. I and II, Antique Collectors' Club, 1991; Franco Cologni and Eric Nussbaum, *Platinum By Cartier, Triumphs of the Jewelers' Art,* Harry N. Abrams, 1996; Genevieve Cummins and Neryvalle Taunton, *Chatelaines*, Antique Collector's Club, 1994.

Lydia Darbyshire and Janet Swarbrick (eds). *Jewelry, The Decorative Arts Library*, Chartwell Books, 1996; Ginny Redington Dawes and Corinne Davidov, *Victorian Jewelry*, Abbeville Press, 1991; Ulysses Grant Dietz, Janet Zapata et. al., *The Glitter & the Gold, Fashioning America's Jewelry,* The Newark Museum, 1997; Janet Drucker, *Georg Jensen, A Tradition of Splendid Silver,*

Schiffer Publishing, 1997; Alastair Duncan, *Paris Salons 1895-1914*, Jewelry, 2 Vols., Antique Collectors' Club, 1994; Martin Eidelberg, (ed.), *Messengers of Modernism, American Studio Jewelry 1940-1960,* Flammarion, 1996; Lodovica Rizzoli Eleuteri, *Twentieth-Century Jewelry*, Electa, Abbeville, 1994; Joan Evans, *History of Jewellery 1100-1870*, Dover Publications, 1988; Stephen Giles, *Jewelry, Miller's Antiques Checklist,* Reed International Books Ltd, 1997; Geza von Habsburg, *Fabergé in America,* Thomas and Hudson, 1996; S. Sylvia Henzel, *Collectible Costume Jewelry, Third Edition,* Krause Publications, 1997; Susan Jonas and Marilyn Nissenor, *Cuff Links*, Harry N. Abrams, 1991; Arthur Guy Kaplan, *Official Identification and Price Guide to Antique Jewelry*, 6th ed., House of Collectibles, 1990, reprinted 1994; Elyse Zorn Karlin, *Jewelry and Metalwork in the Arts and Crafts Tradition*, Schiffer Publishing, 1993; Jack and Pet Kerins, *Collecting Antique Stickpins*, Collector Books, 1995; George Frederick Kunz, *Curious Lore of Precious Stones*, Dover Publications, 1970; ——, *Rings for the Finger*, Dover Publications, n.d.; George Frederick Kunz and Charles Hugh Stevenson, *Book of the Pearl*, Dover Publications, 1973; David Lancaster, *Art Nouveau Jewelry, Christie's Collectibles,* Bulfinch Press, Little Brown and Co., 1996.

Daniel Mascetti and Amanda Triossi, *Bulgari,* Abbeville Press, 1996; Daniel Mascetti and Amanda Triossi, *The Necklace, From Antiquity to the Present,* Harry N. Abrams, Inc., 1997; Antionette Matlins, *The Pearl Book,* GemStone Press, 1996; Patrick Mauries, *Jewelry by Chanel,* Bulfinch Press, 1993; Anna M. Miller, *Cameos Old and New*, Van Nostrand Reinhold, 1991; ——, *Illustrated Guide to Jewelry Appraising: Antique Period & Modern,* Chapman & Hall, 1990; Penny C. Morrill, *Silver Masters of Mexico,* Schiffer Publishing, 1996; Penny Chittim Morrill and Carol A. Beck, *Mexican Silver: 20th Century Handwrought Jewelry and Metalwork,* Schiffer Publishing, 1994; Gabriel Mourey et al., *Art Nouveau Jewellery & Fans*, Dover Publications, n.d.; Clare Phillips, *Jewelry, From Antiquity to the Present,* Thames and Hudson, 1996; Michael Poynder, *Price Guide to Jewellery 3000 B.C.-1950 A.D.*, Antique Collectors' Club, 1990 reprint; Penny Proddow and Marion Fasel, *Diamonds, A Century of Spectacular Jewels,* Harry N. Abrams, 1996; Penny Proddow, Debra Healy, and Marion Fasel, *Hollywood Jewels,* Harry L. Abrams, 1992; Dorothy T. Rainwater, *American Jewelry Manufacturers*, Schiffer Publishing, 1988; Christie Romero, *Warman's Jewelry*, 2nd ed., Krause Publications, 1998; Judy Rudoe, *Cartier 1900-1939,* Harry N. Abrams, 1997; Nancy N. Schiffer, *Silver Jewelry Designs*, Schiffer Publishing, 1996; Peter N. Schiffer, *Indian Jewelry on the Market*, Schiffer Publishing, 1996; Sheryl Gross Shatz, *What's It Made Of? A Jewelry Materials Identification Guide*, 3rd ed., published by author (10931 Hunting Horn Dr., Santa Ana, CA, 92705), 1991; Doris J. Snell, *Antique Jewelry with Prices, Second Edition,* Krause Publications, 1997; Nicholas D. Snider, *Antique Sweetheart Jewelry,* Schiffer Publishing, 1996; Ulrike von Hase-Schmundt et al., *Theodor Fahrner,*

Jewelry...between Avant-Garde and Tradition, Schiffer Publishing, 1991; Ralph Turner, *Jewelry in Europe and America, New Times, New Thinking,* Thames and Hudson, 1995; Fred Ward, *Opals,* Gem Book Publishers, 1997; Janet Zapata, *Jewelry and Enamels of Louis Comfort Tiffany,* Harry N. Abrams, 1993.

Periodicals: *Auction Market Resource for Gems & Jewelry*, P.O. Box 7683, Rego Park, NY 11374; *Gems & Gemology*, Gemological Institute of America, 5355 Armada Drive, Carlsbad CA 92008; *Jewelers' Circular Keystone/Heritage*, P.O. Box 2085, Radnor, PA 19080.

Collectors' Clubs: American Society of Jewelry Historians, Box 103, 1B Quaker Ridge Rd., New Rochelle, NY 10804; Leaping Frog Antique Jewelry and Collectable Club, 4841 Martin Luther Blvd., Sacramento, CA 95820; National Cuff Link Society, P.O. Box 346, Prospect Heights, IL 60070; Society of Antique & Estate Jewelry, Ltd., 570 7th Ave., Suite 1900, New York, NY 10018.

Videotapes: C. Jeanne Bell, *Antique and Collectible Jewelry Video Series*, Vol. I: *Victorian Jewelry, Circa 1837-1901*, Vol. II: *Edwardian, Art Nouveau & Art Deco Jewelry, Circa 1887-1930's*, Antique Images, 1994; Leigh Leshner and Christie Romero, *Hidden Treasures*, Venture Entertainment (P.O. Box 55113, Sherman Oaks, CA 91413), 1992; includes updated printed price guide, 1995.

SPECIAL AUCTIONS

Butterfield & Butterfield
220 San Bruno Ave.
San Francisco, CA 94103
(415) 861-7500

Christie's
502 Park Ave.
New York, NY 10022
(212) 546-1000

Dunning's Auction Service
755 Church Rd.
Elgin, IL 60123
(847) 741-3483

Phillips Fine Art Auctions
406 E. 79th St.
New York, NY 10021
(212) 570-4830

Skinner, Inc.
The Heritage on the Garden
63 Park Plaza
Boston, MA 02116
(617) 350-5400

Sotheby's
1334 York Ave.
New York, NY 10021
(212) 606-7000

Notes: The value of a piece of old jewelry is derived from several criteria, including craftsmanship, scarcity, and the current value of precious metals and gemstones.

Note that antique and period pieces should be set with stones that were cut in the manner in use at the time the piece was made. Antique jewelry is not comparable to contemporary pieces set with modern-cut stones and should not be appraised with the same standards. Nor should old-mine, old-European, or rose-cut stones be replaced with modern brilliant cuts.

The pieces listed here are antique or period and represent fine jewelry (i.e., made from gemstones and/or precious metals). The list contains no new reproduction pieces. Inexpensive and mass-produced costume jewelry is covered in *Warman's Americana & Collectibles*.

Bracelet

Art Deco
  14K yg, 4 sugarloaf cab chrysoprase, alternating prong set rect stones and octagonal links, 7-1/2" l, 1/2" w, 13.1 dwt 690.00
  Platinum, 209 old European cut diamonds, 84 step-cut emeralds, pierced openwork, slight damage to gallery, 7" l, 1/2" w, 24.6 dwt 12,650.00

Art Nouveau
  Bangle, pierced foliate and scroll motifs, 14K yg, not hinged, 2-1/2" x 1/2", maker's mark for "Sloan & Co.," 14.8 dwt 1,035.00
  Link, freshwater pearls, 2 sapphires, 2 peridots, 6.26 and 6.49 mm, 18K yg, 7" l, 3/8" w, 8.5 dwt 2,100.00
  Link, 14K yg, 10 cut bezel set sapphires, maker's mark for "Sloan & Co.," 7-1/8" l, 3/8" w, 12.3 dwt..................2,185.00
  Link, white enamel daisy links, 18K yg, 7-3/4" l, 1/4" w, some enamel loss, 14 dwt....................900.00

Retro
  14K yg, 10 bezel set reverse intaglios, hunting dog motif, double strand, orig box, sgd "Lucien Piccard," 11.7 dwt.........690.00
  18K, 108 full cut diamonds, textured surface, modified bow motif, 8" l, 1-5/8" w, 114 dwt....................................5,750.00

Victorian
  Charm, gold filled chain, 5 fobs with carnelian, bloodstones, sard, onyx, and tiger's eye intaglios, 8" l, 1-1/2" w, 27.1 dwt 320.00
  Diamond, 14K yg, 5 old European cut diamonds hinged bangle, safety chain with key, 11.5 dwt......................1,495.00

Brooch/Pin, early Victorian, double lobed yg floral and scroll motif frame, prong-set with three foil backed oval pink topaz, suspending a floral and scroll motif drop with one prong-set foil backed pear shaped pink topaz, C-catch, tube hinge, c1840, 2" w, 4" l, $1,500. Photo courtesy of E. Foxe Harrell Jewelers.

Brooch

Art Deco
  Platinum, cut-corner rect shape, 18 baguette diamonds, 195 old European cut diamonds, pendant fittings, 2-1/2" x 1-3/8", 11.8 dwt..........................9,200.00
  Platinum, circle, surmounted by bow, millegrain edging, 54 full cut brilliant, single cut and old European diamonds, 1-3/8" d, 5.1 dwt.................................1,485.00
  Silver topped gold, figural lizard, 190 rose and old mine diamonds, 2 cabochon cut rubies as eyes, 3" l, French hallmarks, 11 dwt..........................11,500.00

Art Nouveau
  Enameled pansy suspended from repoussé crescent moon, old European cut diamond, maker's mark for "Whiteside and Blank," 1-1/4" l, 1" w, 4.1 dwt............635.00
  Floral Spray, 139 old European and old mine round and pear cut diamonds, yg, 2-1/2" l, 1-1/4" h, hallmarked, 18.2 dwt...............................7,500.00
  Plique-à-jour enamel, floral spray with open flowers, stem, two buds, silver topped white and yellow gold setting, 250 old European cut diamonds, 3-1/2" l, 2-3/8" h, 45 dwt......................85,500.00
  Prong set amethyst, 4 seed pearls, 1-1/8" l, 1" h, maker's mark for "Krementz," 3.2 dwt................400.00
  Recumbent female, platinum topped gold, 1 old European cut diamond, etched details, 1-3/4" l, 1" h, 6.1 dwt.....2,300.00

Edwardian, platinum topped gold
  Bar, foliate motif, 25 old European cut diamonds, 3" l, 1/2" w, 5.9 dwt....................................1,100.00
  Crown motif, 99 old European cut diamonds, 2" h, 10.7 dwt...............................4,225.00

Retro, 14K yg, 6 circles form flower, 6 peridot and 1 ruby as center, 2-3/4" w 17.5 dwt........................550.00

Victorian
  Pietra Dura, floral motif in curvilinear plaques set in overlapping florentined gold squares, 1-7/8" d, 10.3 dwt....435.00
  Silver topped 18K yellow and white gold, pierced gallery, crescent motif, 21 old European cut diamonds, 2-1/4" l, 4.3 dwt..............................2,555.00

Chain

Art Nouveau
  18K yg, filigree links, French hallmarks, 57" l, 27.3 dwt...................................1,610.00
  Silver, enameled floral and leaf motifs, French hallmarks, 19-1/2" l, 10.8 dwt.................750.00

Edwardian, platinum, openwork navette shaped inks, 18 old European cut diamonds, 20" l, 7.1 dwt........................1,530.00

Cuff Links, pr

Art Nouveau, 14K yg, 3/4" h, 1/2" w
  Double link cluster of grape design, orig fitted box, sgd "Geo. O. Street & Sons," 11.1 dwt...............1,150.00
  Griffin motif, clutching off-white chipped round old European diamond in beak, 6.6 dwt....................690.00

Retro, Chalcedony, round bead style, star motif, connected by gold chain, 9.4 dwt.......................3,450.00

Victorian, 14K yg, chased bulldog motif, maker's mark for Bippart, Griscom & Osborn, 5.3 dwt...................375.00

Earrings, pr

Art Deco, platinum, drop, pearl shaped coral, sgd "Marzo, Paris," 1-5/8" l, 3.2 dwt........................2,530.00

Retro, 18K yg, 2 round bezel cut citrines, swirled design, French hallmarks for Belperron & Herz, 1-3/8" l, 19.3 dwt......4,600.00

Victorian, silvered topped gold, girandole style, 88 old mine and rose diamonds, European backs, 3-1/8" l, 12 dwt......3,450.00

Suite, brooch and earrings, mid-Victorian, rect yg 1-1/2" w x 1-5/8" l, bar with wiretwist, mesh, and beaded dec suspending a woven yg basket filled with sm coral beads, C-catch, tube hinge, 5/8" w x 1-3/4" l pendant earrings, each with a basket with coral beads suspended from coral bead cluster, yg frame and earwire, c1870, $1,000. Photo courtesy of Christie Romero.

Lavaliere

Art Nouveau, 14K yg, 15 cabochon cut moonstones, floral and leaf motif, 15-1/2" l, 2-3/4" w, 5.8 dwt 980.00

Edwardian, platinum, pierced mounting, 39 old European cut diamonds, 2 suspended egg shaped fresh water pearl, round freshwater pearls in center, filigree chain, 17" l, 15.8 dwt 18,975.00

Locket

Art Nouveau

Carved hardstone oval cameo, 14K yg, suspended oval freshwater pearl, engraved "L. S.," 4" l, 2-1/2" w, 15.5 dwt 3,355.00

14K yg, round, profile of woman, enamel dec, one rose cut 2.58 mm diamond, maker's mark for Riker Bros., 1-1/4" d, 6.3 dwt 1,265.00

Victorian

14K yellow and rose gold, 26 old European cut diamonds, diamond monogram "JCS," engraved "JSS" on reverse, 3" l, 66 dwt 3,450.00

18K yg, shakudo, naturalistic scene, Etruscan Revival frame, applied bead and wiretwist, hair compartment, 7.3 dwt 1,325.00

Necklace

Art Deco, 18K and 22K yg, 1 carved and pierced jadeite plaque, 5 freshwater Baroque pearls, 14" l, 8.7 dwt...................990.00

Art Nouveau, 14K yg

Cupid, foliate scene, 1 rose cut diamond, plique-à-jour enamel, maker's mark for Riker Bros., 8.8 dwt...............1,955.00

Opal, 5 cabochon cut blue and green opals, 41 garnets, 17" l, 2" w, 23.5 dwt 7,475.00

Retro

14K yg, snake link style, 16" l, 45.2 dwt 1,200.00

18K yg, 80 full cut brilliant and single cut diamonds, ruffled ribbon on snake link center, sgd "Van Cleef & Arpels, Made in France," 15" l, 104 dwt..31,050.00

Victorian

14K rose gold, 142 rose cut garnets, 14-1/2" l, 15.5 dwt 575.00

Silver topped gold, 64 old European cut round diamonds, 15" l, 14.4 dwt 19,550.00

Pendant

Art Deco, platinum, cabochon cut 37.78 x 29 mm opal, green, blue and slight yellow, 33 old European cut diamonds, bead and bezel set, 1-1/2" l, 8.2 dwt 4,320.00

Art Nouveau, 14K yg, cattails in curvilinear foliate frame, enamel trim, 9 rose cut diamonds, 3 freshwater Baroque pearls, maker's mark for Bippart, Griscom & Osborn, 4.1 dwt 750.00

Victorian, 14K yg, 2 carved coral roses, 2-1/4" l, 6.5 dwt 230.00

Ring

Art Deco, platinum

One 8.15 x 6.27 mm step cut diamond, scroll work on sides, 2.3 dwt 14,920.00

One 21 x 15.3 cabochon cut black opal, prong set, strong play of color, surrounded by 16 old European cut diamonds, 5.1 dwt 13,800.00

Art Nouveau, 14K yg

Cabochon cut, prong set jadeite, 4 cabochon cut opals, 1-1/4" x 3/4", 2.7 dwt 230.00

Freshwater oval pearl flanked by 2 female heads, 5/8" x 1/4", 2.6 dwt 980.00

Edwardian, platinum, 14K yellow and wg, 7.8 x 7.1 mm alexandrite surrounded by 24 old European cut diamonds, 2.7 dwt 2,850.00

Retro, gold, step cut 20 x 15 mm amethyst, prong set, 7.6 dwt 635.00

Victorian, silver topped, 31 old European cut diamonds, marquise shaped dinner ring, 1 diamond chipped, 3.9 dwt......1,610.00

Suite, brooch and earrings, mid-Victorian, micromosaic, oval 1-3/4" w x 1-1/2" brooch depicting scenes of ruins, river, bridge, black glass ground, yg frame, wiretwist border, later added pin assembly, oval 7/8" w x 1-1/8" drop earrings, one depicting the Temple of Vesta, the other the Forum, later added earwires, solder, c1860, $2,250. Photo courtesy of E. Foxe Harrell Jewelers.

Stickpin

Art Deco, 18K yg, 1 cabochon cut bezel set oval moonstone, serpent and lotus blossom frame, 2-1/2" l, 2.5 dwt 435.00
Art Nouveau, 18K yg, 4 colored bezel set colored stone, enameled profile of lady with flowing hair, 3.2 dwt 575.00

Watch Chain

Victorian
14K yg, alternating pattern of rect fancy links, 8-1/2" l, 16.7 dwt 488.00
14K yg, open flat links, 24" l, 45.9 dwt...........................990.00
Shakudo, silver, yellow, and rose gold, round chrysanthemum floral links, swivel hook, 25-1/4" l, 22.1 dwt 3,565.00

JUDAICA

History: Throughout history, Jews have expressed themselves artistically in both the religious and secular spheres. Most Jewish art objects were created as part of the concept of Hiddur Mitzva, i.e., adornment of implements used in performing rituals both in the synagogue and home.

For almost 2,000 years, since the destruction of the Jerusalem Temple in 70 A.D., Jews have lived in many lands. The widely differing environments gave traditional Jewish life and art a multifaceted character. Unlike Greek, Byzantine, or Roman art which have definite territorial and historical boundaries, Jewish art is found throughout Europe, the Middle East, North Africa, and other areas.

Ceremonial objects incorporated not only liturgical appurtenances, but also ethnographic artifacts such as amulets and ritual costumes. The style of each ceremonial object responded to the artistic and cultural milieu in which it was created. Although diverse stylistically, ceremonial objects, whether for Sabbath, holidays, or the life cycle, still possess a unity of purpose.

Reference: Penny Forstner and Lael Bower, *Collecting Religious Artifacts (Christian and Judaic)*, Books Americana, 1996.

Collectors' Club: Judaica Collectors Society, P.O. Box 854, Van Nuys, CA 91408.

Museums: B'nai B'rith Klutznick Museum, Washington, DC; H.U.C., Skirball Museum, Los Angeles, CA; Jewish Museum, New York, NY; Yeshiva University Museum, New York, NY; Judah L. Magnes Museum, Berkeley, CA; Judaic Museum, Rockville, MD; Spertus Museum of Judaica Chicago, IL; Morton B. Weiss Museum of Judaica, Chicago, IL; National Museum of American Jewish History, Philadelphia, PA; Plotkin Judaica Museum of Greater Phoenix, Phoenix, AZ.

Notes: Judaica has been crafted in all media, though silver is the most collectible.

Tabernacle, Russian, silver gilt, Moscow hallmarks, dated 1893, mark's mark in Cyrillic "I.A.," 23" h, 3,300. Photo courtesy of Jackson's Auctioneers & Appraisers.

Amulet, 2-3/4" h, Italian, 18th/19th C, silver and silver filigree, irregular outline, inscribed "Shadai," with pendant chain and fitted leather box..520.00
Beaker, 2-3/4" h, silver, scale motif, German, c1800 ....800.00
Ceremonial Ring, 3-1/4" h, sterling silver, top applied with pavilion, side pierced with door and windows, 3 semi-precious stones, chased Hebrew words......................................425.00
Chalice, 13" h, Continental silver, Herman Lang, Augsburg, 17th C, 29 oz. 2,400.00
Charger, 23" d, Continental silver, repousse floral and figural dec, c1780, 8 oz...1,650.00
Charity Container
3-3/4" h, silver, inverted pear-form, body engraved banding, and molding hinged lid with money slot and hasp, scroll handle, front inscribed "Zeduke für Arme kinder," German, late 19th/20th C 920.00
5" d, cylindrical, sheet copper, German, 1800s............265.00
Circumcision Cup, 5" h, double, silver gilt, mkd "Johanna Becker, Augsburg," 1855-57 ....13,500.00
Comb, 6" w, brass, Burial Society, Hungarian, 1881.......5,800.00
Esther Scroll, cased
9" l, parcel-gilt and filigree, Continental, 19th C, applied jewels, hand-form thumb pc, nicely written ink on vellum scroll, fitted box..9,200.00
10-1/2" l, Austro-Hungarian silver, Vienna, c1846 ....675.00
Etrog Container, silver
6" h, Austrian Wein, c1849, rect, repousse floral work, etrog shaped finial, shell form feet, lacking key 1,610.00
8-1/4" h, Baltic Neoclassical, early 19th C, silver and silver-gilt, possibly Bergen, maker GM in rect, Hebrew inscription, acorn finial 1,035.00

Hanukah Lamp
  6" h, Russian bronze and enamel, late 19th C, arched back-plate with rampant lions and servant lamp, bowed base with candleholders 420.00
  6-1/4 x 6-1/4", Israeli silver, shaped rect, back plate with Meno-rah flanked by figures below Hebrew inscription, fitted with eight oil candle sockets, four paw feet 800.00
  20-1/2" h, sterling silver, circular reeded base, applied grape-vine rising to sq stem, 8 branches, vasiform sconces with pierced covers, central flame finial, matching servant light and oil jug, hand hammered allover, 57 oz., 8 dwt 1,900.00
Hanukah and Sabbath Lamp, 6" h, Bezalel silver, c1930, detach-able bar with 8 candleholders, arched body, domed circular base, applied filigree dec, lacking servant light 920.00
Invalid's Home Medal, 2-7/8" d, paperweight, bronze, Dutch, oc-tagonal, titled "Vredige Levensavond," Star of David above bedridden patient, paper case 260.00
Kiddush Cup, sterling silver
  3" h, George III, double barrel form, Charles Aldridge, Lon-don, 1791-92, inscribed with the seven benedictions of wedlock, pr 7,200.00
  5-1/2" h
    Applied flowers, trellis and medallions, circular floral foot, 4 oz. 150.00
    Swirled fluted lower body, applied foliage at intervals, up-per body chased with scrolls and foliage, circular foliate and beaded foot, 4 oz., 4 dwt 425.00
  6" h, American Coin, second half 19th C, dedicatory inscrip-tion "Presented to Mark L. Hirsch by Solomon Hirsch Feb. 23rd 1863" 550.00
  6" h, repousse, scrolls and foliage on stippled ground, con-forming foot, gilt int., 4 oz., 8 dwt 450.00
  7" h, Wood & Hughes, late 19th C, contemporary enameling af-ter Szyk 1,725.00
Menorah, 20" h, gilt bronze, after Salvador Dali, c1980, set on Jerusalem stone base 2,415.00
Menorah Wall Sconce, 10-1/2" l, Continental silver, heraldic re-pousse back shield, c1858, 18 oz. 2,900.00
Mezuzah, 5-1/2" h, 14K yg, after Ilha Schor, emb and cut-out with figure of Moses, "shin" finial 920.00
Passover Plate, 14" d, pewter, Continental, c1800 .... 225.00
Passover Table Cloth, 76" x 56", linen, rect with shaped edges, white background, multicolored embroidered Passover imple-ments, some staining 920.00
Pendant, 14K yg, enameled, high priest breast plate motif, 12 step-cut multicolored synthetic stones, Retro, 1-1/2" l, 7.4 dwt 70.00

Prayer Book, miniature
  Seder U-Velechtekha Ba-derekh, Feival Monk, Warsaw, 1884, Ashkenazi rite, gilt-stamped calf, faux jewel insets, 60 x 40 mm 490.00
  Sidder Hadrat Zekenim, Y. M. Solomon, Jerusalem, 1845, con-temporary roan gilt, 70 x 53 mm 230.00
Sabbath Candlesticks, pr, 16-1/4" h, Aaron Katz, London, 1894, Polish style 1,000.00
Sabbath Hanging Lamp, 16" h, Continental, 18th/19th C, brass, 8 pointed star-form oval section, plain and turned stem, ratchet suspension hook for adjustable height 375.00
Seal, 5" h, Austrian, Baroque style, silver, for Bassevi von Treufeld, created 1622, formed as a rampant lion holding a shield, the crest 3 stars and 2 lion/leopards 1,840.00
Soap Dish, cov, insert, Star of David finial, cobalt blue, Etruscan majolica, hairline in base 3,025.00
Spice Box, silver, windmill form
  3" h, flanked by house with pierced window and door, shaped rect base, 1 oz., 2 dwt 650.00
  5-1/2" h, applied with floral baskets and birds, sq base, four scroll and foliate feet, 7 oz., 4 dwt 875.00
Spice Tower, 10-3/4" h, Russian silver, sq base, four feet rising to knopped stem, two shaped sq sections, detachable spire, c1865, 13 oz. 1,700.00

Torah Binder, printed linen, typical benediction of Torah, Hupah and Good Deeds, German, late 18th C, minor staining .. 300.00
Torah Pointer, Continental
  6-1/2" l, silver mounted lapis lazuli, 19th C, fitted box .. 8,625.00
  10-1/4" l, silver and silver filigree, Palestine, first half 20th C, Hebrew inscription, dents 345.00
  11" l, gold mounted coral, stem with scrolling vine design, gold hand, openwork knob, beryl finish, fitted box 1,725.00
Traveling Menorah, 3-1/2 x 2-1/2", sterling silver, book form, pierced flowers, animals, center anukah lamp, int. fitted with dividers to form eight oil receptacles, 11 oz., 6 dwt... 1,200.00
Watch, 2-1/2" d, Near Eastern, 19th C, silver-gilt, enamel, and rock crystal, six-sided star, floral enamel work, Hebrew num-bers, rock crystal bezel and backplate, minor damage, enam-el losses 2,415.00
Wine Decanter, sterling silver, Goldman Silversmiths Co., NY, c1940 .... 395.00

JUGTOWN POTTERY

History: In 1920, Jacques and Julianna Busbee left their cos-mopolitan environs and re-turned to North Carolina to revive the state's dying pottery-making craft. Jugtown Pottery, a colorful and somewhat off-beat operation, was located in Moore County, miles away from any large city and accessible only "if mud permits."

Ben Owens, a talented young potter, turned the wares. Jacques Busbee did most of the designing and glazing. Julianna handled promotion.

Utilitarian and decorative items were produced. Al-though many colorful glazes were used, orange predomi-nated. A Chinese blue glaze that ranged from light blue to deep turquoise was a prized glaze reserved for the very finest pieces.

Jacques Busbee died in 1947. Julianna, with the help of Owens, ran the pottery until 1958 when it was closed. After long legal battles, the pottery was reopened in 1960. It now is owned by Country Roads, Inc., a nonprofit organization. The pottery still is operating and using the old mark.

Bowl, 2" h, 4-1/4" d, Chinese blue glaze, imp mark, pr 425.00
Candlesticks, pr, 3" h, Chinese Translation, Chinese blue and red, mkd 85.00
Creamer, cov, 43/4" h, yellow 60.00
Vase
  3-3/4" h, 2-1/2" d, Chinese blue flambé glaze, imp mark 325.00
  4" h, 2-3/4" d, Chinese blue glaze, imp mark 275.00
  6-3/4" h, 6" d, ovoid, thick white semi-matte glaze dripping over brown clay body, imp mark 450.00
  7-1/2" h, 4-1/2" d, ovoid, Chinese blue glaze, tight line to rim, imp mark 850.00
  8-3/4" h, 6-1/2" d, stoneware, 2 small handles, top cov with matte mustard glaze, bottom with clear coating, imp mark 850.00
  11" h, 8-1/2" d, 2 small handles, Chinese blue mottled glaze, imp mark 3,200.00
Vessel
  7-1/4" h, 5" d, ovoid, white satin glaze, hairline to rim, stamped "Jugtown Ware" 300.00
  9" h, 6-1/4" d, 4 small handles, brown speckled luster glaze, red clay body, glaze flakes in making, imp mark 650.00

KPM

History: The "KPM" mark has been used separately and in conjunction with other symbols by many German porcelain manufacturers, among which are the Königliche Porzellan Manufactur in Meissen, 1720s; Königliche Porzellan Manufactur in Berlin, 1832-1847; and Krister Porzellan Manufactur in Waldenburg, mid-19th century.

K.P.M

Collectors now use the term KPM to refer to the high-quality porcelain produced in the Berlin area in the 18th and 19th centuries.

Cheese Board, rose and leaf garland border, pierce for hanging, mkd 48.00
Cup and Saucer, hunting scene, filigree, 19th C 65.00
Dinner Service, Art Deco style, gilt and jeweled in turquoise and pink, flowering plants on speckled gilt and iron-red ground, sea green borders with molded gilt swags, blue scepter, iron-red orb, KPM mark, c1880 ....8,000.00
Dish, 9-1/2" d, leaf shape, painted, birds on flowering branch, burgundy border, gilt drapery, blue scepter, iron-red KPM and orb mark, c1860 ....265.00
Fairy Lamp, 3 faced animal 395.00
Figure, 8-1/2" h, 3-1/2" d, young man with cocked hat, long coat, trousers, and boots, young lady in Empire-style dress, fancy hat and fan, white ground, brown details, gold trim, round base, blue underglaze KPM mark, price for pr 360.00
Luncheon Service, partial, basketweave molded borders, hp enameled floral designs, gilt edging, cov teapot, hot water pot, creamer, 10 teacups, 22 saucers, 10 coffee cups, 7 demitasse cups and saucers, 11 8-3/8" plates, factory marks, damage, repairs 2,415.00

Plaque, Konigin Louise, sgd "A. Schunzel, elaborate carved and gilded Italian frame, 9-1/" h, 6-1/4" w, $1,850. Photo courtesy of Freeman\Fine Arts.

Plaque, polychrome enamel
   7" x 5", oval, Cupid sharpening arrow, sgd 2,700.00
   8-7/8" x 11", rect, St. Anthony holding child, giltwood frame, imp mark, late 19th C 1,380.00
   11" w, 13-1/2" h, rect, Mary in pensive pose holding paper inscribed "Ascetvr de Virgine," giltwood frame 1,600.00
   12-1/2" x 16-1/2", rect, Parting Lovers, figural landscape, giltwood frame, imp "KPM" mark 5,750.00
Plate, 9" d, hp, gold dec, wide scroll reticulated rims, orb mark, 4 pc set...145.00
Scent Bottle, molded scrolls, multicolored painted bouquets of flowers, gilt trim, gilt metal C-scroll stopper, mkd, mid 19th C 175.00
Serving Bowl, 15" l, oval, enamel dec foliate design, gilt border...200.00
Teapot, 6" h, oval, medallion with floral dec, gilt ground......95.00
Vase, 8-1/2" h, baluster, two handles, hp multicolored florals, celery green ground 200.00

KAUFFMANN, ANGELICA

History: Marie Angelique Catherine Kauffmann was a Swiss artist who lived from 1741 until 1807. Many artists who hand-decorated porcelain during the 19th century copied her paintings. The majority of the paintings are neoclassical in style.

References: Susan and Al Bagdade, *Warman's English & Continental Pottery & Porcelain*, 2nd ed., Wallace-Homestead, 1991; Wendy Wassying Roworth (ed.), *Angelica Kauffmann*, Reaktion Books, 1993, distributed by University of Washington Press.

Box, cov, 2-3/4" x 4-1/2", lilac, 2 maidens and child in woods on cov, brass hinges 70.00
Cake Plate, 10" d, ftd, classical scene, 2 maidens and cupid, beehive mark 90.00
Compote, 8" d, classical scene, beehive mark, sgd 85.00
Cup and Saucer, classical scene, heavy gold trim, ftd........90.00
Inkwell, pink luster, classical lady 80.00
Pitcher, 8-1/2" h, garden scene, ladies, children, and flowers, sgd..100.00
Plate, 8" d, cobalt blue border, reticulated rim, classical scene with 2 figures 65.00
Portrait Plate, portrait with cherubs, dark green and cream ground, gold trim, sgd "Carlsbad, Austria, Kaufmann," 4 pc set 495.00
Tobacco Jar, classical ladies and cupid, green ground, SP top, pipe as finial 415.00

KEW BLAS

History: Amory and Francis Houghton established the Union Glass Company, Somerville, Massachusetts, in 1851. The company went bankrupt in 1860, but was reorganized. Between 1870 and 1885 the Union Glass Company made pressed glass and blanks for cut glass.

KEW-BLAS

Art-glass production began in 1893 under the direction of William S. Blake and Julian de Cordova. Two styles were introduced: a Venetian style, which consisted of graceful shapes in colored glass, often flecked with gold; and an iridescent glass, called Kew Blas, made in plain and decorated forms. The pieces are similar in design and form to Quezel products but lack the subtlety of Tiffany items. The company ceased production in 1924.

Museum: Sandwich Glass Museum, Sandwich, MA.

Bowl, 14" d, pulled feather, red ground, sgd 1,400.00
Candlesticks, pr, 8-1/2" h, irid gold, twisted stems 750.00

Vase, pulled feather, sgd, 7" h, $1,600.

Compote, 4-1/2" d, 3-1/2" d, gold irid, flared rim, applied pedestal foot with folded edge, inscribed "Kew Blas" on base ...460.00

Decanter, 14-1/2" h, 4-3/4" d base, gold irid, ribbed and painted stopper, purple-pink highlights, sgd on base 1,450.00

Finger Bowl and Underplate, 5" d bowl, 6" d, plate, ribbed, scalloped border, metallic luster, gold and platinum highlights
....475.00

Pitcher, 4-1/2" h, green pulled feather pattern, deep gold irid int., applied swirl handle, sgd "Kew-Blas" 900.00

Rose Bowl, 4" d, scalloped rim, cased glass sphere, green vertical zipper stripes, orange irid int., inscribed "Kew Blas" on base"
....690.00

Salt, irid gold...220.00

Tumbler, 4" h, pinched sides, irid gold, sgd 225.00

Vase
  6-1/4" h, cylinder, rolled rim, gold and green swags, pale orange ground, early 20th C, sgd, orig paper label 950.00
  6-1/2" h, 7" w, bulbous, oyster white ground, deep green hooked and pulled feathering, gold irid feathers, gold irid rim on neck, sgd...1,450.00

Wine Glass, 4-3/4" h, curving stem, irid gold 250.00

KITCHEN COLLECTIBLES

History: The kitchen was the focal point in a family's environment until the 1960s. Many early kitchen utensils were handmade and prized by their owners. Next came a period of utilitarian products made of tin and other metals. When the housewife no longer wished to work in a sterile environment, enamel and plastic products added color, and their unique design served both aesthetic and functional purposes.

The advent of home electricity changed the type and style of kitchen products. Fads affected many items. High technology already has made inroads into the kitchen, and another revolution seems at hand.

References: E. Townsend Artman, *Toasters: 1909-1960*, Schiffer Publishing, 1996; Ronald S. Barlow, *Victorian*

Houseware, Windmill Publishing, 1992; *Collector's Digest Price Guide to Griswold Mfg. Co. 1918 Catalog Reprint*, L-W Book Sales, 1996; *Collectors Guide to Wagner Ware and Other Companies*, L-W Book Sales, 1994; Gene Florence, *Kitchen Glassware of the Depression Years*, 5th ed., Collector Books, 1997; Linda Campbell Franklin, *300 Years of Housekeeping Collectibles*, Books Americana, 1992; ——, *300 Years of Kitchen Collectibles*, Krause Publications, 1997; Ambrogio Fumagalli, *Coffee Makers*, Chronicle Books, 1995; Michael J. Goldberg, *Collectible Plastic Kitchenware and Dinnerware*, Schiffer Publishing, 1995; ——, *Groovy Kitchen Designs for Collectors*, Schiffer Publishing, 1996; Helen Greguire, *Collector's Guide to Toasters & Accessories*, Collector Books, 1997; Susan E. Grindberg, *Collector's Guide to Porcelier China*, Collector Books, 1996; Jon B. Haussler, *Griswold Muffin Pans,* Schiffer Publishing, 1997; *Griswold Cast Iron*, L-W Book Sales, 1997; Frances Johnson, *Kitchen Antiques*, Schiffer Publishing, 1996; Jan Lindenberger, *The 50s & 60s Kitchen*, Schiffer Publishing, 1994; ——, *Fun Kitchen Collectibles*, Schiffer Publishing, 1996.

Kathryn McNerney, *Kitchen Antiques 1790-1940*, Collector Books, 1991, 1997 value update; Gary Miller and K. M. Mitchell, *Price Guide to Collectible Kitchen Appliances*, Wallace-Homestead, 1991; Jim Moffett, *American Corn Huskers*, Off Beat Books (1345 Poplar Ave., Sunnyvale, CA 94087), 1994; Ellen M. Plante, *Kitchen Collectibles*, Wallace-Homestead, 1991; James Rollband, *American Nutcrackers*, Off Beat Books (1345 Poplar Ave., Sunnyvale, CA 94087), 1996; David G. Smith and Charles Wafford, *Book of Griswold & Wagner*, Schiffer Publishing, 1996; Diane Stoneback, *Kitchen Collectibles*, Wallace-Homestead, 1994; Don Thornton, *Apple Parers,* Off Beat Books, (1345 Poplar Ave., Sunnyvale, CA 94087) 1997; —, *Beat This: The Eggbeater Chronicles*, Off Beat Books, 1994; *Toasters and Small Kitchen Appliances*, L-W Book Sales, 1995; Jean Williams Turner, *Collectible Aunt Jemima*, Schiffer Publishing, 1994; April M. Tvorak, *Fire-King Fever '96*, published by author, 1995.

Periodicals: *Cast Iron Cookware News*, 28 Angela Ave., San Anselmo, CA 94960; *Kettles 'n' Cookware*, P.O. Box B, Perrysburg, NY 14129; *Kitchen Antiques & Collectible News*, 4645 Laurel Ridge Dr., Harrisburg, PA 17110; *Piebirds Unlimited*, 14 Harmony School Rd., Flemington, NJ 08822.

Collectors' Clubs: Cookie Cutter Collectors Club, 1167 Teal Rd., SW, Dellroy, OH 44620; Glass Knife Collectors Club, 711 Kelly Dr., Lebanon, TN 37087; Griswold & Cast Iron Cookware Assoc., 54 Macon Ave., Asheville, NC 28801; International Society for Apple Parer Enthusiasts, 3911 Morgan Center Rd., Utica, OH 43080; National Reamer Collectors Assoc., 47 Midline Court, Gaithersburg, MD 20878.

Museums: Corning Glass Museum, Corning, NY; Kern County Museum, Bakersfield, CA; Landis Valley Farm Museum, Lancaster, PA.

Additional Listings: Baskets; Brass; Butter Prints; Copper; Fruit Jars; Food Molds; Graniteware; Ironware; Tinware; Woodenware. See *Warman's Americana & Collectibles* for more examples including electrical appliances.

Apple Peeler, cast iron, Reading Hardware Co. 90.00
Bill Hook, celluloid cov, Carey Salt Co., 8-1/2" h, 2" w 100.00
Butter Churn, 49" h, old blue paint, America, 19th C, minor imperfections 345.00
Catalog
  Badger Aluminum Ware, Louisville, KY, c1930, 24 pgs, 8-1/2" x 11", kettles, pots, roasters, etc.............................24.00
  Midland Specialties Co., Chicago, IL, 1930, 12 pgs, 8-1/2" x 11", Cat. No. 15, Midland Improved Products, funnels, measures, etc...28.00
  Montgomery Ward & Co., Chicago, IL, 1898, 24 pgs, 10" x 13", Price List No. 430 of Groceries, furnishings, folded in center 21.00
  Sherer-Gillet Co., Chicago, IL, 1928, 4 pgs, 12-1/4" x 18-1/2", departmentalized Food Store, orig mailing envelope ..9.00
Cheese Sieve, 8" d, 7-1/2" h, wood, stave construction, iron band 25.00
Cherry Stoner, 8-1/2" h, hand crank, mkd "Pat'd Nov. 17, 1863" 65.00
Colander, 10-3/4" d, 3" h, copper, punched star design......70.00
Cookie Board, 6-3/4" x 11", oak, relief carved man and woman figures, brown patina..275.00
Dipper, 14-1/4" l, brass and wrought iron, polished...........175.00
Dough Box, pine and turned poplar, PA, 19th C, rect removable top, tapering well, splayed ring-turned legs, ball feet, 38" w, 19-1/4" d, 29-1/2" h 425.00
Flour Sifter, 14" h, 12" w, Tilden's Universal, wood, partial intact paper label 335.00
Food Chopper, 7" w, wrought iron, scalloped edge blade, turned wood handle...270.00
Fork, 11-3/8" l, wrought iron...60.00
Griddle, cast iron, Griswold, No. 10 ....70.00
Ice Shaver, nickel plated steel, mkd "Enterprise," July 4, 1893 patent 42.00
Kettle, cast iron, Griswold No. 4..85.00
Kraut Cutter, 19" l, walnut, worn patina, heart cutout in handle 220.00

Beater, green measuring cup base, mkd "Vidro Prod. Comp. Chicago, IL," patent nos., $20.

Lemon Squeezer, mkd "The Griswold Mfg. Co., Erie, Pa," $165.

Ladle, 15" l, wood, pot hook handle 50.00
Lemon Squeezer, iron, glass insert, mkd "Williams" 50.00
Nutmeg Grater, 7" l, Champion, brass and wood 635.00
Pantry Box, cov, 11-1/2" d, 6-1/2" h, oak, bail handle 175.00
Pastry Board, wood, 3 sided 32.00
Potato Masher, 9" l, turned maple 40.00
Recipe Booklet
  Best War Time Recipes, Royal Baking Powder Co., NY, 1917, 6 pgs..5.00
  Blue Ribbon Malt Extract, 1951, 20 pgs................................6.50
  Carefree Cooking with Frigidaire Electric Range, 1937, General Motors Sales Corp., Dayton, OH 8.00
  Kerr Glass Mfg., Portland, OR, 1909, 20 pgs, 3-1/4" x 8-1/2", Economy Jar Home Recipes 21.00
Recipe File, California Prune Recipe File, 1942, 5" x 3-1/2" envelope with 15 recipe sheets...10.00
Rolling Pin
  15-3/4" l, blown glass, deep amber knopped handles, 19th C 150.00
  22" l, milk glass, cylindrical, turned wood handles, mkd "Imperial Mfg., Co. July 25, 1921" 90.00
  23-1/2" l, curly maple 80.00
Sausage Stuffer, 17-1/2" l, turned wood plunger.................30.00
Skillet, cast iron, Griswold, No. 14....................................165.00
Spatula, 17-3/4" l, brass and wrought iron, polished..........175.00
Taster, 7" l, brass and wrought iron, polished....................150.00
Tin
  Dining Car Brand, Norwine Coffee Co., St. Louis, Ground Black Pepper, fancy int. of train's dining car front and back, cardboard sides, 6-5/8" h, 3-3/4" w, 2-1/2" d............825.00
  Donovan's Baking Powder, Mt. Morris, NY, 1 lb, paper label, 5-1/4" h, 3" d...475.00
  Egg-O Brand Baking Powder, paper label, 2-3/4" h, 1-1/4" d 110.00
  Fairy Queen Marshmallow, Loose-Wiles, 14" x 10" x 8"...90.00
  Fulford Powder, multicolored...25.00
  Kavanaugh's Tea, 1 lb, little girl on porch in dress, talking to doll, mother sipping tea in window, cardboard sides, tin top and bottom, 6" h, 4-1/2" w, 4-1/2" d 500.00
  Maltby's Cocoaut, slip top 40.00
  Miller's Gold Medal Breakfast Cocoa, red and black, c1890, 2" h, 1-5/8" w, 1-1/8" d...250.00
  Opal Powdered Sugar, Hewitt & Sons, Des Moines, 8" h, 4-1/2" w, 3-1/4" d...180.00
  Parrot and Monkey Baking Powder, 4 oz., full, 3-1/4" h, 2-1/8" d 375.00
  Sunshine-Oxford Fruit Cake, early 1900s, sq corners.....20.00
  Three Crow Brand Cream of Tartar, early, #1 ....45.00
  Towle's Log Cabin Brand Maple Syrup, cabin shaped, woman and girl in doorway, 4" h, 3-3/4" l, 2-1/2" d...............110.00
Trivet, 12" l, lyre form, wrought iron frame and turned handle, brass top, replaced foot, stamped maker's mark 45.00
Wafer Iron, cast iron, octagonal, church with steeple and trees dec on one side, pinwheel with plants and star flowers on reverse, wrought iron handles 400.00

KUTANI

History: Kutani originated in the mid-1600s in the Kaga province of Japan. Kutani comes in a variety of color patterns, one of the most popular being Ao Kutani, a green glaze with colors such as green, yellow, and purple enclosed in a black outline. Export wares made since the 1870s are enameled in a wide variety of colors and styles.

Beaker, 4-1/2" h, hp flowers and birds, red, orange, and gold, white ground, mkd "Ao-Kutani" 95.00
Biscuit Jar, cov, Geisha Girl, c1890 ....190.00
Bowl, 6-3/8" d, gilt and bright enamel design, figural, animal, and floral reserves, kinrande ground, base inscribed "Kutani-sei," set of 10 ....400.00
Charter, 18-3/8" d, pomegranate tree, chrysanthemums, and 2 birds on int., birds and flowers between scrolling foliate bands, irregular floral and brocade border, 11 character inscription 600.00
Figure
    12" h, Bodhidhama, standing, long red rope, flywisk in right hand..225.00
    14-1/4" h, Kannon, polychrome and gilt dec, standing, dragon mount, high coiffure, wind-swept rope, inscribed "Kutani-sei" 600.00
Jar, cov, 20-1/2" h, ovoid, fan shaped reserves of warriors, molded ribbon tied tasseled ring handles, shippo-tsunagi ground, multicolored brocade patterned dome lid, pr 1,400.00
Tea Caddy, 6" h, bulbous, hexagonal, Nishikide diapering, figural raised gold reserves of children, red script mark 165.00
Teapot, cov, bulbous, One Thousand Faces 250.00
Tray, 14" l, polychrome and gilt dec, figural scene, red, orange, and gold border..340.00
Vase, 9-3/4" h, ovoid, waisted neck, recessed ring foot, upper portion with enameled reddish-brown wave pattern, underglaze blue wide band of archaistic keyfret design, raised borders, lower section with gilt painted stylized lotus blossoms, green enamel scrolling leafy tendrils, bluish-black ground 395.00

Vase, 9-1/2" h, $250.

LACE AND LINENS

History: Lace, lacy linens, embroidery, and hand-decorated textiles are different from any other antique. They are valued both has a handmade substance and as the thing the substance is made into. Thread is manipulated into stitches, stitches are assembled into lace, lace is made into handkerchiefs, edgings, tablecloths, bedspreads. Things eventually go out of style or are damaged or worn, and just as the diamonds and rubies are taken from old jewelry and placed into new settings, fine stitchery of embroidery and lace is saved and reused. Lace from a handkerchief is used to decorate a blouse, fragments of a bridal veil are made into a scarf; shreds of old lace are remounted onto fine net and used again as a veil.

At each stage in the cycle, different people become interested. Some see fragments as bits and pieces of a collage, and seek raw materials for accent pieces. Others use Victorian whites and turn-of-the-century embroidered linens to complement a life style. Collectors value and admire the stitches themselves, and when those stitches are remarkable enough, they will pay hundreds of dollars for fragments a few inches square.

Until the 1940s, lace collecting was a highly respected avocation of the wealthy. The prosperity of the New World was a magnet for insolvent European royalty, who carried suitcases of old Hapsburg, Bourbon, Stuart, and Romanov laces to suites at New York's Waldorf hotel for dealers to select from. Even Napoleon's bed hangings of handmade Alencon lace, designed for Josephine and finished for Marie Louise, found their way here. In 1932, Fortune magazine profiled socially prominent collectors and lace dealers. For the entire first half of this century, New York City's Needle and Bobbin Club provided a forum for showing off acquisitions.

Until 1940, upscale department stores offered antique lace and lacy linens. Dealers specializing in antique lace and lacy linens had prominent upscale shops, and offered repair, restoration, remodeling, and cleaning services along with the antique linens. In addition to collecting major pieces– intact jabots from the French Ancient Regime, Napoleonic-era Alencon, huge mid-Victorian lace shawls, Georgian bed hangings appliquéd with 17th-century needle lace–collectors assembled study collections of postcard-size samples of each known style of antique lace.

When styles changed round the 1940s and 1950s, and the market for antique lace and linens crashed, some of the best collections did go to museums; others just went into hiding. With renewed interest in a gracious, romantic lifestyle, turn-of-the-century lacy cloths from the linen closets of the barons of the industrial revolution are coming out of hiding. Collectors and wise dealers know that many of the small study-pieces of irreplaceable stitchery–fragments collectors will pay ten to hundreds of dollars for–still emerge in rummage and estate sales.

Very large banquet-sized lace tablecloths, especially those with napkins, continue to be especially popular. Appenzell, a white-on-white embroidered lacework of 19th C Switzerland, has become one of the hottest collector's items. Strong interest continues in patterned silk ribbons, all cotton lace yardage, and other lacy materials for heirloom sewing and fashion.

Those who learn to recognize the artistry and value of old stitchery will not only enhance their lives with beauty, they may find a windfall.

References: Maryanne Dolan, *Old Lace and Linens Including Crochet*, Books Americana, 1989; Pat Earnshaw, *Identification of Lace*, Lubrecht and Cramer, 1989; Frances Johnson, *Collecting Antique Linens, Lace, and Needlework*, Wallace-Homestead, 1991; --, *Collecting More Household Linens,* Schiffer Publishing, 1997; Elizabeth Kurella, *Everybody's Guide To Lace and Linens,* Antique Trader Books, 1997; --, *Secrets of Real Lace,* The Lace Merchant (P.O. Box 222, Plainwell, MI 49080), 1994; ———, *Pocket Guide to Valuable Old Lace and Lacy Linens,* The Lace Merchant (P.O. Box 222, Plainwell, MI 49080), 1996; Marsha L. Manchester, *Vintage White Linens A to Z,* Schiffer Publishing, 1997; Elizabeth Scofield and Peggy Zalamea, *Twentieth Century Linens and Lace,* Schiffer Publishing, 1995.

Periodical: *Old Lace and Linen Merchant,* The Lace Merchant, P.O. Box 222, Plainwell, MI 49080.

Collectors' Club: International Old Lacers, P.O. Box 554, Flanders, NJ 07836.

Museums: Chicago Art Institute, Chicago, IL; Cooper Hewitt (Smithsonian), New York, NY; Metropolitan Museum of Art, New York, NY; Museum of Early Southern Decorative Arts (MESDA), Winston-Salem, NC; Museum of Fine Arts, Boston, MA; Rockwood Museum, Wilmington, DE; Shelburne, Museum, Shelburne, VT; Smithsonian Institution, Washington, DC.

Advisor: Elizabeth M. Kurella.

Bedspread
Crochet, double size, filet crochet grid-style design, scrolling leaves design 85.00
Embroidered, double size, white cloth with red "turkey work" embroidery, cartoon character designs, c1930 ....150.00
Princess Lace (machine tapes appliquéd to machine net) scrolling flower and leaves design..350.00

Bridal Veil
Point De Gaze needle lace in rose and leaf design with scrolls and medallions in 12" edge border on 7' long teardrop shape veil 1,500.00
Princess Lace, 65" x 48" oval, machine net decorated with floral and scroll design 325.00
Bridge Set, linen, embroidered in red and black motifs of playing-card suits, matching napkins 85.00
Collar
Berthe-style, Brussels mixed lace, floral and scroll work of Duchesse bobbin lace with rose inserts of Point de Gauze, many exotic filling stitches of needle lace, 6" deep, 38" l...........625.00
Duchesse bobbin lace, c1870, roses, daisies, and scrollwork design, 5" at center back, 32" l.......................................125.00
Point de Grace, 19th C Belgian needle lace, roses with shaded petals and leaves design, pr of 10" l labels, price for pr 75.00

Curtains
Hand-embroidered machine net, c1900, iris, roses, and filigree elaborate designs, 48" x 96", pr..................................50.00
Machine lace, ecru, 36" x 72" 75.00
Doily
Crochet, roses, raised petals, 8" d round..........................10.00
Flemish bobbin lace, c1900, goldfish design in Petit de Paris ground, 10" d round, 3" deep lace 75.00
Needle lace, rose design, 6" d round..................................20.00
Dresser Scarf
Drawnwork, Victorian, white geometric design, 28" x 48" 45.00
White cotton, flower basket embroidered in bright colors, white crochet edging, c1930, 24" x 38" 10.00
Fragments of Collector's Lace
Gros Point de Venise, c1650, stylized scrolling floral design, motifs defined by raised and padded outlines dec with many styles of picots, 2" x 12" 285.00
Point de Neige, c1680, needle lace with minute stylized design and layers of raised picots, 10" x 18" 285.00
Point de Venise, design of cupid with quiver of arrows, medallions, and scrolling flowers, c1900, 12" x 16" 75.00
Point de Venise a Reseau, stylized floral design, Alencon mesh background, no cordonnet, 3" x 6" fragment of edging 185.00
Handkerchief
Linen
    Edged with colored crochet scallop design, 12" sq..........2.00
    Edged with half inch of white tatting, 12" sq...................6.00
    4" of Irish Youghal needle lace with stylized shamrocks design, background of stitched bars dec with picots, 16" sq 375.00
Whitework, French, 1870s, edged with embroidery, drawnwork, and needle-lace inserts..95.00
Napkin
Cocktail, white, edge with single scallop of needle lace, 1" sq corner inserts of needle lace worked in stylized animal design, price for 6 pc set 45.00
Dinner, linen with needle-lace edging, corner insert, c1900, 24" sq, price for 6 pc set 185.00
Pillowcase
Cotton, embroidered multicolored flower-basket design, crochet edge, c1930, pr...15.00
Linen, white, figural designs in needle-lace inserts, floral design in needle-lace edging, pr 125.00
Maderia, white cotton, flower silhouetted in cutwork, embroidered with satin stitch, pr...15.00
Pillow Cover, linen, white, dec with inserts of needle lace, scrolling floral designs, embroidered in satin stitch, Cluny bobbin lace edging, 18" d round 125.00
Pincushion, white satin, top cov with square of white Italian drawn work in heavy linen, embroidered raised flower and tendril design, corners dec with whimsical knotted tassels, 4" sq, 1" deep 65.00

Table Cloth, Swiss Appenzell, whitework, design of cherubs and lady, dressed in 18th C costume, with parrot, eight matching napkins, 120" x 85", $2,500. Photo courtesy of Elizabeth Kurella.

Runner, Normandy work, patchwork of handmade Valenciennes bobbin lace and other laces, mostly handmade, central motif of French embroidered whitework with birds and flowers, oval, 24" x 18" 145.00

Shawl
Chantilly, flowers, ferns, and scrolls design, 4' x 8' triangle
    Handmade, bobbin lace...................................385.00
    Machine, black 75.00
Machine-made net cov with bouquets and garlands of Brussels bobbin lace and Point de Gaze needle lace, white, c1865, 4' x 8' triangle..675.00

Tablecloth
Crochet, round medallions design, 48" x 68" 75.00
Cutwork
    Floral and scrollwork satin-stitch embroidery, needle-lace inserts, 8" deep border of filet in figural designs, Italian, c1900, 42" sq..175.00
    Floral designs in satin-stitch embroidery, inserts of needle lace with rose designs, 68" x 140", 12 matching napkins, price for set..975.00
Filet, geometric design darned over knotted network, 48" x 72"..125.00
Linen, natural color, Richelieu, all handmade cutwork and embroidery, floral and scroll motif, early 20th C, 68" x 100" 575.00
Swiss Appenzell whitework, with designs of cherubs, and a lady with a parrot dressed in 18th C. costume, 120" x 85", eight napkins, price for set 2,500.00

Yardage
Crochet, white, pinwheel design, 4" deep, per yard 12.00
Ribbons, silk embroidered with floral pattern, 2" wide, still on reel with paper leaf, per yard 10.00
Tatting, white, half inch deep, design of round medallions with picots, per yard 5.00
Valenciennes
    Handmade bobbin lace, strawberries and blossoms design, 4" deep, 4 yards long 850.00
    Machine made, all cotton, floral and scrollwork design, 4" deep, per yard..10.00

LALIQUE

History: René Lalique (1860-1945) first gained prominence as a jewelry designer. Around 1900, he began experimenting with molded-glass brooches and pendants, often embellishing them with semiprecious stones. By 1905, he was devot-

LALIQUE

R.LALIQUE

ing himself exclusively to the manufacture of glass articles.

In 1908, Lalique began designing packaging for the French cosmetic houses. He also produced many objects, especially vases, bowls, and figurines, in the Art Nouveau and Art Deco styles. The full scope of Lalique's genius was seen at the 1925 Paris l'Exposition Internationale des Arts Décorative et Industriels Modernes.

Marks: The mark "R. LALIQUE FRANCE" in block letters is found on pressed articles, tableware, vases, paperweights, and automobile mascots. The script signature, with or without "France," is found on hand-blown objects. Occasionally, a design number is included. The word "France" in any form indicates a piece made after 1926.

The post-1945 mark is generally "Lalique France" without the "R," but there are exceptions.

REPRODUCTION ALERT

The Lalique signature has often been forged, the most common fake includes an "R" with the post-1945 mark.

References: Hugh D. Guinn (ed.), *Glass of René Lalique at Auction*, Guindex Publications, 1992.

Collectors' Club: Lalique Collectors Society, 400 Veterans Blvd., Carlstadt, NJ 07072.

Videotape: Nicholas M. Dawes, *World of Lalique Glass*, Award Video and Film Distributors, 1993.

Ashtray, 5-3/4" d, lion, molded gargoyle form rim, extended mane ridges, engraved script sgd 180.00
Bonbon Box, cov
    8-1/4" d, Boites Ronde Grande Libellulis, irid dragonfly, sgd "R. Lalique No. 51" 1,295.00
    10-1/4" d, Lily of the Valley, mkd "Claire d'Lune," block sgd 695.00

Clock, Muguet, lily of the valley dec, frosted, white enamel dec, c1931, engraved "R. Lalique, France," $4,700.

Bowl

8-1/2" d, 2-1/8" h, Vernon, opalescent, press molded sunflower design, "R. Lalique France" molded below rim, Marcilhac 395, p 296..690.00

9-1/4" d, nesting sparrow rim design, etched signature and paper label 250.00

Center Bowl, 14" d, daisy, broad molded rim, clear, brown patina on floral border 465.00

Coupe, 9-3/8" d, 3-1/4" h, shallow bowl, Vases No. 1, colorless, repeating polished urn-forms alternating frosted stylized bouquets, center molded "R. Lalique," Marcilhac 3216, p 750 ....230.00

Dresser Jar, 3-1/2" h, Epines, domical stopper bottles, molded thornbushes, strong blue patine, molded mark "R. Lalique," one stopper frozen, chip under edge, Marcilhac 593, p 343, price for pr 230.00

Dressing Table Mirror, 12" l, 6-1/2" d, Narcisse Couche, frosted glass frame and handle, molded foliate motif centering male nude above handle, orig gray patine in recesses, inscribed "R. Lalique, France" top rim, mirror slightly stained, Marcilhac 675, p 359..980.00

Medallion, 1-3/8" d, Dana les Fleurs, 1924 model, frosted low relief of nude female under blossoms, made for Fioret perfume box, mkd "R. Lalique/Fioret/Paris," Marcilhac p 931 .....520.00

Perfume Bottle

2-1/2" h, Imprudence, ridged bottle, silver trim, mkd "R. Lalique France," orig Worth box....................................275.00

3-1/2" h, Courer Joie, frosted heart-shaped floral bottle mkd "Bottle Made by Lalique," orig Nina Ricci box 295.00

19" h, Richard Hudnut Master Violet Sec, sq colorless bottle, orig contents, labels intact, some wear, corrosion at rim 145.00

Perfume Flacon

3-3/4" h, Salamandres, colorless flattened oval, polished roundels surrounded by curving lizards, gray-green patine in recesses, motif repeated on stopper, base inscribed "L. Lalique, France," Marcilhac 491, p 328 ....1,495.00

5-1/4" h, Ambre, polished sq bottle, molded draped women recessed at each corner, black sq stopper with floral motif, base mold mark "Lalique/Ambre D'Orsay," small chips inside top, Marcilhac p 929......................................1,380.00

5-1/2" h

Bouchon Fleurs de Pommier, colorless barrel-shaped bottle, green patine in scalloped ridges, molded flawless tiara stopper with matching patine on blossom motif, base inscribed "R. Lalique France N 493," Marcilhac 493, pg 329 ....10,062.50

Bouchon Mures, colorless barrel-shaped bottle, black ribbing, molded flawless matte black tiara stopper with berry clusters, molded "R. Lalique" on base, Marcilhac 495, p 329 ....9,200.00

Powder Box, cov, sepia wash, 2 ladies, arms entwined, fancy scrolls and flowers on cov, sepia washed garlands of flowers on base, sgd "Coty" and "Lalique Depose," c1915 ......600.00

Vase

4-1/2" h, Eglantines, frosted oval, polished thorny branches and rose blossoms in relief, center base inscribed "R. Lalique," Marcilhac 954, p 429 ....400.00

10-1/2" h, frosted colorless oval, molded repeating montage of male archers shooting at birds in flight, gray patine in recessed areas, base inscribed "R. Lalique France N 893," Marcilhac 893, p 415..2,760.00

LAMP SHADES

History: Lamp shades were made to diffuse the harsh light produced by early gas lighting fixtures. These early shades were made by popular Art Nouveau manufacturers including Durand, Quezal, Steuben, and Tiffany. Many shades are not marked.

Quezal, pulled feather dec, 3-1/2" h, $195.

Aladdin

Cased, green...870.00

Satin, white, dogwood dec..65.00

Artichoke, 10" d

Green..1,000.00

White...800.00

Ball, 9-3/4" d...1,500.00

Cased Art glass, 5-1/2" h, 2-1/4" d fitter rim, cased gold, opal glass ruffled bell shade, green pulled feather motif, gold irid luster, price for 4 pc set...435.00

Ceiling Shade, 22" d, 9-1/2" deep, 5" opening, hipped O' Brien dome, leaded green glass segments arranged in brickwork geometric progression, three orig int. bronze reinforcements, rim imp "Tiffany Studios, New York 1501" 10,350.00

Durand, 9-1/2" l, gold Egyptian crackle, blue and white overlay, bulbous, ruffed rim, sgd 225.00

Fenton, 4" d, white opal hobnails, blue ground 90.00

Fostoria, 5-1/2" d, Zipper pattern, green pulled dec, opal ground, gold lining..225.00

Handel

10" d, tam o'shanter, handpainted green silhouette village scene with windmill and harbor, sgd "Handel 2862" 325.00

27-1/2" d, 10" h, octagonal conical shade, leaded green slag panels geometrically arranged, green-amber rippled ladderwork, drop apron dec by bronzed metal scenic tree framework handpainted to enhance forest motif, Handel tag imp on side...2,875.00

Imperial, NuArt, marigold 65.00

Leaded Glass, 17-1/2" d, 3" d opening, narrow topped umbrella-shape, dropped apron, four bright red starburst blossoms with yellow disks on green stems, green slag background segments, conforming motif on apron, some restoration to inside leading..635.00

Lithophane, 12" d, color courting scene......................10,500.00

Loetz, 8-1/2" d, irid green oil spotting, ribbon work, white glass int., c1900..250.00

Lutz Type, 8" sq, 6-1/4" h, opaque white loopings, applied cranberry threading, ribbon edge 195.00

Muller Freres, 6" h, frosted satin, white top, cobalt blue base, yellow highlights, 3 pc set..400.00

Opalescent and amber, optic, Coinspot pattern, c1880......70.00

Pairpoint, 7" h, puffy, flower basket, reverse painted pink and yellow poppies and roses 425.00

Quezal, 5-1/2" d, dark green, platinum feathers, gold lining
....650.00
Rubena, 7-1/4" d, 3-7/8" d fitter ring, cranberry shading to clear,
frosted and clear etched flowers and leaves, ruffled 460.00
Steuben, Aurene, irid brown, platinum applied border 425.00
Tartan, 6" h, 3-1/4" fitter ring, gaslight, bands of white, yellow, and
pink, sgd "Tartan Rd. No. 46498," registered by Henry Geth-
ing Richardson, Wordsley Flint Glass Works, near Stourbridge,
Feb. 24, 1886" 285.00
Tiffany, 51/4" d, bell shape, irid gold ground, 4 pc set ...1,200.00
Verlys, 3-5/8" d, 5-3/4" h, raised birds and fish dec 285.00

LAMPS AND LIGHTING

History: Lighting devices have evolved from simple
stone-age oil lamps to the popular electrified models of
today. Aimé Argand patented the first oil lamp in 1784.
Around 1850, kerosene became a popular lamp-burn-
ing fluid, replacing whale oil and other fluids. In 1879,
Thomas A. Edison invented the electric light, causing
fluid lamps to lose favor and creating a new field for
lamp manufacturers. Companies like Tiffany and Handel became skillful at manufacturing electric lamps, and
their decorators produced beautiful bases and shades.

References: James Edward Black (ed.), *Electric Light-
ing of the 20s-30s* (1988, 1993 value update), *Volume 2
with Price Guide* (1990, 1993 value update), L-W Book
Sales; J. W. Courter, *Aladdin Collectors Manual & Price
Guide #16*, published by author (3935 Kelley Rd., Kevil,
KY 42053), 1996; —, *Aladdin, The Magic Name In
Lamps, Revised Edition,* published by author, 1997; Su-
san E. Grindberg, *Collector's Guide to Porcelier China*,
Collector Books, 1996; Arthur H. Hayward, *Colonial and
Early American Lighting*, 3rd ed., Dover Publications,
1962; Marjorie Hulsebus, *Miniature Victorian Lamps*,
Schiffer Publishing, 1996; Nadja Maril, *American Light-
ing*, Schiffer Publishing, 1995; Richard Miller and John
Solverson, *Student Lamps of the Victorian Era*, Antique
Publications, 1992, 1992-93 value guide; Bill and Linda
Montgomery, *Animated Motion Lamps 1920s to Present*,
L-W Book Sales, 1991; Denys Peter Myers, *Gaslighting
in America*, Dover Publications, 1990; Henry A. Pohs,
Miner's Flame Light Book, Hiram Press, 1995; *Quality
Electric Lamps*, L-W Book Sales, 1992; Catherine M. V.
Thuro, *Oil Lamps*, Wallace-Homestead, 1976, 1992 val-
ue update; —, *Oil Lamps II*, Collector Books, 1983,
1994 value update; Kenneth Wilson, *American Glass
1760-1930*, 2 Vols., Hudson Hills Press and The Toledo
Museum of Art, 1994.

Periodical: *Light Revival*, 35 West Elm Ave., Quincy, MA
02170.

Collectors' Clubs: Aladdin Knights of the Mystic Light,
3935 Kelley Rd., Kevil, KY 42053; Coleman Collector Net-
work, 1822 E Fernwood, Wichita, KS 67216; Historical
Lighting Society of Canada, P.O. Box 561, Postal Station
R, Toronto, Ontario M4G 4EI, Canada; Incandescent
Lamp Collectors Assoc., Museum of Lighting, 717 Wash-
ington Place, Baltimore, MD 21201; Night Light, 38619
Wakefield Ct., Northville, MI 48167; Rushlight Club, Inc.,
Suite 196, 1657 The Fairway, Jenkintown, PA 19046.

Museums: Kerosene Lamp Museum, Winchester Center, CT; Pairpoint Lamp Museum, River Edge, NJ.

REPRODUCTION ALERT

The following is a partial list of reproduction kerosene
lamps. Colors in italics indicate a period color:
Button & Swirl, 8" high–clear, *cobalt blue*, *ruby*
Coolidge Drake (a.k.a. Waterfall), 10" high–clear,
cobalt blue, milk glass, ruby
Lincoln Drape, short, 8-3/4" high–amber, clear,
green, and other colors
Lincoln Drape, tall, 9-3/4" high–amber, clear, cobalt blue, moonstone, ruby
Shield & Star, 7" high–clear, cobalt blue
Sweetheart (a.k.a. Beaded Heart), 10" h–clear, milk
glass, pink, pink cased font with clear base
General clues that help identify a new lamp include
parts that are glued together and hardware that is lacquered solid brass.

SPECIAL AUCTIONS

Green Valley Auctions, Inc.
Rte. 2, Box 434
Mt. Crawford, VA 22841
(540) 434-4260

James D. Julia, Inc.
P.O. Box 830
Fairfield, ME 04937
(207) 453-7125

Astral

American, 19th C
23" h, acid etched shade, foliate standard ending in stepped
marble base, electrified, minor imperfections 460.00
26-1/2" h, acid etched globe, gilt brass lotus font hung with
prisms above overlay shaft cut ruby to clear, stepped mar-
ble base, electrified 865.00
Cornelius & Co., Philadelphia, 24" h, patent date April 18, 1845,
marble base, later blue rimmed wheel cut and acid finish
shade, electrified, gilt wear, minor base chips..............635.00

Boudoir

Aladdin, 14-1/2" h, 8" d, reverse painted bell shade, pine border,
floral molded polychromed metal base.........................225.00
Cut Glass, 9" h, mushroom shade, flared base, sunburst design
....400.00
French, 11" d, 6" d, weighted brass base, crystal glass paneled
insert, brass em leaves and berries, rod curving upward holding night light, brass chains, and mounts, glass night light,
holds candle 215.00
Handel, 14-1/2" h, 8" d ribbed glass domed shade with squared
scalloped rim, obverse painted with snowy winter scene, pastel yellow orange sky, sgd "Handel 5637" on rim, raised on
bronzed metal tree trunk base, threaded Handel label
....3,335.00
Obverse Painted Scenic, 13-1/2" h, closed top mushroom-cap
glass shade with textured surface mounted on gilt metal handled lamp base, weighted foot, handpainted silhouetted for-
ested landscape scenes, rim mkd "Patented April 29th,
1913" 1,150.00

Camphor, pewter, brass caps, 8-3/8" h, $175.

Chandelier

Art glass, 21" drop, 6-1/2" h shade, three scrolling gold metal light arms, flared and bulbed gold irid glass shades, green pulled feather dec 1,150.00

Bradley & Hubbard, 25" d, hand beaten curled heavy brass frame, six caramel colored bent slag glass panels, 19" of heavy brass chain and mounting 980.00

Louis XV, 32" h, gilt bronze and rock crystal, 6-light, open cage form, suspending pear shape drops, applied floral prunts 3,200.00

Regency Style, 45" d, 42" h, gilt bronze, 18-light, c1900 .... 6,800.00

Venetian Glass, 48" d, 58" h, threaded and blown cranberry glass shaft, clear glass scrolled rods suspend faceted swags, 14 scrolled candle arms with molded drip pans 825.00

Desk

Bradley & Hubbard, 13" h, 8-1/2" d adjustable tilt shade, narrow ribbed panels, reverse painted green, blue, and brown Arts and crafts border motif, single socket metal base 460.00

Handel, 15" h, 8" flared glass cylindrical shade, green textured surface cased to reflective opal white, mkd "Mosserine Handel 6010," adjustable bronzed metal weighted base, threaded Handel label on felt liner 1,380.00

Student

22" h, double, brass frame, electrified, cased green shades 605.00

23-1/2" h, brass frame and adjustable arm, white glass shade, early 20th C 260.00

Tiffany

13-1/2" h, 7" d swirl dec irid green ribbed dome Damascene shade cased to white, mkd "L.C.T" on rim, swivel-socket bronze harp frame, rubbed cushion platform, five ball feet, imp "Tiffany Studios New York 419" 3,740.00

17-1/2" h, 7" d swirl dec irid green cased dome Damascene shade, mkd "L.C.T. Favrile," swivel-socket dark patina bronze harp frame with baluster shaft, ribbed cushion platform, five ball feet, imp "Tiffany Studios New York 7907" 4,025.00

18" h, 10-1/2" d gold irid Steuben bell shade, swivel socket dark etched bronze wide harp frame, adjustable shaft above leaf and petal base, imp "Tiffany Studios New York 569" 1,100.00

Early American

Betty Lamp

3-1/2" h wrought iron lamp, stamped "M," 4-1/4" h redware stand with incised wavy lines, minor rim chips 440.00

4-1/4" h, wrought iron, hanger, and pick 300.00

Blown, colorless, 10" h, drop burners, pressed stepped base, chips on base, pr... 385.00

Cage Lamp, 6" d, wrought iron, spherical, self righting gyroscope font, two repaired spout burners 500.00

Candle Holder, 19" h, wrought iron, hanging type, primitive twisted arms and conical socket 385.00

Candle Stand, 57-1/4" h, 24-1/2" w, wrought iron, double arms, brass candleholders and drip pans, attributed to PA, 18th C, pitting, losses to drip pans 8,100.00

Hour Glass, 7" h, clear blown glass, pine and oak frame, whittled baluster posts, old brown finish, glued break in bottom plate 275.00

Loom Light, 14-3/4" h, wrought iron, candle socket, trammel 500.00

Miner's Lamp, 7-3/8" h, cast and wrought iron, chicken finial, replaced hanger 110.00

Rush Light Holder

9" h, wrought iron, turned wooden base, pitted iron 225.00

9-1/2" h, wrought iron, candle socket counter weight, tripod base, penny feet, tooled brass disk at base of stem, simple tooling 470.00

Skater's Lamp, 6-3/4" h, brass, clear glass globe mkd "Perko Wonder Junior," polished, small splint in top of brass cap 160.00

Splint Holder

9-1/2" h, wrought iron, candle socket counter weight, tripod base, diamond shaped feet 415.00

12-1/2" h, wrought iron, tripod base, penny feet, one leg brazed, later added candle socket 250.00

Taper Jack, 5" h, Sheffield silver on copper, old repairs.... 195.00

Student, pewter and brass, glass font, orig shade, new chimney, patent June 4, 1870, 20-1/4" h, $525.

Floor

Bradley and Hubbard, 56" h, 7" d, small domed leaded glass shade, green slag glass, gold key border, open framework adjustable standard, domed circular foot 400.00
Handel, harp base, bronze finish, 2 parrots on yellow ground shade, sgd "Handel #7073 G A" 8,000.00
Tiffany, 55" h, 9-1/2" d linenfold shade, twleve-sided etched bronze shade #1936 with panels of gold-amber favrile fabrique glass, swing socket harp base, tripod legs, spade feet, shade and base imp "Tiffany Studios New York," bronze base hammered "423"...1,380.00
Tiffany/Aladdin, 50" h, 10" d spun bronze shade, reflective white int., mkd "Tiffany Studios New York," adjustable bridge lamp base with Arabian Nights motif, orig dark bronze patina, elaborate platform base, stamped "Tiffany Studios New York 576" 2,990.00

Hanging

American, 19th C
    18" h, patinated metal and cut glass, hall type, candle socket, Gothic arches, diamonds and flowerheads dec ...1,380.00
    23" h, clear blown glass, hall type, elaborate wheel cut dec of birds and deer in landscape, foliate devices, pressed brass mounts 2,415.00
Arts and Crafts, brass washed metal, 4 lanterns, hammered amber glass..1,000.00
Handel, 10" d, hall type, spherical form, acid cut, translucent white, brown, vase and foliate dec, ornate orig hardware.........4,200.00
Perzel, 40-1/4" d, chrome, metal, and glass.....................1,225.00
Tiffany, 18" l, 15" d, attributed to Tiffany Glass and Decorating Co., late 19th C, square green and opalescent diamond-shaped glass jewels arranged as central pendant chandelier drop, twisted wire frame 2,990.00

Piano

Handel, 9" h, 22" l, 7" d conical leaded glass shade with straight apron of green slag and granite glass segments arranged in geometric design, mounted to adjustable socket, curved "dog's leg" shaft above weighed lappet dec base imp "Handel" 1,265.00

Lard, tin, two spouts, hanger, $85.

Tiffany, 6-3/4" h, 19" l tripartite gold amber glass turtleback shade, framed in bronze, three center gold irid turtleback tiles, single-socket swiveling "dog leg" shaft, shade and weighted base imp "Tiffany Studios New York" 4,025.00

Table

Bigelow Kennard, Boston, 26" h, 18" d domed leaded shade, opalescent white segments in geometric progression border, brilliant green leaf forms repeating motif, edge imp "Bigelow Kennard Boston/Bigelow Studios," three socket over Oriental-style bronze base cast with foo dog handles, Japonesque devices 2,875.00
Bradley & Hubbard, 15" sq octagon shade, 21-1/2" h, Prairie School, shade with geometric overlay on green and white slag glass panels with red squares, sgd on base and shade 1,150.00
Duffner and Kimberly, New York
    24" h, 21" d conical leaded glass shade, amber slag background panels, three repeating intricate heraldic elements of lavender-amethyst glass superimposed on crimson red medial band, lower border glass in chevron motif, amber granite and mauve ripple accent colors, three-socket bronzed shaft with cast foliate devices 4,600.00
    26" h, 24-1/2" d dome leaded glass shade with tuck-under irregular rim, multicolored blossoms with yellow centers, green leaves, long stemmed flowers extending to top on segmented white background, three socket bronze lobed shaft with quatraform shaped base.......................7,435.00
Durand, 29-1/2" h, brass, blue glass standard, opaque white and clear feather pattern 300.00
Handel
    15" h, 10" l, 5-1/2" d elongated oval glass shade, glossy irid int., ext. handpainted with colorful woodland scene with center bird in flight on front and back, sgd on rim "Handel 6427," mounted on integrated oval base with "Handel" threaded label 5,462.00
    21" h, 16" d framed bent panel shade, six curved amber slag glass panels overlaid with oak leaf metal framework, conforming applied color, two socket baluster base, orig bronzed finish, work, finial missing, rim repair 920.00
    22" h, 16" d domed shade, shaded green and amber int., obverse painted riverside landscape, muted naturalistic earthen tones, metal rim stamped "Handel," two socket bronzed ribbed base 4,140.00
    23" h, 18" d textured glass dome shade, reverse painted garden bouquet of wild rose blossoms, Schribner pink, red, and yellow, three crystal yellow butterflies in flight, rim sgd "Handel 6688" and by artist, mounted on orig finish bronze metal simulated tree trunk base, threaded Handel label on front liner 14,950.00
    23-1/2" h, 18" d domed glass shade with eight subtle ribs, reverse painted scene of beach front trees and leafy colorful bushes, sailboats and see gulls on blue background ocean, sgd on rim "Handel 6749," mounted on bronzed base with four handles, four splayed feet, mkd "Handel," some metal surface corrosion 5,750.00
Pairpoint
    20-1/2" h, 11-1/2" d domed closed top mushroom-cap glass shade, Vienna, coralene yellow int., painted stylized olive green leaves and red berries, gold outline on ext., ball-decorated ring supported by four arms, quatraform base molded with foliate devices, imp "Pairpoint Mfg Co., 3052" 2,070.00
Steuben, Carder, 23" h, 11" h moss agate angular shouldered oval glass shaft, purple and lavender with mica flecks, green aventurine, amber, red, and blue swirls, gilt metal two socket lamp fittings, catalog #8026 ....1,610.00
Tiffany
    22" h, 16" d dome leaded shade, Bellflower, favrile glass segments leaded as clusters of vivid red and red-orange bellflowers, yellow and fiery-amber scrolling foliate devices against green shaded background, stamped "Tiffany Stu-

dios New York" on rim, dark bronze urn-form lamp base set into three-arm shaft above sq platform, early TS circular imp mark 12,075.00

22-1/2" h, 12" d dome shade, irid swirl dec green Damascene shade cased to reflective white and amber, dark bronze three-arm spider and fluid unit, four-legged base, imp "S1089" on frame and font, also stamped "Tiffany Studios New York" with TG&D Co logo 5,175.00

Wilkinson Co, 27-1/2" h, 20" d scalloped conical leaded glass shade, yellow centered pink and peach colored blossoms, green leaves bordering amber and green slag glass segments arranged in ladderwork progression, locking mechanism with three baluster shaft, bulbed turnings, stepped platform base, imp "Wilkinson Co/Brooklyn, NY" 3,220.00

Williamson, Richard, & Co., Chicago, 25" h, 20" d peaked leaded glass dome, amber slag bordered by red tulips, pink and lavender-blue spring blossoms, green leaf stems, carved glass, mounted on four-socket integrated shaft with stylized tulip blossoms above leafy platform, imp "R. Williamson & Co./Washington & Jefferson Sts./Chicago, Ill," restored cap at top rim 3,220.00

LANTERNS

History: A lantern is an enclosed, portable light source, hand carried or attached to a bracket or pole to illuminate an area. Many lanterns have a protected flame and can be used both indoors and outdoors. Light-producing materials used in early lanterns included candles, kerosene, whale oil, and coal oil, and, later, gasoline, natural gas, and batteries.

References: *Collectible Lanterns*, L-W Book Sales, 1997; Anthony Hobson, *Lanterns That Lit Our World*, Hiram Press, reprinted 1996; Neil S. Wood, *Collectible Dietz Lanterns*, L-W Book Sales, 1996.

Collectors' Club: Coleman Collectors Network, 1822 E. Fernwood, Wichita, KS 67216.

Barn
7-1/4" h, pine, old patina, wire bale, tin heat shield, top plate cracked, old wired repair 385.00

Photographic, tin, kerosene Simplex burner, green, gold lettering, "Common Sense Lantern," two colored pates, burner mkd "E. Miller & Co.," Meriden, CT, c1880, 9-1/4" h, $145.

15-1/4" h, pine and chestnut, scrubbed finish, replaced leather hinges on door 375.00

16-1/2" h, pine and oak, old patina, tin candle socket, heat shield, wire bale handle, crack in top plate 385.00

Candle
10" x 9" x 14-1/4", pine, sliding panel, diamond shaped glass panes on sides, pierced, 3 openings, low strap handle 395.00

16" sq, walnut, 4 glass sides, conical pierced tin top and ring handle, crimped pan and socket 650.00

17-1/2" h, sheet metal, knob feet and finials, glass sides and door, decorative pierced air holes, old black repaint 1,430.00

Dark Room, 17" h, orig black paint, white striping, tin kerosene font and burner "Carbutt's Dry Plate Lantern, PA April 25th 1882" label 75.00

Folding, 10"h, tin, glass sides, em "Stonebridge 1908" 75.00

Japanese, Patterson Bros., Lansing, MI, adv, panes with General U. S. Grant, puppies, young girl, and wilderness scene 195.00

Miner's, 24-1/2" h, tin, orig black paint and kerosene burner, mercury reflector, stenciled label "C. T. Ham Mfg. Co's New No. 8 Tubular Square Lamp Label Registered 1886" 195.00

Miner's, tin, 3 part, leather fitting for head, adapter with brass plate for pole, 2 wire loop handles, adjustable reflector, hinged tin door, em "Ferguson, NY 1878" 195.00

Nautical, 23" h, 11" d, masthead, copper and brass, oil fired, orig burner, label reads "Ellerman, Wilson Line, Hull," mid 19th C 265.00

Paul Revere, 13-1/2" h, tin, punched design with "Burlington," light rust and resoldered door latch, candle socket 715.00

Political Rally, 67" h, gilded wrought iron, flat diamond shape with diamond shaped windows outlined with gilding, amber glass panels," 1842" in gilt, acorn finials, pine carrying staff, mounted on wood base 1,850.00

Skater's
11" h, brass, clear, bulbous globe, wire bail handle 135.00

13-1/2" h, cast iron, lacy base, bulbous clear globe, pierced tin top and wire bail handle 245.00

Wood, 9-1/2" h, pine, old black over red paint, four sides glass, candle access from top, socket pulled by wire bale handle... 690.00

LEEDS CHINA

History: The Leeds Pottery in Yorkshire, England, began production about 1758. Among its products was creamware that was competitive with that of Wedgwood. The original factory closed in 1820, but various subsequent owners continued until 1880. It made enamels, and glazed and unglazed redware.

Marks: Early wares are unmarked. Later pieces are marked "Leeds Pottery," sometimes followed by "Hartley-Green and Co." or the letters "LP."

REPRODUCTION ALERT

Reproductions have the same marks as the antique pieces.

Bowl, cov, floral panels dec, swan finial 185.00

Candlestick, 10" h, spreading sq pedestal pierced shaft, stylized flowers, balustrade nozzle, sq leaf sprig molded bobeche, sq coved leaf spring molded and foliate reticulated base, imp "Leeds Pottery" 250.00

Platter, lady, sheep, and "Faith" in banner, $550.

Charger, 15-3/8" d, multicolored urn of flowers, blue feather edge 450.00
Creamer and Sugar, cov, 4-3/4" h and 5" h, Granite, white dec band, handles, foot, and finial, 19th C, imperfections, edge repair to sugar 550.00
Egg Cup, 2-3/4", creamware, reticulated 150.00
Mug, 5" h, multicolored polychrome floral dec...................250.00
Pitcher, 6-3/4" h, Agate, early 19th C, repaired spout and rim, hairlines 805.00
Plate
    8-1/8" d, pierced edge, mkd on base, early 19th C, minor chips and staining, 6 pc set 805.00
    9-1/2" d, blue feather edge, mkd "Wedgwood," 19th C, minor discoloration 145.00
    9-1/2" d, Chinoiserie design, 19th C, minute rim chips .200.00
    10"d, creamware, molded flutes and edge design, reticulated rim, two imp "Leeds Pottery," some chips, 8 pcs..1,100.00
Sauce Tureen, undertray, ladle, 7-5/8" l, earthenware, green wavy edge, c1800, minor chips, staining 435.00
Teapot, cov, creamware
    4-3/4" h, intertwined ribbed handle, molded floral ends and flower finial, polychrome enameled rose................3,025.00
    5" h, molded spout, intertwined ribbed handle, polychrome enameled portraits of Prince of Orange, completely restored mismatched lid, some flakes, enamel wear ..440.00

LEFTON CHINA

History: China, porcelain, and ceramic with that now familiar "Lefton" mark has been around since the early 1940s and is highly sought by collectors in the secondary marketplace today. The company was founded by George Zoltan Lefton, a Hungarian immigrant. In the 1930s, he was a sportswear designer and manufacturer, but his hobby of collecting fine china and porcelain led him to a new business venture.

After the bombing of Pearl Harbor in 1941, Mr. Lefton aided a Japanese-American friend by helping him to protect his property from anti-Japanese groups. As a result, Lefton came in contact with and began marketing pieces from a Japanese factory owned by Kowa Toki KK.

Figurines and animals, plus many of the whimsical pieces such as the Bluebirds, Dainty Miss, Miss Priss, Cabbage Cutie, Elf Head, Mr. Toodles, and the Dutch Girl, are popular with collectors.

Marks: Until 1980, wares from the Japanese factory include a "KW" in front of the item number.

Reference: Loretta DeLozier, *Collector's Encyclopedia of Lefton China*, Vol. 1 (1995), Vol. 2 (1997), Collector Books.

Collectors' Club: National Society of Lefton Collectors, 1101 Polk St., Bedford, IA 50833.

Advisor: Loretta DeLozier.

Animal
    5", squirrel, bisque...38.00
    8-1/4", bobcat and raccoon.....................................120.00
    8-1/2", tiger, black, white with gold.............................65.00
    10", koala bear with club 180.00
Bank, bluebirds with stones 125.00
Cake Plate, 10" d, server, Hollyberry..............................45.00
Cigarette Set, Elegant Rose, 5 pcs................................200.00
Coffeepot
    Blue Paisley 135.00
    Fleur de Lis 65.00
    Holly Garland 120.00
    Rose Chintz 165.00
Cookie Jar, Bluebirds 300.00
Creamer and Sugar
    Blue Paisley 55.00
    Cuddles 32.00
    Fleur De Lis 38.00
    Holly Garland 65.00
Cup and Saucer
    Christmas Cardinal 25.00
    Roses 45.00
Demitasse Cup and Saucer, Rose Heirloom...................28.00
Figurine
    3-3/4", clown 18.00
    4", Pixie on mushroom watching frog 12.00
    5-1/4", girl on flowers, two pink poodles......................36.00
    5-3/4", ballerina...36.00
    6", Red Boy, Old Masters series 65.00
    6-1/2", Siamese Dancers, pr....................................110.00
    7", cherub on tree, pastel gray, green bisque...............145.00
    8", Rock A Bye Baby in the Treetop 100.00
    8-1/4", nurse...60.00
    11", drummer on horse 195.00
Jam Jar
    Americana 65.00
    Dutch Girl..95.00
Mug
    Hollyberry, 4" 10.00
    Green Holly..18.00
    Poinsettia, white ground 15.00
Planter
    Angel, on cloud, with stones 40.00
    Calico Donkey, 5-1/2"..32.00
Plate
    8" d, Berry Harvest, salad...28.00
    9" d, Magnolia..28.00
    9-1/4" d, To A Wild Rose...28.00
Salt and Pepper Shakers, pr
    Fruit Basket, 2-3/4"...22.00
    Rustic Daisy, 6-3/4"..22.00
    Thumbelina..15.00
Tea Cup and Saucer, ftd, Elegant Rose..........................45.00
Teapot
    Festival..145.00
    Grape Line..85.00
    Honey Bee...125.00
Wall Plaque
    Boy and Girl, oval, bisque, pr....................................120.00
    Rose, black background, 5"...22.00
    Santa's Room, Memories of Home, 6-1/2" 28.00

LENOX CHINA

History: In 1889, Jonathan Cox and Walter Scott Lenox established The Ceramic Art Co. at Trenton, New Jersey. By 1906, Lenox formed his own company, Lenox, Inc. Using potters lured from Belleek, Lenox began making an American version of the famous Irish ware. The firm is still in business.

Marks: Older Lenox china has one of two marks: a green wreath or a palette. The palette mark appears on blanks supplied to amateurs who hand painted china as a hobby. The Lenox company currently uses a gold stamped mark.

References: Susan and Al Bagdade, *Warman's American Pottery and Porcelain*, Wallace-Homestead, 1994; Richard E. Morin, *Lenox Collectibles*, Sixty-Ninth Street Zoo, 1993.

Additional Listings: Belleek.

Bouillon Cup and Saucer, Detroit Yacht Club, palette mark 85.00
Bowl, 2 handles, etched gold trim, M-139, pre-1930 ....45.00
Chocolate Set, cov chocolate pot, 6 cups and saucers, Golden Wheat pattern, cobalt blue ground, 13 pc set................275.00
Cigarette Box, white apple blossoms, green ground, wreath mark 40.00
Compote, 2" h, 5" d, brown rim, white ground, black hp insignia, pre-1930 ....40.00
Cream Soup, Tuxedo, green mark 40.00
Cup and Saucer, Alden...25.00
Honey Pot, 5" h, 6-1/4" d underplate, ivory beehive, gold bee and trim...85.00
Jug, 4" h, hp, grapes and leaves, shaded brown ground, sgd "G. Morley"...250.00
Luncheon Service, partial, burgundy red ground borders with gilt acanthus leaves, 14 10-1/2" d plates, 14 8-1/4" d plates, 12 8-3/8" soup plates, 12 6-1/4" plates, 24 cups and saucers, 20th C 750.00

Mug, 6-1/4" h, monk, smiling, holding up glass of wine, shaded brown ground, SS rim.....................................160.00
Perfume Lamp, 9" h, figural, Marie Antoinette, bisque finish, dated 1929..650.00
Plate, Alden, dinner 20.00
Salt, 3" d, creamy ivory ground, molded seashells and coral, green wreath mark..35.00
Shoe, white, bow trim 190.00
Tea set, cov teapot, creamer, cov sugar, Hawthorne pattern, silver overlay 225.00
Tea Strainer, hp, small pink roses 70.00
Vase
   6" h, pink and roses dec, green leaves, sgd "W. Morley" 195.00
   11-3/4" h, 4-1/2" d, corset shape, pink orchids dec by William Morley, green stamp mark, artist sgd.......................850.00

LIBBEY GLASS

History: Edward Libbey established the Libbey Glass Company in Toledo, Ohio, in 1888 after the New England Glass Works of W. L. Libbey and Son closed in East Cambridge, Massachusetts. The new Libbey company produced quality cut glass which today is considered to belong to the brilliant period.

In 1930, Libbey's interest in art-glass production was renewed, and A. Douglas Nash was employed as a designer in 1931.

The factory continues production today as Libbey Glass Co.

References: Bob Page and Dale Frederickson, *Collection of American Crystal*, Page-Frederickson Publishing, 1995; Kenneth Wilson, *American Glass 1760-1930*, 2 Vols., Hudson Hills Press and The Toledo Museum of Art, 1994.

Additional Listings: Amberina Glass; Cut Glass.

Condiment Set, Maize pattern, opaque ground, green dec, 6-1/4" h, $770. Photo courtesy of Jackson's Auctioneers & Appraisers.

Honey Pot, beehive, ivory, gold bee and trim, 5" h, 6-1/4" saucer, $80.

Banana Boat, 13" x 7" x 7", cut glass, scalloped pedestal base, 24 point hobstar, hobstar, cane, vesica, and fan motifs, sgd 1,500.00
Bell, 5-3/4" h, colorless, acid etched dec "1893 World's Fair," circular logo surrounded by acid-etched florals and banners, shoulder int. molded "1893 World's Columbian Xposition" (sic), twisted frosted handle with star at top, metal clapper 25.00
Bowl
    8" d, cut glass, hobstar, bands of strawberry diamond and fans, sgd 110.00
    9" d, cut glass, Somerset pattern, sgd 150.00
Candy Dish, cov, 7", cut glass, divided, clover shape, hobstar and prism, sgd 90.00
Celery Vase, 6-1/2" h, 5" w, Maize, Pomona dec, amber kernels, blue leaves 395.00
Charger, 14" d, cut glass, hobstar, cane, and wreath motifs, sgd 300.00
Compote, 10-1/2" w, 4" h, colorless, pink Nailsea-type loops, flaring top, sgd "Libbey" 595.00
Cordial, American Prestige pattern, c1930 ....50.00
Ice Cream Tray, 10" x 14", Gloria pattern 275.00
Pitcher, 10" h, copper wheel cut leaves and butterfly dec, sgd 195.00
Plate, 7" d, Gloria pattern..165.00
Rose Bowl, 3-1/2" w, 2-1/2" h, melon ribbed bowl, beige ground, two pansies and leaves, white beads, sgd "Libbey Cut Glass" 550.00
Sherbet, silhouette stem, black rabbit, sgd.......................145.00
Tumble-Up, cut glass, star burst, hobstar, fern, and fan motifs, minor handle check 725.00
Vase
    8" h, oviform, ribbed, wasted neck, wafer and ball stem 720.00
    9" h, bud, elongated, ribbed...615.00
    12" h, trumpet, amberina, ribbed...................................450.00
    13-1/2" h, baluster, emerald green cut flower panels, ftd, sgd base 700.00
Wine, cut glass, Harvard pattern, faceted cut knob stems, sgd, 12 pc set...350.00

LIMITED EDITION COLLECTOR PLATES

History: Bing and Grondahl made the first collector plate in 1895. Royal Copenhagen issued their first Christmas plate in 1908.

In the late 1960s and early 1970s, several potteries, glass factories, mints, and artists began issuing plates commemorating people, animals, and events. Christmas plates were supplemented by Mother's Day plates and Easter plates. Speculation swept the field, fostered in part by flamboyant ads in newspapers and flashy direct-mail promotions.

References: Collectors' Information Bureau Collectibles Market Guide & Price Index, 14th ed., Collectors' Information Bureau (5065 Shoreline Rd., Ste. 200, Barrington, IL 60010), 1996; Beth Dees, *Santa's Price Guide To Contemporary Christmas Collectibles*, Krause Publications, 1997; Carl Luckey, *Luckey's Hummel Figurines & Plates*, 11th Edition, Krause Publications, 1997; Mary Sieber (ed.), *1998 Price Guide to Limited Edition Collectibles*, Krause Publications, 1997.

Periodicals: Collector Editions, 170 Fifth Ave., 12th Floor, New York, NY 10010; Collectors Mart Magazine, 700 E. State St., Iola, WI 54990; Collectors News, 506 Second St., P.O. Box 156, Grundy Center, IA 50638; Insight on Collectibles, 103 Lakeshore Rd., Ste. 202, St.Catharines, Ontario L2N 2T6 Canada; International Collectible Showcase, One Westminster Place, Lake Forest, IL 60045; Plate World, 9200 N. Maryland Ave., Niles, IL 60648; Toybox Magazine, 8393 East Holly Rd., Holly, MI 48442.

Collectors' Clubs: Franklin Mint Collectors Society, US Route 1, Franklin Center, PA 19091; Hummel Collector's Club, Inc., P.O. Box 257, Yardley, PA 19067; International Plate Collectors Guild, P.O. Box 487, Artesia, CA 90702; M. I. Hummel Club, Goebel Plaza, Rte. 31, P.O. Box 11, Pennington, NJ 08534.

Museum: Bradford Museum of Collector's Plates, Niles, IL.

Additional Listings: See *Warman's Americana & Collectibles* for more examples of collector plates plus many other limited edition collectibles.

Notes: The first plate issued in a series (FE) is often favored by collectors. Condition is a critical factor, and price is increased if the original box is available.

Limited edition collector plates, more than any other object in this guide, should be collected for design and pleasure and only secondarily as an investment.

Bing and Grondahl (Denmark)

Christmas Plates, various artists, 7"d
1895 Behind the Frozen Window.....................................3,400.00
1896 New Moon over Snow Covered Trees....................1,975.00
1897 Christmas Meal of the Sparrows..............................725.00
1898 Christmas Roses and Christmas Star.......................700.00
1899 The Crows Enjoying Christmas................................900.00
1900 Church Bells Chiming in Christmas..........................800.00
1901 The Three Wise Men from the East..........................450.00
1902 Interior of a Gothic Church.....................................285.00
1903 Happy Expectation of Children 150.00
1904 View of Copenhagen from Frederiksberg Hill 125.00
1905 Anxiety of the Coming Christmas Night....................130.00
1906 Sleighing to Church on Christmas Eve.......................95.00
1907 The Little Match Girl..125.00
1908 St Petri Church of Copenhagen................................85.00
1909 Happiness Over the Yule Tree................................100.00
1910 The Old Organist..90.00
1911 First It Was Sung by Angels to Shepherds in the Fields 80.00
1912 Going to Church on Christmas Eve...........................80.00
1913 Bringing Home the Yule Tree 85.00
1914 Royal Castle of Amalienborg, Copenhagen...............75.00
1915 Chained Dog Getting Double Meal on Christmas Eve 120.00
1916 Christmas Prayer of the Sparrows...........................85.00
1917 Arrival of the Christmas Boat...................................75.00
1918 Fishing Boat Returning Home for Christmas...............85.00
1919 Outside the Lighted Window....................................80.00
1920 Hare in the Snow...70.00
1921 Pigeons in the Castle Court.....................................55.00
1922 Star of Bethlehem...60.00
1923 Royal Hunting Castle, The Hermitage 55.00
1924 Lighthouse in Danish Waters....................................65.00
1925 The Child's Christmas..70.00
1926 Churchgoers on Christmas Day 65.00
1927 Skating Couple...110.00
1928 Eskimo Looking at Village Church in Greenland.........60.00
1929 Fox Outside Farm on Christmas Eve.........................75.00

1930 Yule Tree in Town Hall Square of Copenhagen 85.00
1931 Arrival of the Christmas Train 75.00
1933 The Korsor-Nyborg Ferry 70.00
1935 Lillebelt Bridge Connecting Funen with Jutland..........65.00
1937 Arrival of Christmas Guests 75.00
1939 Ole Lock-Eye, The Sandman.................................150.00
1941 Horses Enjoying Christmas Meal in Stable................345.00
1943 The Ribe Cathedral..155.00
1945 The Old Water Mill 135.00
1947 Dybbol Mill...70.00
1949 Landsoldaten, 19th Century Danish Soldier................70.00
1951 Jens Bang, New Passenger Boat Running Between Copen-
     hagen and Aalborg...115.00
1953 Royal Boat in Greenland Waters 95.00
1955 Kalundborg Church 115.00
1957 Christmas Candles 155.00
1959 Christmas Eve...120.00
1961 Winter Harmony 115.00
1963 The Christmas Elf..120.00
1965 Bringing Home the Christmas Tree 65.00
1967 Sharing the Joy of Christmas..................................45.00
1969 Arrival of Christmas Guests 30.00
1971 Christmas at Home 20.00
1973 Country Christmas 25.00
1975 The Old Water Mill 25.00
1977 Copenhagen Christmas...25.00
1979 White Christmas...30.00
1981 Christmas Peace 50.00
1983 Christmas in Old Town 55.00
1985 Christmas Eve at the Farmhouse.............................55.00
1987 The Snowman's Christmas Eve 60.00
1989 Christmas Anchorage..65.00
1990 Changing of the Guards 75.00

Mother's Day Plates, Henry Thelander, artist, 6" d
1969 Dog and Puppies...400.00
1971 Cat and Kitten...20.00
1973 Duck and Ducklings 20.00
1975 Doe and Fawns..20.00
1977 Squirrel and Young...25.00
1979 Fox and Cubs..30.00
1981 Hare and Young 40.00
1983 Raccoon and Young...45.00
1985 Bear and Cubs 40.00
1987 Sheep with Lamps 40.00
1989 Cow with Calf 45.00
1990 Hen with Chicks 65.00

Reed & Barton (United States)

Christmas Series, Damascene silver, 11" d through 1978, 8" d
     1979 to present
1970 A Partridge in a Pear Tree, FE.................................200.00
1971 We Three Kings of Orient Are..................................65.00
1973 Adoration of the Kings 75.00
1975 Adoration of the Kings 65.00
1977 Decorating the Church 60.00
1979 Merry Old Santa Claus 65.00
1981 The Shopkeeper at Christmas.................................75.00

Rosenthal (Germany)

Christmas Plates, various artists, 8 1/2" d
1910 Winter Peace 550.00
1911 The Three Wise Men..325.00
1912 Shooting Stars 250.00
1913 Christmas Lights...235.00
1915 Walking to Chruch 180.00
1917 Angel of Peace 200.00
1919 St. Christopher with the Christ Child...........................225.00
1921 Christmas in the Mountains 200.00
1923 Children in the Winter Wood 200.00
1925 The Three Wise Men..200.00

1927 Station on the Way...200.00
1929 Christmas in the Alps...225.00
1931 Path of the Magi..225.00
1933 Through the Night to Light 190.00
1935 Christmas by the Sea 185.00
1937 Berchtesgaden 195.00
1939 Schneekoppe Mountain..195.00
1941 Strassburg Cathedral 250.00
1943 Winter Idyll...300.00
1945 Christmas Peace 400.00
1947 The Dillingen Madonna...975.00
1949 The Holy Family 185.00
1951 Star of Bethlehem 450.00
1953 The Holy Light..185.00
1955 Christmas in a Village 190.00
1957 Christmas by the Sea 195.00
1959 Midnight Mass 195.00
1961 Solitary Christmas 225.00
1963 Silent Night 185.00
1965 Christmas in Munich 185.00
1967 Christmas In Regensburg.......................................185.00
1969 Christmas in Rothenburg..220.00
1971 Christmas in Garmisch 100.00
1973 Christmas in Lubeck-Holstein..................................110.00
1974 Christmas in Wurzburg...100.00

Royal Copenhagen (Denmark)

Christmas Plates, various artists, 6" d 1908, 1909, 1910; 7" 1911
     to present
1908 Madonna and Child..1,750.00
1909 Danish Landscape 150.00
1910 The Magi...120.00
1911 Danish Landscape 135.00
1912 Elderly Couple by Christmas Tree.............................120.00
1913 Spire of Frederik's Church, Copenhagen...................125.00
1914 Sparrows in Tree at Church of the Holy Spirit, Copenhagen
     ....100.00
1915 Danish Landscape 150.00
1916 Shepherd in the Field on Christmas Night..................85.00
1917 Tower of Our Savior's Church, Copenhagen...............90.00
1918 Sheep and Shepherds..80.00
1919 In the Park..80.00
1920 Mary with the Child Jesus.......................................75.00
1921 Aabenraa Marketplace 75.00
1922 Three Singing Angels 70.00
1923 Danish Landscape 70.00
1924 Christmas Star Over the Sea and Sailing Ship 100.00
1925 Street Scene from Christianshavn, Copenhagen 85.00
1926 View of Christmas Canal, Copenhagen......................75.00
1927 Ship's Boy at the Tiller on Christmas Night 140.00
1928 Vicar's Family on Way to Church..............................75.00
1929 Grundtvig Church, Copenhagen..............................100.00
1930 Fishing Boats on the Way to the Harbor....................80.00
1931 Mother and Child 90.00
1932 Frederiksberg Gardens with Statue of Frederik VI 90.00
1933 The Great Belt Ferry 110.00
1934 The Hermitage Castle..115.00
1935 Fishing Boat off Kronborg Castle 145.00
1936 Roskilde Cathedral 130.00
1937 Christmas Scene in Main Street, Copenhagen 135.00
1938 Round Church in Osterlars on Bornholm....................200.00
1939 Expeditional Ship in Pack-Ice of Greenland............180.00
1940 The Good Shepherd 300.00
1941 Danish Village Church..250.00
1943 Flight of Holy Family to Egypt.................................425.00
1945 A Peaceful Motif...325.00
1947 The Good Shepherd 200.00
1949 Our Lady's Cathedral, Copenhagen 165.00
1951 Christmas Angel 300.00
1953 Frederiksborg Castle 120.00

1955 Fano Girl 185.00
1957 The Good Shepherd 115.00
1959 Christmas Night 120.00
1961 Training Ship Danmark 155.00
1963 Hojsager Mill 80.00
1965 Little Skaters 60.00
1967 The Royal Oak 45.00
1969 The Old Farmyard..35.00
1971 Hare in Winter 80.00
1973 Train Homeward Bound for Christmas 85.00
1975 Queen's Palace 85.00
1977 Immervad Bridge 75.00
1979 Choosing the Christmas Tree 60.00
1981 Admiring the Christmas Tree..................................55.00
1983 Merry Christmas 60.00
1985 Snowman..55.00
1987 Winter Birds 55.00
1989 The Old Skating Pond...50.00
1990 Christmas at Tivoli 75.00
Mother's Day Plates, various artists, 6 1/4" d
1971 American Mother 125.00
1973 Danish Mother 60.00
1975 Bird in Nest 50.00
1977 The Twins...50.00
1979 A Loving Mother 30.00
1981 Reunion...40.00

Wedgwood (Great Britain)

Christmas Series, jasper stoneware, 8" d
1969 Windsor Castle, FE...225.00
1970 Christmas in Trafalgar Square................................30.00
1972 St. Paul's Cathedral 40.00
1974 The Houses of Parliament....................................40.00
1976 Hampton Court 45.00
1978 The Horse Guards 55.00
1980 St. James Palace...70.00
1982 Lambeth Palace...80.00
1984 Constitution Hill..80.00
1986 The Albert Memorial 80.00
1988 The Observatory Greenwich....................................90.00
1989 Winchester Cathedral...85.00
Mothers Series, jasper stoneware, 6 1/2"d
1971 Sportive Love, FE...25.00
1972 The Sewing Lesson 20.00
1974 Domestic Employment...30.00
1976 The Spinner 35.00
1978 Swan and Cygnets 35.00
1980 Birds 48.00
1982 Cherubs with Swing 55.00
1984 Musical Cupids...55.00
1986 Cupids Fishing 55.00
1988 Tiger Lily 59.00

LIMOGES

History: Limoges porcelain has been produced in Limoges, France, for over a century by numerous factories in addition to the famed Haviland.

Marks: One of the most frequently encountered marks is "T. & V. Limoges," which is on the wares made by Tressman and Vought. Other identifiable Limoges marks are "A. L." (A. Lanternier), "J. P. L." (J. Pouyat, Limoges), "M. R." (M. Reddon), "Elite," and "Coronet."

References: Susan and Al Bagdade, *Warman's English & Continental Pottery & Porcelain*, 2nd ed., Wallace-Homestead, 1991; Mary Frank Gaston, *Collector's Encyclopedia of Limoges Porcelain*, 2nd ed., Collector Books, 1992, 1998 value update.

Additional Listings: Haviland China.

Salt, white interior, pale blue exterior, gold rim, mkd "Limoges France," 2" x 5/8", $17.50.

Berry Set, 9-1/2" d, master bowl, eight 8" serving bowls, hp, purple berries on ext. white blossoms on int., mkd "T & V" 265.00
Bowl, 4-1/2" h, ftd, hp, wild roses and leaves, sgd "J. E. Dodge, 1892" 85.00
Box, cov, 4-1/4" sq, cobalt blue and white ground, cupids on lid, pate-sur-pate dec 195.00
Cache Pot, 7-1/2" w, 9" h, male and female pheasants on front, mountain scene on obverse, gold handles and 4 ball feet 225.00
Cake Plate, 11-1/2" d, ivory ground, brushed gold scalloped rim, gold medallion, mkd "Limoges T & V"............................75.00
Candy Dish, 6-1/2" d, ftd, 2 handles, silver overlay, white ground, c1920 ....95.00
Chocolate Pot, 13" h, purple violets and green leaves, cream colored ground, gold handle, spout, and base, sgd "Kelly JPL/France" 350.00
Creamer and Sugar, cov, 3-1/4" h, purple flowers, white ground, gold handle and trim 100.00
Cup and Saucer, hp, flowers and leaves, gold trim, artist sgd 75.00
Dessert Service, coffeepot, creamer, sugar, waste bowl, 8 cups and saucers, 10 dessert plates, 12 lemon dishes, 2 10" cake plates, hp gold florals, pale aqua shading to white ground, raised beading and scrollwork 450.00
Dresser Set, pink flowers, pastel blue, green, and yellow ground, large tray, cov powder, cov rouge, pin tray, talc jar, pr candlesticks, 7 pc set..425.00
Figure, 25" h, 13" w, 3 girls, arms entwined, holding basket of flowers, books, and purse, mkd "C & V" and "L & L" 460.00
Hair Receiver, blue flowers and white butterflies, ivory ground, gold trim, mkd "JPL" 80.00
Lemonade Pitcher, matching tray, water lily dec, sgd "Vignard Limoges" 350.00
Mortar and Pestle, 3-1/4" x 2" mortar, 3-1/2" l pestle, hp flowers gold trim, deep rose ground, mkd "GL, Halga, Decor Main, Paris, France, Limoges" 95.00
Mug, corn motif, sgd "T & V Limoges France" 65.00
Nappy, 6 d, curved gold handle, gold scalloped edges, soft pink blossoms, blue-green ground 35.00
Oyster Plate
    7-3/4" w, cut corner sq shape, enameled shell and foliate dec, yellow, blue, green, pink, white, and peach ground colors, light surface and gilt rim wear, 12 pc set 1,150.00
    8" d, 6 wells, ribbed molded, gold tracery, cream and yellow round 125.00
Panel, 4-1/2" x 3-3/8", enameled, Christ with crown of thorns, framed 250.00
Pitcher, 6" h, 5-1/8" d, platinum handle, platinum mistletoe berries and leaves, gray and pink ground, Art Deco style, mkd "J. P. Limoges, Pouyat"...155.00

Plaque, 7-5/8" x 4-1/2", enameled, cavalier, after Meissonier, multicolored garb and banner, late 19th C 460.00
Plate, 9" d, hp, pastel florals, Art Nouveau enameled gold dec, ornate gold scalloped rim..35.00
Punch Bowl, 13" d, scalloped gold rim, fruit blossom dec, gold band pedestal base 245.00
Snuff Box, cov, hp, wildflowers and gold tracery, pink ground, artist sgd, dated 1800...200.00
Tankard Set, 14" h tankard, 4 mugs, hp, grape dec, gold and green ground, 5 pc set..450.00
Vase, 11" h, flamingo, sgd "WG Limoges France," c1890
....150.00

LITHOPHANES

History: Lithophanes are highly translucent porcelain panels with impressed designs. The designs result from differences in the thickness of the plaque; thin parts transmit an abundance of light while thicker parts represent shadows.

Lithophanes were first made by the Royal Berlin Porcelain Works in 1828. Other factories in Germany, France, and England later produced them. The majority of lithophanes on the market today were made between 1850 and 1900.

Collectors' Club: Lithophane Collectors Club, 2030 Robinwood Ave., P.O. Box 4557, Toledo, OH 43620.

Museum: Blair Museum of Lithophanes and Carved Waxes, Toledo, OH.

Candle Shield, 9" h, panel with scene of 2 country boys playing with goat, castle in background 275.00
Cup and Saucer, blue Oriental lady with nude lady...........175.00

Plaque, woman, imp "1812," 5-1/8" x 4-1/4", $150.

Fairy Lamp, 9" h, 3 panels, lady leaning out of tower, rural romantic scenes 1,250.00
Lamp, 20-3/4" h, colored umbrella style shade, 4 panels of outdoor Victorian scenes, bronze and slate standard, German
....675.00
Night Lamp, 5-1/4" h, sq, 4 scenes, irid green porcelain base, gold trim, electrified..650.00
Panel
  KPM
    2-1/2" x 3-1/4", view from West Point 185.00
    3-7/8" x 5-1/4", lake setting, ship and windmill 165.00
  PPM
    3-1/4" x 5-1/4", view of Paterson Falls.....................190.00
    4" x 6", woman and children with hay cart, incised "PPM. 553"..55.00
  PR Sickle, 4-1/4" x 5"
    Cupid and girl fishing 160.00
    Scene of 2 women in doorway, dog and 2 pigeons, sgd, #1320 ....100.00
  Unmarked, 6" x 7-1/2", Madonna and Child 175.00
Pitcher, puzzle type, Victorian scene, nude on bottom......175.00
Stein, regimental, half liter 200.00
Tea Warmer, 5-7/8" h, one pc cylindrical panel, 4 seasonal landscapes with children, copper frame, finger grip and molded base..250.00

LIVERPOOL CHINA

History: Liverpool is the name given to products made at several potteries in Liverpool, England, between 1750 and 1840. Seth and James Pennington and Richard Chaffers were among the early potters who made tin-enameled earthenware.

By the 1780s, tin-glazed earthenware gave way to cream-colored wares decorated with cobalt blue, enameled colors, and blue or black transfers.

The Liverpool glaze is characterized by bubbles and frequent clouding under the foot rims. By 1800 about 80 potteries were working in the town producing not only creamware, but soft paste, soapstone, and bone porcelain.

Reference: Robert McCauley, *Liverpool Transfer Designs on Anglo-American Pottery*, Southworth-Anthoensen Press, out of print.

REPRODUCTION ALERT

Reproduction Liverpool pieces were documented as early as 1942. One example is a black transfer-decorated jug which was made in the 1930s. The jugs vary in height from 8-1/2 to 11 inches. On one side is "The Shipwright's Arms"; on the other, the ship Caroline flying the American flag; and under the spout, a wreath with the words "James Leech."

A transfer of the *Caroline* also was used on a Sunderland bowl about 1936 and reproduction mugs were made bearing the name "James Leech" and an eagle.

The reproduction pieces have a crackled glaze and often age cracks have been artificially produced. When compared to genuine pieces, reproductions are thicker and heavier and have weaker transfers, grayish color (not as crisp and black), ecru or gray body color instead of cream, and crazing that does not spiral upward.

Jug, The Farmer's Arms, The Grave Robbers on reverse, multicolored, 7-3/4" h, $825.

Cup and Saucer, handleless, black transfer, bust of Washington and other gentleman on cup, "Washington, His Country's Father" on saucer, hairlines in cup 330.00

Jug, creamware, transfer print

7-3/4" h, reserve of ships *L'Insurgent* and *Constellation,* reserve of ship yard, cracks, chips, minor losses, transfer imperfections 1,265.00

8-3/4" h, "The Greenwich Pensioner," text underneath, ship on reverse, repairs 460.00

9-1/2" h, "Representation of the British defeat of the French Fleet of Brest by Earl Howe, 1794," reverse "The Flowing Cann," picture of drinking and dancing, descriptive text, minor glaze wear 815.00

9-5/8" h, English hunting scenes "Jos Edge Caldon Grange" inscribed under spout, extensive repairs 345.00

9-3/4" h, oval medallion portrait of John Adams, surrounded by Plenty, Justice and Cupid, circular panel "Peace Plenty and Independence" on reverse flanked by Plenty and Peace destroying the implements of war, surmounted by spread eagle, chips, scratches, minor transfer wear 4,025.00

9-3/4" h, reserves of Thomas Jefferson and James Monroe, misidentified as "Hancock," hp foliate gilt highlights, repairs, hairlines, minor chip, gilt, and enamel wear 20,700.00

10" h, portrait of Thomas Jefferson, American eagle on reverse, chips, glaze wear to handle 21,850.00

Mug

3-3/4" h, dark brown transfer, Hope, allover luster trim, c1829-30 .... 200.00

6" h, creamware, transfer printed three masted ship under sail, figure of Hope, "Jennett Lawson," hairline on base 750.00

Trinket Pot, cov, 5-1/4" d, Delft, blue and white, two handles, chips and hairline in bottom 495.00

LOETZ

History: Loetz is a type of iridescent art glass that was made in Austria by J. Loetz Witwe in the late 1890s. Loetz was a contemporary of L. C. Tiffany's, and he had worked in the Tiffany factory before establishing his own operation; therefore, much of the wares are similar in appearance to Tiffany products. The Loetz factory also produced items with fine cameos on cased glass.

Marks: Some pieces are signed "Loetz," "Loetz, Austria," or "Austria."

Reference: Robert and Deborah Truitt, *Collectible Bohemian Glass: 1880-1940,* R & D Glass, 1995.

Bowl

5" d, 3" h, white, applied punties and rim 130.00

7" d, 4" h, rolled rim, applied green tadpoles, highly irid, white ground 110.00

Center Bowl, 10" d, Onyx, dec 395.00

Compote, 10-5/8" d, 5-1/4" h, bright orange int., deep black ext., white flaring circular rim, 3 ball feet, c1920 .... 310.00

Inkwell, 3-1/2" h, amethyst, sq, irid, web design, bronze mouth 125.00

Oil Lamp, 19-1/2" h, 9-1/2" d, globular shade, bulbous base, all over irid oil-spot dec, orig brass fittings 3,000.00

Pitcher, 8-5/8" h, pinched bulbous body, purple and green irid, applied handle, gilt metal mount with cast foliate motif 650.00

Rose Bowl, 6-1/2" d, ruffled purple irid raindrop dec 265.00

Sweetmeat Jar, cov, 5" h, irid silver spider web dec, green ground, sgd 450.00

Urn, 9-1/4" h, ovoid, irid, blue oil spot dec, inscribed "Loetz, Austria" 1,600.00

Vase

4-1/2" h, 4" w, transparent pink, irid surface with blue and gold highlights, ground pontil 450.00

Vase, elongated bulbous body, shallow collar, flattened rim, irid amber, sgd, 6"h, $195.

6" h, 5" w, irid gold, deep blue and gold highlights, large bronze Raindrop spots, dimpled body, large ground pontil 750.00
6-1/2" h, ruffled trefoil rim, ambergris body, symmetrical dec with three gold and silvery irid pulled feathers, base inscribed "Loetz Austria" 865.00
6-1/2" h, tadpole neck, white irid ground, green rigaree 200.00
7" h
 Melon shape, Carneol 295.00
 Silver plated holder..330.00
7" h, 4-1/2" w, bulbous, three applied loop handles, silver overlay on handles and 2" top band, irid body 975.00
7-1/2" h, 4-1/2" w, ovoid, purple and brown irid ground, large blue and purple pulled raindrops..........................1,150.00
8-3/4" h, Marmorierte, oval body, marbleized green, aubergine, and turquoise blue striations, cased to opal, lined in blue, dec with gilt enamel sunbursts, red glass "jewel" centers...460.00
10-1/2" h, 6" w, bulbous swirl, applied shell handles, Rainbow, white lining, gold trim, cased in crystal, pink, yellow, and blue irid surface, pr 675.00
15-1/4" h, 8-1/2" d, Papillion, lustered gold, purple, and green 750.00
16" h, slender extended neck, bulbous orange body, pulled and coiled gold irid dec, fine colorful luster, polished pontil and base...6,900.00

LUSTER WARE

History: Lustering on a piece of pottery creates a metallic, sometimes iridescent, appearance. Josiah Wedgwood experimented with the technique in the 1790s. Between 1805 and 1840, lustered earthenware pieces were created in England by makers such as Adams, Bailey and Batkin, Copeland and Garrett, Wedgwood, and Enoch Wood.

Copper, pitcher, blue bands, applied floral motif in lower band, scroll hand, 6-1/4" h, $70.

Luster decorations often were used in conjunction with enamels and transfers. Transfers used for luster decoration covered a wide range of public and domestic subjects. They frequently were accompanied by pious or sentimental doggerel as well phrases which reflected on the humors of everyday life.

Copper luster was created by the addition of a copper compound to the glaze. It was very popular in America during the 19th century, and collecting it became a fad from the 1920s to the 1950s. Today it has a limited market.

Pink luster was made by using a gold mixture. Silver luster pieces were first covered completely with a thin coating of a "steel luster" mixture, containing a small quantity of platinum oxide. An additional coating of platinum, worked in water, was then applied before firing.

Sunderland is a coarse type of cream-colored earthenware with a marbled or spotted pink luster decoration which shades from pink to purple. A solution of gold compound applied to the white body developed the many shades of pink.

The development of electroplating in 1840 created a sharp decline in the demands for metal-surfaced earthenware.

REPRODUCTION ALERT

The market stagnation for copper luster can be partially attributed to the large number of reproductions, especially creamers and the "polka" jug, which fool many new buyers. Reproductions are heavier in appearance and weight than the earlier pieces.

Additional Listings: English Soft Paste.

Copper

Creamer
 3-1/8" h, 2 rect panels, Hope transfers, red, green, blue, and purple enamel highlights, pink luster dec handle and mouth int. 90.00
 4" h, polychrome floral dec, French, pr 150.00
Figure, 8" h, spaniels, pr...125.00
Goblet, 4-1/2" h, 3-1/2" d, pink luster band, floral resist dec, copper luster int...50.00
Jug, 8" h, 3 transfers of mother and child playing badminton and writing letters on canary yellow band 185.00
Mug, 4-3/4" h, leaves and berries on orange luster band....60.00
Pepper Shaker, 4-1/4" h, cream colored band.....................45.00
Pitcher
 7-1/2" h, Adam Buck style, two reserves of genre scenes, yellow ground, England, 19th C, minor base chip........175.00
 10" h, wide blue band around body, em greyhound, bull, and urn of flowers in polychrome enamel, pink and purple luster..210.00
Teapot, 6" h, em ribs, polychrome enameled floral dec.....125.00

Pink

Child's Mug, 2" h, pink luster band, reddish hunter and dogs transfer, green highlighted foliate transfer 85.00
Creamer, 4-3/8" h, stylized flower band, pink luster highlights and rim, ftd...75.00
Cup and Saucer, magenta transfers, Faith, Hope, and Charity, applied green enamel highlights, pink luster line borders 60.00

Figure, 4-1/2" h, dogs, white, luster gilt collar, cobalt blue base with gilt trim, Staffordshire, pr 620.00

Pitcher
5-1/2" h, House pattern, ornate pink luster dec.............120.00
5-3/4" h, em ribs, eagle, and flowers in pink and purple luster 150.00

Plate
6-1/4" d, relief figures of dogs running on rim, highlighted with green, red, and pink luster, red, green, and blue stylized floral dec in center.......................................55.00
7-3/4" d, green transfer of "Employ time well," em floral border with polychrome enamel and luster trim.....................75.00
9-3/4" d, painted flowers and leaves, pink, purple, and yellow, green and red overglaze 45.00

Plaque, 9-3/8" l, 8-3/8" h, rect, "The Great Eastern Steam Ship," black transfer with polychrome, pink luster shaped border 450.00
Posset Cup and Saucer, Tray, 5" h, wide luster bands flanked by 2 red bands, 19th C..295.00
Teapot, 12" h, House pattern, Queen Anne style, repaired finial on lid 285.00
Toddy Plate, 5-1/16" d, pink luster House pattern, fern floral sprigs border 45.00
Waste Bowl, 6" d, House pattern 125.00

Silver

Coffee Service, 7-3/8" h cov coffeepot, cov sugar bowl, 6 coffee cups and saucers, silver luster grape and leaves, rust enamel accents, yellow ground 450.00
Creamer, 4" h, 5" w, ribbed loop base, incised band near top, shaped handle...85.00
Cup and Saucer, handleless, overall floral band on cup, scattered florals on saucer 45.00
Figure, 11-7/8" l, standing lion, paw on globe, rect base, early 19th C, repaired..900.00
Goblet, 4-3/8" h, silver luster grapes and vines, white ground, lustered foot..220.00
Jug
4-1/2" h, village scene 100.00
5-1/2" h, blue printed hunting scene, border of flowers and leaves, luster ground, Staffordshire, c1815..............975.00
6-1/2" h, shell detail, minor wear.....................................100.00

Pink, pitcher, curlique and leaf pattern, Wedgwood, Eturia, Barlaston, 3-3/4" h, $60.

Pitcher, 5-1/2" h, squatty body, wide lip, overall silver luster, 19th C 95.00
Spill Vase, 4-1/8" h, gray marbleized applied vines and fruits, silver luster accents, white int., pr......................95.00
Teapot, 5-1/4" h, reeded detail 140.00

Sunderland

Bowl, 8-1/4" d, polychrome highlighted black transfers of ship and verse, pink marble luster, mid 18th C 265.00
Creamer, 5" h, "The Sailor's Tear," outlined in florals, verse with sailing ship and "May Peace and Plenty...," luster trim........275.00
Jug
7-1/2" h, transfer printed, painted polychrome enamels, Iron Bridge in Sunderland on one side, ship on reverse, chips, some wear 300.00
8-3/8" h, transfer printed, painted polychrome enamels, two marine rhymes, chips, some wear...........................245.00
Salt, master, Cloud pattern, ftd..50.00
Mug, 5" h, black transfer of compass on front, "The Sailor's Farewell" on reverse 160.00
Mustard Pot, 4" h, loop handle 150.00
Pitcher, 7-1/8" h, hex panels, black transfers of John Wesley on one side, verse on other, pink marble luster, c1850 .....150.00
Plaque, 8-1/2" l, 7-1/2" w, "Thou God Seeist Me," luster trim, Dixon mark...175.00
Plate, 10" d, center transfer print of Pike and "Be always Ready to Die for your Country," pink luster and yellow banded border, c1820 ....2,650.00

LUTZ-TYPE GLASS

History: Lutz-type glass is an art glass attributed to Nicholas Lutz. He made this type of glass while at the Boston and Sandwich Glass Co. from 1869 until 1888. Since Lutz-type glass was popular, copied by many capable glassmakers, and unsigned, it is nearly impossible to distinguish genuine Lutz products.

Lutz is believed to have made two distinct types of glass: striped and threaded. The striped glass was made by using threaded glass rods in the Venetian manner, and this style is often confused with authentic Venetian glass. Threaded glass was blown and decorated with winding threads of glass.

Bowl, white, amethyst, yellow, goldstone edges, 3" x 3-1/4", $48.

Compote, 8-7/8" x 6-1/2" d, threaded, amberina, colorless hollow stem 500.00
Epergne, 3 pcs, pink threads 275.00
Finger Bowl and Underplate, 7" d, ruffled edge, amber swirls, amethyst latticinio, gold metallic borders...........................165.00
Lamp Shade, 8" sq, 20-1/2" fitter ring, opaque white loopings, applied cranberry threading, ribbon edge 180.00
Punch Cup, 3" x 2-5/8", cranberry threading, colorless ground, circular foot, applied colorless handle 85.00
Tumbler, 3-3/4" d, white and amethyst latticino goldstone highlights 75.00

MAASTRICHT WARE

History: Petrus Regout founded the De Sphinx Pottery in 1836 in Maastricht, Holland. The firm specialized in transfer-printed earthenwares. Other factories also were established in the area, many employing English workmen and adopting their techniques. Maastricht china was exported to the United States in competition with English products.

Bowl
    5-3/4" d, red, green, and blue agate pattern, "Petrous Regout, Maastricht" and lion mark 35.00
    6" d, Sana pattern, black oriental transfer, orange wash, mkd "Sana, Petrous Regout, Maastricht" 20.00
    8-1/4" d, ftd, windmill with people finishing, brown transfer 20.00
Pitcher, 5" h, rooster with iris and leaves, red transfer, mkd "Regout & Co. Haan"...75.00
Plate
    7" d, Fruit pattern, blue transfer, emb woven border, mkd "Petrus Regout & Co., Maastricht" 35.00
    8-1/2" d, gaudy floral design, red, blue, and two shades of green, stick spatter, mkd "Maestricht" 60.00
    8-3/4" d, Ceylon pattern, blue, mkd "Petrous Regout" 40.00
Platter, 11-1/2" d, gaudy polychrome florals, red, yellow, and green white ground 65.00

Bowl, Vlinder, 6" d, 3" h, $35.

MAJOLICA

History: Majolica, an opaque, tin-glazed pottery, has been produced in many countries for centuries. It was named after the Spanish Island of Majorca, where figuline (a potter's clay) is found. Today, however, the term "majolica" denotes a type of pottery which was made during the last half of the 19th century in Europe and America.

Majolica frequently depicts elements of nature: leaves, flowers, birds, and fish. Designs were painted on the soft clay body using vitreous colors and fired under a clear lead glaze to impart the rich color and brilliance characteristic of majolica.

Victorian decorative art philosophy dictated that the primary function of design was to attract the eye; usefulness was secondary. Majolica was a welcome and colorful change from the familiar blue and white wares, creamwares, and white ironstone of the day.

Marks: Wedgwood, George Jones, Holdcraft, and Minton were a few of the English majolica manufacturers who marked their wares. Most of their pieces can be identified through the English Registry mark and/or the potter-designer's mark. Sarreguemines in France and Villeroy and Boch in Baden, Germany, produced majolica that compared favorably with the finer English majolica. Most Continental pieces had an incised number on the base.

Although 600-plus American potteries produced majolica between 1850 and 1900, only a handful chose to identify their wares. Among these manufacturers were George Morley, Edwin Bennett, the Chesapeake Pottery Company, the New Milford-Wannoppee Pottery Company, and the firm of Griffen, Smith, and Hill. The others hoped their unmarked pieces would be taken for English examples.

References: Susan and Al Bagdade, *Warman's American Pottery and Porcelain*, Wallace-Homestead, 1994; ––, *Warman's English & Continental Pottery & Porcelain*, 2nd ed., Wallace-Homestead, 1991; Victoria Bergesen, *Majolica: British, Continental, and American Wares, 1851-1915*, Barrie & Jenkins, 1989; Leslie Bockol, *Victorian Majolica*, Schiffer Publishing, 1996; Helen Cunningham, *Majolica Figures*, Schiffer Publishing, 1997; Nicholas M. Dawes, *Majolica*, Crown, 1990; Marilyn G. Karmason and Joan B. Stacke, *Majolica, A Complete History and Illustrated Survey*, Abrams, 1989; Mariann Katz-Marks, *Collector's Encyclopedia of Majolica*, Collector Books, 1992, 1996 value update; Marshall P. Katz and Robert Lehr, *Palissy Ware: Nineteenth Century French Ceramics from Avisseau to Renoleau*, Athlone Press, 1996; *Price Guide to Majolica*, L-W Book Sales, 1997; Mike Schneider, *Majolica*, Schiffer Publishing, 1990, 1995 value update; Jeffrey B. Snyder and Leslie J. Bockol, *Majolica: European and American Wares*, Schiffer Publishing, 1994.

Periodical: Majolica Market, 2720 N. 45 Rd., Manton, MI 49663.

Collectors' Club: Majolica International Society, 1275 First Ave., Ste. 103, New York, NY 10021.

Advisor: Mary D. Harris.

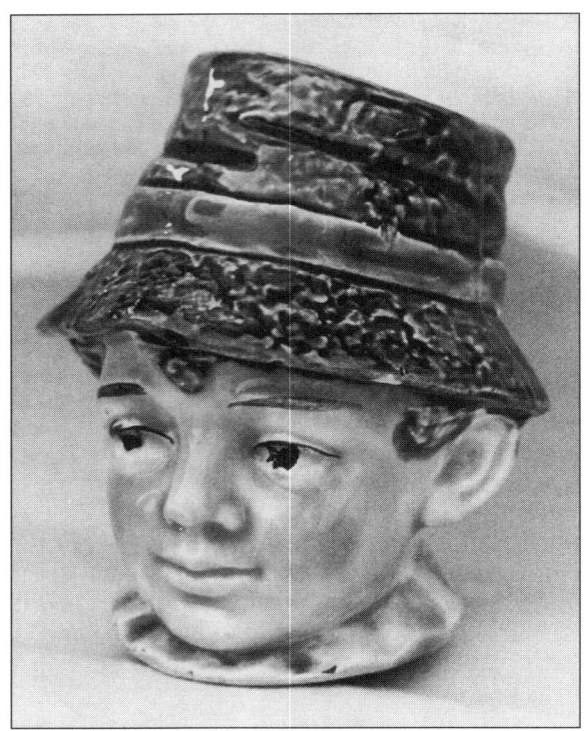

Bank, boy's head, green hat, blue collar, violet band, 3-1/2" h, $45.

Bowl, Shell and Seaweed, Etruscan, 8-1/2" d, minor factory imperfection 385.00
Bowl and Underplate, Daisy, George Jones, cobalt blue, hairline restoration to bowl, rim repair at plate 660.00
Bread Tray
    Ribbon, bow, wheat, and floral, pink border, George Jones, professional rim repair 1,250.00
    Shell and Seaweed, Etruscan 1,300.00
Butter Dish, cov, insert, Shell and Seaweed, Etruscan, minor rim nicks to lid 660.00
Butter Pat
    Astor, Wedgwood, rim wear and nick 70.00
    Butterfly, Fielding, stains 220.00
    Fan and Insect, Fielding type 165.00
    Floral, 4-1/4" d, cobalt blue 175.00
    Grape, Clifton, rim nick 140.00
    Horseshoe, Wedgwood 300.00
    Leaf, turquoise, with vegetable, T. C. Brown Westhead & Moore 200.00
    Shell shape, rim wear 125.00
    Stork in Marsh, cobalt fan 360.00
    Sunflower, Wedgwood 285.00
Cake Stand, Shell and Seaweed, Etruscan, rim repair 660.00
Cake Tray, Napkin, Etruscan, cobalt blue and lavender accents 715.00
Calling Card Tray
    Fox with duck, Continental, rim chips 100.00
    Oak Leaf, Etruscan, rim chips, nicks 165.00
Centerpiece Bowl, Sphinx, George Jones, cobalt blue .. 4,125.00
Clock, Austrian, New Haven Clock works 550.00
Coffeepot, Wild Rose and Trellis, cobalt blue, base, spout, and lid repairs 140.00
Compote
    Double elf, B. Bloch, imp "BB," 13" h, 9" d 1,870.00
    Pinwheel and floral, Samuel Lear, rim nick, hairline 165.00
    Shell and Seaweed, Etruscan, rim repairs 770.00

Creamer
    Birds feeding young, 4" h, minor base chip 200.00
    Blackberry, Holdcroft 150.00
    Pond Lily, Holdcroft, brown ground, minor rim wear 195.00
Shell and Seaweed, Etruscan, rim repairs 175.00
Cuspidor, Shell and Seaweed, Etruscan, professional repaired hairline 550.00
Dessert Dish, napkin strawberry, George Jones, pink, 5-1/2", minor wear 220.00
Epergne, 4 cornucopia vases supported by twigs and vine, George Jones, professional restoration to twigs 2,200.00
Fruit Bowl, Oak Leaf, Etruscan, pink center, rim nick 440.00
Garden Seat, monkey, Minton, pr. 12,075.00
Humidor
    Bulldog, red jacket and pipe, small nicks 440.00
    Shell and Seaweed, Etruscan 1,150.00
Letter Organizer, Art Nouveau style, Continental 1,035.00

Teapot, pink, blue, white, tan, and green seaweed and shell, pink int., 6" h, 10" d, mkd "Etruscan Majolica," $625.

Mustache Cup and Saucer, Shell and Seaweed, Etruscan
....660.00
Oyster Stand, revolving, Minton 8,625.00
Pitcher
   Bird In Hand is Worth Two in the Bush, 7-1/2" h, spout chip
....220.00
   Corn, Shorter & Son, 6-1/2" h...275.00
   Fern, Etruscan, 8" d..325.00
   Shell and Seaweed, Etruscan, 6" h.................................625.00
   Shell and Seaweed, Wardles, coral handle...................900.00
   Wild Rose with butterfly spout, Etruscan, cobalt blue top, 8" h,
      chip to side 110.00
Plate
   Bamboo and butterfly, Fielding, 9" d 145.00
   Banana leaf, pink bow, 8-1/2" d....................................300.00
   Bell Flower, cobalt blue, 8" d...275.00
   Bird and Branch, Eureka, 8" d.......................................175.00
   Deer and Dog, 8" d...165.00
   Geranium, brilliant lavender flowers, 8-1/2" d...............300.00
   Grapes and leaves, angel center, cobalt blue, 9-1/2" d, minor
      rim nicks 165.00
   Merry Christmas and Happy New Year, open wicker border,
      yellow ground, Eureka, 9" d, minor rim nick 275.00
   Morning Glory on napkin, 9" d.......................................135.00
   Pineapple, George Jones, 9" d, small base chip, minor wear
....275.00
   Pinwheel and floral, Samuel Lear, 8" d.........................110.00
   Rabbit, Choisy, 9" d..300.00
   Shell and Seaweed, Etruscan, 9-1/4" d, rim chip on back
....375.00
   Water Lily, George Jones 110.00
Platter
   Fan and floral, Samuel Lear, 14".....................................220.00
   Geranium, Etruscan...350.00
Sardine Box, underplate
   Cobalt blue, acanthus pattern, George Jones 1,100.00
   Turquoise, crab finial, Holdcroft 2,200.00
Spittoon
   Floral, brown...110.00
   Pineapple, Etruscan, rim repair 330.00
   Shell and Seaweed, Etruscan..825.00
   Sunflower, Etruscan, rim repair 550.00
   Wild Rose and Trellis, cobalt blue, hairline 575.00
Spooner, Shell and Seaweed, Etruscan, rim nicks.............250.00
Spoon Warmer, egg shape, Brown-Westhead, Moore & Co
....1,210.00
Syrup, coral, pink..550.00
Teapot
   Cat and Mouse, Minton 13,000.00
   Monkey, Minton 2,400.00
Tea Set
   Beaded Melon, Holdcroft, brown, new spout to teapot, rim re-
      pair to sugar lid, 3 pcs..385.00
   Parrot, Fielding, white ground, turquoise, yellow, gray, and
      red, 3 pcs 385.00
   Shell and Seaweed, Etruscan, teapot, creamer, sugar, spoon-
      er, nicks, glaze flake..935.00
Tray
   Bird and fan, Wardles, 12" l, hairlines............................220.00
   Dragonfly and fan, yellow ground, Eureka, 10" l 330.00
Vase
   4" h, Corn, Etruscan, bud 1,430.00
   10-1/2" h, wicker and twig, triple, George Jones, restoration to
      twig 2,640.00
   13-1/2", cobalt blue, Holdcroft, very minor rim repair......1,430.00
Waste Bowl, Shell and Seaweed, Etruscan.......................650.00

MAPS

History: Maps provide one of the best ways to study the growth of a country or region. From the 16th to the early 20th century, maps were both informative and decorative. Engravers provided ornamental detailing, such as ornate calligraphy and scrolling, especially on bird's-eye views and city maps. Many maps were hand colored to enhance their beauty.

Maps generally were published as plates in books. Many of the maps available today are simply single sheets from cut-apart books.

In the last quarter of the 19th century, representatives from firms in Philadelphia, Chicago, and elsewhere traveled the United States preparing county atlases, often with a sheet for each township and a sheet for each major city or town.

References: *Antique Map Price Record & Handbook for 1996*, available from Spoon River Press (2319C W. Rohmann, Peoria, IL 61604), 1996; Carl Morland and David Bannister, *Antique Maps*, Phaidon Press, 1993; K. A. Sheets, *American Maps 1795-1895*, available from Spoon River Press (2319C W. Rohmann, Peoria, IL 61604), 1995.

Periodical: *Antique Map & Print Quarterly*, P.O. Box 254, Simsbury, CT 06070.

Collectors' Clubs: Assoc. of Map Memorabilia Collectors, 8 Amherst Rd., Pelham, MA 01002; Chicago Map Society, 60 W. Walton St., Chicago, IL 60610.

Museum: Hermon Dunlap Smith Center for the History of Cartography, Newberry Library, Chicago, IL.

Notes: Although mass produced, county atlases are eagerly sought by collectors. Individual sheets sell for $25 to $75. The atlases themselves can usually be purchased in the $200 to $400 range. Individual sheets should be viewed solely as decorative and not as investment material.

"Africa Tertia pars Terrae Septentrio," Heinrich Buenting, Hannover, c1581, double page, wood-engraved, German text on verso, 255 x 335 mm image on 305 x 365 mm sheet....575.00
"Alexandria," Braun and Hogenberg, Amsterdam, c1572, double page, engraved city map, Latin text on verso, hand-colored, wide margins, 365 x 485 mm 575.00
"A Map of North America," Edward Wells, London, 1700, double page, engraved, wide margins, 355 x 480 mm.............635.00
"A Map of the British Empire in America, from the Head of Hudson's Bay to the Southern bounds of Georgia," London, c1750, engraved, folding, hand-colored and in outline, wide margins, 265 x 325 mm 260.00
"A Map of the United States compiled chiefly from The State Maps and other Authentic Information by Samuel Lewis, 1796," Mathew Carey, Philadelphia, 1902, large two sheet, engraved, 645 x 905 mm 1,100.00
"Americae Nova Tabula," Willem Blaeu, Amsterdam, 1633, double page, engraved, wide margins, 365 x 465 mm....2,990.00

Atlas page, Delaware and Maryland, colored, J. H. Colton & Co., NY, 1855, 18-1/2" x 15-1/2", $60.

"An Accurate Map of the West Indies," Emanuel Bowen, London, c1760, double-page, engraved, hand-colored, wide margins, 355 x 425 mm 290.00

"A New and Accurate Map of the World," John Overton, London, 1670, engraved, folding, double-hemispheric, margins trimmed, 390 x 515 mm.............8,625.00

"A New and Accurate Map of the Islands of Newfoundland, Cape Breton, St. John and Anticosta," Emanuel Bowen, London, c1744, engraved, folding, hand-colored, wide margins, 350 x 430 mm 140.00

"A New Chart of the Coast of New England, Nova Scotia, New France or Canada," Jacques Nicholas Bellin, Jeffreys, London, 1746, engraved, folding, hand-colored in outline, no margins, 35 x 465 mm 165.00

"A New Map of America," John Cary, London, 1806, double page, engraved, hand-colored, wide margins, browned along vertical fold, 465 x 525 mm 220.00

"A New Map of Nova Scotia," Thomas Jeffreys, London, 1750, double page, engraved, very wide margins, all edges tissue-backed on verso, 325 x 415 mm 220.00

"A Plan of the Town and Chart of the Harbour of Boston," London, February, 1775, engraved, folding, extracted from 1775 issue of Gentleman's Magazine, 290 x 350 mm 220.00

"Asia," Giovanni Botero, Rome, c1595, small double page, engraved, trimmed margins, 205 x 245 mm 300.00

"Bay of Seven Islands," J. F. Des Barres, London, 1779, double page, engraved, hand-colored, lower margi trimmed, 765 x 545 mm 115.00

"British Dominions in America agreeable to the Treaty of 1763," Thomas Kitchin, Dury, London, 1777, double page, engraved, hand-colored in outline, wide margins, 445 x 540 mm 6,440.00

"Canada et Louisiane," George Louis Le Rouge, Paris, 1755, double page, engraved, wide margins, hand-colored in outlined, 625 x 510 mm 375.00

"Carte de l'Amerique Septentrionale depuis le 28 Degre de Latitude jusqu'au 72," Jacques Nicholas Bellin, Paris, 1755, double page, engraved, wide margins, 585 x 910 mm....2,300.00

"Chart of the Antarctic Polar Circle," Philippe Buache, London, 1763, engraved, folding, hand-colored, margins trimmed, 200 x 230 mm 200.00

"Cruchley's New Plan of London," George Frederick Cruchley, London, 1836, engraved, 30 section map, hand-colored, linen backed, orig board cover with publisher's label, 460 x 855 mm overall 175.00

"Custer's Battle-Field," Charles Becker, c1877, folding, lithographed, 420 x 475 mm 220.00

"Eastern Hemisphere, Western Hemisphere," Anthony Finley, Philadelphia, 1826, from Finley's New General Atlas, engraved, hand-colored, wide margins, 315 x 250 mm, pr 60.00

Globe, 6" terrestrial globe, 11" h ebonized stand, Strand Publications, c1920 ....635.00

"Haemisphaerium Stellatum Astrale Antiquum," Andres Cellarius, Amsterdam, 1660, double page, engraved celestial map, hand-colored, wide margins, clear tear at vertical fold at lower margin just extending into image, 440 x 515 mm 2,530.00

"Jamaica," John Thomson, Edinburgh, 1817, double page, engraved, two insets showing harbors of Bluefields and Kingston, wide margins, hand-colored in outline, 440 x 630 mm 320.00

"Map of Oregon and Upper California," John Charles Fremont, Washington, 1848, folding, lithographed, hand-colored in outline, overall browning, 905 x 755 mm..........2,185.00

"Map of the United States and Territories," Washington, 1866, litho, folding, hand-colored in outline, some minor loss at folds, linen backed, 775 x 1450 mm 550.00

"Marshfield, Massachusetts," litho on paper, John Ford Jr., Survenor, [sic] framed, 30" x 21-1/2" 345.00

"Nouveau Plan de Moscou," G. L. De Lavaur, Auguste Semen, Moscow, c1850, folding, lithographed, hand-colored, early pencil notes, wide margins, 17 Moscow districts, text in French and Cyrillic, linen backed, 560 x 645 mm.........345.00

"Ohio," A J. Johnson, New York, with view of capitol building in corner, from New Illustrated Family Atlas of the World 1864," printed, hand colored, matted, unframed, 23" h, 29" w 75.00

"Plan de la Ville et Rade de Cartagene et du Fort de St. Lazare," Jacques Bureau, April 1701, manuscript map with coloring, sgd "Par Jacques Bureau" in cartouche, cleanly torn in half by vertical tear, 530 x 740 mm sheet size 1,380.00

"Plan de Longuvy," Guerin Cadet, Longuvy, 1686, manuscript map, detailed pen and ink drawing on left portion of map, 420 x 555 mm 345.00

"The Provinces of New York and New Jersey with part of Pensilvania," Thomas Pownall, London, 1776, engraved, 3-sheet map joined, hand-colored and in outline, some browning, bottom margin trimmed, 1355 x 540 mm..........1,610.00

"The State of Ohio," Thomas Cowperthwalt and Company, Philadelphia, 1850, printed, hand colored, matted, unframed, 22" h, 19" w 55.00

"United States of America," W. and D. Lizars, London, c1810, engraved, folding, hand-colored, margins trimmed, several folds closed at lower edge with archival tape, 395 x460 mm 260.00

"West Indies, With Part of Guatemala," David Burr, Colton, NY, 1834, engraved, folding, hand-colored in outline, folds into orig small 12mo roan case, 480 x 575 mm 690.00

MARBLEHEAD POTTERY

History: This hand-thrown pottery was first made in 1905 as part of a therapeutic program introduced by Dr. J. Hall for the patients confined to a sanitarium located in Marblehead, Massachusetts. In 1916, production was removed from the hospital to another site. The factory continued under the directorship of Arthur E. Baggs until it closed in 1936.

Most pieces found today are glazed with a smooth, porous, even finish in a single color. The most desirable pieces have a conventional design in one or more subordinate colors.

Reference: David Rago, *American Art Pottery,* Knickerbocker Press, 1997.

Bulb Bowl, 6" d, slate gray glaze, c1915............................160.00
Centerpiece Bowl, 3-3/4" h, 8-1/4" d, flaring, incised lotus leaf design on ext., dark blue matte glaze, imp sip mark 425.00
Chamberstick, 4" h, 4-1/2" d, bright yellow mate glaze, imp ship mark..275.00
Humidor, 5" h, 4-1/4" d, lightly modeled stylized dark blue flora, speckled sandy ground, rare large paper label, Arthur Baggs, mkd "AEB and MHC/$5.00"..4,100.00
Tile, 6" sq, stylized dark green trees, olive green ground, matte speckled glaze, imp ship mark and paper label........2,000.00
Tile Frieze, two 7-1/2" sq tiles, incised lake scene, matte yellow, browns, and greens, imp mark, paper label, orig price tag on each, orig frame retaining sticker marked "o. 2-64 tiles Poplars with Reflections, Dec by A. E. Baggs, Price $10.00," minor edge nicks, kiln pops, from estate of Dr. Hall, founder of Marblehead Pottery 21,850.00
Trivet
  6" sq, stylized flowers, matte blue, green, yellow, and red, imp mark, paper label, remnant of price label, from estate of Dr. Hall, founder of Marblehead Pottery........................865.00
  6-1/4" sq, red, blue, yellow, green, and orange floral basket, black ground, imp mark, paper label 435.00
Vase
  3-1/2" h, 3" d, cabinet, incised dark green and red berries and leaves, speckled green matte ground, imp ship mark
....1,500.00
  3-1/2" h, 3-1/4" d, circular, tapering outward to base, dripping irid red striations on creamy white/red high glaze ground, imp mark, two paper labels, remnant of orig price tag
....3,450.00
  4-1/4" h, 3-1/4" d, flaring bud, violet speckled matted glass, imp ship mark 250.00
  4-1/2" h, 2-1/2" d, tapering bud vase, incised vertical design, dark blue speckled matte glaze, imp ship mark......425.00
  5" x 3", bulbous, incised stylized leaf design, green, yellow, and blue speckled matte glaze, artist cipher for Arthur Baggs 6,500.00
  5-1/4" h, 3-1/4" d, ovoid, incised design of stylized thistles, matte mauve glaze, incised ship mark..................1,100.00
  5-1/4" h, 4-1/4" d, cylindrical, rolled rim, soft yellow matte glaze, imp ship mark 400.00
  5-1/2" h, 3-1/2" d, ovoid, incised dark green trefoil design, green speckled matte ground, incised ship mark
....2,500.00
  6" h, 5-1/4" d, stylized deep green with red highlights foliate incised design, speckled matte green ground, sgd "H.T." for Hanna Tutt, imp "M.P.," from estate of Dr. Hall, founder of Marblehead Pottery 10,925.00
  6-1/4" h, 4-1/4" d, geometric, lightly tooled, stylized light brown trees, matte speckled sand-colored ground, imp ship mark..4,750.00
  6-1/4" h, 8" d, fan shape, matte blue glaze, imp mark, paper label..320.00
  6-1/2" h, 5-1/2" d, stylized light blue foliate design, dark matte blue ground, imp mark, remnant of orig price tag, from estate of Dr. Hall, founder of Marblehead Pottery 8,050.00
  6-1/2" h, 6" d, incised stylized light brown tree designs on three sides, creamy white ground, imp mark, initials "A.E.B.," two Marblehead Pottery labels, from estate of Dr. Hall, founder of Marblehead Pottery 2,300.00
  7-1/4" h, 4-1/4" d, organic dark brown flowers on tall stems, matte speckled green ground, imp ship mark and "H. T." (Hannah Tutt)..4,000.00
  9" h, 4" d, matte blue glaze, imp mark............................825.00
  13-1/2" h, 5-1/4" d, cylindrical, stylized trees, matte blue glaze over gray-green matte ground, incised ship mark
....12,500.00
Wall Pocket
  5" h, 4" w, blue matte glaze, imp mark 230.00
  8" h, 4" w, fluted rim, matte blue glaze, imp mark 290.00

MARY GREGORY TYPE GLASS

History: The use of enameled decoration on glass, an inexpensive way to imitate cameo glass, developed in Bohemia in the late 19th century. The Boston and Sandwich Glass Co. copied this process in the late 1880s.

Mary Gregory (1856-1908) was employed for two years at the Boston and Sandwich Glass factory when the enameled decorated glass was being manufactured. Some collectors argue that Gregory was inspired to paint her white enamel figures on glass by the work of Kate Greenaway and a desire to imitate pate-sur-pate. However, evidence for these assertions is very weak. Further, it has never been proven that Mary Gregory even decorated glass as part of her job at Sandwich. The result is that "Mary Gregory type" is a better term to describe this glass.

Reference: R. and D. Truitt, *Mary Gregory Glassware,* published by authors, 1992.

Museum: Sandwich Glass Museum, Sandwich, MA.

REPRODUCTION ALERT

Collectors should recognize that most examples of Mary Gregory type glass seen today are either European or modern reproductions.

Barber Bottle, 7-1/8" h, deep sapphire blue, white enameled youngster playing tennis, cylindrical bulbous form, long neck, tooled mouth, pontil scar 150.00
Box, cov
  3-3/4" l, 2-1/4" deep, 3" h, oval, white enameled boy with bunch of flowers in hand, deep amethyst ground, metal fittings, orig key missing..375.00
  6-1/2" d, 6-1/2" h, round, ebony color, white enameled young boy offering nosegay to young girl sitting on bench beneath

Vase, blue, imp mark, 5-1/2" h, 6" d, $185.

Vase, dark blue, white enameled girl, other with boy, broken pontils, ruffled tops, 10-1/4" h, sold as matched pr, $475. Photo courtesy of Gene Harris Antique Auction Center.

overhanging tree, white enamel garland around perimeter, gold colored metal fittings and scrolled legs 1,085.00
Cruet, 8-1/2" h, sapphire blue, sq dimpled sides, white enameled two girls facing each other, blue handle, orig stopper.. 495.00
Dresser Set, pr 10-1/2" h perfume bottles, 7" cov dresser jar, deep cobalt blue, enameled young children and angels, sprays of flowers, crown tops...895.00
Jewel Box, 3" x 3-1/2", cranberry, hinged lid......................420.00
Milk Pitcher, 6" h, cranberry ground, white enameled girl, clear applied handle..50.00
Miniature, pitcher, 1-3/4" h, cranberry ground, white enameled little girl blowing bubbles, clear glass handle with gold highlights 200.00
Mug, 4-1/2" h, amber, ribbed, white enameled girl praying.65.00
Paperweight, 2-1/2" w, 4" l, deep black ground, white enameled young boy and girl in garden setting 295.00
Patch Box, emerald green..295.00
Pitcher, 7-1/2" x 9-1/2", medium green, white enameled boy with bird and trees, girl with bowl and brush dec, pr 275.00
Plate, 6-1/4" d, cobalt blue, white enameled girl with butterfly net 125.00
Salt Shaker, 5" h, blue, paneled, white enameled girl in garden, brass top...190.00
Tumbler, 1-3/4" d, 2-1/2" h, cranberry, white enameled boy on one, girl on other, facing pr 100.00
Vase
   2-1/2" h, 1-1/2" w, cobalt blue ground, white enameled figure of young man standing among foliage, gold trim.....325.00
   4" h, cranberry ground, white enameled boy and wagon 95.00
   4-1/2" h, cranberry ground, 3 ftd, white enameled girl and boy 110.00
   5-1/2" h, cranberry, white enameled girl......................100.00

6-3/4" h, 3" d, pale amber, young girl in forest scene, reverse with spray of flowers and leaves, neck and shoulder with dec band 225.00
7" h, 2-1/2" w, bud, amber, white spatter background, young boy and girl among foliage, facing pr 550.00
8" h, ring, sapphire blue, young boy dec 195.00
8-1/4" h, 3-1/2" d, amber, ruffled top, white enameled young girl 185.00
10-1/2" h, 5" w, cranberry, white enamel of young girl holding a flower, paneled int. 295.00
10-5/8" h, 4" d, cylinder shape, lime green, white enameled young girl carrying butterfly net...............................185.00

MATCH HOLDERS

History: The friction match achieved popularity after 1850. The early matches were packaged and sold in sliding cardboard boxes. To facilitate storage and to eliminate the clumsiness of using the box, match holders were developed.

The first match holders were cast iron or tin, the latter often displaying advertisements. A patent for a wall-hanging match holder was issued in 1849. By 1880, match holders also were being made from glass and china. Match holders began to lose their popularity in the late 1930s with the advent of gas and electric heat and ranges.

Reference: Denis B. Alsford, *Match Holders*, Schiffer Publishing, 1994.

Old Judson, J. C. Stevens, Kansas City, MO, litho tin, farmer and wife, Savage Mfg. Co., Brooklyn, NY, 3-3/8" x 4-7/8", $70.

Advertising
  New Process Gas Range, hanging, tin, gray stove, red
    ground 65.00
  Sharples Separator Co., tin, mother and daughter, farm
    scene 85.00
Bisque, 4" h, 3-5/8" d, natural colored rooster with beige basket,
  two compartments, round base with pink band 135.00
Brass
  2" x 2-1/2", copper colored, hinged lid, Reading PA Fire Hall
    cello insert in lid, early 1900s 45.00
  3" h, bear chained to post, cast, orig gilt trim................225.00
Bronze, 3" h, shoe, mouse in toe..125.00
Cast Iron, figural
  Bird 45.00
  High Button Shoe, 5-1/2" h, black paint, c1890...............50.00
Glass, 3" h, 3-1/4" d, shaded rose to pink overlay satin, ball-
  shape, glossy off-white lining, ground pontil.................155.00
Majolica
  Bull dog, striker, large 440.00
  Dog, striker, Continental, rim chips and repair..............165.00
  Happy Hooligan with suitcase, striker, rim nick to hat ..110.00
  Monk, striker, hairline in base..140.00
Papier-Mâché, 2-3/4" h, black lacquer, Oriental dec.........25.00
Porcelain, seated girl, feeding dog on table, sgd "Elbogen"
  ....125.00
Sterling Silver, 1-3/4" x 2-1/2", hinged lid, diecut striking area, ci-
  gar cutter on one corner, lid inscription "H. R." and diamond,
  inside lid inscribed "Made for Tiffany & Co./Pat 12, 09/Ster-
  ling"...95.00
Tin, 2-3/8" h, top hat, hinged lid, orig green paint, black band
  ....65.00
Torquay Pottery, 2" h, 3-1/8" d, ship scene, reads "A match for any
  Man, Shankin"..65.00

MATCH SAFES

History: Match safes are small containers used to safely
carry matches in one's pocket. They were first used in the
1850s. Match safes are often figural with a hinged lid and
striking surface.

Reference: W. Eugene Sanders Jr., and Christine C.
Sanders, *Pocket Matchsafes, Reflections of Life & Art,
1840-1920,* Schiffer Publishing, 1997; Audrey G. Sullivan,
History of Match Safes in the United States, published by
author, 1978.

REPRODUCTION ALERT

  Reproduction, copycat, and fantasy sterling silver match
safes include:
  Art Nouveau style nude with veil, rectangular case with
  C-scroll edges
  Boot, figural
  Embracing wood nymphs
  Jack Daniels, 1970s fantasy item
  Mermaid, with upper torso out of water, combing her hair
  Owl and Moon
  Many of these match safes are only marked "Sterling."
Any match safe so marked requires careful inspection. Peri-
od American match safes generally are marked with the
name of the manufacturer and/or a patent date. Period En-
glish match safes have the proper hallmarks. Beware of En-
glish reproduction match safes bearing the "DAB" marking.

Note: While not all match safes have a striking surface,
this is one test, besides size, to distinguish a match safe
from a calling card case.

Scallop Shell, brass, 2" l, $135.

Advertising
  Davenport Cigars, 3/4" x 1-1/2" x 2-1/4", tin, cigar, wrap-
    around, red, white, and blue cello..............................60.00
  National Supply Co., Boston, silvered brass, wrap-around cel-
    lo, horse head illus, black and white design and text, early
    1900 ....60.00
  United Hatters Union, 1-1/2" x 2-3/4", silvered brass, black and
    white cello insert panels, union text, 1900-01 ....90.00
  Vacuum Oil Co., Rochester, NY, 1-3/8" x 2-1/4", silvered brass,
    lighthouse with beam and floating barrel of marine oil on
    one side 65.00
Brass
  Billiken, watch chain loop, 1908 ....275.00
  Dragon, Chinese...185.00
  Metamorphic, skull changes to rooster 285.00
  Milk Pail..175.00
  Walnut..200.00
Copper and Brass, figural, baby in shirt 160.00
German Silver, 1-3/8" x 1-5/8", Art Nouveau stylized flowers, loop
  ....80.00
Gun Metal, 3 miniature rose diamond horseshoes, 27 diamonds,
  sapphire, gold button 345.00
Lapis Lazuli, 2-5/8" x 7/8", cylindrical, hinged top, brass
  accents 360.00
Nickel Plated, figural, shoe...125.00
Pewter, figural, pig, silvered..175.00
Silver Plated, playing card dec, King of Hearts, 2 score keeping
  dials, mkd "Gorham" 220.00

McCOY POTTERY

History: The J. W. Mc-
Coy Pottery Co. was es-
tablished in Roseville,
Ohio, in September 1899.
The early McCoy company produced both stoneware
and some art pottery lines, including Rosewood. In Octo-
ber 1911, three potteries merged creating the Brush-Mc-
Coy Pottery Co. This firm continued to produce the
original McCoy lines and added several new art lines.
Much of the early pottery is not marked.

In 1910, Nelson McCoy and his father, J. W. McCoy, founded the Nelson McCoy Sanitary Stoneware Co. In 1925, the McCoy family sold their interest in the Brush-McCoy Pottery Co. and started to expand and improve the Nelson McCoy Co. The new company produced stoneware, earthenware specialties, and artware.

Marks: Most of the pottery marked "McCoy" was made by the Nelson McCoy Co.

References: Susan and Al Bagdade, *Warman's American Pottery and Porcelain*, Wallace-Homestead, 1994; Bob Hanson, Craig Nissen and Margaret Hanson, *McCoy Pottery, Collector's Reference*, Collector Books, 1996; Sharon and Bob Huxford, *Collector's Encyclopedia of Brush-McCoy Pottery*, Collector Books, 1996; ——, *Collectors Encyclopedia of McCoy Pottery*, Collector Books, 1980, 1997 value update; Martha and Steve Sanford, *Sanfords' Guide to Brush-McCoy Pottery*, Book 2, Adelmore Press (230 Harrison Ave., Campbell, CA 95008), 1996; --, *Sanfords Guide to McCoy Pottery*, Adelmore Press, 1997.

REPRODUCTION ALERT

Unfortunately, Nelson McCoy never registered his McCoy trademark, a fact discovered by Roger Jensen of Tennessee. As a result, Jensen began using the McCoy mark on a series of ceramic reproductions made in the early 1990s. While the marks on these recently made pieces copy the original, Jensen made objects which were never produced by the Nelson McCoy Co. The best known example is the Red Riding Hood cookie jar which was originally designed by Hull and also made by Regal China.

The McCoy fakes are a perfect example of how a mark on a piece can be deceptive. A mark alone is not proof that a piece is period or old. Knowing the proper marks and what was and was not made in respect to forms, shapes, and decorative motifs is critical in authenticating a pattern.

Additional Listings: See *Warman's Americana & Collectibles* for more examples.

Basket, Rustic, pine cone dec, 1945...................................35.00
Bird Bath, 6"..38.00
Bowl
    Bird 35.00
    El Rancho Sombero, orig box.......................................335.00
    Mt. Pelee, lava type, charcoal irid, 1902 ....350.00
Canister, Stonecraft, pink and blue bands, cov
    Large 45.00
    Medium...30.00
    Small 25.00
Clock, tambour, vaseline..450.00
Cookie Jar, cov
    Apple Basket 50.00
    Clown..60.00
    Strawberry 45.00
    Wish I Had A Cookie..40.00
Creamer and Sugar, Daisy, brown and green 25.00
Hurricane Lamp, Stonecraft, candle type, ...22.00
Iced Tea Server, El Rancho, orig box.................................200.00
Jardiniere
    4" h, Blossomtime 35.00
    9" h, Rosewood, brown glaze, orange streaks.................70.00
Lamp, Arcanture, bird and foliage dec 290.00

Pitcher, pale tinted green leaves and grapes, cream ground, 9" h, $45.

Mixing Bowl, 12" d, Stonecraft, pink and blue bands...........55.00
Planter
    Flying Duck...170.00
    Hand, ivory 40.00
    Shoe..25.00
    Turtle...40.00
Spittoon, 4-1/2" d, pansies, mkd "Loy-Nel Art"..................100.00
Tankard, corn, mkd "J. W. McCoy" 90.00
Teapot, cov, Stonecraft 40.00
Tea Set, English Ivory pattern, vine handles, 3 pcs 75.00
Vase
    8" h, double tulip..75.00
    8" h, pink..35.00
    9" h, white crackle, band of emb diamonds.....................45.00
    Blossom Lite 45.00
Wall Pocket, lily..75.00

McKEE GLASS

History: The McKee Glass Co. was established in 1843 in Pittsburgh, Pennsylvania. In 1852, it opened a factory to produce pattern glass. In 1888, the factory was relocated to Jeannette, Pennsylvania, and began to produce many types of glass kitchenwares, including several patterns of Depression glass. The factory continued until 1951 when it was sold to the Thatcher Manufacturing Co.

McKee named its colors Chalaine Blue, Custard, Seville Yellow, and Skokie Green. McKee glass may also be found with painted patterns, e.g., dots and ships. A few items were decaled. Many of the canisters and shakers were lettered in black to show the purpose for which they were intended.

Salt and Pepper Shakers, pr, black, Roman Arch sides, range size, 4-1/4" h, $40.

References: Gene Florence, *Kitchen Glassware of the Depression Years*, 6th ed., Collector Books, 1995; ——, *Very Rare Glassware of the Depression Years*, 3rd Series, (1993, 1995 value update), 4th Series (1995), Collector Books.

Additional Listings: See *Warman's Americana & Collectibles* for more examples.

Animal Dish, cov, dove, round base, beaded rim, vaseline, sgd 365.00
Berry Set, Hobnail with Fan pattern, blue, master berry and 8 sauce dishes 170.00
Bowl
  5" d, 4-1/2" h, Skokie Green..8.75
  6-1/2" d, Skokie Green..16.00
Butter Dish, cov, Wiltec pattern, Pre-Cut Ware, frosted.......70.00
Candlesticks, pr, 9" h, Rock Crystal 165.00
Cereal Canister, cov, Skokie Green, 48 oz., round..............35.00
Cheese and Cracker Set, Rock Crystal, red 170.00
Coffee Canister, cov, Skokie Green, 24 oz., faded..............30.00
Egg Beater Bowl, spout, Skokie Green 32.00
Egg Cup, Custard...8.00
Lamp, nude, green..175.00
Measuring Cup, Skokie Green, nested set, 4 pc 125.00
Pitcher, 8" h, Wild Rose and Bowknot, frosted, gilt dec.......65.00
Punch Bowl Set, bowl, 12 mugs, Tom and Jerry, red scroll dec 65.00
Reamer, pointed top, Skokie Green 45.00
Refrigerator Dish, cov, Skokie Green, 4" x 5" 12.00
Ring Box, cov, Seville Yellow..20.00
Salt and Pepper Shakers, pr, Skokie Green, 2-1/4", sq........14.00
Server, center handle, Rock Crystal, red 140.00
Tumbler, Bottoms Up, Skokie Green, orig coaster.............170.00
Vase, 8-1/2" h, nude, Chalaine 175.00
Water Cooler, 21" h, spigot, vaseline, 2 pcs.......................325.00

MEDICAL AND PHARMACEUTICAL ITEMS

History: Modern medicine and medical instruments are well documented. Some instruments are virtually unchanged since their invention; others have changed drastically.

The concept of sterilization phased out decorative handles. Handles on early instruments, which were of-ten carved, were made of materials such as mother-of-pearl, ebony, and ivory. Today's sleek instruments are not as desirable to collectors.

Pharmaceutical items include those things commonly found in a drugstore and used to store or prepare medications.

References: A. Walker Bingham, *Snake-Oil Syndrome: Patent Medicine Advertising*, Christopher Publishing House, 1994; Douglas Congdon-Martin, *Drugstore and Soda Fountain Antiques*, Schiffer Publishing, 1991; Patricia McDaniel, *Drugstore Collectibles*, Wallace-Homestead, 1994; J. William Rosenthal, *Spectacles and Other Vision Aids*, Norman Publishing (720 Market St., 3rd Fl., San Francisco, CA 94102), 1996; Keith Wilbur, *Antique Medical Instruments*: Revised Price Guide Schiffer Publishing, 1987, 1993 value update.

Periodical: *Scientific, Medical & Mechanical Antiques*, 11824 Taneytown Pike, Taneytown, MD 21787.

Collectors' Clubs: Maryland Microscopical Society, 8621 Polk St., McLean, VA 22102; Medical Collectors Assoc., 1685A Eastchester Rd., Bronx, NY 10461.

Museums: Dittrick Museum of Medical History, Cleveland, OH; International Museum of Surgical Science & Hall of Fame, Chicago, IL; National Museum of Health & Medicine, Walter Reed Medical Center, Washington, DC; National Museum of History and Technology, Smithsonian Institution, Washington, DC; Schmidt Apothecary Shop, New England Fire & History Museum, Brewster, MA; Waring Historical Library, Medical University of South Carolina, Charleston, SC.

Amputation Saw, bow blade, ebony handle......................125.00
Apothecary Chest
  6" x 11-3/4" x 21-1/4" l, poplar, gray repaint, 6 drawers, pulls replaced 495.00
  27" w, 12-1/2" d, 32" h, refinished pine and poplar, 24 drawers, wire nail construction, backboards replaced...........550.00
Apothecary Jar, 13-1/4" h, colorless, blown, ground lid.....140.00
Apothecary Shelf, hanging, 50" w, 6-1/4" d, 7-1/2" h, 24 drawers, gray repaint over worn softwood, pressed wood moldings, wire nail construction, edge damage, porcelain knobs..........440.00

Alcohol Burner, brass, sterilizer, 2-1/2", $40.

Jug, "J. L. Moffit/Druggist/Holyoke, Mass," pottery, tall ovoid form, brown and tan glaze, 1860-90, 8-1/2" h, $100. Photo courtesy of Norman C. Heckler & Company.

Book
  Achilles, Rose, MD, *Carbonic Acid in Medicine,* Funk & Wagnalls, 1905, 1st ed., illus 18.00
  Mould Guide For Trubyte New Hue Teeth, The Dentist's Supply Co. of NY, 1920s....................................125.00
  The Physician Hand Book, 1879, leather bound 500.00
Box, 10-1/2" x 11" x 8-1/2", wood, black paint, stenciled "Dr. Greene's Nervura Nerve Tonic"......................................65.00
Capsule Filler, 8" x 16", Sharp and Dohme, chrome, orig wood box and instruction book, 1920-30...............................150.00
Catalog
  Illinois Surgical Supply, Chicago, IL, 1940, 12 pgs, 3-3/4" x 7-1/4", Birth Control Means Freedom, Health & Happiness 20.00
  Ritter Dental Mfg. Co., Rochester, NY, 1919, 112 pgs, 6" x 9", dental equipment...55.00
Condom Tin
  Altex Air Tested Prophylactics, Western Rubber Co, Canada, red and white tin, 1-5/8" x 2-1/8".............................600.00
  Le Transparent Trojan, Eiffel Tower illus, Youngs Rubber Co., 1-3/4" x 2-1/2"..150.00
Counter Display, diecut, cardboard, easel back
  13" h, 5-1/2" w, Kolynos Dental Cream, yellow and green clown outfits, male and female faces, pr 600.00
  19" x 43", Kolynos Dental Cream, folding, window type, baby reaching for tubes of product....................................110.00
  40" h, 19" w, Caldwell's, Syrup Pepsin, "How Are You?" male and female, pr 700.00
Display Case
  Ashton & Parsons Homeopathic Medicines, cherry colored hardwood, curved glass front, reverse etched glass lettering and design on front glass panel, 33" h, 20" w, 13" d 1,200.00
  Dr. Frost's Homeopathic Remedies Build Health, wood, stained, litho tin door panel, lists 38 aliment remedies, 19" h 450.00
  Dr. M. A. Simmons Liver Medicine, wood, stained, imp letter in panels, 30-1/2" h..625.00
  Dr. Morse's Indian Root Pills, 5 diecut cardboard pieces with Indian village, largest pc 27" x 41" 600.00
Dose Glass, clear, Royal Pepsi Stomach Bitters, 1900-10...40.00
Eyelid Retractor, ivory handle, mkd "Hills King St.," c1853.....125.00
Forceps, dental, extracting, SP, handle design, F. Arnold...50.00

Jar, cov, glass, clear, label under glass
  Dr. Kings New Light Pills 325.00
  Dr. Mills Anti Pain Pills Cures Headaches 375.00
Magazine, *The Dental Cosmos,* S. S. White Dental Mfg., Philadelphia, PA, 1904, 164 pgs, 6-3/4" x 9-1/2"........................50.00
Manual, Johnson's First Aid Manual, ed. By Fred B. Kilmer, Johnson & Johnson, NJ, 1918, 8th ed., 8vo, 139 pgs.....22.00
Mortar and Pestle, 9" h, ash burl, turned 130.00
Ophthalmoscope, cased, Morton.....................................120.00
Pill Maker, 12" l, bras, iron and wood, c1900 ....140.00
Scale, chemist's, brass and steel, oak box with drawers, glazed to and sides, Becker's Sons, Rotterdam, c1920 ....225.00
Scalpel, ebony, c1860, 3 pc set......................................400.00
Sign
  Dr. Pierce's Golden Medical Discovery, paper, Indians mixing roots, herbs, and bark for "Dr. Pierce's Golden medical Discovery for the Blood," matted and framed, 38" x 25" 700.00
  Grocery, reverse painted on glass, "Dr. A. C. Daniels Medicines Company," one reverse with bull dog, other reserve with galloping horse, 24" x 9-1/2" 1,150.00
  Hill Liver, frosted glass, lady examining tongue in mirror, "Look At Your Tongue, If Coated You Need Hills Liver Tablets," framed, 9-1/2" x 11-3/4" 150.00
Stethoscope, monaural, metal..120.00
Surgeon's Kit, 17-3/4" w, 9-3/4" d, 3" h orig case, including saws, clamps, needles, etc., 19th C, imperfections.............1,150.00
Tin
  Dr. Scholl's Foot Powder 30.00
  Taylor's Blue Bird Talc sample size, multicolored, 2-1/8" x 1-1/4"...600.00

MEDICINE BOTTLES

History: The local apothecary and his book of formulas played a major role in early America. In 1796, the first patent for a medicine was issued by the U.S. Patent Office. At that time, anyone could apply for a medicinal patent; as long as the dosage was not poisonous, the patent was granted.

Patent medicines were advertised in newspapers and magazines and sold through the general store and at "medicine" shows. In 1907, the Pure Food and Drug Act, requiring an accurate description of contents on a medicine container's label, put an end to the patent medicine industry. Not all medicines were patented.

Most medicines were sold in distinctive bottles, often with the name of the medicine and location of manufacture in relief. Many early bottles were made in the glass-manufacturing area of southern New Jersey. Later, companies in western Pennsylvania and Ohio manufactured bottles.

References: Joseph K. Baldwin, *Collector's Guide to Patent and Proprietary Medicine Bottles of the Nineteenth Century*, Thomas Nelson, 1973; Ralph and Terry Kovel, *Kovels' Bottles Price List*, 10th ed., Crown Publishers, 1996; John Odell, *Digger Odell's Official Antique Bottle and Glass Collector Magazine Price Guide Series*, Vol. 5, published by author (1910 Shawhan Rd., Morrow, OH 45152), 1995.

Periodical: Antique Bottle and Glass Collector, P.O. Box 187, East Greenville, PA 18041.

Collectors' Club: Federation of Historical Bottle Collectors, Inc., 88 Sweetbriar Branch, Longwood, FL 32750.

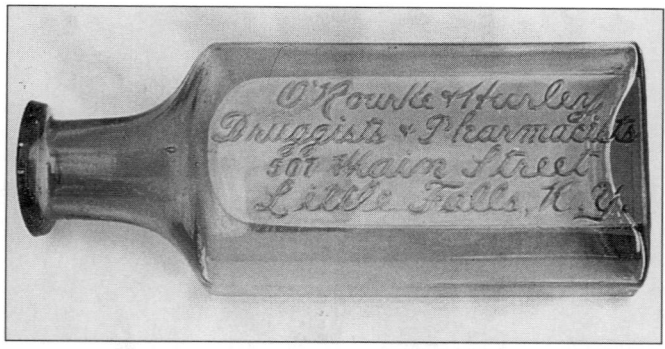

T. H. Taylor, Brattleboro, V.T., rect, beveled corners, indented panels, aquamarine, applied sq collared mouth, tubular pontil scar, 1840-60, 8-1/8" h, $190. Photo courtesy of Norman C. Heckler & Company.

A. B. L. Myers, AM Rock Rose, New Haven, America, 1845-60, rect, beveled corners, indented panels, brilliant rich blue, applied heavy collared mouth, iron pontil mark, 9-3/8" h, some int. stain near base, open shallow burst bubble 1,100.00

American Expectorant, America, 1840-60, octagonal, greenish aquamarine, outward rolled mouth, pontil scar, 5-7/8" h 425.00

Arthurs Renovating Syrup, A. A., American, 1845-60, sq, narrow beveled corners, medium blue green, applied sloping collared mouth, iron pontil mark, 9" h.................................950.00

Booth & Sedgwick's London Cordial Gin, American, 1845-60, sq, beveled corners, deep blue green, applied sloping collared mouth with ring, iron pontil mark, 9-3/4" h 375.00

Brants Indian Balsam, America, 1840-60, octagonal, aquamarine, applied sloping collared mouth, pontil scar, 6-3/4" h 150.00

C. Hemistreet & Co, Troy, N.Y., America, 1840-60, octagonal, medium to deep sapphire blue, applied double collared mouth, pontil scar, 6-3/4" h, minor ext. haze 180.00

Davis & Miller Druggist, Baltimore, attributed to Baltimore Glass Works, Baltimore, MD, 1845-60, cylindrical, brilliant sapphire blue, applied sq collared mouth, iron pontil, mark, 3" d, 7-1/2" h.. 1,800.00

Dr. Bowman's Indian Ointment, America, 1840-60, octagonal, aquamarine, applied sloping collared mouth, pontil scar, 6" h 275.00

Dr. Seymour's Balsam of Wild Cherry & Comfrey, America, 1840-60, octagonal, aquamarine, applied sloping collared mouth, pontil scar, 6-1/2" h 475.00

E. A. Buckhout's Dutch Liniment, Prepared At Mechanicsville, Saratoga Co NY, rect, beveled corners, figure of standing Dutch man, tooled mouth, pontil scar, 4-5/8" h.......................400.00

From The Laboratory of G. W. Merchant, Chemist, Lockport, N. Y., attributed to Lockport Glass Works, Lockport, NY, 1840-60, rect, chamfered corners, deep yellowish green, applied sloping collard mouth, tubular pontil scar, 5-1/2" h..............500.00

Hunt's Liniment Prepared By G. E. Stanton, Sing Sing, N.Y., rect, wide beveled corners, bright yellow green, inward rolled mouth, pontil scar, 4-1/2" h...2,000.00

Iceland Balsam For Pulmonary Consumption, Iceland Balsam, America, 1830-50, rect, beveled corners, emb on 3 sides, yellow olive, short applied sloping collared mouth, pontil scar, 6-1/2" h, professionally cleaned, light emb lettering......5,500.00

I. Newport's Panacea Purifier Of The Blood Norwich, VT, attributed to Stoddard Glasshouse, Stoddard, NH, 1846-60, cylindrical, indented emb panels, yellow olive, applied sloping collared mouth with ring, iron pontil ring, 7-3/8 h, shall chip on sloping collar 1,900.00

J. L. Leavitt, Boston, attributed to Stoddard Glasshouse, Stoddard, NH, 1846-60, cylindrical, yellow olive, applied sloping collard mouth with ring, iron pontil mark, 8-1/8" h 275.00

L. P. Dodge Rheumatic Liniment Newburg, America, 1840-60, rect, beveled corners, light golden amber, applied sloping collared mouth, pontil scar, 6" h, appears to have been cleaned...750.00

Smith's Green Mountain Renovator, attributed to Stoddard Glasshouse, Stoddard, NH, 1846-1850, rect, wide beveled corners, yellow olive amber, applied double collared mouth, iron pontil mark, 6-3/4" h..1,300.00

Swaim's Panacea Philada, America, 1840-60, cylindrical, indented panels, bright grayish green, applied sloping collared mouth with ring, pontil scar, 7-1/2" h, minor ext.wear....400.00

Thorn's Hop & Burdock Tonic, yellow, 6-3/8" h 40.00
Turner's Balsam, eight sided, aqua, 4-7/8" h 65.00
Vaughn's Vegetable Lithontriptic Mixture, aqua, 8" h.........125.00
Web's Carthartic A No. 1 Tonic, amber, 9-1/2" h..................60.00

MERCURY GLASS

History: Mercury glass is a light-bodied, double-walled glass that was "silvered" by applying a solution of silver nitrate to the inside of the object through a hole in its base.

F. Hale Thomas of London patented the method in 1849. In 1855 the New England Glass Co. filed a patent for the same type of process. Other American glassmakers soon followed. The glass reached the height of its popularity in the early 20th century.

Bowl, 4-3/4" d, gold, enameled floral dec 50.00
Cake Stand, 8" d, pedestal base, emb floral dec.................80.00
Candlestick, 10-1/2" h...110.00
Cologne Bottle, 4-1/4" x 71/2", bulbous, flashed amber panel, cut neck, etched grapes and leaves, corked metal stopper, c1840..160.00
Creamer, 6-1/2"h, etched ferns, applied clear handle, attributed to Sandwich 140.00
Curtain Tieback, 2-5/8" d, pewter fitting, starflower dec 65.00
Goblet, 5" d, gold, white lily of the valley dec.......................40.00
Pitcher, 5-1/2" x 9-3/4" h, bulbous, panel cut neck, engraved lacy florals and leaves, applied clear handle, c1840 ....225.00
Salt, 3 x 3", price for pr 100.00

Salt, master, silver, pedestal base, 2-3/4" d, $35.

Sugar Bowl, cov, 4-1/4" x 6-1/4", low foot, enameled white foliage dec, knob finial 65.00
Vase, 9-3/4 h, cylindrical, raised circular foot, everted rim, bright enameled yellow, orange, and blue floral sprays and insects, pr 225.00

METTLACH

History: In 1809, Jean Francis Boch established a pottery at Mettlach in Germany's Moselle Valley. His father had started a pottery at Septfontaines in 1767. Nicholas Villeroy began his pottery career at Wallerfanger in 1789.

In 1841, these three factories merged. They pioneered underglaze printing on earthenware, using transfers from copper plates, and also were among the first companies to use coal-fired kilns. Other factories were developed at Dresden, Wadgassen, and Danischburg. Mettlach decorations include relief and etched designs, prints under the glaze, and cameos.

Marks: The castle and Mercury emblems are the two chief marks although secondary marks are known. The base of each piece also displays a shape mark and usually a decorator's mark.

References: Susan and Al Bagdade, *Warman's English & Continental Pottery & Porcelain*, 2nd ed., Wallace-Homestead, 1991; Gary Kirsner, *Mettlach Book*, 3rd ed., Glentiques (P.O. Box 8807, Coral Springs, FL 33075), 1994.

Periodical: *Beer Stein Journal*, P.O .Box 8807, Coral Springs, FL 33075.

Collectors' Clubs: Stein Collectors International, 281 Shore Dr., Burr Ridge, IL 60521; Sun Steiners, P.O. Box 11782, Fort Lauderdale, FL 33339.

Additional Listings: Villeroy & Boch.

Note: PUG is a common abbreviation for print-underglaze.

Coaster, 5" d, PUG
    #1032, dwarfs, small chip on edge, pr 328.00
    #1264, girl on swing and boy on bicycle, large chip on one, pr 260.00
Jardiniere, 5-1/2" h, 8-3/4 x 10", green ground, off-white cameo figures of Grecian men and women riding in carriage, sitting at table and drinking, base imp "#7000" and "#17" 425.00
Lazy Susan, #1570, PUG, 4 compartments, handle in center, bird design, 1" side hairline, 11" d 130.00
Plaque
    #1044-542, portrait of man, blue delft, 12" d 125.00
    #1044-1067, water wheel on side of building, sgd "F. Reiss," PUG, gold wear on edge, 17" d................................495.00
    #1044-5171, Dutch scene, blue delft, 12" d 90.00
    #1108 enameled incised dec of castle, gilt rim, c1902, 17" d 230.00
    #1168, Cavalier, threading and glaze, sgd "Warth," chip on rear hanging rim, 16-1/2" d............................465.00
    #2196, Stolzensels Castle on the Rhein, 17" d 1,100.00

Stein, #3257, fiddler, rabbit, stamped mark, 8" h, $495.

#2621, man pouring, etched, 7-1/2" d........................185.00
#2625, man singing, etched, small chip repair on edge, 7-1/2" d......................................115.00
#7072, Phanolith, woman, 8" x 6"................................415.00
Stein
    #1027, 1/2 liter, relief, beige, rust, green, inlaid lid, floral, and face 215.00
    #1526, transfer and enameled, Student Society, Amico Pectus Hosti Frontem, dated 1902, roster on either side of crest, pewter lid, slight discoloration to int. 465.00
    #2007, 1/2 liter, etched, black cat, inlaid lid..................660.00
    #2018, 1/2 liter, character, pug dog, inlaid lid 1,100.00
    #2028, 1/2 liter, etched, men in Gasthaus, inlaid lid 550.00
    #2057, 1/2 liter, etched, festive dancing scene, inlaid lid 325.00
    #2093, 1/2 liter, etched and glazed, suit of cards, inlaid lid 700.00
    #2100, 1/3 liter, etched, Germans meeting Romans, inlaid lid, H. Schlitt 495.00
    #2204, 1/2 liter etched and relief, Prussian eagle, inlaid lid 780.00
    #2580, 1/2 liter, etched, Die Kannenburg, conical inlay lid, knight in castle......................................695.00
    #2755, 1/4 liter, cameo and etched, 3 scenes of people at table, Art Nouveau design between scenes, inlaid lid 560.00
    #2811, 1/2 liter, etched, Art Nouveau design, inlaid lid, slight int. discoloration 750.00
    #2922, 1/2 liter, etched, men around campfire, inlaid lid, shallow factory flake on top......................................400.00
    #2950, 1/2 liter, cameo, Bavarian crest, pewter lid with relief crest......................................825.00
    #5001, 4.6 liter, faience type, coat of arms, pewter lid .850.00
Teapot, 3-1/2" h, #3051, etched, Art Deco repeating design, lid missing 95.00
Vase, 10" h, #1808, stoneware, incised foliate dec, imp marks, pr 230.00

MILITARIA

History: Wars have occurred throughout recorded history. Until the mid-19th century, soldiers often had to provide for their own needs, including supplying their own weapons. Even in the 20th century a soldier's uniform and some of his gear are viewed as his personal property, even though issued by a military agency.

Conquering armed forces made a habit of acquiring souvenirs from their vanquished foes. They also brought their own uniforms and accessories home as badges of triumph and service.

Saving militaria may be one of the oldest collecting traditions. Militaria collectors tend to have their own special shows and view themselves outside the normal antiques channels. However, they haunt small indoor shows and flea markets in hopes of finding additional materials.

References: Robert W. D. Ball, *Collector's Guide to British Army Campaign Medals*, Antique Trader Books, 1996; Thomas Berndt, *Standard Catalog of U.S. Military Vehicles*, Krause Publications, 1993; Ray A. Bows, *Vietnam Military Lore 1959-1973*, Bows & Sons, 1988; Gary R. Carpenter, *What's It Worth: A Beginner Collector's Guide to U.S. Army Patches of WW II*, published by author, 1994; W. K. Cross, *Charlton Standard Catalogue of First World War Canadian Corps Badges*, Charlton Press, 1995; ——, *Charlton Standard Catalogue of First World War Canadian Infantry Badges*, 2nd ed., Charlton Press, 1995; Robert Fisch, *Field Equipment of the Infantry 1914-1945*, Greenberg Publications, 1989; Gary Howard, *America's Finest: U.S. Airborne Uniforms, Equipment and Insignia of World War Two* (ETO), Greenhill Books, Stackpole Books, 1994.

Jon A. Maguire, *Silver Wings, Pinks & Greens: Uniforms, Wings, & Insignia of USAAF Airmen in World War II*, Schiffer Publishing, 1994; Jon A. Maguire and John P. Conway, *Art of the Flight Jacket*, Schiffer Publishing, 1995; Ron Manion, *American Military Collectibles Price Guide*, Antique Trader Books, 1995; ——, *German Military Collectibles Price Guide*, Antique Trader Publications, 1995; *North South Trader's Civil War Collector's Price Guide*, 5th ed., North South Trader's Civil War, 1991; Harry Rinker Jr., and Robert Heistand, *World War II Collectibles*, Running Press, Courage Books, 1993; Schuyler, Hartley & Graham *Illustrated Catalog of Civil War Military Goods* (reprint of 1864 catalog), Dover Publications, n.d.; Sydney B. Vernon, *Vernon's Collectors' Guide to Orders, Medals, and Decorations*, published by author, 1986; Ron L. Willis and Thomas Carmichael, *United States Navy Wings of Gold*, Schiffer Publishing, 1995; Richard Windrow and Tim Hawkins, *World War II GI, U.S. Army Uniforms*, Motorbooks International, 1993.

Periodicals: *Men at Arms*, 222 W. Exchange St., Providence, RI 02903; *Militaria Magazine*, P.O. Box 995, Southbury, CT 06488; *Military Collector Magazine*, P.O. Box 245, Lyon Station, PA 19536; *Military Collector News*, P.O. Box 702073, Tulsa, OK 74170; *Military Images*, RD1 Box 99A, Henryville, PA 18332; *Military Trader*, P.O. Box 1050, Dubuque, IA 52004; *North South Trader's Civil War*, P.O. Drawer 631, Orange, VA 22960; *Wildcat Col-*

lectors Journal, 15158 NE. 6th Ave., Miami, FL 33162; *WWII Military Journal*, P.O. Box 28906, San Diego, CA 92198.

Collectors' Clubs: American Society of Military Insignia Collectors, 526 Lafayette Ave., Palmerton, PA 18071; Assoc. of American Military Uniform Collectors, P.O. Box 1876, Elyria, OH 44036; Company of Military Historians, North Main Street, Westbrook, CT, 06498; Imperial German Military Collectors Association, 82 Atlantic St., Keyport, NJ 07735; Karabiner Collector's Network, P.O. Box 5773, High Point, NC 27262; Militaria Collectors Society, 137 S. Almar Dr., Ft. Lauderdale, FL 33334; Orders and Medals Society of America, P.O. Box 484, Glassboro, NJ 08028.

REPRODUCTION ALERT

Pay careful attention to Civil War and Nazi material.

Additional Listings: Firearms; Nazi; Swords. See World War I and World War II in *Warman's Americana & Collectibles* for more examples.

Revolutionary War

Autograph
  Document sgd, promotion of First Lieutenant, by Benjamin Harrison, 1783, paper seal, 6" x 8" 650.00
  Letter sgd, 2 pgs, Camp Springfield, June 1779, to Col. James Abale, orders supplies to be sent, mentions general Washington, by General Nathanael Greene, sgd "Nath Greene Qmr," framed 1,600.00
Pocket Watch, key wound, orig key, inscribed "I Shelby 1802," watch movement by John J. Wilmurt of NY, English silver case with paper label from GW Stewart, Lexington, KY watchmaker, hero Isaac Shelby was first governor of KY 3,520.00

Dirk, folding, locking handle, horn handle, German silver fittings, 4-1/2"blade marked "Wildord Great Western Works," English made, c1850, $935. Photo courtesy of Jackson's Auctioneers & Appraisers.

Snuff Box, cov, 2-7/8" d, gutta percha, round, relief scene of battle, ships, coastline, buildings, French inscription "Prise d'Yorck 1781 (Taking of Yorktown or Battle of Yorktown) 750.00

War of 1812

Cartridge Box, leather, white cloth strap, very worn, missing plate..70.00
Flag, 60-1/2 x 110", 13 stars, Naval, hand sewn 1,100.00
Military Drum, large eagle painted on sides, red, and blue stripes, one drum head, 22" h, 17" d......................................750.00
Shoes, leather, pegged sole, brass buckle, stitching reads "H. S. Shawner, CT"..150.00

Civil War

Autographed Letter Signed, 14-1/2" h, 10" w, from "Camp at Valley Forge 26 miles from Philadelphia May 2, 1778," James Rix to his wife Miriam in Haverhill, West Parish (MA), framed, stains, damage at fold lines...1,540.00
Broadside, 32 x 24", red, white, and blue, recruiting for Philadelphia Brigade of 2nd Army Corps...............................4,400.00
Cabinet Card, Matthew Brady, for Brady's Album Gallery series, identified on label on back
   No. 395, Shipping 1st Conn. Siege train at Yorktown, Union soldiers near vast pile of cannonballs, loading supplies on ship...350.00
   No. 417, 12 lb howitzer, captured by the 7th regiment, N.Y.V., surrounded by Union soldiers 350.00
Canteen, issued to private in Company B, Rome, GA, wooden, copper stamp with name..1,540.00
Diary, Spencer Hall, Guernesy County, Ohio, Union soldier, served in 30th and 185th Companies of Ohio Infantry Volunteers, 12-mo pocket diary, 37 pgs of writing, orig leather-cov boards, begins just before enlistment July 30, 1861, notes marches, details, time spent in Confederate prison camp, accompanied by military discharge, and other family papers 1,900.00

Helmet, Imperial, Officer's Pickelhaube, orig case, scale chin straps, gilded eagle plate, removable spike, $1,980. Photo courtesy of Jackson's Auctioneers & Appraisers.

Drawing, 7-1/4" x 6", titled center top, "Maj. Gen. George B. McClellan," sgd lower right J. S. Kraus (John S.) sgd and dated Jan 21, 1870 on reverse...200.00
Field Desk, 25-1/2" x 18", poplar and pine, four drawers, cherry knobs, seven cubbyholes, drop front writing surface, orig contents included ledgers, 270 General Orders from about 1863, 100 other documents, pressed glass inkwell, Capt. Richard Higgins, 59th Ohio Volunteer infantry.......................7,150.00
Flag, 48" x 108", wool, 34 stars..1,100.00
Personal Effects
   Commodore Charles Green, USN, journals, ledgers, naval medals, wool tuxedo, and beaver top hat.............4,400.00
   Lt. David E Heisey, 63rd Ohio, papers, sword, and beltplate 2,090.00
Photograph
   Ambrotype, sixth-plate, Confederate calvalryman.....1,100.00
   Group portrait of US Navy Midshipman, whole plate image 4,125.00
Presentation Drum, 15" d, 10-1/4" h, silver plaque "Presented to Samuel H. Proctor by the members of Lincoln Guard, June 12th, 1865," also Sergeants frock coat with paper label "Worn by a 14-year-old Drummer Boy in the Civil War/S. H. Proctor," two brass buckles, drum sticks, and letter sgd by C. W. Forrester, Capt..17,250.00
Presentation Pin, gold plated, "Hookers Old Division 1st Reg. Mass. Inf., 1st Brigade, 2nd Divn, 3d Corps," attached bars denoting various battles or campaigns," pendant bullet engraved "Geo. A Dean, Col." 3,740.00
Print, Battles of the Rebellion, 1863, Charles Magnus, lithographer, identified within matrix, litho printed in colors, hand coloring on paper, framed, 26" x 20-1/2".........................400.00
Sword, Model 1850 Presentation Grade Staff and Field Officer's, inscription reads "Lt. F. E. Scripture R.Q.M. 7th N.Y.V. Army/Presented by the members of the Q.M. Dept.," high grade, hilt of gilt cast brass with eagle head quillion, 2 garnet eyes, dec pommel cap, SP metal grip wrapped in wire, etched single etched blade, having U. S. spread eagle and military trophies sold by James P. Fitch, NY, blade by Collins & Co, dated 1862, gun metal scabbard with engraved mounts, presentation located on middle mount, gilt cloth sword knot and leather sword straps attached..3,750.00
Watercolor on Paper, 6-5/8" h, 5-1/8" w, young man in uniform, Union Jack flags at feet, titled "Dr. H. Barnard, 12th Reg. When This You See Remember Me," red, black, blue, yellow, green, and brown, loosely glued down, 11-1/2" h, 10" w bird's eye frame with gilded liner 715.00

Indian War

Bayonet, Model 1873, 3-1/2" w blade...................................80.00
Belt Buckle, Naval officer, brass, stamped "Horstman, Phila" ..120.00
Broadside, Ohio massacre, No. 4, 1791, printed in Boston, 1792, foxed, water stained, modern frame.............................900.00

Spanish American War

Hat Badge, infantry, brass, crossed krag rifles, 2" l.............55.00
Cartridge Box, US Army 125.00
Pinback Button, "Remember the Maine," battleship scene, patent 1896..25.00
Spy Glass, pocket, brass, Naval, round holder, brown leather grip, 16" l..110.00

World War I

Bayonet, British, MK II, No. 4, spike, scabbard 20.00
Book, *Regimental History of the 316 Infantry* 25.00
Buckle, US Balloon Corps, emb hot air balloon 75.00
Compass, mkd "Made in France" 45.00
Dog Tag Stamping Kit, orig wood box, complete 250.00
Flare Pistol, Modele 1918, French.......................................100.00
Gun Sling, soft leather, 1917, for 03 Springfield...................17.50

Helmet, German, Pattern, 1916, painted gray/green 80.00
Map Case, leather, strap, 9 orig French tour maps 50.00
Overcoat, US Army officers, Melton, olive drab, wool, double breasted, 10 bone buttons 65.00
Trench Flashlight and Note Pad, German, black tin container, orig pad and pencil 65.00
Tunic and Trousers, gabardine, pinback, Air Corps and US discs 75.00
Watch Fob, Federal Seal, US officer 15.00

World War II

Armband, Japan, military police, red lettering, white cotton 48.00
Belt and Buckle, German Luftwaffe, silver wash on brass, 1942
.... 55.00
Boots, US Army, double buckle, brown leather, worn 90.00
Cane, 30-3/4" l, Civilian Conservation Corps, fully carved, U-shaped horse head handle, one piece, carved low relief of trees, bathing beauty, alligator, name of carver's friends, Middle Creek Camp F34 Co. 997, 1933, finish removed around later added date 125.00
Cookbook, *Meat Reference Manual for Mess Sergeants and Cooks,* Prepared for the United States Army by the National Live Stock and Meat Board, March, 1943, 36 pgs, soft cover 18.00
Flag, New Zealand PT boat, printed on blue cotton 55.00
Flyers Goggles, Japanese, boxed, gray fur lined cups, yellow lenses 35.00
Gas Mask, German, canister style, rubber mask, canvas straps, carrying container 80.00
Helmet, Italian, steel, leather chip strap 100.00
ID Tag, US Army, oval pattern, instruction envelope, chain 25.00
Overcoat, German, enlisted, late war style, gray, wool, double breasted, 12 buttons 150.00
Telescope, 14" l, Australian, MK 1, heavy leather case and carrying straps 45.00

MILK BOTTLES

History: Milk bottles were known to have been used in the last quarter of the 19th century. Their popularity was enhanced by the inventions of Dr. Hervey Thatcher, who in 1889, developed the bottle with the cap seat holding a cardboard disk following the successful introduction of the Milk Protector system of milk distribution. This system used the now popular Milk Protector bottle with the glass top and picture of a man milking a cow. The use of the bottle was wide spread by the mid teens. With the growth of fluid milk industry, competition resulted in numerous patents. The cream top in 1925, the baby faced and cream separators were popular. Bottles continued well into the 1950s, enhanced by the addition of color and inexpensive manufacturing process. Milk bottles died with the advent of the supermarket and the growing use of fiber board and plastic. There has been a reintroduction recently and a growing number of dairies are now back to using glass.

Milk bottles come in many sizes, colors, and shapes. The beginning collector will very likely collect bottles from the area in which he resides. Other areas can be size, such as quarter pints (gills) or the colorfully painted bottles generally termed "pyro." Other collectors will go to the baby tops, war slogans, or the older tin top closures. Yet even another group may be collected by type, including the modern ones currently in use, or by dairy such as Borden or Carnation. Bottles may be found in shops, at flea markets, or dug in country dumps. History tells us that con-

dition is important and will influence value and collectibility. Regional values will vary.

References: Jeffrey L. Giarde, *Glass Milk Bottles: Their Makers and Marks,* printed by author, Donald E. Lord, *California Milks,* published by author, John Tutton, *Udder Delightful, Udder Fantastic, and Udderly Beautiful,* published by author (Rt. 4, Box 929, Front Royal, VA 22630).

Collectors' Club: The National Association of Milk Bottles Collectors, 4 Ox Bow Road, Westport, CT 06880.

Museums: Billings Farm Museum, Woodstock, VT, National Bottle Museum, Ballston Spa, NY; Southwest Dairy Museum, Arlington, TX.

Advisors: Tony Knipp and Tom Gallagher.

REPRODUCTION ALERT

Milk bottles are being reproduced. Most, by use of blank bottles, then being processed with color slogans, designs, and fictitious farms. Reproduction Elsie the Borden's popular cow, Hopalong Cassidy, and Disney characters have crept into the market. The process has improved and some are virtually undetectable, except to the serious collector. A low price for a very unusual bottle may be a tip off.

Also see: Dairy Items.

Abbots, pint, emb cottage cheese jar 8.00
Alta Crest Farm, Spencer, MA, quart, round, green glass, emb cow's head 1,000.00
Blue Bell Farms, Irvington, NJ, quart, round, orange pyro, Cop-the Cream 140.00
Borden, in script above Elsie, quart, squat, red pyro 18.00
Borden's Condensed Milk, quart, Borden Eagle trademark, clear, emb, tin top 100.00
Borden's, half pint, emb "$.03 deposit," cottage cheese jar .. 8.00
Brookfield Dairy, Hellertown, PA, half pint, round, emb baby top
.... 55.00
Cream Top, generic, quart, sq, dish of ice cream, green/orange
.... 15.00
Crowley's, As good as any better'n some try fresh churned buttermilk, quart, picture of lady, cow, and churn, red pyro
.... 25.00
Dairylea, quart, square, red
   Hopalong Cassidy, black pyro 75.00
   Miss Dairylea, picture of fruit and vegetables 15.00
Dykes' Dairy, Youngsville, PA, our milk for your health, man, woman, 2 children, quart, round, red pyro 18.00
Emmadine Farms, quart, toothache square, orange/black pyro
.... 85.00
Empire State Dairy Co, Brooklyn, half pint, round, emb, state seal in frame 10.00
Fiske, Rumford, RI, qt, round, emb, cream top 15.00
Florida Store Bottle, $.03, quart, picture of state of Florida, round, emb 22.00
Hankin Dairy, 515 3rd Avenue, Brooklyn, quart, clear, emb, tin top 55.00
Hoods, quart, round, cow in framed log, red pyro 12.00
Ingles Dairy, Manchester, NH, Every man's family should have the very best, quart, woman holding child, orange/green pyro
.... 30.00
Jon Alm Dairy, Norwich, NY, quart, sq, tall, picture of girl holding glass, red/blue/orange/brown pyro 30.00
Maple Farms, Brattleboro, VT, quart, sq, amber 8.00
Model Farms, Milford, PA, half pint, round, emb in slug plate, Raw Milk 12.00

Mohawk Farms, Staten Island, NY, quart, large Indian in head-dress, round, emb 40.00
Newport Dairy, quart, squat, round, emb............................10.00
Old Homestead Products, quart, stippled glass, picture of log cabin...40.00
One Quart Liquid Brighton Place Dairy Rochester, N.Y., quart, cylindrical, yellow green, machined mouth, smooth base 550.00
Orange County Milk Association, quart, clear emb, keystone in slug plate, tin top 125.00
Palmerton Sanitary Dairy, Palmerton, PA, quart, sq, emb, cream top..12.00
Palm Mead, The City of Palms, quart, palm tree, green pyro 25.00
Saranac Inn Dairy, quart, clear, emb 30.00
Sheffield Farms, Slawson Decker, NY, quart, logo, round, emb 8.00
State University of New York, Cobleskill, college seal, quart, sq, tall 25.00
Universal Store Bottle, 5¢ deposit, quart, round, emb 8.00
Warner Bros., quart, sq, Bugs Bunny with milk carriers, red/back pyro, modern 10.00
Winona Dairy, Lebanon, NH, for Safety Milk For Health Milk in a Bottle, quart, red pyro..20.00
WW Schultz Sunnyside Farm, Port Jervis in slug plate, round, emb...12.00
Yasgar Farms, Bethel, NY, 25th Anniversary 1994 (Woodstock), quart, sq, brown/yellow pyro 45.00

MILK GLASS

History: Opaque white glass attained its greatest popularity at the end of the 19th century. American glass manufacturers made opaque white tablewares as a substitute for costly European china and glass. Other opaque colors, e.g., blue and green, also were made. Production of milk glass novelties came in with the Edwardian era.

The surge of popularity in milk glass subsided after World War I. However, milk glass continues to be made in the 20th century. Some modern products are reissues and reproductions of earlier forms. This presents a significant problem for collectors, although it is partially obviated by patent dates or company markings on the originals and by the telltale signs of age.

Collectors favor milk glass from the pre-World War I era, especially animal-covered dishes. The most prolific manufacturers of these animal covers were Atterbury, Challinor-Taylor, Flaccus, and McKee.

References: E. McCamley Belknap, *Milk Glass*, Crown Publishers, 1949, out of print; Regis F. and Mary F. Ferson, *Today's Prices for Yesterday's Milk Glass*, published by authors, 1985; ——, *Yesterday's Milk Glass Today*, published by authors, 1981; Everett Grist, *Covered Animal Dishes*, Collector Books, 1988, 1993 value update; Lorraine Kovar, *Westmoreland Glass*, 2 Vols., Antique Publications, 1991; S. T. Millard, *Opaque Glass*, 4th ed., Wallace Homestead, 1975, out of print; Betty and Bill Newbound, *Collector's Encyclopedia of Milk Glass*, Collector Books, 1995.

Collectors' Club: National Milk Glass Collectors Society, 46 Almond Dr., Hershey, PA 17033.

Museum: Houston Antique Museum, Chattanooga, TN.

Notes: There are many so-called "McKee" animal-covered dishes. Caution must be exercised in evaluating

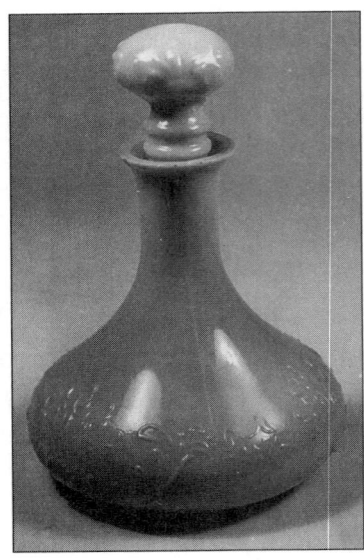
Decanter, blue, orig stopper, 9" h, $65.

pieces because some authentic covers were not signed. Furthermore, many factories have made, and many still are making, split-rib bases with McKee-like animal covers or with different animal covers. The prices below are for authentic McKee pieces with either the cover or base signed.

Numbers in listings prefixed with a letter refer to books listed in the references, wherein the letter identifies the first letter of the author's name.

Animal Dish, cov
Dog, setter, white base, sgd "Flaccus," repair to lid.....150.00
Fish, walking, divided horizontally, 5 central fins support body, detailed scales, red glass eyes (B167b)..................195.00

Miniature Lamp, Pineapple In A Basket pattern, green dec, Smith No. 276, $250.

Hen, marbleized, head turned to left, lacy base, white and deep blue, Atterbury (F8) 165.00

Bowl, 8-1/4" d, Daisy, allover leaves and flower design, open scalloped edge (F165) 85.00

Butter Dish, cov, 4-7/8" l, Roman Cross pattern, sq, ftd base curves outward toward top, cube shape finial (F240) 75.00

Calling Card Receiver, bird, wings extended over fanned tail, head resting on leaf, detailed feather pattern (F669) 150.00

Celery Vase, 6-5/8" h, Blackberry Pattern, scalloped rim, plain band above vertical surface, Hobbs Brockunier (F317)110.00

Compote, Atlas, lacy edge, blue 185.00

Creamer and Sugar, Trumpet Vine, fire painted dec, sgd "SV" 130.00

Egg Cup, cov, 4-1/4" h, bird, round, fluted, Atterbury (F130) 135.00

Lamp, 11" h, Goddess of Liberty, bust, 3 stepped hexagonal bases, clear and frosted font, brass screw connector, patent date, Atterbury (F329) 300.00

Mug, 3" h, Ivy in Snow 40.00

Plate, 6" d, 2 cats form upper edge, bracketed dog head, open work, swirling leaves, emb "He's all right" (B20d) 125.00

Spooner, 5-1/8" h, monkey, scalloped top (F275) 125.00

Syrup, 6" h, Bellflower pattern, single vine, dated, Collins & Wright (F155C0) 245.00

Tumbler, Royal Oak, orig fired paint, green band 50.00

Wine, Feather pattern 40.00

MILLEFIORI

History: Millefiori (thousand flowers) is an ornamental glass composed of bundles of colored glass rods fused together into canes. The canes were pulled to the desired length while still ductile, sliced, arranged in a pattern, and fused together again. The Egyptians developed this technique in the first century B.C. it was revived in the 1880s.

Bowl, 8" d, tricorn, scalloped, folded sides, amethyst and silver deposit 125.00

Creamer, 3" x 4-1/2", white and cobalt blue canes, yellow centers, satin finish 110.00

Cruet, bulbous, multicolored canes, applied camphor handle, matching stopper 120.00

Jar, cov, royal blue, multicolored, 2-1/2" h, 2-3/4" d, $295.

Cup and Saucer, white and cobalt blue canes, yellow center, satin finish 90.00

Decanter, 12" h, deep black ground, all over multicolored flux and canes, including peachblow, and opal, enamel dec, Gundersen 1,450.00

Door Knob, 2-1/2" d, paperweight, center cane dated 1852, New England Glass Co. 395.00

Goblet, 7-1/2" h, multicolored canes, clear stem and base 150.00

Lamp, 14-1/2" h, 8-1/2" d dome shade, glass base, electric 795.00

Pitcher, 6-1/2" h, multicolored canes, applied candy cane handle 195.00

Slipper, 5" l, camphor ruffle and heal 140.00

Sugar, cov, 4" x 4-1/2", white canes, yellow centers, satin finish 125.00

Vase, 4" d, multicolored canes, applied double handles ... 100.00

MINIATURE LAMPS

History: Miniature oil and kerosene lamps, often called "night lamps," are diminutive replicas of larger lamps. Simple and utilitarian in design, miniature lamps found a place in the parlor (as "courting" lamps), hallway, children's rooms, and sickrooms.

Miniature lamps are found in many glass types, from amberina to satin glass. Miniature lamps measure 2-1/2 to 12 inches in height, with the principle parts being the base, collar, burner, chimney, and shade. In 1877, both L. J. Atwood and L. H. Olmsted patented burners for miniature lamps. Their burners made the lamps into a popular household accessory.

References: Marjorie Hulsebus, *Miniature Victorian Lamps*, Schiffer Publishing, 1996; Frank R. and Ruth E. Smith, *Miniature Lamps* (1981), Book II (1982) Schiffer Publishing; John F. Solverson, *Those Fascinating Little Lamps: Miniature Lamps and Their Values*, Antique Publications, 1988, includes prices for Smith numbers.

Collectors' Club: Night Light, 38619 Wakefield Ct., Northville, MI 48167.

Note: The numbers given below refer to the figure numbers found in the Smith books.

Figure III, Artichoke, pink 225.00

Figure VII, Santa Claus 2,700.00

#23-I, time lamp, emb "Time & Light" 75.00

#29-I, nutmeg, white milk glass, brass band and handle 80.00

#50-I, log cabin, blue, handle 1,100.00

#51-I, amber, shoe, applied handle 1,000.00

#68-I, finger lamp, blue with stars, emb "Wide Awake" 115.00

#77-I, nickel, Beauty Night Lamp 55.00

#109-I, Beaded Heart, clear, emb 115.00

#110-I, Bull's Eye, clear, stem 45.00

#125-I, Christmas Tree, white milk glass, gold trim 125.00

#153-I, milk glass, pink and gold, emb 115.00

#171-I, Pond Lily, emb, inside painting 140.00

#177-I, custard glass, rough shade 55.00

#211-I, Medallion, milk glass, emb 45.00

Smith XI, cranberry, applied berries, shortened shade, $520.

#212-I, pink milk glass with shells, base of shade damaged 145.00
#213-I, milk glass, emb, yellow, pink, and white 135.00
#214-I, Maltese Cross, milk glass, emb rough top shade....50.00
#230-I, Acanthus, milk glass, emb. yellow and white.........125.00
#231-I, Drape pattern, pink and white milk glass.................75.00
#286-I, Cosmos, white, chip on shade 75.00
#309-I, Pan American Exposition, 1901, Buffalo, NY, damaged base 150.00
#325-I, pink milk glass, angel dec.....................................165.00
#327-II, swan, milk glass, shade with crack.......................300.00
#330-II, elephant, wrong shade...225.00
#369-I, Beaded Swirl, end of day 300.00
#370-I, cranberry, Beaded Swirl...200.00
#389-I, satin, blue, melon ribbed base, pansy ball shade, chip on shade 155.00
#390-I, melon ribbed, cased, yellow 525.00
#400-I, green beaded...125.00
#474-I, Spanish Lace filigree...750.00
#490-I, Skeleton, 5-1/2" h...8,000.00
#497-I, owl, black, gray, orange eyes 1,100.00
#499-I, swan, annealing marks at neck, pink, no shade 75.00
#502-I, opalescent, amber, pink feet..............................3,000.00
#555-I, glossy satin glass, pink and butterscotch...........1,550.00
#595-I, satin, MOP, DQ, shading from pink to apricot, burner ring damaged 1,050.00
#625-I, glow lamp, white milk glass, floral dec, burner 30.00

MINIATURE PAINTINGS

History: Prior to the advent of the photograph, miniature portraits and silhouettes were the principal way of preserving a person's image. Miniaturists were plentiful, and they often made more than one copy of a drawing. The extras were distributed to family and friends.

Miniaturists worked in watercolors and oil and on surfaces such as paper, vellum, porcelain, and ivory. The miniature paintings were often inserted into jewelry or mounted inside or on the lids of snuff boxes. The artists often supplemented commission work by painting popular figures of the times and copying important works of art.

After careful study miniature paintings have been divided into schools, and numerous artists are now being researched. Many fine examples may be found in today's antiques marketplace.

Reference: Dale T. Johnson, American Portrait Miniatures in the Manney Collection, The Metropolitan Museum of Art, 1990.

Museum: Gibbes Museum of Art, Charleston, SC.

1-1/4" h, 7/8" w, watercolor on ivory, gentleman in oval, framed, American School, 18th C.............290.00
1-7/16" d, watercolor on ivory, round, young child with coral necklace, attributed to Mrs. Moses B. Russell (Clarissa Peters,) framed, very minor pigment loss 4,320.00
2-1/8" h, 1-3/4" w, watercolor on ivory, young gentleman, pendant frame, American School, 19th C................320.00
2-1/4" h x 1-7/8" w, watercolor on ivory, gentleman with clouds in background, pendant frame, American School, 19th C, crack, minor staining 460.00
2-3/8" h, 1-7/8" w, watercolor on ivory, gentleman, framed, Anglo/American School, 19th C, staining, very minor crack 375.00
2-3/8" h, 1-7/8" w, watercolor on ivory, gentleman in blue frock coat, pendant frame, American School, 18th C, very minor pigment loss 1,095.00
2-3/8" h, 1-7/8" w, watercolor on ivory, husband and wife, American School, 19th C, framed, grime.........520.00
2-1/2" h, Agnes Sorel, an Italian Renaissance noblewoman, framed, Continental, 19th C, pr 380.00
2-1/2" h, 2" w, rect, French noblewomen, one sgd "Berry," other sgd "Rene," pr 375.00
2-1/2" h, 2" w, watercolor on ivory, young lady in dark blue dress, pendant frame, American School, 19th C, minor pigment loss, surface abrasions 435.00
2-3/4" h, 2-1/8" d, watercolor on ivory, lady in blue dress, framed, American School, 19th C 490.00
2-3/4" h, 2-1/4" w, young girl holding flowers, American School, 19th C framed, laid down on paper, minor staining and pigment loss 635.00
2-7/8" h, 2-1/4" w, watercolor on ivory, husband and wife, ovals, framed in later gilt gesso frames, mounted on paper, American School, 19th C, very minor surface abrasions.....1,495.00
3" h, watercolor on ivory, Stumer Brothers, c1835, German, pr framed together 425.00
3" h, 2-3/8" w, watercolor on paper, young girl with coral necklace, reverse inscribed "daughter of Isaac Brokaw, clockmaker Band Brook, NJ," framed, American School, 19th C, minor pigment loss, minor toning 490.00
3" h, 2-1/2" w, watercolor on ivory, sea caption seated in Queen Anne chair, telescope in hand, ship in background, 6-3/8" h x 5-7/8" w black lacquer frame with gilded cast brass trim labeled "Portrait of Captain Church, direct descendent of the Indian fighter of that name" 1,320.00
3-1/8" h, 2-3/4" w, watercolor on paper, lady, attributed to Justus Dalee, American School, c1826-47, framed, soiling and minor abrasion 805.00
3-1/4" h, 2-1/2" d, watercolors on ivory, husband and wife, framed, American School, 19th C, very minor pigment loss, pr ..2,070.00
3-1/4" h, 2-3/4" w, watercolor on celluloid, young woman, back of frame labeled "Mrs. Gilchrist a Southern Friend," 5-5/8" h x 5" w wood frame with gilded brass liner 250.00
3-1/4" h, 2-3/4" w, watercolor on paper, lady, giltwood frame, Continental School, 19th C, minor scattered foxing.............520.00
3-1/4" h, 2-7/8" w, watercolor on paper, gentleman, reverse inscribed "Cornelius Lansing Gaston Father of John Wickware

Benjamin Franklin, seated, wearing red coat, gilt metal frame, $750. Photo courtesy of Freeman\Fine Arts.

Gaston," framed, American School, 19th C, minor staining 425.00

3-3/8" h, 2-5/8" w, watercolor on paper, lady in red chair, period gilt frame, American School, 19th C, minor toning, staining, and pigment loss 400.00

3-3/8" h, 2-5/8" w, watercolor on paper, lady with ruffled collar, period wood and stamped brass frame, American School, 19th C, very minor toning 690.00

3-1/2" h, 2-1/2" w, watercolor on ivory, woman with baby holding toy bird, framed, American School, 19th C 6,900.00

3-1/2" h, 2-5/8" w, watercolor on paper, "Mifs [sic] Laura E. Phelps Aged 20," sgd "J. M. Roberts" (John M. Roberts, American School,) lower right, framed, c1831, toning, minor pigment loss 750.00

3-1/2" h, 2-5/8" w, watercolor on paper, portrait of young lady, period frame, eglomise mat, American School, 19th C, minor toning and foxing..460.00

3-1/2" h, 2-3/4" w, 4-1/4" x 3", graphite on paper, J.M. Crowley, identified and dated on reverse "Jany 19, 1839," framed, American School, toning, staining.............................1,495.00

3-1/2" x 4-1/2", watercolor on paper, oval, male and female youths, artist sgd "Sara Cowan," brass frame, fitted case, pr 230.00

3-5/8" x 2-7/8", watercolor on paperboard, gentleman facing left, lady facing right, both initialed and dated "J.E.T. 1819," common frame, Anglo/American School, 19th C, toning, laid down, water staining 150.00

3-5/8" h, 3-1/8" w, pencil and watercolor on paper, child, creases, stains, redone hair, 5-1/8" h x 4-1/8" w gilt frame with eglomise mat..110.00

3-3/4" h, 3" w, watercolor on paper, gentleman, American school, 19th C, eglomise mat, period frame, staining, losses to mat 815.00

3-3/4" h 3-1/4" w, watercolor on paper, Abigail Sawyer, period frame, American School, 19th C, toning, minor staining, foxing..260.00

3-7/8" h, 3" h, watercolor and graphite on paper, portrait of young lady, period gilt frame, American School, 19th C, minor toning and staining 345.00

4-3/8" h, 3-1/2" w, watercolor on ivory, Edward Grant Howe, aged 5, whip and green book, identified on paper label, framed, c1888, minor pigment loss 10,350.00

4-3/8" x 5-7/16", watercolor on paper, girl in gingham dress playing the piano, framed, American school, 19th C, toning, minor staining 425.00

4-3/4" h, 4" w, watercolor on paper, gentleman with gray wig, dark brown frock coat, sgd "HW 1762," water satins, glue stains,

glued to paper backing, 5-7/8" h x 4-7/8" w emb brass frame 440.00

4-7/8" h, 3" w, watercolor on paper, Mr. Sprague of Salem, MA, identified on reverse, framed, American School, 19th C, toning, minor pigment loss 865.00

5-1/4" h, 4" w, watercolor on celluloid, backing labeled "Geo. Washington," faded colors, black lacquer frame, gilt brass fittings 385.00

7-1/4" h, 5-1/2" d, watercolor on paper, young boy with flowers, framed, American School, 19th C, very minor staining ...20.00

7-3/4" h, 6-3/8" w, ink, pencil, and watercolor on paper, young woman seated in chair, rosewood veneer frame with gilded liner..440.00

9-5/8" h, 7-1/2" w, watercolor on paper, full length portrait of boy with hoop, framed, Anglo/American School, 19th C, toning, foxing, surface abrasion 550.00

MINIATURES

History: There are three sizes of miniatures: dollhouse scale (ranging from 1/2 to 1 inch), sample size, and child's size. Since most early material is in museums or is extremely expensive, the most common examples in the marketplace today are from the 20th century.

Many mediums were used for miniatures: silver, copper, tin, wood, glass, and ivory. Even books were printed in miniature. Price ranges are broad, influenced by scarcity and quality of workmanship.

The collecting of miniatures dates back to the 18th century. It remains one of the world's leading hobbies.

References: George M. Beylerian, *Chairmania*, Harry N. Abrams, 1994; Caroline Clifton-Mogg, *Dollhouse Sourcebook*, Abbeville Press, 1993; Nora Earnshaw, *Collecting Dolls' Houses and Miniatures*, Pincushion Press, 1993; Flora Gill Jacobs, *Dolls Houses in America*, Charles Scribner's Sons, 1974; ——, *History of Dolls Houses*, Charles Scribner's Sons; Constance Eileen King, *Dolls and Dolls Houses*, Hamlyn, 1989; Herbert F. Schiffer and Peter B. Schiffer, *Miniature Antique Furniture*, Schiffer Publishing, 1995; Margaret Towner, *Dollhouse Furniture*, Courage Books, Running Press, 1993.

Periodicals: *Doll Castle News*, P.O. Box 247, Washington, NJ 07882; *Miniature Collector*, Scott Publications, 30595 Eight Mile Rd, Livonia, MI 48152; *Nutshell News*, 21027 Crossroads Circle, P.O. Box 1612, Waukesha, WI 53187.

Collectors' Clubs: International Guild Miniature Artisans, P.O. Box 71, Bridgeport, NY 18080; Miniature Industry Assoc. of America Member News, 2270 Jacquelyn Dr., Madison, WI 53711; National Assoc. of Miniature Enthusiasts, P.O. Box 69, Carmel, IN 46032.

Museums: Margaret Woodbury Strong Museum, Rochester, NY; Mildred Mahoney Jubilee Doll House Museum, Fort Erie, Canada; Museums at Stony Brook, Stony Brook, NY; Toy and Miniature Museum of Kansas City, Kansas City, MO; Toy Museum of Atlanta, Atlanta, GA; Washington Dolls' House and Toy Museum, Washington, DC.

Additional Listings: See Dollhouse Furnishings in *Warman's Americana & Collectibles* for more examples.

Doll House Furniture

Armoire, tin litho, purple and black 35.00
Bathroom, wood, painted white, Strombecker 40.00
Bedroom
    French Provincial style, antique white, bed, dressing table,
      bench, pr night stands 195.00
    Victorian style, metal, veneer finish, bed, night stand, com-
      mode with faux marble tops, armoire and mirror, cradle,
      Biedermeier clock, metal washstand 675.00
Bench, wood, rush seat..25.00
Blanket Chest, 7-1/8" l, 4-3/4" h, painted wood, six-board, wallpa-
    per lined int., open till, replaced hinges, lock missing, Ameri-
    ca, 19th C 2,990.00
Buffet Set, stenciled, 3 shelves, column supports, Biedermeier,
    6" h..400.00
Chair
    Golden Oak, center splat, upholstered seat, German, c1875,
      pr 75.00
    Ormolu, ornate, 3" h, c1900, pr 75.00
Cradle, cast iron, painted green, 2" l...................................40.00
Desk, Chippendale style, slant front, drawers open 60.00
Dining Room, Edwardian style, dark red stain, extension table,
    chairs, marble top cupboard, grandfather clock, chandelier,
    candelabra, 5" h bisque shoulder head maid doll, table ser-
    vice for six, Gebruder Schneerass, Waltershausen, Thuringa,
    c1915 ....1,400.00
Hall Rack, walnut, carved fretwork, arched mirror back shelves,
    umbrella holder..450.00

Chest of Drawers, hand made, mirror top, $125.

Kitchen Set, litho tin, Modern Kitchen, all parts and pieces, ani-
    mals, and related items, orig box, Louis Marx 250.00
Living Room
    Empire style, sofa, fainting couch, 2 side chairs, upholstered
      tapestry, matching drapery 350.00
    Victorian style, settee, 2 parlor chairs, footstool, 2 plant stands,
      2 gilt filigree tables, 3 panel screen, upholstered red velvet,
      Gone with the Wind style lamp 650.00
Piano, grand, wood, 8 keys, 5" h..35.00
Rocker, painted tin, lithographed tin seated child holding doll,
    compartment under seat concealed candy storage, Meier,
    Germany, 3" l...275.00
Sewing Table, golden oak, drawer, c1880......................100.00
Table, tin, painted brown, white top, floral design, 1-1/2" x 3/4" h,
    ornate..30.00
Tea Cart, Petite Princess 25.00
Vanity, Biedermeier 90.00

Doll House Accessories

Bird Cage, brass, bird, stand, 7" h......................................65.00
Candelabra, Petite Princess...25.00
Carpet Sweeper, gilt, Victorian...65.00
Christmas Tree, decorated...50.00
Clock, metal...35.00
Coffeepot, brass..25.00
Crock, 2-5/8" h, 3-1/4" d, stoneware, two handles, cobalt blue
    dec, 19th C, minor chips, lid missing 115.00
Cup and Saucer, china, flower design, c1940.....................10.00
Decanter, 2 matching tumblers, Venetian, c1920...............35.00
Fireplace, tin, Britannia metal fretwork, draped mantel, carved
    grate 85.00
Plate, 4-1/4" d, redware, slip dec, America, 19th C, minor rim
    chips, glaze wear 805.00
Radio, Strombecker, c1930...35.00
Refrigerator, Petite Princess..75.00
Silhouettes, Tynietoy, c1930, pr 25.00
Telephone, wall, oak, speaker and bell, German, c1890.....40.00
Towel Stand, golden oak, turned post.................................45.00
Umbrella Stand, brass, ormolu, sq, emb palm fronds 60.00
Urn, silver, handled, ornate 100.00

Child Size

Blanket Chest
    37" w, 13-3/4" d, 15-1/2" h, 6 board, molded lip top, dovetailed
      box, bracket feet, painted light blue, front yellow freehand
      dec, inscribed "J. J. H. 1820" in wreath flanked by tulips
      and meandering vines at ends above pinwheel Schoharie
      County, NY...2,645.00
    26-3/4" w, 11-1/2" d, 22" h, old dark green painted pine and
      poplar, molded hinged top, case with single drawer, cutout
      ends joined by valanced skirt, attributed to New England,
      c1800..2,530.00
Bookcase, hp, scalloped cornice over 4 open shelves, base with
    3 drawers, Peter Hunt dec...1,650.00
Chair
    Arm, Windsor, grain painted and parcel gilt, lowback, PA, first
      half 19th C, reserve scrolling concave crest continuing to
      downswept arms, six bulbous turned supports, plank seat,
      ring-turned tapering legs joined by stretchers, all over
      graining in brown and ochre, gilt highlights 850.00
    Side, 10-3/4" seat, 22" h, worn orig light green paint, black
      striping, gold stenciling, polychrome floral dec, pr ..625.00
Chest of Drawers
    Chinoiserie dec, 19th C, 9-1/4" w, 5-3/4" d, 12" h, minor imper-
      fections 345.00
    Federal, CT, c1790, cherry, rect overhanging top with molded
      edge, case with 4 incised beaded graduated drawers, in-
      laid quarter fans and stringing, ogee bracket feet, old refin-
      ish, 38-3/4" w, 18" d, 34-1/4" h 6,900.00

**Wash bowl and pitcher, cobalt blue, paneled, chips, less than 3"
h, $275. Photo courtesy of Gene Harris Antique Auction Center.**

Federal, Philadelphia or New Jersey, c1800, maple, rect top
with reeded edge, 2 short and 3 long drawers with incised
dec, shaped skirt, straight bracket feet, orig brass knobs,
14" w, 6" d, 13-3/4" h 2,590.00
Sheraton, refinished walnut, scrolled crest, two dovetailed
drawers with cockbeading, turned legs, 15-3/4" w, 9-1/4" d,
16-1/2" h 660.00
Cook Stove, black and white enameled steel, nickel steel fittings,
working gas range, mkd "Estate Fresh Air Oven," break in door
frame, 15" l 2,420.00
Dresser, 23-1/4" h, cottage style, poplar, orig red paint, white
striping, three drawers, high back mirror with shelves, wire nail
construction, minor water damage to paint on feet 300.00
Rocker, Empire style, mahogany, vase shaped splat, rush seat,
scrolled arms, 22" h 225.00
Table, drop leaf, Sheraton, walnut, pine secondary wood, leaves
with decoratively cut corners, one dovetailed drawer, turned
legs, old finish, minor edge damage, hinges replaced, age
crack on top, 23-1/2" l, 12-1/2" w, 10-3/4" l leaves, 19" h
.... 1,100.00
Tub, 5-5/8" d, 2-1/4" h, stave construction, metal bands, wire han-
dles, orig blue paint, black bands 330.00

Doll Size

Bed, 10-7/8" h, 13-1/4" w, 16" d, spool, walnut, miniature brass
and wood bed warmer, orig bedding, pillow cases, and sheets
sgd "Harriet E. Curtis," 19th C, repairs, staining, losses to bedding 150.00
Blanket Chest
11-1/2" l, refinished cherry, dovetailed case, molded edge lid,
two drawers, inlaid escutcheon, short feet, worn ebonized
finish on drawer and lid edges, one drawer rebuilt, other renailed, some deterioration from storage of spaces, feet re-
placed 580.00
13" l, 7" d, 10-1/4" h, grain painted, America, 19th C, minor imperfections 1,495.00
15" l, pine, old worn blue repaint, six board, hinge nail re-
stored 430.00
Chest of Drawers
10" w, 8-1/4" h, poplar, old black paint, six board type construction, cutout feet, two nailed drawers 275.00
13-1/2" w, 7-1/4" d, 13" h, Empire, mahogany and mahogany
veneer, poplar secondary wood, 3 dovetailed drawers, S-
curve pilasters, scrolled feet, some veneer damage
.... 500.00
25" h, 12" 2, 6-1/2" d, Tramp Art, swivel mirror with ornate crest
over top with scalloped sides, 2 drawers over 3 long draw-

ers on base with teardrop pulls, scalloped apron, late
19th/early 20th C, very minor losses 690.00
Cupboard, step back, wall-type, homemade
Pine and poplar, gray paint, wire nail construction, 13-1/2" w,
8-1/4' d, 18-1/4" h 200.00
Poplar, old red paint, white int. with shelves and pencil draw-
ing, back inscribed "To Mary from Papa," 18-1/2" h
.... 200.00
Stove, electric, 8" x 15" x 15", Metal Ware Corp. 66.00
Wash Tub, 5" d, 2-1/2" h, aluminum 12.00

MINTON CHINA

History: In 1793, Thomas
Minton joined other men
to form a partnership and
build a small pottery at
Stoke-on-Trent, Stafford-
shire, England. Production began in 1798 with blue-printed earthenware, mostly in the Willow pattern. In 1798
cream-colored earthenware and bone china were introduced.

A wide range of styles and wares was produced.
Minton introduced porcelain figures in 1826, Parian
wares in 1846, encaustic tiles in the late 1840s, and Majolica wares in 1850. Many famous designers and artists
in the English pottery industry worked for Minton.

In 1883, the modern company was formed and called
Mintons Limited. The "s" was dropped in 1968. Minton
still produces bone-china tablewares and some ornamental pieces.

Marks: Many early pieces are unmarked or have a
Sevres-type marking. The "ermine" mark was used in the
early 19th century. Date codes can be found on tableware and majolica. The mark used between 1873 and
1911 was a small globe with a crown on top and the word
"Minton."

References: Paul Atterbury and Maureen Batkin, *Dictionary of Minton*, Antique Collectors' Club; Susan and Al
Bagdade, *Warman's English & Continental Pottery & Porcelain*, 2nd ed., Wallace-Homestead, 1991; Joan Jones,
*Minton: The First Two Hundred Years of Design and Pro-
duction*, Swan Hill, 1993.

Museum: Minton Museum, Staffordshire, England.

Bowl, 12" x 10", oval, Palissy style, minor base chip 3,080.00
Centerpiece, 16" l, elongated parian vessel, molded scroll handles and feet, pierced rim, 2 brown reserves, white pate-sur-
pate amorini, gilding, dec, attributed to Lawrence Birks, mkd
"Minton," retailer's marks of Thomas Goode & Co., Ltd., Lon-
don, c1889 .... 1,400.00
Dinner Plate, 10-1/8" d, multicolored flowers, light blue edges,
late 19th C, small imperfections, 8 pc set 115.00
Dinner Service
Ancestral pattern, 12 each cups and saucers, 8" plates, 10-
1/2" plates, one open vegetable, 49 pc set 1,200.00
Talbot pattern, floral and foliate dec, 16 bouillon cups, 20
bouillon saucers, 35 bread and butter plates, 2 cereal
bowls, 16 demitasse cups and saucers, 27 dinner plates,
12 fruit bowls, 20 luncheon plates, 34 salad plates, 32 tea-
cups, 29 saucers, price for 252 pc set 1,000.00
Ewer, 21-1/4" h, majolica, heron and fish, after model by J. Protat,
imp mark, 1869 date code 2,400.00

Plate, flower basket center, basketweave rim, green band, scalloped edge with black trim, $12.

Figure, 10-1/2" h, putti, yellow basket and grape vine, 1867, professional repair at rim of basket 2,750.00
Floor Urn, 35" h, 18" d, majolica, Neo-Classical, turquoise, massive foliage handles..12,650.00
Jardiniere, 7" h, molded wooden plants, white vines, lilac int., majolica, matching stands, pr 475.00
Oyster Plate, majolica
   Cobalt blue 1,650.00
   Light green, 9" d 470.00
   Malachite, rim chips 1,210.00
   Mottled..935.00
   Pink, minor rim nick 1,100.00
   Turquoise...495.00
Oyster Server, 4 tier, majolica, green and brown, white wells, turquoise finial, rim damage to 6 wells, mechanical turning mechanism missing 3,575.00
Service Plate, 10-5/8" d, raised gold dec, wide light blue ground banded borders, 2 sets of 12, one with floral dec, other with urn and scrolled leaf dec, printed marks, mid 20th C
....3,450.00
Soup Tureen, Cov, Stand, 14-1/4" l, oval, enamel dec black transfer printed Oriental garden landscape, imp marks, c1882
....420.00
Sweetmeat Dish, 8" d, majolica, blue titmouse on branch, leaf shaped dish, imp mark, 1888..675.00
Tower Pitcher, 12-1/2" h, majolica, castle molded body with relief of dancing villagers in medieval dress, imp marks, c1873, chips to cov thumb rest, spout rim 1,035.00
Vase, 8-1/2" h, Oriental style, pierced scroll formed ivory ground, raised ribbon, enameled and gilt dec, raised and ftd black ground base, printed and imp marks, c1888................950.00

MOCHA

History: Mocha decoration usually is found on utilitarian creamware and stoneware pieces and was produced through a simple chemical action. A color pigment of brown, blue, green, or black was made acidic by an infusion of tobacco or hops. When the acidic colorant was applied in blobs to an alkaline ground, it reacted by spreading in feathery designs resembling sea plants. This type of decoration usually was supplemented with bands of light-colored slip.

Types of decoration vary greatly, from those done in a combination of motifs, such as Cat's Eye and Earthworm, to a plain pink mug decorated with green ribbed bands. Most forms of mocha are hollow, e.g., mugs, jugs, bowls, and shakers.

English potters made the vast majority of the pieces. Collectors group the wares into three chronological periods: 1780-1820, 1820-1840, and 1840-1880.

Marks: Marked pieces are extremely rare.

References: Susan and Al Bagdade, *Warman's English & Continental Pottery & Porcelain*, 2nd ed., Wallace-Homestead, 1991.

Reproduction Alert.

Bowl
   4-3/4" d, 3-1/2" h, green band, canary yellow ground, yellow and black earthworm, partial imp mark "CL & - Mont-," chips and repairs..110.00
   6-1/2" d, band of earthworm dec, late 19th C 235.00
   7-1/4" d, band of earthworm dec, late 19th C 245.00
Chamber Pot
   8-1/2" d, tan band, blue and black stripes, blue, white, and black earthworm, wear, repair, handle replaced 110.00
   8-3/4" d, two tone blue bands, black stripes, black and white earthworm, leaf handle, some wear and edge flakes
   ....125.00
Creamer, 5-1/4" h, black and white checkered band on shoulder medium blue glaze..215.00
Cup, 2-7/8" h, imp border above brown and white earthworm design, blue ground, 19th C, imperfections 375.00
Jar, cov, 5" h, pale blue band, black stripes, white, black, and blue cat's eye and earthworm dec, repairs and hairline in lid
....500.00
Jug
   6-1/8" h, blue and white raise earthworm dec, two blue bands 675.00
   8-1/2" h, 2 black and white checkered bands, blue glaze, foliate handle and spout..345.00
Measure, 5", 6", and 6-1/4" h, tankard, blue, black and tan seaweed dec, one with applied white label "Imperial Pint," other with resist label "Quart," minor stains, wear, and crazing, 3 pc set 440.00
Milk Pitcher
   4-5/8" h, dark bluish-gray band, black stripes, emb band with green and black seaweed, leaf handle, wear and painted over spout flake 440.00

Mug, light tan, white band, 3" d, $85.

4-7/8" h, blue band, black and blue stripes, brown, blue, and black, earthworm dec, repairs 200.00
Mug
3-3/4" h, dark brown band and stripes, blue, white, and tan earthworm, leaf handle, hairlines 550.00
5-3/4" h, large band of pumpkin seaweed dec, 19th C, large rim chip 460.00
Mustard Pot, cov, 2-1/2" h, tan band with black stripes, white, yellow, and black earthworm dec, ribbed handle, chip on rim, small repair to lid 615.00
Pitcher
6-3/4" h, earthworm design, gray, green, and yellow ochre, emb spout, band and leaf handle 500.00
7-1/2" h, blue, orange, tan, black, and white geometric design and stripes, emb leaf handle, crow's foot in bottom 1,500.00
8" h, medium blue, white fluted on bottom, black, and white checkered band in middle 125.00
Salt, 3" d, 2-1/8" h, gray band, black stripes, white wavy lines, stains in foot, rim hairlines 330.00
Shaker
4-1/8" h, tan bands, brown stripes, black seaweed dec, chips 220.00
4-7/8" h, blue band, black stripe, brown, black, and white earthworm dec, blue top, repair 330.00
Tea Canister, 4" h, blue, black, and white band on shoulder, white fluted band on bottom, medium blue glaze 125.00
Teapot, 5-7/8" h, oval shape, medium blue, fluted band on bottom, black and white checkered band on top, acorn finial 500.00
Waste Bowl
4-3/4" d, amber band, black seaweed dec separated into five segments by squiggly lines, green molded lip band, stains and hairlines 275.00
5-5/8" d, 2-7/8" h, orange-tan band, dark brown stripes, emb green band with blue, white, and dark brown earthworm, repairs 550.00
6-1/4" d, 3-1/4" h, tan band with black stripes, seaweed dec, repaired 55.00

MONART GLASS

History: Monart glass is a heavy, simply shaped art glass in which colored enamels are suspended in the glass during the glassmaking process. This technique was originally developed by the Ysart family in Spain in 1923. John Moncrief, a Scottish glassmaker, discovered the glass while vacationing in Spain, recognized the beauty and potential market, and began production in his Perth glassworks in 1924.

Lamp Shade, white opal, 6-1/4" d, $80.

The name "Monart" is derived from the surnames Moncrief and Ysart. Two types of Monart were manufactured: a commercial line which incorporated colored enamels and a touch of aventurine in crystal, and the art line in which the suspended enamels formed designs such as feathers or scrolls.

Marks: Monart glass, in most instances, is not marked. The factory used paper labels.

Basket, brown to light tan opal vertical striations, Cluthra type 600.00
Bowl, 11-1/2" d, mottled orange and green 195.00
Lamp Shade, 6-1/2" d, white opal 95.00
Vase
6-1/2" h, mottled shades of red and blue, white lining .. 225.00
16" h, green, flecked neck, orange body, dark inclusions, gold Cluthra centers 465.00

MONT JOYE GLASS

History: Mont Joye is a type of glass produced by Saint-Hilaire, Touvier, de Varreaux & Company at their glassworks in Pantin, France. Most pieces were lightly acid etched to give them a frosted appearance and were also decorated with enameled florals.

Note: Pieces listed below are frosted unless otherwise noted.

Pitcher, 10" h, amethyst, enameled flowers, aqua, blue, pink, and gold, sgd 350.00
Rose Bowl, 3-3/4" h, 4-1/4" d, pinched sides, acid etched, enameled purple violets, gold stems and dec 295.00
Vase
4" h, pink enameled poppy and gold leaves, frosted textured ground, mkd 275.00
5-1/2" h, swirled shape, green, enameled flowers, c1890, sgd "Mont Joye" 445.00
10" h, bulbous, narrow neck, clear to opalescent green, naturalistic thistle dec, gold highlights 375.00
18" h, green, enameled purple flowers, gold leaves, sgd.... 325.00
Violet Vase, 6" h, frosted etched surface, colorless glass, naturalistic enameled purple violet blossoms, gold highlights, base mkd "Dimier Geneve" 260.00

MOORCROFT

History: William Moorcroft was first employed as a potter by James MacIntyre & Co., Ltd., of Burslem in 1897. He established the Moorcroft pottery in 1913.

The majority of the art pottery wares were hand thrown, resulting in a great variation among similarly styled pieces. Color and marks are keys to determining age.

Walker, William's son, continued the business upon his father's death and made wares in the same style.

Marks: The company initially used an impressed mark, "Moorcroft, Burslem"; a signature mark, "W. Moorcroft" followed. Modern pieces are marked simply "Moorcroft" with export pieces also marked "Made in England."

References: Susan and Al Bagdade, *Warman's English & Continental Pottery & Porcelain*, 2nd ed., Wallace-Homestead, 1991; Frances Salmon, *Collecting Moorcroft*, Francis-Joseph Books, 1994.

Jar, cov, Anemones pattern, light blue ground, imp mark, sgd, c1940, $125.

Museum: Moorcroft Museum, Stoke-on-Trent, England.

Bowl
    10" d, octagonal, grape dec 215.00
    12-1/2" d, grapes and leaves, green ground, Walter Moorcroft facsimile signature, factory mark, c1945..................500.00
Candlesticks, pr, 10" h, tree dec, shades of yellow, cobalt blue ground, script sgd 195.00
Compote, 7-1/4" d, Lily motif, yellow and green ground 150.00
Ginger Jar, cov, 11-1/2" h, pomegranate dec 525.00
Loving Cup, 4-1/4" h, tulip and cornflower dec, green, blue, and red, 3 handles, printed and painted signature, c1900 ....350.00
Marmalade Jar, cov, blue flowers, attached stand, sgd "MacIntyre" 175.00
Pitcher, 5" h, 6" d, bulbous, yellow and pink irises, shaded blue to green ground, imp signature...350.00
Plate
    7-1/4" d, toadstool, blue ground, imp "Moorcroft Claremont" 620.00
    8-1/2" d, Natural Ware, green and blue glaze, pr..........235.00
Potpourri Jar, 3-1/4" h, 3-1/2" d, heart shaped leaves, cinnabar glaze, ink script signature, chip to thread inside 400.00
Vase
    3" h, Pomegranate, cobalt blue ground.........................115.00
    7" h, wide mouth, tapering cylindrical, green tree landscape, blue ground, fitted hammered pewter circular foot, stamped "H Made in England, Tudric, Moorcroft, Made by Liberty & Co." 950.00
    7-1/2" h, 4-1/2" d, ftd, purple grapes, yellow leaves, shaded green to blue ground, die-stamped mark, ink signature 660.00
    8-1/2" h, red, blue, and green floral dec, fluted top, incised and sgd...250.00
    10-1/4" h, red, blue, and yellow floral dec, fluted top, incised and sgd 550.00

MORGANTOWN GLASS WORKS

History: The Morgantown Glass Works, Morgantown, West Virginia, was founded in 1899 and began produc-

tion in 1901. Reorganized in 1903, it operated as the Economy Tumbler Company for 20 years until, in 1923, the word "Tumbler" was dropped from the corporate title. The firm was then known as The Economy Glass Company until reversion to its original name, Morgantown Glass Works, Inc., in 1929, the name it kept until its first closing in 1937. In 1939, the factory was reopened under the aegis of a guild of glassworkers and operated as the Morgantown Glassware Guild from that time until its final closing. Purchased by Fostoria in 1965, the factory operated as a subsidiary of the Moundsville-based parent company until 1971 when Fostoria opted to terminate production of glass at the Morgantown facility. Today, collectors use the generic term, "Morgantown Glass," to include all periods of production from 1901 to 1971.

Morgantown was a 1920s leader in the manufacture of colorful wares for table and ornamental use in American homes. The company pioneered the processes of iridization on glass as well as gold and platinum encrustation of patterns. It enhanced Crystal offerings with contrasting handle and foot of India Black, Spanish Red (ruby), and Ritz Blue (cobalt blue), and other intense and pastel colors for which it is famous. It conceived the use of contrasting shades of fired enamel to add color to its etchings and was the only American company to use a chromatic silk-screen printing process on glass– its two most famous and collectible designs being Queen Louise and Manchester Pheasant.

The company is also known for ornamental "open stems" produced during the late 1920s. Open stems separate to form an open design midway between the bowl and foot, e.g., an open square, a "Y," or two diamond-shaped designs. Many of these open stems were purchased and decorated by Dorothy C. Thorpe in her California studio, and her signed open stems command high prices from today's collectors. Morgantown also produced figural stems for commercial clients such as Koscherak Brothers and Marks & Rosenfeld. Chanticleer (rooster) and Mai Tai (Polynesian bis) cocktails are two of the most popular figurals collected today.

Morgantown is best known for the diversity of design in its stemware patterns, as well as for its four patented optics: Festoon, Palm, Peacock, and Pineapple. These optics were used to embellish stems, jugs, bowls, liquor sets, guest sets, salvers, ivy and witch balls, vases, and smoking items.

Two well-known lines of Morgantown Glass are recognized by most glass collectors today: #758 Sunrise Medallion and #7643 Golf Ball Stem Line. When Economy introduced #758 in 1928, it was originally identified as "Nymph." By 1931, the Morgantown front office had renamed it Sunrise Medallion. Recent publications erred in labeling it "dancing girl." Upon careful study of the medallion, you can see the figure is poised on one tiptoe, musically saluting the dawn with her horn. The second well-known line, #7643 Golf Ball, was patented in 1928; production commenced immediately and continued until the company closed in 1971. More Golf Ball than any other Morgantown product is found on the market today.

References: Jerry Gallagher, *Handbook of Old Morgantown Glass*, Vol. I, published by author (420 First Ave.

NW, Plainview, MN 55964), 1995; ——, Old Morgantown, Catalogue of Glassware, 1931, Morgantown Collectors of America Research Society, n.d.; Ellen Schroy, *Warman's Depression Glass,* Krause Publications, 1997; Hazel Marie Weatherman, *Colored Glassware of the Depression Era*, Book 2 published by author, 1974, available in reprint; ——, *1984 Supplement & Price Trends for Colored Glassware of the Depression Era*, Book 1, published by author, 1984.

Periodical: *Morgantown Newscaster*, Morgantown Collectors of America, 420 First Ave., NW, Plainview, MN 55964.

Collectors' Clubs: Old Morgantown Glass Collectors' Guild, P.O. Box 894, Morgantown, WV 26507.

Advisor: Jerry Gallagher.

Bowl

#1 Berkshire, Crystal w/#90 Starlet Cutting, 8" d.................42.00
#12 Stella, Nanking Blue, #2 Cover, 8" d...........................285.00
#12-1/2 Woodsfield, Pomona Line, 12-1/2" d 550.00
#17 Calypso, Spanish Red, 7-3/4" d................................195.00
#19 Kelsha, Genova Line, 12" d.....................................385.00
#22 Linwood, Topreen Line, Spiral Optic, 10" d...............355.00
#26 Greer, Neubian Line, 10" d......................................645.00
#26 Greer, Topreen Line, 10" d......................................465.00
#35-1/2 Elena, Old Bristol Line, 9-1/2" d...........................745.00
#67 Fantasia, Bristol Blue, 5-1/2" d..................................65.00
#71 Vienna, Steigel Green w/Crystal Italian Base, 12" d ... 1,400.00
#101 Heritage, Gypsy Fire, Matte Finish, 8" d 65.00
#103 Elyse, Steel Blue, 7" d...48.00
#111 Dodd, Bristol Blue, 5" d..65.00
#1102 Crown, Moss Green, 9" d..40.00
#9937 Revere, Ruby, 6" d..65.00
#1933 El Mexicano Console, Ice or Seaweed, 10" d..........245.00
#1933 El Mexicano Ice Tub, Ice or Seaweed, 6" d.............210.0
#4355 Janice, 14K Topaz, Carlton/Madrid, 13" d.............185.00
#4355 Janice, Ritz Blue or Spanish Red, 13" d.................235.00
#4355 Janice, Crystal, #787 Maytime etch, 13" d 195.00
#4355 Janice, Crystal, Glacier Decor w/Snow Flowers, 13" d
....475.00
#7643 Celeste, Spanish Red, Crystal trim, covered, 6" d.....1,200.00
#7643 Truman, Spanish Red, Crystal trim, rare, 10" d 2,500.00

Comport Bowl, #35-1/2 Eleana, Old Bristol Line, Ritz Blue with Alabaster trim, rare, 9-1/2" d, $1,500.

Candleholders, pr, #37, Emperor, Genova Two-Tone Ware, 14K-Topaz with Nanking Blue trim, rare, 8"h, $1,485.

Candleholders, pair

#37 Emperor, Stiegel Green or 14K Topaz, 8" h 585.00
#60 Rhoda Hurricane Lite, plain rim, Lime, 8" h.................110.00
#80 Modern, Moss Green, 7-1/2" h......................................65.00
#81 Bravo, Gypsy Fire, 4-1/2"...68.00
#81 Bravo, Thistle, 4-1/2" h...135.00
#82 Cosmopolitan, Gypsy Fire, slant, 7" h...........................75.00
#87 Hamilton, Evergreen, 5" h..70.00
#88 Classic, Nutmeg, 4-3/4" h..48.00
#105 Coronet, Ebony or Cobalt, slant, 8-3/4" h 118.00
#7620 Fontanne, Ebony filament, #781 Fontinelle etch......575.00
#7643 Dupont, Crystal, rare, 4-5/8" h................................385.00
#7643 Golf Ball, Torch Candle, single, Ritz Blue, 6" h........210.00
#7643 Jacobi, Anna Rose or Venetian Green, rare, 4" h 525.00
#7662 Majesty, Randall Blue, 4" h.....................................425.00
#7662 Majesty, Spanish Red, 4"..395.00
#7690 Monroe, Ritz Blue, 7" h, rare 975.00
#7949 Bertonna, Danube Line, 8-3/4" h 835.00
#7951 Stafford, Crystal w/#25 gold band, 3-1/8" h............625.00
#9923 Colonial, Burgundy, 2-pc hurricane, 8-1/2" h 130.00

Candy Jar

#14 Guilford, Genova Line, #3 cover, 10-3/4" h 500.00
#14 Edmond, Danube Line, #4 cover, rare, 8-1/2" h..........545.00
#15 Lisbon, Crystal w/#734 American Beauty etch, #2 cover, 8-1/2" h...525.00
#16 Rachel, Crystal, Pandora Cutting, 6" h 385.00

#71 Jupiter, Steel Blue, 6" h......................................85.00
#108 Bethann, Topreen Line, 5" h 395.00
#127 Yorktown Steel Blue, 7-1/2" h...........................55.00
    Moss Green, 7-1/2" 8.00
#200, Mansfield, Burgundy matte, 12" h 195.00
#1114 Jerome, Bristol Blue, 11-1/2" h 135.00
#1212 Michael, Spanish Red, Crystal finial, 5-1/2" h..........850.00
#2938 Helga, Anna Rose, Meadow Green finial, 5" h 1,500.00
#7643-1 Alexandra, Randall Blue/Crystal Duo-Tone, 5" h
    ....625.00
#9949 Christmas Tree, Crystal, 4 part stack jar, 11" h 140.00
#9952 Palace, Ruby, 6-12" h 60.00

Champagne

#7565 Astrid, American Beauty etch, 6 oz. 37.50
#7606-1/2 Athena, Ebony filament, #777 Baden etch, 7 oz. 75.00
#7621 Ringer, Aquamarine, 6 oz. 55.00
#7621 Ringer, Anna Rose, 7 oz. 55.00
#7623 Pygon, D.C. Thorpe satin open stem, 6-1/2 oz. 140.00
#7630 Ballerina, #757 Elizabeth etch, 6 oz. 55.00
#7640 Art Moderne, Ebony open stem, 5 oz. 65.00
#7643 Golf Ball, 5-1/2 oz.
    Ritz Blue..345.00
    Spanish Red 325.00
    Stiegel Green 325.00
#7660 Empress, Spanish Red, 6 oz. 48.00
#7664 Queen Anne, Azure, #758 Sunrise Medallion etch, 6-1/2
    oz. 85.00
#7705 Hopkins, Toulon gold decor, 5 oz. 145.00
#7860 Lawton, Azure, Festoon Optic, 5 oz. 48.00

Cocktail

#7577 Venus, Anna Rose or Azure, Palm Optic, 3 oz. 35.00
#7586 Napa, Azure, Festoon Optic, 3-1/2 oz. 48.00
#7620 Fontanne, Ebony filament, #781 Fontinelle etch, 3-1/2 oz.
    ....85.00
#7630 Ballerina, #765 Springtime etch, 3 oz. 45.00
#7643 Golf Ball, 3-1/2 oz.
    Ritz Blue..38.00
    Spanish Red 38.00
    Stiegel Green 38.00
#7654-1/2 Legacy, Spanish Red, 3 oz. 45.00
#7654-1/2 Legacy, Manchester Pheasant Silk Screen, 3-1/2 oz.
    ....165.00

Cordial

#7565 Astrid, Anna Rose, #734 American Beauty etch,
#7570 Horizon, #735 Richmond etch, 1 oz. 45.00
#7577 Venus, Anna Rose, #743 Bramble Rose etch, 1-1/2 oz.
    ....145.00
#7587 Hanover, #733 Virginia etch w/#25 Minton Gold band, 1 oz.
    ....55.00
#7643 Golf Ball, 1-1/2 oz.
    Pastels 48.00
    Ritz Blue..58.00
    Spanish Red 55.00
    Stiegel Green 48.00
#7617 Brilliant
    Ritz Blue, 1-1/2 oz. 135.00
    Spanish Red, 1-1/2 oz. 115.00
#7640 Art Moderne, Ebony stem, 1-1/2 oz. 135.00
#7654 Lorna, Nantucket etch, 1-1/2 oz. 85.00
#7660-1/2 Empress, Spanish red, 1-1/2 oz. 87.50
#7668 Galaxy, Mayfair etch, 1-1/2 oz. 87.50
#7668 Galaxy, #810 Sears' Lace Bouquet etch, 1-1/2 oz.
    ....48.00
#7673 Lexington, Ritz Blue filament, #790 Fairwin etch, 1-1/2 oz.
    ....142.50

Goblet

#7565 Astrid, #734 American Beauty etch, punty cut stem, 10 oz.
    ....58.00
#7568 Horizon, #735 Richmond etch, 10 oz. 48.00
#7577 Venus, Anna Rose
    Azure foot, Tulip Optic, 9 oz. 145.00
    Palm Optic, 9 oz. 48.00
#743 Bramble Rose etch, 9 oz. 125.00
#7577 Venus, Crystal, #743 Bramble Rose etch, 9 oz. 75.00
#7589 Laurette, #735 Richmond etch, 9 oz. 42.00
#7604-1/2 Heirloom, 14-K Topaz, #751 Adonis etch, 9 oz.......95.00
#7614 Hampton
    Anna Rose stem, Queen Louise Silk Screen, 9 oz. 225.00
    Golden iris, Virginia etch, 9 oz. 58.00
#7617 Brilliant
    Ritz Blue, 10 oz. 110.00
    Spanish Red, 10 oz. 95.00
#7623 Pygon, D. C. Thorpe satin open stem, 9 oz. 185.00
#7624 Paragon, Ebony open stem, 10 oz. 165.00
#7625 Paramount, Meadow Green open stem, #765 Springtime
    etch, 10 oz. 165.00
#7630 Ballerina, Aquamarine/Azure, Yukon cutting, 10 oz. 110.00
#7636 Square, open stem, 9 oz. 245.00
#7637 Courtney, D.C. Thorpe satin open stem, 9 oz. 195.00
#7638 Avalon, venetian Green, Peacock Optic, 9 oz. 45.00
#7640 Art Moderne, Ritz Blue, Crystal open stem, 9 oz. ...145.00
#7643 Golf Ball, 9 oz.
    Alabaster 145.00
    Pastels 45.00
    Ritz Blue..55.00
    Spanish Red 50.00
    Stiegel Green 40.00
#7644-1/2 Vernon, Venetian Green, Pineapple Optic, 9 oz. 48.00
#7646 Sophisticate, Picardy etch, 9 oz. 65.00
#7659 Cynthia, #746 Sonoma etch, 10 oz. 65.00
#7664 Queen Anne, #758 Sunrise Medallion etch, 10 oz. ..87.50
#7664 Queen Anne, Manchester Pheasant Silk Screen, 10 oz.
    ....245.00
#7678 Old English, 10 oz.
    Ritz Blue..55.00
    Spanish Red 55.00
    Stiegel Green 45.00
#7690 Monroe, Golden Iris, Amber, 9 oz. 75.00

Guest Set

#23 Trudy, 6-3/8" h
    Alabaster 158.00
    Anna Rose, Palm Optic 87.50
    Baby Blue 65.00
    Baby Blue carafe, India Black tumbler 140.00
    Bristol Blue 125.00
    Jade Green 87.50
    Opaque Yellow carafe, India Black tumbler 165.00
    Venetian Green, Palm Optic 95.00
#24 Margaret, 5-7/8" h
    Azure/Aquamarine, enamel decor 130.00
    Anna Rose, enamel decor 120.00
    Jade Green 185.00
    Golden iris, pulled spout, handled 425.00

Jug

#6 Kaufmann, Old Bristol line, 54 oz. 1,500.00
#6 Kaufmann, #510 Doric Star Sand Blast, 54 oz. 275.00
#8 Orleans, #90 Starlet Cutting, 54 oz. 315.00
#8 Orleans, #131 Brittany Cutting, 54 oz. 385.00
#14 Eiffel, #282 needle etch, 65 oz. 325.00
#33 Martina, 46 oz., 7-piece set, #518 Lily of the Valley Sand
    Blast...585.00
#33 Rawsthorne, Anna Rose, Peacock Optic, 48 oz. 465.00

#36 Bolero, Pomona Two-Tone Line, 54 oz. 975.00
#37 Barry, Anna Rose handle and foot, Palm Optic, 48 oz.
....340.00
#37 Barry, Zurich Two Tone Line, covered, 48 oz.......860.00
#303 Cyrano, #203 needle etch, 54 oz. 365.00
#545 Pickford Spiral, Amber, 54 oz. 135.00
#1933 LMX Del Rey, Randall Blue non-opaque, rare, 54 oz.
....525.00
#1933 LMX Ockner, Ice or Seaweed, 64 oz. 210.00
#1962 Ockner, Crinkle Line, 64 oz.
    Amethyst...125.00
    Pink Champagne....................................115.00
    Pink Champagne, frosted.......................165.00
    Topaz Mist...65.00
#1962 San Juan, Crinkle Line, Amethyst, Tankard, 64 oz. 125.00
#1962 Tijuana, Crinkle Line, Peacock Blue, Juice/Martini, 34 oz.
....80.00
#7622-1/2 Ringling, 54 oz.
    Golden Iris...460.00
    Randall Blue..535.00
    Spanish Red..495.00
#9844 Swirl, Burgundy, 54 oz...................................185.00
#20069 Melon, Alabaster, Ritz Blue trim 650.00

Plate, #1500

Alexandrite, #776 Nasreen etch, dessert, 7" d.............135.00
Anna Rose, #734 American Beauty etch, dessert, 7" d.......48.00
Anna Rose, #743 Bramble Rose etch, salad/luncheon, 8-1/2" d
....55.00
Crystal, Hollywood Platinum/Red band decor, torte, 14" d
....365.00
Crystal, #810 Sear's Lace Bouquet etch, dessert, 7" d........22.00
Meadow Green, #737 Victoria Regina decoration, dessert, 7" d
....22.00
Ritz Blue, Vernay decoration, dessert, 7-1/2" d.................115.00
Old Bristol, dessert, 7-1/4" d.....................................185.00
Stiegel Green, salad/luncheon, 8-1/2" d........................48.00
14-K Topaz, #751 Adonis etch, dessert, 7"d....................58.00
14-K Topaz, Carlton Madrid, liner, 6" d...........................35.00
14-K Topaz, Carlton Madrid, dessert, 7-1/4" d..................48.00
14-K Topaz, #776 Nasreen etch, salad, 7-3/4" d.............55.00

Sherbet

3300 Touraine #509 Essex Cutting
#1962 Crinkle, 6 oz.
    Pineapple...32.50
    Pink...20.00
    Ruby..27.50
#3011 Montego, Peacock Blue, 6-1/2 oz. 24.00
#7620 Fontanne, #781 Fontinelle etch, 6 oz. 135.00
#7640 Aft Moderne, Ritz Blue, 5-1/2 oz.........................65.00
#7643 Golf Ball, 5-1/2 oz.
    Pastels...35.00
    Ritz Blue..45.00
    Spanish Red..38.00
    Stiegel Green.......................................35.00
#7646 Sophisticate, Picardy etch, 5-1/2 oz....................44.00
#7654 Lorna, Meadow Green stem, #766 Nantucket etch, 5-1/2 oz...55.00
#7654-1/2 Legacy, Manchester Pheasant Silk Screen, 6-1/2 oz.
....125.00
#7668 Galaxy, #787-1/2 Mayfair etch, 5-1/2 oz...............30.00
#7690 Monroe, Old Amethyst, 6 oz. 80.00
#7690 Monroe, Spanish red, 6 oz. 70.00
#7780 The President's House, 6 oz..............................15.00

Silk-Screen Color Printing on Crystal

Manchester Pheasant
    #7654-1/2 Legacy, cocktail, 3-1/2 oz. 185.00
    #7664 Queen Anne, goblet, 10 oz................245.00

Queen Louise
    #7614 Hampton, Anna Rose stem, goblet, 9 oz............285.00

Tumbler

#1962 Crinkle, Amberina, flat water, 10 oz. 120.00
#1962 Crinkle, India Black, flat juice, 6 oz. 50.00
#7664 Queen Anne, Azure/Aquamarine, #758 Elizabeth etch, 11 oz. 85.00
#7668 Galaxy, #778 Carlton etch, 9 oz. 22.00
#7703 Sextette, Old Bristol, ftd tea, 11 oz. 185.00
#9074 Belton, Golden Iris, #733 Virginia etch, 12 oz. 48.00
#9074 Belton, Primrose, Vaseline, Pillar Optic, 9 oz. 115.00

Vase

#26 Catherine 10" bud
    Anna Rose, #758 Sunrise Medallion etch.....................395.00
    Azure, #758 Sunrise Medallion etch...........................235.00
    Jade Green, Enamel Floral Decor, crimped..................230.00
#35-1/2 Electra, Continental Line, Old Amethyst, 10".........795.00
#53 Serenade 10" Bud
    Opaque Yellow.....................................390.00
    Spanish Red...215.00
    Venetian Green, #756 Tinker Bell etch.....................395.00
#54 Media, Golden Iris, Pillar Optic, 10".......................190.00
#73 Radio, Ritz Blue, 6"...895.00
#1933 Goydas, LMX Seaweed, 6-1/2".........................465.00
#7643 Kennon, Ivy Ball Vase, Ritz Blue, 4".....................135.00

Wine

#7565 Astrid, Anna Rose, #734 American Beauty etch, 3 oz. ... 95.00
#7560 Horizon, #735 Richmond etch, 3 oz. 45.00
#7577 Venus, Anna Rose, #743 Bramble Rose etch, 3-1/2 oz. 135.00
#7587 Hanover, #733 Virginia etch w/#25 Minton Gold band, 3 oz.
....40.00
#7643 Golf Ball, 3 oz.
    Alabaster...135.00
    Pastels...50.00
    Ritz Blue..65.00
    Spanish Red..56.00
    Stiegel Green.......................................50.00
#7617 Brilliant, Ritz Blue, 2-1/2 oz. 110.00
#7640 Art Moderne, ebony stem, 3 oz. 135.00
#7654 Lorna, Nantucket etch, 3 oz. 85.00
#7660-1/2 Empress, Spanish Red, 3 oz. 85.00
#7668 Galaxy, #810 Sears' Lace Bouquet etch, 2-1/2 oz......48.00
#7673 Lexington, Ritz Blue filament lament, #790 Fairwin etch, 3 oz. 135.00
#7720 Palazzo, Violet, 3-1/2 oz. 120.00
#7721 Panama, Sharon decoration, 3 oz. 195.00
#8445 Plantation, Lotus Green, 3 oz. 115.00
#8446 Summer Cornucopia, Copen Blue bowl, 3 oz. 275.00

MORIAGE, JAPANESE

History: Moriage refers to applied clay (slip) relief decorations used on certain types of Japanese pottery and porcelain.

This decorating was done by one of three methods: 1) hand rolling, hand shaping, and hand application to the biscuit in one or more layers; the design and effect required determine thickness and shape, 2) tubing or slip trailing, which applied decoration from a tube, like decorating a cake, and 3) hakeme which involved reducing the slip to a liquid and decorating the object with a brush. Color was applied either before or after the process.

Vase, two handles, Lotus pattern, yellow and brown ground, pink and green, shallow bulbous body, 7" d, 6" h, $150.

Bowl, 7" d, orange flowers and leaves, green wreath mark
....150.00
Chocolate Pot, cov, 9" h, green ground, 4 floral medallions, heavy Moriage...245.00
Manicure Set, 3 tools, butter and cov trinket box, heavy dec
....195.00
Planter, 3-3/4" h, 3-3/4" l, swan, figural, multicolored enameled dec...95.00
Vase, 9-1/4" h, pedestal base, green ground, white overall slipwork, floral medallions 265.00

MOSER GLASS

Moser   *Moser Karlsbad*

History: Ludwig Moser (1833-1916) founded his polishing and engraving workshop in 1857 in Karlsbad (Karlovy Vary), Czechoslovakia. He employed many famous glass designers, e.g., Johann Hoffmann, Josef Urban, and Rudolf Miller. In 1900 Moser and his sons, Rudolf and Gustav, incorporated Ludwig Moser & Söhne.

Moser art glass included clear pieces with inserted blobs of colored glass, cut colored glass with classical scenes, cameo glass, and intaglio cut items. Many inexpensive enameled pieces also were made.

In 1922, Leo and Richard Moser bought Meyr's Neffe, their biggest Bohemian art glass rival. Moser executed many pieces for the Wiener Werkstätte in the 1920s. The Moser glass factory continues to produce new items.

References: Gary Baldwin and Lee Carno, *Moser–Artistry in Glass*, Antique Publications, 1988; Mural K. Charon and John Mareska, *Ludvik Moser, King of Glass*, published by author, 1984.

Basket, 5-1/2" h, green malachite, molded cherubs dec, pr
....800.00
Beverage Set, 10-1/4" h, frosted and polished smoky topaz decanter, 4 cordials, molded nude women, 5 pc set........265.00
Centerpiece, 5" x 9", green, intaglio cut flowers.................425.00
Cologne Bottle, 7-1/2" h, 3-1/2" d, amethyst shaded to clear, deep intaglio cut flowers and leaves, orig stopper, sgd 695.00
Cup and Saucer, amber, gold scrolls, multicolored enameled flowers 295.00
Demitasse Cup and Saucer, amber shading to white, enameled gilt flowers..100.00

Urn, cov, enameled oak leaves, applied acorns, green ground, 27" h, $8,250. Photo courtesy of Woody Auction.

Ewer, 10-3/4" h, cranberry, gilt surface, applied acorns and clear jewels..2,000.00
Goblet, 8" h, cranberry, Rhine-style, enameled oak leaves, applied acorns, 4 pc set..1,800.00
Perfume, 4-3/4" h, pink-lavender alexandrite, faceted panels, matching stopper, sgd in oval......................................275.00
Pitcher, 6-3/4" h, amberina, IVT, 4 yellow, red, blue, and green applied glass beaded bunches of grapes, pinched in sides, 3 dimensional bird beneath spout, allover enamel and gold leaves, vines, and tendrils 3,200.00
Portrait Vase, 8-1/2" h, woman, gold leaves, light wear 450.00
Urn, 15-3/4" h, cranberry, 2 gilt handles, studded with green, blue, clear, and red stones, highly enameled surface, multicolored and gilt Moorish dec 3,500.00
Vase
   6-1/2", cranberry, heavy applied dec of scrolls, abstract flowers, and butterflies, four ftd, #2208 ....950.00
   7" h, paneled amber baluster body, wide gold medial band of women warriors, base inscribed "Made in Czechoslovakia-Moser Karlsbad"...550.00
   9" h, cranberry, two gilt handles, medallion with hp roses, sgd..1,050.00
   10" h, heavy walled dark amethyst faceted body, etched and gilded medial scene of bear hunt, spear-armed men and dogs pursuing large bear 345.00
   23-1/2" h, cranberry ground, enameled leaf surface, applied acorns, three dimensional eagle and bird, sgd "Moser," stand..8,250.00

MOSS ROSE PATTERN CHINA

History: Several English potteries manufactured china with a Moss Rose pattern in the mid-1800s. Knowles, Taylor and Knowles, an American firm, began production of a Moss Rose pattern in the 1880s.

The moss rose was a common garden flower grown in England. When American consumers tired of English china with Oriental themes, they purchased the Moss Rose pattern as a substitute.

Cake Plate, two emb handles, $35.

Butter Pat, sq, mkd "Meakin"...25.00
Coffee Mug and Saucer, mkd "Meakin" 42.00
Cup and Saucer, mkd "Haviland, Limoges"..........................25.00
Dessert Set, cake plate, eight 7-1/2" plates, cups and saucers,
    creamer and sugar, mkd "Fr. Haviland," price for 28 pc set
    ....295.00
Gravy Boat, matching underplate, mkd "Green & Co., England"
    ....30.00
Nappy, 4-1/2" d, mkd "Edwards"...15.00
Plate
    7-1/2" d, Haviland, Limoges 20.00
    8-1/2" d, mkd "KTK"..25.00
    9-1/2" d, mkd "Haviland" 20.00
Platter, 10" w, 14" l, rect, mkd "Meakin"...............................30.00
Salt and Pepper Shakers, pr, 5" h, sterling silver top and base,
    mkd "Rosenthal" 65.00
Sauce Dish, 4-1/2" d, mkd "Haviland" 20.00
Soup Plate, 9" d, mkd "Meakin"...20.00
Sugar, cov, mkd "Haviland, Limoges"....................................70.00
Tea Service, cov teapot, creamer, sugar, mkd "Meakin"...220.00
Teapot, 8-1/2" h, bulbous, gooseneck spout, basketweave trim,
    mid "T & V" 45.00
Tureen, cov, 12" l, gold trim...75.00

MOUNT WASHINGTON GLASS COMPANY

History: In 1837, Deming Jarves, founder of the Boston and Sandwich Glass Company, established for George D. Jarves, his son, the Mount Washington Glass Company in Boston, Massachusetts. In the following years, the leadership and the name of the company changed several times as George Jarves formed different associations.

In the 1860s, the company was owned and operated by Timothy Howe and William L. Libbey. In 1869, Libbey bought a new factory in New Bedford, Massachusetts. The Mount Washington Glass Company began operating again there under its original name. Henry Libbey became associated with the company early in 1871. He resigned in 1874 during the general depression, and the glassworks was closed. William Libbey had resigned in 1872 when he went to work for the New England Glass Company.

The Mount Washington Glass Company opened again in the fall of 1874 under the presidency of A. H. Seabury and the management of Frederick S. Shirley. In 1894, the glassworks became a part of the Pairpoint Manufacturing Company.

Throughout its history, the Mount Washington Glass Company made different types of glass including pressed, blown, art, lava, Napoli, cameo, cut, Albertine, and Verona.

References: Edward and Sheila Malakoff, *Pairpoint Lamps*, Schiffer Publishing, 1990; John A. Shuman III, *Collector's Encyclopedia of American Art Glass*, Collector Books, 1988, 1994 value update.

Collectors Club: Mount Washington Art Glass Society, P.O. Box 24094, Fort Worth, TX 76124.-1094

Museum: The New Bedford Glass Museum, New Bedford, MA.

Additional Listings: Burmese; Crown Milano; Peachblow; Royal Flemish.

Advisor: Louis O. St. Aubin Jr.

Beverage Set, satin, MOP
    Coralene, yellow sea weed dec, glossy finish, 9" h, bulbous
        water pitcher, three spout top, applied reeded shell handle,
        three matching 4" h tumblers, 2 blisters on pitcher, 3 pc
        set 750.00
    Herringbone, 9" h bulbous water pitcher, 7" w, applied frosted
        handle, deep rose to deep pink to pink, to off white, enameled and painted white wild roses, green, brown, and gold
        leaves, stems, branches, and thorns, 4 3-3/4" h tumblers,
        damage to tumbler, 5 pc set 1,750.00
Bowl, 4-1/2" d, 2-3/4" h, Rose amber, fuchsia, blue swirl bands,
    bell tone flint 295.00
Box, 4-1/2" h, 6-1/2" d, opalware, mint green ground, deep pink
    roses, small red cornflowers, gold trim, blown-out floral and
    ribbon design, #3212/20 ....1,750.00
Collars and Cuffs Box, opalware, shaped as 2 collars with big
    bow in front, cov dec with orange and pink Oriental poppies,
    silver poppy-shaped finial with gold trim, base with poppies,
    white ground, gold trim, bright blue bow, white polka dots,
    buckle on back, sgd "Patent applied for April 10, 1894,"
    #2390/128..950.00
Cracker Jar, 9-1/2" h, 7-1/2" w, opalware, bright yellow ground,
    pink Oriental poppies, green leaves dec, blown-out floral and
    leaf design on base, orig metal hardware, base mkd
    "3930/230," cov mkd "Pairpoint" 525.00
Flower Holder, 5-1/4" d, 3-1/2" h, mushroom shape, white ground,
    blue dot and oak leaf dec..425.00
Fruit Bowl, 10" d, 7-1/2" h, Napoli, solid dark green ground painted on clear glass, outside dec with pale pink and white pond
    lilies, green and pink leaves and blossoms, int. dec with gold
    highlight traceries, silver-plated base with pond lily design, 2
    applied loop handles, 4 buds form feet, base sgd "Pairpoint
    Mfg. Co. B4704" 2,200.00
Humidor, 5-1/2" h, 4-1/2" d top, hinged silver-plated metalwork
    rim and edge, blown-out rococo scroll pattern, brilliant blue
    Delft windmills, ships, and landscape, Pairpoint..........950.00
Jewel Box, 4-1/2" d top, 5-1/4" d base, 3-1/4" h, opalware, Monk
    drinking glass of red wine on lid, solid shaded green background on cover and base, fancy gold-washed, silver-plated
    rim and hinge, orig satin lining, artist sgd "Schindler" ..550.00

Dresser Box, oval, opaque, large hand painted red and yellow roses, silvered mountings, four bracket floral feet sgd with Pairpoint logo, 7-1/4" l, $525. Photo courtesy of Jackson's Auctioneers & Appraisers.

Jug, 6" h, 4" w, satin, Polka Dot, deep peachblow pink, white air traps, DQ, unlined, applied frosted loop handle 475.00
Lamp, parlor, four dec glass oval insert panels, orig dec white opalware ball shade with deep red carnations, sgd "Pairpoint" base, c1890 .... 1,750.00
Lamp Shade, 4-1/4" h, 5" d across top, 2" d fitter, rose amber, ruffled, fuschia shading to deep blue, DQ 575.00
Miniature Lamp, 17" h, 4-1/2" d shade, banquet style, milk glass, bright blue Delft dec of houses and trees, orig metal fittings, attributed to Frank Guba 795.00
Mustard Pot, 4-1/2" h, ribbed, bright yellow and pink background, painted white and magenta wild roses, orig silver-plated hardware 185.00
Perfume Bottle, 5-1/4" h, 3" d, opalware, dark green and brown glossy ground, red and yellow nasturtiums, green leaves, sprinkler top 375.00
Pitcher, 6" h, 3" w, satin, DQ, MOP, large frosted camphor shell loop handle 325.00
Rose Bowl, 4" h, 5" d, satin, bright yellow, enameled red berries, pale orange leaves and branches, 8 large ribbed swirls
.... 145.00
Salt Shaker, fig, white ground, floral dec, orig top 225.00
Tumbler, 4" h, satin, c1880
    Diamond Quilted, heavenly blue 165.00
    Diamond Quilted, shaded yellow to white 165.00
    Herringbone, shaded blue 165.00
Vase
    5" h, 4" w, melon ribbed, ruffled tricorn top, MOP satin, Alice Blue, white lining, applied frosted edge, 1880s 275.00
    5-3/4" h, 4-1/4" h, satin, heavenly blue shading to white, white lining, hobnails, 4 fold, folded in-top 675.00
    6" h, 3-1/4" w, bulbous stick, satin, flaring rim, apricot shading to white, DQ 375.00
    6-1/4" h, 5-1/2" w, satin, melon ribbed, MOP, Bridal White, muslin pattern, applied frosted edge, c1880 .... 425.00
    6-1/2" h, 3" w, satin, Raindrop, Bridal White, MOP, applied frosted edge, pr 550.00
    6-1/2" h, 6" w, satin, bulbous, DQ, deep rose shading to pink, two applied frosted "M" handles with thorns, cut edge, c1880 .... 750.00
    8" h, Ring, black ground, gold storks in flight, gold floral dec, spoke bottom, pr 550.00
    8" h, satin, MOP, Raindrop, butterscotch, applied camphor edge 375.00
    8" h, 7" w, bulbous, satin, MOP, Alice Blue, Muslin pattern, applied frosted edge, 3 petal top 675.00
    8-1/4" h, 5" w, satin, amberina coloration, MOP DQ, deep gold diamonds, white lining, slightly ruffled top 1,250.00

8-1/2" h, 5" d at base, Napoli, int. dec in turquoise, blue, green, and rust, ext. outlined in gold, frog sitting in bulrushes dec, 8 vertical ribs, some paint loss on int. 975.00
9" h, 3-1/2" w at shoulder, MOP satin glass, deep gold, Raindrop pattern sheet lining, applied tightly crimped camphor edge, c1880 .... 285.00
9" h, 5-1/2" w, pink opalware, Delft windmill with person in front, gold trim top and base, Pairpoint 725.00
9-1/4" h, 4-1/4" w, satin, MOP, shaded rose, DQ, ruffled edges, white lining, c1880, pr 875.00
10" h, Neapolitan Ware, yellow, purple, rust, and gold spider mums, green leaves, gold spider webbing on ext., sgd "Napoli," #880 .... 1,450.00
11-1/4" h, gourd shape, 6" l flaring neck, satin, deep brown shading to gold, white lining, enameled seaweed design all over 550.00
11-7/8" h, bulbous stick, Colonial ware, glossy white, gold dec, all over vine and berry dec, two wreath and bow dec at top, sgd, #1010 .... 550.00
12-3/4" h, 5-1/2" w, Colonial ware, shaped like Persian water jug, loop handle on top, small spout, bulbous body, pedestal base, glossy white ground, pale pink and purple lilies, green leaves and stems, overlaid gold dec of leaves, stems, and daisies, sgd and #1022 .... 2,200.00
17-1/2" h, hp floral dec, white satin glass, swirl ribbed tall cylinder body 400.00

MULBERRY CHINA

History: Mulberry china was made primarily in the Staffordshire district of England between 1830 and 1860. The ware often has a flowing effect similar to Flow Blue. It is the color of crushed mulberries, a dark purple, sometimes with a gray tinge or bordering almost on black. The potteries that manufactured Flow Blue also made Mulberry china, and, in fact, frequently made some patterns in both types of wares. To date, there are no known reproductions.

References: Susan and Al Bagdade, *Warman's English & Continental Pottery & Porcelain*, 2nd ed., Wallace-Homestead, 1991; Ellen R. Hill, *Mulberry Ironstone*, published by author, 1993; Petra Williams, *Flow Blue China and Mulberry Ware*, revised ed., Fountain House East, 1993.

Advisor: Ellen G. King.

Bochara, Edwards
    Fruit Compote, cov, pedestal 400.00
    Tea Set, cov teapot (restoration to spout), creamer, cov sugar 350.00
Bryonia, Utzschneider
    Berry/Dessert Bowl, 4" d 35.00
    Plate, 7" d 40.00
    Tea Cup and Saucer 55.00
Calcutta, Challinor
    Gravy Boat 110.00
    Serving Bowl, 10-3/4" d, open 100.00
    Teapot, cov 250.00
Chinese Bells, Meigh, nested platter's, child size, 3 pc set
.... 225.00
Corea, Clementson
    Plate, 9-1/4" d 45.00
    Platter, 14" l 225.00
Corean, Podmore & Walker
    Creamer 120.00
    Platter, 16" l 275.00
    Sauce Tureen, lid, base, tray 400.00

Temple, water pitcher, 12" h, $450. Photo courtesy of Ellen King.

Sydney, plate, 10" d, $55. Photo courtesy of Ellen King.

Sugar Bowl, cov..110.00
Teapot, cov...255.00
Cyprus, Davenport
Creamer...125.00
Platter, 16" l..175.00
Sugar Bowl, cov..225.00
Vegetable Tureen, cov 220.00
Genoa, Davenport, wash basin and pitcher 375.00
Hong, Walker, pitcher, 8" h 250.00
Marble, Avery, tea trivet 135.00
Marble, Wedgwood, creamer 85.00
Medina, Furnival, teapot, cov, child size.........................250.00
Panama, Challinor, platter, 20" l.....................................300.00
Pelew, Challinor
Platter, 12-1/2" l..165.00
Platter, 18" l..350.00
Vegetable Tureen, cov 475.00
Rhone Scenery, Mayer
Plate, 8" d...55.00

Plate, 9-7/8" d 65.00
Teapot, cov, spout restoration.....................................225.00
Shinde, Walker
Plate, 8-1/2" d 45.00
Platter, 15-1/2" d 350.00
Shapoo, Boote, cup plate..85.00
Syndey, Wood & Son, plate, 10" d.................................55.00
Ta-Koo, Moore, plate, 9" d...60.00
Temple, Podmore & Walker
Creamer, 6" d..150.00
Milk Pitcher, 8" h...225.00
Platter, 18" l..185.00
Water Pitcher, 12" h 450.00
Tonquin, Heath, sugar bowl, cov 175.00
Vincennes, Alcock
Cameo Relish 180.00
Pitcher, 9-1/2" d...155.00
Platter, 12-1/2" l..120.00
Platter, 15-1/2" d 175.00
Sauce Tureen, lid, base, tray......................................250.00
Vegetable Tureen, cov 165.00

Bryonia, plate, 7" d, $40. Photo courtesy of Ellen King.

Pitcher, yellow ware ground, floral design, English, c1840-60, 8-1/2" h, $550. Photo courtesy of Ellen King.

Washington Vase, Podmore & Walker

Creamer, 6" h...200.00
Cup and Saucer, handleless.............................100.00
Plate, 8-3/4" d..65.00
Teapot, cov...350.00
Wash Basin and Pitcher..................................675.00

MUSICAL INSTRUMENTS

History: From the first beat of the prehistoric drum to the very latest in electronic music makers, musical instruments have been popular modes of communication and relaxation.

The most popular antique instruments are violins, flutes, oboes, and other instruments associated with the classical music period of 1650 to 1900. Many of the modern instruments, such as trumpets, guitars, and drums, have value on the "used" rather than antiques market.

The collecting of musical instruments is in its infancy. The field is growing very rapidly. Investors and speculators have played a role since the 1930s, especially in early string instruments.

References: Tony Bacon (ed.), *Classic Guitars of the '50s*, Miller Freeman Books (6600 Silacci Way, Gilroy, CA 95020), 1996; S. P. Fjestad (ed.), *Blue Book of Guitar Values*, 2nd ed., Blue Book Publications, 1994; George Gruhn and Walter Carter, *Acoustic Guitars and Other Fretted Instruments*, GPI Books, 1993; ——, *Electric Guitars and Basses*, Miller Freeman Books, GPI Books, 1994; ——, *Gruhn's Guide to Vintage Guitars*, GPI Books, 1991; Mike Longworth, *C. F. Martin & Co.*, 4 Maples Press, 1994; Paul Trynka (ed.), *Electric Guitar*, Chronicle Books, 1993.

Periodicals: *Concertina & Squeezebox*, P.O. Box 6706, Ithaca, NY 14851; *Jerry's Musical Newsletter*, 4624 W. Woodland Rd., Minneapolis, MN 55424; *Piano & Keyboard*, P.O. Box 767, San Anselmo, CA 94979; *Strings*, P.O. Box 767, San Anselmo, CA 94979; *Twentieth Century Guitar*, 135 Oser Ave., Hauppauge, NY 11788; *Vintage Guitar Classics*, P.O. Box 7301, Bismarck, ND 58507.

Collectors' Clubs: American Musical Instrument Society, RD. 3, Box 205-B, Franklin, PA 16323; Automatic Musical Instrument Collectors Assoc., 919 Lantern Glow Trail, Dayton, OH 45431; Fretted Instrument Guild of America, 2344 S. Oakley Ave., Chicago, IL 60608; Musical Box Society International, 887 Orange Ave. E., St. Paul, MN 55106; Reed Organ Society, Inc., P.O. Box 901, Deansboro, NY 13328.

Museums: C. F. Martin Guitar Museum, Nazareth, PA; International Piano Archives at Maryland, Neil Ratliff Music Library, College Park, MD; Miles Musical Museum, Eureka Springs, AR; Museum of the American Piano, New York, NY; Musical Museum, Deansboro, NY; Streitwieser Foundation Trumpet Museum, Pottstown, PA; University of Michigan, Stearns Collection of Musical Instruments, Ann Arbor, MI; Yale University Collection of Musical Instruments, New Haven, CT.

Accordion, 14-1/2" l, black lacquer, brass, silver, and abalone inlay, keys and decorative valve covers in carved mother of pearl, works, needs repair, some damage......................95.00

Banjo

Bacon Banjo Co., Style C, 17 fret neck, hard-shell case
....185.00
Edgemere Banjo, 17 nickel plated hexagonal brackets, nickel, shell, wood lined, birch neck with faux mahogany finish, c1900..300.00
Regina, 18 hook, 17 frets, peghead and fingerboard wood and metal trim, tone ring, metal resonator, 1920 patent date
....125.00

Bassoon, 48-1/4" l, pearwood, 8 keys, brass mounts and keys, Milliam Milhouse, branded "Milhouse/London".............525.00

Bugle, artillery, brass, c1900..150.00

Caliola, Wurlitzer, wooden pipes, decorative front with name "Clancy O'Toole," drums, keyboard for manual play, also roll operation..14,500.00

Clarinet, 11-1/2" l, stained maple, brass mounts, 10 brass keys, stamped "F. Muss/Wien"..425.00

Cymbals, 10" d, leather handles, American, c1900.............90.00

Drum

15" d, 12" h, snare, painted, labeled "Russell & Patee successors to Gilmore & Russell, 61 Court St., Boston, Mass," ink inscription "sold 1849," imperfections......................345.00
16-1/2" d, worn orig varnish and transfer dec of eagle and shield, labeled "Carl Fischer, New York," replaced ropes and leather, old heads, two drum sticks..................330.00
17" d, 13-5/8" h, painted dec, reserve of musical instruments and "H. W. Maynard," labeled "William Sempf Manufacturer of Bass & Snare Drums 209 & 211 Grand Street, New York…," mid 19th C, minor losses............................460.00

Flute, cocoa wood, silver trim, one key, German, late 19th C
....85.00

Guitar, University, rosewood back and sides, with vine and leaf pattern, spruce top, ebony guard plate, mahogany neck, MOP trim, 1905-10..250.00

Harmonica

Hohner, 20 double holes, 80 reeds, c1900.....................30.00
Sousa's Band, 20 holes, 40 brass reeds, c1900.............30.00

Harp, walnut, carved base, gilt traces, partially restored, restrung, Italian, c1620......................................3,500.00

Melodeon, 38" w, 19-1/2" d, 30" h, rosewood veneer, ebony and ivory keyboard, not working..50.00

Nicholodean, Cremona, style G, keyboard style, coin operated player piano, 29 flute pipes, 4 rolls, restored...........12,000.00

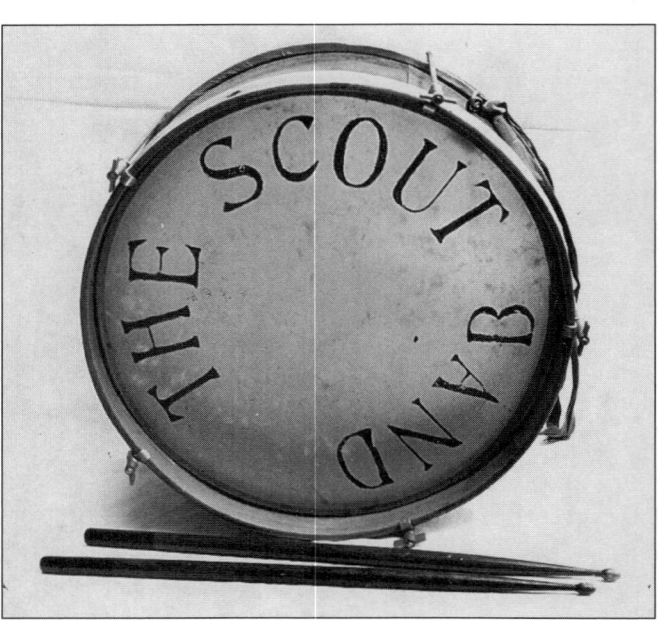

Drum, $80.

Piano

Grand, Classical, Wilkins & Newhall, Boylston St., Boston, early 19th C, mahogany, rosewood veneer piano case bordered by mahogany crossbanding, supported on curule-form base, applied concentric ring bosses, tapered molded feet, 72" w, 31" d, 36" h 1,000.00

Upright, late Empire, Philadelphia, c1850, inlaid and ormolu mounted mahogany, molded cornice, rect case with drapery inset, flanked by turned columns, hinged lid, keys and inlay read "Loud & Brothers/Philadelphia," carved turned legs, casters, 52" w, 26" d, 76" h 3,000.00

Upright, Wurlitzer Style I, nickelodeon, carved oak case, red sharp key, reiterating feature on hammers, 10 rolls 4,500.00

Pitch Pipe, 6" l, walnut, book form, paper label on int. "WN," America, 19th C, crack 200.00

Pump Reed Organ, 43" w, 22-3/4" d, 74" h, oak case, Eastlake detail, old worn finish, backboards incomplete, stop knob labels missing, not in working order 50.00

Saxophone

Dupont, B-flat, baritone, highly polished brass 350.00

Tourville & Co., tenor, silver 350.00

Trombone, Concertone, SP, gold plated bell, satin finish .. 300.00

Trumpet, Holton, B-flat, brass, nickel finish 550.00

Tuba, Dupont, E-flat, bass, nickel plated 475.00

Ukuele, The Serenader, B & G, NY, double binding around edge and hole, celluloid fingerboard and head 225.00

Violin

American, labeled "Henry Richard Knopf New York Anno 1904, No. 139," 2 pc back of strong medium curl, ribs and scroll similar, top of medium grain, red color varnish, 14" l back, with case 2,530.00

English, labeled "Antonius Stradivarius, Anno 1689," 1 pc back of irregular curl, ribs and scroll similar, top of fine to medium grain, gold-brown varnish, 13-7/8" l back, case and silver mounted bow stamped "F" 7,475.00

English, labeled "William Tarr, Fecit No. 56, Manchester 1883," 1 pc back of strong narrow curl, ribs and scroll similar, medium grain top, gold-brown varnish, 14" l back 2,415.00

German, labeled "Ernst" stamped internally, 1 pc back of strong narrow curl, ribs and scroll similar, fine grained top, red-brown varnish, 14-1/6" l back 3,105.00

Milan, labeled "Leandro Bisiach Da Milano Fece L'Anno 1924," 2 pc back of light irregular curl, ribs similar, scroll of broad curl, top of medium to wide grain, orange-brown varnish, 14-1/6" l back, with case 25,300.00

Violincello, labeled "Degani Eugenio, Quatttordici Medagilie Di Metito, Fece Venezia Anno 1891," 2 pc back with strong medium curl, matching ribs and scroll, top with fine grain, orange color varnish, 29-1/16" back length, case and nickel mounted bow 59,700.00

Violincello Bow, silver mounted

Nurnberger, Albet, octagonal stick stamped "Albert Nurnberger" at butt, ebony frog with pearl eye, silver and ebony adjuster with pearl eye, 78 grams 2,415.00

Ouchard, Emile A., Paris, made in the style of J. B. Vuillaume, round stick stamped "Emile A. Ouchard" on both sides of the butt, ebony frog with missing pearl eye, silver and ebony adjuster, 80 grams 10,925.00

Pfretzchner, Hermann Richard, round stick stamped "H. R. Pfretzchner" at the butt, later ebony frog with silver and pearl eye, silver adjuster, 86 grams 500.00

Piernot, Marie Louis, round stick unstamped, ebony frog with parisian eye, plain silver adjuster, 76 grams 1,725.00

Zither, Columbia, 47 strings, c1900 .... 275.00

Music Related

Advertising Sign, 19-1/2" x 27", Mason & Hamlin Grands & Upright Pianos, Boston, New York, Chicago, emb tin, shows grand piano, F. Tuchfarber Co. Mfg., framed 300.00

Book, Davey, *History of English Music*, London, 1895 .... 20.00

Catalog

Daniel F. Beatty, Washington, NJ, 1882, 32 pgs, 6-3/4" x 10", features organs 135.00

H. N. White & Co., Cleveland, OH, c1930, 66 pgs, 9-1/4" x 12-1/4", white Way News #6 .... 50.00

McKinley Music Co, Chicago, IL, 1903, 50 pgs, 6-1/4" x 9-1/2", Catalog No. 22, music books 20.00

Guitar Case, canvas, brown, leather bound edges, strap, buckle, and handle, 1890 .... 20.00

Music Stand, Classical, England, c1830, carved rosewood and rosewood veneer, leaf carved octagonal post, shaped platform base, 3 turned feet, old finish, 18" w, 48" h 1,955.00

MUSIC BOXES

History: Music boxes, invented in Switzerland around 1825, encompass a broad array of forms, from small boxes to huge circus calliopes.

A cylinder box consists of a comb with teeth which vibrate when striking a pin in the cylinder. The music these boxes produce ranges from light tunes to opera and overtures.

The first disc music box was invented by Paul Lochmann of Leipzig, Germany, in 1886. It used an interchangeable steel disc with pierced holes bent to a point which hit the star-wheel as the disc revolved, and thus produced the tune. Discs were easily stamped out of metal, allowing a single music box to play an endless variety of tunes. Disc boxes reached the height of their popularity from 1890 to 1910 when the phonograph replaced them.

Music boxes also were incorporated in many items, e.g., clocks, sewing and jewelry boxes, steins, plates, toys, perfume bottles, and furniture.

References: Gilbert Bahl, *Music Boxes*, Courage Books, Running Press, 1993; Arthur W. J. G. Ord-Hume, *Musical Box*, Schiffer Publishing, 1995.

Collectors' Clubs: Music Box Society of Great Britain, P.O. Box 299, Waterbeach, Cambridge CB4 4DJ England; Musical Box Society International, 887 Orange Ave. E., St. Paul MN 55106.

Museums: Bellms Cars and Music of Yesterday, Sarasota, FL; Lockwood Matthews Mansion Museum, Norwalk, CT; Miles Musical Museum, Eureka Springs, AR; The Musical Museum, Deansboro, NY; The Musical Wonder House Museum, Iscasset, ME.

Additional Listings: See *Warman's Americana & Collectibles* for more examples.

Adler, 14-3/4" disc, walnut inlaid case, crank wind, lithograph cov int. 1,950.00

Baker-Troll, 17" cylinder, walnut case, brass inlaid dec, 6 bells, 3 part comb, matching storage table 2,750.00

Birdcage, singing bird

French, key wound, bird's head moves back and forth while chirping 1,800.00

German 250.00

Bremond, Swiss reed cylinder, works only 3,250.00

Britannia, 9" disc, upright, walnut case, transfer and inlaid dec, double comb 1,250.00

Birdcage, two feathered birds, brass, French, 20-1/2" h, bellows need restoration, $1,150. Photo courtesy of Sanford Alderfer Auction Co.

Continental, 16-1/2" l, 6", 8 tune, cylinder, single comb, bird's eye maple case 345.00
Criterion
    Model 103, 14" disc 3,100.00
    Table, mahogany, carved, to hold Model 103 .... 425.00
Cylinder
    17" x 3", ornate burled wood case, inlaid trim, excellent tone, cabinet need repair 1,500.00
    17" x 5-1/2" x 8", 6" cylinder, coin operated mechanism, mahogany inlaid case, 8 tunes 1,100.00
Ducommon Girod, 11-1/4" cylinder, walnut case, 3 control levers, six tune, c1840 .... 900.00
Edelweiss, 4-1/2" disc, table model, simple case, hand crank 300.00
Euphonia, 15-3/4" disc, mahogany case, metal corners, lithograph female on int. cov 1,200.00
Lochmann, Model 60, sold as is 2,325.00
Mills Vioano-Virtuoso, violin and piano combination, oak cabinet, orig DC motor, restored, converted from coin operated to automatic play 25,000.00
Paillard, NY, four 11" cylinders, full comb and bed, rosewood case with inlaid marquetry, base drawer stenciled "Paillard's Patent Feb 11th 1879, No. 48433", 41" w, 21" d, 16" h 5,500.00
Perfection, 10-1/2" zinc disc, table model, mahogany case 1,250.00
Regina
    Automatic Disc Changing, 15-1/2"
        Commercial Style 36, holds 12 discs, 5¢ coin operated, restored in early 1970s 11,500.00
        Mahogany case, bow front door, stained art glass panel, home model, temp regulator, 12 tune disc, 68" h 19,000.00
    Coin Operated Model, 27" automatic disc changing, walnut case, 12 discs, restored, replaced lower panel glass, mechanism cleaned and regulated 20,000.00

Home Model, short bed plate, mahogany, serpentine case, double comb music box, 12 15-1/2" discs, 22" w, 13" h, 20" d, restored, mechanism cleaned and regulated ... 4,500.00
Model 50, mahogany case, matching base cabinet .. 7,250.00
Snuff Box, early cylindrical musical snuff box, emb scene of Paris on lid, 4 x 1-1/2 x 2-1/2" 550.00
Subline-Harmonie, 15" cylinder, burl walnut on ebony and rosewood case, double comb, matching table with cabriole legs, c1870 .... 7,000.00
Swiss
    12" w, 24" l, 8" h, veneered case, line inlay, 8 tunes, mandolin-harp, serial #17719, 10 bumble bee bell strikes ... 3,300.00
    21-1/2" l, 11", 8 tube, cylinder, single comb, marquetry inlaid case, c1880-1900 .... 825.00
Symphonian, 15-1/2" d disc 2,000.00

NAILSEA-TYPE GLASS

History: Nailsea-type glass is characterized by swirls and loopings, usually white, on a clear or colored ground. One of the first areas where this glass was made was Nailsea, England, 1788-1873, hence the name. Several glass houses, including American factories, made this type of glass.

Bell, 11-3/4" h, white, rose loopings 95.00

Bottle, 8" h, gemel, flattened ovoid body, 2 necks, white casing, red, white, and blue loopings 400.00
Candlestick, 10" h, colorless, white loopings, folded socket rim, hollow blown socket drawn out to a double knop, bulb shaped stem, 2 additional knops, inverted cone shaped base, early 19th C 375.00
Fairy Lamp
    5-1/4" h, 6-1/4" d, frosted blue, opaque white loopings, colorless Clarke insert 695.00
    6-1/2" h, red, sweeping white loops, dome shaped shade, ruffled triangular base, colorless glass candle cup with ruffled edge, orig "Price's Royal Castle Night Light" candle 985.00
Flask
    7-1/4" h, broad oval form, ruby red ground, white herringbone type loopings, applied double collared mouth, pontil scar 400.00

Flask, pocket, deep forest green, milk glass loopings, sheared mouth, pontil scar, Europe, 1800-50, 6-1/2" h, $190. Photo courtesy of Norman C. Heckler & Company.

7-3/4" h, pocket, elongated teardrop form, milk glass ground, blue and rose loopings, sheared mouth, pontil scar 300.00
8-3/4" h, pocket, teardrop form, teal green, profuse white loopings, sheared mouth, pontil scar 240.00
Lamp, 11-1/2" h, colorless ground, pink and white loopings on font and ruffled shade, applied colorless feet, berry prunt....2,500.00
Pitcher, 6-1/2" h, 4" d, colorless ground, white loopings, ftd, solid applied base, triple ribbed solid handle with curled end, flaring formed mouth, attributed t South Jersey, c1840-60 ..... 1,200.00
Rolling Pin, 13-3/4" l, freeblown, rose and white loopings, colorless ground, ground mouth, smooth base, 1850-80 .....220.00
Tumbler, white ground, blue loopings..............................120.00
Vase, 8" h, 5" d, cylindrical, flared mouth and base, colorless, white loopings, plain sheared rim, pontil, attributed to South Jersey 195.00
Witch Ball, 4-3/8" d, white ground, pink and blue loopings 450.00

NANKING

History: Nanking is a type of Chinese porcelain made in Canton, China, from the early 1800s into the 20th century. It was made for export to America and England.

Four elements help distinguish Nanking from Canton, two similar types of ware. Nanking has a spear-and-post border, as opposed to the scalloped-line style of Canton. Second, in the water's edge or Willow pattern, Canton usually has no figures; Nanking includes a standing figure with open umbrella on the bridge. In addition, the blues tend to be darker on the Nanking ware. Finally, Nanking wares often are embellished with gold, Canton is not.

Green and orange variations of Nanking survive, although they are scarce.

REPRODUCTION ALERT

Copies of Nanking ware currently are being produced in China. They are of inferior quality and are decorated in a lighter rather than in the darker blues.

Bowl, 10" d, shaped, 19th C 880.00
Candlesticks, pr, 9-1/2" h 775.00
Cider Jug, 10" h, gilt highlights, 19th C, pr..........................825.00
Cup and Saucer, loop handle 65.00
Ewer, 11" h, small spout, blue and white, mid-19th C 300.00
Pitcher, cov, 9-1/2" h, blue and white, Liverpool shape 550.00
Plate, 9-1/2" d, water's edge scene, c1780-1800.................85.00
Platter
    12-3/4" l, Chinese, 19th C, chips 415.00
    16" l, blue Fitzhugh border, minor chips and knife marks 575.00
Posset Pot, blue and white, intertwined handle, mismatched lid with gilded fruit finial...100.00
Rice Bowl, 19th C 100.00
Salad Bowl, 10" d, 19th C 1,200.00
Soup Tureen, cov, 11-3/4" h, 19th C, imperfections...........475.00
Teapot, 6-1/2" h, globular, diaper border above watery pagoda landscape reserve..125.00
Tray, 9-3/4" l, 19th C 500.00

NAPKIN RINGS, FIGURAL

History: Gracious home dining during the Victorian era required a personal napkin ring for each household member. Figural napkin rings were first patented in 1869. During the remainder of the 19th century, most plating companies, including Cromwell, Eureka, Meriden, and Reed and Barton, manufactured figural rings, many copying and only slightly varying the designs of other companies.

Reference: Lillian Gottschalk and Sandra Whitson, *Figural Napkin Rings*, Collector Books, 1996.

REPRODUCTION ALERT

Quality reproductions do exist.

Additional Listings: See *Warman's Americana & Collectibles* for a listing of non-figural napkin rings.

Notes: Values are determined by the subject matter of the ring, the quality of the workmanship, and the condition.

Baby in cradle, James W. Tufts, Boston.............................300.00
Bird, wings spread over nest of eggs 175.00
Boy, sitting on bench, holding drumstick............................200.00
Brownie, climbing up side of ring, Palmer Cox 185.00
Butterfly, perched on pair of fans 125.00
Cat, glass eyes, ring on back...270.00
Cherries, stems, leaf base, ball feet....................................90.00
Cherub, sitting cross legged on base, candleholder and ring combination 195.00
Chicken, nesting beside ring..150.00
Child, crawling, ring on back..300.00
Dog, sitting next to barrel shaped ring, sgd "Tufts, #1531" 125.00
Dutch Boy, pulling on boots, resilvered 110.00
Frog, holding drumstick, pushing drum-like ring 300.00
Goat, pulling wheeled flower cart.......................................250.00
Horse, standing next to elaborate ring 185.00
Owl, sitting on leafy base, owls perched on upper limbs ..250.00
Parrot, on wheels, Simpson, Hall, Miller & Co. 185.00
Rabbit, sitting alertly next to ring 175.00
Sailor Boy, anchor 220.00
Schoolboy with books, feeding begging puppy 235.00
Squirrel, eating nut, log pile base......................................125.00
Turtle, crawling, ornate ring on back..................................300.00

Cupid, ring on back, 3-1/4" h, 2-3/4" l, $325.

NASH GLASS

History: Nash glass is a type of art glass attributed to Arthur John Nash and his sons, Leslie H. and A. Douglas. Arthur John Nash, originally employed by Webb in Stourbridge, England, came to America and was employed in 1889 by Tiffany Furnaces at its Corona, Long Island, plant.

While managing the plant for Tiffany, Nash designed and produced iridescent glass. In 1928, A. Douglas Nash purchased the facilities of Tiffany Furnaces. The A. Douglas Nash Corporation remained in operation until 1931.

Bowl, 7-3/4" x 2-1/2", Jewel pattern, gold phantom luster ..285.00
Candlestick, 4" h, Chintz, ruby and gray, sgd 450.00
Compote, 7-1/2" d, 4-1/2" h, Chintz, transparent aquamarine, wide flat rim of red and gray-green controlled stripe dec, base inscribed "Nash RD89"..865.00
Cordial, 5-1/2" h, Chintz, green and blue 95.00
Goblet, 6-3/4" h, feathered leaf motif, gilt dec, sgd............295.00
Plate, 8" d, Chintz, green and blue 195.00
Sherbet, bluish-gold texture, ftd, sgd, #417 ....275.00
Vase
  5-1/2" h, Chintz
    Brilliant red oval, controlled black, grown, gray striped dec, base inscribed "Nash" 865.00
    Pastel, transparent oval, internally striped with pastel orange alternating with yellow chintz dec 175.00
  9" h, Polka Dot, deep opaque red oval, molded with prominent sixteen ribs, dec by spaced white opal dots, base inscribed "Nash GD154" 1,100.00

NAUTICAL ITEMS

History: The seas have fascinated man since time began. The artifacts of sailors have been collected and treasured for years. Because of their environment, merchant and naval items, whether factory or handmade, must be of quality construction and long lasting. Many of these items are aesthetically appealing as well.

References: Jon Baddeley, *Nautical Antiques & Collectables*, Sotheby's Publications, 1993; Robert W. D. Ball, *Nautical Antiques*, Schiffer Publishing, 1994.

Periodicals: *Nautical Brass*, P.O. Box 3966, North Ft. Myers, FL 33918; *Nautical Collector*, P.O. Box 949, New London, CT 06320.

Collectors' Club: Nautical Research Guild, 62 Marlboro St., Newburyport, MA 01950.

Museums: Kittery Historical & Naval Museum, Kittery, ME; Lyons Maritime Museum, St. Augustine, FL; Mariners' Museum, Newport News, VA; Maritime Museum of Monterey, Monterey, CA; Museum of Science and Industry, Chicago, IL; Mystic Seaport Museum, Mystic, CT; Peabody Museum of Salem, Salem, MA; Philadelphia Maritime Museum, Philadelphia, PA; San Francisco Maritime National Historical Park, San Francisco, CA; U.S. Naval Academy Museum, Naval Academy, MD.

Account Book, Bark *Arab,* showing purchases and sales from October 1853 to December 1856, 96 pgs, folio, New Bedford or Hawaii, label reads "Purchased of John Kehew at his Navigation Store in New Bedford," Kehew's label mounted on front pastedown, 2 volumes 1,955.00

Account Sheet, financial account for return of bark *Charles W. Morgan,* 8 pgs, folio, New Bedford, 1880-93 ....750.00
Book
  Allyn, Captain Gurdon L., *The Old Sailor's Story, or a Short Account of the Life, Adventures, and Voyages,* Norwich, 1879, 111 pgs, 8vo, orig flexible cloth wrappers 316.00
  Bennett, Frank M., *The Steam Navy of the United States,* Pittsburgh, 1896, 8vo 195.00
  Bligh, William, *Dangerous Voyage of Captain Bligh, in an Open Boat, Over 1200 Leagues of the Ocean, in the Year 1789,* Dublin, 1818, 5 full page woodcut engraved illus, 180 pgs, small 12mo 345.00
  Dexter, Elisha, *Narrative of the Loss of the William and Joseph, of Martha's Vineyard,* Boston, 1842, 5 wood engraved plates, 54 pgs, 8vo 1,370.00
  Dix, William, *Wreck of the Glide, with an Account of Life and Manners in the Fiji Islands,* Boston, 1846, 122 pgs, 12 mo 290.00
  Little, Captain George, *The American Cruiser's Own Book,* New York, 1846, carved wooden binding, ships, paddlewheeler, and inscribed "Capt. JC Pease Oswego 1874," price for 8 volumes 920.00
  Flags of the Maritime Nations, Washington, 1870, second edition, 18 plates, gilt Morocco, rubbed 75.00
Box, cov, 4-3/4" h, 12" l, 6-5/9" d, walnut, dovetailed, ropework handle, polyhedron carved terminals, attributed to New England sailor, early 19th C, 1 terminal missing 460.00
Broadside, 415 x 335 mm, issued as circular to mariners at Table Bay, Robben Island, advising of berthing procedures, 1827 ....345.00
Catalog, William E. Williams, New York, NY, c1927, 445 pgs, 5-1/2" x 7-1/2"..20.00
Children's Book
  On the Seas, a Book for Boys, Boston, c1875, plates, small 8vo 130.00
  Papa's Log or a Voyage to Rio de Janerio, Grant and Griffith, London, 1845, hand colored illus, 28 pgs, small 4to 632.00
  The Adventures of Jack, or a Life on the Wave, Charles L. Newhall, Southbridge, 1859, 134 pgs, 12 mo 230.00
Chronometer
  7-1/2" h, 6-3/4" w, 6-3/4" d, "Morris Tobias, London, Maker to the Admiralty 31 Minories London," c1825, gimbal mounted in brass fitted rosewood case, brass bezel with silver wash dial 1,495.00
  8-1/2" h, 8-1/4" w, 8-1/4" d, "M.F. Dent, 33 Cockspur St. Chronometer Maker to the Queen, London," late 19th C, gimbal mounted in brass fitted mahogany case, brass bezel, silver wash dial, 8 day...5,175.00
Clock, 10-1/2" h, brass, Seth Thomas, one day lever striking movement, circular case, domed bell mounted below on wooden backboard, late 19th C 520.00
Compass, lifeboat, 8" sq, 7-1/4" h, boxed, 20th C.............175.00
Crew List, partly printed, 2 language, *Jireh Swift,* lists 13 additional Hawaiian crew members, Lahaina, March 29, 1865 ....2,070.00
Figurehead, 30" h, carved, Nantucket Island origin, c1830 ....12,000.00
Hourglass, 7" h, 19th C...550.00
Inclinometer, 4-1/2" d, brass, cased, bubble type, Kelvin Bottomley & Baird Ltd. 65.00
Journal, Daniel S. Emmerton of Salem, crewman serving on the *Horsburgh* from March 1852 to March 1853, 146 pgs, folio 1,610.00
Ladle, 9-5/8" l, carved coconut shell, ivory handle, carved eagle, animals, ornaments, and foliate devices, 19th C, cracks 125.00
Log Book, two masted brig *Smyrna,* belonging to Ezra Weston of Duxbury, series of voyages between April 1848 and March 1854, kept by Captain Stephen Sprague, 290 pgs, folio, 2 volumes 635.00

Diving Helmet, US Navy, Mark V, No. 534, manufactured by A. Schrader & Son, Inc., Brooklyn, NY, 1918, $1,900.

Masthead, 16" h, 9-1/2" d, copper and brass, oil fired, complete with burner, 360 degrees, late 19th C 200.00
Model, painted wood
 16-1/2" h, 20-1/2" l, 3 masted schooner, late 19th/20th C, shadowbox frame, repainted..575.00
 21" h, 34" l, *Elia,* mounted in shadowbox frame, losses 2,185.00
 29-1/2" h, gig *Red Rover* 2,185.00
 37" h, 54" l, *Glory of the Seas,* full-rigged, 20th C, minor imperfections 1,725.00
 77-1/2" l, Chesapeake Bay Skip Jack *Carrie Price,* early 20th C, imperfections 3,795.00
Navigational Lesson Book, 12" x 7-1/2", Benjamin Holt, Boston, 1834, watercolor illus of ships, architectural renderings, front papered board detached 865.00
Painting, oil on canvas, craquele
 American ship *Albus* just off port, Marblehead, unsgd, vessel identified on bow, identified on label affixed to reverse, 16" x 24", framed, minor losses and retouch 1,265.00
 Brigantine Off A Distance Coast, Under Gray Skies, sgd "W. Webber" lower left, 22" x 30-1/4", framed..............2,100.00
 Fisherman Making Harbor, sgd "Marshall Johnson" lower left, sgd and titled on reverse, 10" x 14" framed 2,185.00
 Paddle Wheel Bark, unsgd, 20" x 30", framed...........4,600.00
 The American Atlantic Telegraph Steam-Seal Ship *Niagara* and a Second Vessel Laying Transatlantic Cable, unsgd, vessel identified on banner, 24" x 30", repainted period frame..2,875.00
 The Fisherman's Catch, sgd and dated "A. W. Buhler- 1917" lower left, 25-1/2" x 20", framed 2,530.00
Print, Regatta of the New York Yacht Club, June 1st, 1854, Nathaniel Currier, publisher, Charles Parsons, lithographer, identified in inscriptions in matrix, litho printed in black, blue, and tan, hand colored, 20-1/2" x 30-1/4" sheet size, period frame, toning, staining, rippling...................................3,220.00
Quadrant, ebony, cased, mkd "D Booth" and "New Zealand" 330.00

Sailmaker's Kit, 17" l, orig bag with various tools, ornate ropework ties, 19th C..350.00
Sailor's Valentine, 9-5/8" octagonal segmented case, various exotic shells, "For My Love," 19th C, very minor losses....750.00
Sea Chest, 19-1/4" h, 34-3/4" l, 18-3/4" d, painted and carved, rect lift top, polychrome portrait of ship *Molo* on underside of lid, int. fitted with carved mahogany compartments bordered in molding and star corner blocks, ext. carved with leaf panels, stars, and inlaid diamonds, becket handles with carved leaves, berries, and stars, old surface 6,325.00
Ship Picture, 23-1/4" x 35-1/4", woolwork, three-masted steam sailor, 19th C, very minor staining 2,185.00
Telescope, 32-3/4" l, silver plated, one draw, Troughton & Simms, London, mid-19th C, orig leather casing, inscription reads, "Presented by the British Government, Captain Christopher Crowell, Master of the American Ship 'Highland Light' of Boston, in acknowledgment of his humanity and kindness to the Master and the Crew of the Baroque 'Queen of Sheba' when he rescued from their waterlogged vessel, on the 16th, December 1861," damage to leather 980.00
Vessel Registration, *Jireh Swift,* certificate listing owners, specifying their shares, dimensions of the vessel, information on builder, 1 pg, folio, New Bedford, Sept. 1, 1862........2,185.00
Yacht Tender, 11' 3", beam 49", built by Geo. Lawley & Son Corp., Neponset, MA, No. 1615, cedar carved plained oak ribbed, bright finish, mahogany trim, two rowing stations, bronze fastenings and oar locks, equipped with two falls, crack in false keel 4,600.00

NAZI ITEMS

History: The National Socialist German Workers Party (NSDAP) was created on Feb. 24, 1920, by Anton Drexler and Adolf Hitler. Its 25-point nationalistic program was designed to revive the depressed German economy and revitalize the government.

In 1923, after the failed Beer Hall Putsch, Hitler was sentenced to a five-year term in Landsberg Prison. He spent only a year in prison, during which time he wrote the first volume of Mein Kampf.

In the late 1920s and early 1930s, the NSDAP developed from a regional party into a major national party. In the spring of 1933, Hitler became the Reich's chancellor. Shortly after the death of President von Hindenberg in 1934, Hitler combined the offices of president and chancellor into a single position, giving him full control over the German government, as well as NSDAP. From that point until May 1945, the National Socialist German Worker's Party dominated all aspects of German life.

In the mid-1930s, Hitler initiated a widespread plan–ranging from re-arming to territorial acquisition–designed to unite the German-speaking people of Europe into a single nation. Germany's invasion of Poland in 1939 triggered the hostilities that led to the Second World War. The war in Europe ended on VE Day, May 7, 1945.

Reference: Ron Manion, *German Military Collectibles Price Guide,* Antique Trader Publications, 1995.

Periodicals: *Der Gauleiter,* P.O. Box 721288, Houston, TX 77272; *Military Collector Magazine,* P.O. Box 245, Lyon Station, PA 19536; *Military Collectors News,* P.O. Box 702073, Tulsa, OK 74170; *Military History,* 602 S.

King St., Suite 300, Leesburg, VA 22075; *Military Trader*, P.O. Box 1050, Dubuque, IA 52004.

Note: The objects that appear below are associated with the NSDAP as a political party. See the Militaria listing for objects associated with the German military prior to and during World War II.

Arm Band, 20-1/2" l, Ortsgruppenleiter, metal pipe, Bevo NS-DAP patch, gold oak leaves wrapped around band, red wool, blue piping..200.00
Autograph
    Document, Adolf Hitler, typed order sgd, in German, 2 pages, 4 to, Fuhrer's Headquarters, July 12, 1944, "Secret Dispatch" printed in red at top, some coded lines, text relating to sea transport, merchant shipping, Hitler's specific orders relating to situation 8,500.00
    Photograph, Hans Baur, personal pilot and confidant of Hitler, glossy photo in Luftwaffe uniform, inscribed and sgd in German, 1969, folded horizontally 115.00
Banner, 7" x 38", double sided 35.00
Bayonet, police, dress, 13" blade, stag handle, attached police insignia, black leather scabbard, silvered fittings, orig black frog, guard marked "S. MG. 415," matching numbers..175.00
Belt, NSDAP, police officer's, light tan leather belt, clawed buckle 35.00
Cap Badge, RAD, silver finish, enameled, wreath 35.00
Car Pennant, 8-1/2" x 11-12", Teno, printed on both sides, white eagle on blue field, 2 tie strings 75.00
Cigarette Case, presentation, steel, painted, brass plate, emb heads of Mussolini and Hitler, "Vincere" above heads, eagle embracing wreath of swastikas, wreath with Italian emblem 175.00
Collar Tabs, NSDAP, Hauptgemeinschaftsleiter rank, 4 gold pips, gold eagle, double rows of gold ribbon, dark brown, white piping 100.00
Dagger, orange and yellow celluloid grip, SP fittings and scabbard, mkd "E & F Horstaer" 100.00
Emblem, 27" x 16" train engine, eagle with swastika..........250.00
Hat, police officer, black visor, bright eagle and wreath device, green-blue wool, silver cord, leather chin strap, pebbles side buttons 150.00
Holster, P-38, black leather, Nazi acceptance mark, pouch for extra clip..50.00
Magazine, NSDAP Der Schulungsbrief, 1940 ....35.00
Medal, Eastern People's, 2nd Class, silver metal, ribbon 25.00
Membership Pin, swastika in circle, winged NSFK figure 15.00

Pin Cushion, painted plaster, orig paper tag, copyright 1941 Hotzi Nazi, 4-3/4" h, $45.

Pennant, 54" l, 11" h, NSDAP, triangular, painted swastika, double sided...35.00
Photo Album, cigarette company premium, "Adolf Hitler-Bilder Aus Dem Leben Des Fuhrers Herausgegeben von Cigarette Bilder Dienst, Hamburg," 136 pgs with 100 tipped in glossy photocards recording Hitler's rise to power, 1936, 9-1/2" x 12-1/2"...235.00
Poster
    12" x 20", Mein Kampf, portrait of Hitler, black and white25.00
    27" x 40, Imperialists Cannot Stop The Winning Progress Of Our Five Year Plan!," Konstantin Elissev, snaggle-toothed top-hatted capitalist holds bomb throwing Nazi, Pope, French and Eastern European Generals in his raised arm in front of booming factories of industry, red, black, and brown, expert restoration to left corners, 1930.........900.00
Shoulder Boards, police, Wactmeister Rank, black and silver cord, pink piping, removable style 12.00
Sword, dress, eagle and swastika, engraved brass handle, black wire wrapped plastic grip, black painted scabbard 120.00
Tunic, police, green piping, removable shoulder boards, Bevo collar tabs, Bevo green police eagle arm shield on left sleeve, silver pebbled buttons, tailored cuffs, dark brown trim.185.00

NETSUKES

History: The traditional Japanese kimono has no pockets. Daily necessities, such as money and tobacco supplies, were carried in leather pouches, or inros, which hung from a cord with a netsuke toggle. The word netsuke comes from "ne" (to root) and "tsuke" (to fasten).

Netsukes originated in the 14th century and initially were favored by the middle class. By the mid-18th century, all levels of Japanese society used them. Some of the most famous artists, e.g., Shuzan and Yamada Hojitsu, worked in the netsuke form.

Netsukes average from 1 to 2 inches in length and are made from wood, ivory, bone, ceramics, metal, horn, nutshells, etc. The subject matter is broad based, but always portrayed in a lighthearted, humorous manner. A netsuke must have smooth edges and balance in order to hang correctly on the sash.

Reference: Raymond Bushell, *Introduction to Netsuke*, Charles E. Tuttle Co., 1971; George Lazarnick, *The Signature Book of Netsuke, Inro and Ojime Artists in Photographs,* first edition 1976, 2 Volume second edition 1981.

Periodical: *Netsuke & Ivory Carving Newsletter*, 3203 Adams Way, Ambler, PA 19002.

Collectors' Clubs: International Netsuke Society, P.O. Box 471686, San Francisco, CA 94147; Netsuke Kenkyukai Society, P.O. Box 31595, Oakland, CA 94604.

REPRODUCTION ALERT
Recent reproductions are on the market. Many are carved from African ivory.

Notes: Value depends on artist, region, material, and skill of craftsmanship. Western collectors favor katabori, pieces which represent an identifiable object.

Horn
    Lotus leaf, stag horn, 19th C 100.00
    Shishi form, pressed, 19th C 50.00

Ivory
Abalone shell, carved by Tomiharu, 1799.................7,040.00
Boy with fish, sgd, 19th C, 2" h.....................................360.00
Buddha, 19th C, 2-1/4" h 450.00
Chick in egg, 2" l..250.00
Crouched figure, deep folds in clothing, 2 ivory figures with horned
heads in sack over shoulder, carved by Seiji, 2" h 3,450.00
Dragon, curled up, 19th C, 2-1/4" l..............................575.00
Dutchman holding dog, carved by Maskazu 19th C, 3" h....375.00
Entertainer being attacked by his monkey, carved by Masaka,
early 19th C, 1-3/4" h 6,600.00
Lady, carrying jar, folds of robe continue to left and then sweep top
the right, baby boy in Chinese dress playing at her feet, inlaid
horn hair knot on toddler, fingers of lady's left hand and flowers
on her hair band, carved by Anraku, 4-1/4" h 11,550.00
Mouse, carved by Tomokasu, 1-3/4" l 350.00
Pile of fish, stingray, octopus tentacles, and eel, carved by
Kaigyokusai Masatsugu, 1-1/2"d 2,420.00
Plaque, elaborate city scene, carved by Kagetoshi...3,520.00
Shoki, holding oni in left hand, unsgd, 3-1/2" h..........4,400.00
Skull, serpent entwined around toad, black onyx and MOP in-
laid eyes, 2" h 425.00
Woman, flowing gown, cartouche surrounding signature,
carved by Jutsuasi 1,870.00
Ivory and Boxwood, tortoise with small tortoise climbing over
back, opens to reveal sleeping man with gourds and models
of temples, carved by Ho Shu, Yoshihide, 19th C....12,650.00
Mother of Pearl, cat and kitten, 1-15/16" l...........................275.00
Porcelain
Fruit and leaves, red, brown, and celadon, 19th C 60.00
Hotei, mkd "Masakazu," 19th C.......................................60.00
Two puppies, 19th C 85.00
Wood
Boy, seated, reading scroll, boxwood, carved by Masayuki,
19th C 200.00
Geisha, seated, wearing flowing robe, holding tray, carved by
Toshikazu, 19th C 245.00
God, Jurojin stroking crane, silver with tarnished gray patina
as helmet, neck guard, and sash and elbows, ivory face,
hands, and crane's body, ebony feet, Jurojin, and crane,
tortoiseshell sack on back, 2" h 3,850.00
Karasu tengu, seated figure with beaked and fanged face,
holding cucumber, carved by Jugyoko, 19th C 825.00
Monkey, seated, clasping raised left knee, unsgd, first half
19th C 425.00
Noblewoman, wretched beggar form, dying by roadside,
carved by Ichihyo, first half 19th C...........................300.00
Persimmon, stippled skin and leaves, unsgd, 19th C ...295.00
Rat, grooming 24,150.00
Rice Mixer, boxwood, ivory inlaid eyes, teeth, and rice, carved
by Tokoku, 19th C..5,750.00
Scribe, sitting, holding writing slip and brush, carved by Shin-
sai, 195h C..275.00
Snail, crawling from shell, boxwood, 19th C 495.00
Turtle and snake, boxwood, c1800, 2-3/8" l 10,120.00

NEWCOMB POTTERY

History: The Sophie Newcomb Memorial College, an
adjunct of Tulane University in
New Orleans, LA, was origi-
nated as a school to train local women in the decorative
arts. While metal working, painting, and embroidery
were among the classes taught, the production of fine,
hand-crafted art pottery remains their most popular and
collectible pursuit.

Pottery was made by the Newcomb women for nearly
50 years, with earlier work being the rarest and the most
valuable. This is characterized by shiny finishes and
broad, flat-painted and modeled designs. More common, though still quite valuable, are their matte glaze
pieces, often depicting bayou scenes and native flora.
All bear the impressed NC mark.

References: Ralph and Terry Kovel, *Kovels' American
Art Pottery*, Crown Publishers, 1993; Jessie Poesch,
Newcomb Pottery: An Enterprise for Southern Women,
Schiffer Publishing, 1984; David Rago, *American Art
Pottery,* Knickerbocker Press, 1997.

Collectors' Club: American Art Pottery Association,
P.O. Box 525, Cedar Hill, MO 63016.

Museum: Newcomb College, Tulane University, New
Orleans, LA.

Advisor: David Rago.

Bowl
4" d, 5" h, Matte Ware, closed form, stylized yellow flowers,
blue ground, border design 1,200.00
8" d, 3-1/2" h, shoulder dec with yellow, red, and green flowers,
matte blue body, imp "NC, HF, 64, 259" 980.00
Cabinet Vase, 4" h, 4" h, Matte Ware, blue and white molded flowers, blue ground 900.00
Candleholder, 5" h, 5" d, Matte Ware, transitional, green flowers,
blue ground, lightly molded, markings underneath I blue
....1,700.00
Cream Pitcher, 4" x 3", green trefoils, blue leaves, light blue
ground 1,500.00
Inkwell, 4" x 4", stylized yellow flowers and green leaves, cream
ground, orig lid and inkpot 1,500.00

Left, vase, decorated by Sadie Irvine, three
carved blue irises amidst green leaves, $7,250;
right: covered jar, incised band of pink star flowers with green leaves, blue ground, 5-1/2" x 6",
$3,630. Photo courtesy of David Rago Auctions,
Inc.

Left, vase, early high glaze, two hairlines, $22,000; middle: vase, early high glaze, $8,800; right: vase, matte scenic, $7,700. Photo courtesy of David Rago Auctions, Inc.

Match Holder, 4" h, 3" d, Matte Ware, yellow flowers, blue ground 800.00
Pitcher, 5-1/2" h, 4" d, deep gray-green metallic dripping glaze, brown ground, imp "CN, GM" 260.00
Vase
    4-1/2" h, 2" d, crisply molded high relief flowers, mate blue ground, imp "NC RQ3 IS, JH" 1,380.00
    6" h, 6" d, Matte Ware, bulbous, squatty, carved bayou scene in blues, yellow moon 2,000.00
    6" h, 6-3/4" d, slab built, crackle high glaze, base marked with monogram for Leoni Nicholson, minor hairline.........260.00
    7" h, 4" d, stylized flowers, blue and white, shiny finish 2,000.00
    7" h, 6" d, Matte Ware, bulbous, allover design of carved flowers in blue and green, blue ground.......................2,200.00
    10" h, 7" d, Matte Ware, carved iris blossoms in blue and white, blue ground 3,000.00
    11" h, 5" d, bulbous, modeled yellow fleur-de-lis, green leaves, cream ground 20,000.00

NILOAK POTTERY, MISSION WARE

History: Niloak Pottery was made near Benton, Arkansas. Charles Dean Hyten experimented with native clay, trying to preserve its natural colors. By 1911, he perfected Mission Ware, a marbleized pottery in which the cream and brown colors predominate. The company name is the word "kaolin" spelled backwards.

After a devastating fire, the pottery was rebuilt and named Eagle Pottery. This factory included enough space to add a novelty pottery line in 1929. Mr. Hyten left the pottery in 1941, and in 1946 operations ceased.

Marks: The early pieces were marked "Niloak." Eagle Pottery products usually were marked "Hywood-Niloak" until 1934 when the "hywood" was dropped from the mark.

References: Susan and Al Bagdade, *Warman's American Pottery and Porcelain*, Wallace-Homestead, 1994;

Vase, Mission Ware, waisted, 9-7/8" h, $185

David Edwin Gifford, *Collector's Encyclopedia of Niloak*, Collector Books, 1993.

Collectors' Club: Arkansas Pottery Collectors Society, P.O. Box 7617 RD, Little Rock, AR 72217.

Additional Listings: See *Warman's Americana & Collectibles* for more examples, especially the novelty pieces.

Note: Prices listed below are for Mission Ware pieces.

Bowl, 4-1/2" d, marbleized swirls, blue, tan, and brown 65.00
Candlesticks, pr, 8" h, marbleized swirls, blue, cream, terra-cotta, and brown...250.00
Console Set, pr 8-1/2" h candlesticks, 10" d bowl, Mission ware, mkd 275.00
Pot, 2-3/4" x 3-3/4", marbleized swirls, red, brown, and chocolate, early 125.00
Toothpick Holder, marbleized swirls, tan and blue............100.00
Urn, 4-1/2" h, marbleized swirls, brown and blue.................45.00
Vase
    5-1/2" h, bulbous, marbleized swirls, rust, blue, and cream 75.00
    6" h, marbleized swirls, cream, turquoise, rust and brown.. 80.00

NIPPON CHINA, 1891-1921

History: Nippon, Japanese hand-painted porcelain, was made for export between 1891 and 1921. In 1891, when the McKinley tariff act proclaimed that all items of foreign manufacture be stamped with their country of origin, Japan chose to use "Nippon." In 1921, the United States decided the word "Nippon" no longer was acceptable and required all Japanese wares to be marked "Japan," ending the Nippon era.

Marks: There are more than 220 recorded Nippon backstamps or marks; the three most popular are the wreath, maple leaf, and rising sun. Wares with variations of all three marks are being reproduced today. A knowledgeable collector can easily spot the reproductions by the mark variances.

The majority of the marks are found in three different colors: green, blue, or magenta. Colors indicate the quality of the porcelain used: green for first-grade porcelain, blue for second-grade, and magenta for third-grade. Marks were applied by two methods: decal stickers under glaze and imprinting directly on the porcelain.

References: Joan Van Patten, *Collector's Encyclopedia of Nippon Porcelain*, 1st Series (1979, 1997 value update), 2nd Series (1982, 1997 value update), 3rd Series (1986, 1996 value update), 4th Series, (1997), Collector Books; Kathy Wojciechowski, *Wonderful World of Nippon Porcelain*, Schiffer Publishing, 1992.

Collectors' Clubs: ARK-LA-TEX Nippon Club, 6800 Arapaho Rd., #1057, Dallas, TX 75248; Dixieland Nippon Club, P.O. Box 1712, Centerville, VA 22020; International Nippon Collectors Club, 112 Oak Ave. N., Owatonna, MN 55060; Lakes & Plains Nippon Collectors Society, P.O. Box 230, Peotone, IL 60468; Long Island Nippon Collectors Club, 145 Andover Place, W. Hempstead, NY 11552; MD-PA Collectors' Club, 1016 Erwin Dr., Joppa, MD 21085; New England Nippon Collectors Club, 64 Burt Rd., Springfield, MA 01118; Sunshine State Nippon Collectors' Club, 2410 NE. 84th St., Pompano Beach FL 33064; Upstate New York Nippon Collectors' Club, 122 Laurel Ave., Herkimer, NY 13350.

REPRODUCTION ALERT

Distinguishing old marks from New

A common old mark consisted of a central wreath open at the top with the letter M in the center. "Hand Painted" flowed around the top of the wreath; "NIPPON" around the bottom. The modern fake mark reverses the wreath (it is open at the bottom) and places an hourglass form not an "M" in its middle.

An old leaf mark, approximately one-quarter inch wide, has "Hand" with "Painted" below to the left of the stem and "NIPPON" beneath. The newer mark has the identical lettering but the size is now one-half, rather than one-quarter, inch.

An old mark consisted of "Hand Painted" arched above a solid rising sun logo with "NIPPON" in a straight line beneath. The modern fake mark has the same lettering pattern but the central logo looks like a mound with a jagged line enclosing a blank space above it.

Additional Listings: See *Warman's Americana & Collectibles*.

SPECIAL AUCTION

Jackson's Auctioneers & Appraisers
2229 Lincoln St.
Cedar Falls, IA 50613
(319) 277-2256
e-mail:jacksons@corenet.net

Ashtray, 5-1/2" w, Mt Fuji scene, gold beading, mkd "Hand Painted Mt Fujiyama Nippon" 75.00

Basket
    5", tapestry 690.00
    9", tapestry, lake scene 1,870.00
    10", pictorial lake scene 880.00
Bowl, 10" d, hp, flowers, scrolls, and center medallion dec, open handles, green "M" in wreath mark 5.00
Butter dish, cov, floral hand, mkd "Hand Painted RC Nippon" 40.00
Calling Card Tray, 7-3/4" x 6", mythical dragon and bird, blue maple leaf mark 48.00
Candlesticks, pr, 10" h, Galle scene, moriage trees, maple leaf mark 400.00
Celery set, 11-1/2" tray, 4 matching salts, hp, garland of red wild roses and daisies dec, lime green borer, blue rising sun mark 75.00
Charger, 12" d, rose tapestry 2,600.00
Chocolate Pot, 11" h, hp, pale pink, rose, violet, lavender, and yellow, gold beaded dec, turquoise jewels, blue maple leaf mark 90.00
Cigarette Box, cov, horse motif 470.00
Compote, 4-3/8" h, 8-1/2" d, Wedgwood and rose nosegay dec, wreath mark 200.00
Cracker Jar, melon ribbed body, bisque background, Indian in canoe shooting moose on river edge, ftd, wreath mark 425.00
Creamer, doll face 150.00
Demitasse Cup and Saucer, Woodland 110.00
Dresser Set, woodland scene, tray, hatpin holder, power box, and hair receiver, maple leaf mark 950.00
Egg Warmer, holds 4 eggs, stopper, sailboat scene, rising sun mark 115.00
Ferner, 6" w, floral dec, gold beading, 4 handles, green "M" in wreath mark 125.00
Hanging Basket, 4" 990.00
Humidor, cov, 5", elk dec 880.00
Hatpin Holder, 5" h, serpent in relief, mottled ground 175.00
Jam Jar, cov, matching underplate, deep cobalt blue, heavily raised gold cartouches, allover gold dec, pink and pale apricot flowers, 2 handles, blue leaf mark 145.00
Jug, 6-1/2" h, cylindrical, short slender neck, white flat shoulder, stylized dragons and jewels, orig stopper, green "M" in wreath mark 300.00

Vase, two handles, Egyptian Warship, scrolled gold Moriage dec, green M wreath mark, 11" h, $935. Photo courtesy of Jackson's Auctioneers & Appraisers.

Mug, Egyptian motif with warship......................................385.00
Napkin Ring, 4" h, figural, owl on tree stump, wreath mark
....375.00
Nappy, 6-1/2" d, lake scene, forest in distance, moriage trim, gold
beading 70.00
Pitcher, 7" h, slate gray ground, moriage sea gulls, leaf mark
....250.00
Plaque, hanging
   7-3/4" d, Indian portrait, VP 124.....................................325.00
   9" d, quail, enameled leaves and berries, VP 1587.......325.00
   10" d, harbor scene, boats in full sail, shades of beige and
      brown, mkd "Hand Painted Nippon," and "M" in wreath
      mark 275.00
Plate
   8-1/2" d, lake, house, and roses scene, cobalt blue and gold
      trim, leaf mark 185.00
   10" w, gold center, cobalt blue and gold trim, maple leaf
      mark 160.00
   12" d, rose tapestry..2,640.00
Punch Bowl and Stand, 12-1/2" d, 6-1/2" h, bisque, bouquet of
roses scene, wide rim dec with gold and jewels, wreath mark
....350.00
Serving Tray, 11" d, gold and burgundy medallions inside gold
fluted rim, multicolored roses and laves center, gold open
pierced handles, Royal Kinran mark 225.00
Stein, relief molded, dog heads, leash handle, green "M" in
wreath mark 950.00
Sugar Shaker, 4-1/4" h, cobalt blue, floral maple leaf mark
....150.00
Tankard, 11-1/2" h, oval body, ornate gold trim and base bands,
gold handle, large blown out shaded green roses and foliage,
pale green satin ground 250.00
Tea Set, teapot, creamer, and sugar, melon ribbed shape, gold
handles and trim, gold overlay design, pink roses, leaf mark
....265.00
Tea Strainer, pink roses...50.00
Urn
   8" h, floral dec, matching lid 935.00
   11" h, florals, dec scrolling, gold trim, small medallion depict-
      ing "Peace Bringing Abundance" 2,200.00
Vase
   5" h, tapestry, woodland scene, two small handles 690.00
   6" h, tapestry..990.00
   7" h
      Cartoon style ship...470.00
      Cobalt Blue, dec..470.00
   7-1/2" h, handles, bulbous, pedestal foot, cobalt blue, Ma-
      dame Recaimer portrait, three floral inserts, beaded
      ....415.00
   9" h
      Coralene dec 910.00
      Molded rose dec 880.00
Wall Plaque, 10" d, portrait 435.00
Whiskey Jug, 6-1/2" h, Egyptian motif, excessive wear 880.00

NODDERS

History: Nodders are figurines with heads and/or arms attached to the body with wires to enable movement. They are made in a variety of materials–bisque, celluloid, papier-mâché, porcelain, or wood.

Most nodders date from the late 19th century, with Germany being the principal source of supply. Among the American-made nodders, those of Disney and cartoon characters are most eagerly sought.

Reference: Hilma R. Irtz, *Figural Nodders*, Collector Books, 1996.

Bisque
   Buttercup, German 180.00

Monkey, wooden, polychrome dec, $95.

Chinese man, 4-1/2" h, seated, legs crossed, holding in hand,
   pink and beige dec, beading 170.00
Colonial Woman, 7-1/2" h, bisque 190.00
Indian Princess, 3-3/4"h, seated, holding fan, pale blue, gold
   trim..115.00
Kayo, German...145.00
Little Orphan Annie, German...115.00
Monk, 5-3/4" h, standing, holding wine pitcher, German
....150.00
Oriental Couple, 8-3/4" h, pink robes, seated before keyboard
   and music book, gilt dec, Continental, 19th C 500.00
Turkish Girl, 6" h, white beading 300.00
Ceramic
   Old Salt, 7" h sailor, white beard, blue shirt, brown pants, black
      boots..25.00
   Siamese Boy and Girl, 4-1/2" h, salt and pepper shakers,
      black, orange, and gold outfits, orig box mid "A Commo-
      dore Product, Japan" 20.00
Papier-Mâché
   Black Boy, clockwork, felt and cotton suit, 24" h, c1900
....1,265.00
   Japanese Boy and Girl, 5-1/2" h, pr 50.00
   Mother Goose, red cape, black hat, white goose 3,960.00
   Rabbit, 8" h, sitting, light brown.....................................90.00
   Shriner, 7" h..90.00
Wood and Papier-Mâché
   Comical man, 6-3/8" h, top hat, worn orig polychrome . 140.00
   Santa, clockwork, gray mittens, cardboard and wood..900.00
   Santa, replaced red robe and beard.............................910.00

NORITAKE CHINA

History: Morimura Brothers founded Noritake China in 1904 in Nagoya, Japan. They made high-quality chinaware for export to the United States and also produced a line of china blanks for hand painting. In 1910 the company perfected a technique for the production of high-quality dinnerware and introduced streamlined production.

During the 1920s, the Larkin Company of Buffalo, New York, was a prime distributor of Noritake China. Larkin offered Azalea, Briarcliff, Linden, Modjeska, Savory, Sheridan, and Tree in the Meadow patterns as part of their premium line.

The factory was heavily damaged during World War II, and production was reduced. Between 1946 and 1948, the company sold its china under the "Rose China" mark, since the quality of production did not match the earlier Noritake China. Expansion in 1948 brought about the resumption of quality production and the use of the Noritake name once again.

Marks: There are close to 100 different marks for Noritake, the careful study of which can determine the date of production. Most pieces are marked "Noritake" with a wreath, "M," "N," or "Nippon." The use of the letter N was registered in 1953.

References: Aimee Neff Alden, *Collector's Encyclopedia of Early Noritake*, Collector Books, 1995; Joan Van Patten, *Collector's Encyclopedia of Noritake*, 1st Series (1984, 1997 value update), 2nd Series, (1994), Collector Books; David Spain, *Noritake Collectibles A to Z, A Pictorial Record and Guide to Values,* Schiffer Publishing, 1997.

Collectors' Club: Noritake Collectors' Society, 1237 Federal Ave. East, Seattle, WA 98102.

Additional Listings: See *Warman's Americana & Collectibles* for Azalea pattern prices.

Ashtray, Tree in the Meadow, 5-1/4" d, green mark 32.00
Berry Set, Tree in the Meadow, master bowl with pierced handles, 6 sauce bowls...75.00
Bowl, 10" l, oval, Rosewin #6584 pattern...............................30.00
Cake Plate, Tree in the Meadow, 7-1/2" sq 35.00
Candlesticks, pr, 8-1/4" h, gold flowers and bird, blue luster ground, wreath with "M" mark 125.00
Creamer and Sugar
    Art Deco, pink Japanese lanterns, cobalt blue ground, basket type handle on sugar, wreath with "M" mark..............50.00

Demitasse Cup and Saucer, $45.

Tree in the Meadow, scalloped 85.00
Cup and Saucer, Florola, #83374 pattern 24.00
Demitasse Cup and Saucer, Tree in the Meadow.............45.00
Dinner Set, floral motif, gold rimmed, 115 pc set...............375.00
Gravy Boat, Tree in the Meadow...............................50.00
Hair Receiver, 3-1/4" h, 3-1/2" w, art Deco, geometric designs, gold luster, wreath with "M" mark...................................50.00
Inkwell, owl, figural 125.00
Jam Jar, cov, basket style, handle, figural applied cherries on notched lid...55.00
Match Holder, underplate, camel scene, wreath with "M" mark 35.00
Napkin Ring, Art Deco man and woman, wreath with "M" mark, pr 60.00
Place Card Holder, figural, bluebird with butterfly, gold luster, white stripes, wreath with "M" mark, pr 35.00
Plate, 8-1/2" d, Tree in the Meadow..................................15.00
Platter, 11" l, Rosewin, #6584 ....25.00
Salt, 3" l, swan, white, orange luster, pr...........................25.00
Salt and Pepper Shakers, pr, Tree in the Meadow, mkd "Made in Japan"...35.00
Soup Bowl, Florola...15.00
Tea Tile, Tree in the Meadow, 5" w, green mark 35.00
Vegetable Bowl, cov, 9" d, round, Rosewin.......................35.00
Waffle Set, handled serving plate, sugar shaker, Art Deco flowers, wreath with "M" mark...50.00
Wall Pocket, butterfly, wreath with "M" mark.......................75.00

NORTH DAKOTA SCHOOL OF MINES

History: The North Dakota School of Mines was established in 1890. Earle J. Babcock, a chemistry instructor, was impressed with the high purity level of North Dakota potter's clay. In 1898, Babcock received funds to develop his finds. He tried to interest commercial potteries in the North Dakota clay but had limited success.

In 1910, Babcock persuaded the school to establish a Ceramics Department. Margaret Cable, who studied under Charles Binns and Frederick H. Rhead, was appointed head. She remained until her retirement in 1949.

Decorative emphasis was placed on native themes, e.g., flowers and animals. Art Nouveau, Art Deco, and fairly plain pieces were made.

Marks: The pottery is marked with a cobalt blue underglaze circle of the words "University of North Dakota/Grand Forks, N.D./Made at School of Mines/N.D. Clay." Some early pieces are marked only "U.N.D." or "U.N.D./Grand Forks, N.D." Most pieces are numbered (they can be dated from university records) and signed by both the instructor and student. Cable-signed pieces are the most desirable.

References: Susan and Al Bagdade, *Warman's American Pottery and Porcelain*, Wallace-Homestead, 1994; Darlene Hurst Dommel, *Collector's Encyclopedia of the Dakota Potteries*, Collector Books, 1996; Ralph and Terry Kovel, *Kovels' American Art Pottery*, Crown Publishers, 1993.

Collectors' Club: North Dakota Pottery Collectors Society, P.O. Box 14, Beach, ND 58621.

Bookends, pr, 3-3/4" h, 5-1/2" d, planter type, incised ivy leaf design, dark green over moss green matte glaze, ink mark, incised signature of Dora Whitman 750.00

Vase, dark purple, blue flecks, U.N.D. stamp, 2-3/4" h, $145.

Bowl
   2-1/2" h, 8" d, curled edge, brown jonquil and green leaves, soft blue ground, by D. Kane, 1925, circular ink mark 650.00
   3-3/4" h, 6-1/4" d, closed-in, dec by Margaret Cable, meadow larks and rushes, rich lime green matte finish, circular mark "M. Cable/Meadow Lark/155" 600.00
Jar, cov, 6" h, 5-3/4" d, incised oak leaves and acorns, shaded matte green glaze, ink stamp and "M.L.M. 1931" 450.00
Plate, 9-1/2" d, floral and geometric Art Deco yellow and brown pattern, beige ground, ink stamp, incised "JCH/1933"..375.00
Vase, 6-1/2" h, 6-1/2" d, bulbous, carved stylized lotus flowers, glossy blue-gray ground, by A. Berg, ink stamp incised signature...............750.00

WALLACE NUTTING

History: Wallace Nutting (1861-1941) was America's most famous photographer of the early 20th century. A retired minister, Nutting took more than 50,000 pictures, keeping 10,000 of his best and destroying the rest. His popular and best-selling scenes included "Exterior Scenes" (apple blossoms, country lanes, orchards, calm streams, and rural American countrysides), "Interior Scenes" (usually featuring a colonial woman working near a hearth), and "Foreign Scenes" (typically thatch-roofed cottages). Those pictures which were least popular in his day have become the rarest and most highly collectible today and are classified as "Miscellaneous Unusual Scenes." This category encompasses such things as animals, architecturals, children, florals, men, seascapes, and snow scenes.

Nutting sold literally millions of his hand-colored platinotype pictures between 1900 and his death in 1941. Starting first in Southbury, Connecticut, and later moving his business to Framingham, Massachusetts, the peak of Wallace Nutting's picture production was 1915 to 1925. During this period, Nutting employed nearly 200 people, including col-orists, darkroom staff, salesmen, and assorted office personnel. Wallace Nutting pictures proved to be a huge commercial success and hardly an American household was without one by 1925.

While attempting to seek out the finest and best early American furniture as props for his colonial Interior Scenes, Nutting became an expert in American antiques. He published nearly 20 books in his lifetime, including his 10-volume State Beautiful series and various other books on furniture, photography, clocks, and his autobiography. He also contributed many photographs which were published in magazines and books other than his own.

Nutting also became widely known for his reproduction furniture. His furniture shop produced literally hundreds of different furniture forms: clocks, stools, chairs, settles, settees, tables, stands, desks, mirrors, beds, chests of drawers, cabinet pieces, and treenware.

The overall synergy of the Wallace Nutting name, pictures, books, and furniture, has made anything "Wallace Nutting" quite collectible.

Marks: Wallace Nutting furniture is clearly marked with his distinctive paper label (which was glued directly onto the piece) or with a block or script signature brand (which was literally branded into his furniture).

Note: "Process Prints" are 1930s machine-produced reprints of 12 of Nutting's most popular pictures. These have minimal value and can be detected by using a magnifying glass.

References: Michael Ivankovich, *Alphabetical & Numerical Index to Wallace Nutting Pictures*, Diamond Press, 1988; ——, *Collector's Guide to Wallace Nutting Pictures*, Collector Books, 1997; ——, *Guide to Wallace Nutting Furniture*, Diamond Press, 1990; ——, *Wallace Nutting Expansible Catalog* (reprint of 1915 catalog), Diamond Press, 1987; Wallace Nutting, *Wallace Nutting: A Great American Idea* (reprint of 1922 catalog), Diamond Press, 1992; ——, *Wallace Nutting General Catalog* (reprint of 1930 catalog), Schiffer Publishing, 1977; ——, *Wallace Nutting's Windsors* (reprint of 1918 catalog), Diamond Press, 1992.

Collectors' Club: Wallace Nutting Collectors Club, P.O. Box 2458, Doylestown, PA 18901.

Museum: Wadsworth Athenaeum, Hartford, CT.

Advisor: Michael Ivankovich.

Books

American Windsors 85.00
England Beautiful, 1st ed. 125.00
Furniture of the Pilgrim Century, 1st ed...........140.00
Furniture Treasury, Vol. I...............125.00

Furniture Treasury, Vol. II	140.00
Furniture Treasury, Vol. III	105.00
Ireland Beautiful, 1st ed.	45.00
Pathways of the Puritans	85.00
Social Life In Old New England	72.00

State Beautiful Series

Connecticut Beautiful, 1st ed.	72.00
Maine Beautiful, 1st ed.	45.00
Massachusetts Beautiful, 2nd ed.	35.00
New Hampshire Beautiful, 1st ed.	72.00
New York Beautiful, 1st ed.	85.00
Pennsylvania Beautiful, 1st ed.	45.00
Vermont Beautiful, 2nd ed.	40.00
Virginia Beautiful, 1st ed.	60.00
The Cruise of the 800	95.00

Furniture

Chair

Arm, mahogany, chip	1,265.00
Bedroom, mahogany	440.00
Side, Windsor	600.00
Slipper	715.00
Costumer/Coat Rack	415.00
Desk, child's	770.00
Stool, 4 legged, maple, rushed	235.00
Trestle Table	60.00

Miscellaneous

Calendar, 1939, 6" x 10"	75.00

Catalog

Christmas Picture, 1912	135.00
Furniture, 1937	95.00
Christmas Card, 4" x 5"	155.00
Easter Card, 5" x 9"	200.00
Plate, treenware	245.00

Pictures

A Berkshire Cross Road, 14" x 17"	160.00
A Call for More, 10" x 13"	330.00
A Cluster of Zinnias, 13" x 16"	330.00
A Fair Orchard Way, 11" x 14"	105.00
A Gettysburg Crossing, 14" x 17"	200.00
A Keene Road, 13" x 17"	165.00
All the Comforts of Home, 13" x 15"	210.00
A Perkiomen October, 9" x 11"	250.00
Among the Ferns, 14" x 17"	165.00

An Elaborate Dinner, 14" x 17"	200.00
Better than Mowing, 16" x 20"	490.00
Between the Spruces, 10" x 14"	200.00
Birch Hilltop, 15" x 22"	100.00
By the Fireside, 9" x 13"	100.00
California Hilltops, 11" x 14"	165.00
Dog-On-It, 7" x 11"	1,265.00
Elm Drapery, 15" x 22"	385.00
Fleur-de-lis and Spirea, 13" x 16"	685.00
Flume Falls, 12" x 15"	310.00
Four O'Clock, 14" x 17"	855.00
Gloucester Cloister, 16" x 20"	1,100.00
Grandmother's Hollyhocks, 9" x 11"	400.00
Helping Mother, 14" x 17"	410.00
Hesitation, 10" x 16"	220.00
Home Charm, 15" x 22"	315.00
Honeymoon Cottage, 11" x 17"	125.00
Into the West, 10" x 16"	45.00
Mountain Born, 10" x 12"	165.00
On The Heights, 10" x 16"	100.00
Parting at the Gate, 10" x 14"	550.00
Pennsylvania Arches, 14" x 17"	300.00
Priscilla's Cottage, 14" x 17"	360.00
Russet and Gold, 16" x 20"	315.00
Shadowy Orchard Curves, 11" x 14"	85.00
Stepping Stones to Bolton Abbey, 11" x 14"	330.00
The Footbridge by the Ford, 16" x 20"	440.00
The Guardian Mother, 11" x 17"	2,970.00
The Manchester Battenkill, 16" x 20"	245.00
The River Farm, 10" x 12"	180.00
Toward Slumberland, 13" x 17"	770.00
Trumpets, 8" x 10"	580.00
Two Lilies, 9" x 11"	440.00
Village Spires, 10" x 12"	125.00
Watching for Papa, 13" x 16"	420.00
Wilton Waters, 13" x 16"	155.00
Winding an Old Tall clock, 14" x 17"	165.00

Silhouettes

George and Martha Washington, 3" x 4"	90.00
Girl at Vanity Desk, 4" x 4"	79,99
Girl by Garden Urn, 4" x 4"	75.00
Girl by Spider Web, 5" x 4"	50.00
Scenes	40.00

WALLACE NUTTING-LIKE PHOTOGRAPHERS

History: Although Wallace Nutting was widely recognized as the country's leading producer of hand-colored photographs during the early 20th century, he was by no means the only photographer selling this style of picture. Throughout the country, literally hundreds of regional photographers were selling hand-colored photographs from their home regions or travels. The subject matter of these photographers was comparable to Nutting's, including Interior, Exterior, Foreign, And Miscellaneous Unusual scenes.

Several photographers operated large businesses, and, although not as large or well-known as Wallace Nutting, they sold a substantial volume of pictures which can still be readily found today. The vast majority of their work was photographed in their home regions and sold primarily to local residents or visiting tourists. It should come as little surprise that three of the major Wallace Nutting-like photographers–David Davidson, Fred Thompson, and the Sawyer Art Co.–each had ties to Wallace Nutting.

The Meeting Place, $2,255. Photo courtesy of Michael Ivankovich Antiques, Inc.

Hundreds of other smaller local and regional photographers attempted to market hand-colored pictures comparable to Wallace Nutting's from 1900 to the 1930s. Although quite attractive, most were not as appealing to the general public as Wallace Nutting pictures. However, as the price of Wallace Nutting pictures has escalated, the work of these lesser-known Wallace Nutting-like photographers has become increasingly collectible.

A partial listing of some of these minor Wallace Nutting-like photographers includes: Babcock; J. C. Bicknell; Blair; Ralph Blood (Portland, Maine); Bragg; Brehmer; Brooks; Burrowes; Busch; Carlock; Pedro Cacciola; Croft; Currier; Depue Brothers; Derek; Dowly; Eddy; May Farini (hand-colored colonial lithographs); George Forest; Gandara; Gardner (Nantucket, Bermuda, Florida); Gibson; Gideon; Gunn; Bessie Pease Gutmann (hand-colored colonial lithographs); Edward Guy; Harris; C. Hazen; Knoffe; Haynes (Yellowstone Park); Margaret Hennesey; Hodges; Homer; Krabel; Kattleman; La Bushe; Lake; Lamson (Portland, Maine); M. Lightstrum; Machering; Rossiler Mackinae; Merrill; Meyers; William Moehring; Moran; Murrey; Lyman Nelson; J. Robinson Neville (New England); Patterson; Own Perry; Phelps; Phinney; Reynolds; F. Robbins; Royce; Frederick Scheetz (Philadelphia, Pennsylvania); Shelton, Standley (Colorado); Stott; Summers; Esther Svenson; Florence Thompson; Thomas Thompson; M. A. Trott; Sanford Tull; Underhill; Villar; Ward; Wilmot; Edith Wilson; and Wright.

References: Carol Begley Gray, *History of the Sawyer Pictures*, published by author, 1995 (available from Wallace Nutting Collector's Club, P.O. Box 2458, Doylestown, PA 18901); Michael Ivankovich, *Guide to Wallace-Nutting Like Photographers of the Early 20th Century*, Diamond Press, 1991.

Collectors' Club: Wallace Nutting Collector's Club, P.O. Box 2458, Doylestown, PA 18901.

Advisor: Michael Ivankovich.

Notes: The key determinants of value include the collectibility of the particular photographer, subject matter, condition, and size. Exterior Scenes are the most common.

Keep in mind that only the rarest pictures, in the best condition, will bring top prices. Discoloration and/or damage to the picture or matting can reduce value significantly.

David Davidson

Second to Nutting in overall production, Davidson worked primarily in the Rhode and Southern Massachusetts area. While a student at Brown University around 1900, Davidson learned the art of hand-colored photography from Wallace Nutting, who happened to be the Minister at Davidson's church. After Nutting moved to Southbury in 1905, Davidson graduated from Brown and started a successful photography business in Providence, Rhode Island, which he operated until his death in 1967.

A Puritan Lady	70.00
A Real D.A.R.	150.00
Berkshire Sunset	80.00
Christmas Day	160.00
Driving Home The Cows	120.00
Heart's Desire	30.00

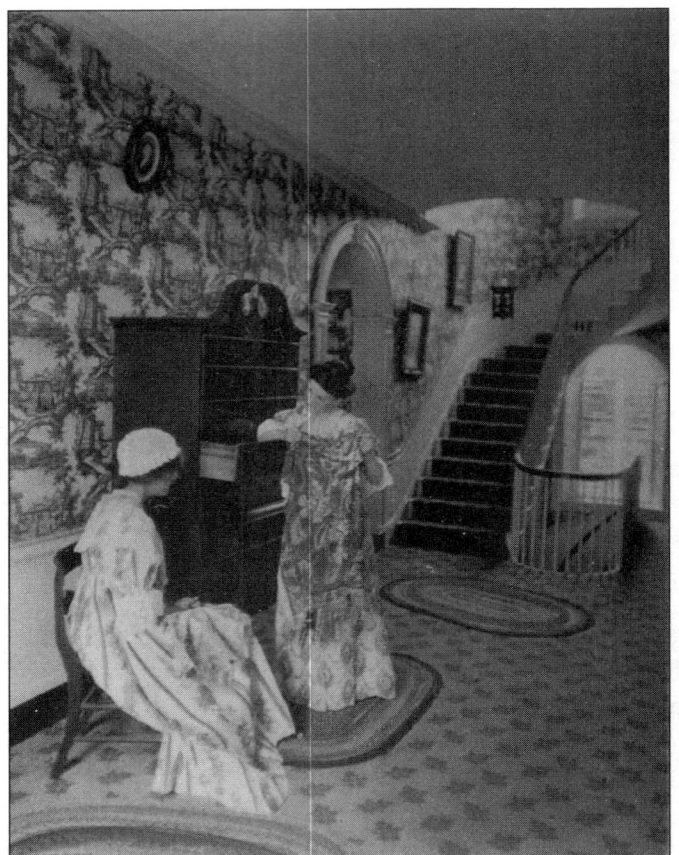

The Heirloom, $100. Photo courtesy of Michael Ivankovich Antiques, Inc.

Her House In Order	75.00
Neighbors	170.00
Old Ironsides	170.00
On A News Hunt	120.00
Plymouth Elm	20.00
Rosemary Club	40.00
Snowbound Brook	55.00
The Brook's Mirro	95.00
The Lamb's May Feast	130.00
The Seine Reel	190.00
The Silent Wave	35.00
Vanity	70.00

Sawyer

A father and son team, Charles H. Sawyer and Harold B. Sawyer, operated the very successful Sawyer Art Company from 1903 until the 1970s. Beginning in Maine, the Sawyer Art Company moved to Concord, New Hampshire, in 1920 to be closer to its primary market–New Hampshire's White Mountains. Charles H. Sawyer briefly worked for Nutting from 1902 to 1903 while living in southern Maine. Sawyer's production volume ranks third behind Wallace Nutting and David Davidson.

A February Morning	210.00
A New England Sugar Birth	300.00
At the Bend of the Road	35.00
Crystal Lake	65.00
Echo Lake, Franconia Notch	50.00
Indian Summer	35.00
Lake Morey	30.00
Lake Willoughby	50.00

Mt. Washington in October	55.00
Newfound Lake	73.00
Old Man of the Mountains	35.00
Original Dennison Plant	100.00
Silver Birches, Lake George	50.00
The Meadow Stream	80.00

Fred Thompson

Frederick H. Thompson and Frederick M. Thompson, another father and son team, operated the Thompson Art Company (TACO) from 1908 to 1923, working primarily in the Portland, Maine, area. We know that Thompson and Nutting had collaborated because Thompson widely marketed an interior scene he had taken in Nutting's Southbury home. The production volume of the Thompson Art Company ranks fourth behind Nutting, Davidson, and Sawyer.

Apple Tree Road	45.00
Blossom Dale	75.00
Brook in Winter	190.00
Calm of Fall	50.00
Fernbank	35.00
Fireside Fancy Work	140.00
High and Dry	45.00
Knitting for the Boys	160.00
Lombardy Poplar	100.00
Nature's Carpet	50.00
Neath the Blossoms	95.00
Peace River	30.00
Six Master	100.00
Sunset on the Suwanee	45.00
The Gossips	80.00
White Head	90.00

Minor Wallace Nutting-Like Photographers

Generally speaking, prices for works by minor Wallace Nutting-like photographers would break down as follows: smaller pictures (5" x 7" to 10" x 12"), $10-$75; medium pictures (11" x 14" to 14" x 17"), $50-$200; larger pictures (larger than 14" x 17"), $75-$200+.

Baker, Florian A., Rushing Waters	50.00
Farini, In Her Boudoir	30.00
Gibson, Mountain Road	20.00
Haynes, Untitled Waterfalls	20.00
Higgins, Charles A., A Colonial Stairway	65.00
Payne, George S., Weekly Letter	25.00

Surf at Pinnacle Rock, $125. Photo courtesy of Michael Ivankovich Antiques, Inc.

OCCUPIED JAPAN

History: The Japanese economy was devastated when World War II ended. To secure necessary hard currency, the Japanese pottery industry produced thousands of figurines and other knickknacks for export. The variety of products is endless—ashtrays, dinnerware, lamps, planters, souvenir items, toys, vases, etc. Initially, the figurines attracted the largest number of collectors; today many collectors focus on other types of pieces.

Marks: From the beginning of the American occupation of Japan until April 28, 1952, objects made in that country were marked "Japan," "Made in Japan," "Occupied Japan," or "Made in Occupied Japan." Only pieces marked with the last two designations are of major interest to Occupied Japan collectors. The first two marks also were used during other time periods.

References: Florence Archambault, *Occupied Japan for Collectors*, Schiffer Publishing, 1992; Gene Florence, *Price Guide to Collector's Encyclopedia of Occupied Japan*, Collector Books, 1997 (updated prices for 5-book series *Collector's Encyclopedia of Occupied Japan*); David C. Gould and Donna Crevar-Donaldson, *Occupied Japan Toys with Prices*, L-W Book Sales, 1993; Anthony Marsella, *Toys from Occupied Japan*, Schiffer Publishing, 1995; Lynette Parmer, *Collecting Occupied Japan*, Schiffer Publishing, 1996; Carole Bess White, *Collector's Guide to Made in Japan Ceramics*, Book I (1996), Book II (1997), Collector Books.

Collectors' Club: The Occupied Japan Club, 29 Freeborn St., Newport, RI 02840.

Additional Listings: See *Warman's Americana & Collectibles* for more examples.

Ashtray, 4-3/4" h, metal, spring-loaded head of young boy smoking cigar 50.00

Bowl, cov, Capo-di-Monte style, double handles, brightly colored enamel dec, winged cherubs in woodland scene, mkd "Occupied Japan" 20.00

Children's Play Dishes, play set, Blue Willow, 18 pc set 375.00

Cigarette Dispenser, mechanical, inlaid wood, spring-operated sliding drawer loads cigarettes into bird's beak 55.00

Clock, 10-1/2" h, bisque, double figure, colonial dancing couple, floral encrusted case 250.00

Cornucopia, 7" x 8", chariot, rearing horse and 2 cherubs, multicolored beading, gold trim, unglazed bisque 80.00

Figure, 4-1/2" h, 5-3/4" l, Chinese couple, woman playing stringed instrument, man smoking pipe 35.00

Finger Bowl, 5-3/4" h, porcelain, winged cherub and raspberries 30.00

Flower Frog, 6" h, figural, girl with bird on shoulder, pastel highlights, gold trim, bisque 45.00

Lamp, Colonial couple, gentleman with guitar, woman holding floral bouquet, floral emb base 25.00

Platter, 16" l, Courley pattern, heavy gold trim, mkd "Meito Norleans China" 30.00

Salt and Pepper Shakers, pr, coffeepots, cobalt blue glass, metal gray with red Bakelite handles, prig presentation box 25.00

Tape Measure, 2-3/8" l, pig, stamped "Occupied Japan" ... 45.00

Shoe, red, blue, orange, and green floral motif, mkd "Made in Occupied Japan," 5-3/4" l, $20.

Vase, 10" h, bisque, figural, young lady and scrolled cornucopia 65.00
Wall Pocket, flying geese, set of 1 large and 3 smaller pockets, 4 pc set...25.00

OHR POTTERY

G.E.OHR,
BILOXI.

History: Ohr pottery was produced by George E. Ohr in Biloxi, Mississippi. There is a discrepancy as to when he actually established his pottery; some say 1878, but Ohr's autobiography indicates 1883. In 1884, Ohr exhibited 600 pieces of his work, suggesting that he had been a potter for some time.

Ohr's techniques included twisting, crushing, folding, denting, and crinkling thin-walled clay into odd, grotesque, and, sometimes, graceful forms. His later pieces were often left unglazed.

In 1906, Ohr closed the pottery and stored more than 6,000 pieces as a legacy to his family. He had hoped the U.S. government would purchase it, which never happened. The entire collection remained in storage until it was rediscovered in 1972.

Today Ohr is recognized as one of the leaders in the American art pottery movement. Some greedy individuals have taken the later unglazed pieces and covered them with poor-quality glazes in hopes of making them more valuable. These pieces do not have stilt marks on the bottom.

Marks: Much of Ohr's early work was signed with an impressed stamp including his name and location in block letters. His later work was often marked with the flowing script designation "G. E. Ohr."

References: Susan and Al Bagdade, *Warman's American Pottery and Porcelain*, Wallace-Homestead, 1994; Garth Clark, Robert Ellison Jr., and Eugene Hecht, *Mad Potter of Biloxi: The Art & Life of George Ohr*, Abbeville Press, 1989; Ralph and Terry Kovel, *Kovels' American Art Pottery*, Crown Publishers, 1993; David Rago, *American Art Pottery,* Knickerbocker Press, 1997.

Candleholder, 6-1/2" h, 4" d, organic, pinched ribbon handle, inbody twist, ribbed base, yellow, green, and raspberry matte mottled glaze, small chip to base, script mark...........3,300.00
Chamberstick, 4" h, 3-3/4" d, deep red, green, and yellow matte mottled glaze, stilt pulls to bottom, hand incised "GE OHR" 1,500.00

Demitasse Cup, 2-1/2" h, 3-3/4" d, ext. with rare green, cobalt blue, and raspberry marbleized glaze, int. with sponged cobalt and raspberry volcanic glaze, die-stamped "G. E. Ohr, Biloxi, Miss" 1,500.00
Jar, cov, 4-1/4" h, 5" d, spherical, gunmetal and green glaze dripping over mottled raspberry ground, shallow storage abrasion, die-stamped "G.E. OHR, Biloxi, Miss" 1,500.00
Mustache Cup, 2-3/4" h, 4" d, hand built as a shirt cuff, ribbon handle, sponged blue glaze, die-stamped "GEO. E. OHR/BILOXI, MISS" 2,000.00
Pitcher, 4" h, 4-1/4" d, pinched handle, pink and green volcanic glaze, die-stamped "G. E. OHR, Biloxi, Miss" 2,200.00
Vase
3" h, 3-1/2" h, bulbous, lobed rim, sponged green, turquoise, and gunmetal glaze, orig price tag, die-stamped "G. E. OHR, Biloxi, Miss"..2,600.00
3-3/4" h, 4-1/3" d, bulbous, cupped top, deep in-body twist, raspberry, turquoise, and amber glaze, minute glaze fleck to rim, die-stamped "G. E. OHR/BILOXI, MISS" 4,500.00
4" h, 2-3/4" d, closed-in rim, dripping mustard gunmetal design, olive and brown ground, stilt pull t base, script mark 475.00
4" h, 4" d, deep in-body twist, gun metal glossy glaze, stamped mark..1,250.00
4" h, 4-3/4" d, corset shape, flaring folded rim, top cov in blue-green glaze, bottom with added mottled raspberry blaze, minor rim abrasion, die-stamped "BILOXI/MISS/GEO. E. OHR" 4,250.00
4-3/4" h, 4-3/4" d, two handles, cupped top, deep in-body twist, pinched ribbon handles, green and purple mottled glaze, die-stamped "G. E. OHR/BILOXI, MISS" 4,250.00
5-1/2" h, 2-1/2" d, bud vase, conical base, in-body twist, dead matte black crystalline glaze, die-stamped "G. E. OHR/BILOXI" 1,400.00
6" h, 4" d, two crimped handles, glossy red finish......4,500.00
7" h, 3-1/4" d, 3 sectioned bottle form, glossy olive glaze, top and bottom sponged dark blue, center purple metallic glaze, die-stamped "G. E. OHR/Biloxi, Miss" 1,200.00

Vase, twisted and compressed base, semi-matte speckled mustard glaze, stove-top pipe ending in folded rim cov in matte gun-metal glaze, imp mark, 6-3/4" x 7", $5,225. Photo courtesy of David Rago Auctions, Inc.

8-1/2" h, 3-3/4" d, bottle shape, brown, green, and amber speckled lustered glaze, restoration to tiny rim chip, die-stamped "G. E. OHR, Biloxi, Miss" 1,200.00

9-1/4" h, 3-3/4" d, bottle shape, mottled raspberry, purple, cobalt blue, and green satin glaze, small abrasion ring around widest part from years of storage at production site, die-stamped "G. E. OHR/Biloxi, Miss" 2,500.00

Vessel

2-3/4" h, 3" d, cupped rim, deep in-body twist, amber speckled glaze, touch up to small base nick, die-stamped "G. E. OHR, Biloxi, Miss" 1,200.00

3-1/2" h, 4-1/2" d, lobed and pinched opening, dark blue-green and gunmetal glaze, script sgd 1,100.00

3-1/2" h, 4-1/2" d, severely pinched sides, lobed rim, dark brown and olive green speckled glaze, die-stamped "G. E. Ohr/Biloxi, Miss" 2,100.00

4-1/4" h, 3-3/4" d, squat base, tapered neck, gunmetal over mottled raspberry glaze, script sgd 1,500.00

4-1/2" h, 6-1/2" d, unglazed scroddled clay, asymmetrically pinched into wave-like folds, script mark 8,750.00

5-1/4" h, 4" d, pinched and bolded top, sponged brown and green glaze, all-over gunmetal drip, die-stamped "G. E. OHR/Biloxi, Miss" 2,100.00

5-1/2" h, 4-1/4" d, bulbous, severely folded and pinched top, leathery gunmetal glaze over amber base, die-stamped "G. E. OHR/BILOXI, MISS" 2,400.00

5-1/2" h, 4-3/4" d, heavily dimpled front and back, folded rim, green speckled glossy glaze, die-stamped "G. E. OHR, Biloxi, Miss" 3,000.00

OLD IVORY CHINA

OLD IVORY
84

History: Old Ivory derives its name from the background color of the china. It was made in Silesia, Germany, during the second half of the 19th century.

Marks: Marked pieces usually have a pattern number (pattern names are not common), a crown, and the word "Silesia."

Reference: Alma Hillman, David Goldschmidt & Adam Szynkiewica, *Collector's Encyclopedia of Old Ivory China, The Mystery Explored,* Collector Books, 1997.

Periodical: *Old Ivory Newsletter*, P.O. Box 1004, Wilsonville, OR 97070.

Collectors' Club: Old Ivory Porcelain Society, P.O. Box 326, Osage, Iowa 50461.

Berry Bowl, individual
#29, 3 pc set 65.00
#40, 3 pc set 75.00
Biscuit Jar, cov, #15 .... 350.00
Bowl
6-1/2" d, #84 .... 65.00
9-1/4" d, #200 .... 195.00
Cake Plate, #13, 10" d, open handles, roses around border, one in center 125.00
Chocolate Set, #84, chocolate pot, 6 cups and saucers ... 850.00
Creamer, #32 .... 50.00
Cup, #16, pr 38.00
Demitasse Pot, cov, #16 .... 395.00
Mustard Pot, cov, #16 .... 110.00
Oyster Bowl, #11 .... 195.00
Place Setting, cup, saucer, and 8" plate, Eglantine pattern
.... 85.00

Cake Plate, mkd "Clairon, Germany," 11" w, $70.

Plate
7-3/4" d, #16, 2 pc set 37.00
8-1/4" d, #16, 3 pc set 44.00
8-3/4" d, #84, 3 pc set 48.00
Sugar Bowl, cov, #75 .... 60.00
Teapot, cov, #15 .... 395.00
Toothpick Holder, #16 .... 195.00

OLD PARIS CHINA

History: Old Paris china is fine-quality porcelain made by various French factories located in and around Paris during the 18th and 19th centuries. Some pieces were marked, but most were not. In addition to its fine quality, this type of ware is characterized by beautiful decorations and gilding. Favored colors are dark maroon, deep cobalt blue, and a dark green.

Additional Listings: Continental China and Porcelain (General).

Basket, reticulated, gold and white dec, c1825 .... 1,400.00
Cake Stand, Honore style, green border, c1845 .... 220.00

Cup and Saucer, blue rim, gold lines, floral band on cup, blurred mark, $45.

Figure, 18-3/4" h, Napoleon, standing, one arm tucked behind back, other tucked into shirt, full military dress, gilt dec, low sq base, inscribed "Roussel-Bardell," late 19th C 700.00

Luncheon Set, light blue ground banding, gilt and iron-red cartouche and monogram, 28 9-1/4" d plates, 18 8-1/4" d plates, 11 6-5/8" d plates, 12 sauce dishes, 11 soup plates, oval 12-1/2" l serving bowl, oval 17-1/2" l platter, 2 circular cov vegetable tureens, cov sauce tureen, cov oval 12-1/4" tureen with underplate, cov jam jar with attached dish, chips, gilt wear 1,610.00

Mantel Vase, bell-like flowered handles, blue ground, paneled enamel portraits of lovers, gilt trim, minor flower damage, pr 350.00

Plate, 9-1/4" d, flower-basket center, gilt vine and borders, ochre ground, c1830, pr...250.00

Tea Set
5-3/4" h cov teapot, creamer, sugar, 8" d waste bowl, 8 cups and saucers, gilt trim, floral design, enameled floral panels, 19th C, gilt wear, creamer handle broken 250.00
8-5/8" h cov teapot, 7-3/4" h cream pitcher, 5-1/2" cov sugar bowl, gilt ground, enamel dec floral bouquets and banding, 19th C, sugar cov damaged....................................460.00

Vase, 13-1/4" h, central medallion with courting couple in landscape, fuchsia border, chartreuse ground, gilt floral, foliate, and lattice dec, price for pr 1,500.00

OLD SLEEPY EYE

History: Sleepy Eye, a Sioux Indian chief who reportedly had a droopy eye, gave his name to Sleepy Eye, Minnesota, and one of its leading flour mills. In the early 1900s, Old Sleepy Eye Flour offered four Flemish-gray heavy stoneware premiums decorated in cobalt blue: a straight-sided butter crock, curved salt bowl, stein, and vase. The premiums were made by Weir Pottery Company, later to become Monmouth Pottery Company, and finally to emerge as the present-day Western Stoneware Company of Monmouth, Illinois.

Additional pottery and stoneware pieces also were issued. Forms included five sizes of pitchers (4, 5-1/2, 6-1/2, 8, and 9 inches), mugs, steins, sugar bowls, and tea tiles (hot plates). Most were cobalt blue on white, but other glaze hues, such as browns, golds, and greens, were used.

Old Sleepy Eye also issued many other items, including bakers' caps, lithographed barrel covers, beanies, fans, multicolored pillow tops, postcards, and trade cards. Regular production of Old Sleepy Eye stoneware ended in 1937.

In 1952, Western Stoneware Company made 22- and 40-ounce steins in chestnut brown glaze with a redesigned Indian's head. From 1961 to 1972, gift editions were made for the board of directors and others within the company. Beginning in 1973, Western Stoneware Company issued an annual limited edition stein for collectors.

Marks: The gift editions made in the 1960s and 1970s were dated and signed with a maple leaf mark. The annual limited edition steins are marked and dated.

References: Susan and Al Bagdade, *Warman's American Pottery and Porcelain*, Wallace-Homestead, 1994; Elinor Meugnoit, *Old Sleepy Eye*, published by author, 1979.

Collectors' Club: Old Sleepy Eye Collectors Club, P.O. Box 12, Monmouth, IL 61462.

REPRODUCTION ALERT

Blue-and-white pitchers, crazed, weighted, and often with a stamp or the word "Ironstone" are the most common reproductions. The stein and salt bowl also have been made. Many reproductions come from Taiwan.

A line of fantasy items, new items which never existed as Old Sleepy Eye originals, includes an advertising pocket mirror with miniature flour-barrel label, small glass plates, fruit jars, toothpick holders, glass and pottery miniature pitchers, and salt and pepper shakers. One mill item has been made: a sack marked as though it was old but of a size that could not possibly hold the amount of flour indicated.

Mill Items

Advertising Premium Cards, 5-1/2" x 9", full-color Indian lore illus, Old Sleepy Eye Indian character trademark, 10 pc set 875.00

Cookbook, Sleepy Eye Milling Co., loaf of bread shape, portrait of chief 150.00

Label, 9-1/4" x 11-1/2" d, egg crate, Sleepy Eye Brand, A. J. Pietrus & Sons Co., Sleepy Eye, MN, red, blue, and yellow 25.00

Letter Opener, bronze, Indian-head handle, mkd "Sleepy Eye Milling Co., Sleepy Eye, MN".....................................750.00

Pinback Button, "Old Sleepy Eye for Me," bust portrait of chief 175.00

Pottery and Stoneware

Mug, cobalt blue on white, Indian head on handle, 1906-37 . 250.00

Pitcher
4" h, gray ground, cobalt blue 300.00
9" h, beige ground, cobalt blue dec, c1906-37.............165.00

Advertising Sign, litho tin over cardboard, New York Metal Sign Works, 13-5/8" x 19", $1,500.

Stein, 22 oz., chestnut brown, 1952 .... 275.00
Tile, cobalt blue and white 950.00

ONION MEISSEN

History: The blue onion or bulb pattern is of Chinese origin and depicts peaches and pomegranates, not onions. Meissen first made it in the 18th century, hence the name Onion Meissen.

Factories in Europe, Japan, and elsewhere copied the pattern. Many still have the pattern in production, including the Meissen factory in Germany.

Marks: Many pieces are marked with a company's logo; after 1891, the country of origin is indicated on imported pieces.

Reference: Robert E. Röntgen, *Book of Meissen*, revised ed., Schiffer Publishing, 1996.

Note: Prices given are for pieces produced between 1870 and 1930. Early Meissen examples bring a high premium.

Ashtray, 5" d, blue crossed swords mark 80.00
Bowl, 8-1/2" d, reticulated, blue crossed swords mark, 19th C
.... 395.00
Box, cov, 4-1/2" d, round, rose finial 80.00
Bread Plate, 6-1/2" d 75.00
Cake Stand, 13-1/2" d, 4-1/2" h 220.00
Candlesticks, pr, 7" h 90.00
Creamer and Sugar, gold edge, c1900 .... 175.00
Demitasse Cup and Saucer, c1890 .... 90.00
Dish, 12" d, circular, divided 175.00
Fruit Compote, 9" h, circular, openwork bowl, 5 oval floral medal-
lions 375.00
Fruit Knives, 6 pc set 75.00
Hot Plate, handles 125.00
Ladle, wooden handle 115.00
Lamp, 22" h, oil, frosted glass globular form shade 475.00
Plate, 10" d 100.00
Platter
    12-1/4" d 175.00
    13" x 10", crossed swords mark 295.00
Pot de Creme 65.00
Serving Dish, 9-1/4" w, 11" l, floral design on handle 200.00
Tray, 17" l, cartouche shape, gilt edge 425.00
Vegetable Dish, cov, 10" w, sq 150.00

OPALESCENT GLASS

History: Opalescent glass, a clear or colored glass with milky white decorations, looks fiery or opalescent when held to light. This effect was achieved by applying bone ash chemicals to designated areas while a piece was still hot and then refiring it at extremely high temperatures.

There are three basic categories of opalescent glass: (1) blown (or mold blown) patterns, e.g., Daisy & Fern and Spanish Lace; (2) novelties, pressed glass patterns made in limited quantity and often in unusual shapes such as corn or a trough; and (3) traditional pattern (pressed) glass forms.

Opalescent glass was produced in England in the 1870s. Northwood began the American production in 1897 at its Indiana, Pennsylvania, plant. Jefferson, National Glass, Hobbs, and Fenton soon followed.

References: Gary Baker et al., *Wheeling Glass 1829-1939*, Oglebay Institute, 1994, distributed by Antique Publications; Bill Banks, *Complete Price Guide for Opalescent Glass*, 2nd ed., published by author, 1996; Bill Edwards, *Standard Encyclopedia of Opalescent Glass*, Collector Books, 1997; William Heacock, *Encyclopedia of Victorian Colored Pattern Glass*, Book II, 2nd ed., Antique Publications, 1977; William Heacock and William Gamble, *Encyclopedia of Victorian Colored Pattern Glass*, Book 9, Antique Publications, 1987; William Heacock, James Measell, and Berry Wiggins, *Dugan/Diamond*, Antique Publications, 1993; ——, *Harry Northwood* (1990), Book 2 (1991) Antique Publications.

Blown

Barber Bottle
    Raised Swirl, cranberry 295.00
    Swirl, blue 225.00
Berry Bowl, master, Chrysanthemum Base Swirl, blue, satin
.... 95.00
Biscuit Jar, cov, Spanish Lace, vaseline 275.00
Bride's Basket, Poinsettia, ruffled top 275.00
Butter Dish, cov, Hobbs Hobnail, vaseline 250.00
Celery Vase, Seaweed, cranberry 250.00
Creamer
    Coin Dot, cranberry 190.00
    Gonterman Swirl, blue, frosted 625.00
    Windows Swirl, cranberry 500.00
Cruet
    Chrysanthemum Base Swirl, white, satin 175.00
    Ribbed Opal Lattice, white 135.00
Finger Bowl, Hobbs Hobnail, cranberry 65.00

Pitcher, tankard, Poinsettia, blue, Hobbs, Brockunier & Co., 13-3/8" h, $265.

Rose Bowl, Pearl and Scale, green, ftd, 4-3/4" d, $65.

Lamp, oil
  Inverted Thumbprint, white, amber fan base 145.00
  Snowflake, cranberry 800.00
Mustard, cov, Reverse Swirl, vaseline....................................65.00
Pickle Castor, Daisy and Fern, blue, emb floral jar, DQ, resilvered
  frame...650.00
Pitcher
  Arabian Nights, white 450.00
  Fern, blue..450.00
  Hobbs Hobnail, cranberry 315.00
  Reverse Swirl, blue, satin, speckled............................495.00
  Seaweed, blue..525.00
  Windows, cranberry..695.00
Rose Bowl, Opal Swirl, white 40.00
Salt Shaker, orig top
  Consolidated Criss-Cross, cranberry 85.00
  Ribbed Opal Lattice, cranberry.....................................95.00
Spooner, Reverse Swirl, cranberry.......................................165.00
Sugar, cov, Reverse Swirl, cranberry...................................350.00
Sugar Shaker
  Coin Spot, cranberry 275.00
  Ribbed Opal Lattice, cranberry....................................325.00
Syrup, Coin Spot, cranberry...175.00
Tumbler
  Acanthus, blue...90.00
  Bubble Lattice, cranberry 135.00
  Christmas Snowflake, blue, ribbed...............................125.00
  Maze, swirling, green 95.00
  Reverse Swirl, cranberry 65.00
  Swirl, blue 95.00
Waste Bowl, Hobbs Hobnail, vaseline....................................75.00

Novelties

Back Bar Bottle, 12-1/4" h, robins egg blue ground, opalescent
  stripes swirled to the right 100.00

Barber Bottle, 8" h, sq, diamond pattern molded form, light cran-
  berry, white vertical stripes...275.00
Bowl
  Grape and Cherry, blue..85.00
  Ruffles and Rings, white 35.00
  Winter Cabbage, white 45.00
Bushel Basket, blue..75.00
Chalice, Maple Leaf, vaseline 45.00
Cruet, Stars and Stripes, cranberry.......................................575.00
Hat, Opal Swirl, white 35.00

Pressed

Berry Bowl, master, Tokyo, green 60.00
Butter Dish, cov, Water Lily and Cattails, blue 300.00
Card Receiver, Fluted Scrolls, white 40.00
Cracker Jar, cov, Wreath and Shell, vaseline....................750.00
Creamer
  Inverted Fan and Feather, blue 125.00
  Swag with Brackets, green...90.00
Cruet, Fluted Scrolls, blue, clear stopper..........................295.00
Jelly Compote, Intaglio, blue..55.00
Salt and Pepper Shakers, pr, Jewel and Flower, canary yellow,
  orig tops 250.00
Sauce
  Alaska, blue 65.00
  Drapery, Northwood, dec, blue 35.00
Spooner, Swag with Brackets, blue...50.00
Toothpick Holder, Ribbed Spiral, blue 90.00
Tumbler
  Alaska, blue 110.00
  Drapery, blue...90.00
  Jackson, green..50.00
  Jeweled Heart, blue...85.00
Vase, Northwood Diamond Point, blue...................................75.00

OPALINE GLASS

History: Opaline glass was a popular mid- to late 19th-century European glass. The glass has a certain amount of translucency and often is found decorated with enamel designs and trimmed in gold.

Biscuit Jar, cov, white ground, hp, florals and birds dec, brass lid
  and bail handle..165.00
Bouquet Holder, 7" h, blue opaline cornucopia shaped gilt dec
  flower holders issuing from bronze stag heads, Belgian black
  marble base, English, Victorian, early 19th C, pr 725.00
Box, cov, gilt metal, blue, Continental, early 20th C
  5-3/8" l, rect, domed 250.00
  7-1/2" l, egg-shaped 295.00
Candelabra, Louis XV style, late 19th C
  18-1/2" h, gilt bronze and blue opaline, scrolled candle arms
  and base, two-light 175.00
  26-1/2" h, gilt metal and blue opaline, five-light 400.00
Chalice, white ground, Diamond Point pattern.........................35.00
Dresser Jar, 5-1/2" d, egg shape, blue ground, heavy gold dec
  ....200.00
Ewer, 13-1/4" h, white ground, Diamond Point pattern.......135.00
Jardinieres, 5-1/4" h, gilt bronze and blue opaline, sq, Empire
  style, tasseled chains, paw feet, early 20th C, pr.......1,610.00
Mantel Lusters, 12-3/4" h, blue, gilt dec, slender faceted prisms,
  Victorian, c1880, damage, pr 250.00
Oil Lamp, 24" h, dolphin-form stepped base, clear glass oil well,
  frosted glass shade, late 19th C, converted to electric, chips
  ....460.00
Oil Lamp Base, 22" h, blue, baluster turned standard on circular
  foot, 20th C, converted to electric, pr............................635.00
Perfume Bottle, 3-1/8" d, 7-3/4" h, tapering cylinder, flat flared
  base white, ring of white opaline around neck and matching
  teardrop stopper, gold trim 115.00

Toothpick Holder, pink cased, ruffled top, 3-3/8" h, $85.

Salt, boat shaped, blue dec, white enamel garland and scrolling 75.00
Water Pitcher, 12-1/4" h, blue, high looped handle, bulbous, early 20th C 230.00

ORIENTALIA

History: Orientalia is a term applied to objects made in the Orient, an area which encompasses the Far East, Asia, China, and Japan. The diversity of cultures produced a variety of objects and styles.

References: Sandra Andacht, *Collector's Guide To Oriental Decorative Arts,* Antique Trader Books, 1997; Christopher Dresser, *Traditional Arts and Crafts of Japan*, Dover Publications, 1994; R. L. Hobson and A L. Hetherington, *Art of the Chinese Potter*, Dover Publications, 1983; Duncan Macintosh, *Chinese Blue and White Porcelain*, Antique Collectors Club, 1994; Gloria and Robert Mascarelli, *Warman's Oriental Antiques*, Wallace-Homestead, 1992; Nancy N. Schiffer, *Imari, Satsuma, and Other Japanese Export Ceramics,* Schiffer Publishing, 1997; Jana Volf, *Treasures of Chinese Glass Work Shops,* Asiantiques, 1997.

Periodical: *Orientalia Journal,* P.O. Box 94, Little Neck, NY 11363.

Collectors' Club: China Student's Club, 59 Standish Rd., Wellesley, MA 02181.

Museums: Art Institute of Chicago, Chicago, IL; Asian Art Museum of San Francisco, San Francisco, CA; George Walter Vincent Smith Art Museum, Springfield, MA; Morikami Museum & Japanese Gardens, Delray Beach, FL; Pacific Asia Museum, Pasadena, CA.

Additional Listings: Canton; Celadon; Cloisonné; Fitzhugh; Nanking; Netsukes; Rose Medallion; Japanese Prints; and other related categories.

Altar Coffer
22" l, 16" d, 12" h, low, elm, rect top over single short drawer over single panel, flanked by shaped edges over shaped apron, block feet, Northern Chinese, mid-19th C 300.00
58" l, 18-1/4" d, 31-1/2" d, cedar, rect top with short curved wings on either end, over three short drawers over two cupboard doors flanked by dragon with bat relief carvings, bracket feet, Chinese, 19th C 550.00
Brush Washer, 5" l, carved green quartz, oval, relief carved vines, hardwood stand, Chinese 45.00
Censor, 7-1/2" d, 5" h, bronze, flared sides, 3 elephant head feet, pierced rect form handles with scrolled corners, brown patination splashed allover with irregular gilded areas, Chinese, 18th C 11,500.00
Cordial, 1-3/4" h, silver, applied chrysanthemum dec, Chinese, minor imperfections, 8 pc set 200.00
Dressing Box, 15" w, 11" d, 9-1/2" h, mother of pearl inlaid rosewood, fitted int. with mirror and drawers, ext. with scrolled foliage inlay, Chinese Export, late 19th C 850.00
Embroidered Picture, 6'8" x 41-1/2", Bird and Butterflies in Landscape with Bamboo and Peonies, silk, Chinese, 19th C... 450.00
Figure
4" l, carved lapis lazuli, water buffalo, recumbent, head turned, fault tines and gold inclusions, fitted wood base 350.00
8" h, carved rose quartz, bird perched on tree trunk, hardwood stand, Chinese 190.00
16-1/2" h, carved and painted wood, horse, standing, saddle and bridle, Chinese, 17th C 475.00
21" h, gilt bronze, Buddha, standing, hand raised, foliate dec tiered stand, Tibetian, 19th C 550.00
38" h, Foo Dog, green and mustard, two parts, glazed pottery, some chips, Chinese 250.00
Furniture
Cabinet
Chinese, 19th C, hardwood and polychrome, rect top over two molded and pierced cupboard doors over three short drawers over geometric pierced panel, sq legs, foliate carved fretwork corners, 36" d, 16-1/4" d, 62-3/4" h 350.00
Korean, mid-19th C, hardwood, rect top over two short drawers over two cupboard doors over two more cupboard doors over two smaller cupboard doors, panels throughout, block feet, 46" l, 21" d, 67" h 500.00
Chair
Asian, side, mother of pearl inlaid rosewood, scrolled and pierced carved crest rail, carved pierced splat, marble inset seat, carved and pierced seat rail, sq molded legs joined by stretchers................................ 150.00
Chinese, arm
Carved, shaped crest rail, carved pear design center splat and arm inserts over customized seat, shaped carved apron, splay legs 90.00
Rosewood, shaped crest rail, carved and pierced splat, geometric carved arms, panel seat, sq molded legs, joined by stretchers, Qing dynasty, 19th C....... 250.00
Chest, Korean, iron bound hardwood, hinged rect top, conforming case, 24" w, 13" d, 14" h 125.00

Armchair, carved rosewood, solid back carved with birds and trees, dragons and figures carved on arms, $625.

Garden Bench, Northern Chinese, 19th C, red lacquered elm, rect top, carved and pierced apron, turned legs, 64-1/2" w, 12-1/2" d, 21" h 450.00

Grain Chest, Northern Chinese, mid 19th C, pine, rect top, two hinged lids, compartments, two cupboard doors, shaped apron, block feet, 37" w, 20-1/4" d, 35" h..................300.00

Incense Table, Chinese, 19th C, walnut, circular top, pierced and shaped apron, six molded cabriole legs, scrolled feet, joined by circular base, 23-1/4" w, 40" h 750.00

Kitchen Cabinet, Northern Chinese, mid 19th C, aspen wood, rect top, two short drawers over two cupboard doors, block feet, 36" w, 24" d, 32-1/2" h..250.00

Nesting Tables, Japan lacquered, rect top, shaped supports, out-curved stretchers, 19-1/2" w, 12" d, 27" h, price for 4 pc set 375.00

Official Arm Chair, Chinese, 19th C, straight crest rail, rect splat, panel seat, turned legs, joined by sq stretchers, price for pr 400.00

Side Table, Northern Chinese, 19th C, chestnut, rect top, molded apron, sq molded legs, 53" w, 17" d, 34" h .475.00

Stand, Chinese
   Low, lacquered elm, rect top, scalloped apron, sq molded legs, Northern, 19th C, 50" l, 14" d, 10" h 150.00
   Two tier, carved, winged griffin supports, carved tops and skirt...350.00

Stool, Northern Chinese, 19th C
   Aspen wood, sq top, molded edge, turned legs jointed by conforming stretcher, 20-3/4" w, 21" h, price for pr .325.00
   Lacquered elm, molded sq top, pierced and carved apron, open corners, turned legs, 18-1/2" w, 19" h...........275.00

Wan Li Cabinet, Northern Chinese, 19th C, elm, rect top over open cabinet, framed with molded geometric designs over

two cupboard doors flanked by two short drawers, molded panel, block feet, 39" w, 18" d, 42" h 650.00

Wine Table, Northern Chinese, early 19th C, elm, rect top, shaped apron, turned legs, joined by double stretchers, 38-1/2" w, 16-1/2" d, 33-1/2" h 250.00

Work Table, Chinese Export, c1840, black lacquer and parcel gilt, rect hinged top, fitted compartment over bag slide, trestle support, carved gilt paw feet, 24-1/2" w, 16-3/4" d, 28-1/2" h..980.00

Inro clock, shitan-wood case, gilded lacquer and MOP insert as grass dec, well-carved ivory ball shaped ojime and netsuke, bell missing..6,900.00

Inro and netsuke, silver and black lacquer plum blossoms cascade over roof and red door of Japanese 4 case inro with ivory and lacquer cord fastener, two wrestlers ivory netsuke, 19th C 24,150.00

Inro, ojime, and netsuke, metal, inro with 5 sections, silver and bronze, inlaid with other bronzes, gold, and copper .6,325.00

Libation Cup, 2-1/2" h, 5" l, rhinoceros horn, ext. carved as chilong crawling among fungi and bamboo, pierced base, rim partially carved with scrolling border, early 18th C....3,220.00

Screen
   19-1/2" x 53-1/4", six panel, Figures in a Landscape, ink and color on paper, sgd, seal, Japanese, 19th C 225.00
   68-3/4" x 17", four panel, Flowering Plants, ink on silk, each panel sgd and sealed, Korean, 19th C 275.00

Scroll Painting, Japanese
   10-1/4" x 11-3/4", hydrangeas and Nasturtiums, color on silk, sgd, Keibun, 1779-1843 ....375.00
   29-1/2" x 17", Dutch Merchant, ink and color on paper, sgd, Nagasaki School, late 18th C 900.00
   32" w, 73" h, two panel, ivory, inlaid lacquer, each inlaid with Japanese women above two smaller figures, black ground, floral dec, verse painted with bird and flowering tree, wood frame carved with phoenix and floral dec 1,500.00

Shigayama, two-fold table screen, Japanese, Meiji period, kinji ground, formal floral arrangements in mother of pearl, horn, and other materials, two panels of maple leaves and enameled metal carp, reverse executed in togisdash lacquer with chicks among flowers, feathers, sgd "Fuchi," ivory frame, engraved silver mounts, some damage and loss, 18-1/4" w, 17-1/2" h, $13,000. Photo courtesy of Freeman\Fine Arts.

Vase, Mandarian Export, c1790, 3-7/8" h, $175.

43" x 26-1/4", Manjursi on a Peacock, ink and color on silk, Kamakura School, 13th-14th C 4,700.00
47" x 22", Tiger, ink on paper, Japanese School, 17th C
.... 900.00
49-1/2" x 22", Bhodiharma, ink on paper, sgd, Kano Tsunenobu, 1636-1713 .... 900.00
Urn, 9" h, 10-1/2" d, bronze, globular, stylized geometric banding, ridged ground, Chinese 275.00
Vase
   19" h, silver plated, ovoid body, tall slender neck, engraved scrolling lotus ground, raised cartouches of scrolling lotus, geometric band around neck, Chinese 1,265.00
   26-1/2" h, black lacquer, baluster form, flying cranes among trees, Chinese Export style, pr 700.00
Water Basket, red lacquered, swan-form, Chinese, price for pr
.... 650.00
Watercolor
   41-1/2" x 15", paper, portrait of lady, Chinese, 19th C .. 150.00
   44" x 21", paper, Buddhist divinities, 19th C 175.00
   48" x 20", silk, female immortal playing flute, Oriental, 19th C
.... 330.00

ORIENTAL RUGS

History: Oriental rugs or carpets date back to 3,000 B.C.; but it was in the 16th century that they became prevalent. The rugs originated in the regions of Central Asia, Iran (Persia), Caucasus, and Anatolia. Early rugs can be classified into basic categories: Iranian, Caucasian, Turkoman, Turkish, and Chinese. Later India, Pakistan, and Iraq produced rugs in the Oriental style.

The pattern name is derived from the tribe, which produced the rug, e.g., Iran is the source for Hamadan, Herez, Sarouk, and Tabriz.

References: George O'Bannon, *Oriental Rugs*, Running Press, Courage Books, 1995; Walter A. Hawley, *Oriental Rugs, Antique and Modern*, Dover Publications, 1970; Charles W. Jacobsen, *Check Points on How to Buy Oriental Rugs*, Charles E. Tuttle Co., 1981; Friedrich Sarre and Hermann Trenkwald, *Oriental Carpet Designs in Full Color*, Dover Publications, 1980.

Periodicals: *HALI*, P.O. Box 4312, Philadelphia, PA 19118; *Oriental Rug Review*, P.O. Box 709, Meredith, NH 03253; *Rug News*, 34 West 37th St., New York, NY 10018.

REPRODUCTION ALERT
Beware! There are repainted rugs on the market.

Notes: When evaluating an Oriental rug, age, design, color, weave, knots per square inch, and condition determine the final value. Silk rugs and prayer rugs bring higher prices than other types.

SPECIAL AUCTION
Skinner Inc. Bolton Gallery 357 Main St. Bolton, MA 01740 (508) 779-6241

Bahktiari, West Persia, early 20th C
   6' 10" x 4' 3", hexagonal lattice with palmette motifs, red, rose, royal blue, camel, gold, and blue-green, on midnight blue field, ivory border, corner and end gouges, moth damage 488.00
   6' 10" x 4' 6", sq grid with floral motifs, midnight and navy blue, red, ivory, pale gold, and light blue-green, navy blue border, even wear, end fraying 750.00
Balkan Kelim, Southeast Europe, early 20th c, 7' 8" x 6' 3" columns of blossoming branches, red, apricot, gold, tan gray, and dark blue-green, on abrashed navy blue field, wide gold border, slightly stained area 5,750.00
Baluch, Northeast Persia, last quarter 19th C, 6' x 3' 5", octagonal lattice, red and aubergine hooked squares, on midnight blue field, midnight blue border, moth damage, creases 345.00
Bergama, West Anatolia, early 19th C, 4' 4" x 4', rows of rosettes, dark red, navy blue, gold, apricot, and dark blue-green, on rosy red field, ivory border, mounted on fabric, wood framed, holes edge gouges 550.00
Chi-Chi, Northeast Caucasus, last quarter 19th C
   5' x 3' 8", diagonal rows of hooked polygons, red, sky blue, gold, rust, ivory and blue-green, on midnight blue field, black border, areas of wear, end fraying 635.00
   5' x 3' 9", rows of palmettes and geometric motifs, navy and sky blue, red, gold, and pale aubergine, on olive field, ivory border, slight even wear, end repairs 1,265.00
Ersari Chuval, West Turkestan, second half 19th C, 5' 4" x 2' 10", ikat design with rows of interlocking hexagons, navy blue, gold, apricot, brown, and blue-green, on rust field, elem of similar coloration, overall war, crease, tears backed with fabric 300.00
Ersari Ensi, West Turkestan, late 19th C, 6' 4" x 4', quarter rust garden plan field, navy blue plant motifs, multicolored border, rust elem, wear in center, crude repair 375.00
Fachralo Kazak, Southwest Caucasus, last quarter 19th C, prayer, 4' 10" x 3' 6", blue-green prayer cartouche inset with concentric gabled sq medallion, red, ivory, royal blue, and gold, on red field, ivory wine glass border, slight moth damage 3,750.00

Prayer, Balouchi, c1915, 2' 10" x 3' 6", $700.

Gendje, South Central Caucasus, third quarter 19th C, 4' 10" x 2' 4", column of 5 squares, red, gold, and blue-green, on narrow royal blue field, wide ivory dragon's tooth border, areas of wear 520.00

Heriz, Northwest Persia, early 20th C, 11' x 8' 6", large gabled sq medallion and floral motifs, midnight, sky, and ice blue, rose, pale gold, and blue-green, on terra cotta red field, sky blue spandrels, midnight blue border, small areas of minor wear 3,450.00

Karabagh, South Caucasus, last quarter 19th C, 6' 5" x 4', 3 lightning medallions and small motifs, rust, red, sky blue, gold, and blue-green, on midnight blue field, ivory border, slight moth damage, small creases 690.00

Karapinar, Central Anatolia, early 19th C, 6' 8" x 4' 5", large diamond medallion and 2 palmettes, midnight and sky blue, light red, deep gold, aubergine, and blue-green, on dark rust field, abrashed brown border, even wear, rewoven areas, small holes 8,625.00

Kazak, Southwest Caucasus, late 19th C, 3' 8" x 3' 2", two serrated diamond medallions, scattered geometric motifs, navy blue, brown, rose, gold, apricot, and blue-green, on red field, abrashed navy and sky blue border, even wear to center 690.00

Kelim

Central Anatolian, early 20th C, 13' x 5' 2", 3 columns of hexagons flanked by pr flowerheads, sky blue, red, rust, gold, apricot, and aubergine, on dark brown field, ivory border small repairs 1,495.00

East Anatolian, last quarter 19th C, 5' 7" x 4' 2", prayer, 2 diamonds in navy and ice blue, tan-gold, cochineal, blue-green field, red spandrels, aubergine border, repairs, small holes 575.00

Kerman, Southeast Persia, late 19th C, 11' 4" x 9", prayer rug design, large flowering shrub, cochineal, rose, apricot, gold, and soft brown, on ivory field, cochineal spandrels, ivory border, areas of wear 2,760.00

Khotan, East Turkestan, early 19th C, 6' 5" x 3' 8", octagonal medallions, rosettes, and floral groups, blue-green, on rd field, light red fretwork border, reduced in length, worn, repairs 345.00

Kurd, Northwest Persia, second half 19th C, 9' 6" x 5' 4", overall Herati design, midnight and sky blue, red, rose, gold, and blue-green, on light brown field, blue-green border, areas of wear, creases 400.00

Lenkoran, Southeast Caucasus, late 19th C, 9' 6" x 3' 2", 2 calyx medallions, 2 squares, 8 small octagons, royal and sky blue, dark red, coral, gold, and green, on midnight sky blue field, ivory border, small rewoven area and patch, slight moth damage..1,100.00

Mahal, West Persia, early 20th C, 13' 2" x 10' 8", overall design of palmettes, rosettes, and boteh-like leaves, dark red, rose, royal blue, camel, and green, on midnight blue field, red border, patch, small holes, small dry area...............................2,645.00

Perepedil, Northeast Caucasus, late 19th C, 6' 4" x 4' 3", serrated hexagons and ram's horn motif, red, rust, royal blue, ivory, and tan-gold, on midnight blue field, midnight blue border, small areas of wear, cat scratch damage...........................2,070.00

Senneh Kelim, Northwest Persia, late 19th C, 6' x 3' 9", rows of paired boteh, red, rose, rust, ice blue, gold, and light blue-green, on brown field, gold border, small repairs in center 1,035.00

Serapi, Northwest Persia, last quarter 19th C, 15' 6" x 11,' large hexagonal medallion and blossoming vines, midnight and sky blue, gold, rose, and blue-green, on terra cotta red field, inscription cartouche inner border, midnight blue main border, all borders missing from both ends, small areas of wear 5,750.00

Shivran, East Caucasus

4' 8" x 4', last quarter 19th C, keyhole medallion inset with 3 octagons, navy and sky blue, red, gold, and dark blue-green, on midnight blue field, ivory border, slight moth damage, minor end fraying...2,185.00

5' x 4', third quarter 19th C, prayer, keyhole medallion surrounded by stepped polygons, red, ivory, navy blue, rust, and tan, midnight blue field, ivory border, even wear, small hole selvage damage 1,955.00

Soumak, Caucasian, late 19th C, 5' 4" x 5', rows of plants with serrated leaves, navy and sky blue, black, dark rust-red, pale tan-ground, and blue-green on plain view ivory field, ivory border, small areas of wear, resewn cut on one side 1,100.00

Tabriz, Northwest Persia, late 19th C

12' 5" x 8' 5", diamond medallion, palmettes, and leafy vines, royal and sky blue, rose red, camel, orange-gold, dark brown, and light blue-green, ivory rosette and blossoming vine border, small areas of wear, brown corrosion 3,450.00

14' x 10' 6", lobed circular medallion, matching spandrels, flowering vines, midnight and sky blue, ivory, rose, aubergine, tan, and pale blue-green, on cochineal field, weeping willow border, areas of wear, moth damage ...2,300.00

Yomaond Asmalik, five-sided, used on camels for wedding processions, 4' x 2'4", $2,200. Photo courtesy of Sanford Alderfer Auction Co.

Tekke, West Turkestan, third quarter 19th C, 9' 10" x 7', four columns of 11 main carpet guls, midnight blue, ivory, apricot, and dark blue-green, on rust field, borders, and elems of similar coloration, areas of wear, moth damage.......................575.00

Uzbek, central Asia, early 20th h, 6' 2" x 2' 8", flatweave saddlebags, diamond lattice with hooked motifs, slate gray, gold, ivory, brown, and blue-green, on rust-red field, red border, small rewoven area.......................................430.00

Yomund Asmalyk, West Turkestan, last quarter 19th C, 3' 9" x 2' 2", hexagonal lattice with ashik guls, midnight blue, red, apricot, ivory, aubergine-brown and blue-green, ivory border, edge gouge, even wear, small repairs..........................230.00

Yuruk, East Anatolia, late 19th C, 8' 6" x 3' 4", 4 concentric hooked diamond medallion, midnight blue, cochineal, ivory, gold, aubergine, and blue-green, on dark red field, deep apricot border, small areas of wear, small creases and repair .690.00

OVERSHOT GLASS

History: Overshot glass was developed in the mid-1800s. To produce overshot glass, a gather of molten glass was rolled over the marver upon which had been placed crushed glass. The piece then was blown into the desired shape. The finished product appeared to be frosted or iced.

Early pieces were made mainly in clear glass. As the demand for colored glass increased, color was added to the base piece and occasionally to the crushed glass.

Pieces of overshot generally are attributed to the Boston and Sandwich Glass Co. although many other companies also made it as it grew in popularity.

Museum: Sandwich Glass Museum, Sandwich, MA.

Basket, 7-1/4" h, 5" d, transparent green shading to colorless, ruffled swirled edge, sq thorn handle, melon-ribbed base with pineapple-like design, entire surface with overshot finish.............285.00

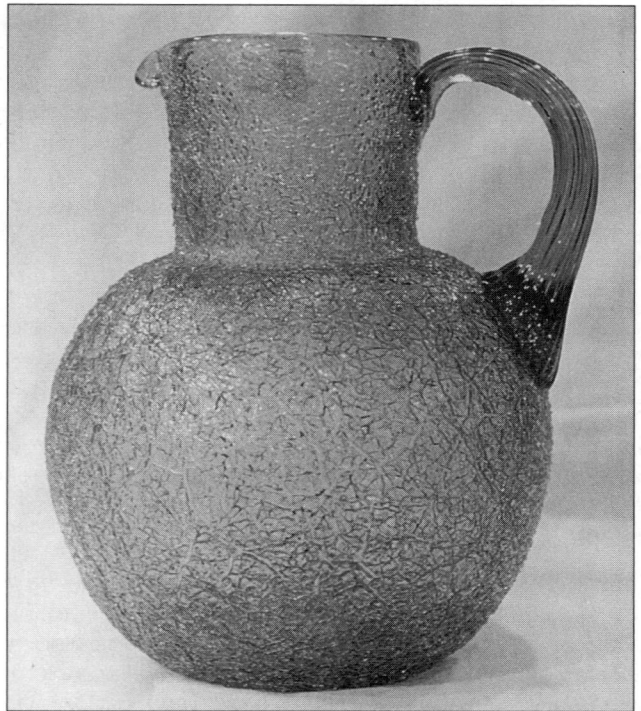

Pitcher, light blue ground, applied amber handle, attributed to Boston & Sandwich, 7-3/4" h, $295.

Bowl, 6" d, 3-7/8" h, pale blue opaque, applied amber rigaree around top, applied green leaves, white, pink, and blue applied flowers 235.00

Celery Vase, 6" h, 3-1/2" d, scalloped top, cranberry ground 90.00

Cheese Dish, dome cov, 8" d, 7" h, cranberry ground, enameled crane and cattails, applied colorless faceted finial.......425.00

Compote, 10" d, 10-1/4" h, cranberry ground, wide rounded bowl, scalloped crown gilt trimmed rim, compressed knob on cylindrical pedestal, wide flaring foot, late 19th C................300.00

Fairy Lamp, 4-1/4" h, 3" d, opalescent, figural, crown shape, colorless pressed "Clark" base..195.00

Pitcher
8-1/4" h, green ground, amber shell handle, Sandwich, c1875, brown age line near lip 225.00
9" h, tankard, cranberry ground, applied colorless reeded handle, hinged metal lid 195.00

Vase, 5-1/2" h, pink ground, applied random amber threading 225.00

PAIRPOINT

History: The Pairpoint Manufacturing Co. was organized in 1880 as a silver-plating firm in New Bedford, Massachusetts. The company merged with Mount Washington Glass Co. in 1894 and became the Pairpoint Corporation. The new company produced specialty glass items often accented with metal frames.

Pairpoint Corp. was sold in 1938 and Robert Gunderson became manager. He operated it as the Gunderson Glass Works until his death in 1952. From 1952 until the plant closed in 1956, operations were maintained under the name Gunderson-Pairpoint. Robert Bryden reopened the glass manufacturing business in 1970, moving it back to the New Bedford area.

References: Edward and Sheila Malakoff, *Pairpoint Lamps*, Schiffer Publishing, 1990; John A. Shumann III, *Collector's Encyclopedia of American Art Glass*, Collector Books, 1988, 1994 value update.

Collectors' Clubs: Mount Washington Art Glass Society, P.O. Box 24094, Fort Worth, TX 76124-1094; Pairpoint Cup Plate Collectors, P.O. Box 890052, East Weymouth, MA 02189.

Museum: Pairpoint Museum, Sagamore, MA.

China

Box, cov, 5" l, 3-1/2" w, 2-1/2" h, raised gold rococo scrolls, reverse on lid with 3 Palmer Cox Brownies playing cards, Pairpoint-Limoges logo, numbered 750.00

Chocolate Pot, 10" h, cream ground, white floral dec, gold trim and scrolls, sgd "Pairpoint Limoges 2500 114" 675.00

Gravy Boat and Underplate, fancy white china with scrolls, Dresden multicolored flowers, elaborate handle, Limoges, 2 pc 175.00

Plate, 7-3/8" d, hp harbor scene, artist sgd "L. Tripp," fuchsia tinted rim, gold highlights, back sgd "Pairpoint Limoges".550.00

Vase
7" h, 6-3/4" w, two handles, pink pond lily dec, soft beige ground, dark green trim on handles and ruffled top, sgd "P.M.C. 2004/261" 425.00
14" h, portrait of little girl, framed by interlocking gold scrolls and stylized florals, fancy scrollwork of base, and rim, mahogany red ground, brushed gold highlights, reverse with well-worn gold dec 835.00

Cake Basket, silver plated, relief cherries in center, pierced bird handles, four pierced floral design feet, mkd, 13-3/4" handle to handle, $165.

Glass

Candlesticks, pr, 9-1/2" h, Mt. Washington opalware glass, silver-plated overlay, deep pink painted ground, white peony dec, fancy Art Nouveau styled silver overlay base and socket, sgd "Pairpoint Mfg. Co" 1,250.00

Console Set, 3 pc set

   12" d bowl, matching 3" h candlesticks, Tavern glass, bouquet of red, white, and green flowers 575.00

   12" d, bowl, matching mushroom candlesticks, Flambo Ware, tomato red, applied black glass foot, c1915 .... 1,950.00

Compote, 10" h, 5-1/2" d, Fine Arts Line, Auroria, brilliant cut deep amber glass bowl, brass and onyx base with full figured cherub holding up bowl, mkd "C1413 Pairpoint" 475.00

Hat, deep red and white, controlled bubbles, orig label, 4-1/4" h, $70.

Cracker Jar, cov

   6-1/2" h, 6" d, 16 panels, gold/beige ground, white and deep pink roses, green leaves, cov sgd "Pairpoint-3932", base sgd "3932/222," fancy metal work 595.00

   6-3/4" h, 7-1/2" w, Mt. Washington opalware, pistachios green top and bottom, 3-1/2" w band of deep pink and red roses, green leaves, gold trim, fancy silver-plated cov, handle, and bail, cov sgd "Pairpoint -3912", base sgd "3912-268" 725.00

Lamp

   27-1/2" h, 17" d Directorie scenic hexagonal heavy walled shade, reverse painted as six continuing panels, colorful landscaped ground with columned waterfront building, irid background coloring, paneled borders above and below, "The Pairpoint Corp." on border, gilt metal, onyx, and cut glass candle lamp form base, imp "Pairpoint Mfg. Co. E30001" 2,645.00

   Mushroom shape, cut glass, dome shade with orig prisms, cut Viscaria pattern, c1915 .... 1,850.00

Vase

   5-1/2" h, 4-1/2" w, Tavern glass, bulbous, enameled floral dec of vase of flowers, base numbered 225.00

   6" h, Tavern glass, bulbous, enameled sailing galleon on wavy sea, sgd "D. 1507," c1900-38 .... 300.00

   14-1/2" h, flared colorless crystal trumpet form, bright-cut floral dec, gilt metal foliate molded weighted pedestal base, imp "Pairpoint C1509" 490.00

PAPER EPHEMERA

History: Maurice Rickards, author of Collecting Paper Ephemera, suggests that ephemera are the "minor transient documents of everyday life," material destined for the wastebasket but never quite making it. This definition is more fitting than traditional dictionary definitions that emphasize time, e.g., "lasting a very short time." A driver's license, which is used for a year or longer, is as much a piece of ephemera as is a ticket to a sporting event or music concert. The transient nature of the object is the key.

Collecting ephemera has a long and distinguished history. Among the English pioneers were John Seldon (1584-1654), Samuel Pepys (1633-1703), and John Bagford (1650-1716). Large American collections can be found at historical societies and libraries across the country, and museums, e.g., Wadsworth Athenaeum, Hartford, CT, and the Museum of the City of New York.

When used by collectors, "ephemera" usually means paper objects, e.g., billheads and letterheads, bookplates, documents, labels, stocks and bonds, tickets, and valentines. However, more and more ephemera collectors are recognizing the transient nature of some three-dimensional material, e.g., advertising tins and pinback buttons. Today's specialized paper shows include dealers selling other types of ephemera in both two- and three-dimensional form.

References: Warren R. Anderson, *Owning Western History*, Mountain Press Publishing, 1993; Patricia Fenn and Alfred P. Malpa, *Rewards of Merit*, Ephemera Society, 1994; Robert Reed, *Paper Collectibles*, Wallace-Homestead, 1995; Kenneth W. Rendell, *Forging History*, University of Oklahoma Press, 1994; Gene Utz, *Collecting Paper*, Books Americana, 1993.

Periodical: *Biblio,* 845 Willamette St., Eugene, OR 87401; *Paper Collectors' Marketplace,* P.O. Box 128, Scandinavia, WI 54977.

Collectors' Clubs: Ephemera Society, 12 Fitzroy Sq., London W1P 5HQ England; Ephemera Society of America, Inc., P.O. Box 95, Cazenovia, NY 13035; The Ephemera Society of Canada, 36 Macauley Dr., Thornhill, Ontario L3T 5S5 Canada; National Assoc. of Paper & Advertising Collectors, P.O. Box 500, Mount Joy, PA 17552.

Additional Listings: See Advertising Trade Cards; Catalogs; Comic Books; Photographs; Sports Cards. Also see Calendars, Catalogs, Magazines, Newspapers, Photographs, Postcards, and Sheet Music in *Warman's Americana & Collectibles.*

Advisor: Norman Martinus.

Blotters

Badger Soap, You Want the Best, attached adv card, multi-colored 15.00
Kellogg's Corn Flakes, multicolored....................................10.00
None Such Mince Meat, factory illus., multicolored 8.00
Prudential Insurance Co., battleship, blue and white.............8.00
Sundial Shoes, Bonnie Laddie, multicolored........................10.00
Wayne Oakland Bank, Santa..12.00

Bookmarks

Advertising
    Austin Young & Co., Biscuits, multicolored, 2" x 7" 5.00
    Bell Pianos, Art Nouveau woman, multicolored...............12.00
    Eastman's Extract, silver gild, multicolored....................10.00
    Palmer Violets Bloom Perfume, gold trim 15.00
    Youth's Companion, 1902, multicolored, 2-3/4" x 6"..........8.00
Cross Stitch on Punched Paper
    Black Emancipation, black couple dancing, 1860s, 3-7/8" x1-1/2" 40.00
    Ever Constant-Ever True, young girl with basket of flowers, 2-5/8" x 7" 10.00
    In God We Trust...10.00

Business Cards

Commercial Hotel, Grand Rapids, MI, $1.00 A day, printed, black and white 10.00
F. A. Howe, Jr., Contracting Freight Agent, MI, Central RR & Blue Line, Chicago, blue on white 12.00
Pfeiffer Brewing Co., Detroit, MI, printed, multicolored..........7.50
Silverthaw & Sons, Dealers in Diamonds & Watches, New Haven, CT, gold lettering, black ground, 1880s, printed 12.00

Calendars

1882, Canada First, The Great Literary-Political Journal, broadside type, 8" x 12" 65.00
1893, Benton Hall Dry Goods, Palmyra, NY, 2-1/2" 12.00
1894, Hoyt's, lady's, perfumed...12.00
1896, Singer Sewing Machines 40.00
1889, Pansies Bright, Taber Prang Art Co., 6 parts, pansy dec on each part 40.00
1900, Hood's, full pad, 2 girls...45.00
1901, Colgate, miniature, flower...20.00
1906, Hiawatha, multiple images of Indian scenes, monthly calendars placed throughout, metal band and grommet at top, metal band missing at bottom, 7-1/2" w, 36" h 125.00
1909, Bank of Waupun, emb lady...32.00
1914, Youth's Companion, marching scene, easel back.....10.00
1916, Putnam Dyes 40.00

1922, Warren National Bank, Norman Rockwell illus 300.00
1923, Winona, F. A. Rettke, Indian Princess on cliff overlooking body of water, full pad, 6-1/2" w, 21-1/2" l......................50.00
1929, Clothesline...65.00
1939, Rogers Statuary 20.00
1940, Columbian Rope..40.00

Coloring Books

Annie Oakley, Whitman, 11" x 14", 1955, unused.................20.00
Blondie, Dell Publishing, 8-1/2" x 11", 1954, unused............24.00
Charlie Chaplin, Donohue & Co., 10" x 17", © 1917.............85.00
Dick Tracy, Saalfield, #2536, 8-1/4" x 11", © 1946.............30.00
Donald Duck, Whitman, 7-1/2" x 8-1/2", 1946, unused.........25.00
Eve Arden, 1953, unused..30.00
Lone Ranger, Whitman, 8-1/2" x 11", Cheerios premium, 1956 ....75.00
Pinky Lee's Health and Safety Cut-Out Coloring Book, Pocket Books, © 1955..20.00
Superman, Whitman, National Periodical Publications, © 1966, unused 25.00

Cookbooks

References: Bob Allen, *Guide to Collecting Cookbooks and Advertising Cookbooks,* Collector Books, 1990, 1995 value update; Mary Barile, *Cookbooks Worth Collecting,* Wallace-Homestead, 1994; Linda Dickinson, *Price Guide to Cookbooks and Recipe Leaflets,* Collector Books, 1990, 1995 value update.

Periodical: Cookbook Collectors' Exchange, P.O. Box 23269, San Jose, CA 95152.

Collectors' Club: CookBook Collectors Club of America, 231 E. James Blvd P.O. Box 85, St. James, MO 65559.

All About Home Baking, General Foods Corporation, 1936, blue and yellow hard cover, black and white and color photos 8.00
American Woman's Cook Book, Ruth Bertolzheimer, ed., Butterick Pub., 1947, 824 pgs..20.00
Better Homes and Gardens New Cook Book, 1953, 5 rings, 416 pgs, indexed tabs, color photos.....................................17.50
Boston Cooking School Cook Book, Fannie Merritt Farmer, 1937, Little Brown Co., 838 pgs..20.00
Choice Receipts from Many Homes, compiled by the Ladies of the Independent Society, Presque Isle, Maine, 1891, advertising, worn cover 15.00
Cutco Cook Book, World's Finest Cutlery, Margaret Mitchel, 1961...8.00
Diet and Cookbook, Dr. Harry Finkel, published by The Society for Public Health Education, NY, 1925, hard cover 15.00
Elisa Celli's Italian Light Cooking, 1987, 263 pgs, photos, dg 18.50
Esquire's Handbook for Hosts, 1949, hard cover, illus and cartoons 20.00
Every Woman's Cookbook, Mrs. Charles Mortiz, Cupples & Leon, 1936, 764 pgs...8.00
Fireside Cookbook, James Beard, Simon & Schuster, 1949, 1st ed., 4to, 322 pgs, 400 color illus 15.00
Gladys Taber's Stillmeadow Cook Book, illus Ann Girfalconi, 1965, 1st ed., 355 pgs, dj...27.50
Gourmet's Menu Cook Book, Egmont H. Petersen, Copenhagen, Denmark, 1967 ....25.00
Helen Corbitt's Cook-Book, 1959, Riverside Press, 388 pgs 17.50
Household Discoveries & Mrs. Curtis's Cook Book, 1913, 1173 pgs 27.50

Little Mother's Cook Book, a Guide to Cooking for Children, Lon Armick, color illus by Jack Ohara, Pixie Press, 1952, inscribed, 11" x 9", matching box 20.00

Meals for Guests: A Book of Unusual, Inexpensive Menus and Recipes, Eveyln Patterson, Abelard-Schuman Pub., 1954, 1st ed.,178 pgs 10.00

Natural Cooking the Finnish Way, Ulla Kakonen, 1974, 209 pgs 16.50

Small World Cook & Color Book, Beverly Frazier, illus by Varian Mace, recipes for kids and dolls from 19 countries 8.00

Southern Cook Book of Fine Old Dixie Recipes, Lillie S. Lustig, Claire Sondheim, Sarah Rensel ed., Culinary Arts Press, 1935, 48 pgs, picture wraps...20.00

The Art of Cooking With Herbs and Spices, Milo Miloradovich, 304 pgs, dj..18.00

The Ford Treasury of Favorite Recipes from Famous Eating Places, Dedicated to the Ford and Lincoln-Mercury Dealers, 1955, owner's name on first page, cartoon type map, hardcover, dj 15.00

The Master Cake Baker, Cleve Carney, published by Calumet Baking Powder, 1927, 99 pgs 14.00

The New Joys of Jell-O, 1973, 128 pgs.................................6.00

The Pecan Cookbook, Koinonia Farm, Americus, GA, 1969, spiral bound, 202 pgs, 2nd printing......................................10.00

Wonderful, Wonderful Danish Cooking, Ingeborg Dahl Jensen, intro by Victor Borge, illus by Edward Kasper, 1965, 335 pgs 18.50

Documents

Arrest Warrants, Marion Co., KY, 1887-1891, 9 pgs, 8" x 12-1/4", 5 warrants ranging from stealing chickens, breach of peace, construction problems, hand written, sgd, dated 24.00

Bill of Laden, Dayton & Michigan R. R. Co., Dayton, OH, March 1865, 1 pg, 8" x 10-3/4", letterhead type, picture of engine of the Express Freight Line, two stamps affixed, filled out for shipping purposes, red, and blue printed ink........................26.00

Invoice

George L. Bidgood, Richmond, VA, 3/4/1872, 7 x 8-1/2", Agents for School Slates used in the Public Schools of Va., Books, Stationery, Piano's, Organs, Music, Chromos, Cold Pens, Writing Desks, & Fancy Articles, illus of sq grand upright piano..15.00

New Jersey Auto Top Mfg., Newark, NJ, 1916, 7 x 8-1/2", company letterhead, illus of 1909 auto with man in it, also 2-3/8" x 4" business card on heavy stock, light green, auto illus 25.00

Letterhead

J. W. Pepper & Son., Philadelphia, PA, 7/8/1912, 8-1/2" x 11" illus of Howard E. Pepper building, typed letter 5.00

Parry Mfg. Co., Indianapolis, IN, 6/15/1906, 1 pg, 8-1/2" x 10-3/4", picture of factory and 4 different styles of buddies down left side of page, typed letter...........................23.00

Studebaker Bros. Mfg. Co., South Bend, IN, 8/21/1907, 1 pg, 8-1/2" x 11", black and white illus of vehicle, harness & automobile mfgrs, typed letter................................16.00

Weekly Bulletin, J. W. Edgerly & Co., Ottumwa, IA, 1892, 4 pgs, 6-1/4" x 9-1/2", listing and prices of products for wholesale druggists and stationers..15.00

Greeting Cards

Birthday

Amos & Andy, brown portraits, message includes song title 'Check and Double Check,' inked birthday note, Rust Craft 25.00

Blondie, Dagwood illus, full color, Hallmark, © 1939 ......18.00

Snow White and the Seven Dwarfs, c1938.....................42.00

Space Patrol Man, diecut, full color, transparent green helmet, orig envelope...25.00

Christmas

A Merry Christmas, 3 children huddled underneath umbrella, Wolf & Co., NY 4.00

Christmas Greetings, emb holly, silver background, The Art Lithographic Co. 7.50

Hearty Greetings, cut-out emb border, holly on front........5.00

Get Well, Amos n' Andy, black and white photo, Hall Bros.,© 1951 ....30.00

Mother's Day, Cracker Jack, diecut puppy, full color, c1920 ....18.00

Invitations and Programs

Camp On White River Col. Dance Program, No. 24, 1881, scrap dec, hand written...12.00

Eddie Cantor, "How To Make A Quack-Quack," program on back, portrait on cov, printed, black and white, four part fold-out 15.00

Grand Masquerade Ball, Marion House Co., NY, 1901, gold trim 10.00

Invitation and Program for Carnival In Honor of George Washington,Request at Opera House, 1893, multicolored cover 12.00

Leap Year Party by Young Ladies, 1888, opens, dance program inside, printed black and white 10.00

Richland Library Literary Society, Benefit Musical, opens, lists musical selections, poems to be read, black and white ...5.00

Sonja Henie Program, white cov, orig tissue cov, 1949.......12.00

St. Patrick's Ball, Lusks Hall, Jacobs City, UT, 1878, red lettering, blue ground, emb, opens 15.00

Menus

Banquet To The Western Michigan Press, Reed City, 1883, fold-over, Robison Engraving Co., 1882, printed, black and white 15.00

Francaise, Art Nouveau design, sgd "Mucha," dated 5 Janvier 1913, 5" x 9" 350.00

Johnson Line 15.00

Metropolitan Hotel, 4 pgs, c1974 ....35.00

SS City of Omaha, Christmas, 1940 ....10.00

United States Hotel, Saratoga Springs, NY, 1892, 7" x 10" ..15.00

Sheet Music

References: Debbie Dillon, *Collectors Guide To Sheet Music,* L-W Promotions, 1988, 1995 Value Update; Anna Marie Guiheen and Marie-Reine A. Pafik, *Sheet Music Reference and Price Guide,* 2nd edition, Collector Books, 1995.

Stock Certificate, Lykens Valley Coal Company, 1864, 5-1/2" x 8-7/8", $25.

Collectors' Clubs: City of Roses Sheet Music Collectors Club, 13447 Bush St., SE, Portland, OR 97236; National Sheet Music Society, 1597 Fair Park, Los Angeles, CA 90041; New York Sheet Music Society, P.O. Box 1214, Great Neck, NY 10023; Remember That Song, 5623 N. 64th St., Glendale, AZ 85301; The Sheet Music Exchange, 1202 12th St., Key West, FL 33040.

American Legion Song-Five Million Strong! J. H. Benson, 1919 .... 10.00

Birds Fly Over White Cliffs of Dover, Glenn Miller, 1941-42 .... 12.00

Break The News To Mother, 1897 .... 18.00

Full Moon & Empty Arms, Frank Sinatra, 1946 .... 10.00

Kokomo, IN, Betty Grable, 1947 .... 8.00

Little Sweetheart of the Ozarks, Sandy Williams, 1937 .... 8.00

Moonlight & Shadows, Dorothy Lamour and Ray Milland, 1936 .... 10.00

Normandy Chimes, Powell, 1913 .... 10.00

Over the Rainbow, cast on cov 30.00

Red River Valley, Gene Autry, photo, 1935 .... 12.00

Song for Me, Bromo-Seltzer, c1890 .... 15.00

Those Ragtime Melodies, Hodgkins, 1912 .... 10.00

You Flew Over/Uncle Sam Takes His Hat Off To You, 9-1/4" x 12-1/4", dedicated to Lindbergh 50.00

Tickets

Boxing, World's Heavyweight Championship, Dempsey vs. Gibbons, July 4, 1923, O'Toole County American Legion, Shelvy, MT, fullticket 50.00

Football, Super Bowl I, 1966, Green Bay and Kansas City 125.00

Lottery
    Kansas State Lottery Co., 1894, multicolored 10.00
    State of New York Medical Science Lottery Promotion, 1915, orange and white, used 8.00

Members, Board of Trade, City of Chicago, 1930, printed, black and white 7.50

Music, Woodstock Music and Art Fair, orange, red letters, orange Globe Ticket background, Friday, Aug. 15, 1969, unused 35.00

PAPERWEIGHTS

History: Although paperweights had their origin in ancient Egypt, it was in the mid-19th century that this art form reached its zenith. The Clichy, Baccarat, and Saint Louis factories produced the finest paperweights between 1834 and 1855 in France. Other weights made in England, Italy, and Bohemia during this period rarely match the quality of the French weights.

In the early 1850s, the New England Glass Co. in Cambridge, Massachusetts, and the Boston and Sandwich Glass Co. in Sandwich, Massachusetts, became the first American factories to make paperweights.

Popularity peaked during the classic period (1845-1855) and faded toward the end of the 19th century. Paperweight production was rediscovered nearly a century later in the mid-1900s. Baccarat, Saint Louis, Perthshire, and many studio craftsmen in the U.S. and Europe still make contemporary weights.

References: *Annual Bulletin of the Paperweight Collectors Association, Inc.*, available from association (P.O. Box 1263, Beltsville, MD 20704), 1996; Monika Flemming and Peter Pommerencke, *Paperweights of the World*, Schiffer Publishing, 1994; John D. Hawley, *Glass Menagerie*, Paperweight Press, 1995; Sibylle Jargstorf, *Paperweights*, Schiffer Publishing, 1991; Paul Jokelson and Dena Tarshis, *Baccarat Paperweights and Related Glass*, Paperweight Press, 1990; Edith Mannoni, *Classic French Paperweights*, Paperweight Press, 1984; Bonnie Pruitt, *St. Clair Glass Collectors Guide*, published by author, 1992; Pat Reilly, *Paperweights*, Running Press, Courage Books, 1994; Lawrence H. Selman, *All About Paperweights*, Paperweight Press, 1992; ——, *Art of the Paperweight*, Paperweight Press, 1988; ——, *Art of the Paperweight, Perthshire*, Paperweight Press, 1983; ——, *Art of the Paperweight, Saint Louis*, Paperweight Press, 1981 (all of the Paperweight Press books are distributed by Charles E. Tuttle Co., 1996).

Collectors' Clubs: Caithness Collectors Club, 141 Lanza Ave, Building 12, Garfield, NJ 07026; International Paperweight Soc., 761 Chestnut St, Santa Cruz, CA 95060; Paperweight Collectors Assoc. Inc, PO Box 1059, Easthampton, MA 01027; Paperweight Collectors Assoc. of Chicago, 535 Delkir Ct, Naperville, IL 60565; Paperweight Collectors Assoc. of Texas, 1631 Aguarena Springs Dr, #408, San Marcos, TX 78666.

Museums: Bergstrom-Mahler Museum, Neenah, WI; Corning Museum of Glass, Corning, NY; Degenhart Paperweight & Glass Museum, Inc., Cambridge, OH; Museum of American Glass at Wheaton Village, Millville, NJ.

Additional Listings: See *Warman's Americana & Collectibles* for examples of advertising paperweights.

Antique

Baccarat
    Butterfly meadow scene 18,700.00
    Silhouette canes, lace ground 2,900.00
Clichy
    Mushroom, close concentric design, large central pink and green rose surrounded by pin, white, cobalt blue, and cadmium green complex millefiori, middle row of canes with 10 green and white roses alternating with pink pastry mold canes, pin and white stems, 2-3/4" d 6,600.00
    Swirled, alternating purple and white pinwheels emanating from white, green, and pink pastry mold cane, minor bubbles, 2-5/8" d 2,200.00
Degenhart, John, window, red crystal cube with yellow and orange upright center lily, one to window, 4 side windows, bubble in center of flower's stamens, 3-3/16" x 2-1/4" x 2-1/4" 1,225.00
Gillinder, orange turtle with moving appendages in hollow center, pale orange ground, molded dome, 3-1/16" d 500.00
Millville, umbrella pedestal, red, white, green, blue, and yellow int., bubble in sphere center, 3-1/8" d, 3-3/8" h 800.00
New England Glass Co, crown, rd, white, blue, and green twists interspersed with white latticinio emanating from a central pink, white, and green complex floret/cog cane, minor bubbles in glass, 2-3/4" d 2,400.00
Pinchbeck, pastoral dancing scene, couple dancing before grouped of onlookers, 3-3/16" d 650.00

Baccarat, Candy, multicolored, sgd, $265.

Saint Louis, close concentric millefiori, central silhouette of couple dancing, chartreuse, cadmium green, white, opaque pink, mauve, salmon, peach, powder blue, and ruby florets, cross canes, cogs, and bull's eyes canes, 3-3/16" d...........5,750.00

Sandwich Glass Co, double poinsettia, red flower with double tier of petals, green and white Lutz rose, green stem and leaves, bubbles between petals, 3" d.....................................1,200.00

Val St. Lambert, patterned millefiori, 4 red, white, blue, pistachio, and turquoise complex canes circlets spaced around central pink, turquoise and cadmium green canes circlet, canes set on stripes of lace encircled by spiraling red and blue torsade, minor blocking crease, 3-1/2" d....................................950.00

Whitefriars, close concentric millefiori, pink, blue, purple, green, white, and yellow cog canes, 1948 date cane, minor bubble in dome, 3-5/8" d 900.00

Modern

Rick Ayotte, yellow finch, perched on branch, faceted, sgd and dated, limited ed. Of 25, 1979, 2-3-16? D 750.00

Baccarat, Gridel pelican cane surrounded by five concentric rings of yellow, pink, green, and white complex canes, pink canes contain 18 Gridel silhouette canes, lace ground, 1973 date cane, signature cane, sgd and dated, limited ed. of 350, 3-1/16" d 850.00

Charles Kaziun, concentric millefiori, heart, turtle silhouette, shamrocks, 6 pointed stars, and floret canes encircled by purple and white torsade, turquoise ground flecked with goldstone, K signature cane, 2-1/16" d 1,200.00

Perthshire, crown, central complex cane with projecting red and blue twisted ribbons alternating with latticinio ribbons, 1985 date cane, signature cane, limited edition of 268, 3" d
....850.00

Paul Stankard, bouquet, yellow meadow wreath, blue forget-me-nots, rd St. Anthony's fire, white bellflowers, and white chokeberry blossom and buds, 1977, 3" d 2,400.00

Debbie Tarsitano, orange and purple bird of paradise flower on stalk, striped green leaves, star cut ground, DT signature cane, 2-15/16" d 550.00

Francis Whittemore, 2 green and brown acorns on branch with 3 brown and yellow oak leaves, translucent cobalt blue ground, circular top facet 5 oval punties on sides, 203/8" d 300.00

Paul Ysart, green fish, yellow eye, yellow and white jasper ground encircled by pink, green, and white complex cane garland, PY signature cane..550.00

PAPIER-MÂCHÉ

History: Papier-mâché is a mixture of wood pulp, glue, resin, and fine sand, which is subjected to great pressure and then dried. The finished product is tough, durable, and heat resistant. Various finishing treatments are used, such as enameling, japanning, lacquering, mother-of-pearl inlaying, and painting.

During the Victorian era, papier-mâché articles such as boxes, trays, and tables were in high fashion. Banks, candy containers, masks, toys, and other children's articles were also made of papier-mâché.

Candy Container
  5-1/2" h, turkey, polychrome dec....................................45.00
  10" h, angel, wax face, fur trim, German 575.00
Cat, 4" h, black, Halloween type, head only......................350.00
Hat Mannequin, 14-1/2" h, French, worn orig polychrome paint, minor damage, bottom mkd "Mme Roland," complete with old blue bonnet...850.00
Mask, 24" h, donkey head, brown and white, upright ears, shoulder cut-outs, polychrome paint 120.00
Nodder, 9-3/4" h, Easter Rabbit, oval cardboard base, orig polychrome paint...65.00
Pip-Squeak, 4-1/4" h, rooster, orig paint, yellow, orange, and black, recovered wooden bellows, faint squeak.............85.00
Plate, 12" d, painted cat, mkd "Patented August 8, 1880"...35.00
Roly Poly, 4-1/8" h, clown, orig white and blue polychrome paint, green ribbon around neck...60.00
Snuff Box, cov
  2-3/4" d, round, portrait of woman 90.00
  2-7/8" d, engraved portrait on lid in black and deep amber, LaFayette, wear, some edge damage......................325.00
  3" d, presentation of dowry scene on top, case and bottom dec, tortoiseshell lining, 18th C 850.00
  3-1/4" d, hand colored engraving of "Gen. Taylor," some damage..150.00
  3-1/2" d, engraved portrait on lid in black and deep amber, wear, some edge damage
    Napoleon 350.00
    Decatur 325.00

Bank, red and gold Oriental dec, black ground, 2" x 3" x 4-3/4", $70.

5" l, shaped like ship's hull 130.00
Table, 24-1/4" d, 28" h, tilt-top, tripod base, painted and mother-of-pearl inlay, Victorian, mid-19th C 375.00
Tray, 30" x 22-1/2", rect, painted flowering still lives, gilt scrolling vine borders, Victorian, mid 19th C, rubbed 250.00

PARIAN WARE

History: Parian ware is a creamy white, translucent porcelain that resembles marble. It originated in England in 1842 and was first called "statuary porcelain." Minton and Copeland have been credited with its development; Wedgwood also made it. In America, Chistopher Fenton in Bennington, Vermont manufactured parian ware objects.

At first parian ware was used only for figures and figural groups. By the 1850s, it became so popular that a vast range of items was manufactured.

References: Kathy Hughes, *Collector's Guide to Nineteenth-Century Jugs* (1985, Routledge & Kegan Paul), Vol. II (1991, Taylor Publishing).

Bust
  9" h, Martha Washington, England, 19th C, very minor chips, firing blemishes 225.00
  10" h, Ulysses S. Grant, civilian dress, inscribed on back "Broome, Sculpt. 1876," and "Ott and Brewer Manufacturers, Trenton, New Jersey" 2,750.00

Vase, figural hand, scalloped base, 8" h, $175.

12-3/4" h, Shakespeare, raised circular base, Robinson and Ledbetter mark, c1875, minor chip to hair 725.00
15-1/2" h, Abraham Lincoln, raised circular base, English, c1860 .... 295.00
Creamer, 5" h, Tulip pattern, relief dec............................ 100.00
Ewer, 10-1/4" h, blue and white, applied grapes dec, Bennington, c1850 .... 215.00
Figure
  11" h, Grecian goddess riding in carriage, pulled by five putti, c1890 .... 450.00
  11-3/4" h, Farmer, modeled seated on rocky freeform base, holding bagpipes, imp Copeland mark, c1875, pipes and fingers restored, small chips to sheaf of wheat 175.00
  15" h, Canova, imp title on circular base, imp Minton marks, c1863, chips to floral garland 750.00
  16-1/2" h, modeled as kneeling maiden, circular base, imp marks, Gustafsberg, Sweden, late 19th C................ 575.00
Plaque, 6" d, relief, angels, brass frames, orig German labels, Boston retailers label, pr.. 275.00
Sculpture, nude riding back of lion, early registry marks, c1860 .... 895.00
Vase, 10" h, applied white monkey type figures, grape clusters at shoulders, blue ground, c1850, pr 265.00

PATE-DE-VERRE

History: The term "pate-de-verre" can be translated simply as "glass paste." It is manufactured by grinding lead glass into a powder or crystal form, making it into a paste by adding a 2% or 3% solution of sodium silicate, molding, firing, and carving. The Egyptians discovered the process as early as 1500 B.C.

In the late 19th century, the process was rediscovered by a group of French glassmakers. Almaric Walter, Henri Cros, Georges Despret, and the Daum brothers were leading manufacturers.

Contemporary sculptors are creating a second renaissance, led by the technical research of Jacques Daum.

Bookends, pr, 6-1/2" h, Buddha, yellow amber pressed molded design, seated in lotus position, inscribed "A Walter Nancy" 2,450.00
Bowl, 4" d, 8-3/4" h, Almeric Walter, designed by Jules Cayette, molded blue green glass, yellow center, green around border, three brown scarab beetles with long black antennae, inscribed "A. Walter Nancy," and also "J. Cayette," "Made in France" on base 4,600.00
Center Bowl, 10-3/8" d, 3-3/4" h, blue, purple, and green press molded design, 7 exotic long legged birds, central multi-pearl blossom, repeating design on ext., raised pedestal foot, sgd "G. Argy-Rousseau" 6,750.00
Clock, 4-1/2" sq, stars within pentagon and tapered sheaves motif, orange and black, molded sgd "G. Argy-Rousseau," clock by J. E. Caldwell.. 2,750.00
Dagger, 12" l, frosted blade, relief design, green horse head handle, script sgd "Nancy France" 1,200.00
Jewelry
  Earrings, pr, 2-3/4" l, teardrop for, molded violet and rose shaded tulip blossom, suspended from rose colored swirl molded circle 2,200.00
  Pendant, 1-1/4" d, molded amethyst portrait of Art Nouveau woman, flowing hair, gilt metal mount 400.00
Paperweight, 2-5/8" h, Papillion de Nuit, cube, internally streaked gray, deep forest green highlights, molded full relief moths, molded "G. Argy-Rousseau," c1923 .... 2,400.00
Sculpture, 9-5/8" l, crab in sea grasses, lemon yellow, chocolate brown, pale mauve, and sea green, sgd "A. Walter/Nancy" and "Berge/SC" 8,500.00

Vase, Apple Picker, yellow apples, red picker, black trees, Greek key motif on base, 9-1/2" h, $18,000.

Tray, 6" x 8", apple green, figural green and yellow duck with orange beak at one end, sgd "Walter, Nancy" 950.00
Vase, 5-1/2" h, press molded and carved, mottled amethyst and frost ground, 3 black and green crabs, red eyes, naturalistic seaweed at rim, center imp "G. Argy-Rousseau," base imp "France"...5,500.00
Veilleuse, 8-1/2" h, Gabriel Argy-Rousseau, press molded oval lamp shade, frosted mottled gray glass, elaborate purple arches with three teardrop-shaped windows of yellow, center teal-green stylized blossoms on black swirling stems, imp "G. Arty-Rousseau" at lower edge, wrought iron frame, three ball feet centering internal lamp socket, conforming iron cover 6,900.00

PATE-SUR-PATE

History: Pate-sur-pate, paste-on-paste, is a 19th-century porcelain-decorating method featuring relief designs achieved by painting layers of thin pottery paste one on top of the other.

About 1880, Marc Solon and other Sevres artists, inspired by a Chinese celadon vase in the Ceramic Museum at Sevres, experimented with this process. Solon emigrated to England at the outbreak of the Franco-Prussian War and worked at Minton, where he perfected pate-sur-pate.

Box, cov, 5-3/4" d, round, white female portrait, blue ground, Limoges, France, late 19th C 690.00
Centerpiece, 16" l, elongated parian vessel, molded scroll handles and feet, pierced rim, 2 brown reserves, white pate-sur-pate amorini, gilding, dec attributed to Lawrence Birks, mkd "Minton," retailer's mark of Thomas Goode & Co., Ltd., London, c1889..1,400.00
Lamp, 19" h, Neoclassical maiden and arabesque motif, pale green ground, circular gilt bronze base, late 19th C 425.00

Vase, aquamarine, white classical lady, flowing robes, beige ground, gold leaf dec, mkd "Made in Germany, Streetz-Marke/Dep," $495.

Plaque
  5-1/4" x 11-1/4", Victoria Ware, Wedgwood, rust ground, gilt florets, applied white figure of Adam, imp mark, c1880, rim chip, framed 2,200.00
  7-5/8" d, one with maiden and cupid spinning web, other with maiden seated on bench with whip in one hand, sunflowers stalked with humanistic snail on other, artist sgd "Louis Solin," both mkd on back, framed, pr 2,500.00
  11" x 16", mottled blue-gray ground, colored slips of partially clad female holding lantern, putt figure lights torch, titled "La Nouvelle Psyche," unsgd, attributed to Louis Solon 27,600.00
  15" l, demi-lune shape, green ground, white slip, central figure of Venus holding mirror in each hand, tending off 2 groups of putti with their reflections, artist sgd Louis Solin, rosewood frame...9,200.00
Plate, 9-1/8" d, deep brown ground, gilt trim, white dec of nude child behind net supported by two small trees, artist monogram sgd "Henry Saunders," printed and imp Moore Brothers factory marks, c1885 ....750.00
Portrait Medallion, 3-7/8" d, circular, blue ground, white slip side self-portrait profile, artist sgd "Louis Solin," dated 1892 ....1,265.00
Vase
  6-1/2" h, cov, 2 handles, deep teal blue ground, gilt framed gray ground panel with white slip dec of reclining maiden, artist sgd Albione Birks, printed Minton factory marks, c1900, shallow restored chip on cov....................1,840.00

6-7/8" h, 2 handles, blue ground, white female subjects within oval mauve ground cartouches, German printed marks, 20th C, pr.................................750.00

7-1/4" h, 5-3/4" w, white flowers, green ground, gold serpent skin twisted handles, gold trim, pr.........................1,100.00

13-3/4" h, cov, dark brown ground, white slip of partially draped female figure holding flowering branch, shaped tripod base, gilt dec at rim, artist sgd Louis Solon, printed and imp marks, 1898, rim cover damage, minor gilt wear 2,300.00

16-1/2" h, cov, deep green ground, circular panels dec in white slip, Psyche being carried heavenly by Mercury, maiden figures applied to shoulder, gilt trim, artist sgd Frederick Schenck, dated 1880, imp George Jones factory marks, cov damaged, hairlines to figures, light gilt wear 3,565.00

37-1/2" h, blue ground, white clip depicting "Cupid's Tollgate," central frieze flanked by blue and green slip dec foliate designs, gold outlines, artist sgd Louis Solin, Minton factory marks, c1890 ....55,200.00

PATTERN GLASS

History: Pattern glass is clear or colored glass pressed into one of hundreds of patterns. Deming Jarves of the Boston and Sandwich Glass Co. invented one of the first successful pressing machines in 1828. By the 1860s, glass-pressing machinery had been improved, and mass production of good-quality matched tableware sets began. The idea of a matched glassware table service (including goblets, tumblers, creamers, sugars, compotes, cruets, etc.) quickly caught on in America. Many pattern glass table services had numerous accessory pieces such as banana stands, molasses cans, and water bottles.

Early pattern glass (flint) was made with a lead formula, giving many items a ringing sound when tapped. Lead became too valuable to be used in glass manufacturing during the Civil War; and in 1864 Hobbs, Brockunier & Co., West Virginia, developed a soda lime (nonflint) formula. Pattern glass also was produced in transparent colors, milk glass, opalescent glass, slag glass, and custard glass.

The hundreds of companies that produced pattern glass experienced periods of development, expansions, personnel problems, material and supply demands, fires, and mergers. In 1899 the National Glass Co. was formed as a combine of 19 glass companies in Pennsylvania, Ohio, Indiana, West Virginia, and Maryland. U.S. Glass, another consortium, was founded in 1891. These combines resulted from attempts to save small companies by pooling talents, resources, and patterns. Because of this pooling, the same pattern often can be attributed to several companies.

Sometimes various companies produced the same patterns at different times and used different names to reflect current fashion trends. U.S. Glass created the States series by using state names for various patterns, several of which were new issues while others were former patterns renamed.

References: Gary Baker et al., *Wheeling Glass 1829-1939*, Oglebay Institute, 1994, distributed by Antique Publications; George and Linda Breeze, *Mysteries of the Moon & Star*, published by authors, 1995; William Heacock, *Encyclopedia of Victorian Colored Pattern Glass: Book 1: Toothpick Holders from A to Z*, 2nd ed. (1976, 1992 value update) *Book 5: U. S. Glass from A to Z* (1980), *Book 7: Ruby Stained Glass from A To Z* (1986), *Book 8: More Ruby Stained Glass* (1987), Antique Publications; ——, *Old Pattern Glass*, Antique Publications, 1981; ——, *1,000 Toothpick Holders*, Antique Publications, 1977; ——, *Rare and Unlisted Toothpick Holders*, Antique Publications, 1984; Kyle Husfloen, *Collector's Guide to American Pressed Glass*, Wallace-Homestead, 1992; Bill Jenks and Jerry Luna, *Early American Pattern Glass—1850 to 1910*, Wallace-Homestead, 1990; Bill Jenks, Jerry Luna, and Darryl Reilly, *Identifying Pattern Glass Reproductions*, Wallace-Homestead, 1993; William J. Jenks and Darryl Reilly, *American Price Guide to Unitt's Canadian & American Goblets Volumes I & II*, Author! Author! Books (P.O. Box 1964, Kingston, PA 18704), 1996.

Minnie Watson Kamm, *Pattern Glass Pitchers*, Books 1 through 8, published by author, 1970, 4th printing; Ruth Webb Lee, *Early American Pressed Glass*, 36th ed., Lee Publications, 1966; ——, *Victorian Glass*, 13th ed., Lee Publications, 1944; Bessie M. Lindsey, *American Historical Glass*, Charles E. Tuttle, 1967; Robert Irwin Lucas, *Tarentum Pattern Glass*, privately printed, 1981; Mollie H. McCain, *Collector's Encyclopedia of Pattern Glass*, Collector Books, 1982, 1994 value update; George P. and Helen McKearin, *American Glass*, Crown Publishers, 1941; James Measell, *Greentown Glass*, Grand Rapids Public Museum Association, 1979, 1992-93 value update, distributed by Antique Publications; Alice Hulett Metz, *Early American Pattern Glass*, published by author, 1958; ——, *Much More Early American Pattern Glass*, published by author, 1965; S. T. Millard, *Goblets I* (1938), *Goblets II* (1940), privately printed, reprinted Wallace-Homestead, 1975; John B. Mordock and Walter L. Adams, *Pattern Glass Mugs*, Antique Publications, 1995.

Arthur G. Peterson, *Glass Salt Shakers*, Wallace-Homestead, 1970; Ellen T. Schroy, *Warman's Pattern Glass*, Wallace-Homestead, 1993; Jane Shadel Spillman, *American and European Pressed Glass in the Corning Museum of Glass*, Corning Museum of Glass, 1981; ——, *Knopf Collectors Guides to American Antiques, Glass*, Vol. 1 (1982), Vol. 2 (1983), Alfred A. Knopf; Doris and Peter Unitt, *American and Canadian Goblets*, Clock House, 1970, reprinted by The Love of Glass Publishing (Box 629, Arthur, Ontario, Canada NOG 1AO), 1996; ——, *Treasury of Canadian Glass*, 2nd ed., Clock House, 1969; Peter Unitt and Anne Worrall, *Canadian Handbook, Pressed Glass Tableware*, Clock House Productions, 1983; Kenneth Wilson, *American Glass 1760-1930*, 2 Vols., Hudson Hills Press and The Toledo Museum of Art, 1994.

Periodical: *Glass Collector's Digest*, The Glass Press, P.O. Box 553, Marietta, OH 45750.

Collectors' Clubs: Early American Pattern Glass Society, P.O. Box 266, Colesburg, IA 52035; The National

Early American Glass Club, P.O. Box 8489, Silver Spring, MD 20907.

Museums: Corning Museum of Glass, Corning, NY; Jones Museum of Glass and Ceramics, Sebago, ME; National Museum of Man, Ottawa, Ontario, Canada; Sandwich Glass Museum, Sandwich, MA; Schminck Memorial Museum, Lakeview, OR.

Additional Listings: Bread Plates; Children's Toy Dishes; Cruets; Custard Glass; Milk Glass; Sugar Shakers; Toothpicks; and specific companies.

Advisors: John and Alice Ahlfeld. Mike Anderton, and Jerry Baker.

REPRODUCTION ALERT

Pattern glass has been widely reproduced.

Notes: Research in pattern glass is continuing. As always, we try to use correct pattern names, histories, and forms. Reflecting the most current thinking, the listing by pattern places colored, opalescent, and clear items together, avoiding duplication.

Items in the listing marked with an * are those for which reproductions are known to exist. Care should be exercised when purchasing such pieces.

Abbreviations:

ah	applied handle
GUTDODB	Give Us This Day Our Daily Bread
hs	high standard
ind	individual
ls	low standard
os	original stopper

SPECIAL AUCTIONS

Bailey's Antiques
102 E. Main St.
Homer, MI 49245
(517) 568-4014

Mike Clum
P.O. Box 2
Rushville, OH 43150
(614) 536-9220

Green Valley Auctions, Inc.
Rt. 2, Box 434
Mt. Crawford, VA 22841
(540) 434-4260

ACTRESS

Made by Adams & Company, Pittsburg, PA, c1880. All clear 20% less. Imperial Glass Co has reproduced some items, including an amethyst pickle dish, in clear and color.

	Clear and Frosted
Bowl	
6", ftd	45.00
7", ftd	50.00
8", Miss Neilson	85.00
9-1/2", ftd	85.00
Bread Plate	
7" x 12", HMS Pinafore	90.00
9" x 13", Miss Neilson	72.00
Butter, cov	90.00
Cake Stand, 10"	145.00
Candlesticks, pr	250.00
Celery Vase	
Actress Head	130.00
HMS Pinafore, pedestal	145.00
Cheese Dish, cov, The Lone Fisherman on cov, Two Dromios on base	250.00
Compote	
Cov, hs, 6" d	250.00
Cov, hs, 12" d	300.00
Open, hs, 10" d	90.00
Open, hs, 12" d	120.00
Open, ls, 5" d	45.00

	Clear and Frosted
Creamer	75.00
Dresser Tray	60.00
Goblet, Kate Claxton (two portraits)	85.00
Marmalade Jar, cov	125.00
Mug, HMS Pinafore	50.00
*Pickle Dish, Love's Request is Pickles	45.00
Pickle Relish, different actresses	
4-1/2" x 7"	35.00
5" x 8"	35.00
5-1/2" x 9"	35.00
Pitcher	
Milk, 6-1/2", HMS Pinafore	295.00
Water, 9", Romeo & Juliet	250.00
Salt, master	70.00
Salt Shaker, orig pewter top	42.50
Sauce	
Flat	15.00
Footed	20.00
Spooner	60.00
Sugar, cov	100.00

ADONIS (Pleat and Tuck, Washboard)

Pattern made by McKee & Bros. of Pittsburgh, PA, in 1897

	Canary	Clear	Deep Blue
Bowl, 5", berry	15.00	10.00	20.00
Butter, cov	70.00	48.00	80.00
Cake Plate, 11"	25.00	20.00	32.00
Cake Stand, 10-1/2"	45.00	30.00	50.00
Celery Vase	35.00	25.00	40.00
Compote			
Cov, hs	65.00	40.00	75.00
Open, hs, 8"	45.00	30.00	50.00
Open, jelly, 4-1/2"	28.00	18.00	32.00
Creamer	28.00	22.50	32.00
Pitcher, water	55.00	35.00	60.00
Plate, 10"	25.00	18.00	32.00
Relish	10.00	15.00	20.00
Salt & Pepper, pr	40.00	35.00	45.00
Sauce, flat, 4"	10.00	8.00	12.00
Spooner	35.00	20.00	40.00
Sugar, cov	40.00	35.00	45.00
Syrup	150.00	50.00	150.00
Tumbler	20.00	16.00	20.00

ALMOND THUMBPRINT (Pointed Thumbprint, Finger Print)

An early flint glass pattern with variants in flint and non-flint. Pattern has been attributed to Bryce, Bakewell, and U.S. Glass Co. Sometimes found in milk glass.

	Flint	Non-Flint
Bowl, 4-1/2" d, ftd	—	20.00
Butter, cov	80.00	40.00
Celery Vase	50.00	25.00
Champagne	60.00	35.00
Compote		
Cov, hs, 4-3/4", jelly	70.00	40.00
Cov, hs, 10"	110.00	45.00
Cov, ls, 4-3/4"	75.00	30.00
Cov, ls, 7"	70.00	25.00
Open, hs, 10-1/2"	70.00	—
Cordial	40.00	30.00
Creamer	60.00	40.00
Cruet, ftd, os	55.00	—
Decanter	70.00	—

	Flint	Non-Flint
Eggcup	45.00	25.00
Goblet	45.00	12.00
Punch Bowl	—	75.00
Salt		
Flat, large	25.00	15.00
Ftd, cov	45.00	25.00
Ftd, open	25.00	10.00
Spooner	20.00	15.00
Sugar, cov	65.00	40.00
Sweetmeat Jar, cov	75.00	50.00
Tumbler	60.00	20.00
Wine	28.00	12.00

APOLLO (Canadian Horseshoe, Shield Band)

Non-flint first made by Adams & Co., Pittsburgh, PA, c1890, and later by U.S. Glass Co. Frosted increases price 20%. Also found in ruby stained and engraved. Lamp found also in blue and yellowed, valued at $250.00

	Clear
Bowl	
4"	10.00
5"	10.00
6"	12.00
7"	15.00
8"	20.00
Butter, cov	40.00
Cake Stand	
8"	35.00
9"	40.00
10"	50.00
Celery Tray, rect	20.00
Celery Vase	35.00
Compote	
Cov, hs	65.00
Open, hs	35.00
Open, ls, 7"	25.00
Creamer	35.00

	Clear
Cruet	60.00
Eggcup	30.00
Goblet	35.00
Lamp, 10"	125.00
Pickle Dish	15.00
Pitcher, water	65.00
Plate, 9-1/2", sq	25.00
Salt	20.00
Salt Shaker	25.00
Sauce	
Flat	10.00
Ftd, 5"	12.00
Spooner	30.00
Sugar, cov	45.00
Syrup	110.00
Tray, water	45.00
Tumbler	30.00
Wine	35.00

ARCHED GRAPE

Non-flint made by Boston and Sandwich Glass Co., Sandwich, MA, c1880.

	Non-Flint		Non-Flint
Butter, cov	45.00	Goblet	25.00
Celery vase	35.00	Pitcher, water, ah	60.00
Champagne	35.00	Sauce, flat	8.00
Compote, cov, hs	50.00	Spooner	30.00
Creamer	40.00	Sugar, cov	45.00
		Wine	25.00

ARGUS

Flint thumbprint-type pattern made by Bakewell, Pears and Co., Pittsburgh, PA, in the early 1860s. Copiously reproduced, some by Fostoria Glass Co. with raised "H.F.M." trademark for Henry Ford Museum, Dearborn, MI. Reproduction colors include clear, red, green and cobalt blue.

	Clear		Clear
Ale Glass	75.00	*Goblet	60.00
Bitters Bottle	60.00	Lamp, ftd	100.00
Bowl, 5-1/2"	30.00	Mug, ah	65.00
*Butter, cov	85.00	Pitcher, water, ah	400.00
Celery vase	90.00	Salt, master, open	30.00
Champagne	65.00	*Spooner	45.00
Compote, open 8", scalloped	50.00	*Sugar, cov	65.00
*Creamer, ah	115.00	*Tumbler, bar	65.00
Decanter, qt	95.00	Whiskey, ah	75.00
Eggcup	30.00	Wine	35.00

ART (Jacob's Tears, Job's Tears, Teardrop and Diamond Block)

Non-flint produced by Adams & Co., Pittsburgh, PA, in the 1880s. Reissued by U.S. Glass Co. in the early 1890s. A reproduced milk glass covered compote is known.

	Clear	Ruby Stained		Clear	Ruby Stained
Banana Stand	90.00	175.00	Regular	55.00	100.00
Biscuit Jar	135.00	175.00	Cruet, os	125.00	250.00
Bowl			Goblet	60.00	—
6" d, 3-1/4" h, ftd	30.00	—	Pitcher		
7", low, collar base	35.00	—	Milk	115.00	175.00
8", berry, one end pointed	50.00	85.00	Water, 2-1/2 qt	100.00	—
Butter, cov	60.00	125.00	Plate, 10"	40.00	—
Cake Stand			Relish	20.00	65.00
9"	55.00	—	Sauce		
10-1/4"	65.00	—	Flat, round, 4"	15.00	—
Celery Vase	40.00	100.00	Pointed end	18.50	—
*Compote			Spooner	25.00	85.00
Cov, hs, 7"	100.00	185.00	Sugar, cov	45.00	125.00
Open, hs, 9"	55.00	—	Tumbler	45.00	—
Open, hs, 9-1/5"	60.00	—	Vinegar Jug, 3 pt	75.00	—
Open, hs, 10"	65.00	—			
Creamer					
Hotel, large, round shape	45.00	90.00			

ASHBURTON

A popular pattern produced by Boston and Sandwich Glass Co. and by McKee & Bros. Glass Co. from the 1850s to the late 1870s with many variations. Originally made in flint by New England Glass Co. and others and later in non-flint. Prices are for flint. Non-flint values 65% less. Also reported are an amber-handled whiskey mug, flint canary celery vase ($750.00), and a scarce emerald green wineglass ($200.00). Some items known in fiery opalescent.

	Clear		Clear
Ale Glass, 5"	90.00	*Claret, 5-1/4"	50.00
Bar Bottle		*Compote, open, ls, 7-1/2"	65.00
Pint	55.00	Cordial, 4-1/4" h	70.00
Quart	75.00	*Creamer, ah	210.00
Bitters Bottle	55.00	Decanter, qt, cut and pressed, os	250.00
*Bowl, 6-1/2"	75.00	Eggcup	
Carafe	175.00	Double	80.00
Celery vase, scalloped top	100.00	Single	30.00
Champagne , cut	85.00	Flip Glass, handled	140.00

	Clear
*Goblet	50.00
Honey Dish	15.00
*Jug, qt	90.00
Lamp	75.00
*Lemonade Glass	55.00
Mug, 7"	100.00
*Pitcher, water	450.00
Plate, 6-5/8"	75.00
Sauce	10.00
*Sugar, cov	90.00

	Clear
Toddy Jar, cov	375.00
*Tumbler	
Bar	75.00
Water	75.00
Whiskey	60.00
Water Bottle, tumble up	95.00
Whiskey, ah	125.00
*Wine	
Cut	65.00
Pressed	40.00

ATLAS (Bullet, Cannon Ball, Crystal Ball)

Non-flint, occasionally ruby stained and etched, made by Adams & Co.; U.S. Glass Co. in 1891; and Bryce Bros., Mt. Pleasant, PA, in 1889.

	Clear	Ruby Stained
Bowl, 9"	20.00	—
Butter, cov, regular	45.00	75.00
Cake Stand		
8"	35.00	—
9"	40.00	95.00
Celery Vase	28.00	—
Champagne, 5-1/2" h	25.00	55.00
Compote		
Cov, hs, 8"	65.00	—
Cov, hs, 5", jelly	50.00	80.00
Open, ls, 7"	40.00	—
Cordial	35.00	—
Creamer		
Table, ah	30.00	55.00
Tankard	25.00	—
Goblet	35.00	65.00

	Clear	Ruby Stained
Marmalade Jar	45.00	—
Molasses Can	65.00	—
Pitcher, water	65.00	—
Salt		
Master	20.00	—
Individual	15.00	—
Salt & Pepper, pr	20.00	—
Sauce		
Flat	10.00	—
Footed	15.00	25.00
Spooner	30.00	45.00
Sugar, cov	40.00	65.00
Syrup	65.00	—
Toothpick	20.00	50.00
Tray, water	75.00	—
Tumbler	28.00	—
Whiskey	20.00	45.00
Wine	25.00	—

AUSTRIAN (Finecut Medallion)

Made by Indiana Tumbler and Goblet Co., Greentown, IN, 1897. Experimental pieces were made in cobalt blue, Nile green, and opaque colors. Some pieces were made in Chocolate glass.

	Amber	Canary	Clear	Emerald Green
Bowl				
8", round	—	150.00	50.00	—
8-1/4", rect	—	150.00	50.00	—
Butter, cov	185.00	300.00	90.00	—
Children's table set	—	550.00	325.00	—
Compote, open, ls	—	150.00	75.00	—
Cordial	145.00	150.00	50.00	150.00
Creamer	120.00	125.00	40.00	120.00
Goblet	—	150.00	40.00	—
Mug, child's	—	—	45.00	—
Nappy, cov	—	135.00	55.00	—
Pitcher, water	—	350.00	100.00	—
Plate, 10"	—	—	40.00	—
Punch Cup	150.00	150.00	18.00	125.00
Rose Bowl	—	150.00	50.00	—
Sauce, 4-5/8" d	—	50.00	20.00	—
Spooner	—	100.00	40.00	—
Sugar, cov	—	175.00	45.00	—
Tumbler	175.00	85.00	25.00	—
Wine	175.00	150.00	30.00	150.00

BALTIMORE PEAR (Double Pear, Fig, Gipsy, Maryland Pear, Twin Pear)

Non-flint originally made by Adams & Company, Pittsburgh, PA, in 1874. Also made by U.S. Glass Company in the 1890s. Compotes were made in 18 different sizes. Given as premiums by different manufacturers and organizations. Heavily reproduced. Reproduced in clear, cobalt blue, and pink milk glass.

	Clear
Bowl	
6"	30.00
9"	35.00
Bread Plate, 12-1/2"	70.00
*Butter, cov	75.00
*Cake Stand, 9"	65.00
Celery vase	50.00
Compote	
Cov, hs, 7"	80.00
Cov, ls, 8-1/2"	45.00
Open, hs	30.00
Open, jelly	25.00
*Creamer	30.00
*Goblet	35.00

	Clear
Pickle	20.00
*Pitcher	
Milk	80.00
Water	95.00
*Plate	
8-1/2"	30.00
10"	40.00
Relish	25.00
*Sauce	
Flat	10.00
Footed	15.00
Spooner	40.00
*Sugar, cov	50.00
Tray, 10-1/2"	35.00

BANDED PORTLAND (Virginia #1, Maiden's Blush)

States pattern, originally named Virginia, by Portland Glass Co., Portland, ME. Painted and fired green, yellow, blue, and possibly pink; ruby stained, and rose-flashed (which Lee notes is Maiden's Blush, referring to the color rather than the pattern, as Metz lists it). Double-flashed refers to color above and below the band, single-flashed refers to color above or below the band only.

	Clear	Color-Flashed	Maiden's Blush Pink
Bowl			
4" d, open	10.00	—	20.00
6" d, cov	40.00	—	55.00
7-1/2" d, shallow	30.00	—	55.00
8"d, cov	50.00	—	75.00
Butter, cov	50.00	195.00	85.00
Cake Stand	55.00	—	90.00
Candlesticks, pr	80.00	—	125.00
Carafe	80.00	—	90.00
Celery Tray	25.00	—	40.00
Celery Vase	35.00	—	45.00
Cologne Bottle	50.00	125.00	85.00
Compote			
Cov, hs, 7"	75.00	—	125.00
Cov, hs, 8"	85.00	—	150.00
Cov, jelly, 6"	40.00	95.00	90.00
Creamer			
Individual, oval	25.00	55.00	40.00
Regular, 6 oz.	35.00	85.00	50.00
Cruet, os	60.00	175.00	300.00
Decanter, handled	50.00	—	100.00
Dresser Tray	50.00	—	65.00
Goblet	40.00	75.00	95.00
Lamp			
Flat	45.00	—	—
Tall	50.00	—	—
Nappy, sq	15.00	55.00	65.00
Olive	18.00	25.00	35.00
Pin Tray	16.00	—	25.00
Pitcher, tankard	75.00	115.00	240.00
Pomade Jar, cov	35.00	75.00	95.00
Punch Bowl, hs	110.00	—	300.00
Punch Cup	20.00	—	30.00
Relish			
6-1/2"	25.00	35.00	25.00
8-1/4"	20.00	40.00	45.00
Ring Holder	75.00	—	125.00
Salt & Pepper, pr	45.00	95.00	75.00
Sardine Box	55.00	—	90.00
Sauce, round, flat, 4 or 4-1/2"	10.00	—	25.00
Spooner	28.00	—	45.00
Sugar, cov	48.00	95.00	75.00
Sugar Shaker, orig top	45.00	—	85.00
Syrup	50.00	—	135.00
Toothpick	40.00	55.00	45.00
Tumbler	25.00	45.00	45.00
Vase			
6"	20.00	—	50.00
9"	35.00	—	65.00
Wine	35.00	—	85.00

BARBERRY (Berry, Olive, Pepper Berry)

Non-flint made by McKee & Bros. Glass Co. in the 1860s. The 6" plates are found in amber, canary, pale green, and pale blue; they are considered scarce. Pattern comes in "9-berry bunch" and "12-berry bunch" varieties.

	Clear
Bowl	
6", oval	20.00
7", oval	25.00
8", oval	25.00
8", round, flat	25.00
9", oval	30.00
Butter	
Cov	50.00
Cov, flange, pattern on edge	80.00
Cake Stand	90.00
Celery vase	55.00
Compote	
Cov, hs, 8", shell finial	85.00
Cov, ls, 8", shell finial	75.00
Open, hs, 8"	35.00

	Clear
Creamer	30.00
Cup Plate	15.00
Eggcup	20.00
Goblet	25.00
Pickle	10.00
Pitcher, water, ah	100.00
Plate, 6"	20.00
Salt, master, ftd	25.00
Sauce	
Flat	10.00
Footed	15.00
Spooner, ftd	30.00
Sugar, cov	45.00
Syrup	150.00
Tumbler, ftd	25.00
Wine	30.00

BASKETWEAVE

Non-flint, c1880. Some covered pieces have a stippled cat's-head finial.

	Amber or Canary	Apple Green	Blue	Clear	Vaseline
Bowl	20.00	—	25.00	15.00	—
Bread Plate, 11"	35.00	—	35.00	10.00	—
Butter, cov	35.00	60.00	40.00	30.00	40.00
Compote, cov, 7"	—	—	—	40.00	—
Cordial	25.00	40.00	28.00	20.00	30.00
Creamer	30.00	50.00	35.00	28.00	36.00
Cup and Saucer	35.00	60.00	35.00	30.00	38.00
Dish, oval	12.00	20.00	15.00	10.00	16.00
Eggcup	20.00	30.00	25.00	15.00	25.00
*Goblet	28.00	50.00	35.00	20.00	35.00
Mug	25.00	40.00	25.00	15.00	30.00
Pickle	20.00	30.00	20.00	15.00	25.00
Pitcher					
Milk	95.00	95.00	95.00	95.00	95.00
*Water	75.00	75.00	75.00	45.00	80.00
Plate, 11", handled	25.00	35.00	25.00	20.00	30.00
Sauce	10.00	10.00	12.00	8.00	12.00
Spooner	30.00	36.00	30.00	20.00	30.00
Sugar, cov	35.00	60.00	35.00	30.00	40.00
Syrup	50.00	75.00	50.00	45.00	55.00
*Tray, water, scenic center	45.00	50.00	60.00	35.00	55.00
Tumbler, ftd	18.00	30.00	20.00	15.00	20.00
Waste Bowl	20.00	35.00	25.00	18.00	25.00
Wine	30.00	50.00	30.00	20.00	30.00

BEADED GRAPE (Beaded Grape and Vine, California, Grape and Vine)

Non-flint made by U.S. Glass Co., Pittsburgh, PA, c1890. Also attributed to Burlington Glass Works, Hamilton, Ontario, and Sydenham Glass Co., Wallaceburg, Ontario, Canada, c1910. Made in clear and emerald green, sometimes with gilt trim. Reproduced in clear, milk glass, and several colors by many, including Westmoreland Glass Co.

	Clear	Emerald Green
Bowl		
5-1/2", sq	17.50	20.00
7-1/2", sq	25.00	35.00
8", round	28.00	35.00
Bread Plate	25.00	45.00
Butter, cov	65.00	85.00
Cake Stand, 9"	65.00	85.00
Celery Tray	30.00	45.00
Celery Vase	40.00	60.00
*Compote		
Cov, hs, 7"	75.00	85.00
Cov, hs, 9"	100.00	110.00

	Clear	Emerald Green
Open, hs, 5", sq	55.00	75.00
Open, hs, 8"	55.00	70.00
Creamer	40.00	50.00
Cruet, os	65.00	125.00
*Goblet	35.00	50.00
Olive, handle	20.00	35.00
Pickle	20.00	30.00
Pitcher		
Milk	75.00	90.00
Water	85.00	120.00
*Plate, 8-1/4", sq	28.00	40.00
Salt & Pepper	45.00	65.00

	Clear	Emerald Green		Clear	Emerald Green
Sauce, 4"	15.00	20.00	Toothpick	40.00	65.00
Spooner	35.00	45.00	*Tumbler	25.00	40.00
Sugar, cov	45.00	55.00	Vase, 6" h	25.00	40.00
			*Wine	35.00	65.00

BEADED LOOP (Oregon # 1)

Non-flint made by U.S. Glass Co., Pittsburgh, PA, as Pattern Line No. 15,073. After the 1891 merger, reissued as one of the States series. Rare in emerald green. Reproduced in clear and color by Imperial.

	Clear		Clear
Berry set, master, 6 sauces	72.00	Cruet	50.00
Bowl		*Goblet	35.00
3-1/2"	10.00	Honey Dish	10.00
6"	12.00	Mug	35.00
7"	15.00	Pickle Dish, boat shape	15.00
Bread Plate	35.00	Pitcher	
Butter, cov		Milk	40.00
English	65.00	Water	60.00
Flanged	50.00	Relish	15.00
Flat	40.00	Salt, master	20.00
Cake Stand		Salt & Pepper Shakers, pr	40.00
8"	40.00	Sauce	
10"	55.00	Flat, 3-1/2" to 4"	5.00
Carafe, water	35.00	Footed, 3-1/2"	10.00
Celery Vase	30.00	Spooner	
Compote		Flat	24.00
Cov, hs, 5", jelly	45.00	Footed	26.00
Cov, hs, 7"	60.00	*Sugar, cov	
Open, hs, 6"	30.00	Flat	25.00
Open, hs, 8"	40.00	Footed	30.00
Creamer		Syrup	55.00
Flat	30.00	Toothpick	55.00
Footed	35.00	Tumbler	25.00
		Wine	50.00

BIGLER

Flint made by Boston and Sandwich Glass Co., Sandwich, MA, and by other early factories. A scarce pattern in which goblets are most common and vary in height, shape and flare. Rare in color. The goblet has been reproduced as a commemorative item for Biglerville, PA.

	Clear		Clear
Ale Glass	65.00	Eggcup, double	50.00
Bar Bottle, qt	95.00	*Goblet	
Bowl, 10" d	40.00	Regular	48.00
Butter, cov	125.00	Short Stem	50.00
Celery Vase	100.00	Lamp, whale oil, monument base	155.00
Champagne	95.00	Mug, ah	60.00
Compote, open, 7" d	40.00	Plate, 6" d	30.00
Cordial	65.00	Salt, master	20.00
Creamer	75.00	Tumbler, water	65.00
Cup Plate	30.00	Whiskey, handled	100.00
		Wine	65.00

BIRD AND STRAWBERRY (Bluebird, Flying Bird and Strawberry, Strawberry and Bird)

Non-flint, c1914. Made by Indiana Glass Co., Dunkirk, IN. Pieces occasionally highlighted by blue birds, pink strawberries, and green leaves, plus the addition of gliding.

	Clear	Colors		Clear	Colors
Bowl			Open, ls, ruffled	65.00	125.00
5"	25.00	45.00	Jelly, cov, hs	150.00	225.00
9-1/2", ftd	50.00	85.00	Creamer	55.00	135.00
10-1/2"	55.00	95.00	Cup	25.00	35.00
Butter, cov	100.00	175.00	Goblet	600.00	1,000.00
Cake Stand	65.00	125.00	Nappy	40.00	65.00
*Celery Vase	45.00	85.00	Pitcher, water	235.00	350.00
Compote			Plate, 12"	125.00	175.00
*Cov, hs	125.00	200.00	Punch Cup	25.00	35.00

	Clear	Colors		Clear	Colors
Relish	20.00	45.00	Sugar, cov	65.00	125.00
Spooner	50.00	120.00	Tumbler	45.00	75.00
			Wine	65.00	100.00

BLEEDING HEART

Non-flint originally made by King Son & Co., Pittsburgh, PA, c1875, and by U.S. Glass Co. c1898. Also found in milk glass. Goblets are found in six variations. Note: A goblet with a tin lid, containing a condiment (mustard, jelly, or baking powder) was made. It is of inferior quality compared to the original goblet.

	Clear		Clear
Bowl		Molded Handle	30.00
7-1/4", oval	30.00	Dish, cov, 7"	55.00
8"	35.00	Eggcup	45.00
9-1/4", oval, cov	65.00	Egg Rack, 3 eggs	350.00
Butter, cov	75.00	Goblet, knob stem	35.00
Cake Stand		Honey Dish	15.00
9"	75.00	Mug, 3-1/4"	40.00
10"	90.00	Pickle, 8-3/4" l, 5" w	30.00
11"	100.00	Pitcher, water, ah	150.00
Compote		Plate	75.00
Cov, hs, 8"	75.00	Platter, oval	65.00
Cov, hs, 9"	95.00	Relish, oval, 5-1/2" x 3-5/8"	35.00
Cov, ls, 7"	60.00	Salt, master, ftd	60.00
Cov, ls, 7-1/2"	60.00	Salt, oval, flat	20.00
Cov, ls, 8"	75.00	Sauce, flat	15.00
Open, ls, 8-1/2"	30.00	Spooner	25.00
Creamer		Sugar, cov	60.00
Applied Handle	60.00	Tumbler, ftd	80.00
		Wine	150.00

BLOCK AND FAN (Red Block and Fan, Romeo)

Non-flint made by Richard and Hartley Glass Co., Tarentum, PA, in the late 1880s. Continued by U.S. Glass Co. after 1891.

	Clear	Ruby Stained		Clear	Ruby Stained
Biscuit Jar, cov	65.00	150.00	Ice Tub	45.00	50.00
Bowl, 4", flat	15.00	—	Orange Bowl	50.00	—
Butter, cov	50.00	85.00	Pickle Dish	20.00	—
Cake Stand			Pitcher		
9"	35.00	—	Milk	35.00	—
10"	42.00	—	Water	48.00	125.00
Carafe	50.00	95.00	Plate		
Celery Tray	30.00	—	6"	15.00	—
Celery Vase	35.00	75.00	10"	18.00	—
Compote, open, hs, 8"	40.00	165.00	Relish, rect	25.00	—
Condiment Set, salt, pepper			Rose Bowl	25.00	—
and cruet on tray	75.00	—	Salt & Pepper	30.00	—
Creamer			Sauce		
Individual	—	35.00	Flat, 5"	8.00	—
Large	30.00	100.00	Ftd, 3-3/4"	12.00	25.00
Regular	25.00	45.00	Spooner	25.00	—
Small	35.00	75.00	Sugar, cov	50.00	—
Cruet, os	35.00	—	Sugar Shaker	40.00	—
Dish, large, rect	25.00	—	Syrup	75.00	95.00
Finger Bowl	55.00	—	Tray, ice cream, rect	75.00	—
Goblet	48.00	120.00	Tumbler	30.00	40.00
			Waste Bowl	30.00	—
			Wine	45.00	80.00

BOW TIE (American Bow Tie)

Non-flint made by Thompson Glass Co., Uniontown, PA, c1889.

	Clear		Clear
Bowl		Butter Pat	25.00
8"	35.00	Cake Stand, large, 9" d	60.00
10-1/4" d, 5" h	65.00	Compote, open	
Butter, cov	65.00	hs, 5-1/2"	60.00

	Clear
hs, 9-1/4"	65.00
ls, 6-1/2"	45.00
ls, 8"	55.00
Creamer	45.00
Goblet	60.00
Honey, cov	55.00
Marmalade Jar	75.00
Orange Bowl, ftd, hs, 10"	110.00
Pitcher	
Milk	85.00
Water	75.00

	Clear
Punch Bowl	100.00
Relish, rect	25.00
Salt	
Individual	20.00
Master	45.00
Salt Shaker	40.00
Sauce, flat	15.00
Spooner	35.00
Sugar	
Cov	55.00
Open	40.00
Tumbler	45.00

BRIDAL ROSETTE (Checkerboard)

Made by Westmoreland Glass Co. in the early 1900s. Add 150% for ruby-stained values. Reproduced since the 1950s in milk glass and, in recent years, with pink satin. The Cambridge Ribbon pattern, usually marked "Nearcut," is similar.

	Clear
Bowl, 9", shallow	20.00
Butter, cov	40.00
Celery Tray	20.00
Celery vase	30.00
Compote, open, ls, 8"	25.00
Creamer	25.00
Cruet, os	40.00
Cup	8.00
Goblet	28.00
Honey Dish, cov, sq, pedestal	45.00
Pitcher	
Milk	40.00

	Clear
Water	35.00
Plate	
7"	15.00
10"	20.00
Punch Cup	5.00
Salt & Pepper	40.00
Sauce, flat	5.00
Spooner	20.00
Sugar, cov	35.00
Tumbler	
Iced tea	25.00
Water	20.00
Wine	15.00

BROKEN COLUMN (Bamboo Irish Column, Notched Rib, Rattan, Ribbed Fingerprint)

Made in Findlay, Ohio, c1888, by Columbia Glass Co.; and later by U.S. Glass Co. Notches may be ruby stained. A cobalt blue cup is known. The square covered compote has been reproduced, as have items for the Metropolitan Museum of Art and the Smithsonian Institution. Those for the Smithsonian are marked with a raised "S.I."

	Clear	Ruby Stained
Banana Stand	185.00	—
Basket, ah, 12" h, 15" l	125.00	
Biscuit Jar	85.00	165.00
Bowl		
4" berry	15.00	20.00
*8"	35.00	—
9"	40.00	—
Bread Plate	60.00	125.00
Butter, cov	85.00	175.00
Cake Stand, 9" or 10"	75.00	225.00
Carafe, water	75.00	150.00
Celery Tray, oval	35.00	85.00
Celery Vase	50.00	135.00
Champagne	100.00	—
Claret	75.00	—
Compote		
Cov, hs, 5-1/4" d, 10-1/4" h	90.00	200.00
Cov, hs, 10"	110.00	400.00
Open, hs, 8" d	75.00	200.00
*Creamer	42.50	125.00

	Clear	Ruby Stained
Cruet, os	85.00	150.00
Decanter	85.00	—
Finger Bowl	30.00	—
*Goblet	55.00	100.00
Marmalade Jar	85.00	—
Pickle Castor, SP frame	225.00	450.00
*Pitcher, water	90.00	230.00
Plate		
4"	25.00	40.00
7-1/2"	40.00	95.00
Punch Cup	15.00	—
Relish	25.00	—
Salt Shaker	45.00	65.00
*Sauce, flat	10.00	20.00
*Spooner	35.00	85.00
*Sugar, cov	70.00	135.00
Sugar Shaker	85.00	200.00
Syrup	165.00	400.00
Toothpick	150.00	—
Tumbler	45.00	55.00
Vegetable, cov	90.00	—
*Wine	80.00	125.00

BUCKLE (Early Buckle)

Flint and non-flint pattern. The original maker is unknown. Shards have been found at the sites of the following glasshouses: Boston and Sandwich Glass Co., Sandwich, MA; Union Glass Co., Somerville, MA; and Burlington Glass Works, Hamilton, Ontario, Canada. Gillinder and Sons, Philadelphia, PA made the non-flint production, in the late 1870s.

	Flint	Non-Flint
Bowl		
8"	60.00	50.00
10"	65.00	50.00
Butter, cov	65.00	60.00
Cake Stand, 9-3/4"	—	30.00
Champagne	60.00	—
Compote		
Cov, hs, 6" d	95.00	40.00
Open, hs, 8-1/2"	40.00	35.00
Open, ls	40.00	35.00
Creamer, ah	120.00	40.00

	Flint	Non-Flint
Eggcup	35.00	25.00
Goblet	40.00	25.00
Pickle	40.00	15.00
Pitcher, water, ah	600.00	85.00
Salt		
flat, oval	30.00	15.00
footed	20.00	18.00
Sauce, flat	10.00	8.00
Spooner	35.00	27.50
Sugar, cov	75.00	55.00
Tumbler	55.00	30.00
Wine	75.00	35.00

BULL'S EYE

Flint made by the New England Glass Co. in the 1850s. Also found in colors and milk glass, which are worth more than double the price of clear.

	Clear
Bitters Bottle	80.00
Butter, cov	150.00
Carafe	45.00
Castor Bottle	35.00
Celery Vase	85.00
Champagne	95.00
Cologne Bottle	85.00
Cordial	75.00
Creamer, ah	125.00
Cruet, os	125.00
Decanter, qt, bar lip	120.00
Eggcup	
Cov	165.00
Open	48.00
*Goblet	65.00

	Clear
Lamp	100.00
Mug, 3-1/2", ah	110.00
Pitcher, water	285.00
Relish, oval	25.00
Salt	
Individual	40.00
Master, ftd	100.00
Spill holder	85.00
Spooner	40.00
Sugar, cov	125.00
Sweetmeat, cov	125.00
Tumbler	85.00
Water Bottle, tumble up	125.00
Whiskey	70.00
Wine	50.00

BULL'S EYE AND DAISY

Made by U.S. Glass Co. in 1909. Also made with amethyst, blue, green, and pink stain in eyes.

	Clear	Emerald Green	Ruby Stained
Bowl	15.00	20.00	30.00
Butter, cov	25.00	45.00	90.00
Celery Vase	20.00	25.00	40.00
Creamer	25.00	25.00	50.00
Decanter	—	110.00	—
Goblet	25.00	25.00	50.00
Pitcher, water	35.00	40.00	95.00
Salt Shaker	20.00	20.00	35.00
Sauce	7.50	10.00	20.00
Spooner	20.00	25.00	40.00
Sugar	22.00	30.00	45.00
Tumbler	15.00	20.00	35.00
Wine	20.00	25.00	40.00

BULL'S EYE WITH DIAMOND POINT (Owl, Union)

Flint made by New England Glass Co. c1869.

	Clear
Butter, cov	250.00
Celery Vase	150.00
Champagne	145.00
Cologne Bottle, os	90.00
Creamer	200.00
Cruet, os	225.00
Decanter, qt, os	200.00
Eggcup	90.00
Goblet	135.00
Honey Dish, flat	25.00
Lamp, finger, ah	165.00

	Clear
Pitcher, water, 10-1/4", tankard	650.00
Salt, master, cov	100.00
Sauce	20.00
Spill	75.00
Spooner	125.00
Sugar, cov	175.00
Syrup	175.00
Tumbler	145.00
Tumble-Up	165.00
Whiskey	150.00
Wine	135.00

BUTTERFLY AND FAN (Bird in Ring, Fan, Grace, Japanese)

Non-flint made by George Duncan & Sons, Pittsburgh, PA, c1880 and by Richards and Hartley Glass Co., Pittsburgh, PA, c1888.

	Clear		Clear
Bowl	30.00	Open, hs	30.00
Bread Plate	50.00	Creamer, ftd	45.00
Butter, cov		Goblet	65.00
Flat	100.00	Marmalade Jar	75.00
Footed	75.00	Pickle Jar, SP frame and cov	80.00
Celery Vase	75.00	Pitcher, water	115.00
Compote		Sauce, ftd	15.00
Cov, hs, 8" d	95.00	Spooner	30.00
Cov, hs, 7" d	95.00	Sugar cov, ftd	50.00

CABBAGE ROSE

Non-flint made by Central Glass Co., Wheeling, WV, c1870. Reproduced in clear and colors by Mosser Glass Co., Cambridge, OH, during the early 1960s.

	Clear		Clear
Basket, handled, 12"	125.00	Open, hs, 7-1/2"	75.00
Bitters Bottle, 6-1/2" h	125.00	Open, hs, 9-1/2"	100.00
Bowl, oval		Creamer, 5-1/2", ah	55.00
7-1/2"	30.00	Eggcup	45.00
9-1/2"	40.00	*Goblet	40.00
Bowl, round		Mug	60.00
6"	25.00	Pickle Dish	35.00
7-1/2", cov	65.00	Pitcher	
Butter, cov	60.00	Milk	150.00
Cake Stand		Water	125.00
11"	40.00	Relish, 8-1/2" l, 5" w, rose-filled	
12-1/2"	50.00	horn of plenty center	35.00
Celery Vase	48.00	Salt, master, ftd	25.00
Champagne	50.00	*Sauce, 4"	10.00
Compote		Spooner	25.00
Cov, hs, 8-1/2"	120.00	Sugar, cov	55.00
Cov, ls, 6"	95.00	Tumbler	40.00
Cov, ls, 7-1/2"	100.00	Wine	40.00

CABLE

Flint, c1860. Made by Boston and Sandwich Glass Co. to commemorate the laying of the Atlantic Cable. Also found with amber-stained panels and in opaque colors and other colors (rare).

	Clear		Clear
Bowl		*Goblet	70.00
8", ftd	45.00	Honey Dish	15.00
9"	70.00	Lamp, 8-3/4"	
Butter, cov	100.00	Glass Base	135.00
Cake Stand, 9"	100.00	Marble Base	100.00
Celery Vase	70.00	Miniature Lamp	500.00
Champagne	250.00	Pitcher, water, rare	650.00
Compote, open		Plate, 6"	75.00
hs, 5-1/2"	65.00	Salt, individual, flat	35.00
ls, 7"	50.00	Salt, master	
ls, 9"	35.00	Cov	95.00
ls, 11"	75.00	Ftd	45.00
Creamer	225.00	Sauce, flat	15.00
Decanter, qt, ground stopper	295.00	Spooner	40.00
Eggcup		Sugar, cov	120.00
Cov	225.00	Syrup	225.00
Open	60.00	Tumbler, ftd	200.00
		Wine	175.00

CANADIAN

Non-flint possibly made by Burlington Glass Works, Hamilton, Ontario, Canada, c1870.

	Clear		Clear
Bowl, 7" d, 4-1/2" h, ftd	65.00	Butter, cov	85.00
Bread Plate, 10"	45.00	Cake Stand, 9-1/4"	85.00

	Clear
Celery Vase	65.00
Compote	
Cov, hs, 6"	90.00
Cov, hs, 7"	100.00
Cov, hs, 8"	110.00
Cov, ls, 6"	50.00
Cov, ls, 8"	75.00
Open, ls, 7"	35.00
Creamer	65.00
Goblet	45.00

	Clear
Mug, small	45.00
Pitcher	
Milk	90.00
Water	125.00
Plate, 6", handles	30.00
Sauce	
Flat	15.00
Footed	20.00
Spooner	45.00
Sugar, cov	90.00
Wine	45.00

CANE (Cane, Insert, Hobnailed Diamond and Star)

Non-flint made by Gillinder and Sons Glass Co., Philadelphia, PA, and by McKee Bros. Glass Co., c1885. Goblets and toddy plates with inverted "buttons" are known.

	Amber	Apple Green	Blue	Clear	Vaseline
Butter, cov	45.00	60.00	75.00	40.00	60.00
Celery Vase	38.00	40.00	50.00	32.50	40.00
Compote, open, ls, 5-3/4"	28.00	30.00	35.00	25.00	35.00
Cordial	—	—	—	25.00	—
Creamer	35.00	40.00	50.00	25.00	30.00
Finger Bowl	20.00	30.00	35.00	15.00	30.00
Goblet	25.00	40.00	35.00	20.00	40.00
Honey Dish	—	—	—	15.00	—
Match Holder, kettle	20.00	—	35.00	30.00	35.00
Pickle	25.00	20.00	25.00	15.00	20.00
Pitcher					
Milk	60.00	55.00	65.00	40.00	55.00
Water	80.00	85.00	80.00	48.00	85.00
Plate, toddy, 4-1/2"	20.00	25.00	30.00	16.50	20.00
Relish	25.00	26.00	25.00	15.00	20.00
Salt & Pepper	60.00	50.00	80.00	30.00	70.00
Sauce, flat	—	10.00	—	7.00	—
Slipper	30.00	—	25.00	15.00	30.00
Spooner	42.00	35.00	30.00	20.00	30.00
Sugar, cov	45.00	45.00	45.00	25.00	45.00
Tray, water	35.00	40.00	50.00	30.00	45.00
Tumbler	24.00	30.00	35.00	20.00	25.00
Waste Bowl, 7-1/2"	32.50	30.00	35.00	20.00	30.00
Wine	35.00	40.00	35.00	20.00	35.00

CAROLINA (Inverness, Mayflower)

Made by Bryce Bros., Pittsburgh, PA, c1890 and later by U.S. Glass Co., as part of the States series, c1903. Ruby-stained pieces often were made as souvenirs. Some clear pieces found with gilt or purple stain.

	Clear	Ruby Stained
Bowl, berry	15.00	—
Butter, cov	35.00	—
Cake Stand	35.00	—
Compote		
Open, hs, 8"	38.50	—
Open, hs, 9-1/2"	20.00	—
Open, jelly	10.00	—
Creamer	20.00	—
Goblet	25.00	45.00
Mug	20.00	35.00

	Clear	Ruby Stained
Pitcher, milk	45.00	—
Plate, 7-1/2"	10.00	—
Relish	10.00	—
Salt Shaker	15.00	35.00
Sauce		
Flat	8.00	—
Footed	10.00	—
Spooner	20.00	—
Sugar, cov	25.00	—
Tumbler	10.00	—
Wine	20.00	35.00

CATHEDRAL (Orion, Waffle and Fine Cut)

Non-flint pattern made by Bryce Bros. Pittsburgh, PA, in the 1880s and by U.S. Glass Co. in 1891. Also found in ruby stained (add 50%).

	Amber	Amethyst	Blue	Clear	Vaseline
Bowl, berry, 8"	40.00	60.00	50.00	45.00	45.00
Butter, cov	60.00	110.00	40.00	45.00	60.00

	Amber	Amethyst	Blue	Clear	Vaseline
Cake Stand	50.00	75.00	65.00	40.00	65.00
Celery Vase	35.00	60.00	40.00	30.00	40.00
Compote					
Cov, hs, 8"	80.00	125.00	100.00	70.00	90.00
Open, hs, 9-1/2"	50.00	85.00	65.00	55.00	—
Open, ls, 7"	45.00	80.00	35.00	25.00	50.00
Open, jelly	—	—	—	25.00	—
Creamer					
Flat, sq	50.00	85.00	—	35.00	50.00
Tall	45.00	80.00	50.00	30.00	45.00
Cruet, os	125.00	—	—	65.00	—
Goblet	50.00	70.00	50.00	40.00	60.00
Lamp, 12-1/4" h	—	—	185.00	—	—
Pitcher, water	75.00	110.00	75.00	60.00	100.00
Relish, fish shape	40.00	50.00	50.00	—	45.00
Salt, boat shape	20.00	30.00	25.00	15.00	25.00
Sauce					
Flat	15.00	30.00	20.00	15.00	20.00
Footed	15.00	35.00	20.00	15.00	20.00
Spooner	40.00	65.00	50.00	35.00	45.00
Sugar, cov	70.00	100.00	60.00	50.00	60.00
Tumbler	40.00	40.00	35.00	25.00	40.00
Wine	40.00	60.00	55.00	30.00	50.00

COLORADO (Lacy Medallion)

Non-flint States pattern made by U.S. Glass Co. in 1898. Made in amethyst stained, ruby stained, and opaque white with enamel floral trim, all of which are scarce. Some pieces found with ornate silver frames or feet. Purists consider these two separate patterns, with the Lacy Medallion restricted to souvenir pieces. Reproductions have been made.

	Blue	Clear	Green
Banana Stand	65.00	35.00	50.00
Bowl			
6"	35.00	25.00	30.00
7-1/2", ftd	40.00	25.00	35.00
8-1/2", ftd	65.00	45.00	60.00
Butter, cov	175.00	60.00	100.00
Cake Stand	70.00	55.00	65.00
Celery Vase	65.00	35.00	75.00
Compote			
Open, ls, 5"	35.00	20.00	30.00
Open, ls, 6"	45.00	20.00	40.00
Open, ls, 9-1/4"	85.00	35.00	65.00
Creamer			
Individual	35.00	30.00	25.00
Regular	95.00	45.00	70.00
Mug	40.00	20.00	30.00
Nappy	40.00	20.00	35.00
Pitcher			
Milk	250.00	—	100.00
Water	375.00	95.00	175.00
Plate			
6"	50.00	15.00	45.00
8"	65.00	20.00	60.00
Punch Cup	30.00	18.00	25.00
Salt Shaker	65.00	30.00	40.00
Sauce, ruffled	30.00	15.00	25.00
Sherbet	50.00	25.00	45.00
Spooner	65.00	40.00	70.00
Sugar			
Cov, regular	75.00	60.00	70.00
Open, individual	35.00	24.00	30.00
*Toothpick	55.00	30.00	35.00
Tray, calling card	45.00	25.00	35.00
Tumbler	35.00	15.00	30.00
Vase, 12"	85.00	35.00	60.00
Violet Bowl	60.00	—	—
Wine	—	25.00	40.00

COMET

Flint, possibly made by Boston and Sandwich Glass Co. in the early 1850s.

	Clear
Butter, cov	200.00
Compote, open, ls	140.00
Creamer	175.00
Goblet	135.00
Mug	135.00

	Clear
Pitcher, water	750.00
Spooner	95.00
Sugar, cov	175.00
Tumbler	110.00
Whiskey, w/handle	250.00

CONNECTICUT

Non-flint, one of the States patterns made by U.S. Glass Co. c1900. Found in plain and engraved. Two varieties of ruby-stained toothpicks ($90.00) have been identified.

	Clear
Biscuit jar	25.00
Bowl	
4"	10.00
8"	15.00
Butter, cov	35.00
Cake Stand	40.00
Celery Tray	20.00
Celery Vase	25.00
Compote	
Cov, hs	40.00
Open, hs, 7"	25.00
Creamer	28.00

	Clear
Dish, 8", oblong	20.00
Lamp, enamel dec	85.00
Lemonade, handled	20.00
Pitcher, water	40.00
Relish	15.00
Salt & Pepper	35.00
Spooner	25.00
Sugar, cov	35.00
Sugar Shaker	35.00
Toothpick	50.00
Tumbler, water	20.00
Wine	35.00

CRYSTAL WEDDING (Collins, Crystal Anniversary)

Non-flint made by Adams Glass Co., Pittsburgh, PA, c1890 and by U.S. Glass Co. in 1891. Also found in frosted, amber stained, and cobalt blue (rare). Heavily reproduced in clear, ruby stained, and milk with enamel.

	Clear	Ruby Stained
Banana Stand	95.00	—
Bowl		
4-1/2", individual berry	15.00	—
7", sq, cov	75.00	85.00
8", sq, berry	50.00	85.00
8", sq, cov	60.00	95.00
Butter, cov	75.00	125.00
Cake Plate, sq	45.00	85.00
Cake Stand, 10"	65.00	—
Celery Vase	45.00	75.00
Compote		
*Cov, hs, 7" x 13"	100.00	110.00
Open, ls, 5", sq	50.00	55.00
Creamer	50.00	75.00
Cruet	125.00	200.00
*Goblet	55.00	85.00
Nappy, handle	25.00	—
Pickle	25.00	40.00

	Clear	Ruby Stained
Pitcher		
Milk, round	110.00	125.00
Milk, sq	125.00	200.00
Water, round	110.00	210.00
Water, sq	165.00	225.00
Plate, 10"	25.00	40.00
Relish	20.00	40.00
Salt		
Individual	25.00	40.00
Master	35.00	65.00
Salt Shaker	65.00	75.00
Sauce	15.00	20.00
Spooner	30.00	60.00
Sugar, cov	70.00	85.00
Syrup	150.00	200.00
Tumbler	35.00	45.00
Vase		
Footed, twisted	25.00	—
Swung	25.00	—
Wine	45.00	70.00

DAISY AND BUTTON

Non-flint made in the 1880s by several companies in many different forms. In continuous production since inception. Original manufacturers include: Bryce Brothers, Doyle & Co., Hobbs, Brockunier & Co., George Duncan & Sons, Boston & Sandwich Glass Co., Beatty & Sons, and U.S. Glass Co. Reproductions have existed since the early 1930s in original and new colors. Several companies, including L.G. Wright, Imperial Glass Co., Fenton Art Glass Co., and Degenhart Glass Co, too, have made reproductions. Also found in amberina, amber stain, and ruby stained.

	Amber	Apple Green	Blue	Clear	Vaseline
Bowl, triangular	40.00	45.00	45.00	25.00	65.00
Bread Plate, 13"	35.00	60.00	35.00	20.00	40.00
*Butter, cov					
Round	70.00	90.00	70.00	65.00	95.00
Square	110.00	115.00	110.00	100.00	120.00
Butter Pat	30.00	40.00	35.00	25.00	35.00
*Canoe					
4"	12.00	24.00	15.00	10.00	24.00

	Amber	Apple Green	Blue	Clear	Vaseline
8-1/2"	30.00	35.00	30.00	25.00	35.00
12"	60.00	35.00	28.00	20.00	40.00
14"	30.00	40.00	35.00	25.00	40.00
*Castor Set					
4 bottle, glass standard	90.00	85.00	95.00	65.00	75.00
5 bottle, metal standard	100.00	100.00	110.00	100.00	95.00
Celery Vase	48.00	55.00	40.00	30.00	55.00
*Compote					
Cov, hs, 6"	35.00	50.00	45.00	25.00	50.00
Open, hs, 8"	75.00	65.00	60.00	40.00	65.00
*Creamer	35.00	40.00	40.00	18.00	35.00
*Cruet, os	100.00	80.00	75.00	45.00	80.00
Eggcup	20.00	30.00	25.00	15.00	30.00
Finger Bowl	30.00	50.00	35.00	30.00	42.00
*Goblet	40.00	50.00	40.00	25.00	40.00
*Hat, 2-1/2"	30.00	35.00	40.00	20.00	40.00
Ice Cream Tray, 14" x 9" x 2"	75.00	50.00	55.00	35.00	55.00
Ice Tub	—	35.00	—	—	75.00
Inkwell	40.00	50.00	45.00	30.00	45.00
Parfait	25.00	35.00	30.00	20.00	35.00
Pickle Castor	125.00	90.00	150.00	75.00	150.00
*Pitcher, water					
Bulbous, reed handle	125.00	95.00	90.00	75.00	90.00
Tankard	62.00	65.00	62.00	60.00	65.00
*Plate					
5", leaf shape	20.00	24.00	12.00	12.00	25.00
6", round	10.00	22.00	15.00	6.50	24.00
7", square	25.00	35.00	25.00	15.00	35.00
Punch Bowl, stand	90.00	100.00	95.00	85.00	100.00
*Salt & Pepper	30.00	40.00	30.00	20.00	35.00
*Sauce, 4"	18.00	25.00	18.00	15.00	25.00
*Slipper					
5"	45.00	48.00	50.00	45.00	50.00
11-1/2"	40.00	50.00	30.00	35.00	50.00
*Spooner	40.00	40.00	45.00	35.00	45.00
*Sugar, cov	45.00	50.00	45.00	35.00	50.00
Syrup	45.00	50.00	45.00	30.00	45.00
*Toothpick					
Round	40.00	55.00	25.00	40.00	45.00
Urn	25.00	30.00	25.00	15.00	30.00
*Tray	65.00	65.00	60.00	35.00	60.00
Tumbler	18.00	30.00	35.00	15.00	25.00
Vase, wall pocket	125.00	—	—	—	—
*Wine	15.00	25.00	20.00	10.00	45.00

DAISY AND BUTTON WITH CROSSBARS (Daisy and Thumbprint Crossbar, Daisy and Button with Crossbar and Thumbprint Band, Daisy with Crossbar, Mikado)

Non-flint made by Richards and Hartley, Tarentum, PA, c1885. Reissued by U.S. Glass Co. after 1891. Shards have been found at Burlington Glass Works, Hamilton, Ontario, Canada.

	Amber	Blue	Clear	Vaseline
Bowl				
6"	25.00	30.00	15.00	25.00
9"	30.00	40.00	25.00	30.00
Bread Plate	30.00	45.00	25.00	35.00
Butter, cov				
Flat	55.00	55.00	45.00	55.00
Footed	—	75.00	25.00	60.00
Celery Vase	36.00	40.00	30.00	50.00
Compote				
Cov, hs, 8"	55.00	65.00	45.00	55.00
Open, hs, 8"	45.00	50.00	30.00	45.00
Open, ls, 7"	30.00	—	20.00	45.00
Creamer				
Individual	30.00	30.00	20.00	30.00
Regular	45.00	45.00	35.00	40.00
Cruet, os	75.00	85.00	35.00	100.00
Goblet	40.00	40.00	25.00	48.00
Mug, 3" h	15.00	18.00	12.50	20.00
Pitcher				
Milk	90.00	95.00	45.00	90.00
Water	145.00	110.00	65.00	125.00

	Amber	Blue	Clear	Vaseline
Salt & Pepper	40.00	50.00	30.00	45.00
Sauce				
Flat	15.00	18.00	10.00	15.00
Footed	18.00	25.00	15.00	24.00
Spooner	35.00	35.00	25.00	35.00
Sugar, cov				
Individual	25.00	35.00	10.00	25.00
Regular	50.00	60.00	25.00	55.00
Syrup	125.00	125.00	65.00	125.00
Toothpick	40.00	40.00	28.00	35.00
Tumbler	20.00	25.00	18.00	25.00
Wine	30.00	35.00	25.00	30.00

DAKOTA (Baby Thumbprint, Thumbprint Band)

Non-flint made by Ripley and Co., Pittsburgh, PA, in the late 1880s and early 1890s. Later reissued by U.S. Glass Co. as one of the States patterns. Prices listed are for etched fern and berry pattern; also found with fern and no berry, and oak-leaf etching, and scarcer grape etching. Other etchings known include fish, swan, peacock, bird and insect, bird and flowers, ivy and berry, stag, spider and insect in web, buzzard on dead tree and crane catching fish. Sometimes ruby stained with or without souvenir markings; ftd. Sauce known in cobalt blue. There is a four-piece table set available in a "hotel" variant. Prices are about 20 percent higher than for the regular type.

	Clear Etched	Clear Plain	Ruby Stained
Basket, 10" x 2"	205.00	175.00	300.00
Bottle, 5-1/2"	85.00	65.00	—
Bowl, berry	45.00	35.00	—
Butter, cov	65.00	40.00	125.00
Cake Cover, 8" d	300.00	200.00	—
Cake Stand, 10-1/2"	95.00	75.00	—
Celery Tray	40.00	25.00	—
Celery Vase	40.00	30.00	—
Compote			
Cov, hs, 5"	60.00	50.00	—
Cov, hs, 7"	70.00	55.00	—
Cov, hs, 10"	125.00	100.00	—
Open, ls, 6"	45.00	35.00	—
Open, ls, 8"	50.00	40.00	—
Open, ls, 10"	75.00	65.00	—
Condiment Tray	—	75.00	—
Creamer	55.00	30.00	—
Cruet	125.00	100.00	175.00
Goblet	35.00	25.00	75.00
Pitcher			
Milk	145.00	80.00	200.00
Water	125.00	75.00	190.00
Plate, 10"	85.00	75.00	—
Salt Shaker	65.00	50.00	125.00
Sauce			
Flat, 4" d	20.00	15.00	30.00
Footed, 5" d	25.00	15.00	35.00
Spooner	30.00	25.00	65.00
Sugar, cov	65.00	55.00	85.00
Tankard	125.00	95.00	205.00
Tray			
Water, 13" d	100.00	75.00	—
Wine, 10" to 12"	125.00	90.00	—
Tumbler	35.00	30.00	55.00
Waste Bowl	65.00	50.00	75.00
Wine	30.00	20.00	55.00

DEER AND PINE TREE (Deer and Doe)

Non-flint made by Belmont Glass Co. and McKee & Bros. Glass Co. c1886. Souvenir mugs with gilt found in clear and olive green. Also made in canary (vaseline). The goblet has been reproduced since 1938. L. G. Wright Glass Co. has reproduced the goblet in clear glass using new molds.

	Amber	Apple Green	Blue	Clear
Bread Plate	90.00	100.00	100.00	65.00
Butter, cov	165.00	165.00	165.00	95.00
Cake Stand	—	—	—	75.00
Celery Vase	—	—	—	75.00

	Amber	Apple Green	Blue	Clear
Compote				
Cov, hs, 8", sq.	—	—	—	100.00
Open, hs, 7"	—	—	—	45.00
Open, hs, 9"	—	—	—	55.00
Creamer	95.00	85.00	90.00	65.00
Finger Bowl	—	—	—	55.00
*Goblet	—	—	—	55.00
Marmalade Jar	—	—	—	90.00
Mug	40.00	45.00	50.00	40.00
Pickle	—	—	—	30.00
Pitcher				
Milk	—	—	—	90.00
Water	165.00	165.00	165.00	100.00
Platter, 8" x 13"	75.00	—	80.00	60.00
Sauce				
Flat	—	—	—	20.00
Footed	—	—	—	25.00
Spooner	—	—	—	65.00
Sugar, cov	—	—	—	85.00
Tray, water	100.00	—	90.00	60.00

DELAWARE (American Beauty, Four Petal Flower)

Non-flint made by U.S. Glass Co., Pittsburgh, PA, 1899-1909. Also made Diamond Glass Co., Montreal, Quebec, Canada, c1902. Also found in amethyst (scarce), clear with rose trim, custard, and milk glass. Prices are for pieces with perfect gold trim.

	Clear	Green with Gold	Rose with Gold
Banana Bowl	40.00	55.00	65.00
Bowl			
8"	30.00	40.00	50.00
9"	25.00	60.00	75.00
Bottle, os	80.00	150.00	185.00
Bride's Basket, SP frame	75.00	115.00	165.00
*Butter, cov	50.00	115.00	150.00
Claret Jug, tankard shape	110.00	195.00	200.00
Celery Vase, flat	75.00	90.00	95.00
*Creamer	45.00	65.00	70.00
Cruet, os	90.00	200.00	250.00
Finger Bowl	25.00	50.00	75.00
Lamp Shade, electric	85.00	—	100.00
Pin Tray	30.00	55.00	95.00
Pitcher, water	50.00	95.00	95.00
Pomade Box, jeweled	100.00	250.00	350.00
Puff Box, bulbous, jeweled	100.00	200.00	315.00
Punch Cup	18.00	30.00	35.00
Sauce, 5-1/2", boat	15.00	35.00	30.00
Spooner	45.00	50.00	55.00
*Sugar, cov	65.00	85.00	100.00
Toothpick	35.00	125.00	155.00
Tumbler	20.00	40.00	45.00
Vase			
6"	25.00	60.00	70.00
8"	25.00	70.00	75.00
9-1/2"	40.00	80.00	85.00

DIAMOND POINT (Diamond Point with Ribs, Pineapple, Sawtooth, Stepped Diamond Point)

Flint originally made by Boston and Sandwich Glass Co. c1850 and by the New England Glass Co., East Cambridge, MA, c1860. Many other companies manufactured this pattern throughout the 19th century. Rare in color.

	Flint	Non-Flint		Flint	Non-Flint
Ale Glass, 6-1/4" h	85.00	—	Butter, cov	95.00	50.00
Bowl			Cake Stand, 14"	185.00	—
7", cov	60.00	20.00	Candlesticks, pr	165.00	—
8", cov	60.00	20.00	Castor Bottle	25.00	15.00
8", open	45.00	15.00	Celery Vase	75.00	30.00

	Flint	Non-Flint		Flint	Non-Flint
Champagne	85.00	35.00	Lemonade	55.00	—
Claret	90.00	—	Mustard, cov	25.00	—
Compote			Pitcher		
Cov, hs, 8"	185.00	60.00	Pint	200.00	—
Open, hs, 10-1/2", flared	100.00	—	Quart	300.00	—
Open, hs, 11",			Plate		
scalloped rim	110.00	—	6"	30.00	—
Open, ls, 7-1/2"	50.00	40.00	8"	50.00	—
Cordial	165.00	—	Salt, master, cov	75.00	—
Creamer, ah	115.00	—	Sauce, flat	15.00	—
Decanter, qt, os	200.00	—	Spill Holder	45.00	—
Eggcup			Spooner	45.00	30.00
Cov	75.00	50.00	Sugar, cov	95.00	55.00
Open	40.00	20.00	Syrup	170.00	—
Goblet	45.00	35.00	Tumbler, bar	65.00	30.00
Honey Dish	15.00	—	Whiskey, ah	85.00	—
			Wine	75.00	30.00

EGG IN SAND (Bean, Stippled Oval)

Non-flint, c1885. Has been reported in colors, including blue and amber, but rare.

	Clear		Clear
Bread Plate, octagonal	25.00	Relish	15.00
Butter, cov	40.00	Salt & Pepper	65.00
Compote, cov, jelly	45.00	Sauce	10.00
Creamer	30.00	Spooner, flat rim	30.00
Dish, swan center	40.00	Sugar, cov	35.00
Goblet	30.00	Tray, water	40.00
Pitcher, water	45.00	Tumbler	30.00
		Wine	35.00

EXCELSIOR

Flint attributed to several firms, including Boston and Sandwich Glass Co., Sandwich, MA; McKee Bros., Pittsburgh, PA; and Ihmsen & Co., Pittsburgh, PA, 1850s-60s. Quality and design vary. Prices are for high-quality flint. Very rare in color.

	Clear		Clear
Ale Glass	50.00	Quart	85.00
Bar Bottle	85.00	Eggcup	
Bitters Bottle	95.00	Double	45.00
Bowl, 10", open	125.00	Single	40.00
Butter, cov	100.00	Goblet	50.00
Candlestick, 9-1/2" h	125.00	Lamp, hand	95.00
Celery Vase, scalloped top	85.00	Mug	30.00
Champagne	60.00	Pickle Jar, cov	45.00
Claret	45.00	Pitcher, water	400.00
Compote		Salt, master	30.00
Cov, ls	125.00	Spillholder	75.00
Open, hs	85.00	Spooner	60.00
Cordial	40.00	Sugar, cov	110.00
Creamer	85.00	Syrup	125.00
Decanter		Tumbler, bar	50.00
Pint	85.00	Whiskey, Maltese Cross	65.00
		Wine	45.00

EYEWINKER (Cannon Ball, Crystal Ball, Winking Eye)

Non-flint made in Findlay, Ohio, in 1889. Reportedly made by Dalzell, Gilmore and Leighton Glass Co., which was organized in 1883 in West Virginia and moved to Findlay in 1888. Made only in clear glass; reproduced in color by several companies, including L. G. Wright Co. A goblet and toothpick were not originally made in this pattern.

	Clear		Clear
Banana Stand, hs	135.00	Cov, hs, 6-1/2"	85.00
Bowl		Cov, hs, 9-1/2"	150.00
6-1/2"	25.00	Open, 7-1/4", fluted	65.00
9", cov	75.00	Open, 4-1/2", jelly	45.00
*Butter, cov	70.00	Creamer	65.00
Cake Stand, 8"	55.00	Cruet	65.00
Celery Vase	45.00	*Honey Dish	40.00
*Compote		Lamp, kerosene	125.00

	Clear
Nappy, folded sides, 7-1/4"	30.00
*Pitcher, water	95.00
Plate	
7"	30.00
9", sq, upturned sides	65.00
10", upturned sides	85.00

	Clear
Salt Shaker	35.00
Sauce	15.00
Spooner	35.00
*Sugar, cov	55.00
Syrup, pewter top	125.00
*Tumbler	45.00

FEATHER (Cambridge Feather, Feather and Quill, Fine Cut and Feather, Indiana Feather, Indiana Swirl, Prince's Feather, Swirl, Swirl and Feather)

Non-flint made by McKee & Bros. Glass Co., Pittsburgh, PA, 1896-1901; Beatty-Brady Glass Co., Dunkirk, IN, c1903; and Cambridge Glass Co., Cambridge, Ohio, c1902-03. Later the pattern was reissued with variations and quality differences. Also found in amber stain (rare).

	Clear	Emerald Green
Banana Boat, ftd	75.00	175.00
Bowl, oval		
7" x 9", ftd	35.00	—
8-1/2"	25.00	—
9-1/4"	20.00	75.00
Bowl, round		
6"	20.00	—
7"	25.00	75.00
8"	30.00	85.00
Butter, cov	55.00	150.00
Cake Plate	65.00	—
Cake Stand		
8"	45.00	175.00
9-1/2"	50.00	175.00
11"	70.00	175.00
Celery Vase	45.00	80.00
Champagne	65.00	—
Compote		
Cov, hs, 8-1/2"	150.00	450.00
Cov, ls, 4-1/4", jelly	100.00	150.00
Cov, ls, 8-1/4"	150.00	—
Open, ls, 4"	20.00	—
Open, ls, 6"	25.00	—

	Clear	Emerald Green
Open, ls, 7"	35.00	—
Open, ls, 8"	40.00	—
Cordial	125.00	—
Creamer	40.00	85.00
Cruet, os	45.00	250.00
Dishes, nest of 3: 7", 8", and 9"	40.00	—
Goblet	55.00	150.00
Honey Dish	15.00	—
Marmalade Jar	125.00	—
Pickle Castor	145.00	—
Pitcher		
Milk	50.00	165.00
Water	75.00	250.00
Plate, 10"	50.00	75.00
Relish	20.00	—
Salt Shaker	35.00	70.00
Sauce	12.00	—
Spooner	25.00	60.00
Sugar, cov	50.00	85.00
Syrup	125.00	300.00
Toothpick	85.00	165.00
Tumbler	50.00	85.00
*Wine		
Scalloped border	40.00	—
Straight border	25.00	—

FINECUT (Flower in Square)

Non-flint made by Bryce Bros., Pittsburgh, PA, c1885, and by U.S. Glass Co. in 1891.

	Amber	Blue	Clear	Vaseline
Bowl, 8-1/4"	15.00	20.00	10.00	15.00
Bread Plate	50.00	60.00	25.00	50.00
Butter, cov	55.00	75.00	45.00	60.00
Cake Stand	—	—	35.00	—
Celery Tray	—	45.00	25.00	40.00
Celery Vase, SP holder	—	—	—	115.00
Creamer	60.00	40.00	35.00	75.00
Goblet	45.00	55.00	22.00	42.00
Pitcher, water	100.00	100.00	60.00	115.00
Plate				
7"	25.00	40.00	15.00	20.00
10"	30.00	50.00	21.00	45.00
Relish	15.00	25.00	10.00	20.00
Sauce, flat	14.00	15.00	10.00	14.00
Spooner	30.00	45.00	18.00	40.00
Sugar, cov	45.00	55.00	35.00	45.00
Tray, water	50.00	55.00	25.00	50.00
Tumbler	—	—	18.00	28.00
Wine	—	—	24.00	30.00

FLAMINGO HABITAT

Non-flint, maker unknown, c1870, etched pattern.

	Clear
Bowl, 10", oval	40.00
Butter, cov	65.00
Celery Vase	45.00
Champagne	45.00
Cheese Dish, blown	110.00
Compote	
Cov, 4-1/2"	75.00
Cov, 6-1/2"	95.00

	Clear
Open, 5", jelly	35.00
Open, 6"	40.00
Creamer	40.00
Goblet	45.00
Sauce, ftd	15.00
Spooner	25.00
Sugar, cov	50.00
Tumbler	30.00
Wine	45.00

FLORIDA (Emerald Green Herringbone, Paneled Herringbone)

Non-flint made by U.S. Glass Co., in the 1890s. One of the States patterns. Goblet reproduced in green, amber, and other colors.

	Clear	Emerald Green
Berry Set	75.00	110.00
Bowl, 7-3/4"	10.00	15.00
Butter, cov	50.00	85.00
Cake Stand		
Large	60.00	75.00
Small	30.00	40.00
Celery Vase	30.00	35.00
Compote, open, hs, 6-1/2", sq	—	40.00
Creamer	30.00	45.00
Cruet, os	40.00	110.00
*Goblet, 5-3/4" h	25.00	40.00
Mustard Pot, attached		
under plate, cov	25.00	45.00

	Clear	Emerald Green
Nappy	15.00	25.00
Pitcher, water	50.00	75.00
Plate		
7-1/2"	12.00	18.00
9-1/4"	15.00	25.00
Relish		
6", sq	10.00	15.00
8-1/2", sq	15.00	20.00
Salt Shaker	25.00	50.00
Sauce	5.00	7.50
Spooner	20.00	35.00
Sugar, cov	35.00	50.00
Syrup	60.00	175.00
Tumbler	20.00	35.00
Wine	25.00	50.00

GALLOWAY (Mirror Plate, U.S. Mirror, Virginia, Woodrow)

Non-flint made by U.S. Glass Co., Pittsburgh, PA, c1904-19. Jefferson Glass Co., Toronto, Canada, produced it from 1900-25. Clear glass with and without gold trim; also known with rose satin and ruby stain. Vases known in emerald green. Toothpick reproduced in several colors.

	Clear with Gold	Rose Stained
Basket, no gold	75.00	125.00
Bowl		
6-1/2", belled	20.00	35.00
8-1/2", oval	35.00	45.00
8-1/2", round	30.00	50.00
9", rect	30.00	45.00
11" d, round	45.00	65.00
Butter, cov	65.00	125.00
Cake Stand	70.00	95.00
Carafe, water	55.00	85.00
Celery Vase	35.00	75.00
Champagne	60.00	175.00
Compote		
Cov, hs, 6"	90.00	125.00
Open, hs, 5-1/2"	25.00	40.00
Open, hs, 10", scalloped	55.00	75.00
Creamer	30.00	50.00
Cruet	45.00	125.00
Eggcup	40.00	60.00
Finger Bowl	40.00	65.00
Goblet	75.00	95.00
Lemonade	35.00	45.00
Mug	40.00	50.00
Nappy, tricorn	25.00	50.00
Olive, 6"	20.00	30.00

	Clear with Gold	Rose Stained
Pickle Castor, sp holder and lid	75.00	200.00
Pitcher		
Milk	60.00	80.00
Tankard	75.00	125.00
Water, ice lip	65.00	175.00
Plate, 8", round	40.00	65.00
Punch Bowl	160.00	225.00
Punch Bowl Plate, 20"	80.00	125.00
Punch Cup	10.00	15.00
Relish	20.00	30.00
Rose Bowl	25.00	60.00
Salt, master	35.00	60.00
Salt & Pepper, pr	40.00	75.00
Sauce		
Flat, 4"	10.00	20.00
Footed, 4-1/2"	10.00	20.00
Sherbet	25.00	30.00
Spooner	30.00	80.00
Sugar, cov	55.00	85.00
Sugar Shaker	40.00	100.00
Syrup	65.00	135.00
*Toothpick	30.00	55.00
Tumbler	35.00	45.00
Vase, swung	30.00	—
Waste Bowl	40.00	65.00
Water Bottle	40.00	85.00
Wine	45.00	65.00

GARFIELD DRAPE (Canadian Drape)

Non-flint issued in 1881 by Adams & Co., Pittsburgh, PA, after the assassination of President Garfield.

	Clear
Bread Plate	
Memorial, portrait of Garfield	65.00
"We Mourn Our Nation's Loss," portrait	75.00
Butter, cov	70.00
Cake Stand, 9-1/2"	70.00
Celery Vase	55.00
Compote	
Cov, hs, 8"	100.00
Cov, ls, 6"	85.00
Open, hs, 8-1/2"	40.00
Creamer	40.00
Goblet	40.00

	Clear
Honey Dish	15.00
Pitcher	
Milk	70.00
Water, ah	75.00
Water, strap handle	100.00
Relish, oval	20.00
Sauce	
Flat	8.50
Footed	12.00
Spooner	35.00
Sugar, cov	60.00
Tumbler	35.00

GEORGIA (Peacock Feather)

Non-flint made by Richards and Hartley Glass Co., Tarentum, PA, and reissued by U.S. Glass Co. in 1902 as part of the States series. Rare in blue. (Chamber lamp, pedestal base, $275.00). No goblet known in pattern.

	Clear
Bonbon, ftd	25.00
Bowl, 8"	30.00
Butter, cov	45.00
Cake Stand, 10"	50.00
Castor Set, 2 bottles	60.00
Celery Tray, 11-3/4"	35.00
Children's	
Cake Stand	35.00
Creamer	35.00
Compote	
Cov, hs, 5"	35.00
Cov, hs, 6"	40.00
Cov, hs, 7"	45.00
Cov, hs, 8"	50.00
Open, hs, 5"	20.00
Open, hs, 6"	25.00
Open, hs, 7"	30.00
Open, hs, 8"	35.00

	Clear
Condiment Set, tray, oil cruet, salt & pepper	75.00
Creamer	35.00
Cruet, os	55.00
Decanter	70.00
Lamp	
Chamber, pedestal	85.00
Hand, oil, 7"	80.00
Mug	25.00
Nappy	25.00
Pitcher, water	70.00
Plate, 5-1/4"	15.00
Relish	15.00
Salt Shaker	40.00
Sauce	10.00
Spooner	35.00
Sugar, cov	45.00
Syrup, metal lid	65.00
Tumbler	35.00

HEART WITH THUMBPRINT (Bull's Eye in Heart, Columbia, Columbian, Heart and Thumbprint)

Non-flint made by Tarentum Glass Co. 1898-1906. Some clear and emerald green pieces have gold trim. Made experimentally in custard, blue custard, opaque Nile green, and cobalt.

	Clear	Emerald Green	Ruby Stain
Banana Boat	75.00	—	145.00
Barber Bottle	115.00	—	—
Bowl			
7" sq	35.00	100.00	95.00
9-1/2" sq	35.00	125.00	100.00
10" scalloped	45.00	100.00	90.00
Butter, cov	125.00	175.00	145.00
Cake Stand, 9"	150.00	—	195.00
Carafe, water	100.00	—	160.00
Card Tray	20.00	55.00	95.00
Celery Vase	65.00	—	110.00
Compote, open, hs			
7-1/2", scalloped	150.00	—	185.00
8-1/2"	100.00	—	200.00
Cordial, 3" h	140.00	175.00	175.00
Creamer			
Individual	30.00	45.00	50.00
Regular	60.00	110.00	175.00
Cruet	75.00	—	—
Finger Bowl	45.00	85.00	95.00
Goblet	65.00	125.00	130.00
Hair Receiver, lid	60.00	100.00	110.00
Ice Bucket	60.00	—	—

	Clear	Emerald Green	Ruby Stain
Lamp			
Finger	95.00	150.00	—
Oil, 8"	125.00	225.00	—
Mustard, SP cov	95.00	100.00	—
Nappy, triangular	30.00	60.00	—
Pitcher, water	200.00	—	—
Plate			
6"	25.00	45.00	50.00
10"	45.00	85.00	90.00
Powder Jar, SP cov	65.00	—	—
Punch Cup	20.00	35.00	40.00
Rose Bowl			
Large	60.00	—	110.00
Small	30.00	—	90.00
Salt & Pepper, pr	95.00	—	—
Sauce, 5"	20.00	35.00	40.00
Spooner	50.00	85.00	90.00
Sugar			
Individual	25.00	35.00	40.00
Table, cov	105.00	—	75.00
Tray, 8-1/4" l, 4-1/4" w	30.00	65.00	75.00
Tumbler	45.00	85.00	75.00
Vase			
6"	35.00	65.00	75.00
10"	65.00	100.00	110.00
Wine	55.00	150.00	165.00

HOLLY

Non-flint, possibly made by Boston and Sandwich Glass Co. in the late 1860s and early 1870s.

	Clear			Clear
Bowl, cov, 8" d	150.00		Pitcher, water, ah	225.00
Butter, cov	150.00		Salt	
Cake Stand, 11"	160.00		Flat, oval	65.00
Celery Vase	90.00		Ftd	60.00
Compote, cov, hs	165.00		Sauce, flat	25.00
Creamer, ah	125.00		Spooner	60.00
Eggcup	95.00		Sugar, cov	135.00
Goblet	135.00		Tumbler	95.00
Pickle, oval	30.00		Wine	165.00

HONEYCOMB

A popular pattern made in flint and non-flint glass by numerous firms, c1850-1900, resulting in many pattern variations. Found with copper-wheel engraving. Rare in color.

	Flint	Non-Flint		Flint	Non-Flint
Ale Glass	50.00	25.00	Quart, os	85.00	65.00
Barber Bottle	45.00	25.00	Eggcup	20.00	15.00
Bowl, cov, 7-1/4" pat'd 1869,			Finger Bowl	45.00	—
acorn finial	100.00	45.00	Goblet	25.00	15.00
Butter, cov	75.00	45.00	Honey Dish, cov	15.00	25.00
Cake Stand	55.00	35.00	Lamp		
Castor Bottle	25.00	18.00	All Glass	—	85.00
Celery Vase	45.00	20.00	Marble base	—	90.00
Champagne	50.00	25.00	Lemonade	40.00	20.00
Claret	35.00	35.00	Mug, half pint	25.00	15.00
Compote, cov, hs			Pitcher, water, ah	165.00	60.00
6-1/2" x 18-1/2" h	60.00	40.00	Plate, 6"	—	12.50
9-1/4" x 11-1/2" h	110.00	65.00	Pomade Jar, cov	50.00	20.00
Compote, open, hs			Relish	30.00	20.00
7" x 7" h	60.00	40.00	Salt, master, cov, ftd	35.00	30.00
7-1/2", scalloped	40.00	25.00	Salt Shaker, orig top	—	35.00
8" x 6-1/4" h	65.00	40.00	Sauce	12.00	7.50
Compote, open, ls			Spillholder	35.00	20.00
6" d, Saucer Bowl	35.00	25.00	Spooner	65.00	35.00
7-1/2", scalloped	40.00	25.00	Sugar		
Cordial, 3-1/2"	35.00	25.00	Frosted rosebud finial	—	50.00
Creamer, ah	35.00	20.00	Regular	75.00	45.00
Decanter			Tumbler		
Pint, os	85.00	45.00	Bar	35.00	—

	Flint	Non-Flint		Flint	Non-Flint
Flat	40.00	12.50	Vase		
Footed	45.00	15.00	7-1/2"	45.00	—
			10-1/2"	75.00	—
			Whiskey, handled	125.00	—
			Wine	35.00	15.00

HORSESHOE (Good Luck, Prayer Rug)

Non-flint made by Adams & Co., Pittsburgh, PA, and others in late 1880s.

	Clear		Clear
Bowl, cov, oval		Marmalade Jar, cov	110.00
7"	150.00	Pitcher	
8"	195.00	Milk	125.00
Bread Plate, 14" x10"		Water	100.00
Double horseshoe handles	65.00	Plate	
Single horseshoe handles	40.00	7"	45.00
Butter, cov	95.00	10"	55.00
Cake Plate	40.00	Relish	
Cake Stand		5" x 7"	20.00
9"	70.00	8", wheelbarrow, pewter wheels	75.00
10"	90.00	Salt	
Celery Vase, knob stem	40.00	Individual, horseshoe shape	20.00
Cheese, cov, woman churning	275.00	Master, horseshoe shape	100.00
Compote		Master, wheelbarrow, pewter wheels	75.00
Cov, hs, 7", horseshoe finial	95.00	Sauce	
Cov, hs, 8" x 12-1/4"	125.00	Flat	10.00
Cov, hs, 11"	135.00	Footed	15.00
Creamer, 6-1/2"	55.00	Spooner	35.00
Doughnut Stand	75.00	Sugar, cov	65.00
Finger Bowl	80.00	Vegetable Dish, oblong	35.00
Goblet		Waste Bowl	45.00
Knob Stem	40.00	Water Tray	125.00
Plain Stem	38.00	Wine	150.00

ILLINOIS (Clarissa, Star of the East)

Non-flint. One of the States patterns made by U.S. Glass Co. c1897. Most forms are square. A few items are known in ruby stained, including a salt ($50.00) and a lidless straw holder with the stain on the inside ($95.00).

	Clear	Emerald Green		Clear	Emerald Green
Basket, ah, 11-1/2"	100.00	—	Pitcher, water, square	65.00	—
Bowl			Plate, 7", sq	25.00	
5", round	20.00	—	Relish		
6", sq	25.00	—	7-1/2" x 4"	10.00	40.00
8", round	25.00	—	8-1/2" x 3"	18.00	
9", sq	35.00	—	Salt		
*Butter, cov	60.00	—	Individual	15.00	—
Candlesticks, pr	95.00	—	Master	25.00	—
Celery Tray, 11"	40.00	—	Salt & Pepper, pr	40.00	—
Cheese, cov	75.00	—	Sauce	15.00	—
Compote, open			Spooner	35.00	—
hs, 5"	40.00	—	Straw Holder, cov	275.00	400.00
hs, 9"	60.00	—	Sugar		
Creamer			Individual	30.00	—
Individual	30.00	—	Table, cov	55.00	—
Table	40.00	—	Sugar Shaker	65.00	—
Cruet	65.00	—	Syrup, pewter top	95.00	—
Finger Bowl	25.00	—	Tankard, SP rim	80.00	135.00
Marmalade Jar	135.00	—	Toothpick		
Olive	18.00	—	Adv emb in base	45.00	—
Pitcher, milk			Plain	30.00	—
Round, SP rim	175.00	—	Tray, 12" x 8", turned up sides	50.00	—
Square	65.00	—	Tumbler	30.00	40.00
			Vase, 6", sq	35.00	45.00
			Vase, 9-1/2"	—	125.00

IOWA (Paneled Zipper)

Non-flint made by U.S. Glass Co. c1902. Part of the States pattern series. Available in clear glass with gold trim (add 20%) and ruby or cranberry stained. Also found in amber (goblet, $65.00), green, canary, and blue. Add 50% to 100% for color.

	Clear			Clear
Bowl, berry	15.00	Olive		15.00
Bread Plate, motto	80.00	Pitcher, water		50.00
Butter, cov	40.00	Punch Cup		15.00
Cake Stand	35.00	Salt Shaker, single		20.00
Carafe	35.00	Sauce, 4-1/2"		6.50
Compote, cov, 8"	40.00	Spooner		30.00
Corn Liquor Jug, os	60.00	Sugar, cov		35.00
Creamer	30.00	Toothpick		
Cruet, os	30.00	Flat		20.00
Cup	15.00	Footed		50.00
Decanter, 1-1/2 pts	40.00	Tumbler		25.00
Goblet	25.00	Vase, 8" h		20.00
Lamp	125.00	Wine		30.00

JACOB'S LADDER (Maltese)

Non-flint made by Bryce Bros., Pittsburgh, PA, in 1876 and by U.S. Glass Co. in 1891. A few pieces found in amber, yellow, blue, pale blue, and pale green. Bowls in variant of pattern found in flint, sometimes in metal holders.

	Clear		Clear
Bowl		Open, hs, 9-1/2", scalloped	38.00
6" x 8-3/4"	15.00	Open, hs, 10"	40.00
6-3/4" x 9-3/4"	20.00	Creamer	35.00
7-1/2" x 10-3/4"	20.00	Cruet, os, ftd	85.00
9", berry, ornate, SP		Goblet	65.00
holder, ftd (variant)	125.00	Honey Dish, 3-1/2"	10.00
Butter, cov	75.00	Marmalade Jar	75.00
Cake Stand		Mug	100.00
8" or 9"	50.00	Pitcher, water, ah	175.00
11" or 12"	60.00	Plate, 6-1/4"	20.00
Castor Bottle	18.00	Relish, 9-1/2" x 5-1/2"	15.00
Castor Set, 4 bottles	100.00	Salt, master, ftd	20.00
Celery Vase	45.00	Sauce	
Cologne Bottle,		Flat, 4" or 5"	8.00
Maltese-cross stopper, ftd	85.00	Footed, 4"	12.00
Compote		Spooner	35.00
Cov, hs, 6"	80.00	Sugar, cov	80.00
Cov, hs, 7-1/2"	100.00	Syrup	
Cov, hs, 9-1/2"	135.00	Knight's Head finial	125.00
Open, hs, 7-1/2"	35.00	Plain top	100.00
Open, hs, 8-1/2", scalloped	30.00	Tumbler, bar	100.00
		Wine	30.00

JERSEY SWIRL (Swirl)

Non-flint made by Windsor Glass Co., Pittsburgh, PA, c1887. Heavily reproduced in color by L. G. Wright Co. The clear goblet is also reproduced.

	Amber	Blue	Canary	Clear
Bowl, 9-1/4"	55.00	55.00	45.00	35.00
Butter, cov	55.00	55.00	50.00	40.00
Cake Stand, 9"	75.00	70.00	45.00	30.00
*Celery Case	42.00	42.00	35.00	30.00
*Compote, hs, 8"	50.00	50.00	45.00	35.00
Creamer	45.00	45.00	40.00	30.00
Cruet, os	—	—	—	25.00
*Goblet				
Buttermilk	40.00	40.00	35.00	30.00
Water	40.00	40.00	35.00	30.00
Marmalade Jar	—	—	—	50.00
Pickle Castor, SP frame and lid	—	—	—	125.00
Pitcher, water	50.00	50.00	45.00	35.00
Plate, round				
6"	25.00	25.00	20.00	15.00
8"	30.00	30.00	25.00	20.00
10"	38.00	38.00	35.00	30.00
*Salt, ind	20.00	20.00	18.00	15.00

	Amber	Blue	Canary	Clear
Salt Shaker	30.00	30.00	25.00	20.00
Sauce, 4-1/2", flat	20.00	20.00	15.00	10.00
Spooner	30.00	30.00	25.00	20.00
Sugar, cov	40.00	40.00	35.00	30.00
Tumbler	30.00	30.00	25.00	20.00
*Wine	50.00	50.00	40.00	15.00

KANSAS (Jewel with Dewdrop)

Non-flint originally produced by Co-Operative Glass Co., Beaver Falls, PA. Later produced as part of the States pattern series by U.S. Glass Co. in 1901 and Jenkins Glass Co. c1915-25. Also known with jewels stained in pink or gold. Mugs (smaller and of inferior quality) have been reproduced in clear, vaseline, amber and blue).

	Clear		Clear
Banana Stand	90.00	Creamer	40.00
Bowl		*Goblet	55.00
7", oval	35.00	*Mug	
8"	40.00	Regular	45.00
Bread Plate, ODB	45.00	Tall	25.00
Butter, cov	65.00	*Pitcher	
Cake Plate	45.00	Milk	80.00
Cake Stand		Water	100.00
7-5/8"	50.00	Relish, 8-1/2", oval	20.00
10"	85.00	Salt Shaker	50.00
Celery Vase	80.00	Sauce, flat, 4"	12.00
Compote		Sugar, cov	65.00
Cov, hs, 6"	60.00	Syrup	125.00
Cov, hs, 8"	85.00	Toothpick	65.00
Cov, ls, 5"	60.00	Tumbler	45.00
Open, hs, 6"	30.00	Whiskey	25.00
Open, hs, 8"	45.00	Wine	50.00

KENTUCKY

Non-flint made by U.S. Glass Co. c1897 as part of the States pattern series. The goblet is found in ruby stained ($50). A footed, square sauce ($30) is known in cobalt blue with gold. A toothpick holder is also known in ruby stained ($150).

	Clear	Emerald Green		Clear	Emerald Green
Bowl, 8" d	20.00	—	Pitcher, water	55.00	—
Butter, cov	50.00	—	Plate, 7", sq	15.00	—
Cake Stand, 9-1/2"	40.00	—	Punch Cup	10.00	15.00
Creamer	25.00	—	Salt Shaker, orig top	10.00	—
Cruet, os	45.00	—	Sauce, ftd, sq	10.00	15.00
Cup	10.00	20.00	Spooner	35.00	—
Goblet	30.00	50.00	Sugar, cov	30.00	—
Nappy	10.00	15.00	Toothpick, sq	35.00	85.00
Olive, handle	25.00	—	Tumbler	20.00	30.00
			Wine	28.00	38.00

KING'S CROWN (Ruby Thumbprint, X.L.C.R.)

Non-flint made by Adams & Co., Pittsburgh, PA, in the 1890s and later. Known as Ruby Thumbprint when pieces are ruby stained. Made in clear and with the thumbprints stained amethyst, gold, green, and cranberry, and in clear with etching and gold trim. It became very popular after 1891 as ruby-stained souvenir ware. Approximately 87 pieces documented. Add 30% for engraved pieces. NOTE: Pattern has been copiously reproduced for the gift-trade market in milk glass, cobalt blue, and other colors. New pieces are easily distinguished: in the case of Ruby Thumbprint, the color is a very pale pinkish red.

	Clear	Ruby Stained		Clear	Ruby Stained
Banana Stand, ftd	85.00	195.00	Celery Vase	40.00	60.00
*Bowl			*Champagne	25.00	35.00
9-1/4" d, pointed	35.00	90.00	*Claret	35.00	50.00
10" d, scalloped	45.00	95.00	*Compote		
Butter, cov, 7-1/2" d	50.00	135.00	Cov, hs, 8"	65.00	245.00
*Cake Stand			Cov, ls, 12"	90.00	225.00
9" d	68.00	195.00	Open, hs, 8-1/4"	75.00	95.00
10" d	75.00	195.00	Open, ls, 5-1/4"	30.00	45.00
Castor Set, glass stand,			*Cordial	45.00	—
four bottles	175.00	300.00	*Creamer, ah, 3-1/4" h		

	Clear	Ruby Stained		Clear	Ruby Stained
Ind, tankard	25.00	35.00	*Plate, 7"	20.00	45.00
Table, 4-7/8" h	50.00	65.00	*Punch Bowl, ftd	275.00	300.00
*Cup and Saucer	55.00	70.00	*Punch Cup	15.00	30.00
Custard Cup	15.00	25.00	Salt		
*Goblet	35.00	45.00	Ind, rect	15.00	35.00
Honey Dish, cov, sq	100.00	175.00	Master, sq	30.00	50.00
*Lamp, oil, 10"	135.00	—	Salt Shaker, 3-1/8" h	30.00	45.00
Mustard, cov, 4" h	35.00	75.00	*Sauce, 4"	15.00	20.00
Preserve, 10" l	35.00	50.00	Spooner, 4-1/4" h	45.00	50.00
*Pitcher			*Sugar		
Milk, tankard	75.00	125.00	Ind, open, 2-3/4" h	25.00	45.00
Water, bulbous	95.00	225.00	Table, cov, 6-3/4" h	55.00	95.00
Water, tankard	110.00	200.00	Toothpick, 2-3/4" h	20.00	35.00
			*Tumbler, 3-3/4" h	20.00	35.00
			*Wine, 4-3/8" h	25.00	40.00

KOKOMO (Bar and Diamond, R and H Swirl Band)

Non-flint made by Richards and Hartley, Tarentum, PA, c1885. Reissued by U.S. Glass Co., c1891 and Kokomo Glass Co., Kokomo, IN, c1901. Found in ruby stained and etched. More than 50 different pieces manufactured.

	Clear	Ruby Stained		Clear	Ruby Stained
Bowl, 8-1/2" ftd	24.00	—	Cruet	35.00	—
Bread Tray	30.00	45.00	Decanter, 9-3/4", wine	65.00	165.00
Butter, cov	35.00	—	Finger Bowl	25.00	35.00
Cake Stand	45.00	165.00	Goblet	30.00	45.00
Celery Vase	30.00	45.00	Lamp, hand, atypical,		
Compote			has no diamonds	50.00	100.00
Cov, hs, 7-1/2"	35.00	165.00	Pitcher, tankard	55.00	100.00
Open, hs, 6"	25.00	—	Sauce, ftd, 5"	8.00	10.00
Open, hs, 8"	35.00	—	Spooner	25.00	45.00
Open, ls, 7-1/2"	20.00	—	Sugar, cov	45.00	65.00
Condiment Set, oblong tray,			Sugar Shaker	35.00	75.00
shakers, cruet	80.00	195.00	Syrup	45.00	135.00
Creamer, ah	35.00	50.00	Tray, water	35.00	90.00
			Tumbler	25.00	35.00
			Wine	25.00	35.00

LION (Frosted Lion)

Made by Gillinder and Sons, Philadelphia, PA, in 1876. Available in clear without frosting (20% less). Many reproductions.

	Frosted		Frosted
Bowl, oblong		Cordial	175.00
6-1/2" x 4-1/4"	55.00	*Creamer	75.00
8" x 5"	50.00	Cup and Saucer, child size	45.00
Bread Plate, 12"	90.00	*Eggcup, 3-1/2" h	65.00
*Butter, cov		*Goblet	70.00
Lion's-head finial	90.00	Marmalade Jar, rampant finial	90.00
Rampant finial	125.00	Pitcher	
Cake Stand	85.00	Milk	375.00
*Celery Vase	85.00	Water	300.00
Champagne	175.00	Relish, lion handles	35.00
Cheese, cov, rampant lion's-head finial	400.00	*Salt, master, rect lid	250.00
Children's Table Set	500.00	*Sauce, 4", ftd	25.00
*Compote		*Spooner	75.00
Cov, hs, 7", rampant finial	150.00	*Sugar, cov	
*Cov, hs, 9", rampant		Lion's-head finial	90.00
finial, oval, collared base	150.00	Rampant finial	110.00
Cov, 9", hs	185.00	Syrup, orig top	350.00
Open, ls, 8"	75.00	Wine	200.00

LOOP AND DART

Clear and stippled flint and non-flint of the late 1860s and early 1870s. Made by Boston and Sandwich Glass Co., Sandwich, MA, and Richards and Hartley, Tarentum, PA. Flint adds 25%.

	Clear
Bowl, 9", oval	30.00
Butter, cov	45.00
Cake Stand, 10"	40.00
Celery Vase	35.00
Compote	
Cov, hs, 8"	85.00
Cov, ls, 8"	65.00
Creamer	35.00
Cruet, os	95.00
Eggcup	25.00
Goblet	25.00

	Clear
Lamp, oil	85.00
Pitcher, water	75.00
Plate, 6"	35.00
Relish	20.00
Salt, master	50.00
Sauce	5.00
Spooner	25.00
Sugar, cov	50.00
Tumbler	
Footed	30.00
Water	25.00
Wine	35.00

LOUISIANA (Sharp Oval and Diamond, Granby)

Made by Bryce Bros., Pittsburgh, PA, in the 1870s. Reissued by U.S. Glass Co. c1898 as one of the States patterns. Available with gold and also comes frosted.

	Clear
Bowl, 9", berry	20.00
Butter, cov	75.00
Cake Stand	65.00
Celery Vase	30.00
Compote	
Cov, hs, 8"	75.00
Open, hs, 5", jelly	40.00
Creamer	30.00
Goblet	30.00

	Clear
Match Holder	35.00
Mug, handled, gold top	25.00
Nappy, 4", cov	30.00
Pitcher, water	65.00
Relish	15.00
Spooner	30.00
Sugar, cov	45.00
Tumbler	25.00
Wine	35.00

MAINE (Paneled Stippled Flower, Stippled Primrose)

Non-flint made by U.S. Glass Co., Pittsburgh, PA, c1899. Researchers dispute if goblet was made originally. Sometimes found with enamel trim or overall turquoise stain.

	Clear	Emerald Green
Bowl, 8"	30.00	40.00
Bread Plate, oval 10" x 7-1/4"	30.00	—
Butter, cov	48.00	—
Cake Stand	40.00	60.00
Compote		
Cov, jelly	50.00	75.00
Open, hs, 7"	20.00	45.00
Open, ls, 8"	38.00	55.00
Open, ls, 9"	30.00	65.00
Creamer	30.00	—
Cruet, os	80.00	—

	Clear	Emerald Green
Mug	35.00	—
Pitcher		
Milk	65.00	85.00
Water	50.00	125.00
Relish	15.00	—
Salt Shaker, single	30.00	—
Sauce	15.00	—
Sugar, cov	45.00	75.00
Syrup	75.00	225.00
Toothpick	125.00	—
Tumbler	30.00	45.00
Wine	50.00	75.00

MANHATTAN

Non-flint with gold made by U.S. Glass Co. c1902. A Depression glass pattern also has the "Manhattan" name. A table-sized creamer and covered sugar are known in true ruby stained, and a goblet is known in old marigold carnival glass. Heavily reproduced by Anchor Hocking Glass Co. and Tiffin Glass Co.

	Clear	Rose Stained
Biscuit jar, cov	60.00	100.00
Bowl		
6"	18.00	—
8-1/4", scalloped	20.00	—
*9-1/2"	20.00	—
10"	22.00	—
12-1/2"	25.00	—
Butter, cov	55.00	—
Cake Stand, 8"	45.00	55.00
Carafe, water	40.00	65.00
Celery Tray, 8"	20.00	—
Celery Vase	25.00	—
Cheese, cov, 8-3/8" d	—	115.00
Compote		

	Clear	Rose Stained
Cov, hs, 9-1/2"	60.00	—
Open, hs, 9-1/2"	45.00	—
Open, hs, 10-1/2"	50.00	—
*Creamer		
Individual	20.00	—
Table	30.00	60.00
Cruet		
Large	65.00	115.00
Small	50.00	—
*Goblet	25.00	—
Ice Bucket	—	65.00
Olive, Gainsborough	30.00	—
Pitcher, water, half gal		
Bulbous, ah	70.00	—

	Clear	Rose Stained		Clear	Rose Stained
Tankard, ah	60.00	125.00	Straw Holder, cov	95.00	150.00
Plate			*Sugar		
5"	10.00	—	Individual, open	15.00	—
6"	10.00	30.00	Table, cov	40.00	65.00
8"	15.00	—	Syrup	48.00	200.00
10-3/4"	20.00	—	*Toothpick	30.00	—
Punch Bowl	125.00	—	Tumbler		
Punch Cup	10.00	—	Iced Tea	30.00	—
Relish, 6"	12.00	—	Water	20.00	—
Salt Shaker, single	20.00	35.00	Vase, 6"	18.00	—
Sauce	14.00	20.00	Violet Bowl	20.00	—
*Spooner	20.00	—	Water Bottle	40.00	—
			*Wine	15.00	—

MARYLAND (Inverted Loop and Fan, Loop and Diamond)

Made originally by Bryce Bros., Pittsburgh, PA. Continued by U.S. Glass Co. as one of its States patterns.

	Clear with Gold	Ruby Stained		Clear with Gold	Ruby Stained
Banana Dish	35.00	105.00	Olive, handled	15.00	—
Bowl, berry	15.00	35.00	Pitcher		
Bread Plate	25.00	—	Milk	42.50	135.00
Butter, cov	65.00	95.00	Water	50.00	100.00
Cake Stand, 8"	40.00	—	Plate, 7", round	25.00	—
Celery Tray	20.00	35.00	Relish, oval	15.00	55.00
Celery Vase	30.00	65.00	Salt Shaker, single	30.00	—
Compote			Sauce, flat	10.00	15.00
Cov, hs	65.00	100.00	Spooner	30.00	55.00
Open, jelly	25.00	45.00	Sugar, cov	45.00	60.00
Creamer	25.00	55.00	Toothpick	125.00	175.00
Goblet	30.00	60.00	Tumbler	25.00	50.00
			Wine	40.00	75.00

MASCOTTE (Dominion, Etched Fern and Waffle, Minor Block)

Non-flint made by Ripley and Co., Pittsburgh, PA, in the 1880s. Reissued by U.S. Glass Co. in 1891. The butter dish shown on Plate 77 of Ruth Webb Lee's *Victorian Glass* is said to go with this pattern. It has a horseshoe finial and was named for the famous "Maude S," "Queen of the Turf" trotting horse during the 1880s. Apothecary jar and pyramid jars made by Tiffin Glass Co. in the 1950s.

	Clear	Etched		Clear	Etched
Bowl			Open, ls, 8"	30.00	45.00
Cov, 5"	—	35.00	Creamer	30.00	45.00
Cov, 7"	—	45.00	Goblet	40.00	45.00
Open 9"	35.00	40.00	Pitcher, water	55.00	65.00
Butter Pat	15.00	20.00	Plate, turned in sides	40.00	45.00
Butter, cov			Pyramid Jar, 7" d, one fits into other		
"Maude S"	100.00	110.00	and forms tall jar-type container		
Regular	50.00	65.00	with lid, three sizes		
Cake Basket, handle	80.00	95.00	with flat separators	50.00	55.00
Cake Stand	35.00	50.00	Salt Dip	25.00	—
Celery Vase	35.00	40.00	Salt Shaker, single	25.00	25.00
Cheese, cov	70.00	80.00	Sauce		
Compote			Flat	8.00	15.00
Cov, hs, 5"	35.00	40.00	Footed	12.00	15.00
Cov, hs, 7"	45.00	55.00	Spooner	30.00	35.00
Cov, hs, 8"	60.00	75.00	Sugar, cov	40.00	45.00
Cov, hs, 9"	65.00	90.00	Tray, water	40.00	55.00
Open, hs, 6"	20.00	25.00	Tumbler	20.00	35.00
Open, hs, 8"	30.00	35.00	Wine	25.00	30.00

MASSACHUSETTS (Arched Diamond Points, Cane Variant, Geneva #2, M2-131, Star and Diamonds)

Made in the 1880s, unknown maker, reissued in 1898 by U.S. Glass Co. as one of the States series. The vase ($45) and wine ($45) are known in emerald green. Some pieces reported in cobalt blue and marigold carnival glass. Reproduced in clear and colors, including cobalt blue.

	Clear		Clear
Bar Bottle, metal shot glass for cover	75.00	Pitcher, water	65.00
Basket, 4-1/2", ah	50.00	Plate, 8"	32.00
Bowl		Punch Cup	15.00
6", sq	17.50	Relish, 8-1/2"	25.00
9", sq	20.00	Rum Jug, various sizes	90.00
*Butter, cov	50.00	Salt Shaker, tall	25.00
Celery Tray	30.00	Sauce, sq, 4"	15.00
Champagne	35.00	Sherry	40.00
Cologne Bottle, os	37.50	Spooner	20.00
Compote, open	35.00	Sugar, cov	40.00
Cordial	55.00	Syrup	65.00
Creamer	28.00	Toothpick	40.00
Cruet, os	45.00	Tumbler	30.00
Goblet	45.00	Vase, trumpet	
Gravy Boat	30.00	6-1/2" h	25.00
Mug	20.00	7" h	25.00
Mustard Jar, cov	35.00	9" h	35.00
Olive	8.50	Whiskey	25.00
		Wine	40.00

MICHIGAN (Loop and Pillar)

Non-flint made by U.S. Glass Co. c1902 as one of the States pattern series. The 10-1/4" bowl ($42) and punch cup ($12) are found with yellow or blue stain. Also found with painted carnations. Other colors include "Sunrise," gold and ruby stained.

	Clear	Rose Stained		Clear	Rose Stained
Bowl			Nappy, Gainsborough handle	35.00	—
7-1/2"	15.00	30.00	Olive, two handles	10.00	25.00
9"	35.00	60.00	Pickle	12.00	20.00
10-1/4"	35.00	62.00	Pitcher		
Butter, cov			8"	50.00	—
Large	60.00	125.00	12", tankard	70.00	150.00
Small	65.00	—	Plate, 5-1/2" d	15.00	—
Celery Vase	40.00	85.00	Punch Bowl, 8"	50.00	—
Compote			Punch Cup	8.00	—
Jelly, 4-1/2"	45.00	75.00	Relish	20.00	35.00
Open, hs, 9-1/4"	65.00	85.00	Salt Shaker, single, 3 types	20.00	30.00
Creamer			Sauce	12.00	22.00
Ind, 6 oz., tankard	20.00	65.00	Sherbet cup, handles	15.00	20.00
Table	30.00	70.00	Spooner	50.00	75.00
Cruet, os	60.00	225.00	Sugar, cov	50.00	85.00
Crushed Fruit Bowl	75.00	—	Syrup	95.00	175.00
Custard Cup	15.00	—	*Toothpick	45.00	100.00
Finger Bowl	15.00	—	Tumbler	30.00	40.00
Goblet	45.00	65.00	Vase		
Honey Dish	10.00	—	Bud	35.00	40.00
Lemonade Mug	24.00	40.00	Ftd, large	45.00	—
			Wine	35.00	50.00

MINERVA (Roman Medallion)

Non-flint made by Boston and Sandwich Glass Co., Sandwich, MA, c1870, as well as other American companies. Shards have been found at Burlington Glass Works, Hamilton, Ontario, Canada.

	Clear		Clear
Bowl		Open, hs, 10-1/2", octagonal ftd	175.00
Footed	40.00	Creamer	45.00
Rectangular		Goblet	95.00
7"	25.00	Marmalade Jar, cov	150.00
8" x 5"	30.00	Pickle	25.00
Bread Plate	65.00	Pitcher, Water	185.00
Butter, cov	75.00	Plate	
Cake Stand		8"	55.00
9" x 6-1/2"	100.00	10", handled	60.00
10-1/2"	120.00	Platter, oval, 13"	65.00
13"	195.00	Sauce	
Champagne	285.00	Flat	185.50
Compote		Footed, 4"	20.00
Cov, hs, 6"	135.00	Spooner	40.00
Cov, hs, 8"	165.00	Sugar, cov	65.00
Cov, ls, 8"	165.00	Waste Bowl	50.00

MINNESOTA

Non-flint made by U.S. Glass Co. in the late 1890s as one of the States patterns.

	Clear	Ruby Stained
Banana Stand	65.00	—
Basket	65.00	—
Biscuit Jar, cov	55.00	150.00
Bonbon, 5"	15.00	—
Butter, cov	50.00	
Carafe	35.00	—
Celery Tray, 13"	25.00	—
Compote		
Open, hs, 10", flared	60.00	—
Open, ls, 9", sq	55.00	—
Creamer		
Individual	20.00	—
Table	30.00	—
Cruet	35.00	—
Cup	18.00	—
Goblet	35.00	75.00
Hair Receiver	30.00	—

	Clear	Ruby Stained
Juice Glass	20.00	—
Match Safe	25.00	—
Mug	25.00	—
Olive	15.00	25.00
Pitcher, tankard	85.00	200.00
Plate		
5", turned up edges	25.00	—
7-3/8" d	15.00	—
Pomade Jar, cov	35.00	—
Relish	20.00	—
Salt Shaker	25.00	—
Sauce, boat shape	10.00	25.00
Spooner	25.00	—
Sugar, cov	35.00	—
Syrup	65.00	—
Toothpick, 3 handles	30.00	150.00
Tray, 8" l	15.00	—
Tumbler	20.00	—
Wine	40.00	—

NEVADA

Non-flint made by U.S. Glass Co., Pittsburgh, PA, c1902 as a States pattern. Pieces are sometimes partly frosted and have enamel decoration. Add 20% for frosted.

	Clear
Biscuit Jar	45.00
Bowl	
6" d, cov	35.00
7" d, open	20.00
8" d, cov	45.00
Butter, cov	70.00
Cake Stand, 10"	35.00
Celery Vase	25.00
Compote	
Cov, hs, 6"	40.00
Cov, hs, 7"	45.00
Cov, hs, 8"	55.00
Open, hs, 6"	20.00
Open, hs, 7"	30.00
Open, hs, 8"	35.00
Creamer	30.00
Cruet	35.00

	Clear
Cup, custard	12.00
Finger Bowl	25.00
Jug	35.00
Pickle, oval	10.00
Pitcher	
Milk, tankard	45.00
Water, bulbous	50.00
Water, tankard	45.00
Salt	
Individual	15.00
Master	20.00
Salt Shaker, table	15.00
Sauce, 4" d	10.00
Spooner	35.00
Sugar, cov	35.00
Syrup, tin top	45.00
Toothpick	35.00
Tumbler	15.00

NEW HAMPSHIRE (Bent Buckle, Modiste)

Non-flint made by U.S. Glass Co., Pittsburgh, PA, c1903 in The States Pattern series.

	Clear with Gold	Rose Stained	Ruby Stained
Biscuit jar, cov	75.00	—	—
Bowl			
Flared, 5-1/2"	10.00	—	25.00
Flared, 8-1/2"	15.00	25.00	—
Round, 8-1/2"	18.00	30.00	—
Square, 8-1/2"	25.00	35.00	—
Butter, cov	45.00	70.00	—
Cake Stand, 8-1/4"	30.00	—	—
Carafe	60.00	—	—
Celery Vase	35.00	50.00	—
Compote			
Cov, hs, 5"	50.00	—	—
Cov, hs, 6"	60.00	—	—
Cov, hs, 7"	65.00	—	—
Open	40.00	55.00	—
Creamer			
Individual	20.00	30.00	—

	Clear with Gold	Rose Stained	Ruby Stained
Table	30.00	45.00	—
Cruet	55.00	135.00	—
Goblet	35.00	45.00	—
Mug, large	20.00	45.00	50.00
Pitcher, water			
Bulbous, ah	90.00	—	—
Straight Sides, molded handle	60.00	90.00	—
Relish	18.00	—	—
Salt & Pepper, pr	35.00	—	—
Sauce	10.00	—	—
Sugar			
Cov, table	45.00	60.00	—
Individual, open	20.00	25.00	—
Syrup	75.00	150.00	175.00
Toothpick	25.00	40.00	40.00
Vase	35.00	50.00	—
Wine	25.00	50.00	—

NEW JERSEY (Loops and Drops)

Non-flint made by U.S. Glass Co., Pittsburgh, PA, c1900-08 in States pattern series. Prices are for items with perfect gold. An emerald green 11" vase is known (value $75).

	Clear with Gold	Ruby Stained
Bowl		
8", flared	25.00	55.00
9", saucer	32.50	70.00
10", oval	30.00	85.00
Bread Plate	30.00	—
Butter, cov		
Flat	75.00	100.00
Footed	125.00	—
Cake Stand, 8"	65.00	—
Carafe	60.00	—
Celery Tray, rect	25.00	45.00
Compote		
Cov, hs, 5", jelly	45.00	65.00
Cov, hs, 8"	65.00	95.00
Open, hs, 6-3/4"	35.00	70.00
Open, hs, 8"	60.00	80.00
Open, hs, 10-1/2", shallow	65.00	—
Creamer	35.00	65.00
Cruet	50.00	—
Fruit bowl, hs, 12-1/2"	55.00	110.00

	Clear with Gold	Ruby Stained
Goblet	40.00	70.00
Molasses Can	90.00	—
Olive	15.00	—
Pickle, rect	15.00	—
Pitcher		
Milk, ah	75.00	185.00
Water		
Applied Handle	80.00	210.00
Pressured Handle	50.00	185.00
Plate, 8" d	30.00	50.00
Salt & Pepper, pr		
Hotel	50.00	120.00
Small	35.00	60.00
Sauce	10.00	35.00
Spooner	27.00	80.00
Sugar, cov	60.00	80.00
Sweetmeat, 8"	70.00	110.00
Syrup	90.00	—
Toothpick	55.00	225.00
Tumbler	30.00	60.00
Water Bottle	55.00	110.00
Wine	45.00	65.00

ONE HUNDRED ONE (Beaded 101)

Non-flint made by Bellaire Goblet Co., Findlay, Ohio, in the late 1880s.

	Clear
Bread Plate, 101 border	
Farm implement center, 11"	75.00
Butter, cov	40.00
Cake Stand, 9"	65.00
Celery Vase	50.00
Compote	
Cov, hs, 7"	60.00
Cov, ls	60.00
Creamer	45.00
*Goblet	50.00
Lamp, hand, oil, 10"	80.00

	Clear
Pickle	20.00
Pitcher, water, ah	125.00
Plate	
6"	20.00
8"	30.00
Relish	15.00
Sauce	
Flat	10.00
Footed	15.00
Spooner	25.00
Sugar, cov	45.00
Wine	60.00

PALMETTE (Hearts and Spades, Spades)

Non-flint, unknown maker, late 1870s. Shards have been found at Burlington Glass Works, Hamilton, Ontario, Canada. Syrup known in milk glass.

	Clear
Bottle, vinegar	80.00
Bowl, scalloped rim	
8"	25.00
9"	20.00
Butter Dish, cov	60.00
Cake Plate, tab handles	35.00
Cake Stand (two sizes)	100.00
Castor Set, 5 bottles, sp holder	125.00
Celery Vase	55.00
Champagne	75.00
Compote	
Cov, hs, 8-1/2"	75.00
Cov, hs, 9-3/4"	85.00
Open, ls, 7"	30.00
Creamer, ah	65.00
Cup Plate	55.00
Eggcup	40.00

	Clear
Goblet	35.00
Lamp, various sizes	95.00
Pickle, scoop shape	20.00
Pitcher, bulbous, ah	
Milk	135.00
Water	125.00
Relish (3 sauces)	18.00
Salt, master, ftd	22.00
Salt Shaker	55.00
Sauce, flat, 6"	10.00
Shaker, saloon, oversize	80.00
Spooner	35.00
Sugar, cov	55.00
Syrup, ah	125.00
Tumbler	
Bar	75.00
Water, ftd	40.00
Wine	110.00

PANELED FORGET-ME-NOT (Regal)

Non-flint, made by Bryce Bros., Pittsburgh, PA, c1880. Reissued by U.S. Glass Co. c1891. Shards have been found at Burlington Glass Works, Hamilton, Ontario, Canada. Made in clear, blue, and amber with limited production in amethyst, vaseline and green.

	Amber	Blue	Clear
Bread Plate	35.00	45.00	30.00
Butter, cov	50.00	60.00	45.00
Cake Stand, 10"	70.00	90.00	45.00
Celery Vase	45.00	70.00	36.00
Compote			
Cov, hs, 7"	90.00	110.00	65.00
Cov, hs, 8"	80.00	100.00	68.00
Open, hs, 8-1/2"	60.00	75.00	50.00
Open, hs, 10"	60.00	80.00	40.00
Creamer	45.00	60.00	35.00
Cruet, os	—	—	45.00
Goblet	50.00	65.00	32.00
Marmalade Jar, cov	80.00	100.00	60.00
Pickle, boat shape	25.00	35.00	15.00
Pitcher			
Milk	90.00	110.00	50.00
Water	90.00	110.00	75.00
Relish, scoop shape	55.00	55.00	65.00
Salt & Pepper, pr	—	—	65.00
Sauce, ftd	18.00	25.00	12.00
Spooner	40.00	50.00	25.00
Sugar, cov	60.00	75.00	40.00
Wine	55.00	65.00	60.00

PENNSYLVANIA (Balder)

Non-flint issued by U.S. Glass Co. in 1898. Also known in ruby stained. A ruffled jelly compote is documented in orange carnival.

	Clear with Gold	Emerald Green
Biscuit Jar, cov	75.00	125.00
Bowl		
4"	20.00	—
8", berry	25.00	35.00
8", sq	20.00	40.00
Butter, cov	60.00	85.00
Carafe	45.00	—
Celery Tray	30.00	—
Celery Vase	45.00	—
Champagne	25.00	—
Cheese Dish, cov	65.00	—
Compote, hs, jelly	50.00	—
Creamer	25.00	50.00
Cruet, os	45.00	—
Decanter, os	100.00	—
Goblet	24.00	—

	Clear with Gold	Emerald Green
Juice Tumbler	10.00	20.00
Molasses Can	75.00	—
Pitcher, water	60.00	—
Punch Bowl	175.00	—
Punch Cup	10.00	—
Salt Shaker	10.00	—
Sauce	7.50	—
*Spooner	24.00	35.00
Sugar, cov	40.00	55.00
Syrup	50.00	—
Tankard	110.00	
Toothpick	35.00	90.00
Tumbler	28.00	40.00
Whiskey	20.00	35.00
Wine	15.00	40.00

PICKET (London, Picket Fence)

Non-flint made by the King, Son and Co., Pittsburgh, PA, c1890. Toothpick holders are known in apple green, vaseline, and purple slag.

	Clear		Clear
Bowl, 9-1/2", sq	30.00	Pitcher, water	95.00
Bread Plate	70.00	Salt	
Butter, cov	65.00	Individual	10.00
Celery Vase	40.00	Master	35.00
Compote		Sauce	
Cov, hs, 8"	135.00	Flat	15.00
Cov, ls, 8"	125.00	Footed	20.00
Open, hs, 7", sq	35.00	Spooner	30.00
Open, hs, 10", sq	70.00	Sugar, cov	50.00
Open, ls, 7"	50.00	Toothpick	35.00
Creamer	50.00	Tray, water	65.00
Goblet	50.00	Waste Bowl	40.00
		Wine	85.00

QUEEN ANNE (Bearded Man)

Non-flint made by LaBelle Glass Co., Bridgeport. Ohio, c1879. Finials are Maltese cross. At least 28 pieces are documented. A table set and water pitcher are known in amber.

	Clear		Clear
Bowl, cov		Eggcup	45.00
8", oval	45.00	Pitcher	
9", oval	55.00	Milk	75.00
Bread Plate	50.00	Water	85.00
Butter, cov	65.00	Salt Shaker	40.00
Celery Vase	35.00	Sauce	15.00
Compote, cov, ls, 9"	85.00	Spooner	40.00
Creamer	45.00	Sugar, cov	55.00
		Syrup	100.00

RED BLOCK (Late Block)

Non-flint with red stain made by Doyle and Co., Pittsburgh, PA. Later made by five companies, plus U.S. Glass Co. in 1892. Prices for clear 50% less.

	Ruby Stained		Ruby Stained
Banana Boat	75.00	Mustard, cov	55.00
Bowl, 8"	75.00	Pitcher, water, 8" h	175.00
Butter, cov	110.00	Relish Tray	25.00
Celery Vase, 6-1/2"	85.00	Rose Bowl	75.00
Cheese Dish, cov	125.00	Salt Dip, individual	50.00
Creamer		Salt Shaker	75.00
Individual	45.00	Sauce, flat, 4-1/2"	20.00
Table	70.00	Spooner	45.00
Decanter, 12", os, variant	175.00	Sugar, cov	90.00
*Goblet	35.00	Tumbler	40.00
Mug	50.00	*Wine	40.00

REVERSE TORPEDO (Bull's Eye Band, Bull's Eye with Diamond Point #2, Pointed Bull's Eye)

Non-flint made by Dalzell, Gilmore and Leighton Glass Co., Findlay, Ohio, c1888-90. Also attributed to Canadian factories. Sometimes found with copper-wheel etching.

	Clear		Clear
Banana Stand, 9-3/4"	100.00	Cov, hs, 7"	80.00
Basket	175.00	Cov, hs, 10"	125.00
Biscuit Jar, cov	135.00	Open, hs, 7"	65.00
Bowl		Open, hs, 8-3/8" d	45.00
8-1/2", shallow	30.00	Open, hs, 10-1/2 d,	
9", fruit, piecrust rim	70.00	V-shaped bowl	165.00
10-1/2", piecrust rim	75.00	Open, hs, jelly	50.00
Butter, cov, 7-1/2", d	75.00	Open, ls, 9-1/4", ruffled	85.00
Cake Stand, hs	85.00	Creamer	55.00
Celery Vase	55.00	Doughnut Tray	90.00
Compote		Goblet	85.00
Cov, hs, 6"	80.00	Honey Dish, sq, cov	145.00

	Clear			Clear
Jam Jar, cov	85.00		Spooner	30.00
Pitcher, tankard, 10-1/4"	160.00		Sugar, cov	85.00
Sauce, flat, 3-3/4"	10.00		Syrup	165.00
			Tumbler	30.00

ROMAN ROSETTE

Non-flint made by Bryce, Walker and Co., Pittsburgh, PA, c1890. Reissued by U.S. Glass Co. in 1892 and 1898. Also seen with English registry mark and known in amber stained.

	Clear	Ruby Stained			Clear	Ruby Stained
Bowl, 8-1/2"	15.00	50.00		Mug	35.00	—
Bread Plate	30.00	75.00		Pitcher		
Butter, cov	50.00	125.00		Milk	50.00	150.00
Cake Stand, 9"	45.00	—		Water	65.00	140.00
Celery Vase	30.00	95.00		Plate, 7-1/2"	35.00	65.00
Compote				Relish, oval, 9"	20.00	40.00
Cov, hs, 4-1/2", jelly	50.00	—		Salt & Pepper, glass tray	40.00	100.00
Cov, hs, 6"	65.00	—		Sauce	15.00	20.00
Cordial	50.00	—		Spooner	25.00	45.00
Creamer	32.00	45.00		Sugar, cov	40.00	80.00
*Goblet	40.00	—		Syrup	85.00	125.00
				Wine	45.00	65.00

ROSE-IN-SNOW (Rose)

Non-flint made by Bryce Bros., Pittsburgh, PA, in the square form c1880. Also made in the more common round form by Ohio Flint Glass Co. and after 1891 by U.S. Glass Co. Both styles reissued by Indiana Glass Co., Dunkirk, IN. Reproductions made by several companies, including Imperial Glass Co., as early as 1930 and continuing through the 1970s.

	Amber and Canary	Blue	Clear
Bowl, 8" sq	40.00	50.00	30.00
Butter, cov			
Round	65.00	125.00	45.00
Square	70.00	150.00	50.00
Cake Stand, 9"	125.00	175.00	90.00
Compote			
Cov, hs, 8"	125.00	175.00	80.00
Cov, ls, 7"	100.00	150.00	75.00
Open, ls, 5-3/4"	65.00	120.00	35.00
Creamer			
Round	60.00	100.00	45.00
Square	65.00	120.00	45.00
*Goblet	40.00	55.00	35.00
Marmalade Jar, cov	70.00	125.00	60.00
*Mug, "In Fond Remembrance"	65.00	125.00	35.00
*Pickle Dish			
Double, 8-1/2" x 7"	85.00	110.00	100.00
Single, oval, handles at end	35.00	95.00	20.00
Pitcher, water, ah	175.00	200.00	125.00
Plate			
5"	40.00	40.00	35.00
6"	30.00	80.00	20.00
7"	30.00	80.00	20.00
*9"	30.00	85.00	20.00
Platter, oval	—	—	125.00
Sauce			
Flat	15.00	20.00	12.00
Footed	8.00	45.00	18.00
Spooner			
Round	30.00	80.00	25.00
Square	40.00	100.00	35.00
Sugar, cov			
Round	55.00	120.00	50.00
*Square	50.00	140.00	45.00
Sweetmeat, cov, 5-3/4" d	80.00	155.00	65.00
Toddy Jar, cov, under plate	150.00	155.00	125.00
Tumbler	60.00	100.00	50.00

SKILTON (Early Oregon)

Made by Richards and Hartley of Tarentum, PA, in 1888 and by U.S. Glass Co. after 1891. This is not one of the U.S. Glass States pattern series and should not be confused with Beaded Loop, which is Oregon #1, named by U.S. Glass Co. It is better as Skilton (named by Millard) to avoid confusion with Beaded Loop.

	Clear	Ruby Stained		Clear	Ruby Stained
Bowl			Olive, handled	20.00	—
5", round	15.00	—	Pickle	15.00	—
7", rect.	20.00	—	Pitcher		
9", rect.	30.00	—	Milk	45.00	125.00
Butter, cov	45.00	110.00	Water	50.00	125.00
Cake Stand	35.00	—	Salt & Pepper, pr	45.00	—
Celery Vase	35.00	95.00	Sauce, ftd	12.00	20.00
Compote			Spooner, flat	25.00	55.00
Cov, hs, 8"	45.00	—	Sugar, cov	35.00	85.00
Open, ls, 8"	30.00	75.00	Tray, water	45.00	—
Creamer	30.00	55.00	Tumbler	25.00	40.00
Dish, oblong, sq	25.00	—	Wine	35.00	50.00
Goblet	35.00	50.00			

SPIREA BAND (Earl, Nailhead Variant, Spirea, Squared Dot)

Non-flint made by Bryce, Higbee and Co., Pittsburgh, PA, c1885.

	Amber	Blue	Clear	Vaseline
Bowl, 8"	25.00	40.00	20.00	30.00
Butter, cov	50.00	55.00	35.00	45.00
Cake Stand, 11"	45.00	55.00	40.00	45.00
Celery Vase	40.00	50.00	25.00	40.00
Compote, cov, hs, 7"	44.00	65.00	40.00	44.00
Cordial	38.00	42.00	20.00	38.00
Creamer	32.50	44.00	35.00	35.00
Goblet	30.00	35.00	25.00	35.00
Pitcher, water	65.00	80.00	35.00	60.00
Platter, 10-1/2"	32.00	42.00	20.00	32.00
Relish	30.00	35.00	18.00	30.00
Sauce				
Flat	10.00	12.00	5.00	10.00
Ftd	15.00	15.00	8.00	15.00
Spooner	30.00	35.00	20.00	35.00
Sugar, open	32.00	40.00	25.00	32.00
Tumbler	24.00	35.00	20.00	30.00
Wine	30.00	35.00	20.00	30.00

STATES, THE (Cane and Star Medallion)

Non-flint made by U.S. Glass Co., Pittsburgh, PA, in 1905. Also found in emerald green (add 50%). Prices given for clear with good gold trim.

	Clear		Clear
Bowl		Plate, 10"	25.00
7", round, 3 handles	25.00	Punch Bowl, 13" d	75.00
9-1/4", round	30.00	Punch Cup	10.00
Butter, cov	65.00	Relish, diamond shape	35.00
Celery Tray	20.00	Salt & Pepper	40.00
Celery Vase	20.00	Sauce, flat, 4", tub shape	15.00
Cocktail	25.00	Spooner	25.00
Compote		Sugar	
Open, hs, 7"	30.00	Individual, open	15.00
Open, hs, 9"	40.00	Regular, cov	40.00
Creamer		Syrup	65.00
Individual, oval	20.00	Toothpick, flat, rectangular, curled lip	45.00
Regular, round	30.00	Tray, 7-1/4" l, 5-1/2" w	20.00
Goblet	35.00	Tumbler	25.00
Pickle Tray	15.00	Wine	30.00
Pitcher, water	45.00		

TENNESSEE (Jewel and Crescent, Jeweled Rosette)

Non-flint made by King, Son & Co., Pittsburgh, PA, and continued by U.S. Glass Co. in 1899 as part of the States series.

	Clear	Colored Jewels		Clear	Colored Jewels
Bowl			Open, hs, 10"	65.00	—
Cov, 7"	40.00	—	Open, ls, 7"	35.00	—
Open, 8"	35.00	40.00	Creamer	30.00	—
Bread Plate	40.00	75.00	Cruet	65.00	—
Butter, cov	55.00	—	Goblet	40.00	—
Cake Stand			Mug	40.00	—
8"	35.00	—	Pitcher		
9-1/2"	38.00	—	Milk	55.00	—
10-1/2"	45.00	—	Water	65.00	—
Celery Vase	35.00	—	Relish	20.00	—
Compote			Salt Shaker	30.00	—
Cov, hs, 5"	40.00	55.00	Spooner	35.00	—
Cov, hs, 7"	50.00	—	Sugar, cov	45.00	—
Open, hs, 6"	30.00	—	Syrup	90.00	—
Open, hs, 8"	40.00	—	Toothpick	75.00	85.00
			Tumbler	35.00	—
			Wine	65.00	85.00

TEXAS (Loop with Stippled Panels)

Non-flint made by U.S. Glass Co., Pittsburgh, PA, c1900, in the States pattern series. Occasionally pieces are found in ruby stained. Reproduced in solid colors, including cobalt blue, by Crystal Art Glass Co. and Boyd Glass Co., Cambridge, Ohio.

	Clear with Gold	Rose Stained		Clear with Gold	Rose Stained
Bowl			Horseradish, cov	50.00	—
7"	20.00	40.00	Pickle, 8-1/2"	25.00	50.00
9", scalloped	35.00	50.00	Pitcher, water	125.00	400.00
Butter, cov	75.00	125.00	Plate, 9"	35.00	60.00
Cake Stand, 9-1/2"	65.00	125.00	Salt Shaker	25.00	—
Celery Tray	30.00	50.00	Sauce		
Celery Vase	40.00	85.00	Flat	10.00	20.00
Compote			Footed	20.00	25.00
Cov, hs, 6"	60.00	125.00	Spooner	35.00	80.00
Cov, hs, 7"	70.00	150.00	Sugar		
Cov, hs, 8"	75.00	175.00	*Individual, cov	45.00	—
Open, hs, 5"	45.00	75.00	Table, cov	75.00	125.00
Creamer			Syrup	75.00	175.00
*Individual	20.00	45.00	Toothpick	25.00	95.00
Table	45.00	85.00	Tumbler	40.00	100.00
Cruet, os	75.00	165.00	Vase		
Goblet	95.00	110.00	6-1/2"	25.00	—
			9"	35.00	—
			*Wine	75.00	140.00

THOUSAND EYE

The original pattern was non-flint made by Adams & Co., Tarentum, PA, in 1875 and by Richards and Hartley in 1888 (pattern No. 103). It was made in two forms: Adams, with a three-knob stem finial, and Richards and Hartley, with a plain stem with a scalloped bottom. Several glass companies made variations of the original pattern and reproductions were made as late as 1981. Crystal Opalescent was produced by Richards and Hartley only in the original pattern. (Opalescent celery vase, $70; open compote, 8", $115; 6" creamer, $85; quarter-gallon water pitcher, $140; half-gallon water pitcher, $180; 4" footed sauce, $40; spooner, $60; and 5" covered sugar, $80). Covered compotes are rare and would command 40% more than open compotes. A 2" mug in blue is known.

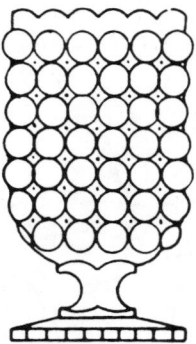

	Amber	Apple Green	Blue	Clear	Vaseline
ABC Plate, 6", clock center	60.00	70.00	60.00	50.00	60.00
Bowl, large, carriage shape	95.00	—	95.00	—	95.00
Butter, cov					
6-1/4"	75.00	85.00	80.00	50.00	100.00
7-1/2"	75.00	85.00	80.00	50.00	105.00
Cake Stand					
10"	60.00	90.00	60.00	35.00	95.00
11"	60.00	95.00	60.00	35.00	95.00
Celery, hat shape	60.00	75.00	70.00	40.00	60.00
Celery Vase, 7"	60.00	70.00	60.00	50.00	60.00
Christmas Light	35.00	50.00	40.00	30.00	45.00
Cologne Bottle	30.00	50.00	40.00	25.00	50.00
Compote, cov, ls, 8", sq	—	115.00	115.00	—	—

	Amber	Apple Green	Blue	Clear	Vaseline
Compote, open					
6"	40.00	45.00	45.00	30.00	45.00
7"	50.00	60.00	50.00	40.00	50.00
8", round	45.00	60.00	50.00	40.00	60.00
8", sq, hs	45.00	60.00	60.00	45.00	60.00
9"	60.00	70.00	60.00	45.00	60.00
10"	60.00	75.00	70.00	50.00	70.00
Cordial	40.00	60.00	45.00	30.00	70.00
Creamer					
4"	40.00	45.00	45.00	30.00	45.00
6"	45.00	85.00	60.00	40.00	85.00
Creamer and Sugar Set	—	170.00	—	115.00	—
*Cruet, 6"	45.00	70.00	60.00	40.00	70.00
Eggcup	75.00	95.00	80.00	50.00	100.00
*Goblet	45.00	50.00	45.00	40.00	50.00
Honey Dish, cov, 6" x 7-1/4"	95.00	110.00	100.00	80.00	95.00
Inkwell, 2" sq	50.00	—	85.00	40.00	90.00
Jelly Glass	30.00	35.00	30.00	20.00	30.00
Lamp, kerosene					
hs, 12"	140.00	170.00	150.00	115.00	160.00
hs, 15"	145.00	180.00	150.00	130.00	170.00
ls, handled	130.00	130.00	130.00	105.00	140.00
Mug					
2-1/2"	30.00	35.00	30.00	25.00	40.00
3-1/2"	30.00	35.00	30.00	25.00	40.00
Nappy					
5"	40.00	—	45.00	35.00	50.00
6"	45.00	—	50.00	40.00	60.00
8"	50.00	—	60.00	50.00	70.00
Pickle	30.00	35.00	35.00	25.00	35.00
Pitcher					
Milk, cov, 7"	95.00	130.00	130.00	85.00	120.00
Water, 1/4 gal	80.00	95.00	90.00	60.00	90.00
Water, 1/2 gal	90.00	110.00	95.00	75.00	95.00
Water, 1 gal	100.00	115.00	110.00	95.00	115.00
*Plate, sq, folded corners					
6"	30.00	35.00	35.00	30.00	35.00
8"	35.00	35.00	35.00	30.00	35.00
10"	40.00	60.00	45.00	30.00	40.00
Platter					
8" x 11", oblong	45.00	60.00	50.00	45.00	50.00
11", oval	85.00	90.00	60.00	45.00	85.00
Salt Shaker, pr					
Banded	70.00	80.00	75.00	70.00	75.00
Plain	60.00	70.00	60.00	45.00	70.00
Salt, ind	90.00	110.00	100.00	60.00	100.00
Salt, open, carriage shape	75.00	95.00	85.00	60.00	85.00
Salt					
Flat, 4"	15.00	25.00	20.00	10.00	20.00
Footed, 4"	20.00	25.00	20.00	15.00	25.00
Spooner	40.00	60.00	45.00	35.00	50.00
*String Holder	40.00	70.00	50.00	35.00	50.00
Sugar, cov, 5"	60.00	85.00	70.00	60.00	70.00
Syrup, pewter top	90.00	115.00	80.00	60.00	80.00
Toothpick					
Hat	45.00	70.00	80.00	40.00	60.00
Plain	40.00	60.00	60.00	30.00	45.00
Thimble	60.00	—	—	—	—
Tray, water					
12-1/2", round	75.00	90.00	85.00	60.00	85.00
14", oval	75.00	90.00	85.00	70.00	85.00
*Tumbler	35.00	75.00	40.00	30.00	35.00
Waste Bowl	—	—	—	75.00	—
*Wine	40.00	60.00	45.00	25.00	45.00

THREE-FACE

Non-flint made by George A. Duncan & Son, Pittsburgh, PA, c1878. Designed by John E. Miller, a designer with Duncan, who later became a member of the firm. It has been heavily reproduced by L. G. Wright Glass Co. and other companies as early as the 1930s. Imperial Glass Co. was commissioned by the Metropolitan Museum of Art, New York, to reproduce a series of Three-Face items, each marked with the "M.M.A." monogram.

	Clear			Clear
Biscuit Jar, cov	300.00		Cov, hs, 10"	225.00
*Butter, cov	165.00		Cov, ls, 6"	160.00
*Cake Stand			Open, hs, 9"	165.00
9"	175.00		Open, ls, 6"	95.00
12-1/2"	225.00		*Creamer	135.00
Celery Vase			*Goblet	85.00
Plain	110.00		*Lamp. Oil	150.00
Scalloped	110.00		Marmalade Jar	275.00
*Champagne			Pitcher, water	325.00
Hollow stem	250.00		*Salt Dip	35.00
Saucer type	150.00		*Salt & Pepper	75.00
*Claret	110.00		*Sauce, ftd	25.00
*Compote			*Spooner	80.00
Cov, hs, 8"	175.00		*Sugar, cov	125.00
Cov, hs, 9"	190.00		*Wine	150.00

TORPEDO (Pigmy)

Non-flint made by Thompson Glass Co., Uniontown, PA, c1889. A black amethyst master salt ($150) is also known.

	Clear	Ruby Stained			Clear	Ruby Stained
Banana Stand	75.00	—		8", plain base, pattern on bowl	85.00	—
Bowl				Marmalade Jar, cov	85.00	—
Cov, 7" d, 7-1/4" h	65.00	—		Pickle Castor, sp holder	125.00	—
Open, 7"	18.00	—		Pitcher		
Open, 9"	20.00	45.00		Milk, 8-1/2"	75.00	150.00
Butter, cov	85.00	—		Water, 10-1/2"	85.00	175.00
Cake Stand, 10"	85.00	—		Punch Cup	25.00	—
Celery Vase, scalloped top	40.00	—		Salt		
Compote				Individual	20.00	—
Cov, hs, 4", jelly	65.00	—		Master	35.00	—
Cov, hs, 13-3/4"	165.00	—		Salt Shaker, single, two types	50.00	—
Creamer	50.00	—		Sauce, 4-1/2", collared base	15.00	—
Cruet, os, ah	80.00	—		Spooner, scalloped top	45.00	—
Cup and Saucer	60.00	—		Sugar, cov	65.00	—
Decanter, os, 8"	85.00	—		Syrup	95.00	175.00
Finger Bowl	55.00	—		Tray, water		
Goblet	45.00	85.00		10", round	85.00	—
Lamp				11-3/4", clover shaped	75.00	—
3", handled	75.00	—		Tumbler	45.00	60.00
				Wine	90.00	—

TRUNCATED CUBE (Thompson's #77)

Non-flint made by Thompson Glass Co., Uniontown, PA, c1894. Also found with copper-wheel engraving.

	Clear	Ruby Stained			Clear	Ruby Stained
Bowl, 8"	—	40.00		Water, 1/2 gal	60.00	115.00
Butter, cov	50.00	90.00		Salt Shaker, single	15.00	30.00
Celery Vase	40.00	55.00		Sauce, 4"	30.00	50.00
Creamer				Spooner	30.00	50.00
Individual	20.00	30.00		Sugar, cov		
Regular	35.00	65.00		Individual	20.00	35.00
Cruet, os, ph	35.00	90.00		Regular	30.00	65.00
Decanter, os, 12" h	60.00	150.00		Syrup	40.00	100.00
Goblet	30.00	50.00		Toothpick	30.00	45.00
Pitcher, ah				Tray, water	20.00	40.00
Milk, 1 qt	50.00	100.00		Tumbler	22.50	35.00
				Wine	25.00	40.00

U.S. COIN

Non-flint frosted, clear, and gilded pattern made by U.S. Glass Co., Pittsburgh, PA, in 1892 for three or four months. The U.S. Treasury stopped production because real coins, dated as early as 1878, were used in the molds. The 1892 coin date is the most common. Lamps with coins on font and stem would be 50% more. Heavily reproduced for the gift-shop trade.

	Clear	Frosted
Ale Glass	250.00	350.00
*Bowl		
6"	170.00	220.00
9"	215.00	325.00
*Bread Plate	175.00	325.00
Butter, cov, dollars and halves	250.00	450.00
Cake Stand, 10"	225.00	400.00
Celery Tray	200.00	—
Celery Vase, quarters	135.00	350.00
Champagne	—	400.00
*Compote		
Cov, hs, 7"	300.00	500.00
Cov, hs, 8",		
quarters and dimes	—	550.00
Open, hs, 7",		
quarters and dimes	200.00	300.00
Open, hs, 7",		
quarters and halves	225.00	350.00
Open, 8-3/8" d, 6-1/2" h	—	240.00
*Creamer	350.00	600.00

	Clear	Frosted
Cruet, os	375.00	500.00
Epergne	—	1,000.00
Goblet	300.00	450.00
Goblet, dimes	200.00	295.00
Lamp		
Round font	275.00	450.00
Square font	300.00	—
Mug, handled	200.00	300.00
Pickle	200.00	—
Pitcher		
Milk	500.00	800.00
Water	400.00	800.00
Sauce, ftd, 4", quarters	100.00	185.00
*Spooner, quarters	225.00	325.00
*Sugar, cov	225.00	450.00
Syrup, dated pewter lid	—	650.00
*Toothpick	180.00	275.00
Tray, water, 10", round	450.00	550.00
*Tumbler	135.00	235.00
Waste Bowl	225.00	250.00
Wine	225.00	375.00

U.S. SHERATON (Greek Key)

Made by U.S. Glass Co., Pittsburgh, PA, in 1912. This pattern was made only in clear, but can be found trimmed with gold or platinum or with a green stain. Some pieces are marked with the intertwined U.S. Glass trademark.

	Clear
Bowl	
6", ftd, sq	15.00
8", flat	12.00
Bureau Tray	30.00
Butter, cov	35.00
Celery Tray	30.00
Compote	
Open, 4", jelly	12.00
Open, 6"	14.00
Creamer	
After dinner, tall, sq ft	12.00
Berry, bulbous, sq ft	15.00
Large	18.00
Cruet, os	25.00
Finger Bowl, under plate	24.00
Goblet	18.00
Iced Tea	20.00
Lamp, miniature	50.00
Marmalade Jar	35.00
Mug	15.00
Mustard Jar, cov	30.00
Pickle	10.00
Pin Tray	12.00
Pitcher, water, 1/2 gal	30.00

	Clear
Squat, medium	30.00
Tankard	35.00
Plate, sq	
4-1/2"	8.00
9"	12.00
Pomade Jar	14.00
Puff Box	14.00
Punch Bowl, cov, 14"	90.00
Ring Tree	25.00
Salt Shaker	
Squat	12.00
Tall	15.00
Salt, individual	17.00
Sardine Box	35.00
Spooner	
Handled	25.00
Tray	12.00
Sugar, cov	
Individual	15.00
Regular	20.00
Sundae Dish	10.00
Syrup, glass lid	35.00
Toothpick	35.00
Tumbler	15.00

VERMONT (Honeycomb with Flower Rim, Inverted Thumbprint with Daisy Band)

Non-flint made by U.S. Glass Co., Pittsburgh, PA, 1899-1903. Also made in custard (usually decorated), chocolate, caramel, novelty slag, milk glass, and blue. Crystal Art Glass Co., Mosser Glass Co., and Degenhart Glass (which marks its colored line) have reproduced toothpick holders.

	Clear with Gold	Green with Gold
Basket, handle	30.00	45.00
Bowl, berry	25.00	45.00
Butter, cov	40.00	75.00
Card Tray	20.00	35.00
Celery Tray	30.00	35.00
Compote, hs		
Cov	55.00	125.00
Open	35.00	65.00
Creamer, 4-1/4"	30.00	55.00
Goblet	40.00	50.00

	Clear with Gold	Green with Gold
Pickle	20.00	30.00
Pitcher, water	50.00	125.00
Salt Shaker	20.00	35.00
Sauce	15.00	20.00
Spooner	25.00	75.00
Sugar, cov	35.00	80.00
*Toothpick	30.00	50.00
Tumbler	20.00	40.00
Vase	20.00	45.00

VIKING (Bearded Head, Bearded Prophet, Hobb's Centennial, Old Man of the Mountain)

Non-flint made by Hobbs, Brockunier, & Co., Wheeling, WV, in 1876 as its Centennial pattern. No tumbler or goblet originally made. Very rare in milk glass.

	Clear		Clear
Apothecary Jar, cov	60.00	Creamer, 2 types	50.00
Bowl		Cup, ftd	35.00
Cov, 8", oval	55.00	Eggcup	40.00
Cov, 9", oval	65.00	Marmalade Jar	85.00
Bread Plate	70.00	Mug, ah	50.00
Butter, cov	75.00	Pickle	20.00
Celery Vase	45.00	Pitcher, water	125.00
Compote		Relish	20.00
Cov, hs, 9"	165.00	Salt, master	40.00
Cov, ls, 8", oval	95.00	Sauce	15.00
Open, hs	60.00	Spooner	35.00
		Sugar, cov	65.00

WAFFLE AND THUMBPRINT (Bull's Eye and Waffle, Palace, Triple Bull's Eye)

Flint made by the New England Glass Co., East Cambridge, MA, c1868 and by Curling, Robertson & Co., Pittsburgh, PA, c1856. Shards have been found at the Boston and Sandwich Glass Co., Sandwich, MA.

	Clear		Clear
Bottle, ftd	135.00	Goblet, knob stem	65.00
Bowl, 5" x 7"	30.00	Lamp	
Butter, cov	95.00	9-1/2"	115.00
Celery Vase	105.00	11", whale oil	175.00
Champagne	90.00	Pitcher, water	500.00
Claret	110.00	Salt, master	45.00
Compote, cov, hs	150.00	Spooner	45.00
Cordial	100.00	Sugar, cov	125.00
Creamer	125.00	Sweetmeat, cov, hs, 6"	150.00
Decanter, os		Tumbler	
Pint	165.00	Flip Glass	125.00
Quart	195.00	Water, ftd	75.00
Eggcup	45.00	Whiskey	75.00
		Wine	70.00

WESTWARD HO! (Pioneer, Tippecanoe)

Non-flint, usually frosted, made by Gillinder and Sons, Philadelphia, PA, c1879. Molds made by Jacobus, who also made Classic. Has been reproduced since the 1930s by L. G. Wright Glass Co., Westmoreland Glass Co., and several others. This pattern was originally made in milk glass (rare) and clear with acid finish as part of the design. Reproductions can be found in several colors and in clear.

	Clear		Clear
Bowl, 5", ftd	125.00	*Goblet	120.00
Bread Plate	175.00	Marmalade Jar, cov	200.00
*Butter, cov	185.00	Mug	
*Celery Vase	125.00	2"	225.00
*Compote		3-1/2", water	175.00
Cov, hs, 5"	225.00	*Pitcher, water	350.00
Cov, hs, 8" d	455.00	*Sauce, ftd, 4-1/2"	35.00
Open, hs, 8"	125.00	*Spooner	95.00
*Creamer	115.00	*Sugar, cov	185.00
		*Wine	200.00

WHEAT AND BARLEY (Duquesne, Hops and Barley, Oats and Barley)

Non-flint made by Bryce Bros., Pittsburgh, PA, c1880. Later made by U.S. Glass Co., Pittsburgh, PA, after 1891.

	Amber	Blue	Clear	Vaseline
Bowl, 8", cov	35.00	40.00	25.00	55.00
Butter, cov	45.00	60.00	35.00	80.00
Cake Stand				
8"	30.00	45.00	20.00	60.00
10"	40.00	50.00	30.00	70.00
Compote				
Cov, hs, 7"	45.00	55.00	40.00	75.00

	Amber	Blue	Clear	Vaseline
Cov, hs, 8"	50.00	55.00	45.00	75.00
Open, hs, jelly	32.50	40.00	30.00	55.00
*Creamer	30.00	40.00	28.00	55.00
*Goblet	40.00	55.00	25.00	75.00
Mug	30.00	40.00	20.00	55.00
Pitcher				
Milk	70.00	85.00	40.00	110.00
Water	85.00	95.00	45.00	125.00
Plate				
7"	20.00	30.00	15.00	40.00
9", closed handles	25.00	35.00	20.00	45.00
Relish	20.00	30.00	15.00	40.00
Salt Shaker	25.00	30.00	20.00	40.00
Sauce				
Flat, handled	15.00	15.00	10.00	20.00
Footed	15.00	15.00	10.00	20.00
Spooner	30.00	40.00	24.00	55.00
Sugar, cov	40.00	50.00	35.00	65.00
Syrup	175.00	195.00	85.00	—
Tumbler	35.00	40.00	20.00	55.00

WILLOW OAK (Acorn, Acorn and Oak Leaf, Bryce's Wreath, Stippled Daisy, Thistle and Sunflower)

Non-flint made by Bryce Bros., Pittsburgh, PA, c1885 and by U.S. Glass Company in 1891.

	Amber	Blue	Canary	Clear
Bowl, 8"	45.00	40.00	50.00	20.00
Butter, cov	65.00	65.00	80.00	40.00
Cake Stand, 8-1/2"	55.00	65.00	70.00	45.00
Celery Vase	45.00	60.00	75.00	35.00
Compote				
Cov, hs, 7-1/2"	50.00	65.00	80.00	40.00
Open, 7"	30.00	40.00	48.00	25.00
Creamer	45.00	50.00	60.00	40.00
Goblet	40.00	50.00	60.00	30.00
Mug	35.00	45.00	54.00	30.00
Pitcher				
Milk	50.00	60.00	70.00	45.00
Water	55.00	60.00	75.00	50.00
Plate				
7"	35.00	45.00	50.00	25.00
9"	35.00	35.00	40.00	25.00
Salt Shaker	25.00	40.00	55.00	20.00
Sauce				
Flat, handled, sq	15.00	20.00	24.00	10.00
Footed, 4"	20.00	25.00	30.00	15.00
Spooner	35.00	40.00	48.00	30.00
Sugar, cov	68.50	70.00	75.00	40.00
Tray, water, 10-1/2"	35.00	50.00	60.00	30.00
Tumbler	35.00	40.00	45.00	30.00
Waste Bowl	35.00	40.00	40.00	30.00

WISCONSIN (Beaded Dewdrop)

Non-flint made by U.S. Glass Co. in Gas City, IN, in 1903. One of the States patterns. Toothpick reproduced in colors

	Clear
Banana Stand	75.00
Bowl	
6", oval, handled, cov	40.00
7", round	42.00
Butter, flat flange	75.00
*Cake Stand	
8-1/2"	60.00
9-1/2"	70.00
Celery Tray	40.00
Celery Vase	60.00
Compote	
Cov, hs, 5"	60.00
Cov, hs, 6"	65.00
Cov, hs, 7"	75.00

	Clear
Cov, hs, 8"	90.00
Open, hs, 6"	35.00
Open, hs, 8"	50.00
Open, hs, 10"	75.00
Condiment Set, salt & pepper, mustard, horseradish, tray	110.00
*Creamer	60.00
Cruet, os	80.00
Cup and Saucer	50.00
*Goblet	75.00
Marmalade Jar, straight sides, glass lid	125.00
Mug	35.00
Pitcher	
Milk	75.00

	Clear			Clear
Water	85.00		Sugar, cov	60.00
Plate, 6-3/4"	25.00		Sugar Shaker	90.00
Punch Cup	12.00		Sweetmeat, 5", ftd, cov	40.00
Relish	25.00		Syrup	110.00
Salt Shaker	30.00		*Toothpick, kettle	55.00
Spooner	30.00		Tumbler	45.00
			Wine	75.00

X-RAY

Non-flint made by Riverside Glass Works, Wellsburgh, WV, 1896-98. Prices are for pieces with gold trim.

	Clear	Emerald Green		Clear	Emerald Green
Bowl, berry, 8", beaded rim	25.00	45.00	Goblet	20.00	35.00
Bread Plate	30.00	50.00	Pitcher, water	40.00	75.00
Butter, cov	40.00	75.00	Salt Shaker	10.00	15.00
Celery Vase	—	50.00	Sauce, flat, 4-1/2" d	8.00	10.00
Compote			Spooner	25.00	40.00
Cov, hs	40.00	65.00	Sugar		
Jelly	—	40.00	Individual, open	20.00	45.00
Creamer			Regular, cov	35.00	65.00
Individual	20.00	50.00	Tumbler shape	—	75.00
Regular	35.00	65.00	Syrup	—	265.00
Cruet Set, 4-leaf clover tray	125.00	350.00	Toothpick	25.00	50.00
			Tumbler	15.00	25.00

YALE (Crow-foot, Turkey Track)

Non-flint made by McKee & Bros. Co., Jeannette, PA, patented in 1887.

	Clear			Clear
Bowl, berry, 10-1/2"	20.00		Goblet	45.00
Butter, cov	45.00		Pitcher, water	65.00
Cake Stand	55.00		Relish, oval	10.00
Celery Vase	40.00		Salt Shaker	30.00
Compote			Sauce, flat	10.00
Cov, hs	50.00		Spooner	45.00
Open, scalloped rim	25.00		Sugar, cov	35.00
Creamer	60.00		Syrup	65.00
			Tumbler	25.00

ZIPPER (Cobb)

Non-flint made by Richards & Hartley, Tarentum, PA, c1888.

	Clear			Clear
Bowl, 7" d	15.00		Pitcher, water, 1/2 gal	40.00
Butter, cov	45.00		Relish, 10" l	15.00
Celery Vase	25.00		Salt Dip	5.00
Cheese, cov	55.00		Sauce	
Compote, cov, ls, 8" d	40.00		Flat	7.50
Creamer	35.00		Footed	12.00
Cruet, os	45.00		Spooner	30.00
Goblet	20.00		Sugar, cov	45.00
Marmalade Jar, cov	45.00		Tumbler	20.00

PAUL REVERE POTTERY

History: Paul Revere Pottery, Boston, Massachusetts, was an outgrowth of a club known as The Saturday Evening Girls. The S.E.G. was composed of young female immigrants who met on Saturday nights to read and participate in craft projects, such as ceramics.

Regular pottery production began in 1908, and the name "Paul Revere" was adopted because the pottery was located near the Old North Church. In 1915 the firm moved to Brighton, Massachusetts. Known as the "Bowl Shop," the pottery grew steadily. In spite of popular acceptance and technical advancements, the pottery required continual subsidies. It finally closed in January 1942.

Items produced range from plain and decorated vases to tablewares to illustrated tiles. Many decorated wares were incised and glazed either in an Art Nouveau matte finish or an occasional high glaze.

Marks: In addition to an impressed mark, paper "Bowl Shop" labels were used prior to 1915. Pieces also can be found with a date and "P.R.P." or "S.E.G." painted on the base.

References: Susan and Al Bagdade, *Warman's American Pottery and Porcelain*, Wallace-Homestead, 1994; Paul Evans, *Art Pottery of the United States*, 2nd ed., Feingold & Lewis Publishing, 1987; Ralph and Terry Kovel, *Kovels' American Art Pottery*, Crown Publishers, 1993; David Rago, *American Art Pottery*, Knickerbocker Press, 1977.

Collectors' Club: American Art Pottery Assoc. P.O. Box 525, Cedar Hill, MO 63016.

Bookends, pr, 4" h, 5" w, night scene of owls, 1921, ink mkd "S.E.G./11-21," flat chip to one base 1,300.00
Bowl
    4-1/4" d, 2-1/4" h, yellow and black band of walking ducks, mkd "S.E.G. 6-21, B.L" 520.00
    5-1/4" d, tree bands with black outline scene, blue sky, green trees, mkd "S.E.G. 4/15, I.G." 275.00
    8-1/4" d, 2-3/4" h, flaring, dripping blue-gray satin glaze, mkd "P. R.P./Lewis/2nd Firing" 275.00
    8-1/2" d, tree bands with black outline scene, blue sky, green trees, mkd "S.E.G. 20/3.15, I.G.," hairline 225.00
Cake Set, Tree pattern, black outline scene, blue sky, green trees, 10" d cake plate, six 8-1/2" d serving plates, each mkd "J.G., S.E.G.," three dated 7/15, three dated 1/4/15, one dated 3/15, price for 7 pc set 1,840.00
Humidor, cov, 6-1/4" h, 5-3/4" d, spherical, blue matte glaze, pink int., minute int. rim nick, sgd in slip "P.R.P. 3/36"..........400.00
Lamp Base, 16" h. 9" d, cuerda seca dec, white Queen Anne's lace, green foliage, white, blue, and green ground, hairline to base comes up side, bruise and short hairline to top rim, ink mark "S.E.G." 15,000.00
Plate
    6-1/2" d, incised white mice, celadon and brown band, ink mark "Dorothy Hopkins/Her Plate," 1911 ....1,300.00
    7-1/2" d
        Blue and green band, incised windmills, white center, 1911, ink S.E.G. mark...950.00

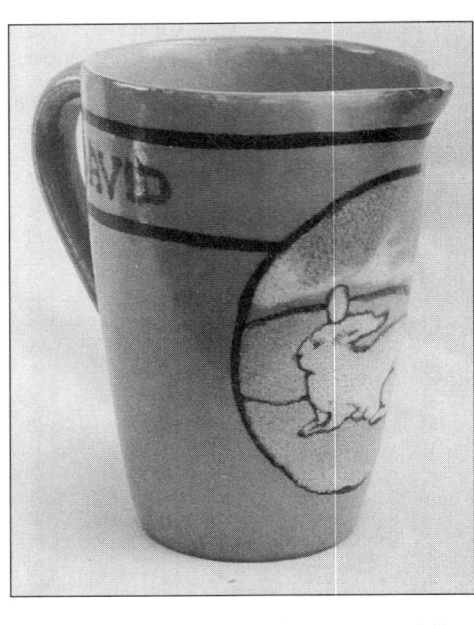

Jug, yellow and brown ground, rabbit medallion, inscribed "David/His Jug," 4-1/2" h, $225.

    Blue and white band, center medallion of blue scene, yellow sky and dock, initials "J.I.T.," mkd "S.E.G. F.L. 7/19" and "S.E.G., F.L. 8/15," price for pr 520.00
    Blue sky, green center, incised landscape of trees, 1912, ink S.E.G. mark...650.00
Ring Tray, 4" d, circular, blue-gray and green band of trees, blue-gray ground, mkd "S.E.G./J.G." 275.00
Teapot, 4-1/2" h, 9" d, brown and white wavy band of sailboats, yellow sky, 1918, restored 700.00
Tile, 3-3/4" sq, Washington Street, blue, white, green, and brown, mkd "H.S. S4 9/1/10," edge chips................................420.00
Trivet
    4-1/4" d, medallion of house against setting sun, blue-gray ground, 1924, imp P.R.P. mark 425.00
    5-1/2" d, medallion of goose standing on hill, dark blue ground, 1924, imp P.R.P. mark 550.00
    5-1/2" d, medallion of poplar trees in landscape, blue-green ground, 1925, imp P.R.P. mark 600.00
Vase
    4-1/4" h, 3" d, bottle shape, glossy orange and matte brown glaze, ink P.R.P. mark...225.00
    6-1/4" h, 3-1/2" d, ovoid, band of green trees, satin blue-gray ground, small glaze bubble on body, imp circular P.R.P. mark, 1924 ....1,300.00
    7" h, 5-1/4" d, baluster shape, band of orange lotus blossoms, frothy green ground, green base, imp P. R. mark.1,300.00
    10-1/2" h, 5-3/4" d, satin green glaze, ink "S.E.G." mark
    ....250.00
    13" h, 8" d, dark blue and green dripping satin glaze, 1926, ink mark "P.R.P." 900.00

PEACHBLOW

History: Peachblow, an art glass which derives its name from a fine Chinese glazed porcelain, resembles a peach or crushed strawberries in color. Three American glass manufacturers and two English firms produced peachblow glass in the late 1880s. A fourth American company resumed the process in the 1950s. The glass from each firm has its own identifying characteristics.

Hobbs, Brockunier & Co., Wheeling peachblow: Opalescent glass, plated or cased with a transparent amber glass; shading from yellow at the base to a deep red at top; glossy or satin finish.

Mt. Washington "Peach Blow": A homogeneous glass, shading from a pale gray-blue to a soft rose color; some pieces enhanced with glass appliqués, enameling, and gilding.

New England Glass Works, New England peachblow (advertised as Wild Rose, but called Peach Blow at the plant): Translucent, shading from rose to white; acid or glossy finish; some pieces enameled and gilded.

Thomas Webb & Sons and Stevens and Williams (English firms): Peachblow-style cased art glass, shading from yellow to red; some pieces with cameo-type relief designs.

Gunderson Glass Co.: Produced peachblow-type art glass to order during the 1950s; shades from an opaque faint tint of pink, which is almost white, to a deep rose.

Marks: Pieces made in England are marked "Peach Blow" or "Peach Bloom."

References: Gary E. Baker et al., *Wheeling Glass 1829-1939*, Oglebay Institute, 1994, distributed by Antique Publications; Neila and Tom Bredehoft, *Hobbs, Brockunier & Co. Glass*, Collector Books, 1997; James Measell, *New Martinsville Glass*, Antique Publications, 1994; John A. Shuman III, *Collector's Encyclopedia of American Glass*, Collector Books, 1988, 1994 value update; Kenneth Wilson, *American Glass 1760-1930*, 2 vols., Hudson Hills Press and The Toledo Museum of Art, 1994.

Gundersen

Cruet, 8" h, 3-1/2" w, matte finish, ribbed shell handle, matching stopper with good color...........875.00
Cup and Saucer 275.00
Decanter, 10" h, 5" w, Pilgrim Canteen form, acid finish, deep raspberry to white, applied peachblow-ribbed handle, deep raspberry stopper...........950.00
Goblet, 701/4" h, 4" d top, glossy finish, deep color, applied Burmese glass base...........285.00
Jug, 4-1/2" h, 4" w, bulbous, applied loop handle, acid finish...........450.00
Pitcher, 5-1/2" h, Hobnail, matte finish, white with hint of pink on int., orig label...........550.00
Plate, 8" d, luncheon, deep raspberry to pale pink, matte finish...........375.00
Punch Cup, acid finish...........275.00
Tumbler, 3-3/4" h, matte finish...........275.00

Gunderson, compote, applied foot, satin finish, 5-5/8" w, 2-3/4" h, $130. Photo courtesy of Gene Harris Antique Auction Center.

Urn, 8-1/2" h, 4-1/2" w, two applied "M" handles, sq cut base, matte finish...........550.00
Vase
  4-1/4" h, 3" d, acid finish...........225.00
  5" h, 6" w, ruffled top, pinched-in base...........525.00
  9" h, 3-1/4" w, Tappan, acid finish...........425.00
Wine Glass, 5" h, glossy finish...........175.00

Mount Washington

Bowl, 3" x 4", shading from deep rose to bluish-white, MOP satin int...........150.00
Pitcher, 6-7/8" h, bulbous, sq handle...........3,750.00
Vase, 8-1/4" h, lily form, satin finish...........1,850.00

New England

Celery Vase, 7" h, 4" w, sq top, deep raspberry with purple highlights shading to white...........785.00
Cruet, 6-3/4" h, 4" d at base, petticoat form, applied white handle and stopper, 3-lip top, acid finish...........1,950.00
Pitcher, 6-3/4" h, 7-1/2" w, 3-1/4" w at top, bulbous, sq top, applied frosted handle, ten rows of hobs, Sandwich...........550.00
Spooner, sq top, acid finish...........825.00
Tumbler
  3-3/4" h, shiny finish, deep color upper third, middle fading to creamy white bottom, thin walls...........445.00
  3-3/4" h, velvety satin finish, deep raspberry red extends 2/3 down, faces to 1/2" pure white band...........400.00
Vase
  3-1/4" h, 2-1/2" d, bulbous bottom, ring around neck, flaring top, matte finish...........550.00
  5-1/2" h, satin finish, bulbous...........485.00
  6-1/2" h, 3" w at top, lily, glossy finish, deep pink shading to white...........650.00
  7" h, lily, satin finish, wafer base...........945.00
  8-3/4" h, 4" w, bulbous stick, deep raspberry to white, matte finish...........950.00
  10-1/2" h, 5" w at base, bulbous, tapering neck, cup top, deep color, orig glossy finish...........1,250.00
  10-1/2" h, 5" w at base, bulbous gourd shape, deep raspberry with fuchsia highlights to white, coloring extends two-thirds way down, 4 dimpled sides...........1,450.00
  15-1/2" h, 6" w at top, lily, deep raspberry pink to white...........1,450.00

Webb

Cologne, 5" h, bulbous, raised gold floral branches, silver hall-marked dome top...........900.00
Creamer, satin finish, coralene dec, rolled rim, flat base...650.00
Finger Bowl, 4-1/2" d, cased...........195.00
Vase
  6" h, satin finish...........375.00
  1-1/4" h, 6-1/2" d, pine needles, boughs, and trailing prunus blossoms, buds, and branches, two butterflies in flight, deep cherry red shading to pink-peach, creamy white lining, gold trim at top and base, dec by Jules Barbe...........750.00

Wheeling

Cruet, 6-1/4" h, ball shaped, mahogany neck and spout, fuchsia shoulders, cream base, Hobbs, Brockunier...........1,950.00
Ewer, 6-3/4" h, 4" w, glossy finish, duck bill top, applied amber loop handle...........3,500.00
Mustard, SP cov and handle...........475.00
Pear, hollow blown
  4-3/4" w, 3" w base, matte finish, bright red and yellow, white lining, very tip of stem gone...........900.00
  5-1/2" h, 3" w base, glossy finish, tip of stem gone...........800.00
Punch Cup, 2-1/2" h, Hobbs, Brockunier...........535.00
Tumbler, shiny finish, deep colored upper third shades to creamy base...........385.00

Vase
9-1/4" h, ball shaped body, 5" slender neck, shape #11
....735.00
13" h, acid finish 975.00

PEKING GLASS

History: Peking glass is a type of cameo glass of Chinese origin. Its production began in the 1700s and continued well into the 19th century. The background color of Peking glass may be a delicate shade of yellow, green, or white. One style of white background is so transparent that it often is referred to as the "snowflake" ground. The overlay colors include a rich garnet red, deep blue, and emerald green.

Bowl
5-3/4" d, rounded form, ext. with cranes and lotus plants, green overlay, whit ground...90.00
6-1/8" d, floral shaped rim, ext. with birds among lotus, lotus leaf form foot, red overly, white ground.................1,150.00
7" d, raised lotus petals on ext., opaque blue with white int., 19th C...375.00
7" d, rounded form, shaped rim, ext. with flowering lotus continuing to a lotus leaf-form foot rim, green overlay, white ground...575.00
Cup, 2-1/2" h, deep form, gently flaring rim, ring foot, continual band of overlapping dragons, cloud collar border, lappet border, red overlay, Snowflake.......................................2,185.00
Dish, 11-3/4" l, flattened round form, bright yellow, 19th C 850.00
Snuff Bottle, green, jade stopper, Chinese 45.00
Vase
7" h, high shouldered form, ducks swimming among tall lotus plants, green overlay, white ground, pr....................500.00
7-1/2" h, ovoid, elongated neck, red overlay, Snowflake pattern, body with 2 dragons and 2 phoenix, neck with dragon and phoenix, Qianlong period, pr 4,600.00
8" h, high shoulder form, red overlay, white ground, female figures in garden, 18th C, pr 1,840.00
9-1/4" h, ovoid, opaque raised yellow flowers, translucent yellow ground, 19th C 525.00

Snuff Bottles, pastel colored leaves, green jade top, 2-3/8" l, $195.

PELOTON

History: Wilhelm Kralik of Bohemia patented Peloton art glass in 1880. Later it was also patented in America and England.

Peloton glass is found with both transparent and opaque grounds, although opaque is more common. Opaque colored glass filaments (strings) are applied by dipping or rolling the hot glass. Generally, the filaments (threads) are pink, blue, yellow, and white (rainbow colors) or a single color. Items also may have a satin finish and enamel decorations.

Biscuit Jar, 7" h, 6-1/2" d, powder blue body, white, yellow, blue, and vivid pink filaments, 48 molded-in vertical ribs, silverplated fittings, barn swallow emb on lid.............................785.00
Bowl, 6-1/2" d, 6" h, white ground, brown and yellow filaments, all-over ribbed surface, 3 applied crystal thorn feet, 8 point star top..325.00
Finger Bowl, colorless, multicolored filaments 75.00
Pitcher, 6-1/2" h, sq blown clear body, applied colorless, pink, yellow, blue and white striped yellow filaments, applied colorless handle 250.00
Punch Cup, turquoise ground, multicolored filaments, enameled florals, set of six 325.00
Rose Bowl
4" h, 4" w, ftd, 4 pulled edges, sq shape, applied crystal edge, 6 shell feet, glossy finish shaded blue ground, yellow, pink, white, blue, and red filaments 395.00
6" h, 5-1/2" w, ftd, 8 point star shaped top, white lining, ribbed and swirled, brown shaded filaments.......................325.00
Toothpick Holder, 3" h, colorless, white filaments.............145.00
Tumbler, 3-3/4" h, colorless ground, yellow, pink, red, light blue, and white filaments...125.00
Vase
3-1/2" h, 3 x 3-7/8" d, orchid pink cased body, emb ribs, pink, blue, and yellow filaments, pinched together in center
....195.00
4" h, 4-3/4" d, bulbous base, folded over tricorn shape top, white ribbed cased body, pink, yellow, blue, and white applied filaments 290.00
6" h, 5" w, ribbed, bright pink ground, yellow, blue, white, red, pink, and purple filaments, white lining, two applied ribbed handles 450.00

PERFUME, COLOGNE, AND SCENT BOTTLES

History: The second half of the 19th century was the golden age for decorative bottles made to hold scents. These bottles were made in a variety of shapes and sizes.

An atomizer is a perfume bottle with a spray mechanism. Cologne bottles usually are larger and have stoppers, which also may be used as applicators. A perfume bottle has a stopper that often is elongated and designed to be an applicator.

Scent bottles are small bottles used to hold a scent or smelling salts. A vinaigrette is an ornamental box or bottle that has a perforated top and is used to hold aromatic vinegar or smelling salts. Fashionable women of the late 18th and 19th centuries carried them in purses or slipped them into gloves in case of a sudden fainting spell.

References: Joanne Dubbs Ball and Dorothy Hehl Torem, *Commercial Fragrance Bottles*, Schiffer Publishing, 1993; ——, *Fragrance Bottle Masterpieces*, Schiffer Publishing, 1996; Carla Bordignon, *Perfume Bottles*, Chronicle Books, 1995; Glinda Bowman, *Miniature Perfume Bottles*, Schiffer Publishing, 1994; ——, *More Miniature Perfume Bottles*, Schiffer Publishing, 1996; Jacquelyne Jones-North, *Commercial Perfume Bottles*, revised and updated ed., Schiffer Publishing, 1996; Christie Mayer Lefkowith, *Art of Perfume*, Thames and Hudson, 1994; Monsen and Baer, *Beauty of Perfume*, published by authors (Box 529, Vienna, VA 22183), 1996; ——, *Legacies of Perfume*, published by authors (Box 529, Vienna, VA 22183), 1997; John Odell, *Digger Odell's Official Antique Bottle and Glass Collector Magazine Price Guide Series*, vol. 6, published by author (1910 Shawhan Rd, Morrow, OH 45152), 1995; Jeri Lyn Ringblum, *Collector's Handbook of Miniature Perfume Bottles*, Schiffer Publishing, 1996.

Periodical: *Perfume & Scent Bottle Quarterly*, P.O. Box 187, Galena, OH 43021.

Collectors' Clubs: International Perfume Bottle Assoc., P.O .Box 529, Vienna, VA 22180; Mini-Scents, 7 Saint John's Rd West Hollywood, CA 90069; Parfum Plus Collections, 1590 Louis-Carrier Ste. 502, Montreal Quebec H4N 2Z1 Canada.

Atomizer

4-1/2" h, Moser, sapphire blue, gold florals, leaves, and swirls, melon ribbed body, orig gold top and bulb 275.00
6-1/4" h, Cambridge, stippled gold, opaque jade, orig silk lined box 140.00

Atomizer, Egyptian motif, gold leafing, Devilbiss, Toledo, orig label, 8" h, $295.

8" h, Galle, cameo, lavender flowers and foliage, shaded yellow and frosted ground 1,250.00

Cologne

3-1/8" h, apple green, pressed base, cut stopper 150.00
4-1/2" h, vaseline, attributed to New England Glass Co., flint, orig stopper 225.00
5-7/8" h, Baccarat, colorless, panel cut, matching stopper .75.00
7" h, cut glass, cranberry cut to colorless, cane cut, matching stopper 250.00
7" h, 5" d, paperweight, double overlay, crimson red over white over colorless squatty bottle, five oval facet windows reveal concentric millefiore cane int., matching stopper 460.00
11" h, art glass, transparent green bottle, delicate floral design, colorless pedestal foot, faceted teardrop stopper 175.00

Perfume

2" h, 1-1/2" d, German, green glass, colored enamel coat of arms, fine enamel trim on body and matching green stopper ..60.00
2-3/8" h, Venetian, globular body, Lion of Venice portrait cane on surface of opaque yellow and silver glass, crowned with ornate cap dec with flowers, no stopper 335.00
3-9/16" h, cherub sulphide surrounded by ornate faceting on all sides, gilded copper cap, glass stopper 365.00
3-11/16" h, Clichy, ext. dec with alternating blue and white swirled bands, stopper and base dec with 16K gold chased with delicate patterns, base mkd "D. J.," fitted leather carrying case 990.00
4-3/8" h, Mary Gregory, cranberry, white enameled girl dec, colorless ball stopper 175.00
4-3/4" h, Steuben, Verre- de Soie, jade green....................310.00
5-1/2" h, Rene Lalique, Sirenes, frosted mermaids with traces of gray patina, molded signature on base, no cover 250.00
6-3/8" h, Baccarat, molded and frosted, acid stamped "Baccarat/France," mid 20th C..650.00

Scent

2-1/2" h, Early American glass, amethyst, teardrop shape, emb sunburst design...225.00
3" h, agate, flattened globe form, silver hinged rim and screw cap, mkd "Black, Starr, & Frost" 260.00
3-1/4" h, porcelain, figural, modeled as male and female, each holding dog, removable heads, Germany, 19th C, pr...435.00
3-3/4" h, ivory, figural, woman holding basket of flowers in one hand, fan in other, polychrome dec, Japan 90.00
3-3/4" h, satin, bridal white, Peacock Eye, MOP, orig glass stopper, push-on silverplated lid with monogram "C"..........435.00

Perfume Bottles, R. S. Germany, pink and green florals, creamy iridescence, gold stoppers, 5" h, pr, $135.

Vinaigrette, stein, enamel and silver, mkd "Grass & München," 1" h, $550.

4" d, satin, bridal white, 24 white vertical stripes, 12 silk ribbons alternating with 12 muted satin ribbons, sterling silver flip top cap, collar stamped "CS, FS, STd, SILr," engraved name 400.00
4-1/8" h, Early American, blown, colorless, cranberry and white stripes, white and gold metallic twist...............................95.00
5-1/2" h, four triangular scenes encased in trelliswork banding, dec gilt metal foliate mounts, cut glass stoppers, French, early 20th C 115.00

Vinaigrette

7/8" l, SS, tooled purse shape, gilded int., John Turner, Birmingham hallmarks, 1792 ....250.00
1-1/4" l, SS, tooled purse shape, gilded int., S. Pemberton, Birmingham hallmarks, 1790 ....220.00
2-1/4" x 1", cranberry, rect, allover cutting, enameled tiny pink roses, green leaves, gold dec, hinged lid, stopper, finger chain 185.00
3-7/8" l, cut glass, cobalt blue, yellow flashing, SS overlay, emb SS cap 125.00

PETERS AND REED POTTERY

History: J. D. Peters and Adam Reed founded their pottery company in South Zanesville, Ohio, in 1900. Common flowerpots, jardinieres, and cooking wares comprised the majority of their early output. Occasionally art pottery was attempted, but it was not until 1912 that their Moss Aztec line was introduced and widely accepted. Other art wares include Chromal, Landsun, Montene, Pereco, and Persian.

Peters retired in 1921 and Reed changed the name of the firm to Zane Pottery Company.

Vase, Art Nouveau, leaf and lily pattern, green striated leaves, purple flowers, high glaze, 5" h, $175.

Marks: Marked pieces of Peters and Reed Pottery are unknown.

Bowl, 10" d, Landsun, shades of blue 90.00
Candlesticks, pr, 10" h, mirror black glaze..........................35.00
Doorstop, cat, yellow 375.00
Ewer, 11" h, orange and yellow raised grapes dec, brown ground 50.00
Jardiniere, #249, Lions 65.00
Mug, blended glaze 30.00
Pitcher, 4" h, green and yellow raised fern leaves, gloss dark brown ground 65.00
Vase
    5" h, Zane Ware, underglaze rose dec............................45.00
    9-3/4" h, pinecones and needles, terra cotta with green wash 65.00
    12" h, Moss Aztec, relief grapes.....................................75.00
Wall Pocket, 9" h, Egyptian...75.00

PEWTER

History: Pewter is a metal alloy consisting mostly of tin with small amounts of lead, copper, antimony, and bismuth added to make the shaping of products easier and to increase the hardness of the material. The metal can be cast, formed around a mold, spun, easily cut, and soldered to form a wide variety of utilitarian articles.

Pewter was known to the ancient Chinese, Egyptians, and Romans. England was the primary source of pewter for the American colonies for nearly 150 years until the American Revolution ended the embargo on raw tin, allowing the small American pewter industry to flourish until the Civil War.

References: Marilyn E. Dragowick (ed.), *Metalwares Price Guide*, Antique Trader Books, 1995; Donald M. Herr, *Pewter in Pennsylvania German Churches*, Vol. XXIX, The Pennsylvania German Society, 1995; Henry J. Kauffman, *American Pewterer*, Astragal Press, 1994.

Collectors' Club: Pewter Collectors Club of America, 504 W. Lafayette St., West Chester, PA 19380.

Museum: The Currier Gallery of Art, Manchester, NH.

Note: The listings concentrate on the American and English pewter forms most often encountered by the collector.

Baptismal Bowl, 9" d, Boardman, Hartford, CT, stamped "BX," mkd "Jacobs," 19th C...950.00
Basin
    6-5/8" d, 1-1/2" h, Blakeslee, Philadelphia, PA, partial eagle touch, wear and battering 175.00
    7-3/4" d, 1-7/8" h, Gershom Jones, Providence, RI, eagle touch, dents, wear, and scratches 375.00
    8" d, 2" h, Thomas Compton, English 220.00
Beaker, 5-1/8" h
    Thomas D. and Sherman Boardman, Hartford, CT, mkd "Laughlin," c1810-30 ....650.00
    Timothy Boardman and Co., NY, mkd "Laughlin," c1825 ....630.00
Candlesticks, pr
    8-3/4" h, mkd "Jacobs," 1822-71 ....950.00
    9-3/4" h, unmarked American, attributed to CT, with bobeches 275.00
Charger
    12" d, London touch, wear...150.00
    13-1/8" d, George Lightner, Baltimore, eagle touch, some wear, minor edge damage 770.00
    13-1/2" d, Nathaniel Austin, MA, c1800.......................750.00
    14" d, David Melville, Newport, RI, 1804-10, dents.......450.00
    15" d, John Townsend, London, smooth rim 250.00
Coffeepot, cov
    7" h, Israel Trask, Beverly, MA, lighthouse, bright cut engraving 350.00
    10-5/8" h, Freeman Porter, Westbrook, ME 470.00
    11" h, R. Dunham...275.00
    13" h, James Dixon, England......................................250.00
    13-1/2" h, Reed and Barton, mkd "Leonard Reed & Barton 3500" 250.00
Communion Chalice, 6-1/4" h, unmarked American, handles removed, pr 200.00
Creamer, 5-7/8" h, unmarked American, teapot shape......250.00
Deep Dish, 13-1/8" d, Stephen Barnes eagle touch, Middletown or Wallingford, CT, minor scratches and wear 415.00
Flagon
    9-1/2" h, thumb piece, engraved floral and amorous couple on bench design, German inscription and "F C S 1809," soldered repair 165.00
    12-1/2" h, attributed to Israel Trask, Beverly, MA, 1807-56, minor dents...300.00
    14" h, Thomas D. and Sherman Boardman, Hartford, CT, mkd "Laughlin," 1810-30 ....3,750.00
Inkstand, 3-1/2" h, 5-1/2" w, 9-1/2" l, unmarked, ftd............175.00
Lamp
    5-3/4" h plus brass and tin whale oil burner, Putnam touch, James Putnam, Madison, MA, some splits in rim of base 315.00
    7" h plus fluid burner, unmarked American, attributed to Meriden, reeded detail on base, ear handle, light pitting 110.00
    8-1/2" h plus burner, Yale and Curtis, NY 1 touch, matching fluid burner missing, snuffers and one brass tube loose 190.00
Measure
    2-3/8" to 8" h, assembled set, bellied, English, minor damage 550.00
    5-3/4" h, John Warne, English, brass rim, battered, old repair, quart 100.00

Plate, Thomas Danforth, Phila, 8-3/4" d, $150.

Mug, quart
    4" h, Thomas Danforth Boardman, Hartford, CT, tankard, partial "T.D.B." touch, some battering, soldered repairs 500.00
    5-7/8" h, Samuel Hamlin, Hartford, Middletown, CT, and Providence RI, dent at base 625.00
Pitcher
    6" h, Freeman Porter, Westbrook, ME, 2 quart 225.00
    6-1/2" h, Continental, swirl design, hinged lid, angel touch 85.00
Plate
    7-3/4" d, Thomas D. Boardman eagle touch, wear and scratches 275.00
    7-3/4" d, S. Kilbourne, Baltimore eagle touch, minor wear and dents...495.00

Porringer, cast crown handle, mkd "I.G.," Boston area, somewhat battered, old repair, 4-3/8" d, $90. Photo courtesy of Garth's Auctions.

7-7/8" d, Asbil Griswold, Meriden, CT, eagle touch some battering and knife scratches 160.00

7-7/8" d, B. Barns, Philada and "B.B." eagle touch, wear and dents...200.00

7-7/8" d, Joseph Danforth lion touch, minor wear 330.00

8" d, rampant lion touch, Edward Danford, Middletown and Hartford, CT, minor wear and scratches 220.00

8-3/8" d, David Melville, Newport, RI, 1776-94, mkd on base, knife marks, minor pitting 520.00

Platter, 28-3/4" l, Townsend and Compton, London, pierced insert, mkd "Cotterell"..2,400.00

Porringer

    3-7/8" d, cast handle, mkd "TD & SB" touch (Thomas Danford Boardman, et al, Hartford)..220.00

    4-3/4" d, cast crown handle, mkd "I.G.," Boston area, pitting, pinpoint hole 140.00

    5-1/2" d, unmarked American, cast flowered handle 150.00

Soup Plate, 8-7/8" d, unmarked Continental, angel touch....75.00

Sugar Bowl, 6" h, Ashril Griswold, Meriden, CT, eagle touch 490.00

Syrup Pitcher, 4-1/2" h, hinged lid, unmarked, American ..220.00

Tablespoon, rattail handle, heart on back of bowl, mkd "L. B.," (Luther Boardman, MA and CT). set of 6 ....330.00

Tea Caddy, 3-3/4" h, B G S & Co, American, 1825-30, almond shape, bright cut designs, touch mark, wear, pitted.....200.00

Teapot

    6-3/4" h, Roswell Gleason, Dorchester, MA, eagle touch 495.00

    6-3/4" h, Ashbil Griswold, Meriden, CT, eagle touch, some battering and repairs 200.00

    7" h, Eben Smith, Beverly, MA, 1813-56, minor pitting and scratches 375.00

    7-1/2" h, L. Boardman, Warranted touch, (Luther Boardman, South Reading, MA,) repairs, spout replaced 200.00

    7-5/8" h, Putnam touch (James H. Putnam, Walden, MA,) repairs...150.00

    7-3/4" h, Smith & Co touch, (Albany, NY,) some battering and damage 175.00

    8-1/8" h, A. Griswold eagle touch, (Ashbil Griswold, Meriden, CT), some battering and repair, splits to bottom......200.00

8-1/2" h, Continental, pear shaped, old soldered repair 160.00

Tobacco Box, 4-3/8" h, Thomas Stanford, cast eagle feet, engraved label with scroll work "Thomas Stanford, Gospel Hill, 1838," wear, final and one foot soldered......................125.00

Tumbler, 2-3/4" h, Thomas Danforth Boardman, Hartford, CT, partial eagle touch 175.00

Warming Platter, 19" l, hot water type, tree and well, mkd "Dixon & Sons," English, repairs 250.00

PHOENIX GLASS

History: Phoenix Glass Company, Beaver, Pennsylvania, was established in 1880. Known primarily for commercial glassware, the firm also produced a molded, sculptured, cameo-type line from the 1930s until the 1950s.

References: Jack D. Wilson, *Phoenix & Consolidated Art Glass*, Antique Publications, 1989.

Collectors' Club: Phoenix & Consolidated Glass Collectors, P.O. Box 81974, Chicago, IL 60681.

Ashtray, Phlox, large, white, frosted 86.00
Bowl, Swallows purple wash 150.00
Cookie Jar, 9" h, Con-Cora, white milk glass, gilt dec..........60.00
Creamer and Sugar, Catalonia, light green........................45.00
Floor Vase, 18" h, Bushberry, light green 450.00
Lamp

    Ceiling, 15" sq, Flying Birds, heavy custard glass, metal mounts 1,500.00

Teapot, Savage, Middletown, CT, 10" h, $375.

Vase, pale green, frosted, 9-1/2" h, $175.

Table, 28" h, Lovebirds, green opalescent glass, brass fixtures 225.00
Umbrella Stand, 18" h, Thistle, pearlized blue ground.......450.00
Vase
6-1/2" h, Line 700, blue crystal 350.00
7" h, Bluebell, brown...125.00
8-3/4" h, clear and frosted, grasshoppers and reeds dec 125.00
10" h, Wild Geese, pearlized white birds, light green ground 195.00
10-1/2" h, Zodiac, raised white figures, peach colored ground 700.00
11" h, Wild rose, blown out, pearlized dec, dark rose ground, orig label..275.00
14" h, Philodendron, blue, ormolu mounts....................400.00

PHONOGRAPHS

History: Early phonographs were commonly called "talking machines." Thomas A. Edison invented the first successful phonograph in 1877; other manufacturers followed with their variations.

References: Timothy C. Fabrizio and George F. Paul, *The Talking Machine: An Illustrated Compendium, 1877-1929,* Schiffer Publishing, 1997; Neil Maker, *Hand-Cranked Phonographs*, Promar Publishing, 1993; Arnold Schwartzman, *Phono-Graphics*, Chronicle Books, 1993.

Periodicals: *Horn Speaker*, P.O. Box 1193, Mabank, TX 75147; *New Amberola Graphic*, 37 Caledonia St., St. Johnsbury, VT 05819.

Collectors' Clubs: Buckeye Radio & Phonograph Club, 4572 Mark Trail, Copley, OH 44321; California Antique Phonograph Society, P.O. Box 67, Duarte, CA 91010; Hudson Valley Antique Radio & Phonograph Society, P.O. Box 207, Campbell Hall, NY 10916; Michigan Antique Phonograph Society, Inc., 2609 Devonshire, Lansing, MI 48910; Vintage Radio & Phonograph Society, Inc., P.O. Box 165345, Irving, TX 75016.

Museums: Edison National Historic Site, West Orange, NJ; Johnson's Memorial, Dover, DE; Seven Acres Antique Village & Museum, Union, IL.

Advisor: Lewis S. Walters.

Graphone
12.5 oak case, metal horn, retailer's mark, cylinder...........450.00
15.0 oak case with columns on corners, nickel plated platform, metal horn, stenciled cast iron parts 725.00
Home Grand, oak case, nickel plated works, #6, spring motor 1,300.00
Columbia, HG cylinder player 2,400.00
Decca, Junior, portable, leather case and handle.............150.00
Edison
Amberola 30 ....350.00
Army-Navy, World War I era..1,200.00
Excelsior, coin operated..2,500.00
Fireside, orig horn...900.00
Gem, maroon, 2//4 minute reproducer 1,700.00
Opera, moving mandrel and fixed reproducer................2,500.00
Standard, Model A, oak case, metal form.........................550.00
Triumph, signet horn, mahogany case.............................2,500.00
S-19 Diamond Disc, floor model, oak case 400.00
Harvard, trumpet style horn 300.00

Edison Gem, orig horn, black, 1904-06, $375.

Kalamazoo, Duplex, reproducer, orig horns with decals, patent date 1904...3,300.00
Odeon, Talking Machine Co., table model, crank wind brass horn, straight tone arm 500.00
Silvertone (Sears), two reproducers 500.00
Sonora
Gothic Deluxe, walnut case, triple spring, gold plated parts, automatic stop and storage...400.00
Luzerne, Renaissance style case with storage 200.00
Talk-O-Phone, Brooke, table model, oak case rope decorations, steel horn..200.00
Victor
Credenza, crank...1,100.00
Monarch, table model, corner columns, brass bell horn 1,500.00
School House 2,500.00
Victor I, mahogany case, corner columns, bell horn.......1,500.00
Victor II, oak case, black bell horn 1,200.00
Victor V, oak case, corner columns, no horn...................1,400.00

PHOTOGRAPHS

History: A vintage print is a positive image developed from the original negative by the photographer or under the photographer's supervision at the time the negative is made. A non-vintage photograph is a print made from an original negative at a later date. It is quite common for a photographer to make prints from the same negative over several decades. Changes between the original and subsequent prints usually can be identified. Limited edition prints must be clearly labeled.

References: Helmut Gernsheim, *Concise History of Photography*, 3rd ed., Dover Publications, 1986; ——, *Creative Photography*, Dover Publications, 1991; Susan Theran (ed.), *Leonard's Annual Price Index of Posters & Photographs*, Auction Index (30 Valentine Park, Newton, MA 02165), 1995.

Periodicals: *CameraShopper*, 313 N. Quaker Lane, P.O. Box 37029, W. Hartford, CT 06137; *History of Photography*, 1900 Frost Rd., Suite 101, Tullytown, PA 19007; *Photograph Collector*, Photographic Arts Center, 163 Amsterdam Ave. #201, New York, NY 10023.

Collectors' Clubs: American Photographic Historical Society, Inc., 1150 Avenue of the Americas, New York, NY 10036; Assoc. of International Photography Art Dealers, 1609 Connecticut Ave. NW. #200, Washington, DC 20009; Daguerrean Society, 625 Liberty Ave., Ste. 1790, Pittsburgh, PA 15222; National Stereoscopic Assoc., P.O. Box 14801, Columbus, OH 43214; Photographic Historical Society, Inc., P.O. Box 39563, Rochester, NY 14604; Photographic Historical Society of Canada, P.O. Box 54620, Toronto, Ontario M5M 4N5 Canada; Photographic Historical Society of New England, P.O. Box 189, Boston, MA 02165; Western Photographic Collectors Assoc. Inc., P.O. Box 4294, Whittier, CA 90607.

Museums: Center for Creative Photography, Tucson, AZ; International Center of Photography, New York, NY; International Museum of Photography at George Eastman House, Rochester, NY; International Photographic Historical Association, San Francisco, CA; National Portrait Gallery, Washington, DC.

Additional Listings: See *Warman's Americana & Collectibles* for more examples.

SPECIAL AUCTION

Swann Galleries, Inc.
104 E. 25th St.
New York, NY 10010
(212) 254-4710

Album
   "A Souvenir of the Harriman Alaska Expedition, Volumes I and II," 251 photographs, more than 100 by Edward Curtin, additional images by Edward H. Harriman, C. Hart Merriam, G.K. Gilbert, D.G. Inverarity, and others, silver prints, various sizes to 6" x 7-1/2", several with handwritten credit and date in negative, others with copyright, album disbound and defective, title pages and map laid in, prints generally in excellent condition, 1899, pr 21,850.00
   "Kodak," 104 photographs of eastern and Midwestern U. S. by Wm. Hoblitzell, prints document his train ride across country from MD to Missoula, MT, unposed glimpses of trains and local stations, Missoulan bicyclists and Native-Americans on horseback, handwritten captions and/or dates on mount rectos, mounted 4 per page recto and verso, oblong 4to, gilt-lettered morocco, spine and edges worn, pgs loose, photographer's handstamp on front and rear pastdowns, ties missing, 1890-91 .... 575.00
Albumen Print
   Lincoln's conspirators having hoods and nooses adjusted, mounted, sgd by Alexander Gardner.................... 7,700.00
   View of the Oswego Harbor, arched top, 13" x 16-1/2", title, photographer, and date printed on label affixed below image, 1869.. 1,380.00
   Ambrotype, William Gannaway Brownlow, known as Parson Brownlow, the fightin' preacher, half plate 3,190.00
Cabinet Card
   Buffalo Bill, albumen photograph 357.50

Chief Thunder, posed holding ceremonial pipe, D. F. Barry and printed title on label affixed to mount recto, Barry's West Superior, Wis., imprint on mount verse, 1891 .... 1,265.00
Oakley, Annie, mounted albumen photograph, facsimile signature.. 2,860.00
Sitting Bull, D. F. Barry, titled, copyrighted, dated, and Barry's imprint on recto, Bismarck D. T. imprint on mount verso, 1885, 7" x 5".. 1,495.00
Wilde, Oscar, age 32, Alfred Ellis & Wallery imprint on mounts recto and verso, period German inscription handwritten on mount verso, 1892, 5" x 4" 1,100.00
CDV, carte de visite
   Davis, Jefferson, President of Confederacy 80.00
   Emancipation Proclamation.. 80.00
   Lincoln, Abraham, taken by Matthew Brady, 1864 .... 1,045.00
   Mrs. Lincoln, portrait with spirit of Abe behind her, Wm. Mumler's Boston imprint on mount verso, c1869 .... 1,725.00
Daguerreotype
   Quarter-plate image, face of deceased man 825.00
   Quarter-plate image, young slave woman holding blond chin on her lap, delicate hand-tinting of child's face, leather case, separated at hinge, 1860s 2,185.00
   Sixth plate, ambrotype, English, harness maker standing outside window of his shop, filled with hanging bridles, ropes, leather harnesses, and tools, leather case, 1950s ... 750.00
   Sixth plate, ambrotype, young Confederate, probably lieutenant, gilt highlights, leather case, early 1860s 1,265.00
   Sixth plate, live chanticleer rooster, delicate hand-tinting, leather case, c1845 .... 6,210.00
   Sixth plate, man and his buggy whip 880.00
   Stereoscopic, 2 sixth plates, Niagara Falls in winter, mat coated with opaque black paint, in Mascher stereo viewing case, Mascher's name and patent printed on lens panel, 1853... 13,800.00
   Ninth plate, ruby glass ambrotype, white cat, paws crossed, posed before dark background, half leather case, 1860s 920.00
   Young man holding his Bible box, found under lid of rosewood and black walnut veneer Bible box 7,700.00
Photograph with Watercolor Detail, 4-15/16" h, 5-9/16" w, seated couple, reverse has another uncolored photo, imp "Paris," minor stains, modern dec frame 220.00
Silver Print, Chief Hairy Chin, dressed as Uncle Same, photographer's (D. F. Barry) blindstamp on recto, 1889, printed c1900, 6-1/4" x 4" 825.00
Tintype, 1-5/8" h gold filled locket, tintype of young woman, swatch of twill from jacket, engraved locket case 85.00

PICKARD CHINA

History: The Pickard China Company was founded by Wilder Pickard in Chicago, Illinois, in 1897. Originally the company imported European china blanks, principally from the Havilands at Limoges, which were then hand painted. The firm presently is located in Antioch, Illinois.

References: Susan and Al Bagdade, *Warman's American Pottery and Porcelain*, Wallace-Homestead, 1994; Alan B. Reed, *Collector's Encyclopedia of Pickard China with Additional Sections on Other Chicago China Studios*, Collector Books, 1996.

Collectors' Club: Pickard Collectors Club, 300 E. Grove St., Bloomington, IL 61701.

Bowl, 9-3/4" d, landscape and bird design, gilded molded rim, sgd "E. Challinor" 300.00
Cake Plate, 10-1/2" d, open gold handles, Desert Garden pattern, black circles, multicolored fruit, shaded ground, gold trim 185.00
Chocolate Pot, cov, 9" h, conical, pink carnations, green leaves, gold arches, pink and white flowers, scrolling, gold handle, rim band and knob 300.00
Creamer and Sugar, 4-1/4" h, Violets, c1898, artist sgd "H. Reury," Silesia blank, pr..325.00
Hatpin Holder, allover gold design of etched flowers, c1925 ....50.00
Lemonade Set, tankard pitcher, 5 tumblers, bluebells and foliate, lemon-yellow ground 120.00
Perfume Bottle, yellow primroses, shaded ground, artist sgd and dated 1905, gold stopper, Limoges blank 200.00
Plate
   7-1/2" d, hp, currants, 1898 ....75.00
   9-1/8" l, hp peaches, gilded and molded border, sgd "S. Heap"..110.00
Platter, 12" d, hp, panted roses, gilded border, sgd "Seidel" 275.00

Mug, gold banding and trim, poinsettia flower, white ground, oil style glaze, artist sgd "N. R. Cifford," Pickard mark, 6-7/8" h, $265.

Punch Bowl, 12" d, orange grapes and plums design, artist sgd "F. Walton" 1,400.00
Tea Set, teapot, creamer, sugar, and cake plate, pink apple blossoms and green leaves, gilded trim, artist sgd 550.00
Tile, 6-3/4" d, Holland, Dutch Merchant Ship, GDA France Mark, c1905..400.00
Urn, 11-1/2" h, allover gold, 3" band of grapes and strawberries, artist sgd, Belleek blank 500.00
Vase
   7-3/4" h, cylindrical, moonlight lake and pine forest scene, artist sgd "Challinor," Nippon blank 265.00
   9-1/2" h, 3-3/4" w, hp, 3 large dark orange poppies, gold, rust, an brown, sgd "Gasper" 365.00

PICKLE CASTORS

History: A pickle castor is a table accessory used to serve pickles. It generally consists of a silver-plated frame fitted with a glass insert, matching silver-plated lid, and matching tongs. Pickle castors were very popular during the Victorian era. Inserts are found in pattern glass and colored art glass.

Amberina, melon ribbed IVT insert, SP lid, ftd frame, lid, tongs, c1875-95..720.00
Bluebird, enameled, resilvered frame 725.00
Colorless, 11-3/4" h, acid etched insert, floral dec with bird medallion, octagonal SP frame, mkd "Meriden Co. 182" ..200.00
Cranberry
   IVT insert, enameled blue and white florals, green leaves, shelf on frame dec with peacocks and other birds...........325.00
   Paneled Spring insert, SP frame, c1875-95 ....450.00
Double
   Colorless inserts, emb fans and flowers, matching cov, fancy tulip finials, Viking head ftd oval handled frame, sgd "Meriden"..275.00
   Vaseline, pickle leaves and pieces, resilvered frame ...800.00
Mt. Washington, 11" h, 6" d, decorated satin glass insert, blue enamel and painted yellow roses, green leaves, orange and yellow blossoms, silver-plated Rogers stand and tongs 875.00
Opalescent
   Daisy & Fern, blue, emb DQ floral jar, resilvered frame 650.00
   Vertical white stripes, colorless ground, resilvered angel frame, elephant's head and trunk feet......................725.00
Pink, shiny pink Florette pattern insert, white int., bowed out frame 325.00

PIGEON BLOOD GLASS

History: Pigeon blood refers to the deep orange-red-colored glassware produced around the turn of the century. Do not confuse it with the many other red glasswares of that period. Pigeon blood has a very definite orange glow.

Berry Bowl, 9" d, master, Torquay, SP rim...........................110.00
Bowl, 4-1/2" d, IVT 50.00
Butter Dish, cov, Venecia, enameled dec 350.00
Celery Vase, 6" h, Torquay, SP rim....................................225.00
Cracker Jar, cov, Quilted Phlox, Consolidated Glass Co, resilvered hardware 325.00
Creamer, Venecia, enameled dec....................................125.00
Decanter, 9-1/2" h, orig stopper 145.00
Hand Cooler, 5" l, cut panels, 2 compartments, SS fittings 145.00

Pickle Castor, Beaded Drape, Consolidated Glass Co, orig SP frame, cov, and tongs..425.00
Pitcher, 9-1/2" h, Bulging Loops, applied clear handle, ground pontil 225.00
Salt and Pepper Shakers, pr, Bulging Loops, orig top.......150.00
Spooner, Torquay, SP rim...225.00
Syrup, Beaded Drape, Consolidated Glass Co., orig hinged lid 250.00
Tumbler, 3-1/4" h, alternating panel and rib 85.00

PINK SLAG

History: True pink slag is found only in the molded Inverted Fan and Feather pattern. Quality pieces shade from pink at the top to white at the bottom.

REPRODUCTION ALERT

Recently, pieces of pink slag made from molds of the now-defunct Cambridge Glass Company have been found in the Inverted Strawberry and Inverted Thistle patterns. This is not considered true pink slag and brings only a fraction of the price of the Inverted Fan and Feather pieces.

Berry Bowl, 10" d 750.00
Butter Dish, cov, 70-5/8" d, 7" h cov, 2-1/4" h base with 4 molded feet, fiery opalescent coloring 1,485.00
Creamer...465.00
Cruet, 6-1/2" h, orig stopper 1,300.00
Jelly Compote, 5" h, 4-1/2" d, scalloped top 375.00
Marmalade Jar, cov..875.00
Pitcher, water..775.00
Punch Cup, 2-1/2" h, ftd 275.00
Salt Shaker...300.00
Sauce Dish, 4-1/4" d, 2-1/2" h, ball feet..............................225.00
Spooner 350.00
Sugar Bowl, cov..550.00
Toothpick Holder 825.00
Tumbler, 4-1/2" h..475.00

Tumbler, Inverted Fan and Feather, 3-7/8" h, 2-3/4" d, $450.

PIPES

History: Pipe making can be traced as far back as 1575. Pipes were made of almost all types of natural and man-made materials, including amber, base metals, clay, cloisonné, glass, horn, ivory, jade, meerschaum, parian, porcelain, pottery, precious metals, precious stones, semiprecious stones, and assorted woods. Some of these materials retain smoke and some do not. Chronologically, the four most popular materials and their generally accepted introduction dates are: clay, c1575; wood, c1700; porcelain, c1710; and meerschaum, c1725.

Pipe styles reflect nationalities all around the world, wherever tobacco smoking is custom or habit. Pipes represent a broad range of themes and messages, e.g., figurals, important personages, commemoration of historical events, mythological characters, erotic and pornographic subjects, the bucolic, the bizarre, the grotesque, and the graceful.

Pipe collecting began in the mid-1880s; William Bragge, F.S.A., Birmingham, England, was an early collector. Although firmly established through the efforts of freelance writers, auction houses, and museums (but not the tobacco industry), the collecting of antique pipes is an amorphous, maligned, and misunderstood hobby. It is amorphous because there are no defined collecting bounds; maligned because it is perceived as an extension of pipe smoking, and now misunderstood because smoking has become socially unacceptable (even though many pipe collectors are avid non-smokers).

References: R. Fresco-Corbu, *European Pipes*, Lutterworth Press, 1982; Benjamin Rapaport, *Complete Guide to Collecting Antique Pipes*, Schiffer Publishing, 1979.

Periodical: *Complete Smoker Magazine*, P.O. Box 7036, Evanston, IL 60204.

Collectors' Clubs: International Assoc. of Pipe Smokers' Clubs, 47758 Hickory, Apt. 22305, Wixom, MI 48393; New York Pipe Club, P.O. Box 265, Gracie Station, New York, NY 10028; North Texas Pipe Club, 1624 East Cherry St., Sherman, TX 75090; Pipe Collectors Club of America, P.O. 5179, Woodbridge, VA 22194; Sherlock Holmes Pipe Club Ltd. USA, P.O. Box 221, Westborough, MA 01581; Society for Clay Pipe Research, P.O. Box 817, Bel Air, MD 21014; Southern California Pipe & Cigar Smokers' Assoc., 1532 South Bundy Dr., Apt. D, Los Angeles, CA 90025.

Museums: Museum of Tobacco Art and History, Nashville, TN; National Tobacco-Textile Museum, Danville, VA; Pipe Smoker's Hall of Fame, Galveston, IN; U.S. Tobacco Museum, Greenwich, CT.

Briar, Queen Victoria, 6-1/4" l, head, carved, silver trim, case, hallmarked..95.00
Clay, 6-5/8" l, red clay, 18 incised presentation signatures, unglazed, chips 55.00
Glass, large ovoid bowl, long shaped stem, red and ivory dec 90.00
Meerschaum, amber stem, fitted case
      4-3/4" l, Meerschaum and amber bowl, gold and silver Art Nouveau ferule 195.00

Lopoldo Weiss, Genoa, orig case, carved Meerschaum bowl, $325.

6" h, man with flower, beard, tasseled hat, fitted case, late 19th
C 2,540.00
8-5/8" l, Bacchanalian scene 660.00
16-3/8" l, presentation model, pierced relief monogram
....200.00
Opium, 7-3/4" l, cranes, red stem, brass fittings, Oriental, c1800
....90.00
Porcelain
9" l, Graf Zeppelin, mkd "P.O.B" 125.00
12" l, floral, relief dec 125.00
19" l, drunken man lying under barrel, small porcelain animal
on bowl lid 280.00
29" l, hunter, sleeping 135.00
Pottery, monk, post war 50.00
Regimental, 41" l, porcelain bowl, 112 Infantry, Sohlettstadt 1888,
named to Res. Huck., two scenes, helmet cover, new spike
and hairline in bowl, minor repair on flexible cord 225.00

POCKET KNIVES

History: Alcas, Case, Colonial, Ka-Bar, Queen, and
Schrade are the best of the modern pocket-knife manufacturers, with top positions enjoyed by Case and Ka-
Bar. Knives by Remington and Winchester, firms no longer in production, are eagerly sought.

References: Jacob N. Jarrett, *Price Guide to Pocket
Knives*, L-W Books, 1993, 1995 value update; Bernard
Levine, *Levine's Guide to Knives and Their Values*,
Krause Publications, 1997; ——, *Pocket Knives*, Apple
Press, 1993; Jack Lewis and Roger Combs, *The Gun Di-
gest Book of Knives,* 5th ed., Krause Publications, 1997;
Jim Sargent, *Sargent's American Premium Guide to
Pocket Knives & Razors*, 4th ed., Books Americana,
1995; Ron Stewart and Roy Ritchie, *Standard Knife Col-
lector's Guide*, 3rd ed., Collector Books, 1993, 1995 val-
ue update; J. Bruce Voyles, *International Blade
Collectors Association's Price Guide to Antique Knives*,
Krause Publications, 1995.

Periodicals: *The Blade*, 700 E. State St., Iola, WI 54990;
Knife World, P.O. Box 3395, Knoxville, TN 37927.

Collectors' Clubs: American Blade Collectors, P.O. Box
22007, Chattanooga, TN 37422; Canadian Knife Collectors Club, Route 1, Milton, Ontario L9T 2X5 Canada; National Knife Collectors Assoc., P.O. Box 21070,
Chattanooga, TN 37421.

Museum: National Knife Collectors Museum, Chattanooga, TN.

Additional Listings: See *Warman's Americana & Collectibles* for more examples.

Notes: Form is a critical collecting element. The most desirable forms are folding hunters (one or two blades),
trappers, peanuts, Barlows, elephant toes, canoes, Texas toothpicks, Coke bottles, gun stocks, and Daddy Barlows. The decorative aspect also heavily influences
prices.

Case

Case uses a numbering code for its knives. The first
number (1-9) is the handle material; the second number
(1-5) designates the number of blades; the third and fourth
numbers (0-99) the knife pattern, stage (5), pearl (8 or 9)
and bone (6) are the most sought handle materials. The
most desirable patterns are 5165–folding hunters; 6185–
doctors; 6445, scout, muskrat–marked muskrat with no
number, and 6254–trappers.

In the Case XX series, a symbol and dot code are used
to designate a year.

3254, yellow composition, 4-1/8", stamped "XX," 1940-65
....150.00
4200, white composition, 5-1/2", serrated master blade, melon
tester, stamped "USA," 1965-70 ....125.00
5265, stag, 5-1/4", saber ground, stamped "USA," 1965-70
....100.00
6265, 5-1/4", flat blade, stamped "Tested XX," green bone, 1920-
40...300.00
8271, genuine pearl, 3-1/4", long pull, stamped "XX," 1940-65
....450.00
9265, imitation pearl, 5-1/4", flat blade, stamped "Tested XX,"
1920-40...450.00
420657, white composition, 3-3/8", "Office Knife" mkd on handle,
1940-56...100.00

Ka-Bar, dog's head, #62156, $550.

Ka-Bar (Union Cut. Co., Olean, N.Y.)

The company was founded by Wallace Brown at Tidiote, PA, in 1892. It was relocated to Olean, NY, in 1912. The products have many stampings, including Union (inside shield); U0R co., Tidoute (variations); Union Cutlery Co. Olean, NY; Aklcut Olean, NY; Kenwell, Olean, NY, and Ka-Bar. The larger knives with a profile of a dog's head on the handle are the most desirable. Pattern numbers rarely appear on a knife prior to the 1940s.

6191L	600.00
6260KF	120.00
24107	1,100.00
31187, 2 blades	185.00
61161, light celluloid handle	125,99
61187, Daddy Barlow	175.00

Keen Kutter (Simons Hardware, St. Louis, Mo.)

K1881, Barlow	85.00
K1920	300.00
6354, Scout	125.00

Remington

R293, Field and Stream Bullet, bone, long pull	1,800.00
R953, toothpick, bone	250.00
R3273, Cattle, brown bone, equal end	275.00

Winchester

1621, Budding, 4-3/4", ebony	150.00
1920, Hunter, 5-3/8", bone, folding	1,000.00
2337, Senator, 3-1/4", pearl	125.00
2703, Barlow, 3-1/2", brown bone	160.00
3944, Whittler, 3-1/4", bone	225.00

POISON BOTTLES

History: The design of poison bottles was meant to serve as a warning in order to prevent accidental intake or misuse of their poisonous contents. Their unique details were especially helpful in the dark. Poison bottles generally were made of colored glass, embossed with "Poison" or a skull and crossbones, and sometimes were coffin-shaped.

John H. B. Howell of Newton, New Jersey, designed the first safety closure in 1866. The idea did not become popular until the 1930s, when bottle designs became simpler and the user had to read the label to identify the contents.

References: Ralph and Terry Kovel, *Kovels' Bottles Price List*, 10th ed., Crown Publishers, 1996; Carlo and Dorothy Sellari, *Standard Old Bottle Price Guide*, Collector Books, 1989.

Periodical: *Antique Bottle and Glass Collector*, P.O. Box 187, East Greenville, PA 18041.

Collectors' Club: Federation of Historical Bottle Collectors, Inc., 88 Sweetbriar Branch, Longwood, FL 32750.

Bowker's Pyrox Poison, colorless	30.00
Carbolic Acid, 3 oz., cobalt blue, hexagonal, flat back	48.00
Chloroform, 5-3/4" h, green, ribbed, label, 1900	80.00
Coffin, 3-1/2" h, cobalt blue, emb, 1890	100.00
Cylindrical, crosshatch dec, cobalt blue, flared mouth with stopper, smooth base, 6-1/4" h	250.00

Poison Tingt Iodine, skull and cross bones, amber, sq, machine made, 3-3/16", $10.

Diamond Antiseptics, 10-3/4" h, triangular shape, golden amber, emb	385.00
Figural, skull, America, 1880-1900, cobalt blue, tooled mouth, smooth base	
2-7/8" h, small hole in nose area	475.00
4-1/8" h	1,800.00
Imperial Fluid Co. Poison, 1 gallon, colorless	95.00
Lysol, 3-1/4" h, cylindrical, amber, emb "Not To Be Taken"	12.00
Melvin & Badger Apothecaries, Boston, Mass, irregular form, cobalt blue, tooled sq mouth, smooth base, 6-1/4" h	140.00
Mercury Bichloride, 2-11/16" h, rect, amber	18.00
Norwich Coffin, 3-3/8" h, amber, emb, tooled lip	95.00
Owl Drug Co., 3-3/8" h, cobalt blue, owl sitting on mortar	70.00
Plumber Drug Co., 7-1/2" h, cobalt blue, lattice and diamond pattern	90.00
Poison, 3-1/2" h, hexagonal, ribbed, cobalt blue	20.00
Tinct Iodine, 3" h, amber, skull and crossbones	45.00
USA Hospital Dept., Acetate Potassa, 6-1/2" h, cylindrical, aqua	65.00

POLITICAL ITEMS

History: Since 1800, the American presidency has been a contest between two or more candidates. Initially, souvenirs were issued to celebrate victories. Items issued during a campaign to show support for a candidate were actively being distributed in the William Henry Harrison election of 1840.

There is a wide variety of campaign items–buttons, bandannas, tokens, pins, etc. The only limiting factor has been the promoter's imagination. The advent of television campaigning has reduced the quantity of individual items, and modern campaigns do not seem to have the variety of materials that were issued earlier.

References: Herbert Collins, *Threads of History*, Smithsonian Institution Press, 1979; Theodore L. Hake, *Encyclopedia of Political Buttons, United States, 1896-1972* (1985), *Book II, 1920-1976* (1977), *Book III, 1789-1916* (1978), revised prices for all three books (1998) Americana & Collectibles Press, (P.O. Box 1444, York, PA 17405); —, *Hake's Guide to Presidential Campaign Collectibles*, Wallace-Homestead, 1992; Edward Krohn (ed.), *National Political Convention Tickets and Other Convention Ephemera*, David G. Phillips Publishing (P.O. Box 611388, N. Miami, FL 33161), 1996; Keith Melder, *Hail to the Candidate*, Smithsonian Institution Press, 1992; James W. Milgram, *Presidential Campaign Illustrated Envelopes and Letter Paper 1840-1872*, David G. Phillips Publishing (P.O. Box 611388, N. Miami, FL 33161), 1996; Edmund B. Sullivan, *American Political Badges and Medalets, 1789-1892*, Quarterman Publications, 1981; –, *Collecting Political Americana*, Christopher Publishing House, 1991; Mark Warda, *100 Years of Political Campaign Collectibles*, Sphinx Publishing (P.O. Box 25, Clearwater, FL 34617), 1996.

Periodicals: *Political Bandwagon*, P.O. Box 348, Leola, PA 17540; *Political Collector*, P.O. Box 5171, York, PA 17405.

Collectors' Clubs: American Political Items Collectors, P.O. Box 340339, San Antonio, TX 78234; Ford Political Items Collectors, 18222 Flower Hill Way #299, Gaithersburg, MD 20879; Indiana Political Collectors Club, P.O. Box 11141, Indianapolis, IN 46201; NIXCO, Nixon Collectors Organization, 975 Maunawili Cr., Kailua, HI 96734; Third Party & Hopefuls, 503 Kings Canyon Blvd., Galesburg, IL 61401.

REPRODUCTION ALERT

Campaign Buttons

The reproduction of campaign buttons is rampant. Many originated as promotional sets from companies such as American Oil, Art Fair/Art Forum, Crackerbarrel, Liberty Mint, Kimberly Clark, and United States Boraxo. Most reproductions began life properly marked on the curl, i.e., the turned-under surface edge.

Look for evidence of disturbance on the curl where someone might try to scratch out the modern mark. Most of the backs of these buttons were bare or had a paper label. Beware of any button with a painted back. Finally, pinback buttons were first made in 1896, and nearly all made between 1896 and 1916 were celluloid covered. Any lithographed tin button from the election of 1916 or earlier is very likely a reproduction or fantasy item.

Museums: National Museum of American History, Smithsonian Institution, Washington, DC; Western Reserve Historical Society, Cleveland, OH.

Additional Listings: See *Warman's Americana & Collectibles* for more examples.

Advisor: Theodore L. Hake.

Badge, 2-1/2" brilliant brass luster, brass shell, jugate portrait of McKinley and Hobart, text "McKinley and Hobart Sound Money and Protection," expertly replaced pin in reverse, 1896 ....40.00

Bandanna
17" sq, Garfield/Arthur, black and white center design, red, white, and blue flag and star edge design, light overall browning, ©1880 ....175.00
17" x 26", T. R. National Progressive, silk, red, white, and blue, moose head design corners, bears with bit stands surround center image of his hat in ring, dated 1912 ...150.00
18" x 19", Harrison, white lettering and star pattern, dark blue background, 1888 ....75.00

Booklet
2-3/4" x 4-3/4", anti-Douglas/Pro-Lincoln, satirical, titled "The Little Giant, His Life, Travels and Death/Published at Chicago, Illinois, 1860," 12 pgs, 6 pgs of cartoons and verses 150.00
5-1/2" x 7-1/2", "Harrison and Morton Songster," 64 pgs, jugate black and white illus of candidates on cover, surrounded by red, white, and blue flag design, 1888, small cover tears, 1" archival tape repair on inside back cover 60.00

Bookmark, 2-1/2" x 10-1/4", Stevensgraph, Grant, inscription "Richmond/1865," bright green and purplish-red 175.00

Bust, 4" x 8" x 8", "Remember Pearl Harbor," FDR, dark brown luster, solid plaster, wearing "V" emblem on label, front incised complete Pledge of Allegiance text and slogan..............75.00

Cabinet Photo, sepia, stiff cardboard
3-1/2" x 5-1/2", Allan G. Thurman, 1888..........................25.00
6-1/2" x 10", Cleveland, mount by Geo. Harris, N.Y., c1888 ....40.00

Calendar, 15" x 21-1/2", T. R. Cigars, 1921, thin cardboard, full color illus of Theodore Roosevelt 100.00

Campaign Button
1-3/4" d, For President Richard M. Nixon, white ground, black and white photo of smiling Nixon in center, red letters at top, white letters on bottom against blue background 4.00
2-1/4" d, For President Herbert Hoover/For Vice-President Charles Curtis, litho jugate, bluetone photos in ovals against pr of draped red, white, and blue flag background 150.00
3-1/2" d, Win with Humphrey, red, white, and blue celluloid, 1968 ....4.00

Campaign Ribbon
2-1/4" x 7", "McKinley and Roosevelt Prosperity Parade," dark blue on white, dinner pail illus, inscribed "Cleveland Nov. 3rd 1900," 95.00
2-1/2" x 4-1/2", Benjamin Harrison, black and white woven silk, red, white, and blue flags, gold eagle, 1888..............38.00
2-1/2" x 7", Taft/Hughes, blue on cream, V-shaped accent at bottom..35.00

2-1/2" x 7", Martin Van Buren, black on light blue, eagle with "Plurbus Unum" ribbon in beak, reading "Liberty and Equality/Fourth of July, 1840/Van Buren, Johnson and Democracy, neatly inked name of orig owner under text, horizontal crease in ribbon, rare...300.00

3" x 7", black and white, inscribed "Clay and Tariff/The Democratic Whig/National Convention, May 2, 1844," some fading..125.00

Campaign Sign

2" x 13", Vote Republican, white letters, blue background, silver reflector dots, early 1930s 10.00

10" x 13", Wilson, cardboard, blue flocked background, raised black and white images of eagle, Washington, Wilson, and Lincoln at center, Wilson surrounded by red, white, and blue star and shield, inscription in white "The Man For The Hour," 1916..250.00

Canvas Bag, Reagan/Bush Inauguration, dark blue and white, fabric handles, each side with design of "RB" initials surrounding inauguration emblem, 1980......................................10.00

Cigar Case, 5-1/2" h, Henry Clay, painted portrait of Clay and inscription "Henry Clay Candidate for 1844 - the American Statesman Come every, your influence bring on this eventful day, And make the western vallies ring with shouts for Henry Clay," varnished 2,185.00

Cloak, 30" h, Garfield and Arthur, painted canvas, flying eagle with banner, c1881, scattered losses, fading 1,100.00

Coloring Book, 10-1/2" x 13", New Frontier, 32 pgs, 1962, Kennedy caricatures, various cabinet members and political friends...30.00

Cup Plate, 3-1/2" d, pressed glass, Henry Clay, clear, scalloped edge, 1844 ....80.00

Curtain Tie Back, 2" d, 2-1/2" l, George Washington, high relief brass, emb portrait, early 1800s, old solder where post meets plaque 300.00

Dexterity Puzzle, 2", "Vote Republican Ticket 1908," glass cover, full color emb cardboard image of black man on pale blue ground 150.00

Fan, 8" x 14-1/2", non-partisan, 1928, black and white, cardboard, wooden handle, one side inserts of every president from Washington to Coolidge, Capitol dome at center, inscription at bottom reads "Who Will Be Next?" reverse side with furniture company advertisement...60.00

Figure, 2" x 2" x 3", plastic, John F. Kennedy seated in gold rocking chair, orig 3" x 7" card, "Hush Up Toys-Rock Chair," Mego, c1963..8.00

Handkerchief

12" sq, Woodrow Wilson, black and white image, 2 vertical and 2 horizontal folds, c1912-16 ....45.00

17" sq, "I Like Ike," silk, red, white, and blue, black and white photo illus insert at 4 corners, black type slogan.......60.00

Hat Pin, Harrison, diecut, beaver hat shape, red and white fabric hat band, brass metallic color, some silver luster remaining on brim, 1888...35.00

Inauguration Book, 9" x 12", Nixon, 100 pgs, titled "The Spirit of '76," first edition, hardcover, black and white and color photos, accompanying text, 1973 ....30.00

Inauguration Medal, bronze

1-3/4" d, McKinley & Hobart, jugate, name of each state surrounding portraits, reverse with large eagle and names of 13 colonies on ribbon design, bronze hanger bar with US Capitol, crossed flags, "Inauguration March 4, 1897," plain beige ribbon, made by Davidson of Philadelphia 150.00

2-3/4" d, raised image on front, Eisenhower inauguration info on reverse 55.00

Jugate, 3-1/2" d, Stevenson, black, white, red, and blue, Philadelphia Badge Co., cardboard reverse 60.00

Key Fob, FDR, silvered brass, name, birth and death dates, reverse shows "Little White House Warm Springs, Ga." 20.00

Lapel Stud

Harrison, red, white, and blue celluloid covered insert, slogan "Reciprocity, Protection," c1892...............................35.00

McKinley/Hobart, jugate, sepia photos, 1896, 3/4" 20.00

Matches, 2" x 2-1/4", red, white, and blue, bluetone photo of Willkie, "For President Wendell Willkie," blue matches held individually by red and white paper covers, back cover reads "Pull for Willkie," 1940 ....15.00

Medalet, brass, luster

Fremont, large bust facing left, name and birthdate, reverse with eagle atop globe, inscribed "Our Country," 1856 ....50.00

Harrison, front with bust, name, and birthdate, reverse has log cabin design, and slogan "The People's Choice in the Year 1840"...35.00

Memorial Ribbon

2-3/4" x 7", "Gen. Andrew Jackson," black and white silk, 2-1/2" x 3" black and white illus of Jackson center, some repairs, c1845...95.00

3" x 8-1/2", dark gold, on black silk, text above and below grave marker reads "In Memory of Wm. H. Harrison, 9th President, U.S. Who Departed This Life, April 4th, A.D. 1841, Aged 68," below "Universally Lamented" is Harrison quotation about principles of government.................85.00

Newspaper, headline edition, New York Times, late city edition

"Agnew Quits," Thursday, Oct .11, 1973.........................10.00

"Ford Sworn In," Aug. 10, 1974 ....10.00

"Nixon Admits," Tuesday, Aug. 6, 1974 ....12.00

Paperweight, 2-3/4" d, 1-1/2" h, Adlai E. Stevenson, Baccarat, sulphite raised image of Stevenson, clear glass dome, small paper "Made in France," sticker on one front facet, orig 3/4" x 4" x 4" fabric lined blue cardboard box, gold trim, 1969...100.00

Pennant, 17" l, red and white felt, from second Eisenhower inauguration...12.00

Pencil, 8" l, Hoover for President, yellow, red 3-dimensional head of Hoover at top, unsharpened, 1928.............................25.00

Philatelic Envelope, 3-1/2" x 6-1/2", slight age tanning

Roosevelt, FD/Garner, jugate, inauguration day, postmark March 4, 1933, bluetone illus on either side of White House illus at center, red type, 3¢ stamp at top right............25.00

Smith, Alfred E./First Day of Issue, stamped Nov. 26, 1945, NY, design at left browntone illus of Smith above governors mansion and brown derby, slogan "East Side West Side All Around The Town," 3¢ Alfred E. Smith stamp at top right 15.00

Wilson First Day Cover, actual glued-on sepia photo on left side, "New Regular Issue-Presidential Series," stamped "Aug. 29, 1938 Washington DC," 1¢ Wilson stamp at top right-hand corner 15.00

Diecut, Harrison and Morton, adv premium from Samuel Clarke, Lancaster, PA, 1888, 11" x 7", $25.

Pin, McKinley, metal "Member" on scrolled banner shaped pin, enameled hanger "McKinley Club, Canton, Ohio," medallion hanger with emb McKinley image, made by Bastian Bros. Co., Rochester, NY, 4" h, 1-3/4" d, $65.

Pillow Cover, 16" x 18", FDR, photo image, black photo of FDR in wicker chair, light peach fabric, pale blue background tint, pink tint on carnation he wears, bright orange fabric back, navy blue piping, bright yellow stitching 60.00

Pinback Button

"For President Wm. H. Taft," 1-1/4" d, gray and black, gray ground 35.00

"Gen. U. S. Grant," ferrotype, brass frame, intertwined rope design surrounding clear and crisp ferrotype with name printed above head, 1868 .... 275.00

"Harding," browntone photo, brown background 50.00

"It's LBJ All The Way," 4" d, red, white, and blue celluloid
.... 8.00

McKinley, 1-1/4" d, black and white photo surrounded by thin gold accents, red, white, and blue star and stripe background, Whitehead & Hoag 70.00

Roosevelt, T., "Washington Party Come With Us," full color, Washington against green background, bright yellow rim, 7/8" d 25.00

"Smith for President," red, white, and blue rim, black and white picture 25.00

"Wilson," full color image, light blue background shades to cream, minor browning of back paper, 1-1/4" d 75.00

Plate

5" d, McKinley, china, full color center image, reverse reads "Made By The American China Co./Toronto, Ohio," c1900
.... 25.00

10" d, J. F. Kennedy and Family, white ceramic, color enhanced photo of family, c1962 .... 18.00

Pocket Mirror, 2" x 3", FDR, full color, celluloid, inaugural, inscription "Our President May He Always Be Right/But Our President Right Or Wrong," reverse has company name and 1933 date on edge, minor aging on mirror side 75.00

Postcard, inaugural

Johnson, Lyndon, 3-1/2" x 5-1/2", full color photo of Johnson seated at desk, wearing blue suit, green background, brown and white reverse "Lyndon Baines Johnson 36th President Of The United States of America," images of Washington DC buildings, A.A.A. Novelty Co., Washington, c1965, unused 2.00

Kennedy, John F., jumbo, color, blue and white imprint on reverse for use as postcard, c1961 .... 3.00

Print, 2-1/2" x 4" card, President Lincoln and Family, sepia
.... 20.00

Ring, "Al Smith," silvered brass, non-adjustable band, top features silver letters against blue enamel 30.00

Scissors, 6" l, mkd "D. Peres Solingen Germany/Magnetic Cutlery Co.," image of Taft and wife inscribed on either side of handles, surrounded by floral design motif, 1908, general wear to silver finish 65.00

Sheet Music

9" x 12", *Hoover Again For Me,"* 4 pg, stiff paper, illus and accomplishments on cov 12.00

9" x 12", *Roosevelt Is On The Job,* 4 pg, glossy sepia photo front, glossy ad on reverse cov, c1933 .... 30.00

10" x 13", *Answer Mr. Wilson's Call,* 4 pgs, portrait and soldiers, red, white, and blue 15.00

Speech Booklet, black and white paper

4" x 9", "President Wilson's Address To The League To Enforce Peace," front cov with 3" x 4" black and white photo of Wilson, 8 pgs 12.00

6" x 9", "The Tariff Speech of Hon. William McKinley Jr., of Ohio, in the House of Representatives, Wed May 8, 1890," 24 pgs 12.00

Plate, Grand Old Party, Standarde Bearers, Wm. Howard Taft and James S. Sherman, 1908, 9-1/2" d, $125.

Stickpin, Hayes & Wheeler, cardboard photo, jugate, mint luster brass rim, bright orange circular cardboard insert surrounds cardboard jugate photo, 1876....................300.00

Trade Card, 3-1/4" x 5-3/4", metamorphic, Presidential Nominee Tilden, inside text relates to possible nomination of Grant, reverse ad for Blackwell's Genuine (Bull) Durham Tobacco 60.00

Tray, litho tin
   Change, 4-1/4" d, Taft/Sherman Inaugural, full color 125.00
   Serving, 13" x 16", oval, Bryan, facsimile signature on bottom edge, 1896, overall wear 75.00

Window Poster, 8-1/2" x 11", FDR, black and white photo, black type "Carry On With Franklin D. Roosevelt" 25.00

POMONA GLASS

History: Pomona glass, produced only by the New England Glass Works and named for the Roman goddess of fruit and trees, was patented in 1885 by Joseph Locke. It is a delicate lead, blown art glass, which has a pale, soft beige ground and a top one-inch band of honey amber.

There are two distinct types of backgrounds. Making fine cuttings through a wax coating followed by an acid bath produced first ground, made only from late 1884 to June 1886. Second ground was made by rolling the piece in acid-resisting particles and acid etching. Second ground was made in Cambridge until 1888 and until the early 1900s in Toledo, where Libbey moved the firm after purchasing New England Glass works. Both methods produced a soft frosted appearance, but fine curlicue lines are more visible on first-ground pieces. Some pieces have designs, which were etched and then stained with a color. The most familiar design is blue cornflowers.

Do not confuse Pomona with Midwestern Pomona, a pressed glass with a frosted body and amber band.

References: Joseph and Jane Locke, *Locke Art Glass*, Dover Publications, 1987; Kenneth Wilson, *American Glass 1760-1930*, 2 Vols., Hudson Hills Press and The Toledo Museum of Art, 1994.

Bowl, 4-1/2" d, 3" h, first ground, rich deep amber staining 275.00

Butter Dish, cov, 4-1/2" h, 8" d underplate, first ground, gold stained acacia leaf dec, reeded curlicue handle.......1,275.00

Bowl, first grind, amber ribbon and crimped foot, ruffled, ground pontil, 5-1/2" d, 3" h, $175.

Celery Vase, 6-1/8" h, 4-1/2" d, first ground, acacia leaf dec 550.00

Champagne, 5" h, stemmed, second ground, amber staining 245.00

Creamer, second ground, Daisy and Butterfly, applied colorless handle, three applied colorless feet.............................275.00

Cruet, 7-1/4" h, first ground, orig ball stopper 365.00

Finger Bowl, first ground 75.00

Goblet, 6" h, first ground, little amber stain remains 115.00

Pitcher, 5-1/2" h, first ground, applied unstained handle, sq mouth 235.00

Punch Cup
   Cornflower, first ground, blue staining 145.00
   Cornflower, second ground..110.00
   Inverted Thumbprint, first ground, amber staining..........85.00

Tankard Pitcher, 6-3/4" h, first ground, optic diamond quilted body, gold stain on clear glass handle and upper border 385.00

Tumbler
   3-3/4" h, 2-5/8" d, Cornflower, second ground, DQ glass, honey amber stain top and bottom, rich blue stained flowers 145.00
   4" h, Cornflower, second ground, DQ, excellent staining 95.00

Vase
   3" h, 6" w, fan, first ground, Cornflower, blue stained flower dec and violet spray 250.00
   6" h, first ground, rigaree around ruffled top and neck ring, etched waisted body, first ground, faded amber stain 215.00

PORTRAIT WARE

History: Plates, vases, and other articles with portraits on them were popular in the second half of the 19th century. Although male subjects, such as Napoleon or Louis XVI, were used, the ware usually depicts a beautiful, and often unidentified, woman.

A large number of English and Continental china manufacturers made portrait ware. Because most was hand painted, an artist's signature often is found.

Cup and Saucer
   3-1/2" h, cup with medallion of Louis XBVI, Madame de Lamballe and Marie Antoinette, blue celeste and jeweled ground, saucer with central crest, Sevres, 19th C, pr 2,200.00
   6-1/2" h cov cup, portrait reserve, floral spray, apple green ground, gilt highlights, Sevres style 250.00

Plaque
   4-1/8" x 6", porcelain, rect, enameled female, artist sgd "Heubach Bros.," German, c1900..................................488.00
   6" d, bronze, Louis XIV, shown in right profile, inscribed "Bertinet Sculp cu privlegio," reverse dec with crowned interlaced L's with drapery and foliage, by Italian sculptor Bertinetti, 17th C 2,530.00

Plate
   8" d, Daphne, green ground, gilt foliate border, titled on verse, Richard Klem, Dresden, Germany marks, late 19th C 300.00
   9-3/8" d, Countess of Harrington, titled on reverse, central enamel portrait sgd "Wagner," raised gilt border, simulated jade medallions, Germany, late 19th/early 20th C ...500.00
   10" d, Napoleon, Louisiana Purchase souvenir, earthenware, blue and white, high glaze, fair buildings on rim, Victoria Art Company, NY 295.00
   12" d, youthful maiden, 3/4 profile, plumed hat, printed marks, elaborate carved giltwood frame, Continental, c1880 ....550.00

Plate, girl, white dress, pink sash, white ground, gold rim, sgd "Mme A-K, France," 8-1/2" d, $180.

14" d, Peter the Great and Catherine, portrait roundels border, Austrian, late 19th C 1,850.00
Vase
    3-1/8" h, 1-5/8" d, green ground, portrait of lady with wine glass, artist sgd "Sontagg," mkd "Royal Schwarzburg" 100.00
    7" h, portrait medallion of young girl, gilt surface dec, cranberry glass, mkd with crown and shield surrounded by oval 350.00
    12" h, gilt ground, white porcelain body, sq enamel dec panels on each side, female taverner, other with topographical landscape with building, Paris, France, 19th C........ 345.00
    14" h, baluster, portrait of elegant young woman by rose bushes, continuous landscape, printed factory Limoges marks, late 19th C... 900.00

POSTERS

History: Posters were a critical and extremely effective method of mass communication, especially in the period before 1920. Enormous quantities were produced, helped in part by the propaganda role posters played in World War I.

Print runs of two million were not unknown. Posters were not meant to be saved; they usually were destroyed once they had served their purpose. The paradox of high production and low survival is one of the fascinating aspects of poster history.

The posters of the late 19th and early 20th centuries represent the pinnacle of American lithography. The advertising posters of firms such as Strobridge or Courier are true classics. Philadelphia was one center for the poster industry.

Europeans pioneered posters with high artistic and aesthetic content, and poster art still plays a key role in Europe. Many major artists of the 20th century designed posters.

References: George Theofiles, *American Posters of World War I*, Dafram House Publishers; Susan Theran (ed.), *Leonard's Annual Price Index of Posters & Photographs*, Auction Index (30 Valentine Park, Newton, MA 02165), 1995; Jon R. Warren, *Collecting Hollywood*, 3rd ed., American Collector's Exchange, 1994; Bruce Lanier Wright, *Yesterday's Tomorrow*, Taylor Publishing, 1993.

Periodicals: *Biblio,* 845 Willamette St., Eugene, OR 87401; *Collecting Hollywood*, American Collectors Exchange, 2401 Broad St., Chattanooga, TN 37408; *Movie Poster Update*, American Collectors Exchange, 2401 Broad St., Chattanooga, TN 37408; Plakat Journal, Oskar-Winter Str. 3 D30160 Hanover, Germany.

Museum: Museé de la Publicité, 107 Rue de Rivoli, Paris, France.

Additional Listings: See *Warman's Americana & Collectibles* for more examples.

Advisor: George Theofiles.

Advertising

Cycles Clement, A Guillaume, women, bikes, fireworks, fine condition, 1903, 37" x 51" 800.00
"Do It Electrically, Comfort, Convenience, Efficiency in the Home…Save Fuel, Food, Time, Money -By Wire," image of angel holding electric motor, period electrical appliances, full color, blue background, expert restoration to edges, c1915, 27" x 35" 600.00
Ediswan Electric Home Iron, full color, showing 1930s electric iron, c1935, 11" x 18" 60.00
Ferry's Seeds, full color image of pretty young lass amid towering hollyhocks, light fold lines, restoration to edges, thin tears, 1925, 21" x 28" 325.00
Fire! Fire! Fire!, "Chicago Lost But J. Dearman of Knoxville, Penna. Continues to Roll Up, Bundle Up, and Box Up As Many Goods As Ever!" red and black, some replacement to border, Oct. 15th, 1871, 22" x 27" 225.00
Granite Iron Ware, paper, woman carrying milking pail, cow, "For Kitchen and Table Use," 12-1/2" x 28" 75.00
Lady Esther Face Cream, printed on board, beautiful young woman in oval vignette, "A Skin Food-An Astringent," c1920, 23 x 36" 325.00
Kix Cereal, Lone Ranger 6-shooter ring, General Mills premium, "Only 15 cents plus Kix box top," c1948, 17" x 22" 225.00
Popcorn Starch, packages and little girl, color litho, c1900, 10" x 13" 200.00
Richfield Gasoline, race driver in car, c1930, 39" x 53" 1,100.00
Royal Portable Typewriter, dark green detailed manual portable typewriter against leafed red and green ground, c1940, 24" x 36" 285.00
Shamrock Tobacco, canvas, seated man holding knife and tobacco, "Plug Smoking-10 cents a Cut," c1900, 17 x 23" 190.00
Waterman's Ideal Fountain Pen, paper, Uncle Sam at Treaty of Portsmouth, early 1900s, 41-1/2 x 19-1/2" 950.00

Circus, Shows, and Acts

Barnum and Bailey Circus, Strobridge Litho, Co., "Jockey Races," 1908, 19" x 28" 900.00
Clyde Beatty-Cole Bros. Combined Circus, The World's Largest Circus, "Clyde Beatty in Person," Roland butler, lion tamer, multicolored, 19" x 26" 90.00
Downey Bros. Big 3 Ring Circus, "Leaps-Revival of that Astounding and Sensational exhibition," group of elephants, camels,

and horses in line, aerial artist leaping overhead, audience background, c1925, 41" x 27" 125.00

Hollywood Peep Show, burlesque strip revue, c1950, 27" x 41" 150.00

Hot From Harlem, black burlesque show, color, Anon, c1947, 22" x 28" 250.00

Hoxie Bros. Old Time Circus Land, One Mile West of Walt Disney World, multicolored view of circus grounds and big top, 20" x 27" 65.00

Larry Breener's Fantasies of 1929, vaudeville and dance revue, Donaldson Litho, 14" x 22" 80.00

Ringling Bros. Barnum & Bailey Liberty Bandwagon, color litho, ornate wagon with Merue Evans portrait, 1943, 30" x 19" 225.00

Tim McCoy's Wild West, circle of riders around red circle, on canvas, 1938, 54" x 41" 900.00

Magic

Buddha and Heartstone, Polish magician performing tricks, English and Polish text, c1914, 14" x 26" 100.00

Carter the Great-A Baffling Chinese Mystery- The Elongated Maiden, Otis Litho, "A pretty Chinese girl tied to a torture rack without seeming discomfort..," life-sized Chinese nobleman looking down on vignettes of complicated rack, stretched maiden, banshees, imps, devils, in color, c1920, 41" x 81" 650.00

Friedlander Stock Magic, Adolph Friedlander #6966, smiling devil holds card-like vignettes of magic acts in one hand, wand in other, yellow ground, c1919, 14" x 19" 150.00

Kar-Mi Swallows a Loaded Gun Barrel, National, "Shoots a cracker from a man's head," Kar-Mi with gun in mouth blasts away at blindfolded assistant, crowd of turbaned Indians, 1914, 42" x28" 350.00

Movie

Action in Arabia, George Sanders and Virginia Bruce, 1944, 27" x 41" 75.00

African Queen, French release of classic Bogart and Hepburn film, color portraits of both above steamy jungle setting, c1960, 22" x 31" 150.00

Alias Boston Blackie, Columbia Pictures, Chester Morris, full color, 1942, 27" x 41" 100.00

Amazing Transparent Man, Miller Consolidated, D Kennedy, Marguerite Chapman, sci-fi silhouette against blue, 1959, 27" x 41" 125.00

Anatomy of a Murder, Columbia, Saul Bass design, 1959, 27" x 41" 125.00

Atlantic City, Republic, Constance Moore, Jerry Colonna in drag, by James Montgomery Flagg, 1941, 14" x 36" 200.00

Blondie in the Dough, Columbia Pictures, Penny Singleton, Chick Young's Blondie cartoon film, full color, 1947, 27" x 41" 95.00

Bad Boy, James Dunn and Louise Fazenda, Fox, 1934, 27" x 41" 150.00

Buck Privates, Relart re-release, Bud Abbott, Lou Costello, the Andrews Sisters, full-color montage, 1953, 27" x 41" 95.00

Cheaters At Play, Thomas Meighan and Charlotte Greenwood, Fox, 1931, 27" x 41" 275.00

Double Danger, Preston Foster and Whitney Bourne, RKO, 1938, 27" x 41" 110.00

Dr. No., United Artist, Sean Connery, Ursula Andress, 1962, 27" x 41" 325.00

13 Rue Madeleine, Fox, James Cagney, Annabella, Cagney coming from behind looming door, printed in US for So American market, 1947, 27" x 41" 225.00

False Paradise, Hopalong Cassidy, United Artists, 1947,27" x 41" 125.00

Farmer's Daughter, RKO, Loretta Young, Joseph Cotton, Ethel Barrymore, Cotton kneeling to pick up blond Young in maid's outfit, 1947, 27" x 41" 125.00

Flipper, MGM, Chuck Connors, 1963 .... 20.00

Goodbye Mr. Chips, Robert Donat and Greer Garson, MGM, 1939, 27" x 41" 450.00

I'll Be Seeing You, Ginger Rogers, Joseph Cotton, and Shirley Temple, United Artists 1945, 27" x 41" 150.00

Letter of Introduction, Universal, Charlie McCarthy, Edgar Bergen, Andrea Leeds, full-color dummy. 1938, 27" x 41" 300.00

Love Takes Flight, Bruce Cabot and Beatrice Roberts, Grand National, 1937, 22" x 28" 135.00

Mule Train, Columbia Pictures, Gene Autry, Champion, full-color portraits, 1950, 27" x 41" 150.00

New York, New York, United Artists, Robert Diniro, Liza Minnelli, 1977 .... 35.00

One-Eyed Jacks, Paramount, Marlon Brando, Karl Malden, full color, 1959, 27" x 41" 85.00

Pursuit Of The Graf Spee, John Gregson and Anthony Quayle, Rank, c1955, 22" x 28" 150.00

Raiders of the Lost Ark, Harrison Ford, Paramount, 1981....65.00

Smoldering Fires, Pauline Frederick and Laura La Plante, Universal, 1925, 14" x 22" 125.00

Political and Patriotic

America Lets Us Worship As We Wish–Attend The Church Of Your Choice, for American Legion sponsored "Americanism Appreciation Month," full color image of praying Uncle Sam, family at dinner table behind him, c1945, 20" x 26" 225.00

Bridge of Peace, Venette Willard Shearer, anti-war poster from American Friends Service Committee, National Council to Prevent War, in color, children of all nations play beneath text of song of peace, c1936, 16" x 22" 125.00

Forgiven, American theater poster, starring Frederick Bryton, c1900, 30" x 40", $750. Photo courtesy of George Theofiles.

Carry On With Franklin D. Roosevelt, portrait in gravure, black letters against white ground, framed, 1936, 9" x 11" 5.00

Confidence, large color portrait of Roosevelt over yacht at sea, "Election Day was our salvation/Franklin Roosevelt is the man/Our ship will reach her destination/Under his command...Bring this depression to an end...," c1933, 18" x 25" 250.00

United Nations Day, blue and white U.N. banner waves over airbrushed stylized brown and yellow globe, minor edge crumple, 1947, 22" x 23" 250.00

Theater

Black Dwarf, Beck & Pauli Litho, Milwaukee, detailed stage set with 9 strutting players, cat-like character, a knight, ladies, etc., folio fold, expert restoration to upper cream border, c1870, 28" x 21" 325.00

Bringing Up Father, McManus, "Jiggs, Maggie, Dinty Moore-George McManus's cartoon comedy with music," early newspaper cartoon characters against New York skyline, c1915, 41" x 81" 425.00

Claudine Clerice Fr, Collette Willy opera, full color, French, 1910, 26" x 35" 275.00

Dangers of a Great City, National show Print, Chicago, play by Oliver North, men fighting in an office, gleaming stock ticker, "Give me the papers or I'll...," c1900, 21" x 28" 150.00

Irene Vanbrugh, Ernest Hamlin Baker, stage actress dressed in purple, grays, yellow, green, and orange hat, fur-collared coat, c1910, 20" x 28" 350.00

Key Largo, window card for play starring Paul Muni, portrait center, black and red motif, c1930, 14" x 22" 65.00

No No Nanette, Tony Gibbons, Theatre Mogador, Paris, European production of American musical, c1925, 15" x 22" 375.00

Transportation

Air France–North Africa, Villemot, stylized imagery of mosques and minarets, lavenders, yellow, and blues against sky blue background, plane and Pegasus logo, c1950, 24" x 39" 225.00

Motorlobene-Fano, Alfred Olsen, Danish auto race, car raising cloud of dust, 1922, 24" x 35" 1,250.00

Royal Mail Atlantis, Padden, tourists in Royal mail motor launch approaching harbor village, mountains in background, c1923, 25" x 38" 675.00

SS France, Bob Peak, launching of French ocean liner, champagne and confection in front of huge, night-lit bow of ship, 1961, 30" x 46" 450.00

SS Michelangelo and SS Raffaello, Astor, detailed cutaway of Italian ocean liners, designed for use in travel office, printed on plasticized stock, metal frame, 1964, 54" x 22" 300.00

SS Rex, P Klodic, advertisement for Italian ocean liner, designed for use in travel office, framed, c1936, 40" x 29" 750.00

Travel

Arizona–Fly TWA, Austin Briggs, full color western lass in 1950s style, c1955, 25" x 40" 300.00

Boston–New Haven Railroad, Nason, full color, stylized montage of Historic Boston by day and night, faint folio folds, c1938, 28" x 42" 275.00

Britain in Winter, Terence Cuneo, color rendering of horseman, hunters, and tourists outside rustic inn, 1948, 19" x 29" 125.00

Come to Ulster, Norman Wilkinson, sailboats and fishermen in front of lighthouse, full color, c1935, 50" x 40" 450.00

Hawaii–United Air Lines, Feher, stylized wahini, island behind her, full color, c1948, 25" x 40" 650.00

Palace Hotel Wengen, Klara Borter, hotel in foothills of Alps, 1928, 27" x 40" 800.00

Paris, Paul Colin, doves floating above stylized Eiffel tower and Arc de Triumph, 1946, 24" x 39" 600.00

World War I

Call to Duty–Join the Army for Home and Country, Cammilli, recruiting image of Army bugler in front of unfurled banner, 1917, 30" x 40" 325.00

Clear the Way!, Howard chandler Christy, Columbia points the way for Naval gun crew, c1918, 20" x 30" 250.00

Follow The Flag–Enlist in the Navy, James Daugherty, sailor plants flag on shore, 1917, 27" x 41" 450.00

Treat 'Em Rough–Join The Tanks, A. Hutaf, window card, electric blue-black cat leaping over tanks in fiery battle, white border, c1917, 14" x 22" 900.00

You Wireless Fans–Help The Navy Get A Hun Submarine–A Thousand Radio Men Wanted, C. B. Falls, wireless operator reaching up to grab lightening bolt, starry night background, blue, green, red, and white, 1918, 27" x 44" 550.00

Which? Soldier Or Mechanic, L.H., "Enlist in the 57th Engineers (Inlaid Waterways) and Be Both... Camp Laurel, Maryland," 1918, 18" x 23" 200.00

Will You Supply Eyes For The Navy? Gordon Grant, "Navy Ships Need Binoculars and Spy-Glasses...Tag Each Article with Your Name and Address, Mail to Hon. Franklin D. Roosevelt, Asst. Sec'y of Navy,..." image of Naval captain ready with blindfold on stormy deck, gun crew at ready behind him, 1918, 21" x 29" 575.00

POT LIDS

History: Pot lids are the lids from pots or small containers, which originally held ointments, pomades, or soap. Although some collectors want both the pot and its lid, lids alone are more often collected. The lids frequently are decorated with multicolored underglaze transfers of rural and domestic scenes, portraits, florals, and landmarks.

F. & R. Pratt, Fenton, Staffordshire, England made the majority of the containers with lids between 1845 and 1920. In 1920, F. & R. Pratt merged with Cauldon Ltd. Several lids were reissued by the firm using the original copper engraving plates. They were used for decoration and never served as actual lids. Reissues by Kirkhams Pottery, England, generally have two holes for hanging. Cauldon, Coalport, and Wedgwood were other firms making reissues.

Marks: Kirkhams Pottery reissues are often marked as such.

References: Susan and Al Bagdade, *Warman's English & Continental Pottery & Porcelain*, 2nd ed., Wallace-Homestead, 1991; A. Ball, *Price Guide to Pot-Lids and Other Underglaze Multicolor Prints on Ware*, 2nd ed., Antique Collectors' Club, 1991 value update.

Note: Sizes given are for actual pot lids; size of any framing not included.

Arctic Expedition, T. J. & J. Mayer, multicolored, 3" d, rim chip 320.00

Bale's Mushroom Savoury, white glaze, brown and black transfer, 3-1/8" d, orig base 95.00

Bloater Paste, black label, white ironstone, 4-1/2" d, mkd "England" 45.00

Burgess's Genuine Anchovy Paste, white glaze, brown and black transfer, 3-1/4" d, shallow chips on reverse 50.00

Cold Cream, white glaze, brown and black transfer, 2-1/2" d 40.00

Dr. Hassall's Hair Restorer, 1-3/4" d 250.00

The Village Wedding, polychrome dec, Pratt, 4-1/4" d, $145.

Dublin Industrial Exhibition, multicolored, 3-3/4" d 65.00
Embarking For The East, Pratt, multicolored, 4-1/8" d, orig jar
....125.00
Golden Eye Ointment, white glaze, brown and black transfer, 1-
3/4" d..50.00
Hazard, Hazard & Co., Violet Cold Cream, 1150 Broadway New
York, white glaze, brown transfer, 2-3/4" d 210.00
Jules Hauel, Saponaeceous Shaving Compound, 120 Chestnut
St., Philadelphia, white glaze, red transfer, 4" d, minor staining,
orig base 190.00
Hide and Seek, multicolored, 4" d, minor chips on reverse
....75.00
Morris's Imperial Eye Ointment...200.00
Mrs. Ellen Hale's Celebrated Heal All Ointment, black on white,
4" d 350.00
Persuasion, multicolored, 4-1/8" d 160.00
Queen Victoria on Balcony, T. J. & J. Mayer, large............275.00
Roussels's Premium Shaving Cream Philadelphia, white glaze,
gray transfer, 3" d, minor age line in rim of lid, orig base
....220.00
Tam O' Sahnger and Souter Johnny, 4" d, framed.............275.00
The Rivals, multicolored, 4" d, minor chips on reverse 85.00
View of Windsor Castle, Pratt, 6-1/2" d 170.00
Walmer Castle, Kent, Tatnell & Son, 4-1/2" d 215.00
Windsor Ointment, Prepared Only By Hooks, bird on branch
....125.00

PRATT WARE

PRATT

PRATT
FENTON

History: The earliest Pratt
earthenware was made in
the late 18th century by Wil-
liam Pratt, Lane Delph, Staffordshire, England. From
1810 to 1818, Felix and Robert Pratt, William's sons, ran
their own firm, F. & R. Pratt, in Fenton in the Staffordshire
district. Potters in Yorkshire, Liverpool, Sunderland,
Tyneside, and Scotland copied the products.

The wares consisted of relief-molded jugs, commercial
pots and tablewares with transfer decoration, commemorative pieces, and figures and figural groups of both people and animals.

Marks: Much of the early ware is unmarked. The mid-
19th century wares bear several different marks in conjunction with the name Pratt, including "& Co."

References: Susan and Al Bagdade, *Warman's English
& Continental Pottery & Porcelain*, 2nd ed., Wallace-
Homestead, 1991; John and Griselda Lewis, *Pratt Ware
1780-1840*, Antique Collectors' Club, 1984.

Additional Listings: Pot Lids.

Creamer, 5-1/4" h, cow and milkmaid, yellow and black sponged
cow, underglaze enamels, translucent green stepped rect
base, horns chipped 450.00
Cup Plate, 3-1/8" d, Dalmatian, white, black spots 95.00
Figure, 5-1/2" h, Summer, pearlware, green, brown, and yellow
ochre, chip on base..385.00
Jar, 7-3/4" h, molded oval panels of peacocks in landscapes,
blue, brown, green, and ochre, lower section with vertical
leaves, band of foliage on rim, c1790 ....620.00
Jug
7-3/4" h, large oval molded reserve, exotic barnyard fowl, still
leaf-tip band at edge of reverse, molded rim band with
flowering branches, base with long stiff leaves alternating
with slender flowering branches, polychrome enamel high-
lights, c1800 ....1,450.00
8" h, molded leaves at neck and base, raised and polychrome
painted hunting scene on colored ground, c1800 ...750.00
Miniature, 4-3/4" l, dish, center molded with sprung of 2 ochre
plums, green leaf, brown stem, feather molded rim, underglaze blue edging, small rim chip, c1800 ....350.00
Mug, 4" h, colorful tavern scene transfer..............................95.00
Mustard Jar, cov, dark blue hunt scene, tan ground 75.00
Pitcher, 7-1/4" h, raised couple, mother, children, and trees dec,
yellow, blue, brown, and green, 18th C.........................350.00
Plaque, 6-1/4" x 7-1/4", Louis XVI portrait, oval form, beaded border, polychrome enamels, c1793, rim nicks, glaze wear
....900.00
Plate, 9" d, Haddon Hall, classical figure border 120.00
Tea Caddy, 6-1/4" h, rect, raised figural panels front and back, fluted and yellow trimmed lid, blue, yellow, orange, and green
dec...350.00

Plate, Phila Public Building, blue ground, 8-1/2" d, $145.

PRINTS

History: Prints serve many purposes. They can be a reproduction of an artist's paintings, drawings, or designs, but often are an original art form. Finally, prints can be developed for mass appeal rather than primarily for aesthetic fulfillment. Much of the production of Currier & Ives fits this latter category. Currier & Ives concentrated on genre, urban, patriotic, and nostalgic scenes.

References: William P. Carl, *Currier's Price Guide to American and European Prints at Auction*, Currier Publications, 1997; --, *Currier & Ives,* Currier Publications, 1997; Clifford P. Catania, *Boudoir Art*, Schiffer Publishing, 1994; Karen Choppa and Paul Humphrey, *Maud Humphrey*, Schiffer Publishing, 1993; Erwin Flacks, *Maxfield Parrish Identification & Price Guide*, 2nd ed., Collectors Press, 1994; Patricia L. Gibson, *R. Atkinson Fox & William M. Thompson Identification & Price Guide*, Collectors Press, 1994; Martin Gordon (ed.), *Gordon's 1995 Print Price Annual*, Gordon and Lawrence Art Reference, 1995; William R. Holland, Clifford P. Catania, and Nathan D. Isen, *Louis Icart*, Schiffer Publishing, 1994; William R. Holland and Douglas L. Congdon-Martin, *Collectible Maxfield Parrish*, Schiffer Publishing, 1993; Robert Kipp, *Currier's Price Guide to Currier & Ives Prints*, 3rd ed., Currier Publications, 1994; Stephanie Lane, *Maxfield Parrish*, L-W Book Sales, 1993; Coy Ludwig, *Maxfield Parrish*, Schiffer Publishing, 1973, 1993 reprint with value guide; *Maxfield Parrish*, Collectors Press, 1995; Rita C. Mortenson, *R. Atkinson Fox, His Life and Work*, Vol. 1 (1991, 1994 value update), Vol. 2 (1992), L-W Book Sales; Norman I. Platnick, *Coles Phillps*, published by author (50 Brentwood Rd., Bay Shore, NY 11706); Kent Steine and Frederick B. Taraba, *J. C. Leyendecker Collection*, Collectors Press, 1996; Susan Theran, *Prints, Posters & Photographs*, Avon Books, 1993; Susan Theran and Katheryn Acerbo (eds.), *Leonard's Annual Price Index of Prints, Posters & Photographs*, Auction Index, published annually.

Periodicals: *Illustrator Collector's News*, P.O. Box 1958, Sequim, WA 98382; *Journal of the Print World*, 1008 Winona Rd., Meredith, NH 03253; *Print Collector's Newsletter*, 119 East 79th St., New York, NY 10021.

Collectors' Clubs: American Antique Graphics Society, 5185 Windfall Rd., Medina, OH 44256; American Historical Print Collectors Society, P.O. Box 201, Fairfield, CT 06430; Gutmann Collector Club, P.O. Box 4743, Lancaster, PA 17604; Prang-Mark Society, P.O. Box 306, Watkins Glen, NY 14891.

Museums: American Museum of Natural History, New York, NY; Audubon Wildlife Sanctuary, Audubon, PA; John James Audubon State Park and Museum, Henderson, KY; Museum of the City of New York, NY; National Portrait Gallery, Washington, DC.

Additional Listings: See Wallace Nutting.

REPRODUCTION ALERT

The reproduction of Maxfield Parrish prints is a continuing process. New reproductions look new, i.e., their surfaces are shiny and the paper crisp and often pure white. The color on older prints develops a mellowing patina. The paper often develops a light brown to dark brown tone, especially if it is acid based or was placed against wooden boards in the back of a frame.

Size is one of the keys to spotting later reproductions. Learn the correct size for the earliest forms. Be alert to earlier examples that have been trimmed to fit into a frame. Check the dimensions before buying any print.

Carefully examine the edges within the print. Any fuzziness indicates a later copy. Also look at the print through a magnifying glass. If the colors separate into dots, this indicates a later version.

Apply the same principles described above for authenticating all prints, especially those attributed to Currier & Ives. Remember, many prints were copied soon after their period introduction. As a result, reproductions can have many of the same aging characteristics as period prints.

Note: Prints are beginning to attract a wide following. This is partially because prices have not matched the rapid rise in oil paintings and other forms of art.

SPECIAL AUCTIONS

Phillips Fine Art Auctions
406 E. 79th St.
New York, NY 10021
(212) 570-4830

Skinner Inc.
Bolton Gallery
357 Main St.
Bolton, MA 01740

Swann Galleries, Inc.
104 E. 25th St.
New York, NY 10010

Appel, Karel, Dutch, 1921-, Nu, color litho on paper, sgd "Appel" in pencil l.r. numbered "44/50" in pencil l.l., 30" x 22-1/4", framed 520.00
Arms, John Taylor, American, 1887-1953, Rodez/The Tower of Notre Dame, etching on paper, edition of 120 plus 6 trial proofs, sgd and dated "John Taylor Arms – 1927" in pencil l.r., inscribed "Arms 1926" and "Rodez 1926" in the plate, 11-7/8" x 4-7/8", framed 230.00
Benson, Frank Weston, American, 1862-1951, sgd "Frank W. Benson" in pencil l.l.
Chickadees, drypoint on paper, 7-7/8" x 5-7/8", deckled edges, matted 460.00
Goose and Teal, etching on paper, 5-7/8" x 7-7/8", matted 750.00
Low Tide, drypoint on Shogun paper with watermark, numbered "11/35" in pencil l.r., 6-3/4" x 10-3/4", matted 1,025.00
Study of Geese, drypoint on Shugon paper with watermark, numbered "54" in pencil l.r., 3-7/8" x 5-7/8", matted 980.00
The Seiner, etching on paper, numbered "47/50" in pencil l.r., 6-3/4" x 10-7/8", framed 2,300.00
The Visitor, etching on paper, numbered "38" in pencil l.r., 3" x 5", matted 435.00

Benton, Thomas Hart, American, 1889-1975, litho on paper, sgd "Benton" in pencil and in matrix, published by Associated American Artists, identified from AAA label affixed to mat

Edge of Town, 1938, edition of 250, 8-7/8" x 10-3/4", full sheet with deckled edges, framed.................................1,670.00

Homestead, 1938, edition of 250, 10-1/4" x 13", matted 980.00

Rainy Day, 1938, edition of 250, 8-3/4" x 13-1/4", full sheet with deckled edges, framed..................................1,100.00

Chagall, Marc, Russian/French, 1887-1985, The Cello, color litho on wove paper, sgd "Marc Chagall" in pencil l.r., numbered "38/50" in pencil ll., 13-1/2" x 9-3/4", framed..............5,750.00

Chase, W. Corwin, color woodcut on paper, sgd and dated "W. Corwin Chase 27" lower right, titled lower left, identified on label "Summerland" on mat, 12-1/2 x 8-1/2" image size, 1/4" or more margins, matted 920.00

Currier & Ives

American Homestead Autumn, C#168, hand colored litho, 10-15/16" h x 13-7/8" w, walnut cross corner 17-1/4" x 20-1/4" frame, gilded liner, minor stains, edge damage, pinpoint hole in image area 415.00

American Homestead Spring, C170, hand colored litho, 10-15/16" h x 13-7/8" w, walnut cross corner 17-1/4" x 20-1/4" frame, gilded liner, stains, edge damage, tear in right margin extends into image, hole in bottom margin 220.00

American Homestead Summer, C#171, hand colored litho, 10-15/16" h x 13-7/8" w, walnut cross corner 17-1/4" x 20-1/4" frame, gilded liner, minor stains 220.00

American Homestead Winter, C#172, hand colored litho, 10-15/16" h x 13-7/8" w, walnut cross corner 17-1/4" x 20-1/4" frame, gilded liner, slightly trimmed, minor stains....600.00

American Winter Scene, C#206, hand colored litho, identified in inscriptions in matrix, 8-1/4" x 10" sheet size, period frame, tear to upper edge, several creases 2,415.00

The Grand Racer Kington, by Spendthrift... 1891, C#2521, hand colored chromolithograph, identified in inscriptions in matrix, 23" x 29-3/4", unmatted, unframed 460.00

The New Brood, C#4411, hand colored litho, 10" h, 14-1/8" w, minor stains, edge damage with tear in top margin, 12-3/4" h, 16-1/2" w frame..200.00

The Old Mill Dam, C#4572, hand colored litho, 10" h, 14" w, margins trimmed, part of title missing, stains, 13-1/2" h x 17-1/4" w frame 200.00

The Soldiers Home, the Vision, C#5599, hand colored litho, 10-13/16" h, 14-7/8" w, margins trimmed and stains, 12-1/4" h x 16" w frame 140.00

Currier, Nathaniel

Snipe Shooting, C#5577, hand colored litho, identified in inscriptions in the matrix, 18-1/2" x 25" sheet size, framed 1,150.00

View of the Park Fountain & City Hall, NY," C#6422, hand colored litho, 9" h, 12-3/8", margins trimmed, stains, and foxing, short tears into image, edge damage, 14-3/9" h x 16-1/2" w frame 200.00

Curry, John Steuart, American, 1897-1946, John Brown, litho on paper, 1939, edition of 250, published by Associated American Artists, sgd "John Steuart Curry" in pencil l.r., initialed and dated in the matrix, titled in pencil l.l., 13-3/4" x 11", framed 2,760.00

Endicott & Co, Hambletonian, 1865, identified within matrix, chromolithograph on paper, 20-1/2" x 26", framed..............230.00

Gearhart, Frances Hammel, color woodcut on paper, sgd "Frances H. Gearhart" in pencil lower right, titled or numbered in pencil l.l., identified on label on mat

A Tatoosh Vista, 10-1/4" x 7-1/2" image size, 1/2" or more margins, matted..1,495.00

Geraniums, 8" x 4-1/4" image size, 1/4" or more margins, matted..575.00

The Peach Orchard, 9" x 10" image size, 1/2" or more margins, matted..2,070.00

The Wave, 7-3/4" x 4-3/4" image size, 1/4" or more margins, matted..690.00

Prints, Kurz & Allison, The Battle of Gettysburg, chromolithograph, bright colors, some margin stains, 22" x 28", $220. Photo courtesy of Garth's Auctions.

Gwathmey, Robert, American, 1903-1989, Sharecropper, litho on paper, sgd "Gwathmey" in pencil l.r., initialed within the matrix l.l., numbered "106/125" in pencil l.l., 29-3/4" x 22", unframed..230.00

Hall, Edith Emma Dorothea, American, 1883-, Still Life/Vegetables, color woodcut on paper, sgd and dated "Emma Hall "54" in pencil lower right, 9-1/4" x 7-1/2", matted 115.00

Hyde, Helen, Moon Bridge at Kameido, color woodcut on paper, sgd "Helen Hyde" in pencil l.r., monogram and clover seals l.l., numbered "67" in pencil l.l., inscribed "Copyright, 1914, by Helen Hyde" in the block l.l., 13-1/4" x 8-7/8", framed 460.00

Indiana, Robert, American, 1928-, Love Cross, color screenprint on paper, sgd and dated "R. Indiana '68" in pencil l.r., titled and numbered "...28/100" in pencil l.l., dedicated lower corner, unmatted, unframed 175.00

Jacquette, Yvonne, 22nd Street, litho with pastel hand coloring on ochre/gray paper, published by Brook Alexander, Inc., NY, sgd "Yvonne Jacquette" in pencil l.r., numbered "A.P. #34" in pencil l.l., 19" x 22-1/4", unmatted, unframed...............850.00

Kasamir, Luigi, Austrian, 1881-, The Magical Island, color etching with aquatint on paper, sgd "Luigi Kasamir" in pencil l.r., numbered and tilted "2/100" in pencil l.l., 11-3/8" x 13-3/4", framed 460.00

Kellogg & Comstock, The Presidents of the United States, Washington to Polk, hand colored litho, 20-1/4" h, 17-1/4" w, gilt frame, light stains 200.00

Kent, Rockwell, America, 1882-1971, Hero, litho on paper, sgd "Rockwell Kent" in pencil l.r., 12-1/8" x 9", framed........345.00

Landeck, Armin, Shadow, litho on paper, 1932, sgd "Landeck" in pencil l.r., numbered "1/10" in pencil l.l., annotated along lower margin, 10-7/8" x 9-1/8", framed................................1,100.00

Lewis, Martin, American, 1881-1962, Chance Meeting, drypoint on laid paper, commission by Society of American Etchers, c1940, edition of 105, sgd "Martin Lewis" in pencil l.r., 10-1/2" x 7-1/2", matted..3,105.00

Lindner, Richard, American, 1901-1978, Composition, color litho on paper, initialed "R.L." in pencil l.r., inscribed "H.C." in pencil l.l., 18-1/2" x 21" 575.00

Lord, Elyse Eshe, British, -1971, Trio, color etching with aquatint on paper, sgd "Elyse Lord" in pencil l.r., chop u.r., numbered "91/100" in pencil l.l., 15-3/4" x 16-1/2", framed 230.00

Marsh, Reginald, American, 1898-1954, Flying Concellos, 1936, etching and engraving on cream wove paper, state 2 of 4, sgd "Reginald Marsh (F.M.M.)" in pencil by the artist's widow l.r., 7-7/8" x 10", matted..750.00

McBey, James, British, 1889-1959, Venice, etching on paper, sgd "James McBey" in pencil l.r., sgd and dated in plate l.r., numbered "LXVII" in pencil l.l., 10-3/4" x 16-7/8", framed 375.00

Picasso, Pablo, Spanish, 1881-1973

Feme au chapeau à fleurs, linocut in black, brown, and tan on Arches wove paper with watermark, 1962, sgd "Picasso" in pencil l.r., numbered "22/50" in pencil l.l., identified on label from the Saidenberg Gallery, NY label affixed to reverse, 13-3/4" x 10-3/4" 18,400.00

Lysistrata, portfolio of "Six Images to Illustrate the Play by Aristophanes," 1934, edition of 150, published by the Limited Editions Club/The Print Club, New York, etchings on Arches paper, each sgd "Picasso" in pencil l.l., numbered "150/15" in pencil l.r., identified on colophon page, 15" x 11-3/4" sheet size, orig folder 18,400.00

Riggs, Robert, American, 1896-1970, litho on wove paper, sgd "Robert Riggs," in pencil l.r. and within the matrix, titled in pencil l.l.

Clown Acrobats, 1934, dedicated in pencil l.c., 14-3/8" x 19", matted...400.00

On the Lot, c1934, 12-1/4" x 17-3/4", matted.................750.00

Ripley, Aiden Lassell, American, 1896-1969, Grouse and Vine, etching and drypoint on paper, sgd "A. Lassell Ripley" in pencil l.l., label from Guild of Boston Artists on reverse, 6-1/2" x 8-3/8", framed 345.00

Sloan, John, America, 1871-1951, Washington Arch, etching on paper, sgd "John Sloan" in pencil l.r., sgd and dated within the plate l.r, titled in pencil l.l., 7-3/4" x 4-3/4", framed 1,265.00

Welsh, Horace Devitt, American, 1888-1942, Brooklyn Bridge-Twilight, etching on paper, sgd "H. Welsh" in pencil l.r., annotated along lower edge, 11-7/8" x 8-7/8", framed 320.00

Wood, Grant, American, 1891-1942, published by Associated American Artists

Tree Planting Group, litho on paper, sgd "Grant Wood–1937" in pencil l.r., 8-3/8" x 10-7/8", matted....................4,025.00

Vegetables, 1938, litho with hand coloring on paper, sgd "Grant Wood" in pencil l.r., identified on label from AAA on reverse, 7" x 9-1/2", framed 550.00

PRINTS, JAPANESE

History: Buying Japanese woodblock prints requires attention to detail and abundant knowledge of the subject. The quality of the impression (good, moderate, or weak), the color, and condition are critical. Various states and strikes of the same print cause prices to fluctuate. Knowing the proper publisher and censor's seals is helpful in identifying an original print.

Most prints were copied and issued in popular versions. These represent the vast majority of the prints found in the marketplace today. These popular versions should be viewed solely as decorative since they have little monetary value.

A novice buyer should seek expert advice before buying. Talk with a specialized dealer, museum curator, or auction division head.

The following terms are used to describe sizes: chuban, 7-1/2 x 10 inches; hosoban, 6 x 12 inches; and oban, 10 x 15 inches. Tat-e is a vertical print; yoko-e a horizontal one.

Collectors' Club: Ukiyo-E Society of America, Inc., FDR Station, P.O .Box 665, New York, NY 10150.

Museum: Honolulu Academy of Fine Arts, Honolulu, HI.

Note: The listings below include the large amount of detail necessary to determine value. Condition and impression are good unless indicated otherwise.

Album

Toyokuni III, Kuniyoshi, Hiroshige, mostly from series *Ogura Imitations of the One Hundred Poets* and *Keniyshi Genji* 2,645.00

Utamaro, Tokoyuni, Koyomine, Eizan, and Kuniyosu, 18 prints of women, trimmed, toned, some stains and wear 2,300.00

Chikanobu, framed triptych of women by lake, c1890, good impression, somewhat faded 125.00

Eishi, four courtesans in elaborate kimonos, 1790s, framed, good impression, somewhat faded 345.00

Eizan

Courtesan at her mirror, c1810, framed, good impression and color...290.00

Courtesan in elaborate kimono with her kamuro, c1810, framed, good impression and color 290.00

Harunobu, pillar print of woman carrying bucket, framed, very good impression, horizontal creases and tears 345.00

Hasui

Oban tate-e, tama seal, signature within image
Autumn at a gorge, publisher's seal in margin.........290.00
Snowstorm at the sacred bridge at Nikko, publisher's seal Tokyo Shobi-do, c1930 ....345.00

Tai-oban, Lake Hakone, 1935, pencil sgd "K. Hasui" lower right, printed signature and seal within image, publisher's information in margin, good color, 20-1/4" x 14-1/4" 575.00

Hiroshige

Scene of small temple, from *Edo Meisho* series, framed, moderate impression and color, soiled 500.00

The Ferry on the Tenryn River near Mitsuke, from *Upright Tokaido,* Meiji printing, framed, good color 90.00

The Outer Bay at Choshi Beach in Simosa Province, from *Sixty Odd Provinces* series, good impression and color, some stains...230.00

Triptych of 3 women, each with umbrella in snowy landscape, c1850, framed 750.00

Hiroshige II, Mimeguiri Embankment and the Sumida River, from "Toto Meisho," 1862, good impression, fine color.........350.00

Hiroshi Yoshida, evening street scene, sgd, Hiroshi seal, 14-1/2" x 19-1/2" 270.00

Hokusai, In The Totomi Mountains, from *Thirty-Six Views of Fuji,* aizuri printing with blue outline, modern impression, wrinkled, torn, stains...1,610.00

Junichiro Sekino, portrait of actor Kichiemon, "il ne etat," printed signature and seal lower right within the image, pencil sgd, 13/50 in lower margin, 22" x 18" 920.00

Kawamishi, the Water Lily Season, sgd and titled in pencil, dated, numbered, framed...425.00

Hiroshige, Gyosho of the Tokaido series, c1840, $195.

Kunihisa, portrait of actor carrying bucket and broom over his shoulder, c1800..425.00
Kunisada, courtesan and two kamuro, landscape in background, printed in blue, c1830, good impression and color 215.00
Kuniyoshi, Beauty with Small Dog, 13-7/8" x 9-5/8" 125.00
Okiie Hashimoto, Village in the Evening, sgd in pencil in margin, dated, Hashi seal, good impression, framed, 17" x 21-1/2" 250.00
Sekino, bridge in snow, sgd in image, seal, good impression, 18" x 12-1/2" 200.00
Shigenobu, surimono of courtesan in an interior, make-up table and mirror to left, fine impression and color..................634.00
Toyokuni II, Kakemono-e portrait of monk peering under blanket on his head, bamboo flute in land, framed, very good impression, somewhat faded 230.00
Toyokuni III
    Pentaptcyh of people in boat feeding goldfish, iris garden, framed, very good impression, missing leaf, somewhat faded..230.00
    Two actors in roles, framed, very good impression and color, slight damage to bottom..115.00
Utamaro II, 3 women in an interior, c1811, good impression, faded, soiled 175.00
Yoshitoshi
    Kakemono-e, vertical diptych, man trying to signal to boat from rocky ledge, framed, stained 210.00
    Woman by moonlight watches geese descending, from *New Forms of Thirty-Six Ghosts,* good impression, stained, trimmed 115.00

PURPLE SLAG (MARBLE GLASS)

History: Challinor, Taylor & Co., Tarantum, Pennsylvania, c1870s-1880s, was the largest producer of purple slag in the United States. Since the quality of pieces varies considerably, there is no doubt other American firms made it as well.

Purple slag also was made in England. English pieces are marked with British Registry marks.

Other slag colors, such as blue, green, and orange, were used, but examples are rare.

Videotape: National Imperial Glass Collectors Society, *Glass of Yesteryears*, The Renaissance of Slag Glass by Imperial, RoCliff Communications, 1994.

REPRODUCTION ALERT

Purple slag has been heavily reproduced over the years and still is reproduced at present.

Additional Listings: Greentown Glass (chocolate slag); Pink Slag.

Ashtray, 6" sq, chocolate slag, Imperial IG mark 25.00
Bowl, 9" d, Rose, caramel slag, Imperial IG mark................50.00
Cake Stand, Flute, purple...75.00
Compote, 4-1/2" d, crimped top, purple..............................70.00
Creamer, Flower and Panel, purple......................................85.00
Goblet, Flute, purple..40.00
Jar, cov, figural, owl, glossy, green slag, Imperial IG mark 60.00
Match Holder, Daisy and Button, green 30.00
Mug, rabbit, purple...65.00
Pitcher, Windmill, glossy, purple slag, Imperial IG mark......45.00
Pate, 10-1/2" d, closed lattice edge, purple........................75.00
Platter, oval, notched rim, wildflowers dec, purple, nick......20.00

Miniature Lamp, Smith # 113, $95.

Spooner, Scroll with Acanthus, purple 65.00
Sugar Bowl, cov, Flute, purple 190.00

PUZZLES

History: The jigsaw puzzle originated in the mid-18th century in Europe. John Spilsbury, a London map maker, was selling dissected-map jigsaw puzzles by the early 1760s. The first jigsaw puzzles in America were English and European imports aimed primarily at children.Prior to the Civil War, several manufacturers, e.g., Samuel L. Hill, W. and S. B. Ives, and McLoughlin Brothers, included puzzles in their lines. However, it was the post-Civil War period that saw the jigsaw puzzle gain a strong foothold among the children of America.

In the late 1890s, puzzles designed specifically for adults first appeared. Both forms–adult and child–have existed side by side ever since. Adult puzzlers were responsible for two 20th-century puzzle crazes: 1908-1909 and 1932-1933.

Prior to the mid-1920s, the vast majority of jigsaw puzzles were cut out of wood for the adult market and composition material for the children's market. In the 1920s, the die-cut, cardboard jigsaw puzzle evolved and was the dominant medium in the 1930s.

Interest in jigsaw puzzles has cycled between peaks and valleys several times since 1933. Mini-revivals occurred during World War II and in the mid-1960s, when Springbok entered the American market.

References: *Dexterity Games and Other Hand-Held Puzzles*, L-W Book Sales, 1995; Jack Matthews, *Toys Go to War*, Pictorial Histories Publishing, 1994; Jerry Slocum and Jack Botermans, *Book of Ingenious & Diabolical Puzzles*, Time Books, 1994.

Collectors' Clubs: American Game Collectors Assoc., P.O. Box 44, Dresher, PA 19025.

Advisor: Bob Armstrong.

Note: Prices listed here are for puzzles which are complete or restored, and in good condition. Most puzzles found in attics do not meet these standards. If evaluating an old puzzle, a discount of 50% should be calculated for moderate damage (1-2 missing pieces, 3-4 broken knobs,) with greater discounts for major damage or missing original box.

Advertising, Rexall Drug Store, Mountain Splendor, 1930s, cardboard, diecut, orig envelope, several pcs missing 4.00

Map

Clemens/Silent Teacher, 1890s, solid wood, adv on back, replaced container
  N.Y./White Sewing Machines, 16-1/4" x 12-1/4", 70 pcs (3 replaced), sq knob, color line cutting, edge-interlocking
  .... 70.00
  U. S./White Sewing Machines, 16-1/4" x 11-1/4", 52 pcs (1 replaced), sq knob, color line cutting, edge-interlocking
  .... 80.00
Milton Bradley, two sided
  U.S. Animals, Work in America, 1900, solid wood, 22-3/4" x 15-3/4", 64 pcs, (6 replaced), push fit, color line cutting, orig wood box 90.00
  U. S./Principal Cities Map of World, 1920-30, cardboard, 20-1/2" x 14-1/2", 63 pcs, diecut, round kb edge, color line cutting, replaced container 15.00

Parker Brothers, Pastime, plywood

Breakfast in Peasant's Home, 1932, 13-1/2" x 9-1/2", 260 pcs (1 replaced), earlets, color line cutting, interlocking, orig box, 29 figures, sawed by #38 .... 70.00
Bridge Over the Stream, artist: L. V. Senger, 1922, 9-1/4" x 11-3/4", 150 pcs, curve knob, color line cutting, interlocking, orig box, 21 figures, sawed by #10 .... 44.00
Bright Angel Trail, 1920-30, 5-3/4" x 7-1/2", 76 pcs (3 replaced), earlets, semi-color line cutting, interlocking, replaced box, 8 figures 18.00
In Picturesque Holland, 1910, 28" x 15-32/4", 630 pcs (4 replaced), curl knob, angular, color line cutting, interlocking, replaced box, 72 figures 175.00
Lovely Thatched Cottage, 1932, 22-3/4" x 16", 539 pcs (2 replaced), random, color line cutting, interlocking, orig box, 60 figures, sawed by #50 .... 140.00
Loves Old Sweet Song, 1920, 10-1/2" x 8-3/4", 100 pcs (1 replaced), curve knob, color line cutting, interlocking, orig box, 16 figures, sawed by #14 .... 28.00
Making Friends-Apple For The Horse, artist: K. Kohler, 1927, 10-3/4" x 14", 200 pcs (2 replaced), round knob, color line cutting, interlocking, orig box, 22 figures 60.00
Now I Lay Me, family type scene, 1929, 7-3/4" x 5.3/4", 65 pcs, curve knob, color line cutting, semi-interlocking, orig box, 8 figures, sawed by #3 .... 18.00

Prize Winners, cows and women, 1930, 8" x 10-1/4", 150 pcs (2 replaced), curl knob/earlets, color line cutting, semi-interlocking, orig box, 18 figures, sawed by #21 .... 40.00
Song of Love, music scene with 1920s dress, 1931, 16-1/2" x 13-3/4", 305 pcs, (2 replaced) earlets curve knob, color line cutting, interlocking, orig box, 39 figures, sawed by #19 .... 85.00
Untitled, Arab Street Scene, artist: Woodward, 1930s, 9" x 14", 212 pcs (1 replaced), curl knob, color line cutting, interlocking, replaced box, 24 figures 55.00
Visiting the Grandparents, artist: Branscombe, 1922, 13-1/4" x 8-3/4", 150 pcs (1 replaced), curl knob, color line cutting, semi-interlocking, orig box, 18 figures, sawed by #8 .... 35.00

Strauss, Joseph K., plywood

Camp Raiders, Schwartz/Spec Cut, 1950-60, 27-3/4" x 21-3/4", 1,000 pcs, random, interlocking, orig box, 20 figures ... 150.00
Cottage By The Winter, artist: Thornton, 1930-40, 12" x 8-3/4", 200 pcs, curve knob, stripcut earlets, interlocking, orig box, variety stripcut 20.00
School is Out, artist: Bollendonk, 1950s, 19-3/4" x 15-3/4", 500 pcs, round knob, stripcut earlets, interlocking, orig box, well cut
  .... 60.00
Silent Winter Night, 1930-40, 12" x 8-3/4", 200 pcs, round knob, stripcut earlets, interlocking, orig box, variety stripcut 22.00
Village and Mountains, 1950s, 11-3/4" x 9", 200 pcs, round knob, stripcut earlets, interlocking, orig box 20.00

Wood and/or Handcut, pre-1930

Ayer, Isabel, Picture Puzzle Exchange, 3 Black Crows and a Fox at TallenSee, artist: Robert Kammerac, 1909, solid wood, 14-3/4" x 20", 400 pcs, push fit, color line cutting, orig box, gloss finish, bright colors 100.00
Derr, Henry (attributed to), Neat Fit, Shade of the Old Apple Tree, artist: Carl Weber, 1910s, plywood, 8" x 24", 311 pcs, push fit, color line cutting, replaced box 70.00
Ullman, Philadelphia Press, Cornered, 1910s, thick plywood, 7-1/2" x 5-3/4", 80 pcs, crooked line, 1-way strip, push fit, replaced box, orig label 20.00
Unknown Makers
  Beating the Storm, canoeing, 1909, plywood, 9-1/4" x 6", 92 pcs, push fit, semi-color line cutting, orig box, back stained red
  .... 22.00
  The New Toys, Christmas, 1910s, plywood, 6-1/2" x 4-1/2", 50 pcs, push fit, semi-color line cutting, orig box, back stained pink, old mfg. box 10.00
  Windmill, artist: W. J. Krola, 1909, solid wood, 5-1/2" x 7", 84 pcs, push fit, color line cutting, orig box, stationary diary 1906 on box 20.00
  Woman and Baby, artist: Olive Rush, Crowell Pub., 1909, solid wood, 10" sq, 168 pcs, push fit, color line cutting, orig box
  .... 35.00

Wood and/or Handcut, 1930-40s

Cape Cod Puzzle Co, Settling the Question, plywood, 10-5" x 6-3/4", 150 pcs, scroll, interlocking, orig box, thick edges, pink stained back 28.00
Foster, Fred, Best O' Luck, In Love with Nature's Perfumed Zephyr, artist: R. Atkinson Fox, plywood, 5-3/4" x 8", 100 pcs, curved knob, interlocking, framed, label on back 50.00
Gold Sea Toy, Locktite, Covered Wagon, plywood, 18" x 12", 400 pcs (2 replaced), earlets, 1-way strip, interlocking, orig box
  .... 75.00
Heddaems, Gib's Jig-Job, Dutch Flower Market, plywood, 20-3/4" x 16", 553 pcs (3 replaced) curved knob, jagged, color line cutting, interlocking orig wood box, 10 figures 140.00
Hodges and Son, Tru Art, Son of Erin, plywood, 8" x 10", 150 pcs, 1-by-1, large knob, interlocking, replaced box, orig label
  .... 30.00

Children's, Little Annie Rooney, 20th C, boxed set of three puzzles, $75.

Jumble Jig Saw Puzzles, A Glistening Sheen, plywood, 20" x 16", 428 pcs (2-1/2 replaced), foot knob, interlocking, 10 figures, trick edges, split corners 75.00

Macy's, The Signing, Declaration of Independence, artist: S. Dodson, plywood, 20" x 14-1/4", 525 pcs (4 replaced), random knob, color line cutting, interlocking, orig box, 48 figures, trick edges.. 130.00

Milton Bradley, Wood Picture Products, 1938, Fisherfolk of Normandy, plywood, 16" x 12", 250 pcs, diecut, round knob strip, interlocking, orig box..25.00

Needham, J. A., School Bus Stop, dogs, artist: R. Sambrook, plywood, 8-1/2" x 11", 216 pcs, random, semi-interlocking, orig box 30.00

Selchow & Righter, Pandora, The Windmill, plywood, 10" x 8", 152 pcs, curve knob, interlocking, orig box, 18 figures, split corners 30.00

Stoughton Studio, Tiz-A-Tee, A Serious Case, humorous children, artist: Norman Rockwell, plywood, 5-3/4" x 7-3/4", 65 pcs (1 replaced), long/knobby, interlocking, orig box...................12.00

Trickey, Harold, A. M., The Old Homestead, 1933, pressboard, 14" x 9-1/2" 263 pcs, long/round knobs, interlocking, orig box, minor discolor to 1 pc..25.00

Tuck, Raphael, Zag-Zaw, The Brush, plywood, 9" x 5-3/4", 90 pcs, earlets, interlocking, orig box, 10 figures 22.00

Unknown Makers
    Autumn Scene, cardboard, 8-1/2" x 6-1/4", 100 pcs, long/round, interlocking, orig box, 4 figures, boot shaped in corners..12.00
    Colonial Sweetheart, plywood, 10-1/2" x 12", 142, long, round, interlocking, replaced box, white border...................20.00
    Sleeping Baby, plywood, 11-3/4" x 9", 219 pcs, random, jagged, semi-color line cutting, interlocking, 20 figures, geometric, relabeled coffee can 40.00
    The Old Barn, plywood, 4-1/4" x 6", 85 pcs, fantasy, semi-color line cutting, interlocking, 6 figures, relabeled coffee can 17.00
    The Old Mill, plywood, 7-1/4" x 10-1/2", 172 pcs, random, jagged, semi-color line cutting, interlocking, 14 figures, relabeled coffee can 35.00

Wood and/or Handcut, post-1950

Browning, James, U-Nit, Miss Innocence, 1950, plywood, 15-3/4" x 19-3/4", 500 pcs (1 replaced), earlets, jagged, interlocking, orig box, 50 figures..135.00

Chesley, Roland, Cavalry, Infantry, Artillery, Revolutionary War, artist: Ogden, 1971, 11-1/2" x 13", 240 pcs, random, interlocking, orig box, 3 figures, American flag in background....32.00

Hayter, Victory Topical, Houses of Parliament and Westminister Abbey, plywood, 15" x 11", 288 pcs, round knob strip, interlocking, orig box, loose cut 30.00

Optimago, Decorative Fowl Round Lake, artist: Jan Van Kessel, 1970s, plywood, 16-1/4" x 12-3/4", 308 pcs (2 replaced), round knob strip, interlocking, orig box.....................................35.00

Playtime House, Fine Arts, Riders Going on Hunt, 1950, cardboard, 27" x 21", 1,000 pcs (2 replaced), diecut, sq knob strip, semi-interlocking, orig box 8.00

Regent Specialties, Deluxe, Awaiting Spring Breezes, 1930s, cardboard, 19-1/2" x 15-1/2", 400 pcs (1 replaced), diecut, sq knob strip, edge-interlocking, orig box 10.00

Russell, Charles, Washington Crossing the Delaware, artist: Currier & Ives, 1976, plywood, 13-1/2" x 8-12", 315 pcs, round knob, color line cutting, interlocking, orig box, 16 figures 60.00

Straley, Sidney L, Lake Louise, 1950s, plywood, 13-1/2" x 9", 311 pcs, semi-strip earlet, interlocking, orig box 36.00

QUEZAL

Quezal

History: The Quezal Art Glass Decorating Company, named for the quetzal–a bird with brilliantly colored feathers–was organized in 1901 in Brooklyn, New York, by Martin Bach and Thomas Johnson, two disgruntled Tiffany workers. They soon hired Percy Britton and William Wiedebine, two more Tiffany employees.

The first products, which are unmarked, were exact Tiffany imitations. Quezal pieces differ from Tiffany pieces in that they are more defined and the decorations are more visible and brighter. No new techniques were developed by Quezal.

Johnson left in 1905. T. Conrad Vahlsing, Bach's son-in-law, joined the firm in 1918, but left with Paul Frank in 1920 to form Lustre Art Glass Company, which copied Quezal pieces. Martin Bach died in 1924 and by 1925 Quezal had ceased operations.

Marks: The "Quezal" trademark was first used in 1902 and was placed on the base of vases and bowls and on the rims of shades. The acid-etched or engraved letters vary in size and may be found in amber, black, or gold. A printed label which includes an illustration of a quetzal was used briefly in 1907.

Bowl, 9-1/2" d, gold calcite ground, stretch rim, pedestal foot, sgd "Quezal"..800.00

Candlesticks, pr, 7-3/4" h, irid blue, sgd 575.00

Chandelier, gilt metal
    14" h, 4 elaborated scroll arms, closed teardrop gold, green, and opal shades, inscribed "Quezal" at collet rim, very minor roughness at rim edge 2,000.00
    16" h, 3 shouldered flared opal shades, rib molded design, gold irid int., collet rim inscribed "Quezal," classic shaped socket, wheel with chain drop 450.00

Cologne Bottle, 7-1/2" h, irid gold ground, Art Deco design, sgd "Q" and "Melba" 250.00

Lamp, desk, 14-1/2" h, gold irid shade with green and white pulled feather dec, inscribed "Quezal" at rim, gilt metal adjustable crook-neck lamp...575.00

Lamp Shade, 5-1/4" h, 2-1/8" outside rim, bell form, gold irid, ribbed, green and white pulled feather design, inscribed "Quezal" on rim, price for pr...345.00

Toothpick Holder, 2-1/4" h, melon ribbed, pinched sides, irid blue, green, purple and gold, sgd 200.00

Vase, trumpet, green feather with gold border, opal ground, highly irid gold, stretched int., sgd "Quezal/J/860," 6-1/2" h, $1,500.

Vase
- 4-5/8" h, double dec opal body, hooked and pulled gold feathers below green hooked elements, medial gold band, gold irid surface above and within flared rim, base inscribed "Quezal 490" 2,070.00
- 4-3/4" h, cased cylinder, five pointed gold irid feathers on opal white body, flared golden foot inscribed "Quezal" on base 575.00
- 5" h, lily, pinched quatraform rim, slender transparent golden bud vase, five subtle green spiked feathers, large partial label covers pontil," Art Quezal - rooklyn"................1,035.00
- 7-3-4" h, 9-1/2" d, large flared bulbous ambergris body cased to opal, dec with green pulled and coiled feathers obscured by lavish overall gold irid, inscribed "Quezal C357" on base 5,175.00
- 9" h, irid ribbon dec, sgd..880.00
Whiskey Taster, 2-3/4" h, oval, gold irid, 4 pinched dimples, sgd "Quezal" on base..200.00

QUILTS

History: Quilts have been passed down as family heirlooms for many generations. Each one is unique. The same pattern may have hundreds of variations in both color and design.

The advent of the sewing machine increased, not decreased, the number of quilts which were made. Quilts are still being sewn today.

References: Cuesta Benberry, *Always There: The African-American Presence in American Quilts*, Kentucky Quilt Project, 1992; Kathryn Berenson, *Quilts of Provence*, Thames and Hudson, 1996; Mary Clare Clark,

Collectible Quilts, Running Press, Courage Books, 1994; Anne Gilbert, *Instant Expert: Collecting Quilts*, Alliance Publishing, 1996; Liz Greenbacker and Kathleen Barach, *Quilts*, Avon Books, 1992; Carter Houck, *Quilt Encyclopedia Illustrated*, Harry N. Abrams and Museum of American Folk Art, 1991; Donald B. Kraybill, Patricia T. Herr, Jonathon Holstein, *A Quiet Spirit: Amish Quilts from the Collection of Cindy Tietze & Stuart Hodosh,* UCLA Fowler Museum of Cultural History (405 Hilgard Ave., Los Angeles, CA 90024); Jeanette Lasansky et. al., *On the Cutting Edge*, Oral Traditions Project, 1994; Patsy and Myron Orlofsky, *Quilts in America*, Abbeville Press, 1992; Nancy and Donald Roan, *Lest I Shall be Forgotten*, Goschenhoppen Historians, Inc. (P.O. Box 476, Green Lane, PA 18054), 1993; Shelly Zegart, *American Quilt Collections/Antique Quilt Masterpieces,* Nihon Vogue Ltd., 1996.

Periodicals: *Quilt Journal*, 635 W. Main St., Louisville, KY 40202; *Quilters Newsletter*, P.O. Box 4101, Golden, CO 80401; *Vintage Quilt Newsletter*, 1305 Morphy St., Great Bend, KS 67530.

Collectors' Clubs: American Quilt Study Group, 660 Mission St., Ste. 400, San Francisco, CA 94105; American Quilter's Society, P.O. Box 3290, Paducah, KY 42001; National Quilting Assoc., Inc., P.O. Box 393, Ellicott City, MD 21043.

Museums: Doll & Quilts Barn, Rocky Ridge, MD; Museum of the American Quilter's Society, Paducah, KY; National Museum of American History, Washington, DC; New England Quilt Museum, Lowell, MA.

Notes: The key considerations for quilt prices are age, condition, aesthetic appeal, and design. Prices are now level, although the very finest examples continue to bring record prices.

Applique
Flower Basket, 77-1/2" x 67", red, green, and yellow calico, white ground, toning, minor staining, fabric wear...................885.00
Floral Medallions, 82" x 90", pastel pink, green, and yellow, swag border, minor stains..415.00

Floral and vine, appliqué, red and green, 25 four floral devices, eight pointed star in center of each, vine and floral border, 97" sq, $440. Photo courtesy of Sanford Alderfer Auction Co.

Pomegranate and Blossom, 80" sq, red, yellow, pink, and green patches, pierced and reverse appliquéd, white cotton ground, Arthur Schuman, Berne, Berks County, PA, late 19th C, top only 460.00

Tree of Life, 112" x 114", Brodene Perse, 19th C, staining 4,600.00

Crazy, 72" x 74", pieced velvet, black, burgundy, purple, red, gold, gray, green, and brown solid and printed shaped patches, arranged in 16 squares, colorful velvet border, late 19th C 885.00

Pieced

Broken Star, 80" x 76", orange, yellow, green, red, brown, blue, and white printed calico patches, red and white calico Flying Geese border, PA, 19th C 460.00

Chinese Lanterns, 82" x 84", green, red, blue, yellow, and white printed calico and solid patches, blue and white ground, red border, diamond and rope quilting, PA, late 19th C, minor staining 1,495.00

Cobweb, 104" x 84", multicolored printed calico triangular patches, yellow, red, and green banded borders, inscribed "A Present from Grandmother, Mary Elizabeth Weider, to Charles Joel Weider, 1886," verso of Nine Patch pattern calico patches 750.00

Compass Star, 88" x 86", red, green, yellow, white, and pink calico patches, reverse triangle border, PA, 19th C 690.00

Courthouse Stems, 74" x 73", red, pink, brown, blue, green, and peach printed calico bars and patches, diagonal patch border, PA, late 19th C 920.00

Four Patch, 84" x 96", green, brown, red, and blue printed calico horizontal panels, diamond and zigzag quilting, Mennonite, PA, 19th C..230.00

Friendship, 102" x 100", red, blue, green, yellow, and brown printed calico, solid white and chintz patches arranged in squares with star, floral, patchwork, and pinwheel designs, sgd and stamped with signatures of Hicksite Quaker members, Middletown, Bucks County, PA, very finely quilted, blue-green and white chintz zigzag borders, discoloration and staining, accompanied by sgd 1950 marriage certificate for Caroline Burton and Pierson Mitchell, for whom the quilt was made 3,450.00

Log Cabin

81" x 74", red, blue, green, orange, yellow, white, and burgundy printed calico and solid patches, yellow and green borders with diagonal line quilting, patches on verso, Mennonite, Bernville, Berks County, PA, 19th C, minor staining 460.00

81" x 81", red, yellow, blue, green, brown, pink, and white bars, broad red and black borders, rope quilting, verso with red, yellow and green calico horizontal bars, some staining 230.00

85" x 98", cotton, wool, and satin, brown, black, red, blue, purple, pink and white printed and solid bars, burgundy border, rope quilting, verso applied with patch with stamped signature "Annie N. Stephen," PA, late 19th C, wear 460.00

Flower Garden, red, white, and brown print, deep gray-green ground, red back, 83" x 86" 175.00

Lone Star, 76" x 79", pink, blue, lavender, and salmon blue ground, quilted with horses, flowers, etc., Mennonite, minor stains 660.00

Nine Patch, 80" x 72", red, blue, yellow, pink, and white printed calico patches, lightning dividers, white and red banded border, PA, 19th C 525.00

Philadelphia Pavements, 84" x 80", blue, red, orange, and white square printed and solid patches, orange and red banded borders with feather and floral fine quilting, PA, late 19th/early 20th C..815.00

Pinwheels

68" x 70", blue and gold ground, minor stains 250.00
100" x 83", brick-red, yellow, blue, pink, brown, and white printed calico patches, 48 pinwheels within broad border printed

Delectable Mountain, pieced, brown and white printed calico, white ground, diamond, rope, and zigzag quilting, sawtooth border, 92" sq, PA, 19th C, $2,100. Photo courtesy of Sotheby's.

in orange and red with leafy vines, diamond quilting, PA, 19th C 175.00

Rolling Stones, 82" x 84", pink, green, blue, and white patches, banded borders, Mennonite, PA, late 19th/early 20th C 425.00

Serrated Square, corresponding border, pink and green calico, shell and diamond quilting, 82" x 84" 320.00

Small Star of Bethlehem, 87" x 84", red, blue, green, and yellow printed calico patches, 9 small stars within green calico borders, diamond quilting, PA, 19th C, some staining 345.00

Spider Web, 82" x 80", pink, red, blue, purple green, peach, and brown printed calico patches, wide purple calico border, diagonal line quilting, Mennonite, PA, late 19th C, some staining...825.00

Squares, 96" x 80-3/4", red, green, yellow, and white printed calico patches, 24 squares, broad brown, blue, green and white floral chintz border, minor staining, PA, 19th C.............460.00

Star of Bethlehem

82" x 73-1/2", purple, green, red, blue, and pink calico, white ground, early 20th C, toning, minor staining, fabric wear 650.00

85" sq, yellow, pink, purple, green, gray, and blue, white ground, pink and greed borders, c1940 ....715.00

Rainbow, pieced, 86" x 84", $975.

Stars
   75" x 76", red, blue, pink, and yellow stars, colorful graphic de-
      sign, some wear and facing, binding frayed in places
      ....275.00
   80" x 82", multicolored prints, red, and blue calico 330.00
   88" x 90", blue, green, yellow, and red printed calico patches,
      white ground, flower, feather, and diagonal line quilting,
      friendship signatures from Boyertown, Berks County, and
      Lehigh County, dated July 16, 1848, initialed and dated "E.
      S. 1848" on verso, fading and staining 460.00
   90" x 86", 8-pointed star, saw tooth border, pink, yellow, and
      green bar back design, feather quilting 400.00
Stars and Squares, 87" x 76", brown, red, blue and yellow printed
   calico, banded borders, Mennonite, PA, 19th C 635.00
Tulips in Square, 94" x 91", red, green, and yellow printed calico
   patches, broad brown, red, green, and white coronation chintz
   and rosevine border, PA, 19th C 920.00
Unknown pattern, 88" x 86", 5 clusters of blossoms alternating
   with stylized flowerheads, red, yellow, and green patches,
   blue calico ground, red and yellow zigzag border, verso with
   red and blue calico bars, PA, 19th C 1,265.00
Windmill, 86" x 76", yellow, red, green, and blue printed calico
   patches, wide red calico with swag quilting, PA, late 19th C
   ....690.00
Pillar, 100" x 102", five panels of printed golden yellow, red, and
   white with pillars of blossoms and leafage on pale olive-green
   ground chintz, diamond quilting, one corner with applied label
   "Harry H. Funk," Lehigh County, PA, 19th C 575.00
Trapunto, white on white, feather wreaths alternating with wavy
   lines, wear and stains, 72" x 46" 495.00

QUIMPER

History: Quimper faience, dating back to the 17th century, is named for Quimper, a French town where numerous potteries were located. Several mergers resulted in the evolution of two major houses–the Jules Henriot and Hubaudière-Bousquet factories.

The peasant design first appeared in the 1860s, and many variations exist. Florals and geometrics, equally popular, also were produced in large quantities. During the 1920s, the Hubaudière-Bousquet factory introduced the Odetta line which utilized a stone body and Art Deco decorations.

The two major houses merged in 1968, the products retaining the individual characteristics and marks of the originals. The concern suffered from labor problems in the 1980s and was purchased by an American group.

Marks: The "HR" and "HR Quimper" marks are found on Henriot pieces prior to 1922. The "Henriot Quimper" mark was used after 1922. The "HB" mark covers a long time span. Numbers or dots and dashes were added for inventory purposes and are found on later pieces. Most marks are in blue or black. Pieces ordered by department stores, such as Macy's and Carson Pirie Scott, carry the store mark along with the factory mark, making them less desirable to collectors. A comprehensive list of marks is found in Bondhus's book.

References: Susan and Al Bagdade, *Warman's English & Continental Pottery & Porcelain*, 3rd ed., Krause, 1998; Sandra V. Bondhus, *Quimper Pottery: A French Folk Art Faience,* printed by author, 1981, revised edition, 1995; Millicent Mali, *French Faience*, United Printing, 1986; Millicent Mali, *Quimper Faience,* Airon, Inc., 1979; Ann Marie O'Neill, *Quimper Pottery*, Schiffer Publishing, 1994; Marjatta Taburet, *La Faience de Quimper*, Editions Sous le Vent, 1979, (French text).

Museums: Musee des Faiences de Quimper, Quimper, France; Musee Departemental Breton, Quimper, France; Victoria and Albert Museum, French Ceramic Dept, London, England.

Advisors: Susan and Al Bagdade.

Additional Terms:
   A la touche border decor–single brush stroke to create floral
   Breton Broderie decor–stylized blue and gold pattern inspired by a popular embroidery pattern often used on Breton costumes, dates from the Art Deco era.
   Croisille–criss-cross pattern
   Decor Riche border–acanthus leaves in two colors
   Fleur de lys–the symbol of France
   Ivoire Corbeille pattern–red dots circled in sponged blue with red touches forming half a floral blossom, all over a tan ground
   Quintal–five-fingered vase.

Asparagus Set, 13-1/2" l, 8-1/2" w serving tray, 4 10" d plates, tray
   with attached drainer, female peasant with basket over arm,
   framed with blue sponged circlet with pink dot center garland
   on yellow band outlined in orange and brown, pale blue dbl.
   brush stroke border alternating with darker blue three line
   stripe, outer brown line with blue sponged rim, "ivoire corbeille" pattern on underside of cradle, 2 plates with males and
   2 plates with females with "ivoire corbeille" decorations and
   same border as tray, "HenRiot Quimper France 75" marks, 5
   pc set...935.00
Bowl
   9-3/4" d, male peasant, green jacket, blue pants, black hat,
      holding whip, flanked by green, red, and blue foliage, blue,
      green, and yellow a la touche border, scalloped edge,
      "HenRiot Quimper France 92" mark 595.00
   14" w handle to handle, 2 musicians playing bagpipe and flute
      beneath Crest of Brittany and crown, decor riche blue on
      pale blue acanthus border, green sponged handles, raised
      yellow and orange seashells, sgd "HR Quimper" on front
      and "HR Quimper 12" on back 495.00
Cake Plate, 9-1/2" d, 4" h, pedestal base, black haired male peasant playing bagpipes, surrounded by floral sprays and floral
   garland border, pattern repeated on underside and base, soft,
   greens, reds, yellows, and blue, "HR Quimper" on front
   ....385.00
Chamberstick, 5-1/2" d, small female peasant, holder in center, 4
   blue dots and a la touche florals, green and blue borders, blue
   line handle, "HenRiot Quimper France 96" mark 295.00
Charger, 11-1/2" d, seated male on mossy rock holding walking
   stick across knees, purple hat and pantaloons, blue jacket,
   green shirt with orange collar, rose cummerbund, red stockings, border with yellow and orange sheaves of wheat, blue
   and green bell flowers, pierced for hanging, sgd "HB
   Quimper" on front, "HB Quimper 224" mark 440.00
Cheese Dish, 9-1/2" d, 4" h, seated female peasant with basket,
   Crest of Brittany with crown, raised yellow handle and floral on

Box, cov, ftd, heart shape, "ivoire corbeille" pattern, female in green shirt, blue skirt, orange apron, green trees, blue sponged circles with rose centers on orange band around cov, rose a la touche strokes and blue sponged circles with orange centers on base, blue sponged and orange borders, tan ground, "HenRiot Quimper Belle Ile" mark, 5-1/4" l, 2-3/4" h, $225. Photo courtesy of Susan and Al Bagdade.

cover, molded bow around cover in blue and light blue bands, green, orange, and rust geometrics with olive green ground, base with 2 sets of ajonc flowers and 2 sets of orange flowers, blue sponged rim with orange line, "HenRiot Quimper 150" mark 725.00

Cruet, 9" l, 7" h, peasant couple on one chamber, male facing front with one hand in cummerbund, other holding walking stick, female with pot on head, hands on hips, yellow and lavender butterfly on top of chamber, other chamber with blue farm house and tower with tree, yellow and red flower on top, 19th C, "HB Quimper" mark 1,018.00

Cup and Saucer, armorial pattern, cup with Crest of Brittany and stylized leaf and blue flower on red croisille and blue dot field, blue polka dots, saucer with shield of Ste. Servan and 2 lions and crown above, gently shaped five sided, 19th C, intersecting 1st Period "PB" mark 363.00

Dish

    7-1/2" l, 4-3/4" w, female peasant in blue blouse, orange skirt, pink apron, leafy sprays and 4 blue dots on each side, scalloped shell with blue edge and feathering topped by mustard-gold bow, pierced for hanging, "HenRiot Quimper 76" 345.00

    12-1/2" d, 6" h, 3-section, center handle, one with young farmer with scythe over shoulder, stick fence with green shrubbery in background, one with fisherman holding nets and basket, daughter beside him, one with mother carrying large basket of fruit, steps, and cottage outline in background, pale blue on soft yellow acanthus border, polka dot twisted rope handle, 19th C, intersecting 1st Period "PB" and "Environs de Quimper" mark 1,210.00

Doll Plate, 3" d, blue breasted strutting rooster, blue, green, red, and yellow tail feathers, blue rim border, "HenRiot Quimper France" mark 149.00

Figure

    5-1/2" h, "Lannic," standing blond lad holding bagpipe, purple hat, green shirt, orange pantaloons, cobalt blue vest with red brush stroke stripes, "HenRiot Quimper France 136" mark 330.00

    10-1/2" h, standing Ste. Anne in yellow dress with black dotted design, blue cape, small Mary next to saint, "HenRiot Quimper" sgd on base 225.00

Gravy Boat, 10-1/2" l, 7-1/2" h, attached underplate, roosters on each side, blue breasts, green head and neck, red cock's comb, green, blue, and yellow tail feathers, floral sprays on each side, alternating red and green dbl. brush stroke chain on underplate, front and back of gravy boat outlined in blue, a la touche work on sculptured handle, "HB Quimper .red x" mark 209.00

Jardiniere, 15" l, 5-1/2" h, 8" w, one side with young couple holding hands dancing, seated flutist, small cottage and trees in background, reverse with seashore scene of 2 barefoot fisherman on rocky beach, small sailing vessel in background, side of scene in orange fleur-de-lys with 5 black ermine tails, handles are figural children's heads, floral sprays to each side, blue scroll and dot border with yellow lines, 19th C, "HB" mark 2,970.00

Knife Rest, 4" l, stylized crown shape, red bud sprig, blue 4 dot design on either side front and back, outlined in orange with single brush strokes on top and sides, set of 6, "HB Quimper" mark 165.00

Menu, 5-1/2" h, 3-1/2" w, female peasant carrying baskets with greenery and stick fence in lower corner, Crest of Brittany with crown beside blue "Menu," 19th C, intersecting 1st Period "PB Quimper" mark 385.00

Pitcher, figural female, orange Celtic design on coif, light brown hair, black border and trim, cream ground, "HB Quimper 228 P.C." mark, 8" h, $195. Photo courtesy of Susan and Al Bagdade.

Nut Bowl, 7" d, 3-3/4" h, seated corner figural female holding distaff, 4 holes in pink apron for picks, 3 holes in blue skirt for picks, green blouse trimmed in yellow and rust, white int., ext. has a la touche green florals, rust cabbage roses, blue flower heads with yellow centers blue and orange rims, "HenRiot Quimper 71 France" mark 525.00

Oyster Plate, 9" d, 6 blue sponged wells with orange bows, a la touche florals in each well, orange and blue chevrons between each well, blue scalloped rim, "HenRiot Quimper 99" mark 275.00

Pitcher, 6-1/2" h, "ivoire corbeille" pattern, male portrait with blue and orange trimmed black hat and jacket, blue sponged circles with rose color dots, orange bands, blue sponged handle and spout rim, tan ground, "HenRiot Quimper 93" mark 245.00

Plate

8" d, 2 of male peasants with pipers, 1 with glass of wine and walking stick, 1 lady with distaff, 1 with milk can on head, 1 with basket of laundry, croisille pattern border interspersed with panels of stylized dogwood blossoms, "Henriot Quimper France" mark and numbers, set of 6 ...... 1,540.00

8-1/2" d, female peasant holding distaff surrounded by floral sprays with forget-me-nots, blue sponged, crimped scalloped edge, pierced for hanging, sgd "HR Quimper" on front...415.00

9-1/4" d, 3 parrot tulips in purple and lavender, pale yellow and red highlights, soft pink and white bud in central panel, yellow linear rim, Botanical, intersecting 1st Period "PB" 1,375.00

9-1/4" d, plump yellow goose with blue head feathers and wings, floral branches to each side, birds flying in blue sky above, border with concentric bands of blue, olive green, and yellow broken by garland of alternating red and olive brush strokes with dbl. blue dot between them, "HB" on front...303.00

9-1/2" d, male peasant facing front, one hand in vest, black hat, cobalt blue jacket, yellow vest with red buttons, green cummerbund, pale blue-striped pantaloons, brown stockings, a la touche rust and green strokes and 4 blue dots on rim, slightly scalloped rim, 19th C, "HB" in blue, "Quimper" in black mark..313.00

Pitcher, male peasant in blue pantaloons, green jacket, black hat, green, yellow, blue and rust florals, green and rust a la touche border with blue dots, yellow, green, and blue lined rim, "HB" mark, 9" h, $300. Photo courtesy of Susan and Al Bagdade.

9-1/2" d, two blond musicians playing bagpipe and flute, shades of deep blue and yellows, touches of greens and pink, border with alternating panels of ajonc and pink bleeding hearts interspersed with 6 cobalt blue panes, small Crests of Brittany, scalloped rim, pierced for hanging, "HenRiot Quimper France 136" mark...440.00

10" d, couple facing forward in front of low stone wall with jug, blond male with purple pantaloons, orange vest, red cummerbund, green shirt, cobalt blue jacket, yellow stockings, holding pipe, walking stick over arm, female in coif with streamers, cobalt blue dress, purple sleeves, green apron, red vest, yellow sash, hand on jug, border alternating sprays of yellow ajonc and pink bleeding hearts with Crests of Brittany on cobalt blue ground, scalloped rim outlined in yellow and orange, "HR Quimper" mark...............................553.00

10" d, young bride in white coif, pink apron over cobalt blue skirt, red petticoat, groom in charcoal hat, blue waistcoat, orange pantaloons with striped stockings, decor riche decor with Crest of Brittany on top, blue acanthus border, scalloped rim, sgd in blue "HR Quimper" on front and back..743.00

Platter

10-1/2" l, 8" w, rect, cut corners, peasant couple with sponged fir tree and greenery on each side, a la touche floral border, "HB Quimper" on front, imp "O" on back 314.00

11" l, 11" w, scene bretonne of "The payment to the lawyer," 4 adults and 1 boy around table with stack of coins in center, green on yellow acanthus border, rolled rims, sgd intersecting 1st Period "PB, Rosporden" mark............. 1,980.00

19-1/4" l, 9" w, oval fish, center with red and blue lattice basket filled with typical Quimper colorful flowers, red buds, and green leaves form garland borders, blue and yellow outline, pierced for hanging, "HenRiot Quimper France" mark 440.00

19-3/4" l, 8-3/4" w, oval fish, "ivoire corbeille" pattern, center with male peasant in blue hat, orange pantaloons, green shirt, blue vest, all over blue sponge circles with rose centers, rose a la touche florals and orange lines, tan ground, pierced for hanging, "HenRiot Quimper France 79" mark 475.00

Porringer, 5-3/4" d, blue bodied rooster, green, blue, and yellow feathers, fence, and greens on each side, int. border with orange lines and blue dots, green sponged handles, "HB Quimper" mark 125.00

Quintal, 5-1/2" h, seated male peasant with pipe, orange pantaloons, blue vest, green shirt, black hat, orange outlined frame, band with orange and blue angles bordered in blue, bottom half with green, rust, blue, and yellow florals, blue and orange bands on base and tubes, florals and 4 blue dots on upper portion, "HenRiot Quimper France 116" mark...............365.00

Snuff Bottle, 3-1/2" l, fleur-de-lys shape, yellow center section with green branches, soft orange outer edges and band, cobalt blue underside edges, cobalt blue outlines 495.00

Teapot, 7" h, 6-1/2" l, male peasant with buggy whip, gray hat, orange jacket, yellow shirt and leggings, blue striped pantaloons on each side, florals on reverse, blue and yellow banded base, blue striped handles on top and side, single blue line rim on pouring spout, sgd "HenRiot Quimper France" on bottom 450.00

Tray

10" l, 5-1/2" w, "breton broderie" pattern, male and female portraits facing each other in center, male in brown and black hat, white collar, blue and mauve jacket, female in white coif and collar, light green dress, wide cobalt blue border with raised orange dashes and dots, scalloped rim, "HB Quimper" mark 320.00

14-1/2" l handle to handle, 9" w, 8 sided, male peasant in center panel, wide border with orange and green florals alternating with circles with rust crosshatches, blue and yellow gold striped rim, striped handles, "HB Quimper" mark 395.00

18" l, 11" w, market scene of 7 peasants in multicolored clothes standing with baskets of cabbages, carrots, and apples, 2 small girls sample apples, tent in background, hunter green decor riche acanthus on blue ground, blue sponged scalloped rim and handles, pierced for hanging, sgd "HR Quimper" on front and back 2,145.00

18-1/2" d, 6 lobed, all over painting of intertwining clematis vines, yellow and pink blossoms, buds and shaded leaves in greens and yellows tones, yellow linear border around raised platform in center and edge, pierced for hanging, 19th C, intersecting 1st Period "PB" mark 1,980.00

Vase

7" h, 6-1/2" w, fleur-de-lys shape, front facing male with walking stick on one side, female knitting on reverse, Crest of Brittany on front foot, powder blue ground, sides in soft red and green geometric lattice on pale yellow ground, "HB" mark 1,075.00

7" h, 7" w, stoneware, one holder on each side of handle, blue and gray enamel geometric designs on gray matte body, "Odetta HB Quimper" mark 320.00

9" h, urn shape, blond male playing flute, blue hat, jacket, and stockings, green shirt trimmed in red, yellow pantaloons, floral sprays on either side of figure, on sides and reverse, green sponged handles and lip, blue scallops and dots on sq base, edges outlined in blue ribbon and dot design, scattered 4 blue dot design, sgd "HR Quimper" on front 468.00

Wall Pocket

4" l, dbl. cornucopia, male and female peasants, red, yellow, and green flower on each opening, 19th C, "AP" mark 413.00

8" l, slipper shaped, female peasant with floral sprays on toe part, large blue bow above female, blue croisille lattice work with red X's at the intersections and green dot in each diamond on back of form, "HenRiot Quimper France" mark...440.00

RADIOS

History: The radio was invented more than 100 years ago. Marconi was the first to assemble and employ the transmission and reception instruments that permitted the sending of electric messages without the use of direct connections. Between 1905 and the end of World War I, many technical advances affected the "wireless," including the invention of the vacuum tube by DeForest. Technology continued its progress, and radios filled the entertainment needs of the average family in the 1920s.

Changes in design, style, and technology brought the radio from the black boxes of the 1920s to the stylish furniture pieces and console models of the 1930s and 1940s, to midget models of the 1950s, and finally to the high-tech radios of the 1980s.

References: Marty and Sue Bunis, *Collector's Guide to Antique Radios*, 4th ed., Collector Books, 1996; ——, *Collector's Guide to Transistor Radios*, Collector Books, 1994; Marty Bunis and Robert Breed, *Collector's Guide to Novelty Radios*, Collector Books, 1995; Philip Collins, *Radio Redux*, Chronicle Books, 1992; Harold Cones, and John Bryant, *Zenith Radio: The Early Years, 1919-1935*, Schiffer Publishing, 1997; Chuck Dachis, *Radios by Hallicrafters*, Schiffer Publishing, 1996; Alan Douglas, *Radio Manufacturers of the 1920s*, Vol. 1 (1988), Vol. 2 (1989), Vol. 3 (1991), Vestal Press; Roger Handy, Maureen Erbe, and Aileen Farnan Antonier, *Made in Japan*, Chronicle

Books, 1993; David and Betty Johnson, *Guide to Old Radios, Pointers, Pictures and Prices*, 2nd ed., Wallace Homestead/Krause, 1995; David R. and Robert A. Lane, *Transistor Radios*, Wallace-Homestead, 1994; Harry Poster, *Poster's Radio & Television Price Guide*, 2nd ed., Wallace-Homestead, 1994; Ron Ramirez, *Philco Radio*, Schiffer Publishing, 1993; B. Eric Rhoads, *Blast from the Past*, available from author (800-226-7857), 1996; Mark Stein, *Machine Age to Jet Age, Radiomania's Guide to Tabletop Radios—1933-1959*, published by author (2109 Carterdale Rd., Baltimore, MD 21209); Eric Wrobbel, *Toy Crystal Radios,* published by author, 1997 (20802 Exhibit Court, Woodland Hills, CA).

Periodicals: *Antique Radio Classified*, P.O. Box 2, Carlisle, MA, 01741; *Horn Speaker*, P.O. Box 1193, Mabank, TX 75147; *Radio Age*, 636 Cambridge Road, Augusta, GA 30909; *Transistor Network*, RR1, Box 36, Bradford, NH 03221.

Collectors' Clubs: Antique Radio Club of America, 300 Washington Trails, Washington, PA 15301; Antique Wireless Assoc., 59 Main St., Bloomfield, NY 14469; New England Antique Radio Club, RR1, Box 36, Bradford, NH 03221; Vintage Radio & Phonograph Society, Inc., P.O. Box 165345, Irving, TX 75016.

Museums: Antique Radio Museum, St. Louis, MO; Antique Wireless Museum, Bloomfield, NY; Caperton's Radio Museum, Louisville, KY; Muchow's Historical Radio Museum, Elgin, IL; Museum of Broadcast Communication, Chicago, IL; Museum of Wonderful Miracles, Minneapolis, MN; New England Wireless and Steam Museum, Inc., East Greenwich, RI; Voice of the Twenties, Orient, NY.

Additional Listings: See *Warman's Americana & Collectibles* for more examples.

Advisor: Lewis S. Walters.

Note: Prices of Catalin radios are dropping by about 10% to 15%. Collectors and dealers feel prices for these radios have reached their high side and are falling into a more realistic range.

Admiral
Portable
#33-35-37 ....30.00
#218, leatherette...40.00
#909, All World 85.00
Y-2127, Imperial 8, c1959 ....45.00
Air King, tombstone, Art Deco......................................3,000.00
Arvin
Hoppy, lariatenna 525.00
Table
#444..100.00
#522A 50.00
Tombstone, #617, Rhythm Maid.................................215.00
Atwater Kent
Breadboard
Model 9A 550.00
Model 10...1,100.00
Model 10C...930.00
Cathedral, 80, c1931...380.00

Table
#55, Keil 225.00
#318, dome 115.00
Tombstone, #854 ....155.00
Bulova, clock radio
#100 ....40.00
#120 ....40.00
Columbia, table, oak 125.00
Crosley
Bandbox, #600, 1927 ....80.00
Gemchest, #609 ....425.00
Litfella, 1N, cathedral 175.00
Pup, with orig box 575.00
Sheraton, cathedral 290.00
Showbox, #706 ....100.00
Super Buddy Boy 125.00
#4-28, battery operated 130.00
#10-135 ....45.00
Dumont, RA346, table, scroll work, 1938 ....110.00
Emerson
AU-190, Catalin tombstone 1,200.00
BT-245 ....1,200.00
#410, Mickey, wood, metal trim, metal grill 1,400.00
#411, Mickey, pressed wood style 1,400.00
#570, Memento 110.00
#640, Portable 30.00
#888, Vanguard 60.00
Fada
#43 ....240.00
#60W 75.00
#115, bullet shape 850.00
#136 ....1,000.00
#252 ....575.00
#625, rounded end, slide rule dial 700.00
Federal
#58DX 500.00
#110 ....425.00
General Electric
#81, c1934 ....200.00
#400 ....30.00
#410 ....30.00
#411 ....30.00
#414 ....30.00
#515, clock radio 25.00
#517, clock radio 25.00

RCA Victor, table model, Art Deco style, curved wrap around louvers, three knobs, 11" x 7-1/4" x 7-1/2", $195.

K-126 ....150.00
Tombstone 250.00
Grebe
CR-12 ....600.00
MU-1 ....200.00
Halicrafters
TW-200 ....125.00
TW-600 ....100.00
Majestic
Charlie McCarthy 1,000.00
#92 ....125.00
#381 ....225.00
Metrodyne, Super 7, 1925 ....265.00
Motorola
#68X11Q, Art Deco 75.00
Jet Plane 55.00
Jewel Box 80.00
M logo 25.00
Pixie 45.00
Ranger
Portable 40.00
Ranger #700 ....45.00
Table, plastic 35.00
Olympic, radio with phonograph 40.00
Paragon
DA-2, table 475.00
RD-5, table 600.00
Philco
T-7, 126 transistor 65.00
T1000, clock radio 80.00
#17-20-38, cathedral 250.00
#37-62, table, 2 tone 75.00
#37-84, cathedral, 1937 ....65.00
#40-180, console, wood 130.00
#46-132, table 20.00
#49-501, Boomerang 475.00
#49-506, Transitone 35.00
$52-544, Transitone 40.00
#551, 1928 ....145.00
Radiobar, glasses and decanters 1,400.00
Radio Corporation of America, RCA
La Siesta 300.00
Radiola
#18 ....55.00
#20 ....165.00
#24 ....170.00
#28, console 200.00
#33 ....40.00
#6X7, table, plastic 25.00
8BT-7LE, portable 35.00
40X56, World's Fair 1,000.00
Silvertone (Sears)
#1, table 75.00
#1582, cathedral, wood 225.00
#1955, tombstone 135.00
#9205, plastic transistor 40.00
Sony, transistor
TFM-151, 1960 ....50.00
TR-63, 1958 ....145.00
Sparton
#506, Blue Bird, Art Deco 3,300.00
#5218 ....95.00
Stewart-Warner, table, slant 175.00
Stromberg Carlson, #636A console 125.00
Westinghouse, Model WR-602
Zenith
Royal
#500, transistor, owl eye 75.00
#500D, transistor 55.00
#750L, transistor, leather case 40.00

Trans-Oceanic 125.00
#6D2615, table, boomerang dial 95.00
Zephyr, multiband 95.00

RAILROAD ITEMS

History: Railroad collectors have existed for decades. The merger of the rail systems and the end of passenger service made many objects available to private collectors. The Pennsylvania Railroad sold its archives at public sale.

References: Susan and Al Bagdade, *Warman's American Pottery and Porcelain*, Wallace-Homestead, 1994; Stanley L. Baker, *Railroad Collectibles*, 4th ed., Collector Books, 1990, 1993 value update; Richard C. Barrett, *Illustrated Encyclopedia of Railroad Lighting*, Vol. 1, Railroad Research Publications, 1994; David Dreimiller, *Dressel Railway Lamp & Signal Company*, Hiram Press, 1995; Joseph F. Farrell, Jr., *Illustrated Guide to Peter Gray Railroad Hardware*, Hiram Press, 1994; Anthony Hobson, *Lanterns That Lit Our World*, Hiram Press, reprinted 1996; Richard Luckin, *Dining on Rails*, RK Publishing, 1994; Don Stewart, *Railroad Switch Keys & Padlocks*, 2nd ed., Key Collectors International, 1993.

Periodicals: *Key, Lock and Lantern*, 3 Berkeley Heights Park, Bloomfield, NJ 07003; *Main Line Journal*, P.O. Box 121, Streamwood, IL 60107.

Collectors' Clubs: Chesapeake & Ohio Historical Society, Inc., P.O. Box 79, Clifton Forge, VA 24422; Illinois Central Railroad Historical Society, 14818 Clifton Park, Midlothian, IL 60445; Railroad Enthusiasts, 102 Dean Rd., Brookline, MA 02146; Railroadiana Collectors Assoc., 795 Aspen Drive, Buffalo Grove, IL 60089; Railway and Locomotive Historical Society, P.O. Box 1418, Westford, MA 01886; Twentieth Century Railroad Club, 329 West 18th St., Ste. 902, Chicago, IL 60616.

Museums: Baltimore and Ohio Railroad, Baltimore, MD; California State Railroad Museum, Sacramento, CA; Frisco Railroad Museum, Van Buren, AR; Museum of Transportation, Brookline, MA; National Railroad Museum, Green Bay, WI; New York Museum of Transportation, West Henrietta, NY; Old Depot Railroad Museum, Dassel, MN.

Additional Listings: See *Warman's Americana & Collectibles* for more examples.

Notes: Railroad enthusiasts have organized into regional and local clubs. Join one if you're interested in this collectible field; your local hobby store can probably point you to the right person. The best pieces pass between collectors and rarely enter the general market.

Baggage Tag, 1-1/2" x 2-1/2", SOO Line, celluloid, leather strap, "Tag Your Grip, Take a trip, the New Train" 20.00
Book
    Fagan, James, *Confessions of a Railroad Signalman,* Boston, 1908, 181 lbs 20.00
    Nock, O. S., *Railways in the Formative Years From 1851-1895,* MacMillian, 1973, 1st ed., 156 pgs, color illus by Clifford and Wendy Meadway, dg 8.50

Ogburn, C., *Railroad The Great American Adventure,* National Geographic Society, 1977, 1st ed., 204 pgs 17.50
Builder's Plate, 15-1/2" l, brass, American Locomotive Works, from NY, New Haven & Hartford engine #573, oval, 1909 .... 1,500.00
Cabinet, American Railway Express, wood, countertop, front door stenciled "AM R.Y. EX. CO," several int. dividers missing, overall varnish loss, 33" x 25" x 11-1/2" 50.00
Calendar, 1938, Burlington Route, litho illus, steam and diesel trains in mountain landscape, vignette of covered wagons above, full pad, 18" x 27" 45.00
Cap Badge, 4-1/4" x 1-1/2" C&O RY, brakeman, emb black enameled lettering pebbled silvered ground, arched top, milled border 32.00
Catalog
    Baldwin Locomotive Works, Philadelphia, PA, c1906, 32 pgs, 6" x 9", walschaerts Valve Gear for Locomotives 32.00
    Hamilton Mfg. Co., Two Rivers, WI, c1910, 42 pgs, 6" x 9" 75.00
China
    Butter Pat, PA RR, backstamp 75.00
    Cereal Bowl, Union Pacific, Challenger pattern, no backstamp, Syracuse China 25.00
    Cup and Saucer, Chicago Burlington & Quincy, Chuck Wagon pattern, backstamp, Syracuse China 250.00
    Ice Cream Dish, B&O, Capitol pattern, ftd, no backstamp 50.00

Oil Lamp, club car, NY Central, tin, repainted base, $85.

Plate, dinner, Wabash RR, Banner pattern, no backstamp, Syracuse China, 9-1/2" d 225.00
Sauce Dish, Atchison Topeka & Santa Fe, Mimbreno pattern, backstamp "Made expressly for Santa Fe dining car service," Syracuse China, 5-1/2" d 80.00
Coach Seat, New Haven 8600 series, double.....................30.00
Engine Status Board, NY&NERR, used in Norwich, CT, engine shop, 60" sq..335.00
Glass, 3-1/2" d, 4-1/2" h, highball, weighted bottom, brown and white streamlined PA passenger train passing by landmarks of Philadelphia, New York City, Washington, DC, single PA Railroad keystone logo, 1930s 20.00
Grade Crossing Sign, wood, circular, black "RR" and white "X," white ground, worn 15.00
Pamphlet, #10033, American Locomotive Co, New York, NY, 1908, 31 pg, 6" x 9", Walschaert Valve Gear, paper read at 8th Biennial Convention of the Brotherhood of Locomotive Engineers...35.00
Lantern
    Atlantic & St Lawrence RR, clear fixed globe, cast lettering, 1859...885.00
    NY&NERR, brass stopped, bell bottom.........................635.00
Napkin, 10-1/2" x 16-1/2", Milwaukee RR, cotton, printed magenta "Hiawatha" and Indian emblem, tan ground 20.00
Pass, 2-1/2" x 4-1/4", annual transportation pass, officer's type, 1889...35.00
Photograph
    Group of 20, silver print photographs of steam locomotives used around the world, from early 1900s to 1940s, 10" x 15-1/2" and smaller, several numbered on negative, others with North British Locomotive Company handstamp and negative number, all with penciled dates and identifying captions on verso, 1904-40 ....2,000.00
    Group of 120 stereoview photographs titled "Pennsylvania Railroad Scenery," view of trains, machine shops, bridges, tracks, tunnels, stations, and scenery, along Delaware Water Gap, Watkin's Glen and waterfalls, gorges, and railroad towns from Philadelphia to Pittsburgh, by W. Purviance, arch topped, album prints, 6 stereo prs per page, mounted recto/verso, most titled and numbered in the negative, gilt bordered mounts with series title, photographer's credit and "Philadelphia" printed recto and verso, folio, linen, contemporary clamshell presentation box, c1875 ....2,400.00
Playing Cards, 1" x 2-3/4" x 3-1/2", cardboard slipcase, complete deck, Southern Pacific Lines, back of each card with full color art of Southern Pacific Daylight streamliner passenger train passing thru scenic landscape, late 1930s....................20.00
Pocket Watch
    American Waltham Watch Co., size 16, open face, gold filled case, damascened Vanguard movement, 23 jewels, wind indicator, adjusted for 6 positions 450.00
    Hamilton Watch Co., model 999, made for the Ball Watch Co., size 18, open face, gold filled case, 21 jewels, damascened plates, inscribed gold lettering, c1895........300.00
Poster
    Eagle Nest Tunnel in the Bitter Root Mountains, Montana, "On the Route of the New Olympian, Chicago, Milwaukee, St. Paul and Pacific Railroad," tinted image of river gorge, c1927, 28" x 22"..250.00
    Fisherman Take Notice, Walt Kuhn, Union Pacific Railway, Sun Valley Lodge, Idaho, view of mountains, happy chef, list of fish to get in center, c1937, 23" x 29" 425.00
    Hoover Dam and Lake Mead, Union Pacific RR, c1947, 25" x 32"..350.00
    Kanawha River Near Montgomery, Adolph Hehn, C & O Railway, color litho, full color panorama of village and river, 1948, 28" x 23"...125.00
    Railroad Jack, comical farmyard scene, hobo riding homemade bicycle, dog, bites tire, matted and framed, 26" x 40" 275.00

Red Man Tobacco, railroad conductor enjoying chew from pack held by engineer, 150s, 11 x 15-1/2"................80.00
Scale Model, NYC&HR, gondola freight car, 69" l, track....250.00
Silver Hollowware
    Coffeepot, Chicago & Northwestern RY, pine cone finial bottom mkd, "International, #05073," 1949, 14 oz. 85.00
    Vase, 7-1/4" h, Great Northern RY, candlestick bud-type, mkd on side and bottom, International #05082, 1951......175.00
Steam Whistle, 19" h, brass..250.00
Timetable, 1946, Charleston and Western Carolina.............15.00
Water Bucket, metal, bail handle...25.00
Whistle Post, black "W," white ground, worn......................25.00

RAZORS

History: Razors date back several thousand years. Early man used sharpened stones; the Egyptians, Greeks, and Romans had metal razors.

Razors made prior to 1800 generally were crudely stamped "Warranted" or "Cast Steel," with the maker's mark on the tang. Until 1870, razors were handmade and almost all razors for the American market were manufactured in Sheffield, England. Most blades were wedge shaped; many were etched with slogans or scenes. Handles were made of natural materials: horn, tortoiseshell, bone, ivory, stag, silver, or pearl.

After 1870, razors were machine made with hollow ground blades and synthetic handle materials. Razors of this period usually were manufactured in Germany (Solingen) or in American cutlery factories. Hundreds of molded-celluloid handle patterns were produced.

Cutlery firms produced boxed sets of two, four, and seven razors. Complete and undamaged sets are very desirable. The most-popular ones are the seven-day sets in which each razor is etched with a day of the week.

References: Ronald S. Barlow, *Vanishing American Barber Shop*, Windmill Publishing, 1993; *Safety Razors: A Price Guide*, L-W Book Sales, 1995; Jim Sargent, *Sargent's American Premium Guide to Pocket Knives & Razors*, 3rd ed., Books Americana, 1992.

Periodical: *Blade Magazine*, P.O. Box 22007, Chattanooga, TN 37422.

Additional Listings: See *Warman's Americana & Collectibles* for more examples.

Notes: The fancier the handle or more intricately etched the blade, the higher the price. Rarest handle materials are pearl, stag, sterling silver, pressed horn, and carved ivory. Rarest blades are those with scenes etched across the entire front. Value is increased by the presence of certain manufacturers' names, e.g., H. Boker, Case, M. Price, Joseph Rogers, Simmons Hardware, Will & Finck, Winchester, and George Wostenholm.

American Blades

Case Bros., Tested XX, Little Valley, NY, hollow point, slick black handles, MOP inlaid tang 400.00
Cattaraugus Cutlery Co., Little Valley, NY, sq point, blue handles with white liners 35.00
Crandall Cutlery Co., Bradford, PA, sq point, blade etched "I. Must Kut," cream colored handles with beaded border 70.00

Celluloid handle, top: Huron eating fish, $75; bottom: peacock,

Kane Cutlery Co., Kane, PA, hollow point, cream and rust twisted rope handles, c1884..45.00
Standard Knife Co., Little Valley, NY, arc mark, round point, yellow mottled handles with beaded borders, 1901-03.....150.00
Union Cutlery Co., Olean, NY, AJ Case Shoo-Fly, tiger-eye handle, c1912..125.00

English Blades, Sheffield

George Wostenholme, etched adv on blade, emb ivory handle 40.00
Joseph Rodgers & Sons, wedge blade, stag handle with inlaid rect escutcheon plate...125.00
Wade & Butcher, hollow ground blade, name etched in ribbon, SS Art Nouveau handle with raised scroll across front and back, monogram 325.00

German Blades

Cosmos Mfg. Co., hollow ground blade, ivory handle, raised nude picking purple grapes, green leaves 125.00
F. A. Koch & Co., ivory handle, colored scene with deer, branches, and oak leaves...50.00
Imperial Razor, blade etched with US Battleship Oregon scene, dark blue celluloid handle 45.00
Wadsworth Razor Co., semi wedge blade, carved bone handle, c1870..60.00

Sets of Razors

Crown & Sword, 7 day set, blades etched "The Crown & Sword Razor Extra Hollow Ground," black handles with raised "Crown and Sword," homemade wood case with felt lining, emb "RAZORS," plaque on top 85.00
G. W. Ruff's Peerless, 2, hollow ground blade, ivory handles, leather over wood case with "Gentlemen's Companion Containing 2 Razors Special Hollow Ground," red lining 70.00
Wilkinson Sword, 7 day, safety, 5" l, 2-1/2" d, 1-5/8" h orig box 125.00

RECORDS

History: With the advent of the more sophisticated recording materials, such as 33-1/3 RPM long-playing records, 8-track tapes, cassettes, and compact discs, earlier phonograph records became collectors' items. Most have little value. The higher-priced items are rare (limited-production) recordings. Condition is critical.

References: Mark Allen Baker, *Goldmine Price Guide to Rock 'n' Roll Memorabilia,* Krause Publications, 1997; Les Docks, *American Premium Record Guide, 1900-1965,* 5th Edition, Krause Publications, 1997; Goldmine Maga-

zine, *Goldmine's 1997 Annual,* Krause Publications, 1996; Ron Lofman, *Goldmine's Celebrity Vocals,* Krause Publications, 1994; William M. Miller, *How to Buy & Sell Used Record Albums,* Loran Publishing, 1994; Tim Neely, *Goldmine Christmas Record Price Guide,* Krause Publications, 1997; *Goldmine's Price Guide to Alternative Records,* Krause Publications, 1996; ——, *Goldmine's Price Guide to 45 RPM Records,* Krause Publications, 1996; Tim Neely and Dave Thompson, *Goldmine British Invasion Record Price Guide,* Krause Publications, 1997; Jerry Osborne (comp.) *Rockin' Records, 1998 Ed.,* Antique Trader Books, 1997; Neal Umphred, *Goldmine's Price Guide to Collectible Jazz Albums,* 1949–1969, 2nd ed., Krause Publications, 1994; ——, *Goldmine's Price Guide to Collectible Record Albums,* 5th ed., Krause Publications, 1996; ——, *Goldmine's Rock 'n' Roll 45 RPM Record Price Guide,* 3rd ed., Krause Publications, 1994.

Periodicals: *Cadence,* Cadence Building, Redwood, NY 13679; *DISCoveries Magazine,* P.O .Box 309, Fraser, MI 48026; *Goldmine,* 700 E. State St., Iola, WI 54990; *Jazz Beat Magazine,* 1206 Decatur St., New Orleans, LA 70116; *Joslin's Jazz Journal,* P.O. Box 213, Parsons, KS 67357; *New Amberola Graphic,* 37 Caledonia St., St. Johnsbury, VT 05819; *Record Collectors Monthly,* P.O. Box 75, Mendham, NJ 07945; *Record Finder,* P.O .Box 1047, Glen Allen, VA 23060.

Collectors' Clubs: Assoc. for Recorded Sound Collections, P.O. Box 453, Annapolis, MD 21404; International Assoc. of Jazz Record Collectors, P.O. Box 75155, Tampa, FL 33605.

Additional Listings: See *Warman's Americana & Collectibles* for more examples.

Note: Most records, especially popular recordings, have a value of less than $3 per disc. The records listed here are classic recordings of their type and are in demand by collectors.

Lounge, LP

Fred Astaire, Another Evening with Fred Astaire, Chrysler 1088 ....12.00
Les Baxter, Passions 10, Capitol LAI-486 ....30.00
Harry Breuer, Mallet Magic, Audio Fidelity 1825.................10.00
Bing Crosby, Jerome Kern Songs, Decca, 5001 ....20.00
Martin Denny, Hawaii Tattoo, Liberty LST-7394 ....10.00
Duke Ellington, Masterpieces by Ellington, Columbia, 4418 ....30.00
Esquivel, The Genius of Esquivel RCA LSP-3697 ....30.00
Eartha Kitt, In Person At the Plaza, CNP Crescento2008.....12.00
Buddy Morrow, Impact, RCA LPM-2042 ....10.00
Mel Torme, California Suite, Capital P-200...........................30.00

Rock

Asylum Choir, Asylum Choir II, Shelber, SW-8910, LP, orig insert 10.00
Beatles, Old Brown Shoe, Apple EPEM-10540, Mexican pcs, 45 rpm 18.00
David Bowie, Man Who Sang, Mercury SR-61325, LP.........18.00
Fat Mattress, Atco SD 33-309, Noel Redding, LP 10.00
Golden Earrings, Greatest Hits, Polydor 236228, Dutch imp, LP 10.00
John Lennon, Roots, Adam Vii-A-80180, orig, LP 200.00

Liverpool Five, Out of Sight, RCA LSP-33682, German imp, LP 8.00
Nirvana, Story of Simon Simopath, Bell, 6015, stereo sleeve, LP 18.00
Pretty Things, Rainin In My Heart, Fontana TE-17422, UK pose 30.00

REDWARE

History: The availability of clay, the same used to make bricks and roof tiles, accounted for the great production of red earthenware pottery in the American colonies. Redware pieces are mainly utilitarian–bowls, crocks, jugs, etc.

Lead-glazed redware retained its reddish color, but a variety of colored glazes were obtained by the addition of metals to the basic glaze. Streaks and mottled splotches in redware items resulted from impurities in the clay and/or uneven firing temperatures.

Slipware is the term used to describe redwares decorated by the application of slip, a semi-liquid paste made of clay. Slipwares were made in England, Germany, and elsewhere in Europe for decades before becoming popular in the Pennsylvania German region and other areas in colonial America.

References: Susan and Al Bagdade, *Warman's American Pottery and Porcelain*, Wallace-Homestead, 1994; William C. Ketchum Jr., *American Pottery and Porcelain*, Avon Books, 1994.

Bank, 3-1/4" h, apple shape, red and yellow paint.............150.00
Bottle, 5-3/4" h, pinched sides and tooling, green glaze, brown flecks, green striping, incised label, "Made by I. S. Stahl, 11-1-1939" 60.00
Bowl
    4" d brown streak dec, red glaze, double handle 225.00
    6-1/2" d, white stripe dec, brown glaze 60.00

12-1/2" d, 2-1/2" h, sgraffito, eagle, flowers, and "1827" 425.00
Charger, 13" d, molded bust of Washington, star ringed medallion, coggled rim, brown fleck glaze 475.00
Cooler, 18" h, ovoid, glaze flaking, mounted as lamp 75.00
Creamer
    4" h, brown dec, yellow glaze, stamped "John Bell" ..2,900.00
    4-3/8" h, yellow slip design, green accents, ribbed strap handle..............450.00
Cup, 3-3/4" h, flared lip, applied handle, clear glaze with mottled amber, minor wear and glaze flakes 90.00
Cuspidor, 8" x 4-1/4", tooled bands, brown and green running glaze, brown dashes, some wear and edge chips 265.00
Figure, 5-3/4" h, painted woman with child, chips..............145.00
Flask, 6-1/2" h, tooled lines and brown spotted glaze, old hairline to side, chip on lid..............225.00
Food Mold, 7-7/8" l, oval, ear of corn, arched sides, crimped edge, four applied feet, clear glaze, sponging on rim, minor flakes 440.00
Jar
    5-1/2" h, ovoid, imp "W. Smith, Womelsdorf," (PA), minor crazing, possible base hairline..............95.00
    6-3/4" h, cream slip stripes, brown glaze, wavy lines, tooled lip 1,650.00
    7-1/2" h, ovoid, int. glaze, imp "John Bell, Waynesboro," chips and hairlines 140.00
    9" h, ovoid, ribbed strap handle, green tint glaze, wear, chips 220.00
Jug
    7" h, bulbous, applied handle, wheel thrown, dark brown slip 110.00
    9" h, ovoid, strap handle, clear glaze, black splotches, small chip on lip, glaze flakes..............110.00
Milk Bowl
    8" d, rim spout..............150.00
    9" d, white slip dec, greenish-amber glaze, surface chips 250.00

Bank, scroodle-glazed, form of miniature Empire chest of drawers, cream colored knobs, paw feet, glazed allover in scroddled brown and yellow glaze, back fitted with coin slot, dated 1883 on underside, repairs to rear feet, 6-1/4" h, $700. Photo courtesy of Sotheby's.

Plate, polychrome and slip dec, flat overhanging rim with wavy green border, shallow bowl dec with three birds and stylized flowers, PA-German inscription and date 1768, dec in tones of green, yellow, white, and brown, orange field, attributed to Ephrata, PA, 18th C, minor chips and losses to dec, 10-1/4" d, $1,380. Photo courtesy of Sotheby's.

Mold, 6" d, brown glaze, black dec.........................85.00
Mug, 5-1/4" h, butter print star design, strap handle, tooled lip, clear glaze with greenish highlights, minor glaze flakes and wear 125.00
Pie Plate
    7-3/8" d, yellow slip wavy lines with green, chips and hairline 275.00
    7-1/2" d, yellow slip dec, minor edge chips 275.00
Pipkin, 8-1/4" h, manganese and colored slip dec, c1800...95.00
Pitcher
    7-1/2" h, wheel thrown, applied handle, coggled top edge and band at top of handle, slip colored with copper oxide (green) at top working down to iron oxide (rust) mottled with manganese (dark brown), attributed to Jacob Medinger, c1900-20...600.00
    8-7/8" h, brown Albany slip, New Geneva 55.00
Plate, 8-1/2" d, sgraffito floral design, white, green, and orange stripes, black German inscription on back, minor wear 660.00
Turk's Head Mold
    8-1/4" d, swirled design, brown sponging, imp "John Bell Waynesboro," minor flakes.......................1,210.00
    8-3/4" d, fluted swirls, scalloped rim, clear glaze, brown sponging, hairline 75.00

RED WING POTTERY

History: The Red Wing pottery category includes several potteries from Red Wing, Minnesota. In 1868, David Hallem started Red Wing Stoneware Co., the first pottery with stoneware as its primary product. The Minnesota Stoneware Co. started in 1883. The North Star Stoneware Co. was in business from 1892 to 1896.

The Red Wing Stoneware Co. and the Minnesota Stoneware Co. merged in 1892. The new company, the Red Wing Union Stoneware Co., made stoneware until 1920 when it introduced a pottery line which it continued until the 1940s. In 1936 the name was changed to Red Wing Potteries, Inc. During the 1930s, this firm introduced several popular patterns of hand-painted dinnerware which were distributed through department stores, mail-order catalogs, and gift-stamp centers. Dinnerware production declined in the 1950s and was replaced with hotel and restaurant china in the early 1960s. The plant closed in 1967.

Marks: Red Wing Stoneware Co. was the first firm to mark pieces with a red wing stamped under the glaze. The North Star Stoneware Co. used a raised star and the words "Red Wing" as its mark.

References: Susan and Al Bagdade, *Warman's American Pottery and Porcelain*, Wallace-Homestead, 1994; Dan and Gail DePasquale and Larry Peterson, *Red Wing Collectibles*, Collector Books, 1985, 1997 value update; –—, *Red Wing Stoneware*, Collector Books, 1983, 1997 value update; B. L. Dollen, *Red Wing Art Pottery*, Collector Books, 1997; Ray Reiss, *Red Wing Art Pottery Includ-*

ing Pottery Made for Rum Rill, published by author (2144 N. Leavitt, Chicago, IL 60647), 1996.

Collectors' Clubs: Red Wing Collectors Society, Inc., P.O. Box 184, Galesburg, IL 61402; RumRill Society, P.O. Box 2161, Hudson, OH 44236.

Additional Listings: See *Warman's Americana & Collectibles* for more examples.

Basket, #1275...45.00
Bean Pot, cov, stoneware, adv.................................85.00
Beater Jar, stoneware, half gallon, "Stanhope, Ia" adv........95.00
Bookends, pr, fan and scroll, green...........................20.00
Bowl, stoneware
    7" d, blue, rust, and cream sponging 75.00
    9-3/4" d, brown and blue sponging, mkd "Red Wing Saffron Ware"...35.00
Butter Crock, 20#, large wing, tight hairline 550.00
Buttermilk Feeder, stoneware.................................75.00
Casserole, cov, 8" d, sponge band, chip on handle..........165.00
Creamer and Sugar, #1376...................................20.00
Crock, stoneware
    One Gallon, large wing.......................................400.00
    Two Gallon, 4" wing...40.00
    Six Gallon, 4" wing...75.00
Ewer, 7" h, #184...55.00
Figure
    Cowboy, rust..175.00
    Cowgirl, #B1414, white.......................................175.00
    Giraffe, 1995 convention commemorative.................90.00
Jug, five gallon, shoulder, large wing, "California White Wine" stencil..135.00
Mixing Bowl, 7" d, stoneware, "Cap," blue sponge dec, white ground...100.00

Vase, Athenian Nude, handles, cobalt blue, shape #249, mkd with Redwing circle ink mark, 11" h, $2,640. Photo courtesy of Jackson's Auctioneers & Appraisers.

Pitcher, 9" h, stoneware, brown glazed grape dec, rick-rack border, waffle ground, "Red Wing North Star Stoneware" mark
....90.00
Planter
    Canoe 25.00
    Puppy 20.00
Salt and Pepper Shakers, pr, Town and Country, dark green
....65.00
Teapot, cov, yellow rooster, gold trim 65.00
Vase
    6-1/2" h, bulbous, leaf design, molded ring handles, shiny jade green glaze, mkd "Red Wing Art Pottery" 80.00
    8" h
        #1103..35.00
        #1357..35.00
    11-1/2" h, handles, #1376.....................................45.00
Water Cooler
    Five gallon, small wing, no lid, small hairline.................275.00
    Six gallon, small wing, no lid 385.00

RELIGIOUS ITEMS

History: Objects used in worship or as expression of man's belief in a superhuman power are collected by many people for many reasons.

This category includes icons since they are religious mementos, usually paintings with a brass encasement. Collecting icons dates from the earliest period of Christianity. Most antique icons in today's market were made in the late 19th century.

Reference: Penny Forstner and Lael Bower, *Collecting Religious Artifacts (Christian and Judaic)*, Books Americana, 1995.

Collectors' Club: Foundation International for Restorers of Religious Medals, P.O. Box 2652, Worcester, MA 01608.

Museum: American Bible Society, New York, NY.

REPRODUCTION ALERT

Icons are frequently reproduced.

Additional Listings: Russian Items.

Altar Cross, 10" x 6", polished brass, 2 pc construction, Russian
....550.00
Altar Gospels, 12" x 14-3/4", silvered and gilded repousse and chased metal, front cover with repousse image of the Resurrection & Descent into Hades in center, corners with Old Testament Prophets, back cover with repousse and chased image of Crucifixion, corners with the 4 Evangelists, matching clasps with double headed eagles, limited edition of the divine and holy Gospel in English.............................675.00
Altar Niche, 41" w, 22" d, 42" h, carved wood, fluted columns, fancy work, polychrome and gilding, 19th C.....................880.00
Altar Shrine, circumference 80", 41" h, Gothic style wood, ext. with applied cherub heads and 4 side mounted votive stands, int. rotates to reveal shine, when closed it exhibits a carved in relief Eucharistic Lamp beneath grapes and wheat, 19th C
....935.00
Bible Cover, 10-1/2" x 7-1/2", vellum cover, front overlaid with massive gilded bronze and silvered plaque with champleve enamel, depicting crucifixion with the 4 Evangelists, back cover with gilded bronze Romanesque style angel and polished stone feet held in

Carving, The Innocents, oak, Karel Hendrik Geerts, sgd and dated on base "C. H. Geerts, 1848," 41" h, $8,030. Photo courtesy of Jackson's Auctioneers & Appraisers.

gilded and enamel frames, spine imp "Santa Biblia," matching bronze clasps 1,100.00
Candlesticks, pr
    15" h, Sabbath, brass, classical and floral design, Polish, minor wear, repair, dents 245.00
    28" h, bronze, Gothic style...935.00
Chair, Worshipful Masters, New Hampshire, 1850, painted black, gold highlights, back with pressed wood rosettes, carpet upholstery, 50-1/4" h 635.00
Doorstop, 6" h, 7-1/2" w, church door, painted cast iron, #9737
....165.00
Figure
    11" h, carved limestone, Madonna and Child, French, 16th C
....2,185.00
    28" h, carved and painted wood, trumpeting angel, attributed to northern Europe, 19th C, minor losses, repairs
....2,185.00
Gospel Cover, 13-1/4" x 15", gilded bronze and champleve enamel, one pc solid wood spine and back cover, hinged wood front with massive plaque, applied border dec, central gilded bronze and enamel Christ, corners with symbols of the 4 Evangelists, back cov with gilded bronze and enamel clover shaped medallions of an arch angel, matching bronze clasps
....880.00
Icon, Greek
    19" x 15", The Mother of God of the Life Bearing Font, tempera on wood panel 1,25.00

Icon, Russian, tempera on wood panel, 19th C
  8-3/4" x 10-1/2", Baptism of Christ 1,155.00
  14" x 12", double sided processional, the Holy Village and
    Baptism of Christ, attributed to Palekh 3,025.00
  16" x 30", The Prophet Elijah with Life Scenes, gold leaf, Elijah
    in the desert in center, fiery ascension at top, surrounded
    by life scenes, overlaid with gilded metal riza 4,125.00
Mosaic, 24" x 36", The Lord Almighty, Venetian colored and gilded glass, attributed to Vatican workshop 3,300.00
Painting, Continental School, oil on canvas
  24" x 38", Abraham and Issac, indistinguishably sgd lower
    right, c1890 .... 420.00
  27" x 23", The Holy Family, nicely framed 330.00
  30" x 38", The Scared Heart of Mary, unsigned 770.00
Plate, 10" d, creamware, hp crucifixion scene, England, 19th C,
  rim chips, knife scratches 115.00
Processional Cross, 27" x 12", silvered and polished bronze, applied corpus, reverse with Mary Magdalene, receptacle base
  .... 715.00
Reliquary Cross, 10" x 15", tempera, gold leaf, porcelain on wood
  cross, reverse with old Slavonic inscription denoting that cross
  was blessed on Mt. Athos at the Russian Monastery of St. Pan-
  teleimon, relic inset on reverse is old square wood fragment, Russian, 19th C 1,650.00
Retablo, Mexican, painted on tin, late 19th C
  9-1/2" x 13-3/4", Our Lady of Sorrows 250.00
  9-3/4" x 13-1/2", Our Lady Refuge of Sinners, black flat iron
    frame 235.00

Icon, Russian, The Archangel Michael, tempura on wood panel, winged warrior holding a sword, c1700, 27-1/2" h, 14-3/4" w, $3,200. Photo courtesy of Jackson's Auctioneers & Appraisers.

Painting, Our Lady of Mt. Carmel, oil on canvas, Cuzco School, late 17th C, 32" h, 26-1/4" w, $6,160. Photo courtesy of Jackson's Auctioneers & Appraisers.

Santos, Philippine, carved and painted wood
  13" h, carved winged angel playing lute 200.00
  14" h, The Christ Child 110.00
  15" h, Saint Martin 110.00
  19" h, Mary 140.00
Sculpture
  10" h, 10" w, Christ with Crown of Thorns, bronze spelter, mar-
    ble plinth 595.00
  10" h, 10" w, Mary Magdalene, bronze spelter, marble plinth
    .... 595.00
  27-1/2" x 24", Saint Elizabeth, carved wood and polychrome,
    German or Italian 1,650.00
  41" h, The Innocents, carved oak, sgd and dated on base
    "C.H. Geerts 1848" 8,100.00
  74" h, The Virgin Mary, carved wood in the round, southern
    Germany, c1870 .... 2,475.00
Shrine, 35-1/2" h, Baroque, painted, gilded wood, and composition, Spanish, early 18th C, extensive worming, losses
  .... 1,955.00
Tabernacle, 26" h, 22" w, 8" x 8" door, cast bronze, form of cross,
  dec with sheaves of wheat, built-in exposition door 110.00
Wall Plaque, 20" x 27", molded cast relief, Virgin & Child, after Giovanni Bastianni, inscribed "Roma 1890" 220.00

REVERSE PAINTING ON GLASS

History: The earliest examples of reverse painting on glass were produced in 13th-century Italy. By the 17th century, the technique had spread to central and eastern Europe. It spread westward as the center of the glass-making industry moved to Germany in the late 17th century.

The Alsace and Black Forest regions developed a unique portraiture style. The half and three-quarter portraits often were titled below the portrait. Women tend to have generic names while most males are likenesses of famous men.

The English used a mezzotint, rather than free-style, method to create their reverse paintings. Landscapes and allegorical figures were popular. The Chinese began working in the medium in the 17th century, eventually favoring marine and patriotic scenes.

Most American reverse painting was done by folk artists and is unsigned. Portraits, patriotic and mourning scenes, floral compositions, landscapes, and buildings are the favorite subjects. Known American artists include Benjamin Greenleaf, A. Cranfield, and Rowley Jacobs.

In the late 19th century, commercially produced reverse paintings, often decorated with mother-of-pearl, became popular. Themes included the Statue of Liberty, the capitol in Washington, D.C., and various worlds' fairs and expositions.

Reference: Shirley Mace, *Encyclopedia of Silhouette Collectibles on Glass*, Shadow Enterprises, 1992.

Portraits

Fredericke, orig frame, 13-1/2" x 10-5/8" 385.00
Geisha, facing pr, geisha seated next to table, vase with flower, bamboo dec, mirrored ground, Chinese Export, 19th C, framed, losses, 16" h, 11-1/2" w, pr 625.00
Lincoln, Abraham, framed, 21-1/2" h, 18" w 425.00
Rosinia, polychrome, dark green ground, orig frame, 9-1/8" h, 6-1/2" w 450.00
Washington, George, silhouette, intricately painted border maple veneer frame, gilded liner with minor damage, 12-3/4" h, 11" w 250.00

Scenes

Country house in winter, gold painted frame, 10-1/2" h, 12-1/2" w 75.00
Perry's Lake Erie Victory, Sept. 10, 1813, naval battle scene, multicolored, 7" x 9" 250.00
Ship, *Ohio,* side wheeler steamship, poplar frame, 10-1/2" h, 12-1/2" w 175.00
Statue of Liberty, mica accents, oval frame 175.00

European scene, house and bridge along river, oval, gilt frame, 19" x 13-1/2", $80.

RIDGWAY

History: Throughout the 19th century, the Ridgway family, through a series of partnerships, held a position of importance in the ceramics industry in Shelton and Hanley, Staffordshire, England. The connection began with Job and George, two brothers, and Job's two sons, John and William. In 1830, John and William dissolved their partnership; John retained the Cauldon Place factory and William the Bell Works. By 1862, the porcelain division of Cauldon was carried on by Coalport China Ltd. William and his heirs continued at the Bell Works and the Church (Hanley) and Bedford (Shelton) works until the end of the 19th century.

Marks: Many early pieces are unmarked. Later marks include the initials of the many different partnerships.

References: Susan and Al Bagdade, *Warman's English & Continental Pottery & Porcelain*, 2nd ed., Wallace-Homestead, 1991; G. A. Godden, *Ridgway Porcelains*, Antique Collectors' Club, 1985.

Additional Listings: Staffordshire, Historical; Staffordshire, Romantic.

Beverage Set, 9-1/2" h pitcher, six 4" h mugs, 12-1/2" d tray, Coaching Days, black coaching scenes, caramel ground, silver luster trim 325.00
Bowl, 9-1/2" d, Coaching Days and Ways, "Henry VII and the Abbot," black and caramel brown 45.00
Cup and Saucer, boy fishing on lake 30.00
Dessert Plate, 9" d, Harlequin patter, molded scalloped rim edge, gilt edge border of white beadwork with 4 clusters of gilt white blossoms, painted with assorted flowers and fruits, iron-red numbers, c1830, 19 pc set.........................2,750.00
Ice Pail, cov, 13" h, horizontal band of gilt edged orange feathery scrollwork reserved on pale yellow ground, above acanthus leaf molding, rope twist handles with trailing vine leaf terminals, cov with finials modeled as rhytons brimming with fruit, finial repaired, c1840, iron-red number 3,500.00
Mug, 4" h, Boating Days, New Haven and Eton, brown body, silver luster trim 45.00
Pitcher, 4-1/4" h, red transfers of family scenes on cream ground in roundels, reserved on cobalt blue ground, c1890, "Humphrey's Clock and William Ridgway" mark...................225.00

Creamer and Sugar, cov, white ground, gray dec, heavy gold trim, $85.

Plate, 8-1/2" d, rose, rust, and purple Oriental-type florals with yellow centers, gray-green branches, raised, ribbed, scalloped edge, white ground, c1830, No. 2004 ....65.00
Teapot, cov, 6" h, 6" l, brown and white whooping cranes and foliage, emb leaves, dated 1877, mkd 125.00
Tray, 9-1/2" l, 7-1/2" w, Pickwick design, silver luster trim, scalloped rim, open handles...50.00

RING TREES

History: A ring tree is a small, generally saucer-shaped object made of glass, porcelain, metal, or wood with a center post in the shape of a hand, branches, or cylinder. It is a convenient object for holding finger rings.

Glass

Black, 3-7/8" d, 4" h, allover dec on saucer and post, lacy gold vines and green enamel leaves, light blue, white, orange, and cream flowers 95.00
Bristol, 3" h, 3-1/4" d, turquoise blue, lacy yellow leaves and large gold leaves dec 85.00
Cameo, 3-1/4" h, 4" d, acid cut, rd flowers, leaves, and stems, leaf ground, St. Louis 160.00
Clear, 3" h, 3-3/4" d, cut floral dec, black enameled bands 65.00
Cranberry, 3-1/4" h, 3-1/2" d, hp, multicolored flowers, gold leaves 115.00
Opalescent, 2-1/2" h, 3-1/2" d, vaseline, striped 65.00
Waterford, crystal 35.00

Porcelain

Austria, hp pink and green floral dec, gold trim, mkd "M. Z. Austria" 70.00
Limoges, multicolored blossoms, white ground, mkd "T. & V. Limoges" 40.00
Minton, 3" h, pastel flowers, gold trim, mkd "Minton England" 45.00

Bear, standing with gun, guarding tree, oval base, Pairpoint, 3-1/4" x 2-1/8" x 3-1/4", $165.

Nippon, gold hand, rim dec 35.00
Royal Worcester, 2-3/4" h, 4-1/2" l, oval dish, 3 pronged holder, hp pink and yellow flowers, beige ground, c1898..............150.00
R. S. Germany, 2-3/4" h, 5-1/2" l, hp, pink flowers, green leaves, told tree, sgd "E. Wolff" 50.00
Wedgwood, 2-3/4" h, jasperware, center post, white cameos of classical ladies, floral border, blue ground, mkd 150.00
Zsolnay, 3-1/2" h, irid gold...85.00

Silver

Tiffany & Co., angel shape 450.00
Wilcox, open hand, saucer base, engraved edge, sgd.......60.00

ROCKINGHAM AND ROCKINGHAM BROWN-GLAZED WARES

History: Rockingham ware can be divided into two categories. The first consists of the fine china and porcelain pieces made between 1826 and 1842 by the Rockingham Company of Swinton, Yorkshire, England, and its predecessor firms: Swinton, Bingley, Don, Leeds, and Brameld. The Bramelds developed the cadogan, a lidless teapot. Between 1826 and 1842, a quality soft-paste product with a warm, silky feel was developed by the Bramelds. Elaborate specialty pieces were made. By 1830, the company employed 600 workers and listed 400 designs for dessert sets and 1,000 designs for tea and coffee services in its catalog. Unable to meet its payroll, the company closed in 1842.

The second category of Rockingham ware includes pieces produced in the famous Rockingham brown glaze that became an intense and vivid purple-brown when fired. It had a dark, tortoiseshell appearance. The glaze was copied by many English and American potteries. American manufacturers, which used Rockingham glaze include D. & J. Henderson of Jersey City, New Jersey; United States Pottery in Bennington, Vermont; potteries in East Liverpool, Ohio; and several potteries in Indiana and Illinois.

References: Susan and Al Bagdade, *Warman's American Pottery and Porcelain*, Wallace-Homestead, 1994; Susan and Al Bagdade, *Warman's English & Continental Pottery & Porcelain*, 2nd ed., Wallace-Homestead, 1991; Mary Brewer, *Collector's Guide to Rockingham,* Collector Books, 1996.

Museum: Bennington Museum, Bennington, VT.

Additional Listings: Bennington and Bennington-Type Pottery.

Bedpan, 15" l, Rockingham glaze, chip 40.00
Bowl
    9-1/2" d, 3-1/4" h 65.00
    10-1/2" d, 4-3/4" h, molded ext. ribs, scalloped band.....50.00
Casserole, cov, 12" l, 10-1/4" h, oval, fruit finial, applied handles 275.00
Creamer, 6-3/4" h, cow-form, 19th C, minor chips............260.00
Dish, 11-1/2" l, octagonal, spotted Rockingham glaze 170.00
Flask, 8" h, molded floral dec, band....................................45.00

Flower Pot, 10-1/4" h, emb acanthus leaves, matching saucer 45.00
Inkwell, 4-1/8" l, shoe shape 60.00
Mixing Bowl, nested set of 3, emb design 95.00
Pie Plate, Rockingham glaze
    8-3/8" d 65.00
    10" d 80.00
Pitcher, Rockingham glaze
    4-3/8" l, squatty, C scroll handle.....................................75.00
    6-3/8" h, molded Gothic Art design 65.00
    8" h, molded peacocks, rim chips 90.00
Plate
    9" d, painted center with exotic bird in landscape, raised C-scroll border with gilt and painting, puce griffin and green number marks..650.00
    9-1/4" d, painted vase of flowers overflowing onto marble table, medium blue ground, gilt line band, shark's tooth and S-scroll border, c1831-42...875.00
Potpourri Vase, 4-3/8" h, waisted rect shape, painted front and reverse with river landscape between gilt formal borders, 4 paw feet, pierced cov with acorn knob, double handles, c1826, iron-red griffin mark..950.00
Scent Bottle, 6" h, onion shape, applied garden flowers, gilt line rims, c1831-40, printed puce griffin mark 465.00
Tray, 8-1/2" x 11", scalloped rim 100.00
Vase
    4-3/8" h, flared, painted view of Larington Yorkshire, figures and sheep, wide gilt border, dark blue ground, restored, c1826-30, iron-red griffin and painted title 420.00
    6-1/2" h, flared hexagon, painted sprays of colored garden flowers alternating with blue panels, gilt scrolls, c1831-42, puce griffin mark...800.00
Washboard, 24-1/4" h, 19th C, imperfections......................350.00

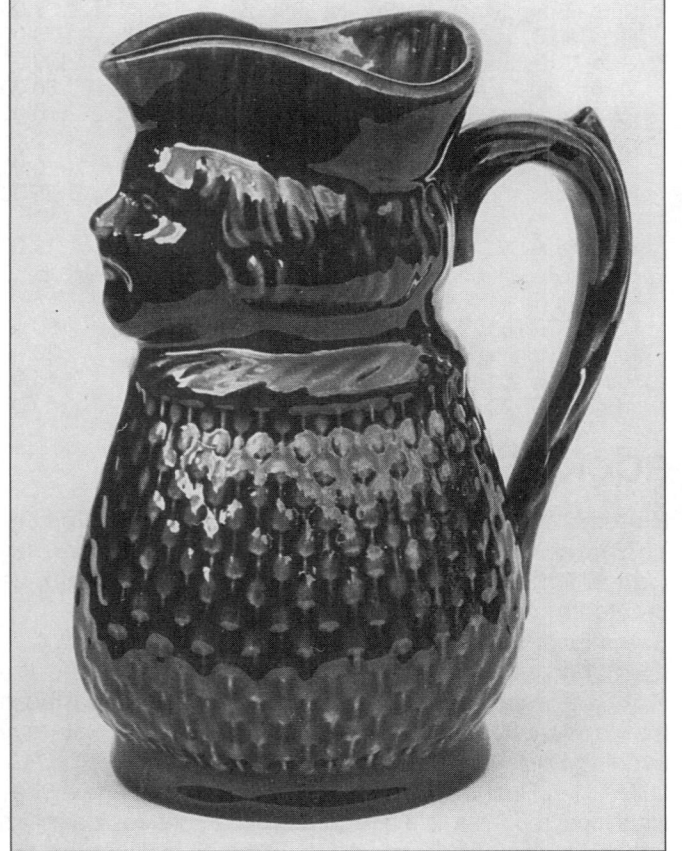

Toby Jug, basketweave body, tricorn hat, 6" h, $275.

ROCK 'N' ROLL

History: Rock music can be traced back to early rhythm and blues. It progressed until it reached its golden age in the 1950s and 1960s. Most of the memorabilia issued during that period focused on individual singers and groups. The largest quantity of collectible material is connected to Elvis Presley and The Beatles.

In the 1980s two areas–clothing and guitars–associated with key rock 'n' roll personalities received special collector attention. Sotheby's and Christie's East regularly feature rock 'n' roll memorabilia as part of their collectibles sales. At the moment, the market is highly speculative and driven by nostalgia.

It is important to identify memorabilia issued during the lifetime of an artist or performing group as opposed to material issued after they died or disbanded. Objects of the latter type are identified as "fantasy" items and will never achieve the same degree of collectibility as period counterparts.

References: Jeff Augsburger, Marty Eck, and Rich Rann, *Beatles Memorabilia Price Guide*, 2nd ed., Wallace-Homestead, 1993; Karen and John Lesniewski, *Kiss Collectibles*, Avon Books, 1993; Stephen Maycock, *Miller's Rock & Pop Memorabilia*, Millers Publications, 1994; Greg Moore, *Price Guide to Rock & Roll Collectibles*, published by author, 1993; Michael Stern, Barbara Crawford, and Hollis Lamon, *The Beatles*, Collector Books, 1994; Neal Umphred, *Goldmine's Price Guide to Collectible Record Albums*, 4th ed., Krause Publications, 1994; ——, *Goldmine's Rock 'n' Roll 45 RPM Record Price Guide*, 3rd ed., Krause Publications, 1994.

Periodicals: Beatlefan, P.O. Box 33515, Decatur, GA 30033; *Good Day Sunshine*, 397 Edgewood Ave., New Haven, CT 06511; *Instant Karma*, P.O. Box 256, Sault Ste. Marie, MI 49783.

Collectors' Clubs: Beatles Connection, P.O. Box 1066, Pinellas Park, FL 34665; Beatles Fan Club of Great Britain, Superstore Productions, 123 Marina St., Leonards on Sea, East Sussex, England TN 38 OBN; Elvis Forever TCB Fan Club, P.O. Box 1066, Pinellas Park, FL 34665; Graceland News Fan Club, P.O. Box 452, Rutherford, NJ 07070; Working Class Hero Club, 3311 Niagara St., Pittsburgh, PA 15213.

REPRODUCTION ALERT

Records, picture sleeves, and album jackets, especially for The Beatles, have been counterfeited. When compared to the original, sound may be inferior, as may be the printing on labels and picture jackets. Many pieces of memorabilia also have been reproduced, often with some change in size, color, and design.

Additional Listings: See The Beatles, Elvis Presley, and Rock 'n' Roll in *Warman's Americana & Collectibles*.

Autograph
    Document, contract, Elvis Presley, contract with MGM Studios, 1961 ....850.00

Letter signed, Frank Zappa, employee dismissal, 5/14/85, typed, to State Unemployment Office regarding employee who quit and who claims he was fired, composed and sgd by Frank Zappa...500.00

Autograph, photo
Greg Allman..40.00
Chuck Berry..75.00
Jon Bon Jovi...40.00
Michael Jackson..195.00
Mick Jagger..135.00
Madonna..195.00
Paul McCartney 275.00
Prince...275.00
Bruce Springsteen.......................................150.00

Backstage Pass, cloth
Aerosmith, Pump Tour '89, afternoon 10.00
Black Sabbath, working personnel.....................9.00
Dylan/Petty, Temples in Flames 20.00
Iron Maiden, World Slavery Tour, '84 ....9.00
Bon Jovi, NJ Guest...7.00
KISS, 10th anniversary, after show, unused........7.00
Cindi Lauper, Crew '86-87.................................6.00
Pink Floyd, Mixer '94..9.00
Rolling Stones, American Tour '81 ....15.00

Cigarette Lighter, Rod Stewart decal, chrome, c1975.........35.00

Cover Artwork
Rolling Stones, R'N'R Comics, orig full color artwork, 1989, 20" x 30", matted and framed, S. Jackson, pencil and ink cover drawing and 13" x 9" back cover H. Ras painting, set 250.00
Frank Zappa, R'N'R Comics, 1994, 8-3/4" x 14-1/2", painting by Scott Jackson, used for front cover of "Via La Bizarre," issue #1........100.00

Counter Display, Rolling Stones, "Made In The Shade," 1976, 21" x 19", 3-D cardboard, bowed diecut, with four previous LP covers at left and "Rolling Stones & Tongue" logo on silver at top right 250.00

Divider Card, Yardbirds, LP bin type, Epic, 1988, 12" x 14" plastic, purple names and logos emb at top 200.00

Drumsticks
Alice in Chains...25.00
Black Crows, concerned used, logo 20.00
Randy Castillo, Ozzy Osbourne 35.00
Iron Maiden, 1985...50.00
Steve Riley, WASP 20.00

Flyer, concert
Aerosmith, 1988, 8" x 6", 2 sided, Whitesnake Def Leppard on back..............45.00
Cramps, Horrible Halloween, Devonshire Fairgrounds, Northridge, CA, 1980s, 6" x 15" 40.00
Led Zeppelin, Tarrant County Convention Center, Ft. Worth, TX, 8/22/70, 8-1/2" x 11-1/2" 60.00
Motley Crue & Others, Glen Dale Civic Auditorium, Glen Dale, CA, 5/7/82, 8-1/2" x 11", two staple holes at top.........35.00

Jacket, Billy Joel, promo, black leather, aviator style, detachable sleeves, keyboard, wings logo embroidered on left breast pocket, 5 outer pockets, size large 325.00

Label Sticker, Deep Purple, promo LP label made for Come Taste The Band 25.00

Menu, Elvis Presley, Las Vegas Hilton Hotel, 8-1/2" x 11" 1,000.00

Merchandising Kit, Queen, Night At The Opera, Elektra, 1985, 24" x 24" cardboard and tin paper poster with LP cover, two 15" x 24" 2 sided thin cardboard "Hanging Arrow" displays, two 9" x 10" oval posters with LP cover art 200.00

Pennant, 29-1/2" l, We Love Lil Richard, felt, white, red design and border, orig 30" l wood stick, 1950s 50.00

Plaque, Bon Jovi, Anytime, Anywhere, with unused tickets from Belgium, Italy, and Istanbul, gold CD, only 45 produced 250.00

Postcard Display, hanging, Allman Brothers Band, Eat A Peach, Capricorn, 1972, 24" x 36"..........200.00

Press Kit, KISS, Casablanca, 1976, custom folder, 3 page bio, 1 page press clipping, five 8" x 10" black and white photos, orig mailing envelope with no writing or postage 500.00

Print, Chuck Berry, by Red Grooms, color screenprint on paper, 1978, edition of 150, published by Marlborough Graphics, NY, sgd "Red Grooms" in pencil lower right, numbered "77/150" in pencil lower left, 24-1/2" x 18-1/2" 345.00

Promotional Standee, Elvis Presley, "Aloha From Hawaii," RA, 1973, 34" x 56" 175.00

Radio Show
Alice Cooper, King Biscuit Flower Hour, Michigan, 197818.00
John Lennon, "What's It All About," 1982, 7", interview, for public service broadcast 95.00

Record Award
Beatles, "20 Greatest Hits," orig RIAA Gold strip plate award, gold wood frame..........795.00
Billy Joel, "Songs from the Attic," RIAA Platinum Strip plate, orig silver wood frame 450.00
Eagles, "The Long Run," RIAA Platinum for 4 million sales 600.00
Hootie & the Blowfish, "Fairweather Johnson," RIAA Gold LP 600.00
KISS, "Alive," Casablanca, in-house Platinum floater ...595.00
Midnight Oil, "Diesel & Dust," RIAA Gold award, with LP and cassette, old style round hologram 250.00

Scarf, Beatles, glossy fabric, half corner design, mkd "The Beatles/Copyright by Ramat & Co., Ltd/London, ECI," 25" sq, c1964..........160.00

Sheet Music, "Elvis Presley Hits," 3 ring binder with every piece of sheet music published by Elvis Presley/Hill & Range Music, 148 songs, custom printed spine, 1964 ....4,500.00

Ticket
Aerosmith, Pacific, 1989..........5.00
Bruce Springsteen, LA Sports, 1988 ....5.00
Elvis, 9/88 ....75.00
Ozzy Osbourne, sgd, last show, 10/92 ....100.00
Yardbirds/Doors, 1967 ....50.00
ZZ Top, sgd, 11/94 ....50.00

Tour Book
Depeche Mode, Devotional Tour 93/94 ....10.00
KISS, 10th anniversary, Vinnie V in makeup.........125.00

T-Shirt
Bob Dylan, XL, True Confession, worn..........10.00
Bon Jovi, L, Slippery When…, never worn 25.00
Deep Purple, L, Perfect Str…'85, never worn..........25.00
Motley Crew, L:, Dr. Feelgood, never worn 20.00
Rolling Stones, XL, Steel Wheels, never worn 20.00
Van Halen, XL, Right Now, never worn..........15.00

Yearbook, Dick Clark, 42 pgs, 1957, 8-1/2" x 11"..........40.00

ROCKWELL, NORMAN

History: Norman Rockwell (Feb. 3, 1894-November 1978) was a famous American artist and illustrator. During the time he painted, from age 18 until his death, he created more than 2,000 works.

His first professional efforts were illustrations for a children's book; his next projects were done for Boy's Life, the Boy Scout magazine. His most famous works are those that appeared as cover illustrations on the Saturday Evening Post.

Norman Rockwell painted everyday people in everyday situations, mixing a little humor with sentiment. His paintings and illustrations are treasured because of this sensitive approach. Rockwell painted people he knew and places with which he was familiar. New England landscapes are found in many of his illustrations.

References: Denis C. Jackson, Norman Rockwell Identification and Value Guide to: Magazines, Posters, Calendars, Books, 2nd ed., published by author, 1985; Karal Ann Marling, Norman Rockwell, Harry N. Abrams, 1997; Mary Moline, Norman Rockwell Collectibles, 6th ed., Green Valley World, 1988.

Collectors' Club: Rockwell Society of America, 597 Saw Mill River Rd., Ardsley, NY 10502.

Museums: Museum of Norman Rockwell Art, Reedsburg, WI; Norman Rockwell Museum, Northbrook, IL; Norman Rockwell Museum, Philadelphia, PA; Norman Rockwell Museum, Stockbridge, MA.

REPRODUCTION ALERT

Because of the popularity of his works, the images have been reproduced on many objects. These new collectibles, which should not be confused with original artwork and illustrations, provide a wide range of collectibles and prices.

Additional Listings: See *Warman's Americana & Collectibles* for more examples.

Historic

Autograph, typed letter sgd, 1 page, 8vo, Stockbridge, April 24, 1973, answering questions relating to his work 450.00

Print, autographed, Check-Up, Saturday Evening Post, Sept. 7, 1957, 11" x 14", $75.

Book
    My Adventures as an Illustrator, Rockwell, 1960.............25.00
    Tom Sawyer, Heritage Press, 1936 ....20.00
Calendar, 1941, boy and dog illus, Hercules Powder Co. adv, 13" x 30-1/2" 175.00
Magazine, cover illus
    Country Gentleman, Oct. 3, 1917..............................60.00
    Literary Digest, Aug. 17, 1918...............................40.00
Magazine Tear Sheet, Jell-O adv, *Country Gentleman,* 1922, matted
....40.00
Poster
    Freedom of Speech, WWII, 1943.................................60.00
    Maxwell House Coffee adv, 1932................................350.00

Modern

Coin, Ford Motor Co., 50th Anniversary 40.00
Figure
    Gorham Fine China, Four Seasons, Childhood, 1973, set of four
....500.00
    Grossman Designs, Inc., Tom Sawyer, Series No. 1, 1976
....95.00
Plate
    Scotty Gets His Tree, Christmas Series, Rockwell Society of America, 1974 ....175.00
    Triple Self Portrait, Gorham 75.00
Print
    Gilding the Eagle, Eleanor Ettinger, Inc., litho, 21" x 25-1/2"
....3,500.00
    Music Hath Charms, Circle Fine Arts, sgd and numbered
....3,000.00
    People Praying, color offset litho, sgd in pencil lower right, numbered, 28-1/4" x 22" 800.00

ROGERS and SIMILAR STATUARY

History: John Rogers, born in America in 1829, studied sculpture in Europe and produced his first plaster-of-paris statue, "The Checker Players," in 1859. It was followed by "The Slave Auction" in 1860.

His works were popular parlor pieces in the Victorian era. He produced at least 80 different statues, and the total number of groups made from the originals is estimated to be more then 100,000.

Casper Hennecke, one of Rogers's contemporaries, operated C. Hennecke & Company from 1881 until 1896 in Milwaukee, Wisconsin. His statuary often is confused with Rogers' work since both are very similar.

References: Paul and Meta Bieier, *John Rogers' Groups of Statuary,* published by author, 1971; Betty C. Haverly, *Hennecke's Florentine Statuary,* published by author, 1972; David H. Wallace, *John Rogers,* Wesleyan University, 1976.

Periodical: *Rogers Group,* 4932 Prince George Ave., Beltsville, MD 20705.

Museums: John Rogers Studio & Museum of the New Canaan Historical Society, New Canaan CT; Lightner Museum, Saint Augustine, FL.

Notes: It is difficult to find a statue in undamaged condition and with original paint. Use the following conversions: 10% off for minor flaking; 10%, chips; 10 to 20%, piece or pieces broken and reglued; 20%, flaking; 50%, repainting.

Council of War, 24" h, $1,300.

Checkers Up At The Farm 525.00
Coming To The Parson's 375.00
Council of War 1,300.00
Faust and Margeurite Leaving the Garden 1,300.00
Going For The Cows...450.00
Ha, I Like Not That...550.00
It Is So Nominated In The Bond...650.00
Parting Promise 400.00
Picket Guard...825.00
Rip Van Winkle at Home, damage.....................................275.00
Speak for Yourself John...550.00
Taking The Oath 650.00
Union Refugee, broken gun 325.00
We Boys..475.00
Weighing The Baby, damage..575.00

ROOKWOOD POTTERY

History: Mrs. Marie Longworth Nicholas Storer, Cincinnati, Ohio, founded Rookwood Pottery in 1880. The name of this outstanding American art pottery came from her family estate, "Rookwood," named for the rooks (crows) which inhabited the wooded grounds.

Though the Rookwood pottery filed for bankruptcy in 1941, it was soon reorganized under new management. Efforts at maintaining the pottery proved futile, and it was sold in 1956 and again in 1959. The pottery was moved to Starkville, Mississippi, in conjunction with the Herschede Clock Co. It finally ceased operating in 1967.

Rookwood wares changed with the times. The variety is endless, in part because of the creativity of the many talented artists responsible for great variations in glazes and designs.

Marks: There are five elements to the Rookwood marking system: the clay or body mark; the size mark; the decorator mark; the date mark; and the factory mark. The best way to date Rookwood art pottery is from factory marks.

From 1880-82, the factory mark was the name "Rookwood" incised or painted on the base. Between 1881-86, the firm name, address, and year appeared in an oval frame. Beginning in 1886, the impressed "RP" monogram appeared and a flame mark was added for each year until 1900. After 1900, a Roman numeral, indicating the last two digits of the year of production, was added at the bottom of the "RP" flame mark. This last mark is the one most often seen on Rookwood pieces in the antiques marketplace.

References: Susan and Al Bagdade, *Warman's American Pottery and Porcelain*, Wallace-Homestead, 1994; Anita J. Ellis, *Rookwood Pottery*, Rizzoli International and Cincinnati Art Museum, 1992; Ralph and Terry Kovel, *Kovels' American Art Pottery*, Crown Publishers, 1993; Herbert Peck, *Book of Rookwood Pottery*, Crown Publishers, 1968; ——, *Second Book of Rookwood Pottery*, published by author, 1985; David Rago, *American Art Pottery,* Knickerbocker Press, 1997.

Videotape: Anita Ellis, *The Collectors Series: Rookwood Pottery*, distributed by Award Video and Film Distributors, Inc., 1994.

Collectors' Club: American Art Pottery Assoc., 125 E. Rose Ave., St. Louis, MO 63119.

Bookends, pr
   Eagle, charcoal, 1934...600.00
   Rook, olive green, c1928..425.00
   St. Francis with bird and fox, brown and cream glaze, "6883," 1945, 5-1/4" w, 7-1/2" h...435.00
Bowl
   6" d, ftd, Arts and Crafts, incised dec, yellow matte 200.00
   6-1/2" d, 3" h, porcelain, stylized paisley teal, mauve, pink, and mustard border, cream ground, Sarah Sax, 1928, uncrazed, flame mark/XXVIII/957D/artist's cipher 800.00
   7-3/4" d, 3-1/2" h, hammered glaze, Limoges style underglaze pink blossoms dec, gold highlights, shape #166, Laura A. Fry 800.00
Box, 4" l, 2-5/8" w, rect, molded head, animals, scrolls, flowers, and leaves, matte green glaze, dated 1929..................135.00

Candlesticks, pr, matte, emb grave leaves under dark and light green glaze, 1922, restored, flame mark/XXII/1193 ...... 250.00
Charger, 12-1/2" d, mauve and ochre galleon center, light blue splashed border, John Wareham, dated 1905 .... 1,500.00
Chocolate Pot, 10" h, standard glaze, oak leaves and across dec, shape #722, Lenore Ashbury, 1904 .... 700.00
Ewer, 8" h, standard glaze over sage clay, #101C, floral design, M. Daley, 1885 .... 650.00
Figure
   Cocker Spaniel, #7024, 4" 275.00
   Crane, #6972, 1954 .... 170.00
Flower Boat, 16" l, standard glaze, pansies dec, shape #3745, Matt A. Daly, 1890 .... 900.00
Flower Frog, #2251, 1915 .... 325.00
Humidor, 6" h, standard glaze, carved and dec salmon pansies, 1889, crazing 500.00
Jug
   7" h, 6" d, bulbous, applied handle, ear of corn dec, brown glaze, imp mark, "676," artist monogram for Josephine Zettel, 1896, some crazing 320.00
   13" h, cov, 4 ears of corn, standard glaze, Sallie Tohey, dated 1896 .... 1,250.00
Mug
   5" h, Chief Goes to War, Sioux portrait, shape #656, Edith R. Felten, 1900 .... 1,275.00
   5" h, 5" w, commemorative, emb mail bag design, standard glaze, imp mark, bottom incised "Compliments of Fifth Division Railway Mail Service to Delegates Attending Annual Convention, Cincinnati, Ohio, 1905," minor glaze nicks 175.00
Paperweight, 3-1/2" d, elephant, 1928 .... 250.00
Pitcher
   4-3/4" h, 6" w, tri-cornered, incised oak leaves, blue ground, Albert Pons, 1900, flame mark/753/D/artist's cipher 425.00
   7-1/2" d, 6-1/2" h, oviform, incised palm leaves, gold and blue highlights, imp "Rookwood, 1883," small kiln, "Y" 13" 230.00

Vase, #1358, matte finish, artist sgd "C. Crabtree," 1923, 5-7/8" h, $695.

Planter, 8-3/4" h, 8-1/2" d, incised stylized leaves, frothy brown-green matte glaze, c12910, flame mark/XI/180C 500.00
Plaque, 11" h, 8-1/2" w, vellum, tall birch trees in landscape, moody grays, ivory sky, E. T. Hurley, 1913, flame mark/XII/E.T.H., Arts and Crafts wood frame 3,600.00
Potter's Tool, 2-1/2" l, Rookwood logo, Roman numeral VX, 1905 .... 260.00
Presentation Stein, cov, 6-3/4" h, standard glaze, stylized ferns dec, presented to Lucian Wulsin by the Commercial Club of Cincinnati, pewter lid, shape #783, Constance A Baker, 1895 .... 1,600.00
Vase
   2-1/4" h, 4-1/2" d, foliate design, standard glaze, imp mark, "798C, W, 1894" 230.00
   2-3/4" h, 5-1/2" d, squatty circular, incised geometric ring, deep blue high glaze, imp mark, "214C," artist monogram for "W. E. Hentschel," 1915 .... 400.00
   5" h, wax matte, yellow, band of flowers, 1931, sgd "Pulman," #1343 .... 450.00
   5-3/4" h, 2-1/2" d, bud, Aerial Blue, sailboat against horizon, shades of light blue, Harriet Strafer, 1895, flame mark/JDW/76523/half moon 3,700.00
   6" h, 3-1/2" d, incised blue, white, and green fish, vellum glaze, imp mark, "913E," artist monogram for Lorinda Epply, 1908 .... 1,610.00

Portrait Mug, Monk, dark glaze, Harriet Wilcox artist, #853, 1899, $1,500.

6" h, 3-1/2" d, Jewel Porcelain, squeezebag dec motif of cactus, Art Deco style, dark blue and aventurine glaze, by William Hentschel, 1931, flamemark/XXXII/924/WH ...4,000.00

6" h, 4" d, Modern, stylized relief foliage, browns, blues, and green, imp mark, "2723," artist monogram for Elizabeth Barrett, 1929 ....490.00

6" h, 4" d, Z Line, 2 female figures languidly draped around rim, smooth matte green glaze, by A. M. Valentien, 1910, flame mark XI/28Z/A.M.V. 3,500.00

6-1/4" h, 3-1/4" d, mat double vellum glaze, stylized flowers, cream green to pink ground, imp ark, 13669, artist monogram for Margaret Heler McDonald, 1926 ....800.00

6-3/4" h, 5" d, bulbous, sgraffito, geometric incised bands, high glaze, imp "Rookwood," artist initials "W.H.B." for W. H. Brever, minor hairlines to rim 375.00

6-3/4" h, 7" w, pillow shape, floral design, standard glaze, imp mark, "297," monogram for Edward Diers................345.00

7" h, Jewel porcelain, floral motif, Jons Jensen S mark 800.00

7" h, 3" d, uncrazed glass, four nicely detailed fish, light orange, yellow, green, and blue ground, imp logo, "951E," obscured initials, possibly Shirayadani. 1906 ......2,160.00

7-1/2" h, 3-1/2" d, oviform, lilies of the valley dec, iris glaze, imp mark, "917," artist monogram for Sara Sax, 1908, hairlines 865.00

8" h, 4" d, Jewel Porcelain, band of stylized purple and green flowers, black ground, Sarah Sax, 1922, uncrazed, flame mark/XXII/536/artist's cipher 8,000.00

8-1/4" h, 4-1/4" d, bulbous base to slightly flaring rim, white flowers on branch, blue ground, vellum glaze, imp mark, "2885," artist initials for Edward T. Hurley, 1927 ......865.00

8-1/2" h, 4" d, bulbous, foliate design, standard glaze, imp mark, "780," artist monogram for Harriet R. Strafer, 1895, minute glaze nick 200.00

9-1/2" h, 5" d, circular tapering to base, blue and white iris, pale blue ground, vellum glaze, imp mark, artist initials, crazing, 1905 ....2,070.00

12" h, 5-1/4" d, Wax Matte, paneled, purple and brown flowers, yellow ground, by Jens Jensen, 1930, flame mark, XXX/2933/JJ 900.00

21-1/2" h, 10" d, oviform, Chinese turquoise glaze, imp mark, "2370," 1921, light crazing 435.00

Wall Sconce, #1760, Arts and Crafts, blue, price for pr.....900.00

ROSE BOWLS

History: A rose bowl is a decorative open bowls with a crimped, scalloped or petal top which turns in at the top, but does not then turn up or back out again. Rose bowls held fragrant rose petals or potpourri which served as an air freshener in the late Victorian period. Practically every glass manufacturer made rose bowls in virtually every glass type, pattern, and style.

Collectors' Club: Rose Bowl Collectors, P.O. Box 244, Danielsville, PA 18038-0244.

REPRODUCTION ALERT

Rose bowls have been widely reproduced. Be especially careful of Italian copies of Victorian art glass, particularly Burmese and Mother-Of-Pearl, imported in the 1960s and early 1970s.

Additional Listings: See specific glass categories.

Advisor: Johanna S. Billings.

Blenko, 3-5/8" h, 4-1/2" w, transparent amethyst, free blown, 30 tight rolled crimps, rough pontil......................................25.00

Bohemian

2" h, 2-1/4" w, transparent amethyst with enameled flowers, polished bottom, six crimps 225.00

3-1/4" h, 3-3/4" w, cranberry, faint vertical ribbing in glass, enameled female figure and gold outlined background, 6 crimps with light gold edging, engraved mark on bottom which looks similar to a scripted E, possibly Rossler 125.00

Dugan, 4" h, 4" w, Japanese line, light yellowish green, three crimps, three indentations on side, decorated with vertical rows of frit, collar base, c1907 ....45.00

Fenton

3-1/4" h, 3-1/2" w, Beaded Melon, white with yellow interior, eight crimps, collar base 45.00

4-1/2" h, 4-1/2" w, vaseline opalescent hobnail, eight crimps, collar base 125.00

Mt. Washington

3" h, 3-1/2" w, mother-of pearl satin, blue, counter clockwise swirl pattern, soft white interior, 9 crimps, polished base 300.00

3-1/4" h, 4-1/4" w, lustreless (white satin), well-done cottage decorated dogwood blossoms in mint condition, nine soft crimps, polished bottom 75.00

Murano

3" h, 3" w, millefiore, glossy white opaque background with individual millefiore scattered throughout the glass, nine uneven crimps, semi-ground bottom, c1960 ....45.00

3-3/8" h, 4-1/4" w, transparent Caribbean blue, diamond optic pattern in glass, applied clear rigaree around base, eight crimps, rough pontil, 1960s 45.00

Porcelain, 2-3/4" h, 3-3/4" w, shaded light heavenly blue to creamy yellow with small bouquet of blue flowers on front, greenish brown stems circling the piece with two smaller bouquets in back, these highlighted with pink flowers, all with green leaves, off-white interior, eight soft crimps with gold edges, marked on bottom with wreath and the words "Q. & E. G. ROYAL Austria"...45.00

Satin

3" h, 3-1/2" w, shaded pink to white, soft white interior, undecorated, eight crimps, ground pontil 45.00

Dugan, Japanese Line, 4" h, 4" w, $45. Photo courtesy Johanna Billings.

Porcelain, Royal Austria, shaded light heavenly blue to creamy yellow, 2-3/4" h, 3-3/4" w, $45. Photo courtesy Johanna Billings.

3" h, 4" w, shaded yellow to white, soft white interior, cherub decal decoration, eight crimps, polished pontil 175.00

3-1/4" h, 3-3/4" w, light green, embossed apple blossoms in glass, eight crimps, ground pontil 150.00

3-7/8" h, 3-3/4" w, apricot, soft white interior, enameled with purple and white violets, gold foliage and scrollwork, eight crimps, ground pontil 175.00

4-3/4" h, 5-3/4" w, Embossed Shell & Seaweed pattern, shaded purple to lavender, white interior, eight crimps, rough pontil, Consolidated Lamp & Glass Co., c1894 ....125.00

Stevens & Williams, 2-1/8" h, 2-3/4" w, jeweled

Cranberry red, threaded in "zipper" pattern, 12 tiny crimps, engraved registry number Rd 55693 on polished bottom 140.00

Sapphire blue, threaded with raindrop effect, 12 tiny crimps, engraved registry number Rd 81051 on polished pontil 160.00

Webb, 2-1/4" h, 2-1/2" w, blue satin with gold prunus blossom decoration, gold butterfly on back, 8 soft crimps, polished pontil 275.00

ROSE CANTON, ROSE MANDARIN AND ROSE MEDALLION

History: The pink rose color has given its name to three related groups of Chinese export porcelain: Rose Mandarin, Rose Medallion, and Rose Canton.

Rose Mandarin, produced from the late 18th century to approximately 1840, derives its name from the Mandarin figure(s) found in garden scenes with women and children. The women often have gold decorations in their hair. Polychrome enamels and birds separate the scenes.

Rose Medallion, which originated in the early 19th century and was made through the early 20th century, has alternating panels of figures and birds and flowers. The elements are four in number, separated evenly around the center medallion. Peonies and foliage fill voids.

Rose Canton, introduced somewhat later than Rose Mandarin and produced through the first half of the 19th century, is similar to Rose Medallion except the figural panels are replaced by flowers. People are present only if

the medallion partitions are absent. Some patterns have been named, e.g., Butterfly and Cabbage and Rooster. Rose Canton actually is a catchall term for any pink enamel ware not fitting into the first two groups.

Rose Canton

Brush Pot, 4-1/2" h, scenic, ladies, reticulated, gilt trim 275.00
Charger, 13" d, floral panels, 19th C 215.00
Platter, 16-1/2" l, 19th C, enamel and gilt wear 200.00
Puzzle Teapot, 6" h, Cadogan, painted birds and foliage, light blue ground, late 19th C, minor chips 150.00
Umbrella Jar, 24-1/4" h, 19th C, minor chips.....................805.00
Urn, cov, 19-1/4" h, minor chips, cracks, gilt wear, pr 2,990.00
Vase, 19th C

6" h, base chips on one, rim chips on other, pr............140.00

14" h, chips, minor cracks, pr......................................1,265.00

Rose Mandarin

Bowl, 9-1/2" d, scalloped edge 300.00
Charger, 16-1/4" d 440.00
Creamer, 3-5/8" h, three feet, plain handle.........................50.00
Cup and Saucer, scalloped edge rim, chips, price for pr....60.00
Cup on Stand, 4-1/4" d, 2-7/8" h, restoration 125.00
Dish, 11" d, kidney shape...440.00
Dish and Underplate, 11" l, oval, reticulated rims, chips ...715.00
Plate

6-1/2" d, mandarin scene 200.00

8-1/4" d, 4 pc set 110.00

8-3/8" d, 4 pc set 110.00

8-1/2" d, fluted rim, scalloped edge, colored-in flake, small hairline 50.00
Platter, 16-1/4" l, chip..250.00
Rice Bowl, 4-5/8" d, scalloped rim, 4 pc set......................110.00
Sauce Boat, 8-1/4" l, intertwined handle...........................110.00
Serving Dish, 9-7/8" d, 19th C, minor chips, enamel wear
....460.00
Soup Plate, 9-3/4" d, three with chips, 6 pc set....................55.00
Sugar Bowl, cov, 4-7/8" h, intertwined handles, fruit finial, minor enamel flaking 50.00

Rose Medallion creamer, helmet shape, hog snout, c1860, 3-1/2" h, 4" d, $250.

Teapot, cov, 8-1/2" h, domed lid 660.00
Tureen, 13-3/4" l, 11-1/4" h, gilded handles and final......1,100.00
Umbrella Stand, 24" h, wrapped bamboo form, 19th C, star
   cracks, gilt and enamel wear 1,495.00
Vase, 10" h, beaker, figural cartouche, chicken skin ground, Qian-
   long, c1775, price for pr 1,900.00
Vegetable Dish, cov, 11-1/2" d, almond shaped, fruit finial, minor
   flakes 200.00

Rose Medallion

Bowl, 9-3/4" d, scalloped edge, 19th C, minor chips, enamel wear
   ....690.00
Box, cov, 7-5/8" l, divided int., 19th C, very minor chips, enamel
   wear 460.00
Fruit Basket, 9-3/4" l, matching undertray, reticulated, 19th C, minor chips 750.00
Garden Seat, 19th C, gilt and enamel wear
   18-1/2" h..1,610.00
   18-3/4" h..1,725.00
Lamp, 13" h, oil, gilt metal fittings, minor imperfections 435.00
Plate, 19th C
   8" d, c, minor chips, gilt and enamel wear, 9 pc set 290.00
   9-1/2" d, chips, 10 pc set..460.00
   9-5/8" d, minor chips, gilt and enamel wear, 10 pc set
      ....460.00
Platter, oval, 19th C
   13-5/8" l, minor chips 410.00
   14-1/8" l, restoration, gilt and enamel wear 290.00
   18-3/8" l, glaze imperfections, gilt and enamel wear.....290.00
Punch Bowl, 19th C
   13-1/4" d 575.00
   15" d, base chips, late 19th C 920.00
   15-3/4" d, minor rim chips, gilt and enamel wear 1,035.00
Serving Dish, 13-5/8" d, circular, 19th C, gilt and enamel wear
   ....400.00
Shrimp Dish, 10-3/8" l, 19th C, minor chips, gilt and enamel wear,
   pr 490.00
Soup Plate, 9-5/8" d, 19th C, chips, cracks, gilt and enamel wear,
   10 pc set 520.00
Teapot, 9-1/4" h, 19th C, minor chips................................375.00
Tureen, 11" h, 14" l, 19th C, gilt and enamel wear, minute chips
   ....2,185.00
Vase
   12-1/4" h, double gourd, 19th C, gilt and enamel wear
      ....805.00
   13-1/2" h, 19th C
      Baluster, restoration and other imperfections, pr 920.00
      Ku-form, gilt and enamel wear 550.00
   37" h, floor type, scalloped rim 4,600.00
Wall Sconce, 8-1/4" h, brass gas fittings, electrified, minor chips
   and cracks, pr 980.00

ROSENTHAL

History: Rosenthal Porcelain Manufactory began operating at Selb, Bavaria, in 1880. Specialties were tablewares
and figurines. The firm is still in operation.

Reference: Dieter Struss, *Rosenthal,* Schiffer Publishing,
1997.

Box, cov, Studio Line, sgd "Peynet" 175.00
Cake Plate, 12" w, grape dec, scalloped ruffled edge, ruffled handles 75.00
Candlestick, 9-1/2" h, Art Deco woman holding candlestick
   ....275.00
Chocolate Set, San Souci pattern, 6 cups and saucers, cov pot,
   creamer and sugar, mkd "Selb Bavaria," c1880, 15 pc set
   ....425.00

**Hatpin Holder, poppies, white ground, gold band at neck, gold
top, 4-7/8" h, $90.**

Creamer and Sugar, pate-sur-pate type blue cherries dec
   ....115.00
Cup and Saucer, San Souci pattern, white 20.00
Demitasse Cup and Saucer, Marie pattern 25.00
Figure
   6" h, clown 225.00
   9" h, ram, mottled gray 200.00
   10-1/2" h, Fairy Queen, sgd "L. Friedrich-Granau"........325.00
   14" h, kneeling nude, sgd "Klimsch" 775.00
Plate
   8" d, Moss Rose pattern, 6 pc set 90.00
   10" d, girl and lamb dec, multicolored 40.00
Portrait Plate, 9-7/8" d, bust portrait of lady, pale yellow and white
   ground, faux green, turquoise, blue, and red hardstone jewels
   ....350.00
Vase
   7" h, modeled owls on branch 165.00
   7-1/4" h, violet cameo, Greek god, cream ground, gold bead
      trim, c1930, pr 140.00
   9-7/8" h, vertical ribs, banded top and base, polychrome floral
      bouquet in center, mkd "Rosenthal"..........................65.00
   11" h, hp, multicolored roses 125.00

ROSEVILLE POTTERY

History: In the late 1880s, a group of investors purchased the J. B. Owens Pottery in Roseville, Ohio, and
made utilitarian stoneware items. In 1892, the firm was in-

corporated and joined by George F. Young who became general manager. Four generations of Youngs controlled Roseville until the early 1950s.

A series of acquisitions began: Midland Pottery of Roseville in 1898, Clark Stoneware Plant in Zanesville (formerly used by Peters and Reed), and Muskingum Stoneware (Mosaic Tile Company) in Zanesville. In 1898, the offices also moved from Roseville to Zanesville.

In 1900, Roseville introduced Rozane, an art pottery. Rozane became a trade name to cover a large series of lines. The art lines were made in limited amounts after 1919.

The success of Roseville depended on its commercial lines, first developed by John J. Herald and Frederick Rhead in the first decades of the 1900s. In 1918, Frank Ferrell became art director and developed more than 80 lines of pottery. The economic depression of the 1930s brought more lines, including Pine Cone.

In the 1940s, a series of high-gloss glazes were tried in an attempt to revive certain lines. In 1952, Raymor dinnerware was produced. None of these changes brought economic success and in November 1954 Roseville was bought by the Mosaic Tile Company.

References: Susan and Al Bagdade, *Warman's American Pottery and Porcelain*, Wallace-Homestead, 1994; Virginia Hillway Buxton, *Roseville Pottery for Love or Money*, updated ed., Tymbre Hill Publishing Co. (P.O. Box 615, Jonesborough, TN 37659), 1996; John W. Humphries, *Price Guide to Roseville Pottery by the Numbers*, published by author, 1993; Sharon and Bob Huxford, *Collectors Encyclopedia of Roseville Pottery*, 1st Series (1976, 1997 value update), 2nd Series (1980, 1997 value update), Collector Books; --, *The Roseville Pottery Price Guide*, Collector Books, 1997; Ralph and Terry Kovel, *Kovels' American Art Pottery*, Crown Publishers, 1993; Randall B. Monsen, *Collectors' Compendium of Roseville Pottery*, Monsen and Baer (Box 529, Vienna, VA 22183), 1995, --, *Collectors' Compendium of Roseville Pottery, Volume II*, Monsen and Baer, 1997; David Rago, *American Art Pottery*, Knickerbocker Press, 1997.

Collectors' Clubs: American Art Pottery Assoc., 125 E. Rose Ave., St. Louis, MO 63119; Rosevilles of the Past, P.O. Box 656, Clarcona, FL 32710.

Additional Listings: See *Warman's Americana & Collectibles* for more examples.

Basket
  Bushberry, 12", blue 400.00
  Magnolia, tan, 384-8...150.00
  Ming Tree, green, 508-8..115.00
  Pine Cone, brown, 408-6...250.00
  White Rose, 8", green 195.00
  Wincraft, blue, 609-12..185.00
Beer Mug, Futura, trial glaze 695.00
Bookends, Bleeding heart, pink, one damaged, price for pr
  ....200.00
Bowl
  Dahlrose, 10" d, handle 185.00
  Earlam, large, tan and blue 275.00
  Mostique, 8" d, rim chip..75.00
  Pine Cone, small, green 105.00

Candleholders, pr, Donatello, early stamp mark, orig sticker, 6-1/4" h, $285.

  Rosecraft, 6-1/2" d, yellow 40.00
  Tourmaline, 6" d, turquoise...65.00
  Vintage, 5" d, brown 110.00
Candlesticks, pr
  Cremona, 1068-4, green..160.00
  Gardenia, 4-1/2" h, gray...115.00
  Magnolia, blue, 1157-4-1/2...150.00
Wincraft
  #251, brown..60.00
  #253, green, triple...250.00
Console Bowl
  Baneda, pink..500.00
  Columbine, #404-10...120.00
  Cremona, 178-8, green, with flower frog......................195.00
  Orian, #275, tan and blue...275.00
  Tuscany, 11" d, turquoise...160.00
Wincraft, 14" d, blue 110.00
Console Set, Cremona, bowl and pr candlesticks, green..250.00
Crocus Pot, Jonquil, 95-6.5...795.00
Cup, #124..210.00
Ewer, Bleeding Heart, 6" h, blue, glaze rub on tip 150.00
Flower Arranger, Tuscany, 5-1/2", gray..........................125.00
Hanging Basket
  Donatello..200.00
  White Rose, blue..295.00
Jardiniere
  Artcraft, 6", green...275.00
  Florentine
    6" h...225.00
    8" h...450.00
  Futura, pink and lavender flowers, gray ground
    6" h, 9" d...400.00
    8" h, 12" d, orig paper label......................................690.00
  Pine Cone, brown, 632-3..140.00
  Rozana, 7" d, cream, 1917...225.00
  Vista, 10-1/4" h, 12" d, green, purple, and gray............550.00
Jardiniere and Pedestal
  Artcraft, 8" d, blue and green, restored small chip on top of
    pedestal...1,995.00
  Dahlrose, 10"...1,325.00
  Freescia, green, #669-8, 24 h....................................1,295.00
  Fuchsia, #645-10, tan, professionally repaired hairline
    ....1,600.00
  Montique, blended 800.00
  Snowberry, 8" d, small nick on pedestal base.............700.00
Lamp
  Orange and green...625.00
  Orian, orange, orig fittings..375.00

Vase, Imperial II, spongeware mottled raspberry glaze, 7-1/2" h, $265.

Plate, Juvenile, rolled edge
    Ducks, 8" d 150.00
    Puppy, 7-1/4" d 115.00
    Rabbits, 8" d 115.00
Urn
    Camelian II, 5" h.......................................165.00
    Earlam, green 185.00
Vase
    Baneda, green, volcano 695.00
    Carnelian II, blue 225.00
    Clemena, 6" h, green 275.00
    Donatello, 8" h...150.00
    Faline, 6" h, blue 695.00
    Florentine, bud, double 175.00
    Foxglove, 15" h, floor type, blue 625.00
    Futura
        7" h, slight repair to bottom...................300.00
        8" h, #386-8, pink and gray, two small chips............450.00

Wall Pocket, Snowberry, blue ground, 5-1/4" h, $275. Photo courtesy of Garth's Auctions.

Imperial II, #478-8, 11" h, brown and tan drip, professionally
    repaired lip 225.00
Iris, 12-1/2" h, pink 425.00
Jonquil, 9" h 550.00
Laurel, #686-6, red 285.00
Magnolia
    14" h, brown, 97-14..................................310.00
    15 h, green, 98-15 ....420.00
Mayfair, #1004-9..95.00
Ming Tree, 8" h...100.00
Morning Glory, 14-1/2" h, 10" d, yellow and purple flowers,
    matte green leaf design.........................1,265.00
Moss, #774-6, tan, pillow shape......................325.00
Mostique, 6" h, stylized flowers, minute chip.............115.00
Pauleo, floor, 18" h, mottled black 1,500.00
Pine Cone, bud, orig label 325.00
Primrose, #769-9, pink 285.00
Rozana, 6" h, teal..85.00
Sunflower, 5" h 600.00
Thornapple, brown, 813-7 ....150.00
Touramaline, blue, 517-6................................150.00
Tuscany, 10" h, pink 250.00
Velmoss, #714-6, blue and brown...................225.00
Vista, 12"..600.00
Wincraft, #247-7, green 185.00
Wisteria, 7", blue 750.00
Wall Pocket
    Bushberry 350.00
    Cherry Blossom, brown 1,100.00
    Donatello, slight hairline near handle 255.00
    Florentine, large.......................................300.00
    Foxglove, blue 425.00
    Iris 575.00
    La Rose..345.00
    Nude, brown 675.00
    Snowberry, pink 200.00
Window Box
    Gardenia, gray, 689-12 ....150.00
    Wincraft, tan..195.00

ROYAL BAYREUTH

History: In 1794, the Royal Bayreuth factory was founded in Tettau, Bavaria. Royal Bayreuth introduced its figural patterns in 1885. Designs of animals, people, fruits, and vegetables decorated a wide array of tablewares and inexpensive souvenir items.

Tapestry wares, in rose and other patterns, were made in the late 19th century. The surface of the piece feels and looks like woven cloth. Tapestry ware was made by covering the porcelain with a piece of fabric tightly stretched over the surface, decorating the fabric, glazing the piece, and firing.

Royal Bayreuth still manufactures dinnerware. It has not maintained production of earlier wares, particularly the figural items. Since thorough records are unavailable, it is difficult to verify the chronology of production.

Marks: The Royal Bayreuth crest used to mark the wares varied in design and color.

References: Susan and Al Bagdade, *Warman's English & Continental Pottery & Porcelain*, 2nd ed., Wallace-

Homestead, 1991; Mary J. McCaslin, *Royal Bayreuth*, Antique Publications, 1994.

Collectors' Club: Royal Bayreuth Collectors Club, 926 Essex Circle, Kalamazoo, MI 49008; Royal Bayreuth International Collectors' Society, P.O. Box 325, Orrville, OH 44667.

Conch Shell
    Creamer, green, lobster handles 125.00
    Match Holder, hanging 225.00
    Mustard, orig spoon 85.00
    Sugar, cov, small flake 85.00
Corinthian
    Chamberstick, 4-1/2" h, enameled Grecian figures, black
        ground 60.00
    Creamer and Sugar, classical figures, black ground 85.00
    Pitcher, 12" h, red ground, pinched spout 225.00
    Vase, 8-1/2" h, conical, black, blue mark 225.00
Devil and Cards
    Ashtray 650.00
    Creamer, 3-3/4" h 195.00
    Mug, large 295.00
    Salt, master 325.00
Lobster
    Ashtray, claw 145.00
    Candy Dish 140.00
    Celery Tray, 12-1/2" l, figural, blue mark 245.00
    Pitcher, 7-3/4" h, figural, orange-red, green handle 175.00
    Salt and Pepper Shakers, pr 150.00
Miscellaneous
    Ashtray, elk 225.00
    Bowl, 6" d, multicolored tavern scene 100.00

Creamer
    Apple 195.00
    Bird of Paradise 225.00
    Bull, gray 225.00
    Cat, black and orange 200.00
    Clown, red 275.00
    Crow, brown bill 200.00
    Duck 200.00
    Eagle 300.00
    Frog, green 225.00
    Lamplighter, green 250.00
    Pear 295.00
    Robin 195.00
    Seal 695.00
    Water Buffalo, black and orange 225.00
Cup and Saucer, yellow and gold, purple and red flowers,
    green leaves, white ground, green mark 80.00
Hatpin Holder, courting couple, cutout base with gold dec,
    blue mark 400.00
Milk Pitcher
    Alligator 450.00
    Butterfly 1,200.00
    Owl 550.00
    Parakeet 495.00
Miniature, pitcher, portrait 95.00
    Plate, 6-1/4" d, musicians 65.00
    Ring Box, cov, pheasant scene, glossy finish 85.00
    Salt and Pepper Shakers, pr, Elk 165.00
    Toothpick Holder, Brittany Girl, 3 ftd, blue mark 150.00
    Vase, 3-1/2" h, peasant ladies and sheep scene, silver rim,
        3 handles, blue mark 60.00
    Wall Pocket, Strawberry 265.00
Nursery Rhyme
    Bell, Ring Around the Rosey, children dancing 295.00
    Planter, Jack and the Beanstalk, round, orig liner 225.00
Plate
    Little Bo Peep, blue mark 90.00
    Little Jack Horner 125.00
    Little Miss Muffet 100.00
Snow Babies
    Bowl, 6" d 325.00
    Creamer, gold trim 110.00
    Jewelry Box, cov 275.00
    Milk Pitcher, corset shape 185.00
    Tea Tile, 6" sq, blue mark 100.00
Sunbonnet Babies
    Cake Plate, 10-1/4" d, babies washing 400.00
    Cup and Saucer, babies fishing 225.00

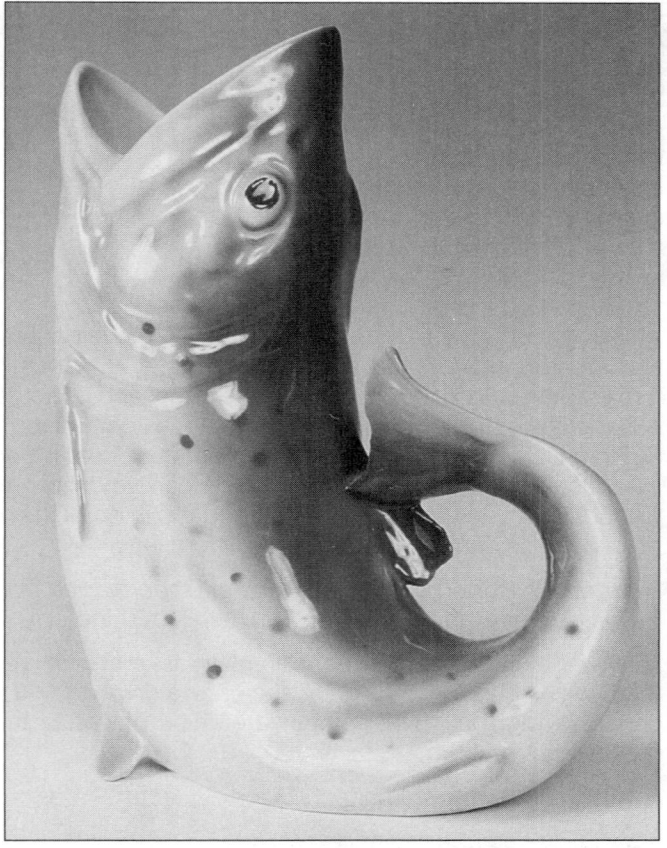

Milk Pitcher, figural, fish, blue mark, 7-1/2" h, $2,100. Photo courtesy of Jackson's Auctioneers & Appraisers.

Tray, Rose Tapestry, pink roses, blue and white background, blue mark, 8" x 11-1/4", $375.

Dish, 8" d, babies ironing, ruffled edge, blue mark.......175.00
Fruit Bowl, 9-3/4" d, babies washing and hanging wash
....95.00
Mustard Pot, cov, babies sweeping, blue mark............395.00
Plate, babies ironing...100.00
Tomato
  Celery Tray 95.00
  Creamer and Sugar, blue mark 190.00
  Milk Pitcher 165.00
  Mustard, cov...125.00
  Salt and Pepper Shakers, pr 85.00
Rose Tapestry
Bowl, 10-1/2" d, pink and yellow roses......................675.00
Cache Pot, 2-3/4" h, 3-12/4" d, ruffled top, gold handles ...200.00
Creamer and Sugar, 3 color roses, blue mark 395.00
Dresser Tray 395.00
Hairpin Box, pink and white..245.00
Nut Dish, 3-1/4" d, 1-3/4" h, 3 color roses, gold feet, green mark
....175.00
Pin Tray, 3 color roses 195.00
Plate, 6" d, 3 color roses, blue mark..............................150.00
Salt and Pepper Shakers, pr, pink roses..........................375.00
Tapestry, Miscellaneous
Bowl, 9-1/2" d, scenic, wheat, girl, and chickens............395.00
Box, 3-3/4" l, 2" w, courting couple, multicolored, blue mark
....245.00
Charger, 13" d, scenic, boy and donkeys.......................300.00
Dresser Tray, goose girl 495.00
Hatpin Holder , swimming swans and sunset, saucer base, blue
  mark..250.00
Match Holder, Arab scene 100.00
Tumbler, 4" h, barrel shape, gazebo, deer standing in stream,
  blue mark...200.00

ROYAL BONN

History: In 1836, Franz Anton Mehlem founded a
Rhineland factory that produced earthenware and
porcelain, including household, decorative, technical,
and sanitary items.

**Vase, bulbous, multicolored florals and wood scene, gold trim,
mkd "Bonn," 10-1/4" h, $795.**

The firm reproduced Hochst figures between 1887 and
1903. These figures, in both porcelain and earthenware,
were made from the original molds from the defunct
Prince-Electoral Mayence Manufactory in Hochst. The factory was purchased by Villeroy and Boch in 1921 and
closed in 1931.

Marks: In 1890, the word "Royal" was added to the mark.
All items made after 1890 include the "Royal Bonn" mark.

Cake Plate, 10-1/4" d, dark blue floral transfer....................35.00
Cheese Dish, cov, multicolored floral dec, cream ground, gold
  trim..90.00
Cup and Saucer, relief luster bands, mkd...........................40.00
Ewer, 10-1/8" h, red and pink flowers, raised gold, fancy handle
....75.00
Plate, 8-1/2" d, red and white roses, green leaves, earthtone
  ground, crazing, c1900 ....20.00
Portrait Vase, 8-1/4" h, central female portrait, floral landscape,
  printed mark, c1900 ....575.00
Tea Tile, 7" d, hp, pink, yellow, and purple pansies, white ground,
  green border, mkd "Bonn-Rhein" 35.00
Urn, cov, 13" h, hp, multicolored flowers, green, and yellow
  ground, 2 gold handles, artist sgd 120.00
Vase
  18-3/4" h, blue ground, gilt and enameled floral designs,
    scrolled handles, printed and imp marks, late 19th C
....400.00
  20" h, 5" d, hp multicolored floral spray with raised gold dec,
    link handles, ftd 240.00

ROYAL COPENHAGEN

History: Franz Mueller established a porcelain factory at Copenhagen in 1775.
When bankruptcy threat-
ened in 1779, the Danish
king acquired ownership,
appointing Mueller manag-
er and selecting the name
"Royal Copenhagen." The
crown sold its interest in
1867; the company remains privately owned today.

Blue Fluted, Royal Copenhagen's most famous pattern,
was created in 1780. It is of Chinese origin and comes in
three styles: smooth edge, closed lace edge, and perforated lace edge (full lace). Many other factories copied it.

Flora Danica, named for a famous botanical work, was
introduced in 1789 and remained exclusive to Royal
Copenhagen. It is identified by its freehand illustrations of
plants and its hand-cut edges and perforations.

Reference: Robert J. Heritage, *Royal Copenhagen Porcelain: Animals and Figurines,* Schiffer Publishing, 1997.

Marks: Royal Copenhagen porcelain is marked with
three wavy lines (which signify ancient waterways) and a
crown (added in 1889). Stoneware does not have the
crown mark.

Additional Listings: Limited Edition Collector Plates.

Bowl, reticulated blue and white
  Round 125.00
  Shell shaped..150.00

Vase, 7" h, sage green and gray crackled glaze 150.00
Vegetable Bowl, #1622, sq 110.00

ROYAL CROWN DERBY

History: Derby Crown Porcelain Co., established in 1875 in Derby, England, had no connection with earlier Derby factories which operated in the late 18th and early 19th centuries. In 189, the company was appointed "Manufacturers of Porcelain to Her Majesty" (Queen Victoria) and since that date has been known as "Royal Crown Derby."

Most of these porcelains, both tableware and figural, were hand decorated. A variety of printing processes were used for additional adornment. Today, Royal Crown Derby is a part of Royal Doulton Tableware, Ltd.

Marks: Derby porcelains from 1878 to 1890 carry only the standard crown printed mark. After 1891, the mark includes the "Royal Crown Derby" wording. In the 20th century, "Made in England" and "English Bone China" were added to the mark.

References: Susan and Al Bagdade, *Warman's English & Continental Pottery & Porcelain*, 2nd ed., Wallace-Homestead, 1991; John Twitchett, *Dictionary of Derby*

Figure, Chimney Sweep and Lady, #1276, 9-3/4" h, $795.

Butter Pat, Symphony pattern, 6 pc set 35.00
Candlesticks, pr, 9" h, blue floral design, white ground, bisque lion heads, floral garlands 160.00
Cream Soup, #1812 .... 75.00
Cup and Saucer, #1870 .... 75.00
Dish, reticulated blue and white 175.00
Figure
    4" h, young girl, traditional dress, holding garland, No. 12418
    .... 250.00
    4-1/2" x 4-1/2, wire haired fox terrier, #3165 .... 150.00
    5-3/4" h, young, native dress, kneeling and holding floral garland, No. 21413, No. 12414, pr 550.00
    6-3/4" h, girl knitting, No. 1314 .... 350.00
    9" h, mermaid on rock, cream, gray base, No. 44318 ..... 50.00
Fish Plate, 10" d, different fish swimming among marine plants, molded and gilt border, light green highlights, gilt dentil edge, crown circular mark, 10 pc set 8,250.00
Inkwell, Blue Fluted pattern, matching tray 150.00
Pickle Tray, 9" l, Half Lace pattern, blue triple wave mark ... 70.00
Plate, 8" d, #1624 .... 50.00
Platter, 14-1/2" l, #1556 .... 140.00
Salad Bowl, 9-7/8" d, Flora Danica, botanical specimen, molded gilt border, dentil edge, pink highlights, blue triple wave and green crown mark 825.00
Soup Tureen, cov, stand, 14-1/2" l, Flora Danica, oval, enamel painted botanical specimens, twin handles, finial, factory marks, botanical identification, modern 5,750.00
Tray, 10" l, Blue Fluted pattern 65.00
Underplate for Cream Soup, #1626 .... 75.00

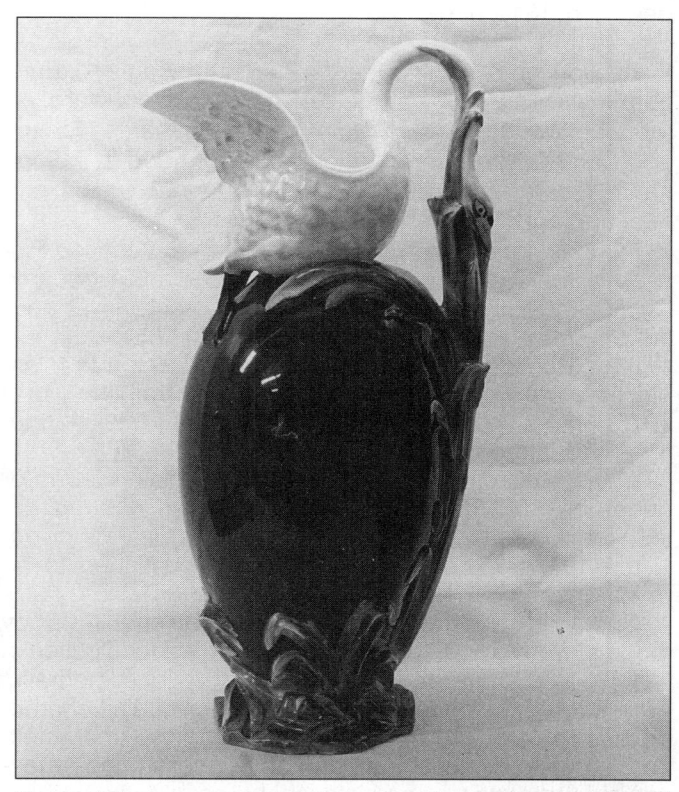

Ewer, white swan, long neck forms handle, maroon egg-shaped body, green foliage on base and handle, mkd "Made for Tiffany & Co.," crown mark, c1878-90, 11-1/2" h, $325.

Porcelain 1748-1848, Antique Collectors' Club; John Twitchett and Betty Bailey, *Royal Crown Derby*, Antique Collectors' Club, 1988.

Cup and Saucer, 5" d saucer, Imari pattern, 20th C 65.00
Dish, 9" d, scattered rose sprays, floral border, late 19th C 160.00
Ewer
  7-1/2" h, cobalt blue, profuse gold gilt and floral dec, sgd 200.00
  12-1/2" h, mottled blue ground, raised gilt and iron-red dec bird and foliate design, pierced handle, shape #409, printed mark, c1888..........690.00
Jug, Imari palette, pink round, gold trim, c1885, pr...........750.00
Plate, 8-1/2" d, Imari palette, shaped rim, printed and imp marks, c1923, 12 pc set 375.00
Potpourri, 6" h, urn form, mounted masks, allover floral and gilt dec, pierced top with finial 85.00
Sauce Dish, Imari pattern, iron-red, cobalt blue and burnished gold, matching stand....................1,200.00
Serving Dish, 11-3/8" l, Japan pattern, Imari palette, painted marks,c1865, slight staining to crazed glaze, gilt rim wear, pr 320.00
Tea Set, Imari pattern, oval 9-1/4" h teapot, 3-1/4" creamer, 6" l cov sugar, c1883, rim repairs, gilt wear 260.00
Urn, 11-1/2" h, cobalt blue, red, and gold floral pattern, painted red crown mark....................400.00
Vase, 7-3/4" h, mottled blue ground, iron-red enhanced gilt bird and foliate design, 1889, gilt wear 575.00

ROYAL DOULTON

ROYAL DOULTON FLAMBE

History: Doulton pottery began in 1815 under the direction of John Doulton at the Doulton & Watts pottery in Lambeth, England. Early output was limited to salt-glazed industrial stoneware. After John Watts retired in 1854, the firm became Doulton and Company, and production was expanded to include hand-decorated stoneware such as figurines, vases, dinnerware, and flasks.

In 1878, John's son, Sir Henry Doulton, purchased Pinder Bourne & Co. in Burslem. The companies became Doulton & Co., Ltd. in 1882. Decorated porcelain was added to Doulton's earthenware production in 1884.

Most Doulton figurines were produced at the Burslem plants where they were made continuously from 1890 until 1978. After a short interruption, a new line of Doulton figurines was introduced in 1979.

Dickens ware, in earthenware and porcelain, was introduced in 1908. The pieces were decorated with characters from Dickens's novels. Most of the line was withdrawn in the 1940s, except for plates, which continued to be made until 1974.

Character jugs, a 20th-century revival of early Toby models, were designed by Charles J. Noke for Doulton in the 1930s. Character jugs are limited to bust portraits, while Royal Doulton toby jugs are full figured. The character jugs come in four sizes and feature fictional characters from Dickens, Shakespeare and other English and American novelists, as well as historical heroes. Marks on both character and toby jugs must be carefully identified to determine dates and values.

Doulton's Rouge Flambé (Veined Sung) is a high-glazed, strong-colored ware noted primarily for the fine modeling and exquisite colorings, especially in the animal items. The process used to produce the vibrant colors is a Doulton secret.

Production of stoneware at Lambeth ceased in 1956; production of porcelain continues today at Burslem.

Marks: Beginning in 1872, the "Royal Doulton" mark was used on all types of wares produced by the company.

Beginning in 1913, an "HN" number was assigned to each new Doulton figurine design. The "HN" numbers, which referred originally to Harry Nixon, a Doulton artist, were chronological until 1940, after which blocks of numbers were assigned to each modeler. From 1928 until 1954, a small number was placed to the right of the crown mark; this number added to 1927 gives the year of manufacture.

References: Susan and Al Bagdade, *Warman's English & Continental Pottery & Porcelain*, 2nd ed., Wallace-Homestead, 1991; Diana and John Callow and Marilyn and Peter Sweet, *Charlton Price Guide to Beswick Animals*, 2nd ed., Charlton Press, 1995; Jean Dale, *Charlton Standard Catalogue of Royal Doulton Animals*, 2nd ed., Charlton Press, 1997; ——, *Charlton Standard Catalogue of Royal Doulton Beswick Jugs*, 4th ed., Charlton Press, 1997; ——, *Charlton Standard Catalogue of Royal Doulton Beswick Storybook Figurines*, Charlton Press, 1994; ——, *Charlton Standard Catalogue of Royal Doulton Figurines*, 4th ed., Charlton Press, 1994; ——, *Charlton Standard Catalogue of Royal Doulton Jugs*, Charlton Press, 1991; Doug Pinchin, *Doulton Figure Collectors Handbook*, 4th ed., Francis-Joseph Books, 1996, distributed by Wallace-Homestead.

Periodicals: *Collecting Doulton*, BBR Publishing, 2 Strattford Ave., Elsecar, Nr Barnsley, S. Yorkshire, S74 8AA, England; *Doulton Divvy*, P.O. Box 2434, Joliet, IL 60434.

Collectors' Clubs: Heartland Doulton Collectors, P.O. Box 2434, Joliet, IL 60434; Mid-America Doulton Collectors, P.O. Box 483, McHenry, IL 60050; Royal Doulton International Collectors Club, P.O. Box 6705, Somerset, NJ 08873; Royal Doulton International Collectors Club, 850 Progress Ave., Scarborough Ontario M1H 3C4 Canada.

Animal
  Alsatian, HN117 ....175.00
  Bonzo Dog, model 883, blue glaze, brown and black detailing
    1-1/2" h, marked "Doulton," cracked 1,344.00
    2" h 1,312.00
  Bull Terrier, K14 ....325.00
  Cocker Spaniel, HN1187 ....160.00
  Dalmatian, HN114 ....250.00
  English Bulldog, HN1074 ....175.00
  English Setter, HN1050 ....150.00
  French Poodle, HN2631 ....150.00
  Greyhound, HN1067...4,325.00
  Irish Setter, HN1055 ....150.00
  Salmon, 12" h, flambé, printed mark 435.00
  Scottish terrier, K18 ....125.00
  Tiger, 14" l, flambé, printed mark 375.00
  Winnie the Pooh Set: Pooh, Kanga, Piglet, Eeyore, Owl, Rabbit, and Tigger, Beswick, boxed set...................650.00

Bowl, 7-3/8" d, stoneware, incised and glazed enamel florals, titled "H. Gibbs 20th Jan 1939," artist sgd, modeled by Vera Huggis, imp marks 175.00
Character jug, large
  Cardinal 150.00
  Poacher, D6781 .... 350.00
  Veteran Motorist 125.00
Character Jug, miniature
  Blacksmith 50.00
  Pickwick 65.00
Character Jug, small
  Pearly King 35.00
  Pirate, no beard, 1967 .... 960.00
  Toby Philpots 85.00
Charger, 12-5/8" d, hp, allover incised leaf, berry, and vine border, central fruits and leaves, attributed to Frank Bragwyn, printed mark, c1930 .... 245.00
Child's Feeding Dish, Bunnykins in country store 135.00
Clock Case, King's are, night watchman, c1905 .... 450.00
Cuspidor, 7" h, Isaac Walton ware, polychrome dec, transfer printed, fisherman on ext., verses on int. lip, printed mark 325.00
Dinnerware
  Covington pattern, cov teapot, 8 bread and butter plates, 8 dessert plates, 6 cups and saucers, 29 pcs 225.00
  English Renaissance pattern, service for 12 .... 450.00
Figure
  Ballet Dancers, 7" h, pink and mauve dec, prototype group attributed to P Davies, c1950, crown and lion mark 2,560.00
  Carolyn, HN 2112, 71/4" h, 3-1/2" d 335.00
  Curly Locks, HN2049 .... 390.00
  Fair Lady, coral pink, HN2835 .... 225.00
  Girl Saying Grace, green floral gown and hairnet, HN 62, 1916-38 .... 4,480.00
  Grace, HN2318 .... 200.00
  Jester, brown and black, black cap, 1929, two bells missing from cap, ... 3,840.00
  Lady Charmain, HN1949 .... 225.00
  King Charles I, dark brown gloves, black flora at boots, imp date 1919 .... 1,312.00
  Marie, HN1370 .... 68.00
  Michelle, HN2234 .... 225.00
  Nicola, HN2839 .... 350.00
  Orange Lady, HN1758 .... 245.00
  Queen Mother's 80th Birthday, HN464, 1980 .... 720.00
  Priscilla, pantaloons showing beneath crinoline, HN1380, 1920-40 .... 288.00
  Rosina, seated, red and blue, HN1364, 1928-38 .... 800.00
  Sandra, HN2275 .... 200.00
  Sweet Sixteen, HN2734 .... 250.00
  The Foaming quart, HM2162 .... 250.00
  The Leisure Hour, HN2055 .... 400.00
  Top of the Hill, HN1833 .... 225.00
  Victorian Lady, HN1208, 1926-38 .... 355.00
  Yardley's Old English Lavender seller, c1925 .... 400.00
Fish Plate, 9" d, swimming fish centers, pale yellow ground, gold bands and rims, sgd "J. Hallmark," 10 pc set 700.00
Flask
  6-1/2" h, triangular, printed, Sydney Harbour, Dewars on reverse, c1914 .... 575.00
  7-1/2" h, King's Ware, Admiral Lord Nelson, Dewars on reverse, c1914 .... 550.00
Humidor, cov, 6" h, Chang Ware, squatty, molded ribs, brilliant shades of red, blue, yellow, and white, thick crackle finish, sgd in overglaze "Chang/Royal/Doulton" and "Noke" with monogram, c1925 .... 1,975.00
Jar, cov, 2-3/4" h, 3-1/4" d, Noke Flambé, crimson-red glass, fully stamped 325.00
Jug, 10-1/2" h, Regency Coach, limited edition, printed marks, 20th C 930.00

Loving Cup
  9-3/4" h, Three Musketeers, limited edition, sgd "Noke, H. Fenton," orig certificate, 20th C 920.00
  10-1/4" d, King George V and Queen Mary, 25 year reign anniversary, c1935 .... 750.00
Mug
  4" h, gladiator, #D6553 .... 300.00
  6-1/2" h, cardinal, A mark 100.00
  8-1/4" h, St. John Falstaff 95.00
Pitcher
  8-3/4" h, flow blue transfer, foliate ground, horseshoe framed panels of deer in landscape setting, printed mark, c1895 .... 245.00
  12-1/2" h, Coaching Days series, continuous scene, dark green rim 265.00
Plate, 10-1/2" d, Gibson Girl, black transfer, each with different titled scene from orig Charles D. Gibson drawings, reserve center, transfer printed cobalt blue stylized foliage border, printed lion and crown mark, c1901, 24 pc set 1,500.00
Spirits Barrel, 7" l, King's Ware, double, silver trim rings and cov, oak stand, c1909 .... 1,200.00
Tankard, 9-1/2" h, hinged pewter lid, incised frieze of herons among reeds, blue slip enamel, imp mark, sgd, c1875 .... 1,600.00
Teacup and Saucer, cobalt blue, heavy gold dec 120.00

Figure, French Peasant, #2075, 9-1/4" h, $425.

Gibson Girl Plate, "Some think that she has remained in retirement too long, others are surprised that she is about so soon," copyright 1900, by Life Publishing Co, $125.

Tobacco Jar, 8" h, incised frieze of cattle, goats, and donkeys, imp mark, sgd, worn SP rim, handle and cover, dated 1880 ....995.00

Toby Jug
    Beefeater, #D6206, 6" h...85.00
    Winston Churchill, #8360.......................................95.00

Umbrella Stand, 23-1/2" h, stoneware, enamel dec, applied floral medallions within diamond formed panels, framed by button motifs, imp mark, glaze crazing, c1910 ....550.00

Vase
    6-3/4" h, Flambé, mottled red and yellow glazes, sgd "Harry Nixon," printed marks, c1930 ....325.00
    7" h, 4-1/4" d, ovoid, Flambé, desert landscape silhouetted against crimson red ground, shallow scratch, stamped "Royal Doulton/Flambé/Made in England" 225.00
    9" h, Luscian Ware, hp, titled "Girlhood," sgd "Leslie Johnson," imp and printed marks, slight rim wear, cover missing 395.00
    10-1/2" h, baluster, stoneware, stylized leaf borders, cartouche with Dartmoor ponies, pr 675.00
    11-1/4" h, Sung Ware Flambé, mottled red and blue glazes, sgd "Noke" and "F. Allen," printed mark 420.00
    11-3/4" h, cov, baluster, Athenic pattern, red glaze, acorn and leaf dec, silver mounted neck, sweeping scroll handle, foliate thumb piece, hinged lid,, ftd. Gorham Mfg. Co., Providence, c1905..1,450.00
    16-3/4" h, Hannah Barlow, central incised frieze of cows gracing, glazed stylized floral and foliate borders, sgd and imp marks, glaze flake to int. edge 635.00
    24-1/2" h, 12" d, natural process dec, imp amber leaves and branches, blue-gray ground, spider-web hairline to base, diestamped mark..250.00

ROYAL DUX

History: Royal Dux porcelain was made in Dux, Bohemia (now the Czech Republic), by E. Eichler at the Duxer Porzellan-Manufaktur, established in 1860. Many items were exported to the United States. By the turn of the century, Royal Dux figurines, vases, and accessories, especially those featuring Art Nouveau designs, were captivating consumers.

Marks: A raised triangle with an acorn and the letter "E" plus "Dux, Bohemia" was used as a mark between 1900 and 1914.

Bowl, 17-1/2" l, modeled as female tending a fishing net, oval shell-form bowl, imp mark, early 20th C 490.00

Bust, 14" h, female portrait, raised leaves and berries on base, Czechoslovakia, early 20th C, unmarked, chips 290.00

Compote, figural
    14-1/2" l, modeled as female atop shell-form bowl, another figure within the wave modeled freeform base, imp mark, early 20th C..750.00
    20-1/4" h, leaf and floral molded bowl mounted to central freeform support, surrounded by three females, imp and printed marks, 20th C 635.00

Figure
    4" x 8", fox, Eichler, post-war, glossy glaze 180.00
    8-1/2" h, dressed in classic Greek style, pre-war "E" mark 335.00
    9" x 8", dog sled team, 3 tethered dogs, pre-war "E" mark 1,295.00
    10" x 13", elephant, trunk up..170.00
    14" l, retriever with duck in jaws, matte finish 400.00
    14" x 8-1/2" x 15-1/2", lady, sedan chair, 2 courtiers, hound 800.00
    14-1/4" h, female with harp, incised scroll banding to raised base, imp mark, early 20th C 175.00
    21" h, peasant couple, "E" mark, pr 1,495.00
    24" h, man and woman at water fountain, price for pr, some base chips 550.00

Bust, female with floral headdress, brown and gold highlights, dress with pink trim, pink triangle mark, #448, 9" h, $415.

Tazza, 19-1/2" h, figural, putti and classically draped woman supporting shell, price for pr, one with hairline in base 880.00
Vase
    11" h, Grecian, "E" mark 595.00
    19-1/4" h, bisque, Art Nouveau style female to one side of leaf and floral molded body, imp mark, early 20th C 290.00

ROYAL FLEMISH

History: Royal Flemish was produced by the Mount Washington Glass Co., New Bedford, Massachusetts. The process was patented by Albert Steffin in 1894.

Royal Flemish is a frosted transparent glass with heavy raised gold enamel lines. These lines form sections–often colored in russet tones–giving the appearance of stained glass windows with elaborate floral or coin medallions.

Collectors' Club: Mount Washington Art Glass Society, 60 President Ave., Providence, RI 02906.

Advisors: Clarence and Betty Maier.

Biscuit Jar, cov, 8" h, ovoid, large Roman coins on stained panels, divided by heavy gold lines, ornate SP cov, rim, and bail handle, orig paper label "Mt. W. G. Co. Royal Flemish" .. 1,750.00
Box, cov, 5-1/2" d, 3-3/4" h, swirled border, gold outlined swirls, gold tracery blossoms, enameled blossom with jeweled center on lid
    .... 1,500.00
Ewer, 10-1/2" h, 9" w, 5" d, circular semi-transparent panel on front with youth thrusting spear into chest of winged creature, reverse panel shows mythical fish created with tail changed into stylized florals, raised gold dec, outlines, and scrolls, rust, purple, and gold curlicues, twisted rope handle with brushed gold encircles neck, hp minute gold florals on neck, burnished gold stripes on rim spout and panels 4,950.00
Jar, 8" h, classical Roman coin medallion dec, simulated stained glass panels, SP rim, bail, and cov, paper label "Mt. W. G. Co. Royal Flemish" 1,650.00

Vase, tapered, bulbous, short flaring neck, pansy dec, gold trim, 6" h, $2,400.

Vase
    6" h, double bulbed, frosted, colorful pansies, allover gold enam-eling..1,210.00
    7-1/2" h, 7-1/2" d, squatty, smaller squatty form as collar, 14 pastel pansies, clear frosted ground, 4 rayed suns, painted foliage-like gold tracery 1,400.00

ROYAL RUDOLSTADT

History: Johann Fredrich von Schwarzburg-Rudolstadt was the patron of a faience factory located in Rudolstadt, Thuringen, Germany, from 1720 to c1790.

In 1854, Ernst Bohne established a factory in Rudolstadt.

The "Royal Rudolstadt" designation originated with wares which Lewis Straus and Sons (later Nathan Straus and Sons) of New York imported from the New York and Rudolstadt Pottery between 1887 and 1918. The factory manufactured several of the Rose O'Neill (Kewpie) items.

Marks: The first mark of the original pottery was a hayfork; later, crossed two-prong hayforks were used in imitation of the Meissen mark.

"EB" was the mark used by Ernst Bohne

A crown over a diamond enclosing the initials "RW" is the mark used by the New York and Rudolstadt Pottery.

Bottle, cov, 9-1/4" h, gourd shape, entrusted flowers, Ernest Bohne Sohne, late 19th/early 20th C, chips, pr.............325.00
Bust, 15" h, classical figure, glazed to simulate marble.....165.00
Cake Plate, 12" d, pink, white roses, gold handles and trim
    .... 75.00

Plate, foliage and scroll motif, gold trim, white background, mkd "Germany//RW//Rudolstadt," 8-7/8"d, $45.

Ewer, 10" h, ivory, floral dec, gold handle and trim............125.00
Figure, 8-1/4", muse Euterpe, wearing classical, garb, flowers in hair, lute at her feet, holding scroll of poetry and flute 225.00
Hatpin Holder lavender and roses 45.00
Nut Set, master bowl, 6 small bowls, white and green roses, fluted, ftd, "B" under crown mark 265.00
Plate, 8-1/2" d, pink, white, and yellow roses, gold molded piecrust rim 35.00
Teapot, cov, 5-1/2" h, hp, ivory, pink, lavender, and green floral dec..95.00
Urn, 10" h, mythological scene, Hector and Andro crowning maiden, cobalt blue ground, gold handles, artist sgd, stand145.00
Vase, 4" h, floral dec, elephant handles 90.00

ROYAL VIENNA

1749-1864

History: Production of hard-paste porcelain in Vienna began in 1720 with Claude Innocentius du Paquier, a runaway employee from the Meissen factory. In 1744, Empress Maria Theresa brought the factory under royal patronage; subsequently the ware became known as Royal Vienna. The firm went through many administrative changes until it closed in 1864. The quality of its workmanship always was maintained.

Marks: Several other Austrian and German firms copied the Royal Vienna products, including the use of the "Beehive" mark. Many of the pieces on today's market are from these firms.

Cabinet Vase
3-1/2" h, children of four seasons, blue beehive mark ..350.00
7" h, oval reserve of Lemiramis, irid red and black ground, gold encrusted, Eolzner, late 19th C 775.00
Chocolate Pot, cov, 10" h, large reserve with artist dec a vase, woman looking on, cream ground, gilt handles and trim, Knoeller 350.00

Charger, painted scene inscribed "Schmuckung Der Venus," (Toilet of Venus,) gold border, artist sgd "Gorner," underglaze blue beehive mark, 16-1/2" d, $2,750. Photo courtesy of Jackson's Auctioneers & Appraisers.

Cup and Saucer, frieze figures and horses dec, cobalt blue border 145.00
Ferner, 7-3/4" w, 4" h, portrait of lady one side, portrait of different lady on other, burgundy, green, and gold, beaded, scalloped edges, ftd, mkd "Royal Vienna, Austria," artist sgd 425.00
Portrait Vase
8" h, Art Nouveau young lady surrounded by rococo swirls and emb flowers, pale yellow, brown, and purple ground, two handles 200.00
10-1/4" h, maiden, green ground, gilt handles and trim, cov, c1900...375.00
Stein, quarter liter, hp, copy of early Meissen Chinese scene, elaborate battle surmounted by gold border, 4 flowers painted in rear, similar scene of harbor of top of lid, floral design painted on underside of lid, eagle thumb lift, beehive mark 2,310.00
Urn, cov
11-1/2" h, hp, elaborate scene of man, women, and cherub, cobalt blue ground, gold trim, beehive mark 1,200.00
30" h, gilt intertwined serpent handles, gilt scroll dec and band, classical figures on cobalt blue ground, sq plinth painted with figural reserves on two sides, repaired, c1900 ....4,000.00

ROYAL WORCESTER

c1876-1891   1891

History: In 1751, the Worcester Porcelain Company, led by Dr. John Wall and William Davis, acquired the Bristol pottery of Benjamin Lund and moved it to Worcester. The first wares were painted blue under the glaze; soon thereafter, decorating was accomplished by painting on the glaze in enamel colors. Among the most-famous 18th-century decorators were James Giles and Jefferys Hamet O'Neale. Transfer-print decoration was developed by the 1760s.

A series of partnerships took place after Davis's death in 1783: Flight (1783-1793); Flight & Barr (1793-1807); Barr, Flight & Barr (1807-1813); and Flight, Barr & Barr (1813-1840). In 1840, the factory was moved to Chamberlain & Co. in Diglis. Decorative wares were discontinued. In 1852, W. H. Kerr and R. W. Binns formed a new company and revived the production of ornamental wares.

In 1862, the firm became the Royal Worcester Porcelain Co. Among the key modelers of the late 19th century were James Hadley, his three sons, and George Owen, an expert with pierced clay pieces. Royal Worcester absorbed the Grainger factory in 1889 and the James Hadley factory in 1905. Modern designers include Dorothy Doughty and Doris Lindner.

References: Susan and Al Bagdade, *Warman's English & Continental Pottery & Porcelain*, 2nd ed., Wallace-Homestead, 1991; Anthony Cast and John Edwards, *Charlton Price Guide to Royal Worcester Figurines*, Charlton Press, 1997; David, John, and Henry Sandon, *Sandon Guide to Royal Worcester Figures*, Alderman Press, 1987; Henry Sandon, *Flight & Barr Worcester*, Antique Collectors' Club, 1992; Henry Sandon and John Sandon, *Dictionary of Worcester Porcelain*, Vol. II, Antique Collectors' Club, 1995; ——, *Grainger's Worcester Porcelain*,

Barrie & Jenkins, 1990; John Sandon, *The Dictionary of Worcester Porcelain*, Vol. I, Antique Collectors' Club, 1993.

Museum: Charles William Dyson Perrins Museum, Worcester, England.

Basket, 8-1/2" d, flaring pierced sides mounted with floral heads, pine cone and floral cluster int., blue and white transfer dec, first period, mid 18th C 550.00

Biscuit Jar, cov, 7-1/4" h, fluted body, raised spear head borders surrounding enamel floral design................................550.00

Bowl, 10" d, scalloped border, shell molded boy, fruit and floral spray, blue and white transfer dec, first period, mid-18th C 320.00

Butter Tub, cov, 4-1/4" d, 3-1/4" h, cylindrical, fully sculpted finial, painted floral sprays below geometric borders, first period, c1765..450.00

Centerpiece, 6-1/4" h, oval, ftd, Royal Lily pattern, first period, c1800, repaired 125.00

Dish, 8" l, leaf form, molded body, underglaze blue floral sprays, branch handle, first period, c1765 ....500.00

Ewer
   12-1/2" h, gilt and enamel floral dec, late 19th C 210.00
   15-3/4" h, scrolled foliate handle, raised gilt and red enamel leaf and floral designs, light gilt wear, 1896..........1,495.00

Figure
   5-1/4" h, politician, white glaze, late 19th C, staining, hat rim chip restored 290.00
   6-1/2" h, Welsh girl, shot enamel porcelain, sgd "Hadley," late 19th C 690.00
   7-3/4" h and 8-1/4" h, lady and gentleman, George III costumes, sgd "Hadley," pr 1,100.00
   8-3/4" h, Cairo water carrier, 1895...............................635.00

Fish Plates, 9-1/4" d, bone china, hp fish, gilt lattice and foliage border, sgd "Harry Ayrton," printed marks, c1930, 13 pc set 2,300.00

Fruit Cooler, 6-1/4" h, cylindrical, Royal Lily pattern, stylized floral reserve, stepped circular foot, first period, c1800 ....225.00

Mustard Pot, 4" h, cylindrical, blue and white transfer, floral clusters, floral finial, first period, mid-18th C.......................325.00

Plate
   7" w, octagonal, landscape fan form reserves, cobalt blue ground, first period, 18th C, pr 350.00
   7-3/4" d, Blind Earl pattern, raised rose spray, polychrome floral sprays, scalloped border, first period, mid-18th C 1,100.00
   8" d, diaper pattern border surrounding floral spray, blue and white transfer dec, first period, mid-19th C 220.00
   10-3/4" d, Tewkesbury, natural colors, gold edge, artist sgd " Nickolis," 1953 mark...190.00

Sauce Boat, 41/4" h, geometric band above foliate molded body, painted floral sprays, oval foot, first period, c1765, pr 275.00

Sweetmeat, 6" l, leaf form, blue and white transfer chinoisiere landscapes, first period, mid-18th C 325.00

Tankard, 6" h, cylindrical, blue and white transfer dec of parrot among fruit, first period, mid-18th C...........................325.00

Teabowl and Saucer, painted chinoisiere vignette, blue border, first period, c1865...185.00

Teapot, cov, 6-1/2" h, globular form body, fully sculpted blossom finial, domed top, painted floral sprays, first period, c1765 ....375.00

Urn, cov, 11-1/2" h, pierced dome top, globular body, painted floral sprays, basketweave molded base, early 20th C 195.00

Vase
   3-1/4" h, reticulated, gilt trimmed oval panels with floral dec, c1891 ....115.00
   8-1/2" h, nautilus shell, staining 230.00
   12-1/4" h, two handles, gilt and enameled leaf, berry, and spider dec 600.00
   15-3/4" h, gilt dragon-form handles, enameled floral sprays, gilt rim wear, 1888 ....750.00

ROYCROFT

History: Elbert Hubbard founded the Roycrofters in East Aurora, New York, at the turn of the century. Considered a genius in his day, he was an author, lecturer, manufacturer, salesman, and philosopher.

Hubbard established a campus, which included a printing plant where he published The Philistine, *The Fra*, and *The Roycrofter*. His most-famous book was *A Message to Garcia*, published in 1899. His "community" also included a furniture manufacturing plant, a metal shop, and a leather shop.

References: Kevin McConnell, *Roycroft Art Metal*, 2nd ed., Schiffer Publishing, 1994; The Roycrofters, *Roycroft Furniture Catalog, 1906*, Dover, 1994; Paul Royka, *Mission Furniture ,from the American Arts & Crafts Movement,* Schiffer Publishing, 1997; Marie Via and Marjorie B. Searl, *Head, Heart and Hand*, University of Rochester Press (34 Administration Bldg, University of Rochester, Rochester, NY 14627), 1994.

Collectors' Clubs: Foundation for the Study of Arts & Crafts Movement, Roycroft Campus, 31 S. Grove St., East Aurora, NY 14052; Roycrofters-at-Large Assoc., P.O. Box 417, East Aurora, NY 14052.

Basket, caneweave base, twisted reed handle, tan, gold highlights, purple mark, reg. #26402/1080, c1891, 5-3/4" h, $495.

Museum: Elbert Hubbard Library-Museum, East Aurora, NY.

Additional Listings: Arts and Crafts Movement; Copper.

Andirons, pr, 13-1/4" w, 27-1/2" h, No. 69, Secessionist-style, twists and curlicues, orig black finish, joined by round-link chain, unmarked 2,400.00
Bookends, pr
    5-1/2" w, 3-1/4" h, line work at edges, ornamental crimping, orig patina, early mark 245.00
    6-1/2" w, 4-1/4" h, open style, applied strap, riveted construction, middle mark 215.00
Bookstand, rect overhanging top, 2 lower shelves, key on tenons, vertical side slats, ftd base, metal tag, top separation, finish wear, 26-1/4" w, 14" d, 26-1/4" h 500.00
Bowl, 10-1/4" d, 4-1/8" h, hammered copper, rolled rim, shouldered bowl, 3 point feet, red patina, imp mark, traces of brass wash 450.00
Candle Lamp, blue art glass, baluster form, flaring foot, stamped "Roycroft," electrified 175.00
Chair
    Arm, 25-1/4" w, 17" d, 51" h, from Grove Park Inn, 1 broad vertical slat incised "G.P.I." replaced tacked-on leather seat, cleaned finish, unmarked 1,700.00
    Straddle, 23-3/4" w, 22" d, 34" h, red leather cushion, brass tacks, mahogany orb and cross mark 7,475.00
Desk Set, hammered copper, paper knife, pen tray, stationery holding, perpetual desk calendar, pr of bookends, flower holder, match holder with nested ashtray, c1915 .... 550.00
Frame
    15" w, 20-1/2" h, orig print, orig finish 450.00
    16-1/4" w, 13-1/2" h, orig watercolor landscape by J. L. Judson, painting sgd 450.00
Goodie Box, 23" w, 12-1/4" d, 9-1/4" h, mahogany, hinged rect lid, iron hardware, imp lock, c1910 .... 500.00
Plaque, motto, 5-1/4" h, 9-1/4" l, carved oak, "Be Yourself," orig dark finish, carved orb and cross mark...................... 3,400.00
Presentation Bowl, 11" d, 3" h, squat-form, broad shoulder engraved "To Boardie from the Squash Crowd 1928," orig dark patina, imp mark... 200.00
Toy, 8" h, 4-1/2" h, Clownie, bean bag, yellow polka-dot outfit, orig paper tag 100.00
Tray
    10" d, octagonal, handles, hand hammered surface, orig dark patina, imp mark, c1906-10...................................... 290.00
    10" w, 22" d, copper, tooled foliate design, two attached handles, orig patina, early orb mark.............................. 690.00
Vase
    4-1/2" h, 3" d, ovoid, hammered copper, orig patina, orb and cross mark, minor wear to base 425.00

Purse, leather, tooled dec, 10-1/8" l, 5-3/4" h, $175.

22" h, 7-1/2" d, hammered copper, American Beauty, from Grove Park Inn, squat base, stovepipe neck, orig dark finish, inscribed "The G.P.I. American Beauty Vase Made Exclusively for Grove Park Inn by the Roycrofters" 2,500.00

RUBENA GLASS

History: Rubena crystal is a transparent blown glass, which shades from clear to red. It also is found as the background for frosted and overshot glass. It was made in the late 1800s by several glass companies, including Northwood and Hobbs, Brockunier & Co. of Wheeling, West Virginia.

Rubena was used for several patterns of pattern glass including Royal Ivy and Royal Oak.

Bowl, 4-1/2" d, Daisy and Scroll 65.00
Butter Dish, cov, Royal Oak, fluted.................................. 250.00
Compote, 14" h, rubena overshot bowl, white metal bronze finished figural standard.. 170.00
Cracker Jar, cov
    Aurora, inverted rib, Northwood 325.00
    Cut fan and strawberry design, fancy sterling silver cov, 7" h, 6" w 1,150.00
Creamer and Sugar Bowl, cov, Royal Ivy............................ 250.00
Decanter, 9" h, bulbous body, narrow neck, applied clear handle 170.00
Finger Bowl, Royal Ivy 65.00
Pickle Castor, enameled daisy dec, ornate sgd frame with 2 handles, pickle fork in front 245.00
Salt Shaker, Coquette... 150.00
Sauce Dish, Royal Ivy... 35.00
Sugar Shaker, Royal Ivy... 250.00
Toothpick Holder, Optic... 150.00
Tumbler, Medallion Sprig... 100.00
Tumble-Up, tumbler and carafe, Baccarat Swirl............... 175.00
Vase, 10" h, ruffled rim, hp enameled flowers, gold trim, Hobbs, Brockunier & Co. 175.00

Pitcher, enameled apple blossoms, 7-1/2" h, $495.

Water Pitcher
  Opal Swirl, Northwood 275.00
  Royal Ivy, frosted 295.00

RUBENA VERDE GLASS

History: Rubena Verde, a transparent glass that shades from red in the upper section to yellow-green in the lower, was made by Hobbs, Brockunier & Co., Wheeling, West Virginia, in the late 1880s. It often is found in the Inverted Thumbprint (IVT) pattern, called "Polka Dot" by Hobbs.

Bride's Basket, miniature, 4-1/2" x 6-1/2", $125.

Bowl, 9-1/2" d, IVT, ruffled 175.00
Butter Dish, cov, Daisy and Button....................................250.00
Celery Vase, 6-1/4" h, IVT 225.00
Creamer and Sugar Bowl, cov, Hobnail, bulbous, applied handle
  ....550.00
Cruet, 7" h, IVT, teepee shape, trefoil spout, vaseline handle and
  faceted stopper, Hobbs, Brockunier 550.00
Finger Bowl, IVT...95.00
Jack In The Pulpit Vase, 8" h 250.00
Pickle Castor, Hobb's Hobnail, SP frame, cov, and tongs.500.00
Salt and Pepper Shakers, pr, IVT 210.00
Tumbler, IVT 125.00
Vase, 9-1/4" h, paneled body, enameled daises dec 85.00
Water Pitcher, Hobb's Hobnail 395.00

RUSSIAN ITEMS

History: During the late 19th and early 20th centuries, craftsmen skilled in lacquer, silver, and enamel wares worked in Russia. During the Czarist era (1880-1917), Fabergé, known for his exquisite enamel pieces, led a group of master craftsmen who were located primarily in Moscow. Fabergé also had an establishment in St. Petersburg and enjoyed the patronage of the Russian Imperial family and royalty and nobility throughout Europe.

ВРАТЬЕВЪ

Baterin's factory
1812-1820

КорНИЛОВЫХЪ

Korniloff's factory
c1835

Almost all enameling was done on silver. Pieces are signed by the artist and the government assayer.

The Russian Revolution in 1917 brought an abrupt end to the century of Russian craftsmanship. The modern Soviet government has exported some inferior enamel and lacquer work, usually lacking in artistic merit. Modern pieces are not collectible.

References: Vladimir Guliayev, *Fine Art of Russian Lacquered Miniatures*, Chronicle Books, 1993; A. Kenneth Snowman, *Fabergé*, Harry N. Abrams, 1993.

Museums: Cleveland Museum of Art, Cleveland, OH; Forbes Magazine Collection, New York, NY; Hillwood, the Marjorie Merriweather Post Collection, Washington, DC; Virginia Museum of Fine Arts, Lillian Thomas Pratt Collection, Richmond, VA; Walters Art Gallery, Baltimore, MD.

Enamels

Cigarette Case, 3-1/2" l, 2-1/4" w, 84 standard, silver gilt, robin's egg blue enamel, feathered guillouche ground, opaque white enamel borders, diamond chips on clasp, gilt in., Ivan Britzin, St. Petersburg, 1908-17, small losses and chips to enamel
  ....1,200.00
Coffee Spoon, blue dot border in bowl, stylized polychrome enamel foliage, gilt stippled ground, twisted gilt stem, crown finial, G Tokmakov, c1890 ....300.00
Egg, silver gilt and shaded enamel ware, 2 pc construction, cabochon stone, makers mark obliterated, 20th C
  3" h, ftd...700.00
  4" h, separate base...800.00
Kovsh, 3" l, silver gilt, Art Nouveau style enameling, pointed prow, hooked handle, Maria Semenaova, Moscow, c1900
  ....1,900.00
Letter Opener, 10-1/2" l, cylindrical handle, enameled translucent green guillouche ground, overlaid gilt trellis dec, horse head finial, red cabochon eyes, seed pearl border, agate glade
  ....925.00
Napkin Ring, 1-3/4" x 1" x 1-1/2", enameled green, blue, pink, brown, white, light blue and maroon, Maria Semenova, Moscow, c1890
  ....700.00
Teaspoon, turquoise ground, filigree cloisons, white enamel dot border, red and white enamel flower in center of bowl, red flower on handle, gilt stern, V Akhimov, 1896 ....300.00
Trinket Box, cov, oval, silver gilt, en plein enameling, slip on lid, Moscow, c1900 ....2,200.00

Icon

8-3/4" x 10-1/2", The Baptism of Christ, 19th C, tempera on wood panel..1,155.00
9-1/2" x 8", Selected Saints, 18th C, Mother of God at top surrounded by saints, including Archangel Michael, tempera and oil on wood panel, overlaid with silver gilt riza, hallmarked Moscow, dated 1798 ....1,375.00
10-1/2" x 8-1/2", The Kazan Mother of God, c1900, oil on wood panel, overlaid with 3 pc silver gilt, repousse and engraved

riza with multicolored enamel haloes and borders, silver drop-let dec on halo, hallmarked Moscow, Cyrillic maker's mark S.E. probably Sergiy Gubkin, son of Imperial silvermaster Ivan Gubkin 3,575.00

10-1/2" x 9", The Kazan Mother of God, c1900, oil on wood panel, overlaid with silver gilt repousse riza with multicolored enam-eled halves, titles plaques and monograms, hallmarked Mos-cow, from the workshop of Sergiv Gubkin..................2,100.00

11" x 9", The Vladimir Mother of God, c1800, Mary and infant Christ in a cheek to cheek embrace, tempera on wood panel, overlaid with silver gilt repousse and chased riza, hallmarked St. Petersburg, dated 1825, from workshop of Ivan Grevoriev 2,300.00

12" x 10", Conversational, late 18th C, visitation of Mary to Sexton Yuri, tempera on wood panel, overlaid with silver gilt riza with indistinguishable maker's mark, cloth covering on reverse in-scribed "With God's Blessing to Duke and Duchess Alexandar Ivanovich Devletkideyew and their daughter Anastasyia from Alandra Michaliovana Drobovaya" 1,375.00

12" x 10", St. Nicholas, 19th C, tempera on wood panel, overlaid with silver riza 1,375.00

12" x 10-1/2", The Resurrection and Descent, 20th C, finely paint-ed, overlaid with late 18th C silver gilt riza dated 1798 ....3,300.00

12-1/2" x 10-1/2", The Vladimir Mother of God, c1800, tempera on wood panel, overlaid with silver gilt repousse riza, hallmarked Moscow and dated 1874, Cyrillic maker's mark I.E. ..1,100.00

13-1/2" x 15-3/4", St. Nicholas with Life Scenes, 18th C, tempera on wood panel, older inserted icon of Nicholas at center, sur-rounded by scenes of his life 1,540.00

Icon, silver and enamel riza by Brothers Zaharov, Weep Not For Me Mother, borders with Saints Barbara, Evdokia, Eliabeth, and the Guardian Angel, Moscow hallmarks, c1900, 13-3/4" h, 11-1/4" w, $3,300. Photo courtesy of Jackson's Auctioneers & Apprais-ers.

Icon, tempera on wood panel, Prophet Elijah, family saints bor-der, 19th C, 14-3/4" h, 12" w, $4,125. Photo courtesy of Jackson's Auctioneers & Appraisers.

14" x 12", The Assembly of the Archangel Michael, 19th C, tem-pera on wood panel, Michael, Gabriel, and all the archangels are gathered supporting Christ Emanual 2,420.00

14" x 12-1/2", The Smolensk Mother of God, 19th C, oil on wood panel, overlaid with silver-gilt engraved riza with applied halo, hallmarked Moscow, dated 1882, from workshop of Alexander Fedorovich Golovin..1,980.00

Metal

Basket, 11" l, silver, oval, foliate border, bail handle 18 ozs. 295.00

Belt, 29" l, turquoise links spaced with silver gilt links, large tur-quoise clasp, hallmarks..185.00

Bonbonniere, 3-3/8" d, 2-3/16" h, orchid guillouche enamel on silver, cylindrical, cast silver bas-relief applied dec on cov and back, applied relief, monogram of Nicholas II set with precious stones, Henrik Wigstrom, workmaster, St., Petersburg, 1908-17, slight damage..4,225.00

Figure, 14-1/2" h, 12" l, bronze, equestrian group, officer and lady riding astride horse, dark brown patina, sgd 20th C....865.00

Safe, 3" l, patinated, applied plaque with Russian characters 125.00

Samovar, 18" h, brass, bowl and tray.................................275.00

Serving Spoon, silver, dated 1857, 4 oz., 4 dwt................200.00

Tabernacle, 23" h, silver gilt, multiple piece, hallmarked Moscow, dated 1893, Cyrillic maker's mark "I.A."......................3,300.00

Tray, 16-1/4" l, silver, pierced border, reeded rim, two reeded handles, mkd "Marvei Kostorv, Moscow, 1806," 26 oz., 4 dwt 2,000.00

Porcelain

Butter Dish, 6" l, modeled as rams, 19th C, pr 400.00

Cabinet Plate, 9" d, cobalt blue, green, and red central rosette, gilt ground 275.00

Cabinet Ornament, Fulda, Moscow, 1851, top surrounded with two gilt classical figures, cabinet door inset with small open face enamel lapel watch with painted porcelain back, int. fitted with gilt mirrored architectural facade, center icon, gilt and enamel coach, rider, and three figures, stepped base, turquoise enameled case, 4" h, $4,500. Photo courtesy of Freeman\Fine Arts.

Cup and Saucer
    3" h, gilt on white designs, F. Gardner, Moscow, early 20th C, set of six..395.00
    4-1/2" h, blue glazed, honoring coronation of Nicholas II, 1878, M. S. Kuznetsov...250.00
Dessert Plate, floral rim, magenta ground, Islamic script, printed mark, I. E. Kuznetsov, 19th C, set of six....................265.00
Egg, 4-1/2" l, floral and foliate polychrome dec, gilt highlights 50.00
Plate
    6-1/4" d, central scene of women peasants in landscape, shaped flower filled panel rim, gilt highlights, Kustentzoff, price for pr 175.00
    9" d, bucolic scene, sepia, A. G. Popov, Moscow, 19th C, minor wear, chips, 10 pc set 690.00
Portrait Plate, 8" d, Empress Elizabeth, Safronov, early 19th C, hairline 315.00
Tankard, 8" h, figural, Turk's head, mkd "F. Gardner, Moscow," 19th C, restored 1,210.00
Urn, 10-3/4" h, baluster, medallion handles, panel with Arab and maiden, polychrome dec, puce ground........................425.00
Vase, 8" h, one green with medallion of Olga, other puce with medallion of Vladimir, allover gilt foliate dec, Gardner, 19th C, drilled, price for pr 250.00

SABINO GLASS

History: Sabino glass, named for its creator Ernest Marius Sabino, originated in France in the 1920s and is an art glass which was produced in a wide range of decorative styles: frosted, clear, opalescent, and colored. Both blown and pressed moldings were used. Hand-sculpted wooden molds that were cast in iron were used and are still in use at the present time.

In 1960, the company introduced fiery opalescent Art Deco style pieces, including a line of one- to eight-inch high figurines. Gold was added to a batch of glass to obtain the fiery glow. These are the Sabino pieces most commonly found today.

Marks: Sabino is marked with the name in the mold, as an etched signature, or both.

Blotter, 6" l, rocker type, crossed American and French flags 275.00
Centerbowl, 10-1/4" d, 4-1/4" h, heavy walled, frosted, three high relief oyster shells, tripod feet, star, and pearls between, center mkd "Sabino France," int. wear..............................500.00
Charger, 11-3/4" d, opalescent, Art Deco molded spiral design, 3 nude women swimming, central molded mark "Sabino Paris" 550.00
Clock, 6-1/8" h, opalescent, arched case, overlapping geometric devices, molded festoons centered by circular chapter ring, molded "SABINO," c1925 ....1,725.00
Figure
    Butterfly, opalescent, relief molded "Sabino"................25.00
    Fish, large 110.00
    Maiden, 7-3/4" h, opalescent, draped in contrapposto with raised right arm, etched "Sabino Paris" 885.00
    Pekinese, 1-1/4" h, begged, opalescent, relief molded "Sabino" 35.00
    Rabbit, 1" x 2" 75.00
    Turkey, 2-1/4" h, 21' l, molded signature "Sabino, France" 45.00
    Venus de Milo, large..75.00
Knife Rest, duck 25.00
Napkin Ring, birds, opalescent...45.00
Powder Box, small 40.00
Scent Bottle, Petalia...50.00
Vase
    9-7/8" h, opalescent, rounded rect form, Art Deco female nude each side, joining hands around vessel, etched 'Sabino Paris" 1,870.00
    15-1/2" h, tall oval body, molded three swallows in flight, fiery amber, base inscribed "Sabino France" in script . 1,035.00

SALOPIAN WARE

C S SALOPIAN

History: Salopian ware was made at Caughley Pot Works, Salop, Shropshire, England, in the 18th century by Thomas Turner. At one time the product was classified "Polychrome Transfer" because of the method of decoration, but the ware is better known by the more popular name "Salopian." Much of the output was sold through Turner's Salopian warehouse in London

Marks: Pieces are impressed or painted under the glaze with an "S" or the word "Salopian."

Bowl, 7-3/4" d, milkmaid milking cow in meadow scene, panels of men at work separated by florals, brown-black transfer with polychromed enamels 250.00
Creamer, 6" h, black transfer of maiden with urn, yellow and burnt orange accents, black and white frieze, black, white, orange, and yellow florals around rim border, c1790.................225.00
Cup and Saucer, Deer pattern, blue, black, yellow, and green transfer, chip on rim...250.00
Milk Jug, 5" h, black transfer of castle and cows, yellow-gold and blue accents, black ad white geometrics on int., blue rim, c1790...35.00

Sugar Bowl, cov, pheasant and floral dec, 5" x 5-1/2", $325.

Plate, 7-1/4" d, white stag center, floral border, black transfer with polychrome enamels 115.00
Posset Pot, 4" h, brown transfer of large and small flowers highlighted by light blue, orange, yellow, and green 350.00
Teabowl and Saucer, brown transfer of farm scene 150.00
Tea Caddy, 4" h, black transfer of deer and cottage, pink and yellow accents.. 275.00
Teapot, 6-7/8" h, Castleford-type shape, Nelson's Victories at Nile, Copenhagen, and Trefalger in scalloped shell, flanked by two half serpents blowing trumpets, green-black transfer with red, yellow, flesh, green, and ochre accents, applied ochre border, swan finial, restored 650.00
Waste Bowl, classical cartouches in brown transfers with 3 maidens, cobalt blue, yellow, green, and ochre flowers, int. with brown transfer of florals 200.00

SALT AND PEPPER SHAKERS

History: Collecting salt and pepper shakers, whether late 19th-century glass forms or the contemporary figural and souvenir types, is becoming more and more popular. The supply and variety is practically unlimited; the price for most sets is within the budget of cost-conscious collectors. In addition, their size offers an opportunity to display a large collection in a relatively small space.

Specialty collections can be by type, form, or maker. Great glass artisans, such as Joseph Locke and Nicholas Kopp, designed salt and pepper shakers in the normal course of their work.

References: Gideon Bosker and Lena Lencer, *Salt and Pepper Shakers*, Avon Books, 1994; Larry Carey and Sylvia Tompkins, *1,002 Salt and Pepper Shakers*, Schiffer Publishing, 1995; ——, *Salt and Pepper*, Schiffer Publishing, 1994; Melva Davern, *Collector's Encyclopedia of Salt & Pepper Shakers*, 1st Series (1985, 1991 value update), 2nd Series (1990, 1995 value update), Collector Books; Helene Guarnaccia, *Salt & Pepper Shakers*, Vol. I (1985, 1996 value update), Vol. II (1989, 1993 value update), Vol. III (1991, 1995 value update), Vol. IV (1993, 1997 value update), Collector Books; Mildred and Ralph Lechner, *World of Salt Shakers*, 2nd ed., Collector Books, 1992,

1996 value update; Arthur G. Peterson, *Glass Salt Shakers*, Wallace-Homestead, 1970, out of print; Mike Schneider, *Complete Salt and Pepper Shaker Book*, Schiffer Publishing, 1993.

Collectors' Clubs: Antique and Art Glass Salt Shaker Collectors Society, 2832 Rapidan Trail, Maitland, FL 32751; Novelty Salt & Pepper Shakers Club, P.O. Box 3617, Lantana, FL 33465.

Museum: Judith Basin Museum, Stanford, MT.

Additional Listings: See *Warman's Americana & Collectibles* for more examples.

Notes: The colored sets, in both transparent and opaque glass, command the highest prices; crystal and white sets the lowest. Although some shakers, e.g., the tomato or fig, have a special patented top and need it to retain their value, it generally is not detrimental to replace the top of a shaker.

The figural and souvenir types are often looked down upon by collectors. Sentiment and whimsy are prime collecting motivations. The large variety and current low prices indicate a potential for long-term price growth.

Generally, older shakers are priced by the piece; figural and souvenir types by the set. Pricing methods are indicated in the listings. All shakers included below are assumed to have original tops unless otherwise noted. Reference numbers are from Arthur Goodwin Peterson's *Glass Salt Shakers*. Peterson made a beginning; there are hundreds, perhaps thousands, of patterns still to be cataloged.

Art Glass (priced individually)

Blue, Inverted Thumbprint, sphere.................................... 125.00
Cobalt Blue, 4" h, deep color, sterling push-on lid with English hallmarks "E.E.," "HH" and a lion facing left, sterling collar mkd "E.E.," anchor, and lion facing left................................ 285.00
Cranberry, Inverted Thumbprint, sphere........................... 175.00
Fig, enameled pansy dec, satin, orig prong top, Mt. Washington
.... 120.00
Peachblow, Wheeling, bulbous....................................... 460.00
Scrollware, blue scrolling 170.00
Wave Crest, Erie Twist body, hp flowers, 2-1/2" h............. 185.00

Figural and Souvenir Types (priced by set)

Christmas, barrel shape
    Amber 80.00
    Amethyst... 145.00
Ducks, 2-1/2" h, sitting, glass, clear bodies, blue heads, sgd "Czechoslovakia".. 45.00
Egg shape
    Opaque white body, holly dec, 23 red raised enameled berries, Mt. Washington 185.00
    Pastel tint, pink enameled blossoms, lid loose................ 65.00
Nipper, RCA Dog, mkd "Lenox" 50.00
Squirrels, 3-1/2" h, standing, metal, SP top 40.00

Opalescent Glass (priced individually)

Argonaut Shell, blue 65.00
Fluted Scrolls, vaseline.. 65.00
Jewel and Flower, blue, (164-J), replaced top..................... 45.00
Seaweed, Hobbs, cranberry 60.00
Windows, Hobbs, blue, pewter top 50.00

Derby China, cream ground, gold branch and bird dec, 3" h, 1-1/2" d, $70.

Opaque Glass (priced individually)

Acorn, Hobbs, shaded pink to white, tin top (21-A) 50.00
Brownie, 2-3/8" h, rounded cube, 4 vertical sides, Palmer Cox Brownies in different poses on each (F-488)...................90.00
Chick on Pedestal, C. F. Monroe, not dec, 3" h.................375.00
Chocolate, Cactus, Greentown 50.00
Creased Waist, yellow 35.00
Chrysanthemum Sprig, custard...150.00
Daisy Sprig 50.00
Egg in Blossom...100.00
Everglades, purple slag, white and gold highlights, pewter (160-K) 85.00
Knobby, heavy opaque white, hp pastel flowers, shading to pale yellow, orig pewter top 45.00
Punty Band, custard 45.00
Winged Scroll, custard 80.00

Pattern Glass (priced individually)

Actress, pewter top 45.00
Beautiful Lady, colorless, 1905 ....25.00
Block and Fan, colorless, 1891 ....20.00
Crown Jewel, c1880, etched 35.00
Flower and Rain, red 425.00
Four Square, Billows...100.00
Franesware, Hobbs, Brockunier Co., c1880, hobnail, frosted, amber stained..45.00
Haines..45.00
Leaf, four feet, berry 115.00
Little Apple, ftd 110.00
Lobe, squatty...120.00
Medallion Sprig, 3-1/4" h, shaded cobalt blue to white, orig base, 33-S 75.00
Tulip 100.00
Twelve Panel, scrolled pink...130.00
Whirligig, colorless, tin top, (177-A) 20.00

SALT-GLAZED WARES

History: Salt-glazed wares have a distinctive pitted surface texture made by throwing salt into the hot kiln during the final firing process. The salt vapors produce sodium oxide and hydrochloric acid, which react on the glaze.

Many Staffordshire potters produced large quantities of this type of ware during the 18th and 19th centuries. A relatively small amount was produced in the United States. Salt-glazed wares still are made today.

Bowl, 11-1/2" l, oval, matching undertray, reticulated, edge wear and hairlines 1,320.00
Cache Pot, 7-1/2" d, taupe, applied classical dec, 1830...450.00
Cream Jug, 5-1/4" h, pear shape, raised rose branch band over drapery, lamb finial on lid...600.00
Creamer, pear shape, lyre handle, 18th C
   3" h, shield design, circular foot 550.00
   3-1/4" h, raised leaf and putti dec, claw feet 750.00
Dish, 9" d, circular, scroll and latticino dec 325.00
Loving Cup, 4-1/4" h, white raised US seal, 2 gold initials on front, Britannia on verse, handles outlined in blue, Castleford
   ....250.00
Plate, shaped reticulated rim
   8-1/4" d, emb border 600.00
   9-3/4" d, emb diaper border 375.00
Platter, 16-3/4" d, molded diaper-work panels, scalloped rim, 18th C...250.00
Salt, helmet shape, latticino star and lion, bird and shell dec, claw feet, c18th C 880.00
Sauce Boat, 3-1/8" l, oval, relief molded diaper, ozier, and scrolling panels, loop handle 425.00
Tea Caddy, 4-1/4" h, pear shape, latticino dec, knob finial, 18th C
   ....375.00
Teapot, cov, 7" h, ball shape, raised branch dec, bird finial on lid, 18th C...2,850.00
Tray, 7-3/4" l, oval, latticino dec, scalloped rim.................350.00

Teapot, sheaf of wheat finial, $175.

SALTS, OPEN

History: When salt was first mined, the supply was limited and expensive. The necessity for a receptacle in which to serve the salt resulted in the first open salt, a crude, hand-carved, wooden trencher.

As time passed, salt receptacles were refined in style and materials. In the 1500s, both master and individual salts existed. By the 1700s, firms such as Meissen, Waterford, and Wedgwood were making glass, china, and porcelain salts. Leading glass manufacturers in the 1800s included Libbey, Mount Washington, New England, Smith Bros., Vallerysthal, Wave Crest, and Webb. Many outstanding silversmiths in England, France, and Germany also produced this form.

Open salts were the only means of serving salt until the appearance of the shaker in the late 1800s. The ease of procuring salt from a shaker greatly reduced the use of and need for the open salts.

References: William Heacock and Patricia Johnson, *5,000 Open Salts*, Richardson Printing Corporation, 1982, 1986 value update; Allan B. and Helen B. Smith have authored and published 10 books on open salts beginning with *One Thousand Individual Open Salts Illustrated* (1972) and ending with *1,334 Open Salts Illustrated: The Tenth Book* (1984). Daniel Snyder did the master salt sections in volumes 8 and 9. In 1987, Mimi Rudnick compiled a revised price list for the 10 Smith Books; Kenneth Wilson, *American Glass 1760-1930*, 2 Vols., Hudson Hills Press and The Toledo Museum of Art, 1994.

Periodical: *Salty Comments*, 401 Nottingham Rd., Newark, DE 19711.

Collectors' Clubs: New England Society of Open Salt Collectors, P.O. Box 177, Sudbury, MA 01776; Open Salt Collectors of the Atlantic Region, 56 Northview Dr., Lancaster, PA 17601.

Note: The numbers in parenthesis refer to plate numbers in the Smiths' books.

Condiment sets with open salts

Bristol Glass, cov mustard pop, pepper shaker with orig lid, open sale, milk white, pink and blue flowers and green leaves dec, 4-1/4" x 5-3/4" SP holder 175.00
Limoges, double salt and mustard, sgd "J. M. Limoges" (388) 80.00
Metal, coolie pulling rickshaw, salt, pepper, and mustard, blown glass liners, Oriental (461)...360.00
Quimper, double salt and mustard, white, blue, and green floral dec, sgd "Quimper" (388) 120.00

Early American Glass

2-3/8" h, 2-3/4" d, pressed vaseline, emb rib, SP ftd holder 55.00
2-5/8" l, colorless, variant, Neal MN3, chips.......................305.00
3" h, cobalt blue, paneled with diamond foot.....................125.00
3" h, colorless, blown, expanded diamond bowl, applied petal foot 145.00
3" l, colorless, lacy, eagle, Neal EE1, chips 200.00
3-1/8" l, cobalt blue, Neal CN 1a, 2 feet replaced, small chips 200.00
3-1/8" l, fiery opalescent, 3-1/8" l, Neal BS2, chips 275.00
3-1/4" l, fiery opalescent, eagles, Neal EE3b, chips...........500.00
3-3/8" h, cobalt blue, facet cut, fan rim, sq foot, edges ground 125.00
3-5/8" l, sapphire blue, Neal BT 2, very minor flakes.......1,075.00

Figurals

Basket, 3" h, 2-3/4" d, coral colored glass, SP basket frame, salt with cut polished facets..55.00
Boat, lacy, colorless, New England, Neal BT-9, slight rim roughness 160.00

Bucket, 2-1/2" d, 1-5/8" h, Bristol glass, turquoise, white, green, and brown enameled bird, butterfly and trees, SP rim and handle 75.00
Sea Horse, Belleek, brilliant turquoise, white base, supports shell salt, first black mark (458) 350.00

Individual

Colored Glass
 Cambridge, Decagon pattern, amber (468)....................40.00
 Cameo, Galle, green pedestal, enamel dec, sgd (205) 295.00
 Moser, cobalt blue, pedestal, gold bands, applied flowers sgd (380) 70.00
 Purple Slag, 3" d, 1-1/4" h, emb shell pattern.................50.00
Cut Glass, 2" d, 1-1/2" h, cut ruby ovals, allover dainty white enameled scrolls, clear ground, gold trim, scalloped top 60.00
German Silver, dolphin feet, 1890-1910 (353) 100.00
Noritake, oval, blue and gold int. dec (382)........................40.00
Pattern glass
 Crystal Wedding 25.00
 Fine Rib, flint 35.00
 Hawaiian Lei, (477)..35.00
 Pineapple and Fan 25.00
 Three Face 40.00
Royal Bayreuth, lobster claw (87)......................................80.00
Russian Enamel, 1-1/4" h, 1-3/4" d, colorless glass liner, gold finished metal, red and white scallop design, Russian hallmarks, c1940..110.00
Sterling Silver, Georg Jensen, Denmark, porringer (238) ..200.00

Intaglios

Niagara Falls, scene (368) 75.00
Tree, six intaglios, Venus and Cupid (423) 115.00

Masters

Colored Glass
 Cobalt blue, master, wafer base, 2-1/6" h, 2-1/16" d.....150.00
 Cranberry, 3" d, 1-3/4" h, emb ribs, applied crystal ruffed rim, SP holder with emb lions heads 160.00
 Green, light, dark green ruffled top, open pontil (449)....90.00

Jacob's Ladder, master, pressed glass, pedestal base, $35.

Raspberry, heavy, sq, Pairpoint (444).............................75.00
Vaseline, 3" d, 2-1/4" h, applied crystal trim around middle, sil-
    verplated stand...125.00
Cut Glass, 2" d, 2" h, green cut to clear, SP holder............115.00
Pattern glass
    Bakewell Pears 30.00
    Barberry, pedestal...40.00
    Basketweave, sleigh (397) 100.00
    Diamond Point, cov 75.00
    Excelsior 30.00
    Snail, ruby stained 75.00
    Sunflower, pedestal..40.00
    Viking 30.00
Pewter, pedestal, cobalt blue liner (349).........................65.00
Sterling Silver, boy with boy and arrow, holding salt on head, Sim-
    pson Hall Miller & Co. (312)................................440.00

SAMPLERS

History: Samplers served many purposes. For a young child, they were a practice exercise and permanent reminder of stitches and patterns. For a young woman, they were a means to demonstrate skills in a "gentle" art and a way to record family genealogy. For the mature woman, they were a useful occupation and method of creating gifts or remembrances, e.g., mourning pieces.

Schools for young ladies of the early 19th century prided themselves on the needlework skills they taught. The Westtown School in Chester County, Pennsylvania, and the Young Ladies Seminary in Bethlehem, Pennsylvania, were two institutions. These schools changed their teaching as styles changed. Berlin work was introduced by the mid-19th century.

Examples of samplers date back to the 1700s. The earliest ones were long and narrow, usually done only with the alphabet and numerals. Later examples were square. At the end of the 19th century, the shape tended to be rectangular.

The same motifs were used throughout the country. The name of the person who stitched the piece is a key factor in determining the region.

References: Ethel Stanwood Bolton and Eva Johnston Coe, *American Samplers*, Dover, 1987; Glee Krueger, *Gallery of American Samplers*, Bonanza Books, 1984; Betty Ring, *American Needlework Treasures*, E. P. Dutton, 1987; Anne Sebba, *Samplers*, Thames and Hudson, 1979.

Museums: Cooper-Hewitt Museum, National Museum of Design, New York, NY; Smithsonian Institution, Washington, DC.

Note: Samplers are assumed to be on linen unless otherwise indicated.

1748, Ann Cushing, Newport, RI, alphabets, horizontal floral vines, "Ann Cushing is my name with my needle I wrought the same in the 9 year of my age July the 10 1847," 10-3/4" h, 7-5/8" w, framed..1,955.00
1770, Barbara Johnson, rows of alphabets above inscription, lower panel with floral motif, "Barbara Johnson Her Sampler Worked in the Fourteenth Year of her Age 1770," 10" x 7", framed 1,725.00
1782, Prisce Gill, blue, green, yellow, gold, white, and brown silk, hem, cross, satin, stem, and bullion stitch, alphabet and nu-

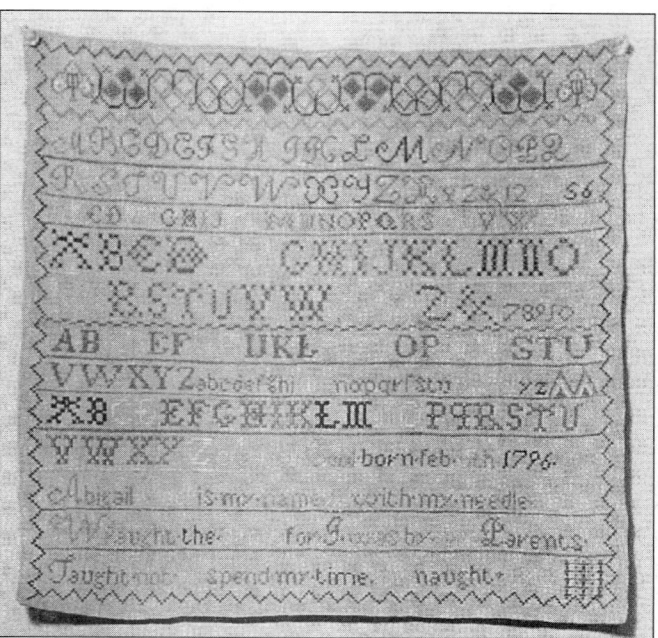

1810, silk on linen homespun, zigzag border, stylized floral band, alphabets and "Abigale Cook born Feb. 6th, 1796, Abigale Cook is my name and with my needle I wrought the same for I was by my parents taught not to spend my time for naught 1810," green, blue, pink, rust, white, unframed, 14-1/2" sq, $2,145. Photo courtesy of Garth's Auctions.

merals surmounted by basket of fruit, 11 years old, under instruction of Mrs. Sarah Fiske Stilvours......................79,500.00
1794, Sarah Mantz, red, blue, brown, and yellow, geometric designs of ladies, birds, flowers, verse about time and the Lord's Prayer, "Finished on March 24, 1794, the eighth year," some loss and staining, framed 525.00
17?2, Susanas Romig, Mennonite, red and green, framed, loss and stains, 10-1/2" x 10-1/4" 90.00
1801, Eliza W Plummer, at Miss Parker's School, Haverhill County, Essex, MA, alphabet and pious verse, outer borders of scrolling vines of leaves, blossoms, and berries issuing from baskets, 17" x 20" 57,500.00
1804, Sarah Share, blue, green, and red, trees, flowers, ivy, and alphabet, framed, 17" x 7-1/2" 275.00
1806
    Elizabeth Smith, silk on linen homespun, alphabets, verse, flowers, some family names and initials, "Elizabeth Smith work done in the 10 year of her age 1806," red, green, brown, blue, some stains and damage, loss of floss, 11-3/4" h, 10" w, matted and framed as 18-1/4" h, 16" w......525.00
    Sarah, silk on homespun, vining border, alphabets, faded blue, green, brown, and black, worn and missing floss, 7-1/2" h, 5" w, unframed...250.00
1810
    Abigale Cook, silk on linen homespun, zig-zag border, stylized floral band, alphabets and "Abigail Cook born Feb. 6th 1796, Abigale Cook is my name and with my needle I wrought the same for I was by my parents taught not to spend my time for naught 1810," green, blue, pink, rust, and white, pristine, 14-1/4" h, 14-1/4" w, unframed
....2,145.00
    Martha West, silk on linen homespun, geometric side border, grassy knolls, pine trees, basket of fruit and flowers, "Martha West wrought this in the 14th year of her age, Haverhill, A. D. 1810," some fading, ground discoloration, 11-1/2 x 14", framed...3,450.00
1813, Elizabeth McMannus, rose sprigs, outer border of meandering strawberry vine, reads "Eliza McMannus, aged 10

years, Female Association School, NY, December, 1813"
and "From Mary Thompson, a member of the Female Association to Elizabeth Thompson," 7-1/2" x 8-3/4" 16,100.00
1814, Ann Louisa Skinner, blue and olive brown silk on linen homespun, family record listing members of Skinner family, "Ann Louisa Skinner born 25th December 1807, Her Sampler, Albany,
March 27, 1814," very work, faded, edges glued down, framed,
17" h, 16-3/4" w 415.00
1817, Abigail Sawyer, upper panel of alphabets above lower panel of three story Federal house flanked by flowering trees, basket of fruit, animals, and other foliate devices, flowering vine
border, "Abigail Sawyer's Sampler Aged 11 years Phillipston
June the 24, 1817. Massachusetts State," framed, 17-1/8" x
17-5/8" 7,475.00

1826
  Braddock, Anna, age 14, blue, green, yellow, brown, and
    white, verse titled "Friendship," floral wreath below West-
    town School Building, Burlington, County, NJ 5,500.00
  Dodge, Mary Wing, age 12, silk on linen homespun, alpha-
    bets, flowers, and fruit, verse and "Mary Wing Dodge, in
    the 12th year of her age, Marietta, Ohio, August 26th,
    1926," green, blue, yellow, white, and black, minor stains,
    old veneered frame, 18-5/8" h, 19-5/8" w 4,400.00
  Kelly, Eleanor, St. Joseph's Academy, silk and watercolor on
    silk ground, St. Joseph's house, approaching carriage, vil-
    lage of Emmitsburg, MD, on left background beneath Ca-
    toctin Mountains, paper label in verso inscribed
    "Emmitsburg, Maryland. Needlework done by Eleanor
    Theresa Kelly, daughter of John and Elizabeth Fitz-Sim-
    mons Kelly of Pittsburgh, Pa, 1826," 16-1/4" x 22-1/2"
    ....46,000.00

1828
  Mary Bournes, silk on linen homespun, Adam and Eve, Quaker
    verse, borders, house, animals, birds in trees, "Mary
    Bournes work aged 12 Anno Domini 1828," minor discolor-
    ation, 20-1/2" h, 16-1/2" w, framed.........................2,300.00
  Sarah J Hildreth, Dracut, MA, age 12, needlework, house,
    trees, and stream, outer border of meandering floral vine,
    cross, crosslet, satin, French knot, chain, stem, and gobe-
    lin stitches, linen ground.....................................19,500.00
1829, Mary Cottoms, silk on linen homespun, vining border,
  verse, house, trees, flowers, animals, hearts and "Mary Cottoms Work Aged 10 Years October 16, 1829, M. Shore Upton
  School," faded green, gold, brown, blue, white, water stain in
  lower right corner, 14-1/2" h, 11-3/4" w, framed 18" h, 13-1/4"
  w 1,100.00

1830
  Rachel Anders, Schwenkfelder, red, green, blue, geometric
    designs of flowers, birds, table, mirror, chair, alphabet,
    provenance on reverse, framed, stains, 17-1/2" x 16-1/2"
    ....360.00
  Margaret Garrigues, white, blue, and green, floral samples,
    various birds, strawberry vine border, pious verse, minor
    stains, framed, 21-1/2" x 16" 935.00
  Elizabeth Sager, Burlington County, NJ, inscribed with verse,
    vining border, building, Quaker cross-stitched floral dis-
    plays, swans, and the "Extract," 17-1/4" h, 17" w, framed,
    scattered losses to ground 1,725.00
1831, Eleanor Hodgson, vining border, alphabets, verse, baskets
  of flowers, name "Eleanor Hodgson 1831" in laurel wreath, 15"
  h, 12-1/2" w, toning to ground 1,380.00
1832, Anna J. Rowell, upper panel with alphabets above lower
  panel of pious verse, flanked by baskets of fruit, geometric floral borders, "Wrought by Anna J. Rowell at the age of 8 years
  1832," framed, 15-1/2" x 17-1/2" 1,495.00
1833, Hannah Boorse, red, green, white, and blue, flowers and
  stars, strawberry border, verse titled "On Death," stitched in
  her 11th year, stains and damage, framed, 18" x 17"
  ....550.00

1835

Sarah Cleggs, English, "Sarah Cleggs Work 1835, a Representation of Solomon's Temple," eglomise mat, 17-1/8" h,
  22-3/4" w, framed, minor losses, toning, fading 550.00
Mary K. Husted, silk on linen homespun, alphabets, house,
  "Mary K. Husted, Sampler, Rushville 1835," faded blue,
  green, yellow, and white, small holes plus larger damage in
  center towards bottom, edges glued down, modern frame,
  19-3/8" h, 18"..440.00
Martha Jane Larcom, linen homespun, alphabets, "Martha
  Jane Larcom Aged 12 Years AD 1935 Born Aug. 18 A.D.
  1823," toning, fading, framed, 17-3/8" h, 17-1/2" w
  ....4,025.00
1836, Hannah Sulton's, blue, brown, and white, alphabet, long
  verse, framed, some staining, 14" x 16-1/2" 825.00
1838, Emilia Hancock, greens and earth tones, flowers, trees, animals, and a building with ivy border, verse, "Finished in her
  ninth year, April 9, 1839, Berry School," framed, 16-1/4" x 12-
  1/2"..970.00
1845, Harriett Webb, greens and earth tones, flowers, bird, butterfly, floral ivy border, center building titled "Panwell Bungalow," alphabet and "Stitched in her thirteenth year, 1845,"
  some staining, 16-1/2" x 18-1/2" 495.00
1846, Dinah Hopkin, upper panel with pious versus, architectural
  facade with putti, lower panel with baskets of flowers, "A Front
  View of the Temple of Solomon Wrought by Dinah Hopkin
  Aged 8, 1846," 22-3/4" x 25", framed, fading, toning, minor
  staining 865.00
1858, Mary Johnson, red, blue, and green, 4 dogs and alphabet,
  framed, 12-1/4" x 8-3/4" 165.00
1868, Fanny Farmer, silk on cotton, alphabets, house, birds, flowers, "Fanny Farmer 1868 Aged 12 Years Old," faded brown,
  blue, green, lavender, worn and stained, some bleeding of
  colors, repairs, modern frame, 10" h, 6-1/2" w 350.00
1877, Hettie Garges, stitched on paper, red, green, black, yellow,
  and blue stitching, geometric figures of potted flowers and floral ivy border, framed, loss.....................................580.00
187-, red and blue wool on coarse linen homespun, alphabets
  and "Kate Battersby 187-," 8-3/4" h, 10-3/4" w..............220.00
Not Dated
  Silk on linen homespun, vining border, alphabets, house, and
    trees, and "Rachael Hopkins," orange, blue, green, and
    black, wear, some colors have run, stains, 8-1/4" x 8-1/4",
    unframed 275.00
  Silk on linen homespun, vining border, stylized trees, flowers,
    animals, verse and "Sarah Whittles Work Aged 9 Years,"
    red, pink, green, yellow, blue, and white, some staining to
    homespun, minor loss of floss, curly frame, 21" h, 20-3/4"
    w 715.00

SANDWICH GLASS

History: In 1818, Deming Jarves was listed in the Boston
Directory as a glass factor. That same year, he was appointed general manager of the newly formed New England Glass Company. In 1824, Jarves toured the
glassmaking factories in Pittsburgh, left New England
Glass Company, and founded a glass factory in Sandwich.

Originally called the Sandwich Manufacturing Company, it was incorporated in April 1826 as the Boston & Sandwich Glass Company. From 1826 to 1858, Jarves served
as general manager. The Boston & Sandwich Glass Company produced a wide variety of wares in differing levels
of quality. The factory used the free-blown, blown three
mold, and pressed glass manufacturing techniques. Both
clear and colored glass were used.

Competition in the American glass industry in the mid-
1850s resulted in lower-quality products. Jarves left the

Boston & Sandwich Company in 1858, founded the Cape Cod Glass Company, and tried to duplicate the high quality of the earlier glass. Meanwhile, at the Boston & Sandwich Glass Company emphasis was placed on mass production. The development of a lime glass (non-flint) led to lower costs for pressed glass. Some free-blown and blown-and-molded pieces, mostly in color, were made. Most of this Victorian-era glass was enameled, painted, or acid etched.

By the 1880s, the Boston & Sandwich Glass Company was operating at a loss. Labor difficulties finally resulted in the closing of the factory on Jan. 1, 1888.

References: Raymond E. Barlow and Joan E. Kaiser, *Glass Industry in Sandwich*, Vol. 1 (1993), Vol. 2 (1989), Vol. 3 (1987), and Vol. 4 (1983), distributed by Schiffer Publishing; ——, *Price Guide for the Glass Industry in Sandwich Vols. 1-4*, Schiffer Publishing, 1993; Ruth Webb Lee, *Sandwich Glass Handbook*, Charles E. Tuttle, 1966; ——, *Sandwich Glass*, Charles E. Tuttle, 1966; George S. and Helen McKearin, *American Glass*, Random House, 1979; Ellen T. Schroy, *Warman's Glass*, 2nd ed., Wallace-Homestead, 1995; Catherine M. V. Thuro, *Oil Lamps II*, Collector Books, 1994 value update; Kenneth Wilson, *American Glass 1760-1930*, 2 Vols., Hudson Hills Press and The Toledo Museum of Art, 1994.

Museum: Sandwich Glass Museum, Sandwich, MA.

Additional Listings: Blown Three Mold; Cup Plates.

Vase, amethyst, tulip, McKearin 201-40, 9-1/2" h, $1,200.

Basket, 5-1/2" h, 5-1/2" w, ruffled box pleated top, White Burmese, candy pink to yellow peachblow-type, applied frosted thorn handle 795.00
Bowl, 7-1/2" d, pressed, lacy, Tulip and Acanthus pattern 45.00
Butter Dish, cov, colorless, flint, Gothic pattern 195.00
Candlesticks, pr
    7" h
        Canary, pressed, loop base, Barlow #3047, very minor chips, gauffering marks 375.00
        Colorless, petal and loop design, slight chip on one petal 425.00
    7-1/2" h, hexagonal base, purple-blue petal socket, translucent white 575.00
    9-3/4" h, opaque blue and white, stepped base 50.00
Compote, 10-1/2" w, 4-3/4" h, cranberry overlay, oval cuts, enameled birds and flowers on inner surface, c1890 ....495.00
Creamer and Sugar, colorless, flint, Gothic pattern 125.00
Cup Plate
    Blue, lacy, ship 125.00
    Violet Blue, lacy, heart 325.00
Decanter, 6-3/4" h, cobalt blue, ribbed, tam o'shanter stopper 195.00
Goblet, colorless, flint, Gothic pattern, 12 pc set..............650.00
Inkwell
    2-3/8" h, sq, honey amber, applied brass collar, hinged cap, smooth base 40.00
    2-9/16", cylindrical domed form, colorless, pink and white stripes, sheared mouth, applied pewter collar and cap, smooth base 2,300.00
Lamp
    11-3/4" h, colorless blown font, sq scrolled pressed base, lion head dec, paw feet, very minor chips and cracks ...290.00
    12-1/2" h, pressed blue glass fonts, clambroth column and stepped base, minor base chips and cracks, pr ..1,840.00
Paperweight, 3-1/2" w, 1-1/4" h, colorless and frosted, portraits of Queen Victoria and Prince Consort, 1851 ....220.00
Pitcher, 10" h
    Amberina Verde, fluted top 325.00
    Electric Blue, enameled floral dec, fluted top, threaded handle 425.00
    Reverse Amberina, fluted top 400.00
Plate
    6" d, lacy, Shell pattern...............165.00
    7" d, Rayed Peacock Eye 125.00
Pomade, cov, figural, bear, imp retailer's name
    3-3/4" h, clambroth, imp "F. B. Strouse, N.Y.," chips 525.00
    4-1/2" h, blue, base imp "X. Bazin, Philada," chips.......300.00
Salt, 2" h, 3-1/8" d, blue, pressed, floral, Barlow 1460, minor chips, mold imperfections 690.00
Spooner, colorless, flint, Gothic pattern 85.00
Toy, lemonade cup, 1-5/8" h, canary, pressed, handle, tooled rim, pontil scar 140.00
Vase
    9-1/4" h, amethyst, Three Printie Block pattern, trumpet shape, gauffered rim, triple ring turned connector, pressed colorless base, hairlines to base 2,900.00
    10" h, dark amethyst, pressed, tulip, octagonal base, few chips to underside of base, pr 2,500.00
Whiskey Taster, cobalt blue, nine panels..........................185.00

SARREGUEMINES CHINA

History: Sarreguemines ware is a faience porcelain, i.e., tin-glazed earthenware. The factory, which made it, was established in Lorraine, France, in 1770, under the supervision of Utzschneider and Fabry. The factory was regarded as one of the three most prominent manufacturers of French faience. Most of the wares found today were made in the 19th century.

Marks: Later wares are impressed "Sarreguemines" and "Germany" as a result of changes in international boundaries.

Basket, 9" h, quilted, green, heavy leopard skin crystallization 250.00
Centerpiece, 14-3/4" h, 14-3/4" d, bowl with pierced ringlets to sides, supported by center stem flanked by sea nymphs either side, mounted atop circular base on 4 scrolled feet, polychrome dec, imp marks, chips, restorations, c1875 .....900.00
Cup and Saucer, Orange, majolica, crack to one cup, nicks, set of 4..200.00
Dinnerware Service, white china, multicolored scenes, 6 luncheon plates, 6 bread and butter plates, 6 demitasse cups, 6 porringers, 2 platters, divided dish 150.00
Face Jug, majolica
　Danish woman, bonnet, minor nick 880.00
　Paul Kruger, repair 110.00
　Smiling face, #3181, 5-1/2" h, minor rim nick 20.00
　Suspicious Eyes, #3320 ....550.00
　Upward Eyes, #3257, hairline......................................220.00
Humidor
　Man with top hat, majolica...165.00
　Pig, 6" h, #481, ear repair, no lid 220.00
Plate, 7-1/2" d, dec with music and characters from French children's songs, 12 pc set 375.00
Tankard, cov, 11" h, stoneware, continuous country scene of dancing and celebrating villagers, branch handle, pewter lid with porcelain medallion and painted polychrome coat of arms, dated 1869 ....325.00
Urn, 31-1/4" h, gilt metal mounted majolica, baluster form, cobalt blue glazed, mounted with the figure of a crowned lion holding sword, lion and mask handled sides, pierced foliate rim, raised on 4 scrolling foliate cast feet, imp "Majolica Sarreguemines," second half 19th C 1,800.00

Character Jug, Lawyer, majolica, mkd, $120.

SARSAPARILLA BOTTLES

History: Sarsaparilla refers to the fragrant roots of a number of tropical American, spiny, woody vines of the lily family. An extract was obtained from these dried roots and used for medicinal purposes. The first containers, which date from the 1840s, were stoneware; glass bottles were used later.

Carbonated water often was added to sarsaparilla to make a soft drink or to make consuming it more pleasurable. For this reason, sarsaparilla and soda became synonymous even though they originally were two different concoctions.

References: Ralph and Terry Kovel, *Kovels' Bottles Price List*, 10th ed., Crown Publishers, 1996; Carlo and Dot Sellari, *Standard Old Bottle Price Guide*, Collector Books, 1989.

Periodical: *Antique Bottle and Glass Collector*, P.O. Box 187, East Greenville, PA 18041.

Additional Listings: See *Warman's Americana & Collectibles* for a list of soda bottles.

Bull's Extract of Sarsaparilla, beveled corners, 7" l 400.00
Compound Extract of Sarsaparilla, amber, gallon 140.00
Dr. Ira Belding's, Honduras Sarsaparilla, colorless, 10-1/2" h 30.00
Dr. Townsend's Sarsaparilla, olive green, pontil 85.00
Foley's Sarsaparilla..20.00
Guysott's Yellow Dock & Sarsaparilla..............................40.00
Lancaster Glassworks, barrel, golden amber 125.00
Skoda's Sarsaparilla, amber..25.00
Warren Allen's Sarsaparilla Beer, tan, pottery..................125.00

SATIN GLASS

History: Satin glass, produced in the late 19th century, is an opaque art glass with a velvety matte (satin) finish achieved through treatment with hydrofluoric acid. A large majority of the pieces were cased or had a white lining.

While working at the Phoenix Glass Company, Beaver, Pennsylvania, Joseph Webb perfected mother-of-pearl (MOP) satin glass in 1885. Similar to plain satin glass in respect to casing, MOP satin glass has a distinctive surface finish and an integral or indented design, the most well known being diamond quilted (DQ).

The most common colors are yellow, rose, or blue. Rainbow coloring is considered choice.

Additional Listings: Cruets; Fairy Lamps; Miniature Lamps; Rose Bowls.

REPRODUCTION ALERT

Satin glass, in both the plain and mother-of-pearl varieties, has been widely reproduced.

Bowl

    5-7/8" d, 4-1/2" h, blue DQ MOP, three applied frosted thorny glass vases forming feet, white lining, ruffled edge
....365.00

    6-1/2" w, 4-1/2" h, bright pink and blue, white lining, Coinspot, scalloped rose bowl like top, 3 thorn feet, berry prunt
....750.00

Celery Vase, Herringbone, MOP, white base shades to raspberry to deep cranberry rim, applied clear frosted ruffled edge, SP holder mkd "Aurora SPMFG" quadruple plate, attributed to Mt. Washington, c1885.. 1,200.00

Cream Pitcher, 4-1/2" h, 3-1/8" d, blue, raindrop pattern, MOP, frosted blue reeded handle, white lining, bulbous, round mouth 195.00

Ewer, 8-1/2" h, pink, MOP, frilly spout, thorn handle 385.00

Finger Bowl and Underplate, blue DQ MOP, sgd "Patent"
....585.00

Mug

    2-3/4" h, 2-1/4" d, barrel shape, deep rose to amber, DQ, creamy white lining, frosted loop handle, English 175.00

    3-1/2" h, pink and gold looping, white ground, applied frosted reeded handle 175.00

Nappy, 6" l, 2-1/2" h, handle, white, MOP, triangular shaped top, applied frosted handle, allover gold dec, DQ design, deeply crimped edge 425.00

Rose Bowl

    3-3/8" d, 4" h, shaded heavenly blue, herringbone pattern, MOP, 6 crimp top 195.00

    3-1/2" d, 2-3/4" h, blue, ground pontil mark...................385.00

Miniature Lamp, Drape pattern, red, Smith #231, 8-5/8" h, $400.

Rose Bowl, light green, emb apple blossoms, ground pontil, 3-1/4" h, 3-3/4" w, $150. Photo courtesy of Johanna Billings.

    3-3/4" d, 2-3/8" h, heavenly blue, ribbon pattern, MOP, nine crimp top, white lining 235.00

    4" h, shaded blue to white, Mezzotint cherub dec, Victorian
....175.00

    4-1/2" d, bright yellow to white, enameled berries, leaves, and stems, Victorian 145.00

    5" d, 4-3/8" h, shaded blue, white lining, 6 crimp top, lavender enameled leaves dec 115.00

    5-1/2" d, 5" h, bright green shading to pale green, enamel blue, pale yellow, and gold floral dec 295.00

Tumbler

    3-1/2" h, rainbow, DQ, MOP, enamel floral dec, 3 white and pink single-petaled blossoms, 4 buds, 4 leaves and grass, gold rim 750.00

    4" h, apricot to pink to white, DQ, MOP, c1880, small blister
....60.00

Vase

    4-1/2" h, 5-5/8" d, light blue, ribbon pattern, MOP, three way top, pinched in side 375.00

    4-3/4" h, 4" d, shaded heavenly blue, heavy gold floral dec, red enameled spider with mark on base "Whitehouse Glass Works, Stourbridge" 260.00

    5-1/2" h, 2-3/4" d, blue raindrop MOP, frosted amber edge ruffled fan top, white lining...145.00

    5-3/4" h, hobnail MOP, pink shades to pale pink base, 4 folded-in sides 500.00

    7" h, 3-5/8" d, shaded pink ground, blue flowers and morning glory dec, bee in flight...125.00

    9" h, 3-1/2" w, swirl, gold to pale pink-white, MOP, Mt. Washington...325.00

    10-1/2" h, 5-1/2" w, bulbous, heavenly blue shading to pale blue, creamy white lining, English 265.00

    11-1/2" h, 4" w, bulbous, deep blue shading to white, four petal top, white flowers and orange branches dec, Victorian
....185.00

SATSUMA

History: Satsuma, named for a war lord who brought skilled Korean potters to Japan in the early 1600s, is a handcrafted Japanese faience (tin-glazed) pottery. It is finely crackled, has a cream, yellow-cream, or gray-cream color, and is decorated with raised enamels in floral, geometric, and figural motifs.

Figural satsuma was made specifically for export in the 19th century. Later satsuma, referred to as satsuma-style ware, is a Japanese porcelain also hand decorated in raised enamels. From 1912 to the present, satsuma-style ware has been mass-produced. Much of the ware on today's market is of this later period.

Reference: Nancy N. Schiffer, *Imari, Satsuma, and Other Japanese Export Ceramics,* Schiffer Publishing, 1997.

Bowl

   4-3/4" d, rounded sides turning in toward hexagonal rim, overlapping floral design, seal on base, sgd, late 19th C 275.00

   5-1/2" d, cobalt blue ground, gilt dec, 19th C, worn gilt 200.00

Box, cov, 3-1/2" d, round, lid dec with group of boys surrounded by floral border, base with band of fluttering butterflies above upright leaf border, int. base and lid with shaped cartouche of boys playing, surrounded by butterflies, sgd "Kinkozan," Meiji period 980.00

Vase, Lo Hans and Dragon, 4-7/8" h, $325.

Censor

   3-1/2" h, ovoid, 3 cabriole legs, 2 shaped handles rising from shoulder, lid with large shi shi seated on top, continual river landscape scene, patterned lappet border above, key fret border below, base sealed "Yabu Meizan," minor loss to one ear on shi shi 2,990.00

   10-1/4" h, tapering rect form, lobed base, 2 squared handles, pierced domed lid, allover dec or Arhats, Meiji period 635.00

Cup and Saucer, bird and floral motif, cobalt blue border, Kinkozan, Japanese 115.00

Dish, 14" d, male and female figures gathered around a goddess, all in landscape, patterned border, Meiji period 115.00

Koro, pierced lid

   2-3/4" h, ovoid, 3 short feet, continual scene of festival with men, women, and children playing games, eating, playing music, brocade shoulder border, 19th C 635.00

   3" h, hexagonal, 6 bracket feet, each side with flowers blooming behind garden fences, domed lid, sgd with Shimazu mon..2,185.00

Miniature

   Jar, cov, 2-1/2" h, square form, small foot, each side with differing panel, musicians, Mt. Fuji, roosters, and women with children visiting a bird vendor, gilt floral designs on blue ground surrounding each panel and on lid, int. liner lid, 19th C, sgd "Kinkozan" 1,495.00

   Teapot, 4" h, round form, panel of samuari and women with boys, blue ground, gilt floral and wave design, woven handle, base sgd "Kinkozan zo," Meiji period 635.00

Tea Cup and Saucer, 1-3/4" h cup, 4-3/4" d saucer, colorful groups of flowerheads with scrolling gilt vines, minor gilt wear, sgd "Yabu Meizan" 900.00

Tea Set, 6-1/2" h teapot, creamer, sugar, 6 cups and saucers, 6 7-1/4" d plates, paneled designs of courtesans in courtyard settings, c1900 ....290.00

Urn, 37-1/2" h, dragon handles, geishas in landscape 295.00

Vase

   2-7/8" h, shouldered form, tall neck gradually flaring to rim, body dec with boys playing games, shoulder and neck with overlapping flowerhead designs, Yabu Meizan seal on base, Meiji period, pr...2,300.00

   4-1/2" h, slender ovoid, continual scene of fishermen in watery landscape, Mount Fuji in distance, floral lappet neck border, Yabu Meizan seal on base, Meiji period 2,100.00

   6-1/4" h, high shouldered form, waisted neck, flared rim, two large panels, one with fisherman, other with immortals, background of shaped cartouches and butterflies, intricate brocade bands, 19th C, sgd "Seikozan"...............1,495.00

   6-1/4" h, ovoid, short waisted necks, flared rims, panels of figures in procession and in courtly pursuits on floral and patterned ground, one with rim damage, Meiji period, pr 750.00

   12" h, geometric banded borders, scene of artist decorating scrolls and birds, floral landscape, attached base, feet repairs, Japanese, late 19th C....................................260.00

   16" h, ovoid, short waisted neck, upturned rim, overlay design of monkeys chasing cabs, eating fruit, scrolling floral ground, black glazed neck, rim and root with sq scroll bands, unsgd, 19th C 11,500.00

   19" h, polychrome figures, gilt, blue ground, minor wear 525.00

SCALES

History: Prior to 1900, the simple balance scale was commonly used for measuring weights. Since then scales have become more sophisticated in design and

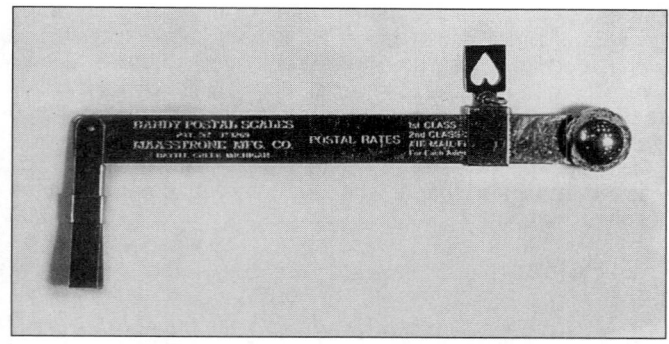

Postal, "Handy Postal Scale," nickel plated, "Maasstrone Mfg. Co.," orig box, $160.

more accurate. There are a wide variety of styles and types, including beam, platform, postal, and pharmaceutical.

Collectors' Club: International Society of Antique Scale Collectors, Ste. 1706, 176 W. Adams St., Chicago, IL 60603.

Baby, wicker basket 50.00
Balance
    Cast Iron, 14" l, orig red paint with black and yellow trim, nickel plated brass pans, mkd "Henry Troemner, Phila. No. 5B, Baker's" 120.00
    Glass and mahogany, mkd "Chainomatic, Christian Becker Inc., NY," c1919...225.00
    Wrought iron, 22" h, cast iron base, tin pans...................65.00
Candy
    Dayton, metallic orange, brass pan 300.00
    National Store Co., tin pan, c1910.................................95.00
Computing, 15-1/4" h, 17-1/2" w, merchant's type, "Computing Scale Co., Dayton, Ohio"...225.00
Counter, blue, chrome with tan, mkd "Toledo"...................175.00
Egg, Oaks Mfg. Co. 20.00
Hand Held, wide side gauge, unusual cylinder, mkd "Chatilion, NY" 30.00
Jeweler, brass pans, brass standard, 10 brass weights, green velvet lined box..160.00
Photographer, brass pans, brass weights, mkd "Made in Germany" 150.00
Postal, 4-1/4" h, desk, SS, cased, monogram, mkd "Shreve & Co.," c1900-22..250.00
Steelyard, wood, weighted bulbous end, turned shaft, 18th C 215.00
Store
    Hanson Weightmaster, 6" x 14" x 10", cast iron, gold case with ground, black lettering and indicator 45.00
    Howe, cast iron, red base, gold highlights, brass pan, 5 weights, patent June 18, 1887 ....75.00

SCHLEGELMILCH PORCELAINS

History: Erdmann Schlegelmilch founded his porcelain factory in Suhl in the Thuringia region in 1861. Reinhold, his brother, established a porcelain factory at Tillowitz in Upper Silesia in 1869. In the 1860s, Prussia controlled Thuringia and Upper Silesia, both rich in the natural ingredients needed for porcelain.

By the late 19th century, an active export business was conducted with the United States and Canada due to a large supply of porcelain at reasonable costs achieved through industrialization and cheap labor.

The Suhl factory ceased production in 1920, unable to recover from the effects of World War I. The Tillowitz plant, located in an area of changing international boundaries, finally came under Polish socialist government control in 1956.

Marks: Both brothers marked their pieces with the "RSP" mark, a designation honoring Rudolph Schlegelmilch, their father. More than 30 mark variations have been discovered.

References: Susan and Al Bagdade, *Warman's English & Continental Pottery & Porcelain*, 2nd ed., Wallace-Homestead, 1991; R. H. Capers, *Capers' Notes on the Marks of Prussia*, Alphabet Printing (667 E. 6th St., El Paso, IL 61738), 1996; Mary Frank Gaston, *Collector's Encyclopedia of R. S. Prussia and Other R. S. and E. S. Porcelain*, 1st Series (1982, 1993 value update), 2nd Series (1986, 1994 value update), 3rd Series (1994), 4th Series (1997), Collector Books; Leland and Carol Marple, *R. S. Prussia: The Early Years,* Schiffer Publishing, 1997.

Collectors' Club: International Assoc. of R. S. Prussia Collectors Inc., 212 Wooded Falls Rd., Louisville, KY 40243.

R.S. Germany

c 1910-1956

Biscuit Jar, cov, 6" h, loop handles, roses dec, satin finish, gold knob 95.00
Bonbon Dish, 7-3/4" l, 4-1/2" w, pink carnations, gold dec, silver-gray ground, looped inside handle 40.00
Bread Plate, iris variant edge mold, blue and white, gold outlined petals and rim, multicolored center flowers, steeple mark 115.00
Bride's Bowl, floral center, ornate ftd stand 95.00
Cake Plate, deep yellow, 2 parrots on hanging leaf vine, open handles, green mark..235.00
Celery Tray, 11" l, 5-3/4" w, lily dec, gold rim, open handles, blue label 120.00
Chocolate Pot, white rose florals, blue mark 95.00
Cup and Saucer, plain mold, swan, blue water, mountain and brown castle background, red mark 225.00
Demitasse Cup and Saucer, 3" h, pink roses, gold stenciled dec, satin finish, blue mark...90.00
Dessert Plate, 6-1/2" d, yellow and cream roses, green and rich brown shaded ground, 6 pc set 135.00
Hatpin Holder, floral dec 85.00
Napkin Ring, green, pink roses, white snowballs.................55.00
Nut Bow, 5-1/4" d, 2-3/4" h, cream, yellow, roses, green scalloped edge 65.00
Pitcher, 5-3/4" h, light blue, chrysanthemums, pink roses, gold trim 85.00
Plate, 9-3/4" d, white flowers, gold leaves, gilded edge, green ground, mkd "RS Germany" in dark green, script sgd "Reinhold Schlegelmilch/Tillowitz/Germany" in red 45.00

Powder Box, cov, green poppies, green mark....................50.00
Punch Bowl, 17-1/4" d, 8" h, mahogany shading to pink, polychrome enameled flowers with gilt, imp fleur-de-lis mark with "J. S. Germany" 275.00
Sauce Dish, underplate, green, yellow roses, blue mark.....45.00
Tea Tile, peach and tan, greenish white snowballs, red mark over faint blue mark 165.00
Vase, 4" h, bottle shape, shaded green to cream, cottage scene,mkd 70.00

R. S. Poland

c 1945-1956

Berry Bowl, 4-1/2" sq, white and pale orange floral design, green leaves, small orange-gold border flowers, mkd 45.00
Creamer, soft green, chain of violets, applied fleur-de-lis feet, red mark..110.00
Flower Holder, pheasants, brass frog insert 675.00
Vase
  8-1/2" h, 4-3/4" d, large white and tan roses, shaded brown and green ground...195.00
  10" h, cottage scene, woman with sheep in foreground, ornate handles, gold trim..650.00
  12" h, 6-1/4" d, white poppies, cream shaded to brown ground, pr 750.00

Sugar Bowl, cov, multicolored floral dec, 5" h, $45.

Sauce Dish, chamfered corners, multicolored floral band, gold highlights, red and green mark, 4-1/2", $35.

R.S. Prussia

Bowl

10" d, Hidden Images, portrait of woman, hair in bun, additional molded florals, pastel green ground 240.00

10-1/2" d, Iris mold, pink poppies and daisies, green ground, red mark 300.00

10-1/2" d, Mold 207, green, white, flowers, red mark....230.00

Butter Dish, cov, porcelain insert, cream and gold shading, pink roses, raised enamel, red mark 715.00

Cake Plate, 10-3/4" d, Art Nouveau, forget-me-not mold, beige flowers, pink luster rim, multicolored floral spray 195.00

Chocolate Set, cov chocolate pot, 6 cups and saucers, pink and red roses, gold luster, angular handles, red mark 995.00

Creamer, floral....................225.00

Demitasse Cup and Saucer, dainty flowers 100.00

Ferner, 7" d, mold 876, florals on purple and green ground, unsgd 165.00

Hair Receiver, green lilies of the valley, white ground, red mark 95.00

Mug, wide steeple mold, purple and orange poppies, steeple mark 82.00

Plate

8-3/4" d, poppies dec, raised molded edge and gilding 75.00

10" d, scalloped, gold beading and chain, satin finish, green foliage and white flowers, open handles, red mark 175.00

Relish Dish, 9" d, blown-out mold, lavender and pink gloss finish, pink and white roses, two handles, red mark 85.00

Pitcher, Poppies, rare mold, blown out base, red mark, 10-1/4" h, $820.

Shaving Mug, with mirror (Gaston Book II, Plate 397)........450.00
Spoon Holder, 14" l, pink and white roses..........................200.00
Toothpick Holder, green shadows, pink and white roses, jeweled, six feet, red mark 250.00
Vase, 4-3/8" h, 2-5/8" d, Pheasant Scene, handle, Mold 918 ....500.00

R. S. Suhl

Coffee Set, 9" h, coffeepot, creamer, sugar, 6 cups and saucers, figural scenes dec, some mkd "Angelica Kauffmann" 1,750.00
Pin Tray, 4-1/2" d, round, Nightwatch..............................375.00
Plate, 8-1/2" d, windmill scene and water, green mark 125.00
Vase, 8" h, 4 pheasants, green mark................................275.00

R. S. Tillowitz

Bowl, 7-3/4" d, slanted sides, open handles, 4 leaf shaped feet, matte finish, pale green ground, roses and violets, gold flowered rim, mkd 125.00
Creamer and Sugar, soft yellow and salmon roses..............65.00

Hatpin Holder, yellow and white roses, gold trim, mkd in red "Reinhold Schlegelmilch/Tillowitz/Germany," 6-3/4" h, $90.

Plate, 6-1/2" d, mixed floral spray, gold beading, emb rim, brown wing mark 120.00
Relish Tray, 8" l, oval, hp, shaded green, white roses, green leaves, center handle, blue mark 45.00
Tea Set, stacking teapot, creamer, and sugar, yellow, rust, and blue flowers, gold trim, ivory ground, mkd "Royal Silesia," green mark in wreath 95.00
Vase, 10" h, pheasants, brown and yellow, 2 curved handles 125.00

SCHNEIDER GLASS

Schneider   *Schneider*

History: Brothers Ernest and Charles Schneider founded a glassworks at Epiney-sur-Seine, France, in 1913. Charles, the artistic designer, previously had worked for Daum and Gallé. Robert, son of Charles, assumed art direction in 1948. Schneider moved to Loris in 1962.

Although Schneider made tablewares, stained glass, and lighting fixtures, its best-known product is art glass, which exhibits simplicity of design and often has bubbles and streaking in larger pieces. Other styles include cameo-cut and hydrofluoric-acid-etched designs.

Marks: Schneider glass was signed with a variety of script and block signatures, "Le Verre Francais," or "Charder."

Bowl, 6" d, amethyst, shallow, sgd 175.00
Centerbowl, 12" d, 3-1/4" h, mottled orange border, yellow and white body, edge inscribed "Schneider," base inscribed "France-Ovington New York," inside wear 345.00
Charger, 15-1/2" d, brilliant orange plate, brown-green amorphous central dec, reverse inscribed "Schneider France/Ovington New York" 525.00
Cigarette Lighter Base, 7-1/2" l, 3" h mottled yellow pear shaped glass, etched purple and rose-pink Art Deco elements, inscribed "Le Verre Francais" on gilt metal atomizer top 375.00
Compote, 10" d, 8-1/2" h, Tango red, mottled blue-black rim, shaped bowl, wrought metal pedestal foot, three glass beads, glass stem inscribed "Schneider France" 690.00
Dish, 13-1/2" x 5-1/2", mottled orange and dark blue, amethyst with white ribbing, pedestal base 275.00
Ewer, 15-1/2" h, ovoid, pointed spout, thick cushion foot, mottled white frosted ground, mottled orange and green overlay, etched floral bands, applied purple angled handle at shoulder, engraved "Charder Le Verre Francais" 1,250.00
Lamp, 15-1/2" d, hanging, creamy glass half-round light bowl, speckled yellow and red, edge inscribed "Schneider," suspended by twisted and knotted cord and wire chain, three matching glass beads 1,380.00
Pitcher, 6-1/2" h, bulbous Tango red body, elongated mottled blue-brown neck and spout, applied purple glass handle, inscribed "Schneider" 635.00
Serving Plate, 14" d, 3" h, transparent green-yellow dish, mottled orange pedestaled foot, inscribed "Schneider France" 345.00
Vase
  4" h, flared rim, pink oval body, amethyst shaded to purple layer, etched stylized sunflower motif, lower edge inscribed "Le Verre Francais France" 520.00
  5-3/8" h, creamy yellow body, orange-brown mottled lower oval, purple disk foot, medial border of aubergine-black olives on leafy branches, ftd sgd "Schneider France" in script 3,450.00

10-1/4" h, ftd oval pink mottled glass body, amethyst shaded to purple overlay, repeating etched stylized sunflower motif, sgd "Le Verre Francais" on foot, "France/Ovington" on base 1,035.00
11" h, oval body, mottled red and yellow glass overlaid, etched stylized leaves and berries, foot inscribed "Le Verre Francais," base mkd "France/Ovington" 1,265.00
12" h, bulbous flared body, mottled red and yellow glass, overlaid and etched stylized leaves and berries, two applied purple handles, lower edge inscribed "Le Verre Francais," base mkd "France-Ovington" 1,380.00
12-1/2" h, flattened oval, mottled pastel blue body, bright royal blue overlay, two stripes of etched foliated elements, sgd "Charder" on cameo at side, foot inscribed "Le Verre Francais France" 1,150.00
15-1/2" h, 12" d, oval colorless and mottled white body, internally decorated with broad orange and purple aubergine strokes and splotches, inscribed "Schneider" mark at side 1,725.00
16-3/4" h, bulbous, elongated neck, translucent orange body with red striations, side inscribed "(vase) Schneider France," some top chips 520.00

SCHOENHUT TOYS

History: Albert Schoenhut, son of a toy maker, was born in Germany in 1849. In 1866, he ventured to America where he worked as a toy-piano repairman for Wanamaker's in Philadelphia, Pennsylvania. Finding the glass sounding bars inadequate, he perfected a toy piano with metal sounding bars. His piano was an instant success, and the A. Schoenhut Company had its beginning.

From that point on, toys seemed to flow out of the factory. Each of his six sons entered the business, and it prospered until 1934, when misfortune forced the company into bankruptcy. In 1935, Otto and George Schoenhut contracted to produce the Pinn Family Dolls.

The Schoenhut Manufacturing Company was formed by two other Schoenhuts. Both companies operated under a partnership agreement that eventually led to O. Schoenhut, Inc., which continues today.

Some dates of interest:

1872–toy piano invented
1903–Humpty Dumpty Circus patented
1911-1924–wooden doll production
1928-1934–composition dolls made.

References: E. Ackerman and F. Keller, *Under the Big Top with Schoenhut's Humpty Dumpty Circus*, published by author (P.O. Box 217, Culver City, CA 90230), 1997; Carol Corson, *Schoenhut Dolls*, Hobby House Press, 1993; Richard O'Brien, *Collecting Toys*, 7th ed., Books Americana, 1995.

Collectors' Clubs: Schoenhut Collectors Club, 1003 W. Huron St., Ann Arbor, MI 48103; Schoenhut Toy Collectors, 1916 Cleveland St., Evanston, IL 60202.

Animal, jointed wood construction
  Alligator, painted green, red mouth, white teeth, leather feet, 13" l 525.00
  Brown Bear, hand painted shades of brown, leather ears, 7-1/2" l on hind legs 275.00
  Buffalo, glass eyes, hand painted dark brown, leather horns, rope tail, 8" l 200.00
  Bulldog, painted white, black spot over eye, leather collar and tail, 5" l 410.00

Camel, painted brown, black hoofs, rope tail, double hump back, 7-1/2" l 250.00

Cat, olive brown, black stripes, white underbelly, leather tail, 4-1/4" h 770.00

Cow, glass eyes, hand painted brown, leather collar, rope tail, horns, and ears, 8-1/2" l 265.00

Donkey, glass eyes, painted brown, gray nose, fabric mane, price for pr 90.00

Elephant, glass eyes, hand painted dark gray, rope tail and tusks, large leather ears, price for pr 315.00

Goat, glass eyes, hand painted black and white, leather ears, horns, beard and tail, 8" l 220.00

Goose, glass eyes, painted white, orange beak and feet, 7" l 360.00

Gorilla, painted brown, leather ears, 11" arm span 3,410.00

Hippo, painted eyes, dark brown, leather tail and ears, wooden carved front teeth, 10" l 185.00

Horse, glass eyes, painted brown, leather ears and saddle, 8" h, missing stirrups, price for pr 110.00

Hyena, Teddy Roosevelt safari animal, hand painted gray with stripes, leather ears, rope tail, 6" l 1,430.00

Kangaroo, painted shades of brown, white underbelly, leather ears, stands on rear legs and tail, 10-1/2" l 440.00

Leopard, painted yellow with brown spots, rope tail, 7-1/4" l 360.00

Pig, glass eyes, painted light brown, leather ears, 8" l 55.00

Polar Bear, painted white, short rope tail, leather ears, 8" l 660.00

Poodle, glass eyes, painted white, rope tail, 7" l 55.00

Rabbit, painted brown, leather ears and tail, 5-1/4" l 715.00

Rhino, painted eyes, hand painted olive brown with black spots, rope tail, leather ears, 9" l, one ear missing 110.00

Seal, painted dark brow, leather flipper hands, 9" l 290.00

Show Horse, glass eyes, ring tail, leather ears, wooden platform mounted on back, 10" l, price for pr 360.00

Tiger, hand painted orange, brown spots, rope tail, 7-1/2" l, some paint flaking 250.00

Wolf, painted shades of brown, red mouth, long carved wooden tail, leather ears 1,980.00

Zebra, painted light brown with dark stripes, leather ears, rope tail, 7-3/4" l 330.00

Balancing Bar, painted wood and metal 550.00

Cage Wagon, 12" x 12", wood, red, gray bars, blue wheels, top mkd "Schoenhut's Humpty Dumpty Circus," contains lion with full mane, rear door opens 990.00

Camera, Spirit of America, wood, painted black, movie camera clicks when turned, 10" h, orig box 935.00

Circus Animal in Cage, wood animal, wire cage
7-1/2" h, brown bear, leather ears, hand painted, shades of brown 220.00

8" l, lion, rope tail, carved head, body painted light to medium brown 415.00

11" h, giraffe, leather ears, wood short horns, rope tail, natural colors 770.00

Circus Pedestals, painted wood and litho paper, price for 5 pc set 470.00

Figure, jointed wood construction
Barney Google and Spark Plug, wood hat, fabric suit, yellow blanket with name on Spark Plug 550.00

Black Dude, hand painted face, leather ears, long purple coat, yellow vest, checkered pants, white top hat, 8-1/2" h 315.00

Circus Performer, bisque head, hand painted, fabric suit
Gent Acrobat, blue and yellow felt suit, red shorts ..300.00
Gert the Acrobat, 9" l 330.00

Farmer, straw hat, bucket and rake, 7" h 110.00

Felix the Cat, black and white, large leather ears 470.00

Hobo, hand painted face, leather ears, felt jacket and hat, fabric pants and scarf around neck 140.00

Maggie and Jiggs, cloth and fabric suits, animated appearance, Maggie holding rolling pin 525.00

Mary and Her Lamb, cloth outfit, straw hat, white lamb, school desk, feeding trough 1,430.00

Ringmaster, hand painted face, red tails, vest, and pants, orig top hat and whip 250.00

Golf Game, indoor, 36" l long wooden handles with golfers, tee area, putting green, sand trap, water well, balls 1,320.00

School Desk, painted wood, for Mary and her lamb set 190.00

Weights, painted wood, lift weights, 50 lb barbells, 100 lb barbells, price for 4 pc set 990.00

Wheelbarrow, painted wood, blue and orange, price for pr 470.00

SCIENTIFIC INSTRUMENTS

History: Chemists, doctors, geologists, navigators, and surveyors used precision instruments as tools of their trade. Such objects were well designed and beautifully crafted. They are primarily made of brass; fancy hardwood cases also are common.

The 1990s have seen a keen interest in scientific instruments, both in the auction market and at antique shows. The number of collectors of this mechanical wonders is increasing as more and more interesting examples are being offered.

References: Florian Cajori, History of the Logarithmic Slide Rule and Allied Instruments, Astragal Press, 1994; Gloria Clifton, Directory of British Scientific Instrument Makers 1550-1851, P. Wilson Publishers, 1994; William H. Skerritt, Catalog of the Charles E. Smart Collection: Antique Surveying Instruments, published by author, (12 Locust Ave., Troy, NY 12180), 1996.

Periodicals: Rittenhouse, P.O. Box 151, Hastings-on-Hudson, NY 10706; Scientific, Medical & Mechanical Antiques, P.O. Box 412, Taneytown, MD 21787.

Collectors' Clubs: International Calculator Collectors Club, 14561 Livingston St., Tustin, CA 92680; Maryland Microscopical Society, 8261 Polk St., McLean VA, 22102; The Oughtred Society, 2160 Middlefield Rd., Palo Alto, CA 94301; Zeiss Historical Society, P.O. Box 631, Clifton, NJ 07012.

Museum: National Museum of American History, Smithsonian Institution, Washington, DC.

Rhinoceros, 9" l, $215.

Anemometer, 6 register, 8 blade, 2-5/8" d, fan drives 2-1/4" d silvered dial, brass, mounting bracket, softwood case, c1875 ....345.00

Astronomical Theodolite, 15-1/2" h, 10-1/2" l telescope, 5-1/2" d, 2 vernier vertical circle, 6", 2 vernier 20" horiz. Circle, telescope and plate vials, microscope vernier readers, detachable alcohol lamp, detachable 4 screw leveling base, trough compass on telescope, orig dovetailed mahogany box with accessories, mkd "Stanley, Great Turnstile, Holborn, London, 7534", c1890, Heller & Brightly label mahogany ext. leg tripod 2,185.00

Astronomical Transit, 20" h, 8-1/2" w, 15-3/4" telescope with rt. Angle prism eyepiece with removable strider level, 7" d double frame, 2 vernier, vertical circle with indexing vial and circle control, 6" d, 2 vernier, 15", silver horizontal scale, plate vial with ivory scale, tribrach leveling base, bright brass finish, pine case, mkd "Blunt, New York," c1860....................7,500.00

Circumferentor, 5-1/4" h, 9" d outside dia., 4-1/8" compass in center, attached to rotating sight vane/vernier arm, inset vial, silvered dial and outer ring, engraved with 8 point star, 2 outer fixed sight vanes, brass, mkd "Dollond London," c1825 ....1,955.00

Drawing Instruments, fitted 6" l x 3" w black shagreen cov wood case, 6" l ivory and brass sector, 6" l ivory scale, 6" ebony and brass parallel rule, 1-3/4" brass protractor, six brass and iron drafting tools with ram's head horn screws, c1800.......445.00

Globe, 8" d, 9-1/2" h, Fitz's, terrestrial, mkd "Ginn & Heath," c1877, dec with revolving cast iron base, adjustable brass daylight/twilight boundary rings, brass moon, minor defects in Arctic Circle 3,220.00

Microscope, compound monocular
12" h, 8-1/4" l, 1-1/8" d tube with 1 obj, fine focus on arm, 3-1/2" d stage with condenser and diaphragm, double mirror on calibrated rotating arm, japanned and lacquered brass, case, extra obj., mkd "3373," c1885 ....575.00
12" h, 8-1/2" l, 1-1/8" d, tube with 1 obj, fine focus on arm, rect stage, 5 hole diaphragm, double mirror on rotating arm, extra eyepiece, orig case, japanned and lacquered brass, sgd "Wm. H. Armstrong & Co., Indianapolis, Ind.," #11737, c1893..635.00
13-1/4" h, 9" l, 1-1/2" d single nosepiece tube with 3-1/2" d. stage, condenser and double mirror revolve on arms centered on stage, against graduated vertical circular silvered dial, 4 obj. and 3 eyepieces, lacquered brass, case, mkd "14668, Pat. Oct. 13, 1885" 1,840.00
15-1/2" h, 10-1/2" l, 1-1/4" d. tube with single nosepiece, fine focus on front of tube, 4-1/2" d stage, 2 sub-stage condenses, double mirror, detachable parabolic mirror, extra 8" l, 1-1/8" d draw tube, detachable stand condenser lens with "B" holder, prism eyepiece, 2 obj., 2 eyepieces, lacquered brass, orig case, mkd "Tolles Boston, 272," c1875" 2,275.00

Nonius Compass, 6 inch
15-1/8" x 6-7/8" x 7-1/8" h, 5-1/4" l detachable sight vanes, top designed to hold 7/8" d telescope, plate vials, silvered dial and edge engraved outer ring, unique 5' vernier moves the

south sight vane by means of worn gear, mahogany case, mkd "J. Hanks," Troy, NY, c1825 ....1,725.00
15-78" x 6-7/8" x 9-1/2" h, 7-1/4" l detachable sight vanes, 4-3/4" rad., 20°, 1' outside vernier ring, also edge graduated, staff adaptor, lacquered brass, mkd "Phelps & Gurley, Troy, N.Y.," c1850..2,530.00

Palmer's Computing Scale, 8-1/2" d computing wheel on 11-1/4" sq outer scale, instructions on reverse, 1 fixed and 1 rotating logarithmic scale, values and gauge points numbered and noted, red, yellow, gold, and black, mkd "Aaron Palmer, 1843 patent" 550.00

Pocket Compass
1-1/2", 2-1/4" x 2-1/4" mahogany case with hinged cov, 1-1/2" needle floats over engraved finely detailed mariner's star inside 2° increment quadrant outer ring, mkd "T. T. Rowe, Lockport, N.Y.," c1825 ....230.00
2", 2-5/8" d, brass, worn silvered dial, full circle, 180° cliometer scale, mkd "Breiothaupt in Cassel," c1800 ....565.00

Sextant, 3" d, brass, pocket, dial engraved "Stanley, Gt. Turnstile London," 19th C..460.00

Sketching Case, 10-1/2" l, 7" w, 4-1/2" x 6-1/8" plotting surface, 5" d graduated plotting scale, 2" l rotating trough compass, 2 paper rollers, varnished hardwood and lacquered brass, mkd "W. & L. E. Gurley, Troy, N.Y., patented Sept. 28, 1897" 750.00

Solar Transit, 17" h, Burt Solar Attachment, hour circle on 6.45" engineer's transit, 11" telescope, 3" rad. vert. arc., 5" compass, telescope and plate vials, 4 screw leveling, brass construction, rubbed bronze finish, dovetailed mahogany case, label, and brass plummet, accessories, mkd "W. & L. E. Gurley, Troy, NY," c1890...3,335.00

Surveyors' Compass
4-7/8" l x 3-1/2" w x 2-1/4" h, 1-9/16" l detachable sight vanes and brass cover, 3" staff type, brass with silvered dial, raised azimuth ring, 4-1/2" x 4-1/2" x 1-5/8" dovetailed, fitted mahogany case, mkd "Edmund Draper Philada Warranted," c1835 ....1,495.00
9-1/2" h, 5-1/2" w, 14-1/2" d, 4-3/4", plain brass, detachable brass slight vanes, brass tripod adapter, dovetailed mahogany box with 1-5/8 x 2-5/8" paper label sgd "Loring & Churchill successors to C. G. King…72 Washington St. …Boston," c1850, minor imperfections.................1,265.00

Surveyors' and Engineers' Transit, 12" h, 11" telescope with vial, vert. arc., 6-1/4", 30" horiz. Circle with inlaid silver scales, plate vials, 4 screw leveling, green leather finish, orig dovetailed mahogany box with labels, mkd "Buff & Berger, Boston, #2149," c1890 ....920.00

Surveyor's compass, L. Beekman Co., Toledo, OH, orig box, complete, $500.

Surveyors' Vernier Transit Compass, 13-1/2" h, 11" telescope with vial, 3-1/2" d vert. circle, 5-3/4" compass, 4" rad. Declination vernier, 2 plate vials, cross sights, 4 screw detachable leveling base, staff adaptor, stiff leg tripod, brass plumb bob, orig case with labels, bronzed brass, mkd "W. & L. E. Gurley, Troy, NY," c1874 .... 1,840.00

Telescope

Brass, E. Vion, Paris, 19th C, brass, oak stand, fitted mahogany case for telescope 7,475.00

Brass and leather, one draw, engraved "G. Young & Co. London Day & Night," England, 19th C, replaced leather, 20-1/4" l 400.00

Brass and mahogany, one draw, 19th C, 21" l 320.00

Brass and wood, replaced objective lens, 18th C, 20-1/4" l 345.00

Webb Adder, 6-3/4" l, 4-7/8" w, brass added attached to mahogany backer, brass wall fasteners, mkd "C. HI Web N.Y. 'The Adder,' PATd March 10, 1868. B1108" 520.00

Wye Level, 8-1/4" h, 4" w, 16-1/4" l, 1-3/8" d reversible telescope with 6-3/4" l, 4 screw leveling base, horiz. motion clamp and screw, eyepiece attachment, mkd "Kuebler & Seelhorst Makers Philada, 597, Oct. 1, 1867 Patent" 500.00

SCRIMSHAW

History: Norman Flayderman defined scrimshaw as "the art of carving or otherwise fashioning useful or decorative articles as practiced primarily by whalemen, sailors, or others associated with nautical pursuits." Many collectors expand this to include the work of Eskimos and French POWs from the War of 1812.

References: Stuard M. Frank, *Dictionary of Scrimshaw Artists*, Mystic Seaport Museum, 1991; Nina Hellman and Norman Brouwer, *Mariner's Fancy*, South Street Seaport Museum, Balsam Press, and the University of Washington Press, 1992; Martha Lawrence, *Scrimshaw*, Schiffer Publishing, 1993.

Museums: Cold Spring Whaling Harbor Museum, Cold Spring Harbor, NY; Kendall Whaling Museum, Sharon, MA; Mystic Seaport Museum, Mystic, CT; National Maritime Museum, San Francisco, CA; New Bedford Whaling Museum, New Bedford, MA; Old Dartmouth Historical Soc, New Bedford, MA; Pacific Whaling Museum, Waimanalo, HI; Sag Harbor Whaling & Historical Museum, Sag Harbor, NY; San Francisco Maritime National Historical Park, San Francisco, CA; South Street Seaport Museum, New York, NY; Whaling Museum, Nantucket, MA.

REPRODUCTION ALERT

The biggest problem in the field is fakes, although there are some clues to spotting them. A very hot needle will penetrate the common plastics used in reproductions but not the authentic material. Ivory will not generate static electricity when rubbed; plastic will. Patina is not a good indicator; it has been faked by applying tea or tobacco juice, burying in raw rabbit hide, and in other ingenious ways. Usually the depth of cutting in an old design will not be consistent since the ship rocked and tools dulled; however, skilled forgers have even copied this characteristic.

Model, ship, ribbed, bone and ivory, detailed, 8-1/2, " $1,400.

Book

Everett, Crosby, *Susan's Teeth and Much About Scrimshaw*, Nantucket, 1955, papered boards, 8 vol, minor rubbing 1,265.00

Flayderman, E. Norman, *Scrimshaw and Scrimshanders*, New Milford, CT, 1972, sgd limited edition, 910/1000, cloth, slipcase 575.00

Busk

11-7/8" l, whalebone, polychrome dec, memorial, foliate and geometric devices, 19th C, cracks 320.00

12-3/4" l, whalebone, polychrome dec, ship, foliate and geometric devices, 19th C, cracks, minor losses 195.00

13-7/8" l, wood, dec with eagle, shield, lovebirds, and ship under sail, heart and foliate devices, inscribed "GC & EW," dated 1840 .... 345.00

Domino Box, 6-7/8" l, bone and wood, shoe form, pierced carved slide top with star and heart dec, domino playing pcs, Prisoner of War, 19th C, cracks, minor insect damage 520.00

Game Box, 5-3/4" x 6-1/2", bone, pierced carved box with geometric dec, 3 slide tops, compartmented int., backgammon and other playing pcs, traces of paint dec, Prisoner of War, 19th C, repair, warping to tops, very minor loses 690.00

Jagging Wheel, 7-1/4" l, dec with building flying American flag, berried vines, 19th C, very minor losses 520.00

Obelisk, 13-3/8" h, inlaid mahogany, inlaid with various exotic woods, abalone and ivory in geometric and star motifs, 19th C, minor losses, minute cracks 815.00

Snuff Box, top inscribed "Capt. N. C. Norten," service dates 1831-1841 on side, other dec, lampwick highlighting, 3" x 1-1/2", $395.

Salt Horn, 5-1/2" l, engraved "John Snow March...1780 by S. H.," crosshatched borders enclosing reserve of ship, geometric, and foliate devices, insect damage 460.00

Seam Rubber, 4" l, whalebone, geometric designs on handle, traces of orig paint, 19th C 850.00

Walrus Tusk

12-1/2" l, polychrome engraving of whales, eagles, displays of arms, ships under sail, figure on horseback, 19th C, restoration, losses, pr 1,265.00

17-3/4" h, reserves of animals, courting couples, ships under sail, memorials, sailors and armaments, later engraved brass presentation caps, "Presented by George M. Chase to Ike B. Dunlap Jan. 25th 1908," cracks, one restored, pr 2,530.00

Watch Hutch, 11-7/8" h, bone, pierce carved floral and figural dec, brass backing, polychrome foliate highlights, Prisoner of War, 19th C, custom made case, minor cracks, losses, repairs 750.00

Whale's Tooth, 19th C

5" h, courting couple on one side, Victorian building on other, geometric and foliate swag border, minor cracks....690.00

5-1/4" h, steamer "C. S. Steamer A. D. Bache," flying American flag, rampart dolphins, reverse with eagle over shield, monogrammed, mahogany stand, minor cracks 690.00

5-1/4" h, young couple and two elegant ladies, cracks 460.00

5-1/2" l, polychrome dec of fashionable lady on one side, other with child and hoop, geometric borders 690.00

5-3/4" h, young girl with jump rope on one side, other with young man, 20th C, cracks 260.00

6" h, engraved dancing sailor, 20th C, chips, minor cracks 635.00

6-1/4" h, dec with three-masted ship "Cyane" and memorial 2,300.00

6-1/2" h, four-masted shaping ship "Clipper Chip Great Republic Built E. Boston 1853" 550.00

6-5/8" h, historic landmarks, dec on both sides, very minor cracks and chips 865.00

6-7/8" h, various ships under sail and young lady, cracks 1,380.00

Whimsey, 5-3/4" h, carved bone, French soldier sharpening his sword on grinding wheel, Prisoner of War, 19th C, minor paint wear 4,715.00

SEVRES

History: The principal patron of the French porcelain industry in early 18th-century France was Jeanne Antoinette Poisson, Marquise de Pompadour. She supported the Vincennes factory of Gilles and Robert Dubois and their successors in their attempt to make soft-paste porcelain in the 1740s. In 1753, she moved the porcelain operations to Sevres, near her home, Chateau de Bellevue.

The Sevres soft-paste formula used sand from Fontainebleau, salt, saltpeter, soda of alicante, powdered alabaster, clay, and soap. Many famous colors were developed, including a cobalt blue. The wonderful scenic designs on the ware were painted by such famous decorators as Watteau, La Tour, and Boucher. In the 18th century, Sevres porcelain was the world's foremost diplomatic gift.

In 1769, kaolin was discovered in France, and a hard-paste formula was developed. The baroque gave way to rococo, a style favored by Jeanne du Barry, Louis XV's next mistress. Louis XVI took little interest in Sevres, and many factories began to turn out counterfeits. In 1876, the factory was moved to St. Cloud and was eventually nationalized.

Marks: Louis XV allowed the firm to use the "double L" in its marks.

Reproduction Alert.

Bowl, 7-1/2" d, pottery, cobalt ground, flared rim, bronze mounts, 3 paw feet, late 19th C...................................575.00

Box, cov, 2" x 3-1/2", floral dec...225.00

Cabinet Plate, 9-1/2" d, wide blue ground banding, gilt border with leafy vine, cartouche of cherubs flanking a Napoleonic "N," print marks, c1868, 3 pc set 488.00

Centerpiece, 20-1/4" h, 4 youths in procession, each supporting basket, mounted on freeform base, white biscuit, imp mark, early 20th C 320.00

Chocolate Cup and Saucer, cov, painted scattered sprays of flowers, blue line and gilt dash borders, gilt dentil rim..275.00

Clock, 14-1/2" h, painted foliage, molded figures, gilt bronze mounts, wear 2,875.00

Compote, 5-1/4" h, polychrome transfer printed figural landscapes, bronze mounts, 20th C, pr 175.00

Dish, 9-3/4" d, central floral design with fruit, border reserve of oval panels painted with floral groups surrounded by gilt floral sprigs and scrolls, green ground, gilt edged rim, c1750 ....195.00

Figure, 12-1/2" h, bisque and blue glazed porcelain, Cupid and youthful Psyche, after model by Falconer, c1872, each inscribed and shaped enamel base, imp and printed factory marks, repairs, both bases with chips, pr 1,380.00

Luncheon Plate, 9-3/4" d, central gilt six-pointed star, border with hunt scenes, price for 6 pc set....................................325.00

Milk Jug, cov, 5" h, pear form, later neoclassical reserve dec, gilt highlights, c1870 ....185.00

Urn, cov, cobalt blue, gold, and turquoise, courting scenes, bouquet of summer flowers, c1870, 17-1/2" h, pr, $1,600.

Pin Box, cov, 6-1/2" l, oval, cartouche of romantic couple on cov, blue ground 275.00

Plate, 9" d, center reserve of pansies, trailing rose border, cobalt blue dec, rim, late 18th C 350.00

Platter, 13-1/4" l, oval, painted military camp scene reserve, scrolling gilt border, cobalt blue scalloped rim.............625.00

Soup Plate, 9-1/2" d, scattered flower springs, 3 kidney shaped flower panes surrounded by apple green border with gilt tooled floral garlands, c1775, 6 pc set........................1,400.00

Tete-A-Tete Service, teapot, cov sugar, 2 teacups and saucers, 13" l, shaped tray, couples in landscapes, jeweled surround, underglaze blue, celeste ground, mid 19th C, set.....6,650.00

Tray, 16" l, oval, putti with bales of wheat center, rim with floral reserves, blue celeste ground, scrolled and rocaille handles, late 18th C 1,500.00

Urn
15" h, pink ground, oval cartouches painted with bawdy peasant scene, mask-form ormolu handles, 19th C, covers missing, pr 3,335.00
18" h, painted courting couple on white ground, ormolu mounts, c1900, cov missing 435.00

Vase
6" h, bud, gilt ground, enamel Art Nouveau stylized leaf and flower design, printed mark 635.00
11" h, pink ground, oval cartouches with figural landscapes and ornaments, metal mount, pr 1,380.00
12" h, cov, enamel and gilt dec, figural landscape, light blue ground borders, late 19th C/early 20th C.................230.00

SEWING ITEMS

History: As recently as 50 years ago, a wide variety of sewing items were found in almost every home in America. Women of every economic and social status were skilled in sewing and dressmaking.

Iron or brass sewing birds, one of the interesting convenience items, which developed, were used to hold cloth (in the bird's beak) while sewing. They could be attached to a table or shelf with a screw-type fixture. Later models included a pincushion.

References: *Advertising & Figural Tape Measures*, L-W Book Sales, 1995; Elizabeth Arbittier et al., *Collecting Figural Tape Measures*, Schiffer Publishing, 1995; Carter Bays, *Encyclopedia of Early American Sewing Machines*, published by author, 1993; Frieda Marion, *China Half-Figures Called Pincushion Dolls*, published by author, 1974, 1994 reprint; Averil Mathias, *Antique and Collectible Thimbles and Accessories*, Collector Books, 1986, 1995 value update; Wayne Muller, *Darn It!*, L-W Book Sales, 1995; James W. Slaten, *Antique American Sewing Machines*, Singer Dealer Museum (3400 Park Blvd., Oakland, CA 94610), 1992; Glenda Thomas, *Toy and Miniature Sewing Machines* (1995), Book II (1997), Collector Books; Helen Lester Thompson, *Sewing Tools & Trinkets*, Collector Books, 1996; Gertrude Whiting, *Old-Time Tools & Toys of Needlework*, Dover Publications, 1970; Estelle Zalkin, *Zalkin's Handbook of Thimbles & Sewing Implements,* Warman Publishing, 1988.

Collectors' Clubs: International Sewing Machine Collectors Society, 1000 E. Charleston Blvd., Las Vegas, NV 89104; The Thimble Guild, P.O. Box 381807, Duncanville, TX 75138; Thimble Collectors International, 6411 Montego Bay Rd., Louisville, KY 40028; Toy Stitchers, 623 Santa Florita Ave., Millbrae, CA 94030.

Museums: Fabric Hall, Historic Deerfield, Deerfield, MA; Museum of American History, Smithsonian Institution, Washington, DC; Sewing Machine Museum, Oakland, CA; Shelburne Museum, Shelburne, VT.

Additional Listings: See Thimbles and *Warman's Americana & Collectibles* for more examples.

Bodkins, whalebone and ivory, sealing wax inlaid scribe lines, 19th C, minor losses, 9 pc set 400.00

Book
History of the Sewing Machine, James Parton, c1867, 44 pgs 35.00
The Standard Work On Cutting, revised, enlarged and improved 6th edition, Jno. J. Mitchell, publ, 1893, 231 pgs, 9 x 11-1/2" 90.00

Calendar
1898, Betsy Ross sewing American flag 25.00
1904, Singer Sewing Machine, diecut, Indian and animal skin 85.00

Catalog
E. Lipman, Beloit, WI, 1910, 32 pgs, 7-1/4" x 10", Spring and Summer Ready Reference, McCall patterns 32.00
The Fashion World, New York, NY, 42 pgs, 1925, 9-1/4" x 12-1/2", Spring and Summer, Every Woman Her Own Dressmaker 25.00
Wm. Horstmann Co., Philadelphia, PA, 160 pgs, 1922, 6-3/4" x 9", Columbia Book of Yarns, illustrations of crochet and knitting needles, various stitches 28.00

Box, black lacquer, gold Oriental scenes and foliage, orig ivory tools, orig key, 1st quarter, 19th C, 14-1/2" x 10" x 6-1/2", $775.

Hem Measure, floral top, sterling and stainless steel, 4-3/4" l,

Folder, 8-3/4" x 14-1/4", wm. R. Moore Dry Goods Co., Memphis, TN, 3 pgs, c1937, heavy weight, "Guaranteed Fast Color No. 10 Batfast Suitings," 10 tipped-in blue Batfast Suiting swatches, 19 1-1/4" x 2" colored swatches tipped in 28.00
Chatelaine, egg shape 80.00
Fan, Singer Ribbonaire, Bakelite 100.00
Magazine
  Home Needlework Magazine, Florence Publishing Co, Florence, MA, 176 pgs, 1899, Vol. 1, No. 2, April 20.00
  Star Needlework Journal, American Thread Co., 1922, Vol. 7, No. 2, published quarterly 20.00
  The Ladies Standard Magazine, Standard Fashion Co., August 1893 ....20.00
Manual, Howe Sewing Machine, NY, 1872, 20 pgs, blue printed wraps 25.00
Sewing Box
  5-3/4" l, figured mahogany veneer on pine, inlay, table clamp, dovetailed drawer, pincushion, wear and edge damage, thumb screw missing 220.00
  6-3/4" l, 5" w, 7" h, mahogany, lift off lid with pin cushion, single drawer, cathedral style 330.00
  13" l, 8" d, 15" h, whalebone and ivory inlaid mahogany, scribed double swift above fist form screw over rect box, ivory escutcheon, repair to screw, finial missing, minor cracks 1,840.00
Sewing Kit, 1-3/4" l, gilded, hinged nut case, slight crack in nut 220.00

Tape Measure, little girl with basket of flowers and puppy, maroon hat, aqua skirt and sleeves, Japan, $100. Photo courtesy of Julie Robinson.

Sewing Stand, 12-5/8" h, pine, old red graining on yellow ground, shiny over varnish, four rotating tiers on turned spindle, wire pins for spools of thread, short cabriole legs and drawer in base, some damage to feet 36.00
Spool Cabinet
  Dexter Fine Yarn, oak, 4 drawers, 18-3/4" h, 18-5/8" w, 16" d 650.00
  Merrick's Spool Cotton, oak, cylindrical, curved glass, 18" d, 22" h 725.00
  Willimantic Spool Cotton, Eastlake style, oak, 4 drawers, adv pulls, side decals, 14-1/4" h 500.00
Tape Measurer
  Adv, round, multicolored litho of young girl with flowers, 1-1/2" d 45.00
  Egg, Chicago World's Fair, red 75.00
  Pig, copper 65.00
  Sentinel, pretty woman 45.00
Thimble
  Brass, fancy band design 15.00
  Cloisonné, China 12.00
  Meissen, hp, c1950 ....25.00
  Scrimshaw, whalebone 95.00
  Silver
    Cupid and garlands, Simons 95.00
    Cupid in high relief, c1900-40 ....120.00
    Engraved, 2 birds on branch 35.00
    Flowers, high relief 45.00

SHAKER

History: The Shakers, so named because of a dance they used in worship, are one of the oldest communal organizations in the United States. This religious group was founded by Mother Ann Lee, who emigrated from England and established the first Shaker community near Albany, New York, in 1784. The Shakers reached their peak in 1850, when there were 6,000 members.

Shakers lived celibate and self-sufficient lives. Their philosophy stressed cleanliness, order, simplicity, and economy. Highly inventive and motivated, the Shakers created many utilitarian household forms and objects. Their furniture reflected a striving for quality and purity in design.

In the early 19th century, the Shakers produced many items for commercial purposes. Chairmaking and the packaged herb and seed business thrived. In every endeavor and enterprise, the members followed Mother Ann's advice: "Put your hands to work and give your heart to God."

References: Michael Horsham, *Art of the Shakers*, Apple Press, 1989; John T. Kirk, *The Shaker World: Art, Life, Belief,* Harry N. Abrams, 1997; Charles R. Muller and Timothy D. Rieman, *The Shaker Chair*, Canal Press, 1984; June Sprigg and Jim Johnson, *Shaker Woodenware*, Berkshire House, 1991; June Sprigg and David Larkin, *Shaker Life*, Work, and Art, Stewart, Tabori & Chang, 1987; Timothy D. Rieman and Jean M. Burks, *Complete Book of Shaker Furniture*, Harry N. Abrams, 1993.

Periodical: *Shaker Messenger*, P.O. Box 1645 Holland, MI 49422.

Museums: Hancock Shaker Village, Pittsfield, MA; Shaker Historical Museum, Shaker Heights, OH; Shaker Museum and Library, Old Chatham, NY; Shaker Village of Pleasant Hill, Harrodsburg, KY 40330.

Apothecary Cabinet, 66" x 14", stained wood, rect, front fitted with 12 small drawers, molded white glazed porcelain handles, identification labels, drawer sides inscribed with various content titles, New England, 19th C 450.00

Blanket Chest, 37" x 24-3/4", red painted wood, hinged rect top with molded edge, int. till, paneled front and sides raised on tapering cylindrical legs, lid int. inscribed in pencil "Bloomsburg, C. B. Hutton, Box 105, Orangeville," Midwestern, 19th C 1,200.00

Bonnet, dark brown palm and straw, black ribbons, 9" flounce, KY 395.00

Book, *How The Shakers Cook & The Noted Cooks of the Country, Feature The Chefs and Their Cooking Recipes*, A. J. White, New York, NY, 1889, 50 pgs, 3-3/8" x 6-1/8', bust of men illus, dusted, chips 15.00

Bottle, 9" h, aqua, emb "Shaker Pickles," base labeled "Portland, Maine, E.D.P. & Co." 90.00

Box, bentwood, oval
4-3/4" l, Harvard, orig black ink graining, faded red ground, copper tacks...250.00
5" l, Harvard, old rosewood graining, gold building with spire on lid, steel tacks 250.00
6" l, Harvard type, iron tacks, old refinishing, traces of green, bottom loose, edge damage 75.00
6-3/8" l, finger construction, iron tacks, two fingers on base, one on lid, worn old bluish green gray paint 660.00
9" l, finger construction, copper tacks, two fingers on base, one on lid, old natural finish......................................550.00
11-1/2" l, finger construction, copper tacks, three fingers on base, one on lid, old worn red paint......................1,430.00

Rocker, arm chair, imp "3" on top slat, orig stenciled label on rocker "Shaker's Trade Mark, T. Lebanon, N.Y.," worn old finish, traces of orig dark finish, replaced woven reed seat has damage, glued split on one rocker, 34-3/4" h, $330. Photo courtesy of Garth's Auctions.

Brush, 10-3/4" l, horsehair, turned wood handle 90.00
Carpet Beater, 41-1/2" l, bent willow, turned beech handle 85.00
Chair, 41" h, 17-1/4" h seat, side, titlers, New England, early 19th C, orig red-brown painted surface, tops of front legs stamped "1," replaced tape seat, surface abrasions................4,315.00
Clothes Rack, 36-1/2" w, 72" h, red painted wood, 3 horizontal bars, top bar mounted on either side with 3 hooks, rect uprights continuing to form arched feet, New England, late 19th C 2,750.00
Display Case, 8" x 10" x 10", pine, red stain, sliding lid, dovetailed, Mt. Lebanon..375.00
Dough Scraper, 4-1/2" l, wrought iron 40.00
Dress, homespun linen, pale brown, wide double collar, 12 later buttons, late 19th C 220.00
Hanger, 24" w, bentwood, chestnut 65.00
Measure, 14-1/2" d, 7-3/4" h, pine, cylindrical bentwood body, nailed end, metal band rim, cast iron semi-circular handles, int. with stenciled Shaker label, late 19th C..................195.00
Rocker, armchair
41" h, 15-1/2" h seat, #7, Mt. Lebanon, NY, decal, shawl bar, old dark varnish, replaced red and black tape seat 1,380.00
41-1/2" h, 15" h seat, #7, attributed to Mt. Lebanon, NY, old finish, replaced red and black tape seat 750.00
42" h, worn old finish, traces of orig dark finish, imp "3" on top slat, orig stenciled label on rocker "Shaker's Trade Mark, Mt Lebanon, N.Y.," damaged replaced woven reed seat, glued splint in on rocker 330.00
Scoop, 11-3/4", walnut...275.00
Sewing Box, 7" h, drawer, spool compartment, worn fabric pin cushion, hardwood, old brown varnish, age cracks and damage...165.00
Sewing Desk, chestnut, pine, and maple, drawers, overhanging base, old refinish 11,500.00
Stand, 29-1/4" h, 19" x 19-3/8" top, South Union Kentucky, c1840, walnut, sq top overhangs base with one drawer, straight chamfered skirt, sq tapering chamfered legs, old refinishing, imperfections 690.00
Table, 34-3/4" x 35-1/2" x 28", maple, drop leaf, rect top, hinged rect leaves, single drawer, sq tapering legs, first half 19th C 6,500.00

SHAVING MUGS

c1908

History: Shaving mugs, which hold the soap, brush, and hot water used to prepare a beard for shaving, come in a variety of materials including tin, silver, glass, and pottery. One style, which has separate compartments for water and soap, is the scuttle, so called because of its coal-scuttle shape.

Shaving mugs were popular between 1880 and 1925, a period of great immigration to the United States. At first barber shops used a common mug for all customers. This led to an epidemic of a type of eczema known as barber itch.

Laws were passed requiring each individual to have his own mug at the barber shop. Initially names and numbers were placed on the mugs for identification purposes, but this did not work well for those who could not read. The occupational mug developed because illiterate workers could identify a picture of their trade or an emblem of its tools. Fraternal emblems also were used and were the most popular of the decorative forms. Immigrants especially liked the heraldry of the fraternal emblems since it reminded them of Europe.

European porcelain blanks were decorated by American barber-supply houses. Prices ranged from 50¢ for a gold name mug to $2.50 for an elaborate occupational design. Most of the artwork was done by German artists who had immigrated to America.

The invention of the safety razor by King C. Gillette, issued to three and one-half million servicemen during World War I, brought about changes in personal grooming–men began to shave on their own rather than visiting the barber shop to be shaved. As a result, the need for personalized shaving mugs declined.

References: Susan and Al Bagdade, *Warman's English & Continental Pottery & Porcelain*, 2nd ed., Wallace-Homestead, 1991; Ronald S. Barlow, *Vanishing American Barber Shop*, Windmill Publishing, 1993; Keith E. Estep, *Shaving Mug & Barber Bottle Book*, Schiffer Publishing, 1995.

Collectors' Club: National Shaving Mug Collectors Assoc., 320 S Glenwood St., Allentown, PA 18104.

Fraternal

ARCIP, Retail Clerks Union, rd star, clasped hands, initials
....195.00
B.L.E.E., Brotherhood of Locomotive Eng., "BLE" monogram
....95.00
B.P.O.E., Elks, double emblem, Dr. title 300.00
F.O.E., Fraternal Order of Eagles, eagle holding F.O.E. plaque
....260.00
IB of PM, International Brotherhood of Paper Makers, paper making machine, clasped hands 275.00

Occupational, butcher, bull, crossed tools, polychrome, gold trim, $90.

I.O.M., International Order of Mechanics, ark ladder.........270.00
Loyal Knights of America, eagle, flags, six-pointed star 275.00

Occupational

Barber, hp, pair of hair clippers, worn name......................145.00
Bartender, hp, bartender pouring drink, mirrored back bar, 2 patrons drinking and smoking 450.00
Butcher, bull's head and butcher cutlery, G. M. Hardendorf, 3-1/4" x 5"..350.00
Chicken Farmer, rooster crowing 200.00
Cooper, man working on wooden barrel 375.00
Fabric Store, colorful hp shop int., owner waiting on well dressed woman, gold trim and name, 3-5/8" x 4-1/2"..................700.00
General Store, pork, flour, and whiskey barrels, Limoges, 4" x 4-3/4"..650.00
Hotel Clerk, clerk at desk, guest signing register 375.00
Ice Cream Parlor, metal dish of strawberry ice cream with spoon, worn gold trim 275.00
Locomotive and Coal Tender, F. M. Briggs, gold base band shows wear, 4" x 5" 105.00
Marksman, crossed rifles, target eagle wreath 200.00
Musical, banjo, owner's name 300.00
Painter, 2 men on scaffold painting house 375.00
Phonograph, outside horn photo..350.00
Photographer, man with beard...250.00
Plasterer, hp, mortar board and 2 trowels, gilt springs, mkd "Teco Co. Semovit" 175.00
Shoemaker, hp, scene of shoemaker in shop, gilt foot and swags around name 195.00
Trolley Repair Wagon, horse drawn, scaffolding 1,250.00
Tugboat, boat in water, crew and captain..........................750.00

Other

Drape and flowers, purple drape, pot of flowers, gold name
....85.00
Fish Shape, scuttle, green and brown.................................75.00
Horses in storm, white and black horses, copied from painting
....100.00
Scuttle, ribbed, multicolored flowers, gold dec...................85.00

SHAWNEE POTTERY

History: The Shawnee Pottery Co. was founded in 1937 in Zanesville, Ohio. The company acquired a 650,000-square-foot plant that had previously housed the American Encaustic Tiling Company. Shawnee produced as many as 100,000 pieces of pottery a day until 1961, when the plant closed.

Shawnee limited its production to kitchenware, decorative art pottery, and dinnerware. Distribution was primarily through jobbers and chain stores.

Marks: Shawnee can be marked "Shawnee," "Shawnee U.S.A.," "USA #——," "Kenwood," or with character names, e.g., "Pat. Smiley" and "Pat. Winnie."

References: Susan and Al Bagdade, *Warman's American Pottery and Porcelain*, Wallace-Homestead, 1994; Pam Curran, *Shawnee Pottery*, Schiffer Publishing, 1995; Jim and Bev Mangus, *Shawnee Pottery*, Collector Books, 1994, 1996 value update; Mark Supnick, *Collecting Shawnee Pottery*, L-W Book Sales, 1997; Duane and Janice Vanderbilt, *Collector's Guide to Shawnee Pottery*, Collector Books, 1992, 1996 value update.

Collectors' Club: Shawnee Pottery Collectors Club, P.O. Box 713, New Smyrna Beach, FL 32170.

Bank, Bulldog 50.00
Casserole, cov, Corn Queen, large 40.00
Cookie Jar, cov
    Dutch Girl, partial label................................150.00
    Puss n' Boots 205.00
    Smiley
        Shamrocks dec.....................................175.00
        Tulip dec 250.00
Creamer
    Elephant..25.00
    Puss n' Boots, green and yellow 65.00
Figure
    Bear 45.00
    Gazelle..45.00
    Puppy 50.00
    Squirrel 30.00
    Rabbit 40.00
Fruit Bowl, Corn Queen 25.00
Mug, Corn King 35.00
Pitcher
    Bo Peep
        Blue bonnet, yellow dress 125.00
        Lilac bonnet 115.00
    Chanticleer 75.00
Planter
    Gazelle..25.00
    Locomotive, black 65.00
Salt and Pepper Shakers, pr
    Chanticleer, large, orig label 45.00
    Dutch Boy and Girl, large 55.00
    Mugsey, small 65.00
    Puss n' Boots, small 30.00
Smiley, small 30.00
Teapot
    Granny Ann, peach apron 105.00
    Tom Tom, blue, red, and yellow 115.00
Utility Jar, Corn King 50.00
Wall Pocket, Bird House.......................................25.00

SILHOUETTES

History: Silhouettes (shades) are shadow profiles produced by hollow cutting, mechanical tracing, or painting. They were popular in the 18th and 19th centuries.

    The name came from Etienne de Silhouette, a French Minister of Finance, who cut "shades" as a pastime. In America, the Peale family was well known for the silhouettes it made.

    Silhouette portraiture lost popularity with the introduction of the daguerreotype prior to the Civil War. In the 1920s and 1930s, a brief revival occurred when tourists to Atlantic City and Paris had their profiles cut as souvenirs.

Marks: An impressed stamp marked "PEALE" or "Peale Museum" identifies pieces made by the Peale family.

References: Shirley Mace, *Encyclopedia of Silhouette Collectibles on Glass*, Shadow Enterprises, 1992.

Museums: Essex Institute, Salem, MA; National Portrait Gallery, Washington, DC.

Children

5-1/8" h, 4-3/4" w, hollow cut, young girl, ink detail on hair and torso, dark blue paper baking, stains, gilt brass frame.....330.00
5-5/8" h, 4-7/8" w, ink silhouette, cut oval and glued to baking, black lacquer frame with gilt brass trim 140.00

Full length cut paper profile silhouette of girl with bird in her hand, sun hat, ink wash background with fence and "Lydia Harris" and "Aug. Edouart fecit 1842," back of figure has ghost image of another silhouette and some pencil sketched lines done before finished cutout, may have been altered and reused by Edouart, shadowbox frame, 10-7/8" h, 8-7/8" w, $2,310. Photo courtesy of Garth's Auctions.

7-3/8" h, 5-1/8" w, cut, child with doll, edges rough, backing paper with laid finish stained, gilt frame 415.00
10-7/8" h, 8-7/8" w, full length paper cup profile of girl with bird in her hand, sun hat, ink wash background with fence and "Lydia Harris," and "Aug Edoart fecit 1842," back of figure has image of another silhouette and some pencil sketched lines done preliminary to finished work, 14-1/4" h, 12-1/4" w shadowbox frame..2,310.00

Groups

6-5/8" h, 10-1/4" w, double, hollow cut man and woman, ink details on man, blue pencil details on woman, black cloth backing, mahogany veneer frame...440.00
13-1/2" h, 9-3/4" w, eight hollow cut silhouettes of family, parents, six daughters, all emb "T. P. Jones fecit," common period frame with gilt and blue eglomise mat, mat repainted
....2,875.00
15" h, 19" w, room setting, aristocratic family, reverse painted on glass, black, red, and blue, old glass with minor imperfections, minor flaking, bird's eye ogee frame with gilded liner...475.00

Men

4" h, 3-1/4" w, black paper cutting, 5-1/4" h x 4-1/2" w emb brass frame with later inscription "Jacobus Ten Eyck Age 19"
....220.00
5-3/4" h, 5" w, hollow cut, faded black cloth backing, tear in paper, black lacquered frame with gilt brass trim 115.00
9-1/2" h, 7-1/2" w, watercolor scene of gentleman in black suit, twig in mouth, standing with cane, drawn at age 18 in 1848, deep Victorian frame 385.00
10-3/4" h, 7-1/4" w, full length, Isaac T. Hopper, pastoral landscape, attributed to August Edouart, late 19th C frame
....865.00

11-1/2" h, 7" w, full length, gentleman reading, bronze highlights, framed, minor foxing, toning...260.00
13" h, 10-1/2" w, full length cut, man with scroll of paper, white painted detail, sgd "W. H. Brown 1845," another hand "James Fenimore Cooper 1945," minor stains and soiling, ogee frame with gilded liner 770.00

Women

3-1/8" l, cut silhouette of young woman, titled "Sister's Present," mounted on book shaped wood, cardboard, printed paper, glass, and gilded paper book-shaped box, some wear 215.00
4" h, 3-1/4" w, hollow cut, young woman in bonnet, 5-1/8" h, 4-1/2" w emb brass frame with later inscription "Margaret Ten Eyck, Age 37, Hurley, N.Y.," water stain at bottom.................220.00
5-1/4" h, 4-1/4" w, hollow cut, brushed ink bodice, tear and stains, old black frame, gilt stenciling.......................................330.00
6-1/4" h, 5-1/4" w, hollow cut, woman, blue hand colored lithographic printed torso, cutout and glued to paper, stains 360.00
6-3/8" h, 5-1/2" w, hollow cut, young woman, faded blue backing, black lacquered frame, gilt brass trim hides part of inscription "Cooper"...90.00
6-3/4" h, 5-1/2" w, hollow cut, laid paper, black cloth backing, stains and tear, bird's eye veneer frame, old label "Sarah Thompson Crissman, March 4, 1788-May 12, 1860"........225.00
7-1/4" h, 4-1/2" w, hollow cut, full length, inscribed "She is like the merchant's ship, She bringeth her food from a jar," framed, toning, staining, minor losses..690.00

SILVER

History: The natural beauty of silver lends itself to the designs of artists and craftsmen. It has been mined and worked into an endless variety of useful and decorative items. Pure silver is too soft to be fashioned into strong, durable, and serviceable utensils. Therefore, a way was found to give silver the required degree of hardness by adding alloys of copper and nickel.

Silversmithing in America goes back to the early 17th century in Boston and New York and the early 18th century in Philadelphia. Boston artisans were influenced by the English styles, New Yorkers by the Dutch.

References: Louise Belden, *Marks of American Silversmiths in the Ineson-Bissell Collection*, University of Virginia Press, 1980; Frederick Bradbury, *Bradbury's Book of Hallmarks*, J. W. Northend, 1987; Bonita Campbell and Nan Curtis (curators), *Depression Silver*, California State University, 1995; Maryanne Dolan, *1830s-1900s American Sterling Silver Flatware*, Books Americana, 1993; Janet Drucker, *Georg Jensen: A Tradition of Splendid Silver*, Schiffer Publishing, 1997; Stephen G. C. Ensko, *American Silversmiths and Their Marks*, Dover Publications, 1983; Rachael Feild, *Macdonald Guide to Buying Antique Silver and Sheffield Plate*, Macdonald & Co., 1988; *Fine Victorian Gold-and Silverplate, Exquisite Designs from the 1882 Catalog of the Meriden-Brittania Co.*, Schiffer Publishing, 1997; Nancy Gluck, *Grosvenor Pattern of Silverplate*, Silver Season, 1996; Tere Hagan, *Silverplated Flatware*, 4th ed., Collector Books, 1990, 1998 value update; Kenneth Crisp Jones (ed.), *Silversmiths of Birmingham and Their Marks*, N.A.G. Press, 1981, distributed by Antique Collectors Club; Henry J. Kaufman, *Colonial Silversmith*, Astragal Press, 1995; Ralph and Terry

Kovel, *Kovels' American Silver Marks*, Crown Publishers, 1989.

Joel Langford, *Silver*, Chartwell Books, 1991; Everett L. Maffett, *Silver Banquet* II, Silver Press, 1990; Penny C. Morrill, *Silver Masters of Mexico*, Schiffer Publishing, 1996; Penny Chittim Morrill and Carole A. Berk, *Mexican Silver 20th Century Handwrought Jewelry & Metalwork*, Schiffer Publishing, 1994; Richard Osterberg, *Silver Hollowware for Dining Elegance*, Schiffer Publishing, 1996; ——, *Sterling Silver Flatware for Dining Elegance*, Schiffer Publishing, 1994; Benton Rabinovitch, *Antique Silver Servers for the Dining Table*, Joslin Hall Publishing, 1991; Dorothy T. Rainwater, *Encyclopedia of American Silver Manufacturers*, 3rd ed., Schiffer Publishing, 1986; Dorothy T. and H. Ivan Rainwater, *American Silverplate*, Schiffer Publishing, 1988; *Sterling Silver, Silverplate, and Souvenir Spoons*, revised ed., L-W Book Sales, 1987, 1994 value update; Charles Truman (ed.), *Sotheby's Concise Encyclopedia of Silver*, Antique Collectors' Club, 1996; Charles Venable, *Silver in America 1840-1940*, Harry Abrams, 1994; Joanna Wissinger, *Arts and Crafts Metalwork and Silver*, Chronicle Books, 1994; Seymour B. Wyler, *Book Of Old Silver*, Crown Publishers, 1937 (available in reprint).

Periodicals: *Silver Magazine*, P.O. Box 9690, Rancho Santa Fe, CA 92067; *Silver News*, 1112 16th St. NW, Ste. 240, Washington, DC 20036; *Silver Update*, P.O. Box 960, Funkstown, MD 21734.

Collectors' Club: New York Silver Society, 242 E. 7th St., #5, New York, NY 10009.

Museums: Bayou Bend Collection, Houston, TX; Boston Museum of Fine Arts, Boston, MA; Currier Gallery of Art, Manchester, NH; Yale University Art Gallery, New Haven, CT; Wadsworth Antheneum, Hartford, CT.

Additional Listings: See Silver Flatware in *Warman's Americana & Collectibles* for more examples.

American, 1790-1840
Mostly Coin

Coin silver is slightly less pure than sterling silver. Coin silver has 900 parts silver to 100 parts alloy. Sterling silver has 925 parts silver. American silversmiths followed the coin standards. Coin silver is also called Pure Coin, Dollar, Standard, or Premium.

Bailey & Co., Chestnut St. Phila, (J. T. Bailey, 1848-50)
Cup, 3-3/8" h, floral rococo repousse, matching cast handle 110.00
Goblet, applied Greek key border, monogrammed "EH," one mkd, 5-3/8" h, 10 troy oz., pr.....................460.00
Bailey, Loring, Hingham, MA, c1780-1814, hot milk jug, vasiform shape, beaded edge, molded circular base, later monogram, mkd twice, very minor dents, 9-7/8" h, 19 troy oz..........865.00
Bard, Conrad and Robert Lamont, Philadelphia, 1841-45, center bowl, baluster, inverted rim, applied leaf banding, engraved crest, ftd, mkd on base, very minor dents, 5-1/4" h, 8-5/8" d, 20 troy oz..345.00
Bogert, Nicholas J., New York City, c1801, water pitcher, baluster form, applied anthemion leaf banding, mkd on base, 13-3/4" h, 37 troy oz...1,495.00

Burt, Benjamin, Boston, 1729-1805, serving spoon, feather edge, webbed shell dec, monogrammed, 8-3/4" l, 2 troy oz 400.00

Connor, John H., New York City, 1833-38, baluster, applied banding of shells and foliage, mkd "J. H. C." twice on base, indistinct monogram, minor dents, wear, 6-7/8" h, 13 troy oz. 320.00

Edwards, Samuel, Boston, 1705-62, tankard, baluster finial, domed molded cov, tapering sides, applied molded base, scroll handle with scroll thumbpiece, molded hinge plate with oval drop, convex terminal, handle engraved "TSA," base with later inscription "Turell Tufts Medford 1835," mkd 3 times, restoration, 7-5/8" h, 23 troy oz. 2,300.00

Edwards, Thomas, Boston, 1701-55, sugar shaker, 5" h, engraved initials "MW," mkd "T. Edwards" 1,200.00

Foster, Joseph, Boston, 1760-12839, mug, applied molded banding, base inscribed "Thomas Hubbart Summer Jan.y 1st 1814," mkd on base, 3-1/2" h 520.00

Gale, W. & Son, ladle, monogrammed, 3 oz., 2 dwt 200.00

Haddock, Lincoln, and Foss, Boston, 1850-65, creamer and sugar basket, handled, beaded rim, Greek key band, shell feet, monogrammed, 3-1/4" h basket, 13 troy oz. 490.00

Hazen, N., soup ladle, monogrammed, 6 oz., 2 dwt..........225.00

Jones, Ball & Poor, Boston, 1847-51, tray, beaded border, engraved foliage design, monogrammed, 15-1/4" l, 30 troy oz. 980.00

Hurd, Jacob, Boston, 1702-58, serving spoon, rat tai bowl, trifid handle, monogrammed "WHS," 7-5/8" l, 3 troy oz., pr 3,740.00

Lincoln, Albert and Charles Foss, Boston, 1848-57, water pitcher, chased floral foliate and scroll devices, inscribed "Elizabeth Shepard from M. Brown," mkd on base, 9-1/8" h, 20 troy oz. 750.00

McGrew, Wilson, Cincinnati, OH, c1850, fork, reeded terminal applied with foliage and floral medallion, 18 oz., price for 12 pc set 140.00

Moulton IV, William, Newburyport, MA, 1772-1861, porringer, underside of handle mkd "W. Moulton" in serrated rect, minor dents, repair to handle, 5-1/4" d, 7 troy oz. 1,150.00

Myers, John, spoon, 9-1/4" l, cast bird on back of bowl, four sets of engraved initials of owners from 1756 to 1876, mkd "J. Myers Phila," dents in bowl 220.00

Richardson, Joseph, Philadelphia, 1711-84, cream pot, pear-shaped body, serrated rim, long wide pouring spout, 3 applied cast cabriole legs, pad feet, body dec in rococo style, C-scrolls and baskets of flowers, mkd on base, buffed, dents, minor tear, 4" h, 4 troy oz..1,495.00

Thompson, William, New York City, 1810-45, tea set, 9-1/4" h teapot, two handled cov sugar, creamer, waste bowl, basket of fruit finial above lobed body, raised loop and diamond design, applied floral borders, approx 100 troy oz. 2,300.00

American, Tiffany & Co., cake tazza, molded circular border chased with shells and cartouche, monogrammed, 12-1/2" d, 38 oz., $1,400. Photo courtesy of Freeman\Fine Arts.

Turner, James, Boston, 1746, tankard, engraved with Derby coat of arms, mkd "R (Richard) M (Mary) Derby," turned finial, domed molded cov above cylindrical tapering body with applied bead, molded base, scroll thumb piece, scroll handle terminates in disc, rococo cartouche surrounds cot of arms of three stags' heads on a diagonal bar, surmounted by a pelican, imperfections, 8-7/8" h, 28 troy oz. 113,600.00

Unknown Maker

Cann, pear-shaped body, double scroll handle, leaf grip, splayed foot, inscribed "Moses Brown to the Church of Christ in Brownville 1823," very minor dents, 5-1/4" h, 13 troy oz. 2,415.00

Tobacco Box, cov, attributed to Hurd, Burt or Coney, Boston area, 1732-35, oval, molded base bad with central engraved Rogers' coat of arms consisting of shield with 3 stags and chevron surrounded by rococo cartouche toped by another stag all surrounded by scrolled ribbon device and Latin script "Ex dono Pupillorum" above and "AD ASTRA PER ASPERA" below, ("A gift from your charges. To stars through adversity," minor imperfections, 2-7/8" w, 3-3/4" d, 3/4" h, 3-1/2 oz.......................................24,150.00

Van Voorhis, Daniel, Philadelphia and NY, 1751-1824, tea set, 6-1/2" h teapot, cov sugar, helmet-form creamer, neoclassical form, urn finials, applied beaded edge, monogrammed "AGL," replaced teapot handle, minor dents, 45 troy oz. 5,175.00

Wilson, Robert and William, Philadelphia, 1824-46, coffeepot, bulbous, acanthus leaf dec, applied foliate banding, acorn leaf finial, mkd on base, minor dents, 10-1/2" h, 31 troy oz. 690.00

Wyer, Eleazer and Charles Farley, Portland, ME, 1828-30, porringer, mkd on base and handle, monogrammed "HB," minor dents, 4-3/4" d, 6 troy oz..750.00

Silver, American, 1840-1920 Mostly Sterling

There are two possible sources for the origin of the word sterling. The first is that it is a corruption of the name Easterling. Easterlings were German silversmiths who came to England in the Middle Ages. The second is that it is named for the starling (little star) used to mark much of the early English silver.

Sterling is 92.5 percent per silver. Copper comprises most of the remaining alloy. American manufacturers began to switch to the sterling standard about the time of the Civil War.

Adams, W., New York, c1842, water pitcher, 17" h, urn shape, all-over floral and scroll repousse dec, C-shape handles with ram's head and leaf dec, circular plinth with loop and date dec, 48 oz..1,900.00

Bailey, Banks & Biddle Co., basket, 9-1/2", Art Nouveau, oval, pierced, flared sides, swing handle, monogram, 11 oz., 11 dwt 385.00

Barbour Silver Co., Hartford, CT, box, cov, 7-1/4" sq, Rococo style rose and foliate dec, handle set with green stone, 4 thread edge feet, gilt int., monogram, 19 troy oz.....................360.00

Bieber, A. A., dish, 5-1/2" d, shaped circular, partly fluted, scalloped, monogram, 11 oz., 4 dwt, price for pr................200.00

Black, Starr & Gorham, cup, 2-1/2" h, plain tapering cylindrical, flaring rim, loop handle, 3 oz., 3 dwt 70.00

Boardman, pitcher, 8-1/4" h, baluster, beads applied at base of spout, curved handled, mkd "By Boardman," 22 oz., 6 dwt 350.00

Caldwell, J. E. & Co, compote, 10" l, octagonal, reeded rim, partly fluted side, cylindrical stem, octagonal shaped foot, rim engraved with two berried laurel wreaths, one with animal in center, 22 oz., 4 dwt...300.00

Dimes, Richard, Boston, Sons of Liberty Bowl, 11-1/4" d, 50 troy oz. 1,035.00

Dominck & Haff, NY
Asparagus Fork, 9-1/4" l, Renaissance pattern, enamel accents, 5 troy oz. 335.00
Entree Dish, 1891, 12" l, rect scrolled rim and feet, foliage handles, 64 troy oz. 3,000.00

Duhme Co., Cincinnati, OH, 1898-1907, punch bowl, 14" d, chased and pierced, floral rim border and feet, 76 troy oz. 800.00

Dunkirk, tea and coffee service, 11" h coffeepot, teapot, 2-handled cov sugar, creamer, waste bowl, plain tapering cylindrical on circular foot, loop handle, ivory stoppers, bombe hinged cov, baluster finial, 81 oz., 4 dwt......800.00

Durgin
Cake Plate, 12-1/2" d, circular, low foot, four panels chased with scrolling foliate, reeded rim, 29 oz. 425.00
Cup, 10" l, 8-1/2" h, ovoid, circular reeded foot, two scroll-capped loop handles, inscribed and dated 1912, 10 oz., 8 dwt 120.00
Dish, 7" l, shaped oval, repousse allover with scrolls, trellis, flowers, putti at play, serpent centering vacant cartouche, rope scalloped rim, also mkd "Cowell & Hubbard," 4 oz., 4 dwt 200.00

Elgin, Silversmith Co., Inc., candelabra, 9-3/4" h, chamfered flaring central shaft supporting arm with nozzle on either side, circular base with engraved cypher monogram, c1945, pr 200.00

Fletcher and Gardiner, Philadelphia, PA, c1820, hot water kettle on stand, 15-1/2" h, domed cov, chased vine band, ovoid body with leafy band, scrolled legs, sq base, paw feet, later Tiffany burner, monogram, dents, 103 troy oz. 3,2500.00

Gorham, Providence, IR
Candlesticks, pr, 10-3/4" h, 1925, vasiform sconces, detachable bobeches, knopped stem with two vacant cartouches flanked by foliate, oval gadrooned and foliate base 600.00
Goblet, 6-1/2" h, tapering circular, reeded band and foliate dec at intervals, flaring rim, gilt int., monogrammed, 27 oz., 4 dwt, price for 6 pc set......350.00
Platter, 20" l, oval, foliage rim, 57 oz. 500.00
Punch Ladle, La Scala pattern, 8 oz. 125.00

Harris & Schafer, pitcher, 9" h, bombe, headed rim at shoulder, circular reeded foot, multi-scroll handle, 23 oz., 2 dwt 600.00

Henckel & Co, basket, 10-1/4" d, shaped circular, piecrust rim, broad pierced border, overhead reeded fixed handle, monogrammed center, 17 oz. 170.00

International, tray, 23" l, oval, pierced handles, monogram "K," 76 oz. 770.00

Kalo Shops, Park Ridge, IL
Compote, 10-5/8" d, 5-1/4" h, shallow bowl, scalloped border, 5 floriform sections, slender neck, circular base, slightly peened finish, mkd "Sterling/Hand Wrought/At/The Kalo Shop," c1920, 23 oz., 12 dwt 1,400.00
Platter, 12" w, 19-1/2" l, oval, folded oval border, convex moldings from handles, applied crescent borders, peened surface, marked "Kalo Shops, Sterling/Hand Beaten," c1905, 34 oz., 8 dwt 5,500.00

Kerr & Co, sauce boat, 7" l, shaped oval, sq foot, applied flowers, angular foliate and scroll handle, monogrammed, 4 oz., 8 dwt......80.00

Kirk, S. & Son, Baltimore, MD
Bowl
9-1/4" d, shaped circular, upper body repousse with flowers and leaves, matted ground, circular foot with conforming dec, scroll rim, 18 oz......1,000.00
9-1/4" d, 7-1/4" h, circular, allover repousse flowers, ferns, and berries, fine stippled ground, scalloped edge, applied scrolls, foliage and flowers, circular foot with applied acanthus, matted ground, 33 oz., 6 dwt 1,600.00
10" d, circular, applied flowers and leaves, matted repousse ground, shaped circular foot with conforming

dec, foliate and scroll rim, 30 oz., 8 dwt 1,800.00
Fruit Bowl, 10-1/4" d, circular, broad floral repousse border on matted ground, circular foot, singular dec, 18 oz. ...350.00
Salver, 15" l, oval, four ball and claw feet, repousse border, leaves on fine stippled ground, center monogrammed cartouche flanked by foliate and flowers, 28 oz., 2 dwt 1,100.00
Serving Spoon, shell form bowl, 4 oz., 2 dwt 125.00

Lebolt, Chicago, IL, early 20th C, salad servers, fork and spoon, hand hammered design, monogram, 8 troy oz. 350.00

Matthews Co., Newark, NJ, 1907-30, child's set, 5-1/2" d plate, mug, and brush, acid etched with scenes and names of nursery rhymes, 6 troy oz. 265.00

Meriden Brittania Co., Meriden, CT
Dessert Plate, 101/2" d, shape circular form, wide applied cast reticulated border with winged masks, foliate scrolls and flowers, 19 troy oz......220.00
Flower Basket, 14-1/2", cylindrical body, wavy open mouth, threaded rim, swelling shoulder, swinging strap handle, pierced with flat chased floral design, monogrammed, 62 troy oz. 1,650.00

Porter, Horace E., creamer and sugar, 7-1/2" w, 3-1/2" h, engraved and cutout foliate pattern on handles, extended spout, hammered surface, monogram, sgd "H. E. Potter, sterling," 11 troy oz. 1,150.00

Reed & Barton
Flatware, Francis I pattern, price for 112 pc set, assorted serving pcs, fitted case, 124 oz., 2 dwt 2,800.00
Water Pitcher, 9-3/4" h, plain tapering cylindrical, circular foot, angular handle, 32 oz., 6 dwt 700.00

Roberts, E. P. & Sons, bread basket, 14-1/2" l, oval, applied scroll border rim, 14 oz., 6 dwt 250.00

Schiebler, tea caddy, 4-1/4" h, circular repousse allover with scrolls and foliage, stippled ground, 9 oz. 500.00

Shreve & Co., San Francisco
Bowl, 4-1/2" d, 7-1/2" d underplate, hammered, strapwork rim border, imp San Francisco marks 4091 and 5100 ...425.00
Cocktail Shaker, 10-1/2" h, cylindrical body, peened surface, fish tail removable pourer, side set with gilt and enameled medallion, bell mark, 20 oz., 4 dwt......600.00
Ice Bucket, Arts and Crafts, 6" h, flaring cylindrical body, applied horizontal staves, swing handle, finger strap below at back, hammered surface, applied monogram on spout, c 1910, 17 oz., 6 dwt 450.00
Teapot, Art Nouveau, 9-1/2" h, undulating vines, 19 oz., 10 dwt 425.00

Smith, Frank W. & Co
Tray, rect, shaped fluted and scrolled rim, 9" l, 7 oz.....200.00
Wine Coaster, applied border with scrolls and flowers, cut glass int., 7" d, price for pr 75.00

Starr, Theodore B., NY, dish, 12" x 12", shaped sq, applied scrolling foliage and flowers, monogrammed, 30 oz. 750.00

Stone, Arthur
Bowl, 8-3/4" w, 1-1/2" h, internally fluted rim, stone logo, initial "T" for Herbert Taylor, monogram, 13 troy oz. each, price for pr 750.00
Pepper Caster, 2" d, 5" h, punched crosses dec, mkd with stone logo, initial "C" with a star, weighted base, 7 troy oz., price for pr 635.00
Platter
11" w, 16" l, oval, simple stepped rim, mkd with stone logo, initial "C," minor scratches, 32 troy oz. 365.00
13-1/4" w, 18" l, internally fluted rim, mkd with stone logo, initial "T" for Herbert Taylor, minor scratches, 49 troy oz. 1,610.00

Spaulding & Co., Chicago, 1888-1920, dish, 11" l, grape leaf form, tendril and leaf handle, 25 troy oz.......400.00

Starr, Theodore, New York, NY, 1900-24, claret jug, 12" h, sterling mounts, globular glass body, peach cut to clear, palmettes, floral repousse rim and stopper, slight base chip......3,200.00

Tuttle, bowl, 11-3/4" d, Onslow pattern, shaped circular partly fluted, circular foot, 31 oz., 4 dwt 350.00
Wallace and Co., serving spoon, 1 oz., 6 dwt 100.00
Whiting, sauce ladle, Dresden pattern, blue enameled flower on white ground at terminal, shell and fluted bowl, 7" l 400.00

Silver, Continental

Generally, Continental silver does not have a strong following in the United States, but Danish pieces by Georg Jensen are eagerly sought. As the antiques marketplace continues to expand globally, Continental silver has become more popular.

Austrian, tray, 19-3/4" l, shaped oval, reeded rim, .800 fine, 44 oz. 700.00
Danish
    Hansen, Hans, flatware service, 107 pcs, 12 place settings, serving pieces, fitted case, mkd "Hans Hansen," 127 oz., 8 dwt 1,900.00
    Jensen, George
        Candy Dish, 5" h, applied grapes and vines attached to base of plain circular bowl, applied balls and beads, swirled stem, circular foot, 8 oz., 4 dwt..............1,100.00

Continental, Russian, chalice, repousse and chased, bell shaped base engraved with 4 Evangelists, bowl engraved with the Deisis, Slavonic inscription, Moscow hallmarks, dated 1860, Cyrillic mark "P.A.," 10.7 oz., 9" h, $1,650. Photo courtesy of Jackson's Auctioneers & Appraisers.

Compote, 9" d, 5-1/4" h, hammered surface, standing on 10 circles, flared base, cut glass insert, imp marks, 1925-32, 12 troy oz.........................575.00
Flatware, Acorn pattern, 75 pc set, 88 oz., 8 dwt 6,000.00
Serving Bowl, 10-1/8" l, 7-1/8" w, designed La Paglia, three-dimensional blossom and stem handles on rim, American mark, 18 troy oz.........................635.00
Unidentified Maker
    Bowl, 6-3/4" d, circular, hand hammered, flared and beaded, four ball feet, 6 oz. 200.00
    Creamer and sugar, hammered design, woven handles, 8 oz.........................175.00
Dutch
    Marrow Scoop, 9-1/4" l, plain design, double ends, Amsterdam, 19th C, 1 troy oz. 375.00
    Tray, 12" l, c1927, oval, molded rim, two ends formed as handles, 11 oz., 2 dwt 325.00
French
    Asparagus Tongs, 10" l, engine turned dec, 950 standard, mkd "JG," late 19th C 200.00
    Dessert Bowl, 4-1/4" x 2-3/4", plain, threaded bands at rim and circular ftd base, monogram, Paris, 950 standard, 82 oz., 6 dwt, set of 12 ....1,800.00
    Wine Taster, 19th C, maker "EP" in lozenge, circular, chased vine dec, inset Louis XV 1737 coin, 4" d, 3 troy oz 395.00
German
    Candlesticks, pr, 11" h, sq base with applied leaves rising to double knopped oval fluted and floral stems, vasiform sconces, detachable bobeches, 11 oz., 6 dwt 400.00
    Creamer, baluster shape, engine turned dec, two vacant cartouches, four foliate feet, loop handle, mkd "750," 3 oz., 8 dwt 80.00
    Cup, 17" h, domed cov, globular, knopped stem, overall Renaissance style design, gilt in., imp "Heisler 800M," c1887, 22 troy oz. 1,200.00
    Plate, shaped scrolling rim, applied crest dec, .800 fine, 18 oz., 6 dwt 200.00
Italian
    Candlestick, 9-1/2" h, Neoclassical, attributed to Naples, early 19th C, knopped shaft, spreading base, engraved diaper bands, mkd "GP," city mark head of woman with "N" over 8, 20 troy oz., pr.........................2,200.00
    Tea and Coffee Service, F. Peruzzi, 20th C, teapot, coffeepot, creamer, and sugar, 26" l tray, twist-fluted pear form, chased rococo finials, 800 fine, 178 troy oz. 1,850.00

Silver, English

From the 17th century to the mid-19th century, English silversmiths set the styles which American silversmiths copied. The work from the period exhibits the highest degree of craftsmanship. English silver is actively collected in the American antiques marketplace.

Charles I, Apostle Spoon, London, 1633, 7-1/2" l, fig shaped bowl, hexagonal stem, surmounted by saint figure, 3 troy oz. 1,600.00
Charles II, tumbler, 3" d, hammered sides, slightly convex bottom, marks rubbed, 2 oz. 275.00
Edwardian
    Caster, 8" h, London, 1909, obscure maker's mark, two handles, 9 oz., 6 dwt 150.00
    Center Bowl, Mapin and Webb, London, c1903, 10" d, 10" h, Baroque style, truncated baluster form, repousse with acanthus leaf tips, scrolling acanthus form lug handles, stepped socle base, 72 troy oz. 2,400.00

Dish Ring, Carrington & Co., London, 1910-11, 7-1/2" d, waisted cylinder, pierced and engraved, 14 troy oz. 500.00

Edward VII, tea set, W. Comyns, London, c1903, teapot, creamer, sugar, and 2 demitasse cups and saucers, silver mounted on Staffordshire Pottery 500.00

Elizabeth II, tray, A. & Bro. Ltd., Birmingham, 1952, 27-1/2" l, octagonal, molded border, 133 troy oz. 2,500.00

George I
  Pepper Pot, John Albright, London, 1721-22, 3" h, cylindrical, molded borders, domed engraved cov, 3 troy oz....550.00
  Spoon, John Le Sage, London, 1718, plain, rattail terminal, monogrammed, 2 oz., 8 dwt...................................350.00

George II
  Candlesticks, J. Café, London, 1751, 7-1/4" h, knopped stem, sq shell and scroll base, engraved crest, 66 troy oz., set of 4 pcs 4,500.00
  Coffeepot, attributed to C. Wright, London, 1769-70, 13" h, baluster form, later chased gadroons, engraved amoral, 40 troy oz. 2,100.00
  Tankard, cov, 8" h, London hallmarks for 1753-54, John Wigman, engraved monogram on side, repair to hinge..............990.00

George III
  Bacon Warming Tray, 5-7/8" x 8-3/8", 5-1/4" handle, London hallmarks for 1770-71, Septimus & Jones Crespell, lid missing...300.00
  Chamber Stick, 4" h, London hallmarks for 1786-87, Daniel Smith and Richard Sharp, small soldered split at handle, faint matching marks on snuffer and bobeches.......660.00
  Salver, 8" d, John Crouch I and Thomas Hannam, London, 1789, shaped circular, shells and scrolls applied to rim, field chased with scrolls and flowers, center crested cartouche, 13 oz., 6 dwt 700.00
  Server, reticulated blade with engraved birds, flowers, and crest on handle, Dublin hallmarks for 1778, "LH" 715.00
  Serving Spoon, London, 1818, obscure maker's mark, fiddle patter, monogrammed, 3 oz., 6 dwt 140.00
  Soup Ladle
    Obscure maker's mark, London, 1802, 6 oz., 4 dwt 250.00
    Piercy, Josion and George, London, 1818, Fiddle pattern, engraved crest, 6 oz., 8 dwt 300.00
  Spoon, London hallmarks for 1778-79, Hester Bateman, 8-1/4" l, tooled handle edge, 6 pc set.........................715.00
  Tea Caddy, 7" h, Charles Hougham, London, 1786, inverted pear shape, partly fluted swirled body, sq feet, detachable circular cov with reeded rim, 7 oz., 8 dwt 800.00
  Tureen, 7-1/4" l, Thomas Robins, London, 1804, shaped rect, four ball feet, reeded rim, two lion ring handles, detachable cov, reeded and foliate handle, engraved crest and armorial, 20 oz., 2 dwt 1,300.00

George IV
  Cup, 3-1/2" h, Edward, John, and William Barnard, London, 1835, baluster, lower body repousse flowers, repousse circular foot with foliage, reeded flaring rim, scroll-capped foliate handles, 5 oz..200.00
  Fruit Basket Robert Hennell, London, 1820, 14-3/4", l, pierced basket with applied border chased with scrolls and fluted garlands, sides of fluted swirls terminating in acanthus leaves, swing openwork handle, pierced band of flowers and scrolls base, central face engraved with rampant cat, inscribed below "Touch Not The Cat Bot A Glove," 45 oz., 16 dwt 5,000.00
  Jug, Rebecca Emes and Edward Barnard, London, 1821, 3-1/2" h, globular, ridged hand, spreading circular foot, 5 troy oz. 150.00
  Salt, Charles Price, London, 1822, 3-3/4" d, double border of scrolls and flowers, tripod hoof feet, gilt int., 15 oz., 4 pc set 375.00
  Stuffing Spoon, W. Welsh, Exeter, 1825-26, 12" l, monogram handle...150.00

George V

Compote, F. N. & S., London, 1913, 5" h, 10" d, round, open-work design, minor dent, 16 troy oz. 425.00
Muffineer, Birmingham, 1934, 8" h, octagonal Queen Anne style, acorn finial, maker's mark "TS" in two ovals, 7 troy oz. 285.00

Queen Anne
  Caudle Cup, Timothy Ley, London, 1705, 4-3/4" h, two handles, stamped and chased designs, engraved initials, mirror dents, 8 troy oz..1,400.00
  Taperstick, M Cooper I, London, 1813-15, 5" h, knobbed stem, octagonal base, later chased, 4 troy oz. 275.00

Victorian
  Claret Jug, 10-1/2" h, Joseph Angell, London, 1846, circular, chased knights on horseback and architectural design, scrolled matted handle, detachable cov, circular foot, 20 oz., 8 dwt 1,900.00
  Cow Creamer, 4-1/4" l, back with hinged flap, repousse bell and chased flowers, 4 oz., 2 dwt............................550.00
  Flower Holder, 5-1/4" l, swan-form, London, 1867, maker's mark "EHS," naturalistically formed, 7 oz., 4 dwt 175.00
  Inkwell, 6" d, Walker & Hall, Sheffield, 1896, circular weighted reeded base, hinged cov with reeded rim, monogrammed 125.00
  Serving Spoon, Exeter, 1858, maker's mark "J.S.," monogrammed, 8 oz., 6 dwt, price for pr 250.00
  Tea and Coffee Service, Birmingham, 1891, plain baluster shape, gadrooned and foliate rim, four ball feet, hinged cover, angular wood handle and finial, 8-1/4" h coffeepot, milk pot, two-handled open sugar, monogrammed, 76 oz., 2 dwt...600.00

William IV, tea service, 6-1/4" h teapot, 2-handle sugar, creamer, bombe lobed body, repousse floral sprays, fine stippled ground, two center vacant cartouches, leaf capped loop handle with ivory stoppers, circular foot, scalloped rim, hinged cov, floral final, 44 oz......................................950.00

Silver, English, Sheffield

Sheffield Silver, or Old Sheffield Plate, has a fusion method of silver-plating that was used from the mid-18th century until the mid-1880s when the process of electroplating silver was introduced.

Sheffield plating was discovered in 1743 when Thomas Boulsover of Sheffield, England, accidentally fused silver and copper. The process consisted of sandwiching a heavy sheet of copper between two thin sheets of silver. The result was a plated sheet of silver, which could be pressed or rolled to a desired thickness. All Sheffield articles are worked from these plated sheets.

Most of the silver-plated items found today marked "Sheffield" are not early Sheffield plate. They are later wares made in Sheffield, England.

Claret Jug, 11" h, cut glass body mounted at neck, hinged cover, baluster finial, multi-scroll foliate handle, c19435 ....500.00
Domed Lid, 22" h, 11" l, engraved armorial whippet, oval handle, early 19th C 575.00
Plate, 9-3/4" d, circular, gadrooned rim, engraved Carlill crest, George III, price for pr...................................175.00
Platter and Meat Cover, 26" l oval tree platter, four ball feet, two wooden handles, gadrooned rim, armorials on both sides, dome cover with gadrooned rim, reeded handles, engraved armorials 2,750.00
Salver, 15-1/4" d, plated, shaped circular, three scroll and floral feet, chased field with scrolls and flowers centering monogrammed cartouche, shell and foliage rim....................155.00
Serving Dish, 10-1/2" d, reservoir, handles 110.00
Vegetable Dish, cov, 13" l, plated, shaped rect, applied grapevine, scroll, and foliage handle, monogrammed 250.00

Wax Jack Bougie Box, 3-1/2" h, cylindrical, pierced dec, flat detachable top, reeded loop handle, snuffer attached by chain 300.00

Wine Bottle Holder, 16" l, wooden base, vintage detail, ivory casters...275.00

Silver, Mexican

The popularity of Mexican Silver is quickly growing with today's collectors. Pieces tend to be well made and easily identified by markings.

Ashtray, Sanborns 65.00

Belt Buckle, Modernistic, Ledeama.....................................185.00

Bottle Holder, 17" l, basket-form, trellis pierced sides, weave pattern bottom and foot, overhead rope handles, 14 oz., 8 dwt 150.00

Box, covered, 4-1/2" l, oval, allover repousse foliage, stippled ground, 8 oz. 175.00

Buttons, 1" d, incised lines, punches, 3 beads at top of lines in center, oxidized, stamped "Made in Taxco," set of 4, 1 oz. 175.00

Ice Bucket, 7-3/4" h, tapering cylindrical, molded scroll rim, applied scroll handles, four feet issuing from applied foliage, inscribed allover, 28 oz., 6 dwt...200.00

Picture Frame, 4" h, 3-1/4" w, oval, scalloped edge, William Spratling, imp early mark, 1931-45 ....490.00

Plate
    10" d, shaped circular, fluted border, 11 oz., 8 dwt........95.00
    11" d, circular, scrolled rim, 14 oz., 4 dwt, price for 6 pc set 700.00

Salad Servers, 9-1/2" l, long tapering geometric handles, foliate design, William Spratling, early imp mark, 1931-45 ... 1,380.00

Toothpick Holder, 2" h, 2-1/4" w, oval, carved primitive figure on front, eagle stamp, Sterling 925, and triangle mark "R. Rodriguez Hecko en Mexico D.F. 925," 2-3/4" oz. 175.00

Silver, Plated

Englishman G. R. and H. Elkington are given credit for being the first to use the electrolytic method of plating silver in 1838.

An electroplated-silver article is completely shaped and formed from a base metal and then coated with a thin layer of silver. In the late 19th century, the base metal was Britannia, an alloy of tin, copper, and antimony. Other bases are copper and brass. Today, the base is nickel silver.

In 1847, the electroplating process was introduced in America by Rogers Bros. of Hartford, Connecticut. By 1855, a number of firms were using the method to produce silver-plated items in large quantities.

The quality of the plating is important. Extensive polishing can cause the base metal to show through. The prices for plated-silver items are low, making them popular items with younger collectors.

Centerpiece, 19" h, oval base, chased border with flowers and birds on four floral feet, circular stem pierced with cherubs and flowers below two winged sitting putti, central circular bowl, partly fluted and applied floral dec, pierced floral border, two branches with bowls, Continental................................1,300.00

Champagne Bucket, 9" d, Simpson, Hall, Miller & Co., cylindrical, bracket handles, applied scroll border band, monogram 265.00

Egg Caddy, Simpson, hall, Miller & Co., emb floral platform holding six egg cups, dec prongs, feet with raised lion's masks, heart shaped ball handle, 6 egg spoons with shell-shaped bowls 250.00

Figure, 22" l, pheasants, naturalistically formed, elongated high raised tail, price for pr 1,000.00

Sugar Bowl/Spooner, urn shape, emb border, horseshoe shaped prongs, bird finial, R & R Mfg. Co., 10" h, $140.

Horn of Plenty, 22-1/4" d, circular mounted foot, four paw and foliate feet, engraved flowers, rim, mid-body, and terminal with floral dec, detachable cov with figural finial, Continental 600.00

Meat Cover, 18" x 10-1/2", Victorian, domed body, bright cut with panel of foliage swags and roses, beaded base edge, twisted branch handle monogram, makers' marks....................250.00

Pitcher, 8-3/4" h, English, Victorian, late 19th C, large pouring lip, compressed circular body, repousse scrollwork and shell motifs, 4 scroll feet..325.00

Punch Bowl, 12" d, cylindrical, reeded circular foot, applied flowers at rim, International Silver 200.00

Tray
    27" l, shaped rect, gadrooned rim, field chased with scrolls, trellis, and foliage, vacant center cartouche, gadrooned and foliate handles, English 140.00
    28" l, oval, two handles, grapevines applied at rim, four feet with conforming dec, field chased with scrolls and foliage centering vacant cartouche, foliate and scroll handles 175.00

Waiter, 18" x 29", Matthew Boulton, George III, early 19th C, rect, shaped gadrooned edge, engraved crest 465.00

SILVER DEPOSIT GLASS

History: Silver deposit glass was popular at the turn of the century. A simple electrical process was used to deposit a thin coating of silver on glass products. After the glass and a piece of silver were placed in a solution, an electric current was introduced which caused the silver to decompose, pass through the solution, and remain on those parts of the glass on which a pattern had been outlined.

Bowl, 10-1/2" d, cobalt blue ground, flowers and foliage, silver scalloped edge..85.00
Cologne Bottle, 3-3/8" h, clear ground, bulbous, floral and flowing leaf motif 165.00
Creamer, 2-3/4" h, clear ground, scrolling silver design......15.00
Decanter, 13-1/4" h, clear ground, Continental silver mounts, grape clusters, and leaves, dec, orig stopper 90.00
Ice Tub, clear ground, floral and foliage dec, closed tab handles, matching sterling silver ice tongs...................................125.00
Perfume Bottle, 4-1/2" h, clear ground, vine and grape leaf dec 60.00
Sugar Shaker, clear ground, vine and grape leaf dec, SP top 65.00

SILVER FLATWARE

History: The silver table service became a hallmark of elegance during the Victorian era. In the homes of the wealthy, sterling silver services made by Gorham, Kirk, Tiffany and Towle were used. Silver place settings became part of a young girl's hope chest and a staple wedding gift. Sterling silver consists of 925 parts silver and 75 parts copper per 1,000 parts sterling.

When electroplating became popular, silver-plated flatware allowed the common man to imitate the wealthy. Silver-plated flatware has a thin layer of silver which has been plated onto a base metal by a chemical process known as electrolysis. The base metal is usually britannia (an alloy of tin, antimony and copper) or white metal (an alloy of tin, copper and lead or bismuth). Leading silver-plate manufacturers are Alvin, Gorham, International Silver Co. (a modern company created by a merger of many older companies), Oneida, Reed & Barton, William Rogers and Wallace.

Collecting Hints: Focus on one pattern by one maker. The same pattern names were sometimes used by several makers for similar pattern designs. Always check the marks carefully; several thousand patterns were manufactured. Popularity of pattern, not necessarily age, is the key to pricing.

A monogram on a piece will reduce its value by at least 50%. Monograms on sterling occasionally can be removed. This, however, is not the case with silver plate. A worn piece of silver plate has virtually no market value.

Silver flatware sold in sets often brings less than pieces sold individually. The reason is that many buyers are looking to replace pieces or add place settings to a pattern they already own. Sterling silver sets certainly retain their value better than silver-plated sets. A number of dealers specializing in replacement services have evolved over the past several years. Many advertise in *The Antique Trader Weekly*.

Alaska Silver, German Silver, Lashar Silver and Nickel Silver are not the same as silver plate. These materials are alloys designed to imitate silver plate. Keep in mind that plated wares have only a very thin surface over the base metal. Once removed, it cannot be easily replaced.

Flatware used by the American railroads is one form of silver flatware that retains its value even when monogrammed. There is a strong market for these pieces among railroad buffs.

References: Bonita Campbell and Nan Curtis (curators), *Depression Silver*, California State University Press, 1995; Maryanne Dolan, *1830's-1990's American Sterling Silver Flatware*, Books Americana, 1993; Marilyn E. Dragowick (ed.), *Metalwares Price Guide*, Antique Trader Books, 1995; Tere Hagan, *Silverplated Flatware*, Revised 4th Edition, Collector Books, 1990, 1995 value update; Joel Langford, *Silver: A Practical Guide to Collecting Silverware and Identifying Hallmarks*, Chartwell Books, 1991; Everett L. Maffet, *Silver Banquet II: A Compendium On Railroad Dining Car Silver Serving Pieces*, Silver Press, 1990; Richard Osterberg, *Sterling Silver Flatware for Dining Elegance*, Schiffer Publishing, 1994; Benton Seymour Rabinovitch, *Antique Silver Servers for the Dining Table*, Joslin Hall, 1991; Dorothy T. and H. Ivan Rainwater, *American Silverplate*, Schiffer Publishing, 1988; *Sterling Silver, Silverplate and Souvenir Spoons with Prices*, Revised Edition, L-W Book Sales, 1987, 1994 value update; Charles Venable, *Silver in America 1840-1940*, Chronicle Books, 1994.

Periodicals: *Silver Magazine*, P.O. Box 9690, Rancho Santa Fe, CA 92067; *Silver News*, 1112 16th St. NW, Ste. 240, Washington, DC 20036; *Silver Update*, P.O. Box 960, Funkstown, MD 21734.

Collectors' Club: New York Silver Society, 242 E. 7th St., #5, New York, NY 10009; Society of American Silversmiths, P.O. Box 3599, Cranston, RI 02910.

Abbreviation: Mono = monogrammed.

Silver Plate: The patterns listed below are among the most desirable of silver plate patterns. The following general prices apply to the more common patterns which are not as eagerly collected:

Cake knife...18.00
Cold meat fork 15.00
Dinner fork 10.00
Dinner knife...10.00
Gravy ladle 15.00
Salad fork 10.00
Soup spoon 8.50
Sugar tongs 18.00
Teaspoon...8.50

Bridal Bouquet, Alvin

Butter pick 55.00
Luncheon fork, mono...25.00
Luncheon knife, mono 25.00
Teaspoon...20.00

Fortun, Oneida, 1939

Butter knife..4.25
Dinner knife...4.00
Serving spoon..4.00
Teaspoon...4.00

Moslem

Cold meat fork 35.00
Dinner fork 20.00
Dinner knife...20.00
Food pusher, mono 95.00
Gravy ladle 40.00
Salad fork 20.00
Soup spoon 27.50

Sugar tongs 38.00
Teaspoon 17.50

Orange Blossom, Alvin
Baby spoon, curved handle 45.00
Bouillon spoon 24.00
Gumbo spoon, mono 40.00
Teaspoon, P.M. 18.00
Youth fork, mono 35.00

Oxford
Cold meat fork 24.00
Dinner fork 15.00
Dinner knife 15.00
Salad Set, fork and spoon 45.00
Soup spoon 12.50
Sugar tongs 24.00
Tablespoon 18.00
Teaspoon 12.00

Remembrance, 1847, Rogers
Butter spreader, individual 9.00
Cold meat fork 20.00
Dinner fork 12.00
Dinner knife 12.00
Gravy ladle 18.00
Iced tea spoon 12.00
Salad fork 7.00
Soup spoon 12.50
Sugar tongs 24.00
Teaspoon 12.00

1776, Dominick & Haff
Bouillon spoon 28.00
Luncheon fork 25.00
Luncheon knife 25.00
Salad fork 22.00
Soup spoon 18.00
Tablespoon 35.00
Teaspoon 15.00

STERLING

Acorn, Jensen
Bottle opener 45.00
Carving set, 2 pcs 300.00
Cheese knife 40.00
Cold meat fork 265.00
Fish fork 45.00
Meat fork 125.00
Pie server 135.00
Salad fork 70.00
Salad serving set 550.00
Salt cellar 135.00
Soup spoon, oval 60.00

Bridal Rose, Alvin
Berry serving spoon 190.00
Butter, master 60.00
Cake server 135.00
Citrus spoon 35.00
Gumbo spoon 38.00
Jelly spoon 55.00
Teaspoon 55.00

Buttercup, Gorham
Bouillon spoon 22.00
Dessert spoon 28.00
Dinner fork 38.00
Fish slice, mono 200.00
Fruit knife 20.00
Gumbo spoon 32.00

Cold meat fork, Astoria, pat. 1868, 1835 R. Wallace, $35.

Ice cream fork 42.00
Iced tea spoon 24.00
Luncheon fork 16.00
Luncheon knife, blunt 18.00
Pickle fork 45.00
Place setting 87.00
Salad fork 25.00
Salad serving fork, mono 90.00
Soup ladle, mono 290.00
Teaspoon 10.00

Cambridge, Gorham
Beef fork 30.00
Berry fork 28.00
Bouillon spoon 10.00
Citrus spoon, mono 25.00
Dessert spoon 25.00
Luncheon fork 20.00
Olive spoon, long, mono 25.00
Pickle fork 25.00
Pie server 40.00
Sugar sifter 78.00
Sugar tongs, mono 30.00

Chantilly, Gorham
Baby fork 18.00
Beef fork 55.00
Bonbon 28.00
Bonbon dish 65.00
Butter fork 25.00
Cheese spreader 30.00
Citrus spoon 25.00
Cold meat fork
    Large 70.00
    Medium 55.00
    Small 50.00
Cream soup spoon 24.00
Fish fork, mono 45.00
Flat spreader 17.00
Food pusher, mono 65.00
Gravy ladle 60.00
Ice cream slice, mono 280.00
Iced tea spoon 26.00
Infant feeding spoon 30.00
Jelly spoon 25.00
Lettuce fork 55.00
Luncheon fork 22.00
Mayonnaise ladle 30.00
Olive fork 18.00
Pie fork, mono 40.00
Preserve spoon 55.00
Salad serving set 225.00
Seafood fork 16.00
Serving fork, mono 25.00
Sugar shell 25.00
Tea strainer 100.00
Teaspoon 50.00
Tomato server 75.00

Chrysanthemum, Durgin
Berry serving spoon 155.00
Cold meat fork 155.00
Dinner fork, mono 35.00
Dinner knife, mono 35.00
Lettuce fork, mono 150.00
Luncheon fork 40.00
Luncheon knife 40.00
Master spreader, mono 50.00
Salad fork 18.00
Teaspoon 30.00

Fairfax, Durgin
Bonbon, mono 25.00
Dinner fork 20.00
Dinner knife 20.00
Flat spreader 16.00
Lemon fork, mono 20.00
Luncheon fork 20.00
Luncheon knife 20.00
Salt spoon, individual 15.00
Seafood fork 17.00
Serving fork 25.00
Teaspoon 18.00
Tomato server, pierced 90.00

Florentine, Alvin
Butter pick 65.00
Dinner fork 25.00
Dinner knife 25.00
Fish fork, 7", mono 55.00
Lemon fork, mono 30.00
Luncheon fork 25.00
Luncheon knife 25.00
Salad fork 25.00
Teaspoon 20.00

Frontenac, International
Berry spoon, mono 225.00
Bonbon 60.00
Cake server, mono 165.00
Cheese spreader, mono 45.00
Coffee spoon 14.00
Cold meat fork, mono 230.00
Demitasse spoon 25.00
Dessert spoon 40.00
Dinner knife 65.00
Gravy ladle, mono 125.00
Ice tongs, large 475.00
Luncheon fork, mono 40.00
Luncheon knife, mono 35.00
Master spreader, mono 65.00
Olive fork, mono 65.00
Sauce ladle 65.00
Serving fork 125.00
Soup ladle, large, mono 525.00
Sugar shell 45.00
Sugar tongs 70.00
Tablespoon, mono 42.00
Teaspoon, mono 16.00

Golden Aegean Wave, Wallace
Butter, master, hollow handle 25.00
Cheese Cleaver 26.00
Cheese Server 27.00
Demitasse spoon 17.00
Place fork 19.00
Salad set, hollow handle, 2 pc 51.00

Grande Baroque, Wallace
Baby set, 2 pc 51.00

Bookmark 13.00
Butter, master, hollow handle 25.00
Butter pick 21.00
Carving set, 32 pc 67.00
Cranberry Server 38.00
Cream Soup spoon 35.00
Demitasse spoon 18.00
Lasagna server 21.00
Pasta scoop 30.00
Pie/Cake server 32.00
Place fork 40.00
Punch ladle, hollow handle 46.00
Rice spoon, hollow handle 39.00
Serving Fork, hollow handle 37.00
Shell, berry, hollow handle 42.00
Soup ladle, hollow handle 45.00
Sugar spoon 26.00
Teaspoon 19.00
Strawberry fork 20.00
Wedding Cake Knife 36.00
Youth set, 3 pcs 78.00

Grande Renaissance, Reed & Barton
Butter knife, hollow handle 17.00
Cold meat fork, large 67.00
Dinner fork 30.00
Gravy ladle 50.00
Jam server 25.00
Luncheon fork 30.00
Pie server 29.00
Place setting 85.00
Place spoon 27.00
Salad fork 22.00
Serving spoon 58.00
Sugar spoon 24.00
Teaspoon 18.00
Tomato server, pierced 60.00

Imperial Queen, Whiting
Berry serving spoon 60.00
Bonbon server 50.00
Butter fork 40.00
Carving set, mono 65.00
Cheese scoop, large, mono 120.00
Cold meat fork, mono 125.00
Demitasse spoon, mono 21.00
Dessert spoon, mono 38.00
Dinner fork 45.00
Dinner knife, mono 60.00
Gravy ladle 70.00
Ice cream spoon, mono 32.00
Jelly slice, mono 100.00
Salad serving fork, mono 100.00
Salt spoon 15.00
Seafood fork 22.00
Spreader, mono 22.00
Tablespoon 35.00
Teaspoon, mono 45.00

Irving, Wallace, 1899
Baked potato serving fork 31.00
Butter fork 11.00
Dinner fork, 7-3/8", mono 30.00
Dinner knife, 9-5/8", SP blade 18.00
Luncheon setting 58.00
Sugar spoon 20.00
Teaspoon 11.00

Teaspoon, Louvain, 1847 Rogers Bros., c1918, $5.

Lancaster, Gorham
Beef fork
    Large 35.00
    Small 25.00
Berry serving spoon, mono 65.00
Cake saw 225.00
Citrus spoon 45.00
Cocktail fork 10.00
Cold meat fork
    Large, mono 65.00
    Medium, mono 45.00
    Small 38.00
Dessert spoon, mono 28.0
Dinner knife 60.00
Gumbo spoon, mono 28.00
Luncheon fork 16.00
Luncheon knife, mono 40.00
Master spreader 25.00
Napkin ring 68.00
Oyster ladle 250.00
Pie server 125.00
Salad fork 65.00
Sardine fork, mono 60.00
Seafood fork, mono 17.00
Serving fork, 7", gold wash, mono 65.00
Spreader, mono 18.00
Sugar tongs
    Large 35.00
    Small 25.00
Tablespoon, mono 26.00
Teaspoon, mono 7.00
Tomato server, mono 125.00

Louis XV, Whiting, 1891
Berry serving spoon, small 45.00
Bouillon ladle, mono 225.00
Bread tray 275.00
Cold meat fork, mono 75.00
Cream ladle 28.00
Crumber 150.00
Demitasse spoon, mono 12.00
Dinner knife, mono 45.00
Fish fork 45.00
Fish knife 58.00
Fish slice, small 110.00
Ice cream server 125.00
Ice spoon 325.00
Lettuce fork, mono 55.00
Luncheon fork, mono 24.00
Luncheon knife, mono 30.00
Macaroni server, mono 240.00
Master salt spoon 20.00
Mustard ladle 45.00
Olive spoon 25.00
Oyster fork 35.00
Pickle fork 24.00
Punch ladle, mono 375.00
Salad serving set 165.00
Soup ladle 295.00

Spreader, mono 20.00
Strawberry fork 30.00
Sugar tongs 30.00
Tea knife 75.00
Teaspoon 45.00

Majestic, Alvin
Bouillon, spoon, mono 14.00
Butter pick 65.00
Dinner fork 40.00
Dinner knife 40.00
Luncheon fork, mono 25.00
Luncheon knife, mono 25.00
Master spreader, mono 45.00
Teaspoon 35.00

Marazin, Dominick & Haff, 1892
Dinner fork 25.00
Dinner knife 25.00
Lemon fork 28.00
Luncheon fork 25.00
Luncheon knife 25.00
Salad serving set, mono 175.00
Tablespoon, mono 38.00
Teaspoon, mono 20.00

Mt. Vernon, Lunt
Bouillon spoon 15.00
Cold meat fork, mono 55.00
Jelly spreader 27.00
Luncheon fork 22.00
Luncheon knife 16.00
Serving fork 23.00
Serving spoon 45.00
Sugar tongs 25.00
Tea strainer on stand, 3 pcs 135.00
Teaspoon 13.00

New King, Dominick & Haff
Demitasse spoon, mono 14.00
Flat spreader, mono 16.00
Seafood fork, mono 16.00
Tea knife, mono 18.00

Normandie, Wallace
Butter, individual, filled handle 11.00
Dinner fork 34.00
Lunch fork 17.00
Sugar spoon 12.00
Teaspoon 10.00

Persian, Tiffany, 1872
Citrus spoon 45.00
Dinner fork 60.00
Dinner knife 58.00
Ice cream fork 50.00
Serving scoop 400.00
Tablespoon 65.00
Teaspoon 60.00

Repoussé, Kirk
Bonbon dish, mono 90.00
Carving set 90.00
Ice tongs 225.00
Iced tea spoon 28.00
Pea spoon 275.00
Relish spoon 30.00

Violet, Wallace
Aspic slice, mono 110.00
Berry serving spoon, mono 85.00
Bonbon, mono 65.00

Bouillon spoon, mono	15.00
Cake saw, mono	100.00
Demitasse spoon, mono	15.00
Dinner fork	30.00
Dinner knife, mono	19.00
Gumbo spoon, mono	36.00
Luncheon fork, mono	22.00
Place setting	45.00
Salad fork, mono	35.00
Spreader, mono	16.00
Sugar tongs, mono	45.00
Teaspoon, mono	13.00

William & Mary, Lunt

Bouillon spoon	18.00
Butter knife, flat handle	15.00
Cream soup spoon	20.00
Lemon fork	15.00
Luncheon fork	25.00
Luncheon knife	18.00
Pickle fork	15.00
Salad fork	18.00
Serving spoon	35.00
Spoon, oval	24.00
Sugar spoon	18.00
Teaspoon	15.00

SILVER OVERLAY

History: Silver overlay is silver applied directly to a finished glass or porcelain object. The overlay is cut and decorated, usually by engraving, prior to being molded around the object.

Vase, pottery, rose, and brown agate, incised "27" on bottom, 4-3/8" h, $150.

Glass usually is of high quality and is either crystal or colored. Lenox used silver overlay on some porcelain pieces. Most designs are from the Art Nouveau and Art Deco periods.

Reference: Lillian F. Potter, *Re-Introduction to Silver Overlay on Glass and Ceramics*, published by author, 1992.

Basket, 5-1/2" l, 6" h, deep cranberry body, allover floral and lattice design, sterling handle 600.00
Decanter, 11-1/2" h, molded, pinched oval bottle, surface bamboo dec overall, base disk imp "Yuan Shun/Sterling," faceted crystal hollow stopper 375.00
Flask, 5" h, clear bottle shaped body, scrolling hallmarked silver, hinged cov 275.00
Inkwell, 3-3/4" x 3", bright green ground, rose, scroll, and lattice overlay, matching cov, monogram 650.00
Perfume Bottle, 6" x 4", deep emerald green ground, abstract scroll sterling overlay, sgd "Sterling Silver Deposit," numbered 600.00
Rose Bowl, 5" w, 4-1/2" h, emerald green ground, heavy floral design of roses, buds, leaves, stems, and scrolls, sgd "999/1000 fine," Alvin mark, patent mark, numbered 725.00
Tea Set, 8-3/4" h, Lenox porcelain body, Reed & Barton silver overlay, 3 pc set 325.00
Vase
    4-1/4" h, burgundy red cased to opal white, oval, overall silver overlay in stylized blossom, leaf, and fence motif, mkd "Sterling" 435.00
    6-3/4" h, faintly ribbed oval bright blue body, lined with silvery green, overlaid foliate silver dec, rim imp "Sterling," Austrian, slight silver rim damage 375.00
    10-1/2" h, dark amethyst, oval body, hammered silver border, Art Deco silver foliate motif, base stamped "Rockwell" in shield, base edge ground 375.00

SMITH BROS. GLASS

History: After establishing a decorating department at the Mount Washington Glass Works in 1871, Alfred and Harry Smith struck out on their own in 1875. Their New Bedford, Mass., firm soon became known worldwide for its fine opalescent decorated wares, similar in style to those of Mount Washington.

Marks: Smith Bros. glass often is marked on the base with a red shield enclosing a rampant lion and the word "Trademark."

References: Kenneth Wilson, *American Glass 1760-1930*, 2 vols., Hudson Hills Press and The Toledo Museum of Art, 1994.

REPRODUCTION ALERT
Beware of examples marked "Smith Bros."

Biscuit Jar, 8-1/2" h, 7-1/2" d
    Pale pink draped over shoulder with hp lacy border, 4 cream colored textured enameled tassels, six-sectioned body, satin finish, metal fittings, lid sgd "S B 4402" 675.00
    Tan, floral dec, melon shaped, matching lid, lion trade mark 275.00
Bowl
    6" d, 2-3/4" h, melon ribbed, two shades of gold prunus dec, beaded white rim 375.00

9" d, 4" h, melon ribbed, beige ground, pink Moss Rose dec, blue flowers, green leaves, white beaded rim..........675.00

Bride's Bowl, 9-1/2" d, 3" h bowl, 16" h overall, opal glass bowl, painted ground, 2" band dec with cranes, fans, vases, and flowers, white and gray dec, fancy silver-plated holder sgd and numbered 2117 ....1,450.00

Cracker Jar, cov, 7" h, 5" d, barrel shape, beige ground, 7 deep brown, rust, maroon, green, and gold pansies, metal cov mkd "S. B. 4412," base also sgd...750.00

Creamer and Sugar, 4" d, 3-3/4" h, shaded blue and beige ground, multicolored violet and leaves dec, fancy silverplated metalware 750.00

Humidor, 6-1/2" h, 4" d, cream ground, 8 blue pansies, melon-ribbed cov 850.00

Juice Tumbler, blue, stork dec 50.00

Mustard Jar, cov, 2" h, ribbed, gold prunus dec, white ground 300.00

Plate, 7-3/4" d, Santa Maria, beige, brown, and pale orange ship 595.00

Rose Bowl
2-1/4" h, 3" d, cream ground, jeweled gold prunus dec, gold beaded top, sgd..285.00
4-1/2" d, fat bulbous shape, beige ground, two sprays of daisy-type flowers, beaded top 325.00

Vase, herons in reeds, light blue ground, 5-1/2" h, $100.

Sugar Shaker
5-3/4" h, pillar ribbed, white ground, pink wild rose and pale blue leaves, blue beaded top, orig cov fair.............495.00
6" h, 2-1/2" d, cylindrical, vertical ribs, opaque white body, stylized dec of pink, blue, and gray summer blossoms, wispy stalks, pewter top 575.00

Toothpick Holder
2" h, ribbed blank, purple and blue violets, beaded top 285.00
2-1/4" h, barrel shape, opaque white body, swag of single petaled blossoms 265.00
2-1/4" h, pillar ribbed, white ground, pink wild rose and pale blue leaves, blue beaded top.................................250.00
2-1/2" h Little Lobe, pale blue body, single petaled rose blossoms, raised blue dots on rim 245.00

Vase
5-1/4" h, 3-1/2" d, pinched-in, apricot ground, white wisteria dec, gold highlights, sgd...375.00
5-1/4" h, 4" d, triangular shape, pale yellow ground, white daisy-like flowers, sgd 425.00
5-1/2" h, petticoat shape, flared base, pink ground, multicolored foliage and herons, stamped mark on base, "Smith brothers- New Bedford, MA," pr..............................850.00
7" h, soft pink ground, inverted dec of white pond lily, blue-green and black leaves, brown stems, maroon trim, c1870, pr...375.00
7-1/4" h, 8" d, double canteen, pink rose sprays centered in 3 decorative reserves, lime-yellow ground, two restored enameled dots, small int. chip.............................325.00
8" h, conical shape, pink, white blossoms and hummingbird dec, script sgd, pr...225.00
8-1/2" h, 3-3/4" w, Verona, colorless ground, painted and enameled pink and yellow orchids, leaves, stems, and buds, int. vertical ribs 495.00
10" h, 6" d, pillow, soft ground, purple wisteria, green, and gold leaves, slight roughage on base 925.00
10" h, 8" w, shaded rust, brown, yellow and gold ground, white apple blossoms, green leaves, and branches, painted beige int..595.00
12-1/2" h, Verona, colorless ground, deep purple and white irises, gold trim, green leaves and stems, int. vertical ribs 550.00

SNOW BABIES

History: Snow babies, small bisque figurines spattered with ground porcelain that resembles snow, were made originally in Germany and marketed in the early 1900s. One theory about their origin is that German doll makers copied the designs from the traditional Christmas candies. While sales were modest at first, demand increased after the birth of Admiral Peary's daughter in Greenland in 1893 and her subsequent popularity as the "Snow Baby," so-named by the Eskimos.

Hertwig and Company, a German manufacturer of china doll heads and bisque figurines, was the first to make these small figures dressed in hooded snowsuits and posed in a variety of positions. They reached their greatest popularity between 1906 and 1910, when they were manufactured by a variety of German firms and imported by many American companies.

Reference: Mary Morrison, *Snow Babies, Santas, and Elves: Collecting Christmas Bisque Figures,* Schiffer Publishing, 1993.

Baby
   In sleigh, sitting, both arms raised, reindeer in front 150.00
   Riding bear, red, white, and maroon, 2-7/8" h 150.00
   Sitting, 2" 195.00
   Sledding
      Single baby pulled by huskies, 2-3/4" h 100.00
      Three seated babies, bisque sled 165.00
   Standing
      Holding tennis racket, stamped "Germany" 115.00
      Playing banjo, stamped "Germany" 135.00
      Waving 160.00
Bear
   On four paws 100.00
   Standing, 2-1/2" h 115.00
Elf, 1-1/2" h 70.00
Girl, seated on snowball, red skirt, arms raised 125.00
Ice Skaters, 2" h, boy and girl, pr 250.00
Sheep, 2" h 75.00
Snowman 65.00

SNUFF BOTTLES

History: Tobacco usage spread from America to Europe to China during the 17th century. Europeans and Chinese preferred to grind the dried leaves into a powder and sniff it into their nostrils. The elegant Europeans carried their snuff in boxes and took a pinch with their fingertips. The Chinese upper class, because of their lengthy fingernails, found this inconvenient and devised a bottle with a fitted stopper and attached spoon. These utilitarian objects soon became objets d'art.

Snuff bottles were fashioned from precious and semi-precious stones, glass, porcelain and pottery, wood, metals, and ivory. Glass and transparent-stone bottles often were enhanced further with delicate hand paintings, some done on the interior of the bottle.

Collectors' Club: International Chinese Snuff Bottle Society, 2601 N. Charles St., Baltimore, MD 21218.

Agate, Chinese
   Baluster, blue, carved and incised birds amid flowering branches, conforming stopper with floral finial, 3" h
      .... 175.00
   Cameo, carved running horse 80.00
   Carved, man rowing boat and pine trees 175.00
   Ovoid, brown relief figure, honey ground, rose quartz stopper, 3" h 175.00
Amber, landscape and figures, caramel inclusions, conforming id, Chinese, late 19th C, 4" l 1,265.00

Seated, one arm extended, $145.

Lapis Lazuli, flattened oviform, carved relief of horse in warrior's armor, wood base, 2-3/8" h, $350.

Celadon
    Light jade, flattened ovoid short neck, 2-1/4" h 185.00
    Mottled jade, gray and brown inclusions, dog mask and ring
        form handles, Qing dynasty, Chinese 400.00
Chrysoprase, flattened ovoid, light green, conforming stopper,
    3" h 215.00
Cinnabar Lacquer, ovoid, continual scene of scholars and boys
    in a pavilion landscape, dark red, conforming stopper,
    3-1/4" h 230.00
Cloisonné, auspicious symbols among clouds, yellow ground,
    lappet base border, ruyi head neck border, conforming stop-
    per with chrysanthemum design, Qianlong 4 character mark
    .... 185.00
Coral, cylindrical, carved kylin, Chinese, 2-1/2" h 175.00
Enameled Glass, each side dec with deer beneath flowing trees,
    seal mark in red on base, 2-3/8" h 920.00
Famille Rose, porcelain, floral and scrolling foliate dec, blue
    ground, Qing dynasty, Chinese 80.00
Ivory, figural, 2 laughing, figures holding lily pad, base mkd with
    Qialong seal mark, Yongzheng seal mark, 3" h 1,840.00
Jade
    Apple-green and celadon, silver mounted, Chinese 750.00
    Black, flattened rect form, relief carved mountains, applied
        white jade figural grouping on one side, rose quartz stop-
        per, wood base, 2-1/2" h 255.00
    Green and brown, Buddha's hand form, relief flowering vine,
        conforming stopper, 3-1/2" h 175.00
    Light green, disc form, enameled silver dec, conforming stop-
        per, stand, 19th C, 2-3/4" h 230.00
    White, flattened ovoid form, short cylindrical neck, raised dou-
        ble character mark on each side, 2-1/4" h 52.00
Lapis Lazuli, ovoid, relief carved, figures beneath tree, Chinese,
    4" h 115.00
Malachite, carved, gourd, Chinese, 3" h 75.00
Opal, carved sage seated before gourd, Ch'ing Dynasty, 3" h
    .... 125.00
Overlay Glass, seven color, one side with floral designs in 2 ar-
    chaic-form vases, reverse with immortal attending a crane and
    deer, bats flying above, each side with animal mask and ring
    handles, green, blue, mauve, coral, brown, and yellow, on
    white ground, 19th C 520.00
Peking Glass, Snowflake
    Blue overlay, each side with prancing deer, head turned with
        a lingshi branch in mouth, 19th C, 2-1/2" h 490.00
    Red overlay, flattened ovoid, one side with serpent and tor-
        toise, other with frog sitting under lily pad, 2-1/4" h
        .... 1,265.00
Porcelain, Chinese
    Blue and white
        Floral dec, wood stand, Qianlong mark 450.00
        Monkey dec, Qing dynasty 150.00
    Red and white, dragon chasing flaming pearl of wisdom, Qing
        dynasty 200.00
    White, molded fish, floral, foliate, and precious objects 275.00
Rose Quartz, flattened ovoid, relief carved leaves and vines, Chi-
    nese, 3" h 45.00
Stag Horn, flattened ovoid, one side with inset ivory panel with 2
    laughing figures, reserve with inset panel with gold archaic
    script, 2-1/8" h 175.00
Turquoise, flattened body, high shoulder, relief carved auspi-
    cious symbol, agate stopper, wood stand, 2-3/8" h 165.00

SOAPSTONE

History: The mineral steatite, known as soapstone because of its greasy feel, has been used for carving figural
groups and designs by the Chinese and others. Utilitarian pieces also were made. Soapstone pieces were very
popular during the Victorian era.

Candlesticks, pr, red tones, flowers and vases, 5-1/8" h, $85.

Reference: *Soapstone*, L-W Book Sales, 1995.

Bookends, pr, 5" h, carved, block form, fu lion resting on top, Chi-
    nese 300.00
Candlesticks, pr, 5-1/8" h, red tones, flowers and foliage 85.00
Figure
    3-1/2" x 3-1/4", geisha, kneeling, Chinese, c1880 .... 125.00
    6-3/4" h, carved bird in flowering tree 50.00
    8-1/2" h, carved loon, green, sgd "Pauloosie" 315.00
    10" l, 8-3/4" h, polar bear, carrying seal, mounted on turntable,
        dated 1,300.00
Plaque, 9-1/2" h, birds, trees, flowers, and rocks 125.00
Sculpture, 11" h, 4 figures dancing in circle 115.00
Toothpick Holder, 2 containers with carved birds, animals, and
    leaves 85.00
Vase, 6" h, carved floral and bird dec 65.00

SOUVENIR AND COMMEMORATIVE CHINA AND GLASS

History: Souvenir, commemorative, and historical china
and glass includes those items produced to celebrate
special events, places, and people.

China plates made by Rowland and Marcellus and
Wedgwood are particularly favored by collectors. Rowland and Marcellus, Staffordshire, England, made a series of blue-and-white historic plates with a wide rolled
edge. Scenes from the Philadelphia Centennial in 1876
through the 1939 New York World's Fair are depicted. In
1910, Wedgwood collaborated with Jones, McDuffee
and Stratton to produce a series of historic dessert-sized
plates showing scenes of places throughout the United
States.

Many localities issued plates, mugs, glasses, etc., for
anniversary celebrations or to honor a local historical
event. These items seem to have greater value when sold
in the region in which they originated.

Commemorative glass includes several patterns of
pressed glass, which celebrate people or events. Historical glass includes campaign and memorial items.

References: Arene Burgess, *Collector's Guide to Souvenir Plates*, Schiffer Publishing, 1996; Bessie M. Lindsey, *American Historical Glass*, Charles E. Tuttle Company, 1967; Lawrence W. Williams, *Collector's Guide To Souvenir China,* Collector Books, 1997.

Periodicals: *Antique Souvenir Collectors News*, Box 562, Great Barrington, MA 01230; *Souvenir Building Collector*, 25 Falls Rd., Roxbury, CT 06783.

Collectors' Club: Statue of Liberty Collectors' Club, 26601 Bernwood Rd., Cleveland, OH 44122.

Additional Listings: Cup Plates; Pressed Glass; Political Items; Staffordshire, Historical. Also see *Warman's Americana & Collectibles* for more examples.

Ale Glass, Centennial 65.00
Bell, 6-1/2" h, Elkhorn Fair, 1913, Button Arches pattern, ruby staining, clear paneled handle 75.00
Bottle, Columbus, oval, lay down, metal screw top............350.00
Bust, Gillinder
    Lincoln, frosted 325.00
    Napoleon, frosted and clear.........................295.00
    Shakespeare, frosted 150.00
Creamer, 6" h, white ground, blue illus of Williamsburg, VA, scenes, English 40.00
Cup and Saucer, 1-3/4" h, creamware, transfer print portraits on cup of George Washington and Lafayette, saucer with portrait titled "Washington His Country's Father," England, early 19th C 490.00
Dish, cov, Remember the *Maine,* green opaque glass......135.00
Goblet
    G.A.R., 1887, 21st Encampment...................................100.00
    Mother, Ruby Thumbprint pattern 35.00
Mug
    Bryan, William Jennings, milk glass 40.00
    Independence Hall, glass 70.00
    Washington and Lafayette, milk glass..........................60.00
Paperweight
    Moses in Bulrushes, frosted center 145.00

Plate, Signing of the Declaration of Independence of United States, blue and white, c1899, Wedgwood, 9-1/4" d, $70.

Plymouth Rock, clear..95.00
Ruth the Cleaner, frosted..125.00
Washington, George, round, frosted center..................295.00
Pitcher, 10-1/2" h, Trans-Atlantic Cable, ironstone, cable form inscribed "To God in the highest, on earth peace, good will towards men, Europe and America are united by telegraph," England, 19th C, cracks and chips to base 345.00
Plate
    Atlantic City, NJ, Rowland and Marcellus, 10-1/2" d 50.00
    Grant, Ulysses, amber glass, emb "Patriot & Soldier," 9-1/2" sq..60.00
    Marietta College 125th Anniversary, 1960, Wedgwood ...25.00
    Old Glory, 5-1/2" d, clear glass 30.00
    Signing of the Declaration of Independence, dark blue transfer, Wedgwood..70.00
Platter, Remember, three presidents, clear and frosted glass 65.00
Stein, Centennial..65.00
Tile, 4" d, Detroit Women's League, multicolored irid glass 135.00
Tumbler, etched
    Lord's Prayer 15.00
    Niagara Falls, Prospect Point, gold rim 20.00
    Ten Commandments 13.00
    Whittier birthplace, waisted, tall.................................60.00
Vase, 6-1/2" h, scrolled enameled panel of Niagara Falls with scenic background, allover enameled pink apple blossoms, purple highlights, brass base 425.00

SOUVENIR AND COMMEMORATIVE SPOONS

History: Souvenir and commemorative spoons have been issued for hundreds of years. Early American silversmiths engraved presentation spoons to honor historical personages or mark key events.

In 1881, Myron Kinsley patented a Niagara Falls spoon, and in 1884 Michael Gibney patented a new flatware design. M. W. Galt, Washington, D.C., issued commemorative spoons for George and Martha Washington in 1889. From these beginnings, a collecting craze for souvenir and commemorative spoons developed in the late 19th and early 20th centuries.

References: George B. James, *Souvenir Spoons (1891)*, reprinted with 1996 price guide by Bill Boyd (7408 Englewood Lane, Raytown, MO 64133), 1996; Dorothy T. Rainwater and Donna H. Fegler, *American Spoons*, Schiffer Publishing, 1990; ——, *Spoons from around the World*, Schiffer Publishing, 1992; *Sterling Silver, Silverplate, and Souvenir Spoons with Prices*, revised ed., L-W Book Sales, 1987, 1994 value update.

Collectors' Clubs: American Spoon Collectors, 7408 Englewood Lane, Raytown, MO 64133; Northeastern Spoon Collectors Guild, 52 Hillcrest Ave., Morristown, NJ 07960; The Scoop Club, 84 Oak Ave., Shelton, CT 06484.

Additional Listings: See *Warman's Americana & Collectibles* for more examples.

Atlantic City, NJ, Steel Pier, chased floral handle, demitasse 35.00
Bar Harbor, ME, emb bowl, fish handle, Shepard mark.......40.00
Boulder, CO, name in bowl, Indian head handle 40.00
California, Golden Gate, emb in bowl, bear handle, mkd "Watson" 20.00

Bermuda, flag, seal, fish, SS, hallmarked, $35.

Decatur, IL, SS	40.00
Denver, mule handle, SS	20.00
Grand Army of the Republic, engraved bowl	70.00
Jamestown Expo	40.00
King Cotton	35.00
Memorial Arch, Brooklyn, NY, round oak stove	40.00
Nebraska, Omaha, high school emb in bowl, SS, Watson	30.00
New Orleans, SS	30.00
Palm Springs, Aerial Tramway, SP, John Brown, mkd "Antico"	100.00
Philadelphia, Independence Hall in bowl, SS	45.00
Portland, OR, SS	40.00
Prophet, veiled	135.00
Richmond, MO, SS	30.00
Rip Van Winkle	30.00
Salem, MA, witch handle	45.00
San Francisco, CA, SS	40.00
Statue of Liberty, NY	40.00
Thousand Islands, fish handle, engraved bowl, SS, Watson	45.00
Winona Hotel, IN, SS	40.00

SPANGLED GLASS

History: Spangled glass is a blown or blown-molded variegated art glass, similar to spatter glass, with the addition of flakes of mica or metallic aventurine. Many pieces are cased with a white or clear layer of glass. Spangled glass was developed in the late 19th century and still is being manufactured.

Originally, spangled glass was attributed only to the Vasa Murrhina Art Glass Company of Hartford, Connecticut, which distributed the glass for Dr. Flower of the Cape Cod Glassworks, Sandwich, Massachusetts. However, research has shown that many companies in Europe, England, and the United States made spangled glass, and attributing a piece to a specific source is very difficult.

Basket
6-1/2" h, 5-1/2" w, bean pot shape, sq top, deep pink int., shaded deep apricot with spangled gold, applied crystal loop handle ... 325.00
7" h, 6" l, ruffled edge, white int., deep apricot with spangled gold, applied crystal loop handle, slight flake ... 225.00
9-1/2" h, 10" l, 8-1/2" w, pink, yellow, and brown-green spatter, silver flecks, white ext., applied crystal twisted rope handle, c1890 ... 325.00
Beverage Set, bulbous pitcher, 6 matching tumblers, rubena, opalescent mottling, silver flecks, attributed to Sandwich, c1850-60 ... 250.00
Bride's Bowl, 10-3/8" d, multicolored, ruby, cranberry, and green, ivory-yellow ground, silver flecks ... 120.00
Candlesticks, pr, 8-1/8" h, pink and white spatter, green Aventurine flecks, cased white int. ... 115.00
Cruet, Leaf Mold pattern, cranberry, mica flakes, white casing, Northwood ... 450.00

Tumbler, rainbow spatter, pink, pale blue, butterscotch, green, beige, and white, silver spangles, cased, white int., 3-3/4" h, $90.

Ewer, 11" h, clear, cased pink, mica flecks, twisted applied handle ... 125.00
Pitcher, 7-1/2" h, bulbous, 4 sided top, apricot, gold mica flecks form diamond pattern, white casing, pontil ... 175.00
Rose Bowl, 3-3/8" d, 3-1/2" h, 8 crimp top, cased deep rose, heavy mica coral like dec, white int. ... 115.00
Sugar Shaker, cranberry, mica flakes, white casing, Northwood ... 115.00
Vase
4-3/4" h, 4" d, amethyst ground, collared scalloped top, goldstone flakes around body ... 145.00
8-1/8" h, 3-5/8" d, cranberry ground, emb swirls, goldstone ... 140.00

SPATTER GLASS

History: Spatter glass is a variegated blown or blown-molded art glass. It originally was called "End-of-Day" glass, based on the assumption that it was made from batches of glass leftover at the end of the day. However, spatter glass was found to be a standard production item for many glass factories.

Spatter glass was developed at the end of the 19th century and is still being produced in the United States and Europe.

References: William Heacock, James Measell and Berry Wiggins, *Harry Northwood*, Antique Publications, 1990.

REPRODUCTION ALERT

Many modern examples come from the area previously called Czechoslovakia.

Basket
6"h, 6-1/2" l, 6" w, pink and bright yellow spatter, white int. lining, clear thorn handle, 8 point star shaped body ... 250.00

6-1/2" h, 6-1/4" l, 5" w, rect, maroon, brown, yellow, blue, red, green spatter, white int. lining, clear thorn loop handle, tightly crimped edge with two rows of hobnails 250.00

7-1/2" h, 5" w, triangular form, bright pink and yellow spatter, white ground, clear twisted thorn handle, ruffled edge, c1890 ....225.00

7-1/2" h, 6" l, brown and jade green spatter, white ground, thorn handle, ruffled star shaped edge, c1890 ....275.00

Bowl, 8-1/2" d, 4-1/4" h, Le Gras, Tigre, cranberry int., spattered cream opaque with goldstone, amber glass applied wishbone feet 220.00

Candlestick, 7-1/2" h, yellow, red, and white streaks, clear overlay, vertical swirled molding, smooth base, flanged socket 60.00

Cologne Bottle, 8-1/2" h, etched adv "Rich Secker Sweet Cologne, New York," applied clear handles 65.00

Creamer, 4-3/4" h, pink and white, applied clear handle, Northwood 50.00

Darning Egg, multicolored, attributed to Sandwich Glass . 125.00

Ewer, cranberry spatter, applied clear handle......................65.00

Salt, 3" l, maroon and pink, white spatter, applied clear feet and handle..........................125.00

Tumbler, 3-3/4"h, emb Swirl pattern, white, maroon, pink, yellow, and green, white int. 65.00

Vase, 7" h, 4-1/2" d, golden yellow and white, enameled bird and flowers, applied clear handles, colored enamel dec 180.00

Water Pitcher, cranberry and yellow, cinched, ground and polished pontil 105.00

SPATTERWARE

History: Spatterware generally was made of common earthenware, although occasionally creamware was used. The earliest English examples were made about 1780. The peak period of production was from 1810 to 1840. Firms known to have made spatterware are Adams, Barlow, and Harvey and Cotton.

The amount of spatter decoration varies from piece to piece. Some objects simply have decorated borders. These often were decorated with a brush, requiring several hundred touches per square inch to achieve the spatter effect. Other pieces have the entire surface covered with spatter.

Marks: Marked pieces are rare.

References: Susan and Al Bagdade, *Warman's English & Continental Pottery & Porcelain*, 2nd ed., Wallace-Homestead, 1991; Kevin McConnell, *Spongeware and Spatterware*, Schiffer Publishing, 1990.

REPRODUCTION ALERT

Cybis spatter is an increasingly collectible ware in its own right. The pieces, made by the Polishman Boleslaw Cybis in the 1940s, have an Adams-type peafowl design. Many contemporary craftsmen also are reproducing spatterware.

Notes: Collectors today focus on the patterns–Cannon, Castle, Fort, Peafowl, Rainbow, Rose, Thistle, Schoolhouse, etc. The decoration on flatware is in the center of the piece; on hollow ware it occurs on both sides.

Aesthetics and the color of spatter are key to determining value. Blue and red are the most common colors; green, purple, and brown are in a middle group; black and yellow are scarce.

Like any soft paste, spatterware is easily broken or chipped. Prices in this listing are for pieces in very good to mint condition.

Creamer, 4-3/8" h, Rainbow, black and brown, wear and stains, tip of spout repaired 440.00

Cup and Saucer, handleless
 Hollyberry, red, green, and black, blue spatter, molded panels, very minor pinpoints............................260.00

Peafowl
 Blue spatter, red, blue, green, and black peafowl, chips on saucer 165.00
 Red spatter, blue, yellow, green, and black peafowl, mismatched, hairline in saucer 150.00
 Red spatter, red, blue, green, and black peafowl, imp "Adams," cup has edge wear, flaking repair on foot 110.00
 Rainbow, green and purple, rim repair 55.00
 Star, red, green, and yellow, blue spatter, minor damage, light overall stain.........................330.00
 Tulip, red and green, purple spatter 525.00

Dish, 6-3/4" l, oblong octagonal, Rose, red, green, and black rose dec, purple spatter, repair 165.00

Miniature
 Cup and Saucer
  Rainbow, blue and purple, repair to saucer 315.00
  Stick Spatter, green and blue, white ground, pinpoints 60.00
 Teapot, cov, 5-3/8" h, design spatter, red and white, minor stains 275.00
 Tea set, 4-1/4" h teapot, creamer, sugar, six cups and saucers, blue spatter, small chips, 9 pcs 650.00

Mug
 Blue, wear, stains, flakes on rim, 3-7/8" h......................45.00
 Green stick spatter, red stripes, crow's foot....................90.00
 Maroon and green, 2-3/4" h.........................250.00

Pitcher
 7" h, leaf handle, blue, minor wear, glaze flake on handle 150.00

Creamer, Rose, blue, slight discoloration, $300.

15-3/4" l, Peafowl, green, yellow, blue, and black peafowl, red
spatter, stains, short hairlines, filled-in back rim chip
....965.00

Plate

6-1/4" d, Peafowl, red, yellow-ochre, green, and black, blue
spatter, short hairline and stains 330.00

7" d, Rainbow, red and blue, small edge damage........165.00

7-1/4" d, Tulip, blue, red, green, and black, blue spatter, wear,
stains, crazing, small rim chips 385.00

8-1/4" d, Thistle, red and green, red spatter, red touched up on
flower 140.00

8-1/2" d

Castle, brown, wear and crazing.........................275.00

Peafowl, red, blue, yellow-ochre, and black, blue spatter,
molded rim 615.00

Pomegranate, red, blue, green, and black, blue spatter,
wear and rim chips.......................................385.00

Rose, red, green, blue, and black rose, blue design spatter
border...275.00

Rose, red, green, blue, and black rose, green design spatter border, red stripes, ...310.00

8-5/8" d, Holly, red and green, minor stains 100.00

8-7/8" d, Tulip, red, green, yellow, and black, blue spatter
....385.00

9" d, Tulip, red spatter border, red, green, and black, stains,
small flakes, short hairline 250.00

9-1/8" d, Peafowl, red, blue, green, yellow, and black, red
spatter, light stains 630.00

9-1/4" d, brown rabbit transfer, yellow stick spatter, gaudy red,
blue, and green floral border.............................385.00

9-3/8" d, gaudy floral dec, red, blue, and green, minor wear
and scratches, minor glaze wear on edge...............220.00

10-1/8" d, black rabbit transfer rim, yellow and green stick
spatter, gaudy red, blue, and green floral center, stains
....385.00

Platter

12-3/8" l, Columbine, green, purple, red, blue, and black, red
border, stains..550.00

13-5/8" l, Rainbow, blue and purple, oval bull's eye center,
wear, stains, poorly executed edge repair...............615.00

Saucer, Peafowl, red, blue, yellow-ochre, and black, red spatter
....275.00

Soup Plate

10-1/2" d, Columbine, green, purple, red, blue, and black flower, red spatter, stains..330.00

10-3/4" d, gaudy stick spatter, red, blue, green, and yellow, floral design center, zigzag spatter border with stripes, mkd
"Nimy, Made in Belgium," 3 pc set.............185.00

Sugar, cov

4-3/8" h, Rainbow, red and green, rim hairline 250.00

4-1/2" h, Tulip, blue, red, green, and black, married lid, yellowed repairs 165.00

4-5/8" h, Peafowl, blue, red, yellow-ochre, and black, stains,
small chips on lid, rim repaired 135.00

7-3/4" h, Peafowl, blue, green, red, and black, red spatter,
paneled body, finial and rim poorly repaired 165.00

8" h, Peafowl, red, dark yellow ochre, green, and black, blue
spatter, octagonal body, mismatched lid repaired, small
flakes on base 110.00

Teapot, cov

6" h, Tree, green and black tree design, blue spatter, molded
flower finial and handle, minor stains 330.00

9-1/4" h, Hollyberry, red, green, and black, blue spatter, molded panels, minor chips, stains, heavily repaired lid .525.00

Waste Bowl, 5-3/8" d, Rainbow, red, blue, and green, hairlines,
stains, and chips 150.00

SPONGEWARE

History: Spongeware is a specific type of decoration, not
a type of pottery or glaze.

Spongeware decoration is found on many kinds of pottery bodies: ironstone, redware, stoneware, yellowware,
etc. It was made in both England and the United States.
Pieces were marked after 1815, and production extended into the 1880s.

Decoration is varied. On some pieces the sponging is
minimal with the white underglaze dominant. Other pieces appear to be solidly sponged on both sides. Pieces
made between 1840 and 1860 have circular or horizontally streaked sponging.

Blue and white are the most common colors, but
browns, greens, ochres, and a greenish blue also were
used. The greenish blue results from blue sponging with
a pale yellow overglaze. A red overglaze produces a
black or navy color. Blue and red were used on English
creamware and American earthenware of the 1880s. Other spongeware colors include gray, grayish green, red,
dark green on stark white, dark green on mellow yellow,
and purple.

References: Susan and Al Bagdade, *Warman's Ameri-
can Pottery and Porcelain*, Wallace-Homestead, 1994; –
—, *Warman's English & Continental Pottery & Porcelain*,
2nd ed., Wallace-Homestead, 1991; William C. Ketchum,
Jr., *American Pottery and Porcelain*, Avon Books, 1994;
Kevin McConnell, *Spongeware and Spatterware*, Schiffer
Publishing, 1990.

Bowl, 7" d, fluted, brown and blue sponge, cream ground
....60.00

Creamer, 3" h, green, blue and cream 100.00

Cup and Saucer, blue flower dec on cup 60.00

Dish, 6-1/2" x 8-1/2", blue and white, serpentine rim..........200.00

Marble, 2" d, gray, blue sponge, late 19th C.....................220.00

Milk Pitcher, 7-1/2" h, black sponge, white ground............185.00

Mush Cup and Saucer, blue and white, worn gilt trim, slight hairline in cup base 85.00

Pitcher

7 1/8" h, brown and blue sponge, cream ground, molded vintage band 65.00

8-1/4" h, blue and white dec, blue stripes 225.00

10" h, barrel shape, green, gold, and brown sponge ...110.00

Plate, 9-1/2" d, red, green, and black central flower dec, red and
green sponged border 190.00

Platter, 13-1/4" l, octagonal, central red and blue foliate chain,
blue band border, cream ground, imp factory mark, Elsmore &
Foster, Tunstall, 19th C 115.00

Sugar Bowl, cov, 4" h, floral reserve, brown sponge, English, 19th
C 95.00

Umbrella Stand, 21" h, American, 19th C...........................600.00

SPORTS CARDS

History: Baseball cards were first printed in the late 19th
century. By 1900, the most common cards, known as "T"
cards, were those made by tobacco companies such as
American Tobacco Co. The majority of the tobacco-relat-
ed cards were produced between 1909 and 1915. During the 1920s American Caramel, National Caramel, and
York Caramel candy companies issued cards identified
in lists as "E" cards.

During the 1930s, Goudey Gum Co. of Boston (from
1933 to 1941) and Gum Inc. (in 1939) were prime producers of baseball cards. Following World War II, Bowman Gum of Philadelphia (B.G.H.L.I.), the successor to

Gum, Inc., lead the way. Topps, Inc. (T.C.G.) of Brooklyn, New York, followed. Topps bought Bowman in 1956 and enjoyed almost a monopoly in card production until 1981.

In 1981, Topps was challenged by Fleer of Philadelphia and Donruss of Memphis. All three companies annually produce sets numbering 600 cards or more.

Football cards have been printed since the 1890s. However, it was not until 1933 that the first bubble gum football card appeared in the Goudey Sport Kings set. In 1935, National Chickle of Cambridge, Massachusetts, produced the first full set of gum cards devoted exclusively to football.

Both Leaf Gum of Chicago and Bowman Gum of Philadelphia produced sets of football cards in 1948. Leaf discontinued production after its 1949 issue; Bowman continued until 1955.

Topps Chewing Gum entered the market in 1950 with its college-stars set. Topps became a fixture in the football card market with its 1955 All-American set. From 1956 thorough 1963, Topps printed card sets of National Football League players, combining them with the American Football League players in 1961.

Topps produced sets with only American Football League players from 1964 to 1967. The Philadelphia Gum Company made National Football League card sets during this period. Beginning in 1968 and continuing to the present, Topps has produced sets of National Football League cards, the name adopted after the merger of the two leagues.

References: *All Sports Alphabetical Price Guide*, Krause Publications, 1995; Mark Allen Baker, *All-Sport Autograph Guide*, Krause Publications, 1995; Tol Broome, *From Ruth to Ryan*, Krause Publications, 1994; *Charlton Standard Catalogue of Canadian Baseball & Football Cards*, 4th ed., The Charlton Press, 1995; *Charlton Standard Catalogue of Hockey Cards*, 7th ed., Charlton Press, 1995; Gene Florence, *Florence's Standard Baseball Card Price Guide*, 6th ed., Collector Books, 1995.

Jeff Kurowski and Tony Prudom, *Sports Collectors Digest Pre-War Baseball Card Price Guide*, Krause Publications, 1993; Mark Larson, *Complete Guide to Baseball Memorabilia*, 3rd ed., Krause Publications, 1996; --, *Complete Guide to Football, Basketball & Hockey Memorabilia*, Krause Publications, 1995; --, *Sports Collectors Digest Minor League Baseball Card Price Guide*, Krause Publications, 1993; Mark Larson (ed.), *Sports Card Explosion*, Krause Publications, 1993; Bob Lemke and Sally Grace, *Sportscard Counterfeit Detector*, 3rd ed., Krause Publications, 1994; Michael McKeever, *Collecting Sports Cards*, Alliance Publishing, 1996; Alan Rosen, *True Mint*, Krause Publications, 1994; *Sports Collectors Digest, Baseball Card Price Guide*, 11th ed., Krause Publications, 1997; ——, *Premium Insert Sports Cards*, Krause Publications, 1995; ——, *Standard Catalog of Baseball Cards*, 7th ed., Krause Publications, 1997; --, *1998 Standard Catalog of Basketball Cards*, Krause Publications, 1997; --, *1998 Standard Catalog of Football Cards*, Krause Publications, 1997; ——, *Standard Catalog of*

Football, Basketball, & Hockey Cards, 2nd ed., Krause Publications, 1996.

Periodicals: *Allan Kaye's Sports Cards News & Price Guides*, 10300 Watson Rd., St. Louis, MO 63127; *Baseball Update*, Suite 284, 220 Sunrise Hwy, Rockville Centre, NY 11570; *Beckett Baseball Card Monthly*, 15850 Dallas Pkwy, Dallas, TX 75248; *Beckett Football Card Magazine*, 15850 Dallas Pkwy, Dallas, TX 75248; *Canadian Sportscard Collector*, P.O. Box 1299, Lewiston, NY 14092; *The Old Judge*, P.O. Box 137, Centerbeach, NY 11720; *Sport Card Economizer*, RFD 1 Box 350, Winthrop, ME 04364; *Sports Cards Magazine & Price Guide*, 700 E. State St., Iola, WI 54490; *Sports Card Trader*, P.O. Box 443, Mt Morris, IL 61054; *Sports Collectors Digest*, 700 E. State St., Iola, WI 54990; *Tuff Stuff*, P.O. Box 1637, Glen Allen, VA 23060; *Your Season Ticket*, 106 Liberty Rd., Woodsboro, MD 21798.

Sports Cards Language

As in a dictionary, new terms and abbreviations are added to various antiques and collectibles categories. Here are some commonly used Sports Cards terms.

ACC–American Card Catalog, edited by Jefferson Burdick, Nostalgia Press, 1960. Lists alphabetical and numerical designations as it identifies card sets. It has devised a set of sub-abbreviations, such as F for food inserts. The one-, two-, or three-digit number which follows the letter prefix identifies the company and the series.

AS–All Star Card. A special card for players of the all star teams of the National League, American League, or Major League.

AU–Card with autograph.

Blank Back–refers to a card with no printing at all on the back.

Borders–white space, although sometimes colored, which surrounds the picture, used in establishing grading.

Brick–a wrapped group of cards, often of only one year.

Centering–the player should be centered on the card with even borders; an important grading factor.

Chipping–wearing away of a dark-colored border.

Combination Card–shows two or more players but not an entire team.

Common Card–ordinary player, lowest-valued card in a set.

CO–abbreviation for coach.

COR–corrected card.

CY–Cy Young award.

Ding–slight damage to the edge or corner of a card.

DP–double-quantity print run.

DR–draft choice.

ERR–error card. Card with a known mistake, misspelling, etc. When a variation card has been issued, the value of an error card goes down.

First Card–first card of a player in a national set, not necessarily a rookie card.

Foil–foil embossed stamp on card.

F/S–father and son on card.

Gloss–the amount of shine on a card, again a value determination.

Grade–condition that helps determine value.

Key Card–most important cards in a set.

Reverse Negative–common error in which picture negative is flipped so the picture comes out backward.

ROY–Rookie of the Year.

SP–single or short print, printed in lesser amounts than rest of series.

Team Card–card showing entire team.

Wrapper–paper wrapper surrounding wax packs.

YL–yellow letters, Topps, 1958.

Baseball

Allen & Ginter, N28, Cap Anson, 1887, PSA 5, framed
....1,995.00

American Caramel, E90-1, 1909-11, Keeler, throwing, even corner wear 695.00

American Tobacco Cards
0, Cobb, 1909, T-206, PSA Grade 5...............................2,000.00
0, Cobb, 1910, T-206, PSA Grade 5...............................2,500.00
0, Cobb, 1910, T-206, PSA Grade 5...............................2,000.00
0, Cobb, red, 1911, T-206, PSA Grade 3 ....1,500.00
86, Jackson, 1915, M101-5 SN, PSA Grade 5 ....5,500.00
87, Jackson, 1916 M101-4 SN, PSA Grade 4 ....5,500.00

Berk Ross, 1952
0, Mantle, PSA Grade 8...3,500.00
0, Williams, PSA Grade 8..1,000.00

Bowman
1948
1, Eliot, PSA Grade 8 ....325.00
8, Rizzuto, PSA Grade 8 ....750.00
14, Reynolds, PSA Grade 7...100.00
24, Leonard, PSA Grade 8 ....75.00
1949
36, Reese, PSA Grade 7..2,750.00
50, Robinson, PSA Grade 8..2,000.00
84, Campanella, PSA Grade 8 ....1,500.00
131, Lather, PSA Grade 8..35.00
186, Kerr, PSA Grade 7 ....75.00
208, Trout, PSA Grade 8...175.00
1950
98, Williams, PSA Grade 5...500.00
157, Roe, PSA Grade 8 ....150.00
194, Cox, PSA Grade 8 ....125.00
215, Looat, PSA Grade 8..125.00
1951
1, Ford, PSA Grade 7 ....850.00
3, Roberts, PSA Grade 8 ....325.00
26, Rizzuto, PSA Grade 8 ....475.00
56, Branca, PSA Grade 7 ....125.00
152, Abrams, PSA 8 ....100.00
203, Law, PSA 8 ....100.00
253, Mantle, PSA 7 ....8,500.00
259, Dressen, PSA 8...200.00
1952
4, Roberts, PSA Grade 8 ....275.00
33, McDougald, PSA Grade 7..100.00
43, Feller, PSA Grade 8 ....500.00
101, Mantel, PSA Grade 7 ....2,500.00
217, Stengel, PSA Grade 8..425.00
232, Slaughter, PSA Grade 7 ....200.00
1953, color
6, Ginsburg, PSA Grade 7 ....50.00
9, Rizzuto, PSA Grade 7 ....275.00
18, Fox, PSA Grade 7 ....200.00
19, Dark, PSA Grade 8 ....125.00
32, Musial, PSA Grade 7 ....1,000.00

33, Reese, PSA Grade 6...675.00
46, Campanella, PSA Grade 7 ....525.00
59, Mantle, PSA Grade 4 ....1,250.00
68, Reynolds, PSA Grade 7 ....125.00
74, Mueller, PSA Grade 7 ....65.00
1954
19, Shantz..12.00
98, Kinder 17.00
171, Bernier 17.00
201, Thomson 10.00
Complete Set
1948, very good..1,100.00
1949, very good..4,250.00
1950, very good/excellent 1,750.00
1951, very good..3,000.00
1952, very good..2,000.00
1953, color, excellent/mint..5,750.00
1954, very good to excellent..5,750.00
1955, excellent/mint..3,500.00
Cracker Jack, 30, Ty Cobb, 1914, PSA 8, framed 24,950.00
Diamond Star, Ott, 50, 1935, PSA Grade 5......................875.00
Fleer, complete sets
1959, near mint...1,750.00
1960, good to excellent 200.00
1961, excellent/mint...400.00
1963, good to excellent, mkd...750.00
1982, near mint..70.00
1984, near mint..100.00
1986, near mint..90.00
Goudey
75, Kamm, 1933, PSA Grade 7 ....125.00
87, O'Rouke, 1933, PSA Grade 5.....................................75.00
91, Zachary, 1933, PSA Grade 6.....................................100.00
92, Gehrig, 1933, PSA Grade 6.....................................3,000.00
93, Welsh, 1933, PSA Grade 5...65.00
101, Coffman, 1933, PSA Grade 5....................................65.00
144, Ruth, 1933, PSA Grade 3......................................1,750.00
Sheet, uncut, 1933, printed backs, framed..................6,995.00
Leaf
1, DiMaggio, PSA Grade 4 ....1,000.00
4, Musial, PSA Grade 6 ....750.00
76, Williams, PSA Grade 6..750.00
Playball
14, Williams, 1941, PSA Grade 5.................................1,750.00
27, DiMaggio, 1939, PSA Grade 7 ....2,500.00
27, DiMaggio, 1940, PSA Grade 7 ....2,500.00
71, DiMaggio, 1941, PSA Grade 5 ....2,000.00
92, Williams, 1939, PSA Grade 8 ....4,500.00
103, Berg, 1939, PSA Grade 3 ....300.00
Topps
1951
3, Ashburn, PSA Grade 8 ....325.00
20, Branca, PSA Grade 9 ....250.00
50, Mize, PSA Grade 8 ....250.00
52, Chapman, PSA Grade 8 ....175.00
1952
37, Snider, PSA Grade 7 ....425.00
44, Dempsey, PSA Grade 8 ....100.00
88, Feller, PSA Grade 7 ....325.00
124, Kennedy, PSA Grade 8 ....100.00
195, Minoso, PSA Grade 8 ....250.00
261, Mays, PSA Grade 5 ....1,750.00
311, Mantle, PSA Grade 5 ....11,000.00
312, Robinson, PSA Grade 6..1,250.00
313, Thompson, PSA Grade 7 ....425.00
314, Campanella, PSA Grade 8 ....5,000.00
333, Reese, PSA Grade 7 ....2,000.00
356, Atwell, PSA Grade 7 ....275.00
384, Crosetti, PSA Grade 6 ....375.00
392, Wilhelm, PSA Grade 7 ....900.00

1953
1, Robinson ,PSA Grade 7 ....750.00
4, Wade, PSA Grade 7 ....75.00
1954
11, Smith 15.00
22, Greengrass 24.00
65, Swift 24.00
94, Banks 250.00
Complete Sets
1951, blue 750.00
1952, good to very good/excellent 15,000.00
1953, good to very good/excellent 3,750.00
1954, good to very good 2,500.00
1955, very good to excellent 2,250.00
1956, good to very good 1,750.00
1957, very good to excellent 2,500.00
1958, good to very good 1,500.00
1959, good to very good/excellent 1,500.00
1960, excellent/mint 2,500.00
W. W. Gum
55, Gehrig, 1933, PSA Grade 4 ....2,500.00
78, Ruth, 1935, PSA Grade 5 ....3,250.00
80, Ruth, 1933, PSA Grade 5 ....5,000.00

Basketball
Bowman
1948
2, Hamilton 18.00
3, Bishop 18.00
19, Ehliers 45.00
20, Vance 35.00
27, Norlander 18.00
31, Gilmur 35.00
Topps
1957
1, Cufton 90.00
2, Yardley 20.00
4, Braun 15.00
5, Sharman 60.00
12, Martin 50.00
19, Heinsohn 105.00
20, Thieben 25.00
21, Meineke 25.00
52, Spoelstra 25.00
58, Colin 15.00
77, Russel 675.00
1974-75
1, Jabbar 25.00
10, Maravich 18.00
39, Walton 50.00
200, Irving 40.00

Football
Bowman, 1950
80, Wildung 30.00
81, Rote 30.00
Fleer
1961
30, Unitas 18.00
197, Otto 25.00
204, Burford 4.00
1963
1, Garron 18.00
6, Long 95.00
36, Blanda 30.00
59, Powell 12.00
72, Alworth 175.00
Topps
1955, All Americans
4, Pinkert 5.00

12, Graham 75.00
22, Muller 12.00
65, Donchess 15.00
1959
44, Johnson 3.00
118, Cardinal team 6.00
126, Rams Pennant 4.00
161, Brown Team 6.00
1960
1, Unitas 27.00
4, Berry 10.00
23, Brown 120.00
31, Starr 23.00
60, Packer team 5.00
62, Ryan 7.00
1961, 166, Kemp 95.00
1964, 30, Kemp 110.00
1966, 96, Namath 60.00

Hockey
Topps
1966, 73, Beliveau 40.00
1966, 109, Howe 190.00
1971, 100, Orr 45.00
1973, 17, Dionne 10.00
1973, 88, Gilbert 5.00

SPORTS COLLECTIBLES

History: People have been saving sports-related equipment since the inception of sports. Some was passed down from generation to generation for reuse; the rest was stored in dark spaces in closets, attics, and basements.

In the 1980s, two key trends brought collectors' attention to sports collectibles. First, decorators began using old sports items, especially in restaurant decor. Second, card collectors began to discover the thrill of owning the "real" thing. By the beginning of the 1990s, all sport categories were collectible, with baseball items paramount and golf and football running close behind.

References: Mark Allen Baker, *Sports Collectors Digest Complete Guide to Boxing Collectibles*, Krause Publications, 1995; Don Bevans and Ron Menchine, *Baseball Team Collectibles*, Wallace-Homestead, 1994; David Bushing, *Guide to Spalding Bats 1908-1938*, published by author; ——, *Sports Equipment Price Guide*, Krause Publications, 1995; Dave Bushing and Joe Phillips, *1996 Vintage Baseball Glove Pocket Price Guide*, No. 4, published by authors (217 Homewood, Libertyville, IL 60048), 1996; ——, *Vintage Baseball Bat 1994 Pocket Price Guide*, published by authors, 1994; Bruce Chadwick and David M. Spindel authored a series of books on major-league teams published by Abbeville Press between 1992 and 1995; Duncan Chilcott, *Miller's Soccer Memorabilia*, Miller's Publications, 1994; Douglas Congdon-Martin and John Kashmanian, *Baseball Treasures*, Schiffer Publishing, 1993; Ralf Coykendall, Jr., *Coykendall's Complete Guide to Sporting Collectibles*, Wallace-Homestead, 1996; Sarah Fabian-Baddiel, *Miller's Golf Memorabilia*, Millers Publications, 1994; Chuck Furjanic, *Antique Golf Collectibles, A Price and Reference Guide*, Krause Publications, 1997; John F. Hotchkiss, *500 Years* *of Golf Balls,* Antique Trader Books, 1997; Mark K. Larson, *Complete Guide to Baseball Memorabilia,* 3rd ed., Krause Publications, 1996; Mark Larson, Rick Hines and David Platta (eds.), *Mickey Mantle Memorabilia,* Krause Publications, 1993; Carl Luckey, *Old Fishing Lures and Tackle,* 4th ed., Books Americana, 1996; Roderick A. Malloy, *Malloy's Sports Collectibles Value Guide,* Attic Books Ltd, Wallace-Homestead, 1993; Michael McKeever, *Collecting Sports Memorabilia,* Alliance Publishing (P.O. Box 080377, Brooklyn, NY 11208), 1966; Dudley Murphy and Rick Edmisten, *Fishing Lure Collectibles,* 1995, 1997 value update, Collector Books; *1996 Vintage Baseball Glove Catalog Source Book,* The Glove Collector (14057 Rolling Hills Lane, Dallas, TX 75240), 1996; John M. and Morton W. Olman, *Golf Antiques & Other Treasures of the Game,* Market Street Press, 1993; George Richey, *Made in Michigan Fishing Lures,* published by author (Rte. 1, Box 280, Honor, MI 49640), 1995; George Sanders, Helen Sanders, and Ralph Roberts, *Sanders Price Guide to Sports Autographs,* 1994 ed., Scott Publishing, 1993; Harold E. Smith, *Collector's Guide to Creek Chub Lures & Collectibles,* Collector Books, 1996; Mark Wilson (ed.), *Golf Club Identification and Price Guide III,* Ralph Maltby Enterprises, 1993.

Periodicals: *Baseball Hobby News,* 4540 Kearney Villa Rd., San Diego, CA 92123; *Beckett Focus on Future Stars,* 15850 Dallas Pkwy, Dallas, TX 75248; *Boxing Collectors Newsletter,* 59 Boston St., Revere, MA 02151; *Button Pusher,* P.O. Box 4, Coopersburg, PA 18036; *Diamond Angle,* P.O. Box 409, Kaunakakai, HI 97648; *Diamond Duds,* P.O. Box 10153, Silver Spring, MD 20904; *Fantasy Baseball,* 700 E. State St., Iola, WI 54990; *Golfiana Magazine,* P.O. Box 688, Edwardsville, IL 62025; *Old Tyme Baseball News,* P.O. Box 833, Petoskey, MI 49770; *Sports Collectors Digest,* 700 E. State St., Iola, WI 54990; *Tuff Stuff,* P.O. Box 1637, Glen Allen, VA 23060; *US Golf Classics & Heritage Hickories,* 5407 Pennock Point Rd., Jupiter, FL 33458.

Collectors' Clubs: The (Baseball) Glove Collector, 14507 Rolling Hills Lane, Dallas, TX, 75240; Boxiana & Pugilistica Collectors International, P.O. Box 83135, Portland, OR 97203; Golf Club Collectors Assoc., 640 E. Liberty St., Girard, OH 44420; Golf Collectors Society, P.O. Box 491, Shawnee Mission, KS 66202; Logo Golf Ball Collector's Assoc., 4552 Barclay Fairway, Lake Worth, FL 33467; Rose Bowl Collectors, 1111 Delps Rd., Daneilsville, PA 18038; Society for American Baseball Research, P.O. Box 93183, Cleveland, OH 44101.

Museums: Aiken Thoroughbred Racing Hall of Fame & Museum, Aiken, SC; International Boxing Hall of Fame, Canastota, NY; Kentucky Derby Museum, Louisville, KY; Metropolitan Museum of Art, The Jefferson Burdich Collection, New York, NY; Naismith Memorial Basketball Hall of Fame, Springfield, MA; National Baseball Hall of Fame & Museum, Inc., Cooperstown, NY; National Bowling Hall of Fame & Museum, St. Louis, MO; New England Sports Museum, Boston, MA; PGA/World Golf Hall of Fame, Pinehurst, NC; University of New Haven National Art Museum of Sport, W Haven, CT.

Baseball

Autograph, photo, sgd
  Hank Aaron 35.00
  Wade Boggs 30.00
  Joe DiMaggio 110.00
  Mickey Mantle 110.00
  Mike Piazza 30.00
  Bernie Williams 25.00
Baseball, autographed by seven Hall of Famers, 1920s
  .... 4,495.00
Cabinet Card, John Clarkson, 1888, N173, Old Judge/Dogs Head 6,495.00
Jersey, game used
  1955, Ken Griffey 2,800.00
  1987, Reggie Jackson 700.00
  1988, Mark McQwire 1,500.00
Magazine, *Baseball,* December, 1926, cover with Ruby and Hornsby shaking hands during 1926 world Series 295.00
Pennant, felt
  Brooklyn Dodgers, Ebbert Field, blue, 1940s 190.00
  Cooperstown, blue, multicolored Braves style Indian head, 1940s 75.00
  Minnesota Twins A. L. Champs World Series, photo, 1965 .... 125.00
  New York Yankees, photo "M&M Boys Last Year Together!," 1966 .... 90.00
Program
  All Star, Philadelphia, 1943 .... 495.00
  All Star, St. Louis, 1948 .... 325.00
  New York Yankees, 1937 .... 195.00
  New York Yankees, 1951 .... 195.00
  World Series, 1938, at New York, Yankees and Chicago Cubs 550.00
  World Series, 1950, at Philadelphia 250.00

Basketball

Autograph, photo, sgd
  Charles Barkley 50.00
  Wilt Chamberlain 60.00
  Michael Jordan 110.00
  Shawn Kemp 35.00
  Shaquille O'Neal 75.00
Bumper Sticker, Kentucky Colonels, 4" x 15", ABA ball, team logo, name in blue and white, unused, 1974-75 .... 20.00
Magazine, *Sports Illustrated,* February 1949, Ralph Beard, Kentucky cover 95.00
Pin, Chicago Americans Tournament Championship, brass, 1935 .... 75.00
Program
  Basketball Hall of Fame Commemoration Day Program, orig invitation, 1961 .... 75.00
  NCAA Final Four Championship, Louisville, KY, 1967 .. 175.00
  World Series of Basketball, 1951, Harlem Globetrotters and College All-Americans 55.00
Souvenir Book, *Los Angeles Lakers,* with 2 records, Jerry West and Elgin Baylor on action cover 75.00

Ticket
　NBA Finals Boston Celtics at Los Angeles Lakers, 1963
　..95.00
　San Antonio Spurs ABA Phantom Playoff, 1975, unused
　..15.00
　St. Louis Hawks at San Francisco Warriors, Dec. 17, 1963
　..50.00
Yearbook
　1961-62, Boston Celtics 150.00
　1965-66, Boston Celtics 85.00
　1969-70, Milwaukee Bucks...40.00

Boxing

Autograph, photo, sgd
　Max Baer, 8" x 10"...180.00
　Mike Tyson..60.00
Badge, 4" d, Larry Holmes, black and white photo, red and black
　inscriptions, 1979 copyright Don King Productions........25.00
Boxing Gloves, 35 readable autographs............................380.00
Cabinet Card, 4" x 6"
　Corbett, James F., dressed in suit...............................375.00
　Ryan, Paddy, full boxing post, dark brown border........395.00
　Sullivan, John L., dark brown border, "John L. Sullivan, Cham-
　　pion of the World" 495.00
Flipbook, 1-7/8" x 2-1/2", copyright 1897 by Cies & Co., 91 black
　and white pictures 60.00

Fishing

Book
　Oberrecht, Kenn, *The Practical Anglers Guide to Successful
　　Fishing,* Wince Press, 1978, 271 pgs, illus, dg 7.00
　Walton, Issac (1st) and Charles Cotton (2nd), *The Complete
　　Angler: or Contemplative Man's Recreation: A Discourse
　　on Rivers, Fish-Ponds, Fish & Fishing in 2 Parts,* supple-
　　mentary and explanatory Sir John Hawkins 125.00
Catalog
　Evinrude Motors, Milwaukee, WI, 1961, 24 pgs, 8-1/4" x 11",
　　Cat. Of Outboard Motors 32.00
　Shakespeare Co., Kalamazoo, MI, 1942, 86 pgs, 5-1/2" x 8-
　　1/2", Shakespeare's Wondereel Long Casts, No Backlash &
　　No Thumbing, Angler Catalog....................................55.00
　The National Fisherman, 1951, 16 pgs, 8" x 10", Tackle
　　...35.00
　Wallsten Tackle Co., Chicago, IL, 1940s, 20 pgs, 5-1/2" x 8-
　　1/4", Fishing Tips, Courtesy of Cisco Kid Lures 21.00
Sign, "The Flatfish, World's largest selling fishing plug," Helen
　Tackle Co., Detroit, metal framed glass, 8" x 16" 350.00
Tobacco Tin, Forest & Stream, pocket size, 4-1/4" x 3" x 7/8"
　..600.00

Football

Autograph, photo, sgd
　Terry Bradshaw 40.00
　Eddie George 25.00
　Howie Long..35.00
　Joe Montana 50.00
Game, Tom Hamilton's Navy Football Game, 1940s............45.00
Pennant, felt, A.F.L.
　Boston Patriots, white on red, multicolored Patriot..........75.00
　Buffalo Bills, white on blue, pink buffaloes 95.00
　Houston Oilers, white on light blue..................................75.00
Pinback Button, 1-1/4" d, Philadelphia Eagles, logo, football dan-
　gle, early 1950s..45.00
Playoff Guide, 1965 NFL, Green Bay Packers vs. St. Louis Cardi-
　nals 40.00
Program
　Army vs. Duke, at the Polo Grounds, 1946 ....40.00
　Army vs. Navy, Michie Stadium, 1952............................25.00
　Fordham vs. St. Mary's, at Polo Grounds, 1938.............40.00

　Heisman Trophy, 1957, John David Crow.......................30.00
　Pennsylvania vs. Cornell at Franklin Field 30.00
　Rose Bowl, 1974, USC vs. Ohio State 40.00

Golf

Autograph, photo, sgd, Tiger Woods 60.00
Book
　George Fullerton Carnegie, *Golfiana: or Niceties Connected
　　with the Game of Golf,* Edinburgh, 1833, 18 pgs of poetry
　　...21,850.00
　The Architectural Side of Golf, London, 1925 ....14,950.00
Magazine, *American Golfer,* June 1932.............................10.00
Noisemaker, 2-3/4" d, 6-1/2" l, litho tin, full color image of male
　golfer, mkd "Germany" on handle, 1930s 35.00
Print, Charles Crombie, *The Rules of Golf Illustrated,* 24 humorous
　lithographs of golfers in medieval clothes, London, 1905
　..1,265.00
Program, Fort Worth Open Golf Championship, Glen Garden
　Country Club, Ft. Worth, TX, 1945 ....100.00

Hockey

Autograph, photo, sgd, Eric Lindros 45.00
Jersey, game used, Wayne Gretzky, Rangers, autographed
　..415.00
Magazine, *Sport Revue,* Quebec publication, February 1956,
　Bert Olmstead, Hall of Fame cov...................................15.00
Program, Boston Bruins, Sports News, 1937-38................250.00
Stick, game used, autographed
　Bondra, Peter, Sherwood 90.00
　Lindros, Eric, Bauer Supreme 295.00

Golf, vase, purple hat yellow jacket, red paints, blue base, green top, pink flowers, 6" h, $125.

Hunting

Badge, Western Cartridge Co., plant type, emb metal, pin back, 1-3/4" x 1-3/8"..100.00
Box, Peters High Velocity, 2 pc cardboard shotgun shells, multicolored graphics, 25 16 gauge shells..........................250.00
Calendar Top, Winchester, paper, man atop rock ledge, hunting rams, artist sgd "Philip R. Goodwin," metal top rim, 20" x 14" 125.00
Sign
    Paul Jones Whiskey, game hunting scene, orig gold gilt frame, 43" x 57"..750.00
    Remington UMC, diecut cardboard
        15" x 14", oversized shell next to box of ammunition 200.00
        15-1/2" x 9", Nitro Club Shells, English Setter atop pile of Remington Shotgun Shells......................100.00
    L. C. Smith Guns, paper, two setters pointing to prey, 14" x 14-3/4"..1,200.00
Winchester, diecut, cardboard, stand-up, Indian Chief with Winchester shotgun in one hand, additional barrels in other hand, 24" x 60"..200.00
Tin, Kentucky Rifle Gunpowder..70.00
Watch Fob, Savage Revolver, figural, metal......................110.00

STAFFORDSHIRE, HISTORICAL

History: The Staffordshire district of England is the center of the English pottery industry. There were 80 different potteries operating there in 1786, with the number increasing to 179 by 1802. The district includes Burslem, Cobridge, Etruria, Fenton, Foley, Hanley, Lane, Lane End, Longport, Shelton, Stoke, and Tunstall. Among the many famous potters were Adams, Davenport, Spode, Stevenson, Wedgwood, and Wood.

References: David and Linda Arman, *Historical Staffordshire* (1974), 1st Supplement (1977), published by authors, out of print; Susan and Al Bagdade, *Warman's English & Continental Pottery & Porcelain*, 2nd ed., Wallace-Homestead, 1991; A. W. Coysh and R. K. Henrywood, *Dictionary of Blue and White Printed Pottery* (1982), Vol. II (1989), Antique Collectors' Club; Mary J. Finegan, *Johnson Brothers Dinnerware*, published by author, 1993; Jeffrey B. Snyder, *Historical Staffordshire*, Schiffer Publishing, 1995.

Museum: Hershey Museum, Hershey, PA.

SPECIAL AUCTION
The Armans Collector's Sales and Services
P.O. Box 4037
Middletown, RI 02842
(401) 849-5012

Notes: The view is the most critical element when establishing the value of historical Staffordshire; American collectors pay much less for non-American views. Dark blue pieces are favored; light views continue to remain underpriced. Among the forms, soup tureens have shown the largest price increases.

Prices listed below are for mint examples. Reduce prices by 20% for a hidden chip, a faint hairline, or an invisible professional repair; by 35% for knife marks through the glaze and a visible professional repair; by 50% for worn glaze and major repairs.

The numbers in parentheses refer to items in the Armans' books, which constitute the most detailed list of American historical views and their forms.

Adams

W.ADAMS&SONS ADAMS

The Adams family has been associated with ceramics since the mid-17th century. In 1802, William Adams of Stoke-on-Trent produced American views.

In 1819, a fourth William Adams, son of William of Stoke, became a partner with his father and was later joined by his three brothers. The firm became William Adams & Sons. The father died in 1829 and William, the eldest son, became manager.

The company operated four potteries at Stoke and one at Tunstall. American views were produced at Tunstall in black, light blue, sepia, pink, and green in the 1830-40 period. William Adams died in 1865. All operations were moved to Tunstall. The firm continues today under the name of Wm. Adams & Sons, Ltd.

Creamer, 5-3/8" d, English scene, imp "Adams," dark blue 175.00
Pitcher, 7-1/2" h, Seal of the United States, dark blue (443) 1,200.00
Plate
    8-7/8" d, English scene, imp "Adams," dark blue, chip on table ring..250.00
    10-1/4" d, Mitchell & Freeman's China & Glass Warehouse, Chatham Street, Boston, imp "Adams," dark blue...715.00
Teapot, Log Cabin, medallions of Gen. Harrison on border, pink (458)...450.00

Adams, plate, pink transfer, Headquarters of the Juniata, U. S. Views series, 10-1/2" d, $140.

Clews

From sketchy historical accounts that are available, it appears that James Clews took over the closed plant of A. Stevenson in 1819. His brother Ralph entered the business later. The firm continued until about 1836, when James Clews came to America to enter the pottery business at Troy, Indiana. The venture was a failure because of the lack of skilled workmen and the proper type of clay. He returned to England but did not re-enter the pottery business.

Bowl, Landing of Lafayette, 9" d, ext. floral design, rim repair 410.00
Cup Plate, Landing of Lafayette at Castle Garden, dark blue 400.00
Plate
  7-7/8" d, Winter View of Pittsfield, Mass, imp "Clews," dark blue, hairline and glued repair 55.00
  7-7/8" d, Welcome Lafayette the Nations Guest and Our Country's Glory, molded rim with blue edge, imp "Clews," dark blue..1,155.00
  8-7/8" d, States, America and Independence, sheep in lawn, imp "Clews," dark blue, wear and scratches 220.00
  8-7/8" d, States, America and Independence, building, curved drive, imp "Clews," dark blue, minor glaze wear 360.00
  10" d, Landing of General Lafayette, imp "Clews," dark blue, very minor wear 350.00
  10-1/4" d, Landing of General Lafayette, imp "Clews," dark blue...360.00
  10-1/4" d, Peace and Plenty, imp "Clews,"" dark blue ..715.00
  10-5/8" d, States series, America and Independence, fisherman with net, imp "Clews," dark blue, small rim flake 440.00
Platter, 17" d, Landing of Lafayette, imp "Clews," dark blue, scratches and wear 1,100.00
Soup Plate
  10-3/8" d, Winter View of Pittsfield, Mass, imp "Clews," dark blue..440.00

Clews, platter, dark blue transfer of Landing of General Lafayette, imp mark, scratches and wear, 17" l, $1,100. Photo courtesy of Garth's Auctions.

10-1/2" d, Picturesque Views, Hudson, Hudson River, imp "Clews," black transfer 165.00
10-1/2" d, Picturesque Views, Pittsburgh, PA, imp "Clews," steam ships with "Home, Nile, Larch," black transfer, chips on table ring..330.00

J. & J. Jackson

J.&J. JACKSON

Job and John Jackson began operations at the Churchyard Works, Burslem, about 1830. The works formerly were owned by the Wedgwood family. The firm produced transfer scenes in a variety of colors, such as black, light blue, pink, sepia, green, maroon, and mulberry. More than 40 different American views of Connecticut, Massachusetts, Pennsylvania, New York, and Ohio were issued. The firm is believed to have closed about 1844.

Deep Disk, American Beauty Series, Yale College (493)...125.00
Plate, 10-3/8" d, The President's House, Washington, purple transfer...275.00
Platter, American Beauty Series
  12" l, Iron Works at Saugerties (478) 275.00
  17-1/2" l, View of Newburgh, black transfer (463).........575.00
Soup Plate, 10" d, American Beauty Series, Hartford, CT, black transfer (476) 150.00

Joseph Heath & Co., platter, lavender, The Riverside Residence of the late Richard Jordan, New Jersey, 15-1/2" l, $270.

Thomas Mayer

In 1829, Thomas Mayer and his brothers, John and Joshua, purchased Stubbs's Dale Hall Works of Burslem. They continued to produce a superior grade of ceramics.

Cream Pitcher, 4" h, Lafayette at Franklin's Tomb, dark blue 550.00
Gravy Tureen, Arms of the American States, CT, dark blue (498) 3,800.00
Plate, 8-1/2" d, Arms of the American States, RI, dark blue (507) 800.00

Platter

8-1/4" l, Lafayette at Franklin's Tomb, dark blue 525.00
19" l, Arms of the American States, NJ, dark blue (503)
....7,200.00
Sugar Bowl, cov, Lafayette at Franklin's Tomb, dark blue (510)
....850.00

Mellor, Veneables & Co.

Little information is recorded on Mellor, Veneables & Co., except that it was listed as potters in Burslem in 1843. Its Scenic Views with the Arms of the States Border does include the arms for New Hampshire. This state is missing from the Mayer series.

Plate, 7-1/2" d, Tomb of Washington, Mt. Vernon, Arms of States
border 125.00
Platter, 15" l, Scenic Views, Arms of States border, Albany, light
blue (516) 265.00
Sugar Bowl, cov, Arms of States, PA, dark blue 350.00
Teapot, 9-1/2" h, Windsor pattern, dark blue.....................200.00

J. & W. Ridgway and William Ridgway & Co.

John and William Ridgway, sons of Job Ridgway and nephews of George Ridgway, who owned Bell Bank Works and Cauldon Place Works, produced the popular Beauties of America series at the Cauldon plant. The partnership between the two brothers was dissolved in 1830. John remained at Cauldon.

William managed the Bell Bank Works until 1854. Two additional series were produced based upon the etchings of Bartlett's American Scenery. The first series had various borders including narrow lace. The second series is known as Catskill Moss.

Beauties of America is in dark blue. The other series are found in light transfer colors of blue, pink, brown, black, and green.

Plate

6" d, Catskill Moss, Anthony's Nose (925) 85.00
7" d, American Scenery, Valley of the Shenandoah from Jefferson's Rock, brown (289) 120.00
10" h, Beauties of America, City Hall, NY, dark blue (260)
....225.00
10-1/4" h, Columbian Star, Harrison's Log Cabin, side view,
green (277) 250.00
Platter, 19" l, Catskill Moss, Boston and Bunker's Hill, imp "William
Ridgway Son & Co.," medium blue, dated 1844, minor chips,
knife marks, edge wear 525.00
Soup Plate, 9-7/8" d, Octagon Church Boston, imp "Ridgway,"
dark medium blue...330.00
Vegetable Dish, 1-" l, open, American Scenery, Peekskill Landing,
Hudson River, purple (287) 195.00
Wash Bowl, American Scenery, Albany (279)...................325.00

Rogers

John Rogers and his brother George established a pottery near Longport in 1782.

After George's death in 1815, John's son Spencer became a partner, and the firm operated under the name of John Rogers & Sons. John died in 1916. His son continued the use of the name until he dissolved the pottery in 1842.

Cup and Saucer, Boston Harbor, dark blue (441) 650.00
Cup Plate, Boston Harbor, dark blue (441) 1,400.00
Plate, 9-5/8" d, The Canal at Buffalo, lace border, purple transfer,
int. hairline 55.00
Platter, 16-5/8" l, Boston State House, medium dark blue (442)
....1,000.00
Waste Bowl, Boston Harbor, dark blue (441)...................850.00

Stevenson

As early as the 17th century, the name Stevenson has been associated with the pottery industry. Andrew Stevenson of Cobridge introduced American scenes with the flower and scroll border. Ralph Stevenson, also of Cobridge, used a vine and leaf border on his dark blue historical views and a lace border on his series in light transfers.

The initials R. S. & W. indicate Ralph Stevenson and Williams are associated with the acorn and leaf border. It has been reported that Williams was Ralph's New York agent and the wares were produced by Ralph alone.

Cup and Saucer, New Orleans, floral and scroll border 95.00
Jug, 8-1/4" h, dark blue print 750.00
Plate
6-1/2" d, Catholic Cathedral, NY, floral and scroll border, dark
blue (395) 1,650.00
6-7/8" d, Battery, NY, vine border (367) 800.00
7-1/2" d, Columbia College, NY, acorn and oak leaves border,
dark blue (350) 450.00
Soup Plate, 10" d, Erie Canal at Buffalo, lace border (386)
....95.00
Wash bowl, Riceborough, GA, lace border (388) 375.00

Stubbs

In 1790, Stubbs established a pottery works at Burslem, England. He operated it until 1829 when he retired and sold the pottery to the Mayer brothers. He probably produced his American views about 1825. Many of his scenes were from Boston, New York, New Jersey, and Philadelphia.

Pitcher, 6-1/2" h, Boston State House and New York City Hall, rose
border, dark blue (335) 1,100.00
Plate
6-1/2" d, City Hall, NY, spread eagle border, medium blue
(323) 275.00
10-1/4" d, Fairmount Near Philadelphia, imp "Stubbs," medium
blue..220.00

Unknown maker, platter, dark blue transfer of Sandusky, very minor scratches, 16-5/8" l, $8,525. Photo courtesy of Garth's Auctions.

Platter, 14-1/2" l, State House, Boston, spread eagle border, dark blue (331) 750.00
Salt Shaker, Hoboken in NJ, spread eagle border, dark blue (326) 700.00

Unknown

Plate
    6" d, Entrance of the Erie Canal into the Hudson at Albany, dark blue...700.00
    7" d, Junction of the Sacandaga & Hudson River, black transfer, small rim glaze defect 95.00
    7-3/4" d, Near Fishkill, small chip on table ring 100.00
    9" d, The Residence of the late Richard Jordon, New Jersey," brown, minor wear and stains 250.00
    9-3/4" d, British Views, dark blue, minor wear and pinpoints 215.00
    10" d, Knighthood Confer'd on Don Quixote, dark blue, minor wear and scratches 150.00
    10-1/8" d
        Harvard College, medium blue, minor edge roughness, light stains 110.00
        Park Theatre, New York, dark blue...........................330.00
    10-5/8" d, Picturesque Views Near Fishkill, Hudson River, purple transfer..110.00
Platter, 16-5/8" l, Sandusky, dark blue, very minor scratches 8,525.00
Saucer, 5-7/8" d, scene of early railroad, engine and one car, floral border, dark blue..275.00
Soup Plate, 10-1/4" d, ---burgs, Yorkshire, medium blue...220.00
Teapot, 8-1/4" h, The Residence of the Late Richard Jordan, New Jersey, brown transfer, small chip, stain and repair to lid 715.00

Wood

Enoch Wood, sometimes referred to as the father of English pottery, began operating a pottery at Fountain Place, Burslem, in 1783. A cousin, Ralph Wood, was associated with him. In 1790, James Caldwell became a partner and the firm was

known as Wood and Caldwell. In 1819, Wood and his sons took full control.

Enoch died in 1840. His sons continued under the name of Enoch Wood & Sons. The American views were first made in the mid-1820s and continued through the 1840s.

It is reported that the pottery produced more signed historical views than any other Staffordshire firm. Many of the views attributed to unknown makers probably came from the Woods.

Marks vary, although always include the name Wood. The establishment was sold to Messrs. Pinder, Bourne & Hope in 1846.

Creamer, 5-3/4" h, horse drawn sleigh, imp "Wood," dark blue, minor hairline in base 550.00
Cup and Saucer, handleless
    Commodore MacDonnough's Victory, imp "Wood & Sons," dark blue, pinpoints on cup table ring 605.00
    Ship with American flag, Chancellor Livingston, imp "Wood & Sons" 770.00
Plate
    6-1/2" d, Catskill House, Hudson, imp "Wood & Sons," dark blue, white spot near center, pinpoint rim flake 495.00
    7-5/8" d, The Capitol Washington, shell border, imp "Wood & Sons," dark blue 935.00
    8-3/8" d, Chief Justice Marshall, Troy, imp "Wood & Sons," dark blue, small chip 600.00
    9-1/4" d, Commodore MacDonnough's Victory, imp "Wood," dark blue..385.00
    9-1/4" d, The Baltimore & Ohio Railroad, (incline), imp "Enoch Wood," dark blue..770.00
    10-1/8" d, Cadmus, imp "Wood & Sons," dark blue......495.00
    10-1/4" d, Boston State House, imp "Wood & Sons," medium blue...165.00
    10-1/4" d, The Baltimore & Ohio Railroad, (straight), imp "Wood," dark blue, minor scratches........................825.00

Wood & Son, plate, dark blue, The Residence of Marquis Lafayette, 10-1/4" d, $225.

10-3/8" d, Constitution and Guerriere, imp "Wood," dark blue minor scratches 1,760.00

Platter, 16-5/8" l, London Views, St. George's Chapel, Regents Street, imp "Wood," dark blue, minor wear, scratches, pinpoint flakes 660.00

Toddy Plate

5-3/4" d, ship scene, shell border, scene not identified, imp "Wood," dark blue 330.00

6-1/2" d, dark blue transfer, Catskill House, Hudson, imp "Wood," minor wear and stains 525.00

STAFFORDSHIRE ITEMS

History: A wide variety of ornamental pottery items originated in England's Staffordshire district, beginning in the 17th century and still continuing today. The height of production took place from 1820 to 1890.

These naive pieces are considered folk art by many collectors. Most items were not made carefully; some even were made and decorated by children.

The types of objects are varied, e.g., animals, cottages, and figurines (chimney ornaments).

References: Susan and Al Bagdade, *Warman's English & Continental Pottery & Porcelain*, 2nd ed., Wallace-Homestead, 1991; Pat Halfpenny, *English Earthenware Figures*, Antique Collectors' Club, 1992; Adele Kenny, *Staffordshire Spaniels*, Schiffer Publishing, 1997; P. D. Gordon Pugh, *Staffordshire Portrait Figures of the Victorian Era*, Antique Collectors' Club, 1987; Dennis G. Rice, *English Porcelain Animals of the 19th Century*, Antique Collectors' Club, 1989.

REPRODUCTION ALERT

Early Staffordshire figurines and hollowware forms were molded. Later examples were made using a slip-casting process. Slip casting leaves telltale signs that are easy to spot. Look in the interior. Hand molding created a smooth interior surface. Slip casting produces indentations that conform to the exterior design. Holes occur where handles meet the body of slip-cast pieces. There is not hole in a hand-molded piece.

A checkpoint on figurines is the firing or vent hole, which is a necessary feature on these forms. Early figurines had small holes; modern reproductions feature large holes often the size of a dime or quarter. Vent holes are found on the sides or hidden among the decoration in early Staffordshire figurines; most modern reproductions have them in the base.

These same tips can be used to spot modern reproductions of Flow Blue, Majolica, Old Sleepy Eye, Stoneware, Willow, and other ceramic pieces.

Note: The key to price is age and condition. As a general rule, the older the piece, the higher the price.

Bank, 5-1/4" h, cottage shape, repairs 195.00

Bowl, 14" x 8", rect, handles, all over cobalt floral dec, c1860 .... 150.00

Cheese Plate, cov, triangular, blue and white transfer, painted floral dec, ironstone 225.00

Child's Plate, 4-1/2" d, molded dressed goose, green, brown, and black enamel 55.00

Figure, George Washington, holding tricorn hat and document, 14-1/4" h, $1,100. Photo courtesy of Freeman\Fine Arts.

Cup and Saucer, handleless, vase with flower, imp "Clews," dark blue, wear, small chips 95.00

Figure

3-1/4" h, rabbit, black and white, brown and green base, wear and enamel flaking 315.00

4" h, dogs, seated, white, polychrome, orange pots in mouth, one with hairlines and chip to base, pr 400.00

4-1/4" h, Spring, pearlware, brown and green glaze, small flakes, old repair 220.00

4-1/2" h, Spring, canary, wear, small flakes 770.00

4-5/8" h, Winter, canary, minor wear, small flakes........660.00

5-1/2" h, 3-1/2" l, boy and girl under tree canopy, sheep and dog, oval base, 2 small nicks 90.00

6-1/2" h, 3-1/4" d, lad up in tree, bird in hand, nest nearby, girl seated below, oval base, repairs 65.00

7" h, squirrel, sitting upright holding nut, naturalistic stump base, ear repaired 125.00

8-1/8" h, seated gentleman, book and spectacles, polychrome enamel, damaged, old repairs 275.00

11" h, seated cats, crazing, pr................................... 3,110.00

Hen on Nest, 10-1/2" l, polychrome, good color, minor edge wear and chips on inner flange of base 715.00

Mantel Ornament, 9" h, cottage, Potash Farm, hairlines 175.00

Pitcher, 4-7/8" h, mask, pink luster rim, glaze wear, hairline to spout..175.00

Plate, 10" d, feather edge, blue, emb rim design.................55.00

Platter

16" l, 12" w, orchid ground, large colonial transfer scene, c1850... 195.00

19" l, Cambrian, Phillips, brown transfer........................415.00

Sauce Boat, 7-7/8" l, fruit and flowers, molded feet and handle, dark blue, rim chips..330.00

Sauce Tureen, 7-1/2" l, blue transfer, pastoral scene, chips 345.00

Teapot, 6-1/2" h, blue transfer, central dec of bird's nest with eggs..460.00

Waste Bowl, 5-5/8" d, Forget Me Not, red transfer, edge roughness 60.00

STAFFORDSHIRE, ROMANTIC

History: In the 1830s, two factors transformed the blue-and-white printed wares of the Staffordshire potters into what is now called "Romantic Staffordshire." Technical innovations expanded the range of transfer-printed colors to light blue, pink, purple, black, green, and brown. There was also a shift from historical to imaginary scenes with less printed detail and more white space, adding to the pastel effect.

Shapes from the 1830s are predominately rococo with rounded forms, scrolled handles, and floral finials. Over time, patterns and shapes became simpler and the earthenware bodies coarser. The late 1840s and 1850s saw angular gothic shapes and pieces with the weight and texture of ironstone.

The most dramatic post-1870 change was the impact of the craze for all things Japanese. Staffordshire designs adopted zigzag border elements and motifs such as bamboo, fans, and cranes. Brown printing dominated this style, sometimes with polychrome enamel highlights.

Marks: Wares are often marked with pattern or potter's names, but marking was inconsistent and many authentic, unmarked examples exist. The addition of "England" as a country of origin mark in 1891 helps to distinguish 20th-century wares made in the romantic style.

References: Susan and Al Bagdade, *Warman's English & Continental Pottery & Porcelain*, 2nd ed., Wallace-Homestead, 1991; Jeffrey B. Snyder, *Romantic Staffordshire Ceramics,* Schiffer Publishing, 1997; Petra Williams, *Staffordshire: Romantic Transfer Patterns* (1978), *Staffordshire II* (1986), *Staffordshire III* (1996), Fountain House East (P.O. Box 99298, Jeffersontown, KY 40269).

Caledonia, Williams Adams, 1830s
    Plate, 9-1/2" d, purple transfer, imp "Adams"...................60.00
    Platter, 17" l...500.00
    Soup Plate, two color.......................................175.00

Plate, Parisian Chateau, R. Hall, 10-1/2" d, $60.

Canova, Thomas Mayer, c1835; G. Phillips, c1840
    Plate, 10-1/2" d 95.00
    Pudding Bowl, two color..................................200.00
    Vegetable, cov..325.00
Columbia, W. Adams & Sons, 1850
    Creamer..115.00
    Cup and Saucer 65.00
    Cup Plate..65.00
    Plate, 10" d...60.00
    Relish...65.00
Dado, Ridgways, 1880s
    Creamer, brown..75.00
    Cup and Saucer, polychrome 80.00
    Plate
        7-1/2" d, brown 35.00
        10-1/2" d, polychrome 70.00
Delzoni, plate, 8-3/4" d, brown transfer 60.00
India, plate, 9" d, red transfer scene, floral border...............65.00
Japonica, creamer and sugar 275.00
Marmora, William Ridgway & Co., 1830s
    Platter, 16-1/2" l..325.00
    Sauce Tureen, matching tray 350.00
    Soup Plate 100.00
Millenium, Ralph Stevenson & Son, 1830s, plate, 10-1/2" d
    ....145.00
Palestine, William Adams, 1836
    Creamer and Sugar 265.00
    Cup and Saucer, two color...............................135.00
    Cup Plate..75.00
    Plate
        5" d...45.00
        7" d...60.00
        9-1/2" d 65.00
    Platter, 13" l...325.00
    Vegetable, open, 12" l....................................200.00
Union, William Ridgway Son & Co., 1840s
    Plate, 10-1/2" d 70.00
    Platter, 15" l...165.00
Venus, Podmore, Walker & Co., 1850s, plate, 7-1/2" d........50.00

STAINED AND/OR LEADED GLASS PANELS

History: American architects in the second half of the 19th century and the early 20th century used stained- and leaded-glass panels as a chief decorative element. Skilled glass craftsmen assembled the designs, the best known being Louis C. Tiffany.

The panels are held together with soft lead cames or copper wraps. When purchasing a panel, protect your investment by checking the lead and making any necessary repairs.

Reference: Web Wilson, *Great Glass in American Architecture,* E. P. Dutton, New York, 1986.

Periodicals: *Glass Art Magazine*, P.O. Box 260377, Highlands Ranch, CO 80126; *Glass Patterns Quarterly*, P.O. Box 131, Westport, NY 40077; *Professional Stained Glass*, P.O. Box 69, Brewster, NY 10509; *Stained Glass*, 6 SW. 2nd St., #7, Lees Summit, MO 64063.

Collectors' Club: Stained Glass Assoc. of America, P.O. Box 22462, Kansas City, MO 64113.

Museum: Corning Museum of Glass, Corning, NY.

Leaded

Firescreen, 48-1/2" w, 32" h, 3 panels, clear glass top half, hammered white glass lower half, central applied Art Nouveau floral design, green bull's eye highlights 2,750.00

Panel, 96" h, 20" w, rect, rippled, and opaque glass, turquoise, white, and avocado, clear glass ground, stylized flowering plant motif, c1910, 6 panels 6,000.00

Window

Center design of music lyre, squared ribbon border, orig condition...400.00

3 sections, large center with 5 squares across, 8 down, flanked by side lights each with 2 sq across, 8 panes down, wisteria and foliage design, orig condition, couple of broken sections...1,000.00

Stained

Panel

24" x 14", red, white, green, pink, and blue floral design, 2 layers of striated and fractured glass, green patinated bronze frame, stamped "Tiffany Studios New York" pr 2,400.00

26" x 21", Richard the Lion-Hearted on horseback, 1883 ....675.00

Window

32" x 24", Art Nouveau, yellow, blue, and orange geometric, oak frame, c1900 ....275.00

Multicolored cartouche center, green border, red sq, custard band, wood frame, 47" l, 22-1/2" w, $265.

61-1/2" h, 61" l, over entry door type, blue and orange shield and geometric design, c1920 ....490.00

Sketch for leaded glass window

Charcoal on paper, The Cruxification, 26" d, America, c1920 ....170.00

Charcoal on paper, The Temptation, 26" d, America, c1920 ....150.00

Watercolor, garden scene, mother and child before Christ figure, sgd on mat "Louis Comfort Tiffany," 6-3/4 x 4-1/2" 1,725.00

STANGL POTTERY BIRDS

History: Stangl ceramic birds were produced from 1940 until the Stangl factory closed in 1978. The birds were produced at Stangl's Trenton plant and either decorated there or shipped to their Flemington, New Jersey, outlet for hand painting.

During World War II, the demand for these birds, and other types of Stangl pottery as well, was so great that 40 to 60 decorators could not keep up with the demand. Orders were contracted out to be decorated by individuals in their own homes. These orders then were returned for firing and finishing. Colors used to decorate these birds varied according to the artist.

Marks: As many as 10 different trademarks were used. Almost every bird is numbered; many are signed by the artist. However, the signatures are used only for dating purposes and add very little to the value of the birds.

References: Susan and Al Bagdade, *Warman's American Pottery and Porcelain*, Wallace-Homestead, 1994; Harvey Duke, *Stangl Pottery*, Wallace-Homestead, 1992; Mike Schneider, *Stangl and Pennsbury Birds*, Schiffer Publishing, 1994.

Collectors' Club: Stangl/Fulper Collectors Club, P.O. Box 538, Flemington, NJ 08822.

Additional Listings: See *Warman's Americana & Collectibles* for more examples.

Advisor: Bob Perzel.

Note: Several birds were reissued between 1972 and 1977. These reissues are dated on the bottom and are worth approximately the same as older birds if well decorated.

3250C, Preening duck, natural colors 110.00
3250D, Gazing duck, black, gold...45.00
3276, Bluebird 75.00
3285, Rooster, early, black spots 90.00
3286, Hen, late, all white body 50.00
3401, Wren, old, tan 200.00
3401, Wren, revised brown..50.00
3402, Oriole, old, beak down 150.00
3406, Kingfishers, pr, blue 150.00
3407, Owl..350.00
3431, Duck, standing 500.00
3433, Rooster, 16" h 2,200.00
3443, Flying Duck, gray..300.00
3444, Cardinal, pink gloss 100.00
3444, Cardinal, red matte 125.00
3447, Prothonartary Warbler...65.00
3450, Passenger Pigeon 1,250.00
3451, Willow Ptmarigan 2,500.00

3452, Painted Bunting	110.00
3453, Mountain Bluebird	1,100.00
3455, Shoveler Duck	1,400.00
3459, Fishhawk, Osprey, Falcon	2,500.00
3490, Redstarts, pr	200.00
3580, Cockatoo, medium	125.00
3582, Parakeets, pr, blue	250.00
3582, Parakeets, pr, green	200.00
3586, Delaware Pheasant, natural colors	600.00
3586, Delaware Pheasant, terra rose colors	400.00
3590, Chat, Carolina Wren	175.00
3591, Brewers Blackbird	125.00
3599, Hummingbirds, pr	300.00
3625, Bird of Paradise, 13-1/2" h	2,200.00
3717, Blue Jays, pr	3,500.00
3749, Scarlett Tanager	325.00
3750, Western Tanagers, pr	425.00
3755, Audubon Warbler	175.00
3810, Blackpoll Warbler	175.00
3814, Black Throated Green Warbler	150.00
3815, Western bluebird	450.00
3853, Group of Cedar Waxwings	600.00
3868, Summer Tanager	550.00
3921, Yellow Headed Verdin	1,250.00

STATUES

History: Beginning with primitive cultures, man created statues in the shape of people and animals. During the Middle Ages, most works were religious and symbolic in character and form. During the Renaissance the human and secular forms were preferred.

During the 18th and 19th centuries, it was fashionable to have statues in the home. Many famous works were copied for use by the general public.

Allegory of Wine, gilded bronze, Etienne A. Stella, French, sgd, foundry marks, 36" h, $3,410. Photo courtesy of Jackson's Auctioneers & Appraisers.

Reference: Lynne and Fritz Weber (eds.), *Jacobsen's Thirteenth Painting and Bronze Price Guide*, Weber Publications, 1994.

Bacchi Dance, Pietro Caproni, after orig, housed in National Museum, Naples, plaster cast, 30-1/2" h, 30" w 275.00

Blackamoors, 45" h, man and woman, each holding bracket aloft, carved wood, polychrome paint, Venetian, 19th C, later black and yellow painted 24" sq pedestal base, areas of repaint, pr 6,625.00

Children in Cradle, 10-1/2" h, unknown 19th C Continental artist, bronze, brown-green patina, stepped marble base ..2,200.00

Circus Wagon, painted and carved pine, classically draped maiden, design attributed to Jacob Sebastian; carving attributed to Robb or Peter Breit, NY, c1880, cracks, losses, paint wear, 59" h 2,300.00

Madonna Nursing Child, 33" h, carved stone, unknown 18th C German artist, some remaining polychrome paint 2,000.00

Master of the Hounds, 30" h, Hippolyte Moreau, sgd in case, "Hippolyte Moreau, Lecourtier," dark brown patina 4,500.00

Mermaid, 17" h, 34" l, carved by Bill Jackman, cherry and oak, lounging back, sitting on 54" carved wooden pedestal 420.00

Man under sunflower, brass, copper, and mixed metals, Richard Gerhart, Montgomery County, PA, 6'8" h, $5,500. Photo courtesy of Sanford Alderfer Auction Co.

Nude Woman, 58" h, 45" l, bronze, ballet pose, large green marble base, figure sgd "V. Salmones 88 B-20 PA" 3,300.00
St. Paul, 60" h, Perie Sons, c1890, stone...........................375.00
Stehender Torso, 47-3/4" h, Herman Hubacher, sgd "Hubacher," dated "24," stamped foundry mark, "M. Pastori, cire perdue, Geneva," bronze lost wax process, greenish-black patina 3,750.00
Three Graces, 63-1/2" h, marble, Continental, artist unknown, after the antique..2,500.00
Young Neptune, 53" h, marble, sgd, located, and dated "Pio fede, Sculp, Firenze, 1859," restorations............................2,500.00
William Tell and Son, 23" h, carved walnut, Continental, 19th C, losses...1,100.00
Winged Nymph, sgd "E. Laurent," bronze, black marble base, French, 19th C, pitting 460.00

STEIFF

History: Margarete Steiff, GmbH, established in Germany in 1880, is known for very fine-quality stuffed animals and dolls, as well as other beautifully made collectible toys. It is still in business, and its products are highly respected.

The company's first products were wool-felt elephants made by Margarete Steiff. In a few years, the animal line was expanded to include a donkey, horse, pig, and camel.

By 1903, the company also was producing a jointed mohair teddy bear, whose production dramatically increased to more than 970,000 units in 1907. Margarete's nephews took over the company at this point.

Newly designed animals were added: Molly and Bully, the dogs; and Fluffy, the cat. Pull toys and kites also were produced, as well as larger animals, on which children could ride or play.

Marks: The bear's-head label became the symbol for the firm in about 1907, and the famous "Button in the Ear" round, metal trademark was added.

References: Peter Consalvi, Sr., *2nd Collector Steiff Values*, Hobby House Press, 1996; Margaret and Gerry Grey, *Teddy Bears*, Running Press, Courage Books, 1994; Margaret Fox Mandel, *Teddy Bears and Steiff Animals*, 1st Series (1984, 1997 value update), 2nd Series (1987, 1996 value update), Collector Books; ——, *Teddy Bears, Annalee Animals & Steiff Animals*, 3rd Series, Collector Books, 1990, 1996 value update; Dee Hockenberry, *Big Bear Book*, Schiffer Publishing, 1996; Linda Mullins, *Teddy Bear & Friends Price Guide*, 4th ed., Hobby House Press, 1993.

Collectors' Clubs: Steiff Club USA, 225 Fifth Ave., Ste. 1033, New York, NY 10010; Steiff Collectors Club, P.O. Box 798, Holland, OH 43528.

Additional Listings: Teddy Bears. See also Stuffed Toys in *Warman's Americana & Collectibles* for more examples.

Notes: Become familiar with genuine Steiff products before purchasing an antique stuffed animal. Plush in old Steiff animals was mohair; trimmings usually were felt or velvet. Unscrupulous individuals have attached the famil-

Bear on wheels, ear button, cloth label "Made in U. S. Zone Germany," worn brown mohair coat, red wheels, eyes missing, voice box works, 36-1/2" l, 26" h, $750. Photo courtesy of Garth's Auctions.

iar Steiff metal button to animals that are not Steiff.

Bear, 36-1/2" l, 26" h, brown mohair coat worn, eyes missing, working voice box, red wheels, ear button, cloth label "Made in U. S. Zone Germany"................................750.00
Camel, cast iron wheels, orig button, c1913 ....695.00
Cat, 5-1/4" h, mohair, green plastic eyes, movable head and legs, c1950..50.00
Cow, 19" l, pull toy, gold and white pieced mohair, suede horns and hooves, bead eyes, wood wheels, ear button........475.00
Fox, 5-1/2 h, 10-1/4" l, mohair, fully jointed excelsior stuffing, glass eyes, embroidered nose, mouth, and claws, button missing, slight moth damage, c1913..425.00
Goat, 6-1/2" h, standing, white, brown felt horns..................65.00
Hen, 7" h, gold and black spotted feathers, yellow plush head, felt tail, black button eyes, c1949................................75.00
Lamb, 11-1/8" h, 12-1/2" l, pull toy, curly wool coat, felt face, ears, and legs, glass eyes, ear button, metal frame and wheels, excelsior stuffing, some moth damage, c1913 ....1,600.00
Lion, 20" l, mohair, glass eyes, ear button, voice box 350.00
Rabbit, 12" h, sitting up, blond mohair, fully jointed, excelsior stuffing, pink glass eyes, slight moth damage, c1913..800.00
Teddy Bear
    17", center seam, blank button, near mint condition, mohair 7,000.00
    17", center seam, unmarked, cinnamon mohair, very good condition, huge hump..7,200.00
    22", early golden mohair, c1905, ear button, center seam 10,062.50

STEINS

History: Steins, mugs especially made to hold beer or ale, range in size from the smaller 3/10 and 1/4 liter to the larger 1, 1-1/2, 2, 3, 4, and 5 liters, and in rare cases to 8 liters. (A liter is 1.05 liquid quarts.)

Master steins or pouring steins hold 3 to 5 liters and are called krugs. Most steins are fitted with a metal hinged lid with thumb lift. The earthenware character-type steins usually are German in origin.

References: Susan and Al Bagdade, *Warman's English & Continental Pottery & Porcelain*, 2nd ed., Wallace-Homestead, 1991; Gary Kirsner, *German Military Steins*, 2nd ed., Glentiques (P.O. Box 8807, Coral Springs, FL 33075), 1996; ——, *Mettlach Book*, 3rd ed., Glentiques (P.O. Box 8807, Coral Springs, FL 33075), 1994.

Periodical: *Regimental Quarterly*, P.O. Box 793, Frederick, MD 21705.

Collectors' Clubs: Stein Collectors International, P.O. Box 5005, Laurel, MD 20726; Sun Steiners, P.O. Box 11782, Fort Lauderdale, FL 33339.

SPECIAL AUCTION

Andre Ammelounx
P.O. Box 136
Palantine, IL 60078
(708) 991-5927

Character

Beethoven, half liter, porcelain, lire on side of body and on porcelain inlaid lid, E. Bohne & Sohn.....................570.00
Cat with Hangover, 1/2 liter, porcelain, inlaid lid, Schierholz, repaired chip on ribbon head bandage 330.00
Drunken Monkey, 1/2 liter, porcelain, inlaid lid, mkd "RPM" 220.00

Relief glazed earthenware, Bacchanalian scene in brown, tan, and beige, "Colln Meissen," 1 liter, $195. Photo courtesy of Susan and Al Bagdade.

Frederick III, in uniform, 1/2 liter, porcelain, porcelain lid, Schierholz, chips on lid repaired, int. color yellowing 1,735.00
Hunter Rabbit, 1/2 liter, inlaid lid, mkd "RPM"......................295.00
Indian, 1/4 liter, porcelain, inlaid lid, E. Bohne & Sohn 440.00
L.A.W. high wheel bicycle, half liter, porcelain, lithophane of man falling onto woman, inlaid lid, Schierholz 440.00
Monk, 1/2 liter, pewter, pewter lid, heaving casting...........350.00
Monk, 1/3 liter, design by Frank Ringer, mkd "J. Reinemann, Munchen" on underside of base, inlaid lid, 5" h............580.00
Singing Pig, 1/2 liter, porcelain, Schierholz, inlaid lid 580.00
Skull, 1/3 liter, porcelain, large jaw, inlaid lid, E. Bohne & Sohn, pewter slightly bent 550.00

Faience

Thuringen, 1 liter, 9-1/2" h, hp, floral design on front, purple trees on sides, pewter top rim and lid, pewter base ring, 18th C, tight hairline on side 1,155.00

Glass

9-1/2" h, 1 liter, blown, wedding type, hp floral design and verse, pewter lid with earlier date of 1779, pewter brass ring, c1850 ....925.00
15-1/4" h, 6-1/2" d, amber, encased in fancy French pewter frame, ram's heads around stein, hinged top lid.....................495.00

Ivory, hand carved, c1850-70

11-1/2" h, elaborate battle scene with approx. 100 figures, carving around entire body, silver top with figural knight finial, cherub bases and fruit in repousse o lid, figural handle of man in armor, silver base with touch marks, discoloration to ivory 6,700.00
13-1/2" h, elaborate hunting scene, four men on horseback, 15 dogs, ivory lid with various animals carved around border, 3-1/2" h finial of man blowing trumpet with dog, figural handle of bare breasted woman with crown, dog head thumblift, left arm and trumpet missing 11,550.00

Porcelain

Delft, 1/2 liter, elaborate scene of two people playing lawn tennis, porcelain inlaid lid of sail boat, mkd "Delft, Germany" 1,390.00
Meissen, 1 liter, 7" h, hp, scene of three people in forest, floral design around sides, porcelain lid with berry finial and painted flowers, closed hinge, cross swords and "S" mark, c1820, strap repoured 3,100.00
Schierholz, Musterchultz, Sad Radish,...............................295.00

Pottery

1/4 liter, transfer and enameled, color, Ulmer Splatz!, The Bird from the City of Ulm, pewter lid 115.00
1/2 liter, relief, tan, brown, and green, chicken with egg body design, relief pewter lid with bust of Bismarck, repaired tear in pewter, 2" hairline I body 130.00

Regimental, 1/2 liter, porcelain

2 Schwer. Reit. Regt. Erzh. Fz, Ferd u. Osterr-Este5 Esk Landshut 1899-02, named to Friederich Schmidt, 2 side scenes, lion thumblift, old tear on lid repaired, minor scruffs, 11-1/2" h 675.00
11 Armee Corps, Mainz 1899, names to Res. Doring, two side scenes, plain thumblift, strap tear repaired, lines in lithophane, 10" h...485.00
30 Field Artillery, Rastatt 1897-99, named to Freund Hilfstromp, two side scenes, roster, thumblift missing 375.00
50 Field Artillery, Karlsruhe 1899-01, named to Knonier Hillenbrand, two side scenes, roster, Griffin thumblift, minor pewter tear, 10-1/2" h 550.00
61 Field Artillery, Dartmstadt 1910-12, named to Kanonier Boxheimer, four side sides, roster worn, lion thumblift............415.00
120 Infantry, Ulm 1899-01, named to Tambour Wurst, two side scenes, Wurttemberg thumblift, 10-1/2" h 520.00
123 Grenadier, Ulm 1908-10, named to Grenadier Schindler, four side scenes, roster, bird thumblift, open blister on int. base, finial missing 550.00
127 Infantry, Ulm 1910-12, named to Musketier Vollm, four side scenes, roster, bird thumblift, 11-1/2" h.......................475.00

Wood and Pewter, Daubenkrug
1/2 liter, 6-1/2" h, pewter scene of deer, vines and leaves on sides, pewter handle and lid, c1820, some separations to pewter 925.00
1/3 liter, 5-1/2" h, floral design on sides, oval with crown on front, pewter handle and lid, 18th C, splints in pewter and wood 1,270.00

STEUBEN GLASS

1903–32

History: Frederick Carder, an Englishman, and Thomas G. Hawkes of Corning, New York, established the Steuben Glass Works in 1904. In 1918, the Corning Glass Company purchased the Steuben company. Carder remained with the firm and designed many of the pieces bearing the Steuben mark. Probably the most widely recognized wares are Aurene, Verre De Soie, and Rosaline, but many other types were produced.

The firm is still operating, producing glass of exceptional quality.

References: Paul Gardner, *Glass of Frederick Carder*, Crown Publishers, 1971; Paul Perrot, Paul Gardner, and James S. Plaut, *Steuben*, Praeger Publishers, 1974; Kenneth Wilson, *American Glass 1760–1930*, 2 Vols., Hudson Hills Press and The Toledo Museum of Art, 1994.

Museums: Corning Museum of Glass, Corning, NY; Rockwell Museum, Corning, NY.

Animal, colorless crystal
Angel Fish, 10-1/2" h, 10" w, sgd 750.00
Koala Bear, 5-1/4" h, designed by Lloyd Atkins, solid glass, applied appendages, mkd "Steuben" on base 920.00
Owl, 7-3/4" h, design by James Houston, 18kt figural owl on curvilinear glass perch 1,840.00
Partridge in a Pear Tree, designed by Lloyd Atkins, 18K gold on central bird and fruit laden tree, mkd "Steuben" on base 1,840.00

Aurene

AURENE

Atomizer, 7-1/4" h, catalog #6136, gold, tapered bottle fitted with gilt metal cap and tube for atomizer bulb 520.00
Basket, 6-3/4" h, 6-1/4" w, irid gold, brilliant gold, purple, and blue highlights, applied loop handle, applied berry prunts, sgd "Aurene 453" 1,750.00
Bonbon, 4-1/2" d, 1-1/4" h, catalog #138, blue, scalloped design, silvery blue luster, base inscribed "Aurene 138" 550.00
Candlestick, 12" h, catalog #6405, blue, twisted shafts, price for mated pr 575.00
Centerbowl, 8" d, 4" h, gold, deeply pinched scalloped rim manipulated into eight apertures 550.00
Lamp, 12" h, vase catalog #429, opaque white alabaster glass oval, gold Aurene heart and vine dec, elaborate gilt metal base, electrified cap, three Art Nouveau women as fittings, not drilled 3,737.00
Plate, 8-1/2" d, catalog #3059, gold, shallow bowl-form, fine irid lustrous surface, inscribed "Aurene 3059," price for pr 345.00
Salt, 1-1/2" h, 2-1/2" w, gold aurene on calcite, pedestal foot 375.00

Sherbet Set, 6" d, 3-3/4" h, catalog #2960, gold stemmed bowl with calcite stem, matching undertray, sgd "F. Carder Aurene" on base 290.00
Vase
4-1/4" h, catalog #131, gold, early quatraform, ruffled rim, dimpled body, platinum gold irid, base inscribed "Aurene 131" 550.00
4-1/2" h, pointed quatraform rim, dimpled body, platinum gold irid surface dec by subtle green swirls on ext., base inscribed "Aurene 131B" 1,265.00
7" h, 6-3/4" d, catalog #1952, gold Aurene, six ruffled rim, white calcite body, fine gold veining on ext. gold irid int., shades from dark to light 375.00
9" h, catalog #260, gourd-shaped green oval body cased to irid opal, gold Aurene blossoms, vertical stems, inscribed "Aurene 260" on base 865.00
12-1/2" h, catalog #273, six ruffle rim, smooth oval opaque white body, four green eye peacock feathers, gold Aurene dec, inscribed "Aurene 273" on base 4,600.00

Celeste Blue
Urn, cov, fruit dec, white prints 600.00
Vase, 6" h, catalog #6287, fan, optic ribbed version, triple wafer stem, pedestal base stamped with fleur-de-lis mark 320.00

Cluthra
Vase
8-1/4" h, catalog #6882, angular Art Deco form, two color, rose at rim shading to white base, elongated bubbles throughout 575.00

Aurene, vase, irid gold, vine and leaf dec, mkd, 9-1/2" h, $3,000.

12-1/4" h, catalog #8494, colored oval cluthra body, yellow at top shading to bright rose-pink base, overlaid in Rosa, etched in Carder's Cliftwood pattern, quintessential Art Deco elements 3,737.00

Flemish Blue

Bowl, 8" l, 4-1/2" l, catalog #6380, rect body, optic ridges swirled to right, four applied feet, fleur-de-lis mark on base 490.00

Perfume Jar, 3-3/4" h, catalog #6887 variant, swirled optic ribbing and threading, conforming stoppers, fleur-de-lis mark on back, price for pr 460.00

Ivorine

Candleholders, 3" h, catalog #7564, irid opaque white glass, ruffled and folded bobeche about integrated disk foot 435.00

Centerbowl, 10" d, 4-1/4" h, catalog #7023, classic flared bowl, integrated disk foot, applied rim wrap of lustrous blue Aurene, satin irid, some minor int. wear 900.00

Lamp, 15" h, 11" d shade, catalog #2384, matching 12-rib base and shade, irid opaque Calcite white, engraved floral motif interspersed through wheel-cut geometric medial design, minimal chipping at top under shade cap 2,070.00

Vase, 5" h, 5" d, catalog #2533, flared body, 10 prominent optic ridges...460.00

Jade

Bowl

7-1/2" d, 2" h, catalog #5062, light blue, wide flattened rim, cased glass body 375.00

12" d, 3-1/4" h, catalog #6774, bulbed and flared jade centerbowl, int. and ext. iridescence, wide Aurene threading 865.00

Centerbowl, 16" d, 5-1/2" h, catalog #3200 variant, broad, flared, opaque yellow, bulbed integrated foot, two small sand grain spots on int. 230.00

Compote, 7" d, 3" h, catalog #3234, translucent light blue jade above applied opal white alabaster stem and disk foot 575.00

Cornucopia, 8-1/4" h, 4-1/2" w at top, green, doomed alabaster foot, sgd, pr 1,150.00

Vase, 6-1/4" h, catalog #7311, green, modified four-pillar grotesque design, vertical shading 400.00

Matsu Noke

Candlestick, 10-1/2" h, colorless crystal, applied rim wraps, handles, and Matsu Noke dec in light Pomona Green glass 520.00

Glass, catalog #2239, green handle 290.00

Vase, catalog #3359, rose dec 340.00

Mirror Black

Bowl, 8" d, 3-1/4" h, catalog #5023, opaque flared form, fleur-de-lis mark on foot, minor scratches 435.00

Vase

6-1/4" h, 8" l, catalog #7564, modified four pillar grotesque form, ivory bowl raised on capped black foot 460.00

10-1/2" h, catalog #6873, prong-type, three triangular holders applied to conforming oval pad foot, one with fleur-de-lis stamp mark, price for pr 920.00

12-1/4" h, catalog #6989/7008, classic oval, curved rim flare, base gold foil triangular label "Steuben Made in Corning, NY"...635.00

Miscellaneous

Bonbon, 4-1/2" d, 6-3/4" h, catalog #5128, pear-shaped Citron Yellow body, Celeste Blue twisted stem, full bodied, ribbed leaf finial, partial triangular Steuben paper label on base 920.00

Bowl

11" d, 6" h, open flower form, Grotesque, deep green shading to colorless, sgd 550.00

12" l, 7-1/4" h, catalog #7535, Grotesque, topaz, four-pillar ruffled oval body, light topaz color, "Steuben" inscribed on base foot...400.00

Catalog #2896, topaz and cobalt blue, weave effect.........325.00

Cologne

Catalog #6605, 5-3/4" h, bright Antique Green squared bottles, matching random threading and faceted stoppers, minor chips at base edges, price for pr 345.00

Catalog #6887, light amethyst 325.00

Catalog #6887, Rosa 240.00

Compote, 7-1/4" d, 6-1/4" h, catalog #7171, green, two line pillar molded design, grotesque suggestion in scalloped rim, hollow flared colorless base, fleur-de-lis mark, price for pr 490.00

Lamp, 25" h overall, catalog #8431, Rose Quartz, 10" h covered urn-forms, heavy walled cased rose quartz glass, etched in dragon motif front and back, conforming etched removable cover, lighted within, intricately mounted in gilt bronze lamp fittings, offset dragon shaft, adjustable finial, price for pr 1,725.00

Perfume Bottle, 10-1/2" h, 1-1/2" d, Cerise Ruby, swirl rocket shape, orig long colorless dauber, clear base..............550.00

Urn, cov, catalog #3134, cobalt blue 495.00

Vase

6" h, 4" w at top, Selenium, red dome foot, rolled edge, deep color..295.00

10" h, Bristol Yellow, catalog #6030, flared oval optic ribbed design, strong twist to the right, fleur-de-lis mark on bulbed foot, small sand grain bubble at side 200.00

Moss Agate

Lamp, 30" h overall, catalog #8026, 11" h angular shouldered oval glass shaft of purple and lavender with mica flecks, swirls of green aventurine, amber, red, and blue, mounted to gilt metal single-socket lamp fittings...1,610.00

Torchere, 15" h, flared glass shade, eight scalloped rim, mottled amber, green, yellow, rust, red swirled with cluthra bubbles and crackling, black painted cast iron lamp base 1,200.00

Oriental Poppy

Lamp, catalog #6501...1,500.00

Vase, 10-1/4" h, catalog #8422, flared oval body, vertical opal ribstripes, rosy-pink surround, applied Pomona Green pedestal foot...1,495.00

Pomona Green

Centerbowl, 10" d, 5-1/4" h, catalog #3080, air trap bubbled variation, four hollow stems around central opening 345.00

Pitcher, 8-1/2" h, catalog #6232, ribbed oval green body, applied amber handle 230.00

Vase

6-3/4" h, catalog #6031 variant, ribbed sphere 200.00

11" h, 9" d, broad flared ftd oval, five repeating foliate elements centering wheel-cut vertical designs........................345.00

Verre de Soie, sherbet and underplate, light green irid, $95.

11" h, 10" d, catalog #6914 variant, wide flared oval, Silverina decoration of mica flecks in diamond pattern, stamped "Steuben"......490.00

12" h, ribbed conical body, wide grapevine dec border, applied topaz flared foot, fleur-de-lis mark on base.....460.00

Roseline

Compote, 12" d, 2-3/4" h, catalog #506, elegant pink bowl, applied alabaster glass foot, int. bubble 375.00

Vase, 4-3/4" h, catalog #1500 variant, diminutive oval ginger jar form, double etched Chinese pattern surface, alabaster ground 1,265.00

Silverina

Candlesticks, pr, 12" h, catalog #3328 variant, colorless crystal internally dec by diamond patterned air-trap mica flecks, mirror black cupped bases stamped "Steuben"......900.00

Vase, 12" h, topaz bulbous bud vase, decorative mica flecks throughout, applied Pomona Green disk foot 400.00

Spanish Green

Candlestick, 12" h, catalog #2596, optic ribbed baluster form, double ball below candle cup, fleur-de-lis mark on base 250.00

Champagne Goblet, 6-1/4" h, floriform, five applied ribbed leaves under bubbled bowl, raised on nubby stem, folded rim pedestal foot, stamped mark on base, price for 10 pc set .. 1,380.00

Threaded

Compote, catalog #2018, crystal, green machine threading, engraved 285.00

Dresser Jar, catalog #1169, colorless puff jars, one with ruby random threads, one with black threads, price for pr 325.00

Verre de Soie

Tumbler, 4" h, 3-1/4" w at top, flaring rim, sgd "F. Carder Steuben" 450.00

Vase, 12-3/4" h, catalog #334, baluster candlestick form, irid colorless frosted glass, triangular gold foil label on base..435.00

STEVENS AND WILLIAMS

History: In 1824, Joseph Silvers and Joseph Stevens leased the Moor Lane Glass House at Briar Lea Hill (Brierley Hill), England, from the Honey-Borne family.

19th C

In 1847, William Stevens and Samuel Cox Williams took over, giving the firm its present name. In 1870, the company moved to its Stourbridge plant. In the 1880s, the firm employed such renowned glass artisans as Frederick C. Carder, John Northwood, other Northwood family members, James Hill, and Joshua Hodgetts.

Stevens and Williams made cameo glass. Hodgetts developed a more commercial version using thinner-walled blanks, acid etching, and the engraving wheel. Hodgetts, an amateur botanist, was noted for his brilliant floral designs.

Other glass products and designs manufactured by Stevens and Williams include intaglio ware, Peach Bloom (a form of peachblow), moss agate, threaded ware, "jewell" ware, tapestry ware, and Silveria. Stevens and Williams made glass pieces covering the full range of late Victorian fashion.

After World War I, the firm concentrated on refining the production of lead crystal and achieving new glass colors. In 1932, Keith Murray came to Stevens and Williams as a designer. His work stressed the pure nature of the glass form. Murray stayed with Stevens and Williams until World War II and later followed a career in architecture.

Additional Listings: Cameo Glass.

Bowl, 6" d, 3" h, Matsu No Ke, creamy yellow satin bowl, branch of twisted, knurled, and thorny frosted crystal glass winds around perimeter, 36 florets, three feet, one slight chip on one flower 1,250.00

Ewer, 5-1/4" h, Silveria, silver foil sandwiched between layers of glass, crimson, ruby-red, and gold on upper half, large areas of vivid purple accented by splotches of gold on lower portion, clear green glass entwining vertical trailing overlaid, applied handle, sgd "S&W" in pontil mark 3,450.00

Perfume Bottle, 6-1/2" h, 3-3/4" w, Pompeian Swirl, deep gold, brown to red, turquoise blue lining, orig cut frosted stopper 895.00

Pitcher, 6" h, 5" d, yellow opalescent, vertical stripes, shell reeded handle......225.00

Rose Bowl, 5-1/4" d, 5" h, Pompeian Swirl, shaded brown to gold, robin's egg blue lining, box pleated top, 6 ruffles.........850.00

Vase

6" h, 6" w, 4-3/4" w at top, applied dec, Matso Nuke style, ftd, pink-peach peachblow ground, bright cream-yellow lining, colorless applied band of shell-like rigaree at top, three rosettes, three large 5-1/4" l leaf feet, applied raspberry prunt over pontil 750.00

6-1/2" h, 5-1/2" d, amber ruffled top edge, amber loop feet, rose lined cream opaque body, three applique amber, green, and cranberry ruffled leaves 260.00

7-1/4" h, Pompeian Swirl, MOP, powder blue body, pink air-traps, shiny pink ribbons swirl down neck to body, two small ext. flakes 545.00

7-1/2" h, 5" w, striped Swirl, frosted deep pink, rose, and yellow stripes, frosted ground, 36 vertical ribs......425.00

7-3/4" h, 3-3/4" w, double gourd, Pompeian Swirl, light brown shading to gold......475.00

8" h, 4-1/2" w, bulbous, Pompeian Swirl, deep rose, white int. 575.00

10-3/4" h, 5-3/4" w, bulbous, pedestal base, Pompeian Swirl, MOP, pale lime green, white lining......850.00

11" h, 6-1/2" base, stick with bulbous base, Pompeian Swirl, deep amber to bright red 950.00

Rose Bowl, cranberry, Zipper pattern, 12 tiny crimps at top, engraved registry no. RD 55693 on polished base, 2-1/8" h, 2-3/4" w, $140. Photo courtesy of Johanna Billings.

11-1/2" h, 4" w, rose shading to pink, white and colorless applied flowers and leaves, ruffled top, flaring ribbed neck 225.00

12" h, 6-1/2" w, gourd, Pompeian Swirl, brilliant blue, brown swirls, bright yellow lining 1,750.00

STICKLEYS

History: There were five Stickley brothers: Albert, Gustav, Leopold, George, and John George. Gustav often is credited with creating the Mission style, a variant of the Arts and Crafts style. Gustav headed Craftsman Furniture, a New York firm, much of whose actual production took place near Syracuse. A characteristic of Gustav's furniture is exposed tenon ends. Gustav published The Craftsman, a magazine espousing his antipathy to machines.

Originally Leopold and Gustav worked together. In 1902, Leopold and John George formed the L. and J. G. Stickley Furniture Company. This firm made Mission-style furniture and cherry and maple early-American style pieces.

George and Albert organized the Stickley Brothers Company, located in Grand Rapids, Michigan.

References: Donald A. Davidoff and Robert L. Zarrow, *Early L. & J. G. Stickley Furniture*, Dover Publications, 1992; *Furniture of the Arts & Crafts Period*, L-W Book Sales, 1992, 1995 value update; Thomas K. Maher, *The Kaufmann Collection: The Early Furniture of Gustav Stickley*, Treadway Gallery (2029 Madison Rd., Cincinnati, OH 45208), 1996; Paul Royka, *Mission Furniture ,from the American Arts & Crafts Movement,* Schiffer Publishing, 1997.

Periodical: *Style 1900,* 333 Main St., Lambertville, NJ 08530.

Collectors' Club: Foundation for the Study of Arts & Crafts Movement, Roycroft Campus, 31 S. Grove St., East Aurora, NY 14052.

Museum: Craftsman Farms Foundation, Inc., Morris Plains, NJ.

Gustav denotes Gustav Stickley and Craftsman Furniture.

L. & J. G. denotes L. and J. G. Stickley Furniture Company.

Andirons, pr, Gustav, #315, wrought iron, each signed with imp mark, 13-1/2" w, 18" d, 16" h 9,775.00

Bed, Gustav, 58-1/4" w, 51" h, full sized, paneled headboard and footboard, inverted V crest rails, orig finish, large red decal 4,500.00

Bench, 41-1/2" w, 24" d, 36" h, Gustav, #212, V-back, 12 vertical slats, orig leather, orig worn finish..............................1,955.00

Bookcase, L. & J. G.
22" w, 11" d, 50" h, single door, three shelves, through tenons and arched toe board, orig finish, good repair to back leg 1,840.00

55-1/4" x 48" x 12", double door, gallery top, each door with 12 panes, hammered copper pulls, keyed through tenons, minor cleaning to orig finish, Handcraft decal 5,750.00

Book Rack, 42-1/4" w, 12" d, 36" h, Gustav, similar to #74, 2 V-board shelves over straight shelf, key and tenons, paper label, orig finish 1,955.00

Cabinet, 20" w, 14" d, 29" h, Gustav, #78, single drawer over strap hinged door, overhand top, arched base with through tenons, orig dark finish, signed with Gustav red mark, minor repairs and losses 3,105.00

Chair
Arm, L. & J. G.
#334, 25-1/2" w, 20-3/4" d, 37-3/4" h, two vertical slats, orig finish, Handcraft decal 230.00
#822, 27" w, 20-3/4" h, 36" h, U-form back, five vertical back slats, orig medium brown finish 290.00

Dining
Arm, Gustav, #353A, 25" w, 21" d, 41-1/2" d, 3 vertical slats, arched apron, orig finish, old overcoat, sgd with red mark 290.00

Side
Gustav, #353, 17" w, 16-1/2" d, 39-1/2" h, 3 vertical slats, arched apron, orig finish, old overcoat, sgd with red mark, price for pr..865.00
L. & J. G., #341, 19" w, 16" d, 36" h, 2 horizontal slats, orig finish, Handcraft decal, partial paper label, price for set of five..2,185.00

Morris
Gustav, 29" w, 32" d, 43" h, #346, V-sided paddle arms, orig worn finish, sgd Gustav red mark, replaced brown leather upholstery, missing corbel 1,955.00
L. & J. G., #471, 31-1/2" w, 35" d, 46" h, six vertical slats at sides, adjustable pegs, orig finish, replaced cushion 2,760.00

Reclining, Gustav, 32-1/2" w, 27-1/2" d, 40" h, Gustav, #369, drop arms over five vertical slats, through tenons, orig cushions, refinished, overall sanding marks, unmarked, adjusting peg replaced 5,750.00

Side, L. & J. G., #820, 19-3/4" w, 17" d, 36" h, U-form back, five vertical back slats, orig overcoated medium brown finish, replaced brown vinyl cushions, price for pr 920.00

Chest of Drawers, Gustav Stickley, by Harvey Ellis, unusual golden finish, $9,350. Photo courtesy of David Rago Auctions, Inc.

China Cabinet
    41-1/4" w, 15" d, 64-1/2" h, Gustav, double door, each with eight panes of glass, eight panes on each side, gallery top, through tenon construction, V pulls, lightly oiled orig finish, mkd 5,750.00
    42" w, 15-1/4" d, 62-1/2" h, Gustav, double door, each with 8 panes of glass, 4 panes to each side, orig finish, paper label, 1 side glass pane cracked 5,175.00
Costumer (clothes tree), shoe feet, four double hooks, orig reddish brown finish, co-joined label, 72" h, 24" w 800.00
Day Bed
    Gustav
        #191, 74" l, 30" w, 29" h, five vertical slats, orig finish, early mark, minor wear..2,990.00
        #216, 80" l, 31" w, 29" h, five vertical slats at sides, orig finish replaced brown leather cushion...................4,025.00
    L. & J. G., attributed, similar to #292, 80" l, 30" d, 28-1/4" h, four vertical side slats, reverse tapered splined posts, orig worn finish, missing cushions, splits to seams, nicks to frame 1,840.00
Desk
    32" l, 12" d, 46" h, Gustav, #824, lady's, paneled, trimmed in hand-wrought iron, orig black finish, int. with 11 pigeonholes and drawer, sgd with large Gustav red mark 29,900.00
    39-3/4" l, 22-1/2" h, 36" h, Gustav, #708, two drawers over open shelf, orig finish, sgd Gustav red mark, loss to seam on top 1,955.00
    42" l, 28-1/4" d, 30-1/4" h, Gustav, bookshelf sides, two vertical slats on each side, orig finish, branded mark 805.00
    59-1/2" l, 33-1/2" d, 30-1/4" h, L. & J. G., double bank, three drawers on each side of center drawer, orig worn finish, minor veneer chips, missing center pull 3,740.00
Drink Stand, L. and J. G., circular overhanging top, arched cross-stretchers, lower circular shelf, refinished top, unmarked, 18" d, 29" h...950.00
Inkwell, 5-1/2" d, 2-1/4" h, Gustav, copper, hand hammered finish, fine orig patina, imp marks, insert missing....................200.00
Lamp, table, 18" h, 16" d, Gustav, hammered copper base, orig wicker shade, orig patina, stamped mark on side, damage to wicker 2,000.00
Mirror
    Gustav, hall, six triple hooks, crested top rail, skinned finish, 36-1/2" l, 28" h...2,100.00
    L. and J. G., hall, four double hooks, arched frame top, corbeled sides, hanging chains, orig medium finish, 39" w x 23-1/4" h. 1,800.00
    Stickley Brothers, 37-1/2" w, 20-1/2" h, orig coat hanger hooks, refinished 635.00
Night Stand, Stickley Brothers, 24" w, 22" d, 25-3/4" h, 3 vertical slats on either side, drawer containing writing tablet, refinished 1,950.00
Plant Stand, Gustav, No. 41, 14" sq, 28" h, arched apron, orig finish, early mark 2,415.00
Rocker
    Gustav, sewing, H-back, one broad cut-out backslat, inset new rush seat, orig dark finish, red decal, 16-3/4" w, 15" d, 34-1/2" h...375.00
    L. & J. G., similar to #485, oak, arm, U-shaped back, five horizontal back slats, one horizontal side slat, orig medium brown finish, replaced leather cushions, 31-3/4" w, 30" d, 42-1/2" h..1,380.00
Settle, L. and J. G., cube, five board vertical slats across the back, one to each side, orig Japan leather drop-in spring seat, new dark finish, Handcraft decal, 28" x 72" x 27".......2,200.00
Server, Gustav, backsplash, overhanging top, two drawers with copper V-pulls, orig medium dark finish, red decal, 38-1/2" x 42" x 19"..2,800.00

Sideboard
    Gustav
        #814, 67" l, 24" d, 48" h, three center drawers, one lined with Ooze leather, flanked by doors, over one long drawer, orig finish, some veneer loss on doors 4,025.00
        #816, 48" l, 18-1/2" d, 47" h, long drawer over three center drawers flanked by doors, arched apron, casters, orig finish, sgd Gustav red mark...................................2,415.00
    L. & J. G.
        46-1/2" l, 22" d, 45" h, two drawers over one long drawer over two paneled doors, refinished, replaced hardware, int. painted green, custom ordered by NY architect Emory Ruth...3,335.00
        60" w, 23" d, 45" h, three graduated center drawers flanked by two paneled doors over one long drawer, refinished, replaced hardware, int. painted green, custom ordered by NY architect Emory Ruth 4,660.00
Stock Certificate, 11-1/2" x 8", Gustav, unsigned, specimen for a $100 share, Jan. 1, 1919...175.00
Table
    Book, 23" sq, 29" h, Gustav, spindled, flush sq top, each side with two shelves, six spindles over slightly tapered sq legs, refinished, remnant of paper label 3,000.00
    Dining
        54" d, Gustav, corbel-form base, four leaves, orig finish, sgd, veneer missing from apron seams..............3,740.00
        54" d, 29" h, L. & J. G., #713, four long corbels mounted on pedestal base, two hide-away legs, one leaf, refinished, brand mark..3,105.00
    Lamp, 36" d, 29-1/4" h, L. & J. G., No. 579, round second tier, arched cross-stretchers, refinished, slight stains to top, unmarked...800.00
    Library, Gustav, #653, 48" w, 30-1/4" d, 29" h, single drawer overhang top with stretcher base, orig worn finish 1,380.00
    Occasional, L. and J. G., No. 562, clip-corner, one broad slat, arched stretcher on each side, new medium finish, touch-up, 22" x 20" sq...1,200.00
Tabouret
    15" sq top, 17" h, L. & J. G., #558, through tenons on top, arched stretcher sgd "The Work of ...," orig finish, retail tag, minor staining to top 1,725.00
    18" d, 20" h, Gustav, #602, arched cross stretcher base, cleaned finish, stain on top, unsigned......................517.30
Tray, 12" w, 17-1/2" l, Gustav, copper, twisted brass handles, imp mark, cleaned patina, some scratches 375.00
Umbrella Stand, 11-1/4" d, 24" h, Gustav, slanted, slats riveted to int. wrought bands, orig finish, drop pan missing 900.00
Waste Basket, 12" d, 14" h, Gustav, slats riveted to int. wrought bands, orig finish, unmarked....................................1,700.00

Table, Gustav Stickley, rare hexagonal form, $3,575. Photo courtesy of David Rago Auctions, Inc.

STIEGEL-TYPE GLASS

History: Baron Henry Stiegel founded America's first flint-glass factory at Manheim, Pennsylvania, in the 1760s. Although clear glass was the most common color made, amethyst, blue (cobalt), and fiery opalescent pieces also are found. Products included bottles, creamers, flasks, flips, perfumes, salts, tumblers, and whiskeys. Prosperity was short-lived; Stiegel's extravagant lifestyle forced the factory to close.

It is very difficult to identify a Stiegel-made item. As a result, the term "Stiegel-type" is used to identify glass made during the time period of Stiegel's firm and in the same shapes and colors as used by that company.

Enamel-decorated ware also is attributed to Stiegel. True Stiegel pieces are rare; an overwhelming majority is of European origin.

References: Frederick W. Hunter, *Stiegel Glass*, 1950, available in Dover reprint; Kenneth Wilson, *American Glass 1760-1930*, 2 Vols., Hudson Hills Press and The Toledo Museum of Art, 1994.

Tumbler, running animal dec, 4" h, 3-5/8" d, $475. Photo courtesy of Sanford Alderfer Auction Co.

Bottle, flattened globular, colorless, polychrome enameled love-birds with heart, German inscription and "America" .. 1,595.00
Bottle, half post, colorless, pewter lip, minor enamel flaking
  5-1/8" h, polychrome enameled flowers and birds, stain
  ....110.00
  5-3/8" h, polychrome enameled flowers and birds........360.00
  5-3/8" h, polychrome enameled flowers, man with wine glass
  ....165.00
  5-1/2" h, polychrome enameled flowers, bird in medallion, some residue, threads incomplete 250.00
  5-3/4" h, polychrome enameled flowers, man with bell, threads on lip incomplete, broken blister on man's arm 55.00
  5-7/8" h, polychrome enameled flowers, inscription, fox with birds in basket 300.00
  6-3/4" h, polychrome enameled flowers, man with yoke, and buckets 175.00
Flip Glass, colorless, sheared rim, pontil scar, form similar to McKearin plate 22, #2
  3-1/2" h, handle, engraved repeating swag motif around rim, lower body emb with graduated panels...................210.00
  6-1/4" h, engraved floral motif and sunflower 300.00
  7" h, engraved basket and floral motif..........................350.00
  7" h, engraved bird in heart dec within sunburst motif
  ....400.00
  7-7/8" h, engraved pair of birds perched on heart within sunburst motif...475.00
  8" h, engraved large flower and floral motif...................325.00
Flask
  4-3/4" h, amethyst diamond and daisy 495.00
  5" h, amethyst, globular, 20 molded ribs, minute rim chip
  ....1,380.00
Jar, cov, 10-1/2" h, colorless, engraved sunflower and floral motifs, repeating dot and vine dec on cov, applied finial, sheared rim, pontil scar, form similar to McKearin plate 35, #2 and 3
  ....750.00
Miniature, flip glass, 3" h, colorless, engraved bird within sunburst motif, seared mouth, pontil scar 325.00

Tankard, handle, cylindrical, applied solid reeded handle, flared foot, sheared rim, pontil scar, form similar to McKearin plate 22, #4
  5-1/2" h, milk glass, red, yellow, blue, and green enameled dec of house on mountain with floral motif, old meandering fissure around body of vessel 150.00
  5-3/4" h, colorless, engraved with bird in elaborate sunburst motif 500.00
  6-1/4" h, colorless, engraved elaborate bird and tulip dec
  ....475.00
Tumbler, 2-7/8" h, colorless, paneled, polychrome enameled flowers 220.00

STONEWARE

History: Made from dense kaolin and commonly salt-glazed, stonewares were hand-thrown and high-fired to produce a simple, bold, vitreous pottery. Stoneware crocks, jugs, and jars were made to store products and fill other utilitarian needs. These intended purposes dictated shape and design–solid, thick-walled forms with heavy rims, necks, and handles and with little or no embellishment. Any decorations were simple: brushed cobalt oxide, incised, slip trailed, stamped, or tooled.

Stoneware has been made for centuries. Early American settlers imported stoneware items at first. As English and European potters refined their earthenware, colonists began to produce their own wares. Two major North American traditions emerged based only on location or type of clay. North Jersey and parts of New York comprise the first area; the second was eastern Pennsylvania spreading westward and into Maryland, Virginia, and West Virginia. These two distinct geographical boundaries, style of decoration, and shape are discernible factors in classifying and dating early stoneware.

By the late 18th century, stoneware was manufactured in all sections of the country. This vigorous industry flourished during the 19th century until glass fruit jars appeared and the use of refrigeration became widespread.

By 1910, commercial production of salt-glazed stone-ware came to an end.

References: Susan and Al Bagdade, *Warman's American Pottery and Porcelain*, Wallace-Homestead, 1994; Georgeanna H. Greer, *American Stoneware*, revised ed., Schiffer Publishing, 1996; William C. Ketchum Jr., *American Pottery and Porcelain*, 1994; Jim Martin and Bette Cooper, *Monmouth-Western Stoneware*, published by authors, 1983, 1993 value update; Don and Carol Raycraft, *Collector's Guide to Country Stoneware & Pottery*, 1st Series (1985, 1995 value update), 2nd Series (1990, 1996 value update), Collector Books; —, *Stoneware*, Wallace-Homestead, 1995; Terry G. Taylor and Terry and Kay Lowrance, *Collector's Encyclopedia of Salt Glaze Stoneware*, Collector Books, 1996.

Collectors' Clubs: American Stoneware Assoc., 208 Crescent Ct., Mars, PA 16066; Federation of Historical Bottle Collectors, Inc., 88 Sweetbriar Branch, Longwood, FL 32750.

Museum: Museum of Ceramics at East Liverpool, East Liverpool, OH.

Batter Pail, gallon, Cowden & Wilcos, Harrisburg, PA, bold brushed cobalt blue floral dec on front and back, cobalt blue around spout and ears, bail handle, chip on spout in making 1,870.00

Butter Crock, 12" d, 6-1/2" h plus lid, brushed cobalt blue foliage, imp label "R.C.R. Phila.," applied handles, chips, filled in base chip 600.00

Canning Jar, 9-1/2" h, cobalt blue stenciled and freehand blue, "Excelsior Works, Isaac Hewitt Jr., Rices Landing, PA" 330.00

Churn, N. A. White & Son, Utica, NY, 5 gallon, large paddletail bird on flower, c1885 ...... 4,620.00

Cream Pot

John Burger, Rochester, NY, three-gallon, large double flower dec, c1865 ...... 880.00

T. Harrington, Lyons, four-gallon, company's signature star-face design, c1860, professional restoration to some cracks, right ear missing 2,310.00

Crock

A. K. Ballard, Burlington, VT, two-gallon, running deer and trees, full-length crack and some smaller cracks in front 1,485.00

Belmont Ave. Pottery, cobalt blue quill work bird on branch and "3," imp label, applied handles, hairline and small chips, 10-1/4" h 200.00

Brady & Ryan, Ellenville, NY, four-gallon, dog ready to pounce at bird on stump, c1880, large crack through dec ...910.00

C. W. Braun, Buffalo, NY, two-gallon, applied handles, cobalt blue quill work roses, imp label 220.00

C. W .Braun, Buffalo, NY, three-gallon, dotted bird perched on branch, minor damage 750.00

G. Apley & Co, three-gallon, double flower, c1860 ...... 330.00

Jonathan Fenton, two handles, cobalt incised label "Jonathan Fenton, Boston, 1794-97," two codfish on front, "Boston" and "JF" monogram on reverse, minor chips, 13" h 6,325.00

J. & E. Norton, Bennington, VT

two-gallon, large tailed rooster on round cov, tree in background, c1859, minor cracks 1,815.00

six-gallon, ovoid, thick blue compote of flowers, house, and fence in background, c1859, bottom incised in script "Benning" and "Bennington" 3,850.00

Butter Churn, N. A. White & Son, Utica, NY, five gal., large paddletail bird on flower, c1885, 18" h, $935. Photo courtesy of Bruce and Vicki Waasdorp Stoneware Auction.

Cream Pot, John Burger, Rochester, two gal., large cabbage flower in dark blue cobalt, long age spider on side, c1865, 10-1/2" h, $715. Photo courtesy of Bruce and Vicki Waasdorp Stoneware Auction.

Macumber & Tannahill, Ithaca, NY, three-gallon, double flower on flowering tree dec, c1875 ....495.00

M. Woodruff, Cortland, three-gallon, single stem with four large flowers, c1860, rim chip, some line staining ...990.00

New York Stoneware Co, Fort Edward, NY, flying chicken dec, c1865, extensive glaze flaking 860.00

Unsigned, two-gallon, crude profile of man smoking a pipe, c1860, some chips 1,925.00

Unsigned, three-gallon, imp "3," cobalt blue quill work pecking chicken, applied handles, hairlines and chips ...580.00

R. O. Whittemore, Havana, NY, 1860, cobalt blue cottage dec, minor cracks and chips, 8-3/8" d, 7-3/4" h 1,035.00

Harvest Jug, Clark & Fox, Athens, NY, one-gallon, tooled dec, cobalt blue highlights around body and stoneware handle, sgd 6,270.00

Lid, 10-5/8" d, brown Albany slip, three molded eagles, branch handle imp "S. S. Perry, Troy," minor flakes 195.00

Jar

Amboy S., ovoid, tooled shoulder and rim bands, imp label and two leaf shaped designs highlighted in cobalt blue, "S. Amboy N. Jersy (sic) Warne," 12-5/8" h, minor flakes 1,595.00

Edmands & Co, three-gallon, eagle holding flag, c1870, professionally repaired crack 1,870.00

Hamilton & Jones, Greensboro, PA, ovoid, applied shoulder handles, cobalt blue brushed and stenciled label, 14-1/2" h...500.00

J. & E. Norton, Bennington, VT, three-gallon, crossed peacocks in a tree, c1855, cracked base 4,290.00

S. Purdy, Portage Co, Ohio, applied shoulder handles, imp label, blue at label and handle, 10" h, chips 315.00

T. F. Reppert, Successor to James Hamilton & Co., Greensboro, PA, cobalt blue freehand and stenciled label, applied shoulder handles, glued crack in base, 13-1/2" h 330.00

Unknown Maker, ovoid, applied shoulder handles, incised bird on flowering tree, cobalt blue at handles, highlighted dec, brushed foliage design on back, 13-3/4" h, chips on bottom edge 3,190.00

Jug

C. W. Braun, Buffalo, NY, three-gallon, heavy cobalt blue large dotted and ribbed flower, c1860, chipped spout, glued breaks to handle...990.00

N. Clark Jr., Athens, NY, 3, bluish-brown floral dec, gray salt glaze, golden highlights, strap handle, imp label, slightly bubbled glaze on dec, 14-1/2" h 330.00

Cowden & Wilcox, Harrisburg, PA, 4, cobalt blue brushed flower at handle and label, imp label base hairline, flake on lip, 16" h 275.00

Haxstun Ottman & Co., Fort Edward, NY, cobalt blue quill work bird on branch, imp label, strap handle, 13-3/4" h...445.00

Haxstun Ottman & Co., Fort Edward, NY, 5, cobalt blue quill work bird on branch, imp label, strap handle, 18-1/2" h 595.00

Rogers & Co. Boston, 3, cobalt blue quill work floral dec, imp label, strap handle, hairlines in neck and handle.....415.00

R. W. Martin & Bros, globular, one handle molded on each side with smiling face, glazed in dark and warm brown, incised "RW Martin Bros., London & Southall 1708-1879," 8" h, 7" w 1,265.00

Seymour & Bosworth, Hartford, Conn, 3, cobalt blue quill work bird on branch, imp label, strap handle, hairline in base, 15-1/2" h 330.00

Jug, C. W. Braun, Buffalo, NY, three gal., dotted and ribbed floral dec, dark and heavy blue cobalt, surface chip at spout, glued breaks in handle, c1860, 16" h, $690. Photo courtesy of Bruce and Vicki Waasdorp Stoneware Auction.

Water Cooler, W. H. Farrar Factory, Geddes, NY, six gal., large dotted bird, dated "1860," dots of blue cobalt highlight the date, bird, and scribe lines, glaze kiln burn on side, c1860, 15" h, $580. Photo courtesy of Bruce and Vicki Waasdorp Stoneware Auction.

N. A. White & Son, Utica, NY, two-gallon, paddletail bird, extended dotted wings..2,420.00
Unmarked
  Attributed to New York City, two-gallon, ovoid, incised double flower, two flying birds, c1810 ....1,100.00
  Attributed to Red Wing, five-gallon, beehive shape, cloverleaf dec, freehand gallonage number...................990.00
Pitcher, unmarked, attributed to Edmands & Co., one-gallon, dotted bird on fence, tree in background........................1,100.00
Poultry Fountain
  9-3/4" h, cobalt blue trim, imp "1," chips and hairline ...215.00
  13-3/4" h, cobalt blue trim, chips on one handle, imp "2"
  ....330.00
Preserve Jar
  Cobalt blue stenciled and brushed dec, red clay, chips, 8" h
  ....215.00
  Cobalt blue stenciled flowers and brushed stripes, small flakes, 8" h 225.00
  Cobalt blue stenciled rose, 6" h....................................315.00
  Lyons, attributed to Harrington factory, bold triple flower dec, c1860...2,420.00
Water Cooler
  W. H. Farrar Factory, Geddes, NY, six-gallon, large freehand cobalt blue dec of dotted bird, dated 1860, gallonage number and four rows of multiple dots, glaze kiln burn on one side 6,050.00
  Unmarked, double ear handles, cobalt blue quill work, "8" with flourish, gray salt glaze, green pebbled highlights, hairline in lip, wooden spigot and turned plug, 20" h............165.00

STRETCH GLASS

History: Stretch glass was produced by many glass manufacturers in the United States between the early 1900s and the 1920s. The most prominent makers were Cambridge, Fenton (which probably manufactured more stretch glass than any of the others), Imperial, Northwood, and Steuben. Stretch glass can be identified by its iridescent, onionskin-like effect. Look for mold marks. Imported pieces are blown and show a pontil mark.

References: Berry Wiggins, *Stretch Glass*, Antique Publications, 1972, 1987 value update.

Collectors' Club: Stretch Glass Society, P.O. Box 573, Hampshire, IL 60140.

Bowl
  9" d, low, blue irid 45.00
  10" d, green, rolled rim 25.00
Candy Dish, cov, topaz, Fenton 60.00
Compote, 6-1/2" d, 5-1/2" h, bright green, zipper notched pedestal base...50.00
Console Bowl, 11-1/2" d, orange, rolled rim........................40.00
Creamer and Sugar, tangerine, Rings pattern 75.00
Hat, 4" h, purple, Imperial...55.00
Nappy, 7" w, vaseline, Fenton 40.00
Plate, 8-1/2" d, blue 35.00
Sandwich Service, sq, green, center handle 30.00
Vase
  5-1/2" h, baluster, pink, Imperial.....................................75.00
  6" h, fan, green, ribbed...45.00

STRING HOLDERS

History: The string holder developed as a useful tool to assist the merchant or manufacturer who needed tangle-free string or twine to tie packages. The early holders were made of cast iron, some patents dating to the 1860s.

When the string holder moved into the household, lighter and more attractive forms developed, many made of chalkware. The string holder remained a key kitchen element until the early 1950s.

Reference: Sharon Ray Jacobs, *Collector's Guide to Stringholders*, L-W Book Sales, 1996.

Advertising
  Chase & Sanborn's Coffee, tin, 13-3/4" x 10-1/4" sign, 4" d wire basket string holder insert, hanging chain 825.00
  Dutch Boy Paints, diecut tin, Dutch Boy painting door frame, hanging bucket string holder, American Art Sign Co., 13-3/4" x 30"...2,000.00
  Es-Ki-Mo Rubbers, tin, cutout center holds string spool, hanging boot moves up and down on sign, 17" x 19-3/4" h
  ....2,500.00
  Heinz, diecut tin, pickle, hanging, "57 Varieties," 17" x 14"
  ....1,650.00
  Lowney's Cocoa, tin, cutout center holds string spool, cup and saucer hanger, 16" x 24"......................................3,000.00

Tin, counter type, enamel cat playing with string dec, 4-1/2" h, 4" d, $25.

Mail Pouch Tobacco, metal, 2 pc, string held between two
    sections, hanging chains, hanging Mail Pouch tobacco tin,
    15" x 31" h 2,000.00
Ball of String, cast iron, figural, hinged, 6-1/2" x 5" h 100.00
Black Boy, 8-1/2" h, cardboard head and arms, fabric body holds
    string, felt feet 50.00

SUGAR SHAKERS

History: Sugar shakers, sugar castors, or muffineers all
served the same purpose: to "sugar" muffins, scones, or
toast. They are larger than salt and pepper shakers, were
produced in a variety of materials, and were in vogue in
the late Victorian era.

Reference: William Heacock, *Encyclopedia of Victorian
Colored Pattern Glass*, Book III, Antique Publications,
1976, 199-92 value update.

China

Nippon, white, gold beading 60.00
R. S. Prussia, Schlegelmilch, 5" h, scalloped base, pearl finish,
    shaded roses, green leaves, red mark..........................245.00
Wedgwood, jasperware, white classical design, dark blue
    ground 50.00

Glass

Bristol, 6-1/4" h, tall tapering cylinder, pink, blue flowers and
    green leaves dec...75.00
Cranberry, Parian Swirl...185.00
Crown Milano, melon shape, ribbed, dec, Mt. Washington two pc
    top..395.00
Custard, Paneled Teardrop 110.00
Cut Glass, Russian pattern alternating with clear panels, orig SS
    top..375.00
Green Opaque, Parian Swirl, dec.......................................110.00
Opalescent
    Beatty Rib, blue 250.00
    Bubble Lattice, blue, bulbous ring neck, orig top 225.00
    Daisy and Fern, Parian Swirl mold, cranberry 385.00

Leaf Umbrella, orig top, Northwood 295.00
    Spanish Lace, cranberry, orig top................................150.00
Satin, Leaf Mold, cased blue, orig top, Northwood...........285.00
Smith Bros, Ribbed Pillar, dec..375.00

SWANSEA

History: This superb pottery and porcelain was made at
Swansea (Glamorganshire, Wales) as early as the 1760s,
with production continuing until 1870.

Marks: Marks on Swansea vary. The earliest marks were
"Swansea" impressed under glaze and "Dillwan" under
glaze after 1805. "Cambrian Pottery" was stamped in red
under glaze from 1803 to 1805. Many fine examples, including the botanical series in pearlware, are not marked
but may have the name of the botanical species stamped
underglaze.

REPRODUCTION ALERT

Swansea porcelain has been copied for many decades
in Europe and England. Marks should be studied carefully.

Note: Fine examples of Swansea often may show imperfections such as firing cracks. These pieces are considered mint because they left the factory in this condition.

Bowl, 6-3/8" d, gilt cartouches with idyllic landscape scenes, gilt
    line borders, William Billingsley, c1815, red Swansea mark
    ....750.00
Cup and Saucer, ribbed, gold fluted border and handle, white
    int., c1820 ....175.00
Plate, wild rose and trailing blue flowers, elaborate gilt diaper and
    foliage well, molded flower wreath and C-scroll border, re-
    served with gilt green berried foliage, gilt line rim, William Pol-
    lard, red stencil mark, c1820.......................................990.00
Vase, 6-3/4" h, floral band, gilt borders, flared base with painted
    flowers, applied bee handles, imp "Swansea" and triden mark,
    c1815-20, restored, pr..4,750.00

**Mt. Washington, peachblow colored melon body shades to light
blue, painted dots, raised enamel floral motif, pewter top with relief leaf design, $375.**

Plate, floral, underglaze mark, c1812, 8-1/2" d, $120.

SWORDS

History: The first swords used in America came from Europe. The chief cities for sword manufacturing were Solingen in Germany, Klingenthal in France, and Hounslow and Shotley Bridge in England. Among the American importers of these foreign blades was Horstmann, whose name is found on many military weapons.

New England and Philadelphia were the early centers for American sword manufacturing. By the Franco-Prussian War, the Ames Manufacturing Company of Chicopee, Massachusetts, was exporting American swords to Europe.

Sword collectors concentrate on a variety of styles: commissioned vs. non-commissioned officers' swords, presentation swords, naval weapons, and swords from a specific military branch, such as cavalry or infantry. The type of sword helped identify a person's military rank and, depending on how he had it customized, his personality as well.

Following the invention of repeating firearms in the mid-19th century, the sword lost its functional importance as a combat weapon and became a military dress accessory.

References: *Swords and Hilt Weapons*, Barnes & Noble Books, 1993; Gerald Welond, *Collector's Guide to Swords, Daggers & Cutlasses*, Chartwell Books, 1991.

Museum: Fort Ticonderoga Museum, Ticonderoga, NY.

Note: Condition is key to determining value.

American
32" l blade, cavalry officer's saber, c1870, slender curved highly polished black stuck maker's mark, sgd by retailer "The M. C. Liley & Co., Columbus, O.," finely etched o matted panels both sides, owner's name "Capt. L. P. Hunt, 10th Cavalry U.S.A.," gilt brass hilt cast in relief, three bar guard, orig wire bound fish skin guard, orig nickel plated scabbard with presentation quality gilt brass mounts, orig sword knot and belt...2,100.00
33" l, 1842 pattern light artillery, moderately curved blade, 1-3/8" at ricasso, single wide fuller, left ricasso mkd with early Ames logo, and right "1862," surcharged "Conn," handle leather wrapped with braided brass wire, large oval plain pommel cap, single D-guard with ball quillion, plain nickel plated scabbard with two hangers...........................450.00
34" l Spanish-American War skinny blade, light cavalry saber, 1872 Pattern, wide unstopped fuller, etched "US" and eagle, presented to "Capt. Alexander Wilson Norris," further engraved "Camp McKenzie," Ass't Adj. Gen'l, USV," right side of blade mkd "Camp Hastings-Camp Alger-Camp Meade" along cutting edge, fitted with light three branch brass hand guard, dec pommel and pommel cap with leather wrap handle, twisted brass wire, nickel plated scabbard with brass throat and tip, two dec hangers, leather wrapped scuffed, wear to scabbard....................200.00
34-1/2" slightly curved blade, heavy saber, officer's hanger, Revolutionary War, three unstopped fullers, 1-7/16" wide at the handguard, each side of blade engraved with half moon and sun, each with face and stars around arm holding sword, handguard pierced brass centered over blade with single D knuckle guard, round handle of dark wood with brass ferrules at each end, round turned brass pommel cap..1,500.00

U.S. Civil War, presentation officer's sword, Schulyer, Harlety & Graham, double engraved blade, also mkd "Clauberg-Solingen" and "Iron Proof," fancy basket and grip, bronze scabbard, ornate acorn and oak leaf hangers and drag, $1,870. Photo courtesy of Jackson's Auctioneers & Appraisers.

35" blade, light cavalry saber, Lansfield & Lamb, one wide and one unstopped narrow fullers, ricasso mkd with maker's name on wide side and "US/JCW/1864" on other, leather washer, 3-branch brass handguard, plain pommel cap, leather wrapped handle with twisted wire, plain nickeled iron scabbard 375.00
36-1/2" blade, heavy cavalry saber, S & K, spine mkd "FM 47"ith proofmarks, 1-3/8" at ricasso, with one fuller and one unstopped narrow fuller, three-branch handguard, leather wrapped with twisted brass wire and plain pommel cap, plain iron scabbard 350.00
40" very curved blade, heavy saber, 1806 Virginia Manufactory, 1-1/8" at ricasso with two unstopped fullers, one narrow, other more narrow, pierced flat iron knuckle guard with eight holes of varying size plus a portapee slot, plain leather wrapped handle with single strand iron wire wrap, smooth iron backing, plain iron scabbard with small brazed tip, screwed on throat with fixed hangar button, dark even peppery brown patina 2,000.00
French, 37" l, officer's, regulation, dated 1816, curved fullered dated Klingenthal blade etched on one side of the forte with fleur-de-lis above and below the inscription "Gardes du Corps Monsuier," martial trophies below, other side with radiant human mask, further trophies, Royal Arms of France between, brass hilt including semi-basket guard, orig grip and steel scabbard 1,200.00
German, 42-1/2" l, processional, early 17th C, two handles, blade formed by two lugs ahead of leather cov ricasso, writhen and straight guillons with fish tail terminals, small inner and outer rings, wooden grip, spirally fluted pommel 2,750.00
Japanese
Katana, 27" cutting edge blade, Tachi style mountings, late Koto to Shinto period, Nakago displays one mekugi-ana, blade displays deep sori and Choki Hamon, unclear Hada, blade displays number of kizo and openings, 19th C mountings, Tsuka wrapped in green it-maki with matching pr of gold lacquered menunk of floral design 700.00
Waharyahi Samuari, suba, short................................1,400.00
Polish, officer's, WWII period, cast brass dec hilt with Polish crest, single edged curved etched Solingen blade, mkd "W. Kralka," brass mounted leather scabbard 150.00
Scottish or English, mid 18th C, unmarked 34" double edge blade with wear, staining, full basket hilt of iron with two small breaks in iron work and one or two razed repairs, handle twisted wire, large fluted octagonal pommel with peened rivet slightly loose 850.00

TEA CADDIES

History: Tea once was a precious commodity and was stored in special boxes or caddies. These containers were made to accommodate different teas and included a special cup for blending.

Around 1700, silver caddies appeared in England. Other materials, such as Sheffield plate, tin, wood, china, and pottery, also were used. Some tea caddies are very ornate.

4-1/2" h, 7" w, 4-1/2" d, late Georgian, early 19th C, satinwood, fan inlay, oval amboyna panels, crossbanded, losses 320.00

5" h, 11-3/4" l, 5" d, Regency, silver mounted blond tortoiseshell, rect, two oval topped int. caddies, mixing bowl area, early 19th C, losses, mixing bowl missing 1,265.00

5-1/4" h, creamware, red and green enamel floral dec, wear and small chips, pr 1,420.00

5-3/8" h, 15-1/2" w, fan shaped, lacquer, reserves of Chinoiserie courtyard scenes, bat form feet, int. fitted with 2 engraved pewter caddies, imperfections 550.00

5-1/2" h, 6-1/4" w, 4" d, George III, mahogany, octagonal, inlaid oval reserve of shell, checkered banding and lines, late 18th C, minor losses 460.00

5-1/2" h, 6-3/4" w, 4-1/2" d, George III, boxwood and harewood, three foliate inlaid oval panels, late 18th c 320.00

5-1/2" h, 10" w, 6" d, painted papier-mâché and mother-of-pearl, serpentine front, fitted int., gilt borders, floral still life, Victorian, mid-19th C, minor losses................ 415.00

6-1/4" w, 13" l at top, 7-1/4" h, walnut veneer, inlaid edging, tapered shape, two side brass rings with lion mounts, ornate brass claw feet, two removable side compartments, center cylinder 420.00

6-1/2" h, 8-3/4" w, 4-3/4" d, Victorian, c1850, burl walnut, brass mounted, domed top, two lidded wells, each with tea name plaque, ext. with openwork straps, minor losses 750.00

7-1/8" l, dome top, figured wood veneer, colorful inlay, two int. lids, damage to veneer.................. 110.00

8" h, 15-1/2" w, 10" d, Victorian, mid-19th C, papier-mâché, double, ext. with foil, painted and gilded folite designs, flattened serpentine feet, int. with two lidded containers, mixing bowl 230.00

8-1/2" l, Victorian, 19th C, burl walnut, rect, int. with two lidded wells, minor losses........... 150.00

9" l, mahogany, old finish, orig brass bale and escutcheon, int. with double lids, some alterations 500.00

9" h, 14-1/2" w, 10" d, William IV, c1835, mahogany, stepped and beaded rect case, fitted with four lidded wells, two mixing wells (bowls missing), flattened bun feet 150.00

9-1/2" w, 5" d, 7" h, mahogany, small bun feet, caddy style top, missing top handle 360.00

TEA LEAF IRONSTONE CHINA

History: Tea Leaf Ironstone flowed into America from England in great quantities from the mid-1850s through the turn-of-the-century to grace the tables of working-class America famililies. It traveled to California and Texas in wagons and down the Mississippi River by boat to Kentucky and Missouri. It was too plain for the rich homes; its simplicity and durability appealed to wives forced to watch pennies. Tea Leaf found its way into the kitchen of Lincoln's Springfield home; sailors ate from it aboard the *Star of India*, (now moored in San Diego and still displaying Tea Leaf), and numerous historical sites display Tea Leaf as part of everyday American pioneer life.

Anthony Shaw is credited with introducing Tea Leaf. The most prolific Tea Leaf makers were Anthony Shaw and Alfred Meakin, Johnson Bros., Henry Burgess, Enoch Wecgwood, and Arthur J. Wilkinson, all of whom shipped much of their ware to America.

Although most of the English Tea Leaf is copper luster, Powell and Bishop and their successors, Bishop and Stonier, worked primarily in gold luster. Beautiful examples of gold luster were also made by H. Burgess; Mellor, Taylor & Co. used it on children's tea sets. Other English potters also were known to use gold luster, including W. & E. Corn, Thomas Elsmore, and Thomas Hughes, companies which have been recently identified as makers of this type of ware.

Contrary to popular belief, Tea Leaf was not manufactured exclusively by English potters in Staffordshire. Although there were more than 35 English potters producing Tea Leaf, at least 26 American potters helped satisfy the demand.

J. & E. Mayer, Beaver Falls, PA, founded by English potters who immigrated to America, produced a large amount of copper luster Tea Leaf. The majority of the American potters decorated with both gold and copper luster. East Liverpool, Ohio, potters such as Cartwright Bros., East End Pottery and Knowles, Taylor & Knowles decorated only in gold luster. This also is a true of Trenton, N.J., potters such as Glasgow Pottery, American Crockery Co., and Fell & Thropp Co. Since no underglazing was used with the gold, much of it has been washed away.

By the 1900s, Tea Leaf's popularity had waned. The sturdy ironstone did not disappear; it was stored in barns and relegated to attics and basements. While the manufacture of Tea Leaf did experience a brief resurgence from the late 1950s through the 1970s by potters such as Red Cliff (American) and Wm. Adams (English), copper

Burl mahogany, two compartments, string inlay on compartment covers, ivory key inlay, chamfered corners, brass hinges, 4-3/8" x 7-1/2" x 4-3/4", $595.

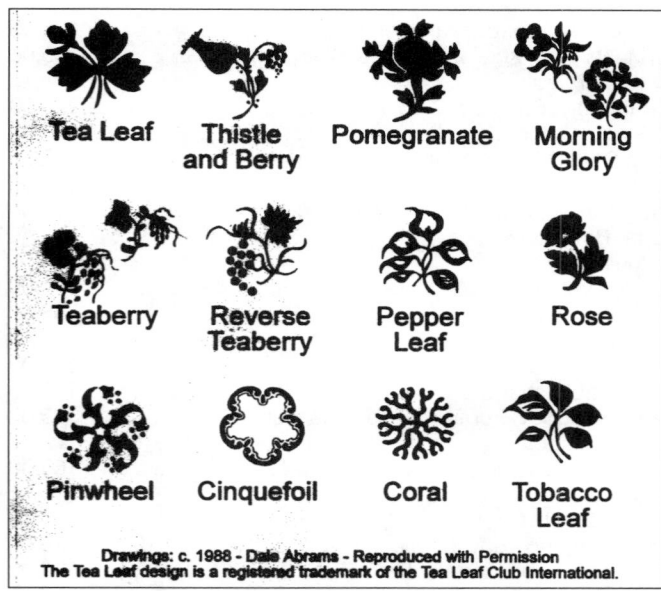

Tea Leaf | Thistle and Berry | Pomegranate | Morning Glory
Teaberry | Reverse Teaberry | Pepper Leaf | Rose
Pinwheel | Cinquefoil | Coral | Tobacco Leaf

Drawings: c. 1988 - Dale Abrams - Reproduced with Permission
The Tea Leaf design is a registered trademark of the Tea Leaf Club International.

Tea Leaf Ironstone

lustre Tea Leaf didn't recapture the hearts of the American consumer as it had a generation before.

Tea Leaf collectors recognize a number of "variant" decorative motifs as belonging to the Tea Leaf family: Teaberry, Morning Glory, Coral, Cinquefoil, Rose, Pre-Tea Leaf, Tobacco Leaf, Pepper Leaf, Pinwheel, Pomegranate, and Thistle & Berry, as well as white ironstone decorated with copper lustre bands and floral and geometric motifs. Once considered the stepchildren of Tea leaf, these variants are now prized by collectors and generally bring strong prices.

Today's collectors eagerly seek out Tea Leaf and all of its variant motifs, and copper-luster decorated white ironstone has once again become prized for its durability, beauty, simplicity, craft, and style.

References: Annise Doring Heaivilin, *Grandma's Tea Leaf Ironstone*, Wallace-Homestead, 1981, 1996 reprint distributed by L-W Book Sales; Jean Wetherbee, *White Ironstone, A Collector's Guide*, Antique Trader Books, 1996; *Handbook of Tea Leaf Body Styles*, Tea Leaf Club International (324 Powderhorn Dr., Houghton Lake, MI 48629), 1995; Dawn Stolzfus & Jeffrey B. Snyder, *White Ironstone, A Survey of its Many Forms, Undecorated, Flow Blue, Mulberry, Copper Lustre*, Schiffer Publishing, 1997.

Collectors' Club: Tea Leaf Club International, 324 Powderhorn Dr., Houghton Lake, MI 48629. Web site: http://ourworld.compuserve.com/homepages/da

Museums: Lincoln Home, Springfield, IL; Ox Barn Museum, Aurora, OR; Sherman Davidson House, Newark OH.

Advisor: Dale Abrams. Tea Leaf Antiques, Columbus, Ohio.

Notes: Tea Leaf values have increased steadily for the last decade, but there are some general rules of thumb for the knowledgeable collector. English Tea Leaf is still more collectible than American, except for rare pieces. The earlier the Tea Leaf production (1850s–1860s), the harder it is to find pieces and, therefore, the more expensive they are. Children's pieces are highly collectible, especially those with copper lustre decorative motifs. Hard-to-find Tea Leaf pieces include mustache cups, egg-cups, covered syrup pitchers, ladles, oversized serving pieces, and pieces with significant embossing. Common pieces (plates, platters) of later production (1880–1900) need to be in excellent condition or should be priced accordingly as they are not that difficult to find.

Bone Dish
  Meakin
    Crescent shape 55.00
    Scalloped edge 65.00
  Shaw, fluted edge..60.00
Brush Vase
  Burgess, Pagoda..215.00
  Meakin, Fishhook...200.00
  Shaw
    Basketweave 425.00
    Plain round, drain hole..225.00
Butter Dish, 3 pc, base, cover, liner
  Meakin, Fishhook..185.00
  Wedgwood, simple square..185.00
Butter Dish Liner, sq...25.00
Butter Pat, Meakin
  Square 15.00
  Round, Chelsea 25.00
Cake Plate
  Edwards, Peerless (Feather), sq, handles 185.00
  Meakin, Bamboo, 8-3/4" with handles 85.00
  Wilkinson, Senate shape, oval......................................150.00
Chamber Pot, Meakin
  Bamboo, 2 pc 265.00
  Scroll, 2 pc..285.00
Children's Dishes
  Mug, child's, Shaw 375.00
  Tea Set, Knowles, Taylor & Knowles, four cups and saucers, teapot, creamer and sugar 850.00
  Tea Set, Mellor-Taylor, round bottom, gold luster, six cups and saucers, six plates, teapot, creamer, sugar, waste bowl 1,850.00
Coffeepot, cov
  Furnival, Gentle Square (Rooster) 325.00

Butter dish, John Edwards, Peerless shape, 3 piece (includes insert); $195.

Meakin
    Bamboo 210.00
    Chelsea 295.00
    Fishhook 185.00
  Shaw, Lily-of-the-Valley 475.00
Compote
  Mellor Taylor, sq, ridged 325.00
  Red Cliff, simple square, 1960s 150.00
  Shaw, plain, round 310.00
  Unmarked, unusually deep bowl, 8" d, 5" h 435.00
Creamer
  Edwards, Peerless (Feather) 285.00
  Meakin, Bamboo 185.00
  Red Cliff, Chinese shape, 1960s 80.00
  Shaw
    Cable 250.00
    Lily-of-the Valley 375.00
Cup and Saucer
  Adams, Empress shape, 1950s 30.00
  Meakin 65.00
  Shaw
    Basketweave 90.00
    Lily-of-the-Valley 125.00
Egg Cup
  Meakin, Boston Egg Cup, 4" d, 1-3/4" h 395.00
  Unmarked, 3-1/2" h 325.00
Gravy Boat
  Johnson Bros, Acanthus, with stand 160.00
  Mayer, American 90.00
  Meakin, Bamboo 85.00
  Shaw, Basketweave, with stand 185.00
  Wedgwood, simple square 65.00
Mug
  Meakin, Scroll 195.00
  Shaw
    Chinese shape 115.00
    Lily-of-the-Valley 350.00
Mush Bowl, Meakin 85.00
Nappy
  Meakin
    Chelsea, round 22.00
    Fishhook, 4-1/4" sq 18.00
  Wedgwood, 4-1/4" sq, scalloped edge 20.00
Pitcher and Bowl Set
  Furnival, Cable 495.00
  Meakin, Fishhook 285.00
  Shaw, Cable 525.00
Pitcher/Jug
  Meakin
    Chelsea 375.00
    Fishhook 285.00
  Shaw
    Cable shape, 7" h 295.00
    Chinese shape, 7-1/2" 500.00
Plate
  Furnival, plain, round, 8-1/4" 12.00
  Johnson Bros., Acanthus, 9" d 22.00
  Meakin, plain, round, 6-3/4" d 10.00
  Shaw, plain, round, 10" d 25.00
  Wedgwood, plain, round, 9-1/4" d 17.00
Platter
  Meakin
    Chelsea, 10" x 14", oval 65.00
    Plain, 9" x 13", rect 35.00
  Shaw, Lily-of-the-Valley, 13" 150.00
Punch Bowl, Shaw, Cable 525.00
Relish Dish, Shaw, Chinese shape 265.00
Sauce Tureen
  Furnival, Cable, 3 pc 185.00
  Meakin, Bamboo, 4 pc, including ladle 425.00
  Red Cliff, 4 pc, including ladle 175.00

Serving Bowl, open
  Grindley, round, scalloped edge 135.00
  Meakin, sq, scalloped edge, 6" sq 45.00
Soap Dish, cov
  Grindley, Bamboo, 3 pc, liner, rect 225.00
  Shaw, Cable, 3 pc, liner, oval 300.00
Soup Bowl, Meakin, plain, round, 8-3/4" d 25.00
Soup Plate, Meakin, plain, round, 10" d 50.00
Soup Tureen, Meakin, Bamboo, 4 pc with ladle ... 1,500.00
Sugar Bowl, cov
  Meakin
    Bamboo 95.00
    Fishhook 85.00
  Shaw
    Bullet 135.00
    Cable shape 145.00
Vanity Box, cov, Furnival, Cable, horizontal 325.00
Vegetable, cov
  Meakin, Bamboo 165.00
  Shaw
    Basketweave 325.00
    Hanging Leaves 450.00
  Wilkinson, Maidenhair Fern 275.00
Waste Bowl
  Meakin, plain, round 95.00
  Shaw, Niagara Fan 120.00

TEAPOTS

History: The origins of the teapot have been traced to China in the late 16th century. Early Yixing teapots were no bigger than the tiny cups previously used for drinking tea. By the 17th century, tea had spread to civilized nations of the world. The first recorded advertisement for tea in London is dated 1658 and called a "China drink,...call Tcha, by other Nations Tay, alias Tee..." Although coffee houses were already established, they began to add tea to their selections.

While the Chinese had long been producing teapots and other tea items, the English were receiving these wares along with shipments of tea. By the early 1700s, British china and stoneware producers were manufacturing teapots. It was in 1706 that Thomas Twining bought his own coffeehouse and thwarted the competition of the many other such establishments by offering a variety of quality teas. Coffeehouses were exclusively for males; thus women would wait outside, sending their footmen inside for purchases. For the majority of the 1700s, teapots were Oriental imports. British factories continued experimenting with the right combination of materials which would make a teapot durable enough to withstand the daily rigors of boiling water. Chinese Export Porcelain was an inspiration to the British and by the end of the 1700s, many companies found the necessary combinations of china clay and stone, fired at high temperature, which could withstand boiling water needed to brew precious pots of tea.

From the very first teapots, figural shapes have always been a favorite with tea drinkers. The Victorian era saw a change from more utilitarian teapots towards beautiful, floral, and Rococo designs, yet figural pots continued to be manufactured.

Early American manufacturers mimicked Oriental and British designs. While the new land demanded sturdy teapots in the unsettled land, potteries were established steadily in the Eastern states. Rockingham teapots were produced by many companies, deriving this term from British companies manufacturing a strong, shiny brown glaze on heavy pottery. The best known are from the Bennington, Vermont, potteries.

By the 1800s and the turn-of-the-century, many pottery companies were well established in the U. S., producing a lighter dinnerware and china including teapots. Figural teapots from this era are highly desired by collectors while others concentrate on collecting all known patterns produced by a company.

The last 20 years has seen a renewed interest in teapots and collectors' desires– not only older examples, but high-priced, specialty manufactured teapots such as those from the Lomonosov factory in Russia or individual artist creations commanding hundreds of dollars.

References: Edward Bramah, *Novelty Teapots,* Quiller Press, London, 1992; Tina M. Carter, *Teapots,* Running Press, 1995; Robin Emmerson, *British Teapots & Tea Drinking,* HMSO, London, 1992.

Periodicals: *Tea, A Magazine,* P.O. Box 348, Scotland, CT 06264; *Tea Talk,* P.O. Box 860, Sausalito, CA 94966; *Tea Time Gazette,* P.O. Box 40276, St. Paul, MN 55104.

REPRODUCTION ALERT

Teapots and other ware with blurry mark of shield and two animals, ironstone, celadon colored body background, design made to look like flow blue, are new products, possibly from China. Yixing teapots have been reproduced or made in similar styles for centuries, study this type of teapot to help determine the old from the new.

Advisor: Tina M. Carter.

Automobile, figural, shaped like Austin, Carlton Ware, England 500.00
Blue Canton, reproduction of Chinese export porcelain, 1970s 150.00
Clarice Cliff, teepee, 1946 ....850.00

Automobile, Austin, made by Carltonware, England, $500. Photo courtesy of The Antique Gallery.

Parian Ware, Mistletoe pattern, Brownfield, England, registry diamond mark, c1870, $450. Photo courtesy of Tina Carter.

Cloisonné, panel with butterflies and flowers, Chinese, late 19th C 450.00
Copper, spun, E. W. Allen, 1940s 550.00
Flow Blue, Scinde pattern, Alcock, octagonal, 8-1/2" h 950.00
Lenox, Art Deco, applied sterling silver dec, c1930, 3 pc set 400.00
Meissen, tea service, puce-mosaic, birds, highly detailed, c1750 ....20,000.00
Old Worcester, first period, Old Japan Star, 1765-70 .....5,250.00
Parian Ware, Brownfield, Mistletoe pattern 450.00
Sheffield, silver and ebony details, c1912 ....1,500.00
Silver, repousse, S. Kirk & Sons, 6 pc set 8,000.00
Wedgwood, earthenware, cabbage, lettuce, melon, various designs 650.00
Yixing, bamboo handle, Chinese "chop mark" or signature, c1880 ....450.00
Zurich porcelain, dragon spout, china series, rococo style, c1770 ....6,000.00

TEDDY BEARS

History: Originally thought of as "Teddy's Bears," in reference to President Theodore Roosevelt, these stuffed toys are believed to have originated in Germany. The first ones to be made in the United States were produced about 1902.

Most of the earliest teddy bears had humps on their backs, elongated muzzles, and jointed limbs. The fabric used was generally mohair; the eyes were either glass with pin backs or black shoe buttons. The stuffing was usually excelsior. Kapok (for softer bears) and wood-wool (for firmer bears) also were used as stuffing materials.

Quality older bears often have elongated limbs, sometimes with curved arms, oversized feet, and felt paws. Noses and mouths are black and embroidered onto the fabric.

The earliest teddy bears are believed to have been made by the original Ideal Toy Corporation in America and by a German company, Margarete Steiff, GmbH. Bears made in the early 1900s by other companies can be difficult to identify because they were all similar in appearance and most identifying tags or labels were lost during childhood play.

References: Pauline Cockrill, *Teddy Bear Encyclopedia*, Dorling Kindersley, 1993; Margaret and Gerry Grey, *Teddy Bears*, Courage Books, 1994; Pam Hebbs, *Collecting Teddy Bears*, Pincushion Press, 1992; Dee Hockenberry, *Bear Memorabilia*, Hobby House Press, 1992; ——, *Big Bear Book*, Schiffer Publishing, 1996; Margaret Fox Mandel, *Teddy Bears and Steiff Animals*, 1st Series (1984, 1997 value update), 2nd Series (1987, 1996 value update), Collector Books; ——, *Teddy Bears, Annalee Animals & Steiff Animals*, 3rd Series, Collector Books, 1990, 1996 value update; Linda Mullins, *Teddy Bear & Friends Price Guide*, 4th ed., Hobby House Press, 1993; ——, *Raikes Bear & Doll Story*, Hobby House, 1991; ——, *Teddy Bears Past & Present*, Vol. II, Hobby House Press, 1992; ——, *Tribute to Teddy Bear Artists*, Series 2, Hobby House Press, 1996; Jesse Murray, *Teddy Bear Figurines Price Guide*, Hobby House, 1996; Sue Pearson and Dottie Ayers, *Teddy Bears: A Complete Guide to History, Collecting, and Care*, McMillan, 1995; Cynthia Powell, *Collector's Guide to Miniature Teddy Bears*, Collector Books, 1994; Carol J. Smith, *Identification & Price Guide to Winnie the Pooh Collectibles*, Hobby House Press, 1994.

Periodicals: *Antiques & Collectbles*, P.O. Drawer 1565, El Cajon, CA 92022; *National Doll & Teddy Bear Collector*, P.O. Box 4032, Portland, OR 97208; *Teddy Bear and Friends*, 6405 Flank Dr., Harrisburg, PA 17112; *Teddy Bear Review*, 170 Fifth Ave., New York, NY 10010.

Collectors' Clubs: Good Bears of the World, P.O. Box 13097, Toledo, OH 43613; My Favorite Bear: Collectors Club for Classic Winnie the Pooh, 468 W Alpine #10, Upland, CA 91786.

Museum: Teddy Bear Museum of Naples, Naples, FL.

Additional Listings: See Steiff.

Notes: Teddy bears are rapidly increasing as collectibles and their prices are rising proportionately. As in other fields, desirability should depend upon appeal, quality, uniqueness, and condition. One modern bear already has been firmly accepted as a valuable collectible among its antique counterparts: the Steiff teddy put out in 1980 for the company's 100th anniversary. This is a reproduction of that company's first teddy and has a special box, signed certificate, and numbered ear tag; 11,000 of these were sold worldwide.

3-1/2" h, Schuco, Cinnamon, 3-1/2" h 145.00
3-7/8" h, blond mohair, fully jointed, black bead eyes, embroidered nose and mouth, Steiff 250.00
10" h, Tyford, white, mohair, English 110.00
10-1/2" h, Electric Eye, red, mohair, American 675.00
12" h, light apricot, fully jointed, black steel eyes, embroidered snout, blank button, Steiff, 1903-04 .... 850.00
13" l, yellowish-gold mohair, reticulated limbs, felt paw pads, metal nose, glass eyes, red, white, and blue ribbon 250.00
15" h, blond mohair, fully jointed, triangular face, long snout, shoe button eyes, embroidered nose and claws, excelsior and soft stuffing, c1910 .... 345.00
15-1/2" h, English, Merry Thoughts in England, worn gold mohair, reticulated limbs, oil cloth paw pads, glass eyes, restored embroidered nose and mouth, dressed in white lace dress, white straw hat 250.00

18" h, English, Oxford, worn gold mohair, reticulated limbs, velvet paw pads, bakelite nose, glass eyes, red ribbon 220.00
22" h, red mohair, articulated front limbs, blue eyes light when tongue is pulled, worn pads, starched collar 110.00
25" h, gold mohair, articulated limbs, glass eyes, embroidered features, replaced foot pads 275.00
26" h, gold mohair, articulated limbs, glass eyes, repairs .. 200.00
35" h, brown mohair, fully jointed, glass eyes, velveteen pads, excelsior stuffing, mid-20th C 575.00
36" h, dark brown mohair, fully jointed, glass eyes, embroidered nose and mouth, velveteen pads, c1910 .... 750.00

TEPLITZ CHINA

History: Around 1900, there were 26 ceramic manufacturers located in Teplitz, a town in the Bohemian province of what was then known as Czechoslovakia. Other potteries were located in the nearby town of Turn. Wares from these factories were molded, cast, and hand decorated. Most are in the Art Nouveau and Art Deco styles.

Marks: The majority of pieces do not carry a specific manufacturer's mark; they are simply marked "Teplitz," "Turn-Teplitz," or "Turn."

Vase, enameled soldiers holding long rifle, blue-gray ground, double handle, gold Stellmacher mark, 8-1/2" h, $150. Photo courtesy of Susan and Al Bagdade.

Basket, Arab motif 70.00
Bowl, 6-3/4" d, ecru, enameled flowers, c1912 ....175.00
Box, cov, turtle shape, children on cov, green, gray, and natural colors, satin finish, mkd "Ernest Wahliss Turn Vienna," c1918 ....385.00
Bust, 22-1/2" h, young woman, elaborate dress, fan, flowers and hat with reticulated border, putto on shoulder, Ernst Wahliss, c1900, repaired 1,650.00
Candlestick, 5-1/4" h, figural, woman in flowing gown, c1905 ....145.00
Ewer
 6-1/2" h, hp, pink and gold flowers, light green ground, light pink neck, gold twig handle 95.00
 9-1/2" h, cream, red roses, gold trim, mkd "Royal Teplitz" 65.00
Figure
 12-1/2" h, young girl, peasant costume, basket resting on tree stump 350.00
 15" h, man and woman, court dress, multicolored, pr...265.00
Pitcher, 9-1/2" h, lily pad dec, green and pink, c1895 ....195.00
Tobacco Jar, 8" h, Boxer dog dec 400.00
Vase
 5" h, bud, relief rooster head in medallion, multicolored geometric dec 100.00
 7" h, 4 handles, pierced rim panels of poppies, drip enamel cobalt blue and green dec, gold trim 265.00
Window Box, 12" l, 3" w, 4" h, boat shape, rose dec, spider web ground, orig liner 125.00

TERRA-COTTA WARE

History: Terra-cotta is ware made of hard, semi-fired ceramic. The color of the pottery ranges from a light orange-brown to a deep brownish red. It is usually unglazed, but some pieces are partially glazed and have incised, carved, or slip designs. Utilitarian objects, as well as statuettes and large architectural pieces, were made. Fine early Chinese terra-cotta pieces recently have sold for substantial prices.

Figure, boy leaning on fence, Italian, 4-1/2" h,

Bust, 30" h, court lady, Louis XVI style, sgd "Coustou" 600.00
Cigar Holder, 12" x 10", figural dog, glazed brown, Victorian 75.00
Figure
 3-3/4" h, Lekythos, squatty, winged figure, flowerheads, and palmette, painted black, Corinthian, c600 B.C. 345.00
 19-3/4" h, seated, folding fragments of serpents, stepped shaped plinth, inscribed "R. J. Auguste F. 1744," remnants of paper label and wax seal, some restoration ...20,000.00
Jug, 7-1/2" h, mkd "Cambridge Ale" 150.00
Pipe Holder, 5" x 9", Chinese boy, black glaze 90.00
Tobacco Jar, 11" h, figural, Bismarck, sitting in easy chair 250.00
Tray, 9" x 7", hp, pilgrims resting, 1920 ....85.00
Vase, 6" h, raised daisy dec, green glazed int. 45.00

TEXTILES

History: Textiles is the generic term for cloth or fabric items, especially anything woven or knitted. Antique textiles that have survived are usually those that were considered the "best" by their original owners, since these were the objects that were used and stored carefully by the housewife.

Textiles are collected for many reasons: to study fabrics, to understand the elegance of a historical period, for decorative purposes, or to use as was originally intended. The renewed interest in antique clothing has sparked a revived interest in period textiles of all forms.

References: Gideon Bosker, Michele Mancini, John Gramstad, *Fabulous Fabrics of the 50s, and Other Terrific Textiles of the 20s, 30s, and 40s*, Chronicle Books, 1992; M. Dupont-Auberville, *Full-Color Historic Textile Designs*, Dover Publications, 1996; Frances Johnson, *Collecting Household Linens*, Schiffer Publishing, 1997; Sheila Paine, *Embroidered Textiles: Traditional Patterns from Five Continents, With a Worldwide Guide To Identification,* Thames & Hudson, 1997; Pamela Smith, *Vintage Fashion and Fabrics*, Alliance Publishing, 1995; Jessie A. Turbayne, *Hooked Rug Treasury*, Schiffer Publishing, 1997; ——, *Hookers' Art: Evolving Designs in Hooked Rugs*, Schiffer Publishing, 1993; Sigrid Wortmann Weltge, *Women's Work*, Chronicle Press, 1993.

Periodicals: *International Old Lacers Bulletin*, P.O. Box 481223, Denver, CO 80248; *Lace Collector*, P.O. Box 222, Plainwell, MI 49080; *Textile Museum Newsletter*, The Textile Museum, 2320 S. St. NW, Washington, DC 20008.

Collectors' Clubs: Costume Society of America, 55 Edgewater Dr., P.O. Box 73, Earleville, MD 21919; Stumpwork Society, P.O. Box 122, Bogota, NJ 07603.

Museums: Cooper-Hewitt Museum, New York, NY; Currier Gallery of Art, Manchester, NH; Ipswich Historical Society, Ipswich, MA; Lace Museum, Mountain View, CA; Museum of American Textile History, North Andover, MA; Museum of Art, Rhode Island School of Design, Providence, RI; Philadelphia College of Textiles & Science, Philadelphia, PA; Textile Museum, Washington, DC; Valentine Museum, Richmond, VA.

Additional Listings: See Clothing; Lace and Linens; Quilts; Samplers.

Bed Rug, 80" x 70", hooked, loose weave, butternut dyed wool ground, hooked green, cerise, and coral wool floral design, northern New England, 19th C, minor losses, tears, repairs 575.00

Coverlet, Jacquard

One piece, double weave, 79" x 99", star center, floral borders, corners labeled "Made by E. Hausman, Trexlertown, PA, 1851," red, green, and blue 635.00

One piece, single weave

76" x 90", vintage center, Christian and Heathen border on sides, bird border on end, corners labeled "Daniel Bury Cornersburgh, Ohio, 1850," purple, gold, blue back, and white.....................................860.00

86" x 87", four rose medallions, stars and compote borders, corners labeled "Made by D. Crosley, Xenia, Ohio 1859," olive green, deep red, and natural white, very minor wear and stains...........................1,320.00

Two piece, double weave

70" x 85", geometric floral design, stars and basket of flowers, building borders, corners dated 1852, black and white, minor stains, some edge wear at top, bottom fringe incomplete.....................1,100.00

74" x 84", four part floral medallions with tree and building border, corners labeled "J. Klein, Hamilton, Co. Indiana 1858," deep navy blue and natural white, minor edge damage and fringe loss 910.00

86" x 92", floral medallions and lion border, corners labeled "Permela Gardner 1838, B. French weaver in Clinton," wear, stains, two small holes, no fringe 1,980.00

Two piece, single weave

62 x 86", geometric floral center and borders, rose border at bottom edge, corners labeled "W. Minster, Allen Co, 1848," with rooster, navy blue, tomato red, olive green, natural white, minor wear and stains, two small holes at top 470.00

Coverlet, jacquard, double weave, two pc, geometric floral design with stars and basket of flowers, building borders with corners dated "1852," black and white, minor stains, some edge wear, bottom fringe incomplete, 70"x 85", $1,100. Photo courtesy of Garth's Auctions.

70" x 85", four rose medallions and birds, rose and bird borders, corners labeled "W. Shank, Shelby Co, Ohio 1842," navy blue, light blue, tomato red, bleached white 770.00

70" x 88", floral medallions and stripes, rose border, corners labeled "Manufacturd by C. K. Hinkel, Shippensburg, PA, 1843, Caroline Helt," burgundy red, gold, deep blue, and natural white.....................425.00

70" x 88", peacock and young with urns of flowers, vintage and floral border, corners labeled "Made 1862," attributed to Bucyrus, Crawford County, OH, tomato red, navy blue, natural white, minor stains.....................500.00

71" x 89", four rose and star medallions, bird borders, corners labeled "Austintown 1841," navy blue, royal blue, olive green, deep pink, natural white, some wear and stains, fringe loss, small holes 330.00

74" x 99", floral medallions, building borders, corners labeled "Made by J. Witmer, Manor Township for Elizabeth Plantz 1845," (Lancaster, PA), navy blue, olive green, tomato red, natural white.....................1,320.00

76" x 79", floral and star flower medallions, bird borders, corners labeled "Peace and Plenty 1847," navy blue and white, top edge turned and rebound 600.00

81" x 88", four rose and compass star medallions, bird borders with swags, corners labeled "Mathias Klein 1844," (Jefferson, Montgomery County), tomato red and natural white, very minor stain.........................825.00

Coverlet, Overshot, two piece woven, 82" x 90", Optical pattern, salmon red and black wool, faded blue cotton warp, wear and damage 175.00

Globe, 12-1/4" h, 5" d, terrestrial globe embroidered with gild silk threads, inscribed with black ink, celestial globe similarly dec with additional watercolor highlights, both with cream silk ground, turned wood stands, attributed to Westtown School, Chester County, PA, fiber wear, minor losses, fading, pr 8,625.00

Hooked Rug, America, 19th C

22" h, 32" w, checkerboard, floral border, red, pink, black, green, yellow, gray ground, black cloth covered stretcher 330.00

23" x 40", semi-circular, urn of flowers, green, red, yellow, gray ground, black border, some fading and repairs, edges rebound, mounted on board.........................220.00

28" x 48-1/2", figural, linen ground, striated border, center reserve of two horses and foliate device, black, rust, blue, purple, and brown yarns, taupe field, framed, minor fiber wear and losses, fading 520.00

28-1/2" x 52", figural, band border enclosing reserve of bird hunting scene, gray, black, safe, red, and ecru yarns, cream field, minor repair, fading, staining.................865.00

29" x 39-1/2", figural, striped, scalloped, and foliate border, center reserve of trotting horse, black, gray, brown, red, blue, and purple yarns, green field, dated "Feb. 14, 1922," framed 1,095.00

30-1/2" h, 51" l, pictorial, saddled horse, variegated ground with grass, trees, plants, sky, New England, mounted, repairs.............................2,185.00

31" x 63", Fishscale, red, green, brown, and black, minor professional repair 770.00

32" x 39", figural, geometric border enclosing reserve of prancing horse, purple, taupe, gray, and green, on black field, framed.............................920.00

34-1/4" x 40", figural, striped border, center reserved of domestic animal and vase of flowers, worked in blue, purple, red, brown, taupe, and gray yarn, framed, fiber wear, minor losses, fading 400.00

35-1/2" x 24", star border enclosing reserve of American field with crossed arrows and "Centennial 1776-1876," taupe, red, white, blue, and black yarn, minor losses.........460.00

40" x 49", figural, border of stars and hearts, center reserve of horse, black, pink, and blue yarns, striated field, framed, fiber wear, fading, minor losses 1,380.00

40-1/2" d, florals, celery, sage, pink, red, navy, and light brown wool yarns.. 1,750.00

41" x 33", flowerheads, striated border, slate blue, cream, ivory, red, navy, and brown yarn, losses, fading, staining 230.00

66" x 98", repeating flowerheads design and other foliate devices, blue, sage, terra-cotta, and green on tobacco brown field, very minor wear, minor staining 980.00

Mattress Cover, blue and white check homespun, machine sewn, 54" x 75" 275.00

Mourning Picture, silk embroidery, sgd "Penelope Howland, Mary Balch's School, Providence, RI, 1802," two large weeping willows over two center urns and biographical information 14,950.00

Needlework Picture

6-3/4" h, 12-1/2" l, tent stitch, polychrome wool threads, linen ground, Renaissance maiden surrounded by florals, squirrel, England, 17th C, framed 1,840.00

10-1/2" h, 8-1/2" w, oval, Hope, attributed to Balch School, Providence, RI, early 19th C, replaced eglomise mat, framed 1,265.00

12-1/4" x 16-1/4", "Joseph Meeting His New Wife," watercolor highlights, eglomise mat, England, early 19th C, toning, minor losses, tears 300.00

6-7/8" x 25-1/4", England, 1746, depicts events in a seamstress's life, family, home, tending sheep, playing with dogs, three draped and swagged white tents, peaked tops contain winged cherub heads, an hour glass beside each, two tents marked with skulls and crossbones, one tent with bodies of twins and other two with single bodies 101,500.00

9" x 19-1/2", chenille, "Angelique L. C. Picot aged 9, Richmond, 1-1819," two men duck hunting from small boat, framed 7,500.00

9" x 20" oval, Landing of Columbus, attributed to Susanna Rowson's Academy, Boston, watercolor and metallic threads on silk, framed, minor staining 1,380.00

Panel, embroidered, England

8" h, 9-1/2" w, stumpwork, two figures and child beside building with portcullis and stylized trees, flowers, animals, very work satin foundation tattered, blue, green, white, red, and brown, 10-1/8" h x 12" w frame 550.00

8-1/2" h, 13-1/2" w, two figures, stylized trees, deer, leopard, flowers, building, silk and metallic thread on satin, mica overlay on windows of buildings, green, gold, yellow, blue, white, brown, and black, some wear and minor damage, 12" h x 17-1/4" w frame 2,750.00

Pocketbook, 8-1/4" l, flame stitch needlework, blue glazed chintz lining, America, late 18th/19th C, minor losses 750.00

Tablecloth, 58" w, 100" l, Irish linen, masks and griffins dec 330.00

Table Rug, 74-1/2" l, 39-1/2" w, appliqued and embroidered, 32 tan and black blocks in checkerboard pattern, colored appliqued birds and flowers, framed by flowers and hearts, New England, mid-19th C, minor imperfections................. 4,025.00

THREADED GLASS

History: Threaded glass is glass decorated with applied threads of glass. Before the English invention of a glass-threading machine in 1876, threads were applied by hand. After this invention, threaded glass was produced in quantity by practically every major glass factory.

Threaded glass was revived by the art glass manufacturers such as Durand and Steuben, and it is still made today.

Bowl, 7" d, 3" h, light pink, green threaded swirl design 45.00

Claret Jug, 11-1/2" h, 3-1/2" d, chartreuse green, emb scrolled French pewter hinged top, handle, and pedestal foot 245.00

Creamer, 4-3/4" h, colorless with slight blue tint, threaded neck and lip, applied ribbed handle, Pittsburgh....................170.00

Finger Bowl and Underplate, 2-3/4" h, 7" d, cranberry optic diamond quilted design, fine closely spaced cranberry threads 295.00

Rug, hooked, rag, circular compass star design, red, gray, black, blue, and yellow, 55" d, $415. Photo courtesy of Garth's Auctions.

Lamp Shade, pinched rim, pink threading, 5" d, 2" h, $45.

Mug, 4-3/4" h, colorless, second gather of glass with swirled ribs, applied handle, copper wheel engraved initials and wreath, threaded neck, attributed to New England Glass Co. 1,550.00

Pitcher
3-7/8" h, colorless, applied threading at neck, applied handle 145.00
7" h, Lily Pad, aqua, threaded neck and lip, applied hollow handle..550.00

Vase, 11-1/2" h, 5-3/4" w, 6" h stick neck, Herringbone satin, bridal white, bright pink int., allover clear threading, Victorian 750.00

TIFFANY

History: Louis Comfort Tiffany (1849-1934) established a glass house in 1878 primarily to make stained glass windows. In 1890, in order to utilize surplus materials at the plant, Tiffany began to design and produce "small glass," such as iridescent glass lamp shades, vases, stemware, and tableware in the Art Nouveau manner. Commercial production began in 1896.

Tiffany developed a unique type of colored iridescent glass called Favrile, which differs from other art glass in that it was a composition of colored glass worked together while hot. The essential characteristic is that the ornamentation is found within the glass; Favrile was never further decorated. Different effects were achieved by varying the amount and position of colors.

Louis Tiffany and the artists in his studio also are well known for their fine work in other areas—bronzes, pottery, jewelry, silver and enamels.

Marks: Most Tiffany wares are signed with the name "L. C. Tiffany" or the initials "L.C.T." Some pieces also are marked "Favrile" along with a number. A variety of other marks can be found, e.g., "Tiffany Studios" and "Louis C. Tiffany Furnaces."

REPRODUCTION ALERT

A large number of brass belt buckles and badges bearing Tiffany markings were imported into the United States and sold at flea markets and auctions in the late 1960s. The most common marking is "Tiffany Studios, New York." Now, more than 25 years later, many of these items are resurfacing and deceiving collectors and dealers.

A partial list of belt buckles includes the Wells Fargo guard dog, Wells Fargo & Company mining stage, Coca-Cola Bottling, Southern Comfort Whiskey, Currier and Ives express train, and U.S. Mail. Beware of examples that have been enhanced through color enameling.

An Indian police shield is among the fake Tiffany badges. The badge features an intertwined "U" and "S" at the top and a bow and arrow motif separating "INDIAN" and "POLICE."

References: Victor Arwas, *Glass, Art Nouveau and Art Deco*, Rizzoli International Publications, 1977; Alastair Duncan, *Louis Comfort Tiffany*, Harry N. Abrams, 1992; Robert Koch, *Louis C. Tiffany, Rebel in Glass*, Crown Publishers, 1966; David Rago, *American Art Pottery*, Knickerbocker Press, 1997; John A. Shuman III, *Collector's Encyclopedia of American Art Glass*, Collector Books, 1988, 1994 value update.

Museums: Chrysler Museum, Norfolk, VA; Corning Glass Museum, Corning, NY; University of Connecticut, The William Benton Museum of Art, Storrs, CT.

Bronze

Calling Card Receiver, mkd "Tiffany Studios" 75.00
Candlesticks, pr, 20-1/2" h, slit candlecups, blown-out green Favrile glass inserts, raised on tall bronze stems, dark orig patina, beaded bobeches, imp "S 1457" 2,300.00
Clock, 5-1/2" h, offset triangular cast bronze frame, geometric motif enhanced by red and pink enamel, base imp "Louis C. Tiffany Furnaces Inc. 360," keywind Chelsea movement, dial imp "Tiffany & Co, New York" 1,495.00
Desk Set, Zodiac, etched matte finish, gold patina, calendar frame, #929; rocker blotter, #990; large blotter ends, #988; pen tray, #1000; memo pad, #1090; paper knife #1095, each imp "Tiffany Studios New York," price for 6 pc set........520.00
Floor Ashtray
24-1/12" h, trifid, platform base with ribbed tripartite shaft supporting tray and holder for metal ash receiver, base imp "Tiffany Studios, New York, 1658" 1,265.00
25-1/2" h, bright gold patina, etched surface, artichoke pattern on platform base and shaft, supporting hinged and conforming gilt metal ash receiver bowl, base imp "Tiffany Studios New York 1651" 1,035.00
Inkstand, 9-3/4" x 10-3/4", gilt bronze, Zodiac, etched gold patina, partner's type, hinged cover, compartmented integrated undertray, imp "Tiffany Studios New York 1073"...............920.00
Lamp Base
10" h, model #201, pumpkin base, translucent etched brown amber eight ribbed glass body, eight conforming metal legs, opal favrile glass curved inserts, rim fitted with four shade support arms spaced by twelve integrated opal glass jewels 9,200.00
22" h, amphora-shaped 10" red Cypriote favrile glass shaft, mottled irid red, yellow, and blue surface cased to opal white, inscribed "Louis C. Tiffany Favrile" at side, two socket gilt bronze Cassidy lamp fittings 1,725.00
Memo Book Cover, 4-5/8" x 7-5/8", gilded, inlaid abalone shell, imp "Tiffany Studios, New York" 300.00
Paper Rack, 12" l, 8" h, Chinese pattern, dark patina, some green wash in pattern recesses, three-tier letter holder, imp "Tiffany Studios New York 1756," some metal corrosion 260.00

Glass

Basket, 10" h, pedestaled parfait base, flared rim folded and applied with ambergris transparent basket handle, base inscribed "L.C.T. Favrile 1849"....................................1,955.00
Bonbon, 6" d, 1-3/4" h, gold amber bowl, three applied shell feet, intaglio cut leaf border, inscribed "L. C. Tiffany, Favrile" 865.00
Bowl
4-1/4" d, 2-1/2" h, squared dimpled form, transparent aquamarine, foot inscribed "L. C. Tiffany Favrile," one numbered V493, price for pr...490.00
4-1/2" d, 2-1/2" h, ten ribbed transparent pale green jar form, irid gold int., inscribed "L. C. T. H1802," stained int.320.00
6-1/4" d, 2-1/2" h, irid gold, eight rib scalloped body, inscribed "L.C.T." 435.00
Candlestick, 6-3/4" h, heavy walled amber stick, ten prominent swirled ribs on shaft, fine gold luster, inscribed "L.C.T." and labeled...400.00

Compote, irid blue, mkd "1710/L.C. Tiffany, Favrile," 8" d, 4-1/2" h, $1,200.

6-1/2" d, 3" h, folded flared rim on half-round, bright purple lustered int., blue irid ext., inscribed "L. C. Tiffany Inc." Favrile, numbered 42233M and 8169M, price for pr 1,500.00
12-1/2" d, 4-1/4" h, 10 ribbed flared and scalloped favrile bowl with opal ext., emerald green int. stretched and irid at flared rim, base inscribed "L. C. Tiffany Favrile," some int. wear 865.00

Clock, 12" w, 14" h, archtectonic structure of alabaster, center multicolored geometric and curvilinear motif glass segments, dial inscribed "Tiffany & Co.," wooden clock frame with Chelsea keywind movement 20,700.00

Compote
6-1/4" d, 6" h, optic 10 ribbed scalloped bowl, tapered stem, folded foot, lustrous purple-blue surface, inscribed "L.C.T. Favrile 1725," gold foil label 1,036.00
8" d, 4-1/2" d, flared bowl, baluster stem, disk foot, bright purple lustrous color stretched at edges, base inscribed "L. C. Tiffany Inc. Favrile 1710" 1,200.00
9-1/4" d, 2-3/4" h, molded diamond quilted pattern on flared pastel opal bowl, dark gold amber int., stretched irid luster tinted pink, ftd pedestal base inscribed "L. C. Tiffany Inc. Favrile 1561" 635.00

Flower Bowl, 7-1/4" d, 2-3/4" h, cornflower blue rolled rim, white opal bowl, internally dec in molded herringbone leaf design, unsigned 920.00

Medallion, 2-3/4" d, end of World War I commemorative pressed Favrile glass medallion, spread wing eagle perched on Liberty Bell, ocean background above "Victory 1918" ribbon, gilt metal frame 800.00

Tile
4" x 4", press molded irid blue glass, stylized blossom motif, imp "Patent Applied For," small chip 375.00
17" x 18", architectural, square stylized geometric inlaid with opal, green, and gold glass tiles, jewels, and tesserae 1,840.00

Vase
2" h, 2-1/2" w, bean pot shake, two pulled handles, pale oyster white shading to vaseline, sgd "L.C.T" 575.00
3-1/4" h, 2-1/2" w, double shoulder, rim top, bright gold, purple highlights, jade green pulled feather, sgd "L.C.T.," #2413 .... 1,250.00
4-1/2" h, golden-brown bulbous oval body cased to opal white favrile glass, swirling pulled feather medial design, inscribed "L. C. T. Y2284" 1,610.00

4-3/4" h, strong shouldered colorless crystal body, applied purple blossoms, green leaf pads, intaglio cut and carved in blossom laden scrolls and swags, base inscribed "L. C. T. L342" 2,530.00
5" h
Cased, red to yellow, translucent body, five elongated oval quilted depressions, base inscribed "L. C. T. 1097A" 4,320.00
Millefiore, gold oval body, green heart-shaped leaves on amber vines, subtle white millefiore canes in blossom form, base inscribed "L. C. Tiffany Favrile 4927G" 1,150.00
5" h, 7-1/2" d, squat three-layered body, opal and ambergris favrile, five gold and green coiled feather elements, distressed irid surface, base pontil inscribed "L.C.T. Favrile 1972" 1,150.00
5-1/2" h, honey brown ftd oval, lined in irid opal white, gold irid border, stretched ruffled rim, imp "L. C. Tiffany Favrile 8719G" 3,740.00
5-3/4" h, teal blue oval body lined in opal white glass, smooth matte lustrous surface, inscribed "L. C. Tiffany Favrile 1753E" 750.00
6" h, swelled baluster, dark emerald green favrile with aventurine flecks, black irid surface dec by silver-gold lustered double chain matching rim wrap above, inscribed "L. C. Tiffany Favrile" 2,875.00
7" h, paperweight-type, baluster, aquamarine favrile glass cased to bright irid red-orange dec internally with six red centered white dogwood blossoms and green leaves, base inscribed "L.C. Tiffany Favrile 5779C," chips on button pontil 5,465.00
7-1/4" h, elongated bulbous body, 10 prominent ribs below flattened rim, gold irid, inscribed "L. C. Tiffany Favrile 9356M1835" 520.00
7-3/4" h, oval form, dark mahogany red cased to lime yellow int., smooth glossy surface, base inscribed "L. C. T. Favrile" 1,160.00
8" h, slender flared trumpet, purple favrile, blue irid luster, inscribed "L. C. Tiffany Favrile 6219K" 920.00
9" h
Bulbed oval, chimney-form, 16 subtle vertical ribs, dark translucent blue, inscribed "L. C. T. Favrile" 920.00
Tapered cylinder, Cypriote, metallic inclusions, rough textured surface, golden purple luster, imp "L. C. Tiffany Favrile 8500" 1,610.00
10-1/4" h, floriform, ribbed amber glass blossom, stretched gold luster, bulbed stem, disk foot inscribed "L. C. T. Favrile 1268A" 2,530.00
12" h, elongated oval 18 ribbed amber bud vase, applied disk foot, inscribed "L. C. Tiffany Inc. Favrile S-7496 N-1547," paper label 865.00
13" h, elongated oval amber body, 10 prominent vertical ribs, fine gold luster, base inscribed "L. C. Tiffany Inc. Favrile 1093 6030 M," slight int. stain 1,035.00
15" h, flared conical irid gold glass insert mkd "L. C. T," ribbed bronze pedestal foot, imp "Louis C. Tiffany Furnaces Inc. 160" 865.00

Wine, 3-1/2" d, 5" h, transparent amber stem, gold irid luster, inscribed "L. C. T." and "N8639," "N8623," "8630," and "8642," price for 6 pc set 980.00

Lamp

Candle
6-1/2" h, 7" d w, bronze and turtleback, Favrile glass, Gimbal-style, adjustable ball-form candleholder, dark irid leaded glass segments affixed to dark patinated bronze framework, bobeche designed to hold shade, imp "Tiffany Studios," early logo, shade and candlesnuffer missing 8,100.00

13" h, gold irid diamond patterned shade mkd "L. C. T.," single socket electrolier, nine green glass jewel inserts in candlecup, bronze base imp "Tiffany Studios New York 1810," worn dark patina, converted 3,450.00

Ceiling, 16" h, 14" d leaded turtleback shade, scalloped, beaded rim, fiery golden translucent leaded curving segments, intricate arrangement ending in hinged "trap door" framing opalescent glass turtleback, orig hooks on rim attach to bronze beaded chain, single-socket ceiling mount 8,050.00

Chandelier, 30" h, Moorish, arched bronze ceiling mount supports twisted wire double ring suspending bronze beading, decorative balls, and six sockets with gold irid ribbed favrile glass shades, each inscribed "L. C. T.," center medial drop with triple bulbed matching shade marked "L. C. Tiffany Favrile" at rim, adjustable 18,400.00

Desk

10" h, Lily, floriform white shade, green leaf dec, rim inscribed "L. C. T," Queen Anne's lace platform base, single crookneck stem, base imp "Tiffany Studios New York D674," TG&D Co. logo 3,335.00

14" h, Nautilus, natural shell shade with silver trim, dark bronze adjustable split shaft on ribbed platform base, five ball feet, imp "Tiffany Studios New York 403" 3,450.00

Floor, 56" h, 10" d gold Favrile shade, #425, standard with six buds form circular bronze base with gold/brown patina, eight scrolled feet, damage to standard near bud closes to shade 2,950.00

Table

19" h, 16" d dome shade, Dogwood, leaded favrile glass segments arranged as yellow centered pink and white flowers, buds, and green leaves, diachronic and mottled glass interspersed, rim imp "Tiffany Studios New York 1446-5," dark bronze converted fluid lamp base with swirl motif on foot and base, three integrated shall ribbed supports, base imp "25778" 20,700.00

Serving Tray, scroll and lozenge border, copper inlay of shell design on front with central LCT monogram, back inscribed "Tiffany & Co. Makers, 12037, 927 silver and copper inlay, made special for Charles Stanford," 13-3/4" d, 39 oz., $3,100. Photo courtesy of Freeman\Fine Arts.

24" h, 16" d leaded favrile glass dome shade, Pansy Blossoms, clusters of multicolored pansies in purples, opalescent, yellow, orange, red, and mottled combinations, green background, rim imp "Tiffany Studios New York 1448," converted urn-form fluid lamp base, held by three curved legs ending in paw feet, platform, and font imp "Tiffany Studios New York 190," socket replaced 24,150.00

25" h, 18" d raised pagoda rim on dome shade, Tyler, swirling medial band of orange and yellow Tyler motif, honey amber arched arrow border, green, green-amber, and green slag background, wide bronze border rim tagged "Tiffany Studios New York," orig finish converted fluid lamp base, three-arm spider, 12 organic blossoms forms repeated on font and base, font imp "Tiffany Studios New York 25780," TG&D Co logo 13,800.00

28" h, 32" d, Zodiac six round green turtlebacks centrally spaced against diachronic blue reserves framed by green segments, interspersed with twelve gilt cut-out signs of the zodiac depicted in favrile glass leaded segments, imp at rim "Tiffany Studios New York," raised on bright gold bronze twisted stem lamp shaft with integrated platform foot...68,500.00

Silver

Basket, 12" d, reticulated, swing handle, #3908/69, monogrammed, mkd "Made for Tiffany & Co." 800.00

Beaker, 3-3/4" h, flared rim, reeded foot, 4 oz....................100.00

Bowl

7-1/4" d, lobed side, circular base, mkd "Tiffany & Co.," 17 oz., 8 dwt 400.00

9" d, circular, plain, circular foot, mkd "Tiffany & Co.," 24 oz. 650.00

Cake Dish, 10-1/2" d, shaped circular, gadrooned and reeded rim, circular foot, c1925..450.00

Child's Set, 4" d bowl, 6-3/16" d tray, acid etched Noah's Ark and animal borders, engraved name, 1907, 15 troy oz. 750.00

Desk Set, blotter holders, pen tray, inkwell, clipper, and paper clip holder, pierced grapevine dec, caramel and white slag glass liners..1,200.00

Dish, 8" d, circular, reeded rim, center monogram, 10 oz., 8 dwt 175.00

Flatware Service, Hamilton pattern, 60 pc set, monogrammed, 81 oz., 2 dwt 2,000.00

Pitcher, 8-1/2" h, c1880, bombe, repousse allover flowers and leaves, fine stippled ground, spout and rim repousse with acanthus, 31 oz., 6 dwt 3,000.00

Salver

10-1/4" d, 1891-1902, circular, floral and scroll repousse border, four paw feet issuing from scrolls, 20 oz., 2 dwt 400.00

12" d, reproduction orig by Robert Abercromby, London, 1735, circular, pie crust edge, four hoof feet, central monogrammed armorial, 27 oz., 2 dwt..............................900.00

Serving Fork, Wave Edge pattern, 3 oz., 4 dwt..................150.00

Tea and Coffee Service, made by Moore, c1860, coffeepot, 16" h kettle on stand with four hoof feet and later dated burner, teapot, two-handled cov sugar, creamer, waste bowl, compressed ovoid, allover applied leaves and berries, fine stippled ground, hinged cov, finial, angular handle, applied foliate and berries on circular foot, 217 oz. 12,000.00

Tray

13" d, plain circular, reeded rim, c1923, 27 oz., 8 dwt 750.00

18" d, plain oval, reeded rim, 38 oz..........................1,100.00

TIFFIN GLASS

History: A. J. Beatty & Sons built a glass manufacturing plant in Tiffin, Ohio, in 1888. On Jan. 1, 1892, the firm joined the U. S. Glass Co. and was known as factory R. Fine-quality Depression-era items were made at this high-production factory.

From 1923 to 1936, Tiffin produced a line of black glassware called Black Satin. The company discontinued operation in 1980.

Marks: Beginning in 1916, wares were marked with a paper label.

References: Fred Bickenheuser, *Tiffin Glassmasters*, Book I (1979), Book II (1981), Book III (1985), Glassmasters Publications; Bob Page and Dale Fredericksen, *Tiffin is Forever*, Page-Fredericksen, 1994; Jerry Gallagher and Leslie Piña, *Tiffin Glass*, Schiffer Publishing, 1996.

Collectors' Club: Tiffin Glass Collectors Club, P.O. Box 554, Tiffin, OH 44883.

Ashtray, Twilight, cloverleaf
   3", #9123-96 ....25.00
   5", #9123-97 ....45.00
Basket
   Emerald Green, #15151, satin, 7" 55.00
   Satin, #9574, sky blue, 6" 45.00
   Twilight, 9" h, 5-1/2" w 295.00
Bowl, Twilight, ftd, wishbone, 6-1/2" 135.00
Bud Vase
   Cherokee Rose, 8" h 45.00
   Fuchsia, 10" h 45.00
   Isabella, 10" h 195.00
   June Night, 10-1/2" h 45.00
Candelabrum, #5831, crystal, pr 38.00
Candlesticks, #5902, double, pr
   Cherokee Rose 135.00
   Fuchsia 125.00
   June Night 125.00
   Williamsburg 75.00
Candy Jar, cov, Emerald Green, satin, 10" h 65.00
Cake Plate, Jack Frost, canary yellow, handle, 9-1/2" d 65.00
Centerpiece, Fontaine, green, slight use 85.00
Champagne
   Byzantine, crystal 18.00
   Consul, #17679 ....18.00
   Flanders, crystal 14.75
   June Night 22.50
Claret
   Twilight, panel optic, 2-1/2 oz 28.00
   Wisteria, #17477 ....25.00
Cocktail
   Byzantine, crystal 14.00
   Cherokee Rose, #17399 ....16.00
   Flanders, crystal 22.00
   June Night 28.00
   Persian Pheasant, crystal, #15083 ....22.50
Compote
   Cherokee Rose, ball stem 115.00
   Emerald Green, satin, 4-3/4" 35.00
   Persian Pheasant, crystal, blown, 6" 85.00
Cordial
   Byzantine, crystal 32.50
   Flanders, crystal 150.00
   Fontaine, #15033, green, crystal 35.00

Fuchsia, #15083 ....45.00
June Night 45.00
Queen Astrid, crystal 35.00
Cream Soup
   Flanders, pink 45.00
   La Fleure, yellow 40.00
Creamer and Sugar
   Cherokee Rose, beaded 60.00
   Flanders, yellow 225.00
Cup and Saucer
   Flanders, yellow 100.00
   Fontaine, twilight, blown 125.00
Dahlia Vase, Black Satin, 8" h, gold dec 125.00
Flower Basket, Open, #6553, blue and crystal, 13" 165.00
Fruit Bowl, Open Work, line #310, sky blue, 12" d 75.00
Goblet
   Draped Nude, satin stem 150.00
   Festival, #17640 ....24.00
   June Night, crystal 32.00
   Line #011, crystal, green stem, wheel cut 38.00
   Psyche, #15106, crystal, green stem 45.00
   Shamrock, dark green 22.00
   Thistle 22.00
   Twilight, #17492 ....35.00
   Wisteria, #17477 ....27.00
Iced Tea Tumbler, ftd, green, crystal
   Flying Nun 60.00
   Fontaine, #15033 ....33.00
Juice Tumbler, ftd
   Byzantine, crystal 16.00
   June Night 25.00
Martini Jug, Twilight, 11-1/2" 450.00
Pitcher
   Flanders 350.00
   Threaded Optic, cornflower blue, 4-3/4" h, 32 oz. pitcher crystal handle, four 2-5/8" 4 oz. tumblers 95.00

Paperweight, Standing Elephant, controlled bubbles, Twilight core, 6-1/2" h, $475.

Plate
  Byzantine, crystal, 8-1/2" d 7.50
  Cadena, yellow, dinner 45.00
  Classic, dinner, 10-1/2" d 125.00
  Flanders, crystal, diner 195.00
  June Night, 8" d 9.75
  Juno, yellow, 9-1/2" d..40.00
Relish
  Cherokee Rose
       6-1/2" d, round, 3 part..47.50
       12"...80.00
  June Night, 12", 3 part...80.00
Salt Shaker, June Night 85.00
Sherbet
  Flanders, crystal, high...28.00
  Fontaine, #15033, rose pink 33.00
  Forever Yours, #17507 ....8.00
  Pink, #15018, wire optic, high 36.00
  Wisteria, #17477...18.00
Sherry, June Night, 2 oz. 45.00
Sweet Pea Vase, Swedish Modern, Copen Blue and crystal, 7" h
  ....58.00
Tumbler, Wide Optic, #017, rose pink, 4-3/4", 9-1/2 oz., ftd
  ....18.00
Vase
  Black Satin, 10" h, U. S. Glass sticker 45.00
  Modern, yellow, ball shaped, Saturn optic 50.00
Wine
  Byzantine, crystal 22.50
  Flanders, crystal 90.00
  Fontaine, #15033, 1-1/2 oz
       Green, crystal 38.00
       Rose Pink..38.00
  Thistle 17.00
  Twilight, #17507...38.00

TILES

History: The use of decorat-
ed tiles peaked during the
latter part of the 19th century.
More than 100 companies in
England alone were produc-
ing tiles by 1880. By 1890,
companies had opened in
Belgium, France, Australia,
Germany, and the United
States.

Tiles were not used only as fireplace adornments.
Many were installed into furniture, such as washstands,
hall stands, and folding screens. Since tiles were easily
cleaned and, hence, hygienic, they were installed on the
floors and walls of entry halls, hospitals, butcher shops,
or any place where sanitation was a concern. Many public buildings and subways also employed tiles to add interest and beauty.

References: Susan and Al Bagdade, *Warman's American Pottery and Porcelain*, Wallace-Homestead, 1994; –
—, *Warman's English & Continental Pottery & Porcelain*,
2nd ed., Wallace-Homestead, 1991; Ralph and Terry
Kovel, *Kovels' American Art Pottery*, Crown Publishers,
1993; Ralph Moore and Dinah Tanner, *Porcelain & Pottery Tea Tiles*, Antique Publications, 1994; Richard and
Hilary Myers, *William Morris Tiles*, Richard Dennis (distributed by Antique Collectors' Club), 1996; David Rago,

American Art Pottery, Knickerbocker Press, 1997; Ronald
L. Rindge et al., *Ceramic Art of the Malibu Potteries*, Malibu Lagoon Museum, 1994.

Periodical: *Flash Point*, P.O. Box 1850, Healdsburg, CA
95448.

Collectors' Club: Tiles & Architectural Ceramics Society, Ironbridge Gorge Museum, Ironbridge, Telford,
Shropshire, England.

Notes: Condition is an important factor in determining
price. A cracked, badly scuffed and scratched, or heavily
chipped tile has very little value. Slight chipping around
the outer edges of a tile is, at times, considered acceptable by collectors, especially if these chips can be covered by a frame.

It is not uncommon for the highly glazed surface of
some tiles to have become crazed. Crazing is not considered detrimental as long as it does not detract from the
overall appearance of the tile.

Advertising
  Baker's Chocolate, 6-1/4" sq, lady carrying serving tray, blue,
       white, yellow, green, and lavender, tan ground, Grueby
       ....365.00
  Northwestern Terra Cotta Works, 4" x -1/4", detailed, rough
       corners...250.00
American Encaustic Tiling Co., Zanesville, OH
  4-1/4" sq, white, black design of horseman riding through
       brush...45.00
  6" sq, Cherub band, highly emb, brown.........................175.00
  6" sq, Ulysses Grant bust, peacock green glaze, framed
       ....300.00

**Claycraft from CA, Aztec design, brown, blue, and green, imp
mark, 1920, $48.**

Art Pottery
 6" h, 12" w, landscape with birds and moose in foreground, dark green high gloss glaze 175.00
 6" h, 12" w, landscape with moose, dark green high gloss glaze 175.00
Batchelder, 6" sq, imp bird design, blue ground, imp mark, price for pr 175.00
California Art
 5-3/4" sq, landscape, tan and green 65.00
 7-1/2" x 11-1/2", peacock and grapes, multicolored 145.00
Cambridge Art Tile, Covington, KY, 6" x 18"
 Goddess and Cherub, amber, pr 250.00
 Night and Morning, pr 500.00
J. & J. G. Low, Chelsea, MA
 4-1/4" sq, putti carrying grapes, blue, pr........................75.00
 6" d, circular, yellow, minor edge nicks and glaze wear .35.00
 6" sq, woman wearing hood, brown 95.00
 6-1/8" x 4-1/2", rect, blue-green, woman, titled "Autumn"
 ....90.00
KPM, 5-3/4" x 3-3/8", portrait of monk, titled "Hieronymous of Ferrara sends this image to the prophet to God," small nicks to corners..245.00
Marblehead, 4-5/8" sq, ships, blue and white, pr..............125.00
Minton China Works
 6" sq, Aesops Fables, Fox and Crow, black and white ...75.00
 6" sq, Cows crossing stream, brown and cream............85.00
 6" x 12", wild roses, polychrome slip dec........................50.00
 8" sq, Rob Roy, Waverly Tales, brown and cream 95.00
Minton Hollins & Co.
 6" sq, urn and floral relief, green ground........................45.00
 8" sq, Morning, blue and white 100.00
Mosaic Tile Co., Zanesville, OH
 6" sq, Fortune and the Boy, polychrome 80.00
 8" sq, Delft windmill, blue and white, framed 55.00
Pardee, C.
 4-1/4" sq, chick and griffin, blue-green matte 175.00
 6" sq, portrait of Grover Cleveland, gray-lavender........125.00
Providential Tile Works, Trenton, N.J., round, stove type, hold in center, flowered...20.00
Rookwood, 5-3/4" d, circular, seagulls in flight, two colors, 1943
 ....75.00
Sherwin & Cotton
 6" sq, dog head, brown, artist sgd 100.00
 6" x 12", Quiltmaker and Ledger, orange, pr 145.00
Trent, 6" sq, head of Michelangelo, sea green glaze, sgd by Isaac Broome, imp mark 115.00
U. S. Encaustic Tile Works, Indianapolis, IN
 6" sq, wreath, flowered, emb, light green.......................20.00
 6" x 18", panel, Dawn, green, framed 150.00
Wedgwood, England
 6" sq, Red Riding Hood, black and white......................110.00
 6" sq, calendar, November, boy at seashore, peacock blue
 ....95.00
 8" sq, Tally Ho, man riding horse, blue and white 85.00

TINWARE

History: Beginning in the 1700s, many utilitarian household objects were made of tin. Because it is nontoxic, rust resistant, and fairly durable, tin can be used for storing food; and because it was cheap, tinware and tin-plated wares were in the price range of most people. It often was plated to iron to provide strength.

An early center of tinware manufacture in the United States was Berlin, Connecticut, but almost every small town and hamlet had its own tinsmith, tinner, or whitesmith. Tinsmiths used patterns to cut out the pieces, hammered and shaped them, and soldered the parts. If a piece was to be used with heat, a copper bottom was added because of the low melting point of tin. The industrial revolution brought about machine-made, mass-produced tinware pieces. The handmade era had ended by the late 19th century.

References: Dover Stamping Co., *1869 Illustrated Catalog*, Astragal Press, 1994 reprint; Marilyn E. Dragowick (ed.), *Metalwares Price Guide*, Antique Trader Books, 1995; John Player, *Origins and Craft of Antique Tin & Tole*, Norwood Publishing, 1995 (available from Christie & Christie Assoc., P.O. Box 392, Cookstown, Ontario, Canada LOL 1LO).

Museum: Cooper-Hewitt Museum, New York, NY.

Additional Listings: See Advertising; Kitchen Collectibles; Lanterns; Lamps and Lighting; and Tinware, Decorated.

Note: This category is a catchall for tin objects, which do not fit into other categories in this book.

Candle Box, 14-1/2" h, cylindrical, hanging, some battering
 ....220.00
Candle Mold
 5-1/43" h, four tube, half mold, ear handle, light rust 310.00
 10-1/2" h, 14-3/4" l, 48 tubes, ear handle, curved foot, minor separation of end seams in top gallery 470.00
 11-1/4" h, eight tubes, curved feet, ear handle 315.00

Candle mold, rect dished top, 10 tapering cylindrical molds, applied ring and applied strap handle, bracket base, 10-3/4" h, PA, 19th C, $435. Photo courtesy of Sotheby's.

Candle Sconce
  9-1/2" d, round reflector with 3-D stamped cutouts in bright tin under glass, two socket candle arm soldered in place 1,815.00
  10-1/2" d, round reflector backs with mirror mosaic, slight damage to one, pr 990.00
  13-1/2" h, sunburst crest, star and two leaves, PA.....1,265.00
  14" h, raised vine and curved scalloped crest on back, slight rust 500.00
Candle Screen, 10" h, 10" w, girls with cats, painted in naturalistic colors, Victorian, 19th C, restorations, pr 1,610.00
Cheese Sieve, 6" h, heart shape, resoldered hanging ring 360.00
Cookie Cutter, eagle, 4" wing span 50.00
Foot Warmer, 8" x 9" x 5-3/4" h, punched panels in circle and heart design, mortised wood frame with traces of red paint, turned corner posts......200.00
Lamp
  Grease, 1-5/8" h, colorful glaze 165.00
  Petticoat, 4" h, orig whale oil burner, orig black paint 65.00
  Skater's, 6-3/8" h, light teal-green globe 225.00
Lantern
  7-5/8" h, mkd "Dietz Scout" 75.00
  9-1/2" h, font with single spout burner, clear pressed paneled globe, ring handle 195.00
Match Box, 2-1/2" h, English post office dec, ivory socket 90.00
Muffin Pan, heart shaped wells 45.00
Roaster, 12" w, 9-1/4" h, hearth type 185.00
Sconce, 14" h, pr, candle, crimped circular crests............350.00

TINWARE, DECORATED

History: The art of decorating sheet iron, tin, and tin-coated sheet iron dates back to the mid-18th century. The Welsh called the practice pontypool; the French, töle peinte. In America, the center for tin-decorated ware in the late 1700s was Berlin, Connecticut.

Several styles of decorating techniques were used: painting, japanning, and stenciling. Designs were done by both professionals and itinerants. English and Oriental motifs strongly influenced both form and design.

A special type of decoration was the punch work on unpainted tin practiced by the Pennsylvania tinsmiths. Forms included coffeepots, spice boxes, and grease lamps.

Reference: Marilyn E. Dragowick (ed), *Metalwares Price Guide*, Antique Trader Books, 1995.

Apple Tray, 13-1/4" l, painted dec, attributed to PA, 19th C 920.00
Box, 4-7/8" l, blue japanning, yellow striping, silver stenciling 50.00
Bread Tray, 12-3/4" l, oblong, painted fruit and leaf motif border, brown ground 19th C......3,100.00
Canister, 5-1/2" d, 4-3/4" h, red, green, and yellow floral dec, white band, orig alligatored dark brown japanning.......410.00
Chamberstick, 6-1/2" d, orig dark brown japanning, red, green, yellow, and white floral dec, wear at base 1,705.00
Chocolate Pot, 10-1/2" h, painted dec, inscribed "Lizzie Lefever 1875" 1,600.00
Coffeepot, 11" h, punched dec, potted tulip design above double twisted band, hinged lid with brass finial, PA, early 19th C 1,425.00

Coffepot, tapered body, hinged dome lid, pointed ball finial, strap handle, tapering projecting spout, dec on one side with solider with plumed hat holding a sword, bird, and tulips, revere dec with wing-spread American eagle, flag, and tulips below swags and tassels, lid with initials "AC" and tulips and leaves, serpent dec on handle, PA, c1810, lacks finger grip under handle, old repairs to base, 9-1/2" h, $13,800. Photo courtesy of Sotheby's.

Document Box, 12-1/2" w, 6" d, 7-1/2" h, black ground, red and yellow dec, domed hinged lid, top brass handle 470.00
Foot Warmer, punched diamonds and circles
  6-3/4" x 8-1/2", mortised hardwood case, turned corner posts, old cherry finish 150.00
  12-1/2" x 15", mortised cherry frame, turned corner posts 375.00
Lantern, pierced, 14" h, fitted handle holder on outside 150.00
Mug, 5-5/8" h, red, yellow, green, and white oval stylized floral design, orig brown japanning......625.00
Needle Case, 9" l, red and yellow stylized foliage dec, orig dark brown japanning......120.00
Spice Caddy, 3-3/4" x 5-1/2", orig brown japanning, yellow stripe, six canisters 110.00
Tea Caddy, 4" h, orig dark brown japanning, floral dec, white band, mismatched lid......125.00
Tray, 30" l, capriccio amidst ruins, Continental, early 19th C 1,955.00
Wall Pocket, 7-3/4" h, punched heart design 250.00

TOBACCO CUTTERS

History: Before pre-packaging, tobacco was delivered to merchants in bulk form. Tobacco cutters were used to cut the tobacco into desired sizes.

Brown's Mule, iron, counter top......65.00
Climax, 17" l......60.00
Cupples, Arrow & Superb......50.00
Drummond Tobacco C......75.00
John Finzer & Brothers, Louisville, KY......50.00
Griswold Tobacco Cutter, Erie, PA......70.00
Keen Kutter, E. C. Simmons 225.00
Lorillards Chew Climax Plus, brass, Penn Hardware Co., Reading, PA 100.00

Sprague Warner & Co. 75.00
Unmarked, graduated 6-1/4" to 7-1/2" w, 10-/12" l, cast iron cutter,
    wood base 45.00

TOBACCO JARS

History: A tobacco jar is a container for storing tobacco. Tobacco humidors were made of various materials and in many shapes, including figurals. The earliest jars date to the early 17th century; however, most examples seen in the antiques market today were made in the late 19th or early 20th centuries.

Collectors' Club: Society of Tobacco Jar Collectors, 6370 Kirby Ridge Cove, Memphis, TN 38119.

Bear with beehive, 6-1/2" h, majolica, Continental 770.00
Black Boy, red hat with tassel, majolica, repainted, nicks
    ....275.00
Bull Dog, porcelain, German 275.00
Creamware, 9" h, 6" d, plum colored transfers on side, one titled "Success to the British Fleet," striped orange, blue, and yellow molding, domed lid..900.00
Dog's Head, with pipe and green hat and collar, majolica, professional repairs 165.00
Dwarf in Sack, 8" h, terra cotta, multicolor dec, mkd "JM3478," chips, wear 255.00
Girl on side, pipe on lid, majolica, Continental.....................75.00
Indian, 5-1/2" h, black, majolica 330.00
Jasperware, raised white Indian chief on cov, Indian regalia on front, green ground..195.00
Mandarin, papier-mâché...95.00
Man with Pipe, large bow tie, with match holder and striker, rim chips, hairline 165.00
Man with Top Hat, majolica, Sarreguemines, hairline in base
    ....165.00
Moose, porcelain, Austrian..200.00
Owl, 11" h, majolica, brown, yellow glass eyes 825.00
Skull, mkd "Carlsbad, Austria" 175.00
Toby Type, Shorter and Sons..55.00
Wavecrest, 5" sq, white opaque body, SP fittings..............450.00

Dog's head, green hunting cap, pipe in mouth, multicolored, high glaze, 5" h, $195.

TOBY JUGS

History: Toby jugs are drinking vessels that usually depict a full-figured, robust, genial drinking man. They originated in England in the late 18th century. The term "Toby" probably is related to the character Uncle Toby from *Tristram Shandy* by Laurence Sterne.

Reference: Susan and Al Bagdade, *Warman's English & Continental Pottery & Porcelain*, 2nd ed., Wallace-Homestead, 1991.

Additional Listings: Royal Doulton.

REPRODUCTION ALERT

During the last 100 years or more, tobies have been copiously reproduced by many potteries in the United States and England.

Delft, 11-1/4" h, man seated on barrel, green hat, green and black sponged coat, blue and yellow pants, old cork stopper, c19th C 365.00
Minton, 11-1/4" h, majolica, Quaker man and woman, polychrome dec, imp mark, pr 4,600.00
Portobello Pottery, 10" h, standing, spatter enamel dec, orig cov, c1840..275.00
Pratt
    9-1/4" h, pearlware glaze, typical blue, brown, and ochre palette, hat inset, small chips 425.00
    10-3/4" h, Hearty Good Fellow, blue jacket, yellow-green vest, blue and yellow striped pants, blue and ochre sponged base and handle, stopper missing, slight glaze wear, c1770-80..1,500.00
Royal Doulton
    6-1/2" h, stoneware, blue coat, double XX, Harry Simson
        ....395.00
    7" h, Baccachus, wreath of grapes and leaves on head, twisted vine handle 95.00
Staffordshire
    9" h, pearlware, seated figure, sponged blue jacket, ochre buttons, ochre and lavender speckled vest and trousers, brown hair and hat, green glazed base, shallow flake inside hat rim, attributed to Ralph Wood, c1770-80 ....1,950.00
    9-1/4" h, Martha Gunn, translucent brown and ochre glazes, pearl body, brim repaired at hairline 1,265.00
    9-1/4" h, Thin Man, full chair, green, blue and brown, holding pipe and foaming mug, attributed to Ralph Wood, c1765-75 ....5,000.00
    9-3/4" h, mottled and translucent glazes, cream colored body, small foot rim chips..460.00
    10-1/2" h, King Charles Spaniel, enamel dec, restored hat, late 19th C 275.00
    10-3/4" h, cat, enameled dec, holding letter, restored hat, late 19th C 300.00
    11-3/4" h, Rodent's Sailor, black hat, green coat, white trousers with blue stripes, imp "65," on base, Ralph Wood, lid missing, c1765-75 ....5,900.00
Whieldon, 9-1/2" h, pearlware, seated figure, yellow greatcoat, green vest, blue trousers, holding brow jug in left hand, raises foaming glass of ale towards mouth, lid missing, c1770-80
    ....1,600.00
Wilkinson
    10" h, Marshall Joffre, modeled by Sir Francis Carruthers Gould, titled "75mm Ce que joffre," printed mark, c1918, hat brim restored 345.00

Old Staffo, Shorter & Son, Ltd., Staffordshire, 5-3/8" h, $65.

10-3/4" h, Field Marshall Haig, modeled by Sir Francis Carruthers Gould, titled "Push and Go," printed marks, c1917 ....460.00
11-3/4" h, Marshall Foch, modeled by Sir Francis Carruthers Gould, titled "Au Diable Le Kaiser," printed marks, c1918 ....345.00
11-3/4" h, Winston Churchill, multicolored, designed by Clarice Cliff, black printed marks, number and facsimile signature, c1940..825.00
Yorkshire-Type, 7-3/4" h, caryatid form handle, Pratt palette dec, sponged base and hat brim int. 750.00

TOOLS

History: Before the advent of the assembly line and mass production, practically everything required for living was handmade at home or by a local tradesman or craftsman. The cooper, the blacksmith, the cabinet maker, and the carpenter all had their special tools.

Early examples of these hand tools are collected for their workmanship, ingenuity, place of manufacture, or design. Modern-day craftsman often search out and use old hand tools in order to authentically recreate the manufacture of an object.

References: Ronald S. Barlow, *Antique Tool Collector's Guide to Value*, Windmill Publishing (2147 Windmill View Rd., El Cajon, CA 92020), 3rd ed., 1991; Kenneth L. Cope, *American Machinist's Tools*, Astragal Press, 1993; Martin J. Donnelly, *Catalogue of Antique Tools*, published by author (31 Rumsey St., Bath, NY 14810), 1997; Garrett Hack, *The Handplane Book,* Taunton Press, 1997; Jerry & Elaine Heuring, *Keen Kutter Collectibles,* Collector Books, 1996; Herbert P. Kean and Emil S. Pollak, *Price Guide to Antique Tools*, Astragal Press, 1992; ——, *Collecting Antique Tools*, Astragal Press, 1990; Kathryn McNerney, *Antique Tools, Our American Heritage*, Collector Books, 1979, 1997 value update; Emil and Martyl Pollak, *Guide to American Wooden Planes and Their Makers*, 3rd ed., The Astragal Press, 1994; ——, *Prices Realized on Rare Imprinted American Wood Planes, 1979-1992*, Astragal Press, 1993; John Walter, *Antique & Collectible Stanley Tools, Guide to Identity & Value*, 2nd ed.., The Tool Merchant, 1996; John M. Whelan, *The Wooden Plane*, Astragal Press, 1993; Jack Wood, *Town-Country Old Tools*, 6th ed., L-W Book Sales, 1997.

Periodicals: *Fine Tool Journal*, P.O. Box 4001, Pittsford, VT 05763; *Plumb Line*, 10023 St. Clair's Retreat, Fort Wayne, IN 46825; *Stanley Tool Collector News*, 208 Front St., P.O. Box 227, Marietta, OH 45750; *Tool Ads*, P.O. Box 33, Hamilton, MT 59840.

Collectors' Clubs: Blow Torch Collectors Club, 3328 258th Ave. SE, Issaquah, WA 98027-9173; Collectors of Rare & Familiar Tools Society, 38 Colony Ct., Murray Hill, NJ 07974; Early American Industries Assoc., P.O. Box 2128, Empire State Plaza Station, Albany, NY 12220; Early American Industries-West, 8476 West Way Dr., La Jolla, CA 92038; Mid-West Tool Collectors Assoc., 808 Fairway Dr., Columbia, MO 65201; Missouri Valley Wrench Club, 613 N. Long St., Shelbyville, IL 62565; New England Tool Collectors Assoc., 303 Fisher Rd., Fitchburg, MA 01420; Ohio Tool Collectors Assoc., P.O. Box 261, London, OH 43140; Pacific Northwest Tool Collectors, 2132 NE 81st St., Seattle, WA 98115; Potomac Antique Tools & Industries Assoc., 6802 Newbitt Pl, McLean, VA 22101; Rocky Mountain Tool Collectors, 2024 Owens Ct., Denver, CO 80227; Society of Workers in Early Arts & Trades, 606 Lake Lena Blvd., Auburndale, FL 33823; Southwest Tool Collectors Assoc., 7032 Oak Bluff Dr., Dallas, TX 75240; Three Rivers Tool Collectors, 39 S. Rolling Hills, Irwin, PA 15642; Tool Group of Canada, 7 Tottenham Rd., Ontario MC3 2J3 Canada.

Museums: American Precision Museum Association, Windsor, VT; Mercer Museum, Doylestown, PA; Shelburne Museum, Shelburne, VT; World of Tools Museum, Waverly, TN.

SPECIAL AUCTION

Fine Tool Journal
27 Fickett Rd.
Pownal, ME 04069

Anvil, hand forged, 8" 60.00
Bench Press, Sherman, solid brass, 12 lbs, 9-1/2" x 6"........65.00
Clamp, wood, jaws, 13-1/2" l, pr..115.00

Bit brace, ultimatum type, brass framed ebony, maple, British, $400.

Chisel, blade stamped "E. Connor," 22-1/2" l 45.00
Cooper's Howel, L. & I. J. White, Buffalo, NY, No. 20, beechwood, 15" l 225.00
Drill
    Bow, ivory, brass, rosewood, Erlandsen type, 13" l 845.00
    Hand, Goodel and Pratt, brass ferrules..........................28.00
File, half round, 20" l 15.00
Hammer, claw type
    Iron, wood handle, c180....................................35.00
    Winchester...55.00
Key Hole Saw, British, 15-1/2" l 30.00
Level, wood and brass
    Davis & Cook, patent "Dec., 1886" 45.00
    Goodell-Pratt, brass bound mahogany, orig decal, 24" l
    ....225.00
Mallet, burl, hickory handle, 34" l..200.00
Marking Gauge, Stanley, Williams' Patent, patented May 26, 1857, 7" l 445.00
Mitre Box, laminated maple, birch, and oak, graduated quadrant, Stanley 45.00
Plane
    Keen Kutter, K110 ....40.00
    Ohio Tool Co., walnut, inscribed with carpenter's name, 9-1/2" l..20.00
    Pond, W. H., New Haven, CT, carriage maker's molding planes, 1840s, 7" l, 4 pc set 595.00
    Sandusky, 7/8" dado molding, No. 62, 9-1/2" l..............115.00
    Stanley, #10-1/2..120.00
    Varvill & Son, York, England, boxed bead molding planes, 9-1/2" l, 10 pc set 595.00
    Winchester Repeating Arms Co. No. 3208, smoothing, metallic, mahogany handles, 9" l......................................185.00
Pruning Knife, hand forged iron blade, wood handle, c1800
    ....35.00
Router, Stanley, #71-1/2", patent date 1901 ....40.00
Rule, Stanley, folding..20.00
Saw
    Band, mortised and pinned wood frame, orig red paint with blue and white striping, black and lade guides, laminated cherry and maple top, 76" 300.00
    Buck, wood, worn varnish finish, mkd "W. T. Banres," 30"
    ....45.00
    Dovetail, Hague, Clegg & Barton, brass back, 9" l 95.00
    Turning, W. Johnson, Newark, NJ, Richardson blade, 21" l
    ....165.00
Screwdriver, flat wood handle, round sides, 9" blade..........35.00
Scribe, curly maple adjustable fence and arm, 21" l...........75.00
Shoot Board, Stanley, No. 51/52, orig decal, 14" l 1,295.00
Square, cherry, iron, brass bound blade, mkd "Set Tray" ...50.00
Wheel Measure, wrought iron, 14-1/2" l................................45.00

TOOTHPICK HOLDERS

History: Toothpick holders, indispensable table accessories of the Victorian era, are small containers made specifically to hold toothpicks.

They were made in a wide range of materials: china (bisque and porcelain), glass (art, blown, cut, opalescent, pattern, etc.), and metals, especially silver plate. Makers include both American and European firms.

By applying a decal or transfer, a toothpick holder became a souvenir item; by changing the decal or transfer, the same blank could become a memento for any number of locations.

References: William Heacock, *Encyclopedia of Victorian Colored Pattern Glass*, Book I, 2nd ed., Antique Publications, 1976, 1992 value update; ——, *1,000 Toothpick Holders*, Antique Publications, 1977; ——, *Rare & Unlisted Toothpick Holders*, Antique Publications, 1984; National Toothpick Holders Collectors Society, *Toothpick Holders*, Antique Publications, 1992.

Collectors' Club: National Toothpick Holder Collectors, P.O. Box 246, Sawyer, MI 49221.

Additional Listings: See *Warman's Americana & Collectibles* for more examples.

Advisor: Judy Knauer.

Bisque, skull, blue anchor shape mark 65.00
China
    Meissen, clown..65.00
    Royal Bayreuth, elk...120.00
    Royal Doulton, Santa scene, green handles 75.00
    R. S. Germany, Schlegelmilch, MOP luster 40.00
Glass
    Amberina, DQ, sq top..350.00
    Cameo, Daum Nancy, winter scene, sgd.........750.00
    Cranberry, coralene beaded flowers............................285.00
    Cut, pedestal, chain of hobstars 145.00

Pomona glass, Flower & Pleat, first ground, yellow stain, 2-1/4" h, $250.

Milk
    Alligator, c1885..70.00
    Florette, turquoise..110.00
    Parrot and Top Hat, c1895 ....45.00
    Scroll, claw ftd, light pink and blue dec, c1900 ....555.00
Opalescent, Reverse Swirl, blue 85.00
Pattern Glass
    Daisy and Button, blue 75.00
    Delaware, rose stain, gold dec....................................175.00
    Florida, ruby amber 265.00
    Kansas...45.00
    Michigan, clear, yellow stain 175.00
    Spearpoint Band, ruby stained....................................195.00
    Texas, gold trim 50.00
    Truncated Cube, ruby stained.......................................75.00

TORTOISESHELL ITEMS

History: For many years, amber and mottled tortoiseshell has been used in the manufacture of small items such as boxes, combs, dresser sets, and trinkets.

Note: Anyone dealing in the sale of tortoiseshell objects should be familiar with the Endangered Species Act and Amendment in its entirety. As of November 1978, antique tortoiseshell objects can be legally imported and sold with some restrictions.

Box, cov
    3" d, circular, painted figure by riverscape, French, late 19th C, minor losses 488.00
    3-3/4" l, miniature painting with figures salvaging wrecked schooner, Continental, 18th C, losses....................1,380.00
Calligraphy Brush, tortoiseshell handle and cup, inscribed Chinese characters, horn tip, sable brush, Chinese, 19th C
    ....2,300.00
Calling Card Case, 4" x 3", MOP and ivory inlaid dec, c1825
    ....225.00
Eyeglass and Case, 5" l, rounded lens, worn ear pieces, case with rounded ends 175.00
Glove Box, 3-1/2" h, domed lid, ornate ivory strapping, sandalwood int. 375.00
Letter Opener, 12" l, silver fox head handle 245.00
Model, 8" l, ricksaw, hinged hood, spoked wheels, metal poles
    ....120.00
Patch Box, 2" l, rect, slightly domed lid, ivory trim 200.00
Pin Box, 3-1/2" w, silver corner dec, inscribed "Pin" on top
    ....225.00
Scent Bottle Case, 2-1/2" h, arched cov, convex front and back, Georgian 115.00
Snuff Box, 1-1/2" x 2", oval, silver dec 325.00
Tea Caddy, 7-3/4" w, serpentine, MOP panels, ivory trim and escutcheon, Regency 1,450.00
Violin Bow, gold and tortoiseshell mounted
    Tourte, Francois, c1800, round unstamped stick, tortoiseshell frog with pearl eye, gold adjuster with pearl eye, 59 grams, frog and adjuster not orig to bow 9,775.00
    Vignernon, Joseph Arthur, c1895, round stick faintly stamped "J. A. Vigneron A. Paris" at the butt, tortoiseshell frog with parisian eye, gold and ebony adjuster with pearl eye, 56 grams..10,925.00

TOYS

History: The first cast iron toys began to appear in America shortly after the Civil War. Leading 19th-century manufacturers include Hubley, Dent, Kenton, and Schoenhut. In the first decades of the 20th century, Arcade, Buddy L., Marx, and Tootsie Toy joined these earlier firms.

Wooden toys were made by George Brown and other manufacturers who did not sign or label thei work.

Nuremberg, Germany, was the European center for the toy industry from the late 18th through the mid-20th centuries. Companies such as Lehman and Marklin produced high-quality toys.

References: Linda Baker, *Modern Toys, American Toys*, Collector Books, 1985, 1993 value update; Bill Bruegman, *Toys of the Sixties*, Cap'n Penny Productions, 1991; Dana Cain, *Collecting Monsters of Film and TV,* Krause Publications, 1997; Jurgen and Marianne Cieslik, *Lehmann Toys*, New Cavendish Books, 1982; *Collector's Digest Price Guide to Pull Toys*, L-W Book Sales, 1996; Don Cranmer, *Collectors Encyclopedia, Toys–Banks*, L-W Books, 1986, 1993 value update; Charles F. Donovan Jr., *Renwal, World's Finest Toys*, published by author (11877 U.S. Hwy 431, Ohatchee, AL 36271), 1994; Elmer Duellman, *Elmer's Price Guide to Toys*, Vol. 2, L-W Book Sales, 1996; James L. Dundas, *Gap Guns with Values*, Schiffer Publishing, 1996; Edward Force, *Lledo Toys*, Schiffer Publishing, 1996; Tom Frey, *Toy Bop: Kid Classics of the 50s & 60s*, Fuzzy Dice Productions, 1994.

Christine Gentry and Sally Gibson-Downs, *Motorcycle Toys*, Collector Books, 1994; David C. Gould and Donna Crevar-Donaldson, *Occupied Japan Toys with Prices*, L-W Book Sales, 1993; Morton Hirschberg, *Steam Toys*, Schiffer Publishing, 1996; Andrew Gurka, *Pedal Car Restoration and Price Guide,* Krause Publications, 1996; Dee Hockenberry, *Big Bear Book*, Schiffer Publishing, 1996; Don Hultzman, *Collecting Battery Toys*, Books Americana, 1994; Ken Hutchison & Greg Johnson, *Golden Age of Automotive Toys, 1925-1941*, Collector Books, 1996; Charles M. Jacobs, *Kenton Cast Iron Toys*, Schiffer Publishing, 1996; Alan Jaffe, *J. Chein and Co., A Collector's Guide to an American Toymaker,* Schiffer Publishing, 1997; Dana Johnson, *Matchbox Toys 1947-1996*, 2nd ed., Collector Books, 1996; Dale Kelley, *Die Cast Price Guide, Post-War: 1946-Present,* Antique Trader Books, 1997 Lisa Kerr, *American Tin-Litho Toys*, Collectors Press, 1995; Constance King, *Metal Toys & Automata*, Chartwell Books, 1989; Sharon Korbeck, *Toys & Prices, 1998*, 5th ed., Krause Publications, 1997.

Cynthia Boris Liljeblad, *TV Toys and the Shows that Inspired Them*, Krause Publications, 1996; Jerrell Little, *Collector's Digest Price Guide to Cowboy Cap Guns and Guitars*, L-W Book Sales, 1996; David Longest, *Antique & Collectible Toys 1870-1950*, Collector Books, 1994; ——, *Character Toys and Collectibles* (1984, 1992 value update), 2nd Series (1987), Collector Books; ——, *Toys*, Collector Books, 1990, 1994 value update; Charlie Mack, *Encyclopedia of Matchbox Toys, 1947-1996*, Schiffer Publishing, 1997; Bill Manzke, *The Encyclopedia of Corgi Toys*, Schiffer Publishing, 1997; Brian Moran, *Battery Toys*, Schiffer Publishing, 1984; Richard O'Brien, *Collecting Toys*, 8th ed., Krause Publications, 1997; --, *Collecting Toy Cars & Trucks*, 2nd ed., Krause Publications, 1997; ——,*Collecting American Made Toy Soldiers*, Krause Publications, 1997; --, *Collecting Foreign-Made Toy Soldiers*, Krause Publications, 1997; Bob Parker, *Hot*

Wheels, revised ed., Schiffer Publishing, 1996; ——, *Marx Toys*, Schiffer Publishing, 1996.

John Ramsay, *British Diecast Model Toys*, 6th ed., available from Tim Arthurs (Ralston Gallery, 109 Gover Ave., Norwalk, CT 06850), 1996; David E. Richter, *Collector's Guide to Tootsietoys*, 2nd ed., Collector Books, 1996; Vincent Santelmo, *The Complete Encyclopedia to G. I. Joe*, 2nd ed., Krause Publications, 1997; Martyn L. Schorr, *Guide to Mechanical Toy Collecting*, Performance Media, 1979; *Schroeder's Collectible Toys*, 3rd ed., Collector Books, 1996; Carole and Richard Smith, *Pails by Comparison*, published by author (P.O. Box 2068, Huntington, NY 11743), 1996; Craig Strange, *Collector's Guide to Tinker Toys*, Collector Books, 1996; Carl P. Stirn, *Turn-of-the-Century Dolls, Toys and Games* (1893 catalog reprint), Dover Publications, 1990; Jack Tempest, *Post-War Tin Toys*, Wallace-Homestead, 1991; Carol Turpen, *Baby Boomer Toys and Collectibles*, Schiffer Publishing, 1993; Gerhard G. Walter, *Metal Toys from Nuremberg*, Schiffer Publishing, 1992.

Periodicals: *Antique Toy World*, P.O. Box 34509, Chicago, IL 60634; *Canadian Toy Mania*, P.O. Box 489, Rocanville, Saskatchewan SOA 3LO Canada; *Die Cast & Tin Toy Report*, 559 North Park Ave., Easton, CT 06612; *Model & Toy Collector Magazine*, 137 Casterton Ave., Akron, OH 44303; *Plane News*, P.O. Box 845, Greenwich, CT 06836; *Robot World & Price Guide*, P.O. Box 184, Lenox Hill Station, New York, NY 10021; *Toy Cannon News*, P.O. Box 2052-N, Norcross, GA 30071; *Toy Collector & Price Guide*, 700 E. State St., Iola, WI 54990; *Toy Collector Marketplace*, 1550 Territorial Rd., Benton Harbor, MI 49022; *Toy Gun Collectors of America Newsletter*, 312 Starling Way, Anaheim, CA 92807; *Toy Shop*, 700 East State St., Iola, WI 54990; *Toy Trader*, P.O. Box 1050, Dubuque, IA 52004; Toybox Magazine, 8393 E. Holly Rd., Holly, MI 48442; *U.S. Toy Collector Magazine*, P.O. Box 4244, Missoula, MT 59806; *Yo-Yo Times*, P.O. Box 1519, Herndon, VA 22070.

Collectors' Clubs: American Game Collectors Assoc., P.O. Box 44, Dresher, PA 19025; Antique Engine, Tractor & Toy Club, Inc, 5731 Paradise Rd., Slatington, PA 18080; Antique Toy Collectors of America, 13th Floor, Two Wall St, New York, NY 10005; Capitol Miniature Auto Collectors Club, 10207 Greenacres Dr., Silver Spring, MD 20903; Diecast Exchange Club, P.O. Box 1066, Pineallas Park, FL 34665; Ertl Collectors Club, Highways 136 & 120, Dyersville, IA 52040; Farm Toy Collectors Club, P.O. Box 38, Boxholm, IA 50040; Majorette Diecast Toy Collectors Assoc., 13447 NW. Albany Ave., Bend, OR 97701; Miniature Piano Enthusiast Club, 633 Pennsylvania Ave, Hagerstown, MD 21740; San Francisco Bay Brooklin Club, P.O. Box 61018, Palo Alto, CA 94306; Schoenhut Collectors Club, 45 Louis Ave, West Seneca, NY 14224; Southern California Toy Collectors Club, Ste. 300, 1760 Termino, Long Beach, CA 90804;

Museums: American Museum of Automobile Miniatures, Andover, MA; Eugene Field House & Toy Museum, St. Louis, MO; Evanston Historical Society, Evanston, IL 60201; Forbes Magazine Collection, New York, NY; Hobby City Doll & Toy Museum, Anaheim, CA; Margaret Woodbury Strong Museum, Rochester, NY; Matchbox & Lesney Toy Museum, Durham, CT; Matchbox Road Museum, Newfield, NJ; Museum of the City of New York, New York, NY; Smithsonian Institution, Washington, DC; Spinning Top Exploratory Museum, Burlington, WI; Toy & Miniature Museum of Kansas City, Kansas City, MO; Toy Museum of Atlanta, Atlanta, GA; Washington Dolls' House & Toy Museum, Washington, DC; Western Reserve Historical Society, Cleveland, OH.

Additional Listings: Characters; Disneyana; Dolls; Schoenhut. Also see *Warman's Americana & Collectibles* for more examples.

SPECIAL AUCTIONS

Bill Bertoia Auctions
1881 Spring Rd.
Vineland, NJ 08360
(609) 692-1881

Jackson's Auctioneers & Appraisers
2229 Lincoln St.
Cedar Falls, IA 50613
(319) 277-2256
email: jacksons@corenet.net

James D. Julia, Inc.
P.O. Box 830
Fairfield, ME 04937
(207) 453-7125

Richard Opfer Auctioneering, Inc.
1919 Greenspring Dr.
Timonium, MD 21093
(410) 252-5035

Phillips Fine Art Auctions
406 E. 79th St.
New York, NY 10021
(212) 570-4830

Lloyd Ralston Toys
173 Post Rd.
Fairfield, CT 06432
(203) 255-1233

Skinner Inc.
Bolton Gallery
357 Main St.
Bolton, MA 01740
(508) 779-6241

Stout Auctions
11 W. Third St.
Williamsport, IN 47993-1119
(765) 764-6901

Toy Scouts, Inc.
137 Casterton Ave.
Akron, OH 44303
(330) 836-0068
email: toyscout@salamander.net

Notes: Every toy is collectible; the key is condition. Good working order is important when considering mechanical toys. Examples in this listing are considered to be at least in good condition, if not better, unless otherwise specified.

Arcade

Airplane, cast iron, Air France Fighter, 1941, painted blue fuselage, yellow pressed steel wings, nickeled propeller, 10" wingspan 250.00

Auto, cast iron

Chevrolet

Coupe, 1928, painted gray and black, classic styling, full running boards, nickeled wheels, spare mounted on trunk, 8-1/4" l 1,320.00

Utility Coupe, 1925, painted black, nickeled driver, rubber tires, spoked wheels, 7" l...825.00

Desoto, sedan, painted gray, nickeled grill and bumper, decal on trunk reads "Sundial Shoes," rubber tires, 4" l 130.00

Pontiac, sedan, painted red, nickeled grill and rubber tires, 6" l, repainted, replaced tires....................................125.00

Runabout, open seat touring car, wood, pressed steel seat, painted blue, red cast iron spoke wheels, seated driver, 9" l 500.00

Sedan and Red Cap Trailer, sedan painted red, pulling small Mullens Red Cap trailer, lift-up hood, 8-3/4" l...........220.00

Touring Coupe, Model T, painted black, spoke wheels, 5" l 470.00

Bread Truck, cast iron, painted black and white, side panel decals with children, side doors contain International decals, Hathaway's, replaced tires 1,650.00

Car Carrier, Austin, cast iron truck, painted green, pulling red sheet metal flat bed containing three Austin coupes, 14" l, some replaced tires 460.00

Car Hauler

Cast iron tractor, painted green, pulling two tier pressed steel carriers containing three small scale cast iron vehicles, 11" l, missing rear wheels 165.00

Cast iron tractor, painted green, pulling two tiers, pressed steel body, four cast iron vehicles, 1939, large size, 15-3/8" l...440.00

Cast iron tractor, painted green, nickeled grill, two tier orange sheet metal trailer, four small cast iron vehicles, 1939, 15-3/4" l 605.00

Cast iron truck, cast headlights, painted green, pulling red pressed steel flat bed trailer, three cast iron couples, 19" l, replaced trailer, repaired cars 360.00

Cast iron truck, nickel spoke wheels, pulling pressed steel flat bed trailer with four cast iron vehicles of various colors, 1921, 23-1/2" l, new tires, few restored cars 880.00

Cast iron truck, painted green, pulling red pressed steel flat bed narrow bed with three Model "A" autos in various colors, 20" l, replaced nickeled wheels......................1,320.00

Cast iron truck, painted green, pulling red sheet metal trailer, four coupes in various colors, nickeled spoked wheels, 24" l..715.00

Chester Gump Card, cast iron, pulled by single horse, red spoke wheels, 7-1/2" l, repainted 200.00

City Ambulance, cast iron, painted white, red cross, emb on sides, black rubber tires, 5-7/8" l, over painted............240.00

Dump Truck, cast iron

8-1/4" l, painted red, enclosed cab, cast chain drive, side lever controls dump bed, seated figure, spoke wheels 385.00

10" l, red, "Coal" stenciled on body, Mack, high body tilts for dumping 1,320.00

10-1/2" l, painted green, red chassis, dual rubber tires on rear, seated nickel drive, decals on doors, 1932, repainted 440.00

11-1/4" l, International Harvester, painted green, red chassis, yellow pressed steel dump body 275.00

12" l, Mack

Painted blue, Mack "T" bar, emb "Mack" on side doors, spoke wheels, painted centers, 1928, two replaced wheels 550.00

Painted gray, white spoke wheels, chromed winch, "Mack" decals on doors, seated driver 2,750.00

Fire Truck

Mack, cast iron, painted red, hose reels, two ladders, cast driver, spoke wheels, 9-3/4" l....................................935.00

Pontiac, cast iron, painted red, nickeled grills and hoods, rubber tires

Pumper and ladder truck, decals on sides, 6" l 630.00

Pumper, 8-5/8" l, missing one headlight........................250.00

Ice Truck, cast iron, painted blue

6-3/4" l

Nickeled grill and headlights, emb emblems on doors, hood ornament, railed side open body, rear platform, rubber tires, repainted..200.00

Studebaker, nickeled grill, bumper, and headlights, tailed open bed platform, orig tong and ice cubes, 1938 ....470.00

6-7/8" l, Mack, railed open bed body, rear platform, rubber tires, emb sides 275.00

8-1/2" l, Mack, railed open bed body, rear platform, stenciled "ICE" on sides, cast chain drive frame, nickeled spoke wheels...275.00

Milk truck, cast iron, painted green, classic milk bottle design, rubber tires, Borden's..1,430.00

Pick-Up Truck, cast iron, painted bright yellow, "International" decals on door, black rubber tires, 9-1/4" l, some rust on left side 330.00

Racer, Bullet, cast iron, classic bullet shaped body, painted red, nickeled driver and mechanic, side pipes, and disc wheels, emb "#9" on side 550.00

Red Baby Truck, cast iron, painted red, International

10" l, rubber tires, stationary bed, decals on doors, driver missing...660.00

10-1/2" l, nickeled driver and winch, disc wheels with painted centers, decals on doors, 1923................................495.00

Stake Truck, cast iron

6-7/8" l, painted blue, open stake side body, nickeled spoke wheels...220.00

7-3/8" l, painted green, emb cab, stake side body, nickeled spoke wheels, decal on door, driver missing...........310.00

8-3/4" l, painted green, cast chain drive, enclosed cab, high stake sides, nickeled spoke wheels, Mack, repainted 330.00

11-3/4" l, painted green, nickeled grill and bumper, International decal on side doors, rubber wheels, 1936 .....495.00

Tank, cast iron, camouflage painting, large metal wheels, 7-1/4" l 330.00

Taxi, cast iron

5-1/8" l, painted orange and black, nickeled spare on rear and wheels...615.00

8-1/4" l, painted blue, black trim, emb luggage rack, seated driver and passenger, rubber tires.........................660.00

9" l, painted orange and black, nickel seated driver, painted wheels and center, cast spare on rear, replaced radiator and driver 470.00

Thresher, McCormick Deering, cast iron

9-1/2" l, painted yellow, replaced straw shoot................715.00

11" l, painted gray, red striping, yellow spoke wheels ..330.00

Touring Car, cast iron, 1923 Ford, painted black, spoke wheels, 6-1/2" l..320.00

Tractor, cast iron

Caterpillar, 1929, crawler, orig chain tracks, green, nickel plated driver, trade mark decal

5-1/2" l 1,760.00

6-1/2" l 385.00

Cultivision, painted red, gold highlights, rubber tread tires, nickel driver and steering post, decal on hood, includes McCormick Deering Manure Spreader, 7-1/2" l 485.00

Fordson, painted gray, disc wheels, stenciled "Thorndike Co, Sioux City, Iowa," seated nickel driver, pulling tin land scraper, 5-3/4" l..525.00

Yellow Cab, cast iron, stenciled "Yellow Cab" on doors 7-3/4" l

Painted orange and black, nickeled wheels with painted centers, seated driver, chip off fender, new radiator screw 275.00

Painted orange body, black roof, full running boards, seated nickel driver, rubber tires, two replaced tires...........415.00

8-1/4" l, painted yellow, black trim, emb luggage rack, rubber tires, seated driver, missing clicker, repainted 100.00

9" l, painted orange and black, seated driver, painted disc wheels..1,100.00

Wrecker, cast iron

Baby Weaver, red, green, Weaver Wrecker boom, International Harvester decals on each door, nickel plated drive and drank, rubber tires on disc wheels, 12" l, replaced tires 440.00

Ford

8" l, red cab and body, green Weaver crane, nickeled driver, wheels, and hoist parts, crane stenciled "Weaver" on side..660.00

10" l, red cab and body, green Weaver Crane, nickeled crank, spoke wheels, seated driver 470.00

11" l, red cab and body, green Weaver Crane on rear, nickeled crank and spoke wheels, driver missing........385.00

Mack, red, emb cab and rail side body, green crane, spoked wheels, stenciled "Wrecker" on sides, 12-1/2" l 615.00

B & R Co.

Kid Flyer, litho tin, pull string, boy pedaling crate on wheels, 8" l 415.00

Bing, Germany

Auto, tin, clockwork, center door model, black, seated driver, radiator cap ornament, spare tire on rear, 6-1/4" l............385.00

Garage, litho tin, double doors, extensive graphics, houses sedan and roadster 550.00

Limousine, litho tin windup, red, maroon and orange striping, orig driver, c1910, 5-1/4" l.....................................690.00

Taxi Limousine, hp tin, clockwork, beveled glass windows, kilometer taxi meter, nickel-plated carriage lights, rubber wheels, orig key, wooden storage box, c1910, 14-1/4" l.......21,850.00

Buddy L.

Army Truck, pressed steel, painted army green, cloth covered bodies, rubber tires, mkd "Army" on canopy, 31" l 145.00

Bucket Loader, pressed steel, gray, black loading buckets, cast iron, wheels, all chain driver, side cranks, 16-1/2" l 200.00

Dump Truck, pressed steel, black cab with opening doors, painted red dump body, rubber tires, simulated spoke wheels, 25" l..990.00

Express Truck, green enclosed hard plastic cab, open slat side delivery body painted green, large decal depicting milk and young girl, rubber tires, disc wheels, 21-1/2" l 440.00

Fire Truck, hydraulic water tower, pressed steel, red, silver latticework water tower, headlights, brass gong, red disc, emb spoke wheels, air pressure propelled water from long tank inside body, filler cap on tank 2,420.00

Flivver, pressed steel, black, simulated soft top, single bench seat, spoked aluminum wheels, 10-3/4" l 580.00

Greyhound Bus, pressed steel, clockwork, bright blue and white, "Greyhound Lines" on sides, rubber tires, 16" l 275.00

Carette, Germany, battleship, red, light green tin litho, paint flanked, dented, 9" l, $395.

Parcel Delivery Truck, pressed steel, brown and beige, large slat back body, rear doors, decals on sides, solid rubber wheels, 24" l, rooftop missing 275.00

Railway Express, van body, large decal advertising ice cream, cab painted green, side decal reads "Railway Express Agency," 23" l, missing one headlight 330.00

Robotoy, pressed steel, electrical, red tractor, green dump body, black chassis, moves forwards and backwards, automatically dumps cargo, 21-5/8" l 660.00

Scarab, pressed steel, wind-up, red, chromed lights, grill trim, rubber tires, 10" l, minor scratches...............................250.00

Tank Truck, pressed steel, black cab, body painted green, brass rear faucet, red disc aluminum wheels, professionally restored..715.00

Train Set, all pressed steel, green locomotive, red coal car, rack car, platform car, rocker dump car, and dump side car, sections of track 470.00

Buffalo Toys

See-Saw, litho tin, boy and girl seated at each end of plank, 14" l 275.00

Carette, Germany

Lighthouse, handpainted tin, clockwork, central lighthouse, railed deck on each side hovers over tin water basin where boat with seated driver circles, 11" h, 10" d..................................715.00

Champion

Auto, cast iron, coupe, painted red, nickeled grill and headlights, rumble seat, rubber tires, spare mounted on trunk, 7" l, repainted..250.00

Gasoline Truck, cast iron, painted red, Mack "C" cab, tanker body, emb on sides, rubber tires, 8-1/8" l 385.00

Panel Truck, cast iron, enclosed panel van, cast spare tires and headlights, traces of orig blue paint, spoked metal wheels, 7-1/2" l, poor condition..180.00

Racer, cast iron

7-1/4" l, red body, long green hood, seated driver painted blue, emb on rear, replaced black rubber tires 525.00

8-1/2" l, painted red, silver trim, wind deflector on rear, separately cast driver painted blue, nickeled disc wheels 1,815.00

Stake Truck, cast iron, painted red, Mack "C" cab, stake side body, nickeled spoke wheels, 7" l 660.00

Truck, cast iron, "C" Mack cab, blue body, 7-3/4" l, replaced wheels..195.00

Wrecker, cast iron, red C-cab with crane, nickel plated crank and barrel, rubber tires, 8-1/4" l................................330.00

Chein

Rocket Ride, litho tin, clockwork, four tin rocket ships with figures, 17-1/2" h..................910.00

Cor-Cor

Automobile, Graham, 1936, 20" l, pressed steel
Brown and beige, full running boards, black rooftop, electric headlights, spare disc wheels, emb "Cor-Cor Toys," chromed grill and rubber tires, restored 935.00
Green, electric headlights, switch on side, rubber tires, metal wheels, chromed grill, restored 660.00
Bus, sheet metal construction, green, orange wheels, "Inter City" decals on side, bench seats diecut from window wells, 23-1/2" l.....................990.00
Dump Truck, sheet metal construction, enclosed black cab, green dump body, large painted metal wheels, 23" l....715.00
Stake Truck, sheet metal construction, black, brown stake body and rear platform, rubber tires, emb "Cor-Cor" on sides 770.00
Truck, sheet metal construction, enclosed black cab, green van body, rear platform, large painted metal wheels, 23" l..825.00

Cowdery Works

Sedan, Flivver, center door, painted black, disc wheels, includes orig button and box, #123 in series, 11" l.......650.00

Dayton Friction Co.

Patrol Wagon, pressed metal and wood, friction driven, painted red, stenciled "Police Patrol" on front panel, seated driver on open bench seat, spoke wheels, 10" l.....200.00
Touring Car, pressed metal, painted red, gold spoke wheels, open sides, friction driver, 12" l.....470.00

Dent

Auto, sedan, 1930, cast iron, painted blue, partial black paint on roof, nickeled wheels, spare on rear, 7-1/2" l, repainted 330.00
Contractor's Truck, cast iron, Mack, painted red, dual dump gondolas, open frame, nickeled disc wheels, painted centers, emb on sides, 7-1/2" l.....1,050.00
Fire Patrol, cast iron, open seat truck, rail sided open bed body, rear platform, disc wheels, 5-3/4" l.....220.00
Ice Cream Can, cast iron, painted yellow, "Breyers Ice Cream" emb on side, three removable ice cream doors on other side, 1921, old store stock, 8-1/2" l, repainted.....275.00
Taxi, cast iron, painted orange and black
Repainted seated driver, replaced painted disc wheels 315.00
Seated figure, painted disc wheels, spare disc wheel on rear, 7-1/2" l.....385.00
Transfer Wagon, cast iron, open seat, wagon painted orange, flared sides, seated driver on full width bench set and splash board sides, mkd "Transfer," yellow spoked wheels, pulled by three horses, 18" l.....1,100.00

Fisher Price

American Airlines Plane, paper litho over wood, bright orange and blue, extensive graphics, two propellers, 20" wingspan 500.00

Freidag

Fire Truck, cast iron, painted red and silver, emb hoses on sides, open bed body, rear platform and cast bell on hood, 7" l 935.00
Racer, Midget, cast iron, painted green, stenciled "#23" on doors, seated nickeled driver, disc wheels, 4-1/2" l.....220.00
Stake Truck, cast iron, open door cab, stake side body, spoked wheels, painted gray and black, 7-1/2" l, repainted......360.00

Gilbert, A. C.

Truck, tin wind-up, driver, c1915, 10-1/2" l.....320.00

Girard

Auto, 1934 Pierce Arrow, pressed steel, clockwork, colorful orange, green and beige top, electric headlights, luggage rack, rubber tires, 13-1/2" l.....330.00

Gong Bell

Columbus Bell, cast iron, Columbus standing, men rowing ornate ship mounted to spoke wheels, bell rings, emb on side "Landing of Columbus," 7-1/4" l, replaced figure 420.00
See Saw, pull type, cast iron, figures of black man on one end, clown on other end, spoked wheel platform, central bell rings when figures articulate, 6-1/2" l.....660.00

Gundka & Kelpert, Germany

Jackie, litho tin, clockwork, articulated ostrich pulling boy in cart, 9-1/2" l.....550.00

Harris

Foxy Grandpa Cart, open bed, steel cart painted green, standing cast iron figure of Grandpa, cast iron donkey, cart supported by cast iron spoke wheels, 7-1/4" l.....300.00
Goat Cart, cast iron, painted deep red, emb upholstered seating, arm rests, low splash board, yellow spoke wheels, drawn by goat, 9-1/4" l, cart and figure repainted.....275.00

Hercules

Wrecker, sheet metal open bench seat truck, hoist crane on body, painted black, red body, large metal balloon wheels, 19" l.....935.00

Hess, Germany

Germany, Ambulance, early litho, penny toy, brightly colored, seated driver, disc wheels, 4" l.....290.00

Hubley

Airplane, cast iron
Bremen, painted green, nickeled wheels, propeller, and figure, 7" l, repainted 330.00
Lindy
Glider, painted red, yellow wings, driver seated on front, emb wings, 6-1/2" l.....1,210.00
NR-211, Lockheed Sirius, rubber tires, nickeled propeller, repainted 2,860.00
Auto, cast iron
Airflow
6-1/4" l, painted blue, nickeled grill, bumper and running boards, spare on trunk, rubber tires 250.00
8" l, painted green, nickeled grill and bumpers, electric headlights, rubber tires 2,200.00

Hubley Packard, $27,500. Photo courtesy of James Julia Auctions.

Chrysler Airflow, 1932, painted red, nickeled grill and bumpers, electric lights, spare tired mounted on trunk, rubber tires, 7-7/8" l, replaced tires, repainted 525.00
Lincoln Zephyr and Trailer, painted green, nickeled grill and bumper, 13-1/2" l 825.00
Sedan and Trailer, painted red sedan, trailer panted silver and red, rubber tires, factory sample tag, 9-1/2" l...........715.00
Studebaker
  6-1/2" l, painted green, take-apart nickeled frame, lights and grill, open front driver's seat, rubber tires.......580.00
  6-5/8" l, sedan, painted red, nickeled grill, bumper, lights, and running boards, rubber tires, spare on trunk 470.00
  6-3/4" l, roadster, painted red, nickeled front grill with headlights, front and rear bumpers, side running boards, rubber tires, trunk mounted spare 640.00
  7-1/4" l, painted blue, open seat, electric headlights, nickeled grill, bumper, windshield, running boards, rubber tires, spare on trunk 2,090.00
Bell Telephone, cast iron
  8-1/4" l, painted green, silver sides, emb company name, Mack "C" cab, nickeled ladders, long handled shovels, pole carrier, spoked wheels, repainted....................250.00
  9-1/4" l, painted green, winch, auger, nickel water barrel on side, ladders, and pole carrier, fatigued rubber tires 660.00
Boat, cast iron, painted red, emb "Static" on sides, sleet form, seated driver, hand on throttle of attached motor, chromed air cleaner, painted orange, three tires, clicker, 9-1/2" l, over painted...1,650.00
Boxed Set, Taxi Cab Assortment, three colorful cast iron taxies, three red cast iron street signs, orig box, 8 x 11-1/2"....935.00
Car Hauler, cast iron
  Cab over two tiered carrier, 1938 Modern, four small scale cast iron vehicles, 10-1/4" l, fatigued tires................350.00
  Nu Car Transport, painted red, separate silver trailer bed, cab, and driver, emb lettering trimmed in gold, rubber tires, 16" l 525.00
  Truck pulling flat bed ramp car trailing, painted red, two small scale coupes, 11-3/4" l 715.00
Cement Mixer Truck, cast iron, red and green, nickel tank, rubber wheels, Mack, 8" l, restored.......................................1,760.00
Fire Truck, cast iron, painted red, nickeled grill, headlamps, painted silver full running boards, railed rear platform, rubber tires
  Ladder Truck, drivers, 8" l, ladders missing..................110.00
  Pumper Truck, hose reel, boiler rim, two seated figures, 10" l 525.00
Gasoline Truck, cast iron, painted silver, red spoked wheels, cast figure, round tank body, rear facets, c1920, 6" l 495.00
Grasshopper, cast iron, painted green
  4-1/2" l, nickeled arms and wheels...............................770.00
  9" l, articulated legs, orig pull string 250.00
Milk Truck, cast iron, painted white, emb "Borden's" on side panel, rear opening door, nickeled grill, headlights, and spoke wheels, 7-1/2" l, repaired headlights 1,980.00
Motorcycle, cast iron
  Harley Davidson, sidecar, olive green, driver and rider, orig decal on gas tank, 9" l 3,410.00
  Hillclimber, painted blue, black tank and motor, "2" emb on driver, 6-1/2" l...1,210.00
  Indian, pained red, "Indian" emb on tank, "Crash Car" emb on open trailer, seated policeman holding handle bars, rubber tires, spoke wheels, 6-1/2" l 660.00
Panama Steam Shovel, cast iron, painted red and green, large scale, nickeled shovel, cast people on trailer, dual rubbers on rear, 12" l...935.00
Pull Toy, Old Dutch Girl, cast iron, white and blue dress, holding yellow can of cleanser, rubber tires, c1932, 9" l, repaired stick, orig checker floor...4,100.00

Racer, cast iron
  5-1/2" l, painted red, curved tail fin, rubber tires, cast driver, "No. 8" emb on sides..200.00
  6-1/2" l, painted green, seated driver painted black, rubber tires 220.00
  7" l, painted red, seated driver, emb "8" on sides, rubber tires 385.00
  7-3/4" l, painted red, seated driver, emb "#1" on sides, rubber tires 385.00
  8-1/2" l, painted silver and red, eight piston articulated racer, seated driver, hi-tail fin design, rubber tires.............935.00
  9-1/2" l
    Painted green, red emb "5" on sides, hood opens on both sides to show extensively cast engine, disc wheels, seated driver, replaced hood doors 1,100.00
    Painted red, "Red Devil," hood doors open to reveal engine, seated driver in sleek aluminum body, nickeled grill, emb "5" on doors, rubber tires with spoke wheels 2,145.00
  10-1/2" l, painted blue, painted red articulated pistons, seated driver, black tires, spoked wheels 1,760.00
Road Roller, Huber, cast iron, 7-1/2" l
  Painted green, large fancy spoke wheels painted red, figure stands on rear platform 1,320.00
  Painted orange, nickel chains and wheels, restored 145.00
Stake Truck, cast iron, two piece mold, chassis and hood painted red, stake body and cab painted blue, six rubber tires, 6-1/2" l 375.00
Steam Shovel Truck, cast iron, painted green and red
  8-1/4" l, nickeled shovel, fatigued rubber tires 385.00
  9-3/4" l, silver painted shove, replaced dual rubber tires, new shovel 330.00
Take Apart Wrecker, cast iron, painted red and yellow, low hook and rubber tires, 6-1/4" l, fatigued tires 220.00
Taxi Cab, painted orange and black, separate driver chassis and luggage rack, rubber tires, yellow cab stencil on rear doors, 8-1/4" l, professionally restored 470.00
Ten Ton Stake Truck, cast iron, painted orange, nickeled grill, headlights and stake sides emb "10 Ton" on sides, replaced rubber tires, 8-1/2" l 330.00
Yellow Cab, cast iron Lincoln Zephyr, painted orange, black trim, rear luggage rack, seated figure, silver bumper and under carriage, new rubber tires, 8" l 415.00

Katz Toys

Airplane, litho tin, clockwork, three propellers, green and gold, black motors, question marks, and name on wings, red disc wheels, 18" wingspan 880.00

K Co., Japan

Exploration Train, litho, locomotive, transmitter car, radar car, other carriers, battery operated, orig box, 12" l..................800.00

Kenton

Ambulance, nickeled cast iron, open sided drivers compartment, emb on sides, spoke wheels, 7-1/4" l, replaced roof 715.00
Auto, coupe, cast iron, painted red...................................600.00
Car Hauler, cast iron tractor, painted red, pulling black cast iron flat ramp car trailer, four small cast iron vehicles of various colors and manufacturers, 18" l.....................................1,540.00
Cement Mixer, Jaeger, cast iron
  6" l, painted red, blue, and green, nickel plated operating pieces, rubber tires, c1935 ....300.00
  6-1/2" l, painted orange, aluminum drum and scope, spoked wheels..500.00
  7" l, painted red and green, nickel cast cement drum, levers and scoop, nickeled disc wheels 385.00
  7-5/8" l, painted silver, red and green frame, large mixing drum and scoop, rubber tires, nickeled wheel crank 615.00

9-1/4" l, painted orange, blue frame, large aluminum drum and scoop, nickeled disc wheels 770.00
Coal Tractor and Trailer, cast iron, truck pulling open bed coal trailer emb on sides, painted red, nickeled disc wheels, 8-1/2" l.................................330.00
Coal Truck, cast iron
6-1/2" l, painted red, open bed, coal bed body, emb sides, nickeled disc wheels, driver missing........................440.00
7-3/4" l, enclosed red cab, separate grill, open bed coal body, emb on sides, rubber tires, missing driver..............825.00
Coal Wagon, cast iron, painted green, emb sides, yellow spoke wheels, pulled by white horse, 13" l...........................385.00
Contractor's Truck, cast iron, three open dump buckets on bed, emb "Contractors" on sides, balloon rubber tires, 10" l, re-painted....................................440.00
Digger, cast iron, painted red and green, c1930
Buckeye Ditch Digger, chain drive, nickel plated crank, dig-ger, and wheels, 12" l, missing chain threads on one side 470.00
Buckeye Ditcher, nickeled chain drive digger, cast wheels with chain tread, 9" l 635.00
Fairfield Ditcher, chain drive, rubber tires, 9-1/2" l, missing gear chain....................................2,090.00
Dray Wagon, cast iron, seated driver on open bench seat, pulled by two horses, one painted black, other painted white
10" l, painted green, stake side wagon, red spoke wheels 190.00
14-1/2" l, painted red, low stake side wagon, green spoke wheels....................................125.00
Fire Truck, cast iron, painted red
Extension Ladder Truck, open frame body, separate extension ladder, side cranks, seated driver, disc wheels, 9-1/4" l 935.00
Pumper, gold highlights on boiler, spoke wheels, cast driver, chrome bumper, 10-1/2" l 400.00
Gas Truck, cast iron, painted green, gold highlights, emb side cans and filler caps, seated driver, painted wheels, 8" l, re-painted....................................360.00
Ice Truck, cast iron, emb cab painted red, pulling two open railed body ice trailers, emb on sides, nickeled disc wheels, 10-1/2" l....................................660.00
Overland Circus, cast iron, painted red, ornate casting, emb gold trim
Band Wagon, yellow spoked wheels, six seated musicians, driver, and parade figure mounted on white horses, 15" l 825.00
Cage Wagon, yellow spoked wheels, roof bench seat, pulled by two white horses, 14-1/4" l....................................385.00
Truck, cage body houses two elephants, painted white disc wheels, seated driver, 8" l....................................1,320.00
Plantation Cart, cast iron, horse drawn cart, yellow spoke wheels, pulled by horse, 13" l....................................550.00
Road Roller, cast iron, Galion Master, painted red, emb lettering on sides, wooden roller, nickeled cast iron spoke wheels, 7-1/2" l....................................200.00
Stake Truck, cast iron, enclosed red cab pulling open green stake trailer emb "Speed" on sides, rubber tires, 9" l, mis-matched wheels 330.00
State Highway Truck, cast iron, open bed dump truck, emb "State Highway" on sides, side lever activates dumping, red en-closed cab, disc wheels, front bumper, 10-1/4", repainted 2,805.00
Tanker Truck, cast iron, tandem tractor and tanker
8-1/4" l, painted orange, rubber tires....................................385.00
10" l, Texaco, painted green, emb name on sides, nickel driv-er, rubber tires 2,255.00
Tractor Trailer Set, all cast iron, tractor painted red, orange tank-er, two speed stake trailers, nickeled disc wheels, 22" l 1,210.00
Touring Car, cast iron, painted white spoke wheels, cast head-lamps and lanterns, 7-3/4" l, replaced figures..............250.00

Yellow Cab, cast iron, painted orange and black, white disc wheels, orange centers, 6-1/2" l....................................495.00

Kilgore, Canada

Airplane, cast iron, Seagull, painted red, nickeled wheels and wing mounted propeller, 7-3/4" l....................................880.00
Auto, open roadster, 1928, cast iron, painted blue, nickeled wheels and driver, decal reads "Kilgore, Made in Canada," 6-1/8" l....................................825.00
Delivery Truck, cast iron, Toy Town, painted red, emb on side panels, gold highlights, silver disc wheels, 6-1/8" l, repainted 360.00
Dump Truck, cast iron, painted blue enclosed cab, red dump body, lever to lift, nickeled disc wheels, 8-1/2" l....................................330.00
Ice Cream Truck, cast iron, enclosed cab painted blue, orange body, emb "Arctic Ice Cream" on sides, disc wheels, 8" l 420.00

Kingsbury

Auto, pressed steel, 1935 Desoto, classic airflow design, red, chromed grill and trim, electric headlights, 13" l, some rust at battery box....................................990.00
Ladder Truck, pressed steel, open bed truck, yellow ladders on frame supports, hose reel, and two chemical containers, 37" l, restored 825.00

Kyser & Rex

Hay Wagon, cast iron, open seat farm wagon, flared stake sides, seated driver, mounted on two red spoked wheels, pulled by black and brown steer....................................525.00

Lehmann, Germany

Alabama Coon Jigger, litho tin, clockwork, orig box..........965.00
Bulky Mule, litho tin, clockwork, 7-1/4" l....................................230.00
Crawling Beetle, litho tin, clockwork, deep green wings, 4" x 4-1/2" l....................................190.00
Military Plane, litho tin, combat camouflage paint, iron cross markings, orig box, 5-3/4" wingspan....................................315.00
Motor Car, litho tin, steering by front wheels....................................315.00
New Century, litho tin, clockwork, man holding umbrella for driver, red and white striped umbrella, blue and yellow car, 5" l 360.00
Oho, litho tin, clockwork, open cab automobile, 3-3/4" l....................................250.00
Paak-Pak, litho tin, clockwork, duck cart, ducklings, 7" l....................................275.00
Performing Sea Lion, litho tin, clockwork, 8" l....................................160.00
Sailor, handpainted tin face, dressed in blue fabric sailor's suit, walks with clockwork activated, 7-1/2" l....................................500.00
Susi The Turtle, litho tin, clockwork, crawling turtle, orig box, 4" l 715.00
Tap-Tap, litho and handpainted tin, clockwork, walking gardener, wheelbarrow, c1920....................................315.00
Tut-Tut, litho tin auto, suited gentleman blowing horn........715.00
Zig-Zag, litho and handpainted tin, clockwork, rocking car, 4-1/4" l....................................1,045.00
Zulu, litho tin, clockwork, ostrich mail, 7" l....................................440.00

Linemar, Japan

Minnie Mouse Knitter, litho tin, clockwork, Minnie seated on rock-ing chair, knitting, 6-1/2" h, spring sprung....................................360.00

Lineol, Germany

Armored Car, litho tin clockwork, camouflage colors, revolving turret with gun, opening doors, spring lever for gun, wire guard covers vehicle, rubber tires, 10" l, symbols repainted, minor paint loss....................................935.00
Cannon, 88MM, litho tin, camouflage colors, stabilizer arms, ele-vation cranks, 4 tire open frame, tow hook, 14-1/2" l.....935.00
Motorcycle with Side Car, composition figures, tin fenders, disc wheels, 4-1/2" l....................................300.00

Lionel

Mickey Mouse Hand Car, red metal base, clockwork, handpainted, orig box, 9 x 6" box, Minnie with replaced legs 880.00

Marx, Louis Co.

Amos and Andy Fresh Air Car, litho tin, clockwork, orange and black, pair seated with pet dog, horseshoe hood ornament 495.00
Buck Rogers Rocket Ship, litho tin, clockwork, colorful, sleep wings on side, fin tail, 11-3/4" l 615.00
Charlie McCarthy, litho tin, clockwork, 8" l 275.00
Circus Set, litho tin, tent, signs, platforms, flags, accessories, circus props, orig box 275.00
Climbing Fireman, litho tin, clockwork, colorful fireman on extension ladder, 22" h 200.00
Contractors Dump Truck, pressed steel, cab and chassis painted red, blue dump body, yellow dump gate, litho tin wheels, decals on body, 17" l 250.00
Coo Coo Car, litho tin, clockwork, orig driver, 7-1/2" l 315.00
Cowboy Rider, litho tin wind-up, cowboy on horse with lasso, orig box, 1930s, 7" h 435.00
G-Man Pursuit Car, litho tin, clockwork, colorful police car, protruding gun through windshield held by seated figure, rubber tires, extensive graphics, 14" l 715.00
Harold Lloyd Walter, litho tin, clockwork, 10-1/2" l 385.00
Honeymoon Express, litho tin wind-up, 1920s, 9-1/2" d 175.00
Joy Rider, litho tin funny car, clockwork, comical driver, humorous graphics, 7-1/2" l 360.00
Limping Lizzie Auto, litho tin, clockwork, black, humorous graphics, seated figure, orig box, 7" l 360.00
Mortimer Snerd Walker, litho tin, clockwork, plaid suit, walks, hat flips up, 8-1/2" l 220.00
Pluto Drum Major, litho tin, Pluto wearing hat, holding baton in hand, whistle in mouth, 6" l 275.00
Police Patrol Car, painted green, clockwork, graphics depict siren and 1st Pct Police Patrol, rubber tires, battery box for front headlights, 13" l, some rust on battery box 800.00
Rookie Pilot, litho tin, clockwork, pilot's head peering from cockpit, 8" wingspan 285.00
Sparkling Soldier Motorcycle, litho tin, clockwork, camouflaged shield, seated driver, 1940, 8" l 360.00

Marx, Popeye pushing cart, litho tin wind-up, $650.

Tank, litho tin wind-up, pop-op solider, orange and blue, 1930s, 9" l 150.00
Travel Bureau, litho tin, station with large base, graphics depict cab stand, people waiting for buses, tin ad placard, 11" w, 17" l 90.00

Meier, Germany

Ambulance, horse drawn, litho tin, 2 horses, spoke wheels, 4-1/2" l 260.00
Cart and Canon, litho tin, 2 horses pulling cart with seated soldier, trailing cannon, 6" l 175.00
Field Bakery Truck, litho tin, open driver's seat, boiler style field bakery body, tall stack, spoke wheels, 4-1/4" l 210.00
Field Kitchen Truck, litho tin, open bench seat, spoke wheels, replaced stack, 4" l 125.00

Model Toys

Bucket Loader, pressed steel, green, chain driven loading buckets painted black, traction treads, chain activated levers on sides, orig box, 18" h 330.00

Modern Toys

Delivery Truck, cast iron, painted yellow, enclosed cab, wire mesh body sides, well cast, rubber tires, nickeled spoke wheels, orig box, 8-1/4" l 220.00
Huckster Truck, Motorcade series, cast iron, painted green, colorful painted open side body, rubber tires, nickeled spoke wheels, orig box, 8-1/4" l 280.00
Ice Cream Truck, Motorcade series, cast iron, van body, white and black large decal on side panels, rubber tires, spoke wheels, orig box, 7-1/2" l 360.00

Pratt & Letchworth

Dray Wagon, cast iron, open bed wagon, single slat slides, wooden floor, standing figure, red spoke wheels, one horse, 10-1/4" l 175.00
Surrey, cast iron, open carriage, low splash board, two full width seams with arm and back rests, emb upholstering mounted on two prs of spoked wheels, pulled by one horse, c1900, 14" l 990.00

Schieble Toys

Roaster, pressed steel, fly wheel motion, blue, large rubber tires, spare mounted on truck, full running boards, 18" l 385.00

Skoglund & Olson, Sweden

Coupe, cast iron, painted gray, spare tire mounted on rear, rubber tires, red disc wheels, 8" l, repainted 550.00
Farm Tractor, cast iron, painted blue, red traction wheel, seated nickel driver, replaced steering wheel 1,100.00
Gasoline Truck, cast iron, painted red, enclosed cab, two cast fill caps on tank body, rubber tires, blue disc wheels, 10" l, repainted 615.00
Ladder Truck, cast iron, painted red, black cast side boxes, nickeled supports, rubber tires, removable house reel on open frame, one tin ladder, 16" l, repainted 715.00
Pick-Up Truck, cast iron, painted yellow, enclosed cab, low side body, removable tailgate, rubber tires, red disc wheels, 10-3/4" l, repaired 950.00
Sedan and Ramp, cast iron, green touring sedan with spare tire, resting in gray car ramp, 7-1/4" to 14-1/4" l, overpainted 1,870.00
Wrecker, cat iron, painted white, red winch and crane on open body, rubber tires, painted red disc wheels, sides emb "Central-Garage," 11-3/4" l 1,540.00

Straus, Jenny, the Bulking Mule, litho tin wind-up, $250.

Steel Craft

Fire Truck, pressed steel, all red, open drivers seat, "Mack Model," low side hose wheel, ladders, supporting rails, rear mounted extension ladders, hand lever action, wire side railing to rear step, gong on radiator, disc wheels, rubber tires, decals read "City Fire Dept.," Mack stickers on sides, 25" l.....625.00

Stevens, J. & E. Co.

Sulky, cast iron, donkey pulling black man in fancy cart, man's arm moves in whipping motion when pulled forward, c1895, cart repainted 440.00

Strauss, Ferdinand

Derrick Truck, litho tin, clockwork, open bed body, tin winch, "Derrick Truck" on sides, 8-1/2" l..............715.00
Ham & Sam, Minstrel Team, litho tin, clockwork, piano player and banjo player, orig box, 1921, 6-1/2" l..............1,210.00
Leaping Lena, litho tin, clockwork, black, wording all over, front end appears to break in half when wound, 8" l..............200.00
Zeppelin, litho tin, clockwork, 1930s, 9-1/2" l..............225.00

Structo

Dump Truck, diecast cab painted white, red sheet metal body lifts on scissors extension frame, dual rubber tires, side decals, orig box, 12" l, mint..............200.00

TN, Japan

Trumpet Player, mechanical, full figured character resembling Louis Armstrong, standing on base, trumpet in hand, orig box, 10-1/2" l..............420.00

Turner Mfg

Automobile, Lincoln, 1928, pressed steel, light green, black roof and sun visor, chromed radiator, rubber tires, green painted disc wheels, 26" l, professionally restored 1,045.00

Unique Art

Jazzbo Jim, litho tin, clockwork, boy violinist, orig box, 1920s, 10" h..............825.00
Lil' Abner & His Dog Patch Band, litho tin, wind-up, four figures, 1945, orig box, 5-3/4 x 9"..............770.00

Unknown Manufacturer

Circus Wagon Pip-Squeak, 13-1/2" l wooden cage, cast iron wheels, 4 composition animals, bear in center cage no longer roars, mkd "Made in Germany," damage to animals 415.00
Crawling Buttercup, litho tin wind-up, Germany, mid 1920s, 7-1/2" l..............260.00

Vindex

John Deere Harvester, cast iron, detailed casting, painted silver, green trim, combine, top railed platform housing standing figure, open engine front end mounted, harvest hopper mounted, realistic brackets, combine attachment with spoked wheels, 13-1/2" l..............7,150.00

Williams, A. C.

Airplane, cast iron, UX166, painted silver, nickeled prop and motor, spoked wheels, emb on wings, 6" wingspan 200.00
Auto, cast iron
  Airflow
    4-3/4" l, painted bright orange, nickeled grill and bumper, rubber tires..............415.00
    7" l, painted red, nickeled chassis extending to grill and bumpers, rubber tires 935.00
  Sedan, futuristic, stream lined, painted green, rubber tires, 8-1/2" l..............245.00
  Take-Apart Sedan, cast iron, painted red, blue chassis, white rubber tires, 7-1/4" l, red repainted 235.00
Car Carrier, Austin, cast iron
  Tractor, painted green, pulling slant front trailer, three small Austin sedans in various colors, 12-3/8" l, repaired truck 470.00
  Tractor pulling cast iron flat bed, slant front, three small Austin sedans in various colors, 12-3/8" l..............835.00
Coast to Coast Truck, cast iron, tractor, green open stake cartage trailer, emb on sides, nickeled spoke wheels, 10-1/8" l, tractor repainted 250.00
Delivery Truck, take-apart, cat iron, simulated wood side truck, painted yellow, black chassis, rubber tires, 7-1/4" l......500.00
Gasoline Truck, cast iron, Ford semi-trailer, painted blue, emb "Gasoline-Motor Oil," on tanker, spoke wheels, 10-1/8" l, over painted..............290.00
Racer, cast iron
  7-1/2" l, painted black, open seat, seated driver, emb on side, spoke wheels, made in Canada 220.00
  8-1/2" l, painted red, high tail fan, cast cylinders on front hood, nickeled driver, rubber tires 580.00
Stake Truck, cast iron, Mack "C" cab, painted red, open stake body, nickeled spoke wheels, 6-3/4" l..............165.00
Take-Apart Stake Truck, cast iron
  7" l, painted orange, nickeled grill and lights, replaced black chassis..............160.00
  7-1/4" l, painted yellow, black chassis, rubber tires 910.00

Wolverine Supply Co.

Rooster, litho tin, rooster plucks worm from tree truck as baby chick looks on, colorful wheeled base, orig pull string and box, 10" l..............880.00
Ziltone, litho tin, clockwork, seven records, not working....315.00

TRAINS, TOY

History: Railroading has always been an important part of childhood, largely because of the romance associated with the railroad and the prominence of toy trains.

The first toy trains were cast iron and tin; wind-up motors added movement. The golden age of toy trains was 1920 to 1955, when electric-powered units and high-quality rolling stock were available and names such as Ives, American Flyer, and Lionel were household words. The advent of plastic in the late 1950s resulted in considerably lower quality.

Toy trains are designated by a model scale or gauge. The most popular are HO, N, O and standard. Narrow gauge was a response to the modern capacity to miniaturize. Its popularity has decreased in the last few years.

References: Paul V. Ambrose, *Greenberg's Guide to Lionel Trains, 1945-1969*, Vol. III, Greenberg Publishing, 1990; Paul V. Ambrose and Joseph P. Algozzini, *Greenberg's Guide to Lionel Trains 1945-1969*, Vol. IV, *Uncatalogued Sets* (1992), Vol. V, *Rare and Unusual* (1993), Greenberg Publishing; Susan and Al Bagdade, *Collector's Guide to American Toy Trains*, Wallace-Homestead, 1990; John O. Bradshaw, *Greenberg's Guide to Kusan Trains*, Greenberg Publishing, 1987; Pierce Carlson, *Collecting Toy Trains*, Pincushion Press, 1993; W. G. Claytor Jr., P. Doyle, and C. McKenney, *Greenberg's Guide to Early American Toy Trains*, Greenberg Publishing, 1993; Joe Deger, *Greenberg's Guide to American Flyer S. Gauge*, Vol. I, 4th ed. (1991), Vol. II (1991), Vol. III (1992), Greenberg Publishing; Cindy Lee Floyd (comp.), *Greenberg's Marx Train Catalogues*, Greenberg Publishing, 1993; John Glaab, *Brown Book of Brass Locomotives*, 3rd ed., Chilton, 1993.

Bruce Greenberg, *Greenberg's Guide to Ives Trains*, Vol. I (1991), Vol. II (1992), Greenberg Publishing; —— (Christian F. Rohlfing, ed.), *Greenberg's Guide to Lionel Trains: 1901-1942*, Vol. 1 (1988), Vol. 2 (1988), Greenberg Publishing; ——, *Greenberg's Guide To Lionel Trains: 1945-1969*, Vol. 1, 8th ed. (1992), Vol. 2, 2nd ed. (1993), Greenberg Publishing; *Greenberg's Lionel Catalogues*, Vol. V, Greenberg Publishing, 1992; *Greenberg's Marx Train Catalogues*, Greenberg Publishing, 1992; George Horan, *Greenberg's Guide to Lionel HO*, Vol. II, Greenberg Publishing, 1993; George Horan and Vincent Rosa, *Greenberg's Guide to Lionel HO*, Vol. I, 2nd ed., Greenberg Publishing, 1993; John Hubbard, *Story of Williams Electric Trains*, Greenberg Publishing, 1987; Steven H. Kimball, *Greenberg's Guide to American Flyer Prewar O Gauge*, Greenberg Publishing, 1987; Roland La Voie, *Greenberg's Guide to Lionel Trains, 1970-1991*, Vol. I (1991), Vol. II (1992), Greenberg Publishing.

Lionel Book Committee, *Lionel Trains: Standard Of The World, 1900-1943*, Train Collectors Association, 1989; Dallas J. Mallerich III, *Greenberg's American Toy Trains: From 1900 with Current Values*, Greenberg Publishing, 1990; ——, *Greenberg's Guide to Athearn Trains*, Greenberg Publishing, 1987; Eric J. Matzke, *Greenberg's Guide to Marx Trains*, Vol. 1 (1989), Vol. II (1990), Greenberg Publishing; Robert P. Monaghan, *Greenberg's Guide to Marklin OO/HO*, Greenberg Publishing, 1989; Richard O'Brien, *Collecting Toy Trains*, No. 3, Books Americana, 1991; John R. Ottley, *Greenberg's Guide to LGB Trains*, Greenberg Publishing, 1989; Alan R. Schuweiler, *Greenberg's Guide to American Flyer*, Wide Gauge, Greenberg Publishing, 1989; John D. Spanagel, *Greenberg's Guide to Varney Trains*, Greenberg Publishing, 1991; Robert C. Whitacre, *Greenberg's Guide to Marx Trains Sets*, Vol. III, Greenberg Publishing, 1992.

Periodicals: *Classic Toy Trains*, 21027 Crossroads Cr., P.O. Box 1612, Waukesha, WI 53187; *Lionel Collector Series Marketmaker*, Trainmaster, P.O. Box 1499, Gainesville, FL 32602.

Collectors' Clubs: American Flyer Collectors Club, P.O. Box 13269, Pittsburgh, PA 15234; Lionel Collectors Club of America, P.O. Box 479, LaSalle, IL 61301; Lionel Operating Train Society, 18 Eland Ct., Fairfield, OH 45014; Marklin Club-North America, P.O. Box 51559, New Berlin, WI 53151; Marklin Digital Special Interest Group, P.O. Box 51319, New Berlin, WI 53151; The National Model Railroad Assoc., 4121 Cromwell Road, Chattanooga, TN 37421; The Toy Train Operating Society, Inc., Suite 308, 25 West Walnut St., Pasadena, CA 91103; Train Collector's Assoc., P.O. Box 248, Strasburg, PA 17579.

Museum: Toy Train Museum of the Train Collectors Assoc., Strasburg, PA.

Additional Listings: See *Warman's Americana & Collectibles* for more examples.

Notes: Condition of trains is critical when establishing price. Items in fair condition and below (scratched, chipped, dented, rusted or warped) generally have little value to a collector. Accurate restoration is accepted and may enhance the price by one or two grades. Prices listed below are for trains in very good to mint condition unless otherwise noted.

SPECIAL AUCTIONS

**Greenberg Auctions
7566 Main St.
Sykesville, MD 21784
(410) 795-7447**

**Lloyd Ralston Toys
173 Post Rd.
Fairfield, CT 06432
(203) 255-1233**

**Stout Auctions
11 W. Third St.
Williamsport, IN 47993-1119
(765) 764-6901**

American Flyer

Car
    910 Gilbert Chemicals Tank Car 185.00
    3007 gondola, HO gauge..35.00
    23743 track maintenance car.......................................100.00
Locomotive
    3110, AFL rubber stamped tender, nickel trim, HO gauge
    ....100.00
    21910, 21910-1, and 21910-2, SF PA ABA 950.00
Set
    433 PA switcher and tender, 512 NH box car, 502 MKT stock, 503 transformer car, 516 NYC caboose, 621 switch, HO gauge, orig boxes 180.00
    322AC locomotive and tender, 718 mail car, three 650 NH coaches, red..300.00
    322DC UP Northern locomotive and tender, 653 combine, two 652 pullmans, 654 observation, dark green, several broken couplers 850.00
    3116 Potomac locomotive 3180 combine, 3181 pullman, 3182 observation, minor fatigue, buff and green, orig box with partial end label only 875.00

Buddy L., pressed steel, from Outdoor Railroad set

Box Car, painted red, black trucks, sliding center door, ladders on one end, 22-1/2" l...360.00
Caboose, red, black trucks, ladders on ends, cupola on roof, 20-1/4" l, over painted...330.00
Coal Car, black, ladders on one end, decal "68502," black trucks, 22-1/2" l, new couplers 250.00
Gondola Car, black, dual bottom dump doors, inside compartment angled for gravity feed dumping, black trucks, decals on sides, couplers missing..................................470.00
Locomotive and Tender, black lid on tender, water tank opens, 26" l locomotive, 18-3/4" l tender 1,100.00
Stock Car, red, black trucks, sliding center door, ladders on one end, 22-1/2" l..360.00
Tank Car, tank and dome painted yellow, frame and trucks in black, decals on sides, 19-1/2" l, couplers missing 990.00

Ives

Car
    125 box, white litho, red roof 450.00
    184 club, olive, c1927 ....100.00
Locomotive
    3, litho tin, black and gold striped roof, clockwork, tender, orig box for locomotive 1,650.00
    20, black, painted cast iron, 3 bands, #25 tender 450.00
Set
    #1 locomotive, windup, boiler needs reattaching, coal bunker tender, gondola, hp, green, orig box with inserts .3,000.00
    #4 locomotive, painted cast iron, working clockwork LVE #11 tender, 50 baggage, 52 Buffalo coach, white and red litho 1,950.00
    3253 locomotive, 131 baggage, 130 combine, 129 coach, 132 observation, orange litho, orange roofs, minor paper crazing, wheels fatigued on locomotive 750.00

Lionel

Car
    211 lumber car, orig box 135.00
    219 derrick, yellow cab, pea green boom, red roof 400.00
    514 Reefer, standard gauge, ivory and peacock..........420.00
    2559 Budd Trailer, orig box...475.00
Locomotive
    42, standard gauge, mojave, double motor 1,300.00
    51 Navy yard switcher, orig box....................................290.00
    247 B & O, tender, orig box, minor repair 400.00

Lionel, Santa Fe diesel engine and #233-B unit, $660. Photo courtesy of Jackson's Auctioneers & Appraisers.

252X locomotive, two 607 pullmans, 608 observation, peacock and orange, brass trim 200.00
736 Berkshire, 2046W-50 tender 280.00
773 Hudson, 773W NYC tender, orig box 1,150.00
2055, minor bend to cab corner, 2046 tender, one orig box 100.00
Set
    390E locomotive, 390T black with orange stripes tender, 512 gondola, 513 orange and pea green stock, 517 pea green, rd, and brass caboose 615.00
    1623W, 2349 NP GP9, 3512 fire ladder car, 3435 aquarium car with gold lettering, 6062 gondola with reels, 6425-11- flat with 2 autos, 6017-1 caboose, orig boxes, minor damage 675.00
    19510, 241 diecast loco, 234W tender, 6076 LV black hopper, 6473 dark yellow and maroon horse transport, 3362 lumber dump, 6142 green gondola with canisters, 6130 SF work caboose, inserts, peripherals 400.00
    State, standard gauge, 381E rewheeled logo with restored cap, 412 and 413 pullman, 416 observation, missing 4 handrails, minor fatigue 2,800.00

TRAMP ART

History: Tramp art was an internationally practiced craft, brought to the United States by European immigrants. Its span of popularity was between the late 1860s to the 1940s.

Made with simple tools–usually a pocketknife, and from scrap woods–non-reusable cigar box wood and crate wood, this folk art form can be seen in small boxes to large pieces of furniture. Usually identifiable by the composition of thin layered pieces of wood with chip-carved edges assembled in built-up pyramids, circles, hearts, stars, etc. At times, pieces included velvet, porcelain buttons, brass tacks, glass knobs, shards of china, etc., that the craftsmen used to embellish his work. The pieces were predominantly stained or painted. Collected as folk art, most of the work was attributed to anonymous makers. A premium is placed on the more whimsical artistic forms, pieces in original painted surfaces, or pieces verified to be from an identified maker.

Reference: Clifford A. Wallach and Michael Cornish, *Tramp Art, One Notch At A Time,* Wallach-Irons Publishing, (277 W. 10th St., NY NY 10014) 1998.

Advisor: Clifford Wallach

Bank, coin, 6" h x 4" w x 4" d, secret access to coins 335.00
Bird Cage, 28" h x 22" w x 13-1/2" d, house with 2 compartments 775.00
Box, ftd, 11-1/2" h x 15"w x 14"d, brass lions, date, and clasp for lock 265.00
Cabinet, 44" h x 22-1/2" w x 14" d, scratch built cabinet, embellished with pyramids, floral pattern on blue doors, crest and secret compartment 6,500.00
Chest of Drawers, 40" h x 29" w x 20" d, scratch built from crates with four drawers, 10 layers deep 2,400.00
Clock, mantel, 22" h x 14" w x 7" d, red stain with drawers at base...475.00
Comb Case, 27" h x 17" w x 4"d, adorned with horseshoes, hearts, birds, 2 drawers and mirrors 700.00
Crucifix, 16" h x 7" w x 4-1/2" d, wooden pedestal base, wooden carved figure 185.00
Document Box, 14" h x 9-1/2" w x 9" d, diamond designs, sgd and date...375.00

Clock, mantel, red stain, drawers in base, 14" w, 7" d, 22" h, $475. Photo courtesy of Clifford Wallach.

Doll Furniture
    Chair, 10" h, 7" w, 12" d, dec with brass tacks 450.00
    Bureau, 14" h x 12" w x 9" d, drawers and mirror 650.00
Frame
    9" h, 6-3/4" w, photograph of maker, signed and dated "1906"
    ....275.00
    13" h x 12" w, horseshoe shape, light and dark wood ..465.00
    14" x 12", hearts and diamonds, painted gold 255.00
    14" h x 24" w, double opening frame with oval opening for pho-
    tos 325.00
    16" h x 18" w x 4-3/4" d, crown of thorns, multiple opening
    frame with minor losses, dark stain 495.00
    16" h, 22" w, block corner style, with painted hearts, pair of
    frames by same maker 225.00
    26" h x 24" w, velvet panels and sq corners.................350.00
    48" h x 34" w, large, ornately carved, star decorated crown, 18
    layers 2,200.00
Jewelry Box
    6" h x 11" w x 6" d, covered with hearts painted silver over gold,
    velvet lined...595.00
    6-3/4" h x 11-1/2" w x 7" d, hinged jewelry box with velvet top
    and sides 175.00
    8" h x 11" w x 7" d, hinged, pedestal, dark stain 175.00
    8-3/4" h x 13 3-4" w x 9" d, lock, mirrored top and int
    ....425.00
    9" h x 11-1/2" w x 7" d, large, dated "1898," metal lion pulls
    ....300.00
    16" h x 14" w x 10"d , shallow drawers and carved finial on
    top..395.00
Lamp
    24" h, 10" w, 10" d, table, double socket 550.00
    68" h, 17" w, 17" d, floor, heavy pedestal base, no shade
    ....1,200.00

Frame, horseshoe shape, light and dark wood, 12" w, 13" h, $465. Photo courtesy of Clifford Wallach.

Match Safe, 9" h x 2" w x 2" d, strike surface, open holder for
    matches 75.00
Medicine Cabinet, 22" h x 18" w x 10" d, light and dark woods
    ....675.00
Miniature
    Chair, 8" h x 6" w x 5-1/2" d, crown of thorns................245.00
    Chest of Drawers, 14" h x 5" w x 4" d, made of cigar boxes
    ....375.00
Music Box , 3" h x 7" w x 6" d, velvet sides.........................425.00
Night Stand, 37" h x 22" w x 14"d, dark stain, drawer on top and
    cabinet on bottom, no losses 1,600.00
Pedestal
    6 1-2" h x 10" w x 7" d, lift off lid, velvet lined.................225.00
    14 1-2" h x 12" w x 8" d, multi-level, 6 draw 675.00
    16" h x 7" w x 4-1/2" d, polychromed in green and black paint
    ....950.00

Pocket Watch Holder, ftd, 6-1/2" w, 5-1/2" d, 9" h, $375. Photo courtesy of Clifford Wallach.

Wall Pocket, shelf, diamonds motif, 16" w, 4-3/4" d, 8-1/2" h, $125. Photo courtesy of Clifford Wallach.

Pedestal Box
    8-1/4" h x 9" w x 6-1/2" d, double, bar connecting top pyramids, velvet lined, precise notching....................................325.00
    29-1/2" h x 16" w x 15" d, light and dark stained, made from fruit crates 1,850.00
Plant Stand, 22" h x 11" w x 11" d, painted gold, heavily layered
    ....675.00
Pocket Watch Holder, 9" h x 6-1/2" w x 5-1/2" d, ftd...........375.00
Radio Cabinet, 50" h x 33" w x 16" d, box type radio encased behind doors, ornate 3,600.00
Sewing Box
    8-1/2" h x 11-1/2" w x 8-1/2"d, velvet pin cushion on top
    ....265.00
    9" h x 16-1/2" w x 8" d, painted red, white and blue sewing box, Uncle Sam cigar label under lid 1,600.00
Sewing Cabinet, 27" h x 16" w x 9"d, lift top and three drawers made from crate wood 1,400.00
Side by Side, bookcase/desk, 49" h x 29" w x 20" d, glass cabinet door with shelves on one side, other side is drop front desk
    ....3,200.00
Vanity Mirror, 26" h, 14" d, 10" d, table top, heart on top and drawer..375.00
Wall Pocket
    7" h x 9" w x 4" d, open work and porcelain buttons 95.00
    8-1/2" h x 16" w x 4-3/4" d, shelf and diamonds for design
    ....125.00
    14" h x 11" w x 7" d, painted with hearts and stars, pr
    ....700.00
    20" h x 18" w x 5-1/2" d, carved leaves and acorns surrounding mirror 1,400.00

TRANSPORTATION MEMORABILIA

History: Most of the income for the first airlines in the United States came from government mail-carrying subsidies. The first non-Post Office Department flight to carry mail was in 1926 between Detroit and Chicago. By 1930, there were 38 domestic and five international airlines operating in the United States. A typical passenger load was 10. After World War II, four-engine planes with a capacity of 100 or more passengers were introduced.

The jet age was launched in the 1950s. In 1955, Capitol Airlines used British-made turboprop airliners for domestic service. In 1958, National Airlines began domestic jet passenger service. The giant Boeing 747 went into operation in 1970 as part of the Pan American fleet. The Civil Aeronautics Board, which regulates the airline industry, ended control of routes in 1982 and fares in 1983.

Transoceanic travel falls into two distinct periods: the era of the great clipper ships and the era of the diesel-powered ocean liners. The golden age of the later craft took place between 1900 and 1940.

An ocean liner is a city unto itself. Many have their own printing rooms to produce a wealth of daily memorabilia. Companies such as Cunard, Holland-America, and others encouraged passengers to acquire souvenirs with the company logo and ship name.

Certain ships acquired a unique mystic. The *Queen Elizabeth*, *Queen Mary*, and *United States* became symbols of elegance and style. Today the cruise ship dominates the world of the ocean liner.

References: Leila Dunbar, *Motorcycle Collectibles*, Schiffer Publishing, 1996; Lynn Johnson and Michael O'Leary, *En Route*, Chronicle Books, 1993; Karl D. Spence, *How to Identify and Price Ocean Liner Collectibles*, published by author, 1991; ——, *Oceanliner Collectibles*, published by author, 1992; Richard R. Wallin, *Commercial Aviation Collectibles: An Illustrated Price Guide*, Wallace-Homestead, 1990.

Periodical: *Airliners*, P.O. Box 52-1238, Miami, FL 33152.

Collectors' Clubs: Aeronautic & Air Label Collectors Club, P.O. Box 1239, Elgin, IL 60121; Gay Airline Club, P.O Box 69A04, West Hollywood, CA 90069; National Assoc. of Timetable Collectors, 125 American Inn Rd., Villa Ridge, MO 63089; Oceanic Navigation Research Society, P.O. Box 8005, Studio City, CA 91608-0005; Steamship Historical Society of America, Inc., Ste. #4, 300 Ray Drive, Providence, RI 02906; Titanic Historical Society, P.O. Box 51053, Indian Orchard, MA 01151; Titanic International, P.O. Box 7007, Freehold, NJ 07728; Transport Ticket Society, 4 Gladridge Close, Earley, Reading Berks RG6 2DL England; World Airline Historical Society, 3381 Apple Tree Lane, Erlanger, KY 41018.

Museums: Owls Head Transportation Museum, Owls Head, ME; South Street Seaport Museum, New York, NY, University of Baltimore, Steamship Historical Society Collection, Baltimore, MD.

Additional Listings: See Automobilia; Railroad Items. See also Aviation Collectibles, Ocean Liner Collectibles, and Railroad Items in *Warman's Americana & Collectibles*.

By Air

Advertising, fan, Air India 4.00
Baggage Label, 4-1/4" x 6", full color paper, *Graf Zeppelin,* German lettering for South Atlantic flight, c1929, unused.....60.00
Counter Display Figure, 6-1/4" x 9" x 16" h, Air-India, painted composition, c1970 ....185.00
Game, 13" x 14-1/2", United Air Lines Skyways, cardboard folder opens to 14-1/2" x 26" playing board, 1937 copyright, "Approved by United Air Lines," distributed by Levi & Gade, Chicago, Mainliner, 2 engine plan on cov 70.00
Paperweight, 2-1/2" d, dark luster lead, "Aero Club of America," raised image of eagle soaring beneath sun rays above world globe nestled in cloud banks, also inscribed "13th Annual Banquet Feb. 19, 1919, Waldorf-Astoria"........................20.00
Photo Card, 3-1/2" x 5-1/2", browntone, real photo, hovering over York Fairgrounds, airship suspends web and rudder, reverse

Zeppelin, folk art bird house, mounted on bicycle pedal, blue, gray, and red, 40" l, $935. Photo courtesy of Sanford Alderfer Auction Co.

with post card imprint and "AZO" marking at stamp, unused, 1900s 60.00
Ticket
    2-1/2" x 3-1/2", black, white, and red, German zeppelin, c1930 ....70.00
    3-1/4" x 5-1/2", passenger, *Hindenburg*, US to Germany flight in connection with Transatlantic Airship Demonstration, 1936, inked name, unused 125.00

By Land

Blotter, 3" x 5-1/4", Firestone Bicycle tiers, black, white, orange and blue, unused, 1920s 20.00
Box Bed Wagon..575.00
Cap Badge, Pacific Greyhound Bus Line, chrome, blue and green cloisonné enameling, 2-1/2" x 2" 325.00
Milk and Ice Delivery Wagon, 1926, horse drawn, Cambridge City, IN 2,500.00
Horse and Pony Buggy, St. Paris, OH, orig parasol and wicker seat 1,900.00
Luggage Tag, Canadian Pacific, stringed cardstock, red, white, and blue ship signs, c1930, 5" x 3" 15.00
Pin, 1" d, Schwinn Bicycles, dark maroon, world glove with "Ride the World Cycles" inscription on one side, other with "Arnold Schwinn & Co/Chicago," 1930s 35.00
Pinback Button, Tilton's Trolley Trip, multicolored, trolley excursion from CA, early 1900s 25.00
Poster, Cleveland Cycles, Indian riding bicycle looking back, 58" x 43" 525.00
Schedule and Timetable, New England Bus Transportation Co., 1955, 3" x 4-1/2" folded 12.00
Sign, National Trailways Bus Depot, porcelain, two-sided, multicolored, 18" x 22" 300.00
Stickpin, brass, bug pedaling bicycle, mkd "Compliments of United States Tire Co.," 1920s..25.00
Stock Certificate, Brooklyn Rapid Transit Co., engraved, rear of street car vignette, c1910..35.00
Wagon Wheel, wood...70.00

By Sea

Advertising Trade Card
    Lund's Pioneer Lion, 1860s Florida steam, red and black lettering..75.00
    National Line Steamships, *S.S. The Queen,* entire ship line and rates on reverse 150.00
Booklet, *St. Lawrence Route to Europe,* Canadian Pacific, 1930, 16 pgs, 8" x 11" 25.00
Deck Plan, *S. S. Hamburg,* fold out, 1930............................35.00
Lighter, *R.M.S. Queen Elizabeth,* 1/2" x 1-3/4" x 2" h, chrome, metal disk official insignia on one side with red, blue, and copper enamel accents, 1950s 35.00

Manifest/Broadside, *Ship Dido,* hand colored, sgd by 28 crew members, 1822, 18" x 23"..450.00
Poster
    Allez En Corse, Ed. Collin, steamship, harbor village as seen through Corsican cave, c1950, 16" x 25" 200.00
    American Line-Red Star Line St. Louis and St. Paul, Orcutt Co. Litho, Chicago, *SS St. Louis* shown in black and green gravure, c1900, 37" x 20" 400.00
    Canada- Anchor Donaldson Line, *Odin Rosenvinge,* multicolor lithograph of steamer with Anchor Line logo at top, c1912, 25" x 40" 1,650.00
Sign
    Cunard Line, tin, *Aquitana* steam ship, old time paddle boat and sail boat sailing along side, artist sgd "A. F. Bishop," new frame with Cunard Line plaque, 33" x 43".........100.00
    Cunard Line, tin, ocean liner in New York Bay, Statue of Liberty in background, *Berengaria,* sgd on lower right corner "Bishop 1924," 43-1/2" x 34"....................................300.00
    Scandinavian-American, self framed tin, ocean liner in bay, *Frederick VIII,* 41 x 31"..1,200.00
Vase, 10-1/2" h, *Normandie,* silvered metal, trumpet form, sq base with beaded foot, Compagnie generale Translantique monogram, imp "E. Brandt" and "G. Bastard" 1,200.00

Dance Card, Europa, Nord Deutscher Lloyd Bremen Line, printed, black and white, gold emb logo, 1930s, 3-1/2" x 6", $10.

TRUNKS

History: Trunks are portable containers that clasp shut and are used for the storage or transportation of personal possessions. Normally "trunk" means the ribbed flat- or domed-top models of the second half of the 19th century.

References: Martin and Maryann Labuda, *Price & Identification Guide to Antique Trunks*, published by authors, 1980; Jacquelyn Peake, *How to Recognize and Refinish Antiques for Pleasure and Profit*, 3rd ed., Globe Pequot Press (P.O. Box 833, Old Saybrook, CT 06475), 1995.

Notes: Unrestored trunks sell for between $50 and $150. Refinished and relined, the price rises to $200 to $400, with decorators being a principal market.

Early trunks frequently were painted, stenciled, grained, or covered with wallpaper. These are collected for their folk-art qualities and, as such, demand high prices.

Chinese, brass bound camphor wood, 19th C, minor imperfections
 16" h, 36" w, 18" d, polychrome foliate dec on top, nailhead trim 1,035.00
 16-1/2" h, 36-1/4" w, 18-1/4" d, nailhead dec, monogrammed brass plaque...865.00
Dome Top
 8" h, 20" w, 10-1/8" d, paint dec, foliate devices and swags with tassels, ochre and red on black ground, bail handle, America, 19th C, minor imperfections............................1,610.00
 11" h, 22" w, 12" d, paint dec, blue stamped flowers on black ground, lined with 1811 newspaper, wear.............230.00
 11" h, 24" w, 13" d, paint dec, poplar, top with central floral device within yellow and green painted oval bordered by green, tan, and black, front initialed "PG" within foliate painted escutcheon rimmed by painted oval, light tan background, New England, early 19th C.............1,035.00
 11-1/2" h, 28" w, 14" d, paint dec, black painted ground, central vined pinwheel bordered by meandering floral and arched vines, front with tassel and drape border, central MA, early 19th C...1,035.00
Flat Top
 10-1/4" h, 14" w, 27" d, marbleized, black graining on gray-white ground, American, dated 1825, some wear ...805.00
 14" x 8", Chinese, pigskin, red, painted Oriental maidens and landscapes within quatrefoils, brass loop handles and lock, 19th C 125.00

Leather covered, initialed with nail heads, iron hardware and rivets, 26-1/2" l x 15" d, 12-1/2" h, $185.

29-1/4" x 15-1/2" x 16-1/4", tin over wood, brass banded ends, wood rim, int. shelf missing 100.00
Steamer, 21-3/4" h, 45" w, 21-1/2" d, Louis Vuitton, early 20th C, pigskin lining...2,100.00

TUCKER CHINA

History: William Ellis Tucker (1800-1832) was the son of a Philadelphia schoolmaster who had a small shop on Market Street, where he sold imported French china. William helped in the shop and became interested in the manufacture of china.

In 1820, kaolin, a white clay which is the prime ingredient for translucence in porcelain, was discovered on a farm in Chester County, Pennsylvania, and William earnestly began producing his own products with the plentiful supply of kaolin close at hand. The business prospered but not without many trials and financial difficulties. He had many partners, a fact reflected in the various marks found on Tucker china including "William Ellis Tucker," "Tucker and Hulme," and "Joseph Hemphill," as well as workmen's incised initials which are sometimes found.

The business operated between 1825 and 1838, when Thomas Tucker, William's brother, was forced by business conditions to close the firm. There are very few pieces available for collectors today, and almost all known pieces are in collections or museums. But you can never tell!

Museum: Pennsylvania Historical Museum, Harrisburg, PA.

Coffee Cup and Saucer, large size, floral spray, green band dec, gilt edges and handle, from set made for Atherton family of Chester County, PA, monogram "A".........................1,500.00
Creamer and Sugar, black transfer dec, landscape with house, c1830, sugar repaired 500.00
Fruit Dish, 11" l, oval, serpentine, gilt border, c1830.......1,150.00
Miniature, tea service
 Hot water pot with lid, head spout (handle and rim repaired), teapot with bird's head spout, creamer, four straight sided cups with loop handles, three saucers, classical form, Li-beat pattern, white, gold trim...............................1,900.00
 Teapot with bird's head spout, creamer (handle repaired), open sugar bowl, four flaring rim tea cups with scroll handles (one cup with rim repair), four saucers, white, gold trim...1,800.00
Plate, 10" d, gold band and peach border, three gilt leaf dec, centered monogram "EMW," incised letter view on bottom
 ....625.00
Pitcher
 Classical, gold trim, two side bouquets of flowers, reeded base, 9-1/4" h..1,100.00
 Grecian shape, gold trim, polychrome floral sprays, hand repaired, bottom inscribed "W & N" (Andrew Craig Walker)
 ....800.00
 Oblong pear shape, reeded, squared C-form handle, polychrome floral band at center, gilt rims, front inscribed "Wm. Bokius 1828," sgd on bottom "Tucker and H China Manufacturers, Philadelphia 1828," 7-1/4" h, repairs to handle and rim side...2,800.00
 Urn shape, loop handle, gold trim, two floral bouquets I gold floral wreaths, reeded base, 9-1/4" h, crack to rim
 ....3,200.00
 Urn shape, loop handle, gold trim, two sepia landscape reserves on water, ribbed base, 9-7/8" h, chip to lip ...825.00

Vases, one with view of Sedgley Park, other view of Schuylkill, 21" h, pr, $291,500. Photo courtesy of Freeman\Fine Arts.

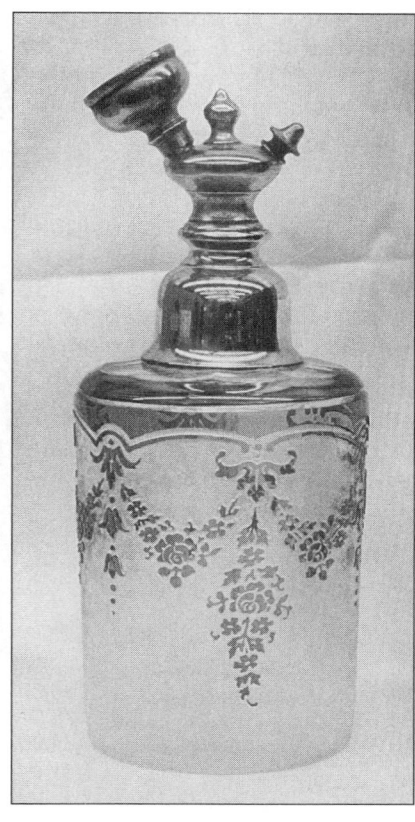

Atomizer, acid etched, raised floral garland flashed in light cranberry, cranberry rim, gold wash mechanism, bulb missing, 6-3/4" h, $295.

Teapot, 9" h, pink and green floral dec, white ground, gold bands, restored 100.00
Tea Service, teapot, creamer, sugar, waste bowl, 10 7" plates, seven cups, nine saucers, Forget-Me-Not pattern, white ground, gold band, wear, slight damage, 30 pc set 365.00
Vase, 21" h, matching pair, one painted with scene of county house identified as "Sedgley Park, Seat of Mr. James Fisher," reverse with view of Schuylkill River, other painted with two dramatic scenes, one with man rescuing women in red dress and turning to shoot three men, reverse with man on horseback, another on foot holding life line, trying to rescue survivor from shipwreck in distance, two part construction, loosely bolted together, cast gilt bronze handles, gold trim rubbed, price for pr $291,500.00

VAL ST. LAMBERT

History: Val St. Lambert, a 12th-century Cistercian abbey, was located during different historical periods in France, Netherlands, and Belgium (1930 to present). In 1822, Francois Kemlin and Auguste Lelievre, along with a group of financiers, bought the abbey and opened a glassworks. In 1846, Val St.-Lambert merged with the Socété Anonyme des Manufactures de Glaces, Verres à Vitre, Cristaux et Gobeletaries. The company bought many other glassworks.

Val St.-Lambert developed a reputation for technological progress in the glass industry. In 1879, Val St.-Lambert became an independent company employing 4,000 workers. The firm concentrated on the export market, making table glass, cut, engraved, etched, and molded pieces,

and chandeliers. Some pieces were finished in other countries, e.g., silver mounts were added in the United States.

Val St.-Lambert executed many special commissions for the artists of the Art Nouveau and Art Deco periods. The tradition continues. The company also made cameo-etched vases, covered boxes, and bowls. The firm celebrated its 150th anniversary in 1975.

Bowl
    6-1/2" d, cov, cameo, deep cut purple florals, frosted ground, sgd "Val St. Lambert" 750.00
    10" d, 4" h, red flashed overlay, sgd 350.00
Compote, 3-1/2" d, amberina, ruby rim, mottled glass bow, applied amber foot and handles 175.00
Dresser Box, colored 100.00
Finger Bowl, 4-1/2" d, crystal, half pentagon, cut edge, sgd
.... 45.00
Pitcher, crystal, paneled, cut diamond design, sgd 95.00
Tumble-Up, decanter and matching tumbler, amber-crystal, mkd 95.00
Vase, 10" h, cranberry cut to clear, 3" acid cut band of Renaissance style chariots and people, Gothic arch panels, notched rim 300.00

VALENTINES

History: Early cards were handmade, often containing both handwritten verses and hand-drawn pictures. Many cards also were hand colored and contained cutwork.

Mass production of machine-made cards featuring chromolithography began after 1840. In 1847, Esther Howland of Worcester, Massachusetts, established a company to make valentines which were hand decorated with paper lace and other materials imported from England. They had a small "H" stamped in red in the top left corner. Howland's company eventually became the New England Valentine Company (N.E.V. Co.).

The company George C. Whitney and his brother founded after the Civil War dominated the market from the 1870s through the first decades of the 20th century. They bought out several competitors, one of which was the New England Valentine Company.

Lace paper was invented in 1834. The golden age of lacy cards took place between 1835 and 1860.

Embossed paper was used in England after 1800. Embossed lithographs and woodcuts developed between 1825 and 1840, and early examples were hand colored.

References: Dan & Pauline Campanelli, *Romantic Valentines*, L-W Book Sales, 1996; Roberta B. Etter, *Tokens of Love*, Abbeville Press, 1990; Katherine Kreider, *Valentines with Values*, Schiffer Publishing, 1996.

Collectors' Club: National Valentine Collectors Assoc., Box 1404, Santa Ana, CA 92702.

Advisor: Evalene Pulati.

Animated, large
    Felix, half tone, German......22.00
    Jumping Jack, Tuck, 1900 ......65.00
Bank True Love note, England, 1865 ......75.00
Bank of Love note, Nister, 1914 ......35.00
Charm String
    Brundage, 3 pcs......45.00
    Four hearts, ribbon 45.00
Comic
    Sheet, 8" x 10", Park, London 20.00
    Sheet, 9" x 14", McLoughlin Co., USA, 1915 ......15.00
    Woodcut, Strong, USA, 1845......25.00
Diecut foldout
    Brundage, flat, cardboard 20.00
    Cherubs, 2 pcs......35.00
    Clapsaddle, 1911 ......55.00
Documentary
    Passport, love, 1910......45.00
    Wedding certificate, 1914 ......45.00
Engraved
    5" x 7", American, verse......35.00
    8" x 10" sheet, English, emb, pg......65.00
    8" x 10" sheet, English, hand colored 45.00
Handmade
    Calligraphy, envelope, 1885......135.00

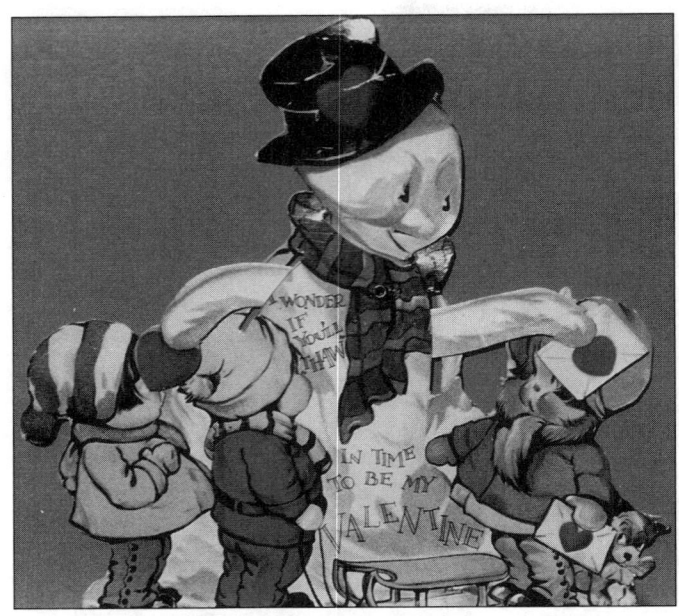

Child's, mechanical, Charles Twelvtrees design, 1920s, 8" x 7", $22.50.

    Cutwork, hearts, 6" x 6", 1855......250.00
    Fraktur, cutwork, 1800 ......950.00
    Pen and ink loveknot, 1820 ......275.00
    Puzzle, purse, 14" x 14", 1855......450.00
    Theorem, 9" x 14", c1885......325.00
    Woven heart, hand, 1840 ......55.00
Honeycomb
    American, kids, tunnel of love 45.00
    American, wide-eyed kids, 9" 37.50
    German, 1914, white and pink, 11" 75.00
    Simple, 1920, Beistle, 8" 17.50
Lace Paper
    American, B & J Cameo Style
        Large 75.00
        Small, 1865 ......45.00
    American, layered, McLoughlin Co., c1880 ......35.00
    Cobweb center, c1855 ......250.00
    English, fancy
        3" x 5", 1865 ......35.00
        5" x 7", 1855 ......75.00
        8" x 10", 1840 ......135.00
    Hand Layered, scraps, 1855......65.00
    Layered, in orig box
        1875, Howland......75.00
        1910, McLoughlin Co. 45.00
    Orig box, c1890......55.00
    Simple, small pc, 1875 ......22.50
    Tiny mirror center, 4" x 6" 75.00
    Whitney, 1875, 5" x 7" 35.00
Pulldown, German
    Airplane, 1914, 8" x 14" 175.00
    Auto, 1910, 8" x 11" x 4" 150.00
    Car and kids, 1920s 35.00
    Dollhouse, large, 1935......45.00
    Rowboat, small, honeycomb paper puff 65.00
    Seaplane, 1934, 8" x 9"......75.00
    Tall Ship, 8" x 16"......175.00
Silk Fringed
    Prang, double sided, 3" x 5"......18.50
    Triple layers, orig box......35.00
Standup Novelty
    Cupid, orig box......45.00
    Hands, heart, without orig box 35.00

Howland, N.E.V. Co, 1870-80, each $35.

Animal Dish, cov, duck, brown top, green base, 4-1/2" h, $95.

Pullout, mechanical, German, HCPP as center, 1914-20 era, air brushed color, 12" h, 7" w, $55.

Salt, cov, hen on nest, white opal 65.00
Sugar, cov, 5" h, Strawberry pattern, opaque white, gold trim, salamander finial 85.00
Tumbler, 4" h, blue..40.00
Vase, 8" h, flared folded burgundy red rim, oval pale green body, matching red enamel berry bush on front, inscribed "Vallerysthal" on base..490.00

Parchment
    Banjo, small, with ribbon 65.00
    Violin, large, boxed..125.00

VALLERYSTHAL GLASS

History: Vallerysthal (Lorraine), France, has been a glass-producing center for centuries. In 1872, two major factories, Vallerysthal glassworks and Portieux glassworks, merged and produced art glass until 1898. Later, pressed glass animal-covered dishes were introduced. The factory continues to operate today.

Animal Dish, cov
    Hen on nest, opaque aqua, sgd..75.00
    Rabbit, white, frosted..65.00
    Swan, blue opaque glass 100.00
Box, cov, 5" x 3", cameo, dark green, applied and cut dec, sgd
    ....950.00
Butter Dish, cov, turtle, opaque white, snail finial...............100.00
Candlesticks, pr, Baroque pattern, amber 75.00
Compote, 6-1/4" sq, blue opaque glass............................75.00
Dish, cov, figural, lemon, opaque white, sgd 70.00
Mustard, cov, swirled ribs, scalloped blue opaque, matching cover with slot for spoon 35.00
Plate, 6" d, Thistle pattern, green 65.00

VAN BRIGGLE POTTERY

History: Artus Van Briggle, born in 1869, was a talented Ohio artist. He joined Rookwood in 1887 and studied in Paris under Rookwood's sponsorship from 1893 until 1896. In 1899, he moved to Colorado for his health and established his own pottery in Colorado Springs in 1901.

Van Briggle's work was heavily influenced by the Art Nouveau schools he had seen in France. He produced a great variety of matte-glazed wares in this style. Colors varied.

Artus died in 1904. Anne Van Briggle continued the pottery until 1912.

Marks: The "AA" mark, a date, and "Van Briggle" were incised on all pieces prior to 1907 and on some pieces into the 1920s. After 1920, "Colorado Springs, Colorado" or an abbreviation was added. Dated pieces are the most desirable.

References: Susan and Al Bagdade, *Warman's American Pottery and Porcelain*, Wallace-Homestead, 1994; Carol and Jim Carlton, *Colorado Pottery*, Collector Books, 1994; Ralph and Terry Kovel, *Kovels' American Art Pottery*, Crown Publishers, 1993; Richard Sasicki and Josie Fania, *Collector's Encyclopedia of Van Briggle Art Pot-*

tery, Collector Books, 1993, 1998 value update; David Rago, *American Art Pottery,* Knickerbocker Press, 1997.

Collectors' Club: American Art Pottery Assoc., 125 E. Rose Ave., St. Louis, MO 63119.

Museum: Pioneer Museum, Colorado Springs, CO.

1901-1920

Bowl, 6-1/4" d, 3-1/4" h, No. 735, flaring shoulder, interlocking and repeating rig and X raised in relief on body, tapering to cylindrical foot, dark blue mottled matte glaze, incised mark 376.00
Chamberstick, 5-1/2" h, molded leaf shape, hood over candle socket, green glaze 115.00
Figure, 7" h, female nude holding shell, matte Persian blue glaze, incised "Van Briggle"....................................250.00
Night Light, 8-1/2" h, figural, stylized owl, bulb cavity, light refracting glass eyes, turquoise blue matte glaze, unsgd.......425.00
Vase
    5-1/2" h, 3" d, tapering, emb stylized flowers and leaves, soft rose and pale green, cream ground, marks obscured by glaze, 1903 ....900.00
    7-1/4" h, 3-1/2" d, shape No. 830, crisply carved poppy pods, sinewy stems, matte purple glaze, green ground, incised "AA/Van Briggle/Colo.Spgs./830" 1,600.00

Vase, stylized spiderwort, light green matte, blue/green leaves, slight brown peppering, pinched handles, incised logo, date "1903," shape #165, incised "III," 6" h, $1,375. Photo courtesy of Jackson's Auctioneers & Appraisers.

Vase, Dos Cabewzas, two molded figures of women in flowing gowns, rich mulberry glaze, slight blue overspray, dated 1919, incised logo and date, 7-3/4" h, $2,970. Photo courtesy of Jackson's Auctioneers & Appraisers.

7-1/2" j, 5" d, Dos Cabezas, two emb Art Nouveau women, flowing hair and garments, matte light green glaze, 1902, incised "AA/Van Briggle/1902/III 19,000.00
8-1/2" h, 7" d, bulbous, shape No. 164, emb stylized leaves and berries, matte green, light brown ground, incised "AA/VAN BRIGGLE/1903/III/164" 5,600.00
10" h, 4" d, corset, shape No. 671, emb stylized iris, smooth microcrystalline French blue matte glaze, clay showing through, incised "AA/Van Briggle/Colo.Spgs.671," c1908-11 ....850.00
10" h, 4-1/2" d, Lorelei, diaphoanously clad woman wrapped around side, soft green and cream matte finish, incised "AA/Van Briggle/17/1902/III" 27,000.00
14" h, 5-1/2" d, emb daffodils, frothy periwinkle blue glaze, incised "AA/VAN BRIGGLE/1903/111/110" 7,450.00

1928-1968

Ashtray, 6-1/2" w, Hopi Indian maiden kneeling, grinding corn, turquoise Ming glaze.......................................75.00
Bust, 6-1/2" h, child reading book 60.00
Paperweight, 3" d, rabbit, maroon..65.00
Tile, 18" x 12", six tile frieze, cuenca with stylized trees against blue sky, framed 250.00
Vase, 9-1/4" h, 4-1/2" h, Lorelei, woman wrapped around rim, cadmium yellow matte glaze, restoration to small base chip, incised "AA/VAN BRIGGLE/COLO. SPRINGS" 3,000.00

VENETIAN GLASS

History: Venetian glass has been made on the island of Murano, near Venice, since the 13th century. Most of the wares are thin walled. Many types of decoration have been used: embedded gold dust, lacework, and applied fruits or flowers.

Candlestick, opal ribbon twist, canary, brass rings, 11-1/4" h, 5-1/4" d, $150.

Boch, managed a pottery at Mettlach; Nicholas Villeroy also had a pottery nearby.

In 1841, the three potteries merged into the firm of Villeroy & Boch. Early production included a hard-paste earthenware comparable to English ironstone. The factory continues to use this hard-paste formula for its modern tablewares.

References: Susan and Al Bagdade, *Warman's English & Continental Pottery & Porcelain*, 2nd ed., Wallace-Homestead, 1991; Gary Kirsner, *Mettlach Book*, 3rd ed., Glentiques (P.O. Box 8807, Coral Springs, FL 33075), 1994.

Additional Listings: Mettlach.

Beaker, quarter liter, couple at feast, multicolored, printed underglaze 115.00

Bowl, 8" d, 3-3/4" h, gaudy floral dec, blue, red, green, purple, and yellow, mkd "Villeroy & Boch," minor wear and stains 50.00

Charger, 15-1/2" d, gentleman on horseback, sgd "Stocke" 600.00

Ewer, 17-3/4" h, central frieze of festive beer hall, band playing white couples dance and drink, neck and foot with formal panels between leaf molded borders, subdued tones, c1884, imp shape number, production number and date codes 900.00

Figure, 53" h, Venus, scantily clad seated figure, ribbon tied headdress, left arm raised across chest, resting on rock, inscribed "Villeroy & Boch, damage to foot and base ..1,900.00

Plaque, 10-1/4" d, blue and white harbor scene, Mercury mark 90.00

Platter, 17" l, elongated oval, black transfer, red, blue, green, and yellow Gaudy Ironstone dec..55.00

Tray, 11-1/4" d, metal gallery with geometric cut-outs, ceramic base with border and stylized geometric pattern, white ground, soft gray high gloss glaze, blue accents, base mkd 200.00

Vase, 15" h, bulbous, cylindrical, deep cobalt blue glaze, splashes of drizzled white, three handled SP mount cast with leaves, berries, and blossoms, molded, pierced foot, vase imp "V" & "B," "S" monogram, numbered, c1900, pr 2,750.00

Beverage Set, 10-1/2" h, pitcher, applied striped handle, eight flared tumblers, six spherical glasses, each striped with opaque orange, transparent yellow-amber, and clear crystal, design attributed to Fulvio Bianconi, 15 pc set 1,950.00

Bowl, 7-1/2" w, 6-1/8" w, deep quatraform bowl, applied quatraform rim, blue, clear internal dec, trapped air bubble square, circles, and gold inclusions, c1950...................360.00

Centerpiece Set, two 8-1/2" baluster ftd ewers, seven 8-1/2" ftd compote, red and white latticino stripes with gold flecks, applied clear handles and feet, 3 pc set...........................150.00

Decanter, 13" h, figural clown, bright red, yellow, black, and white, aventurine swirls, orig stopper 250.00

Goblet, 7" h, etched, enameled biblical scenes.................200.00

Sherbet, 4" d, 4-1/2" h, ruby bowl, clear stem, gold knob ..195.00

Sherry, amber swirled bowls, blue beaded stems, 8 pc set 495.00

Tableware, green, applied blue ruffle and prunts, 12 champagnes, compote, 11 dessert plates, 13 sherbets with 12 underplates, 11 tumblers, 10 wines, 70 pc set 2,500.00

Vase, 8" h, handkerchief shape, pale green and white pulled stripe, applied clear rope base, attributed to Barovier, 1930s 65.00

VILLEROY & BOCH

History: Pierre Joseph Boch established a pottery near Luxembourg, Germany, in 1767. Jean Francis, his son, introduced the first coal-fired kiln in Europe and perfected a water-power-driven potter's wheel. Pierre's grandson, Eugene

Plate, Onion pattern, imp "Dresden, Saxony," 10" d, $22.

WARWICK

History: Warwick China Manufacturing Co., Wheeling, West Virginia, was incorporated in 1887 and remained in business until 1951. The company was one of the first manufacturers of vitreous glazed wares in the United States. Production was extensive and included tableware, garden ornaments, and decorative and utilitarian items.

Pieces were hand painted or decorated with decals. Collectors seek portrait items and fraternal pieces from groups such as the Elks, Eagles, and Knights of Pythias.

Some experimental, eggshell-type porcelain was made before 1887. A few examples are found in the antiques market.

Beer Pitcher, 7-5/8" h, decal bust of monk, shaded brown ground, gold trim, IOGA mark..90.00
Bowl, 8" d, 4" h, red poinsettia, shaded brown ground, IOGA mark..70.00
Chocolate Pot, cov, 7-1/2" h, cherries design 65.00
Cup and Saucer, Chateau pattern 10.00
Dresser Tray, 10" l, 6" w, fluted, small blue and yellow flowers, pale blue and yellow ground, mkd "Warwick China" 35.00
Mug, monk reading paper, unsgd...40.00
Pitcher, 9-1/2" h, poppies, IOGA Mark 120.00
Plate
  8-1/4" d, swimming fish decal..50.00
  10" d, coach scene, yellow and gold bands 95.00
Platter, 15" l, raised matte gold ribbed border design, scalloped trim, green helmet mark...45.00
Spirit Jug, 6" h, Dickens character with guitar, shaded brown ground 95.00
Tray, 11-1/4" l, scattered bunches of pink and red roses, gold rim, open handles...25.00
Vase
  8-3/4" h, bud, rose design, helmet mark 125.00
  9-1/2" h, bulbous oval base, narrow neck, flared rim with gold outline, two tapered loop handles, open red flower, green leaves, shaded brown ground, IOGA mark..............155.00
  10-1/2" h, red roses, blue-green ground 95.00
Vegetable Bowl, cov, Chateau pattern................................30.00

WATCHES, POCKET

History: Pocket watches can be found in many places–from flea markets to the specialized jewelry auctions. Condition of movement is the first priority; design and detailing of the case is second.

Descriptions of pocket watches may include the size (16/0 to 20), number of jewels in the movement, whether the face is open or closed (hunter), and the composition (gold, gold filled, or some other metal). The movement is the critical element since cases often were switched. However, an elaborate case, especially if gold, adds significantly to value.

Pocket watches designed to railroad specifications are desirable. They are between 16 and 18 in size, have a minimum of 17 jewels, adjust to at least five positions, and conform to many other specifications. All are openfaced.

Study the field thoroughly before buying. There is a vast amount of literature, including books and newsletters from clubs and collectors.

References: Roy Ehrhardt, *European Pocket Watches*, Book 2, Heart of America Press, 1993; Roy Ehrhardt and Joe Demsey, *Cartier Wrist & Pocket Watches*, Clocks, Heart of America Press, 1992; ——, *Patek Phillipe*, Heart of America Press, 1992; ——, *American Pocket Watch Serial Number Grade Book*, Heart of America Press, 1993; Cooksey Shugart and Richard E. Gilbert, *Complete Price Guide to Watches*, No. 17, Collector Books, 1997.

Periodical: *Watch & Clock Review*, 2403 Champa St., Denver, CO 80205.

Collectors' Clubs: American Watchmakers Institute Chapter 102, 3 Washington Sq., Apt. 3C, Larchmont, NY 10538; Early American Watch Club Chapter 149, P.O. Box 5499, Beverly Hills, CA 90210; National Assoc. of Watch & Clock Collectors, 514 Poplar St., Columbia, PA 17512.

Museums: American Clock & Watch Museum, Bristol, CT; Hoffman Clock Museum, Newark, NY; National Association of Watch and Clock Collectors Museum, Columbia, PA; The Time Museum, Rockford, IL.

Abbreviations:

gf	gold filled
j	jewels
S	size
yg	yellow gold

Baree, Neuchatel, No. 18332, 14k yg, repeater, Roman numerals, subsidiary dial for seconds, hairline to dial 500.00
Bautte, Jq Fd. Geneve, 18k yg, white dial, Roman numerals, chased case with bi-color floral bouquet on one side, mixed meal and enamel dec on other, scalloped edges, enamel damage 260.00
Bijou Watch Co., lady's label, 14k yg, dec dial with ornate hands, subsidiary seconds hand and dial, diamond-set engraved crescent moon and star on case, 14k yg ribbon shaped watch pin, c1900..390.00
Bourquin, Ami, Locle, #30993, 18k yg, key wind, white porcelain dial, black Roman numerals, subsidiary seconds dial, engraved case with black and blue enamel, accented with rose-cut diamonds, fitted wooden box with inlaid dec.......1,100.00
Boutte, #277389, 14k yg, 10 rubies, white dial, black Roman numerals, chased case with red and blue enamel star dec, Russian hallmarks, 29" l ropetwist chain, enamel loss 300.00
Champney, S. P., Worcester, MA, 18k yg, openface, gilt movement, #8063, key wind, white dial, Roman numerals, subsidiary seconds dial, hallmarks, orig key, c1850, dial cracked, nicks to crystal...250.00

Elgin, hunter, 12 size, gold filled case, 17 jewel, $175.

Jacot, Charles E., 18k yg hunter case, nickel jeweled movement, #9562, numbered on dust cov, case and movement, white porcelain dial, Roman numerals, subsidiary dial for seconds, monogrammed case, orig wood case with extra spring, 14k yg chain 750.00

Jurgensen, J. Alfred, Copenhagen, #784, 18k yd hunter case, highly jeweled movement, patent 1865, white porcelain dial, subsidiary dial for seconds, fancy hands, elaborate monogram 3,300.00

Kaston, Eye of Time, brooch, figural eye set with round and baguette diamonds, blue enamel clock for pupil, platinum mount, sgd "Dali"...5,290.00

Moard, Remontoir Cylindre, 14k yg, engraved hunter case, white dial with Roman numerals, 56" l ropetwist chain, small slide, Russian hallmarks...375.00

Patek Philippe & Co, Geneve, 18k yg, open face, movement and case No. 161442, white dial, Roman numerals, bail missing 575.00

Pendant

    Edwardian, octagonal shaped pendant, one side with classical female framed in rose-cut diamonds, other side with goldtone dial with black Arabic numerals, allover green and white enamel dec, some enamel loss 1,380.00

    Eterna, 18k yg, rushed gold, rect form, black line indicators, hallmark, 23.10 dwt 230.00

    Figural, insect, 18k yg, rose-cut diamond accents, blue enamel hinged wings opening to reveal white dial, Roman numerals, flat 23-1/2" trace link chain........................4,500.00

    Swiss, gold filled, repeated, white dial, Arabic numerals, fancy hands, subsidiary seconds dial....................................300.00

U. S. Watch Co., Waltham, 14k yg, hunter, size 6, white dial, black Roman numerals, subsidiary seconds dial, engraved floral and scroll motifs on case...230.00

WATCHES, WRIST

History: The definition of a wristwatch is simply "a small watch that is attached to a bracelet or strap and is worn around the wrist." However, a watch on a bracelet is not necessarily a wristwatch. The key is the ability to read the time. A true wristwatch allows you to read the time at a glance, without making any other motions. Early watches on an arm bracelet had the axis of their dials, from 6 to 12, perpendicular to the band. Reading them required some extensive arm movements.

The first true wristwatch appeared about 1850. However, the key date is 1880 when the stylish, decorative wristwatch appeared and almost universal acceptance occurred. The technology to create the wristwatch existed in the early 19th century with Brequet's shock-absorbing "Parachute System" for automatic watches and Ardien Philipe's winding stem.

The wristwatch was a response to the needs of the entrepreneurial age with its emphasis on punctuality and planned free time. Sometime around 1930 the sales of wristwatches surpassed that of pocket watches. Swiss and German manufacturers were quickly joined by American makers.

The wristwatch has undergone many technical advances during the 20th century including self-winding (automatic), shock-resistance, and electric movements.

References: Hy Brown and Nancy Thomas, *Comic Character Timepieces*, Schiffer Publishing, 1992; Gisbert L. Brunner and Christian Pfeiffer-Belli, *Wristwatches, A Handbook and Price Guide*, Schiffer Publishing, 1997; James M. Dowling and Jeffrey P. Hess, *The Best of Time: Rolex Wristwatches, An Unauthorized History*, Schiffer Publishing, 1996; Roy Ehrhardt and Joe Demsey, *Cartier Wrist & Pocket Watches, Clocks*, Heart of America Press, 1992; ——, *Patek Phillipe*, Heart of America Press, 1992; ——, *Rolex Identification and Price Guide*, Heart of America Press, 1993; Sherry and Roy Ehrhardt and Joe Demsey, *Vintage American & European Wrist Watch Price Guide*, Book 6, Heart of America Press, 1993; Edward Faber and Stewart Unger, *American Wristwatches*, revised ed., Schiffer Publishing, 1996 Anton Kreuzer, *Omega Wristwatches*, Schiffer Publishing, 1996; Heinz Hampel, *Automatic Wristwatches from Switzerland*, Schiffer Publishing, 1997; Fritz von Osterhausen, *Movado History*, Schiffer Publishing, 1996; --, *Wristwatch Chronometers*, Schiffer Publishing, 1997; Cooksey Shugart and Richard E. Gilbert, *Complete Price Guide to Watches*, No. 17, Collector Books, 1997.

Periodical: *International Wrist Watch*, 242 West Ave., Darien, CT 06820.

Collectors' Clubs: International Wrist Watch Collectors Chapter 146, 5901C Westheimer, Houston, TX 77057; National Assoc. of Watch & Clock Collectors, 514 Poplar St., Columbia, PA 17512; The Swatch Collectors Club, P.O. Box 7400, Melville, NY 11747.

Museums: American Clock & Watch Museum, Bristol, CT; Hoffman Clock Museum, Newark, NY; National Association of Watch and Clock Collectors Museum, Columbia, PA; The Time Museum, Rockford, IL.

Borel, gentleman's, cocktail, 14k yg, 17 jewel, black dial with kaleidoscope like center, goldtone Arabic numerals, abstract indicators, leather Borel strap 400.00

Boucheron, gentleman's, dress tank, A250565, white gold, reeded bezel and dial, invisible clasp, black leather Boucheron strap, French hallmarks, orig leather pouch...............2,150.00

Buccellati, Gianmaria, gentleman's, dress, 18k yg, fancy engrave dial, black tracery enamel, black leather strap, 18k yg clasp, Italian hallmarks......................................6,900.00

Bueche Girod, lady's, 18k yg, elongated oval goldtone dial, rect bezel with stylized hinge lucks, satin band, c1970 ....980.00

Bucherer, Lady's, 18k yg, Swiss movement, 17 jewel, designed as double-hinged engraved bangle, center covered watch, cream dial, applied goldtone Arabic and abstract indicators, Swiss hallmarks 165.00

Cartier, gentleman's, 18k yg, rect convex white dial, black Roman numerals, round gold bezel, black leather strap........1,380.00

Chopard, Geneve, lady's, 18k yg, goldtone oval dial framed in carved coral with flanking pave-set diamond accents, gold mesh bracelet, buckle with "C" logo...........................1,725.00

Elgin, lady's, 14k yg, MOP dial, black abstract and Arabic numeral indicators, hinged freeform cover with diamonds and cultured pearl accent, tapering link bracelet with mesh edges, 33.80 dwt 500.00

Hamilton Watch Co., lady's
    Art Deco, bezel and shoulders set with round baguette diamonds, platinum mount, black chord strap, white gold-filled clasp, minor discoloration to dial 460.00
    Dress, silvertone rect dial, applied Arabic numerals, flanked by four graduating collet set diamonds, diamond-set platinum bracelet, 2.16 cts...2,300.00

Herna, lady's, 14k yg, 17 jewel, sq cream dial, applied gold indicators, heavy mesh bracelet, 22.70 dwt 320.00

Jurgensen, Jules, gentleman's, dress, 14k white gold, Swiss movement, silvertone brushed dial, abstract indicators, diamond-set bevel, black faux alligator strap 290.00

Le Coultre, gentleman's, Futurematic, goldtone dial, subsidiary seconds dial, power reserve indicator, 10k yg-filled mount, lizard strap, 1950s 435.00

Lehman, lady's, Retro, Uti movement, 18k yg, round goldtone dial with ruby indicators, one half framed in graduated calibre-cut channel-set rubies, snake like bracelet, French hallmarks, slight discoloration to dial...1,495.00

Lucien Piccard, lady's, Retro, 14k yg, MOP dial, Arabic numeral and abstract indicators, framed in channel0-set rubies, bracelet of circular links centered by gold discs framed in rubies, orig box...980.00

Movado
    Gentleman's, 14k yg, tank, stepped lugs, slightly bowed sides, goldtone dial, Roman numerals and abstract indicators, subsidiary seconds dial, worn leather strap, crystal loose 230.00
    Lady's, 14k yg, square dial, integral link bracelet, 17.00 dwt 265.00
    Lady's, 18k yg, goldtone dial, abstract indicators, 14k yg mesh bracelet 260.00

Nardin, Ulysse
    Gentleman's, 14k yg, chronometer, goldtone dial, luminescent quarter sections, applied abstract and Arabic numeral indicators, subsidiary seconds dial, lugs with scroll accents, leather strap, discoloration and scratches to dial 290.00
    Lady's, Retro, bi-color gold, stylized buckle motif, calibre-cut rubies and diamonds accent, snake link bracelet, slight discoloration to dial 2,185.00

Omega, gentleman's, 18k yg, round cream dial, goldtone Arabic numeral and abstract indicators
    Heavy mesh bracelet, mild soil to dial, 44.80 dwt........460.00
    Subsidiary seconds dial 225.00

Rolex, Oyster Perpetual
    Gentleman's, 14k yg, goldtone dial, abstract indicators, sweep second hand, ostrich strap, slight spotting to dial 850.00
    Gentleman's, stainless steel, Air King, silvertone dial, applied abstract indicators, sweep second hand, oyster bracelet with clasp, discoloration to dial, scratches to crystal 575.00
    Lady's, stainless steel, date, crenelated bezel, silvertone dial, abstract indicators, sweep second hand, magnifying glass on date aperture, jubilee bracelet 1,035.00
    Lady's, stainless steel, precision, cream dial, abstract indicators with phosphorescent, subsidiary seconds dial, slight discoloration to dial 1,380.00

Swiss, lady's, 18k yg, Swiss movement, manual wind, domed bezel, goldtone dial, black Roman numerals, hallmark, leather strap...920.00

Tiffany & Co
    Gentleman's, 18k yg, lapis lazuli color dial, stepped bezel, black crocodile strap...............................635.00
    Lady's, 14k yg, oval goldtone dial, black line indicators, fix tail chain bracelet, 10.50 dwt...450.00
    Lady's, 14k yg, Retro, white sq dial, black Arabic numerals, applied gold indicators, domed crystal, flanked by 10 diamonds, 2 aquamarines, two rect link chains 1,035.00
    Lady's, 18k yg, Atlas, Roman numerals on bezel, orig leather strap, blue felt pouch...980.00
    Lady's, 18k yg, back wind, textured gold dial with black Roman numerals and abstract indicators, diamond frame, textured gold bracelet, boxed...920.00

Ullman, M. & W, Art Deco, Swiss movement, 17 jewel, cartouche form, set with diamonds, accented with blue stones, cream dial, Arabic numerals, platinum mount, stainless steel band 200.00

Universal, Geneve, Uni-Compax, gentleman's, 18k yg, 2 dial chronograph, silver-tone dial, sweep seconds hand, black lizard strap 980.00

Uti, Paris, Spritzer and Furhmann, lady's, 18k yg, silvertone dial, applied goldtone indicators, leather strap with keyhole form closure, hallmarks, wear to strap...........................575.00

Vacheron & Constantin, Geneve, gentleman's, 18k yg, black dial, goldtone abstract and Arabic numeral indicators, subsidiary seconds dial, black leather strap 1,725.00

WATERFORD

History: Waterford crystal is high-quality flint glass commonly decorated with cuttings. The original factory was established at Waterford, Ireland, in 1729. Glass made before 1830 is darker than the brilliantly clear glass of later production. The factory closed in 1852. One hundred years later it reopened and continues in production today.

Bowl
    6" d, allover diamond cutting...70.00
    8" d, DQ, thumbprint stem...125.00
    10" d, ftd, Benjamin Franklin Liberty Bowl, American Heritage collection 275.00

Cake Plate, 10" d, 5-1/4" h, sunburst center, geometric design 85.00

Cake Server, cut glass handle, orig box 80.00

Champagne Flute, 6" h, Coleen pattern, 12 pc set 450.00

Compote, 5-1/2" h, allover diamond cutting above double wafer stem, pr...400.00

Creamer and Sugar, 4" h creamer, 3-3/4" d sugar, Tralee pattern 85.00

Decanter, orig stopper
   10" h, ship's, diamond cutting 200.00
   12-3/4" h, allover diamond cutting, monogram, pr 300.00
Honey Jar, cov 70.00
Lamp, 23" h, 13" d umbrella shade, blunt diamond cutting, Pattern
   L-1122 ....450.00
Napkin Ring, 2" h, 12 pc set 225.00
Old Fashioned Tumbler, 3-1/2" h, Comeragh pattern, pr 70.00
Ring Dish, 5" d, colorless, cut glass, price for 3 pc set......110.00
Vase, 8" h, alternating diamond cut panels and horizontal notches
Wine
   5-1/2" h, Patrick, 8 pc set...220.00
   7-3/8" h, Coleen, 12 pc set 725.00

WAVE CREST

WAVE CREST WARE

c1892

History: The C. F. Monroe Company of Meriden, Connecticut, produced the opal glassware known as Wave Crest from 1898 until World War I. The company bought the opaque, blown-molded glass blanks from the Pairpoint Manufacturing Co. of New Bedford, Massachusetts, and other glassmakers, including European factories. The Monroe Company then decorated the blanks, usually with floral patterns. Trade names used were "Wave Crest Ware," "Kelva," and "Nakara."

References: Wilfred R. Cohen, *Wave Crest*, Collector Books, out-of-print; Elsa H. Grimmer, *Wave Crest Ware*, Wallace-Homestead, out-of-print.

Salt Shaker, Erie Twist, pink flowers, green, blue highlights, 2-1/4" h, 1-3/4" w, $90.

Biscuit Jar, cov, unmarked
   5-1/2" d, 5-1/2" h, pink and white background, melon ribbed, hp flowers 250.00
   8" h, blue and white ground, swirled, cherry blossoms dec, lid with handle 150.00
   8" h, white ground, fern dec 200.00
Bonbon, 7" h, 6" w, Venetian scene, multicolored landscape, dec rim, satin lining missing 1,200.00
Box, cov
   4" d, shell, blue, ftd 325.00
   4-1/4" d, bright blue ground, pink and white flowers, emb shell pattern, hinged 425.00
   4-1/4" d, 3-1/2" h, Bishop's Hat shape, brown-orange ground, pink flowers on lid, no lining, stamped "Nakara"......340.00
   4-1/2" d, 3" h, round, blue and white ground, swirled, wild flowers on lid, unmarked 225.00
   5-1/2" d, 3-1/2" h, Bishop's Hat shape, gray-blue ground, pink and purple floral dec, orig lining, stamped "C.F.M. Co. Nakara" 425.00
   7" d, 4" h, round, irid crystal, holly dec, Cohen, page 51 ....750.00
   7-1/4" d, 3-3/4" h, Baroque Shell, raised pink-gold rococo shells, fancy Arabic pale turquoise dec, opaque white ground, lace-like network of hundreds of precisely placed raised white enamel beads, shiny metal work, satin lining missing 1,450.00
Cigar Humidor, 8-3/4" h, blue body, single-petaled pink rose, pink "Cigar" signature, pewter collar, bail, and lid, flame-shaped finial, sgd "Kelva" 685.00
Cracker Jar, cov
   10-1/2" h, 6" d, barrel shape, green-blue ground, yellow emb crests, hp yellow and brown wild roses, leaves, and stems, silver-plated cover and handle 675.00
   11-1/4" h, 5" w, square, four sides with blown-out dec, pink roses and buds, leaves, medium blue ground, emb metal hardware, sgd "Wave Crest" in pink banner 675.00
Ewer
   14-1/2" h, fishing scene, unmarked 110.00
   16" h, blue ground, melon ribbed, courting scene, unmarked, pr 250.00
Ferner, 7" d, 2-1/2" h, pale blue, swirled, yellow flowers, unmarked 150.00
Jewel Stand, 4" d, 3" h, green and white ground, scroll design, pink floral dec, unmarked 90.00
Mustard Jar, cov, spoon, green ground, floral dec, unmarked 140.00
Pickle Castor, 5-1/2" h, white ground, floral dec, fork holder on both sides of SP holder, unmarked 150.00
Pin Dish, open
   3-1/2" d, 1-1/2" h, pink and white, swirled, floral dec, unmarked..35.00
   4-1/4" d, 2" h, pink and white, eggcrate mold, blue violets dec, mkd..80.00
   5" d, 1-1/2" h, white, scrolls, pink floral dec, marked.......80.00
Plate, 7" d, reticulated border, pond lily dec, shaded pale blue ground 750.00
Salt and Pepper Shakers, pr
   Shape No. 6, blue and white ground, fox and hound dec 75.00
   Swirled, light yellow ground, floral dec, unmarked 75.00
   Tulip, brown and white ground, birds and floral dec 60.00
Sugar Shaker, 3" h, 31/4" d, 8 Helmschmied Swirls, creamy pink ground, hp Johnny Jump-Up sprigs, SP metal cov with emb blossoms and leaves...585.00
Syrup Pitcher, Helmschmied Swirl, ivory colored body, blue and white floral dec, smoky-gray leafy branches, SP lid and collar 485.00
Trinket Dish, 1-1/2" x 5", blue and red flowers....................175.00
Vase, 10" h, pale pink accents on white, pink and orange chrysanthemums, enameled foliage, beaded white top 600.00

WEATHER VANES

History: A weather vane indicates wind direction. The earliest known examples were found on late 17th-century structures in the Boston area. The vanes were handcrafted of wood, copper, or tin. By the last half of the 19th century, weather vanes adorned farms and houses throughout the nation. Mass-produced vanes of cast iron, copper, and sheet metal were sold through mail-order catalogs or at country stores.

The champion vane is the rooster–in fact, the name weathercock is synonymous with weather vane–but the styles and patterns are endless. Weathering can affect the same vane differently; for this reason, patina is a critical element in collectible vanes.

Whirligigs are a variation of the weather vane. Constructed of wood and metal, often by the unskilled, whirligigs indicate the direction of the wind and its velocity. Watching their unique movements also provides entertainment.

References: Robert Bishop and Patricia Coblentz, *Gallery of American Weathervanes and Whirligigs*, E. P. Dutton, 1981; Ken Fitzgerald, *Weathervanes and Whirligigs*, Clarkson N. Potter, 1967; A. B. & W. T. Westervelt, *American Antique Weathervanes* (1883 catalog reprint), Dover Publications, 1982.

REPRODUCTION ALERT

Reproductions of early models exist, are being aged, and then sold as originals.

Weather Vane

Arrow, 39-1/2" l, gilt iron and copper, America, late 19th/early 20th C, repainted, very minor losses 815.00
Arrow Banner, 42" l, gilt zinc, America, 19th C, bullet hole, minor dents 2,530.00
Arrow and Star Banneret, 22" l, painted wood, America, 19th C, cracks, minor losses, paint wear 1,380.00
Beaver, 48" l, painted over giltwood, America, early 20th C, wear 460.00
Bull, copper, orig gilding, New England, late 19th C 6,500.00
Cow, 29" l, molded zinc, America, late 19th C, dents, repainted, very minor holes 230.00
Fish, 35-1/2" l, gilt copper, America, late 19th C, regilt, dents, seam splints 1,380.00
Half Moon with Face, decorative wrought iron, 67" h, some bending 5,550.00
Horse, America, 19th C
  17-3/4" l, running, gilt molded copper, imperfections
  ....1,840.00
  18" h, 27" l, Blackhawk, copper, fine verdigris and bole surface, bullet holes 2,530.00
  20" h, 25" l, tin, galloping, wooden base 1,100.00
  24" h, 17" h, Blackhawk, molded copper, verdigris, repaired bullet hole, dents, seam splits, minor losses 2,645.00
  25" l, running, gilt molded copper, regilt, minor dents, seam splits 805.00
  25-1/2" h, 34" l, prancing, gilt copper, attributed to W. A. Snow, Boston, minor dents, splits repairs, surface imperfections
  ....2,415.00
  26" l, Blackhawk, gilt molded copper, imperfections . 1,380.00

Horse and rider, sheet iron, orig surface, forged iron support straps, late 19th or early 20th C, 40" l, 33" h, $500. Photo courtesy of Aston Macek Auctioneers & Appraisers.

  29" l, running horse, gilded copper, traces of verdigris, regilt, minor dents 4,025.00
  30" l, running horse, molded copper, verdigris, repaired bullet holes, seam splits, minor losses 750.00
  30-1/2" l, running, molded copper, verdigris, imperfections
  ....1,725.00
  41" l, Colonel Patchen, cast zinc head, full bodied copper body, white wash over vestiges of gilt, repair 3,105.00
Lyre, 36" h, 59" l, copper and zinc, America, 19th C, dents
  ....4,890.00
Ram, Merino, "Ethan Allen," molded and gilded copper, full bodied figure, molded zinc head, sheet metal repousse horns and ears, attributed to J. W. Fiske & Co., New York, late 19th C, from Abbot Worsted Co, Westford, MA, weathered gilding and verdigris surface...68,500.00
Rooster, 28-1/2" h, 24" l, gilt over copper on iron stand, bullet holes 770.00
Schooner, 29" h, 41" l, painted wood and zinc, Martha's Vineyard, MA, early 20th C, minor cracks, losses, corrosion 1,150.00
Stag, 25" h, 30" h, leaping, gilt copper, attributed to Harris & Co., Boston, c1885, gilt bole surface, minor imperfections
  ....13,800.00

Whirligig

Locomotive, 10" h, 28-1/8" w, 10" d, painted and carved wood and metal, mechanized engine and signal man, old weathered surface, minor imperfections, America, early 20th C 750.00

WEBB, THOMAS & SONS

History: Thomas Webb & Sons was established in 1837 in Stourbridge, England. The company probably is best known for its very beautiful English cameo glass. However, many other types of colored art glass were produced, including enameled, iridescent, heavily ornamented, and cased.

References: Charles R. Hajdamach, *British Glass, 1800-1914*, Antique Collectors' Club, 1991.

Additional Listings: Burmese; Cameo; Peachblow.

Basket, 8" l, 6-1/2" h, vaseline opalescent shading to pink, petal edge, twisted pink handle, DQ pattern, c1890 ....265.00
Beverage Set, 11-3/4" h x 6" w pitcher, four 3-3/4" tumblers, pale cream ext., brilliant cranberry cased int., large cranberry loop

handle, white, yellow, and magenta roses and leaves dec 875.00

Bowl

5-1/2" w, 5" h, Rainbow MOP satin, triangular, deep pink, yellow, blue, and white, applied thorn feet, raspberry prunt, sgd "Patent"..1,500.00

5-3/4" d, 4-1/2" h, avocado green, sapphire blue stripes, mica flakes, crystal applied fancy drippings on sides, applied crystal rigaree around top edge, applied clear feet, clear berry pontil..235.00

Cologne Bottle, 6" h, cameo, spherical, clear frosted body, overlaid white and red, carved blossoms, buds, leafy stems, and butterfly, linear pattern, hallmarked silver dec, molded and chased blossoms dec 3,200.00

Cream Pitcher

3-1/4" h, sepia to pale tan ground, heavy gold burnished prunus blossoms, butterfly on back, gold rim and base, clear glass handle with brushed gold 385.00

3-3/4" h, 2-1/2" d, bulbous, round mouth, brown satin, cream lining, applied frosted handle.....................................210.00

Ewer, 9" h, 4" d, satin, deep green shading to off-white, gold enameled leaves and branches, 3 naturalistic applies, applied ivory handle, long spout, numbered base.....................425.00

Perfume Bottle, 4-1/4" h, undulating body, yellow overlaid in white, cut and carved as swimming dolphin, inscribed registry mark, "Rd. 18100," rim and cap missing....................4,950.00

Rose Bowl, 2-3/4" h, 3-1/2" d, deep rose, ground pontil, shiny signature "Patent"..385.00

Vase

3-1/2" h, 5-1/2" w, pocket type, Flower and Acorn pattern, MOP satin, bridal white, gold flowers and leaves 650.00

5" h, 6" w, 18" circumference, shaded blue, sky blue to pale white cream, applied crystal edge, enameled gold and yellow dec of flowers, leaves, and buds, full butterfly, entire surface acid-cut in basketweave design...................425.00

5-1/4" h, 3-1/2" d, opaque ivory, cut leaves and berries, brown staining, circular cameo mark on base "Simulated Ivory English Cameo Glass," hallmarked silver rim and frosted ball feet...625.00

7" h, gourd-shaped body, butterscotch yellow shaded to turquoise blue, cased to opal white, outer layer etched and carved as five-petaled rose on front, ornamental grasses on back, linear borders above and below.............1,955.00

Rose Bowl, blue satin, gold prunus blossom dec, gold butterfly on back, polished pontil, 2-1/4" h, 2-1/2" w, $275. Photo courtesy of Johanna Billings.

7" h, 4" d, satin, robin's egg blue, leaves, berries, and vines dec, flowing gold and scroll design, white lining 450.00

7" h, 5" w, satin, basketweave mother of pearl, bulbous base shading from deep blue to pale blue, creamy lining 750.00

7-1/4" h, 4" w at shoulder, Rainbow MOP satin, pink, yellow, blue, and white, DQ, flaring top, broad shoulder, tapered body, glossy white int., sgd "Patent"....................1,250.00

7-1/4" h, Japanesque, pale oval heat reactive body, white Burmese to pink at top, overall delicate oriental sepia scenes 345.00

7-1/2" h, 5-5/8" d, shaded orange overlay, off-white lining, gold flowers and fern-like leaves, gold butterfly on back, applied bronze-colored glass handles..................................255.00

8" h, 4" w, satin, pink and white stripes, fancy frilly top, bulbous base, unlined 425.00

10" h, 4" w, satin, pulled down edges, deep rose shading to pink, creamy lining, ruffled top, dome foot, pr 550.00

10-1/2" h, gourd shape, satin, bright yellow shading to pale yellow, creamy white lining, bleed-through in pontil 285.00

10-1/2" h, 4" w, bulbous, gold floral prunus blossoms, leaves, branches, pine needles, and insect, satin ground shaded brown to gold, creamy white lining, Jules Barbe dec 450.00

20" h, 7" w, banjo shape, bright yellow-green ground, pink and white azalea dec, green and white leaves, gold highlights, allover small enameled flowers on neck, painted and enameled collar, dome foot, two applied thorn handles, slight roughness to handles 895.00

WEDGWOOD

History: In 1754, Josiah Wedgwood and Thomas Whieldon of Fenton Vivian, Staffordshire, England, became partners in a pottery enterprise. Their products included marbled, agate, tortoiseshell, green glaze, and Egyptian black wares. In 1759, Wedgwood opened his own pottery at the Ivy House works, Burslem. In 1764, he moved to the Brick House (Bell Works) at Burslem. The pottery concentrated on utilitarian pieces.

Between 1766 and 1769, Wedgwood built the famous works at Etruria. Among the most-renowned products of this plant were the Empress Catherina of Russia dinner service (1774) and the Portland Vase (1790s). The firm also made caneware, unglazed earthenwares (drabwares), piecrust wares, variegated and marbled wares, black basalt (developed in 1768), Queen's or creamware, and Jasperware (perfected in 1774).

Bone china was produced under the direction of Josiah Wedgwood II between 1812 and 1822 and revived in 1878. Moonlight luster was made from 1805 to 1815. Fairyland luster began in 1920. All luster production ended in 1932.

A museum was established at the Etruria pottery in 1906. When Wedgwood moved to its modern plant at Barlaston, North Staffordshire, the museum was expanded.

References: Susan and Al Bagdade, *Warman's English & Continental Pottery & Porcelain*, 2nd ed., Wallace-Homestead, 1991; Diana Edwards, *Black Basalt*, Antique Collectors Club, 1994; Robin Reilly, *Wedgwood*, Antique

Collectors Club, 1994; Peter Williams, *Wedgwood*, Wallace-Homestead, 1992.

Periodical: *ARS Ceramica*, 5 Dogwood Court, Glen Head, NY 11545.

Collectors' Clubs: Wedgwood Collectors Society, P.O. Box 14013, Newark, NJ 07198; The Wedgwood Society, The Roman Villa, Rockbourne, Fordingbridge, Hants, SP6 3PG, England.

Museums: Art Institute of Chicago, Chicago, IL; Birmingham Museum of Art, Birmingham, AL; Cincinnati Museum of Art, Cincinnati, OH; Cleveland Museum of Art, Cleveland, OH; Henry E. Huntington Library and Art Gallery, San Marino, CA; Nassau County Museum System, Long Island, NY; Nelson-Atkins Museum of Art, Kansas City, MO; Potsdam Public Museum, Potsdam, NY; Rose Museum, Brandeis University, Waltham, MA; Wadsworth Atheneum, Hartford, CT.

SPECIAL AUCTION

Skinner Inc.
Bolton Gallery
357 Main St.
Bolton, MA 01740
(508) 779-6241

Agate Ware

Candleholder, 6-1/2" h, surface agate, applied creamware drapery swags, black basalt base, wafer Wedgwood & Bentley mark, c1775, restored chip to socle 1,495.00
Vase, cov, 9-1/2" h, solid agate, creamware sibyl finials, traces of gilding, black basalt base, imp wafer Wedgwood & Bentley marks, c1770, gilt rim wear, covers with rim chips, nicks to bases, pr 7,500.00

Basalt

Bust
  7-3/4" h, Locke, raised base, imp title and mark, c1865 ....525.00
  18" h, Minerva, imp mark and title, imp as lamp, chips restored to nose 1,610.00
Crater Urn, 11-1/2" d, pierced disc cover, inset lid, polychrome enamel floral designs, iron-red trim, imp mark, restored rim chips 1,265.00
Crocus Pot and Tray, 9-3/4" l, hedgehog shape, imp marks, c1800, repaired chips 920.00
Figure
  5-1/8" h, reclining baby, after Della Robbia, imp mark, mid-19th C, foot rim chips 690.00
  5-1/4" h, Toucan group, two birds with glass eyes, freeform circular base, modeled by Ernest Light, c1913, imp marks 1,380.00
  7-1/2" h, Cupid and Psyche, seated figures, oval base, imp mark and title 1,380.00
Incense Burner, 5-1/2" h, pierced cover seated on bowl supported by three dolphins, triangular base, imp "Josiah Wedgwood Feb. 2, 1805," cov chips restored 1,610.00
Pitcher, 6-1/2" h, Club, enameled floral dec, imp mark, c1860 ....345.00
Plaque, 10-3/4" x 19-1/4", black, "Death of a Roman Warrior," high relief, warrior figures carrying body of Meleanger, imp mark, small restored chips 2,875.00

Basalt, sugar bowl, seated woman finial, 5-1/4" w, $375.

Vase
  9-3/4" h, engine turned, fixed lid, applied bacchus head handles and drapery swags, Wedgwood & Bentley wafer mark, handles restored 1,200.00
  12-1/2" h, two handles, iron-red, black, and white classical figures on one side, stylized palmette design on reverse, gadroon and dot, palmette, laurel, and dot, and spearhead and dot borders, imp mark, c1800 .... 4,325.00
  14" h, cov, serpent handles terminating to satyr masks, relief of Venus and Cupid, engine turning to base, shoulders, neck and cover, imp Wedgwood & Bentley wafer mark, c1775 .... 1,725.00
Wine and Water Ewers, 15-1/2" h, water ewer with triton seated on shoulders and head of marine monster below the spout, wine with bacchus seated on shoulder's, ram's head below spout, imp marks, mid-19th C, base restored to water ewer, pr 1,955.00

Blue Transfer Printed Earthenware

Platter
  12-1/2" x 16-1/2", Corinth pattern, imp mark, early 19th C, rim chips on back 160.00
  15-5/8" x 20-1/4", botanical flowers pattern, imp mark, early 19th C, glaze wear spots 200.00
Sink, 13-3/4" d, Chinese Temple pattern, brass drain, collar, imp mark, c1830, chips at drain, glaze wear 375.00
Slop Pail, cov, 9-1/4" h, Willow Ware pattern, rattan handle, printed and imp marks, c1913 .... 460.00
Teapot, 7-3/4" h, Oaklands pattern, imp and printed marks, 1909, spout chips, cover stained and dated 200.00
Tiles, each 6" sq, set of 12 showing different months, designed by Helen J. A. Miles, each titled, set in wood and lucite backed frame, raised marks, c1877, light edge wear 815.00

Bone China, First period, c1820

Celery Dish, gilt diamond border, printed mark, foot rim, light gilt war 175.00
Lithophane, 2-5/8" x 3-3/4", matte black glazed ground, muse subjects, printed marks, c1900, price for pr 550.00
Tea Set, 11" cov teapot, 51/2" l creamer, 5-1/2" cup and saucer, 6-1/2" cov sugar, 5-1/2" d waste bowl, blue transfer printed Chinese figural landscape, printed marks, slight damage, 5 pc 435.00
Tureen, cov, underplate, 7-1/8" l, oval, polychrome floral dec, printed mark, rim chip to cov 346.00

Vase, 5-1/2" h, trumpet form, deep blue ground, gilt trimmed cartouche of youth to one side, floral spray on reverse, sgd "J. Thorley," printed factory mark, c1901, slight rim restoration 260.00

Caneware

Game Pie, 7" l, oval, liner, molded, rabbit finial, imp mark, 1865, liner cracked..435.00
Pie Dish, 12" l, oval, liner, leaf molded cover, imp marks, 1863 ....920.00
Potpourri Basket, 4-1/4" h, black basalt fruiting grapevine relief, imp mark, rim staining 575.00
Teapot
    4-1/2" h, bamboo form, five-sided body, imp Wedgwood and Bentley mark, c1780, slight nicks to spout............2,990.00
    Cov, 7" l, white fruiting grapevine relief, imp mark, c1830, base rim chip 175.00

Cream Ware

Bowl, 8-1/8" l, reticulated, molded fiddleback ladle, imp "Wedgwood," stains, edge chip..160.00
Plate, 9-1/8" d, scenic, little girl and mother buying buns from the Bun Man, back titled "Buns!, Buns!, Buns!," 1863 mark and artist sgd "Lessore" 335.00
Vase, 6" h, molded grape vines and foliage, painted band of strawberries, mid 19th C, minor damage 90.00

Drab Ware

Bowl, 7" d, lilac, imp mark, 19th C.......................................200.00
Chess Figure, 4-1/4" h, robed warrior representing King with child grasping at his side, imp mark, c1800 ....815.00
Sugar, cov, 5-1/4" l, applied grapevines in relief, imp mark, 19th C 275.00
Teapot
    5-3/4" l, unglazed, scrolled floral relief, orange peel body, imp mark, c1830, spaniel finial, spout restored 175.00
    6-3/4" l, glazed and molded gothic shape, faceted sides, imp mark, c1830..200.00

Jasper

Barber Bottle, 11" h, three color, green ground, white relief and lilac ground medallions, bacchus head reliefs to shoulder, imp mark, mid 19th C, cover insert damaged....................2,100.00
Bowl, 5" d, solid light blue, white foliate relief, polished int., imp mark, c1800...550.00
Door Knobs, 1-7/8" x 2-5/8" oval, solid light blue, white relief classical subject, 19th C, pr..400.00
Jardiniere, 4-1/2" h, black, white classical figures, imp marks, early 20th C..435.00
Letter Box, 8-1/4" l, 5" d, 6" h, seven blue jasper plaques with white classical reliefs, ormolu mounts 1,955.00
Medallion, 3-1/2" x 4-1/4", light green dip, oval, portrait of Admiral Richard Howe, imp title and mark, ...260.00
Oenochoe Jug, 7-1/2" h, solid light blue, white ring mounts to neck and socle, bacchus mask relief to handle terminal, imp mark, 19th C, handle repairs 575.00
Perfume Bottle, 4-3/4" h, oval, green jasper dip, white classical relief, SP screw top 690.00
Plaque
    3" x 8", rect, solid black, applied white classical relief of muses, imp mark, 19th C, wood frame 490.00
    6-1/4" d, circular, solid blue, white relief palmette border, figural frieze from Achilles in Scyros among the Daughters of Lycomedes, imp marks, mounted in ebonized wood frame, pr 1,610.00
    6-1/2" x 8-1/2", rect, solid blue, white relief of the Sacrifice to Hymen, imp mark, crazing lines 460.00
Pot, cov, 3-1/2" h, light green jasper dip, white classical and foliate relief, imp mark, late 19th C...............................425.00

Capri Ware, inkwell, 2-5/8" d, $650.

Vase
    8-3/4" h, cov, "Apollo," light blue, white jasper relief and raised Latin verse, "CC Posnatum Conditorem Anno Viget Ars Eturiae Redilnegrata," designed by John Goodwin to commemorate 200th anniversary of birth of Joseph Wedgwood, limited edition of 50, mounted on ebonized wood base, imp marks, 1930, cover restored...................................1,100.00
    9-1/2" h, black, white relief, satyr mask handles, classical subjects, foliate borders, imp mark, 19th C, ...1,100.00
    10-1/2" h, solid black, white classical relief, base with half-length figure wearing Phrygian cap, imp "T. Lovatt," factory mark, c1877 ....1,955.00
    15-3/4" h, solid pale blue, white relief of children playing Blind Man's Bluff, mounted to white marble base set with oval Wedgwood pale blue jasper medallion with white relief of children playing, modern cov, imp mark, late 18th C, minor damage 1,850.00

Lusters

Butterfly, Melba bowl, 8" d, butterflies on MOP ext., orange luster int., Pattern Z4832, printed mark, c1920 ....550.00
Dragon
    Bowl, 6-5/8" d, octagonal, mottled blue ext., MOP int., ornament center, paneled Oriental landscape border, printed mark, c1920 ....375.00
    Cup, 2" h, 3 handles, blue ext., gilt reptiles, eggshell int. with central dragon, printed mark, c1920 ....275.00
Fairyland
Bowl
    5-1/2" d, pattern Z4968, leap-frogging elves ext., mother-of-pearl int. with elves and butterflies, printed mark, c1920, restored 690.00
    6-1/2" d, shape 3227, Daventry, ext. with Springbok border, int. with wide gnome border, center
    8-3/4" d, Firbolgs III ext., washed ruby color ground, MOP int., fish border, Thumbelina central medallion, printed marks, c1925...2,750.00
    from White Pagodas, c1920 ....6,900.00
    9" d, circular, ext. with Poplar Trees, flame sky, int. with Elves and Bell Branch, printed mark, c1920, restored 1,725.00
Chalice Bowl, 10-1/2" d, pattern Z5360, ext. with Twyford Garlands, Fairy Gondola int., printed mark, c1920 ...13,800.00

Malfrey Pot, cov, 8-1/8" h, black, Candlemas design, printed mark, cov restored 2,300.00
Punch Bowl
9-1/2" d, pattern Z4968, ext. with Poplar Trees, black sky, int., with daylight background and Fairy with large hat, printed marks, c1920, int. wear 4,025.00
11" d, Firbolgs, ruby ext., MOP Thumbelina int., printed mark and no., c1920 .... 3,600.00
Vase, 9-3/4" h, black, trumpet, shape 2810, Z4968, Butterfly Women, printed marks, c1920, pr 4,000.00
Hummingbird
Bowl, blue mottled ext., orange int., printed mark, c1920
4-3/4" d, octagonal, pattern Z5294 .... 420.00
8" d, octagonal 750.00
9-1/2" d, circular, pattern Z5294 .... 690.00
Vase, 8-7/8" h, pattern Z5294, blue mottled ext., orange mottled int., shape 2351, printed mark, c1920 .... 690.00
Moonlight
Coffeepot, cov, 5-1/2" h, imp mark, c1810, small chips to spout and cover 690.00
Teapot, cov, 3" h, drum form, imp mark, c1810, rim chips restored, nicks to spout rim 575.00
Wall Pocket, 10" l, nautilus shell, c1810, restorations, pr 575.00

Majolica

Bowl, 11" d, cauliflower, multicolored, cobalt blue, rim nick on back 495.00
Caterer Jug 770.00
Compote
8-1/2" d, 8-1/2" h, cherub, cattails and flowers 770.00
11" l, Argenta Ware, oval, pierced gallery, fruiting grapevine border, base with 4 hoofed legs, imp marks, c1871, light staining 260.00
Creamer and Sugar, cov, 4-1/2" h creamer, 4-3/4" h sugar, Argenta Ware, molded arched panels of flowers, imp marks, c1882 .... 550.00
Cup and Saucer, 5-1/8" d saucer, molded flower design, imp marks, c1879, 4 pc set 865.00
Cuspidor, 7" d, mottled blue, brown, and yellow glaze, imp marks, 1885 .... 345.00
Dessert Plate, Argenta, 5-3/4" d 250.00
Dish, Argenta Ware
7-1/2" l, shaped square form, molded rope border, central basket of flowers, imp marks, c1880 .... 575.00
13" l, oval, flowering berry pattern, imp marks, c1870 .... 375.00
Floor Urn, 26" h, cobalt blue, ladies seated at top of bulbous vase, drapes of laurel wreaths and ladies head at base, turquoise, yellow, white, brown, green, and pink, repair to one base, minor nicks and repair to feet of ladies, pr 5,500.00
Fruit Plate, 6-1/2" d, turquoise basketweave 250.00
Garden Seat, 17-3/4" h, Argenta Ware, Rubens, pillow-form square seat, side panels of flowers and scrolled fines, scrolled legs leaf molded and supporting fruiting festoons, imp marks, c1875, glaze wear, one festoon repaired, chips to feet 5,750.00
Jug
5-3/8" h, Centennial commemorative, dark blue ground, titled portraits on each side of Lincoln and Washington, imp marks, c1875, rim lines and chips 500.00
7" h, Reed pattern, dark blue ground, molded and colored design, imp mark, c1868 .... 865.00
8-1/2" h, cobalt blue, green ivy and grapes, brown ground, hinged silver top, handle re-attached 715.00
9-1/4" h, Caterer, raised jewels and banded motto, imp factory mark, incised monogram "FBR" for designer Frederick Bret Russel, c1870, rim restored 345.00
Oyster Plate, brown basketweave and shell 1,210.00
Pitcher, 7" h, sunflower and urn, turquoise 770.00

Plate
8-3/4" d, mottled, reticulated 165.00
9" d, Argenta, bird and fan, rim wear, slight hairline 110.00
9" d, crane 690.00
9" d, wicker, minor rim nicks on back 200.00
Platter, 25-3/4" l, Argenta Ware, Ocean, oval, light staining, c1875 .... 2,100.00
Salad Compote, 10-1/4" d, 7" h, Argenta Ware, fork and spoon framed ovoid panels with variety of vegetables, cruet bottles surrounding base, imp mark, c1877 .... 980.00
Salt, 5-1/4" d, figural, child holding basket on irregular rocky base, imp marks, c1875, slight glaze loss to basket rim 550.00
Strawberry Dish, 9-3/4" l, Argenta Ware, heart-shaped dish, molded strawberries and leaves, imp mark, 1871 date letters 550.00
Sugar, Argenta, bird and fan, repair to lid, hairline in base 125.00
Umbrella Stand, 24" h, Argenta Fan, hairlines 1,760.00
Vase
11" h, cov, Louis XV, scrolled leaf handles, raised vines and leaves on shoulder and neck, laurel framed oval medallions on each side, one side with portrait of Contesse Du Barry, other with trophy, imp mark, c1880, chip to cov, edge wear 575.00
12" h, sunflower, deep blue ground, raised leaves and flowers, imp mark, c1875 .... 1,725.00
Wall Pocket, 9" h, modeled as bird's nest with oak branches, bird perched to one side, imp mark, 1874 .... 1,725.00

Miscellaneous

Mortar and Pestle, 6" h, 3-1/8" d, "Vitreous Stoneware," wood handle, imp marks, mid-19th C 225.00
Pitcher, 6-1/4" h, Etruria, horse and hound hunting scene, hound handle 175.00
Plate, luncheon, hunt scene, copper luster border, Etruria, 6 pc set 600.00
Wine Cooler, 10" h, redware, fruiting vine molded body, raised mask handles, imp mark, early 19th C 550.00

Pearlware

Display Teapot, cov, 18-1/2" h, gray enhanced gilt dec, leaf design to spout, banded borders, central knot emblems, imp mark and "pearl,"c1850, finial restored at join, handle restored, slight gilt wear 1,380.00
Potpourri Vase
Cov, 16" h, globular form, green ground body, red enhanced blue transfers of floral sprays, birds, and butterflies, insert lid, imp mark, 19th C 1,725.00
Pierced cov, blue ground, white relief floral swags, band above engine-turned fluting, imp mark, c1800, body restoration, married cover 230.00
Teapot, 5-1/2" h, blue transfer peony printed design, imp and printed marks, c1908, cover repairs 345.00

Queen's Ware

Basket, 9" l, oval, undertray, basketweave molded bodies, pierced galleries, green and black enamel oak leaves and trim lines, imp mark, early 19th C 290.00
Bidet, 21-1/2" l, fitted mahogany stand with cov, imp mark 425.00
Child's Tea Set, brown feather banding with red trim lines, circular 14-1/4" d tray, 5-1/4" h cov coffeepot, 2-1/2" h cov teapot, 3-1/4" creamer, 2-1/2" h cov sugar, 4" h cov tea canister, five 2" d tea bowls, five coffee cups, four 3-3/8" d saucers, imp marks, late 18th C, nicks, rim chips 3,740.00
Compote, 11-3/4" l, ftd, oval, banded border pattern 32, brown laurel, imp mark, late 18th C 345.00

Custard Cup Set, six 3-1/2" h cov two-handled custard cup, enameled leaf and berry border, 8-1/2" x 13" rect tray with cut corners, imp marks, printed retailer James Powell & Sons mark, c1909, some enamel flaking to finials 865.00
Dish, 12-1/4" d, ftd, Armorial, enamel dec with central crest titled "Noli Irritare Leones," wide border in Imari-type palette and design, printed mark "Marie Lyons Brighton 1883," imp factory mark, c1883, rim chip 175.00
Egg Tray, 6-1/4" x 9-1/4", black enamel trim, cut corner rect form, six pierced egg cups, raised oval salt cellar, imp mark, c1800, two cups damaged......................................520.00
Figure, 8-1/2" h, Psyche, nude figure seated on freeform rock, pierced circular base, 20th C 345.00
Jug, 11-1/2" h, enamel dec scallop and thistle borders, thistle sprays on body, imp mark, 20th C 115.00
Plate, 9" d, octagonal, raised oak leaf border, central enameled dec figural landscape, artist sgd "Emile Lessore," imp mark, c1872....................................320.00
Pitcher and Bowl Set, 8-3/4" h pitcher, 15" d bowl, banded lag and feather pattern in brown and iron red, imp marks and date letters, c1877-79, rim line 300.00
Pitcher, 12-1/2" h, barrel form, banded body, imp mark, late 18th C 300.00
Platter
    5-3/4" x 20-3/8", oval, polychrome bird and floral dec in Chelsea style, imp mark, 1871 ....375.00
    18-7/8" d, circular, green strawberry leaf and drop pattern with black dots and lines, #197, imp marks, early 19th C 375.00
Slop Pail, cov, 9-7/8" h, brown transfer printed botanical flowers, imp mark and date letters, c1885................750.00
Teapot, cov
    4-1/2" h, globular, black transfer printed Tea Party and Shepherd, cabbage leaf molded spout, double entwined handle, rose finial, imp upper and lower case mark, c1780, slight nicks to cover rim 1,265.00
    5-3/4" h, globular, double twisted handle, leaf molded spout, enameled body with Chinese figures in courtyard setting, imp mark, c1775, finial and chip to spout lip restored 1,725.00
Vase, cov, 11" h, drapery swags in relief, enameled painted botanical border, imp mark, 19th C, rim line to cover 690.00
Veilleuse, 3-3/8" h, cover and stand, iron-red and blue enamel banding, imp mark, early 19th C, staining, rim wear.....460.00

Rosso Antico

Bust, 7-1/4" h, Matthew Prior, mounted on raised circular base, imp mark and title, restorations 420.00
Crater Potpourri, pierced disc cover and insert lid, black basalt vine relief, imp mark, early 19th C, foot rim and insert flakes 1,150.00
Cup and Saucer, 5" d, undecorated, imp mark, 19th C, set of 4 ....300.00
Inkstand, 4" h, applied black basalt leaf and berry border on stand, supported by three dolphin feet, central pot insert, imp mark, early 19th C, foot rim restored 550.00
Jug, 3-1/2" h, Egyptian, globular form, banded black basalt relief of hieroglyphs, imp mark, early 19th C........................920.00
Plate, Egyptian, banded black basalt relief of hieroglyphs, imp mark, early 19th C
    6-3/8" d 635.00
    7-7/8" d 635.00
    8-1/4" d 815.00
Sugar Bowl, cov
    4-1/2" h, classical black basalt relief between foliate panels, widow finial, imp mark, c1820 ....450.00
    5" d, Egyptian, banded black basalt relief of hieroglyphs, bowl with meander banding, crocodile finial, imp mark, c1810 ....1,265.00

6-3/4" l, parapet form, white Chinese flowers in relief, imp mark, early 19th C, shallow chips to cov..................690.00
Teapot, cov
    5" h, Cabbage Leaf mold, globular form, imp mark, early 19th C, chips to finial and edge of spout 1,495.00
    7-1/4" l, banded black basalt relief of hieroglyphs above meander, crocodile finial, imp mark, early 19th C......1,725.00
    9" w from handle to spout, banded hieroglyphs in relief including winged discs, sphinx, Apis, and a canopic urn above strapwork border, crocodile finial, imp mark, c1810 ....1,840.00
Vase, 6-1/2" h, modeled as open mouth fish, enamel and gilt dec squid designs, imp marks and date letters, c1870, rim chips, restoration, pr 1,900.00

Stoneware

Bowl, 7-1/8" d, white smear glaze, applied blue fruiting grapevine banding, imp mark, c1820 ....165.00
Candlesticks, pr, 4-3/4" h, white ground, blue relief of wreathed laurel to columns, imp marks, c1825..........................750.00
Jug
    7-1/4" h, white smear glaze, blue slip to neck and handle tops, scenes of hunt scenes in relief, imp mark, c1920, rim chips 150.00
    8" h, white smear glaze, Gothic shape, paneled sides, blue classical figures in relief, imp mark, c1825 ....220.00
Plant Pot, 6-3/4" h, basketweave molded body, white, imp mark, early 19th C 425.00
Teapot, cov
    6-5/8" h, molded gothic shape, white smear glaze, imp mark, c1820....................................250.00
    7" h, smear glaze, arabesque molded, spaniel finial, imp mark, c1830, slight damage..............................200.00

WELLER POTTERY

History: In 1872, Samuel A. Weller opened a small factory in Fultonham, near Zanesville, Ohio. There he produced utilitarian stoneware, such as milk pans and sewer tile. In 1882, he moved his facilities to Zanesville. Then, in 1890, Weller built a new plant in the Putnam section of Zanesville along the tracks of the Cincinnati and Muskingum Railway. Additions followed in 1892 and 1894.

In 1894, Weller entered into an agreement with William A. Long to purchase the Lonhuda Faience Company, which had developed an art pottery line under the guidance of Laura A. Fry, formerly of Rookwood. Long left in 1895, but Weller continued to produce Lonhuda under the new name "Louwelsa." Replacing Long as art director was Charles Babcock Upjohn. He, along with Jacques Sicard, Frederick Hurten Rhead, and Gazo Fudji, developed Weller's art pottery lines.

At the end of World War I, many prestige lines were discontinued and Weller concentrated on commercial wares. Rudolph Lorber joined the staff and designed lines such as Roma, Forest, and Knifewood. In 1920 Weller purchased the plant of the Zanesville Art Pottery and claimed to produce more pottery than anyone else in the country.

Art pottery enjoyed a revival when the Hudson Line was introduced in the early 1920s. The 1930s saw Coppertone and Graystone Garden ware added. However, the Depression forced the closing of the Putnam plant and one on Marietta Street in Zanesville. After World War II, inexpensive Japanese imports took over Weller's market. In 1947, Essex Wire Company of Detroit bought the controlling stock, but early in 1948 operations ceased.

References: Susan and Al Bagdade, *Warman's American Pottery and Porcelain*, Wallace-Homestead, 1994; Sharon and Bob Huxford, *Collectors Encyclopedia of Weller Pottery*, Collector Books, 1979, 1998 value update; Ralph and Terry Kovel, *Kovels' American Art Pottery*, Crown Publishers, 1993.

Collectors' Club: American Art Pottery Assoc., 125 E. Rose Ave., St. Louis, MO 63119.

Additional Listings: See *Warman's Americana & Collectibles* for more examples.

Ashtray
    Coppertone, frog seated at end 95.00
    Roma, 2-1/2" d 35.00
    Woodcraft, 3" d 75.00
Basket
    Florenzo, 5-1/2" 75.00
    Melrose, 10" 145.00
    Sabrinian...165.00
    Silvertone, 8" 350.00

Vase, Hudson, gray and white, yellow daffodil dec, imp, 11-1/4" h, $195.

Batter Bowl, Mammy..895.00
Bowl
    Bonito, underplate 110.00
    Cameo, 6" d, 3-1/4" h, all-over crazing 85.00
    Claremont 325.00
    Claywood, 4" d..40.00
    Cornish, light orange, 7-1/4" d..75.00
    Fleron, 3", all green 80.00
    Hudson dec 200.00
    Knifewood, swans, dark ground....................................255.00
    Marbleized, 5-3/4" d, 1-5/8" d, shades of rose, pink and
        mauve 55.00
    Sabrinian, 6-1/2" x 3" h..240.00
    Sunflower 250.00
Bud Vase, Eocean, 6"...150.00
Candlesticks, pr
    Euclid, 12-1/2" h, orange luster 85.00
    Glendale 165.00
    Lorbeek, 2-1/2" h, shape #1 ....125.00
    Pumila 65.00
Cigarette Holder, figural, frog, Coppertone..........................200.00
Compote, Bonito, 4" h..75.00
Console Bowl
    Sydonia, 17" x 6" 95.00
    Warwick, 10-1/2" d..75.00
Cornucopia
    Lido, mauve 55.00
    Softone, light blue...45.00
    Wild Rose...75.00
Cookie Jar, Mammy, bow on head, chip on back, 2 hairlines
    ....1,100.00
Creamer and Sugar, Pierre, seafoam...................................45.00
Ewer
    Barcelona Ware, orig label..250.00
    Cameo, 10" h, white rose, blue ground 65.00
    Louwelsa, red and orange clover dec, 5-1/2" h, artist sgd
        ....190.00
    Panella..55.00
Figure
    Brighton Kingfisher 350.00
    Brighton Woodpecker, 6" h, orig base 375.00
    Elephant, bug-eyed, Cactus line, yellow 145.00
    Turtle, Coppertone, 5-1/2" l...95.00
Flower Frog
    Marvo, blue..55.00
    Muskota starfish...135.00
Fountain Frog, 5-1/2" h, 6-1/2" w, Coppertone, bright green and
    brown glaze, hole in base and mouth for tube, mkd "12," glaze
    thinning at base 635.00
Ginger Jar, Greora..195.00
Hanging Basket
    Forest, 10" d, orig chains...225.00
    Scenic Green, orig chains..100.00
Jardiniere
    7" h, 7-3/4" d, architectural form, four buttresses and four
        squares on each panel, eggplant glaze with green high-
        lights, mkd "Weller" 435.00
    Claywood, 8", cherries and trees...................................95.00
    Ivory, 5" 45.00
    L'Art Nouveau, 10" h, pheasant motif 400.00
    Marvo, rust, 7-1/2" 85.00
    Roma, cat chasing canary..175.00
Jug, Louwelsa, small 140.00
Lamp, owl 600.00
Mug
    Claywood, star shaped flowers 65.00
    Dickensware, dolphin handle and band, sgraffito ducks
    ....250.00
    Ivory, brown accents, cream ground 55.00
    Louwelsa, raspberries, 6" h 200.00

Pitcher
   Bouquet, 6" h, ruffled top, lavender flower, white ground, artist sgd "M".............60.00
   Louwelsa, 14" h, artist sgd, #750................600.00
   Pansy, 6-1/2" h....................110.00
   Pierre, 5" h.....................50.00
   Zona , kingfisher, green, 7-1/2" h.........150.00
Planter
   Blue Drapery......................60.00
   Forest Tub, 4"....................135.00
   Klyro, small......................45.00
   Sabrinian, 5" x 5"................170.00
   Woodrose, 9" h....................60.00
Salad Plate, Zona, 7-1/2" d.............40.00
Teapot, cov, pink, 5-1/2" h, gold trim, all-over crazing.........75.00
Towel Bar, 12" l, Flemish..............1,750.00
Tub, Flemish...........................85.00
Tumbler, Bonito, multicolored flowers, 4-1/4" h.........70.00
Umbrella Stand, Ivory, 20" h...........225.00
Vase
   Ardsley, 9" h.....................90.00
   Aurelian, 24-1/2" h, 13" d, oviform, flaring rim, four blossoming iriises, high gloss glaze, sgd "L. J. Dibowski," base mkd "Weller, Aurelian No. 52," minor glaze nicks.........1,955.00
   Chase, 9" h......................375.00
   Chengtu, 8" h....................125.00
   Claywood, 9" h...................150.00
   Coppertone, 10-1/2" h............400.00
   Cornish, brown, 10" h............150.00
   Eocean
      8" h..........................300.00
      Sgd "Pillsbury"..............725.00
   Faience, Frederick Rhead
      7-1/2" h, 6-1/2" d, oviform, white and green birds wearing hats on one foot, tobacco brown glaze, sgd "Rhead, Weller, Faience, V509".........1,840.00
      9-1/2" h, 7" d, bulbous, incised standing rabbits playing trumpets, tobacco brown and yellow ground, high glaze, sgd "Rhead, Weller, Faience B489, 7".........1,840.00
   Goldenglow, ftd, 7" h............145.00
   Greora, 9" h.....................190.00
   Hudson
      9-1/2" h, 4" d, white, blue, and green blooming iris, blue ground, sgd "Walch, Weller Pottery".........550.00
      13" h, 4-1/4" d, tall cylinder, white floral blossoms, pink to blue ground, painted paper label, imp "Weller," sgd "Pillsbury".........690.00
   Indian, polychrome, green shaded putty matte glaze, sgd "L. J. Burgess," 10-1/4" h.........600.00
   Iris, polychrome, shaded brown ground artist sgd "D. England," imp "Weller," 8-3/4" h.........775.00
   LaSa, 4" h, bulbous................250.00
   Louwelsa, acorns and oak leaves, olive and dark brown ground, imp "Louwelsa Weller," incised "C. Bloomeri," 11-3/4" h.........220.00
   Lustre, 6" h, bud.................40.00
   Marbleized, 12" h................125.00
   Sicard
      4-1/2" h......................550.00
      5" h, 3" d, triangular form, foliate dec, irid glaze, sgd "Weller, Sicard".........490.00
      7" h, 6" d, circular, foliate dec, rich irid glaze, imp "Weller".........2,415.00
      8" h, 5" d, six rubbed sides tapering outward to base, green clover dec, irid glaze, mkd "27".........1,100.00
      9" h, 4-1/4" d, cylinder, tapering outward to base, irid glaze, stylized peacock feathers, sgd "Weller, Sicard".........1,035.00
   Silvertone, 8-1/2" h.............275.00
   Solitone, 10" h, blue............160.00
   Tutone, Art Deco, 9"............285.00

Warwick
   Bud, 7" h........................50.00
   Double, 5".......................60.00
Woodcraft, 18" h, 7" d, owl and squirrel, green and brown tree trunk, imp "Weller".........750.00
Woodland, Apple Blossom, 10-1/4" x 4-1/4".........250.00
Wall Pocket
   Pearl, 8-1/2" l..................150.00
   Roma 195.00
   Sabrinian.......................475.00
   Suevo...........................195.00
   Sydonia, blue...................225.00
Woodcraft
   9" h, tree-trunk shape, molded leaves, purple plus.........400.00
   10" h, conical, molded owl's head in trunk opening.........300.00
Woodrose, lilac.....................85.00

WESTERN AMERICANA

History: From the Great Plains to the Golden West and from the mid-19th century to the early 20th century, the American West was viewed as the land of opportunity by settlers. Key events caused cataclysmic changes: the 1848 Gold Rush, the opening of the Transcontinental railroad, the silver strikes in Nevada, the Indian massacres and the Oklahoma land rush. By 1890, the West of the cowboy and cattle was dead; Indians had been relocated onto reservations.

The romance did not die. Novels, movies and television, whether through the Ponderosa or Southfork, keep the romance of the West alive. Oil may have replaced cattle, but the legend remains.

References: Warren R. Anderson, *Owning Western History*, Mountain Press Publishing, 1993; Robert W.D. Ball, *Western Memorabilia and Collectibles*, Schiffer Publishing, 1993; Robert W.D. Ball and Edward Vebell, *Cowboy Collectibles and Western Memorabilia*, Schiffer Publishing, 1991, 1993 value update; James Lynn Bartz, *Company Property of Wells, Fargo & Co.'s Express 1852-1918*, Westbound Stage Co., 1993; Judy Crandall, *Cowgirls*, Schiffer Publishing, 1994; *Cowboy Clothing and Gear: The Complete Hamley Catalog of 1942*, Dover Publications, 1995 reprint; Michael Friedman, *Cowboy Culture*, Schiffer Publishing, 1992; R.C. House, *Official Price Guide to Old West Collectibles*, House of Collectibles, 1994; William C. Ketchum Jr., *Collecting the West*, Crown Publishers, 1993; ——, *Western Memorabilia*, Avon Books, 1993; Hunter and Shelkie Montana, *Cowboy Ties*, Gibbs Smith, 1994; Joice I. Overton, *Cowbits and Spurs*, Schiffer Publishing, 1997; Richard C. Rattenbury, *Packing Iron*, Zon International Publishing, 1993; Jim Schleyer, *Collecting Toy Western Guns*, Krause Publications, 1996.

Periodicals: *American Cowboy*, P.O. Box 12830, Wichita, KS 67277; *Boots*, Lone Pine Rd., P.O. Box 766, Challis, ID 83226; *Cowboy Collector Newsletter*, P.O. Box 7486, Long Beach, CA 90807; *Cowboy Guide*, P.O. Box 47, Millwood, NY 10546; *Texas Monthly*, P.O. Box 7088, Red Oak, IA 51591; *The Westerner*, P.O. Box 5253, Vienna, WV, 26105; *Wild West*, 6405 Flank Dr., Harrisburg, PA

17112; *Yippy Yi Yea Magazine*, 8393 E. Holly Rd., Holly, MI 48442.

Collectors' Club: American Barb Wire Collector's Society, 1023 Baldwin Rd., Bakersfield, CA 93304; National Bit, Spur & Saddle Collectors Association, P.O. Box 3098, Colorado Springs, CO 80934; Western American Collectors Society, P.O. Box 620417, Woodside, CA 94062.

Museums: Cowboy & Gunfighter Museum, Craig, CO; Gene Autry Western Heritage Museum, Los Angeles, CA; National Cowgirl Hall of Fame & Western Heritage Center, Hereford, TX; Pony Express Museum, St. Joseph, MO; Rockwell Museum, Corning, NY; Wells Fargo History Museum, Los Angeles, CA; Round Up Hall of Fame & Museum, Pendleton, OR 97801; Seven Acres Antique Village & Museum, Union, IL; Texas Ranger Hall of Fame & Museum, Waco, TX.

Additional Listings: Cowboy Heroes.

Advertising
Banner, 19-1/2" x 29", Winchester, horse-and-rider center, "Headquarters for Winchester Rifles & Shotguns," fringed hem, wood rod..150.00
Sign, Moccasin Agency, fierce Indian with full headdress, emb tin 50.00
Artwork
Buffalo Bill, drawn and burnt by Albert J. Seigfried, Seneca Falls, NY, 1907..120.00
Wells Fargo Depot and Office Building, Moron Taft, CA, 1910, orig ink drawing, 20" x 30", framed............................400.00
Autograph, photo, "Louise Getchell from W.F. Cody, Cauifro Bonito, Feb. 20, 1906" 1,430.00
Bit
J.F. Echaverria, silver inlay, spade bit, full engraving of kissing-birds design, minor restoration 1,870.00
G.S. Garcia, silver inlaid high-port style, curved-snake cheeks, large 2" domed conchos 1,320.00
Phillips and Gutierrez, #20, engraved silver eagle shank style, sgd "Blake Miller" 5,610.00
Jesus Tapia, half-breed, eagle and shield engraved design, c1916..7,700.00
Unmarked, CA spade, silver overlay on brass, narrow mouth, 1850s..3,300.00
Bolo, 3" d, found, filigreed and engraved SS, ruby-eyed steer in yellow, pink and green gold, 1930 ....1,540.00
Book
Allen, A. J., compiler, *Ten Years in Oregon. Travels and Adventures of Doctor E. White and Lady,* Ithaca, 1848, 8vo, orig cloth, first edition, second issue, 430 pgs.........175.00
Beeler, Joe, *Cowboys and Indians: Characters in Oil and Bronze,* Norman, 1967, 8vo, cloth, dust jacket, with pine and ink sketch of Indian, sgd inscription by Beeler on half title 175.00
Brown, John P., *Old Frontiers: The Story of the Cherokee Indians,* Kingsport, 1938, plates, 8vo, cloth 70.00
Custer, Elizabeth B., Tenting on the Plains, 1893 ....20.00
Douglas, Claude L., *Cattle Kings of Texas,* Cecil Baugh, Dallas, 1939, 8vo, pictorial cloth, remnants of dust jacket, many photographic illus 60.00
Farnham, T. J., *Life, Adventures and Travels in California,* New York, 1850, 8vo, publisher's gilt-pictorial cloth, large hand-colored folding map, plates, scattered foxing..........140.00
Greenhow, Robert, *The History of Oregon and California,* Boston, 1844, large folding map, 8vo, early half calf, scattered foxing and browning..460.00
Hamilton, W. T., *My Sixty Years on the Plains: Trapping, Trading, and Indian Fighting,* New York, 1905, portrait frontis-

piece, plates by Charles M. Russell, 8vo, publisher's gilt-lettered cloth, cover portrait label, first edition 150.00
McKenney, Thomas and James Hall, *The Indian Tribes of North America,* Edinburgh, Grant, 1933-34, thick 8vo, orig cloth, 3 volumes..490.00
McKenney-Hall, History of the Indian Tribes of North America, Grant, 1934, 123 color plates, 3-vol set 125.00
Zeisberger, David, *Zeisberger's Indian Dictionary,* Cambridge, 1887, small 4to, orig cloth.............................70.00
Cabinet Card, W.F. Cody, Woodbury-type card, wood frame 1,375.00
Chaps
Bohlin, batwin style, brown, tooled billet (belt), engraved SS buckle, mounted with eight 1878 silver dollars 1,980.00
Hamley, wide, over 1,000 metal studs, c1919 ....4,510.00
Clothing Rack, Tales of Wells Fargo, 1-1/2" x 20" x 20", wood rack, 2 metal hanger loops at top, light oak finish, brown lettering across top, 6 attached black-finished metal horseshoe hangers, 1959 Overland Products, 2 wood pegs missing 90.00
Cuffs, shirt type, tooled leather, c1915.............................500.00
Ephemera
Abert, James W., *Report...in Answer to a resolution of the Senate, a report and map of the examination of New Mexico,* Washington, 1848, large folding map, 24 lithographed plates, 8vo, discount, for the 30th Congress, First Session, Senate Executive Doc. 23 ....550.00
Brown, Samuel R., *The Western Gazetteer; or Emigrant's Directory,* Auburn, 1817, 8vo, first edition, third issue, 360 pgs..290.00
Figure, cowboy, Stetson...35.00
Gun Belt and Holster, Bohlin, 2-tone floral carved, large engraved SS buckle..1,260.00
Headstall (bridle) and bit
Keystone Bros., scalloped, engraved SS horsehead conchos trimmed in gold, 1930s, bit missing 550.00
Visalia, silver mounted, round silver-ferruled cheeks, star-face drop matching silver-mounted spade bit 1,925.00
Holster and Gun
Fast draw, Colt SA 38-40 revolver, used by stunt man Mark Swain 2,200.00
Visalia, .38-caliber Smith & Wesson revolver, made for Alamedo County Sheriff's Posse, 1930s.........................3,850.00
Magic Lantern Slides, set of 60, "Colorado by a Tenderfoot," railroad, mining towns, Pikes Peak, waterfalls, Denver, c1907 ....225.00
Map, *J. J. Sage & Sons New & Reliable Rail Road Map, Travellers Edition, Western,* Buffalo, 1859, engraved, folding, 420 x 600 mm, folds into orig 12mo board case..........................920.00
Newspaper Adv, Dr. Carver's, illus, 1883 ....30.00
Parade Outfit, Bohlin, silver mounted
c1937, Cottam model, made for Eleanor Montana...16,700.00
c1950, black, silver mounted, wool corona roll, matching breast collar and bridle 29,700.00
Party Set, covered wagon bean pot, ceramic coffeepot, beverage barrel, chip-and-dip bowl with cowboy hat lid, tan, ranch scenes, McCoy Pottery, price for set 1,045.00
Pinback Button
Niagara County Pioneers Association, multicolored Indian portrait, c1918..90.00
Redpath Chautauqua Indian, multicolored illus, red ground, c1907-20..80.00
Photograph Album, *California Illustrated in Photo-Gravure,* 18 photogravure plates, including scenes of Yosemite, oblong 8vo, publisher's gilt lettered cloth, New York and San Francisco, 1894 ....50.00
Photograph
Adobe Houses, silver print by Clarence Sinclair Bull, parchment paper, dated, various notations written in pencil, 1925, 9-3/4" x 12-3/4"..900.00

Canon de Chelly, orotone by Edward S. Curtis, photographer's signature in the negative, orig Curtis studio frame, 1904-05, 10-1/2" x 13-1/2" 20,700.00

Chief of the Desert, platinum-palladium print by Edward S. Curtis, photographer's signature on recto, orig mount, period wood frame with emb dec leaf motif, 1904, 8" x 6-1/2" 4,140.00

Corn Maiden, silver print by Karl Moon, c1905, 4-1/2" x 6-3/4" 500.00

Death Valley, silver print by Wynn Bullock, penciled signature on mount recto, titled, dated, and numerical notation, 1940, 7-1/2" x 9-1/2" 1,380.00

Hart, William S., photo by Hartsook of Los Angeles, profile torso view, in cowboy attire, brandishing two revolvers, inscribed in black ink, 7-1/2" x 9" 230.00

Loti, Laguna Girl, silver print by Karl Moon, typed caption on verso, c1905, 6" x 4" 865.00

Oasis in the Badlands, Red Hawk, orotone by Edward s. Curtis, copyright in negative, orig Curtis studio frame, c1904, 11" x 14" 7,475.00

Poster
Levi's, Round-Up of Cowboy Lore, by Joe Mora, 1930
....395.00
101 Ranch Wild West Show, 1915, 28" x 42" 2,200.00

Program, 101 Ranch Wild West Show...............................330.00

Saddle
20" l, rawhide and tooled tanned leather, brass fittings, wood stirrups, some wear and damage............................165.00

Bohlin, youth, 11" seat, small silver diamond-shaped spots, 1920s...5,500.00

Tibercio Carlos, loop, slick fork working style, large sq skirts, minor restoration..4,100.00

Child's, unknown maker, c1950 ....400.00

J.C. Higgins, black silver-trimmed parade, 15" seat, factory floral stamping 1,100.00

Mexican, stock, tapaderos and exposed wood tree, floral carved and buck stitched, raised leather flowers, silver thread trim, tooled bull-roping scene, c1900 ....3,850.00

Texas Ranger, stock, floral stamped, Cheyenne roll cantle, nickel horn, double rigging, 1930s......................1,100.00

Saddle Bags, pr, R.T. Frazier, woolly angora trim...........1,870.00
Saddle Blanket 225.00
Saddle Stand 100.00

Spittoon
Brass and iron turtle, Victorian 935.00
Copper, 13" d, saloon-type, 1870s...............................275.00

Spurs, silver mounted
Bohlin/Hollywood, McChesney, #125-2, tooled leather Bohlin straps..3,400.00

Cox, John, Canon City, prisoner #4307, 4" l shanks, fancy nickel-spotted leather straps by R.T. Frazier Saddlery Co., CO 13,200.00

Garcia, G.S., #44, early mark, 14-point rowels...........7,150.00

Eddie Hulbert, Montana, Cheyenne-style heel band, engraved button design, 2-1/4" 18-point rowels..................11,600.00

Mike Morales, CA-style, engraved shield, snowshoes and eagle motif 5,500.00

Phillips & Gutierrez, eagle bit 5,610.00

Qualey Bros., fully engraved, card-suit design, raised silver buttons, tooled leather straps..............................12,100.00

L.D. Stone, mkd "1900," silver-mounted drop shank, engraved button heel band, silver inlaid rowels, orange 2-1/4" domed-button beaded conchos, basketweave leather straps..6,050.00

Jesus Tapia, c1916 ....23,650.00

Wauley Bros...12,100.00

Stereograph
Group of 40, Northern Pacific Views, Northern Pacific Railroad, Black Hills Views, and Yellowstone National Park series, views by F. J. Haynes, many titled and numbered in the negative, all with series titles and Haynes' extended cap-

tion printed on mount recto, some with handwritten captions and/or dates..2,760.00

Group of 57, documenting life and customs among Native American tribes of the west, southwest and Pacific northwest, photographers include Jackson, Savage, and Hillers, several from U.S. Geographical and Geological Survey of the Rocky Mountains, albumen prints, several hand-colored, some with series titles, and/or caption printed on mount recto, label with printed photographer's credit, caption, etc., on mount verso, some with handwritten titles 3,450.00

Group of 280, views of Yosemite, Napa, and San Gabriel Valleys, Columbia River, urban scenes of San Francisco, Stockton, Fresno, Marysville, and Venice, 44 by Watkins, 28 by Helios/Muybridge, 4 by Alfred Hart, 21 by Houseworth/Lawrence & Houseworth, scenes by local photographers, assorted misc views, several hand tinted, c1860 to c1910..3,220.00

Thermometer, Dr. Cox's Barbed Wire Liniment.................225.00

Toy Chest, cowboy and Indian motif, burnt-wood designs, 1950s 350.00

Trunk, Miller Bros., rawhide cov, "101" and "MB" in brass nailheads, from Cody's 101 Ranch Show 1,650.00

Vase, 7" h, 7-1/2" h, green fan, paper label, blue stamp "Alamo Pottery, San Antonio, Texas" 35.00

Watch Band, Bohlin, SS filigree, 10k and 18k yellow and pink gold, rubies...4,400.00

WHALING

History: Whaling items are a specialized part of nautical collecting. Provenance is of prime importance since collectors want assurances that their pieces are from a whaling voyage. Since ship's equipment seldom carries the ship's identification, some individuals have falsely attributed a whaling provenance to general nautical items. Know the dealer, auction house, or collector from whom you buy.

Special tools, e.g., knives, harpoons, lances, and spades, do not overlap the general nautical line. Makers' marks and condition determine value for these items.

References: Nina Hellman and Norman Brouwer, *Mariner's Fancy*, South Street Seaport Museum, Balsam Press, and University of Washington Press, 1992; Martha Lawrence, *Scrimshaw*, Schiffer Publishing, 1993.

Museums: Cold Spring Harbor Whaling Museum, Cold Spring Harbor, NY; Kendall Whaling Museum, Sharon, MA; Mystic Seaport Museum, Mystic, CT; National Maritime Museum Library, San Francisco, CA; New Bedford Whaling Museum, New Bedford, MA; Pacific Whaling Museum, Waimanalo, HI; Sag Harbor Whaling & Historical Museum, Sag Harbor, NY; South Street Seaport Museum, New York, NY.

Additional Listings: Nautical Items; Scrimshaw.

Alphabet Game Set, whalebone and ivory, slide top box, 19th C, minor imperfections 195.00

Billet Head, 18-1/4" l, carved and painted wood, scrolling design, 19th C 920.00

Bill of Sale, Whaleship *William Rotch*, October 29, 1819, New Bedford, hull purchase 125.00

Binnacle Lamp, bark, *Ben Avon*, brass, oil burner, 1885...220.00

Block, carved whalebone, 19th C, pr
2-1/2" l..575.00
3-1/4" l...1,095.00

Blubber Knife, 67" l, sheath, minor losses 550.00

Book

Andrews, Roy C., *Whale Hunting with Gun and Camera,* NY, 1925, 8vo, cloth 90.00

Ashley, Clifford W., *The Yankee Whaler,* Boston, 1938, illus, gilt buckram, minor rubbing 125.00

Beale, Thomas, *The Natural History of the Sperm Whale,* London, 1838, 393 pgs, three plates, illus, 12 mo 690.00

Bennett, Frederick Debell, *Narrative of a Whaling Voyage round the Globe, from the Year 1833 to 1836,* London, 1840, folding map, two plates, two volumes, 8vo
....1,620.00

Brown, John Ross, *Etchings of a Whaling Cruise, with Notes of a Sojourn on the Island of Zanzibar,* NY, 1846, plates and illus, 8vo...815.00

Draper, Seth, *Voyage of the Bark Orion from Boston,* Providence, 1870, 8vo, orig letter press wrappers 375.00

Stern, Edward, *Sketch of the Old New Bedford Whaling Bark "Stafford,"* Philadelphia, c1892, 30 pgs, 8vo, orig pictorial wrappers..420.00

Broadside

255 x 175 mm, *Land of the West, Greenland Whale Fishery,* 12 stanza poem, London, second half 19th C 110.00

490 x 580 mm, *List of Shipping Owned in the District of New Bedford, Jan. 1, 1832, Employed in the Whale Fishery and Foreign Trade,* lists vessels, tonnage, managing owners, New Bedford, 1832..575.00

Chart Square, 29-7/8", brass and wood, inscribed "MST," 19th C
....200.00

Club, 11-7/8" l, whalebone, 19th C.....................................950.00

Crimper, 9-1/4" l, whalebone, baleen and abalone inlay, 19th C, old repair to handle 980.00

Ditty Box, 5-7/8" l, whalebone, oval, single finger construction, 19th C 1,150.00

Doll bed, 10-3/8" h, 7-7/8" w, 10-5/8" d, whalebone, tall post, 19th C, very minor cracks...3,740.00

Domino Set, whalebone and baleen, sliding top box, 19th C, minor imperfections...190.00

Duster, 15-1/2" l, whalebone and carved wood, 19th C.....415.00

Fid, 16" l, whalebone, 19th C, minor cracks......................490.00

Figure, 16-3/8" l, carved baleen, whale, whalebone inlaid eye, 19th C, repair to tail 865.00

Game Board, 9-1/4" sq, whalebone and mahogany, 19th C, minor edge roughness 1,035.00

Harpoon

39" l, double flue, inscribed "Alpha," 19th C, pitting, minor corrosion 290.00

60" l, double-tined, cracks, loss to pole 285.00

99-1/2" l, toggle, mounted on pole, 19th C.................1,265.00

Horn Book, 3-7/8" l, whalebone, miniature 175.00

Ladle, 14" l, whalebone, coconut, and copper, 19th C......345.00

Lance, 103-1/2" l, minor corrosion....................................600.00

Cribbage Board, walrus tusk, scrimshaw dec, c1920, 14-3/4" l, $195.

Lantern, 10-1/2" h, whalebone, pierced arched copper top, pierced base, ball feet, 19th C, replaced glass, minor loss
....1,380.00

Log Book

Bark *Otranto,* commences at New Bedford January 17, 1847, through April 30, 1848, contains whale stamps and ship stamps 3,200.00

Whaleship *Phoenix,* October 4, 1847, through October 18, 1847..660.00

Photograph, 10" x 12-1/2", whaleship under sail, orig wood frame, tan matting 75.00

Marking Gauge, 9-1/8" l, whalebone, 19th C...................1,035.00

Miniature, stool, 4-3/4" h, engraved whalebone, compass star and heart motif, top with lightly inscribed names, dates, and initials, baleen inlaid exotic wood, turned legs, 19th C, repair
....1,150.00

Pan Bone, 2-1/4" x 3-1/4", double sided engravings of three-masted ships under sail, 19th C, crack, gouges 375.00

Parceling Tool, 5-7/8" l, whale ivory, crossbanded design, engraved "N. D. 1829," repair 175.00

Pickwick, 3-3/4" h, whale ivory, green and red sealing wax inlaid scribe line dec, 19th C, minute chip to finial 1,495.00

Picture Frame, 6-1/4" h, 4" w, whalebone, pierce carved bird, star, and heart motif, 19th C, minute chip 4,600.00

Print, Sperm Whaling with its Varieties, John H. Bufford, 1870, identified within matrix, chromolithograph on paper, 18-3/4" x 34-1/2" sheet size, framed 1,725.00

Rattle and Whistle, 5-3/4" l, whalebone and whale ivory, 19th C, minor cracks 575.00

Rubber, whalebone, 19th C...425.00

Scribe, 8" l, whalebone, 19th C 1,150.00

Sewing Carrier, 6-7/8" h, 7" l, reticulated whalebone and pine, 19th C, repair, minor cracks....................................1,150.00

Ship Log Book, 13-1/2" h, 8-1/2" w, Bark *Mercury,* New Bedford, outlining trip to North Pacific, entries from Dec 1876 to May 1878, staining, toning 2,415.00

Spool Stand, 3 tiers, ftd, 19th C

6-3/8" h, whale ivory and exotic wood, cup finial above three graduated circular tiers, five bun feet, 19th C, minor cracks 575.00

7-1/8" h, whalebone, ivory, and wood, doughnut shaped ivory thimble holder above three graduated scalloped tiers, sealing wax inlaid scribe lines, tripod base, traces of blue pigment, missing three spool holders, very minor losses, minor cracks 750.00

Swift, 19th C

22-5/8" l, whalebone and ivory, red and black sealing wax inlaid scribe lines, cup finial, barrel form clasp, cracks, minor losses..920.00

23" l, whalebone, ivory, and wood, ball final, clamp carved with crosshatched diamond motif, minor losses, old repair
....460.00

Try-Square, 9-3/8" l, whalebone, 19th C, very minor crack
....290.00

Watch Hutch

7-1/2" h, 5" w, 3-3/4" d, hanging, whalebone, arched crest pierce carved with star and crescent motifs, backed with painted cloth, 19th C, minor cracks, minute losses
....8,625.00

9-1/8" h, whalebone and cherry, scrolled crest above ring turned posts, kidney shaped base, scribed bun feet, 19th C, minor cracks 690.00

13-3/4" h, tall case clock form, baleen and ivory inlaid walnut, star and heart motif, 19th C, very minor losses 4,025.00

Whip, 24-1/4" l, whalebone handle, 19th C, losses to leather
....175.00

Yardstick, 35-7/8" l, whalebone, 19th C............................490.00

WHIELDON

History: Thomas Whieldon, a Staffordshire potter, established his shop in 1740. He is best known for his mottled ware, molded in the shapes of vegetables, fruits, and leaves. Josiah Spode and Josiah Wedgwood, in different capacities, had connections with Whieldon.

WHIELDON

Whieldon ware is a generic term. His wares were never marked, and other potters made similar items. Whieldon ware is agate-tortoiseshell earthenware, in limited shades of green, brown, blue and yellow. Most pieces are utilitarian items, e.g., dinnerware and plates, but figurines and other decorative pieces also were made.

Coffeepot, cov, 7-1/2" h, molded spout and strap handle, brown tortoise shell glaze, blue and green, mismatched lid, old professional repair 475.00
Creamer, 4-1/4" h, Cauliflower, molded design green and clear laze, applied handle, old yellowed repair on spout, wear, stains, minor edge damage..385.00
Pitcher, 4-3/4" h 350.00
Plate
    9" d, shaped, late 18th C, hairlines, pr 290.00
    9-1/4" d, majolica, rim nick 165.00
    9-1/2" d, rim nick, hairline 140.00
    9-5/8" d, green, blue, and brown, black tortoiseshell glaze, emb rim..250.00
    9-3/4" d, mottled, rim nick...250.00
Platter, 10-3/8" l, blue and green, brown tortoiseshell glaze, emb rim..315.00

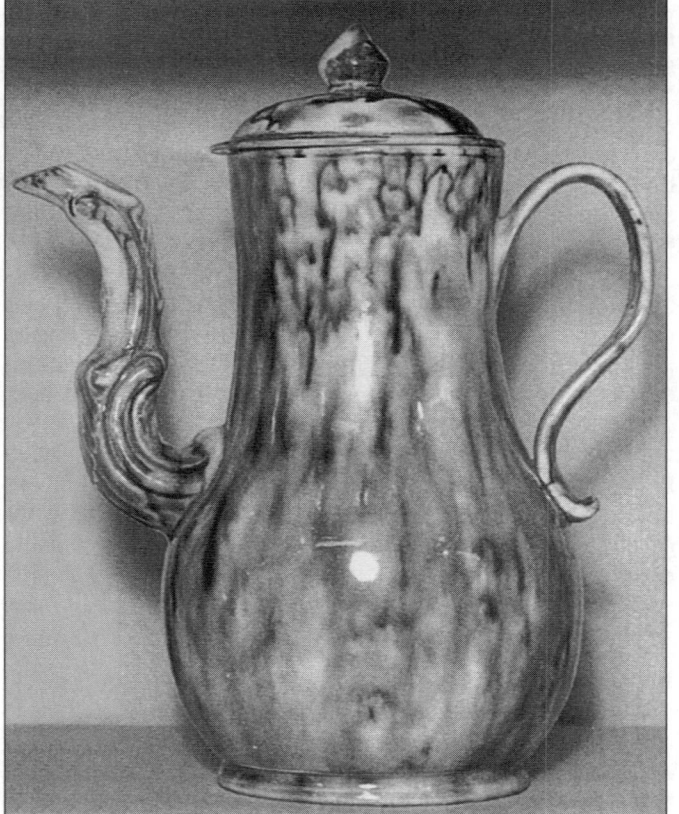

Coffeepot, molded spout and strap handle, brown tortoiseshell glaze with blue and green, mismatched lid, old professional repair, 7-1/2" h plus lid, $475. Photo courtesy of Garth's Auctions.

Teapot, Grape pattern, 4" h, $1,200.

Sugar, cov, 4-3/8" d, 3-5/8" h, cauliflower, molded design, green and clear glaze, wear, stains, edge chips 3,245.00
Tea Caddy, 4-1/4" h, Cauliflower, molded design, green and clear glaze, lid missing, wear, light stains..............................550.00
Teapot, cov, 3-3/4" h, creamware body, Cauliflower, cream glazed florets, green glazed leaves, 18th C, restorations 475.00

WHIMSIES, GLASS

History: During lunch or after completing their regular work schedule, glassworkers occasionally spent time creating unusual glass objects known as whimsies, e.g. candy-striped canes, darners, hats, paperweights, pipes, and witch balls. Whimsies were taken home and given as gifts to family and friends.

Because of their uniqueness and infinite variety, whimsies can rarely be attributed to a specific glass house or glassworker. Whimsies were created wherever glass was made, from New Jersey to Ohio and westward. Some have suggested that style and color can be used to pinpoint region or factory, but no one has yet developed an identification key that is adequate.

Glass canes are among the most collectible types of whimsies. These range in length from very short (under one foot) to 10 feet or more. They come in both hollow and solid form. Hollow canes can have a bulb-type handle or the rarer C- or L-shaped handle. Canes are found in many fascinating colors, with the candy striped being a regular favorite with collectors. Many canes are also filled with various colored powders, gold and white being the most common and silver being harder to find. Sometimes they were even used as candy containers.

References: Gary Baker et al., *Wheeling Glass 1829-1939*, Oglebay Institute, 1994, distributed by Antique Publications; Joyce E. Blake, *Glasshouse Whimsies*, published by author, 1984; Joyce E. Blake and Dale Murschell, *Glasshouse Whimsies: An Enhanced Reference*, published by authors, 1989.

Collectors' Club: Whimsey Club, 20 William St., Dansville, KY 14437.

Advisors: Lon Knickerbocker.

Bracelet
    2" to 3" d, Lutz type, clear, multicolored twists and spirals, gold...85.00
    3" d, solid glass, varied colored stripes 65.00
Buttonhook
    5" to 10" l, plain
        Bottle green 35.00
        Colorless..25.00
    7" h, bottle green, elaborately twisted body, amber ends
    ....75.00
Cane, solid
    46-1/2" l, aqua, spiraled, mid-19th C.........................175.00
    48" l, cobalt blue, shepherd's crook handle.................265.00
    60" l, bottle green, finely twisted, curved handle...........150.00
Darner
    5" l, amber head, applied colorless handle..................200.00
    6" l, Aurene, gold, Steuben...300.00
    7" l, white ground, blue Nailsea loopings 165.00

Witch Ball, matching goblet, Lutz-type lattice, pink, white, and gold design, 4" d ball, $375.

Egg, hollow, milk glass, various colored splotches
    2" h..65.00
    4-1/2" h...85.00
Hat, free blown
    1-1/2" h, milk glass, c1910...50.00
    1-1/2" h, 4" d, amber, attributed to Keene, c1860 ....165.00
Horn
    8-1/2" l, French horn type, candy stripes.....................300.00
    20" l, trumpet type, red, white, yellow, purple, and green candy stripes 175.00
Ladle, 10" l, hollow, gold powder filled, colored splotches, curved handles 65.00
Pen
    Elaborate, green, finely twisted applied bird finial 85.00
    Simple design, amber, colorless nib, 7" l 35.00
Pipe
    20" l, spatter, large bowl, English 250.00
    36" l, long twisted stem, small hollow bowl, aqua, America, c1900...120.00
Potichomanie Ball, 12" d, blown, aqua, paper cut-outs of flowers, etc., matching 24" h stand, attributed to Lancaster NY 600.00
Rolling Pin
    14" l, black or deep olive green, white dec, early Keene or Stoddard 150.00
    15" l, Nailsea type, cobalt blue ground, white loopings 165.00
Witch Ball, 3-1/2" d, freeblown, attributed to Boston and Sandwich Glass Works,1850-80, rose and green loops on white milk glass background, ground moth, smooth base 375.00

WHISKEY BOTTLES, COLLECTOR'S SPECIAL EDITIONS

History: The Jim Beam Distillery began the practice of issuing novelty (collectors' special edition) bottles for the 1953 Christmas trade. By the late 1960s, more than 100 other distillers and wine manufacturers followed suit. The Jim Beam Distillery remains the most prolific issuer of the bottle. Lionstone, McCormick and Ski Country are the other principal suppliers today. One dealer, Jon-Sol, Inc., has distributed his own line of collector bottles.

The golden age of the special edition bottle was the early 1970s. Interest waned in the late 1970s and early 1980s as the market became saturated with companies trying to join the craze. Prices fell from record highs and many manufacturers dropped special-edition bottle production altogether.

A number of serious collectors, clubs and dealers have brought stability to the market. Realizing that instant antiques cannot be created by demand alone, they have begun to study and classify their bottles. Most importantly, collectors have focused on those special-edition bottles which show quality workmanship and design and which are true limited editions.

References: Hugh Cleveland, *Bottle Pricing Guide*, 3rd Edition, 1988, 1993 value update; Ralph and Terry Kovel, *Kovels' Bottles Price List*, 10th Edition, Crown Publishers, 1996; Jim Megura, *Official Price Guide Bottles*, House of Collectibles, 1991; Michael Polak, *Bottles*, Avon Books, 1994.

Collectors' Clubs: Cape Codders Jim Beam Bottle & Specialty Club, 80 Lincoln Rd., Rockland, MA 02370; Hoffman National Collectors Club, P.O. Box 37341, Cincinnati, OH 45222; International Association of Jim Beam Bottle & Specialties Clubs, 5013 Chase Ave., Downers Grove, IL 60515; National Ski Country Bottle Club, 1224 Washington Ave., Golden, CO 80401; Space Coast Jim Beam Bottle & Specialties Club, 2280 Cox Rd., Cocoa, FL 32926.

Museum: American Outpost, James B. Beam Distillery, Clermont, KY.

Aesthetic Specialties, Inc., World's Greatest Hunter, 1979 ....34.00

ALPA, Warner Bros. Characters
    Bugs Bunny, 1977 .... 10.00
    Tweety Bird, 1978 ....20.00
Anniversary, Lincoln, 1973 ....15.50
Ballantine
    Golf Bag, 1969.. 9.50
    Mallard, 1969 ....18.00
    Zebra, 1970 .... 14.00

Jim Beam

Beam Clubs and Conventions
Akron, Rubber Capital, 1973.............................. 24.00
    Conventions
        First, Denver, 1971 .... 16.00
        Fifth, Sacramento, 1975........................ 14.00
        Thirteenth, St. Louis, 1983 ....48.00
Evergreen State Club, 1974 .... 15.50
Twin Bridges Club, 1971 ....50.00
Beam on Wheels
    Cable car, 1983 ....66.00
    Caboose, 1980 ....39.00
    Ernie's Flower Car, 1976..............................35.00
    Stutz Bearcat, yellow, 1977 ....38.00
Casino Series
    Barney's Slot Machine, 1978........................20.00
    Harold's Club, Covered Wagon, green, 1969 ....6.00
Centennial Series, first issued 1960
Alaska Purchase, 1966.......................................9.00
    Civil War, 1961, South 53.00
    Hawaii, 200th, 1978 ....20.00
    Reidsville, 1973 .... 7.50
    San Diego, 1968 ....7.00
Clubs and Organizations
    Ahepa, 1972 ....5.00
    BPO Does, 1971 ....5.00
    Ducks Unlimited, #5, 1979 ....22.00
    Pennsylvania Dutch Club, 1974 ....12.00
    Shriners, Western Association, 1980.............30.00
Customer Specialties
    Armanetti, fun shopper, 1971 ....7.50
    Katz Cat, black, 1968 ....13.00
    Ralph's Market, 1973 ....13.00
    Zimmerman, vase, brown, 1972 ....20.00
Executive Series, first issue 1955
    1957, Royal DiMonte 73.00
    1960, Blue Cherub..120.00
    1969, Sovereign...14.00
    1972, Regency 14.00
    1982, Executive 30.00
Foreign Countries
    Australia, Sydney Opera, 1978......................22.50
    Thailand, 1969 ....5.00
People Series
    Cowboy, 1981..15.50
    Emmet Kelly, Kansas autograph, 1973 ....68.00
    John Henry, 1972 ....72.00
    Paul Bunyan, 1970 ....10.00
    Viking, 1973..12.00

Political Series
    Kansas City Convention Elephant, 1976 ....14.00
    Spiro Agnew Elephant, 1970 ....2,200.00
Regal China Series
    Green China Jug, 1965 ....7.00
    Las Vegas, 1969 ....5.00
    London Bridge, 1971 ....5.50
    New Hampshire Golden Eagle, 1971 ....44.00
Sports Series
    Fiesta Bowl, 1970 ....13.00
    Hawaiian Open, golf ball, 1983 ....16.00
    Kentucky Derby, 100th, 1974 ....10.00
    Louisiana Superdome, 1975 ....9.00
State Series
    Colorado, 1959 ....33.00
    New Hampshire, 1968 ....7.00
    New Jersey, blue, 1963 ....68.00
    Ohio, 1966 ....14.00
    South Carolina, 1970 ....7.50
Trophy Series
    Bird, pheasant, 1960 ....30.00
    Coho Salmon, 1976 ....12.00
    Dog, poodle, gray, 1970................................7.00
    Horse, brown, 1967-68 ....21.50
    Rabbit, 1971 ....13.50

Beneagle

Barrel, thistle...4.50
Chess Pawn, John Knox, black, miniature 12.00

Bischoff

Chinese Boy, 1962 ....36.00
Grecian Vase, 1969 ....15.50
Pirate..20.00

Ezra Brooks

Animal Series
    Elephant, Big Bertha, 1970............................8.00
    Hereford, 1971 ....14.00
    Panda, 1972 ....18.00
Automotive/Transportation Series
    Motorcycle, 1971 ....13.50
    Ontario Racer, #10, 1970 ....21.00
    Train, Iron Horse, 1969.................................12.00
Fish Series, trout and fly, 1970 ....10.00
Heritage China Series, silver dollar, black base, 1969 ....9.00
Institutional Series
    Bucket of Blood, 1970 ....8.00
    Club Bottle #1, Distillery, 1970 ....12.50
    Iowa Farmers Elevator, 1978 ....36.00
    Wichita Centennial, 1970...............................7.50
People Series
    Clown with balloons, 1973..............................22.00
    Max "The Hat" Zimmerman, 1976 ....32.00
    Mr. Merchant, 1970 ....10.00
    Oliver Hardy, 1976...17.50
    Stonewall Jackson, 1974 ....32.00
Sports Series
    Basketball Players, 1974 ....10.00
    Casey at Bat, 1973 ....16.00
    Go Big Red #3, Rooter, 1972 ....14.00
    Greensboro Open, cup, 1975 ....50.00

Collector's Art

Bird Series, cardinal, miniature 30.00
Cattle Series, Texas Longhorn, 1974 ....35.00
Dog Series, miniature
    Basset Hound 25.50
    Poodle, white 21.00

Cyrus Noble

Animal Series
   Buffalo Cow & Calf, Nevada ed, 1977 ....88.00
   Moose & Calf, 2nd ed, 1977 ....80.00
Carousel Series, pipe organ, 1980 ....45.00
Mine Series, mine shaft, 1978 ....35.00
Sea Animals
   Harp Seal, 1979 ....50.00
   Sea Turtle, 1979 ....50.00

J.W. Dant

Boeing 747 ....14.00
Field Birds, 1969, #4, mountain quail 9.00
Patrick Henry, 1969 ....5.00

Double Springs

Bicentennial Series
   Iowa 50.00
   Washington, DC 14.00
Car Series
   Mercedes Benz, 1975 ....28.00
   Rolls Royce, 1971 ....40.00

Early Times, 1976

Cannon Fire
   Delaware 22.00
   Nevada 22.00
   New Mexico 28.00
Drum and Fife
   Florida 17.00
   Kansas 20.00
Minuteman
   Alaska 35.50
   Oklahoma 24.00
Paul Revere, Arizona 21.00
Washington Crossing the Delaware, South Dakota..............17.00

Famous Firsts

Airplane Series, Winnie Mae, large, 1972 ....88.00
Animal Series
   Bears, miniature, 1981..36.00
   Hippo, baby, 1980...50.00
   Panda, baby, 1980 ....50.00
Car/Transportation Series
   Balloon, 1971...65.00
   Corvette, 1963 Stingray, white, miniature, 1979.............13.50
   Porsche Targa, 1979 ....44.00
Miscellaneous
   Fireman, 1980...53.50
   Hurdy Gurdy, miniature, 1979 ....15.50
   Phonograph, 1969 ....36.00
   Sewing Machine, 1979 ....35.00

Garnier (France)

Christmas Tree, 1956 ....67.00
Locomotive, 1969 ....14.00
Soccer Shoe, 1962 ....37.00

Grenadier

American Revolution Series
   Second Maryland, 1969...37.50
   Third New York, 1970 ....22.00
British Army Series, Kings African Rifle Crops, 5th, 1970....20.00
Civil War Series, General Robert E. Lee, 1/2 gal, 1977......150.00
Miscellaneous
   Jester Mirth King, 1977...56.00

San Fernando Electric Mfg Co., 1976 ....66.00
Napoleonic Series, Eugene, 1970.................................21.00

Hoffman

Aesop's Fables Series, music, 6 types, 1978.....................30.00
Band Series, Accordion player, miniature, 1987.................13.50
Bird Series, eagle, open wing, miniature, 1979.................18.00
Cheerleaders, Rams, miniature, 1980 ....20.00
Mr. Lucky Series, music
   Barber, 1980..38.00
   Cobbler, 1973...25.00
   Fiddler, 1974...25.00
   Mailman, miniature, 1976 ....12.50
School Series
   Kentucky Wildcats, football, 1979 ....38.00
   Tennessee Volunteers 28.00
Wildlife Series, doe & fawn, 1975 ....50.00

Japanese Firms

House of Koshu
   Geisha, chrysanthemum, 1969...23.50
   Sake God, white, 1969 ....14.00
Kamotsuru, treasure tower, 1966 ....18.00
Kikukawa
   Eisenhower, 1970 ....17.00
   Royal couple, pr 32.00

Lewis and Clark

Clark, miniature, 1971..15.50
General Custer, 1974 ....71.00
Lewis, 1971...88.00
Troll Family, grandmother troll, 1979 ....29.00

Lionstone

Bird Series, dove of peace, 1977 ....40.00
Car/Transportation Series
   Stutz Bearcat, miniature, 1978 ....15.00
   Turbo Car STP, red, 1972...25.00
Clown Series, #6, Lampy, 1979.......................................34.00
European Workers Series, 1974, 6 types, each 24.00
Firefighter Series, fireman, #8, fire alarm box, 1983............57.00
Old West Series
   Bartender, 1969 ....30.00
   Dance Hall Girl, 1973 ....67.00
   Indian, squaw, 1973 ....25.00
   Riverboat Captain, 1969 ....14.00
   Telegrapher, 1969 ....20.00
Sports Series
   Baseball Player, 1974 ....27.50
   Hockey Player, 1974 ....20.00
   Tennis Player, male, 1980 ....45.00

Luxardo

Apple, figural 14.00
Bizantina 26.00
Calypso Girl, 1962 ....15.50
Frog, miniature...15.00
Tower of Flowers, 1968 ....18.00
Zodiac, 1970..31.50

McCormick

Bicentennial Series, Betsy Ross, miniature, 1976 ....48.00
Bull Series
   Brahma, 1973 ....40.00
   Texas Longhorn, 1974..36.50
Entertainment Series, Jimmie Durante, 1981 ....50.00

Football Mascots
    Drake Bulldogs, 1974 ....23.00
    Indiana Hoosiers, 1974...17.00
Frontiersmen Series, Kit Carson, 1975 ....15.00
Great American Series
    Ulysses S. Grant, 1976 ....29.00
    Mark Twain, 1977 ....32.00
Sports Series
    Air Racy Pylon, 1970 ....14.00
    Nebraska Football Player, 1972 ....24.00
Train Series, wood tender, 1969..22.00
Warrior Series, Centurion, 1969...20.00

OBR

Caboose, 1973 ....21.00
River Queen, 1967 ....10.00
W.C. Fields, top hat, 1976 ....16.00

Old Commonwealth

Apothecary Series, North Carolina University, 1979 ....30.00
Coal Miners
    #3, with shovel, 1977 ....41.50
    #5, coal shooter, 1983 ....44.00
Fireman Series, modern, #5, Lifesaver, 1983.....................72.50
Miscellaneous
    Indian Chief Illini, University of Illinois, 1979 ....60.00
    Lumberjack, old time, 1979 ....20.00
    Kentucky Thoroughbreds, 1977 ....39.00

Old Fitzgerald

America's Cup, 1970 ....27.00
Blarney, Irish toast, 1970 ....16.00
Davidson, NC, 1972 ....40.00
Hospitality, 1958 ....9.00
Rip Van Winkle, 1971..34.50
West Virginia Forest Festival, 1973....................................22.00

Old Mr. Boston

Concord Coach, 1976 ....17.00
Deadwood, SD, 1975 ....16.00
Hawk, 1975 ....18.00
Nebraska, #1, gold, 1970 ....20.00
Paul Revere, 1974 ....15.50
Town Crier, 1976 ....10.00

Pacesetter

Camaro, Z28, yellow, 1982...42.00
Corvette, red, 1975..40.00
Tractor Series, No. 2, Big Green Machine, International Harvester,
    1983...66.00
Vokovich, #2, 1974 ....30.00

Ski Country

Christmas Series, Ebenezer Scrooge, 1979, miniature........24.00
Circus Series
    Clown, bust, 1974, miniature 17.00
    Ringmaster, 1975, miniature..26.50
Customer Specialties
    Eagle, paperweight 190.00
    Mill River Country Club, 1977 ....44.00
    Submarine, 1976, miniature...29.00
Domestic Animal Series
    Bassett, miniature, 1978 ....20.00
    Labrador with mallard, 1977, miniature.........................49.00
Indian Series, Cigar Store Indian, 1974..............................40.00
Waterfowl Series, duck, mallard, 1973, miniature 40.00
Wildlife Series
    Antelope, pronghorn...70.00

Jaguar, miniature..33.00
Koala, 1973...42.00
Mountain Lion, 1973, miniature 30.00
Woodpecker, ivory bill, 1974 ....66.00

Wild Turkey

Crystal Anniversary, 1955...2,000.00
Mack Truck 20.00
Series #1
    2, female, 1972 ....150.00
    5, with flags, 1975 ....40.00
    8, strutting, 1978 ....45.00
Turkey Lore Series
    #1, 1979 ....65.00
    #4, 1982 ....50.00

WHISKEY BOTTLES, EARLY

History: The earliest American whiskey bottles were generic in shape and were blown by pioneer glass makers in the 18th century. The Biningers (1820-1880s) were the first bottles specifically designed for whiskey. After the 1860s, distillers favored the cylindrical "fifth" design.

The first embossed brand-name bottle was the amber E. G. Booz Old Cabin Whiskey bottle which was issued in 1860. Many stories have been told about this classic bottle; unfortunately, most are not true. Research has proven that "booze" was a corruption of the words "bouse" and "boosy" from the 16th and 17th centuries. It was only a coincidence that the Philadelphia distributor also was named "Booz." This bottle has been reproduced extensively.

Prohibition (1920-1933) brought the legal whiskey industry to a standstill. Whiskey was marked "medicinal purposes only" and distributed by private distillers in unmarked or paper-labeled bottles.

The size and shape of whiskey bottles are standard. Colors are limited to amber, amethyst, clear, green, and cobalt blue (rare). Corks were the common closure in the early period, with the inside screw top being used between 1880 and 1910.

Bottles made prior to 1880 are the most desirable. When purchasing a bottle with a label, condition of that label is a critical factor. In the 1950s, distillers began to issue collectors' special-edition bottles to help increase sales.

References: Ralph & Terry Kovel, *Kovels' Bottles Price List*, 10th ed., Crown Publishers, 1996; John Odell, *Digger Odell's Official Antique Bottle and Glass Collector Magazine Price Guide Series*, Vol. 8, published by author (1910 Shawhan Rd., Morrow, OH 45152), 1995 Carlo and Dorothy Sellari, *Standard Old Bottle Price Guide*, Collector Books, 1989.

Periodicals: *Antique Bottle and Glass Collector*, P.O. Box 187, East Greenville, PA 18041; *Bottles & Extras*, P.O. Box 154, Happy Camp, CA 96039.

Museum: The Seagram Museum, Waterloo, Ontario, Canada.

Additional Listings: See *Warman's Americana & Collectibles* for a listing of Collectors' Special Edition Whiskey Bottles.

Mount Vernon, bottled 1933, orig box, $90.

A. M. Bininger & Co, No. 19 Broad St., New York, c1860-80, cylindrical, applied handle, yellowish-olive green, applied double collared mouth, smooth base, 7-7/8" h 1,400.00
Bininger's Regular, 19 Broad St., New York, 1840-50, clock shape, deep gold amber, applied double collared mouth, pontil scar, 5-7/8" h 300.00
Bininger's Travelers Guide, A. M. Bininger & Co, No. 19 Broad St., NY, 1860-80, teardrop form, golden amber, applied double collared mouth, smooth base, 6-3/4" h 200.00
C. A. Richards & Co., 99 Washington St., Boston, Mass, 1860-80, sq with beveled corners, yellow green, applied sloping collared mouth, smooth base, 9-1/2" h, 3/8" potstone........550.00
Caspers Whiskey, Made by Honest North Carolina People, 1870-90, cylindrical, paneled shoulder, cobalt blue, tooled sloping collared mouth with ring, smooth base, 11-3/4" h 325.00
Chestnut Grove Whiskey, 1840-60, flattened chestnut form, applied handle, golden amber, applied mouth with ring, pontil scar, 9" h...110.00
Freeblown Jug, applied handle, America, 1840-60
    6-1/8" h, pear form, red amber, applied sloping collared mouth, pontil scar 220.00
    8" h, cylindrical corseted form, golden amber, applied double collared mouth, pontil scar 350.00
    8" h, flattened chestnut, golden amber, applied mouth with ring, pontil scar, 8" h......................................475.00
Griffith Hyatt & Co., Baltimore, 1840-80, globular, flattened label panels, applied handle, golden amber with olive tone, applied sq collared mouth, pontil scar, 7" h 375.00
H. Pharazyn/Phila/Right Secured, 1860-80, Indian Warrior form, brilliant light yellow amber, inward rolled mouth, smooth base, 12-1/2" h, incomplete mouth with roughness, some minor int. residue..800.00
Lancaster Glassworks, Lancaster, NY, 1860-80, barrel, puce amber, applied double collared mouth, smooth base, 9-5/8" h
....180.00
Old Continental Whiskey, yellow amber, 9-1/4" h...............650.00
Ridgeway Straight Corn Whiskey, miniature, stoneware......50.00
Weeks Glass Works, Stoddard, NH, 1860-70, emb base, cylindrical, yellow amber with olive tone, applied sloping collared mouth with ring, smooth base, 11-1/2" h, retains cork and some int. residue 200.00

WHITE-PATTERNED IRONSTONE

History: White-patterned ironstone is a heavy earthenware, first patented under the name "Patent Ironstone China" in 1813 by Charles Mason, Staffordshire, England. Other English potters soon began copying this opaque, feldspathic, white china.

All-white ironstone dishes first became available in the American market in the early 1840s. The first patterns had simple Gothic lines similar to the shapes used in transfer wares. Pattern shapes, such as New York, Union, and Atlantic, were designed to appeal to the American housewife. Motifs, such as wheat, corn, oats, and poppies, were embossed on the pieces as the American prairie influenced design. Eventually, more than 200 shapes and patterns, with variations on finials and handles, were made.

White-patterned ironstone is identified by shape names and pattern names. Many potters only identified the shape in their catalogs. Pattern names usually refer to the decorative motif.

References: Annise Doring Heaivilin, *Grandma's Tea Leaf Ironstone*, Updated Price Guide, L-W Book Sales, 1996; Dawn Stolzfus & Jeffrey B. Snyder, *White Ironstone, A Survey of its Many Forms, Undecorated, Flow Blue, Mulberry, Copper Lustre,* Schiffer Publishing, 1997; Jean Wetherbee, *White Ironstone*, Antique Trader Books, 1996.

Collectors' Clubs: Mason's Ironstone Collectors' Club, 542 Seskeyon Blvd., Ashland, OR 97520; White Ironstone China Assoc., RD #1, Box 23, Howes Cave, NY 12092.

Butter Dish, cov, Athens, Podmore Walker, c1857 ....85.00
Cake Plate, 9" d, Brocade, Mason, handled 140.00
Chamber Pot, cov, emb Fleur-De-Lis & Daisy o handle, 1883-1913, mkd "Johnson Bros." 135.00
Coffeepot, cov, Wheat and Blackberry, Clementson Bros.
....120.00
Creamer
    Fig, Davenport..65.00
    Wheat in the Meadow, Powell & Bishop, 1870...............45.00
Cup and Saucer
    Acorn and Tiny Oak, Parkhurst.....................................35.00
    Grape and Medallion, Challinor......................................40.00
Ewer, Scalloped Decagon, Wedgwood 150.00
Gravy Boat
    Bordered Fuchsia, Anthony Shaw 45.00
    Wheat & Blackberry, Meakin 35.00
Nappy, Prairie Flowers, Livesley & Powell............................20.00
Pancake Server, octagonal, Botte, 1851 ....40.00
Pitcher
    Berlin Swirl, Mayer & Elliot...120.00

Tureen, Wheat and Ivy, mkd "Stone China (W. Taylor) Hanley," 11-1/2" l, $75.

Japan, Mason, c1915 ....275.00
Syndenhaum, T. & R. Boote 195.00
Wheat, W. E. Corn 85.00
Plate
    Ceres, Elsmore & Forster, 8-1/2" d 15.00
    Corn, Davenport, 10-1/2" d 20.00
    Fluted Pearl, Wedgwood, 9-1/2" d 15.00
    Gothic, Adams, 9-1/2" d 20.00
    Prairie, Clemenston, Hanley, 6-5/8" d 12.00
    Wheat and Clover, Turner & Tomkinson 18.00
Platter
    Columbia, 20" x 15" 125.00
    Wheat, Meakin, 20-3/4" x 15-3/4" 75.00
Punch Bowl, Berry Cluster, J. Furnival 175.00
Relish
    Ceres, Elsmore & Forster, 1960 ....40.00
    Wheat, W. E. corn 30.00
Sauce Tureen, cov
    Columbia, underplate, Joseph Goodwin, 1855 ....115.00
    Prize Bloom, T.J. & J. Mayer, Dale Hall Pottery 220.00
    Wheat & Blackberry, Clementson Bros. 175.00
Soap Dish, Bordered Hyacinth, cov, insert, W. Baker & Co.,
    1860s 150.00
Soup Plate, Fig, Davenport, 9-1/2" d 25.00
Sugar Bowl, cov
    Hyacinth, Wedgwood 45.00
    Fuchsia, Meakin 40.00
Teapot, cov, Ivy, Wm. Adams, 10" h 85.00
Toothbrush Holder
    Bell Flower, Burgess 50.00
    Cable and Ring, Cockson & Seddon 40.00
Vegetable, cov
    Blackberry 50.00
    Prairie Flowers, Livesley & Powell 85.00

WILLOW PATTERN CHINA

History: Josiah Spode developed the first "traditional" willow pattern in 1810. The components, all motifs taken from Chinese export china, are a willow tree, "apple" tree, two pagodas, fence, two birds, and three figures crossing a bridge. The legend, in its many versions, is an English invention based on this scenic design.

By 1830, there were more than 200 makers of willow pattern china in England. The pattern has remained in continuous production. Some of the English firms that still produce it are Burleigh, Johnson Bros. (Wedgwood Group), Royal Doulton (continuing production of the Booths' pattern), and Wedgwood.

By the end of the 19th century, production of this pattern spread to France, Germany, Holland, Ireland, Sweden, and the United States. Buffalo Pottery made the first willow pattern in the United States beginning in 1902. Many other companies followed, developing willow variants using rubber-stamp simplified patterns as well as overglaze decals. The largest American manufacturers of the traditional willow pattern were Royal China and Homer Laughlin, usually preferred because it is dated. Shenango pieces are the most desirable among restaurant-quality wares.

Japan began producing large quantities of willow pattern china in the early 20th century. Noritake began about 1902. Most Japanese pieces are porous earthenware with a dark blue pattern using the traditional willow design, usually with no inner border. Noritake did put the pattern on china bodies. Unusual forms include salt and pepper shakers, one-quarter pound butter dishes, and canisters. The most desirable Japanese willow is the fine quality NKT Co. ironstone with a copy of the old Booths pattern. Recent Japanese willow is a paler shade of blue on a porcelain body.

The most common dinnerware color is blue. However, pieces can also be found in black (with clear glaze or mustard-colored glaze by Royal Doulton), brown, green, mulberry, pink (red), and polychrome.

The popularity of the willow design has resulted in a large variety of willow-decorated products: candles, fabric, glass, graniteware, linens, needlepoint, plastic, tinware, stationery, watches, and wall coverings. All this material has collectible value.

Marks: Early pieces of Noritake have a Nippon "Royal Sometuke" mark. "Occupied Japan" may add a small percentage to the value of common table wares. Pieces marked "Maruta" or "Moriyama" are especially valued.

References: Robert Copeland, *Spode's Willow Pattern and Other Designs after the Chinese*, Studio Vista, 1980, 1990 reprint; Mary Frank Gaston, *Blue Willow*, 2nd ed., Collector Books, 1990, 1996 value update.

Periodicals: *American Willow Report*, P.O. Box 900, Oakridge, OR 97463; *Willow Word*, P.O. Box 13382, Arlington, TX 76094.

Collectors' Clubs: International Willow Collectors, 2903 Blackbird Rd., Petoskey, MI 49770; Willow Society, 39 Medhurst Rd., Toronto Ontario M4B 1B2 Canada.

REPRODUCTION ALERT

The Scio Pottery, Scio, Ohio, currently manufactures a willow pattern set sold in variety stores. The pieces have no marks or backstamps, and the transfer is of poor quality. The plates are flatter in shape than those of other manufacturers.

Note: Although colors other than blue are hard to find, there is less demand; thus, prices may not necessarily be higher priced.

Berry Bowl, small
    Blue, Homer Laughlin Co. 6.50
    Pink, mkd "Japan" 5.00
Bowl, 9" d, Mason 45.00
Cake Plate, tab handles, Royal China Co. 20.00
Charger, 13" d 35.00
Chop Plate, Royal China Co. 20.00
Creamer and Sugar, Royal China Co. 20.00
Cup and Saucer
    Booths 30.00
    Buffalo Pottery 25.00
    Homer Laughlin 10.00
    Japanese, decal inside cup, pink 25.00
    Shenango 15.00
Gravy Boat, orig ladle, Royal China Co. 25.00
Pie Plate, 10" d 50.00
Plate, dinner
    Allerton, 10" d 25.00
    Buffalo Pottery, 9" d 20.00

Berry Bowl, Allerton, 5-1/4" d, $12.

Johnson Bros., 10" d	15.00
Royal China Co., 9" d	8.00
Platter, 12" l, Homer Laughlin	25.00
Soup Bowl, Royal China Co.	7.50
Sugar, cov, Allerton	65.00
Tea Cup and Saucer, scalloped, Allerton	45.00
Vegetable Dish, cov, wear to knob	115.00

WOMEN'S CAUSES

History: The accent on women's rights is not new—in 1792, Mary Wollstonecraft published *A Vindication of the Rights of Women*. But the First Woman's Rights Convention, in Seneca Falls, NY, wasn't until 1848. By the late 19th century and into early 20th century, there was a major thrust to give women the right to vote. After decades of work, the suffrage movement saw its efforts rewarded when the 19th amendment was ratified in 1920.

Women's involvement in World War II broke down more barriers. However, it was Betty Friedan's *The Feminine Mystic*, that heralded the modern women's liberation movement. In addition to concern about their own rights, many women in the 19th century were also conscious of injustices to others and became involved in the abolition and social reform movements. Women pioneers wrote and published accounts of their role in settling the American West, became involved in American industrial growth and explored foreign lands.

References: Eleanor Flexner, *Century of Struggle: The Woman's Rights Movement in the United States*, Revised Edition, Belknap Press, 1975; *Notable American Women*, 4 vols., Belknap Press, 1971-1980.

Autograph
  Barton, Clara, Civil War nurse, founder of American Red Cross, ALS, 4-pg small 8vo, Glen Echo, MD, May 5, 1906, to Miss Kensel, regarding organizational business and praise of 2 younger women who are enthusiastic and devoted to first-aid work 485.00
  Moore, Marianne, manuscript sgd, inscribed, fair copy of poem "What Are Yours," three 9-line stanzas, 1 page, tall 4to, New York, 1942 .... 575.00
  Nightingale, Florence, letter, sgd in pencil, regarding health of Mr. Verney, commenting on her own health, 1 page, 8vo, integral blank leaf, February 1888 .... 635.00
  O'Keeffe, Georgia, letter, sgd in black ink, sending thanks to Flora for record and book, 2 pgs on versos of separate 4to sheets, Abiquin, New Mexico, June, 1961 .... 1,265.00
  O'Neill, Rose, illustrated letter, sgd, to Margaret Cathbert of NBC, referred to Witter Bynner and Edna St. Vincent Millay, 2 pgs, calligraphic style writing, single tall 8vo sheet, Saugatuck, July 1931 .... 490.00
  Roosevelt, Eleanor, book, *This I Remember,* 8vo, cloth, dust jacket, warmly inscribed and sgd, New York, 1949 .... 320.00
  Stowe, Harriet Beecher, quotation sgd, dated, card, "Trust in the Lord and/do good/Your friend/H. B. Stowe," Nov. 23, 1885 .... 460.00
Book
  American Feminists, Robert E. Riegel, University of Kansas Press, 1963, 233 pgs 28.00
  Marking A Trail, Texas Women's University Press, hardcover, orig dust jacket 20.00
  The Female Spy of the Union Army, 1864 .... 35.00
Ephemera
  Check, sgd by Mary Baker Eddy, for $1,000, Bay State Trust Co., sgd by E. A. Kimball, Boston, Oct. 17, 1903, 2-3/4" x 6" l, cancellation perforations do not affect signature 750.00
  Legal Document, incorporation papers of the Young Woman's Aid Association, 3 pgs, folio, two notarized attachments with city seals, New York City, 1872-73 .... 175.00
Fan, Women's Christian Temperance Union 10.00
Lapel Stud, 7/8" l, I Am for Allison Are You, b&w, 1896 .... 10.00
Miniature Ax, 4" l, nickel plated cast iron, face of Carry Nation on one side with inscription "Axe Of All Nations/Cut Out The Whiskey," other side imprinted "Laurel Stoves And Ranges/Art Stove Co., Detroit, Mich.," c1901 .... 70.00
Photo, woman on motorcycle, 4" x 5" 25.00
Pin, Angela Davis, gold-finished brass, black image, red letters "Libertad Para," inscribed "Hecho En Cuba" 50.00
Pinback Button
  "Angela Davis Day," black and white, "Free Angela/Bail Now/Central Park Sept. 25, 1971" 25.00
  "Black Women United To Save Our Children, Inc." black and white, young black child with dates "1974-75" 15.00
  Don't Let Us Suffer, b&w cigarette premium, Rube Goldberg cartoon of woman singing 50.00
  Equality, b&w litho, c1960 .... 20.00
  Equal Suffrage, 6 stars, 3/4" d, black letters, dark gold ground 85.00
  Frances Willard, softly tinted sepia, c1900 .... 40.00
  I Gave My Blood for the Equal Rights Amendment, 1-3/4" d, bright red on white 25.00
  I Vote Dry, purple type, purple diamond design, white ground 20.00
  "Lesbian and Gay Rights Now," orange and red lettering, white ground, March on UN/August 20/C.L.G.R. 12.00
  "Lesbian Pride 75," stylized illus of sunburst and Egyptian women in yellow, dark blue ground 15.00
  Mamie/Pat, 3-1/2" d, red, white and blue, b&w photos, 1952 .... 30.00
  Opposed to Woman Suffrage, black and white, red center 20.00
  President Carter/Barbara Walters, 3-1/2" d, white, yellow, b&w portraits, Balloon coming from Walters' head that says "Be Wise with Us...Be Good to Us," Dec. 1976 .... 15.00

Take Delmar Garden Cars to Camp Lewis, City of Tents and Woman's Magazine Building 35.00

"Tell Anita You're Against Discrimination," blue on orange 10.00

Time for Repeal, dark blue on gold ground, Liberty Bell, designed as clock face 15.00

United Nations Decade for Women, white lettering, dark blue ground, peach dove and female symbols, dated 1976-1986 ....25.00

Vote No for My Sake, prohibition, young girl, faded red rim 10.00

Votes for Women
    Black letter, gold ground 40.00
    Red, white and blue sunburst, 1915...............150.00

Ribbon
    2-1/4" x 6-1/2", black and white, inscribed "We Mourn Our Loss," Women's Christian Temperance Association and Benevolent Society, thick heavy fringed bottom 30.00
    2-1/2" x 6-1/2", blue and white, "For the Prohibitory Amendment," slight wear at edges......................................20.00

WOODENWARE

History: Many utilitarian household objects and farm implements were made of wood. Although they were subjected to heavy use, these implements were made of the strongest woods and were well cared for by their owners.

References: Arene Burgess, *19th Century Wooden Boxes,* Schiffer Publishing, 1997; George C. Neumann, *Early American Antique Country Furnishing*, L-W Book Sales, 1984, 1993 reprint.

Additional Listings: See *Warman's Americana & Collectibles* for more examples.

Note: This category serves as a catchall for wooden objects which do not fit into other categories.

Apple Box, 9-3/4" x 10" x 4" h, pine, old red paint, conical feet 310.00

Artist's Model, articulated, late 19th C, minor losses and breaks 1,100.00

Barber Pole, 59" h, acorn finials, old red and white repaint 470.00

Basket Tree, 37-1/4" h, walnut, old finish, turned detail, round base, three legs, column with finial, three arms, acorn ends 1,210.00

Bowl
    6" d, treen, poplar, old worn brown finish, tight age cracks 165.00
    7-1/2" x 9" x 3-3/8" h, burl, worn scrubbed int., ext. with traces of old blue, by Solomon Jackson, American Indian, accompanied by old photo post card of Mr. Jackson 220.00
    9-1/2" d, 73/8" h, treen, cov, poplar, worn orig red sponged graining, age cracks, finial chipped.........................495.00
    15" d, 4-3/4" h, ash, burl, turned rings, old refinishing, worn int. 500.00
    21" d, 7" h, ask, worn patina int., old red and white ext 330.00
    21-1/2" d, carved burl, 19th C 230.00

Box, 16-1/4" l, pine, worn orig brown graining, yellow ground, wire nails, machine dovetail 200.00

Busk, 11-3/4" l, carved, all over geometric and pinwheel design, 19th C, minor losses 345.00

Butter Paddle, 8-5/8" l, burl, old dark patina, minor edge wear 360.00

Candle Box, hanging
    10-1/4" w, 10-1/2" h, pine, hardwood, old worn gray paint, unsymmetrical backboard with cutout hanging, some edge damage 330.00

12" w, 6-1/2" d, 19-1/2" h, stained pine, New England, early 19th C, old refinish, cracks......................................575.00

13-1/2" w, 7-1/4" d, 24" h, pine, old charcoal colored paint over earlier red, shaped crest, two shelves, some edge damage..1,065.00

Candle Shelf, 12" h, 7-1/2" w, 5-1/4" h, corner, stained cherry, diamond form mirrored panels 345.00

Churn, 21-1/2" h, stave construction, metal bands, turned lid, dasher, old refinishing 110.00

Coffin, 78" l, 23-1/4" w, 19" h, rect box, grain painted, glazed hinged top, oval opening, chamfered plinth base, old brown graining to resemble exotic wood, back sgd "W. P. Whitney Blossom St. Boston, Mass," early 19th C 460.00

Dipper, 5-1/2" l, horse head handle, worn patina...............230.00

Drying Rack, 24-1/2" w, 29-1/2" h, mortised construction, chamfered, shoe feet, old blue repaint over yellow 220.00

Footwarmer, 6-1/4" x 8" x 8-1/2" h, walnut, old finish, dovetailed, sliding front panel, drilled holes in circular design on sides and back, alternate diagonal rows on top, initials "L. F." and punched date 1814 on door, cat iron pan, age cracks, scorched spot on base and door, small nail repairs, wire bale handle..780.00

Cutting Board, round top, shaped base, metal blade, 6-5/8" x 18", $35.

Jar, cov
    4-1/2" h, treen, dec, poplar, worn orig green and yellow vinegar paint, glued chip on rim of lid 330.00
    5-5/8" h, green, Pease, old soft finish, age cracks 215.00
Lap Desk, 13-3/4" w, 9" d, 5-1/2" h, bird's eye maple and mahogany veneer, compartmented int., inlaid leather writing surface, minor imperfections 575.00
Lighting Stand
    12" h, adjustable arm on threaded post, two candle sockets, hardwood, worn finish 440.00
    38-1/2" h, Windsor, hard wood, old black paint over earlier red, threaded spindle with adjustable round dish turned shelf and candle arm with 2 sockets, 3 turned legs, round base, minor edge damage 2,860.00
Mortar and Pestle, 8-1/2" h, turned, old patina..................140.00
Niddy Noddy, 18-1/4" l, hardwood, old yellow paint, one end with age crack at mortise..110.00
Noggin, 4-7/8" h, primitive, worn patina, short age crack 125.00
Press, 17" h, hardware, patina, dovetailed construction, carved spout..140.00
Printing Block, 7-1/4" x 12", pine, attributed to MA, 18th C, carved alternating bands of foliate, geometric, and vine motif, minor losses..815.00
Shoe, 5-7/8" h, old worn black paint over turquoise, red and yellow striping, red, white, green, and yellow flowers, edge damage...165.00
Snuff Box, cov
    2" d, burl, round, inset hand colored engraving of woman, glass cracked, some damage....................................50.00
    3" l, shoe shaped, curved toe, worn black lacquer, inlaid pewter...225.00
    3-3/8" d, burl, round, carved ext. with well detailed relief scene of banquet aboard ship, French inscription "Party given for the King of Portugal on the Lena, long give France," tortoise shell int. 220.00
Spinning Wheel, 36" h, refinished oak and hardwood, turned detail, repairs and replacements.......................................300.00
Swift, 27-1/2" h, "X" base, old patina...................................130.00
Table Top Organizer, 17-1/4" w, 7" d, 7" h, pine, orig reddish brown graining, two tiers, four drawers 330.00
Tankard, 8-1/2" h, fruitwood, animal carved top and hinge, notched handle, beast form feet, Continental, 19th C...230.00
Towel Bar, 37-1/2" h, 29" h, walnut, three horizontal bars on tapering squared posts, scrolled trestle feet, New England, early 19th C 175.00
Wool Wheel, 44" d wheel, hardwood, old dark patina, traces of old red paint, turned and chip carved detail......................250.00

WORLD'S FAIRS AND EXPOSITIONS

History: The Great Exhibition of 1851 in London marked the beginning of the World's Fair and Exposition movement. The fairs generally featured exhibitions from nations around the world displaying the best of their industrial and scientific achievements.

Many important technological advances have been introduced at world's fairs, including the airplane, telephone, and electric lights. Ice cream cones, hot dogs, and iced tea were first sold by vendors at fairs. Art movements often were closely connected to fairs, with the Paris Exhibition of 1900 generally considered to have assembled the best of the works of the Art Nouveau artists.

References: *Crystal Palace Exhibition Illustrated Catalogue* (London, 1851), Dover Publications, n.d.; Robert L. Hendershott, *1904 St. Louis World's Fair Mementos and Memorabilia*, Kurt R. Krueger Publishing (160 N. Wash-

ington, Iola, WI 54945), 1994; Frederick and Mary Megson, *American Exposition Postcards*, The Postcard Lovers, 1992; Howard Rusen and John Kaduck *Columbia World's Fair Collectibles*; Zim, Lernez, Rolfes, *1939 World's Fair, World of Tomorrow*, Harper and Row.

Collectors' Clubs: 1904 World's Fair Society, 529 Barcia Dr., St. Louis, MO 63119; World's Fair Collectors' Society Inc., P.O. Box 20806, Sarasota, FL 34276.

Museums: Buffalo & Erie County Historical Society, Buffalo, NY; California State University, Madden Library, Fresno, CA; 1893 Chicago World's Fair Columbian Exposition Museum, Columbus, WI; Museum of Science & Industry, Chicago, IL; Presidio Army Museum, San Francisco, CA; The Queens Museum, Flushing, NY.

Advisor: Herbert Rolfes.

Crystal Palace, 1851
Pipe, white clay Pipe, 6" l, Crystal Palace on bowl 100.00
Pot Lid, Pratt, 5" d 200.00
Crystal Palace, NY 1853
Dollar, so called, 1-3/4" d, shows seated Liberty and Crystal Palace..75.00
Print, Currier and Ives, Crystal Palace................................400.00
Centennial, 1876
Bank, still, cast iron, Independence Hall, 9" h x 7" w 350.00
Glass Slipper, Gillinder
    Clear 35.00
    Frosted 40.00
Medal, wooden, Main Building, 3" d.....................................60.00
Scarf, 19 x 34", Memorial Hall, Art Gallery colorful.............100.00
Columbian Exposition, 1893
Book, *Harper's Chicago and the World's Fair*, Julian Ralph, NY, Harper and Brothers, 1893, clothbound, 244 pgs, 70 illus 45.00
Brochure, Mammoth Redwood Plank, Owned by the Berry Bros., Ltd., 4 pgs, 4" x 5"...25.00
Clock, shaped like sailing ship, cast iron, bronzed............225.00
Crumb Tray and Scraper, SP 30.00

Crystal Palace, 1851, pot lid, Pratt, 5" d, $200. Photo courtesy of Herb Rolfes.

Folder, 5-1/2" x 9-3/4", views 40.00
Guide Book , Official..45.00
Plate, Wedgwood, dark blue and white, Administration Building in
    middle...45.00
Playing Cards 45.00
Sheet Music, *World's Columbian Expo March* 75.00
Souvenir Book, *Official Guide to the World's Columbian Exposi-
    tion,* 5" x 7", 192 pgs 50.00
Tablecloth, 11" sq, Machinery Hall, fringed border, small stain
    and damage 70.00
Watch Case Opener, Keystone Watch Case Co. 15.00
California Mid-Winter Exposition, **1894**, souvenir spoon, bowl with
    drawing of ornate pavilion, SP, mkd "AMN Sterling Co."
    ....25.00

Trans-Mississippi, 1898, change purse, leather and mother of
    pearl, showing fair name on side 45.00
Pan American, 1901
Bandanna, 20" sq, silk, Electrical Tower illus 195.00
Cigar Case, hinged aluminum 2-1/2" x 5-1/2".....................35.00
Frying Pan, pictures North and South America, 6" long 75.00
Match Holder, hanging type...25.00
Plate, frosted glass, three cats painted on dec, 7-1/2" d 35.00
Souvenir Spoon
    4-1/2" l, SP, Machinery & Transportation Building on bowl
    ....13.00
    6" l, SP, buffalo sitting on earth on top of handle, waterfalls on
    bowl 15.00
St. Louis, 1904
Bowl, Grant log cabin 165.00
Coffee Tin, Hanley & Kinsella 30.00
Letter Opener, emb buildings on handle 45.00
Medal, silvered brass, 2-3/4" d....................................60.00
Souvenir Book, *Souvenir Book of the Louisiana Purchase Exposi-
tion,* day-and-night scenes, published by the Official Photo-
graphic Co., 11" x 8-1/2"...45.00
Stamp holder, aluminum, 1-1/8" x 1-3/8".........................35.00
Tumbler 4" high, copper plated base, metal, shows Louisiana
    Purchase Monument, Cascades, Union Station and Liberal
    Arts Bldg...35.00
Alaska-Yukon, 1909, fob, 3 pc, State Building, Totem Pole, Fair
    Logo in Center, 4" lg 75.00
Hudson-Fulton, 1909, pinback, color pictures profiles of Hudson
    and Fulton, 1-1/4" d 25.00
Panama-Pacific, 1915
Booklet, Panama-Pacific International Exposition, compliments of
    Remington Typewriter, 30 pgs, 7-1/4" x 11" 40.00
Handbook, *The Sculpture & Murals of the Panama-Pacific Inter-
national Exposition,* Stella S. G Perry, 1915, 104 pgs, 5" x 6-
3/4", ex-library copy...45.00
Pocket Watch, official, silver plated, 2" d 300.00
Post Card...5.00
Tray, 3-1/2" x 5-1/2, hammered metal, bear figural, emb "Tower of
    Jewels, Panama Pacific International/San Francisco, Cal
    1915," dark finish..45.00
Watch Fob, brass, orig black leather strap 95.00

Chicago, 1934

Automobile Accessory, rear-view mirror, no glare, orig box
    ....90.00
Bracelet, copper, scenic 35.00
Brochure
    Baltimore and Ohio Railroad World's Fair Exhibit 1934, 20 pag-
    es, 4-1/2" x 9-3/4"...25.00
    57 at the Fair, Heinz 57 Exhibit, Agricultural Building, 16 pgs
    ....22.00
    How! And Where! At Chicago and the World's Fair, Chicago
    and Northwestern (Railroad) Line, 16-pg guide to Chicago
    ....20.00
Official Pictures, Reuben H. Donnelly, b&w, 7" x 10" 35.00
Sky-Ride, See the Fair from the Air, 4 pgs, 3-1/2" x 5-3/4" ...12.00

Columbian Exposition, 1893, clock, shaped like sailing ship, bronzed cast iron, $225. Photo courtesy of Herb Rolfes.

The Why-What-and When of a Century of Progress, 10 pgs
    ....10.00
Certificate of Attendance, Closing Day, Oct. 31, 1934, 3" x 5-1/4"
    ....15.00
Coffee Mug, Stewart's 50.00
Coin, flattened
    1-3/8" l, Fort Dearborn 15.00
    1-1/2" x 3/4", General Motors Exhibit 15.00
Good Luck Key, 2" l, Master Lock, pavilions on shank 20.00
Handkerchief, 11" sq, painted silk, small stains 40.00
Magazine, *Marshall Field & Co.,* 9-1/2" x 13", 44 pgs, photos and
    articles 20.00

New York, 1939, stamp, blue, tan, green, and orange, $2. Photo courtesy of Herb Rolfes.

Map, City of Chicago and Century of Progress fairgrounds, Shell Oil 16.00
Needle Case, 6-3/4" x 4-1/2", A Century of Progress 27.00
Playing Cards, gold-leaf edges, orig red leather case 30.00
Pocket Mirror 25.00
Puzzle, 16-1/2", aerial view of fair opening, 300 pcs...........50.00
Snowdome..50.00
Souvenir Book
    1933 Century of Progress Souvenir Book, 8-1/2" x 11-1/2"
    ....20.00
    Official Guide Book of the Fair, foldout map and Firestone col-
        ored adv insert...25.00
Souvenir Spoon, SP
    Electrical Group on bowl, Fort Dearborn on handle, dated
        1934 ....10.00
    Travel & Transport on bowl, Hall of Science on handle, dated
        1933 ....8.00
Tray, Hall of Science, emb buildings, bridge 30.00
View Book, 9" x 12", A Century of Progress Exhibition Official Book
    of Views, watercolor views and painting reproductions, pub-
    lished by Donnelly 30.00
Wings 25.00
Century of Progress, 1937
Playing Cards, full deck, showing views of the fair, all different,
    black and white 45.00
Poker Chip, red, white, or blue, 1-1/2" d.............................15.00
Ring , silver plated, blue and white, comet and star, adjustable
    ....20.00
Toy Wagon, red or blue with white wheels, decal of Transportation
    Bldg in middle approx 3-1/2" lg....................................175.00
Great Lakes, 1936, pin back, Florida, with state flag on the face,
    1-1/2" d 18.00
Texas Centennial, 1936, playing cards, colorful with Texas state
    flag on back, boxed...40.00
Golden Gate, 1939
Ashtray, 1939 Golden Gate Expo, Homer Laughlin Pottery
    ....125.00
Bookmark, typical view, 4" l..20.00
Handkerchief, 12-1/2" sq, Treasure Island, minor stains......40.00
Label, luggage type, Greyhound, 3-1/2" d 15.00
Match Book, orig matches, pictures Pacifica........................10.00
Match Cover, Golden Gate Bridge scenes, pr.......................25.00
Pinback Button, 1-1/4" d, yellow, blue and white 25.00
Plate, 10" d, Homer Laughlin 125.00
Ticket
    Elephant Train Ticket, 3-1/2" x 2", slight glue and paper on
        back...15.00
    General Admission, 3-1/2" x 2-1/4", slight glue and paper on
        back...15.00
Token, shows Sun Tower and Bridge, 1-1/8" d 15.00
New York, 1939
Ashtray, 3" x 3-1/2", Trylon and Perisphere, Almar, Point Marian,
    PA...60.00
Banner, 10" x 8", multicolored paint on blue felt..................45.00
Belt Buckle, goldtone, enameled Trylon and Perisphere.....20.00
Bookends, pr, alabaster, figural, Trylon and Perisphere....110.00
Booklet
    General Motors Highway & Horizons, 20 pgs 24.00
    The Foods of Tomorrow, Birdseye....................................8.00
    Bowl, spring, Homer Laughlin Pottery 55.00
Brochure, 12 pgs, foldout, Trylon and Perisphere 16.00
Cake Knife 45.00
Candy Tin, miniature, by Bagatele, very colorful, 4-1/4" x 6-1/2"
    ....65.00
Cane, 34" l, wood, blue, round wood knob, Trylon and Perisphere
    decal...85.00
Cigarette Holder, Lenox, pink, yellow, blue, green, white, 2-1/2"
    h...350.00
Clock, travel, 1-2/ x 1-1/4" x 1-1/2", chrome-silver case, Trylon,
    Perisphere and fair buildings on cover, blue and orange
    enamel accents 125.00

Coin, flattened, World of Tomorrow, Trylon and Perisphere. 13.00
Commemorative Plate 150.00
Compact, 2-3/4" d, metal, full-color celluloid insert, ivory white
    enameling...40.00
Cuff Links, pr, Trylon and Perisphere 45.00
Cup 25.00
Glass, 4-1/4" h
    Business Administration Building, dark blue top and center,
        orange base, "NYWF 39" and row of stars at base 20.00
    Textile Building, yellow top and center, green base, center
        shows building...25.00
Guide Book, *Official Guide to World of Tomorrow*, first ed, 1939
    ....25.00
Hat, employee, wool, navy, orange Trylon and Perisphere and
    "1940" on front 42.00
Hot Plate, silver, engraved fair scenes................................15.00
Identification Check, Greyhound Bus, Sightseeing Bus Trip Thru
    Grounds...7.50
Kerchief, 20" sq, deep blue, cluttered yellow, green and red art-
    work of Fair buildings, Trylon and Perisphere 65.00
Key Ring 20.00
Magazine, *Life*, Trylon and Perisphere on cover.................30.00
Map, Transit Map of Greater New York, Compliments of Franklin
    Fire Insurance Co. 25.00
Match Case, 1-1/2" x 2", leather, Trylon and Perisphere 35.00
Music Box...65.00
Night-Light, ceramic, oval base with Trylon and Perisphere, ivory
    white finish, gold accents 100.00
Photo, 25" x 20", American Jubilee, dry mounted 55.00
Pin
    I Have Seen the Future..25.00
    Shield-shaped logo, 5/8" h, 3/8" w, 1-1/2" chain to "39" on
        smaller shield, blue enamel on brass 25.00
    Red enameled, from Russian Pavilion...........................150.00
Pipe, when standing on bowl looks like Trylon and Perisphere, 5-
    1/2" lg..125.00
Plate
    7-1/4" d, Joint Exhibit of Capital & Labor, The American Potter,
        New York World's Fair, 1940, National Brotherhood Coop-
        erative Potteries 45.00
    9" d, Homer Laughlin Pottery, potter, turquoise 38.00
    10" d, Cronin, crazed 85.00
Playing Cards, 2 decks, orig box, U.S. Playing Card Co. 50.00
Post Card
    Photo type...6.00
    Set of 10 double-faced cards, orig folder, unused 18.00
Postage Stamps, 54 licensed stamps in orig envelope, unused
    ....25.00
Potholder, 7-1/2" x 8-1/2", woven terry cloth, blue and white de-
    sign, inscribed "Macy's Pot Holder"...............................50.00
Program, Opening Day, April 30, 1939 ....150.00
Ring, 5/8" d, 3/8" x 5/8" top with Trylon and Perisphere, SS
    ....45.00
Rug, 9" x 13", woven Oriental type, image of Trylon and Peri-
    sphere surrounded by flowers, shades of green, yellow, red
    and orange highlights, Italian 95.00
Salt and Pepper Shakers, pr, figural, Trylon and Perisphere, or-
    ange and blue 25.00
Scarf, 18" x 17", white, orange, yellow and maroon, blue ground,
    trees and buildings, Trylon and Perisphere around edge,
    clouds center...45.00
Souvenir Spoon, SP, Trylon and Perisphere on handle, different
    exhibit on bowl, Wm. Rogers, set of 12 ....240.00
Table Mat, 11" x 21", red felt, yellow, green and white graphics,
    Statue of Liberty, Fair Administration Building, Empire State
    Building, Trylon and Perisphere 95.00
Tape Measure, 2-1/2" w, egg shape, metal, blue finish, bee figure
    on both sides, orange Trylon and Perisphere on 1 side, mkd
    "New York World's Fair 1939"...60.00
Teapot, white glazed china, blue Trylon and Perisphere 50.00
Thermometer, 8-1/4" l, key shape, aerial view.....................32.00

Thermos, 10" h, steel, threaded aluminum cap, orange Trylon and Perisphere, Universal Thermos 100.00

Ticket, 3" x 4", b&w photo, starched black fabric holder......45.00

Tie Clip, 2-3/4" w, brass, raised center emblem of Trylon and Perisphere...25.00

Valet Holder, clothes-brush holder and tie rack, sirocco, raised Trylon and Perisphere, orig brush 50.00

View-Master, set of 3 reels, orig booklet and envelope 40.00

Brussels, 1958, paperweight, Atomaton, chrome plated on marble base, 4-1/2" x 4-1/2" x 4-1/2".......................................75.00

Seattle, 1962

Glasses, frosted, Space Needle.................................15.00

Glass, set of eight...80.00

Pinback Button, 1-1/4" d, red, white and blue, Space Needle scene 17.50

Token, gold...10.00

Tray, metal, Space Needle scene 12.00

New York, 1964

Ashtray

4" x 5", glass, white, orange and blue graphics, 2 Fair Kids, Unisphere, 1964...25.00

5" h, ceramic, Unisphere shape 35.00

Backpack, vinyl 15.00

Bank, dime register, orig card................................40.00

Change Tray 12.00

Coaster, 4" d, plastic, white, emb gold Unisphere, title and date, price for 4-pc set...32.00

Comic Book, Flintstones.......................................20.00

Envelope, Unisphere as Christmas tree ornament, unused 10.00

Flash Card Set, New York World's Fair Attractions

Full Size, 3-1/2" x 6", 28 cards 25.00

Miniature Size, 24 cards 20.00

Fork and Spoon Display, 11" l, mounted on wood plaque, Unisphere decals on handles 45.00

Hat, black felt, Unisphere emblem, white cord trim, feather, name "Richard" embroidered on front 25.00

Mug, 3-1/4" h, milk glass, red inscription 17.50

Place Mat, 11" x 17-1/2", plastic, full-color illus, Swiss Sky Ride and Lunar Fountain, price for pr...........................25.00

Postcard, 10 miniature pictures, 20 natural color reproductions, unused 20.00

Salt and Pepper Shakers, pr, figural 12.00

Souvenir Book, *Official Souvenir Book of the New York World's Fair,* 1965...25.00

Stein, 6" h, ceramic, blue, German-style, emb Unisphere, German village scene, beer drinkers 25.00

Thermometer, 6" x 6", diamond shape, metal and plastic, full-color fair buildings and attractions 25.00

Ticket

Belgian Village...7.50

General Admission, adult, unused 20.00

Pavilion of American Interiors, unused prepaid ticket, courtesy of International Silver Co.................................15.00

Travelers Pavilion, The Travelers Insurance Companies stockholders' courtesy card...................................12.00

Tray, 10-1/2" x 11-1/2", oval, plastic, raised fair attractions 42.00

Tumbler, Science Hall, 6-1/2" h 17.50

Seattle, 1964

Beer Glass, Shaefer..15.00

Compact, varied attractions on cover, 3-1/2" d...............30.00

Salt and Pepper Shakers, pr, Peter and Wendy................35.00

Magazine, *Life,* May 1, 1964, Unisphere at night on cover 20.00

Tray, chrome plated steel tray, U.S. Steel, 10" x 14-1/2"......25.00

Waste Paper Basket, blue, Unisphere.........................125.00

Montreal, 1967

Lapel Pin, brass, repeated motif around edge, threaded post fastener on back..12.00

Tab, 1-1/2" l, litho tin, blue and white, U.S. Pavilion, Compliments of Avis Car Rental..6.00

Knoxville, 1982

Glass, 5-1/2" h, clear, tapered, Energy Turns the World theme, trademark for McDonald's and Coca-Cola..................8.00

Sailor Cap, black and red inscription on brim..................5.00

YARD-LONG PRINTS

History: In the early 1900s, many yard-long prints could be had for a few cents postage and a given number of wrappers or box tops. Others were premiums for renewing a subscription to a magazine or newspaper. A large number were advertising items created for a store or company and had calendars on the front or back. Many people believe that the only true yard-long print is 36 inches long and titled "A Yard of Kittens," etc. But lately collectors feel that any long and narrow print, horizontal or vertical, can be included in this category. It is a matter of personal opinion.

Untitled, birds, copyrighted 1899 by American Lithographic Co., artist sgd F. Giacomelli (or Hiacomelli) (3-20) $300. Photo courtesy of Joan Rhoden.

Values are listed for full-length prints in near-mint condition, nicely framed, and with original glass.

References: C. G. and J. M. Rhoden and W. D. and M. J. Keagy, *Those Wonderful Yard-Long Prints and More,* Book 1 (1989), Book 2 (1992), Book 3 (1995), published by authors (605 No. Main, Georgetown, IL 61846).

Calendar, Howard Chandler Christie, orig calendar (removed) from 1926, adv Selz Good Shoes, (1-45) $350. Photo courtesy of Joan Rhoden.

Advisors: Charles G. and Joan M. Rhoden, W. D. and M. J. Keagy.

Note: Numbers in parentheses below indicate the Rhoden and Keagy book number and page on which the item is illustrated, e.g. (3-52) refers to Book 3, page 52.

Calendar

1904, Pabst Extract, different nationality baby for each month of calendar, roll at bottom (2-100) 350.00

1909, Schlitz, Malt Extract "Indian Girl," adv for products on back (3-64) 400.00

1911, Pabst Extra, "American Girl," by C. W. Henning, full length, cardboard roll at bottom (2-81) 350.00

1915, Selz Good Shoes, lady and child in swing, calendar at bottom (2-102) 300.00

1917, "The Walk-Over Shoe" at top of print, full calendar pd at bottom (3-78) 400.00

1918, American Farming Magazine, sgd "W. H. Lister," lovely lady with parasol, holding basket of flowers in right hand, date and info on back (1-9) 350.00

1919, Pompeian, "Liberty Girl," by Forbes, pretty girl clutching drape with her soldier's picture in star, date and info on back (1-28) 300.00

1927, Pompeian, "The Bride," sgd "Rolf Armstrong," gorgeous bride in all her wedding attire (1-36) 350.00

Print

Battle of the Chicks, by Ben Austrian, © 1920 by The Art Interchange Co. of New York (2-17) 250.00

Cupid's Festival, by M. Delecrolk, © by The Art Interchange Co. of New York (3-109) 350.00

Down on the Congo, #1036, © 1904 by Jos. Hoover & Son, Philadelphia (3-17) 350.00

Easter Greetings, by Paul DeLongpre, © 1894 by Knapp Co. Litho. (3-107) 400.00

Hula Girl, sgd "Gene Pressler," lovely lady dancing, palm trees all around, wearing grass skirt, flowers across bosom and in hair, bangles on ankles and arms (1-96)..............................350.00

La France Roses, by Paul DeLongpre, © 1903, advertising Spiehler's Perfume (3-32) 300.00

Study of Chrysanthemums, by Paul DeLongpre, © 1900 by The Art Interchange Co. (2-35)...250.00

Study of Sweet Peas, by Grace Barton Allen, © 1900 by The Art Interchange Co. of New York (2-62).............................200.00

YELLOWWARE

History: Yellowware is a heavy earthenware which varies in color from a rich pumpkin to lighter shades, which are more tan than yellow. The weight and strength varies from piece to piece. Although plates, nappies, and custard cups are found, kitchen bowls and other cooking utensils are most prevalent.

The first American yellowware was produced at Bennington, Vermont. English yellowware has additional ingredients which make its body much harder. Derbyshire and Sharp's were foremost among the English manufacturers.

Humidor, banded, c1930, 6" h, $75.

References: Susan and Al Bagdade, *Warman's American Pottery and Porcelain*, Wallace-Homestead, 1994; William C. Ketchum Jr., *American Pottery and Porcelain*, Avon Books, 1994; Joan Leibowitz, *Yellow Ware*, Schiffer Publishing, 1985, 1993 value update; Lisa S. McAllister, *Collector's Guide to Yellow Ware*, Collector Books, 1996; Lisa S. McAllister and John L. Michael, *Collecting Yellow Ware*, Collector Books, 1993.

Bank, 3-5/8" h, house shape, molded detail highlighted in black, roof mkd "For My Dear Girl," firing crack at chimney 660.00
Canning Jar, 6-3/4" h, barrel shape....................................110.00
Creamer
    3-7/8" h, black stripes, white band, green seaweed dec, hairline at base of handle 165.00
    4-3/4" h, brown stripes, white band, blue seaweed dec, shallow flake on inside edge of table ring......................440.00
Flask, 11" x 6", fish shape 1,000.00
Food Mold
    3-3/4" d, 1-1/4" h, miniature, Yellow Rock, Phila mark ...185.00
    7-1/2" d, 2-3/4" h, turk's head 145.00
Measure, 5-3/4" h, 6-1/2"d, Spearpoint & Trellis.................300.00
Mug, 3" h, flared sides, white slip dec................................150.00
Nappy, 10" d, Jeffords blue diamond mark.......................225.00
Pepper Pot, 4-1/2" h, blue seaweed dec, band dec 475.00
Pie Funnel, 2-1/2" h, unmarked..125.00
Pie Plate, 10" d, unmarked 90.00
Rolling Pin, wood handles, adv 125.00
Syllabub Cub, 3" h..125.00
Wash Board, 12-3/4" x 25" h wooden frame, yellow ware insert with brown striping, gray weathered surface, wear and chips to pottery..200.00
Wash Bowl and Pitcher, 9-1/2" d bowl, 7-3/4" h pitcher, brown and blue sponged dec, brown stripe on pitcher ....335.

ZANE POTTERY

History: In 1921, Adam Reed and Harry McClelland bought the Peters and Reed Pottery in Zanesville, Ohio. The firm continued production of garden wares and intro-

Vase, daisy dec, unglazed terra cotta, glazed green int., 6" h, $40.

duced several new art lines: Sheen, Powder Blue, Crystalline, and Drip. The factory was sold in 1941 to Lawton Gonder.

Reference: Jeffrey, Sherrie, and Barry Hersone, *Peters and Reed and Zane Pottery Experience*, published by authors, 1990.

Additional Listings: Gonder; Peters and Reed.

Bowl
    5" d, brown and blue 45.00
    6-1/2" d, blue, mkd "Zanesware" 35.00
Figure, 10-1/8" h, cat, black, green eyes..........................500.00
Jardiniere, 34" h, green matte glaze, matching pedestal, artist sgd "Frank Ferreu" 375.00
Vase
    5" h, green, cobalt blue drip glaze 30.00
    7" h, flowing medium green over dark forest green ground
    ....85.00

ZANESVILLE POTTERY   LA MORO

History: Zanesville Art Pottery, one of several potteries located in Zanesville, Ohio, began production in 1900. At first, a line of utilitarian products was made; art pottery was introduced shortly thereafter. The major line was La Moro, which was hand painted and decorated under glaze. The firm was bought by S. A. Weller in 1920 and became known as Weller Plant No. 3.

Marks: The impressed block-print mark "La Moro" appears on the high-glazed and matte-glazed decorated ware.

References: Louise and Evan Purviance and Norris F. Schneider, *Zanesville Art Pottery in Color*, Mid-America Book Company, 1968; Evan and Louise Purviance, *Zanesville Art Tile in Color*, Wallace-Homestead, 1972, out-of-print.

Bowl, 6-1/2" d, fluted edge, mottled blue glaze 45.00
Jardiniere
   7-1/8" h, 8-1/2" d, waisted cylindrical form, landscape scene, blue, green, and maroon matte glaze, c1908 .... 175.00
   8-1/4" h, ruffled rim, cream to light amber peony blossoms, shaded brown ground 75.00
Plate, 4-1/2" d, applied floral dec 25.00
Vase
   8-3/4" h, cone shaped top, bulbous base, La Morro, mkd "2/802/4" 350.00
   10-1/4" h, light gray horse portrait, light olive green to blue-green ground, matte ext., glossy brown int., sgd "R. G. Turner" 825.00

ZSOLNAY POTTERY

History: Vilmos Zsolnay (1828-1900) assumed control of his brother's factory in Pécs, Hungary, in the mid-19th century. In 1899, Miklos, Vilmos's son, became manager. The firm still produces ceramic ware.

The early wares are highly ornamental, glazed, and have a cream-colored ground. Eosin glaze, a deep rich play of colors reminiscent of Tiffany's iridescent wares, received a gold medal at the 1900 Paris exhibition. Zsolnay Art Nouveau pieces show great creativity.

Marks: Originally, no trademark was used; but in 1878 the company began to use a blue mark depicting the five towers of the cathedral at Pécs. The initials "TJM" represent the names of Miklos's three children.

Note: Zsolnay's recent series of iridescent glazed figurines, which initially were inexpensive, now are being sought by collectors and are steadily increasing in value.

Bowl, 6" d, reticulated Persian design, gold, burgundy, and blue 95.00
Cache Pot, 13" d, young girls dance holding hands around stylized tree form, blue, pale silver, and pale lilac glazes 4,250.00
Chalice, 6" h, four flower stems as handles attached to upper body, flowers and berries in relief as terminals, green and blue Eosin glazes, red int., form #5668, c1899, millennium factory mark, ext. rim chip repaired 1,650.00
Compote, 11" d, ribbed, four caryatids molded as angels supports, blue-green irid glaze 1,100.00
Dish, 8-1/2" w, fan shape, reticulated, beige, gold, and pink dec, rolled in edge, steeple mark 195.00
Ewer
   7-1/2" h, cream, yellow, and beige dec, gold base, gold reticulated neck band, ornate handle 125.00
   17" h, polychrome, highly ornate, chipped scroll and base, craquelure, price for pr 150.00

Figure, 7-1/2" w, 4-1/2" h, polar bears, irid purple and green 225.00
Garden Seat, 18-1/2" h, form #1105, c1882, wear to top surface, repairs to applied dec 1,850.00
Jardiniere, 16" l, ovoid, multicolored florals, protruding pierced roundels, cream ground, blue steep mark 450.00
Jug, 10-1/2" h, yellow glaze, worn gilt highlights, form #109, c1882 .... 500.00
Mug, 4-1/2" h, irid blue luster 90.00
Pitcher
   7-1/2" h, form #5064, red/maroon metallic Eosin ground, cream and pale brown flower dec, c1898, millennium factory mark 750.00
   15" h, Art Nouveau style, floriform, winding stem handle, peacock-green irid glaze, imp "Zsolnay Pecs-5517/1003" 4,200.00
Plate
   8-1/2" d, shell shape, reticulated, red and gold flowers, beige ground, steeple mark 190.00
   12" d, pink and blue flowers, light yellow center, reticulated gold trimmed border extending to rim, mkd "Zsolnay Pecs" 250.00
Puzzle Jug, 6-1/2" h, pierced roundels, irid dec, cream ground, castle mark, imp "Zsolnay" 195.00
Sculpture, 8-1/2" h, mother and child, irid green glaze 325.00
Vase
   3-3/4" h, all over hp flower and leaf design, red, cream and gold-green metallic Eosin glazes, sgd "Flora Nici," dated Nov. 14, 1923 .... 1,200.00
   4-1/4" h, form #2289, hand drawn factory mark and name, c1882 .... 1,500.00
   5-7/8" h, irid gold and blue swirl glaze, raised medallion mark, c1903 .... 315.00
   6-7/8" h, double gourd shape, four mice dec, red, and mustard irid glaze, four handles, imp mark and "6020" 990.00
   8" h, irid blue and green, six handles 800.00
   9" h, tapering reeded baluster, gold and cobalt blue irid finish 225.00
   11-3/4" h, cylindrical, 3 dark olive frogs sitting under water, mottled purplish spotted irid ground 5,500.00
   14" h, baluster, white spider webs, black ground 150.00
Wine Flask, 6-1/2" h, relief dec, putty ground, c1902 .... 450.00

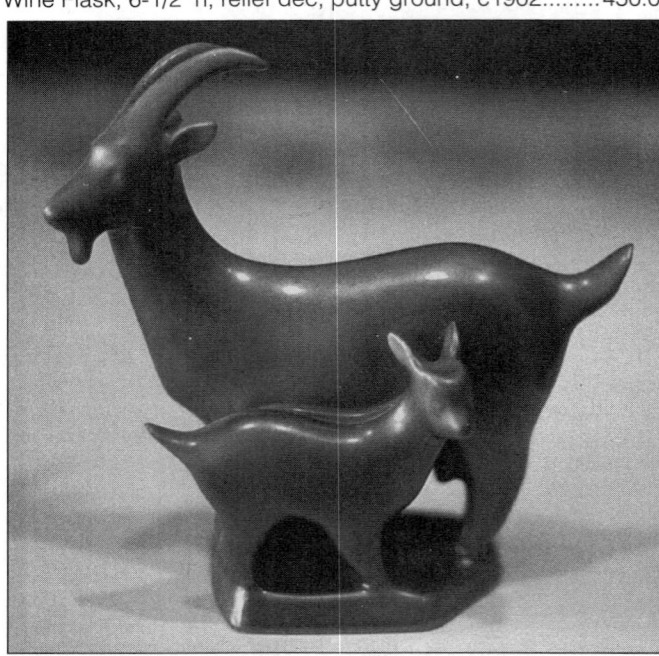

Figure, mountain goat and kid, irid blue, mkd "3 Castle Pecs, Hungary," c1930, 6" h, $190.

INDEX

B

C

Look to These Resource Guides for All Your Collecting Needs

Warman's Americana & Collectibles
8th Edition
by Ellen Schroy, editor
   Get the latest prices on today's hottest collectibles in this brand-new edition. From Pez to Hot Wheels to golf collectibles, and from Depression-era to Baby Boomer to Generation X, the 1930s to current day collectibles, this diverse value guide has it all.
Softcover • 8-1/2 x 11 • 400 pages • 250 b&w photos
WAMC8 • $17.95

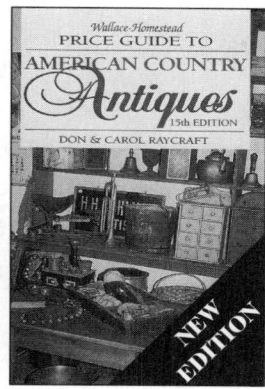

Wallace-Homestead Price Guide to American Country Antiques
15th Edition
by Don and Carol Raycraft
   The venerable "bible" of country antiques, this is your link to country collectibles of every sort baskets, furniture, graniteware, stoneware, textiles, and more. Collecting and pricing guidelines, antique markets reviews, and overviews of the hottest collectibles.
Softcover • 7-1/4x9 • 256 pages • 700 photos • 8-page color section
WACA15 • $19.95

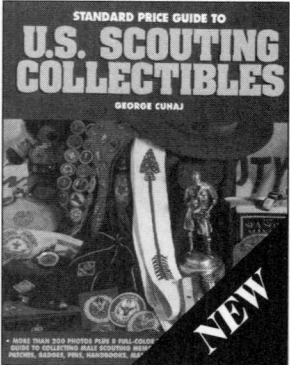

Standard Price Guide to U.S. Scouting Collectibles
ID & Price Guide for Cub, Scout and Explorer Programs
by George Cuhaj
   This easy-to-use book is the ultimate guide to Cub Scouts and Boy Scouts collectibles. Detailed descriptions and current market prices in two pricing grades for more than 5,000 items including rank and office patches and badges, pins, award medals, handbooks and manuals, medallions, uniforms, storybooks, and unusual items like cameras, games, and calendars is quick and easy.
Softcover • 8-1/2 x 11 • 328 pages • 200+ b&w photos • 32 color photos •
SCOUT • $24.95 • AVAIL 6/98

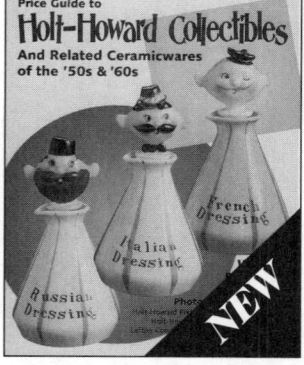

Price Guide to Holt-Howard Collectibles and Other Related Ceramicwares of the 50s & 60s
by Walter Dworkin
   The first-ever price guide devoted to Holt-Howard "Pixie-wares" and similar items from other companies, includes the whimsical items, intended for daily use in the home, featured the heads of impish Pixies on condiment jars of all types, liquor bottles and salt-and-pepper shakers. Historical information on Holt-Howard, full-color photos of almost every piece of the firm's Pixie-ware and current prices for 350 items make this a must-have guide.
Softcover • 8-1/4 x 10-7/8 • 160 pages • 300 color photos
HHCK • $24.95

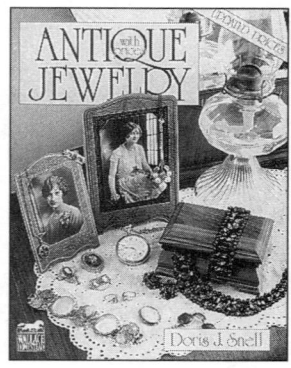

Antique Jewelry with Prices
2nd edition
by Doris J. Snell
   Uncover this gem of a guide to antique jewelry, long considered the standard reference in the field. This new edition contains updated prices, information and additional illustrations for hundreds of bracelets, brooches, chains, earrings, lockets, rings, watches and more. Inspect over 100 years of beautiful jewelry, from the Victorian era to the Art Moderne period. Beautiful stones and settings are displayed for you in photos, catalog reprints, and a special color section.
Softcover • 8-1/2 x 11 • 160 pages • 8-page color section
AJP2 • $19.95

krause publications

700 E. State Street • Iola, WI 54990-0001

Visit and order from our secure web site: www.krause.com

Credit Card Calls Toll-Free

800-258-0929 Dept. BPB1

Monday-Friday, 7 a.m. - 8 p.m. • Saturday, 8 a.m. - 2 p.m., CST

Managerial Accounting for Managers

Managerial Accounting for Managers

Fourth Edition

Eric W. Noreen, Ph.D., CMA

Professor Emeritus
University of Washington

Peter C. Brewer, Ph.D.

Wake Forest University

Ray H. Garrison, D.B.A., CPA

Professor Emeritus
Brigham Young University

Mc
Graw
Hill
Education

MANAGERIAL ACCOUNTING FOR MANAGERS, FOURTH EDITION

Published by McGraw-Hill Education, 2 Penn Plaza, New York, NY 10121. Copyright © 2017 by McGraw-Hill Education. All rights reserved. Printed in the United States of America. Previous editions © 2014, 2011, and 2008. No part of this publication may be reproduced or distributed in any form or by any means, or stored in a database or retrieval system, without the prior written consent of McGraw-Hill Education, including, but not limited to, in any network or other electronic storage or transmission, or broadcast for distance learning.

Some ancillaries, including electronic and print components, may not be available to customers outside the United States.

This book is printed onacid-free paper.

1 2 3 4 5 6 7 8 9 0 DOW/DOW1 0 9 8 7 6

ISBN 978-1-259-57854-0
MHID 1-259-57854-2

Senior Vice President, Products & Markets: *Kurt L. Strand*
Vice President, General Manager, Products & Markets: *Marty Lange*
Vice President, Content Design & Delivery: *Kimberly Meriwether David*
Managing Director: *Tim Vertovec*
Brand Manager: *Nichole Pullen*
Director, Product Development: *Rose Koos*
Product Developer: *Erin Quinones*
Marketing Manager: *Cheryl Osgood*
Digital Product Developer: *Kevin Moran*
Director, Content Design & Delivery: *Linda Avenarius*
Program Manager: *Daryl Horrocks*
Lead Content Project Managers: *Pat Frederickson* and *Brian Nacik*
Buyer: *Laura M. Fuller*
Senior Designer: *Srdjan Savanovic*
Content Licensing Specialists: *Carrie Burger* and *Jacob Sullivan*
Cover and Chapter Opener Image: © *narvikk/Getty Images*
Compositor: *SPi Global*
Printer: *R. R. Donnelley*

All credits appearing on page xxvi are considered to be an extension of the copyright page.

Library of Congress Cataloging-in-Publication Data

Noreen, Eric W., author.
  Managerial accounting for managers / Eric W. Noreen, Peter C. Brewer, Ray H.
Garrison. — Fourth Edition.
    pages cm
  ISBN 978-1-259-57854-0 (alk. paper)
  1. Managerial accounting. I. Brewer, Peter C., author. II. Garrison, Ray H., author. III. Title.
HF5657.4.N668 2017
658.15'11—dc23
                                                                2015030580

The Internet addresses listed in the text were accurate at the time of publication. The inclusion of a website does not indicate an endorsement by the authors or McGraw-Hill Education, and McGraw-Hill Education does not guarantee the accuracy of the information presented at these sites.

mheducation.com/highered

About the Authors

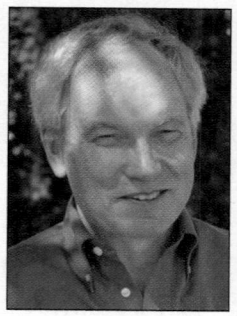

Eric W. Noreen has held appointments at institutions in the United States, Europe, and Asia. He is emeritus professor of accounting at the University of Washington.

His BA degree is from the University of Washington and his MBA and PhD degrees are from Stanford University. A Certified Management Accountant, he was awarded a Certificate of Distinguished Performance by the Institute of Certified Management Accountants.

Professor Noreen has served as associate editor of *The Accounting Review* and the *Journal of Accounting and Economics*. He has numerous articles in academic journals, including the *Journal of Accounting Research; The Accounting Review;* the *Journal of Accounting and Economics; Accounting Horizons; Accounting, Organizations and Society; Contemporary Accounting Research;* the *Journal of Management Accounting Research;* and the *Review of Accounting Studies.* Professor Noreen has won a number of awards from students for his teaching.

In his spare time, Eric organizes and leads annual hut-to-hut hiking treks for friends in the Alps in Italy, Switzerland, and Austria. ■

Peter C. Brewer is a Lecturer in the Department of Accountancy at Wake Forest University. Prior to joining the faculty at Wake Forest, he was an accounting professor at Miami University for 19 years. He holds a BS degree in accounting from Penn State University, an MS degree in accounting from the University of Virginia, and a PhD from the University of Tennessee. He has published more than 40 articles in a variety of journals, including *Management Accounting Research;* the *Journal*

of *Information Systems; Cost Management; Strategic Finance;* the *Journal of Accountancy; Issues in Accounting Education;* and the *Journal of Business Logistics.*

Professor Brewer is a member of the editorial board of the *Journal of Accounting Education* and has served on the editorial board of *Issues in Accounting Education.* His article "Putting Strategy into the Balanced Scorecard" won the 2003 International Federation of Accountants' Articles of Merit competition, and his articles "Using Six Sigma to Improve the Finance Function" and "Lean Accounting: What's It All About?" were awarded the Institute of Management Accountants' Lybrand Gold and Silver Medals in 2005 and 2006. He has received Miami University's Richard T. Farmer School of Business Teaching Excellence Award.

Prior to joining the faculty at Miami University, Professor Brewer was employed as an auditor for Touche Ross in the firm's Philadelphia office. He also worked as an internal audit manager for the Board of Pensions of the Presbyterian Church (USA).

Pete's recreational interests include fishing, bow hunting, golf, and gardening, He also enjoys biking with his wife spending quality time with his two daughters; and spoiling his two labrador retrievers, Genevieve and Sweet Baby. ■

Ray H. Garrison is emeritus professor of accounting at Brigham Young University, Provo, Utah. He received his BS and MS degrees from Brigham Young University and his DBA degree from Indiana University.

As a certified public accountant, Professor Garrison has been involved in management consulting work with both national and regional accounting firms. He has published articles in *The Accounting Review, Management Accounting,* and other professional journals. Innovation in the classroom has earned Professor Garrison the Karl G. Maeser Distinguished Teaching Award from Brigham Young University. ■

Dedication

To our families and to our many colleagues who use this book.

—*Eric W. Noreen, Peter C. Brewer, and Ray H. Garrison*

Focus on the Future Manager

with Noreen/Brewer/Garrison

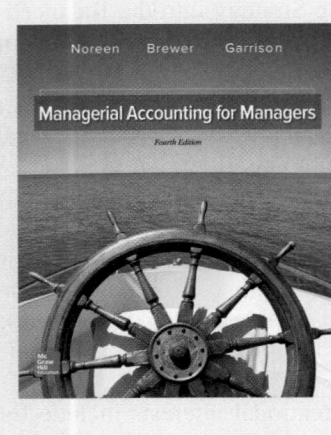

In ***Managerial Accounting for Managers,*** the authors have crafted a streamlined managerial accounting book that is perfect for non-accounting majors who intend to move into managerial positions. The traditional Process Costing, Statement of Cash Flows, and Financial Statement Analysis chapters have been dropped to enable instructors to **focus their attention on the bedrocks of managerial accounting**—planning, control, and decision making. Noreen/Brewer/Garrison focuses on the fundamentals, allowing students to develop the conceptual framework managers need to succeed. In its fourth edition, *Managerial Accounting for Managers* continues to adhere to three core standards:

FOCUS.
Noreen/Brewer/Garrison pinpoint the key managerial concepts students will need in their future careers. With no journal entries or financial accounting topics to worry about, students can focus on the fundamental principles of managerial accounting. The manager approach in Noreen allows students to develop the conceptual framework needed to succeed, with a focus on decision making and analytical skills.

RELEVANCE.
Building student interest with its insightful Business Focus vignettes opening each chapter, current In Business examples throughout the text, and tried-and-true end-of-chapter material, students will always see the real-world applicability of Noreen/Brewer/Garrison.

BALANCE.
There is more than one type of business, and so Noreen/Brewer/Garrison covers a variety of business models, including non-profit, retail, service, wholesale, and manufacturing organizations. Service company examples are highlighted with icons in the margins of the text.

"It's a very clear book with a healthy focus on decision making and service businesses. Great for non-majors."
—Mark Holtzman, Seton Hall University

"Very well-written and compatible with a user-based approach."
—Kay Poston, University of Indianapolis

"The best introductory management accounting book I have used. It is complete, concise, and written at a level beginning students can understand."
—Christine Haynes, University of West Georgia

New in the Fourth Edition

All Chapters

All chapters (except Chapter 1) have a new Foundational 15 feature.

Chapter 1

This chapter has a new section titled Managerial Accounting: Beyond the Numbers. It has expanded coverage of leadership skills and an expanded set of end-of-chapter exercises.

Chapter 2

The learning objective pertaining to direct and indirect costs has been moved to the front of the chapter to improve the students' ability to understand the material. Appendix 2A has been overhauled to simplify the explanation of how to use Microsoft Excel to perform least-squares regression analysis.

Chapter 3

The assumptions of CVP analysis have been moved from the end of the chapter to the beginning of the chapter. The target profit analysis and break-even analysis learning objectives have been reversed.

Chapter 4

This chapter has added Appendix 3A: Activity-Based Absorption Costing. This material was formerly Appendix 7B in the previous edition of the book. Moving this material to Chapter 3 offers instructors greater flexibility when determining how to cover activity-based costing.

Chapter 5

This chapter has added a new learning objective related to calculating companywide and segment break-even points for companies with traceable fixed costs. It has also added a new appendix related to super-variable costing.

Chapter 6

This chapter has added a new exhibit and accompanying text to better explain key concepts and terminology within the chapter.

Chapter 7

A section illustrating the meaning of a constraint has been added. Also, several new In Business boxes have been created.

Chapter 8

The learning objective pertaining to the payback period has been moved to the front of the chapter. Adopted a Microsoft Excel-based approach for depicting net present value calculations. Added a discussion of the behavioral implications of the simple rate of return method. Completely overhauled Appendix 8C so that students can more easily grasp the impact of income taxes on net present value analysis.

Chapter 9

We added new text and an exhibit to help students better understand how and why a master budget is created and how Microsoft Excel can be used to create a financial planning model that answers "what-if" questions. Two new end-of-chapter exercises that enable students to use Microsoft Excel to answer "what-if" questions have also been added.

Chapter 10

The discussion of the variance analysis cycle and management by exception have been moved into the front of this chapter. This material was previously included in the standard costing chapter. In response to customer feedback, we reversed the headings in the flexible budget performance report. The actual results are shown in the far-left column, and the planning budget is shown in the far-right column.

Chapter 11

In response to customer feedback, we reversed the headings in the general model for standard cost variance analysis. The actual results (AQ × AP) are shown in the far-left column and the flexible budget (SQ × SP) is shown in the far-right column.

Chapter 12

This chapter a new Business Focus feature and two new In Business boxes were added.

Noreen's Powerful Pedagogy

Managerial Accounting for Managers is full of pedagogy designed to make studying productive and hassle-free.

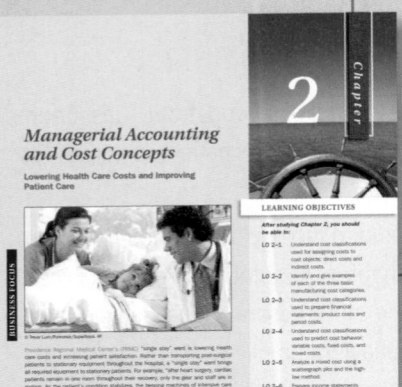

Opening Vignette

Each chapter opens with a **Business Focus** feature that provides a real-world example for students, allowing them to see how the chapter's information and insights apply to the world outside the classroom. **Learning Objectives** alert students to what they should expect as they progress through the chapter.

> *"Many concepts in accounting are rather abstract if not given some type of context to understand them in. The business focus features help to provide this context and can lead to discussions in class if the instructor wishes."*
>
> —Jeffrey Wong, University of Nevada, Reno

Applying Excel

This exciting end-of-chapter feature **links the power of Excel with managerial accounting concepts** by illustrating how Excel functionality can be used to better understand accounting data. Applying Excel goes beyond plugging numbers into a template by providing students with an opportunity to build their own Excel worksheets and formulas. Students are then asked "what if" questions in which they analyze not only **how** related pieces of accounting data affect each other but **why** they do. Applying Excel immediately precedes the Exercises in eleven of the twelve chapters in the book and is also **integrated with Connect,** allowing students to practice their skills online with algorithmically generated datasets and to watch animated, narrated tutorials on how to use formulas in Excel.

> *"An excellent pedagogical feature that helps further reinforce students' knowledge of key concepts in the text book, while strengthening students' Excel skills that are so important in the work place."*
>
> —Marianne L. James, California State University, Los Angeles

> *"[Applying Excel is] an excellent way for students to programmatically develop spreadsheet skills without having to be taught spreadsheet techniques by the instructor. A significant associated benefit is that students gain more exposure to the dynamics of accounting information by working with what-if scenarios."*
>
> —Earl Godfrey, Gardner–Webb University

The Foundational 15

NEW to the fourth edition of Noreen!

Each chapter now contains one Foundational 15 exercise that includes 15 "building-block" questions related to one concise set of data. These exercises can be used for in-class discussion or as homework assignments. They are found before the Exercises and are available in **Connect.**

Additional student resources are available with Connect. **≡ connect** The Foundational 15

Martinez Company's relevant range of production is 7,500 units to 12,500 units. When it produces and sells 10,000 units, its unit costs are as follows:

LEARNING OBJECTIVES 2–1, 2–2, 2–3, 2–4, 2–6, 2–7

	Amount Per Unit
Direct materials.............................	$6.00
Direct labor...............................	$3.50
Variable manufacturing overhead..........	$1.50
Fixed manufacturing overhead............	$4.00
Fixed selling expense....................	$3.00
Fixed administrative expense.............	$2.00
Sales commissions.......................	$1.00
Variable administrative expense..........	$0.50

In Business Boxes

These helpful boxed features offer a glimpse into how real companies use the managerial accounting concepts discussed within the chapter. Each chapter contains from three to fourteen of these current examples.

IN BUSINESS

© Digital Vision/PunchStock, RF

FOOD PRICES HIT RECORD HIGHS FOR RESTAURANTS

Direct material costs are critically important to restaurants and fast-food chains. In recent years, some food costs have spiked to record highs. For example, unexpected freezing temperatures in the southwestern portion of the United States caused the cost of lettuce to increase 290%. Similarly, the costs of green peppers, tomatoes, and cucumbers jumped 145%, 85%, and 30%, respectively. A large chain such as Subway can withstand these price increases better than smaller competitors because of its buying power and long-term contracts.

Source: Anne VanderMey, "Food For Thought," *Fortune*, May 9, 2011, p. 12.

"I love these. Again, a connection to the real world that adds credence to the course."

—Larry N.Bitner, Shippensburg University

Managerial Accounting in Action Vignettes

These vignettes depict cross-functional teams working together in real-life settings. Using products and services students recognize from their own lives increases engagement and enhances problem-solving skills. Students are shown step-by-step how accounting concepts are implemented in organizations and how these concepts are applied to solve everyday business problems. First, "The Issue" is introduced through a dialogue; the student then walks through the implementation process; finally, "The Wrap-up" summarizes the big picture.

Job-Order Costing—An Example

To introduce job-order costing, we will follow a specific job as it progresses through the manufacturing process. This job consists of two experimental couplings that Yost Precision Machining has agreed to produce for Loops Unlimited, a manufacturer of roller coasters. Couplings connect the cars on the roller coaster and are a critical component in the performance and safety of the ride. Before we begin our discussion, recall from a previous chapter that companies generally classify manufacturing costs into three broad categories: (1) direct materials, (2) direct labor, and (3) manufacturing overhead. As we study the operation of a job-order costing system, we will see how each of these three types of costs is recorded and accumulated.

Yost Precision Machining is a small company in Michigan that specializes in fabricating precision metal parts that are used in a variety of applications ranging from deep-sea exploration vehicles to the inertial triggers in automobile air bags. The company's top managers gather every morning at 8:00 A.M. in the company's conference room for the daily planning meeting. Attending the meeting this morning are: Jean Yost, the company's president; David Cheung, the marketing manager; Debbie Turner, the production manager; and Marc White, the company controller. The president opened the meeting:

MANAGERIAL ACCOUNTING IN ACTION
The Issue

YOST
Precision Machining

Jean: The production schedule indicates we'll be starting Job 2B47 today. Isn't that the special order for experimental couplings, David?
David: That's right. That's the order from Loops Unlimited for two couplings for their new roller coaster ride for Magic Mountain.
Debbie: Why only two couplings? Don't they need a coupling for every car?
David: Yes. But this is a completely new roller coaster. The cars will go faster and will be subjected to more twists, turns, drops, and loops than on any other existing roller coaster. To hold up under these stresses, Loops Unlimited's engineers completely

"This element is exceptional. The situations truly reflect real life issues business people would face—not just "textbook" manufactured examples that always have black-and-white answers."

—Ann E. Selk, University of Wisconsin–Green Bay

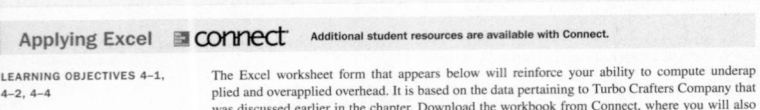

Applying Excel ⬛ **connect** Additional student resources are available with Connect.

LEARNING OBJECTIVES 4-1, 4-2, 4-4

The Excel worksheet form that appears below will reinforce your ability to compute underapplied and overapplied overhead. It is based on the data pertaining to Turbo Crafters Company that was discussed earlier in the chapter. Download the workbook from Connect, where you will also receive instructions about how to use this worksheet.

Exercises ⬛ **connect** Additional student resources are available with Connect.

EXERCISE 4-1 Compute the Predetermined Overhead Rate [LO4-1]
Logan Products computes its predetermined overhead rate annually on the basis of direct labor-hours. At the beginning of the year, it estimated that 40,000 direct labor-hours would be required for the period's estimated level of production. The company also estimated $466,000 of fixed manufacturing overhead expenses for the coming period and variable manufacturing overhead of

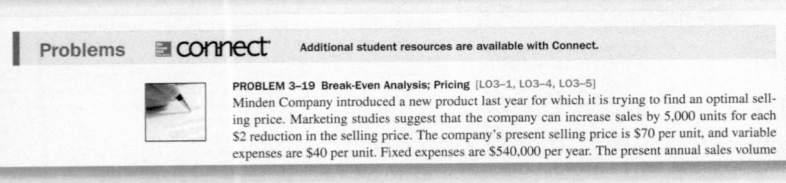

Problems ⬛ **connect** Additional student resources are available with Connect.

PROBLEM 3-19 Break-Even Analysis; Pricing [LO3-1, LO3-4, LO3-5]
Minden Company introduced a new product last year for which it is trying to find an optimal selling price. Marketing studies suggest that the company can increase sales by 5,000 units for each $2 reduction in the selling price. The company's present selling price is $70 per unit, and variable expenses are $40 per unit. Fixed expenses are $540,000 per year. The present annual sales volume

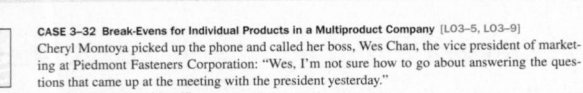

Cases ⬛ **connect** Additional student resources are available with Connect.

CASE 3-32 Break-Evens for Individual Products in a Multiproduct Company [LO3-5, LO3-9]
Cheryl Montoya picked up the phone and called her boss, Wes Chan, the vice president of marketing at Piedmont Fasteners Corporation: "Wes, I'm not sure how to go about answering the questions that came up at the meeting with the president yesterday."
"What's the problem?"

> *"The problem material is still the best I can find."*
> —Noel McKeon, Florida State College–Jacksonville

> *"The teaching supplementary materials are excellent for new professors as well as seasoned professors."*
> —Terence Pitre, University of St. Thomas

End-of-Chapter Material

Building on Garrison/Noreen/Brewer's reputation for having the best end-of-chapter review and discussion material of any text on the market, Noreen's problem and case material continues to conform to AACSB recommendations and makes a great starting point for class discussions and group projects.

Applying Excel integrates key course concepts and Excel—a software students will encounter in the workplace, whether they go into accounting or any other business major. With Applying Excel, students not only gain practice working with Excel software, they also learn how Excel can be used to present accounting data and how that data is interrelated.

Author-Written Supplements

Unlike other managerial accounting texts, the book's authors write all of the major supplements, ensuring a perfect fit between text and supplements. For more information on *Managerial Accounting for Managers'* supplements package.

- Instructor's Resource Guide
- Test Bank
- Solutions Manual

Utilizing the Icons

 To reflect our service-based economy, the text is replete with examples from service-based businesses. A helpful icon distinguishes service-related examples in the text.

 Ethics assignments and examples serve as a reminder that good conduct is vital in business. Icons call out content that relates to ethical behavior for students.

 The writing icon denotes problems that require students to use critical thinking as well as writing skills to explain their decisions.

 The IFRS icon highlights content that may be affected by the impending change to IFRS and possible convergence between U.S. GAAP and IFRS.

"I strongly recommend this book to colleagues [for the] introductory course in managerial accounting. It fits students without a background in managerial accounting. It is the best textbook in managerial accounting."

—Yousef Jahmani, Savannah State University

"Excellent, comprehensive book. Easy for students to read and understand."

—Sandy Copa, North Hennepin College

"Students can easily understand the book. [Noreen] covers all the pertinent topics needed in Managerial Accounting in a concise, easy to understand format."

—Linda Malgeri, Kennesaw State University

Education is changing . . . and so are we.

McGraw-Hill's Connect is a digital teaching and learning environment that support student's skills in the classroom and beyond. With Connect, instructors use technology to enhance learning by delivering interactive assignments, quizzes, and tests easily online. Connect digital assets focus on concepts, application, and assessment. Students can practice important skills at their own pace and on their own schedule.

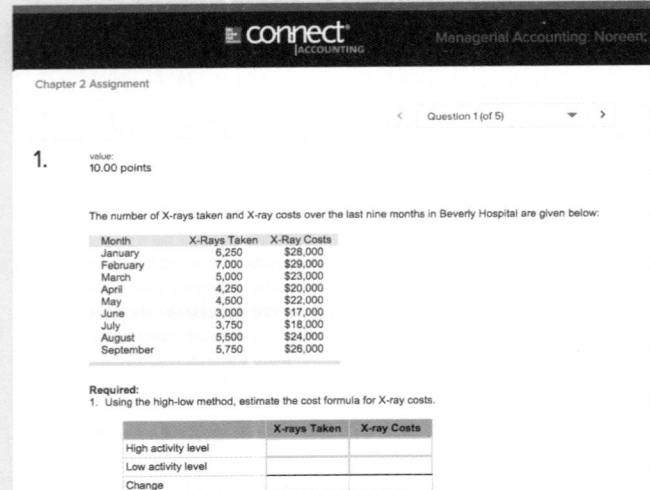

Online Assignments

Connect helps students learn more efficiently by providing feedback and practice material when and where they need it. Connect grades homework automatically, and students benefit from the immediate feedback that they receive, particularly on any questions they may have missed. Furthermore, algorithmic questions provide students with unlimited opportunities for practice.

NEW! Excel Simulations

Simulated Excel questions, assignable within Connect, allow students to practice their Excel skills—such as basic formulas and formatting—within the content of financial accounting. These questions feature animated, narrated Help and Show Me tutorials (when enabled), as well as automatic feedback and grading for both students and professors.

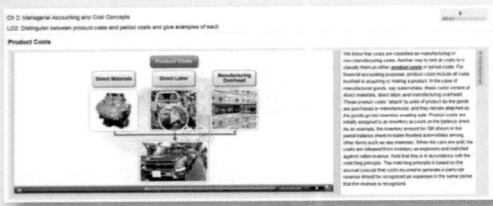

Interactive Presentations

Interactive Presentations, assignable by individual learning objective within Connect, teach the core concepts of the text in an animated, narrated, and interactive multimedia format, bringing the key concepts of the course to life—particularly helpful for online courses and for those audio and visual learners who struggle reading the textbook page by page.

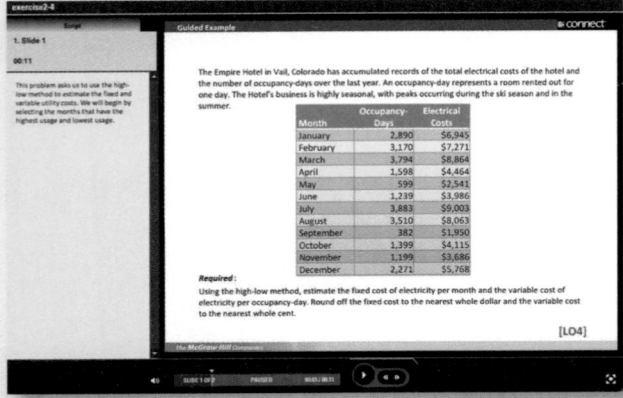

Guided Examples

Guided Examples, available as hints within Connect when enabled by the instructor, provide a narrated, animated, step-by-step walkthrough of select exercises similar to those assigned. These short presentations provide reinforcement when students need it most.

Less Managing. More Teaching. Greater Learning.

Connect offers a number of powerful tools and features to make managing assignments easier, so faculty can spend more time teaching. With *Connect,* students can engage with their coursework anytime, anywhere, making the learning process more accessible and efficient. Please see the previous page for a description of the student tools available within *Connect.*

connect *Connect* for Instructors

Simple Assignment Management and Smart Grading. With *Connect,* creating assignments is easier than ever, so you can spend more time teaching and less time managing. *Connect* enables you to:

- Create and deliver assignments and assessments easily with selectable static and algorithmic end-of-chapter questions and test bank items.

- Go paperless with online submission and grading of student assignments and by sharing notes through the media-rich eBook.

- Have assignments scored automatically, giving students immediate feedback on their work and comparisons with correct answers and explanations.

- Reinforce classroom concepts by assigning Guided Examples, LearnSmart modules, and Interactive Presentations.

Instructor Library

The *Connect* Instructor Library is your repository for additional resources to improve student engagement in and out of class. You can select and use any asset that enhances your lecture. The *Connect* Instructor Library includes access to the textbook's Solutions Manual, Test Bank, Instructor PowerPoint® Slides, Instructor's Resource Guide, Applying Excel Solutions, Sample Syllabus, and Media-rich eBook.

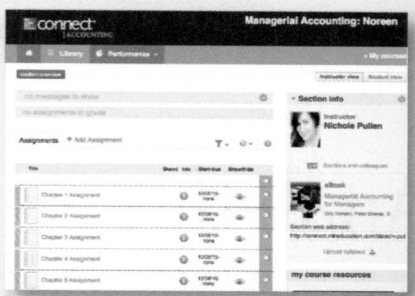

Connect

McGraw-Hill reinvents the textbook learning experience for the modern student with *Connect,* which provides a seamless integration of the eBook and *Connect. Connect* provides all of the *Connect* features, as well as:

- An integrated eBook, allowing for any time, anywhere access to the textbook.

- Dynamic links between the problems or questions you assign to your students and the location in the eBook where the concept related to that problem or question is covered.

- A powerful search function to pinpoint and connect key concepts in a snap.

- Highlighting, note-taking and sharing, and other media-rich capabilities.

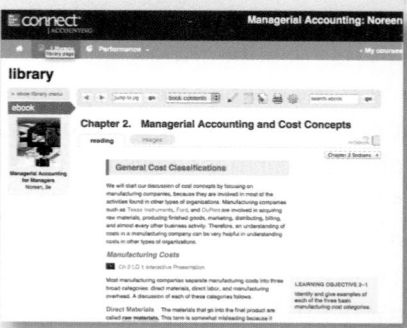

For more information about *Connect,* go to **www.mcgrawhillconnect.com**, or contact your local McGraw-Hill sales representative.

McGraw-Hill Customer Experience

At McGraw-Hill, we understand that getting the most from new technology can be challenging. That's why our services don't stop after you purchase our products. You can e-mail our Product Specialists 24 hours a day to get product training online. Or you can search our knowledge bank of Frequently Asked Questions on our support website. For Customer Support, call 800-331-5094 or visit **www.mhhe.com/support**. One of our Technical Support Analysts will be able to assist you in a timely fashion.

Required=Results

McGraw-Hill Connect®
Learn Without Limits

Connect is a teaching and learning platform that is proven to deliver better results for students and instructors.

Connect empowers students by continually adapting to deliver precisely what they need, when they need it, and how they need it, so your class time is more engaging and effective.

Course outcomes improve with Connect.

	With Connect	Without Connect
Exam Scores	80.4%	74.7%
Pass Rates	83.7%	72.9%
Attendance Rates	92.5%	74.5%
Retention Rates	87.5%	71.1%

Using **Connect** improves passing rates by **10.8%** and retention by **16.4%**.

88% of instructors who use **Connect** require it; instructor satisfaction **increases** by 38% when **Connect** is required.

Analytics

Connect Insight®

Connect Insight is Connect's new one-of-a-kind visual analytics dashboard—that provides at-a-glance information regarding student performance, which is immediately actionable. By presenting assignment, assessment, and topical performance results together with a time metric that is easily visible for aggregate or individual results, Connect Insight gives the user the ability to take a just-in-time approach to teaching and learning, which was never before available. Connect Insight presents data that helps instructors improve class performance in a way that is efficient and effective.

Connect helps students achieve better grades

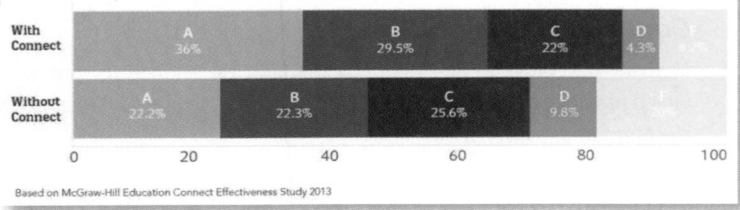

	A	B	C	D	F
With Connect	36%	29.5%	22%	4.3%	
Without Connect	22.2%	22.3%	25.6%	9.8%	

Based on McGraw-Hill Education Connect Effectiveness Study 2013

Adaptive

THE FIRST AND ONLY **ADAPTIVE READING EXPERIENCE** DESIGNED TO TRANSFORM THE WAY STUDENTS READ

More students earn **A's** and **B's** when they use McGraw-Hill Education **Adaptive** products.

SmartBook®

Proven to help students improve grades and study more efficiently, SmartBook contains the same content within the print book, but actively tailors that content to the needs of the individual. SmartBook's adaptive technology provides precise, personalized instruction on what the student should do next, guiding the student to master and remember key concepts, targeting gaps in knowledge and offering customized feedback, and driving the student toward comprehension and retention of the subject matter. Available on smartphones and tablets, SmartBook puts learning at the student's fingertips—anywhere, anytime.

Over **4 billion questions** have been answered, making McGraw-Hill Education products more intelligent, reliable, and precise.

STUDENTS WANT

SMARTBOOK®

95% of students reported **SmartBook** to be a more effective way of reading material

100% of students want to use the Practice Quiz feature available within **SmartBook** to help them study

100% of students reported having reliable access to off-campus wifi

90% of students say they would purchase **SmartBook** over print alone

95% reported that **SmartBook** would impact their study skills in a positive way

McGraw Hill Education

*Findings based on a 2015 focus group survey at Pellissippi State Community College administered by McGraw-Hill Education

Acknowledgments

Suggestions have been received from many of our colleagues throughout the world. Each of those who have offered comments and suggestions has our thanks.

The efforts of many people are needed to develop and improve a text. Among these people are the reviewers and consultants who point out areas of concern, cite areas of strength, and make recommendations for change. In this regard, the following professors provided feedback that was enormously helpful in preparing the fourth edition of *Managerial Accounting for Managers:*

Wagdy Abdallah, *Seton Hall University*
Linda Abernathy, *Kirkwood Community College*
James Andrews, *Central New Mexico Community College*
Rick Andrews, *Sinclair Community College*
Frank Aquilino, *Montclair State University*
Jane Austin, *Oklahoma City University*
Kashi R. Balachandran, *New York University*
Linda Benz, *Jefferson Technical College*
Surasakdi Bhamornsiri, *University of North Carolina–Charlotte*
Larry N. Bitner, *Shippensburg University*
Jorja Bradford, *Alabama State University*
Janet Butler, *Texas State University-San Marcos*
Jennifer Cainas, *University of South Florida*
Rusty Calk, *New Mexico State University*
Dana Carpenter, *MATC Truax*
Chiaho Chang, *Montlcair State University*
Cathy Claiborne, *University of Colorado–Colorado*
Robert Clarke, *Brigham Young University–Idaho*
Darlene Coarts, *University of Northern Iowa*
Elizabeth Connors, *University of Massachusetts–Boston*
Sandy Copa, *North Hennepin Community College*
Deb Cosgrove, *University of Nebraska–Lincoln*
Nancy Coulmas, *Bloomsburg University of Pennsylvania*
Jean Crawford, *Alabama State University*
Patricia Doherty, *Boston University*
David L. Doyon, *Southern New Hampshire University*
Andrea Drake, *Louisiana Tech University*
Jan Duffy, *Iowa State University*
Cindy Easterwood, *Virginia Tech*
Gene Elrod, *University of North Texas*
Rebecca Evans, *Florida State College–Jacksonville*

Janice Fergusson, *University of South Carolina*
Annette Fisher, *Glendale Community College*
Ananda Ganguly, *Claremont College*
J. Marie Gibson, *University of Nevada Reno*
Olen Greer, *Missouri State University*
Cynthia Greeson, *Ivy Tech Community College*
Richard O. Hanson, *Southern New Hampshire University*
Ken Harmon, *Kennesaw State University*
Christine Haynes, *University of West Georgia*
David Henderson, *College of Charleston*
Kathy Ho, *Niagara University*
Mark Holtzman, *Seton Hall University*
Maggie Houston, *Wright State University*
Tom Hrubec, *Franklin University*
Chuo-Hsuan Lee, *SUNY–Plattsburgh*
Ronald Huefner, *SUNY Buffalo*
Yousef Jahmani, *Savannah State University*
Robyn Jarnagin, *Montana State University*
Iris Jenkel, *St. Norbert College*
Randy Johnston, *Michigan State University*
Nancy Jones, *California State University*
Jai Kang, *San Francisco State University*
Catherine Katagiri, *College of Saint Rose*
Carl Keller, *Indiana Purdue University/Fort Wayne*
Cynthia Khanlarian, *University of North Carolina–Greensboro*
James Kinard, *Ohio State University–Columbus*
Gary Kleinman, *Montclair State University*
Leon Korte, *The University of South Dakota*
Christy Land, *Catawba Valley Community College*
Ron Lazer, *University of Houston*
Candace Leuck, *Clemson University*
Natasha Librizzi, *Milwaukee Area Technical College*
William R. Link, *University of Missouri–St. Louis*

Kathy Long, *University of Tennessee–Chattanooga*
Patti Lopez, *Valencia Community College East*
Mary Loretta Manktelow, *James Madison University*
Jim Lukawitz, *University of Memphis*
Anna Lusher, *Slippery Rock University*
Linda Malgeri, *Kennesaw State University*
Steve Markoff, *Montclair State University*
Melissa Martin, *Arizona State University–Tempe*
Gary McCombs, *College of Charleston*
Noel McKeon, *Florida State College–Jacksonville*
Jim McKittrick, *University of Portland*
Laurie McWhorter, *Mississippi State University*
James Meddaugh, *Ohio University*
Tammy Metzke, *Milwaukee Area Technical College–West Allis*
Tony Mifsud, *Catawba Valley Community College*
Tim Mills, *Eastern Illinois University*
Mark E. Motluck, *Anderson University*
Dennis Mullen, *City College of San Francisco*
Gerald M. Myers, *Pacific Lutheran University*
Michael Newman, *University of Houston–Houston*
Joseph M. Nicassio, *Westmoreland County Community College*
Alfonso R. Oddo, *Niagara University*
Tamara Phelan, *Northern Illinois University*
JoAnn Pinto, *Montclair State University*
Terence Pitre, *University of St. Thomas*
Shirley Polejewski, *University of St. Thomas*
Kay Poston, *University of Indianapolis*
Les Price, *Pierce College*
Kamala Raghavan, *Robert Morris University*
Raul Ramos, *Lorain County Community College*

John Reisch, *East Carolina University*
Michelle Reisch, *East Carolina University*
Therese Rice, *North Hennepin Community College*
Luther L. Ross, Sr., *Central Piedmont Community College*
Pamela Rouse, *Butler University*
Amy Santos, *Manatee Community College*
Rex Schildhouse, *Miramar College*
Ann E. Selk, *University of Wisconsin–Green Bay*
Daniel Sevall, *Lincoln University*
Ken Snow, *Florida State College–Jacksonville*
Vic Stanton, *University of California–Berkeley*
Ellen Sweatt, *Georgia Perimeter College*
Rick Tabor, *Auburn University*
Diane Tanner, *University of North Florida*
Samantha Ternes, *Kirkwood Community College*
Chuck Thompson, *University of Massachusetts*
Dorothy Thompson, *North Central Texas College*
Terri Walsh, *Seminole State College of Florida*
James White, *Boston University*
Michael Wilson, *University of Indianapolis*
Janet Woods, *Macon State College*
Christine Wright, *Seminole State College of Florida*
James Yang, *Montclair State University*
Marjorie Yuschak, *Rutgers University*
Ronald Zhao, *Monmouth University*
Kiran Verma, *University of Massachusetts–Boston*
Jeffrey Wong, *University of Nevada–Reno*
Peter Woodlock, *Youngstown State University*

We are grateful for the outstanding support from McGraw-Hill. In particular, we would like to thank Tim Vertovec, Director; Nichole Pullen, Brand Manager; Erin Quinones, Product Developer; Pat Plumb, Director of Digital Content; Pat Frederickson and Brian Nacik, Lead Content Project Managers; Laura Fuller, Buyer; Srdj Savanovic, Designer; and Carrie Burger and Jacob Sullivan, Content Licensing Specialists.

Thank you to the following individuals who helped prepare the supplements: Jon A. Booker of Tennessee Technological University, Cynthia J. Rooney of the University of New Mexico, and Susan C. Galbreath of Lipscomb University for crafting the Instructor and Student PowerPoint Slides; Ilene Persoff of CW Post Campus/Long Island University for updating the Quizzes and Exams.

Thank you to our Digital Contributor, Margaret Shackell-Dowell (Cornell University), for her many contributions to Connect for Noreen 4e, including Guided Example content, Interactive Presentation review, and accuracy checking. Thank you to Julie Hankins for acting as Lead subject matter expert on Connect content. Patti Lopez (Valencia College) for her efforts as lead subject matter expert on LearnSmart and Jeannie Folk for her review of LearnSmart. Finally, we would like to thank Beth Woods and Helen Roybark for working so hard to ensure an error-free fourth edition.

We are grateful to the Institute of Certified Management Accountants for permission to use questions and/or unofficial answers from past Certificate in Management Accounting (CMA) examinations. Likewise, we thank the American Institute of Certified Public Accountants, the Society of Management Accountants of Canada, and the Chartered Institute of Management Accountants (United Kingdom) for permission to use (or to adapt) selected problems from their examinations. These problems bear the notations CPA, SMA, and CIMA respectively.

Eric W. Noreen • Peter C. Brewer • Ray H. Garrison

Brief Contents

Contents

Chapter 3

Cost-Volume-Profit Relationships 70

Chapter 4

Job-Order Costing 117

**Variable Costing and Segment
Reporting: Tools for Management   170**

**Activity-Based Costing: A Tool
to Aid Decision Making   223**

Chapter 7

Differential Analysis: The Key to Decision Making   280

Chapter 8

Capital Budgeting Decisions   333

Chapter 9

Master Budgeting 386

Chapter 10

**Flexible Budgets and Performance
Analysis 438**

Chapter 11

Standard Costs and Variances 475

Chapter 12

Performance Measurement in Decentralized Organizations 521

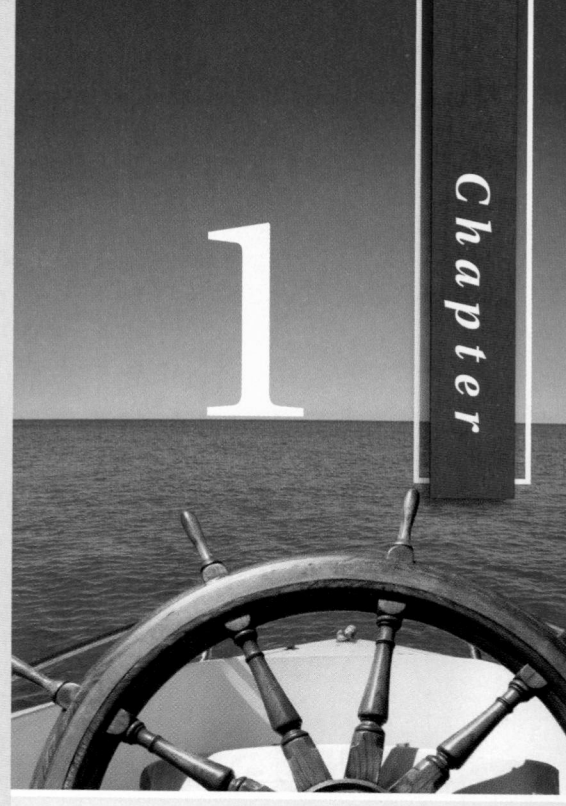

Managerial Accounting: An Overview

Managerial Accounting: It's More Than Just Crunching Numbers

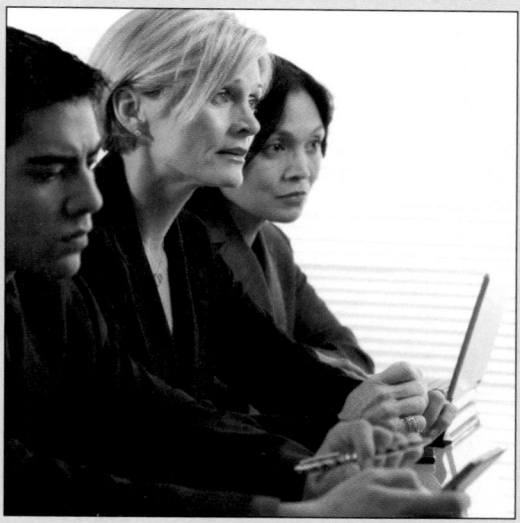

© Corbis/Superstock, RF

"Creating value through values" is the credo of today's management accountant. It means that management accountants should maintain an unwavering commitment to ethical values while using their knowledge and skills to influence decisions that create value for organizational stakeholders. These skills include managing risks and implementing strategy through planning, budgeting and forecasting, and decision support. Management accountants are strategic business partners who understand the financial and operational sides of the business. They not only report and analyze financial measures, but also nonfinancial measures of process performance and corporate social performance. Think of these responsibilities as profits (financial statements), process (customer focus and satisfaction), people (employee learning and satisfaction), and planet (environmental stewardship). ■

Source: Conversation with Jeff Thomson, president and CEO of the Institute of Management Accountants.

This chapter explains why managerial accounting is important to the future careers of all business students. It begins by answering two questions: (1) What is managerial accounting? and (2) Why does managerial accounting matter to your career? It concludes by discussing six topics—ethics, strategic management, enterprise risk management, corporate social responsibility, process management, and leadership—that define the business context for applying the quantitative aspects of managerial accounting.

What Is Managerial Accounting?

Many students enrolled in this course will have recently completed an introductory *financial accounting* course. **Financial accounting** is concerned with reporting financial information to external parties, such as stockholders, creditors, and regulators. **Managerial accounting** is concerned with providing information to managers for use within the organization. Exhibit 1–1 summarizes seven key differences between financial and managerial accounting. It recognizes that the fundamental difference between financial and managerial accounting is that financial accounting serves the needs of those

EXHIBIT 1–1
Comparison of Financial and Managerial Accounting

Accounting

- Recording
- Estimating
- Organizing
- Summarizing
} Financial and Operational Data

Financial Accounting

- Reports to those outside the organization:
  Owners
  Creditors
  Tax authorities
  Regulators

- Emphasizes financial consequences of past activities.

- Emphasizes objectivity and verifiability.

- Emphasizes precision.

- Emphasizes companywide reports.

- Must follow GAAP/IFRS.

- Mandatory for external reports.

Managerial Accounting

- Reports to managers inside the organization for:
  Planning
  Controlling
  Decision making

- Emphasizes decisions affecting the future.

- Emphasizes relevance.

- Emphasizes timeliness.

- Emphasizes segment reports.

- Need not follow GAAP/IFRS.

- Not mandatory.

outside the organization, whereas managerial accounting serves the needs of managers employed *inside* the organization. Because of this fundamental difference in users, financial accounting emphasizes the financial consequences of past activities, objectivity and verifiability, precision, and companywide performance, whereas managerial accounting emphasizes decisions affecting the future, relevance, timeliness, and *segment* performance. A **segment** is a part or activity of an organization about which managers would like cost, revenue, or profit data. Examples of business segments include product lines, customer groups (segmented by age, ethnicity, gender, volume of purchases, etc.), geographic territories, divisions, plants, and departments. Finally, financial accounting is mandatory for external reports and it needs to comply with rules, such as generally accepted accounting principles (GAAP) and international financial reporting standards (IFRS), whereas managerial accounting is not mandatory and it does not need to comply with externally imposed rules.

As mentioned in Exhibit 1–1, managerial accounting helps managers perform three vital activities—*planning, controlling,* and *decision making.* **Planning** involves establishing goals and specifying how to achieve them. **Controlling** involves gathering feedback to ensure that the plan is being properly executed or modified as circumstances change. **Decision making** involves selecting a course of action from competing alternatives. Now let's take a closer look at these three pillars of managerial accounting.

Planning

Assume that you work for Procter & Gamble (P&G) and that you are in charge of the company's campus recruiting for all undergraduate business majors. In this example, your planning process would begin by establishing a goal such as: our goal is to recruit the "best and brightest" college graduates. The next stage of the planning process would require specifying how to achieve this goal by answering numerous questions such as:

- How many students do we need to hire in total and from each major?
- What schools do we plan to include in our recruiting efforts?
- Which of our employees will be involved in each school's recruiting activities?
- When will we conduct our interviews?
- How will we compare students to one another to decide who will be extended job offers?
- What salary will we offer our new hires? Will the salaries differ by major?
- How much money can we spend on our recruiting efforts?

As you can see, there are many questions that need to be answered as part of the planning process. Plans are often accompanied by a *budget.* A **budget** is a detailed plan for the future that is usually expressed in formal quantitative terms. As the head of recruiting at P&G, your budget would include two key components. First, you would have to work with other senior managers inside the company to establish a budgeted amount of total salaries that can be offered to all new hires. Second, you would have to create a budget that quantifies how much you intend to spend on your campus recruiting activities.

Controlling

Once you established and started implementing P&G's recruiting plan, you would transition to the control process. This process would involve gathering, evaluating, and responding to feedback to ensure that this year's recruiting process meets expectations. It would also include evaluating the feedback in search of ways to run a more effective recruiting campaign next year. The control process would involve answering questions such as:

- Did we succeed in hiring the planned number of students within each major and at each school?
- Did we lose too many exceptional candidates to competitors?
- Did each of our employees involved in the recruiting process perform satisfactorily?

- Is our method of comparing students to one another working?
- Did the on-campus and office interviews run smoothly?
- Did we stay within our budget in terms of total salary commitments to new hires?
- Did we stay within our budget regarding spending on recruiting activities?

As you can see, there are many questions that need to be answered as part of the control process. When answering these questions your goal would be to go beyond simple yes or no answers in search of the underlying reasons why performance exceeded or failed to meet expectations. Part of the control process includes preparing *performance reports.* A **performance report** compares budgeted data to actual data in an effort to identify and learn from excellent performance and to identify and eliminate sources of unsatisfactory performance. Performance reports can also be used as one of many inputs to help evaluate and reward employees.

Although this example focused on P&G's campus recruiting efforts, we could have described how planning enables FedEx to deliver packages across the globe overnight, or how it helped Apple develop and market the iPad. We could have discussed how the control process helps Pfizer, Eli Lilly, and Abbott Laboratories ensure that their pharmaceutical drugs are produced in conformance with rigorous quality standards, or how Kroger relies on the control process to keep its grocery shelves stocked. We also could have looked at planning and control failures such as BP's massive oil spill in the Gulf of Mexico. In short, all managers (and that probably includes you someday) perform planning and controlling activities.

Decision Making

Perhaps the most basic managerial skill is the ability to make intelligent, data-driven decisions. Broadly speaking, many of those decisions revolve around the following three questions. *What* should we be selling? *Who* should we be serving? *How* should we execute? Exhibit 1–2 provides examples of decisions pertaining to each of these three categories.

The left-hand column of Exhibit 1–2 suggests that every company must make decisions related to the products and services that it sells. For example, each year Procter & Gamble must decide how to allocate its marketing budget across 23 brands that each generates over $1 billion in sales as well as other brands that have promising growth potential. Mattel must decide what new toys to introduce to the market. Southwest Airlines must decide what ticket prices to establish for each of its thousands of flights per day. General Motors must decide whether to discontinue certain models of automobiles.

EXHIBIT 1–2
Examples of Decisions

What should we be selling?	Who should we be serving?	How should we execute?
What products and services should be the focus of our marketing efforts?	Who should be the focus of our marketing efforts?	How should we supply our parts and services?
What new products and services should we offer?	Who should we start serving?	How should we expand our capacity?
What prices should we charge for our products and services?	Who should pay price premiums or receive price discounts?	How should we reduce our capacity?
What products and services should we discontinue?	Who should we stop serving?	How should we improve our efficiency and effectiveness?

The middle column of Exhibit 1–2 indicates that all companies must make decisions related to the customers that they serve. For example, Sears must decide how to allocate its marketing budget between products that tend to appeal to male versus female customers. FedEx must decide whether to expand its services into new markets across the globe. Hewlett-Packard must decide what price discounts to offer corporate clients that purchase large volumes of its products. A bank must decide whether to discontinue customers that may be unprofitable.

The right-hand column of Exhibit 1–2 shows that companies also make decisions related to how they execute. For example, Boeing must decide whether to rely on outside vendors such as Goodrich, Saab, and Rolls-Royce to manufacture many of the parts used to make its airplanes. Cintas must decide whether to expand its laundering and cleaning capacity in a given geographic region by adding square footage to an existing facility or by constructing an entirely new facility. In an economic downturn, a manufacturer might have to decide whether to eliminate one 8-hour shift at three plants or to close one plant. Finally, all companies have to decide among competing improvement opportunities. For example, a company may have to decide whether to implement a new software system, to upgrade a piece of equipment, or to provide extra training to its employees.

This portion of the chapter has explained that the three pillars of managerial accounting are planning, controlling, and decision making. This book helps prepare you to become an effective manager by explaining how to make intelligent data-driven decisions, how to create financial plans for the future, and how to continually make progress toward achieving goals by obtaining, evaluating, and responding to feedback.

Why Does Managerial Accounting Matter to Your Career?

Many students feel anxious about choosing a major because they are unsure if it will provide a fulfilling career. To reduce these anxieties, we recommend deemphasizing what you cannot control about the future, instead focusing on what you can control right now. More specifically, concentrate on answering the following question: What can you do now to prepare for success in an unknown future career? The best answer is to learn skills that will make it easier for you to adapt to an uncertain future. You need to become adaptable!

Whether you end up working in the United States or abroad, for a large corporation, a small entrepreneurial company, a nonprofit organization, or a governmental entity, you'll need to know how to plan for the future, how to make progress toward achieving goals, and how to make intelligent decisions. In other words, managerial accounting skills are useful in just about any career, organization, and industry. If you commit energy to this course, you'll be making a smart investment in your future— even though you cannot clearly envision it. Next, we will elaborate on this point by explaining how managerial accounting relates to the future careers of business majors and accounting majors.

Business Majors

Exhibit 1–3 provides examples of how planning, controlling, and decision making affect three majors other than accounting—marketing, supply chain management, and human resource management.

The left-hand column of Exhibit 1–3 describes some planning, controlling, and decision-making applications in the marketing profession. For example, marketing managers make planning decisions related to allocating advertising dollars across various communication mediums and to staffing new sales territories. From a control standpoint, they may closely track sales data to see if a budgeted price cut is generating an anticipated increase in unit sales, or they may study inventory levels during the holiday shopping

EXHIBIT 1–3
Relating Managerial Accounting to Three Business Majors

	Marketing	Supply Chain Management	Human Resource Management
Planning	How much should we budget for TV, print, and Internet advertising?	How many units should we plan to produce next period?	How much should we plan to spend for occupational safety training?
	How many salespeople should we plan to hire to serve a new territory?	How much should we budget for next period's utility expense?	How much should we plan to spend on employee recruitment advertising?
Controlling	Is the budgeted price cut increasing unit sales as expected?	Did we spend more or less than expected for the units we actually produced?	Is our employee retention rate exceeding our goals?
	Are we accumulating too much inventory during the holiday shopping season?	Are we achieving our goal of reducing the number of defective units produced?	Are we meeting our goal of completing timely performance appraisals?
Decision Making	Should we sell our services as one bundle or sell them separately?	Should we transfer production of a component part to an overseas supplier?	Should we hire an on-site medical staff to lower our health care costs?
	Should we sell directly to customers or use a distributor?	Should we redesign our manufacturing process to lower inventory levels?	Should we hire temporary workers or full-time employees?

season so that they can adjust prices as needed to optimize sales. Marketing managers also make many important decisions such as whether to bundle services together and sell them for one price or to sell each service separately. They may also decide whether to sell products directly to the customer or to sell to a distributor, who then sells to the end consumer.

The middle column of Exhibit 1–3 states that supply chain managers have to plan how many units to produce to satisfy anticipated customer demand. They also need to budget for operating expenses such as utilities, supplies, and labor costs. In terms of control, they monitor actual spending relative to the budget, and closely watch operational measures such as the number of defects produced relative to the plan. Supply chain managers make numerous decisions, such as deciding whether to transfer production of a component part to an overseas supplier. They also decide whether to invest in redesigning a manufacturing process to reduce inventory levels.

The right-hand column of Exhibit 1–3 explains how human resource managers make a variety of planning decisions, such as budgeting how much to spend on occupational safety training and employee recruitment advertising. They monitor feedback related to numerous management concerns, such as employee retention rates and the timely completion of employee performance appraisals. They also help make many important decisions such as whether to hire on-site medical staff in an effort to lower health care costs, and whether to hire temporary workers or full-time employees in an uncertain economy.

For brevity, Exhibit 1–3 does not include all business majors, such as finance, management information systems, and economics. Can you explain how planning, controlling, and decision-making activities would relate to these majors?

Accounting Majors

Many accounting graduates begin their careers working for public accounting firms that provide a variety of valuable services for their clients. Some of these graduates will build successful and fulfilling careers in the public accounting industry; however, most will leave public accounting at some point to work in other organizations. In fact, the Institute of Management Accountants (IMA) estimates that more than 80% of professional accountants in the United States work in nonpublic accounting environments (**www.imanet.org/ about_ima/our_mission.aspx**).

The public accounting profession has a strong financial accounting orientation. Its most important function is to protect investors and other external parties by assuring them that companies are reporting historical financial results that comply with applicable accounting rules. Managerial accountants also have strong financial accounting skills. For example, they play an important role in helping their organizations design and maintain financial reporting systems that generate reliable financial disclosures. However, the primary role of managerial accountants is to partner with their co-workers within the organization to improve performance.

Given the 80% figure mentioned above, if you are an accounting major there is a very high likelihood that your future will involve working for a nonpublic accounting employer. Your employer will expect you to have strong financial accounting skills, but more importantly, it will expect you to help improve organizational performance by applying the planning, controlling, and decision-making skills that are the foundation of managerial accounting.

IN BUSINESS

A NETWORKING OPPORTUNITY

The Institute of Management Accountants (IMA) is a network of more than 70,000 accounting and finance professionals from over 120 countries. Every year the IMA hosts a student leadership conference that attracts 300 students from over 50 colleges and universities. Guest speakers at past conferences have discussed topics such as leadership, advice for a successful career, how to market yourself in a difficult economy, and excelling in today's multigenerational workforce. One student who attended the conference said, "I liked that I was able to interact with professionals who are in fields that could be potential career paths for me." For more information on this worthwhile networking opportunity, contact the IMA at the phone number and website shown below.

Source: Conversation with Jodi Ryan, the Institute of Management Accountants' Director, Education/Corporate Partnerships. (201) 474-1556 or visit its website at www.imanet.org.

Professional Certification—A Smart Investment If you plan to become an accounting major, the Certified Management Accountant (CMA) designation is a globally respected credential (sponsored by the IMA) that will increase your credibility, upward mobility, and compensation. Exhibit 1–4 summarizes the topics covered in the two-part CMA exam. For brevity, we are not going to define all the terms included in this exhibit. Its purpose is simply to emphasize that the CMA exam focuses on the planning, controlling, and decision-making skills that are critically important to nonpublic accounting employers. The CMA's internal management orientation is a complement to the highly respected Certified Public Accountant (CPA) exam that focuses on rule-based compliance—assurance standards, financial accounting standards, business law, and the tax code. Information about becoming a CMA is available on the IMA's website (www.imanet.org) or by calling 1-800-638-4427.

EXHIBIT 1–4
CMA Exam Content
Specifications

Part 1	Financial Reporting, Planning, Performance and Control
	External financial reporting decisions
	Planning, budgeting, and forecasting
	Performance management
	Cost management
	Internal controls
Part 2	Financial Decision Making
	Financial statement analysis
	Corporate finance
	Decision analysis
	Risk management
	Investment decisions
	Professional ethics

IN BUSINESS

HOW'S THE PAY?

The Institute of Management Accountants has created the following table that allows individuals to estimate what their salary would be as a management accountant.

			Your Calculation
Start with this base amount................		$75,879	$75,879
If you are top-level management	ADD	$48,471	
OR, if you are senior-level management.....	ADD	$26,516	
OR, if you are entry-level management......	SUBTRACT	$22,137	
Number of years in the field _____	TIMES	$ 7	
If you have an advanced degree	ADD	$14,662	
If you hold the CMA	ADD	$19,992	
If you hold the CPA......................	ADD	$15,837	
Your estimated salary level			

For example, if you make it to top-level management in 10 years, have an advanced degree and a CMA, your estimated salary would be $159,074 [$75,879 + $48,471 + (10 × 7) + $14,662 + $19,992].

Source: Lee Schiffel, and Coleen Wilder, "IMA 2013 Salary Survey. Rainy Days Persist," *Strategic Finance* June 2014, pp. 23–39.

Managerial Accounting: Beyond the Numbers

Exhibit 1–5 summarizes how each chapter of the book teaches measurement skills that managers use on the job every day. For example, Chapter 9 teaches you the measurement skills that managers use to answer the question—how should I create a financial plan for next year? Chapters 10 and 11 teach you the measurement skills that managers use to answer the question—how well am I performing relative to my plan? Chapter 6 teaches you measurement skills related to product, service, and customer profitability. However, it is vitally important that you also understand managerial accounting involves more than just "crunching numbers." To be successful, managers must complement their

Chapter Number	The Key Question from a Manager's Perspective
Chapter 2	What cost classifications do I use for different management purposes?
Chapter 3	How will my profits change if I change my selling price, sales volume, or costs?
Chapter 4	What is the value of our ending inventory and cost of goods sold for external reporting purposes?
Chapter 5	How should the income statement be presented?
Chapter 6	How profitable is each of our products, services, and customers?
Chapter 7	How do I quantify the profit impact of pursuing one course of action versus another?
Chapter 8	How do I make long-term capital investment decisions?
Chapter 9	How should I create a financial plan for next year?
Chapters 10 & 11	How well am I performing relative to my plan?
Chapter 12	What performance measures should we monitor to ensure that we achieve our strategic goals?

EXHIBIT 1–5
Measurement Skills: A Manager's Perspective

measurement skills with six business management perspectives that "go beyond the numbers" to enable intelligent planning, control, and decision making.

An Ethics Perspective

Ethical behavior is the lubricant that keeps the economy running. Without that lubricant, the economy would operate much less efficiently—less would be available to consumers, quality would be lower, and prices would be higher. In other words, without fundamental trust in the integrity of business, the economy would operate much less efficiently. Thus, for the good of everyone—including profit-making companies—it is vitally important that business be conducted within an ethical framework that builds and sustains trust.

Code of Conduct for Management Accountants The Institute of Management Accountants (IMA) of the United States has adopted an ethical code called the *Statement of Ethical Professional Practice* that describes in some detail the ethical responsibilities of management accountants. Even though the standards were developed specifically for management accountants, they have much broader application. The standards consist of two parts that are presented in full in Exhibit 1–6. The first part provides general guidelines for ethical behavior. In a nutshell, a management accountant has ethical responsibilities in four broad areas: first, to maintain a high level of professional competence; second, to treat sensitive matters with confidentiality; third, to maintain personal integrity; and fourth, to disclose information in a credible fashion. The second part of the standards specifies what should be done if an individual finds evidence of ethical misconduct.

The ethical standards provide sound, practical advice for management accountants and managers. Most of the rules in the ethical standards are motivated by a very practical consideration—if these rules were not generally followed in business, then the economy and all of us would suffer. Consider the following specific examples of the consequences of not abiding by the standards:

- Suppose employees could not be trusted with confidential information. Then top managers would be reluctant to distribute such information within the company and, as a result, decisions would be based on incomplete information and operations would deteriorate.

EXHIBIT 1–6
IMA Statement of Ethical Professional Practice

Members of IMA shall behave ethically. A commitment to ethical professional practice includes: overarching principles that express our values, and standards that guide our conduct.

PRINCIPLES

IMA's overarching ethical principles include: Honesty, Fairness, Objectivity, and Responsibility. Members shall act in accordance with these principles and shall encourage others within their organizations to adhere to them.

STANDARDS

A member's failure to comply with the following standards may result in disciplinary action.

I. COMPETENCE

Each member has a responsibility to:
1. Maintain an appropriate level of professional expertise by continually developing knowledge and skills.
2. Perform professional duties in accordance with relevant laws, regulations, and technical standards.
3. Provide decision support information and recommendations that are accurate, clear, concise, and timely.
4. Recognize and communicate professional limitations or other constraints that would preclude responsible judgment or successful performance of an activity.

II. CONFIDENTIALITY

Each member has a responsibility to:
1. Keep information confidential except when disclosure is authorized or legally required.
2. Inform all relevant parties regarding appropriate use of confidential information. Monitor subordinates' activities to ensure compliance.
3. Refrain from using confidential information for unethical or illegal advantage.

III. INTEGRITY

Each member has a responsibility to:
1. Mitigate actual conflicts of interest. Regularly communicate with business associates to avoid apparent conflicts of interest. Advise all parties of any potential conflicts.
2. Refrain from engaging in any conduct that would prejudice carrying out duties ethically.
3. Abstain from engaging in or supporting any activity that might discredit the profession.

IV. CREDIBILITY

Each member has a responsibility to:
1. Communicate information fairly and objectively.
2. Disclose all relevant information that could reasonably be expected to influence an intended user's understanding of the reports, analyses, or recommendations.
3. Disclose delays or deficiencies in information, timeliness, processing, or internal controls in conformance with organization policy and/or applicable law.

RESOLUTION OF ETHICAL CONFLICT

In applying the Standards of Ethical Professional Practice, you may encounter problems identifying unethical behavior or resolving an ethical conflict. When faced with ethical issues, you should follow your organization's established policies on the resolution of such conflict. If these policies do not resolve the ethical conflict, you should consider the following courses of action:
1. Discuss the issue with your immediate supervisor except when it appears that the supervisor is involved. In that case, present the issue to the next level. If you cannot achieve a satisfactory resolution, submit the issue to the next management level. If your immediate superior is the chief executive officer or equivalent, the acceptable reviewing authority may be a group such as the audit committee, executive committee, board of directors, board of trustees, or owners. Contact with levels above the immediate superior should be initiated only with your superior's knowledge, assuming he or she is not involved. Communication of such problems to authorities or individuals not employed or engaged by the organization is not considered appropriate, unless you believe there is a clear violation of the law.
2. Clarify relevant ethical issues by initiating a confidential discussion with an IMA Ethics Counselor or other impartial advisor to obtain a better understanding of possible courses of action.
3. Consult your own attorney as to legal obligations and rights concerning the ethical conflict.

- Suppose employees accepted bribes from suppliers. Then contracts would tend to go to the suppliers who pay the highest bribes rather than to the most competent suppliers. Would you like to fly in aircraft whose wings were made by the subcontractor who paid the highest bribe? Would you fly as often? What would happen to the airline industry if its safety record deteriorated due to shoddy workmanship on contracted parts and subassemblies?

- Suppose the presidents of companies routinely lied in their annual reports and financial statements. If investors could not rely on the basic integrity of a company's financial statements, they would have little basis for making informed decisions. Suspecting the worst, rational investors would pay less for securities issued by companies and may not be willing to invest at all. As a consequence, companies would have less money for productive investments—leading to slower economic growth, fewer goods and services, and higher prices.

© Irene Alastruey/Author's Image/
Punchstock, RF

IN BUSINESS

TOYOTA ENCOUNTERS MAJOR PROBLEMS

When Toyota Motor Corporation failed to meet its profit targets, the company set an aggressive goal of reducing the cost of its auto parts by 30%. The quality and safety of the company's automobiles eventually suffered mightily resulting in recalls, litigation, incentive campaigns, and marketing efforts that analysts estimate will cost the company more than $5 billion. The car maker's president, Akio Toyoda, blamed his company's massive quality lapses on an excessive focus on profits and market share. Similarly, Jim Press, Toyota's former top U.S. executive, said the problems were caused by "financially-oriented pirates who didn't have the character to maintain a customer-first focus."

Sources: Yoshio Takahashi, "Toyota Accelerates Its Cost-Cutting Efforts," *The Wall Street Journal*, December 23, 2009, p. B4; Mariko Sanchanta and Yoshio Takahashi, "Toyota's Recall May Top $5 Billion," *The Wall Street Journal*, March 10, 2010, p. B2; and Norihiko Shirouzu, "Toyoda Rues Excessive Profit Focus," *The Wall Street Journal*, March 2, 2010, p. B3.

Not only is ethical behavior the lubricant for our economy, it is the foundation of managerial accounting. The numbers that managers rely on for planning, control, and decision making are meaningless unless they have been competently, objectively, and honestly gathered, analyzed, and reported. As your career unfolds, you will inevitably face decisions with ethical implications. Before making such decisions, consider performing the following steps. First, define your alternative courses of action. Second, identify all of the parties that will be affected by your decision. Third, define how each course of action will favorably or unfavorably impact each affected party. Once you have a complete understanding of the decision context, seek guidance from external sources such as the IMA Statement of Ethical Professional Practice, the IMA Ethics Helpline at (800) 245-1383, or a trusted confidant. Before executing your decision ask yourself one final question—would I be comfortable disclosing my chosen course of action on the front page of *The Wall Street Journal?*

A Strategic Management Perspective

Companies do not succeed by sheer luck; instead, they need to develop a *strategy* that defines how they intend to succeed in the marketplace. A **strategy** is a "game plan" that enables a company to attract customers by distinguishing itself from competitors. The focal point of a company's strategy should be its target customers. A company can only succeed if it creates a reason for its target customers to choose it over a competitor. These reasons, or what are more formally called *customer value propositions,* are the essence of strategy.

Customer value propositions tend to fall into three broad categories—*customer intimacy, operational excellence,* and *product leadership.* Companies that adopt a *customer intimacy* strategy are in essence saying to their customers, "You should choose us because we can customize our products and services to meet your individual needs better than our competitors." Ritz-Carlton, Nordstrom, and Virtuoso (a premium service travel agency) rely primarily on a customer intimacy value proposition for their success. Companies that pursue the second customer value proposition, called *operational excellence,* are saying to their target customers, "You should choose us because we deliver products and services faster, more conveniently, and at a lower price than our competitors." Southwest Airlines, Walmart, and Google are examples of companies that succeed first and foremost because of their operational excellence. Companies pursuing the third customer value proposition, called *product leadership,* are saying to their target customers, "You should choose us because we offer higher quality products than our competitors." Apple, Cisco Systems, and W.L. Gore (the creator of GORE-TEX® fabrics) are examples of companies that succeed because of their product leadership.[1]

The plans managers set forth, the variables they seek to control, and the decisions they make are all influenced by their company's strategy. For example, Walmart would not make plans to build ultra-expensive clothing boutiques because these plans would conflict with the company's strategy of operational excellence and "everyday low prices." Apple would not seek to control its operations by selecting performance measures that focus solely on cost-cutting because those measures would conflict with its product leadership customer value proposition. Finally, it is unlikely that Rolex would decide to implement drastic price reductions for its watches even if a financial analysis indicated that establishing a lower price might boost short-run profits. Rolex would oppose this course of action because it would diminish the luxury brand that forms the foundation of the company's product leadership customer value proposition.

© John Foxx Images/Imagestate Media (John Foxx)/Imagestate, RF

IN BUSINESS

A FOUR-YEAR WAITING LIST AT VANILLA BICYCLES

Sacha White started Vanilla Bicycles in Portland, Oregon, in 2001. After eight years in business, he had a four-year backlog of customer orders. He limits his annual production to 40–50 bikes per year that sell for an average of $7,000 each. He uses a silver alloy that costs 20 times as much as brass (which is the industry standard) to join titanium tubes together to form a bike frame. White spends three hours taking a buyer's measurements to determine the exact dimensions of the bike frame. He has resisted expanding production because it would undermine his strategy based on product leadership and customer intimacy. As White said, "If I ended up sacrificing what made Vanilla special just to make more bikes, that wouldn't be worth it to me."

Source: Christopher Steiner, "Heaven on Wheels," *Forbes,* April 13, 2009, p. 75.

An Enterprise Risk Management Perspective

Every strategy, plan, and decision involves risks. **Enterprise risk management** is a process used by a company to identify those risks and develop responses to them that enable it to be reasonably assured of meeting its goals. The left-hand column of Exhibit 1–7 provides 12 examples of the types of business risks that companies face. They range from risks that relate to the weather to risks associated with computer hackers, complying with the law, employee theft, and products harming customers. The right-hand column of Exhibit 1–7 provides an example of a control that could be implemented to help reduce each of the risks mentioned in the left-hand column of the exhibit.[2] Although these types of controls

---

[1] These three customer value propositions were defined by Michael Treacy and Fred Wiersema in "Customer Intimacy and Other Value Disciplines," *Harvard Business Review,* Volume 71 Issue 1, pp. 84–93.

[2] Besides using controls to reduce risks, companies can also chose other risk responses, such as accepting or avoiding a risk.

Examples of Business Risks	Examples of Controls to Reduce Business Risks	EXHIBIT 1–7 Identifying and Controlling Business Risks
• Intellectual assets being stolen from computer files	• Create firewalls that prohibit computer hackers from corrupting or stealing intellectual property	
• Products harming customers	• Develop a formal and rigorous new product testing program	
• Losing market share due to the unforeseen actions of competitors	• Develop an approach for legally gathering information about competitors' plans and practices	
• Poor weather conditions shutting down operations	• Develop contingency plans for overcoming weather-related disruptions	
• A website malfunctioning	• Thoroughly test the website before going "live" on the Internet	
• A supplier strike halting the flow of raw materials	• Establish a relationship with two companies capable of providing needed raw materials	
• A poorly designed incentive compensation system causing employees to make bad decisions	• Create a balanced set of performance measures that motivates the desired behavior	
• Financial statements inaccurately reporting the value of inventory	• Count the physical inventory on hand to make sure that it agrees with the accounting records	
• An employee stealing assets	• Segregate duties so that the same employee does not have physical custody of an asset and the responsibility of accounting for it	
• An employee accessing unauthorized information	• Create password-protected barriers that prohibit employees from obtaining information not needed to do their jobs	
• Inaccurate budget estimates causing excessive or insufficient production	• Implement a rigorous budget review process	
• Failing to comply with equal employment opportunity laws	• Create a report that tracks key metrics related to compliance with the laws	

cannot completely eliminate risks, they enable companies to proactively manage their risks rather than passively reacting to unfortunate events that have already occurred.

In managerial accounting, companies use controls to reduce the risk that their plans will not be achieved. For example, if a company plans to build a new manufacturing facility within a predefined budget and time frame, it will establish and monitor control measures to ensure that the project is concluded on time and within the budget. Risk management is also a critically important aspect of decision making. For example, when a company quantifies the labor cost savings that it can realize by sending jobs overseas, it should complement its financial analysis with a prudent assessment of the accompanying risks. Will the overseas manufacturer use child labor? Will the product's quality decline, thereby leading to more warranty repairs, customer complaints, and lawsuits? Will the elapsed time from customer order to delivery dramatically increase? Will terminating domestic employees diminish morale within the company and harm perceptions within the community? These are the types of risks that managers should incorporate into their decision-making processes.

MANAGING THE RISK OF A POWER OUTAGE

Between January and April of 2010, the United States had 35 major power outages. For business owners, these power outages can be costly. For example, a New York night club called the Smoke Jazz and Supper Club lost an estimated $1,500 in revenue when a power outage shut down its on-line reservation system for one night. George Pauli, the owner of Great Embroidery LLC in Mesa, Arizona, estimates that his company has an average of six power outages every year. Since Pauli's sewing machines cannot resume exactly where they leave off when abruptly shut down, each power outage costs him $120 in lost inventory. Pauli decided to buy $700 worth of batteries to keep his sewing machines running during power outages. The batteries paid for themselves in less than one year.

Source: Sarah E. Needleman, "Lights Out Means Lost Sales," *The Wall Street Journal*, July 22, 2010, p. B8.

A Corporate Social Responsibility Perspective

Companies are responsible for creating strategies that produce financial results that satisfy stockholders. However, they also have a *corporate social responsibility* to serve other stakeholders—such as customers, employees, suppliers, communities, and environmental and human rights advocates—whose interests are tied to the company's performance. **Corporate social responsibility** (CSR) is a concept whereby organizations consider the needs of all stakeholders when making decisions. CSR extends beyond legal compliance to include voluntary actions that satisfy stakeholder expectations. Numerous companies, such as Procter & Gamble, 3M, Eli Lilly and Company, Starbucks, Microsoft, Genentech, Johnson & Johnson, Baxter International, Abbott Laboratories, KPMG, PNC Bank, Deloitte, Southwest Airlines, and Caterpillar, prominently describe their corporate social performance on their websites.

Exhibit 1–8 presents examples of corporate social responsibilities that are of interest to six stakeholder groups.[3] If a company fails to meet the needs of these six stakeholder groups it can adversely affect its financial performance. For example, if a company pollutes the environment or fails to provide safe and humane working conditions for its employees, the negative publicity from environmental and human rights activists could cause the company's customers to defect and its "best and brightest" job candidates to apply elsewhere—both of which are likely to eventually harm financial performance. This explains why in managerial accounting a manager must establish plans, implement controls, and make decisions that consider impacts on all stakeholders.

GREENPEACE LEVERAGES THE POWER OF SOCIAL MEDIA

When Nestlé purchased palm oil from an Indonesian supplier to manufacture Kit-Kat candy bars, Greenpeace International used social media to express its disapproval. Greenpeace claimed that the Indonesian company destroyed rainforest to create its palm oil plantation; therefore, Nestlé's actions were contributing to global warming and endangering orangutans. Greenpeace posted YouTube videos, added comments to Nestlé's Facebook page, and sent Twitter Tweets to communicate its message to supporters. At one point, the number of fans on Nestlé's Facebook page grew to 95,000, most of them being protesters. Nestlé terminated its relationship with the supplier, which provided 1.25% of Nestlé's palm oil needs. A Nestlé spokesperson says the difficulty in responding to social media is to "show that we are listening, which we obviously are, while not getting involved in a shouting match."

Source: Emily Steel, "Nestlé Takes a Beating on Social-Media Sites," *The Wall Street Journal*, March 29, 2010, p. B5.

---

[3] Many of the examples in Exhibit 1-8 were drawn from Terry Leap and Misty L. Loughry, "The Stakeholder-Friendly Firm," *Business Horizons*, March/April 2004, pp. 27–32.

EXHIBIT 1–8
Examples of Corporate Social
Responsibilities

Companies should provide *customers* with:
- Safe, high-quality products that are fairly priced.
- Competent, courteous, and rapid delivery of products and services.
- Full disclosure of product-related risks.
- Easy-to-use information systems for shopping and tracking orders.

Companies should provide *suppliers* with:
- Fair contract terms and prompt payments.
- Reasonable time to prepare orders.
- Hassle-free acceptance of timely and complete deliveries.
- Cooperative rather than unilateral actions.

Companies should provide *stockholders* with:
- Competent management.
- Easy access to complete and accurate financial information.
- Full disclosure of enterprise risks.
- Honest answers to knowledgeable questions.

Companies and their suppliers should provide *employees* with:
- Safe and humane working conditions.
- Nondiscriminatory treatment and the right to organize and file grievances.
- Fair compensation.
- Opportunities for training, promotion, and personal development.

Companies should provide *communities* with:
- Payment of fair taxes.
- Honest information about plans such as plant closings.
- Resources that support charities, schools, and civic activities.
- Reasonable access to media sources.

Companies should provide *environmental and human rights advocates* with:
- Greenhouse gas emissions data.
- Recycling and resource conservation data.
- Child labor transparency.
- Full disclosure of suppliers located in developing countries.

A Process Management Perspective

Most companies organize themselves by functional departments, such as the Marketing Department, the Research and Development Department, and the Accounting Department. These departments tend to have a clearly defined "chain of command" that specifies superior and subordinate relationships. However, effective managers understand that *business processes,* more so than functional departments, serve the needs of a company's most important stakeholders—its customers. A **business process** is a series of steps that are followed in order to carry out some task in a business. These steps often span departmental boundaries, thereby requiring managers to cooperate across functional departments. The term *value chain* is often used to describe how an organization's functional departments interact with one another to form business processes. A **value chain**, as shown in Exhibit 1–9, consists of the major business functions that add value to a company's products and services.

EXHIBIT 1–9
Business Functions Making Up
the Value Chain

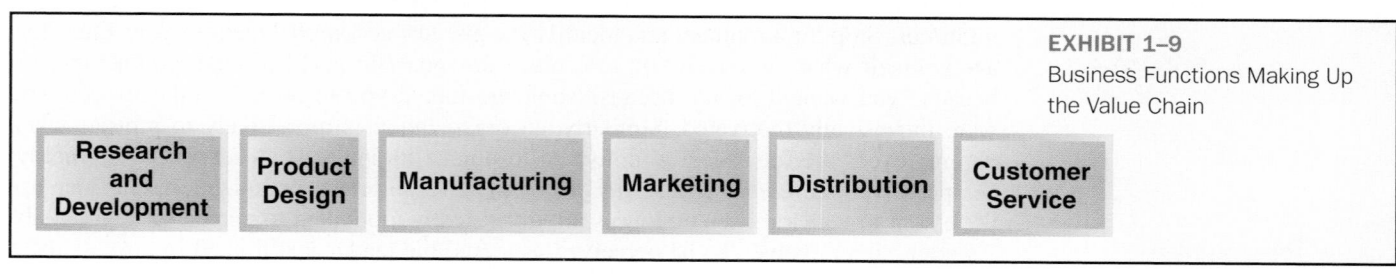

Research and Development → Product Design → Manufacturing → Marketing → Distribution → Customer Service

Managers need to understand the value chain to be effective in terms of planning, control, and decision making. For example, if a company's engineers plan to design a new product, they must communicate with the Manufacturing Department to ensure that the product can actually be produced, the Marketing Department to ensure that customers will buy the product, the Distribution Department to ensure that large volumes of the product can be cost-effectively transported to customers, and the Accounting Department to ensure that the product will increase profits. From a control and decision-making standpoint, managers also need to focus on process excellence instead of functional performance. For example, if the Purchasing Department focuses solely on minimizing the cost of purchased materials, this narrowly focused attempt at cost reduction may lead to greater scrap and rework in the Manufacturing Department, more complaints in the Customer Service Department, and greater challenges in the Marketing Department because dissatisfied customers are turning their attention to competitors.

Managers frequently use a process management method known as *lean thinking,* or what is called *Lean Production* in the manufacturing sector. **Lean Production** is a management approach that organizes resources such as people and machines around the flow of business processes and that only produces units in response to customer orders. It is often called *just-in-time* production (or *JIT*) because products are only manufactured in response to customer orders and they are completed just-in-time to be shipped to customers. Lean thinking differs from traditional manufacturing methods, which organize work departmentally and encourage departments to maximize their output even if it exceeds customer demand and bloats inventories. Because lean thinking only allows production in response to customer orders, the number of units produced tends to equal the number of units sold, thereby resulting in minimal inventory. The lean approach also results in fewer defects, less wasted effort, and quicker customer response times than traditional production methods.

A Leadership Perspective

An organization's employees bring diverse needs, beliefs, and goals to the workplace. Therefore, an important role for organizational leaders is to unite the behaviors of their fellow employees around two common themes—pursuing strategic goals and making optimal decisions. To fulfill this responsibility, leaders need to understand how *intrinsic motivation, extrinsic incentives,* and *cognitive bias* influence human behavior.

Intrinsic Motivation Intrinsic motivation refers to motivation that comes from within us. Stop for a moment and identify the greatest accomplishment of your life. Then ask yourself what motivated you to achieve this goal? In all likelihood, you achieved it because you wanted to, not because someone forced you to do it. In other words, you were intrinsically motivated. Similarly, an organization is more likely to prosper when its employees are intrinsically motivated to pursue its interests. A leader, who employees perceive as *credible* and *respectful* of their value to the organization, can increase the extent to which those employees are intrinsically motivated to pursue strategic goals. As your career evolves, to be perceived as a credible leader you'll need to possess three attributes—technical competence (that spans the value chain), personal integrity (in terms of work ethic and honesty), and strong communication skills (including oral presentation skills and writing skills). To be perceived as a leader who is respectful of your co-workers' value to the organization, you'll need to possess three more attributes—strong mentoring skills (to help others realize their potential), strong listening skills (to learn from your co-workers and be responsive to their needs), and personal humility (in terms of deferring recognition to all employees who contribute to the organization's success). If you possess these six traits, then you'll have the potential to become a leader who inspires others to readily and energetically channel their efforts toward achieving organizational goals.

Extrinsic Incentives Many organizations use *extrinsic incentives* to highlight important goals and to motivate employees to achieve them. For example, assume a company establishes the goal of reducing the time needed to perform a task by 20%. In addition, assume the company agrees to pay bonus compensation to its employees if they achieve the goal within three months. In this example, the company is using a type of extrinsic incentive known as a bonus to highlight a particular goal and to presumably motivate employees to achieve it.

While proponents of extrinsic incentives rightly assert that these types of rewards can have a powerful influence on employee behavior, many critics warn that they can also produce dysfunctional consequences. For example, suppose the employees mentioned above earned their bonuses by achieving the 20% time reduction goal within three months. However, let's also assume that during those three months the quality of the employees' output plummeted, thereby causing a spike in the company's repair costs, product returns, and customer defections. In this instance, did the extrinsic incentive work properly? The answer is yes and no. The bonus system did motivate employees to attain the time reduction goal; however, it also had the unintended consequences of causing employees to neglect product quality, thereby increasing repair costs, product returns, and customer defections. In other words, what may have seemed like a well-intended extrinsic incentive actually produced dysfunctional results for the company. This example highlights an important leadership challenge that you are likely to face someday—designing financial compensation systems that fairly reward employees for their efforts without inadvertently creating extrinsic incentives that motivate them to take actions that harm the company.

Cognitive Bias Leaders need to be aware that all people (including themselves) possess *cognitive biases,* or distorted thought processes, that can adversely affect planning, controlling, and decision making. To illustrate how cognitive bias works, let's consider the scenario of a television "infomercial" where someone is selling a product with a proclaimed value of $200 for $19.99 if viewers call within the next 30 minutes. Why do you think the seller claims that the product has a $200 value? The seller is relying on a cognitive bias called *anchoring bias* in an effort to convince viewers that a $180 discount is simply too good to pass up. The "anchor" is the false assertion that the product is actually worth $200. If viewers erroneously attach credibility to this contrived piece of information, their distorted analysis of the situation may cause them to spend $19.99 on an item whose true economic value is much less than that amount.

While cognitive biases cannot be eliminated, effective leaders should take two steps to reduce their negative impacts. First, they should acknowledge their own susceptibility to cognitive bias. For example, a leader's judgment might be clouded by optimism bias (being overly optimistic in assessing the likelihood of future outcomes) or self-enhancement bias (overestimating ones strengths and underestimating ones weaknesses relative to others). Second, they should acknowledge the presence of cognitive bias in others and introduce techniques to minimize their adverse consequences. For example, to reduce the risks of confirmation bias (a bias where people pay greater attention to information that confirms their preconceived notions, while devaluing information that contradicts them) or groupthink bias (a bias where some group members support a course of action solely because other group members do), a leader may routinely appoint independent teams of employees to assess the credibility of recommendations set forth by other individuals and groups.

Summary

This chapter defined managerial accounting and explained why it is relevant to business and accounting majors. It also discussed six topics—ethics, strategic management, enterprise risk management, corporate social responsibility, process management, and leadership—that define the context for applying the quantitative aspects of managerial accounting. The most important goal of this chapter was to help you understand that managerial accounting matters to your future career regardless of your major. Accounting is the language of business and you'll need to speak it to communicate effectively with and influence fellow managers.

Glossary

Budget A detailed plan for the future that is usually expressed in formal quantitative terms. (p. 3)

Business process A series of steps that are followed in order to carry out some task in a business. (p. 15)

Controlling The process of gathering feedback to ensure that a plan is being properly executed or modified as circumstances change. (p. 3)

Corporate social responsibility A concept whereby organizations consider the needs of all stakeholders when making decisions. (p. 14)

Decision making Selecting a course of action from competing alternatives. (p. 3)

Enterprise risk management A process used by a company to identify its risks and develop responses to them that enable it to be reasonably assured of meeting its goals. (p. 12)

Financial accounting The phase of accounting that is concerned with reporting historical financial information to external parties, such as stockholders, creditors, and regulators. (p. 2)

Lean Production A management approach that organizes resources such as people and machines around the flow of business processes and that only produces units in response to customer orders. (p. 16)

Managerial accounting The phase of accounting that is concerned with providing information to managers for use within the organization. (p. 2)

Performance report A report that compares budgeted data to actual data to highlight instances of excellent and unsatisfactory performance. (p. 4)

Planning The process of establishing goals and specifying how to achieve them. (p. 3)

Segment A part or activity of an organization about which managers would like cost, revenue, or profit data. (p. 3)

Strategy A company's "game plan" for attracting customers by distinguishing itself from competitors. (p. 11)

Value chain The major business functions that add value to a company's products and services, such as research and development, product design, manufacturing, marketing, distribution, and customer service. (p. 15)

Questions

1–1 How does managerial accounting differ from financial accounting?

1–2 Pick any major television network and describe some planning and control activities that its managers would engage in.

1–3 If you had to decide whether to continue making a component part or to begin buying the part from an overseas supplier, what quantitative and qualitative factors would influence your decision?

1–4 Why do companies prepare budgets?

1–5 Why is managerial accounting relevant to business majors and their future careers?

1–6 Why is managerial accounting relevant to accounting majors and their future careers?

1–7 Pick any large company and describe its strategy using the framework in the chapter.

1–8   Why do management accountants need to understand their company's strategy?

1–9   Pick any large company and describe three risks that it faces and how it responds to those risks.

1–10 Provide three examples of how a company's risks can influence its planning, controlling, and decision-making activities.

1–11 Pick any large company and explain three ways that it could segment its companywide performance.

1–12 Locate the website of any company that publishes a corporate social responsibility report (also referred to as a sustainability report). Describe three nonfinancial performance measures included in the report. Why do you think the company publishes this report?

1–13 Why do companies that implement Lean Production tend to have minimal inventories?

1–14 Why are leadership skills important to managers?

1–15 Why is ethical behavior important to business?

Multiple-choice questions are available with Connect.

Additional student resources are available with Connect. **Exercises**

EXERCISE 1–1 Planning and Control

Many companies use budgets for three purposes. First, they use them to plan how to deploy resources to best serve customers. Second, they use them to establish challenging goals, or stretch targets, to motivate employees to strive for exceptional results. Third, they use them to evaluate and reward employees.

Assume that you are a sales manager working with your boss to create a sales budget for next year. Once the sales budget is established, it will influence how other departments within the company plan to deploy their resources. For example, the manufacturing manager will plan to produce enough units to meet budgeted unit sales. The sales budget will also be instrumental in determining your pay raise, potential for promotion, and bonus. If actual sales exceed the sales budget, it bodes well for your career. If actual sales are less than budgeted sales, it will diminish your financial compensation and potential for promotion.

Required:

1. Do you think it would be appropriate for your boss to establish the sales budget without any input from you? Why?

2. Do you think the company would be comfortable with allowing you to establish the sales budget without any input from your boss? Why?

3. Assume the company uses its sales budget for only one purpose—planning to deploy resources in a manner that best serves customers. What thoughts would influence your estimate of future sales as well as your boss's estimate of future sales?

4. Assume the company uses its sales budget for only one purpose—motivating employees to strive for exceptional results. What thoughts would influence your estimate of future sales as well as your boss's estimate of future sales?

5. Assume the company uses its sales budget for only one purpose—to determine your pay raise, potential for promotion, and bonus. What thoughts would influence your estimate of future sales as well as your boss's estimate of future sales?

6. Assume the sales budget is used for all three purposes described in requirements 3–5. Describe any conflicts or complications that might arise when using the sales budget for these three purposes.

EXERCISE 1–2 Controlling

Assume that you work for an airline unloading luggage from airplanes. Your boss has said that, on average, each airplane contains 100 pieces of luggage. Furthermore, your boss has stated that you should be able to unload 100 pieces of luggage from an airplane in 10 minutes. Today an airplane arrived with 150 pieces of luggage and you unloaded all of it in 13 minutes. After finishing with the 150 pieces of luggage, your boss yelled at you for exceeding the 10-minute allowance for unloading luggage from an airplane.

Required:

1. How would you feel about being yelled at for taking 13 minutes to unload 150 pieces of luggage?
2. How does this scenario relate to the larger issue of how companies design control systems?

EXERCISE 1–3   Decision Making

Exhibit 1–2 includes 12 questions related to 12 types of decisions that companies often face. In the chapter, these 12 decisions were discussed within the context of for-profit companies; however, they are also readily applicable to nonprofit organizations. To illustrate this point, assume that you are a senior leader, such as a president, provost, or dean, in a university setting.

Required:

For each of the 12 decisions in Exhibit 1–2, provide an example of how that type of decision might be applicable to a university setting.

EXERCISE 1–4   Ethics and the Manager

Richmond, Inc., operates a chain of 44 department stores. Two years ago, the board of directors of Richmond approved a large-scale remodeling of its stores to attract a more upscale clientele.

Before finalizing these plans, two stores were remodeled as a test. Linda Perlman, assistant controller, was asked to oversee the financial reporting for these test stores, and she and other management personnel were offered bonuses based on the sales growth and profitability of these stores. While completing the financial reports, Perlman discovered a sizable inventory of outdated goods that should have been discounted for sale or returned to the manufacturer. She discussed the situation with her management colleagues; the consensus was to ignore reporting this inventory as obsolete because reporting it would diminish the financial results and their bonuses.

Required:

1. According to the IMA's Statement of Ethical Professional Practice, would it be ethical for Perlman *not* to report the inventory as obsolete?
2. Would it be easy for Perlman to take the ethical action in this situation? (CMA, adapted)

EXERCISE 1–5   Strategy

The table below contains the names of six companies.

Required:

For each company, categorize its strategy as being focused on customer intimacy, operational excellence, or product leadership. If you wish to improve your understanding of each company's customer value proposition before completing the exercise, review its most recent annual report. To obtain electronic access to this information, perform an Internet search on each company's name followed by the words "annual report."

Company	Strategy
1. Deere.........................	?
2. FedEx.........................	?
3. State Farm Insurance	?
4. BMW..........................	?
5. Amazon.com...................	?
6. Charles Schwab.	?

EXERCISE 1–6   Enterprise Risk Management

The table below refers to seven industries.

Required:

For each industry, identify one important risk faced by the companies that compete within that industry. Also, describe one control that companies could use to reduce the risk that you have identified.

Industry	Type of Risk	Control to Reduce the Risk
1. Airlines (e.g., Delta Airlines)........................		
2. Pharmaceutical drugs (e.g., Merck)		
3. Package delivery (e.g., United Parcel Service)........		
4. Banking (e.g., Bank of America)		
5. Oil & gas (e.g., ExxonMobil).......................		
6. E-commerce (e.g., eBay)...........................		
7. Automotive (e.g., Toyota)		

EXERCISE 1–7 Ethics in Business

Consumers and attorney generals in more than 40 states accused a prominent nationwide chain of auto repair shops of misleading customers and selling them unnecessary parts and services, from brake jobs to front-end alignments. Lynn Sharpe Paine reported the situation as follows in "Managing for Organizational Integrity," *Harvard Business Review,* Volume 72, Issue 3:

> In the face of declining revenues, shrinking market share, and an increasingly competitive market . . . management attempted to spur performance of its auto centers. . . . The automotive service advisers were given product-specific sales quotas—sell so many springs, shock absorbers, alignments, or brake jobs per shift—and paid a commission based on sales. . . . [F]ailure to meet quotas could lead to a transfer or a reduction in work hours. Some employees spoke of the "pressure, pressure, pressure" to bring in sales.
>
> This pressure-cooker atmosphere created conditions under which employees felt that the only way to satisfy top management was by selling products and services to customers that they didn't really need.

Suppose all automotive repair businesses routinely followed the practice of attempting to sell customers unnecessary parts and services.

Required:

1.   How would this behavior affect customers? How might customers attempt to protect themselves against this behavior?
2.   How would this behavior probably affect profits and employment in the automotive service industry?

EXERCISE 1–8 Cognitive Bias

In the 1970s, 1 million college-bound students were surveyed and asked to compare themselves to their peers. Some of the key findings of the survey were as follows:

a.   70% of the students rated themselves as above average in leadership ability, while only 2% rated themselves as below average in this regard.
b.   With respect to athletic skills, 60% of the students rated their skills as above the median and only 6% of students rated themselves as below the median.
c.   60% of the students rated themselves in the top 10% in terms of their ability to get along with others, while 25% of the students felt that they were in the top 1% in terms of this interpersonal skill.

Required:

What type of cognitive bias reveals itself in the data mentioned above? How might this cognitive bias adversely influence a manager's planning, controlling, and decision-making activities? What steps could managers take to reduce the possibility that this cognitive bias would adversely influence their actions?

Source: Dan Lovallo and Daniel Kahneman, "Delusions of Success: How Optimism Undermines Executives' Decisions," *Harvard Business Review,* July 2003, pp. 56–63.

EXERCISE 1–9 Ethics and Decision Making

Assume that you are the chairman of the Department of Accountancy at Mountain State University. One of the accounting professors in your department, Dr. Candler, has been consistently and uniformly regarded by students as an awful teacher for more than 10 years. Other accounting professors within your department have observed Dr. Candler's classroom teaching and they concur that his teaching skills are very poor. However, Dr. Candler was granted tenure 12 years ago, thereby ensuring him life-long job security at Mountain State University.

Much to your surprise, today you received a phone from an accounting professor at Oregon Coastal University. During this phone call you are informed that Oregon Coastal University is on the verge of making a job offer to Dr. Candler. However, before extending the job offer, the faculty at Oregon Coastal wants your input regarding Dr. Candler's teaching effectiveness while at Mountain State University.

Required:

How would you respond to the professor from Oregon Coastal University? What would you say about Dr. Candler's teaching ability? Would you describe your answer to this inquiry as being ethical? Why?

EXERCISE 1–10 Corporate Social Responsbility

In his book *Capitalism and Freedom,* economist Milton Friedman wrote on page 133: "There is one and only one social responsibility of business—to use its resources and engage in activities designed to increase its profits so long as it . . . engages in open and free competition, without deception or fraud."

Required:

Explain why you agree or disagree with this quote.

EXERCISE 1–11 Intrinsic Motivation and Extrinsic Incentives

In a *Harvard Business Review* article titled "Why Incentive Plans Cannot Work," (Volume 71, Issue 5) author Alfie Kohn wrote: "Research suggests that, by and large, rewards succeed at securing one thing only: temporary compliance. When it comes to producing lasting change in attitudes and behavior, however, rewards, like punishment, are strikingly ineffective. Once the rewards run out, people revert to their old behaviors. . . . Incentives, a version of what psychologists call extrinsic motivators, do not alter the attitudes that underlie our behaviors. They do not create an enduring *commitment* to any value or action. Rather, incentives merely—and temporarily—change what we do."

Required:

1. Do you agree with this quote? Why?
2. As a manager, how would you seek to motivate your employees?
3. As a manager, would you use financial incentives to compensate your employees? If so, what would be the keys to using them effectively? If not, then how would you compensate your employees?

EXERCISE 1–12 Cognitive Bias and Decision Making

During World War II, the U.S. military was studying its combat-tested fighter planes to determine the parts of the plane that were most vulnerable to enemy fire. The purpose of the study was to identify the most vulnerable sections of each plane and then take steps to reinforce those sections to improve pilot safety and airplane durability. The data gathered by the U.S. military showed that certain sections of its combat-tested fighter planes were consistently hit more often with enemy fire than other sections of the plane.

Required:

1. Would you recommend reinforcing the sections of the plane that were hit most often by enemy fire, or would you reinforce the sections that were hit less frequently by enemy fire? Why?
2. Do you think cognitive bias had the potential to influence the U.S. military's decision-making process with respect to reinforcing its fighter planes?

Source: Jerker Denrell, "Selection Bias and the Perils of Benchmarking," *Harvard Business Review,* Volume 83, Issue 4, pp. 114–119.

EXERCISE 1–13 Ethics and Decision Making

Assume that you just completed a December weekend vacation to a casino within the United States. During your trip you won $10,000 gambling. When the casino exchanged your chips for cash they did not record any personal information, such as your driver's license number or social security number. Four months later while preparing your tax returns for the prior year, you stop to contemplate the fact that the Internal Revenue Service requires taxpayers to report all gambling winnings on Form 1040.

Required:

Would you report your gambling winnings to the Internal Revenue Service so that you could pay federal income taxes on those winnings? Do you believe that your actions are ethical? Why?

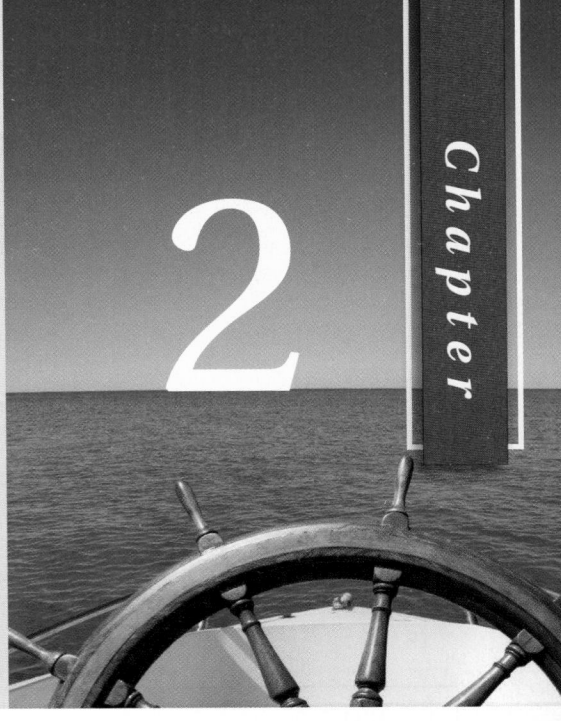

Chapter 2

Managerial Accounting and Cost Concepts

Lowering Health Care Costs and Improving Patient Care

© Trevor Lush/Purestock/SuperStock, RF

Providence Regional Medical Center's (PRMC) "single stay" ward is lowering health care costs and increasing patient satisfaction. Rather than transporting post-surgical patients to stationary equipment throughout the hospital, a "single stay" ward brings all required equipment to stationary patients. For example, "after heart surgery, cardiac patients remain in one room throughout their recovery, only the gear and staff are in motion. As the patient's condition stabilizes, the beeping machines of intensive care are removed and physical therapy equipment is added." The results of this shift in orientation have been impressive. Patient satisfaction scores have skyrocketed and the average length of a patient's stay in the hospital has declined by more than a day. ∎

Source: Catherine Arnst, "Radical Surgery," *Bloomberg Businessweek*, January 18, 2010, pp. 40–45.

LEARNING OBJECTIVES

After studying Chapter 2, you should be able to:

LO 2–1 Understand cost classifications used for assigning costs to cost objects: direct costs and indirect costs.

LO 2–2 Identify and give examples of each of the three basic manufacturing cost categories.

LO 2–3 Understand cost classifications used to prepare financial statements: product costs and period costs.

LO 2–4 Understand cost classifications used to predict cost behavior: variable costs, fixed costs, and mixed costs.

LO 2–5 Analyze a mixed cost using a scattergraph plot and the high-low method.

LO 2–6 Prepare income statements for a merchandising company using the traditional and contribution formats.

LO 2–7 Understand cost classifications used in making decisions: differential costs, opportunity costs, and sunk costs.

LO 2–8 (Appendix 2A) Analyze a mixed cost using a scattergraph plot and the least-squares regression method.

This chapter explains that in managerial accounting the term *cost* is used in many different ways. The reason is that there are many types of costs, and these costs are classified differently according to the immediate needs of management. For example, managers may want cost data to prepare external financial reports, to prepare planning budgets, or to make decisions. Each different use of cost data demands a different classification and definition of costs. For example, the preparation of external financial reports requires the use of historical cost data, whereas decision making may require predictions about future costs. This notion of *different costs for different purposes* is a critically important aspect of managerial accounting.

Exhibit 2–1 summarizes the cost classifications that will be defined in this chapter, namely cost classifications (1) for assigning costs to cost objects, (2) for manufacturing companies, (3) for preparing financial statements, (4) for predicting cost behavior, and (5) for making decisions. As we begin defining the cost terminology related to each of these cost classifications, please refer back to this exhibit to help improve your understanding of the overall organization of the chapter.

EXHIBIT 2–1
Summary of Cost Classifications

Purpose of Cost Classification	Cost Classifications
Assigning costs to cost objects	• Direct cost (can be easily traced) • Indirect cost (cannot be easily traced)

Accounting for costs in manufacturing companies	• Manufacturing costs
	  • Direct materials
	  • Direct labor
	  • Manufacturing overhead
	• Nonmanufacturing costs
	  • Selling costs
	  • Administrative costs

Preparing financial statements	• Product costs (inventoriable) • Period costs (expensed)
Predicting cost behavior in response to changes in activity	• Variable cost (proportional to activity) • Fixed cost (constant in total) • Mixed cost (has variable and fixed elements)
Making decisions	• Differential cost (differs between alternatives) • Sunk cost (should be ignored) • Opportunity cost (foregone benefit)

Cost Classifications for Assigning Costs to Cost Objects

LEARNING OBJECTIVE 2–1
Understand cost classifications used for assigning costs to cost objects: direct costs and indirect costs.

Costs are assigned to cost objects for a variety of purposes including pricing, preparing profitability studies, and controlling spending. A **cost object** is anything for which cost data are desired—including products, customers, jobs, and organizational subunits. For purposes of assigning costs to cost objects, costs are classified as either *direct* or *indirect*.

Direct Cost

A **direct cost** is a cost that can be easily and conveniently traced to a specified cost object. For example, if Reebok is assigning costs to its various regional and national sales offices, then the salary of the sales manager in its Tokyo office would be a direct cost of that office. If a printing company made 10,000 brochures for a specific customer, then the cost of the paper used to make the brochures would be a direct cost of that customer.

Indirect Cost

An **indirect cost** is a cost that cannot be easily and conveniently traced to a specified cost object. For example, a Campbell Soup factory may produce dozens of varieties of canned soups. The factory manager's salary would be an indirect cost of a particular variety such as chicken noodle soup. The reason is that the factory manager's salary is incurred as a consequence of running the entire factory—it is not incurred to produce any one soup variety. *To be traced to a cost object such as a particular product, the cost must be caused by the cost object.* The factory manager's salary is called a *common cost* of producing the various products of the factory. A **common cost** is a cost that is incurred to support a number of cost objects but cannot be traced to them individually. A common cost is a type of indirect cost.

A particular cost may be direct or indirect, depending on the cost object. While the Campbell Soup factory manager's salary is an *indirect* cost of manufacturing chicken noodle soup, it is a *direct* cost of the manufacturing division. In the first case, the cost object is chicken noodle soup. In the second case, the cost object is the entire manufacturing division.

Cost Classifications for Manufacturing Companies

Manufacturing companies such as Texas Instruments, Ford, and DuPont separate their costs into two broad categories—manufacturing and nonmanufacturing costs.

Manufacturing Costs

Most manufacturing companies further separate their manufacturing costs into two direct cost categories, direct materials and direct labor, and one indirect cost category, manufacturing overhead. A discussion of each of these categories follows.

LEARNING OBJECTIVE 2–2
Identify and give examples of each of the three basic manufacturing cost categories.

Direct Materials The materials that go into the final product are called **raw materials**. This term is somewhat misleading because it seems to imply unprocessed natural resources like wood pulp or iron ore. Actually, raw materials refer to any materials that are used in the final product; and the finished product of one company can become the raw materials of another company. For example, the plastics produced by Du Pont are a raw material used by Hewlett-Packard in its personal computers.

Raw materials may include both *direct* and *indirect materials*. **Direct materials** are those materials that become an integral part of the finished product and whose costs can be conveniently traced to the finished product. This would include, for example, the seats that Airbus purchases from subcontractors to install in its commercial aircraft and the electronic components that Apple uses in its iPhones.

Sometimes it isn't worth the effort to trace the costs of relatively insignificant materials to end products. Such minor items would include the solder used to make electrical connections in a Samsung HDTV or the glue used to assemble an Ethan Allen chair. Materials such as solder and glue are called **indirect materials** and are included as part of manufacturing overhead, which is discussed shortly.

Direct Labor **Direct labor** consists of labor costs that can be easily (i.e., physically and conveniently) traced to individual units of product. Direct labor is sometimes

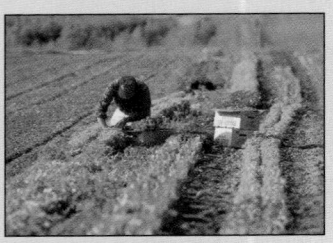
FOOD PRICES HIT RECORD HIGHS FOR RESTAURANTS

Direct material costs are critically important to restaurants and fast-food chains. In recent years, some food costs have spiked to record highs. For example, unexpected freezing temperatures in the southwestern portion of the United States caused the cost of lettuce to increase 290%. Similarly, the costs of green peppers, tomatoes, and cucumbers jumped 145%, 85%, and 30%, respectively. A large chain such as Subway can withstand these price increases better than smaller competitors because of its buying power and long-term contracts.

Source: Anne VanderMey, "Food For Thought," *Fortune,* May 9, 2011, p. 12.

called *touch labor* because direct labor workers typically touch the product while it is being made. Examples of direct labor include assembly-line workers at Toyota, carpenters at the home builder KB Home, and electricians who install equipment on aircraft at Bombardier Learjet.

Labor costs that cannot be physically traced to particular products, or that can be traced only at great cost and inconvenience, are termed **indirect labor**. Just like indirect materials, indirect labor is treated as part of manufacturing overhead. Indirect labor includes the labor costs of janitors, supervisors, materials handlers, and night security guards. Although the efforts of these workers are essential, it would be either impractical or impossible to accurately trace their costs to specific units of product. Hence, such labor costs are treated as indirect labor.

Manufacturing Overhead **Manufacturing overhead**, the third manufacturing cost category, includes all manufacturing costs except direct materials and direct labor. Manufacturing overhead includes items such as indirect materials; indirect labor; maintenance and repairs on production equipment; and heat and light, property taxes, depreciation, and insurance on manufacturing facilities. A company also incurs costs for heat and light, property taxes, insurance, depreciation, and so forth, associated with its selling and administrative functions, but these costs are not included as part of manufacturing overhead. Only those costs associated with *operating the factory* are included in manufacturing overhead.

Various names are used for manufacturing overhead, such as *indirect manufacturing cost, factory overhead,* and *factory burden.* All of these terms are synonyms for *manufacturing overhead.*

Nonmanufacturing Costs

Nonmanufacturing costs are often divided into two categories: (1) *selling costs* and (2) *administrative costs.* **Selling costs** include all costs that are incurred to secure customer orders and get the finished product to the customer. These costs are sometimes called *order-getting* and *order-filling costs.* Examples of selling costs include advertising, shipping, sales travel, sales commissions, sales salaries, and costs of finished goods warehouses. Selling costs can be either direct or indirect costs. For example, the cost of an advertising campaign dedicated to one specific product is a direct cost of that product, whereas the salary of a marketing manager who oversees numerous products is an indirect cost with respect to individual products.

Administrative costs include all costs associated with the *general management* of an organization rather than with manufacturing or selling. Examples of administrative costs include executive compensation, general accounting, secretarial, public relations, and similar costs involved in the overall, general administration of the organization *as a whole.* Administrative costs can be either direct or indirect costs. For example, the salary of an accounting manager in charge of accounts receivable collections in the East region is a direct cost of that region, whereas the salary of a chief financial officer who oversees all of a company's regions is an indirect cost with respect to individual regions.

Nonmanufacturing costs are also often called selling, general, and administrative (SG&A) costs or just selling and administrative costs.

Cost Classifications for Preparing Financial Statements

When preparing a balance sheet and an income statement, companies need to classify their costs as *product costs* or *period costs*. To understand the difference between product costs and period costs, we must first discuss the matching principle from financial accounting.

Generally, costs are recognized as expenses on the income statement in the period that benefits from the cost. For example, if a company pays for liability insurance in advance for two years, the entire amount is not considered an expense of the year in which the payment is made. Instead, one-half of the cost would be recognized as an expense each year. The reason is that both years—not just the first year—benefit from the insurance payment. The unexpensed portion of the insurance payment is carried on the balance sheet as an asset called prepaid insurance.

The *matching principle* is based on the *accrual* concept that *costs incurred to generate a particular revenue should be recognized as expenses in the same period that the revenue is recognized.* This means that if a cost is incurred to acquire or make something that will eventually be sold, then the cost should be recognized as an expense only when the sale takes place—that is, when the benefit occurs. Such costs are called *product costs.*

LEARNING OBJECTIVE 2–3
Understand cost classifications used to prepare financial statements: product costs and period costs.

Product Costs

For financial accounting purposes, **product costs** include all costs involved in acquiring or making a product. In the case of manufactured goods, these costs consist of direct materials, direct labor, and manufacturing overhead.[1] Product costs "attach" to units of product as the goods are purchased or manufactured, and they remain attached as the goods go into inventory awaiting sale. Product costs are initially assigned to an inventory account on the balance sheet. When the goods are sold, the costs are released from inventory as expenses (typically called cost of goods sold) and matched against sales revenue on the income statement. Because product costs are initially assigned to inventories, they are also known as **inventoriable costs**.

We want to emphasize that product costs are not necessarily recorded as expenses on the income statement in the period in which they are incurred. Rather, as explained above, they are recorded as expenses in the period in which the related products *are sold.*

Period Costs

Period costs are all the costs that are not product costs. *All selling and administrative expenses are treated as period costs.* For example, sales commissions, advertising, executive salaries, public relations, and the rental costs of administrative offices are all period costs. Period costs are not included as part of the cost of either purchased or manufactured goods; instead, period costs are expensed on the income statement in the period in which they are incurred using the usual rules of accrual accounting. Keep in mind that the period in which a cost is incurred is not necessarily the period in which cash changes

---

[1] For internal management purposes, product costs may exclude some manufacturing costs. For example, see Appendix 4B and the discussion in Chapter 5.

hands. For example, as discussed earlier, the costs of liability insurance are spread across the periods that benefit from the insurance—regardless of the period in which the insurance premium is paid.

Prime Cost and Conversion Cost

Two more cost categories are often used in discussions of manufacturing costs—*prime cost* and *conversion cost*. **Prime cost** is the sum of direct materials cost and direct labor cost. **Conversion cost** is the sum of direct labor cost and manufacturing overhead cost. The term *conversion cost* is used to describe direct labor and manufacturing overhead because these costs are incurred to convert materials into the finished product.

To improve your understanding of these definitions, consider the following scenario: A company has reported the following costs and expenses for the most recent month:

Direct materials	$69,000
Direct labor	$35,000
Manufacturing overhead	$14,000
Selling expenses	$29,000
Administrative expenses	$50,000

These costs and expenses can be categorized in a number of ways, including product costs, period costs, conversion costs, and prime costs:

$$
\begin{aligned}
\text{Product cost} &= \text{Direct materials} + \text{Direct labor} + \text{Manufacturing overhead} \\
&= \$69,000 + \$35,000 + \$14,000 \\
&= \$118,000 \\
\text{Period cost} &= \text{Selling expenses} + \text{Administrative expenses} \\
&= \$29,000 + \$50,000 \\
&= \$79,000 \\
\text{Conversion cost} &= \text{Direct labor} + \text{Manufacturing overhead} \\
&= \$35,000 + \$14,000 \\
&= \$49,000 \\
\text{Prime cost} &= \text{Direct materials} + \text{Direct labor} \\
&= \$69,000 + \$35,000 \\
&= \$104,000
\end{aligned}
$$

© Zoonar/Michael Roseb/AGE Fotostock

WALMART LOOKS TO REDUCE ITS SHIPPING COSTS

Walmart hopes to lower its shipping costs, thereby enabling it to reduce its "everyday low prices." In years past, suppliers would ship their merchandise to Walmart's distribution centers, and then Walmart would use its own fleet of trucks to ship goods from its distribution centers to its retail store locations. However, now Walmart wants to assume control of transporting merchandise from its suppliers' manufacturing facilities to its distribution centers. Walmart believes it can lower these shipping costs by carrying more merchandise per truck and by taking advantage of volume purchase price discounts for fuel. In exchange for assuming these shipping responsibilities, Walmart is seeking price reductions from suppliers that it can pass along, at least in part, to its customers.

Source: Chris Burritt, Carol Wolf, and Matthew Boyle, "Why Wal-Mart Wants to Take the Driver's Seat," *Bloomberg Businessweek*, May 31–June 6, 2010, pp. 17–18.

Cost Classifications for Predicting Cost Behavior

It is often necessary to predict how a certain cost will behave in response to a change in activity. For example, a manager at Under Armour may want to estimate the impact a 5 percent increase in sales would have on the company's total direct materials cost. **Cost behavior** refers to how a cost reacts to changes in the level of activity. As the activity level rises and falls, a particular cost may rise and fall as well—or it may remain constant. For planning purposes, a manager must be able to anticipate which of these will happen; and if a cost can be expected to change, the manager must be able to estimate how much it will change. To help make such distinctions, costs are often categorized as *variable, fixed,* or *mixed.* The relative proportion of each type of cost in an organization is known as its **cost structure**. For example, an organization might have many fixed costs but few variable or mixed costs. Alternatively, it might have many variable costs but few fixed or mixed costs.

LEARNING OBJECTIVE 2–4
Understand cost classifications used to predict cost behavior: variable costs, fixed costs, and mixed costs.

Variable Cost

A **variable cost** varies, in total, in direct proportion to changes in the level of activity. Common examples of variable costs include cost of goods sold for a merchandising company, direct materials, direct labor, variable elements of manufacturing overhead, such as indirect materials, supplies, and power, and variable elements of selling and administrative expenses, such as commissions and shipping costs.[2]

For a cost to be variable, it must be variable *with respect to something.* That "something" is its *activity base.* An **activity base** is a measure of whatever causes the incurrence of a variable cost. An activity base is sometimes referred to as a *cost driver.* Some of the most common activity bases are direct labor-hours, machine-hours, units produced, and units sold. Other examples of activity bases (cost drivers) include the number of miles driven by salespersons, the number of pounds of laundry cleaned by a hotel, the number of calls handled by technical support staff at a software company, and the number of beds occupied in a hospital. *While there are many activity bases within organizations, throughout this textbook, unless stated otherwise, you should assume that the activity base under consideration is the total volume of goods and services provided by the organization. We will specify the activity base only when it is something other than total output.*

To provide an example of a variable cost, consider Nooksack Expeditions, a small company that provides daylong whitewater rafting excursions on rivers in the North Cascade Mountains. The company provides all of the necessary equipment and experienced guides, and it serves gourmet meals to its guests. The meals are purchased from a caterer for $30 a person for a daylong excursion. The behavior of this variable cost, on both a per unit and a total basis, is shown below:

Number of Guests	Cost of Meals per Guest	Total Cost of Meals
250	$30	$7,500
500	$30	$15,000
750	$30	$22,500
1,000	$30	$30,000

[2] Direct labor costs often can be fixed instead of variable for a variety of reasons. For example, in some countries, such as France, Germany, and Japan, labor regulations and cultural norms may limit management's ability to adjust the labor force in response to changes in activity. In this textbook, always assume that direct labor is a variable cost unless you are explicitly told otherwise.

COST DRIVERS IN THE ELECTRONICS INDUSTRY

Accenture Ltd. estimates that the U.S. electronics industry spends $13.8 billion annually to rebox, restock, and resell returned products. Conventional wisdom is that customers only return products when they are defective, but the data show that this explanation only accounts for 5% of customer returns. The biggest cost drivers that cause product returns are that customers often inadvertently buy the wrong products and that they cannot understand how to use the products that they have purchased. Television manufacturer Vizio Inc. has started including more information on its packaging to help customers avoid buying the wrong product. Seagate Technologies is replacing thick instruction manuals with simpler guides that make it easier for customers to begin using their products.

Source: Christopher Lawton, "The War on Returns," *The Wall Street Journal*, May 8, 2008, pp. D1 and D6.

FOOD COSTS AT A LUXURY HOTEL

© Sandee Noreen

The Sporthotel Theresa (http://www.theresa.at/), owned and operated by the Egger family, is a four star hotel located in Zell im Zillertal, Austria. The hotel features access to hiking, skiing, biking, and other activities in the Ziller Alps as well as its own fitness facility and spa.

Three full meals a day are included in the hotel room charge. Breakfast and lunch are served buffet-style while dinner is a more formal affair with as many as six courses. The chef, Stefan Egger, believes that food costs are roughly proportional to the number of guests staying at the hotel; that is, they are a variable cost. He must order food from suppliers two or three days in advance, but he adjusts his purchases to the number of guests who are currently staying at the hotel and their consumption patterns. In addition, guests make their selections from the dinner menu early in the day, which helps Stefan plan which foodstuffs will be required for dinner. Consequently, he is able to prepare just enough food so that all guests are satisfied and yet waste is held to a minimum.

Source: Conversation with Stefan Egger, chef at the Sporthotel Theresa.

While total variable costs change as the activity level changes, it is important to note that a variable cost is constant if expressed on a *per unit* basis. For example, the per unit cost of the meals remains constant at $30 even though the total cost of the meals increases and decreases with activity. The graph in the first part of Exhibit 2–2 illustrates that the total variable cost rises and falls as the activity level rises and falls. At an activity level of 250 guests, the total meal cost is $7,500. At an activity level of 1,000 guests, the total meal cost rises to $30,000.

Fixed Cost

A **fixed cost** is a cost that remains constant, in total, regardless of changes in the level of activity. Examples of fixed costs include straight-line depreciation, insurance, property taxes, rent, supervisory salaries, administrative salaries, and advertising. Unlike variable costs, fixed costs are not affected by changes in activity. Consequently, as the activity level rises and falls, total fixed costs remain constant unless influenced by some outside force, such as a landlord increasing your monthly rental expense. To continue the Nooksack Expeditions example, assume the company rents a building for $500 per month to store its equipment. The total amount of rent paid is the same regardless of the number of guests the company takes on its expeditions during any given month. The concept of a fixed cost is shown graphically in the second part of Exhibit 2–2.

Because total fixed costs remain constant for large variations in the level of activity, the average fixed cost *per unit* becomes progressively smaller as the level of activity

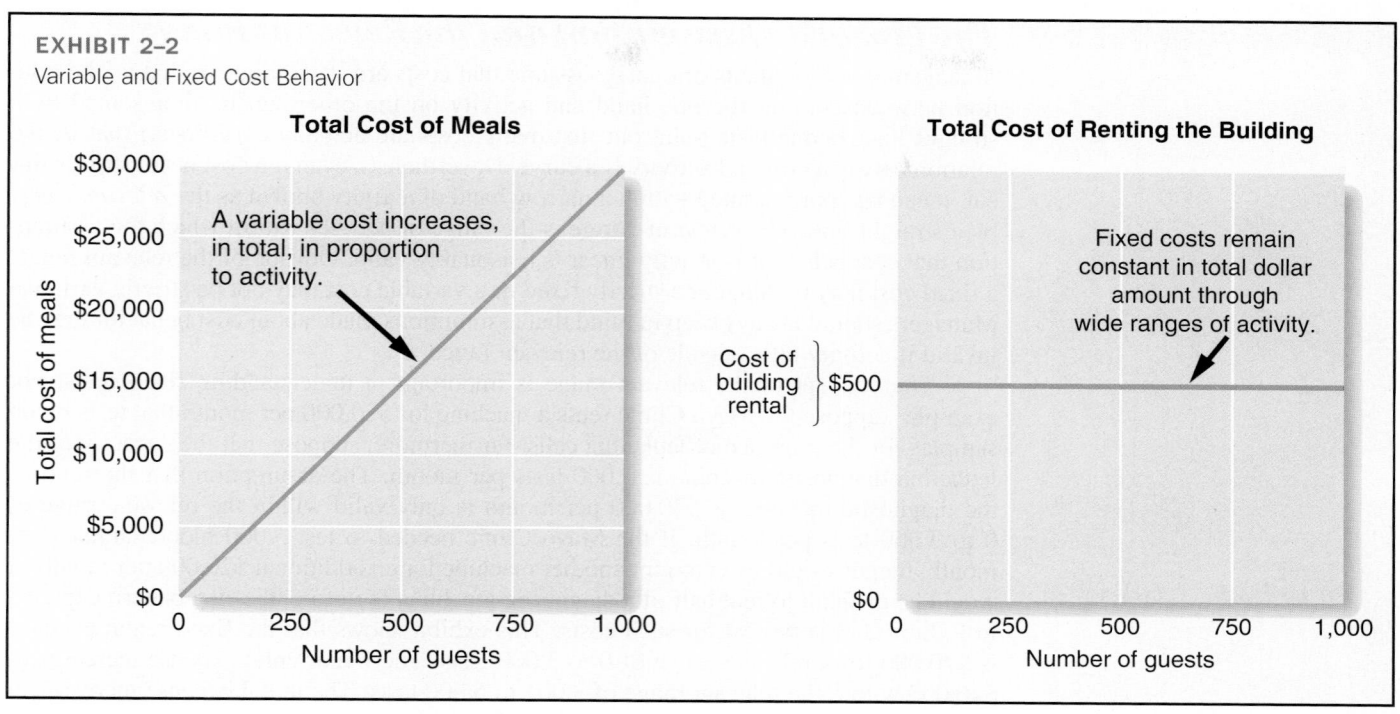

EXHIBIT 2–2
Variable and Fixed Cost Behavior

Total Cost of Meals

A variable cost increases, in total, in proportion to activity.

Total Cost of Renting the Building

Fixed costs remain constant in total dollar amount through wide ranges of activity.

Cost of building rental } $500

increases. If Nooksack Expeditions has only 250 guests in a month, the $500 fixed rental cost would amount to an average of $2 per guest. If there are 1,000 guests, the fixed rental cost would average only 50 cents per guest. The table below illustrates this aspect of the behavior of fixed costs. Note that as the number of guests increase, the average fixed cost per guest drops.

Monthly Rental Cost	Number of Guests	Average Cost per Guest
$500.......	250	$2.00
$500.......	500	$1.00
$500.......	750	$0.67
$500.......	1,000	$0.50

As a general rule, *we caution against expressing fixed costs on an average per unit basis in internal reports because it creates the false impression that fixed costs are like variable costs and that total fixed costs actually change as the level of activity changes.*

For planning purposes, fixed costs can be viewed as either *committed* or *discretionary*. **Committed fixed costs** represent organizational investments with a *multiyear* planning horizon that can't be significantly reduced even for short periods of time without making fundamental changes. Examples include investments in facilities and equipment, as well as real estate taxes, insurance expenses, and salaries of top management. Even if operations are interrupted or cut back, committed fixed costs remain largely unchanged in the short term because the costs of restoring them later are likely to be far greater than any short-run savings that might be realized. **Discretionary fixed costs** (often referred to as *managed fixed costs*) usually arise from *annual* decisions by management to spend on certain fixed cost items. Examples of discretionary fixed costs include advertising, research, public relations, management development programs, and internships for students. Discretionary fixed costs can be cut for short periods of time with minimal damage to the long-run goals of the organization.

The Linearity Assumption and the Relevant Range

Management accountants ordinarily assume that costs are strictly linear; that is, the relation between cost on the one hand and activity on the other can be represented by a straight line. Economists point out that many costs are actually curvilinear; that is, the relation between cost and activity is a curve. Nevertheless, even if a cost is not strictly linear, it can be approximated within a narrow band of activity known as the *relevant range* by a straight line. The **relevant range** is the range of activity within which the assumption that cost behavior is strictly linear is reasonably valid. Outside of the relevant range, a fixed cost may no longer be strictly fixed or a variable cost may not be strictly variable. Managers should always keep in mind that assumptions made about cost behavior may be invalid if activity falls outside of the relevant range.

The concept of the relevant range is important in understanding fixed costs. For example, suppose the Mayo Clinic rents a machine for $20,000 per month that tests blood samples for the presence of leukemia cells. Furthermore, suppose that the capacity of the leukemia diagnostic machine is 3,000 tests per month. The assumption that the rent for the diagnostic machine is $20,000 per month is only valid within the relevant range of 0 to 3,000 tests per month. If the Mayo Clinic needed to test 5,000 blood samples per month, then it would need to rent another machine for an additional $20,000 per month. It would be difficult to rent half of a diagnostic machine; therefore, the step pattern depicted in Exhibit 2–3 is typical for such costs. This exhibit shows that the fixed rental expense is $20,000 for a relevant range of 0 to 3,000 tests. The fixed rental expense increases to $40,000 within the relevant range of 3,001 to 6,000 tests. The rental expense increases in discrete steps or increments of 3,000 tests, rather than increasing in a linear fashion per test.

This step-oriented cost behavior pattern can also be used to describe other costs, such as some labor costs. For example, salaried employee expenses can be characterized using a step pattern. Salaried employees are paid a fixed amount, such as $40,000 per year, for providing the capacity to work a prespecified amount of time, such as 40 hours per week for 50 weeks a year (= 2,000 hours per year). In this example, the total salaried employee expense is $40,000 within a relevant range of 0 to 2,000 hours of work. The total salaried employee expense increases to $80,000 (or two employees) if the organization's work requirements expand to a relevant range of 2,001 to 4,000 hours of work. Cost behavior patterns such as salaried employees are often called *step-variable costs*. Step-variable costs can often be adjusted quickly as conditions change. Furthermore, the width of the steps for step-variable costs is generally so narrow that these costs can be treated essentially as variable costs for most purposes. The width of the steps for fixed costs, on the other hand, is so wide that these costs should be treated as entirely fixed within the relevant range.

EXHIBIT 2–3
Fixed Costs and the Relevant Range

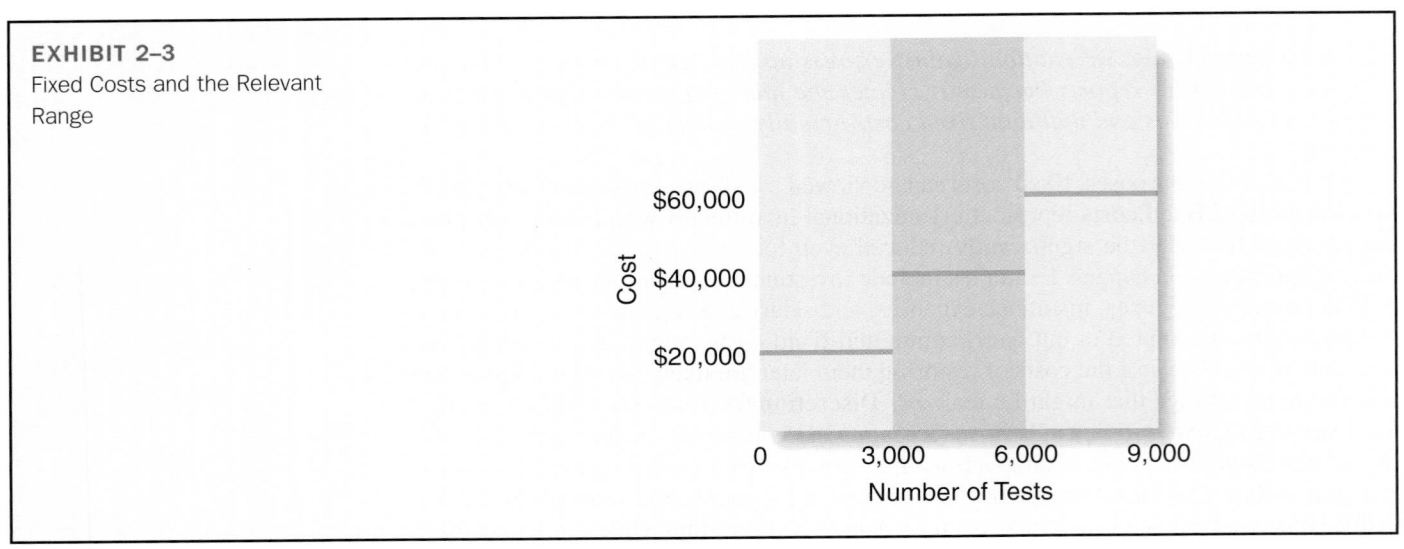

EXHIBIT 2–4

Summary of Variable and Fixed Cost Behavior

	Behavior of the Cost (within the relevant range)	
Cost	**In Total**	**Per Unit**
Variable cost	Total variable cost increases and decreases in proportion to changes in the activity level	Variable cost per unit remains constant
Fixed cost	Total fixed cost is not affected by changes in the activity level within the relevant range	Fixed cost per unit decreases as the activity level rises and increases as the activity level falls

Exhibit 2–4 summarizes four key concepts related to variable and fixed costs. Study it carefully before reading further.

HOW MANY GUIDES?

Majestic Ocean Kayaking, of Ucluelet, British Columbia, is owned and operated by Tracy Morben-Eeftink. The company offers a number of guided kayaking excursions ranging from three-hour tours of the Ucluelet harbor to six-day kayaking and camping trips in Clayoquot Sound. One of the company's excursions is a four-day kayaking and camping trip to The Broken Group Islands in the Pacific Rim National Park. Special regulations apply to trips in the park—including a requirement that one certified guide must be assigned for every five guests or fraction thereof. For example, a trip with 12 guests must have at least three certified guides. Guides are not salaried and are paid on a per-day basis. Therefore, the cost to the company of the guides for a trip is a step-variable cost rather than a fixed cost or a strictly variable cost. One guide is needed for 1 to 5 guests, two guides for 6 to 10 guests, three guides for 11 to 15 guests, and so on.

Sources: Tracy Morben-Eeftink, owner, Majestic Ocean Kayaking. For more information about the company, see www.oceankayaking.com.

Mixed Costs

A **mixed cost** contains both variable and fixed cost elements. Mixed costs are also known as semivariable costs. To continue the Nooksack Expeditions example, the company incurs a mixed cost called fees paid to the state. It includes a license fee of $25,000 per year plus $3 per rafting party paid to the state's Department of Natural Resources. If the company runs 1,000 rafting parties this year, then the total fees paid to the state would be $28,000, made up of $25,000 in fixed cost plus $3,000 in variable cost. Exhibit 2–5 depicts the behavior of this mixed cost.

Even if Nooksack fails to attract any customers, the company will still have to pay the license fee of $25,000. This is why the cost line in Exhibit 2–5 intersects the vertical cost axis at the $25,000 point. For each rafting party the company organizes, the total cost of the state fees will increase by $3. Therefore, the total cost line slopes upward as the variable cost of $3 per party is added to the fixed cost of $25,000 per year.

Because the mixed cost in Exhibit 2–5 is represented by a straight line, the next equation for a straight line can be used to express the relationship between a mixed cost and the level of activity.

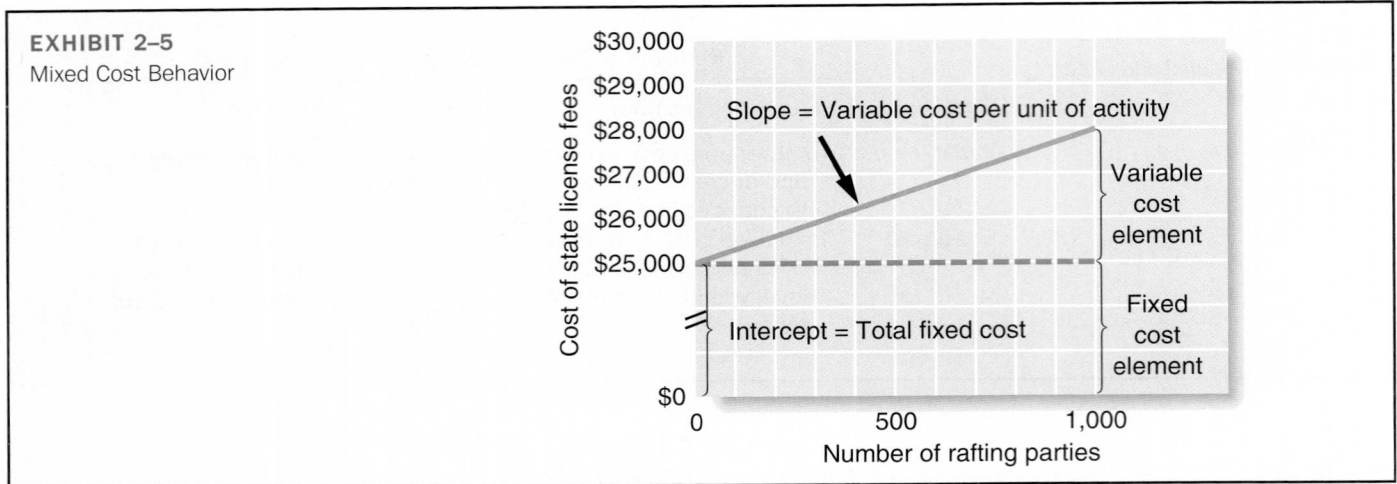

EXHIBIT 2–5
Mixed Cost Behavior

$$Y = a + bX$$

In this equation,

Y = The total mixed cost

a = The total fixed cost (the vertical intercept of the line)

b = The variable cost per unit of activity (the slope of the line)

X = The level of activity

Because the variable cost per unit equals the slope of the straight line, the steeper the slope, the higher the variable cost per unit.

In the case of the state fees paid by Nooksack Expeditions, the equation is written as follows:

$$Y = \$25,000 + \$3.00X$$

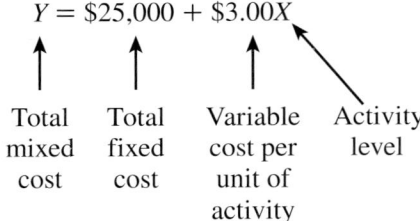

Total	Total	Variable	Activity
mixed	fixed	cost per	level
cost	cost	unit of	
		activity	

This equation makes it easy to calculate the total mixed cost for any level of activity within the relevant range. For example, suppose that the company expects to organize 800 rafting parties in the next year. The total state fees would be calculated as follows:

$$Y = \$25,000 + (\$3.00 \text{ per rafting party} \times 800 \text{ rafting parties})$$

$$= \$27,400$$

The Analysis of Mixed Costs

Mixed costs are very common. For example, the overall cost of providing X-ray services to patients at the Harvard Medical School Hospital is a mixed cost. The costs of equipment depreciation and radiologists' and technicians' salaries are fixed, but the costs of X-ray film, power, and supplies are variable. At Southwest Airlines, maintenance costs are a mixed cost. The company incurs fixed costs for renting maintenance facilities and for keeping skilled mechanics on the payroll, but the costs of replacement parts, lubricating oils, tires, and so forth, are variable with respect to how often and how far the company's aircraft are flown.

The fixed portion of a mixed cost represents the minimum cost of having a service *ready and available* for use. The variable portion represents the cost incurred for *actual consumption* of the service, thus it varies in proportion to the amount of service actually consumed.

Managers can use a variety of methods to estimate the fixed and variable components of a mixed cost such as *account analysis,* the *engineering approach,* the *high-low method,* and *least-squares regression analysis.* In **account analysis**, an account is classified as either variable or fixed based on the analyst's prior knowledge of how the cost in the account behaves. For example, direct materials would be classified as variable and a building lease cost would be classified as fixed because of the nature of those costs. The **engineering approach** to cost analysis involves a detailed analysis of what cost behavior should be, based on an industrial engineer's evaluation of the production methods to be used, the materials specifications, labor requirements, equipment usage, production efficiency, power consumption, and so on.

The high-low and least-squares regression methods estimate the fixed and variable elements of a mixed cost by analyzing past records of cost and activity data. We will use an example from Brentline Hospital to illustrate the high-low method calculations and to compare the resulting high-low method cost estimates to those obtained using least-squares regression. Appendix 2A demonstrates how to use Microsoft Excel to perform least-squares regression computations.

Diagnosing Cost Behavior with a Scattergraph Plot

Assume that Brentline Hospital is interested in predicting future monthly maintenance costs for budgeting purposes. The senior management team believes that maintenance cost is a mixed cost and that the variable portion of this cost is driven by the number of patient-days. Each day a patient is in the hospital counts as one patient-day. The hospital's chief financial officer gathered the following data for the most recent seven-month period:

LEARNING OBJECTIVE 2–5
Analyze a mixed cost using a scattergraph plot and the high-low method.

Month	Activity Level: Patient-Days	Maintenance Cost Incurred
January	5,600	$7,900
February	7,100	$8,500
March	5,000	$7,400
April	6,500	$8,200
May	7,300	$9,100
June	8,000	$9,800
July	6,200	$7,800

The first step in applying the high-low method or the least-squares regression method is to diagnose cost behavior with a scattergraph plot. The scattergraph plot of maintenance costs versus patient-days at Brentline Hospital is shown in Exhibit 2–6. Two things should be noted about this scattergraph:

1. The total maintenance cost, *Y,* is plotted on the vertical axis. Cost is known as the **dependent variable** because the amount of cost incurred during a period depends on the level of activity for the period. (That is, as the level of activity increases, total cost will also ordinarily increase.)
2. The activity, *X* (patient-days in this case), is plotted on the horizontal axis. Activity is known as the **independent variable** because it causes variations in the cost.

From the scattergraph plot, it is evident that maintenance costs do increase with the number of patient-days in an approximately *linear* fashion. In other words, the points lie more or less along a straight line that slopes upward and to the right. Cost behavior is considered **linear** whenever a straight line is a reasonable approximation for the relation between cost and activity.

EXHIBIT 2–6
Scattergraph Method of Cost
Analysis

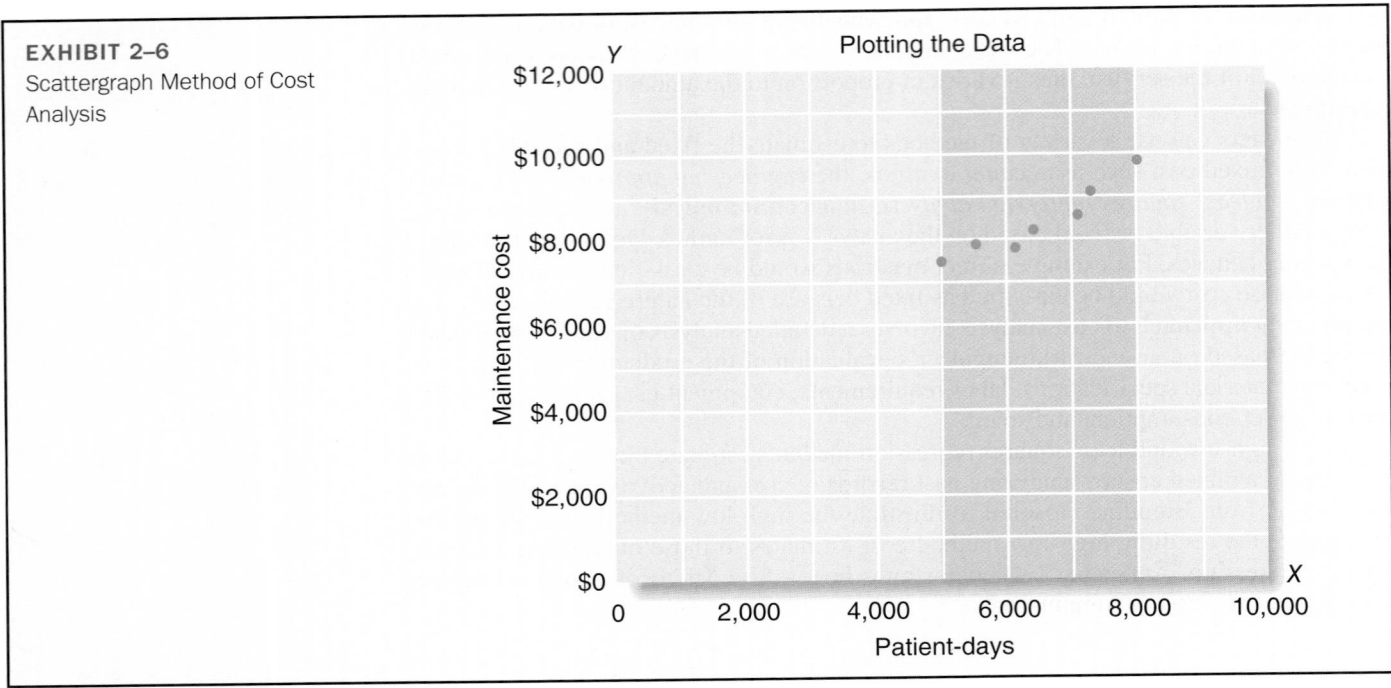

Plotting the data on a scattergraph is an essential diagnostic step that should be performed before performing the high-low method or least-squares regression calculations. If the scattergraph plot reveals linear cost behavior, then it makes sense to perform the high-low or least-squares regression calculations to separate the mixed cost into its variable and fixed components. If the scattergraph plot does not depict linear cost behavior, then it makes no sense to proceed any further in analyzing the data.

The High–Low Method

Assuming that the scattergraph plot indicates a linear relation between cost and activity, the fixed and variable cost elements of a mixed cost can be estimated using the *high-low method* or the *least-squares regression method.* The high-low method is based on the rise-over-run formula for the slope of a straight line. As previously discussed, if the relation between cost and activity can be represented by a straight line, then the slope of the straight line is equal to the variable cost per unit of activity. Consequently, the following formula can be used to estimate the variable cost:

$$\text{Variable cost} = \text{Slope of the line} = \frac{\text{Rise}}{\text{Run}} = \frac{Y_2 - Y_1}{X_2 - X_1}$$

To analyze mixed costs with the **high-low method**, begin by identifying the period with the lowest level of activity and the period with the highest level of activity. The period with the lowest activity is selected as the first point in the above formula and the period with the highest activity is selected as the second point. Consequently, the formula becomes:

$$\text{Variable cost} = \frac{Y_2 - Y_1}{X_2 - X_1} = \frac{\text{Cost at the high activity level} - \text{Cost at the low activity level}}{\text{High activity level} - \text{Low activity level}}$$

or

$$\text{Variable cost} = \frac{\text{Change in cost}}{\text{Change in activity}}$$

Therefore, when the high-low method is used, the variable cost is estimated by dividing the difference in cost between the high and low levels of activity by the change in activity between those two points.

To return to the Brentline Hospital example, using the high-low method, we first identify the periods with the highest and lowest *activity*—in this case, June and March. We then use the activity and cost data from these two periods to estimate the variable cost component as follows:

	Patient-Days	Maintenance Cost Incurred
High activity level (June)	8,000	$9,800
Low activity level (March)	5,000	7,400
Change	3,000	$2,400

$$\text{Variable cost} = \frac{\text{Change in cost}}{\text{Change in activity}} = \frac{\$2,400}{3,000 \ \text{patient-days}} = \$0.80 \ \text{per patient-day}$$

Having determined that the variable maintenance cost is 80 cents per patient-day, we can now determine the amount of fixed cost. This is done by taking the total cost at *either* the high or the low activity level and deducting the variable cost element. In the computation below, total cost at the high activity level is used in computing the fixed cost element:

Fixed cost element = Total cost − Variable cost element

$$= \$9,800 - (\$0.80 \ \text{per patient-day} \times 8,000 \ \text{patient-days})$$

$$= \$3,400$$

Both the variable and fixed cost elements have now been isolated. The cost of maintenance can be expressed as $3,400 per month plus 80 cents per patient-day or as:

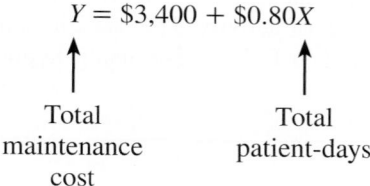

$$Y = \$3,400 + \$0.80X$$

Total maintenance cost	Total patient-days

The data used in this illustration are shown graphically in Exhibit 2–7. Notice that a straight line has been drawn through the points corresponding to the low and high levels of activity. In essence, that is what the high-low method does—it draws a straight line through those two points.

Sometimes the high and low levels of activity don't coincide with the high and low amounts of cost. For example, the period that has the highest level of activity may not have the highest amount of cost. Nevertheless, the costs at the highest and lowest levels of *activity* are always used to analyze a mixed cost under the high-low method. The reason is that the analyst would like to use data that reflect the greatest possible variation in activity.

The high-low method is very simple to apply, but it suffers from a major (and sometimes critical) defect—it utilizes only two data points. Generally, two data points are not enough to produce accurate results. Additionally, the periods with the highest and lowest activity tend to be unusual. A cost formula that is estimated solely using data from these unusual periods may misrepresent the true cost behavior during normal periods. Such a distortion is evident in Exhibit 2–7. The straight line should probably be shifted down somewhat so that it is closer to more of the data points. For these reasons, least-squares regression will generally be more accurate than the high-low method.

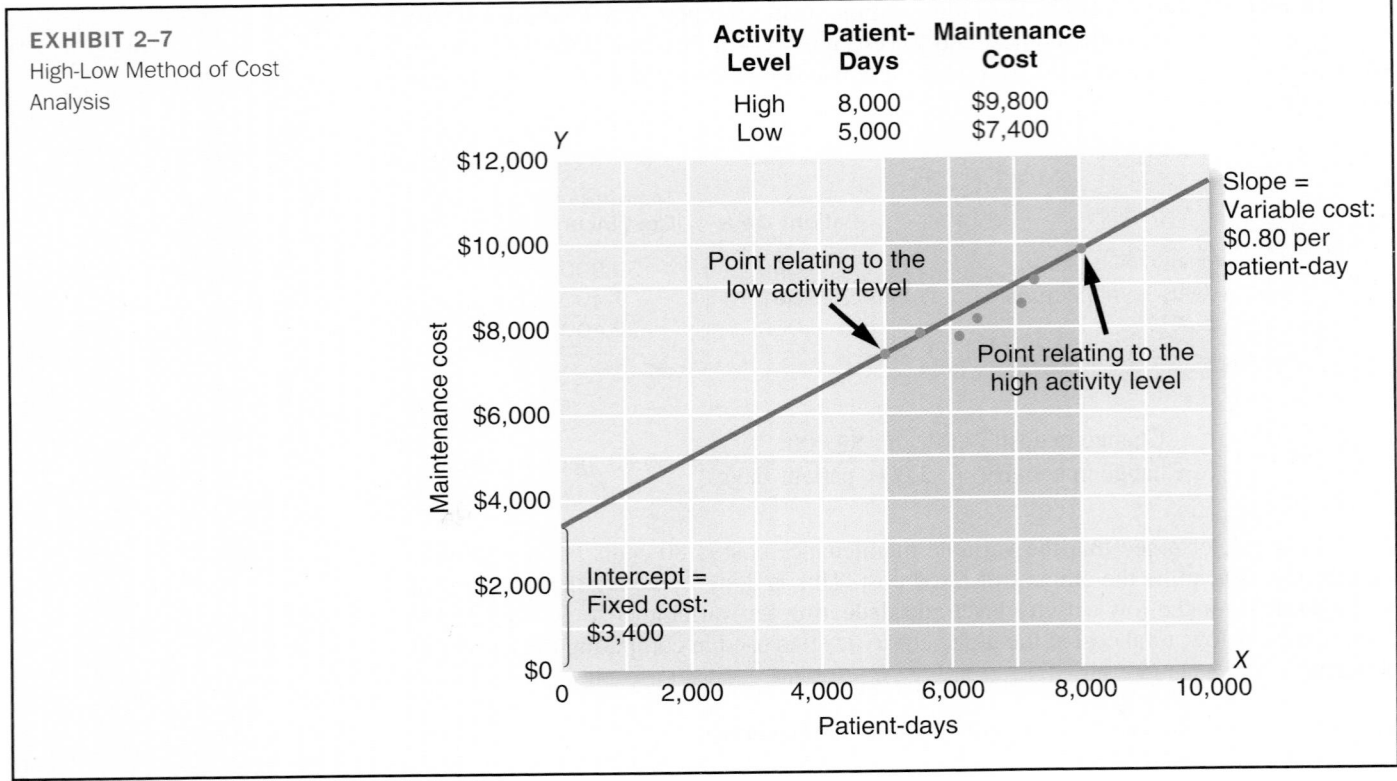

EXHIBIT 2–7
High-Low Method of Cost
Analysis

Activity Level	Patient-Days	Maintenance Cost
High	8,000	$9,800
Low	5,000	$7,400

Slope = Variable cost: $0.80 per patient-day

Point relating to the low activity level

Point relating to the high activity level

Intercept = Fixed cost: $3,400

Maintenance cost

Patient-days

The Least–Squares Regression Method

The **least-squares regression method**, unlike the high-low method, uses all of the data to separate a mixed cost into its fixed and variable components. A *regression line* of the form $Y = a + bX$ is fitted to the data, where a represents the total fixed cost and b represents the variable cost per unit of activity. The basic idea underlying the least-squares regression method is illustrated in Exhibit 2–8 using hypothetical data points. Notice

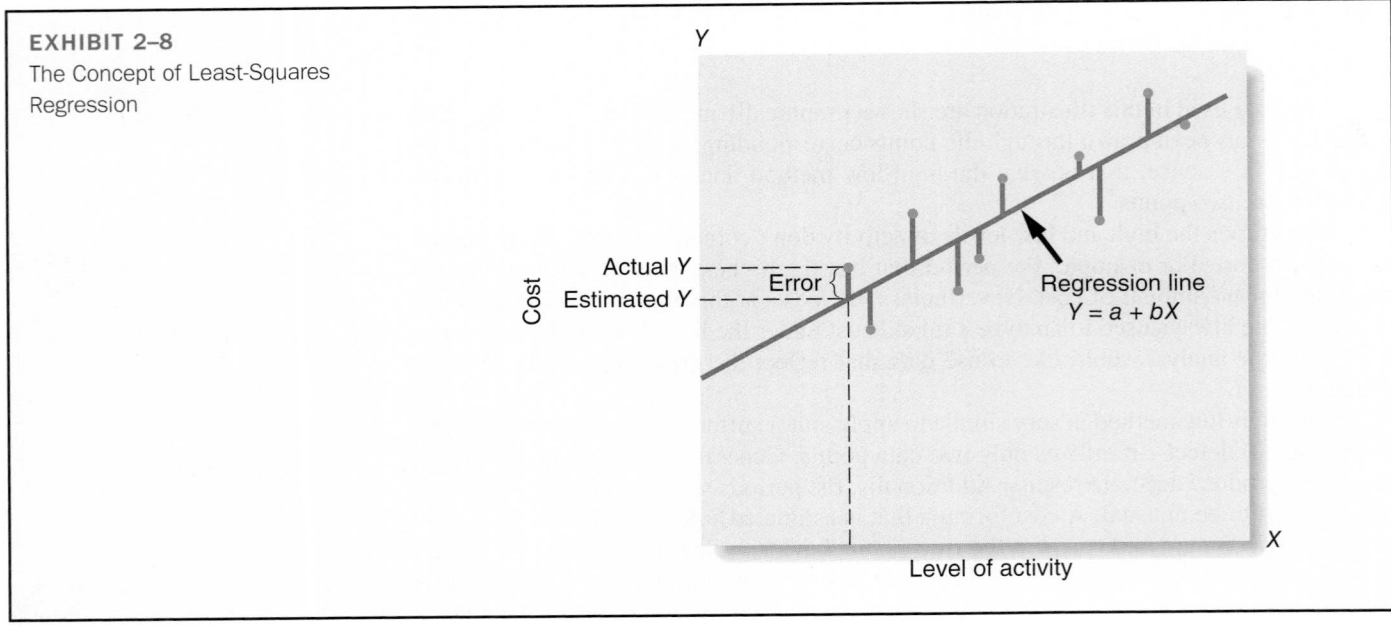

EXHIBIT 2–8
The Concept of Least-Squares
Regression

Actual Y
Estimated Y
Error

Regression line
$Y = a + bX$

Cost

Level of activity

from the exhibit that the deviations from the plotted points to the regression line are measured vertically on the graph. These vertical deviations are called the regression errors. There is nothing mysterious about the least-squares regression method. It simply computes the regression line that minimizes the sum of these squared errors. The formulas that accomplish this are fairly complex and involve numerous calculations, but the principle is simple.

Fortunately, computers are adept at carrying out the computations required by the least-squares regression formulas. The data—the observed values of X and Y—are entered into the computer, and software does the rest. In the case of the Brentline Hospital maintenance cost data, a statistical software package on a personal computer can calculate the following least-squares regression estimates of the total fixed cost (a) and the variable cost per unit of activity (b):

$$a = \$3,431$$

$$b = \$0.759$$

Therefore, using the least-squares regression method, the fixed element of the maintenance cost is $3,431 per month and the variable portion is 75.9 cents per patient-day.

In terms of the linear equation $Y = a + bX$, the cost formula can be written as

$$Y = \$3,431 + \$0.759X$$

where activity (X) is expressed in patient-days.

Appendix 2A discusses how to use Microsoft Excel to perform least-squares regression calculations. For now, you only need to understand that least-squares regression analysis generally provides more accurate cost estimates than the high-low method because, rather than relying on just two data points, it uses all of the data points to fit a line that minimizes the sum of the squared errors. The table below compares Brentline Hospital's cost estimates using the high-low method and the least-squares regression method:

	High-Low Method	Least-Squares Regression Method
Variable cost estimate per patient-day..........	$0.800	$0.759
Fixed cost estimate per month.................	$3,400	$3,431

When Brentline uses the least-squares regression method to create a straight line that minimizes the sum of the squared errors, it results in estimated fixed costs that are $31 higher than the amount derived using the high-low method. It also decreases the slope of the straight line resulting in a lower variable cost estimate of $0.759 per patient-day rather than $0.80 per patient-day as derived using the high-low method.

THE ZIPCAR COMES TO COLLEGE CAMPUSES

Zipcar is a car sharing service based in Cambridge, Massachusetts. The company serves 13 cities and 120 university campuses. Members pay a $50 annual fee plus $7 an hour to rent a car. They can use their iPhones to rent a car, locate it in the nearest Zipcar parking lot, unlock it using an access code, and drive it off the lot. This mixed cost arrangement is attractive to customers who need a car infrequently and wish to avoid the large cash outlay that comes with buying or leasing a vehicle.

Source: Jefferson Graham, "An iPhone Gets Zipcar Drivers on Their Way," USA Today, September 30, 2009, p. 3B.

© Michael Philip O'Malley/Flickr RF/ Getty Images, RF

Chapter 2

Traditional and Contribution Format Income Statements

LEARNING OBJECTIVE 2–6
Prepare income statements for a merchandising company using the traditional and contribution formats.

In this section of the chapter, we discuss how to prepare traditional and contribution format income statements for a merchandising company.[3] Merchandising companies do not manufacture the products that they sell to customers. For example, Lowe's and Home Depot are merchandising companies because they buy finished products from manufacturers and then resell them to end consumers.

The Traditional Format Income Statement

Traditional income statements are prepared primarily for external reporting purposes. The left-hand side of Exhibit 2–9 shows a traditional income statement format for merchandising companies. This type of income statement organizes costs into two categories—cost of goods sold and selling and administrative expenses. Sales minus cost of goods sold equals the *gross margin*. The gross margin minus selling and administrative expenses equals net operating income.

The cost of goods sold reports the *product costs* attached to the merchandise sold during the period. The selling and administrative expenses report all *period costs* that have been expensed as incurred. The cost of goods sold for a merchandising company can be computed directly by multiplying the number of units sold by their unit cost or indirectly using the equation below:

$$\text{Cost of goods sold} = \text{Beginning merchandise inventory} + \text{Purchases} - \text{Ending merchandise inventory}$$

For example, let's assume that the company depicted in Exhibit 2–9 purchased $3,000 of merchandise inventory during the period and had beginning and ending merchandise inventory balances of $7,000 and $4,000, respectively. The equation above could be used to compute the cost of goods sold as follows:

EXHIBIT 2–9
Comparing Traditional and Contribution Format Income Statements for Merchandising Companies (all numbers are given)

Traditional Format			Contribution Format		
Sales		$12,000	Sales		$12,000
Cost of goods sold*		6,000	Variable expenses:		
Gross margin		6,000	Cost of goods sold	$6,000	
Selling and administrative expenses:			Variable selling	600	
Selling	$3,100		Variable administrative	400	7,000
Administrative	1,900	5,000	Contribution margin		5,000
Net operating income		$ 1,000	Fixed expenses:		
			Fixed selling	2,500	
			Fixed administrative	1,500	4,000
			Net operating income		$ 1,000

*For a manufacturing company, the cost of goods sold would include some variable costs, such as direct materials, direct labor, and variable overhead, and some fixed costs, such as fixed manufacturing overhead. Income statement formats for manufacturing companies will be explored in greater detail in a subsequent chapter.

---

[3] Subsequent chapters compare the income statement formats for manufacturing companies.

$$\text{Cost of goods sold} = \text{Beginning merchandise inventory} + \text{Purchases} - \text{Ending merchandise inventory}$$

$$= \$7{,}000 + \$3{,}000 - \$4{,}000$$

$$= \$6{,}000$$

Although the traditional income statement is useful for external reporting purposes, it has serious limitations when used for internal purposes. It does not distinguish between fixed and variable costs. For example, under the heading "Selling and administrative expenses," both variable administrative costs ($400) and fixed administrative costs ($1,500) are lumped together ($1,900). Internally, managers need cost data organized by cost behavior to aid in planning, controlling, and decision making. The contribution format income statement has been developed in response to these needs.

The Contribution Format Income Statement

The crucial distinction between fixed and variable costs is at the heart of the **contribution approach** to constructing income statements. The unique thing about the contribution approach is that it provides managers with an income statement that clearly distinguishes between fixed and variable costs and therefore aids planning, controlling, and decision making. The right-hand side of Exhibit 2–9 shows a contribution format income statement for merchandising companies.

The contribution approach separates costs into fixed and variable categories, first deducting variable expenses from sales to obtain the *contribution margin*. For a merchandising company, cost of goods sold is a variable cost that gets included in the "Variable expenses" portion of the contribution format income statement. The **contribution margin** is the amount remaining from sales revenues after variable expenses have been deducted. This amount *contributes* toward covering fixed expenses and then toward profits for the period.

The contribution format income statement is used as an internal planning and decision-making tool. Its emphasis on cost behavior aids cost-volume-profit analysis (such as we shall be doing in a subsequent chapter), management performance appraisals, and budgeting. Moreover, the contribution approach helps managers organize data pertinent to numerous decisions such as product-line analysis, pricing, use of scarce resources, and make or buy analysis. All of these topics are covered in later chapters.

Cost Classifications for Decision Making

Costs are an important feature of many business decisions. In making decisions, it is essential to have a firm grasp of the concepts *differential cost, opportunity cost,* and *sunk cost.*

LEARNING OBJECTIVE 2–7
Understand cost classifications used in making decisions: differential costs, opportunity costs, and sunk costs.

Differential Cost and Revenue

Decisions involve choosing between alternatives. In business decisions, each alternative will have costs and benefits that must be compared to the costs and benefits of the other available alternatives. A difference in costs between any two alternatives is known as a **differential cost**. A difference in revenues (usually just sales) between any two alternatives is known as **differential revenue**.

A differential cost is also known as an **incremental cost**, although technically an incremental cost should refer only to an increase in cost from one alternative to another; decreases in cost should be referred to as *decremental costs*. Differential cost is a broader term, encompassing both cost increases (incremental costs) and cost decreases (decremental costs) between alternatives.

The accountant's differential cost concept can be compared to the economist's marginal cost concept. In speaking of changes in cost and revenue, the economist uses the terms *marginal cost* and *marginal revenue*. The revenue that can be obtained from selling one more unit of product is called marginal revenue, and the cost involved in producing one more unit of product is called marginal cost. The economist's marginal concept is basically the same as the accountant's differential concept applied to a single unit of output.

Differential costs can be either fixed or variable. To illustrate, assume that Natural Cosmetics, Inc., is thinking about changing its marketing method from distribution through retailers to distribution by a network of neighborhood sales representatives. Present costs and revenues are compared to projected costs and revenues in the following table:

	Retailer Distribution (present)	Sales Representatives (proposed)	Differential Costs and Revenues
Sales (Variable).....................	$700,000	$800,000	$100,000
Cost of goods sold (Variable).........	350,000	400,000	50,000
Advertising (Fixed)...................	80,000	45,000	(35,000)
Commissions (Variable).............	0	40,000	40,000
Warehouse depreciation (Fixed)......	50,000	80,000	30,000
Other expenses (Fixed)...............	60,000	60,000	0
Total expenses......................	540,000	625,000	85,000
Net operating income	$160,000	$175,000	$ 15,000

According to the above analysis, the differential revenue is $100,000 and the differential costs total $85,000, leaving a positive differential net operating income of $15,000 in favor of using sales representatives.

In general, only the differences between alternatives are relevant in decisions. Those items that are the same under all alternatives and that are not affected by the decision can be ignored. For example, in the Natural Cosmetics, Inc., example above, the "Other expenses" category, which is $60,000 under both alternatives, can be ignored because it has no effect on the decision. If it were removed from the calculations, the sales representatives would still be preferred by $15,000. This is an extremely important principle in management accounting that we will revisit in later chapters.

Opportunity Cost and Sunk Cost

Opportunity cost is the potential benefit that is given up when one alternative is selected over another. For example, assume that you have a part-time job while attending college that pays $200 per week. If you spend one week at the beach during spring break without pay, then the $200 in lost wages would be an opportunity cost of taking the week off to be at the beach. Opportunity costs are not usually found in accounting records, but they are costs that must be explicitly considered in every decision a manager makes. Virtually every alternative involves an opportunity cost.

A **sunk cost** is a cost *that has already been incurred* and that cannot be changed by any decision made now or in the future. Because sunk costs cannot be changed by any decision, they are not differential costs. And because only differential costs are relevant in a decision, sunk costs should always be ignored.

To illustrate a sunk cost, assume that a company paid $50,000 several years ago for a special-purpose machine. The machine was used to make a product that is now obsolete and is no longer being sold. Even though in hindsight purchasing the machine may have been unwise, the $50,000 cost has already been incurred and cannot be undone. And it would be folly to continue making the obsolete product in a misguided attempt to "recover" the original cost of the machine. In short, the $50,000 originally paid for the machine is a sunk cost that should be ignored in current decisions.

THE ECONOMICS OF DRIVING YOUR DREAM CAR

The costs of buying, insuring, repairing, and garaging ultra-luxury vehicles can be very expensive. For example, the purchase price alone for a new Lamborghini or Bentley can easily exceed $300,000. Thus, Gotham Dream Cars offers an alternative to customers who want to drive ultra-luxury cars while avoiding the exorbitant costs of ownership. It sells fractional shares in luxury cars—the minimum price starts at $9,000 for 20 driving-days. George Johnson is a Gotham Dream Cars customer who spent $30,000 for 90 driving-days in two types of ultra-luxury vehicles. He noted that "it's not worth it to buy one of these cars when you have to fix them." In essence, Johnson compared the costs of ownership with the rental costs and decided to rent.

Source: David Kiley, "My Lamborghini—Today, Anyway," *BusinessWeek*, January 14, 2008, p. 17.

© AP Photo/Damian Dovarganes

Summary

In this chapter, we have discussed ways in which managers classify costs. How the costs will be used—for assigning costs to cost objects, preparing external reports, predicting cost behavior, or decision making—will dictate how the costs are classified.

For purposes of assigning costs to cost objects such as products or departments, costs are classified as direct or indirect. Direct costs can be conveniently traced to cost objects. Indirect costs cannot be conveniently traced to cost objects.

For external reporting purposes, costs are classified as either product costs or period costs. Product costs are assigned to inventories and are considered assets until the products are sold. At the point of sale, product costs become cost of goods sold on the income statement. In contrast, period costs are taken directly to the income statement as expenses in the period in which they are incurred.

For purposes of predicting how costs will react to changes in activity, costs are classified into three categories—variable, fixed, and mixed. Variable costs, in total, are strictly proportional to activity. The variable cost per unit is constant. Fixed costs, in total, remain the same as the activity level changes within the relevant range. The average fixed cost per unit decreases as the activity level increases. Mixed costs consist of variable and fixed elements and can be expressed in equation form as $Y = a + bX$, where X is the activity, Y is the total cost, a is the fixed cost element, and b is the variable cost per unit of activity.

If the relation between cost and activity appears to be linear based on a scattergraph plot, then the variable and fixed components of a mixed cost can be estimated using the high-low method, which implicitly draws a straight line through the points of lowest activity and highest activity, or the least-squares regression method, which uses all of the data points to compute a regression line that minimizes the sum of the squares errors.

The traditional income statement format is used primarily for external reporting purposes. It organizes costs using product and period cost classifications. The contribution format income statement aids decision making because it organizes costs using variable and fixed cost classifications.

For purposes of making decisions, the concepts of differential cost and revenue, opportunity cost, and sunk cost are vitally important. Differential costs and revenues are the costs and revenues that differ between alternatives. Opportunity cost is the benefit that is forgone when one alternative is selected over another. Sunk cost is a cost that occurred in the past and cannot be altered. Differential costs and opportunity costs should be carefully considered in decisions. Sunk costs are always irrelevant in decisions and should be ignored.

Review Problem 1: Cost Terms

Many new cost terms have been introduced in this chapter. It will take you some time to learn what each term means and how to properly classify costs in an organization. Consider the following example: Porter Company manufactures furniture, including tables. Selected costs are given below:

1. The tables are made of wood that costs $100 per table.
2. The tables are assembled by workers, at a wage cost of $40 per table.
3. Workers assembling the tables are supervised by a factory supervisor who is paid $38,000 per year.
4. Electrical costs are $2 per machine-hour. Four machine-hours are required to produce a table.
5. The depreciation on the machines used to make the tables totals $10,000 per year. The machines have no resale value and do not wear out through use.
6. The salary of the president of the company is $100,000 per year.
7. The company spends $250,000 per year to advertise its products.
8. Salespersons are paid a commission of $30 for each table sold.
9. Instead of producing the tables, the company could rent its factory space for $50,000 per year.

Required:

Classify these costs according to the various cost terms used in the chapter. *Carefully study the classification of each cost.* If you don't understand why a particular cost is classified the way it is, reread the section of the chapter discussing the particular cost term. The terms *variable cost* and *fixed cost* refer to how costs behave with respect to the number of tables produced in a year.

Solution to Review Problem 1

	Variable Cost	Fixed Cost	Period (Selling and Administrative) Cost	Product Cost — Direct Materials	Product Cost — Direct Labor	Product Cost — Manufacturing Overhead	Sunk Cost	Opportunity Cost
1. Wood used in a table ($100 per table).........	X			X				
2. Labor cost to assemble a table ($40 per table) ...	X				X			
3. Salary of the factory supervisor ($38,000 per year)		X				X		
4. Cost of electricity to produce tables ($2 per machine-hour)...........	X					X		
5. Depreciation of machines used to produce tables ($10,000 per year)		X				X	X*	
6. Salary of the company president ($100,000 per year)		X	X					
7. Advertising expense ($250,000 per year)		X	X					
8. Commissions paid to salespersons ($30 per table sold)	X		X					
9. Rental income forgone on factory space...........								X†

*This is a sunk cost because the outlay for the equipment was made in a previous period.

†This is an opportunity cost because it represents the potential benefit that is lost or sacrificed as a result of using the factory space to produce tables. Opportunity cost is a special category of cost that is not ordinarily recorded in an organization's accounting records. To avoid possible confusion with other costs, we will not attempt to classify this cost in any other way except as an opportunity cost.

Review Problem 2: High-Low Method

The administrator of Azalea Hills Hospital would like a cost formula linking the administrative costs involved in admitting patients to the number of patients admitted during a month. The Admitting Department's costs and the number of patients admitted during the immediately preceding eight months are given in the following table:

Month	Number of Patients Admitted	Admitting Department Costs
May.................	1,800	$14,700
June................	1,900	$15,200
July................	1,700	$13,700
August.............	1,600	$14,000
September..........	1,500	$14,300
October............	1,300	$13,100
November...........	1,100	$12,800
December..........	1,500	$14,600

Required:
1. Use the high-low method to estimate the fixed and variable components of admitting costs.
2. Express the fixed and variable components of admitting costs as a cost formula in the form $Y = a + bX$.

Solution to Review Problem 2

1. The first step in the high-low method is to identify the periods of the lowest and highest activity. Those periods are November (1,100 patients admitted) and June (1,900 patients admitted).

   The second step is to compute the variable cost per unit using those two data points:

Month	Number of Patients Admitted	Admitting Department Costs
High activity level (June).............	1,900	$15,200
Low activity level (November).........	1,100	12,800
Change...........................	800	$ 2,400

$$\text{Variable cost} = \frac{\text{Change in cost}}{\text{Change in activity}} = \frac{\$2,400}{800 \text{ patients admitted}} = \$3 \text{ per patient admitted}$$

The third step is to compute the fixed cost element by deducting the variable cost element from the total cost at either the high or low activity. In the computation below, the high point of activity is used:

Fixed cost element = Total cost − Variable cost element

= $15,200 − ($3 per patient admitted × 1,900 patients admitted)

= $9,500

2. The cost formula is $Y = \$9,500 + \$3X$.

Glossary

Account analysis A method for analyzing cost behavior in which an account is classified as either variable or fixed based on the analyst's prior knowledge of how the cost in the account behaves. (p. 35)

Activity base A measure of whatever causes the incurrence of a variable cost. For example, the total cost of X-ray film in a hospital will increase as the number of X-rays taken increases. Therefore, the number of X-rays is the activity base that explains the total cost of X-ray film. (p. 29)

Administrative costs All executive, organizational, and clerical costs associated with the general management of an organization rather than with manufacturing or selling. (p. 26)

Committed fixed costs Investments in facilities, equipment, and basic organizational structure that can't be significantly reduced even for short periods of time without making fundamental changes. (p. 31)

Common cost A cost that is incurred to support a number of cost objects but that cannot be traced to them individually. For example, the wage cost of the pilot of a 747 airliner is a common cost of all of the passengers on the aircraft. Without the pilot, there would be no flight and no passengers. But no part of the pilot's wage is caused by any one passenger taking the flight. (p. 25)

Contribution approach An income statement format that organizes costs by their behavior. Costs are separated into variable and fixed categories rather than being separated into product and period costs for external reporting purposes. (p. 41)

Contribution margin The amount remaining from sales revenues after all variable expenses have been deducted. (p. 41)

Conversion cost Direct labor cost plus manufacturing overhead cost. (p. 28)

Cost behavior The way in which a cost reacts to changes in the level of activity. (p. 29)

Cost object Anything for which cost data are desired. Examples of cost objects are products, customers, jobs, and parts of the organization such as departments or divisions. (p. 24)

Cost structure The relative proportion of fixed, variable, and mixed costs in an organization. (p. 29)

Dependent variable A variable that responds to some causal factor; total cost is the dependent variable, as represented by the letter Y, in the equation $Y = a + bX$. (p. 35)

Differential cost A difference in cost between two alternatives. Also see *Incremental cost*. (p. 41)

Differential revenue The difference in revenue between two alternatives. (p. 41)

Direct cost A cost that can be easily and conveniently traced to a specified cost object. (p. 24)

Direct labor Factory labor costs that can be easily traced to individual units of product. Also called *touch labor*. (p. 25)

Direct materials Materials that become an integral part of a finished product and whose costs can be conveniently traced to it. (p. 25)

Discretionary fixed costs Those fixed costs that arise from annual decisions by management to spend on certain fixed cost items, such as advertising and research. (p. 31)

Engineering approach A detailed analysis of cost behavior based on an industrial engineer's evaluation of the inputs that are required to carry out a particular activity and of the prices of those inputs. (p. 35)

Fixed cost A cost that remains constant, in total, regardless of changes in the level of activity within the relevant range. If a fixed cost is expressed on a per unit basis, it varies inversely with the level of activity. (p. 30)

High-low method A method of separating a mixed cost into its fixed and variable elements by analyzing the change in cost between the high and low activity levels. (p. 36)

Incremental cost An increase in cost between two alternatives. Also see *Differential cost*. (p. 41)

Independent variable A variable that acts as a causal factor; activity is the independent variable, as represented by the letter X, in the equation $Y = a + bX$. (p. 35)

Indirect cost A cost that cannot be easily and conveniently traced to a specified cost object. (p. 25)

Indirect labor The labor costs of janitors, supervisors, materials handlers, and other factory workers that cannot be conveniently traced to particular products. (p. 26)

Indirect materials Small items of material such as glue and nails that may be an integral part of a finished product, but whose costs cannot be easily or conveniently traced to it. (p. 25)

Inventoriable costs Synonym for product costs. (p. 27)

Least-squares regression method A method of separating a mixed cost into its fixed and variable elements by fitting a regression line that minimizes the sum of the squared errors. (p. 38)

Linear cost behavior Cost behavior is said to be linear whenever a straight line is a reasonable approximation for the relation between cost and activity. (p. 35)

Manufacturing overhead All manufacturing costs except direct materials and direct labor. (p. 26)

Mixed cost A cost that contains both variable and fixed cost elements. (p. 33)

Opportunity cost The potential benefit that is given up when one alternative is selected over another. (p. 42)

Period costs Costs that are taken directly to the income statement as expenses in the period in which they are incurred or accrued. (p. 27)

Prime cost Direct materials cost plus direct labor cost. (p. 28)

Product costs All costs that are involved in acquiring or making a product. In the case of manu-factured goods, these costs consist of direct materials, direct labor, and manufacturing over-head. Also see *Inventoriable costs*. (p. 27)

Raw materials Any materials that go into the final product. (p. 25)

Relevant range The range of activity within which assumptions about variable and fixed cost behavior are valid. (p. 32)

Selling costs All costs that are incurred to secure customer orders and get the finished product or service into the hands of the customer. (p. 26)

Sunk cost A cost that has already been incurred and that cannot be changed by any decision made now or in the future. (p. 42)

Variable cost A cost that varies, in total, in direct proportion to changes in the level of activity. A variable cost is constant per unit. (p. 29)

Questions

2–1   What are the three major elements of product costs in a manufacturing company?
2–2   Define the following: (*a*) direct materials, (*b*) indirect materials, (*c*) direct labor, (*d*) indirect labor, and (*e*) manufacturing overhead.
2–3   Explain the difference between a product cost and a period cost.
2–4   Distinguish between (*a*) a variable cost, (*b*) a fixed cost, and (*c*) a mixed cost.
2–5   What effect does an increase in volume have on—
   a.   Unit fixed costs?
   b.   Unit variable costs?
   c.   Total fixed costs?
   d.   Total variable costs?
2–6   Define the following terms: (*a*) cost behavior and (*b*) relevant range.
2–7   What is meant by an *activity base* when dealing with variable costs? Give several exam-ples of activity bases.
2–8   Managers often assume a strictly linear relationship between cost and volume. How can this practice be defended in light of the fact that many costs are curvilinear?
2–9   Distinguish between discretionary fixed costs and committed fixed costs.
2–10 Does the concept of the relevant range apply to fixed costs? Explain.
2–11 What is the major disadvantage of the high-low method?
2–12 Give the general formula for a mixed cost. Which term represents the variable cost? The fixed cost?
2–13 What is meant by the term *least-squares regression?*
2–14 What is the difference between a contribution format income statement and a traditional format income statement?
2–15 What is the contribution margin?
2–16 Define the following terms: differential cost, opportunity cost, and sunk cost.
2–17 Only variable costs can be differential costs. Do you agree? Explain.

Multiple-choice questions are available with Connect.

Applying Excel

LEARNING OBJECTIVE 2–6

The Excel worksheet form that appears below is to be used to recreate Exhibit 2–9. Download the workbook from Connect, where you will also receive instructions about how to use this worksheet.

	A	B	C	D
1	Chapter 2: Applying Excel			
2				
3	**Data**			
4	Sales	$12,000		
5	Variable costs:			
6	Cost of goods sold	$6,000		
7	Variable selling	$600		
8	Variable administrative	$400		
9	Fixed costs:			
10	Fixed selling	$2,500		
11	Fixed administrative	$1,500		
12				
13	*Enter a formula into each of the cells marked with a ? below*			
14	**Exhibit 2-9**			
15				
16	**Traditional Format Income Statement**			
17	Sales		?	
18	Cost of goods sold		?	
19	Gross margin		?	
20	Selling and administrative expenses:			
21	Selling	?		
22	Administrative	?	?	
23	Net operating income		?	
24				
25	**Contribution Format Income Statement**			
26	Sales		?	
27	Variable expenses:			
28	Cost of goods sold	?		
29	Variable selling	?		
30	Variable administration	?	?	
31	Contribution margin		?	
32	Fixed expenses:			
33	Fixed selling	?		
34	Fixed administrative	?	?	
35	Net operating income		?	
36				

Chapter 2 Form   FIled in Chapter 2 Fo

Required:

1. Check your worksheet by changing the variable selling cost in the Data area to $900, keeping all of the other data the same as in Exhibit 2–9. If your worksheet is operating properly, the net operating income under the traditional format income statement and under the contribution format income statement should now be $700 and the contribution margin should now be $4,700. If you do not get these answers, find the errors in your worksheet and correct them.

    How much is the gross margin? Did it change? Why or why not?

2. Suppose that sales are 10% higher as shown below:

Sales....................................	$13,200
Variable costs:	
Cost of goods sold....................	$ 6,600
Variable selling........................	$ 990
Variable administrative	$ 440
Fixed costs:	
Fixed selling	$ 2,500
Fixed administrative..................	$ 1,500

Enter this new data into your worksheet. Make sure that you change all of the data that are different—not just the sales. Print or copy the income statements from your worksheet.

    What happened to the variable costs and to the fixed costs when sales increased by 10%? Why? Did the contribution margin increase by 10%? Why or why not? Did the net operating income increase by 10%? Why or why not?

The Foundational 15

Martinez Company's relevant range of production is 7,500 units to 12,500 units. When it produces and sells 10,000 units, its unit costs are as follows:

LEARNING OBJECTIVES 2–1, 2–2, 2–3, 2–4, 2–6, 2–7

	Amount Per Unit
Direct materials.........................	$6.00
Direct labor	$3.50
Variable manufacturing overhead.........	$1.50
Fixed manufacturing overhead	$4.00
Fixed selling expense	$3.00
Fixed administrative expense............	$2.00
Sales commissions......................	$1.00
Variable administrative expense	$0.50

Required:

1. For financial accounting purposes, what is the total amount of product costs incurred to make 10,000 units?
2. For financial accounting purposes, what is the total amount of period costs incurred to sell 10,000 units?
3. If 8,000 units are sold, what is the variable cost per unit sold?
4. If 12,500 units are sold, what is the variable cost per unit sold?
5. If 8,000 units are sold, what is the total amount of variable costs related to the units sold?
6. If 12,500 units are sold, what is the total amount of variable costs related to the units sold?
7. If 8,000 units are produced, what is the average fixed manufacturing cost per unit produced?
8. If 12,500 units are produced, what is the average fixed manufacturing cost per unit produced?
9. If 8,000 units are produced, what is the total amount of fixed manufacturing cost incurred to support this level of production?
10. If 12,500 units are produced, what is the total amount of fixed manufacturing cost incurred to support this level of production?
11. If 8,000 units are produced, what is the total amount of manufacturing overhead cost incurred to support this level of production? What is this total amount expressed on a per unit basis?
12. If 12,500 units are produced, what is the total amount of manufacturing overhead cost incurred to support this level of production? What is this total amount expressed on a per unit basis?
13. If the selling price is $22 per unit, what is the contribution margin per unit sold?
14. If 11,000 units are produced, what are the total amounts of direct and indirect manufacturing costs incurred to support this level of production?
15. What total incremental cost will Martinez incur if it increases production from 10,000 to 10,001 units?

  Exercises

EXERCISE 2–1 Identifying Direct and Indirect Costs [LO 2–1]

Northwest Hospital is a full-service hospital that provides everything from major surgery and emergency room care to outpatient clinics.

Required:

For each cost incurred at Northwest Hospital, indicate whether it would most likely be a direct cost or an indirect cost of the specified cost object by placing an X in the appropriate column.

Cost		Cost Object	Direct Cost	Indirect Cost
Ex.	Catered food served to patients	A particular patient	X	
1.	The wages of pediatric nurses	The pediatric department		
2.	Prescription drugs	A particular patient		
3.	Heating the hospital	The pediatric department		
4.	The salary of the head of pediatrics	The pediatric department		
5.	The salary of the head of pediatrics	A particular pediatric patient		
6.	Hospital chaplain's salary	A particular patient		
7.	Lab tests by outside contractor	A particular patient		
8.	Lab tests by outside contractor	A particular department		

EXERCISE 2–2 Classifying Manufacturing Costs [LO 2–2]

The PC Works assembles custom computers from components supplied by various manufacturers. The company is very small and its assembly shop and retail sales store are housed in a single facility in a Redmond, Washington, industrial park. Listed below are some of the costs that are incurred at the company.

Required:

For each cost, indicate whether it would most likely be classified as direct labor, direct materials, manufacturing overhead, selling, or an administrative cost.
1. The cost of a hard drive installed in a computer.
2. The cost of advertising in the *Puget Sound Computer User* newspaper.
3. The wages of employees who assemble computers from components.
4. Sales commissions paid to the company's salespeople.
5. The wages of the assembly shop's supervisor.
6. The wages of the company's accountant.
7. Depreciation on equipment used to test assembled computers before release to customers.
8. Rent on the facility in the industrial park.

EXERCISE 2–3 Classification of Costs as Product or Period Cost [LO 2–3]

Suppose that you have been given a summer job as an intern at Issac Aircams, a company that manufactures sophisticated spy cameras for remote-controlled military reconnaissance aircraft. The company, which is privately owned, has approached a bank for a loan to help it finance its growth. The bank requires financial statements before approving such a loan. You have been asked to help prepare the financial statements and were given the following list of costs:
 1. Depreciation on salespersons' cars.
 2. Rent on equipment used in the factory.
 3. Lubricants used for machine maintenance.
 4. Salaries of personnel who work in the finished goods warehouse.
 5. Soap and paper towels used by factory workers at the end of a shift.
 6. Factory supervisors' salaries.
 7. Heat, water, and power consumed in the factory.
 8. Materials used for boxing products for shipment overseas. (Units are not normally boxed.)
 9. Advertising costs.
10. Workers' compensation insurance for factory employees.
11. Depreciation on chairs and tables in the factory lunchroom.
12. The wages of the receptionist in the administrative offices.
13. Cost of leasing the corporate jet used by the company's executives.
14. The cost of renting rooms at a Florida resort for the annual sales conference.
15. The cost of packaging the company's product.

Required:

Classify the above costs as either product costs or period costs for the purpose of preparing the financial statements for the bank.

EXERCISE 2–4 Fixed and Variable Cost Behavior [LO 2–4]

Espresso Express operates a number of espresso coffee stands in busy suburban malls. The fixed weekly expense of a coffee stand is $1,200 and the variable cost per cup of coffee served is $0.22.

Required:

1. Fill in the following table with your estimates of total costs and cost per cup of coffee at the indicated levels of activity for a coffee stand. Round off the cost of a cup of coffee to the nearest tenth of a cent.

	Cups of Coffee Served in a Week		
	2,000	2,100	2,200
Fixed cost.....................................	?	?	?
Variable cost	?	?	?
Total cost	?	?	?
Average cost per cup of coffee served	?	?	?

2. Does the average cost per cup of coffee served increase, decrease, or remain the same as the number of cups of coffee served in a week increases? Explain.

EXERCISE 2–5 High-Low Method [LO 2–5]

The Cheyenne Hotel in Big Sky, Montana, has accumulated records of the total electrical costs of the hotel and the number of occupancy-days over the last year. An occupancy-day represents a room rented out for one day. The hotel's business is highly seasonal, with peaks occurring during the ski season and in the summer.

Month	Occupancy-Days	Electrical Costs
January	1,736	$4,127
February	1,904	$4,207
March.............	2,356	$5,083
April..............	960	$2,857
May	360	$1,871
June..............	744	$2,696
July...............	2,108	$4,670
August............	2,406	$5,148
September	840	$2,691
October...........	124	$1,588
November.........	720	$2,454
December.........	1,364	$3,529

Required:

1. Using the high-low method, estimate the fixed cost of electricity per month and the variable cost of electricity per occupancy-day. Round off the fixed cost to the nearest whole dollar and the variable cost to the nearest whole cent.
2. What other factors other than occupancy-days are likely to affect the variation in electrical costs from month to month?

EXERCISE 2–6 Traditional and Contribution Format Income Statements [LO 2–6]

Cherokee Inc. is a merchandiser that provided the following information:

	Amount
Number of units sold	20,000
Selling price per unit	$30
Variable selling expense per unit	$4
Variable administrative expense per unit.	$2
Total fixed selling expense	$40,000
Total fixed administrative expense	$30,000
Beginning merchandise inventory.	$24,000
Ending merchandise inventory	$44,000
Merchandise purchases	$180,000

Required:

1. Prepare a traditional income statement.
2. Prepare a contribution format income statement.

EXERCISE 2–7 Differential, Opportunity, and Sunk Costs [LO 2–7]

Northwest Hospital is a full-service hospital that provides everything from major surgery and emergency room care to outpatient clinics. The hospital's Radiology Department is considering replacing an old inefficient X-ray machine with a state-of-the-art digital X-ray machine. The new machine would provide higher quality X-rays in less time and at a lower cost per X-ray. It would also require less power and would use a color laser printer to produce easily readable X-ray images. Instead of investing the funds in the new X-ray machine, the Laboratory Department is lobbying the hospital's management to buy a new DNA analyzer.

Required:

For each of the items below, indicate by placing an *X* in the appropriate column whether it should be considered a differential cost, an opportunity cost, or a sunk cost in the decision to replace the old X-ray machine with a new machine. If none of the categories apply for a particular item, leave all columns blank.

Item	Differential Cost	Opportunity Cost	Sunk Cost
Ex. Cost of X-ray film used in the old machine.	X		
1. Cost of the old X-ray machine			
2. The salary of the head of the Radiology Department. . . .			
3. The salary of the head of the Pediatrics Department . . .			
4. Cost of the new color laser printer.			
5. Rent on the space occupied by Radiology.			
6. The cost of maintaining the old machine			
7. Benefits from a new DNA analyzer			
8. Cost of electricity to run the X-ray machines			

EXERCISE 2–8 Cost Behavior; High-Low Method [LO 2–4, LO 2–5]

Hoi Chong Transport, Ltd., operates a fleet of delivery trucks in Singapore. The company has determined that if a truck is driven 105,000 kilometers during a year, the average operating cost is 11.4 cents per kilometer. If a truck is driven only 70,000 kilometers during a year, the average operating cost increases to 13.4 cents per kilometer.

Required:

1. Using the high-low method, estimate the variable and fixed cost elements of the annual cost of the truck operation.
2. Express the variable and fixed costs in the form $Y = a + bX$.
3. If a truck were driven 80,000 kilometers during a year, what total cost would you expect to be incurred?

EXERCISE 2–9 Cost Terminology for Manufacturers [LO 2–2, LO 2–3]

Arden Company reported the following costs and expenses for the most recent month:

Direct materials.	$80,000
Direct labor	$42,000
Manufacturing overhead.	$19,000
Selling expenses	$22,000
Administrative expenses.	$35,000

Required:

1. What is the total amount of product costs?
2. What is the total amount of period costs?
3. What is the total amount of conversion costs?
4. What is the total amount of prime costs?

EXERCISE 2–10 Cost Behavior; Contribution Format Income Statement [LO 2–4, LO 2–6]

Harris Company manufactures and sells a single product. A partially completed schedule of the company's total and per unit costs over the relevant range of 30,000 to 50,000 units produced and sold annually is given below:

	Units Produced and Sold		
	30,000	40,000	50,000
Total costs:			
Variable costs	$180,000	?	?
Fixed costs.	300,000	?	?
Total costs	$480,000	?	?
Cost per unit:			
Variable cost	?	?	?
Fixed cost	?	?	?
Total cost per unit.	?	?	?

Required:

1. Complete the schedule of the company's total and unit costs above.
2. Assume that the company produces and sells 45,000 units during the year at a selling price of $16 per unit. Prepare a contribution format income statement for the year.

EXERCISE 2–11 High-Low Method; Scattergraph Analysis [LO 2–4, LO 2–5]

The following data relating to units shipped and total shipping expense have been assembled by Archer Company, a wholesaler of large, custom-built air-conditioning units for commercial buildings:

Month	Units Shipped	Total Shipping Expense
January.	3	$1,800
February.	6	$2,300
March	4	$1,700
April.	5	$2,000
May	7	$2,300
June	8	$2,700
July	2	$1,200

Required:

1. Prepare a scattergraph using the data given above. Plot cost on the vertical axis and activity on the horizontal axis. Is there an approximately linear relationship between shipping expense and the number of units shipped?

2. Using the high-low method, estimate the cost formula for shipping expense. Draw a straight line through the high and low data points shown in the scattergraph that you prepared in requirement 1. Make sure your line intersects the Y axis.
3. Comment on the accuracy of your high-low estimates assuming a least-squares regression analysis estimated the total fixed costs to be $910.71 per month and the variable cost to be $217.86 per unit. How would the straight line that you drew in requirement 2 differ from a straight line that minimizes the sum of the squared errors?
4. What factors, other than the number of units shipped, are likely to affect the company's shipping expense? Explain.

EXERCISE 2–12 Cost Classification [LO 2–2, LO 2–3, LO 2–4, LO 2–7]

Wollogong Group Ltd. of New South Wales, Australia, acquired its factory building about 10 years ago. For several years, the company has rented out a small annex attached to the rear of the building. The company has received a rental income of $30,000 per year on this space. The renter's lease will expire soon, and rather than renewing the lease, the company has decided to use the space itself to manufacture a new product.

Direct materials cost for the new product will total $80 per unit. To have a place to store finished units of product, the company will rent a small warehouse nearby. The rental cost will be $500 per month. In addition, the company must rent equipment for use in producing the new product; the rental cost will be $4,000 per month. Workers will be hired to manufacture the new product, with direct labor cost amounting to $60 per unit. The space in the annex will continue to be depreciated on a straight-line basis, as in prior years. This depreciation is $8,000 per year.

Advertising costs for the new product will total $50,000 per year. A supervisor will be hired to oversee production; her salary will be $1,500 per month. Electricity for operating machines will be $1.20 per unit. Costs of shipping the new product to customers will be $9 per unit.

To provide funds to purchase materials, meet payrolls, and so forth, the company will have to liquidate some temporary investments. These investments are presently yielding a return of about $3,000 per year.

Required:

Prepare an answer sheet with the following column headings:

Name of the Cost	Variable Cost	Fixed Cost	Product Cost			Period (Selling and Administrative) Cost	Opportunity Cost	Sunk Cost
			Direct Materials	Direct Labor	Manufacturing Overhead			

List the different costs associated with the new product decision down the extreme left column (under Name of the Cost). Then place an X under each heading that helps to describe the type of cost involved. There may be X's under several column headings for a single cost. (For example, a cost may be a fixed cost, a period cost, and a sunk cost; you would place an X under each of these column headings opposite the cost.)

EXERCISE 2–13 Traditional and Contribution Format Income Statements [LO 2–6]

The Alpine House, Inc., is a large retailer of snow skis. The company assembled the information shown below for the quarter ended March 31:

	Amount
Total sales revenue	$150,000
Selling price per pair of skis	$750
Variable selling expense per pair of skis	$50
Variable administrative expense per pair of skis	$10
Total fixed selling expense	$20,000
Total fixed administrative expense	$20,000
Beginning merchandise inventory	$30,000
Ending merchandise inventory	$40,000
Merchandise purchases	$100,000

Required:

1. Prepare a traditional income statement for the quarter ended March 31.
2. Prepare a contribution format income statement for the quarter ended March 31.
3. What was the contribution toward fixed expenses and profits for each pair of skis sold during the quarter? (State this figure in a single dollar amount per pair of skis.)

EXERCISE 2–14 High-Low Method; Predicting Cost [LO 2–4, LO 2–5]

The Lakeshore Hotel's guest-days of occupancy and custodial supplies expense over the last seven months were:

Month	Guest-Days of Occupancy	Custodial Supplies Expense
March	4,000	$7,500
April.	6,500	$8,250
May	8,000	$10,500
June	10,500	$12,000
July	12,000	$13,500
August	9,000	$10,750
September.	7,500	$9,750

Guest-days is a measure of the overall activity at the hotel. For example, a guest who stays at the hotel for three days is counted as three guest-days.

Required:

1. Using the high-low method, estimate a cost formula for custodial supplies expense.
2. Using the cost formula you derived above, what amount of custodial supplies expense would you expect to be incurred at an occupancy level of 11,000 guest-days?
3. Prepare a scattergraph using the data given above. Plot custodial supplies expense on the vertical axis and the number of guest-days occupied on the horizontal axis. Draw a straight line through the two data points that correspond to the high and low levels of activity. Make sure your line intersects the Y-axis.
4. Comment on the accuracy of your high-low estimates assuming a least-squares regression analysis estimated the total fixed costs to be $3,973.10 per month and the variable cost to be $0.77 per guest-day. How would the straight line that you drew in requirement 3 differ from a straight line that minimizes the sum of the squared errors?
5. Using the least-squares regression estimates given in requirement 4, what custodial supplies expense would you expect to be incurred at an occupancy level of 11,000 guest-days?

EXERCISE 2–15 Classification of Costs as Variable or Fixed and as Product or Period [LO 2–3, LO 2–4]

Below are listed various costs that are found in organizations.

1. Hamburger buns in a Wendy's outlet.
2. Advertising by a dental office.
3. Apples processed and canned by Del Monte.
4. Shipping canned apples from a Del Monte plant to customers.
5. Insurance on a Bausch & Lomb factory producing contact lenses.
6. Insurance on IBM's corporate headquarters.
7. Salary of a supervisor overseeing production of printers at Hewlett-Packard.
8. Commissions paid to automobile salespersons.
9. Depreciation of factory lunchroom facilities at a General Electric plant.
10. Steering wheels installed in BMWs.

Required:

Classify each cost as being either variable or fixed with respect to the number of units produced and sold. Also classify each cost as either a selling and administrative cost or a product cost. Prepare your answer sheet as shown below. Place an X in the appropriate columns to show the proper classification of each cost.

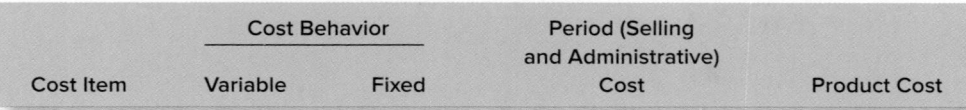

	Cost Behavior		Period (Selling and Administrative)	
Cost Item	Variable	Fixed	Cost	Product Cost

PROBLEM 2–16 Cost Behavior; High-Low Method; Contribution Format Income Statement [LO 2–4, LO 2–5, LO 2–6]

Morrisey & Brown, Ltd., of Sydney is a merchandising company that is the sole distributor of a product that is increasing in popularity among Australian consumers. The company's income statements for the three most recent months follow:

Morrisey & Brown, Ltd Income Statements For the Three Months Ended September 30			
	July	August	September
Sales in units	4,000	4,500	5,000
Sales.....................................	$400,000	$450,000	$500,000
Cost of goods sold........................	240,000	270,000	300,000
Gross margin	160,000	180,000	200,000
Selling and administrative expenses:			
Advertising expense	21,000	21,000	21,000
Shipping expense	34,000	36,000	38,000
Salaries and commissions................	78,000	84,000	90,000
Insurance expense	6,000	6,000	6,000
Depreciation expense......................	15,000	15,000	15,000
Total selling and administrative expenses......	154,000	162,000	170,000
Net operating income.....................	$ 6,000	$ 18,000	$ 30,000

Required:

1. Identify each of the company's expenses (including cost of goods sold) as either variable, fixed, or mixed.
2. Using the high-low method, separate each mixed expense into variable and fixed elements. State the cost formula for each mixed expense.
3. Redo the company's income statement at the 5,000-unit level of activity using the contribution format.

PROBLEM 2–17 High-Low Method; Predicting Cost [LO 2–4, LO 2–5]

Sawaya Co., Ltd., of Japan is a manufacturing company whose total factory overhead costs fluctuate considerably from year to year according to increases and decreases in the number of direct labor-hours worked in the factory. Total factory overhead costs at high and low levels of activity for recent years are given below:

	Level of Activity	
	Low	High
Direct labor-hours	50,000	75,000
Total factory overhead costs	$14,250,000	$17,625,000

The factory overhead costs above consist of indirect materials, rent, and maintenance. The company has analyzed these costs at the 50,000-hour level of activity as follows:

Indirect materials (variable)...............	$ 5,000,000
Rent (fixed).............................	6,000,000
Maintenance (mixed)	3,250,000
Total factory overhead costs	$14,250,000

To have data available for planning, the company wants to break down the maintenance cost into its variable and fixed cost elements.

Required:

1. Estimate how much of the $17,625,000 factory overhead cost at the high level of activity consists of maintenance cost. (*Hint:* To do this, it may be helpful to first determine how much of the $17,625,000 consists of indirect materials and rent. Think about the behavior of variable and fixed costs!)
2. Using the high-low method, estimate a cost formula for maintenance.
3. What total factory overhead costs would you expect the company to incur at an operating level of 70,000 direct labor-hours?

PROBLEM 2–18 Variable and Fixed Costs; Subtleties of Direct and Indirect Costs [LO 2–1, LO 2–4]

Madison Seniors Care Center is a nonprofit organization that provides a variety of health services to the elderly. The center is organized into a number of departments, one of which is the Meals-On-Wheels program that delivers hot meals to seniors in their homes on a daily basis. Below are listed a number of costs of the center and the Meals-On-Wheels program.

example	The cost of groceries used in meal preparation
a.	The cost of leasing the Meals-On-Wheels van
b.	The cost of incidental supplies such as salt, pepper, napkins, and so on
c.	The cost of gasoline consumed by the Meals-On-Wheels van
d.	The rent on the facility that houses Madison Seniors Care Center, including the Meals-On-Wheels program
e.	The salary of the part-time manager of the Meals-On-Wheels program
f.	Depreciation on the kitchen equipment used in the Meals-On-Wheels program
g.	The hourly wages of the caregiver who drives the van and delivers the meals
h.	The costs of complying with health safety regulations in the kitchen
i.	The costs of mailing letters soliciting donations to the Meals-On-Wheels program

Required:

For each cost listed above, indicate whether it is a direct or indirect cost of the Meals-On-Wheels program, whether it is a direct or indirect cost of particular seniors served by the program, and whether it is variable or fixed with respect to the number of seniors served. Use the form below for your answer.

		Direct or Indirect Cost of the Meals-on-Wheels Program		Direct or Indirect Cost of Particular Seniors Served by the Meals-on-Wheels Program		Variable or Fixed with Respect to the Number of Seniors Served by the Meals-on-Wheels Program	
Item	Description	Direct	Indirect	Direct	Indirect	Variable	Fixed
Example	The cost of groceries used in meal preparation........	X		X		X	

PROBLEM 2–19 Contribution Format versus Traditional Income Statement [LO 2–6]

Marwick's Pianos, Inc., purchases pianos from a large manufacturer and sells them at the retail level. The pianos cost, on the average, $2,450 each from the manufacturer. Marwick's Pianos, Inc., sells the pianos to its customers at an average price of $3,125 each. The selling and administrative costs that the company incurs in a typical month are presented below:

Costs	Cost Formula
Selling:	
Advertising	$700 per month
Sales salaries and commissions	$950 per month, plus 8% of sales
Delivery of pianos to customers	$30 per piano sold
Utilities	$350 per month
Depreciation of sales facilities	$800 per month
Administrative:	
Executive salaries.	$2,500 per month
Insurance	$400 per month
Clerical	$1,000 per month, plus $20 per piano sold
Depreciation of office equipment	$300 per month

During August, Marwick's Pianos, Inc., sold and delivered 40 pianos.

Required:

1. Prepare an income statement for Marwick's Pianos, Inc., for August. Use the traditional format, with costs organized by function.
2. Redo requirement 1 above, this time using the contribution format, with costs organized by behavior. Show costs and revenues on both a total and a per unit basis down through contribution margin.
3. Refer to the income statement you prepared in requirement 2 above. Why might it be misleading to show the fixed costs on a per unit basis?

PROBLEM 2–20 High-Low Method; Predicting Cost [LO 2–4, LO 2–5]

Nova Company's total overhead cost at various levels of activity are presented below:

Month	Machine-Hours	Total Overhead Cost
April.	70,000	$198,000
May	60,000	$174,000
June	80,000	$222,000
July	90,000	$246,000

Assume that the total overhead cost above consists of utilities, supervisory salaries, and maintenance. The breakdown of these costs at the 60,000 machine-hour level of activity is:

Utilities (variable)	$ 48,000
Supervisory salaries (fixed)	21,000
Maintenance (mixed)	105,000
Total overhead cost	$174,000

Nova Company's management wants to break down the maintenance cost into its variable and fixed cost elements.

Required:

1. Estimate how much of the $246,000 of overhead cost in July was maintenance cost. (*Hint:* to do this, it may be helpful to first determine how much of the $246,000 consisted of utilities and supervisory salaries. Think about the behavior of variable and fixed costs!)
2. Using the high-low method, estimate a cost formula for maintenance.
3. Express the company's *total* overhead cost in the linear equation form $Y = a + bX$.
4. What *total* overhead cost would you expect to be incurred at an activity level of 75,000 machine-hours?

PROBLEM 2–21 Cost Classification [LO 2–1, LO 2–3, LO 2–4]

Listed below are costs found in various organizations.

1. Property taxes, factory.
2. Boxes used for packaging detergent produced by the company.
3. Salespersons' commissions.

4. Supervisor's salary, factory.
5. Depreciation, executive autos.
6. Wages of workers assembling computers.
7. Insurance, finished goods warehouses.
8. Lubricants for production equipment.
9. Advertising costs.
10. Microchips used in producing calculators.
11. Shipping costs on merchandise sold.
12. Magazine subscriptions, factory lunchroom.
13. Thread in a garment factory.
14. Billing costs.
15. Executive life insurance.
16. Ink used in textbook production.
17. Fringe benefits, assembly-line workers.
18. Yarn used in sweater production.
19. Wages of receptionist, executive offices.

Required:

Prepare an answer sheet with column headings as shown below. For each cost item, indicate whether it would be variable or fixed with respect to the number of units produced and sold; and then whether it would be a selling cost, an administrative cost, or a manufacturing cost. If it is a manufacturing cost, indicate whether it would typically be treated as a direct cost or an indirect cost with respect to units of product. Three sample answers are provided for illustration.

Cost Item	Variable or Fixed	Selling Cost	Administrative Cost	Manufacturing (Product) Cost Direct	Manufacturing (Product) Cost Indirect
Direct labor	V			X	
Executive salaries	F		X		
Factory rent	F				X

PROBLEM 2–22 High-Low and Scattergraph Analysis [LO 2–4, LO 2–5]

Pleasant View Hospital of British Columbia has just hired a new chief administrator who is anxious to employ sound management and planning techniques in the business affairs of the hospital. Accordingly, she has directed her assistant to summarize the cost structure of the various departments so that data will be available for planning purposes.

The assistant is unsure how to classify the utilities costs in the Radiology Department because these costs do not exhibit either strictly variable or fixed cost behavior. Utilities costs are very high in the department due to a CAT scanner that draws a large amount of power and is kept running at all times. The scanner can't be turned off due to the long warm-up period required for its use. When the scanner is used to scan a patient, it consumes an additional burst of power. The assistant has accumulated the following data on utilities costs and use of the scanner since the first of the year.

Month	Number of Scans	Utilities Cost
January	60	$2,200
February	70	$2,600
March	90	$2,900
April	120	$3,300
May	100	$3,000
June	130	$3,600
July	150	$4,000
August	140	$3,600
September	110	$3,100
October	80	$2,500

The chief administrator has informed her assistant that the utilities cost is probably a mixed cost that will have to be broken down into its variable and fixed cost elements by use of a scattergraph. The assistant feels, however, that if an analysis of this type is necessary, then the high-low method should be used, since it is easier and quicker. The controller has suggested that there may be a better approach.

Required:
1. Using the high-low method, estimate a cost formula for utilities. Express the formula in the form $Y = a + bX$. (The variable rate should be stated in terms of cost per scan.)
2. Prepare a scattergraph by plotting the number of scans and utility cost on a graph. Draw a straight line though the two data points that correspond to the high and low levels of activity. Make sure your line intersects the Y-axis.
3. Comment on the accuracy of your high-low estimates assuming a least-squares regression analysis estimated the total fixed costs to be $1,170.90 per month and the variable cost to be $18.18 per scan. How would the straight line that you drew in requirement 2 differ from a straight line that minimizes the sum of the squared errors?

PROBLEM 2–23 High-Low Method; Contribution Format Income Statement [LO 2–5, LO 2–6]
Milden Company has an exclusive franchise to purchase a product from the manufacturer and distribute it on the retail level. As an aid in planning, the company has decided to start using a contribution format income statement. To have data to prepare such a statement, the company has analyzed its expenses and has developed the following cost formulas:

Cost	Cost Formula
Cost of good sold	$35 per unit sold
Advertising expense.	$210,000 per quarter
Sales commissions	6% of sales
Shipping expense	?
Administrative salaries.	$145,000 per quarter
Insurance expense	$9,000 per quarter
Depreciation expense	$76,000 per quarter

Management has concluded that shipping expense is a mixed cost, containing both variable and fixed cost elements. Units sold and the related shipping expense over the last eight quarters follow:

Quarter	Units Sold	Shipping Expense
Year 1:		
First	10,000	$119,000
Second.	16,000	$175,000
Third	18,000	$190,000
Fourth.	15,000	$164,000
Year 2:		
First	11,000	$130,000
Second.	17,000	$185,000
Third	20,000	$210,000
Fourth.	13,000	$147,000

Milden Company's president would like a cost formula derived for shipping expense so that a budgeted contribution format income statement can be prepared for the next quarter.

Required:
1. Using the high-low method, estimate a cost formula for shipping expense.
2. In the first quarter of Year 3, the company plans to sell 12,000 units at a selling price of $100 per unit. Prepare a contribution format income statement for the quarter.

PROBLEM 2–24 Ethics and the Manager [LO 2–3]

M. K. Gallant is president of Kranbrack Corporation, a company whose stock is traded on a national exchange. In a meeting with investment analysts at the beginning of the year, Gallant had predicted that the company's earnings would grow by 20% this year. Unfortunately, sales have been less than expected for the year, and Gallant concluded within two weeks of the end of the fiscal year that it would be impossible to ultimately report an increase in earnings as large as predicted unless some drastic action was taken. Accordingly, Gallant has ordered that wherever possible, expenditures should be postponed to the new year—including canceling or postponing orders with suppliers, delaying planned maintenance and training, and cutting back on end-of-year advertising and travel. Additionally, Gallant ordered the company's controller to carefully scrutinize all costs that are currently classified as period costs and reclassify as many as possible as product costs. The company is expected to have substantial inventories at the end of the year.

Required:
1. Why would reclassifying period costs as product costs increase this period's reported earnings?
2. Do you believe Gallant's actions are ethical? Why or why not?

PROBLEM 2–25 Cost Classification and Cost Behavior [LO 2–1, LO 2–2, LO 2–3, LO 2–4]

The Dorilane Company specializes in producing a set of wood patio furniture consisting of a table and four chairs. The set enjoys great popularity, and the company has ample orders to keep production going at its full capacity of 2,000 sets per year. Annual cost data at full capacity follow:

Direct labor	$118,000
Advertising	$50,000
Factory supervision	$40,000
Property taxes, factory building	$3,500
Sales commissions	$80,000
Insurance, factory	$2,500
Depreciation, administrative office equipment	$4,000
Lease cost, factory equipment	$12,000
Indirect materials, factory	$6,000
Depreciation, factory building	$10,000
Administrative office supplies (billing)	$3,000
Administrative office salaries	$60,000
Direct materials used (wood, bolts, etc.)	$94,000
Utilities, factory	$20,000

Required:
1. Prepare an answer sheet with the column headings shown below. Enter each cost item on your answer sheet, placing the dollar amount under the appropriate headings. As examples, this has been done already for the first two items in the list above. Note that each cost item is classified in two ways: first, as variable or fixed with respect to the number of units produced and sold; and second, as a selling and administrative cost or a product cost. (If the item is a product cost, it should also be classified as either direct or indirect as shown.)

Cost Item	Cost Behavior		Period (Selling or Administrative) Cost	Product Cost	
	Variable	Fixed		Direct	Indirect*
Direct labor	$118,000			$118,000	
Advertising		$50,000	$50,000		
*To units of product.					

2. Total the dollar amounts in each of the columns in requirement 1 above. Compute the average product cost of one patio set.
3. Assume that production drops to only 1,000 sets annually. Would you expect the average product cost per set to increase, decrease, or remain unchanged? Explain. No computations are necessary.

Chapter 2

4. Refer to the original data. The president's brother-in-law has considered making himself a patio set and has priced the necessary materials at a building supply store. The brother-in-law has asked the president if he could purchase a patio set from the Dorilane Company "at cost," and the president agreed to let him do so.

   a. Would you expect any disagreement between the two men over the price the brother-in-law should pay? Explain. What price does the president probably have in mind? The brother-in-law?

   b. Because the company is operating at full capacity, what cost term used in the chapter might be justification for the president to charge the full, regular price to the brother-in-law and still be selling "at cost"?

Cases **connect** Additional student resources are available with Connect.

CASE 2–26 Mixed Cost Analysis and the Relevant Range [LO 2–4, LO 2–5]

The Ramon Company is a manufacturer that is interested in developing a cost formula to estimate the fixed and variable components of its monthly manufacturing overhead costs. The company wishes to use machine-hours as its measure of activity and has gathered the data below for this year and last year:

Month	Last Year Machine-Hours	Last Year Overhead Costs	This Year Machine-Hours	This Year Overhead Costs
January..................	21,000	$84,000	21,000	$86,000
February.................	25,000	$99,000	24,000	$93,000
March....................	22,000	$89,500	23,000	$93,000
April.....................	23,000	$90,000	22,000	$87,000
May......................	20,500	$81,500	20,000	$80,000
June	19,000	$75,500	18,000	$76,500
July......................	14,000	$70,500	12,000	$67,500
August	10,000	$64,500	13,000	$71,000
September................	12,000	$69,000	15,000	$73,500
October	17,000	$75,000	17,000	$72,500
November	16,000	$71,500	15,000	$71,000
December	19,000	$78,000	18,000	$75,000

The company leases all of its manufacturing equipment. The lease arrangement calls for a flat monthly fee up to 19,500 machine-hours. If the machine-hours used exceeds 19,500, then the fee becomes strictly variable with respect to the total number of machine-hours consumed during the month. Lease expense is a major element of overhead cost.

Required:

1. Using the high-low method, estimate a manufacturing overhead cost formula.

2. Prepare a scattergraph using all of the data for the two-year period. Fit a straight line or lines to the plotted points using a ruler. Describe the cost behavior pattern revealed by your scattergraph plot.

3. Assume a least-squares regression analysis using all of the given data points estimated the total fixed costs to be $40,102 and the variable costs to be $2.13 per machine-hour. Do you have any concerns about the accuracy of the high-low estimates that you have computed or the least-squares regression estimates that have been provided?

4. Assume that the company consumes 22,500 machine-hours during a month. Using the high-low method, estimate the total overhead cost that would be incurred at this level of activity. Be sure to consider only the data points contained in the relevant range of activity when performing your computations.

5. Comment on the accuracy of your high-low estimates assuming a least-squares regression analysis using only the data points in the relevant range of activity estimated the total fixed costs to be $10,090 and the variable costs to be $3.53 per machine-hour.

CASE 2–27 Scattergraph Analysis; Selection of an Activity Base [LO 2–5]

Angora Wraps of Pendleton, Oregon, makes fine sweaters out of pure angora wool. The business is seasonal, with the largest demand during the fall, the winter, and Christmas holidays. The company must increase production each summer to meet estimated demand.

The company has been analyzing its costs to determine which costs are fixed and variable for planning purposes. Below are data for the company's activity and direct labor costs over the last year.

Month	Thousands of Units Produced	Number of Paid Days	Direct Labor Cost
January....................	98	20	$14,162
February..................	76	20	$12,994
March.....................	75	21	$15,184
April......................	80	22	$15,038
May.......................	85	22	$15,768
June	102	21	$15,330
July	52	19	$13,724
August	136	21	$14,162
September.................	138	22	$15,476
October	132	23	$15,476
November	86	18	$12,972
December	56	21	$14,074

The number of workdays varies from month to month due to the number of weekdays, holidays, and days of vacation in the month. The paid days include paid vacations (in July) and paid holidays (in November and December). The number of units produced in a month varies depending on demand and the number of workdays in the month.

The company has eight workers who are classified as direct labor.

Required:

1. Plot the direct labor cost and units produced on a scattergraph. (Place cost on the vertical axis and units produced on the horizontal axis.)
2. Plot the direct labor cost and number of paid days on a scattergraph. (Place cost on the vertical axis and the number of paid days on the horizontal axis.)
3. Which measure of actievity—number of units produced or paid days—should be used as the activity base for explaining direct labor cost? Explain.

Appendix 2A: Least-Squares Regression Computations

The least-squares regression method for estimating a linear relationship is based on the equation for a straight line:

$$Y = a + bX$$

As explained in the chapter, least-squares regression selects the values for the intercept a and the slope b that minimize the sum of the squared errors. The following formulas, which are derived in statistics and calculus texts, accomplish that objective:

$$b = \frac{n(\Sigma XY) - (\Sigma X)(\Sigma Y)}{n(\Sigma X^2) - (\Sigma X)^2}$$

$$a = \frac{(\Sigma Y) - b(\Sigma X)}{n}$$

LEARNING OBJECTIVE 2–8

Analyze a mixed cost using a scattergraph plot and the least-squares regression method.

where:

X = The level of activity (independent variable)
Y = The total mixed cost (dependent variable)
a = The total fixed cost (the vertical intercept of the line)
b = The variable cost per unit of activity (the slope of the line)
n = Number of observations
Σ = Sum across all n observations

Manually performing the calculations required by the formulas is tedious at best. Fortunately, Microsoft® Excel can be used to estimate the intercept (fixed cost) and slope (variable cost per unit) that minimize the sum of the squared errors. Excel also provides a statistic called the R^2, which is a measure of "goodness of fit." The $\textbf{R}^2$ tells us the percentage of the variation in the dependent variable (cost) that is explained by variation in the independent variable (activity). The R^2 varies from 0% to 100%, and the higher the percentage, the better. You should always plot the data in a scattergraph, but it is particularly important to check the data visually when the R^2 is low. A quick look at the scattergraph can reveal that there is little relation between the cost and the activity or that the relation is something other than a simple straight line. In such cases, additional analysis would be required.

To illustrate how Excel can be used to prepare a scattergraph plot and to calculate the intercept a, the slope b, and the R^2, we will use the Brentline Hospital data for patient-days and maintenance costs that was given earlier in the chapter and that is now recreated in Exhibit 2A–1.[1]

To prepare a scattergraph plot, begin by highlighting the data in cells B4 through C10. From the Charts group within the Insert tab, select the "Scatter" subgroup and then click on the choice that has no lines connecting the data points. This should produce a scattergraph plot similar to the one shown in Exhibit 2A–2. Notice that the number of patient-days is plotted on the X-axis and the maintenance costs are plotted on the Y-axis.[2]

EXHIBIT 2A–1
The Least-Squares Regression Worksheet for Brentline Hospital

	A	B	C
1		Patient	Maintenance
2		Days	Cost
3	*Month*	*X*	*Y*
4	January	5,600	$ 7,900
5	February	7,100	$ 8,500
6	March	5,000	$ 7,400
7	April	6,500	$ 8,200
8	May	7,300	$ 9,100
9	June	8,000	$ 9,800
10	July	6,200	$ 7,800
11			

Least-squares regression

[1] The authors wish to thank Don Schwartz, Professor of Accounting at National University, for providing suggestions that were instrumental in creating this appendix.
[2] To insert labels for the X-axis and Y-axis, go to the Layout tab in Excel. Then, within the Labels group, select Axis Titles.

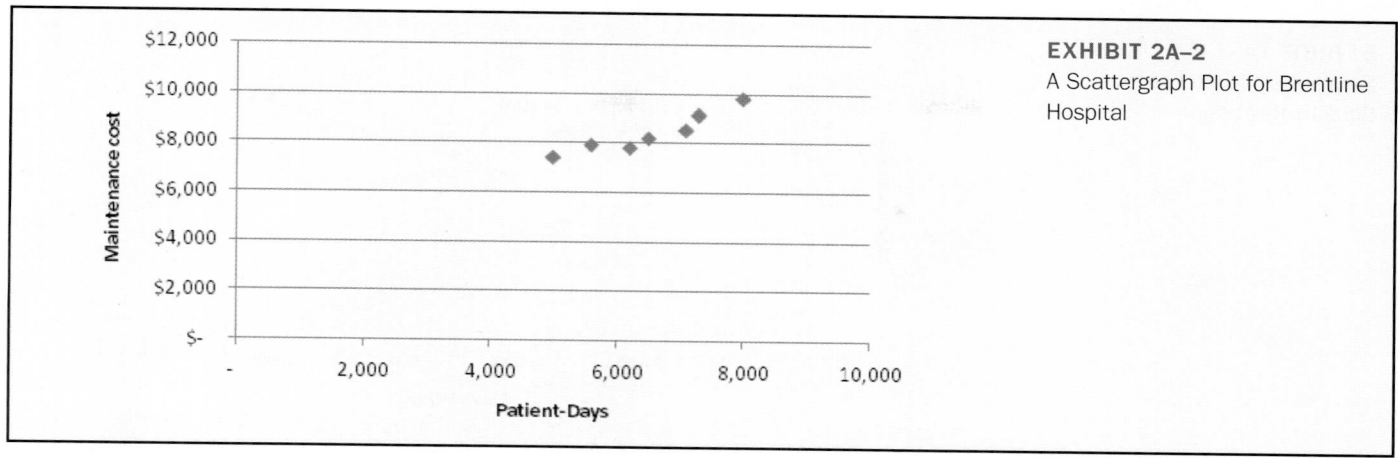

EXHIBIT 2A–2
A Scattergraph Plot for Brentline Hospital

The data is approximately linear, so it makes sense to proceed with estimating a regression equation that minimizes the sum of the squared errors.

To determine the intercept a, the slope b, and the R^2, begin by right clicking on any data point in the scattergraph plot and selecting "Add Trendline." This should produce the screen that is shown in Exhibit 2A–3. Notice that under "Trend/Regression Type" you should select "Linear." Similarly, under "Trendline Name" you should select "Automatic." Next to the word "Backward" you should input the lowest value for the independent variable, which in this example is 5000 patient-days. Taking this particular step instructs Excel to extend your fitted line until it intersects the Y-axis. Finally, you should check the two boxes at the bottom of Exhibit 2A–3 that say "Display Equation on chart" and "Display R-squared value on chart."

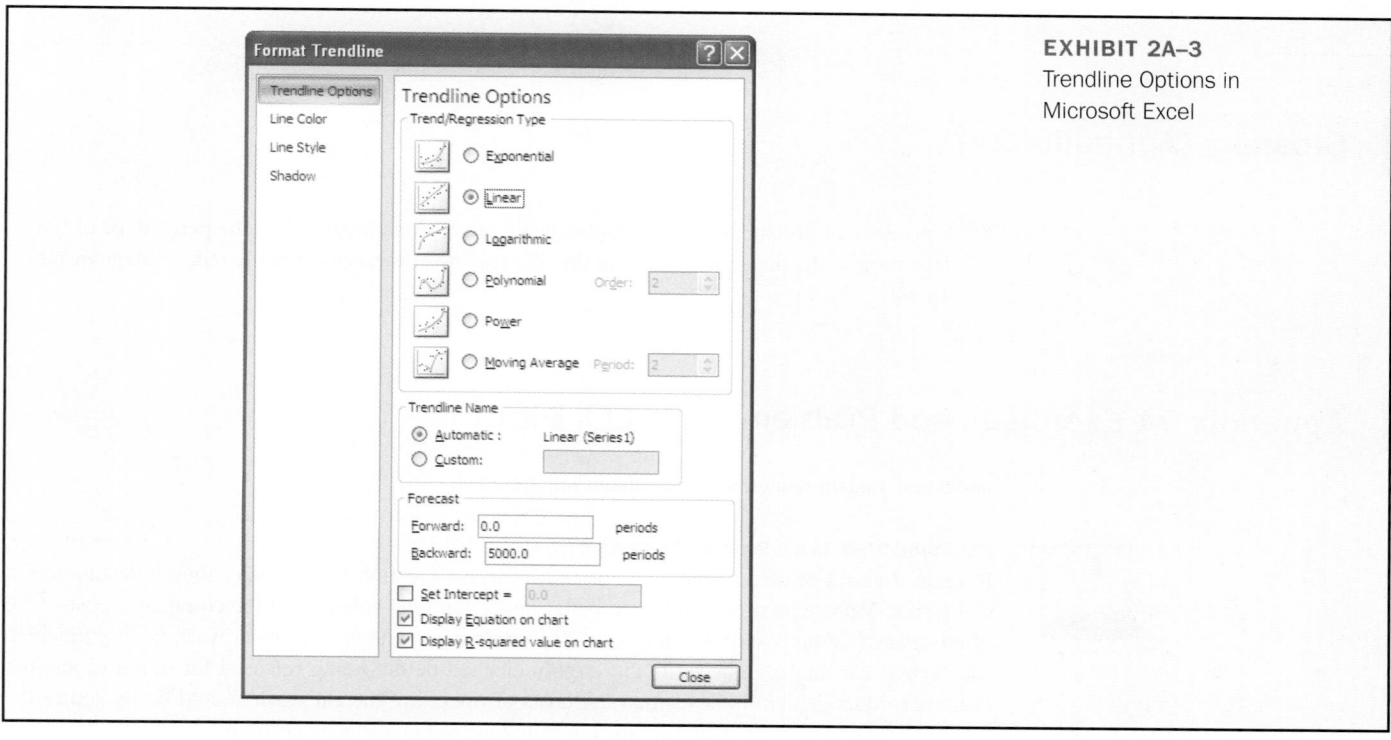

EXHIBIT 2A–3
Trendline Options in Microsoft Excel

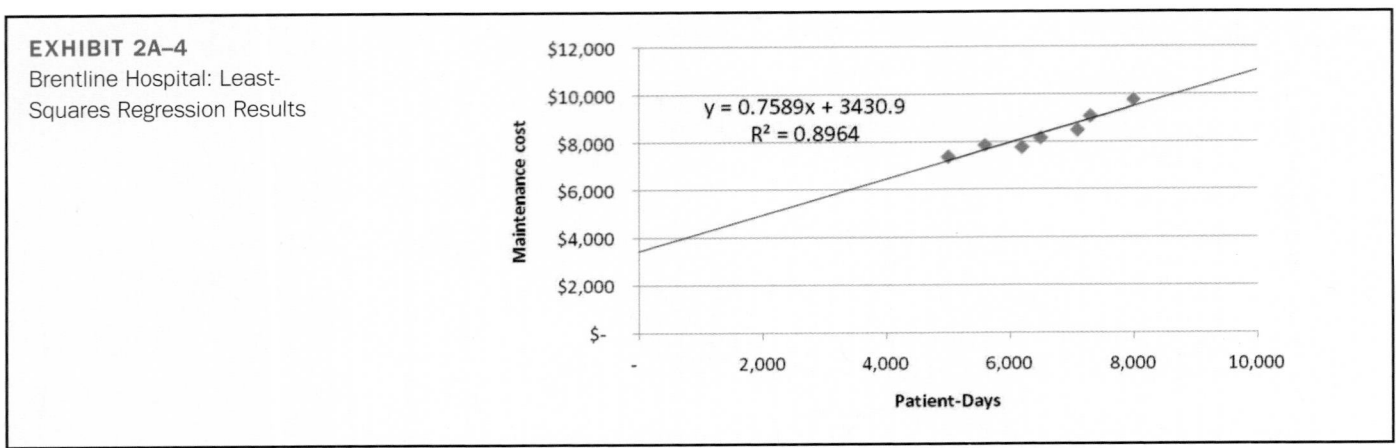

EXHIBIT 2A–4
Brentline Hospital: Least-Squares Regression Results

$y = 0.7589x + 3430.9$
$R^2 = 0.8964$

Once you have established these settings, then click "Close." As shown in Exhibit 2A–4, this will automatically insert a line within the scattergraph plot that minimizes the sum of the squared errors. It will also cause the estimated least-squares regression equation and R^2 to be inserted into your scattergraph plot. Instead of depicting the results using the form $Y = a + bX$, Excel uses an equivalent form of the equation depicted as $Y = bX + a$. In other words, Excel reverses the two terms shown to the right of the equals sign. So, in Exhibit 2A–4, Excel shows a least-squares regression equation of $y = 0.7589x + 3,430.9$. The slope b in this equation of $0.7589 represents the estimated variable maintenance cost per patient-day. The intercept a in this equation of $3,430.90 (or approximately $3,431) represents the estimated fixed monthly maintenance cost. Note that the R^2 is approximately 0.90, which is quite good and indicates that 90% of the variation in maintenance costs is explained by the variation in patient-days.

Glossary (Appendix 2A)

R^2 A measure of goodness of fit in least-squares regression analysis. It is the percentage of the variation in the dependent variable that is explained by variation in the independent variable. (p. 64)

Appendix 2A Exercises and Problems connect

Additional student resources are available with Connect.

EXERCISE 2A–1 Least-Squares Regression [LO 2–8]
Bargain Rental Car offers rental cars in an off-airport location near a major tourist destination in California. Management would like to better understand the behavior of the company's costs. One of those costs is the cost of washing cars. The company operates its own car wash facility in which each rental car that is returned is thoroughly cleaned before being released for rental to another customer. Management believes that the costs of operating the car wash should be related to the number of rental returns. Accordingly, the following data have been compiled:

Month	Rental Returns	Car Wash Costs
January..............	2,380	$10,825
February.............	2,421	$11,865
March	2,586	$11,332
April................	2,725	$12,422
May..................	2,968	$13,850
June	3,281	$14,419
July	3,353	$14,935
August	3,489	$15,738
September............	3,057	$13,563
October	2,876	$11,889
November	2,735	$12,683
December	2,983	$13,796

Required:
1. Prepare a scattergraph plot. (Place car wash costs on the vertical axis and rental returns on the horizontal axis.)
2. Using least-squares regression, estimate the fixed cost and variable cost elements of monthly car wash costs. The fixed cost element should be estimated to the nearest dollar and the variable cost element to the nearest cent.

EXERCISE 2A–2 Least-Squares Regression [LO 2–4, LO 2–8]
George Caloz & Frères, located in Grenchen, Switzerland, makes prestige high-end custom watches in small lots. One of the company's products, a platinum diving watch, goes through an etching process. The company has observed etching costs as follows over the last six weeks:

Week	Units	Total Etching Cost
1...............	4	$ 18
2...............	3	17
3...............	8	25
4...............	6	20
5...............	7	24
6...............	2	16
	30	$120

For planning purposes, management would like to know the amount of variable etching cost per unit and the total fixed etching cost per week.

Required:
1. Prepare a scattergraph plot. (Place etching costs on the vertical axis and units on the horizontal axis.)
2. Using the least-squares regression method, estimate the variable and fixed elements of etching cost. Express these estimates in the form $Y = a + bX$.
3. If the company processes five units next week, what would be the expected total etching cost?

PROBLEM 2A–3 Least-Squares Regression; Scattergraph; Comparison of Activity Bases [LO 2–4, LO 2–8]
The Hard Rock Mining Company is developing cost formulas for management planning and decision-making purposes. The company's cost analyst has concluded that utilities cost is a mixed cost, and he is attempting to find a base with which the cost might be closely correlated. The controller has suggested that tons mined might be a good base to use in developing a cost formula. The production superintendent disagrees; she thinks that direct labor-hours

would be a better base. The cost analyst has decided to try both bases and has assembled the following information:

Quarter	Tons Mined	Direct Labor-Hours	Utilities Cost
Year 1:			
First....................	15,000	5,000	$50,000
Second................	11,000	3,000	$45,000
Third...................	21,000	4,000	$60,000
Fourth.................	12,000	6,000	$75,000
Year 2:			
First....................	18,000	10,000	$100,000
Second................	25,000	9,000	$105,000
Third...................	30,000	8,000	$85,000
Fourth.................	28,000	11,000	$120,000

Required:
1. Using tons mined as the independent variable, prepare a scattergraph that plots tons mined on the horizontal axis and utilities cost on the vertical axis. Determine a cost formula for utilities cost using least-squares regression. Express this cost formula in the form $Y = a + bX$.

2. Using direct labor-hours as the independent variable, prepare a scattergraph that plots direct labor-hours on the horizontal axis and utilities cost on the vertical axis. Determine a cost formula for utilities cost using least-squares regression. Express this cost formula in the form $Y = a + bX$.

3. Would you recommend that the company use tons mined or direct labor-hours as a base for planning utilities cost?

PROBLEM 2A–4 Least-Squares Regression Method; Scattergraph; Cost Behavior [LO 2–4, LO 2–8]
Professor John Morton has just been appointed chairperson of the Finance Department at Westland University. In reviewing the department's cost records, Professor Morton has found the following total cost associated with Finance 101 over the last several terms:

Term	Number of Sections Offered	Total Cost
Fall, last year........................	4	$10,000
Winter, last year	6	$14,000
Summer, last year...................	2	$7,000
Fall, this year........................	5	$13,000
Winter, this year	3	$9,500

Professor Morton knows that there are some variable costs, such as amounts paid to graduate assistants, associated with the course. He would like to have the variable and fixed costs separated for planning purposes.

Required:
1. Prepare a scattergraph plot. (Place total cost on the vertical axis and number of sections offered on the horizontal axis.)
2. Using the least-squares regression method, estimate the variable cost per section and the total fixed cost per term for Finance 101. Express these estimates in the linear equation form $Y = a + bX$.
3. Assume that because of the small number of sections offered during the Winter Term this year, Professor Morton will have to offer eight sections of Finance 101 during the Fall Term. Compute the expected total cost for Finance 101. Can you see any problem with using the cost formula from requirement 2 above to derive this total cost figure? Explain.

CASE 2A–5 Analysis of Mixed Costs in a Pricing Decision [LO 2–4, LO 2–8]

Maria Chavez owns a catering company that serves food and beverages at parties and business functions. Chavez's business is seasonal, with a heavy schedule during the summer months and holidays and a lighter schedule at other times.

One of the major events Chavez's customers request is a cocktail party. She offers a standard cocktail party and has estimated the cost per guest as follows:

Food and beverages	$15.00
Labor (0.5 hrs. @ $10.00/hr.)	5.00
Overhead (0.5 hrs. @ $13.98/hr.).	6.99
Total cost per guest	$26.99

The standard cocktail party lasts three hours and Chavez hires one worker for every six guests, so that works out to one-half hour of labor per guest. These workers are hired only as needed and are paid only for the hours they actually work.

When bidding on cocktail parties, Chavez adds a 15% markup to yield a price of about $31 per guest. She is confident about her estimates of the costs of food and beverages and labor but is not as comfortable with the estimate of overhead cost. The $13.98 overhead cost per labor-hour was determined by dividing total overhead expenses for the last 12 months by total labor-hours for the same period. Monthly data concerning overhead costs and labor-hours follow:

Month	Labor-Hours	Overhead Expenses
January.	2,500	$ 55,000
February.	2,800	59,000
March	3,000	60,000
April.	4,200	64,000
May	4,500	67,000
June	5,500	71,000
July	6,500	74,000
August	7,500	77,000
September.	7,000	75,000
October	4,500	68,000
November	3,100	62,000
December	6,500	73,000
Total	57,600	$805,000

Chavez has received a request to bid on a 180-guest fund-raising cocktail party to be given next month by an important local charity. (The party would last the usual three hours.) She would like to win this contract because the guest list for this charity event includes many prominent individuals that she would like to land as future clients. Maria is confident that these potential customers would be favorably impressed by her company's services at the charity event.

Required:

1. Prepare a scattergraph plot that puts labor-hours on the X-axis and overhead expenses on the Y-axis. What insights are revealed by your scattergraph?
2. Use the least-squares regression method to estimate the fixed and variable components of overhead expenses. Express these estimates in the form $Y = a + bX$.
3. Estimate the contribution to profit of a standard 180-guest cocktail party if Chavez charges her usual price of $31 per guest. (In other words, by how much would her overall profit increase?)
4. How low could Chavez bid for the charity event in terms of a price per guest and still not lose money on the event itself?
5. The individual who is organizing the charity's fund-raising event has indicated that he has already received a bid under $30 from another catering company. Do you think Chavez should bid below her normal $31 per guest price for the charity event? Why or why not?

(CMA, adapted)

LEARNING OBJECTIVES

After studying Chapter 3, you should be able to:

LO3–1 Explain how changes in activity affect contribution margin and net operating income.

LO3–2 Prepare and interpret a cost-volume-profit (CVP) graph and a profit graph.

LO3–3 Use the contribution margin ratio (CM ratio) to compute changes in contribution margin and net operating income resulting from changes in sales volume.

LO3–4 Show the effects on net operating income of changes in variable costs, fixed costs, selling price, and volume.

LO3–5 Determine the break-even point.

LO3–6 Determine the level of sales needed to achieve a desired target profit.

LO3–7 Compute the margin of safety and explain its significance.

LO3–8 Compute the degree of operating leverage at a particular level of sales and explain how it can be used to predict changes in net operating income.

LO3–9 Compute the break-even point for a multiproduct company and explain the effects of shifts in the sales mix on contribution margin and the break-even point.

Cost–Volume–Profit Relationships

Moreno Turns Around the Los Angeles Angels

© Comstock/Getty Images, RF

When Arturo Moreno bought Major League Baseball's Los Angeles Angels in 2003, the team was drawing 2.3 million fans and losing $5.5 million per year. Moreno immediately cut prices to attract more fans and increase profits. In his first spring training game, he reduced the price of selected tickets from $12 to $6. By increasing attendance, Moreno understood that he would sell more food and souvenirs. He dropped the price of draft beer by $2 and cut the price of baseball caps from $20 to $7.

The Angels now consistently draw about 3.4 million fans per year. This growth in attendance helped double stadium sponsorship revenue to $26 million, and it motivated the Fox Sports Network to pay the Angels $500 million to broadcast all of its games for the next ten years. Since Moreno bought the Angels, annual revenues have jumped from $127 million to $212 million, and the team's operating loss of $5.5 million has been transformed to a profit of $10.3 million.

Source: Matthew Craft, "Moreno's Math," *Forbes,* May 11, 2009, pp. 84–87.

Cost–volume–profit (CVP) analysis helps managers make many important decisions such as what products and services to offer, what prices to charge, what marketing strategy to use, and what cost structure to maintain. Its primary purpose is to estimate how profits are affected by the following five factors:

1. Selling prices.
2. Sales volume.
3. Unit variable costs.
4. Total fixed costs.
5. Mix of products sold.

To simplify CVP calculations, managers typically adopt the following assumptions with respect to these factors[1]:

1. Selling price is constant. The price of a product or service will not change as volume changes.
2. Costs are linear and can be accurately divided into variable and fixed elements. The variable element is constant per unit. The fixed element is constant in total over the entire relevant range.
3. In multiproduct companies, the mix of products sold remains constant.

While these assumptions may be violated in practice, the results of CVP analysis are often "good enough" to be quite useful. Perhaps the greatest danger lies in relying on simple CVP analysis when a manager is contemplating a large change in sales volume that lies outside the relevant range. However, even in these situations the CVP model can be adjusted to take into account anticipated changes in selling prices, variable costs per unit, total fixed costs, and the sales mix that arise when the estimated sales volume falls outside the relevant range.

To help explain the role of CVP analysis in business decisions, we'll now turn our attention to the case of Acoustic Concepts, Inc., a company founded by Prem Narayan.

Prem, who was a graduate student in engineering at the time, started Acoustic Concepts to market a radical new speaker he had designed for automobile sound systems. The speaker, called the Sonic Blaster, uses an advanced microprocessor and proprietary software to boost amplification to awesome levels. Prem contracted with a Taiwanese electronics manufacturer to produce the speaker. With seed money provided by his family, Prem placed an order with the manufacturer and ran advertisements in auto magazines.

The Sonic Blaster was an immediate success, and sales grew to the point that Prem moved the company's headquarters out of his apartment and into rented quarters in a nearby industrial park. He also hired a receptionist, an accountant, a sales manager, and a small sales staff to sell the speakers to retail stores. The accountant, Bob Luchinni, had worked for several small companies where he had acted as a business advisor as well as accountant and bookkeeper. The following discussion occurred soon after Bob was hired:

Prem: Bob, I've got a lot of questions about the company's finances that I hope you can help answer.
Bob: We're in great shape. The loan from your family will be paid off within a few months.
Prem: I know, but I am worried about the risks I've taken on by expanding operations. What would happen if a competitor entered the market and our sales slipped? How far could sales drop without putting us into the red? Another question I've been trying to resolve is how much our sales would have to increase to justify the big marketing campaign the sales staff is pushing for.
Bob: Marketing always wants more money for advertising.
Prem: And they are always pushing me to drop the selling price on the speaker. I agree with them that a lower price will boost our sales volume, but I'm not sure the increased volume will offset the loss in revenue from the lower price.

MANAGERIAL
ACCOUNTING IN
ACTION
The Issue

ACOUSTIC
concepts

inc

---

[1] One additional assumption often used in manufacturing companies is that inventories do not change. The number of units produced equals the number of units sold.

Bob: It sounds like these questions are all related in some way to the relationships among our selling prices, our costs, and our volume. I shouldn't have a problem coming up with some answers.

Prem: Can we meet again in a couple of days to see what you have come up with?

Bob: Sounds good. By then I'll have some preliminary answers for you as well as a model you can use for answering similar questions in the future.

The Basics of Cost-Volume-Profit (CVP) Analysis

Bob Luchinni's preparation for his forthcoming meeting with Prem begins with the contribution income statement. The contribution income statement emphasizes the behavior of costs and therefore is extremely helpful to managers in judging the impact on profits of changes in selling price, cost, or volume. Bob will base his analysis on the following contribution income statement he prepared last month:

	Total	Per Unit
Acoustic Concepts, Inc.		
Contribution Income Statement		
For the Month of June		
Sales (400 speakers)	$100,000	$250
Variable expenses	60,000	150
Contribution margin	40,000	$100
Fixed expenses	35,000	
Net operating income	$ 5,000	

Notice that sales, variable expenses, and contribution margin are expressed on a per unit basis as well as in total on this contribution income statement. The per unit figures will be very helpful to Bob in some of his calculations. Note that this contribution income statement has been prepared for management's use inside the company and would not ordinarily be made available to those outside the company.

Contribution Margin

LEARNING OBJECTIVE 3–1

Explain how changes in activity affect contribution margin and net operating income.

Contribution margin is the amount remaining from sales revenue after variable expenses have been deducted. Thus, it is the amount available to cover fixed expenses and then to provide profits for the period. Notice the sequence here—contribution margin is used *first* to cover the fixed expenses, and then whatever remains goes toward profits. If the contribution margin is not sufficient to cover the fixed expenses, then a loss occurs for the period. To illustrate with an extreme example, assume that Acoustic Concepts sells only one speaker during a particular month. The company's income statement would appear as follows:

	Total	Per Unit
Contribution Income Statement		
Sales of 1 Speaker		
Sales (1 speaker)	$ 250	$250
Variable expenses	150	150
Contribution margin	100	$100
Fixed expenses	35,000	
Net operating loss	$ (34,900)	

Cost-Volume-Profit Relationships 73

For each additional speaker the company sells during the month, $100 more in contribution margin becomes available to help cover the fixed expenses. If a second speaker is sold, for example, then the total contribution margin will increase by $100 (to a total of $200) and the company's loss will decrease by $100, to $34,800:

Contribution Income Statement
Sales of 2 Speakers

	Total	Per Unit
Sales (2 speakers)	$ 500	$250
Variable expenses	300	150
Contribution margin	200	$100
Fixed expenses.	35,000	
Net operating loss	$ (34,800)	

If enough speakers can be sold to generate $35,000 in contribution margin, then all of the fixed expenses will be covered and the company will *break even* for the month—that is, it will show neither profit nor loss but just cover all of its costs. To reach the break-even point, the company will have to sell 350 speakers in a month because each speaker sold yields $100 in contribution margin:

Contribution Income Statement
Sales of 350 Speakers

	Total	Per Unit
Sales (350 speakers)	$87,500	$250
Variable expenses	52,500	150
Contribution margin	35,000	$100
Fixed expenses.	35,000	
Net operating income	$ 0	

Computation of the break-even point is discussed in detail later in the chapter; for the moment, note that the **break-even point** is the level of sales at which profit is zero.

Once the break-even point has been reached, net operating income will increase by the amount of the unit contribution margin for each additional unit sold. For example, if 351 speakers are sold in a month, then the net operating income for the month will be $100 because the company will have sold 1 speaker more than the number needed to break even:

Contribution Income Statement
Sales of 351 Speakers

	Total	Per Unit
Sales (351 speakers)	$87,750	$250
Variable expenses	52,650	150
Contribution margin	35,100	$100
Fixed expenses.	35,000	
Net operating income	$ 100	

If 352 speakers are sold (2 speakers above the break-even point), the net operating income for the month will be $200. If 353 speakers are sold (3 speakers above the break-even point), the net operating income for the month will be $300, and so forth. To estimate the profit at any sales volume above the break-even point, multiply the number of units sold in excess of the break-even point by the unit contribution margin. The result represents the anticipated profits for the period. Or, to estimate the effect of a planned increase in sales on profits, simply multiply the increase in units sold by the unit contribution margin. The result will be the expected increase in profits. To illustrate, if Acoustic Concepts is currently selling 400 speakers per month and plans to increase sales to 425 speakers per month, the anticipated impact on profits can be computed as follows:

Increased number of speakers to be sold	25
Contribution margin per speaker.	× $100
Increase in net operating income	$2,500

These calculations can be verified as follows:

	Sales Volume			
	400 Speakers	425 Speakers	Difference (25 Speakers)	Per Unit
Sales (@ $250 per speaker)	$100,000	$106,250	$6,250	$250
Variable expenses (@ $150 per speaker)	60,000	63,750	3,750	150
Contribution margin	40,000	42,500	2,500	$100
Fixed expenses.	35,000	35,000	0	
Net operating income	$ 5,000	$ 7,500	$2,500	

To summarize, if sales are zero, the company's loss would equal its fixed expenses. Each unit that is sold reduces the loss by the amount of the unit contribution margin. Once the break-even point has been reached, each additional unit sold increases the company's profit by the amount of the unit contribution margin.

CVP Relationships in Equation Form

The contribution format income statement can be expressed in equation form as follows:

$$\text{Profit} = (\text{Sales} - \text{Variable expenses}) - \text{Fixed expenses}$$

For brevity, we use the term *profit* to stand for net operating income in equations.

When a company has only a *single* product, as at Acoustic Concepts, we can further refine the equation as follows:

$$\text{Sales} = \text{Selling price per unit} \times \text{Quantity sold} = P \times Q$$

$$\text{Variable expenses} = \text{Variable expenses per unit} \times \text{Quantity sold} = V \times Q$$

$$\text{Profit} = (P \times Q - V \times Q) - \text{Fixed expenses}$$

We can do all of the calculations of the previous section using this simple equation. For example, on the previous page we computed that the net operating income (profit) at sales of 351 speakers would be $100. We can arrive at the same conclusion using the above equation as follows:

$$\text{Profit} = (P \times Q - V \times Q) - \text{Fixed expenses}$$

$$\text{Profit} = (\$250 \times 351 - \$150 \times 351) - \$35,000$$

$$= (\$250 - \$150) \times 351 - \$35,000$$

$$= (\$100) \times 351 - \$35,000$$

$$= \$35,100 - \$35,000 = \$100$$

It is often useful to express the simple profit equation in terms of the unit contribution margin (Unit CM) as follows:

Unit CM = Selling price per unit − Variable expenses per unit = $P - V$

Profit = $(P \times Q - V \times Q)$ − Fixed expenses

Profit = $(P - V) \times Q$ − Fixed expenses

Profit = Unit CM $\times Q$ − Fixed expenses

We could also have used this equation to determine the profit at sales of 351 speakers as follows:

Profit = Unit CM $\times Q$ − Fixed expenses

$= \$100 \times 351 - \$35,000$

$= \$35,100 - \$35,000 = \$100$

For those who are comfortable with algebra, the quickest and easiest approach to solving the problems in this chapter may be to use the simple profit equation in one of its forms.

CVP Relationships in Graphic Form

The relationships among revenue, cost, profit, and volume are illustrated on a **cost-volume-profit (CVP) graph**. A CVP graph highlights CVP relationships over wide ranges of activity. To help explain his analysis to Prem Narayan, Bob Luchinni prepared a CVP graph for Acoustic Concepts.

LEARNING OBJECTIVE 3–2
Prepare and interpret a cost-volume-profit (CVP) graph and a profit graph.

Preparing the CVP Graph In a CVP graph (sometimes called a *break-even chart*), unit volume is represented on the horizontal (X) axis and dollars on the vertical (Y) axis. Preparing a CVP graph involves the three steps depicted in Exhibit 3–1:

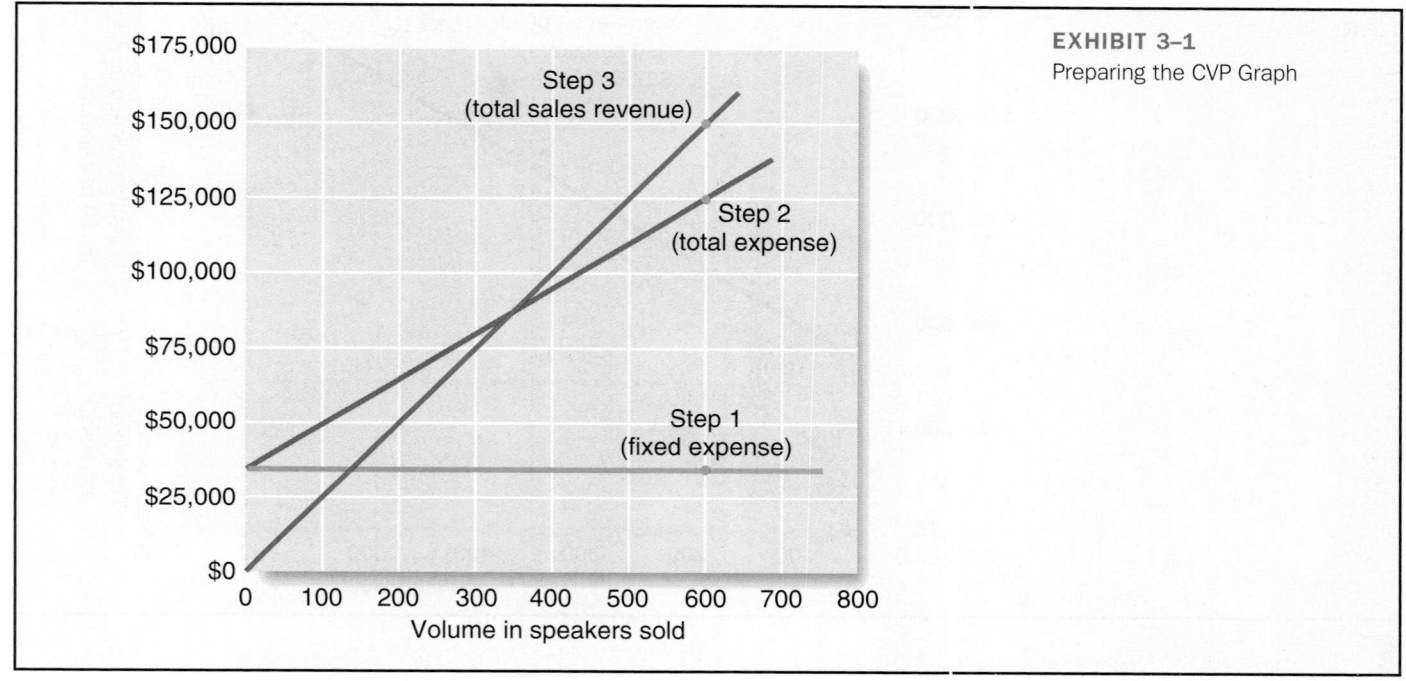

EXHIBIT 3–1
Preparing the CVP Graph

1. Draw a line parallel to the volume axis to represent total fixed expense. For Acoustic Concepts, total fixed expenses are $35,000.
2. Choose some volume of unit sales and plot the point representing total expense (fixed and variable) at the sales volume you have selected. In Exhibit 3–1, Bob Luchinni chose a volume of 600 speakers. Total expense at that sales volume is:

Fixed expense.	$ 35,000
Variable expense (600 speakers × $150 per speaker)	90,000
Total expense	$125,000

After the point has been plotted, draw a line through it back to the point where the fixed expense line intersects the dollars axis.

3. Again choose some sales volume and plot the point representing total sales dollars at the activity level you have selected. In Exhibit 3–1, Bob Luchinni again chose a volume of 600 speakers. Sales at that volume total $150,000 (600 speakers × $250 per speaker). Draw a line through this point back to the origin.

The interpretation of the completed CVP graph is given in Exhibit 3–2. The anticipated profit or loss at any given level of sales is measured by the vertical distance between the total revenue line (sales) and the total expense line (variable expense plus fixed expense).

The break-even point is where the total revenue and total expense lines cross. The break-even point of 350 speakers in Exhibit 3–2 agrees with the break-even point computed earlier.

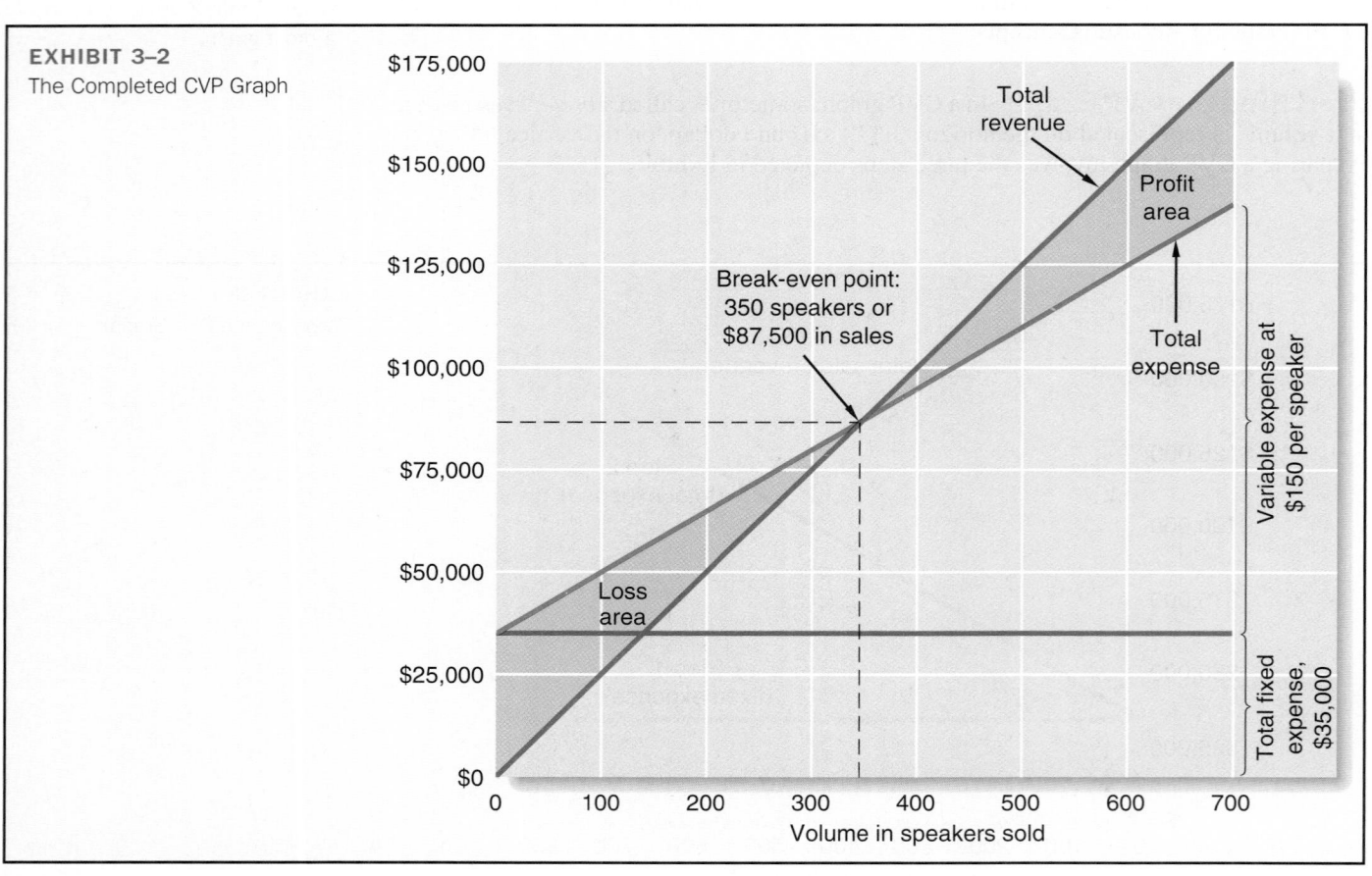

EXHIBIT 3–2
The Completed CVP Graph

As discussed earlier, when sales are below the break-even point—in this case, 350 units—the company suffers a loss. Note that the loss (represented by the vertical distance between the total expense and total revenue lines) gets bigger as sales decline. When sales are above the break-even point, the company earns a profit and the size of the profit (represented by the vertical distance between the total revenue and total expense lines) increases as sales increase.

An even simpler form of the CVP graph, which we call a profit graph, is presented in Exhibit 3–3. That graph is based on the following equation:

$$\text{Profit} = \text{Unit CM} \times Q - \text{Fixed expenses}$$

In the case of Acoustic Concepts, the equation can be expressed as:

$$\text{Profit} = \$100 \times Q - \$35,000$$

Because this is a linear equation, it plots as a single straight line. To plot the line, compute the profit at two different sales volumes, plot the points, and then connect them with a straight line. For example, when the sales volume is zero (i.e., $Q = 0$), the profit is $-\$35,000$ ($= \$100 \times 0 - \$35,000$). When Q is 600, the profit is $\$25,000$ ($= \$100 \times 600 - \$35,000$). These two points are plotted in Exhibit 3–3 and a straight line has been drawn through them.

The break-even point on the profit graph is the volume of sales at which profit is zero and is indicated by the dashed line on the graph. Note that the profit steadily increases to the right of the break-even point as the sales volume increases and that the loss becomes steadily worse to the left of the break-even point as the sales volume decreases.

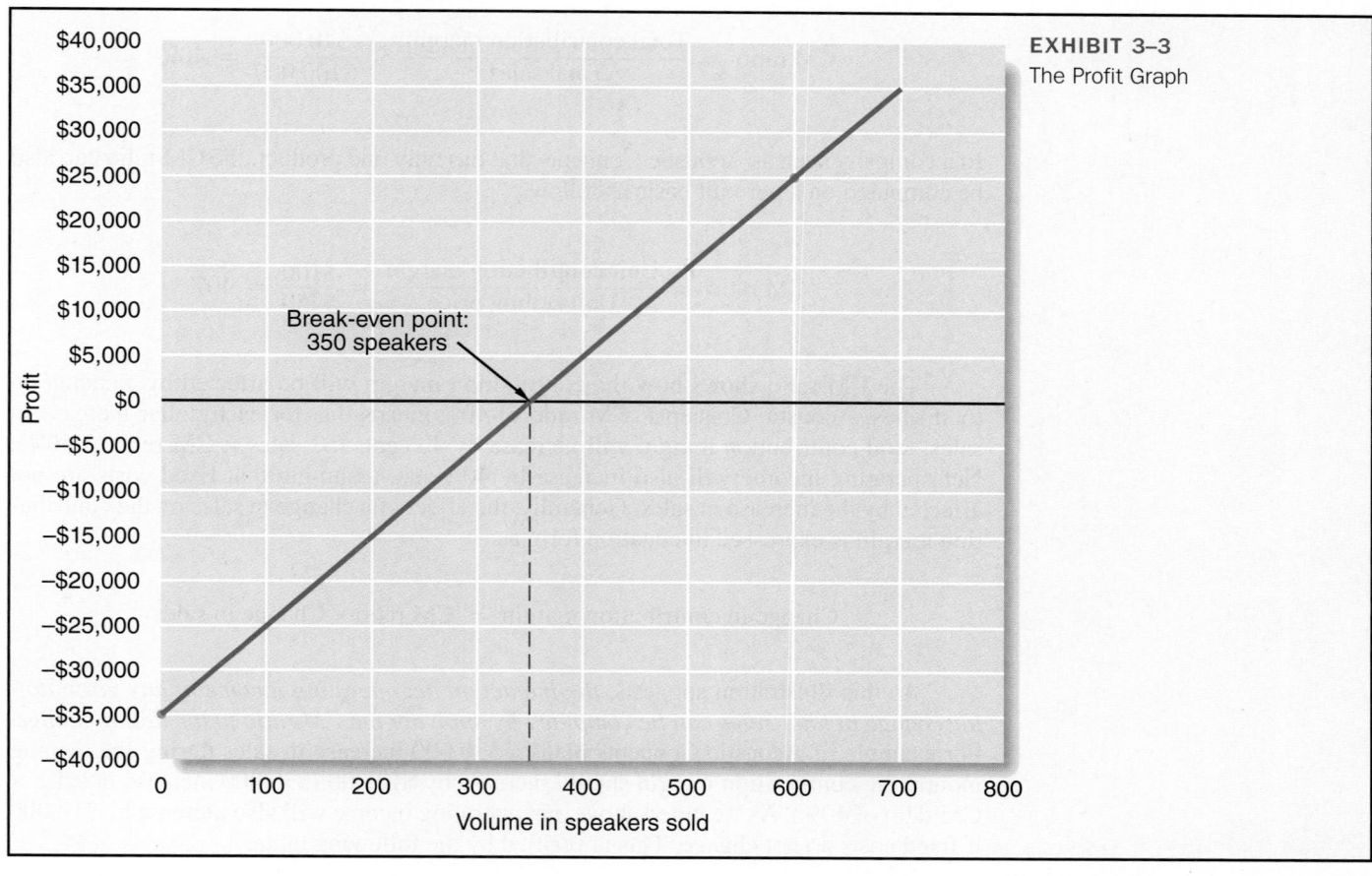

EXHIBIT 3–3
The Profit Graph

Contribution Margin Ratio (CM Ratio)

In the previous section, we explored how cost-volume-profit relationships can be visualized. In this section, we show how the *contribution margin ratio* can be used in cost-volume-profit calculations. As the first step, we have added a column to Acoustic Concepts' contribution format income statement in which sales revenues, variable expenses, and contribution margin are expressed as a percentage of sales:

	Total	Per Unit	Percent of Sales
Sales (400 speakers)	$100,000	$250	100%
Variable expenses	60,000	150	60%
Contribution margin	40,000	$100	40%
Fixed expenses	35,000		
Net operating income	$ 5,000		

The contribution margin as a percentage of sales is referred to as the **contribution margin ratio (CM ratio)**. This ratio is computed as follows:

$$CM\ ratio = \frac{Contribution\ margin}{Sales}$$

For Acoustic Concepts, the computations are:

$$CM\ ratio = \frac{Total\ contribution\ margin}{Total\ sales} = \frac{\$40,000}{\$100,000} = 40\%$$

In a company such as Acoustic Concepts that has only one product, the CM ratio can also be computed on a per unit basis as follows:

$$CM\ ratio = \frac{Unit\ contribution\ margin}{Unit\ selling\ price} = \frac{\$100}{\$250} = 40\%$$

The CM ratio shows how the contribution margin will be affected by a change in total sales. Acoustic Concepts' CM ratio of 40% means that for each dollar increase in sales, total contribution margin will increase by 40 cents ($1 sales × CM ratio of 40%). Net operating income will also increase by 40 cents, assuming that fixed costs are not affected by the increase in sales. Generally, the effect of a change in sales on the contribution margin is expressed in equation form as:

$$Change\ in\ contribution\ margin = CM\ ratio \times Change\ in\ sales$$

As this illustration suggests, *the impact on net operating income of any given dollar change in total sales can be computed by applying the CM ratio to the dollar change.* For example, if Acoustic Concepts plans a $30,000 increase in sales during the coming month, the contribution margin should increase by $12,000 ($30,000 increase in sales × CM ratio of 40%). As we noted above, net operating income will also increase by $12,000 if fixed costs do not change. This is verified by the following table:

	Sales Volume			Percent of Sales
	Present	**Expected**	**Increase**	
Sales....................	$100,000	$130,000	$30,000	100%
Variable expenses.......	60,000	78,000*	18,000	60%
Contribution margin......	40,000	52,000	12,000	40%
Fixed expenses	35,000	35,000	0	
Net operating income ...	$ 5,000	$ 17,000	$12,000	

* $130,000 expected sales ÷ $250 per unit = 520 units. 520 units × $150 per unit = $78,000.

The relation between profit and the CM ratio can also be expressed using the following equations:

$$\text{Profit} = \text{CM ratio} \times \text{Sales} - \text{Fixed expenses}[2]$$

or, in terms of changes,

$$\text{Change in profit} = \text{CM ratio} \times \text{Change in sales} - \text{Change in fixed expenses}$$

For example, at sales of $130,000, the profit is expected to be $17,000 as shown below:

$$\text{Profit} = \text{CM ratio} \times \text{Sales} - \text{Fixed expenses}$$
$$= 0.40 \times \$130,000 - \$35,000$$
$$= \$52,000 - \$35,000 = \$17,000$$

Again, if you are comfortable with algebra, this approach will often be quicker and easier than constructing contribution format income statements.

The CM ratio is particularly valuable in situations where the dollar sales of one product must be traded off against the dollar sales of another product. In this situation, products that yield the greatest amount of contribution margin per dollar of sales should be emphasized.

Some Applications of CVP Concepts

Bob Luchinni, the accountant at Acoustic Concepts, wanted to demonstrate to the company's president Prem Narayan how the concepts developed on the preceding pages can be used in planning and decision making. Bob gathered the following basic data:

	Per Unit	Percent of Sales
Selling price.................	$250	100%
Variable expenses	150	60%
Contribution margin	$100	40%

LEARNING OBJECTIVE 3–4

Show the effects on net operating income of changes in variable costs, fixed costs, selling price, and volume.

---

[2] This equation can be derived using the basic profit equation and the definition of the CM ratio as follows:

$$\text{Profit} = (\text{Sales} - \text{Variable expenses}) - \text{Fixed expenses}$$
$$\text{Profit} = \text{Contribution margin} - \text{Fixed expenses}$$
$$\text{Profit} = \frac{\text{Contribution margin}}{\text{Sales}} \times \text{Sales} - \text{Fixed expenses}$$
$$\text{Profit} = \text{CM ratio} \times \text{Sales} - \text{Fixed expenses}$$

Recall that fixed expenses are $35,000 per month. Bob Luchinni will use these data to show the effects of changes in variable costs, fixed costs, sales price, and sales volume on the company's profitability in a variety of situations.

Before proceeding further, however, we need to introduce another concept—the *variable expense ratio*. The **variable expense ratio** is the ratio of variable expenses to sales. It can be computed by dividing the total variable expenses by the total sales, or in a single product analysis, it can be computed by dividing the variable expenses per unit by the unit selling price. In the case of Acoustic Concepts, the variable expense ratio is 0.60; that is, variable expense is 60% of sales. Expressed as an equation, the definition of the variable expense ratio is:

$$\text{Variable expense ratio} = \frac{\text{Variable expenses}}{\text{Sales}}$$

This leads to a useful equation that relates the CM ratio to the variable expense ratio as follows:

$$\text{CM ratio} = \frac{\text{Contribution margin}}{\text{Sales}}$$

$$\text{CM ratio} = \frac{\text{Sales} - \text{Variable expenses}}{\text{Sales}}$$

$$\text{CM ratio} = 1 - \text{Variable expense ratio}$$

Change in Fixed Cost and Sales Volume Acoustic Concepts is currently selling 400 speakers per month at $250 per speaker for total monthly sales of $100,000. The sales manager feels that a $10,000 increase in the monthly advertising budget would increase monthly sales by $30,000 to a total of 520 units. Should the advertising budget be increased? The table below shows the financial impact of the proposed change in the monthly advertising budget.

	Current Sales	Sales with Additional Advertising Budget	Difference	Percent of Sales
Sales.	$100,000	$130,000	$30,000	100%
Variable expenses	60,000	78,000*	18,000	60%
Contribution margin.	40,000	52,000	12,000	40%
Fixed expenses.	35,000	45,000†	10,000	
Net operating income	$ 5,000	$ 7,000	$ 2,000	

*520 units × $150 per unit = $78,000.
†$35,000 + additional $10,000 monthly advertising budget = $45,000.

Assuming no other factors need to be considered, the increase in the advertising budget should be approved because it would increase net operating income by $2,000. There are two shorter ways to arrive at this solution. The first alternative solution follows:

Alternative Solution 1

Expected total contribution margin:	
$130,000 × 40% CM ratio	$52,000
Present total contribution margin:	
$100,000 × 40% CM ratio	40,000
Increase in total contribution margin.	12,000
Change in fixed expenses:	
Less incremental advertising expense	10,000
Increased net operating income.	$ 2,000

Because in this case only the fixed costs and the sales volume change, the solution can also be quickly derived as follows:

Alternative Solution 2

Incremental contribution margin:	
$30,000 × 40% CM ratio.....................	$12,000
Less incremental advertising expense...........	10,000
Increased net operating income...............	$ 2,000

Notice that this approach does not depend on knowledge of previous sales. Also note that it is unnecessary under either shorter approach to prepare an income statement. Both of the alternative solutions involve **incremental analysis**—they consider only the costs and revenues that will change if the new program is implemented. Although in each case a new income statement could have been prepared, the incremental approach is simpler and more direct and focuses attention on the specific changes that would occur as a result of the decision.

Change in Variable Costs and Sales Volume Refer to the original data. Recall that Acoustic Concepts is currently selling 400 speakers per month. Prem is considering the use of higher-quality components, which would increase variable costs (and thereby reduce the contribution margin) by $10 per speaker. However, the sales manager predicts that using higher-quality components would increase sales to 480 speakers per month. Should the higher-quality components be used?

The $10 increase in variable costs would decrease the unit contribution margin by $10—from $100 down to $90.

Solution

Expected total contribution margin with higher-quality components:	
480 speakers × $90 per speaker	$43,200
Present total contribution margin:	
400 speakers × $100 per speaker	40,000
Increase in total contribution margin	$ 3,200

According to this analysis, the higher-quality components should be used. Because fixed costs would not change, the $3,200 increase in contribution margin shown above should result in a $3,200 increase in net operating income.

Change in Fixed Cost, Selling Price, and Sales Volume Refer to the original data and recall again that Acoustic Concepts is currently selling 400 speakers per month. To increase sales, the sales manager would like to cut the selling price by $20 per speaker and increase the advertising budget by $15,000 per month. The sales manager believes that if these two steps are taken, unit sales will increase by 50% to 600 speakers per month. Should the changes be made?

A decrease in the selling price of $20 per speaker would decrease the unit contribution margin by $20 down to $80.

Solution

According to this analysis, the changes should not be made. The $7,000 reduction in net operating income that is shown above can be verified by preparing comparative income statements as shown below.

	Expected total contribution margin with lower selling price:		
	600 speakers × $80 per speaker	$48,000
	Present total contribution margin:	
	400 speakers × $100 per speaker	40,000
	Incremental contribution margin.	8,000
	Change in fixed expenses:	
	Less incremental advertising expense	15,000
	Reduction in net operating income.	$ (7,000)

	Present 400 Speakers per Month		Expected 600 Speakers per Month		
	Total	Per Unit	Total	Per Unit	Difference
Sales.	$100,000	$250	$138,000	$230	$38,000
Variable expenses	60,000	150	90,000	150	30,000
Contribution margin.	40,000	$100	48,000	$ 80	8,000
Fixed expenses	35,000		50,000*		15,000
Net operating income (loss)	$ 5,000		$ (2,000)		$ (7,000)

*35,000 + Additional monthly advertising budget of $15,000 = $50,000.

Change in Variable Cost, Fixed Cost, and Sales Volume

Refer to Acoustic Concepts' original data. As before, the company is currently selling 400 speakers per month. The sales manager would like to pay salespersons a sales commission of $15 per speaker sold, rather than the flat salaries that now total $6,000 per month. The sales manager is confident that the change would increase monthly sales by 15% to 460 speakers per month. Should the change be made?

Solution Changing the sales staff's compensation from salaries to commissions would affect both fixed and variable expenses. Fixed expenses would decrease by $6,000, from $35,000 to $29,000. Variable expenses per unit would increase by $15, from $150 to $165, and the unit contribution margin would decrease from $100 to $85.

	Expected total contribution margin with sales staff on commissions:		
	460 speakers × $85 per speaker	$39,100
	Present total contribution margin:	
	400 speakers × $100 per speaker	40,000
	Decrease in total contribution margin	(900)
	Change in fixed expenses:	
	Add salaries avoided if a commission is paid.	6,000
	Increase in net operating income.	$ 5,100

According to this analysis, the changes should be made. Again, the same answer can be obtained by preparing comparative income statements:

Change in Selling Price

Refer to the original data where Acoustic Concepts is currently selling 400 speakers per month. The company has an opportunity to make a bulk sale of 150 speakers to a wholesaler if an acceptable price can be negotiated. This sale would not disturb the company's regular sales and would not affect the company's total fixed expenses. What price per speaker should be quoted to the wholesaler if Acoustic Concepts is seeking a profit of $3,000 on the bulk sale?

	Present 400 Speakers per Month		Expected 460 Speakers per Month		
	Total	Per Unit	Total	Per Unit	Difference
Sales....................	$100,000	$250	$115,000	$250	$15,000
Variable expenses........	60,000	150	75,900	165	15,900
Contribution margin.......	40,000	$100	39,100	$ 85	900
Fixed expenses	35,000		29,000		(6,000)*
Net operating income.....	$ 5,000		$ 10,100		$ 5,100

*Note: A *reduction* in fixed expenses has the effect of *increasing* net operating income.

Solution

Variable cost per speaker.........	$150
Desired profit per speaker:	
$3,000 ÷ 150 speakers	20
Quoted price per speaker	$170

Notice that fixed expenses are not included in the computation. This is because fixed expenses are not affected by the bulk sale, so all of the additional contribution margin increases the company's profits.

MANAGING RISK IN THE BOOK PUBLISHING INDUSTRY

Greenleaf Book Group is a book publishing company in Austin, Texas, that attracts authors who are willing to pay publishing costs and forgo up-front advances in exchange for a larger royalty rate on each book sold. For example, assume a typical publisher prints 10,000 copies of a new book that it sells for $12.50 per unit. The publisher pays the author an advance of $20,000 to write the book and then incurs $60,000 of expenses to market, print, and edit the book. The publisher also pays the author a 20% royalty (or $2.50 per unit) on each book sold above 8,000 units. In this scenario, the publisher must sell 6,400 books to break even (= $80,000 in fixed costs ÷ $12.50 per unit). If all 10,000 copies are sold, the author earns $25,000 (= $20,000 advance + 2,000 copies × $2.50) and the publisher earns $40,000 (= $125,000 − $60,000 − $20,000 × $5,000).

Greenleaf alters the financial arrangement described above by requiring the author to assume the risk of poor sales. It pays the author a 70% royalty on all units sold (or $8.75 per unit), but the author forgoes the $20,000 advance and pays Greenleaf $60,000 to market, print, and edit the book. If the book flops, the author fails to recover her production costs. If all 10,000 units are sold, the author earns $27,500 (= $10,000 units × $8.75 − $60,000) and Greenleaf earns $37,500 (= 10,000 units × ($12.50 − $8.75)).

Source: Christopher Steiner, "Book It," *Forbes*, September 7, 2009, p. 58.

© Yellow Dog Productions/Digital Vision/ Getty Images, RF

Break-Even and Target Profit Analysis

Managers use break-even and target profit analysis to answer questions such as how much would we have to sell to avoid incurring a loss or how much would we have to sell to make a profit of $10,000 per month? We'll discuss break-even analysis first followed by target profit analysis.

Break—Even Analysis

LEARNING OBJECTIVE 3–5
Determine the break-even point.

Earlier in the chapter we defined the break-even point as *the level of sales at which the company's profit is zero.* To calculate the break-even point (in unit sales and dollar sales), managers can use either of two approaches, the equation method or the formula method. We'll demonstrate both approaches using the data from Acoustic Concepts.

The Equation Method The equation method relies on the basic profit equation introduced earlier in the chapter. Since Acoustic Concepts has only one product, we'll use the contribution margin form of this equation to perform the break-even calculations. Remembering that Acoustic Concepts' unit contribution margin is $100, and its fixed expenses are $35,000, the company's break-even point is computed as follows:

$$\text{Profit} = \text{Unit CM} \times Q - \text{Fixed expense}$$

$$\$0 = \$100 \times Q - \$35,000$$

$$\$100 \times Q = \$0 + \$35,000$$

$$Q = \$35,000 \div \$100$$

$$Q = 350$$

Thus, as we determined earlier in the chapter, Acoustic Concepts will break even (or earn zero profit) at a sales volume of 350 speakers per month.

The Formula Method The formula method is a shortcut version of the equation method. It centers on the idea discussed earlier in the chapter that each unit sold provides a certain amount of contribution margin that goes toward covering fixed expenses. In a single product situation, the formula for computing the unit sales to break even is:

$$\text{Unit sales to break even} = \frac{\text{Fixed expenses}^3}{\text{Unit CM}}$$

In the case of Acoustic Concepts, the unit sales needed to break even is computed as follows:

$$\text{Unit sales to break even} = \frac{\text{Fixed expenses}}{\text{Unit CM}}$$

$$= \frac{\$35,000}{\$100}$$

$$= 350$$

Notice that 350 units is the same answer that we got when using the equation method. This will always be the case because the formula method and equation method are mathematically equivalent. The formula method simply skips a few steps in the equation method.

Break—Even in Dollar Sales In addition to finding the break-even point in unit sales, we can also find the break-even point in dollar sales using three methods. First, we could solve for the break-even point in *unit* sales using the equation method or formula method and then simply multiply the result by the selling price. In the case of Acoustic Concepts, the break-even point in dollar sales using this approach would be computed as 350 speakers × $250 per speaker, or $87,500 in total sales.

---

[3] This formula can be derived as follows:

$$\begin{aligned}\text{Profit} &= \text{Unit CM} \times Q - \text{Fixed expenses} \\ \$0 &= \text{Unit CM} \times Q - \text{Fixed expenses} \\ \text{Unit CM} + Q &= \$0 + \text{Fixed expenses} \\ Q &= \text{Fixed expenses} \div \text{Unit CM}\end{aligned}$$

Second, we can use the equation method to compute the break-even point in dollar sales. Remembering that Acoustic Concepts' contribution margin ratio is 40% and its fixed expenses are $35,000, the equation method calculates the break-even point in dollar sales as follows:

$$\text{Profit} = \text{CM ratio} \times \text{Sales} - \text{Fixed expenses}$$

$$\$0 = 0.40 \times \text{Sales} - \$35,000$$

$$0.40 \times \text{Sales} = \$0 + \$35,000$$

$$\text{Sales} = \$35,000 \div 0.40$$

$$\text{Sales} = \$87,500$$

Third, we can use the formula method to compute the dollar sales needed to break even as shown below:

$$\text{Dollar sales to break even} = \frac{\text{Fixed expenses}^4}{\text{CM ratio}}$$

In the case of Acoustic Concepts, the computations are performed as follows:

$$\text{Dollar sales to break even} = \frac{\text{Fixed expenses}}{\text{CM ratio}}$$

$$= \frac{\$35,000}{0.40}$$

$$= \$87,500$$

Again, you'll notice that the break-even point in dollar sales ($87,500) is the same under all three methods. This will always be the case because these methods are mathematically equivalent.

Target Profit Analysis

Target profit analysis is one of the key uses of CVP analysis. In **target profit analysis**, we estimate what sales volume is needed to achieve a specific target profit. For example, suppose Prem Narayan of Acoustic Concepts would like to estimate the sales needed to attain a target profit of $40,000 per month. To determine the unit sales and dollar sales needed to achieve a target profit, we can rely on the same two approaches that we have been discussing thus far, the equation method or the formula method.

LEARNING OBJECTIVE 3–6
Determine the level of sales needed to achieve a desired target profit.

The Equation Method To compute the unit sales required to achieve a target profit of $40,000 per month, Acoustic Concepts can use the same profit equation that was used for its break-even analysis. Remembering that the company's contribution margin per unit is $100 and its total fixed expenses are $35,000, the equation method could be applied as follows:

$$\text{Profit} = \text{Unit CM} \times Q - \text{Fixed expense}$$

$$\$40,000 = \$100 \times Q - \$35,000$$

$$\$100 \times Q = \$40,000 + \$35,000$$

$$Q = \$75,000 \div \$100$$

$$Q = 750$$

---

[4] This formula can be derived as follows:

$$
\begin{aligned}
\text{Profit} &= \text{CM ratio} \times \text{Sales} - \text{Fixed expenses} \\
\$0 &= \text{CM ratio} \times \text{Sales} - \text{Fixed expenses} \\
\text{CM ratio} \times \text{Sales} &= \$0 + \text{Fixed expenses} \\
\text{Sales} &= \text{Fixed expenses} \div \text{CM ratio}
\end{aligned}
$$

Thus, the target profit can be achieved by selling 750 speakers per month. Notice that the only difference between this equation and the equation used for Acoustic Concepts' break-even calculation is the profit figure. In the break-even scenario, the profit is $0, whereas in the target profit scenario the profit is $40,000.

The Formula Method In general, in a single product situation, we can compute the sales volume required to attain a specific target profit using the following formula:

$$\text{Unit sales to attain the target profit} = \frac{\text{Target profit} + \text{Fixed expenses}}{\text{Unit CM}}$$

In the case of Acoustic Concepts, the unit sales needed to attain a target profit of 40,000 is computed as follows:

$$\text{Unit sales to attain the target profit} = \frac{\text{Target profit} + \text{Fixed expenses}}{\text{Unit CM}}$$

$$= \frac{\$40,000 + \$35,000}{\$100}$$

$$= 750$$

Target Profit Analysis in Terms of Dollar Sales When quantifying the dollar sales needed to attain a target profit we can apply the same three methods that we used for calculating the dollar sales needed to break even. First, we can solve for the *unit* sales needed to attain the target profit using the equation method or formula method and then simply multiply the result by the selling price. In the case of Acoustic Concepts, the dollar sales to attain its target profit would be computed as 750 speakers × $250 per speaker, or $187,500 in total sales.

Second, we can use the equation method to compute the dollar sales needed to attain the target profit. Remembering that Acoustic Concepts' target profit is $40,000, its contribution margin ratio is 40%, and its fixed expenses are $35,000, the equation method calculates the answer as follows:

$$\text{Profit} = \text{CM ratio} \times \text{Sales} - \text{Fixed expenses}$$

$$\$40,000 = 0.40 \times \text{Sales} - \$35,000$$

$$0.40 \times \text{Sales} = \$40,000 + \$35,000$$

$$\text{Sales} = \$75,000 \div 0.40$$

$$\text{Sales} = \$187,500$$

Third, we can use the formula method to compute the dollar sales needed to attain the target profit as shown below:

$$\text{Dollar sales to attain a target profit} = \frac{\text{Target profit} + \text{Fixed expenses}}{\text{CM ratio}}$$

In the case of Acoustic Concepts, the computations would be:

$$\text{Dollar sales to attain a target profit} = \frac{\text{Target profit} + \text{Fixed expenses}}{\text{CM ratio}}$$

$$= \frac{\$40,000 + \$35,000}{0.40}$$

$$= \$187,500$$

Again, you'll notice that the answers are the same regardless of which method we use. This is because all of the methods discussed are simply different roads to the same destination.

SNAP FITNESS GROWS IN A WEAK ECONOMY

When Bally's Total Fitness was filing for bankruptcy, Snap Fitness was expanding to more than 900 clubs in the United States with 400,000 members. The secret to Snap Fitness' success is its "no frills" approach to exercise. Each club typically has five treadmills, two stationary bikes, five elliptical machines, and weight equipment while bypassing amenities such as on-site child care, juice bars, and showers. Each club is usually staffed only 25–40 hours per week and it charges a membership fee of $35 per month.

   To open a new Snap Fitness location, each franchise owner has an initial capital outlay of $120,000 for various types of equipment and a one-time licensing fee of $15,000. The franchisee also pays Snap (the parent company) a royalty fee of $400 per month plus $0.50 for each membership. Snap also collects one-time fees of $5 for each new member's "billing setup" and $5 for each security card issued. If a new club attracts 275 members, it can break even in as little as three months. Can you estimate the underlying calculations related to this break-even point?

Source: Nicole Perlroth, "Survival of the Fittest," *Forbes,* January 12, 2009, pp. 54–55.

© AP Images/LM Otero

The Margin of Safety

The **margin of safety** is the excess of budgeted or actual sales dollars over the break-even volume of sales dollars. It is the amount by which sales can drop before losses are incurred. The higher the margin of safety, the lower the risk of not breaking even and incurring a loss. The formula for the margin of safety is:

$$\text{Margin of safety in dollars} = \text{Total budgeted (or actual) sales} - \text{Break-even sales}$$

   The margin of safety can also be expressed in percentage form by dividing the margin of safety in dollars by total dollar sales:

$$\text{Margin of safety percentage} = \frac{\text{Margin of safety in dollars}}{\text{Total budgeted (or actual) sales in dollars}}$$

   The calculation of the margin of safety for Acoustic Concepts is:

Sales (at the current volume of 400 speakers) (a).	$100,000
Break-even sales (at 350 speakers).	87,500
Margin of safety in dollars (b)	$ 12,500
Margin of safety percentage, (b) ÷ (a).	12.5%

This margin of safety means that at the current level of sales and with the company's current prices and cost structure, a reduction in sales of $12,500, or 12.5%, would result in just breaking even.

   In a single-product company like Acoustic Concepts, the margin of safety can also be expressed in terms of the number of units sold by dividing the margin of safety in dollars by the selling price per unit. In this case, the margin of safety is 50 speakers ($12,500 ÷ $250 per speaker = 50 speakers).

COMPUTING MARGIN OF SAFETY FOR A SMALL BUSINESS

Sam Calagione owns Dogfish Head Craft Brewery, a microbrewery in Rehobeth Beach, Delaware. He charges distributors as much as $100 per case for his premium beers such as World Wide Stout. The high-priced microbrews bring in $800,000 in operating income on revenue of $7 million. Calagione reports that his raw ingredients and labor costs for one case of World Wide Stout are $30 and $16, respectively. Bottling and packaging costs are $6 per case. Gas and electric costs are about $10 per case.

If we assume that World Wide Stout is representative of all Dogfish microbrews, then we can compute the company's margin of safety in five steps. First, variable cost as a percentage of sales is 62% [($30 + $16 + $6 + $10)/$100]. Second, the contribution margin ratio is 38% (1 − 0.62). Third, Dogfish's total fixed cost is $1,860,000 [($7,000,000 × 0.38) − $800,000]. Fourth, the break-even point in dollar sales is $4,894,737 ($1,860,000/0.38). Fifth, the margin of safety is $2,105,263 ($7,000,000 − $4,894,737).

Source: Patricia Huang, "Château Dogfish," *Forbes*, February 28, 2005, pp. 57–59.

MANAGERIAL ACCOUNTING IN ACTION

The Wrap-Up

ACOUSTIC
concepts
inc

Prem Narayan and Bob Luchinni met to discuss the results of Bob's analysis.

Prem: Bob, everything you have shown me is pretty clear. I can see what impact the sales manager's suggestions would have on our profits. Some of those suggestions are quite good and others are not so good. I am concerned that our margin of safety is only 50 speakers. What can we do to increase this number?

Bob: Well, we have to increase total sales or decrease the break-even point or both.

Prem: And to decrease the break-even point, we have to either decrease our fixed expenses or increase our unit contribution margin?

Bob: Exactly.

Prem: And to increase our unit contribution margin, we must either increase our selling price or decrease the variable cost per unit?

Bob: Correct.

Prem: So what do you suggest?

Bob: Well, the analysis doesn't tell us which of these to do, but it does indicate we have a potential problem here.

Prem: If you don't have any immediate suggestions, I would like to call a general meeting next week to discuss ways we can work on increasing the margin of safety. I think everyone will be concerned about how vulnerable we are to even small downturns in sales.

CVP Considerations in Choosing a Cost Structure

Cost structure refers to the relative proportion of fixed and variable costs in an organization. Managers often have some latitude in trading off between these two types of costs. For example, fixed investments in automated equipment can reduce variable labor costs. In this section, we discuss the choice of a cost structure. We also introduce the concept of *operating leverage.*

Cost Structure and Profit Stability

Which cost structure is better—high variable costs and low fixed costs, or the opposite? No single answer to this question is possible; each approach has its advantages. To show what we mean, refer to the following contribution format income statements for two blueberry farms. Bogside Farm depends on migrant workers to pick its berries by hand, whereas Sterling Farm has invested in expensive berry-picking machines. Consequently, Bogside Farm has higher variable costs, but Sterling Farm has higher fixed costs:

	Bogside Farm		Sterling Farm	
	Amount	Percent	Amount	Percent
Sales	$100,000	100%	$100,000	100%
Variable expenses	60,000	60%	30,000	30%
Contribution margin	40,000	40%	70,000	70%
Fixed expenses	30,000		60,000	
Net operating income	$ 10,000		$ 10,000	

Which farm has the better cost structure? The answer depends on many factors, including the long-run trend in sales, year-to-year fluctuations in the level of sales, and the attitude of the owners toward risk. If sales are expected to exceed $100,000 in the future, then Sterling Farm probably has the better cost structure. The reason is that its CM ratio is higher, and its profits will therefore increase more rapidly as sales increase. To illustrate, assume that each farm experiences a 10% increase in sales without any increase in fixed costs. The new income statements would be as follows:

	Bogside Farm		Sterling Farm	
	Amount	Percent	Amount	Percent
Sales	$110,000	100%	$110,000	100%
Variable expenses	66,000	60%	33,000	30%
Contribution margin	44,000	40%	77,000	70%
Fixed expenses	30,000		60,000	
Net operating income	$ 14,000		$ 17,000	

Sterling Farm has experienced a greater increase in net operating income due to its higher CM ratio even though the increase in sales was the same for both farms.

What if sales drop below $100,000? What are the farms' break-even points? What are their margins of safety? The computations needed to answer these questions are shown below using the formula method:

	Bogside Farm	Sterling Farm
Fixed expenses	$ 30,000	$ 60,000
Contribution margin ratio	÷ 0.40	÷ 0.70
Dollar sales to break even	$ 75,000	$ 85,714
Total current sales (a)	$100,000	$100,000
Break-even sales	75,000	85,714
Margin of safety in sales dollars (b)	$ 25,000	$ 14,286
Margin of safety percentage (b) ÷ (a)	25.0%	14.3%

Bogside Farm's margin of safety is greater and its contribution margin ratio is lower than Sterling Farm. Therefore, Bogside Farm is less vulnerable to downturns than Sterling Farm. Due to its lower contribution margin ratio, Bogside Farm will not lose contribution margin as rapidly as Sterling Farm when sales decline. Thus, Bogside Farm's profit will be less volatile. We saw earlier that this is a drawback when sales increase, but it provides more protection when sales drop. And because its break-even point is lower, Bogside Farm can suffer a larger sales decline before losses emerge.

To summarize, without knowing the future, it is not obvious which cost structure is better. Both have advantages and disadvantages. Sterling Farm, with its higher fixed costs and lower variable costs, will experience wider swings in net operating income as sales fluctuate, with greater profits in good years and greater losses in bad years. Bogside Farm, with its lower fixed costs and higher variable costs, will enjoy greater profit stability and will be more protected from losses during bad years, but at the cost of lower net operating income in good years.

Operating Leverage

LEARNING OBJECTIVE 3–8

Compute the degree of operating leverage at a particular level of sales and explain how it can be used to predict changes in net operating income.

A lever is a tool for multiplying force. Using a lever, a massive object can be moved with only a modest amount of force. In business, *operating leverage* serves a similar purpose. **Operating leverage** is a measure of how sensitive net operating income is to a given percentage change in dollar sales. Operating leverage acts as a multiplier. If operating leverage is high, a small percentage increase in sales can produce a much larger percentage increase in net operating income.

Operating leverage can be illustrated by returning to the data for the two blueberry farms. We previously showed that a 10% increase in sales (from $100,000 to $110,000 in each farm) results in a 70% increase in the net operating income of Sterling Farm (from $10,000 to $17,000) and only a 40% increase in the net operating income of Bogside Farm (from $10,000 to $14,000). Thus, for a 10% increase in sales, Sterling Farm experiences a much greater percentage increase in profits than does Bogside Farm. Therefore, Sterling Farm has greater operating leverage than Bogside Farm.

The **degree of operating leverage** at a given level of sales is computed by the following formula:

$$\text{Degree of operating leverage} = \frac{\text{Contribution margin}}{\text{Net operating income}}$$

The degree of operating leverage is a measure, at a given level of sales, of how a percentage change in sales volume will affect profits. To illustrate, the degree of operating leverage for the two farms at $100,000 sales would be computed as follows:

$$\text{Bogside Farm:} \frac{\$40,000}{\$10,000} = 4$$

$$\text{Sterling Farm:} \frac{\$70,000}{\$10,000} = 7$$

Because the degree of operating leverage for Bogside Farm is 4, the farm's net operating income grows four times as fast as its sales. In contrast, Sterling Farm's net operating income grows seven times as fast as its sales. Thus, if sales increase by 10%, then we can expect the net operating income of Bogside Farm to increase by four times this amount, or by 40%, and the net operating income of Sterling Farm to increase by seven times this amount, or by 70%. In general, this relation between the percentage change in sales and the percentage change in net operating income is given by the following formula:

$$\frac{\text{Percentage change in}}{\text{net operating income}} = \frac{\text{Degree of}}{\text{operating leverage}} \times \frac{\text{Percentage}}{\text{change in sales}}$$

Bogside Farm: Percentage change in net operating income $= 4 \times 10\% = 40\%$

Sterling Farm: Percentage change in net operating income $= 7 \times 10\% = 70\%$

What is responsible for the higher operating leverage at Sterling Farm? The only difference between the two farms is their cost structure. If two companies have the same total revenue and same total expense but different cost structures, then the company with the higher proportion of fixed costs in its cost structure will have higher operating leverage. Referring back to the original example on page 206, when both farms have sales of $100,000 and total expenses of $90,000, one-third of Bogside Farm's costs are fixed but two-thirds of Sterling Farm's costs are fixed. As a consequence, Sterling's degree of operating leverage is higher than Bogside's.

The degree of operating leverage is not a constant; it is greatest at sales levels near the break-even point and decreases as sales and profits rise. The following table shows the degree of operating leverage for Bogside Farm at various sales levels. (Data used earlier for Bogside Farm are shown in color.)

Sales	$75,000	$80,000	$100,000	$150,000	$225,000
Variable expenses	45,000	48,000	60,000	90,000	135,000
Contribution margin (a)	30,000	32,000	40,000	60,000	90,000
Fixed expenses	30,000	30,000	30,000	30,000	30,000
Net operating income (b)	$ 0	$ 2,000	$ 10,000	$ 30,000	$ 60,000
Degree of operating leverage, (a) ÷ (b)	∞	16	4	2	1.5

Thus, a 10% increase in sales would increase profits by only 15% (10% × 1.5) if sales were previously $225,000, as compared to the 40% increase we computed earlier at the $100,000 sales level. The degree of operating leverage will continue to decrease the farther the company moves from its break-even point. At the break-even point, the degree of operating leverage is infinitely large ($30,000 contribution margin ÷ $0 net operating income = ∞).

The degree of operating leverage can be used to quickly estimate what impact various percentage changes in sales will have on profits, without the necessity of preparing detailed income statements. As shown by our examples, the effects of operating leverage can be dramatic. If a company is near its break-even point, then even small percentage increases in sales can yield large percentage increases in profits. *This explains why management will often work very hard for only a small increase in sales volume.* If the degree of operating leverage is 5, then a 6% increase in sales would translate into a 30% increase in profits.

IN BUSINESS

THE DANGERS OF A HIGH DEGREE OF OPERATING LEVERAGE

In recent years, computer chip manufacturers have poured more than $75 billion into constructing new manufacturing facilities to meet the growing demand for digital devices such as iPhones and BlackBerrys. Because 70% of the costs of running these facilities are fixed, a sharp drop in customer demand forces these companies to choose between two undesirable options. They can slash production levels and absorb large amounts of unused capacity costs, or they can continue producing large volumes of output in spite of shrinking demand, thereby flooding the market with excess supply and lowering prices. Either choice distresses investors who tend to shy away from computer chip makers in economic downturns.

Source: Bruce Einhorn, "Chipmakers on the Edge," *BusinessWeek*, January 5, 2009, pp. 30–31.

© Digital Stock/Corbis, RF

Structuring Sales Commissions

Companies usually compensate salespeople by paying them a commission based on sales, a salary, or a combination of the two. Commissions based on sales dollars can lead to lower profits. To illustrate, consider Pipeline Unlimited, a producer of surfing equipment. Salespersons sell the company's products to retail sporting goods stores throughout North America and the Pacific Basin. Data for two of the company's surfboards, the XR7 and Turbo models, appear below:

	Model	
	XR7	Turbo
Selling price..............	$695	$749
Variable expenses.........	344	410
Contribution margin........	$351	$339

Which model will salespeople push hardest if they are paid a commission of 10% of sales revenue? The answer is the Turbo because it has the higher selling price and hence the larger commission. On the other hand, from the standpoint of the company, profits will be greater if salespeople steer customers toward the XR7 model because it has the higher contribution margin.

To eliminate such conflicts, commissions can be based on contribution margin rather than on selling price. If this is done, the salespersons will want to sell the mix of products that maximizes contribution margin. Providing that fixed costs are not affected by the sales mix, maximizing the contribution margin will also maximize the company's profit.[5] In effect, by maximizing their own compensation, salespersons will also maximize the company's profit.

Sales Mix

LEARNING OBJECTIVE 3–9
Compute the break-even point for a multiproduct company and explain the effects of shifts in the sales mix on contribution margin and the break-even point.

Before concluding our discussion of CVP concepts, we need to consider the impact of changes in *sales mix* on a company's profit.

The Definition of Sales Mix

The term **sales mix** refers to the relative proportions in which a company's products are sold. The idea is to achieve the combination, or mix, that will yield the greatest profits. Most companies have many products, and often these products are not equally profitable. Hence, profits will depend to some extent on the company's sales mix. Profits will be greater if high-margin rather than low-margin items make up a relatively large proportion of total sales.

Changes in the sales mix can cause perplexing variations in a company's profits. A shift in the sales mix from high-margin items to low-margin items can cause total profits to decrease even though total sales may increase. Conversely, a shift in the sales mix from low-margin items to high-margin items can cause the reverse effect—total profits may increase even though total sales decrease. It is one thing to achieve a particular sales volume; it is quite another to sell the most profitable mix of products.

---

[5] This also assumes the company has no production constraint. If it does, the sales commissions should be modified. See the Profitability Appendix at the end of the book.

NETBOOK SALES CANNIBALIZE PC SALES

When computer manufacturers introduced the "netbook," they expected it to serve as a consumer's third computer—complementing home and office personal computers (PCs) rather than replacing them. However, when the economy soured, many customers decided to buy lower-priced netbooks instead of PCs, which in turn adversely affected the financial performance of many companies. For example, when Microsoft failed to achieve its sales goals, the company partially blamed growing netbook sales and declining PC sales for its troubles. Microsoft's Windows operating system for netbooks sells for $15–$25 per device, which is less than half the cost of the company's least expensive Windows operating system for PCs.

Source: Olga Kharif, "Small, Cheap—and Frighteningly Popular," *BusinessWeek*, December 8, 2008, p. 64.

Sales Mix and Break–Even Analysis

If a company sells more than one product, break-even analysis is more complex than discussed to this point. The reason is that different products will have different selling prices, different costs, and different contribution margins. Consequently, the break-even point depends on the mix in which the various products are sold. To illustrate, consider Virtual Journeys Unlimited, a small company that sells two DVDs: the Monuments DVD, a tour of the United States' most popular National Monuments; and the Parks DVD, which tours the United States' National Parks. The company's September sales, expenses, and break-even point are shown in Exhibit 3–4.

As shown in the exhibit, the break-even point is $60,000 in sales, which was computed by dividing the company's fixed expenses of $27,000 by its overall CM ratio of 45%. However, this is the break-even only if the company's sales mix does not change. Currently, the Monuments DVD is responsible for 20% and the Parks DVD for 80% of the company's dollar sales. Assuming this sales mix does not change, if total sales are $60,000, the sales of the Monuments DVD would be $12,000 (20% of $60,000) and the sales of the Parks DVD would be $48,000 (80% of $60,000). As shown in Exhibit 3–4, at these levels of sales, the company would indeed break even. But $60,000 in sales represents the break-even point for the company only if the sales mix does not change. *If the sales mix changes, then the break-even point will also usually change.* This is illustrated by the results for October in which the sales mix shifted away from the more profitable Parks DVD (which has a 50% CM ratio) toward the less profitable Monuments CD (which has a 25% CM ratio). These results appear in Exhibit 3–5.

Although sales have remained unchanged at $100,000, the sales mix is exactly the reverse of what it was in Exhibit 3–4, with the bulk of the sales now coming from the less profitable Monuments DVD. Notice that this shift in the sales mix has caused both the overall CM ratio and total profits to drop sharply from the prior month even though total sales are the same. The overall CM ratio has dropped from 45% in September to only 30% in October, and net operating income has dropped from $18,000 to only $3,000. In addition, with the drop in the overall CM ratio, the company's break-even point is no longer $60,000 in sales. Because the company is now realizing less average contribution margin per dollar of sales, it takes more sales to cover the same amount of fixed costs. Thus, the break-even point has increased from $60,000 to $90,000 in sales per year.

In preparing a break-even analysis, an assumption must be made concerning the sales mix. Usually the assumption is that it will not change. However, if the sales mix is expected to change, then this must be explicitly considered in any CVP computations.

EXHIBIT 3–4
Multiproduct Break-Even Analysis

Virtual Journeys Unlimited
Contribution Income Statement
For the Month of September

	Monuments DVD		Parks DVD		Total	
	Amount	Percent	Amount	Percent	Amount	Percent
Sales	$20,000	100%	$80,000	100%	$100,000	100%
Variable expenses...............	15,000	75%	40,000	50%	55,000	55%
Contribution margin	$ 5,000	25%	$40,000	50%	45,000	45%
Fixed expenses					27,000	
Net operating income............					$ 18,000	

Computation of the break-even point:

$$\frac{\text{Fixed expenses}}{\text{Overall CM ratio}} = \frac{\$27,000}{0.45} = \$60,000$$

Verification of the break-even point:

	Monuments DVD	Parks DVD	Total
Current dollar sales.................	$20,000	$80,000	$100,000
Percentage of total dollar sales	20%	80%	100%
Sales at the break-even point	$12,000	$48,000	$60,000

	Monuments DVD		Parks DVD		Total	
	Amount	Percent	Amount	Percent	Amount	Percent
Sales	$12,000	100%	$ 48,000	100%	$60,000	100%
Variable expenses...............	9,000	75%	24,000	50%	33,000	55%
Contribution margin	$ 3,000	25%	$ 24,000	50%	27,000	45%
Fixed expenses					27,000	
Net operating income............					$ 0	

EXHIBIT 3–5
Multiproduct Break-Even Analysis: A Shift in Sales Mix (see Exhibit 3–4)

Virtual Journeys Unlimited
Contribution Income Statement
For the Month of October

	Monuments DVD		Parks DVD		Total	
	Amount	Percent	Amount	Percent	Amount	Percent
Sales	$80,000	100%	$20,000	100%	$100,000	100%
Variable expenses...............	60,000	75%	10,000	50%	70,000	70%
Contribution margin	$20,000	25%	$10,000	50%	30,000	30%
Fixed expenses					27,000	
Net operating income............					$ 3,000	

Computation of the break-even point:

$$\frac{\text{Fixed expenses}}{\text{Overall CM ratio}} = \frac{\$27,000}{0.30} = \$90,000$$

Summary

CVP analysis is based on a simple model of how profits respond to prices, costs, and volume. This model can be used to answer a variety of critical questions such as what is the company's break-even volume, what is its margin of safety, and what is likely to happen if specific changes are made in prices, costs, and volume.

A CVP graph depicts the relationships between unit sales on the one hand and fixed expenses, variable expenses, total expenses, total sales, and profits on the other hand. The profit graph is simpler than the CVP graph and shows how profits depend on sales. The CVP and profit graphs are useful for developing intuition about how costs and profits respond to changes in sales.

The contribution margin ratio is the ratio of the total contribution margin to total sales. This ratio can be used to quickly estimate what impact a change in total sales would have on net operating income. The ratio is also useful in break-even analysis.

Break-even analysis is used to estimate how much sales would have to be to just break even. The unit sales required to break even can be estimated by dividing the fixed expense by the unit contribution margin. Target profit analysis is used to estimate how much sales would have to be to attain a specified target profit. The unit sales required to attain the target profit can be estimated by dividing the sum of the target profit and fixed expense by the unit contribution margin.

The margin of safety is the amount by which the company's current sales exceeds break-even sales.

The degree of operating leverage allows quick estimation of what impact a given percentage change in sales would have on the company's net operating income. The higher the degree of operating leverage, the greater is the impact on the company's profits. The degree of operating leverage is not constant—it depends on the company's current level of sales.

The profits of a multiproduct company are affected by its sales mix. Changes in the sales mix can affect the break-even point, margin of safety, and other critical factors.

Review Problem: CVP Relationships

Voltar Company manufactures and sells a specialized cordless telephone for high electromagnetic radiation environments. The company's contribution format income statement for the most recent year is given below:

	Total	Per Unit	Percent of Sales
Sales (20,000 units)	$1,200,000	$60	100%
Variable expenses	900,000	45	? %
Contribution margin	300,000	$15	? %
Fixed expenses	240,000		
Net operating income	$ 60,000		

Management is anxious to increase the company's profit and has asked for an analysis of a number of items.

Required:

1. Compute the company's CM ratio and variable expense ratio.
2. Compute the company's break-even point in both unit sales and dollar sales. Use the equation method.
3. Assume that sales increase by $400,000 next year. If cost behavior patterns remain unchanged, by how much will the company's net operating income increase? Use the CM ratio to compute your answer.

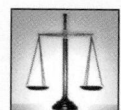

4. Refer to the original data. Assume that next year management wants the company to earn a profit of at least $90,000. How many units will have to be sold to meet this target profit?
5. Refer to the original data. Compute the company's margin of safety in both dollar and percentage form.
6. *a.* Compute the company's degree of operating leverage at the present level of sales.
    b. Assume that through a more intense effort by the sales staff, the company's sales increase by 8% next year. By what percentage would you expect net operating income to increase? Use the degree of operating leverage to obtain your answer.
    c. Verify your answer to (*b*) by preparing a new contribution format income statement showing an 8% increase in sales.
7. In an effort to increase sales and profits, management is considering the use of a higher-quality speaker. The higher-quality speaker would increase variable costs by $3 per unit, but management could eliminate one quality inspector who is paid a salary of $30,000 per year. The sales manager estimates that the higher-quality speaker would increase annual sales by at least 20%.
    a. Assuming that changes are made as described above, prepare a projected contribution format income statement for next year. Show data on a total, per unit, and percentage basis.
    b. Compute the company's new break-even point in both unit sales and dollar sales. Use the formula method.
    c. Would you recommend that the changes be made?

Solution to Review Problem

1.

$$\text{CM ratio} = \frac{\text{Unit contribution margin}}{\text{Unit selling price}} = \frac{\$15}{\$60} = 25\%$$

$$\text{Variable expense ratio} = \frac{\text{Variable expense}}{\text{Selling price}} = \frac{\$45}{\$60} = 75\%$$

2.

$$\text{Profit} = \text{Unit CM} \times Q - \text{Fixed expenses}$$

$$\$0 = (\$60 - \$45) \times Q - \$240,000$$

$$\$15Q = \$240,000$$

$$Q = \$240,000 \div \$15$$

$$Q = 16,000 \text{ units; or at } \$60 \text{ per unit, } \$960,000$$

3.

Increase in sales...............................	$400,000
Multiply by the CM ratio.........................	× 25%
Expected increase in contribution margin	$100,000

Because the fixed expenses are not expected to change, net operating income will increase by the entire $100,000 increase in contribution margin computed above.

4. Equation method:

$$\text{Profit} = \text{Unit CM} \times Q - \text{Fixed expenses}$$

$$\$90,000 = (\$60 - \$45) \times Q - \$240,000$$

$$\$15Q = \$90,000 + \$240,000$$

$$Q = \$330,000 \div \$15$$

$$Q = 22,000 \text{ units}$$

Formula method:

$$\frac{\text{Unit sales to attain}}{\text{the target profit}} = \frac{\text{Target profit} + \text{Fixed expenses}}{\text{Contribution margin per unit}} = \frac{\$90,000 + \$240,000}{\$15 \text{ per unit}} = 22,000 \text{ units}$$

5.   Margin of safety in dollars $=$ Total sales $-$ Break-even sales

$$= \$1,200,000 - \$960,000 = \$240,000$$

Margin of safety percentage $= \dfrac{\text{Margin of safety in dollars}}{\text{Total sales}} = \dfrac{\$240,000}{\$1,200,000} = 20\%$

6.   *a.*   Degree of operating leverage $= \dfrac{\text{Contribution margin}}{\text{Net operating income}} = \dfrac{\$300,000}{\$60,000} = 5$

b.

Expected increase in sales	8%
Degree of operating leverage	× 5
Expected increase in net operating income	40%

c.   If sales increase by 8%, then 21,600 units (20,000 × 1.08 = 21,600) will be sold next year. The new contribution format income statement would be as follows:

	Total	Per Unit	Percent of Sales
Sales (21,600 units)	$1,296,000	$60	100%
Variable expenses..............	972,000	45	75%
Contribution margin	324,000	$15	25%
Fixed expenses	240,000		
Net operating income...........	$ 84,000		

Thus, the $84,000 expected net operating income for next year represents a 40% increase over the $60,000 net operating income earned during the current year:

$$\frac{\$84,000 - \$60,000}{\$60,000} = \frac{\$24,000}{\$60,000} = 40\% \text{ increase}$$

Note that the increase in sales from 20,000 to 21,600 units has increased *both* total sales and total variable expenses.

7.   *a.*   A 20% increase in sales would result in 24,000 units being sold next year: 20,000 units × 1.20 = 24,000 units.

	Total	Per Unit	Percent of Sales
Sales (24,000 units)	$1,440,000	$60	100%
Variable expenses	1,152,000	48*	80%
Contribution margin	288,000	$12	20%
Fixed expenses	210,000†		
Net operating income...........	$ 78,000		

*$45 + $3 = $48; $48 ÷ $60 = 80%.
†$240,000 − $30,000 = $210,000.

Note that the change in per unit variable expenses results in a change in both the per unit contribution margin and the CM ratio.

b.   Unit sales to break even $= \dfrac{\text{Fixed expenses}}{\text{Unit contribution margin}}$

$$= \frac{\$210,000}{\$12 \text{ per unit}} = 17,500 \text{ units}$$

Dollar sales to break even $= \dfrac{\text{Fixed expenses}}{\text{CM ratio}}$

$$= \frac{\$210,000}{0.20} = \$1,050,000$$

c.   Yes, based on these data, the changes should be made. The changes increase the company's net operating income from the present $60,000 to $78,000 per year. Although the changes also result in a higher break-even point (17,500 units as compared to the present 16,000 units), the company's margin of safety actually becomes greater than before:

$$\text{Margin of safety in dollars} = \text{Total sales} - \text{Break-even sales}$$
$$= \$1,440,000 - \$1,050,000 = \$390,000$$

As shown in (5) above, the company's present margin of safety is only $240,000. Thus, several benefits will result from the proposed changes.

Glossary

Break-even point   The level of sales at which profit is zero. (p. 73)

Contribution margin ratio (CM ratio)   A ratio computed by dividing contribution margin by dollar sales. (p. 78)

Cost-volume-profit (CVP) graph   A graphical representation of the relationships between an organization's revenues, costs, and profits on the one hand and its sales volume on the other hand. (p. 75)

Degree of operating leverage   A measure, at a given level of sales, of how a percentage change in sales will affect profits. The degree of operating leverage is computed by dividing contribution margin by net operating income. (p. 90)

Incremental analysis   An analytical approach that focuses only on those costs and revenues that change as a result of a decision. (p. 81)

Margin of safety   The excess of budgeted or actual dollar sales over the break-even dollar sales. (p. 87)

Operating leverage   A measure of how sensitive net operating income is to a given percentage change in dollar sales. (p. 90)

Sales mix   The relative proportions in which a company's products are sold. Sales mix is computed by expressing the sales of each product as a percentage of total sales. (p. 92)

Target profit analysis   Estimating what sales volume is needed to achieve a specific target profit. (p. 85)

Variable expense ratio   A ratio computed by dividing variable expenses by dollar sales. (p. 80)

Questions

3–1   What is meant by a product's contribution margin ratio? How is this ratio useful in planning business operations?

3–2   Often the most direct route to a business decision is an incremental analysis. What is meant by an *incremental analysis?*

3–3   In all respects, Company A and Company B are identical except that Company A's costs are mostly variable, whereas Company B's costs are mostly fixed. When sales increase, which company will tend to realize the greatest increase in profits? Explain.

3–4   What is meant by the term *operating leverage?*

3–5   What is meant by the term *break-even point?*

3–6   In response to a request from your immediate supervisor, you have prepared a CVP graph portraying the cost and revenue characteristics of your company's product and operations. Explain how the lines on the graph and the break-even point would change if (*a*) the selling price per unit decreased, (*b*) fixed cost increased throughout the entire range of activity portrayed on the graph, and (*c*) variable cost per unit increased.

3–7   What is meant by the margin of safety?

3–8   What is meant by the term *sales mix?* What assumption is usually made concerning sales mix in CVP analysis?

3–9   Explain how a shift in the sales mix could result in both a higher break-even point and a lower net income.

Multiple-choice questions are available with Connect.

Applying Excel

The Excel worksheet form that appears below is to be used to recreate portions of the Review Problem pertaining to Voltar Company that was presented earlier. Download the workbook from Connect, where you will also receive instructions about how to use this worksheet.

LEARNING OBJECTIVES 3–6, 3–7, 3–8

	A	B	C	D
1	Chapter 3: Applying Excel			
2				
3	**Data**			
4	Unit sales	20,000	units	
5	Selling price per unit	$60	per unit	
6	Variable expenses per unit	$45	per unit	
7	Fixed expenses	$240,000		
8				
9	*Enter a formula into each of the cells marked with a ? below*			
10	**Review Problem: CVP Relationships**			
11				
12	*Compute the CM ratio and variable expense ratio*			
13	Selling price per unit	?	per unit	
14	Variable expenses per unit	?	per unit	
15	Contribution margin per unit	?	per unit	
16				
17	CM ratio	?		
18	Variable expense ratio	?		
19				
20	*Compute the break-even*			
21	Break-even in unit sales	?	units	
22	Break-even in dollar sales	?		
23				
24	*Compute the margin of safety*			
25	Margin of safety in dollars	?		
26	Margin of safety percentage	?		
27				
28	*Compute the degree of operating leverage*			
29	Sales	?		
30	Variable expenses	?		
31	Contribution margin	?		
32	Fixed expenses	?		
33	Net operating income	?		
34				
35	Degree of operating leverage	?		
36				

⏮ ◀ ▶ ⏭   Chapter 3 Form   Filled in Chapter 3 Form

You should proceed to the requirements below only after completing your worksheet.

Required:

1. Check your worksheet by changing the fixed expenses to $270,000. If your worksheet is operating properly, the degree of operating leverage should be 10. If you do not get this answer, find the errors in your worksheet and correct them. How much is the margin of safety percentage? Did it change? Why or why not?

2. Enter the following data from a different company into your worksheet:

Unit sales	10,000 units
Selling price per unit	$120 per unit
Variable expenses per unit	$72 per unit
Fixed expenses	$420,000

What is the margin of safety percentage? What is the degree of operating leverage?

3. Using the degree of operating leverage and without changing anything in your worksheet, calculate the percentage change in net operating income if unit sales increase by 15%.

4. Confirm the calculations you made in requirement 3 above by increasing the unit sales in your worksheet by 15%. What is the new net operating income and by what percentage did it increase?

5. Thad Morgan, a motorcycle enthusiast, has been exploring the possibility of relaunching the Western Hombre brand of cycle that was popular in the 1930s. The retro-look cycle would be sold for $10,000 and at that price, Thad estimates 600 units would be sold each year. The variable cost to produce and sell the cycles would be $7,500 per unit. The annual fixed cost would be $1,200,000.

    a. Using your worksheet, what would be the break-even unit sales, the margin of safety in dollars, and the degree of operating leverage?

    b. Thad is worried about the selling price. Rumors are circulating that other retro brands of cycles may be revived. If so, the selling price for the Western Hombre would have to be reduced to $9,000 to compete effectively. In that event, Thad would also reduce fixed expenses by $300,000 by reducing advertising expenses, but he still hopes to sell 600 units per year. Do you think this is a good plan? Explain. Also, explain the degree of operating leverage that appears on your worksheet.

The Foundational 15   connect   Additional student resources are available with Connect.

LEARNING OBJECTIVES 3–1, 3–3, 3–4, 3–5, 3–6, 3–7, 3–8

Oslo Company prepared the following contribution format income statement based on a sales volume of 1,000 units (the relevant range of production is 500 units to 1,500 units):

Sales..........................	$20,000
Variable expenses	12,000
Contribution margin............	8,000
Fixed expenses.................	6,000
Net operating income	$ 2,000

Required:
(Answer each question independently and always refer to the original data unless instructed otherwise.)

1. What is the contribution margin per unit?
2. What is the contribution margin ratio?
3. What is the variable expense ratio?
4. If sales increase to 1,001 units, what would be the increase in net operating income?
5. If sales decline to 900 units, what would be the net operating income?
6. If the selling price increases by $2 per unit and the sales volume decreases by 100 units, what would be the net operating income?
7. If the variable cost per unit increases by $1, spending on advertising increases by $1,500, and unit sales increase by 250 units, what would be the net operating income?
8. What is the break-even point in unit sales?
9. What is the break-even point in dollar sales?
10. How many units must be sold to achieve a target profit of $5,000?
11. What is the margin of safety in dollars? What is the margin of safety percentage?
12. What is the degree of operating leverage?
13. Using the degree of operating leverage, what is the estimated percent increase in net operating income of a 5% increase in sales?
14. Assume that the amounts of the company's total variable expenses and total fixed expenses were reversed. In other words, assume that the total variable expenses are $6,000 and the total fixed expenses are $12,000. Under this scenario and assuming that total sales remain the same, what is the degree of operating leverage?
15. Using the degree of operating leverage that you computed in the previous question, what is the estimated percent increase in net operating income of a 5% increase in sales?

EXERCISE 3–1 Preparing a Contribution Format Income Statement [LO3–1]
Whirly Corporation's most recent income statement is shown below:

	Total	Per Unit
Sales (10,000 units).................	$350,000	$35.00
Variable expenses	200,000	20.00
Contribution margin.................	150,000	$15.00
Fixed expenses.....................	135,000	
Net operating income...............	$ 15,000	

Required:
Prepare a new contribution format income statement under each of the following conditions (consider each case independently):
1. The sales volume increases by 100 units.
2. The sales volume decreases by 100 units.
3. The sales volume is 9,000 units.

EXERCISE 3–2 Prepare a Cost-Volume-Profit (CVP) Graph [LO3–2]
Karlik Enterprises distributes a single product whose selling price is $24 and whose variable expense is $18 per unit. The company's monthly fixed expense is $24,000.

Required:
1. Prepare a cost-volume-profit graph for the company up to a sales level of 8,000 units.
2. Estimate the company's break-even point in unit sales using your cost-volume-profit graph.

EXERCISE 3–3 Prepare a Profit Graph [LO3–2]
Jaffre Enterprises distributes a single product whose selling price is $16 and whose variable expense is $11 per unit. The company's fixed expense is $16,000 per month.

Required:
1. Prepare a profit graph for the company up to a sales level of 4,000 units.
2. Estimate the company's break-even point in unit sales using your profit graph.

EXERCISE 3–4 Computing and Using the CM Ratio [LO3–3]
Last month when Holiday Creations, Inc., sold 50,000 units, total sales were $200,000, total variable expenses were $120,000, and fixed expenses were $65,000.

Required:
1. What is the company's contribution margin (CM) ratio?
2. Estimate the change in the company's net operating income if it were to increase its total sales by $1,000.

EXERCISE 3–5 Changes in Variable Costs, Fixed Costs, Selling Price, and Volume [LO3–4]
Data for Hermann Corporation are shown below:

	Per Unit	Percent of Sales
Selling price	$90	100%
Variable expenses.................	63	70%
Contribution margin	$27	30%

Fixed expenses are $30,000 per month and the company is selling 2,000 units per month.

Required:

1. The marketing manager argues that a $5,000 increase in the monthly advertising budget would increase monthly sales by $9,000. Should the advertising budget be increased?
2. Refer to the original data. Management is considering using higher-quality components that would increase the variable expense by $2 per unit. The marketing manager believes that the higher-quality product would increase sales by 10% per month. Should the higher-quality components be used?

EXERCISE 3–6 Compute the Break-Even Point [LO3–5]

Mauro Products distributes a single product, a woven basket whose selling price is $15 and whose variable expense is $12 per unit. The company's monthly fixed expense is $4,200.

Required:

1. Solve for the company's break-even point in unit sales using the equation method.
2. Solve for the company's break-even point in dollar sales using the equation method and the CM ratio.
3. Solve for the company's break-even point in unit sales using the formula method.
4. Solve for the company's break-even point in dollar sales using the formula method and the CM ratio.

EXERCISE 3–7 Compute the Level of Sales Required to Attain a Target Profit [LO3–6]

Lin Corporation has a single product whose selling price is $120 and whose variable expense is $80 per unit. The company's monthly fixed expense is $50,000.

Required:

1. Using the equation method, solve for the unit sales that are required to earn a target profit of $10,000.
2. Using the formula method, solve for the unit sales that are required to earn a target profit of $15,000.

EXERCISE 3–8 Compute the Margin of Safety [LO3–7]

Molander Corporation is a distributor of a sun umbrella used at resort hotels. Data concerning the next month's budget appear below:

Selling price	$30 per unit
Variable expenses	$20 per unit
Fixed expenses	$7,500 per month
Unit sales	1,000 units per month

Required:

1. Compute the company's margin of safety.
2. Compute the company's margin of safety as a percentage of its sales.

EXERCISE 3–9 Compute and Use the Degree of Operating Leverage [LO3–8]

Engberg Company installs lawn sod in home yards. The company's most recent monthly contribution format income statement follows:

	Amount	Percent of Sales
Sales	$ 80,000	100%
Variable expenses	32,000	40%
Contribution margin	48,000	60%
Fixed expenses	38,000	
Net operating income	$ 10,000	

Required:

1. Compute the company's degree of operating leverage.
2. Using the degree of operating leverage, estimate the impact on net operating income of a 5% increase in sales.
3. Verify your estimate from part (2) above by constructing a new contribution format income statement for the company assuming a 5% increase in sales.

EXERCISE 3–10 Compute the Break-Even Point for a Multiproduct Company [LO3–9]

Lucido Products markets two computer games: Claimjumper and Makeover. A contribution format income statement for a recent month for the two games appears below:

	Claimjumper	Makeover	Total
Sales...........................	$ 30,000	$70,000	$100,000
Variable expenses	20,000	50,000	70,000
Contribution margin..................	$ 10,000	$20,000	30,000
Fixed expenses			24,000
Net operating income...............			$ 6,000

Required:

1. Compute the overall contribution margin (CM) ratio for the company.
2. Compute the overall break-even point for the company in dollar sales.
3. Verify the overall break-even point for the company by constructing a contribution format income statement showing the appropriate levels of sales for the two products.

EXERCISE 3–11 Missing Data; Basic CVP Concepts [LO3–1, LO3–9]

Fill in the missing amounts in each of the eight case situations below. Each case is independent of the others. (*Hint:* One way to find the missing amounts would be to prepare a contribution format income statement for each case, enter the known data, and then compute the missing items.)

a. Assume that only one product is being sold in each of the four following case situations:

Case	Units Sold	Sales	Variable Expenses	Contribution Margin per Unit	Fixed Expenses	Net Operating Income (Loss)
1......	15,000	$180,000	$120,000	?	$50,000	?
2......	?	$100,000	?	$10	$32,000	$8,000
3......	10,000	?	$70,000	$13	?	$12,000
4......	6,000	$300,000	?	?	$100,000	$(10,000)

b. Assume that more than one product is being sold in each of the four following case situations:

Case	Sales	Variable Expenses	Average Contribution Margin Ratio	Fixed Expenses	Net Operating Income (Loss)
1......	$500,000	?	20%	?	$7,000
2......	$400,000	$260,000	?	$100,000	?
3......	?	?	60%	$130,000	$20,000
4......	$600,000	$420,000	?	?	$(5,000)

EXERCISE 3–12 Multiproduct Break-Even Analysis [LO3–9]

Olongapo Sports Corporation distributes two premium golf balls—the Flight Dynamic and the Sure Shot. Monthly sales and the contribution margin ratios for the two products follow:

	Product		
	Flight Dynamic	Sure Shot	Total
Sales..........................	$150,000	$250,000	$400,000
CM ratio......................	80%	36%	?

Fixed expenses total $183,750 per month.

Required:

1. Prepare a contribution format income statement for the company as a whole. Carry computations to one decimal place.
2. Compute the break-even point for the company based on the current sales mix.
3. If sales increase by $100,000 a month, by how much would you expect net operating income to increase? What are your assumptions?

EXERCISE 3–13 Using a Contribution Format Income Statement [LO3–1, LO3–4]

Miller Company's most recent contribution format income statement is shown below:

	Total	Per Unit
Sales (20,000 units)	$300,000	$15.00
Variable expenses	180,000	9.00
Contribution margin	120,000	$ 2.00
Fixed expenses.................	70,000	
Net operating income............	$ 50,000	

Required:

Prepare a new contribution format income statement under each of the following conditions (consider each case independently):

1. The number of units sold increases by 15%.
2. The selling price decreases by $1.50 per unit, and the number of units sold increases by 25%.
3. The selling price increases by $1.50 per unit, fixed expenses increase by $20,000, and the number of units sold decreases by 5%.
4. The selling price increases by 12%, variable expenses increase by 60 cents per unit, and the number of units sold decreases by 10%.

EXERCISE 3–14 Break-Even and Target Profit Analysis [LO3–3, LO3–4, LO3–5, LO3–6]

Lindon Company is the exclusive distributor for an automotive product that sells for $40 per unit and has a CM ratio of 30%. The company's fixed expenses are $180,000 per year. The company plans to sell 16,000 units this year.

Required:

1. What are the variable expenses per unit?
2. Using the equation method:
   a. What is the break-even point in unit sales and in dollar sales?
   b. What amount of unit sales and dollar sales is required to earn an annual profit of $60,000?
   c. Assume that by using a more efficient shipper, the company is able to reduce its variable expenses by $4 per unit. What is the company's new break-even point in unit sales and in dollar sales?
3. Repeat requirement 2 above using the formula method.

EXERCISE 3–15 Operating Leverage [LO3–4, LO3–8]

Magic Realm, Inc., has developed a new fantasy board game. The company sold 15,000 games last year at a selling price of $20 per game. Fixed expenses associated with the game total $182,000 per year, and variable expenses are $6 per game. Production of the game is entrusted to a printing contractor. Variable expenses consist mostly of payments to this contractor.

Required:

1. Prepare a contribution format income statement for the game last year and compute the degree of operating leverage.
2. Management is confident that the company can sell 18,000 games next year (an increase of 3,000 games, or 20%, over last year). Compute:
    a. The expected percentage increase in net operating income for next year.
    b. The expected total dollar net operating income for next year. (Do not prepare an income statement; use the degree of operating leverage to compute your answer.)

EXERCISE 3–16 Break-Even Analysis and CVP Graphing [LO3–2, LO3–4, LO3–5]

The Hartford Symphony Guild is planning its annual dinner-dance. The dinner-dance committee has assembled the following expected costs for the event:

Dinner (per person)........................	$18
Favors and program (per person)	$2
Band.....................................	$2,800
Rental of ballroom........................	$900
Professional entertainment during intermission .	$1,000
Tickets and advertising	$1,300

The committee members would like to charge $35 per person for the evening's activities.

Required:

1. Compute the break-even point for the dinner-dance (in terms of the number of persons who must attend).
2. Assume that last year only 300 persons attended the dinner-dance. If the same number attend this year, what price per ticket must be charged in order to break even?
3. Refer to the original data ($35 ticket price per person). Prepare a CVP graph for the dinner-dance from zero tickets up to 600 tickets sold.

EXERCISE 3–17 Break-Even and Target Profit Analysis [LO3–4, LO3–5, LO3–6]

Outback Outfitters sells recreational equipment. One of the company's products, a small camp stove, sells for $50 per unit. Variable expenses are $32 per stove, and fixed expenses associated with the stove total $108,000 per month.

Required:

1. Compute the break-even point in unit sales and in dollar sales.
2. If the variable expenses per stove increase as a percentage of the selling price, will it result in a higher or a lower break-even point? Why? (Assume that the fixed expenses remain unchanged.)
3. At present, the company is selling 8,000 stoves per month. The sales manager is convinced that a 10% reduction in the selling price would result in a 25% increase in monthly sales of stoves. Prepare two contribution format income statements, one under present operating conditions, and one as operations would appear after the proposed changes. Show both total and per unit data on your statements.
4. Refer to the data in requirement 3 above. How many stoves would have to be sold at the new selling price to yield a minimum net operating income of $35,000 per month?

EXERCISE 3–18 Break-Even and Target Profit Analysis; Margin of Safety; CM Ratio [LO3–1, LO3–3, LO3–5, LO3–6, LO3–7]

Menlo Company distributes a single product. The company's sales and expenses for last month follow:

	Total	Per Unit
Sales..........................	$450,000	$30
Variable expenses..............	180,000	12
Contribution margin............	270,000	$18
Fixed expenses	216,000	
Net operating income...........	$ 54,000	

Required:
1. What is the monthly break-even point in unit sales and in dollar sales?
2. Without resorting to computations, what is the total contribution margin at the break-even point?
3. How many units would have to be sold each month to earn a target profit of $90,000? Use the formula method. Verify your answer by preparing a contribution format income statement at the target sales level.
4. Refer to the original data. Compute the company's margin of safety in both dollar and percentage terms.
5. What is the company's CM ratio? If sales increase by $50,000 per month and there is no change in fixed expenses, by how much would you expect monthly net operating income to increase?

Problems **Additional student resources are available with Connect.**

PROBLEM 3–19 Break-Even Analysis; Pricing [LO3–1, LO3–4, LO3–5]

Minden Company introduced a new product last year for which it is trying to find an optimal selling price. Marketing studies suggest that the company can increase sales by 5,000 units for each $2 reduction in the selling price. The company's present selling price is $70 per unit, and variable expenses are $40 per unit. Fixed expenses are $540,000 per year. The present annual sales volume (at the $70 selling price) is 15,000 units.

Required:
1. What is the present yearly net operating income or loss?
2. What is the present break-even point in unit sales and in dollar sales?
3. Assuming that the marketing studies are correct, what is the maximum annual profit that the company can earn? At how many units and at what selling price per unit would the company generate this profit?
4. What would be the break-even point in unit sales and in dollar sales using the selling price you determined in requirement 3 above (e.g., the selling price at the level of maximum profits)? Why is this break-even point different from the break-even point you computed in requirement 2 above?

PROBLEM 3–20 Various CVP Questions: Break-Even Point; Cost Structure; Target Sales [LO3–1, LO3–3, LO3–4, LO3–5, LO3–6, LO3–8]

Northwood Company manufactures basketballs. The company has a ball that sells for $25. At present, the ball is manufactured in a small plant that relies heavily on direct labor workers. Thus, variable expenses are high, totaling $15 per ball, of which 60% is direct labor cost.

Last year, the company sold 30,000 of these balls, with the following results:

Sales (30,000 balls).....................	$750,000
Variable expenses........................	450,000
Contribution margin	300,000
Fixed expenses..........................	210,000
Net operating income	$ 90,000

Required:

1. Compute (a) the CM ratio and the break-even point in balls, and (b) the degree of operating leverage at last year's sales level.

2. Due to an increase in labor rates, the company estimates that variable expenses will increase by $3 per ball next year. If this change takes place and the selling price per ball remains constant at $25, what will be the new CM ratio and break-even point in balls?

3. Refer to the data in requirement 2 above. If the expected change in variable expenses takes place, how many balls will have to be sold next year to earn the same net operating income, $90,000, as last year?

4. Refer again to the data in requirement 2 above. The president feels that the company must raise the selling price of its basketballs. If Northwood Company wants to maintain the same CM ratio as last year, what selling price per ball must it charge next year to cover the increased labor costs?

5. Refer to the original data. The company is discussing the construction of a new, automated manufacturing plant. The new plant would slash variable expenses per ball by 40%, but it would cause fixed expenses per year to double. If the new plant is built, what would be the company's new CM ratio and new break-even point in balls?

6. Refer to the data in requirement 5 above.
   a. If the new plant is built, how many balls will have to be sold next year to earn the same net operating income, $90,000, as last year?
   b. Assume the new plant is built and that next year the company manufactures and sells 30,000 balls (the same number as sold last year). Prepare a contribution format income statement and compute the degree of operating leverage.
   c. If you were a member of top management, would you have been in favor of constructing the new plant? Explain.

PROBLEM 3–21 Sales Mix; Multiproduct Break-Even Analysis [LO3–9]

Gold Star Rice, Ltd., of Thailand exports Thai rice throughout Asia. The company grows three varieties of rice—Fragrant, White, and Loonzain. Budgeted sales by product and in total for the coming month are shown below:

	Product							
	White		**Fragrant**		**Loonzain**		**Total**	
Percentage of total sales	20%		52%		28%		100%	
Sales......................	$150,000	100%	$390,000	100%	$210,000	100%	$750,000	100%
Variable expenses.................	108,000	72%	78,000	20%	84,000	40%	270,000	36%
Contribution margin................	$ 42,000	28%	$312,000	80%	$126,000	60%	480,000	64%
Fixed expenses							449,280	
Net operating income..............							$ 30,720	

$$\text{Dollar sales to breakeven} = \frac{\text{Fixed expenses}}{\text{CM ratio}} = \frac{\$449{,}280}{0.64} = \$702{,}000$$

As shown by these data, net operating income is budgeted at $30,720 for the month and break-even sales at $702,000.

Assume that actual sales for the month total $750,000 as planned. Actual sales by product are: White, $300,000; Fragrant, $180,000; and Loonzain, $270,000.

Required:
1. Prepare a contribution format income statement for the month based on actual sales data. Present the income statement in the format shown above.
2. Compute the break-even point in dollar sales for the month based on your actual data.
3. Considering the fact that the company met its $750,000 sales budget for the month, the president is shocked at the results shown on your income statement in requirement 1 above. Prepare a brief memo for the president explaining why both the operating results and the break-even point in dollar sales are different from what was budgeted.

PROBLEM 3–22 Basics of CVP Analysis; Cost Structure [LO3–1, LO3–3, LO3–4, LO3–5, LO3–6]
Due to erratic sales of its sole product—a high-capacity battery for laptop computers—PEM, Inc., has been experiencing difficulty for some time. The company's contribution format income statement for the most recent month is given below:

Sales (19,500 units × $30 per unit).	$585,000
Variable expenses.	409,500
Contribution margin	175,500
Fixed expenses.	180,000
Net operating income.	$ (4,500)

Required:
1. Compute the company's CM ratio and its break-even point in both unit sales and dollar sales.
2. The president believes that a $16,000 increase in the monthly advertising budget, combined with an intensified effort by the sales staff, will result in an $80,000 increase in monthly sales. If the president is right, what will be the effect on the company's monthly net operating income or loss? (Use the incremental approach in preparing your answer.)
3. Refer to the original data. The sales manager is convinced that a 10% reduction in the selling price, combined with an increase of $60,000 in the monthly advertising budget, will double unit sales. What will the new contribution format income statement look like if these changes are adopted?
4. Refer to the original data. The Marketing Department thinks that a fancy new package for the laptop computer battery would help sales. The new package would increase packaging costs by 75 cents per unit. Assuming no other changes, how many units would have to be sold each month to earn a profit of $9,750?
5. Refer to the original data. By automating, the company could reduce variable expenses by $3 per unit. However, fixed expenses would increase by $72,000 each month.
   a. Compute the new CM ratio and the new break-even point in both unit sales and dollar sales.
   b. Assume that the company expects to sell 26,000 units next month. Prepare two contribution format income statements, one assuming that operations are not automated and one assuming that they are. (Show data on a per unit and percentage basis, as well as in total, for each alternative.)
   c. Would you recommend that the company automate its operations? Explain.

PROBLEM 3–23 Basics of CVP Analysis [LO3–1, LO3–3, LO3–4, LO3–5, LO3–8]
Feather Friends, Inc., distributes a high-quality wooden birdhouse that sells for $20 per unit. Variable expenses are $8 per unit, and fixed expenses total $180,000 per year.

Required:
Answer the following independent questions:
1. What is the product's CM ratio?
2. Use the CM ratio to determine the break-even point in dollar sales.
3. Due to an increase in demand, the company estimates that sales will increase by $75,000 during the next year. By how much should net operating income increase (or net loss decrease) assuming that fixed expenses do not change?

4. Assume that the operating results for last year were:

Sales	$400,000
Variable expenses	160,000
Contribution margin	240,000
Fixed expenses	180,000
Net operating income	$ 60,000

   a. Compute the degree of operating leverage at the current level of sales.
   b. The president expects sales to increase by 20% next year. By what percentage should net operating income increase?
5. Refer to the original data. Assume that the company sold 18,000 units last year. The sales manager is convinced that a 10% reduction in the selling price, combined with a $30,000 increase in advertising, would increase annual unit sales by one-third. Prepare two contribution format income statements, one showing the results of last year's operations and one showing the results of operations if these changes are made. Would you recommend that the company do as the sales manager suggests?
6. Refer to the original data. Assume again that the company sold 18,000 units last year. The president does not want to change the selling price. Instead, he wants to increase the sales commission by $1 per unit. He thinks that this move, combined with some increase in advertising, would increase annual sales by 25%. By how much could advertising be increased with profits remaining unchanged? Do not prepare an income statement; use the incremental analysis approach.

PROBLEM 3–24 Break-Even and Target Profit Analysis [LO3–5, LO3–6]

The Shirt Works sells a large variety of tee shirts and sweatshirts. Steve Hooper, the owner, is thinking of expanding his sales by hiring high school students, on a commission basis, to sell sweatshirts bearing the name and mascot of the local high school.

These sweatshirts would have to be ordered from the manufacturer six weeks in advance, and they could not be returned because of the unique printing required. The sweatshirts would cost Hooper $8 each with a minimum order of 75 sweatshirts. Any additional sweatshirts would have to be ordered in increments of 75.

Since Hooper's plan would not require any additional facilities, the only costs associated with the project would be the costs of the sweatshirts and the costs of the sales commissions. The selling price of the sweatshirts would be $13.50 each. Hooper would pay the students a commission of $1.50 for each shirt sold.

Required:

1. To make the project worthwhile, Hooper would require a $1,200 profit for the first three months of the venture. What level of unit sales and dollar sales would be required to reach this target net operating income? Show all computations.
2. Assume that the venture is undertaken and an order is placed for 75 sweatshirts. What would be Hooper's break-even point in unit sales and in dollar sales? Show computations and explain the reasoning behind your answer.

PROBLEM 3–25 Changes in Fixed and Variable Expenses; Break-Even and Target Profit Analysis
[LO3–4, LO3–5, LO3–6]

Neptune Company produces toys and other items for use in beach and resort areas. A small, inflatable toy has come onto the market that the company is anxious to produce and sell. The new toy will sell for $3 per unit. Enough capacity exists in the company's plant to produce 16,000 units of the toy each month. Variable expenses to manufacture and sell one unit would be $1.25, and fixed expenses associated with the toy would total $35,000 per month.

The company's Marketing Department predicts that demand for the new toy will exceed the 16,000 units that the company is able to produce. Additional manufacturing space can be rented from another company at a fixed expense of $1,000 per month. Variable expenses in the rented facility would total $1.40 per unit, due to somewhat less efficient operations than in the main plant.

Required:

1. Compute the monthly break-even point for the new toy in unit sales and in dollar sales.
2. How many units must be sold each month to make a monthly profit of $12,000?
3. If the sales manager receives a bonus of 10 cents for each unit sold in excess of the break-even point, how many units must be sold each month to earn a return of 25% on the monthly investment in fixed expenses?

PROBLEM 3–26 Basic CVP Analysis; Graphing [LO3–1, LO3–2, LO3–4, LO3–5]

The Fashion Shoe Company operates a chain of women's shoe shops that carry many styles of shoes that are all sold at the same price. Sales personnel in the shops are paid a substantial commission on each pair of shoes sold (in addition to a small base salary) in order to encourage them to be aggressive in their sales efforts.

The following worksheet contains cost and revenue data for Shop 48 and is typical of the company's many outlets:

	Per Pair of Shoes
Selling price....................	$30.00
Variable expenses:	
Invoice cost.................	$13.50
Sales commission............	4.50
Total variable expenses.........	$18.00

	Annual
Fixed expenses:	
Advertising	$ 30,000
Rent.......................	20,000
Salaries....................	100,000
Total fixed expenses	$150,000

Required:

1. Calculate the annual break-even point in unit sales and in dollar sales for Shop 48.
2. Prepare a CVP graph showing cost and revenue data for Shop 48 from zero shoes up to 17,000 pairs of shoes sold each year. Clearly indicate the break-even point on the graph.
3. If 12,000 pairs of shoes are sold in a year, what would be Shop 48's net operating income or loss?
4. The company is considering paying the store manager of Shop 48 an incentive commission of 75 cents per pair of shoes (in addition to the salesperson's commission). If this change is made, what will be the new break-even point in unit sales and in dollar sales?
5. Refer to the original data. As an alternative to requirement 4 above, the company is considering paying the store manager 50 cents commission on each pair of shoes sold in excess of the break-even point. If this change is made, what will be the shop's net operating income or loss if 15,000 pairs of shoes are sold?
6. Refer to the original data. The company is considering eliminating sales commissions entirely in its shops and increasing fixed salaries by $31,500 annually. If this change is made, what will be the new break-even point in unit sales and in dollar sales for Shop 48? Would you recommend that the change be made? Explain.

PROBLEM 3–27 Sales Mix; Break-Even Analysis; Margin of Safety [LO3–7, LO3–9]

Island Novelties, Inc., of Palau makes two products, Hawaiian Fantasy and Tahitian Joy. Present revenue, cost, and sales data for the two products follow:

	Hawaiian Fantasy	Tahitian Joy
Selling price per unit...................	$15	$100
Variable expenses per unit.............	$ 9	$ 20
Number of units sold annually..........	20,000	5,000

Fixed expenses total $475,800 per year.

Required:

1. Assuming the sales mix given above, do the following:
   a. Prepare a contribution format income statement showing both dollar and percent columns for each product and for the company as a whole.
   b. Compute the break-even point in dollar sales for the company as a whole and the margin of safety in both dollars and percent.
2. The company has developed a new product to be called Samoan Delight. Assume that the company could sell 10,000 units at $45 each. The variable expenses would be $36 each. The company's fixed expenses would not change.
   a. Prepare another contribution format income statement, including sales of the Samoan Delight (sales of the other two products would not change).
   b. Compute the company's new break-even point in dollar sales and the new margin of safety in both dollars and percent.
3. The president of the company examines your figures and says, "There's something strange here. Our fixed expenses haven't changed and you show greater total contribution margin if we add the new product, but you also show our break-even point going up. With greater contribution margin, the break-even point should go down, not up. You've made a mistake somewhere." Explain to the president what has happened.

PROBLEM 3–28 Sales Mix; Commission Structure; Multiproduct Break-Even Analysis [LO3–9]

Carbex, Inc., produces cutlery sets out of high-quality wood and steel. The company makes a standard cutlery set and a deluxe set and sells them to retail department stores throughout the country. The standard set sells for $60, and the deluxe set sells for $75. The variable expenses associated with each set are given below.

	Standard	Deluxe
Production costs	$15.00	$30.00
Sales commissions (15% of sales price)	$ 9.00	$11.25

The company's fixed expenses each month are:

Advertising.......................................	$105,000
Depreciation.....................................	$ 21,700
Administrative...................................	$ 63,000

Salespersons are paid on a commission basis to encourage them to be aggressive in their sales efforts. Mary Parsons, the financial vice president, watches sales commissions carefully and has noted that they have risen steadily over the last year. For this reason, she was shocked to find that even though sales have increased, profits for the current month—May—are down substantially from April. Sales, in sets, for the last two months are given below:

	Standard	Deluxe	Total
April.....................	4,000	2,000	6,000
May	1,000	5,000	6,000

Required:

1. Prepare contribution format income statements for April and May. Use the following headings:

	Standard		Deluxe		Total	
	Amount	Percent	Amount	Percent	Amount	Percent
Sales...						
Etc.....						

Chapter 3

Place the fixed expenses only in the Total column. Do not show percentages for the fixed expenses.

2. Explain the difference in net operating incomes between the two months, even though the same total number of sets was sold in each month.

3. What can be done to the sales commissions to improve the sales mix?
   a. Using April's sales mix, what is the break-even point in dollar sales?
   b. Without doing any calculations, explain whether the break-even points would be higher or lower with May's sales mix than April's sales mix.

PROBLEM 3–29 Changes in Cost Structure; Break-Even Analysis; Operating Leverage; Margin of Safety [LO3–4, LO3–5, LO3–7, LO3–8]
Morton Company's contribution format income statement for last month is given below:

Sales (15,000 units × $30 per unit)	$450,000
Variable expenses	315,000
Contribution margin	135,000
Fixed expenses	90,000
Net operating income	$ 45,000

The industry in which Morton Company operates is quite sensitive to cyclical movements in the economy. Thus, profits vary considerably from year to year according to general economic conditions. The company has a large amount of unused capacity and is studying ways of improving profits.

Required:

1. New equipment has come onto the market that would allow Morton Company to automate a portion of its operations. Variable expenses would be reduced by $9 per unit. However, fixed expenses would increase to a total of $225,000 each month. Prepare two contribution format income statements, one showing present operations and one showing how operations would appear if the new equipment is purchased. Show an Amount column, a Per Unit column, and a Percent column on each statement. Do not show percentages for the fixed expenses.

2. Refer to the income statements in requirement 1 above. For both present operations and the proposed new operations, compute (a) the degree of operating leverage, (b) the break-even point in dollar sales, and (c) the margin of safety in both dollar and percentage terms.

3. Refer again to the data in requirement 1 above. As a manager, what factor would be paramount in your mind in deciding whether to purchase the new equipment? (Assume that enough funds are available to make the purchase.)

4. Refer to the original data. Rather than purchase new equipment, the marketing manager argues that the company's marketing strategy should be changed. Rather than pay sales commissions, which are currently included in variable expenses, the company would pay salespersons fixed salaries and would invest heavily in advertising. The marketing manager claims this new approach would increase unit sales by 30% without any change in selling price; the company's new monthly fixed expenses would be $180,000; and its net operating income would increase by 20%. Compute the break-even point in dollar sales for the company under the new marketing strategy. Do you agree with the marketing manager's proposal?

PROBLEM 3–30 Graphing; Incremental Analysis; Operating Leverage [LO3–2, LO3–4, LO3–5, LO3–6, LO3–8]
Angie Silva has recently opened The Sandal Shop in Brisbane, Australia, a store that specializes in fashionable sandals. Angie has just received a degree in business and she is anxious to apply the principles she has learned to her business. In time, she hopes to open a chain of sandal shops. As a first step, she has prepared the following analysis for her new store:

Required:

1. How many pairs of sandals must be sold each year to break even? What does this represent in total sales dollars?

Sales price per pair of sandals....................	$40
Variable expenses per pair of sandals.............	16
Contribution margin per pair of sandals............	$24
Fixed expenses per year:	
Building rental	$15,000
Equipment depreciation	7,000
Selling.......................................	20,000
Administrative	18,000
Total fixed expense	$60,000

2. Prepare a CVP graph or a profit graph for the store from zero pairs up to 4,000 pairs of sandals sold each year. Indicate the break-even point on your graph.

3. Angie has decided that she must earn at least $18,000 the first year to justify her time and effort. How many pairs of sandals must be sold to reach this target profit?

4. Angie now has two salespersons working in the store—one full time and one part time. It will cost her an additional $8,000 per year to convert the part-time position to a full-time position. Angie believes that the change would bring in an additional $25,000 in sales each year. Should she convert the position? Use the incremental approach. (Do not prepare an income statement.)

5. Refer to the original data. During the first year, the store sold only 3,000 pairs of sandals and reported the following operating results:

Sales (3,000 pairs)........................	$ 120,000
Variable expenses........................	48,000
Contribution margin	72,000
Fixed expenses...........................	60,000
Net operating income	$ 12,000

 a. What is the store's degree of operating leverage?
 b. Angie is confident that with a more intense sales effort and with a more creative advertising program she can increase sales by 50% next year. What would be the expected percentage increase in net operating income? Use the degree of operating leverage to compute your answer.

PROBLEM 3–31 Interpretive Questions on the CVP Graph [LO3–2, LO3–5]
A CVP graph such as the one shown below is a useful technique for showing relationships among an organization's costs, volume, and profits.

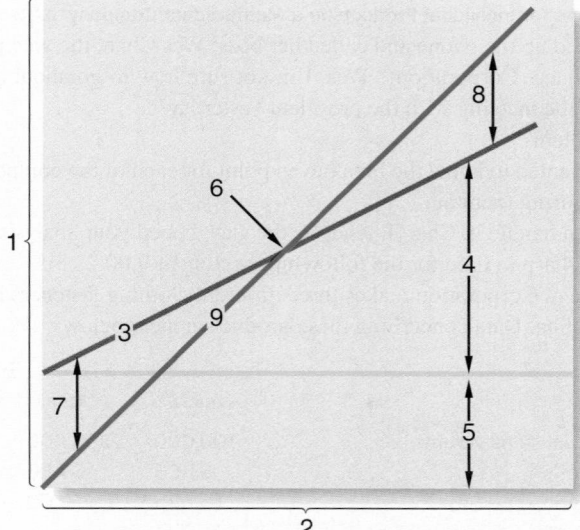

Total fixed expenses are $400,000 per year.

All three products are sold in highly competitive markets, so the company is unable to raise its prices without losing unacceptable numbers of customers.

The company has an extremely effective lean production system, so there are no beginning or ending work in process or finished goods inventories.

Required:

1. What is the company's overall break-even point in dollar sales?
2. Of the total fixed expenses of $400,000, $20,000 could be avoided if the Velcro product is dropped, $80,000 if the Metal product is dropped, and $60,000 if the Nylon product is dropped. The remaining fixed expenses of $240,000 consist of common fixed expenses such as administrative salaries and rent on the factory building that could be avoided only by going out of business entirely.
   a. What is the break-even point in unit sales for each product?
   b. If the company sells exactly the break-even quantity of each product, what will be the overall profit of the company? Explain this result.

CASE 3–33 Cost Structure; Break-Even and Target Profit Analysis [LO3–4, LO3–5, LO3–6]

Pittman Company is a small but growing manufacturer of telecommunications equipment. The company has no sales force of its own; rather, it relies completely on independent sales agents to market its products. These agents are paid a sales commission of 15% for all items sold.

Barbara Cheney, Pittman's controller, has just prepared the company's budgeted income statement for next year. The statement follows:

Pittman Company Budgeted Income Statement For the Year Ended December 31		
Sales......................................		$16,000,000
Manufacturing expenses:		
Variable	$7,200,000	
Fixed overhead...................	2,340,000	9,540,000
Gross margin		6,460,000
Selling and administrative expenses:		
Commissions to agents...........	2,400,000	
Fixed marketing expenses.........	1,20,000*	
Fixed administrative expenses.....	1,800,000	4,320,000
Net operating income...............		2,140,000
Fixed interest expenses.............		540,000
Income before income taxes		1,600,000
Income taxes (30%).................		480,000
Net income		$ 1,120,000

*Primarily depreciation on storage facilities.

As Barbara handed the statement to Karl Vecci, Pittman's president, she commented, "I went ahead and used the agents' 15% commission rate in completing these statements, but we've just learned that they refuse to handle our products next year unless we increase the commission rate to 20%."

"That's the last straw," Karl replied angrily. "Those agents have been demanding more and more, and this time they've gone too far. How can they possibly defend a 20% commission rate?"

"They claim that after paying for advertising, travel, and the other costs of promotion, there's nothing left over for profit," replied Barbara.

"I say it's just plain robbery," retorted Karl. "And I also say it's time we dumped those guys and got our own sales force. Can you get your people to work up some cost figures for us to look at?"

"We've already worked them up," said Barbara. "Several companies we know about pay a 7.5% commission to their own salespeople, along with a small salary. Of course, we would have to handle all promotion costs, too. We figure our fixed expenses would increase by $2,400,000 per year, but that would be more than offset by the $3,200,000 (20% × $16,000,000) that we would avoid on agents' commissions."

The breakdown of the $2,400,000 cost follows:

Salaries:	
Sales manager................	$ 100,000
Salespersons	600,000
Travel and entertainment.........	400,000
Advertising	1,300,000
Total..........................	$2,400,000

"Super," replied Karl. "And I noticed that the $2,400,000 is just what we're paying the agents under the old 15% commission rate."

"It's even better than that," explained Barbara. "We can actually save $75,000 a year because that's what we're having to pay the auditing firm now to check out the agents' reports. So our overall administrative expenses would be less."

"Pull all of these numbers together and we'll show them to the executive committee tomorrow," said Karl. "With the approval of the committee, we can move on the matter immediately."

Required:

1. Compute Pittman Company's break-even point in dollar sales for next year assuming:
   a. The agents' commission rate remains unchanged at 15%.
   b. The agents' commission rate is increased to 20%.
   c. The company employs its own sales force.
2. Assume that Pittman Company decides to continue selling through agents and pays the 20% commission rate. Determine the volume of sales that would be required to generate the same net income as contained in the budgeted income statement for next year.
3. Determine the volume of sales at which net income would be equal regardless of whether Pittman Company sells through agents (at a 20% commission rate) or employs its own sales force.
4. Compute the degree of operating leverage that the company would expect to have on December 31 at the end of next year assuming:
   a. The agents' commission rate remains unchanged at 15%.
   b. The agents' commission rate is increased to 20%.
   c. The company employs its own sales force.
   Use income *before* income taxes in your operating leverage computation.
5. Based on the data in requirements 1–4 above, make a recommendation as to whether the company should continue to use sales agents (at a 20% commission rate) or employ its own sales force. Give reasons for your answer.

(CMA, adapted)

Job–Order Costing

University Tees: Serving Over 150 Campuses Nationwide

Courtesy of University Tees, Inc.

University Tees was founded in 2003 by two Miami University college students to provide screen-printing, embroidery, and promotional products for fraternities, sororities, and student organizations. Today, the company, which is headquartered in Cleveland, Ohio, employs as many as four Campus Managers on each of over 150 college campuses across America.

Accurately calculating the cost of each potential customer order is critically important to University Tees because the company needs to be sure that the sales price exceeds the cost associated with satisfying the order. The costs include the cost of the blank t-shirts themselves, printing costs (which vary depending on the quantity of shirts produced and the number of colors per shirt), screen costs (which also vary depending on the number of colors included in a design), shipping costs, and the artwork needed to create a design. The company also takes into account its competitors' pricing strategies when developing its own prices.

Given its success on college campuses, University Tees has introduced a sister company called On Point Promos to serve for-profit companies and nonprofit organizations. ∎

Source: Conversation with Joe Haddad, cofounder of University Tees.

LEARNING OBJECTIVES

After studying Chapter 4, you should be able to:

LO 4–1 Compute a predetermined overhead rate.

LO 4–2 Apply overhead cost to jobs using a predetermined overhead rate.

LO 4–3 Compute the total cost and average cost per unit of a job.

LO 4–4 Compute underapplied or overapplied overhead cost.

LO 4–5 Use the direct method to determine cost of goods sold.

LO 4–6 Use the indirect method to determine cost of goods sold.

LO 4–7 (Appendix 4A) Use activity-based absorption costing to compute unit product costs.

LO 4–8 (Appendix 4B) Understand the implications of basing the predetermined overhead rate on activity at capacity rather than on estimated activity for the period.

The way in which product and service costs are determined can have a substantial impact on reported profits, as well as on key management decisions.

A managerial costing system should provide cost data to help managers plan, control, and make decisions. Nevertheless, external financial reporting and tax reporting requirements often heavily influence how costs are accumulated and summarized on managerial reports. This is true of product costing. In this chapter we use *absorption costing* to determine product costs. In **absorption costing**, all manufacturing costs, both fixed and variable, are assigned to units of product—units are said to *fully absorb manufacturing costs.*

Most countries—including the United States—require some form of absorption costing for both external financial reports and for tax reports. In addition, the vast majority of companies throughout the world also use absorption costing in their management reports. Because absorption costing is the most common approach to product costing throughout the world, we discuss it first and then discuss the alternatives in subsequent chapters.

Job-Order Costing—An Overview

Under absorption costing, product costs include all manufacturing costs. Some manufacturing costs, such as direct materials, can be directly traced to particular products. For example, the cost of the airbags installed in a Toyota Camry can be easily traced to that particular auto. But what about manufacturing costs like factory rent? Such costs do not change from month to month, whereas the number and variety of products made in the factory may vary dramatically from one month to the next. Because these costs remain unchanged from month to month regardless of what products are made, they are clearly not caused by—and cannot be directly traced to—any particular product. Therefore, these types of costs are assigned to products and services by averaging across time and across products. The type of production process influences how this averaging is done.

Job-order costing is used in situations where many *different* products, each with individual and unique features, are produced each period. For example, a Levi Strauss clothing factory would typically make many different types of jeans for both men and women during a month. A particular order might consist of 1,000 boot-cut men's blue denim jeans, style number A312. This order of 1,000 jeans is called a *job.* In a job-order costing system, costs are traced and allocated to jobs and then the costs of the job are divided by the number of units in the job to arrive at an average cost per unit.

Other examples of situations where job-order costing would be used include large-scale construction projects managed by Bechtel International, commercial aircraft produced by Boeing, greeting cards designed and printed by Hallmark, and airline meals prepared by LSG SkyChefs. All of these examples are characterized by diverse outputs. Each Bechtel project is unique and different from every other—the company may be simultaneously constructing a dam in the Republic of Congo and a bridge in Indonesia. Likewise, each airline orders a different type of meal from LSG SkyChefs' catering service.

Job-order costing is also used extensively in service industries. For example, hospitals, law firms, movie studios, accounting firms, advertising agencies, and repair shops all use a variation of job-order costing to accumulate costs. Although the detailed example of job-order costing provided in the following section deals with a manufacturing company, the same basic concepts and procedures are used by many service organizations.

IS THIS REALLY A JOB?

VBT Bicycling Vacations of Bristol, Vermont, offers deluxe bicycling vacations in the United States, Canada, Europe, and other locations throughout the world. For example, the company offers a 10-day tour of the Puglia region of Italy—the "heel of the boot." The tour price includes international airfare, 10 nights of lodging, most meals, use of a bicycle, and ground transportation as needed. Each tour is led by at least two local tour leaders, one of whom rides with the guests along the tour route. The other tour leader drives a "sag wagon" that carries extra water, snacks, and bicycle repair equipment and is available for a shuttle back to the hotel or up a hill. The sag wagon also transports guests' luggage from one hotel to another.

Each specific tour can be considered a job. For example, Giuliano Astore and Debora Trippetti, two natives of Puglia, led a VBT tour with 17 guests over 10 days in late April. At the end of the tour, Giuliano submitted a report, a sort of job cost sheet, to VBT headquarters. This report detailed the on the ground expenses incurred for this specific tour, including fuel and operating costs for the van, lodging costs for the guests, the costs of meals provided to guests, the costs of snacks, the cost of hiring additional ground transportation as needed, and the wages of the tour leaders. In addition to these costs, some costs are paid directly by VBT in Vermont to vendors. The total cost incurred for the tour is then compared to the total revenue collected from guests to determine the gross profit for the tour.

Sources: Giuliano Astore and Gregg Marston, President, VBT Bicycling Vacations. For more information about VBT, see www.vbt.com.

© Sandee Noreen

© Sandee Noreen

Job-Order Costing—An Example

To introduce job-order costing, we will follow a specific job as it progresses through the manufacturing process. This job consists of two experimental couplings that Yost Precision Machining has agreed to produce for Loops Unlimited, a manufacturer of roller coasters. Couplings connect the cars on the roller coaster and are a critical component in the performance and safety of the ride. Before we begin our discussion, recall from a previous chapter that companies generally classify manufacturing costs into three broad categories: (1) direct materials, (2) direct labor, and (3) manufacturing overhead. As we study the operation of a job-order costing system, we will see how each of these three types of costs is recorded and accumulated.

Yost Precision Machining is a small company in Michigan that specializes in fabricating precision metal parts that are used in a variety of applications ranging from deep-sea exploration vehicles to the inertial triggers in automobile air bags. The company's top managers gather every morning at 8:00 A.M. in the company's conference room for the daily planning meeting. Attending the meeting this morning are: Jean Yost, the company's president; David Cheung, the marketing manager; Debbie Turner, the production manager; and Marc White, the company controller. The president opened the meeting:

Jean: The production schedule indicates we'll be starting Job 2B47 today. Isn't that the special order for experimental couplings, David?

David: That's right. That's the order from Loops Unlimited for two couplings for their new roller coaster ride for Magic Mountain.

Debbie: Why only two couplings? Don't they need a coupling for every car?

David: Yes. But this is a completely new roller coaster. The cars will go faster and will be subjected to more twists, turns, drops, and loops than on any other existing roller coaster. To hold up under these stresses, Loops Unlimited's engineers completely

YOST
Precision Machining

EXHIBIT 4–1
Materials Requisition Form

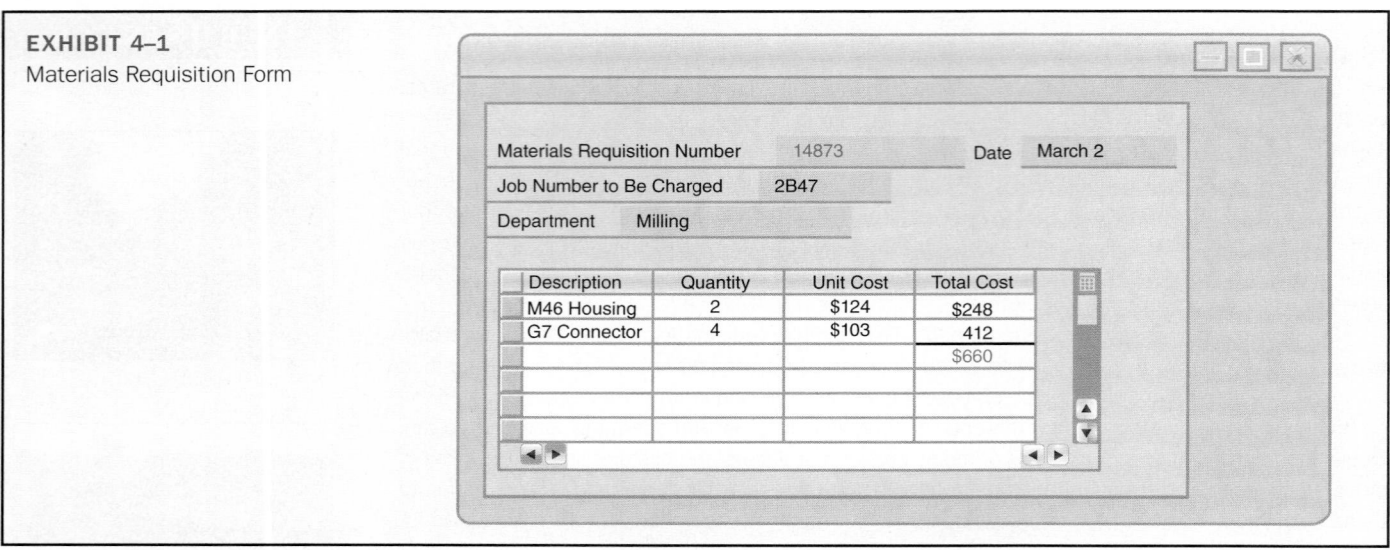

Materials Requisition Number	14873	Date	March 2
Job Number to Be Charged	2B47		
Department	Milling		

Description	Quantity	Unit Cost	Total Cost
M46 Housing	2	$124	$248
G7 Connector	4	$103	412
			$660

redesigned the cars and couplings. They want us to make just two of these new couplings for testing purposes. If the design works, then we'll have the inside track on the order to supply couplings for the whole ride.

Jean: We agreed to take on this initial order at our cost just to get our foot in the door. Marc, will there be any problem documenting our cost so we can get paid?

Marc: No problem. The contract with Loops stipulates that they will pay us an amount equal to our cost of goods sold. With our job-order costing system, I can tell you the cost on the day the job is completed.

Jean: Good. Is there anything else we should discuss about this job at this time? No? Well then let's move on to the next item of business.

Measuring Direct Materials Cost

The blueprints submitted by Loops Unlimited indicate that each experimental coupling will require three parts that are classified as direct materials: two G7 Connectors and one M46 Housing. Since each coupling requires two connectors and one housing, the production of two couplings requires four connectors and two housings. This is a custom product that is being made for the first time, but if this were one of the company's standard products, it would have an established *bill of materials*. A **bill of materials** is a document that lists the type and quantity of each type of direct material needed to complete a unit of product.

When an agreement has been reached with the customer concerning the quantities, prices, and shipment date for the order, a *production order* is issued. The Production Department then prepares a *materials requisition form* similar to the form in Exhibit 4–1. The **materials requisition form** is a document that specifies the type and quantity of materials to be drawn from the storeroom and identifies the job that will be charged for the cost of the materials. The form is used to control the flow of materials into production and also for making entries in the accounting records.

The Yost Precision Machining materials requisition form in Exhibit 4–1 shows that the company's Milling Department has requisitioned two M46 Housings and four G7 Connectors for the Loops Unlimited job, which has been designated as Job 2B47.

Job Cost Sheet

After a production order has been issued, the Accounting Department's job-order costing software system automatically generates a *job cost sheet* like the one presented in Exhibit 4–2. A **job cost sheet** records the materials, labor, and manufacturing overhead costs charged to that job.

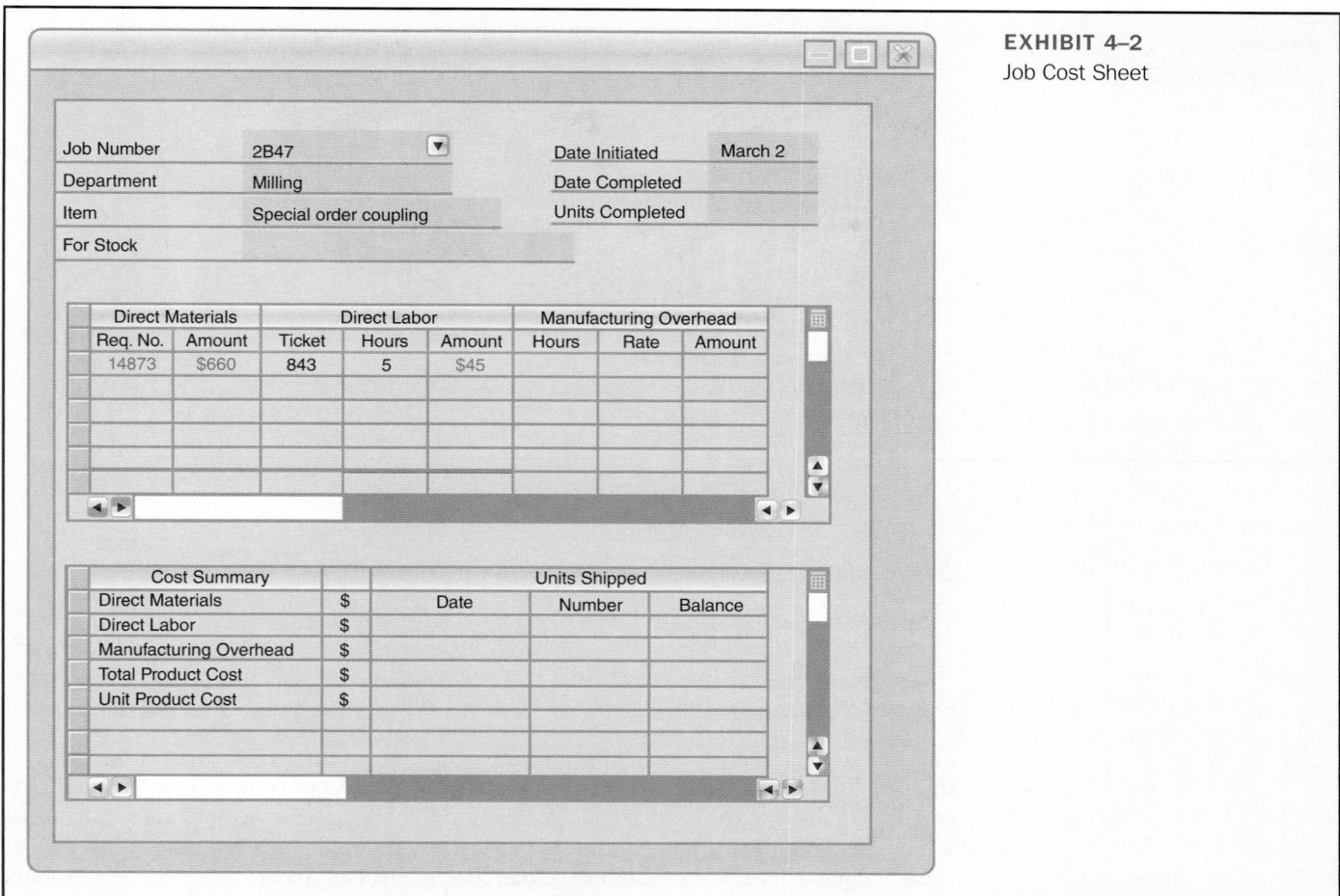

EXHIBIT 4–2
Job Cost Sheet

IN BUSINESS

SUPPLY AND DEMAND INFLUENCE LUMBER PRICES

When the housing market crumbled between 2005 and 2009, lumber mills responded by slashing output by 45%. However, in 2010 many home builders decided to expand speculative construction on the belief that an expiring federal tax credit would entice more customers to purchase new homes. The result of plummeting supply coupled with an uptick in demand was predictable-the price of lumber spiked to $279 per thousand board feet, thereby adding about $1,000 to the price of a typical new home. Pulte Homes told investors that it would attempt to offset the increase in direct materials cost by reducing its labor costs.

Home builders use job-order costing systems to accumulate the costs incurred to build each new home. When materials and labor costs fluctuate, job-order costing systems can measure these impacts on each customer's new home construction costs.

Source: Liam Pleven and Lester Aldrich, "Builders Nailed by Lumber Prices," *The Wall Street Journal*, February 16, 2010, pp. C1 and C4.

After direct materials are issued, the cost of these materials are automatically recorded on the job cost sheet. Note from Exhibit 4–2, for example, that the $660 cost for direct materials shown earlier on the materials requisition form has been charged to Job 2B47 on its job cost sheet. The requisition number 14873 from the materials requisition form appears on the job cost sheet to make it easier to identify the source document for the direct materials charge.

EXHIBIT 4–3
Employee Time Ticket

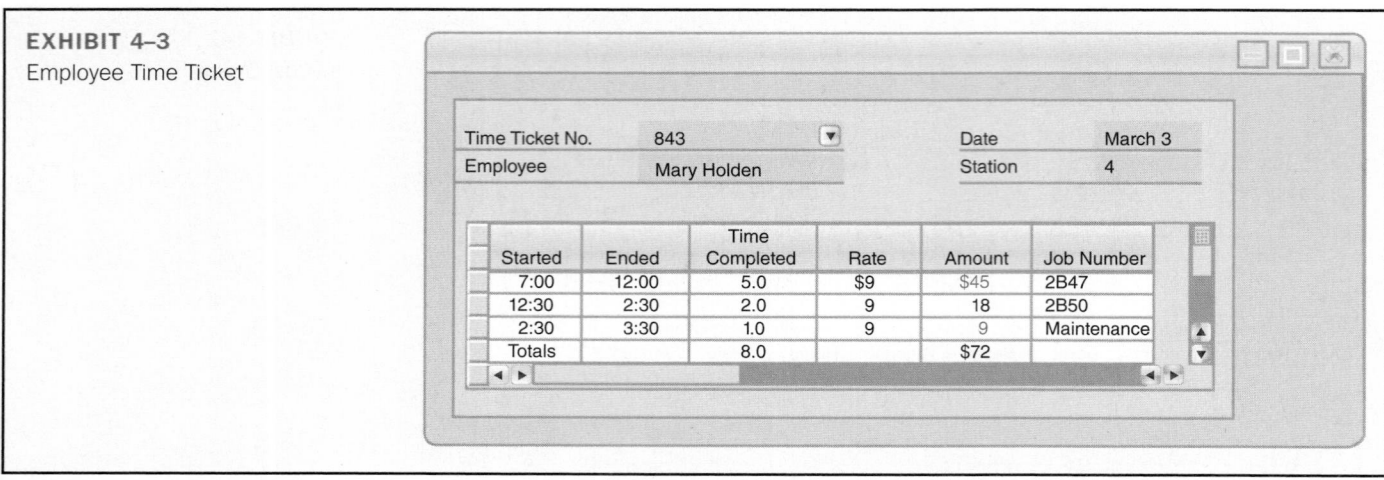

| Time Ticket No. | 843 | | | Date | March 3 |
| Employee | Mary Holden | | | Station | 4 |

Started	Ended	Time Completed	Rate	Amount	Job Number
7:00	12:00	5.0	$9	$45	2B47
12:30	2:30	2.0	9	18	2B50
2:30	3:30	1.0	9	9	Maintenance
Totals		8.0		$72	

Measuring Direct Labor Cost

Direct labor consists of labor charges that can be easily traced to a particular job. Labor charges that cannot be easily traced directly to any job are treated as part of manufacturing overhead. As discussed in a previous chapter, this latter category of labor costs is called *indirect labor* and includes tasks such as maintenance, supervision, and cleanup.

Today many companies rely on computerized systems (rather than paper and pencil) to maintain employee *time tickets*. A completed **time ticket** is an hour-by-hour summary of the employee's activities throughout the day. One computerized approach to creating time tickets uses bar codes to capture data. Each employee and each job has a unique bar code. When beginning work on a job, the employee scans three bar codes using a handheld device much like the bar code readers at grocery store checkout stands. The first bar code indicates that a job is being started; the second is the unique bar code on the employee's identity badge; and the third is the unique bar code of the job itself. This information is fed automatically via an electronic network to a computer that notes the time and records all of the data. When the task is completed, the employee scans a bar code indicating the task is complete, the bar code on his or her identity badge, and the bar code attached to the job. This information is relayed to the computer that again notes the time, and a time ticket, such as the one shown in Exhibit 4–3, is automatically prepared. Because all of the source data is already in computer files, the labor costs can be automatically posted to job cost sheets. For example, Exhibit 4–3 shows $45 of direct labor cost related to Job 2B47. This amount is automatically posted to the job cost sheet shown in Exhibit 4–2. The time ticket in Exhibit 4–3 also shows $9 of indirect labor costs related to performing maintenance. This cost is treated as part of manufacturing overhead and does not get posted on a job cost sheet.

Computing Predetermined Overhead Rates

LEARNING OBJECTIVE 4–1

Compute a predetermined overhead rate.

Recall that product costs include manufacturing overhead as well as direct materials and direct labor. Therefore, manufacturing overhead also needs to be recorded on the job cost sheet. However, assigning manufacturing overhead to a specific job involves some difficulties. There are three reasons for this:

1. Manufacturing overhead is an *indirect cost*. This means that it is either impossible or difficult to trace these costs to a particular product or job.
2. Manufacturing overhead consists of many different types of cost ranging from the grease used in machines to the annual salary of the production manager. Some of these costs are variable overhead costs because they vary in direct proportion to changes in the level of production (e.g., indirect materials, supplies, and power) and

some are fixed overhead costs because they remain constant as the level of production fluctuates (e.g., heat and light, property taxes, and insurance).

3. Because of the fixed costs in manufacturing overhead, total manufacturing overhead costs tend to remain relatively constant from one period to the next even though the number of units produced can fluctuate widely. Consequently, the average cost per unit will vary from one period to the next.

Given these problems, allocation is used to assign overhead costs to products. Allocation is accomplished by selecting an *allocation base* that is common to all of the company's products and services. An **allocation base** is a measure such as direct labor-hours (DLH) or machine-hours (MH) that is used to assign overhead costs to products and services. The most widely used allocation bases in manufacturing are direct labor-hours, direct labor cost, machine-hours and (where a company has only a single product) units of product.

Manufacturing overhead is commonly assigned to products using *a predetermined overhead rate*. The **predetermined overhead rate** is computed by dividing the total estimated manufacturing overhead cost for the period by the estimated total amount of the allocation base for the period as follows:

$$\text{Predetermined overhead rate} = \frac{\text{Estimated total manufacturing overhead cost}}{\text{Estimated total amount of the allocation base}}$$

The predetermined overhead rate is computed *before* the period begins using a four-step process. The first step is to estimate the total amount of the allocation base (the denominator) that will be required for next period's estimated level of production. The second step is to estimate the total fixed manufacturing overhead cost for the coming period and the variable manufacturing overhead cost per unit of the allocation base. The third step is to use the cost formula shown below to estimate the total manufacturing overhead cost (the numerator) for the coming period:

$$Y = a + bX$$

where,

Y = The estimated total manufacturing overhead cost
a = The estimated total fixed manufacturing overhead cost
b = The estimated variable manufacturing overhead cost per unit of the allocation base
X = The estimated total amount of the allocation base

The fourth step is to compute the predetermined overhead rate. Notice, the estimated amount of the allocation base is determined before estimating the total manufacturing overhead cost. This needs to be done because total manufacturing overhead cost includes variable overhead costs that depend on the amount of the allocation base.

Applying Manufacturing Overhead

To repeat, the predetermined overhead rate is computed *before* the period begins. The predetermined overhead rate is then used to apply overhead cost to jobs throughout the period. The process of assigning overhead cost to jobs is called **overhead application**. The formula for determining the amount of overhead cost to apply to a particular job is:

$$\text{Overhead applied to a particular job} = \text{Predetermined overhead rate} \times \text{Amount of the allocation base incurred by the job}$$

For example, if the predetermined overhead rate is $8 per direct labor-hour, then $8 of overhead cost is *applied* to a job for each direct labor-hour incurred on the job. When the allocation base is direct labor-hours, the formula becomes:

$$\text{Overhead applied to a particular job} = \text{Predetermined overhead rate} \times \text{Actual direct labor-hours charged to the job}$$

LEARNING OBJECTIVE 4–2
Apply overhead cost to jobs using a predetermined overhead rate.

Manufacturing Overhead—A Closer Look

To illustrate the steps involved in computing and using a predetermined overhead rate, let's return to Yost Precision Machining and make the following assumptions. In step one, the company estimated that 40,000 direct labor-hours would be required to support the production planned for the year. In step two, it estimated $220,000 of total fixed manufacturing overhead cost for the coming year and $2.50 of variable manufacturing overhead cost per direct labor-hour. Given these assumptions, in step three the company used the cost formula shown below to estimate its total manufacturing overhead cost for the year:

$Y = a + bX$

$Y = \$220,000 + (\$2.50 \text{ per direct labor-hour} \times 40,000 \text{ direct labor-hours})$

$Y = \$220,000 + \$100,000$

$Y = \$320,000$

In step four, Yost Precision Machining computed its predetermined overhead rate for the year of $8 per direct labor-hour as shown below:

$$\text{Predetermined overhead rate} = \frac{\text{Estimated total manufacturing overhead cost}}{\text{Estimated total amount of the allocation base}}$$

$$= \frac{\$320,000}{40,000 \text{ direct labor-hours}}$$

$$= \$8 \text{ per direct labor-hour}$$

The job cost sheet in Exhibit 4–4 indicates that 27 direct labor-hours (i.e., DLHs) were charged to Job 2B47. Therefore, a total of $216 of manufacturing overhead cost would be applied to the job:

$$\begin{array}{c}\text{Overhead applied to} \\ \text{Job 2B47}\end{array} = \begin{array}{c}\text{Predetermined} \\ \text{overhead rate}\end{array} \times \begin{array}{c}\text{Actual direct labor-hours} \\ \text{charged to Job 2B47}\end{array}$$

$$= \$8 \text{ per DLH} \times 27 \text{ DLHs}$$

$$= \$216 \text{ of overhead applied to Job 2B47}$$

This amount of overhead has been entered on the job cost sheet in Exhibit 4–4. Note that this is *not* the actual amount of overhead caused by the job. Actual overhead costs are *not* assigned to jobs—if that could be done, the costs would be direct costs, not overhead. The overhead assigned to the job is simply a share of the total overhead that was estimated at the beginning of the year. A **normal cost system**, which we have been describing, applies overhead to jobs by multiplying a predetermined overhead rate by the actual amount of the allocation base incurred by the jobs.

The Need for a Predetermined Rate

Instead of using a predetermined rate based on estimates, why not base the overhead rate on the *actual* total manufacturing overhead cost and the *actual* total amount of the allocation base incurred on a monthly, quarterly, or annual basis? If an actual rate is computed monthly or quarterly, seasonal factors in overhead costs or in the allocation base can produce fluctuations in the overhead rate. For example, the costs of heating and cooling a factory in Illinois will be highest in the winter and summer months and lowest in the spring and fall. If the overhead rate is recomputed at the end of each month or each quarter based on actual costs and activity, the overhead rate would go up in the winter and summer and down in the spring and fall. As a result, two identical jobs, one completed in the winter and one completed in the spring, would be assigned different manufacturing overhead costs. Many managers believe that such fluctuations in product costs serve no useful purpose. To avoid such fluctuations, actual overhead rates could be computed on an annual or less-frequent basis. However, if the overhead rate is computed annually based on the actual costs and activity for the year, the manufacturing overhead assigned

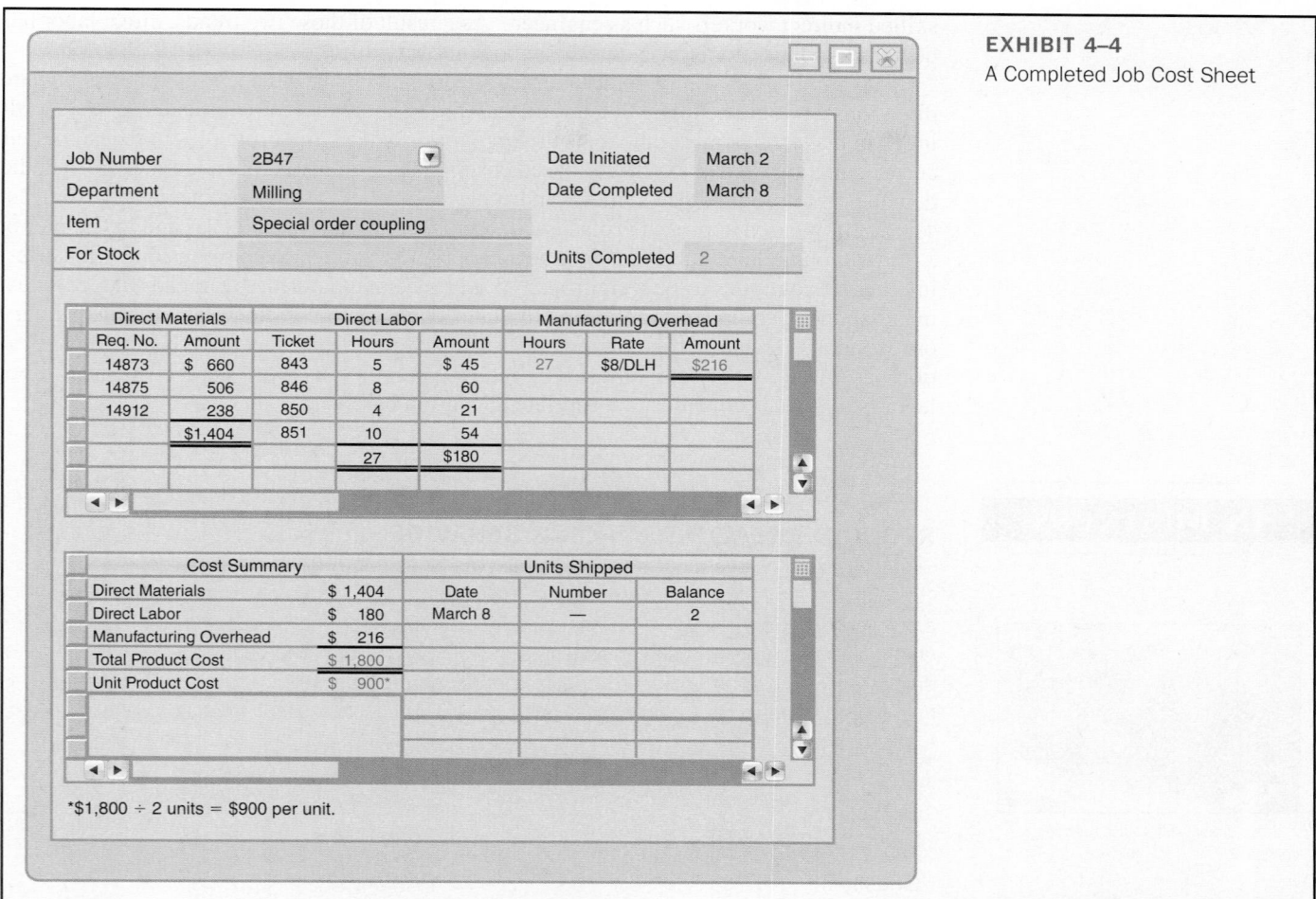

EXHIBIT 4–4
A Completed Job Cost Sheet

to any particular job would not be known until the end of the year. For example, the cost of Job 2B47 at Yost Precision Machining would not be known until the end of the year, even though the job will be completed and shipped to the customer in March. For these reasons, most companies use predetermined overhead rates rather than actual overhead rates in their cost accounting systems.

Choice of an Allocation Base for Overhead Cost

Ideally, the allocation base in the predetermined overhead rate should *drive* overhead cost. A **cost driver** is a factor, such as machine-hours, beds occupied, computer time, or flight-hours, that causes overhead costs. If the base in the predetermined overhead rate does not "drive" overhead costs, product costs will be distorted. For example, if direct labor-hours is used to allocate overhead, but in reality overhead has little to do with direct labor-hours, then products with high direct labor-hour requirements will be overcosted.

Most companies use direct labor-hours or direct labor cost as the allocation base for manufacturing overhead. In the past, direct labor accounted for up to 60% of the cost of many products, with overhead cost making up only a portion of the remainder. This situation has changed for two reasons. First, sophisticated automated equipment has taken over functions that used to be performed by direct labor workers. Because the costs of acquiring and maintaining such equipment are classified as overhead, this increases overhead while decreasing direct labor. Second, products are becoming more sophisticated and complex and are modified more frequently. This increases the need for highly skilled indirect workers such as engineers. As a result of these two trends, direct labor has decreased relative to overhead as a component of product costs.

In companies where direct labor and overhead costs have been moving in opposite directions, it would be difficult to argue that direct labor "drives" overhead costs. Accordingly, managers in some companies use *activity-based costing* principles to redesign their cost accounting systems. Activity-based costing is designed to more accurately reflect the demands that products, customers, and other cost objects make on overhead resources. The activity-based approach is discussed in more detail in Appendix 4A and in Chapter 6.

Although direct labor may not be an appropriate allocation base in some industries, in others it continues to be a significant driver of manufacturing overhead. Indeed, most manufacturing companies in the United States continue to use direct labor as the primary or secondary allocation base for manufacturing overhead. The key point is that the allocation base used by the company should really drive, or cause, overhead costs, and direct labor is not always the most appropriate allocation base.

IN BUSINESS

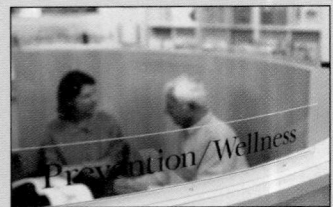

© Keith Brofsky/Photodisc/Getty Images, RF

REDUCING HEALTH-DAMAGING BEHAVIORS

Cianbro is an industrial construction company headquartered in Pittsfield, Maine, whose goal is "to be the healthiest company in America." It introduced a corporate wellness program to attack employee behaviors that drive up health-care costs. The table below summarizes the number of employees in five health risk categories as of 2003 and 2005. The decreases in the number of employees in these high-risk categories are evidence that the wellness program was effective in helping employees make positive lifestyle changes. This should result in reduced health-care costs for the company.

Health Risk Category	Number of Employees		
	January 2003	March 2005	Decrease
Obesity	432	353	79
High cholesterol	637	515	122
Tobacco use.	384	274	110
Inactivity	354	254	100
High blood pressure.	139	91	48

Source: Cianbro, WELCOA's *Absolute Advantage* Magazine, 2006.

Computation of Unit Costs

LEARNING OBJECTIVE 4–3
Compute the total cost and average cost per unit of a job.

With the application of Yost Precision Machining's $216 of manufacturing overhead to the job cost sheet in Exhibit 4–4, the job cost sheet is complete except for two final steps. First, the totals for direct materials, direct labor, and manufacturing overhead are transferred to the Cost Summary section of the job cost sheet and added together to obtain the total cost for the job.[1] Then the total product cost ($1,800) is divided by the number of units (2) to obtain the unit product cost ($900). This unit product cost information is used for valuing unsold units in ending inventory and for determining cost of goods sold. As indicated earlier, *this unit product cost is an average cost and should not be interpreted as the cost that would actually be incurred if another unit were produced.* The incremental cost of an additional unit is something less than the average unit cost of $900 because much of the actual overhead costs would not change if another unit were produced.

---

[1] Notice, we are assuming that Job 2B47 required direct materials and direct labor beyond the charges shown in Exhibits 4–1 and 4–3.

In the 8:00 A.M. daily planning meeting on March 9, Jean Yost, the president of Yost Precision Machining, once again drew attention to Job 2B47, the experimental couplings:

Jean: I see Job 2B47 is completed. Let's get those couplings shipped immediately to Loops Unlimited so they can get their testing program under way. Marc, how much are we going to bill Loops for those two units?

Marc: Because we agreed to sell the experimental couplings at cost, we will be charging Loops Unlimited just $900 a unit.

Jean: Fine. Let's hope the couplings work out and we make some money on the big order later.

**MANAGERIAL
ACCOUNTING IN
ACTION**

The Wrap-Up

IN BUSINESS

ONE-OF-A-KIND MASTERPIECE

In a true job-order costing environment, every job is unique. For example, Purdey manufactures 80–90 shotguns per year with each gun being a specially commissioned one-of-a-kind masterpiece. The prices start at $110,000 because every detail is custom built, engraved, assembled, and polished by a skilled craftsman. The hand engraving can take months to complete and may add as much as $100,000 to the price. The guns are designed to shoot perfectly straight and their value increases over time even with heavy use. One Purdey gun collector said "when I shoot my Purdeys I feel like an orchestra conductor waving my baton."

Source: Eric Arnold, "Aim High," *Forbes,* December 28, 2009, p. 86.

Job-Order Costing—The Flow of Costs

We are now ready to discuss the flow of costs through a job-order costing system. Exhibit 4–5 provides a conceptual overview of these cost flows. It highlights the fact that *product costs* flow through inventories on the balance sheet and then on to cost of goods sold in the income statement. More specifically, raw materials purchases are recorded in the *Raw Materials* inventory account. **Raw materials** include any materials that go into the final product. When raw materials are used in production, their costs are transferred to the *Work in Process* inventory account as direct materials.[2] **Work in process** consists of units of product that are only partially complete and will require further work before they are ready for sale to the customer. Notice that direct labor costs are added directly to Work in Process—they do not flow through Raw Materials inventory. Manufacturing overhead costs are applied to Work in Process by multiplying the predetermined overhead rate by the actual quantity of the allocation base consumed by each job.[3] When goods are completed, their costs are transferred from Work in Process to *Finished Goods.* **Finished goods** consist of completed units of product that have not yet been sold to customers. The amount transferred from Work in Process to Finished Goods is referred to as the *cost of goods manufactured.* The **cost of goods manufactured** includes the manufacturing costs associated with the goods that were finished during the period. As goods are sold, their costs are transferred from Finished Goods to Cost of Goods Sold. At this point, the various costs required to make the product are finally recorded as an expense. Until that point, these costs are in inventory accounts on the balance sheet. Period costs (or selling and administrative expenses) do not flow through inventories on the balance sheet. They are recorded as expenses on the income statement in the period incurred.

---

[2] Indirect material costs are accounted for as part of manufacturing overhead.

[3] For simplicity, Exhibit 4–5 assumes that Cost of Goods Sold does not need to be adjusted as discussed later in the chapter.

EXHIBIT 4–5
Cost Flows and Classifications in a Manufacturing Company

Job cost sheets are the basis for valuing inventory in a job-order costing system. Before a job is completed, its cost from the job cost sheet is included in work in process inventory. When a job is completed, it is part of finished goods inventory. When completed products are sold, their costs from their job cost sheets become part of cost of goods sold.

We are now ready to take a more detailed look at the flow of costs in job-order costing. To illustrate, let's consider activity for the month of April at Rand Company, a producer of gold and silver commemorative medallions. At the beginning of the month, Rand Company had no finished goods inventory and one job in process—Job A, a special minting of 1,000 gold medallions commemorating the invention of motion pictures. Some work had been completed on this job prior to April; therefore, a total of $30,000 in manufacturing costs had already been recorded on Job A's cost sheet. This job will be completed in April. In addition, Job B, an order for 10,000 silver medallions commemorating the fall of the Berlin Wall, will be started in April and completed in a subsequent month.

In this example, we will track the flow of Rand Company's raw materials, labor, and overhead costs for April and prepare an income statement for the month.

Direct and Indirect Materials

During April, $52,000 in raw materials were requisitioned from the storeroom for use in production. These raw materials included $28,000 of direct materials for Job A, $22,000 of direct materials for Job B, and $2,000 of indirect materials. As shown in Exhibit 4–6, these costs are recorded on the appropriate job cost sheets and in an account we will call Manufacturing Overhead Incurred. Specifically, $28,000 of direct materials is charged to Job A's cost sheet and $22,000 is charged to Job B's cost sheet. Note that the $2,000 of indirect materials has *not* been assigned to either of the two jobs—instead, it is charged to the account we call Manufacturing Overhead Incurred. We will be charging all of the actual manufacturing overhead costs that are incurred to this account.

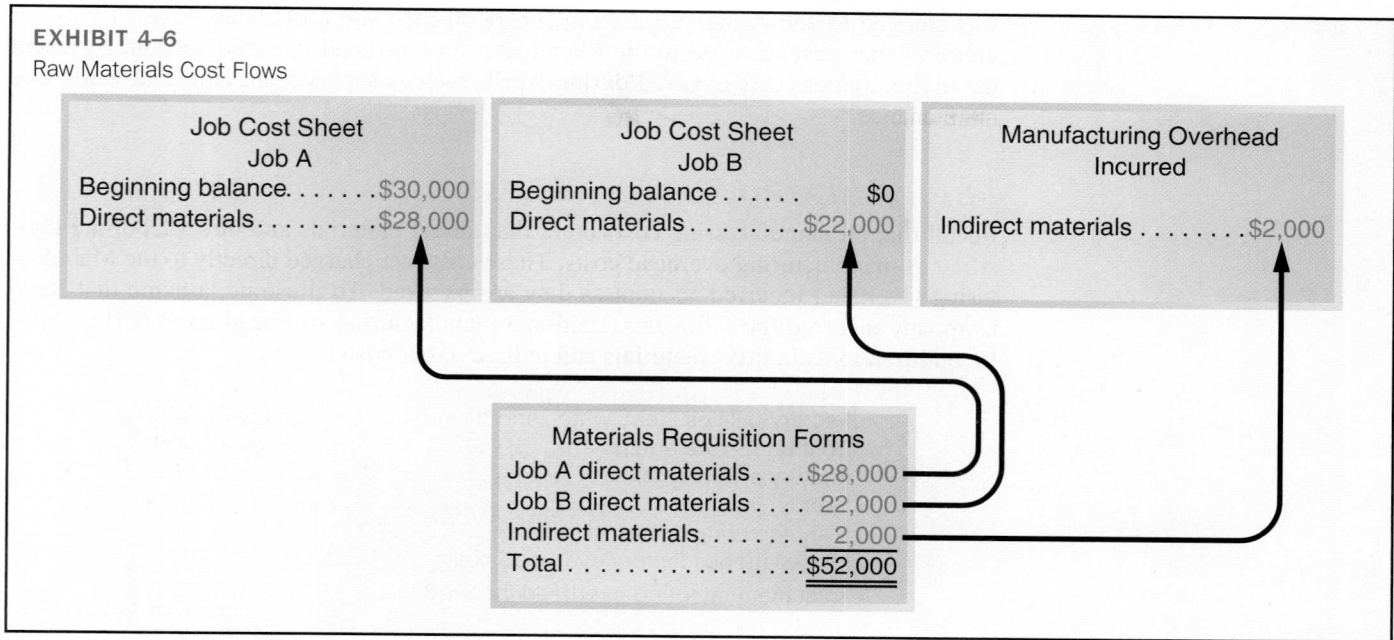

EXHIBIT 4–6
Raw Materials Cost Flows

Notice from Exhibit 4–6 that the job cost sheet for Job A contains a beginning balance of $30,000. We stated earlier that this balance represents the cost of work done on this job prior to April. This cost would be classified on the company's balance sheet as Work in Process inventory at the beginning of April.

Labor Cost

Employee time tickets are filled out by workers, collected, and forwarded to the Accounting Department. In the Accounting Department, wages are computed and the resulting costs are classified as either direct or indirect labor. In April, Rand Company incurred $40,000 of direct labor cost for Job A, $20,000 of direct labor cost for Job B, and $15,000 of indirect labor cost. Exhibit 4–7 shows that during April, $40,000 of direct labor cost

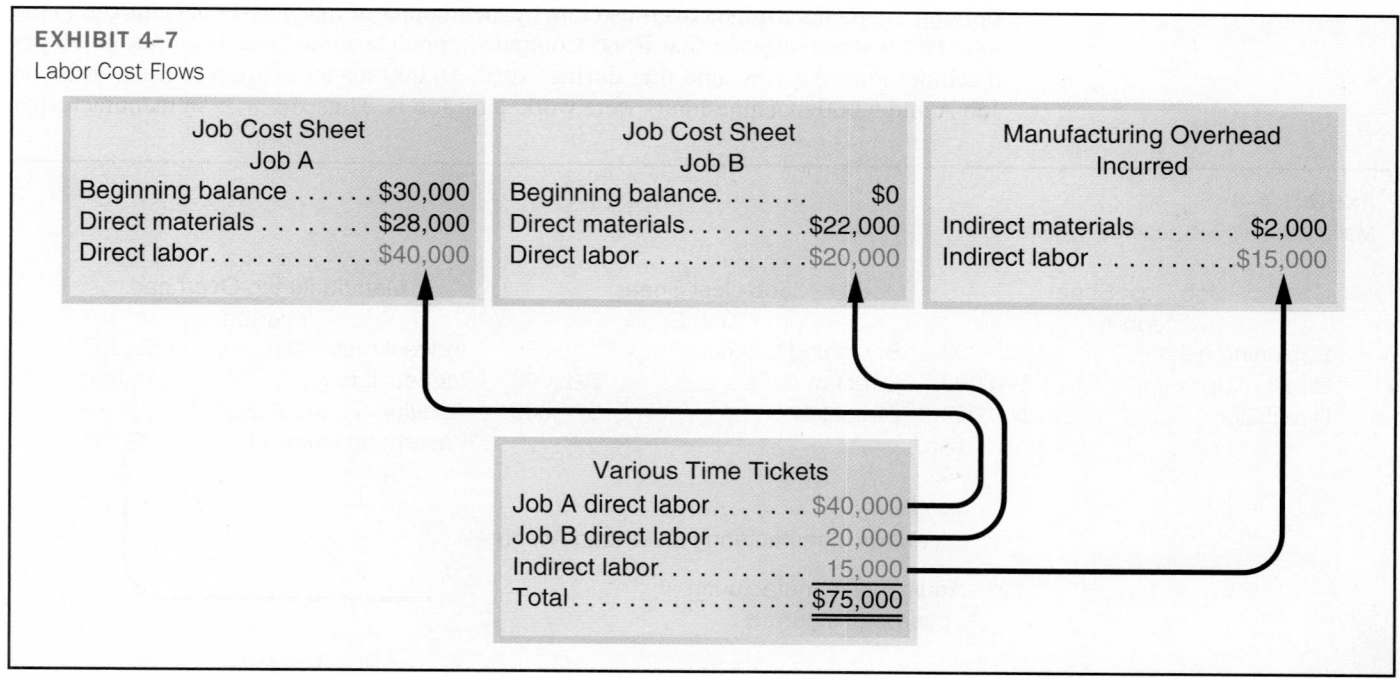

EXHIBIT 4–7
Labor Cost Flows

was charged to Job A and $20,000 to Job B on their job cost sheets. The $15,000 of indirect labor costs charged to the Manufacturing Overhead Incurred account represent the indirect labor costs incurred during April, such as supervision, janitorial work, and maintenance.

Manufacturing Overhead Cost

Recall that all manufacturing costs other than direct materials and direct labor are classified as manufacturing overhead costs. These costs are charged directly to the Manufacturing Overhead Incurred account as they are incurred. To illustrate, assume that Rand Company incurred the following additional manufacturing overhead costs during April (in addition to its indirect materials and indirect labor costs):

Factory utilities (heat, water, and power)	$21,000
Rent on factory equipment	16,000
Factory property taxes	13,000
Factory insurance	7,000
Manufacturing depreciation	18,000
Miscellaneous factory overhead costs	3,000
Total manufacturing overhead incurred	$78,000

Exhibit 4–8 shows how these costs are recorded.

Applying Manufacturing Overhead

Because actual manufacturing costs are charged to the Manufacturing Overhead Incurred account rather than to the job cost sheets, how are manufacturing overhead costs assigned to jobs? The answer is, by means of the predetermined overhead rate. Recall from our discussion earlier in the chapter that a predetermined overhead rate is established at the beginning of each year. The rate is calculated by dividing the estimated total manufacturing overhead cost for the year by the estimated amount of the allocation base (measured in machine-hours, direct labor-hours, or some other base). The predetermined overhead rate is then used to apply overhead costs to jobs. For example, if machine-hours is the allocation base, overhead cost is applied to each job by multiplying the predetermined overhead rate by the number of machine-hours charged to the job. To illustrate, assume that Rand Company's predetermined overhead rate is $6 per machine-hour. Also assume that during April, 10,000 machine-hours were worked on Job A and 5,000 machine-hours were worked on Job B. Thus, $60,000 in manufacturing

EXHIBIT 4–8
Manufacturing Overhead Cost Flows

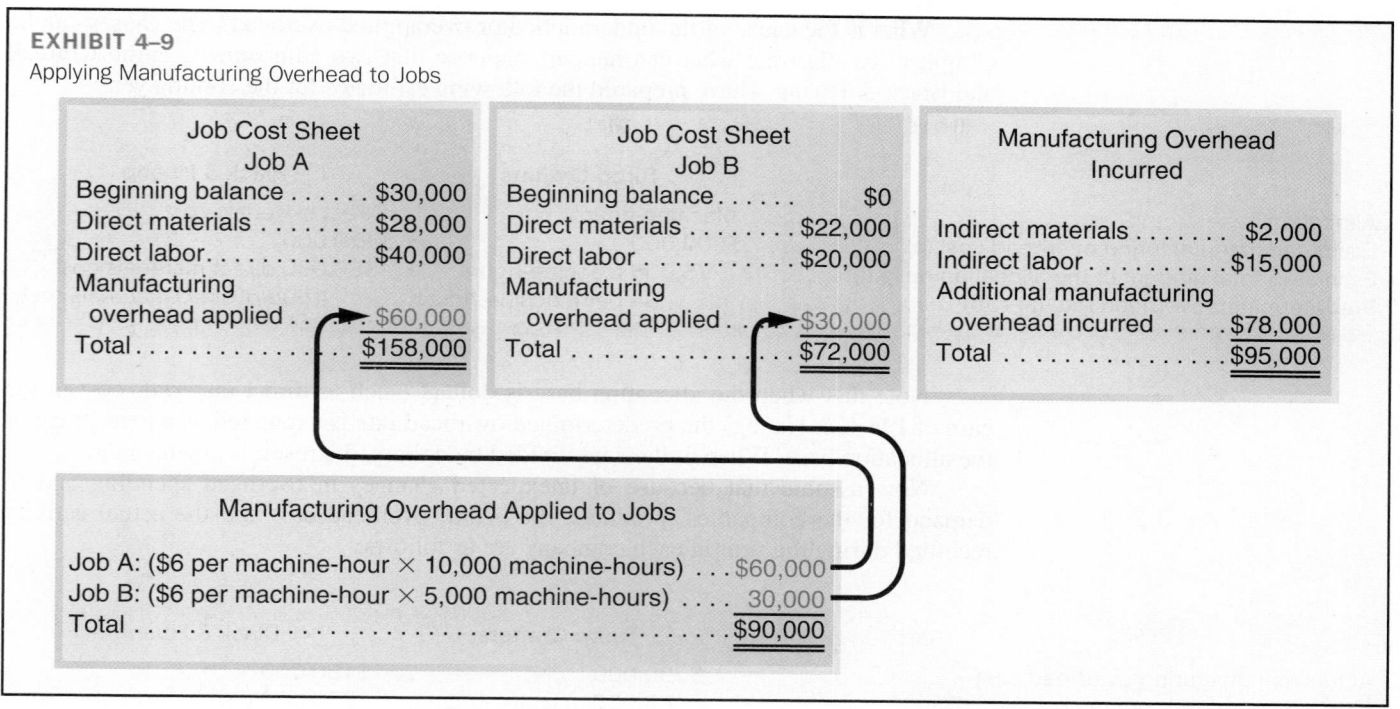

EXHIBIT 4–9
Applying Manufacturing Overhead to Jobs

overhead cost ($6 per machine-hour × 10,000 machine-hours) would be applied to Job A and $30,000 in manufacturing overhead cost ($6 per machine-hour × 5,000 machine-hours) would be applied to Job B. Exhibit 4–9 shows how these costs are applied to jobs.

Notice that Job A has been assigned total manufacturing costs of $158,000. Since Job A was completed in April, we can now compute the unit product cost for each of the 1,000 gold medallions included in the job. The unit product cost for Job A is $158 ($158,000 ÷ 1,000 units). This figure will be referred to later when we turn our attention to computing Rand Company's cost of goods sold. Also notice in Exhibit 4–9 that Job B has been assigned $72,000 of manufacturing costs; however, its unit product cost cannot be determined yet because the job is still in progress at the end of April. The $72,000 assigned to Job B will be reported as Work in Process inventory on the balance sheet at the end of April.

Underapplied or Overapplied Overhead

You may have noticed a discrepancy in Exhibit 4–9. The actual manufacturing overhead incurred during April was $95,000, but only $90,000 in manufacturing overhead cost was applied to the two jobs in process during the month. This discrepancy occurs because the manufacturing overhead applied to jobs is based on the predetermined overhead rate, which is itself based on estimates of the total manufacturing overhead cost and the total machine-hours that were made before the month began. Except under very special circumstances, if either of these estimates is off, the actual manufacturing overhead costs that are incurred will not equal the manufacturing overhead cost that is applied to jobs using the predetermined overhead rate.

The difference between the manufacturing overhead cost applied to jobs and the actual manufacturing overhead costs of a period is called either **underapplied** or **overapplied overhead**. For Rand Company, overhead was underapplied by $5,000 because the applied cost ($90,000) was $5,000 less than the actual cost ($95,000). If the situation had been reversed and the company had applied $95,000 in manufacturing overhead cost to jobs while incurring actual manufacturing overhead costs of only $90,000, then the overhead would have been overapplied.

LEARNING OBJECTIVE 4–4
Compute underapplied or overapplied overhead cost.

What is the cause of the underapplied or overapplied overhead? The causes can be complex. To illustrate what can happen, suppose that two companies—Turbo Crafters and Black & Huang—have prepared the following estimates for the coming year:

	Turbo Crafters	Black & Huang
Allocation base	Machine-hours	Direct materials cost
Estimated manufacturing overhead cost (a)	$300,000	$120,000
Estimated total amount of the allocation base (b)	75,000 machine-hours	$80,000 direct materials cost
Predetermined overhead rate (a) ÷ (b)	$4 per machine-hour	150% of direct materials cost

Note that when the allocation base is dollars (such as direct materials cost in the case of Black & Huang) the predetermined overhead rate is expressed as a percentage of the allocation base. When dollars are divided by dollars, the result is a percentage.

Now assume that because of unexpected changes in overhead spending and in demand for the companies' products, the *actual* overhead cost and the actual activity recorded during the year in each company are as follows:

	Turbo Crafters	Black & Huang
Actual manufacturing overhead cost	$290,000	$130,000
Actual total amount of the allocation base	68,000 machine-hours	$90,000 direct materials cost

For each company, note that the actual data for both the cost and the allocation base differ from the estimates used in computing the predetermined overhead rate. This results in underapplied and overapplied overhead as follows:

	Turbo Crafters	Black & Huang
Actual manufacturing overhead cost	$290,000	$130,000
Manufacturing overhead cost applied to jobs during the year:		
Predetermined overhead rate (a)	$4 per machine-hour	150% of direct materials cost
Actual total amount of the allocation base (b)	68,000 machine-hours	$ 90,000 direct materials cost
Manufacturing overhead applied (a) × (b)	$272,000	$135,000
Underapplied (overapplied) manufacturing overhead ...	$ 18,000	$ (5,000)

For Turbo Crafters, the $272,000 of manufacturing overhead cost applied to jobs is less than the $290,000 actual manufacturing overhead cost for the year. Therefore, overhead is underapplied. Notice that the original $300,000 estimate of manufacturing overhead for Turbo Crafters is not directly involved in this computation. Its impact is felt only through the $4 predetermined overhead rate.

For Black & Huang, the $135,000 of manufacturing overhead cost applied to jobs is greater than the $130,000 actual manufacturing overhead cost for the year, so overhead is overapplied. A summary of the concepts discussed above is presented in Exhibit 4–10.

Disposition of Underapplied or Overapplied Overhead

Note that the manufacturing overhead cost that is applied to jobs is an estimate—it does not represent actual costs incurred. The company's accounts must be adjusted at the end of the period so that they reflect actual costs rather than this estimate. This is accomplished in one of two ways: either (1) the underapplied or overapplied overhead at the

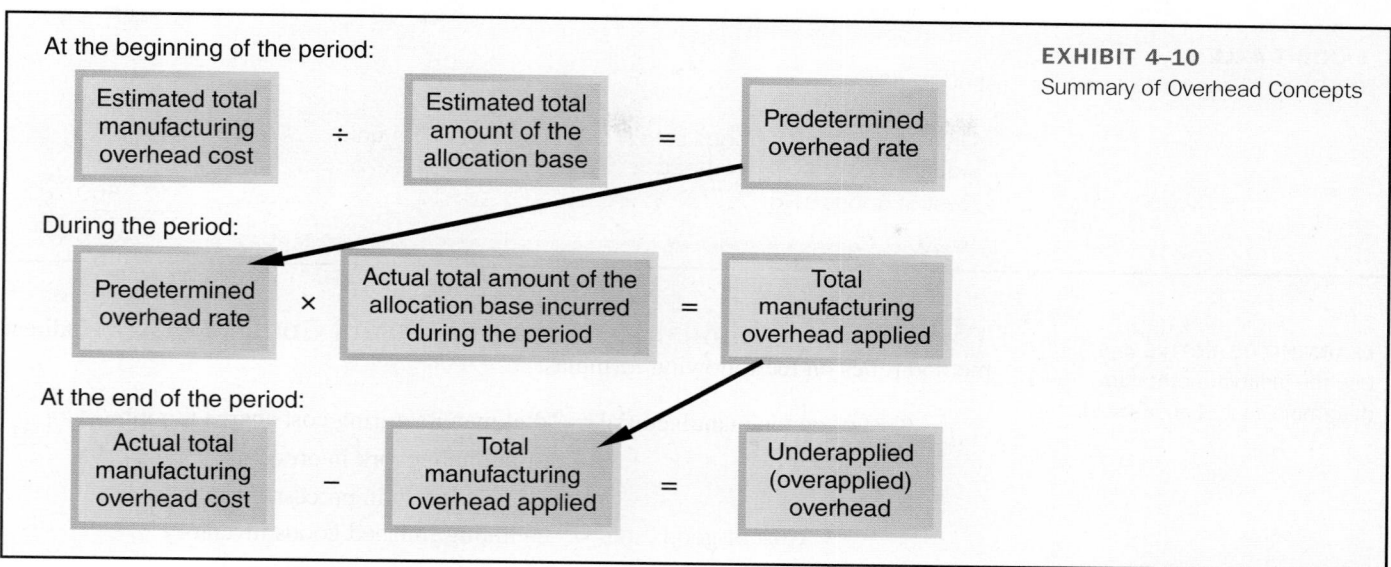

EXHIBIT 4–10
Summary of Overhead Concepts

end of a period is closed out to Cost of Goods Sold; or (2) it is allocated among Work in Process, Finished Goods, and Cost of Goods Sold in proportion to the overhead applied during the current period that is in the ending balances of these accounts. The latter method takes us further into the details of bookkeeping than we would like to go in this book, so we will always assume that the underapplied or overapplied overhead is closed out to Cost of Goods Sold. In other words, Cost of Goods Sold is adjusted for the amount of underapplied or overapplied overhead.

The procedure for closing out underapplied or overapplied overhead to Cost of Goods Sold is quite simple. Underapplied overhead is added to Cost of Goods Sold. Overapplied overhead is deducted from Cost of Goods Sold. The reasoning is that if overhead is underapplied, not enough manufacturing overhead was applied to jobs and hence their costs are understated. Therefore, Cost of Goods Sold must be increased to compensate for this understatement. Likewise, if overhead is overapplied, too much manufacturing overhead was applied to jobs and hence their costs are overstated. Therefore, Cost of Goods Sold must be decreased to compensate for this overstatement. In short, adding to or deducting from Cost of Goods Sold corrects the misstatement of cost that occurs as a result of using a predetermined overhead rate.

Prepare an Income Statement

Cost of Goods Sold

Recall from Chapter 2 that Cost of Goods Sold consists of the costs of the products sold to customers. It can be determined directly or indirectly. The direct method is simpler and quicker when the necessary data are available. We will illustrate both approaches for Rand Company.

LEARNING OBJECTIVE 4–5
Use the direct method to determine cost of goods sold.

The Direct Method of Determining Cost of Goods Sold Recall that Job A, which consisted of 1,000 gold medallions, was completed during April, but Job B was not completed. Also recall that the unit product cost for each of the 1,000 gold medallions included in Job A was $158 ($158,000 ÷ 1,000 units). If we assume that 750 of the 1,000 gold medallions included in Job A were shipped to customers by the end of April, then the cost of the medallions sold to customers was $118,500 (750 units × $158 per unit). This amount must be adjusted for the $5,000 underapplied overhead to arrive at the cost of goods sold for the period. Exhibit 4–11 illustrates the direct method of determining the cost of goods sold.

EXHIBIT 4–11
The Direct Method of Determining Cost of Goods Sold

Unadjusted cost of goods sold (750 units × $158 per unit)	$118,500
Add: Underapplied overhead	5,000
Cost of goods sold	$123,500

LEARNING OBJECTIVE 4–6
Use the indirect method to determine cost of goods sold.

The Indirect Method of Determining Cost of Goods Sold
The indirect method relies on the following formulas:

Cost of goods manufactured = Total manufacturing cost charged to jobs
+ Beginning work in process inventory
− Ending work in process inventory

Cost of goods sold = Beginning finished goods inventory
+ Cost of goods manufactured
− Ending finished goods inventory

To determine the cost of goods sold with these formulas, we will need to know five items: (1) the beginning work in process inventory; (2) the total manufacturing cost charged to jobs for the period; (3) the ending work in process inventory; (4) the beginning finished goods inventory; and (5) the ending finished goods inventory. These costs for Rand Company are detailed below:

1. The beginning work in process inventory was $30,000—the beginning balance on Job A's job cost sheet from Exhibit 4–6.
2. The total manufacturing cost charged to jobs consists of direct materials, direct labor, and manufacturing overhead charged to jobs during the period. From Exhibit 4–9, the total manufacturing cost can be determined as follows:

	Job A	Job B	Total
Direct materials	$28,000	$22,000	$ 50,000
Direct labor.	$40,000	$20,000	60,000
Manufacturing overhead applied	$60,000	$30,000	90,000
Total manufacturing cost charged to jobs. . . .			$200,000

3. The ending work in process inventory consists of $72,000—the accumulated cost of Job B from Exhibit 4–9.
4. At the start of the Rand Company example, we stated that the company had no beginning finished goods inventories.
5. The ending finished goods inventory consists of the costs of any completed units that have not been sold at the end of the month. Job A consisted of 1,000 units, 750 of which were sold. Therefore, the ending finished goods inventory consists of 250 units (1,000 units – 750 units). Recall that the unit product cost of Job A is $158 per unit. Consequently, the total cost of these 250 unsold, but completed, units is $39,500 (250 units × $158 per unit).

Using these data, Exhibit 4–12 illustrates the indirect method of determining the cost of goods sold.

Note two things from Exhibit 4–11 and Exhibit 4–12. First, the cost of goods sold is identical under the two methods—and always will be. Second, under both methods,

EXHIBIT 4–12
The Indirect Method of
Determining Cost of Goods Sold

Manufacturing costs charged to jobs:	
Direct materials	$ 50,000
Direct labor	60,000
Manufacturing overhead applied	90,000
Total manufacturing cost charged to jobs	200,000
Add: Beginning work in process inventory	30,000
	230,000
Deduct: Ending work in process inventory	72,000
Cost of goods manufactured	$158,000
Beginning finished goods inventory	$ 0
Add: Cost of goods manufactured (see above)	158,000
Goods available for sale	158,000
Deduct: Ending finished goods inventory	39,500
Unadjusted cost of goods sold	118,500
Add: Underapplied overhead	5,000
Cost of goods sold	$123,500

the underapplied overhead is added to the unadjusted cost of goods sold to determine the cost of goods sold. Remember the reason for this. Underapplied overhead means that not enough overhead was applied to jobs—the actual manufacturing overhead exceeded the amount of manufacturing overhead applied to jobs using the predetermined overhead rate. We must add the underapplied overhead to the unadjusted cost of goods sold to remove this discrepancy.

Income Statement

Now that we know the cost of goods sold ($123,500), all we need to construct the company's income statement for April is the total sales revenue and the selling and administrative expenses. We will assume that Rand Company's total sales revenue is $225,000 and that it has supplied the following data concerning its selling and administrative expenses in April:

Rand Company Selling and Administrative Expenses For the Month Ending April 30	
Salaries expense	$30,000
Depreciation expense	7,000
Advertising expense	42,000
Other expense	8,000
Total selling and administrative expense	$87,000

Exhibit 4–13 combines these selling and administrative expenses with the sales and cost of goods sold data to create the company's income statement for the month.

EXHIBIT 4–13
Income Statement

Rand Company Income Statement For the Month Ending April 30	
Sales	$225,000
Cost of goods sold	123,500
Gross margin	101,500
Selling and administrative expense	87,000
Net operating income	$ 14,500

Multiple Predetermined Overhead Rates

Our discussion in this chapter has assumed that there is a single predetermined overhead rate for an entire factory called a **plantwide overhead rate**. This is a fairly common practice—particularly in smaller companies. But in larger companies, *multiple predetermined overhead rates* are often used. In a **multiple predetermined overhead rate** system each production department may have its own predetermined overhead rate. Such a system, while more complex, is more accurate because it can reflect differences across departments in how overhead costs are incurred. For example, in departments that are relatively labor intensive overhead might be allocated based on direct labor-hours and in departments that are relatively machine intensive overhead might be allocated based on machine-hours. When multiple predetermined overhead rates are used, overhead is applied in each department according to its own overhead rate as jobs proceed through the department.

Job-Order Costing in Service Companies

Job-order costing is used in service organizations such as law firms, movie studios, hospitals, and repair shops, as well as in manufacturing companies. In a law firm, for example, each client is a "job," and the costs of that job are accumulated on a job cost sheet as the client's case is handled by the firm. Legal forms and similar inputs represent the direct materials for the job; the time expended by attorneys is like direct labor; and the costs of secretaries and legal aids, rent, depreciation, and so forth, represent the overhead.

In a movie studio such as Columbia Pictures, each film produced by the studio is a "job," and costs of direct materials (costumes, props, film, etc.) and direct labor (actors, directors, and extras) are charged to each film's job cost sheet. A share of the studio's overhead costs, such as utilities, depreciation of equipment, wages of maintenance workers, and so forth, is also charged to each film.

In sum, job-order costing is a versatile and widely used costing method that may be encountered in virtually any organization that provides diverse products or services.

IN BUSINESS

COMPUTING JOB COSTS AT FAST WRAP

In 2007, Michael Enos founded Fast Wrap, a company that shrink-wraps everything from jet skis and recreation vehicles (RVs) to entire buildings. Today, the company has 64 locations across America and generates more $6 million in annual sales. The company's revenues far-exceed its direct materials and direct labor costs. For example, Fast Wrap charges customers $400 to wrap a 20-foot boat that requires $25 worth of plastic and $30 worth of labor. Larger jobs are even more profitable. For example, Fast Wrap signed a $250,000 contract to shrink-wrap a 244,000-square-foot hospital under construction in Fontana, California. The materials and labor for this job cost Fast Wrap $44,000.

Source: Susan Adams, "It's a Wrap," *Forbes,* March 15, 2010, pp. 36–38.

Summary

Job-order costing is used to cost products in situations where the organization offers many different products or services, such as in furniture manufacturing, hospitals, and legal firms.

Materials requisition forms and labor time tickets are used to assign direct materials and direct labor costs to jobs in a job-order costing system. Manufacturing overhead costs are assigned to jobs using a predetermined overhead rate. All of the costs are recorded on a job cost sheet.

The predetermined overhead rate is determined before the period begins by dividing the estimated total manufacturing cost for the period by the estimated total amount of the allocation base for the period. The most frequently used allocation bases are direct labor-hours and machine-hours. Overhead is applied to jobs by multiplying the predetermined overhead rate by the actual amount of the allocation base recorded for the job.

Because the predetermined overhead rate is based on estimates, the actual overhead cost incurred during a period may be more or less than the amount of overhead cost applied to production. Such a difference is referred to as underapplied or overapplied overhead. The underapplied or overapplied overhead for a period can be either closed out to Cost of Goods Sold or allocated between Work in Process, Finished Goods, and Cost of Goods Sold. When overhead is underapplied, manufacturing overhead costs have been understated and therefore inventories and/or expenses must be adjusted upwards. When overhead is overapplied, manufacturing overhead costs have been overstated and therefore inventories and/or expenses must be adjusted downward.

Review Problem: Job-Order Costing

Hogle Corporation uses job-order costing and applies overhead cost to jobs on the basis of machine-hours worked. For the just completed year, the company estimated that it would work 75,000 machine-hours and incur $450,000 in manufacturing overhead cost. The company actually worked 80,000 machine-hours.

The company has provided the following financial data concerning its actual operations for the year:

Direct materials	$360,000
Indirect materials	$20,000
Direct labor	$75,000
Indirect labor	$110,000
Sales commissions	$90,000
Administrative salaries	$200,000
General selling expenses	$17,000
Factory utility costs	$43,000
Advertising costs	$180,000
Factory depreciation	$280,000
Selling and administrative depreciation	$70,000
Factory insurance	$7,000
Selling and administrative insurance	$3,000
Cost of goods sold (not adjusted for underapplied or overapplied overhead)	$ 870,000
Sales	$1,500,000

Required:

1. Is overhead underapplied or overapplied for the year? By how much?
2. Prepare an income statement for the year.

Solution to Review Problem

1. To determine the underapplied or overapplied overhead for the year, we must know the actual manufacturing overhead cost incurred and the manufacturing overhead applied to jobs. The actual manufacturing overhead cost incurred can be determined by adding together all of the manufacturing overhead items in the financial data provided by the company as follows:

Manufacturing overhead costs incurred:	
Indirect materials	$ 20,000
Indirect labor	110,000
Factory utility costs	43,000
Factory depreciation	280,000
Factory insurance	7,000
Total manufacturing overhead cost incurred	$460,000

The predetermined overhead rate for the year is computed as follows:

$$\text{Predetermined overhead rate} = \frac{\text{Estimated total manufacturing overhead cost}}{\text{Estimated total amount of the allocation base}}$$

$$= \frac{\$450,000}{75,000 \text{ machine-hours}}$$

$$= \$6 \text{ per machine-hour}$$

Based on the 80,000 machine-hours actually worked during the year, the company applied $480,000 in overhead cost to production ($6 per machine-hour × 80,000 machine hours). The actual manufacturing overhead cost incurred was $460,000, whereas the manufacturing overhead applied to jobs using the company's predetermined overhead rate was $480,000. Therefore, overhead was overapplied by $20,000 ($480,000 – $460,000).

2. To construct the income statement, we will need the sales (which is given), the adjusted cost of goods sold, and the total selling and administrative expenses. The latter can be determined as follows:

Selling and administrative expenses incurred:	
Sales commissions	$ 90,000
Administrative salaries	200,000
General selling expenses	17,000
Advertising costs	180,000
Selling and administrative depreciation	70,000
Selling and administrative insurance	3,000
Total selling and administrative expense	$560,000

The adjusted cost of goods sold is determined as follows:

Unadjusted cost of goods sold	$870,000
Deduct: Overapplied overhead	20,000
Cost of goods sold	$850,000

Finally, the income statement is constructed as follows:

Hogle Corporation Income Statement	
Sales	$1,500,000
Cost of goods sold	850,000
Gross margin	650,000
Selling and administrative expense	560,000
Net operating income	$ 90,000

Absorption costing A costing method that includes all manufacturing costs—direct materials, direct labor, and both variable and fixed manufacturing overhead—in unit product costs. (p. 118)

Allocation base A measure of activity such as direct labor-hours or machine-hours that is used to assign costs to cost objects. (p. 123)

Bill of materials A document that shows the quantity of each type of direct material required to make a product. (p. 120)

Cost driver A factor, such as machine-hours, beds occupied, computer time, or flight-hours, that causes overhead costs. (p. 125)

Cost of goods manufactured The manufacturing costs associated with the goods that were finished during the period. (p. 127)

Finished goods Units of product that have been completed but not yet sold to customers. (p. 127)

Job cost sheet A form that records the materials, labor, and manufacturing overhead costs charged to a job. (p. 120)

Job-order costing A costing system used in situations where many different products, jobs, or services are produced each period. (p. 118)

Materials requisition form A document that specifies the type and quantity of materials to be drawn from the storeroom and that identifies the job that will be charged for the cost of those materials. (p. 120)

Multiple predetermined overhead rates A costing system with multiple overhead cost pools and a different predetermined overhead rate for each cost pool, rather than a single predetermined overhead rate for the entire company. Each production department may be treated as a separate overhead cost pool. (p. 136)

Normal cost system A costing system in which overhead costs are applied to a job by multiplying a predetermined overhead rate by the actual amount of the allocation base incurred by the job. (p. 124)

Overapplied overhead A credit balance in the Manufacturing Overhead account that occurs when the amount of overhead cost applied to Work in Process exceeds the amount of overhead cost actually incurred during a period. (p. 131)

Overhead application The process of charging manufacturing overhead cost to job cost sheets and to the Work in Process account. (p. 123)

Plantwide overhead rate A single predetermined overhead rate that is used throughout a plant. (p. 136)

Predetermined overhead rate A rate used to charge manufacturing overhead cost to jobs that is established in advance for each period. It is computed by dividing the estimated total manufacturing overhead cost for the period by the estimated total amount of the allocation base for the period. (p. 123)

Raw materials Any materials that go into the final product. (p. 127)

Time ticket A document that is used to record the amount of time an employee spends on various activities. (p. 122)

Underapplied overhead A debit balance in the Manufacturing Overhead account that occurs when the amount of overhead cost actually incurred exceeds the amount of overhead cost applied to Work in Process during a period. (p. 131)

Work in process Units of product that are only partially complete and will require further work before they are ready for sale to the customer. (p. 127)

4–1 Why aren't actual manufacturing overhead costs traced to jobs just as direct materials and direct labor costs are traced to jobs?

4–2 What is the purpose of the job cost sheet in a job-order costing system?

4–3 What is a predetermined overhead rate, and how is it computed?

4–4 Explain how a sales order, a production order, a materials requisition form, and a labor time ticket are involved in producing and costing products.

4–5   Explain why some production costs must be assigned to products through an allocation process.

4–6   Why do companies use predetermined overhead rates rather than actual manufacturing overhead costs to apply overhead to jobs?

4–7   What factors should be considered in selecting a base to be used in computing the predetermined overhead rate?

4–8   If a company fully allocates all of its overhead costs to jobs, does this guarantee that a profit will be earned for the period?

4–9   Would you expect the amount of overhead applied for a period to equal the actual overhead costs of the period? Why or why not?

4–10   What is underapplied overhead? Overapplied overhead? What disposition is made of these amounts at the end of the period?

4–11   Provide two reasons why overhead might be underapplied in a given year.

4–12   What adjustment to cost of goods sold is made for underapplied overhead? What adjustment is made for overapplied overhead?

4–13   What is a plantwide overhead rate? Why are multiple overhead rates, rather than a plantwide overhead rate, used in some companies?

4–14   What happens to overhead rates based on direct labor when automated equipment replaces direct labor?

Multiple-choice questions are available with Connect.

Applying Excel   connect   Additional student resources are available with Connect.

LEARNING OBJECTIVES 4–1, 4–2, 4–4

The Excel worksheet form that appears below will reinforce your ability to compute underapplied and overapplied overhead. It is based on the data pertaining to Turbo Crafters Company that was discussed earlier in the chapter. Download the workbook from Connect, where you will also receive instructions about how to use this worksheet.

	A	B	C	D
1	Chapter 4: Applying Excel			
2				
3	**Data**			
4	Allocation base	Machine-hours		
5	Estimated manufacturing overhead cost	$300,000		
6	Estimated total amount of the allocation base	75,000 machine-hours		
7	Actual manufacturing overhead cost	$290,000		
8	Actual total amount of the allocation base	68,000 machine-hours		
9				
10	*Enter a formula into each of the cells marked with a ? below*			
11				
12	**Computation of the predetermined overhead rate**			
13	Estimated manufacturing overhead cost	?		
14	Estimated total amount of the allocation base	? machine-hours		
15	Predetermined overhead rate	? per machine-hour		
16				
17	**Computation of underapplied or overapplied manufacturing overhead**			
18	Actual manufacturing overhead cost	?		
19	Manufacturing overhead cost applied to Work in Process during the year:			
20	Predetermined overhead rate	? per machine-hour		
21	Actual total amount of the allocation base	? machine-hours		
22	Manufacturing overhead applied	?		
23	Underapplied (overapplied) manufacturing overhead	?		
24				

Chapter 4 Form / Filled in Chapter 4 Form / Chapter 4 Formulas

You should proceed to the requirements below only after completing your worksheet.

Required:

1. Check your worksheet by changing the estimated total amount of the allocation base in the Data area to 60,000 machine-hours, keeping all of the other data the same as in the original example. If your worksheet is operating properly, the predetermined overhead rate should now be $5.00 per machine-hour. If you do not get this answer, find the errors in your worksheet and correct them.

   How much is the underapplied (overapplied) manufacturing overhead? Did it change? Why or why not?

2. Determine the underapplied (overapplied) manufacturing overhead for a different company with the following data:

Allocation base	Machine-hours
Estimated manufacturing overhead cost	$100,000
Estimated total amount of the allocation base.............	50,000 machine-hours
Actual manufacturing overhead cost	$90,000
Actual total amount of the allocation base	40,000 machine-hours

3. What happens to the underapplied (overapplied) manufacturing overhead from part (2) if the estimated total amount of the allocation base is changed to 40,000 machine-hours and everything else remains the same? Why is the amount of underapplied (overapplied) manufacturing overhead different from part (2)?

4. Change the estimated total amount of the allocation base back to 50,000 machine-hours so that the data look exactly like they did in part (2). Now change the actual manufacturing overhead cost to $100,000. What is the underapplied (overapplied) manufacturing overhead now? Why is the amount of underapplied (overapplied) manufacturing overhead different from part (2)?

Additional student resources are available with Connect. **connect** **The Foundational 15**

Sweeten Company had no jobs in progress at the beginning of March and no beginning inventories. It started only two jobs during March—Job P and Job Q. Job P was completed and sold by the end of March and Job Q was incomplete at the end of March. The company uses a plantwide predetermined overhead rate based on direct labor-hours. The following additional information is available for the company as a whole and for Jobs P and Q (all data and questions relate to the month of March):

LEARNING OBJECTIVES 4–1, 4–2, 4–3, 4–4, 4–5, 4–6

Estimated total fixed manufacturing overhead.............	$10,000
Estimated variable manufacturing overhead per direct labor-hour......................................	$1.00
Estimated total direct labor hours to be worked...........	2,000
Total actual manufacturing overhead costs incurred	$12,500

	Job P	Job Q
Direct materials	$13,000	$8,000
Direct labor cost	$21,000	$7,500
Actual direct labor hours worked..........	1,400	500

(Answer each question independently by always referring to the original data.)

1. What is the company's predetermined overhead rate?
2. How much manufacturing overhead was applied to Job P and Job Q?
3. What is the direct labor hourly wage rate?
4. If Job P includes 20 units, what is its unit product cost?

5. What is the total amount of manufacturing cost assigned to Job Q as of the end of March (including applied overhead)?
6. What is the amount of underapplied or overapplied overhead?
7. Will your answer to question 6 increase or decrease unadjusted cost of goods sold?
8. If Sweeten Company requisitioned $24,000 from raw materials inventory during March, then how much indirect materials cost would be included in Manufacturing Overhead Incurred?
9. If Sweeten Company's labor time tickets totaled $33,000 for the month of March, then how much indirect labor cost would be included in Manufacturing Overhead Incurred?
10. Calculate the cost of goods sold using the direct method.
11. Calculate the cost of goods manufactured using the indirect method.
12. Calculate the cost of goods sold using the indirect method.
13. How would you revise your answer to question 11 if the company had beginning work in process inventory of $8,000?
14. How would you revise your answer to question 12 if the company had beginning finished goods inventory of $12,000?
15. Assume that Job P includes 20 units that each sell for $3,000 and that the company's selling and administrative expenses in March were $14,000. Prepare an absorption costing income statement for March.

Exercises Additional student resources are available with Connect.

EXERCISE 4–1 Compute the Predetermined Overhead Rate [LO4–1]
Logan Products computes its predetermined overhead rate annually on the basis of direct labor-hours. At the beginning of the year, it estimated that 40,000 direct labor-hours would be required for the period's estimated level of production. The company also estimated $466,000 of fixed manufacturing overhead expenses for the coming period and variable manufacturing overhead of $3.00 per direct labor-hour. Logan's actual manufacturing overhead for the year was $713,400 and its actual total direct labor was 41,000 hours.

Required:
Compute the company's predetermined overhead rate for the year.

EXERCISE 4–2 Apply Overhead [LO4–2]
Westan Corporation uses a predetermined overhead rate of $23.10 per direct labor-hour. This predetermined rate was based on a cost formula that estimated $277,200 of total manufacturing overhead for an estimated activity level of 12,000 direct labor-hours.

The company incurred actual total manufacturing overhead costs of $266,000 and 12,600 total direct labor-hours during the period.

Required:
Determine the amount of manufacturing overhead that would have been applied to all jobs during the period.

EXERCISE 4–3 Computing Job Costs [LO4–3]
Weaver Company's predetermined overhead rate is $18.00 per direct labor-hour and its direct labor wage rate is $12.00 per hour. The following information pertains to Job A-200:

Direct materials	$200
Direct labor.	$120

Required:
1. What is the total manufacturing cost assigned to Job A-200?
2. If Job A-200 consists of 50 units, what is the average cost assigned to each unit included in the job?

EXERCISE 4–4 Determine Underapplied or Overapplied Overhead [LO4–4]

Kirkaid Company recorded the following transactions for the just completed month:

a. $84,000 in raw materials were requisitioned for use in production. Of this amount, $72,000 was for direct materials and the remainder was for indirect materials.

b.   Total labor wages of $108,000 were incurred. Of this amount, $105,000 was for direct labor and the remainder was for indirect labor.

c.   Additional actual manufacturing overhead costs of $197,000 were incurred.

d.   A total of $218,000 in manufacturing overhead was applied to jobs.

Required:

Determine the underapplied or overapplied overhead for the month.

EXERCISE 4–5 Direct Method of Determining Cost of Goods Sold [LO4–5]

Morrow Corporation had only one job in process during May—Job X32Z—and had no finished goods inventory on May 1. Job X32Z was started in April and finished during May. Data concerning that job appear below:

	Job X32Z
Beginning balance......................	$5,000
Charged to the job during May	
Direct materials......................	$8,000
Direct labor	$2,000
Manufacturing overhead applied........	$4,000
Units completed	100
Units in process at the end of May	0
Units sold during May	40

In May, overhead was overapplied by $300. The company adjusts its cost of goods sold every month for the amount of the overhead that was underapplied or overapplied.

Required:

1.   Using the direct method, what is the cost of goods sold for May?

2.   What is the total value of the finished goods inventory at the end of May?

3.   What is the total value of the work in process inventory at the end of May?

EXERCISE 4–6 Indirect Method of Determining Cost of Goods Sold [LO4–6]

Refer to the data for Morrow Corporation in Exercise 4–5.

Required:

Using the indirect method, determine the cost of goods sold for May.

EXERCISE 4–7 Predetermined Overhead Rate; Applying Overhead; Underapplied or Overapplied
Overhead [LO4–1, LO4–2, LO4–4]

Medusa Products uses a job-order costing system. Overhead costs are applied to jobs on the basis of machine-hours. At the beginning of the year, management estimated that the company would work 85,000 machine-hours and incur $170,000 in manufacturing overhead costs for the year.

Required:

1.   Compute the company's predetermined overhead rate.

2.   Assume that during the year the company actually worked only 80,000 machine-hours and incurred $168,000 of manufacturing overhead costs. Compute the amount of underapplied or overapplied overhead for the year.

3.   Explain why the manufacturing overhead was underapplied or overapplied for the year.

EXERCISE 4–8 Computing Predetermined Overhead Rates and Job Costs [LO4–1, LO4–2,
LO4–3, LO4–4]

Kody Corporation uses a job-order costing system with a plantwide overhead rate based on machine-hours. At the beginning of the year, the company made the following estimates:

Machine-hours required to support estimated production	150,000
Fixed manufacturing overhead cost.....................................	$750,000
Variable manufacturing overhead cost per machine-hour...............	$4.00

Required:

1. Compute the predetermined overhead rate.
2. During the year Job 500 was started and completed. The following information was available with respect to this job:
   Compute the total manufacturing cost assigned to Job 500.

Direct materials requisitioned...................	$350
Direct labor cost	$230
Machine-hours used...........................	30

3. During the year the company worked a total of 147,000 machine-hours on all jobs and incurred actual manufacturing overhead costs of $1,325,000. What is the amount of underapplied or overapplied overhead for the year? If this amount were closed out entirely to Cost of Goods Sold, would net operating income increase or decrease?

EXERCISE 4–9 Departmental Overhead Rates [LO4–1, LO4–2, LO4–3]

Diewold Company has two departments, Milling and Assembly. The company uses a job-order costing system and computes a predetermined overhead rate in each department. The Milling Department bases its rate on machine-hours, and the Assembly Department bases its rate on direct labor-hours. At the beginning of the year, the company made the following estimates:

	Department	
	Milling	Assembly
Direct labor-hours	8,000	80,000
Machine-hours...	60,000	3,000
Total fixed manufacturing overhead cost	$390,000	$500,000
Variable manufacturing overhead per machine-hour..............	$2.00	—
Variable manufacturing overhead per direct labor-hour	—	$3.75

Required:

1. Compute the predetermined overhead rate to be used in each department.
2. Assume that the overhead rates you computed in requirement 1 are in effect. The job cost sheet for Job 407, which was started and completed during the year, showed the following:

	Department	
	Milling	Assembly
Direct labor-hours	5	20
Machine-hours........................	90	4
Materials requisitioned................	$800	$370
Direct labor cost	$45	$160

Compute the total manufacturing cost assigned to Job 407.
3. Would you expect substantially different amounts of overhead cost to be charged to some jobs if the company used a plantwide overhead rate based on direct labor-hours instead of using departmental rates? Explain. No computations are necessary.

EXERCISE 4–10 Applying Overhead; Computing Unit Product Cost [LO4–2, LO4–3]

A company assigns overhead cost to completed jobs on the basis of 120% of direct labor cost. The job cost sheet for Job 413 shows that $12,000 in direct materials has been used on the job and that $8,000 in direct labor cost has been incurred. A total of 200 units were produced in Job 413.

Required:

What is the total manufacturing cost assigned to Job 413? What is the unit product cost for Job 413?

EXERCISE 4–11 Underapplied and Overapplied Overhead [LO4–4]

Cretin Enterprises uses a predetermined overhead rate of $21.40 per direct labor-hour. This predetermined rate was based on a cost formula that estimated $171,200 of total manufacturing overhead for an estimated activity level of 8,000 direct labor-hours.

The company incurred actual total manufacturing overhead costs of $172,500 and 8,250 total direct labor-hours during the period.

Required:

1. Determine the amount of underapplied or overapplied manufacturing overhead for the period.
2. Assuming that the entire amount of the underapplied or overapplied overhead is closed out to cost of goods sold, what would be the effect of the underapplied or overapplied overhead on the company's gross margin for the period?

EXERCISE 4–12 Applying Overhead; Cost of Goods Manufactured [LO4–2, LO4–4, LO4–6]

The following cost data relate to the manufacturing activities of Black Company during the just completed year:

Manufacturing overhead costs incurred:	
Property taxes, factory.	$ 3,000
Utilities, factory	5,000
Indirect labor	10,000
Depreciation, factory.	24,000
Insurance, factory	6,000
Total actual manufacturing overhead costs.	$48,000
Other costs incurred:	
Purchases of raw materials.	$32,000
Direct labor cost	$40,000
Inventories:	
Raw materials, beginning	$ 8,000
Raw materials, ending	$ 7,000
Work in process, beginning	$ 6,000
Work in process, ending	$ 7,500

The company uses a predetermined overhead rate to apply overhead cost to jobs. The rate for the year was $5 per machine-hour; a total of 10,000 machine-hours was recorded for the year. All raw materials ultimately become direct materials—none are classified as indirect materials.

Required:

1. Compute the amount of underapplied or overapplied overhead cost for the year.
2. Prepare a schedule of cost of goods manufactured for the year using the indirect method.

EXERCISE 4–13 Varying Predetermined Overhead Rates [LO4–1, LO4–2, LO4–3]

Javadi Company makes a single product that is subject to wide seasonal variations in demand. The company uses a job-order costing system and computes predetermined overhead rates on a quarterly basis using the number of units to be produced as the allocation base. Its estimated costs, by quarter, for the coming year are given below:

	Quarter			
	First	Second	Third	Fourth
Direct materials.	$240,000	$120,000	$ 60,000	$180,000
Direct labor.	96,000	48,000	24,000	72,000
Manufacturing overhead	228,000	204,000	192,000	?
Total manufacturing costs (a).	$564,000	$372,000	$276,000	$?
Number of units to be produced (b).	80,000	40,000	20,000	60,000
Estimated unit product cost (a) ÷ (b).	$7.05	$9.30	$13.80	?

Management finds the variation in quarterly unit product costs to be confusing and difficult to work with. It has been suggested that the problem lies with manufacturing overhead because it is the largest element of total manufacturing cost. Accordingly, you have been asked to find a more appropriate way of assigning manufacturing overhead cost to units of product.

Required:
1. Using the high-low method, estimate the fixed manufacturing overhead cost per quarter and the variable manufacturing overhead cost per unit. Create a cost formula to estimate the total manufacturing overhead cost for the fourth quarter. Compute the total manufacturing cost and unit product cost for the fourth quarter.
2. What is causing the estimated unit product cost to fluctuate from one quarter to the next?
3. How would you recommend stabilizing the company's unit product cost? Support your answer with computations that adapt the cost formula you created in requirement 1.

EXERCISE 4–14 Apply Overhead to a Job [LO4–2]
Winston Company applies overhead cost to jobs on the basis of direct labor cost. Job X, which was started and completed during the current period, shows charges of $18,000 for direct materials, $10,000 for direct labor, and $15,000 for overhead on its job cost sheet. Job Q, which is still in process at year-end, shows charges of $20,000 for direct materials, and $8,000 for direct labor.

Required:
Should any overhead cost be added to Job Q at year-end? If so, how much? Explain.

EXERCISE 4–15 Plantwide and Departmental Overhead Rates; Job Costs [LO4–1, LO4–2, LO4–3]
Smithson Company uses a job-order costing system and has two manufacturing departments—Molding and Fabrication. The company provided the following estimates at the beginning of the year:

	Molding	Fabrication	Total
Machine-hours.	20,000	30,000	50,000
Fixed manufacturing overhead costs.	$800,000	$300,000	$1,100,000
Variable manufacturing overhead per machine-hour	$5.00	$5.00	

During the year, the company had no beginning or ending inventories and it started, completed, and sold only two jobs—Job D-75 and Job C-100. It provided the following information related to those two jobs:

Job D-75:	Molding	Fabrication	Total
Direct materials cost	$375,000	$325,000	$700,000
Direct labor cost	$200,000	$160,000	$360,000
Machine-hours.	15,000	5,000	20,000

Job C-100:	Molding	Fabrication	Total
Direct materials cost	$300,000	$250,000	$550,000
Direct labor cost	$175,000	$225,000	$400,000
Machine-hours.	5,000	25,000	30,000

Smithson had no overapplied or underapplied manufacturing overhead during the year.

Required:

1. Assume Smithson uses a plantwide overhead rate based on machine-hours.
    a. Compute the predetermined plantwide overhead rate.
    b. Compute the total manufacturing costs assigned to Job D-75 and Job C-100.
    c. If Smithson establishes bid prices that are 150% of total manufacturing costs, what bid price would it have established for Job D-75 and Job C-100?
    d. What is Smithson's cost of goods sold for the year?

2. Assume Smithson uses departmental overhead rates based on machine-hours.
    a. Compute the predetermined departmental overhead rates.
    b. Compute the total manufacturing costs assigned to Job D-75 and Job C-100.
    c. If Smithson establishes bid prices that are 150% of total manufacturing costs, what bid price would it have established for Job D-75 and Job C-100?
    d. What is Smithson's cost of goods sold for the year?

3. What managerial insights are revealed by the computations that you performed in this problem? (*Hint:* Do the cost of goods sold amounts that you computed in requirements 1 and 2 differ from one another? Do the bid prices that you computed in requirements 1 and 2 differ from one another? Why?)

Additional student resources are available with Connect.   **Problems**

PROBLEM 4–16 Applying Overhead in a Service Company [LO4–1, LO4–2, LO4–3]

Pearson Architectural Design uses a job-order costing system and applies studio overhead to jobs on the basis of direct staff costs. Because Pearson Architectural Design is a service firm, the names of the accounts it uses are different from the names used in manufacturing companies. The following costs were recorded in January:

Cost of subcontracted work (comparable to direct materials)	$90,000
Direct staff costs (comparable to direct labor)	$200,000
Studio overhead (comparable to manufacturing overhead cost applied)	$320,000
Cost of work completed (comparable to cost of goods manufactured)	$570,000

There were no beginning inventories in January.

At the end of January, only job was still in process. This job (the Krimmer Corporation Headquarters project) had been charged with $13,500 in direct staff costs.

Required:

1. Compute the predetermined overhead rate that was used during January.
2. Complete the following job cost sheet for the partially completed Krimmer Corporation Headquarters project. (*Hint:* Cost of goods manufactured equals beginning work in process inventory plus manufacturing costs incurred less ending work in process inventory.)

Job Cost Sheet	
Krimmer Corporation Headquarters Project	
Costs of subcontracted work	$?
Direct staff costs	?
Studio overhead	?
Total cost to January 31	$?

PROBLEM 4–17 Applying Overhead; Underapplied or Overapplied Overhead; Income Statement [LO4–2, LO4–4, LO4–5]

Durham Company uses a job-order costing system. The following transactions took place last year:

a. Raw materials requisitioned for use in production, $40,000 (80% direct and 20% indirect).

b.   Factory utility costs incurred, $14,600.
c.   Depreciation recorded on plant and equipment, $28,000. Three-fourths of the depreciation relates to factory equipment, and the remainder relates to selling and administrative equipment.
d.   Costs for salaries and wages were incurred as follows:

Direct labor.........................	$40,000
Indirect labor	$18,000
Sales commissions	$10,400
Administrative salaries	$25,000

e.   Insurance costs incurred, $3,000 (80% relates to factory operations, and 20% relates to selling and administrative activities).
f.   Miscellaneous selling and administrative expenses incurred, $18,000.
g.   Manufacturing overhead was applied to production. The company applies overhead on the basis of 150% of direct labor cost.
h.   Goods that cost $130,000 to manufacture according to their job cost sheets were transferred to the finished goods warehouse.
i.   Goods that had cost $120,000 to manufacture according to their job cost sheets were sold for $200,000.

Required:
1.   Determine the underapplied or overapplied overhead for the year.
2.   Prepare an income statement for the year. (**Hint:** No calculations are required to determine the cost of goods sold before any adjustment for underapplied or overapplied overhead.)

PROBLEM 4–18 Applying Overhead in a Service Company [LO4–2, LO4–4, LO4–5]
Heritage Gardens provides complete garden design and landscaping services. The company uses a job-order costing system to track the costs of its landscaping projects. The table below provides data concerning the three landscaping projects that were in progress during May. There was no work in process at the beginning of May.

	Project		
	Williams	Chandler	Nguyen
Designer-hours	200	80	120
Direct materials...........	$4,800	$1,800	$3,600
Direct labor	$2,400	$1,000	$1,500

Actual overhead costs were $16,000 for May. Overhead costs are applied to projects on the basis of designer-hours because most of the overhead is related to the costs of the garden design studio. The predetermined overhead rate is $45 per designer-hour. The Williams and Chandler projects were completed in May; the Nguyen project was not completed by the end of the month. No other jobs were in process during May.

Required:
1.   Compute the amount of overhead cost that would have been applied to each project during May.
2.   Determine the cost of goods manufactured for May.
3.   What is the accumulated cost of the work in process at the end of the month?
4.   Determine the underapplied or overapplied overhead for May.

PROBLEM 4–19 Predetermined Overhead Rate; Applying Overhead; Underapplied or Overapplied Overhead [LO4–2, LO4–4, LO4–5]
Ravsten Company uses a job-order costing system.

The company applies overhead cost to jobs on the basis of machine-hours. For the current year, the company estimated that it would work 36,000 machine-hours and incur $153,000 in manufacturing overhead cost. The following transactions occurred during the year:

a. Raw materials requisitioned for use in production, $190,000 (80% direct and 20% indirect).
b. The following costs were incurred for employee services:

Direct labor.	$160,000
Indirect labor	$18,000
Sales commissions	$10,000
Administrative salaries	$25,000

c. Heat, power, and water costs incurred in the factory, $42,000.
d. Insurance costs, $10,000 (90% relates to factory operations, and 10% relates to selling and administrative activities).
e. Advertising costs incurred, $50,000.
f. Depreciation recorded for the year, $60,000 (85% relates to factory operations, and 15% relates to selling and administrative activities).
g. The company used 40,000 machine-hours during the year.
h. Goods that cost $480,000 to manufacture according to their job cost sheets were transferred to the finished goods warehouse.
i. Sales for the year totaled $700,000. The total cost to manufacture these goods according to their job cost sheets was $475,000.

Required:
1. Determine the underapplied or overapplied overhead for the year.
2. Prepare an income statement for the year. (**Hint:** No calculations are required to determine the cost of goods sold before any adjustment for underapplied or overapplied overhead.)

PROBLEM 4–20 Predetermined Overhead Rate; Disposition of Underapplied or Overapplied Overhead [LO4–1, LO4–4, LO4–5]
Savallas Company is highly automated and uses computers to control manufacturing operations. The company uses a job-order costing system and applies manufacturing overhead cost to products on the basis of computer-hours. The following estimates were used in preparing the predetermined overhead rate at the beginning of the year:

Computer-hours	85,000
Fixed manufacturing overhead cost.	$1,275,000
Variable manufacturing overhead per computer-hour.	$3.00

During the year, a severe economic recession resulted in cutting back production and a buildup of inventory in the company's warehouse. The company's cost records revealed the following actual cost and operating data for the year:

Computer-hours	60,000
Manufacturing overhead cost	$1,350,000
Inventories at year-end:	
Raw materials.	$400,000
Work in process	$160,000
Finished goods	$1,040,000
Cost of goods sold	$2,800,000

Required:
1. Compute the company's predetermined overhead rate for the year.
2. Compute the underapplied or overapplied overhead for the year.
3. Determine the cost of goods sold for the year after any adjustment for underapplied or overapplied overhead.

PROBLEM 4–21 Multiple Departments; Applying Overhead [LO4–1, LO4–2, LO4–3, LO4–4]

WoodGrain Technology makes home office furniture from fine hardwoods. The company uses a job-order costing system and predetermined overhead rates to apply manufacturing overhead cost to jobs. The predetermined overhead rate in the Preparation Department is based on machine-hours, and the rate in the Fabrication Department is based on direct labor-hours. At the beginning of the year, the company's management made the following estimates for the year:

	Department	
	Preparation	Fabrication
Machine-hours...	80,000	21,000
Direct labor-hours.......................................	35,000	50,000
Direct materials cost....................................	$190,000	$400,000
Direct labor cost..	$280,000	$530,000
Fixed manufacturing overhead cost	$256,000	$520,000
Variable manufacturing overhead per machine-hour	$2.00	—
Variable manufacturing overhead per direct labor-hour	—	$4.00

Job 127 was started on April 1 and completed on May 12. The company's cost records show the following information concerning the job:

	Department	
	Preparation	Fabrication
Machine-hours......................	350	70
Direct labor-hours..................	80	130
Direct materials cost...............	$940	$1,200
Direct labor cost	$710	$980

Required:
1. Compute the predetermined overhead rate used during the year in the Preparation Department. Compute the rate used in the Fabrication Department.
2. Compute the total overhead cost applied to Job 127.
3. What would be the total cost recorded for Job 127? If the job contained 25 units, what would be the unit product cost?
4. At the end of the year, the records of WoodGrain Technology revealed the following *actual* cost and operating data for all jobs worked on during the year:

	Department	
	Preparation	Fabrication
Machine-hours......................	73,000	24,000
Direct labor-hours	30,000	54,000
Direct materials cost...............	$165,000	$420,000
Manufacturing overhead cost	$390,000	$740,000

What was the amount of underapplied or overapplied overhead in each department at the end of the year?

PROBLEM 4–22 Multiple Departments; Overhead Rates; Underapplied or Overapplied Overhead
[LO4–1, LO4–2, LO4–3, LO4–4]

Winkle, Kotter, and Zale is a small law firm that contains 10 partners and 10 support persons. The firm employs a job-order costing system to accumulate costs chargeable to each client, and it is organized into two departments—the Research and Documents Department and the Litigation

Department. The firm uses predetermined overhead rates to charge the costs of these departments to its clients. At the beginning of the current year, the firm's management made the following estimates for the year:

	Department	
	Research and Documents	Litigation
Research-hours	20,000	—
Direct attorney-hours	9,000	16,000
Materials and supplies	$18,000	$5,000
Direct attorney cost.................	$430,000	$800,000
Departmental overhead cost.........	$700,000	$320,000

The predetermined overhead rate in the Research and Documents Department is based on research-hours, and the rate in the Litigation Department is based on direct attorney cost.

The costs charged to each client are made up of three elements: materials and supplies used, direct attorney costs incurred, and an applied amount of overhead from each department in which work is performed on the case.

Case 618-3 was initiated on February 10 and completed on June 30. During this period, the following costs and time were recorded on the case:

	Department	
	Research and Documents	Litigation
Research-hours	18	—
Direct attorney-hours	9	42
Materials and supplies	$50	$30
Direct attorney cost.................	$410	$2,100

Required:

1. Compute the predetermined overhead rates used during the year in the Research and Documents Department and the Litigation Department.
2. Using the rates you computed in requirement 1, compute the total overhead cost applied to Case 618–3.
3. What would be the total cost charged to Case 618–3? Show computations by department and in total for the case.
4. At the end of the year, the firm's records revealed the following *actual* cost and operating data for all cases handled during the year:

	Department	
	Research and Documents	Litigation
Research-hours	23,000	—
Direct attorney-hours	8,000	15,000
Materials and supplies	$19,000	$6,000
Direct attorney cost.................	$400,000	$775,000
Departmental overhead cost.........	$770,000	$300,000

Determine the amount of underapplied or overapplied overhead cost in each department for the year.

PROBLEM 4–23 Direct Method of Determining Cost of Goods Sold [LO4–5]

Techuxia Corporation worked on four jobs during October: Job A256, Job A257, Job A258, and Job A260. At the end of October, the job cost sheets for these jobs contained the following data:

	Job A256	Job A257	Job A258	Job A260
Beginning balance	$1,200	$500	$0	$0
Charged to the jobs during October:				
Direct materials	$2,600	$3,500	$1,400	$3,500
Direct labor........................	$800	$1,000	$600	$400
Manufacturing overhead applied	$1,200	$1,500	$900	$600
Units completed	100	0	200	0
Units in process at the end of October	0	400	0	500
Units sold during October	80	0	40	0

Jobs A256 and A258 were completed during October. The other two jobs had not yet been completed at the end of October. There was no finished goods inventory on October 1.

In October, overhead was overapplied by $800. The company adjusts its cost of goods sold every month for the amount of the underapplied or overapplied overhead.

Required:

1. Using the direct method, what is the cost of goods sold for October?
2. What is the total value of the finished goods inventory at the end of October?
3. What is the total value of the work in process inventory at the end of October?

PROBLEM 4–24 Indirect Method of Determining Cost of Goods Sold [LO4–6]

Refer to the data for Techuxia Corporation in Problem 4–23.

Required:

Using the indirect method, what is the cost of goods sold for October?

Cases Mc Graw Hill **connect** Additional student resources are available with Connect.

CASE 4–25 Plantwide versus Departmental Overhead Rates; Underapplied or Overapplied Overhead [LO4–1, LO4–2, LO4–3, LO4–4]

"Don't tell me we've lost another bid!" exclaimed Sandy Kovallas, president of Lenko Products, Inc. "I'm afraid so," replied Doug Martin, the operations vice president. "One of our competitors underbid us by about $10,000 on the Hastings job." "I just can't figure it out," said Kovallas. "It seems we're either too high to get the job or too low to make any money on half the jobs we bid anymore. What's happened?"

Lenko Products manufactures specialized goods to customers' specifications and operates a job-order costing system. Manufacturing overhead cost is applied to jobs on the basis of direct labor cost. The following estimates were made at the beginning of the year:

	Department			
	Cutting	Machining	Assembly	Total Plant
Direct labor...................	$300,000	$200,000	$400,000	$ 900,000
Manufacturing overhead	$540,000	$800,000	$100,000	$1,440,000

Jobs require varying amounts of work in the three departments. The Hastings job, for example, would have required manufacturing costs in the three departments as follows:

	Department			
	Cutting	Machining	Assembly	Total Plant
Direct materials..............	$12,000	$900	$5,600	$18,500
Direct labor..................	$6,500	$1,700	$13,000	$21,200
Manufacturing overhead	?	?	?	?

The company uses a plantwide overhead rate to apply manufacturing overhead cost to jobs.

Required:

1. Assuming the use of a plantwide overhead rate:
    a.   Compute the rate for the current year.
    b.   Determine the amount of manufacturing overhead cost that would have been applied to the Hastings job.
2. Suppose that instead of using a plantwide overhead rate, the company had used a separate predetermined overhead rate in each department. Under these conditions:
    a.   Compute the rate for each department for the current year.
    b.   Determine the amount of manufacturing overhead cost that would have been applied to the Hastings job.
3. Explain the difference between the manufacturing overhead that would have been applied to the Hastings job using the plantwide rate in requirement 1(b) and using the departmental rates in requirement 2(b).
4. Assume that it is customary in the industry to bid jobs at 150% of total manufacturing cost (direct materials, direct labor, and applied overhead). What was the company's bid price on the Hastings job? What would the bid price have been if departmental overhead rates had been used to apply overhead cost?
5. At the end of the year, the company assembled the following *actual* cost data relating to all jobs worked on during the year:

	Department			
	Cutting	Machining	Assembly	Total Plant
Direct materials	$760,000	$ 90,000	$ 410,000	$1,260,000
Direct labor......................	$320,000	$ 210,000	$340,000	$870,000
Manufacturing overhead	$560,000	$830,000	$92,000	$1,482,000

Compute the underapplied or overapplied overhead for the year (*a*) assuming that a plantwide overhead rate is used, and (*b*) assuming that departmental overhead rates are used.

CASE 4–26 Ethics and the Manager [LO4–1, LO4–2, LO4–4]

Cristin Madsen has recently been transferred to the Appliances Division of Solequin Corporation. Shortly after taking over her new position as divisional controller, she was asked to develop the division's predetermined overhead rate for the upcoming year. The accuracy of the rate is important because it is used throughout the year and any overapplied or underapplied overhead is closed out to Cost of Goods Sold at the end of the year. Solequin Corporation uses direct labor-hours in all of its divisions as the allocation base for manufacturing overhead.

To compute the predetermined overhead rate, Cristin divided her estimate of the total manufacturing overhead for the coming year by the production manager's estimate of the total direct labor-hours for the coming year. She took her computations to the division's general manager for approval but was quite surprised when he suggested a modification in the base. Her conversation with the general manager of the Appliances Division, Lance Jusic, went like this:

Madsen: Here are my calculations for next year's predetermined overhead rate. If you approve, we can enter the rate into the computer on January 1 and be up and running in the job-order costing system right away this year.

Jusic: Thanks for coming up with the calculations so quickly, and they look just fine. There is, however, one slight modification I would like to see. Your estimate of the total direct labor-hours for the year is 110,000 hours. How about cutting that to about 105,000 hours?

Madsen: I don't know if I can do that. The production manager says she will need about 110,000 direct labor-hours to meet the sales projections for next year. Besides, there are going to be over 108,000 direct labor-hours during the current year and sales are projected to be higher next year.

Jusic: Cristin, I know all of that. I would still like to reduce the direct labor-hours in the base to something like 105,000 hours. You probably don't know that I had an agreement with your predecessor as divisional controller to shave 5% or so off the estimated direct labor-hours every year. That way, we kept a reserve that usually resulted in a big boost to net operating income at the end of the fiscal year in December. We called it our Christmas bonus.

Corporate headquarters always seemed as pleased as punch that we could pull off such a miracle at the end of the year. This system has worked well for many years, and I don't want to change it now.

Required:
1. Explain how shaving 5% off the estimated direct labor-hours in the base for the predetermined overhead rate usually results in a big boost in net operating income at the end of the fiscal year.
2. Should Cristin Madsen go along with the general manager's request to reduce the direct labor-hours in the predetermined overhead rate computation to 105,000 direct labor-hours?

CASE 4–27 Critical Thinking; Interpretation of Manufacturing Overhead Rates [LO4–1, LO4–2]
Sharpton Fabricators Corporation manufactures a variety of parts for the automotive industry. The company uses a job-order costing system with a plantwide predetermined overhead rate based on direct labor-hours. On December 10, 2015, the company's controller made a preliminary estimate of the predetermined overhead rate for 2016. The new rate was based on the estimated total manufacturing overhead cost of $2,475,000 and the estimated 52,000 total direct labor-hours for 2016:

$$\text{Predetermined overhead rate} = \frac{\$2,475,000}{52,000 \text{ hours}}$$

$$= \$47.60 \text{ per direct labor-hour}$$

This new predetermined overhead rate was communicated to top managers in a meeting on December 11. The rate did not cause any comment because it was within a few pennies of the overhead rate that had been used during 2015. One of the subjects discussed at the meeting was a proposal by the production manager to purchase an automated milling machine built by Central Robotics. The president of Sharpton Fabricators, Kevin Reynolds, agreed to meet with the regional sales representative from Central Robotics to discuss the proposal.

On the day following the meeting, Mr. Reynolds met with Jay Warner, Central Robotics' sales representative. The following discussion took place:

Reynolds: Larry Winter, our production manager, asked me to meet with you because he is interested in installing an automated milling machine. Frankly, I am skeptical. You're going to have to show me this isn't just another expensive toy for Larry's people to play with.

Warner: That shouldn't be too difficult, Mr. Reynolds. The automated milling machine has three major advantages. First, it is much faster than the manual methods you are using. It can process about twice as many parts per hour as your present milling machines. Second, it is much more flexible. There are some up-front programming costs, but once those have been incurred, almost no setup is required on the machines for standard operations. You just punch in the code of the standard operation, load the machine's hopper with raw material, and the machine does the rest.

Reynolds: Yeah, but what about cost? Having twice the capacity in the milling machine area won't do us much good. That center is idle much of the time anyway.

Warner: I was getting there. The third advantage of the automated milling machine is lower cost. Larry Winters and I looked over your present operations, and we estimated that the automated equipment would eliminate the need for about 6,000 direct labor-hours a year. What is your direct labor cost per hour?

Reynolds: The wage rate in the milling area averages about $21 per hour. Fringe benefits raise that figure to about $30 per hour.

Warner: Don't forget your overhead.

Reynolds: Next year the overhead rate will be about $48 per hour.

Warner: So including fringe benefits and overhead, the cost per direct labor-hour is about $78.

Reynolds: That's right.

Warner: Since you save 6,000 direct labor-hours per year, the cost savings would amount to about $468,000 a year.

Reynolds: That's pretty impressive, but you aren't giving away this equipment are you?

Warner: Several options are available, including leasing and outright purchase. Just for comparison purposes, our 60-month lease plan would require payments of only $300,000 per year.

Reynolds: Sold! When can you install the equipment?

Shortly after this meeting, Mr. Reynolds informed the company's controller of the decision to lease the new equipment, which would be installed over the Christmas vacation period. The controller realized that this decision would require a recomputation of the predetermined overhead rate for the year 2016 since the decision would affect both the manufacturing overhead and the direct labor-hours for the year. After talking with both the production manager and the sales representative from Central Robotics, the controller discovered that in addition to the annual lease cost of $300,000, the new machine would also require a skilled technician/programmer who would have to be hired at a cost of $45,000 per year to maintain and program the equipment. Both of these costs would be included in factory overhead. There would be no other changes in total manufacturing overhead cost, which is almost entirely fixed. The controller assumed that the new machine would result in a reduction of 6,000 direct labor-hours for the year from the levels that had initially been planned.

When the revised predetermined overhead rate for the year 2016 was circulated among the company's top managers, there was considerable dismay.

Required:

1. Recompute the predetermined overhead rate assuming that the new machine will be installed. Explain why the new predetermined overhead rate is higher (or lower) than the rate that was originally estimated for the year 2016.
2. What effect (if any) would this new rate have on the cost of jobs that do not use the new automated milling machine?
3. Why would managers be concerned about the new overhead rate?
4. After seeing the new predetermined overhead rate, the production manager admitted that he probably wouldn't be able to eliminate all of the 6,000 direct labor-hours. He had been hoping to accomplish the reduction by not replacing workers who retire or quit, but that would not be possible. As a result, the real labor savings would be only about 2,000 hours—one worker. Given this additional information, evaluate the original decision to acquire the automated milling machine from Central Robotics.

Appendix 4A: Activity-Based Absorption Costing

LEARNING OBJECTIVE 4–7
Use activity-based absorption costing to compute unit product costs.

Chapter 4 described how manufacturing companies use traditional absorption costing systems to calculate unit product costs for the purpose of valuing inventories and determining cost of goods sold for external financial reports. In this appendix, we contrast traditional absorption costing with an alternative approach called *activity-based absorption costing*. **Activity-based absorption costing** assigns all manufacturing overhead costs to products based on the *activities* performed to make those products. An **activity** is an event that causes the consumption of manufacturing overhead resources. Rather than relying on plantwide or departmental cost pools, the activity-based approach accumulates each activity's overhead costs in *activity cost pools*. An **activity cost pool** is a "bucket" in which costs are accumulated that relate to a single activity. Each activity cost pool has one *activity measure*. An **activity measure** is an allocation base that is used as the denominator for an activity cost pool. The costs accumulated in the numerator of an activity cost pool divided by the quantity of the activity measure in its denominator equals what is called an *activity rate*. An activity rate is used to assign costs from an activity cost pool to products.

Activity-based absorption costing differs from traditional absorption costing in two ways. First, the activity-based approach uses more cost pools than a traditional approach. Second, the activity-based approach includes some activities and activity measures that *do not* relate to the volume of units produced, whereas the traditional approach relies exclusively on allocation bases that are driven by the volume of production. For example, the activity-based approach may include *batch-level activities*. A **batch-level activity** is performed each time a batch is handled or processed, regardless of how many units are in the batch. Batch-level activities include tasks such as placing purchase orders, setting up equipment, and transporting batches of component parts. Costs at the batch level depend on the number of batches processed rather than the number of units produced. The activity-based approach may also include *product-level activities*. A **product-level activity** relates to specific products and typically must be carried out regardless of how many batches are run or units of product are produced and sold. Product-level activities include tasks such as designing a product and making engineering design changes to a product. Costs at the product-level depend on the number of products supported rather than the number of batches run or the number of units of product produced and sold.

To illustrate the differences between traditional and activity-based absorption costing, we'll use an example focused on Maxtar Industries, a manufacturer of high-quality smoker/barbecue units. The company has two product lines—Premium and Standard. The company has traditionally applied manufacturing overhead costs to these products using a plantwide predetermined overhead rate based on direct labor-hours. Exhibit 4A–1 details how the unit product costs of the two product lines are computed using the company's traditional costing system. The unit product cost of the Premium product line is $71.60 and the unit product cost of the Standard product line is $53.70 according to this traditional costing system.

Maxtar Industries has recently experimented with an activity-based absorption costing system that has three activity cost pools: (1) supporting direct labor; (2) setting up machines; and (3) parts administration. The top of Exhibit 4A–2 displays basic data concerning these activity cost pools. Note that the total estimated overhead cost in these three costs pools, $1,520,000, agrees with the total estimated overhead cost in the company's traditional costing system. The company's activity-based approach simply provides an alternative way to allocate the company's manufacturing overhead across the two products.

EXHIBIT 4A–1
Maxtar Industries' Traditional Costing System

Basic Data

Total estimated manufacturing overhead cost.....		$1,520,000
Total estimated direct labor-hours		400,000 DLHs

	Premium	Standard
Direct materials per unit.......................	$40.00	$30.00
Direct labor per unit	$24.00	$18.00
Direct labor-hours per unit.....................	2.0 DLHs	1.5 DLHs
Units produced	50,000 units	200,000 units

Computation of the Predetermined Overhead Rate

$$\text{Predetermined overhead rate} = \frac{\text{Total estimated manufacturing overhead}}{\text{Total estimated amount of the allocation base}}$$

$$= \frac{\$1,520,000}{400,000 \text{ DLHs}}$$

$$= \$3.80 \text{ per DLH}$$

Traditional Unit Product Costs

	Premium	Standard
Direct materials	$40.00	$30.00
Direct labor...................................	24.00	18.00
Manufacturing overhead (2.0 DLHs × $3.80 per DLH; 1.5 DLHs × $3.80 per DLH)	7.60	5.70
Unit product cost..............................	$71.60	$53.70

EXHIBIT 4A–2
Maxtar Industries' Activity-Based Absorption Costing System

Basic Data

Activity Cost Pools and Activity Measures	Estimated Overhead Cost	Expected Activity		
		Premium	Standard	Total
Supporting direct labor (DLHs)................	$ 800,000	100,000	300,000	400,000
Setting up machines (setups).................	480,000	600	200	800
Parts administration (part types)...............	240,000	140	60	200
Total manufacturing overhead cost.............	$1,520,000			

Computation of Activity Rates

Activity Cost Pools	(a) Estimated Overhead Cost	(b) Total Expected Activity	(a) ÷ (b) Activity Rate
Supporting direct labor	$800,000	400,000 DLHs	$2 per DLH
Setting up machines.........................	$480,000	800 setups	$600 per setup
Parts administration	$240,000	200 part types	$1,200 per part type

Assigning Overhead Costs to Products

Overhead Cost for the Premium Product

Activity Cost Pools	(a) Activity Rate	(b) Activity	(a) × (b) ABC Cost
Supporting direct labor	$2 per DLH	100,000 DLHs	$200,000
Setting up machines.........................	$600 per setup	600 setups	360,000
Parts administration	$1,200 per part type	140 part types	168,000
Total..			$728,000

Overhead Cost for the Standard Product

Activity Cost Pools	(a) Activity Rate	(b) Activity	(a) × (b) ABC Cost
Supporting direct labor	$2 per DLH	300,000 DLHs	$600,000
Setting up machines.........................	$600 per setup	200 setups	120,000
Parts administration	$1,200 per part type	60 part types	72,000
Total..			$792,000

Activity-Based Absorption Costing Product Costs

	Premium	Standard
Direct materials...	$40.00	$30.00
Direct labor	24.00	18.00
Manufacturing overhead ($728,000 ÷ 50,000 units; $792,000 ÷ 200,000 units)	14.56	3.96
Unit product cost	$78.56	$51.96

The activity rates for the three activity cost pools are computed in the second table in Exhibit 4A–2. For example, the total cost in the "setting up machines" activity cost pool, $480,000, is divided by the total activity associated with that cost pool, 800 setups, to determine the activity rate of $600 per setup.

The activity rates are used to allocate overhead costs to the two products in the third table in Exhibit 4A–2. For example, the activity rate for the "setting up machines" activity cost pool, $600 per setup, is multiplied by the Premium product line's 600 setups to determine the $360,000 machine setup cost allocated to the Premium product line.

The table at the bottom of Exhibit 4A–2 displays the overhead costs per unit and the activity-based unit product costs. The overhead cost per unit is determined by dividing the total overhead cost by the number of units produced. For example, the Premium product line's total overhead cost of $728,000 is divided by 50,000 units to determine the $14.56 overhead cost per unit. Note that the unit product costs differ from those computed using the company's traditional costing system in Exhibit 4A–1. Because the activity-based approach contains both a batch-level (setting up machines) and a product-level (parts administration) activity cost pool, the unit product costs under the activity-based approach follow the usual pattern in which overhead costs are shifted from the high-volume to the low-volume product. The unit product cost of the Standard product line, the high-volume product, has gone down from $53.70 under the traditional costing system to $51.96 under activity-based costing. In contrast, the unit product cost of the Premium product line, the low-volume product, has increased from $71.60 under the traditional costing system to $78.56 under activity-based costing. Instead of using direct labor-hours (which moves in tandem with the volume of the production) to assign all manufacturing overhead costs to products, the activity-based approach uses a batch-level activity measure and a product-level activity measure to assign the batch-level and product-level activity cost pools to the two products.

Glossary (Appendix 4A)

Activity An event that causes the consumption of overhead resources in an organization. (p. 155)

Activity-based absorption costing A costing method that assigns all manufacturing overhead costs to products based on the *activities* performed to make those products. (p. 155)

Activity cost pool A "bucket" in which costs are accumulated that relate to a single activity measure in an activity-based costing system. (p. 155)

Activity measure An allocation base in an activity-based costing system; ideally, a measure of the amount of activity that drives the costs in an activity cost pool. (p. 155)

Batch-level activity An activity that is performed each time a batch is handled or processed, regardless of how many units are in the batch. The amount of resources consumed depends on the number of batches run rather than on the number of units in the batch. (p. 155)

Product-level activity An activity that relates to specific products and typically must be carried out regardless of how many batches are run or units of product are produced and sold. (p. 156)

Appendix 4A Exercises, Problems, and Case   connect

Additional student resources are available with Connect.

EXERCISE 4A–1 Activity-Based Absorption Costing [LO4–7]

Fogerty Company makes two products, titanium Hubs and Sprockets. Data regarding the two products follow:

	Direct Labor-Hours per Unit	Annual Production
Hubs.................	0.80	10,000 units
Sprockets.............	0.40	40,000 units

Additional information about the company follows:

a. Hubs require $32 in direct materials per unit, and Sprockets require $18.

b. The direct labor wage rate is $15 per hour.

c. Hubs are more complex to manufacture than Sprockets and they require special processing.

d. The company's activity-based absorption costing system has the following activity cost pools:

Activity Cost Pool (and Activity Measure)	Estimated Overhead Cost	Expected Activity		
		Hubs	Sprockets	Total
Machine setups (number of setups)....	$72,000	100	300	400
Special processing (machine-hours) ...	$200,000	5,000	0	5,000
General factory (direct labor-hours)....	$ 816,000	8,000	16,000	24,000

Required:

1. Compute the activity rate for each activity cost pool.
2. Compute the unit product cost for Hubs and Sprockets using activity-based absorption costing.

EXERCISE 4A–2 Activity-Based Absorption Costing as an Alternative to Traditional Product Costing [LO4–7]

Harrison Company makes two products and uses a traditional costing system in which a single plantwide predetermined overhead rate is computed based on direct labor-hours. Data for the two products for the upcoming year follow:

	Rascon	Parcel
Direct materials cost per unit	$13.00	$22.00
Direct labor cost per unit	$6.00	$3.00
Direct labor-hours per unit.............	0.40	0.20
Number of units produced.............	20,000	80,000

These products are customized to some degree for specific customers.

Required:

1. The company's manufacturing overhead costs for the year are expected to be $576,000. Using the company's traditional costing system, compute the unit product costs for the two products.
2. Management is considering an activity-based absorption costing system in which half of the overhead would continue to be allocated on the basis of direct labor-hours and half would be allocated on the basis of engineering design time. This time is expected to be distributed as follows during the upcoming year:

	Rascon	Parcel	Total
Engineering design time (in hours)	3,000	3,000	6,000

Compute the unit product costs for the two products using the proposed activity-based absorption costing system.

3. Explain why the product costs differ between the two systems.

EXERCISE 4A–3 Activity-Based Absorption Costing as an Alternative to Traditional Product Costing [LO4–7]

Stillicum Corporation makes ultra light-weight backpacking tents. Data concerning the company's two product lines appear below:

	Deluxe	Standard
Direct materials per unit............	$72.00	$53.00
Direct labor per unit	$ 12.00	$9.60
Direct labor-hours per unit..........	1.0 DLHs	0.8 DLHs
Estimated annual production........	10,000 units	50,000 units

The company has a traditional costing system in which manufacturing overhead is applied to units based on direct labor-hours. Data concerning manufacturing overhead and direct labor-hours for the upcoming year appear below:

Estimated total manufacturing overhead.........	$325,000
Estimated total direct labor-hours..............	50,000 DLHs

Required:
1. Determine the unit product costs of the Deluxe and Standard products under the company's traditional costing system.
2. The company is considering replacing its traditional costing system with an activity-based absorption costing system that would have the following three activity cost pools:

Activity Cost Pools and Activity Measures	Estimated Overhead Cost	Expected Activity Deluxe	Standard	Total
Supporting direct labor (direct labor-hours)......	$200,000	10,000	40,000	50,000
Batch setups (setups).........................	75,000	200	100	300
Safety testing (tests).........................	50,000	30	70	100
Total manufacturing overhead cost.............	$325,000			

Determine the unit product costs of the Deluxe and Standard products under the activity-based absorption costing system.

PROBLEM 4A–4 Activity-Based Absorption Costing as an Alternative to Traditional Product Costing [LO4–7]
Ellix Company manufactures two models of ultra-high fidelity speakers, the X200 model and the X99 model. Data regarding the two products follow:

Product	Direct Labor-Hours	Annual Production	Total Direct Labor-Hours
X200....	1.8 DLHs per unit	5,000 units	9,000 DLHs
X99.....	0.9 DLHs per unit	30,000 units	27,000 DLHs
			36,000 DLHs

Additional information about the company follows:
a. Model X200 requires $72 in direct materials per unit, and model X99 requires $50.
b. The direct labor rate is $10 per hour.
c. The company has always used direct labor-hours as the base for applying manufacturing overhead cost to products.
d. Model X200 is more complex to manufacture than model X99 and requires the use of special equipment.
e. Because of the special work required in part (d) above, the company is considering the use of activity-based absorption costing to apply manufacturing overhead cost to products. Three activity cost pools have been identified as follows:

Activity Cost Pool	Activity Measure	Estimated Total Cost	Estimated Total Activity X200	X99	Total
Machine setups	Number of setups	$ 360,000	50	100	150
Special processing	Machine-hours	180,000	12,000	0	12,000
General factory	Direct labor-hours	1,260,000	9,000	27,000	36,000
		$1,800,000			

Required:

1. Assume that the company continues to use direct labor-hours as the base for applying overhead cost to products.
   a. Compute the predetermined overhead rate.
   b. Compute the unit product cost of each model.
2. Assume that the company decides to use activity-based absorption costing to apply overhead cost to products.
   a. Compute the activity rate for each activity cost pool and determine the amount of overhead cost that would be applied to each model using the activity-based approach.
   b. Compute the unit product cost of each model.
3. Explain why overhead cost shifted from the high-volume model to the low-volume model under the activity-based approach.

PROBLEM 4A–5 Activity-Based Absorption Costing as an Alternative to Traditional Product Costing [LO4–7]

Siegel Company manufactures a product that is available in both a deluxe model and a regular model. The company has manufactured the regular model for years. The deluxe model was introduced several years ago to tap a new segment of the market. Since introduction of the deluxe model, the company's profits have steadily declined and management has become increasingly concerned about the accuracy of its costing system. Sales of the deluxe model have been increasing rapidly.

Manufacturing overhead is assigned to products on the basis of direct labor-hours. For the current year, the company has estimated that it will incur $900,000 in manufacturing overhead cost and produce 5,000 units of the deluxe model and 40,000 units of the regular model. The deluxe model requires two hours of direct labor time per unit, and the regular model requires one hour. Material and labor costs per unit are as follows:

	Model	
	Deluxe	Regular
Direct materials.....................	$40	$25
Direct labor	$14	$7

Required:

1. Using direct labor-hours as the base for assigning overhead cost to products, compute the predetermined overhead rate. Using this rate and other data from the problem, determine the unit product cost of each model.
2. Management is considering using activity-based absorption costing to apply manufacturing overhead cost to products. The activity-based system would have the following four activity cost pools:

Activity Cost Pool	Activity Measure	Estimated Overhead Cost
Purchasing.........	Purchase orders issued	$204,000
Processing.........	Machine-hours	182,000
Scrap/rework.......	Scrap/rework orders issued	379,000
Shipping...........	Number of shipments	135,000
		$900,000

	Expected Activity		
Activity Measure	Deluxe	Regular	Total
Purchase orders issued.............	200	400	600
Machine-hours	20,000	15,000	35,000
Scrap/rework orders issued.........	1,000	1,000	2,000
Number of shipments	250	650	900

Determine the predetermined overhead rate for each of the four activity cost pools.

3. Using the predetermined overhead rates you computed in requirement 2, do the following:
   a. Compute the total amount of manufacturing overhead cost that would be applied to each model using the activity-based absorption costing system. After these totals have been computed, determine the amount of manufacturing overhead cost per unit of each model.
   b. Compute the unit product cost of each model (direct materials, direct labor, and manufacturing overhead).

4. From the data you have developed in parts requirements 1 through 3, identify factors that may account for the company's declining profits.

CASE 4A–6 Activity-Based Absorption Costing and Pricing [LO4–7]

Java Source, Inc. (JSI), is a processor and distributor of a variety of blends of coffee. The company buys coffee beans from around the world and roasts, blends, and packages them for resale. JSI offers a large variety of different coffees that it sells to gourmet shops in one-pound bags. The major cost of the coffee is raw materials. However, the company's predominantly automated roasting, blending, and packing processes require a substantial amount of manufacturing overhead. The company uses relatively little direct labor.

Some of JSI's coffees are very popular and sell in large volumes, while a few of the newer blends sell in very low volumes. JSI prices its coffees at manufacturing cost plus a markup of 25%, with some adjustments made to keep the company's prices competitive.

For the coming year, JSI's budget includes estimated manufacturing overhead cost of $2,200,000. JSI assigns manufacturing overhead to products on the basis of direct labor-hours. The expected direct labor cost totals $600,000, which represents 50,000 hours of direct labor time. Based on the sales budget and expected raw materials costs, the company will purchase and use $5,000,000 of raw materials (mostly coffee beans) during the year.

The expected costs for direct materials and direct labor for one-pound bags of two of the company's coffee products appear below.

	Kenya Dark	Viet Select
Direct materials.....................	$4.50	$2.90
Direct labor (0.02 hours per bag).........	$0.24	$0.24

JSI's controller believes that the company's traditional costing system may be providing misleading cost information. To determine whether or not this is correct, the controller has prepared an analysis of the year's expected manufacturing overhead costs, as shown in the following table:

Activity Cost Pool	Activity Measure	Expected Activity for the Year	Expected Cost for the Year
Purchasing............	Purchase orders	2,000 orders	$ 560,000
Material handling......	Number of setups	1,000 setups	193,000
Quality control.........	Number of batches	500 batches	90,000
Roasting..............	Roasting hours	95,000 roasting hours	1,045,000
Blending..............	Blending hours	32,000 blending hours	192,000
Packaging	Packaging hours	24,000 packaging hours	120,000
Total manufacturing overhead cost.......			$2,200,000

Data regarding the expected production of Kenya Dark and Viet Select coffee are presented below.

	Kenya Dark	Viet Select
Expected sales	80,000 pounds	4,000 pounds
Batch size	5,000 pounds	500 pounds
Setups	2 per batch	2 per batch
Purchase order size	20,000 pounds	500 pounds
Roasting time per 100 pounds	1.5 roasting hours	1.5 roasting hours
Blending time per 100 pounds	0.5 blending hour	0.5 blending hour
Packaging time per 100 pounds	0.3 packaging hour	0.3 packaging hour

Required:

1. Using direct labor-hours as the base for assigning manufacturing overhead cost to products, do the following:

    a. Determine the predetermined overhead rate that will be used during the year.

    b. Determine the unit product cost of one pound of the Kenya Dark coffee and one pound of the Viet Select coffee.

2. Using activity-based absorption costing as the basis for assigning manufacturing overhead cost to products, do the following:

    a. Determine the total amount of manufacturing overhead cost assigned to the Kenya Dark coffee and to the Viet Select coffee for the year.

    b. Using the data developed in requirement 2a, compute the amount of manufacturing overhead cost per pound of the Kenya Dark coffee and the Viet Select coffee. Round all computations to the nearest whole cent.

    c. Determine the unit product cost of one pound of the Kenya Dark coffee and one pound of the Viet Select coffee.

3. Write a brief memo to the president of JSI explaining what you have found in requirements 1 and 2 above and discussing the implications to the company of using direct labor as the base for assigning manufacturing overhead cost to products.

(CMA, adapted)

Appendix 4B: The Predetermined Overhead Rate and Capacity

Companies typically base their predetermined overhead rates on the estimated, or budgeted, amount of the allocation base for the upcoming period. This is the method that is used in the chapter, but it is a practice that is often criticized based on the accounting for fixed manufacturing overhead costs.[1] As we shall see, the critics argue that, in general, too much fixed manufacturing overhead cost is applied to products. To focus on this issue, we will make two simplifying assumptions in this appendix: (1) we will consider only fixed manufacturing overhead; and (2) we will assume that the actual fixed manufacturing overhead at the end of the period is the same as the estimated, or budgeted, fixed manufacturing overhead at the beginning of the period. Neither of these assumptions is entirely realistic. Ordinarily, some manufacturing overhead is variable and even fixed costs can differ from what was expected at the beginning of the period, but making those assumptions enables us to focus on the primary issues the critics raise.

An example will help us to understand the controversy. Prahad Corporation manufactures music CDs for local recording studios. The company's CD duplicating machine is capable of producing a new CD every 10 seconds from a master CD. The company leases the CD duplicating machine for $180,000 per year, and this is the company's only manufacturing overhead cost. With allowances for setups and maintenance, the machine is theoretically capable of producing up to 900,000 CDs per year. However, due to weak retail sales of CDs, the company's commercial customers are unlikely to order more than 600,000 CDs next year. The company uses machine time as the allocation base for applying manufacturing overhead to CDs. These data are summarized below:

> **LEARNING OBJECTIVE 4–8**
> Understand the implications of basing the predetermined overhead rate on activity at capacity rather than on estimated activity for the period.

Prahad Corporation Data	
Total manufacturing overhead cost	$180,000 per year
Allocation base—machine time per CD	10 seconds per CD
Capacity	900,000 CDs per year
Budgeted output for next year	600,000 CDs

---

[1] Statement of Financial Accounting Standards No. 151: *Inventory Costs* and International Accounting Standard 2: *Inventories* require allocating fixed manufacturing overhead costs to products based on normal capacity. Normal capacity reflects the level of output expected to be produced over numerous periods under normal circumstances. This definition mirrors the language used in this book that refers to basing the predetermined overhead rate on the estimated, or budgeted, amount of the allocation base for the upcoming period.

If Prahad follows common practice and computes its predetermined overhead rate using estimated or budgeted figures, then its predetermined overhead rate for next year would be $0.03 per second of machine time computed as follows:

$$\text{Predetermined overhead rate} = \frac{\text{Estimated total manufacturing overhead cost}}{\text{Estimated total amount of the allocation base}}$$

$$= \frac{\$180,000}{600,000 \text{ CDs} \times 10 \text{ seconds per CD}}$$

$$= \$0.03 \text{ per second}$$

Because each CD requires 10 seconds of machine time, each CD will be charged for $0.30 of overhead cost.

Critics charge that there are two problems with this procedure. First, if predetermined overhead rates are based on budgeted activity and overhead includes significant fixed costs, then the unit product costs will fluctuate depending on the budgeted level of activity for the period. For example, if the budgeted output for the year was only 300,000 CDs, the predetermined overhead rate would be $0.06 per second of machine time or $0.60 per CD rather than $0.30 per CD. In general, if budgeted output falls, the overhead cost per unit will increase; it will appear that the CDs cost more to make. Managers may then be tempted to increase prices at the worst possible time—just as demand is falling.

Second, critics charge that under the traditional approach, products are charged for resources that they don't use. When the fixed costs of capacity are spread over estimated activity, the units that are produced must shoulder the costs of unused capacity. That is why the applied overhead cost per unit increases as the level of activity falls. The critics argue that products should be charged only for the capacity that they use; they should not be charged for the capacity they don't use. This can be accomplished by basing the predetermined overhead rate on capacity as follows:

$$\frac{\text{Predetermined overhead}}{\text{rate based on capacity}} = \frac{\text{Estimated total manufacturing overhead cost at capacity}}{\text{Estimated total amount of the allocation base at capacity}}$$

$$= \frac{\$180,000}{900,000 \text{ CDs} \times 10 \text{ seconds per CD}}$$

$$= \$0.02 \text{ per second}$$

It is important to realize that the numerator in this predetermined overhead rate is the estimated total manufacturing overhead cost *at capacity*. In general, the numerator in a predetermined overhead rate is the estimated total manufacturing overhead cost for the level of activity in the denominator. Ordinarily, the estimated total manufacturing overhead cost *at capacity* will be larger than the estimated total manufacturing overhead cost *at the estimated level of activity*. The estimated level of activity in this case was 600,000 CDs (or 6 million seconds of machine time), whereas capacity is 900,000 CDs (or 9 million seconds of machine time). The estimated total manufacturing overhead cost at 600,000 CDs was $180,000. This also happens to be the estimated total manufacturing overhead cost at 900,000 CDs, but that only happens because we have assumed that the manufacturing overhead is entirely fixed. If manufacturing overhead contained any variable element, the total manufacturing overhead would be larger at 900,000 CDs than at 600,000 CDs and, in that case, the predetermined overhead rate should reflect that fact.

At any rate, returning to the computation of the predetermined overhead rate based on capacity, the predetermined overhead rate is $0.02 per second and so the overhead cost applied to each CD would be $0.20. This charge is constant and would not be affected by the level of activity during a period. If output falls, the charge would still be $0.20 per CD.

This method will almost certainly result in underapplied overhead. If actual output at Prahad Corporation is 600,000 CDs, then only $120,000 of overhead cost would be applied to products ($0.20 per CD × 600,000 CDs). Because the actual overhead cost is $180,000, overhead would be underapplied by $60,000. Because we are assuming that manufacturing overhead is entirely fixed and that actual manufacturing overhead equals the manufacturing overhead as estimated at the beginning of the year, the underapplied overhead represents the cost of unused capacity. In other words, if there had been no unused capacity, there would have been no underapplied overhead. The critics suggest that the underapplied overhead that results from unused capacity should be separately disclosed on the income statement as the Cost of Unused Capacity—a period expense. Disclosing this cost as a lump sum on the income statement, rather than burying it in Cost of Goods Sold or ending inventories, makes it much more visible to managers. An example of such an income statement appears below:

Prahad Corporation Income Statement For the Year Ended December 31		
Sales[1]		$1,200,000
Cost of goods sold[2]		1,080,000
Gross margin		120,000
Other expenses:		
Cost of unused capacity[3]	$60,000	
Selling and administrative expenses[4]	90,000	150,000
Net operating loss		$ (30,000)

[1] Assume sales of 600,000 CDs at $2 per CD.
[2] Assume the unit product cost of the CDs is $1.80, including $0.20 for manufacturing overhead.
[3] See the calculations in the text above. Underapplied overhead is $60,000.
[4] Assume selling and administrative expenses total $90,000.

---

connect Appendix 4B Exercises, Problem, and Case

Additional student resources are available with Connect.

EXERCISE 4B–1 Overhead Rate Based on Capacity [LO 4–8]
Samanca Cabinets makes custom wooden cabinets for high-end stereo systems from specialty woods. The company uses a job-order costing system. The capacity of the plant is determined by the capacity of its constraint, which is time on the automated bandsaw that makes finely beveled cuts in wood according to the preprogrammed specifications of each cabinet. The bandsaw can operate up to 150 hours per month. The estimated total manufacturing overhead at capacity is $11,000 per month. The company bases its predetermined overhead rate on capacity, so its predetermined overhead rate is $74 per hour of bandsaw use.
The results of a recent month's operations appear below:

Sales	$39,860
Beginning inventories	$0
Ending inventories	$0
Direct materials	$4,820
Direct labor (all variable)	$9,640
Manufacturing overhead incurred	$10,870
Selling and administrative expense	$9,350
Actual hours of bandsaw use	124

Required:

1. Prepare an income statement following the example in Appendix 4B in which any under-applied overhead is directly recorded on the income statement as an expense.
2. Why is overhead ordinarily underapplied when the predetermined overhead rate is based on capacity?

EXERCISE 4B–2 Overhead Rates and Capacity Issues [LO 4–1, LO 4–2, LO 4–4, LO 4–8]

Estate Pension Services helps clients to set up and administer pension plans that are in compliance with tax laws and regulatory requirements. The firm uses a job-order costing system in which over-head is applied to clients' accounts on the basis of professional staff hours charged to the accounts. Data concerning two recent years appear below:

	2016	2017
Estimated professional staff hours to be charged to clients' accounts	2,400	2,250
Estimated overhead cost	$144,000	$144,000
Professional staff hours available	3,000	3,000

"Professional staff hours available" is a measure of the capacity of the firm. Any hours available that are not charged to clients' accounts represent unused capacity. All of the firm's overhead is fixed.

Required:

1. Jennifer Miyami is an established client whose pension plan was set up many years ago. In both 2016 and 2017, only five hours of professional staff time were charged to Ms. Miyami's account. If the company bases its predetermined overhead rate on the estimated overhead cost and the estimated professional staff hours to be charged to clients, how much overhead cost would have been applied to Ms. Miyami's account in 2016? In 2017?
2. Suppose that the company bases its predetermined overhead rate on the estimated overhead cost and the estimated professional staff hours to be charged to clients as in requirement 1. Also suppose that the actual professional staff hours charged to clients' accounts and the actual overhead costs turn out to be exactly as estimated in both years. By how much would the overhead be underapplied or overapplied in 2016? In 2017?
3. Refer back to the data concerning Ms. Miyami in requirement 1. If the company bases its pre-determined overhead rate on the professional staff hours available, how much overhead cost would have been applied to Ms. Miyami's account in 2016? In 2017?
4. Suppose that the company bases its predetermined overhead rate on the professional staff hours available as in requirement 3. Also, suppose that the actual professional staff hours charged to clients' accounts and the actual overhead costs turn out to be exactly as estimated in both years. By how much would the overhead be underapplied or overapplied in 2016? In 2017?

PROBLEM 4B–3 Predetermined Overhead Rate and Capacity [LO 4–1, LO 4–2, LO 4–4, LO 4–8]

Skid Road Recording, Inc., is a small audio recording studio located in Seattle. The company handles work for advertising agencies—primarily for radio ads—and has a few singers and bands as clients. Skid Road Recording handles all aspects of recording from editing to making a digital master from which CDs can be copied. The competition in the audio recording industry in Seattle has always been tough, but it has been getting even tougher over the last several years. The studio has been losing customers to newer studios that are equipped with more up-to-date equipment and that are able to offer very attractive prices and excellent service. Summary data concerning the last two years of operations follow:

	2016	2017
Estimated hours of studio service	1,000	750
Estimated studio overhead cost	$90,000	$90,000
Actual hours of studio service provided	900	600
Actual studio overhead cost incurred	$90,000	$90,000
Hours of studio service at capacity	1,800	1,800

The company applies studio overhead to recording jobs on the basis of the hours of studio service provided. For example, 30 hours of studio time were required to record, edit, and master the Slug Fest music CD for a local band. All of the studio overhead is fixed, and the actual overhead cost incurred was exactly as estimated at the beginning of the year in both 2016 and 2017.

Required:

1. Skid Road Recording computes its predetermined overhead rate at the beginning of each year based on the estimated studio overhead and the estimated hours of studio service for the year. How much overhead would have been applied to the Slug Fest job if it had been done in 2016? In 2017? By how much would overhead have been underapplied or overapplied in 2016? In 2017?

2. The president of Skid Road Recording has heard that some companies in the industry have changed to a system of computing the predetermined overhead rate at the beginning of each year based on the hours of studio service that could be provided at capacity. He would like to know what effect this method would have on job costs. How much overhead would have been applied using this method to the Slug Fest job if it had been done in 2016? In 2017? By how much would overhead have been underapplied or overapplied in 2016 using this method? In 2017?

3. How would you interpret the underapplied or overapplied overhead that results from using studio hours at capacity to compute the predetermined overhead rate?

4. What fundamental business problem is Skid Road Recording facing? Which method of computing the predetermined overhead rate is likely to be more helpful in facing this problem? Explain.

CASE 4B–4 Ethics; Predetermined Overhead Rate and Capacity [LO 4–2, LO 4–4, LO 4–8]

Melissa Ostwerk, the new controller of TurboDrives, Inc., has just returned from a seminar on the choice of the activity level in the predetermined overhead rate. Even though the subject did not sound exciting at first, she found that there were some important ideas presented that should get a hearing at her company. After returning from the seminar, she arranged a meeting with the production manager, Jan Kingman, and the assistant production manager, Lonny Chan.

Melissa: I ran across an idea that I wanted to check out with both of you. It's about the way we compute predetermined overhead rates.

Jan: We're all ears.

Melissa: We compute the predetermined overhead rate by dividing the estimated total factory overhead for the coming year, which is all a fixed cost, by the estimated total units produced for the coming year.

Lonny: We've been doing that as long as I've been with the company.

Jan: And it has been done that way at every other company I've worked at, except at most places they divide by direct labor-hours.

Melissa: We use units because it is simpler and we basically make one product with minor variations. But, there's another way to do it. Instead of basing the overhead rate on the estimated total units produced for the coming year, we could base it on the total units produced at capacity.

Lonny: Oh, the Marketing Department will love that. It will drop the costs on all of our products. They'll go wild over there cutting prices.

Melissa: That is a worry, but I wanted to talk to both of you first before going over to Marketing.

Jan: Aren't you always going to have a lot of underapplied overhead?

Melissa: That's correct, but let me show you how we would handle it. Here's an example based on our budget for next year.

Budgeted (estimated) production....................	80,000 units
Budgeted sales	80,000 units
Capacity	100,000 units
Selling price.......................................	$70 per unit
Variable manufacturing cost	$18 per unit
Total manufacturing overhead cost (all fixed)...........	$2,000,000
Selling and administrative expenses (all fixed)..........	$1,950,000
Beginning inventories................................	$0

Traditional approach to computing the predetermined overhead rate:

$$\text{Predetermined overhead rate} = \frac{\text{Estimated total manufacturing overhead cost}}{\text{Estimated total amount of the allocation base}}$$

$$= \frac{\$2,000,000}{80,000 \text{ units}} = \$25 \text{ per unit}$$

Budgeted Income Statement		
Revenue (80,000 units × $70 per unit)		$5,600,000
Cost of goods sold:		
Variable manufacturing		
(80,000 units × $18 per unit)	$1,440,000	
Manufacturing overhead applied		
(80,000 units × $25 per unit)	2,000,000	3,440,000
Gross margin		2,160,000
Selling and administrative expenses		1,950,000
Net operating income		$ 210,000

New approach to computing the predetermined overhead rate using capacity in the denominator:

$$\text{Predetermined overhead rate} = \frac{\text{Estimated total manufacturing overhead cost at capacity}}{\text{Estimated total amount of the allocation base at capacity}}$$

$$= \frac{\$2,000,000}{100,000 \text{ units}} = \$20 \text{ per unit}$$

Budgeted Income Statement		
Revenue (80,000 units × $70 per unit)		$5,600,000
Cost of goods sold:		
Variable manufacturing		
(80,000 units × $18 per unit)	$1,440,000	
Manufacturing overhead applied		
(80,000 units × $20 per unit)	1,600,000	3,040,000
Gross margin		2,560,000
Cost of unused capacity		
[(100,000 units − 80,000 units) × $20 per unit]		400,000
Selling and administrative expenses		1,950,000
Net operating income		$ 210,000

Jan: Whoa!! I don't think I like the looks of that "Cost of unused capacity." If that thing shows up on the income statement, someone from headquarters is likely to come down here looking for some people to lay off.

Lonny: I'm worried about something else, too. What happens when sales are not up to expectations? Can we pull the "hat trick"?

Melissa: I'm sorry, I don't understand.

Jan: Lonny's talking about something that happens fairly regularly. When sales are down and profits look like they are going to be lower than the president told the owners they were going to be, the president comes down here and asks us to deliver some more profits.

Lonny: And we pull them out of our hat.

Jan: Yeah, we just increase production until we get the profits we want.

Melissa: I still don't understand. You mean you increase sales?

Jan: Nope, we increase production. We're the production managers, not the sales managers.
Melissa: I get it. Because you have produced more, the sales force has more units it can sell.
Jan: Nope, the marketing people don't do a thing. We just build inventories and that does the trick.

Required:

In all of the forthcoming questions, assume that the predetermined overhead rate under the traditional method is $25 per unit, and under the new method it is $20 per unit. Also, assume that under the traditional method any underapplied or overapplied overhead is taken directly to the income statement as an adjustment to Cost of Goods Sold.

1. Suppose actual production is 80,000 units. Compute the net operating incomes that would be realized under the traditional and new methods if actual sales are 75,000 units and everything else turns out as expected.

2. How many units would have to be produced under each of the methods in order to realize the budgeted net operating income of $210,000 if actual sales are 75,000 units and everything else turns out as expected?

3. What effect does the new method based on capacity have on the volatility of net operating income?

4. Will the "hat trick" be easier or harder to perform if the new method based on capacity is used?

5. Do you think the "hat trick" is ethical?

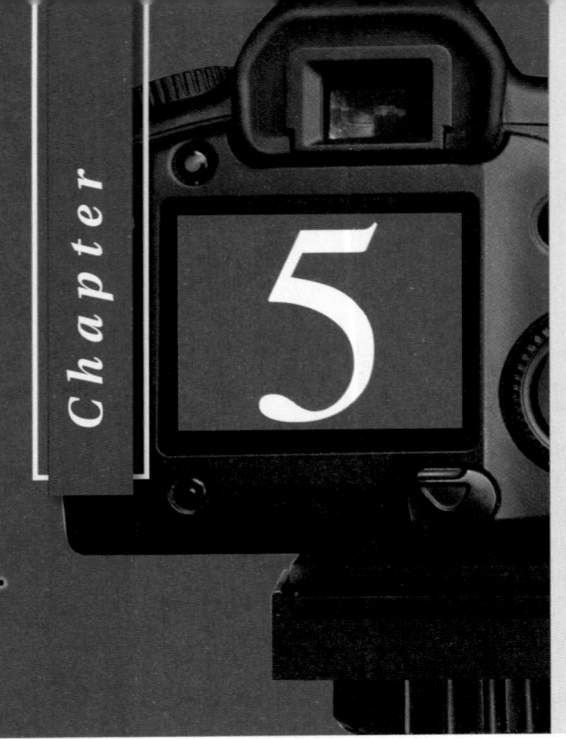

5

Variable Costing and Segment Reporting: Tools for Management

Misguided Incentives in the Auto Industry

After studying Chapter 5, you should be able to:

LO 5–1 Explain how variable costing differs from absorption costing and compute unit product costs under each method.

LO 5–2 Prepare income statements using both variable and absorption costing.

LO 5–3 Reconcile variable costing and absorption costing net operating incomes and explain why the two amounts differ.

LO 5–4 Prepare a segmented income statement that differentiates traceable fixed costs from common fixed costs and use it to make decisions.

LO 5–5 Compute companywide and segment break-even points for a company with traceable fixed costs.

LO 5–6 *(Appendix 5A)* Prepare an income statement using super-variable costing and reconcile this approach with variable costing.

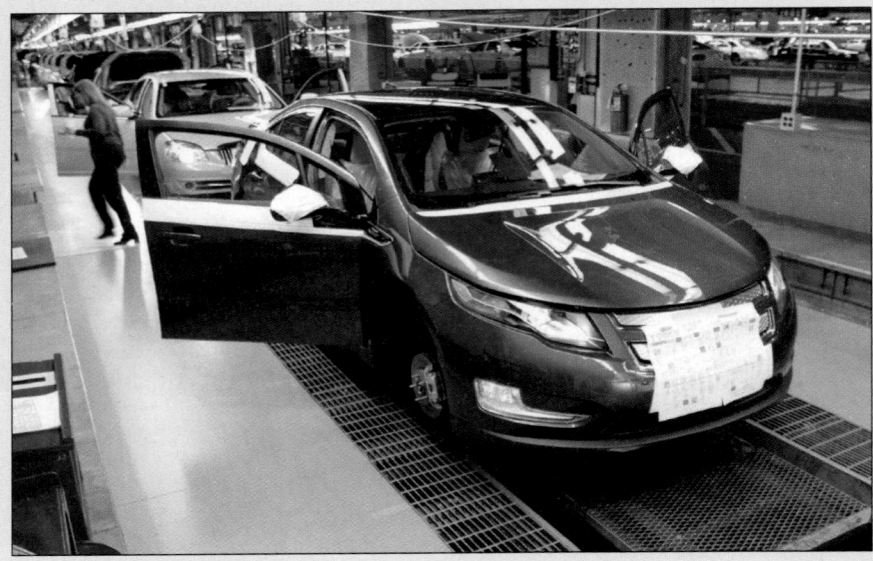

© Jeff Kowalsky/Bloomberg/Getty Images

BUSINESS FOCUS

When the economy tanks, automakers, such as General Motors and Chrysler, often "flood the market" with a supply of vehicles that far exceeds customer demand. They pursue this course of action even though it tarnishes their brand image and increases their auto storage costs, tire replacement costs, customer rebate costs, and advertising costs. This begs the question why would managers knowingly produce more vehicles than are demanded by customers?

In the auto industry, a manager's bonus is often influenced by her company's reported profits; thus, there is a strong incentive to boost profits by producing more units. How can this be done you ask? It would seem logical that producing more units would have no impact on profits unless the units were sold, right? Wrong! As we will discover in this chapter, absorption costing—the most widely used method of determining product costs—can artificially increase profits when managers choose to increase the quantity of units produced. ■

Source: Marielle Segarra, *"Lots of Trouble,"* CFO, March 2012, pp. 29–30.

This chapter describes two applications of the contribution format income statements that were introduced in earlier chapters. First, it explains how manufacturing companies can prepare *variable costing* income statements, which rely on the contribution format, for internal decision making purposes. The variable costing approach will be contrasted with *absorption costing* income statements, which were discussed in Chapter 4 and are generally used for external reports. Ordinarily, variable costing and absorption costing produce different net operating income figures, and the difference can be quite large. In addition to showing how these two methods differ, we will describe the advantages of variable costing for internal reporting purposes and we will show how management decisions can be affected by the costing method chosen.

Second, the chapter explains how the contribution format can be used to prepare segmented income statements. In addition to companywide income statements, managers need to measure the profitability of individual *segments* of their organizations. A **segment** is a part or activity of an organization about which managers would like cost, revenue, or profit data. This chapter explains how to create contribution format income statements that report profit data for business segments, such as divisions, individual stores, geographic regions, customers, and product lines.

Overview of Variable and Absorption Costing

As you begin to read about variable and absorption costing income statements in the coming pages, focus your attention on three key concepts. First, both income statement formats include product costs and period costs, although they define these cost classifications differently. Second, variable costing income statements are grounded in the contribution format. They categorize expenses based on cost behavior—variable expenses are reported separately from fixed expenses. Absorption costing income statements ignore variable and fixed cost distinctions. Third, as mentioned in the paragraph above, variable and absorption costing net operating income figures often differ from one another. The reason for these differences always relates to the fact the variable costing and absorption costing income statements account for fixed manufacturing overhead differently. *Pay very close attention to the two different ways that variable costing and absorption costing account for fixed manufacturing overhead.*

LEARNING OBJECTIVE 5–1
Explain how variable costing differs from absorption costing and compute unit product costs under each method.

Variable Costing

Under **variable costing**, only those manufacturing costs that vary with output are treated as product costs. This would usually include direct materials, direct labor, and the variable portion of manufacturing overhead. Fixed manufacturing overhead is not treated as a product cost under this method. Rather, fixed manufacturing overhead is treated as a period cost and, like selling and administrative expenses, it is expensed in its entirety each period. Consequently, the cost of a unit of product in inventory or in cost of goods sold under the variable costing method does not contain any fixed manufacturing overhead cost. Variable costing is sometimes referred to as *direct costing* or *marginal costing*.

Absorption Costing

As discussed in Chapter 4, **absorption costing** treats *all* manufacturing costs as product costs, regardless of whether they are variable or fixed. The cost of a unit of product under the absorption costing method consists of direct materials, direct labor, and *both* variable and fixed manufacturing overhead. Thus, absorption costing allocates a portion of fixed manufacturing overhead cost to each unit of product, along with the variable manufacturing costs. Because absorption costing includes all manufacturing costs in product costs, it is frequently referred to as the *full cost* method.

Selling and Administrative Expenses

Selling and administrative expenses are never treated as product costs, regardless of the costing method. Thus, under absorption and variable costing, variable and fixed selling and administrative expenses are always treated as period costs and are expensed as incurred.

Summary of Differences   The essential difference between variable costing and absorption costing, as illustrated in Exhibit 5–1, is how each method accounts for fixed manufacturing overhead costs—all other costs are treated the same under the two methods. In absorption costing, fixed manufacturing overhead costs are included as part of the costs of work in process inventories. When units are completed, these costs are transferred to finished goods and only when the units are sold do these costs flow through to the income statement as part of cost of goods sold. In variable costing, fixed manufacturing overhead costs are considered to be period costs—just like selling and administrative costs—and are taken immediately to the income statement as period expenses.

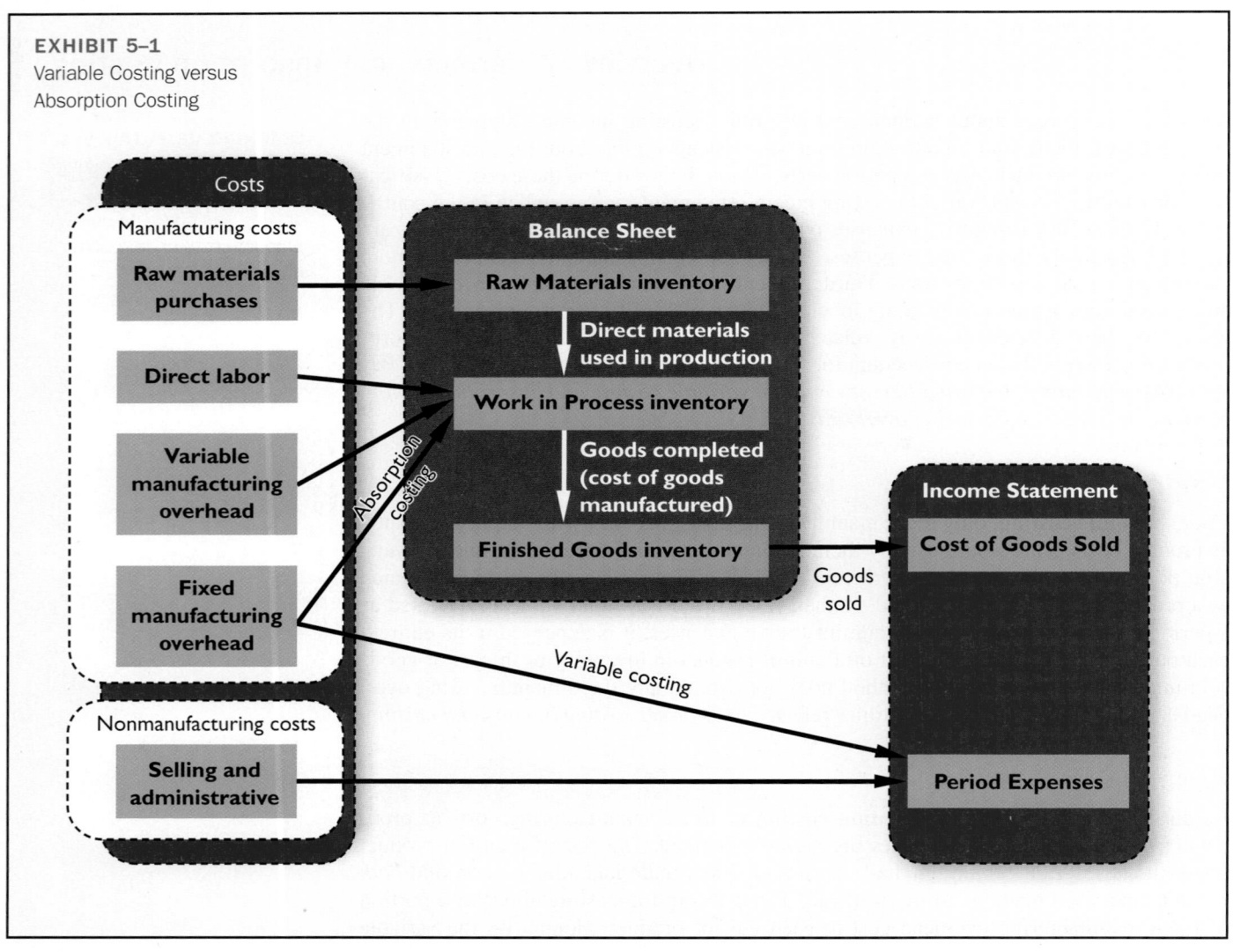

EXHIBIT 5–1
Variable Costing versus
Absorption Costing

Variable and Absorption Costing—An Example

To illustrate the difference between variable costing and absorption costing, consider Weber Light Aircraft, a company that produces light recreational aircraft. Data concerning the company's operations appear below:

	Per Aircraft	Per Month
Selling price..................................	$100,000	
Direct materials..............................	$19,000	
Direct labor.................................	$5,000	
Variable manufacturing overhead	$1,000	
Fixed manufacturing overhead		$70,000
Variable selling and administrative expenses......	$10,000	
Fixed selling and administrative expenses		$20,000

	January	February	March
Beginning inventory...........................	0	0	1
Units produced	1	2	4
Units sold...................................	1	1	5
Ending inventory.............................	0	1	0

As you review the data above, it is important to realize that for the months of January, February, and March, the selling price per aircraft, variable cost per aircraft, and total monthly fixed expenses never change. The only variables that change in this example are the number of units produced (January = 1 unit produced; February = 2 units produced; March = 4 units produced) and the number of units sold (January = 1 unit sold; February = 1 unit sold; March = 5 units sold).

We will first construct the company's variable costing income statements for January, February, and March. Then we will show how the company's net operating income would be determined for the same months using absorption costing.

Variable Costing Contribution Format Income Statement

To prepare the company's variable costing income statements for January, February, and March we begin by computing the unit product cost. Under variable costing, product costs consist solely of variable production costs. At Weber Light Aircraft, the variable production cost per unit is $25,000, determined as follows:

LEARNING OBJECTIVE 5–2
Prepare income statements using both variable and absorption costing.

Variable Costing Unit Product Cost	
Direct materials	$19,000
Direct labor...	5,000
Variable manufacturing overhead........................	1,000
Variable costing unit product cost	$25,000

Since each month's variable production cost is $25,000 per aircraft, the variable costing cost of goods sold for all three months can be easily computed as follows:

Variable Costing Cost of Goods Sold			
	January	February	March
Variable production cost (a)	$25,000	$25,000	$25,000
Units sold (b).................................	1	1	5
Variable cost of goods sold (a) × (b)	$25,000	$25,000	$125,000

And the company's total selling and administrative expense would be derived as follows:

Selling and Administrative Expenses			
	January	February	March
Variable selling and administrative expense (@ $10,000 per unit sold)...............	$10,000	$10,000	$50,000
Fixed selling and administrative expense.....	20,000	20,000	20,000
Total selling and administrative expense......	$30,000	$30,000	$70,000

Putting it all together, the variable costing income statements would appear as shown in Exhibit 5–2. Notice, the contribution format has been used in these income statements. Also, the monthly fixed manufacturing overhead costs ($70,000) have been recorded as a period expense in the month incurred.

EXHIBIT 5–2
Variable Costing Income Statements

Variable Costing Contribution Format Income Statements			
	January	February	March
Sales	$100,000	$100,000	$500,000
Variable expenses:			
Variable cost of goods sold..............	25,000	25,000	125,000
Variable selling and administrative expense	10,000	10,000	50,000
Total variable expenses	35,000	35,000	175,000
Contribution margin......................	65,000	65,000	325,000
Fixed expenses:			
Fixed manufacturing overhead	70,000	70,000	70,000
Fixed selling and administrative expense....	20,000	20,000	20,000
Total fixed expenses.....................	90,000	90,000	90,000
Net operating income (loss)	$ (25,000)	$ (25,000)	$235,000

A simple method for understanding how Weber Light Aircraft computed its variable costing net operating income figures is to focus on the contribution margin per aircraft sold, which is computed as follows:

Contribution Margin per Aircraft Sold		
Selling price per aircraft.......................................		$100,000
Variable production cost per aircraft	$25,000	
Variable selling and administrative expense per aircraft	10,000	35,000
Contribution margin per aircraft............................		$ 65,000

The variable costing net operating income for each period can always be computed by multiplying the number of units sold by the contribution margin per unit and then subtracting total fixed costs. For Weber Light Aircraft these computations would appear as follows:

	January	February	March
Number of aircraft sold	1	1	5
Contribution margin per aircraft......	× $ 65,000	× $ 65,000	× $ 65,000
Total contribution margin	$ 65,000	$ 65,000	$325,000
Total fixed expenses................	90,000	90,000	90,000
Net operating income (loss)	$(25,000)	$(25,000)	$235,000

Notice, January and February have the same net operating loss. This occurs because one aircraft was sold in each month and, as previously mentioned, the selling price per aircraft, variable cost per aircraft, and total monthly fixed expenses remain constant.

Absorption Costing Income Statement

As we begin the absorption costing portion of the example, remember that the only reason absorption costing income differs from variable costing is that the methods account for fixed manufacturing overhead differently. Under absorption costing, fixed manufacturing overhead is included in product costs. In variable costing, fixed manufacturing overhead is not included in product costs and instead is treated as a period expense just like selling and administrative expenses.

The first step in preparing Weber's absorption costing income statements for January, February, and March is to determine the company's unit product costs for each month as follows[1]:

Absorption Costing Unit Product Cost			
	January	February	March
Direct materials	$19,000	$19,000	$19,000
Direct labor	5,000	5,000	5,000
Variable manufacturing overhead	1,000	1,000	1,000
Fixed manufacturing overhead ($70,000 ÷ 1 unit produced in January; $70,000 ÷ 2 units produced in February; $70,000 ÷ 4 units produced in March) . . .	70,000	35,000	17,500
Absorption costing unit product cost	$95,000	$60,000	$42,500

Notice that in each month, Weber's fixed manufacturing overhead cost of $70,000 is divided by the number of units produced to determine the fixed manufacturing overhead cost per unit.

Given these unit product costs, the company's absorption costing net operating income in each month would be determined as shown in Exhibit 5–3.

The sales for all three months in Exhibit 5–3 are the same as the sales shown in the variable costing income statements. The January cost of goods sold consists of one unit produced during January at a cost of $95,000 according to the absorption costing system. The February cost of goods sold consists of one unit produced during February at a cost of $60,000 according to the absorption costing system. The March cost of goods

Absorption Costing Income Statements			
	January	February	March
Sales	$100,000	$100,000	$500,000
Cost of goods sold ($95,000 × 1 unit; $60,000 × 1 unit; $60,000 × 1 unit + $42,500 × 4 units)	95,000	60,000	230,000
Gross margin	5,000	40,000	270,000
Selling and administrative expenses	30,000	30,000	70,000
Net operating income (loss).	$ (25,000)	$ 10,000	$200,000

EXHIBIT 5–3
Absorption Costing Income Statements

---

[1] For simplicity, we assume in this section that an actual costing system is used in which actual costs are spread over the units produced during the period. If a predetermined overhead rate were used, the analysis would be similar, but more complex.

sold ($230,000) consists of one unit produced during February at an absorption cost of $60,000 plus four units produced in March with a total absorption cost of $170,000 (= 4 units produced × $42,500 per unit). The selling and administrative expenses equal the amounts reported in the variable costing income statements; however they are reported as one amount rather than being separated into variable and fixed components.

Note that even though sales were exactly the same in January and February and the cost structure did not change, net operating income was $35,000 higher in February than in January under absorption costing. This occurs because one aircraft produced in February is not sold until March. This aircraft has $35,000 of fixed manufacturing overhead attached to it that was incurred in February, but will not be recorded as part of cost of goods sold until March.

Contrasting the variable costing and absorption costing income statements in Exhibits 5–2 and 5–3, note that net operating income is the same in January under variable costing and absorption costing, but differs in the other two months. We will discuss this in some depth shortly. Also note that the format of the variable costing income statement differs from the absorption costing income statement. An absorption costing income statement categorizes costs by function—manufacturing versus selling and administrative. All of the manufacturing costs flow through the absorption costing cost of goods sold and all of the selling and administrative expenses are listed separately as period expenses. In contrast, in the contribution approach, costs are categorized according to how they behave. All of the variable expenses are listed together and all of the fixed expenses are listed together. The variable expenses category includes manufacturing costs (i.e., variable cost of goods sold) as well as selling and administrative expenses. The fixed expenses category also includes both manufacturing costs and selling and administrative expenses.

IN BUSINESS

THE BEHAVIORAL SIDE OF CALCULATING UNIT PRODUCT COSTS

Andreas STIHL, a manufacturer of chain saws and other landscaping products, asked its U.S. subsidiary, STIHL Inc., to replace its absorption costing income statements with the variable costing approach. From a computer systems standpoint, the change was not disruptive because STIHL used an enterprise system called SAP that accommodates both absorption and variable costing. However, from a behavioral standpoint, STIHL felt the change could be very disruptive. For example, STIHL's senior managers were keenly aware that the variable costing approach reported lower unit product costs than the absorption costing approach. Given this reality, the sales force might be inclined to erroneously conclude that each product had magically become more profitable, thereby justifying ill-advised price reductions. Because of behavioral concerns such as this, STIHL worked hard to teach its employees how to interpret a variable costing income statement.

Source: Carl S. Smith, "Going for GPK: STIHL Moves Toward This Costing System in the United States," *Strategic Finance*, April 2005, pp. 36–39.

Reconciliation of Variable Costing with Absorption Costing Income

LEARNING OBJECTIVE 5–3

Reconcile variable costing and absorption costing net operating incomes and explain why the two amounts differ.

As noted earlier, variable costing and absorption costing net operating incomes may not be the same. In the case of Weber Light Aircraft, the net operating incomes are the same in January, but differ in the other two months. These differences occur because under absorption costing some fixed manufacturing overhead is capitalized in inventories (i.e., included in product costs) rather than being immediately expensed on the income statement. If inventories increase during a period, under absorption costing some of the fixed manufacturing overhead of the current period will be *deferred* in ending inventories. For example, in February two aircraft were produced and each carried with it $35,000 (= $70,000 ÷ 2 aircraft produced) in fixed manufacturing overhead. Since only one aircraft was sold, $35,000 of this fixed manufacturing overhead was on February's absorption costing income statement as part of cost of goods sold, but $35,000 would have been on the balance sheet as part of finished goods inventories. In contrast, under variable costing *all* of the $70,000 of fixed manufacturing overhead appeared on the February income statement as a period expense. Consequently, net operating income was higher under absorption costing than under variable costing by $35,000 in February. This was reversed in March when four units were produced, but five were sold. In March, under absorption costing $105,000 of fixed manufacturing overhead was included in cost of goods sold ($35,000 for the unit produced in February and sold in March plus $17,500 for each of the four units produced and sold in March), but only $70,000 was recognized as a period expense under variable costing. Hence, the net operating income in March was $35,000 lower under absorption costing than under variable costing.

In general, when the units produced exceed unit sales and hence inventories increase, net operating income is higher under absorption costing than under variable costing. This occurs because some of the fixed manufacturing overhead of the period is *deferred* in inventories under absorption costing. In contrast, when unit sales exceed the units produced and hence inventories decrease, net operating income is lower under absorption costing than under variable costing. This occurs because some of the fixed manufacturing overhead of previous periods is *released* from inventories under absorption costing. When the units produced and unit sales are equal, no change in inventories occurs and absorption costing and variable costing net operating incomes are the same.[2]

Variable costing and absorption costing net operating incomes can be reconciled by determining how much fixed manufacturing overhead was deferred in, or released from, inventories during the period:

Fixed Manufacturing Overhead Deferred in, or Released from, Inventories under Absorption Costing			
	January	February	March
Fixed manufacturing overhead in ending inventories..........................	$0	$35,000	$ 0
Fixed manufacturing overhead in beginning inventories	0	0	35,000
Fixed manufacturing overhead deferred in (released from) inventories...................	$0	$35,000	$(35,000)

In equation form, the fixed manufacturing overhead that is deferred in or released from inventories can be determined as follows:

$$\begin{array}{c}\text{Manufacturing overhead} \\ \text{deferred in} \\ \text{(released from) inventory}\end{array} = \begin{array}{c}\text{Fixed manufacturing} \\ \text{overhead in} \\ \text{ending inventories}\end{array} - \begin{array}{c}\text{Fixed manufacturing} \\ \text{overhead in} \\ \text{beginning inventories}\end{array}$$

The reconciliation would then be reported as shown in Exhibit 5–4.

Again note that the difference between variable costing net operating income and absorption costing net operating income is entirely due to the amount of fixed manufacturing overhead that is deferred in, or released from, inventories during the period under absorption costing. Changes in inventories affect absorption costing net operating income—they do not affect variable costing net operating income, providing that variable manufacturing costs per unit are stable.

---

[2] These general statements about the relation between variable costing and absorption costing net operating income assume LIFO is used to value inventories. Even when LIFO is not used, the general statements tend to be correct. Although U.S. GAAP allows LIFO and FIFO inventory flow assumptions, International Financial Reporting Standards do not allow a LIFO inventory flow assumption.

EXHIBIT 5–4

Reconciliation of Variable Costing and Absorption Costing Net Operating Incomes

Reconciliation of Variable Costing and Absorption Costing Net Operating Incomes	January	February	March
Variable costing net operating income (loss)	$(25,000)	$(25,000)	$235,000
Add (deduct) fixed manufacturing overhead deferred in (released from) inventory under absorption costing	0	35,000	(35,000)
Absorption costing net operating income (loss)	$(25,000)	$ 10,000	$200,000

The reasons for differences between variable and absorption costing net operating incomes are summarized in Exhibit 5–5. When the units produced equal the units sold, as in January for Weber Light Aircraft, absorption costing net operating income will equal variable costing net operating income. This occurs because when production equals sales, all of the fixed manufacturing overhead incurred in the current period flows through to the income statement under both methods. For companies that use Lean Production, the number of units produced tends to equal the number of units sold. This occurs because goods are produced in response to customer orders, thereby eliminating finished goods inventories and reducing work in process inventory to almost nothing. So, when a company uses Lean Production differences in variable costing and absorption costing net operating income will largely disappear.

When the units produced exceed the units sold, absorption costing net operating income will exceed variable costing net operating income. This occurs because inventories have increased; therefore, under absorption costing some of the fixed manufacturing overhead incurred in the current period is deferred in ending inventories on the balance sheet, whereas under variable costing all of the fixed manufacturing overhead incurred in the current period flows through to the income statement. In contrast, when the units produced are less than the units sold, absorption costing net operating income will be less than variable costing net operating income. This occurs because inventories have

EXHIBIT 5–5

Comparative Income Effects— Absorption and Variable Costing

Relation between Production and Sales for the Period	Effect on Inventories	Relation between Absorption and Variable Costing Net Operating Incomes
Units produced = Units sold	No change in inventories	Absorption costing net operating income = Variable costing net operating income
Units produced > Units sold	Inventories increase	Absorption costing net operating income > Variable costing net operating income*
Units produced < Units sold	Inventories decrease	Absorption costing net operating income < Variable costing net operating income†

*Net operating income is higher under absorption costing because fixed manufacturing overhead cost is *deferred* in inventory under absorption costing as inventories increase.
†Net operating income is lower under absorption costing because fixed manufacturing overhead cost is *released* from inventory under absorption costing as inventories decrease.

decreased; therefore, under absorption costing fixed manufacturing overhead that had been deferred in inventories during a prior period flows through to the current period's income statement together with all of the fixed manufacturing overhead incurred during the current period. Under variable costing, just the fixed manufacturing overhead of the current period flows through to the income statement.

LEAN MANUFACTURING SHRINKS INVENTORIES

Conmed, a surgical device maker in Utica, New York, switched to lean manufacturing by replacing its assembly lines with U-shaped production cells. It also started producing only enough units to satisfy customer demand rather than producing as many units as possible and storing them in warehouses. The company calculated that its customers use one of its disposable surgical devices every 90 seconds, so that is precisely how often it produces a new unit. Its assembly area for fluid-injection devices used to occupy 3,300 square feet of space and contained $93,000 worth of parts. Now the company produces its fluid-injection devices in 660 square feet of space while maintaining only $6,000 of parts inventory.

When Conmed adopted lean manufacturing, it substantially reduced its finished goods inventories. What impact do you think this initial reduction in inventories may have had on net operating income? Why?

Source: Pete Engardio, "Lean and Mean Gets Extreme," *BusinessWeek*, March 23 and 30, 2009, pp. 60–62.

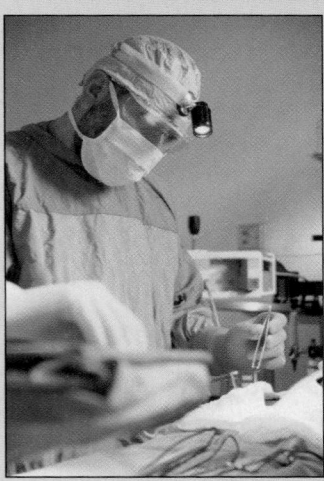

© Photodisc/Getty Images, RF

Advantages of Variable Costing and the Contribution Approach

Variable costing, together with the contribution approach, offers appealing advantages for internal reports. This section discusses three of those advantages.

Enabling CVP Analysis

CVP analysis requires that we break costs down into their fixed and variable components. Because variable costing income statements categorize costs as fixed and variable, it is much easier to use this income statement format to perform CVP analysis than attempting to use the absorption costing format, which mixes together fixed and variable costs.

Moreover, absorption costing net operating income may or may not agree with the results of CVP analysis. For example, let's suppose that you are interested in computing the sales that would be necessary to generate a target profit of $235,000 at Weber Light Aircraft. A CVP analysis based on the January variable costing income statement from Exhibit 5–2 would proceed as follows:

Sales (a).	$100,000
Contribution margin (b).	$65,000
Contribution margin ratio (b) ÷ (a).	65%
Total fixed expenses.	$90,000

$$\text{Dollar sales to attain target profit} = \frac{\text{Target profit} + \text{Fixed expenses}}{\text{CM ratio}}$$

$$= \frac{\$235,000 + \$90,000}{0.65} = \$500,000$$

Thus, a CVP analysis based on the January variable costing income statement predicts that the net operating income would be $235,000 when sales are $500,000. And indeed, the net operating income under variable costing *is* $235,000 when the sales are $500,000 in March. However, the net operating income under absorption costing is *not* $235,000 in March, even though the sales are $500,000. Why is this? The reason is that under absorption costing, net operating income can be distorted by changes in inventories. In March, inventories decreased, so some of the fixed manufacturing overhead that had been deferred in February's ending inventories was released to the March income statement, resulting in a net operating income that is $35,000 lower than the $235,000 predicted by CVP analysis. If inventories had increased in March, the opposite would have occurred— the absorption costing net operating income would have been higher than the $235,000 predicted by CVP analysis.

Explaining Changes in Net Operating Income

The variable costing income statements in Exhibit 5–2 are clear and easy to understand. All other things the same, when sales go up, net operating income goes up. When sales go down, net operating income goes down. When sales are constant, net operating income is constant. The number of units produced does not affect net operating income.

Absorption costing income statements can be confusing and are easily misinterpreted. Look again at the absorption costing income statements in Exhibit 5–3; a manager might wonder why net operating income went up from January to February even though sales were exactly the same. Was it a result of lower selling costs, more efficient operations, or was it some other factor? In fact, it was simply because the number of units produced exceeded the number of units sold in February and so some of the fixed manufacturing overhead costs were deferred in inventories in that month. These costs have not gone away—they will eventually flow through to the income statement in a later period when inventories go down. There is no way to tell this from the absorption costing income statements.

To avoid mistakes when absorption costing is used, readers of financial statements should be alert to changes in inventory levels. Under absorption costing, if inventories increase, fixed manufacturing overhead costs are deferred in inventories, which in turn increases net operating income. If inventories decrease, fixed manufacturing overhead costs are released from inventories, which in turn decreases net operating income. Thus, when absorption costing is used, fluctuations in net operating income can be caused by changes in inventories as well as changes in sales.

Supporting Decision Making

The variable costing method correctly identifies the additional variable costs that will be incurred to make one more unit. It also emphasizes the impact of fixed costs on profits. The total amount of fixed manufacturing costs appears explicitly on the income statement, highlighting that the whole amount of fixed manufacturing costs must be covered for the company to be truly profitable. In the Weber Light Aircraft example, the variable costing income statements correctly report that the cost of producing another unit is $25,000 and they explicitly recognize that $70,000 of fixed manufactured overhead must be covered to earn a profit.

Under absorption costing, fixed manufacturing overhead costs appear to be variable with respect to the number of units sold, but they are not. For example, in January, the absorption unit product cost at Weber Light Aircraft is $95,000, but the variable portion of this cost is only $25,000. The fixed overhead costs of $70,000 are commingled with variable production costs, thereby obscuring the impact of fixed overhead costs on profits. Because absorption unit product costs are stated on a per unit basis, managers may mistakenly believe that if another unit is produced, it will cost the company $95,000. But of course it would not. The cost of producing another unit would be only $25,000. Misinterpreting absorption unit product costs as variable can lead to many problems, including inappropriate pricing decisions and decisions to drop products that are in fact profitable.

Segmented Income Statements and the Contribution Approach

In the remainder of the chapter, we'll learn how to use the contribution approach to construct income statements for business segments. These segmented income statements are useful for analyzing the profitability of segments, making decisions, and measuring the performance of segment managers.

Traceable and Common Fixed Costs and the Segment Margin

You need to understand three new terms to prepare segmented income statements using the contribution approach—*traceable fixed cost, common fixed cost,* and *segment margin.*

A **traceable fixed cost** of a segment is a fixed cost that is incurred because of the existence of the segment—if the segment had never existed, the fixed cost would not have been incurred; and if the segment were eliminated, the fixed cost would disappear. Examples of traceable fixed costs include the following:

- The salary of the Fritos product manager at PepsiCo is a *traceable* fixed cost of the Fritos business segment of PepsiCo.
- The maintenance cost for the building in which Boeing 747s are assembled is a *traceable* fixed cost of the 747 business segment of Boeing.
- The liability insurance at Disney World is a *traceable* fixed cost of the Disney World business segment of The Walt Disney Corporation.

A **common fixed cost** is a fixed cost that supports the operations of more than one segment, but is not traceable in whole or in part to any one segment. Even if a segment were entirely eliminated, there would be no change in a true common fixed cost. For example:

- The salary of the CEO of General Motors is a *common* fixed cost of the various divisions of General Motors.
- The cost of heating a Safeway or Kroger grocery store is a *common* fixed cost of the store's various departments—groceries, produce, bakery, meat, and so forth.
- The cost of the receptionist's salary at an office shared by a number of doctors is a *common* fixed cost of the doctors. The cost is traceable to the office, but not to individual doctors.

To prepare a segmented income statement, variable expenses are deducted from sales to yield the contribution margin for the segment. The contribution margin tells us what happens to profits as volume changes—holding a segment's capacity and fixed costs constant. The contribution margin is especially useful in decisions involving temporary uses of capacity such as special orders. These types of decisions often involve only variable costs and revenues—the two components of contribution margin.

The **segment margin** is obtained by deducting the traceable fixed costs of a segment from the segment's contribution margin. It represents the margin available after a segment has covered all of its own costs. *The segment margin is the best gauge of the long-run profitability of a segment* because it includes only those costs that are caused by the segment. If a segment can't cover its own costs, then that segment probably should be dropped (unless it has important side effects on other segments). Notice, common fixed costs are not allocated to segments.

From a decision-making point of view, the segment margin is most useful in major decisions that affect capacity such as dropping a segment. By contrast, as we noted earlier, the contribution margin is most useful in decisions involving short-run changes in volume, such as pricing special orders that involve temporary use of existing capacity.

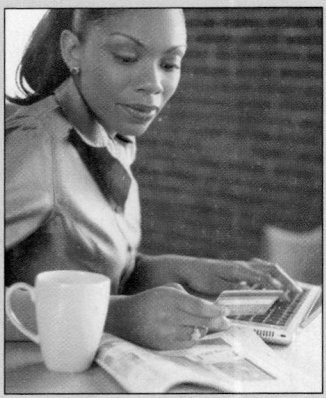

HAS THE INTERNET KILLED CATALOGS?

Smith & Hawken, an outdoor-accessories retailer, has experienced growing Internet sales and declining catalog sales. These trends seem consistent with conventional wisdom, which suggests that the Internet will make catalogs obsolete. Yet, Smith & Hawken, like many retailers with growing Internet sales, has no plans to discontinue its catalogs. In fact, the total number of catalogs mailed in the United States by all companies has jumped from 16.6 billion in 2002 to 19.2 billion in 2005. Why?

Catalog shoppers and Internet shoppers are not independent customer segments. Catalog shoppers frequently choose to complete their sales transactions online rather than placing telephone orders. This explains why catalogs remain a compelling marketing medium even though catalog sales are declining for many companies. If retailers separately analyze catalog sales and Internet sales, they may discontinue the catalogs segment while overlooking the adverse impact of this decision on Internet segment margins.

Source: Louise Lee, "Catalogs, Catalogs, Everywhere," *BusinessWeek,* December 4, 2006, pp. 32–34.

Identifying Traceable Fixed Costs

The distinction between traceable and common fixed costs is crucial in segment reporting because traceable fixed costs are charged to segments and common fixed costs are not. In an actual situation, it is sometimes hard to determine whether a cost should be classified as traceable or common.

The general guideline is to treat as traceable costs *only those costs that would disappear over time if the segment itself disappeared.* For example, if one division within a company were sold or discontinued, it would no longer be necessary to pay that division manager's salary. Therefore the division manager's salary would be classified as a traceable fixed cost of the division. On the other hand, the president of the company undoubtedly would continue to be paid even if one of many divisions was dropped. In fact, he or she might even be paid more if dropping the division was a good idea. Therefore, the president's salary is common to the company's divisions and should not be charged to them.

When assigning costs to segments, the key point is to resist the temptation to allocate costs (such as depreciation of corporate facilities) that are clearly common and that will continue regardless of whether the segment exists or not. *Any allocation of common costs to segments reduces the value of the segment margin as a measure of long-run segment profitability and segment performance.*

Traceable Costs Can Become Common Costs

Fixed costs that are traceable to one segment may be a common cost of another segment. For example, United Airlines might want a segmented income statement that shows the segment margin for a particular flight from Chicago to Paris further broken down into first-class, business-class, and economy-class segment margins. The airline must pay a substantial landing fee at Charles DeGaulle airport in Paris. This fixed landing fee is a traceable cost of the flight, but it is a common cost of the first-class, business-class, and economy-class segments. Even if the first-class cabin is empty, the entire landing fee must be paid. So the landing fee is not a traceable cost of the first-class cabin. But on the other hand, paying the fee is necessary in order to have any first-class, business-class, or economy-class passengers. So the landing fee is a common cost of these three classes.

SEGMENT REPORTING AT THE VILAR PERFORMING ARTS CENTER

The Vilar Performing Arts Center is a 535-seat theater located in Beaver Creek, Colorado, that presents an unusually wide variety of performances categorized into six business segments—Family Series, Broadway Series, Theatre/Comedy Series, Dance Series, Classical Series, and Concert Series. The executive director of the Vilar, Kris Sabel, must decide which shows to book, what financial terms to offer to the artists, what contributions are likely from underwriters (i.e., donors), and what prices to charge for tickets. He evaluates the profitability of the segments using segmented income statements that include traceable costs (such as the costs of transporting, lodging, and feeding the artists) and exclude common costs (such as the salaries of Kris and his staff, depreciation on the theater, and general marketing expenses).

Data concerning the Classical Series segment for one season appears below:

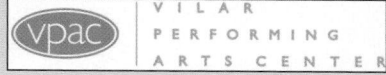

Number of shows	4
Number of seats budgeted	863
Number of seats sold	655
Average seats sold per show	164
Ticket sales	$ 46,800
Underwriting (donors)	65,000
Total income	$ 111,800
Artists fees	78,870
Other traceable expenses	11,231
Classical Series segment margin	$ 21,699

Although the Classical Series sold an average of only 164 seats per show, its overall segment margin ($21,699) is positive thanks to $65,000 of underwriting revenues from donors. Had common costs been allocated to the Classical Series, it may have appeared unprofitable and been discontinued—resulting in fewer shows during the season; less diverse programming; disappointment among a small, but dedicated, number of fans; and lower overall income for the Vilar due to the loss of its Classical Series segment margin.

Segmented Income Statements—An Example

ProphetMax, Inc., is a rapidly growing computer software company. Exhibit 5–6 shows its variable costing income statement for the most recent month. As the company has grown, its senior managers have asked for segmented income statements that could be used to make decisions and evaluate managerial performance. ProphetMax's controller

ProphetMax, Inc.
Variable Costing Income Statement

Sales	$500,000
Variable expenses:	
Variable cost of goods sold	180,000
Other variable expenses	50,000
Total variable expenses	230,000
Contribution margin	270,000
Fixed expenses	256,500
Net operating income	$ 13,500

EXHIBIT 5–6
ProphetMax, Inc. Variable Costing Income Statement

responded by creating examples of contribution format income statements segmented by the company's divisions, product lines, and sales channels. She created Exhibit 5–7 to explain that ProphetMax's profits can be segmented into its two divisions—the Business Products Division and the Consumer Products Division. The Consumer Products Division's profits can be further segmented into the Clip Art and Computer Games product lines. Finally, the Computer Games product line's profits (within the Consumer Products Division) can be segmented into the Online and Retail Stores sales channels.

Levels of Segmented Income Statements

Exhibit 5–8 contains the controller's segmented income statements for the segments depicted in Exhibit 5–7. The contribution format income statement for the entire company appears at the very top of the exhibit under the column labeled Total Company. Notice, the net operating income shown in this column ($13,500) is the same as the net operating income shown in Exhibit 5–6. Immediately to the right of the Total Company column are two columns—one for each of the two divisions. We can see that the Business Products Division's traceable fixed expenses are $90,000 and the Consumer Products Division's are $81,000. These $171,000 of traceable fixed expenses (as shown in the Total Company column) plus the $85,500 of common fixed expenses not traceable to individual divisions equals ProphetMax's total fixed expenses ($256,500) as shown in Exhibit 5–6. We can also see that the Business Products Division's segment margin is $60,000 and the Consumer Products Division's is $39,000. These segment margins show the company's divisional managers how much each of their divisions is contributing to the company's profits.

The middle portion of Exhibit 5–8 further segments the Consumer Products Division into its two product lines, Clip Art and Computer Games. The dual nature of some

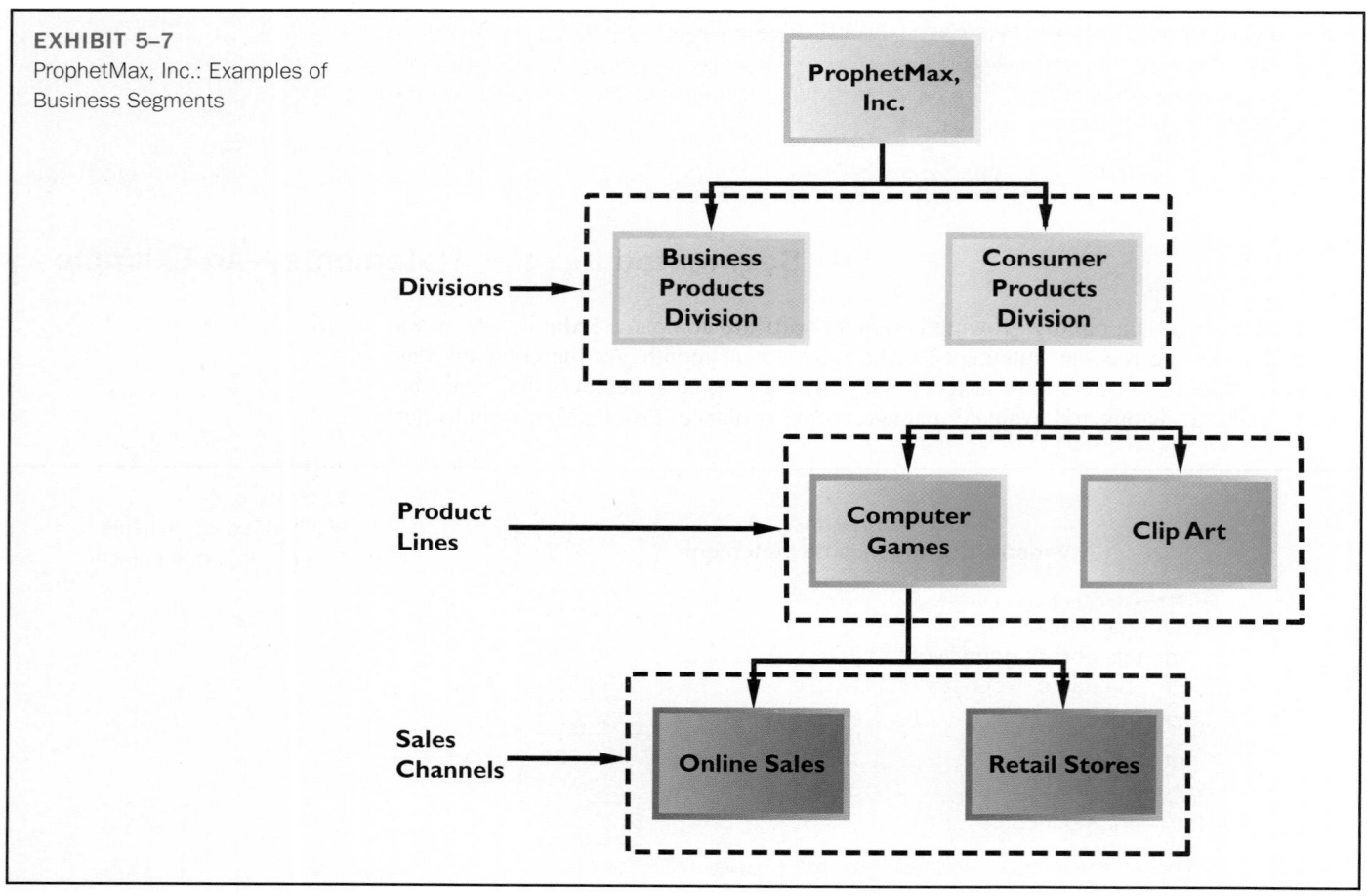

EXHIBIT 5–7
ProphetMax, Inc.: Examples of Business Segments

Segments Defined as Divisions

EXHIBIT 5–8
ProphetMax, Inc.—Segmented Income Statements in the Contribution Format

	Total Company	Divisions	
		Business Products Division	Consumer Products Division
Sales	$500,000	$300,000	$200,000
Variable expenses:			
Variable cost of goods sold	180,000	120,000	60,000
Other variable expenses	50,000	30,000	20,000
Total variable expenses	230,000	150,000	80,000
Contribution margin	270,000	150,000	120,000
Traceable fixed expenses	171,000	90,000	81,000
Divisional segment margin	99,000	$ 60,000	$ 39,000
Common fixed expenses not traceable to individual divisions	85,000		
Net operating income	$ 13,500		

Segments Defined as Product Lines of the Consumer Products Division

	Consumer Products Division	Product Line	
		Clip Art	Computer Games
Sales	$200,000	$75,000	$125,000
Variable expenses:			
Variable cost of goods sold	60,000	20,000	40,000
Other variable expenses	20,000	5,000	15,000
Total variable expenses	80,000	25,000	55,000
Contribution margin	120,000	50,000	70,000
Traceable fixed expenses	70,000	30,000	40,000
Product-line segment margin	50,000	$20,000	$ 30,000
Common fixed expenses not traceable to individual product lines	11,000		
Divisional segment margin	$ 39,000		

Segments Defined as Sales Channels for One Product Line, Computer Games, of the Consumer Products Division

	Computer Games	Sales Channels	
		Online Sales	Retail Stores
Sales	$125,000	$100,000	$25,000
Variable expenses:			
Variable cost of goods sold	40,000	32,000	8,000
Other variable expenses	15,000	5,000	10,000
Total variable expenses	55,000	37,000	18,000
Contribution margin	70,000	63,000	7,000
Traceable fixed expenses	25,000	15,000	10,000
Sales-channel segment margin	45,000	$ 48,000	$ (3,000)
Common fixed expenses not traceable to individual sales channels	15,000		
Product-line segment margin	$ 30,000		

fixed costs can be seen in this portion of the exhibit. Notice, in the top portion of Exhibit 5–8 when segments are defined as divisions, the Consumer Products Division has $81,000 in traceable fixed expenses. However, when we drill down to the product lines (in the middle portion of the exhibit), only $70,000 of the $81,000 cost that was traceable to the Consumer Products Division is traceable to the product lines. The other $11,000 becomes a common fixed cost of the two product lines of the Consumer Products Division.

Why would $11,000 of traceable fixed costs become a common fixed cost when the division is divided into product lines? The $11,000 is the monthly depreciation expense on a machine that is used to encase products in tamper-proof packages for the consumer market. The depreciation expense is a traceable cost of the Consumer Products Division as a whole, but it is a common cost of the division's two product lines. Even if one of the product lines were discontinued entirely, the machine would still be used to wrap the remaining products. Therefore, none of the depreciation expense can really be traced to individual products. Conversely, the $70,000 traceable fixed cost can be traced to the individual product lines because it consists of the costs of product-specific advertising. A total of $30,000 was spent on advertising clip art and $40,000 was spent on advertising computer programs.

The bottom portion of Exhibit 5–8 further segments the Computer Games product line into two sales channels, Online Sales and Retail Stores. The dual nature of some fixed costs can also be seen in this portion of the exhibit. In the middle portion of Exhibit 5–8 when segments are defined as product lines, the Computer Games product line has $40,000 in traceable fixed expenses. However, when we look at the sales channels in the bottom portion of the exhibit, only $25,000 of the $40,000 that was traceable to Computer Games is traceable to the sales channels. The other $15,000 becomes a common fixed cost of the two sales channels for the Computer Games product line.

Segmented Income Statements—Decision Making and Break-Even Analysis

Once a company prepares contribution format segmented income statements, it can use those statements to make decisions and perform break-even analysis.

Decision Making

Let's refer again to the bottom portion of Exhibit 5–8 to illustrate how segmented income statements support decision making. Notice that the Online Sales segment has a segment margin of $48,000 and the Retail Stores segment has a segment margin of $(3,000). Let's assume that ProphetMax wants to know the profit impact of discontinuing the sale of computer games through its Retail Stores sales channel. The company believes that online sales of its computer games will increase 10% if it discontinues the Retail Stores sales channel. It also believes that the Business Products Division and Clip Art product line will be unaffected by this decision. How would you compute the profit impact of this decision?

The first step is to calculate the profit impact of the Retail Stores sales channel disappearing. If this sales channel disappears, we assume its sales, variable expenses, and traceable fixed expenses would all disappear. The quickest way to summarize these financial impacts is to focus on the Retail Stores' segment margin. In other words, if the Retail Stores sales channel disappears, then its negative segment margin of $3,000 would also disappear. This would increase ProphetMax's net operating income by $3,000. The second step is to calculate the profit impact of increasing online sales of computer games by 10%. To perform this calculation, we assume that the Online Sales total traceable fixed expenses ($15,000) remain constant and its contribution margin ratio remains constant at 63% (= $63,000 ÷ $100,000). If online sales increase $10,000 (= $100,000 × 10%), then the Online Sales segment's contribution margin will increase by $6,300 (= $10,000 × 63%). The overall profit impact of discontinuing the Retail Stores sales channel can be summarized as follows:

Avoidance of the retail segment's loss	$3,000
Online Sales additional contribution margin	6,300
Increase in ProphetMax's net operating income	$9,300

Break–Even Analysis

LEARNING OBJECTIVE 5–5
Compute companywide and segment break-even points for a company with traceable fixed costs.

In Chapter 3, we learned how to compute a companywide break-even point for a multi-product company with no traceable fixed expenses. Now we are going to use the Prophet-Max, Inc., data in Exhibit 5–8 to explain how to compute companywide and segment break-even points for a company with traceable fixed expenses. The formula for computing a companywide break-even point is as follows:

$$\text{Dollar sales for company to break even} = \frac{\text{Traceable fixed expenses} + \text{Common fixed expenses}}{\text{Overall CM ratio}}$$

In the case of ProphetMax, we should begin by reviewing the information in the Total Company column in the top portion of Exhibit 5–8. This column of data indicates that ProphetMax's total traceable fixed expenses are $171,000 and its total common fixed expenses are $85,500. Furthermore, the company's overall contribution margin of $270,000 divided by its total sales of $500,000 equals its overall CM ratio of 0.54. Given this information, ProphetMax's companywide break-even point is computed as follows:

$$\text{Dollar sales for company to break even} = \frac{\text{Traceable fixed expenses} + \text{Common fixed expenses}}{\text{Overall CM ratio}}$$

$$= \frac{\$171,000 + \$85,500}{0.54}$$

$$= \frac{\$256,500}{0.54}$$

$$= \$475,000$$

It is important to emphasize that this computation assumes a constant sales mix. In other words, in the ProphetMax example, it assumes that 60% of the total sales ($300,000 ÷ $500,000) will always come from the Business Products Division and 40% of the total sales ($200,000 ÷ $500,000) will always come from the Consumer Products Division.

To compute the break-even point for a business segment, the formula is as follows:

$$\text{Dollar sales for a segment to break even} = \frac{\text{Segment traceable fixed expenses}}{\text{Segment CM ratio}}$$

In the case of ProphetMax's Business Products Division, we should begin by reviewing the information in the Business Products Division column in the top portion of Exhibit 5–8. This column of data indicates that the Business Products Division's traceable fixed expenses are $90,000 and its CM ratio is 0.50 ($150,000 ÷ $300,000). Given this information, the Business Products Division's break-even point is computed as follows:

$$\text{Dollar sales for a segment to break even} = \frac{\text{Segment traceable fixed expenses}}{\text{Segment CM ratio}}$$

$$= \frac{\$90,000}{0.50}$$

$$= \$180,000$$

The same calculation can be performed for the Consumer Products Division using data from the Consumer Products Division column in the top portion of Exhibit 5–8.

Given that the Consumer Products Division's traceable fixed expenses are $81,000 and its CM ratio is 0.60 ($120,000 ÷ $200,000), its break-even point is computed as follows:

$$\text{Dollar sales for a segment to break even} = \frac{\text{Segment traceable fixed expenses}}{\text{Segment CM ratio}}$$

$$= \frac{\$81,000}{0.60}$$

$$= \$135,000$$

Notice that the sum of the segment break-even sales figures of $315,000 ($180,000 + $135,000) is less than the companywide break-even point of $475,000. This occurs because the segment break-even calculations *do not include the company's common fixed expenses.* The exclusion of the company's common fixed expenses can be verified by preparing income statements based on each segment's break-even dollar sales as follows:

	Total Company	Business Products Division	Consumer Products Division
Sales.....................	$315,000	$180,000	$135,000
Variable expenses	144,000	90,000	54,000
Contribution margin........	171,000	90,000	81,000
Traceable fixed expenses...	171,000	90,000	81,000
Segment margin...........	0	$ 0	$ 0
Common fixed expenses ...	85,500		
Net operating loss	$ (85,500)		

When each segment achieves its break-even point, the company's overall net operating loss of $85,500 equals its common fixed expenses of $85,500. This reality can often lead managers astray when making decisions. In an attempt to "cover the company's common fixed expenses," managers will often allocate common fixed expenses to business segments when performing break-even calculations and making decisions. *This is a mistake!* Allocating common fixed expenses to business segments artificially inflates each segment's break-even point. This may cause managers to erroneously discontinue business segments where the inflated break-even point appears unobtainable. The decision to retain or discontinue a business segment should be based on the sales and expenses that would disappear if the segment were dropped. Because common fixed expenses *will persist even if a business segment is dropped,* they should not be allocated to business segments when making decisions.

Segmented Income Statements—Common Mistakes

All of the costs attributable to a segment—and only those costs—should be assigned to the segment. Unfortunately, companies often make mistakes when assigning costs to segments. They omit some costs, inappropriately assign traceable fixed costs, and arbitrarily allocate common fixed costs.

Omission of Costs

The costs assigned to a segment should include all costs attributable to that segment from the company's entire value chain. All of these functions, from research and development, through product design, manufacturing, marketing, distribution, and customer service, are required to bring a product or service to the customer and generate revenues.

However, only manufacturing costs are included in product costs under absorption costing, which is widely regarded as required for external financial reporting. To avoid having to maintain two costing systems and to provide consistency between internal and external reports, many companies also use absorption costing for their internal reports such as segmented income statements. As a result, such companies omit from their profitability analysis part or all of the "upstream" costs in the value chain, which consist of research and development and product design, and the "downstream" costs, which consist of marketing, distribution, and customer service. Yet these nonmanufacturing costs are just as essential in determining product profitability as are the manufacturing costs. These upstream and downstream costs, which are usually included in selling and administrative expenses on absorption costing income statements, can represent half or more of the total costs of an organization. If either the upstream or downstream costs are omitted in profitability analysis, then the product is undercosted and management may unwittingly develop and maintain products that in the long run result in losses.

Inappropriate Methods for Assigning Traceable Costs among Segments

In addition to omitting costs, many companies do not correctly handle traceable fixed expenses on segmented income statements. First, they do not trace fixed expenses to segments even when it is feasible to do so. Second, they use inappropriate allocation bases to allocate traceable fixed expenses to segments.

Failure to Trace Costs Directly Costs that can be traced directly to a specific segment should be charged directly to that segment and should not be allocated to other segments. For example, the rent for a branch office of an insurance company should be charged directly to the branch office rather than included in a companywide overhead pool and then spread throughout the company.

Inappropriate Allocation Base Some companies use arbitrary allocation bases to allocate costs to segments. For example, some companies allocate selling and administrative expenses on the basis of sales revenues. Thus, if a segment generates 20% of total company sales, it would be allocated 20% of the company's selling and administrative expenses as its "fair share." This same basic procedure is followed if cost of goods sold or some other measure is used as the allocation base.

Costs should be allocated to segments for internal decision-making purposes only when the allocation base actually drives the cost being allocated (or is very highly correlated with the real cost driver). For example, sales should be used to allocate selling and administrative expenses only if a 10% increase in sales will result in a 10% increase in selling and administrative expenses. To the extent that selling and administrative expenses are not driven by sales volume, these expenses will be improperly allocated—with a disproportionately high percentage of the selling and administrative expenses assigned to the segments with the largest sales.

Arbitrarily Dividing Common Costs among Segments

The third business practice that leads to distorted segment costs is the practice of assigning nontraceable costs to segments. For example, some companies allocate the common costs of the corporate headquarters building to products on segment reports. However, in a multiproduct company, no single product is likely to be responsible for any significant amount of this cost. Even if a product were eliminated entirely, there would usually be no significant effect on any of the costs of the corporate headquarters building. In short, there is no cause-and-effect relation between the cost of the corporate headquarters building and the existence of any one product. As a consequence, any allocation of the cost of the corporate headquarters building to the products must be arbitrary.

Common costs like the costs of the corporate headquarters building are necessary, of course, to have a functioning organization. The practice of arbitrarily allocating common costs to segments is often justified on the grounds that "someone" has to "cover the common costs." While it is undeniably true that a company must cover its common costs to earn a profit, arbitrarily allocating common costs to segments does not ensure that this will happen. In fact, adding a share of common costs to the real costs of a segment may make an otherwise profitable segment appear to be unprofitable. If a manager eliminates the apparently unprofitable segment, the real traceable costs of the segment will be saved, but its revenues will be lost. And what happens to the common fixed costs that were allocated to the segment? They don't disappear; they are reallocated to the remaining segments of the company. That makes all of the remaining segments appear to be less profitable—possibly resulting in dropping other segments. The net effect will be to reduce the overall profits of the company and make it even more difficult to "cover the common costs."

Additionally, common fixed costs are not manageable by the manager to whom they are arbitrarily allocated; they are the responsibility of higher-level managers. When common fixed costs are allocated to managers, they are held responsible for those costs even though they cannot control them.

Income Statements—An External Reporting Perspective

Companywide Income Statements

Practically speaking, absorption costing is required for external reports according to U.S. generally accepted accounting principles (GAAP).[3] Furthermore, International Financial Reporting Standards (IFRS) explicitly require companies to use absorption costing. Probably because of the cost and possible confusion of maintaining two separate costing systems—one for external reporting and one for internal reporting—most companies use absorption costing for their external and internal reports.

With all of the advantages of the contribution approach, you may wonder why the absorption approach is used at all. While the answer is partly due to adhering to tradition, absorption costing is also attractive to many accountants and managers because they believe it better matches costs with revenues. Advocates of absorption costing argue that *all* manufacturing costs must be assigned to products in order to properly match the costs of producing units of product with their revenues when they are sold. The fixed costs of depreciation, taxes, insurance, supervisory salaries, and so on, are just as essential to manufacturing products as are the variable costs.

Advocates of variable costing argue that fixed manufacturing costs are not really the costs of any particular unit of product. These costs are incurred to have the *capacity* to make products during a particular period and will be incurred even if nothing is made during the period. Moreover, whether a unit is made or not, the fixed manufacturing costs will be exactly the same. Therefore, variable costing advocates argue that fixed manufacturing costs are not part of the costs of producing a particular unit of product, and thus, the matching principle dictates that fixed manufacturing costs should be charged to the current period.

---

[3] The Financial Accounting Standards Board (FASB) has created a single source of authoritative non-governmental U.S. generally accepted accounting principles (GAAP) called the FASB Accounting Standards Codification (FASB codification). Although the FASB codification does not explicitly disallow variable costing, it does explicitly prohibit companies from excluding all manufacturing overhead costs from product costs. It also provides an in-depth discussion of fixed overhead allocation to products, thereby implying that absorption costing is required for external reports. Although some companies expense significant elements of fixed manufacturing costs on their external reports, practically speaking, U.S. GAAP requires absorption costing for external reports.

Segmented Financial Information

U.S. GAAP and IFRS require that publicly traded companies include segmented financial and other data in their annual reports and that the segmented reports prepared for external users *must use the same methods and definitions that the companies use in internal segmented reports that are prepared to aid in making operating decisions.* This is a very unusual stipulation because companies are not ordinarily required to report the same data to external users that are used for internal decision-making purposes. This requirement creates incentives for publicly traded companies to avoid using the contribution format for internal segmented reports. Segmented contribution format income statements contain vital information that companies are often very reluctant to release to the public (and hence competitors). In addition, this requirement creates problems in reconciling internal and external reports.

3M REPORTS SEGMENTED PROFITABILITY TO SHAREHOLDERS

In 2009, 3M Company reported segmented profitability to its shareholders by product lines and geographic areas. A portion of the company's segmented information is summarized below (all numbers are in millions):

	Net Sales	Net Operating Income
Product Lines:		
Industrial and transportation	$7,116	$1,238
Health care................................	$4,294	$1,350
Consumer and office......................	$3,471	$748
Safety, security, and protection services	$3,180	$745
Display and graphics	$3,132	$590
Electro and communications................	$2,276	$322
Geographic Areas:		
United States.............................	$8,509	$1,640
Asia Pacific	$6,120	$1,528
Europe, Middle East, and Africa.............	$5,972	$1,003
Latin America and Canada..................	$2,516	$631

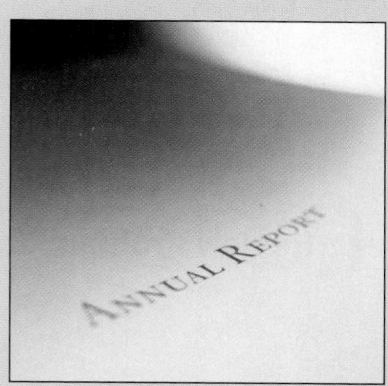

© Duncan Smith/Photodisc/Getty Images, RF

3M's annual report does not report the gross margins or contribution margins for its business segments. Why do you think this is the case?

Source: 3M Company, 2009 Annual Report.

Variable and absorption costing are alternative methods of determining unit product costs. Under variable costing, only those manufacturing costs that vary with output are treated as product costs. This includes direct materials, variable overhead, and ordinarily direct labor. Fixed manufacturing overhead is treated as a period cost and it is expensed on the income statement as incurred. By contrast, absorption costing treats fixed manufacturing overhead as a product cost, along with direct materials, direct labor, and variable overhead. Under both costing methods, selling and administrative expenses are treated as period costs and they are expensed on the income statement as incurred.

Because absorption costing treats fixed manufacturing overhead as a product cost, a portion of fixed manufacturing overhead is assigned to each unit as it is produced. If units of product are unsold at the end of a period, then the fixed manufacturing overhead cost attached to those units is carried with them into the inventory account and deferred to a future period. When these units are later sold, the fixed manufacturing overhead cost attached to them is released from the inventory account and charged against income as part of cost of goods sold. Thus, under absorption costing, it is possible to defer a portion of the fixed manufacturing overhead cost from one period to a future period through the inventory account.

Unfortunately, this shifting of fixed manufacturing overhead cost between periods can cause erratic fluctuations in net operating income and can result in confusion and unwise decisions. To guard against mistakes when they interpret income statement data, managers should be alert to changes in inventory levels or unit product costs during the period.

Segmented income statements provide information for evaluating the profitability and performance of divisions, product lines, sales territories, and other segments of a company. Under the contribution approach, variable costs and fixed costs are clearly distinguished from each other and only those costs that are traceable to a segment are assigned to the segment. A cost is considered traceable to a segment only if the cost is caused by the segment and could be avoided by eliminating the segment. Fixed common costs are not allocated to segments. The segment margin consists of revenues, less variable expenses, less traceable fixed expenses of the segment.

The dollar sales required for a segment to break even is computed by dividing the segment's traceable fixed expenses by its contribution margin ratio. A company's common fixed expenses should not be allocated to segments when performing break-even calculations because they will not change in response to segment-level decisions.

Review Problem 1: Contrasting Variable and Absorption Costing

Dexter Corporation produces and sells a single product, a wooden hand loom for weaving small items such as scarves. Selected cost and operating data relating to the product for two years are given below:

Selling price per unit.............................	$50
Manufacturing costs:	
Variable per unit produced:	
Direct materials..............................	$11
Direct labor	$6
Variable manufacturing overhead.............	$3
Fixed manufacturing overhead per year..........	$120,000
Selling and administrative expenses:	
Variable per unit sold	$4
Fixed per year	$70,000

	Year 1	Year 2
Units in beginning inventory................	0	2,000
Units produced during the year.............	10,000	6,000
Units sold during the year	8,000	8,000
Units in ending inventory	2,000	0

Required:
1. Assume the company uses absorption costing.
   a. Compute the unit product cost in each year.
   b. Prepare an income statement for each year.
2. Assume the company uses variable costing.
   a. Compute the unit product cost in each year.
   b. Prepare an income statement for each year.
3. Reconcile the variable costing and absorption costing net operating incomes.

Solution to Review Problem 1

1. *a.* Under absorption costing, all manufacturing costs, variable and fixed, are included in unit product costs:

	Year 1	Year 2
Direct materials	$11	$11
Direct labor	6	6
Variable manufacturing overhead	3	3
Fixed manufacturing overhead		
($120,000 ÷ 10,000 units)	12	
($120,000 ÷ 6,000 units)		20
Absorption costing unit product cost	$32	$40

b. The absorption costing income statements follow:

	Year 1	Year 2
Sales (8,000 units × $50 per unit)	$400,000	$400,000
Cost of goods sold (8,000 units × $32 per unit);		
(2,000 units × $32 per unit) +		
(6,000 units × $40 per unit)	256,000	304,000
Gross margin	144,000	96,000
Selling and administrative		
expenses (8,000 units × $4 per		
unit + $70,000)	102,000	102,000
Net operating income (loss)	$ 42,000	$ (6,000)

2. *a.* Under variable costing, only the variable manufacturing costs are included in unit product costs:

	Year 1	Year 2
Direct materials	$11	$11
Direct labor	6	6
Variable manufacturing overhead	3	3
Variable costing unit product cost	$20	$20

b. The variable costing income statements follow:

	Year 1		Year 2	
Sales (8,000 units × $50 per unit)		$400,000		$400,000
Variable expenses:				
Variable cost of goods sold				
(8,000 units × $20 per unit)	$160,000		$160,000	
Variable selling and administrative				
expenses (8,000 units ×				
$4 per unit)	32,000	192,000	32,000	192,000
Contribution margin		208,000		208,000
Fixed expenses:				
Fixed manufacturing overhead	120,000		120,000	
Fixed selling and administrative				
expenses	70,000	190,000	70,000	190,000
Net operating income		$ 18,000		$ 18,000

3. The reconciliation of the variable and absorption costing net operating incomes follows:

	Year 1	Year 2
Fixed manufacturing overhead in ending inventories	$24,000	$ 0
Fixed manufacturing overhead in beginning inventories.	0	24,000
Fixed manufacturing overhead deferred in		
(released from) inventories	$24,000	$(24,000)

	Year 1	Year 2
Variable costing net operating income.	$18,000	$18,000
Add fixed manufacturing overhead costs deferred		
in inventory under absorption costing		
(2,000 units × $12 per unit).	24,000	
Deduct fixed manufacturing overhead costs released		
from inventory under absorption costing		
(2,000 units × $12 per unit).		(24,000)
Absorption costing net operating income (loss)	$42,000	$ (6,000)

Review Problem 2: Segmented Income Statements

The business staff of the law firm Frampton, Davis & Smythe has constructed the following report that breaks down the firm's overall results for last month into two business segments—family law and commercial law:

	Company Total	Family Law	Commercial Law
Revenues from clients	$1,000,000	$400,000	$600,000
Variable expenses	220,000	100,000	120,000
Contribution margin	780,000	300,000	480,000
Traceable fixed expenses	670,000	280,000	390,000
Segment margin.	110,000	20,000	90,000
Common fixed expenses.	60,000	24,000	36,000
Net operating income (loss)	$ 50,000	$ (4,000)	$ 54,000

However, this report is not quite correct. The common fixed expenses such as the managing partner's salary, general administrative expenses, and general firm advertising have been allocated to the two segments based on revenues from clients.

Required:

1. Redo the segment report, eliminating the allocation of common fixed expenses. Would the firm be better off financially if the family law segment were dropped? (**Note:** Many of the firm's commercial law clients also use the firm for their family law requirements such as drawing up wills.)

2. The firm's advertising agency has proposed an ad campaign targeted at boosting the revenues of the family law segment. The ad campaign would cost $20,000, and the advertising agency claims that it would increase family law revenues by $100,000. The managing partner of Frampton, Davis & Smythe believes this increase in business could be accommodated without any increase in fixed expenses. Estimate the effect this ad campaign would have on the family law segment margin and on the firm's overall net operating income.

3. Compute the companywide break-even point in dollar sales and the dollar sales required for each business segment to break even.

Solution to Review Problem 2

1. The corrected segmented income statement appears below:

	Company Total	Family Law	Commercial Law
Revenues from clients...........	$1,000,000	$400,000	$600,000
Variable expenses	220,000	100,000	120,000
Contribution margin.............	780,000	300,000	480,000
Traceable fixed expenses........	670,000	280,000	390,000
Segment margin.................	110,000	$ 20,000	$ 90,000
Common fixed expenses	60,000		
Net operating income	$ 50,000		

No, the firm would not be financially better off if the family law practice were dropped. The family law segment is covering all of its own costs and is contributing $20,000 per month to covering the common fixed expenses of the firm. While the segment margin for family law is much lower than for commercial law, it is still profitable. Moreover, family law may be a service that the firm must provide to its commercial clients in order to remain competitive.

2. The ad campaign would increase the family law segment margin by $55,000 as follows:

Increased revenues from clients	$100,000
Family law contribution margin ratio ($300,000 ÷ $400,000)	× 75%
Incremental contribution margin	$ 75,000
Less cost of the ad campaign................................	20,000
Increased segment margin....................................	$ 55,000

Because there would be no increase in fixed expenses (including common fixed expenses), the increase in overall net operating income is also $55,000.

3. The companywide break-even point is computed as follows:

$$\text{Dollar sales for company to break even} = \frac{\text{Traceable fixed expenses} + \text{Common fixed expenses}}{\text{Overall CM ratio}}$$

$$= \frac{\$670,000 + \$60,000}{0.78}$$

$$= \frac{\$730,000}{0.78}$$

$$= \$935,897 \text{ (rounded)}$$

The break-even point for the family law segment is computed as follows:

$$\text{Dollar sales for a segment to break even} = \frac{\text{Segment traceable fixed expenses}}{\text{Segment CM ratio}}$$

$$= \frac{\$280,000}{0.75}$$

$$= \$373,333 \text{ (rounded)}$$

The break-even point for the commercial law segment is computed as follows:

$$\text{Dollar sales for a segment to break even} = \frac{\text{Segment traceable fixed expenses}}{\text{Segment CM ratio}}$$

$$= \frac{\$390,000}{0.80}$$

$$= \$487,500$$

Glossary

Absorption costing A costing method that includes all manufacturing costs—direct materials, direct labor, and both variable and fixed manufacturing overhead—in unit product costs. (p. 171)

Common fixed cost A fixed cost that supports more than one business segment, but is not traceable in whole or in part to any one of the business segments. (p. 181)

Segment Any part or activity of an organization about which managers seek cost, revenue, or profit data. (p. 171)

Segment margin A segment's contribution margin less its traceable fixed costs. It represents the margin available after a segment has covered all of its own traceable costs. (p. 181)

Traceable fixed cost A fixed cost that is incurred because of the existence of a particular business segment and that would be eliminated if the segment were eliminated. (p. 181)

Variable costing A costing method that includes only variable manufacturing costs—direct materials, direct labor, and variable manufacturing overhead—in unit product costs. (p. 171)

Questions

5–1 What is the basic difference between absorption costing and variable costing?

5–2 Are selling and administrative expenses treated as product costs or as period costs under variable costing?

5–3 Explain how fixed manufacturing overhead costs are shifted from one period to another under absorption costing.

5–4 What are the arguments in favor of treating fixed manufacturing overhead costs as product costs?

5–5 What are the arguments in favor of treating fixed manufacturing overhead costs as period costs?

5–6 If the units produced and unit sales are equal, which method would you expect to show the higher net operating income, variable costing or absorption costing? Why?

5–7 If the units produced exceed unit sales, which method would you expect to show the higher net operating income, variable costing or absorption costing? Why?

5–8 If fixed manufacturing overhead costs are released from inventory under absorption costing, what does this tell you about the level of production in relation to the level of sales?

5–9 Under absorption costing, how is it possible to increase net operating income without increasing sales?

5–10 How does Lean Production reduce or eliminate the difference in reported net operating income between absorption and variable costing?

5–11 What is a segment of an organization? Give several examples of segments.

5–12 What costs are assigned to a segment under the contribution approach?

5–13 Distinguish between a traceable cost and a common cost. Give several examples of each.

5–14 Explain how the segment margin differs from the contribution margin.

5–15 Why aren't common costs allocated to segments under the contribution approach?

5–16 How is it possible for a cost that is traceable to a segment to become a common cost if the segment is divided into further segments?

5–17 Should a company allocate its common fixed expenses to business segments when computing the break-even point for those segments? Why?

Multiple-choice questions are provided in Connect.

Applying Excel   CONNECT   Additional student resources are available with Connect.

LEARNING OBJECTIVE 5–2

The Excel worksheet form that follows is to be used to recreate portions of Review Problem 1. Download the workbook containing this form from Connect. *On the website you will also receive instructions about how to use this worksheet form.*

	A	B	C	D	E	F
1	Chapter 5: Applying Excel					
2						
3	Data					
4	Selling price per unit	$50				
5	Manufacturing costs:					
6	Variable per unit produced:					
7	Direct materials	$11				
8	Direct labor	$6				
9	Variable manufacturing overhead	$3				
10	Fixed manufacturing overhead per year	$120,000				
11	Selling and administrative expenses:					
12	Variable per unit sold	$4				
13	Fixed per year	$70,000				
14						
15		Year 1	Year 2			
16	Units in beginning inventory	0				
17	Units produced during the year	10,000	6,000			
18	Units sold during the year	8,000	8,000			
19						
20	Enter a formula into each of the cells marked with a ? below					
21	Review Problem 1: Contrasting Variable and Absorption Costing					
22						
23	Compute the Ending Inventory					
24		Year 1	Year 2			
25	Units in beginning inventory	0	?			
26	Units produced during the year	?	?			
27	Units sold during the year	?	?			
28	Units in ending inventory	?	?			
29						
30	Compute the Absorption Costing Unit Product Cost					
31		Year 1	Year 2			
32	Direct materials	?	?			
33	Direct labor	?	?			
34	Variable manufacturing overhead	?	?			
35	Fixed manufacturing overhead	?	?			
36	Absorption costing unit product cost	?	?			
37						
38	Construct the Absorption Costing Income Statement					
39		Year 1	Year 2			
40	Sales	?	?			
41	Cost of goods sold	?	?			
42	Gross margin	?	?			
43	Selling and administrative expenses	?	?			
44	Net operating income	?	?			
45						
46	Compute the Variable Costing Unit Product Cost					
47		Year 1	Year 2			
48	Direct materials	?	?			
49	Direct labor	?	?			
50	Variable manufacturing overhead	?	?			
51	Variable costing unit product cost	?	?			
52						
53	Construct the Variable Costing Income Statement					
54		Year 1		Year 2		
55	Sales		?		?	
56	Variable expenses:					
57	Variable cost of goods sold	?		?		
58	Variable selling and administrative expenses	?	?	?	?	
59	Contribution margin		?		?	
60	Fixed expenses:					
61	Fixed manufacturing overhead	?		?		
62	Fixed selling and administrative expenses	?	?	?	?	
63	Net operating income		?		?	
64						

◄ ◄ ► ►│ Chapter 5 Form / Filled in Chapter 5 Form / Chapter 5 │◄

You should proceed to the requirements below only after completing your worksheet. The LIFO inventory flow assumption is used throughout this problem.

Required:

1. Check your worksheet by changing the units sold in the Data to 6,000 for Year 2. The cost of goods sold under absorption costing for Year 2 should now be $240,000. If it isn't, check cell C41. The formula in this cell should be =IF(C26 < C27,C26*C36+(C27-C26)*B36,C27*C36). If your worksheet is operating properly, the net operating income under both absorption costing and variable costing should be $(34,000) for Year 2. That is, the loss in Year 2 is $34,000 under both systems. If you do not get these answers, find the errors in your worksheet and correct them.

    Why is the absorption costing net operating income now equal to the variable costing net operating income in Year 2?

2. Enter the following data from a different company into your worksheet:

Data		
Selling price per unit.	$75	
Manufacturing costs:		
Variable per unit produced:		
Direct materials	$12	
Direct labor	$5	
Variable manufacturing overhead	$7	
Fixed manufacturing overhead per year. .	$150,000	
Selling and administrative expenses:		
Variable per unit sold	$1	
Fixed per year	$60,000	
	Year 1	Year 2
Units in beginning inventory	0	
Units produced during the year	15,000	10,000
Units sold during the year.	12,000	12,000

Is the net operating income under variable costing different in Year 1 and Year 2? Why or why not? Explain the relation between the net operating income under absorption costing and variable costing in Year 1. Explain the relation between the net operating income under absorption costing and variable costing in Year 2.

3. At the end of Year 1, the company's board of directors set a target for Year 2 of net operating income of $500,000 under absorption costing. If this target is met, a hefty bonus would be paid to the CEO of the company. Keeping everything else the same from requirement 2, change the units produced in Year 2 to 50,000 units. Would this change result in a bonus being paid to the CEO? Do you think this change would be in the best interests of the company? What is likely to happen in Year 3 to the absorption costing net operating income if sales remain constant at 12,000 units per year?

The Foundational 15   connect   Additional student resources are available with Connect.

LEARNING OBJECTIVE 5–1, 5–2, 5–3, 5–4

Diego Company manufactures one product that is sold for $80 per unit in two geographic regions— the East and West regions. The following information pertains to the company's first year of operations in which it produced 40,000 units and sold 35,000 units.

Variable costs per unit:		
Manufacturing:		
Direct materials		$24
Direct labor.		$14
Variable manufacturing overhead		$2
Variable selling and administrative.		$4
Fixed costs per year:		
Fixed manufacturing overhead.	$800,000	
Fixed selling and administrative expenses.	$496,000	

The company sold 25,000 units in the East region and 10,000 units in the West region. It determined that $250,000 of its fixed selling and administrative expenses is traceable to the West region, $150,000 is traceable to the East region, and the remaining $96,000 is a common fixed cost. The company will continue to incur the total amount of its fixed manufacturing overhead costs as long as it continues to produce any amount of its only product.

Required:

Answer each question independently based on the original data unless instructed otherwise. You do not need to prepare a segmented income statement until requirement 13.

1. What is the unit product cost under variable costing?
2. What is the unit product cost under absorption costing?
3. What is the company's total contribution margin under variable costing?
4. What is the company's net operating income under variable costing?
5. What is the company's total gross margin under absorption costing?
6. What is the company's net operating income under absorption costing?
7. What is the amount of the difference between the variable costing and absorption costing net operating incomes? What is the cause of this difference?
8. What is the company's break-even point in unit sales? Is it above or below the actual sales volume? Compare the break-even sales volume to your answer for requirement 6 and comment.
9. If the sales volumes in the East and West regions had been reversed, what would be the company's overall break-even point in unit sales?
10. What would have been the company's variable costing net operating income if it had produced and sold 35,000 units? You do not need to perform any calculations to answer this requirement.
11. What would have been the company's absorption costing net operating income if it had produced and sold 35,000 units? You do not need to perform any calculations to answer this requirement.
12. If the company produces 5,000 fewer units than it sells in its second year of operations, will absorption costing net operating income be higher or lower than variable costing net operating income in Year 2? Why? No calculations are necessary.
13. Prepare a contribution format segmented income statement that includes a Total column and columns for the East and West regions.
14. Diego is considering eliminating the West region because an internally generated report suggests the region's total *gross margin* in the first year of operations was $50,000 less than its traceable fixed selling and administrative expenses. Diego believes that if it drops the West region, the East region's sales will grow by 5% in Year 2. Using the contribution approach for analyzing segment profitability and assuming all else remains constant in Year 2, what would be the profit impact of dropping the West region in Year 2?
15. Assume the West region invests $30,000 in a new advertising campaign in Year 2 that increases its unit sales by 20%. If all else remains constant, what would be the profit impact of pursuing the advertising campaign?

Additional student resources are available with Connect.   **Exercises**

EXERCISE 5–1 Variable and Absorption Costing Unit Product Costs [LO 5–1]

Ida Sidha Karya Company is a family-owned company located in the village of Gianyar on the island of Bali in Indonesia. The company produces a handcrafted Balinese musical instrument called a gamelan that is similar to a xylophone. The gamelans are sold for $850. Selected data for the company's operations last year follow:

Units in beginning inventory	0
Units produced	250
Units sold	225
Units in ending inventory	25
Variable costs per unit:	
Direct materials	$100
Direct labor.	$320
Variable manufacturing overhead	$40
Variable selling and administrative.	$20
Fixed costs:	
Fixed manufacturing overhead.	$60,000
Fixed selling and administrative	$20,000

Required:

1. Assume that the company uses absorption costing. Compute the unit product cost for one gamelan.
2. Assume that the company uses variable costing. Compute the unit product cost for one gamelan.

EXERCISE 5–2 Variable Costing Income Statement; Explanation of Difference in Net Operating Income [LO 5–2]

Refer to the data in Exercise 5–1 for Ida Sidha Karya Company. The absorption costing income statement prepared by the company's accountant for last year appears below:

Sales	$191,250
Cost of goods sold	157,500
Gross margin	33,750
Selling and administrative expense.........	24,500
Net operating income....................	$ 9,250

Required:

1. Determine how much of the ending inventory consists of fixed manufacturing overhead cost deferred in inventory to the next period.
2. Prepare an income statement for the year using variable costing. Explain the difference in net operating income between the two costing methods.

EXERCISE 5–3 Reconciliation of Absorption and Variable Costing Net Operating Incomes [LO 5–3]

Jorgansen Lighting, Inc., manufactures heavy-duty street lighting systems for municipalities. The company uses variable costing for internal management reports and absorption costing for external reports to shareholders, creditors, and the government. The company has provided the following data:

	Year 1	Year 2	Year 3
Inventories:			
Beginning (units)	200	170	180
Ending (units).........................	170	180	220
Variable costing net operating income	$1,080,400	$1,032,400	$996,400

The company's fixed manufacturing overhead per unit was constant at $560 for all three years.

Required:

1. Determine each year's absorption costing net operating income. Present your answer in the form of a reconciliation report.
2. In Year 4, the company's variable costing net operating income was $984,400 and its absorption costing net operating income was $1,012,400. Did inventories increase or decrease during Year 4? How much fixed manufacturing overhead cost was deferred or released from inventory during Year 4?

EXERCISE 5–4 Basic Segmented Income Statement [LO 5–4]

Royal Lawncare Company produces and sells two packaged products, Weedban and Greengrow. Revenue and cost information relating to the products follow:

	Product	
	Weedban	Greengrow
Selling price per unit..................	$6.00	$7.50
Variable expenses per unit	$2.40	$5.25
Traceable fixed expenses per year.......	$45,000	$21,000

Common fixed expenses in the company total $33,000 annually. Last year the company produced and sold 15,000 units of Weedban and 28,000 units of Greengrow.

Required:

Prepare a contribution format income statement segmented by product lines.

EXERCISE 5–5 Companywide and Segment Break-Even Analysis [LO 5–5]

Piedmont Company segments its business into two regions—North and South. The company prepared the contribution format segmented income statement shown below:

	Total Company	North	South
Sales	$600,000	$400,000	$200,000
Variable expenses.........................	360,000	280,000	80,000
Contribution margin	240,000	120,000	120,000
Traceable fixed expenses	120,000	60,000	60,000
Segment margin	120,000	$ 60,000	$ 60,000
Common fixed expenses....................	50,000		
Net operating income.....................	$ 70,000		

Required:

1. Compute the companywide break-even point in dollar sales.
2. Compute the break-even point in dollar sales for the North region.
3. Compute the break-even point in dollar sales for the South region.

EXERCISE 5–6 Variable and Absorption Costing Unit Product Costs and Income Statements [LO 5–1, LO 5–2]

Lynch Company manufactures and sells a single product. The following costs were incurred during the company's first year of operations:

Variable costs per unit:	
Manufacturing:	
Direct materials	$6
Direct labor..................................	$9
Variable manufacturing overhead	$3
Variable selling and administrative.................	$4
Fixed costs per year:	
Fixed manufacturing overhead...................	$300,000
Fixed selling and administrative................	$190,000

During the year, the company produced 25,000 units and sold 20,000 units. The selling price of the company's product is $50 per unit.

Required:

1. Assume that the company uses absorption costing:
   a. Compute the unit product cost.
   b. Prepare an income statement for the year.
2. Assume that the company uses variable costing:
   a. Compute the unit product cost.
   b. Prepare an income statement for the year.

EXERCISE 5–7 Segmented Income Statement [LO 5–4]

Shannon Company segments its income statement into its North and South Divisions. The company's overall sales, contribution margin ratio, and net operating income are $500,000, 46%, and $10,000, respectively. The North Division's contribution margin and contribution margin ratio are $150,000 and 50%, respectively. The South Division's segment margin is $30,000. The company has $90,000 of common fixed expenses that cannot be traced to either division.

Required:

Prepare an income statement for Shannon Company that uses the contribution format and is segmented by divisions. In addition, for the company as a whole and for each segment, show each item on the segmented income statements as a percent of sales.

EXERCISE 5–8 Deducing Changes in Inventories [LO 5–3]

Parker Products Inc, a manufacturer, reported $123 million in sales and a loss of $18 million in its annual report to shareholders. According to a CVP analysis prepared for management, the company's break-even point is $115 million in sales.

Required:

Assuming that the CVP analysis is correct, is it likely that the company's inventory level increased, decreased, or remained unchanged during the year? Explain.

EXERCISE 5–9 Variable and Absorption Costing Unit Product Costs and Income Statements [LO 5–1, LO 5–2, LO 5–3]

Walsh Company manufactures and sells one product. The following information pertains to each of the company's first two years of operations:

Variable costs per unit:	
Manufacturing:	
Direct materials	$25
Direct labor..................................	$15
Variable manufacturing overhead	$5
Variable selling and administrative...............	$2
Fixed costs per year:	
Fixed manufacturing overhead..................	$250,000
Fixed selling and administrative expenses.........	$80,000

During its first year of operations, Walsh produced 50,000 units and sold 40,000 units. During its second year of operations, it produced 40,000 units and sold 50,000 units. The selling price of the company's product is $60 per unit.

Required:

1. Assume the company uses variable costing:
   a. Compute the unit product cost for Year 1 and Year 2.
   b. Prepare an income statement for Year 1 and Year 2.
2. Assume the company uses absorption costing:
   a. Compute the unit product cost for Year 1 and Year 2.
   b. Prepare an income statement for Year 1 and Year 2.
3. Explain the difference between variable costing and absorption costing net operating income in Year 1. Also, explain why the two net operating income figures differ in Year 2.

EXERCISE 5–10 Companywide and Segment Break-Even Analysis [LO 5–5]

Crossfire Company segments its business into two regions—East and West. The company prepared the contribution format segmented income statement shown below:

	Total Company	East	West
Sales	$900,000	$600,000	$300,000
Variable expenses........................	675,000	480,000	195,000
Contribution margin	225,000	120,000	105,000
Traceable fixed expenses	141,000	50,000	91,000
Segment margin	84,000	$ 70,000	$ 14,000
Common fixed expenses..................	59,000		
Net operating income.....................	$ 25,000		

Required:

1. Compute the companywide break-even point dollar in sales.
2. Compute the break-even point in dollar sales for the East region.
3. Compute the break-even point in dollar sales for the West region.
4. Prepare a new segmented income statement based on the break-even dollar sales that you computed in requirements 2 and 3. Use the same format as shown above. What is Crossfire's net operating income in your new segmented income statement?
5. Do you think that Crossfire should allocate its common fixed expenses to the East and West regions when computing the break-even points for each region? Why?

EXERCISE 5–11 Segmented Income Statement [LO 5–4]

Wingate Company, a wholesale distributor of electronic equipment, has been experiencing losses for some time, as shown by its most recent monthly contribution format income statement, which follows:

Sales.......................................	$1,000,000
Variable expenses	390,000
Contribution margin.......................	610,000
Fixed expenses............................	625,000
Net operating income (loss)...............	$ (15,000)

In an effort to isolate the problem, the president has asked for an income statement segmented by division. Accordingly, the Accounting Department has developed the following information:

	Division		
	East	Central	West
Sales......................................	$250,000	$400,000	$350,000
Variable expenses as a percentage of sales...............................	52%	30%	40%
Traceable fixed expenses................	$160,000	$200,000	$175,000

Required:

1. Prepare a contribution format income statement segmented by divisions, as desired by the president.
2. As a result of a marketing study, the president believes that sales in the West Division could be increased by 20% if monthly advertising in that division were increased by $15,000. Would you recommend the increased advertising? Show computations to support your answer.

EXERCISE 5–12 Variable Costing Income Statement; Reconciliation [LO 5–2, LO 5–3]

Whitman Company has just completed its first year of operations. The company's absorption costing income statement for the year appears below:

Whitman Company Income Statement	
Sales (35,000 units × $25 per unit)	$875,000
Cost of goods sold (35,000 units × $16 per unit).................	560,000
Gross margin	315,000
Selling and administrative expenses..........................	280,000
Net operating income..	$ 35,000

The company's selling and administrative expenses consist of $210,000 per year in fixed expenses and $2 per unit sold in variable expenses. The $16 per unit product cost given above is computed as follows:

Direct materials...	$5
Direct labor..	6
Variable manufacturing overhead...............................	1
Fixed manufacturing overhead ($160,000 ÷ 40,000 units).........	4
Absorption costing unit product cost...........................	$16

Required:

1. Redo the company's income statement in the contribution format using variable costing.
2. Reconcile any difference between the net operating income on your variable costing income statement and the net operating income on the absorption costing income statement above.

EXERCISE 5–13 Inferring Costing Method; Unit Product Cost [LO 5–1]

Sierra Company incurs the following costs to produce and sell a single product.

Variable costs per unit:	
Direct materials	$9
Direct labor..	$10
Variable manufacturing overhead	$5
Variable selling and administrative expenses	$3
Fixed costs per year:	
Fixed manufacturing overhead.....................	$150,000
Fixed selling and administrative expenses...........	$400,000

During the last year, 25,000 units were produced and 22,000 units were sold. The Finished Goods inventory account at the end of the year shows a balance of $72,000 for the 3,000 unsold units.

Required:

1. Is the company using absorption costing or variable costing to cost units in the Finished Goods inventory account? Show computations to support your answer.
2. Assume that the company wishes to prepare financial statements for the year to issue to its stockholders.
   a. Is the $72,000 figure for Finished Goods inventory the correct amount to use on these statements for external reporting purposes? Explain.
   b. At what dollar amount *should* the 3,000 units be carried in the inventory for external reporting purposes?

EXERCISE 5–14 Variable Costing Unit Product Cost and Income Statement; Break-Even [LO 5–1, LO 5–2]

Chuck Wagon Grills, Inc., makes a single product—a handmade specialty barbecue grill that it sells for $210. Data for last year's operations follow:

Units in beginning inventory	0
Units produced	20,000
Units sold	19,000
Units in ending inventory	1,000
Variable costs per unit:	
Direct materials	$ 50
Direct labor...............................	80
Variable manufacturing overhead	20
Variable selling and administrative..........	10
Total variable cost per unit.................	$160
Fixed costs:	
Fixed manufacturing overhead.............	$700,000
Fixed selling and administrative	285,000
Total fixed costs...........................	$985,000

Required:

1. Assume that the company uses variable costing. Compute the unit product cost for one barbecue grill.
2. Assume that the company uses variable costing. Prepare a contribution format income statement for the year.
3. What is the company's break-even point in terms of the number of barbecue grills sold?

EXERCISE 5–15 Absorption Costing Unit Product Cost and Income Statement [LO 5–1, LO 5–2]
Refer to the data in Exercise 5–14 for Chuck Wagon Grills. Assume in this exercise that the company uses absorption costing.

Required:

1. Compute the unit product cost for one barbecue grill.
2. Prepare an income statement.

EXERCISE 5–16 Working with a Segmented Income Statement; Break-Even Analysis [LO 5–4, LO 5–5]
Raner, Harris, & Chan is a consulting firm that specializes in information systems for medical and dental clinics. The firm has two offices—one in Chicago and one in Minneapolis. The firm classifies the direct costs of consulting jobs as variable costs. A contribution format segmented income statement for the company's most recent year is given below:

	Total Company		Office			
			Chicago		Minneapolis	
Sales..........................	$450,000	100%	$150,000	100%	$300,000	100%
Variable expenses	225,000	50%	45,000	30	180,000	60
Contribution margin	225,000	50%	105,000	70	120,000	40
Traceable fixed expenses	126,000	28%	78,000	52	48,000	16
Office segment margin..........	99,000	22%	$ 27,000	18%	$ 72,000	24%
Common fixed expenses not traceable to offices	63,000	14%				
Net operating income...........	$ 36,000	8%				

Required:

1. Compute the companywide break-even point in dollar sales. Also, compute the break-even point for the Chicago office and for the Minneapolis office. Is the companywide break-even point greater than, less than, or equal to the sum of the Chicago and Minneapolis break-even points? Why?
2. By how much would the company's net operating income increase if Minneapolis increased its sales by $75,000 per year? Assume no change in cost behavior patterns.
3. Refer to the original data. Assume that sales in Chicago increase by $50,000 next year and that sales in Minneapolis remain unchanged. Assume no change in fixed costs.
   a. Prepare a new segmented income statement for the company using the above format. Show both amounts and percentages.
   b. Observe from the income statement you have prepared that the contribution margin ratio for Chicago has remained unchanged at 70% (the same as in the above data) but that the segment margin ratio has changed. How do you explain the change in the segment margin ratio?

EXERCISE 5–17 Working with a Segmented Income Statement [LO 5–4]
Refer to the data in Exercise 5–16. Assume that Minneapolis' sales by major market are:

The company would like to initiate an intensive advertising campaign in one of the two market segments during the next month. The campaign would cost $5,000. Marketing studies indicate that such a campaign would increase sales in the Medical market by $40,000 or increase sales in the Dental market by $35,000.

	Minneapolis		Market			
			Medical		Dental	
Sales	$300,000	100%	$200,000	100%	$100,000	100%
Variable expenses...........	180,000	60%	128,000	64%	52,000	52%
Contribution margin	120,000	40%	72,000	36%	48,000	48%
Traceable fixed expenses	33,000	11%	12,000	6%	21,000	21%
Market segment margin.......	87,000	29%	$ 60,000	30%	$ 27,000	27%
Common fixed expenses not traceable to markets	15,000	5%				
Office segment margin........	$ 72,000	24%				

Required:

1. In which of the markets would you recommend that the company focus its advertising campaign? Show computations to support your answer.
2. In Exercise 5–16, Minneapolis shows $48,000 in traceable fixed expenses. What happened to the $48,000 in this exercise?

Problems Additional student resources are available with Connect.

PROBLEM 5–18 Variable and Absorption Costing Unit Product Costs and Income Statements [LO 5–1, LO 5–2]

Haas Company manufactures and sells one product. The following information pertains to each of the company's first three years of operations:

Variable costs per unit:	
Manufacturing:	
Direct materials	$20
Direct labor	$12
Variable manufacturing overhead	$4
Variable selling and administrative.................	$2
Fixed costs per year:	
Fixed manufacturing overhead....................	$960,000
Fixed selling and administrative expenses	$240,000

During its first year of operations, Haas produced 60,000 units and sold 60,000 units. During its second year of operations, it produced 75,000 units and sold 50,000 units. In its third year, Haas produced 40,000 units and sold 65,000 units. The selling price of the company's product is $58 per unit.

Required:

1. Compute the company's break-even point in units sold.
2. Assume the company uses variable costing:
   a. Compute the unit product cost for Year 1, Year 2, and Year 3.
   b. Prepare an income statement for Year 1, Year 2, and Year 3.
3. Assume the company uses absorption costing:
   a. Compute the unit product cost for Year 1, Year 2, and Year 3.
   b. Prepare an income statement for Year 1, Year 2, and Year 3.
4. Compare the net operating income figures that you computed in requirements 2 and 3 to the break-even point that you computed in requirement 1. Which net operating income figures seem counterintuitive? Why?

PROBLEM 5–19 Variable Costing Income Statement; Reconciliation [LO 5–2, LO 5–3]

During Heaton Company's first two years of operations, the company reported absorption costing net operating income as follows:

	Year 1	Year 2
Sales (@ $25 per unit)......................	$1,000,000	$1,250,000
Cost of goods sold (@ $18 per unit)..........	720,000	900,000
Gross margin	280,000	350,000
Selling and administrative expenses*.........	210,000	230,000
Net operating income........................	$ 70,000	$ 120,000

*$2 per unit variable; $130,000 fixed each year.

The company's $18 unit product cost is computed as follows:

Direct materials	$ 4
Direct labor...	7
Variable manufacturing overhead	1
Fixed manufacturing overhead ($270,000 ÷ 45,000 units)......	6
Absorption costing unit product cost.......................	$18

Forty percent of fixed manufacturing overhead consists of wages and salaries; the remainder consists of depreciation charges on production equipment and buildings.
   Production and cost data for the two years are:

	Year 1	Year 2
Units produced	45,000	45,000
Units sold	40,000	50,000

Required:
1. Prepare a variable costing contribution format income statement for each year.
2. Reconcile the absorption costing and the variable costing net operating income figures for each year.

PROBLEM 5–20 Variable and Absorption Costing Unit Product Costs and Income Statements; Explanation of Difference in Net Operating Income [LO 5–1, LO 5–2, LO 5–3]

High Country, Inc., produces and sells many recreational products. The company has just opened a new plant to produce a folding camp cot that will be marketed throughout the United States. The following cost and revenue data relate to May, the first month of the plant's operation:

Beginning inventory	0
Units produced	10,000
Units sold	8,000
Selling price per unit..............................	$75
Selling and administrative expenses:	
Variable per unit	$6
Fixed (per month)	$200,000
Manufacturing costs:	
Direct materials cost per unit	$20
Direct labor cost per unit........................	$8
Variable manufacturing overhead cost per unit.......	$2
Fixed manufacturing overhead cost (per month)......	$100,000

Management is anxious to see how profitable the new camp cot will be and has asked that an income statement be prepared for May.

Required:
1. Assume that the company uses absorption costing.
   a. Determine the unit product cost.
   b. Prepare an income statement for May.

208

Chapter 5

2. Assume that the company uses variable costing.
   a. Determine the unit product cost.
   b. Prepare a contribution format income statement for May.
3. Explain the reason for any difference in the ending inventory balances under the two costing methods and the impact of this difference on reported net operating income.

PROBLEM 5–21 Segment Reporting and Decision-Making [LO 5–4]
Vulcan Company's contribution format income statement for June is given below:

Vulcan Company Income Statement For the Month Ended June 30	
Sales..........................	$750,000
Variable expenses	336,000
Contribution margin.............	414,000
Fixed expenses..................	378,000
Net operating income...........	$ 36,000

Management is disappointed with the company's performance and is wondering what can be done to improve profits. By examining sales and cost records, you have determined the following:

a. The company is divided into two sales territories—Northern and Southern. The Northern territory recorded $300,000 in sales and $156,000 in variable expenses during June; the remaining sales and variable expenses were recorded in the Southern territory. Fixed expenses of $120,000 and $108,000 are traceable to the Northern and Southern territories, respectively. The rest of the fixed expenses are common to the two territories.

b. The company is the exclusive distributor for two products—Paks and Tibs. Sales of Paks and Tibs totaled $50,000 and $250,000, respectively, in the Northern territory during June. Variable expenses are 22% of the selling price for Paks and 58% for Tibs. Cost records show that $30,000 of the Northern territory's fixed expenses are traceable to Paks and $40,000 to Tibs, with the remainder common to the two products.

Required:
1. Prepare contribution format segmented income statements first showing the total company broken down between sales territories and then showing the Northern territory broken down by product line. In addition, for the company as a whole and for each segment, show each item on the segmented income statements as a percent of sales.
2. Look at the statement you have prepared showing the total company segmented by sales territory. What insights revealed by this statement should be brought to the attention of management?
3. Look at the statement you have prepared showing the Northern territory segmented by product lines. What insights revealed by this statement should be brought to the attention of management?

PROBLEM 5–22 Prepare and Reconcile Variable Costing Statements [LO 5–1, LO 5–2, LO 5–3]
Denton Company manufactures and sells a single product. Cost data for the product are given below:

Variable costs per unit:	
Direct materials	$ 7
Direct labor..............................	10
Variable manufacturing overhead	5
Variable selling and administrative.........	3
Total variable costs per unit..............	$25
Fixed costs per month:	
Fixed manufacturing overhead.............	$315,000
Fixed selling and administrative...........	245,000
Total fixed cost per month	$560,000

The product sells for $60 per unit. Production and sales data for July and August, the first two months of operations, follow:

	Units Produced	Units Sold
July...................	17,500	15,000
August...............	17,500	20,000

The company's Accounting Department has prepared absorption costing income statements for July and August as presented below:

	May	June
Sales	$900,000	$1,200,000
Cost of goods sold	600,000	800,000
Gross margin	300,000	400,000
Selling and administrative expenses	290,000	305,000
Net operating income....................	$ 10,000	$ 95,000

Required:
1. Determine the unit product cost under:
    a. Absorption costing.
    b. Variable costing.
2. Prepare contribution format variable costing income statements for July and August.
3. Reconcile the variable costing and absorption costing net operating income figures.
4. The company's Accounting Department has determined the company's break-even point to be 16,000 units per month, computed as follows:

$$\frac{\text{Fixed cost per month}}{\text{Unit contribution margin}} = \frac{\$560,000}{\$35 \text{ per unit}} = 16,000 \text{ units}$$

"I'm confused," said the president. "The accounting people say that our break-even point is 16,000 units per month, but we sold only 15,000 units in July, and the income statement they prepared shows a $10,000 profit for that month. Either the income statement is wrong or the break-even point is wrong." Prepare a brief memo for the president, explaining what happened on the July absorption costing income statement.

PROBLEM 5–23 Absorption and Variable Costing; Production Constant, Sales Fluctuate [LO 5–1, LO 5–2, LO 5–3]

Tami Tyler opened Tami's Creations, Inc., a small manufacturing company, at the beginning of the year. Getting the company through its first quarter of operations placed a considerable strain on Ms. Tyler's personal finances. The following income statement for the first quarter was prepared by a friend who has just completed a course in managerial accounting at State University.

Tami's Creations, Inc. Income Statement For the Quarter Ended March 31		
Sales (28,000 units)		$1,120,000
Variable expenses:		
Variable cost of goods sold...................	$462,000	
Variable selling and administrative.............	168,000	630,000
Contribution margin		490,000
Fixed expenses:		
Fixed manufacturing overhead................	300,000	
Fixed selling and administrative	200,000	500,000
Net operating loss		$ (10,000)

Ms. Tyler is discouraged over the loss shown for the quarter, particularly because she had planned to use the statement as support for a bank loan. Another friend, a CPA, insists that the company should be using absorption costing rather than variable costing and argues that if absorption costing had been used the company probably would have reported at least some profit for the quarter.

At this point, Ms. Tyler is manufacturing only one product, a swimsuit. Production and cost data relating to the swimsuit for the first quarter follow:

Units produced	30,000
Units sold	28,000
Variable costs per unit:	
Direct materials	$3.50
Direct labor	$12.80
Variable manufacturing overhead	$1.00
Variable selling and administrative	$6.00

Required:
1. Complete the following:
   a. Compute the unit product cost under absorption costing.
   b. Redo the company's income statement for the quarter using absorption costing.
   c. Reconcile the variable and absorption costing net operating income (loss) figures.
2. Was the CPA correct in suggesting that the company really earned a "profit" for the quarter? Explain.
3. During the second quarter of operations, the company again produced 30,000 units but sold 32,000 units. (Assume no change in total fixed costs.)
   a. Prepare a contribution format income statement for the quarter using variable costing.
   b. Prepare an income statement for the quarter using absorption costing.
   c. Reconcile the variable costing and absorption costing net operating incomes.

PROBLEM 5–24 Companywide and Segment Break-Even Analysis; Decision Making [LO 5–4, LO 5–5]
Toxaway Company is a merchandiser that segments its business into two divisions—Commercial and Residential. The company's accounting intern was asked to prepare segmented income statements that the company's divisional managers could use to calculate their break-even points and make decisions. She took the prior month's companywide income statement and prepared the absorption format segmented income statement shown below:

	Total Company	Commercial	Residential
Sales	$750,000	$250,000	$500,000
Cost of goods sold	500,000	140,000	360,000
Gross margin	250,000	110,000	140,000
Selling and administrative expenses	240,000	104,000	136,000
Net operating income	$ 10,000	$ 6,000	$ 4,000

In preparing these statements, the intern determined that Toxaway's only variable selling and administrative expense is a 10% sales commission on all sales. The company's total fixed expenses include $72,000 of common fixed expenses that would continue to be incurred even if the Commercial or Residential segments are discontinued, $38,000 of fixed expenses that would be avoided if the Residential segment is dropped, and $55,000 of fixed expenses that would be avoided if the Commericial segment is dropped.

Required:
1. Do you agree with the intern's decision to use an absorption format for her segmented income statement? Why?

2. Based on the intern's segmented income statement, can you determine how she allocated the company's common fixed expenses to the Commercial and Residential segments? Do you agree with her decision to allocate the common fixed expenses to the Commercial and Residential segments?

3. Redo the intern's segmented income statement using the contribution format.

4. Compute the companywide break-even point in dollar sales.

5. Compute the break-even point in dollar sales for the Commercial Division and for the Residential Division.

6. Assume the company decided to pay its sales representatives in the Commercial and Residential Divisions a total monthly salary of $15,000 and $30,000, respectively, and to lower its companywide sales commission percentage from 10% to 5%. Calculate the new break-even point in dollar sales for the Commercial Division and the Residential Division.

PROBLEM 5–25 Prepare and Interpret Income Statements; Changes in Both Sales and Production; Lean Production [LO 5–1, LO 5–2, LO 5–3]

Starfax, Inc., manufactures a small part that is widely used in various electronic products such as home computers. Operating results for the first three years of activity were as follows (absorption costing basis):

	Year 1	Year 2	Year 3
Sales.....................................	$800,000	$640,000	$800,000
Cost of goods sold	580,000	400,000	620,000
Gross margin..................................	220,000	240,000	180,000
Selling and administrative expenses	190,000	180,000	190,000
Net operating income (loss)	$ 30,000	$ 60,000	$ (10,000)

In the latter part of Year 2, a competitor went out of business and in the process dumped a large number of units on the market. As a result, Starfax's sales dropped by 20% during Year 2 even though production increased during the year. Management had expected sales to remain constant at 50,000 units; the increased production was designed to provide the company with a buffer of protection against unexpected spurts in demand. By the start of Year 3, management could see that inventory was excessive and that spurts in demand were unlikely. To reduce the excessive inventories, Starfax cut back production during Year 3, as shown below:

	Year 1	Year 2	Year 3
Production in units	50,000	60,000	40,000
Sales in units	50,000	40,000	50,000

Additional information about the company follows:

a. The company's plant is highly automated. Variable manufacturing expenses (direct materials, direct labor, and variable manufacturing overhead) total only $2 per unit, and fixed manufacturing overhead expenses total $480,000 per year.

b. Fixed manufacturing overhead costs are applied to units of product on the basis of each year's production. That is, a new fixed manufacturing overhead rate is computed each year.

c. Variable selling and administrative expenses were $1 per unit sold in each year. Fixed selling and administrative expenses totaled $140,000 per year.

d. The company uses a FIFO inventory flow assumption.

Starfax's management can't understand why profits doubled during Year 2 when sales dropped by 20% and why a loss was incurred during Year 3 when sales recovered to previous levels.

Required:
1. Prepare a contribution format variable costing income statement for each year.
2. Refer to the absorption costing income statements above.
   a. Compute the unit product cost in each year under absorption costing. (Show how much of this cost is variable and how much is fixed.)
   b. Reconcile the variable costing and absorption costing net operating income figures for each year.
3. Refer again to the absorption costing income statements. Explain why net operating income was higher in Year 2 than it was in Year 1 under the absorption approach, in light of the fact that fewer units were sold in Year 2 than in Year 1.
4. Refer again to the absorption costing income statements. Explain why the company suffered a loss in Year 3 but reported a profit in Year 1 although the same number of units was sold in each year.
5. a. Explain how operations would have differed in Year 2 and Year 3 if the company had been using Lean Production, with the result that ending inventory was zero.
   b. If Lean Production had been used during Year 2 and Year 3 and the predetermined over-head rate is based on 50,000 units per year, what would the company's net operating income (or loss) have been in each year under absorption costing? Explain the reason for any differences between these income figures and the figures reported by the company in the statements above.

PROBLEM 5–26 Restructuring a Segmented Income Statement [LO 5–4]
Losses have been incurred at Millard Corporation for some time. In an effort to isolate the problem and improve the company's performance, management has requested that the monthly income statement be segmented by sales region. The company's first effort at preparing a segmented statement is given below. This statement is for May, the most recent month of activity.

	Sales Region		
	West	Central	East
Sales	$450,000	$800,000	$ 750,000
Regional expenses (traceable):			
Cost of goods sold	162,900	280,000	376,500
Advertising.....................................	108,000	200,000	210,000
Salaries..	90,000	88,000	135,000
Utilities	13,500	12,000	15,000
Depreciation..................................	27,000	28,000	30,000
Shipping expense............................	17,100	32,000	28,500
Total regional expenses......................	418,500	640,000	795,000
Regional income (loss)			
before corporate expenses..................	31,500	160,000	(45,000)
Corporate expenses:			
Advertising (general)..........................	18,000	32,000	30,000
General administrative expense..............	50,000	50,000	50,000
Total corporate expenses	68,000	82,000	80,000
Net operating income (loss)	$ (36,500)	$ 78,000	$(125,000)

Cost of goods sold and shipping expense are both variable; other costs are all fixed.

Millard Corporation is a wholesale distributor of office products. It purchases office products from manufacturers and distributes them in the three regions given above. The three regions are about the same size, and each has its own manager and sales staff. The products that the company distributes vary widely in profitability.

Required:

1. List any disadvantages or weaknesses that you see to the statement format illustrated on the previous page.
2. Explain the basis that is apparently being used to allocate the corporate expenses to the regions. Do you agree with these allocations? Explain.
3. Prepare a new contribution format segmented income statement for May. Show a Total column as well as data for each region. In addition, for the company as a whole and for each sales region, show each item on the segmented income statement as a percent of sales.
4. Analyze the statement that you prepared in requirement 3. What points that might help to improve the company's performance would you bring to management's attention?

PROBLEM 5–27 Incentives Created by Absorption Costing; Ethics and the Manager [LO 5–2]

Carlos Cavalas, the manager of Echo Products' Brazilian Division, is trying to set the production schedule for the last quarter of the year. The Brazilian Division had planned to sell 3,600 units during the year, but by September 30 only the following activity had been reported:

	Units
Inventory, January 1	0
Production.	2,400
Sales.	2,000
Inventory, September 30	400

The division can rent warehouse space to store up to 1,000 units. The minimum inventory level that the division should carry is 50 units. Mr. Cavalas is aware that production must be at least 200 units per quarter in order to retain a nucleus of key employees. Maximum production capacity is 1,500 units per quarter.

Demand has been soft, and the sales forecast for the last quarter is only 600 units. Due to the nature of the division's operations, fixed manufacturing overhead is a major element of product cost.

Required:

1. Assume that the division is using variable costing. How many units should be scheduled for production during the last quarter of the year? (The basic formula for computing the required production for a period in a company is: Expected sales + Desired ending inventory − Beginning inventory = Required production.) Show computations and explain your answer. Will the number of units scheduled for production affect the division's reported income or loss for the year? Explain.
2. Assume that the division is using absorption costing and that the divisional manager is given an annual bonus based on divisional operating income. If Mr. Cavalas wants to maximize his division's operating income for the year, how many units should be scheduled for production during the last quarter? [See the formula in requirement 1.] Explain.
3. Identify the ethical issues involved in the decision Mr. Cavalas must make about the level of production for the last quarter of the year.

PROBLEM 5–28 Basic Segment Reporting; Activity-Based Cost Assignment [LO 5–4]

Diversified Products, Inc., has recently acquired a small publishing company that offers three books for sale—a cookbook, a travel guide, and a handy speller. Each book sells for $10. The publishing company's most recent monthly income statement follows.

The following additional information is available about the company:

a. Only printing costs and sales commissions are variable; all other costs are fixed. The printing costs (which include materials, labor, and variable overhead) are traceable to the three product lines as shown in the statement above. Sales commissions are 10% of sales for any product.
b. The same equipment is used to produce all three books, so the equipment depreciation cost has been allocated equally among the three product lines. An analysis of the company's activities indicates that the equipment is used 30% of the time to produce cookbooks, 50% of the time to produce travel guides, and 20% of the time to produce handy spellers.

			Product Line	
	Total Company	Cookbook	Travel Guide	Handy Speller
Sales	$300,000	$90,000	$150,000	$60,000
Expenses:				
Printing costs.................	102,000	27,000	63,000	12,000
Advertising....................	36,000	13,500	19,500	3,000
General sales.................	18,000	5,400	9,000	3,600
Salaries......................	33,000	18,000	9,000	6,000
Equipment depreciation.........	9,000	3,000	3,000	3,000
Sales commissions	30,000	9,000	15,000	6,000
General administration..........	42,000	14,000	14,000	14,000
Warehouse rent................	12,000	3,600	6,000	2,400
Depreciation—office facilities	3,000	1,000	1,000	1,000
Total expenses..................	285,000	94,500	139,500	51,000
Net operating income (loss).........	$ 15,000	$ (4,500)	$ 10,500	$ 9,000

c.   The warehouse is used to store finished units of product, so the rental cost has been allocated to the product lines on the basis of sales dollars. The warehouse rental cost is $3 per square foot per year. The warehouse contains 48,000 square feet of space, of which 7,200 square feet is used by the cookbook line, 24,000 square feet by the travel guide line, and 16,800 square feet by the handy speller line.

d.   The general sales cost above includes the salary of the sales manager and other sales costs not traceable to any specific product line. This cost has been allocated to the product lines on the basis of sales dollars.

e.   The general administration cost and depreciation of office facilities both relate to administration of the company as a whole. These costs have been allocated equally to the three product lines.

f.   All other costs are traceable to the three product lines in the amounts shown on the statement above.

The management of Diversified Products, Inc., is anxious to improve the publishing company's 5% return on sales.

Required:

1.   Prepare a new contribution format segmented income statement for the month. Adjust allocations of equipment depreciation and of warehouse rent as indicated by the additional information provided.

2.   After seeing the income statement in the main body of the problem, management has decided to eliminate the cookbook because it is not returning a profit, and to focus all available resources on promoting the travel guide.

   a.   Based on the statement you have prepared, do you agree with the decision to eliminate the cookbook? Explain.

   b.   Based on the statement you have prepared, do you agree with the decision to focus all available resources on promoting the travel guide? Assume that an ample market is available for all three product lines. (*Hint:* Compute the contribution margin ratio for each product.)

Cases   📘**connect**   Additional student resources are available with Connect.

CASE 5–29 Variable and Absorption Costing Unit Product Costs and Income Statements [LO 5–1, LO 5–2]
O'Brien Company manufactures and sells one product. The following information pertains to each of the company's first three years of operations:

Variable costs per unit:	
Manufacturing	
Direct materials	$32
Direct labor	$20
Variable manufacturing overhead	$4
Variable selling and administrative.	$3
Fixed costs per year:	
Fixed manufacturing overhead.	$660,000
Fixed selling and administrative expenses.	$120,000

During its first year of operations, O'Brien produced 100,000 units and sold 80,000 units. During its second year of operations, it produced 75,000 units and sold 90,000 units. In its third year, O'Brien produced 80,000 units and sold 75,000 units. The selling price of the company's product is $75 per unit.

Required:

1. Assume the company uses variable costing and a FIFO inventory flow assumption (FIFO means first-in first-out. In other words, it assumes that the oldest units in inventory are sold first):
   a. Compute the unit product cost for Year 1, Year 2, and Year 3.
   b. Prepare an income statement for Year 1, Year 2, and Year 3.
2. Assume the company uses variable costing and a LIFO inventory flow assumption (LIFO means last-in first-out. In other words, it assumes that the newest units in inventory are sold first):
   a. Compute the unit product cost for Year 1, Year 2, and Year 3.
   b. Prepare an income statement for Year 1, Year 2, and Year 3.
3. Assume the company uses absorption costing and a FIFO inventory flow assumption (FIFO means first-in first-out. In other words, it assumes that the oldest units in inventory are sold first):
   a. Compute the unit product cost for Year 1, Year 2, and Year 3.
   b. Prepare an income statement for Year 1, Year 2, and Year 3.
4. Assume the company uses absorption costing and a LIFO inventory flow assumption (LIFO means last-in first-out. In other words, it assumes that the newest units in inventory are sold first):
   a. Compute the unit product cost for Year 1, Year 2, and Year 3.
   b. Prepare an income statement for Year 1, Year 2, and Year 3.

CASE 5–30 Service Organization; Segment Reporting [LO 5–4]

Music Teachers, Inc., is an educational association for music teachers that has 20,000 members. The association operates from a central headquarters but has local membership chapters throughout the United States. Monthly meetings are held by the local chapters to discuss recent developments on topics of interest to music teachers. The association's journal, Teachers' Forum, is issued monthly with features about recent developments in the field. The association publishes books and reports and also sponsors professional courses that qualify for continuing professional education credit. The association's statement of revenues and expenses for the current year is presented below.

Music Teachers, Inc. Statement of Revenues and Expenses For the Year Ended November 30	
Revenues	$3,275,000
Expenses:	
Salaries.	920,000
Personnel costs	230,000
Occupancy costs	280,000
Reimbursement of member costs to local chapters . . .	600,000
Other membership services.	500,000
Printing and paper	320,000
Postage and shipping.	176,000
Instructors' fees	80,000
General and administrative	38,000
Total expenses	3,144,000
Excess of revenues over expenses.	$ 131,000

The board of directors of Music Teachers, Inc., has requested that a segmented income statement be prepared showing the contribution of each segment to the association. The association has four segments: Membership Division, Magazine Subscriptions Division, Books and Reports Division, and Continuing Education Division. Mike Doyle has been assigned responsibility for preparing the segmented income statement, and he has gathered the following data prior to its preparation.

a. Membership dues are $100 per year, of which $20 is considered to cover a one-year subscription to the association's journal. Other benefits include membership in the association and chapter affiliation. The portion of the dues covering the magazine subscription ($20) should be assigned to the Magazine Subscription Division.

b. One-year subscriptions to Teachers' Forum were sold to nonmembers and libraries at $30 per subscription. A total of 2,500 of these subscriptions were sold last year. In addition to subscriptions, the magazine generated $100,000 in advertising revenues. The costs per magazine subscription were $7 for printing and paper and $4 for postage and shipping.

c. A total of 28,000 technical reports and professional texts were sold by the Books and Reports Division at an average unit selling price of $25. Average costs per publication were $4 for printing and paper and $2 for postage and shipping.

d. The association offers a variety of continuing education courses to both members and nonmembers. The one-day courses had a tuition cost of $75 each and were attended by 2,400 students. A total of 1,760 students took two-day courses at a tuition cost of $125 for each student. Outside instructors were paid to teach some courses.

e. Salary costs and space occupied by division follow:

	Salaries	Space Occupied (square feet)
Membership	$210,000	2,000
Magazine Subscriptions	150,000	2,000
Books and Reports	300,000	3,000
Continuing Education	180,000	2,000
Corporate staff	80,000	1,000
Total	$920,000	10,000

Personnel costs are 25% of salaries in the separate divisions as well as for the corporate staff. The $280,000 in occupancy costs includes $50,000 in rental cost for a warehouse used by the Books and Reports Division for storage purposes.

f. Printing and paper costs other than for magazine subscriptions and for books and reports relate to the Continuing Education Division.

g. General and administrative expenses include costs relating to overall administration of the association as a whole. The company's corporate staff does some mailing of materials for general administrative purposes.

The expenses that can be traced or assigned to the corporate staff, as well as any other expenses that are not traceable to the segments, will be treated as common costs. It is not necessary to distinguish between variable and fixed costs.

Required:

1. Prepare a contribution format segmented income statement for Music Teachers, Inc. This statement should show the segment margin for each division as well as results for the association as a whole.

2. Give arguments for and against allocating all costs of the association to the four divisions.

(CMA, adapted)

Appendix 5A: Super-Variable Costing

In the discussion of variable costing in this chapter we have assumed that direct labor and a portion of manufacturing overhead are variable costs that should be attached to products. However, these assumptions about cost behavior may not be true. For example, it may be easier and more accurate to assume that *all* manufacturing overhead costs are fixed costs because the variable portion of these costs is insignificant or too difficult to estimate. Furthermore, many companies' labor costs (including direct and indirect labor) are more fixed than variable due to labor regulations, labor contracts, or management policy. In countries such as France, Germany, Spain, and Japan, management often has little flexibility in adjusting the labor force to changes in business activity. Even in countries such as the United States and the United Kingdom, where management usually has greater latitude to adjust the size of its labor force, many managers choose to view labor as a fixed cost. They make this choice because the cost savings from terminating or laying off employees during a short-term business downturn may be swamped by the negative effects on employee morale and by the costs of later finding and training suitable replacements. Moreover, treating employees as variable costs subtly fosters the attitude that employees are expendable and replaceable like materials rather than unique, difficult-to-replace assets.

Super-variable costing is a variation on variable costing in which direct labor and manufacturing overhead costs are considered to be fixed. **Super-variable costing** classifies all direct labor and manufacturing overhead costs as fixed period costs and *only direct materials as a variable product cost.* To simplify, in this appendix we also assume that selling and administrative expenses are entirely fixed.

LEARNING OBJECTIVE 5–6
Prepare an income statement using super-variable costing and reconcile this approach with variable costing.

Super–Variable Costing and Variable Costing—An Example

To illustrate the difference between treating direct labor as a fixed cost (as in super-variable costing) and treating direct labor as a variable cost (as in variable costing), we will use a modified version of the Weber Light Aircraft example from the main body of the chapter. Data concerning the company's operations appear below:

	Per Aircraft	Per Month
Selling price	$100,000	
Direct materials	$19,000	
Direct labor		$20,000
Fixed manufacturing overhead		$74,000
Fixed selling and administrative expense		$40,000

	January	February	March
Beginning inventory	0	0	1
Units produced	2	2	2
Units sold	2	1	3
Ending inventory	0	1	0

The key thing to notice here is that direct labor is a fixed cost—$20,000 per month. Also, notice that Weber Light Aircraft has no variable manufacturing overhead costs and no variable selling and administrative expenses. For the months of January, February, and March, the company's selling price per aircraft, variable cost per aircraft, monthly production in units, and total monthly fixed expenses never change. The only thing that changes in this example is the number of units sold (January = 2 units sold; February = 1 unit sold; March = 3 units sold).

We will first construct the company's super-variable costing income statements for January, February, and March. Then we will show how the company's net operating income would be determined for the same months using variable costing if it were incorrectly assumed that direct labor is a variable cost. As you'll see, both income statements rely on the contribution format.

Super–Variable Costing Income Statements

To prepare the company's super-variable costing income statements for each month we follow four steps. First, we compute sales by multiplying the number of units sold by the selling price per unit, which in this example is $100,000 per unit. Second, we compute the variable cost of goods sold by multiplying the number of units sold by the unit product cost, which in this example is the direct materials cost of $19,000 per unit. Third, we compute the contribution margin by subtracting the variable cost of goods sold from sales. Fourth, we compute net operating income by subtracting all fixed expenses from the contribution margin.

Using these four steps, Weber's super-variable costing income statements for each month would appear as shown in Exhibit 5A–1. Notice that the only variable expense is variable cost of goods sold, which is the $19,000 of direct materials per unit sold. For example, in March, the unit product cost of $19,000 is multiplied by three units sold to obtain the variable cost of goods sold of $57,000. The total monthly fixed manufacturing expenses of $94,000 include $20,000 of direct labor and $74,000 of fixed manufacturing overhead.

EXHIBIT 5A–1
Super-Variable Costing Income Statements

	January	February	March
Sales (@ $100,000 per unit)............	$200,000	$100,000	$300,000
Variable cost of goods sold (@ $19,000 per unit)	38,000	19,000	57,000
Contribution margin	162,000	81,000	243,000
Fixed expenses:			
Fixed manufacturing expenses......	94,000	94,000	94,000
Fixed selling and administrative expenses	40,000	40,000	40,000
Total fixed expenses.................	134,000	134,000	134,000
Net operating income (loss)...........	$ 28,000	$ (53,000)	$109,000

Variable Costing Income Statements

The variable costing income statements in this example differ from the super-variable costing income statements in one important respect—we will assume that direct labor is incorrectly classified as a variable cost and is included in unit product costs. Because the monthly direct labor cost is $20,000 and two aircraft are produced each month, if direct labor costs are included in unit product costs, then Weber Light Aircraft will assign $10,000 of direct labor cost to each aircraft that it produces. Thus, the company's unit product costs under variable costing would be computed as follows:

	January	February	March
Direct materials	$19,000	$19,000	$19,000
Direct labor...............	10,000	10,000	10,000
Unit product cost..........	$29,000	$29,000	$29,000

Given these unit product cost figures, the company's variable costing income statements would be computed as shown in Exhibit 5A–2. For example, in March, the unit product cost of $29,000 is multiplied by three units sold to obtain the variable cost of goods sold of $87,000. The total fixed manufacturing overhead of $74,000 and total fixed selling and administrative expenses of $40,000 are both recorded as period expenses.

	January	February	March	
				EXHIBIT 5A–2
	January	**February**	**March**	Variable Costing Income
Sales (@ $100,000 per unit)............	$200,000	$100,000	$300,000	Statements
Variable cost of goods sold				
(@ $29,000 per unit)...............	58,000	29,000	87,000	
Contribution margin	142,000	71,000	213,000	
Fixed expenses:				
Fixed manufacturing overhead......	74,000	74,000	74,000	
Fixed selling and administrative				
expenses	40,000	40,000	40,000	
Total fixed expenses.................	114,000	114,000	114,000	
Net operating income (loss)...........	$ 28,000	$(43,000)	$ 99,000	

Reconciliation of Super–Variable Costing and Variable Costing Income

The super-variable costing and variable costing net operating incomes are both $28,000 in January. However, in February, the super-variable costing income is $10,000 lower than the variable costing income and the opposite holds true in March. In other words, the super-variable costing income in March is $10,000 higher than the variable costing income.

Why do these two costing methods produce different net operating incomes? The answer can be found in the accounting for direct labor costs. Super-variable costing treats direct labor as a fixed period expense whereas variable costing treats direct labor as a variable product cost. In other words, super-variable costing records the entire direct labor cost of $20,000 as an expense on each month's income statement. Conversely, variable costing assigns $10,000 of direct labor cost to each unit produced. The $10,000 assigned to each unit produced remains in inventory on the balance sheet until the unit is sold—at which point the $10,000 assigned to it is transferred to variable cost of goods sold on the income statement. Given this background, the super-variable costing and variable costing incomes for each month can be reconciled as follows:

	January	February	March
Direct labor cost in ending inventory			
(@ $10,000 per unit)	$ 0	$10,000	$ 0
– Direct labor cost in beginning inventory			
(@ $10,000 per unit)	0	0	10,000
= Direct labor cost deferred in			
(released from) inventory.................	$ 0	$10,000	$(10,000)

	January	February	March
Super-variable costing net			
operating income (loss)...................	$28,000	$(53,000)	$109,000
Direct labor deferred in (released from)			
inventory	0	10,000	(10,000)
Variable costing net operating			
income (loss)	$28,000	$(43,000)	$ 99,000

In January, both costing methods report the same net operating income ($28,000). This occurs because each method expenses $20,000 of direct labor in the income statement. In February, super-variable costing income is $10,000 less than variable costing income. This difference arises because super-variable costing expenses $20,000 of direct labor in the income statement, whereas variable costing expenses only $10,000 of direct labor in the income statement ($10,000 per unit × 1 unit sold) and defers $10,000 of direct labor on the balance sheet ($10,000 per unit × 1 unit produced but not sold). In March, super-variable costing income is $10,000 greater than variable costing income. This difference arises because super-variable costing expenses $20,000 of direct labor on the income statement, whereas variable costing expenses $30,000 of direct labor on the income statement ($10,000 per unit × 3 unit sold). Notice that one of the units sold in March was actually produced in February. Under variable costing, the $10,000 of direct labor attached to the unit produced in February is released from inventory and included in variable cost of goods sold for March.

In summary, the key issue considered in this appendix is how a company treats direct labor costs. If a company treats direct labor as a variable cost, the cost system may encourage managers to treat labor costs as an expense to be minimized when sales decline and this may result in reduced morale and eventual problems when business picks up. Second, in practice management may have little ability to adjust the direct labor force even if they wanted to, resulting in a situation in which direct labor costs are in fact fixed. In either case, treating direct labor costs as variable can lead to bad decisions. The super-variable costing approach overcomes this problem by treating labor costs as fixed costs.

Glossary (Appendix 5A)

Super-variable costing A costing method that classifies all direct labor and manufacturing overhead costs as fixed period costs and *only direct materials as a variable product cost.* (p. 217)

Appendix 5A Exercises and Problems   connect

Additional student resources are available with Connect.

EXERCISE 5A–1 Super-Variable Costing Income Statement [LO 5–6]
Zola Company manufactures and sells one product. The following information pertains to the company's first year of operations:

Variable cost per unit:	
Direct materials.	$18
Fixed costs per year:	
Direct labor	$200,000
Fixed manufacturing overhead	$250,000
Fixed selling and administrative expenses	$80,000

The company does not incur any variable manufacturing overhead costs or variable selling and administrative expenses. During its first year of operations, Zola produced 25,000 units and sold 20,000 units. The selling price of the company's product is $50 per unit.

Required:
1. Assume the company uses super-variable costing:
    a. Compute the unit product cost for the year.
    b. Prepare an income statement for the year.

EXERCISE 5A–2 Super-Variable Costing and Variable Costing Unit Product Costs and Income Statements [LO 5–2, LO 5–6]
Lyons Company manufactures and sells one product. The following information pertains to the company's first year of operations:

Variable cost per unit:	
Direct materials	$13
Fixed costs per year:	
Direct labor.	$750,000
Fixed manufacturing overhead.	$420,000
Fixed selling and administrative expenses.	$110,000

The company does not incur any variable manufacturing overhead costs or variable selling and administrative expenses. During its first year of operations, Lyons produced 60,000 units and sold 52,000 units. The selling price of the company's product is $40 per unit.

Required:

1. Assume the company uses super-variable costing:
   a. Compute the unit product cost for the year.
   b. Prepare an income statement for the year.
2. Assume the company uses a variable costing system that assigns $12.50 of direct labor cost to each unit produced:
   a. Compute the unit product cost for the year.
   b. Prepare an income statement for the year.
3. Prepare a reconciliation that explains the difference between the super-variable costing and variable costing net operating incomes.

EXERCISE 5A–3 Super-Variable Costing and Variable Costing Unit Product Costs and Income Statements [LO 5–2, LO 5–6]

Kelly Company manufactures and sells one product. The following information pertains to each of the company's first two years of operations:

Variable cost per unit:	
Direct materials	$12
Fixed costs per year:	
Direct labor.	$500,000
Fixed manufacturing overhead.	$450,000
Fixed selling and administrative expenses.	$180,000

The company does not incur any variable manufacturing overhead costs or variable selling and administrative expenses. During its first year of operations, Kelly produced 50,000 units and sold 40,000 units. During its second year of operations, it produced 50,000 units and sold 60,000 units. The selling price of the company's product is $50 per unit.

Required:

1. Assume the company uses super-variable costing:
   a. Compute the unit product cost for Year 1 and Year 2.
   b. Prepare an income statement for Year 1 and Year 2.
2. Assume the company uses a variable costing system that assigns $10 of direct labor cost to each unit produced:
   a. Compute the unit product cost for Year 1 and Year 2.
   b. Prepare an income statement for Year 1 and Year 2.
3. Prepare a reconciliation that explains the difference between the super-variable costing and variable costing net operating incomes in Years 1 and 2.

PROBLEM 5A–4 Super-Variable Costing and Variable Costing Unit Product Costs and Income Statements [LO 5–2, LO 5–6]

Ogilvy Company manufactures and sells one product. The following information pertains to each of the company's first three years of operations:

Variable cost per unit:	
Direct materials	$16
Fixed costs per year:	
Direct labor.	$540,000
Fixed manufacturing overhead.	$822,000
Fixed selling and administrative expenses.	$370,000

The company does not incur any variable manufacturing overhead costs or variable selling and administrative expenses. During its first year of operations, Ogilvy produced 60,000 units and sold 60,000 units. During its second year of operations, it produced 60,000 units and sold 55,000 units. In its third year, Ogilvy produced 60,000 units and sold 65,000 units. The selling price of the company's product is $45 per unit.

Required:

1. Assume the company uses super-variable costing:
   a. Compute the unit product cost for Year 1, Year 2, and Year 3.
   b. Prepare an income statement for Year 1, Year 2, and Year 3.
2. Assume the company uses a variable costing system that assigns $9 of direct labor cost to each unit produced:
   a. Compute the unit product cost for Year 1, Year 2, and Year 3.
   b. Prepare an income statement for Year 1, Year 2, and Year 3.
3. Prepare a reconciliation that explains the difference between the super-variable costing and variable costing net operating incomes in Years 1, 2, and 3.

PROBLEM 5A–5 Super-Variable Costing, Variable Costing, and Absorption Costing Income Statements [LO 5–2, LO 5–6]

Bracey Company manufactures and sells one product. The following information pertains to the company's first year of operations:

Variable cost per unit:	
Direct materials	$19
Fixed costs per year:	
Direct labor.	$250,000
Fixed manufacturing overhead.	$300,000
Fixed selling and administrative expenses.	$90,000

The company does not incur any variable manufacturing overhead costs or variable selling and administrative expenses. During its first year of operations, Bracey produced 20,000 units and sold 18,000 units. The selling price of the company's product is $55 per unit.

Required:

1. Assume the company uses super-variable costing:
   a. Compute the unit product cost for the year.
   b. Prepare an income statement for the year.
2. Assume the company uses a variable costing system that assigns $12.50 of direct labor cost to each unit produced:
   a. Compute the unit product cost for the year.
   b. Prepare an income statement for the year.
3. Assume the company uses an absorption costing system that assigns $12.50 of direct labor cost and $15.00 of fixed manufacturing overhead cost to each unit produced:
   a. Compute the unit product cost for the year.
   b. Prepare an income statement for the year.
4. Prepare a reconciliation that explains the difference between the super-variable costing and variable costing net operating incomes. Prepare another reconciliation that explains the difference between the super-variable costing and absorption costing net operating incomes.

Chapter

6

Activity–Based Costing: A Tool to Aid Decision Making

Managing Product Complexity

BUSINESS FOCUS

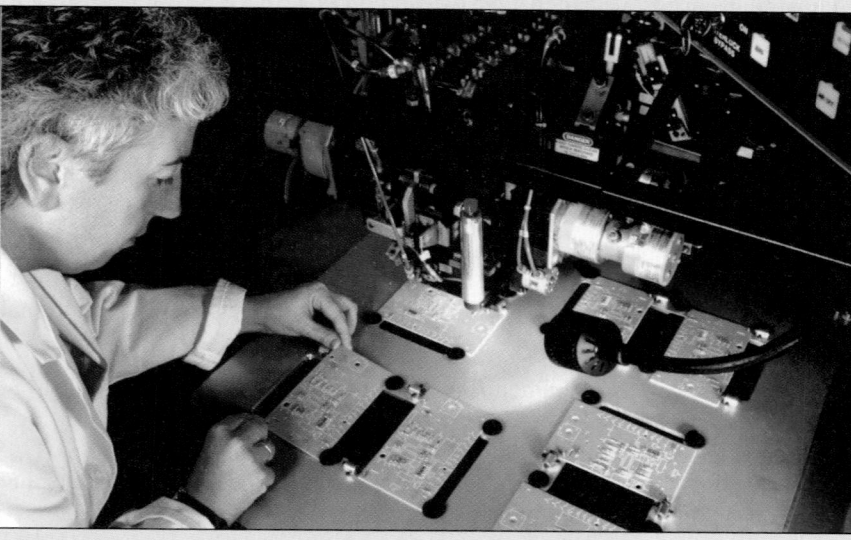

© Brand X Pictures/PunchStock, RF

Managers often understand that increasing the variety of raw material inputs used in their products increases costs. For example, General Mills studied its 50 varieties of Hamburger Helper and concluded that it could lower costs by discontinuing half of them without alienating customers. Seagate studied seven varieties of its computer hard drives and found that only 2% of their parts could be shared by more than one hard drive. The engineers fixed the problem by redesigning the hard drives so that they used more common component parts. Instead of using 61 types of screws to make the hard drives, the engineers reduced the number of screws needed to 19. Eventually all Seagate products were designed so that 75% of their component parts were shared with other product lines.

Activity-based costing systems quantify the increase in costs, such as procurement costs, material handling costs, and assembly costs that are caused by inefficient product designs and other factors. ■

Sources: Mina Kimes, "Cereal Cost Cutters," *Fortune*, November 10, 2008, p. 24; Erika Brown, "Drive Fast, Drive Hard," *Forbes*, January 9, 2006, pp. 92–96.

LEARNING OBJECTIVES

After studying Chapter 6, you should be able to:

LO 6–1 Understand activity-based costing and how it differs from a traditional costing system.

LO 6–2 Assign costs to cost pools using a first-stage allocation.

LO 6–3 Compute activity rates for cost pools.

LO 6–4 Assign costs to a cost object using a second-stage allocation.

LO 6–5 Use activity-based costing to compute product and customer margins.

LO 6–6 (Appendix 6A) Prepare an action analysis report using activity-based costing data and interpret the report.

223

This chapter introduces the concept of *activity-based costing,* which has been embraced by a wide variety of organizations including Charles Schwab, Citigroup, Lowe's, Coca-Cola, J&B Wholesale, Fairchild Semiconductor, Assan Aluminum, Sysco Foods, Fisher Scientific International, and Peregrine Outfitters. **Activity-based costing (ABC)** is a costing method that is designed to provide managers with cost information for strategic and other decisions that potentially affect capacity and therefore "fixed" as well as variable costs. Activity-based costing is ordinarily used as a supplement to, rather than as a replacement for, a company's usual costing system. Most organizations that use activity-based costing have two costing systems—the official costing system that is used for preparing external financial reports and the activity-based costing system that is used for internal decision making and for managing activities.

This chapter focuses primarily on ABC applications in manufacturing to provide a contrast with the material presented in earlier chapters. More specifically, Chapter 4 focused on traditional absorption costing systems used by manufacturing companies to calculate unit product costs for the purpose of valuing inventories and determining cost of goods sold for external financial reports. In contrast, this chapter explains how manufacturing companies can use activity-based costing rather than traditional methods to calculate unit product costs for the purposes of managing overhead and making decisions. Chapter 5 had a similar purpose. That chapter focused on how to use variable costing to aid decisions that do not affect fixed costs. This chapter extends that idea to show how activity-based costing can be used to aid decisions that potentially affect fixed costs as well as variable costs.

Activity-Based Costing: An Overview

LEARNING OBJECTIVE 6–1
Understand activity-based costing and how it differs from a traditional costing system.

As stated above, traditional absorption costing is designed to provide data for external financial reports. In contrast, activity-based costing is designed to be used for internal decision making. As a consequence, activity-based costing differs from traditional absorption costing in three ways. In activity-based costing:

1. Nonmanufacturing as well as manufacturing costs may be assigned to products, but only on a cause-and-effect basis.
2. Some manufacturing costs may be excluded from product costs.
3. Numerous overhead cost pools are used, each of which is allocated to products and other cost objects using its own unique measure of activity.

Each of these departures from traditional absorption costing will be discussed in turn.

Nonmanufacturing Costs and Activity–Based Costing

In traditional absorption costing, manufacturing costs are assigned to products and nonmanufacturing costs are not assigned to products. Conversely, in activity-based costing, we recognize that many nonmanufacturing costs relate to selling, distributing, and servicing specific products. Thus, ABC includes manufacturing *and* nonmanufacturing costs when calculating the entire cost of a product rather than just its manufacturing cost.

There are two types of nonmanufacturing costs that ABC systems assign to products. First, ABC systems trace all direct nonmanufacturing costs to products. Commissions paid to salespersons, shipping costs, and warranty repair costs are examples of nonmanufacturing costs that can be directly traced to individual products. Second, ABC systems allocate indirect nonmanufacturing costs to products whenever the products have presumably caused the costs to be incurred. In fact, in this chapter, we emphasize this point by expanding the definition of *overhead* to include all indirect costs—manufacturing and nonmanufacturing.

In summary, ABC product cost calculations include all direct costs that can be traced to products and all indirect costs that are caused by products. The need to distinguish between manufacturing and nonmanufacturing costs disappears—which is very different from earlier chapters that focused solely on determining the manufacturing cost of a product.

Manufacturing Costs and Activity–Based Costing

In traditional absorption costing systems, *all* manufacturing costs are assigned to products—even manufacturing costs that are not caused by the products. For example, in Chapter 4 we learned that a predetermined plantwide overhead rate is computed by dividing *all* budgeted manufacturing overhead costs by a measure of budgeted activity such as direct labor-hours. This approach spreads *all* manufacturing overhead costs across products based on each product's direct labor-hour usage. In contrast, activity-based costing systems purposely do not assign two types of manufacturing overhead costs to products.

Manufacturing overhead includes costs such as the factory security guard's wages, the plant controller's salary, and the cost of supplies used by the plant manager's secretary. These types of costs are assigned to products in a traditional absorption costing system even though they are totally unaffected by which products are made during a period. In contrast, activity-based costing systems do not arbitrarily assign these types of costs, which are called *organization-sustaining* costs, to products. Activity-based costing treats these types of costs as period expenses rather than product costs.

Additionally, in a traditional absorption costing system, the costs of unused, or idle, capacity are assigned to products. If the budgeted level of activity declines, the overhead rate and unit product costs increase as the increasing costs of idle capacity are spread over a smaller base. In contrast, in activity-based costing, products are only charged for the costs of the capacity they use—not for the costs of capacity they don't use. This provides more stable unit product costs and is consistent with the goal of assigning to products only the costs of the resources that they use.[1]

Exhibit 6–1 summarizies the two departures from traditional absorption costing that we have discussed thus far. The top portion of the exhibit shows that traditional absorption costing treats all manufacturing costs as product costs and all nonmanufacturing costs as period costs. The bottom portion of the exhibit shows that activity-based costing expands the definition of *overhead* to include all indirect costs—manufacturing and nonmanufacturing. The overhead costs that are caused by products are allocated to them, whereas any overhead costs that are not caused by products are treated as period costs. It also shows that ABC treats direct nonmanufacturing costs as product costs rather than period costs.

Now we turn our attention to the third and final difference between traditional absorption costing and activity-based costing.

Cost Pools, Allocation Bases, and Activity–Based Costing

Throughout the 19th century and most of the 20th century, cost system designs were simple and satisfactory. Typically, either one plantwide overhead cost pool or a number of departmental overhead cost pools were used to assign overhead costs to products. The plantwide and departmental approaches always had one thing in common—they relied on allocation bases such as direct labor-hours and machine-hours for allocating overhead costs to products. In the labor-intensive production processes of many years ago, direct labor was the most common choice for an overhead allocation base because it represented a large component of product costs, direct labor-hours were closely tracked, and many managers believed that direct labor-hours, the total volume of units produced, and overhead costs were highly correlated. (Three variables, such as direct labor-hours, the total

---

[1] Appendix 4B discusses how the costs of idle capacity can be accounted for as a period cost in an income statement. This treatment highlights the cost of idle capacity rather than burying it in inventory and cost of goods sold. The procedures laid out in this chapter for activity-based costing have the same end effect.

EXHIBIT 6–1

Differences between Traditional Absorption Costing and Activity-Based Costing

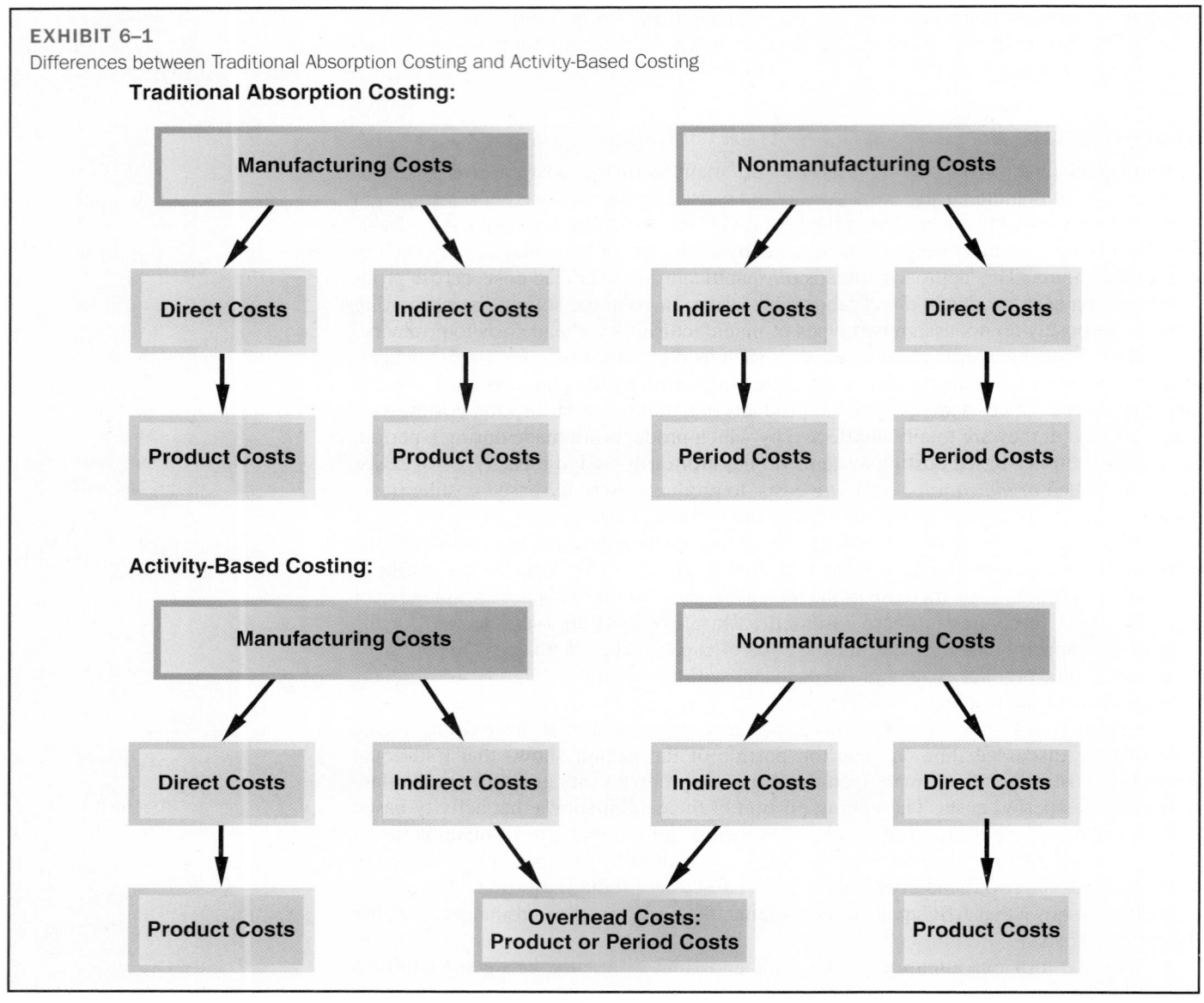

volume of units produced, and overhead costs, are highly correlated if they tend to move together.) Given that most companies at the time were producing a very limited variety of products that required similar resources to produce, allocation bases such as direct labor-hours, or even machine-hours, worked fine because, in fact, there was probably little difference in the overhead costs attributable to different products.

Then conditions began to change. As a percentage of total cost, direct labor began declining and overhead began increasing. Many tasks previously done by direct laborers were being performed by automated equipment—a component of overhead. Companies began creating new products and services at an ever-accelerating rate that differed in volume, batch size, and complexity. Managing and sustaining this product diversity required investing in many more overhead resources, such as production schedulers and product design engineers, that had no obvious connection to direct labor-hours or machine-hours. In this new environment, continuing to rely exclusively on a limited number of overhead cost pools and traditional allocation bases posed the risk that reported unit product costs would be distorted and, therefore, misleading when used for decision-making purposes.

Activity-based costing, thanks to advances in technology that make more complex cost systems feasible, provides an alternative to the traditional plantwide and departmental approaches to defining cost pools and selecting allocation bases. The activity-based approach has appeal in today's business environment because it uses more cost pools and unique measures of activity to better understand the costs of managing and sustaining product diversity.

In activity-based costing, an **activity** is any event that causes the consumption of overhead resources. An **activity cost pool** is a "bucket" in which costs are accumulated that relate to a single activity measure in the ABC system. An **activity measure** is an allocation base in an activity-based costing system. The term *cost driver* is also used to refer to an activity measure because the activity measure should "drive" the cost being allocated. The two most common types of activity measures are *transaction drivers* and *duration drivers*. **Transaction drivers** are simple counts of the number of times an activity occurs, such as the number of bills sent out to customers. **Duration drivers** measure the amount of time required to perform an activity, such as the time spent preparing individual bills for customers. In general, duration drivers are more accurate measures of resource consumption than transaction drivers, but they take more effort to record. For that reason, transaction drivers are often used in practice.

IN BUSINESS

A CRITICAL PERSPECTIVE OF ABC

Marconi is a Portuguese telecommunications company that encountered problems with its ABC system. The company's production managers felt that 23% of the costs included in the system were common costs that should not be allocated to products and that allocating these costs to products was not only inaccurate, but also irrelevant to their operational cost reduction efforts. Furthermore, Marconi's front-line workers resisted the ABC system because they felt it might be used to weaken their autonomy and to justify downsizing, outsourcing, and work intensification. They believed that ABC created a "turkeys queuing for Christmas syndrome" because they were expected to volunteer information to help create a cost system that could eventually lead to their demise. These two complications created a third problem—the data necessary to build the ABC cost model was provided by disgruntled and distrustful employees. Consequently, the accuracy of the data was questionable at best. In short, Marconi's experiences illustrate some of the challenges that complicate real-world ABC implementations.

Source: Maria Major and Trevor Hopper, "Managers Divided: Implementing ABC in a Portuguese Telecommunications Company," *Management Accounting Research*, June 2005, pp. 205–229.

Traditional cost systems rely exclusively on allocation bases that are driven by the volume of production. On the other hand, activity-based costing defines five levels of activity—unit-level, batch-level, product-level, customer-level, and organization-sustaining—that largely do *not* relate to the volume of units produced. The costs and corresponding activity measures for unit-level activities do relate to the volume of units produced; however, the remaining categories do not. These levels are described as follows:[2]

1. **Unit-level activities** are performed each time a unit is produced. The costs of unit-level activities should be proportional to the number of units produced. For example, providing power to run processing equipment would be a unit-level activity because power tends to be consumed in proportion to the number of units produced.
2. **Batch-level activities** are performed each time a batch is handled or processed, regardless of how many units are in the batch. For example, tasks such as placing

---

[2] Robin Cooper, "Cost Classification in Unit-Based and Activity-Based Manufacturing Cost Systems," *Journal of Cost Management*, Fall 1990, pp. 4–14.

purchase orders, setting up equipment, and arranging for shipments to customers are batch-level activities. They are incurred once for each batch (or customer order). Costs at the batch level depend on the number of batches processed rather than on the number of units produced, the number of units sold, or other measures of volume. For example, the cost of setting up a machine for batch processing is the same regardless of whether the batch contains one or thousands of items.

3. **Product-level activities** relate to specific products and typically must be carried out regardless of how many batches are run or units of product are produced or sold. For example, activities such as designing a product, advertising a product, and maintaining a product manager and staff are all product-level activities.

4. **Customer-level activities** relate to specific customers and include activities such as sales calls, catalog mailings, and general technical support that are not tied to any specific product.

5. **Organization-sustaining activities** are carried out regardless of which customers are served, which products are produced, how many batches are run, or how many units are made. This category includes activities such as heating the factory, cleaning executive offices, providing a computer network, arranging for loans, preparing annual reports to shareholders, and so on.

Many companies throughout the world continue to base overhead allocations on direct labor-hours or machine-hours. In situations where overhead costs and direct labor-hours are highly correlated or in situations where the goal of the overhead allocation process is to prepare external financial reports, this practice makes sense. However, if plantwide overhead costs do not move in tandem with plantwide direct labor-hours or machine-hours, product costs will be distorted—with the potential of distorting decisions made within the company.

IN BUSINESS

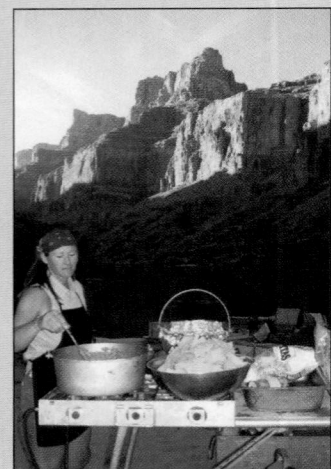

© Sandee Noreen

DINING IN THE CANYON

Western River Expeditions (www.westernriver.com) runs river rafting trips on the Colorado, Green, and Salmon rivers. One of its most popular trips is a six-day trip down the Grand Canyon, which features famous rapids such as Crystal and Lava Falls as well as the awesome scenery accessible only from the bottom of the Grand Canyon. The company runs trips of one or two rafts, each of which carries two guides and up to 18 guests. The company provides all meals on the trip, which are prepared by the guides.

In terms of the hierarchy of activities, a guest can be considered as a unit and a raft as a batch. In that context, the wages paid to the guides are a batch-level cost because each raft requires two guides regardless of the number of guests in the raft. Each guest is given a mug to use during the trip and to take home at the end of the trip as a souvenir. The cost of the mug is a unit-level cost because the number of mugs given away is strictly proportional to the number of guests on a trip.

What about the costs of food served to guests and guides—is this a unit-level cost, a batch-level cost, a product-level cost, or an organization-sustaining cost? At first glance, it might be thought that food costs are a unit-level cost—the greater the number of guests, the higher the food costs. However, that is not quite correct. Standard menus have been created for each day of the trip. For example, the first night's menu might consist of shrimp cocktail, steak, cornbread, salad, and cheesecake. The day before a trip begins, all of the food needed for the trip is taken from the central warehouse and packed in modular containers. It isn't practical to finely adjust the amount of food for the actual number of guests planned to be on a trip—most of the food comes prepackaged in large lots. For example, the shrimp cocktail menu may call for two large bags of frozen shrimp per raft and that many bags will be packed regardless of how many guests are expected on the raft. Consequently, the costs of food are not a unit-level cost that varies with the number of guests actually on a trip. Instead, the costs of food are a batch-level cost.

Source: Conversations with Western River Expeditions personnel.

Designing an Activity-Based Costing (ABC) System

There are three essential characteristics of a successful activity-based costing implementation. First, top managers must strongly support the ABC implementation because their leadership is instrumental in properly motivating all employees to embrace the need to change. Second, top managers should ensure that ABC data is linked to how people are evaluated and rewarded. If employees continue to be evaluated and rewarded using traditional (non-ABC) cost data, they will quickly get the message that ABC is not important and they will abandon it. Third, a cross-functional team should be created to design and implement the ABC system. The team should include representatives from each area that will use ABC data, such as the marketing, production, engineering, and accounting departments. These cross-functional employees possess intimate knowledge of many parts of an organization's operations that is necessary for designing an effective ABC system. Furthermore, tapping the knowledge of cross-functional managers lessens their resistance to ABC because they feel included in the implementation process. Time after time, when accountants have attempted to implement an ABC system on their own without top-management support and cross-functional involvement, the results have been ignored.

IMPLEMENTING ACTIVITY-BASED COSTING IN CHINA

IN BUSINESS

Xu Ji Electric Company is publicly traded on China's Shen Zhen Stock Exchange. From 2001–2003, it successfully implemented an activity-based costing (ABC) system because top-level managers continuously supported the new system—particularly during a challenging phase when the ABC software encountered problems. The ABC adoption was also aided by Xu Ji's decision to drive the implementation using a top-down approach, which is aligned with the company's cultural norm of deferring to and supporting the hierarchical chain of command.

Xu Ji's experience is similar to Western ABC implementations that have consistently recognized the necessity of top-level management support. However, contrary to Xu Ji's experience, many Western managers do not readily support the top-down implementation of new management innovations in their organizations. They prefer to be involved in the decision-making processes that introduce change into their organizations.

Source: Lana Y.J. Liu and Fei Pan, "The Implementation of Activity-Based Costing in China: An Innovation Action Research Approach," *The British Accounting Review* 39, 2007, pp. 249–264.

Classic Brass, Inc., makes two main product lines for luxury yachts—standard stanchions and custom compass housings. The president of the company, John Towers, recently attended a management conference at which activity-based costing was discussed. Following the conference, he called a meeting of the company's top managers to discuss what he had learned. Attending the meeting were production manager Susan Richter, the marketing manager Tom Olafson, and the accounting manager Mary Goodman. He began the conference by distributing the company's income statement that Mary Goodman had prepared a few hours earlier (see Exhibit 6–2):

MANAGERIAL ACCOUNTING IN ACTION

The Issue

John: Well, it's official. Our company has sunk into the red for the first time in its history—a loss of $1,250.

Tom: I don't know what else we can do! Given our successful efforts to grow sales of the custom compass housings, I was expecting to see a boost to our bottom line, not a net loss. Granted, we have been losing even more bids than usual for standard stanchions because of our recent price increase, but . . .

John: Do you think our prices for standard stanchions are too high?

Tom: No, I don't think our prices are too high. I think our competitors' prices are too low. In fact, I'll bet they are pricing below their cost.

Susan: Why would our competitors price below their cost?

Tom: They are out to grab market share.

EXHIBIT 6–2

Classic Brass Income
Statement

Classic Brass
Income Statement
Year Ended December 31, 2016

Sales......................................		$3,200,000
Cost of goods sold:		
Direct materials.........................	$ 975,000	
Direct labor	351,250	
Manufacturing overhead*................	1,000,000	2,326,250
Gross margin............................		873,750
Selling and administrative expenses:		
Shipping expenses......................	65,000	
General administrative expenses	510,000	
Marketing expenses	300,000	875,000
Net operating loss.......................		$ (1,250)

*The company's traditional cost system allocates manufacturing overhead
to products using a plantwide overhead rate and machine-hours as the
allocation base. Inventory levels did not change during the year.

Susan: What good is more market share if they are losing money on every unit sold?

John: I think Susan has a point. Mary, what is your take on this?

Mary: If our competitors are pricing standard stanchions below cost, shouldn't they be losing money rather than us? If our company is the one using accurate information to make informed decisions while our competitors are supposedly clueless, then why is our "bottom line" taking a beating? Unfortunately, I think we may be the ones relying on distorted cost data, not our competitors.

John: Based on what I heard at the conference that I just attended, I am inclined to agree. One of the presentations at the conference dealt with activity-based costing. As the speaker began describing the usual insights revealed by activity-based costing systems, I was sitting in the audience getting an ill feeling in my stomach.

Mary: Honestly John, I have been claiming for years that our existing cost system is okay for external reporting, but it is dangerous to use it for internal decision making. It sounds like you are on board now, right?

John: Yes.

Mary: Well then, how about if all of you commit the time and energy to help me build a fairly simple activity-based costing system that may shed some light on the problems we are facing?

John: Let's do it. I want each of you to appoint one of your top people to a special "ABC team" to investigate how we cost products.

Like most other ABC implementations, the ABC team decided that its new ABC system would supplement, rather than replace, the existing cost accounting system, which would continue to be used for external financial reports. The new ABC system would be used to prepare special reports for management decisions such as bidding on new business.

The accounting manager drew the chart appearing in Exhibit 6–3 to explain the general structure of the ABC model to her team members. Cost objects such as products generate activities. For example, a customer order for a custom compass housing requires the activity of preparing a production order. Such an activity consumes resources. A production order uses a sheet of paper and takes time to fill out. And consumption of resources causes costs. The greater the number of sheets used to fill out production orders and the greater the amount of time devoted to filling out such orders, the greater the cost. Activity-based costing attempts to trace through these relationships to identify how products and customers affect costs.

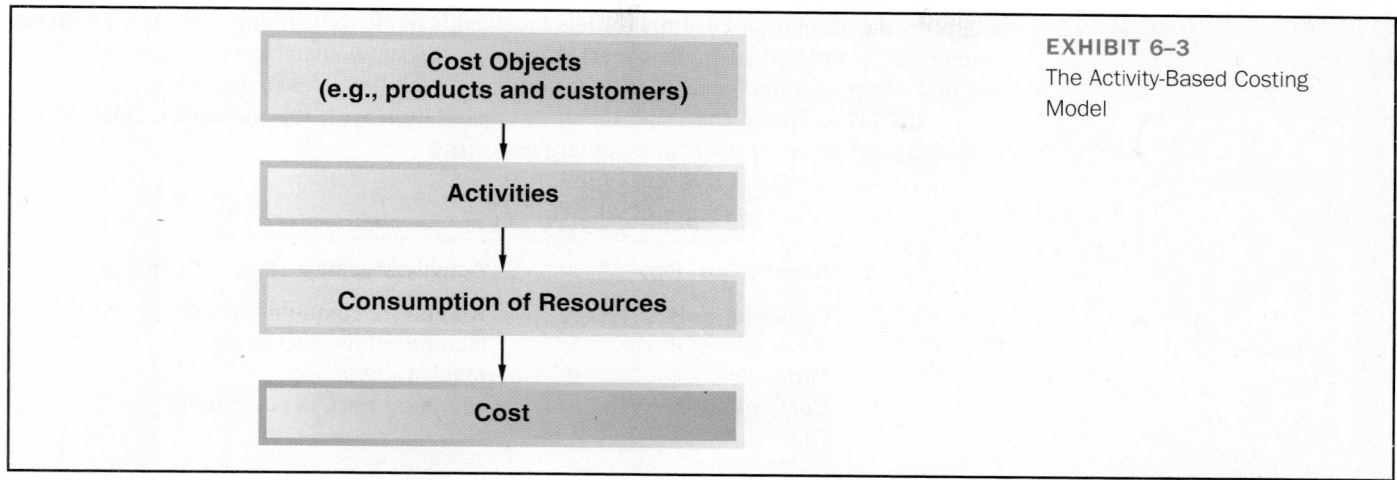

EXHIBIT 6–3
The Activity-Based Costing Model

As in most other companies, the ABC team at Classic Brass felt that the company's traditional cost accounting system adequately measured the direct materials and direct labor costs of products because these costs are directly traced to products. Therefore, the ABC study would be concerned solely with the other costs of the company—manufacturing overhead and selling and administrative costs.

The team felt it was important to carefully plan how it would go about implementing the new ABC system at Classic Brass. Accordingly, it broke down the implementation process into five steps:

Steps for Implementing Activity–Based Costing:

1. Define activities, activity cost pools, and activity measures.
2. Assign overhead costs to activity cost pools.
3. Calculate activity rates.
4. Assign overhead costs to cost objects using the activity rates and activity measures.
5. Prepare management reports.

Step 1: Define Activities, Activity Cost Pools, and Activity Measures

The first major step in implementing an ABC system is to identify the activities that will form the foundation for the system. This can be difficult and time-consuming and involves a great deal of judgment. A common procedure is for the individuals on the ABC implementation team to interview people who work in overhead departments and ask them to describe their major activities. Ordinarily, this results in a very long list of activities.

The length of such lists of activities poses a problem. On the one hand, the greater the number of activities tracked in the ABC system, the more accurate the costs are likely to be. On the other hand, a complex system involving large numbers of activities is costly to design, implement, maintain, and use. Consequently, the original lengthy list of activities is usually reduced to a handful by combining similar activities. For example, several actions may be involved in handling and moving raw materials—from receiving raw materials on the loading dock to sorting them into the appropriate bins in the storeroom. All of these activities might be combined into a single activity called material handling.

When combining activities in an ABC system, activities should be grouped together at the appropriate level. Batch-level activities should not be combined with unit-level activities or product-level activities with batch-level activities and so on. In general, it is best to combine only those activities that are highly correlated with each other within a level. For example, the number of customer orders received is likely to be highly correlated with the number of completed customer orders shipped, so these two batch-level activities (receiving and shipping orders) can usually be combined with little loss of accuracy.

At Classic Brass, the ABC team, in consultation with top managers, selected the following *activity cost pools* and *activity measures:*

Activity Cost Pools at Classic Brass	
Activity Cost Pool	**Activity Measure**
Customer orders..........	Number of customer orders
Product design	Number of product designs
Order size...............	Machine-hours
Customer relations	Number of active customers
Other...................	Not applicable

The *Customer Orders* cost pool will be assigned all costs of resources that are consumed by taking and processing customer orders, including costs of processing paperwork and any costs involved in setting up machines for specific orders. The activity measure for this cost pool is the number of customer orders received. This is a batch-level activity because each order generates work that occurs regardless of whether the order is for one unit or 1,000 units.

The *Product Design* cost pool will be assigned all costs of resources consumed by designing products. The activity measure for this cost pool is the number of products designed. This is a product-level activity because the amount of design work on a new product does not depend on the number of units ultimately ordered or batches ultimately run.

The *Order Size* cost pool will be assigned all costs of resources consumed as a consequence of the number of units produced, including the costs of miscellaneous factory supplies, power to run machines, and some equipment depreciation. This is a unit-level activity because each unit requires some of these resources. The activity measure for this cost pool is machine-hours.

The *Customer Relations* cost pool will be assigned all costs associated with maintaining relations with customers, including the costs of sales calls and the costs of entertaining customers. The activity measure for this cost pool is the number of customers the company has on its active customer list. The Customer Relations cost pool represents a customer-level activity.

The *Other* cost pool will be assigned all overhead costs that are not associated with customer orders, product design, the size of the orders, or customer relations. These costs mainly consist of organization-sustaining costs and the costs of unused, idle capacity. These costs *will not* be assigned to products because they represent resources that are *not* consumed by products.

It is unlikely that any other company would use exactly the same activity cost pools and activity measures that were selected by Classic Brass. Because of the amount of judgment involved, the number and definitions of the activity cost pools and activity measures used by companies vary considerably.

The Mechanics of Activity-Based Costing

LEARNING OBJECTIVE 6–2
Assign costs to cost pools using a first-stage allocation.

Step 2: Assign Overhead Costs to Activity Cost Pools

Exhibit 6–4 shows the annual overhead costs (both manufacturing and nonmanufacturing) that Classic Brass intends to assign to its activity cost pools. Notice the data in the exhibit are organized by department (e.g., Production, General Administrative, and Marketing). This is because the data have been extracted from the company's general ledger. General ledgers usually classify costs within the departments where the costs are incurred. For example,

Production Department:

Indirect factory wages	$500,000	
Factory equipment depreciation	300,000	
Factory utilities	120,000	
Factory building lease	80,000	$1,000,000

General Administrative Department:

Administrative wages and salaries	400,000	
Office equipment depreciation	50,000	
Administrative building lease	60,000	510,000

Marketing Department:

Marketing wages and salaries	250,000	
Selling expenses	50,000	300,000
Total overhead cost		$1,810,000

EXHIBIT 6–4
Annual Overhead Costs
(Both Manufacturing and
Nonmanufacturing) at Classic
Brass

salaries, supplies, rent, and so forth incurred in the marketing department are charged to that department. The functional orientation of the general ledger mirrors the presentation of costs in the absorption income statement in Exhibit 6–2. In fact, you'll notice the total costs for the Production Department in Exhibit 6–4 ($1,000,000) equal the total manufacturing overhead costs from the income statement in Exhibit 6–2. Similarly, the total costs for the General Administrative and Marketing Departments in Exhibit 6–4 ($510,000 and $300,000) equal the marketing and general and administrative expenses shown in Exhibit 6–2.

Three costs included in the income statement in Exhibit 6–2: direct materials, direct labor, and shipping—are excluded from the costs shown in Exhibit 6–4. The ABC team purposely excluded these costs from Exhibit 6–4 because the existing cost system can accurately trace direct materials, direct labor, and shipping costs to products. There is no need to incorporate these direct costs in the activity-based allocations of indirect costs.

Classic Brass's activity-based costing system will divide the nine types of overhead costs in Exhibit 6–4 among its activity cost pools via an allocation process called *first-stage allocation*. The **first-stage allocation** in an ABC system is the process of assigning functionally organized overhead costs derived from a company's general ledger to the activity cost pools.

First-stage allocations are usually based on the results of interviews with employees who have first-hand knowledge of the activities. For example, Classic Brass needs to allocate $500,000 of indirect factory wages to its five activity cost pools. These allocations will be more accurate if the employees who are classified as indirect factory workers (e.g., supervisors, engineers, and quality inspectors) are asked to estimate what percentage of their time is spent dealing with customer orders, with product design, with processing units of product (i.e., order size), and with customer relations. These interviews are conducted with considerable care. Those who are interviewed must thoroughly understand what the activities encompass and what is expected of them in the interview. In addition, departmental managers are typically interviewed to determine how the non-personnel costs should be distributed across the activity cost pools. For example, the Classic Brass production manager would be interviewed to determine how the $300,000 of factory equipment depreciation (shown in Exhibit 6–4) should be allocated to the activity cost pools. The key question that the production manager would need to answer is "What percentage of the available machine capacity is consumed by each activity such as the number of customer orders or the number of units processed (i.e., size of orders)?"

The results of the interviews, at Classic Brass are displayed in Exhibit 6–5. For example, factory equipment depreciation is distributed 20% to Customer Orders, 60% to Order Size, and 20% to the Other cost pool. The resource in this instance is machine time. According to the estimates made by the production manager, 60% of the total available machine time was used to actually process units to fill orders. This percentage is entered in the Order Size column. Each customer order requires setting up, which also requires machine time. This activity consumes 20% of the total available machine time and is entered under the Customer Orders column. The remaining 20% of available machine time represents idle time and is entered under the Other column.

AN ABC APPLICATION IN THE CONSTRUCTION INDUSTRY

Researchers from the United States and the Republic of Korea studied how a Korean manufacturer assigned the indirect costs of supplying reinforced steel bars (also called *rebar*) to various construction projects. The company's traditional cost system assigned all indirect costs to projects using rebar tonnage as the allocation base. Its ABC system had 10 activities that assigned indirect costs to projects using activity measures such as number of orders, number of sheets, number of distributing runs, number of production runs, and number of inspections.

The traditional and ABC systems assigned the following overhead costs to three construction projects called Commercial, High-Rise Condo, and Heavy Civil:

	Commercial	High-Rise Condo	Heavy Civil
Traditional cost system allocations	$ 64,587	$ 50,310	$91,102
ABC allocations........................	90,466	61,986	53,548
Difference	$(25,879)	$(11,676)	$37,554

Notice that the traditional cost system was undercosting the Commercial and High-Rise Condo projects relative to the ABC system. It was also overcosting the Heavy Civil project by $37,554 when compared to the ABC system.

Source: Yong-Woo Kim, Seungheon Han, "Sungwon Shin, and Kunhee Choi, "A Case Study of Activity-Based Costing in Allocation Rebar Fabrication Costs to Projects," *Construction Management and Economics,* May 2010, pp. 449–461.

Exhibit 6–5 and many of the other exhibits in this chapter are presented in the form of Excel spreadsheets. All of the calculations required in activity-based costing can be done by hand. Nevertheless, setting up an activity-based costing system on a spreadsheet or using special ABC software can save a lot of work—particularly in situations involving many activity cost pools and in organizations that periodically update their ABC systems.

We will not go into the details of how all of the percentages in Exhibit 6–5 were determined. However, note that 100% of the factory building lease has been assigned to the Other cost pool. Classic Brass has a single production facility. It has no plans to expand or to sublease any excess space. The cost of this production facility is treated as an organization-sustaining cost because there is no way to avoid even a portion of this cost if a particular product or customer were to be dropped. (Remember that organization-sustaining costs are assigned to the Other cost pool and are not allocated to products.) In contrast, some companies have separate facilities for manufacturing specific products. The costs of these separate facilities could be directly traced to the specific products.

Once the percentage distributions in Exhibit 6–5 have been established, it is easy to allocate costs to the activity cost pools. The results of this first-stage allocation are displayed in Exhibit 6–6. Each cost is allocated across the activity cost pools by multiplying it by the percentages in Exhibit 6–5. For example, the indirect factory wages of $500,000 are multiplied by the 25% entry under Customer Orders in Exhibit 6–5 to arrive at the $125,000 entry under Customer Orders in Exhibit 6–6. Similarly, the indirect factory wages of $500,000 are multiplied by the 40% entry under Product Design in Exhibit 6–5 to arrive at the $200,000 entry under Product Design in Exhibit 6–6. All of the entries in Exhibit 6–6 are computed in this way.

Now that the first-stage allocations to the activity cost pools have been completed, the next step is to compute the activity rates.

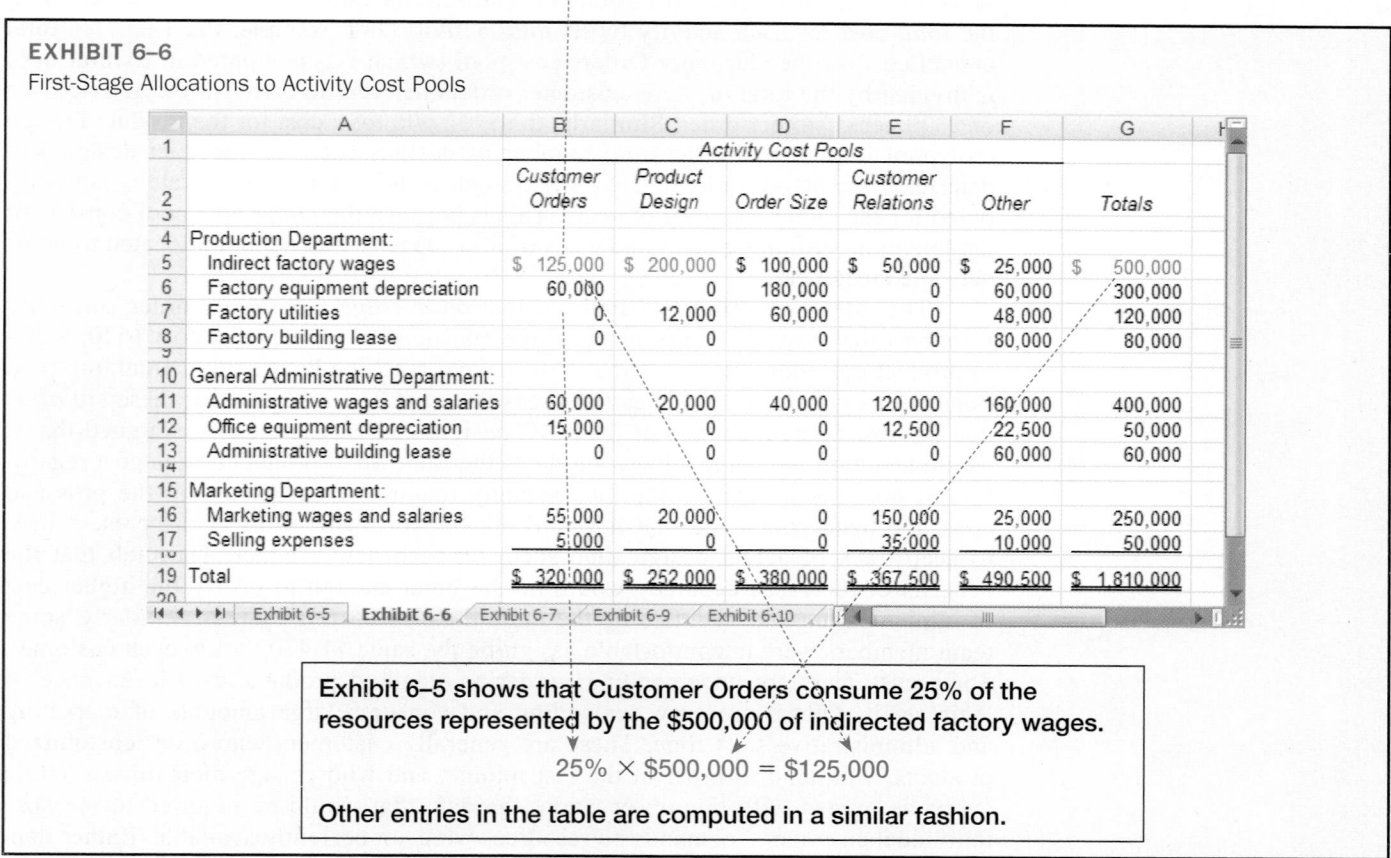

EXHIBIT 6–5

Results of Interviews: Distribution of Resource Consumption across Activity Cost Pools

	Customer Orders	Product Design	Order Size	Customer Relations	Other	Totals
	Activity Cost Pools					
Production Department:						
Indirect factory wages	25%	40%	20%	10%	5%	100%
Factory equipment depreciation	20%	0%	60%	0%	20%	100%
Factory utilities	0%	10%	50%	0%	40%	100%
Factory building lease	0%	0%	0%	0%	100%	100%
General Administrative Department:						
Administrative wages and salaries	15%	5%	10%	30%	40%	100%
Office equipment depreciation	30%	0%	0%	25%	45%	100%
Administrative building lease	0%	0%	0%	0%	100%	100%
Marketing Department:						
Marketing wages and salaries	22%	8%	0%	60%	10%	100%
Selling expenses	10%	0%	0%	70%	20%	100%

Exhibit 6-5 Exhibit 6-6 Exhibit 6-7 Exhibit 6-9 Exhibit 6-10

EXHIBIT 6–6

First-Stage Allocations to Activity Cost Pools

	Customer Orders	Product Design	Order Size	Customer Relations	Other	Totals
	Activity Cost Pools					
Production Department:						
Indirect factory wages	$ 125,000	$ 200,000	$ 100,000	$ 50,000	$ 25,000	$ 500,000
Factory equipment depreciation	60,000	0	180,000	0	60,000	300,000
Factory utilities	0	12,000	60,000	0	48,000	120,000
Factory building lease	0	0	0	0	80,000	80,000
General Administrative Department:						
Administrative wages and salaries	60,000	20,000	40,000	120,000	160,000	400,000
Office equipment depreciation	15,000	0	0	12,500	22,500	50,000
Administrative building lease	0	0	0	0	60,000	60,000
Marketing Department:						
Marketing wages and salaries	55,000	20,000	0	150,000	25,000	250,000
Selling expenses	5,000	0	0	35,000	10,000	50,000
Total	$ 320,000	$ 252,000	$ 380,000	$ 367,500	$ 490,500	$ 1,810,000

Exhibit 6-5 **Exhibit 6-6** Exhibit 6-7 Exhibit 6-9 Exhibit 6-10

Exhibit 6–5 shows that Customer Orders consume 25% of the resources represented by the $500,000 of indirected factory wages.

25% × $500,000 = $125,000

Other entries in the table are computed in a similar fashion.

Step 3: Calculate Activity Rates

The activity rates that will be used for assigning overhead costs to products and customers are computed in Exhibit 6–7. The ABC team determined the total activity for each cost pool that would be required to produce the company's present product

LEARNING OBJECTIVE 6–3

Compute activity rates for cost pools.

EXHIBIT 6–7
Computation of Activity Rates

	A	B	C	D	E	F
		(a)	*(b)*		*(a) ÷ (b)*	
1	*Activity Cost Pools*	*Total Cost**	*Total Activity*		*Activity Rate*	
2	Customer orders	$320,000	1,000	orders	$320	per order
3	Product design	$252,000	400	designs	$630	per design
4	Order size	$380,000	20,000	MHs	$19	per MH
5	Customer relations	$367,500	250	customers	$1,470	per customer
6	Other	$490,500	Not applicable		Not applicable	
8	*From Exhibit 6-6.					

Exhibit 6-5 Exhibit 6-6 **Exhibit 6-7** Exhibit 6-9

mix and to serve its present customers. These numbers are listed in Exhibit 6–7. For example, the ABC team found that 400 new product designs are required each year to serve the company's present customers. The activity rates are computed by dividing the *total* cost for each activity by its *total* activity. For example, the $320,000 total annual cost for the Customer Orders cost pool (which was computed in Exhibit 6–6) is divided by the total of 1,000 customer orders per year to arrive at the activity rate of $320 per customer order. Similarly, the $252,000 *total* cost for the Product Design cost pool is divided by the *total* number of designs (i.e., 400 product designs) to determine the activity rate of $630 per design. Note that an activity rate is not computed for the Other category of costs. This is because the *Other* cost pool consists of organization-sustaining costs and costs of idle capacity that are not allocated to products and customers.

The rates in Exhibit 6–7 indicate that *on average* a customer order consumes resources that cost $320; a product design consumes resources that cost $630; a unit of product consumes resources that cost $19 per machine-hour; and maintaining relations with a customer consumes resources that cost $1,470. Note that these are *average* figures. Some members of the ABC design team at Classic Brass argued that it would be unfair to charge all new products the same $630 product design cost regardless of how much design time they actually require. After discussing the pros and cons, the team concluded that it would not be worth the effort at the present time to keep track of actual design time spent on each new product. They felt that the benefits of increased accuracy would not be great enough to justify the higher cost of implementing and maintaining the more detailed costing system. Similarly, some team members were uncomfortable assigning the same $1,470 cost to each customer. Some customers are undemanding—ordering standard products well in advance of their needs. Others are very demanding and consume large amounts of marketing and administrative staff time. These are generally customers who order customized products, who tend to order at the last minute, and who change their minds. While everyone agreed with this observation, the data that would be required to measure individual customers' demands on resources were not currently available. Rather than delay implementation of the ABC system, the team decided to defer such refinements to a later date.

Before proceeding further, it would be helpful to get a better idea of the overall process of assigning costs to products and other cost objects in an ABC system. Exhibit 6–8 provides a visual perspective of the ABC system at Classic Brass. We recommend that you carefully go over this exhibit. In particular, note that the Other category, which contains organization-sustaining costs and costs of idle capacity, is not allocated to products or customers.

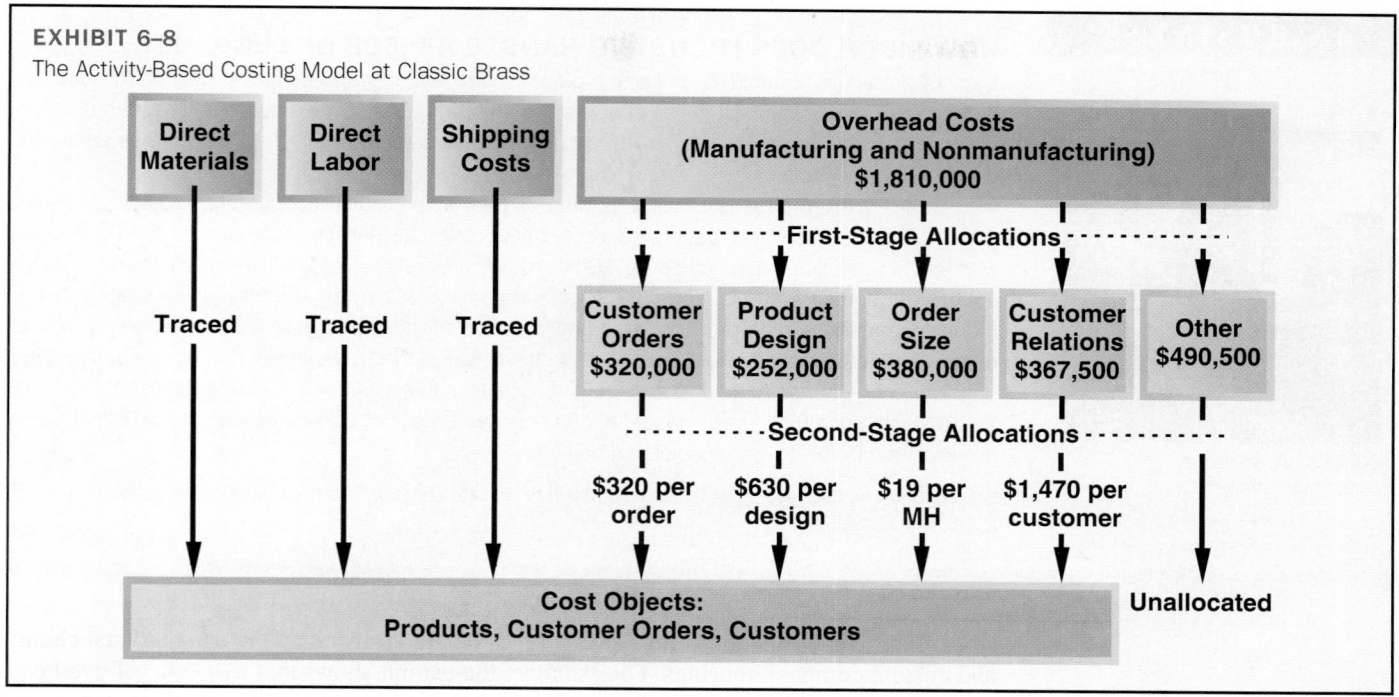

EXHIBIT 6–8
The Activity-Based Costing Model at Classic Brass

Step 4: Assign Overhead Costs to Cost Objects

The fourth step in the implementation of activity-based costing is called *second-stage allocation.* In the **second-stage allocation,** activity rates are used to apply overhead costs to products and customers. First, we will illustrate how to assign costs to products followed by an example of how to assign costs to customers.

The data needed by the ABC team to assign overhead costs to Classic Brass's two products—standard stanchions and custom compass housings—are as follows:

LEARNING OBJECTIVE 6–4
Assign costs to a cost object using a second-stage allocation.

Standard Stanchions

1. This product line does not require any new design resources.
2. 30,000 units were ordered during the year, comprising 600 separate orders.
3. Each stanchion requires 35 minutes of machine time for a total of 17,500 machine-hours.

Custom Compass Housings

1. This is a custom product that requires new design resources.
2. There were 400 orders for custom compass housings. Orders for this product are placed separately from orders for standard stanchions.
3. There were 400 custom designs prepared. One custom design was prepared for each order.
4. Because some orders were for more than one unit, a total of 1,250 custom compass housings were produced during the year. A custom compass housing requires an average of 2 machine-hours for a total of 2,500 machine-hours.

Notice, 600 customer orders were placed for standard stanchions and 400 customer orders were placed for custom compass housings, for a total of 1,000 customer orders. All 400 product designs related to custom compass housings; none related to standard stanchions. Producing 30,000 standard stanchions required 17,500 machine-hours and producing 1,250 custom compass housings required 2,500 machine-hours, for a total of 20,000 machine-hours.

HOW MUCH DOES IT COST TO HANDLE A PIECE OF LUGGAGE?

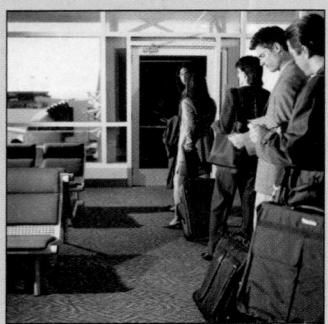

© Ryan McVay/Photodisc/
Getty Images, RF

It costs an airline about $15 to carry a piece of checked luggage from one destination another. The activity "transporting luggage" consists of numerous sub-activities such as tagging bags, sorting them, placing them on carts, transporting bags planeside, loading them into the airplane, and delivering them to carousels and connecting flights.

A variety of employees invest a portion of their labor hours "transporting luggage" including ground personnel, check-in agents, service clerks, baggage service managers, and maintenance workers. In total, labor costs comprise $9 per bag. Airlines also spend millions of dollars on baggage equipment, sorting systems, carts, tractors, and conveyors, as well as rental costs related to bag rooms, carousels, and offices. They also pay to deliver misplaced bags to customers' homes and to compensate customers for lost bags that are never found. These expenses add up to about $4 per bag. The final expense related to transporting luggage is fuel costs, which average about $2 per bag.

Many major airlines now charge fees for checked bags. United Airlines expects to collect $275 million annually for its first and second bag fees.

Source: Scott McCartney, "What It Costs an Airline to Fly Your Luggage," *The Wall Street Journal*, November 25, 2008, p. D1 and D8.

Exhibit 6–9 illustrates how overhead costs are assigned to the standard stanchions and custom compass housings. For example, the exhibit shows that $192,000 of overhead costs are assigned from the Customer Orders activity cost pool to the standard stanchions ($320 per order × 600 orders). Similarly, $128,000 of overhead costs are assigned from the Customer Orders activity cost pool to the custom compass housings ($320 per order × 400 orders). The Customer Orders cost pool contained a total of $320,000 (see Exhibit 6–6 or 6–7) and this total amount has been assigned to the two products ($192,000 + $128,000 = $320,000).

Exhibit 6–9 shows that a total of $952,000 of overhead costs is assigned to Classic Brass's two product lines—$524,500 to standard stanchions and $427,500 to custom compass housings. This amount is less than the $1,810,000 of overhead costs included in the ABC system. Why? The total amount of overhead assigned to products does not match the total amount of overhead cost in the ABC system because the ABC team purposely did not assign the $367,500 of Customer Relations and $490,500 of Other costs to products. The Customer Relations activity is a customer-level activity and the Other activity is an organization-sustaining activity—neither activity is caused by products. As shown below, when the Customer Relations and Other activity costs are added to the $952,000 of overhead costs assigned to products, the total is $1,810,000.

	Standard Stanchions	Custom Compass Housings	Total
Overhead Costs Assigned to Products			
Customer orders	$192,000	$128,000	$ 320,000
Product design	0	252,000	252,000
Order size	332,500	47,500	380,000
Subtotal	$524,500	$427,500	952,000
Overhead Costs Not Assigned to Products			
Customer relations			367,500
Other			490,500
Subtotal			858,000
Total overhead cost			$1,810,000

EXHIBIT 6–9
Assigning Overhead Costs to Products

	A	B	C	D	E	F
1	**Overhead Cost for the Standard Stanchions**					
2	*Activity Cost Pools*	*(a)* *Activity Rate**		*(b)* *Activity*		*(a) × (b)* *ABC Cost*
3	Customer orders	$320	per order	600	orders	$ 192,000
4	Product design	$630	per design	0	designs	0
5	Order size	$19	per MH	17,500	MHs	332,500
6	Total					$ 524,500
7						
8	**Overhead Cost for the Custom Compass Housing**					
9	*Activity Cost Pools*	*(a)* *Activity Rate**		*(b)* *Activity*		*(a) × (b)* *ABC Cost*
10	Customer orders	$320	per order	400	orders	$ 128,000
11	Product design	$630	per design	400	designs	252,000
12	Order size	$19	per MH	2,500	MHs	47,500
13	Total					$ 427,500
14						
15	*From Exhibit 6-7.					
16						

Exhibit 6-6　Exhibit 6-7　**Exhibit 6-9**　Exhibit 6-10

Next, we describe another example of second-stage allocation—assigning activity costs to customers. The data needed by Classic Brass to assign overhead costs to one of its customers—Windward Yachts—are as follows:

Windward Yachts

1. The company placed a total of three orders.
   a. Two orders were for 150 standard stanchions per order.
   b. One order was for a single custom compass housing unit.
2. A total of 177 machine-hours were used to fulfill the three customer orders.
   a. The 300 standard stanchions required 175 machine-hours.
   b. The custom compass housing required 2 machine-hours.
3. Windward Yachts is one of 250 customers served by Classic Brass.

Exhibit 6–10 illustrates how the ABC system assigns overhead costs to this customer. As shown in Exhibit 6–10, the ABC team calculated that $6,423 of overhead costs should be assigned to Windward Yachts. The exhibit shows that Windward Yachts is assigned $960 ($320 per order × 3 orders) of overhead costs from the Customer Orders activity cost pool; $630 ($630 per design × 1 design) from the Product Design cost pool; $3,363 ($19 per machine-hour × 177 machine-hours) from the Order Size cost pool; and $1,470 ($1,470 per customer × 1 customer) from the Customer Relations cost pool.

With second-stage allocations complete, the ABC design team was ready to turn its attention to creating reports that would help explain the company's first ever net operating loss.

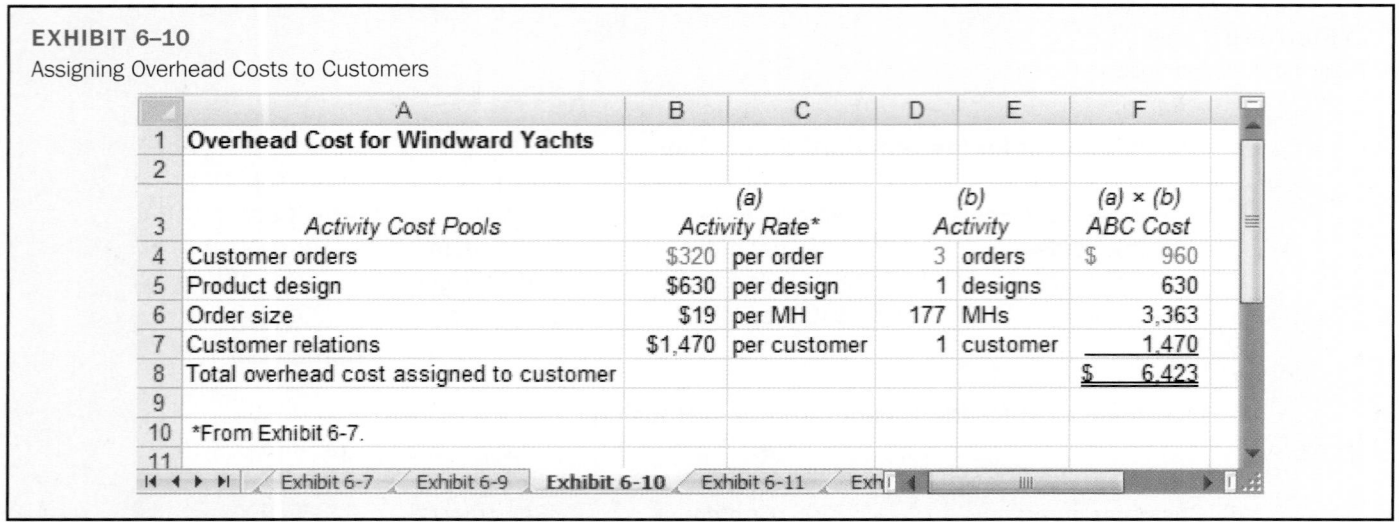

EXHIBIT 6–10
Assigning Overhead Costs to Customers

	A	B	C	D	E	F
1	**Overhead Cost for Windward Yachts**					
2						
3	*Activity Cost Pools*		*(a)* *Activity Rate**		*(b)* *Activity*	*(a) × (b)* *ABC Cost*
4	Customer orders		$320 per order	3	orders	$ 960
5	Product design		$630 per design	1	designs	630
6	Order size		$19 per MH	177	MHs	3,363
7	Customer relations		$1,470 per customer	1	customer	1,470
8	Total overhead cost assigned to customer					$ 6,423
9						
10	*From Exhibit 6-7.					
11						

H ◄ ► H / Exhibit 6-7 / Exhibit 6-9 / **Exhibit 6-10** / Exhibit 6-11 / Exh ◄

Step 5: Prepare Management Reports

LEARNING OBJECTIVE 6–5
Use activity-based costing
to compute product and
customer margins.

The most common management reports prepared with ABC data are product and customer profitability reports. These reports help companies channel their resources to their most profitable growth opportunities while at the same time highlighting products and customers that drain profits. We begin by illustrating a product profitability report followed by a customer profitability report.

The Classic Brass ABC team realized that the profit from a product, also called the *product margin,* is a function of the product's sales and the direct and indirect costs that the product causes. The ABC cost allocations shown in Exhibit 6–9 only summarize each product's indirect (i.e., overhead) costs. Therefore, to compute a product's profit (i.e., product margin), the design team needed to gather each product's sales and direct costs in addition to the overhead costs previously computed. The pertinent sales and direct cost data for each product are shown below. Notice the numbers in the total column agree with the income statement in Exhibit 6–2.

	Standard Stanchions	Custom Compass Housings	Total
Sales....................	$2,660,000	$540,000	$3,200,000
Direct costs:			
Direct materials	$905,500	$69,500	$975,000
Direct labor.............	$263,750	$87,500	$351,250
Shipping..............	$60,000	$5,000	$65,000

Having gathered the above data, the design team created the product profitability report shown in Exhibit 6–11. The report revealed that standard stanchions are profitable, with a positive product margin of $906,250, whereas the custom compass housings are unprofitable, with a negative product margin of $49,500. Keep in mind that the product profitability report purposely does not include the costs in the Customer Relations and Other activity cost pools. These costs, which total $858,000, were excluded from the report because they are not caused by the products. Customer Relations costs are caused by customers, not products. The Other costs are organization-sustaining costs and unused capacity costs that are not caused by any particular product.

EXHIBIT 6–11

Product Margins—Activity-Based Costing

	A	B	C	D	E	F
1	**Product Margins—Activity-Based Costing**					
2			*Standard Stanchions*		*Custom Compass Housings*	
3	Sales		$ 2,660,000			$ 540,000
4	Costs:					
5	Direct materials	$ 905,500			$ 69,500	
6	Direct labor	263,750			87,500	
7	Shipping	60,000			5,000	
8	Customer orders (from Exhibit 6-9)	192,000			128,000	
9	Product design (from Exhibit 6-9)	-			252,000	
10	Order size (from Exhibit 6-9)	332,500			47,500	
11	Total cost		1,753,750			589,500
12	Product margin		$ 906,250			$ (49,500)
13						

Exhibit 6-7   Exhibit 6-9   Exhibit 6-10   **Exhibit 6-11**   Exhibit 6-[

The product margins can be reconciled with the company's net operating loss as follows:

	Standard Stanchions	Custom Compass Housings	Total
Sales (See Exhibit 6–11).................	$2,660,000	$540,000	$3,200,000
Total costs (See Exhibit 6–11)..............	1,753,750	589,500	2,343,250
Product margins (See Exhibit 6–11)	$ 906,250	$ (49,500)	856,750
Overhead costs not assigned to products:			
Customer relations......................			367,500
Other			490,500
Total			858,000
Net operating loss			$ (1,250)

Next, the design team created a customer profitability report for Windward Yachts. Similar to the product profitability report, the design team needed to gather data concerning sales to Windward Yachts and the direct material, direct labor, and shipping costs associated with those sales. Those data are presented below:

	Windward Yachts
Sales	$11,350
Direct costs:.................	
Direct material costs........	$2,123
Direct labor costs	$1,900
Shipping costs.............	$205

Using these data and the data from Exhibit 6–10, the design team created the customer profitability report shown in Exhibit 6–12. The report revealed that the customer margin for Windward Yachts is $699. A similar report could be prepared for each of Classic Brass's 250 customers, thereby enabling the company to cultivate relationships with its most profitable customers, while taking steps to reduce the negative impact of unprofitable customers.

IN BUSINESS

IS ACTIVITY-BASED COSTING STILL BEING USED?

Researchers surveyed 348 managers to determine which costing methods their companies use. The table below shows the percentage of respondents whose companies use the various costing methods to assign departmental costs to cost objects such as products.

			Departments				
Costing Method	Research and Development	Product and Process Design	Production	Sales and Marketing	Distribution	Customer Service	Shared Services
Activity-based	13.0%	14.7%	18.3%	17.3%	17.2%	21.8%	23.0%
Standard[1]	17.6%	20.7%	42.0%	18.1%	28.4%	18.5%	23.0%
Normal[2]	4.6%	8.6%	9.9%	7.9%	6.0%	8.1%	5.6%
Actual[3]	23.1%	25.0%	23.7%	23.6%	26.7%	16.9%	15.9%
Other	1.9%	0.9%	0.0%	0.8%	0.9%	1.6%	2.4%
Not allocated	39.8%	30.2%	6.1%	32.3%	20.7%	33.1%	30.2%

[1]Standard costing is used for the variance computations in Chapter 10.
[2]Normal costing is used for the job-order costing computations in Chapter 3.
[3]Actual costing is used to create the absorption and variable costing income statements in Chapter 6.

The results show that 18.3% of respondents use ABC to allocate production costs to cost objects and 42% use standard costing for the same purpose. ABC is used by at least 13% of respondents within all functional departments across the value chain. Many companies do not allocate nonproduction costs to cost objects.

Source: William O. Stratton, Denis Desroches, Raef Lawson, and Toby Hatch, "Activity-Based Costing: Is It Still Relevant?" *Management Accounting Quarterly*, Spring 2009, pp. 31–40.

EXHIBIT 6–12
Customer Margin—Activity-Based Costing

	A	B	C
1	**Customer Margin—Activity-Based Costing**		
2			*Windward Yachts*
3	Sales		$ 11,350
4	Costs:		
5	Direct materials	$ 2,123	
6	Direct labor	1,900	
7	Shipping	205	
8	Customer orders (from Exhibit 6-10)	960	
9	Product design (from Exhibit 6-10)	630	
10	Order size (from Exhibit 6-10)	3,363	
11	Customer relations (from Exhibit 6-10)	1,470	10,651
12	Customer margin		$ 699
13			

|◄ ◄ ► ►| Exhibit 6-12 / Exhibit 6-13 / Exhibit 6-14 / Exhibit 6A|

Comparison of Traditional and ABC Product Costs

The ABC team used a two-step process to compare its traditional and ABC product costs. First, the team reviewed the product margins reported by the traditional cost system. Then, it contrasted the differences between the traditional and ABC product margins.

Product Margins Computed Using the Traditional Cost System

Classic Brass's traditional cost system assigns only manufacturing costs to products—this includes direct materials, direct labor, and manufacturing overhead. Selling and administrative costs are not assigned to products. Exhibit 6–13 shows the product margins reported by Classic Brass's traditional cost system. We will explain how these margins were calculated in three steps. First, the sales and direct materials and direct labor cost data are the same numbers used by the ABC team to prepare Exhibit 6–11. In other words, the traditional cost system and the ABC system treat these three pieces of revenue and cost data identically.

Second, the traditional cost system uses a plantwide overhead rate to assign manufacturing overhead costs to products. The numerator for the plantwide overhead rate is $1,000,000, which is the total amount of manufacturing overhead shown on the income statement in Exhibit 6–2. The footnote in Exhibit 6–2 mentions that the traditional cost system uses machine-hours to assign manufacturing overhead costs to products. The Order Size activity in Exhibit 6–7 used 20,000 machine-hours as its level of activity. These same 20,000 machine-hours would be used in the denominator of the plantwide overhead rate, which is computed as follows:

$$\text{Plantwide overhead rate} = \frac{\text{Total estimated manufacturing overhead}}{\text{Total estimated machine-hours}}$$

$$= \frac{\$1,000,000}{20,000 \text{ machine-hours}}$$

$$= \$50 \text{ per machine-hour}$$

Because 17,500 machine-hours were worked on standard stanchions, this product line is assigned $875,000 (17,500 machine-hours × $50 per machine-hour) of manufacturing overhead cost. Similarly, the custom compass housings required 2,500 machine-hours, so this product line is assigned $125,000 (2,500 machine-hours × $50 per machine-hour) of manufacturing overhead cost. The sales of each product minus its cost of goods sold equals the product margin of $615,750 for standard stanchions and $258,000 for custom compass housings.

Notice, the net operating loss of $1,250 shown in Exhibit 6–13 agrees with the loss reported in the income statement in Exhibit 6–2 and with the loss shown in the table beneath Exhibit 6–11. The company's *total* sales, *total* costs, and its resulting net operating loss are the same regardless of whether you are looking at the absorption income statement in Exhibit 6–2, the ABC product profitability analysis, or the traditional

---

EXHIBIT 6–13

Product Margins—Traditional Costing System

	A	B	C	D	E	F	G	H	I
1	Product Margins—Traditional Cost System								
2			Standard Stanchions			Custom Compass Housings			Total
3	Sales		$2,660,000			$ 540,000			$3,200,000
4	Cost of goods sold:								
5	Direct materials	$ 905,500			$ 69,500			$ 975,000	
6	Direct labor	263,750			87,500			351,250	
7	Manufacturing overhead	875,000	2,044,250		125,000	282,000		1,000,000	2,326,250
8	Product margin		$ 615,750			$ 258,000			873,750
9	Selling and administrative								875,000
10	Net operating income								$ (1,250)
11									

Exhibit 6-12   **Exhibit 6-13**   Exhibit 6-14   Exhibit 6A-1   Exhibit 6A-2   Exhibit 6A-3A

product profitability analysis in Exhibit 6–13. Although the "total pie" remains constant across the traditional and ABC systems, what differs is how the pie is divided between the two product lines. The traditional product margin calculations suggest that standard stanchions are generating a product margin of $615,750 and the custom compass housings a product margin of $258,000. However, these product margins differ from the ABC product margins reported in Exhibit 6–11. Indeed, the traditional cost system is sending misleading signals to Classic Brass's managers about each product's profitability. Let's explain why.

The Differences between ABC and Traditional Product Costs

The changes in product margins caused by switching from the traditional cost system to the activity-based costing system are shown below:

	Standard Stanchions	Custom Compass Housings
Product margins—traditional	$615,750	$ 258,000
Product margins—ABC	906,250	(49,500)
Change in reported product margins	$290,500	$(307,500)

The traditional cost system overcosts the standard stanchions and consequently reports an artificially low product margin for this product. The switch to an activity-based view of product profitability increases the product margin on standard stanchions by $290,500. In contrast, the traditional cost system undercosts the custom compass housings and reports an artificially high product margin for this product. The switch to activity-based costing decreases the product margin on custom compass housings by $307,500.

The reasons for the change in reported product margins between the two costing methods are revealed in Exhibit 6–14. The top portion of the exhibit shows each product's direct and indirect cost assignments as reported by the traditional cost system in Exhibit 6–13. For example, Exhibit 6–14 includes the following costs for standard stanchions: direct materials, $905,500; direct labor, $263,750; and manufacturing overhead, $875,000. Each of these costs corresponds with those reported in Exhibit 6–13. Notice, the selling and administrative costs of $875,000 are purposely not allocated to products because these costs are considered to be period costs when using traditional costing. Similarly, the bottom portion of Exhibit 6–14 summarizes the direct and indirect cost assignments as reported by the activity-based costing system in Exhibit 6–11. The only new information in Exhibit 6–14 is shown in the two columns of percentages. The first column of percentages shows the percentage of each cost assigned to standard stanchions. For example, the $905,500 of direct materials cost traced to standard stanchions is 92.9% of the company's total direct materials cost of $975,000. The second column of percentages does the same thing for custom compass housings.

There are three reasons why the traditional and activity-based costing systems report different product margins. First, Classic Brass's traditional cost system allocates all manufacturing overhead costs to products. This forces both products to absorb all manufacturing overhead costs regardless of whether they actually consumed the costs that were allocated to them. The ABC system does not assign the manufacturing overhead costs consumed by the Customer Relations activity to products because these costs are caused by customers, not specific products. It also does not assign the manufacturing overhead costs included in the Other activity to products because these organization-sustaining and unused capacity costs are not caused by any particular

EXHIBIT 6–14
A Comparison of Traditional and Activity-Based Cost Assignments

	A	B	C	D	E	F	G	H	I
1			Standard Stanchions			Custom Compass Housings			
			(a)	(a) ÷ (c)		(b)	(b) ÷ (c)		(c)
2	**Traditional Cost System**		Amount	%*		Amount	%*		Total
3	Direct materials		$ 905,500	92.9%		$ 69,500	7.1%		$ 975,000
4	Direct labor		263,750	75.1%		87,500	24.9%		351,250
5	Manufacturing overhead		875,000	87.5%		125,000	12.5%		1,000,000
6	Total cost assigned to products		$2,044,250			$282,000			2,326,250
7	Selling and administrative								875,000
8	Total cost								$3,201,250
9									
10	**Activity-Based Costing System**								
11	Direct costs:								
12	Direct materials		$ 905,500	92.9%		$ 69,500	7.1%		$ 975,000
13	Direct labor		263,750	75.1%		87,500	24.9%		351,250
14	Shipping		60,000	92.3%		5,000	7.7%		65,000
15	Indirect costs:								
16	Customer orders		192,000	60.0%		128,000	40.0%		320,000
17	Product design		-	0.0%		252,000	100.0%		252,000
18	Order size		332,500	87.5%		47,500	12.5%		380,000
19	Total cost assigned to products		$1,753,750			$589,500			2,343,250
21	Costs not assigned to products:								
22	Customer relations								367,500
23	Other								490,500
24	Total cost								$3,201,250
25									
26	*The percentages are rounded to the nearest tenth of a percent.								

product. From an ABC point of view, assigning these costs to products is inherently arbitrary and counterproductive.

Second, Classic Brass's traditional cost system allocates all of the manufacturing overhead costs using a volume-related allocation base—machine-hours—that may or may not reflect what actually causes the costs. In other words, in the traditional system, 87.5% of each manufacturing overhead cost is implicitly assigned to standard stanchions and 12.5% is assigned to custom compass housings. For example, the traditional cost system inappropriately assigns 87.5% of the costs of the Customer Orders activity (a batch-level activity) to standard stanchions even though the ABC system revealed that standard stanchions caused only 60% of these costs. Conversely, the traditional cost system assigns only 12.5% of these costs to custom compass housings even though this product caused 40% of these costs. Similarly, the traditional cost system assigns 87.5% of the costs of the Product Design activity (a product-level activity) to standard stanchions even though the standard stanchions caused none (0%) of these costs. All (100%) of the costs of the Product Design activity, rather than just 12.5%, should be assigned to custom compass housings. The result is that traditional cost systems overcost high-volume products (such as the standard stanchions) and undercost low-volume products (such as the custom compass housings) because they assign batch-level and product-level costs using volume-related allocation bases.

The third reason the product margins differ between the two cost systems is that the ABC system assigns the nonmanufacturing overhead costs caused by products to those products on a cause-and-effect basis. The traditional cost system disregards these costs because they are classified as period costs. The ABC system directly traces shipping costs to products and includes the nonmanufacturing overhead costs caused by products in the activity cost pools that are assigned to products.

The ABC design team presented the results of its work in a meeting attended by all of the top managers of Classic Brass, including the president John Towers, the production manager Susan Richter, the marketing manager Tom Olafson, and the accounting manager Mary Goodman. The ABC team brought with them copies of the chart showing the ABC design (Exhibit 6–8), and the table comparing the traditional and ABC cost assignments (Exhibit 6–14). After the formal presentation by the ABC team, the following discussion took place:

John: I would like to personally thank the ABC team for all of the work they have done and for an extremely interesting presentation. I am now beginning to wonder about a lot of the decisions we have made in the past using our old cost accounting system. According to the ABC analysis, we had it all backwards. We are losing money on the custom products and making a fistful on the standard products.

Mary: I have to admit that I had no idea that the Product Design work for custom compass housings was so expensive! I knew burying these costs in our plantwide overhead rate was penalizing standard stanchions, but I didn't understand the magnitude of the problem.

Susan: I never did believe we were making a lot of money on the custom jobs. You ought to see all of the problems they create for us in production.

Tom: I hate to admit it, but the custom jobs always seem to give us headaches in marketing, too.

John: If we are losing money on custom compass housings, why not suggest to our customers that they go elsewhere for that kind of work?

Tom: Wait a minute, we would lose a lot of sales.

Susan: So what, we would save a lot more costs.

Mary: Maybe yes, maybe no. Some of the costs would not disappear if we were to drop the custom business.

Tom: Like what?

Mary: Well Tom, I believe you said that about 10% of your time is spent dealing with new products. As a consequence, 10% of your salary was allocated to the Product Design cost pool. If we were to drop all of the products requiring design work, would you be willing to take a 10% pay cut?

Tom: I trust you're joking.

Mary: Do you see the problem? Just because 10% of your time is spent on custom products doesn't mean that the company would save 10% of your salary if the custom products were dropped. Before we take a drastic action like dropping the custom products, we should identify which costs are really relevant.

John: I think I see what you are driving at. We wouldn't want to drop a lot of products only to find that our costs really haven't changed much. It is true that dropping the products would free up resources like Tom's time, but we had better be sure we have some good use for those resources *before* we take such an action.

As this discussion among the managers of Classic Brass illustrates, caution should be exercised before taking action based on an ABC analysis such as the one shown in Exhibit 6–11 and Exhibit 6–12. The product and customer margins computed in these exhibits are a useful starting point for further analysis, but managers need to know what costs are really affected before taking any action such as dropping a product or customer or changing the prices of products or services. Appendix 6A shows how an *action analysis report* can be constructed to help managers make such decisions. An **action analysis report** provides more detail about costs and how they might adjust to changes in activity than the ABC analysis presented in Exhibit 6–11 and Exhibit 6–12.

AN ABC IMPLEMENTATION IN THAILAND

APS, a parawood furniture factory located in the Songkhla Province of Southern Thailand, employs over 250 workers to make more than 100 types of furniture. The company's traditional cost system assigns indirect manufacturing costs to products based on each product's total sales. Its ABC system relies on various volume-related and non–volume-related activity measures, such as direct labor-hours, number of setups, and number of trips, to assign overhead costs to products.

The company's traditional and ABC systems assigned per-unit overhead costs to its five best-selling products as follows:

	Tile Top Table	Side Chair	Telephone Table	Plant Tree with Grooves	Computer Desk
Traditional cost system allocations	$7.08	$2.21	$3.53	$3.65	$ 4.53
ABC allocations	2.18	1.13	1.32	1.80	6.07
Difference...	$4.90	$1.08	$2.21	$1.85	$(1.54)

Given that all five of these products have high sales volumes, it is not surprising to see that the traditional cost system has overcosted four of them.

Source: Sakesun Suthummanon, Wanida Ratanamanee, Nirachara Boonyanuwat, and Pieanpon Saritprit, "Applying Activity-Based Costing (ABC) to a Parawood Furniture Factory," *The Engineering Economist*, Volume 56 (2011), pp. 80–93.

Targeting Process Improvements

Activity-based costing can also be used to identify activities that would benefit from process improvements. When used in this way, activity-based costing is often called *activity-based management*. Basically, **activity-based management (ABM)** involves focusing on activities to eliminate waste, decrease processing time, and reduce defects. Activity-based management is used in organizations as diverse as manufacturing companies, hospitals, and the U.S. Marine Corps.

The first step in any improvement program is to decide what to improve. The activity rates computed in activity-based costing can provide valuable clues concerning where there is waste and opportunity for improvement. For example, looking at the activity rates in Exhibit 6–7, managers at Classic Brass may conclude that $320 to process a customer order is far too expensive for an activity that adds no value to the product. As a consequence, they may target their process improvement efforts toward the Customer Orders activity.[3]

Benchmarking is another way to leverage the information in activity rates. **Benchmarking** is a systematic approach to identifying the activities with the greatest room for improvement. It is based on comparing the performance in an organization with the performance of other, similar organizations known for their outstanding performance. If a particular part of the organization performs far below the world-class standard, managers will be likely to target that area for improvement.

Activity-Based Costing and External Reports

Although activity-based costing generally provides more accurate product costs than traditional costing methods, it is infrequently used for external reports for a number of reasons. First, external reports are less detailed than internal reports prepared for decision

---

[3] In Chapter 7, we introduce the Theory of Constraints, which is a powerful tool that helps companies target their process improvement efforts on the most profitable opportunities.

making. On the external reports, individual product costs are not reported. Cost of goods sold and inventory valuations are disclosed, but they are not broken down by product. If some products are undercosted and some are overcosted, the errors tend to offset each other when the product costs are added together.

Second, it is often very difficult to make changes in a company's accounting system. The official cost accounting systems in most large companies are usually embedded in complex computer programs that have been modified in-house over the course of many years. It is extremely difficult to make changes in such computer programs without causing numerous bugs.

Third, an ABC system such as the one described in this chapter does not conform to generally accepted accounting principles (GAAP). As discussed in prior chapters, product costs computed for external reports must include all of the manufacturing costs and only manufacturing costs; but in an ABC system as described in this chapter, product costs exclude some manufacturing costs and include some nonmanufacturing costs. It is possible to adjust the ABC data at the end of the period to conform to GAAP, but that requires more work.

Fourth, auditors are likely to be uncomfortable with allocations that are based on interviews with the company's personnel. Such subjective data can be easily manipulated by management to make earnings and other key variables look more favorable.

For all of these reasons, most companies confine their ABC efforts to special studies for management, and they do not attempt to integrate activity-based costing into their formal cost accounting systems.

The Limitations of Activity-Based Costing

Implementing an activity-based costing system is a major project that requires substantial resources. And once implemented, an activity-based costing system is more costly to maintain than a traditional costing system—data concerning numerous activity measures must be periodically collected, checked, and entered into the system. The benefits of increased accuracy may not outweigh these costs.

Activity-based costing produces numbers, such as product margins, that are at odds with the numbers produced by traditional costing systems. But managers are accustomed to using traditional costing systems to run their operations and traditional costing systems are often used in performance evaluations. Essentially, activity-based costing changes the rules of the game. It is a fact of human nature that changes in organizations, particularly those that alter the rules of the game, inevitably face resistance. This underscores the importance of top management support and the full participation of line managers, as well as the accounting staff, in any activity-based costing initiative. If activity-based costing is viewed as an accounting initiative that does not have the full support of top management, it is doomed to failure.

In practice, most managers insist on fully allocating all costs to products, customers, and other costing objects in an activity-based costing system—including the costs of idle capacity and organization-sustaining costs. This results in overstated costs and understated margins and mistakes in pricing and other critical decisions.

Activity-based costing data can easily be misinterpreted and must be used with care when used in making decisions. Costs assigned to products, customers, and other cost objects are only *potentially* relevant. Before making any significant decisions using activity-based costing data, managers must identify which costs are really relevant for the decision at hand. See Appendix 6A for more details.

As discussed in the previous section, reports generated by the best activity-based costing systems do not conform to external reporting requirements. Consequently, an organization involved in activity-based costing should have two cost systems—one for internal use and one for preparing external reports. This is costlier than maintaining just one system and may cause confusion about which system is to be believed and relied on.

Summary

Traditional cost accounting methods suffer from several defects that can result in distorted costs for decision-making purposes. All manufacturing costs—even those that are not caused by any specific product—are allocated to products. Nonmanufacturing costs that are caused by products are not assigned to products. And finally, traditional methods tend to place too much reliance on unit-level allocation bases such as direct labor and machine-hours. This results in overcosting high-volume products and undercosting low-volume products and can lead to mistakes when making decisions.

Activity-based costing estimates the costs of the resources consumed by cost objects such as products and customers. The activity-based costing approach assumes that cost objects generate activities that in turn consume costly resources. Activities form the link between costs and cost objects. Activity-based costing is concerned with overhead—both manufacturing overhead and selling and administrative overhead. The accounting for direct labor and direct materials is usually the same under traditional and ABC costing methods.

To build an ABC system, companies typically choose a small set of activities that summarize much of the work performed in overhead departments. Associated with each activity is an activity cost pool. To the extent possible, overhead costs are directly traced to these activity cost pools. The remaining overhead costs are allocated to the activity cost pools in the first-stage allocation. Interviews with managers often form the basis for these allocations.

An activity rate is computed for each cost pool by dividing the costs assigned to the cost pool by the measure of activity for the cost pool. Activity rates provide useful information to managers concerning the costs of performing overhead activities. A particularly high cost for an activity may trigger efforts to improve the way the activity is carried out in the organization.

In the second-stage allocation, activity rates are used to apply costs to cost objects such as products and customers. The costs computed under activity-based costing are often quite different from the costs generated by a company's traditional cost accounting system. While the ABC system is almost certainly more accurate, managers should nevertheless exercise caution before making decisions based on the ABC data. Some of the costs may not be avoidable and hence would not be relevant.

Review Problem: Activity-Based Costing

Ferris Corporation makes a single product—a fire-resistant commercial filing cabinet—that it sells to office furniture distributors. The company has a simple ABC system that it uses for internal decision making. The company has two overhead departments whose costs are listed below:

Manufacturing overhead.	$500,000
Selling and administrative overhead.	300,000
Total overhead costs	$800,000

The company's ABC system has the following activity cost pools and activity measures:

Activity Cost Pool	Activity Measure
Assembling units	Number of units
Processing orders	Number of orders
Supporting customers	Number of customers
Other.	Not applicable

Costs assigned to the "Other" activity cost pool have no activity measure; they consist of the costs of unused capacity and organization-sustaining costs—neither of which are assigned to orders, customers, or the product.

Ferris Corporation distributes the costs of manufacturing overhead and selling and administrative overhead to the activity cost pools based on employee interviews, the results of which are reported below:

Distribution of Resource Consumption across Activity Cost Pools					
	Assembling Units	Processing Orders	Supporting Customers	Other	Total
Manufacturing overhead	50%	35%	5%	10%	100%
Selling and administrative overhead	10%	45%	25%	20%	100%
Total activity	1,000 units	250 orders	100 customers		

Required:

1. Perform the first-stage allocation of overhead costs to the activity cost pools as in Exhibit 6–6.
2. Compute activity rates for the activity cost pools as in Exhibit 6–7.
3. OfficeMart is one of Ferris Corporation's customers. Last year, OfficeMart ordered filing cabinets four different times. OfficeMart ordered a total of 80 filing cabinets during the year. Construct a table as in Exhibit 6–10 showing the overhead costs attributable to OfficeMart.
4. The selling price of a filing cabinet is $595. The cost of direct materials is $180 per filing cabinet, and direct labor is $50 per filing cabinet. What is the customer margin of OfficeMart? See Exhibit 6–12 for an example of how to complete this report.

Solution to Review Problem

1. The first-stage allocation of costs to the activity cost pools appears below:

	Activity Cost Pools				
	Assembling Units	Processing Orders	Supporting Customers	Other	Total
Manufacturing overhead	$250,000	$175,000	$ 25,000	$ 50,000	$500,000
Selling and administrative overhead..................	30,000	135,000	75,000	60,000	300,000
Total cost....................	$280,000	$310,000	$100,000	$110,000	$800,000

2. The activity rates for the activity cost pools are:

Activity Cost Pools	(a) Total Cost	(b) Total Activity	(a) ÷ (b) Activity Rate
Assembling units	$280,000	1,000 units	$280 per unit
Processing orders............	$310,000	250 orders	$1,240 per order
Supporting customers.........	$100,000	100 customers	$1,000 per customer

3. The overhead cost attributable to OfficeMart would be computed as follows:

Activity Cost Pools	(a) Activity Rate	(b) Activity	(a) × (b) ABC Cost
Assembling units	$280 per unit	80 units	$22,400
Processing orders............	$1,240 per order	4 orders	$4,960
Supporting customers.........	$1,000 per customer	1 customer	$1,000

4. The customer margin can be computed as follows:

Sales ($595 per unit × 80 units)		$47,600
Costs:		
Direct materials ($180 per unit × 80 units)	$14,400	
Direct labor ($50 per unit × 80 units)	4,000	
Assembling units (above)	22,400	
Processing orders (above)	4,960	
Supporting customers (above)	1,000	46,760
Customer margin		$ 840

Glossary

Action analysis report A report showing what costs have been assigned to a cost object, such as a product or customer, and how difficult it would be to adjust the cost if there is a change in activity. (p. 246)

Activity An event that causes the consumption of overhead resources in an organization. (p. 227)

Activity-based costing (ABC) A costing method based on activities that is designed to provide managers with cost information for strategic and other decisions that potentially affect capacity and therefore fixed as well as variable costs. (p. 224)

Activity-based management (ABM) A management approach that focuses on managing activities as a way of eliminating waste and reducing delays and defects. (p. 247)

Activity cost pool A "bucket" in which costs are accumulated that relate to a single activity measure in an activity-based costing system. (p. 227)

Activity measure An allocation base in an activity-based costing system; ideally, a measure of the amount of activity that drives the costs in an activity cost pool. (p. 227)

Batch-level activities Activities that are performed each time a batch of goods is handled or processed, regardless of how many units are in the batch. The amount of resource consumed depends on the number of batches run rather than on the number of units in the batch. (p. 227)

Benchmarking A systematic approach to identifying the activities with the greatest potential for improvement. (p. 247)

Customer-level activities Activities that are carried out to support customers, but that are not related to any specific product. (p. 228)

Duration driver A measure of the amount of time required to perform an activity. (p. 227)

First-stage allocation The process by which overhead costs are assigned to activity cost pools in an activity-based costing system. (p. 233)

Organization-sustaining activities Activities that are carried out regardless of which customers are served, which products are produced, how many batches are run, or how many units are made. (p. 228)

Product-level activities Activities that relate to specific products that must be carried out regardless of how many units are produced and sold or batches run. (p. 228)

Second-stage allocation The process by which activity rates are used to apply costs to products and customers in activity-based costing. (p. 237)

Transaction driver A simple count of the number of times an activity occurs. (p. 227)

Unit-level activities Activities that are performed each time a unit is produced. (p. 227)

Questions

6–1 In what fundamental ways does activity-based costing differ from traditional costing methods such as job-order costing as described in Chapter 4?

6–2 Why is direct labor a poor base for allocating overhead in many companies?

6–3 Why are top management support and cross-functional involvement crucial when attempting to implement an activity-based costing system?

6–4 What are unit-level, batch-level, product-level, customer-level, and organization-sustaining activities?

6–5 What types of costs should not be assigned to products in an activity-based costing system?

6–6 Why are there two stages of allocation in activity-based costing?

6–7 Why is the first stage of the allocation process in activity-based costing often based on interviews?

6–8 When activity-based costing is used, why do manufacturing overhead costs often shift from high-volume products to low-volume products?

6–9 How can the activity rates (i.e., cost per activity) for the various activities be used to target process improvements?

6–10 Why is the activity-based costing described in this chapter unacceptable for external financial reports?

Multiple-choice questions are available with Connect.

| Applying Excel | | Additional student resources are available with Connect. |

LEARNING OBJECTIVES 6–1, 6–2, 6–3, 6–4

The Excel worksheet form that follows is to be used to recreate the Review Problem relating to Ferris Corporation that was presented earlier. Download the workbook containing this form from Connect. *On the website you will also receive instructions about how to use this worksheet form.*
You should proceed to the requirements below only after completing your worksheet.

Required:

1. Check your worksheet by doubling the units ordered in cell B16 to 160. The customer margin under activity-based costing should now be $7,640 and the traditional costing product margin should be $(21,600). If you do not get these results, find the errors in your worksheet and correct them.

   a. Why has the customer margin under activity-based costing more than doubled when the number of units ordered is doubled?

   b. Why has the traditional costing product margin exactly doubled from a loss of $10,800 to a loss of $21,600?

   c. Which costing system, activity-based costing or traditional costing, provides a more accurate picture of what happens to profits as the number of units ordered increases? Explain.

2. Let's assume that OfficeMart places different orders next year, purchasing higher-end filing cabinets more frequently, but in smaller quantities per order. Enter the following data into your worksheet:

Data				
Manufacturing overhead...............	$500,000			
Selling and administrative overhead......	$300,000			
	Assembling Units	**Processing Orders**	**Supporting Customers**	**Other**
Manufacturing overhead	50%	35%	5%	10%
Selling and administrative overhead	10%	45%	25%	20%
Total activity..........................	1,000 units	250 orders	100 customers	
OfficeMart orders:				
Customers............................	1 customer			
Orders	20 orders			
Total number of filing cabinets ordered . . .	80 units			
Selling price..........................	$795			
Direct materials.......................	$185			
Direct labor..........................	$90			

	A	B	C	D	E	F
1	Chapter 6: Applying Excel					
2						
3	Data					
4	Manufacturing overhead	$500,000				
5	Selling and administrative overhead	$300,000				
6						
7		Assembling Units	Processing Orders	Supporting Customers	Other	
8	Manufacturing overhead	50%	35%	5%	10%	
9	Selling and administrative overhead	10%	45%	25%	20%	
10	Total activity	1,000	250	100		
11		units	orders	customers		
12						
13	OfficeMart orders:					
14	Customers	1	customer			
15	Orders	4	orders			
16	Number of filing cabinets ordered in total	80	units			
17	Selling price	$595				
18	Direct materials	$180				
19	Direct labor	$50				
20						
21	Enter a formula into each of the cells marked with a ? below					
22	Review Problem: Activity-Based Costing					
23						
24	Perform the first stage allocations					
25		Assembling Units	Processing Orders	Supporting Customers	Other	Total
26	Manufacturing overhead	?	?	?	?	?
27	Selling and administrative overhead	?	?	?	?	?
28	Total cost	?	?	?	?	?
29						
30	Compute the activity rates					
31	Activity Cost Pools	Total Cost	Total Activity		Activity Rate	
32	Assembling units	?	? units		? per unit	
33	Processing orders	?	? orders		? per order	
34	Supporting customers	?	? customers		? per customer	
35						
36	Compute the overhead cost attributable to the OfficeMart orders					
37	Activity Cost Pools	Activity Rate		Activity		ABC Cost
38	Assembling units	? per unit		? units		?
39	Processing orders	? per order		? orders		?
40	Supporting customers	? per customer		? customer		?
41						
42	Determine the customer margin for the OfficeMart orders under Activity-Based Costing					
43	Sales		?			
44	Costs:					
45	Direct materials	?				
46	Direct labor	?				
47	Unit-related overhead	?				
48	Order-related overhead	?				
49	Customer-related overhead	?	?			
50	Customer margin		?			
51						
52	Determine the product margin for the OfficeMart orders under a traditional cost system					
53	Manufacturing overhead	?				
54	Total activity	? units				
55	Manufacturing overhead per unit	? per unit				
56						
57	Sales		?			
58	Costs:					
59	Direct materials	?				
60	Direct labor	?				
61	Manufacturing overhead	?	?			
62	Traditional costing product margin		?			

K ◀ ▶ ▶l Chapter 6 Form / Filled in Chapter 6 Form / Chapter 6 Formulas

a. What is the customer margin under activity-based costing?
b. What is the product margin under the traditional cost system?
c. Explain why the profitability picture looks much different now than it did when OfficeMart was ordering less expensive filing cabinets less frequently, but in larger quantities per order.

3. Using the data you entered in requirement 2, change the percentage of selling and administrative overhead attributable to processing orders from 45% to 30% and the percentage attributable to supporting customers from 25% to 40%. That portion of the worksheet should look like this:

	Assembling Units	Processing Orders	Supporting Customers	Other
Manufacturing overhead...............	50%	35%	5%	10%
Selling and administrative overhead......	10%	30%	40%	20%
Total activity...........................	1,000 units	250 orders	100 customers	

   a. Relative to the results from requirement 2, what has happened to the customer margin under activity-based costing? Why?

   b. Relative to the results from requirement 2, what has happened to the product margin under the traditional cost system? Why?

The Foundational 15 Additional student resources are available with Connect.

Hickory Company manufactures two products—14,000 units of Product Y and 6,000 units of Product Z. The company uses a plantwide overhead rate based on direct labor-hours. It is considering implementing an activity-based costing (ABC) system that allocates all of its manufacturing overhead to four cost pools. The following additional information is available for the company as a whole and for Products Y and Z:

Activity Cost Pool	Activity Measure	Estimated Overhead Cost	Expected Activity
Machining	Machine-hours	$200,000	10,000 MHs
Machine setups.........	Number of setups	$100,000	200 setups
Product design	Number of products	$84,000	2 products
General factory.........	Direct labor-hours	$300,000	12,000 DLHs

Activity Measure	Product Y	Product Z
Machine-hours..............	7,000	3,000
Number of setups	50	150
Number of products	1	1
Direct labor-hours	8,000	4,000

Required:
1. What is the company's plantwide overhead rate?
2. Using the plantwide overhead rate, how much manufacturing overhead cost is allocated to Product Y? How much is allocated to Product Z?
3. What is the activity rate for the Machining activity cost pool?
4. What is the activity rate for the Machine Setups activity cost pool?
5. What is the activity rate for the Product Design activity cost pool?
6. What is the activity rate for the General Factory activity cost pool?
7. Which of the four activities is a batch-level activity? Why?
8. Which of the four activities is a product-level activity? Why?

9. Using the ABC system, how much total manufacturing overhead cost would be assigned to Product Y?

10. Using the ABC system, how much total manufacturing overhead cost would be assigned to Product Z?

11. Using the plantwide overhead rate, what percentage of the total overhead cost is allocated to Product Y? What percentage is allocated to Product Z?

12. Using the ABC system, what percentage of the Machining costs is assigned to Product Y? What percentage is assigned to Product Z? Are these percentages similar to those obtained in requirement 11? Why?

13. Using the ABC system, what percentage of Machine Setups cost is assigned to Product Y? What percentage is assigned to Product Z? Are these percentages similar to those obtained in requirement 11? Why?

14. Using the ABC system, what percentage of the Product Design cost is assigned to Product Y? What percentage is assigned to Product Z? Are these percentages similar to those obtained in requirement 11? Why?

15. Using the ABC system, what percentage of the General Factory cost is assigned to Product Y? What percentage is assigned to Product Z? Are these percentages similar to those obtained in requirement 11? Why?

Additional student resources are available with Connect. **Exercises**

EXERCISE 6–1 ABC Cost Hierarchy [LO6–1]

The following activities occur at Greenwich Corporation, a company that manufactures a variety of products.

a. Receive raw materials from suppliers.
b. Manage parts inventories.
c. Do rough milling work on products.
d. Interview and process new employees in the personnel department.
e. Design new products.
f. Perform periodic preventive maintenance on general-use equipment.
g. Use the general factory building.
h. Issue purchase orders for a job.

Required:

Classify each of the activities above as either a unit-level, batch-level, product-level, or organization-sustaining activity.

EXERCISE 6–2 First Stage Allocation [LO6–2]

SecuriCorp operates a fleet of armored cars that make scheduled pickups and deliveries in the Los Angeles area. The company is implementing an activity-based costing system that has four activity cost pools: Travel, Pickup and Delivery, Customer Service, and Other. The activity measures are miles for the Travel cost pool, number of pickups and deliveries for the Pickup and Delivery cost pool, and number of customers for the Customer Service cost pool. The Other cost pool has no activity measure because it is an organization-sustaining activity. The following costs will be assigned using the activity-based costing system:

Driver and guard wages.........................	$ 720,000
Vehicle operating expense	280,000
Vehicle depreciation............................	120,000
Customer representative salaries and expenses.....	160,000
Office expenses................................	30,000
Administrative expenses.........................	320,000
Total cost.....................................	$1,630,000

The distribution of resource consumption across the activity cost pools is as follows:

	Travel	Pickup and Delivery	Customer Service	Other	Totals
Driver and guard wages..............	50%	35%	10%	5%	100%
Vehicle operating expense	70%	5%	0%	25%	100%
Vehicle depreciation...................	60%	15%	0%	25%	100%
Customer representative salaries and expenses	0%	0%	90%	10%	100%
Office expenses......................	0%	20%	30%	50%	100%
Administrative expenses...............	0%	5%	60%	35%	100%

Required:

Complete the first stage allocations of costs to activity cost pools as illustrated in Exhibit 6–6.

EXERCISE 6–3 Compute Activity Rates [LO6–3]

Green Thumb Gardening is a small gardening service that uses activity-based costing to estimate costs for pricing and other purposes. The proprietor of the company believes that costs are driven primarily by the size of customer lawns, the size of customer garden beds, the distance to travel to customers, and the number of customers. In addition, the costs of maintaining garden beds depends on whether the beds are low maintenance beds (mainly ordinary trees and shrubs) or high maintenance beds (mainly flowers and exotic plants). Accordingly, the company uses the five activity cost pools listed below:

Activity Cost Pool	Activity Measure
Caring for lawn	Square feet of lawn
Caring for garden beds—low maintenance.........	Square feet of low maintenance beds
Caring for garden beds—high maintenance	Square feet of high maintenance beds
Travel to jobs....................................	Miles
Customer billing and service	Number of customers

The company has already completed its first stage allocations of costs and has summarized its annual costs and activity as follows:

Activity Cost Pool	Estimated Overhead Cost	Expected Activity
Caring for lawn..............	$72,000	150,000 square feet of lawn
Caring for garden beds—low maintenance	$26,400	20,000 square feet of low maintenance beds
Caring for garden beds—high maintenance	$41,400	15,000 square feet of high maintenance beds
Travel to jobs	$3,250	12,500 miles
Customer billing and service ...	$8,750	25 customers

Required:

Compute the activity rate for each of the activity cost pools.

EXERCISE 6–4 Second-Stage Allocation [LO6–4]

Klumper Corporation is a diversified manufacturer of industrial goods. The company's activity-based costing system contains the following six activity cost pools and activity rates:

Activity Cost Pool	Activity Rates
Supporting direct labor........................	$6.00 per direct labor-hour
Machine processing	$4.00 per machine-hour
Machine setups	$50.00 per setup
Production orders..........................	$90.00 per order
Shipments	$14.00 per shipment
Product sustaining.........................	$840.00 per product

Activity data have been supplied for the following two products:

	Total Expected Activity	
	K425	M67
Number of units produced per year....	200	2,000
Direct labor-hours	80	500
Machine-hours......................	100	1,500
Machine setups	1	4
Production orders	1	4
Shipments	1	10
Product sustaining..................	1	1

Required:

Determine the total overhead cost that would be assigned to each of the products listed above in the activity-based costing system.

EXERCISE 6–5 Product and Customer Profitability Analysis [LO6–4, LO6–5]

Thermal Rising, Inc., makes paragliders for sale through specialty sporting goods stores. The company has a standard paraglider model, but also makes custom-designed paragliders. Management has designed an activity-based costing system with the following activity cost pools and activity rates:

Activity Cost Pool	Activity Rate
Supporting direct labor.................	$26 per direct labor-hour
Order processing	$284 per order
Custom design processing.............	$186 per custom design
Customer service	$379 per customer

Management would like an analysis of the profitability of a particular customer, Big Sky Outfitters, which has ordered the following products over the last 12 months:

	Standard Model	Custom Design
Number of gliders	20	3
Number of orders	1	3
Number of custom designs	0	3
Direct labor-hours per glider.................	26.35	28.00
Selling price per glider......................	$1,850	$2,400
Direct materials cost per glider	$564	$634

The company's direct labor rate is $19.50 per hour.

Required:

Using the company's activity-based costing system, compute the customer margin of Big Sky Outfitters.

EXERCISE 6–6 Cost Hierarchy [LO6–1]

CD Express, Inc., provides CD duplicating services to software companies. The customer provides a master CD from which CD Express makes copies. An order from a customer can be for a single copy or for thousands of copies. Most jobs are broken down into batches to allow smaller jobs, with higher priorities, to have access to the machines.

A number of activities carried out at CD Express are listed below.

a. Sales representatives' periodic visits to customers to keep them informed about the services provided by CD Express.
b. Ordering labels from the printer for a particular CD.
c. Setting up the CD duplicating machine to make copies from a particular master CD.
d. Loading the automatic labeling machine with labels for a particular CD.
e. Visually inspecting CDs and placing them by hand into protective plastic cases prior to shipping.
f. Preparation of the shipping documents for the order.
g. Periodic maintenance of equipment.
h. Lighting and heating the company's production facility.
i. Preparation of quarterly financial reports.

Required:

Classify each of the activities above as either a unit-level, batch-level, product-level, customer-level, or organization-sustaining activity. An order to duplicate a particular CD is a product-level activity. Assume the order is large enough that it must be broken down into batches.

EXERCISE 6–7 First-Stage Allocations [LO6–2]

The operations vice president of Security Home Bank has been interested in investigating the efficiency of the bank's operations. She has been particularly concerned about the costs of handling routine transactions at the bank and would like to compare these costs at the bank's various branches. If the branches with the most efficient operations can be identified, their methods can be studied and then replicated elsewhere. While the bank maintains meticulous records of wages and other costs, there has been no attempt thus far to show how those costs are related to the various services provided by the bank. The operations vice president has asked your help in conducting an activity-based costing study of bank operations. In particular, she would like to know the cost of opening an account, the cost of processing deposits and withdrawals, and the cost of processing other customer transactions.

The Westfield branch of Security Home Bank has submitted the following cost data for last year:

Teller wages.....................	$160,000
Assistant branch manager salary ...	75,000
Branch manager salary...........	80,000
Total.........................	$315,000

Virtually all other costs of the branch—rent, depreciation, utilities, and so on—are organization-sustaining costs that cannot be meaningfully assigned to individual customer transactions such as depositing checks.

In addition to the cost data above, the employees of the Westfield branch have been interviewed concerning how their time was distributed last year across the activities included in the activity-based costing study. The results of those interviews appear below:

	Distribution of Resource Consumption across Activities				
	Opening Accounts	Processing Deposits and Withdrawals	Processing Other Customer Transactions	Other Activities	Totals
Teller wages...........	5%	65%	20%	10%	100%
Assistant branch manager salary	15%	5%	30%	50%	100%
Branch manager salary..............	5%	0%	10%	85%	100%

Required:

Prepare the first-stage allocation for the activity-based costing study. (See Exhibit 6–6 for an example of a first-stage allocation.)

EXERCISE 6–8 Computing and Interpreting Activity Rates [LO6–3]

(This exercise is a continuation of Exercise 6–7; it should be assigned *only* if Exercise 6–7 is also assigned.) The manager of the Westfield branch of Security Home Bank has provided the following data concerning the transactions of the branch during the past year:

Activity	Total Activity at the Westfield Branch
Opening accounts	500 new accounts opened
Processing deposits and withdrawals	100,000 deposits and withdrawals processed
Processing other customer transactions . . .	5,000 other customer transactions processed

The lowest costs reported by other branches for these activities are displayed below:

Activity	Lowest Cost among All Security Home Bank Branches
Opening accounts	$26.75 per new account
Processing deposits and withdrawals	$1.24 per deposit or withdrawal
Processing other customer transactions	$11.86 per other customer transaction

Required:

1. Using the first-stage allocation from Exercise 6–7 and the above data, compute the activity rates for the activity-based costing system. (Use Exhibit 6–7 as a guide.) Round all computations to the nearest whole cent.
2. What do these results suggest to you concerning operations at the Westfield branch?

EXERCISE 6–9 Second-Stage Allocation to an Order [LO6–4]

Durban Metal Products, Ltd., of the Republic of South Africa makes specialty metal parts used in applications ranging from the cutting edges of bulldozer blades to replacement parts for Land Rovers. The company uses an activity-based costing system for internal decision-making purposes. The company has four activity cost pools as listed below:

Activity Cost Pool	Activity Measure	Activity Rate
Order size	Number of direct labor-hours	$16.85 per direct labor-hour
Customer orders	Number of customer orders	$320.00 per customer order
Product testing	Number of testing hours	$89.00 per testing hour
Selling	Number of sales calls	$1,090.00 per sales call

The managing director of the company would like information concerning the cost of a recently completed order for heavy-duty trailer axles. The order required 200 direct labor-hours, 4 hours of product testing, and 2 sales calls.

Required:

Prepare a report summarizing the overhead costs assigned to the order for heavy-duty trailer axles. What is the total overhead cost assigned to the order?

EXERCISE 6–10 Customer Profitability Analysis [LO6–3, LO6–4, LO6–5]

Worley Company buys surgical supplies from a variety of manufacturers and then resells and delivers these supplies to hundreds of hospitals. Worley sets its prices for all hospitals by marking up its cost of goods sold to those hospitals by 5%. For example, if a hospital buys supplies from Worley that had cost Worley $100 to buy from manufacturers, Worley would charge the hospital $105 to purchase these supplies.

For years, Worley believed that the 5% markup covered its selling and administrative expenses and provided a reasonable profit. However, in the face of declining profits Worley decided to implement an activity-based costing system to help improve its understanding of customer profitability. The company broke its selling and administrative expenses into five activities as shown below:

Activity Cost Pool (Activity Measure)	Total Cost	Total Activity
Customer deliveries (Number of deliveries)	$ 500,000	5,000 deliveries
Manual order processing (Number of manual orders).	248,000	4,000 orders
Electronic order processing (Number of electronic orders).	200,000	12,500 orders
Line item picking (Number of line items picked)	450,000	450,000 line items
Other organization-sustaining costs (None)	602,000	
Total selling and administrative expenses	$2,000,000	

Worley gathered the data below for two of the many hospitals that it serves—University and Memorial (both hospitals purchased a total quantity of medical supplies that had cost Worley $30,000 to buy from its manufacturers):

	Activity	
Activity Measure	University	Memorial
Number of deliveries	10	25
Number of manual orders	0	30
Number of electronic orders	15	0
Number of line items picked	120	250

Required:

1. Compute the total revenue that Worley would receive from University and Memorial.
2. Compute the activity rate for each activity cost pool.
3. Compute the total activity costs that would be assigned to University and Memorial.
4. Compute Worley's customer margin for University and Memorial. (*Hint:* Do not overlook the $30,000 cost of goods sold that Worley incurred serving each hospital.)
5. Describe the purchasing behaviors that are likely to characterize Worley's least profitable customers.

EXERCISE 6–11 Second-Stage Allocation and Margin Calculations [LO6–4, LO6–5]

Foam Products, Inc., makes foam seat cushions for the automotive and aerospace industries. The company's activity-based costing system has four activity cost pools, which are listed below along with their activity measures and activity rates:

Activity Cost Pool	Activity Measure	Activity Rate
Supporting direct labor	Number of direct labor-hours	$5.55 per direct labor-hour
Batch processing.	Number of batches	$107.00 per batch
Order processing.	Number of orders	$275.00 per order
Customer service.	Number of customers	$2,463.00 per customer

The company just completed a single order from Interstate Trucking for 1,000 custom seat cushions. The order was produced in two batches. Each seat cushion required 0.25 direct labor-hours. The selling price was $20 per unit, the direct materials cost was $8.50 per unit, and the direct labor cost was $6.00 per unit. This was Interstate Trucking's only order during the year.

Required:

Using Exhibit 6–12 as a guide, prepare a report showing the customer margin on sales to Interstate Trucking for the year.

EXERCISE 6–12 Activity Measures [LO6–1]

Various activities at Ming Corporation, a manufacturing company, are listed below. Each activity has been classified as a unit-level, batch-level, product-level, or customer-level activity.

	Activity	Level of Activity	Examples of Activity Measures
a.	Direct labor workers assemble a product...........	Unit	
b.	Products are designed by engineers...............	Product	
c.	Equipment is set up	Batch	
d.	Machines are used to shape and cut materials	Unit	
e.	Monthly bills are sent out to regular customers......	Customer	
f.	Materials are moved from the receiving dock to production lines...............................	Batch	
g.	All completed units are inspected for defects	Unit	

Required:

Complete the table by providing an example of an activity measure for each activity.

EXERCISE 6–13 Computing ABC Product Costs [LO6–3, LO6–4]

Fogerty Company makes two products, titanium Hubs and Sprockets. Data regarding the two products follow:

	Direct Labor-Hours per Unit	Annual Production
Hubs	0.80	10,000 units
Sprockets	0.40	40,000 units

Additional information about the company follows:

a. Hubs require $32 in direct materials per unit, and Sprockets require $18.
b. The direct labor wage rate is $15 per hour.
c. Hubs are more complex to manufacture than Sprockets and they require special equipment.
d. The ABC system has the following activity cost pools:

Activity Cost Pool (Activity Measure)	Estimated Overhead Cost	Hubs	Sprockets	Total
Machine setups (number of setups)........	$72,000	100	300	400
Special processing (machine-hours)	$200,000	5,000	0	5,000
General factory (organization-sustaining) ...	$816,000	NA	NA	NA

Required:

1. Compute the activity rate for each activity cost pool. Did you compute an activity rate for all of the activity cost pools? Why?
2. Determine the unit product cost of each product according to the ABC system.

EXERCISE 6–14 Calculating and Interpreting Activity-Based Costing Data [LO6–3, LO6–4]

Hiram's Lakeside is a popular restaurant located on Lake Washington in Seattle. The owner of the restaurant has been trying to better understand costs at the restaurant and has hired a student intern to conduct an activity-based costing study. The intern, in consultation with the owner, identified three major activities and then completed the first-stage allocations of costs to the activity cost pools. The results appear below.

Activity Cost Pool	Activity Measure	Total Cost	Total Activity
Serving a party of diners	Number of parties served	$33,000	6,000 parties
Serving a diner.	Number of diners served	$138,000	15,000 diners
Serving a drink.	Number of drinks ordered	$24,000	10,000 drinks

The above costs include all of the costs of the restaurant except for organization-sustaining costs such as rent, property taxes, and top-management salaries.

A group of diners who ask to sit at the same table are counted as a party. Some costs, such as the costs of cleaning linen, are the same whether one person is at a table or the table is full. Other costs, such as washing dishes, depend on the number of diners served.

Prior to the activity-based costing study, the owner knew very little about the costs of the restaurant. She knew that the total cost for the month (including organization-sustaining costs) was $240,000 and that 15,000 diners had been served. Therefore, the average cost per diner was $16.

Required:

1. According to the activity-based costing system, what is the total cost of serving each of the following parties of diners?
    a. A party of four diners who order three drinks in total.
    b. A party of two diners who do not order any drinks.
    c. A lone diner who orders two drinks.
2. Convert the total costs you computed in (1) above to costs per diner. In other words, what is the average cost per diner for serving each of the following parties?
    a. A party of four diners who order three drinks in total.
    b. A party of two diners who do not order any drinks.
    c. A lone diner who orders two drinks.
3. Why do the costs per diner for the three different parties differ from each other and from the overall average cost of $16 per diner?

EXERCISE 6–15 Comprehensive Activity-Based Costing Exercise [LO6–2, LO6–3, LO6–4, LO6–5]
Advanced Products Corporation has supplied the following data from its activity-based costing system:

Overhead Costs	
Wages and salaries.	$300,000
Other overhead costs	100,000
Total overhead costs	$400,000

Activity Cost Pool	Activity Measure	Total Activity for the Year
Supporting direct labor. . . .	Number of direct labor-hours	20,000 DLHs
Order processing	Number of customer orders	400 orders
Customer support	Number of customers	200 customers
Other	This is an organization-sustaining activity	Not applicable

	Distribution of Resource Consumption across Activities				
	Supporting Direct Labor	Order Processing	Customer Support	Other	Total
Wages and salaries.	40%	30%	20%	10%	100%
Other overhead costs.	30%	10%	20%	40%	100%

During the year, Advanced Products completed one order for a new customer, Shenzhen Enterprises. This customer did not order any other products during the year. Data concerning that order follow:

Data Concerning the Shenzhen Enterprises Order	
Units ordered...................	10 units
Direct labor-hours...............	2 DLHs per unit
Selling price	$300 per unit
Direct materials	$180 per unit
Direct labor.....................	$50 per unit

Required:

1. Using Exhibit 6–6 as a guide, prepare a report showing the first-stage allocations of overhead costs to the activity cost pools.
2. Using Exhibit 6–7 as a guide, compute the activity rates for the activity cost pools.
3. Prepare a report showing the overhead costs for the order from Shenzhen Enterprises including customer support costs.
4. Using Exhibit 6–12 as a guide, prepare a report showing the customer margin for Shenzhen Enterprises.

Additional student resources are available with Connect. **Problems**

PROBLEM 6–16 Comparing Traditional and Activity-Based Product Margins [LO6–1, LO6–3, LO6–4, LO6–5]
Hi-Tek Manufacturing Inc. makes two types of industrial component parts—the B300 and the T500. An absorption costing income statement for the most recent period is shown below:

Hi-Tek Manufacturing Inc. Income Statement	
Sales......................................	$2,100,000
Cost of goods sold	1,600,000
Gross margin..............................	500,000
Selling and administrative expenses	550,000
Net operating loss	$ (50,000)

Hi-Tek produced and sold 70,000 units of B300 at a price of $20 per unit and 17,500 units of T500 at a price of $40 per unit. The company's traditional cost system allocates manufacturing overhead to products using a plantwide overhead rate and direct labor dollars as the allocation base. Additional information relating to the company's two product lines is shown below:

	B300	T500	Total
Direct materials............	$436,300	$251,700	$ 688,000
Direct labor...............	$200,000	$104,000	304,000
Manufacturing overhead ...			608,000
Cost of goods sold			$1,600,000

The company has created an activity-based costing system to evaluate the profitability of its products. Hi-Tek's ABC implementation team concluded that $50,000 and $100,000 of the company's advertising expenses could be directly traced to B300 and T500, respectively. The remainder of the selling and administrative expenses was organization-sustaining in nature.

The ABC team also distributed the company's manufacturing overhead to four activities as shown below:

Activity Cost Pool (and Activity Measure)	Manufacturing Overhead	Activity		
		B300	T500	Total
Machining (machine-hours)...............	$213,500	90,000	62,500	152,500
Setups (setup hours)	157,500	75	300	375
Product-sustaining (number of products) ...	120,000	1	1	2
Other (organization-sustaining costs)......	117,000	NA	NA	NA
Total manufacturing overhead cost........	$608,000			

Required:

1. Using Exhibit 6–13 as a guide, compute the product margins for the B300 and T500 under the company's traditional costing system.
2. Using Exhibit 6–11 as a guide, compute the product margins for B300 and T500 under the activity-based costing system.
3. Using Exhibit 6–14 as a guide, prepare a quantitative comparison of the traditional and activity-based cost assignments. Explain why the traditional and activity-based cost assignments differ.

PROBLEM 6–17 Comparing Traditional and Activity-Based Product Margins [LO6–1, LO6–3, LO6–4, LO6–5]
Smoky Mountain Corporation makes two types of hiking boots—Xtreme and the Pathfinder. Data concerning these two product lines appear below:

	Xtreme	Pathfinder
Selling price per unit	$140.00	$99.00
Direct materials per unit.....................	$72.00	$53.00
Direct labor per unit.........................	$24.00	$12.00
Direct labor-hours per unit	2.0 DLHs	1.0 DLHs
Estimated annual production and sales	20,000 units	80,000 units

The company has a traditional costing system in which manufacturing overhead is applied to units based on direct labor-hours. Data concerning manufacturing overhead and direct labor-hours for the upcoming year appear below:

Estimated total manufacturing overhead	$1,980,000
Estimated total direct labor-hours	120,000 DLHs

Required:

1. Using Exhibit 6–13 as a guide, compute the product margins for the Xtreme and the Pathfinder products under the company's traditional costing system.
2. The company is considering replacing its traditional costing system with an activity-based costing system that would assign its manufacturing overhead to the following four activity cost pools (the Other cost pool includes organization-sustaining costs and idle capacity costs):

Activities (and Activity Measures)	Estimated Overhead Cost	Expected Activity		
		Xtreme	Pathfinder	Total
Supporting direct labor (direct labor-hours)....	$ 783,600	40,000	80,000	120,000
Batch setups (setups)	495,000	200	100	300
Product sustaining (number of products)	602,400	1	1	2
Other	99,000	NA	NA	NA
Total manufacturing overhead cost..........	$1,980,000			

Using Exhibit 6–11 as a guide, compute the product margins for the Xtreme and the Path-finder products under the activity-based costing system.

3. Using Exhibit 6–14 as a guide, prepare a quantitative comparison of the traditional and activity-based cost assignments. Explain why the traditional and activity-based cost assignments differ.

PROBLEM 6–18 Activity-Based Costing and Bidding on Jobs [LO6–2, LO6–3, LO6–4]

Mercer Asbestos Removal Company removes potentially toxic asbestos insulation and related products from buildings. There has been a long-simmering dispute between the company's estimator and the work supervisors. The on-site supervisors claim that the estimators do not adequately distinguish between routine work such as removal of asbestos insulation around heating pipes in older homes and nonroutine work such as removing asbestos-contaminated ceiling plaster in industrial buildings. The on-site supervisors believe that nonroutine work is far more expensive than routine work and should bear higher customer charges. The estimator sums up his position in this way: "My job is to measure the area to be cleared of asbestos. As directed by top management, I simply multiply the square footage by $2.50 to determine the bid price. Since our average cost is only $2.175 per square foot, that leaves enough cushion to take care of the additional costs of nonroutine work that shows up. Besides, it is difficult to know what is routine or not routine until you actually start tearing things apart."

To shed light on this controversy, the company initiated an activity-based costing study of all of its costs. Data from the activity-based costing system follow:

Activity Cost Pool	Activity Measure	Total Activity
Removing asbestos...............	Thousands of square feet	800 thousand square feet
Estimating and job setup	Number of jobs	500 jobs
Working on nonroutine jobs	Number of nonroutine jobs	100 nonroutine jobs
Other (costs of idle capacity and organization-sustaining costs).....	None	

Note: The 100 nonroutine jobs are included in the total of 500 jobs. Both nonroutine jobs and routine jobs require estimating and setup.

Costs for the Year

Wages and salaries.........................	$ 300,000
Disposal fees	700,000
Equipment depreciation....................	90,000
On-site supplies............................	50,000
Office expenses............................	200,000
Licensing and insurance	400,000
Total cost..................................	$1,740,000

Distribution of Resource Consumption across Activities

	Removing Asbestos	Estimating and Job Setup	Working on Nonroutine Jobs	Other	Total
Wages and salaries.............	50%	10%	30%	10%	100%
Disposal fees	60%	0%	40%	0%	100%
Equipment depreciation.........	40%	5%	20%	35%	100%
On-site supplies...............	60%	30%	10%	0%	100%
Office expenses................	10%	35%	25%	30%	100%
Licensing and insurance........	30%	0%	50%	20%	100%

Required:

1. Using Exhibit 6–6 as a guide, perform the first-stage allocation of costs to the activity cost pools.
2. Using Exhibit 6–7 as a guide, compute the activity rates for the activity cost pools.
3. Using the activity rates you have computed, determine the total cost and the average cost per thousand square feet of each of the following jobs according to the activity-based costing system.
    a. A routine 1,000-square-foot asbestos removal job.
    b. A routine 2,000-square-foot asbestos removal job.
    c. A nonroutine 2,000-square-foot asbestos removal job.
4. Given the results you obtained in (3) above, do you agree with the estimator that the company's present policy for bidding on jobs is adequate?

PROBLEM 6–19 Second Stage Allocations and Product Margins [LO6–4, LO6–5]

Pixel Studio, Inc., is a small company that creates computer-generated animations for films and television. Much of the company's work consists of short commercials for television, but the company also does realistic computer animations for special effects in movies.

The young founders of the company have become increasingly concerned with the economics of the business—particularly since many competitors have sprung up recently in the local area. To help understand the company's cost structure, an activity-based costing system has been designed. Three major activities are carried out in the company: animation concept, animation production, and contract administration. The animation concept activity is carried out at the contract proposal stage when the company bids on projects. This is an intensive activity that involves individuals from all parts of the company in creating story boards and prototype stills to be shown to the prospective client. Once a project is accepted by the client, the animation goes into production and contract administration begins. Almost all of the work involved in animation production is done by the technical staff, whereas the administrative staff is largely responsible for contract administration. The activity cost pools and their activity measures are listed below:

Activity Cost Pool	Activity Measure	Activity Rate
Animation concept.............	Number of proposals	$6,040 per proposal
Animation production	Minutes of completed animation	$7,725 per minute
Contract administration.........	Number of contracts	$6,800 per contract

These activity rates include all of the company's costs, except for the costs of idle capacity and organization-sustaining costs. There are no direct labor or direct materials costs.

Preliminary analysis using these activity rates has indicated that the local commercial segment of the market may be unprofitable. This segment is highly competitive. Producers of local commercials may ask three or four companies like Pixel Studio to bid, which results in an unusually low ratio of accepted contracts to bids. Furthermore, the animation sequences tend to be much shorter for local commercials than for other work. Since animation work is billed at fairly standard rates according to the running time of the completed animation, this means that the revenues from these short projects tend to be below average. Data concerning activity in the local commercial market appear below:

Activity Measure	Local Commercials
Number of proposals..............	25
Minutes of completed animation....	5
Number of contracts	10

The total sales from the 10 contracts for local commercials was $180,000.

Required:

1. Determine the cost of serving the local commercial market.
2. Prepare a report showing the margin earned serving the local commercial market. (Remember, this company has no direct materials or direct labor costs.)
3. What would you recommend to management concerning the local commercial market?

PROBLEM 6–20 Evaluating the Profitability of Services [LO6–2, LO6–3, LO6–4, LO6–5]

Gallatin Carpet Cleaning is a small, family-owned business operating out of Bozeman, Montana. For its services, the company has always charged a flat fee per hundred square feet of carpet cleaned. The current fee is $28 per hundred square feet. However, there is some question about whether the company is actually making any money on jobs for some customers—particularly those located on remote ranches that require considerable travel time. The owner's daughter, home for the summer from college, has suggested investigating this question using activity-based costing. After some discussion, a simple system consisting of four activity cost pools seemed to be adequate. The activity cost pools and their activity measures appear below:

Activity Cost Pool	Activity Measure	Activity for the Year
Cleaning carpets	Square feet cleaned (00s)	20,000 hundred square feet
Travel to jobs....................	Miles driven	60,000 miles
Job support.....................	Number of jobs	2,000 jobs
Other (costs of idle capacity and organization-sustaining costs) ...	None	Not applicable

The total cost of operating the company for the year is $430,000, which includes the following costs:

Wages.............................	$150,000
Cleaning supplies	40,000
Cleaning equipment depreciation........	20,000
Vehicle expenses	80,000
Office expenses......................	60,000
President's compensation	80,000
Total cost...........................	$430,000

Resource consumption is distributed across the activities as follows:

	Distribution of Resource Consumption across Activities				
	Cleaning Carpets	Travel to Jobs	Job Support	Other	Total
Wages............................	70%	20%	0%	10%	100%
Cleaning supplies	100%	0%	0%	0%	100%
Cleaning equipment depreciation......	80%	0%	0%	20%	100%
Vehicle expenses	0%	60%	0%	40%	100%
Office expenses.....................	0%	0%	45%	55%	100%
President's compensation	0%	0%	40%	60%	100%

Job support consists of receiving calls from potential customers at the home office, scheduling jobs, billing, resolving issues, and so on.

Required:

1. Using Exhibit 6–6 as a guide, prepare the first-stage allocation of costs to the activity cost pools.
2. Using Exhibit 6–7 as a guide, compute the activity rates for the activity cost pools.
3. The company recently completed a 5 hundred square foot carpet-cleaning job at the Flying N ranch—a 75-mile round-trip journey from the company's offices in Bozeman. Compute the cost of this job using the activity-based costing system.
4. The revenue from the Flying N ranch was $140 (5 hundred square feet @ $28 per hundred square feet). Using Exhibit 6–12 as a guide, prepare a report showing the margin from this job.
5. What do you conclude concerning the profitability of the Flying N ranch job? Explain.
6. What advice would you give the president concerning pricing jobs in the future?

Appendix 6A: ABC Action Analysis

A conventional ABC analysis, such as the one presented in Exhibit 6–11 and Exhibit 6–12 in the chapter, has several important limitations. Referring back to Exhibit 6–11, recall that the custom compass housings show a negative product margin of $49,500. Because of this apparent loss, managers were considering dropping this product. However, as the discussion among the managers revealed, it is unlikely that all of the $589,500 cost of the product would be avoided if it were dropped. Some of these costs would continue even if the product were totally eliminated. *Before* taking action, it is vital to identify which costs would be avoided and which costs would continue. Only those costs that can be avoided are relevant in the decision. Moreover, many of the costs are managed costs that would require explicit management action to eliminate. If the custom compass housings product line were eliminated, the direct materials cost would be avoided without any explicit management action—the materials simply wouldn't be ordered. On the other hand, if the custom compass housings were dropped, explicit management action would be required to eliminate the salaries of overhead workers that are assigned to this product.

Simply shifting these managed costs to other products would not solve anything. These costs would have to be eliminated or redeployed to increase sales to have any benefit to the company. While eliminating the cost is obviously beneficial, redeploying the resources is only beneficial if the resources are used to expand the output of a work center that has been operating at full capacity. If the resources are redeployed to a work center with idle capacity, the additional resources would only increase the excess capacity in that work center—which has no direct benefit to the company.

In addition, if some overhead costs need to be eliminated as a result of dropping a product, specific managers must be held responsible for eliminating those costs or the reductions are unlikely to occur. If no one is specifically held responsible for eliminating the costs, they will almost certainly continue to be incurred. Without external pressure, managers usually avoid cutting costs in their areas of responsibility. The action analysis report developed in this appendix is intended to help top managers identify what costs are relevant in a decision and to place responsibility for the elimination of those costs on the appropriate managers.

Activity Rates—Action Analysis Report

Constructing an action analysis report begins with the results of the first-stage allocation, which is reproduced as Exhibit 6A–1. In contrast to the conventional ABC analysis covered in the chapter, the calculation of the activity rates for an action analysis report is a bit more involved. In addition to computing an overall activity rate for each activity cost pool, an activity rate is computed for each cell in Exhibit 6A–1. The computations of activity rates for the action analysis are carried out in Exhibit 6A–2. For example, the $125,000 cost of indirect factory wages for the Customer Orders cost pool is divided by the total activity for that cost pool—1,000 orders—to arrive at the activity rate of $125 per customer order for indirect factory wages. Similarly, the $200,000 cost of indirect factory wages for the Product Design cost pool is divided by the total activity for that cost pool—400 designs—to arrive at the activity rate of $500 per design for indirect factory wages. Note that the totals at the bottom of Exhibit 6A–2 agree with the overall activity rates in Exhibit 6–7 in the chapter. Exhibit 6A–2, which shows the activity rates for the action analysis report, contains more detail than Exhibit 6–7, which contains the activity rates for the conventional ABC analysis.

Assignment of Overhead Costs to Products—Action Analysis Report

Computing the overhead costs to be assigned to products for an action analysis report also involves more detail than for a conventional ABC analysis. The computations for Classic Brass are carried out in Exhibit 6A–3. For example, the activity rate of $125 per customer

EXHIBIT 6A–1

First-Stage Allocations to Activity Cost Pools

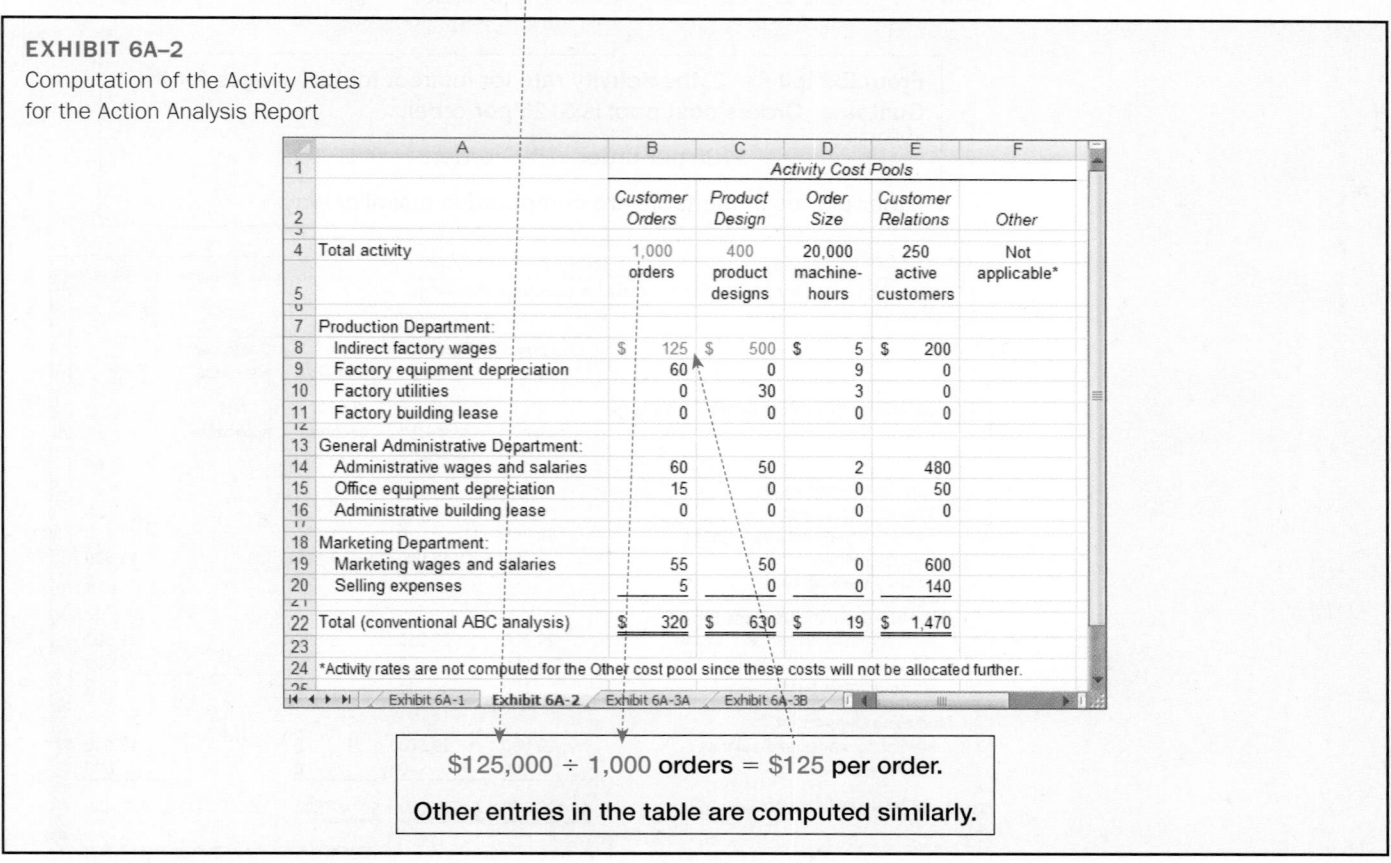

	A	B	C	D	E	F	G
1		Activity Cost Pools					
2		Customer Orders	Product Design	Order Size	Customer Relations	Other	Total
4	Production Department:						
5	Indirect factory wages	$ 125,000	$ 200,000	$ 100,000	$ 50,000	$ 25,000	$ 500,000
6	Factory equipment depreciation	60,000	0	180,000	0	60,000	300,000
7	Factory utilities	0	12,000	60,000	0	48,000	120,000
8	Factory building lease	0	0	0	0	80,000	80,000
10	General Administrative Department:						
11	Administrative wages and salaries	60,000	20,000	40,000	120,000	160,000	400,000
12	Office equipment depreciation	15,000	0	0	12,500	22,500	50,000
13	Administrative building lease	0	0	0	0	60,000	60,000
15	Marketing Department:						
16	Marketing wages and salaries	55,000	20,000	0	150,000	25,000	250,000
17	Selling expenses	5,000	0	0	35,000	10,000	50,000
19	Total cost	$ 320,000	$ 252,000	$ 380,000	$ 367,500	$ 490,500	$ 1,810,000

Exhibit 6A-1 Exhibit 6A-2 Exhibit 6A-3A Exhibit 6A-3B Exhibit 6A-5 Act◄

EXHIBIT 6A–2

Computation of the Activity Rates
for the Action Analysis Report

	A	B	C	D	E	F
1		Activity Cost Pools				
2		Customer Orders	Product Design	Order Size	Customer Relations	Other
4	Total activity	1,000 orders	400 product designs	20,000 machine-hours	250 active customers	Not applicable*
7	Production Department:					
8	Indirect factory wages	$ 125	$ 500	$ 5	$ 200	
9	Factory equipment depreciation	60	0	9	0	
10	Factory utilities	0	30	3	0	
11	Factory building lease	0	0	0	0	
13	General Administrative Department:					
14	Administrative wages and salaries	60	50	2	480	
15	Office equipment depreciation	15	0	0	50	
16	Administrative building lease	0	0	0	0	
18	Marketing Department:					
19	Marketing wages and salaries	55	50	0	600	
20	Selling expenses	5	0	0	140	
22	Total (conventional ABC analysis)	$ 320	$ 630	$ 19	$ 1,470	
24	*Activity rates are not computed for the Other cost pool since these costs will not be allocated further.					

Exhibit 6A-1 Exhibit 6A-2 Exhibit 6A-3A Exhibit 6A-3B

$125,000 ÷ 1,000 **orders** = $125 **per order.**

Other entries in the table are computed similarly.

order for indirect factory wages is multiplied by 600 orders for the standard stanchions to arrive at the cost of $75,000 for indirect factory wages in Exhibit 6A–3. Instead of just a single cost number for each cost pool as in the conventional ABC analysis, we now have an entire cost matrix showing much more detail. Note that the column totals for the cost matrix in Exhibit 6A–3 agree with the ABC costs for standard stanchions in Exhibit 6–9. Indeed, the conventional ABC analysis of Exhibit 6–11 can be easily constructed using the column totals at the bottom of the cost matrices in Exhibit 6A–3. In contrast, the

EXHIBIT 6A–3
Action Analysis Cost Matrices

	A	B	C	D	E	F
1	**Action Analysis Cost Matrix for Standard Stanchions**					
3		*Activity Cost Pools*				
4		*Customer Orders*	*Product Design*	*Order Size*	*Customer Relations*	*Total*
6	Total activity for stanchions	600 orders	product designs	17,500 machine-hours	Not applicable	
9	Production Department:					
10	Indirect factory wages	$ 75,000	$ 0	$ 87,500		$ 162,500
11	Factory equipment depreciation	36,000	0	157,500		193,500
12	Factory utilities	0	0	52,500		52,500
13	Factory building lease	0	0	0		0
15	General Administrative Department:					
16	Administrative wages and salaries	36,000	0	35,000		71,000
17	Office equipment depreciation	9,000	0	0		9,000
18	Administrative building lease	0	0	0		0
20	Marketing Department:					
21	Marketing wages and salaries	33,000	0	0		33,000
22	Selling expenses	3,000	0	0		3,000
24	Total (conventional ABC analysis)	$ 192,000	$ 0	$ 332,500		$ 524,500

Exhibit 6A-3A Exhibit 6A-3B Exhibit 6A-5 Activity rates

From Exhibit 6A–2, the activity rate for indirect factory wages for the Customer Orders cost pool is $125 per order.

$125 per order × 600 orders = $75,000

Other entries in the table are computed in a similar way.

	A	B	C	D	E	F
1	**Action Analysis Cost Matrix for the Custom Compass Housings**					
3		*Activity Cost Pools*				
4		*Customer Orders*	*Product Design*	*Order Size*	*Customer Relations*	*Total*
6	Total activity for custom compass housings	400 order	400 product design	2,500 machine-hours	Not applicable	
9	Production Department:					
10	Indirect factory wages	$ 50,000	$ 200,000	$ 12,500		$ 262,500
11	Factory equipment depreciation	24,000	0	22,500		46,500
12	Factory utilities	0	12,000	7,500		19,500
13	Factory building lease	0	0	0		0
15	General Administrative Department:					
16	Administrative wages and salaries	24,000	20,000	5,000		49,000
17	Office equipment depreciation	6,000	0	0		6,000
18	Administrative building lease	0	0	0		0
20	Marketing Department:					
21	Marketing wages and salaries	22,000	20,000	0		42,000
22	Selling expenses	2,000	0	0		2,000
24	Total (conventional ABC analysis)	$ 128,000	$ 252,000	$ 47,500		$ 427,500

Exhibit 6A-3A Exhibit 6A-3B Exhibit 6A-5 Activity rates

From Exhibit 6A–2, the activity rate for indirect factory wages for the Customer Orders cost pool is $125 per order.

$125 per order × 400 orders = $50,000

Other entries in the table are computed in a similar way.

action analysis report will be based on the row totals at the right of the cost matrices in Exhibit 6A–3. In addition, the action analysis report will include a simple color-coding scheme that will help managers identify how easily the various costs can be adjusted.

Ease of Adjustment Codes

The ABC team constructed Exhibit 6A–4 to aid managers in the use of the ABC data. In this exhibit, each cost has been assigned an *ease of adjustment code*—Green, Yellow, or Red. The **ease of adjustment code** reflects how easily the cost could be adjusted to changes in activity.[4] "Green" costs are those costs that would adjust more or less automatically to changes in activity without any action by managers. For example, direct materials costs would adjust to changes in orders without any action being taken by managers. If a customer does not order stanchions, the direct materials for the stanchions would not be required and would not be ordered. "Yellow" costs are those costs that could be adjusted in response to changes in activity, but such adjustments require management action; the adjustment is not automatic. The ABC team believes, for example, that direct labor costs should be included in the Yellow category. Managers must make difficult decisions and take explicit action to increase or decrease, in aggregate, direct labor costs—particularly because the company has a no lay-off policy. "Red" costs are costs that could be adjusted to changes in activity only with a great deal of difficulty, and the adjustment would require management action. The building leases fall into this category because it would be very difficult and expensive to break the leases.

The Action Analysis View of the ABC Data

Looking at Exhibit 6A–3, the totals on the right-hand side of the table indicate that the $427,500 of overhead cost for the custom compass housings consists of $262,500 of indirect factory wages, $46,500 of factory equipment depreciation, and so on. These data are displayed in Exhibit 6A–5, which shows an action analysis of the custom compass housings product. An action analysis report shows what costs have been assigned to the

EXHIBIT 6A–4
Ease of Adjustment Codes

Green: Costs that adjust automatically to changes in activity without management action.
  Direct materials
  Shipping costs
Yellow: Costs that could, in principle, be adjusted to changes in activity, but management action would be required.
  Direct labor
  Indirect factory wages
  Factory utilities
  Administrative wages and salaries
  Office equipment depreciation
  Marketing wages and salaries
  Selling expenses
Red: Costs that would be very difficult to adjust to changes in activity and management action would be required.
  Factory equipment depreciation
  Factory building lease
  Administrative building lease

[4] The idea of using colors to code how easily costs can be adjusted was suggested to us at a seminar put on by Boeing and by an article by Alfred King, "Green Dollars and Blue Dollars: The Paradox of Cost Reduction," *Journal of Cost Management,* Fall 1993, pp. 44–52.

EXHIBIT 6A–5

Action Analysis of Custom
Compass Housings: Activity-
Based Costing System

	A	B	C
1	**Custom Compass Housings**		
2	Sales (from Exhibit 6-11)		$ 540,000
3			
4	Green costs:		
5	Direct materials (from Exhibit 6-11)	$ 69,500	
6	Shipping (from Exhibit 6-11)	5,000	74,500
7	Green margin		465,500
8			
9	Yellow costs:		
10	Direct labor (from Exhibit 6-11)	87,500	
11	Indirect factory wages (from Exhibit 6A-3)	262,500	
12	Factory utilities (from Exhibit 6A-3)	19,500	
13	Administrative wages and salaries (from Exhibit 6A-3)	49,000	
14	Office equipment depreciation (from Exhibit 6A-3)	6,000	
15	Marketing wages and salaries (from Exhibit 6A-3)	42,000	
16	Selling expenses (from Exhibit 6A-3)	2,000	468,500
17	Yellow margin		(3,000)
18			
19	Red costs:		
20	Factory equipment depreciation (from Exhibit 6A-3)	46,500	
21	Factory building lease (from Exhibit 6A-3)	0	
22	Administrative building lease (from Exhibit 6A-3)	0	46,500
23	Red margin		$ (49,500)
24			

Exhibit 6A-5 / Activity rates / Stanchions / Co

cost object, such as a product or customer, and how difficult it would be to adjust the cost if there is a change in activity. Note that the Red margin at the bottom of Exhibit 6A–5, $(49,500), is exactly the same as the product margin for the custom compass housings in Exhibit 6–11 in the chapter.

The cost data in the action analysis in Exhibit 6A–5 are arranged by the color coded ease of adjustment. All of the Green costs—those that adjust more or less automatically to changes in activity—appear together at the top of the list of costs. These costs total $74,500 and are subtracted from the sales of $540,000 to yield a Green margin of $465,500. The same procedure is followed for the Yellow and Red costs. This action analysis indicates what costs would have to be cut and how difficult it would be to cut them if the custom compass housings product were dropped. Prior to making any decision about dropping products, the managers responsible for the costs must agree to either eliminate the resources represented by those costs or to transfer the resources to an area in the organization that really needs the resources. If managers do not make such a commitment, it is likely that the costs would continue to be incurred. As a result, the company would lose the sales from the products without really eliminating the costs.

After the action analysis was prepared by the ABC team, top management at Classic Brass met once again to review the results of the ABC analysis.

**MANAGERIAL
ACCOUNTING IN
ACTION**

The Wrap-Up

John: When we last met, we had discussed the advisability of discontinuing the custom compass housings product line. I understand that the ABC team has done some additional analysis to help us in making this decision.

Mary: That's right. The action analysis report we put together indicates how easy it would be to adjust each cost and where specific cost savings would have to come from if we were to drop the custom compass housings.

John: What's this red margin at the bottom of the action analysis? Isn't that a product margin?

Mary: Yes, it is. However, we call it a red margin because we should stop and think very, very carefully before taking any actions based on that margin.

John: Why is that?

Mary: As an example, we subtracted the costs of factory equipment depreciation to arrive at that red margin. We doubt that we could avoid any of that cost if we were to drop custom orders. We use the same machines on custom orders that we use on standard products. The factory equipment has no resale value, and it does not wear out through use.

John: What about this yellow margin?

Mary: Yellow means proceed with a great deal of caution. To get to the yellow margin we deducted from sales numerous costs that could be adjusted only if the managers involved are willing to eliminate resources or shift them to another department in an effort to grow sales.

John: If I understand the yellow margin correctly, the apparent loss of $3,000 on the custom compass housings is the result of the indirect factory wages of $262,500.

Susan: Right, that's basically the wages of our design engineers.

John: I am uncomfortable with the idea of laying off any of our designers for numerous reasons. So where does that leave us?

Mary: What about raising prices on our custom products?

Tom: We should be able to do that. We have been undercutting the competition to make sure that we won bids on custom work because we thought it was a very profitable thing to do.

John: Why don't we just charge directly for design work?

Tom: Some of our competitors already do that. However, I don't think we would be able to charge enough to cover our design costs.

John: Can we do anything to make our design work more efficient so it costs us less? I'm not going to lay anyone off, but if we make the design process more efficient, we could lower the charge for design work and spread those costs across more customers.

Susan: That may be possible. I'll form a process improvement team to look at it.

John: Let's get some benchmark data on design costs. If we set our minds to it, I'm sure we can be world class in no time.

Susan: Okay. Mary, will you help with the benchmark data?

Mary: Sure.

John: Let's meet again in about a week to discuss our progress. Is there anything else on the agenda for today?

The points raised in the preceding discussion are extremely important. By measuring the resources consumed by products (and other cost objects), an ABC system provides a much better basis for decision making than a traditional cost accounting system that spreads overhead costs around without much regard for what might be causing the overhead. A well-designed ABC system provides managers with estimates of potentially relevant costs that can be a very useful starting point for management analysis.

Summary (Appendix 6A)

The action analysis report illustrated in this appendix is a valuable addition to the ABC toolkit. An action analysis report provides more information for decision making than a conventional ABC analysis. The action analysis report makes it clear where costs would have to be adjusted in the organization as a result of an action. In a conventional ABC analysis, a cost such as $320 for processing an order represents costs from many parts of the organization. If an order is dropped, there will be little pressure to actually eliminate the $320 cost unless it is clear where the costs are incurred and which managers would be responsible for reducing the cost. In contrast, an action analysis report traces the costs to where they are incurred in the organization and makes it much easier to assign responsibility to managers for reducing costs. In addition, an action analysis report provides information concerning how easily a cost can be adjusted. Costs that cannot be adjusted are not relevant in a decision.

EXHIBIT 6A–6
Summary of the Steps to
Produce an Action Analysis
Report

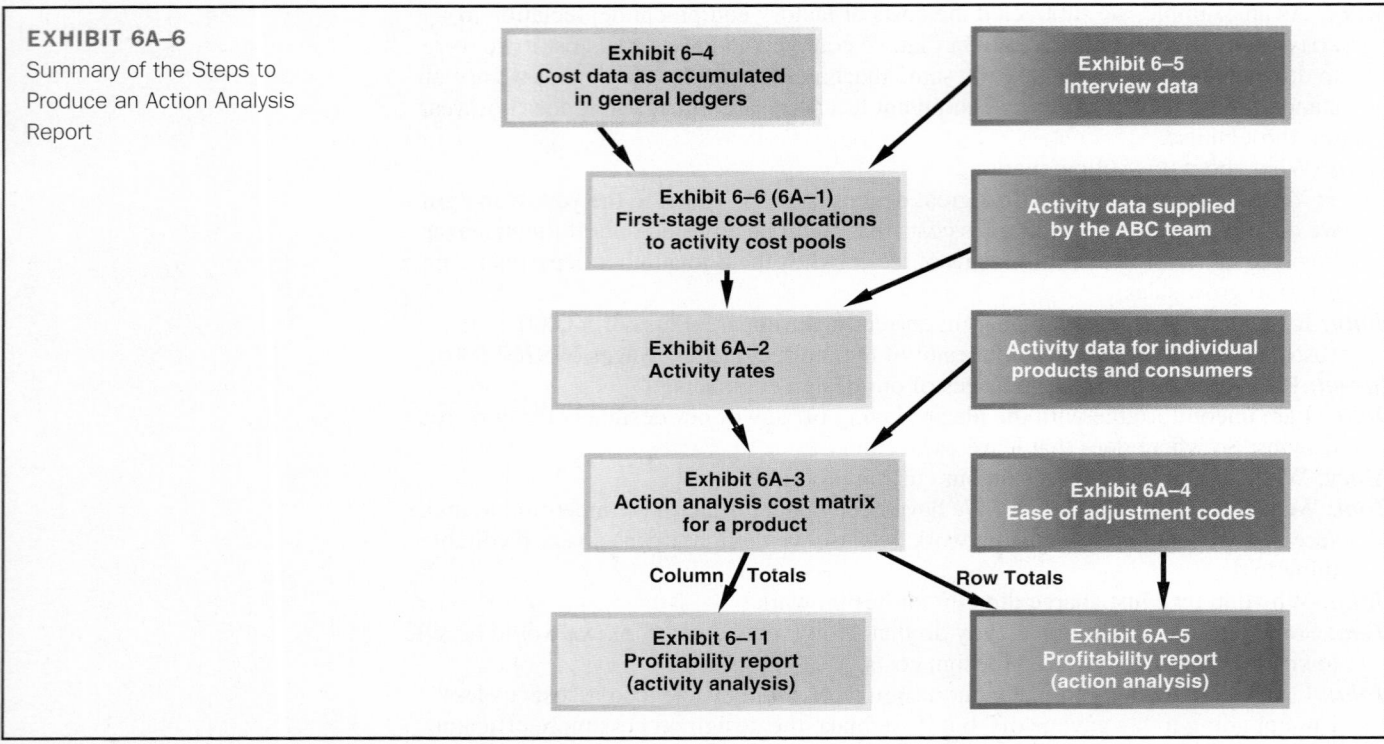

Exhibit 6A–6 summarizes all of the steps required to create both an action analysis report as illustrated in this appendix and an activity analysis as shown in the chapter.

Review Problem: Activity Analysis Report

Refer to the data for Ferris Corporation in the Review Problem at the end of the chapter.

Required:
1. Compute activity rates for Ferris Corporation as in Exhibit 6A–2.
2. Using Exhibit 6A–3 as a guide, construct a table showing the overhead costs for the OfficeMart orders described in requirement (3) of the Review Problem at the end of the chapter.
3. The management of Ferris Corporation has assigned ease of adjustment codes to costs as follows:

Cost	Ease of Adjustment Code
Direct materials.......................	Green
Direct labor	Yellow
Manufacturing overhead	Yellow
Selling and administrative overhead	Red

Using Exhibit 6A–5 as a guide, prepare an action analysis of the OfficeMart orders.

Solution to Review Problem

1. The activity rates for the activity cost pools are:

	Assembling Units	Processing Orders	Supporting Customers
Total activity..........................	1,000 units	250 orders	100 customers
Manufacturing overhead	$250	$ 700	$ 250
Selling and administrative overhead	30	540	750
Total	$280	$1,240	$1,000

2. The overhead cost for the four orders of a total of 80 filing cabinets would be computed as follows:

	Assembling Units	Processing Orders	Supporting Customers	Total
Activity	80 units	4 orders	1 customer	
Manufacturing overhead	$20,000	$2,800	$ 250	$23,050
Selling and administrative overhead...............	2,400	2,160	750	5,310
Total......................	$22,400	$4,960	$1,000	$28,360

3. The action analysis report is:

Sales		$47,600
Green costs:		
Direct materials..........................	$14,400	14,400
Green margin..............................		33,200
Yellow costs:		
Direct labor.............................	4,000	
Manufacturing overhead..................	23,050	27,050
Yellow margin..............................		6,150
Red costs:		
Selling and administrative overhead.......	5,310	5,310
Red margin................................		$ 840

Glossary (Appendix 6A)

Ease of adjustment codes Costs are coded as Green, Yellow, or Red—depending on how easily the cost could be adjusted to changes in activity. "Green" costs adjust automatically to changes in activity. "Yellow" costs could be adjusted in response to changes in activity, but such adjustments require management action; the adjustment is not automatic. "Red" costs could be adjusted to changes in activity only with a great deal of difficulty and would require management action. (p. 271)

Appendix 6A Exercises and Problems   connect

Additional student resources are available with Connect.

EXERCISE 6A–1 Preparing an Action Analysis Report [LO6–6]

Fairway Golf Corporation produces private label golf clubs for pro shops throughout North America. The company uses activity-based costing to evaluate the profitability of serving its customers. This analysis is based on categorizing the company's costs as follows, using the ease of adjustment color coding scheme described in Appendix 6A:

	Ease of Adjustment Code
Direct materials	Green
Direct labor.	Yellow
Indirect labor	Yellow
Factory equipment depreciation.	Red
Factory administration.	Red
Selling and administrative wages and salaries	Red
Selling and administrative depreciation	Red
Marketing expenses.	Yellow

Management would like to evaluate the profitability of a particular customer—Shaker Run Golf Club of Lebanon, Ohio. Over the last twelve months this customer submitted one order for 100 golf clubs that had to be produced in four batches due to differences in product labeling requested by the customer. Summary data concerning the order appear below:

Number of clubs	100
Number of orders	1
Number of batches.	4
Direct labor-hours per club.	0.3
Selling price per club.	$50.00
Direct materials cost per club	$29.50
Direct labor rate per hour	$20.50

A cost analyst working in the controller's office at the company has already produced the action analysis cost matrix for the Shaker Run Golf Club that appears below:

Action Analysis Cost Matrix for Shaker Run Golf Club

	Activity Cost Pools				
	Supporting Direct labor	Batch Processing	Order Processing	Customer Service	Total
Activity	30 direct labor-hours	4 batches	1 order	1 customer	
Manufacturing overhead:					
Indirect labor	$ 35.40	$53.70	$ 6.80	$ 0.00	$ 95.90
Factory equipment depreciation.	102.80	0.90	0.00	0.00	103.70
Factory administration.	18.50	0.50	12.00	228.00	259.00
Selling and administrative overhead:					
Wages and salaries	11.00	0.00	36.00	382.00	429.00
Depreciation	0.00	0.00	6.00	24.00	30.00
Marketing expenses	117.70	0.00	54.00	369.00	540.70
Total	$285.40	$55.10	$114.80	$1,003.00	$1,458.30

Required:
Prepare an action analysis report showing the profitability of the Shaker Run Golf Club. Include direct materials and direct labor costs in the report. Use Exhibit 6A–5 as a guide for organizing the report.

EXERCISE 6A–2 Second-Stage Allocation Using the Action Analysis Approach [LO6–4, LO6–6]
This exercise should be assigned in conjunction with Exercise 6–9.

The results of the first-stage allocation of the activity-based costing system at Durban Metal Products, Ltd., in which the activity rates were computed, appear below:

	Order Size	Customer Orders	Product Testing	Selling
Manufacturing overhead:				
Indirect labor	$ 8.25	$180.00	$30.00	$ 0.00
Factory depreciation	8.00	0.00	40.00	0.00
Factory utilities	0.10	0.00	1.00	0.00
Factory administration........	0.00	48.00	18.00	30.00
Selling and administrative:				
Wages and salaries	0.50	80.00	0.00	800.00
Depreciation	0.00	12.00	0.00	40.00
Taxes and insurance	0.00	0.00	0.00	20.00
Selling expenses.............	0.00	0.00	0.00	200.00
Total overhead cost	$16.85	$320.00	$89.00	$1,090.00

Required:
1. Using Exhibit 6A–3 as a guide, prepare a report showing the overhead cost of the order for heavy-duty trailer axles discussed in Exercise 6–9. What is the total overhead cost of the order according to the activity-based costing system?
2. Explain the two different perspectives this report gives to managers concerning the nature of the overhead costs involved in the order. (*Hint:* Look at the row and column totals of the report you have prepared.)

EXERCISE 6A–3 Second-Stage Allocations and Margin Calculations Using the Action Analysis Approach [LO6–4, LO6–6]
Refer to the data for Foam Products, Inc., in Exercise 6–11 and the following additional details concerning the activity rates in the activity-based costing system:

	Activity Rates			
	Supporting Direct Labor	Batch Processing	Order Processing	Customer Service
Manufacturing overhead:				
Indirect labor....................	$0.60	$ 60.00	$ 20.00	$ 0.00
Factory equipment depreciation ...	4.00	17.00	0.00	0.00
Factory administration............	0.10	7.00	25.00	150.00
Selling and administrative overhead:				
Wages and salaries	0.40	20.00	160.00	1,600.00
Depreciation....................	0.00	3.00	10.00	38.00
Marketing expenses	0.45	0.00	60.00	675.00
Total	$5.55	$107.00	$275.00	$2,463.00

Management has provided its ease of adjustment codes for the purpose of preparing action analyses.

	Ease of Adjustment Codes
Direct materials............................	Green
Direct labor.................................	Yellow
Manufacturing overhead:	
Indirect labor............................	Yellow
Factory equipment depreciation...........	Red
Factory administration....................	Red
Selling and administrative overhead:	
Wages and salaries	Red
Depreciation	Red
Marketing expenses	Yellow

Required:

Using Exhibit 6A–5 as a guide, prepare an action analysis report for Interstate Trucking similar to those prepared for products.

EXERCISE 6A–4 Comprehensive Activity-Based Costing Exercise [LO6–2, LO6–3, LO6–4, LO6–6]

Refer to the data for Advanced Products Corporation in Exercise 6–15.

Required:

1. Using Exhibit 6A–1 as a guide, prepare a report showing the first-stage allocations of overhead costs to the activity cost pools.
2. Using Exhibit 6A–2 as a guide, compute the activity rates for the activity cost pools.
3. Using Exhibit 6A–3 as a guide, prepare a report showing the overhead costs for the order from Shenzhen Enterprises including customer support costs.
4. Using Exhibit 6–12 as a guide, prepare a report showing the customer margin for Shenzhen Enterprises.
5. Using Exhibit 6A–5 as a guide, prepare an action analysis report showing the customer margin for Shenzhen Enterprises. Direct materials should be coded as a Green cost, direct labor and wages and salaries as Yellow costs, and other overhead costs as a Red cost.
6. What action, if any, do you recommend as a result of the above analyses?

EXERCISE 6A–5 Second Stage Allocations and Product Margins [LO6–4, LO6–6]

Refer to the data for Pixel Studio, Inc., in PROBLEM 6–19. In addition, the company has provided the following details concerning its activity rates:

	Activity Rates		
	Animation Concept	Animation Production	Contract Administration
Technical staff salaries....................	$4,000	$6,000	$1,600
Animation equipment depreciation	360	1,125	0
Administrative wages and salaries........	1,440	150	4,800
Supplies costs	120	300	160
Facility costs............................	120	150	240
Total	$6,040	$7,725	$6,800

Management has provided the following ease of adjustment codes for the various costs:

	Ease of Adjustment Code
Technical staff salaries......................	Red
Animation equipment depreciation	Red
Administrative wages and salaries...........	Yellow
Supplies costs	Green
Facility costs...............................	Red

These codes created some controversy. In particular, some administrators objected to coding their own salaries Yellow, while the technical staff salaries were coded Red. However, the founders of the firm overruled these objections by pointing out that "our technical staff is our most valuable asset. Good animators are extremely difficult to find, and they would be the last to go if we had to cut back."

Required:

1. Using Exhibit 6A–3 as a guide, determine the cost of the local commercials market. (Think of the local commercial market as a product.)
2. Using Exhibit 6A–5 as a guide, prepare an action analysis report concerning the local commercial market. (This company has no direct materials or direct labor costs.)
3. What would you recommend to management concerning the local commercial market?

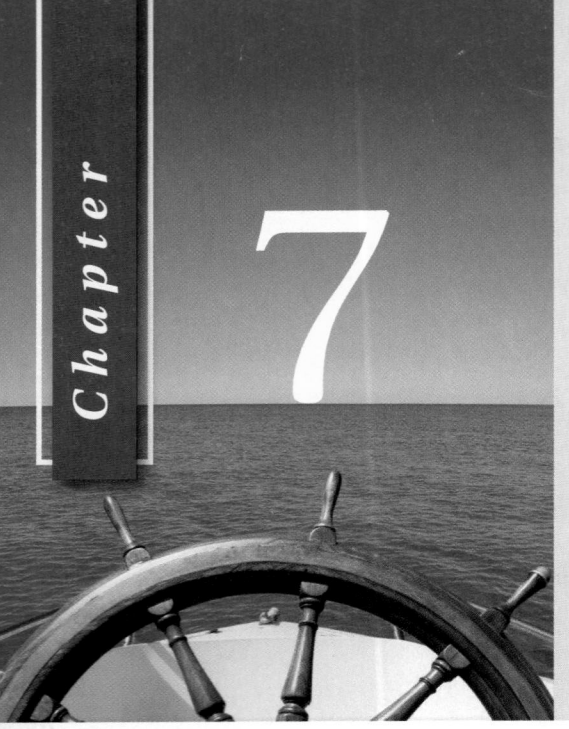

Differential Analysis: The Key to Decision Making

Moving Manufacturing Operations Overseas

LEARNING OBJECTIVES

After studying Chapter 7, you should be able to:

LO 7–1   Identify relevant and irrelevant costs and benefits in a decision.

LO 7–2   Prepare an analysis showing whether a product line or other business segment should be added or dropped.

LO 7–3   Prepare a make or buy analysis.

LO 7–4   Prepare an analysis showing whether a special order should be accepted.

LO 7–5   Determine the most profitable use of a constrained resource.

LO 7–6   Determine the value of obtaining more of the constrained resource.

LO 7–7   Prepare an analysis showing whether joint products should be sold at the split-off point or processed further.

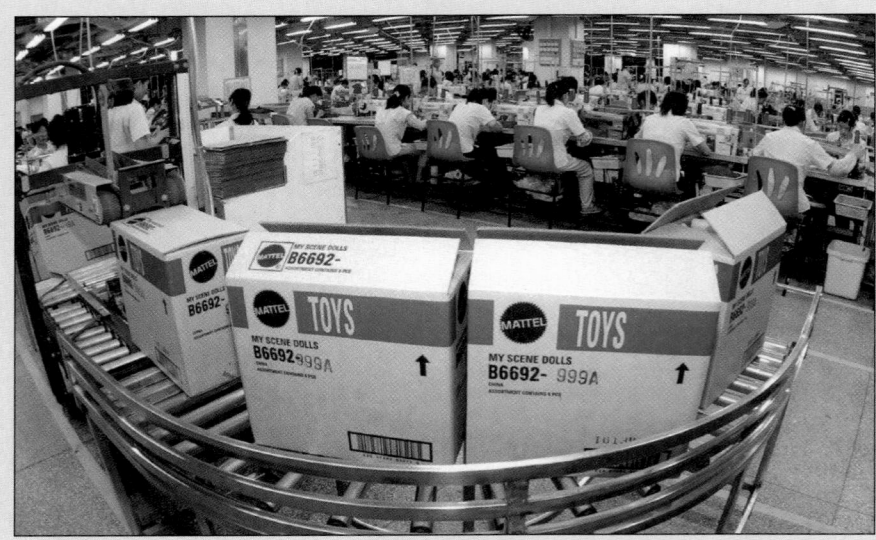

© AP Images/Imaginechina/Jhphoto

BUSINESS FOCUS

A survey from Ventoro Institute LLC found that many companies expect to realize an 80% cost savings when moving manufacturing operations overseas. However, in this same survey, companies reported an average actual cost savings of less than 10%. Some of the problems encountered by these companies included miscommunications with offshore manufacturers, shipping delays, intellectual property infringement, and substandard product quality. William Botts, vice chairman of Vegas Valley Angels (an angel-investing group), suggests that companies with labor-intensive manufacturing processes are most likely to benefit from sending manufacturing operations overseas because the bulk of potential cost savings relate to labor costs. ∎

Source: Small Talk, "Kelly Spors Answers Questions on Protecting Ideas, Cutting Off Junk Mail, and Overseas Manufacturing," *The Wall Street Journal*, March 17, 2008, p. R2.

Managers must decide what products to sell, whether to make or buy component parts, what prices to charge, what channels of distribution to use, whether to accept special orders at special prices, and so forth. Making such decisions is often a difficult task that is complicated by numerous alternatives and massive amounts of data, only some of which may be relevant.

Every decision involves choosing from among at least two alternatives. In making a decision, the costs and benefits of one alternative must be compared to the costs and benefits of other alternatives. The key to making such comparisons is *differential analysis*—focusing on the costs and benefits that *differ* between the alternatives. A difference in cost between any two alternatives is known as a **differential cost**. A difference in revenue between any two alternatives is known as **differential revenue**. Differential costs and revenues are relevant to decision making, whereas costs and revenues that do not differ between alternatives are irrelevant to decision making. Because differential costs and differential revenues are the only inputs that are relevant to decision making, they are also often referred to as **relevant costs** and **relevant benefits**.

Distinguishing between relevant and irrelevant costs and benefits is critical for two reasons. First, irrelevant data can be ignored—saving decision makers tremendous amounts of time and effort. Second, bad decisions can easily result from erroneously including irrelevant costs and benefits when analyzing alternatives. To be successful in decision making, managers must be able to tell the difference between relevant and irrelevant data and must be able to correctly use the relevant data in analyzing alternatives. The purpose of this chapter is to develop these skills by illustrating their use in a wide range of decision-making situations. These decision-making skills are as important in your personal life as they are to managers. After completing your study of this chapter, you should be able to think more clearly about decisions in many facets of your life.

Cost Concepts for Decision Making

Identifying Relevant Costs and Benefits

Only those costs and benefits that differ in total between alternatives are relevant in a decision. If the total amount of a cost will be the same regardless of the alternative selected, then the decision has no effect on the cost, so the cost can be ignored. To elaborate on this point, we'd like to define the terms *avoidable cost, sunk cost,* and *opportunity cost,* and illustrate the concept of *future costs that do not differ between alternatives.*

Assume you are trying to decide whether to go to a movie or rent a DVD for the evening. The rent on your apartment is irrelevant. Whether you go to a movie or rent a DVD, the rent on your apartment will be exactly the same and is therefore irrelevant to the decision. On the other hand, the cost of the movie ticket and the cost of renting the DVD would be relevant in the decision because they are *avoidable costs.*

An **avoidable cost** is a cost that can be eliminated by choosing one alternative over another. By choosing the alternative of going to the movie, the cost of renting the DVD can be avoided. By choosing the alternative of renting the DVD, the cost of the movie ticket can be avoided. Therefore, the cost of the movie ticket and the cost of renting the DVD are both avoidable costs. On the other hand, the rent on your apartment is not an avoidable cost of either alternative. You would continue to rent your apartment under either alternative. Avoidable costs are relevant costs. Unavoidable costs are irrelevant costs.

To refine the notion of relevant costs a little further, two broad categories of costs are never relevant in decisions—sunk costs and future costs that do not differ between the alternatives. As we learned in Chapter 2, **sunk cost** is a cost that has already been incurred and cannot be avoided regardless of what a manager decides to do. For example, suppose a company purchased a five-year-old truck for $12,000. The amount paid for the truck is a sunk cost because it has already been incurred and the transaction cannot be undone. Even though it is perhaps counterintuitive, the amount the company paid for the truck is irrelevant in making decisions such as whether to keep, sell, or replace the truck. Furthermore, any depreciation expense related to the truck is *irrelevant in making decisions.* This is true because depreciation is a noncash expense that simply spreads the cost of the truck over its useful life.[1] Sunk costs are always the same no matter what alternatives are being considered; therefore, they are irrelevant and should be ignored when making decisions.

Future costs that do not differ between alternatives should also be ignored. Continuing with the example discussed earlier, suppose you plan to order a pizza after you go to the movie theater or you rent a DVD. If you are going to buy the same pizza regardless of your choice of entertainment, the cost of the pizza is irrelevant to the choice of whether you go to the movie theater or rent a DVD. Notice, the cost of the pizza is not a sunk cost because it has not yet been incurred. Nonetheless, the cost of the pizza is irrelevant to the entertainment decision because it is a future cost that does not differ between the alternatives.

Opportunity costs also need to be considered when making decisions. An **opportunity cost** is the potential benefit that is given up when one alternative is selected over another. For example, if you were considering giving up a high-paying summer job to travel overseas, the forgone wages would be an opportunity cost of traveling abroad. Opportunity costs are not usually found in accounting records, but they are costs that must be explicitly considered in every decision a manager makes.

To summarize, only those costs and benefits that differ between alternatives are relevant in a decision. Differential costs are also referred to as relevant costs or avoidable costs. The key to successful decision making is to focus on relevant costs and benefits as well as opportunity costs while ignoring everything else—including sunk costs and future costs and benefits that do not differ between the alternatives.

INDUSTRIAL MOTION HEADS EAST

Eric Kozlowski and Brian Pfeifer founded Industrial Motion Inc. in Rancho Santa Margarita, California; however, after 10 years in California, they decided to cut costs by relocating the company to Mooresville, North Carolina. In Mooresville, the company's 42 employees are paid salaries of $35,000–$45,000 instead of the $60,000 paid to employees in California; furthermore, workers' compensation insurance is one-tenth of the amount paid in California. Property taxes and the cost of real estate are 50% less in Mooresville compared to Rancho Santa Margarita. Even the company's security system in Mooresville costs only $25 per month instead of $280 per month in California.

Source: Simona Covel, "Moving Across the Country to Cut Costs," *The Wall Street Journal,* January 10, 2008, p. B4.

Different Costs for Different Purposes

We need to recognize a fundamental concept from the outset of our discussion—costs that are relevant in one decision situation are not necessarily relevant in another. This means that *managers need different costs for different purposes.* For one purpose, a particular group of costs may be relevant; for another purpose, an entirely different group of costs may be relevant. Thus, *each* decision situation must be carefully analyzed to isolate the relevant costs. Otherwise, irrelevant data may cloud the situation and lead to a bad decision.

The concept of "different costs for different purposes" is basic to managerial accounting; we shall frequently see its application in the pages that follow.

An Example of Identifying Relevant Costs and Benefits

Cynthia is currently a student in an MBA program in Boston and would like to visit a friend in New York City over the weekend. She is trying to decide whether to drive or take the train. Because she is on a tight budget, she wants to carefully consider the costs of the two alternatives. If one alternative is far less expensive than the other, that may be decisive in

---

[1] See Appendix 8C for a discussion of how depreciation expense impacts decisions when tax implications are considered.

her choice. By car, the distance between her apartment in Boston and her friend's apartment in New York City is 230 miles. Cynthia has compiled the following list of items to consider:

Automobile Costs

Item	Annual Cost of Fixed Items	Cost per Mile (based on 10,000 miles per year)
(a) Annual straight-line depreciation on car [($24,000 original cost − $10,000 estimated resale value in 5 years)/5 years]	$2,800	$0.280
(b) Cost of gasoline ($3.30 per gallon ÷ 33 miles per gallon)		0.100
(c) Annual cost of auto insurance and license	$1,380	0.138
(d) Maintenance and repairs		0.065
(e) Parking fees at school ($45 per month × 8 months)	$360	0.036
(f) Total average cost per mile		$0.619

Additional Data

Item	
(g) Reduction in the resale value of car due solely to wear and tear	$0.026 per mile
(h) Cost of round-trip train ticket from Boston to New York City	$104
(i) Benefit of relaxing and being able to study during the train ride rather than having to drive	?
(j) Cost of putting the dog in a kennel while gone	$40
(k) Benefit of having a car available in New York City	?
(l) Hassle of parking the car in New York City	?
(m) Cost of parking the car in New York City	$25 per day

Which costs and benefits are relevant in this decision? Remember, only those costs and benefits that differ between alternatives are relevant. Everything else is irrelevant and can be ignored.

Start at the top of the list with item (a): the original cost of the car is a sunk cost. This cost has already been incurred and therefore can never differ between alternatives. Consequently, it is irrelevant and should be ignored. The same is true of the accounting depreciation of $2,800 per year, which simply spreads the sunk cost across five years.

Item (b), the cost of gasoline consumed by driving to New York City, is a relevant cost. If Cynthia takes the train, this cost would not be incurred. Hence, the cost differs between alternatives and is therefore relevant.

Item (c), the annual cost of auto insurance and license, is not relevant. Whether Cynthia takes the train or drives on this particular trip, her annual auto insurance premium and her auto license fee will remain the same.[2]

Item (d), the cost of maintenance and repairs, is relevant. While maintenance and repair costs have a large random component, over the long run they should be more or less proportional to the number of miles the car is driven. Thus, the average cost of $0.065 per mile is a reasonable estimate to use.

---

[2] If Cynthia has an accident while driving to New York City or back, this might affect her insurance premium when the policy is renewed. The increase in the insurance premium would be a relevant cost of this particular trip, but the normal amount of the insurance premium is not relevant in any case.

Item (e), the monthly fee that Cynthia pays to park at her school during the academic year is not relevant. Regardless of which alternative she selects—driving or taking the train—she will still need to pay for parking at school.

Item (f) is the total average cost of $0.619 per mile. As discussed above, some elements of this total are relevant, but some are not relevant. Because it contains some irrelevant costs, it would be incorrect to estimate the cost of driving to New York City and back by simply multiplying the $0.619 by 460 miles (230 miles each way × 2). This erroneous approach would yield a cost of driving of $284.74. Unfortunately, such mistakes are often made in both personal life and in business. Because the total cost is stated on a per-mile basis, people are easily misled. Often people think that if the cost is stated as $0.619 per mile, the cost of driving 100 miles is $61.90. But it is not. Many of the costs included in the $0.619 cost per mile are sunk and/or fixed and will not increase if the car is driven another 100 miles. The $0.619 is an average cost, not an incremental cost. Beware of such unitized costs (i.e., costs stated in terms of a dollar amount per unit, per mile, per direct labor-hour, per machine-hour, and so on)—they are often misleading.

Item (g), the decline in the resale value of the car that occurs as a consequence of driving more miles, is relevant in the decision. Because she uses the car, its resale value declines, which is a real cost of using the car that should be taken into account. Cynthia estimated this cost by accessing the *Kelly Blue Book* website at www.kbb.com. The reduction in resale value of an asset through use or over time is often called *real* or *economic depreciation*. This is different from accounting depreciation, which attempts to match the sunk cost of an asset with the periods that benefit from that cost.

Item (h), the $104 cost of a round-trip ticket on the train, is relevant in this decision. If she drives, she would not have to buy the ticket.

Item (i) is relevant to the decision, even if it is difficult to put a dollar value on relaxing and being able to study while on the train. It is relevant because it is a benefit that is available under one alternative but not under the other.

Item (j), the cost of putting Cynthia's dog in the kennel while she is gone, is irrelevant in this decision. Whether she takes the train or drives to New York City, she will still need to put her dog in a kennel.

Like item (i), items (k) and (l) are relevant to the decision even if it is difficult to measure their dollar impacts.

Item (m), the cost of parking in New York City, is relevant to the decision.

Bringing together all of the relevant data, Cynthia would estimate the relevant costs of driving and taking the train as follows:

Relevant financial cost of driving to New York City:

Gasoline (460 miles × $0.100 per mile)	$ 46.00
Maintenance and repairs (460 miles × $0.065 per mile)	29.90
Reduction in the resale value of car due solely to wear and tear (460 miles × $0.026 per mile)	11.96
Cost of parking the car in New York City (2 days × $25 per day)	50.00
Total	$137.86

Relevant financial cost of taking the train to New York City:

Cost of round-trip train ticket from Boston to New York City	$104.00

What should Cynthia do? From a purely financial standpoint, it would be cheaper by $33.86 ($137.86 − $104.00) to take the train than to drive. Cynthia has to decide if the convenience of having a car in New York City outweighs the additional cost and the disadvantages of being unable to relax and study on the train and the hassle of finding parking in the city.

In this example, we focused on identifying the relevant costs and benefits—everything else was ignored. In the next example, we include all of the costs and benefits—relevant or not. Nonetheless, we'll still get the correct answer because the irrelevant costs and benefits will cancel out when we compare the alternatives.

UNDERSTANDING THE IMPORTANCE OF QUALITATIVE FACTORS

SAS is a privately held $2.26 billion company located on a 200-acre campus in Cary, North Carolina. The company has an on-site medical facility (including a lab for blood tests) that is staffed by doctors, nurse practitioners, physical therapists, and a nutritionist. The company also has an infant day care, a Montessori school, a hair salon, a dry cleaning shop, a fitness center, and jogging and biking trails on campus. Employees that use the day care pay $360 per month per child for the service and SAS covers the remaining $720 per month per child that it costs to retain 120 teachers and staffers.

Although it may be difficult to quantify the benefits of these investments, SAS firmly believes that retaining happy and healthy employees is instrumental to its success. Mary Simmons, a SAS software developer says, "At lunch I will go out and bike 20 miles. Then I'll get back and all of a sudden a thought comes to my brain, and I solve something I was struggling with."

Source: Christopher Tkaczyk, "Offer Affordable (Awesome) Day Care," *Fortune*, August 17, 2009, p. 26.

Reconciling the Total and Differential Approaches

Oak Harbor Woodworks is considering a new labor-saving machine that rents for $3,000 per year. The machine will be used on the company's butcher block production line. Data concerning the company's annual sales and costs of butcher blocks with and without the new machine are shown below:

	Current Situation	Situation with the New Machine
Units produced and sold	5,000	5,000
Selling price per unit.	$40	$40
Direct materials cost per unit	$14	$14
Direct labor cost per unit	$8	$5
Variable overhead cost per unit	$2	$2
Fixed expenses, other	$62,000	$62,000
Fixed expenses, rental of new machine	—	$3,000

Given the data above, the net operating income for the product under the two alternatives can be computed as shown in Exhibit 7–1.

Note that the net operating income is $12,000 higher with the new machine, so that is the better alternative. Note also that the $12,000 advantage for the new machine can be obtained in two different ways. It is the difference between the $30,000 net operating income with the new machine and the $18,000 net operating income for the current situation. It is also the sum of the differential costs and benefits as shown in the last column of Exhibit 7–1 ($15,000 + $(3,000) = $12,000). A positive number in the Differential Costs and Benefits column indicates that the difference between the alternatives favors the new machine; a negative number indicates that the difference favors the current situation. A zero in that column simply means that the total amount for the item is exactly the same for both alternatives. Thus, because the difference in the net operating incomes equals the sum of the differences for the individual items, any cost or benefit that is the same for both alternatives will have no impact on which alternative is preferred. This is the reason that costs and benefits that do not differ between alternatives are irrelevant and can be ignored. If we properly account for them, they will cancel out when we compare the alternatives.

EXHIBIT 7–1
Total and Differential Costs

	Current Situation	Situation with New Machine	Differential Costs and Benefits
Sales (5,000 units × $40 per unit).........	$200,000	$200,000	$ 0
Variable expenses:			
Direct materials (5,000 units × $14 per unit)	70,000	70,000	0
Direct labor (5,000 units × $8 per unit; 5,000 units × $5 per unit)............	40,000	25,000	15,000
Variable overhead (5,000 units × $2 per unit)........................	10,000	10,000	0
Total variable expenses	120,000	105,000	
Contribution margin	80,000	95,000	
Fixed expenses:			
Other...............................	62,000	62,000	0
Rental of new machine................	0	3,000	(3,000)
Total fixed expenses....................	62,000	65,000	
Net operating income..................	$ 18,000	$ 30,000	$12,000

We could have arrived at the same solution much more quickly by completely ignoring the irrelevant costs and benefits.

- The selling price per unit and the number of units sold do not differ between the alternatives. Therefore, the total sales revenues are exactly the same for the two alternatives as shown in Exhibit 7–1. Because the sales revenues are exactly the same, they have no effect on the difference in net operating income between the two alternatives. That is shown in the last column in Exhibit 7–1, which shows a $0 differential benefit.
- The direct materials cost per unit, the variable overhead cost per unit, and the number of units produced and sold do not differ between the alternatives. Consequently, the total direct materials cost and the total variable overhead cost are the same for the two alternatives and can be ignored.
- The "other" fixed expenses do not differ between the alternatives, so they can be ignored as well.

Indeed, the only costs that do differ between the alternatives are direct labor costs and the fixed rental cost of the new machine. Hence, the two alternatives can be compared based only on these relevant costs:

Net Advantage of Renting the New Machine	
Decrease in direct labor costs (5,000 units at a cost savings of $3 per unit)..	$15,000
Increase in fixed expenses	(3,000)
Net annual cost savings from renting the new machine.................	$12,000

If we focus on just the relevant costs and benefits, we get exactly the same answer as when we listed all of the costs and benefits—including those that do not differ between the alternatives and, hence, are irrelevant. We get the same answer because the only costs and benefits that matter in the final comparison of the net operating incomes are those that differ between the two alternatives and, hence, are not zero in the last column of

Exhibit 7–1. Those two relevant costs are both included in the above analysis that quantifies the net advantage of renting the new machine.

Why Isolate Relevant Costs?

In the preceding example, we used two different approaches to analyze the alternatives. First, we considered all costs, both those that were relevant and those that were not; and second, we considered only the relevant costs. We obtained the same answer under both approaches. It would be natural to ask, "Why bother to isolate relevant costs when total costs will do the job just as well?" Isolating relevant costs is desirable for at least two reasons.

First, only rarely will enough information be available to prepare a detailed income statement for both alternatives. Assume, for example, that you are called on to make a decision relating to a portion of a single business process in a multidepartmental, multiproduct company. Under these circumstances, it would be virtually impossible to prepare an income statement of any type. You would have to rely on your ability to recognize which costs are relevant and which are not in order to assemble the data necessary to make a decision.

Second, mingling irrelevant costs with relevant costs may cause confusion and distract attention from the information that is really critical. Furthermore, the danger always exists that an irrelevant piece of data may be used improperly, resulting in an incorrect decision. The best approach is to ignore irrelevant data and base the decision entirely on relevant data.

Relevant cost analysis, combined with the contribution approach to the income statement, provides a powerful tool for making decisions. We will investigate various uses of this tool in the remaining sections of this chapter.

Adding and Dropping Product Lines and Other Segments

Decisions relating to whether product lines or other segments of a company should be dropped and new ones added are among the most difficult that a manager has to make. In such decisions, many qualitative and quantitative factors must be considered. Ultimately, however, any final decision to drop a business segment or to add a new one hinges primarily on the impact the decision will have on net operating income. To assess this impact, costs must be carefully analyzed.

LEARNING OBJECTIVE 7–2
Prepare an analysis showing whether a product line or other business segment should be added or dropped.

An Illustration of Cost Analysis

Exhibit 7–2 provides sales and cost information for the preceding month for the Discount Drug Company and its three major product lines—drugs, cosmetics, and housewares. A quick review of this exhibit suggests that dropping the housewares segment would increase the company's overall net operating income by $8,000. However, this would be a flawed conclusion because the data in Exhibit 7–2 do not distinguish between fixed expenses that can be avoided if a product line is dropped and common fixed expenses that cannot be avoided by dropping any particular product line.

In this scenario, the two alternatives under consideration are keeping the housewares product line and dropping the housewares product line. Therefore, only those costs that differ between these two alternatives (i.e., that can be avoided by dropping the housewares product line) are relevant. In deciding whether to drop housewares, it is crucial to identify which costs can be avoided, and hence are relevant to the decision, and which costs cannot be avoided, and hence are irrelevant. The decision should be analyzed as follows.

If the housewares line is dropped, then the company will lose $20,000 per month in contribution margin, but by dropping the line it may be possible to avoid some fixed costs such as salaries or advertising costs. If dropping the housewares line enables the company to avoid more in fixed costs than it loses in contribution margin, then its overall

EXHIBIT 7–2
Discount Drug Company
Product Lines

	Total	Drugs	Cosmetics	Housewares
			Product Line	
Sales	$250,000	$125,000	$75,000	$50,000
Variable expenses	105,000	50,000	25,000	30,000
Contribution margin	145,000	75,000	50,000	20,000
Fixed expenses:				
Salaries	50,000	29,500	12,500	8,000
Advertising	15,000	1,000	7,500	6,500
Utilities	2,000	500	500	1,000
Depreciation—fixtures	5,000	1,000	2,000	2,000
Rent	20,000	10,000	6,000	4,000
Insurance	3,000	2,000	500	500
General administrative	30,000	15,000	9,000	6,000
Total fixed expenses	125,000	59,000	38,000	28,000
Net operating income (loss)	$ 20,000	$ 16,000	$12,000	$ (8,000)

net operating income will improve by eliminating the product line. On the other hand, if the company is not able to avoid as much in fixed costs as it loses in contribution margin, then the housewares line should be kept. In short, the manager should ask, "What costs can I avoid if I drop this product line?"

As we have seen from our earlier discussion, not all costs are avoidable. For example, some of the costs associated with a product line may be sunk costs. Other costs may be allocated fixed costs that will not differ in total regardless of whether the product line is dropped or retained.

To show how to proceed in a product-line analysis, suppose that Discount Drug Company has analyzed the fixed costs being charged to the three product lines and determined the following:

1. The salaries expense represents salaries paid to employees working directly on the product. All of the employees working in housewares would be discharged if the product line is dropped.
2. The advertising expense represents advertisements that are specific to each product line and are avoidable if the line is dropped.
3. The utilities expense represents utilities costs for the entire company. The amount charged to each product line is an allocation based on space occupied and is not avoidable if the product line is dropped.
4. The depreciation expense represents depreciation on fixtures used to display the various product lines. Although the fixtures are nearly new, they are custom-built and will have no resale value if the housewares line is dropped.
5. The rent expense represents rent on the entire building housing the company; it is allocated to the product lines on the basis of sales dollars. The monthly rent of $20,000 is fixed under a long-term lease agreement.
6. The insurance expense is for insurance carried on inventories within each of the three product lines. If housewares is dropped, the related inventories will be liquidated and the insurance premiums will decrease proportionately.
7. The general administrative expense represents the costs of accounting, purchasing, and general management, which are allocated to the product lines on the basis of sales dollars. These costs will not change if the housewares line is dropped.

With this information, management can determine that $15,000 of the fixed expenses associated with the housewares product line are avoidable and $13,000 are not:

Fixed Expenses	Total Cost Assigned to Housewares	Not Avoidable*	Avoidable
Salaries	$ 8,000		$ 8,000
Advertising	6,500		6,500
Utilities	1,000	$ 1,000	
Depreciation—fixtures	2,000	2,000	
Rent	4,000	4,000	
Insurance	500		500
General administrative	6,000	6,000	
Total	$28,000	$13,000	$15,000

*These fixed costs represent either sunk costs or future costs that will not change whether the housewares line is retained or discontinued.

As stated earlier, if the housewares product line were dropped, the company would lose the product's contribution margin of $20,000, but would save its associated avoidable fixed expenses. We now know that those avoidable fixed expenses total $15,000. Therefore, dropping the housewares product line would result in a $5,000 *reduction* in net operating income as shown below:

Contribution margin lost if the housewares line is discontinued (see Exhibit 7–2)	$(20,000)
Fixed expenses that can be avoided if the housewares line is discontinued (see above).......................................	15,000
Decrease in overall company net operating income	$ (5,000)

In this case, the fixed costs that can be avoided by dropping the housewares product line ($15,000) are less than the contribution margin that will be lost ($20,000). Therefore, based on the data given, the housewares line should not be discontinued unless a more profitable use can be found for the floor and counter space that it is occupying.

A Comparative Format

This decision can also be approached by preparing comparative income statements showing the effects of either keeping or dropping the product line. Exhibit 7–3 contains such an analysis for the Discount Drug Company. As shown in the last column of the exhibit, if the housewares line is dropped, then overall company net operating income will decrease by $5,000 each period. This is the same answer, of course, as we obtained when we focused just on the lost contribution margin and avoidable fixed costs.

Beware of Allocated Fixed Costs

Go back to Exhibit 7–2. Does this exhibit suggest that the housewares product line should be kept—as we have just concluded? No, it does not. Exhibit 7–2 suggests that the housewares product line is losing money. Why keep a product line that is showing a loss? The explanation for this apparent inconsistency lies in part with the common fixed costs that are being allocated to the product lines. One of the great dangers in allocating common fixed costs is that such allocations can make a product line (or other business segment) look less profitable than it really is. In this instance, allocating the common fixed costs among all product lines makes the housewares product line appear to be unprofitable. However, as we have just shown, dropping the product line would result in a decrease in the company's overall net operating income. This point can be seen clearly if we redo Exhibit 7–2 by eliminating the allocation of the common fixed costs. Exhibit 7–4 uses the segmented approach from Chapter 6 to estimate the profitability of the product lines.

EXHIBIT 7–3

A Comparative Format for Product-Line Analysis

	Keep Housewares	Drop Housewares	Difference: Net Operating Income Increase (or Decrease)
Sales	$50,000	$ 0	$(50,000)
Variable expenses	30,000	0	30,000
Contribution margin	20,000	0	(20,000)
Fixed expenses:			
Salaries	8,000	0	8,000
Advertising	6,500	0	6,500
Utilities	1,000	1,000	0
Depreciation—fixtures	2,000	2,000	0
Rent	4,000	4,000	0
Insurance	500	0	500
General administrative	6,000	6,000	0
Total fixed expenses	28,000	13,000	15,000
Net operating loss	$ (8,000)	$(13,000)	$ (5,000)

Exhibit 7–4 gives us a much different perspective of the housewares line than does Exhibit 7–2. As shown in Exhibit 7–4, the housewares line is covering all of its own traceable fixed costs and generating a $3,000 segment margin toward covering the common

EXHIBIT 7–4

Discount Drug Company Product Lines—Recast in Contribution Format (from Exhibit 7–2)

	Total	Product Line Drugs	Cosmetics	Housewares
Sales	$250,000	$125,000	$75,000	$50,000
Variable expenses	105,000	50,000	25,000	30,000
Contribution margin	145,000	75,000	50,000	20,000
Traceable fixed expenses:				
Salaries	50,000	29,500	12,500	8,000
Advertising	15,000	1,000	7,500	6,500
Depreciation—fixtures	5,000	1,000	2,000	2,000
Insurance	3,000	2,000	500	500
Total traceable fixed expenses	73,000	33,500	22,500	17,000
Product-line segment margin	72,000	$ 41,500	$27,500	$ 3,000*
Common fixed expenses:				
Utilities	2,000			
Rent	20,000			
General administrative	30,000			
Total common fixed expenses	52,000			
Net operating income	$ 20,000			

*If the housewares line is dropped, the company will lose the $3,000 segment margin generated by this product line. In addition, we have seen that the $2,000 depreciation on the fixtures is a sunk cost that cannot be avoided. The sum of these two figures ($3,000 + $2,000 = $5,000) would be the decrease in the company's overall profits if the housewares line were discontinued. Of course, the company may later choose to drop the product if circumstances change—such as a pending decision to replace the fixtures.

fixed costs of the company. Unless another product line can be found that will generate a segment margin greater than $3,000, the company would be better off keeping the housewares line. By keeping the product line, the company's overall net operating income will be higher than if the product line were dropped.

Additionally, managers may choose to retain an unprofitable product line if the line helps sell other products, or if it serves as a "magnet" to attract customers. Bread, for example, may not be an especially profitable line in some food stores, but customers expect it to be available, and many of them would undoubtedly shift their buying elsewhere if a particular store decided to stop carrying it.

POOR ECONOMY LEADS TO SEGMENT DISCONTINUATIONS

When the economy declines, many companies must decide whether to retain or discontinue struggling products and services. For example, Condé Nast Publications reacted to a steep drop in advertising revenues by cutting 180 jobs and discontinuing four magazines—*Gourmet, Modern Bride, Elegant Bride,* and *Cookie.* It also cut the budgets of its remaining magazines by 20–25%. Pioneer Corp.'s annual plasma television sales dropped from 460,000 units to 290,000 units. The company responded to its shrinking customer demand by cutting thousands of jobs and withdrawing from the plasma television business.

Sources: Russell Adams, "Ax Falls on Four Condé Nast Titles," *The Wall Street Journal,* October 6, 2009, p. B1; and Daisuke Wakabayashi, "Pioneer Unplugs Its TV Business," *The Wall Street Journal,* February 13, 2009, p. B1.

The Make or Buy Decision

LEARNING OBJECTIVE 7–3
Prepare a make or buy analysis.

Providing a product or service to a customer involves many steps. For example, consider all of the steps that are necessary to develop and sell a product such as tax preparation software in retail stores. First the software must be developed, which involves highly skilled software engineers and a great deal of project management effort. Then the product must be put into a form that can be delivered to customers. This involves burning the application onto a blank CD or DVD, applying a label, and packaging the result in an attractive box. Then the product must be distributed to retail stores. Then the product must be sold. And finally, help lines and other forms of after-sale service may have to be provided. And we should not forget that the blank CD or DVD, the label, and the box must of course be made by someone before any of this can happen. All of these activities, from development, to production, to after-sales service are called a *value chain.*

Separate companies may carry out each of the activities in the value chain or a single company may carry out several. When a company is involved in more than one activity in the entire value chain, it is **vertically integrated**. Some companies control all of the activities in the value chain from producing basic raw materials right up to the final distribution of finished goods and provision of after-sales service. Other companies are content to integrate on a smaller scale by purchasing many of the parts and materials that go into their finished products. A decision to carry out one of the activities in the value chain internally, rather than to buy externally from a supplier, is called a **make or buy decision**. Quite often these decisions involve whether to buy a particular part or to make it internally. Make or buy decisions also involve decisions concerning whether to outsource development tasks, after-sales service, or other activities.

Strategic Aspects of the Make or Buy Decision

Vertical integration provides certain advantages. An integrated company is less dependent on its suppliers and may be able to ensure a smoother flow of parts and materials for production than a nonintegrated company. For example, a strike against a major parts supplier can interrupt the operations of a nonintegrated company for many months, whereas an integrated company that is producing its own parts would be able to continue operations. Also, some companies feel that they can control quality better by producing their own parts and materials, rather than by relying on the quality control standards of outside suppliers. In addition, an integrated company realizes profits from the parts and materials that it is "making" rather than "buying," as well as profits from its regular operations.

The advantages of vertical integration are counterbalanced by the advantages of using external suppliers. By pooling demand from a number of companies, a supplier may be able to enjoy economies of scale. These economies of scale can result in higher quality and lower costs than would be possible if the company were to attempt to make the parts or provide the service on its own. A company must be careful, however, to retain control over activities that are essential to maintaining its competitive position. For example, Hewlett-Packard controls the software for laser printers that it makes in cooperation with Canon Inc. of Japan. The present trend appears to be toward less vertical integration, with companies like Oracle and Hewlett-Packard concentrating on hardware and software design and relying on outside suppliers for almost everything else in the value chain.

An Example of Make or Buy

To provide an illustration of a make or buy decision, consider Mountain Goat Cycles. The company is now producing the heavy-duty gear shifters used in its most popular line of mountain bikes. The company's Accounting Department reports the following costs of producing 8,000 units of the shifter internally each year:

	Per Unit	8,000 Units
Direct materials	$ 6	$ 48,000
Direct labor.	4	32,000
Variable overhead.	1	8,000
Supervisor's salary	3	24,000
Depreciation of special equipment . .	2	16,000
Allocated general overhead	5	40,000
Total cost.	$21	$168,000

An outside supplier has offered to sell 8,000 shifters a year to Mountain Goat Cycles for a price of only $19 each, or a total of $152,000 (= 8,000 shifters × $19 each). Should the company stop producing the shifters internally and buy them from the outside supplier? As always, the focus should be on the relevant costs—those that differ between the alternatives. And the costs that differ between the alternatives consist of the costs that could be avoided by purchasing the shifters from the outside supplier. If the costs that can be avoided by purchasing the shifters from the outside supplier total less than $152,000, then the company should continue to manufacture its own shifters and reject the outside supplier's offer.

© Asia Images Group/PictureIndia/Getty Images, RF

OUTSOURCING TASKS RATHER THAN JOBS

Pfizer saved 4,000 of its managers 66,500 hours of work by enabling them to outsource their tedious, time-consuming tasks to companies in India. With the click of a mouse the managers go to a website called PfizerWorks to prepare online work orders for services such as PowerPoint slide preparation, spreadsheet preparation, or basic market research. The requests are sent overseas and completed by a services-outsourcing firm. This outsourcing enables Pfizer's managers to spend their time on higher value work such as motivating teams, creating new products, and strategy formulation.

Source: Jena McGregor, "The Chore Goes Offshore," *BusinessWeek,* March 23 & 30, 2009, p. 50–51.

On the other hand, if the costs that can be avoided by purchasing the shifters from the outside supplier total more than $152,000 the outside supplier's offer should be accepted.

Note that depreciation of special equipment is listed as one of the costs of producing the shifters internally. Because the equipment has already been purchased, this depreciation is a sunk cost and is therefore irrelevant. If the equipment could be sold, its salvage value would be relevant. Or if the machine could be used to make other products, this could be relevant as well. However, we will assume that the equipment has no salvage value and that it has no other use except making the heavy-duty gear shifters.

Also note that the company is allocating a portion of its general overhead costs to the shifters. Any portion of this general overhead cost that would actually be eliminated if the gear shifters were purchased rather than made would be relevant in the analysis. However, it is likely that the general overhead costs allocated to the gear shifters are in fact common to all items produced in the factory and would continue unchanged even if the shifters were purchased from the outside. Such allocated common costs are not relevant costs (because they do not differ between the make or buy alternatives) and should be eliminated from the analysis along with the sunk costs.

The variable costs of producing the shifters can be avoided by buying the shifters from the outside supplier so they are relevant costs. We will assume in this case that the variable costs include direct materials, direct labor, and variable overhead. The supervisor's salary is also relevant if it could be avoided by buying the shifters. Exhibit 7–5 contains the relevant cost analysis of the make or buy decision assuming that the supervisor's salary can indeed be avoided.

	Total Relevant Costs—8,000 units	
	Make	**Buy**
Direct materials (8,000 units × $6 per unit)	$ 48,000	
Direct labor (8,000 units × $4 per unit)	32,000	
Variable overhead (8,000 units × $1 per unit)	8,000	
Supervisor's salary	24,000	
Depreciation of special equipment (not relevant)		
Allocated general overhead (not relevant)		
Outside purchase price		$152,000
Total cost.	$112,000	$152,000
Difference in favor of continuing to make.	$40,000	

EXHIBIT 7–5
Mountain Goat Cycles
Make or Buy Analysis

Because the avoidable costs related to making the shifters is $40,000 less than the total amount that would be paid to buy them from the outside supplier, Mountain Goat Cycles should reject the outside supplier's offer. However, the company may wish to consider one additional factor before coming to a final decision—the opportunity cost of the space now being used to produce the shifters.

Opportunity Cost

If the space now being used to produce the shifters *would otherwise be idle,* then Mountain Goat Cycles should continue to produce its own shifters and the supplier's offer should be rejected, as stated above. Idle space that has no alternative use has an opportunity cost of zero.

But what if the space now being used to produce shifters could be used for some other purpose? In that case, the space would have an opportunity cost equal to the segment margin that could be derived from the best alternative use of the space.

To illustrate, assume that the space now being used to produce shifters could be used to produce a new cross-country bike that would generate a segment margin of $60,000 per year. Under these conditions, Mountain Goat Cycles should accept the supplier's offer and use the available space to produce the new product line:

	Make	Buy
Total annual cost (see Exhibit 7–5)...................	$112,000	$152,000
Opportunity cost—segment margin forgone on a potential new product line	60,000	
Total cost...	$172,000	$152,000
Difference in favor of purchasing from the outside supplier...		$20,000

Opportunity costs are not recorded in the organization's general ledger because they do not represent actual dollar outlays. Rather, they represent economic benefits that are *forgone* as a result of pursuing some course of action. The opportunity cost for Mountain Goat Cycles is sufficiently large in this case to change the decision.

Special Orders

LEARNING OBJECTIVE 7–4
Prepare an analysis showing whether a special order should be accepted.

Managers must often evaluate whether a *special order* should be accepted, and if the order is accepted, the price that should be charged. A **special order** is a one-time order that is not considered part of the company's normal ongoing business. To illustrate, Mountain Goat Cycles has just received a request from the Seattle Police Department to produce 100 specially modified mountain bikes at a price of $558 each. The bikes would be used to patrol some of the more densely populated residential sections of the city. Mountain Goat Cycles can easily modify its City Cruiser model to fit the specifications of the Seattle Police. The normal selling price of the City Cruiser bike is $698, and its unit product cost is $564 as shown below:

Direct materials	$372
Direct labor..........................	90
Manufacturing overhead	102
Unit product cost....................	$564

The variable portion of the above manufacturing overhead is $12 per unit. The order would have no effect on the company's total fixed manufacturing overhead costs.

The modifications requested by the Seattle Police Department consist of welded brackets to hold radios, nightsticks, and other gear. These modifications would require $34 in incremental variable costs. In addition, the company would have to pay a graphics design studio $2,400 to design and cut stencils that would be used for spray painting the Seattle Police Department's logo and other identifying marks on the bikes.

This order should have no effect on the company's other sales. The production manager says that she can handle the special order without disrupting any of the company's regular scheduled production.

What effect would accepting this order have on the company's net operating income?

Only the incremental costs and benefits are relevant. Because the existing fixed manufacturing overhead costs would not be affected by the order, they are not relevant. The incremental net operating income can be computed as follows:

	Per Unit	Total 100 Bikes
Incremental revenue......................	$558	$55,800
Less incremental costs:		
Variable costs:		
Direct materials......................	372	37,200
Direct labor.........................	90	9,000
Variable manufacturing overhead	12	1,200
Special modifications..................	34	3,400
Total variable cost......................	$508	50,800
Fixed cost:		
Purchase of stencils		2,400
Total incremental cost....................		53,200
Incremental net operating income...........		$ 2,600

Therefore, even though the $558 price on the special order is below the normal $564 unit product cost and the order would require additional costs, the order would increase net operating income. In general, a special order is profitable if the incremental revenue from the special order exceeds the incremental costs of the order. However, it is important to make sure that there is indeed idle capacity and that the special order does not cut into normal unit sales or undercut prices on normal sales. For example, if the company was operating at capacity, opportunity costs would have to be taken into account, as well as the incremental costs that have already been detailed above.

Utilization of a Constrained Resource

What Is a Constraint?

A **constraint** is anything that prevents you from getting more of what you want. Every individual and every organization faces at least one constraint, so it is not difficult to find examples of constraints. You may not have enough time to study thoroughly for every subject *and* to go out with your friends on the weekend, so time is your constraint. United Airlines has only a limited number of loading gates available at its busy Chicago O'Hare hub, so its constraint is loading gates. Vail Resorts has only a limited amount of land to develop as homesites and commercial lots at its ski areas, so its constraint is land.

As an example, long waiting periods for surgery are a chronic problem in the National Health Service (NHS), the government-funded provider of health care in the United Kingdom. A simplified version of the steps followed by an NHS surgery patient accompanied by a summary of the number of patients who can be processed through each of these steps is shown below:

Step	Steps for Processing Patients	Number of Patients That Can Be Processed per Day
1.	General practitioner referral	100
2.	Appointment made	100
3.	Outpatient visit.	50
4.	Add to surgery waiting list	150
5.	Surgery	15
6.	Follow-up visit	60
7.	Discharge	140

The constraint, or **bottleneck**, in the NHS system is determined by the step that limits total output because it has the smallest capacity—in this case surgery (step 5). The total number of patients processed through the entire system cannot exceed 15 per day—the maximum number of patients who can be treated in surgery. No matter how hard managers, doctors, and nurses try to improve the processing rate elsewhere in steps 1 through 4 or steps 6 and 7, they will never succeed in driving down wait lists until the capacity of surgery is increased. In fact, improvements elsewhere in the system—particularly before the constraint in steps 1 through 4—are likely to result in even longer waiting times and more frustrated patients and health care providers. Thus, to be effective, improvement efforts must be focused on the constraint. A business process, such as the process for serving surgery patients, is like a chain. If you want to increase the strength of a chain, what is the most effective way to do this? Should you concentrate your efforts on strengthening the strongest link, all the links, or the weakest link? Clearly, focusing your effort on the weakest link will bring the biggest benefit.

The procedure to follow to strengthen the chain is clear. First, identify the weakest link, which is the constraint. In the case of the NHS, the constraint is surgery. Second, do not place a greater strain on the system than the weakest link can handle—if you do, the chain will break. In the case of the NHS, more referrals than surgery can accommodate lead to unacceptably long waiting lists. Third, concentrate improvement efforts on strengthening the weakest link. In the case of the NHS, this means finding ways to increase the number of surgeries that can be performed in a day. Fourth, if the improvement efforts are successful, eventually the weakest link will improve to the point where it is no longer the weakest link. At that point, the new weakest link (i.e., the new constraint) must be identified, and improvement efforts must be shifted over to that link. This simple sequential process provides a powerful strategy for optimizing business processes.

Contribution Margin per Unit of the Constrained Resource

Managers routinely face the problem of deciding how constrained resources are going to be used. A department store, for example, has a limited amount of floor space and therefore cannot stock every product that may be available. A manufacturer has a limited number of machine-hours and a limited number of direct labor-hours at its disposal. Because the company cannot fully satisfy demand, managers must decide which products or services should be cut back. In other words, managers must decide which products or services make the best use of the constrained resource. Fixed costs are usually unaffected by such choices, so the course of action that will maximize the company's total contribution margin should ordinarily be selected.

If some products must be cut back because of a constraint, the key to maximizing the total contribution margin may seem obvious—favor the products with the highest unit contribution margins. Unfortunately, that is not quite correct. Rather, the correct solution is to favor the products that provide the highest *contribution margin per unit of the constrained resource.* To illustrate, in addition to its other products, Mountain Goat Cycles makes saddlebags for bicycles called *panniers*. These panniers come in two models—a touring model and a mountain model. Cost and revenue data for the two models of panniers follow:

	Mountain Pannier	Touring Pannier
Selling price per unit.	$25	$30
Variable cost per unit	10	18
Contribution margin per unit	$15	$12
Contribution margin (CM) ratio . .	60%	40%

The mountain pannier appears to be much more profitable than the touring pannier. It has a $15 per unit contribution margin as compared to only $12 per unit for the touring model, and it has a 60% CM ratio as compared to only 40% for the touring model.

But now let us add one more piece of information—the plant that makes the panniers is operating at capacity. This does not mean that every machine and every person in the plant is working at the maximum possible rate. Because machines have different capacities, some machines will be operating at less than 100% of capacity. However, if the plant as a whole cannot produce any more units, some machine or process must be operating at capacity. The machine or process that is limiting overall output is called the bottleneck—it is the constraint.

At Mountain Goat Cycles, the bottleneck (i.e., constraint) is a stitching machine. The mountain pannier requires two minutes of stitching time per unit, and the touring pannier requires one minute of stitching time per unit. The stitching machine is available for 12,000 minutes per month, and the company can sell up to 4,000 mountain panniers and 7,000 touring panniers per month. Producing up to this demand for both products would require 15,000 minutes, as shown below:

	Mountain Pannier	Touring Pannier	Total
Monthly demand (a)	4,000 units	7,000 units	
Stitching machine time required to produce one unit (b)	2 minutes	1 minute	
Total stitching time required (a) × (b)	8,000 minutes	7,000 minutes	15,000 minutes

Producing up to demand would require 15,000 minutes, but only 12,000 minutes are available. This simply confirms that the stitching machine is the bottleneck. By definition, because the stitching machine is a bottleneck, the stitching machine does not have enough capacity to satisfy the existing demand for mountain panniers and touring panniers Therefore, some orders for the products will have to be turned down. Naturally, managers will want to know which product is less profitable. To answer this question, they should focus on the contribution margin per unit of the constrained resource. This figure is computed by dividing a product's contribution margin per unit by the amount of the constrained resource required to make a unit of that product. These calculations are carried out below for the mountain and touring panniers:

	Mountain Pannier	Touring Pannier
Contribution margin per unit (a)	$15.00	$12.00
Stitching machine time required to produce one unit (b)	2 minutes	1 minute
Contribution margin per unit of the constrained resource, (a) ÷ (b)	$7.50 per minute	$12.00 per minute

It is now easy to decide which product is less profitable and should be deemphasized. Each minute on the stitching machine that is devoted to the touring pannier results in an increase of $12.00 in contribution margin and profits. The comparable figure for the mountain pannier is only $7.50 per minute. Therefore, the touring model should be emphasized. Even though the mountain model has the larger contribution margin per unit and the larger CM ratio, the touring model provides the larger contribution margin in relation to the constrained resource.

To verify that the touring model is indeed the more profitable product, suppose an hour of additional stitching time is available and that unfilled orders exist for both products. The additional hour on the stitching machine could be used to make either 30 mountain panniers (60 minutes ÷ 2 minutes per mountain pannier) or 60 touring panniers (60 minutes ÷ 1 minute per touring pannier), with the following profit implications:

	Mountain Pannier	Touring Pannier
Contribution margin per unit	$ 15	$ 12
Additional units that can be processed in one hour	× 30	× 60
Additional contribution margin	$450	$720

Because the additional contribution margin would be $720 for the touring panniers and only $450 for the mountain panniers, the touring panniers make the most profitable use of the company's constrained resource—the stitching machine.

The stitching machine is available for 12,000 minutes per month, and producing the touring panniers is the most profitable use of the stitching machine. Therefore, to maximize profits, the company should produce all of the touring panniers the market will demand (7,000 units) and use any remaining capacity to produce mountain panniers. The computations to determine how many mountain panniers can be produced are as follows:

Monthly demand for touring panniers (a)	7,000 units
Stitching machine time required to produce one touring pannier (b)	1 minute
Total stitching time required to produce touring panniers (a) × (b)	7,000 minutes
Remaining stitching time available (12,000 minutes − 7,000 minutes) (c)	5,000 minutes
Stitching machine time required to produce one mountain pannier (d)	2 minutes
Production of mountain panniers (c) ÷ (d)	2,500 units

© McGraw-Hill Education/Andrew Resek

BOEING IS CONSTRAINED BY A SUPPLIER

Boeing Co. had to delay delivery of its model 777 airplanes to Emirates airline because the German supplier Sell GmbH could not provide the equipment for cooking galleys to Boeing on time. The production bottleneck forced Emirates to repeatedly postpone its planned expansion into the U.S. west coast. It also forced Boeing to accept payment delays for airplanes that sell for more than $200 million apiece. In response, Sell GmbH hired 250 more employees and invested millions of euros in new machine tools and factory space to expand its production capacity.

Source: Daniel Michaels and J. Lynn Lunsford, "Lack of Seats, Galleys Stalls Boeing, Airbus," *The Wall Street Journal,* August 8, 2008, pp. B1 and B4.

Therefore, profit would be maximized by producing 7,000 touring panniers and then using the remaining capacity to produce 2,500 mountain panniers.

This example clearly shows that looking at each product's unit contribution margin alone is not enough; the contribution margin must be viewed in relation to the amount of the constrained resource each product requires.

Managing Constraints

Effectively managing an organization's constraints is a key to increased profits. As discussed above, when a constraint exists in the production process, managers can increase profits by producing the products with the highest contribution margin per unit of the constrained resource. However, they can also increase profits by increasing the capacity of the bottleneck operation.

LEARNING OBJECTIVE 7–6
Determine the value of obtaining more of the constrained resource.

When a manager increases the capacity of the bottleneck, it is called **relaxing (or elevating) the constraint**. In the case of Mountain Goat Cycles, the company is currently working one eight-hour shift. To relax the constraint, the stitching machine operator could be asked to work overtime. No one else would have to work overtime. Because all of the other operations involved in producing panniers have excess capacity, up to a point, the additional panniers processed through the stitching machine during overtime could be finished during normal working hours in the other operations.

The benefits from relaxing the constraint are often enormous and can be easily quantified—the key is the contribution margin per unit of the constrained resource that we have already computed. This number, which was originally stated in terms of minutes in the Mountain Goat Cycles example, is restated below in terms of hours for easier interpretation:

	Mountain Pannier	Touring Pannier
Contribution margin per unit of the constrained resource (in minutes) . . .	$7.50 per minute × 60 minutes per hour	$12.00 per minute × 60 minutes per hour
Contribution margin per unit of the constrained resource (in hours)	= $450 per hour	= $720 per hour

So what is the value of relaxing the constraint—the time on the stitching machine? The manager should first ask, "What would I do with additional capacity at the bottleneck if it were available?" If the time were to be used to make additional mountain panniers, it would be worth $450 per hour. If the time were to be used to make additional touring panniers, it would be worth $720 per hour. In this latter case, the company should be willing to pay an overtime *premium* to the stitching machine operator of up to $720 per hour! Suppose, for example, that the stitching machine operator is paid $20 per hour during normal working hours and time-and-a-half, or $30 per hour, for overtime. In this case, the premium for overtime is only $10 per hour, whereas in principle, the company should be willing to pay a premium of up to $720 per hour. The difference between what the company should be willing to pay as a premium, $720 per hour, and what it would actually have to pay, $10 per hour, is pure profit of $710 per hour.

To reinforce this concept, suppose that there are only unfilled orders for the mountain pannier. How much would it be worth to the company to run the stitching machine overtime in this situation? Because the additional capacity would be used to make the mountain pannier, the value of that additional capacity would drop to $7.50 per minute or $450 per hour. Nevertheless, the value of relaxing the constraint would still be quite high and the company should be willing to pay an overtime premium of up to $450 per hour.

These calculations indicate that managers should pay great attention to the bottleneck operation. If a bottleneck machine breaks down or is ineffectively utilized, the losses to the company can be quite large. In our example, for every minute the stitching machine is down due to breakdowns or setups, the company loses between $7.50 and $12.00.[3] The losses on an hourly basis are between $450 and $720! In contrast, there is no such loss of contribution margin if time is lost on a machine that is not a bottleneck—such machines have excess capacity anyway.

The implications are clear. Managers should focus much of their attention on managing the bottleneck. As we have discussed, managers should emphasize products that most profitably utilize the constrained resource. They should also make sure that products are processed smoothly through the bottleneck, with minimal lost time due to breakdowns and setups. And they should try to find ways to increase the capacity at the bottleneck.

The capacity of a bottleneck can be effectively increased in a number of ways, including:

- Working overtime on the bottleneck.
- Subcontracting some of the processing that would be done at the bottleneck.
- Investing in additional machines at the bottleneck.
- Shifting workers from processes that are not bottlenecks to the process that is the bottleneck.
- Focusing business process improvement efforts on the bottleneck.
- Reducing defective units. Each defective unit that is processed through the bottleneck and subsequently scrapped takes the place of a good unit that could have been sold.

The last three methods of increasing the capacity of the bottleneck are particularly attractive because they are essentially free and may even yield additional cost savings.

The Problem of Multiple Constraints

What does a company do if it has more than one potential constraint? For example, a company may have limited raw materials, limited direct labor-hours available, limited floor space, and limited advertising dollars to spend on product promotion. How would it determine the right combination of products to produce? The proper combination or "mix" of products can be found by use of a quantitative method known as *linear programming,* which is covered in quantitative methods and operations management courses.

Joint Product Costs and the Contribution Approach

LEARNING OBJECTIVE 7–7
Prepare an analysis showing whether joint products should be sold at the split-off point or processed further.

In some industries, a number of end products are produced from a single raw material input. For example, in the petroleum refining industry a large number of products are extracted from crude oil, including gasoline, jet fuel, home heating oil, lubricants, asphalt, and various organic chemicals. Another example is provided by the Santa Maria Wool Cooperative of New Mexico. The company buys raw wool from local sheepherders, separates the wool into three grades—coarse, fine, and superfine—and then dyes the wool using traditional methods that rely on pigments from local materials. Exhibit 7–6 contains a diagram of the production process.

At Santa Maria Wool Cooperative, coarse wool, fine wool, and superfine wool are produced from one input—raw wool. Two or more products that are produced from a common input are known as **joint products**. The **split-off point** is the point in the manufacturing process at which the joint products can be recognized as separate products. This does not occur at Santa Maria Wool Cooperative until the raw wool has gone through the separating process. The term **joint cost** is used to describe the costs incurred up to the split-off point. At Santa Maria Wool Cooperative, the joint costs are the $200,000 cost of

---

[3] Setups are required when production switches from one product to another. For example, consider a company that makes automobile side panels. The panels are painted before shipping them to an automobile manufacturer for final assembly. The customer might require 100 blue panels, 50 black panels, and 20 yellow panels. Each time the color is changed, the painting equipment must be purged of the old paint color, cleaned with solvents, and refilled with the new paint color. This takes time. In fact, some equipment may require such lengthy and frequent setups that it is unavailable for actual production more often than not.

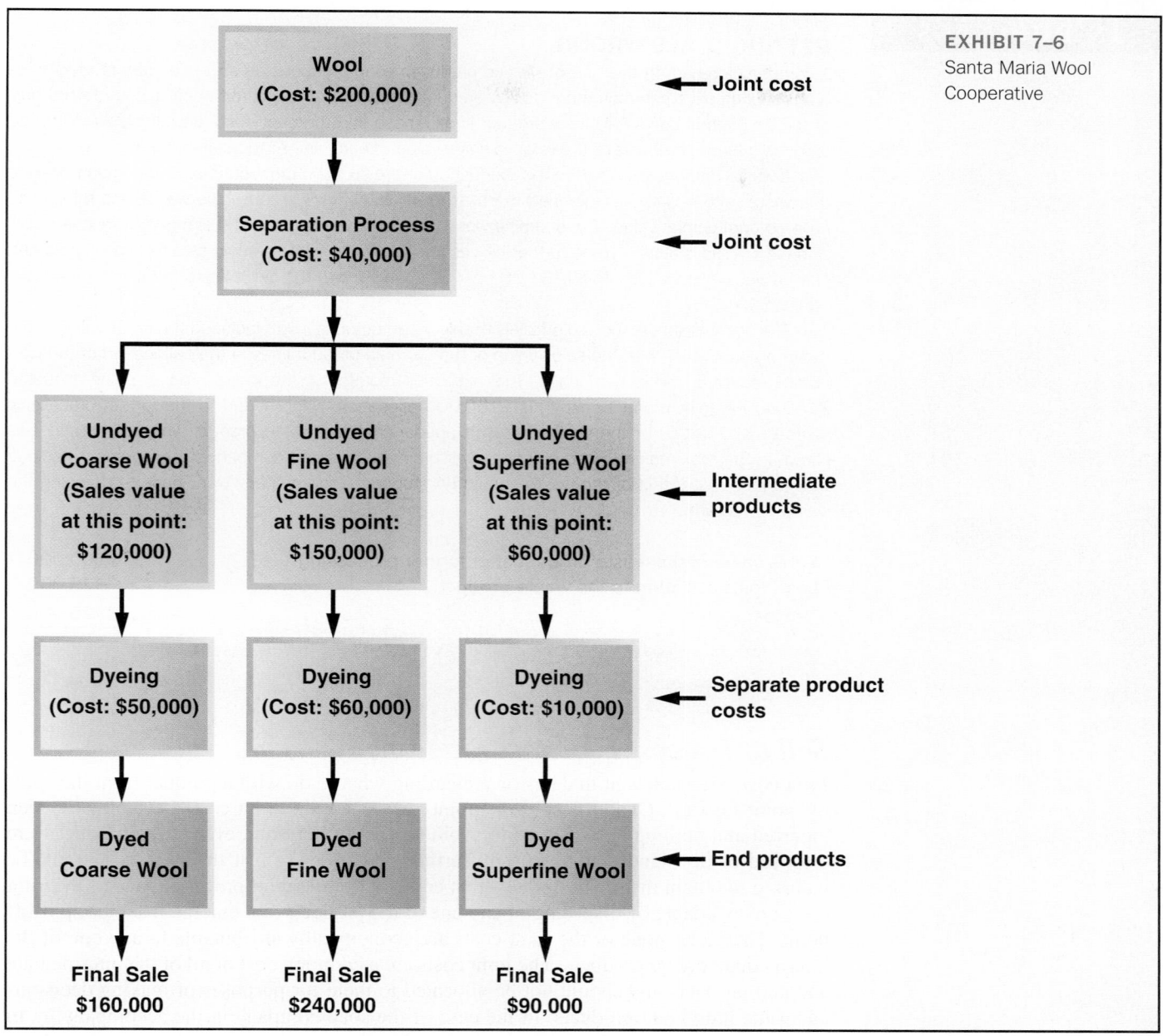

EXHIBIT 7–6
Santa Maria Wool
Cooperative

the raw wool and the $40,000 cost of separating the wool. The undyed wool is called an *intermediate product* because it is not finished at this point. Nevertheless, a market does exist for undyed wool—although at a significantly lower price than finished, dyed wool.

The Pitfalls of Allocation

Joint costs are common costs that are incurred to simultaneously produce a variety of end products. These joint costs are often allocated among the different products at the split-off point. A typical approach is to allocate the joint costs according to the relative sales value of the end products.

Although allocation of joint product costs is needed for some purposes, such as balance sheet inventory valuation, allocations of this kind are extremely misleading for decision making. The In Business box "Getting It All Wrong" (see below) illustrates an incorrect decision that resulted from using such an allocated joint cost. You should stop now and read that box before proceeding further.

IN BUSINESS

GETTING IT ALL WRONG

A company located on the Gulf of Mexico produces soap products. Its six main soap product lines are produced from common inputs. Joint product costs up to the split-off point constitute the bulk of the production costs for all six product lines. These joint product costs are allocated to the six product lines on the basis of the relative sales value of each line at the split-off point.

A waste product results from the production of the six main product lines. The company loaded the waste onto barges and dumped it into the Gulf of Mexico because the waste was thought to have no commercial value. The dumping was stopped, however, when the company's research division discovered that with some further processing the waste could be sold as a fertilizer ingredient. The further processing costs $175,000 per year. The waste was then sold to fertilizer manufacturers for $300,000.

The accountants responsible for allocating manufacturing costs included the sales value of the waste product along with the sales value of the six main product lines in their allocation of the joint product costs at the split-off point. This allocation resulted in the waste product being allocated $150,000 in joint product cost. This $150,000 allocation, when added to the further processing costs of $175,000 for the waste, made it appear that the waste product was unprofitable—as shown in the table below. When presented with this analysis, the company's management decided that further processing of the waste should be stopped. The company went back to dumping the waste in the Gulf.

Sales value of the waste product after further processing.	$300,000
Less costs assigned to the waste product	325,000
Net loss	$ (25,000)

Sell or Process Further Decisions

Joint costs are irrelevant in decisions regarding what to do with a product from the split-off point forward. Once the split-off point is reached, the joint costs have already been incurred and nothing can be done to avoid them. Furthermore, even if the product were disposed of in a landfill without any further processing, all of the joint costs must be incurred to obtain the other products that come out of the joint process. None of the joint costs are avoidable by disposing of any one of the products that emerge from the split-off point. Therefore, none of the joint costs are economically attributable to any one of the intermediate or end products. The joint costs are a common cost of all of the intermediate and end products and should not be allocated to them for purposes of making decisions about the individual products. In the case of the soap company in the accompanying In Business box "Getting It All Wrong," the $150,000 in allocated joint costs should not have influenced what was done with the waste product from the split-off point forward. Even ignoring the negative environmental impact of dumping the waste in the Gulf of Mexico, a correct analysis would have shown that the company was making money by further processing the waste into a fertilizer ingredient. The analysis should have been done as follows:

	Dump in Gulf	Process Further
Sales value of fertilizer ingredient	0	$300,000
Additional processing costs	0	175,000
Contribution margin	0	$125,000
Advantage of processing further		$125,000

Decisions of this type are known as **sell or process further decisions**. It is profitable to continue processing a joint product after the split-off point *so long as the incremental revenue from such processing exceeds the incremental processing cost incurred after the split-off point.* Joint costs that have already been incurred up to the split-off point are always irrelevant in decisions concerning what to do from the split-off point forward.

To provide a detailed example of the sell or process further decision, return to the data for Santa Maria Wool Cooperative in Exhibit 7–6. We can answer several important questions using this data. First, is the company making money if it runs the entire process from beginning to end? Assuming there are no costs other than those displayed in Exhibit 7–6, the company is indeed making money as follows:

Analysis of the profitability of the overall operation:

Combined final sales value ($160,000 + $240,000 + $90,000)..		$490,000
Less costs of producing the end products:		
Cost of wool.....................................	$200,000	
Cost of separating wool...........................	40,000	
Combined costs of dyeing ($50,000 + $60,000 + $10,000).......................................	120,000	360,000
Profit		$130,000

Note that the joint costs of buying the wool and separating the wool *are* relevant when considering the profitability of the entire operation. This is because these joint costs *could* be avoided if the entire operation were shut down. However, these joint costs are *not* relevant when considering the profitability of any one product. As long as the process is being run to make the other products, no additional joint costs are incurred to make the specific product in question.

Even though the company is making money overall, it may be losing money on one or more of the products. If the company buys wool and runs the separation process, it will get all three intermediate products. Nothing can be done about that. However, each of these products can be sold *as is* without further processing. It may be that the company would be better off selling one or more of the products prior to dyeing to avoid the dyeing costs. The appropriate way to make this choice is to compare the incremental revenues to the incremental costs from further processing as follows:

Analysis of sell or process further:

	Coarse Wool	Fine Wool	Superfine Wool
Final sales value after further processing ...	$160,000	$240,000	$90,000
Less sales value at the split-off point.......	120,000	150,000	60,000
Incremental revenue from further processing	40,000	90,000	30,000
Less cost of further processing (dyeing)	50,000	60,000	10,000
Profit (loss) from further processing........	$ (10,000)	$ 30,000	$20,000

As this analysis shows, the company would be better off selling the undyed coarse wool as is rather than processing it further. The other two products should be processed further and dyed before selling them.

Note that the joint costs of the wool ($200,000) and of the wool separation process ($40,000) play no role in the decision to sell or further process the intermediate products. These joint costs are relevant in a decision of whether to buy wool and to run the wool separation process, but they are not relevant in decisions about what to do with the intermediate products once they have been separated.

Activity-Based Costing and Relevant Costs

As discussed in an earlier chapter, activity-based costing can be used to help identify potentially relevant costs for decision-making purposes. Activity-based costing improves the traceability of costs by focusing on the activities caused by a product or other segment. However, managers should exercise caution against reading more into this "traceability" than really exists. People have a tendency to assume that if a cost is traceable to a segment, then the cost is automatically an avoidable cost. That is not true because the costs provided by a well-designed activity-based costing system are only *potentially* relevant. Before making a decision, managers must still decide which of the potentially relevant costs are actually avoidable. Only those costs that are avoidable are relevant and the others should be ignored.

To illustrate, refer again to the data relating to the housewares line in Exhibit 7–4. The $2,000 fixtures depreciation is a traceable cost of the housewares lines because it directly relates to activities in that department. We found, however, that the $2,000 is not avoidable if the housewares line is dropped. The key lesson here is that the method used to assign a cost to a product or other segment does not change the basic nature of the cost. A sunk cost such as depreciation of old equipment is still a sunk cost regardless of whether it is traced directly to a particular segment on an activity basis, allocated to all segments on the basis of labor-hours, or treated in some other way in the costing process. Regardless of the method used to assign costs to products or other segments, the principles discussed in this chapter must be applied to determine the costs that are avoidable in each situation.

Summary

Everything in this chapter consists of applications of one simple but powerful idea—only those costs and benefits that differ between alternatives are relevant in a decision. All other costs and benefits are irrelevant and should be ignored. In particular, sunk costs are irrelevant as are future costs that do not differ between alternatives.

This simple idea was applied in a variety of situations including decisions that involve adding or dropping a product line, making or buying a component, accepting or rejecting a special order, using a constrained resource, and processing a joint product further. This list includes only a small sample of the possible applications of the relevant cost concept. Indeed, any decision involving costs hinges on the proper identification and analysis of the costs that are relevant. We will continue to focus on the concept of relevant costs in the following chapter where long-term investment decisions are considered.

Review Problem: Relevant Costs

Charter Sports Equipment manufactures round, rectangular, and octagonal trampolines. Sales and expense data for the past month follow:

Management is concerned about the continued losses shown by the round trampolines and wants a recommendation as to whether or not the line should be discontinued. The special equipment used to produce the trampolines has no resale value. If the round trampoline model is dropped, the two line supervisors assigned to the model would be discharged.

Required:

1. Should production and sale of the round trampolines be discontinued? The company has no other use for the capacity now being used to produce the round trampolines. Show computations to support your answer.
2. Recast the above data in a format that would be more useful to management in assessing the profitability of the various product lines.

| | Total | Trampoline | | |
		Round	Rectangular	Octagonal
Sales.........................	$1,000,000	$140,000	$500,000	$360,000
Variable expenses	410,000	60,000	200,000	150,000
Contribution margin.............	590,000	80,000	300,000	210,000
Fixed expenses:				
Advertising—traceable	216,000	41,000	110,000	65,000
Depreciation of special				
equipment.................	95,000	20,000	40,000	35,000
Line supervisors' salaries	19,000	6,000	7,000	6,000
General factory overhead*	200,000	28,000	100,000	72,000
Total fixed expenses	530,000	95,000	257,000	178,000
Net operating income (loss)	$ 60,000	$ (15,000)	$ 43,000	$ 32,000

*A common fixed cost that is allocated on the basis of sales dollars.

Solution to Review Problem

1. No, production and sale of the round trampolines should not be discontinued. Computations to support this answer follow:

Contribution margin lost if the round trampolines are discontinued...		$(80,000)
Less fixed expenses that can be avoided:		
Advertising—traceable	$41,000	
Line supervisors' salaries	6,000	47,000
Decrease in net operating income for the company as a whole		$(33,000)

The depreciation of the special equipment is a sunk cost, and therefore, it is not relevant to the decision. The general factory overhead is allocated and will presumably continue regardless of whether or not the round trampolines are discontinued; thus, it is not relevant.

2. If management wants a clearer picture of the profitability of the segments, the general factory overhead should not be allocated. It is a common cost and, therefore, should be deducted from the total product-line segment margin. A more useful income statement format would be as follows:

| | Total | Trampoline | | |
		Round	Rectangular	Octagonal
Sales.........................	$1,000,000	$140,000	$500,000	$360,000
Variable expenses	410,000	60,000	200,000	150,000
Contribution margin.............	590,000	80,000	300,000	210,000
Traceable fixed expenses:				
Advertising—traceable	216,000	41,000	110,000	65,000
Depreciation of special				
equipment.................	95,000	20,000	40,000	35,000
Line supervisors' salaries	19,000	6,000	7,000	6,000
Total traceable fixed expenses.....	330,000	67,000	157,000	106,000
Product-line segment margin......	260,000	$ 13,000	$143,000	$104,000
Common fixed expenses..........	200,000			
Net operating income	$ 60,000			

Avoidable cost A cost that can be eliminated by choosing one alternative over another in a decision. This term is synonymous with *differential cost* and *relevant cost*. (p. 281)

Bottleneck A machine or some other part of a process that limits the total output of the entire system. (p. 296)

Constraint A limitation under which a company must operate, such as limited available machine time or raw materials, that restricts the company's ability to satisfy demand. (p. 295)

Differential cost A difference in cost between two alternatives. Also see *Incremental cost.* (p. 281)

Differential revenue A difference in revenue between two alternatives. (p. 281)

Joint costs Costs that are incurred up to the split-off point in a process that produces joint products. (p. 300)

Joint products Two or more products that are produced from a common input. (p. 300)

Make or buy decision A decision concerning whether an item should be produced internally or purchased from an outside supplier. (p. 291)

Opportunity cost The potential benefit that is given up when one alternative is selected over another. (p. 282)

Relaxing (or elevating) the constraint An action that increases the amount of a constrained resource. Equivalently, an action that increases the capacity of the bottleneck. (p. 299)

Relevant benefit A benefit that differs between alternatives in a decision. *Differential revenue* is a *relevant benefit.* (p. 281)

Relevant cost A difference in cost between any two alternatives. Synonyms are *avoidable cost, differential cost,* and *incremental cost.* (p. 281)

Sell or process further decision A decision as to whether a joint product should be sold at the split-off point or sold after further processing. (p. 303)

Special order A one-time order that is not considered part of the company's normal ongoing business. (p. 294)

Split-off point That point in the manufacturing process where some or all of the joint products can be recognized as individual products. (p. 300)

Sunk cost A cost that has already been incurred and that cannot be changed by any decision made now or in the future. (p. 281)

Vertical integration The involvement by a company in more than one of the activities in the entire value chain from development through production, distribution, sales, and after-sales service. (p. 291)

Questions

7–1 What is a *relevant cost?*

7–2 Define the following terms: *incremental cost, opportunity cost,* and *sunk cost.*

7–3 Are variable costs always relevant costs? Explain.

7–4 "Sunk costs are easy to spot—they're the fixed costs associated with a decision." Do you agree? Explain.

7–5 "Variable costs and differential costs mean the same thing." Do you agree? Explain.

7–6 "All future costs are relevant in decision making." Do you agree? Why?

7–7 Prentice Company is considering dropping one of its product lines. What costs of the product line would be relevant to this decision? What costs would be irrelevant?

7–8 "If a product is generating a loss, then it should be discontinued." Do you agree? Explain.

7–9 What is the danger in allocating common fixed costs among products or other segments of an organization?

7–10 How does opportunity cost enter into a make or buy decision?

7–11 Give at least four examples of possible constraints.

7–12 How will relating product contribution margins to the amount of the constrained resource they consume help a company maximize its profits?

7–13 Define the following terms: *joint products, joint costs,* and *split-off point.*

7–14 From a decision-making point of view, should joint costs be allocated among joint products?

7–15 What guideline should be used in determining whether a joint product should be sold at the split-off point or processed further?

7–16 Airlines sometimes offer reduced rates during certain times of the week to members of a businessperson's family if they accompany him or her on trips. How does the concept of relevant costs enter into the decision by the airline to offer reduced rates of this type?

Multiple-choice questions are available with Connect.

The Excel worksheet form that appears below is to be used to recreate an example earlier in the chapter. Download the workbook containing this form from Connect. *On the website you will also receive instructions about how to use this worksheet form.*

LEARNING OBJECTIVE 7–7

	A	B	C	D	E
1	Chapter 7: Applying Excel				
2					
3	Data				
4	Exhibit 7-6 Santa Maria Wool Cooperative				
5	Cost of wool	$200,000			
6	Cost of separation process	$40,000			
7	Sales value of intermediate products at split-off point:				
8	Undyed coarse wool	$120,000			
9	Undyed fine wool	$150,000			
10	Undyed superfine wool	$60,000			
11	Costs of further processing (dyeing) intermediate products:				
12	Undyed coarse wool	$50,000			
13	Undyed fine wool	$60,000			
14	Undyed superfine wool	$10,000			
15	Sales value of end products:				
16	Dyed coarse wool	$160,000			
17	Dyed fine wool	$240,000			
18	Dyed superfine wool	$90,000			
19					
20	Enter a formula into each of the cells marked with a ? below				
21	Example: Joint Product Costs and the Contribution Approach				
22					
23	Analysis of the profitability of the overall operation:				
24	Combined final sales value		?		
25	Less costs of producing the end products:				
26	Cost of wool	?			
27	Cost of separation process	?			
28	Combined costs of dyeing	?	?		
29	Profit		?		
30					
31	Analysis of sell or process further:				
32		Coarse	Fine	Superfine	
33		Wool	Wool	Wool	
34	Final sales value after further processing	?	?	?	
35	Less sales value at the split-off point	?	?	?	
36	Incremental revenue from further processing	?	?	?	
37	Less cost of further processing (dyeing)	?	?	?	
38	Profit (loss) from further processing	?	?	?	
39					

◄ ► ►│ **Chapter 7 Form** / Filled in Chapter 7 Form / Chapter 7

You should proceed to the requirements below only after completing your worksheet.

Required:

1. Check your worksheet by changing the cost of further processing undyed coarse wool in cell B12 to $30,000. The overall profit from processing all intermediate products into final products should now be $150,000 and the profit from further processing coarse wool should now be $10,000. If you do not get these answers, find the errors in your worksheet and correct them.

    How should operations change in response to this change in cost?

2. In industries that process joint products, the costs of the raw materials inputs and the sales values of intermediate and final products are often volatile. Change the data area of your worksheet to match the following:

    a. What is the overall profit if all intermediate products are processed into final products?

    b. What is the profit from further processing each of the intermediate products?

    c. With these new costs and selling prices, what recommendations would you make concerning the company's operations? If your recommendation is followed, what should be the overall profit of the company?

Data
Exhibit 7–6 Santa Maria Wool Cooperative

Cost of wool	$290,000
Cost of separation process.	$40,000
Sales value of intermediate products at split-off point:	
Undyed coarse wool	$100,000
Undyed fine wool.	$110,000
Undyed superfine wool.	$90,000
Costs of further processing (dyeing) intermediate products:	
Undyed coarse wool	$50,000
Undyed fine wool.	$60,000
Undyed superfine wool.	$10,000
Sales value of end products:	
Dyed coarse wool	$180,000
Dyed fine wool	$210,000
Dyed superfine wool	$90,000

The Foundational 15 ▮**connect** Additional student resources are available with Connect.

LEARNING OBJECTIVES 7–2, 7–3, 7–4, 7–5, 7–6

Cane Company manufactures two products called Alpha and Beta that sell for $120 and $80, respectively. Each product uses only one type of raw material that costs $6 per pound. The company has the capacity to annually produce 100,000 units of each product. Its unit costs for each product at this level of activity are given below:

	Alpha	Beta
Direct materials.	$ 30	$12
Direct labor	20	15
Variable manufacturing overhead	7	5
Traceable fixed manufacturing overhead.	16	18
Variable selling expenses	12	8
Common fixed expenses.	15	10
Total cost per unit.	$100	$68

The company considers its traceable fixed manufacturing overhead to be avoidable, whereas its common fixed expenses are deemed unavoidable and have been allocated to products based on sales dollars.

Required:
(Answer each question independently unless instructed otherwise.)
1. What is the total amount of traceable fixed manufacturing overhead for the Alpha product line and for the Beta product line?
2. What is the company's total amount of common fixed expenses?
3. Assume that Cane expects to produce and sell 80,000 Alphas during the current year. One of Cane's sales representatives has found a new customer that is willing to buy 10,000 additional Alphas for a price of $80 per unit. If Cane accepts the customer's offer, how much will its profits increase or decrease?
4. Assume that Cane expects to produce and sell 90,000 Betas during the current year. One of Cane's sales representatives has found a new customer that is willing to buy 5,000 additional Betas for a price of $39 per unit. If Cane accepts the customer's offer, how much will its profits increase or decrease?
5. Assume that Cane expects to produce and sell 95,000 Alphas during the current year. One of Cane's sales representatives has found a new customer that is willing to buy 10,000 additional Alphas for a price of $80 per unit. If Cane accepts the customer's offer, it will decrease Alpha sales to regular customers by 5,000 units. Should Cane accept this special order?
6. Assume that Cane normally produces and sells 90,000 Betas per year. If Cane discontinues the Beta product line, how much will profits increase or decrease?

7. Assume that Cane normally produces and sells 40,000 Betas per year. If Cane discontinues the Beta product line, how much will profits increase or decrease?

8. Assume that Cane normally produces and sells 60,000 Betas and 80,000 Alphas per year. If Cane discontinues the Beta product line, its sales representatives could increase sales of Alpha by 15,000 units. If Cane discontinues the Beta product line, how much would profits increase or decrease?

9. Assume that Cane expects to produce and sell 80,000 Alphas during the current year. A supplier has offered to manufacture and deliver 80,000 Alphas to Cane for a price of $80 per unit. If Cane buys 80,000 units from the supplier instead of making those units, how much will profits increase or decrease?

10. Assume that Cane expects to produce and sell 50,000 Alphas during the current year. A supplier has offered to manufacture and deliver 50,000 Alphas to Cane for a price of $80 per unit. If Cane buys 50,000 units from the supplier instead of making those units, how much will profits increase or decrease?

11. How many pounds of raw material are needed to make one unit of Alpha and one unit of Beta?

12. What contribution margin per pound of raw material is earned by Alpha and Beta?

13. Assume that Cane's customers would buy a maximum of 80,000 units of Alpha and 60,000 units of Beta. Also assume that the company's raw material available for production is limited to 160,000 pounds. How many units of each product should Cane produce to maximize its profits?

14. If Cane follows your recommendation in requirement 13, what total contribution margin will it earn?

15. If Cane uses its 160,000 pounds of raw materials as you recommended in requirement 13, up to how much should it be willing to pay per pound for additional raw materials?

Additional student resources are available with Connect. **Exercises**

EXERCISE 7–1 Identifying Relevant Costs [LO 7–1]

A number of costs are listed below that may be relevant in decisions faced by the management of Svahn, AB, a Swedish manufacturer of sailing yachts:

	Case 1		Case 2	
Item	Relevant	Not Relevant	Relevant	Not Relevant
a. Sales revenue........................				
b. Direct materials.....................				
c. Direct labor				
d. Variable manufacturing overhead.......				
e. Depreciation—Model B100 machine				
f. Book value—Model B100 machine......				
g. Disposal value—Model B100 machine...				
h. Market value—Model B300 machine (cost)...............................				
i. Fixed manufacturing overhead (general).				
j. Variable selling expense..............				
k. Fixed selling expense				
l. General administrative overhead				

Required:

Copy the information above onto your answer sheet and place an X in the appropriate column to indicate whether each item is relevant or not relevant in the following situations. Requirement 1 relates to Case 1 above, and requirement 2 relates to Case 2.

1. The company chronically has no idle capacity and the old Model B100 machine is the company's constraint. Management is considering purchasing a Model B300 machine to use in addition to the company's present Model B100 machine. The old Model B100 machine will continue to be used to capacity as before, with the new Model B300 machine being used to expand production. This will increase the company's production and sales. The increase in

volume will be large enough to require increases in fixed selling expenses and in general administrative overhead, but not in the fixed manufacturing overhead.

2. The old Model B100 machine is not the company's constraint, but management is considering replacing it with a new Model B300 machine because of the potential savings in direct materials with the new machine. The Model B100 machine would be sold. This change will have no effect on production or sales, other than some savings in direct materials costs due to less waste.

EXERCISE 7–2 Dropping or Retaining a Segment [LO 7–2]
The Regal Cycle Company manufactures three types of bicycles—a dirt bike, a mountain bike, and a racing bike. Data on sales and expenses for the past quarter follow:

	Total	Dirt Bikes	Mountain Bikes	Racing Bikes
Sales	$300,000	$90,000	$150,000	$60,000
Variable manufacturing and selling expenses	120,000	27,000	60,000	33,000
Contribution margin	180,000	63,000	90,000	27,000
Fixed expenses:				
Advertising, traceable	30,000	10,000	14,000	6,000
Depreciation of special equipment	23,000	6,000	9,000	8,000
Salaries of product-line managers	35,000	12,000	13,000	10,000
Allocated common fixed expenses*	60,000	18,000	30,000	12,000
Total fixed expenses	148,000	46,000	66,000	36,000
Net operating income (loss)	$ 32,000	$17,000	$ 24,000	$ (9,000)

*Allocated on the basis of sales dollars.

Management is concerned about the continued losses shown by the racing bikes and wants a recommendation as to whether or not the line should be discontinued. The special equipment used to produce racing bikes has no resale value and does not wear out.

Required:
1. Should production and sale of the racing bikes be discontinued? Explain. Show computations to support your answer.
2. Recast the above data in a format that would be more usable to management in assessing the long-run profitability of the various product lines.

EXERCISE 7–3 Make or Buy a Component [LO 7–3]
Troy Engines, Ltd., manufactures a variety of engines for use in heavy equipment. The company has always produced all of the necessary parts for its engines, including all of the carburetors. An outside supplier has offered to sell one type of carburetor to Troy Engines, Ltd., for a cost of $35 per unit. To evaluate this offer, Troy Engines, Ltd., has gathered the following information relating to its own cost of producing the carburetor internally:

	Per Unit	15,000 Units per Year
Direct materials	$14	$210,000
Direct labor	10	150,000
Variable manufacturing overhead	3	45,000
Fixed manufacturing overhead, traceable	6*	90,000
Fixed manufacturing overhead, allocated	9	135,000
Total cost	$42	$630,000

*One-third supervisory salaries; two-thirds depreciation of special equipment (no resale value).

Required:

1. Assuming that the company has no alternative use for the facilities that are now being used to produce the carburetors, should the outside supplier's offer be accepted? Show all computations.

2. Suppose that if the carburetors were purchased, Troy Engines, Ltd., could use the freed capacity to launch a new product. The segment margin of the new product would be $150,000 per year. Should Troy Engines, Ltd., accept the offer to buy the carburetors for $35 per unit? Show all computations.

EXERCISE 7–4 Evaluating a Special Order [LO 7–4]

Imperial Jewelers is considering a special order for 20 handcrafted gold bracelets to be given as gifts to members of a wedding party. The normal selling price of a gold bracelet is $189.95 and its unit product cost is $149.00 as shown below:

Direct materials.	$ 84.00
Direct labor	45.00
Manufacturing overhead.	20.00
Unit product cost	$149.00

Most of the manufacturing overhead is fixed and unaffected by variations in how much jewelry is produced in any given period. However, $4.00 of the overhead is variable with respect to the number of bracelets produced. The customer who is interested in the special bracelet order would like special filigree applied to the bracelets. This filigree would require additional materials costing $2.00 per bracelet and would also require acquisition of a special tool costing $250 that would have no other use once the special order is completed. This order would have no effect on the company's regular sales and the order could be fulfilled using the company's existing capacity without affecting any other order.

Required:

What effect would accepting this order have on the company's net operating income if a special price of $169.95 per bracelet is offered for this order? Should the special order be accepted at this price?

EXERCISE 7–5 Utilizing a Constrained Resource [LO 7–5]

Outdoor Luggage Inc. makes high-end hard-sided luggage for sports equipment. Data concerning three of the company's most popular models appear below.

	Ski Guard	Golf Guard	Fishing Guard
Selling price per unit	$200	$300	$255
Variable cost per unit.	$60	$140	$55
Plastic injection molding machine processing time required to produce one unit.	2 minutes	5 minutes	4 minutes
Pounds of plastic pellets per unit.	7 pounds	4 pounds	8 pounds

Required:

1. The total time available on the plastic injection molding machine is the constraint in the production process. Which product would be the most profitable use of this constraint? Which product would be the least profitable use of this constraint?

2. A severe shortage of plastic pellets has required the company to cut back its production so much that the plastic injection molding machine is no longer the bottleneck. Instead, the constraint is the total available pounds of plastic pellets. Which product would be the most profitable use of this constraint? Which product would be the least profitable use of this constraint?

3. Which product has the largest unit contribution margin? Why wouldn't this product be the most profitable use of the constrained resource in either case?

EXERCISE 7–6 Managing a Constrained Resource [LO 7–6]

Portsmouth Company makes fine colonial reproduction furniture. Upholstered furniture is one of its major product lines and the bottleneck on this production line is time in the upholstery shop. Upholstering is a craft that takes years of experience to master and the demand for upholstered furniture far exceeds the company's capacity in the upholstering shop. Information concerning three of the company's upholstered chairs appears below:

	Recliner	Sofa	Love Seat
Selling price per unit	$1,400	$1,800	$1,500
Variable cost per unit.	$800	$1,200	$1,000
Upholstery shop time required to produce one unit	8 hours	10 hours	5 hours

Required:

1. More time could be made available in the upholstery shop by asking the employees who work in this shop to work overtime. Assuming that this extra time would be used to produce sofas, up to how much should the company be willing to pay per hour to keep the upholstery shop open after normal working hours?

2. A small nearby upholstering company has offered to upholster furniture for Portsmouth at a fixed charge of $45 per hour. The management of Portsmouth is confident that this upholstering company's work is high quality and their craftsmen should be able to work about as quickly as Portsmouth's own craftsmen on the simpler upholstering jobs such as the love seat. Should management accept this offer? Explain.

EXERCISE 7–7 Sell or Process Further [LO 7–7]

Dorsey Company manufactures three products from a common input in a joint processing operation. Joint processing costs up to the split-off point total $350,000 per quarter. The company allocates these costs to the joint products on the basis of their relative sales value at the split-off point. Unit selling prices and total output at the split-off point are as follows:

Product	Selling Price	Quarterly Output
A	$16 per pound	15,000 pounds
B	$8 per pound	20,000 pounds
C	$25 per gallon	4,000 gallons

Each product can be processed further after the split-off point. Additional processing requires no special facilities. The additional processing costs (per quarter) and unit selling prices after further processing are given below:

Product	Additional Processing Costs	Selling Price
A	$63,000	$20 per pound
B	$80,000	$13 per pound
C	$36,000	$32 per gallon

Required:

Which product or products should be sold at the split-off point and which product or products should be processed further? Show computations.

EXERCISE 7–8 Utilization of a Constrained Resource [LO 7–5, LO 7–6]

Barlow Company manufactures three products: A, B, and C. The selling price, variable costs, and contribution margin for one unit of each product follow:

	Product		
	A	B	C
Selling price.	$180	$270	$240
Variable expenses:			
Direct materials.	24	72	32
Other variable expenses.	102	90	148
Total variable expenses.	126	162	180
Contribution margin.	$ 54	$108	$ 60
Contribution margin ratio	30%	40%	25%

The same raw material is used in all three products. Barlow Company has only 5,000 pounds of raw material on hand and will not be able to obtain any more of it for several weeks due to a strike in its supplier's plant. Management is trying to decide which product(s) to concentrate on next week in filling its backlog of orders. The material costs $8 per pound.

Required:

1. Compute the amount of contribution margin that will be obtained per pound of material used in each product.
2. Which orders would you recommend that the company work on next week—the orders for product A, product B, or product C? Show computations.
3. A foreign supplier could furnish Barlow with additional stocks of the raw material at a substantial premium over the usual price. If there is unfilled demand for all three products, what is the highest price that Barlow Company should be willing to pay for an additional pound of materials? Explain.

EXERCISE 7–9 Special Order [LO 7–4]

Delta Company produces a single product. The cost of producing and selling a single unit of this product at the company's normal activity level of 60,000 units per year is:

Direct materials.	$5.10
Direct labor	$3.80
Variable manufacturing overhead.	$1.00
Fixed manufacturing overhead	$4.20
Variable selling and administrative expense.	$1.50
Fixed selling and administrative expense	$2.40

The normal selling price is $21 per unit. The company's capacity is 75,000 units per year. An order has been received from a mail-order house for 15,000 units at a special price of $14.00 per unit. This order would not affect regular sales.

Required:

1. If the order is accepted, by how much will annual profits be increased or decreased? (The order will not change the company's total fixed costs.)
2. Assume the company has 1,000 units of this product left over from last year that are inferior to the current model. The units must be sold through regular channels at reduced prices. What unit cost is relevant for establishing a minimum selling price for these units? Explain.

EXERCISE 7–10 Make or Buy a Component [LO 7–3]

For many years Futura Company has purchased the starters that it installs in its standard line of farm tractors. Due to a reduction in output, the company has idle capacity that could be used to produce the starters. The chief engineer has recommended against this move, however, pointing out that the cost to produce the starters would be greater than the current $8.40 per unit purchase price:

	Per Unit	Total
Direct materials.............................	$3.10	
Direct labor	2.70	
Supervision	1.50	$60,000
Depreciation	1.00	$40,000
Variable manufacturing overhead...............	0.60	
Rent..	0.30	$12,000
Total production cost.........................	$9.20	

A supervisor would have to be hired to oversee production of the starters. However, the company has sufficient idle tools and machinery that no new equipment would have to be purchased. The rent charge above is based on space utilized in the plant. The total rent on the plant is $80,000 per period. Depreciation is due to obsolescence rather than wear and tear.

Required:

Prepare computations showing how much profits will increase or decrease as a result of making the starters.

EXERCISE 7–11 Make or Buy a Component [LO 7–3]

Han Products manufactures 30,000 units of part S-6 each year for use on its production line. At this level of activity, the cost per unit for part S-6 is:

Direct materials................................	$ 3.60
Direct labor	10.00
Variable manufacturing overhead................	2.40
Fixed manufacturing overhead	9.00
Total cost per part.............................	$25.00

An outside supplier has offered to sell 30,000 units of part S-6 each year to Han Products for $21 per part. If Han Products accepts this offer, the facilities now being used to manufacture part S-6 could be rented to another company at an annual rental of $80,000. However, Han Products has determined that two-thirds of the fixed manufacturing overhead being applied to part S-6 would continue even if part S-6 were purchased from the outside supplier.

Required:

Prepare computations showing how much profits will increase or decrease if the outside supplier's offer is accepted.

EXERCISE 7–12 Utilization of a Constrained Resource [LO 7–5]

Benoit Company produces three products, A, B, and C. Data concerning the three products follow (per unit):

	Product		
	A	B	C
Selling price............................	$80	$56	$70
Variable expenses:			
Direct materials........................	24	15	9
Other variable expenses................	24	27	40
Total variable expenses..................	48	42	49
Contribution margin......................	$32	$14	$21
Contribution margin ratio	40%	25%	30%

Demand for the company's products is very strong, with far more orders each month than the company can produce with the available raw materials. The same material is used in each product. The material costs $3 per pound with a maximum of 5,000 pounds available each month.

Required:

Which orders would you advise the company to accept first, those for A, for B, or for C? Which orders second? Third?

EXERCISE 7–13 Sell or Process Further [LO 7–7]

Wexpro, Inc., produces several products from processing 1 ton of clypton, a rare mineral. Material and processing costs total $60,000 per ton, one-fourth of which is allocated to product X15. Seven thousand units of product X15 are produced from each ton of clypton. The units can either be sold at the split-off point for $9 each, or processed further at a total cost of $9,500 and then sold for $12 each.

Required:

Should product X15 be processed further or sold at the split-off point?

EXERCISE 7–14 Identification of Relevant Costs [LO 7–1]

Kristen Lu purchased a used automobile for $8,000 at the beginning of last year and incurred the following operating costs:

Depreciation ($8,000 ÷ 5 years).	$1,600
Insurance.	$1,200
Garage rent.	$360
Automobile tax and license	$40
Variable operating cost.	$0.14 per mile

The variable operating cost consists of gasoline, oil, tires, maintenance, and repairs. Kristen estimates that, at her current rate of usage, the car will have zero resale value in five years, so the annual straight-line depreciation is $1,600. The car is kept in a garage for a monthly fee.

Required:

1. Kristen drove the car 10,000 miles last year. Compute the average cost per mile of owning and operating the car.
2. Kristen is unsure about whether she should use her own car or rent a car to go on an extended cross-country trip for two weeks during spring break. What costs above are relevant in this decision? Explain.
3. Kristen is thinking about buying an expensive sports car to replace the car she bought last year. She would drive the same number of miles regardless of which car she owns and would rent the same parking space. The sports car's variable operating costs would be roughly the same as the variable operating costs of her old car. However, her insurance and automobile tax and license costs would go up. What costs are relevant in estimating the incremental cost of owning the more expensive car? Explain.

EXERCISE 7–15 Dropping or Retaining a Segment [LO 7–2]

Thalassines Kataskeves, S.A., of Greece makes marine equipment. The company has been experiencing losses on its bilge pump product line for several years. The most recent quarterly contribution format income statement for the bilge pump product line follows:

Discontinuing the bilge pump product line would not affect sales of other product lines and would have no effect on the company's total general factory overhead or total Purchasing Department expenses.

Thalassines Kataskeves, S.A.
Income Statement—Bilge Pump
For the Quarter Ended March 31

Sales..		$850,000
Variable expenses:		
Variable manufacturing expenses.........................	$330,000	
Sales commissions......................................	42,000	
Shipping...	18,000	
Total variable expenses.......................................		390,000
Contribution margin..		460,000
Fixed expenses:		
Advertising..	270,000	
Depreciation of equipment (no resale value)...............	80,000	
General factory overhead...............................	105,000*	
Salary of product-line manager..........................	32,000	
Insurance on inventories...............................	8,000	
Purchasing department..................................	45,000†	
Total fixed expenses..		540,000
Net operating loss..		$ (80,000)

*Common costs allocated on the basis of machine-hours.
†Common costs allocated on the basis of sales dollars.

Required:

Would you recommend that the bilge pump product line be discontinued? Support your answer with appropriate computations.

EXERCISE 7–16 Identification of Relevant Costs [LO 7–1]

Bill has just returned from a duck hunting trip. He has brought home eight ducks. Bill's friend, John, disapproves of duck hunting, and to discourage Bill from further hunting, John has presented him with the following cost estimate per duck:

Camper and equipment:	
Cost, $12,000; usable for eight seasons; 10 hunting trips per season..........	$150
Travel expense (pickup truck):	
100 miles at $0.31 per mile (gas, oil, and tires—$0.21 per mile; depreciation	
and insurance—$0.10 per mile).......................................	31
Shotgun shells (two boxes).......................................	20
Boat:	
Cost, $2,320, usable for eight seasons; 10 hunting trips per season.........	29
Hunting license:	
Cost, $30 for the season; 10 hunting trips per season......................	3
Money lost playing poker:	
Loss, $24 (Bill plays poker every weekend).............................	24
Bottle of whiskey:	
Cost, $15 (used to ward off the cold).................................	15
Total cost..	$272
Cost per duck ($272 ÷ 8 ducks)..	$ 34

Required:

1. Assuming that the duck hunting trip Bill has just completed is typical, what costs are relevant to a decision as to whether Bill should go duck hunting again this season?
2. Suppose that Bill gets lucky on his next hunting trip and shoots 10 ducks in the amount of time it took him to shoot 8 ducks on his last trip. How much would it have cost him to shoot the last two ducks? Explain.
3. Which costs are relevant in a decision of whether Bill should give up hunting? Explain.

EXERCISE 7–17 Dropping or Retaining a Segment [LO 7–2]

Bed & Bath, a retailing company, has two departments, Hardware and Linens. The company's most recent monthly contribution format income statement follows:

	Total	Department Hardware	Linens
Sales...........................	$4,000,000	$3,000,000	$1,000,000
Variable expenses	1,300,000	900,000	400,000
Contribution margin.............	2,700,000	2,100,000	600,000
Fixed expenses.................	2,200,000	1,400,000	800,000
Net operating income (loss)	$ 500,000	$ 700,000	$ (200,000)

A study indicates that $340,000 of the fixed expenses being charged to Linens are sunk costs or allocated costs that will continue even if the Linens Department is dropped. In addition, the elimination of the Linens Department will result in a 10% decrease in the sales of the Hardware Department.

Required:

If the Linens Department is dropped, what will be the effect on the net operating income of the company as a whole?

Additional student resources are available with Connect. **Problems**

PROBLEM 7–18 Relevant Cost Analysis in a Variety of Situations [LO 7–2, LO 7–3, LO 7–4]

Andretti Company has a single product called a Dak. The company normally produces and sells 60,000 Daks each year at a selling price of $32 per unit. The company's unit costs at this level of activity are given below:

Direct materials...............................	$10.00	
Direct labor	4.50	
Variable manufacturing overhead................	2.30	
Fixed manufacturing overhead	5.00	($300,000 total)
Variable selling expenses......................	1.20	
Fixed selling expenses	3.50	($210,000 total)
Total cost per unit............................	$26.50	

A number of questions relating to the production and sale of Daks follow. Each question is independent.

Required:

1. Assume that Andretti Company has sufficient capacity to produce 90,000 Daks each year without any increase in fixed manufacturing overhead costs. The company could increase its sales by 25% above the present 60,000 units each year if it were willing to increase the fixed selling expenses by $80,000. Would the increased fixed selling expenses be justified?

2. Assume again that Andretti Company has sufficient capacity to produce 90,000 Daks each year. A customer in a foreign market wants to purchase 20,000 Daks. Import duties on the Daks would be $1.70 per unit, and costs for permits and licenses would be $9,000. The only selling costs that would be associated with the order would be $3.20 per unit shipping cost. Compute the per unit break-even price on this order.

3. The company has 1,000 Daks on hand that have some irregularities and are therefore considered to be "seconds." Due to the irregularities, it will be impossible to sell these units at the normal price through regular distribution channels. What unit cost figure is relevant for setting a minimum selling price? Explain.

4. Due to a strike in its supplier's plant, Andretti Company is unable to purchase more material for the production of Daks. The strike is expected to last for two months. Andretti Company

has enough material on hand to operate at 30% of normal levels for the two-month period. As an alternative, Andretti could close its plant down entirely for the two months. If the plant were closed, fixed manufacturing overhead costs would continue at 60% of their normal level during the two-month period and the fixed selling expenses would be reduced by 20%. What would be the impact on profits of closing the plant for the two-month period?

5. An outside manufacturer has offered to produce Daks and ship them directly to Andretti's customers. If Andretti Company accepts this offer, the facilities that it uses to produce Daks would be idle; however, fixed manufacturing overhead costs would be reduced by 75%. Because the outside manufacturer would pay for all shipping costs, the variable selling expenses would be only two-thirds of their present amount. Compute the unit cost that is relevant for comparison to the price quoted by the outside manufacturer.

 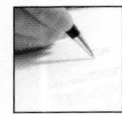

PROBLEM 7–19 Dropping or Retaining a Segment [LO 7–2]

Jackson County Senior Services is a nonprofit organization devoted to providing essential services to seniors who live in their own homes within the Jackson County area. Three services are provided for seniors—home nursing, Meals On Wheels, and housekeeping. Data on revenue and expenses for the past year follow:

	Total	Home Nursing	Meals On Wheels	House-keeping
Revenues..........................	$900,000	$260,000	$400,000	$240,000
Variable expenses	490,000	120,000	210,000	60,000
Contribution margin.................	410,000	140,000	190,000	80,000
Fixed expenses:				
Depreciation	68,000	8,000	40,000	20,000
Liability insurance.................	42,000	20,000	7,000	15,000
Program administrators' salaries	115,000	40,000	38,000	37,000
General administrative overhead*...	180,000	52,000	80,000	48,000
Total fixed expenses	405,000	120,000	165,000	120,000
Net operating income (loss)	$ 5,000	$ 20,000	$ 25,000	$ (40,000)

*Allocated on the basis of program revenues.

The head administrator of Jackson County Senior Services, Judith Miyama, is concerned about the organization's finances and considers the net operating income of $5,000 last year to be razor-thin. (Last year's results were very similar to the results for previous years and are representative of what would be expected in the future.) She feels that the organization should be building its financial reserves at a more rapid rate in order to prepare for the next inevitable recession. After seeing the above report, Ms. Miyama asked for more information about the financial advisability of perhaps discontinuing the housekeeping program.

The depreciation in housekeeping is for a small van that is used to carry the housekeepers and their equipment from job to job. If the program were discontinued, the van would be donated to a charitable organization. None of the general administrative overhead would be avoided if the housekeeping program were dropped, but the liability insurance and the salary of the program administrator would be avoided.

Required:

1. Should the Housekeeping program be discontinued? Explain. Show computations to support your answer.

2. Recast the above data in a format that would be more useful to management in assessing the long-run financial viability of the various services.

PROBLEM 7–20 Sell or Process Further [LO 7–7]

(Prepared from a situation suggested by Professor John W. Hardy.) Lone Star Meat Packers is a major processor of beef and other meat products. The company has a large amount of T-bone steak on hand, and it is trying to decide whether to sell the T-bone steaks as they are initially cut or to process them further into filet mignon and the New York cut.

If the T-bone steaks are sold as initially cut, the company figures that a 1-pound T-bone steak would yield the following profit:

Selling price ($2.25 per pound).......................................	$2.25
Less joint costs incurred up to the split-off point where T-bone steak can be identified as a separate product	1.80
Profit per pound	$0.45

As mentioned above, instead of being sold as initially cut, the T-bone steaks could be further processed into filet mignon and New York cut steaks. Cutting one side of a T-bone steak provides the filet mignon, and cutting the other side provides the New York cut. One 16-ounce T-bone steak cut in this way will yield one 6-ounce filet mignon and one 8-ounce New York cut; the remaining ounces are waste. The cost of processing the T-bone steaks into these cuts is $0.25 per pound. The filet mignon can be sold for $4.00 per pound, and the New York cut can be sold for $2.80 per pound.

Required:
1. Determine the profit per pound from processing the T-bone steaks into filet mignon and New York cut steaks.
2. Would you recommend that the T-bone steaks be sold as initially cut or processed further? Why?

PROBLEM 7–21 Dropping or Retaining a Flight [LO 7–2]

Profits have been decreasing for several years at Pegasus Airlines. In an effort to improve the company's performance, consideration is being given to dropping several flights that appear to be unprofitable.

A typical income statement for one round-trip of one such flight (flight 482) is as follows:

Ticket revenue (175 seats × 40% occupancy × $200 ticket price)..	$14,000	100.0%
Variable expenses ($15 per person)............................	1,050	7.5
Contribution margin.......................................	12,950	92.5%
Flight expenses:		
Salaries, flight crew	1,800	
Flight promotion..	750	
Depreciation of aircraft	1,550	
Fuel for aircraft	5,800	
Liability insurance...	4,200	
Salaries, flight assistants.....................................	1,500	
Baggage loading and flight preparation......................	1,700	
Overnight costs for flight crew and assistants at destination	300	
Total flight expenses	17,600	
Net operating loss	$ (4,650)	

The following additional information is available about flight 482:
a. Members of the flight crew are paid fixed annual salaries, whereas the flight assistants are paid based on the number of round trips they complete.
b. One-third of the liability insurance is a special charge assessed against flight 482 because in the opinion of the insurance company, the destination of the flight is in a "high-risk" area. The remaining two-thirds would be unaffected by a decision to drop flight 482.
c. The baggage loading and flight preparation expense is an allocation of ground crews' salaries and depreciation of ground equipment. Dropping flight 482 would have no effect on the company's total baggage loading and flight preparation expenses.
d. If flight 482 is dropped, Pegasus Airlines has no authorization at present to replace it with another flight.
e. Aircraft depreciation is due entirely to obsolescence. Depreciation due to wear and tear is negligible.
f. Dropping flight 482 would not allow Pegasus Airlines to reduce the number of aircraft in its fleet or the number of flight crew on its payroll.

Required:

1. Prepare an analysis showing what impact dropping flight 482 would have on the airline's profits.

2. The airline's scheduling officer has been criticized because only about 50% of the seats on Pegasus' flights are being filled compared to an industry average of 60%. The scheduling officer has explained that Pegasus' average seat occupancy could be improved considerably by eliminating about 10% of its flights, but that doing so would reduce profits. Explain how this could happen.

PROBLEM 7–22 Accept or Reject a Special Order [LO 7–4]

Polaski Company manufactures and sells a single product called a Ret. Operating at capacity, the company can produce and sell 30,000 Rets per year. Costs associated with this level of production and sales are given below:

	Unit	Total
Direct materials..........................	$15	$ 450,000
Direct labor	8	240,000
Variable manufacturing overhead...........	3	90,000
Fixed manufacturing overhead	9	270,000
Variable selling expense...................	4	120,000
Fixed selling expense	6	180,000
Total cost...............................	$45	$1,350,000

The Rets normally sell for $50 each. Fixed manufacturing overhead is constant at $270,000 per year within the range of 25,000 through 30,000 Rets per year.

Required:

1. Assume that due to a recession, Polaski Company expects to sell only 25,000 Rets through regular channels next year. A large retail chain has offered to purchase 5,000 Rets if Polaski is willing to accept a 16% discount off the regular price. There would be no sales commissions on this order; thus, variable selling expenses would be slashed by 75%. However, Polaski Company would have to purchase a special machine to engrave the retail chain's name on the 5,000 units. This machine would cost $10,000. Polaski Company has no assurance that the retail chain will purchase additional units in the future. Determine the impact on profits next year if this special order is accepted.

2. Refer to the original data. Assume again that Polaski Company expects to sell only 25,000 Rets through regular channels next year. The U.S. Army would like to make a one-time-only purchase of 5,000 Rets. The Army would pay a fixed fee of $1.80 per Ret, and it would reimburse Polaski Company for all costs of production (variable and fixed) associated with the units. Because the army would pick up the Rets with its own trucks, there would be no variable selling expenses associated with this order. If Polaski Company accepts the order, by how much will profits increase or decrease for the year?

3. Assume the same situation as that described in requirement 2, except that the company expects to sell 30,000 Rets through regular channels next year. Thus, accepting the U.S. Army's order would require giving up regular sales of 5,000 Rets. If the Army's order is accepted, by how much will profits increase or decrease from what they would be if the 5,000 Rets were sold through regular channels?

PROBLEM 7–23 Make or Buy Decision [LO 7–3]

Silven Industries, which manufactures and sells a highly successful line of summer lotions and insect repellents, has decided to diversify in order to stabilize sales throughout the year. A natural area for the company to consider is the production of winter lotions and creams to prevent dry and chapped skin.

After considerable research, a winter products line has been developed. However, Silven's president has decided to introduce only one of the new products for this coming winter. If the product is a success, further expansion in future years will be initiated.

The product selected (called Chap-Off) is a lip balm that will be sold in a lipstick-type tube. The product will be sold to wholesalers in boxes of 24 tubes for $8 per box. Because of excess capacity, no additional fixed manufacturing overhead costs will be incurred to produce the product. However, a $90,000 charge for fixed manufacturing overhead will be absorbed by the product under the company's absorption costing system.

Using the estimated sales and production of 100,000 boxes of Chap-Off, the Accounting Department has developed the following cost per box:

Direct material............................	$3.60
Direct labor	2.00
Manufacturing overhead...................	1.40
Total cost	$7.00

The costs above include costs for producing both the lip balm and the tube that contains it. As an alternative to making the tubes, Silven has approached a supplier to discuss the possibility of purchasing the tubes for Chap-Off. The purchase price of the empty tubes from the supplier would be $1.35 per box of 24 tubes. If Silven Industries accepts the purchase proposal, direct labor and variable manufacturing overhead costs per box of Chap-Off would be reduced by 10% and direct materials costs would be reduced by 25%.

Required:
1. Should Silven Industries make or buy the tubes? Show calculations to support your answer.
2. What would be the maximum purchase price acceptable to Silven Industries? Explain.
3. Instead of sales of 100,000 boxes, revised estimates show a sales volume of 120,000 boxes. At this new volume, additional equipment must be acquired to manufacture the tubes at an annual rental of $40,000. Assuming that the outside supplier will not accept an order for less than 120,000 boxes, should Silven Industries make or buy the tubes? Show computations to support your answer.
4. Refer to the data in requirement 3. Assume that the outside supplier will accept an order of any size for the tubes at $1.35 per box. How, if at all, would this change your answer? Show computations.
5. What qualitative factors should Silven Industries consider in determining whether they should make or buy the tubes?

(CMA, adapted)

PROBLEM 7–24 Shutting Down or Continuing to Operate a Plant [LO 7–2]
(Note: This type of decision is similar to keeping or dropping a product line.)

Birch Company normally produces and sells 30,000 units of RG-6 each month. RG-6 is a small electrical relay used as a component part in the automotive industry. The selling price is $22 per unit, variable costs are $14 per unit, fixed manufacturing overhead costs total $150,000 per month, and fixed selling costs total $30,000 per month.

Employment-contract strikes in the companies that purchase the bulk of the RG-6 units have caused Birch Company's sales to temporarily drop to only 8,000 units per month. Birch Company estimates that the strikes will last for two months, after which time sales of RG-6 should return to normal. Due to the current low level of sales, Birch Company is thinking about closing down its own plant during the strike, which would reduce its fixed manufacturing overhead costs by $45,000 per month and its fixed selling costs by 10%. Start-up costs at the end of the shutdown period would total $8,000. Because Birch Company uses Lean Production methods, no inventories are on hand.

Required:
1. Assuming that the strikes continue for two months, would you recommend that Birch Company close its own plant? Explain. Show computations.
2. At what level of sales (in units) for the two-month period should Birch Company be indifferent between closing the plant or keeping it open? Show computations. (*Hint:* This is a type of break-even analysis, except that the fixed cost portion of your break-even computation should include only those fixed costs that are relevant [i.e., avoidable] over the two-month period.)

PROBLEM 7–25 Utilization of a Constrained Resource [LO 7–5, LO 7–6]

The Walton Toy Company manufactures a line of dolls and a doll dress sewing kit. Demand for the dolls is increasing, and management requests assistance from you in determining an economical sales and production mix for the coming year. The company has provided the following data:

Product	Demand Next Year (units)	Selling Price per Unit	Direct Materials	Direct Labor
Debbie	50,000	$13.50	$4.30	$3.20
Trish	42,000	$5.50	$1.10	$2.00
Sarah	35,000	$21.00	$6.44	$5.60
Mike	40,000	$10.00	$2.00	$4.00
Sewing kit	325,000	$8.00	$3.20	$1.60

The following additional information is available:

a. The company's plant has a capacity of 130,000 direct labor-hours per year on a single-shift basis. The company's present employees and equipment can produce all five products.

b. The direct labor rate of $8 per hour is expected to remain unchanged during the coming year.

c. Fixed costs total $520,000 per year. Variable overhead costs are $2 per direct labor-hour.

d. All of the company's nonmanufacturing costs are fixed.

e. The company's finished goods inventory is negligible and can be ignored.

Required:

1. Determine the contribution margin per direct labor-hour expended on each product.

2. Prepare a schedule showing the total direct labor-hours that will be required to produce the units estimated to be sold during the coming year.

3. Examine the data you have computed in requirements 1 and 2. How would you allocate the 130,000 direct labor-hours of capacity to Walton Toy Company's various products?

4. What is the highest total contribution margin that the company can earn if it makes optimal use of its constrained resource?

5. What is the highest price, in terms of a rate per hour, that Walton Toy Company would be willing to pay for additional capacity (that is, for added direct labor time)?

6. Assume again that the company does not want to reduce sales of any product. Identify ways in which the company could obtain the additional output.

(CMA, adapted)

PROBLEM 7–26 Close or Retain a Store [LO 7–2]

Superior Markets, Inc., operates three stores in a large metropolitan area. A segmented absorption costing income statement for the company for the last quarter is given below:

Superior Markets, Inc. Income Statement For the Quarter Ended September 30				
	Total	North Store	South Store	East Store
Sales.	$3,000,000	$720,000	$1,200,000	$1,080,000
Cost of goods sold.	1,657,200	403,200	660,000	594,000
Gross margin.	1,342,800	316,800	540,000	486,000
Selling and administrative expenses:				
Selling expenses	817,000	231,400	315,000	270,600
Administrative expenses. . . .	383,000	106,000	150,900	126,100
Total expenses	1,200,000	337,400	465,900	396,700
Net operating income (loss) . . .	$ 142,800	$ (20,600)	$ 74,100	$ 89,300

The North Store has consistently shown losses over the past two years. For this reason, management is giving consideration to closing the store. The company has asked you to make a recommendation as to whether the store should be closed or kept open. The following additional information is available for your use:

a.   The breakdown of the selling and administrative expenses is as follows:

	Total	North Store	South Store	East Store
Selling expenses:				
Sales salaries...............	$239,000	$ 70,000	$ 89,000	$ 80,000
Direct advertising	187,000	51,000	72,000	64,000
General advertising*...........	45,000	10,800	18,000	16,200
Store rent	300,000	85,000	120,000	95,000
Depreciation of store fixtures	16,000	4,600	6,000	5,400
Delivery salaries	21,000	7,000	7,000	7,000
Depreciation of delivery equipment	9,000	3,000	3,000	3,000
Total selling expenses	$817,000	$231,400	$315,000	$270,600

*Allocated on the basis of sales dollars.

	Total	North Store	South Store	East Store
Administrative expenses:				
Store management salaries	$ 70,000	$ 21,000	$ 30,000	$ 19,000
General office salaries*.........	50,000	12,000	20,000	18,000
Insurance on fixtures and inventory...................	25,000	7,500	9,000	8,500
Utilities	106,000	31,000	40,000	35,000
Employment taxes	57,000	16,500	21,900	18,600
General office—other*	75,000	18,000	30,000	27,000
Total administrative expenses	$383,000	$106,000	$150,900	$126,100

*Allocated on the basis of sales dollars.

b.   The lease on the building housing the North Store can be broken with no penalty.
c.   The fixtures being used in the North Store would be transferred to the other two stores if the North Store were closed.
d.   The general manager of the North Store would be retained and transferred to another position in the company if the North Store were closed. She would be filling a position that would otherwise be filled by hiring a new employee at a salary of $11,000 per quarter. The general manager of the North Store would be retained at her normal salary of $12,000 per quarter. All other employees in the store would be discharged.
e.   The company has one delivery crew that serves all three stores. One delivery person could be discharged if the North Store were closed. This person's salary is $4,000 per quarter. The delivery equipment would be distributed to the other stores. The equipment does not wear out through use, but does eventually become obsolete.
f.   The company's employment taxes are 15% of salaries.
g.   One-third of the insurance in the North Store is on the store's fixtures.
h.   The "General office salaries" and "General office—other" relate to the overall management of Superior Markets, Inc. If the North Store were closed, one person in the general office could be discharged because of the decrease in overall workload. This person's compensation is $6,000 per quarter.

Required:
1.   Prepare a schedule showing the change in revenues and expenses and the impact on the company's overall net operating income that would result if the North Store were closed.

2. Assuming that the store space can't be subleased, what recommendation would you make to the management of Superior Markets, Inc.?
3. Disregard requirement 2. Assume that if the North Store were closed, at least one-fourth of its sales would transfer to the East Store, due to strong customer loyalty to Superior Markets. The East Store has enough capacity to handle the increased sales. You may assume that the increased sales in the East Store would yield the same gross margin as a percentage of sales as present sales in that store. What effect would these factors have on your recommendation concerning the North Store? Show all computations to support your answer.

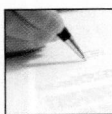

PROBLEM 7–27 Sell or Process Further [LO 7–7]

Come-Clean Corporation produces a variety of cleaning compounds and solutions for both industrial and household use. While most of its products are processed independently, a few are related, such as the company's Grit 337 and its Sparkle silver polish.

Grit 337 is a coarse cleaning powder with many industrial uses. It costs $1.60 a pound to make, and it has a selling price of $2.00 a pound. A small portion of the annual production of Grit 337 is retained in the factory for further processing. It is combined with several other ingredients to form a paste that is marketed as Sparkle silver polish. The silver polish sells for $4.00 per jar.

This further processing requires one-fourth pound of Grit 337 per jar of silver polish. The additional direct costs involved in the processing of a jar of silver polish are:

Other ingredients	$0.65
Direct labor	1.48
Total direct cost.	$2.13

Overhead costs associated with processing the silver polish are:

Variable manufacturing overhead cost.	25% of direct labor cost
Fixed manufacturing overhead cost (per month):	
Production supervisor	$3,000
Depreciation of mixing equipment	$1,400

The production supervisor has no duties other than to oversee production of the silver polish. The mixing equipment is special-purpose equipment acquired specifically to produce the silver polish. Its resale value is negligible and it does not wear out through use.

Direct labor is a variable cost at Come-Clean Corporation.

Advertising costs for the silver polish total $4,000 per month. Variable selling costs associated with the silver polish are 7.5% of sales.

Due to a recent decline in the demand for silver polish, the company is wondering whether its continued production is advisable. The sales manager feels that it would be more profitable to sell all of the Grit 337 as a cleaning powder.

Required:

1. What is the incremental contribution margin per jar from further processing of Grit 337 into silver polish?
2. What is the minimum number of jars of silver polish that must be sold each month to justify the continued processing of Grit 337 into silver polish? Explain. Show all computations.

(CMA, adapted)

PROBLEM 7–28 Make or Buy Analysis [LO 7–3]

"In my opinion, we ought to stop making our own drums and accept that outside supplier's offer," said Wim Niewindt, managing director of Antilles Refining, N.V., of Aruba. "At a price of $18 per drum, we would be paying $5 less than it costs us to manufacture the drums in our own plant. Since we use 60,000 drums a year, that would be an annual cost savings of $300,000." Antilles Refining's current cost to manufacture one drum is given below (based on 60,000 drums per year):

Direct materials...	$10.35
Direct labor	6.00
Variable overhead	1.50
Fixed overhead ($2.80 general company overhead, $1.60 depreciation and, $0.75 supervision)	5.15
Total cost per drum	$23.00

A decision about whether to make or buy the drums is especially important at this time because the equipment being used to make the drums is completely worn out and must be replaced. The choices facing the company are:

Alternative 1:   Rent new equipment and continue to make the drums. The equipment would be rented for $135,000 per year.

Alternative 2:   Purchase the drums from an outside supplier at $18 per drum.

The new equipment would be more efficient than the equipment that Antilles Refining has been using and, according to the manufacturer, would reduce direct labor and variable overhead costs by 30%. The old equipment has no resale value. Supervision cost ($45,000 per year) and direct materials cost per drum would not be affected by the new equipment. The new equipment's capacity would be 90,000 drums per year.

The company's total general company overhead would be unaffected by this decision.

Required:

1. To assist the managing director in making a decision, prepare an analysis showing the total cost and the cost per drum for each of the two alternatives given above. Assume that 60,000 drums are needed each year. Which course of action would you recommend to the managing director?

2. Would your recommendation in requirement 1 be the same if the company's needs were: (a) 75,000 drums per year or (b) 90,000 drums per year? Show computations to support your answer, with costs presented on both a total and a per unit basis.

3. What other factors would you recommend that the company consider before making a decision?

Additional student resources are available with Connect.   Cases

CASE 7–29 Sell or Process Further Decision [LO 7–7]

The Scottie Sweater Company produces sweaters under the "Scottie" label. The company buys raw wool and processes it into wool yarn from which the sweaters are woven. One spindle of wool yarn is required to produce one sweater. The costs and revenues associated with the sweaters are given below:

		Per Sweater
Selling price...........................		$30.00
Cost to manufacture:		
Raw materials:		
Buttons, thread, lining	$ 2.00	
Wool yarn.........................	16.00	
Total raw materials..................	18.00	
Direct labor	5.80	
Manufacturing overhead..............	8.70	32.50
Manufacturing profit (loss).............		$ (2.50)

Originally, all of the wool yarn was used to produce sweaters, but in recent years a market has developed for the wool yarn itself. The yarn is purchased by other companies for use in production of wool blankets and other wool products. Since the development of the market for the wool yarn, a continuing dispute has existed in the Scottie Sweater Company as to whether the yarn should be sold simply as yarn or processed into sweaters. Current cost and revenue data on the yarn are given below:

		Per Spindle of Yarn
Selling price..............................		$20.00
Cost to manufacture:		
Raw materials (raw wool)................	$7.00	
Direct labor	3.60	
Manufacturing overhead................	5.40	16.00
Manufacturing profit.....................		$ 4.00

The market for sweaters is temporarily depressed, due to unusually warm weather in the western states where the sweaters are sold. This has made it necessary for the company to discount the selling price of the sweaters to $30 from the normal $40 price. Since the market for wool yarn has remained strong, the dispute has again surfaced over whether the yarn should be sold outright rather than processed into sweaters. The sales manager thinks that the production of sweaters should be discontinued; she is upset about having to sell sweaters at a $2.50 loss when the yarn could be sold for a $4.00 profit. However, the production superintendent does not want to close down a large portion of the factory. He argues that the company is in the sweater business, not the yarn business, and that the company should focus on its core strength.

All of the manufacturing overhead costs are fixed and would not be affected even if sweaters were discontinued. Manufacturing overhead is assigned to products on the basis of 150% of direct labor cost. Materials and direct labor costs are variable.

Required:

1. Would you recommend that the wool yarn be sold outright or processed into sweaters? Support your answer with appropriate computations and explain your reasoning.
2. What is the lowest price that the company should accept for a sweater? Support your answer with appropriate computations and explain your reasoning.

CASE 7–30 Ethics and the Manager; Shut Down or Continue Operations [LO 7–2]

Haley Romeros had just been appointed vice president of the Rocky Mountain Region of the Bank Services Corporation (BSC). The company provides check processing services for small banks. The banks send checks presented for deposit or payment to BSC, which records the data on each check in a computerized database. BSC then sends the data electronically to the nearest Federal Reserve Bank check-clearing center where the appropriate transfers of funds are made between banks. The Rocky Mountain Region has three check processing centers, which are located in Billings, Montana; Great Falls, Montana; and Clayton, Idaho. Prior to her promotion to vice president, Ms. Romeros had been the manager of a check processing center in New Jersey.

Immediately after assuming her new position, Ms. Romeros requested a complete financial report for the just-ended fiscal year from the region's controller, John Littlebear. Ms. Romeros specified that the financial report should follow the standardized format required by corporate headquarters for all regional performance reports. That report follows:

Upon seeing this report, Ms. Romeros summoned John Littlebear for an explanation.

Romeros: What's the story on Clayton? It didn't have a loss the previous year did it?
Littlebear: No, the Clayton facility has had a nice profit every year since it was opened six years ago, but Clayton lost a big contract this year.
Romeros: Why?
Littlebear: One of our national competitors entered the local market and bid very aggressively on the contract. We couldn't afford to meet the bid. Clayton's costs—particularly their facility expenses—are just too high. When Clayton lost the contract, we had to lay off a lot of employees, but we could not reduce the fixed costs of the Clayton facility.
Romeros: Why is Clayton's facility expense so high? It's a smaller facility than either Billings or Great Falls and yet its facility expense is higher.
Littlebear: The problem is that we are able to rent suitable facilities very cheaply at Billings and Great Falls. No such facilities were available at Clayton; we had them built. Unfortunately, there were big cost overruns. The contractor we hired was inexperienced at this kind of work and in fact went bankrupt before the project was completed. After hiring another contractor

Bank Services Corporation (BSC) Rocky Mountain Region Financial Performance				
		Check Processing Centers		
	Total	Billings	Great Falls	Clayton
Sales	$50,000,000	$20,000,000	$18,000,000	$12,000,000
Operating expenses:				
Direct labor.	32,000,000	12,500,000	11,000,000	8,500,000
Variable overhead.	850,000	350,000	310,000	190,000
Equipment depreciation. .	3,900,000	1,300,000	1,400,000	1,200,000
Facility expense.	2,800,000	900,000	800,000	1,100,000
Local administrative expense*.	450,000	140,000	160,000	150,000
Regional administrative expense†.	1,500,000	600,000	540,000	360,000
Corporate administrative expense‡.	4,750,000	1,900,000	1,710,000	1,140,000
Total operating expense. . . .	46,250,000	17,690,000	15,920,000	12,640,000
Net operating income (loss)	$ 3,750,000	$ 2,310,000	$ 2,080,000	$ (640,000)

*Local administrative expenses are the administrative expenses incurred at the check processing centers.
†Regional administrative expenses are allocated to the check processing centers based on sales.
‡Corporate administrative expenses are charged to segments of the company such as the Rocky Mountain Region and the check processing centers at the rate of 9.5% of their sales.

to finish the work, we were way over budget. The large depreciation charges on the facility didn't matter at first because we didn't have much competition at the time and could charge premium prices.

Romeros: Well we can't do that anymore. The Clayton facility will obviously have to be shut down. Its business can be shifted to the other two check processing centers in the region.

Littlebear: I would advise against that. The $1,200,000 in depreciation at the Clayton facility is misleading. That facility should last indefinitely with proper maintenance. And it has no resale value; there is no other commercial activity around Clayton.

Romeros: What about the other costs at Clayton?

Littlebear: If we shifted Clayton's business over to the other two processing centers in the region, we wouldn't save anything on direct labor or variable overhead costs. We might save $90,000 or so in local administrative expense, but we would not save any regional administrative expense and corporate headquarters would still charge us 9.5% of our sales as corporate administrative expense.

In addition, we would have to rent more space in Billings and Great Falls in order to handle the work transferred from Clayton; that would probably cost us at least $600,000 a year. And don't forget that it will cost us something to move the equipment from Clayton to Billings and Great Falls. And the move will disrupt service to customers.

Romeros: I understand all of that, but a money-losing processing center on my performance report is completely unacceptable.

Littlebear: And if you shut down Clayton, you are going to throw some loyal employees out of work.

Romeros: That's unfortunate, but we have to face hard business realities.

Littlebear: And you would have to write off the investment in the facilities at Clayton.

Romeros: I can explain a write-off to corporate headquarters; hiring an inexperienced contractor to build the Clayton facility was my predecessor's mistake. But they'll have my head at headquarters if I show operating losses every year at one of my processing centers. Clayton has to go. At the next corporate board meeting, I am going to recommend that the Clayton facility be closed.

Required:
1. From the standpoint of the company as a whole, should the Clayton processing center be shut down and its work redistributed to other processing centers in the region? Explain.
2. Do you think Haley Romeros's decision to shut down the Clayton facility is ethical? Explain.
3. What influence should the depreciation on the facilities at Clayton have on prices charged by Clayton for its services?

CASE 7–31 Integrative Case: Relevant Costs; Pricing [LO 7–1, LO 7–4]

Wesco Incorporated's only product is a combination fertilizer/weedkiller called GrowNWeed. GrowNWeed is sold nationwide to retail nurseries and garden stores.

Zwinger Nursery plans to sell a similar fertilizer/weedkiller compound through its regional nursery chain under its own private label. Zwinger does not have manufacturing facilities of its own, so it has asked Wesco (and several other companies) to submit a bid for manufacturing and delivering a 20,000-pound order of the private brand compound to Zwinger. While the chemical composition of the Zwinger compound differs from that of GrowNWeed, the manufacturing processes are very similar.

The Zwinger compound would be produced in 1,000-pound lots. Each lot would require 25 direct labor-hours and the following chemicals:

Chemicals	Quantity in Pounds
AG-5	300
KL-2	200
CW-7	150
DF-6	175

The first three chemicals (AG-5, KL-2, and CW-7) are all used in the production of GrowNWeed. DF-6 was used in another compound that Wesco discontinued several months ago. The supply of DF-6 that Wesco had on hand when the other compound was discontinued was not discarded. Wesco could sell its supply of DF-6 at the prevailing market price less $0.10 per pound selling and handling expenses.

Wesco also has on hand a chemical called BH-3, which was manufactured for use in another product that is no longer produced. BH-3, which cannot be used in GrowNWeed, can be substituted for AG-5 on a one-for-one basis without affecting the quality of the Zwinger compound. The BH-3 in inventory has a salvage value of $600.

Inventory and cost data for the chemicals that can be used to produce the Zwinger compound are shown below:

Raw Material	Pounds in Inventory	Actual Price per Pound When Purchased	Current Market Price per Pound
AG-5	18,000	$1.15	$1.20
KL-2	6,000	$1.10	$1.05
CW-7	7,000	$1.35	$1.35
DF-6	3,000	$0.80	$0.70
BH-3	3,500	$0.90	(Salvage)

The current direct labor wage rate is $14 per hour. The predetermined overhead rate is based on direct labor-hours (DLH). The predetermined overhead rate for the current year, based on a two-shift capacity with no overtime, is as follows:

Variable manufacturing overhead	$ 3.00 per DLH
Fixed manufacturing overhead	10.50 per DLH
Combined predetermined overhead rate	$13.50 per DLH

Wesco's production manager reports that the present equipment and facilities are adequate to manufacture the Zwinger compound. Therefore, the order would have no effect on total fixed manufacturing overhead costs. However, Wesco is within 400 hours of its two-shift capacity this month. Any additional hours beyond the 400 hours must be done in overtime. If need be, the Zwinger compound could be produced on regular time by shifting a portion of GrowNWeed production to overtime. Wesco's direct labor wage rate for overtime is $21 per hour. There is no allowance for any overtime premium in the predetermined overhead rate.

Required:

1. Wesco has decided to submit a bid for the 20,000 pound order of Zwinger's new compound. The order must be delivered by the end of the current month. Zwinger has indicated that this is a one-time order that will not be repeated. Calculate the lowest price that Wesco could bid for the order without reducing its net operating income.
2. Refer to the original data. Assume that Zwinger Nursery plans to place regular orders for 20,000-pound lots of the new compound. Wesco expects the demand for GrowNWeed to remain strong. Therefore, the recurring orders from Zwinger would put Wesco over its two-shift capacity. However, production could be scheduled so that 90% of each Zwinger order could be completed during regular hours. As another option, some GrowNWeed production could be shifted temporarily to overtime so that the Zwinger orders could be produced on regular time. Current market prices are the best available estimates of future market prices.

    Wesco's standard markup policy for new products is 40% of the full manufacturing cost, including fixed manufacturing overhead. Calculate the price that Wesco, Inc., would quote Zwinger Nursery for each 20,000 pound lot of the new compound, assuming that it is to be treated as a new product and this pricing policy is followed.

(CMA, adapted)

CASE 7–32 Make or Buy; Utilization of a Constrained Resource [LO 7–1, LO 7–3, LO 7–5]

TufStuff, Inc., sells a wide range of drums, bins, boxes, and other containers that are used in the chemical industry. One of the company's products is a heavy-duty corrosion-resistant metal drum, called the WVD drum, used to store toxic wastes. Production is constrained by the capacity of an automated welding machine that is used to make precision welds. A total of 2,000 hours of welding time is available annually on the machine. Because each drum requires 0.4 hours of welding machine time, annual production is limited to 5,000 drums. At present, the welding machine is used exclusively to make the WVD drums. The accounting department has provided the following financial data concerning the WVD drums:

WVD Drums		
Selling price per drum		$149.00
Cost per drum:		
Direct materials	$52.10	
Direct labor ($18 per hour)	3.60	
Manufacturing overhead	4.50	
Selling and administrative expense	29.80	90.00
Margin per drum		$ 59.00

Management believes 6,000 WVD drums could be sold each year if the company had sufficient manufacturing capacity. As an alternative to adding another welding machine, management has considered buying additional drums from an outside supplier. Harcor Industries, Inc., a supplier of quality products, would be able to provide up to 4,000 WVD-type drums per year at a price of $138 per drum, which TufStuff would resell to its customers at its normal selling price after appropriate relabeling.

Megan Flores, TufStuff's production manager, has suggested that the company could make better use of the welding machine by manufacturing bike frames, which would require only 0.5 hours of welding machine time per frame and yet sell for far more than the drums. Megan believes that TufStuff could sell up to 1,600 bike frames per year to bike manufacturers at a price of $239 each. The accounting department has provided the following data concerning the proposed new product:

Bike Frames		
Selling price per frame		$239.00
Cost per frame:		
Direct materials.	$99.40	
Direct labor ($18 per hour).	28.80	
Manufacturing overhead.	36.00	
Selling and administrative expense	47.80	212.00
Margin per frame		$ 27.00

The bike frames could be produced with existing equipment and personnel. Manufacturing overhead is allocated to products on the basis of direct labor-hours. Most of the manufacturing overhead consists of fixed common costs such as rent on the factory building, but some of it is variable. The variable manufacturing overhead has been estimated at $1.35 per WVD drum and $1.90 per bike frame. The variable manufacturing overhead cost would not be incurred on drums acquired from the outside supplier.

Selling and administrative expenses are allocated to products on the basis of revenues. Almost all of the selling and administrative expenses are fixed common costs, but it has been estimated that variable selling and administrative expenses amount to $0.75 per WVD drum whether made or purchased and would be $1.30 per bike frame.

All of the company's employees—direct and indirect—are paid for full 40-hour workweeks and the company has a policy of laying off workers only in major recessions.

Required:
1. Would you be comfortable relying on the financial data provided by the accounting department for making decisions related to the WVD drums and bike frames? Why?
2. Compute the contribution margin per unit for:
    a. Purchased WVD drums.
    b. Manufactured WVD drums.
    c. Manufactured bike frames.
3. Determine the number of WVD drums (if any) that should be purchased and the number of WVD drums and/or bike frames (if any) that should be manufactured. What is the increase in net operating income that would result from this plan over current operations?

    As soon as your analysis was shown to the top management team at TufStuff, several managers got into an argument concerning how direct labor costs should be treated when making this decision. One manager argued that direct labor is always treated as a variable cost in textbooks and in practice and has always been considered a variable cost at TufStuff. After all, "direct" means you can directly trace the cost to products. "If direct labor is not a variable cost, what is?" Another manager argued just as strenuously that direct labor should be considered a fixed cost at TufStuff. No one had been laid off in over a decade, and for all practical purposes, everyone at the plant is on a monthly salary. Everyone classified as direct labor works a regular 40-hour workweek and overtime has not been necessary since the company adopted Lean Production techniques. Whether the welding machine is used to make drums or frames, the total payroll would be exactly the same. There is enough slack, in the form of idle time, to accommodate any increase in total direct labor time that the bike frames would require.
4. Redo requirements (2) and (3) making the opposite assumption about direct labor from the one you originally made. In other words, if you treated direct labor as a variable cost, redo the analysis treating it as a fixed cost. If you treated direct labor as a fixed cost, redo the analysis treating it as a variable cost.
5. What do you think is the correct way to treat direct labor cost in this situation—as variable or as fixed? Explain.

CASE 7–33 Plant Closing Decision [LO 7–1, LO 7–2]
QualSupport Corporation manufactures seats for automobiles, vans, trucks, and various recreational vehicles. The company has a number of plants around the world, including the Denver Cover Plant, which makes seat covers.

Ted Vosilo is the plant manager of the Denver Cover Plant but also serves as the regional production manager for the company. His budget as the regional manager is charged to the Denver Cover Plant.

Vosilo has just heard that QualSupport has received a bid from an outside vendor to supply the equivalent of the entire annual output of the Denver Cover Plant for $35 million. Vosilo was astonished at the low outside bid because the budget for the Denver Cover Plant's operating costs for the upcoming year was set at $52 million. If this bid is accepted, the Denver Cover Plant will be closed down.

The budget for Denver Cover's operating costs for the coming year is presented below.

Denver Cover Plant Annual Budget for Operating Costs		
Materials..............................		$14,000,000
Labor:		
Direct	$13,100,000	
Supervision	900,000	
Indirect plant......................	4,000,000	18,000,000
Overhead:		
Depreciation—equipment.............	3,200,000	
Depreciation—building	7,000,000	
Pension expense	5,000,000	
Plant manager and staff	800,000	
Corporate expenses*................	4,000,000	20,000,000
Total budgeted costs		$52,000,000

*Fixed corporate expenses allocated to plants and other operating units based on total budgeted wage and salary costs.

Additional facts regarding the plant's operations are as follows:

a. Due to Denver Cover's commitment to use high-quality fabrics in all of its products, the Purchasing Department was instructed to place blanket purchase orders with major suppliers to ensure the receipt of sufficient materials for the coming year. If these orders are canceled as a consequence of the plant closing, termination charges would amount to 20% of the cost of direct materials.

b. Approximately 400 plant employees will lose their jobs if the plant is closed. This includes all of the direct laborers and supervisors as well as the plumbers, electricians, and other skilled workers classified as indirect plant workers. Some would be able to find new jobs while many others would have difficulty. All employees would have difficulty matching Denver Cover's base pay of $18.80 per hour, which is the highest in the area. A clause in Denver Cover's contract with the union may help some employees; the company must provide employment assistance to its former employees for 12 months after a plant closing. The estimated cost to administer this service would be $1.5 million for the year.

c. Some employees would probably choose early retirement because QualSupport has an excellent pension plan. In fact, $3 million of the annual pension expense would continue whether Denver Cover is open or not.

d. Vosilo and his staff would not be affected by the closing of Denver Cover. They would still be responsible for administering three other area plants.

e. If the Denver Cover Plant were closed, the company would realize about $3.2 million salvage value for the equipment and building. If the plant remains open, there are no plans to make any significant investments in new equipment or buildings. The old equipment is adequate and should last indefinitely.

Required:

1. Without regard to costs, identify the advantages to QualSupport Corporation of continuing to obtain covers from its own Denver Cover Plant.

2. QualSupport Corporation plans to prepare a financial analysis that will be used in deciding whether or not to close the Denver Cover Plant. Management has asked you to identify:

    a.   The annual budgeted costs that are relevant to the decision regarding closing the plant (show the dollar amounts).

    b.   The annual budgeted costs that are *not* relevant to the decision regarding closing the plant and explain why they are not relevant (again show the dollar amounts).

    c.   Any nonrecurring costs that would arise due to the closing of the plant, and explain how they would affect the decision (again show any dollar amounts).

3.   Looking at the data you have prepared in requirement 2, should the plant be closed? Show computations and explain your answer.

4.   Identify any revenues or costs not specifically mentioned in the problem that QualSupport should consider before making a decision.

(CMA, adapted)

Chapter 8

Capital Budgeting Decisions

Commercial Delivery Fleets Adopt Electric Trucks

BUSINESS FOCUS

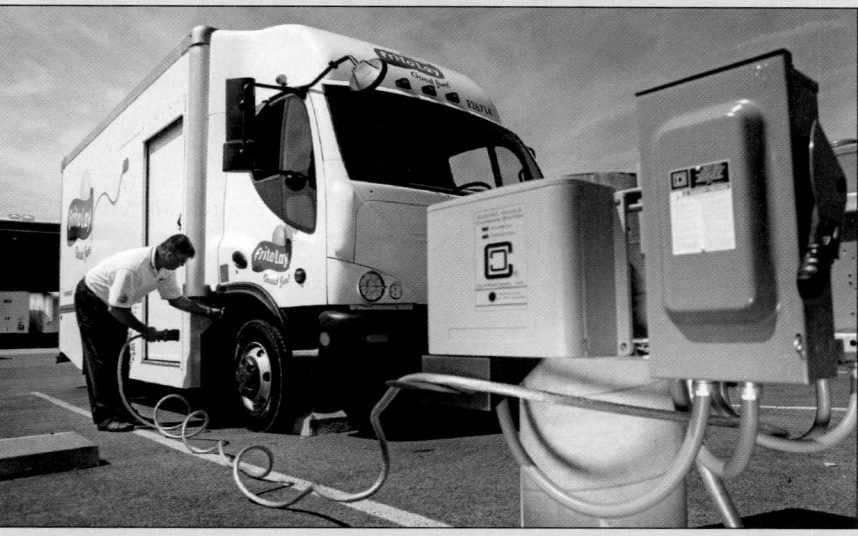

© AP Images/David Goldman

Staples, Frito-Lay, and AT&T have begun purchasing electric delivery trucks even though they cost $30,000 more than diesel delivery trucks. Staples is willing to make the more expensive up-front investment because it expects each electric truck to incur lower operating costs. For example, it estimates that electric trucks will save $2,450 per year in maintenance costs and $6,500 per year in fuel costs. It also expects to replace each electric truck's brakes every four or five years instead of every one or two years with diesel trucks. In total, Staples expects each electric delivery truck to save $60,000 over its 10-year useful life. ■

Source: Mike Ramsey, "As Electric Vehicles Arrive, Firms See Payback in Trucks," *The Wall Street Journal*, December 8, 2010, pp. B1–B2.

LEARNING OBJECTIVES

After studying Chapter 8, you should be able to:

LO 8–1 Determine the payback period for an investment.

LO 8–2 Evaluate the acceptability of an investment project using the net present value method.

LO 8–3 Evaluate the acceptability of an investment project using the internal rate of return method.

LO 8–4 Evaluate an investment project that has uncertain cash flows.

LO 8–5 Rank investment projects in order of preference.

LO 8–6 Compute the simple rate of return for an investment.

LO 8–7 (Appendix 8A) Understand present value concepts and the use of present value tables.

LO 8–8 (Appendix 8C) Include income taxes in a net present value analysis.

Managers often consider decisions that involve an investment today in the hope of realizing future profits. For example, Yum! Brands, Inc., makes an investment when it opens a new Pizza Hut restaurant. L.L. Bean makes an investment when it installs a new computer to handle customer billing. Ford makes an investment when it redesigns a vehicle such as the F-150 pickup truck. Merck & Co. invests in medical research. Amazon.com makes an investment when it redesigns its website. All of these investments require spending now with the expectation of additional future net cash inflows.

The term **capital budgeting** is used to describe how managers plan significant investments in projects that have long-term implications such as the purchase of new equipment or the introduction of new products. Most companies have many more potential projects than can actually be funded. Hence, managers must carefully select those projects that promise the greatest future return. How well managers make these capital budgeting decisions is a critical factor in the long-run financial health of the organization. This chapter discusses four methods for making capital budgeting decisions—the *payback method,* the *net present value method,* the *internal rate of return method,* and the *simple rate of return method.*

Capital Budgeting—An Overview

Typical Capital Budgeting Decisions

Any decision that involves a cash outlay now in order to obtain a future return is a capital budgeting decision. Typical capital budgeting decisions include:

1. Cost reduction decisions. Should new equipment be purchased to reduce costs?
2. Expansion decisions. Should a new plant, warehouse, or other facility be acquired to increase capacity and sales?
3. Equipment selection decisions. Which of several available machines should be purchased?
4. Lease or buy decisions. Should new equipment be leased or purchased?
5. Equipment replacement decisions. Should old equipment be replaced now or later?

Capital budgeting decisions fall into two broad categories—*screening decisions* and *preference decisions.* **Screening decisions** relate to whether a proposed project is acceptable—whether it passes a preset hurdle. For example, a company may have a policy of accepting projects only if they provide a return of at least 20% on the investment. The required rate of return is the minimum rate of return a project must yield to be acceptable. **Preference decisions**, by contrast, relate to selecting from among several acceptable alternatives. To illustrate, a company may be considering several different machines to replace an existing machine on the assembly line. The choice of which machine to purchase is a preference decision.

Cash Flows versus Net Operating Income

The first three capital budgeting methods discussed in the chapter—the payback method, the net present value method, and internal rate of return method—all focus on analyzing the *cash flows* associated with capital investment projects, whereas the simple rate of return method focuses on *incremental net operating income.* To better prepare you to apply the payback, net present value, and internal rate of return methods, we'd like to define the most common types of cash outflows and cash inflows that accompany capital investment projects.

Typical Cash Outflows Most projects have at least three types of cash outflows. First, they often require an immediate cash outflow in the form of an initial investment in equipment, other assets, and installation costs. Any salvage value realized from the sale of old equipment can be recognized as a reduction in the initial investment or as a cash inflow. Second, some projects require a company to expand its working capital. **Working capital** is current assets (e.g., cash, accounts receivable, and inventory) less current liabilities. When a company takes on a new project, the balances in the current asset accounts often increase. For example, opening a new Nordstrom's department store requires additional cash in sales registers and more inventory. These additional working capital needs are treated as part of the initial investment in a project. Third, many projects require periodic outlays for repairs and maintenance and additional operating costs.

Typical Cash Inflows Most projects also have at least three types of cash inflows. First, a project will normally increase revenues or reduce costs. Either way, the amount involved should be treated as a cash inflow for capital budgeting purposes. Notice that from a cash flow standpoint, a reduction in costs is equivalent to an increase in revenues. Second, cash inflows are also frequently realized from selling equipment for its salvage value when a project ends, although the company may actually have to pay to dispose of some low-value or hazardous items. Third, any working capital that was tied up in the project can be released for use elsewhere at the end of the project and should be treated as a cash inflow at that time. Working capital is released, for example, when a company sells off its inventory or collects its accounts receivable.

The Time Value of Money

Beyond defining a capital project's cash outflows and inflows, it is also important to consider when those cash flows occur. For example, if someone offered to give you $1,000 dollars today that you could save toward your eventual retirement or $1,000 dollars a year from now that you could save toward your future retirement, which alternative would you choose? In all likelihood, you would choose to receive $1,000 today because you could invest it and have more than $1,000 dollars a year from now. This simple example illustrates an important capital budgeting concept known as *the time value of money*. The **time value of money** recognizes that a dollar today is worth more than a dollar a year from now if for no other reason than you could put the dollar in a bank today and have more than a dollar a year from now. Because of the time value of money, capital investments that promise earlier cash flows are preferable to those that promise later cash flows.

Although the payback method focuses on cash flows, it does not recognize the time value of money. In other words, it treats a dollar received today as being of equal value to a dollar received at any point in the future. Conversely, the net present value and internal rate of return methods not only focus on cash flows, but they also recognize the time value of those cash flows. These two methods use a technique called *discounting cash flows* to translate the value of future cash flows to their lesser present value. If you are not familiar with the concept of discounting cash flows and the use of present value tables, you should read Appendix 8A: The Concept of Present Value, at the end of the chapter, before studying the net present value and internal rate of return methods.

INVESTING IN A VINEYARD: A CASH FLOWS PERSPECTIVE

When Michael Evans was contemplating moving to Buenos Aires, Argentina, to start a company called the Vines of Mendoza, he had to estimate the project's initial cash outlays and compare them to its future net cash inflows. The initial cash outlays included $2.9 million to buy 1,046 acres of land and to construct a tasting room, $300,000 for a well and irrigation system, $30,000 for underground power lines, and $285,000 for 250,000 grape plants. The annual operating costs included $1,500 per acre for pruning, mowing, and irrigation and $114 per acre for harvesting.

In terms of future cash inflows, Evans hopes to sell his acreage to buyers who want to grow their own grapes and make their own wine while avoiding the work involved with doing so. He intends to charge buyers a one-time fee of $55,000 per planted acre. The buyers would also reimburse Evans for his annual operating costs per acre plus a 25% markup. In a good year, buyers should be able to get 250 cases of wine from their acre of grapevines.

© Digital Stock/Corbis, RF

Source: Helen Coster, "Planting Roots," *Forbes,* March 1, 2010, pp. 42–44.

The Payback Method

LEARNING OBJECTIVE 8–1

Determine the payback period for an investment.

The payback method of evaluating capital budgeting projects focuses on the *payback period*. The **payback period** is the length of time that it takes for a project to recover its initial cost from the net cash inflows that it generates. This period is sometimes referred to as "the time that it takes for an investment to pay for itself." The basic premise of the payback method is that the more quickly the cost of an investment can be recovered, the more desirable is the investment.

The payback period is expressed in years. *When the annual net cash inflow is the same every year,* the following formula can be used to compute the payback period:

$$\text{Payback period} = \frac{\text{Investment required}}{\text{Annual net cash inflow}} \qquad (1)$$

To illustrate the payback method, consider the following data:

Example A: York Company needs a new milling machine. The company is considering two machines: machine A and machine B. Machine A costs $15,000, has a useful life of ten years, and will reduce operating costs by $5,000 per year. Machine B costs only $12,000, will also reduce operating costs by $5,000 per year, but has a useful life of only five years.

Required:
Which machine should be purchased according to the payback method?

$$\text{Machine A payback period} = \frac{\$15,000}{\$5,000} = 3.0 \text{ years}$$

$$\text{Machine B payback period} = \frac{\$12,000}{\$5,000} = 2.4 \text{ years}$$

According to the payback calculations, York Company should purchase machine B because it has a shorter payback period than machine A.

Evaluation of the Payback Method

The payback method is not a true measure of the profitability of an investment. Rather, it simply tells a manager how many years are required to recover the original investment. Unfortunately, a shorter payback period does not always mean that one investment is more desirable than another.

To illustrate, refer back to Example A on the previous page. Machine B has a shorter payback period than machine A, but it has a useful life of only 5 years rather than 10 years for machine A. Machine B would have to be purchased twice—once immediately and then again after the fifth year—to provide the same service as just one machine A. Under these circumstances, machine A would probably be a better investment than machine B, even though machine B has a shorter payback period. Unfortunately, the payback method ignores all cash flows that occur after the payback period.

A further criticism of the payback method is that it does not consider the time value of money. A cash inflow to be received several years in the future is weighed the same as a cash inflow received right now. To illustrate, assume that for an investment of $8,000 you can purchase either of the two following streams of cash inflows:

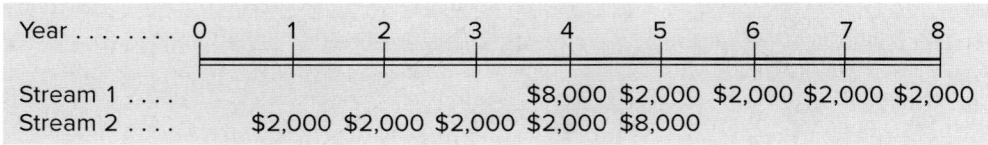

Which stream of cash inflows would you prefer to receive in return for your $8,000 investment? Each stream has a payback period of 4.0 years. Therefore, if payback alone is used to make the decision, the streams would be considered equally desirable. However, from a time value of money perspective, stream 2 is much more desirable than stream 1.

On the other hand, under certain conditions the payback method can be very useful. For one thing, it can help identify which investment proposals are in the "ballpark." That is, it can be used as a screening tool to help answer the question, "Should I consider this proposal further?" If a proposal doesn't provide a payback within some specified period, then there may be no need to consider it further. In addition, the payback period is often important to new companies that are "cash poor." When a company is cash poor, a project with a short payback period but a low rate of return might be preferred over another project with a high rate of return but a long payback period. The reason is that the company may simply need a faster return of its cash investment. And finally, the payback method is sometimes used in industries where products become obsolete very rapidly—such as consumer electronics. Because products may last only a year or two, the payback period on investments must be very short.

THE ECONOMICS OF HYBRID VEHICLES

The table below shows the price premiums (after tax credits) that customers must pay to buy four types of hybrid vehicles. It also depicts the annual gas savings that customers realize by driving a hybrid version of the vehicle instead of a standard model of the same vehicle (assuming the vehicles are driven 15,000 miles per year and gas costs $2.79 a gallon). Dividing the price premium by the annual gas savings yields the payback period when purchasing the hybrid version of the vehicle.

Make and Model	Price Premium	Annual Gas Savings	Payback Period
Ford Escape	$1,364	$438	3.1
Honda Civic	$1,482	$317	4.7
Toyota Camry	$3,763	$310	12.1
Toyota Highlander	$4,372	$388	11.3

The above payback figures highlight the dilemma faced by customers who want to make environmentally friendly purchases, but are constrained by limited financial resources.

Source: Mike Spector, "The Economics of Hybrids," *The Wall Street Journal,* October 29, 2007, pp. R5–R6.

An Extended Example of Payback

As shown by formula (1) above, the payback period is computed by dividing the investment in a project by the project's annual net cash inflows. If new equipment is replacing old equipment, then any salvage value to be received when disposing of the old equipment should be deducted from the cost of the new equipment, and only the *incremental* investment should be used in the payback computation. In addition, any depreciation deducted in arriving at the project's net operating income must be added back to obtain the project's expected annual net cash inflow. To illustrate, consider the following data:

Example B: Goodtime Fun Centers, Inc., operates amusement parks. Some of the vending machines in one of its parks provide very little revenue, so the company is considering removing the machines and installing equipment to dispense soft ice cream. The equipment would cost $80,000 and have an eight-year useful life with no salvage value. Incremental annual revenues and costs associated with the sale of ice cream would be as follows:

Sales	$150,000
Variable expenses	90,000
Contribution margin	60,000
Fixed expenses:	
Salaries	27,000
Maintenance	3,000
Depreciation	10,000
Total fixed expenses	40,000
Net operating income	$ 20,000

The vending machines can be sold for a $5,000 scrap value. The company will not purchase equipment unless it has a payback period of three years or less. Does the ice cream dispenser pass this hurdle?

Exhibit 8–1 computes the payback period for the ice cream dispenser. Several things should be noted. First, depreciation is added back to net operating income to obtain the annual net cash inflow from the new equipment. Depreciation is not a cash outlay; thus, it must be added back to adjust net operating income to a cash basis. Second, the payback computation deducts the salvage value of the old machines from the cost of the new equipment so that only the incremental investment is used in computing the payback period.

Because the proposed equipment has a payback period of less than three years, the company's payback requirement has been met.

Payback and Uneven Cash Flows

When the cash flows associated with an investment project change from year to year, the simple payback formula that we outlined earlier cannot be used. Instead, the payoff period can be computed as follows (assuming that cash inflows occur evenly throughout the year): Payback period = Number of years up to the year in which the investment is paid off + (Unrecovered investment at the beginning of the year in which the investment

---

EXHIBIT 8–1
Computation of the Payback Period

Step 1: *Compute the annual net cash inflow.* Because the annual net cash inflow is not given, it must be computed before the payback period can be determined:

Net operating income	$20,000
Add: Noncash deduction for depreciation	10,000
Annual net cash inflow	$30,000

Step 2: *Compute the payback period.* Using the annual net cash inflow from above, the payback period can be determined as follows:

Cost of the new equipment	$80,000
Less salvage value of old equipment	5,000
Investment required	$75,000

$$\text{Payback period} = \frac{\text{Investment required}}{\text{Annual net cash inflow}}$$

$$= \frac{\$75,000}{\$30,000} = 2.5 \text{ years}$$

is paid off ÷ Cash inflow in the period in which the investment is paid off). To illustrate how to apply this formula, consider the following data:

Year	Investment	Cash Inflow
1	$4,000	$1,000
2		$0
3		$2,000
4	$2,000	$1,000
5		$500
6		$3,000
7		$2,000

What is the payback period on this investment? The answer is 5.5 years, computed as follows: 5 + ($1,500 ÷ $3,000) = 5.5 years. In essence, we are tracking the unrecovered investment year by year as shown in Exhibit 8–2. By the middle of the sixth year, sufficient cash inflows will have been realized to recover the entire investment of $6,000 ($4,000 + $2,000).

Year	Investment	Cash Inflow	Unrecovered Investment*
1	$4,000	$1,000	$3,000
2		$0	$3,000
3		$2,000	$1,000
4	$2,000	$1,000	$2,000
5		$500	$1,500
6		$3,000	$0
7		$2,000	$0

*Year X unrecovered investment = Year X-1 unrecovered investment + Year X investment − Year X cash inflow

EXHIBIT 8–2
Payback and Uneven Cash Flows

The Net Present Value Method

As previously mentioned, the *net present value method* and the *internal rate of return method* use discounted cash flows to analyze capital budgeting decisions. The net present value method is discussed in this section followed by a discussion of the internal rate of return method.

LEARNING OBJECTIVE 8–2
Evaluate the acceptability of an investment project using the net present value method.

The Net Present Value Method Illustrated

The net present value method compares the present value of a project's cash inflows to the present value of its cash outflows. The difference between the present value of these cash flows, called the **net present value**, determines whether or not a project is an acceptable investment.

When performing net present value analysis, managers usually make two important assumptions. First, they assume that all cash flows other than the initial investment occur at the end of periods. This assumption is somewhat unrealistic because cash flows typically occur *throughout* a period rather than just at its end; however, it simplifies the computations considerably. Second, managers assume that all cash flows generated by an investment project are immediately reinvested at a rate of return equal to the rate used to discount the future cash flows, also known as the *discount rate*. If this condition is not met, the net present value computations will not be accurate.

To illustrate net present analysis, consider the following data:

Example C: Harper Company is contemplating the purchase of a machine capable of performing some operations that are now performed manually. The machine will cost $50,000, and it will last for five years. At the end of the five-year period, the machine will be sold for its salvage value of $5,000. Use of the machine will reduce labor costs by $18,000 per year. Harper Company requires a minimum pretax return of 18% on all investment projects.[1]

Should the machine be purchased? Harper Company must determine whether a cash investment now of $50,000 can be justified if it will result in an $18,000 reduction in cost in each of the next five years. It may appear that the answer is obvious because the total cost savings is $90,000 ($18,000 per year × 5 years). However, the company can earn an 18% return by investing its money elsewhere. It is not enough that the cost reductions cover just the original cost of the machine; they must also yield a return of at least 18% or the company would be better off investing the money elsewhere.

To determine whether the investment is desirable, the stream of annual $18,000 cost savings and the machine's salvage value of $5,000 should be discounted to their present values and then compared to the cost of the new machine. Exhibit 8–3 demonstrates a four-step approach for performing these computations. First, it calculates the present value of the initial investment by multiplying $50,000 by 1.000, the present value factor for any cash flow that occurs immediately. Second, it calculates the present value of the annual cost savings by multiplying $18,000 by 3.127, the present value factor of a five-year annuity at the discount rate of 18%, to obtain $56,286. Third, it calculates the present value of the machine's salvage value by multiplying $5,000 by 0.437, the present value factor of a single sum to be received in five years at the discount rate of 18%, to obtain $2,185. Finally, cells B8 through D8 are added together to derive the net present value of $8,471.[2]

Exhibit 8–4 demonstrates an alternative approach for performing these same calculations. This alternative approach also begins by calculating the present value of the initial investment by multiplying $50,000 by 1.000, the present value factor for any cash flow that occurs immediately. However, rather than calculating the present value of the annual cost savings using a discount factor of 3.127 from Exhibit 8B–2, it discounts the annual cost savings in Years 1–5 and the machine's salvage value in Year 5 to their present values using the discount factors from Exhibit 8B–1. For example, the $18,000 cost savings in Year 3 is multiplied by the discount factor of 0.609 to derive this future

EXHIBIT 8–3

Net Present Value Analysis Using Discount Factors from Exhibits 8B–1 and 8B–2 in Appendix 8B

	A	B	C	D
1			Year(s)	
2		Now	1-5	5
3	Initial investment	$ (50,000)		
4	Annual cost savings		$ 18,000	
5	Salvage value of the new machine			$ 5,000
6	Total cash flows (a)	$ (50,000)	$ 18,000	$ 5,000
7	Discount factor (18%) (b)	1.000	3.127	0.437
8	Present value of the cash flows (a) × (b)	$ (50,000)	$ 56,286	$ 2,185
9	Net present value (SUM B8:D8)	$ 8,471		
10				
11	Note: The discount factors comes from Exhibits 8B-1 and 8B-2 in Appendix 8B.			
12				

Exhibit 8-3 / Exhibit 8-4 / Exhibit 8-5

---

[1] For simplicity, we ignore inflation and taxes. The impact of income taxes on capital budgeting decisions is discussed in Appendix 8C.

[2] In this chapter, we use the discount factors from Appendix 8B, which have been rounded to three decimal places, for all present value calculations. However, Microsoft Excel can also be used to calculate discount factors that are not rounded to three decimal places. These unrounded discount factors provide solutions that slightly differ from those derived using the tables in Appendix 8B.

EXHIBIT 8–4

Net Present Value Analysis Using Discount Factors from Exhibit 8B–1 in Appendix 8B

	A	B	C	D	E	F	G
1					Year		
2		Now	1	2	3	4	5
3	Initial investment	$ (50,000)					
4	Annual labor cost savings		$ 18,000	$ 18,000	$ 18,000	$ 18,000	$ 18,000
5	Salvage value of new machine						$ 5,000
6	Total cash flows (a)	$ (50,000)	$ 18,000	$ 18,000	$ 18,000	$ 18,000	$ 23,000
7	Discount factor (18%) (b)	1.000	0.847	0.718	0.609	0.516	0.437
8	Present value of cash flows (a) × (b)	$ (50,000)	$ 15,246	$ 12,924	$ 10,962	$ 9,288	$ 10,051
9	Net present value (SUM B8:G8)	$ 8,471					
10							
11	Note: The discount factors come from Exhibit 8B-1 in Appendix 8B.						
12							

Exhibit 8-3   **Exhibit 8-4**   Exhibit 8-5   Exhibit 8-6   Exhibit 8-7   Exhibit 8

---

cash flow's present value of $10,962. As another example, the $23,000 of total cash flows in Year 5 is multiplied by the discount factor of 0.437 to determine these future cash flows' present value of $10,051. The present values in cells B8 through G8 are then added together to compute the project's net present value of $8,471.

The methods described in Exhibits 8–3 and 8–4 are mathematically equivalent—they both produced a net present value of $8,471. The only difference between these two exhibits relates to the discounting of the annual labor cost savings. In Exhibit 8–3, the labor cost savings are discounted to their present value using the annuity factor of 3.127, whereas in Exhibit 8–4, these cost savings are discounted using five separate factors that sum to 3.127 (0.847 + 0.718 + 0.609 + 0.516 + 0.437 = 3.127). In other words, the calculations are equivalent.

While you should feel free to use either of these methods when performing net present value calculations, from this point forward we'll be emphasizing the approach used in Exhibit 8–4 for two reasons. First, most managers use an approach similar to Exhibit 8–4 when performing net present value calculations. They use Microsoft Excel to summarize each year's cash flows in a separate column and then they discount each year's cash flows to their present values using the factors shown in Exhibit 8B–1. Second, many students believe that the approach shown in Exhibit 8–4 is easier to understand than competing methods when the net present value computations become increasingly complex.

Once you have computed a net present value using either of the approaches that we just demonstrated, you'll need to interpret your findings. For example, because Harper Company's proposed project has a positive net present value of $8,471, it implies that the company should purchase the new machine. A positive net present value indicates that the project's return exceeds the discount rate. A negative net present value indicates that the project's return is less than the discount rate. Therefore, if the company's minimum required rate of return is used as the discount rate, a project with a positive net present value has a return that exceeds the minimum required rate of return and is acceptable. Conversely, a project with a negative net present value has a return that is less than the minimum required rate of return and is unacceptable. In sum:

If the Net Present Value Is . . .	Then the Project Is . . .
Positive	Acceptable because its return is greater than the required rate of return.
Zero	Acceptable because its return is equal to the required rate of return.
Negative	Not acceptable because its return is less than the required rate of return.

To improve your understanding of the minimum required rate of return, it bears emphasizing that a company's *cost of capital* is usually regarded as its minimum required rate of return. The **cost of capital** is the average rate of return that the company must pay to its long-term creditors and its shareholders for the use of their funds. If a project's rate of return is less than the cost of capital, the company does not earn enough to compensate its creditors and shareholders. Therefore, any project with a rate of return less than the cost of capital should be rejected.

The cost of capital serves as a *screening device*. When the cost of capital is used as the discount rate in net present value analysis, any project with a negative net present value does not cover the company's cost of capital and should be discarded as unacceptable.

Recovery of the Original Investment

The net present value method automatically provides for return of the original investment. Whenever the net present value of a project is positive, the project will recover the original cost of the investment plus sufficient excess cash inflows to compensate the organization for tying up funds in the project. To demonstrate this point, consider the following situation:

Example D: Carver Hospital is considering the purchase of an attachment for its X-ray machine that will cost $3,169. The attachment will be usable for four years, after which time it will have no salvage value. It will increase net cash inflows by $1,000 per year in the X-ray department. The hospital's board of directors requires a rate of return of at least 10% on such investments.

A net present value analysis of the desirability of purchasing the X-ray attachment is presented in Exhibit 8–5. Notice that the attachment has exactly a 10% return on the original investment because the net present value is zero at a 10% discount rate.

Each annual $1,000 cash inflow arising from use of the attachment is made up of two parts. One part represents a recovery of a portion *of* the original $3,169 paid for the attachment, and the other part represents a return *on* this investment. The breakdown of each year's $1,000 cash inflow between recovery *of* investment and return *on* investment is shown in Exhibit 8–6.

The first year's $1,000 cash inflow consists of a return *on* investment of $317 (a 10% return *on* the $3,169 original investment), plus a $683 return *of* that investment. Because the amount of the unrecovered investment decreases each year, the dollar amount of the return on investment also decreases each year. By the end of the fourth year, all $3,169 of the original investment has been recovered.

EXHIBIT 8–5

Carver Hospital—Net Present Value Analysis of X-Ray Attachment

	A	B	C	D	E	F
1				Year		
2		Now	1	2	3	4
3	Initial investment	$ (3,169)				
4	Annual net cash inflow		$ 1,000	$ 1,000	$ 1,000	$ 1,000
5	Total cash flows (a)	$ (3,169)	$ 1,000	$ 1,000	$ 1,000	$ 1,000
6	Discount factor (10%) (b)	1.000	0.909	0.826	0.751	0.683
7	Present value of cash flows (a) × (b)	$ (3,169)	$ 909	$ 826	$ 751	$ 683
8	Net present value (SUM B7:F7)	$ 0				
9						
10	Note: The discount factors come from Exhibit 8B-1 in Appendix 8B.					
11						

Exhibit 8-3   Exhibit 8-4   Exhibit 8-5

EXHIBIT 8–6

Carver Hospital—Breakdown of Annual Cash Inflows

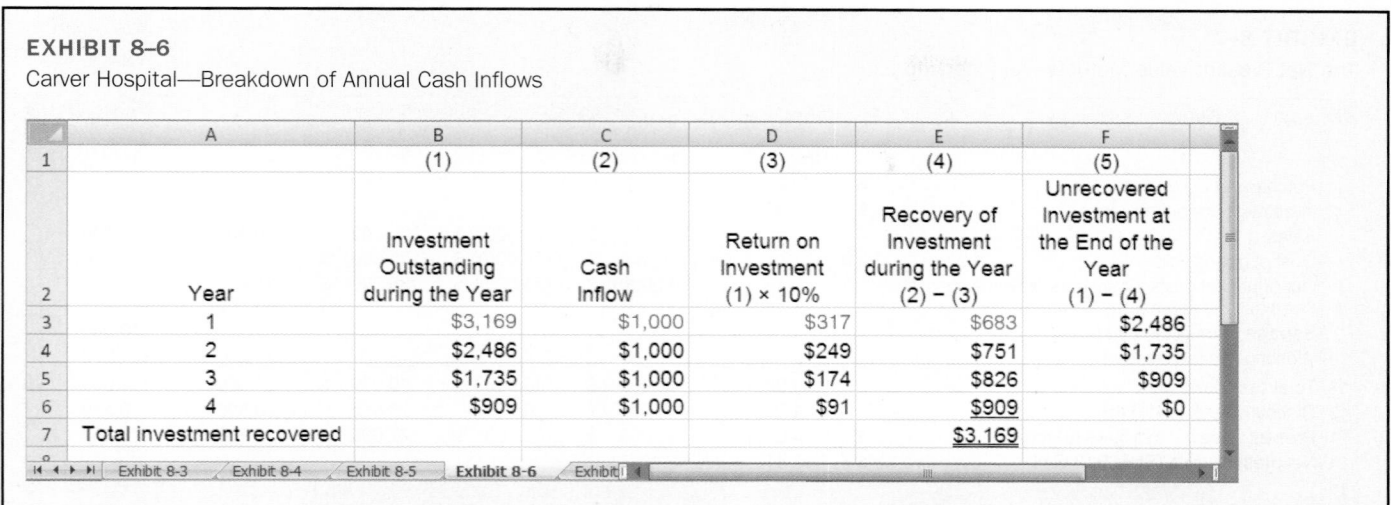

	A	B	C	D	E	F
1		(1)	(2)	(3)	(4)	(5)
2	Year	Investment Outstanding during the Year	Cash Inflow	Return on Investment (1) × 10%	Recovery of Investment during the Year (2) − (3)	Unrecovered Investment at the End of the Year (1) − (4)
3	1	$3,169	$1,000	$317	$683	$2,486
4	2	$2,486	$1,000	$249	$751	$1,735
5	3	$1,735	$1,000	$174	$826	$909
6	4	$909	$1,000	$91	$909	$0
7	Total investment recovered				$3,169	

Exhibit 8-3   Exhibit 8-4   Exhibit 8-5   **Exhibit 8-6**   Exhibit

COOLING SERVERS NATURALLY

Google consumes more than 2 terawatt hours of electricity per year, which is greater than the annual electricity consumption of 200,000 American homes. A large part of Google's electricity consumption relates to running and cooling its huge number of servers. In an effort to lower its electricity bill, Google invested €200 million to build a server storage facility in the Baltic Sea coastal community of Hamina, Finland. Hamina's low electricity rates coupled with its persistently low ambient air temperatures will lower Google's annual electricity bills considerably. Shortly after Google's facility opened in Hamina, Facebook opened a five-acre data center in Luleå, Sweden, where the average temperature is 35 degrees Fahrenheit.

Source: Sven Grunberg and Niclas Rolander, "For Data Center, Google Goes for the Cold," *The Wall Street Journal,* September 12, 2011, p. B10.

An Extended Example of the Net Present Value Method

Example E provides an extended example of how the net present value method is used to analyze a proposed project. This example helps tie together and reinforce many of the ideas discussed thus far.

Example E: Under a special licensing arrangement, Swinyard Corporation has an opportunity to market a new product for a five-year period. The product would be purchased from the manufacturer, with Swinyard responsible for promotion and distribution costs. The licensing arrangement could be renewed at the end of the five-year period. After careful study, Swinyard estimated the following costs and revenues for the new product:

Cost of equipment needed	$60,000
Working capital needed	$100,000
Overhaul of the equipment in four years	$5,000
Salvage value of the equipment in five years	$10,000
Annual revenues and costs:	
Sales revenues	$200,000
Cost of goods sold	$125,000
Out-of-pocket operating costs (for salaries,	
advertising, and other direct costs)	$35,000

EXHIBIT 8–7
The Net Present Value Method—An Extended Example

	A	B	C	D	E	F	G
1					Year		
2		Now	1	2	3	4	5
3	Purchase of equipment	$ (60,000)					
4	Investment in working capital	$ (100,000)					
5	Sales		$ 200,000	$ 200,000	$ 200,000	$ 200,000	$ 200,000
6	Cost of goods sold		$ (125,000)	$ (125,000)	$ (125,000)	$ (125,000)	$ (125,000)
7	Out-of-pocket costs for salaries, advertising, etc.		$ (35,000)	$ (35,000)	$ (35,000)	$ (35,000)	$ (35,000)
8	Overhaul of equipment					$ (5,000)	
9	Salvage value of the equipment						$ 10,000
10	Working capital released						$ 100,000
11	Total cash flows (a)	$ (160,000)	$ 40,000	$ 40,000	$ 40,000	$ 35,000	$ 150,000
12	Discount factor (14%) (b)	1.000	0.877	0.769	0.675	0.592	0.519
13	Present value of cash flows (a) × (b)	$ (160,000)	$ 35,080	$ 30,760	$ 27,000	$ 20,720	$ 77,850
14	Net present value (SUM B13:G13)	$ 31,410					
15							
16	Note: The discount factors come from Exhibit 8B-1 in Appendix 8B.						
17							

Exhibit 8-4   Exhibit 8-5   Exhibit 8-6   **Exhibit 8-7**   Exhibit 8-8

At the end of the five-year period, if Swinyard decides not to renew the licensing arrangement the working capital would be released for investment elsewhere. Swinyard uses a 14% discount rate. Would you recommend that the new product be introduced?

This example involves a variety of cash inflows and cash outflows. The solution is given in Exhibit 8–7.

Notice how the working capital is handled in this exhibit. It is counted as a cash outflow at the beginning of the project and as a cash inflow when it is released at the end of the project. Also notice how the sales revenues, cost of goods sold, and out-of-pocket costs are handled. **Out-of-pocket costs** are actual cash outlays for salaries, advertising, and other operating expenses.

Because the net present value of the proposal is positive, the new product is acceptable.

IN BUSINESS

ECONOMIC WOES SHRINK CAPITAL BUDGETS

When the health of the economy is uncertain, capital spending declines. Rite Aid CEO Mary Sammons cut her company's capital budget by $50 million due to uncertain economic conditions. PetroHawk Energy responded to a weak economy by slashing its $1.5 billion capital budget by one-third. Estee Lauder tightened its belt by challenging managers to defend what they must have and define what they can give up. YUM! Brands (owner of Pizza Hut, KFC, and Taco Bell) navigated the difficult economy by abandoning projects that "might come true" in favor of a "must have" capital budgeting mentality.

Source: Matthew Boyle, "The Budget Knives Come Out," *BusinessWeek*, October 13, 2008, p. 30.

The Internal Rate of Return Method

LEARNING OBJECTIVE 8–3
Evaluate the acceptability of an investment project using the internal rate of return method.

The **internal rate of return** is the rate of return of an investment project over its useful life. The internal rate of return is computed by finding the discount rate that equates the present value of a project's cash outflows with the present value of its cash inflows. In other words, the internal rate of return is the discount rate that results in a net present value of zero.

The Internal Rate of Return Method Illustrated

To illustrate the internal rate of return method, consider the following data:

Example F: Glendale School District is considering the purchase of a large tractor-pulled lawn mower. At present, the lawn is mowed using a small hand-pushed gas mower. The large, tractor-pulled mower will cost $21,630 and will have a useful life of 5 years. It will have a negligible scrap value, which can be ignored. The tractor-pulled mower would do the job faster than the old mower, resulting in labor savings of $6,000 per year.

To compute the internal rate of return of the new mower, we must find the discount rate that will result in a zero net present value. How do we do this? The simplest and most direct approach *when the net cash inflow is the same every year* is to divide the investment in the project by the expected annual net cash inflow. This computation yields a factor from which the internal rate of return can be determined. The formula is as follows:

$$\text{Factor of the internal rate of return} = \frac{\text{Investment required}}{\text{Annual net cash inflow}} \qquad (2)$$

The factor derived from formula (2) is then located in the present value tables to see what rate of return it represents. Using formula (2) and the data for the Glendale School District's proposed project, we get:

$$\frac{\text{Investment required}}{\text{Annual net cash inflow}} = \frac{\$21,630}{\$6,000} = 3.605$$

Thus, the discount factor that will equate a series of $6,000 cash inflows with a present investment of $21,630 is 3.605. Now we need to find this factor in Exhibit 8B–2 in Appendix 8B to see what rate of return it represents. We should use the 5-period line in Exhibit 8B–2 because the cash flows for the project continue for 5 years. If we scan along the 5-period line, we find that a factor of 3.605 represents a 12% rate of return. Therefore, the internal rate of return of the mower project is 12%. We can verify this by computing the project's net present value using a 12% discount rate as shown in Exhibit 8–8.

Notice that the net present value in Exhibit 8–8 is zero, confirming that the project's internal rate of return equals 12%. However, you'll also notice that the discount factors used in Exhibit 8–8 come from Exhibit 8B–1 in Appendix 8B, whereas the discount factor cited above (3.605) comes from Exhibit 8B–2 in Appendix 8B. Although these approaches to discounting cash flows appear to differ from one another, they are actually mathematically equivalent. To prove this fact, notice that the sum of the discount factors used in Exhibit 8–8 equals 3.605 (0.893 + 0.797 + 0.712 + 0.636 + 0.567 = 3.605). The five discount factors in Exhibit 8–8 are being used to discount five annual cash flows of $6,000 per year to their present value of $21,630, whereas the discount factor of 3.605 discounts the entire five-year annuity stream to its present value of $21,630.

EXHIBIT 8–8

Evaluation of the Mower Using a 12% Discount Rate

	A	B	C	D	E	F	G
1					Year		
2		Now	1	2	3	4	5
3	Initial investment	$ (21,630)					
4	Annual labor cost savings	_____	$ 6,000	$ 6,000	$ 6,000	$ 6,000	$ 6,000
5	Total cash flows (a)	$ (21,630)	$ 6,000	$ 6,000	$ 6,000	$ 6,000	$ 6,000
6	Discount factor (12%) (b)	1.000	0.893	0.797	0.712	0.636	0.567
7	Present value of cash flows (a) × (b)	$ (21,630)	$ 5,358	$ 4,782	$ 4,272	$ 3,816	$ 3,402
8	Net present value (SUM B7:G7)	$ 0					
9							
10	Note: The discount factors come from Exhibit 8B-1 in Appendix 8B.						

Exhibit 8-5 | Exhibit 8-6 | Exhibit 8-7 | Exhibit 8-8

Once the Glendale School District computes the project's internal rate of return of 12%, it would accept or reject the project by comparing this percentage to the school district's minimum required rate of return. If the internal rate of return is equal to or greater than the required rate of return, then the project is acceptable. If the internal rate of return is less than the required rate of return, then the project is rejected. For example, if we assume that Glendale's minimum required rate of return is 15%, then the school district would reject this project because the 12% internal rate of return does not clear the 15% *hurdle rate*.

Comparison of the Net Present Value and Internal Rate of Return Methods

This section compares the net present value and internal rate of return methods in three ways. First, both methods use the cost of capital to screen out undesirable investment projects. When the internal rate of return method is used, the cost of capital is used as the hurdle rate that a project must clear for acceptance. If the internal rate of return of a project is not high enough to clear the cost of capital hurdle, then the project is ordinarily rejected. When the net present value method is used, the cost of capital is the discount rate used to compute the net present value of a proposed project. Any project yielding a negative net present value is rejected unless other factors are significant enough to warrant its acceptance.

Second, the net present value method is often simpler to use than the internal rate of return method, particularly when a project does not have identical cash flows every year. For example, if a project has some salvage value at the end of its life in addition to its annual cash inflows, the internal rate of return method requires a trial-and-error process to find the rate of return that will result in a net present value of zero. While computer software can be used to perform this trial-and-error process in seconds, it is still a little more complex than using spreadsheet software to perform net present value analysis.

Third, the internal rate of return method makes a questionable assumption. Both methods assume that cash flows generated by a project during its useful life are immediately reinvested elsewhere. However, the two methods make different assumptions concerning the rate of return that is earned on those cash flows. The net present value method assumes the rate of return is the discount rate, whereas the internal rate of return method assumes the rate of return earned on cash flows is the internal rate of return on the project. Specifically, if the internal rate of return of the project is high, this assumption may not be realistic. It is generally more realistic to assume that cash inflows can be reinvested at a rate of return equal to the discount rate—particularly if the discount rate is the company's cost of capital or an opportunity rate of return. For example, if the discount rate is the company's cost of capital, this rate of return can be actually realized by paying off the company's creditors and buying back the company's stock with cash flows from the project. In short, when the net present value method and the internal rate of return method do not agree concerning the attractiveness of a project, it is best to go with the net present value method. Of the two methods, it makes the more realistic assumption about the rate of return that can be earned on cash flows from the project.

Expanding the Net Present Value Method

So far, all of our examples have involved an evaluation of a single investment project. In the following section we use the *total-cost approach* to explain how the net present value method can be used to evaluate two alternative projects.

The total-cost approach is the most flexible method for comparing competing projects. To illustrate the mechanics of the approach, consider the following data:

Example G: Harper Ferry Company operates a high-speed passenger ferry service across the Mississippi River. One of its ferryboats is in poor condition. This ferry can be renovated at an immediate cost of $200,000. Further repairs and an overhaul of the motor will be needed three years from now at a cost of $80,000. In all, the ferry will be usable for 5 years if this work is done. At the end of 5 years, the ferry will have to be scrapped at a salvage value of

EXHIBIT 8–9

The Total-Cost Approach to Project Selection

	A	B	C	D	E	F	G
1	Keep the old ferry:				Year		
2		Now	1	2	3	4	5
3	Renovation	$ (200,000)					
4	Annual revenues		$ 400,000	$ 400,000	$ 400,000	$ 400,000	$ 400,000
5	Annual cash operating costs		$ (300,000)	$ (300,000)	$ (300,000)	$ (300,000)	$ (300,000)
6	Repairs in three years				$ (80,000)		
7	Salvage value of old ferry						$ 60,000
8	Total cash flows (a)	$ (200,000)	$ 100,000	$ 100,000	$ 20,000	$ 100,000	$ 160,000
9	Discount factor (14%) (b)	1.000	0.877	0.769	0.675	0.592	0.519
10	Present value of cash flows (a) × (b)	$ (200,000)	$ 87,700	$ 76,900	$ 13,500	$ 59,200	$ 83,040
11	Net present value (SUM B10:G10)	$ 120,340					
12							
13	Buy the new ferry:				Year		
14		Now	1	2	3	4	5
15	Initial investment	$ (360,000)					
16	Salvage value of the old ferry	$ 70,000					
17	Annual revenues		$ 400,000	$ 400,000	$ 400,000	$ 400,000	$ 400,000
18	Annual cash operating costs		$ (210,000)	$ (210,000)	$ (210,000)	$ (210,000)	$ (210,000)
19	Repairs in three years				$ (30,000)		
20	Salvage value of new ferry						$ 60,000
21	Total cash flows (a)	$ (290,000)	$ 190,000	$ 190,000	$ 160,000	$ 190,000	$ 250,000
22	Discount factor (14%) (b)	1.000	0.877	0.769	0.675	0.592	0.519
23	Present value of cash flows (a) × (b)	$ (290,000)	$ 166,630	$ 146,110	$ 108,000	$ 112,480	$ 129,750
24	Net present value (SUM B23:G23)	$ 372,970					
25							
26	Net present value in favor of buying the new ferry (B24-B11)	$ 252,630					
27							
28	Note: The discount factors come from Exhibit 8B-1 in Appendix 8B.						
29							

Exhibit 8-7 Exhibit 8-8 **Exhibit 8-9** Exhibit 8-10 Exhibit 8-11 Ex...

$60,000. The scrap value of the ferry right now is $70,000. It will cost $300,000 each year to operate the ferry, and revenues will total $400,000 annually.

As an alternative, Harper Ferry Company can purchase a new ferryboat at a cost of $360,000. The new ferry will have a life of 5 years, but it will require some repairs costing $30,000 at the end of 3 years. At the end of 5 years, the ferry will have a scrap value of $60,000. It will cost $210,000 each year to operate the ferry, and revenues will total $400,000 annually.

Harper Ferry Company requires a return of at least 14% on all investment projects.

Should the company purchase the new ferry or renovate the old ferry? Exhibit 8–9 shows the solution using the total-cost approach.

Two points should be noted from the exhibit. First, *all* cash inflows and *all* cash outflows are included in the solution under each alternative. No effort has been made to isolate those cash flows that are relevant to the decision and those that are not relevant. The inclusion of all cash flows associated with each alternative gives the approach its name—the *total-cost* approach.

Second, notice that a net present value is computed for each alternative. This is a strength of the total-cost approach because an unlimited number of alternatives can be compared side by side to determine the best option. For example, another alternative for Harper Ferry Company would be to get out of the ferry business entirely. If management desired, the net present value of this alternative could be computed to compare with the alternatives shown in Exhibit 8–9. Still other alternatives might be available to the company. In the case at hand, given only two alternatives, the data indicate that the net present value in favor of buying the new ferry is $252,630.[3]

Least–Cost Decisions

Some decisions do not involve any revenues. For example, a company may be trying to decide whether to buy or lease an executive jet. The choice would be made on the basis of

---

[3] The alternative with the highest net present value is not always the best choice, although it is the best choice in this case. For further discussion, see the section Preference Decisions—The Ranking of Investment Projects.

which alternative—buying or leasing—would be least costly. In situations such as these, where no revenues are involved, the most desirable alternative is the one with the *least total cost* from a present value perspective. Hence, these are known as least-cost decisions. To illustrate a least-cost decision, consider the following data:

Example H: Val-Tek Company is considering replacing an old threading machine with a new threading machine that would substantially reduce annual operating costs. Selected data relating to the old and new machines are presented below:

	Old Machine	New Machine
Purchase cost when new	$200,000	$250,000
Salvage value now	$30,000	—
Annual cash operating costs	$150,000	$90,000
Overhaul needed immediately	$40,000	—
Salvage value in six years	$0	$50,000
Remaining life	6 years	6 years

Val-Tek Company uses a 10% discount rate.

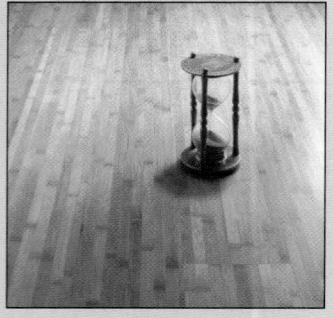

IN BUSINESS

HOME CONSTRUCTION GOES GREEN—OR DOES IT?

Many homebuyers like the idea of building environmentally friendly homes until they get the bill. Specpan, an Indianapolis research firm, estimates a "green" home costs 10%–19% more than a comparable conventional home. For example, installing solar-electric glass-faced tiles on a roof costs $15,000 per 100 square feet compared to $1,200 per 100 square feet for standard fiber-cement tiles. Environmentally friendly interior paint costs $35–$42 per gallon compared to $20–$32 per gallon for standard latex paint. To further complicate this least-cost decision, the average homeowner lives in a house only seven years before moving. Within this time frame, many green investments appear to be financially unattractive. Nonetheless, the American Institute of Architects reports that 63% of their clients expressed an interest in renewable flooring materials such as cork and bamboo, up from 53% a year earlier.

Source: June Fletcher, "The Price of Going Green," *The Wall Street Journal,* February 29, 2008, p. W8.

Exhibit 8–10 analyzes the alternatives using the total-cost approach. Because this is a least-cost decision, the present values are negative for both alternatives. However, the present value of the alternative of buying the new machine is $109,440 higher than the other alternative. Therefore, buying the new machine is the less costly alternative.

Uncertain Cash Flows

LEARNING OBJECTIVE 8–4
Evaluate an investment project that has uncertain cash flows.

Thus far, we have assumed that all future cash flows are known with certainty. However, future cash flows are often uncertain or difficult to estimate. A number of techniques are available for handling this complication. Some of these techniques are quite technical—involving computer simulations or advanced mathematical skills—and are beyond the scope of this book. However, we can provide some very useful information to without getting too technical.

An Example

As an example of difficult-to-estimate future cash flows, consider the case of investments in automated equipment. The up-front costs of automated equipment and the tangible

EXHIBIT 8–10
Least-Cost Decision: A Net Present Value Analysis

	A	B	C	D	E	F	G	H
1	Keep the old machine:					Year		
2		Now	1	2	3	4	5	6
3	Overhaul needed now	$ (40,000)						
4	Annual cash operating costs		$ (150,000)	$ (150,000)	$ (150,000)	$ (150,000)	$ (150,000)	$ (150,000)
5	Total cash flows (a)	$ (40,000)	$ (150,000)	$ (150,000)	$ (150,000)	$ (150,000)	$ (150,000)	$ (150,000)
6	Discount factor (10%) (b)	1.000	0.909	0.826	0.751	0.683	0.621	0.564
7	Present value of cash flows (a) × (b)	$ (40,000)	$ (136,350)	$ (123,900)	$ (112,650)	$ (102,450)	$ (93,150)	$ (84,600)
8	Net present value (SUM B7:H7)	$ (693,100)						
9								
10	Buy the new machine:					Year		
11		Now	1	2	3	4	5	6
12	Initial investment	$ (250,000)						
13	Salvage value of the old machine	$ 30,000						
14	Annual cash operating costs		$ (90,000)	$ (90,000)	$ (90,000)	$ (90,000)	$ (90,000)	$ (90,000)
15	Salvage value of new machine							$ 50,000
16	Total cash flows (a)	$ (220,000)	$ (90,000)	$ (90,000)	$ (90,000)	$ (90,000)	$ (90,000)	$ (40,000)
17	Discount factor (10%) (b)	1.000	0.909	0.826	0.751	0.683	0.621	0.564
18	Present value of cash flows (a) × (b)	$ (220,000)	$ (81,810)	$ (74,340)	$ (67,590)	$ (61,470)	$ (55,890)	$ (22,560)
19	Net present value (SUM B18:H18)	$ (583,660)						
20								
21	Net present value in favor of buying the new machine	$ 109,440						
22								
23	Note: The discount factors come from Exhibit 8B-1 in Appendix 8B.							
24								

Exhibit 8-7 Exhibit 8-8 Exhibit 8-9 Exhibit 8-10 Exhibit 8-11 Exhibit 8

benefits, such as reductions in operating costs and waste, tend to be relatively easy to estimate. However, the intangible benefits, such as greater reliability, greater speed, and higher quality, are more difficult to quantify in terms of future cash flows. These intangible benefits certainly impact future cash flows—particularly in terms of increased sales and perhaps higher selling prices—but the cash flow effects are difficult to estimate. What can be done?

A fairly simple procedure can be followed when the intangible benefits are likely to be significant. Suppose, for example, that a company with a 12% discount rate is considering purchasing automated equipment that would have a 10-year useful life. Also suppose that a discounted cash flow analysis of just the tangible costs and benefits shows a negative net present value of $226,000. Clearly, if the intangible benefits are large enough, they could turn this negative net present value into a positive net present value. In this case, the amount of additional cash flow per year from the intangible benefits that would be needed to make the project financially attractive can be computed as follows:

> Net present value excluding the
> intangible benefits (negative) .... $(226,000)
> Present value factor for an annuity at 12%
> for 10 periods (from Exhibit 8B–2 in Appendix 8B) 5.650

$$\frac{\text{Negative net present value to be offset, } \$226,000}{\text{Present value factor, } 5.650} = \$40,000$$

Thus, if the intangible benefits of the automated equipment are worth at least $40,000 a year to the company, then the automated equipment should be purchased. If, in the judgment of management, these intangible benefits are not worth $40,000 a year, then the automated equipment should not be purchased.

This technique can be used in other situations in which future cash flows are difficult to estimate. For example, this technique can be used when the salvage value is difficult to estimate. To illustrate, suppose that all of the cash flows from an investment in a supertanker have been estimated—other than its salvage value in 20 years. Using a discount rate of 12%, management has determined that the net present value of all of these cash flows is a negative $1.04 million. This negative net present value would be offset by the salvage value of the supertanker. How large would the salvage value have to be to make this investment attractive?

Net present value excluding salvage value (negative)	$(1,040,000)
Present value factor at 12% for 20 periods (from Exhibit 8B–1 in Appendix 8B)	0.104

$$\frac{\text{Negative net present value to be offset, } \$1,040,000}{\text{Present value factor, } 0.104} = \$10,000,000$$

Thus, if the salvage value of the tanker in 20 years is at least $10 million, its net present value would be positive and the investment would be made. However, if management believes the salvage value is unlikely to be as large as $10 million, the investment should not be made.

Preference Decisions—The Ranking of Investment Projects

LEARNING OBJECTIVE 8–5
Rank investment projects in order of preference.

Recall that when considering investment opportunities, managers must make two types of decisions—screening decisions and preference decisions. Screening decisions, which come first, pertain to whether or not a proposed investment is acceptable. Preference decisions come *after* screening decisions and attempt to answer the following question: "How do the remaining investment proposals, all of which have been screened and provide an acceptable rate of return, rank in terms of preference? That is, which one(s) would be *best* for the company to accept?"

Sometimes preference decisions are called rationing decisions, or ranking decisions. Limited investment funds must be rationed among many competing alternatives. Hence, the alternatives must be ranked. Either the internal rate of return method or the net present value method can be used in making preference decisions. However, as discussed earlier, if the two methods are in conflict, it is best to use the net present value method, which is more reliable.

Internal Rate of Return Method

When using the internal rate of return method to rank competing investment projects, the preference rule is: *The higher the internal rate of return, the more desirable the project.* An investment project with an internal rate of return of 18% is usually considered preferable to another project that has a return of only 15%. Internal rate of return is widely used to rank projects.

Net Present Value Method

The net present value of one project cannot be directly compared to the net present value of another project unless the initial investments are equal. For example, assume that a company is considering two competing investments, as shown below:

	Investment A	Investment B
Investment required	$(10,000)	$(5,000)
Present value of cash inflows	11,000	6,000
Net present value	$ 1,000	$ 1,000

Although each project has a net present value of $1,000, the projects are not equally desirable if the funds available for investment are limited. The project requiring an investment of only $5,000 is much more desirable than the project requiring an investment of $10,000. This fact can be highlighted by dividing the net present value of the project by the investment required. The result, shown below in equation form, is called the **project profitability index**.

$$\text{Project profitability index} = \frac{\text{Net present value of the project}}{\text{Investment required}} \qquad (3)$$

The project profitability indexes for the two investments above would be computed as follows:

	Investment	
	A	B
Net present value (a)	$1,000	$1,000
Investment required (b).	$10,000	$5,000
Project profitability index, (a) ÷ (b).	0.10	0.20

When using the project profitability index to rank competing investments projects, the preference rule is: *The higher the project profitability index, the more desirable the project.*[4] Applying this rule to the two investments above, investment B should be chosen over investment A.

The project profitability index is an application of the techniques for utilizing constrained resources discussed in an earlier chapter. In this case, the constrained resource is the limited funds available for investment, and the project profitability index is similar to the contribution margin per unit of the constrained resource.

A few details should be clarified with respect to the computation of the project profitability index. The "Investment required" refers to any cash outflows that occur at the beginning of the project, reduced by any salvage value recovered from the sale of old equipment. The "Investment required" also includes any investment in working capital that the project may need.

The Simple Rate of Return Method

The **simple rate of return** method is the final capital budgeting technique discussed in the chapter. This method is also often referred to as the accounting rate of return or the unadjusted rate of return. We will begin by explaining how to compute the simple rate of return followed by a discussion of this method's limitations and its impact on the behavior of investment center managers.

To obtain the simple rate of return, the annual incremental net operating income generated by a project is divided by the initial investment in the project, as shown below.

LEARNING OBJECTIVE 8–6
Compute the simple rate of return for an investment.

$$\text{Simple rate of return} = \frac{\text{Annual incremental net operating income}}{\text{Initial investment}} \qquad (4)$$

The annual incremental net operating income included in the numerator should be reduced by the depreciation charges that result from making the investment. Furthermore,

---

[4] Because of the "lumpiness" of projects, the project profitability index ranking may not be perfect. Nevertheless, it is a good starting point. For further details, see the Profitability Analysis Appendix at the end of the book.

the initial investment shown in the denominator should be reduced by any salvage value realized from the sale of old equipment.

Example I: Brigham Tea, Inc., is a processor of low-acid tea. The company is contemplating purchasing equipment for an additional processing line that would increase revenues by $90,000 per year. Incremental cash operating expenses would be $40,000 per year. The equipment would cost $180,000 and have a nine-year life with no salvage value.

To apply the formula for the simple rate of return, we must first determine the annual incremental net operating income from the project:

Annual incremental revenues		$90,000
Annual incremental cash operating expenses	$40,000	
Annual depreciation ($180,000 – $0)/9	20,000	
Annual incremental expenses		60,000
Annual incremental net operating income		$30,000

Given that the annual incremental net operating income from the project is $30,000 and the initial investment is $180,000, the simple rate of return is 16.7% as shown below:

$$\text{Simple rate of return} = \frac{\text{Annual incremental net operating income}}{\text{Initial investment}}$$

$$= \frac{\$30,000}{\$180,000}$$

$$= 16.7\%$$

Example J: Midwest Farms, Inc., hires people on a part-time basis to sort eggs. The cost of hand sorting is $30,000 per year. The company is investigating an egg-sorting machine that would cost $90,000 and have a 15-year useful life. The machine would have negligible salvage value, and it would cost $10,000 per year to operate and maintain. The egg-sorting equipment currently being used could be sold now for a scrap value of $2,500.

This project is slightly different from the preceding project because it involves cost reductions with no additional revenues. Nevertheless, the annual incremental net operating income can be computed by treating the annual cost savings as if it were incremental revenues as follows:

Annual incremental cost savings		$30,000
Annual incremental cash operating expenses	$10,000	
Annual depreciation ($90,000 – $0)/15	6,000	
Annual incremental expenses		16,000
Annual incremental net operating income		$14,000

Thus, even though the new equipment would not generate any additional revenues, it would reduce costs by $14,000 a year. This would have the effect of increasing net operating income by $14,000 a year.

Finally, the salvage value of the old equipment offsets the initial cost of the new equipment as follows:

Cost of the new equipment	$90,000
Less salvage value of the old equipment	2,500
Initial investment	$87,500

Given the annual incremental net operating income of $14,000 and the initial investment of $87,500, the simple rate of return is 16.0% computed as follows:

$$\text{Simple rate of return} = \frac{\text{Annual incremental net operating income}}{\text{Initial investment}}$$

$$= \frac{\$14,000}{\$87,500}$$

$$= 16.0\%$$

The simple rate of return suffers from two important limitations. First, it focuses on accounting net operating income rather than cash flows. Thus, if a project does not have constant incremental revenues and expenses over its useful life, the simple rate of return will fluctuate from year to year, thereby possibly causing the same project to appear desirable in some years and undesirable in others. Second, the simple rate of return method does not involve discounting cash flows. It considers a dollar received 10 years from now to be as valuable as a dollar received today.

Given these limitations, it is reasonable to wonder why we bothered discussing this method. First of all, in spite of its limitations, some companies use the simple rate of return to evaluate capital investment proposals. Therefore, you should be familiar with this approach so that you can properly critique it in the event that you encounter it in practice. More importantly, you need to understand how the simple rate of return method influences the behavior of investment center managers who are evaluated and rewarded based on their return on investment (ROI).

For example, assume the following three facts. First, assume that you are an investment center manager whose pay raises are based solely on ROI. Second, assume that last year your division had an ROI of 20%. Third, assume that your division has the chance to pursue a capital budgeting project that will have a positive net present value and a simple rate of return of 17%. Given these three assumptions, would you choose to accept this project or reject it? Although the company would want you to accept it because of its positive net present value, you would probably choose to reject it because the simple rate of return of 17% is less than your prior year's ROI of 20%. This basic example illustrates how a project's simple rate of return can influence the decisions made by investment center managers. It also highlights an important challenge faced by organizations, namely designing performance measurement systems that align employee actions with organizational goals.

Postaudit of Investment Projects

After an investment project has been approved and implemented, a *postaudit* should be conducted. A **postaudit** involves checking whether or not expected results are actually realized. This is a key part of the capital budgeting process because it helps keep managers honest in their investment proposals. Any tendency to inflate the benefits or downplay the costs in a proposal should become evident after a few postaudits have been conducted. The postaudit also provides an opportunity to reinforce and possibly expand successful projects and to cut losses on floundering projects.

The same capital budgeting method should be used in the postaudit as was used in the original approval process. That is, if a project was approved on the basis of a net present value analysis, then the same procedure should be used in performing the postaudit. However, the data used in the postaudit analysis should be *actual observed data* rather than estimated data. This gives management an opportunity to make a side-by-side comparison to see how well the project has succeeded. It also helps assure that estimated data received on future proposals will be carefully prepared because the persons submitting the data knows that their estimates will be compared to actual results in the postaudit process. Actual results that are far out of line with original estimates should be carefully reviewed.

ROYAL CARIBBEAN CRUISES LAUNCHES *OASIS OF THE SEAS*

Royal Caribbean Cruises invested $1.4 billion to build the *Oasis of the Seas,* a cruise ship that carries 5,400 passengers and stands 20 stories above the sea. The vessel is a third larger than any other cruise ship and contains 21 pools, 24 restaurants, 13 retail shops, and 300-foot water slides. The company hopes the ship's extraordinary amenities will attract large numbers of customers willing to pay premium prices. However, the economic downturn has caused many customers to refrain from spending on lavish vacations.

Source: Mike Esterl, "Huge Cruise Ships Prepare for Launch but Face Uncertain Waters," *The Wall Street Journal,* December 4, 2009, pp. B1–B2.

Summary

The payback method of evaluating capital investment projects focuses on the payback period. The payback period is the length of time that it takes for a project to recover its initial cost from the net cash inflows that it generates. The basic premise of the payback method is that the more quickly the cost of an investment can be recovered, the more desirable is the investment.

Investment decisions should take into account the time value of money because a dollar today is more valuable than a dollar received in the future. The net present value and internal rate of return methods both reflect this fact. In the net present value method, future cash flows are discounted to their present value. The difference between the present value of the cash inflows and the present value of the cash outflows is called a project's net present value. If the net present value of a project is negative, the project is rejected. The discount rate in the net present value method is usually based on a minimum required rate of return such as a company's cost of capital.

The internal rate of return is the rate of return that equates the present value of the cash inflows and the present value of the cash outflows, resulting in a zero net present value. If the internal rate of return is less than a company's minimum required rate of return, the project is rejected.

After rejecting projects whose net present values are negative or whose internal rates of return are less than the minimum required rate of return, more projects may remain than can be supported with available funds. The remaining projects can be ranked using either the project profitability index or internal rate of return. The project profitability index is computed by dividing the net present value of the project by the required initial investment.

The simple rate of return is determined by dividing a project's accounting net operating income by the initial investment in the project. While this method has important limitations, it can influence the decision-making process of investment center managers who are evaluated and rewarded based on their return on investment (ROI).

Review Problem: Comparison of Capital Budgeting Methods

Lamar Company is considering a project that would have a five-year life and require a $2,400,000 investment in equipment. At the end of five years, the project would terminate and the equipment would have no salvage value. The project would provide net operating income each year as follows:

Sales		$3,200,000
Variable expenses		1,800,000
Contribution margin		1,400,000
Fixed expenses:		
Advertising, salaries, and other		
fixed out-of-pocket costs	$700,000	
Depreciation	300,000	
Total fixed expenses		1,000,000
Net operating income		$ 400,000

The company's discount rate is 12%.

Required:
1. Compute the annual net cash inflow from the project.
2. Compute the project's net present value. Is the project acceptable?
3. Find the project's internal rate of return to the nearest whole percent.
4. Compute the project's payback period.
5. Compute the project's simple rate of return.

Solution to Review Problem

1. The annual net cash inflow can be computed by deducting the cash expenses from sales:

Sales	$3,200,000
Variable expenses	1,800,000
Contribution margin	1,400,000
Advertising, salaries, and	
other fixed out-of-pocket costs	700,000
Annual net cash inflow	$ 700,000

Or the annual net cash inflow can be computed by adding depreciation back to net operating income:

Net operating income	$400,000
Add: Noncash deduction for depreciation	300,000
Annual net cash inflow	$700,000

2. The net present value is computed as follows:

	A	B	C	D	E	F	G
1					Year		
2		Now	1	2	3	4	5
3	Initial investment	$ (2,400,000)					
4	Sales		$ 3,200,000	$ 3,200,000	$ 3,200,000	$ 3,200,000	$ 3,200,000
5	Variable expenses		$ (1,800,000)	$ (1,800,000)	$ (1,800,000)	$ (1,800,000)	$ (1,800,000)
6	Fixed out-of-pocket costs		$ (700,000)	$ (700,000)	$ (700,000)	$ (700,000)	$ (700,000)
7	Total cash flows (a)	$ (2,400,000)	$ 700,000	$ 700,000	$ 700,000	$ 700,000	$ 700,000
8	Discount factor (12%) (b)	1.000	0.893	0.797	0.712	0.636	0.567
9	Present value of cash flows (a) × (b)	$ (2,400,000)	$ 625,100	$ 557,900	$ 498,400	$ 445,200	$ 396,900
10	Net present value (SUM B9:G9)	$ 123,500					
11							
12	Note: The discount factors comes from Exhibit 8B-1 in Appendix 8B.						

Sheet1 Sheet2 Sheet3

Or, it can also be computed as follows:

	A	B	C
1			Years
2		Now	1-5
3	Initial investment	$ (2,400,000)	
4	Sales		$ 3,200,000
5	Variable expenses		$ (1,800,000)
6	Fixed out-of-pocket costs		$ (700,000)
7	Total cash flows (a)	$ (2,400,000)	$ 700,000
8	Discount factor (12%) (b)	1.000	3.605
9	Present value of the cash flows (a) × (b)	$ (2,400,000)	$2,523,500
10	Net present value (SUM B9:C9)	$123,500	
11			
12	Note: The discount factors comes from Exhibit 8B-2 in Appendix 8B.		
13			

Sheet1 Sheet2 Sheet3

Yes, the project is acceptable because it has a positive net present value.

3. The formula for computing the factor of the internal rate of return is:

$$\text{Factor of the internal rate of return} = \frac{\text{Investment required}}{\text{Annual net cash inflow}}$$

$$= \frac{\$2,400,000}{\$700,000} = 3.429$$

Looking in Exhibit 8B–2 in Appendix 8B at the end of the chapter and scanning along the 5-period line, we find that a factor of 3.429 represents a rate of return of about 14%.

4. The formula for the payback period is:

$$\text{Payback period} = \frac{\text{Investment required}}{\text{Annual net cash flow}}$$

$$= \frac{\$2,400,000}{\$700,000}$$

$$= 3.4 \text{ years}$$

5. The formula for the simple rate of return is:

$$\text{Simple rate of return} = \frac{\text{Annual incremental net operating income}}{\text{Initial investment}}$$

$$= \frac{\$400,000}{\$2,400,000}$$

$$= 16.7\%$$

Glossary

Capital budgeting The process of planning significant investments in projects that have long-term implications such as the purchase of new equipment or the introduction of a new product. (p. 334)

Cost of capital The average rate of return a company must pay to its long-term creditors and shareholders for the use of their funds. (p. 342)

Internal rate of return The discount rate at which the net present value of an investment project is zero; the rate of return of a project over its useful life. (p. 344)

Net present value The difference between the present value of an investment project's cash inflows and the present value of its cash outflows. (p. 339)

Out-of-pocket costs Actual cash outlays for salaries, advertising, repairs, and similar costs. (p. 344)

Payback period The length of time that it takes for a project to fully recover its initial cost out of the net cash inflows that it generates. (p. 336)

Postaudit The follow-up after a project has been approved and implemented to determine whether expected results were actually realized. (p. 353)

Preference decision A decision in which the alternatives must be ranked. (p. 334)

Project profitability index The ratio of the net present value of a project's cash flows to the investment required. (p. 351)

Screening decision A decision as to whether a proposed investment project is acceptable. (p. 334)

Simple rate of return The rate of return computed by dividing a project's annual incremental accounting net operating income by the initial investment required. (p. 351)

Time value of money The concept that a dollar today is worth more than a dollar a year from now. (p. 335)

Working capital Current assets less current liabilities. (p. 335)

Questions

8–1 What is the difference between capital budgeting screening decisions and capital budgeting preference decisions?

8–2 What is meant by the term *time value of money?*

8–3 What is meant by the term *discounting?*

8–4 Why isn't accounting net income used in the net present value and internal rate of return methods of making capital budgeting decisions?

8–5 Why are discounted cash flow methods of making capital budgeting decisions superior to other methods?

8–6 What is net present value? Can it ever be negative? Explain.

8–7 Identify two simplifying assumptions associated with discounted cash flow methods of making capital budgeting decisions.

8–8 If a company has to pay interest of 14% on long-term debt, then its cost of capital is 14%. Do you agree? Explain.

8–9 What is meant by an investment project's internal rate of return? How is the internal rate of return computed?

8–10 Explain how the cost of capital serves as a screening tool when using (*a*) the net present value method and (*b*) the internal rate of return method.

8–11 As the discount rate increases, the present value of a given future cash flow also increases. Do you agree? Explain.

8–12 Refer to Exhibit 8–7. Is the return on this investment proposal exactly 14%, more than 14%, or less than 14%? Explain.

8–13 How is the project profitability index computed, and what does it measure?

8–14 What is meant by the term *payback period?* How is the payback period determined? How can the payback method be useful?

8–15 What is the major criticism of the payback and simple rate of return methods of making capital budgeting decisions?

Multiple-choice questions are available with Connect.

Additional student resources are available with Connect. **connect**

Applying Excel

The Excel worksheet form that follows is to be used to recreate Example E and Exhibit 8–7. Download the workbook containing this form from Connect. *On the website you will also receive instructions about how to use this worksheet form.*

LEARNING OBJECTIVES 8–1, 8–3

	A	B	C	D	E	F	G
1	Chapter 8: Applying Excel						
2							
3	**Data**						
4	**Example E**						
5	Cost of equipment needed	$60,000					
6	Working capital needed	$100,000					
7	Overhaul of equipment in four years	$5,000					
8	Salvage value of the equipment in five years	$10,000					
9	Annual revenues and costs:						
10	Sales revenues	$200,000					
11	Cost of goods sold	$125,000					
12	Out-of-pocket operating costs	$35,000					
13	Discount rate	14%					
14							
15	*Enter a formula into each of the cells marked with a ? below*						
16	**Exhibit 8-6**						
17					Years		
18		Now	1	2	3	4	5
19	Purchase of equipment	?					
20	Investment in working capital	?					
21	Sales		?	?	?	?	?
22	Cost of goods sold		?	?	?	?	?
23	Out-of-pocket operating costs		?	?	?	?	?
24	Overhaul of equipment					?	
25	Salvage value of the equipment						?
26	Working capital released						?
27	Total cash flows (a)	?	?	?	?	?	?
28	Discount factor (14%) (b)	?	?	?	?	?	?
29	Present value of cash flows (a) x (b)	?	?	?	?	?	?
30	Net present value	?					
31							
32	*Use the formulas from Appendix 13B:						
33	Present value of $1 = 1/(1+r)^n						
34	Present value of an annuity of $1 = (1/r)*(1-(1/(1+r)^n))						
35	where n is the number of years and r is the discount rate						
36							

Chapter 8 Form | Filled in Chapter 8 Form | Chapter 8 Formulas | Cha

You should proceed to the requirements below only after completing your worksheet. Note that you may get a slightly different net present value from that shown in the text due to the precision of the calculations.

Required:

1. Check your worksheet by changing the discount rate to 10%. The net present value should now be between $56,495 and $56,518—depending on the precision of the calculations. If you do not get an answer in this range, find the errors in your worksheet and correct them.

   Explain why the net present value has increased as a result of reducing the discount rate from 14% to 10%.

2. The company is considering another project involving the purchase of new equipment. Change the data area of your worksheet to match the following:

   a. What is the net present value of the project?

Data	
Example E	
Cost of equipment needed	$120,000
Working capital needed	$80,000
Overhaul of equipment in four years . . .	$40,000
Salvage value of the equipment in five years	$20,000
Annual revenues and costs:	
Sales revenues	$255,000
Cost of goods sold	$160,000
Out-of-pocket operating costs	$50,000
Discount rate	14%

   b. Experiment with changing the discount rate in one percent increments (e.g., 13%, 12%, 15%, etc.). At what interest rate does the net present value turn from negative to positive?

c. The internal rate of return is between what two whole discount rates (e.g., between 10% and 11%, between 11% and 12%, between 12% and 13%, between 13% and 14%, etc.)?

d. Reset the discount rate to 14%. Suppose the salvage value is uncertain. How large would the salvage value have to be to result in a positive net present value?

Additional student resources are available with Connect. Mc Graw Hill Education **connect** **The Foundational 15**

Cardinal Company is considering a five-year project that would require a $2,975,000 investment in equipment with a useful life of five years and no salvage value. The company's discount rate is 14%. The project would provide net operating income in each of five years as follows:

LEARNING OBJECTIVES 8–1, 8–2, 8–3, 8–5, 8–6

Sales	$2,735,000
Variable expenses	1,000,000
Contribution margin	1,735,000
Fixed expenses:	
Advertising, salaries, and other fixed out-of-pocket costs ... $735,000	
Depreciation ... 595,000	
Total fixed expenses	1,330,000
Net operating income	$ 405,000

Required:

(Answer each question by referring to the original data unless instructed otherwise.)

1. Which item(s) in the income statement shown above will not affect cash flows?
2. What are the project's annual net cash inflows? Using the correct discount factor from Exhibit 8B–2 in Appendix 8B, what is the present value of the project's annual net cash inflows?
3. Using the format shown in Exhibit 8–7, what is the project's net present value?
4. Does your answer to requirement 2 differ from the present value of the annual net cash inflows that you computed in requirement 3? Why?
5. What is the project profitability index for this project? (Round your answer to the nearest whole percent.)
6. What is the project's internal rate of return to the nearest whole percent?
7. What is the project's payback period?
8. What is the project's simple rate of return for each of the five years?
9. If the company's discount rate was 16% instead of 14%, would you expect the project's net present value to be higher than, lower than, or the same as your answer to requirement 4? No computations are necessary
10. If the equipment had a salvage value of $300,000 at the end of five years, would you expect the project's payback period to be higher than, lower than, or the same as your answer to requirement 7? No computations are necessary.
11. If the equipment had a salvage value of $300,000 at the end of five years, would you expect the project's net present value to be higher than, lower than, or the same as your answer to requirement 3? No computations are necessary.
12. If the equipment had a salvage value of $300,000 at the end of five years, would you expect the project's simple rate of return to be higher than, lower than, or the same as your answer to requirement 8? No computations are necessary.
13. Assume a postaudit showed that all estimates (including total sales) were exactly correct except for the variable expense ratio, which actually turned out to be 45%. What was the project's actual net present value?
14. Assume a postaudit showed that all estimates (including total sales) were exactly correct except for the variable expense ratio, which actually turned out to be 45%. What was the project's actual payback period?
15. Assume a postaudit showed that all estimates (including total sales) were exactly correct except for the variable expense ratio, which actually turned out to be 45%. What was the project's actual simple rate of return?

EXERCISE 8–1 Payback Method [LO 8–1]

The management of Unter Corporation, an architectural design firm, is considering an investment with the following cash flows:

Year	Investment	Cash Inflow
1	$15,000	$1,000
2	$8,000	$2,000
3		$2,500
4		$4,000
5		$5,000
6		$6,000
7		$5,000
8		$4,000
9		$3,000
10		$2,000

Required:
1. Determine the payback period of the investment.
2. Would the payback period be affected if the cash inflow in the last year were several times as large?

EXERCISE 8–2 Net Present Value Method [LO 8–2]

The management of Kunkel Company is considering the purchase of a $27,000 machine that would reduce operating costs by $7,000 per year. At the end of the machine's five-year useful life, it will have zero scrap value. The company's required rate of return is 12%.

Required:
1. Determine the net present value of the investment in the machine.
2. What is the difference between the total, undiscounted cash inflows and cash outflows over the entire life of the machine?

EXERCISE 8–3 Internal Rate of Return [LO 8–3]

Wendell's Donut Shoppe is investigating the purchase of a new $18,600 donut-making machine. The new machine would permit the company to reduce the amount of part-time help needed, at a cost savings of $3,800 per year. In addition, the new machine would allow the company to produce one new style of donut, resulting in the sale of 1,000 dozen more donuts each year. The company realizes a contribution margin of $1.20 per dozen donuts sold. The new machine would have a six-year useful life.

Required:
1. What would be the total annual cash inflows associated with the new machine for capital budgeting purposes?
2. Find the internal rate of return promised by the new machine to the nearest whole percent.
3. In addition to the data given previously, assume that the machine will have a $9,125 salvage value at the end of six years. Under these conditions, compute the internal rate of return to the nearest whole percent. (**Hint:** You may find it helpful to use the net present value approach; find the discount rate that will cause the net present value to be closest to zero.)

EXERCISE 8–4 Uncertain Future Cash Flows [LO 8–4]

Lukow Products is investigating the purchase of a piece of automated equipment that will save $400,000 each year in direct labor and inventory carrying costs. This equipment costs $2,500,000 and is expected to have a 15-year useful life with no salvage value. The company's required rate of return is 20% on all equipment purchases. Management anticipates that this equipment will provide intangible benefits such as greater flexibility and higher-quality output that will result in additional future cash inflows.

Required:

What dollar value per year would these intangible benefits have to have to make the equipment an acceptable investment?

EXERCISE 8–5 Preference Ranking [LO 8–5]

Information on four investment proposals is given below:

	Investment Proposal			
	A	B	C	D
Investment required	$(90,000)	$(100,000)	$(70,000)	$(120,000)
Present value of cash inflows	126,000	138,000	105,000	160,000
Net present value	$ 36,000	$ 38,000	$ 35,000	$ 40,000
Life of the project	5 years	7 years	6 years	6 years

Required:

1. Compute the project profitability index for each investment proposal.
2. Rank the proposals in terms of preference.

EXERCISE 8–6 Simple Rate of Return Method [LO 8–6]

The management of Ballard MicroBrew is considering the purchase of an automated bottling machine for $120,000. The machine would replace an old piece of equipment that costs $30,000 per year to operate. The new machine would cost $12,000 per year to operate. The old machine currently in use could be sold now for a scrap value of $40,000. The new machine would have a useful life of 10 years with no salvage value.

Required:

Compute the simple rate of return on the new automated bottling machine.

EXERCISE 8–7 Net Present Value Analysis of Two Alternatives [LO 8–2]

Perit Industries has $100,000 to invest. The company is trying to decide between two alternative uses of the funds. The alternatives are:

	Project A	Project B
Cost of equipment required	$100,000	$0
Working capital investment required	$0	$100,000
Annual cash inflows	$21,000	$16,000
Salvage value of equipment in six years	$8,000	$0
Life of the project 6 years	6 years	6 years

The working capital needed for project B will be released at the end of six years for investment elsewhere. Perit Industries' discount rate is 14%.

Required:

Which investment alternative (if either) would you recommend that the company accept? Show all computations using the net present value format. Prepare separate computations for each project.

EXERCISE 8–8 Payback Period and Simple Rate of Return [LO 8–1, LO 8–6]

Nick's Novelties, Inc., is considering the purchase of new electronic games to place in its amusement houses. The games would cost a total of $300,000, have an eight-year useful life, and have a total salvage value of $20,000. The company estimates that annual revenues and expenses associated with the games would be as follows:

Revenues		$200,000
Less operating expenses:		
Commissions to amusement houses	$100,000	
Insurance	7,000	
Depreciation	35,000	
Maintenance	18,000	160,000
Net operating income		$ 40,000

Required:
1. Assume that Nick's Novelties, Inc., will not purchase new games unless they provide a payback period of five years or less. Would the company purchase the new games?
2. Compute the simple rate of return promised by the games. If the company requires a simple rate of return of at least 12%, will the games be purchased?

EXERCISE 8–9 Net Present Value Analysis and Simple Rate of Return [LO 8–2, LO 8–6]
Derrick Iverson is a divisional manager for Holston Company. His annual pay raises are largely determined by his division's return on investment (ROI), which has been above 20% each of the last three years. Derrick is considering a capital budgeting project that would require a $3,000,000 investment in equipment with a useful life of five years and no salvage value. Holston Company's discount rate is 15%. The project would provide net operating income each year for five years as follows:

Sales		$2,500,000
Variable expenses		1,000,000
Contribution margin		1,500,000
Fixed expenses:		
Advertising, salaries, and other fixed		
out-of-pocket costs	$600,000	
Depreciation	600,000	
Total fixed expenses		1,200,000
Net operating income		$ 300,000

Required:
1. Compute the project's net present value.
2. Compute the project's simple rate of return.
3. Would the company want Derrick to pursue this investment opportunity? Would Derrick be inclined to pursue this investment opportunity? Explain.

EXERCISE 8–10 Basic Net Present Value Analysis [LO 8–2]
Kathy Myers frequently purchases stocks and bonds, but she is uncertain how to determine the rate of return that she is earning. For example, three years ago she paid $13,000 for 200 shares of Malti Company's common stock. She received a $420 cash dividend on the stock at the end of each year for three years. At the end of three years, she sold the stock for $16,000. Kathy would like to earn a return of at least 14% on all of her investments. She is not sure whether the Malti Company stock provided a 14% return and would like some help with the necessary computations.

Required:
Using the net present value method, determine whether or not the Malti Company stock provided a 14% return. Round all computations to the nearest whole dollar.

EXERCISE 8–11 Preference Ranking of Investment Projects [LO 8–5]
Oxford Company has limited funds available for investment and must ration the funds among four competing projects. Selected information on the four projects follows:

Project	Investment Required	Net Present Value	Life of the Project (years)	Internal Rate of Return (percent)
A	$160,000	$44,323	7	18%
B	$135,000	$42,000	12	16%
C	$100,000	$35,035	7	20%
D	$175,000	$38,136	3	22%

The net present values above have been computed using a 10% discount rate.

The company wants your assistance in determining which project to accept first, second, and so forth.

Required:

1. Compute the project profitability index for each project.
2. In order of preference, rank the four projects in terms of:
   a. Net present value.
   b. Project profitability index.
   c. Internal rate of return.
3. Which ranking do you prefer? Why?

EXERCISE 8–12 Uncertain Cash Flows [LO 8–4]

The Cambro Foundation, a nonprofit organization, is planning to invest $104,950 in a project that will last for three years. The project will produce net cash inflows as follows:

Year 1	$30,000
Year 2	$40,000
Year 3	?

Required:

Assuming that the project will yield exactly a 12% rate of return, what is the expected net cash inflow for Year 3?

EXERCISE 8–13 Basic Payback Period and Simple Rate of Return Computations [LO 8–1, LO 8–6]

A piece of laborsaving equipment has just come onto the market that Mitsui Electronics, Ltd., could use to reduce costs in one of its plants in Japan. Relevant data relating to the equipment follow:

Purchase cost of the equipment	$432,000
Annual cost savings that will be provided	
by the equipment	$90,000
Life of the equipment	12 years

Required:

1. Compute the payback period for the equipment. If the company requires a payback period of four years or less, would the equipment be purchased?
2. Compute the simple rate of return on the equipment. Use straight-line depreciation based on the equipment's useful life. Would the equipment be purchased if the company's required rate of return is 14%?

EXERCISE 8–14 Comparison of Projects Using Net Present Value [LO 8–2]

Labeau Products, Ltd., of Perth, Australia, has $35,000 to invest. The company is trying to decide between two alternative uses for the funds as follows:

	Invest in Project X	Invest in Project Y
Investment required	$35,000	$35,000
Annual cash inflows	$12,000	$90,000
Single cash inflow at the end of 6 years		$90,000
Life of the project	6 years	6 years

The company's discount rate is 18%.

Required:
Which alternative would you recommend that the company accept? Show all computations using the net present value approach. Prepare separate computations for each project.

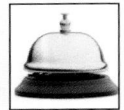

EXERCISE 8–15 Internal Rate of Return and Net Present Value [LO 8–2, LO 8–3]
Henrie's Drapery Service is investigating the purchase of a new machine for cleaning and blocking drapes. The machine would cost $137,280, including freight and installation. Henrie's has estimated that the new machine would increase the company's cash inflows, net of expenses, by $40,000 per year. The machine would have a five-year useful life and no salvage value.

Required:
1. Compute the machine's internal rate of return to the nearest whole percent.
2. Compute the machine's net present value. Use a discount rate of 14%. Why do you have a zero net present value?
3. Suppose that the new machine would increase the company's annual cash inflows, net of expenses, by only $37,150 per year. Under these conditions, compute the internal rate of return to the nearest whole percent.

Problems connect   Additional student resources are available with Connect.

PROBLEM 8–16 Basic Net Present Value Analysis [LO 8–2]
Windhoek Mines, Ltd., of Namibia, is contemplating the purchase of equipment to exploit a mineral deposit on land to which the company has mineral rights. An engineering and cost analysis has been made, and it is expected that the following cash flows would be associated with opening and operating a mine in the area:

Cost of new equipment and timbers	$275,000
Working capital required	$100,000
Annual net cash receipts	$120,000*
Cost to construct new roads in three years	$40,000
Salvage value of equipment in four years	$65,000

*Receipts from sales of ore, less out-of-pocket costs for salaries, utilities, insurance, and so forth.

The mineral deposit would be exhausted after four years of mining. At that point, the working capital would be released for reinvestment elsewhere. The company's required rate of return is 20%.

Required:
Determine the net present value of the proposed mining project. Should the project be accepted? Explain.

PROBLEM 8–17 Net Present Value Analysis; Internal Rate of Return; Simple Rate of Return [LO 8–2, LO 8–3, LO 8–6]
Casey Nelson is a divisional manager for Pigeon Company. His annual pay raises are largely determined by his division's return on investment (ROI), which has been above 20% each of the last three years. Casey is considering a capital budgeting project that would require a $3,500,000 investment in equipment with a useful life of five years and no salvage value. Pigeon Company's

discount rate is 16%. The project would provide net operating income each year for five years as follows:

Sales		$3,400,000
Variable expenses		1,600,000
Contribution margin		1,800,000
Fixed expenses:		
Advertising, salaries, and other fixed out-of-pocket costs	$700,000	
Depreciation	700,000	
Total fixed expenses		1,400,000
Net operating income		$ 400,000

Required:

1. What is the project's net present value?
2. What is the project's internal rate of return to the nearest whole percent?
3. What is the project's simple rate of return?
4. Would the company want Casey to pursue this investment opportunity? Would Casey be inclined to pursue this investment opportunity? Explain.

PROBLEM 8–18 Net Present Value Analysis [LO 8–2]

Oakmont Company has an opportunity to manufacture and sell a new product for a four-year period. The company's discount rate is 15%. After careful study, Oakmont estimated the following costs and revenues for the new product:

Cost of equipment needed	$130,000
Working capital needed	$60,000
Overhaul of the equipment in two years	$8,000
Salvage value of the equipment in four years	$12,000
Annual revenues and costs:	
Sales revenues	$250,000
Variable expenses	$120,000
Fixed out-of-pocket operating costs	$70,000

When the project concludes in four years the working capital will be released for investment elsewhere within the company.

Required:

Calculate the net present value of this investment opportunity.

PROBLEM 8–19 Simple Rate of Return; Payback [LO 8–1, LO 8–6]

Paul Swanson has an opportunity to acquire a franchise from The Yogurt Place, Inc., to dispense frozen yogurt products under The Yogurt Place name. Mr. Swanson has assembled the following information relating to the franchise:

a. A suitable location in a large shopping mall can be rented for $3,500 per month.
b. Remodeling and necessary equipment would cost $270,000. The equipment would have a 15-year life and an $18,000 salvage value. Straight-line depreciation would be used, and the salvage value would be considered in computing depreciation.
c. Based on similar outlets elsewhere, Mr. Swanson estimates that sales would total $300,000 per year. Ingredients would cost 20% of sales.
d. Operating costs would include $70,000 per year for salaries, $3,500 per year for insurance, and $27,000 per year for utilities. In addition, Mr. Swanson would have to pay a commission to The Yogurt Place, Inc., of 12.5% of sales.

Required:

1. Prepare a contribution format income statement that shows the expected net operating income each year from the franchise outlet.

2. Compute the simple rate of return promised by the outlet. If Mr. Swanson requires a simple rate of return of at least 12%, should he acquire the franchise?

3. Compute the payback period on the outlet. If Mr. Swanson wants a payback of four years or less, will he acquire the franchise?

PROBLEM 8–20 Net Present Value Analysis; Uncertain Cash Flows [LO 8–2, LO 8–4]

"I'm not sure we should lay out $250,000 for that automated welding machine," said Jim Alder, president of the Superior Equipment Company. "That's a lot of money, and it would cost us $80,000 for software and installation, and another $3,000 every month just to maintain the thing. In addition, the manufacturer admits that it would cost $45,000 more at the end of three years to replace worn-out parts."

"I admit it's a lot of money," said Franci Rogers, the controller. "But you know the turnover problem we've had with the welding crew. This machine would replace six welders at a cost savings of $108,000 per year. And we would save another $6,500 per year in reduced material waste. When you figure that the automated welder would last for six years, I'm sure the return would be greater than our 16% required rate of return."

"I'm still not convinced," countered Mr. Alder. "We can only get $12,000 scrap value out of our old welding equipment if we sell it now, and in six years the new machine will only be worth $20,000 for parts. But have your people work up the figures and we'll talk about them at the executive committee meeting tomorrow."

Required:

1. Compute the annual net cost savings promised by the automated welding machine.

2. Using the data from requirement 1 and other data from the problem, compute the automated welding machine's net present value. Would you recommend purchasing the automated welding machine? Explain.

3. Assume that management can identify several intangible benefits associated with the automated welding machine, including greater flexibility in shifting from one type of product to another, improved quality of output, and faster delivery as a result of reduced throughput time. What dollar value per year would management have to attach to these intangible benefits in order to make the new welding machine an acceptable investment?

PROBLEM 8–21 Preference Ranking of Investment Projects [LO 8–5]

The management of Revco Products is exploring four different investment opportunities. Information on the four projects under study follows:

	Project Number			
	1	2	3	4
Investment required	$(270,000)	$(450,000)	$(360,000)	$(480,000)
Present value of cash inflows at a				
10% discount rate	336,140	522,970	433,400	567,270
Net present value	$ 66,140	$ 72,970	$ 73,400	$ 87,270
Life of the project	6 years	3 years	12 years	6 years
Internal rate of return	18%	19%	14%	16%

Because the company's required rate of return is 10%, a 10% discount rate has been used in the present value computations above. Limited funds are available for investment, so the company can't accept all of the available projects.

Required:

1. Compute the project profitability index for each investment project.

2. Rank the four projects according to preference, in terms of:
   a. Net present value
   b. Project profitability index
   c. Internal rate of return

3. Which ranking do you prefer? Why?

PROBLEM 8–22 Basic Net Present Value Analysis [LO 8–2]

The Sweetwater Candy Company would like to buy a new machine that would automatically "dip" chocolates. The dipping operation is currently done largely by hand. The machine the company is considering costs $120,000. The manufacturer estimates that the machine would be usable for five years but would require the replacement of several key parts at the end of the third year. These parts would cost $9,000, including installation. After five years, the machine could be sold for $7,500.

The company estimates that the cost to operate the machine will be $7,000 per year. The present method of dipping chocolates costs $30,000 per year. In addition to reducing costs, the new machine will increase production by 6,000 boxes of chocolates per year. The company realizes a contribution margin of $1.50 per box. A 20% rate of return is required on all investments.

Required:
1. What are the annual net cash inflows that will be provided by the new dipping machine?
2. Compute the new machine's net present value. Round all dollar amounts to the nearest whole dollar.

PROBLEM 8–23 Comprehensive Problem [LO 8–1, LO 8–2, LO 8–3, LO 8–5, LO 8–6]

Lou Barlow, a divisional manager for Sage Company, has an opportunity to manufacture and sell one of two new products for a five-year period. His annual pay raises are determined by his division's return on investment (ROI), which has exceeded 18% each of the last three years. He has computed the cost and revenue estimates for each product as follows:

	Product A	Product B
Initial investment:		
Cost of equipment (zero salvage value)	$170,000	$380,000
Annual revenues and costs:		
Sales revenues	$250,000	$350,000
Variable expenses	$120,000	$170,000
Depreciation expense	$34,000	$76,000
Fixed out-of-pocket operating costs	$70,000	$50,000

The company's discount rate is 16%.

Required:
1. Calculate the payback period for each product.
2. Calculate the net present value for each product.
3. Calculate the internal rate of return for each product.
4. Calculate the project profitability index for each product.
5. Calculate the simple rate of return for each product.
6. Which of the two products should Lou's division pursue? Why?

PROBLEM 8–24 Simple Rate of Return; Payback; Internal Rate of Return [LO 8–1, LO 8–3, LO 8–6]

The Elberta Fruit Farm of Ontario has always hired transient workers to pick its annual cherry crop. Francie Wright, the farm manager, has just received information on a cherry picking machine that is being purchased by many fruit farms. The machine is a motorized device that shakes the cherry tree, causing the cherries to fall onto plastic tarps that funnel the cherries into bins. Ms. Wright has gathered the following information to decide whether a cherry picker would be a profitable investment for the Elberta Fruit Farm:

a. Currently, the farm is paying an average of $40,000 per year to transient workers to pick the cherries.

b. The cherry picker would cost $94,500, and it would have an estimated 12-year useful life. The farm uses straight-line depreciation on all assets and considers salvage value in computing depreciation deductions. The estimated salvage value of the cherry picker is $4,500.

c. Annual out-of-pocket costs associated with the cherry picker would be: cost of an operator and an assistant, $14,000; insurance, $200; fuel, $1,800; and a maintenance contract, $3,000.

Required:

1. Determine the annual savings in cash operating costs that would be realized if the cherry picker were purchased.
2. Compute the simple rate of return expected from the cherry picker. Would the cherry picker be purchased if Elberta Fruit Farm's required rate of return is 16%?
3. Compute the payback period on the cherry picker. The Elberta Fruit Farm will not purchase equipment unless it has a payback period of five years or less. Would the cherry picker be purchased?
4. Compute (to the nearest whole percent) the internal rate of return promised by the cherry picker. Based on this computation, does it appear that the simple rate of return is an accurate guide in investment decisions?

PROBLEM 8–25 Net Present Value Analysis of a Lease or Buy Decision [LO 8–2]

The Riteway Ad Agency provides cars for its sales staff. In the past, the company has always purchased its cars from a dealer and then sold the cars after three years of use. The company's present fleet of cars is three years old and will be sold very shortly. To provide a replacement fleet, the company is considering two alternatives:

Annual cost of servicing, taxes, and licensing	$3,000
Repairs, first year	$1,500
Repairs, second year	$4,000
Repairs, third year	$6,000

Purchase alternative: The company can purchase the cars, as in the past, and sell the cars after three years of use. Ten cars will be needed, which can be purchased at a discounted price of $17,000 each. If this alternative is accepted, the following costs will be incurred on the fleet as a whole:

At the end of three years, the fleet could be sold for one-half of the original purchase price.

Lease alternative: The company can lease the cars under a three-year lease contract. The lease cost would be $55,000 per year (the first payment due at the end of Year 1). As part of this lease cost, the owner would provide all servicing and repairs, license the cars, and pay all the taxes. Riteway would be required to make a $10,000 security deposit at the beginning of the lease period, which would be refunded when the cars were returned to the owner at the end of the lease contract.

Riteway Ad Agency's required rate of return is 18%.

Required:

1. Use the total-cost approach to determine the present value of the cash flows associated with each alternative. Round all dollar amounts to the nearest whole dollar.
2. Which alternative should the company accept?

PROBLEM 8–26 Simple Rate of Return; Payback [LO 8–1, LO 8–6]

Sharkey's Fun Center contains a number of electronic games as well as a miniature golf course and various rides located outside the building. Paul Sharkey, the owner, would like to construct a water slide on one portion of his property. Mr. Sharkey has gathered the following information about the slide:

a. Water slide equipment could be purchased and installed at a cost of $330,000. According to the manufacturer, the slide would be usable for 12 years after which it would have no salvage value.
b. Mr. Sharkey would use straight-line depreciation on the slide equipment.
c. To make room for the water slide, several rides would be dismantled and sold. These rides are fully depreciated, but they could be sold for $60,000 to an amusement park in a nearby city.
d. Mr. Sharkey has concluded that about 50,000 more people would use the water slide each year than have been using the rides. The admission price would be $3.60 per person (the same price that the Fun Center has been charging for the old rides).

e.   Based on experience at other water slides, Mr. Sharkey estimates that annual incremental operating expenses for the slide would be: salaries, $85,000; insurance, $4,200; utilities, $13,000; and maintenance, $9,800.

Required:

1.   Prepare an income statement showing the expected net operating income each year from the water slide.
2.   Compute the simple rate of return expected from the water slide. Based on this computation, would the water slide be constructed if Mr. Sharkey requires a simple rate of return of at least 14% on all investments?
3.   Compute the payback period for the water slide. If Mr. Sharkey accepts any project with a payback period of five years or less, would the water slide be constructed?

PROBLEM 8–27 Net Present Value Analysis [LO 8–2]

In five years, Kent Duncan will retire. He is exploring the possibility of opening a self-service car wash. The car wash could be managed in the free time he has available from his regular occupation, and it could be closed easily when he retires. After careful study, Mr. Duncan has determined the following:

a.   A building in which a car wash could be installed is available under a five-year lease at a cost of $1,700 per month.
b.   Purchase and installation costs of equipment would total $200,000. In five years the equipment could be sold for about 10% of its original cost.
c.   An investment of an additional $2,000 would be required to cover working capital needs for cleaning supplies, change funds, and so forth. After five years, this working capital would be released for investment elsewhere.
d.   Both a wash and a vacuum service would be offered with a wash costing $2.00 and the vacuum costing $1.00 per use.
e.   The only variable costs associated with the operation would be 20 cents per wash for water and 10 cents per use of the vacuum for electricity.
f.   In addition to rent, monthly costs of operation would be: cleaning, $450; insurance, $75; and maintenance, $500.
g.   Gross receipts from the wash would be about $1,350 per week. According to the experience of other car washes, 60% of the customers using the wash would also use the vacuum.
       Mr. Duncan will not open the car wash unless it provides at least a 10% return.

Required:

1.   Assuming that the car wash will be open 52 weeks a year, compute the expected annual net cash receipts (gross cash receipts less cash disbursements) from its operation. (Do not include the cost of the equipment, the working capital, or the salvage value in these computations.)
2.   Would you advise Mr. Duncan to open the car wash? Show computations using the net present value method of investment analysis. Round all dollar figures to the nearest whole dollar.

PROBLEM 8–28 Net Present Value [LO 8–2]

Bilboa Freightlines, S.A., of Panama, has a small truck that it uses for intracity deliveries. The truck is worn out and must be either overhauled or replaced with a new truck. The company has assembled the following information:

	Present Truck	New Truck
Purchase cost new	$21,000	$30,000
Remaining book value	$11,500	
Overhaul needed now	$7,000	
Annual cash operating costs	$10,000	$6,500
Salvage value-now	$9,000	
Salvage value-five years from now	$1,000	$4,000

If the company keeps and overhauls its present delivery truck, then the truck will be usable for five more years. If a new truck is purchased, it will be used for five years, after which it will be traded in on another truck. The new truck would be diesel-operated, resulting in a substantial reduction in annual operating costs, as shown above.

The company computes depreciation on a straight-line basis. All investment projects are evaluated using a 16% discount rate.

Required:

Should Bilboa Freightlines keep the old truck or purchase the new one? Use the total-cost approach to net present value in making your decision. Round to the nearest whole dollar.

PROBLEM 8–29 Net Present Value Analysis of Securities [LO 8–2]

Linda Clark received $175,000 from her mother's estate. She placed the funds into the hands of a broker, who purchased the following securities on Linda's behalf:

a.   Common stock was purchased at a cost of $95,000. The stock paid no dividends, but it was sold for $160,000 at the end of three years.

b.   Preferred stock was purchased at its par value of $30,000. The stock paid a 6% dividend (based on par value) each year for three years. At the end of three years, the stock was sold for $27,000.

c.   Bonds were purchased at a cost of $50,000. The bonds paid annual interest of $6,000. After three years, the bonds were sold for $52,700.

The securities were all sold at the end of three years so that Linda would have funds available to open a new business venture. The broker stated that the investments had earned more than a 16% return, and he gave Linda the following computations to support his statement:

Common stock:	
Gain on sale ($160,000 − $95,000)	$65,000
Preferred stock:	
Dividends paid (6% × $30,000 × 3 years)	5,400
Loss on sale ($27,000 − $30,000)	(3,000)
Bonds:	
Interest paid ($6,000 × 3 years)	18,000
Gain on sale ($52,700 − $50,000)	2,700
Net gain on all investments	$88,100

$$\frac{\$88,100 \div 3 \text{ years}}{\$172,000} = 16.8\%$$

Required:

1.   Using a 16% discount rate, compute the net present value of each of the three investments. On which investment(s) did Linda earn a 16% rate of return? (Round computations to the nearest whole dollar.)

2.   Considering all three investments together, did Linda earn a 16% rate of return? Explain.

3.   Linda wants to use the $239,700 proceeds ($160,000 + $27,000 + $52,700 = $239,700) from sale of the securities to open a retail store under a 12-year franchise contract. What annual net cash inflow must the store generate for Linda to earn a 14% return over the 12-year period? Round computations to the nearest whole dollar.

PROBLEM 8–30 Net Present Value; Uncertain Future Cash Flows; Postaudit [LO 8–2, LO 8–4]

Saxon Products, Inc., is investigating the purchase of a robot for use on the company's assembly line. Selected data relating to the robot are provided below:

Cost of the robot	$1,600,000
Installation and software	$450,000
Annual savings in labor costs	?
Annual savings in inventory carrying costs	$210,000
Monthly increase in power and maintenance costs	$2,500
Salvage value in 5 years	$70,000
Useful life	5 years

Engineering studies suggest that use of the robot will result in a savings of 25,000 direct labor-hours each year. The labor rate is $16 per hour. Also, the smoother work flow made possible by the use of automation will allow the company to reduce the amount of inventory on hand by $400,000. This inventory reduction will take place at the end of the first year of operation; the released funds will be available for use elsewhere in the company. Saxon Products has a 20% required rate of return.

Shelly Martins, the controller, has noted that all of Saxon's competitors are automating their plants. She is pessimistic, however, about whether Saxon's management will allow it to automate. In preparing the proposal for the robot, she stated to a colleague, "Let's just hope that reduced labor and inventory costs can justify the purchase of this automated equipment. Otherwise, we'll never get it. You know how the president feels about equipment paying for itself out of reduced costs."

Required:

1. Determine the *annual net* cost savings if the robot is purchased. (Do not include the $400,000 inventory reduction or the salvage value in this computation.)
2. Compute the net present value of the proposed investment in the robot. Based on these data, would you recommend that the robot be purchased? Explain.
3. Assume that the robot is purchased. At the end of the first year, Shelly Martins has found that some items didn't work out as planned. Due to unforeseen problems, software and installation costs were $75,000 more than estimated and direct labor has been reduced by only 22,500 hours per year, rather than by 25,000 hours. Assuming that all other cost data were accurate, does it appear that the company made a wise investment? Show computations using the net present value format as in requirement 2. (***Hint:*** It might be helpful to place yourself back at the beginning of the first year with the new data.)
4. Upon seeing your analysis in requirement 3, Saxon's president stated, "That robot is the worst investment we've ever made. And now we'll be stuck with it for years."
    a. Explain to the president what benefits other than cost savings might accrue from using the new automated equipment.
    b. Compute for the president the dollar amount of cash inflow that would be needed each year from the benefits in part (*a*) for the automated equipment to yield a 20% rate of return.

Additional student resources are available with Connect. **Cases**

CASE 8–31 ETHICS AND THE MANAGER

The Fore Corporation is an integrated food processing company that has operations in over two dozen countries. Fore's corporate headquarters is in Chicago, and the company's executives frequently travel to visit Fore's foreign and domestic facilities.

Fore has a fleet of aircraft that consists of two business jets with international range and six smaller turboprop aircraft that are used on shorter flights. Company policy is to assign aircraft to trips on the basis of minimizing cost, but the practice is to assign the aircraft based on the organizational rank of the traveler. Fore offers its aircraft for short-term lease or for charter by other organizations whenever Fore itself does not plan to use the aircraft. Fore surveys the market often in order to keep its lease and charter rates competitive.

William Earle, Fore's vice president of finance, has claimed that a third business jet can be justified financially. However, some people in the controller's office have surmised that the real reason for a third business jet was to upgrade the aircraft used by Earle. Presently, the people outranking Earle keep the two business jets busy with the result that Earle usually flies in smaller turboprop aircraft.

The third business jet would cost $11 million. A capital expenditure of this magnitude requires a formal proposal with projected cash flows and net present value computations using Fore's minimum required rate of return. If Fore's president and the finance committee of the board of directors approve the proposal, it will be submitted to the full board of directors. The board has final approval on capital expenditures exceeding $5 million and has established a firm policy of rejecting any discretionary proposal that has a negative net present value.

Earle asked Rachel Arnett, assistant corporate controller, to prepare a proposal on a third business jet. Arnett gathered the following data:

- Acquisition cost of the aircraft, including instrumentation and interior furnishing.
- Operating cost of the aircraft for company use.
- Projected avoidable commercial airfare and other avoidable costs from company use of the plane.
- Projected value of executive time saved by using the third business jet.
- Projected contribution margin from incremental lease and charter activity.
- Estimated resale value of the aircraft.

When Earle reviewed Arnett's completed proposal and saw the large negative net present value figure, he returned the proposal to Arnett. With a glare, Earle commented, "You must have made an error. The proposal should look better than that."

Feeling some pressure, Arnett went back and checked her computations; she found no errors. However, Earle's message was clear. Arnett discarded her projections that she believed were reasonable and replaced them with figures that had a remote chance of actually occurring but were more favorable to the proposal. For example, she used first-class airfares to refigure the avoidable commercial airfare costs, even though company policy was to fly coach. She found revising the proposal to be distressing.

The revised proposal still had a negative net present value. Earle's anger was evident as he told Arnett to revise the proposal again, and to start with a $100,000 positive net present value and work backwards to compute supporting projections.

Required:
1. Explain whether Rachel Arnett's revision of the proposal was in violation of the IMA's Statement of Ethical Professional Practice.
2. Was William Earle in violation of the IMA's Statement of Ethical Professional Practice by telling Arnett specifically how to revise the proposal? Explain your answer.
3. Identify specific internal controls that Fore Corporation could implement to prevent unethical behavior on the part of the vice president of finance.

(CMA, adapted)

CASE 8–32 Net Present Value Analysis of a New Product [LO 8–2]
Matheson Electronics has just developed a new electronic device that it believes will have broad market appeal. The company has performed marketing and cost studies that revealed the following information:
a. New equipment would have to be acquired to produce the device. The equipment would cost $315,000 and have a six-year useful life. After six years, it would have a salvage value of about $15,000.
b. Sales in units over the next six years are projected to be as follows:

Year	Sales in Units
1	9,000
2	15,000
3	18,000
4–6	22,000

c. Production and sales of the device would require working capital of $60,000 to finance accounts receivable, inventories, and day-to-day cash needs. This working capital would be released at the end of the project's life.
d. The devices would sell for $35 each; variable costs for production, administration, and sales would be $15 per unit.
e. Fixed costs for salaries, maintenance, property taxes, insurance, and straight-line depreciation on the equipment would total $135,000 per year. (Depreciation is based on cost less salvage value.)

f. To gain rapid entry into the market, the company would have to advertise heavily. The advertising program would be:

Year	Amount of Yearly Advertising
1–2	$180,000
3	$150,000
4–6	$120,000

g. The company's required rate of return is 14%.

Required:

1. Compute the net cash inflow (cash receipts less yearly cash operating expenses) anticipated from sale of the device for each year over the next six years.
2. Using the data computed in (1) above and other data provided in the problem, determine the net present value of the proposed investment. Would you recommend that Matheson accept the device as a new product?

Appendix 8A: The Concept of Present Value

A dollar received today is more valuable than a dollar received a year from now for the simple reason that if you have a dollar today, you can put it in the bank and have more than a dollar a year from now. Because dollars today are worth more than dollars in the future, cash flows that are received at different times must be valued differently.

LEARNING OBJECTIVE 8–7
Understand present value concepts and the use of present value tables.

The Mathematics of Interest

If a bank pays 5% interest, then a deposit of $100 today will be worth $105 one year from now. This can be expressed as follows:

$$F_1 = P(1 + r) \qquad (1)$$

where F_1 = the balance at the end of one period, P = the amount invested now, and r = the rate of interest per period.

In the case where $100 is deposited in a savings account that earns 5% interest, P = $100 and r = 0.05. Under these conditions, F_1 = $105.

The $100 present outlay is called the **present value** of the $105 amount to be received in one year. It is also known as the *discounted value* of the future $105 receipt. The $100 represents the value in present terms of $105 to be received a year from now when the interest rate is 5%.

Compound Interest What if the $105 is left in the bank for a second year? In that case, by the end of the second year the original $100 deposit will have grown to $110.25:

Original deposit	$100.00
Interest for the first year: $100 × 0.05	5.00
Balance at the end of the first year	105.00
Interest for the second year: $105 × 0.05	5.25
Balance at the end of the second year	$110.25

Notice that the interest for the second year is $5.25, as compared to only $5.00 for the first year. This difference arises because interest is being paid on interest during the second year. That is, the $5.00 interest earned during the first year has been left in the account and has been added to the original $100 deposit when computing interest for the second year. This is known as **compound interest**. In this case, the compounding is annual. Interest can be compounded on a semiannual, quarterly, monthly, or even more frequent basis. The more frequently compounding is done, the more rapidly the balance will grow.

We can determine the balance in an account after n periods of compounding using the following equation:

$$F_n = P(1 + r)^n \qquad (2)$$

where n = the number of periods of compounding.

If $n = 2$ years and the interest rate is 5% per year, then the balance in two years will be computed as follows:

$$F_2 = \$100(1 + 0.05)^2$$
$$F_2 = \$110.25$$

Present Value and Future Value Exhibit 8A–1 shows the relationship between present value and future value. As shown in the exhibit, if $100 is deposited in a bank at 5% interest compounded annually, it will grow to $127.63 by the end of five years.

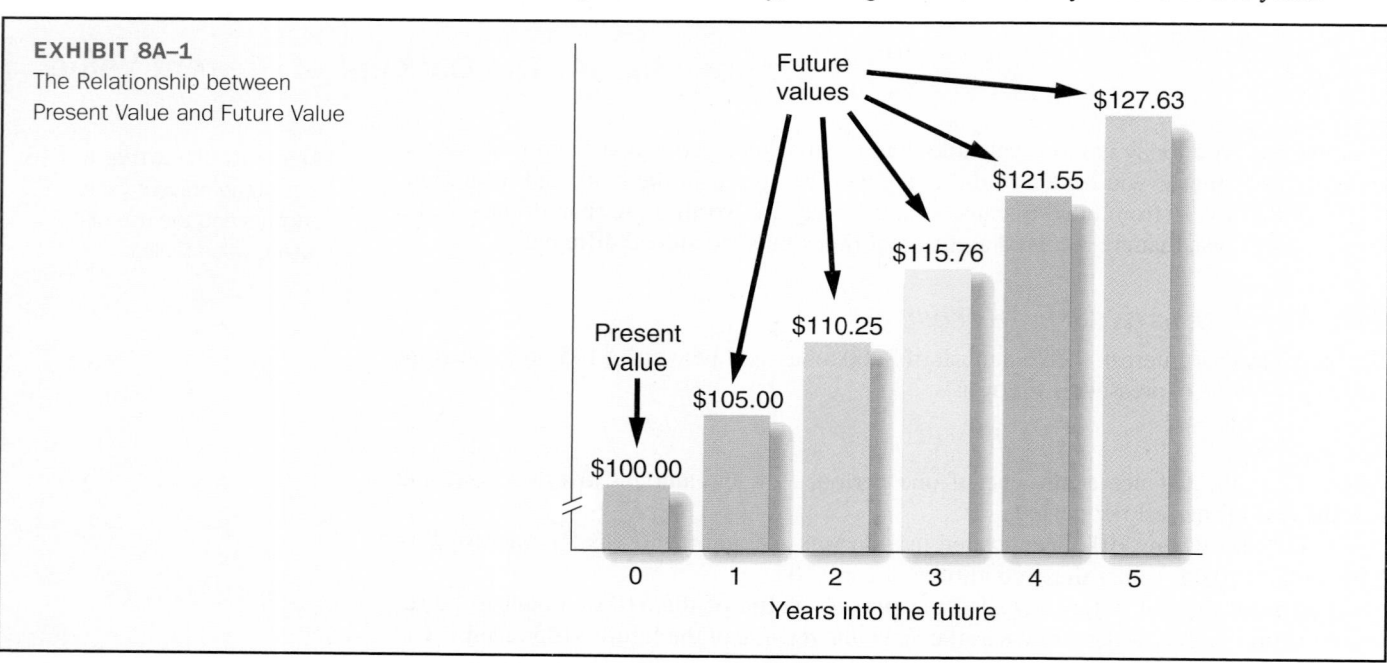

EXHIBIT 8A–1
The Relationship between
Present Value and Future Value

Computation of Present Value

An investment can be viewed in two ways—either in terms of its future value or in terms of its present value. We have seen from our computations above that if we know the present value of a sum (such as our $100 deposit), the future value in n years can be computed by using equation (2). But what if the situation is reversed and we know the *future* value of some amount but we do not know its present value?

For example, assume that you are to receive $200 two years from now. You know that the future value of this sum is $200 because this is the amount that you will be receiving in two years. But what is the sum's present value—what is it worth *right now?* The present value of any sum to be received in the future can be computed by turning equation (2) around and solving for *P:*

$$P = \frac{F_n}{(1 + r)^n} \qquad (3)$$

In our example, $F_n = \$200$ (the amount to be received in the future), $r = 0.05$ (the annual rate of interest), and $n = 2$ (the number of years in the future that the amount will be received).

$$P = \frac{\$200}{(1 + 0.05)^2}$$

$$P = \frac{\$200}{1.1025}$$

$$P = \$181.40$$

As shown by the computation above, the present value of a $200 amount to be received two years from now is $181.40 if the interest rate is 5%. In effect, $181.40 received *right now* is equivalent to $200 received two years from now.

The process of finding the present value of a future cash flow, which we have just completed, is called **discounting**. We have *discounted* the $200 to its present value of $181.40. The 5% interest that we have used to find this present value is called the **discount rate**. Discounting future sums to their present value is a common practice in business, particularly in capital budgeting decisions.

If you have a power key (y^x) on your calculator, the above calculations are fairly easy. However, some of the present value formulas we will be using are more complex. Fortunately, tables are available in which many of the calculations have already been done. For example, Exhibit 8B–1 in Appendix 8B shows the discounted present value of $1 to be received at various periods in the future at various interest rates. The table indicates that the present value of $1 to be received two periods from now at 5% is 0.907. Because in our example we want to know the present value of $200 rather than just $1, we need to multiply the factor in the table by $200:

$$\$200 \times 0.907 = \$181.40$$

This answer is the same as we obtained earlier using the formula in equation (3).

Present Value of a Series of Cash Flows

Although some investments involve a single sum to be received (or paid) at a single point in the future, other investments involve a *series* of cash flows. A series of identical cash flows is known as an **annuity**. To provide an example, assume that a company has just purchased some government bonds. The bonds will yield interest of $15,000 each year and will be held for five years. What is the present value of the stream of interest receipts from the bonds? As shown in Exhibit 8A–2, if the discount rate is 12%, the present value of this stream is $54,075. The discount factors used in this exhibit were taken from Exhibit 8B–1 in Appendix 8B.

Exhibit 8A–2 illustrates two important points. First, the present value of the $15,000 interest declines the further it is into the future. The present value of $15,000 received a year from now is $13,395, as compared to only $8,505 if received five years from now. This point underscores the time value of money.

Year	Factor at 12% (Exhibit 8B–1)	Interest Received	Present Value
1	0.893	$15,000	$13,395
2	0.797	$15,000	11,955
3	0.712	$15,000	10,680
4	0.636	$15,000	9,540
5	0.567	$15,000	8,505
			$54,075

EXHIBIT 8A–2
Present Value of a Series of Cash Receipts

The second point is that the computations used in Exhibit 8A–2 involved unnecessary work. The same present value of $54,075 could have been obtained more easily by referring to Exhibit 8B–2 in Appendix 8B. Exhibit 8B–2 contains the present value of $1 to be received each year over a *series* of years at various interest rates. Exhibit 8B–2 has been derived by simply adding together the factors from Exhibit 8B–1, as follows:

Year	Factors at 12% (from Exhibit 8B–1)
1	0.893
2	0.797
3	0.712
4	0.636
5	0.567
	3.605

The sum of these five factors is 3.605. Notice from Exhibit 8B–2 that the factor for $1 to be received each year for five years at 12% is also 3.605. If we use this factor and multiply it by the $15,000 annual cash inflow, then we get the same $54,075 present value that we obtained earlier in Exhibit 8A–2.

$$\$15{,}000 \times 3.605 = \$54{,}075$$

Therefore, when computing the present value of a series of equal cash flows that begins at the end of period 1, Exhibit 8B–2 should be used.

To summarize, the present value tables in Appendix 8B should be used as follows:

Exhibit 8B–1: This table should be used to find the present value of a single cash flow (such as a single payment or receipt) occurring in the future.

Exhibit 8B–2: This table should be used to find the present value of a series of identical cash flows beginning at the end of the current period and continuing into the future.

The use of both of these tables is illustrated in various exhibits in the main body of the chapter. *When a present value factor appears in an exhibit, you should take the time to trace it back into either or to get acquainted with the tables and how they work.*

Review Problem: Basic Present Value Computations

Each of the following situations is independent. Work out your own solution to each situation, and then check it against the solution provided.

1. John plans to retire in 12 years. Upon retiring, he would like to take an extended vacation, which he expects will cost at least $40,000. What lump-sum amount must he invest now to have $40,000 at the end of 12 years if the rate of return is:
   a. 8%?
   b. 12%?

2. The Morgans would like to send their daughter to a music camp at the end of each of the next five years. The camp costs $1,000 a year. What lump-sum amount would have to be invested now to have $1,000 at the end of each year if the rate of return is:
   a. 8%?
   b. 12%?

3. You have just received an inheritance from a relative. You can either receive a $200,000 lump-sum amount at the end of 10 years or receive $14,000 at the end of each year for the next 10 years. If your discount rate is 12%, which alternative would you prefer?

Solution to Review Problem

1. *a.* The amount that must be invested now would be the present value of the $40,000, using a discount rate of 8%. From Exhibit 8B–1 in Appendix 8B, the factor for a discount rate of 8% for 12 periods is 0.397. Multiplying this discount factor by the $40,000 needed in 12 years will give the amount of the present investment required: $40,000 × 0.397 = $15,880.

   b. We will proceed as we did in (*a*) above, but this time we will use a discount rate of 12%. From Exhibit 8B–1 in Appendix 8B, the factor for a discount rate of 12% for 12 periods is 0.257. Multiplying this discount factor by the $40,000 needed in 12 years will give the amount of the present investment required: $40,000 × 0.257 = $10,280.

   Notice that as the discount rate (desired rate of return) increases, the present value decreases.

2. This part differs from part (1) in that we are now dealing with an annuity rather than with a single future sum. The amount that must be invested now is the present value of the $1,000 needed at the end of each year for five years. Because we are dealing with an annuity, or a series of annual cash flows, we must refer to Exhibit 8B–2 in Appendix 8B for the appropriate discount factor.

   a. From Exhibit 8B–2 in Appendix 8B, the discount factor for 8% for five periods is 3.993. Therefore, the amount that must be invested now to have $1,000 available at the end of each year for five years is $1,000 × 3.993 = $3,993.

   b. From Exhibit 8B–2 in Appendix 8B, the discount factor for 12% for five periods is 3.605. Therefore, the amount that must be invested now to have $1,000 available at the end of each year for five years is $1,000 × 3.605 = $3,605.

   Again, notice that as the discount rate increases, the present value decreases. When the rate of return increases, less must be invested today to yield a given amount in the future.

3. For this part we will need to refer to both Exhibits 8B–1 and 8B–2 in Appendix 8B. From Exhibit 8B–1, we will need to find the discount factor for 12% for 10 periods, then apply it to the $200,000 lump sum to be received in 10 years. From Exhibit 8B–2, we will need to find the discount factor for 12% for 10 periods, then apply it to the series of $14,000 payments to be received over the 10-year period. Whichever alternative has the higher present value is the one that should be selected.

$$\$200,000 \times 0.322 = \$64,400$$

$$\$14,000 \times 5.650 = \$79,100$$

   Thus, you should prefer to receive the $14,000 per year for 10 years rather than the $200,000 lump sum. This means that you could invest the $14,000 received at the end of each year at 12% and have *more* than $200,000 at the end of 10 years.

Glossary (Appendix 8A)

Annuity A series of identical cash flows. (p. 375)
Compound interest The process of paying interest on interest in an investment. (p. 374)
Discount rate The rate of return that is used to find the present value of a future cash flow. (p. 375)
Discounting The process of finding the present value of a future cash flow. (p. 375)
Present value The value now of an amount that will be received in some future period. (p. 373)

 ## Appendix 8A Exercises

Additional student resources are available with Connect.

EXERCISE 8A–1 Basic Present Value Concepts [LO 8–7]
Annual cash inflows that will arise from two competing investment projects are given below:

Year	Investment A	Investment B
1	$ 3,000	$12,000
2	6,000	9,000
3	9,000	6,000
4	12,000	3,000
	$30,000	$30,000

The discount rate is 18%.

Required:

Compute the present value of the cash inflows for each investment.

EXERCISE 8A–2 Basic Present Value Concepts [LO 8–7]

Julie has just retired. Her company's retirement program has two options as to how retirement benefits can be received. Under the first option, Julie would receive a lump sum of $150,000 immediately as her full retirement benefit. Under the second option, she would receive $14,000 each year for 20 years plus a lump-sum payment of $60,000 at the end of the 20-year period.

Required:

If she can invest money at 12%, which option would you recommend that she accept? Use present value analysis.

EXERCISE 8A–3 Basic Present Value Concepts [LO 8–7]

In three years, when he is discharged from the Air Force, Steve wants to buy an $8,000 power boat.

Required:

What lump-sum amount must Steve invest now to have the $8,000 at the end of three years if he can invest money at:

1. 10%?
2. 14%?

EXERCISE 8A–4 Basic Present Value Concepts [LO 8–7]

Fraser Company will need a new warehouse in five years. The warehouse will cost $500,000 to build.

Required:

What lump-sum amount should the company invest now to have the $500,000 available at the end of the five-year period? Assume that the company can invest money at:

1. 10%.
2. 14%.

EXERCISE 8A–5 Basic Present Value Concepts [LO 8–7]

The Atlantic Medical Clinic can purchase a new computer system that will save $7,000 annually in billing costs. The computer system will last for eight years and have no salvage value.

Required:

Up to how much should the Atlantic Medical Clinic be willing to pay for the new computer system if the clinic's required rate of return is:

1. 16%?
2. 20%?

EXERCISE 8A–6 Basic Present Value Concepts [LO 8–7]

The Caldwell Herald newspaper reported the following story: Frank Ormsby of Caldwell is the state's newest millionaire. By choosing the six winning numbers on last week's state lottery, Mr. Ormsby has won the week's grand prize totaling $1.6 million. The State Lottery Commission has indicated that Mr. Ormsby will receive his prize in 20 annual installments of $80,000 each.

Required:

1. If Mr. Ormsby can invest money at a 12% rate of return, what is the present value of his winnings?
2. Is it correct to say that Mr. Ormsby is the "state's newest millionaire"? Explain your answer.

EXHIBIT 8B–1

Present Value of \$1; $\dfrac{1}{(1+r)^n}$

Periods	4%	5%	6%	7%	8%	9%	10%	11%	12%	13%	14%	15%	16%	17%	18%	19%	20%	21%	22%	23%	24%	25%
1	0.962	0.952	0.943	0.935	0.926	0.917	0.909	0.901	0.893	0.885	0.877	0.870	0.862	0.855	0.847	0.840	0.833	0.826	0.820	0.813	0.806	0.800
2	0.925	0.907	0.890	0.873	0.857	0.842	0.826	0.812	0.797	0.783	0.769	0.756	0.743	0.731	0.718	0.706	0.694	0.683	0.672	0.661	0.650	0.640
3	0.889	0.864	0.840	0.816	0.794	0.772	0.751	0.731	0.712	0.693	0.675	0.658	0.641	0.624	0.609	0.593	0.579	0.564	0.551	0.537	0.524	0.512
4	0.855	0.823	0.792	0.763	0.735	0.708	0.683	0.659	0.636	0.613	0.592	0.572	0.552	0.534	0.516	0.499	0.482	0.467	0.451	0.437	0.423	0.410
5	0.822	0.784	0.747	0.713	0.681	0.650	0.621	0.593	0.567	0.543	0.519	0.497	0.476	0.456	0.437	0.419	0.402	0.386	0.370	0.355	0.341	0.328
6	0.790	0.746	0.705	0.666	0.630	0.596	0.564	0.535	0.507	0.480	0.456	0.432	0.410	0.390	0.370	0.352	0.335	0.319	0.303	0.289	0.275	0.262
7	0.760	0.711	0.665	0.623	0.583	0.547	0.513	0.482	0.452	0.425	0.400	0.376	0.354	0.333	0.314	0.296	0.279	0.263	0.249	0.235	0.222	0.210
8	0.731	0.677	0.627	0.582	0.540	0.502	0.467	0.434	0.404	0.376	0.351	0.327	0.305	0.285	0.266	0.249	0.233	0.218	0.204	0.191	0.179	0.168
9	0.703	0.645	0.592	0.544	0.500	0.460	0.424	0.391	0.361	0.333	0.308	0.284	0.263	0.243	0.225	0.209	0.194	0.180	0.167	0.155	0.144	0.134
10	0.676	0.614	0.558	0.508	0.463	0.422	0.386	0.352	0.322	0.295	0.270	0.247	0.227	0.208	0.191	0.176	0.162	0.149	0.137	0.126	0.116	0.107
11	0.650	0.585	0.527	0.475	0.429	0.388	0.350	0.317	0.287	0.261	0.237	0.215	0.195	0.178	0.162	0.148	0.135	0.123	0.112	0.103	0.094	0.086
12	0.625	0.557	0.497	0.444	0.397	0.356	0.319	0.286	0.257	0.231	0.208	0.187	0.168	0.152	0.137	0.124	0.112	0.102	0.092	0.083	0.076	0.069
13	0.601	0.530	0.469	0.415	0.368	0.326	0.290	0.258	0.229	0.204	0.182	0.163	0.145	0.130	0.116	0.104	0.093	0.084	0.075	0.068	0.061	0.055
14	0.577	0.505	0.442	0.388	0.340	0.299	0.263	0.232	0.205	0.181	0.160	0.141	0.125	0.111	0.099	0.088	0.078	0.069	0.062	0.055	0.049	0.044
15	0.555	0.481	0.417	0.362	0.315	0.275	0.239	0.209	0.183	0.160	0.140	0.123	0.108	0.095	0.084	0.074	0.065	0.057	0.051	0.045	0.040	0.035
16	0.534	0.458	0.394	0.339	0.292	0.252	0.218	0.188	0.163	0.141	0.123	0.107	0.093	0.081	0.071	0.062	0.054	0.047	0.042	0.036	0.032	0.028
17	0.513	0.436	0.371	0.317	0.270	0.231	0.198	0.170	0.146	0.125	0.108	0.093	0.080	0.069	0.060	0.052	0.045	0.039	0.034	0.030	0.026	0.023
18	0.494	0.416	0.350	0.296	0.250	0.212	0.180	0.153	0.130	0.111	0.095	0.081	0.069	0.059	0.051	0.044	0.038	0.032	0.028	0.024	0.021	0.018
19	0.475	0.396	0.331	0.277	0.232	0.194	0.164	0.138	0.116	0.098	0.083	0.070	0.060	0.051	0.043	0.037	0.031	0.027	0.023	0.020	0.017	0.014
20	0.456	0.377	0.312	0.258	0.215	0.178	0.149	0.124	0.104	0.087	0.073	0.061	0.051	0.043	0.037	0.031	0.026	0.022	0.019	0.016	0.014	0.012
21	0.439	0.359	0.294	0.242	0.199	0.164	0.135	0.112	0.093	0.077	0.064	0.053	0.044	0.037	0.031	0.026	0.022	0.018	0.015	0.013	0.011	0.009
22	0.422	0.342	0.278	0.226	0.184	0.150	0.123	0.101	0.083	0.068	0.056	0.046	0.038	0.032	0.026	0.022	0.018	0.015	0.013	0.011	0.009	0.007
23	0.406	0.326	0.262	0.211	0.170	0.138	0.112	0.091	0.074	0.060	0.049	0.040	0.033	0.027	0.022	0.018	0.015	0.012	0.010	0.009	0.007	0.006
24	0.390	0.310	0.247	0.197	0.158	0.126	0.102	0.082	0.066	0.053	0.043	0.035	0.028	0.023	0.019	0.015	0.013	0.010	0.008	0.007	0.006	0.005
25	0.375	0.295	0.233	0.184	0.146	0.116	0.092	0.074	0.059	0.047	0.038	0.030	0.024	0.020	0.016	0.013	0.010	0.009	0.007	0.006	0.005	0.004
26	0.361	0.281	0.220	0.172	0.135	0.106	0.084	0.066	0.053	0.042	0.033	0.026	0.021	0.017	0.014	0.011	0.009	0.007	0.006	0.005	0.004	0.003
27	0.347	0.268	0.207	0.161	0.125	0.098	0.076	0.060	0.047	0.037	0.029	0.023	0.018	0.014	0.011	0.009	0.007	0.006	0.005	0.004	0.003	0.002
28	0.333	0.255	0.196	0.150	0.116	0.090	0.069	0.054	0.042	0.033	0.026	0.020	0.016	0.012	0.010	0.008	0.006	0.005	0.004	0.003	0.002	0.002
29	0.321	0.243	0.185	0.141	0.107	0.082	0.063	0.048	0.037	0.029	0.022	0.017	0.014	0.011	0.008	0.006	0.005	0.004	0.003	0.002	0.002	0.002
30	0.308	0.231	0.174	0.131	0.099	0.075	0.057	0.044	0.033	0.026	0.020	0.015	0.012	0.009	0.007	0.005	0.004	0.003	0.003	0.002	0.002	0.001
40	0.208	0.142	0.097	0.067	0.046	0.032	0.022	0.015	0.011	0.008	0.005	0.004	0.003	0.002	0.001	0.001	0.001	0.000	0.000	0.000	0.000	0.000

EXHIBIT 8B–2

Present Value of an Annuity of $1 in Arrears; $\frac{1}{r}\left[1 - \frac{1}{(1+r)^n}\right]$

Periods	4%	5%	6%	7%	8%	9%	10%	11%	12%	13%	14%	15%	16%	17%	18%	19%	20%	21%	22%	23%	24%	25%
1	0.962	0.952	0.943	0.935	0.926	0.917	0.909	0.901	0.893	0.885	0.877	0.870	0.862	0.855	0.847	0.840	0.833	0.826	0.820	0.813	0.806	0.800
2	1.886	1.859	1.833	1.808	1.783	1.759	1.736	1.713	1.690	1.668	1.647	1.626	1.605	1.585	1.566	1.547	1.528	1.509	1.492	1.474	1.457	1.440
3	2.775	2.723	2.673	2.624	2.577	2.531	2.487	2.444	2.402	2.361	2.322	2.283	2.246	2.210	2.174	2.140	2.106	2.074	2.042	2.011	1.981	1.952
4	3.630	3.546	3.465	3.387	3.312	3.240	3.170	3.102	3.037	2.974	2.914	2.855	2.798	2.743	2.690	2.639	2.589	2.540	2.494	2.448	2.404	2.362
5	4.452	4.329	4.212	4.100	3.993	3.890	3.791	3.696	3.605	3.517	3.433	3.352	3.274	3.199	3.127	3.058	2.991	2.926	2.864	2.803	2.745	2.689
6	5.242	5.076	4.917	4.767	4.623	4.486	4.355	4.231	4.111	3.998	3.889	3.784	3.685	3.589	3.498	3.410	3.326	3.245	3.167	3.092	3.020	2.951
7	6.002	5.786	5.582	5.389	5.206	5.033	4.868	4.712	4.564	4.423	4.288	4.160	4.039	3.922	3.812	3.706	3.605	3.508	3.416	3.327	3.242	3.161
8	6.733	6.463	6.210	5.971	5.747	5.535	5.335	5.146	4.968	4.799	4.639	4.487	4.344	4.207	4.078	3.954	3.837	3.726	3.619	3.518	3.421	3.329
9	7.435	7.108	6.802	6.515	6.247	5.995	5.759	5.537	5.328	5.132	4.946	4.772	4.607	4.451	4.303	4.163	4.031	3.905	3.786	3.673	3.566	3.463
10	8.111	7.722	7.360	7.024	6.710	6.418	6.145	5.889	5.650	5.426	5.216	5.019	4.833	4.659	4.494	4.339	4.192	4.054	3.923	3.799	3.682	3.571
11	8.760	8.306	7.887	7.499	7.139	6.805	6.495	6.207	5.938	5.687	5.453	5.234	5.029	4.836	4.656	4.486	4.327	4.177	4.035	3.902	3.776	3.656
12	9.385	8.863	8.384	7.943	7.536	7.161	6.814	6.492	6.194	5.918	5.660	5.421	5.197	4.988	4.793	4.611	4.439	4.278	4.127	3.985	3.851	3.725
13	9.986	9.394	8.853	8.358	7.904	7.487	7.103	6.750	6.424	6.122	5.842	5.583	5.342	5.118	4.910	4.715	4.533	4.362	4.203	4.053	3.912	3.780
14	10.563	9.899	9.295	8.745	8.244	7.786	7.367	6.982	6.628	6.302	6.002	5.724	5.468	5.229	5.008	4.802	4.611	4.432	4.265	4.108	3.962	3.824
15	11.118	10.380	9.712	9.108	8.559	8.061	7.606	7.191	6.811	6.462	6.142	5.847	5.575	5.324	5.092	4.876	4.675	4.489	4.315	4.153	4.001	3.859
16	11.652	10.838	10.106	9.447	8.851	8.313	7.824	7.379	6.974	6.604	6.265	5.954	5.668	5.405	5.162	4.938	4.730	4.536	4.357	4.189	4.033	3.887
17	12.166	11.274	10.477	9.763	9.122	8.544	8.022	7.549	7.120	6.729	6.373	6.047	5.749	5.475	5.222	4.990	4.775	4.576	4.391	4.219	4.059	3.910
18	12.659	11.690	10.828	10.059	9.372	8.756	8.201	7.702	7.250	6.840	6.467	6.128	5.818	5.534	5.273	5.033	4.812	4.608	4.419	4.243	4.080	3.928
19	13.134	12.085	11.158	10.336	9.604	8.950	8.365	7.839	7.366	6.938	6.550	6.198	5.877	5.584	5.316	5.070	4.843	4.635	4.442	4.263	4.097	3.942
20	13.590	12.462	11.470	10.594	9.818	9.129	8.514	7.963	7.469	7.025	6.623	6.259	5.929	5.628	5.353	5.101	4.870	4.657	4.460	4.279	4.110	3.954
21	14.029	12.821	11.764	10.836	10.017	9.292	8.649	8.075	7.562	7.102	6.687	6.312	5.973	5.665	5.384	5.127	4.891	4.675	4.476	4.292	4.121	3.963
22	14.451	13.163	12.042	11.061	10.201	9.442	8.772	8.176	7.645	7.170	6.743	6.359	6.011	5.696	5.410	5.149	4.909	4.690	4.488	4.302	4.130	3.970
23	14.857	13.489	12.303	11.272	10.371	9.580	8.883	8.266	7.718	7.230	6.792	6.399	6.044	5.723	5.432	5.167	4.925	4.703	4.499	4.311	4.137	3.976
24	15.247	13.799	12.550	11.469	10.529	9.707	8.985	8.348	7.784	7.283	6.835	6.434	6.073	5.746	5.451	5.182	4.937	4.713	4.507	4.318	4.143	3.981
25	15.622	14.094	12.783	11.654	10.675	9.823	9.077	8.422	7.843	7.330	6.873	6.464	6.097	5.766	5.467	5.195	4.948	4.721	4.514	4.323	4.147	3.985
26	15.983	14.375	13.003	11.826	10.810	9.929	9.161	8.488	7.896	7.372	6.906	6.491	6.118	5.783	5.480	5.206	4.956	4.728	4.520	4.328	4.151	3.988
27	16.330	14.643	13.211	11.987	10.935	10.027	9.237	8.548	7.943	7.409	6.935	6.514	6.136	5.798	5.492	5.215	4.964	4.734	4.524	4.332	4.154	3.990
28	16.663	14.898	13.406	12.137	11.051	10.116	9.307	8.602	7.984	7.441	6.961	6.534	6.152	5.810	5.502	5.223	4.970	4.739	4.528	4.335	4.157	3.992
29	16.984	15.141	13.591	12.278	11.158	10.198	9.370	8.650	8.022	7.470	6.983	6.551	6.166	5.820	5.510	5.229	4.975	4.743	4.531	4.337	4.159	3.994
30	17.292	15.372	13.765	12.409	11.258	10.274	9.427	8.694	8.055	7.496	7.003	6.566	6.177	5.829	5.517	5.235	4.979	4.746	4.534	4.339	4.160	3.995
40	19.793	17.159	15.046	13.332	11.925	10.757	9.779	8.951	8.244	7.634	7.105	6.642	6.233	5.871	5.548	5.258	4.997	4.760	4.544	4.347	4.166	3.999

Appendix 8C: Income Taxes and the Net Present Value Method

This appendix discusses the impact of income taxes on the net present value method of making capital budgeting decisions. We ignored income taxes throughout the chapter for two reasons. First, many organizations do not pay income taxes. Nonprofit organizations, such as hospitals and charitable foundations, and government agencies are exempt from income taxes. Second, capital budgeting is complex and best absorbed in small doses. Now that we have a solid foundation in the concept of discounting cash flows, we can explore the impact of income taxes on the net present value method.

To keep this discussion within reasonable bounds, we make a number of simplifying assumptions. We assume that a company's taxable income equals its net income for financial reporting purposes and that straight-line depreciation with zero salvage value is used. We also assume that the tax rate is a flat percentage of taxable income and that there are no gains or losses on the sale of noncurrent assets.

LEARNING OBJECTIVE 8–8
Include income taxes in a capital budgeting analysis.

Key Concepts

This appendix takes everything that you have already learned about the net present value method and simply adds one more type of cash flow to the computations—it adds income tax expense as a *cash outflow*. To calculate the amount of income tax expense associated with a capital budgeting project, we'll be using a two-step process. The first step is to calculate the incremental net income earned during each year of the project. The second step is to multiply each year's incremental net income by the tax rate to determine the income tax expense. Each year's income tax expense is then discounted to its present value along with all other cash flows realized over the life of the project.

A capital budgeting project's incremental net income computation *includes* annual revenues minus annual cash operating expenses (including variable expenses and fixed out-of-pocket costs), annual depreciation expense, and any one-time expenses. Notice that *depreciation expense is included in the computation of incremental net income*. Although depreciation expense is a noncash expense, it does impact the computation of taxable income, which in turn affects the cash outflows pertaining to income tax expense. A capital budgeting project's incremental net income computation *does not include* immediate cash outflows in the form of initial investments in equipment, other assets, and installation costs. It also *does not include* investments in working capital, the release of working capital at the end of a project, and the proceeds from selling a noncurrent asset when no gain or loss is realized on the sale. To summarize, the items that should be included and excluded from a capital budgeting project's incremental net income computations are as follows:

Include in the computation of incremental net income:
Annual revenues
Annual cash operating expenses
Annual depreciation expense
One-time expenses

Exclude from the computation of incremental net income:
Initial investments in equipment, other assets, and installation costs
Investment in working capital
Release of working capital at the end of a project
Proceeds from selling noncurrent assets when no gain or loss is realized

Income Taxes and Net Present Value Analysis: An Example

Holland Company owns the mineral rights to land that has a deposit of ore. The company is uncertain if it should purchase equipment and open a mine on the property. After careful study, the company gathered the following data:

Initial investment in equipment	$275,000
Initial investment in working capital	$50,000
Estimated annual sales of ore	$250,000
Estimated annual cash operating expenses	$150,000
Cost of road repairs needed in 3 years	$30,000

The ore in the mine would be exhausted after five years, at which time the mine would be closed and the working capital would be released and redeployed by the company. The equipment has a useful life of five years and a salvage value of zero. The company uses straight-line depreciation for financial reporting and tax purposes. Its after-tax cost of capital is 12% and its tax rate is 30%. To be consistent, when we take the net present value of after-tax cash flows, we use the *after-tax* cost of capital as the discount rate.

Should Holland Company purchase the equipment and open a mine on the property? Exhibit 8C–1 shows a net present value analysis that incorporates the impact of income taxes on this decision. The top portion of the exhibit computes the project's incremental net income for Years 1–5 and the income tax expense for each of those years. The incremental net income computations include the annual sales ($250,000), the annual cash operating expenses ($150,000), the road repairs in Year 3 ($30,000), and the annual depreciation expense of $55,000 ($275,000 ÷ 5 years = $55,000 per year). Each year's incremental net income is multiplied by the tax rate of 30% to determine the income tax expense.

The bottom portion of Exhibit 8C–1 calculates the net present value of the mining project. The cash flows summarized in this portion of the exhibit include the initial outlays for the purchase of equipment ($275,000) and the investment in working capital

EXHIBIT 8C–1

Holland Company: Income Taxes and Net Present Value Analysis

	A	B	C	D	E	F	G
					Year		
1							
2		Now	1	2	3	4	5
3	*Calculate the annual tax expense:*						
4	Sales		$ 250,000	$ 250,000	$ 250,000	$ 250,000	$ 250,000
5	Cash operating expenses		$(150,000)	$(150,000)	$(150,000)	$(150,000)	$(150,000)
6	Road repairs				$ (30,000)		
7	Depreciation expense		$ (55,000)	$ (55,000)	$ (55,000)	$ (55,000)	$ (55,000)
8	Incremental net income		$ 45,000	$ 45,000	$ 15,000	$ 45,000	$ 45,000
9	Tax rate		30%	30%	30%	30%	30%
10	Income tax expense		$ (13,500)	$ (13,500)	$ (4,500)	$ (13,500)	$ (13,500)
11							
12	*Calculate the net present value:*						
13	Purchase of equipment	$(275,000)					
14	Investment in working capital	$ (50,000)					
15	Sales		$ 250,000	$ 250,000	$ 250,000	$ 250,000	$ 250,000
16	Cash operating expenses		$(150,000)	$(150,000)	$(150,000)	$(150,000)	$(150,000)
17	Road repairs				$ (30,000)		
18	Release of working capital						$ 50,000
19	Income tax expense		$ (13,500)	$ (13,500)	$ (4,500)	$ (13,500)	$ (13,500)
20	Total cash flows (a)	$(325,000)	$ 86,500	$ 86,500	$ 65,500	$ 86,500	$ 136,500
21	Discount factor (12%) (b)	1.000	0.893	0.797	0.712	0.636	0.567
22	Present value of cash flows (a) × (b)	$(325,000)	$ 77,245	$ 68,941	$ 46,636	$ 55,014	$ 77,396
23	Net present value (SUM B22:G22)	$ 231					
24							
25	Note: The discount factors come from Exhibit 8B-1 in Appendix 8B.						
26							

Exhibit 8-9   Exhibit 8-10   Exhibit 8-11   Exhibit 8C-1

($50,000), the annual sales ($250,000), the annual cash operating expenses ($150,000), the road repairs in Year 3 ($30,000), the release of working capital in Year 5 ($50,000), and the annual income tax expense. Notice that the amounts of income tax expense shown in cells C19 through G19 come directly from the calculations previously performed in cells C10 through G10. Each year's total cash flows in cells B20 through G20 are multiplied by the appropriate discount factor for 12% to compute their present value. The present values in cells B22 through G22 are combined to determine the project's net present value of $231. Because the net present value is positive, it indicates that Holland Company should proceed with the mining project.

Summary (Appendix 8C)

Unless the organization is tax-exempt, such as a nonprofit school or a governmental body, income taxes should be considered when using net present value analysis to make capital budgeting decisions. Calculating the amount of income tax expense associated with a capital budgeting project is a two-step process. The first step is to calculate the incremental net income earned during each year of the project. The second step is to multiply each year's incremental net income by the tax rate to determine the income tax expense. Each year's income tax expense is then discounted to its present value along with all other cash flows realized over the life of the project.

A capital budgeting project's incremental net income computation includes annual revenues minus annual cash operating expenses, annual depreciation expense, and any one-time expenses. It does not include immediate cash outflows in the form of initial investments in equipment, other assets, and installation costs, as well as investments in working capital, the release of working capital at the end of a project, and the proceeds from selling a noncurrent asset where no gain or loss is realized on the sale.

Mc Graw Hill connect   Appendix 8C Exercises and Problems

Additional student resources are available with Connect.

EXERCISE 8C–1 Income Taxes and Net Present Value Analysis [LO 8–8]
Gaston Company is considering a capital budgeting project that would require a $2,000,000 investment in equipment with a useful life of five years and no salvage value. The company's tax rate is 30% and its after-tax cost of capital is 13%. It uses the straight-line depreciation method for financial reporting and tax purposes. The project would provide net operating income each year for five years as follows:

Sales		$2,800,000
Variable expenses		1,600,000
Contribution margin		1,200,000
Fixed expenses:		
Advertising, salaries, and other fixed out-of-pocket costs	$500,000	
Depreciation	400,000	
Total fixed expenses		900,000
Net operating income		$ 300,000

Required:

Compute the project's net present value.

EXERCISE 8C–2 Income Taxes and Net Present Value Analysis [LO 8–8]

Winthrop Company has an opportunity to manufacture and sell a new product for a five-year period. To pursue this opportunity, the company would need to purchase a piece of equipment for $130,000. The equipment would have a useful life of five years and zero salvage value. It would be depreciated for financial reporting and tax purposes using the straight-line method. After careful study, Winthrop estimated the following annual costs and revenues for the new product:

Annual revenues and costs:	
Sales revenues	$250,000
Variable expenses	$120,000
Fixed out-of-pocket operating costs	$70,000

The company's tax rate is 30% and its after-tax cost of capital is 15%.

Required:

Calculate the net present value of this investment opportunity.

PROBLEM 8C–3 Income Taxes and Net Present Value Analysis [LO 8–8]

Lander Company has an opportunity to pursue a capital budgeting project with a five-year time horizon. After careful study, Lander estimated the following costs and revenues for the project:

Cost of equipment needed	$250,000
Working capital needed	$60,000
Overhaul of the equipment in two years	$18,000
Annual revenues and costs:	
Sales revenues	$350,000
Variable expenses	$180,000
Fixed out-of-pocket operating costs	$80,000

The piece of equipment mentioned above has a useful life of five years and zero salvage value. Lander uses straight-line depreciation for financial reporting and tax purposes. The company's tax rate is 30% and its after-tax cost of capital is 12%. When the project concludes in five years the working capital will be released for investment elsewhere within the company.

Required:

Calculate the net present value of this investment opportunity.

PROBLEM 8C–4 Income Taxes and Net Present Value Analysis [LO 8–8]

Rosman Company has an opportunity to pursue a capital budgeting project with a five-year time horizon. After careful study, Rosman estimated the following costs and revenues for the project:

Cost of new equipment needed	$420,000
Sale of old equipment no longer needed	$80,000
Working capital needed	$65,000
Equipment maintenance in each of Years 3 and 4	$20,000
Annual revenues and costs:	
Sales revenues	$410,000
Variable expenses	$175,000
Fixed out-of-pocket operating costs	$100,000

The new piece of equipment mentioned above has a useful life of five years and zero salvage value. The old piece of equipment mentioned above would be sold at the beginning of the project and there would be no gain or loss realized on its sale. Rosman uses the straight-line depreciation method for financial reporting and tax purposes. The company's tax rate is 30% and its after-tax cost of capital is 12%. When the project concludes in five years the working capital will be released for investment elsewhere within the company.

Required:
Calculate the net present value of this investment opportunity.

PROBLEM 8C–5 Income Taxes and Net Present Value Analysis [LO 8–5, LO 8–8]

Shimano Company has an opportunity to manufacture and sell one of two new products for a five-year period. The company's tax rate is 30% and its after-tax cost of capital is 14%. The cost and revenue estimates for each product are as follows:

	Product A	Product B
Initial investment in equipment	$400,000	$550,000
Initial investment in working capital	$85,000	$60,000
Annual sales	$370,000	$390,000
Annual cash operating expenses	$200,000	$170,000
Cost of repairs needed in three years	$45,000	$70,000

The equipment pertaining to both products has a useful life of five years and no salvage value. The company uses the straight-line depreciation method for financial reporting and tax purposes. At the end of five years, each product's working capital will be released for investment elsewhere within the company.

Required:
1. What is the net present value of each investment opportunity?
2. Which of the two products should the company pursue? Why?

Master Budgeting

Planning for a Crisis—Civil War Trust

The Civil War Trust (CWT) is a private, nonprofit organization with 70,000 members that works to preserve the nation's remaining Civil War battlefields—many of which are threatened by commercial development such as shopping centers, houses, industrial parks, and casinos. To forestall development, the CWT typically purchases the land or development rights to the land. The CWT has saved over 25,000 acres from development, including, for example, 698 acres of battlefield at Gettysburg.

CWT's management team was particularly concerned about the budget proposal for 2009, which was to be presented to the board of directors in the fall of 2008. The CWT is wholly supported by contributions from its members and many of those members had been adversely affected by the ongoing financial crisis that followed the collapse of the subprime mortgage market. Consequently, the funds that would be available for operations in 2009 were particularly difficult to predict. Accordingly, the budget for 2009 contained three variations based on progressively pessimistic economic assumptions. The more pessimistic budgets were called contingent budgets. As 2008 progressed and member contributions declined somewhat from previous levels, CWT switched to the first contingent budget. This contingent budget required a number of actions to reduce costs including a hiring freeze and a salary freeze, but maintained an aggressive program of protecting battlefield acreage through purchases of land and development rights. Fortunately, the CWT did not have to switch to the most pessimistic budget—which would have involved layoffs and other extraordinary cost-saving measures.

Instead of reacting in a panic mode to unfavorable developments, CWT used the budgeting process to carefully plan in advance for a number of possible contingencies. ■

Source: Communications with James Lighthizer, president, and David Duncan, director of membership and development, Civil War Trust; and the CWT website, www.civilwar.org.

BUSINESS FOCUS

LEARNING OBJECTIVES

After studying Chapter 9, you should be able to:

LO 9–1 Understand why organizations budget and the processes they use to create budgets.

LO 9–2 Prepare a sales budget, including a schedule of expected cash collections.

LO 9–3 Prepare a production budget.

LO 9–4 Prepare a direct materials budget, including a schedule of expected cash disbursements for purchases of materials.

LO 9–5 Prepare a direct labor budget.

LO 9–6 Prepare a manufacturing overhead budget.

LO 9–7 Prepare a selling and administrative expense budget.

LO 9–8 Prepare a cash budget.

LO 9–9 Prepare a budgeted income statement.

LO 9–10 Prepare a budgeted balance sheet.

In this chapter, we describe how organizations strive to achieve their financial goals by preparing a number of budgets that together form an integrated business plan known as the *master budget*. The master budget is an essential management tool that communicates management's plans throughout the organization, allocates resources, and coordinates activities.

What Is a Budget?

A **budget** is a detailed plan for the future that is usually expressed in formal quantitative terms. Individuals sometimes create household budgets that balance their income and expenditures for food, clothing, housing, and so on while providing for some savings. Once the budget is established, actual spending is compared to the budget to make sure the plan is being followed. Companies use budgets in a similar way, although the amount of work and underlying details far exceed a personal budget.

> **LEARNING OBJECTIVE 9–1**
> Understand why organizations budget and the processes they use to create budgets.

Budgets are used for two distinct purposes—*planning* and *control*. **Planning** involves developing goals and preparing various budgets to achieve those goals. **Control** involves gathering feedback to ensure that the plan is being properly executed or modified as circumstances change. To be effective, a good budgeting system must provide for both planning and control. Good planning without effective control is a waste of time and effort.

Advantages of Budgeting

Organizations realize many benefits from budgeting, including:

1. Budgets *communicate* management's plans throughout the organization.
2. Budgets force managers to *think about* and *plan* for the future. In the absence of the necessity to prepare a budget, many managers would spend all of their time dealing with day-to-day emergencies.
3. The budgeting process provides a means of *allocating resources* to those parts of the organization where they can be used most effectively.
4. The budgeting process can uncover potential *bottlenecks* before they occur.
5. Budgets *coordinate* the activities of the entire organization by *integrating* the plans of its various parts. Budgeting helps to ensure that everyone in the organization is pulling in the same direction.
6. Budgets define goals and objectives that can serve as *benchmarks* for evaluating subsequent performance.

IN BUSINESS

EXECUTING STRATEGY WITH BUDGETS

Robert DeMartini, the CEO of New Balance, set a goal of tripling his company's revenues to $3 billion in four years. He tripled the company's annual advertising budget and doubled its consumer research budget in an effort to attract more young customers. These decisions represented a strategic shift for New Balance, which usually spends less than $20 million per year in advertising compared to competitors such as Nike and Adidas, which annually invest $184 million and $80 million, respectively.

One reason companies prepare budgets is to allocate resources across departments in a manner that supports strategic priorities. DeMartini used the budget to send a clear signal that his marketing department was expected to play a huge role in achieving the company's revenue growth targets. As time progresses, he will compare the company's actual revenue growth from young consumers to the marketing department's expenditures to see if his strategy is working or requires adjustment.

Source: Stephanie Kang, "New Balance Steps up Marketing Drive," *The Wall Street Journal*, March 21, 2008, p. B3.

Responsibility Accounting

Most of what we say in this chapter and in the next three chapters is concerned with *responsibility accounting*. The basic idea underlying? **responsibility accounting** is that a manager should be held responsible for those items—and *only* those items—that the manager can actually control to a significant extent. Each line item (i.e., revenue or cost) in the budget is the responsibility of a manager who is held responsible for subsequent deviations between budgeted goals and actual results. In effect, responsibility accounting *personalizes* accounting information by holding individuals responsible for revenues and costs. This concept is central to any effective planning and control system. Someone must be held responsible for each cost or else no one will be responsible and the cost will inevitably grow out of control.

What happens if actual results do not measure up to the budgeted goals? The manager is not necessarily penalized. However, the manager should take the initiative to understand the sources of significant favorable or unfavorable discrepancies, should take steps to correct unfavorable discrepancies and to exploit and replicate favorable discrepancies, and should be prepared to explain discrepancies and the steps taken to correct or exploit them to higher management. The point of an effective responsibility accounting system is to make sure that nothing "falls through the cracks," that the organization reacts quickly and appropriately to deviations from its plans, and that the organization learns from the feedback it gets by comparing budgeted goals to actual results. The point is *not* to penalize individuals for missing targets.

IN BUSINESS

SMALL BUSINESSES ARE CUTTING THE NUMBER OF EMPLOYEES

Costume Specialists had to decrease its workforce by 20% when the economy tanked. However, when sales began to surge the company did not budget for a workforce expansion because it had learned to function more efficiently with fewer employees. Many other small businesses have also "tightened their budgeting belts" by choosing to operate with fewer employees. In some cases, these companies have used methods such as cross-training their employees to improve efficiency. However, in other cases they are using contract workers instead of hiring full-time employees to avoid the cost of providing full-time employees with fringe benefits such as health insurance.

Source: Sarah E. Needleman, "Entrepreneurs Prefer to Keep Staffs Lean," *The Wall Street Journal*, March 2, 2010, p. B5.

Choosing a Budget Period

Operating budgets ordinarily cover a one-year period corresponding to the company's fiscal year. Many companies divide their budget year into four quarters. The first quarter is then subdivided into months, and monthly budgets are developed. The last three quarters may be carried in the budget as quarterly totals only. As the year progresses, the figures for the second quarter are broken down into monthly amounts, then the third-quarter figures are broken down, and so forth. This approach has the advantage of requiring periodic review and reappraisal of budget data throughout the year.

Continuous or *perpetual budgets* are sometimes used. A **continuous** or **perpetual budget** is a 12-month budget that rolls forward one month (or quarter) as the current month (or quarter) is completed. In other words, one month (or quarter) is added to the end of the budget as each month (or quarter) comes to a close. This approach keeps managers focused at least one year ahead so that they do not become too narrowly focused on short-term results.

In this chapter, we will look at one-year operating budgets. However, using basically the same techniques, operating budgets can be prepared for periods that extend over many years. It may be difficult to accurately forecast sales and other data much beyond a year, but even rough estimates can be invaluable in uncovering potential problems and opportunities that would otherwise be overlooked.

The Self–Imposed Budget

The success of a budget program is largely determined by the way a budget is developed. Oftentimes, the budget is imposed from above, with little participation by lower-level managers. However, in the most successful budget programs, managers actively participate in preparing their own budgets. Imposing expectations from above and then penalizing employees who do not meet those expectations will generate resentment rather than cooperation and commitment. In fact, many managers believe that being empowered to create their own *self-imposed budgets* is the most effective method of budget preparation. A **self-imposed** or **participative budget** is a budget that is prepared with the full cooperation and participation of managers at all levels.

Self-imposed budgets have a number of advantages:

1. Individuals at all levels of the organization are recognized as members of the team whose views and judgments are valued by top management.
2. Budget estimates prepared by front-line managers are often more accurate and reliable than estimates prepared by top managers who have less intimate knowledge of markets and day-to-day operations.
3. Motivation is generally higher when individuals participate in setting their own goals than when the goals are imposed from above. Self-imposed budgets create commitment.
4. A manager who is not able to meet a budget that has been imposed from above can always say that the budget was unrealistic and impossible to meet. With a self-imposed budget, this claim cannot be made.

Self-imposed budgeting has two important limitations. First, lower-level managers may make suboptimal budgeting recommendations if they lack the broad strategic perspective possessed by top managers. Second, self-imposed budgeting may allow lower-level managers to create too much *budgetary slack*. Because the manager who creates the budget will be held accountable for actual results that deviate from the budget, the manager will have a natural tendency to submit a budget that is easy to attain (i.e., the manager will build slack into the budget). For this reason, budgets prepared by lower-level managers should be scrutinized by higher levels of management. Questionable items should be discussed and modified as appropriate. Without such a review, self-imposed budgets may fail to support the organization's strategy or may be too slack, resulting in suboptimal performance.

Unfortunately, many companies do not use self-imposed budgeting. Instead, top managers often initiate the budgeting process by issuing profit targets. Lower-level managers are directed to prepare budgets that meet those targets. The difficulty is that the targets set by top managers may be unrealistically high or may allow too much slack. If the targets are too high and employees know they are unrealistic, motivation will suffer. If the targets allow too much slack, waste will occur. Unfortunately, top managers are often not in a position to know whether the targets are appropriate. Admittedly, a self-imposed budgeting system may lack sufficient strategic direction and lower-level managers may be tempted to build slack into their budgets. Nevertheless, because of the motivational advantages of self-imposed budgets, top managers should be cautious about imposing inflexible targets from above.

Human Factors in Budgeting

The success of a budget program also depends on whether top management uses the budget to pressure or blame employees. Using budgets to blame employees breeds hostility, tension, and mistrust rather than cooperation and productivity. Unfortunately, the budget is too often used as a pressure device and excessive emphasis is placed on "meeting the budget" under all circumstances. Rather than being used as a weapon, the budget should be used as a positive instrument to assist in establishing goals, measuring operating results, and isolating areas that need attention.

The budgeting process is also influenced by the fact that bonuses are often based on meeting and exceeding budgets. Typically, no bonus is paid unless the budget is met. The bonus often increases when the budget target is exceeded, but the bonus is usually capped out at some level. For obvious reasons, managers who have such a bonus plan or whose performance is evaluated based on meeting budget targets usually prefer to be evaluated based on highly achievable budgets. Moreover, highly achievable budgets may help build a manager's confidence and generate greater commitment to the budget while also reducing the likelihood that a manager will engage in undesirable behavior at the end of budgetary periods to secure bonus compensation. So, while some experts argue that budget targets should be very challenging and should require managers to stretch to meet their goals, in practice, most companies set their budget targets at "highly achievable" levels.

The Master Budget: An Overview

The **master budget** consists of a number of separate but interdependent budgets that formally lay out the company's sales, production, and financial goals. The master budget culminates in a cash budget, a budgeted income statement, and a budgeted balance sheet. Exhibit 9–1 provides an overview of the various parts of the master budget and how they are related.

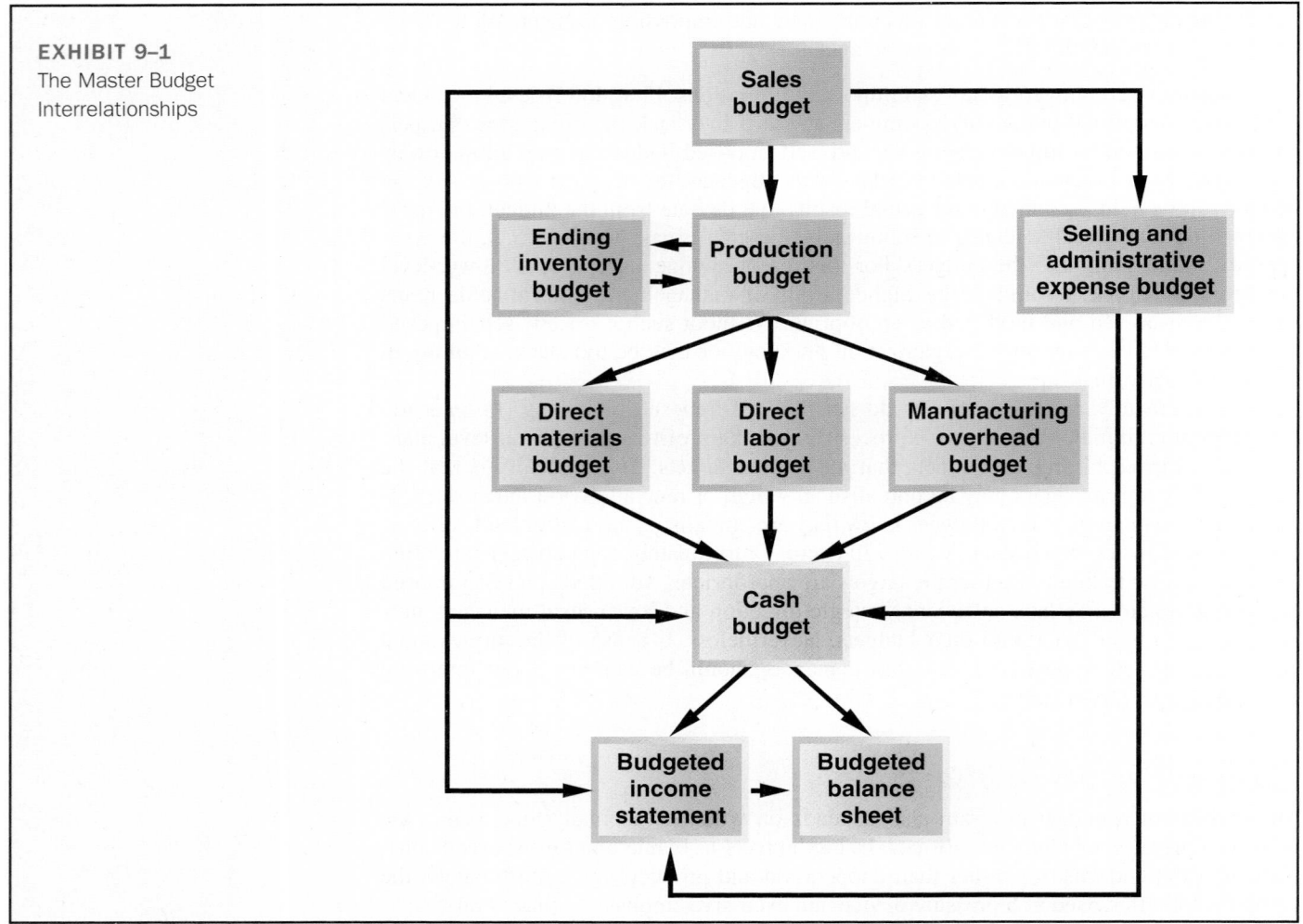

EXHIBIT 9–1
The Master Budget
Interrelationships

The first step in the budgeting process is the preparation of the **sales budget**, which is a detailed schedule showing the expected sales for the budget period. An accurate sales budget is the key to the entire budgeting process. As illustrated in Exhibit 9–1, all other parts of the master budget depend on the sales budget. If the sales budget is inaccurate, the rest of the budget will be inaccurate. The sales budget is based on the company's sales forecast, which may require the use of sophisticated mathematical models and statistical tools that are beyond the scope of this course.

The sales budget influences the variable portion of the selling and administrative expense budget and it feeds into the production budget, which defines how many units need to be produced during the budget period. The production budget in turn is used to determine the direct materials, direct labor, and manufacturing overhead budgets. Once a company has prepared these three manufacturing cost budgets, it can prepare the ending finished goods inventory budget.

The master budget concludes with the preparation of a cash budget, income statement, and balance sheet. Information from the sales budget, selling and administrative expense budget, and the manufacturing cost budgets all influence the preparation of the *cash budget*. A **cash budget** is a detailed plan showing how cash resources will be acquired and used. The budgeted income statement provides an estimate of net income for the budget period and it relies on information from the sales budget, ending finished goods inventory budget, selling and administrative expense budget, and the cash budget. The final schedule of the master budget is the balance sheet, which estimates a company's assets, liabilities, and stockholders' equity at the end of a budget period.

Seeing the Big Picture

The 10 schedules contained in a master budget can be overwhelming; therefore, it is important to see the big picture in two respects. First, a master budget for a manufacturing company is designed to answer 10 key questions as follows:

1. How much sales revenue will we earn?
2. How much cash will we collect from customers?
3. How much raw material will we need to purchase?
4. How much manufacturing cost (including direct materials, direct labor, and manufacturing overhead) will we incur?
5. How much cash will we pay to our suppliers and our direct laborers, and how much will we pay for manufacturing overhead resources?
6. What is the total cost that will be transferred from finished goods inventory to cost of goods sold?
7. How much selling and administrative expense will we incur and how much cash will we pay related to those expenses?
8. How much money will we borrow from or repay to lenders—including interest?
9. How much net operating income will we earn?
10. What will our balance sheet look like at the end of the budget period?

Second, it is important to understand that many of the schedules in a master budget hinge on a variety of estimates and assumptions that managers must make when preparing those schedules. Exhibit 9–2 summarizes the questions that underlie these estimates and assumptions for seven of the schedules included in a master budget. As you study the forthcoming budget schedules, keep these two "big picture" insights in mind—that the budget is designed to answer 10 key questions and that it is based on various estimates and assumptions—because they will help you understand *why* and *how* a master budget is created.

EXHIBIT 9–2
Estimates and Assumptions for a Master Budget

Sales budget:
1. What are the budgeted unit sales?
2. What is the budgeted selling price per unit?
3. What percentage of accounts receivable will be collected in the current and subsequent periods?

Production budget:
1. What percentage of next period's unit sales needs to be maintained in ending finished goods inventory?

Direct materials budget:
1. How many units of raw material are needed to make one unit of finished goods?
2. What is the budgeted cost for one unit of raw material?
3. What percentage of next period's production needs should be maintained in ending raw materials inventory?
4. What percentage of raw material purchases will be paid in the current and subsequent periods?

Direct labor budget:
1. How many direct labor-hours are required per unit of finished goods?
2. What is the budgeted direct labor wage rate per hour?

Manufacturing overhead budget:
1. What is the budgeted variable overhead cost per unit of the allocation base?
2. What is the total budgeted fixed overhead cost per period?
3. What is the budgeted depreciation expense on factory assets per period?

Selling and administrative expense budget:
1. What is the budgeted variable selling and administrative expense per unit sold?
2. What is the total budgeted fixed selling and administrative expense per period?
3. What is the budgeted depreciation expense on non-factory assets per period?

Cash budget:
1. What is the budgeted minimum cash balance?
2. What are our estimated expenditures for noncurrent asset purchases and dividends?
3. What is the estimated interest rate on borrowed funds?

Preparing the Master Budget

MANAGERIAL ACCOUNTING IN ACTION

The Issue

Tom Wills is the majority stockholder and chief executive officer of Hampton Freeze, Inc., a company he started in 2015. The company makes premium popsicles using only natural ingredients and featuring exotic flavors such as tangy tangerine and minty mango. The company's business is highly seasonal, with most of the sales occurring in spring and summer.

In 2016, the company's second year of operations, a major cash crunch in the first and second quarters almost forced the company into bankruptcy. In spite of this cash crunch, 2016 turned out to be a very successful year in terms of both cash flow and net income. Partly as a result of that harrowing experience, Tom decided toward the end of 2016 to hire a professional financial manager. Tom interviewed several promising candidates for the job and settled on Larry Giano, who had considerable experience in the packaged foods industry. In the job interview, Tom questioned Larry about the steps he would take to prevent a recurrence of the 2016 cash crunch:

Tom: As I mentioned earlier, we are going to end 2016 with a very nice profit. What you may not know is that we had some very big financial problems this year.
Larry: Let me guess. You ran out of cash sometime in the first or second quarter.
Tom: How did you know?

Larry: Most of your sales are in the second and third quarter, right?

Tom: Sure, everyone wants to buy popsicles in the spring and summer, but nobody wants them when the weather turns cold.

Larry: So you don't have many sales in the first quarter?

Tom: Right.

Larry: And in the second quarter, which is the spring, you are producing like crazy to fill orders?

Tom: Sure.

Larry: Do your customers, the grocery stores, pay you the day you make your deliveries?

Tom: Are you kidding? Of course not.

Larry: So in the first quarter, you don't have many sales. In the second quarter, you are producing like crazy, which eats up cash, but you aren't paid by your customers until long after you have paid your employees and suppliers. No wonder you had a cash problem. I see this pattern all the time in food processing because of the seasonality of the business.

Tom: So what can we do about it?

Larry: The first step is to predict the magnitude of the problem before it occurs. If we can predict early in the year what the cash shortfall is going to be, we can go to the bank and arrange for credit before we really need it. Bankers tend to be leery of panicky people who show up begging for emergency loans. They are much more likely to make the loan if you look like you are in control of the situation.

Tom: How can we predict the cash shortfall?

Larry: You can put together a cash budget. In fact, while you're at it, you might as well do a master budget. You'll find it well worth the effort because we can use a master budget to estimate the financial statement implications of numerous "what-if" questions. For example, with the click of a mouse we can answer questions such as: What-if unit sales are 10% less than our original forecast, what will be the impact on profits? Or, what if we increase our selling price by 15% and unit sales drop by 5%, what will be the impact on profits?

Tom: That sounds great Larry! Not only do we need a cash budget, but I would love to have a master budget that could quickly answer the types of "what-if" questions that you just described. As far as I'm concerned, the sooner you get started, the better.

With the full backing of Tom Wills, Larry Giano set out to create a master budget for the company for the year 2017. In his planning for the budgeting process, Larry drew up the following list of documents that would be a part of the master budget:

1. A sales budget, including a schedule of expected cash collections.
2. A production budget (a merchandise purchases budget would be used in a merchandising company).
3. A direct materials budget, including a schedule of expected cash disbursements for purchases of materials.
4. A direct labor budget.
5. A manufacturing overhead budget.
6. An ending finished goods inventory budget.
7. A selling and administrative expense budget.
8. A cash budget.
9. A budgeted income statement.
10. A budgeted balance sheet.

Larry felt it was important to have everyone's cooperation in the budgeting process, so he asked Tom to call a companywide meeting to explain the budgeting process. At the meeting there was initially some grumbling, but Tom was able to convince nearly everyone of the necessity for planning and getting better control over spending. It helped that the cash crisis earlier in the year was still fresh in everyone's minds. As much as some people disliked the idea of budgets, they liked their jobs more.

In the months that followed, Larry worked closely with all of the managers involved in the master budget, gathering data from them and making sure that they understood and fully supported the parts of the master budget that would affect them.

The interdependent documents that Larry Giano prepared for Hampton Freeze are Schedules 1 through 10 of the company's master budget. In this section, we will study these schedules as well as the beginning balance sheet and the budgeting assumptions that Larry included in his master budget to help answer the types of "what-if" questions that he discussed with Tom Wills.

The Beginning Balance Sheet

Exhibit 9–3 shows the first tab included in Larry's Microsoft Excel master budget file. It contains Hampton Freeze's beginning balance sheet as of December 31, 2016. Larry included this balance sheet in his master budget file so that he could link some of this data to subsequent schedules. For example, as you'll eventually see, he used cell references within Excel to link the beginning accounts receivable balance of $90,000 to the schedule of expected cash collections. He also used cell references to link the beginning cash balance of $42,500 to the cash budget.

The Budgeting Assumptions

Exhibit 9–4 shows the second tab included in Larry's master budget file. It is labeled Budgeting Assumptions and it contains all of Hampton Freeze's answers to the questions summarized in Exhibit 9–2. The data included in Exhibit 9–4 summarize the estimates and assumptions that provide the foundation for Hampton Freeze's entire master budget,

EXHIBIT 9–3

Hampton Freeze: The Beginning Balance Sheet

	A	B	C
1	**Hampton Freeze, Inc.**		
2	**Balance Sheet**		
3	**December 31, 2016**		
4			
5	**Assets**		
6	Current assets:		
7	Cash	$ 42,500	
8	Accounts receivable	90,000	
9	Raw materials inventory (21,000 pounds)	4,200	
10	Finished goods inventory (2,000 cases)	26,000	
11	Total current assets		$162,700
12	Plant and equipment:		
13	Land	80,000	
14	Buildings and equipment	700,000	
15	Accumulated depreciation	(292,000)	
16	Plant and equipment, net		488,000
17	Total assets		$650,700
18			
19	**Liabilities and Stockholders' Equity**		
20	Current liabilities:		
21	Accounts payable		$ 25,800
22	Stockholders' equity:		
23	Common stock	$ 175,000	
24	Retained earnings	449,900	
25	Total stockholders' equity		624,900
26	Total liabilities and stockholders' equity		$650,700
27			

EXHIBIT 9–4
Hampton Freeze: Budgeting Assumptions

	A	B	C	D	E	F
1	Hampton Freeze, Inc.					
2	Budgeting Assumptions					
3	For the Year Ended December 31, 2017					
4						
5		All 4 Quarters		Quarter		
6	Sales Budget		1	2	3	4
7	Budgeted sales in cases		10,000	30,000	40,000	20,000
8	Selling price per case	$ 20.00				
9	Percentage of sales collected in the quarter of sale	70%				
10	Percentage of sales collected in the quarter after sale	30%				
11						
12	Production Budget					
13	Percentage of next quarter's sales in ending finished goods inventory	20%				
14						
15	Direct Materials Budget					
16	Pounds of sugar per case	15				
17	Cost per pound of sugar	$ 0.20				
18	Percentage of next quarter's production needs in ending inventory	10%				
19	Percentage of purchases paid in the quarter purchased	50%				
20	Percentage of purchases paid in the quarter after purchase	50%				
21						
22	Direct Labor Budget					
23	Direct labor-hours required per case	0.40				
24	Direct labor cost per hour	$ 15.00				
25						
26	Manufacturing Overhead Budget					
27	Variable manufacturing overhead per direct labor-hour	$ 4.00				
28	Fixed manufacturing overhead per quarter	$ 60,600				
29	Depreciation per quarter	$ 15,000				
30						
31						
32	Selling and Administrative Expense Budget					
33	Variable selling and administrative expense per case	$ 1.80				
34	Fixed selling and administrative expense per quarter:					
35	Advertising	$ 20,000				
36	Executive salaries	$ 55,000				
37	Insurance	$ 10,000				
38	Property tax	$ 4,000				
39	Depreciation	$ 10,000				
40						
41	Cash Budget					
42	Minimum cash balance	$ 30,000				
43	Equipment purchases		$ 50,000	$ 40,000	$ 20,000	$ 20,000
44	Dividends	$ 8,000				
45	Simple interest rate per quarter	3%				
46						

Beginning Balance Sheet | **Budgeting Assumptions** | Schedule 1 | Schedule 2 | Sche

*For simplicity, we assume that all quarterly estimates, except quarterly unit sales and equipment purchases, will be the same for all four quarters.

so it is important to familiarize yourself with this information now. Beginning with the estimates underlying the sales budget, Exhibit 9–4 shows that Hampton Freeze's budgeted quarterly unit sales are 10,000, 30,000, 40,000, and 20,000 cases. Its budgeted selling price is $20 per case. The company expects to collect 70% of its credit sales in the quarter of sale, and the remaining 30% of credit sales will be collected in the quarter after sale.

Exhibit 9–4 also shows that the production budget is based on the assumption that Hampton Freeze will maintain ending finished goods inventory equal to 20% of the next quarter's unit sales. In terms of the company's only direct material, high fructose sugar, it budgets 15 pounds of sugar per case of popsicles at a cost of $0.20 per pound.[1] It expects to maintain ending raw materials inventory equal to 10% of the raw materials needed to

---

[1] While popsicle manufacturing is likely to involve other raw materials, such as popsicle sticks and packaging materials, for simplicity, we have limited our scope to high fructose sugar.

satisfy the following quarter's production. In addition, the company plans to pay for 50% of its material purchases within the month of purchase and the remaining 50% in the following month.

Continuing with a summary of Exhibit 9–4, the two key assumptions underlying the direct labor budget are that 0.40 direct labor-hours are required per case of popsicles and the direct labor cost per hour is $15. The manufacturing overhead budget is based on three underlying assumptions—the variable overhead cost per direct labor-hour is $4.00, the total fixed overhead per quarter is $60,600, and the quarterly depreciation on factory assets is $15,000. Exhibit 9–4 also shows that the budgeted variable selling and administrative expense per case of popsicles is $1.80 and the fixed selling and administrative expenses per quarter include advertising ($20,000), executive salaries ($55,000), insurance ($10,000), property tax ($4,000), and depreciation expense ($10,000). The remaining budget assumptions depicted in Exhibit 9–4 pertain to the cash budget. The company expects to maintain a minimum cash balance each quarter of $30,000; it plans to make quarterly equipment purchases of $50,000, $40,000, $20,000, and $20,000;[2] it plans to pay quarterly dividends of $8,000; and it expects to pay simple interest on borrowed money of 3% per quarter.

Before reading further, it is important to understand why Larry created the Budgeting Assumptions tab shown in Exhibit 9–4. He did it because it simplifies the process of using a master budget to answer "what-if" questions. For example, assume that Larry wanted to answer the question: What-if we increase the selling price per unit by $2 and expect sales to drop by 1,000 units per quarter, what would be the impact on profits? With a properly constructed Budgeting Assumptions tab, Larry would only need to make a few adjustments to the data within this tab and the formulas embedded in each of the budget schedules would automatically update the projected financial results. This is much simpler than attempting to adjust data inputs within each of the master budget schedules.

The Sales Budget

LEARNING OBJECTIVE 9–2
Prepare a sales budget, including a schedule of expected cash collections.

Schedule 1 contains Hampton Freeze's sales budget for 2017. As you study this schedule, keep in mind that all of its numbers are derived from cell references to the Budgeting Assumptions tab and formulas—none of the numbers appearing in the schedule were actually keyed into their respective cells. Furthermore, it bears emphasizing that all remaining schedules in the master budget are prepared in the same fashion—they rely almost exclusively on cell references and formulas.

For the year, Hampton Freeze expects to sell 100,000 cases of popsicles at a price of $20 per case for total budgeted sales of $2,000,000. The budgeted unit sales for each quarter (10,000, 30,000, 40,000, and 20,000) come from cells C7 through F7 in the Budgeting Assumptions tab shown in Exhibit 9–4, and the selling price per case ($20.00) comes from cell B8 in the Budgeting Assumptions tab. Schedule 1 also shows that the company's expected cash collections for 2017 are $1,970,000. The accounts receivable balance of $90,000 that is collected in the first quarter comes from cell B8 of the beginning balance sheet shown in Exhibit 9–3. All other cash collections rely on the estimated cash collection percentages from cells B9 and B10 of the Budgeting Assumptions tab. For example, Schedule 1 shows that the budgeted sales for the first quarter equal $200,000. In the first quarter, Hampton Freeze expects to collect 70% of this amount, or $140,000. In the second quarter, the company expects to collect the remaining 30% of this amount, or $60,000.

The Production Budget

LEARNING OBJECTIVE 9–3
Prepare a production budget.

The production budget is prepared after the sales budget. The **production budget** lists the number of units that must be produced to satisfy sales needs and to provide for the desired ending finished goods inventory. Production needs can be determined as follows:

---

[2] For simplicity, we assume that depreciation on these newly acquired assets is included in the quarterly depreciation estimates included in the Budgeting Assumptions tab.

SCHEDULE 1

	A	B	C	D	E	F
1		Hampton Freeze, Inc.				
2		Sales Budget				
3		For the Year Ended December 31, 2017				
4						
5				Quarter		
6		1	2	3	4	Year
7	Budgeted unit sales (in cases)	10,000	30,000	40,000	20,000	100,000
8	Selling price per unit	$ 20.00	$ 20.00	$ 20.00	$ 20.00	$ 20.00
9	Total sales	$200,000	$600,000	$800,000	$400,000	$2,000,000
10						
11		70%	30%			
12		Schedule of Expected Cash Collections				
13	Beginning accounts receivable[1]	$ 90,000				$ 90,000
14	First-quarter sales[2]	140,000	$ 60,000			200,000
15	Second-quarter sales[3]		420,000	$180,000		600,000
16	Third-quarter sales[4]			560,000	$240,000	800,000
17	Fourth-quarter sales[5]	-	-	-	280,000	280,000
18	Total cash collections[6]	$230,000	$480,000	$740,000	$520,000	$1,970,000

Budgeting Assumptions | Schedule 1 | Schedule 2 | Schedule 3 | Sc

[1]Cash collections from last year's fourth-quarter sales. See the beginning balance sheet in Exhibit 9–3.
[2]$200,000 × 70%; $200,000 × 30%.
[3]$600,000 × 70%; $600,000 × 30%.
[4]$800,000 × 70%; $800,000 × 30%.
[5]$400,000 × 70%.
[6]Uncollected fourth-quarter sales ($120,000) appear as accounts receivable on the company's end-of-year budgeted balance sheet (see Schedule 10).

Budgeted unit sales	XXXX
Add desired units of ending finished goods inventory	XXXX
Total needs.	XXXX
Less units of beginning finished goods inventory	XXXX
Required production in units	XXXX

Note the production requirements are influenced by the desired level of the ending finished goods inventory. Inventories should be carefully planned. Excessive inventories tie up funds and create storage problems. Insufficient inventories can lead to lost sales or last-minute, high-cost production efforts.

Schedule 2 contains the production budget for Hampton Freeze. The budgeted sales data come from cells B7 through E7 of the sales budget. The desired ending finished goods inventory for the first quarter of 6,000 cases is computed by multiplying budgeted sales from the second quarter (30,000 cases) by the desired ending finished goods inventory percentage (20%) shown in cell B13 of the Budgeting Assumptions tab. The total needs for the first quarter (16,000 cases) are determined by adding together the budgeted sales of 10,000 cases for the quarter and the desired ending inventory of 6,000 cases. As discussed above, the ending inventory is intended to provide some cushion in the event that problems develop in production or sales increase unexpectedly. Because the company already has 2,000 cases in beginning finished goods inventory (as shown in the beginning balance sheet in Exhibit 9–3), only 14,000 cases need to be produced in the first quarter.

SCHEDULE 2

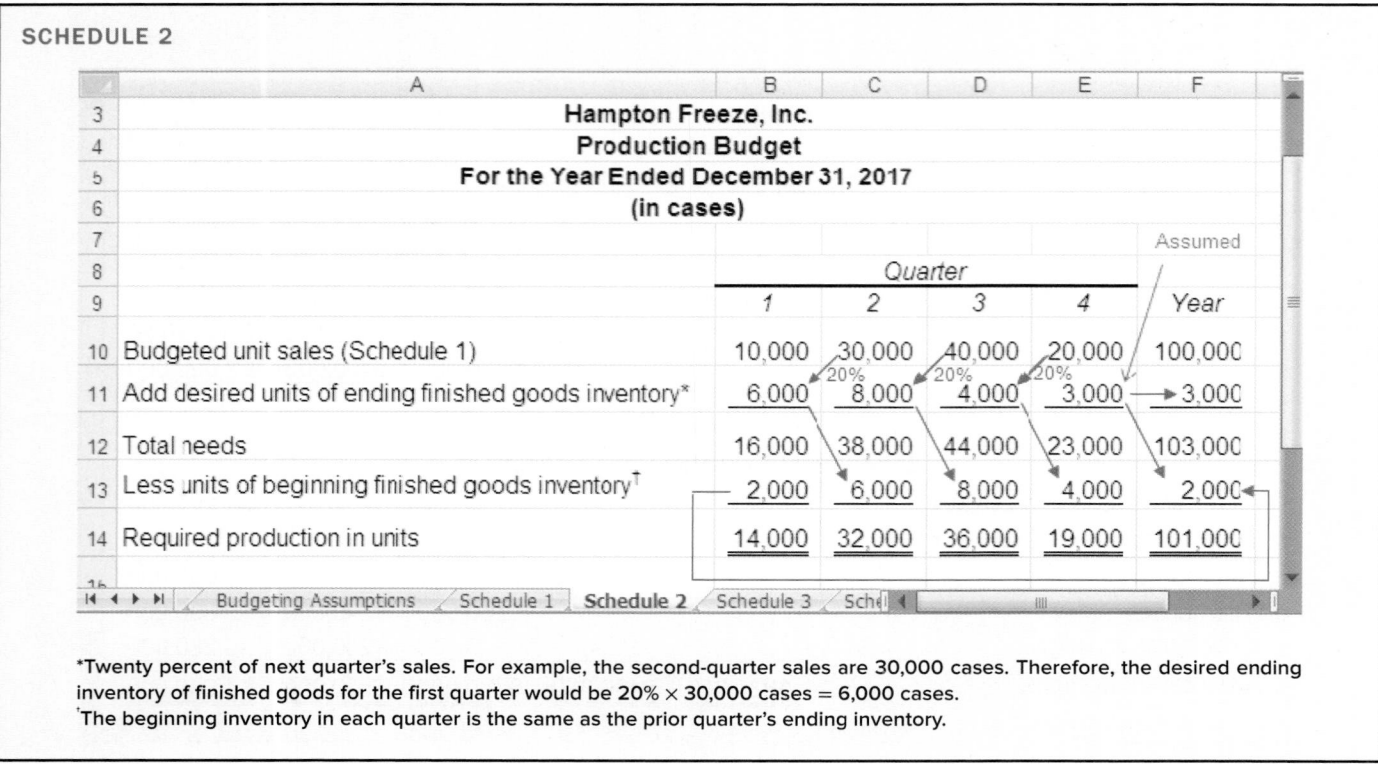

	1	2	3	4	Assumed Year
		Quarter			
Budgeted unit sales (Schedule 1)	10,000	30,000	40,000	20,000	100,000
Add desired units of ending finished goods inventory*	6,000	8,000	4,000	3,000	3,000
Total needs	16,000	38,000	44,000	23,000	103,000
Less units of beginning finished goods inventory†	2,000	6,000	8,000	4,000	2,000
Required production in units	14,000	32,000	36,000	19,000	101,000

Budgeting Assumptions | Schedule 1 | **Schedule 2** | Schedule 3 | Sche...

*Twenty percent of next quarter's sales. For example, the second-quarter sales are 30,000 cases. Therefore, the desired ending inventory of finished goods for the first quarter would be 20% × 30,000 cases = 6,000 cases.
†The beginning inventory in each quarter is the same as the prior quarter's ending inventory.

Pay particular attention to the Year column to the right of the production budget in Schedule 2. In some cases (e.g., budgeted sales, total needs, and required production), the amount listed for the year is the sum of the quarterly amounts for the item. In other cases, (e.g., desired units of ending finished goods inventory and units of beginning finished goods inventory), the amount listed for the year is not simply the sum of the quarterly amounts. From the standpoint of the entire year, the beginning finished goods inventory is the same as the beginning finished goods inventory for the first quarter—it is *not* the sum of the beginning finished goods inventories for all four quarters. Similarly, from the standpoint of the entire year, the ending finished goods inventory, which Larry Giano assumed to be 3,000 units, is the same as the ending finished goods inventory for the fourth quarter—it is *not* the sum of the ending finished goods inventories for all four quarters. It is important to pay attention to such distinctions in all schedules that follow.

Inventory Purchases—Merchandising Company

Hampton Freeze prepares a production budget because it is a *manufacturing* company. If it were a *merchandising* company, instead it would prepare a **merchandise purchases budget** showing the amount of goods to be purchased from suppliers during the period. The format of the merchandise purchases budget is shown below:

Budgeted cost of goods sold.	XXXX
Add desired ending merchandise inventory.	XXXX
Total needs.	XXXX
Less beginning merchandise inventory	XXXX
Required purchases	XXXX

A merchandising company would prepare a merchandise purchases budget, such as the one above, for each item carried in stock. The merchandise purchases budget can be expressed in dollars (as shown above) or in units. The top line of a merchandise purchases budget based on units would say Budgeted unit sales instead of Budgeted cost of goods sold.

A merchandise purchases budget is usually accompanied by a schedule of expected cash disbursements for merchandise purchases. The format of this schedule mirrors the approach used for the schedule of expected cash disbursements for purchases of materials that is illustrated at the bottom of Schedule 3.

The Direct Materials Budget

A *direct materials budget* is prepared after the production requirements have been computed. The **direct materials budget** details the raw materials that must be purchased to fulfill the production budget and to provide for adequate inventories. The required purchases of raw materials are computed as follows:

LEARNING OBJECTIVE 9–4
Prepare a direct materials budget, including a schedule of expected cash disbursements for purchases of materials.

Required production in units of finished goods	XXXX
Units of raw materials needed per unit of finished goods	XXXX
Units of raw materials needed to meet production	XXXX
Add desired units of ending raw materials inventory	XXXX
Total units of raw materials needed	XXXX
Less units of beginning raw materials inventory	XXXX
Units of raw materials to be purchased	XXXX
Unit cost of raw materials	XXXX
Cost of raw materials to be purchased	XXXX

Schedule 3 contains the direct materials budget for Hampton Freeze. The first line of this budget contains the required production for each quarter, which is taken directly from cells B14 through E14 of the production budget (Schedule 2). The second line of the direct materials budget recognizes that 15 pounds of sugar (see cell B16 from the Budgeting Assumptions tab) are required to make one case of popsicles. The third line of the budget presents the raw materials needed to meet production. For example, in the first quarter, the required production of 14,000 cases is multiplied by 15 pounds to equal 210,000 pounds of sugar needed to meet production. The fourth line shows the desired units of ending raw materials inventory. For the first quarter this amount is computed by multiplying the raw materials needed to meet production in the second quarter of 480,000 pounds by the desired ending inventory percentage of 10% as shown in cell B18 of the Budgeting Assumptions tab. The desired units of ending raw materials inventory of 48,000 pounds is added to 210,000 pounds to provide the total units of raw materials needed of 258,000 pounds. However, because the company already has 21,000 pounds of sugar in beginning inventory (as shown in cell A9 in the beginning balance sheet in Exhibit 9–3), only 237,000 pounds of sugar need to be purchased in the first quarter. Because the budgeted cost of raw materials per pound is $0.20 (see cell B17 from the Budgeting Assumptions tab), the cost of raw material to be purchased in the first quarter is $47,400. For the entire year, the company plans to purchase $303,300 of raw materials.

Schedule 3 also shows that the company's expected cash disbursements for material purchases for 2017 are $301,200. The accounts payable balance of $25,800 that is paid in the first quarter comes from cell C21 of the beginning balance sheet shown in Exhibit 9–3. All other cash disbursement computations rely on the estimated cash payment percentages (both of which are 50%) from cells B19 and B20 of the Budgeting Assumptions tab. For example, Schedule 3 shows that the budgeted raw material purchases for the first quarter equal $47,400. In the first quarter, Hampton Freeze expects to pay 50% of this amount, or $23,700. In the second quarter, the company expects to pay the remaining 50% of this amount, or $23,700.

SCHEDULE 3

A	B	C	D	E	F
	Hampton Freeze, Inc.				
	Direct Materials Budget				
	For the Year Ended December 31, 2017				
					Assumed
			Quarter		
	1	2	3	4	Year
9 Required production in cases (Schedule 2)	14,000	32,000	36,000	19,000	101,000
10 Units of raw materials needed per case	15	15	15	15	15
11 Units of raw materials needed to meet production	210,000	480,000	540,000	285,000	1,515,000
12 Add desired units of ending raw materials inventory[1]	48,000	54,000	28,500	22,500	22,500
13 Total units of raw materials needed	258,000	534,000	568,500	307,500	1,537,500
14 Less units of beginning raw materials inventory	21,000	48,000	54,000	28,500	21,000
15 Units of raw materials to be purchased	237,000	486,000	514,500	279,000	1,516,500
16 Cost of raw materials per pound	$ 0.20	$ 0.20	$ 0.20	$ 0.20	$ 0.20
17 Cost of raw materials to be purchased	$47,400	$97,200	$102,900	$55,800	$ 303,300
19		50%	50%		
20	**Schedule of Expected Cash Disbursements for Purchases of Materials**				
22 Beginning accounts payable[2]	$25,800				$ 25,800
23 First-quarter purchases[3]	23,700	$23,700			47,400
24 Second-quarter purchases[4]		48,600	$ 48,600		97,200
25 Third-quarter purchases[5]			51,450	$51,450	102,900
26 Fourth-quarter purchases[6]				27,900	27,900
27 Total cash disbursements for materials	$49,500	$72,300	$100,050	$79,350	$ 301,200

Schedule 3 / Schedule 4 / Schedule 5 / Schedule 6 / Schedule 7 / S

[1]Ten percent of the next quarter's production needs. For example, the second-quarter production needs are 480,000 pounds. Therefore, the desired ending inventory for the first quarter would be 10% × 480,000 pounds = 48,000 pounds.

[2]Cash payments for last year's fourth-quarter purchases. See the beginning-of-year balance sheet in Exhibit 9–3 on page 394.

[3]$47,400 × 50%; $47,400 × 50%.

[4]$97,200 × 50%; $97,200 × 50%.

[5]$102,900 × 50%; $102,900 × 50%.

[6]$55,800 × 50%. Unpaid fourth-quarter purchases ($27,900) appear as accounts payable on the company's end-of-year budgeted balance sheet (see Schedule 10).

The Direct Labor Budget

The **direct labor budget** shows the direct labor-hours required to satisfy the production budget. By knowing in advance how much labor time will be needed throughout the budget year, the company can develop plans to adjust the labor force as the situation requires. Companies that neglect the budgeting process run the risk of facing labor shortages or having to hire and lay off workers at awkward times. Erratic labor policies lead to insecurity, low morale, and inefficiency.

The direct labor budget for Hampton Freeze is shown in Schedule 4. The first line in the direct labor budget consists of the required production for each quarter, which is taken directly from cells B14 through E14 of the production budget (Schedule 2). The direct labor requirement for each quarter is computed by multiplying the number of units to be produced in each quarter by the 0.40 direct labor-hours required to make one unit (see cell B23 from the Budgeting Assumptions tab). For example, 14,000 cases are to be produced in the first quarter and each case requires 0.40 direct labor-hours, so a total of 5,600 direct labor-hours (14,000 cases × 0.40 direct labor-hours per case) will be required in the first quarter. The direct labor requirements are then translated into budgeted direct labor costs. How this is done will depend on the company's labor policy. In Schedule 4, Hampton Freeze has assumed that the direct labor force will be adjusted as the work requirements change from quarter to quarter. In that case, the direct labor cost is computed by simply multiplying the direct labor-hour requirements by the direct labor rate of $15 per hour

	A	B	C	D	E	F	G		SCHEDULE 4
1		Hampton Freeze, Inc.							
2		Direct Labor Budget							
3		For the Year Ended December 31, 2017							
4									
5				Quarter					
6		1	2	3	4	Year			
7	Required production in cases (Schedule 2)	14,000	32,000	36,000	19,000	101,000			
8	Direct labor-hours per case	0.40	0.40	0.40	0.40	0.40			
9	Total direct labor-hours needed	5,600	12,800	14,400	7,600	40,400			
10	Direct labor cost per hour	$ 15.00	$ 15.00	$ 15.00	$ 15.00	$ 15.00			
11	Total direct labor cost	$ 84,000	$ 192,000	$ 216,000	$ 114,000	$ 606,000			
12									

Schedule 1 / Schedule 2 / Schedule 3 / **Schedule 4** / Schedule 5 / Schedule

*This schedule assumes that the direct labor workforce will be fully adjusted to the total direct labor-hours needed each quarter.

(see cell B24 from the Budgeting Assumptions tab). For example, the direct labor cost in the first quarter is $84,000 (5,600 direct labor-hours × $15 per direct labor-hour).

However, many companies have employment policies or contracts that prevent them from laying off and rehiring workers as needed. Suppose, for example, that Hampton Freeze has 25 workers who are classified as direct labor, but each of them is guaranteed at least 480 hours of pay each quarter at a rate of $15 per hour. In that case, the minimum direct labor cost for a quarter would be computed as follows:

25 workers × 480 hours per worker × $15 per hour = $180,000

Note that in this case the direct costs shown in the first and fourth quarters of Schedule 4 would have to be increased to $180,000.

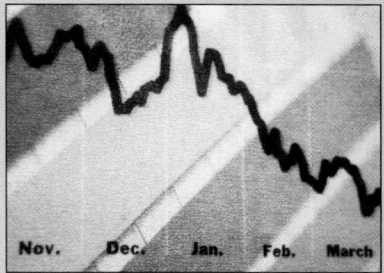

MANAGING LABOR COSTS IN A DIFFICULT ECONOMY

When the economy sours, many companies choose to lay off employees. While this tactic lowers costs in the short run, it also lowers the morale and productivity of retained employees, sacrifices the institutional knowledge possessed by terminated employees, and increases future recruiting and training costs. Hypertherm Inc. has not fired a permanent employee since its founding in 1968, instead responding to economic hardship by eliminating overtime, cutting temporary staff, delaying capital investments, shifting cross-trained employees to new job responsibilities, and implementing a four-day work week. Hypertherm's employees regularly share their process improvement ideas with the company because they know if they eliminate non-value-added portions of their job responsibilities the company will redeploy them rather than eliminate non-value-added labor costs by firing them.

Source: Cari Tuna, "Some Firms Cut Costs Without Resorting to Layoffs," *The Wall Street Journal,* December 15, 2008, p. B4.

© Ryan McVay/Photodisc/Getty Images, RF

The Manufacturing Overhead Budget

LEARNING OBJECTIVE 9–6
Prepare a manufacturing overhead budget.

The **manufacturing overhead budget** lists all costs of production other than direct materials and direct labor. Schedule 5 shows the manufacturing overhead budget for Hampton Freeze. At Hampton Freeze, manufacturing overhead is separated into variable and fixed components. As shown in the Budgeting Assumptions tab (Exhibit 9–4), the variable component is $4 per direct labor-hour and the fixed component is $60,600 per quarter. Because the variable component of manufacturing overhead depends on direct labor, the first line in the manufacturing overhead budget consists of the budgeted direct labor-hours from cells B9 through E9 of the direct labor budget (Schedule 4). The budgeted direct labor-hours in each quarter are multiplied by the variable rate to determine the variable component of manufacturing overhead. For example, the variable manufacturing

SCHEDULE 5

	A	B	C	D	E	F
1	Hampton Freeze, Inc.					
2	Manufacturing Overhead Budget					
3	For the Year Ended December 31, 2017					
4						
5				Quarter		
6		1	2	3	4	Year
7	Budgeted direct labor-hours (Schedule 4)	5,600	12,800	14,400	7,600	40,400
8	Variable manufacturing overhead rate	$ 4.00	$ 4.00	$ 4.00	$ 4.00	$ 4.00
9	Variable manufacturing overhead	$ 22,400	$ 51,200	$ 57,600	$ 30,400	$ 161,600
10	Fixed manufacturing overhead	60,600	60,600	60,600	60,600	242,400
11	Total manufacturing overhead	83,000	111,800	118,200	91,000	404,000
12	Less depreciation	15,000	15,000	15,000	15,000	60,000
13	Cash disbursements for manufacturing overhead	$ 68,000	$ 96,800	$ 103,200	$ 76,000	$ 344,000
14						
15	Total manufacturing overhead (a)					$ 404,000
16	Budgeted direct labor-hours (b)					40,400
17	Predetermined overhead rate for the year (a)÷(b)					$10.00
18						

Schedule 3 / Schedule 4 / **Schedule 5** / Schedule 6 / Schedule 7 / Schedule 8

overhead for the first quarter is $22,400 (5,600 direct labor-hours × $4.00 per direct labor-hour). This is added to the fixed manufacturing overhead for the quarter to determine the total manufacturing overhead for the quarter of $83,000 ($22,400 + $60,600).

A few words about fixed costs and the budgeting process are in order. In most cases, fixed costs are the costs of supplying capacity to make products, process purchase orders, handle customer calls, and so on. The amount of capacity that will be required depends on the expected level of activity for the period. If the expected level of activity is greater than the company's current capacity, then fixed costs may have to be increased. Or, if the expected level is appreciably below the company's current capacity, then it may be desirable to decrease fixed costs if possible. However, once the level of the fixed costs has been determined in the budget, the costs really are fixed. The time to adjust fixed costs is during the budgeting process. An activity-based costing system can help to determine the appropriate level of fixed costs at budget time by answering questions like, "How many clerks will we need to process the anticipated number of purchase orders next year?" For simplicity, all of the budgeting examples in this book assume that the appropriate levels of fixed costs have already been determined.

The last line of Schedule 5 for Hampton Freeze shows the budgeted cash disbursements for manufacturing overhead. Because some of the overhead costs are not cash outflows, the total budgeted manufacturing overhead costs must be adjusted to determine the cash disbursements for manufacturing overhead. At Hampton Freeze, the only significant noncash manufacturing overhead cost is depreciation, which is $15,000 per quarter (see cell B29 in the Budgeting Assumptions tab). These noncash depreciation charges are deducted from the total budgeted manufacturing overhead to determine the expected cash disbursements. Hampton Freeze pays all overhead costs involving cash disbursements in the quarter incurred. Note that the company's predetermined overhead rate for the year is $10 per direct labor-hour, which is determined by dividing the total budgeted manufacturing overhead for the year by the total budgeted direct labor-hours for the year.

The Ending Finished Goods Inventory Budget

After completing Schedules 1–5, Larry Giano had all of the data he needed to compute the unit product cost for the units produced during the budget year. This computation was needed for two reasons: first, to help determine cost of goods sold on the budgeted income statement; and second, to value ending inventories on the budgeted balance

SCHEDULE 6

	A	B	C	D	E	F	G	H	I
1			Hampton Freeze, Inc.						
2			Ending Finished Goods Inventory Budget						
3			(absorption costing basis)						
4			For the Year Ended December 31, 2017						
5									
6	*Item*		*Quantity*			*Cost*		*Total*	
7	Production cost per case:								
8	Direct materials	15.00	pounds		$ 0.20	per pound		$ 3.00	
9	Direct labor	0.40	hours		$ 15.00	per hour		6.00	
10	Manufacturing overhead	0.40	hours		$ 10.00	per hour		4.00	
11	Unit product cost							$ 13.00	
12									
13	Budgeted finished goods inventory:								
14	Ending finished goods inventory in cases (Schedule 2)							3,000	
15	Unit product cost (see above)							$ 13.00	
16	Ending finished goods inventory in dollars							$ 39,000	
17									

Schedule 3 / Schedule 4 / Schedule 5 / **Schedule 6** / Sch

sheet. The cost of unsold units is computed on the **ending finished goods inventory budget**.[3]

Larry Giano considered using variable costing to prepare Hampton Freeze's budget statements, but he decided to use absorption costing instead because the bank would very likely require absorption costing. He also knew that it would be easy to convert the absorption costing financial statements to a variable costing basis later. At this point, the primary concern was to determine what financing, if any, would be required in 2017 and then to arrange for that financing from the bank.

The unit product cost computations are shown in Schedule 6. For Hampton Freeze, the absorption costing unit product cost is $13 per case of popsicles—consisting of $3 of direct materials, $6 of direct labor, and $4 of manufacturing overhead. The manufacturing overhead is applied to units of product at the rate of $10 per direct labor-hour. The budgeted carrying cost of the ending inventory is $39,000.

The Selling and Administrative Expense Budget

The **selling and administrative expense budget** lists the budgeted expenses for areas other than manufacturing. In large organizations, this budget would be a compilation of many smaller, individual budgets submitted by department heads and other persons responsible for selling and administrative expenses. For example, the marketing manager would submit a budget detailing the advertising expenses for each budget period.

Schedule 7 contains the selling and administrative expense budget for Hampton Freeze. Like the manufacturing overhead budget, the selling and administrative expense budget is divided into variable and fixed cost components. Consequently, budgeted sales in cases for each quarter are entered at the top of the schedule. These data are taken from

LEARNING OBJECTIVE 9–7
Prepare a selling and administrative expense budget.

---

[3] For simplicity, the beginning balance sheet and the ending finished goods inventory budget both report a unit product cost of $13. For purposes of answering "what-if" questions, this schedule would assume a FIFO inventory flow. In other words, the ending inventory would consist solely of units that are produced during the budget year.

SCHEDULE 7

	A	B	C	D	E	F
		Hampton Freeze, Inc.				
		Selling and Administrative Expense Budget				
		For the Year Ended December 31, 2017				
4						
5				Quarter		
6		1	2	3	4	Year
7	Budgeted units sales (Schedule 1)	10,000	30,000	40,000	20,000	100,000
8	Variable selling and administrative expense per case	$ 1.80	$ 1.80	$ 1.80	$ 1.80	$ 1.80
9	Variable selling and administrative expense	$ 18,000	$ 54,000	$ 72,000	$ 36,000	$180,000
10	Fixed selling and administrative expenses:					
11	Advertising	20,000	20,000	20,000	20,000	80,000
12	Executive salaries	55,000	55,000	55,000	55,000	220,000
13	Insurance	10,000	10,000	10,000	10,000	40,000
14	Property taxes	4,000	4,000	4,000	4,000	16,000
15	Depreciation	10,000	10,000	10,000	10,000	40,000
16	Total fixed selling and administrative expenses	99,000	99,000	99,000	99,000	396,000
17	Total selling and administrative expenses	117,000	153,000	171,000	135,000	576,000
18	Less depreciation	10,000	10,000	10,000	10,000	40,000
19	Cash disbursements for selling and administrative expenses	$107,000	$143,000	$161,000	$125,000	$536,000

Schedule 5 / Schedule 6 / **Schedule 7** / Schedule 8 / Schedule 9 / Schedule 10

cells B7 through E7 of the sales budget (Schedule 1). The budgeted variable selling and administrative expenses are determined by multiplying the budgeted cases sold by the variable selling and administrative expense of $1.80 per case (see cell B33 from the Budgeting Assumptions tab). For example, the budgeted variable selling and administrative expense for the first quarter is $18,000 (10,000 cases × $1.80 per case). The fixed selling and administrative expenses of $99,000 per quarter (see cells B35 through B39 from the Budgeting Assumptions tab) are then added to the variable selling and administrative expenses to arrive at the total budgeted selling and administrative expenses. Finally, to determine the cash disbursements for selling and administrative items, the total budgeted selling and administrative expense is adjusted by subtracting any noncash selling and administrative expenses (in this case, just depreciation).[4]

The Cash Budget

The cash budget is composed of four major sections:

1. The receipts section.
2. The disbursements section.
3. The cash excess or deficiency section.
4. The financing section.

The receipts section lists all of the cash inflows, except from financing, expected during the budget period. Generally, the major source of receipts is from sales. The disbursements section summarizes all cash payments that are planned for the budget period. These payments include raw materials purchases, direct labor payments, manufacturing overhead costs, and so on, as contained in their respective budgets. In addition, other cash disbursements such as equipment purchases and dividends are listed.

---

[4] Other adjustments might need to be made for differences between cash flows on the one hand and revenues and expenses on the other hand. For example, if property taxes are paid twice a year in installments of $8,000 each, the expense for property tax would have to be "backed out" of the total budgeted selling and administrative expenses and the cash installment payments added to the appropriate quarters to determine the cash disbursements. Similar adjustments might also need to be made in the manufacturing overhead budget. We generally ignore these complications in this chapter.

MISMATCHED CASH FLOWS—CLIMBING THE HILLS AND VALLEYS

The Washington Trails Association (WTA) is a private, nonprofit organization primarily concerned with protecting and maintaining hiking trails in the state of Washington. Some 2,000 WTA volunteer workers donate more than 80,000 hours per year maintaining trails in rugged landscapes on federal, state, and private lands. The organization is supported by membership dues, voluntary contributions, grants, and some contract work for government.

The organization's income and expenses are erratic—although somewhat predictable—over the course of the year as shown in the chart below. Expenses tend to be highest in the spring and summer when most of the trail maintenance work is done. However, income spikes in December well after the expenses have been incurred. With cash outflows running ahead of cash inflows for much of the year, it is very important for the WTA to carefully plan its cash budget and to maintain adequate cash reserves to be able to pay its bills.

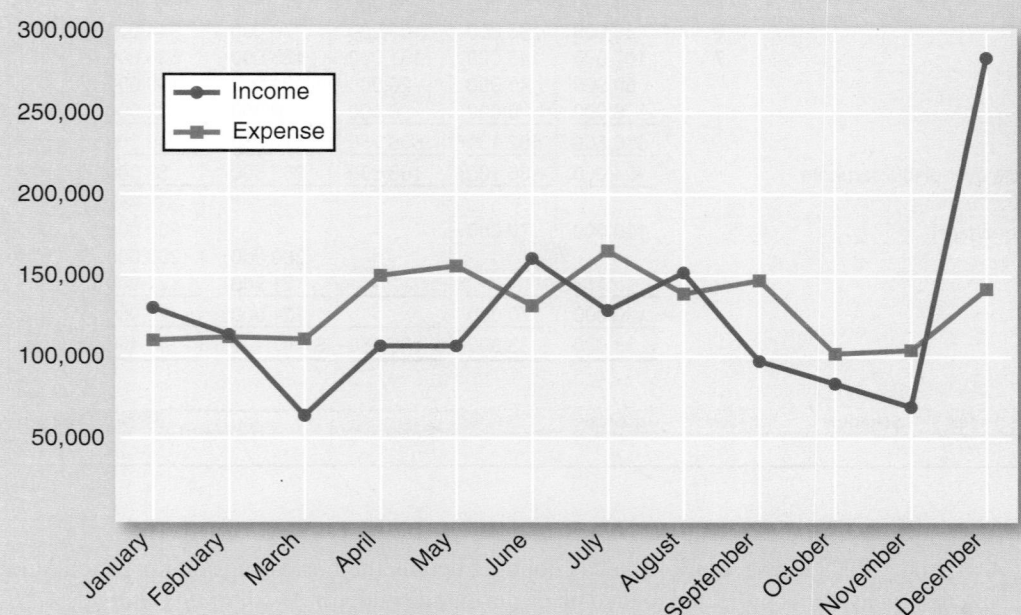

Note: Total income and total expense are approximately equal over the course of the year.

Sources: Conversation with Elizabeth Lunney, President of the Washington Trails Association; WTA documents; and the WTA website **www.wta.org**.

The cash excess or deficiency section is computed as follows:

Beginning cash balance	XXXX
Add cash receipts	XXXX
Total cash available	XXXX
Less cash disbursements	XXXX
Excess (deficiency) of cash available over disbursements	XXXX

If a cash deficiency exists during any budget period or if there is a cash excess during any budget period that is less than the minimum required cash balance, the company will need to borrow money. Conversely, if there is a cash excess during any budget period that is greater than the minimum required cash balance, the company can invest the excess funds or repay principal and interest to lenders.

SCHEDULE 8

	A	B	C	D	E	F	G	H
1			Hampton Freeze, Inc.					
2			Cash Budget					
3			For the Year Ended December 31, 2017					
4								
5					Quarter			
6		Schedule	1	2	3	4	Year	
7	Beginning cash balance		$ 42,500	$ 36,000	$ 33,900	$ 165,650	$ 42,500	
8	Add cash receipts:							
9	Collections from customers	1	230,000	480,000	740,000	520,000	1,970,000	
10	Total cash available		272,500	516,000	773,900	685,650	2,012,500	
11	Less cash disbursements:							
12	Direct materials	3	49,500	72,300	100,050	79,350	301,200	
13	Direct labor	4	84,000	192,000	216,000	114,000	606,000	
14	Manufacturing overhead	5	68,000	96,800	103,200	76,000	344,000	
15	Selling and administrative	7	107,000	143,000	161,000	125,000	536,000	
16	Equipment purchases		50,000	40,000	20,000	20,000	130,000	
17	Dividends		8,000	8,000	8,000	8,000	32,000	
18	Total cash disbursements		366,500	552,100	608,250	422,350	1,949,200	
19	Excess (deficiency) of cash available over disbursements		(94,000)	(36,100)	165,650	263,300	63,300	
20	Financing:							
21	Borrowings (at the beginnings of quarters)		130,000	70,000	-	-	200,000	
22	Repayments (at end of the year)		-	-	-	(200,000)	(200,000)	
23	Interest		-	-	-	(21,900)	(21,900)	
24	Total financing		130,000	70,000	-	(221,900)	(21,900)	
25	Ending cash balance		$ 36,000	$ 33,900	$ 165,650	$ 41,400	$ 41,400	
26								
27								

Schedule 5 / Schedule 6 / Schedule 7 / **Schedule 8** / Schedule 9 / Schedule 10

The financing section of the cash budget details the borrowings and principal and interest repayments projected to take place during the budget period. *In this chapter, we'll always assume that all borrowings take place on the first day of the borrowing period and all repayments take place on the last day of the final period included in the cash budget.* To calculate borrowings and interest payments, you'll need to pay attention to the company's desired minimum cash balance and to the terms of the company's loan agreement with the bank. For example, Hampton Freeze's desired minimum cash balance is $30,000 (see cell B42 in the Budgeting Assumptions tab). Furthermore, *we are going to assume that Hampton Freeze's loan agreement stipulates that it must borrow money in increments of $10,000* and that it must pay simple interest of 3% per quarter (as shown in cell B43 of the Budgeting Assumptions tab).[5]

The cash balances at both the beginning and end of the year may be adequate even though a serious cash deficit occurs at some point during the year. Consequently, the cash budget should be broken down into time periods that are short enough to capture major fluctuations in cash balances. While a monthly cash budget is most common, some organizations budget cash on a weekly or even daily basis. At Hampton Freeze, Larry Giano has prepared a quarterly cash budget that can be further refined as necessary. This budget appears in Schedule 8.[6]

---

[5] We use simple interest rather than compound interest throughout the chapter for simplicity.

[6] The format for the statement of cash flows, which is discussed in a later chapter, may also be used for the cash budget.

The beginning cash balance in the first quarter of $42,500 agrees with cell B7 of the beginning balance sheet in Exhibit 9–3. Each quarter's collections from customers come from cells B18 through E18 of the schedule of expected cash collections in Schedule 1. Each quarter's beginning cash balance plus the collections from customers equals the total cash available. For example, in the first quarter, the beginning cash balance of $42,500 plus the collections from customers of $230,000 equals the total cash available of $272,500.

The disbursements section of the cash budget includes six types of cash disbursements. Each quarter's cash disbursements for direct materials come from cells B27 through E27 of the schedule of expected cash disbursements for materials (see Schedule 3). The quarterly cash payments for direct labor were calculated in cells B11 through E11 of the direct labor budget (see Schedule 4), whereas the quarterly cash payments related to manufacturing overhead were calculated in cells B13 through E13 of the manufacturing overhead budget (see Schedule 5). The quarterly cash payments for selling and administrative expenses come from cells B19 through E19 of the selling and administrative expense budget (see Schedule 7). So putting it all together, in the first quarter, the cash disbursements for direct materials ($49,500), direct labor ($84,000), manufacturing overhead ($68,000), and selling and administrative expenses ($107,000), plus equipment purchases of $50,000 and a dividend of $8,000 (see cells C43 and B44 from the Budgeting Assumptions tab) equals the total cash disbursements of $366,500.

Each quarter's total cash available minus its total disbursements equals the excess (deficiency) of cash available over disbursements. For example, in the first quarter the total cash available of $272,500 minus the total disbursements of $366,500 results in a cash deficiency of $94,000. The excess or deficiency of cash directly influences whether Hampton Freeze will need to borrow money as shown in the Financing section of the cash budget.

The first row in the financing section of the cash budget relates to projected borrowings. In any period where a company's excess of cash available over disbursements is greater than its desired minimum cash balance, the company will not need to borrow money during that period. In the case of Hampton Freeze, the company wants to maintain a minimum cash balance of $30,000; therefore, it will not need to borrow money in any quarter where its excess of cash available over disbursements is greater than $30,000. However, in the first quarter of 2017 Hampton Freeze estimates that it will have a cash deficiency of $94,000; consequently, the company's minimum required borrowings at the beginning of the first quarter would be computed as follows:

Required Borrowings at the Beginning of the First Quarter

Desired ending cash balance	$ 30,000
Plus deficiency of cash available over disbursements	94,000
Minimum required borrowings	$124,000

Recall that the bank requires that loans be made in increments of $10,000. Because Hampton Freeze needs to borrow at least $124,000, it will have to borrow $130,000.

In the second quarter of 2017 Hampton Freeze estimates that it will have another cash deficiency of $36,100; therefore, the company's minimum required borrowings at the beginning of the second quarter would be computed as follows:

Required Borrowings at the Beginning of the Second Quarter

Desired ending cash balance	$30,000
Plus deficiency of cash available over disbursements	36,100
Minimum required borrowings	$66,100

Again, recall that the bank requires that loans be made in increments of $10,000. Because Hampton Freeze needs to borrow at least $66,100 at the beginning of the second quarter, the company will have to borrow $70,000 from the bank.

In the third and fourth quarters, Hampton Freeze has an excess of cash available over disbursements that is greater than $30,000, so it will not need to borrow money in these two quarters. Notice that in the third quarter Hampton Freeze has excess cash of $165,650, yet the cash budget does not include any principal or interest repayments during this quarter. This occurs because in this chapter, we always assume that the company will, as far as it is able, repay the loan plus accumulated interest on the *last day of the final period* included in the cash budget. Because Hampton Freeze has excess cash of $263,300 in the fourth quarter, on the last day of the fourth quarter, it would be able to repay the $200,000 that it borrowed from the lender plus $21,900 of interest computed as follows:

Interest on the $130,000 borrowed at the beginning of the first quarter:	
$130,000 × 0.01 per month × 12 months*	$15,600
Interest on the $70,000 borrowed at the beginning of the second quarter:	
$70,000 × 0.01 per month × 9 months*	6,300
Total interest accrued to the end of the fourth quarter.................	$21,900

* Simple, rather than compounded, interest is assumed for simplicity.

The ending cash balance for each period is computed by taking the excess (deficiency) of cash available over disbursements plus the total financing. For example, in the first quarter, Hampton Freeze's cash deficiency of $(94,000) plus its total financing of $130,000 equals its ending cash balance of $36,000. The ending cash balance for each quarter then becomes the beginning cash balance for the next quarter. Also notice that the amounts under the Year column in the cash budget are not always the sum of the amounts for the four quarters. In particular, the beginning cash balance for the year is the same as the beginning cash balance for the first quarter and the ending cash balance for the year is the same as the ending cash balance for the fourth quarter.

NEW INSPECTIONS PINCH CASH FLOWS

Herald Metal and Plastic Works is a Chinese toy manufacturer that produces Star Wars action figures and G.I. Joes for Hasbro Inc. in the United States. The company used to ship its toys to America immediately after they rolled off the production line. However, this changed when American consumers discovered that some Chinese companies were using poisonous lead-based paint in their manufacturing processes. The Chinese government now requires toy manufacturers to store finished goods in warehouses for anywhere from three weeks to two months until its inspectors certify them for export.

Herald Metal and Plastic Works borrows money from lenders to buy raw materials and pay laborers to make its toys. The company is struggling to repay its loans because the government's inspection process delays cash receipts from customers.

Source: Chi-Chu Tschang, "Bottlenecks in Toyland," *BusinessWeek*, October 15, 2007, p. 52.

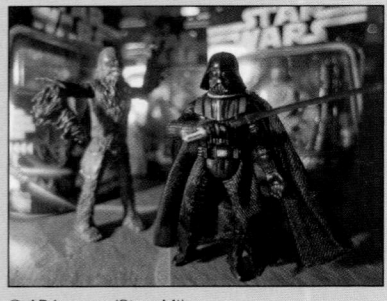

© AP Images/Stew Milne

The Budgeted Income Statement

LEARNING OBJECTIVE 9–9
Prepare a budgeted income statement.

Schedule 9 contains the budgeted income statement for Hampton Freeze. All of the revenues and expenses shown on the budgeted income statement come from the data in the beginning balance sheet and the data developed in Schedules 1–8. The sales of $2,000,000 come from cell F9 of the sales budget (Schedule 1). The cost of goods sold of $1,300,000 is computed in two steps. First, cost of goods sold includes the 2,000 units of finished goods inventory from the beginning balance sheet, which have a total cost of $26,000 (see Exhibit 9–3). Second, it includes 98,000 units produced and sold in 2014 multiplied by $13 per unit (see Schedule 6), for a total of $1,274,000. Combining these

SCHEDULE 9

	A	B	C
	Hampton Freeze, Inc.		
1			
2	**Budgeted Income Statement**		
3	**For the Year Ended December 31, 2017**		
4			
5		*Schedules*	
6	Sales	1	$ 2,000,000
7	Cost of goods sold	1, 6	1,300,000
8	Gross margin		700,000
9	Selling and administrative expenses	7	576,000
10	Net operating Income		124,000
11	Interest expense	8	21,900
12	Net Income		$ 102,100
13			

Schedule 8 | **Schedule 9** | Schedule 10

two steps, the total cost of the 100,000 units sold (see Schedule 1) is $1,300,000 ($26,000 + $1,274,000).[7] The selling and administrative expenses of $576,000 come from cell F17 of the selling and administrative expenses budget (Schedule 7). Finally, the interest expense of $21,900 comes from cell G23 of the cash budget (Schedule 8).

The budgeted income statement is one of the key schedules in the budget process. It shows the company's planned profit and serves as a benchmark against which subsequent company performance can be measured. Because Larry Giano created a Budgeting Assumptions tab in his Excel file and linked all of his budget schedules together using properly constructed Excel formulas, he can make changes to his underlying budgeting assumptions and instantly see the impact of the change on all of the schedules and on net income. For example, if Larry wanted to estimate the profit impact if fourth quarter sales are 18,000 cases instead of 20,000 cases, he would simply change the 20,000 cases shown in cell F7 of his Budgeting Assumptions worksheet to 18,000 cases. The revised net income of $87,045 would instantly appear in cell C12 of the budgeted income statement.

The Budgeted Balance Sheet

The budgeted balance sheet is developed using data from the balance sheet from the beginning of the budget period (see Exhibit 9–3) and data contained in the various schedules. Hampton Freeze's budgeted balance sheet accompanied by explanations of how the numbers were derived is presented in Schedule 10.

After completing the master budget, Larry Giano took the documents to Tom Wills, chief executive officer of Hampton Freeze, for his review.

Larry: Here's the budget. Overall, the income is excellent, and the net cash flow for the entire year is positive.

Tom: Yes, but I see on this cash budget that we have the same problem with negative cash flows in the first and second quarters that we had last year.

Larry: That's true. I don't see any way around that problem. However, there is no doubt in my mind that if you take this budget to the bank today, they'll approve an open line of credit that will allow you to borrow enough money to make it through the first two quarters without any problem.

LEARNING OBJECTIVE 9–10
Prepare a budgeted balance sheet.

MANAGERIAL ACCOUNTING IN ACTION
The Wrap-Up

---

[7] This explanation assumes a FIFO inventory flow assumption.

SCHEDULE 10

	A	B	C	D	E
1	Hampton Freeze, Inc.				
2	Budgeted Balance Sheet				
3	December 31, 2017				
4					
5	*Assets*				
6	Current assets:				
7	Cash	$ 41,400	(a)		
8	Accounts receivable	120,000	(b)		
9	Raw materials inventory	4,500	(c)		
10	Finished goods inventory	39,000	(d)		
11	Total current assets			$ 204,900	
12	Plant and equipment:				
13	Land	80,000	(e)		
14	Buildings and equipment	830,000	(f)		
15	Accumulated depreciation	(392,000)	(g)		
16	Plant and equipment, net			518,000	
17	Total assets			$ 722,900	
18					
19	*Liabilities and Stockholders' Equity*				
20	Current liabilities:				
21	Accounts payable (raw materials)			$ 27,900	(h)
22	Stockholders' equity:				
23	Common stock, no par	$ 175,000	(i)		
24	Retained earnings	520,000	(j)		
25	Total stockholders' equity			695,000	
26	Total liabilities and stockholders' equity			$ 722,900	
27					

Schedule 8   Schedule 9   **Schedule 10**

Explanations of December 31, 2017, balance sheet figures:
(a) From cell G25 of the cash budget (Schedule 8).
(b) Thirty percent of fourth-quarter sales, from Schedule 1 ($400,000 × 30% = $120,000).
(c) From the direct materials budget (Schedule 3). Cell E12 multiplied by cell E16. In other words, 22,500 pounds × $0.20 per pound = $4,500.
(d) From cell H16 of the ending finished goods inventory budget (Schedule 6).
(e) From cell B13 of the beginning balance sheet (Exhibit 9–3).
(f) Cell B14 of the beginning balance sheet (Exhibit 9–3) plus cell G16 from the cash budget (Schedule 8). In other words, $700,000 + $130,000 = $830,000.
(g) The beginning balance of $292,000 (from cell B15 of the beginning balance sheet in Exhibit 9–3) plus the depreciation of $60,000 included in cell F12 of the manufacturing overhead budget (Schedule 5) plus depreciation expense of $40,000 included in cell F18 in the selling and administrative expense budget (Schedule 8). In other words, $292,000 + $60,000 + $40,000 = $392,000.
(h) One-half of fourth-quarter raw materials purchases, from Schedule 3.
(i) From cell B23 of the beginning balance sheet (Exhibit 9–3).
(j)

December 31, 2016, balance.	$449,900
Add net income, from cell C12 of Schedule 9	102,100
	552,000
Deduct dividends paid, from cell G17 of Schedule 8	32,000
December 31, 2017, balance	$520,000

Tom: Are you sure? They didn't seem very happy to see me last year when I came in for an emergency loan.

Larry: Did you repay the loan on time?

Tom: Sure.

Larry: I don't see any problem. You won't be asking for an emergency loan this time. The bank will have plenty of warning. And with this budget, you have a solid plan that shows when and how you are going to pay off the loan. Trust me, they'll go for it. Also, keep in mind that the master budget contains all the embedded formulas you'll need to answer the types of "what-if" questions that we discussed earlier. If you want to calculate the financial impact of changing any of your master budget's underlying estimates or assumptions, you can do it with the click of a mouse!

Tom: This sounds fabulous Larry. Thanks for all of your work on this project.

IN BUSINESS

LOCAL MUNICIPALITIES CLOSE BUDGET DEFICITS

Municipalities across the Unites States face a combined budget deficit of $56 to $86 billion. Many cities are responding to their budget shortfalls by outsourcing services to avoid the crushing cost of providing employee benefits. For example, San Jose, California, decided to put a dent in its $118 million budget deficit by outsourcing its janitorial services. The town of Lakewood, California, contracts 40% of its municipal services to outside vendors. Maywood, California, took the drastic step of outsourcing all of its public services to outside contractors. This small town of 40,000 residents terminated all municipal employees and hired the Los Angeles County Sheriff to oversee public safety.

Sources: Tamara Audi, "Cities Rent Police, Janitors to Save Cash," *The Wall Street Journal,* July 19, 2010, p. A3.

Summary

This chapter describes the budgeting process and shows how the various operating budgets relate to each other. The sales budget is the foundation for a master budget. Once the sales budget has been set, the production budget and the selling and administrative expense budget can be prepared because they depend on how many units are to be sold. The production budget determines how many units are to be produced, so after it is prepared, the various manufacturing cost budgets can be prepared. All of these budgets feed into the cash budget and the budgeted income statement and balance sheet. The parts of the master budget are connected in many ways. For example, the schedule of expected cash collections, which is completed in connection with the sales budget, provides data for both the cash budget and the budgeted balance sheet.

The material in this chapter is just an introduction to master budgeting. In later chapters, we will see how budgets are used to control day-to-day operations and how they are used in performance evaluation.

Review Problem: Budget Schedules

Mynor Corporation manufactures and sells a seasonal product that has peak sales in the third quarter. The following information concerns operations for Year 2—the coming year—and for the first two quarters of Year 3:

a. The company's single product sells for $8 per unit. Budgeted unit sales for the next six quarters are as follows (all sales are on credit):

	Year 2 Quarter				Year 3 Quarter	
	1	2	3	4	1	2
Budgeted unit sales.........	40,000	60,000	100,000	50,000	70,000	80,000

b. Sales are collected in the following pattern: 75% in the quarter the sales are made, and the remaining 25% in the following quarter. On January 1, Year 2, the company's balance sheet showed $65,000 in accounts receivable, all of which will be collected in the first quarter of the year. Bad debts are negligible and can be ignored.

c. The company desires an ending finished goods inventory at the end of each quarter equal to 30% of the budgeted unit sales for the next quarter. On December 31, Year 1, the company had 12,000 units on hand.

d. Five pounds of raw materials are required to complete one unit of product. The company requires ending raw materials inventory at the end of each quarter equal to 10% of the following quarter's production needs. On December 31, Year 1, the company had 23,000 pounds of raw materials on hand.

e. The raw material costs $0.80 per pound. Raw material purchases are paid for in the following pattern: 60% paid in the quarter the purchases are made, and the remaining 40% paid in the following quarter. On January 1, Year 2, the company's balance sheet showed $81,500 in accounts payable for raw material purchases, all of which will be paid for in the first quarter of the year.

Required:

Prepare the following budgets and schedules for the year, showing both quarterly and total figures:
1. A sales budget and a schedule of expected cash collections.
2. A production budget.
3. A direct materials budget and a schedule of expected cash payments for purchases of materials.

Solution to Review Problem

1. The sales budget is prepared as follows:

	Year 2 Quarter				Year
	1	2	3	4	
Budgeted unit sales.........	40,000	60,000	100,000	50,000	250,000
Selling price per unit	× $8	× $8	× $8	× $8	× $8
Total sales	$320,000	$480,000	$800,000	$400,000	$2,000,000

Based on the budgeted sales above, the schedule of expected cash collections is prepared as follows:

	Year 2 Quarter				Year
	1	2	3	4	
Beginning accounts receivable	$ 65,000				$ 65,000
First-quarter sales ($320,000 × 75%, 25%)............	240,000	$ 80,000			320,000
Second-quarter sales ($480,000 × 75%, 25%)		360,000	$120,000		480,000
Third-quarter sales ($800,000 × 75%, 25%)...........			600,000	$200,000	800,000
Fourth-quarter sales ($400,000 × 75%)				300,000	300,000
Total cash collections.............................	$305,000	$440,000	$720,000	$500,000	$1,965,000

2. Based on the sales budget in units, the production budget is prepared as follows:

	Year 2 Quarter					Year 3 Quarter	
	1	2	3	4	Year	1	2
Budgeted unit sales................................	40,000	60,000	100,000	50,000	250,000	70,000	80,000
Add desired ending finished goods inventory*.........	18,000	30,000	15,000	21,000⁺	21,000	24,000	
Total needs	58,000	90,000	115,000	71,000	271,000	94,000	
Less beginning finished goods inventory..............	12,000	18,000	30,000	15,000	12,000	21,000	
Required production	46,000	72,000	85,000	56,000	259,000	73,000	

*30% of the following quarter's budgeted unit sales.
⁺30% of the budgeted Year 3 first-quarter sales.

3. Based on the production budget, raw materials will need to be purchased during the year as follows:

	Year 2 Quarter					Year 3 Quarter
	1	2	3	4	Year 2	1
Required production in units of finished goods..................	46,000	72,000	85,000	56,000	259,000	73,000
Units of raw materials needed per unit of finished goods	× 5	× 5	× 5	× 5	× 5	× 5
Units of raw materials needed to meet production..............	230,000	360,000	425,000	280,000	1,295,000	365,000
Add desired units of ending raw materials inventory*	36,000	42,500	28,000	36,500'	36,500	
Total units of raw materials needed	266,000	402,500	453,000	316,500	1,331,500	
Less units of beginning raw materials inventory	23,000	36,000	42,500	28,000	23,000	
Units of raw materials to be purchased	243,000	366,500	410,500	288,500	1,308,500	
Unit cost of raw materials....................................	× $0.80	× $0.80	× $0.80	× $0.80	× $0.80	
Cost of raw materials to be purchased........................	$194,400	$293,200	$328,400	$230,800	$1,046,800	

*10% of the following quarter's production needs in pounds.
'10% of the Year 3 first-quarter production needs in pounds.

Based on the raw material purchases above, expected cash payments are computed as follows:

	Year 2 Quarter				
	1	2	3	4	Year 2
Beginning accounts payable	$ 81,500				$ 81,500
First-quarter purchases ($194,400 × 60%, 40%)...................	116,640	$ 77,760			194,400
Second-quarter purchases ($293,200 × 60%, 40%)..............		175,920	$117,280		293,200
Third-quarter purchases ($328,400 × 60%, 40%)................			197,040	$131,360	328,400
Fourth-quarter purchases ($230,800 × 60%)...................				138,480	138,480
Total cash disbursements..	$198,140	$253,680	$314,320	$269,840	$1,035,980

Glossary

Budget A detailed plan for the future that is usually expressed in formal quantitative terms. (p. 387)

Cash budget A detailed plan showing how cash resources will be acquired and used over a specific time period. (p. 391)

Continuous budget A 12-month budget that rolls forward one month as the current month is completed. (p. 388)

Control The process of gathering feedback to ensure that a plan is being properly executed or modified as circumstances change. (p. 387)

Direct labor budget A detailed plan that shows the direct labor-hours required to fulfill the production budget. (p. 400)

Direct materials budget A detailed plan showing the amount of raw materials that must be purchased to fulfill the production budget and to provide for adequate inventories. (p. 399)

Ending finished goods inventory budget A budget showing the dollar amount of unsold finished goods inventory that will appear on the ending balance sheet. (p. 403)

Manufacturing overhead budget A detailed plan showing the production costs, other than direct materials and direct labor, that will be incurred over a specified time period. (p. 401)

Master budget A number of separate but interdependent budgets that formally lay out the company's sales, production, and financial goals and that culminates in a cash budget, budgeted income statement, and budgeted balance sheet. (p. 390)

Merchandise purchases budget A detailed plan used by a merchandising company that shows the amount of goods that must be purchased from suppliers during the period. (p. 398)

Participative budget See *Self-imposed budget.* (p. 389)

Perpetual budget See *Continuous budget.* (p. 388)

Planning Developing goals and preparing budgets to achieve those goals. (p. 387)

Production budget A detailed plan showing the number of units that must be produced during a period in order to satisfy both sales and inventory needs. (p. 396)

Responsibility accounting A system of accountability in which managers are held responsible for those items of revenue and cost—and only those items—over which they can exert significant control. The managers are held responsible for differences between budgeted and actual results. (p. 388)

Sales budget A detailed schedule showing expected sales expressed in both dollars and units. (p. 391)

Self-imposed budget A method of preparing budgets in which managers prepare their own budgets. These budgets are then reviewed by higher-level managers, and any issues are resolved by mutual agreement. (p. 389)

Selling and administrative expense budget A detailed schedule of planned expenses that will be incurred in areas other than manufacturing during a budget period. (p. 403)

Questions

9–1 What is a budget? What is budgetary control?

9–2 Discuss some of the major benefits to be gained from budgeting.

9–3 What is meant by the term *responsibility accounting?*

9–4 What is a master budget? Briefly describe its contents.

9–5 Why is the sales forecast the starting point in budgeting?

9–6 "As a practical matter, planning and control mean exactly the same thing." Do you agree? Explain.

9–7 Why is it a good idea to create a "Budgeting Assumptions" tab when creating a master budget in Microsoft Excel?

9–8 What is a self-imposed budget? What are the major advantages of self-imposed budgets? What caution must be exercised in their use?

9–9 How can budgeting assist a company in planning its workforce staffing levels?

9–10 "The principal purpose of the cash budget is to see how much cash the company will have in the bank at the end of the year." Do you agree? Explain.

Multiple-choice questions are available with Connect.

Applying Excel

The Excel worksheet form that follows is to be used to recreate the Review Problem related to Mynor Corporation. Download the workbook containing this form at from Connect. *On the website you will also receive instructions about how to use this worksheet form.*

LEARNING OBJECTIVES 9–2, 9–3, 9–4

	A	B	C	D	E	F	G	H	I
1	Chapter 9: Applying Excel								
2									
3	Data			Year 2 Quarter			Year 3 Quarter		
4			1	2	3	4	1	2	
5	Budgeted unit sales		40,000	60,000	100,000	50,000	70,000	80,000	
6									
7	• Selling price per unit		$8 per unit						
8	• Accounts receivable, beginning balance	$65,000							
9	• Sales collected in the quarter sales are made	75%							
10	• Sales collected in the quarter after sales are made	25%							
11	• Desired ending finished goods inventory is	30% of the budgeted unit sales of the next quarter							
12	• Finished goods inventory, beginning	12,000 units							
13	• Raw materials required to produce one unit	5 pounds							
14	• Desired ending inventory of raw materials is	10% of the next quarter's production needs							
15	• Raw materials inventory, beginning	23,000 pounds							
16	• Raw material costs	$0.80 per pound							
17	• Raw materials purchases are paid	60% in the quarter the purchases are made							
18	and	40% in the quarter following purchase							
19	• Accounts payable for raw materials, beginning balance	$81,500							
20									
21	Enter a formula into each of the cells marked with a ? below								
22	**Review Problem: Budget Schedules**								
23									
24	*Construct the sales budget*			Year 2 Quarter			Year 3 Quarter		
25			1	2	3	4	1	2	
26	Budgeted unit sales		?	?	?	?	?	?	
27	Selling price per unit		?	?	?	?	?	?	
28	Total sales		?	?	?	?	?	?	
29									
30	*Construct the schedule of expected cash collections*			Year 2 Quarter					
31			1	2	3	4	Year		
32	Accounts receivable, beginning balance	?				?			
33	First-quarter sales	?	?			?			
34	Second-quarter sales		?	?		?			
35	Third-quarter sales			?	?	?			
36	Fourth-quarter sales				?	?			
37	Total cash collections	?	?	?	?	?			
38									
39	*Construct the production budget*			Year 2 Quarter				Year 3 Quarter	
40			1	2	3	4	Year	1	2
41	Budgeted unit sales		?	?	?	?	?	?	?
42	Add desired finished goods inventory		?	?	?	?	?	?	
43	Total needs		?	?	?	?	?	?	
44	Less beginning inventory		?	?	?	?	?	?	
45	Required production		?	?	?	?	?	?	
46									
47	*Construct the raw materials purchases budget*			Year 2 Quarter				Year 3 Quarter	
48			1	2	3	4	Year	1	
49	Required production (units)		?	?	?	?	?	?	
50	Raw materials required to produce one unit		?	?	?	?	?	?	
51	Production needs (pounds)		?	?	?	?	?	?	
52	Add desired ending inventory of raw materials (pounds)		?	?	?	?	?		
53	Total needs (pounds)		?	?	?	?	?		
54	Less beginning inventory of raw materials (pounds)		?	?	?	?	?		
55	Raw materials to be purchased		?	?	?	?	?		
56	Cost of raw materials per pound		?	?	?	?	?		
57	Cost of raw materials to be purchased		?	?	?	?	?		
58									
59	*Construct the schedule of expected cash payments*			Year 2 Quarter					
60			1	2	3	4	Year		
61	Accounts payable, beginning balance	?				?			
62	First-quarter purchases	?	?			?			
63	Second-quarter purchases		?	?		?			
64	Third-quarter purchases			?	?	?			
65	Fourth-quarter purchases				?	?			
66	Total cash disbursements	?	?	?	?	?			
67									

Chapter 9 Form / Filled in Chapter 9 Form / Chapter 9 Formulas / Chapter 9 Requirement

You should proceed to the requirements below only after completing your worksheet.

Required:

1. Check your worksheet by changing the budgeted unit sales in Quarter 2 of Year 2 in cell C5 to 75,000 units. The total expected cash collections for the year should now be $2,085,000. If you do not get this answer, find the errors in your worksheet and correct them. Have the total cash disbursements for the year changed? Why or why not?

2. The company has just hired a new marketing manager who insists that unit sales can be dramatically increased by dropping the selling price from $8 to $7. The marketing manager would like to use the following projections in the budget:

Data	Year 2 Quarter				Year 3 Quarter	
	1	2	3	4	1	2
Budgeted unit sales.......	50,000	70,000	120,000	80,000	90,000	100,000
Selling price per unit......	$7					

a. What are the total expected cash collections for the year under this revised budget?
b. What is the total required production for the year under this revised budget?
c. What is the total cost of raw materials to be purchased for the year under this revised budget?
d. What are the total expected cash disbursements for raw materials for the year under this revised budget?
e. After seeing this revised budget, the production manager cautioned that due to the limited availability of a complex milling machine, the plant can produce no more than 90,000 units in any one quarter. Is this a potential problem? If so, what can be done about it?

The Foundational 15   connect   Additional student resources are available with Connect.

LEARNING OBJECTIVES 9–2, 9–3, 9–4, 9–5, 9–7, 9–9, 9–10

Morganton Company makes one product and it provided the following information to help prepare the master budget for its first four months of operations:

a. The budgeted selling price per unit is $70. Budgeted unit sales for June, July, August, and September are 8,400, 10,000, 12,000, and 13,000 units, respectively. All sales are on credit.
b. Forty percent of credit sales are collected in the month of the sale and 60% in the following month.
c. The ending finished goods inventory equals 20% of the following month's unit sales.
d. The ending raw materials inventory equals 10% of the following month's raw materials production needs. Each unit of finished goods requires 5 pounds of raw materials. The raw materials cost $2.00 per pound.
e. Thirty percent of raw materials purchases are paid for in the month of purchase and 70% in the following month.
f. The direct labor wage rate is $15 per hour. Each unit of finished goods requires two direct labor-hours.
g. The variable selling and administrative expense per unit sold is $1.80. The fixed selling and administrative expense per month is $60,000.

Required:
1. What are the budgeted sales for July?
2. What are the expected cash collections for July?
3. What is the accounts receivable balance at the end of July?
4. According to the production budget, how many units should be produced in July?
5. If 61,000 pounds of raw materials are needed to meet production in August, how many pounds of raw materials should be purchased in July?
6. What is the estimated cost of raw materials purchases for July?
7. If the cost of raw material purchases in June is $88,880, what are the estimated cash disbursements for raw materials purchases in July?
8. What is the estimated accounts payable balance at the end of July?
9. What is the estimated raw materials inventory balance at the end of July?
10. What is the total estimated direct labor cost for July assuming the direct labor workforce is adjusted to match the hours required to produce the forecasted number of units produced?
11. If the company always uses an estimated predetermined plantwide overhead rate of $10 per direct labor-hour, what is the estimated unit product cost?
12. What is the estimated finished goods inventory balance at the end of July?
13. What is the estimated cost of goods sold and gross margin for July?
14. What is the estimated total selling and administrative expense for July?
15. What is the estimated net operating income for July?

EXERCISE 9–1 Schedule of Expected Cash Collections [LO9–2]

Silver Company makes a product that is very popular as a Mother's Day gift. Thus, peak sales occur in May of each year, as shown in the company's sales budget for the second quarter given below:

	April	May	June	Total
Budgeted sales (all on account)........	$300,000	$500,000	$200,000	$1,000,000

From past experience, the company has learned that 20% of a month's sales are collected in the month of sale, another 70% are collected in the month following sale, and the remaining 10% are collected in the second month following sale. Bad debts are negligible and can be ignored. February sales totaled $230,000, and March sales totaled $260,000.

Required:

1. Prepare a schedule of expected cash collections from sales, by month and in total, for the second quarter.
2. Assume that the company will prepare a budgeted balance sheet as of June 30. Compute the accounts receivable as of that date.

EXERCISE 9–2 Production Budget [LO9–3]

Down Under Products, Ltd., of Australia has budgeted sales of its popular boomerang for the next four months as follows:

	Sales in Units
April..........................	50,000
May...........................	75,000
June	90,000
July...........................	80,000

The company is now in the process of preparing a production budget for the second quarter. Past experience has shown that end-of-month inventory levels must equal 10% of the following month's sales. The inventory at the end of March was 5,000 units.

Required:

Prepare a production budget for the second quarter; in your budget, show the number of units to be produced each month and for the quarter in total.

EXERCISE 9–3 Direct Materials Budget [LO9–4]

Three grams of musk oil are required for each bottle of Mink Caress, a very popular perfume made by a small company in western Siberia. The cost of the musk oil is $1.50 per gram. Budgeted production of Mink Caress is given below by quarters for Year 2 and for the first quarter of Year 3:

	Year 2				Year 3
	First	Second	Third	Fourth	First
Budgeted production, in bottles........	60,000	90,000	150,000	100,000	70,000

Musk oil has become so popular as a perfume ingredient that it has become necessary to carry large inventories as a precaution against stock-outs. For this reason, the inventory of musk oil at the end of a quarter must be equal to 20% of the following quarter's production needs. Some 36,000 grams of musk oil will be on hand to start the first quarter of Year 2.

Required:

Prepare a direct materials budget for musk oil, by quarter and in total, for Year 2. At the bottom of your budget, show the amount of purchases for each quarter and for the year in total.

EXERCISE 9–4 Direct Labor Budget [LO9–5]

The production manager of Rordan Corporation has submitted the following forecast of units to be produced by quarter for the upcoming fiscal year:

	1st Quarter	2nd Quarter	3rd Quarter	4th Quarter
Units to be produced	8,000	6,500	7,000	7,500

Each unit requires 0.35 direct labor-hours, and direct laborers are paid $12.00 per hour.

Required:

1. Construct the company's direct labor budget for the upcoming fiscal year, assuming that the direct labor workforce is adjusted each quarter to match the number of hours required to produce the forecasted number of units produced.

2. Construct the company's direct labor budget for the upcoming fiscal year, assuming that the direct labor workforce is not adjusted each quarter. Instead, assume that the company's direct labor workforce consists of permanent employees who are guaranteed to be paid for at least 2,600 hours of work each quarter. If the number of required direct labor-hours is less than this number, the workers are paid for 2,600 hours anyway. Any hours worked in excess of 2,600 hours in a quarter are paid at the rate of 1.5 times the normal hourly rate for direct labor.

EXERCISE 9–5 Manufacturing Overhead Budget [LO9–6]

The direct labor budget of Yuvwell Corporation for the upcoming fiscal year contains the following details concerning budgeted direct labor-hours:

	1st Quarter	2nd Quarter	3rd Quarter	4th Quarter
Budgeted direct labor-hours	8,000	8,200	8,500	7,800

The company's variable manufacturing overhead rate is $3.25 per direct labor-hour and the company's fixed manufacturing overhead is $48,000 per quarter. The only noncash item included in fixed manufacturing overhead is depreciation, which is $16,000 per quarter.

Required:

1. Construct the company's manufacturing overhead budget for the upcoming fiscal year.

2. Compute the company's manufacturing overhead rate (including both variable and fixed manufacturing overhead) for the upcoming fiscal year. Round off to the nearest whole cent.

EXERCISE 9–6 Selling and Administrative Expense Budget [LO9–7]

The budgeted unit sales of Weller Company for the upcoming fiscal year are provided below:

	1st Quarter	2nd Quarter	3rd Quarter	4th Quarter
Budgeted unit sales	15,000	16,000	14,000	13,000

The company's variable selling and administrative expense per unit is $2.50. Fixed selling and administrative expenses include advertising expenses of $8,000 per quarter, executive salaries of $35,000 per quarter, and depreciation of $20,000 per quarter. In addition, the company will make insurance payments of $5,000 in the first quarter and $5,000 in the third quarter. Finally, property taxes of $8,000 will be paid in the second quarter.

Required:

Prepare the company's selling and administrative expense budget for the upcoming fiscal year.

EXERCISE 9–7 Cash Budget [LO9–8]

Garden Depot is a retailer that is preparing its budget for the upcoming fiscal year. Management has prepared the following summary of its budgeted cash flows:

	1st Quarter	2nd Quarter	3rd Quarter	4th Quarter
Total cash receipts	$180,000	$330,000	$210,000	$230,000
Total cash disbursements	$260,000	$230,000	$220,000	$240,000

The company's beginning cash balance for the upcoming fiscal year will be $20,000. The company requires a minimum cash balance of $10,000 and may borrow any amount needed from a local bank at a quarterly interest rate of 3%. The company may borrow any amount at the beginning of any quarter and may repay its loans, or any part of its loans, at the end of any quarter. Interest payments are due on any principal at the time it is repaid. For simplicity, assume that interest is not compounded.

Required:

Prepare the company's cash budget for the upcoming fiscal year.

EXERCISE 9–8 Budgeted Income Statement [LO9–9]

Gig Harbor Boating is the wholesale distributor of a small recreational catamaran sailboat. Management has prepared the following summary data to use in its annual budgeting process:

Budgeted unit sales	460
Selling price per unit	$1,950
Cost per unit..	$1,575
Variable selling and administrative expenses (per unit)	$75
Fixed selling and administrative expenses (per year)	$105,000
Interest expense for the year	$14,000

Required:

Prepare the company's budgeted income statement. Use the absorption costing income statement format shown in Schedule 9.

EXERCISE 9–9 Budgeted Balance Sheet [LO9–10]

The management of Mecca Copy, a photocopying center located on University Avenue, has compiled the following data to use in preparing its budgeted balance sheet for next year:

	Ending Balances
Cash	?
Accounts receivable	$8,100
Supplies inventory..................	$3,200
Equipment.........................	$34,000
Accumulated depreciation	$16,000
Accounts payable	$1,800
Common stock	$5,000
Retained earnings..................	?

The beginning balance of retained earnings was $28,000, net income is budgeted to be $11,500, and dividends are budgeted to be $4,800.

Required:

Prepare the company's budgeted balance sheet.

EXERCISE 9–10 Production and Direct Materials Budgets [LO9–3, LO9–4]

Pearl Products Limited of Shenzhen, China, manufactures and distributes toys throughout South East Asia. Three cubic centimeters (cc) of solvent H300 are required to manufacture each unit of Supermix, one of the company's products. The company is now planning raw materials needs for the third quarter, the quarter in which peak sales of Supermix occur. To keep production and sales moving smoothly, the company has the following inventory requirements:

a.   The finished goods inventory on hand at the end of each month must be equal to 3,000 units of Supermix plus 20% of the next month's sales. The finished goods inventory on June 30 is budgeted to be 10,000 units.

b.   The raw materials inventory on hand at the end of each month must be equal to one-half of the following month's production needs for raw materials. The raw materials inventory on June 30 is budgeted to be 54,000 cc of solvent H300.

c.   The company maintains no work in process inventories.

A sales budget for Supermix for the last six months of the year follows.

	Budgeted Sales in Units
July	35,000
August....................	40,000
September	50,000
October....................	30,000
November..................	20,000
December..................	10,000

Required:

1.   Prepare a production budget for Supermix for the months July, August, September, and October.

2.   Examine the production budget that you prepared in requirement 1. Why will the company produce more units than it sells in July and August, and fewer units than it sells in September and October?

3.   Prepare a direct materials budget showing the quantity of solvent H300 to be purchased for July, August, and September, and for the quarter in total.

EXERCISE 9–11 Cash Budget Analysis [LO9–8]

A cash budget, by quarters, is given below for a retail company (000 omitted). The company requires a minimum cash balance of at least $5,000 to start each quarter.

	Quarter				
	1	2	3	4	Year
Cash balance, beginning......................	$ 6	$?	$?	$?	$?
Add collections from customers	?	?	96	?	323
Total cash available	71	?	?	?	?
Less disbursements:					
Purchase of inventory	35	45	?	35	?
Selling and administrative expenses	?	30	30	?	113
Equipment purchases	8	8	10	?	36
Dividends....................................	2	2	2	2	?
Total disbursements.........................	?	85	?	?	?
Excess (deficiency) of cash available over disbursements	(2)	?	11	?	?
Financing:					
Borrowings	?	15	—	—	?
Repayments (including interest)*..............	—	—	(?)	(17)	(?)
Total financing...............................	?	?	?	?	?
Cash balance, ending	$?	$?	$?	$?	$?

*Interest will total $1,000 for the year.

Required:

Fill in the missing amounts in the above table.

EXERCISE 9–12 Schedules of Expected Cash Collections and Disbursements; Income Statement; Balance Sheet [LO9–2, LO9–4, LO9–9, LO9–10]

Beech Corporation is a merchandising company that is preparing a master budget for the third quarter of the calendar year. The company's balance sheet as of June 30 is shown below:

Beech Corporation Balance Sheet June 30	
Assets	
Cash.	$ 90,000
Accounts receivable.	136,000
Inventory.	62,000
Plant and equipment, net of depreciation.	210,000
Total assets	$498,000
Liabilities and Stockholders' Equity	
Accounts payable	$ 71,100
Common stock.	327,000
Retained earnings.	99,900
Total liabilities and stockholders' equity	$498,000

Beech's managers have made the following additional assumptions and estimates:

1. Estimated sales for July, August, September, and October will be $210,000, $230,000, $220,000, and $240,000, respectively.

2. All sales are on credit and all credit sales are collected. Each month's credit sales are collected 35% in the month of sale and 65% in the month following the sale. All of the accounts receivable at June 30 will be collected in July.

3. Each month's ending inventory must equal 30% of the cost of next month's sales. The cost of goods sold is 60% of sales. The company pays for 40% of its merchandise purchases in the month of the purchase and the remaining 60% in the month following the purchase. All of the accounts payable at June 30 will be paid in July.

4. Monthly selling and administrative expenses are always $60,000. Each month $5,000 of this total amount is depreciation expense and the remaining $55,000 relates to expenses that are paid in the month they are incurred.

5. The company does not plan to borrow money or pay or declare dividends during the quarter ended September 30. The company does not plan to issue any common stock or repurchase its own stock during the quarter ended September 30.

Required:

1. Prepare a schedule of expected cash collections for July, August, and September. Also compute total cash collections for the quarter ended September 30.

2. *a.* Prepare a merchandise purchases budget for July, August, and September. Also compute total merchandise purchases for the quarter ended September 30.

   b. Prepare a schedule of expected cash disbursements for merchandise purchases for July, August, and September. Also compute total cash disbursements for merchandise purchases for the quarter ended September 30.

3. Prepare an income statement for the quarter ended September 30. Use the absorption format shown in Schedule 9.

4. Prepare a balance sheet as of September 30.

EXERCISE 9–13 Schedules of Expected Cash Collections and Disbursements; Income Statement; Balance Sheet [LO9–2, LO9–4, LO9–9, LO9–10]

Refer to the data for Beech Corporation in Exercise 9–12. The company is considering making the following changes to the assumptions underlying its master budget:

1. Each month's credit sales are collected 45% in the month of sale and 55% in the month following the sale.
2. Each month's ending inventory must equal 20% of the cost of next month's sales.
3. The company pays for 30% of its merchandise purchases in the month of the purchase and the remaining 70% in the month following the purchase.

All other information from Exercise 9–12 that is not mentioned above remains the same.

Required:

Using the new assumptions described above, complete the following requirements:

1. Prepare a schedule of expected cash collections for July, August, and September. Also compute total cash collections for the quarter ended September 30.
2. *a.* Prepare a merchandise purchases budget for July, August, and September. Also compute total merchandise purchases for the quarter ended September 30.
    b. Prepare a schedule of expected cash disbursements for merchandise purchases for July, August, and September. Also compute total cash disbursements for merchandise purchases for the quarter ended September 30.
3. Prepare an income statement for the quarter ended September 30. Use the absorption format shown in Schedule 9.
4. Prepare a balance sheet as of September 30.

EXERCISE 9–14 Sales and Production Budgets [LO9–2, LO9–3]

The marketing department of Jessi Corporation has submitted the following sales forecast for the upcoming fiscal year (all sales are on account):

	1st Quarter	2nd Quarter	3rd Quarter	4th Quarter
Budgeted unit sales	11,000	12,000	14,000	13,000

The selling price of the company's product is $18.00 per unit. Management expects to collect 65% of sales in the quarter in which the sales are made, 30% in the following quarter, and 5% of sales are expected to be uncollectible. The beginning balance of accounts receivable, all of which is expected to be collected in the first quarter, is $70,200.

The company expects to start the first quarter with 1,650 units in finished goods inventory. Management desires an ending finished goods inventory in each quarter equal to 15% of the next quarter's budgeted sales. The desired ending finished goods inventory for the fourth quarter is 1,850 units.

Required:

1. Prepare the company's sales budget and schedule of expected cash collections.
2. Prepare the company's production budget for the upcoming fiscal year.

EXERCISE 9–15 Direct Labor and Manufacturing Overhead Budgets [LO9–5, LO9–6]

The Production Department of Hruska Corporation has submitted the following forecast of units to be produced by quarter for the upcoming fiscal year:

	1st Quarter	2nd Quarter	3rd Quarter	4th Quarter
Units to be produced	12,000	10,000	13,000	14,000

Each unit requires 0.2 direct labor-hours and direct laborers are paid $12.00 per hour.

In addition, the variable manufacturing overhead rate is $1.75 per direct labor-hour. The fixed manufacturing overhead is $86,000 per quarter. The only noncash element of manufacturing overhead is depreciation, which is $23,000 per quarter.

Required:

1. Prepare the company's direct labor budget for the upcoming fiscal year, assuming that the direct labor workforce is adjusted each quarter to match the number of hours required to produce the forecasted number of units produced.
2. Prepare the company's manufacturing overhead budget.

EXERCISE 9–16 Direct Materials and Direct Labor Budgets [LO9–4, LO9–5]

The production department of Zan Corporation has submitted the following forecast of units to be produced by quarter for the upcoming fiscal year:

	1st Quarter	2nd Quarter	3rd Quarter	4th Quarter
Units to be produced	5,000	8,000	7,000	6,000

In addition, the beginning raw materials inventory for the 1st Quarter is budgeted to be 6,000 grams and the beginning accounts payable for the 1st Quarter is budgeted to be $2,880.

Each unit requires 8 grams of raw material that costs $1.20 per gram. Management desires to end each quarter with an inventory of raw materials equal to 25% of the following quarter's production needs. The desired ending inventory for the 4th Quarter is 8,000 grams. Management plans to pay for 60% of raw material purchases in the quarter acquired and 40% in the following quarter. Each unit requires 0.20 direct labor-hours and direct laborers are paid $11.50 per hour.

Required:

1. Prepare the company's direct materials budget and schedule of expected cash disbursements for purchases of materials for the upcoming fiscal year.
2. Prepare the company's direct labor budget for the upcoming fiscal year, assuming that the direct labor workforce is adjusted each quarter to match the number of hours required to produce the forecasted number of units produced.

Additional student resources are available with Connect.   **Problems**

PROBLEM 9–17 Cash Budget; Income Statement; Balance Sheet [LO9–2, LO9–4, LO9–8, LO9–9, LO9–10]

Minden Company is a wholesale distributor of premium European chocolates. The company's balance sheet as of April 30 is given below:

Minden Company Balance Sheet April 30	
Assets	
Cash...	$ 9,000
Accounts receivable......................	54,000
Inventory....................................	30,000
Buildings and equipment, net of depreciation........	207,000
Total assets................................	$300,000
Liabilities and Stockholders' Equity	
Accounts payable	$ 63,000
Note payable	14,500
Common stock..............................	180,000
Retained earnings..........................	42,500
Total liabilities and stockholders' equity	$300,000

The company is in the process of preparing a budget for May and has assembled the following data:

a.   Sales are budgeted at $200,000 for May. Of these sales, $60,000 will be for cash; the remainder will be credit sales. One-half of a month's credit sales are collected in the month the sales are made, and the remainder is collected in the following month. All of the April 30 accounts receivable will be collected in May.

b.   Purchases of inventory are expected to total $120,000 during May. These purchases will all be on account. Forty percent of all purchases are paid for in the month of purchase; the remainder are paid in the following month. All of the April 30 accounts payable to suppliers will be paid during May.

c.   The May 31 inventory balance is budgeted at $40,000.

d.   Selling and administrative expenses for May are budgeted at $72,000, exclusive of depreciation. These expenses will be paid in cash. Depreciation is budgeted at $2,000 for the month.

e.   The note payable on the April 30 balance sheet will be paid during May, with $100 in interest. (All of the interest relates to May.)

f.   New refrigerating equipment costing $6,500 will be purchased for cash during May.

g.   During May, the company will borrow $20,000 from its bank by giving a new note payable to the bank for that amount. The new note will be due in one year.

Required:

1.   Prepare a cash budget for May. Support your budget with a schedule of expected cash collections from sales and a schedule of expected cash disbursements for merchandise purchases.

2.   Prepare a budgeted income statement for May. Use the absorption costing income statement format as shown in Schedule 9.

3.   Prepare a budgeted balance sheet as of May 31.

PROBLEM 9–18 Cash Budget; Income Statement; Balance Sheet; Changing Assumptions [LO9–2, LO9–4, LO9–8, LO9–9, LO9–10]

Refer to the data for Minden Company in Problem 9–17. The company is considering making the following changes to the assumptions underlying its master budget:

1.   Sales are budgeted for $220,000 for May.

2.   Each month's credit sales are collected 60% in the month of sale and 40% in the month following the sale.

3.   The company pays for 50% of its merchandise purchases in the month of the purchase and the remaining 50% in the month following the purchase.

All other information from Problem 9–17 that is not mentioned above remains the same.

Required:

Using the new assumptions described above, complete the following requirements:

1.   Prepare a cash budget for May. Support your budget with a schedule of expected cash collections from sales and a schedule of expected cash disbursements for merchandise purchases.

2.   Prepare a budgeted income statement for May. Use the absorption costing income statement format as shown in Schedule 9.

3.   Prepare a budgeted balance sheet as of May 31.

PROBLEM 9–19 Schedules of Expected Cash Collections and Disbursements [LO9–2, LO9–4, LO9–8]

You have been asked to prepare a December cash budget for Ashton Company, a distributor of exercise equipment. The following information is available about the company's operations:

a.   The cash balance on December 1 is $40,000.

b.   Actual sales for October and November and expected sales for December are as follows:

	October	November	December
Cash sales	$65,000	$70,000	$83,000
Sales on account........	$400,000	$525,000	$600,000

Sales on account are collected over a three-month period as follows: 20% collected in the month of sale, 60% collected in the month following sale, and 18% collected in the second month following sale. The remaining 2% is uncollectible.

c. Purchases of inventory will total $280,000 for December. Thirty percent of a month's inventory purchases are paid during the month of purchase. The accounts payable remaining from November's inventory purchases total $161,000, all of which will be paid in December.

d. Selling and administrative expenses are budgeted at $430,000 for December. Of this amount, $50,000 is for depreciation.

e. A new web server for the Marketing Department costing $76,000 will be purchased for cash during December, and dividends totaling $9,000 will be paid during the month.

f. The company maintains a minimum cash balance of $20,000. An open line of credit is available from the company's bank to bolster the cash position as needed.

Required:

1. Prepare a schedule of expected cash collections for December.
2. Prepare a schedule of expected cash disbursements for merchandise purchases for December.
3. Prepare a cash budget for December. Indicate in the financing section any borrowing that will be needed during the month. Assume that any interest will not be paid until the following month.

PROBLEM 9–20 Evaluating a Company's Budget Procedures [LO9–1]

Springfield Corporation operates on a calendar-year basis. It begins the annual budgeting process in late August, when the president establishes targets for total sales dollars and net operating income before taxes for the next year.

The sales target is given to the Marketing Department, where the marketing manager formulates a sales budget by product line in both units and dollars. From this budget, sales quotas by product line in units and dollars are established for each of the corporation's sales districts.

The marketing manager also estimates the cost of the marketing activities required to support the target sales volume and prepares a tentative marketing expense budget.

The executive vice president uses the sales and profit targets, the sales budget by product line, and the tentative marketing expense budget to determine the dollar amounts that can be devoted to manufacturing and corporate office expense. The executive vice president prepares the budget for corporate expenses, and then forwards to the Production Department the product-line sales budget in units and the total dollar amount that can be devoted to manufacturing.

The production manager meets with the factory managers to develop a manufacturing plan that will produce the required units when needed within the cost constraints set by the executive vice president. The budgeting process usually comes to a halt at this point because the Production Department does not consider the financial resources allocated to it to be adequate.

When this standstill occurs, the vice president of finance, the executive vice president, the marketing manager, and the production manager meet to determine the final budgets for each of the areas. This normally results in a modest increase in the total amount available for manufacturing costs, while the marketing expense and corporate office expense budgets are cut. The total sales and net operating income figures proposed by the president are seldom changed. Although the participants are seldom pleased with the compromise, these budgets are final. Each executive then develops a new detailed budget for the operations in his or her area.

None of the areas has achieved its budget in recent years. Sales often run below the target. When budgeted sales are not achieved, each area is expected to cut costs so that the president's profit target can still be met. However, the profit target is seldom met because costs are not cut enough. In fact, costs often run above the original budget in all functional areas. The president is disturbed that Springfield has not been able to meet the sales and profit targets. He hired a consultant with considerable relevant industry experience. The consultant reviewed the budgets for the past four years. He concluded that the product-line sales budgets were reasonable and that the cost and expense budgets were adequate for the budgeted sales and production levels.

Required:

1. Discuss how the budgeting process as employed by Springfield Corporation contributes to the failure to achieve the president's sales and profit targets.
2. Suggest how Springfield Corporation's budgeting process could be revised to correct the problem.
3. Should the functional areas be expected to cut their costs when sales volume falls below budget? Explain your answer.

(CMA, adapted)

PROBLEM 9–21 Schedule of Expected Cash Collections; Cash Budget [LO9–2, LO9–8]

The president of the retailer Prime Products has just approached the company's bank with a request for a $30,000, 90-day loan. The purpose of the loan is to assist the company in acquiring inventories. Because the company has had some difficulty in paying off its loans in the past, the loan officer has asked for a cash budget to help determine whether the loan should be made. The following data are available for the months April through June, during which the loan will be used:

a. On April 1, the start of the loan period, the cash balance will be $24,000. Accounts receivable on April 1 will total $140,000, of which $120,000 will be collected during April and $16,000 will be collected during May. The remainder will be uncollectible.

b. Past experience shows that 30% of a month's sales are collected in the month of sale, 60% in the month following sale, and 8% in the second month following sale. The other 2% represents bad debts that are never collected. Budgeted sales and expenses for the three-month period follow:

	April	May	June
Sales (all on account)	$300,000	$400,000	$250,000
Merchandise purchases........	$210,000	$160,000	$130,000
Payroll	$20,000	$20,000	$18,000
Lease payments..............	$22,000	$22,000	$22,000
Advertising..................	$60,000	$60,000	$50,000
Equipment purchases..........	—	—	$65,000
Depreciation.................	$15,000	$15,000	$15,000

c. Merchandise purchases are paid in full during the month following purchase. Accounts payable for merchandise purchases during March, which will be paid during April, total $140,000.

d. In preparing the cash budget, assume that the $30,000 loan will be made in April and repaid in June. Interest on the loan will total $1,200.

Required:

1. Prepare a schedule of expected cash collections for April, May, and June, and for the three months in total.

2. Prepare a cash budget, by month and in total, for the three-month period.

3. If the company needs a minimum cash balance of $20,000 to start each month, can the loan be repaid as planned? Explain.

PROBLEM 9–22 Cash Budget with Supporting Schedules [LO9–2, LO9–4, LO9–8]

Garden Sales, Inc., sells garden supplies. Management is planning its cash needs for the second quarter. The company usually has to borrow money during this quarter to support peak sales of lawn care equipment, which occur during May. The following information has been assembled to assist in preparing a cash budget for the quarter:

a. Budgeted monthly absorption costing income statements for April–July are:

	April	May	June	July
Sales.....................	$ 600,000	$900,000	$500,000	$400,000
Cost of goods sold.....	420,000	630,000	350,000	280,000
Gross margin............	180,000	270,000	150,000	120,000
Selling and administrative expenses:				
Selling expense	79,000	120,000	62,000	51,000
Administrative expense*.....	45,000	52,000	41,000	38,000
Total selling and administrative expenses ...	124,000	172,000	103,000	89,000
Net operating income	$ 56,000	$ 98,000	$ 47,000	$ 31,000

*Includes $20,000 of depreciation each month.

b. Sales are 20% for cash and 80% on account.
c. Sales on account are collected over a three-month period with 10% collected in the month of sale; 70% collected in the first month following the month of sale; and the remaining 20% collected in the second month following the month of sale. February's sales totaled $200,000, and March's sales totaled $300,000.
d. Inventory purchases are paid for within 15 days. Therefore, 50% of a month's inventory purchases are paid for in the month of purchase. The remaining 50% is paid in the following month. Accounts payable at March 31 for inventory purchases during March total $126,000.
e. Each month's ending inventory must equal 20% of the cost of the merchandise to be sold in the following month. The merchandise inventory at March 31 is $84,000.
f. Dividends of $49,000 will be declared and paid in April.
g. Land costing $16,000 will be purchased for cash in May.
h. The cash balance at March 31 is $52,000; the company must maintain a cash balance of at least $40,000 at the end of each month.
i. The company has an agreement with a local bank that allows the company to borrow in increments of $1,000 at the beginning of each month, up to a total loan balance of $200,000. The interest rate on these loans is 1% per month and for simplicity we will assume that interest is not compounded. The company would, as far as it is able, repay the loan plus accumulated interest at the end of the quarter.

Required:
1. Prepare a schedule of expected cash collections for April, May, and June, and for the quarter in total.
2. Prepare the following for merchandise inventory:
   a. A merchandise purchases budget for April, May, and June.
   b. A schedule of expected cash disbursements for merchandise purchases for April, May, and June, and for the quarter in total.
3. Prepare a cash budget for April, May, and June as well as in total for the quarter.

PROBLEM 9–23 Cash Budget with Supporting Schedules; Changing Assumptions [LO9–2, LO9–4, LO9–8]
Refer to the data for Garden Sales, Inc., in Problem 9–22. The company's president is interested in knowing how reducing inventory levels and collecting accounts receivable sooner will impact the cash budget. He revises the cash collection and ending inventory assumptions as follows:
1. Sales continue to be 20% for cash and 80% on credit. However, credit sales from April, May, and June are collected over a three-month period with 25% collected in the month of sale, 65% collected in the month following sale, and 10% in the second month following sale. Credit sales from February and March are collected during the second quarter using the collection percentages specified in Problem 9–22.
2. The company maintains its ending inventory levels for April, May, and June at 15% of the cost of merchandise to be sold in the following month. The merchandise inventory at March 31 remains $84,000 and accounts payable for inventory purchases at March 31 remains $126,000.

All other information from Problem 9–22 that is not referred to above remains the same.

Required:
1. Using the president's new assumptions in requirement 1, prepare a schedule of expected cash collections for April, May, and June and for the quarter in total.
2. Using the president's new assumptions in requirement 2, prepare the following for merchandise inventory:
   a. A merchandise purchases budget for April, May, and June.
   b. A schedule of expected cash disbursements for merchandise purchases for April, May, and June and for the quarter in total.
3. Using the president's new assumptions, prepare a cash budget for April, May, and June, and for the quarter in total.
4. Prepare a brief memorandum for the president explaining how his revised assumptions affect the cash budget.

PROBLEM 9–24 Behavioral Aspects of Budgeting; Ethics and the Manager [LO9–1]
Norton Company, a manufacturer of infant furniture and carriages, is in the initial stages of preparing the annual budget for next year. Scott Ford has recently joined Norton's accounting staff and

is interested to learn as much as possible about the company's budgeting process. During a recent lunch with Marge Atkins, sales manager, and Pete Granger, production manager, Ford initiated the following conversation.

Ford: Since I'm new around here and am going to be involved with the preparation of the annual budget, I'd be interested to learn how the two of you estimate sales and production numbers.

Atkins: We start out very methodically by looking at recent history, discussing what we know about current accounts, potential customers, and the general state of consumer spending. Then, we add that usual dose of intuition to come up with the best forecast we can.

Granger: I usually take the sales projections as the basis for my projections. Of course, we have to make an estimate of what this year's ending inventories will be, which is sometimes difficult.

Ford: Why does that present a problem? There must have been an estimate of ending inventories in the budget for the current year.

Granger: Those numbers aren't always reliable because Marge makes some adjustments to the sales numbers before passing them on to me.

Ford: What kind of adjustments?

Atkins: Well, we don't want to fall short of the sales projections so we generally give ourselves a little breathing room by lowering the initial sales projection anywhere from 5% to 10%.

Granger: So, you can see why this year's budget is not a very reliable starting point. We always have to adjust the projected production rates as the year progresses and, of course, this changes the ending inventory estimates. By the way, we make similar adjustments to expenses by adding at least 10% to the estimates; I think everyone around here does the same thing.

Required:

1. Marge Atkins and Pete Granger have described the use of what is sometimes called *budgetary slack.*
   a. Explain why Atkins and Granger behave in this manner and describe the benefits they expect to realize from the use of budgetary slack.
   b. Explain how the use of budgetary slack can adversely affect Atkins and Granger.

2. As a management accountant, Scott Ford believes that the behavior described by Marge Atkins and Pete Granger may be unethical. By referring to the IMA's Statement of Ethical Professional Practice in Chapter 1, explain why the use of budgetary slack may be unethical.

(CMA, adapted)

PROBLEM 9–25 Schedule of Expected Cash Collections; Cash Budget [LO9–2, LO9–8]
Herbal Care Corp., a distributor of herb-based sunscreens, is ready to begin its third quarter, in which peak sales occur. The company has requested a $40,000, 90-day loan from its bank to help meet cash requirements during the quarter. Since Herbal Care has experienced difficulty in paying off its loans in the past, the loan officer at the bank has asked the company to prepare a cash budget for the quarter. In response to this request, the following data have been assembled:

a. On July 1, the beginning of the third quarter, the company will have a cash balance of $44,500.

b. Actual sales for the last two months and budgeted sales for the third quarter follow (all sales are on account):

May (actual)	$250,000
June (actual)	$300,000
July (budgeted)	$400,000
August (budgeted)	$600,000
September (budgeted)	$320,000

Past experience shows that 25% of a month's sales are collected in the month of sale, 70% in the month following sale, and 3% in the second month following sale. The remainder is uncollectible.

c. Budgeted merchandise purchases and budgeted expenses for the third quarter are given below:

	July	August	September
Merchandise purchases..............	$240,000	$350,000	$175,000
Salaries and wages.................	$45,000	$50,000	$40,000
Advertising.......................	$130,000	$145,000	$80,000
Rent payments.....................	$9,000	$9,000	$9,000
Depreciation......................	$10,000	$10,000	$10,000

Merchandise purchases are paid in full during the month following purchase. Accounts payable for merchandise purchases on June 30, which will be paid during July, total $180,000.

d. Equipment costing $10,000 will be purchased for cash during July.

e. In preparing the cash budget, assume that the $40,000 loan will be made in July and repaid in September. Interest on the loan will total $1,200.

Required:

1. Prepare a schedule of expected cash collections for July, August, and September and for the quarter in total.

2. Prepare a cash budget, by month and in total, for the third quarter.

3. If the company needs a minimum cash balance of $20,000 to start each month, can the loan be repaid as planned? Explain.

PROBLEM 9–26 Cash Budget with Supporting Schedules [LO9–2, LO9–4, LO9–7, LO9–8]

Westex Products is a wholesale distributor of industrial cleaning products. When the treasurer of Westex Products approached the company's bank late in the current year seeking short-term financing, he was told that money was very tight and that any borrowing over the next year would have to be supported by a detailed statement of cash collections and disbursements. The treasurer also was told that it would be very helpful to the bank if borrowers would indicate the quarters in which they would be needing funds, as well as the amounts that would be needed, and the quarters in which repayments could be made.

Because the treasurer is unsure as to the particular quarters in which bank financing will be needed, he has assembled the following information to assist in preparing a detailed cash budget:

a. Budgeted sales and merchandise purchases for next year, as well as actual sales and purchases for the last quarter of the current year, are:

	Sales	Merchandise Purchases
Current Year:		
Fourth quarter actual	$200,000	$126,000
Next year:		
First quarter estimated............	$300,000	$186,000
Second quarter estimated.........	$400,000	$246,000
Third quarter estimated	$500,000	$305,000
Fourth quarter estimated..........	$200,000	$126,000

b. All sales are on account. The company normally collects 65% of a quarter's sales before the quarter ends and another 33% in the following quarter. The remainder is uncollectible. This pattern of collections is now being experienced in the current year's fourth-quarter actual data.

c. Eighty percent of a quarter's merchandise purchases are paid for within the quarter. The remainder is paid for in the following quarter.

d. Selling and administrative expenses for next year are budgeted at $50,000 per quarter plus 15% of sales. Of the fixed amount, $20,000 each quarter is depreciation.

e. The company will pay $10,000 in dividends each quarter.

f. Land purchases of $75,000 will be made in the second quarter, and purchases of $48,000 will be made in the third quarter. These purchases will be for cash.

g. The Cash account contained $10,000 at the end of the current year. The treasurer feels that this represents a minimum balance that must be maintained.

h. The company has an agreement with a local bank that allows the company to borrow in increments of $1,000 at the beginning of each quarter, up to a total loan balance of $100,000. The interest rate on these loans is 2.5% per quarter and for simplicity we will assume that interest is not compounded. The company would, as far as it is able, repay the loan plus accumulated interest at the end of the year.

i. At present, the company has no loans outstanding.

Required:

1. Prepare the following by quarter and in total for next year:
    a. A schedule of expected cash collections.
    b. A schedule of expected cash disbursements for merchandise purchases.
2. Compute the expected cash disbursements for selling and administrative expenses, by quarter and in total, for next year.
3. Prepare a cash budget, by quarter and in total, for next year.

PROBLEM 9–27 Completing a Master Budget [LO9–2, LO9–4, LO9–7, LO9–8, LO9–9, LO9–10]

The following data relate to the operations of Shilow Company, a wholesale distributor of consumer goods:

Current assets as of March 31:	
Cash	$8,000
Accounts receivable................	$20,000
Inventory..........................	$36,000
Buildings and equipment, net...........	$120,000
Accounts payable	$21,750
Capital stock........................	$150,000
Retained earnings....................	$12,250

a. The gross margin is 25% of sales.
b. Actual and budgeted sales data:

March (actual)	$50,000
April..................................	$60,000
May	$72,000
June..................................	$90,000
July	$48,000

c. Sales are 60% for cash and 40% on credit. Credit sales are collected in the month following sale. The accounts receivable at March 31 are a result of March credit sales.

d. Each month's ending inventory should equal 80% of the following month's budgeted cost of goods sold.

e. One-half of a month's inventory purchases is paid for in the month of purchase; the other half is paid for in the following month. The accounts payable at March 31 are the result of March purchases of inventory.

f. Monthly expenses are as follows: commissions, 12% of sales; rent, $2,500 per month; other expenses (excluding depreciation), 6% of sales. Assume that these expenses are paid monthly. Depreciation is $900 per month (includes depreciation on new assets).

g. Equipment costing $1,500 will be purchased for cash in April.

h. Management would like to maintain a minimum cash balance of at least $4,000 at the end of each month. The company has an agreement with a local bank that allows the company to borrow in increments of $1,000 at the beginning of each month, up to a total loan balance of $20,000. The interest rate on these loans is 1% per month and for simplicity we will assume that interest is not compounded. The company would, as far as it is able, repay the loan plus accumulated interest at the end of the quarter.

Required:

Using the preceding data:

1. Complete the following schedule:

Schedule of Expected Cash Collections				
	April	May	June	Quarter
Cash sales	$36,000			
Credit sales............	20,000			
Total collections........	$56,000			

2. Complete the following:

Merchandise Purchases Budget				
	April	May	June	Quarter
Budgeted cost of goods sold	$45,000*	$54,000		
Add desired ending inventory...........	43,200†			
Total needs............................	88,200			
Less beginning inventory...............	36,000			
Required purchases	$52,200			

*For April sales: $60,000 sales × 75% cost ratio = $45,000.
†$54,000 × 80% = $43,200

Schedule of Expected Cash Disbursements—Merchandise Purchases				
	April	May	June	Quarter
March purchases......................	$21,750			$21,750
April purchases	26,100	$26,100		52,200
May purchases........................				
June purchases.......................				
Total disbursements	$47,850			

3. Complete the following cash budget:

Cash Budget				
	April	May	June	Quarter
Beginning cash balance................	$8,000			
Add cash collections..................	56,000			
Total cash available	64,000			
Less cash disbursements:				
For inventory	47,850			
For expenses	13,300			
For equipment	1,500			
Total cash disbursements..............	62,650			
Excess (deficiency) of cash............	1,350			
Financing				
Etc.				

4. Prepare an absorption costing income statement, similar to the one shown in Schedule 9 in the chapter, for the quarter ended June 30.
5. Prepare a balance sheet as of June 30.

PROBLEM 9–28 Integration of the Sales, Production, and Direct Materials Budgets [LO9–2, LO9–3, LO9–4]

Milo Company manufactures beach umbrellas. The company is preparing detailed budgets for the third quarter and has assembled the following information to assist in the budget preparation:

a. The Marketing Department has estimated sales as follows for the remainder of the year (in units):

July	30,000	October	20,000
August	70,000	November	10,000
September	50,000	December	10,000

The selling price of the beach umbrellas is $12 per unit.

b. All sales are on account. Based on past experience, sales are collected in the following pattern:

> 30% in the month of sale
> 65% in the month following sale
> 5% uncollectible

Sales for June totaled $300,000.

c. The company maintains finished goods inventories equal to 15% of the following month's sales. This requirement will be met at the end of June.

d. Each beach umbrella requires 4 feet of Gilden, a material that is sometimes hard to acquire. Therefore, the company requires that the ending inventory of Gilden be equal to 50% of the following month's production needs. The inventory of Gilden on hand at the beginning and end of the quarter will be:

June 30	72,000 feet
September 30	? feet

e. Gilden costs $0.80 per foot. One-half of a month's purchases of Gilden is paid for in the month of purchase; the remainder is paid for in the following month. The accounts payable on July 1 for purchases of Gilden during June will be $76,000.

Required:

1. Prepare a sales budget, by month and in total, for the third quarter. (Show your budget in both units and dollars.) Also prepare a schedule of expected cash collections, by month and in total, for the third quarter.
2. Prepare a production budget for each of the months July–October.
3. Prepare a direct materials budget for Gilden, by month and in total, for the third quarter. Also prepare a schedule of expected cash disbursements for Gilden, by month and in total, for the third quarter.

PROBLEM 9–29 Completing a Master Budget [LO9–2, LO9–4, LO9–7, LO9–8, LO9–9, LO9–10]

Hillyard Company, an office supplies specialty store, prepares its master budget on a quarterly basis. The following data have been assembled to assist in preparing the master budget for the first quarter:

---

a. As of December 31 (the end of the prior quarter), the company's general ledger showed the following account balances:

	Debits	Credits
Cash	$ 48,000	
Accounts receivable	224,000	
Inventory	60,000	
Buildings and equipment (net)	370,000	
Accounts payable		$ 93,000
Common stock		500,000
Retained earnings		109,000
	$702,000	$702,000

b. Actual sales for December and budgeted sales for the next four months are as follows:

December (actual)	$280,000
January	$400,000
February	$600,000
March	$300,000
April	$200,000

c. Sales are 20% for cash and 80% on credit. All payments on credit sales are collected in the month following sale. The accounts receivable at December 31 are a result of December credit sales.

d. The company's gross margin is 40% of sales. (In other words, cost of goods sold is 60% of sales.)

e. Monthly expenses are budgeted as follows: salaries and wages, $27,000 per month: advertising, $70,000 per month; shipping, 5% of sales; other expenses, 3% of sales. Depreciation, including depreciation on new assets acquired during the quarter, will be $42,000 for the quarter.

f. Each month's ending inventory should equal 25% of the following month's cost of goods sold.

g. One-half of a month's inventory purchases is paid for in the month of purchase; the other half is paid in the following month.

h. During February, the company will purchase a new copy machine for $1,700 cash. During March, other equipment will be purchased for cash at a cost of $84,500.

i. During January, the company will declare and pay $45,000 in cash dividends.

j. Management wants to maintain a minimum cash balance of $30,000. The company has an agreement with a local bank that allows the company to borrow in increments of $1,000 at the beginning of each month. The interest rate on these loans is 1% per month and for simplicity we will assume that interest is not compounded. The company would, as far as it is able, repay the loan plus accumulated interest at the end of the quarter.

Required:
Using the data above, complete the following statements and schedules for the first quarter:
1. Schedule of expected cash collections:

	January	February	March	Quarter
Cash sales	$ 80,000			
Credit sales	224,000			
Total cash collections	$304,000			

2. *a.*   Merchandise purchases budget:

	January	February	March	Quarter
Budgeted cost of goods sold........	$240,000*	$360,000		
Add desired ending inventory	90,000†			
Total needs	330,000			
Less beginning inventory	60,000			
Required purchases...............	$270,000			

*$400,000 sales × 60% cost ratio = $240,000.
†$360,000 × 25% = $90,000.

b.   Schedule of expected cash disbursements for merchandise purchases:

	January	February	March	Quarter
December purchases	$ 93,000			$ 93,000
January purchases................	135,000	135,000		270,000
February purchases...............	—			
March purchases	—			
Total cash disbursements for purchases	$228,000			

3. Cash budget:

	January	February	March	Quarter
Beginning cash balance	$48,000			
Add cash collections	304,000			
Total cash available	352,000			
Less cash disbursements:				
Purchases of inventory	228,000			
Selling and administrative expenses....................	129,000			
Purchases of equipment..........	—			
Cash dividends..................	45,000			
Total cash disbursements	402,000			
Excess (deficiency) of cash..........	(50,000)			
Financing:				
Etc				

4. Prepare an absorption costing income statement for the quarter ending March 31 as shown in Schedule 9 in the chapter.
5. Prepare a balance sheet as of March 31.

Cases   connect   **Additional student resources are available with Connect.**

CASE 9–30 Evaluating a Company's Budget Procedures [LO9–1]
Tom Emory and Jim Morris strolled back to their plant from the administrative offices of Ferguson & Son Manufacturing Company. Tom is manager of the machine shop in the company's factory; Jim is manager of the equipment maintenance department.

The men had just attended the monthly performance evaluation meeting for plant department heads. These meetings had been held on the third Tuesday of each month since Robert Ferguson, Jr., the president's son, had become plant manager a year earlier.

As they were walking, Tom Emory spoke: "Boy, I hate those meetings! I never know whether my department's accounting reports will show good or bad performance. I'm beginning to expect the worst. If the accountants say I saved the company a dollar, I'm called 'Sir,' but if I spend even a little too much—boy, do I get in trouble. I don't know if I can hold on until I retire."

Tom had just been given the worst evaluation he had ever received in his long career with Ferguson & Son. He was the most respected of the experienced machinists in the company. He had been with Ferguson & Son for many years and was promoted to supervisor of the machine shop when the company expanded and moved to its present location. The president (Robert Ferguson, Sr.) had often stated that the company's success was due to the high-quality work of machinists like Tom. As supervisor, Tom stressed the importance of craftsmanship and told his workers that he wanted no sloppy work coming from his department.

When Robert Ferguson, Jr., became the plant manager, he directed that monthly performance comparisons be made between actual and budgeted costs for each department. The departmental budgets were intended to encourage the supervisors to reduce inefficiencies and to seek cost reduction opportunities. The company controller was instructed to have his staff "tighten" the budget slightly whenever a department attained its budget in a given month; this was done to reinforce the plant manager's desire to reduce costs. The young plant manager often stressed the importance of continued progress toward attaining the budget; he also made it known that he kept a file of these performance reports for future reference when he succeeded his father.

Tom Emory's conversation with Jim Morris continued as follows:

Emory: I really don't understand. We've worked so hard to meet the budget, and the minute we do so they tighten it on us. We can't work any faster and still maintain quality. I think my men are ready to quit trying. Besides, those reports don't tell the whole story. We always seem to be interrupting the big jobs for all those small rush orders. All that setup and machine adjustment time is killing us. And quite frankly, Jim, you were no help. When our hydraulic press broke down last month, your people were nowhere to be found. We had to take it apart ourselves and got stuck with all that idle time.

Morris: I'm sorry about that, Tom, but you know my department has had trouble making budget, too. We were running well behind at the time of that problem, and if we'd spent a day on that old machine, we would never have made it up. Instead we made the scheduled inspections of the forklift trucks because we knew we could do those in less than the budgeted time.

Emory: Well, Jim, at least you have some options. I'm locked into what the scheduling department assigns to me and you know they're being harassed by sales for those special orders. Incidentally, why didn't your report show all the supplies you guys wasted last month when you were working in Bill's department?

Morris: We're not out of the woods on that deal yet. We charged the maximum we could to other work and haven't even reported some of it yet.

Emory: Well, I'm glad you have a way of getting out of the pressure. The accountants seem to know everything that's happening in my department, sometimes even before I do. I thought all that budget and accounting stuff was supposed to help, but it just gets me into trouble. It's all a big pain. I'm trying to put out quality work; they're trying to save pennies.

Required:

1. Identify the problems that appear to exist in Ferguson & Son Manufacturing Company's budgetary control system and explain how the problems are likely to reduce the effectiveness of the system.

2. Explain how Ferguson & Son Manufacturing Company's budgetary control system could be revised to improve its effectiveness.

(CMA, adapted)

CASE 9–31 Master Budget with Supporting Schedules [LO9–2, LO9–4, LO9–8, LO9–9, LO9–10]

You have just been hired as a new management trainee by Earrings Unlimited, a distributor of earrings to various retail outlets located in shopping malls across the country. In the past, the company has done very little in the way of budgeting and at certain times of the year has experienced a shortage of cash.

Since you are well trained in budgeting, you have decided to prepare comprehensive budgets for the upcoming second quarter in order to show management the benefits that can be gained from an integrated budgeting program. To this end, you have worked with accounting and other areas to gather the information assembled below.

The company sells many styles of earrings, but all are sold for the same price—$10 per pair. Actual sales of earrings for the last three months and budgeted sales for the next six months follow (in pairs of earrings):

January (actual)...........	20,000	June (budget).................	50,000
February (actual).........	26,000	July (budget).................	30,000
March (actual)	40,000	August (budget)..............	28,000
April (budget).............	65,000	September (budget)	25,000
May (budget).............	100,000		

The concentration of sales before and during May is due to Mother's Day. Sufficient inventory should be on hand at the end of each month to supply 40% of the earrings sold in the following month.

Suppliers are paid $4 for a pair of earrings. One-half of a month's purchases is paid for in the month of purchase; the other half is paid for in the following month. All sales are on credit, with no discount, and payable within 15 days. The company has found, however, that only 20% of a month's sales are collected in the month of sale. An additional 70% is collected in the following month, and the remaining 10% is collected in the second month following sale. Bad debts have been negligible.

Monthly operating expenses for the company are given below:

Variable:	
Sales commissions..................	4% of sales
Fixed:	
Advertising	$200,000
Rent...............................	$18,000
Salaries............................	$106,000
Utilities	$7,000
Insurance..........................	$3,000
Depreciation	$14,000

Insurance is paid on an annual basis, in November of each year.

The company plans to purchase $16,000 in new equipment during May and $40,000 in new equipment during June; both purchases will be for cash. The company declares dividends of $15,000 each quarter, payable in the first month of the following quarter.

A listing of the company's ledger accounts as of March 31 is given below:

Assets

Cash	$ 74,000
Accounts receivable ($26,000 February sales;	
$320,000 March sales)	346,000
Inventory	104,000
Prepaid insurance	21,000
Property and equipment (net).......................	950,000
Total assets	$1,495,000

Liabilities and Stockholders' Equity

Accounts payable..................................	$ 100,000
Dividends payable	15,000
Common stock	800,000
Retained earnings	580,000
Total liabilities and stockholders' equity..............	$1,495,000

The company maintains a minimum cash balance of $50,000. All borrowing is done at the beginning of a month; any repayments are made at the end of a month.

The company has an agreement with a bank that allows the company to borrow in increments of $1,000 at the beginning of each month. The interest rate on these loans is 1% per month and for simplicity we will assume that interest is not compounded. At the end of the quarter, the company would pay the bank all of the accumulated interest on the loan and as much of the loan as possible (in increments of $1,000), while still retaining at least $50,000 in cash.

Required:

Prepare a master budget for the three-month period ending June 30. Include the following detailed budgets:

1. *a.* A sales budget, by month and in total.
   b. A schedule of expected cash collections from sales, by month and in total.
   c. A merchandise purchases budget in units and in dollars. Show the budget by month and in total.
   d. A schedule of expected cash disbursements for merchandise purchases, by month and in total.
2. A cash budget. Show the budget by month and in total. Determine any borrowing that would be needed to maintain the minimum cash balance of $50,000.
3. A budgeted income statement for the three-month period ending June 30. Use the contribution approach.
4. A budgeted balance sheet as of June 30.

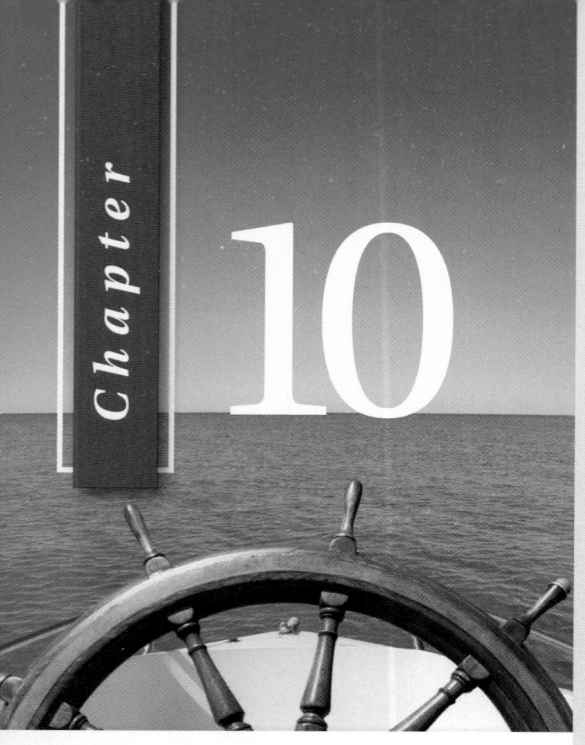

Flexible Budgets and Performance Analysis

Why Do Companies Need Flexible Budgets?

© Michael Sears/MCT/Newscom

BUSINESS FOCUS

The difficulty of accurately predicting future financial performance can be readily understood by reading the annual report of any publicly traded company. For example, Nucor Corporation, a steel manufacturer headquartered in Charlotte, North Carolina, cites numerous reasons why its actual results may differ from expectations, including the following: (1) changes in the supply and cost of raw materials; (2) changes in the availability and cost of electricity and natural gas; (3) changes in the market demand for steel products; (4) fluctuations in currency conversion rates; (5) significant changes in laws or government regulations; and (6) the cyclical nature of the steel industry. ■

Source: Nucor Corporation 2011 Annual Report, p. 3.

In the last chapter we explored how budgets are developed before a period begins. In this chapter, we explain how budgets can be adjusted to help guide actual operations and influence the performance evaluation process. For example, an organization's actual expenses will rarely equal its budgeted expenses as estimated at the beginning of the period. The reason is that the actual level of activity (such as unit sales) will rarely be the same as the budgeted activity; therefore, many actual expenses and revenues will naturally differ from what was budgeted. Should a manager be penalized for spending 10% more than budgeted for a variable expense like direct materials if unit sales are 10% higher than budgeted? Of course not. After studying this chapter, you'll know how to adjust a budget to enable meaningful comparisons to actual results.

The Variance Analysis Cycle

Companies use the *variance analysis cycle,* as illustrated in Exhibit 10–1, to evaluate and improve performance. The cycle begins with the preparation of performance reports in the accounting department. These reports highlight variances, which are the differences between the actual results and what should have occurred according to the budget. The variances raise questions. Why did this variance occur? Why is this variance larger than it was last period? The significant variances are investigated so that their root causes can be either replicated or eliminated. Then, next period's operations are carried out and the cycle begins again with the preparation of a new performance report for the latest period. The emphasis should be on highlighting superior and unsatisfactory results, finding the root causes of these outcomes, and then replicating the sources of superior achievement and eliminating the sources of unsatisfactory performance. The variance analysis cycle should not be used to assign blame for poor performance.

Managers frequently use the concept of *management by exception* in conjunction with the variance analysis cycle. Management by exception is a management system that compares actual results to a budget so that significant deviations can be flagged as exceptions and investigated further. This approach enables managers to focus on the most important variances while bypassing trivial discrepancies between the budget and actual results. For example, a variance of $5 is probably not big enough to warrant attention, whereas a variance of $5,000 might be worth tracking down. Another clue is the size of the variance relative to the amount of spending. A variance that is only 0.1% of spending on an item is probably caused by random factors. On the other hand, a variance of 10% of spending is much more likely to be a signal that something is wrong. In addition to

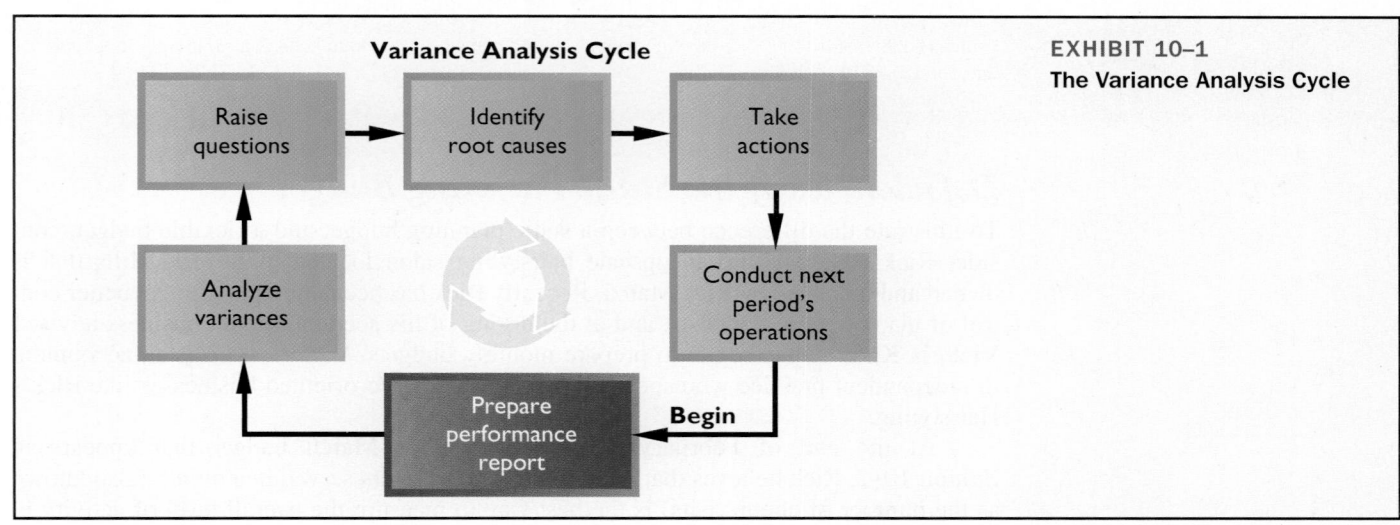

EXHIBIT 10–1
The Variance Analysis Cycle

watching for unusually large variances, the pattern of the variances should be monitored. For example, a run of steadily mounting variances should trigger an investigation even though none of the variances is large enough by itself to warrant investigation.

Next, we explain how organizations use flexible budgets to compare actual results to what should have occurred according to the budget.

Flexible Budgets

Characteristics of a Flexible Budget

The budgets that we explored in the last chapter were *planning budgets*. A **planning budget** is prepared before the period begins and is valid for only the planned level of activity. A static planning budget is suitable for planning but is inappropriate for evaluating how well costs are controlled. If the actual level of activity differs from what was planned, it would be misleading to compare actual costs to the static, unchanged planning budget. If activity is higher than expected, variable costs should be higher than expected; and if activity is lower than expected, variable costs should be lower than expected.

Flexible budgets take into account how changes in activity affect costs. A **flexible budget** is an estimate of what revenues and costs should have been, given the actual level of activity for the period. When a flexible budget is used in performance evaluation, actual costs are compared to what the costs *should have been for the actual level of activity during the period* rather than to the static planning budget. This is a very important distinction. If adjustments for the level of activity are not made, it is very difficult to interpret discrepancies between budgeted and actual costs.

IN BUSINESS

WINNERS AND LOSERS FROM THE NBA LOCKOUT

A company's actual net operating income can deviate from the budget for numerous and often uncontrollable reasons. For example, when the National Basketball Association (NBA) decided to suspend play because of a dispute between its team owners and players, many small businesses suffered—caterers, sports bars, apparel retailers, and parking lot owners all experienced a drop in revenues. BestSportsApparel.com experienced a substantial drop in NBA apparel sales due to the work stoppage. Rather than hiring 12 extra employees for the NBA season, the company reduced the size of its workforce.

While some companies lost revenues when the NBA shut down, others benefited from the situation. Andrew Zimbalist, professor of economics at Smith College, notes that "local economies are not impacted by sports work stoppages" because people choose to spend their entertainment dollars at other venues such as the theater, the zoo, or the museum.

Source: Emily Maltby and Sarah E. Needleman, "NBA Lockout: Local Firms Lose Big," *The Wall Street Journal,* October 13, 2011, p. B5.

Deficiencies of the Static Planning Budget

To illustrate the difference between a static planning budget and a flexible budget, consider Rick's Hairstyling, an upscale hairstyling salon located in Beverly Hills that is owned and managed by Rick Manzi. Recently Rick has been attempting to get better control of his revenues and costs, and at the urging of his accounting and business adviser, Victoria Kho, he has begun to prepare monthly budgets. Victoria Kho is an accountant in independent practice who specializes in small service-oriented businesses like Rick's Hairstyling.

At the end of February, Rick prepared the March budget that appears in Exhibit 10–2. Rick believes that the number of customers served in a month (also known as the number of client-visits) is the best way to measure the overall level of activity in

EXHIBIT 10–2
Planning Budget

Rick's Hairstyling
Planning Budget
For the Month Ended March 31

Budgeted client-visits (q)	1,000
Revenue ($180.00q).............................	$180,000
Expenses:	
Wages and salaries ($65,000 + $37.00q)..........	102,000
Hairstyling supplies ($1.50q)....................	1,500
Client gratuities ($4.10q)	4,100
Electricity ($1,500 + $0.10q)	1,600
Rent ($28,500)................................	28,500
Liability insurance ($2,800)	2,800
Employee health insurance ($21,300).............	21,300
Miscellaneous ($1,200 + $0.20q)................	1,400
Total expense.....................................	163,200
Net operating income.............................	$ 16,800

his salon. A customer who comes into the salon and has his or her hair styled is counted as one client-visit.

Note that the term *revenue* is used in the planning budget rather than *sales*. We use the term revenue throughout the chapter because some organizations have sources of revenue other than sales. For example, donations, as well as sales, are counted as revenue in nonprofit organizations.

Rick has identified eight major categories of costs—wages and salaries, hairstyling supplies, client gratuities, electricity, rent, liability insurance, employee health insurance, and miscellaneous. Client gratuities consist of flowers, candies, and glasses of champagne that Rick gives to his customers while they are in the salon.

Working with Victoria, Rick estimated a cost formula for each cost. For example, the cost formula for electricity is $1,500 + $0.10q$, where q equals the number of client-visits. In other words, electricity is a mixed cost with a $1,500 fixed element and a $0.10 per client-visit variable element. Once the budgeted level of activity was set at 1,000 client-visits, Rick computed the budgeted amount for each line item in the budget. For example, using the cost formula, he set the budgeted cost for electricity at $1,600 (= $1,500 + $0.10 \times 1,000$). To finalize his budget, Rick computed his expected net operating income for March of $16,800.

At the end of March, Rick prepared the income statement in Exhibit 10–3, which shows that 1,100 clients actually visited his salon in March and that his actual net operating income for the month was $21,230. It is important to realize that the actual results are *not* determined by plugging the actual number of client-visits into the revenue and cost formulas. The formulas are simply estimates of what the revenues and costs should be for a given level of activity. What actually happens usually differs from what is supposed to happen.

The first thing Rick noticed when comparing Exhibits 10–2 and 10–3 is that the actual profit of $21,230 (from Exhibits 10–3) was substantially higher than the budgeted profit of $16,800 (from Exhibit 10–2). This was, of course, good news, but Rick wanted to know more. Business was up by 10%—the salon had 1,100 client-visits instead of the budgeted 1,000 client-visits. Could this alone explain the higher net operating income? The answer is no. An increase in net operating income of 10% would have resulted in net operating income of only $18,480 (= $1.1 \times $16,800$), not the $21,230 actually earned during the month. What is responsible for this better outcome? Higher prices? Lower costs? Something else? Whatever the cause, Rick would like to know the answer and then hopefully repeat the same performance next month.

EXHIBIT 10–3
Actual Results—Income Statement

Rick's Hairstyling
Income Statement
For the Month Ended March 31

Actual client-visits	1,100
Revenue	$194,200
Expenses:	
Wages and salaries	106,900
Hairstyling supplies	1,620
Client gratuities	6,870
Electricity	1,550
Rent	28,500
Liability insurance	2,800
Employee health insurance	22,600
Miscellaneous	2,130
Total expense	172,970
Net operating income	$ 21,230

In an attempt to analyze what happened in March, Rick prepared the report comparing actual to budgeted costs that appears in Exhibit 10–4. Note that most of the variances in this report are labeled unfavorable (U) rather than favorable (F) even though net operating income was actually higher than expected. For example, wages and salaries show an unfavorable variance of $4,900 because the actual wages and salaries expense was $106,900, whereas the budget called for wages and salaries of $102,000. The problem with the report, as Rick immediately realized, is that it compares revenues and costs at

EXHIBIT 10–4
Comparison of Actual Results to the Static Planning Budget

Rick's Hairstyling
Comparison of Actual Results to the Planning Budget
For the Month Ended March 31

	Actual Results	Planning Budget	Variances*
Client-visits	1,100	1,000	
Revenue	$194,200	$180,000	$14,200 F
Expenses:			
Wages and salaries	106,900	102,000	4,900 U
Hairstyling supplies	1,620	1,500	120 U
Client gratuities	6,870	4,100	2,770 U
Electricity	1,550	1,600	50 F
Rent	28,500	28,500	0
Liability insurance	2,800	2,800	0
Employee health insurance	22,600	21,300	1,300 U
Miscellaneous	2,130	1,400	730 U
Total expense	172,970	163,200	9,770 U
Net operating income	$ 21,230	$ 16,800	$ 4,430 F

*The revenue variance is labeled favorable (unfavorable) when the actual revenue is greater than (less than) the planning budget. The expense variances are labeled favorable (unfavorable) when the actual expense is less than (greater than) the planning budget.

one level of activity (1,000 client-visits) to revenues and costs at a different level of activity (1,100 client-visits). This is like comparing apples to oranges. Because Rick had 100 more client-visits than expected, some of his costs should be higher than budgeted. From Rick's standpoint, the increase in activity was good; however, it appears to be having a negative impact on most of the costs in the report. Rick knew that something would have to be done to make the report more meaningful, but he was unsure of what to do. So he made an appointment to meet with Victoria Kho to discuss the next step.

Victoria: How is the budgeting going?

Rick: Pretty well. I didn't have any trouble putting together the budget for March. I also prepared a report comparing the actual results for March to the budget, but that report isn't giving me what I really want to know.

Victoria: Because your actual level of activity didn't match your budgeted activity?

Rick: Right. I know the level of activity shouldn't affect my fixed costs, but we had more client-visits than I had expected and that had to affect my other costs.

Victoria: So you want to know whether the higher actual costs are justified by the higher level of activity?

Rick: Precisely.

Victoria: If you leave your reports and data with me, I can work on it later today, and by tomorrow I'll have a report to show you.

MANAGERIAL
ACCOUNTING IN
ACTION
The Issue

How a Flexible Budget Works

A flexible budget approach recognizes that a budget can be adjusted to show what costs *should be* for the actual level of activity. To illustrate how flexible budgets work, Victoria prepared the report in Exhibit 10–5 that shows what the *revenues and costs should have been given the actual level of activity* in March. Preparing the report is straightforward. The cost formula for each cost is used to estimate what the cost should have been for 1,100 client-visits—the actual level of activity for March. For example, using the cost formula $1,500 + $0.10q, the cost of electricity in March *should have been* $1,610 (= $1,500 + $0.10 × 1,100). Also, notice that the amounts of rent ($28,500), liability insurance ($2,800), and employee health insurance ($21,300) in the flexible budget equal the corresponding amounts in the planning budget (see Exhibit 10–2). This occurs because fixed costs are not affected by the activity level.

Rick's Hairstyling Flexible Budget For the Month Ended March 31	
Actual client-visits (q)	1,100
Revenue ($180.00q)	$198,000
Expenses:	
Wages and salaries ($65,000 + $37.00q)	105,700
Hairstyling supplies ($1.50q)	1,650
Client gratuities ($4.10q)	4,510
Electricity ($1,500 + $0.10q)	1,610
Rent ($28,500)	28,500
Liability insurance ($2,800)	2,800
Employee health insurance ($21,300)	21,300
Miscellaneous ($1,200 + $0.20q)	1,420
Total expense	167,490
Net operating income	$ 30,510

EXHIBIT 10–5
Flexible Budget Based on Actual Activity

We can see from the flexible budget that the net operating income in March *should have been* $30,510, but recall from Exhibit 10–3 that the net operating income was actually only $21,230. The results are not as good as we thought. Why? We will answer that question shortly.

To summarize to this point, Rick had budgeted for a profit of $16,800. The actual profit was quite a bit higher—$21,230. However, Victoria's analysis shows that given the actual number of client-visits in March, the profit should have been even higher—$30,510. What are the causes of these discrepancies? Rick would certainly like to build on the positive factors, while working to reduce the negative factors. But what are they?

Flexible Budget Variances

To answer Rick's questions concerning the discrepancies between budgeted and actual costs, Victoria broke down the variances shown in Exhibit 10–4 into two types of variances—activity variances and revenue and spending variances. We explain how she did it in the next two sections.

Activity Variances

LEARNING OBJECTIVE 10–2
Prepare a report showing activity variances.

Part of the discrepancy between the budgeted profit and the actual profit is due to the fact that the actual level of activity in March was higher than expected. How much of this discrepancy was due to this single factor? Victoria prepared the report in Exhibit 10–6 to answer this question. In that report, the flexible budget based on the actual level of

---

EXHIBIT 10–6
Activity Variances from Comparing the Flexible Budget Based on Actual Activity to the Planning Budget

Rick's Hairstyling
Activity Variances
For the Month Ended March 31

	Flexible Budget	Planning Budget	Activity Variances*
Client-visits	1,100	1,000	
Revenue ($180.00q)	$198,000	$180,000	$18,000 F
Expenses:			
Wages and salaries			
($65,000 + $37.00q)	105,700	102,000	3,700 U
Hairstyling supplies ($1.50q)	1,650	1,500	150 U
Client gratuities ($4.10q)	4,510	4,100	410 U
Electricity ($1,500 + $0.10q)	1,610	1,600	10 U
Rent ($28,500)	28,500	28,500	0
Liability insurance ($2,800)	2,800	2,800	0
Employee health insurance ($21,300)	21,300	21,300	0
Miscellaneous ($1,200 + $0.20q)	1,420	1,400	20 U
Total expense	167,490	163,200	4,290 U
Net operating income	$ 30,510	$ 16,800	$13,710 F

*The revenue variance is labeled favorable (unfavorable) when the revenue in the flexible budget is greater than (less than) the planning budget. The expense variances are labeled favorable (unfavorable) when the expense in the flexible budget is less than (greater than) the planning budget.

activity for the period is compared to the planning budget from the beginning of the period. The flexible budget shows what should have happened at the actual level of activity, whereas the planning budget shows what should have happened at the budgeted level of activity. Therefore, the differences between the flexible budget and the planning budget show what should have happened solely because the actual level of activity differed from what had been expected.

For example, the flexible budget based on 1,100 client-visits shows revenue of $198,000 (= $180 per client-visit × 1,100 client-visits). The planning budget based on 1,000 client-visits shows revenue of $180,000 (= $180 per client-visit × 1,000 client-visits). Because the salon had 100 more client-visits than anticipated in the budget, actual revenue should have been higher than budgeted revenue by $18,000 (= $198,000 − $180,000). This activity variance is shown on the report as $18,000 F (favorable). Similarly, the flexible budget based on 1,100 client-visits shows electricity costs of $1,610 (= $1,500 + $0.10 per client-visit × 1,100 client-visits). The planning budget based on 1,000 client-visits shows electricity costs of $1,600 (= $1,500 + $0.10 per client-visit × 1,000 client-visits). Because the salon had 100 more client-visits than anticipated in the budget, actual electricity costs should have been higher than budgeted costs by $10 (= $1,610 − $1,600). The activity variance for electricity is shown on the report as $10 U (unfavorable). Note that in this case, the label "unfavorable" may be a little misleading. Costs *should* be $10 higher for electricity simply because business was up by 100 client-visits; therefore, is this variance really unfavorable if it was a necessary cost of serving more customers? For reasons such as this, we would like to caution you against assuming that unfavorable variances always indicate bad performance and favorable variances always indicate good performance.

Because all of the variances on this report are solely due to the difference between the actual level of activity and the level of activity in the planning budget from the beginning of the period, they are called **activity variances.** For example, the activity variance for revenue is $18,000 F, the activity variance for electricity is $10 U, and so on. The most important activity variance appears at the very bottom of the report; namely, the $13,710 F (favorable) variance for net operating income. This variance says that because activity was higher than expected in the planning budget, the net operating income should have been $13,710 higher. We caution against placing too much emphasis on any other single variance in this report. As we have said above, one would expect some costs to be higher as a consequence of more business. It is misleading to think of these unfavorable variances as indicative of poor performance.

On the other hand, the favorable activity variance for net operating income is important. Let's explore this variance a bit more thoroughly. First, as we have already noted, activity was up by 10%, but the flexible budget indicates that net operating income should have increased much more than 10%. A 10% increase in net operating income from the $16,800 in the planning budget would result in net operating income of $18,480 (= 1.1 × $16,800); however, the flexible budget shows much higher net operating income of $30,510. Why? The short answer is: Because of the presence of fixed costs. When we apply the 10% increase to the budgeted net operating income to estimate the profit at the higher level of activity, we implicitly assume that the revenues and *all* of the costs increase by 10%. But they do not. Note that when the activity level increases by 10%, three of the costs—rent, liability insurance, and employee health insurance—do not increase at all. These are all purely fixed costs. So while sales do increase by 10%, these costs do not increase. This results in net operating income increasing by more than 10%. A similar effect occurs with the mixed costs, which contain fixed cost elements—wages and salaries, electricity, and miscellaneous. While sales increase by 10%, these mixed costs increase by less than 10%, resulting in an overall increase in net operating income of more than 10%. Because of the existence of fixed costs, net operating income does not change in proportion to changes in the level of activity. There is a leverage effect. The percentage changes in net operating income are ordinarily larger than the percentage increases in activity.

LEARNING OBJECTIVE 10–3
Prepare a report showing revenue and spending variances.

Revenue and Spending Variances

In the last section we answered the question "What impact did the change in activity have on our revenues, costs, and profit?" In this section we will answer the question "How well did we control our revenues, our costs, and our profit?"

Recall that the flexible budget based on the actual level of activity in Exhibit 10–5 shows what *should have happened given the actual level of activity.* Therefore, Victoria's next step was to compare actual results to the flexible budget—in essence comparing what actually happened to what should have happened. Her work is shown in Exhibit 10–7.

Focusing first on revenue, the actual revenue totaled $194,200. However, the flexible budget indicates that, given the actual level of activity, revenue should have been $198,000. Consequently, revenue was $3,800 less than it should have been, given the actual number of client-visits for the month. This discrepancy is labeled as a $3,800 U (unfavorable) variance and is called a *revenue variance.* A **revenue variance** is the difference between the actual total revenue and what the total revenue should have been, given the actual level of activity for the period. If actual revenue exceeds what the revenue should have been, the variance is labeled favorable. If actual revenue is less than what the revenue should have been, the variance is labeled unfavorable. Why would actual revenue be less than or more than it should have been, given the actual level of activity? Basically, the revenue variance is favorable if the average selling price is greater than expected; it is unfavorable if the average selling price is less than expected. This could happen for a variety of reasons including a change in selling price, a different mix of products sold, a change in the amount of discounts given, poor accounting controls, and so on.

EXHIBIT 10–7
Revenue and Spending Variances from Comparing Actual Results to the Flexible Budget

Rick's Hairstyling
Revenue and Spending Variances
For the Month Ended March 31

	Actual Results	Flexible Budget	Revenue and Spending Variances*
Client-visits	1,100	1,100	
Revenue ($180.00q)	$194,200	$198,000	$3,800 U
Expenses:			
Wages and salaries ($65,000 + $37.00q)	106,900	105,700	1,200 U
Hairstyling supplies ($1.50q)	1,620	1,650	30 F
Client gratuities ($4.10q)	6,870	4,510	2,360 U
Electricity ($1,500 + $0.10q)	1,550	1,610	60 F
Rent ($28,500)	28,500	28,500	0
Liability insurance ($2,800)	2,800	2,800	0
Employee health insurance ($21,300)	22,600	21,300	1,300 U
Miscellaneous ($1,200 + $0.20q)	2,130	1,420	710 U
Total expense	172,970	167,490	5,480 U
Net operating income	$ 21,230	$ 30,510	$9,280 U

*The revenue variance is labeled favorable (unfavorable) when the actual revenue is greater than (less than) the flexible budget. The expense variances are labeled favorable (unfavorable) when the actual expense is less than (greater than) the flexible budget.

STATE OF THE UNION SPEECH HURTS CORPORATE JET INDUSTRY

In December 2008, Detroit auto executives flew private corporate jets to Washington D.C. to plead for billions of taxpayer dollars to save their companies. The public outcry was loud and clear: How could companies on the verge of bankruptcy afford to transport their executives in private corporate jets? One month later President Obama's State of the Union speech included criticism of CEOs who "disappear on a private jet."

The impact of these events on the corporate jet manufacturing industry was swift and severe. Dassault Aviation had 27 more order cancellations than new orders in the first quarter of 2009. Cessna Aircraft had 92 first-quarter order cancellations and laid off 42% of its workforce. Approximately 3,100 jets flooded the resale market compared to 1,800 jets for resale in the first quarter of the prior year. The CEO of Cessna and the president of Gulfstream Aerospace went to the White House in May 2009 to seek an end to the rhetoric that was destroying their sales.

These facts illustrate how an activity variance can be affected by uncontrollable events. The actual first-quarter sales at these companies were substantially lower than their budgeted sales due to reasons that they could not foresee or control.

Source: Carol Matlack, "Public Flak Grounds Private Jets," *BusinessWeek*, June 8, 2009, p. 13.

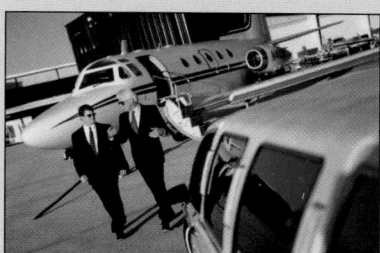
© Francisco Cruz/Purestock/Superstock

Focusing next on costs, the actual electricity cost was $1,550; however, the flexible budget indicates that electricity costs should have been $1,610 for the 1,100 client-visits in March. Because the cost was $60 less than we would have expected for the actual level of activity during the period, it is labeled as a favorable variance, $60 F. This is an example of a *spending variance*. By definition, a **spending variance** is the difference between the actual amount of the cost and how much a cost should have been, given the actual level of activity. If the actual cost is greater than what the cost should have been, the variance is labeled as unfavorable. If the actual cost is less than what the cost should have been, the variance is labeled as favorable. Why would a cost have a favorable or unfavorable variance? There are many possible explanations including paying a higher price for inputs than should have been paid, using too many inputs for the actual level of activity, a change in technology, and so on. In the next chapter we will explore these types of explanations in greater detail.

Note from Exhibit 10–7 that the overall net operating income variance is $9,280 U (unfavorable). This means that given the actual level of activity for the period, the net operating income was $9,280 lower than it should have been. There are a number of reasons for this. The most prominent is the unfavorable revenue variance of $3,800. Next in line is the $2,360 unfavorable variance for client gratuities. Looking at this in another way, client gratuities were more than 50% larger than they should have been according to the flexible budget. This is a variance that Rick would almost certainly want to investigate further. He may find that this unfavorable variance is not necessarily a bad thing. It is possible, for example, that more lavish use of gratuities led to the 10% increase in client-visits.

Exhibit 10–7 also includes a $1,300 unfavorable variance related to employee health insurance, thereby highlighting how a fixed cost can have a spending variance. While fixed costs do not depend on the level of activity, the actual amount of a fixed cost can differ from the estimated amount included in a flexible budget. For example, perhaps Rick's employee health insurance premiums unexpectedly increased by $1,300 during March.

In conclusion, the revenue and spending variances in Exhibit 10–7 will help Rick better understand why his actual net operating income differs from what should have happened given the actual level of activity.

A Performance Report Combining Activity and Revenue and Spending Variances

Exhibit 10–8 displays Victoria's performance report that combines the activity variances (from Exhibit 10–6) with the revenue and spending variances (from Exhibit 10–7). The report brings together information from those two earlier exhibits in a way that makes it easier to interpret what happened during the period. The format of this report is a bit different from the format of the previous reports in that the variances appear between the amounts being compared rather than after them. For example, the activity variances appear between the flexible budget amounts and the planning budget amounts. In Exhibit 10–6, the activity variances appeared after the flexible budget and the planning budget.

Note two numbers in particular in the performance report—the activity variance for net operating income of $13,710 F (favorable) and the overall revenue and spending variance for net operating income of $9,280 U (unfavorable). It is worth repeating what those two numbers mean. The $13,710 favorable activity variance occurred because actual activity (1,100 client-visits) was greater than the budgeted level of activity (1,000 client-visits). The $9,280 unfavorable overall revenue and spending variance occurred because the profit was not as large as it should have been for the actual level of activity for the period. These two different variances mean very different things and call for different types of actions. To generate a favorable activity variance for net operating income, managers must take actions to increase client-visits. To generate a favorable overall revenue and spending variance, managers must take actions to protect selling prices, increase operating efficiency, and reduce the prices of inputs.

The performance report in Exhibit 10–8 provides much more useful information to managers than the simple comparison of budgeted to actual results in Exhibit 10–4. In Exhibit 10–4, the effects of changes in activity were jumbled together with the effects of how well prices were controlled and operations were managed. The performance report in Exhibit 10–8 clearly separates these effects, allowing managers to take a much more focused approach in evaluating operations.

EXHIBIT 10–8

Performance Report Combining Activity Variances with Revenue and Spending Variances

Rick's Hairstyling
Flexible Budget Performance Report
For the Month Ended March 31

	(1) Actual Results	Revenue and Spending Variances (1) – (2)	(2) Flexible Budget	Activity Variances (2) – (3)	(3) Planning Budget
Client-visits.	1,100		1,100		1,000
Revenue ($180.00q).	$194,200	$3,800 U	$198,000	$18,000 F	$180,000
Expenses:					
Wages and salaries ($65,000 + $37.00q)	106,900	1,200 U	105,700	3,700 U	120,000
Hairstyling supplies ($1.50q).	1,620	30 F	1,650	150 U	1,500
Client gratuities ($4.10q)	6,870	2,360 U	4,510	410 U	4,100
Electricity ($1,500 + $0.10q).	1,550	60 F	1,610	10 U	1,600
Rent ($28,500)	28,500	0	28,500	0	28,500
Liability insurance ($2,800)	2,800	0	2,800	0	2,800
Employee health insurance ($21,300).	22,600	1,300 U	21,300	0	21,300
Miscellaneous ($1,200 + $0.20q)	2,130	710 U	1,420	20 U	1,400
Total expense	172,970	5,480 U	167,490	4,290 U	163,200
Net operating income	$ 21,230	$9,280 U	$ 30,510	$13,710 F	$ 16,800

To get a better idea of how the performance report accomplishes this task, look at hairstyling supplies in the performance report. The actual cost of hairstyling supplies was $1,620 for the period, whereas in the planning budget, this cost was $1,500. In the comparison of the actual results to the planning budget in Exhibit 10–4, this difference is shown as an unfavorable variance of $120. Exhibit 10–4 uses a static planning budget approach that compares actual costs at one level of activity to budgeted costs at a different level of activity. As we said before, this is like comparing apples to oranges. This variance is actually a mixture of two different effects. This becomes clear in the performance report in Exhibit 10–8. The $120 difference between the actual results and the budgeted amount is composed of two different variances—a favorable spending variance of $30 and an unfavorable activity variance of $150. The favorable spending variance occurred because less was spent on hairstyling supplies than one would have expected, given the actual level of activity for the month. The activity variance occurs because activity was greater than anticipated in the planning budget, which naturally resulted in a higher total cost for this variable cost.

The flexible budget performance report in Exhibit 10–8 provides a more valid assessment of performance than simply comparing actual costs to static planning budget costs because actual costs are compared to what costs should have been at the actual level of activity. In other words, apples are compared to apples. When this is done, we see that the spending variance for hairstyling supplies is $30 F (favorable) rather than $120 U (unfavorable) as it was in the original static planning budget performance report (see Exhibit 10–4). In some cases, as with hairstyling supplies in Rick's report, an unfavorable static planning budget variance may be transformed into a favorable revenue or spending variance when an increase in activity is properly taken into account. The following discussion took place the next day at Rick's salon.

Victoria: Let me show you what I've got. [Victoria shows Rick the flexible budget performance report in Exhibit 10–8.] I simply used the cost formulas to update the budget to reflect the increase in client-visits you experienced in March. That allowed me to come up with a better benchmark for what the costs should have been.

Rick: That's what you labeled the "flexible budget based on 1,100 client-visits"?

Victoria: That's right. Your original budget was based on 1,000 client-visits, so it understated what some of the costs should have been when you actually served 1,100 customers.

Rick: That's clear enough. These spending variances aren't quite as shocking as the variances on my first report.

Victoria: Yes, but you still have an unfavorable variance of $2,360 for client gratuities.

Rick: I know how that happened. In March there was a big political fundraising dinner that I forgot about when I prepared the March budget. To fit all of our regular clients in, we had to push them through here pretty fast. Everyone still got top-rate service, but I felt bad about not being able to spend as much time with each customer. I wanted to give my customers a little extra something to compensate them for the less personal service, so I ordered a lot of flowers, which I gave away by the bunch.

Victoria: With the prices you charge, Rick, I am sure the gesture was appreciated.

Rick: One thing bothers me about the report. When we discussed my costs before, you called rent, liability insurance, and employee health insurance fixed costs. How can I have a variance for a fixed cost? Doesn't fixed mean that it doesn't change?

Victoria: We call these costs *fixed* because they shouldn't be affected by *changes in the level of activity.* However, that doesn't mean that they can't change for other reasons. Also, the use of the term *fixed* also suggests to people that the cost can't be controlled, but that isn't true. It is often easier to control fixed costs than variable costs. For example, it would be fairly easy for you to change your insurance bill by adjusting the amount of insurance you carry. It would be much more difficult for you to significantly reduce your spending on hairstyling supplies—a variable cost that is a necessary part of serving customers.

Rick: I think I understand, but it *is* confusing.

R I C K ' S
Hairstyling Salon

Victoria: Just remember that a cost is called variable if it is proportional to activity; it is called fixed if it does not depend on the level of activity. However, fixed costs can change for reasons unrelated to changes in the level of activity. And controllability has little to do with whether a cost is variable or fixed. Fixed costs are often more controllable than variable costs.

© Janis Christie/Photodisc/Getty Images

HOTELS MANAGE REVENUE AND COST LEVERS AMID RECESSION

When the economy spiraled downward in 2009, it forced hotel chains to make tough decisions in an effort to achieve their profit goals. For example, Wyndham Hotels and Resorts decided to take sewing kits, mouthwash, and showercaps out of its rooms—instead, requiring customers to ask for these amenities at the front desk. Intercontinental Hotels Group stopped delivering newspapers to loyalty-program members' rooms; Marriott International cut back its breakfast offerings; and the Ritz-Carlton reduced operating hours at its restaurants, spas, and retail shops. In addition, many hotel chains reduced their rental rates.

A flexible budget performance report can help hotel managers analyze how the changes described above impact net operating income. It isolates activity, revenue, and spending variances that help identify the underlying reasons for differences between budgeted and actual net operating income.

Source: Sarah Nassauer, "No Showercaps at the Inn," *The Wall Street Journal,* January 22, 2009, pp. D1–D2.

Performance Reports in Nonprofit Organizations

The performance reports in nonprofit organizations are basically the same as the performance reports we have considered so far—with one prominent difference. Nonprofit organizations usually receive a significant amount of funding from sources other than sales. For example, universities receive their funding from sales (i.e., tuition charged to students), from endowment income and donations, and—in the case of public universities—from state appropriations. This means that, like costs, the revenue in governmental and nonprofit organizations may consist of both fixed and variable elements. For example, the Seattle Opera Company's revenue in a recent year consisted of grants and donations of $12,719,000 and ticket sales of $8,125,000 (or about $75.35 per ticket sold). Consequently, the revenue formula for the opera can be written as:

$$\text{Revenue} = \$12,719,000 + \$75.35q$$

where q is the number of tickets sold. In other respects, the performance report for the Seattle Opera and other nonprofit organizations would be similar to the performance report in Exhibit 10–8.

Performance Reports in Cost Centers

Performance reports are often prepared for organizations that do not have any source of outside revenue. In particular, in a large organization a performance report may be prepared for each department—including departments that do not sell anything to outsiders. For example, a performance report is very commonly prepared for production departments in manufacturing companies. Such reports should be prepared using the same principles we have discussed and should look very much like the performance report in Exhibit 10–8—with the exception that revenue, and consequently net operating income, will not appear on the report. Because the managers in these departments are responsible for costs, but not revenues, they are often called *cost centers.*

Flexible Budgets with Multiple Cost Drivers

LEARNING OBJECTIVE 10–5
Prepare a flexible budget with more than one cost driver.

At Rick's Hairstyling, we have thus far assumed that there is only one cost driver—the number of client-visits. However, in the activity-based costing chapter, we found that more than one cost driver might be needed to adequately explain all of the costs in an organization. For example, some of the costs at Rick's Hairstyling probably depend more on the number of hours that the salon is open for business than the number of client-visits. Specifically, most of Rick's employees are paid salaries, but some are paid on an hourly basis. None of the employees is paid on the basis of the number of customers actually served. Consequently, the cost formula for wages and salaries would be more accurate if it were stated in terms of the hours of operation rather than the number of client-visits. The cost of electricity is even more complex. Some of the cost is fixed—the heat must be kept at some minimum level even at night when the salon is closed. Some of the cost depends on the number of client-visits—the power consumed by hair dryers depends on the number of customers served. Some of the cost depends on the number of hours the salon is open—the costs of lighting the salon and heating it to a comfortable temperature. Consequently, the cost formula for electricity would be more accurate if it were stated in terms of both the number of client-visits and the hours of operation rather than just in terms of the number of client-visits.

Exhibit 10–9 shows a flexible budget in which these changes have been made. In that flexible budget, two cost drivers are listed—client-visits and hours of operation—where q_1 refers to client-visits and q_2 refers to hours of operation. For example, wages and salaries depend on the hours of operation and its cost formula is $65,000 + $220q_2$. Because the salon actually operated 190 hours, the flexible budget amount for wages and salaries is $106,800 (= $65,000 + $220 × 190). The electricity cost depends on both client-visits and the hours of operation and its cost formula is $390 + $0.10q_1 + $6.00q_2$. Because the actual number of client-visits was 1,100 and the salon actually operated for 190 hours, the flexible budget amount for electricity is $1,640 (= $390 + $0.10 × 1,100 + $6.00 × 190). Notice that the net operating income in the flexible budget based on two cost drivers is $29,380, whereas the net operating income in the flexible budget based on one cost driver (see Exhibit 10–5) is $30,510. These two amounts differ because the flexible budget based on two cost drivers is more accurate than the flexible budget based on one driver.

EXHIBIT 10–9
Flexible Budget Based on More than One Cost Driver

Rick's Hairstyling
Flexible Budget
For the Month Ended March 31

Actual client-visits (q_1)	1,100
Actual hours of operation (q_2)	190
Revenue ($180.00q_1$)	$198,000
Expenses:	
Wages and salaries ($65,000 + $220q_2$)	106,800
Hairstyling supplies ($1.50q_1$)	1,650
Client gratuities ($4.10q_1$)	4,510
Electricity ($390 + $0.10q_1 + $6.00q_2$)	1,640
Rent ($28,500)	28,500
Liability insurance ($2,800)	2,800
Employee health insurance ($21,300)	21,300
Miscellaneous ($1,200 + $0.20q_1$)	1,420
Total expense	168,620
Net operating income	$ 29,380

HOSPITALS TURN TO FLEXIBLE BUDGETS

Mary Wilkes, a senior managing director with Phase 2 Consulting, says that hospitals may have to pay as much as $300,000 to install a flexible budgeting system, but the investment should readily pay for itself by enabling "more efficient use of hospital resources, particularly when it comes to labor." One of the keys to creating an effective flexible budgeting system is to recognize the existence of multiple cost drivers. Many hospitals frequently use patient volume as a cost driver when preparing flexible budgets; however, other variables can influence revenues and costs. For example, the percentage of patients covered by private insurance, Medicaid, or Medicare, as well as the proportion of uninsured patients all influence revenues and costs. A flexible budgeting system that incorporates patient volume and these other variables will be more accurate than one based solely on patient volume.

Source: Paul Barr, "Flexing Your Budget," *Modern Healthcare*, September 12, 2005, pp. 24–26.

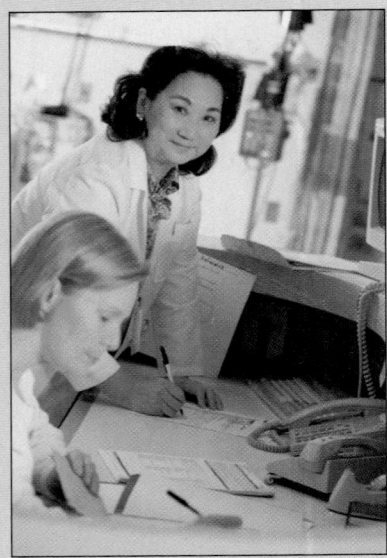

© Comstock Images/Jupiter Images

The revised flexible budget based on both client-visits and hours of operation can be used exactly like we used the earlier flexible budget based on just client-visits to compute activity variances as in Exhibit 10–6, revenue and spending variances as in Exhibit 10–7, and a performance report as in Exhibit 10–8. The difference is that because the cost formulas based on more than one cost driver are more accurate than the cost formulas based on just one cost driver, the variances will also be more accurate.

Some Common Errors

LEARNING OBJECTIVE 10–6
Understand common errors made in preparing performance reports based on budgets and actual results.

We started this chapter by discussing the need for managers to understand the difference between what actually happened and what was expected to happen—formalized by the planning budget. To meet this need, we developed a flexible budget that allowed us to isolate activity variances and revenue and spending variances. Unfortunately, this approach is not always followed in practice—resulting in misleading and difficult-to-interpret reports. The most common errors in preparing performance reports are to implicitly assume that all costs are fixed or to implicitly assume that all costs are variable. These erroneous assumptions lead to inaccurate benchmarks and incorrect variances.

We have already discussed one of these errors—assuming that all costs are fixed. This is the error that is made when static planning budget costs are compared to actual costs without any adjustment for the actual level of activity. Such a comparison appeared in Exhibit 10–4. For convenience, the comparison of actual to budgeted revenues and costs is repeated in Exhibit 10–10. Looking at that exhibit, note that the actual cost of hairstyling supplies of $1,620 is directly compared to the budgeted cost of $1,500, resulting in an unfavorable variance of $120. But this comparison only makes sense if the cost of hairstyling supplies is fixed. If the cost of hairstyling supplies isn't fixed (and indeed it is not), one would *expect* the cost to go up because of the increase in activity over the budget. Comparing actual costs to static planning budget costs only makes sense if the cost is fixed. If the cost isn't fixed, it needs to be adjusted for any change in activity that occurs during the period.

Rick's Hairstyling For the Month Ended March 31	Actual Results	Planning Budget	Variances
Client-visits.....................	1,100	1,000	
Revenue.........................	$194,200	$180,000	$14,200 F
Expenses:			
Wages and salaries	106,900	102,000	4,900 U
Hairstyling supplies..............	1,620	1,500	120 U
Client gratuities.................	6,870	4,100	2,770 U
Electricity	1,550	1,600	50 F
Rent	28,500	28,500	0
Liability insurance..............	2,800	2,800	0
Employee health insurance........	22,600	21,300	1,300 U
Miscellaneous...................	2,130	1,400	730 U
Total expense	172,970	163,200	9,770 U
Net operating income	$ 21,230	$ 16,800	$ 4,430 F

EXHIBIT 10–10
Faulty Analysis Comparing Actual Amounts to Budgeted Amounts (Implicitly Assumes All Income Statement Items Are Fixed)

Rick's Hairstyling For the Month Ended March 31	(1) Actual Results	(2) Planning Budget × (1,100/1,000)	Variances (1) − (2)
Client-visits....................	1,100		
Revenue.....................	$194,200	$198,000	$ 3,800 U
Expenses:			
Wages and salaries	106,900	112,200	5,300 F
Hairstyling supplies...........	1,620	1,650	30 F
Client gratuities..............	6,870	4,510	2,360 U
Electricity	1,550	1,760	210 F
Rent.......................	28,500	31,350	2,850 F
Liability insurance............	2,800	3,080	280 F
Employee health insurance....	21,600	23,430	830 F
Miscellaneous	2,130	1,540	590 U
Total expense	172,970	179,520	6,550 F
Net operating income	$ 21,230	$ 18,480	$2,750 F

EXHIBIT 10–11
Faulty Analysis That Assumes All Budget Items Are Variable

The other common error when comparing budgets to actual results is to assume that all costs are variable. A report that makes this error appears in Exhibit 10–11. The variances in this report are computed by comparing actual results to the amounts in the second numerical column where *all* of the budget items have been inflated by 10%—the percentage by which activity increased. This is a perfectly valid adjustment to make if an item is strictly variable—like sales and hairstyling supplies. It is *not* a valid adjustment if the item contains any fixed element. Take, for example, rent. If the salon serves 10% more customers in a given month, would you expect the rent to increase by 10%? The answer is no. Ordinarily, the rent is fixed in advance and does not depend on the volume of business. Therefore, the amount shown in the second numerical column of $31,350 is incorrect, which leads to the erroneous favorable variance of $2,850. In fact, the actual rent paid was exactly equal to the budgeted rent, so there should be no variance at all on a valid report.

SNOW REMOVAL BUDGETS GET PLOWED UNDER

The District of Columbia budgeted $6.2 million for its annual snow removal needs based on an expectation of 15 inches of snow per year. So, when it received 28 inches of snow in one weekend, its snow removal budget got plowed under. During this same weekend, the Virginia Department of Transportation estimated that 500,000 tons of snow dropped on its northern Virginia roadways, leading to historic cost overruns in its $79 million snow removal budget.

In these types of situations, a flexible budget can help managers assess operational efficiency. For example, a manager could create a cost formula such as "the snow removal cost per inch of snow" to estimate what the total variable snow removal costs should be for the actual inches of snowfall. This "flexed" snow removal cost could be compared to the actual snow removal cost in an effort to identify sources of exceptional performance or opportunities for process improvement.

Source: Sudeep Reddy and Clare Ansberry, "States Face Big Costs to Dig Out From Blizzard," *The Wall Street Journal,* February 9, 2010, p. A6.

Summary

Directly comparing actual revenues and costs to static planning budget revenues and costs can easily lead to erroneous conclusions. Actual revenues and costs differ from budgeted revenues and costs for a variety of reasons, but one of the biggest is a change in the level of activity. One would expect actual revenues and costs to increase or decrease as the activity level increases or decreases. Flexible budgets enable managers to isolate the various causes of the differences between budgeted and actual costs.

A flexible budget is a budget that is adjusted to the actual level of activity. It is the best estimate of what revenues and costs should have been, given the actual level of activity during the period. The flexible budget can be compared to the budget from the beginning of the period or to the actual results.

When the flexible budget is compared to the budget from the beginning of the period, activity variances are the result. An activity variance shows how a revenue or cost should have changed in response to the difference between actual and budgeted activity.

When actual results are compared to the flexible budget, revenue and spending variances are the result. A favorable revenue variance indicates that revenue was larger than should have been expected, given the actual level of activity. An unfavorable revenue variance indicates that revenue was less than it should have been, given the actual level of activity. A favorable spending variance indicates that the cost was less than expected, given the actual level of activity. An unfavorable spending variance indicates that the cost was greater than it should have been, given the actual level of activity.

A flexible budget performance report combines activity variances and revenue and spending variances on one report.

Common errors in comparing actual costs to budgeted costs are to assume all costs are fixed or to assume all costs are variable. If all costs are assumed to be fixed, the variances for variable and mixed costs will be incorrect. If all costs are assumed to be variable, the variances for fixed and mixed costs will be incorrect. The variance for a cost will only be correct if the actual behavior of the cost is used to develop the flexible budget benchmark.

Review Problem: Variance Analysis Using a Flexible Budget

Harrald's Fish House is a family-owned restaurant that specializes in Scandinavian-style seafood. Data concerning the restaurant's monthly revenues and costs appear below (q refers to the number of meals served):

	Formula
Revenue..................	$16.50q$
Cost of ingredients.........	$6.25q$
Wages and salaries	$10,400
Utilities	$800 + $0.20q$
Rent	$2,200
Miscellaneous.............	$600 + $0.80q$

Required:

1. Prepare the restaurant's planning budget for April assuming that 1,800 meals are served.
2. Assume that 1,700 meals were actually served in April. Prepare a flexible budget for this level of activity.
3. The actual results for April appear below. Prepare a flexible budget performance report for the restaurant for April.

Revenue......................	$27,920
Cost of ingredients.............	$11,110
Wages and salaries	$10,130
Utilities	$1,080
Rent	$2,200
Miscellaneous.................	$2,240

Solution to Review Problem

1. The planning budget for April appears below:

Harralds Fish House Planning Budget For the Month Ended April 30	
Budgeted meals served(q)	1,800
Revenue ($16.50q$)	$29,700
Expenses:	
Cost of ingredients ($6.25q$)..............	11,250
Wages and salaries ($10,400)............	10,400
Utilities ($800 + $0.20q$)	1,160
Rent ($2,200)	2,200
Miscellaneous ($600 + $0.80q$)	2,040
Total expense	27,050
Net operating income	$ 2,650

2. The flexible budget for April appears below:

Harralds Fish House Flexible Budget For the Month Ended April 30	
Actual meals served (q).....................	1,700
Revenue ($16.50q$)	$28,050
Expenses:	
Cost of ingredients ($6.25q$)..............	10,625
Wages and salaries ($10,400)............	10,400
Utilities ($800 + $0.20q$)	1,140
Rent ($2,200)	2,200
Miscellaneous ($600 + $0.80q$)	1,960
Total expense	26,325
Net operating income	$ 1,725

3. The flexible budget performance report for April appears below:

	Harralds Fish House Flexible Budget Performance Report For the Month Ended April 30					
	(1) Actual Results	Revenue and Spending Variances (1) – (2)	(2) Flexible Budget	Activity Variances (2) – (3)	(3) Planning Budget
Meals served..............	1,700		1,700		1,800
Revenue ($16.50q)	$27,920	$130 U	$28,050	$1,650 U	$29,700
Expenses:					
Cost of ingredients ($6.25q)...............	11,110	485 U	10,625	625 F	11,250
Wages and salaries ($10,400).............	10,130	270 F	10,400	0	10,400
Utilities ($800 + $0.20q) ..	1,080	60 F	1,140	20 F	1,160
Rent ($2,200)	2,200	0	2,200	0	2,200
Miscellaneous ($600 + $0.80q)................	2,240	280 U	1,960	80 F	2,040
Total expense	26,760	435 U	26,325	725 F	27,050
Net operating income	$ 1,160	$565 U	$ 1,725	$ 925 U	$ 2,650

Glossary

Activity variance The difference between a revenue or cost item in the flexible budget and the same item in the static planning budget. An activity variance is due solely to the difference between the actual level of activity used in the flexible budget and the level of activity assumed in the planning budget. (p. 445)

Flexible budget A report showing estimates of what revenues and costs should have been, given the actual level of activity for the period. (p. 440)

Planning budget A budget created at the beginning of the budgeting period that is valid only for the planned level of activity. (p. 440)

Revenue variance The difference between the actual revenue for the period and how much the revenue should have been, given the actual level of activity. A favorable (unfavorable) revenue variance occurs because the revenue is higher (lower) than expected, given the actual level of activity for the period. (p. 446)

Spending variance The difference between the actual amount of the cost and how much the cost should have been, given the actual level of activity. A favorable (unfavorable) spending variance occurs because the cost is lower (higher) than expected, given the actual level of activity for the period. (p. 447)

Questions

10–1 What is a static planning budget?

10–2 What is a flexible budget and how does it differ from a static planning budget?

10–3 What are some of the possible reasons that actual results may differ from what had been budgeted at the beginning of a period?

10–4 Why is it difficult to interpret a difference between how much expense was budgeted and how much was actually spent?

10–5 What is an activity variance and what does it mean?

10–6 What is a revenue variance and what does it mean?

10–7 What is a spending variance and what does it mean?

10–8 What does a flexible budget performance report do that a simple comparison of budgeted to actual results does not do?

10–9 How does a flexible budget based on two cost drivers differ from a flexible budget based on a single cost driver?

10–10 What assumption is implicitly made about cost behavior when actual results are directly compared to a static planning budget? Why is this assumption questionable?

10–11 What assumption is implicitly made about cost behavior when all of the items in a static planning budget are adjusted in proportion to a change in activity? Why is this assumption questionable?

Multiple-choice questions are available with Connect.

Additional student resources are available with Connect.   **connect**   **Applying Excel**

LEARNING OBJECTIVES 10–1, 10–2, 10–3, 10–4

The Excel worksheet form that appears below is to be used to recreate the Review Problem related to Harrald's Fish House. Download the workbook containing this from Connect. *On the website you will also receive instructions about how to use this worksheet form.*

You should proceed to the requirements below only after completing your worksheet.

Required:

1. Check your worksheet by changing the revenue in cell D4 to $16.00; the cost of ingredients in cell D5 to $6.50; and the wages and salaries in cell B6 to $10,000. The activity variance for net operating income should now be $850 U and the spending variance for total expenses should be $410 U. If you do not get these answers, find the errors in your worksheet and correct them.

   a. What is the activity variance for revenue? Explain this variance.

   b. What is the spending variance for the cost of ingredients? Explain this variance.

	A	B	C	D	E	F	G	H	I
1	Chapter 10: Applying Excel								
2									
3	**Data**								
4	Revenue			$16.50 q					
5	Cost of ingredients			$6.25 q					
6	Wages and salaries	$10,400							
7	Utilities	$800	+	$0.20 q					
8	Rent	$2,200							
9	Miscellaneous	$600	+	$0.80 q					
10									
11	Actual results:								
12	Revenue	$27,920							
13	Cost of ingredients	$11,110							
14	Wages and salaries	$10,130							
15	Utilities	$1,080							
16	Rent	$2,200							
17	Miscellaneous	$2,240							
18									
19	Planning budget activity	1,800	meals served						
20	Actual activity	1,700	meals served						
21									
22	*Enter a formula into each of the cells marked with a ? below*								
23	**Review Problem: Variance Analysis Using a Flexible Budget**								
24									
25	*Construct a flexible budget performance report*								
26						Revenue			
27						and			
28		Planning	Activity		Flexible	Spending		Actual	
29		Budget	Variances		Budget	Variances		Results	
30	Meals served	?			?			?	
31	Revenue	?	?		?	?		?	
32	Expenses:								
33	Cost of ingredients	?	?		?	?		?	
34	Wages and salaries	?	?		?	?		?	
35	Utilities	?	?		?	?		?	
36	Rent	?	?		?	?		?	
37	Miscellaneous	?	?		?	?		?	
38	Total expenses	?	?		?	?		?	
39	Net operating income	?	?		?	?		?	
40									

I◀ ◀ ▶ ▶I **Chapter 10 Form** Filled in Chapter 10 Form Chapter 10 Form

2. Revise the data in your worksheet to reflect the results for the following year:

Data

Revenue.................		$16.50q
Cost of ingredients........		$6.25q
Wages and salaries	$10,400	
Utilities	$800 +	$0.20q
Rent.....................	$2,200	
Miscellaneous...........	$600 +	$0.80q

Actual results:

Revenue.................	$28,900
Cost of ingredients........	$11,300
Wages and salaries	$10,300
Utilities	$1,120
Rent.....................	$2,300
Miscellaneous...........	$2,020
Planning budget activity ...	1,700 meals served
Actual activity	1,800 meals served

Using the flexible budget performance report, briefly evaluate the company's performance for the year and indicate where attention should be focused.

The Foundational 15 Additional student resources are available with Connect.

LEARNING OBJECTIVES 10–1, 10–2, 10–3,

Adger Corporation is a service company that measures its output based on the number of customers served. The company provided the following fixed and variable cost estimates that it uses for budgeting purposes and the actual results for May as shown below:

	Fixed Element per Month	Variable Element per Customer Served	Actual Total for May
Revenue..........		$5,000	$160,000
Employee salaries and wages.....	$50,000	$1,100	$88,000
Travel expenses ..		$600	$19,000
Other expenses ..	$36,000		$34,500

When preparing its planning budget the company estimated that it would serve 30 customers per month; however, during May the company actually served 35 customers.

Required:

1. What amount of revenue would be included in Adger's flexible budget for May?
2. What amount of employee salaries and wages would be included in Adger's flexible budget for May?
3. What amount of travel expenses would be included in Adger's flexible budget for May?
4. What amount of other expenses would be included in Adger's flexible budget for May?
5. What net operating income would appear in Adger's flexible budget for May?
6. What is Adger's revenue variance for May?
7. What is Adger's employee salaries and wages spending variance for May?
8. What is Adger's travel expenses spending variance for May?
9. What is Adger's other expenses spending variance for May?
10. What amount of revenue would be included in Adger's planning budget for May?
11. What amount of employee salaries and wages would be included in Adger's planning budget for May?
12. What amount of travel expenses would be included in Adger's planning budget for May?
13. What amount of other expenses would be included in Adger's planning budget for May?
14. What activity variance would Adger report in May with respect to its revenue?
15. What activity variances would Adger report with respect to each of its expenses?

Exercises

EXERCISE 10–1 Prepare a Flexible Budget [LO 10–1]

Puget Sound Divers is a company that provides diving services such as underwater ship repairs to clients in the Puget Sound area. The company's planning budget for May appears below:

Puget Sound Divers Planning Budget For the Month Ended May 31	
Budgeted diving-hours (q)	100
Revenue ($365.00q)	$36,500
Expenses:	
Wages and salaries ($8,000 + $125.00q) . . .	20,500
Supplies ($3.00q)	300
Equipment rental ($1,800 + $32.00q)	5,000
Insurance ($3,400)	3,400
Miscellaneous ($630 + $1.80q)	810
Total expense	30,010
Net operating income	$ 6,490

Required:

During May, the company's activity was actually 105 diving-hours. Prepare a flexible budget for that level of activity.

EXERCISE 10–2 Prepare a Report Showing Activity Variances [LO 10–2]

Flight Café is a company that prepares in-flight meals for airlines in its kitchen located next to the local airport. The company's planning budget for July appears below:

Flight Café Planning Budget For the Month Ended July 31	
Budgeted meals (q)	18,000
Revenue ($4.50q)	$ 81,000
Expenses:	
Raw materials ($2.40q)	43,200
Wages and salaries ($5,200 + $0.30q)	10,600
Utilities ($2,400 + $0.05q)	3,300
Facility rent ($4,300)	4,300
Insurance ($2,300)	2,300
Miscellaneous ($680 + $0.10q)	2,480
Total expense	66,180
Net operating income	$ 14,820

In July, 17,800 meals were actually served. The company's flexible budget for this level of activity appears below:

Flight Café Flexible Budget For the Month Ended July 31	
Budgeted meals (q)	17,800
Revenue ($4.50q)	$80,100
Expenses:	
Raw materials ($2.40q)	42,720
Wages and salaries ($5,200 + $0.30q)	10,540
Utilities ($2,400 + $0.05q)	3,290
Facility rent ($4,300)	4,300
Insurance ($2,300)	2,300
Miscellaneous ($680 + $0.10q)	2,460
Total expense	65,610
Net operating income	$14,490

Required:

1. Prepare a report showing the company's activity variances for July.
2. Which of the activity variances should be of concern to management? Explain.

EXERCISE 10–3 Prepare a Report Showing Revenue and Spending Variances [LO 10–3]

Quilcene Oysteria farms and sells oysters in the Pacific Northwest. The company harvested and sold 8,000 pounds of oysters in August. The company's flexible budget for August appears below:

Quilcene Oysteria Flexible Budget For the Month Ended August 31	
Actual pounds (*q*)	8,000
Revenue ($4.00*q*).	$32,000
Expenses:	
Packing supplies ($0.50*q*).	4,000
Oyster bed maintenance ($3,200)	3,200
Wages and salaries ($2,900 + $0.30*q*) . .	5,300
Shipping ($0.80*q*).	6,400
Utilities ($830).	830
Other ($450 + $0.05*q*).	850
Total expense	20,580
Net operating income	$11,420

The actual results for August appear below:

Quilcene Oysteria Income Statement For the Month Ended August 31	
Actual pounds.	8,000
Revenue.	$35,200
Expenses:	
Packing supplies.	4,200
Oyster bed maintenance.	3,100
Wages and salaries	5,640
Shipping.	6,950
Utilities	810
Other	980
Total expense	21,680
Net operating income	$13,520

Required:

Prepare a report showing the company's revenue and spending variances for August.

EXERCISE 10–4 Prepare a Flexible Budget Performance Report [LO 10–4]

Vulcan Flyovers offers scenic overflights of Mount St. Helens, the volcano in Washington State that explosively erupted in 1982. Data concerning the company's operations in July appear below:

Vulcan Flyovers Operating Data For the Month Ended July 31	Actual Results	Flexible Budget	Planning Budget
Flights (q)	48	48	50
Revenue ($320.00q)	$13,650	$15,360	$16,000
Expenses:			
Wages and salaries ($4,000 + $82.00q).	8,430	7,936	8,100
Fuel ($23.00q)	1,260	1,104	1,150
Airport fees ($650 + $38.00q)	2,350	2,474	2,550
Aircraft depreciation ($7.00q)	336	336	350
Office expenses ($190 + $2.00q).	460	286	290
Total expense	12,836	12,136	12,440
Net operating income	$ 814	$ 3,224	$ 3,560

The company measures its activity in terms of flights. Customers can buy individual tickets for overflights or hire an entire plane for an overflight at a discount.

Required:
1. Prepare a flexible budget performance report for July.
2. Which of the variances should be of concern to management? Explain.

EXERCISE 10–5 Prepare a Flexible Budget with More Than One Cost Driver [LO 10–5]
Alyeski Tours operates day tours of coastal glaciers in Alaska on its tour boat the Blue Glacier. Management has identified two cost drivers—the number of cruises and the number of passengers—that it uses in its budgeting and performance reports. The company publishes a schedule of day cruises that it may supplement with special sailings if there is sufficient demand. Up to 80 passengers can be accommodated on the tour boat. Data concerning the company's cost formulas appear below:

	Fixed Cost per Month	Cost per Cruise	Cost per Passenger
Vessel operating costs	$5,200	$480.00	$2.00
Advertising.	$1,700		
Administrative costs.	$4,300	$24.00	$1.00
Insurance.	$2,900		

For example, vessel operating costs should be $5,200 per month plus $480 per cruise plus $2 per passenger. The company's sales should average $25 per passenger. The company's planning budget for July is based on 24 cruises and 1,400 passengers.

Required:
Prepare the company's planning budget for July.

EXERCISE 10–6 Critique a Variance Report [LO 10–6]
The Terminator Inc. provides on-site residential pest extermination services. The company has several mobile teams who are dispatched from a central location in company-owned trucks. The company uses the number of jobs to measure activity. At the beginning of April, the company budgeted for 100 jobs, but the actual number of jobs turned out to be 105. A report comparing the budgeted revenues and costs to the actual revenues and costs appears below:

The Terminator Inc. Variance Report For the Month Ended April 30			
	Actual Results	Planning Budget	Variances
Jobs	105	100	
Revenue..............................	$20,520	$19,500	$1,020 F
Expenses:			
Mobile team operating costs	10,320	10,000	320 U
Exterminating supplies	960	1,800	840 F
Advertising	800	800	0
Dispatching costs....................	2,340	2,200	140 U
Office rent	1,800	1,800	0
Insurance............................	2,100	2,100	0
Total expense	18,320	18,700	380 F
Net operating income	$ 2,200	$ 800	$1,400 F

Required:

Is the above variance report useful for evaluating how well revenues and costs were controlled during April? Why, or why not?

EXERCISE 10–7 Critique a Variance Report [LO 10–6]

Refer to the data for The Terminator Inc. in Exercise 10–6. A management intern has suggested that the budgeted revenues and costs should be adjusted for the actual level of activity in April before they are compared to the actual revenues and costs. Because the actual level of activity was 5% higher than budgeted, the intern suggested that all budgeted revenues and costs should be adjusted upward by 5%. A report comparing the budgeted revenues and costs, with this adjustment, to the actual revenues and costs appears below.

The Terminator Inc. Variance Report For the Month Ended April 30			
	Actual Results	Adjusted Planning Budget	Variances
Jobs	105	105	
Revenue..............................	$20,520	$20,475	$ 45 F
Expenses:			
Mobile team operating costs	10,320	10,500	180 F
Exterminating supplies	960	1,890	930 F
Advertising	800	840	40 F
Dispatching costs....................	2,340	2,310	30 U
Office rent	1,800	1,890	90 F
Insurance...........................	2,100	2,205	105 F
Total expense	18,320	19,635	1,315 F
Net operating income	$ 2,200	$ 840	$1,360 F

Required:

Is the above variance report useful for evaluating how well revenues and costs were controlled during April? Why, or why not?

EXERCISE 10–8 Flexible Budgets and Activity Variances [LO 10–1, LO 10–2]

Jake's Roof Repair has provided the following data concerning its costs:

	Fixed Cost per Month	Cost per Repair-Hour
Wages and salaries	$23,200	$16.30
Parts and supplies		$8.60
Equipment depreciation	$1,600	$0.40
Truck operating expenses	$6,400	$1.70
Rent.	$3,480	
Administrative expenses.	$4,500	$0.80

For example, utilities should be $1,400 per month plus $0.05 per machine-hour. The company expects to work 5,000 machine-hours in June. Note that the company's direct labor is a fixed cost.

Required:

Prepare a report showing the company's activity variances for May.

EXERCISE 10–9 Flexible Budget [LO 10–1]

Wyckam Manufacturing Inc. has provided the following information concerning its manufacturing costs:

	Fixed Cost per Month	Cost per Machine-Hour
Direct materials.		$4.25
Direct labor	$36,800	
Supplies		$0.30
Utilities	$1,400	$0.05
Depreciation	$16,700	
Insurance.	$12,700	

For example, utilities should be $1,400 per month plus $0.05 per machine-hour. The company expects to work 5,000 machine-hours in June. Note that the company's direct labor is a fixed cost.

Required:

Prepare the company's planning budget for manufacturing costs for June.

EXERCISE 10–10 Flexible Budget [LO 10–1]

Lavage Rapide is a Canadian company that owns and operates a large automatic carwash facility near Montreal. The following table provides data concerning the company's costs:

	Fixed Cost per Month	Cost per Car Washed
Cleaning supplies.		$0.80
Electricity	$1,200	$0.15
Maintenance		$0.20
Wages and salaries	$5,000	$0.30
Depreciation	$6,000	
Rent.	$8,000	
Administrative expenses.	$4,000	$0.10

For example, electricity costs are $1,200 per month plus $0.15 per car washed. The company expects to wash 9,000 cars in August and to collect an average of $4.90 per car washed.

Required:

Prepare the company's planning budget for August.

EXERCISE 10–11 Flexible Budget [LO 10–1]

Refer to the data for Lavage Rapide in Exercise 10–10. The company actually washed 8,800 cars in August.

Required:
Prepare the company's flexible budget for August.

EXERCISE 10–12 Prepare a Report Showing Activity Variances [LO 10–2]
Refer to the data for Lavage Rapide in Exercise 10–10. The actual operating results for August appear below.

Lavage Rapide Income Statement For the Month Ended August 31	
Actual cars washed.	8,800
Revenue	$43,080
Expenses:	
Cleaning supplies	7,560
Electricity	2,670
Maintenance	2,260
Wages and salaries	8,500
Depreciation	6,000
Rent	8,000
Administrative expenses	4,950
Total expense	39,940
Net operating income	$ 3,140

Required:
Prepare a report showing the company's activity variances for August.

EXERCISE 10–13 Prepare a Report Showing Revenue and Spending Variances [LO 10–3]
Refer to the data for Lavage Rapide in Exercise 10–10 and Exercise 10–12.
Required:
Prepare a report showing the company's revenue and spending variances for August.

EXERCISE 10–14 Prepare a Flexible Budget Performance Report [LO 10–4]
Refer to the data for Lavage Rapide in Exercises 10–10 and Exercises 10–12.
Required:
Prepare a flexible budget performance report that shows the company's revenue and spending variances and activity variances for August

EXERCISE 10–15 Flexible Budget Performance Report in a Cost Center [LO 10–1, LO 10–4]
Packaging Solutions Corporation manufactures and sells a wide variety of packaging products. Performance reports are prepared monthly for each department. The planning budget and flexible budget for the Production Department are based on the following formulas, where q is the number of labor-hours worked in a month:

	Cost Formulas
Direct labor	$15.80q
Indirect labor	$8,200 + $1.60q
Utilities	$6,400 + $0.80q
Supplies	$1,100 + $0.40q
Equipment depreciation	$23,000 + $3.70q
Factory rent	$8,400
Property taxes	$2,100
Factory administration	$11,700 + $1.90q

The actual costs incurred in March in the Production Department are listed below:

	Actual Cost Incurred in March
Direct labor	$134,730
Indirect labor	$19,860
Utilities	$14,570
Supplies	$4,980
Equipment depreciation	$54,080
Factory rent	$8,700
Property taxes	$2,100
Factory administration	$26,470

Required:
1. The company had budgeted for an activity level of 8,000 labor-hours in March. Prepare the Production Department's planning budget for the month.
2. The company actually worked 8,400 labor-hours in March. Prepare the Production Department's flexible budget for the month.
3. Prepare the Production Department's flexible budget performance report for March, including both the spending and activity variances.
4. What aspects of the flexible budget performance report should be brought to management's attention? Explain.

EXERCISE 10–16 Flexible Budgets and Revenue and Spending Variances [LO 10–1 , LO 10–3]
Via Gelato is a popular neighborhood gelato shop. The company has provided the following data concerning its operations:

	Fixed Element per Month	Variable Element per Liter	Actual Total for June
Revenue		$12.00	$71,540
Raw materials		$4.65	$29,230
Wages	$5,600	$1.40	$13,860
Utilities	$1,630	$0.20	$3,270
Rent	$2,600		$2,600
Insurance	$1,350		$1,350
Miscellaneous	$650	$0.35	$2,590

While gelato is sold by the cone or cup, the shop measures its activity in terms of the total number of liters of gelato sold. For example, wages should be $5,600 plus $1.40 per liter of gelato sold and the actual wages for June were $13,860. Via Gelato expected to sell 6,000 liters in June, but actually sold 6,200 liters.

Required:
Prepare a report showing Via Gelato revenue and spending variances for June.

EXERCISE 10–17 Flexible Budget Performance Report [LO 10–1, LO 10–4]
AirQual Test Corporation provides on-site air quality testing services. The company has provided the following data concerning its operations:

	Fixed Component per Month	Variable Component per Job	Actual Total for February
Revenue		$360	$18,950
Technician wages	$6,400		$6,450
Mobile lab operating expenses	$2,900	$35	$4,530
Office expenses....................	$2,600	$2	$3,050
Advertising expenses................	$970		$995
Insurance	$1,680		$1,680
Miscellaneous expenses	$500	$3	$465

The company uses the number of jobs as its measure of activity. For example, mobile lab operating expenses should be $2,900 plus $35 per job, and the actual mobile lab operating expenses for February were $4,530

The company expected to work 50 jobs in February, but actually worked 52 jobs.

Required:

Prepare a flexible budget performance report showing AirQual Test Corporation's revenue and spending variances and activity variances for February.

EXERCISE 10–18 Working with More Than One Cost Driver [LO 10–4, LO 10–5]

The Gourmand Cooking School runs short cooking courses at its small campus. Management has identified two cost drivers that it uses in its budgeting and performance reports—the number of courses and the total number of students. For example, the school might run two courses in a month and have a total of 50 students enrolled in those two courses. Data concerning the company's cost formulas appear below:

	Fixed Cost per Month	Cost per Course	Cost per Student
Instructor wages		$3,080	
Classroom supplies..................			$260
Utilities	$870	$130	
Campus rent.......................	$4,200		
Insurance	$1,890		
Administrative expenses	$3,270	$15	$4

For example, administrative expenses should be $3,270 per month plus $15 per course plus $4 per student. The company's sales should average $800 per student.

The actual operating results for September appear below:

	Actual
Revenue	$32,400
Instructor wages	$9,080
Classroom supplies...........	$8,540
Utilities	$1,530
Campus rent..................	$4,200
Insurance	$1,890
Administrative expenses	$3,790

Required:

1. The Gourmand Cooking School expects to run three courses with a total of 45 students in September. Prepare the company's planning budget for this level of activity.
2. The school actually ran three courses with a total of 42 students in September. Prepare the company's flexible budget for this level of activity.
3. Prepare a flexible budget performance report that shows both revenue and spending variances and activity variances for September.

PROBLEM 10–19 Activity and Spending Variances [LO 10–1, LO 10–2, LO 10–3]

You have just been hired by FAB Corporation, the manufacturer of a revolutionary new garage door opening device. The president has asked that you review the company's costing system and "do what you can to help us get better control of our manufacturing overhead costs." You find that the company has never used a flexible budget, and you suggest that preparing such a budget would be an excellent first step in overhead planning and control.

After much effort and analysis, you determined the following cost formulas and gathered the following actual cost data for March:

	Cost Formula	Actual Cost in March
Utilities	$20,600 plus $0.10 per machine-hour	$24,200
Maintenance	$40,000 plus $1.60 per machine-hour	$78,100
Supplies	$0.30 per machine-hour	$8,400
Indirect labor	$130,000 plus $0.70 per machine-hour	$149,600
Depreciation.	$70,000	$71,500

During March, the company worked 26,000 machine-hours and produced 15,000 units. The company had originally planned to work 30,000 machine-hours during March.

Required:

1. Prepare a report showing the activity variances for March. Explain what these variances mean.
2. Prepare a report showing the spending variances for March. Explain what these variances mean.

PROBLEM 10–20 More than One Cost Driver [LO 10–4, LO 10–5]

Milano Pizza is a small neighborhood pizzeria that has a small area for in-store dining as well as offering take-out and free home delivery services. The pizzeria's owner has determined that the shop has two major cost drivers—the number of pizzas sold and the number of deliveries made.

Data concerning the pizzeria's costs appear below:

	Fixed Cost per Month	Cost per Pizza	Cost per Delivery
Pizza ingredients		$3.80	
Kitchen staff.	$5,220		
Utilities	$630	$0.05	
Delivery person			$3.50
Delivery vehicle	$540		$1.50
Equipment depreciation	$275		
Rent	$1,830		
Miscellaneous.	$820	$0.15	

In November, the pizzeria budgeted for 1,200 pizzas at an average selling price of $13.50 per pizza and for 180 deliveries.

Data concerning the pizzeria's operations in November appear below:

	Actual Results
Pizzas	1,240
Deliveries.	174
Revenue.	$17,420
Pizza ingredients	$4,985
Kitchen staff.	$5,281
Utilities	$984
Delivery person.	$609
Delivery vehicle	$655
Equipment depreciation	$275
Rent.	$1,830
Miscellaneous.	$954

Required:
1. Prepare a flexible budget performance report that shows both revenue and spending variances and activity variances for the pizzeria for November.
2. Explain the activity variances.

 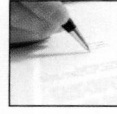

PROBLEM 10–21 Critique a Report; Prepare a Performance Report [LO 10–1, LO 10–4, LO 10–6]

TipTop Flight School offers flying lessons at a small municipal airport. The school's owner and manager has been attempting to evaluate performance and control costs using a variance report that compares the planning budget to actual results. A recent variance report appears below:

TipTop Flight School Variance Report For the Month Ended July 31			
	Actual Results	Planning Budget	Variances
Lessons	155	150	
Revenue	$33,900	$33,000	$900 F
Expenses:			
Instructor wages	9,870	9,750	120 U
Aircraft depreciation	5,890	5,700	190 U
Fuel	2,750	2,250	500 U
Maintenance	2,450	2,330	120 U
Ground facility expenses	1,540	1,550	10 F
Administration	3,320	3,390	70 F
Total expense	25,820	24,970	850 U
Net operating income	$ 8,080	$ 8,030	$ 50 F

After several months of using such variance reports, the owner has become frustrated. For example, she is quite confident that instructor wages were very tightly controlled in July, but the report shows an unfavorable variance.

The planning budget was developed using the following formulas, where *q* is the number of lessons sold:

	Cost Formulas
Revenue	$220q
Instructor wages	$65q
Aircraft depreciation	$38q
Fuel	$15q
Maintenance	$ 530 + $12q
Ground facility expenses	$1,250 + $2q
Administration	$3,240 + $1q

Required:
1. Should the owner feel frustrated with the variance reports? Explain.
2. Prepare a flexible budget performance report for the school for July.
3. Evaluate the school's performance for July.

PROBLEM 10–22 Performance Report for a Nonprofit Organization [LO 10–1, LO 10–4, LO 10–6]

The St. Lucia Blood Bank, a private charity partly supported by government grants, is located on the Caribbean island of St. Lucia. The blood bank has just finished its operations for September, which was a particularly busy month due to a powerful hurricane that hit neighboring islands causing many injuries. The hurricane largely bypassed St. Lucia, but residents of St. Lucia willingly donated their blood to help people on other islands. As a consequence, the blood bank collected and processed over 20% more blood than had been originally planned for the month.

A report prepared by a government official comparing actual costs to budgeted costs for the blood bank appears below. Continued support from the government depends on the blood bank's ability to demonstrate control over its costs.

St. Lucia Blood Bank Cost Control Report For the Month Ended September 30	Actual Results	Planning Budget	Variances
Liters of blood collected	620	500	
Medical supplies	$ 9,250	$ 7,500	$1,750 U
Lab tests	6,180	6,000	180 U
Equipment depreciation	2,800	2,500	300 U
Rent	1,000	1,000	0
Utilities	570	500	70 U
Administration	11,740	11,250	490 U
Total expense	$31,540	$28,750	$2,790 U

The managing director of the blood bank was very unhappy with this report, claiming that his costs were higher than expected due to the emergency on the neighboring islands. He also pointed out that the additional costs had been fully covered by payments from grateful recipients on the other islands. The government official who prepared the report countered that all of the figures had been submitted by the blood bank to the government; he was just pointing out that actual costs were a lot higher than promised in the budget.

The following cost formulas were used to construct the planning budget:

	Cost Formulas
Medical supplies	$15.00q
Lab tests	$12.00q
Equipment depreciation	$2,500
Rent	$1,000
Utilities	$500
Administration	$10,000 + $2.50q

Required:
1. Prepare a new performance report for September using the flexible budget approach.
2. Do you think any of the variances in the report you prepared should be investigated? Why?

PROBLEM 10–23 Critiquing a Report; Preparing a Performance Budget [LO 10–1, LO 10–4, LO 10–6]
Exchange Corp. is a company that acts as a facilitator in tax-favored real estate swaps. Such swaps, know as 1031 exchanges, permit participants to avoid some or all of the capital gains taxes that would otherwise be due. The bookkeeper for the company has been asked to prepare a report for the company to help its owner/manager analyze performance. The first such report appears below:

Exchange Corp Analysis of Revenues and Costs For the Month Ended May 31	Actual Unit Revenues and Costs	Planning Budget Unit Revenues and Costs	Variances
Exchanges completed	50	40	
Revenue	$385	$395	$10 U
Expenses:			
Legal and search fees	184	165	19 U
Office expenses	112	135	23 F
Equipment depreciation	8	10	2 F
Rent	36	45	9 F
Insurance	4	5	1 F
Total expense	344	360	16 F
Net operating income	$ 41	$ 35	$ 6 F

Note that the revenues and costs in the above report are *unit* revenues and costs. For example, the average office expense is $135 per exchange completed on the planning budget; whereas, the average actual office expense is $112 per exchange completed.

Legal and search fees is a variable cost; office expenses is a mixed cost; and equipment depreciation, rent, and insurance are fixed costs. In the planning budget, the fixed component of office expenses was $5,200.

All of the company's revenues come from fees collected when an exchange is completed.

Required:
1. Evaluate the report prepared by the bookkeeper.
2. Prepare a performance report that would help the owner/manager assess the performance of the company in May.
3. Using the report you created, evaluate the performance of the company in May.

PROBLEM 10–24 Critiquing a Variance Report; Preparing a Performance Report [LO 10–1, LO 10–4, LO 10–6]

Several years ago, Westmont Corporation developed a comprehensive budgeting system for planning and control purposes. While departmental supervisors have been happy with the system, the factory manager has expressed considerable dissatisfaction with the information being generated by the system.

A typical departmental cost report for a recent period follows:

	Actual Results	Planning Budget	Variances
Assembly Department Cost Report For the Month Ended March 31			
Machine-hours	35,000	40,000	
Variable costs:			
Supplies	$ 29,700	$ 32,000	$ 2,300 F
Scrap	19,500	20,000	500 F
Indirect materials	51,800	56,000	4,200 F
Fixed costs:			
Wages and salaries	79,200	80,000	800 F
Equipment depreciation	60,000	60,000	—
Total cost	$240,200	$248,000	$ 7,800 F

After receiving a copy of this cost report, the supervisor of the Assembly Department stated, "These reports are super. It makes me feel really good to see how well things are going in my department. I can't understand why those people upstairs complain so much about the reports."

For the last several years, the company's marketing department has chronically failed to meet the sales goals expressed in the company's monthly budgets.

Required:
1. The company's president is uneasy about the cost reports and would like you to evaluate their usefulness to the company.
2. What changes, if any, should be made in the reports to give better insight into how well departmental supervisors are controlling costs?
3. Prepare a new performance report for the quarter, incorporating any changes you suggested in requirement 2.
4. How well were costs controlled in the Assembly Department in March?

PROBLEM 10–25 Critiquing a Cost Report; Preparing a Performance Report [LO 10–1, LO 10–4, LO 10–6]

Frank Weston, supervisor of the Freemont Corporation's Machining Department, was visibly upset after being reprimanded for his department's poor performance over the prior month. The department's cost control report is given below:

Freemont Corporation–Machining Department Cost Control Report For the Month Ended June 30	Actual Results	Planning Budget	Variances
Machine-hours	38,000	35,000	
Direct labor wages	$ 86,100	$ 80,500	$ 5,600 U
Supplies	23,100	21,000	2,100 U
Maintenance	137,300	134,000	3,300 U
Utilities	15,700	15,200	500 U
Supervision	38,000	38,000	0
Depreciation	80,000	80,000	0
Total	$380,200	$368,700	$11,500 U

"I just can't understand all of these unfavorable variances," Weston complained to the supervisor of another department. "When the boss called me in, I thought he was going to give me a pat on the back because I know for a fact that my department worked more efficiently last month than it has ever worked before. Instead, he tore me apart. I thought for a minute that it might be over the supplies that were stolen out of our warehouse last month. But they only amounted to a couple of hundred dollars, and just look at this report. Everything is unfavorable."

Direct labor wages and supplies are variable costs; supervision and depreciation are fixed costs; and maintenance and utilities are mixed costs. The fixed component of the budgeted maintenance cost is $92,000; the fixed component of the budgeted utilities cost is $11,700.

Required:
1. Evaluate the company's cost control report and explain why the variances were all unfavorable.
2. Prepare a performance report that will help Mr. Weston's superiors assess how well costs were controlled in the Machining Department.

Additional student resources are available with Connect.   Cases

CASE 10–26 Ethics and the Manager [LO 10–3]
Tom Kemper is the controller of the Wichita manufacturing facility of Prudhom Enterprises, Inc.

The annual cost control report is one of the many reports that must be filed with corporate headquarters and is due at corporate headquarters shortly after the beginning of the New Year. Kemper does not like putting work off to the last minute, so just before Christmas he prepared a preliminary draft of the cost control report. Some adjustments would later be required for transactions that occur between Christmas and New Year's Day. A copy of the preliminary draft report, which Kemper completed on December 21, follows:

Wichita Manufacturing Facility Cost Control Report December 21 Preliminary Draft	Actual Results	Flexible Budget	Spending Variances
Labor-hours	18,000	18,000	
Direct labor	$ 326,000	$ 324,000	$ 2,000 U
Power	19,750	18,000	1,750 U
Supplies	105,000	99,000	6,000 U
Equipment depreciation	343,000	332,000	11,000 U
Supervisory salaries	273,000	275,000	2,000 F
Insurance	37,000	37,000	0
Industrial engineering	189,000	210,000	21,000 F
Factory building lease	60,000	60,000	0
Total expense	$1,352,750	$1,355,000	$ 2,250 F

Melissa Ilianovitch, the general manager at the Wichita facility, asked to see a copy of the preliminary draft report. Kemper carried a copy of the report to her office where the following discussion took place:

Ilianovitch: Ouch! Almost all of the variances on the report are unfavorable. The only favorable variances are for supervisory salaries and industrial engineering. How did we have an unfavorable variance for depreciation?

Kemper: Do you remember that milling machine that broke down because the wrong lubricant was used by the machine operator?

Ilianovitch: Yes.

Kemper: We couldn't fix it. We had to scrap the machine and buy a new one.

Ilianovitch: This report doesn't look good. I was raked over the coals last year when we had just a few unfavorable variances.

Kemper: I'm afraid the final report is going to look even worse.

Ilianovitch: Oh?

Kemper: The line item for industrial engineering on the report is for work we hired Ferguson Engineering to do for us. The original contract was for $210,000, but we asked them to do some additional work that was not in the contract. We have to reimburse Ferguson Engineering for the costs of that additional work. The $189,000 in actual costs that appears on the preliminary draft report reflects only their billings up through December 21. The last bill they had sent us was on November 28, and they completed the project just last week. Yesterday I got a call from Laura Sunder over at Ferguson and she said they would be sending us a final bill for the project before the end of the year. The total bill, including the reimbursements for the additional work, is going to be . . .

Ilianovitch: I am not sure I want to hear this.

Kemper: $225,000

Ilianovitch: Ouch!

Kemper: The additional work added $15,000 to the cost of the project.

Ilianovitch: I can't turn in a report with an overall unfavorable variance! They'll kill me at corporate headquarters. Call up Laura at Ferguson and ask her not to send the bill until after the first of the year. We have to have that $21,000 favorable variance for industrial engineering on the report.

Required:

What should Tom Kemper do? Explain.

CASE 10–27 Plantwide versus Departmental Overhead Rates; Underapplied or Overapplied Overhead [LO 10–3, LO 10–5, LO 10–6]

Boyne University offers an extensive continuing education program in many cities throughout the state. For the convenience of its faculty and administrative staff and to save costs, the university operates a motor pool. The motor pool's monthly planning budget is based on operating 20 vehicles; however, for the month of March the university purchased one additional vehicle. The motor pool furnishes gasoline, oil, and other supplies for its automobiles. A mechanic does routine maintenance and minor repairs. Major repairs are performed at a nearby commercial garage.

The following cost control report shows actual operating costs for March of the current year compared to the planning budget for March.

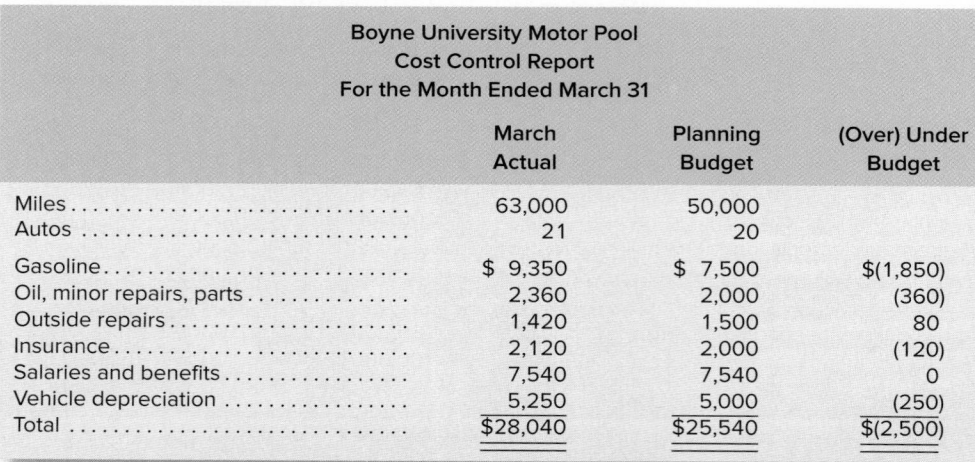

Boyne University Motor Pool Cost Control Report For the Month Ended March 31			
	March Actual	Planning Budget	(Over) Under Budget
Miles	63,000	50,000	
Autos	21	20	
Gasoline	$ 9,350	$ 7,500	$(1,850)
Oil, minor repairs, parts	2,360	2,000	(360)
Outside repairs	1,420	1,500	80
Insurance	2,120	2,000	(120)
Salaries and benefits	7,540	7,540	0
Vehicle depreciation	5,250	5,000	(250)
Total	$28,040	$25,540	$(2,500)

The planning budget was based on the following assumptions:

a. $0.15 per mile for gasoline.
b. $0.04 per mile for oil, minor repairs, and parts.
c. $75 per automobile per month for outside repairs.
d. $100 per automobile per month for insurance.
e. $7,540 per month for salaries and benefits.
f. $250 per automobile per month for depreciation.

The supervisor of the motor pool is unhappy with the report, claiming it paints an unfair picture of the motor pool's performance.

Required:

1. Prepare a new performance report for March based on a flexible budget that shows spending variances.
2. What are the deficiencies in the original cost control report? How does the report that you prepared in requirement 1 overcome these deficiencies?
    (CMA, adapted)

CASE 10–28 Performance Report with More than One Cost Driver [LO 10–4, LO 10–5]

The Little Theatre is a nonprofit organization devoted to staging plays for children. The theater has a very small full-time professional administrative staff. Through a special arrangement with the actors' union, actors and directors rehearse without pay and are paid only for actual performances.

The costs from the current year's planning budget appear below. The Little Theatre had tentatively planned to put on six different productions with a total of 108 performances. For example, one of the productions was *Peter Rabbit,* which had a six-week run with three performances on each weekend.

The Little Theatre Costs from the Planning Budget For the Year Ended December 31	
Budgeted number of productions	6
Budgeted number of performances	108
Actors' and directors' wages	$216,000
Stagehands' wages	32,400
Ticket booth personnel and ushers' wages.	16,200
Scenery, costumes, and props.	108,000
Theater hall rent.	54,000
Printed programs	27,000
Publicity	12,000
Administrative expenses.	43,200
Total	$508,800

Some of the costs vary with the number of productions, some with the number of performances, and some are fixed and depend on neither the number of productions nor the number of performances. The costs of scenery, costumes, props, and publicity vary with the number of productions. It doesn't make any difference how many times *Peter Rabbit* is performed, the cost of the scenery is the same. Likewise, the cost of publicizing a play with posters and radio commercials is the same whether there are 10, 20, or 30 performances of the play. On the other hand, the wages of the actors, directors, stagehands, ticket booth personnel, and ushers vary with the number of performances. The greater the number of performances, the higher the wage costs will be. Similarly, the costs of renting the hall and printing the programs will vary with the number of performances. Administrative expenses are more difficult to pin down, but the best estimate is that approximately 75% of the budgeted costs are fixed, 15% depend on the number of productions staged, and the remaining 10% depend on the number of performances.

After the beginning of the year, the board of directors of the theater authorized expanding the theater's program to seven productions and a total of 168 performances. Not surprisingly, actual costs were considerably higher than the costs from the planning budget. (Grants from donors and ticket sales were also correspondingly higher, but are not shown here.) Data concerning the actual costs appear below:

The Little Theatre Actual Costs For the Year Ended December 31	
Actual number of productions	7
Actual number of performances	168
Actors' and directors' wages	$341,800
Stagehands' wages	49,700
Ticket booth personnel and ushers' wages.	25,900
Scenery, costumes, and props.	130,600
Theater hall rent	78,000
Printed programs	38,300
Publicity	15,100
Administrative expenses.	47,500
Total	$726,900

Required:

1. Prepare a flexible budget for The Little Theatre based on the actual activity of the year.
2. Prepare a flexible budget performance report for the year that shows both spending variances and activity variances.
3. If you were on the board of directors of the theater, would you be pleased with how well costs were controlled during the year? Why, or why not?
4. The cost formulas provide figures for the average cost per production and average cost per performance. How accurate do you think these figures would be for predicting the cost of a new production or of an additional performance of a particular production?

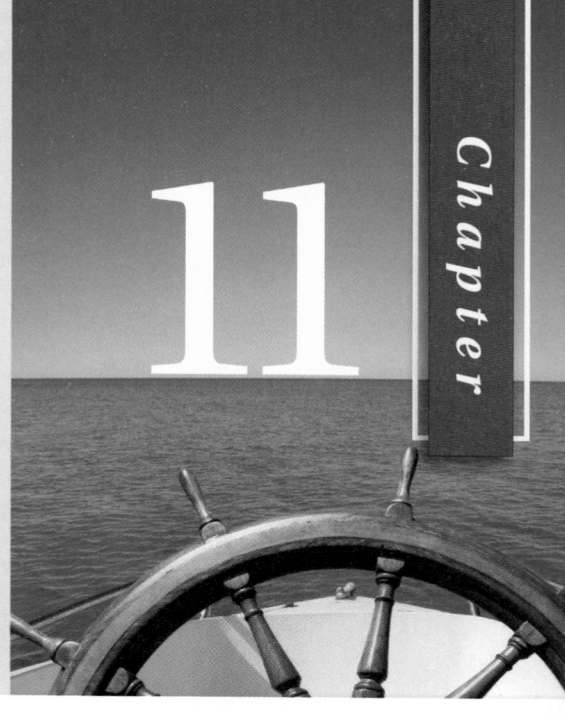

Standard Costs and Variances

Managing Materials and Labor

© Fabrice Dimier/Bloomberg/Getty Images

BUSINESS FOCUS

Schneider Electric's Oxford, Ohio, plant manufactures *busways* that transport electricity from its point of entry into a building to remote locations throughout the building. The plant's managers pay close attention to direct material costs because they are more than half of the plant's total manufacturing costs. To help control scrap rates for direct materials such as copper, steel, and aluminum, the accounting department prepares direct materials quantity variances. These variances compare the amount of direct materials that were actually used to the standard quantity of direct materials that should have been used to make a product (according to computations by the plant's engineers). Keeping a close eye on these differences helps to identify and deal with the causes of excessive scrap, such as an inadequately trained machine operator, poor quality raw material inputs, or a malfunctioning machine.

Because direct labor is also a significant component of the plant's total manufacturing costs, the management team daily monitors the direct labor efficiency variance. This variance compares the actual amount of labor time used to the standard amount of labor time allowed to make a product. When idle workers cause an unfavorable labor efficiency variance, managers temporarily move workers from departments with slack to departments with a backlog of work to be done. ∎

Source: Author's conversation with Doug Taylor, plant controller, Schneider Electric's Oxford, Ohio, plant.

LEARNING OBJECTIVES

After studying Chapter 11, you should be able to:

LO 11–1 Compute the direct materials price and quantity variances and explain their significance.

LO 11–2 Compute the direct labor rate and efficiency variances and explain their significance.

LO 11–3 Compute the variable manufacturing overhead rate and efficiency variances and explain their significance.

LO 11–4 (Appendix 11A) Compute and interpret the fixed overhead budget and volume variances.

In the last chapter, we investigated flexible budget variances. These variances provide feedback concerning how well an organization performed in relation to its budget. The impact on profit of a change in the level of activity is captured in the overall net operating income activity variance. The revenue and spending variances indicate how well revenues and costs were controlled—given the actual level of activity. In the case of many of the spending variances, we can get even more detail about how well costs were controlled. For example, at Rick's Hairstyling, an unfavorable spending variance for hairstyling supplies could be due to paying too much for the supplies or to using too many supplies, or some combination of the two. It would be useful to separate those two different effects, particularly if different people are responsible for purchasing the supplies and for using them. In this chapter, we learn how to use standard costs to decompose spending variances into two parts—a part that measures how well the acquisition prices of resources were controlled and a part that measures how efficiently those resources were used.

Standard Costs—Setting the Stage

A *standard* is a benchmark for measuring performance. Standards are found everywhere. Auto service centers like Firestone and Sears, for example, often set specific labor time standards for the completion of certain tasks, such as installing a carburetor or doing a valve job, and then measure actual performance against these standards. Fast-food outlets such as McDonald's and Subway have exacting standards for the quantity of meat going into a sandwich, as well as standards for the cost of the meat. Your doctor evaluates your weight using standards for individuals of your age, height, and gender. The buildings we live in conform to standards set in building codes.

Standards are also widely used in managerial accounting where they relate to the *quantity* and acquisition *price* of inputs used in manufacturing goods or providing services. *Quantity standards* specify how much of an input should be used to make a product or provide a service. *Price standards* specify how much should be paid for each unit of the input. If either the quantity or acquisition price of an input departs significantly from the standard, managers investigate the discrepancy to find the cause of the problem and eliminate it.

Next we'll demonstrate how a company can establish quantity and price standards for direct materials, direct labor, and variable manufacturing overhead and then we'll discuss how those standards can be used to calculate variances and manage operations.

MANAGERIAL ACCOUNTING IN ACTION

The Issue

Colonial
Pewter
Company

The Colonial Pewter Company makes only one product—an elaborate reproduction of an 18th century pewter statue. The statue is made largely by hand, using traditional metalworking tools. Consequently, the manufacturing process is labor intensive and requires a high level of skill.

Colonial Pewter has recently expanded its workforce to take advantage of unexpected demand for the statue as a gift. The company started with a small cadre of experienced pewter workers but has had to hire less experienced workers as a result of the expansion. The president of the company, J. D. Wriston, has called a meeting to discuss production problems. Attending the meeting are Tom Kuchel, the production manager; Janet Warner, the purchasing manager; and Terry Sherman, the corporate controller.

J. D.: I've got a feeling that we aren't getting the production we should out of our new people.

Tom: Give us a chance. Some of the new people have been with the company for less than a month.

Janet: Let me add that production seems to be wasting an awful lot of material—particularly pewter. That stuff is very expensive.

Tom: What about the shipment of defective pewter that you bought—the one with the iron contamination? That caused us major problems.

Janet: How was I to know it was off-grade? Besides, it was a great deal.

J. D.: Calm down everybody. Let's get the facts before we start attacking each other.

Tom: I agree. The more facts the better.

J. D.: Okay, Terry, it's your turn. Facts are the controller's department.

Terry: I'm afraid I can't provide the answers off the top of my head, but if you give me about a week I can set up a system that can routinely answer questions relating to worker productivity, material waste, and input prices.

J. D.: Let's mark it on our calendars.

Setting Direct Materials Standards

Terry Sherman's first task was to prepare quantity and price standards for the company's only significant raw material, pewter ingots. The **standard quantity per unit** defines the amount of direct materials that should be used for each unit of finished product, including an allowance for normal inefficiencies, such as scrap and spoilage.[1] After consulting with the production manager, Tom Kuchel, Terry set the quantity standard for pewter at 3.0 pounds per statue.

The **standard price per unit** defines the price that should be paid for each unit of direct materials and it should reflect the final, delivered cost of those materials. After consulting with purchasing manager Janet Warner, Terry set the standard price of pewter at $4.00 per pound.

Once Terry established the quantity and price standards he computed the standard direct materials cost per statue as follows:

3.0 pounds per statue × $4.00 per pound = $12.00 per statue

MANAGING RAW MATERIAL COSTS IN THE APPAREL INDUSTRY

A company's raw material costs can rise for numerous and often uncontrollable reasons. For example, severe weather in China, which is the world's largest producer of cotton, can influence the cotton prices paid by Abercrombie & Fitch. Rising fuel costs can influence what Maidenform Brands pays for its petroleum-based synthetic fabrics. When farmers stop producing cotton in favor of soybeans, it increases the price Jones Apparel Group pays for a shrinking supply of cotton.

When faced with rising raw material costs, companies can respond three ways. First, they can maintain existing selling prices and consequently operate with lower margins. Second, they can pass the cost increases along to customers in the form of higher prices. Third, they can try to lower their raw material costs. For example, Hanesbrands buys hedging contracts that lock in its cotton prices, thereby insulating the company from future cost increases. JCPenney is changing the blend of raw materials used in its garments, whereas Maidenform has started buying some of its raw materials from lower-cost producers in Bangladesh.

Source: Elizabeth Holmes and Rachel Dodes, "Cotton Tale: Apparel Prices Set to Rise," *The Wall Street Journal*, May 19, 2010, p. B8.

© David Sucsy/Getty Images

Setting Direct Labor Standards

Direct labor quantity and price standards are usually expressed in terms of labor-hours or a labor rate. The **standard hours per unit** defines the amount of direct labor-hours that should be used to produce one unit of finished goods. One approach used to determine this standard is for an industrial engineer to do a time and motion study, actually

---

[1] Although companies often create "practical" rather than "ideal" materials quantity standards that include allowances for normal inefficiencies such as scrap, spoilage, and rejects, this practice is often criticized because it contradicts the zero defects goal that underlies many process improvement programs. If these types of allowances are built into materials quantity standards, they should be periodically reviewed and reduced over time to reflect improved processes, better training, and better equipment.

clocking the time required for each task. Throughout the chapter, we'll assume that "tight but attainable" labor standards are used rather than "ideal" standards that can only be attained by the most skilled and efficient employees working at peak effort 100% of the time. Therefore, after consulting with the production manager and considering reasonable allowances for breaks, personal needs of employees, cleanup, and machine downtime, Terry set the standard hours per unit at 0.50 direct labor-hours per statue.

The **standard rate per hour** defines the company's expected direct labor wage rate per hour, including employment taxes and fringe benefits. Using wage records and in consultation with the production manager, Terry Sherman established a standard rate per hour of $22.00. This standard rate reflects the expected "mix" of workers, even though the actual hourly wage rates may vary somewhat from individual to individual due to differing skills or seniority.

Once Terry established the time and rate standards, he computed the standard direct labor cost per statue as follows:

0.50 direct labor-hours per statue × $22.00 per direct labor-hour = $11.00 per statue

Setting Variable Manufacturing Overhead Standards

As with direct labor, the quantity and price standards for variable manufacturing overhead are usually expressed in terms of hours and a rate. The *standard hours per unit* for variable overhead measures the amount of the allocation base from a company's predetermined overhead rate that is required to produce one unit of finished goods. In the case of Colonial Pewter, we will assume that the company uses direct labor-hours as the allocation base in its predetermined overhead rate. Therefore, the standard hours per unit for variable overhead is exactly the same as the standard hours per unit for direct labor—0.50 direct labor-hours per statue.

The *standard rate per unit* that a company expects to pay for variable overhead equals *the variable portion of the predetermined overhead rate*. At Colonial Pewter, the variable portion of the predetermined overhead rate is $6.00 per direct labor-hour. Therefore, Terry computed the standard variable manufacturing overhead cost per statue as follows:

0.50 direct labor-hours per statue × $6.00 per direct-labor hour = $3.00 per statue

This $3.00 per unit cost for variable manufacturing overhead appears along with direct materials ($12 per unit) and direct labor ($11 per unit) on the *standard cost card* in Exhibit 11–1. A **standard cost card** shows the standard quantity (or hours) and standard price (or rate) of the inputs required to produce a unit of a specific product. The **standard cost per unit** for all three variable manufacturing costs is computed the same way. The standard quantity (or hours) per unit is multiplied by the standard price (or rate) per unit to obtain the standard cost per unit.

EXHIBIT 11–1
Standard Cost Card—
Variable Manufacturing
Costs

Inputs	(1) Standard Quantity or Hours	(2) Standard Price or Rate	Standard Cost (1) × (2)
Direct materials.	3.0 pounds	$4.00 per pound	$ 12.00
Direct labor	0.50 hours	$22.00 per hour	11.00
Variable manufacturing overhead	0.50 hours	$6.00 per hour	3.00
Total standard cost per unit			$26.00

Using Standards in Flexible Budgets

Once Terry Sherman created the standard cost card shown in Exhibit 11–1, he was ready to use this information to calculate direct materials, direct labor, and variable manufacturing overhead variances. Therefore, he gathered the following data for the month of June:

Originally budgeted output in June	2,100 statues
Actual output in June	2,000 statues
Actual direct materials cost in June*	$24,700
Actual direct labor cost in June?	$22,680
Actual variable manufacturing overhead cost in June	$7,140

*The revenue variance is labeled favorable (unfavorable) when the actual revenue is greater than (less than) the planning budget. The expense variances are labeled favorable (unfavorable) when the actual expense is less than (greater than) the planning budget.

Using the above data and the standard cost data from Exhibit 11–1, Terry computed the spending and activity variances shown in Exhibit 11–2. Notice that the actual results and flexible budget columns are each based on the actual output of 2,000 statues. The planning budget column is based on the planned output of 2,100 statues. The standard costs of $12.00 per unit for materials, $11.00 per unit for direct labor, and $3.00 per unit for variable manufacturing overhead are each multiplied by the actual output of 2,000 statues to compute the amounts in the flexible budget column. For example, the standard direct labor cost per unit of $11.00 multiplied by 2,000 statues equals the direct labor flexible budget of $22,000. Similarly, the three standard variable cost figures are multiplied by 2,100 units to compute the amounts in the planning budget column. For example, the direct labor cost for the planning budget is $23,100 (= $11.00 per unit × 2,100 units).

The spending variances shown in Exhibit 11–2 are computed by taking the amounts in the actual results column and subtracting the amounts in the flexible budget column. For all three variable manufacturing costs, this computation results in a positive number because the actual amount of the cost incurred to produce 2,000 statues exceeds the standard cost allowed for 2,000 statues. Because, in all three instances, the actual cost incurred exceeds the standard cost allowed for the actual level of output, the variance is labeled unfavorable (U). Had any of the actual costs incurred been less than the standard cost allowed for the actual level of output, the corresponding variances would have been labeled favorable (F).

The activity variances shown in the exhibit are computed by taking the amounts in the flexible budget column and subtracting the amounts in the planning budget column. For all three variable manufacturing costs, these computations result in negative numbers and what are labeled as favorable (F) variances. The label favorable is used in these instances because the standard cost allowed for the actual output is less than the standard cost allowed for the planned

---

EXHIBIT 11–2

Flexible Budget Performance Report for Variable Manufacturing Costs

Colonial Pewter
Flexible Budget Performance Report—Manufacturing Costs Only
For the Month Ended June 30

	Actual Results	Spending Variances	Flexible Budget	Activity Variances	Planning Budget
Statues produced (q).	2,000		2,000		2,100
Direct materials ($12.00q).	$24,700	$ 700 U	$24,000	$1,200 F	$25,200
Direct labor ($11.00q)	$22,680	$ 680 U	$22,000	$ 1,100 F	$23,100
Variable manufacturing overhead ($3.00q).	$7,140	$1,140 U	$6,000	$300 F	$6,300

output. Had the actual level of activity been greater than the planned level of activity, all of the computations would have resulted in positive numbers and unfavorable (U) activity variances.

While the performance report in Exhibit 11–2 is useful, it would be even more useful if the spending variances could be broken down into their price-related and quantity-related components. For example, the direct materials spending variance in the report is $700 unfavorable. This means that, given the actual level of production for the period, direct materials costs were too high by $700—at least according to the standard costs. Was this due to higher than expected prices for materials? Or was it due to too much material being used? The standard cost variances we will be discussing in the rest of the chapter are designed to answer these questions.

A General Model for Standard Cost Variance Analysis

Standard cost variance analysis decomposes spending variances from the flexible budget into two elements—one due to the price paid for the input and the other due to the amount of the input that is used. A **price variance** is the difference between the actual amount paid for an input and the standard amount that should have been paid, multiplied by the actual amount of the input purchased. A **quantity variance** is the difference between how much of an input was actually used and how much should have been used and is stated in dollar terms using the standard price of the input.

Why are standards separated into two categories—price and quantity? Price variances and quantity variances usually have different causes. In addition, different managers are usually responsible for buying and using inputs. For example, in the case of a raw material, the purchasing manager is responsible for its price and the production manager is responsible for the amount of the raw material actually used to make products. Therefore, it is important to clearly distinguish between deviations from price standards (the responsibility of the purchasing manager) and deviations from quantity standards (the responsibility of the production manager).

Exhibit 11–3 presents a general model that can be used to decompose the spending variance for a variable cost into a *price variance* and a *quantity variance.*[2] Column (1) in this exhibit corresponds with the Actual Results column in Exhibit 11–2. Column (3) corresponds with the Flexible Budget column in Exhibit 11–2. Column (2) has been inserted into Exhibit 11–3 to enable separating the spending variance into a price variance and a quantity variance.

EXHIBIT 11–3
A General Model for Standard Cost Variance Analysis—Variable Manufacturing Costs

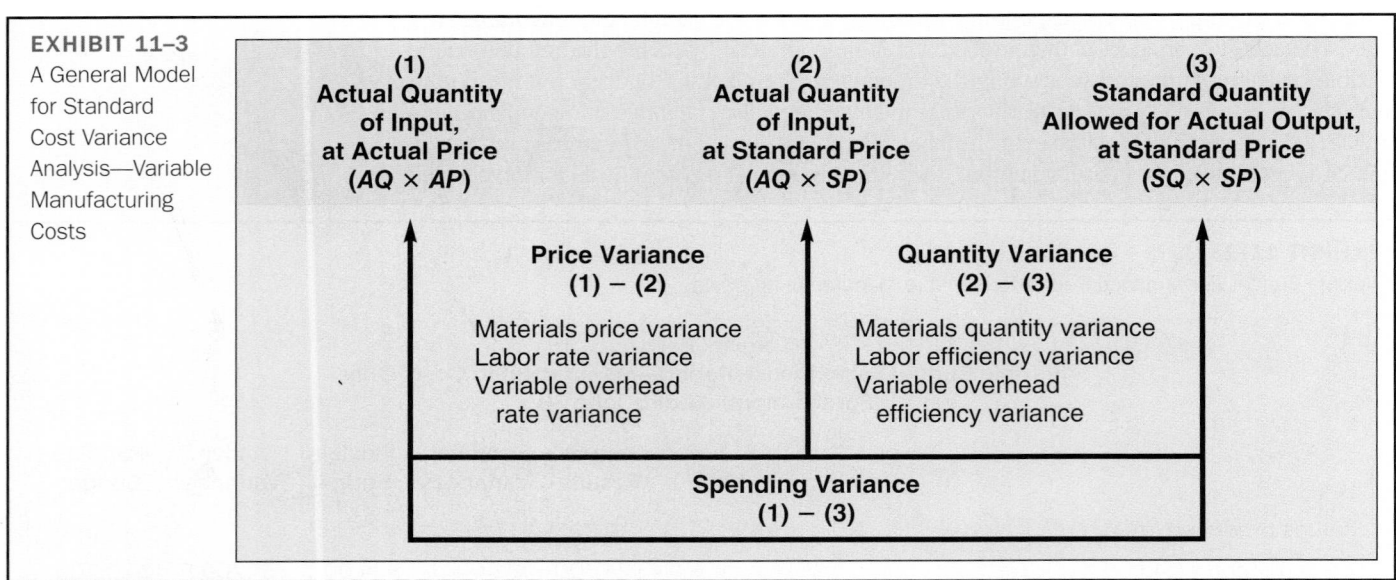

---

[2] This general model can always be used to compute direct labor and variable manufacturing overhead variances. However, it can be used to compute direct materials variances only when the actual quantity of materials purchased equals the actual quantity of materials used in production. Later in the chapter, we will explain how to compute direct materials variances when these quantities differ.

Three things should be noted from Exhibit 11–3. First, it can be used to compute a price variance and a quantity variance for each of the three variable cost elements—direct materials, direct labor, and variable manufacturing overhead—even though the variances have different names. A price variance is called a *materials price variance* in the case of direct materials, a *labor rate variance* in the case of direct labor, and a *variable overhead rate variance* in the case of variable manufacturing overhead. A quantity variance is called a *materials quantity variance* in the case of direct materials, a *labor efficiency variance* in the case of direct labor, and a *variable overhead efficiency variance* in the case of variable manufacturing overhead.

Second, all three columns in the exhibit are based on the *actual amount of output* produced during the period. Even the flexible budget column depicts the standard cost allowed for the *actual amount of output* produced during the period. The key to understanding the flexible budget column in Exhibit 11–3 is to grasp the meaning of the term *standard quantity allowed (SQ)*. The **standard quantity allowed** (when computing direct materials variances) or **standard hours allowed** (when computing direct labor and variable manufacturing overhead variances) refers to the amount of an input *that should have been used* to manufacture the actual output of finished goods produced during the period. It is computed by multiplying the actual output by the standard quantity (or hours) per unit. The standard quantity (or hours) allowed is then multiplied by the standard price (or rate) per unit of the input to obtain the total cost according to the flexible budget. For example, if a company actually produced 100 units of finished goods during the period and its standard quantity per unit of finished goods for direct materials is 3 pounds, then its *standard quantity allowed (SQ)* would be 300 pounds (= 100 units × 3 pounds per unit). If the company's standard cost per pound of direct materials is $2.00, then the total direct materials cost in its flexible budget would be $600 (= 300 pounds × $2.00 per pound).

Third, the spending, price, and quantity variances—regardless of what they are called—are computed exactly the same way regardless of whether one is dealing with direct materials, direct labor, or variable manufacturing overhead. The spending variance is computed by taking the total cost in column (1) and subtracting the total cost in column (3). The price variance is computed by taking the total cost in column (1) and subtracting the total cost in column (2). The quantity variance is computed by taking the total cost in column (2) and subtracting the total cost in column (3). In all of these variance calculations, a positive number should be labeled as an unfavorable (U) variance and a negative number should be labeled as a favorable (F) variance. An unfavorable price variance indicates that the actual price (AP) per unit of the input was greater than the standard price (SP) per unit. A favorable price variance indicates that the actual price (AP) of the input was less than the standard price per unit (SP). An unfavorable quantity variance indicates that the actual quantity (AQ) of the input used was greater than the standard quantity allowed (SQ). Conversely, a favorable quantity variance indicates that the actual quantity (AQ) of the input used was less than the standard quantity allowed (SQ).

With this general model as the foundation, we will now calculate Colonial Pewter's price and quantity variances.

Using Standard Costs—Direct Materials Variances

After determining Colonial Pewter Company's standard costs for direct materials, direct labor, and variable manufacturing overhead, Terry Sherman's next step was to compute the company's variances for June. As discussed in the preceding section, variances are computed by comparing actual costs to standard costs. Terry referred to the standard cost card in Exhibit 11–1 that shows the standard direct materials cost per statue was computed as follows:

LEARNING OBJECTIVE 11–1
Compute the direct materials price and quantity variances and explain their significance.

3.0 pounds per statue × $4.00 per pound = $12.00 per statue

Colonial Pewter's records for June showed that the actual quantity (AQ) of pewter purchased was 6,500 pounds at an actual price (AP) of $3.80 per pound, for a total cost of $24,700. All of the material purchased was used during June to manufacture

EXHIBIT 11-4

Standard Cost Variance Analysis—Direct Materials

(Note: The quantity of materials purchased equals the quantity used in production.)

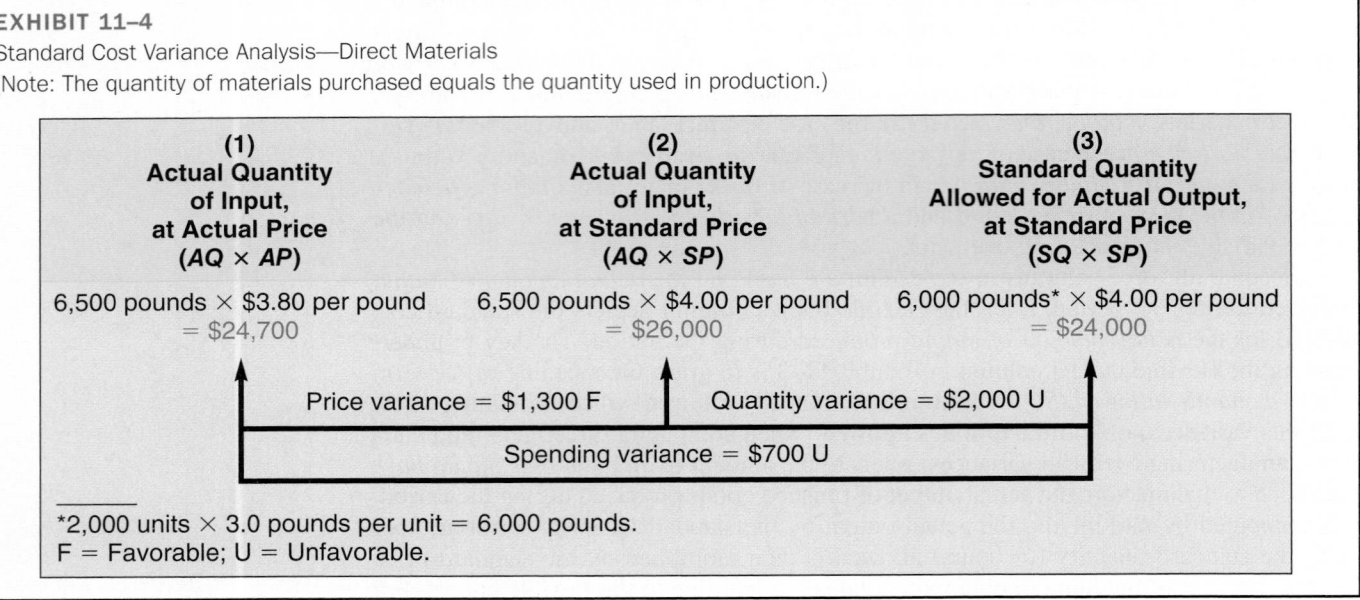

(1) Actual Quantity of Input, at Actual Price ($AQ \times AP$)	(2) Actual Quantity of Input, at Standard Price ($AQ \times SP$)	(3) Standard Quantity Allowed for Actual Output, at Standard Price ($SQ \times SP$)
6,500 pounds $\times$ \$3.80 per pound = \$24,700	6,500 pounds $\times$ \$4.00 per pound = \$26,000	6,000 pounds* $\times$ \$4.00 per pound = \$24,000

Price variance = \$1,300 F   Quantity variance = \$2,000 U

Spending variance = \$700 U

*2,000 units $\times$ 3.0 pounds per unit = 6,000 pounds.
F = Favorable; U = Unfavorable.

2,000 statues.[3] Using these data and the standard costs from Exhibit 11–1, Terry computed the price and quantity variances shown in Exhibit 11–4.

Notice that the variances in this exhibit are based on three different total costs— $24,700, $26,000, and $24,000. The first, $24,700, is the actual amount paid for the actual amount of pewter purchased. The third total cost figure, $24,000, refers to how much should have been spent on pewter to produce the actual output of 2,000 statues. The standards call for 3 pounds of pewter per statue. Because 2,000 statues were produced, 6,000 pounds of pewter should have been used. This is referred to as the *standard quantity allowed* for the actual output and its computation can be stated in formula form as follows:

Standard quantity allowed for actual output = Actual output × Standard quantity

If 6,000 pounds of pewter had been purchased at the standard price of $4.00 per pound, the company would have spent $24,000. This is the amount that appears in the company's flexible budget for the month. The difference between the $24,700 actually spent and the $24,000 that should have been spent is the spending variance for the month of $700 U. This variance is unfavorable (denoted by U) because the amount that was actually spent exceeds the amount that should have been spent.

The second total cost figure in Exhibit 11–4, $26,000, is the key that allows us to decompose the spending variance into two distinct elements—one due to price and one due to quantity. It represents how much the company should have spent if it had purchased the actual amount of input, 6,500 pounds, at the standard price of $4.00 a pound rather than the actual price of $3.80 a pound.

The Materials Price Variance

Using the $26,000 total cost figure in column (2) of Exhibit 11–4, we can make two comparisons—one with the total cost of $24,700 in column (1) and one with the total cost of $24,000 in column (3). The difference between the $24,700 in column (1) and the $26,000 in column (2) is the *materials price variance* of $1,300, which is labeled as favorable (denoted by F). A **materials price variance** measures the difference between an input's actual price and its standard price, multiplied by the actual quantity purchased.

---

[3] Throughout this section, we assume zero beginning and ending inventories of materials and that all materials purchased during the period are used during that period. The more general case in which there are beginning and ending inventories of materials and materials are not necessarily used during the period in which they are purchased is considered later in the chapter.

To understand the price variance, note that the actual price of $3.80 per pound of pewter is $0.20 less than the standard price of $4.00 per pound. Because 6,500 pounds were purchased, the total amount of the variance is $1,300 (= $0.20 per pound × 6,500 pounds). This variance is labeled favorable (F) because the actual purchase price per pound is less than the standard purchase price per pound. A price variance is labeled unfavorable (U) if the actual purchase price exceeds the standard purchase price.

Generally speaking, the purchasing manager has control over the price paid for goods and is therefore responsible for the materials price variance. Many factors influence the prices paid for goods including how many units are ordered, how the order is delivered, whether the order is a rush order, and the quality of materials purchased. If any of these factors deviates from what was assumed when the standards were set, a price variance can result. For example, purchasing second-grade materials rather than top-grade materials may result in a favorable price variance because the lower-grade materials may be less costly. However, the lower-grade materials may create production problems. It also bears emphasizing that someone other than the purchasing manager could be responsible for a materials price variance. For example, due to production problems beyond the purchasing manager's control, the purchasing manager may have to use express delivery. In these cases, the production manager should be held responsible for the resulting price variances.

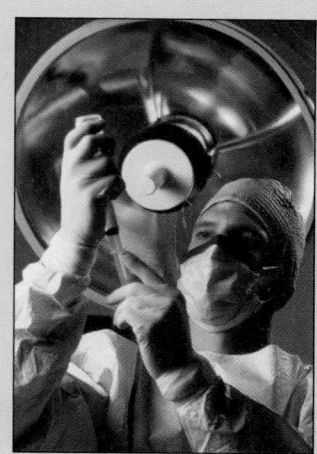
The Materials Quantity Variance

Referring again to Exhibit 11–4, the difference between the $26,000 in column (2) and the $24,000 in column (3) is the *materials quantity variance* of $2,000, which is labeled as unfavorable (denoted by U). The **materials quantity variance** measures the difference between the actual quantity of materials used in production and the standard quantity of materials allowed for the actual output, multiplied by the standard price per unit of materials. It is labeled as unfavorable (favorable) when the actual quantity of material used in production is greater than (less than) the quantity of material that should have been used according to the standard.

To understand the materials quantity variance, note that the actual amount of pewter used in production was 6,500 pounds. However, the standard amount of pewter allowed for the actual output is 6,000 pounds. Therefore, too much pewter was used to produce the actual output—by a total of 500 pounds. To express this in dollar terms, the 500 pounds is multiplied by the standard price of $4.00 per pound to yield the quantity variance of $2,000 U. Why is the standard price of pewter, rather than the actual price, used in this calculation? The production manager is ordinarily responsible for the quantity variance. If the actual price were used in the calculation of the quantity variance, the production

EXHIBIT 11–5
Direct Materials Variances:
The Equations-Based
Approach

Materials Price Variance:

Materials price variance = $(AQ \times AP) - (AQ \times SP)$
Materials price variance = $AQ(AP - SP)$
Materials price variance = 6,500 pounds($3.80 per pound − $4.00 per pound)
Materials price variance = $1,300 F

Materials Quantity Variance:

Materials quantity variance = $(AQ \times SP) - (SQ \times SP)$
Materials quantity variance = $SP(AQ - SQ)$
Materials quantity variance = $4.00 per pound(6,500 pounds − 6,000 pounds)
Materials quantity variance = $2,000 U
where:
AQ = Actual quantity of pounds purchased and used in production
SQ = Standard quantity of pounds allowed for the actual output
AP = Actual price per unit of the input
SP = Standard price per unit of the input

manager's performance evaluation would be unfairly influenced by the efficiency or inefficiency of the purchasing manager.

Excessive materials usage can result from many factors, including faulty machines, inferior materials quality, untrained workers, and poor supervision. Generally speaking, it is the responsibility of the production manager to see that material usage is kept in line with standards. There may be times, however, when the *purchasing* manager is responsible for an unfavorable materials quantity variance. For example, if the purchasing manager buys inferior materials at a lower price, the materials may be unsuitable for use and may result in excessive waste. Thus, the purchasing manager rather than the production manager would be responsible for the quantity variance.

Thus far, we have shown how to compute direct materials variances using the general model depicted in Exhibit 11–4; however, these variances can also be calculated using basic mathematical equations. Exhibit 11–5 shows how Colonial Pewter can compute its direct materials variances using the equations-based approach.

IN BUSINESS

CUSTOMERS SPEAK LOUD AND CLEAR

When ConAgra Foods raised the price of its Banquet frozen dinners from $1.00 to $1.25, many customers stopped buying the product. The resulting drop in sales contributed to a 40% decline in the company's stock price. It also presented ConAgra with an interesting challenge—lowering its raw material costs so that Banquet frozen dinners could be profitable at the customer-mandated price of $1.00. ConAgra responded by replacing expensive entrees such as barbecued chicken and country-fried pork with less costly choices such as meat patties and rice and beans. It also shrank standard portion sizes and expanded the use of cheaper side items such as mashed potatoes and brownies. However, the company did not sacrifice on variety—it still offers more than 100 Banquet-branded products.

Source: Joseph Weber, "Over a Buck for Dinner? Outrageous," *BusinessWeek*, March 9, 2009, p. 57.

Using Standard Costs—Direct Labor Variances

LEARNING OBJECTIVE 11–2
Compute the direct labor rate and efficiency variances and explain their significance.

Terry Sherman's next step in determining Colonial Pewter's variances for June was to compute the direct labor variances for the month. Recall from Exhibit 11–1 that the standard direct labor cost per statue is $11, computed as follows:

0.50 hours per statue × $22.00 per hour = $11.00 per statue

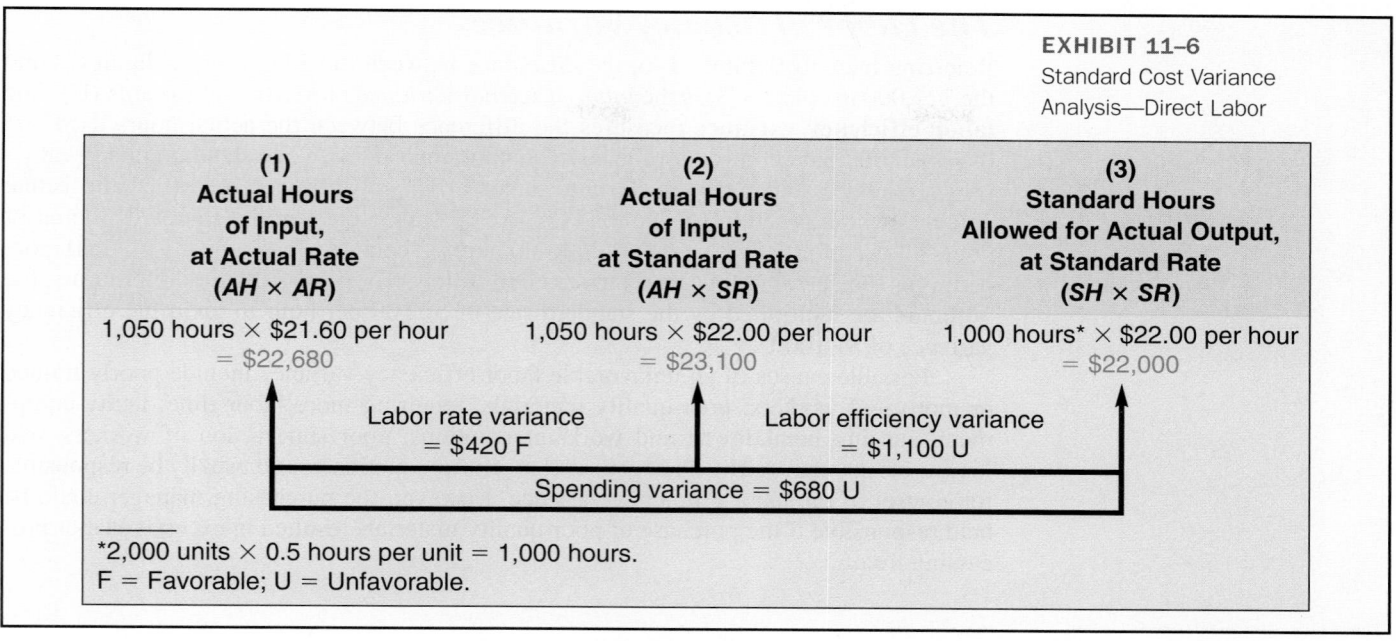

EXHIBIT 11–6
Standard Cost Variance
Analysis—Direct Labor

(1) Actual Hours of Input, at Actual Rate (AH × AR)	(2) Actual Hours of Input, at Standard Rate (AH × SR)	(3) Standard Hours Allowed for Actual Output, at Standard Rate (SH × SR)
1,050 hours × $21.60 per hour = $22,680	1,050 hours × $22.00 per hour = $23,100	1,000 hours* × $22.00 per hour = $22,000

Labor rate variance = $420 F

Labor efficiency variance = $1,100 U

Spending variance = $680 U

*2,000 units × 0.5 hours per unit = 1,000 hours.
F = Favorable; U = Unfavorable.

In addition, Colonial Pewter's records for June showed that 1,050 direct labor-hours were actually worked. Given that the company paid its direct labor workers a total of $22,680 (including payroll taxes and fringe benefits), the average actual wage rate was $21.60 per hour (= $22,680 ÷ 1,050 hours). Using these data and the standard costs from Exhibit 11–1, Terry computed the direct labor rate and efficiency variances that appear in Exhibit 11–6.

Notice that the column headings in Exhibit 11–6 are the same as those used Exhibits 11–3 and 10–4, except that in Exhibit 11–6 the terms *rate* and *hours* are used in place of the terms *price* and *quantity*.

The Labor Rate Variance

Using the $23,100 total cost figure in column (2) of Exhibit 11–6, we can make two comparisons—one with the total cost of $22,680 in column (1) and one with the total cost of $22,000 in column (3). The difference between the 22,680 in column (1) and the $23,100 in column (2) is the *labor rate variance* of $420 F. The **labor rate variance** measures the difference between the actual hourly rate and the standard hourly rate, multiplied by the actual number of hours worked during the period.

To understand the labor rate variance, note that the actual hourly rate of $21.60 is $0.40 less than the standard rate of $22.00 per hour. Because 1,050 hours were actually worked, the total amount of the variance is $420 (= $0.40 per hour × 1,050 hours). The variance is labeled favorable (F) because the actual hourly rate is less than the standard hourly rate. If the actual hourly rate had been greater than the standard hourly rate, the variance would have been labeled unfavorable (U).

In most companies, the wage rates paid to workers are quite predictable. Nevertheless, rate variances can arise based on how production supervisors use their direct labor workers. Skilled workers with high hourly rates of pay may be given duties that require little skill and call for lower hourly rates of pay. This will result in an unfavorable labor rate variance because the actual hourly rate of pay will exceed the standard rate specified for the particular task. In contrast, a favorable rate variance would result when workers who are paid at a rate lower than specified in the standard are assigned to the task. However, the lower-paid workers may not be as efficient. Finally, overtime work at premium rates will result in an unfavorable labor rate variance if the overtime premium is charged to the direct labor account.

486   Chapter 11

The Labor Efficiency Variance

Referring back to Exhibit 11–6, the difference between the $23,100 in column (2) and the $22,000 in column (3) is the *labor efficiency variance* of $1,100 unfavorable (U). The **labor efficiency variance** measures the difference between the actual hours used and the standard hours allowed for the actual output, multiplied by the standard hourly rate.

To understand Colonial Pewter's labor efficiency variance, note that the actual amount of hours used in production was 1,050 hours. However, the standard amount of hours allowed for the actual output is 1,000 hours. Therefore, the company used 50 more hours for the actual output than the standards allow. To express this in dollar terms, the 50 hours are multiplied by the standard rate of $22.00 per hour to yield the efficiency variance of $1,100 U.

Possible causes of an unfavorable labor efficiency variance include poorly trained or motivated workers; poor-quality materials, requiring more labor time; faulty equipment, causing breakdowns and work interruptions; poor supervision of workers; and inaccurate standards. The managers in charge of production would usually be responsible for control of the labor efficiency variance. However, the purchasing manager could be held responsible if the purchase of poor-quality materials resulted in excessive labor processing time.

Another important cause of an unfavorable labor efficiency variance may be insufficient demand for the company's products. Managers in some companies argue that it is difficult, and perhaps unwise, to constantly adjust the workforce in response to changes in the amount of work that needs to be done. In such companies, the direct labor workforce is essentially fixed in the short run. If demand is insufficient to keep everyone busy, workers are not laid off and an unfavorable labor efficiency variance will often be recorded.

If customer orders are insufficient to keep the workers busy, the work center manager has two options—either accept an unfavorable labor efficiency variance or build inventory. A central lesson of Lean Production is that building inventory with no immediate prospect of sale is a bad idea. Excessive inventory—particularly work in process inventory—leads to high defect rates, obsolete goods, and inefficient operations. As a consequence, when the workforce is basically fixed in the short term, managers must be cautious about how labor efficiency variances are used. Some experts advocate eliminating labor efficiency variances in such situations—at least for the purposes of motivating and controlling workers on the shop floor.

Direct labor variances can also be computed using equations instead of the general model depicted in Exhibit 11–6. Exhibit 11–7 shows how Colonial Pewter can compute its direct labor variances using the equations-based approach.

Labor Rate Variance:

Labor rate variance = $(AH \times AR) - (AH \times SR)$
Labor rate variance = $AH(AR - SR)$
Labor rate variance = 1,050 hours($21.60 per hour − $22.00 per hour)
Labor rate variance = $420 F

Labor Efficiency Variance:

Labor efficiency variance = $(AH \times SR) - (SH \times SR)$
Labor efficiency variance = $SR(AH - SH)$
Labor efficiency variance = $22.00 per hour(1,050 hours − 1,000 hours)
Labor efficiency variance = $1,100 U
where:
AH = Actual quantity of hours used in production
SH = Standard quantity of hours allowed for the actual output
AR = Actual rate per direct labor-hour
SR = Standard rate per direct labor-hour

EXHIBIT 11–7
Direct Labor Variances: The Equations-Based Approach

Using Standard Costs—Variable Manufacturing Overhead Variances

The final step in Terry Sherman's analysis of Colonial Pewter's variances for June was to compute the variable manufacturing overhead variances. The variable portion of manufacturing overhead can be analyzed using the same basic formulas that we used to analyze direct materials and direct labor. Recall from Exhibit 11–1 that the standard variable manufacturing overhead is $3.00 per statue, computed as follows:

LEARNING OBJECTIVE 11–3
Compute the variable manufacturing overhead rate and efficiency variances and explain their significance.

0.50 hours per statue × $6.00 per hour = $3.00 per statue

Also recall that Colonial Pewter's cost records showed that the total actual variable manufacturing overhead cost for June was $7,140 and that 1,050 direct labor-hours were worked in June to produce 2,000 statues. Terry's analysis of this overhead data appears in Exhibit 11–8.

EXHIBIT 11–8
Standard Cost Variance Analysis—Variable Manufacturing Overhead

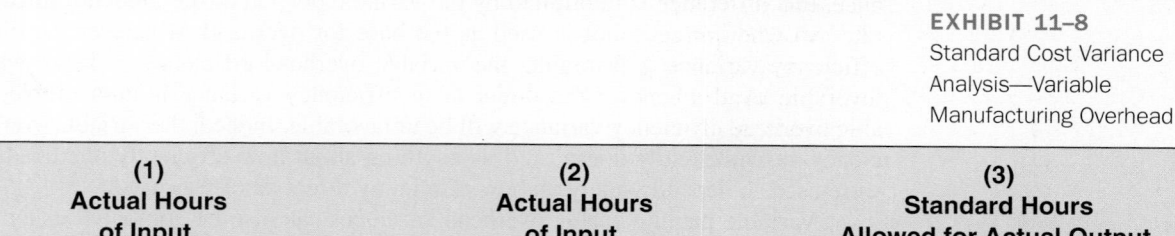

(1) Actual Hours of Input, at Actual Rate ($AH \times AR$)	(2) Actual Hours of Input, at Standard Rate ($AH \times SR$)	(3) Standard Hours Allowed for Actual Output, at Standard Rate ($SH \times SR$)
1,050 hours × $6.80 per hour† = $7,140	1,050 hours × $6.00 per hour = $6,300	1,000 hours* × $6.00 per hour = $6,000

Variable overhead rate variance = $840 U   Variable overhead efficiency variance = $300 U

Spending Variance = $1,140 U

*2,000 units × 0.5 hours per unit = 1,000 hours.
†$7,140 ÷ 1,050 hours = $6.80 per hour.
F = Favorable; U = Unfavorable.

Notice the similarities between Exhibits 11–6 and 11–8. These similarities arise from the fact that direct labor-hours are being used as the base for allocating overhead cost to units of product; thus, the same hourly figures appear in Exhibit 11–8 for variable manufacturing overhead as in Exhibit 11–6 for direct labor. The main difference between the two exhibits is in the standard hourly rate being used, which in this company is much lower for variable manufacturing overhead than for direct labor.

The Variable Manufacturing Overhead Rate and Efficiency Variances

Using the $6,300 total cost figure in column (2) of Exhibit 11–8, we can make two comparisons—one with the total cost of $7,140 in column (1) and one with the total cost of $6,000 in column (3). The difference between the $7,140 in column (1) and the $6,300 in column (2) is the *variable overhead rate variance* of $840 U. The **variable overhead rate variance** measures the difference between the actual variable overhead cost incurred during the period and the standard cost that should have been incurred based on the actual activity of the period. The difference between the $6,300 in column (2) and the $6,000 in column (3) is the *variable overhead efficiency variance* of $300 U. The **variable overhead efficiency variance** measures the difference between the actual level of activity and the standard activity allowed for the actual output, multiplied by the variable part of the predetermined overhead rate.

To understand Colonial Pewter's variable overhead efficiency variance, note that the actual amount of hours used in production was 1,050 hours. However, the standard amount of hours allowed for the actual output is 1,000 hours. Therefore, the company used 50 more hours for the actual output than the standards allow. To express this in dollar terms, the 50 hours are multiplied by the variable part of the predetermined overhead rate of $6.00 per hour to yield the variable overhead efficiency variance of $300 U.

The interpretation of the variable overhead variances is not as clear as the direct materials and direct labor variances. In particular, the variable overhead efficiency variance is exactly the same as the direct labor efficiency variance except for one detail—the rate that is used to translate the variance into dollars. In both cases, the variance is the difference between the actual hours worked and the standard hours allowed for the actual output. In the case of the direct labor efficiency variance, this difference is multiplied by the standard direct labor rate. In the case of the variable overhead efficiency variance, this difference is multiplied by the variable portion of the predetermined overhead rate. So when direct labor is used as the base for overhead, whenever the direct labor efficiency variance is favorable, the variable overhead efficiency variance will also be favorable. And whenever the direct labor efficiency variance is unfavorable, the variable overhead efficiency variance will be unfavorable. Indeed, the variable overhead efficiency variance really doesn't tell us anything about how efficiently overhead resources were used. It depends solely on how efficiently direct labor was used.

Variable manufacturing overhead variances can also be computed using equations instead of the general model depicted in Exhibit 11–8. Exhibit 11–9 shows how Colonial Pewter can compute its variable overhead variances using the equations-based approach.

MANAGERIAL ACCOUNTING IN ACTION

The Wrap-Up

Colonial Pewter Company

In preparation for the scheduled meeting to discuss his analysis of Colonial Pewter's standard costs and variances, Terry distributed his computations to the management group of Colonial Pewter. This included J. D. Wriston, the president of the company; Tom Kuchel, the production manager; and Janet Warner, the purchasing manager. J. D. Wriston opened the meeting with the following question:

J. D.: Terry, I think I understand what you have done, but just to make sure, would you mind summarizing the highlights of what you found?

Terry: As you can see, the biggest problems are the unfavorable materials quantity variance of $2,000 and the unfavorable labor efficiency variance of $1,100.

EXHIBIT 11–9
Variable Manufacturing
Overhead Variances: The
Equations-Based Approach

Variable Overhead Rate Variance:

Variable overhead rate variance = $(AH \times AR) - (AH \times SR)$
Variable overhead rate variance = $AH(AR - SR)$
Variable overhead rate variance = 1,050 hours($6.80 - $6.00)
Variable overhead rate variance = $840 U

Variable Overhead Efficiency Variance:

Variable overhead efficiency variance = $(AH \times SR) - (SH \times SR)$
Variable overhead efficiency variance = $SR(AH - SH)$
Variable overhead efficiency variance = $6.00 per hour(1,050 hours − 1,000 hours)
Variable overhead efficiency variance = $300 U
where:
AH = Actual quantity of hours used in production
SH = Standard quantity of hours allowed for the actual output
AR = Actual rate per direct labor-hour
SR = Standard rate per direct labor-hour

J. D.: Tom, you're the production boss. What do you think is causing the unfavorable labor efficiency variance?

Tom: It has to be the new production workers. Our experienced workers shouldn't have much problem meeting the standard of half an hour per unit. We all knew that there would be some inefficiency for a while as we brought new people on board. My plan for overcoming the problem is to pair up each of the new guys with one of our old-timers and have them work together for a while. It would slow down our older guys a bit, but I'll bet the unfavorable variance disappears and our new workers would learn a lot.

J. D.: Sounds good. Now, what about that $2,000 unfavorable materials quantity variance?

Terry: Tom, are the new workers generating a lot of scrap?

Tom: Yeah, I guess so.

J. D.: I think that could be part of the problem. Can you do anything about it?

Tom: I can watch the scrap closely for a few days to see where it's being generated. If it is the new workers, I can have the old-timers work with them on the problem when I team them up.

J. D.: Janet, the favorable materials price variance of $1,300 isn't helping us if it is contributing to the unfavorable materials quantity and labor efficiency variances. Let's make sure that our raw material purchases conform to our quality standards.

Janet: Will do.

J. D.: Good. Let's reconvene in a few weeks to see what has happened. Hopefully, we can get those unfavorable variances under control.

An Important Subtlety in the Materials Variances

Most companies use the *quantity of materials purchased* to compute the materials price variance and the *quantity of materials used* in production to compute the materials quantity variance. There are two reasons for this practice. First, delaying the computation of the price variance until the materials are used would result in less timely variance reports. Second, computing the price variance when the materials are purchased allows materials to be carried in the inventory accounts at their standard cost. This greatly simplifies bookkeeping.

When we computed materials price and quantity variances for Colonial Pewter in Exhibit 11–4, we assumed that 6,500 pounds of materials were purchased and used in production. However, it is very common for a company's quantity of materials purchased to differ from its quantity used in production. When this happens, the materials price variance is computed using the *quantity of materials purchased,* whereas the materials quantity variance is computed using the *quantity of materials used* in production.

To illustrate, assume that during June Colonial Pewter purchased 7,000 pounds of materials at $3.80 per pound instead of 6,500 pounds as assumed earlier in the chapter. Also assume that the company continued to use 6,500 pounds of materials in production and that the standard price remained at $4.00 per pound.

Given these assumptions, Exhibit 11–10 shows how to compute the materials price variance of $1,400 F and the materials quantity variance of $2,000 U. Note that the price variance is based on the amount of the input purchased whereas the quantity variance is based on the quantity of the input used in production. Column (2) of Exhibit 11–10 contains two different total costs for this reason. When the price variance is computed, the total cost used from column (2) is $28,000—which is the cost of the input *purchased,* evaluated at the standard price. When the quantity variance is computed, the total cost used from column (2) is $26,000—which is the cost of the actual input *used,* evaluated at the standard price.

Exhibit 11–10 shows that the price variance is computed on the entire amount of material purchased (7,000 pounds), whereas the quantity variance is computed only on the amount of materials used in production during the month (6,500 pounds). What about the other 500 pounds of material that were purchased during the period, but that have not yet been used? When those materials are used in future periods, a quantity variance will be computed. However, a price variance will not be computed when the materials are finally used because the price variance was computed when the materials were purchased.

Because the price variance is based on the amount purchased and the quantity variance is based on the amount used, the two variances do not generally sum to the spending variance from the flexible budget, which is wholly based on the amount used. We would also like to emphasize that the variances depicted in Exhibit 11–10 can also be computed

EXHIBIT 11–10
Standard Cost Variance Analysis—Direct Materials
(Note: The quantity of materials purchased does not equal the quantity used in production.)

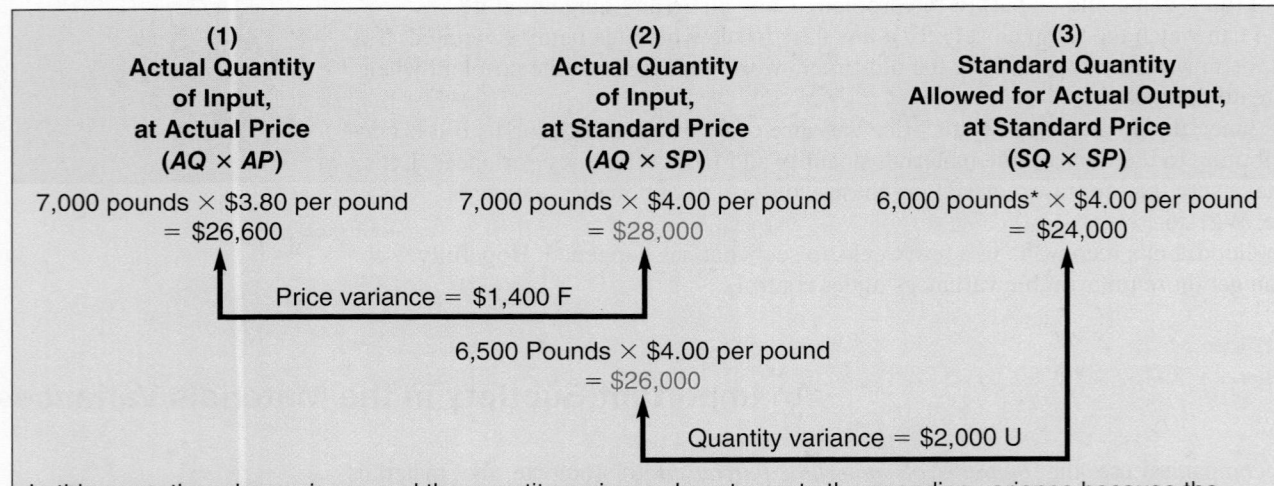

In this case, the price variance and the quantity variance do not sum to the spending variance because the price variance is based on the quantity purchased whereas the quantity variance is based on the quantity used in production, and the two numbers differ.

---
*2,000 units × 3.0 pounds per unit = 6,000 pounds.
F = Favorable; U = Unfavorable.

Materials Price Variance:

Materials price variance = $(AQ \times AP) - (AQ \times SP)$
Materials price variance = $AQ(AP - SP)$
Materials price variance = 7,000 pounds($3.80 per pound - $4.00 per pound)
Materials price variance = $1,400 F
where:
AQ = Actual quantity of pounds *purchased*
AP = Actual price per unit of the input
SP = Standard price per unit of the input

Materials Quantity Variance:

Materials quantity variance = $(AQ = SP) - (SQ \times SP)$
Materials quantity variance = $SP(AQ - SQ)$
Materials quantity variance = $4.00 per pound(6,500 pounds - 6,000 pounds)
Materials quantity variance = $2,000 U
where:
AQ = Actual quantity of pounds *used in production*
SQ = Standard quantity of pounds allowed for the actual output
SP = Standard price per unit of the input

EXHIBIT 11–11
Direct Materials Variances: The Equations-Based Approach (when the quantity of materials purchased does not equal the quantity used in production)

using the equations shown in Exhibit 11–11. The approaches shown in *Exhibits 11–10 and 11–11 can always be used to compute direct materials variances.* However, *Exhibits 11–4 and 11–5 can only be used in the special case when the quantity of materials purchased equals the quantity of materials used.*

Standard Costs—Managerial Implications

Advantages of Standard Costs

Standard cost systems have a number of advantages.

1. Standard costs are a key element in a management by exception approach as defined in the previous chapter. If costs conform to the standards, managers can focus on other issues. When costs are significantly outside the standards, managers are alerted that problems may exist that require attention. This approach helps managers focus on important issues.
2. Standards that are viewed as reasonable by employees can promote economy and efficiency. They provide benchmarks that individuals can use to judge their own performance.
3. Standard costs can greatly simplify bookkeeping. Instead of recording actual costs for each job, the standard costs for direct materials, direct labor, and overhead can be charged to jobs.
4. Standard costs fit naturally in an integrated system of "responsibility accounting." The standards establish what costs should be, who should be responsible for them, and whether actual costs are under control.

Potential Problems with Standard Costs

The improper use of standard costs can present a number of potential problems.

1. Standard cost variance reports are usually prepared on a monthly basis and often are released days or even weeks after the end of the month. As a consequence, the

information in the reports may be so outdated that it is almost useless. Timely, frequent reports that are approximately correct are better than infrequent reports that are very precise but out of date by the time they are released. Some companies are now reporting variances and other key operating data daily or even more frequently.

2. If managers use variances only to assign blame and punish subordinates, morale may suffer. Furthermore, subordinates may be tempted to cover up unfavorable variances or take actions that are not in the best interests of the company to make sure the variances are favorable.

3. Labor-hour standards and efficiency variances make two important assumptions. First, they assume that the production process is labor-paced; if labor works faster, output will go up. However, output in many companies is not determined by how fast labor works; rather, it is determined by the processing speed of machines. Second, the computations assume that labor is a variable cost. However, direct labor may be essentially fixed. If labor is fixed, then an undue emphasis on labor efficiency variances creates pressure to build excess inventories.

4. In some cases, a "favorable" variance can be worse than an "unfavorable" variance. For example, McDonald's has a standard for the amount of hamburger meat that should be in a Big Mac. A "favorable" variance would mean that less meat was used than the standard specifies. The result is substandard Big Macs and possibly numerous dissatisfied customers.

5. Too much emphasis on meeting the standards may overshadow other important objectives such as maintaining and improving quality, on-time delivery, and customer satisfaction. This tendency can be reduced by using supplemental performance measures that focus on these other objectives.

6. Just meeting standards is not sufficient because companies need to continually improve to remain competitive. For this reason, some companies focus on the trends in the standard cost variances—aiming for continual improvement rather than just meeting the standards. In other companies, engineered standards are replaced either by a rolling average of actual costs, which is expected to decline, or by very challenging target costs.

In sum, managers should exercise considerable care when using a standard cost system. It is particularly important that managers go out of their way to focus on the positive, rather than just on the negative, and to be aware of possible unintended consequences.

Summary

A standard is a benchmark for measuring performance. Standards are set for both the quantity and the cost of inputs needed to manufacture goods or to provide services. Quantity standards indicate how much of an input, such as labor time or raw materials, should be used to make a product or provide a service. Cost standards indicate what the cost of the input should be.

When standards are compared to actual performance, the difference is referred to as a *variance*. Variances are computed and reported to management on a regular basis for both the quantity and the price elements of direct materials, direct labor, and variable overhead. Price variances are computed by taking the difference between actual and standard prices and multiplying the result by the amount of input purchased. Quantity variances are computed by taking the difference between the actual amount of the input used and the amount of input that is allowed for the actual output, and then multiplying the result by the standard price of the input.

Standard cost systems provide companies with a number of advantages, such as supporting the management by exception approach, simplifying bookkeeping, and providing a benchmark that employees can use to judge their own performance. However, critics of standard cost systems argue that they provide information that is outdated, they can motivate employees to make poor decisions in an effort to generate favorable variances, and they fail to adequately embrace the mindset of continuous process improvement.

Traditional standard cost variance reports are often supplemented with other performance measures to ensure that overemphasis on standard cost variances does not lead to problems in other critical areas such as product quality, inventory levels, and on-time delivery.

Review Problem: Standard Costs

Xavier Company produces a single product. Variable manufacturing overhead is applied to products on the basis of direct labor-hours. The standard costs for one unit of product are as follows:

Direct material: 6 ounces at $0.50 per ounce	$ 3.00
Direct labor: 0.6 hours at $30.00 per hour	18.00
Variable manufacturing overhead: 0.6 hours at $10.00 per hour.........	6.00
Total standard variable cost per unit.	$27.00

During June, 2,000 units were produced. The costs associated with June's operations were as follows:

Material purchased: 18,000 ounces at $0.60 per ounce	$10,800
Material used in production: 14,000 ounces.....................	—
Direct labor: 1,100 hours at $30.50 per hour....................	$33,550
Variable manufacturing overhead costs incurred	$12,980

Required:
Compute the direct materials, direct labor, and variable manufacturing overhead variances.

Solution to Review Problem

Direct Materials Variances

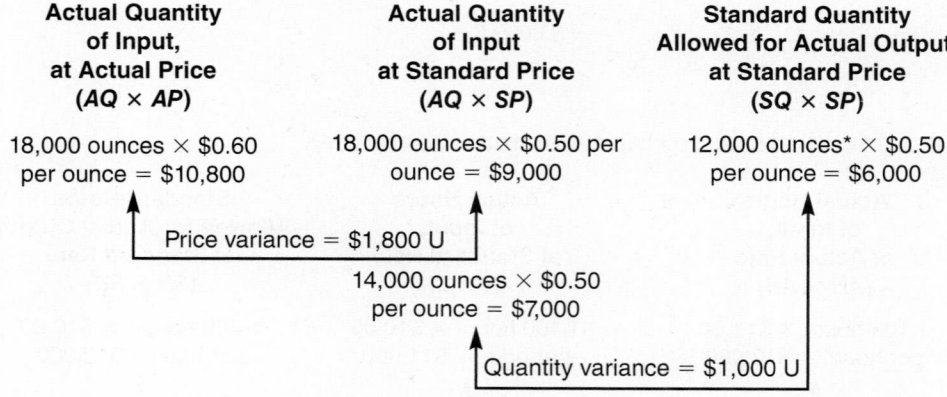

Actual Quantity of Input, at Actual Price ($AQ \times AP$)	Actual Quantity of Input at Standard Price ($AQ \times SP$)	Standard Quantity Allowed for Actual Output, at Standard Price ($SQ \times SP$)
18,000 ounces × $0.60 per ounce = $10,800	18,000 ounces × $0.50 per ounce = $9,000	12,000 ounces* × $0.50 per ounce = $6,000

Price variance = $1,800 U

14,000 ounces × $0.50 per ounce = $7,000

Quantity variance = $1,000 U

——————
*2,000 units × 6 ounces per unit = 12,000 ounces.

Using the formulas in the chapter, the same variances would be computed as follows:

$$\text{Materials price variance} = (AQ \times AP) - (AQ \times SP)$$
$$= AQ(AP - SP)$$
$$= 18,000 \text{ ounces } (\$0.60 \text{ per ounce} \times \$0.50 \text{ per ounce})$$
$$= \$1,800 \text{ U}$$

$$\text{Materials quantity variance} = (AQ \times SP) - (SQ \times SP)$$
$$= SP(AQ - SQ)$$
$$= \$0.50 \text{ per ounce } (14,000 \text{ ounces} \times 12,000 \text{ ounces})$$
$$= \$1,000 \text{ U}$$

Direct Labor Variances

*2,000 units $\times$ 0.6 hours per unit =1,200 hours.
F = Favorable; U = Unfavorable.

Using the formulas in the chapter, the same variances can be computed as follows:

$$\text{Labor rate variance} = (AH \times AR) - (AH \times SR)$$
$$= AH(AR - SR)$$
$$= 1,100 \text{ hours } (\$30.50 \text{ per hour} - \$30.00 \text{ per hour})$$
$$= \$550 \text{ U}$$
$$\text{Labor efficiency variance} = (AH \times SR) - (SH \times SR)$$
$$= SR(AH - SH)$$
$$= \$30.00 \text{ per hour } (1,100 \text{ hours} - 1,200 \text{ hours})$$
$$= \$3,000 \text{ F}$$

Variable Manufacturing Overhead Variances

*2,000 units $\times$ 0.6 hours per unit = 1,200 hours.
†\$12,980 ÷ 1,100 hours = \$11.80 per hour.
F = Favorable; U = Unfavorable.

Using the formulas in the chapter, the same variances can be computed as follows:

$$\begin{aligned} \text{Variable overhead rate variance} &= (AH \times AR) - (AH \times SR) \\ &= AH(AR - SR) \\ &= 1{,}100 \text{ hours } (\$11.80 \text{ per hour} - \$10.00 \text{ per hour}) \\ &= \$\,1{,}980 \text{ U} \end{aligned}$$

$$\begin{aligned} \text{Variable overhead efficiency variance} &= (AH \times SR) - (SH \times SR) \\ &= SR(AH - SH) \\ &= \$10.00 \text{ per hour } (1{,}100 \text{ hours} - 1{,}200 \text{ hours}) \\ &= \$1{,}000 \text{ F} \end{aligned}$$

Glossary

Labor efficiency variance The difference between the actual hours taken to complete a task and the standard hours allowed for the actual output, multiplied by the standard hourly labor rate. (p. 486)

Labor rate variance The difference between the actual hourly labor rate and the standard rate, multiplied by the number of hours worked during the period. (p. 485)

Materials price variance The difference between the actual unit price paid for an item and the standard price, multiplied by the quantity purchased. (p. 482)

Materials quantity variance The difference between the actual quantity of materials used in production and the standard quantity allowed for the actual output, multiplied by the standard price per unit of materials. (p. 483)

Price variance A variance that is computed by taking the difference between the actual price and the standard price and multiplying the result by the actual quantity of the input. (p. 480)

Quantity variance A variance that is computed by taking the difference between the actual quantity of the input used and the amount of the input that should have been used for the actual level of output and multiplying the result by the standard price of the input. (p. 480)

Standard cost card A detailed listing of the standard amounts of inputs and their costs that are required to produce one unit of a specific product. (p. 478)

Standard cost per unit The standard quantity allowed of an input per unit of a specific product, multiplied by the standard price of the input. (p. 478)

Standard hours allowed The time that should have been taken to complete the period's output. It is computed by multiplying the actual number of units produced by the standard hours per unit. (p. 481)

Standard hours per unit The amount of direct labor time that should be required to complete a single unit of product, including allowances for breaks, machine downtime, cleanup, rejects, and other normal inefficiencies. (p. 477)

Standard price per unit The price that should be paid for an input. (p. 477)

Standard quantity allowed The amount of an input that should have been used to complete the period's actual output. It is computed by multiplying the actual number of units produced by the standard quantity per unit. (p. 481)

Standard quantity per unit The amount of an input that should be required to complete a single unit of product, including allowances for normal waste, spoilage, rejects, and other normal inefficiencies. (p. 477)

Standard rate per hour The labor rate that should be incurred per hour of labor time, including employment taxes and fringe benefits. (p. 478)

Variable overhead efficiency variance The difference between the actual level of activity
(direct labor-hours, machine-hours, or some other base) and the standard activity allowed,
multiplied by the variable part of the predetermined overhead rate. (p. 488)

Variable overhead rate variance The difference between the actual variable overhead cost
incurred during a period and the standard cost that should have been incurred based on the
actual activity of the period. (p. 488)

Questions

11–1 What is a quantity standard? What is a price standard?

11–2 Why are separate price and quantity variances computed?

11–3 Who is generally responsible for the materials price variance? The materials quantity
variance? The labor efficiency variance?

11–4 The materials price variance can be computed at what two different points in time?
Which point is better? Why?

11–5 If the materials price variance is favorable but the materials quantity variance is unfavorable, what might this indicate?

11–6 Should standards be used to identify who to blame for problems?

11–7 "Our workers are all under labor contracts; therefore, our labor rate variance is bound to
be zero." Discuss.

11–8 What effect, if any, would you expect poor-quality materials to have on direct labor
variances?

11–9 If variable manufacturing overhead is applied to production on the basis of direct labor-
hours and the direct labor efficiency variance is unfavorable, will the variable overhead
efficiency variance be favorable or unfavorable, or could it be either? Explain.

11–10 Why can undue emphasis on labor efficiency variances lead to excess work in process
inventories?

Multiple-choice questions are available with Connect.

Applying Excel   Additional student resources are available with Connect.

**LEARNING OBJECTIVES 11–1,
11–2, 11–3**

The Excel worksheet form that follows is to be used to recreate the main example in the text related
to the Colonial Pewter Company. Download the workbook containing this from Connect. *On the
website you will also receive instructions about how to use this worksheet form.*

You should proceed to the requirements below only after completing your worksheet.

Required:

1. Check your worksheet by changing the direct materials standard quantity in cell B6 to 2.9
    pounds, the direct labor quantity standard quantity in cell B7 to 0.6 hours, and the variable
    manufacturing overhead in cell B8 to 0.6 hours. The materials spending variance should now
    be $1,500 U, the labor spending variance should now be $3,720 F, and the variable overhead
    spending variance should now be $60 F. If you do not get these answers, find the errors in
    your worksheet and correct them.

    a. What is the materials quantity variance? Explain this variance.

    b. What is the labor rate variance? Explain this variance.

	A	B	C	D	E	F	G
1	Chapter 11: Applying Excel						
2							
3	**Data**						
4	*Exhibit 11-1: Standard Cost Card*						
5	Inputs	*Standard Quantity*		*Standard Price*			
6	Direct materials	3.0	pounds	$4.00	per pound		
7	Direct labor	0.50	hours	$22.00	per hour		
8	Variable manufacturing overhead	0.50	hours	$6.00	per hour		
9							
10	Actual results:						
11	Actual output	2,000	units				
12	Actual variable manufacturing overhead cost	$7,140					
13		*Actual Quantity*		*Actual price*			
14	Actual direct materials cost	6,500	pounds	$3.80	per pound		
15	Actual direct labor cost	1,050	hours	$21.60	per hour		
16							
17	*Enter a formula into each of the cells marked with a ? below*						
18	**Main Example: Chapter 11**						
19							
20	*Exhibit 11-4: Standard Cost Variance Analysis – Direct Materials*						
21	Standard Quantity Allowed for the Actual Output, at Standard Price	?	pounds ×	?	per pound =	?	
22	Actual Quantity of Input, at Standard Price	?	pounds ×	?	per pound =	?	
23	Actual Quantity of Input, at Actual Price	?	pounds ×	?	per pound =	?	
24	Direct materials variances:						
25	Materials quantity variance	?					
26	Materials price variance	?					
27	Materials spending variance	?					
28							
29	*Exhibit 11-6: Standard Cost Variance Analysis – Direct Labor*						
30	Standard Hours Allowed for the Actual Output, at Standard Rate	?	hours ×	?	per hour =	?	
31	Actual Hours of Input, at Standard Rate	?	hours ×	?	per hour =	?	
32	Actual Hours of Input, at Actual Rate	?	hours ×	?	per hour =	?	
33	Direct labor variances:						
34	Labor efficiency variance	?					
35	Labor rate variance	?					
36	Labor spending variance	?					
37							
38	*Exhibit 11-8: Standard Cost Variance Analysis – Variable Manufacturing Overhead*						
39	Standard Hours Allowed for the Actual Output, at Standard Rate	?	hours ×	?	per hour =	?	
40	Actual Hours of Input, at Standard Rate	?	hours ×	?	per hour =	?	
41	Actual Hours of Input, at Actual Rate	?	hours ×	?	per hour =	?	
42	Variable overhead variances:						
43	Variable overhead efficiency variance	?					
44	Variable overhead rate variance	?					
45	Variable overhead spending variance	?					
46							

Chapter 11 Form / Filled in Chapter 11 Form / Chapter 11 Formulas

2.   Revise the data in your worksheet to reflect the results for the subsequent period:

Data
Exhibit 11–1: Standard Cost Card

Inputs	Standard Quantity	Standard Price
Direct materials	3.0 pounds	$4.00 per pound
Direct labor.....................................	0.50 hours	$22.00 per hour
Variable manufacturing overhead	0.50 hours	$6.00 per hour
Actual results:		
Actual output	2,100 units	
Actual variable manufacturing overhead cost ...	$5,100	
	Actual Quantity	Actual Price
Actual direct materials cost....................	6,350 pounds	$4.10 per pound
Actual direct labor cost......................	1,020 hours	$22.10 per hour

a.   What is the materials quantity variance? What is the materials price variance?
b.   What is the labor efficiency variance? What is the labor rate variance?
c.   What is the variable overhead efficiency variance? What is the variable overhead rate variance?

The Foundational 15   **connect**   Additional student resources are available with Connect.

LEARNING OBJECTIVES 11–1,
11–2, 11–3

Preble Company manufactures one product. Its variable manufacturing overhead is applied to production based on direct labor-hours and its standard cost card per unit is as follows:

Direct materials: 5 pounds at $8.00 per pound....................	$40.00
Direct labor: 2 hours at $14 per hour.............................	28.00
Variable overhead: 2 hours at $5 per hour.......................	10.00
Total standard cost per unit.....................................	$78.00

The planning budget for March was based on producing and selling 25,000 units. However, during March the company actually produced and sold 30,000 units and incurred the following costs:

a. Purchased 160,000 pounds of raw materials at a cost of $7.50 per pound. All of this material was used in production.

b. Direct laborers worked 55,000 hours at a rate of $15.00 per hour.

c. Total variable manufacturing overhead for the month was $280,500.

Required:
1. What raw materials cost would be included in the company's planning budget for March?
2. What raw materials cost would be included in the company's flexible budget for March?
3. What is the materials price variance for March?
4. What is the materials quantity variance for March?
5. If Preble had purchased 170,000 pounds of materials at $7.50 per pound and used 160,000 pounds in production, what would be the materials price variance for March?
6. If Preble had purchased 170,000 pounds of materials at $7.50 per pound and used 160,000 pounds in production, what would be the materials quantity variance for March?
7. What direct labor cost would be included in the company's planning budget for March?
8. What direct labor cost would be included in the company's flexible budget for March?
9. What is the labor rate variance for March?
10. What is the labor efficiency variance for March?
11. What is the labor spending variance for March?
12. What variable manufacturing overhead cost would be included in the company's planning budget for March?
13. What variable manufacturing overhead cost would be included in the company's flexible budget for March?
14. What is the variable overhead rate variance for March?
15. What is the variable overhead efficiency variance for March?

Exercises   **connect**   Additional student resources are available with Connect.

EXERCISE 11–1 Direct Materials Variances [LO11–1]
Bandar Industries Berhad of Malaysia manufactures sporting equipment. One of the company's products, a football helmet for the North American market, requires a special plastic. During the quarter ending June 30, the company manufactured 35,000 helmets, using 22,500 kilograms of plastic. The plastic cost the company $171,000.

According to the standard cost card, each helmet should require 0.6 kilograms of plastic, at a cost of $8 per kilogram.

Required:
1. According to the standards, what cost for plastic should have been incurred to make 35,000 helmets? How much greater or less is this than the cost that was incurred?

2. Break down the difference computed in requirement 1 into a materials price variance and a materials quantity variance.

EXERCISE 11–2 Direct Labor Variances [LO11–2]

SkyChefs, Inc., prepares in-flight meals for a number of major airlines. One of the company's products is grilled salmon in dill sauce with baby new potatoes and spring vegetables. During the most recent week, the company prepared 4,000 of these meals using 960 direct labor-hours. The company paid these direct labor workers a total of $9,600 for this work, or $10.00 per hour.

According to the standard cost card for this meal, it should require 0.25 direct labor-hours at a cost of $9.75 per hour.

Required:

1. According to the standards, what direct labor cost should have been incurred to prepare 4,000 meals? How much does this differ from the actual direct labor cost?
2. Break down the difference computed in requirement 1 into a labor rate variance and a labor efficiency variance.

EXERCISE 11–3 Variable Overhead Variances [LO11–3]

Logistics Solutions provides order fulfillment services for dot.com merchants. The company maintains warehouses that stock items carried by its dot.com clients. When a client receives an order from a customer, the order is forwarded to Logistics Solutions, which pulls the item from storage, packs it, and ships it to the customer. The company uses a predetermined variable overhead rate based on direct labor-hours.

In the most recent month, 120,000 items were shipped to customers using 2,300 direct labor-hours. The company incurred a total of $7,360 in variable overhead costs.

According to the company's standards, 0.02 direct labor-hours are required to fulfill an order for one item and the variable overhead rate is $3.25 per direct labor-hour.

Required:

1. According to the standards, what variable overhead cost should have been incurred to fill the orders for the 120,000 items? How much does this differ from the actual variable overhead cost?
2. Break down the difference computed in requirement 1 into a variable overhead rate variance and a variable overhead efficiency variance.

EXERCISE 11–4 Direct Labor and Variable Manufacturing Overhead Variances [LO11–2, LO11–3]

Erie Company manufactures a small mp3 player called the Jogging Mate. The company uses standards to control its costs. The labor standards that have been set for one Jogging Mate mp3 player are as follows:

Standard Hours	Standard Rate per Hour	Standard Cost
18 minutes	$12.00	$3.60

During August, 5,750 hours of direct labor time were needed to make 20,000 units of the Jogging Mate. The direct labor cost totaled $73,600 for the month.

Required:

1. According to the standards, what direct labor cost should have been incurred to make 20,000 units of the Jogging Mate? By how much does this differ from the cost that was incurred?
2. Break down the difference in cost from requirement 1 into a labor rate variance and a labor efficiency variance.
3. The budgeted variable manufacturing overhead rate is $4 per direct labor-hour. During August, the company incurred $21,850 in variable manufacturing overhead cost. Compute the variable overhead rate and efficiency variances for the month.

EXERCISE 11–5 Working Backwards from Labor Variances [LO11–2]

The auto repair shop of Quality Motor Company uses standards to control the labor time and labor cost in the shop. The standard labor cost for a motor tune-up is given below:

Job	Standard Hours	Standard Rate	Standard Cost
Motor tune-up	2.5	$9.00	$22.50

The record showing the time spent in the shop last week on motor tune-ups has been misplaced. However, the shop supervisor recalls that 50 tune-ups were completed during the week, and the controller recalls the following variance data relating to tune-ups:

Labor rate variance	$87 F
Labor spending variance	$93 U

Required:
1. Determine the number of actual labor-hours spent on tune-ups during the week.
2. Determine the actual hourly rate of pay for tune-ups last week.

(*Hint:* A useful way to proceed would be to work from known to unknown data either by using the variance formulas in Exhibit 11–7 or by using the columnar format shown in Exhibit 11–6.)

EXERCISE 11–6 Direct Materials and Direct Labor Variances [LO11–1, LO11–2]

Huron Company produces a commercial cleaning compound known as Zoom. The direct materials and direct labor standards for one unit of Zoom are given below:

	Standard Quantity or Hours	Standard Price or Rate	Standard Cost
Direct materials	4.6 pounds	$2.50 per pound	$11.50
Direct labor	0.2 hours	$12.00 per hour	$2.40

During the most recent month, the following activity was recorded:
a. Twenty thousand pounds of material were purchased at a cost of $2.35 per pound.
b. All of the material purchased was used to produce 4,000 units of Zoom.
c. 750 hours of direct labor time were recorded at a total labor cost of $10,425.

Required:
1. Compute the materials price and quantity variances for the month.
2. Compute the labor rate and efficiency variances for the month.

EXERCISE 11–7 Direct Materials Variances [LO11–1]

Refer to the data in Exercise 11–6. Assume that instead of producing 4,000 units during the month, the company produced only 3,000 units, using 14,750 pounds of material. (The rest of the material purchased remained in raw materials inventory.)

Required:
Compute the materials price and quantity variances for the month.

EXERCISE 11–8 Direct Materials and Direct Labor Variances [LO11–1, LO11–2]

Dawson Toys, Ltd., produces a toy called the Maze. The company has recently established a standard cost system to help control costs and has established the following standards for the Maze toy:

Direct materials: 6 microns per toy at $0.50 per micron
Direct labor: 1.3 hours per toy at $8 per hour

During July, the company produced 3,000 Maze toys. Production data for the month on the toy follow:

Direct materials: 25,000 microns were purchased at a cost of $0.48 per micron. 5,000 of these microns were still in inventory at the end of the month.

Direct labor: 4,000 direct labor-hours were worked at a cost of $36,000.

Required:
1. Compute the following variances for July:
    a.   The materials price and quantity variances.
    b.   The labor rate and efficiency variances.
2. Prepare a brief explanation of the possible causes of each variance.

Additional student resources are available with Connect.   **connect**   **Problems**

PROBLEM 11–9 Comprehensive Variance Analysis [LO11–1, LO11–2, LO11–3]

Marvel Parts, Inc., manufactures auto accessories. One of the company's products is a set of seat covers that can be adjusted to fit nearly any small car. The company has a standard cost system in use for all of its products. According to the standards that have been set for the seat covers, the factory should work 2,850 hours each month to produce 1,900 sets of covers. The standard costs associated with this level of production are:

	Total	Per Set of Covers
Direct materials	$42,560	$22.40
Direct labor.......................................	$17,100	9.00
Variable manufacturing overhead		
(based on direct labor-hours)	$6,840	3.60
		$35.00

During August, the factory worked only 2,800 direct labor-hours and produced 2,000 sets of covers. The following actual costs were recorded during the month:

	Total	Per Set of Covers
Direct materials (12,000 yards)	$45,600	$22.80
Direct labor.......................................	$18,200	9.10
Variable manufacturing overhead	$7,000	3.50
		$35.40

At standard, each set of covers should require 5.6 yards of material. All of the materials purchased during the month were used in production.

Required:
Compute the following variances for August:
1. The materials price and quantity variances.
2. The labor rate and efficiency variances.
3. The variable overhead rate and efficiency variances.

PROBLEM 11–10 Multiple Products, Materials, and Processes [LO11–1, LO11–2]

Mickley Corporation produces two products, Alpha6s and Zeta7s, which pass through two operations, Sintering and Finishing. Each of the products uses two raw materials, X442 and Y661. The company uses a standard cost system, with the following standards for each product (on a per unit basis):

Product	Raw Material		Standard Labor Time	
	X442	Y661	Sintering	Finishing
Alpha6	1.8 kilos	2.0 liters	0.20 hours	0.80 hours
Zeta7	3.0 kilos	4.5 liters	0.35 hours	0.90 hours

Information relating to materials purchased and materials used in production during May follows:

Material	Purchases	Purchase Cost	Standard Price	Used in Production
X442	14,500 kilos	$52,200	$3.50 per kilo	8,500 kilos
Y661.............	15,500 liters	$20,925	$1.40 per liter	13,000 liters

The following additional information is available:
a. The company recognizes price variances when materials are purchased.
b. The standard labor rate is $19.80 per hour in Sintering and $19.20 per hour in Finishing.
c. During May, 1,200 direct labor-hours were worked in Sintering at a total labor cost of $27,000, and 2,850 direct labor-hours were worked in Finishing at a total labor cost of $59,850.
d. Production during May was 1,500 Alpha6s and 2,000 Zeta7s.

Required:
1. Prepare a standard cost card for each product, showing the standard cost of direct materials and direct labor.
2. Compute the materials price and quantity variances for each material.
3. Compute the labor rate and efficiency variances for each operation.

PROBLEM 11–11 Direct Materials and Direct Labor Variances; Computations from Incomplete Data [LO11–1, LO11–2]
Sharp Company manufactures a product for which the following standards have been set:

	Standard Quantity or Hours	Standard Price or Rate	Standard Cost
Direct materials	3 feet	$5 per foot	$15
Direct labor.........................	? hours	? per hour	?

During March, the company purchased direct materials at a cost of $55,650, all of which were used in the production of 3,200 units of product. In addition, 4,900 hours of direct labor time were worked on the product during the month. The cost of this labor time was $36,750. The following variances have been computed for the month:

Materials quantity variance..................	$4,500 U
Labor spending variance	$1,650 F
Labor efficiency variance	$800 U

Required:
1. For direct materials:
   a. Compute the actual cost per foot for materials for March.
   b. Compute the price variance and the spending variance.
2. For direct labor:
   a. Compute the standard direct labor rate per hour.
   b. Compute the standard hours allowed for the month's production.
   c. Compute the standard hours allowed per unit of product.
(*Hint:* In completing the problem, it may be helpful to move from known to unknown data either by using the columnar format shown in Exhibits 11–4 and 11–6 or by using the variance formulas in Exhibits 11–5 and 11–7.)

PROBLEM 11–12 Variance Analysis in a Hospital [LO11–1, LO11–2, LO11–3]

John Fleming, chief administrator for Valley View Hospital, is concerned about the costs for tests in the hospital's lab. Charges for lab tests are consistently higher at Valley View than at other hospitals and have resulted in many complaints. Also, because of strict regulations on amounts reimbursed for lab tests, payments received from insurance companies and governmental units have not been high enough to cover lab costs.

Mr. Fleming has asked you to evaluate costs in the hospital's lab for the past month. The following information is available:

a. Two types of tests are performed in the lab—blood tests and smears. During the past month, 1,800 blood tests and 2,400 smears were performed in the lab.

b. Small glass plates are used in both types of tests. During the past month, the hospital purchased 12,000 plates at a cost of $28,200. 1,500 of these plates were unused at the end of the month; no plates were on hand at the beginning of the month.

c. During the past month, 1,150 hours of labor time were recorded in the lab at a cost of $13,800.

d. The lab's variable overhead cost last month totaled $7,820.

Valley View Hospital has never used standard costs. By searching industry literature, however, you have determined the following nationwide averages for hospital labs:

Plates: Two plates are required per lab test. These plates cost $2.50 each and are disposed of after the test is completed.

Labor: Each blood test should require 0.3 hours to complete, and each smear should require 0.15 hours to complete. The average cost of this lab time is $14 per hour.

Overhead: Overhead cost is based on direct labor-hours. The average rate for variable overhead is $6 per hour.

Required:

1. Compute a materials price variance for the plates purchased last month and a materials quantity variance for the plates used last month.

2. For labor cost in the lab:

   a. Compute a labor rate variance and a labor efficiency variance.

   b. In most hospitals, one-half of the workers in the lab are senior technicians and one-half are assistants. In an effort to reduce costs, Valley View Hospital employs only one-fourth senior technicians and three-fourths assistants. Would you recommend that this policy be continued? Explain.

3. Compute the variable overhead rate and efficiency variances. Is there any relation between the variable overhead efficiency variance and the labor efficiency variance? Explain.

PROBLEM 11–13 Basic Variance Analysis; the Impact of Variances on Unit Costs [LO11–1, LO11–2, LO11–3]

Koontz Company manufactures a number of products. The standards relating to one of these products are shown below, along with actual cost data for May.

	Standard Cost per Unit	Actual Cost per Unit
Direct materials:		
Standard: 1.80 feet at $3.00 per foot...............	$ 5.40	
Actual: 1.80 feet at $3.30 per foot.................		$ 5.94
Direct labor:		
Standard: 0.90 hours at $18.00 per hour...........	16.20	
Actual: 0.92 hours at $17.50 per hour..............		16.10
Variable overhead:		
Standard: 0.90 hours at $5.00 per hour............	4.50	
Actual: 0.92 hours at $4.50 per hour..............		4.14
Total cost per unit	$26.10	$26.18
Excess of actual cost over standard cost per unit	$0.08	

The production superintendent was pleased when he saw this report and commented: "This $0.08 excess cost is well within the 2 percent limit management has set for acceptable variances. It's obvious that there's not much to worry about with this product."

Actual production for the month was 12,000 units. Variable overhead cost is assigned to products on the basis of direct labor-hours. There were no beginning or ending inventories of materials.

Required:

1. Compute the following variances for May:
   a. Materials price and quantity variances.
   b. Labor rate and efficiency variances.
   c. Variable overhead rate and efficiency variances.
2. How much of the $0.08 excess unit cost is traceable to each of the variances computed in requirement 1?
3. How much of the $0.08 excess unit cost is traceable to apparent inefficient use of labor time?
4. Do you agree that the excess unit cost is not of concern?

PROBLEM 11–14 Basic Variance Analysis [LO11–1, LO11–2, LO11–3]

Becton Labs, Inc., produces various chemical compounds for industrial use. One compound, called Fludex, is prepared using an elaborate distilling process. The company has developed standard costs for one unit of Fludex, as follows:

	Standard Quality	Standard Price or Rate	Standard Cost
Direct materials	2.5 ounces	$20.00 per ounce	$50.00
Direct labor.	1.4 hours	$12.50 per hour	17.50
Variable manufacturing overhead	1.4 hours	$3.50 per hour	4.90
			$72.40

During November, the following activity was recorded related to the production of Fludex:

a. Materials purchased, 12,000 ounces at a cost of $225,000.

b. There was no beginning inventory of materials; however, at the end of the month, 2,500 ounces of material remained in ending inventory.

c. The company employs 35 lab technicians to work on the production of Fludex. During November, they worked an average of 160 hours at an average rate of $12 per hour.

d. Variable manufacturing overhead is assigned to Fludex on the basis of direct labor-hours. Variable manufacturing overhead costs during November totaled $18,200.

e. During November, 3,750 good units of Fludex were produced.

Required:

1. For direct materials:
   a. Compute the price and quantity variances.
   b. The materials were purchased from a new supplier who is anxious to enter into a long-term purchase contract. Would you recommend that the company sign the contract? Explain.
2. For direct labor:
   a. Compute the rate and efficiency variances.
   b. In the past, the 35 technicians employed in the production of Fludex consisted of 20 senior technicians and 15 assistants. During November, the company experimented with fewer senior technicians and more assistants in order to save costs. Would you recommend that the new labor mix be continued? Explain.
3. Compute the variable overhead rate and efficiency variances. What relation can you see between this efficiency variance and the labor efficiency variance?

PROBLEM 11–15 Comprehensive Variance Analysis [LO11–1, LO11–2, LO11–3]

Miller Toy Company manufactures a plastic swimming pool at its Westwood Plant. The plant has been experiencing problems as shown by its June contribution format income statement below:

	Budgeted	Actual
Sales (15,000 pools)	$450,000	$450,000
Variable expenses:		
Variable cost of goods sold*..............	180,000	196,290
Variable selling expenses................	20,000	20,000
Total variable expenses..................	200,000	216,290
Contribution margin.....................	250,000	233,710
Fixed expenses:		
Manufacturing overhead.................	130,000	130,000
Selling and administrative...............	84,000	84,000
Total fixed expenses	214,000	214,000
Net operating income	$ 36,000	$ 19,710

*The revenue variance is labeled favorable (unfavorable) when the revenue in the flexible budget is greater than (less than) the planning budget. The expense variances are labeled favorable (unfavorable) when the expense in the flexible budget is less than (greater than) the planning budget.

Janet Dunn, who has just been appointed general manager of the Westwood Plant, has been given instructions to "get things under control." Upon reviewing the plant's income statement, Ms. Dunn has concluded that the major problem lies in the variable cost of goods sold. She has been provided with the following standard cost per swimming pool:

	Standard Quantity or Hours	Standard Price or Rate	Standard Cost
Direct materials......................	3.0 pounds	$2.00 per pound	$ 6.00
Direct labor	0.8 hours	$6.00 per hour	4.80
Variable manufacturing overhead......	0.4 hours*	$3.00 per hour	1.20
Total standard cost...................			$12.00

*The revenue variance is labeled favorable (unfavorable) when the actual revenue is greater than (less than) the flexible budget. The expense variances are labeled favorable (unfavorable) when the actual expense is less than (greater than) the flexible budget.

During June the plant produced 15,000 pools and incurred the following costs:

a. Purchased 60,000 pounds of materials at a cost of $1.95 per pound.
b. Used 49,200 pounds of materials in production. (Finished goods and work in process inventories are insignificant and can be ignored.)
c. Worked 11,800 direct labor-hours at a cost of $7.00 per hour.
d. Incurred variable manufacturing overhead cost totaling $18,290 for the month. A total of 5,900 machine-hours was recorded.

It is the company's policy to close all variances to cost of goods sold on a monthly basis.

Required:

1. Compute the following variances for June:
   a. Materials price and quantity variances.
   b. Labor rate and efficiency variances.
   c. Variable overhead rate and efficiency variances.
2. Summarize the variances that you computed in requirement 1 by showing the net overall favorable or unfavorable variance for the month. What impact did this figure have on the company's income statement? Show computations.
3. Pick out the two most significant variances that you computed in requirement 1. Explain to Ms. Dunn possible causes of these variances.

PROBLEM 11–16 Comprehensive Variance Analysis [LO11–1, LO11–2, LO11–3]
Highland Company produces a lightweight backpack that is popular with college students. Standard variable costs relating to a single backpack are given below:

	Standard Quantity or Hours	Standard Price or Rate	Standard Cost
Direct materials..................	?	$6 per yard	$?
Direct labor	?	?	?
Variable manufacturing overhead...	?	$3 per direct labor-hour	?
Total standard cost................			$?

Overhead is applied to production on the basis of direct labor-hours. During March, 1,000 backpacks were manufactured and sold. Selected information relating to the month's production is given below:

	Materials Used	Direct Labor	Variable Manufacturing Overhead
Total standard cost allowed*...........	$16,800	$10,500	$4,200
Actual costs incurred.................	$15,000	?	$3,600
Materials price variance	?		
Materials quantity variance...........	$1,200 U		
Labor rate variance		?	
Labor efficiency variance		?	
Variable overhead rate variance			?
Variable overhead efficiency variance ...			?

*For the month's production.

The following additional information is available for March's production:

Actual direct labor-hours...............................	1,500
Difference between standard and actual cost per backpack produced during March.................	$0.15 F

Required:
1. What is the standard cost of a single backpack?
2. What was the actual cost per backpack produced during March?
3. How many yards of material are required at standard per backpack?
4. What was the materials price variance for March if there were no beginning or ending inventories of materials?
5. What is the standard direct labor rate per hour?
6. What was the labor rate variance for March? The labor efficiency variance?
7. What was the variable overhead rate variance for March? The variable overhead efficiency variance?
8. Prepare a standard cost card for one backpack.

Cases   Additional student resources are available with Connect.

CASE 11–17 Working Backwards from Variance Data [LO11–1, LO11–2, LO11–3]
You have recently accepted a position with Vitex, Inc., the manufacturer of a popular consumer product. During your first week on the job, the vice president has been favorably impressed with your work. She has been so impressed, in fact, that yesterday she called you into her office and asked you to attend the executive committee meeting this morning for the purpose of leading a discussion on the variances reported for last period. Anxious to favorably impress the executive committee, you took the variances and supporting data home last night to study.

On your way to work this morning, the papers were laying on the seat of your new, red convertible. As you were crossing a bridge on the highway, a sudden gust of wind caught the papers and blew them over the edge of the bridge and into the stream below. You managed to retrieve only one page, which contains the following information:

Standard Cost Card		
Direct materials, 6 pounds at $3 per pound		$18.00
Direct labor, 0.8 direct labor-hours at $15 per direct labor-hour		$12.00
Variable manufacturing overhead, 0.8 direct labor-hours at		$2.40
$3 per direct labor-hour		

		Variances Reported	
	Total Standard Cost*	Price or Rate	Quantity or Efficiency
Direct materials.	$405,000	$6,900 F	$9,000 U
Direct labor	$270,000	$14,550 U	$21,000 U
Variable manufacturing overhead	$54,000	$1,300 F	$?† U

*Applied to Work in Process during the period.
†Entry obliterated.

You recall that manufacturing overhead cost is applied to production on the basis of direct labor-hours and that all of the materials purchased during the period were used in production. Work in process inventories are insignificant and can be ignored.

It is now 8:30 A.M. The executive committee meeting starts in just one hour; you realize that to avoid looking like a bungling fool you must somehow generate the necessary "backup" data for the variances before the meeting begins. Without backup data it will be impossible to lead the discussion or answer any questions.

Required:
1. How many units were produced last period?
2. How many pounds of direct material were purchased and used in production?
3. What was the actual cost per pound of material?
4. How many actual direct labor-hours were worked during the period?
5. What was the actual rate paid per direct labor-hour?
6. How much actual variable manufacturing overhead cost was incurred during the period?

Appendix 11A: Predetermined Overhead Rates and Overhead Analysis in a Standard Costing System

In this appendix, we will investigate how the predetermined overhead rates that we discussed in the job-order costing chapter earlier in the book can be used in a standard costing system. Throughout this appendix, we assume that an absorption costing system is used in which *all* manufacturing costs—both fixed and variable—are included in product costs.

LEARNING OBJECTIVE 11–4
Compute and interpret the fixed overhead budget and volume variances.

Predetermined Overhead Rates

The data in Exhibit 11A–1 pertain to MicroDrive Corporation, a company that produces miniature electric motors. Note that the company budgeted for 50,000 machine-hours based on production of 25,000 motors. At this level of activity, the budgeted variable manufacturing overhead was $75,000 and the budgeted fixed manufacturing overhead was $300,000.

Recall from the job-order costing chapter that the following formula is used to set the predetermined overhead rate at the beginning of the period:

$$\frac{\text{Predetermined}}{\text{overhead rate}} = \frac{\text{Estimated total manufacturing overhead cost}}{\text{Estimated total amount of the allocation base}}$$

The estimated total amount of the allocation base in the formula for the predetermined overhead rate is called the **denominator activity**.

As discussed in the job-order costing chapter, once the predetermined overhead rate has been determined, it remains unchanged throughout the period, even if the actual level of activity differs from what was estimated. Consequently, the amount of overhead applied to each unit of product is the same regardless of when it is produced during the period.

EXHIBIT 11A–1
MicroDrive Corporation Data

Budgeted production	25,000 motors
Standard machine-hours per motor	2 machine-hours per motor
Budgeted machine-hours (2 machine-hours per motor 3 25,000 motors).	50,000 machine-hours
Actual production	20,000 motors
Standard machine-hours allowed for the actual production (2 machine-hours per motor × 20,000 motors).	40,000 machine-hours APPLIED
Actual machine-hours.	42,000 machine-hours
Budgeted variable manufacturing overhead . . .	$75,000
Budgeted fixed manufacturing overhead	$300,000
Total budgeted manufacturing overhead	$375,000
Actual variable manufacturing overhead	$71,400
Actual fixed manufacturing overhead	$308,000
Total actual manufacturing overhead.	$379,400

MicroDrive Corporation uses budgeted machine-hours as its denominator activity in the predetermined overhead rate. Consequently, the company's predetermined overhead rate would be computed as follows:

$$\frac{\text{Predetermined}}{\text{overhead rate}} = \frac{\$375,000}{50,000 \text{ MHs}} = \$7.50 \text{ per MH}$$

This predetermined overhead rate can be broken down into its variable and fixed components as follows:

$$\frac{\text{Variable component of the}}{\text{predetermined overhead rate}} = \frac{\$75,000}{50,000 \text{ MHs}} = \$1.50 \text{ per MH}$$

$$\frac{\text{Fixed component of the}}{\text{predetermined overhead rate}} = \frac{\$300,000}{50,000 \text{ MHs}} = \$6.00 \text{ per MH}$$

For every standard machine-hour recorded, work in process is charged with $7.50 of manufacturing overhead, of which $1.50 represents variable manufacturing overhead and $6.00 represents fixed manufacturing overhead. In total, MicroDrive Corporation would apply $300,000 of overhead to work in process as shown below:

$$\text{Overhead applied} = \frac{\text{Predetermined}}{\text{overhead rate}} \times \frac{\text{Standard hours allowed}}{\text{for the actual output}}$$

$$= \$7.50 \text{ per machine–hour} \times 40,000 \text{ machine–hours}$$

$$= \$300,000$$

Overhead Application in a Standard Cost System

To understand fixed overhead variances, we first have to understand how overhead is applied to work in process in a standard cost system. Recall that in the job-order costing chapter we applied overhead to work in process on the basis of the actual level of activity. This procedure was correct because at the time we were dealing with a normal cost system.[1] However, we are now dealing with a standard cost system. In such a system, overhead is applied to work in process on the basis of the *standard hours allowed for the actual output of the period* rather than on the basis of the actual number of hours worked. Exhibit 11A–2 illustrates this point. In a standard cost system, every unit of a particular product is charged with the same amount of overhead cost, regardless of how much time the unit actually requires for processing.

Normal Cost System		Standard Cost System	
Manufacturing Overhead		**Manufacturing Overhead**	
Actual overhead costs incurred.	Applied overhead costs: Actual hours × Pre-determined overhead rate.	Actual overhead costs incurred.	Applied overhead costs: Standard hours allowed for actual output × Pre-determined overhead rate.
Underapplied or overapplied overhead		Underapplied or overapplied overhead	

EXHIBIT 11A–2
Applied Overhead Costs: Normal Cost System versus Standard Cost System

Budget Variance

Two fixed manufacturing overhead variances are computed in a standard costing system—a *budget variance* and a *volume variance*. These variances are computed in Exhibit 11A–3. The **budget variance** is simply the difference between the actual fixed manufacturing overhead and the budgeted fixed manufacturing overhead for the period. The formula is:

Budget variance = Actual fixed overhead + Budgeted fixed overhead

If the actual fixed overhead cost exceeds the budgeted fixed overhead cost, the budget variance is labeled unfavorable. If the actual fixed overhead cost is less than the budgeted fixed overhead cost, the budget variance is labeled favorable.

Applying the formula to the MicroDrive Corporation data, the budget variance is computed as follows:

Budget variance = $308,000 – $300,000 = $8,000 U

According to the budget, the fixed manufacturing overhead should have been $300,000, but it was actually $308,000. Because the actual cost exceeds the budget by $8,000, the

---

[1] Normal cost systems are discussed in the job-order costing chapter.

EXHIBIT 11A–3
Fixed Overhead Variances

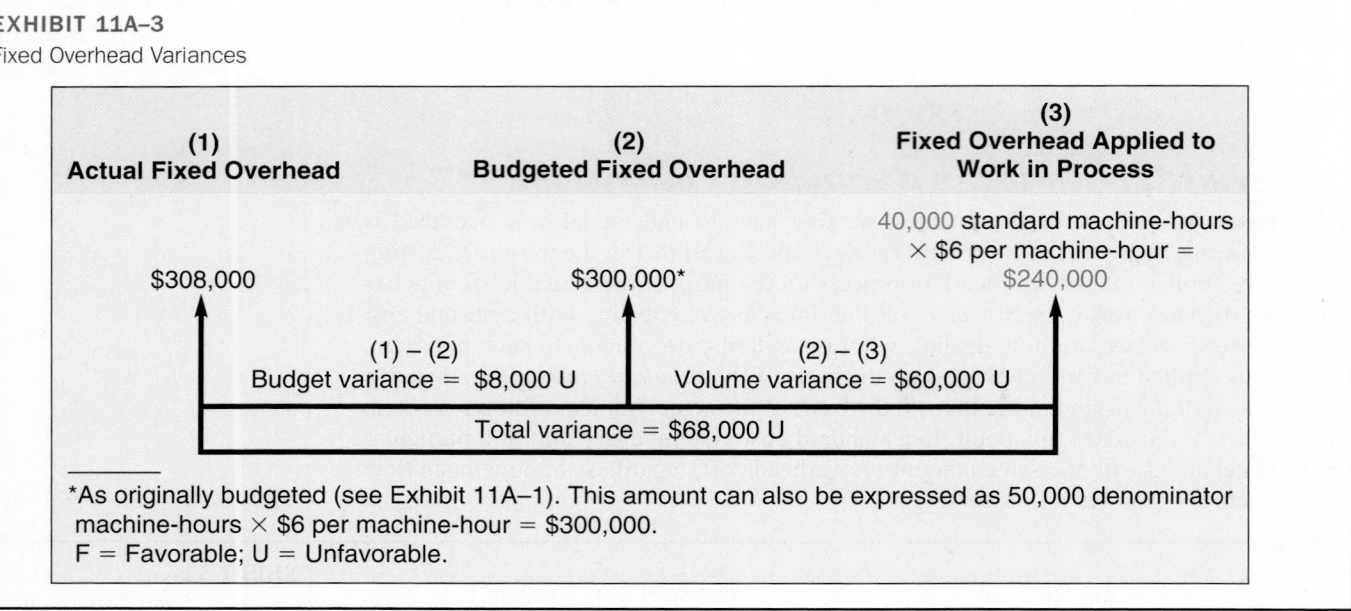

(1) Actual Fixed Overhead	(2) Budgeted Fixed Overhead	(3) Fixed Overhead Applied to Work in Process
		40,000 standard machine-hours × $6 per machine-hour = $240,000
$308,000	$300,000*	

(1) – (2)
Budget variance = $8,000 U

(2) – (3)
Volume variance = $60,000 U

Total variance = $68,000 U

*As originally budgeted (see Exhibit 11A–1). This amount can also be expressed as 50,000 denominator machine-hours × $6 per machine-hour = $300,000.
F = Favorable; U = Unfavorable.

variance is labeled as unfavorable; however, this label does not automatically signal ineffective managerial performance. For example, this variance may be the result of waste and inefficiency, or it may be due to an unforeseen yet prudent investment in fixed overhead resources that improves product quality or manufacturing cycle efficiency.

Volume Variance

The **volume variance** is defined by the following formula:

$$\text{Volume variance} = \frac{\text{Budgeted fixed}}{\text{overhead}} - \frac{\text{Fixed overhead applied}}{\text{to work in process}}$$

When the budgeted fixed manufacturing overhead exceeds the fixed manufacturing overhead applied to work in process, the volume variance is labeled as unfavorable. When the budgeted fixed manufacturing overhead is less than the fixed manufacturing overhead applied to work in process, the volume variance is labeled as favorable. As we shall see, caution is advised when interpreting this variance.

To understand the volume variance, we need to understand how fixed manufacturing overhead is applied to work in process in a standard costing system. As discussed earlier, fixed manufacturing overhead is applied to work in process on the basis of the standard hours allowed for the actual output of the period. In the case of MicroDrive Corporation, the company produced 20,000 motors and the standard for each motor is 2 machine-hours. Therefore, the standard hours allowed for the actual output is 40,000 machine-hours (= 20,000 motors × 2 machine-hours). As shown in Exhibit 11A–3, the predetermined fixed manufacturing overhead rate of $6.00 per machine-hour is multiplied by the 40,000 standard machine-hours allowed for the actual output to arrive at $240,000 of fixed manufacturing overhead applied to work in process. Another way to think of this is that the standard for each motor is 2 machine-hours. Because the predetermined fixed manufacturing overhead rate is $6.00 per machine-hour, each motor is assigned $12.00 (= 2 machine-hours × $6.00 per machine-hour) of fixed manufacturing overhead.

Consequently, a total of $240,000 of fixed manufacturing overhead is applied to the 20,000 motors that are actually produced. Under either explanation, the volume variance according to the formula is:

$$\text{Volume variance} = \$300{,}000 - \$240{,}000 = \$60{,}000 \text{ U}$$

The key to interpreting the volume variance is to understand that it depends on the difference between the hours used in the denominator to compute the predetermined overhead rate and the standard hours allowed for the actual output of the period. While it is not obvious, the volume variance can also be computed using the following formula:

$$\frac{\text{Volume}}{\text{variance}} = \frac{\text{Fixed component of the}}{\text{predetermined overhead rate}} \times \left(\frac{\text{Denominator}}{\text{hours}} - \frac{\text{Standard hours allowed}}{\text{for the actual output}} \right)$$

In the case of MicroDrive Corporation, the volume variance can be computed using this formula as follows:

$$\text{Volume variance} = \frac{\$6.00 \text{ per}}{\text{machine-hour}} \times \left(\frac{50{,}000}{\text{machine-hours}} - \frac{40{,}000}{\text{machine-hours}} \right)$$

$$= \$6.00 \text{ per machine-hour} \times (10{,}000 \text{ machine-hours})$$

$$= \$60{,}000 \text{ U}$$

Note that this agrees with the volume variance computed using the earlier formula.

Focusing on this new formula, if the denominator hours exceed the standard hours allowed for the actual output, the volume variance is unfavorable. If the denominator hours are less than the standard hours allowed for the actual output, the volume variance is favorable. Stated differently, the volume variance is unfavorable if the actual level of activity is less than expected. The volume variance is favorable if the actual level of activity is greater than expected. It is important to note that the volume variance does not measure overspending or underspending. A company should incur the same dollar amount of fixed overhead cost regardless of whether the period's activity was above or below the planned (denominator) level.

The volume variance is often viewed as a measure of the utilization of facilities. If the standard hours allowed for the actual output are greater than (less than) the denominator hours, it signals efficient (inefficient) usage of facilities. However, other measures of utilization—such as the percentage of capacity utilized—are easier to compute and understand. Perhaps a better interpretation of the volume variance is that it is the error that occurs when the level of activity is incorrectly estimated and the costing system assumes fixed costs behave as if they are variable. This interpretation may be clearer in the next section that graphically analyzes the fixed manufacturing overhead variances.

Graphic Analysis of Fixed Overhead Variances

Exhibit 11A–4 shows a graphic analysis that offers insights into the fixed overhead budget and volume variances. As shown in the graph, fixed overhead cost is applied to work in process at the predetermined rate of $6.00 for each standard hour of activity. (The applied-cost line is the upward-sloping line on the graph.) Because a denominator level of 50,000 machine-hours was used in computing the $6.00 rate, the applied-cost line crosses the budget-cost line at exactly 50,000 machine-hours. If the denominator hours and the standard hours allowed for the actual output are the same, there is no volume variance. It is only when the standard hours differ from the denominator hours that a volume variance arises.

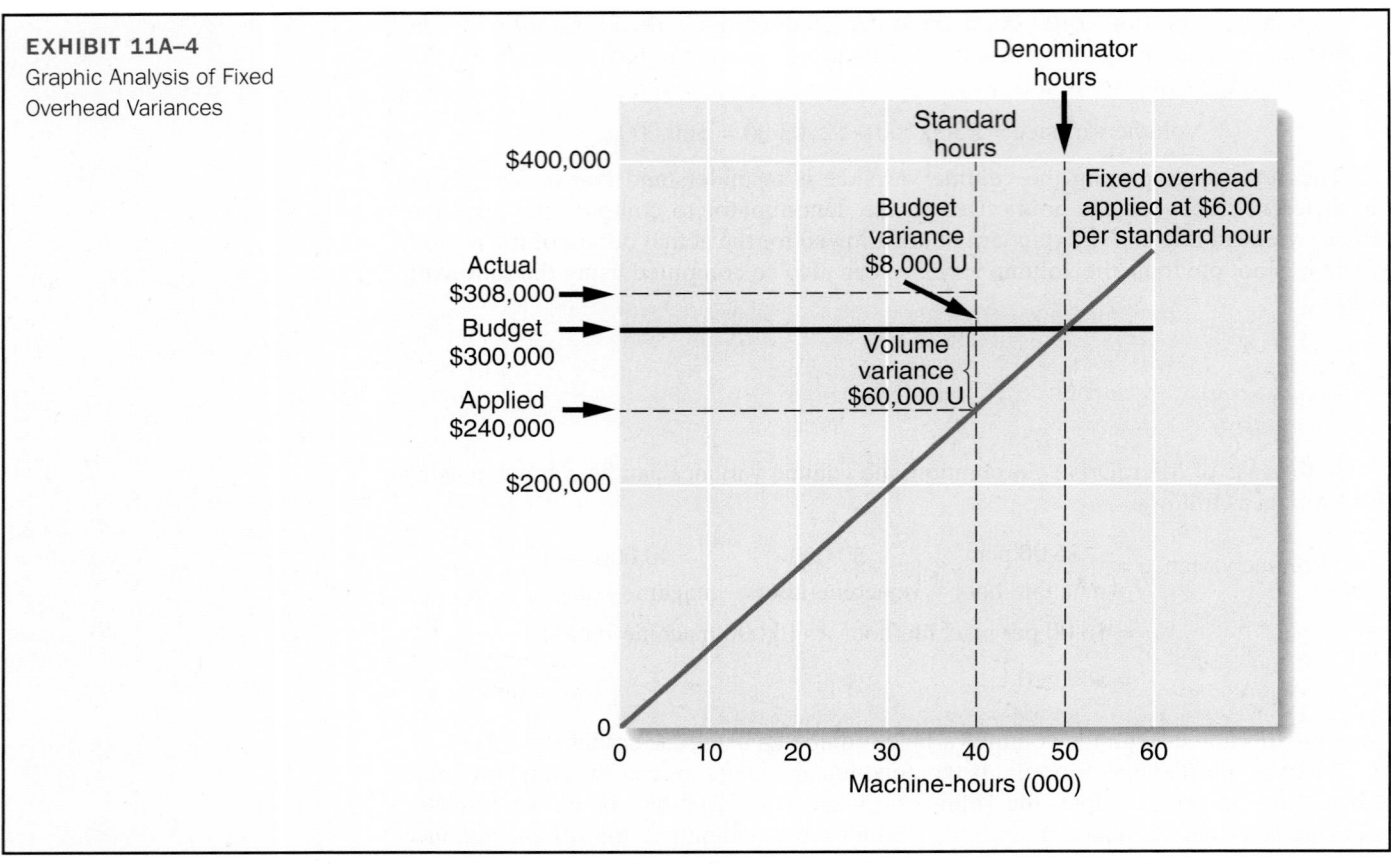

EXHIBIT 11A–4
Graphic Analysis of Fixed
Overhead Variances

In MicroDrive's case, the standard hours allowed for the actual output (40,000 hours) are less than the denominator hours (50,000 hours). The result is an unfavorable volume variance because less cost was applied to production than was originally budgeted. If the situation had been reversed and the standard hours allowed for the actual output had exceeded the denominator hours, then the volume variance on the graph would have been favorable.

Cautions in Fixed Overhead Analysis

A volume variance for fixed overhead arises because when applying the costs to work in process, we act *as if* the fixed costs are variable. The graph in Exhibit 11A–4 illustrates this point. Notice from the graph that fixed overhead costs are applied to work in process at a rate of $6 per hour *as if* they are variable. Treating these costs as if they are variable is necessary for product costing purposes, but some real dangers lurk here. Managers can easily be misled into thinking that fixed costs are *in fact* variable.

Keep clearly in mind that fixed overhead costs come in large chunks. Expressing fixed costs on a unit or per hour basis, though necessary for product costing for external reports, is artificial. Increases or decreases in activity in fact have no effect on total fixed costs within the relevant range of activity. Even though fixed costs are expressed on a unit or per hour basis, they are *not* proportional to activity. In a sense, the volume variance is the error that occurs as a result of treating fixed costs as variable costs in the costing system.

Reconciling Overhead Variances and Underapplied or Overapplied Overhead

In a standard cost system, the underapplied or overapplied overhead for a period equals the sum of the overhead variances. To see this, we will return to the MicroDrive Corporation example.

As discussed earlier, in a standard cost system, overhead is applied to work in process on the basis of the standard hours allowed for the actual output of the period. The following table shows how the underapplied or overapplied overhead for MicroDrive is computed.

Predetermined overhead rate (a)	$7.50 per machine-hour
Standard hours allowed for the actual output [Exhibit 11A–1] (b)	40,000 machine-hours
Manufacturing overhead applied (a) × (b).	$300,000
Total Actual manufacturing overhead [Exhibit 11A–1]	$379,400
Manufacturing overhead underapplied or overapplied	$79,400 underapplied

We have already computed the budget variance and the volume variance for this company. We will also need to compute the variable manufacturing overhead variances. The data for these computations are contained in Exhibit 11A–1. Recalling the formulas for the variable manufacturing overhead variances from Exhibit 11–9, we can compute the variable overhead rate and efficiency variances as follows:

Variable overhead rate variance $= (AH \times AR) - (AH \times SR)$

$$= AH(AR - SR)$$

$$= \begin{pmatrix} 42,000 \\ \text{machine-hours} \end{pmatrix} - \begin{pmatrix} \$1.70 \text{ per} \\ \text{machine-hours}^2 \end{pmatrix} - \begin{pmatrix} \$1.50 \text{ per} \\ \text{machine-hours} \end{pmatrix}$$

$$= \$8.400 \text{ U}$$

Variable overhead efficiency variance $= (AH \times SR) - (SH \times SR)$

$$= SR(AH - SH)$$

$$= \begin{pmatrix} \$1.50 \text{ per} \\ \text{machine-hours} \end{pmatrix} - \begin{pmatrix} 42,000 \\ \text{machine-hours} \end{pmatrix} - \begin{pmatrix} 40,000 \text{ per} \\ \text{machine-hours} \end{pmatrix}$$

$$= \$3,000 \text{ U}$$

We can now compute the sum of all of the overhead variances as follows:

Variable overhead rate variance	$ 8,400 U
Variable overhead efficiency variance	3,000 U
Fixed overhead budget variance	8,000 U
Fixed overhead volume variance.	60,000 U
Total of the overhead variances	$79,400 U

Note that the total of the overhead variances is $79,000, which equals the underapplied overhead of $79,000. In general, if the overhead is underapplied, the total of the standard cost overhead variances is unfavorable. If the overhead is overapplied, the total of the standard cost overhead variances is favorable.

---

[2] AR = $780,400 ÷ 42,000 machine-hours = $1.70 per machine-hour.

Glossary   ![McGraw Hill] **connect**

Budget variance The difference between the actual fixed overhead costs and the budgeted fixed overhead costs for the period. (p. 509)

Denominator activity The level of activity used to compute the predetermined overhead rate. (p. 508)

Volume variance The variance that arises whenever the standard hours allowed for the actual output of a period are different from the denominator activity level that was used to compute the predetermined overhead rate. It is computed by multiplying the fixed component of the predetermined overhead rate by the difference between the denominator hours and the standard hours allowed for the actual output. (p. 510)

Appendix 11A Exercises and Problems   Additional student resources are available with Connect.

EXERCISE 11A–1 Fixed Overhead Variances [LO11–4]

Primara Corporation has a standard cost system in which it applies overhead to products based on the standard direct labor-hours allowed for the actual output of the period. Data concerning the most recent year appear below:

Total budgeted fixed overhead cost for the year	$250,000
Actual fixed overhead cost for the year	$254,000
Budgeted standard direct labor-hours (denominator level of activity)	25,000
Actual direct labor-hours	27,000
Standard direct labor-hours allowed for the actual output	26,000

Required:

1. Compute the fixed portion of the predetermined overhead rate for the year.
2. Compute the fixed overhead budget variance and volume variance.

EXERCISE 11A–2 Predetermined Overhead Rate; Overhead Variances [LO11–3, LO11–4]

Norwall Company's variable manufacturing overhead should be $3.00 per standard machine-hour and its fixed manufacturing overhead should be $300,000 per month.

The following information is available for a recent month:

a. The denominator activity of 60,000 machine-hours is used to compute the predetermined overhead rate.

b. At the 60,000 standard machine-hours level of activity, the company should produce 40,000 units of product.

c. The company's actual operating results were:

Number of units produced	42,000
Actual machine-hours	64,000
Actual variable manufacturing overhead cost	$185,600
Actual fixed manufacturing overhead cost	$302,400

Required:

1. Compute the predetermined overhead rate and break it down into variable and fixed cost elements.
2. Compute the standard hours allowed for the actual production.
3. Compute the variable overhead rate and efficiency variances and the fixed overhead budget and volume variances.

EXERCISE 11A–3 Applying Overhead in a Standard Costing System [LO11–4]

Privack Corporation has a standard cost system in which it applies overhead to products based on the standard direct labor-hours allowed for the actual output of the period. Data concerning the most recent year appear below:

Variable overhead cost per direct labor-hour	$2.00
Total fixed overhead cost per year	$250,000
Budgeted standard direct labor-hours (denominator level of activity)	40,000
Actual direct labor-hours...	39,000
Standard direct labor-hours allowed for the actual output	38,000

Required:

1. Compute the predetermined overhead rate for the year.
2. Determine the amount of overhead that would be applied to the output of the period.

EXERCISE 11A–4 Fixed Overhead Variances [LO11–4]

Selected operating information on three different companies for a recent year is given below:

	Company		
	A	B	C
Full-capacity machine-hours............................	10,000	18,000	20,000
Budgeted machine-hours*	9,000	17,000	20,000
Actual machine-hours	9,000	17,800	19,000
Standard machine-hours allowed for actual production	9,500	16,000	20,000

*Denominator activity for computing the predetermined overhead rate.

Required:

For each company, state whether the company would have a favorable or unfavorable volume variance and why.

EXERCISE 11A–5 Using Fixed Overhead Variances [LO11–4]

The standard cost card for the single product manufactured by Cutter, Inc., is given below:

Standard Cost Card—per Unit	
Direct materials, 3 yards at $6.00 per yard	$ 18
Direct labor, 4 hours at $15.50 per hour	62
Variable overhead, 4 hours at $1.50 per hour	6
Fixed overhead, 4 hours at $5.00 per hour............	20
Total standard cost per unit	$106

Manufacturing overhead is applied to production on the basis of standard direct labor-hours. During the year, the company worked 37,000 hours and manufactured 9,500 units of product. Selected data relating to the company's fixed manufacturing overhead cost for the year are shown below:

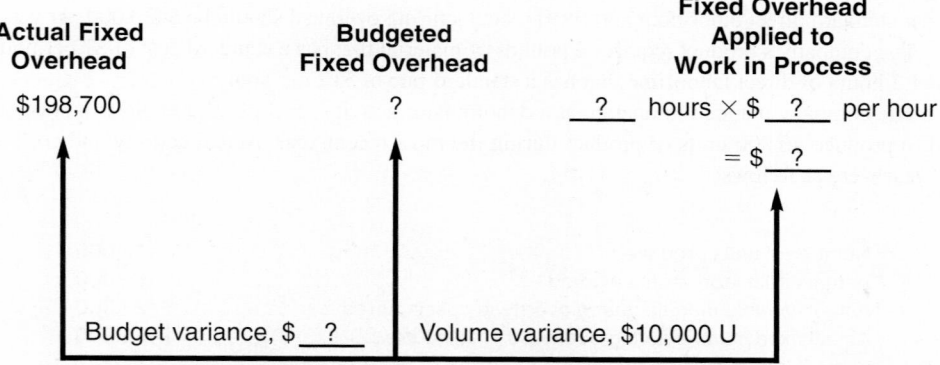

Required:
1.   What were the standard hours allowed for the year's production?
2.   What was the amount of budgeted fixed overhead cost for the year?
3.   What was the fixed overhead budget variance for the year?
4.   What denominator activity level did the company use in setting the predetermined overhead rate for the year?

EXERCISE 11A–6 Predetermined Overhead Rate [LO11–4]
Operating at a normal level of 30,000 direct labor-hours, Lasser Company produces 10,000 units of product each year. The direct labor wage rate is $12 per hour. Two and one-half yards of direct materials go into each unit of product; the material costs $8.60 per yard. Variable manufacturing overhead should be $1.90 per standard direct labor-hour. Fixed manufacturing overhead should be $168,000 per period.

Required:
1.   Using 30,000 direct labor-hours as the denominator activity, compute the predetermined overhead rate and break it down into variable and fixed elements.
2.   Complete the standard cost card below for one unit of product:

Direct materials, 2.5 yards at $8.60 per yard	$21.50
Direct labor, ?	?
Variable manufacturing overhead, ?	?
Fixed manufacturing overhead, ?	?
Total standard cost per unit	$?

EXERCISE 11A–7 Relations Among Fixed Overhead Variances [LO11–4]
Selected information relating to Yost Company's operations for the most recent year is given below:

Activity:	
Denominator activity (machine-hours)	45,000
Standard hours allowed per unit	3
Number of units produced	14,000
Costs:	
Actual fixed overhead costs incurred	$267,000
Fixed overhead budget variance	$3,000 F

The company applies overhead cost to products on the basis of standard machine-hours.

Required:
1.   What were the standard machine-hours allowed for the actual production?
2.   What was the fixed portion of the predetermined overhead rate?
3.   What was the volume variance?

PROBLEM 11A–8 Applying Overhead; Overhead Variances [LO11–3, LO11–4]
Lane Company manufactures a single product that requires a great deal of hand labor. Overhead cost is applied on the basis of standard direct labor-hours. Variable manufacturing overhead should be $2 per standard direct labor-hour and fixed manufacturing overhead should be $480,000 per year.

The company's product requires 3 pounds of material that has a standard cost of $7 per pound and 1.5 hours of direct labor time that has a standard rate of $12 per hour.

The company planned to operate at a denominator activity level of 60,000 direct labor-hours and to produce 40,000 units of product during the most recent year. Actual activity and costs for the year were as follows:

Number of units produced	42,000
Actual direct labor-hours worked	65,000
Actual variable manufacturing overhead cost incurred	$123,500
Actual fixed manufacturing overhead cost incurred	$483,000

Required:

1. Compute the predetermined overhead rate for the year. Break the rate down into variable and fixed elements.
2. Prepare a standard cost card for the company's product; show the details for all manufacturing costs on your standard cost card.
3. Do the following:
   a. Compute the standard direct labor-hours allowed for the year's production.
   b. Complete the following Manufacturing Overhead T-account for the year:

Manufacturing Overhead

?	?
?	?

4. Determine the reason for any underapplied or overapplied overhead for the year by computing the variable overhead rate and efficiency variances and the fixed overhead budget and volume variances.
5. Suppose the company had chosen 65,000 direct labor-hours as the denominator activity rather than 60,000 hours. State which, if any, of the variances computed in requirement 4 would have changed, and explain how the variance(s) would have changed. No computations are necessary.

PROBLEM 11A–9 Applying Overhead; Overhead Variances [LO11–3, LO11–4]

Chilczuk, S.A., of Gdansk, Poland, is a major producer of classic Polish sausage. The company uses a standard cost system to help control costs. Manufacturing overhead is applied to production on the basis of standard direct labor-hours. According to the company's flexible budget, the following manufacturing overhead costs should be incurred at an activity level of 35,000 labor-hours (the denominator activity level):

Variable manufacturing overhead cost....	$ 87,500
Fixed manufacturing overhead cost	210,000
Total manufacturing overhead cost.......	$ 297,500

During the most recent year, the following operating results were recorded:

Activity:	
Actual labor-hours worked.....	30,000
Standard labor-hours allowed for output...	32,000
Cost:	
Actual variable manufacturing overhead cost incurred...	$78,000
Actual fixed manufacturing overhead cost incurred....	$209,400

At the end of the year, the company's Manufacturing Overhead account contained the following data:

Manufacturing Overhead

Actual	287,400	Applied	272,000
	15,400		

Management would like to determine the cause of the $15,400 underapplied overhead.

Required:

1. Compute the predetermined overhead rate. Break the rate down into variable and fixed cost elements.
2. Show how the $272,000 Applied figure in the Manufacturing Overhead account was computed.
3. Analyze the $15,400 underapplied overhead figure in terms of the variable overhead rate and efficiency variances and the fixed overhead budget and volume variances.
4. Explain the meaning of each variance that you computed in requirement 3.

PROBLEM 11A–10 Comprehensive Standard Cost Variances [LO11–1, LO11–2, LO11–3, LO11–4]
"Wonderful! Not only did our salespeople do a good job in meeting the sales budget this year, but our production people did a good job in controlling costs as well," said Kim Clark, president of Martell Company. "Our $18,300 overall manufacturing cost variance is only 1.2% of the $1,536,000 standard cost of products made during the year. That's well within the 3% parameter set by management for acceptable variances. It looks like everyone will be in line for a bonus this year."

The company produces and sells a single product. The standard cost card for the product follows:

Standard Cost Card—per Unit	
Direct materials, 2 feet at $8.45 per foot..	$16.90
Direct labor, 1.4 direct labor-hours at $16 per direct labor-hour.................	22.40
Variable overhead, 1.4 direct labor-hours at $2.50 per direct labor-hour.........	3.50
Fixed overhead, 1.4 direct labor-hours at $6 per direct labor-hour	8.40
Standard cost per unit..	$51.20

The following additional information is available for the year just completed:

a.   The company manufactured 30,000 units of product during the year.
b.   A total of 64,000 feet of material was purchased during the year at a cost of $8.55 per foot. All of this material was used to manufacture the 30,000 units. There were no beginning or ending inventories for the year.
c.   The company worked 43,500 direct labor-hours during the year at a direct labor cost of $15.80 per hour.
d.   Overhead is applied to products on the basis of standard direct labor-hours. Data relating to manufacturing overhead costs follow:

Denominator activity level (direct labor-hours)	35,000
Budgeted fixed overhead costs.........................	$210,000
Actual variable overhead costs incurred	$108,000
Actual fixed overhead costs incurred	$211,800

Required:
1.   Compute the materials price and quantity variances for the year.
2.   Compute the labor rate and efficiency variances for the year.
3.   For manufacturing overhead compute:
     a.   The variable overhead rate and efficiency variances for the year.
     b.   The fixed overhead budget and volume variances for the year.
4.   Total the variances you have computed, and compare the net amount with the $18,300 mentioned by the president. Do you agree that bonuses should be given to everyone for good cost control during the year? Explain.

PROBLEM 11A–11 Comprehensive Standard Cost Variances [LO11–1, LO11–2, LO11–3, LO11–4]
Flandro Company uses a standard cost system and sets predetermined overhead rates on the basis of direct labor-hours. The following data are taken from the company's budget for the current year:

Denominator activity (direct labor-hours)...........	5,000
Variable manufacturing overhead cost.............	$25,000
Fixed manufacturing overhead cost	$59,000

The standard cost card for the company's only product is given below:

Direct materials, 3 yards at $4.40 per yard	$13.20
Direct labor, 1 hour at $12 per hour	12.00
Manufacturing overhead, 140% of direct labor cost	16.80
Standard cost per unit.............................	$42.00

During the year, the company produced 6,000 units of product and incurred the following costs:

Materials purchased, 24,000 yards at $4.80 per yard.................	$115,200
Materials used in production (in yards)...............................	18,500
Direct labor cost incurred, 5,800 hours at $13 per hour................	$75,400
Variable manufacturing overhead cost incurred........................	$29,580
Fixed manufacturing overhead cost incurred	$60,400

Required:

1. Redo the standard cost card in a clearer, more usable format by detailing the variable and fixed overhead cost elements.
2. Prepare an analysis of the variances for direct materials and direct labor for the year.
3. Prepare an analysis of the variances for variable and fixed overhead for the year.
4. What effect, if any, does the choice of a denominator activity level have on unit standard costs? Is the volume variance a controllable variance from a spending point of view? Explain.

PROBLEM 11A–12 Selection of a Denominator; Overhead Analysis; Standard Cost Card [LO11–3, LO11–4]

Morton Company's variable manufacturing overhead should be $4.50 per standard direct labor-hour and fixed manufacturing should be $270,000 per year.

The company manufactures a single product that requires two direct labor-hours to complete. The direct labor wage rate is $15 per hour. Four feet of raw material are required for each unit of product; the standard cost of the material is $8.75 per foot.

Although normal activity is 30,000 direct labor-hours each year, the company expects to operate at a 40,000-hour level of activity this year.

Required:

1. Assume that the company chooses 30,000 direct labor-hours as the denominator level of activity. Compute the predetermined overhead rate, breaking it down into variable and fixed cost elements.
2. Assume that the company chooses 40,000 direct labor-hours as the denominator level of activity. Repeat the computations in requirement 1.
3. Complete two standard cost cards as outlined below.

Denominator Activity: 30,000 Direct Labor-Hours	
Direct materials, 4 feet at $8.75 per foot........	$35.00
Direct labor, ?	?
Variable manufacturing overhead, ?............	?
Fixed manufacturing overhead, ?	?
Standard cost per unit.......................	$?

Denominator Activity: 40,000 Direct Labor-Hours	
Direct materials, $4 feet at $8.75 per foot.......	$35.00
Direct labor, ?	?
Variable manufacturing overhead, ?............	?
Fixed manufacturing overhead, ?	?
Standard cost per unit.......................	$?

4. Assume that the company actually produces 18,000 units and works 38,000 direct labor-hours during the year. Actual manufacturing overhead costs for the year are:

Variable manufacturing overhead cost.......	$174,800
Fixed manufacturing overhead cost	271,600
Total manufacturing overhead cost..........	$446,400

Do the following:

a. Compute the standard direct labor-hours allowed for this year's production.

b. Complete the Manufacturing Overhead account below. Assume that the company uses 30,000 direct labor-hours (normal activity) as the denominator activity figure in computing predetermined overhead rates, as you have done in requirement 1.

Manufacturing Overhead

Actual costs	446,400	Applied	?
	?		?

c. Determine the cause of the underapplied or overapplied overhead for the year by computing the variable overhead rate and efficiency variances and the fixed overhead budget and volume variances.

5. Looking at the variances you have computed, what appears to be the major disadvantage of using normal activity rather than expected actual activity as a denominator in computing the predetermined overhead rate? What advantages can you see to offset this disadvantage?

Performance Measurement in Decentralized Organizations

Performance Measures That Drive Financial Results

© ZUMA Press, Inc/Alamy

Companies that wish to achieve strong financial results need to be responsive to employee and customer needs. For example, Papa John's uses mystery shoppers and a 10-point scale to measure the quality of 10,000 pizzas per month. The mystery shopper scores, which are tied to executive bonuses, help Papa John's meet the customers' need for high-quality pizza. American Express asked its 26,000 call-center employees what they needed to achieve higher job satisfaction—then it responded by delivering flexible schedules, more career development, and higher pay. Collectively, these changes increased the company's service margins by 10%.

This chapter discusses financial measures that companies use to track performance. It also introduces some nonfinancial performance measures, related to customers, employees, and business processes, that companies use to drive financial results. ■

Sources: Scott Cendrowski, "Papa John's John Schnatter," *Fortune*, September 28, 2009, p. 34; Christopher Tkaczyk, "No. 73: American Express," *Fortune*, August 16, 2010, p. 14.

LEARNING OBJECTIVES

After studying Chapter 12, you should be able to:

LO 12–1 Compute return on investment (ROI) and show how changes in sales, expenses, and assets affect ROI.

LO 12–2 Compute residual income and understand its strengths and weaknesses.

LO 12–3 Compute delivery cycle time, throughput time, and manufacturing cycle efficiency (MCE).

LO 12–4 Understand how to construct and use a balanced scorecard.

LO 12–5 (Appendix 12A) Determine the range, if any, within which a negotiated transfer price should fall.

LO 12–6 (Appendix 12B) Charge operating departments for services provided by service departments.

Except in very small organizations, top managers must delegate some decisions. For example, the CEO of the Hyatt Hotel chain cannot be expected to decide whether a particular hotel guest at the Hyatt Hotel on Maui should be allowed to check out later than the normal checkout time. Instead, employees at Maui are authorized to make this decision. As in this example, managers in large organizations have to delegate some decisions to those who are at lower levels in the organization.

Decentralization in Organizations

In a **decentralized organization**, decision-making authority is spread throughout the organization rather than being confined to a few top executives. As noted above, out of necessity all large organizations are decentralized to some extent. Organizations do differ, however, in the extent to which they are decentralized. In strongly centralized organizations, decision-making authority is reluctantly delegated to lower-level managers who have little freedom to make decisions. In strongly decentralized organizations, even the lowest-level managers are empowered to make as many decisions as possible. Most organizations fall somewhere between these two extremes.

Advantages and Disadvantages of Decentralization

The major advantages of decentralization include:

1. By delegating day-to-day problem solving to lower-level managers, top management can concentrate on bigger issues, such as overall strategy.
2. Empowering lower-level managers to make decisions puts the decision-making authority in the hands of those who tend to have the most detailed and up-to-date information about day-to-day operations.
3. By eliminating layers of decision making and approvals, organizations can respond more quickly to customers and to changes in the operating environment.
4. Granting decision-making authority helps train lower-level managers for higher-level positions.
5. Empowering lower-level managers to make decisions can increase their motivation and job satisfaction.

The major disadvantages of decentralization include:

1. Lower-level managers may make decisions without fully understanding the company's overall strategy.
2. If lower-level managers make their own decisions independently of each other, coordination may be lacking.
3. Lower-level managers may have objectives that clash with the objectives of the entire organization.[1] For example, a manager may be more interested in increasing the size of his or her department, leading to more power and prestige, than in increasing the department's effectiveness.

---

[1] Similar problems exist with top-level managers as well. The shareholders of the company delegate their decision-making authority to the top managers. Unfortunately, top managers may abuse that trust by rewarding themselves and their friends too generously, spending too much company money on palatial offices, and so on. The issue of how to ensure that top managers act in the best interests of the company's owners continues to challenge experts. To a large extent, the owners rely on performance evaluation using return on investment and residual income measures, as discussed later in the chapter, and on bonuses and stock options. The stock market is also an important disciplining mechanism. If top managers squander the company's resources, the price of the company's stock will almost surely fall—possibly resulting in a loss of prestige, bonuses, and a job. And, of course, particularly outrageous self-dealing may land a CEO in court.

4. Spreading innovative ideas may be difficult in a decentralized organization. Someone in one part of the organization may have a terrific idea that would benefit other parts of the organization, but without strong central direction the idea may not be shared with, and adopted by, other parts of the organization.

Responsibility Accounting

Decentralized organizations need *responsibility accounting systems* that link lower-level managers' decision-making authority with accountability for the outcomes of those decisions. The term **responsibility center** is used for any part of an organization whose manager has control over and is accountable for cost, profit, or investments. The three primary types of responsibility centers are *cost centers, profit centers,* and *investment centers.*

Cost, Profit, and Investment Centers

Cost Center The manager of a **cost center** has control over costs, but not over revenue or the use of investment funds. Service departments such as accounting, finance, general administration, legal, and personnel are usually classified as cost centers. In addition, manufacturing facilities are often considered to be cost centers. The managers of cost centers are expected to minimize costs while providing the level of products and services demanded by other parts of the organization. For example, the manager of a manufacturing facility would be evaluated at least in part by comparing actual costs to how much costs should have been for the actual level of output during the period. Standard cost variances and flexible budget variances, such as those discussed in earlier chapters, are often used to evaluate cost center performance.

Profit Center The manager of a **profit center** has control over both costs and revenue, but not over the use of investment funds. For example, the manager in charge of a Six Flags amusement park would be responsible for both the revenues and costs, and hence the profits, of the amusement park, but may not have control over major investments in the park. Profit center managers are often evaluated by comparing actual profit to targeted or budgeted profit.

Investment Center The manager of an **investment center** has control over cost, revenue, and investments in operating assets. For example, General Motors' vice president of manufacturing in North America would have a great deal of discretion over investments in manufacturing—such as investing in equipment to produce more fuel-efficient engines. Once General Motors' top-level managers and board of directors approve the vice president's investment proposals, he is held responsible for making them pay off. As discussed in the next section, investment center managers are often evaluated using return on investment (ROI) or residual income measures.

Evaluating Investment Center Performance—Return on Investment

An investment center is responsible for earning an adequate return on investment. The following two sections present two methods for evaluating this aspect of an investment center's performance. The first method, covered in this section, is called *return on investment* (ROI). The second method, covered in the next section, is called *residual income.*

LEARNING OBJECTIVE 12–1
Compute return on investment (ROI) and show how changes in sales, expenses, and assets affect ROI.

The Return on Investment (ROI) Formula

Return on investment (ROI) is defined as net operating income divided by average operating assets:

$$ROI = \frac{\text{Net operating income}}{\text{Average operating assets}}$$

The higher a business segment's return on investment (ROI), the greater the profit earned per dollar invested in the segment's operating assets.

Net Operating Income and Operating Assets Defined

Note that *net operating income,* rather than net income, is used in the ROI formula. **Net operating income** is income before interest and taxes and is sometimes referred to as EBIT (earnings before interest and taxes). Net operating income is used in the formula because the base (i.e., denominator) consists of *operating assets.* To be consistent, we use net operating income in the numerator.

Operating assets include cash, accounts receivable, inventory, plant and equipment, and all other assets held for operating purposes. Examples of assets that are not included in operating assets (i.e., examples of nonoperating assets) include land held for future use, an investment in another company, or a building rented to someone else. These assets are not held for operating purposes and therefore are excluded from operating assets. The operating assets base used in the formula is typically computed as the average of the operating assets between the beginning and the end of the year.

Most companies use the net book value (i.e., acquisition cost less accumulated depreciation) of depreciable assets to calculate average operating assets. This approach has drawbacks. An asset's net book value decreases over time as the accumulated depreciation increases. This decreases the denominator in the ROI calculation, thus increasing ROI. Consequently, ROI mechanically increases over time. Moreover, replacing old depreciated equipment with new equipment increases the book value of depreciable assets and decreases ROI. Hence, using net book value in the calculation of average operating assets results in a predictable pattern of increasing ROI over time as accumulated depreciation grows and discourages replacing old equipment with new, updated equipment. An alternative to using net book value is the gross cost of the asset, which ignores accumulated depreciation. Gross cost stays constant over time because depreciation is ignored; therefore, ROI does not grow automatically over time, and replacing a fully depreciated asset with a comparably priced new asset will not adversely affect ROI.

Nevertheless, most companies use the net book value approach to computing average operating assets because it is consistent with their financial reporting practices of recording the net book value of assets on the balance sheet and including depreciation as an operating expense on the income statement. In this text, we will use the net book value approach unless a specific exercise or problem directs otherwise.

Understanding ROI

The equation for ROI, net operating income divided by average operating assets, does not provide much help to managers interested in taking actions to improve their ROI. It only offers two levers for improving performance—net operating income and average operating assets. Fortunately, ROI can also be expressed in terms of **margin** and **turnover** as follows:

$$\text{ROI} = \text{Margin} \times \text{Turnover}$$

where

$$\text{Margin} = \frac{\text{Net operating income}}{\text{Sales}}$$

and

$$\text{Turnover} = \frac{\text{Sales}}{\text{Average operating assets}}$$

Note that the sales terms in the margin and turnover formulas cancel out when they are multiplied together, yielding the original formula for ROI stated in terms of net operating income and average operating assets. So either formula for ROI will give the same answer. However, the margin and turnover formulation provides some additional insights.

Margin and turnover are important concepts in understanding how a manager can affect ROI. All other things the same, margin is ordinarily improved by increasing selling prices, reducing operating expenses, or increasing unit sales. Increasing selling prices and reducing operating expenses both increase net operating income and therefore margin. Increasing unit sales also ordinarily increases the margin because of operating leverage. As discussed in a previous chapter, because of operating leverage, a given percentage increase in unit sales usually leads to an even larger percentage increase in net operating income. Therefore, an increase in unit sales ordinarily has the effect of increasing margin. Some managers tend to focus too much on margin and ignore turnover. However, turnover incorporates a crucial area of a manager's responsibility—the investment in operating assets. Excessive funds tied up in operating assets (e.g., cash, accounts receivable, inventories, plant and equipment, and other assets) depress turnover and lower ROI. In fact, excessive operating assets can be just as much of a drag on ROI as excessive operating expenses, which depress margin.

© John Burke/Getty Images

A STRATEGY OF SCARCITY

IN BUSINESS

Old Rip Van Winkle Distillery employs two people, Julian Van Winkle III and his son Preston. Its annual sales of $2 million pale in comparison to larger competitors such as Makers' Mark and Wild Turkey. Although the company could easily triple its sales volume, it chooses to limit sales to 7,000 cases of bourbon per year. Given that the company's 20-year-old aged whiskey once achieved an unprecedented "99" rating from the Beverage Tasting Institute of Chicago, demand for the company's products far exceeds its supply—thereby enabling regular price increases. For example, a fifth of 20-year-old Pappy Van Winkle bourbon sells for $110. In accounting terms, the Old Rip Van Winkle Distillery purposely foregoes turnover in favor of earning large margins on its award-winning products.

Source: Brian Dumaine, "Creating the Ultimate Cult Brand," *Fortune*, February 28, 2011, pp. 21–24.

Many actions involve combinations of changes in sales, expenses, and operating assets. For example, a manager may make an investment in (i.e., increase) operating assets to reduce operating expenses or increase sales. Whether the net effect is favorable or not is judged in terms of its overall impact on ROI.

For example, suppose that the Montvale Burger Grill expects the following operating results next month:

Sales	$100,000
Operating expenses	$90,000
Net operating income	$10,000
Average operating assets	$50,000

The expected return on investment (ROI) for the month is computed as follows:

$$\text{ROI} = \frac{\text{Net operating income}}{\text{Sales}} \times \frac{\text{Sales}}{\text{Average operating assets}}$$

$$= \frac{\$10,000}{\$100,000} \times \frac{\$100,000}{\$50,000}$$

$$= 10\% \times 2 = 20\%$$

Suppose that the manager of the Montvale Burger Grill is considering investing $2,000 in a state-of-the-art soft-serve ice cream machine that can dispense a number of different flavors. This new machine would boost sales by $4,000, but would require additional operating expenses of $1,000. Thus, net operating income would increase by $3,000, to $13,000. The new ROI would be:

$$ROI = \frac{\text{Net operating income}}{\text{Sales}} \times \frac{\text{Sales}}{\text{Average operating assets}}$$

$$= \frac{\$13,000}{\$104,000} \times \frac{\$104,000}{\$52,000}$$

$$= 12.5\% \times 2 = 25\% \text{ (as compared to 20\% originally)}$$

In this particular example, the investment increases ROI, but that will not always happen.

E.I. du Pont de Nemours and Company (better known as DuPont) pioneered the use of ROI and recognized the importance of looking at both margin and turnover in assessing a manager's performance. ROI is now widely used as the key measure of investment center performance. ROI reflects in a single figure many aspects of the manager's responsibilities. It can be compared to the returns of other investment centers in the organization, the returns of other companies in the industry, and to the past returns of the investment center itself. DuPont also developed the diagram that appears in Exhibit 12–1. This exhibit helps managers understand how they can improve ROI.

EXHIBIT 12–1
Elements of Return on Investment (ROI)

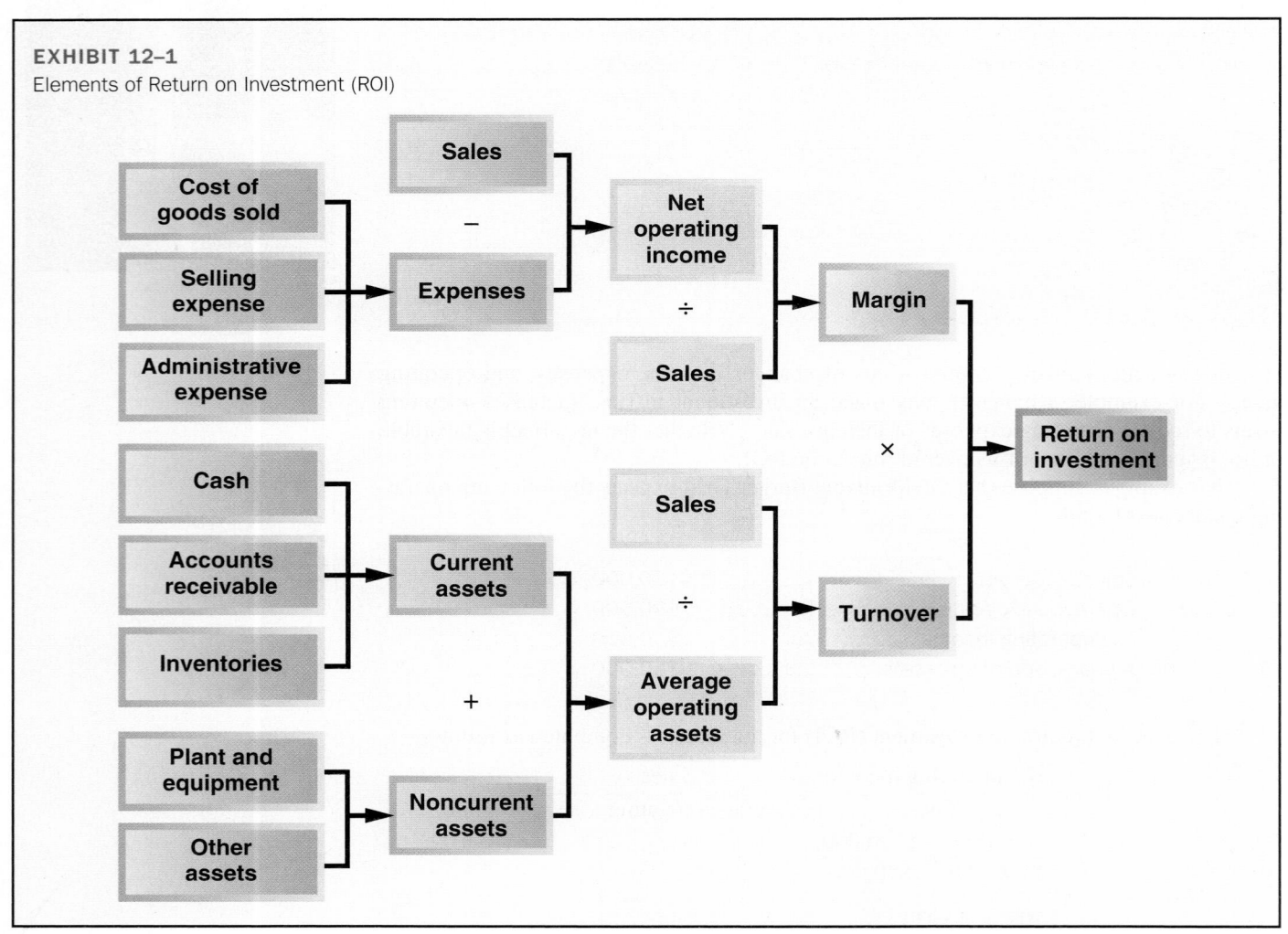

MICROSOFT MANAGES IN AN ECONOMIC DOWNTURN

Microsoft responded to tough economic times by lowering its prices, thereby accepting lower margins per unit sold in exchange for higher turnover. For example, Microsoft lowered the price of its Office software from $150 to $100 (after promotional discounts) and realized a 415% increase in unit sales. In China, the company combated huge piracy problems by dropping the price of Office to $29, resulting in an 800% increase in sales. Microsoft established a selling price of $200 for its Windows 7 PC operating system, which was $40 less than the price the company charged for its predecessor Vista PC operating system.

Source: Peter Burrows, "Microsoft's Aggressive New Pricing Strategy," *BusinessWeek*, July 27, 2009, p. 51.

Criticisms of ROI

Although ROI is widely used in evaluating performance, it is subject to the following criticisms:

1. Just telling managers to increase ROI may not be enough. Managers may not know how to increase ROI; they may increase ROI in a way that is inconsistent with the company's strategy; or they may take actions that increase ROI in the short run but harm the company in the long run (such as cutting back on research and development). This is why ROI is best used as part of a balanced scorecard, as discussed later in this chapter. A balanced scorecard can provide concrete guidance to managers, making it more likely that their actions are consistent with the company's strategy and reducing the likelihood that they will boost short-run performance at the expense of long-term performance.
2. A manager who takes over a business segment typically inherits many committed costs over which the manager has no control. These committed costs may be relevant in assessing the performance of the business segment as an investment but they make it difficult to fairly assess the performance of the manager.
3. As discussed in the next section, a manager who is evaluated based on ROI may reject investment opportunities that are profitable for the whole company but would have a negative impact on the manager's performance evaluation.

Residual Income

LEARNING OBJECTIVE 12–2
Compute residual income and understand its strengths and weaknesses.

Residual income is another approach to measuring an investment center's performance. **Residual income** is the net operating income that an investment center earns above the minimum required return on its operating assets. In equation form, residual income is calculated as follows:

$$\text{Residual income} = \text{Net operating income} - \left(\text{Average operating assets} \times \text{Minimum required rate of return} \right)$$

Economic Value Added (EVA®) is an adaptation of residual income that has been adopted by many companies.[2] Under EVA, companies often modify their accounting principles in various ways. For example, funds used for research and development are often treated as investments rather than as expenses.[3] These complications are best dealt

---

[2] The basic idea underlying residual income and economic value added has been around for over 100 years. Economic value added has been popularized and trademarked by the consulting firm Stern Stewart & Co.

[3] Over 100 different adjustments could be made for deferred taxes. LIFO reserves, provisions for future liabilities, mergers and acquisitions, gains or losses due to changes in accounting rules, operating leases, and other accounts, but most companies make only a few. For further details, see John O'Hanlon and Ken Peasnell, "Wall Street's Contribution to Management Accounting: the Stern Stewart EVA® Financial Management System," *Management Accounting Research* 9, 1998. pp. 421–444.

with in a more advanced course; in this text we will not draw any distinction between residual income and EVA.

When residual income or EVA is used to measure performance, the objective is to maximize the total amount of residual income or EVA, not to maximize ROI. This is an important distinction. If the objective were to maximize ROI, then every company should divest all of its products except the single product with the highest ROI.

A wide variety of organizations have embraced some version of residual income or EVA, including Bausch & Lomb, Best Buy, Boise Cascade, Coca-Cola, Dun and Bradstreet, Eli Lilly, Federal Mogul, Georgia-Pacific, Hershey Foods, Husky Injection Molding, J.C. Penney, Kansas City Power & Light, Olin, Quaker Oats, Silicon Valley Bank, Sprint, Toys R Us, Tupperware, and the United States Postal Service.

For purposes of illustration, consider the following data for an investment center—the Ketchikan Division of Alaskan Marine Services Corporation.

Alaskan Marine Services Corporation	
Ketchikan Division	
Basic Data for Performance Evaluation	
Average operating assets	$100,000
Net operating income.	$20,000
Minimum required rate of return	15%

Alaskan Marine Services Corporation has long had a policy of using ROI to evaluate its investment center managers, but it is considering switching to residual income. The controller of the company, who is in favor of the change to residual income, has provided the following table that shows how the performance of the division would be evaluated under each of the two methods:

Alaskan Marine Services Corporation		
Ketchikan Division		
	Alternative Performance Measures	
	ROI	Residual Income
Average operating assets (a).	$100,000	$100,000
Net operating income (b).	$20,000	$20,000
ROI, (b) ÷ (a)	20%	
Minimum required return (15% × $100,000)		15,000
Residual income.		$ 5,000

The reasoning underlying the residual income calculation is straightforward. The company is able to earn a rate of return of at least 15% on its investments. Because the company has invested $100,000 in the Ketchikan Division in the form of operating assets, the company should be able to earn at least $15,000 (15% × $100,000) on this investment. Because the Ketchikan Division's net operating income is $20,000, the residual income above and beyond the minimum required return is $5,000. If residual income is adopted as the performance measure to replace ROI, the manager of the Ketchikan Division would be evaluated based on the growth in residual income from year to year.

Motivation and Residual Income

One of the primary reasons why the controller of Alaskan Marine Services Corporation would like to switch from ROI to residual income relates to how managers view new investments under the two performance measurement methods. The residual income approach encourages managers to make investments that are profitable for the entire company but that would be rejected by managers who are evaluated using the ROI formula.

To illustrate this problem with ROI, suppose that the manager of the Ketchikan Division is considering purchasing a computerized diagnostic machine to aid in servicing marine diesel engines. The machine would cost $25,000 and is expected to generate additional operating income of $4,500 a year. From the standpoint of the company, this would be a good investment because it promises a rate of return of 18% ($4,500 ÷ $25,000), which exceeds the company's minimum required rate of return of 15%.

If the manager of the Ketchikan Division is evaluated based on residual income, she would be in favor of the investment in the diagnostic machine as shown below:

Alaskan Marine Services Corporation
Ketchikan Division
Performance Evaluated Using Residual Income

	Present	New Project	Overall
Average operating assets	$100,000	$25,000	$125,000
Net operating income	$20,000	$4,500	$24,500
Minimum required return	15,000	3,750*	18,750
Residual income	$ 5,000	$ 750	$ 5,750

*The revenue variance is labeled favorable (unfavorable) when the actual revenue is greater than (less than) the planning budget. the expense variances are labeled favorable (unfavorable) when the actual expense is less than (greater than) the planning budget.

Because the project would increase the residual income of the Ketchikan Division by $750, the manager would choose to invest in the new diagnostic machine.

Now suppose that the manager of the Ketchikan Division is evaluated based on ROI. The effect of the diagnostic machine on the division's ROI is computed below:

Alaskan Marine Services Corporation
Ketchikan Division
Performance Evaluated Using ROI

	Present	New Project	Overall
Average operating assets (a)	$100,000	$25,000	$125,000
Net operating income (b)	$20,000	$4,500	$24,500
ROI, (b) ÷ (a)	20%	18%	19.6%

The new project reduces the division's ROI from 20% to 19.6%. This happens because the 18% rate of return on the new diagnostic machine, while above the company's 15% minimum required rate of return, is below the division's current ROI of 20%. Therefore, the new diagnostic machine would decrease the division's ROI even though it would be a good investment from the standpoint of the company as a whole. If the manager of the division is evaluated based on ROI, she will be reluctant to even propose such an investment.

Generally, a manager who is evaluated based on ROI will reject any project whose rate of return is below the division's current ROI even if the rate of return on the project is above the company's minimum required rate of return. In contrast, managers who are evaluated using residual income will pursue any project whose rate of return is above the minimum required rate of return because it will increase their residual income. Because it is in the best interests of the company as a whole to accept any project whose rate of return is above the minimum required rate of return, managers who are evaluated based on residual income will tend to make better decisions concerning investment projects than managers who are evaluated based on ROI.

Divisional Comparison and Residual Income

The residual income approach has one major disadvantage. It can't be used to compare the performance of divisions of different sizes. Larger divisions often have more residual income than smaller divisions, not necessarily because they are better managed but simply because they are bigger.

As an example, consider the following residual income computations for the Wholesale Division and the Retail Division of Sisal Marketing Corporation:

	Wholesale Division	Retail Division
Average operating assets (a)..............	$1,000,000	$250,000
Net operating income	$120,000	$40,000
Minimum required return: 10% × (a)	100,000	25,000
Residual income.........................	$ 20,000	$15,000

Observe that the Wholesale Division has slightly more residual income than the Retail Division, but that the Wholesale Division has $1,000,000 in operating assets as compared to only $250,000 in operating assets for the Retail Division. Thus, the Wholesale Division's greater residual income is probably due to its larger size rather than the quality of its management. In fact, it appears that the smaller division may be better managed because it has been able to generate nearly as much residual income with only one-fourth as much in operating assets. When comparing investment centers, it is probably better to focus on the percentage change in residual income from year to year rather than on the absolute amount of the residual income.

Operating Performance Measures

LEARNING OBJECTIVE 12–3
Compute delivery cycle time, throughput time, and manufacturing cycle efficiency (MCE).

In addition to financial performance measures, organizations use many nonfinancial performance measures. While financial measures pick up the *results* of what people in the organization do, they do not measure what *drives* organizational performance. For example, activity and revenue variances pick up the results of efforts aimed at increasing sales, but they do not measure the actions that actually drive sales such as improving quality, exposing more potential customers to the product, filling customer orders on time, and so on. Consequently, many organizations use a variety of nonfinancial performance measures in addition to financial measures. In this section we will discuss three examples of such measures that are critical to success in many organizations—delivery cycle time, throughput time, and manufacturing cycle efficiency (MCE). Note that while these examples focus on manufacturers, very similar measures can be used by any service organization that experiences a delay between receiving a customer request and responding to that request.

Delivery Cycle Time

The amount of time from when a customer order is received to when the completed order is shipped is called **delivery cycle time**. This time is an important concern to many customers, who would like the delivery cycle time to be as short as possible. Cutting the delivery cycle time may give a company a key competitive advantage—and may be necessary for survival. The formula for computing delivery cycle time is as follows:

$$\text{Delivery cycle time} = \text{Wait time} + \text{Throughput time}$$

Throughput (Manufacturing Cycle) Time

The amount of time required to turn raw materials into completed products is called **throughput time**, or *manufacturing cycle time*. The relation between the delivery cycle time and the throughput (manufacturing cycle) time is illustrated in Exhibit 12–2.

As shown in Exhibit 12–2, the throughput time, or manufacturing cycle time, is made up of process time, inspection time, move time, and queue time. *Process time* is the amount of time work is actually done on the product. *Inspection time* is the amount of time spent ensuring that the product is not defective. *Move time* is the time required to move materials or partially completed products from workstation to workstation. *Queue time* is the amount of time a product spends waiting to be worked on, to be moved, to be inspected, or to be shipped.

As shown at the bottom of Exhibit 12–2, only one of these four activities adds value to the product—process time. The other three activities—inspecting, moving, and queuing—add no value and should be eliminated as much as possible. The formula for computing throughput (manufacturing cycle) time is as follows:

$$\text{Throughput (manufacturing cycle) time} =$$
$$\text{Process time} + \text{Inspection time} + \text{Move time} + \text{Queue time}$$

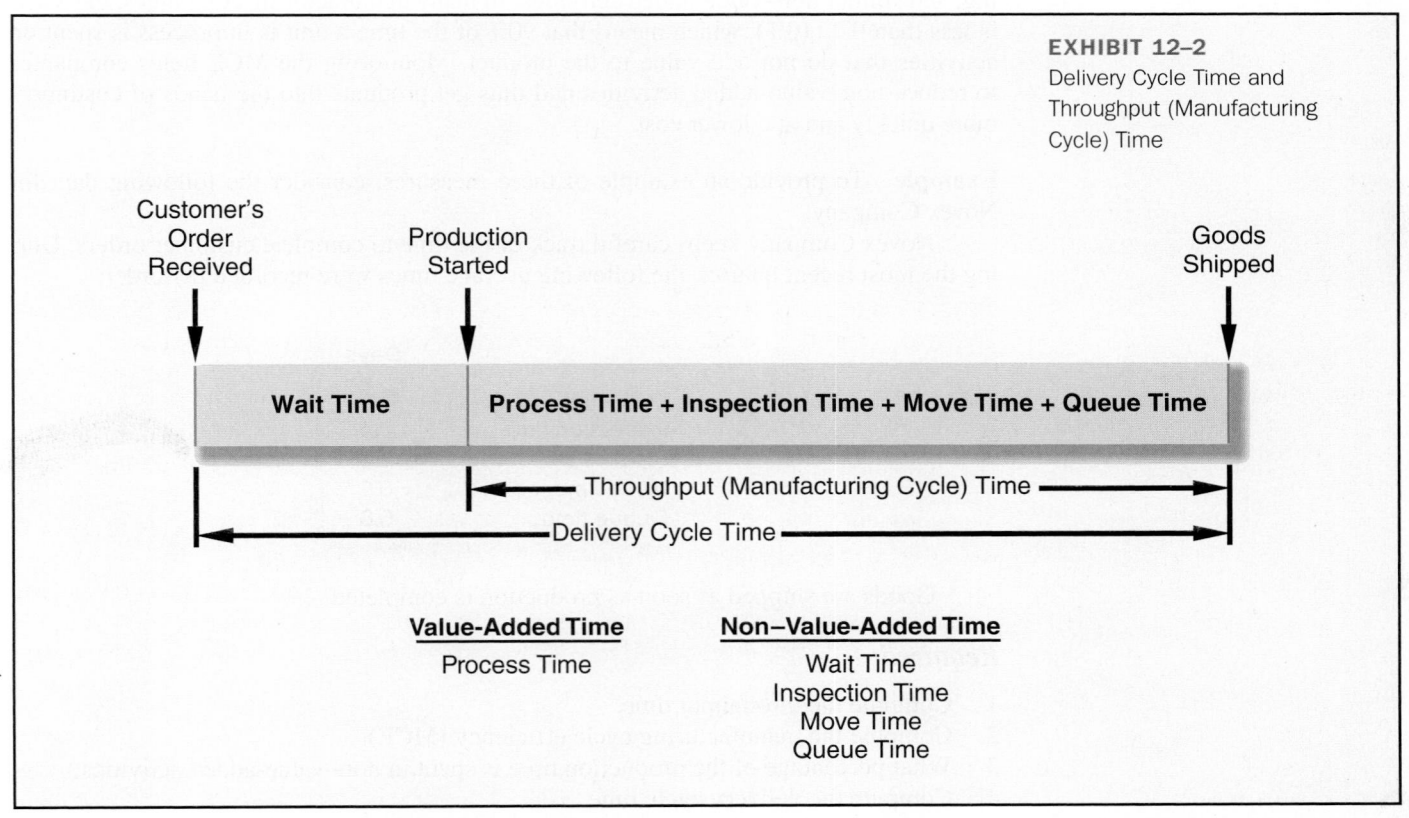

EXHIBIT 12–2
Delivery Cycle Time and Throughput (Manufacturing Cycle) Time

---

IN BUSINESS

THE DOCTOR WILL SEE YOU . . . LATER

When medical care reimbursement rates drop, doctors often respond by packing more patients into each day, thereby increasing patient wait times. Press Ganey Associates surveyed 2.4 million patients at more than 10,000 locations and determined an average wait time to see a doctor of 22 minutes. While these delays inconvenience patients, they also have financial implications for doctors. For example, Laurie Green, an obstetrician-gynecologist in San Francisco, prides herself on running an efficient medical practice because "she needs to bring in $75 every 15 minutes just to meet her office overhead."

If your doctor's office is overrun with delays, consider getting the first appointment of the day because the "early bird" not only gets the worm, but it also avoids wait time at the doctor's office!

Source: Melinda Beck, "The Doctor Will See You Eventually," *The Wall Street Journal,* October 19, 2010, pp. D1 and D4.

Manufacturing Cycle Efficiency (MCE)

Through concerted efforts to eliminate the *non–value-added* activities of inspecting, moving, and queuing, some companies have reduced their throughput time to only a fraction of previous levels. In turn, this has helped to reduce the delivery cycle time from months to only weeks or hours. Throughput time, which is a key measure in delivery performance, can be put into better perspective by computing the **manufacturing cycle efficiency (MCE)**. The MCE is computed by relating the value-added time to the throughput time. The formula is:

$$\text{MCE} = \frac{\text{Value-added time (Process time)}}{\text{Throughput (manufacturing cycle) time}}$$

Any non–value-added time results in an MCE of less than 1. An MCE of 0.5, for example, would mean that half of the total production time consists of inspection, moving, and similar non–value-added activities. In many manufacturing companies, the MCE is less than 0.1 (10%), which means that 90% of the time a unit is in process is spent on activities that do not add value to the product. Monitoring the MCE helps companies to reduce non–value-added activities and thus get products into the hands of customers more quickly and at a lower cost.

Example To provide an example of these measures, consider the following data for Novex Company:

Novex Company keeps careful track of the time to complete customer orders. During the most recent quarter, the following average times were recorded per order:

	Days
Wait time	17.0
Inspection time	0.4
Process time	2.0
Move time	0.6
Queue time	5.0

Goods are shipped as soon as production is completed.

Required:

1. Compute the throughput time.
2. Compute the manufacturing cycle efficiency (MCE).
3. What percentage of the production time is spent in non–value-added activities?
4. Compute the delivery cycle time.

Solution

1. Throughput time = Process time + Inspection time + Move time + Queue time
$$= 2.0 \text{ days} + 0.4 \text{ days} + 0.6 \text{ days} + 5.0 \text{ days}$$
$$= 2.0 \text{ days}$$

2. Only process time represents value-added time; therefore, MCE would be computed as follows:
$$\text{MCE} = \frac{\text{Value-added time}}{\text{Throughput time}} = \frac{2.0 \text{ days}}{8.0 \text{ days}}$$
$$= 0.25$$

Thus, once put into production, a typical order is actually being worked on only 25% of the time.

3. Because the MCE is 25%, 75% (100% − 25%) of total production time is spent in non–value-added activities.

4. Delivery cycle time = Wait time + Throughput time
$$= 17.0 \text{ days} + 8.0 \text{ days}$$
$$= 25.0 \text{ days}$$

IN BUSINESS

LEAN OPERATING PERFORMANCE MEASURES

Watlow Electric Manufacturing Company implemented *lean accounting* to support its lean manufacturing methods. The company stopped providing standard cost variance reports to operating managers because the information was generated too late (at the end of each month) and it could not be understood by frontline employees. Instead, the company began reporting daily and hourly process-oriented measures that helped frontline workers improve performance.

Examples of lean operating performance measures are shown in the table below:

Measure	Description of Measure
On-time delivery percentage	Measures the percentage of orders that customers would define as being delivered on time.
Day-by-the-hour	Measures the quantity of production on an hourly basis to ensure that it is synchronized with customer demand.
First time through percentage	Measures the percentage of completed units that are free of defects.
Number of accidents and injuries	Measures the number of accidents and injuries on the manufacturing floor.
5S audit	Measures the cell workers' ability to keep their work area organized and clean.

Note: 5S stands for Sort, Straighten, Shine, Standardize, and Sustain

Sources: Jan Brosnahan, "Unleash the Power of Lean Accounting," *Journal of Accountancy*, July 2008, pp. 60–66; and Brian Maskell and Frances Kennedy, "Why Do We Need Lean Accounting and How Does It Work?" *Journal of Corporate Accounting and Finance*, March/April 2007, pp. 59–73.

Balanced Scorecard

Financial measures, such as ROI and residual income, and operating measures, such as those discussed in the previous section, may be included in a *balanced scorecard*. A **balanced scorecard** consists of an integrated set of performance measures that are derived from and support a company's strategy. A strategy is essentially a theory about how

LEARNING OBJECTIVE 12–4
Understand how to construct and use a balanced scorecard.

to achieve the organization's goals. For example, Southwest Airlines' strategy is to offer an *operational excellence* customer value proposition that has three key components—low ticket prices, convenience, and reliability. The company operates only one type of aircraft, the Boeing 737, to reduce maintenance and training costs and simplify scheduling. It further reduces costs by not offering meals, seat assignments, or baggage transfers and by booking a large portion of its passenger revenue over the Internet. Southwest also uses point-to-point flights rather than the hub-and-spoke approach of its larger competitors, thereby providing customers convenient, nonstop service to their final destination. Because Southwest serves many less-congested airports such as Chicago Midway, Burbank, Manchester, Oakland, and Providence, it offers quicker passenger check-ins and reliable departures, while maintaining high asset utilization (i.e., the company's average gate turnaround time of 25 minutes enables it to function with fewer planes and gates). Overall, the company's strategy has worked. At a time when Southwest Airlines' larger competitors are struggling, it continues to earn substantial profits.

Under the balanced scorecard approach, top management translates its strategy into performance measures that employees can understand and influence. For example, the amount of time passengers have to wait in line to have their baggage checked might be a performance measure for the supervisor in charge of the Southwest Airlines check-in counter at the Burbank airport. This performance measure is easily understood by the supervisor, and can be improved by the supervisor's actions.

Common Characteristics of Balanced Scorecards

Performance measures used in balanced scorecards tend to fall into the four groups illustrated in Exhibit 12–3: financial, customer, internal business processes, and learning and growth. Internal business processes are what the company does in an attempt to satisfy customers. For example, in a manufacturing company, assembling a product is an internal

EXHIBIT 12–3
From Strategy to Performance Measures: The Balanced Scorecard

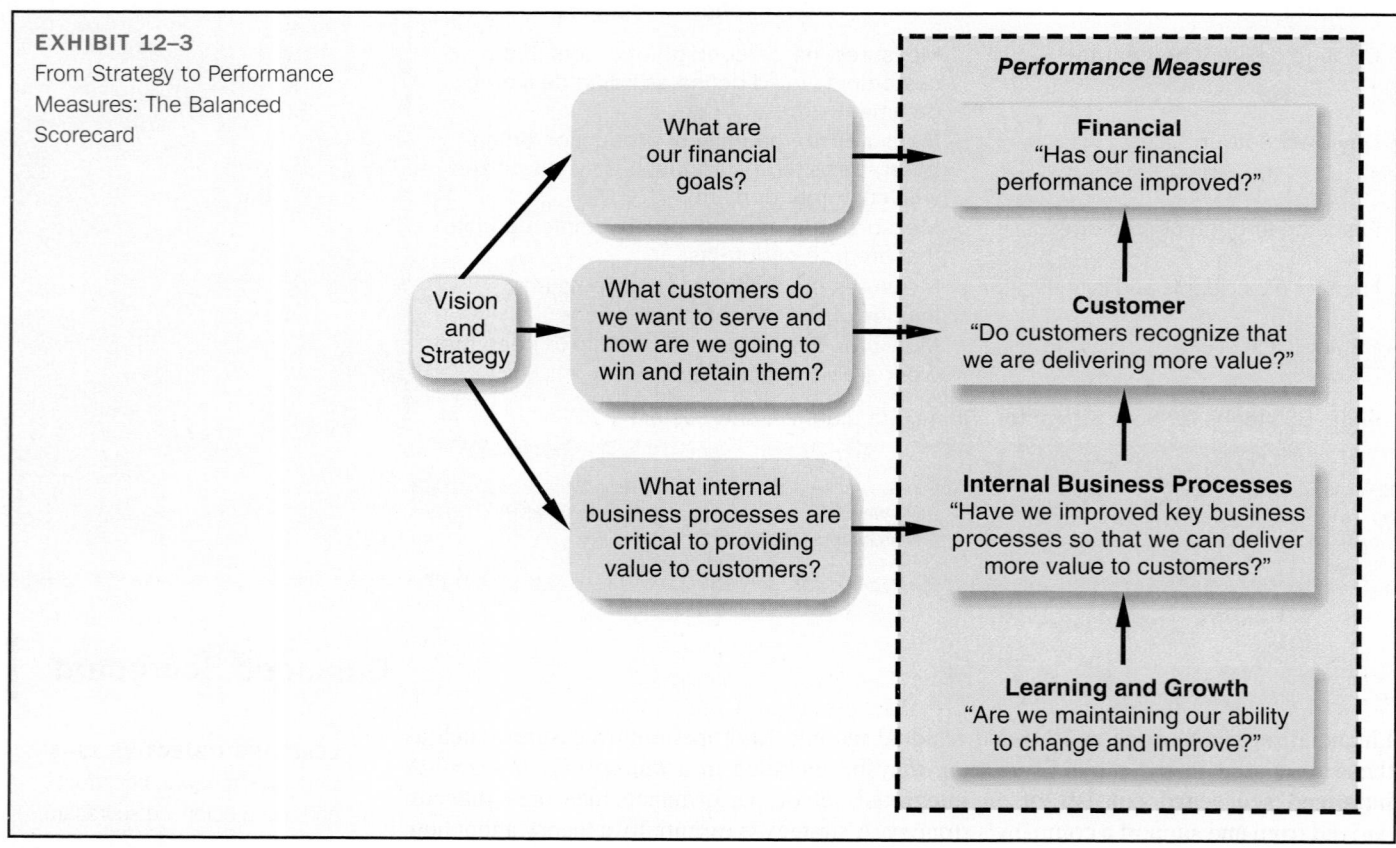

business process. In an airline, handling baggage is an internal business process. The idea underlying these groupings (as indicated by the vertical arrows in Exhibit 12–3) is that learning is necessary to improve internal business processes; improving business processes is necessary to improve customer satisfaction; and improving customer satisfaction is necessary to improve financial results.

Note that the emphasis in Exhibit 12–3 is on *improvement*—not on just attaining some specific objective such as profits of $10 million. In the balanced scorecard approach, continual improvement is encouraged. If an organization does not continually improve, it will eventually lose out to competitors that do.

Financial performance measures appear at the top of Exhibit 12–3. Ultimately, most companies exist to provide financial rewards to owners. There are exceptions. Some companies—for example, The Body Shop—may have loftier goals such as providing environmentally friendly products to consumers. However, even nonprofit organizations must generate enough financial resources to stay in operation.

For several reasons, financial performance measures are not sufficient in themselves—they should be integrated with nonfinancial measures in a well-designed balanced scorecard. First, financial measures are lag indicators that report on the results of past actions. In contrast, nonfinancial measures of key success drivers such as customer satisfaction are leading indicators of future financial performance. Second, top managers are ordinarily responsible for the financial performance measures—not lower-level managers. The supervisor in charge of checking in passengers can be held responsible for how long passengers have to wait in line. However, this supervisor cannot reasonably be held responsible for the entire company's profit. That is the responsibility of the airline's top managers.

IN BUSINESS

WHY DO COMPANIES FAIL TO EXECUTE THEIR STRATEGIES?

Robert Paladino served as the vice president and global leader of the Telecommunications and Utility Practice for the Balanced Scorecard Collaborative—a consulting organization that works with companies to implement balanced scorecards. He offers four reasons why nine out of ten organizations fail to execute their business strategies.

First, only 5% of a company's workforce understands their organization's strategy. Paladino commented "if employees don't understand the strategic objectives, then they could be focused on closing the wrong performance gaps." Second, 85% of management teams spend less than one hour per month discussing strategy. Managers cannot effectively implement strategies if they do not spend enough time talking about them. Third, 60% of organizations do not link their budgets to strategy. The inevitable result is that companies pursue "financial strategies that differ from or, worse, may be in conflict with their business and customer quality strategies." Finally, only 25% of managers have their incentives linked to strategy. Thus, most managers are working to maximize their compensation by improving strategically misguided metrics.

Paladino says the balanced scorecard overcomes these four barriers because it helps employees focus their actions on executing organizational strategies.

Source: Robert E. Paladino, "Balanced Forecasts Drive Value," *Strategic Finance*, January 2005, pp. 37–42.

Exhibit 12–4 lists some examples of performance measures that can be found on the balanced scorecards of companies. However, few companies, if any, would use all of these performance measures, and almost all companies would add other performance measures. Managers should carefully select performance measures for their own company's balanced scorecard, keeping the following points in mind. First and foremost, the performance measures should be consistent with, and follow from, the company's strategy. If the performance measures are not consistent with the company's strategy, people will find themselves working at cross-purposes. Second, the performance measures should be understandable and controllable to a significant extent by those being

EXHIBIT 12–4

Examples of Performance Measures for Balanced Scorecards

Customer Perspective

Performance Measure	Desired Change
Customer satisfaction as measured by survey results	+
Number of customer complaints	−
Market share	+
Product returns as a percentage of sales	−
Percentage of customers retained from last period	+
Number of new customers	+

Internal Business Processes Perspective

Performance Measure	Desired Change
Percentage of sales from new products	+
Time to introduce new products to market	−
Percentage of customer calls answered within 20 seconds	+
On-time deliveries as a percentage of all deliveries	+
Work in process inventory as a percentage of sales	−
Unfavorable standard cost variances	−
Defect-free units as a percentage of completed units	+
Delivery cycle time	−
Throughput time	−
Manufacturing cycle efficiency	+
Quality costs	−
Setup time	−
Time from call by customer to repair of product	−
Percent of customer complaints settled on first contact	+
Time to settle a customer claim	−

Learning and Growth Perspective

Performance Measure	Desired Change
Suggestions per employee	+
Employee turnover	−
Hours of in-house training per employee	+

evaluated. Third, the performance measures should be reported on a frequent and timely basis. For example, data about defects should be reported to the responsible manager at least once a day so that problems can be resolved quickly. Fourth, the scorecard should not have too many performance measures. This can lead to a lack of focus and confusion.

While the entire organization will have an overall balanced scorecard, each responsible individual will have his or her own personal scorecard as well. This scorecard should consist of items the individual can personally influence that relate directly to the performance measures on the overall balanced scorecard. The performance measures on this personal scorecard should not be overly influenced by actions taken by others in the company or by events that are outside of the individual's control. And, focusing on the performance measure should not lead an individual to take actions that are counter to the organization's objectives.

With those broad principles in mind, we will now take a look at how a company's strategy affects its balanced scorecard.

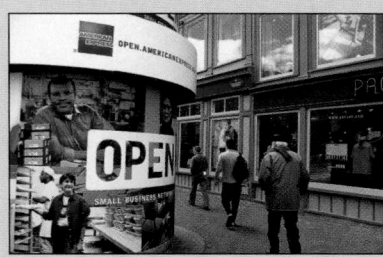
A Company's Strategy and the Balanced Scorecard

Returning to the performance measures in Exhibit 12–3, each company must decide which customers to target and what internal business processes are crucial to attracting and retaining those customers. Different companies, having different strategies, will target different customers with different kinds of products and services. Take the automobile industry as an example. BMW stresses engineering and handling; Volvo, safety; Jaguar, luxury detailing; and Honda, reliability. Because of these differences in emphasis, a one-size-fits-all approach to performance measurement won't work even within this one industry. Performance measures must be tailored to the specific strategy of each company.

Suppose, for example, that Jaguar's strategy is to offer distinctive, richly finished luxury automobiles to wealthy individuals who prize handcrafted, individualized products. To deliver this customer intimacy value proposition to its wealthy target customers, Jaguar might create such a large number of options for details, such as leather seats, interior and exterior color combinations, and wooden dashboards, that each car becomes virtually one of a kind. For example, instead of just offering tan or blue leather seats in standard cowhide, the company may offer customers the choice of an almost infinite palette of colors in any of a number of different exotic leathers. For such a system to work effectively, Jaguar would have to be able to deliver a completely customized car within a reasonable amount of time—and without incurring more cost for this customization than the customer is willing to pay. Exhibit 12–5 suggests how Jaguar might reflect this strategy in its balanced scorecard.

If the balanced scorecard is correctly constructed, the performance measures should be linked together on a cause-and-effect basis. Each link can then be read as a hypothesis in the form "If we improve this performance measure, then this other performance measure should also improve." Starting from the bottom of Exhibit 12–5, we can read the links between performance measures as follows. If employees acquire the skills to install new options more effectively, then the company can offer more options and the options can be installed in less time. If more options are available and they are installed in less time, then customer surveys should show greater satisfaction with the range of options available. If customer satisfaction improves, then the number of cars sold should increase. In addition, if customer satisfaction improves, the company should be able to

EXHIBIT 12–5
A Possible Strategy at Jaguar and the Balanced Scorecard

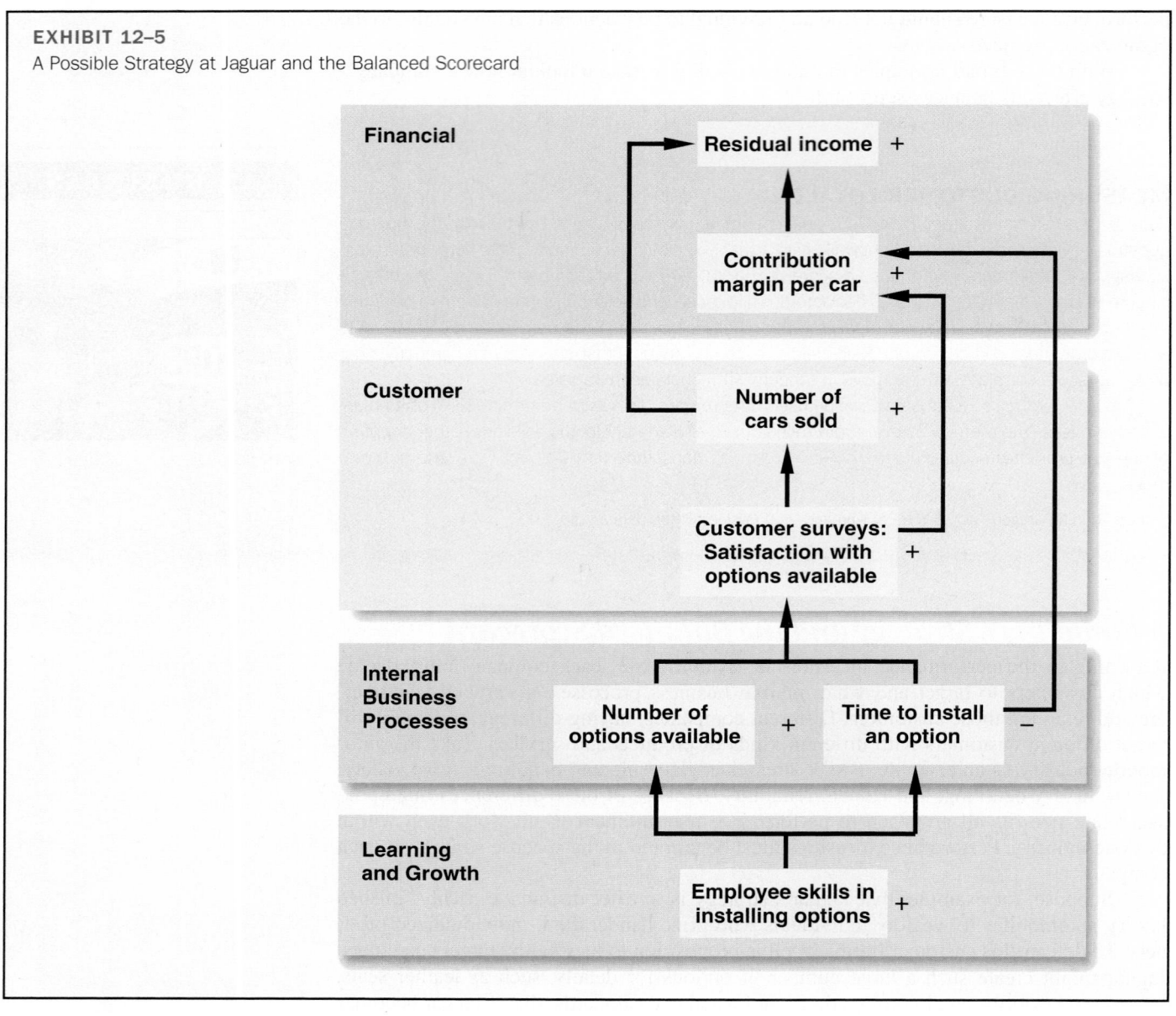

maintain or increase its selling prices, and if the time to install options decreases, the costs of installing the options should decrease. Together, this should result in an increase in the contribution margin per car. If the contribution margin per car increases and more cars are sold, the result should be an increase in residual income.

In essence, the balanced scorecard lays out a theory of how the company can take concrete actions to attain its desired outcomes (financial, in this case). The strategy laid out in Exhibit 12–5 seems plausible, but it should be regarded as only a theory. For example, if the company succeeds in increasing the number of options available and in decreasing the time required to install options and yet there is no increase in customer satisfaction, the number of cars sold, the contribution margin per car, or residual income, the strategy would have to be reconsidered. One of the advantages of the balanced scorecard is that it continually tests the theories underlying management's strategy. If a strategy is not working, it should become evident when some of the predicted effects (i.e., more car sales) don't occur. Without this feedback, the organization may drift on indefinitely with an ineffective strategy based on faulty assumptions.

THE WELLNESS SCORECARD

Towers Watson estimates that America's average annual health care spending per employee now exceeds $10,000, up from $5,386 in 2002. However, companies that have implemented high-performing corporate wellness programs have annual health care costs that are $1,800 per employee less than other organizations. These high-performing companies create and track wellness performance measures as an important part of managing their programs.

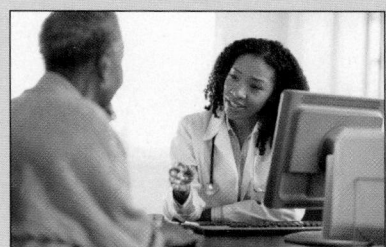

© JGI/Tom Grill/Blend Images/Getty Images

The wellness scorecard is one framework for measuring corporate wellness performance. It has four categories of measures—attitudes, participation, physical results, and financial results—that are connected on a cause-and-effect basis. If employee attitudes toward the company's wellness program improve, then it should increase the rate of employee participation in wellness activities. If employees increase their participation rates, then it should produce physical results, such as lower obesity rates, lower incidents of diabetes, and increased smoking cessation rates. These physical improvements should produce positive financial results for the company, such as lower medical, pharmaceutical, and disability disbursements.

Sources: Towers Perrin, "2010 Health Care Cost Survey," www.towerswatson.com; and Peter C. Brewer, Angela Gallo, and Melanie R. Smith, "Getting Fit with Corporate Wellness Programs," *Strategic Finance,* May 2010, pp. 27–33.

Tying Compensation to the Balanced Scorecard

Incentive compensation for employees, such as bonuses, can, and probably should, be tied to balanced scorecard performance measures. However, this should be done only after the organization has been successfully managed with the scorecard for some time—perhaps a year or more. Managers must be confident that the performance measures are reliable, sensible, understood by those who are being evaluated, and not easily manipulated. As Robert Kaplan and David Norton, the originators of the balanced scorecard concept point out, "compensation is such a powerful lever that you have to be pretty confident that you have the right measures and have good data for the measures before making the link."[4]

SUSTAINABILITY AND THE BALANCED SCORECARD

The Sustainable Investment Research Analyst Network (SIRAN) studied changes in the sustainability reporting practices of the Standard & Poor's (S&P) 100 companies from 2005 to 2007. Eighty-six of the S&P 100 companies had corporate sustainability websites as of 2007, an increase of 48% since 2005. Forty-nine of the S&P 100 companies published sustainability reports in 2007, up 26% from 2005.

Graham Hubbard, a professor at the University of Adelaide, recommends incorporating sustainability reporting into the balanced scorecard by adding two categories of measures related to social performance and environmental performance. Social performance measures focus on a company's philanthropic investments, community service, and employee safety and satisfaction. Environmental measures focus on a company's energy and water use per unit of output and its waste generation and disposal performance.

Sources: "Rise in Sustainability Reporting by S&P 100 Companies," *Business and the Environment with ISO14000 Updates,* October 2008, pp. 5–6; and Graham Hubbard, "Measuring Organizational Performance: Beyond the Triple Bottom Line," *Business Strategy and the Environment,* March 2009, pp. 177–191.

---

[4] Lori Calabro. "On Balance: A CFO Interview," *CFO,* February 2001, pp. 73–78.

Summary

For purposes of evaluating performance, business units are classified as cost centers, profit centers, and investment centers. Cost and profit centers are commonly evaluated using standard cost and flexible budget variances as discussed in prior chapters. Investment centers are evaluated using the techniques discussed in this chapter.

Return on investment (ROI) and residual income and its cousin EVA are widely used to evaluate the performance of investment centers. ROI suffers from the underinvestment problem—managers are reluctant to invest in projects that would decrease their ROI but whose returns exceed the company's required rate of return. The residual income and EVA approaches solve this problem by giving managers full credit for any returns in excess of the company's required rate of return.

A balanced scorecard is an integrated system of performance measures designed to support an organization's strategy. The various measures in a balanced scorecard should be linked on a plausible cause-and-effect basis from the very lowest level up through the organization's ultimate objectives. The balanced scorecard is essentially a theory about how specific actions taken by various people in the organization will further the organization's objectives. The theory should be viewed as tentative and subject to change if the actions do not in fact result in improvements in the organization's financial and other goals. If the theory changes, then the performance measures on the balanced scorecard should also change. The balanced scorecard is a dynamic measurement system that evolves as an organization learns more about what works and what doesn't work and refines its strategy accordingly.

Review Problem: Return on Investment (ROI) and Residual Income

The Magnetic Imaging Division of Medical Diagnostics, Inc., has reported the following results for last year's operations:

Sales..........................	$25 million
Net operating income	$3 million
Average operating assets	$10 million

Required:

1. Compute the Magnetic Imaging Division's margin, turnover, and ROI.
2. Top management of Medical Diagnostics, Inc., has set a minimum required rate of return on average operating assets of 25%. What is the Magnetic Imaging Division's residual income for the year?

Solution to Review Problem

1. The required calculations follow:

$$\text{Margin} = \frac{\text{Net operating income}}{\text{Sales}}$$

$$= \frac{\$3,000,000}{\$25,000,000}$$

$$= 12\%$$

$$\text{Turnover} = \frac{\text{Sales}}{\text{Average operating assets}}$$

$$= \frac{\$25,000,000}{\$10,000,000}$$

$$= 2.5$$

$$\text{ROI} = \text{Margin} \times \text{Turnover}$$

$$= 12\% \times 2.5$$

$$= 30\%$$

2. The Magnetic Imaging Division's residual income is computed as follows:

Average operating assets.	$10,000,000
Net operating income.	$3,000,000
Minimum required return (25% × $10,000,000).	2,500,000
Residual income	$ 500,000

Glossary

Balanced scorecard An integrated set of performance measures that are derived from and support the organization's strategy. (p. 533)

Cost center A business segment whose manager has control over cost but has no control over revenue or investments in operating assets. (p. 523)

Decentralized organization An organization in which decision-making authority is not confined to a few top executives but rather is spread throughout the organization. (p. 522)

Delivery cycle time The elapsed time from receipt of a customer order to when the completed goods are shipped to the customer. (p. 530)

Economic Value Added (EVA®) A concept similar to residual income in which a variety of adjustments may be made to GAAP financial statements for performance evaluation purposes. (p. 527)

Investment center A business segment whose manager has control over cost, revenue, and investments in operating assets. (p. 523)

Manufacturing cycle efficiency (MCE) Process (value-added) time as a percentage of throughput time. (p. 532)

Margin Net operating income divided by sales. (p. 524)

Net operating income Income before interest and income taxes have been deducted. (p. 524)

Operating assets Cash, accounts receivable, inventory, plant and equipment, and all other assets held for operating purposes. (p. 524)

Profit center A business segment whose manager has control over cost and revenue but has no control over investments in operating assets. (p. 523)

Residual income The net operating income that an investment center earns above the minimum required return on its operating assets. (p. 527)

Responsibility center Any business segment whose manager has control over costs, revenues, or investments in operating assets. (p. 523)

Return on investment (ROI) Net operating income divided by average operating assets. It also equals margin multiplied by turnover. (p. 523)

Throughput time The amount of time required to turn raw materials into completed products. (p. 531)

Turnover Sales divided by average operating assets. (p. 524)

Questions

12–1 What is meant by the term *decentralization?*
12–2 What benefits result from decentralization?
12–3 Distinguish among a cost center, a profit center, and an investment center.
12–4 What is meant by the terms *margin* and *turnover* in ROI calculations?

12–5   What is meant by residual income?

12–6   In what way can the use of ROI as a performance measure for investment centers lead to bad decisions? How does the residual income approach overcome this problem?

12–7   What is the difference between delivery cycle time and throughput time? What four elements make up throughput time? What elements of throughput time are value-added and what elements are non–value-added?

12–8   What does a manufacturing cycle efficiency (MCE) of less than 1 mean? How would you interpret an MCE of 0.40?

12–9   Why do the measures used in a balanced scorecard differ from company to company?

12–10 Why does the balanced scorecard include financial performance measures as well as measures of how well internal business processes are doing?

Multiple-choice questions are available with Connect.

Applying Excel ☰ connect   Additional student resources are available with Connect.

LEARNING OBJECTIVES 12–1, 12–2

The Excel worksheet form that follows is to be used to recreate the Review Problem related to Medical Diagnostics, Inc. Download the workbook containing this from Connect. *On the website you will also receive instructions about how to use this worksheet form.*

	A	B	C	D	E
1	Chapter 12: Applying Excel				
2					
3	Data				
4	Sales	$25,000,000			
5	Net operating income	$3,000,000			
6	Average operating assets	$10,000,000			
7	Minimum required rate of return	25%			
8					
9	Enter a formula into each of the cells marked with a ? below				
10	Review Problem: Return on Investment (ROI) and Residual Income				
11					
12	Compute the ROI				
13	Margin	?			
14	Turnover	?			
15	ROI	?			
16					
17	Compute the residual income				
18	Average operating assets	?			
19	Net operating income	?			
20	Minimum required return	?			
21	Residual income	?			
22					

◄ ◄ ► ► Chapter 12 Form   Filled in Chapter 12 Form

You should proceed to the requirements below only after completing your worksheet.

Required:

1. Check your worksheet by changing the average operating assets in cell B6 to $8,000,000. The ROI should now be 38% and the residual income should now be $1,000,000. If you do not get these answers, find the errors in your worksheet and correct them.

    Explain why the ROI and the residual income both increase when the average operating assets decrease.

2. Revise the data in your worksheet as follows:

Data	
Sales..........................	$1,200
Net operating income	$72
Average operating assets.............	$500
Minimum required rate of return	15%

a. What is the ROI?
b. What is the residual income?
c. Explain the relationship between the ROI and the residual income?

Additional student resources are available with Connect. **The Foundational 15**

Westerville Company reported the following results from last year's operations:

LEARNING OBJECTIVES 12–1, 12–2

Sales.....................................	$1,000,000
Variable expenses	300,000
Contribution margin.....................	700,000
Fixed expenses..........................	500,000
Net operating income	$ 200,000
Average operating assets.................	$625,000

This year, the company has a $120,000 investment opportunity with the following cost and revenue characteristics:

Sales.....................................	$200,000
Contribution margin ratio	60% of sales
Fixed expenses..........................	$90,000

The company's minimum required rate of return is 15%.

Required:

1. What is last year's margin?
2. What is last year's turnover?
3. What is last year's return on investment (ROI)?
4. What is the margin related to this year's investment opportunity?
5. What is the turnover related to this year's investment opportunity?
6. What is the ROI related to this year's investment opportunity?
7. If the company pursues the investment opportunity and otherwise performs the same as last year, what margin will it earn this year?
8. If the company pursues the investment opportunity and otherwise performs the same as last year, what turnover will it earn this year?
9. If the company pursues the investment opportunity and otherwise performs the same as last year, what ROI will it earn this year?
10. If Westerville's chief executive officer will earn a bonus only if her ROI from this year exceeds her ROI from last year, would she pursue the investment opportunity? Would the owners of the company want her to pursue the investment opportunity?
11. What is last year's residual income?
12. What is the residual income of this year's investment opportunity?
13. If the company pursues the investment opportunity and otherwise performs the same as last year, what residual income will it earn this year?

14. If Westerville's chief executive officer will earn a bonus only if her residual income from this year exceeds her residual income from last year, would she pursue the investment opportunity?

15. Assume that the contribution margin ratio of the investment opportunity was 50% instead of 60%. If Westerville's chief executive officer will earn a bonus only if her residual income from this year exceeds her residual income from last year, would she pursue the investment opportunity? Would the owners of the company want her to pursue the investment opportunity?

Additional student resources are available with Connect.   **Exercises**

EXERCISE 12–1 Compute the Return on Investment (ROI) [LO 12–1]

Alyeska Services Company, a division of a major oil company, provides various services to the operators of the North Slope oil field in Alaska. Data concerning the most recent year appear below:

Sales.	$7,500,000
Net operating income	$600,000
Average operating assets	$5,000,000

Required:

1. Compute the margin for Alyeska Services Company.
2. Compute the turnover for Alyeska Services Company.
3. Compute the return on investment (ROI) for Alyeska Services Company.

EXERCISE 12–2 Residual Income [LO 12–2]

Juniper Design Ltd. of Manchester, England, is a company specializing in providing design services to residential developers. Last year the company had net operating income of $600,000 on sales of $3,000,000. The company's average operating assets for the year were $2,800,000 and its minimum required rate of return was 18%.

Required:

Compute the company's residual income for the year.

EXERCISE 12–3 Measures of Internal Business Process Performance [LO 12–3]

Management of Mittel Rhein AG of Köln, Germany, would like to reduce the amount of time between when a customer places an order and when the order is shipped. For the first quarter of operations during the current year the following data were reported:

Inspection time	0.3 days
Wait time (from order to start of production)	14.0 days
Process time	2.7 days
Move time	1.0 days
Queue time	5.0 days

Required:

1. Compute the throughput time.
2. Compute the manufacturing cycle efficiency (MCE) for the quarter.
3. What percentage of the throughput time was spent in non–value-added activities?
4. Compute the delivery cycle time.
5. If by using Lean Production all queue time during production is eliminated, what will be the new MCE?

EXERCISE 12–4 Building a Balanced Scorecard [LO 12–4]

Lost Peak ski resort was for many years a small, family-owned resort serving day skiers from nearby towns. Lost Peak was recently acquired by Western Resorts, a major ski resort operator. The new owners have plans to upgrade the resort into a destination resort for vacationers. As part of this plan, the new owners would like to make major improvements in the Powder 8 Lodge, the resort's on-the-hill cafeteria. The menu at the lodge is very limited—hamburgers, hot dogs, chili, tuna fish sandwiches, pizzas, french fries, and packaged snacks. With little competition, the previous owners of the resort had felt no urgency to upgrade the food service at the lodge. If skiers want lunch on the mountain, the only alternatives are the Powder 8 Lodge or a brown bag lunch brought from home.

As part of the deal when acquiring Lost Peak, Western Resorts agreed to retain all of the current employees of the resort. The manager of the lodge, while hardworking and enthusiastic, has very little experience in the restaurant business. The manager is responsible for selecting the menu, finding and training employees, and overseeing daily operations. The kitchen staff prepare food and wash dishes. The dining room staff take orders, serve as cashiers, and clean the dining room area.

Shortly after taking over Lost Peak, management of Western Resorts held a day-long meeting with all of the employees of the Powder 8 Lodge to discuss the future of the ski resort and the new management's plans for the lodge. At the end of this meeting, management and lodge employees created a balanced scorecard for the lodge that would help guide operations for the coming ski season. Almost everyone who participated in the meeting seemed to be enthusiastic about the scorecard and management's plans for the lodge.

The following performance measures were included on the balanced scorecard for the Powder 8 Lodge:
a. Weekly Powder 8 Lodge sales
b. Weekly Powder 8 Lodge profit
c. Number of menu items
d. Dining area cleanliness as rated by a representative from Western Resorts management
e. Customer satisfaction with menu choices as measured by customer surveys
f. Customer satisfaction with service as measured by customer surveys
g. Average time to take an order
h. Average time to prepare an order
i. Percentage of kitchen staff completing basic cooking course at the local community college
j. Percentage of dining room staff completing basic hospitality course at the local community college

Western Resorts will pay for the costs of staff attending courses at the local community college.

Required:
1. Using the above performance measures, construct a balanced scorecard for the Powder 8 Lodge. Use Exhibit 12–5 as a guide. Use arrows to show causal links and indicate with a + or − whether the performance measure should increase or decrease.
2. What hypotheses are built into the balanced scorecard for the Powder 8 Lodge? Which of these hypotheses do you believe are most questionable? Why?
3. How will management know if one of the hypotheses underlying the balanced scorecard is false?

EXERCISE 12–5 Return on Investment (ROI) [LO 12–1]
Provide the missing data in the following table for a distributor of martial arts products:

	Division		
	Alpha	Bravo	Charlie
Sales	$?	$11,500,000	$?
Net operating income	$?	$920,000	$210,000
Average operating assets	$800,000	$?	$?
Margin	4%	?	7%
Turnover	5	?	?
Return on investment (ROI)	?	20%	14%

EXERCISE 12–6 Contrasting Return on Investment (ROI) and Residual Income [LO 12–1, LO 12–2]

Meiji Isetan Corp. of Japan has two regional divisions with headquarters in Osaka and Yokohama. Selected data on the two divisions follow:

	Division	
	Osaka	Yokohama
Sales	$3,000,000	$9,000,000
Net operating income	$210,000	$720,000
Average operating assets	$1,000,000	$4,000,000

Required:

1. For each division, compute the return on investment (ROI) in terms of margin and turnover. Where necessary, carry computations to two decimal places.
2. Assume that the company evaluates performance using residual income and that the minimum required rate of return for any division is 15%. Compute the residual income for each division.
3. Is Yokohama's greater amount of residual income an indication that it is better managed? Explain.

EXERCISE 12–7 Creating a Balanced Scorecard [LO 12–4]

Ariel Tax Services prepares tax returns for individual and corporate clients. As the company has gradually expanded to 10 offices, the founder Max Jacobs has begun to feel as though he is losing control of operations. In response to this concern, he has decided to implement a performance measurement system that will help control current operations and facilitate his plans of expanding to 20 offices.

Jacobs describes the keys to the success of his business as follows:

"Our only real asset is our people. We must keep our employees highly motivated and we must hire the 'cream of the crop.' Interestingly, employee morale and recruiting success are both driven by the same two factors—compensation and career advancement. In other words, providing superior compensation relative to the industry average coupled with fast-track career advancement opportunities keeps morale high and makes us a very attractive place to work. It drives a high rate of job offer acceptances relative to job offers tendered."

"Hiring highly qualified people and keeping them energized ensures operational success, which in our business is a function of productivity, efficiency, and effectiveness. Productivity boils down to employees being billable rather than idle. Efficiency relates to the time required to complete a tax return. Finally, effectiveness is critical to our business in the sense that we cannot tolerate errors. Completing a tax return quickly is meaningless if the return contains errors."

"Our growth depends on acquiring new customers through word-of-mouth from satisfied repeat customers. We believe that our customers come back year after year because they value error-free, timely, and courteous tax return preparation. Common courtesy is an important aspect of our business! We call it service quality, and it all ties back to employee morale in the sense that happy employees treat their clients with care and concern."

"While sales growth is obviously important to our future plans, growth without a corresponding increase in profitability is useless. Therefore, we understand that increasing our profit margin is a function of cost-efficiency as well as sales growth. Given that payroll is our biggest expense, we must maintain an optimal balance between staffing levels and the revenue being generated. As I alluded to earlier, the key to maintaining this balance is employee productivity. If we can achieve cost-efficient sales growth, we should eventually have 20 profitable offices!"

Required:

1. Create a balanced scorecard for Ariel Tax Services. Link your scorecard measures using the framework from Exhibit 12–5. Indicate whether each measure is expected to increase or decrease. Feel free to create measures that may not be specifically mentioned in the chapter, but make sense given the strategic goals of the company.
2. What hypotheses are built into the balanced scorecard for Ariel Tax Services? Which of these hypotheses do you believe are most questionable and why?

3. Discuss the potential advantages and disadvantages of implementing an internal business process measure called *total dollar amount of tax refunds generated*. Would you recommend using this measure in Ariel's balanced scorecard?

4. Would it be beneficial to attempt to measure each office's individual performance with respect to the scorecard measures that you created? Why or why not?

EXERCISE 12–8 Computing and Interpreting Return on Investment (ROI) [LO 12–1]

Selected operating data for two divisions of Outback Brewing, Ltd., of Australia are given below:

	Division	
	Queensland	New South Wales
Sales..	$4,000,000	$7,000,000
Average operating assets........................	$2,000,000	$2,000,000
Net operating income	$360,000	$420,000
Property, plant, and equipment (net).............	$950,000	$800,000

Required:

1. Compute the rate of return for each division using the return on investment (ROI) formula stated in terms of margin and turnover.

2. Which divisional manager seems to be doing the better job? Why?

EXERCISE 12–9 Return on Investment (ROI) and Residual Income Relations [LO 12–1, LO 12–2]

A family friend has asked your help in analyzing the operations of three anonymous companies operating in the same service sector industry. Supply the missing data in the table below:

	Company		
	A	B	C
Sales...............................	$9,000,000	$7,000,000	$4,500,000
Net operating income	$?	$280,000	$?
Average operating assets............	$3,000,000	$?	$1,800,000
Return on investment (ROI)..........	18%	14%	?
Minimum required rate of return:			
Percentage	16%	?	15%
Dollar amount....................	$?	$320,000	$?
Residual income....................	$?	$?	$90,000

EXERCISE 12–10 Cost-Volume-Profit Analysis and Return on Investment (ROI) [LO 12–1]

Posters.com is a small Internet retailer of high-quality posters. The company has $1,000,000 in operating assets and fixed expenses of $150,000 per year. With this level of operating assets and fixed expenses, the company can support sales of up to $3,000,000 per year. The company's contribution margin ratio is 25%, which means that an additional dollar of sales results in additional contribution margin, and net operating income, of 25 cents.

Required:

1. Complete the following table showing the relation between sales and return on investment (ROI).

Sales	Net Operating Income	Average Operating Assets	ROI
$2,500,000	$475,000	$1,000,000	?
$2,600,000	$?	$1,000,000	?
$2,700,000	$?	$1,000,000	?
$2,800,000	$?	$1,000,000	?
$2,900,000	$?	$1,000,000	?
$3,000,000	$?	$1,000,000	?

2. What happens to the company's return on investment (ROI) as sales increase? Explain.

EXERCISE 12–11 Effects of Changes in Profits and Assets on Return on Investment (ROI) [LO 12–1]
Fitness Fanatics is a regional chain of health clubs. The managers of the clubs, who have authority to make investments as needed, are evaluated based largely on return on investment (ROI). The company's Springfield Club reported the following results for the past year:

Sales............................	$1,400,000
Net operating income.............	$70,000
Average operating assets..........	$350,000

Required:
The following questions are to be considered independently. Carry out all computations to two decimal places.
1. Compute the Springfield club's return on investment (ROI).
2. Assume that the manager of the club is able to increase sales by $70,000 and that, as a result, net operating income increases by $18,200. Further assume that this is possible without any increase in operating assets. What would be the club's return on investment (ROI)?
3. Assume that the manager of the club is able to reduce expenses by $14,000 without any change in sales or operating assets. What would be the club's return on investment (ROI)?
4. Assume that the manager of the club is able to reduce operating assets by $70,000 without any change in sales or net operating income. What would be the club's return on investment (ROI)?

EXERCISE 12–12 Evaluating New Investments Using Return on Investment (ROI) and Residual Income [LO 12–1, LO 12–2]
Selected sales and operating data for three divisions of different structural engineering firms are given as follows:

	Division A	Division B	Division C
Sales............................	$12,000,000	$14,000,000	$25,000,000
Average operating assets..........	$3,000,000	$7,000,000	$5,000,000
Net operating income	$600,000	$560,000	$800,000
Minimum required rate of return	14%	10%	16%

Required:
1. Compute the return on investment (ROI) for each division using the formula stated in terms of margin and turnover.
2. Compute the residual income for each division.
3. Assume that each division is presented with an investment opportunity that would yield a 15% rate of return.
   a. If performance is being measured by ROI, which division or divisions will probably accept the opportunity? Reject? Why?

b. If performance is being measured by residual income, which division or divisions will probably accept the opportunity? Reject? Why?

EXERCISE 12–13 Effects of Changes in Sales, Expenses, and Assets on ROI [LO 12–1]

CommercialServices.com Corporation provides business-to-business services on the Internet. Data concerning the most recent year appear below:

Sales	$3,000,000
Net operating income.	$150,000
Average operating assets	$750,000

Required:

Consider each question below independently. Carry out all computations to two decimal places.

1. Compute the company's return on investment (ROI).
2. The entrepreneur who founded the company is convinced that sales will increase next year by 50% and that net operating income will increase by 200%, with no increase in average operating assets. What would be the company's ROI?
3. The chief financial officer of the company believes a more realistic scenario would be a $1,000,000 increase in sales, requiring a $250,000 increase in average operating assets, with a resulting $200,000 increase in net operating income. What would be the company's ROI in this scenario?

Additional student resources are available with Connect.   **Problems**

PROBLEM 12–14 Measures of Internal Business Process Performance [LO 12–3]

DataSpan, Inc., automated its plant at the start of the current year and installed a flexible manufacturing system. The company is also evaluating its suppliers and moving toward Lean Production. Many adjustment problems have been encountered, including problems relating to performance measurement. After much study, the company has decided to use the performance measures below, and it has gathered data relating to these measures for the first four months of operations.

	Month			
	1	2	3	4
Throughput time (days)	?	?	?	?
Delivery cycle time (days)	?	?	?	?
Manufacturing cycle efficiency (MCE)	?	?	?	?
Percentage of on-time deliveries	91%	86%	83%	79%
Total sales (units).	3,210	3,072	2,915	2,806

Management has asked for your help in computing throughput time, delivery cycle time, and MCE. The following average times have been logged over the last four months:

	Average per Month (in days)			
	1	2	3	4
Move time per unit	0.4	0.3	0.4	0.4
Process time per unit	2.1	2.0	1.9	1.8
Wait time per order before start of production	16.0	17.5	19.0	20.5
Queue time per unit	4.3	5.0	5.8	6.7
Inspection time per unit	0.6	0.7	0.7	0.6

Required:

1. For each month, compute the following:
    a.   The throughput time.
    b.   The MCE.
    c.   The delivery cycle time.
2. Evaluate the company's performance over the last four months.
3. Refer to the move time, process time, and so forth, given above for month 4.
    a.   Assume that in month 5 the move time, process time, and so forth, are the same as in month 4, except that through the use of Lean Production the company is able to completely eliminate the queue time during production. Compute the new throughput time and MCE.
    b.   Assume in month 6 that the move time, process time, and so forth, are again the same as in month 4, except that the company is able to completely eliminate both the queue time during production and the inspection time. Compute the new throughput time and MCE.

PROBLEM 12–15 Return on Investment (ROI) and Residual Income [LO 12–1, LO 12–2]

Financial data for Joel de Paris, Inc., for last year follow:

	Joel de Paris, Inc. Balance Sheet	
	Beginning Balance	Ending Balance
Assets		
Cash	$ 140,000	$ 120,000
Accounts receivable....................	450,000	530,000
Inventory	320,000	380,000
Plant and equipment, net	680,000	620,000
Investment in Buisson, S.A.	250,000	280,000
Land (undeveloped)	180,000	170,000
Total assets	$2,020,000	$2,100,000
Liabilities and Stockholders' Equity		
Accounts payable.......................	$ 360,000	$ 310,000
Long-term debt	1,500,000	1,500,000
Stockholders' equity....................	160,000	290,000
Total liabilities and stockholders' equity...	$2,020,000	$2,100,000

	Joel de Paris, Inc. Income Statement	
Sales		$4,050,000
Operating expenses....................		3,645,000
Net operating income..................		405,000
Interest and taxes:		
Interest expense	$150,000	
Tax expense.........................	110,000	260,000
Net income............................		$ 145,000

The company paid dividends of $15,000 last year. The "Investment in Buisson, S.A.," on the balance sheet represents an investment in the stock of another company.

Required:

1. Compute the company's margin, turnover, and return on investment (ROI) for last year.

2. The board of directors of Joel de Paris, Inc., has set a minimum required rate of return of 15%. What was the company's residual income last year?

PROBLEM 12–16 Creating a Balanced Scorecard [LO 12–4]

Mason Paper Company (MPC) manufactures commodity grade papers for use in computer printers and photocopiers. MPC has reported net operating losses for the last two years due to intense price pressure from much larger competitors. The MPC management team—including Kristen Townsend (CEO), Mike Martinez (vice president of Manufacturing), Tom Andrews (vice president of Marketing), and Wendy Chen (CFO)—is contemplating a change in strategy to save the company from impending bankruptcy. Excerpts from a recent management team meeting are shown below:

Townsend: As we all know, the commodity paper manufacturing business is all about economies of scale. The largest competitors with the lowest cost per unit win. The limited capacity of our older machines prohibits us from competing in the high-volume commodity paper grades. Furthermore, expanding our capacity by acquiring a new paper-making machine is out of the question given the extraordinarily high price tag. Therefore, I propose that we abandon cost reduction as a strategic goal and instead pursue manufacturing flexibility as the key to our future success.

Chen: Manufacturing flexibility? What does that mean?

Martinez: It means we have to abandon our "crank out as many tons of paper as possible" mentality. Instead, we need to pursue the low-volume business opportunities that exist in the nonstandard, specialized paper grades. To succeed in this regard, we'll need to improve our flexibility in three ways. First, we must improve our ability to switch between paper grades. Right now, we require an average of four hours to change over to another paper grade. Timely customer deliveries are a function of changeover performance. Second, we need to expand the range of paper grades that we can manufacture. Currently, we can only manufacture three paper grades. Our customers must perceive that we are a "one-stop shop" that can meet all of their paper grade needs. Third, we will need to improve our yields (e.g., tons of acceptable output relative to total tons processed) in the nonstandard paper grades. Our percentage of waste within these grades will be unacceptably high unless we do something to improve our processes. Our variable costs will go through the roof if we cannot increase our yields!

Chen: Wait just a minute! These changes are going to destroy our equipment utilization numbers!

Andrews: You're right Wendy; however, equipment utilization is not the name of the game when it comes to competing in terms of flexibility. Our customers don't care about our equipment utilization. Instead, as Mike just alluded to, they want just-in-time delivery of smaller quantities of a full range of paper grades. If we can shrink the elapsed time from order placement to order delivery and expand our product offerings, it will increase sales from current customers and bring in new customers. Furthermore, we will be able to charge a premium price because of the limited competition within this niche from our cost-focused larger competitors. Our contribution margin per ton should drastically improve!

Martinez: Of course, executing the change in strategy will not be easy. We'll need to make a substantial investment in training because ultimately it is our people who create our flexible manufacturing capabilities.

Chen: If we adopt this new strategy, it is definitely going to impact how we measure performance. We'll need to create measures that motivate our employees to make decisions that support our flexibility goals.

Townsend: Wendy, you hit the nail right on the head. For our next meeting, could you pull together some potential measures that support our new strategy?

Required:

1. Contrast MPC's previous manufacturing strategy with its new manufacturing strategy.
2. Generally speaking, why would a company that changes its strategic goals need to change its performance measurement system as well? What are some examples of measures that would have been appropriate for MPC prior to its change in strategy? Why would those measures fail to support MPC's new strategy?

3. Construct a balanced scorecard that would support MPC's new manufacturing strategy. Use arrows to show the causal links between the performance measures and show whether the performance measure should increase or decrease over time. Feel free to create measures that may not be specifically mentioned in the chapter, but nonetheless make sense given the strategic goals of the company.
4. What hypotheses are built into MPC's balanced scorecard? Which of these hypotheses do you believe are most questionable and why?

PROBLEM 12–17 Comparison of Performance Using Return on Investment (ROI) [LO 12–1]
Comparative data on three companies in the same service industry are given below:

	Company		
	A	B	C
Sales.........................	$600,000	$500,000	$?
Net operating income	$84,000	$70,000	$?
Average operating assets.............	$300,000	$?	$1,000,000
Margin	?	?	3.5%
Turnover...........................	?	?	2
ROI	?	7%	?

Required:
1. What advantages are there to breaking down the ROI computation into two separate elements, margin and turnover?
2. Fill in the missing information above, and comment on the relative performance of the three companies in as much detail as the data permit. Make *specific recommendations* about how to improve the ROI.

(Adapted from National Association of Accountants, *Research Report No. 35,* p. 34)

PROBLEM 12–18 Return on Investment (ROI) and Residual Income [LO 12–1, LO 12–2]
"I know headquarters wants us to add that new product line," said Dell Havasi, manager of Billings Company's Office Products Division. "But I want to see the numbers before I make any move. Our division's return on investment (ROI) has led the company for three years, and I don't want any letdown."

Billings Company is a decentralized wholesaler with five autonomous divisions. The divisions are evaluated on the basis of ROI, with year-end bonuses given to the divisional managers who have the highest ROIs. Operating results for the company's Office Products Division for the most recent year are given below:

	Total
Sales	$10,000,000
Variable expenses..................	6,000,000
Contribution margin	4,000,000
Fixed expenses	3,200,000
Net operating income...............	$ 800,000
Divisional operating assets	$ 4,000,000

The company had an overall return on investment (ROI) of 15% last year (considering all divisions). The Office Products Division has an opportunity to add a new product line that would require an additional investment in operating assets of $1,000,000. The cost and revenue characteristics of the new product line per year would be:

Sales	$2,000,000
Variable expenses	60% of sales
Fixed expenses	$640,000

Required:

1. Compute the Office Products Division's ROI for the most recent year; also compute the ROI as it would appear if the new product line is added.
2. If you were in Dell Havasi's position, would you accept or reject the new product line? Explain.
3. Why do you suppose headquarters is anxious for the Office Products Division to add the new product line?
4. Suppose that the company's minimum required rate of return on operating assets is 12% and that performance is evaluated using residual income.
    a. Compute the Office Products Division's residual income for the most recent year; also compute the residual income as it would appear if the new product line is added.
    b. Under these circumstances, if you were in Dell Havasi's position, would you accept or reject the new product line? Explain.

PROBLEM 12–19 Internal Business Process Performance Measures [LO 12–3]

Tombro Industries is in the process of automating one of its plants and developing a flexible manufacturing system. The company is finding it necessary to make many changes in operating procedures. Progress has been slow, particularly in trying to develop new performance measures for the factory.

In an effort to evaluate performance and determine where improvements can be made, management has gathered the following data relating to activities over the last four months:

	Month			
	1	2	3	4
Quality control measures:				
Number of defects	185	163	124	91
Number of warranty claims	46	39	30	27
Number of customer complaints	102	96	79	58
Material control measures:				
Purchase order lead time	8 days	7 days	5 days	4 days
Scrap as a percent of total cost	1%	1%	2%	3%
Machine performance measures:				
Machine downtime as a percentage of availability	3%	4%	4%	6%
Use as a percentage of availability	95%	92%	89%	85%
Setup time (hours)	8	10	11	12
Delivery performance measures:				
Throughput time	?	?	?	?
Manufacturing cycle efficiency (MCE)	?	?	?	?
Delivery cycle time	?	?	?	?
Percentage of on-time deliveries	96%	95%	92%	89%

The president has read in industry journals that throughput time, MCE, and delivery cycle time are important measures of performance, but no one is sure how they are computed. You have been asked to assist the company, and you have gathered the following data relating to these measures:

	Average per Month (in days)			
	1	2	3	4
Wait time per order before start of production............	9.0	11.5	12.0	14.0
Inspection time per unit	0.8	0.7	0.7	0.7
Process time per unit	2.1	2.0	1.9	1.8
Queue time per unit	2.8	4.4	6.0	7.0
Move time per unit	0.3	0.4	0.4	0.5

Required:

1. For each month, compute the following performance measures:
   a. Throughput time.
   b. MCE.
   c. Delivery cycle time.
2. Using the performance measures given in the main body of the problem and the performance measures computed in requirement 1, do the following:
   a. Identify areas where the company seems to be improving.
   b. Identify areas where the company seems to be deteriorating.
3. Refer to the inspection time, process time, and so forth, given for month 4.
   a. Assume that in month 5 the inspection time, process time, and so forth, are the same as for month 4, except that the company is able to completely eliminate the queue time during production using Lean Production. Compute the new throughput time and MCE.
   b. Assume that in month 6 the inspection time, process time, and so forth, are the same as in month 4, except that the company is able to eliminate both the queue time during production and the inspection time using Lean Production. Compute the new throughput time and MCE.

PROBLEM 12–20 Return on Investment (ROI) Analysis [LO 12–1]

The contribution format income statement for Huerra Company for last year is given below:

	Total	Unit
Sales...........................	$4,000,000	$80.00
Variable expenses	2,800,000	56.00
Contribution margin................	1,200,000	24.00
Fixed expenses....................	840,000	16.80
Net operating income	360,000	7.20
Income taxes @ 30%	108,000	2.16
Net operating income	$ 252,000	$ 5.04

The company had average operating assets of $2,000,000 during the year.

Required:

1. Compute the company's return on investment (ROI) for the period using the ROI formula stated in terms of margin and turnover.

   For each of the following questions, indicate whether the margin and turnover will increase, decrease, or remain unchanged as a result of the events described, and then compute the new ROI figure. Consider each question separately, starting in each case from the data used to compute the original ROI in requirement 1.
2. Using Lean Production, the company is able to reduce the average level of inventory by $400,000. (The released funds are used to pay off short-term creditors.)
3. The company achieves a cost savings of $32,000 per year by using less costly materials.
4. The company issues bonds and uses the proceeds to purchase $500,000 in machinery and equipment at the beginning of the period. Interest on the bonds is $60,000 per year. Sales remain unchanged. The new, more efficient equipment reduces production costs by $20,000 per year.
5. As a result of a more intense effort by salespeople, sales are increased by 20%; operating assets remain unchanged.

6. Obsolete inventory carried on the books at a cost of $40,000 is scrapped and written off as a loss.
7. The company uses $200,000 of cash (received on accounts receivable) to repurchase and retire some of its common stock.

PROBLEM 12–21 Creating Balanced Scorecards that Support Different Strategies [LO 12–4]

The Midwest Consulting Group (MCG) helps companies build balanced scorecards. As part of its marketing efforts, MCG conducts an annual balanced scorecard workshop for prospective clients. As MCG's newest employee, your boss has asked you to participate in this year's workshop by explaining to attendees how a company's strategy determines the measures that are appropriate for its balanced scorecard. Your boss has provided you with the excerpts below from the annual reports of two current MCG clients. She has asked you to use these excerpts in your portion of the workshop.

Excerpt from Applied Pharmaceuticals' annual report:

The keys to our business are consistent and timely new product introductions and manufacturing process integrity. The new product introduction side of the equation is a function of research and development (R&D) yield (e.g., the number of marketable drug compounds created relative to the total number of potential compounds pursued). We seek to optimize our R&D yield and first-to-market capability by investing in state-of-the-art technology, hiring the highest possible percentage of the "best and the brightest" engineers that we pursue, and providing world-class training to those engineers. Manufacturing process integrity is all about establishing world-class quality specifications and then relentlessly engaging in prevention and appraisal activities to minimize defect rates. Our customers must have an awareness of and respect for our brand image of being "first to market and first in quality." If we deliver on this pledge to our customers, then our financial goal of increasing our return on stockholders' equity should take care of itself.

Excerpt from Destination Resorts International's annual report:

Our business succeeds or fails based on the quality of the service that our front-line employees provide to customers. Therefore, it is imperative that we strive to maintain high employee morale and minimize employee turnover. In addition, it is critical that we train our employees to use technology to create one seamless worldwide experience for our repeat customers. Once an employee enters a customer preference (e.g., provide two extra pillows in the room, deliver fresh brewed coffee to the room at 8:00 A.M., etc.) into our database, our worldwide workforce strives to ensure that a customer will never need to repeat it at any of our destination resorts. If we properly train and retain a motivated workforce, we should see continuous improvement in our percentage of error-free repeat customer check-ins, the time taken to resolve customer complaints, and our independently assessed room cleanliness. This in turn should drive improvement in our customer retention, which is the key to meeting our revenue growth goals.

Required:
1. Based on the excerpts above, compare and contrast the strategies of Applied Pharmaceuticals and Destination Resorts International.
2. Select balanced scorecard measures for each company and link the scorecard measures using the framework from Exhibit 12–5. Use arrows to show the causal links between the performance measures and show whether the performance measure should increase or decrease over time. Feel free to create measures that may not be specifically mentioned in the chapter, but nonetheless make sense given the strategic goals of each company.
3. What hypotheses are built into each balanced scorecard? Why do the hypotheses differ between the two companies?

PROBLEM 12–22 Perverse Effects of Some Performance Measures [LO 12–4]

There is often more than one way to improve a performance measure. Unfortunately, some of the actions taken by managers to make their performance look better may actually harm the organization. For example, suppose the marketing department is held responsible only for increasing the performance measure "total revenues." Increases in total revenues may be achieved by working harder and smarter, but they can also usually be achieved by simply cutting prices. The increase in volume from cutting prices almost always results in greater total revenues; however, it does not always lead to greater total profits. Those who design performance measurement systems need to keep in mind that managers who are under pressure to perform may take actions to improve performance measures that have negative consequences elsewhere.

Required:

For each of the following situations, describe actions that managers might take to show improvement in the performance measure but which do not actually lead to improvement in the organization's overall performance.

1. Concerned with the slow rate at which new products are brought to market, top management of a consumer electronics company introduces a new performance measure—speed-to-market. The research and development department is given responsibility for this performance measure, which measures the average amount of time a product is in development before it is released to the market for sale.

2. The CEO of an airline company is dissatisfied with the amount of time that her ground crews are taking to unload luggage from airplanes. To solve the problem, she decides to measure the average elapsed time from when an airplane parks at the gate to when all pieces of luggage are unloaded from the airplane. For each month that an airport's ground crew can lower its "average elapsed time" relative to the prior month, the CEO pays a lump-sum bonus to be split equally among members of the crew.

3. A manufacturing company has been plagued by the chronic failure to ship orders to customers by the promised date. To solve this problem, the production manager has been given the responsibility of increasing the percentage of orders shipped on time. When a customer calls in an order, the production manager and the customer agree to a delivery date. If the order is not completed by that date, it is counted as a late shipment.

4. Concerned with the productivity of employees, the board of directors of a large multinational corporation has dictated that the manager of each subsidiary will be held responsible for increasing the revenue per employee of his or her subsidiary.

 Cases   Additional student resources are available with Connect.

CASE 12–23 Balanced Scorecard [LO 12–4]

Haglund Department Store is located in the downtown area of a small city. While the store had been profitable for many years, it is facing increasing competition from large national chains that have set up stores on the outskirts of the city. Recently the downtown area has been undergoing revitalization, and the owners of Haglund Department Store are somewhat optimistic that profitability can be restored.

In an attempt to accelerate the return to profitability, management of Haglund Department Store is in the process of designing a balanced scorecard for the company. Management believes the company should focus on two key problems. First, customers are taking longer and longer to pay the bills they incur using the department store's charge card, and the company has far more bad debts than are normal for the industry. If this problem were solved, the company would have more cash to make much needed renovations. Investigation has revealed that much of the problem with late payments and unpaid bills results from customers disputing incorrect charges on their bills. These incorrect charges usually occur because salesclerks incorrectly enter data on the charge account slip. Second, the company has been incurring large losses on unsold seasonal apparel. Such items are ordinarily resold at a loss to discount stores that specialize in such distress items.

The meeting in which the balanced scorecard approach was discussed was disorganized and ineffectively led—possibly because no one other than one of the vice presidents had read anything about how to build a balanced scorecard. Nevertheless, a number of potential performance measures were suggested by various managers. These potential performance measures are:

a. Percentage of charge account bills containing errors.

b. Percentage of salesclerks trained to correctly enter data on charge account slips.

c. Average age of accounts receivables.

d. Profit per employee.

e. Customer satisfaction with accuracy of charge account bills from monthly customer survey.

f. Total sales revenue.

g. Sales per employee.

h. Travel expenses for buyers for trips to fashion shows.

i. Unsold inventory at the end of the season as a percentage of total cost of sales.

j. Courtesy shown by junior staff members to senior staff members based on surveys of senior staff.

k. Percentage of suppliers making just-in-time deliveries.

l. Sales per square foot of floor space.

m. Written-off accounts receivable (bad debts) as a percentage of sales.

n. Quality of food in the staff cafeteria based on staff surveys.

o. Percentage of employees who have attended the city's cultural diversity workshop.

p. Total profit.

Required:

1. As someone with more knowledge of the balanced scorecard than almost anyone else in the company, you have been asked to build an integrated balanced scorecard. In your scorecard, use only performance measures listed previously. You do not have to use all of the performance measures suggested by the managers, but you should build a balanced scorecard that reveals a strategy for dealing with the problems with accounts receivable and with unsold merchandise. Construct the balanced scorecard following the format used in Exhibit 12–5. Do not be concerned with whether a specific performance measure falls within the learning and growth, internal business process, customer, or financial perspective. However, use arrows to show the causal links between performance measures within your balanced scorecard and explain whether the performance measures should show increases or decreases.

2. Assume that the company adopts your balanced scorecard. After operating for a year, some performance measures show improvements, but not others. What should management do next?

3. a. Suppose that customers express greater satisfaction with the accuracy of their charge account bills but the performance measures for the average age of accounts receivable and for bad debts do not improve. Explain why this might happen.

    b. Suppose that the performance measures for the average age of accounts receivable, bad debts, and unsold inventory improve, but total profits do not. Explain why this might happen. Assume in your answer that the explanation lies within the company.

Appendix 12A: Transfer Pricing

Divisions in a company often supply goods and services to other divisions within the same company. For example, the truck division of Toyota supplies trucks to other Toyota divisions to use in their operations. When the divisions are evaluated based on their profit, ROI, or residual income, a price must be established for such a transfer—otherwise, the division that produces the good or service will receive no credit. The price in such a situation is called a *transfer price*. A **transfer price** is the price charged when one segment of a company provides goods or services to another segment of the same company. For example, most companies in the oil industry, such as Shell, have petroleum refining and retail sales divisions that are evaluated on the basis of ROI or residual income. The petroleum refining division processes crude oil into gasoline, kerosene, lubricants, and other end products. The retail sales division takes gasoline and other products from the refining division and sells them through the company's chain of service stations. Each product has a price for transfers within the company. Suppose the transfer price for gasoline is $0.80 a gallon. Then the refining division gets credit for $0.80 a gallon of revenue on its segment report and the retailing division must deduct $0.80 a gallon as an expense on its segment report. Clearly, the refining division would like the transfer price to be as high as possible, whereas the retailing division would like the transfer price to be as low as possible. However, the transaction has no direct effect on the entire company's reported profit. It is like taking money out of one pocket and putting it into the other.

Managers are intensely interested in how transfer prices are set because they can have a dramatic effect on the reported profitability of their divisions. Three common approaches are used to set transfer prices:

1. Allow the managers involved in the transfer to negotiate the transfer price.
2. Set transfer prices at cost using either variable cost or full (absorption) cost.
3. Set transfer prices at the market price.

We will consider each of these transfer pricing methods in turn, beginning with negotiated transfer prices. Throughout the discussion, keep in mind that *the fundamental objective in setting transfer prices is to motivate the managers to act in the best interests of the overall company.* In contrast, **suboptimization** occurs when managers do not act in the best interests of the overall company or even in the best interests of their own division.

Negotiated Transfer Prices

LEARNING OBJECTIVE 12–5
Determine the range, if any, within which a negotiated transfer price should fall.

A **negotiated transfer price** results from discussions between the selling and buying divisions. Negotiated transfer prices have several important advantages. First, this approach preserves the autonomy of the divisions and is consistent with the spirit of decentralization. Second, the managers of the divisions are likely to have much better information about the potential costs and benefits of the transfer than others in the company.

When negotiated transfer prices are used, the managers who are involved in a proposed transfer within the company meet to discuss the terms and conditions of the transfer. They may decide not to go through with the transfer, but if they do, they must agree to a transfer price. Generally speaking, we cannot predict what transfer price they will agree to. However, we can confidently predict two things: (1) the selling division will agree to the transfer only if its profits increase as a result of the transfer, and (2) the buying division will agree to the transfer only if its profits also increase as a result of the transfer. This may seem obvious, but it is an important point.

Clearly, if the transfer price is below the selling division's cost, the selling division will incur a loss on the transaction and it will refuse to agree to the transfer. Likewise, if the transfer price is set too high, it will be impossible for the buying division to make any profit on the transferred item. For any given proposed transfer, the transfer price has both a lower limit (determined by the situation of the selling division) and an upper limit (determined by the situation of the buying division). The actual transfer price agreed to by the two division managers can fall anywhere between those two limits. These limits determine the **range of acceptable transfer prices**—the range of transfer prices within which the profits of both divisions participating in a transfer would increase.

An example will help us to understand negotiated transfer prices. Harris & Louder, Ltd., owns fast-food restaurants and snack food and beverage manufacturers in the United Kingdom. One of the restaurants, Pizza Maven, serves a variety of beverages along with pizzas. One of the beverages is ginger beer, which is served on tap. Harris & Louder has just purchased a new division, Imperial Beverages, that produces ginger beer. The managing director of Imperial Beverages has approached the managing director of Pizza Maven about purchasing Imperial Beverages' ginger beer to sell at Pizza Maven restaurants rather than its usual brand of ginger beer. Managers at Pizza Maven agree that the quality of Imperial Beverages' ginger beer is comparable to the quality of their regular brand. It is just a question of price. The basic facts are as follows:

Imperial Beverages:

Ginger beer production capacity per month	10,000 barrels
Variable cost per barrel of ginger beer	$8 per barrel
Fixed costs per month	$70,000
Selling price of Imperial Beverages ginger beer on the outside market	$20 per barrel

Pizza Maven:

Purchase price of regular brand of ginger beer.	$18 per barrel
Monthly consumption of ginger beer.	2,000 barrels

The Selling Division's Lowest Acceptable Transfer Price The selling division, Imperial Beverages, will be interested in a proposed transfer only if its profit increases. Clearly, the transfer price must not fall below the variable cost per barrel of $8. In addition, if Imperial Beverages does not have sufficient capacity to fill the Pizza Maven order while supplying its regular customers, then it would have to sacrifice some of its regular sales. Imperial Beverages would expect to be compensated for the contribution margin on any lost sales. In sum, if the transfer has no effect on fixed costs, then from the selling division's standpoint, the transfer price must cover both the variable costs of producing the transferred units and any opportunity costs from lost sales.

Seller's perspective:

$$\frac{\text{Transfer}}{\text{price}} \geq \frac{\text{Variable cost}}{\text{per unit}} + \frac{\text{Total contribution margin on lost sales}}{\text{Number of units transferred}}$$

The Buying Division's Highest Acceptable Transfer Price The buying division, Pizza Maven, will be interested in a transfer only if its profit increases. In cases like this where a buying division has an outside supplier, the buying division's decision is simple. Buy from the inside supplier if the price is less than the price offered by the outside supplier.

Purchaser's perspective:

$$\text{Transfer price} \leq \text{Cost of buying from outside supplier}$$

Or, if an outside supplier does not exist:

$$\text{Transfer price} \leq \text{Profit to be earned per unit sold (not including the transfer price)}$$

We will consider several different hypothetical situations and see what the range of acceptable transfer prices would be in each situation.

Selling Division with Idle Capacity Suppose that Imperial Beverages has sufficient idle capacity to satisfy Pizza Maven's demand for ginger beer without sacrificing sales of ginger beer to its regular customers. To be specific, let's suppose that Imperial Beverages is selling only 7,000 barrels of ginger beer a month on the outside market. That leaves unused capacity of 3,000 barrels a month—more than enough to satisfy Pizza Maven's requirement of 2,000 barrels a month. What range of transfer prices, if any, would make both divisions better off with the transfer of 2,000 barrels a month?

1. The selling division, Imperial Beverages, will be interested in the transfer only if:

$$\frac{\text{Transfer}}{\text{price}} \geq \frac{\text{Variable cost}}{\text{per unit}} + \frac{\text{Total contribution margin on lost sales}}{\text{Number of units transferred}}$$

Because Imperial Beverages has enough idle capacity, there are no lost outside sales. And because the variable cost per unit is $8, the lowest acceptable transfer price for the selling division is $8.

$$\text{Transfer price} \geq \$8 + \frac{\$0}{2,000} = \$8$$

2. The buying division, Pizza Maven, can buy similar ginger beer from an outside vendor for $18. Therefore, Pizza Maven would be unwilling to pay more than $18 per barrel for Imperial Beverages' ginger beer.

$$\text{Transfer price} \leq \text{Cost of buying from outside supplier} = \$18$$

3. Combining the requirements of both the selling division and the buying division, the acceptable range of transfer prices in this situation is:

$$\$8 \leq \text{Transfer price} \leq \$18$$

Assuming that the managers understand their own businesses and that they are cooperative, they should be able to agree on a transfer price within this range.

Selling Division with No Idle Capacity Suppose that Imperial Beverages has *no* idle capacity; it is selling 10,000 barrels of ginger beer a month on the outside market at $20 per barrel. To fill the order from Pizza Maven, Imperial Beverages would have to divert 2,000 barrels from its regular customers. What range of transfer prices, if any, would make both divisions better off transferring the 2,000 barrels within the company?

1. The selling division, Imperial Beverages, will be interested in the transfer only if:

$$\text{Transfer price} \geq \frac{\text{Variable cost}}{\text{per unit}} + \frac{\text{Total contribution margin on lost sales}}{\text{Number of units transferred}}$$

Because Imperial Beverages has no idle capacity, there *are* lost outside sales. The contribution margin per barrel on these outside sales is $12 ($20 − $8).

$$\text{Transfer price} \geq \$8 + \frac{(\$20 - \$8) \times 2,000}{2,000} = \$8 + (\$20 - \$8) - \$20$$

Thus, as far as the selling division is concerned, the transfer price must at least cover the revenue on the lost sales, which is $20 per barrel. This makes sense because the cost of producing the 2,000 barrels is the same whether they are sold on the inside market or on the outside. The only difference is that the selling division loses the revenue of $20 per barrel if it transfers the barrels to Pizza Maven.

2. As before, the buying division, Pizza Maven, would be unwilling to pay more than the $18 per barrel it is already paying for similar ginger beer from its regular supplier.

$$\text{Transfer price} \leq \text{Cost of buying from outside supplier} = \$18$$

3. Therefore, the selling division would insist on a transfer price of at least $20. But the buying division would refuse any transfer price above $18. It is impossible to satisfy both division managers simultaneously; there can be no agreement on a transfer price and no transfer will take place. Is this good? The answer is yes. From the standpoint of the entire company, the transfer doesn't make sense. Why give up sales of $20 to save costs of $18?

Basically, the transfer price is a mechanism for dividing between the two divisions any profit the entire company earns as a result of the transfer. If the company as a whole loses money on the transfer, there will be no profit to divide up, and it will be impossible for the two divisions to come to an agreement. On the other hand, if the company as a whole makes money on the transfer, there will be a profit to share, and it will always be possible for the two divisions to find a mutually agreeable transfer price that increases the profits of both divisions. If the pie is bigger, it is always possible to divide it up in such a way that everyone has a bigger piece.

Selling Division Has Some Idle Capacity Suppose now that Imperial Beverages is selling 9,000 barrels of ginger beer a month on the outside market. Pizza Maven can only sell one kind of ginger beer on tap. It cannot buy 1,000 barrels from Imperial Beverages and 1,000 barrels from its regular supplier; it must buy all of its ginger beer from one source.

To fill the entire 2,000-barrel a month order from Pizza Maven, Imperial Beverages would have to divert 1,000 barrels from its regular customers who are paying $20 per barrel. The other 1,000 barrels can be made using idle capacity. What range of transfer prices, if any, would make both divisions better off transferring the 2,000 barrels within the company?

1. As before, the selling division, Imperial Beverages, will insist on a transfer price that at least covers its variable cost and opportunity cost:

$$\text{Transfer price} \geq \frac{\text{Variable cost}}{\text{per unit}} + \frac{\text{Total contribution margin on lost sales}}{\text{Number of units transferred}}$$

Because Imperial Beverages does not have enough idle capacity to fill the entire order for 2,000 barrels, there *are* lost outside sales. The contribution margin per barrel on the 1,000 barrels of lost outside sales is $12 ($20 − $8).

$$\text{Transfer price} \geq \$8 + \frac{(\$20 - \$8) \times 2,000}{2,000} = \$8 + (\$20 - \$8) = \$20$$

Thus, as far as the selling division is concerned, the transfer price must cover the variable cost of $8 plus the average opportunity cost of lost sales of $6.

2. As before, the buying division, Pizza Maven, would be unwilling to pay more than the $18 per barrel it pays its regular supplier.

$$\text{Transfer price} \leq \text{Cost of buying from outside supplier} = \$18$$

3. Combining the requirements for both the selling and buying divisions, the range of acceptable transfer prices is:

$$\$14 \leq \text{Transfer price} \leq \$18$$

Again, assuming that the managers understand their own businesses and that they are cooperative, they should be able to agree on a transfer price within this range.

No Outside Supplier If Pizza Maven has no outside supplier for the ginger beer, the highest price the buying division would be willing to pay depends on how much the buying division expects to make on the transferred units—excluding the transfer price. If, for example, Pizza Maven expects to earn $30 per barrel of ginger beer after paying its own expenses, then it should be willing to pay up to $30 per barrel to Imperial Beverages. Remember, however, that this assumes Pizza Maven cannot buy ginger beer from other sources.

Evaluation of Negotiated Transfer Prices As discussed earlier, if a transfer within the company would result in higher overall profits for the company, there is always a range of transfer prices within which both the selling and buying division would also have higher profits if they agree to the transfer. Therefore, if the managers understand their own businesses and are cooperative, then they should always be able to agree on a transfer price if it is in the best interests of the company that they do so.

Unfortunately, not all managers understand their own businesses and not all managers are cooperative. As a result, negotiations often break down even when it would be in the managers' own best interests to come to an agreement. Sometimes that is the fault of the way managers are evaluated. If managers are pitted against each other rather than against their own past performance or reasonable benchmarks, a noncooperative atmosphere is almost guaranteed. Nevertheless, even with the best performance evaluation system, some people by nature are not cooperative.

Given the disputes that often accompany the negotiation process, many companies rely on some other means of setting transfer prices. Unfortunately, as we will see below, all of the alternatives to negotiated transfer prices have their own serious drawbacks.

Transfers at the Cost to the Selling Division

Many companies set transfer prices at either the variable cost or full (absorption) cost incurred by the selling division. Although the cost approach to setting transfer prices is relatively simple to apply, it has some major defects.

First, the use of cost—particularly full cost—as a transfer price can lead to bad decisions and thus suboptimization. Return to the example involving the ginger beer. The full cost of ginger beer can never be less than $15 per barrel ($8 per barrel variable cost + $7 per barrel fixed cost at capacity). What if the cost of buying the ginger beer from an outside supplier is less than $15—for example, $14 per barrel? If the transfer price were set at full cost, then Pizza Maven would never want to buy ginger beer from Imperial Beverages because it could buy its ginger beer from an outside supplier at a lower price. However, from the standpoint of the company as a whole, ginger beer should be transferred from Imperial Beverages to Pizza Maven whenever Imperial Beverages has idle capacity. Why? Because when Imperial Beverages has idle capacity, it only costs the company $8 in variable cost to produce a barrel of ginger beer, but it costs $14 per barrel to buy from outside suppliers.

Second, if cost is used as the transfer price, the selling division will never show a profit on any internal transfer. The only division that shows a profit is the division that makes the final sale to an outside party.

Third, cost-based prices do not provide incentives to control costs. If the actual costs of one division are simply passed on to the next, there is little incentive for anyone to work to reduce costs. This problem can be overcome by using standard costs rather than actual costs for transfer prices.

Despite these shortcomings, cost-based transfer prices are often used in practice. Advocates argue that they are easily understood and convenient to use.

Transfers at Market Price

Some form of competitive **market price** (i.e., the price charged for an item on the open market) is sometimes advocated as the best approach to the transfer pricing problem—particularly if transfer price negotiations routinely become bogged down.

The market price approach is designed for situations in which there is an *outside market* for the transferred product or service; the product or service is sold in its present form to outside customers. If the selling division has no idle capacity, the market price is the correct choice for the transfer price. This is because, from the company's perspective, the real cost of the transfer is the opportunity cost of the lost revenue on the outside sale. Whether the item is transferred internally or sold on the outside market, the production costs are exactly the same. If the market price is used as the transfer price, the selling division manager will not lose anything by making the transfer, and the buying division manager will get the correct signal about how much it really costs the company for the transfer to take place.

While the market price works well when the selling division has no idle capacity, difficulties occur when the selling division has idle capacity. Recalling once again the ginger beer example, the outside market price for the ginger beer produced by Imperial Beverages is $20 per barrel. However, Pizza Maven can purchase all of the ginger beer it wants from outside suppliers for $18 per barrel. Why would Pizza Maven ever buy from Imperial Beverages if Pizza Maven is forced to pay Imperial Beverages' market price? In some market price-based transfer pricing schemes, the transfer price would be lowered to $18, the outside vendor's market price, and Pizza Maven would be directed to buy from Imperial Beverages as long as Imperial Beverages is willing to sell. This scheme can work reasonably well, but a drawback is that managers at Pizza Maven will regard the cost of ginger beer as $18 rather than the $8, which is the real cost to the company when the selling division has idle capacity. Consequently, the managers of Pizza Maven will make pricing and other decisions based on an incorrect cost.

Unfortunately, none of the possible solutions to the transfer pricing problem are perfect—not even market-based transfer prices.

Divisional Autonomy and Suboptimization

The principles of decentralization suggest that companies should grant managers autonomy to set transfer prices and to decide whether to sell internally or externally. It may be very difficult for top managers to accept this principle when their subordinate managers are about to make a suboptimal decision. However, if top management intervenes, the purposes of decentralization are defeated. Furthermore, to impose the correct transfer price, top managers would have to know details about the buying and selling divisions' outside market, variable costs, and capacity utilization. The whole premise of decentralization is that local managers have access to better information for operational decisions than top managers at corporate headquarters.

Of course, if a division manager consistently makes suboptimal decisions, the performance of the division will suffer. The offending manager's compensation will be adversely affected and promotion will become less likely. Thus, a performance evaluation system based on divisional profits, ROI, or residual income provides some built-in checks and balances. Nevertheless, if top managers wish to create a culture of autonomy and independent profit responsibility, they must allow their subordinate managers to control their own destiny—even to the extent of granting their managers the right to make mistakes.

International Aspects of Transfer Pricing

The objectives of transfer pricing change when a multinational corporation is involved and the goods and services being transferred cross international borders. In this context, the objectives of international transfer pricing focus on minimizing taxes, duties, and foreign exchange risks, along with enhancing a company's competitive position and improving its relations with foreign governments. Although domestic objectives such as managerial motivation and divisional autonomy are always important, they often become secondary when international transfers are involved. Companies will focus instead on charging a transfer price that reduces its total tax bill or that strengthens a foreign subsidiary.

For example, charging a low transfer price for parts shipped to a foreign subsidiary may reduce customs duty payments as the parts cross international borders, or it may help the subsidiary to compete in foreign markets by keeping the subsidiary's costs low. On the other hand, charging a high transfer price may help a multinational corporation draw profits out of a country that has stringent controls on foreign remittances, or it may allow a multinational corporation to shift income from a country that has high income tax rates to a country that has low rates.

Review Problem: Transfer Pricing

Situation A

Collyer Products, Inc., has a Valve Division that manufactures and sells a standard valve:

Capacity in units	100,000
Selling price to outside customers.	$30
Variable costs per unit	$16
Fixed costs per unit (based on capacity)	$9

The company has a Pump Division that could use this valve in one of its pumps. The Pump Division is currently purchasing 10,000 valves per year from an overseas supplier at a cost of $29 per valve.

Required:
1. Assume that the Valve Division has enough idle capacity to handle all of the Pump Division's needs. What is the acceptable range, if any, for the transfer price between the two divisions?
2. Assume that the Valve Division is selling all of the valves that it can produce to outside customers. What is the acceptable range, if any, for the transfer price between the two divisions?
3. Assume again that the Valve Division is selling all of the valves that it can produce to outside customers. Also assume that $3 in variable expenses can be avoided on transfers within the company, due to reduced selling costs. What is the acceptable range, if any, for the transfer price between the two divisions?

Solution to Situation A

1. Because the Valve Division has idle capacity, it does not have to give up any outside sales to take on the Pump Division's business. Applying the formula for the lowest acceptable transfer price from the viewpoint of the selling division, we get:

$$\text{Transfer price} \geq \frac{\text{Variable cost}}{\text{per unit}} + \frac{\text{Total contribution margin on lost sales}}{\text{Number of units transferred}}$$

$$\text{Transfer price} \geq \$16 + \frac{\$0}{10,000} = \$16$$

The Pump Division would be unwilling to pay more than $29, the price it is currently paying an outside supplier for its valves. Therefore, the transfer price must fall within the range:

$$\$16 \leq \text{Transfer price} \leq \$29$$

2. Because the Valve Division is selling all of the valves that it can produce on the outside market, it would have to give up some of these outside sales to take on the Pump Division's business. Thus, the Valve Division has an opportunity cost, which is the total contribution margin on lost sales:

$$\text{Transfer price} \geq \frac{\text{Variable cost}}{\text{per unit}} + \frac{\text{Total contribution margin on lost sales}}{\text{Number of units transferred}}$$

$$\text{Transfer price} \geq \$16 + \frac{(\$30 - \$16) \times 10,000}{10,000} = \$16 + \$14 = \$30$$

Because the Pump Division can purchase valves from an outside supplier at only $29 per unit, no transfers will be made between the two divisions.

3. Applying the formula for the lowest acceptable transfer price from the viewpoint of the selling division, we get:

$$\text{Transfer price} \geq \frac{\text{Variable cost}}{\text{per unit}} + \frac{\text{Total contribution margin on lost sales}}{\text{Number of units transferred}}$$

$$\text{Transfer price} \geq (\$16 - \$3) + \frac{(\$30 - \$16) \times 10,000}{10,000} = \$16 + \$14 = \$30$$

In this case, the transfer price must fall within the range:

$$\$27 \leq \text{Transfer price} \leq \$29$$

Situation B

Refer to the original data in situation A above. Assume that the Pump Division needs 20,000 special high-pressure valves per year. The Valve Division's variable costs to manufacture and ship the special valve would be $20 per unit. To produce these special valves, the Valve Division would have to reduce its production and sales of regular valves from 100,000 units per year to 70,000 units per year.

Required:
As far as the Valve Division is concerned, what is the lowest acceptable transfer price?

Solution to Situation B

To produce the 20,000 special valves, the Valve Division will have to give up sales of 30,000 regular valves to outside customers. Applying the formula for the lowest acceptable transfer price from the viewpoint of the selling division, we get:

$$\text{Transfer price} \geq \frac{\text{Variable cost}}{\text{per unit}} + \frac{\text{Total contribution margin on lost sales}}{\text{Number of units transferred}}$$

$$\text{Transfer price} \geq \$20 + \frac{(\$30 - \$16) \times 30,000}{20,000} = \$20 + \$21 = \$41$$

Glossary (Appendix 12A)

Market price The price charged for an item on the open market. (p. 562)
Negotiated transfer price A transfer price agreed on between buying and selling divisions. (p. 558)
Range of acceptable transfer prices The range of transfer prices within which the profits of both the selling division and the buying division would increase as a result of a transfer. (p. 558)
Suboptimization An overall level of profits that is less than a segment or a company is capable of earning. (p. 558)
Transfer price The price charged when one division or segment provides goods or services to another division or segment of an organization. (p. 557)

■ connect Appendix 12A Exercises and Problems

Additional student resources are available with Connect.

EXERCISE 12A–1 Transfer Pricing Basics [LO 12–5]
Sako Company's Audio Division produces a speaker that is used by manufacturers of various audio products. Sales and cost data on the speaker follow:

Selling price per unit on the intermediate market	$60
Variable costs per unit	$42
Fixed costs per unit (based on capacity)	$8
Capacity in units	25,000

Sako Company has a Hi-Fi Division that could use this speaker in one of its products. The Hi-Fi Division will need 5,000 speakers per year. It has received a quote of $57 per speaker from another manufacturer. Sako Company evaluates division managers on the basis of divisional profits.

Required:
1. Assume that the Audio Division is now selling only 20,000 speakers per year to outside customers.
   a. From the standpoint of the Audio Division, what is the lowest acceptable transfer price for speakers sold to the Hi-Fi Division?
   b. From the standpoint of the Hi-Fi Division, what is the highest acceptable transfer price for speakers acquired from the Audio Division?

    c.   If left free to negotiate without interference, would you expect the division managers to voluntarily agree to the transfer of 5,000 speakers from the Audio Division to the Hi-Fi Division? Why or why not?

    d.   From the standpoint of the entire company, should the transfer take place? Why or why not?

2. Assume that the Audio Division is selling all of the speakers it can produce to outside customers.

    a.   From the standpoint of the Audio Division, what is the lowest acceptable transfer price for speakers sold to the Hi-Fi Division?

    b.   From the standpoint of the Hi-Fi Division, what is the highest acceptable transfer price for speakers acquired from the Audio Division?

    c.   If left free to negotiate without interference, would you expect the division managers to voluntarily agree to the transfer of 5,000 speakers from the Audio Division to the Hi-Fi Division? Why or why not?

    d.   From the standpoint of the entire company, should the transfer take place? Why or why not?

EXERCISE 12A–2 Transfer Pricing from the Viewpoint of the Entire Company [LO 12–5]

Division A manufactures electronic circuit boards. The boards can be sold either to Division B of the same company or to outside customers. Last year, the following activity occurred in Division A:

Selling price per circuit board	$125
Variable cost per circuit board	$90
Number of circuit boards:	
Produced during the year	20,000
Sold to outside customers	16,000
Sold to Division B	4,000

Sales to Division B were at the same price as sales to outside customers. The circuit boards purchased by Division B were used in an electronic instrument manufactured by that division (one board per instrument). Division B incurred $100 in additional variable cost per instrument and then sold the instruments for $300 each.

Required:

1. Prepare income statements for Division A, Division B, and the company as a whole.

2. Assume that Division A's manufacturing capacity is 20,000 circuit boards. Next year, Division B wants to purchase 5,000 circuit boards from Division A rather than 4,000. (Circuit boards of this type are not available from outside sources.) From the standpoint of the company as a whole, should Division A sell the 1,000 additional circuit boards to Division B or continue to sell them to outside customers? Explain.

EXERCISE 12A–3 Transfer Pricing Situations [LO 12–5]

In each of the cases below, assume that Division X has a product that can be sold either to outside customers or to Division Y of the same company for use in its production process. The managers of the divisions are evaluated based on their divisional profits.

	Case A	Case B
Division X:		
Capacity in units	200,000	200,000
Number of units being sold to outside customers	200,000	160,000
Selling price per unit to outside customers	$90	$75
Variable costs per unit	$70	$60
Fixed costs per unit (based on capacity)	$13	$8
Division Y:		
Number of units needed for production	40,000	40,000
Purchase price per unit now being paid to an outside supplier	$86	$74

Required:

1. Refer to the data in case A above. Assume in this case that $3 per unit in variable selling costs can be avoided on intracompany sales. If the managers are free to negotiate and make decisions on their own, will a transfer take place? If so, within what range will the transfer price fall? Explain.
2. Refer to the data in case B above. In this case, there will be no savings in variable selling costs on intracompany sales. If the managers are free to negotiate and make decisions on their own, will a transfer take place? If so, within what range will the transfer price fall? Explain.

PROBLEM 12A–4 Transfer Price with an Outside Market [LO 12–5]

Hrubec Products, Inc., operates a Pulp Division that manufactures wood pulp for use in the production of various paper goods. Revenue and costs associated with a ton of pulp follow:

Selling price		$70
Expenses:		
Variable.	$42	
Fixed (based on a capacity of		
50,000 tons per year)	18	60
Net operating income.		$10

   Hrubec Products has just acquired a small company that manufactures paper cartons. This company will be treated as a division of Hrubec with full profit responsibility. The newly formed Carton Division is currently purchasing 5,000 tons of pulp per year from a supplier at a cost of $70 per ton, less a 10% purchase discount. Hrubec's president is anxious for the Carton Division to begin purchasing its pulp from the Pulp Division if an acceptable transfer price can be worked out.

Required:

For requirements 1 and 2, assume that the Pulp Division can sell all of its pulp to outside customers for $70 per ton.

1. Are the managers of the Carton and Pulp Divisions likely to voluntarily agree to a transfer price for 5,000 tons of pulp next year? Why or why not?
2. If the Pulp Division meets the price that the Carton Division is currently paying to its supplier and sells 5,000 tons of pulp to the Carton Division each year, what will be the effect on the profits of the Pulp Division, the Carton Division, and the company as a whole?

For requirements 3–6, assume that the Pulp Division is currently selling only 30,000 tons of pulp each year to outside customers at the stated $70 price.

3. Are the managers of the Carton and Pulp Divisions likely to voluntarily agree to a transfer price for 5,000 tons of pulp next year? Why or why not?
4. Suppose that the Carton Division's outside supplier drops its price (net of the purchase discount) to only $59 per ton. Should the Pulp Division meet this price? Explain. If the Pulp Division does *not* meet the $59 price, what will be the effect on the profits of the company as a whole?
5. Refer to requirement 4. If the Pulp Division refuses to meet the $59 price, should the Carton Division be required to purchase from the Pulp Division at a higher price for the good of the company as a whole?
6. Refer to requirement 4. Assume that due to inflexible management policies, the Carton Division is required to purchase 5,000 tons of pulp each year from the Pulp Division at $70 per ton. What will be the effect on the profits of the company as a whole?

PROBLEM 12A–5 Market-Based Transfer Price [LO 12–5]

Stavos Company's Screen Division manufactures a standard screen for high-definition televisions (HDTVs). The cost per screen is:

Variable cost per screen.	$ 70
Fixed cost per screen*	30
Total cost per screen	$100

*Based on a capacity of 10,000 screens per year.

Part of the Screen Division's output is sold to outside manufacturers of HDTVs and part is sold to Stavos Company's Quark Division, which produces an HDTV under its own name. The Screen Division charges $140 per screen for all sales.

The costs, revenue, and net operating income associated with the Quark Division's HDTV are given below:

Selling price per unit..............................		$480
Variable cost per unit:		
Cost of the screen............................	$140	
Variable cost of electronic parts.................	210	
Total variable costs		350
Contribution margin		130
Fixed costs per unit...............................		80*
Net operating income per unit		$ 50

*Based on a capacity of 3,000 units per year.

The Quark Division has an order from an overseas source for 1,000 HDTVs. The overseas source wants to pay only $340 per unit.

Required:
1. Assume that the Quark Division has enough idle capacity to fill the 1,000-unit order. Is the division likely to accept the $340 price or to reject it? Explain.
2. Assume that both the Screen Division and the Quark Division have idle capacity. Under these conditions, would it be advantageous for the company as a whole if the Quark Division rejects the $340 price? Show computations to support your answer.
3. Assume that the Quark Division has idle capacity but that the Screen Division is operating at capacity and could sell all of its screens to outside manufacturers. Compute the profit impact to the Quark Division of accepting the 1,000-unit order at the $340 unit price.
4. What conclusions do you draw concerning the use of market price as a transfer price in intra-company transactions?

PROBLEM 12A–6 Basic Transfer Pricing [LO 12–5]
Alpha and Beta are divisions within the same company. The managers of both divisions are evaluated based on their own division's return on investment (ROI). Assume the following information relative to the two divisions:

	Case			
	1	2	3	4
Alpha Division:				
Capacity in units	80,000	400,000	150,000	300,000
Number of units now being sold to outside				
customers.................................	80,000	400,000	100,000	300,000
Selling price per unit to outside customers	$30	$90	$75	$50
Variable costs per unit......................	$18	$65	$40	$26
Fixed costs per unit (based on capacity)	$6	$15	$20	$9
Beta Division:				
Number of units needed annually	5,000	30,000	20,000	120,000
Purchase price now being paid to an outside				
supplier....................................	$27	$89	$75*	—

*Before any purchase discount.

Managers are free to decide if they will participate in any internal transfers. All transfer prices are negotiated.

Required:

1. Refer to case 1 shown above. Alpha Division can avoid $2 per unit in commissions on any sales to Beta Division. Will the managers agree to a transfer, and if so, within what range will the transfer price be? Explain.

2. Refer to case 2 shown above. A study indicates that Alpha Division can avoid $5 per unit in shipping costs on any sales to Beta Division.

   a. Would you expect any disagreement between the two divisional managers over what the transfer price should be? Explain.

   b. Assume that Alpha Division offers to sell 30,000 units to Beta Division for $88 per unit and that Beta Division refuses this price. What will be the loss in potential profits for the company as a whole?

3. Refer to case 3 shown above. Assume that Beta Division is now receiving an 8% price discount from the outside supplier.

   a. Will the managers agree to a transfer? If so, what is the range within which the transfer price would be?

   b. Assume that Beta Division offers to purchase 20,000 units from Alpha Division at $60 per unit. If Alpha Division accepts this price, would you expect its ROI to increase, decrease, or remain unchanged? Why?

4. Refer to case 4 shown above. Assume that Beta Division wants Alpha Division to provide it with 120,000 units of a *different* product from the one that Alpha Division is now producing. The new product would require $21 per unit in variable costs and would require that Alpha Division cut back production of its present product by 45,000 units annually. What is the lowest acceptable transfer price from Alpha Division's perspective?

CASE 12A–7 Transfer Pricing; Divisional Performance [LO 12–5]

Weller Industries is a decentralized organization with six divisions. The company's Electrical Division produces a variety of electrical items, including an X52 electrical fitting. The Electrical Division (which is operating at capacity) sells this fitting to its regular customers for $7.50 each; the fitting has a variable manufacturing cost of $4.25.

The company's Brake Division has asked the Electrical Division to supply it with a large quantity of X52 fittings for only $5 each. The Brake Division, which is operating at 50% of capacity, will put the fitting into a brake unit that it will produce and sell to a large commercial airline manufacturer. The cost of the brake unit being built by the Brake Division follows:

Purchased parts (from outside vendors)	$22.50
Electrical fitting X52	5.00
Other variable costs	14.00
Fixed overhead and administration	8.00
Total cost per brake unit	$49.50

Although the $5 price for the X52 fitting represents a substantial discount from the regular $7.50 price, the manager of the Brake Division believes that the price concession is necessary if his division is to get the contract for the airplane brake units. He has heard "through the grapevine" that the airplane manufacturer plans to reject his bid if it is more than $50 per brake unit. Thus, if the Brake Division is forced to pay the regular $7.50 price for the X52 fitting, it will either not get the contract or it will suffer a substantial loss at a time when it is already operating at only 50% of capacity. The manager of the Brake Division argues that the price concession is imperative to the well-being of both his division and the company as a whole.

Weller Industries uses return on investment (ROI) to measure divisional performance.

Required:

1. Assume that you are the manager of the Electrical Division. Would you recommend that your division supply the X52 fitting to the Brake Division for $5 each as requested? Why or why not? Show all computations.

2. Would it be profitable for the company as a whole for the Electrical Division to supply the fittings to the Brake Division if the airplane brakes can be sold for $50? Show all computations, and explain your answer.

3. In principle, should it be possible for the two managers to agree to a transfer price in this particular situation? If so, within what range would that transfer price lie?
4. Discuss the organizational behavior problems, if any, inherent in this situation. What would you advise the company's president to do in this situation?

(CMA, adapted)

Appendix 12B: Service Department Charges

LEARNING OBJECTIVE 12–6
Charge operating departments for services provided by service departments.

Most large organizations have both *operating departments* and *service departments*. The central purposes of the organization are carried out in the **operating departments**. In contrast, **service departments** do not directly engage in operating activities. Instead, they provide services or assistance to the operating departments. Examples of service departments include Cafeteria, Internal Auditing, Human Resources, Cost Accounting, and Purchasing.

Service department costs are charged to operating departments for a variety of reasons, including:

- To encourage operating departments to make wise use of service department resources. If the services were provided for free, operating managers would be inclined to waste these resources.
- To provide operating departments with more complete cost data for making decisions. Actions taken by operating departments have impacts on service department costs. For example, hiring another employee will increase costs in the human resources department. Such service department costs should be charged to the operating departments, otherwise the operating departments will not take them into account when making decisions.
- To help measure the profitability of operating departments. Charging service department costs to operating departments provides a more complete accounting of the costs incurred as a consequence of activities in the operating departments.
- To create an incentive for service departments to operate efficiently. Charging service department costs to operating departments provides a system of checks and balances in the sense that cost-conscious operating departments will take an active interest in keeping service department costs low.

In Appendix 12A, we discussed *transfer prices* that are charged within an organization when one part of an organization provides a product to another part of the organization. The service department charges considered in this appendix can be viewed as transfer prices that are charged for services provided by service departments to operating departments.

Charging Costs by Behavior

Whenever possible, variable and fixed service department costs should be charged to operating departments separately to provide more useful data for planning and control of departmental operations.

Variable Costs

Variable costs vary in total in proportion to changes in the level of service provided. For example, the cost of food in a cafeteria is a variable cost that varies in proportion to the number of persons using the cafeteria or the number of meals served.

A variable cost should be charged to consuming departments according to whatever activity causes the incurrence of the cost. For example, variable costs of a maintenance department that are caused by the number of machine-hours worked in the operating departments should be charged to the operating departments on the basis of machine-hours. This will ensure that these costs are properly traced to departments, products, and customers.

Fixed Costs

The fixed costs of service departments represent the costs of making capacity available for use. These costs should be charged to consuming departments in *predetermined lump-sum amounts* that are determined in advance and do not change. The lump-sum amount charged to a department can be based either on the department's peak-period or long-run average servicing needs.

The logic behind lump-sum charges of this type is as follows: When a service department is first established, its capacity will be determined by the needs of the departments that it will serve. This capacity may reflect the peak-period needs of the other departments, or it may reflect their long-run average or "normal" servicing needs. Depending on how much servicing capacity is provided for, it will be necessary to make a commitment of resources, which will be reflected in the service department's fixed costs. These fixed costs should be borne by the consuming departments in proportion to the amount of capacity each consuming department requires. That is, if available capacity in the service department has been provided to meet the peak-period needs of consuming departments, then the fixed costs of the service department should be charged in predetermined lump-sum amounts to consuming departments on that basis. If available capacity has been provided only to meet "normal" or long-run average needs, then the fixed costs should be charged on that basis.

Once set, charges should not vary from period to period, because they represent the cost of having a certain level of service capacity available for each operating department. The fact that an operating department does not need the peak level or even the "normal" level of service every period is immaterial; the capacity to deliver this level of service must be available. The operating departments should bear the cost of that availability.

Should Actual or Budgeted Costs Be Charged?

The *budgeted,* rather than actual, costs of a service department should be charged to operating departments. This ensures that service departments remain solely responsible for explaining any differences between their actual and budgeted costs. If service departments could base their charges on actual costs, then operating departments would be unfairly held accountable for cost overruns in the service departments.

Guidelines for Service Department Charges

The following summarizes how service department costs should be charged to operating departments:
- Variable and fixed service department costs should be charged separately.
- Variable service department costs should be charged using a predetermined rate applied to the actual quantity of services consumed.
- Fixed costs represent the costs of having service capacity available. These costs should be charged in lump sums to each operating department in proportion to their peak-period needs or long-run average needs. The lump-sum amounts should be based on budgeted fixed costs, not actual fixed costs.

Example

Seaboard Airlines has two operating divisions: a Freight Division and a Passenger Division. The company has a Maintenance Department that services both divisions. Variable servicing costs are budgeted at $10 per flight-hour. The department's fixed costs are budgeted at $750,000 for the year. The fixed costs of the Maintenance Department are budgeted based on the peak-period demand, which occurs during the Thanksgiving to New Year's holiday period. The airline wants to make sure that none of its aircraft are grounded during this key period due to unavailability of maintenance facilities. Approximately 40% of the maintenance during this period is performed on the Freight Division's equipment, and 60% is performed on the Passenger Division's equipment. These figures and the budgeted flight-hours for the coming year are as follows:

	Percent of Peak Period Capacity Required	Budgeted Flight-Hours
Freight Division	40%	9,000
Passenger Division	60	15,000
Total.	100%	24,000

Year-end records show that actual variable and fixed costs in the aircraft Maintenance Department for the year were $260,000 and $780,000, respectively. One division logged more flight-hours during the year than planned, and the other division logged fewer flight-hours than planned, as shown below:

	Flight-Hours	
	Budgeted	Actual
Freight Division	9,000	8,000
Passenger Division	15,000	17,000
Total flight-hours	24,000	25,000

The amount of Maintenance Department cost charged to each division for the year would be as follows:

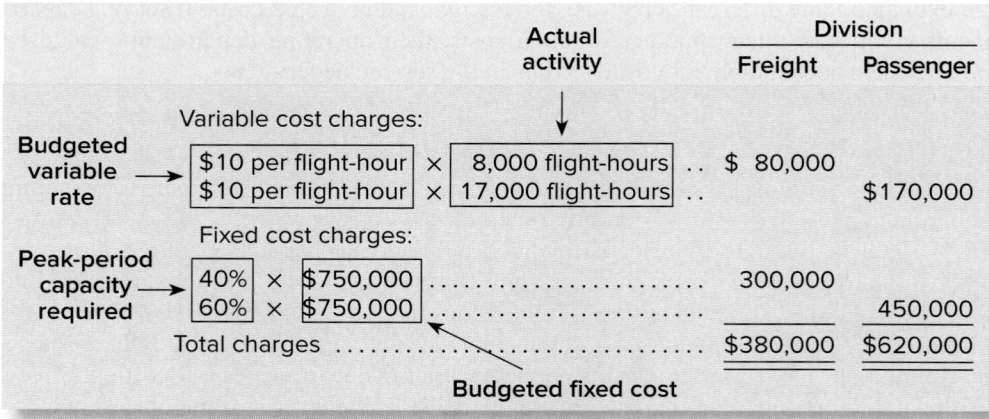

Notice that variable servicing costs are charged to the operating divisions based on the budgeted rate ($10 per hour) and the *actual activity* for the year. In contrast, the charges for fixed costs are based entirely on budgeted data. Also note that the two operating divisions are *not* charged for the actual costs of the service department, which are influenced by how well the service department is managed. Instead, the service department is held responsible for the actual costs not charged to other departments as shown below:

	Variable	Fixed
Total actual costs incurred	$260,000	$780,000
Total charges to operating departments	250,000*	750,000
Spending variance—responsibility of the Maintenance Department	$ 10,000	$ 30,000

*$10 per flight-hour × 25,000 actual flight-hours = $250,000.

Some Cautions in Allocating Service Department Costs

Pitfalls in Allocating Fixed Costs

Rather than charge fixed costs to operating departments in predetermined lump-sum amounts, some companies allocate them using a *variable* allocation base that fluctuates from period to period. This practice can distort decisions and create serious inequities between departments. The inequities arise from the fact that the fixed costs allocated to one department are heavily influenced by what happens in *other* departments.

Sales dollars is an example of a variable allocation base that is often used to allocate fixed costs from service departments to operating departments. Using sales dollars as a base is simple, straightforward, and easy to work with. Furthermore, people tend to view sales dollars as a measure of ability to pay, and, hence, as a measure of how readily costs can be absorbed from other parts of the organization.

Unfortunately, sales dollars are often a very poor base for allocating or charging costs because sales dollars vary from period to period, whereas the costs are often largely *fixed.* Therefore, a letup in sales effort in one department will shift allocated costs from that department to other, more successful departments. In effect, the departments putting forth the best sales efforts are penalized in the form of higher allocations. The result is often bitterness and resentment on the part of the managers of the better departments.

For example, let's assume that a large men's clothing store has one service department and three sales departments—Suits, Shoes, and Accessories. The service department's costs total $60,000 per period and are allocated to the three sales departments according to sales dollars. A recent period showed the following allocation:

	Departments			
	Suits	Shoes	Accessories	Total
Sales by department.	$260,000	$40,000	$100,000	$400,000
Percentage of total sales	65%	10%	25%	100%
Allocation of service department costs, based on percentage of total sales.	$39,000	$6,000	$15,000	$60,000

In the following period, let's assume the manager of the Suits Department launched a successful program to expand sales in his department by $100,000. Furthermore, let's assume that sales in the other two departments remained unchanged, total service department costs remained unchanged, and the sales departments' expected usage of service department resources remained unchanged. Given these assumptions, the service department cost allocations to the sales departments would change as shown below:

| | Departments | | | |
	Suits	Shoes	Accessories	Total
Sales by department.............	$360,000	$40,000	$100,000	$500,000
Percentage of total sales..........	72%	8%	20%	100%
Allocation of service department costs, based on percentage of total sales.....................	$43,200	$4,800	$12,000	$60,000
Increase (or decrease) from prior allocation.................	$4,200	$(1,200)	$(3,000)	$0

After seeing these allocations, the manager of the Suits Department is likely to complain, because by growing sales in his department, he is being forced to carry a larger share of the service department costs. In essence, this manager is being punished for his outstanding performance by being saddled with a greater proportion of service department costs. On the other hand, the managers of the departments that showed no sales growth are being relieved of a portion of the costs they had been carrying. Yet, there was no change in the amount of services provided for any department across the two periods.

This example shows why a variable allocation base such as sales dollars should only be used as a base for allocating or charging costs in those cases where service department costs actually vary with the chosen allocation base. When service department costs are fixed, they should be charged to operating departments according to the guidelines mentioned earlier.

Glossary (Appendix 12B)

Operating department A department in which the central purposes of the organization are carried out. (p. 570)

Service department A department that does not directly engage in operating activities; rather, it provides services or assistance to the operating departments. (p. 570)

Appendix 12B Exercises and Problems   connect

Additional student resources are available with Connect.

EXERCISE 12B–1 Service Department Charges [LO 12–6]
Hannibal Steel Company has a Transport Services Department that provides trucks to haul ore from the company's mine to its two steel mills—the Northern Plant and the Southern Plant. Budgeted costs for the Transport Services Department total $350,000 per year, consisting of $0.25 per ton variable cost and $300,000 fixed cost. The level of fixed cost is determined by peak-period requirements. During the peak period, the Northern Plant requires 70% of the Transport Services Department's capacity and the Southern Plant requires 30%.

During the year, the Transport Services Department actually hauled the following amounts of ore for the two plants: Northern Plant, 130,000 tons; Southern Plant, 50,000 tons. The Transport Services Department incurred $364,000 in cost during the year, of which $54,000 was variable cost and $310,000 was fixed cost.

Required:
1. Determine how much of the $54,000 in variable cost should be charged to each plant.
2. Determine how much of the $310,000 in fixed cost should be charged to each plant.
3. Should any of the $364,000 in the Transport Services Department cost not be charged to the plants? Explain.

EXERCISE 12B–2 Sales Dollars as an Allocation Base for Fixed Costs [LO 12–6]

Konig Enterprises, Ltd., owns and operates three restaurants in Vancouver, B.C. The company allocates its fixed administrative expenses to the three restaurants on the basis of sales dollars. During 2013, the fixed administrative expenses totaled $2,000,000. These expenses were allocated as follows:

	Restaurants			
	Rick's Harborside	Imperial Garden	Ginger Wok	Total
Total sales—2013...........	$16,000,000	$15,000,000	$9,000,000	$40,000,000
Percentage of total sales....	40%	37.5%	22.5%	100%
Allocation (based on the above percentages)	$800,000	$750,000	$450,000	$2,000,000

During 2014, the following year, the Imperial Garden restaurant increased its sales by $10 million. The sales levels in the other two restaurants remained unchanged. The company's 2014 sales data were as follows:

	Restaurants			
	Rick's Harborside	Imperial Garden	Ginger Wok	Total
Total sales—2014...........	$16,000,000	$25,000,000	$9,000,000	$50,000,000
Percentage of total sales....	32%	50%	18%	100%

Fixed administrative expenses remained unchanged at $2,000,000 during 2014.

Required:
1. Using sales dollars as an allocation base, show the allocation of the fixed administrative expenses among the three restaurants for 2014.
2. Compare your allocation from requirement 1 to the allocation for 2013. As the manager of the Imperial Garden, how would you feel about the amount that has been charged to you for 2014?
3. Comment on the usefulness of sales dollars as an allocation base.

EXERCISE 12B–3 Service Department Charges [LO 12–6]

Korvanis Corporation operates a Medical Services Department for its employees. Charges to the company's operating departments for the variable costs of the Medical Services Department are based on the actual number of employees in each department. Charges for the fixed costs of the Medical Services Department are based on the long-run average number of employees in each operating department.

Variable Medical Services Department costs are budgeted at $80 per employee. Fixed Medical Services Department costs are budgeted at $400,000 per year. Actual Medical Services Department costs for the most recent year were $41,000 for variable costs and $408,000 for fixed costs. Data concerning employees in the three operating departments follow:

	Cutting	Milling	Assembly
Budgeted number of employees	170	100	280
Actual number of employees for the most recent year	150	80	270
Long-run average number of employees	180	120	300

Required:

1. Determine the Medical Services Department charges for the year to each of the operating departments—Cutting, Milling, and Assembly.
2. How much, if any, of the actual Medical Services Department costs for the year should not be charged to the operating departments?

PROBLEM 12B–4 Service Department Charges [LO 12–6]

Sharp Motor Company has two operating divisions—an Auto Division and a Truck Division. The company has a cafeteria that serves the employees of both divisions. The costs of operating the cafeteria are budgeted at $40,000 per month plus $3 per meal served. The company pays all the cost of the meals.

The fixed costs of the cafeteria are determined by peak-period requirements. The Auto Division is responsible for 65% of the peak-period requirements, and the Truck Division is responsible for the other 35%.

For June, the Auto Division estimated that it would need 35,000 meals served, and the Truck Division estimated that it would need 20,000 meals served. However, due to unexpected layoffs of employees during the month, only 20,000 meals were served to the Auto Division. Another 20,000 meals were served to the Truck Division as planned.

Cost records in the cafeteria show that actual fixed costs for June totaled $42,000 and that actual meal costs totaled $128,000.

Required:

1. How much cafeteria cost should be charged to each division for June?
2. Assume that the company follows the practice of allocating *all* cafeteria costs incurred each month to the divisions in proportion to the number of meals served to each division during the month. On this basis, how much cost would be allocated to each division for June?
3. What criticisms can you make of the allocation method used in requirement 2?
4. If managers of operating departments know that fixed service costs are going to be allocated on the basis of peak-period requirements, what will be their probable strategy as they report their estimate of peak-period requirements to the company's budget committee? As a member of top management, what would you do to neutralize such strategies?

PROBLEM 12B–5 Service Department Charges [LO 12–6]

Tasman Products, Ltd., of Australia has a Maintenance Department that services the equipment in the company's Forming Department and Assembly Department. The cost of this servicing is charged to the operating departments on the basis of machine-hours. Cost and other data relating to the Maintenance Department and to the other two departments for the most recent year are presented below.

Data for the Maintenance Department follow:

	Budget	Actual
Variable costs for lubricants	$96,000*	$110,000
Fixed costs for salaries and other.	$150,000	$153,000

*Budgeted at $0.40 per machine-hour.

Data for the Forming and Assembly departments follow:

	Percent of Peak-Period Capacity Required	Machine-Hours	
		Budget	Actual
Forming Department.	70%	160,000	190,000
Assembly Department . . .	30%	80,000	70,000
Total.	100%	240,000	260,000

The level of fixed costs in the Maintenance Department is determined by peak-period requirements.

Required:

Management would like data to assist in comparing actual performance to planned performance in the Maintenance Department and in the other departments.

1. How much Maintenance Department cost should be charged to the Forming Department and to the Assembly Department? Show all computations.
2. Should any portion of the actual Maintenance Department costs not be charged to the other departments? If all costs should be charged, explain why; if a portion should not be charged, compute the amount and explain why it should not be charged.

Pricing Products and Services

LEARNING OBJECTIVES

After studying Appendix A, you should be able to:

LO A–1 Compute the profit-maximizing price of a product or service using the price elasticity of demand and variable cost.

LO A–2 Compute the selling price of a product using the absorption costing approach.

LO A–3 Compute the target cost for a new product or service.

Some products have an established market price. Consumers will not pay more than this price and there is no reason for a supplier to charge less—the supplier can sell all that it produces at this price. Under these circumstances, the supplier simply charges the prevailing market price for the product. Markets for basic raw materials such as farm products and minerals follow this pattern.

In this appendix, we are concerned with the more common situation in which a business is faced with the problem of setting its own prices. Clearly, the pricing decision can be critical. If the price is set too high, customers won't buy the company's products. If the price is set too low, the company's costs won't be covered.

The usual approach in pricing is to *mark up* cost.[1] A product's **markup** is the difference between its selling price and its cost and is usually expressed as a percentage of cost.

$$\text{Selling price} = (1+ \text{Markup percentage}) \times \text{Cost}$$

For example, a company that uses a markup of 50% adds 50% to the costs of its products to determine selling prices. If a product costs $10, then the company would charge $15 for the product. This approach is called **cost-plus pricing** because a predetermined markup percentage is applied to a cost base to determine the selling price.

Two key issues must be addressed with the cost-plus approach to pricing. First, what cost should be used? Second, how should the markup be determined? Several alternative approaches are considered in this appendix, starting with the approach generally favored by economists.

THE BUSINESS OF ART SCULPTURE

Shidoni Foundry, located in Tesuque, New Mexico, is a fine art casting and fabrication facility. The process of creating a bronze or other metal sculpture is complex. The artist creates the sculpture using modeling clay and then hires a foundry such as Shidoni to produce the actual metal sculpture. Shidoni craftspeople make a rubber mold from the clay model then use that mold to make a wax version of the original. The wax is in turn used to make a ceramic casting mold, and finally the bronze version is cast. Both the wax and the ceramic casting mold are destroyed in the process of making the metal casting, but the rubber mold is not and can be reused to make additional castings.

The surface of the metal sculpture can be treated with various patinas. One of the accompanying photos shows Harry Gold, the shop's patina artist, applying a patina to a metal sculpture with brush and blowtorch. The other photo shows a finished sculpture with patinas applied.

The artist is faced with a difficult business decision. The rubber mold for a small figure such as the seated Indian in the accompanying photo costs roughly $500; the mold for a life-size figure such as the cowboy costs $3,800 to $5,000. This is just for the mold! Fortunately, as discussed above, a number of metal castings can be made from each mold. However, each life-size casting costs $8,500 to $11,000. In contrast, a casting of the much smaller Indian sculpture would cost about $750. Given the fixed costs of the mold and variable costs of the casting, finish treatments, and bases, the artist must decide how many castings to produce and how to price them. The fewer the castings, the greater the rarity factor, and hence the higher the price that can be charged to art lovers. However, in that case, the fixed costs of making the mold must be spread across fewer items. The artist must make sure not to price the sculptures so high that the investment in molds and in the castings cannot be recovered.

Source: Conversations with Shidoni personnel, including Bill Rogers and Harry Gold, and Shidoni literature. See www.shidoni.com for more information concerning the company.

© Eric Noreen

© Eric Noreen

---

[1] There are some legal restrictions on prices. Antitrust laws prohibit "predatory" prices, which are generally interpreted by the courts to mean a price below average variable cost. "Price discrimination"—charging different prices to customers in the same market for the same product or service—is also prohibited by the law.

The Economists' Approach to Pricing

LEARNING OBJECTIVE A–1
Compute the profit-
maximizing price of a product
or service using the price
elasticity of demand and
variable cost.

If a company raises the price of a product, unit sales ordinarily fall. Because of this, pricing is a delicate balancing act in which the benefits of higher revenues per unit are traded off against the lower volume that results from charging a higher price. The sensitivity of unit sales to changes in price is called the *price elasticity of demand.*

Elasticity of Demand

A product's price elasticity should be a key element in setting its price. The **price elasticity of demand** measures the degree to which a change in price affects the unit sales of a product or service. Demand for a product is said to be *inelastic* if a change in price has little effect on the number of units sold. The demand for designer perfumes sold by trained personnel at cosmetic counters in department stores is relatively inelastic. Raising or lowering prices on these luxury goods has little effect on unit sales. On the other hand, demand for a product is *elastic* if a change in price has a substantial effect on the volume of units sold. An example of a product whose demand is elastic is gasoline. If a gas station raises its price for gasoline, unit sales will drop as customers seek lower prices elsewhere.

Price elasticity is very important in determining prices. Managers should set higher markups over cost when customers are relatively insensitive to price (i.e., demand is inelastic) and lower markups when customers are relatively sensitive to price (i.e., demand is elastic). This principle is followed in department stores. Merchandise sold in the bargain basement has a much lower markup than merchandise sold elsewhere in the store because customers who shop in the bargain basement are much more sensitive to price (i.e., demand is elastic).

The price elasticity of demand for a product or service, ε_d, can be estimated using the following formula.[2,3]

$$\varepsilon_d = \frac{\ln\,(1\,+\,\%\text{ change in quantity sold})}{\ln(1\,+\,\%\text{ change in price})}$$

For example, suppose that the managers of Nature's Garden believe that a 10% increase in the selling price of their apple-almond shampoo would result in a 15% decrease in the number of bottles of shampoo sold.[4] The price elasticity of demand for this product would be computed as follows:

$$\varepsilon_d = \frac{\ln[1\,+\,(-0.15)]}{\ln[1\,+\,(0.10)]} = \frac{\ln(0.85)}{\ln(1.10)} = -1.71$$

For comparison purposes, the managers of Nature's Garden believe that another product, strawberry glycerin soap, would experience a 20% drop in unit sales if its price is increased by 10%. (Purchasers of this product are more sensitive to price than the purchasers of the apple-almond shampoo.) The price elasticity of demand for the strawberry glycerin soap is:

$$\varepsilon_d = \frac{\ln[1\,+\,(-0.20)]}{\ln[1\,+\,(0.10)]} = \frac{\ln(0.80)}{\ln(1.10)} = -2.34$$

Both of these products, like other normal products, have a price elasticity that is less than −1.

---

[2]   The term "ln()" is the natural log function. You can compute the natural log of any number using the LN or In*x* key on your calculator. For example, In(0.85) = –0.1625.

[3]   This formula assumes that the price elasticity of demand is constant. This occurs when the relation between the selling price, *p*, and the unit sales, *q* can be expressed in the following form: In(q) = a + ε_d. Even if this is not precisely true, the formula provides a useful way to estimate a product's price elasticity.

[4]   The estimated change in unit sales should take into account competilors' responses to a price change.

Note that the price elasticity of demand for the strawberry glycerin soap is larger (in absolute value) than the price elasticity of demand for the apple-almond shampoo. This indicates that the demand for strawberry glycerin soap is more elastic than the demand for apple-almond shampoo.

In the next subsection, the price elasticity of demand will be used to compute the selling price that maximizes the profits of the company.

The Profit–Maximizing Price

Under certain conditions, the profit-maximizing price can be determined by marking up *variable cost* using the following formula:[5]

$$\text{Profit-maximizing markup on variable cost} = \frac{-1}{1 + \varepsilon_d}$$

Using the above markup, the selling price would be set using the formula:

$$\text{Profit-maximizing price} = (1 + \text{Profit-maximizing markup on variable cost}) \times \text{Variable cost per unit}$$

The profit-maximizing prices for the two Nature's Garden products are computed below using these formulas:

Apple-Almond Shampoo

$$\text{Profit-maximizing markup on variable cost} = \left(\frac{-1}{1 + (-1.71)} \right) = 1.41$$

$$\text{Profit-maximizing price} = (1 + 1.41)\$2.00 = \$4.82$$

Strawberry Glycerin Soap

$$\text{Profit-maximizing markup on variable cost} = \left(\frac{-1}{1 + (-2.34)} \right) = 0.75$$

$$\text{Profit-maximizing price} = (1 + 0.75)\$0.40 = \$0.70$$

Note that the 75% markup for the strawberry glycerin soap is lower than the 141% markup for the apple-almond shampoo. The reason for this is that the purchasers of strawberry glycerin soap are more sensitive to price than the purchasers of apple-almond shampoo. Strawberry glycerin soap is a relatively common product with close substitutes available in nearly every grocery store.

Exhibit A–1 shows how the profit-maximizing markup is generally affected by how sensitive unit sales are to price. For example, if a 10% increase in price leads to a 20% decrease in unit sales, then the optimal markup on variable cost according to the exhibit is 75%—the figure computed above for the strawberry glycerin soap. Note that the optimal markup drops as unit sales become more sensitive to price.

Caution is advised when using these formulas to establish a selling price. The formulas rely on simplifying assumptions and the estimate of the percentage change in unit sales that would result from a given percentage change in price is likely to be inexact. Nevertheless, the formulas can provide valuable clues regarding whether prices should be increased or decreased. Suppose, for example, that the strawberry glycerin soap is currently being sold for $0.60 per bar. The formula indicates that the profit-maximizing price

---

[5] The formula assumes that (a) the price elasticity of demand is constant; (b) Total cost = Total fixed cost + Variable cost per unit × Quantity sold: and (c) the price of the product has no effect on the sales or costs of any other product. The formula can be derived using calculus.

EXHIBIT A–1

The Optimal Markup on
Variable Cost as a Function
of the Sensitivity of Unit Sales
to Price

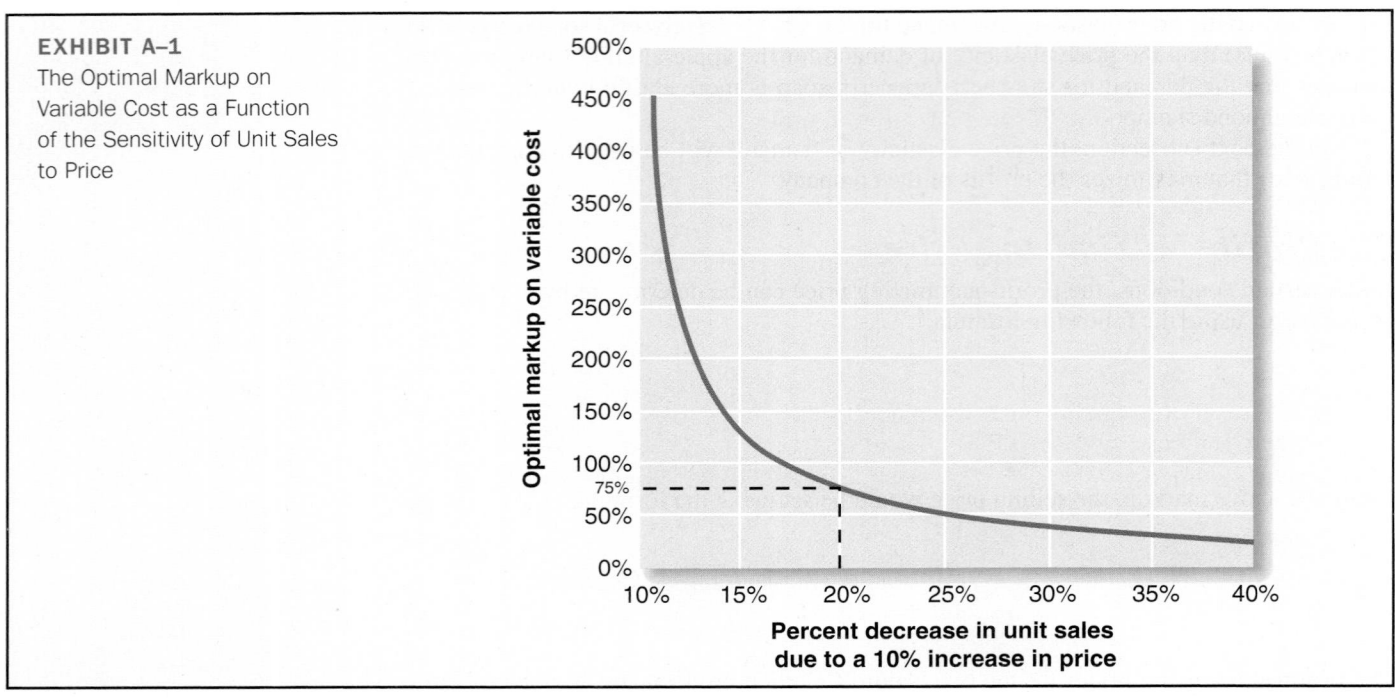

is $0.70 per bar. Rather than increasing the price by $0.10, it would be prudent to increase the price by a more modest amount to observe what happens to unit sales and to profits.

The formula for the profit-maximizing price conveys a very important lesson. If the total fixed costs are the same whether the company charges $0.60 or $0.70, they cannot be relevant in the decision of which price to charge for the soap. The optimal selling price should depend on two factors—the variable cost per unit and how sensitive unit sales are to changes in price. Fixed costs play no role in setting the optimal price. Fixed costs are relevant when deciding whether to offer a product but are not relevant when deciding how much to charge for the product.

We can directly verify that an increase in selling price for the strawberry glycerin soap from the current price of $0.60 per bar is warranted, based just on the forecast that a 10% increase in selling price would lead to a 20% decrease in unit sales. Suppose, for example, that Nature's Garden is currently selling 200,000 bars of the soap per year at the price of $0.60 a bar. If the change in price has no effect on the company's fixed costs or on other products, the effect on profits of increasing the price by 10% can be computed as follows:

	Present Price	Higher Price
Selling price (a)	$0.60	$0.60 + (0.10 × $0.60) = $0.66
Unit sales (b)	200,000	200,000 − (0.20 × 200,000) = 160,000
Sales (a) × (b)	$120,000	$105,600
Variable cost ($0.40 per unit)	80,000	64,000
Contribution margin	$ 40,000	$ 41,600

Despite the apparent optimality of prices based on marking up variable costs according to the price elasticity of demand, surveys consistently reveal that most managers approach the pricing problem from a completely different perspective. They prefer to mark up some version of full, not variable, costs, and the markup is based on desired profits rather than on factors related to demand. This approach is called the *absorption costing approach to cost-plus pricing.*

The Absorption Costing Approach to Cost-Plus Pricing

The absorption costing approach to cost-plus pricing differs from the economists' approach both in what costs are marked up and in how the markup is determined. Under the absorption approach to cost-plus pricing, the cost base is the absorption costing unit product cost, as defined in Chapter 3, rather than variable cost.

LEARNING OBJECTIVE A–2
Compute the selling price of a product using the absorption costing approach.

Setting a Target Selling Price Using the Absorption Costing Approach

To illustrate, assume that the management of Ritter Company wants to set the selling price on a product that has just undergone some design modifications. The accounting department has provided cost estimates for the redesigned product as shown below:

	Per Unit	Total
Direct materials.	$6	
Direct labor.	$4	
Variable manufacturing overhead.	$3	
Fixed manufacturing overhead		$70,000
Variable selling and administrative expenses.	$2	
Fixed selling and administrative expenses		$60,000

The first step in the absorption costing approach to cost-plus pricing is to compute the unit product cost. For Ritter Company, this amounts to $20 per unit at a volume of 10,000 units, as computed below:

Direct materials.	$ 6
Direct labor.	4
Variable manufacturing overhead.	3
Fixed manufacturing overhead ($70,000 ÷ 10,000 units)	7
Unit product cost	$20

Ritter Company has a general policy of marking up unit product costs by 50%. A price quotation sheet for the company prepared using the absorption approach is presented in Exhibit A–2. Note that selling and administrative expenses are not included in the cost base. Instead, the markup is supposed to cover these expenses.

Direct materials	$ 6	**EXHIBIT A–2**
Direct labor.	4	Price Quotation Sheet—
Variable manufacturing overhead.	3	Absorption Basis (10,000 Units)
Fixed manufacturing overhead (based on 10,000 units)	7	
Unit product cost	20	
Markup to cover selling and administrative expenses and desired profit—50% of unit manufacturing cost	10	
Target selling price	$30	

Determining the Markup Percentage

Ritter Company's markup percentage of 50% could be a widely used rule of thumb in the industry or just a company tradition that seems to work. The markup percentage may also be the result of an explicit computation. As we have discussed, the markup over cost should be largely determined by market conditions. However, many companies base their markup on cost and desired profit. The reasoning goes like this. The markup must be large enough to cover selling and administrative expenses and provide an adequate return on investment (ROI). Given the forecasted unit sales, the markup can be computed as follows:

$$\text{Markup percentage on absorption cost} = \frac{(\text{Required ROI} \times \text{Investment}) + \text{Selling and administrative expenses}}{\text{Unit product cost} \times \text{Unit sales}}$$

To show how this formula is applied, assume Ritter Company invests $100,000 in operating assets such as equipment to produce and market 10,000 units of the product each year. If Ritter Company requires a 20% ROI, then the markup for the product would be determined as follows:

$$\text{Markup percentage on absorption cost} = \frac{(20\% \times \$100,000) + (\$2 \text{ per unit} \times 10,000 \text{ units} + \$60,000)}{\$20 \text{ per unit} \times 10,000 \text{ units}}$$

$$= \frac{(\$20,000) + (\$80,000)}{\$200,000} = 50\%$$

As shown earlier, this markup of 50% leads to a target selling price of $30 for Ritter Company. *If the company actually sells 10,000 units* of the product at this price, the company's ROI on this product will indeed be 20%. This is verified in Exhibit A–3. However,

EXHIBIT A–3
Income Statement and ROI Analysis—Ritter Company Actual Unit Sales = 10,000 Units; Selling Price = $30

Direct materials	$ 6
Direct labor	4
Variable manufacturing overhead	3
Fixed manufacturing overhead ($70,000 ÷ 10,000 units)	7
Unit product cost	$20

Ritter Company
Absorption Costing Income Statement

Sales ($30 per unit × 10,000 units)	$300,000
Cost of goods sold ($20 per unit × 10,000 units)	200,000
Gross margin	100,000
Selling and administrative expenses ($2 per unit × 10,000 units + $60,000)	80,000
Net operating income	$ 20,000

ROI

$$\text{ROI} = \frac{\text{Net operating income}}{\text{Average operating assets}}$$

$$= \frac{\$20,000}{\$100,000}$$

$$= 20\%$$

if it turns out that more than 10,000 units are sold at this price, the ROI will be greater than 20%. If less than 10,000 units are sold, the ROI will be less than 20%. *The required ROI will be attained only if the forecasted unit sales volume is attained.*

Problems with the Absorption Costing Approach

The absorption costing approach makes pricing decisions look deceptively simple. All a company needs to do is compute its unit product cost, decide how much profit it wants, and then set its price. It appears that a company can ignore demand and arrive at a price that will safely yield whatever profit it wants. However, as noted above, the absorption costing approach relies on a forecast of unit sales. Neither the markup nor the unit product cost can be computed without such a forecast.

The absorption costing approach essentially assumes that customers *need* the forecasted unit sales and will pay whatever price the company decides to charge. However, customers have a choice. If the price is too high, they can buy from a competitor or they may choose not to buy at all. Suppose, for example, that when Ritter Company sets its price at $30, it sells only 7,000 units rather than the 10,000 units forecasted. As shown in Exhibit A–4, the company would then have a loss of $25,000 on the product instead of a profit of $20,000.[6] Some managers believe that the absorption costing approach to pricing is safe. This is an illusion. The absorption costing approach is safe only if customers choose to buy at least as many units as managers forecasted they would buy.

Direct materials	$ 6
Direct labor	4
Variable manufacturing overhead	3
Fixed manufacturing overhead ($70,000 ÷ 7,000 units)	10
Unit product cost	$23

EXHIBIT A–4
Income Statement and ROI Analysis—Ritter Company Actual Unit Sales = 7,000 Units; Selling Price = $30

Ritter Company
Absorption Costing Income Statement

Sales ($30 per unit × 7,000 units)	$210,000
Cost of goods sold ($23 per unit × 7,000 units)	161,000
Gross margin	49,000
Selling and administrative expenses ($2 per unit × 7,000 units + $60,000)	74,000
Net operating loss	$ (25,000)

ROI

$$\text{ROI} = \frac{\text{Net operating income}}{\text{Average operating assets}}$$

$$= \frac{-\$25,000}{\$100,000}$$

$$= -25\%$$

---

[6] It may be *impossible* to break even using an absorption costing approach when the company has more than one product—even when it would be possible to make substantial profits using the economists' approach to pricing. For details, see Eric Noreen and David Burgstahler. "Full Cost Pricing and the Illusion of Satisficing," *Journal of Management Accounting Research* 9 (1997).

Target Costing

Our discussion thus far has presumed that a product has already been developed, has been costed, and is ready to be marketed as soon as a price is set. In many cases, the sequence of events is just the reverse. That is, the company already *knows* what price should be charged, and the problem is to *develop* a product that can be marketed profitably at the desired price. Even in this situation, where the normal sequence of events is reversed, cost is still a crucial factor. The company can use an approach called *target costing*. **Target costing** is the process of determining the maximum allowable cost for a new product and then developing a prototype that can be profitably made for that maximum target cost figure. A number of companies have used target costing, including Compaq, Culp, Cummins Engine, Daihatsu Motors, Chrysler, Ford, Isuzu Motors, ITT Automotive, Komatsu, Matsushita Electric, Mitsubishi Kasei, NEC, Nippodenso, Nissan, Olympus, Sharp, Texas Instruments, and Toyota.

The target cost for a product is computed by starting with the product's anticipated selling price and then deducting the desired profit, as follows:

$$\text{Target cost} = \text{Anticipated selling price} - \text{Desired profit}$$

The product development team is then given the responsibility of designing the product so that it can be made for no more than the target cost.

Reasons for Using Target Costing

The target costing approach was developed in recognition of two important characteristics of markets and costs. The first is that many companies have less control over price than they would like to think. The market (i.e., supply and demand) really determines price, and a company that attempts to ignore this does so at its peril. Therefore, the anticipated market price is taken as a given in target costing. The second observation is that most of a product's cost is determined in the design stage. Once a product has been designed and has gone into production, not much can be done to significantly reduce its cost. Most of the opportunities to reduce cost come from designing the product so that it is simple to make, uses inexpensive parts, and is robust and reliable. If the company has little control over market price and little control over cost once the product has gone into production, then it follows that the major opportunities for affecting profit come in the design stage where valuable features that customers are willing to pay for can be added and where most of the costs are really determined. So that is where the effort is concentrated—in designing and developing the product. The difference between target costing and other approaches to product development is profound. Instead of designing the product and then finding out how much it costs, the target cost is set first and then the product is designed so that the target cost is attained.

An Example of Target Costing

To provide a simple example of target costing, assume the following situation: Handy Company wishes to invest $2,000,000 to design, develop, and produce a new hand mixer. The company's Marketing Department surveyed the features and prices of competing products and determined that a price of $30 would enable Handy to sell an estimated 40,000 hand mixers per year. Because the company desires a 15% ROI, the target cost to manufacture, sell, distribute, and service one mixer is $22.50 as computed below:

Projected sales (40,000 mixers × $30 per mixer)	$1,200,000
Less desired profit (15% × $2,000,000).	300,000
Target cost for 40,000 mixers	$ 900,000
Target cost per mixer ($900,000 ÷ 40,000 mixers).	$22.50

This $22.50 target cost would be broken down into target costs for the various functions: manufacturing, marketing, distribution, after-sales service, and so on. Each functional area would be responsible for keeping its actual costs within target.

Summary

Pricing involves a delicate balancing act. Higher prices result in more revenue per unit but drive down unit sales. Exactly where to set prices to maximize profit is a difficult problem, but, in general, the markup over cost should be highest for those products where customers are least sensitive to price. The demand for such products is said to be price inelastic.

Managers often rely on cost-plus formulas to set target prices. From the economists' point of view, the cost base for the markup should be variable cost. In contrast, in the absorption costing approach the cost base is the absorption costing unit product cost and the markup is computed to cover both nonmanufacturing costs and to provide an adequate return on investment. With the absorption approach, costs will not be covered and return on investment will not be adequate unless the unit sales forecast used in the cost-plus formula is accurate. If applying the cost-plus formula results in a price that is too high, the unit sales forecast will not be attained.

Some companies take a different approach to pricing. Instead of starting with costs and then determining prices, they start with prices and then determine allowable costs. Companies that use target costing estimate what a new product's market price is likely to be based on its anticipated features and prices of products already on the market. They subtract desired profit from the estimated market price to arrive at the product's target cost. The design and development team is then given the responsibility of ensuring that the actual cost of the new product does not exceed the target cost.

Glossary

Cost-plus pricing A pricing method in which a predetermined markup is applied to a cost base to determine the target selling price. (p. 579)

Markup The difference between the selling price of a product or service and its cost. The markup is usually expressed as a percentage of cost. (p. 579)

Price elasticity of demand A measure of the degree to which a change in price affects the unit sales of a product or service. (p. 580)

Target costing The process of determining the maximum allowable cost for a new product and then developing a prototype that can be profitably made for that maximum target cost figure. (p. 586)

Questions

A–1 What is cost-plus pricing?

A–2 What does the price elasticity of demand measure? What is inelastic demand? What is elastic demand?

A–3 According to the economists' approach to setting prices, the profit-maximizing price should depend on what two factors?

A–4 Which product should have a larger markup over variable cost, a product whose demand is elastic or a product whose demand is inelastic?

A–5 When the absorption costing approach to cost-plus pricing is used, what is the markup supposed to cover?

A–6 What assumption does the absorption costing approach make about how consumers react to prices?

A–7   Discuss the following statement: "Full cost can be viewed as a floor of protection. If a company always sets its prices above full cost, it will never have to worry about operating at a loss."

A–8   What is target costing? How do target costs enter into the pricing decision?

Multiple-choice questions are available with Connect.

Exercises   Additional student resources are available with Connect.

EXERCISE A–1 The Economists' Approach to Pricing [LO A–1]
Maria Lorenzi owns an ice cream stand that she operates during the summer months in West Yellowstone, Montana. Her store caters primarily to tourists passing through town on their way to Yellowstone National Park.

   Maria is unsure of how she should price her ice cream cones and has experimented with two prices in successive weeks during the busy August season. The number of people who entered the store was roughly the same each week. During the first week, she priced the cones at $1.89 and 1,500 cones were sold. During the second week, she priced the cones at $1.49 and 2,340 cones were sold. The variable cost of a cone is $0.43 and consists solely of the costs of the ice cream and of the cone itself. The fixed expenses of the ice cream stand are $675 per week.

Required:
1.   Did Maria make more money selling the cones for $1.89 or for $1.49?
2.   Estimate the price elasticity of demand for the ice cream cones.
3.   Estimate the profit-maximizing price for ice cream cones.

EXERCISE A–2 Absorption Costing Approach to Setting a Selling Price [LO A–2]
Martin Company is considering the introduction of a new product. To determine a selling price, the company has gathered the following information:

Number of units to be produced and sold each year	14,000
Unit product cost	$25
Projected annual selling and administrative expenses	$50,000
Estimated investment required by the company	$750,000
Desired return on investment (ROI)	12%

Required:
The company uses the absorption costing approach to cost-plus pricing.
1.   Compute the markup required to achieve the desired ROI.
2.   Compute the selling price per unit.

EXERCISE A–3 Target Costing [LO A–3]
Shimada Products Corporation of Japan is anxious to enter the electronic calculator market. Management believes that in order to be competitive in world markets, the price of the electronic calculator that the company is developing cannot exceed $15. Shimada's required rate of return is 12% on all investments. An investment of $5,000,000 would be required to purchase the equipment needed to produce the 300,000 calculators that management believes can be sold each year at the $15 price.

Required:
Compute the target cost of one calculator.

EXERCISE A–4 The Economists' Approach to Pricing [LO A–1]
The postal service of St. Vincent, an island in the West Indies, obtains a significant portion of its revenues from sales of special souvenir sheets to stamp collectors. The souvenir sheets usually contain several high-value St. Vincent stamps depicting a common theme, such as the life of

Princess Diana. The souvenir sheets are designed and printed for the postal service by Imperial Printing, a stamp agency service company in the United Kingdom. The souvenir sheets cost the postal service $0.80 each. St. Vincent has been selling these souvenir sheets for $7.00 each and ordinarily sells about 100,000 units. To test the market, the postal service recently priced a new souvenir sheet at $8.00 and sales dropped to 85,000 units.

Required:
1. Does the postal service of St. Vincent make more money selling souvenir sheets for $7.00 each or $8.00 each?
2. Estimate the price elasticity of demand for the souvenir sheets.
3. Estimate the profit-maximizing price for souvenir sheets.
4. If Imperial Printing increases the price it charges to the St. Vincent postal service for souvenir sheets to $1.00 each, how much should the St. Vincent postal service charge its customers for the souvenir sheets?

Additional student resources are available with Connect.   **Problems**

PROBLEM A–5 Standard Costs; Absorption Costing Approach to Setting Prices [LO A–2]
Wilderness Products, Inc., has designed a self-inflating sleeping pad for use by backpackers and campers. The following information is available about the new product:
a. An investment of $1,350,000 will be necessary to carry inventories and accounts receivable and to purchase some new equipment needed in the manufacturing process. The company's required rate of return is 24% on all investments.
b. A standard cost card has been prepared for the sleeping pad, as shown below:

	Standard Quantity or Hours	Standard Price or Rate	Standard Cost
Direct materials	4.0 yards	$2.70 per yard	$ 10.80
Direct labor............................	2.4 hours	$8.00 per hour	19.20
Manufacturing overhead (⅕ variable).......	2.4 hours	$12.50 per hour	30.00
Total standard cost per jacket			$60.00

c. The only variable selling and administrative expense will be a sales commission of $9 per pad. Fixed selling and administrative expenses will be (per year):

Salaries.........................	$ 82,000
Warehouse rent..................	50,000
Advertising and other.............	600,000
Total...........................	$732,000

d. Because the company manufactures many products, no more than 38,400 direct labor-hours per year can be devoted to production of the new sleeping pads.
e. Manufacturing overhead costs are allocated to products on the basis of direct labor-hours.

Required:
1. Assume that the company uses the absorption approach to cost-plus pricing.
   a. Compute the markup that the company needs on the pads to achieve a 24% return on investment (ROI) if it sells all of the pads it can produce.
   b. Using the markup you have computed, prepare a price quotation sheet for a single sleeping pad.
   c. Assume that the company is able to sell all of the pads that it can produce. Prepare an income statement for the first year of activity and compute the company's ROI for the year on the pads, using the ROI formula from Chapter 11.

2. After marketing the sleeping pads for several years, the company is experiencing a falloff in demand due to an economic recession. A large retail outlet will make a bulk purchase of pads if its label is sewn in and if an acceptable price can be worked out. What is the minimum acceptable price for this special order?

PROBLEM A–6 Missing Data; Markup Computations: Return on Investment (ROI); Pricing [LO A–2]

South Seas Products, Inc., has designed a new surfboard to replace its old surfboard line. Because of the unique design of the new surfboard, the company anticipates that it will be able to sell all the boards that it can produce. On this basis, the following incomplete budgeted income statement for the first year of activity is available:

Sales (? boards at ? per board)	$?
Cost of goods sold (? boards at ? per board)	1,600,000
Gross margin	?
Selling and administrative expenses	1,130,000
Net operating income	$?

Additional information on the new surfboard follows:

a. An investment of $1,500,000 will be necessary to carry inventories and accounts receivable and to purchase some new equipment. The company's required rate of return is 18% on all investments.

b. A partially completed standard cost card for the new surfboard follows:

	Standard Quantity or Hours	Standard Price or Rate	Standard Cost
Direct materials	6 feet	$4.50 per foot	$27
Direct labor	2 hours	? per hour	?
Manufacturing overhead	? hours	? per hour	?
Total standard cost per surfboard			$?

c. The company will employ 20 workers to make the new surfboards. Each will work a 40-hour week, 50 weeks a year.

d. Other information relating to production and costs follows:

Variable manufacturing overhead cost (per board)	$5
Variable selling expense (per board)	$10
Fixed manufacturing overhead cost (total)	$600,000
Fixed selling and administrative expense (total)	$?
Number of boards produced and sold (per year)	?

e. Overhead costs are allocated to production on the basis of direct labor-hours.

Required:

1. Complete the standard cost card for a single surfboard.

2. Assume that the company uses the absorption costing approach to cost-plus pricing.

a. Compute the markup that the company needs on the surfboards to achieve an 18% return on investment (ROI).

b. Using the markup you have computed, prepare a price quotation sheet for a single surfboard.

c. Assume, as stated, that the company is able to sell all of the surfboards that it can produce. Complete the income statement for the first year of activity, and then compute the company's ROI for the year.

3. Assuming that direct labor is a variable cost, how many units would the company have to sell at the price you computed in (2) above to achieve the 18% ROI? How many units would have to be sold to just break even?

PROBLEM A–7 The Economists' Approach to Pricing; Absorption Costing Approach to Cost-Plus Pricing [LO A–1, LO A–2]

Software Solutions, Inc., was started by two young software engineers to market SpamBlocker, a software application they had written that screens incoming e-mail messages and eliminates unsolicited mass mailings. Sales of the software have been good at 50,000 units a month, but the company has been losing money as shown below:

Sales (50,000 units × $25 per unit)	$1,250,000
Variable cost (50,000 units × $6 per unit)	300,000
Contribution margin	950,000
Fixed expenses	960,000
Net operating loss	$ (10,000)

The company's only variable cost is the $6 fee it pays to another company to reproduce the software on CDs, print manuals, and package the result in an attractive box for sale to consumers. Monthly fixed selling and administrative expenses are $960,000.

The company's marketing manager has been arguing for some time that the software is priced too high. She estimates that every 5% decrease in price will yield an 8% increase in unit sales. The marketing manager would like your help in preparing a presentation to the company's owners concerning the pricing issue.

Required:

1. To help the marketing manager prepare for her presentation, she has asked you to fill in the blanks in the following table. The selling prices in the table were computed by successively decreasing the selling price by 5%. The estimated unit sales were computed by successively increasing the unit sales by 8%. For example, $23.75 is 5% less than $25.00 and 54,000 units is 8% more than 50,000 units.

Selling Price	Estimated Unit Sales	Sales	Variable Cost	Fixed Expenses	Net Operating Income
$25.00	50,000	$1,250,000	$300,000	$960,000	$(10,000)
$23.75	54,000	$1,282,500	$324,000	$960,000	$(1,500)
$22.56	58,320	?	?	?	?
$21.43	62,986	?	?	?	?
$20.36	68,025	?	?	?	?
$19.34	73,467	?	?	?	?
$18.37	79,344	?	?	?	?
$17.45	85,692	?	?	?	?
$16.58	92,547	?	?	?	?
$15.75	99,951	?	?	?	?

2. Using the data from the table, construct a chart that shows the net operating income as a function of the selling price. Put the selling price on the X-axis and the net operating income on the Y-axis. Using the chart, determine the approximate selling price at which net operating income is maximized.

3. Compute the price elasticity of demand for the SpamBlocker software. Based on this calculation, what is the profit-maximizing price?

4. The owners have invested $2,000,000 in the company and feel that they should be earning at least 2% per month on these funds. If the absorption costing approach to pricing were used, what would be the target selling price based on the current sales of 50,000 units? What do you think would happen to the net operating income of the company if this price were charged?

5. If the owners of the company are dissatisfied with the net operating income and return on investment at the selling price you computed in requirement 3, should they increase the selling price? Explain.

PROBLEM A–8 Target Costing [LO A–3]

National Restaurant Supply, Inc., sells restaurant equipment and supplies throughout most of the United States. Management is considering adding a machine that makes sorbet to its line of ice cream making machines. Management will negotiate the price of the sorbet machine with its Swedish manufacturer.

Management of National Restaurant Supply believes the sorbet machine can be sold to its customers in the United States for $4,950. At that price, annual sales of the sorbet machine should be 100 units. If the sorbet machine is added to National Restaurant Supply's product lines, the company will have to invest $600,000 in inventories and special warehouse fixtures. The variable cost of selling the sorbet machines would be $650 per machine.

Required:

1. If National Restaurant Supply requires a 15% return on investment (ROI), what is the maximum amount the company would be willing to pay the Swedish manufacturer for the sorbet machines?

2. The manager who is flying to Sweden to negotiate the purchase price of the machines would like to know how the purchase price of the machines would affect National Restaurant Supply's ROI. Construct a chart that shows National Restaurant Supply's ROI as a function of the purchase price of the sorbet machine. Put the purchase price on the X-axis and the resulting ROI on the Y-axis. Plot the ROI for purchase prices between $3,000 and $4,000 per machine.

3. After many hours of negotiations, management has concluded that the Swedish manufacturer is unwilling to sell the sorbet machine at a low enough price so that National Restaurant Supply is able to earn its 15% required ROI. Apart from simply giving up on the idea of adding the sorbet machine to National Restaurant Supply's product lines, what could management do?

Profitability Analysis

LEARNING OBJECTIVES

After studying Appendix B, you should be able to:

LO B–1   Compute the profitability index and use it to select from among possible actions.

LO B–2   Compute and use the profitability index in volume trade-off decisions.

LO B–3   Compute and use the profitability index in other business decisions.

Introduction

Perhaps more than any other information, managers would like to know the profitability of their products, customers, and other business segments. They want this information so that they know what segments to drop and add and which to emphasize. This appendix provides a coherent framework for measuring profitability, bringing together relevant materials from several chapters. After studying this appendix you should have a firm grasp of the principles underlying profitability analysis. The first step is to distinguish between *absolute profitability* and *relative profitability*.

Absolute Profitability

Absolute profitability is concerned with the impact on the organization's overall profits of adding or dropping a particular segment such as a product or customer—without making any other changes. For example, if Coca-Cola were considering closing down its operations in the African country of Zimbabwe, managers would be interested in the absolute profitability of those operations. Measuring the absolute profitability of an existing segment is conceptually straightforward—compare the revenues that would be lost from dropping the segment to the costs that would be avoided. When considering a new potential segment, compare the additional revenues from adding the segment to the additional costs that would be incurred. In each case, include only the additional costs that would actually be avoided or incurred. All other costs are irrelevant and should be ignored.

In practice, figuring out what costs would change and what costs would not change if a segment were dropped (or added) can be very difficult. Activity-based costing can help in identifying such costs, but all costs should be carefully analyzed to determine whether they would really change. For example, an activity-based costing study of Coca-Cola's Zimbabwe operations might include charges for staff support provided to the Zimbabwe operations by Coca-Cola's corporate headquarters in Atlanta. However, if eliminating the Zimbabwe operations would have no impact on actual costs in Atlanta, then these costs are not relevant and should be excluded when measuring the absolute profitability of the Zimbabwe operations.

For examples of the measurement of absolute profitability, see "Appendix 6A: ABC Action Analysis," the section "Segmented Income Statements and the Contribution Approach" in Chapter 5, and the section "Adding and Dropping Product Lines and Other Segments" in Chapter 7.

Relative Profitability

LEARNING OBJECTIVE B–1
Compute the profitability index and use it to select from among possible actions.

Even when every segment is *absolutely* profitable, managers often want to know which segments are most and least profitable. **Relative profitability** is concerned with ranking products, customers, and other business segments to determine which should be emphasized.

Why are managers interested in ranking segments or determining the relative profitability of segments? The answer to this deceptively simple question provides the key to measuring relative profitability. The only reason to rank segments is if something forces you to make trade-offs among them. If trade-offs are not necessary, the solution is simple—keep every segment that is absolutely profitable. What would force a manager to make trade-offs among profitable segments? There is only one answer—a *constraint*. In the absence of a constraint, all segments that are absolutely profitable should be pursued. On the other hand, if a constraint is present, then by definition the company cannot pursue every profitable opportunity. Choices have to be made. Thus, measuring relative profitability makes sense only when a constraint exists that forces trade-offs. This point cannot be overemphasized; constraints are fundamental to understanding and measuring relative profitability.

How should relative profitability be measured? Divide each segment's measure of absolute profitability, which is the incremental profit from that segment, by the amount of the constraint required by the segment. For example, refer to the data below for two of the many segments within a company:

	Segment A	Segment B
Incremental profit	$100,000	$200,000
Amount of constrained resource required.	100 hours	400 hours

Segment B may seem more attractive than Segment A because its incremental profit is twice as large, but it requires four times as much of the constrained resource. In fact, Segment B would not be the best use of the constrained resource because it generates only $500 of incremental profit per hour ($200,000 ÷ 400 hours), whereas Segment A generates $1,000 of incremental profit per hour ($100,000 ÷ 100 hours). Another way to look at this is to suppose that 400 hours of the constrained resource are available. Would you rather use the hours on four segments like Segment A, generating a total incremental profit of $400,000, or on one segment like Segment B, which generates $200,000 in incremental profit?

In general, the relative profitability of segments should be measured by the **profitability index** as defined below:

$$\text{Profitability index} = \frac{\text{Incremental profit from the segment}}{\text{Amount of the constrained resource required by the segment}}$$

The profitability index is computed below for the two segments in the example:

	Segment A	Segment B
Incremental profit (a).	$100,000	$200,000
Amount of constrained resource required (b)	100 hours	400 hours
Profitability index (a) ÷ (b)	$1,000 per hour	$500 per hour

We have already encountered several examples of the profitability index in previous chapters. For example, in Chapter 8 the project profitability index was defined as:

$$\text{Project profitability index} = \frac{\text{Net present value of the project}}{\text{Amount of investment required by the project}}$$

The project profitability index is used when a company has more long-term projects with positive net present values than it can fund. In this case, the incremental profit from the segment is the net present value of the project. And because the investment funds are the constraint, the amount of the constrained resource required by the segment is the amount of investment required by the project.

As an example of the use of the profitability index, consider the case of Quality Kitchen Design, a small company specializing in designing kitchens for upscale homes. Management is considering the 10 short-term projects listed in Panel A of Exhibit B–1. The incremental profit from each project is listed in the second column. For example, the incremental profit from Project A is $9,180. This incremental profit consists of the revenues from the project less any costs that would be incurred by the company as a consequence of accepting the project. The company's constraint is the lead designer's time. Project A would require 17 hours of the lead designer's time. If all of the projects were accepted, they would require a total of 100 hours. Unfortunately, only 46 hours are available. Consequently, management will have to turn down some projects. The profitability index will be used in deciding which projects to accept and which to turn down. The profitability index for a project is computed by dividing its incremental profit by the amount of the lead designer's time required for the project. In the case of Project A, the profitability index is $540 per hour.

EXHIBIT B–1

Ranking Segments Based on the Profitability Index

Panel A: Computation of the Profitability Index

	Incremental Profit (A)	Amount of the Constrained Resource Required (B)	Profitability Index (A) ÷ (B)
Project A	$9,180	17 hours	$540 per hour
Project B	$7,200	9 hours	$800 per hour
Project C	$7,040	16 hours	$440 per hour
Project D	$5,680	8 hours	$710 per hour
Project E	$5,330	13 hours	$410 per hour
Project F	$4,280	4 hours	$1,070 per hour
Project G	$4,160	13 hours	$320 per hour
Project H	$3,720	12 hours	$310 per hour
Project I	$3,650	5 hours	$730 per hour
Project J	$2,940	3 hours	$980 per hour
		100 hours	

Panel B: Ranking Based on the Profitability Index

	Profitability Index	Amount of the Constrained Resource Required	Cumulative Amount of the Constrained Resource Used
Project F	$1,070 per hour	4 hours	4 hours
Project J	$980 per hour	3 hours	7 hours
Project B	$800 per hour	9 hours	16 hours
Project I	$730 per hour	5 hours	21 hours
Project D	$710 per hour	8 hours	29 hours
Project A	$540 per hour	17 hours	46 hours
Project C	$440 per hour	16 hours	62 hours
Project E	$410 per hour	13 hours	75 hours
Project G	$320 per hour	13 hours	88 hours
Project H	$310 per hour	12 hours	100 hours

Panel C: The Optimal Plan

	Incremental Profit
Project F	$ 4,280
Project J	2,940
Project B	7,200
Project I	3,650
Project D	5,680
Project A	9,180
	$32,930

The projects are ranked in order of the profitability index in Panel B of Exhibit B–1. The last column in that panel shows the cumulative amount of the constrained resource (i.e., lead designer's time) required to do the projects at that point in the list and higher. For example, the 7 hours listed to the right of Project J in the cumulative column represents the sum of the 4 hours required for Project F plus the 3 hours required for Project J.

To find the best combination of projects within the limits of the constrained resource, go down the list in Panel B to the point where all of the available constrained resource is used. In this case, because 46 hours of lead designer time are available, that would be the point above the solid line drawn in Panel B of Exhibit B–1. Projects F, J, B, I, D, and A lie above that line and would require a total of exactly 46 hours of lead designer time. The optimal plan consists of accepting these six projects and turning down the others. The total incremental profit from accepting these projects would be $32,930 as shown in Panel C of Exhibit B–1. No other feasible combination of projects would yield a higher total incremental profit.[1]

We should reinforce a very important point that may be forgotten in the midst of these details. The profitability index is based on *incremental* profit. When computing the incremental profit for a segment such as a product, customer, or project, only the *incremental* costs of the segment should be included. Those are the costs that could be avoided—whether fixed or variable—if the segment is eliminated. All other costs are not relevant and should be ignored—including allocations of common costs.

Volume Trade-Off Decisions

Earlier we stated that you have already encountered several examples of the profitability index in this book. One was the project profitability index in Chapter 8. The other example of the profitability index is in the section "Utilization of a Constrained Resource" in Chapter 7. That section deals with situations in which a company does not have enough capacity to satisfy demand for all of its products. Therefore, the company must produce less than the market demands of some products. This is called a volume trade-off decision because the decision, at the margin, consists of trading off units of one product for units of another. Fixed costs are typically unaffected by such decisions—capacity will be fully utilized, it is just a question of how it will be utilized. In volume trade-off decisions where fixed costs are irrelevant, the profitability index takes the special form:

$$\text{Profitability index for a volume trade-off decision} = \frac{\text{Unit contribution margin}}{\text{Amount of the constrained resource required by one unit}}$$

This profitability index is identical to the "contribution margin per unit of the constrained resource" that was used in Chapter 7 to decide which products should be emphasized. An example of a volume trade-off decision is presented in Exhibit B–2. In this example, the company makes three products that use the constrained resource—a machine that is available 2,200 minutes per week. As shown in Panel B of Exhibit B-2, producing all

---

[1] In this example, the top projects exactly consumed all of the available constrained resource. That won't always happen. For example, assume that only 45 hours of lead designer time are available. This small change complicates matters considerably. Because of the "lumpiness" of the projects, the optimal plan isn't necessarily to do projects F, J, B, I, and D—slopping at Project D on the list and a cumulative requirement of 29 hours. That would leave 16 hours of unused lead designer time. The best use of this time may be Project C, which has an incremental profit of $7,040. However, other possibilities exist too. Finding and evaluating all of the most likely possibilities can take a lot of lime and ingenuity. When the constrained resource is not completely exhausted by the top projects on the list, some tinkering with the solution may be necessary. For this reason, the list generated by ranking based on the profitability index should be viewed as a starting point rather than as a definitive solution when the projects are "lumpy" and take big chunks of the constrained resource.

EXHIBIT B–2
Using the Profitability Index in a
Volume Trade-Off Decision

Panel A: Product Data

	Products		
	RX200	VB30	SQ500
Unit contribution margin	$15 per unit	$10 per unit	$16 per unit
Demand per week	300 units	400 units	100 units
Amount of the constrained resource required..................	5 minutes per unit	2 minutes per unit	4 minutes per unit

Panel B: Total Demand on the Constrained Resource

	Products			
	RX200	VB30	SQ500	Total
Demand per week (a).................	300 units	400 units	100 units	
Amount of the constrained resource required (b)	5 minutes per unit	2 minutes per unit	4 minutes per unit	
Total amount of the constraint required per week to meet demand (a) × (b).................	1,500 minutes	800 minutes	400 minutes	2,700 minutes

Panel C: Computation of the Profitability Index

	Products		
	RX200	VB30	SQ500
Unit contribution margin (a)	$15 per unit	$10 per unit	$16 per unit
Amount of the constrained resource required (b)	5 minutes per unit	2 minutes per unit	4 minutes per unit
Profitability index (contribution margin per unit of the constrained resource) (a) × (b).................	$3 per minute	$5 per minute	$4 per minute

Panel D: The Optimal Plan

Amount of constrained resource available.....................................	2,200 minutes
Less: Constrained resource required for production of 400 units of VB30	800 minutes
Remaining constrained resource available......................................	1,400 minutes
Less: Constrained resource required for production of 100 units of SQ500	400 minutes
Remaining constrained resource available.....................................	1,000 minutes
Less: Constrained resource required for production of 200 units of RX200*.......	1,000 minutes
Remaining constrained resource available	0 minutes

*1,000 minutes available ÷ 5 minutes per unit of RX200 = 200 units of RX200.

Panel E: The Total Contribution Margin under the Optimal Plan

	Products			
	RX200	VB30	SQ500	Total
Unit contribution margin (a).........	$15 per unit	$10 per unit	$16 per unit	
Optimal production plan (b).........	200 units	400 units	100 units	
Contribution margin (a) × (b)........	$3,000	$4,000	$1,600	$8,600

three products up to demand would require 2,700 minutes per week—500 more minutes than are available. Consequently, the company cannot fully satisfy demand for these three products and some product or products must be cut back.

The profitability index for this decision is computed in Panel C of Exhibit B–2. For example, the profitability index for product RX200 is $3 per minute. The comparable figure for product VB30 is $5 per minute and for product SQ500 is $4 per minute. Consequently, the correct ranking of the products is VB30 followed by SQ500, then followed by RX200.

The optimal production plan is laid out in Panel D of Exhibit B–2. The most profitable products, VB30 and SQ500, are produced up to demand and the remaining time on the constraint is used to make 200 units of RX200 (1,000 available minutes ÷ 5 minutes per unit).

The total contribution margin from following this plan is computed in Panel E of Exhibit B–2. The total contribution margin of $8,600 is higher than the contribution margin that could be realized from following any other feasible plan. Assuming that fixed costs are not affected by the decision of which products to emphasize, this plan will also yield a higher total profit than any other feasible plan.

Managerial Implications

In addition to the add-or-drop and volume trade-off decisions discussed above, the profitability index can be used in other ways. For example, which products would you rather have your salespersons emphasize—those with a low profitability index or those with a high profitability index? The answer is, of course, that salespersons should be encouraged to emphasize sales of the products with the highest profitability indexes. However, if salespersons are paid commissions based on sales, what products will they try to sell? The selling prices of products RX200, VB30, and SQ500 appear below:

LEARNING OBJECTIVE B–3
Compute and use the profitability index in other business decisions.

		Products	
	RX200	VB30	SQ500
Unit selling price	$40	$30	$35

If salespersons are paid a commission based on gross sales, they will prefer to sell product RX200, which has the highest selling price. But that is the *least* profitable product given the current constraint. It has a profitability index of only $3 per minute compared to $5 per minute for VB30 and $4 per minute for SQ500.

This suggests that salespersons should be paid commissions based on the profitability index and the amount of constraint time sold rather than on sales revenue. This would encourage them to sell the most profitable products, rather than the products with the highest selling prices. How would such a compensation system work? Prior to making a sales call, a salesperson would receive an up-to-date report indicating how much of the constrained resource is currently available and a listing of all products showing the amount of the constraint each requires and the profitability index. Such a report would appear as follows:

Marketing Data Report

		Products	
	RX200	VB30	SQ500
Unit selling price	$40	$30	$35
Unit variable cost	25	20	19
Unit contribution margin (a).	$15	$10	$16
Amount of the constrained resource required per unit (b).	5 minutes	2 minutes	4 minutes
Profitability index (a) ÷ (b).	$3 per minute	$5 per minute	$4 per minute

Total available time on the constrained resource: 100 minutes

The key here is to realize that the salesperson is, in essence, selling time on the constraint. A salesperson who is paid based on the profitability index will prefer to sell product VB30 because the salesperson would get credit for sales of $500 if all 100 minutes are used on product VB30 ($5 per minute × 100 minutes), whereas the credit would be only $300 for product RX200 or $400 for product SQ500.[2]

The profitability index also has implications for pricing new products. Suppose that the company has designed a new product, WR6000, whose variable cost is $30 per unit and that requires 6 minutes of the constrained resource per unit. Because the company is currently using all of its capacity, the new product would necessarily displace production of existing products. Consequently, the price of the new product should cover not only its variable cost, but it should also cover the opportunity cost of displacing existing products. What product would be displaced? Production of RX200 should be cut first because it is the least profitable existing product. And how much is a minute of the constrained resource worth if it would otherwise be used to make product RX200? A minute of the constrained resource is worth $3 per minute, the profitability index of product RX200. Therefore, the selling price of the new product should at least cover the costs laid out below:[3]

$$\begin{matrix} \text{Selling price of} \\ \text{new product} \end{matrix} \geq \begin{matrix} \text{Variable cost of} \\ \text{the new product} \end{matrix} + \left(\begin{matrix} \text{Opportunity} \\ \text{cost per unit of} \\ \text{the constrained} \\ \text{resource} \end{matrix} \times \begin{matrix} \text{Amount of the} \\ \text{constrained resource} \\ \text{required by a unit of} \\ \text{the new product} \end{matrix} \right)$$

In the case of the new product WR6000, the calculations would be:

$$\text{Selling price of WR6000} \geq \$ + (\$3 \text{ per minute} \times 6 \text{ minutes}) = \$30 + \$18 = \$48$$

WR6000 should sell for at least $48 or the company would be better off continuing to use the available capacity to produce RX200.[4]

---

[2] Equivalent incentives would be provided by commissions based on total coniribution margin. If all 100 available minutes are used to make product VB30, 50 units could be produced (100 minutes ÷ 2 minutes per unit), for which the total contribution margin would be $500 ($10 per unit × 50 units). Likewise, the total contribution margin for products RX200 and SQ500 would be $300 and $400. Respectively, if all available minutes were used to make just those products.

[3] In addition, the selling price of a new product should cover any avoidable fixed costs of the product. This is easier said than done, however, because achieving this goal involves estimating how many units will be sold—which in turn depends on the selling price.

[4] If production of WR6000 eventually completely displaces production of RX200. the opportunity cost would change. It would increase to $4 per minute, the profitability index of the next product in line to be cut back.

Summary

A strong distinction should be made between absolute profitability and relative profitability. A segment is considered profitable in an absolute sense if dropping it would result in lower overall profits. Absolute profitability is measured by the segment's incremental profit, which is the difference between the revenues from the segment and the costs that could be avoided by dropping the segment.

A relative profitability measure is used to rank segments. Such rankings are necessary only if a constraint forces the organization to make trade-offs among segments. To appropriately measure relative profitability, three things must be known. First, the constraint must be identified. Second, the incremental profit associated with each segment must be computed. Third, the amount of the constrained resource required by each segment must be determined. Relative profitability is measured by the profitability index, which is the incremental profit from the segment divided by the amount of the constrained resource required by the segment. The profitability index can be used in a variety of situations, including selections of projects and volume trade-off decisions.

Glossary

Absolute profitability The impact on the organization's overall profits of adding or dropping a particular segment such as a product or customer—without making any other changes. (p. 594)
Profitability index The measure of relative profitability, which is computed by dividing the incremental profit from a segment by the amount of the constrained resource required by the segment. (p. 595)
Relative profitability A ranking of products, customers, or other business segments for purposes of making trade-offs among segments. This is necessary when a constraint exists. (p. 594)

Questions

B–1 What is meant by *absolute* profitability?
B–2 What is meant by *relative* profitability?
B–3 A successful owner of a small business stated: "We have the best technology, the best products, and the best people in the world. We have no constraints." Do you agree?
B–4 What information is needed to measure the *absolute* profitability of a segment?
B–5 What information is needed to measure the *relative* profitability of a product?
B–6 How should the relative profitability of products be determined in a volume trade-off decision?
B–7 What costs should be covered by the selling price of a new product?

Multiple-choice questions are available with Connect.

Additional student resources are available with Connect.

Exercises

EXERCISE B–1 Ranking Projects Based on the Profitability Index [LO B–1]
MidWest Amusements is in the process of reviewing 10 proposals for new rides at its theme parks in cities scattered throughout the American heartland. The company's only experienced safety engineer must carefully review plans and monitor the construction of all new rides. However, she is only available to work on new rides for 1,590 hours during the year. The net present values and the amount of safety engineer time required for the proposed rides are listed below:

Proposed Ride	Net Present Value	Safety Engineer Time Required (hours)
Ride 1	$1,268,200	340
Ride 2	1,152,000	360
Ride 3	649,600	320
Ride 4	644,100	190
Ride 5	540,000	250
Ride 6	539,200	160
Ride 7	462,000	110
Ride 8	457,200	360
Ride 9	403,200	180
Ride 10	387,500	250
Total	$6,503,000	2,520

Required:

1. Which of the proposed rides should the company build this year? (Note: The incremental profit of a long-term project such as constructing a new ride is its net present value.)
2. What would be the total net present value of the rides built under your plan?

EXERCISE B–2 Volume Trade-Off Decision [LO B–2]

Heritage Watercraft makes reproductions of classic wooden boats. The bottleneck in the production process is fitting wooden planks to build up the curved sections of the hull. This process requires the attention of the shop's most experienced craftsman. A total of 1,800 hours is available per year in this bottleneck operation. Data concerning the company's four products appear below:

Adirondack	Adirondack	Lake Huron	Oysterman	Voyageur
Unit contribution margin.	$485	$268	$385	$600
Annual demand (units)	80	120	100	140
Hours required in the bottleneck operation per unit	5	4	7	8

No fixed costs could be avoided by modifying how many units are produced of any product or even by dropping any one of the products.

Required:

1. Is there sufficient capacity in the bottleneck operation to satisfy demand for all products?
2. What is the optimal production plan for the year?
3. What would be the total contribution margin for the optimal production plan you have proposed?

EXERCISE B–3 Pricing a New Product [LO B–3]

Seattle's Top Coffee owns and operates a chain of popular coffee stands that serve over 30 different coffee-based beverages. The constraint at the coffee stands is the amount of time required to fill an order, which can be considerable for the more complex beverages. Sales are often lost because customers leave after seeing a long waiting line to place an order. Careful analysis of the company's existing products has revealed that the opportunity cost of order filling time is $2.70 per minute.

The company is considering introducing a new product, praline cappuccino, to be made with pecan extract and molasses. The variable cost of the standard size praline cappuccino would be $0.30 and the time required to fill an order for the beverage would be 40 seconds.

Required:

What is the minimum acceptable selling price for the new praline cappuccino product?

Problems   Additional student resources are available with Connect.

PROBLEM B–4 Customer Profitability and Managerial Decisions [LO B–1, LO B–3]

Advanced Pharmaceuticals, Inc., is a wholesale distributor of prescription drugs to independent retail and hospital-based pharmacies. Management believes that top-notch customer representatives are the key factor in determining whether the company will be successful in the future. Customer representatives serve as the company's liaison with customers—helping pharmacies monitor their stocks, delivering drugs when customer stocks run low, and providing up-to-date information on drugs from many different companies. Customer representatives must be ultra-reliable and are highly trained. Good customer representatives are hard to come by and are not easily replaced.

Customer representatives routinely record the amount of time they spend serving each pharmacy. This time includes travel time to and from the company's central warehouse as well as time spent replenishing stocks, dealing with complaints, answering questions about drugs, informing pharmacists of the latest developments and newest products, reviewing bills, explaining procedures, and so on. Some pharmacies require more hand-holding and attention than others and consequently they consume more of the representatives' time.

Recently, customer representatives have made more frequent complaints that it is impossible to do their jobs without working well beyond normal working hours. This has led to an alarming increase in the number of customer representatives quitting for jobs in other organizations. As a consequence, management is considering dropping some customers to reduce the workload on customer representatives. Data concerning a representative sample of the company's customers appears below:

	Leafcrest Pharmacy	Providence Hospital Pharmacy	Madison Clinic Pharmacy	Jenkins Pharmacy
Total revenues	$272,650	$2,948,720	$1,454,880	$155,280
Cost of drugs sold	$211,470	$2,234,480	$1,119,440	$115,920
Customer service costs..............	$10,640	$74,400	$42,000	$4,480
Customer representative time........	190	1,240	560	80

Customer service costs include all of the costs—other than the costs of the drugs themselves—that could be avoided by dropping the customer. These costs include the hourly wages of the customer representatives, their sales commissions, the mileage-related costs of the customer representatives' company-provided vehicles, and so on.

Required:
1. Rank the four customers in terms of their profitability.
2. Customer representatives are currently paid $25 per hour plus a commission of 1% of sales revenues. If these four pharmacies are indeed representative of the company's customers, could the company afford to pay its customer representatives more in order to retain them?

PROBLEM B–5 Volume Trade-Off Decision; Managing the Constraint [LO B–2, LO B–3]
Sammamish Brick, Inc., manufactures bricks using clay deposits on the company's property. Raw clays are blended and then extruded into molds to form unfired bricks. The unfired bricks are then stacked onto movable metal platforms and rolled into the kiln where they are fired until dry. The dried bricks are then packaged and shipped to retail outlets and contractors. The bottleneck in the production process is the kiln, which is available for 2,000 hours per year. Data concerning the company's four main products appear below. Products are sold by the pallet.

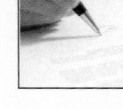

	Traditional Brick	Textured Facing	Cinder Block	Roman Brick
Gross revenue per pallet...............	$756	$1,356	$589	$857
Contribution margin per pallet..........	$472	$632	$376	$440
Annual demand (pallets)	90	110	100	120
Hours required in the kiln per pallet......	8	8	4	5

No fixed costs could be avoided by modifying how much is produced of any product.

Required:
1. Is there sufficient capacity in the kiln to satisfy demand for all products?
2. What is the production plan for the year that would maximize the company's profit?
3. What would be the total contribution margin for the production plan you have proposed?
4. The kiln could be operated for more than 2,000 hours per year by running it after normal working hours. Up to how much per hour should the company be willing to pay in overtime wages, energy costs, and other incremental costs to operate the kiln additional hours?
5. The company is considering introducing a new product, glazed Venetian bricks, whose variable cost would be $820 per pallet and that would require 10 hours in the kiln per pallet. What is the minimum acceptable selling price for this new product?
6. Salespersons are currently paid a commission of 5% of gross revenues. Will this motivate the salespersons to make the right choices concerning which products to sell most aggressively?

PROBLEM B–6 Interpreting Common Practice [LO B–1]

In practice, many organizations measure the relative profitability of their segments by dividing the segments' margins by their revenues. The segment margin for this purpose is the segment's revenue less its fully allocated costs—including allocations of fixed common costs. For example, a hospital might compute the relative profitability of its major segments as follows:

St. Ignatius Hospital Profitability Report (in thousands of dollars)				
	Emergency Room	Surgery	Acute Care	Total
Revenue...........................	$10,630	$21,470	$18,840	$50,940
Fully allocated cost.................	10,060	21,090	18,550	49,700
Margin	$ 570	$ 380	$ 290	$ 1,240
Profitability (Margin ÷ Revenue)	5.4%	1.8%	1.5%	2.4%

The hospital's net operating income for this period was $1,240,000.

Required:

1. Evaluate the use of the margin, as defined above, in the numerator of the profitability measure.
2. Evaluate the use of revenue in the denominator of the profitability measure.

PROBLEM B–7 Ranking Alternatives and Managing with a Constraint [LO B–1, LO B–3]

Luxus Baking Company has developed a reputation for producing superb, one-of-a-kind wedding cakes in addition to its normal fare of breads and pastries. While the wedding cake business is a major moneymaker, it creates some problems for the bakery's owner, Kari Therau, particularly in June. The company's reputation for wedding cakes is largely based on the skills of Regina Yesterman, who decorates all of the cakes. Unfortunately, last year the company accepted too many cake orders for some June weekends, with the result that Regina was worked to a frazzle and almost quit. To prevent a recurrence, Kari has promised Regina that she will not have to work more than 27 hours in any week to prepare the wedding cakes for the upcoming weekend. (Regina also has other duties at the bakery, so even with the 27-hour limitation, she would be working more than full-time in June.)

A number of reservations for wedding cakes for the first weekend in June had already been received from customers by early May. When a customer makes a reservation, Ms. Therau gets enough information concerning the size of the wedding party and the desires of the customer to determine the cake's price, the cost to make it, and the amount of time that Regina will need to spend decorating it. The reservations for the first weekend in June are listed below:

Customer	Incremental Profit	Reginas Time Required (hours)
Afonso.............	$ 195	5
Carloni.............	259	7
Cullins	105	3
Frese	170	5
Gerst	117	3
Jelovich.............	124	4
Klarr...............	192	6
Melby..............	144	4
Rideau.............	150	5
Towner	256	8
Total..............	$1,712	50

For example, the Afonso cake would require 5 hours of Regina's time and would generate a profit of $195 for the bakery. Following industry practice, pricing for the cakes is based on their size and standard formulas and does not reflect how much decorating would be required.

Required:

1. Ms. Therau feels that she must cancel enough cake reservations to reduce Regina's workload to the promised level. She knows that customers whose reservations have been cancelled will be disappointed, but she intends to refer all of those customers to an excellent bakery across town. If the sole objective is to maximize the company's total profit, which reservations should be cancelled?
2. What would be the total profit if your recommendation in requirement 1 is followed?
3. Assume that for competitive reasons it would not be practical for Luxus Bakery to change the pricing of its wedding cakes. What recommendations would you make to Ms. Therau concerning taking reservations in the future?
4. Assume that Luxus Bakery could change the way it prices its wedding cakes. What recommendations would you make to Ms. Therau concerning how she should set the prices of wedding cakes in the future?
5. What might Ms. Therau be able to do to keep both Regina and her customers happy while increasing her profits? Be creative. (Hint: Review the section on managing constraints in Chapter 7.)

Additional student resources are available with Connect. **Cases**

CASE B–8 Redirecting Effort [LO B–2]

Vectra Corporation recently suffered its fourth straight decline in quarterly earnings—despite a modest increase in sales. Unfortunately, Vectra's industry is highly competitive, so the company is reluctant to increase its prices. However, management believes that profits would improve if the efforts of its sales force were redirected toward the company's most profitable products.

Several years ago Vectra decided that its core competencies were strategy, design, and marketing and that production should be outsourced. Consequently, Vectra subcontracts all of its production.

Vectra's salespersons are paid salaries and commissions. All of the company's salespersons sell the company's full line of products. The commissions are 5% of the revenue generated by a salesperson and average about 60% of a salesperson's total compensation. There has been some discussion of increasing the size of the sales force, but management prefers for the present to redirect the efforts of salespersons toward the more profitable products. While management is reluctant to tinker with the sales compensation scheme, revenue targets for the various products will be set for the regional sales managers based on the products that management wants to push most aggressively. The regional sales managers will be paid a bonus if the sales targets are met. The company computes product margins for all of its products using the following formula:

> Selling price
> Less: Sales commissions
> Less: Cost of sales
> Less: Operating expenses
> Product margin

The cost of sales in the product margin formula is the amount Vectra pays to its production subcontractors. The operating expenses represent fixed costs. Each product is charged a fair share of those costs, calculated this year as 34.6% of the product's selling price.

Management is convinced that the best way to improve overall profits is to redirect the efforts of the company's salespersons. There are no plans to add or drop any products.

Required:

How would you measure the relative profitability of the company's products in this situation? Assume that it is not feasible to change the way salespersons are compensated. Also assume that the only data you have available are the selling price, the sales commissions, the cost of sales, the operating expenses, and the product margin for each product.